15⁰⁰/mij

Rugged design minimum maintenance.

NOHAB-GM type T44 diesel-electric 1670 HP locomotives for Sweden.

Another 15 T44 locomotives with the GM 12-cylinder, 1670 HP EMD 645 engine are now under manufacture for the Swedish State Railways.

B BOFORS
NOHAB LOCOMOTIVE

AB BOFORS-NOHAB
S-461 01 TROLLHÄTTAN SWEDEN
Tel. 0520/180 00 Telex: 42084 Cables: NOHAB

JANE'S
WORLD RAILWAYS
1980-81

METCALFE-BSI (Bergische-Stahl Industrie)
Dependable Disc Brakes

METCALFE-BSI disc brakes with high thermal capacity and cooling by self ventilation to give long efficient service life

Hundreds of thousands of sets in service under all operating conditions providing **safe, reliable braking**

METCALFE-BSI disc brakes for rail vehicles are backed by 50 years experience, expertise and understanding of the thermal and metallurgical problems encountered in this specialised field. They are available in a wide range of styles and sizes to suit all applications including wheel mounted styles for hub or rim fixing and axle mounted styles with BSI patented connection between hub and disc. For further information please write for catalogue E7.

Reader Enquiry Form No. **65**

Rolling stock custom-built just for you

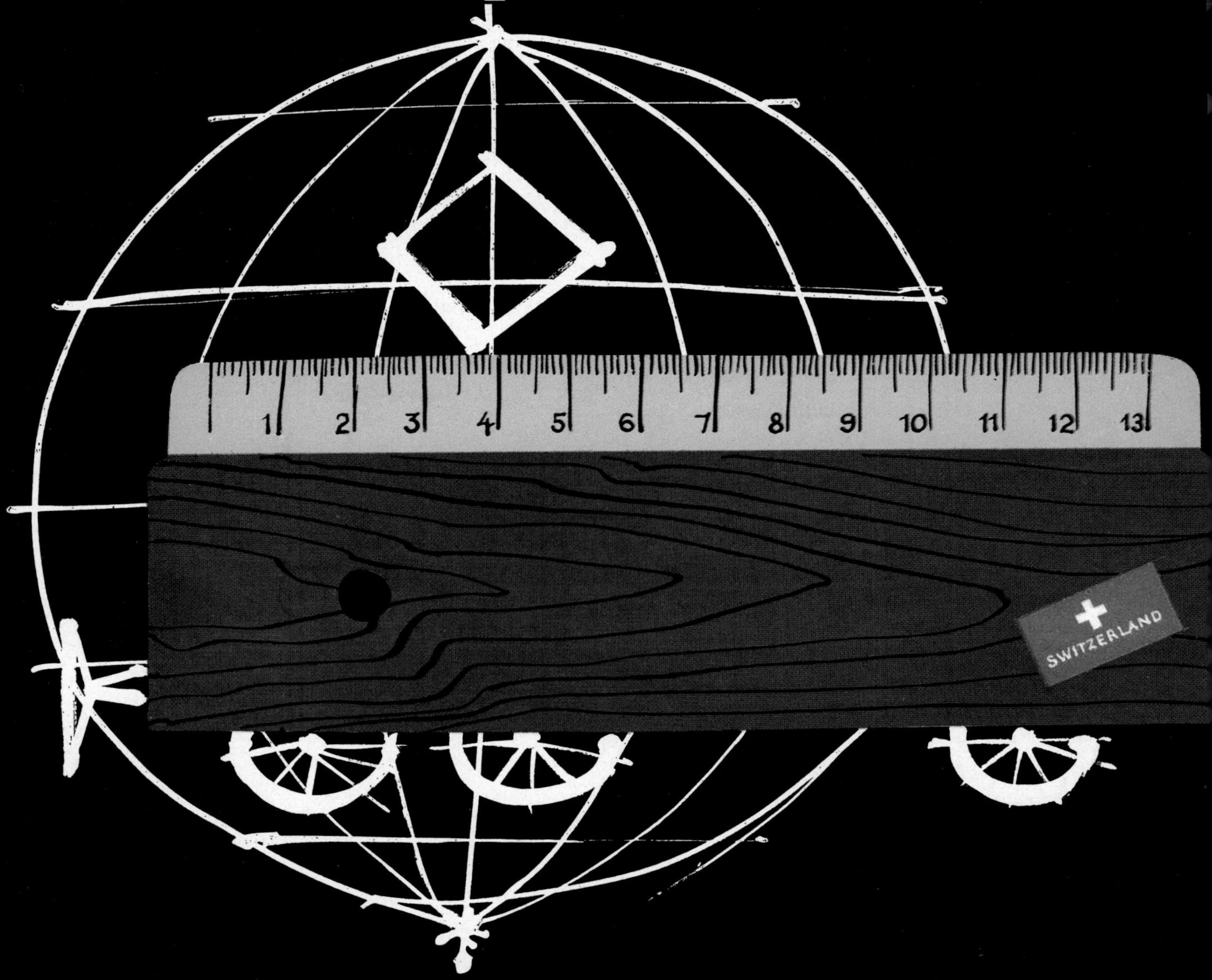

For modern rail rolling stock ESW is a must. Our specialities are design and manufacture to your particular requirements. Experience in AAR and UIC Standards, in body structures in light alloy, stainless and mild steel, in bogies for high speeds, with tilting system, conventional and air suspension. ESW-built rolling stock successfully operates on all continents, on main lines, in cities, through deserts, in high mountain as well as in tropical areas. Ask ESW also about long term financing, after sale, maintenance and railway consultancy services. We have the answer.
Products:
Electric and diesel railcars - Urban and suburban train sets - L. R. V./tramways - Passenger coaches - Dining cars - Sleeping cars - Mail/luggage vans - Rack and pinion rolling stock - Goods wagons - Motor and trailer bogies - High speed bogies - Tilting suspension system - Intercar cross-overs - etc.

Alphabetical list of advertisers

Motive power on a world scale.

On the one hand, the range of requirements for the world's railways is vast—on the other, there is our equally vast experience at solving these problems. In fact, when you weigh it up, we have a great deal to offer the railway motive power business.

Our technical expertise goes back to the very first locomotives whilst today, our range covers the complete spectrum of railway electrification.

Since the turn of the century, we have supplied electric and diesel traction to 70 countries for high speed services and heavy freight, from sea level to the world's highest railway and in all climatic regions.

Our specialists are always pleased to talk and advise on every aspect of motive power.

So, for a balanced view, phone our number, 061-872 2431. International Code for the U.K.—44.

GEC Traction Limited, Trafford Park, Manchester M17 1PR England. Telex: 667152 GEC MCR G Telegrams: 'Assocelect', Manchester.

GEC TRACTION

There's nothing we like better than a challenge

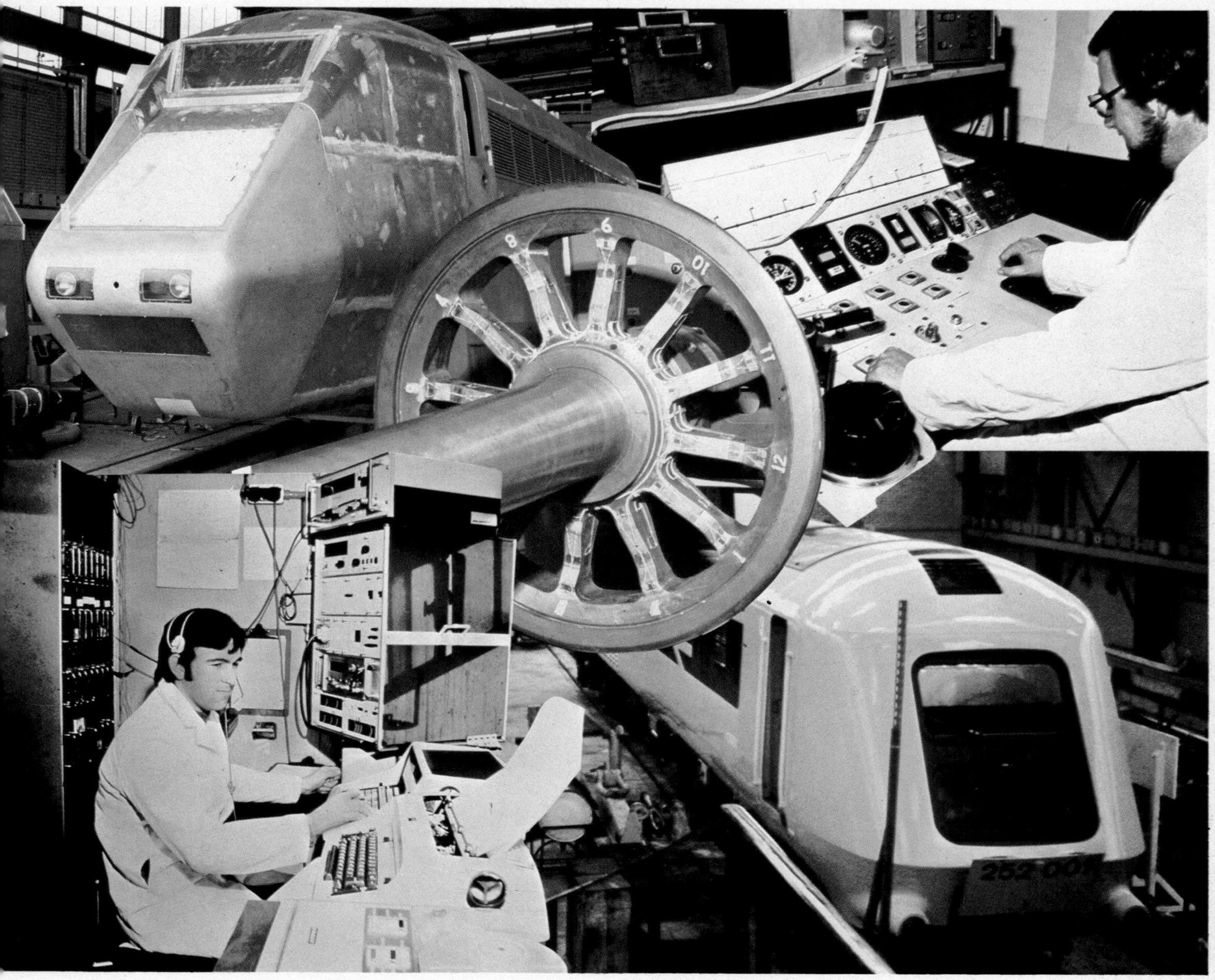

BRE-Metro
for Rail Transport Research

BRE-Metro is supported by probably the most comprehensive and successful rail transport Research Design and Development organisation in the world. Calling on years of practical experience and the latest scientific aids the highly skilled team of professionals are dedicated to breaking new ground in all aspects of railway operation and to finding cost effective solutions to modern railway problems.

In addition you are offered extensive manufacturing facilities, years of experience in Freight and Passenger transport, and complete design and installation facilities of Rapid Transit Systems.

For further information contact General Manager BRE-Metro Limited, 274/280 Bishopsgate, London, EC2M 4XQ
Telex 885353 BREBIS-G
Telephone 01-247 5444

BRE-Metro for Inter-City Stock
BRE-Metro for Manufacture
BRE-Metro for Freight Wagons
BRE-Metro for Rapid Transit Systems
BRE-Metro for Rail Transport Research

The joint export sales company of British Rail Engineering Limited and Metro-Cammell Limited

[7]

Classified list of advertisers

The companies advertising in this publication have informed us that they are involved in the fields of manufacture indicated below:

Air brake equipment
Knorr-Bremse
Kolmex
Mitsubishi
Oerlikon-Bührle

Air-conditioned carriages
BRE-Metro
Breda
Brown Boveri
Ganz Mavag
Hawker Siddeley Canada
Kolmex
SIG
Snia Viscosa

Air-conditioning equipment
Mitsubishi
Pintsch Bamag
Toshiba

Air filters
Ganz Mavag
Knorr-Bremse

Aluminium semis
Swiss Aluminium

Audible signals and alarms
Velec-Sefat

Automatic couplers
AEG-Telefunken
Dresser
GEC Traction
Knorr-Bremse
Kolmex
Socimi

Automatic wagon identification
AEG-Telefunken

Autopilots for trams, underground railways, etc
AEG-Telefunken
Ansaldo
Mitsubishi

Auxiliary motors
AEG-Telefunken
Ansaldo
GEC Traction
Mitsubishi

Axle-box liner plates
Ganz Mavag

Axle-boxes and bearings
Ganz Mavag
Kolmex

Axle boxes and cylindrical roller bearers
Kolmex

Axle drive for diesel-hydraulic locomotives
Ganz Mavag
Fried Krupp
Voith Getriebe

Axle gears
SOCIMI

Axles, railway
Kolmex

Ballast cleaners
Kolmex
Plasser & Theurer

Ballast compactors
Plasser & Theurer

Ballast regulators
Plasser & Theurer

Ballast tampers
Plasser & Theurer

Battery locomotives
GEC Industrial Locomotives

Bogies
Breda
BRE-Metro
Dresser
Flug-und Fahrzeugwerke
Ganz Mavag
GEC Traction
Hawker Siddeley Canada
Kolmex
Fried Krupp
MAN
SIG
Societe Franco Belge
SOCIMI
Sulzer Bros
Swiss Aluminium
Toshiba
Wickham, D

Bogies, especially air suspension type
Breda
BRE-Metro
Ganz Mavag
Hawker Siddeley Canada
MAN
SIG

Boxes, battery
Flug-und Fahrzeugwerke
GEC Traction
Pintsch-Bamag

Brake equipment
Knorr-Bremse
Kolmex
Miner
Mitsubishi
Oerlikon-Bührle
SOCIMI

Brake equipment (hydraulic disc)
Knorr-Bremse

Brake equipment (hydrodynamic braking system)
Voith Getriebe

Brake slack adjusters
Knorr-Bremse
Kolmex

Brake units for disc brakes
Knorr-Bremse
SOCIMI

Brake units for tread brakes
Knorr-Bremse

Buffer friction
Kolmex
Miner

Cables, electric
AEG-Telefunken
Siemens

Car body tilting equipment
BRE-Metro
MAN
SIG

Cardan shafts
Voith Getriebe

Carriages and wagons
Breda
BRE-Metro
CIMT
Flug-und Fahrzeugwerke
Ganz Mavag
Hawker Siddeley Canada
Kolmex
MAN
Ortner
SIG
Snia Viscosa
Societe Franco Belge

Castings, aluminium and aluminium alloy
BRE-Metro
Dresser
Ganz Mavag

Castings, iron
Dresser
Ganz Mavag
Krauss-Maffei

Coach heaters
AEG-Telefunken
Ganz Mavag
GEC Traction
Mitsubishi
Pintsch Bamag

Coal wagons
BRE-Metro
Kolmex
Ortner
SIG
Snia Viscosa
Societe Franco Belge
Swiss Aluminium

Compressed air drying equipment
Ansaldo
Knorr-Bremse
Mitsubishi

Compressor motors
Ansaldo
Ganz Mavag
Mitsubishi

Compressors
Ansaldo
Brown Boveri
Ganz Mavag
Knorr-Bremse
Mitsubishi

WICKHAM

In addition to a well known range of powered track inspection and maintenance vehicles, Wickham design and build:

Diesel and diesel-electric railcars and trailers.

Railbuses and senior officials' luxury cars.

Driving and trailing bogies incorporating radius arm controlled suspension, a principle pioneered by Wickham.

A 'power pack' vehicle, which makes possible the economical revival of D.M.U. cars rendered non-operational by time-worn power units and transmissions.

Enquiries related to your own particular problem or requirement will be welcomed.

D. WICKHAM & COMPANY LTD.
WARE · HERTFORDSHIRE · ENGLAND

TEL: WARE 2491-7   CABLES: WICKHAM WARE   TELEX: 81340

CLASSIFIED LIST OF ADVERTISERS

Computer controlled district control centres and marshalling yards
AEG-Telefunken
Ansaldo
Mitsubishi

Concrete sleepers/manufacturing plant and equipment
Monier

Concrete sleepers/ties
Monier

Containers
Breda
Flug-und Fahrzeugwerke
Interfrigo
Kolmex
SNAV
Snia Viscosa
Toshiba

Control equipment, locomotive
AEG-Telefunken
Ansaldo
BRE-Metro
Brown Boveri
Deuta-Werke
GEC Traction
General Motors
Holec
Knorr-Bremse
Mitsubishi
Siemens

Control equipment, signal etc
AEG-Telefunken
Ansaldo
BRE-Metro
GEC Traction
Knorr-Bremse
Pintsch Bamag
Siemens

Conveyors for ballast
Plasser & Theurer

Cooling Units
Voith Getriebe

Couplings
AEG-Telefunken
BRE-Metro
Dresser
Kolmex
Mitsubishi
SOCIMI
Toshiba
Voith Getriebe

Cranes, electric
Ganz Mavag
Holec
MAN

Crankshafts
Ganz Mavag

Crossings
Elektro-Thermit
Pintsch-Bamag

Current Collectors
AEG-Telefunken
BRE-Metro
Brown Boveri
GEC Traction
Toshiba

Diesel-electric cars (shunting and transfer)
AEG-Telefunken

Diesel-electric locomotives
AEG-Telefunken
Ansaldo
Breda
BRE-Metro
Brown Boveri
Fried Krupp
Ganz Mavag
GEC Industrial Locomotives
GEC Traction
General Motors
Kolmex
Krauss-Maffei
Mitsubishi
SIG
Sulzer Bros
Toshiba

Diesel-electric railcars
AEG-Telefunken
Ansaldo
Breda
BRE-Metro
Brown Boveri
CIMT
Ganz Mavag
GEC Traction
Hawker Siddeley Canada
Kolmex
MAN
SIG
Toshiba
Wickham, D

**Diesel-electric cars,
shunting & transfer**
Breda
Ganz Mavag
GEC Industrial Locomotives
GEC Traction
Kolmex

Diesel engine parts
Brown Boveri
Ganz Mavag
Kolmex
MAN
SACM

Diesel engines
Alsthom-Atlantique
Ganz Mavag
General Motors
MAN
Motoren-und Turbinen-Union
SACM

Diesel-hydraulic coaches
Breda
Ganz Mavag
MAN

Diesel-hydraulic locomotives
Fried Krupp

Diesel-hydraulic railcars
Breda
CIMT
Ganz Mavag
MAN
Wickham, D

Diesel locomotives
Breda
BRE-Metro
Ganz Mavag
GEC Industrial Locomotives
GEC Traction
Kolmex
Krauss-Maffei
Sulzer Bros

Diesel mechanical
GEC Industrial locomotives

Diesel-mechanical railcars
Breda
Ganz Mavag
GEC Traction
Kolmex
MAN
Wickham, D
Windhoff

Diesel passenger rail buses (trolleys)
Breda
BRE-Metro
MAN
Wickham, D

Diesel railcars
Breda
BRE-Metro
Ganz-Mavag
Wickham, D

**Disc brake equipment for trams,
locomotives, etc**
Knorr-Bremse

Disc brakes
Knorr-Bremse
SOCIMI

Discharge gates
Miner

Door and window fittings
Ganz Mavag
Kolmex
Snia Viscosa

Door control equipment
Pintsch Bamag

Draught (draw) gears
Dresser
Kolmex
Miner

Draw springs
BRE-Metro

Driver's safety and vigilance equipment
AEG-Telefunken
Ganz Mavag
GEC Traction
Knorr-Bremse
Mitsubishi

Electric couplers
AEG-Telefunken
Kolmex
Mitsubishi
Toshiba

Electric locomotive equipment
AEG-Telefunken
Ansaldo
GEC Traction
Holec
Kolmex
Mitsubishi
Pintsch Bamag
Siemens
Sulzer Bros
Toshiba

Electric propulsion equipment
AEG-Telefunken
GEC Traction
Holec

Electric railcars
AEG-Telefunken
Ansaldo
Breda
BRE-Metro
CIMT
Flug-und Fahrzeugwerke
Ganz Mavag
GEC Traction
Holec
Kolmex
MAN
Mitsubishi
Siemens
SIG
Societe Franco Belge
Toshiba

Electric subway cars
AEG-Telefunken
Breda
BRE-Metro
CIMT
Daewoo Heavy Industries
Ganz Mavag
GEC Traction
Holec

Electric tractors
AEG-Telefunken
Ansaldo
GEC Industrial Locomotives
SIG

Electric trailer cars
AEG-Telefunken
Ansaldo
Breda
BRE-Metro
Flug-und Fahrzeugwerke
Ganz Mavag
GEC Traction
Hawker Siddeley Canada
MAN
Mitsubishi
SIG

Electric transmission systems
GEC Traction
Holec

Electrical equipment
AEG-Telefunken
Ansaldo
Holec
Mitsubishi
Pintsch Bamag
Siemens
Toshiba

Electric traction equipment
SOCIMI

Electromagnetic rail brakes
AEG-Telefunken
Knorr-Bremse
Kolmex
Oerlikon-Bührle

Electronic control systems for diesel locomotives including adaptation for radio control
AEG-Telefunken
Ansaldo
Fried-Krupp
GEC Traction
Krauss-Maffei
Mitsubishi

Electronic protection equipment for rail vehicles (slip and spin protection)
AEG-Telefunken
Ansaldo
Deuta-Werke
GEC Traction
Holec
Knorr-Bremse
Krauss Maffei
Mitsubishi
Oerlikon-Bührle

Electronic testing equipment
AEG-Telefunken
BRE-Metro
Mitsubishi
Pintsch Bamag
Siemens

Electro pneumatic brake
Kolmex
Knorr-Bremse

Engine parts, diesel
Ganz Mavag
General Motors
MAN

Engine testing equipment
AEG-Telefunken
Ganz Mavag

Engineers
Grant Lyon Eagre

Exhausters
Knorr-Bremse

Exhaust motors
AEG-Telefunken

Explosion-proof locomotive
Ganz Mavag

Fail-safe warning systems
AEG-Telefunken
Deuta-Werke
Knorr-Bremse
Mitsubishi
Pintsch-Bamag

Filters (air)
Ganz Mavag
Knorr-Bremse
Mitsubishi

Filters, oil
Knorr-Bremse

Flame-proof mining locomotives
Ganz Mavag
GEC Industrial Locomotives
GEC Traction
Kolmex

Fluorescent lighting
AEG-Telefunken
Brown Boveri
Mitsubishi
Pintsch Bamag

Forgings, steel
BRE-Metro

Freight cars
BRE-Metro
Daewoo Heavy Industries
Hawker Siddeley Canada
Kolmex
MAN
Ortner
SIG
Snia Viscosa
Société Franco-Belge

Gang warning systems
Pintsch Bamag

Gears and gearboxes
AEG-Telefunken
Ganz Mavag
GEC Traction
Mitsubishi
Sulzer Bros
Voith Getriebe

Generators
AEG-Telefunken
Ansaldo
Brown Boveri
GEC Traction
General Motors
Holec
Mitsubishi
Oerlikon-Bührle
Pintsch Bamag
Siemens

Convincing arguments for SLM motive power

Firstly, SLM designs are purpose-oriented. The employment of a low-level tractive device and axle-load compensation facilitate optimal adhesion utilization and the transmission of maximum tractive forces. The well-balanced lightweight construction means an increase in the specific power to locomotive weight

ratio. The interbogie coupling, the lateral spring centering of the axle and, last but not least, correct selection of the axle arrangement result in optimal tracking and minimum horizontal forces between wheel and rail. Favourable matching of the spring suspension, damping devices and suitable arrangement of the running gear ensure excellent operating characteristics. These are only some aspects of SLM technology.

tain railways. The experts are well acquainted with the extremely stringent requirements for gear units and braking systems.

About 60% of the world's rack traction vehicles have been built by SLM. You will find them in the Swiss Alps, the Rocky Mountains, the High Tatras, in

Brazil, Chile, the Federal Republic of Germany and in France.

Fourthly, SLM railed vehicles are economical, ensure low maintenance costs and idle times of short duration, as well as low wear of rail and wheel. Irrespective of whether it concerns a line or shunting locomotive, railcar or railcar set, adhesion or rack-rail drive, electric or thermal operation, narrow, standard or wide gauge—the operating requirements of the railway are always fully considered. Our customers are aware of this. Licensees have acquired the rights to build complete vehicles, major assemblies and detail parts. A reflection of the confidence placed in SLM and its developments.

Finally, SLM is always at your disposal with expert advice and a world-wide network of contacts. Why not ask for our documentation or better still arrange a personal meeting?

SLM®

Swiss Locomotive and Machine Works
CH-8401 Winterthur, Switzerland
Telephone 052 85 41 41
Telex 76131 slm ch

Member of the SULZER Group

80.24 e

Secondly, the quality and stringent testing of the materials, meticulous fabrication and continuous quality control provide SLM vehicles with their recognized ruggedness and ensure the durability needed for the exacting duties over a great many years, even in alpine regions.

Thirdly, safety and reliability have been the essential features of SLM products for over a century. This is demonstrated not only by the vehicles built for adhesion railways, but also very impressively by rack locomotives and railcars for moun-

Generators, portable
Mitsubishi
Plasser & Theurer
Siemens

Hand brakes
Breda
Knorr-Bremse
Miner

Heat exchangers
Ganz Mavag
Pintsch Bamag
Windhoff

Heating equipment (switch)
AEG-Telefunken
Mitsubishi
Pintsch Bamag

Hoists
LOC Manutention

Hopper cars
BRE-Metro
Kolmex
MAN
Ortner
Snia Viscosa

Hose and couplings
Knorr-Bremse

Hydraulic pumps
Voith Getriebe

Inspection, track
Ford, Bacon & Davis
Plasser & Theurer

Instruments
AEG-Telefunken
Mitsubishi
Siemens

Insulated rail joints
Elektro-Thermit

Insulation, electric
AEG-Telefunken

Intercommunication equipment
AEG-Telefunken
Mitsubishi
Siemens
SIG
Velac-Sefat

Interlocking signalling equipment
AEG-Telefunken
Ansaldo
Siemens

Level crossing barriers, automatic & manual
Pintsch Bamag

Light rail vehicles
AEG-Telefunken
Breda
BRE-Metro
GEC Traction

Lighting equipment, locomotives
AEG-Telefunken
Brown Boveri
Fried Krupp
Mitsubishi
Pintsch Bamag

Lighting equipment, trains
AEG-Telefunken
Fried Krupp
Mitsubishi
Pintsch Bamag
Toshiba

Lighting equipment, station buildings
Mitsubishi

Load braking devices
Knorr-Bremse
Mitsubishi

Locomotive equipment
AEG-Telefunken
Ansaldo
Brown Boveri
Daewoo Heavy Industries
Ganz Mavag
Mitsubishi
Siemens
Sulzer Bros
Toshiba

Locomotive equipment electric
AEG-Telefunken
Ansaldo
Brown Boveri
Daewoo Heavy Industries
GEC Traction
Mitsubishi
Siemens

Locomotives, diesel-electric
AEG-Telefunken
Ansaldo
Breda
BRE-Metro
Brown Boveri
Daewoo Heavy Industries
Fiat
Fried Krupp
Ganz Mavag
GEC Industrial Locomotives
GEC Traction
General Motors
Hyundai
Kolmex
Krauss-Maffei
Siemens
SIG
Sulzer Bros

Locomotives, diesel-hydraulic
Breda
BRE-Metro
Daewoo Heavy Industries
Fried Krupp
Ganz Mavag
GEC Industrial Locomotives
GEC Traction
Kolmex
Krauss-Maffei
Fried Krupp
Sulzer Bros

Locomotives, diesel-mechanical
Breda
BRE-Metro
Daewoo Heavy Industries
Ganz Mavag
GEC Industrial Locomotives
Kolmex
Sulzer Bros

Locomotives, electric
AEG-Telefunken
Ansaldo
Breda
BRE-Metro
Brown Boveri
Daewoo Heavy Industries
Fiat
Fried Krupp
Ganz Mavag
GEC Industrial Locomotives
GEC Traction
General Motors
Hyundai
Kolmex
Krauss-Maffei
Fried Krupp
Mitsubishi
Siemens
Sulzer Bros

Locomotives, industrial and mining
AEG-Telefunken
Brown Boveri
Ganz Mavag
GEC Industrial Locomotives
GEC Traction
Krauss-Maffei
Siemens
SIG

Loudspeakers
AEG-Telefunken

Locomotives, tilting body
Fiat

Locomotive washing equipment
Wickham, D.

Manriding cars for underground mines
Kolmex
Wickham, D.

Materials handling equipment
Plasser and Theurer
SIG

Metro/subway cars
AEG-Telefunken
Ansaldo
Breda
BRE-Metro
CIMT
Flug-und Fahrzeugwerke
Ganz Mavag
GEC Traction
Hawker Siddeley Canada
MAN
Siemens
Societe Franco Belge

Motor coaches
AEG-Telefunken
Ansaldo
BRE-Metro
Flug-und Fahrzeugwerke
Ganz Mavag
GEC Traction
MAN
Siemens
SIG

Motors, electric
AEG-Telefunken
Ansaldo
Brown Boveri
Holec
Mitsubishi
Pintsch Bamag
Siemens

[14]

 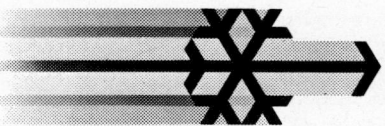

Driving always entails braking.

With running speed in rail transport increasing all the time, it is the brake equipment above all that needs to remain in step. Take disc brakes, for example: featuring short response times and stopping distances, they are capable of braking a train silently and smoothly.

The exacting requirements call for a special concept – the Knorr concept:
- thermal separation of the friction ring from the hub or supporting ring
- single or double axle-mounted or wheel-mounted brake discs of wear-resistant cast iron
- hubs or supporting rings of cast steel.

Knorr brake discs are available also with split friction rings which considerably simplify replacement.

Knorr thus contributes towards shortening travelling as well as replacement times.

Let Knorr tell you more.

 KNORR-BREMSE GMBH MUNICH

CLASSIFIED LIST OF ADVERTISERS

Roller bearing axle-boxes
Ganz Mavag
Kolmex

Rolling stock, railway
BRE-Metro
Daewoo Heavy Industries
GEC Traction
Hawker Siddeley Canada
Hyundai
Kolmex
MAN
Ortner
SIG
Societe Franco Belge
Snia Viscosa
Sulzer Bros
Toshiba

Sanding devices
Ansaldo
Ganz Mavag
Knorr-Bremse
Krauss-Maffei

Seats, passenger
BRE-Metro
Flug-und Fahrzeugwerke
Ganz Mavag
SIG
Snia Viscosa

Signalling systems and apparatus
AEG-Telefunken
Ansaldo
Pintsch Bamag
Siemens

Simulation methodologies
Ansaldo
Ford, Bacon & Davis

Sleepers
Monier

Snow removers
Beilhack

Snow switch cleaners
Zweiweg-Fahrzeug

Special purpose self-propelled railway vehicles
Flug-und Fahrzeugwerke
GEC Industrial Locomotives
Hawker Siddeley Canada
Kolmex
Wickham, D.

Speed control devices
AEG-Telefunken
Brown Boveri
Deuta-Werke
Ganz Mavag
GEC Traction
Holec
Mitsubishi
Siemens

Speed indications
AEG-Telefunken
Deuta-Werke
GEC Traction
Mitsubishi

Standby diesel generators
AEG-Telefunken
MAN

Steam heating apparatus
Pintsch Bamag

Steel castings
BRE-Metro
Dresser
Ganz Mavag

Steel sleepers
Le Materiel de Voie
Pandrol

Steel structures
Breda
BRE-Metro
MAN
SIG

Surface and underground battery and trolley locomotives
AEG-Telefunken
Ansaldo
BRE-Metro
GEC Industrial Locomotives
GEC Traction
Siemens
SIG

Suspension components
Flug-und Fahrzeugwerke

Switchgear, electric
AEG-Telefunken
Ansaldo
Holec
Mitsubishi
Pintsch Bamag
Toshiba

Switch heaters
Brown Boveri
Pintsch Bamag

Switches, trackwork
BRE-Metro

Tank cars
Breda
BRE-Metro
Flug-und Fahrzeugwerke
Kolmex
MAN
SIG
Snia Viscosa
Societe Franco Belge

Telecommunications
AEG-Telefunken
Mitsubishi
Toshiba

Thyristors and thyristor equipment
AEG-Telefunken
Ansaldo
Brown Boveri
GEC Traction
Mitsubishi
Toshiba

Ties
Le Materiel de Voie

Torpedo cars for liquid iron transport
Fried Krupp

Track inspection cars
Kolmex
Wickham, D.

Track liners
Plasser and Theurer

Track maintenance equipment
Elektro-Thermit
Kolmex
Mitsubishi
Monier
Pandrol
Plasser and Theurer
Wickham, D.

Track measuring vehicle (cars & coaches)
Flug-und Fahrzeugwerke
Plasser and Theurer

Track renewal train (gantry cranes)
Plasser and Theurer

Track undercutters
Plasser and Theurer

Trackwork
Grant Lyon Eagre
Pandrol

Traffic control systems
AEG-Telefunken
Ansaldo
Deuta-Werke
Mitsubishi
Pintsch Bamag
Toshiba

Trailers
Flug-und Fahrzeugwerke
Ganz Mavag
MAN
SIG

Tramcars
AEG-Telefunken
Ansaldo
Breda
Brown Boveri
Flug-und Fahrzeugwerke
Ganz Mavag
Hawker Siddeley Canada
Kolmex
MAN
Mitsubishi
Siemens
SIG
SOCIMI

Transformers
AEG-Telefunken
Ansaldo
Mitsubishi
Pintsch Bamag
Toshiba

Trucks
Breda
BRE-Metro
Dresser
Flug-und Fahrzeugwerke
Hawker Siddeley Canada
MAN
SIG
Swiss Aluminium

Turbo-chargers
Brown Boveri
Hispano Suiza

Turbo-generators
AEG-Telefunken
Siemens

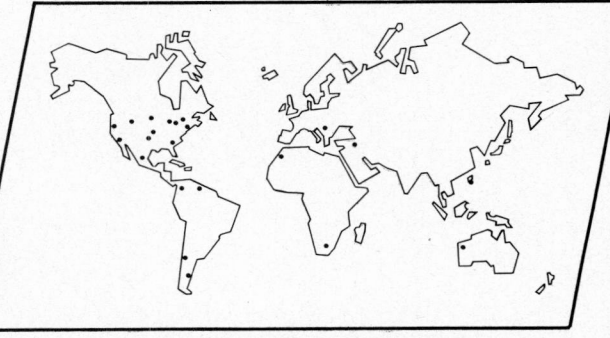

CLASSIFIED LIST OF ADVERTISERS

Two-way vehicles
Siemens
Wickham, D.
Zweiweg-Fahrzeug

Tyres (railway)
Kolmex
Valdunes

Tyres (tramways)
Kolmex

Ultrasonic testing equipment
BRE-Metro
Mitsubishi

Underground supplies vehicles
Siemens
Societe Franco Belge

Vacuum brake equipment
Knorr-Bremse
Toshiba

Vacuum brake testing equipment
Knorr-Bremse

Valves, pneumatic
Knorr-Bremse
Kolmex
Oerlikon-Bührle

Ventilation equipment
Brown Boveri
Mitsubishi
Pintsch Bamag
Toshiba
Voith Getriebe

Ventilators
Toshiba
Voith Getriebe

Video surveillance
Velec-Sefat

Video surveillance with motor carriage monitors
Velec-Sefat

Wagons and carriages
Breda
BRE-Metro
Flug-und Fahrzeugwerke
Hawker Siddeley Canada
Kolmex
MAN
Ortner
SIG
Societe Franco Belge
Snia Viscosa

Water heaters
Mitsubishi
Pintsch Bamag

Welded fabrications
Breda
BRE-Metro
Flug-und Fahrzeugwerke
Ganz Mavag
MAN
Mitsubishi
Wickham, D.

Wheels and axles
Kolmex
SOCIMI
Valdunes

Wheel and axle testing equipment
BRE-Metro
Mitsubishi
Valdunes
Zweiweg-Fahrzeug

Windscreen wipers
Knorr-Bremse

GRUPPO/G

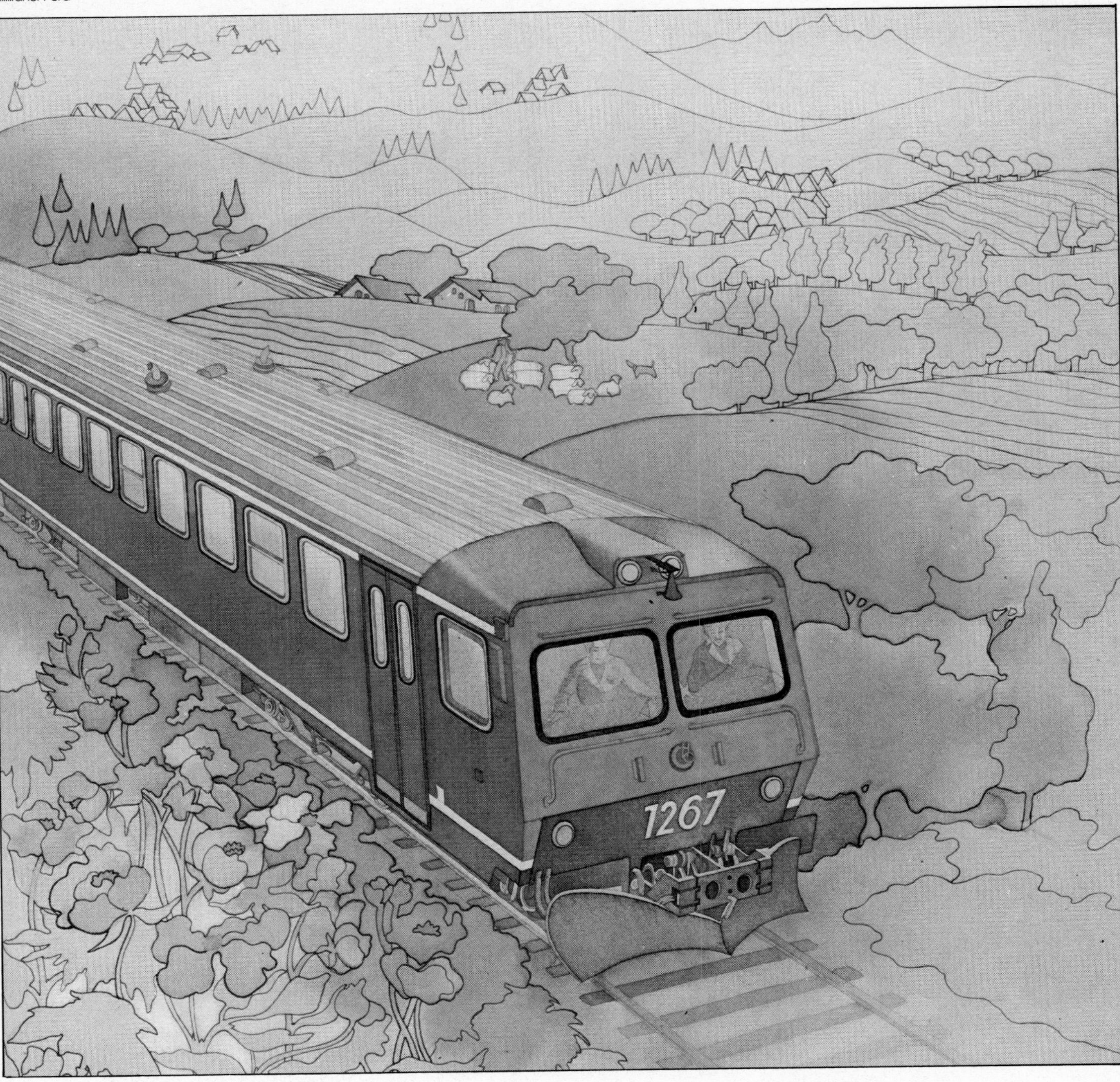

The human dimension.

When the problem is one of choosing a type of transport to cater for emerging needs with respect to the environment, land conservation and human comfort the train's the thing. All over the world.

And Fiat pursues its tradition with a type of diesel railcar that forms a response to the demands of interurban-commuter service, as well as for long journeys: the Aln 668.

Outstanding acceleration, great adaptability to both high and low temperatures, an engine that is the offspring of Fiat's vast experience: with these qualities, the Aln 668 is already travelling the rails of Italy, Sweden, the USA, Mexico, Jugoslavia, Algeria, and many other countries.

Railcar Sweden: features
Twin engine diesel type, 294 Kw

weight about 42 tonnes - 76 seats
max speed 130 k.p.h. (over 80 m.p.h.)

FIAT *FERROVIARIA SAVIGLIANO*

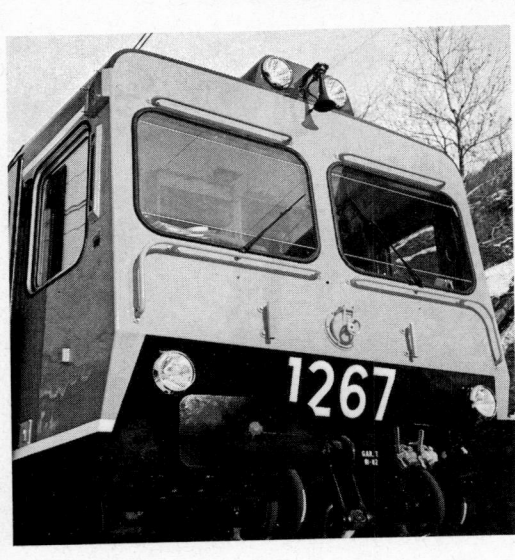

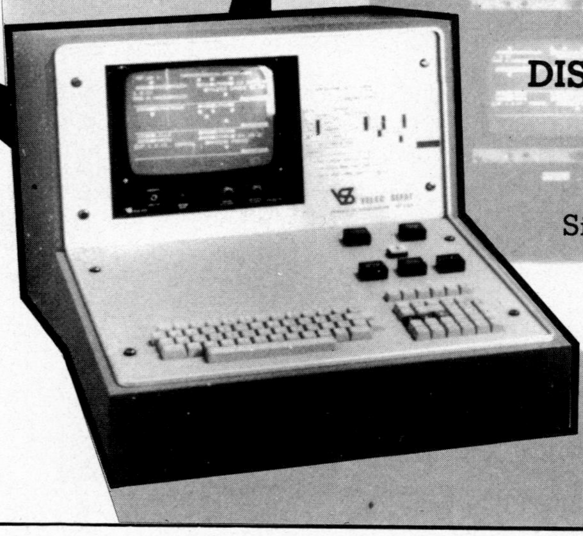

We are travelling years ahead.

High speeds can be a severe trial for passengers, especially on long journeys. It's not enough to provide carriage roominess and efficient function. Comfort starts from below.

That is why Fiat Ferroviaria Savigliano has built a bogie with superior friction-abolishing elasticity that revolutionizes previous technologies.

A bogie already adopted by many countries and which enables you to travel - and arrive - safely and protected at speeds of up to 200 k.p.h. (124 m.p.h.)

Y0270S bogie Eurofima | 2000 units already in service.

FIAT *FERROVIARIA SAVIGLIANO*

Pattern of Progress

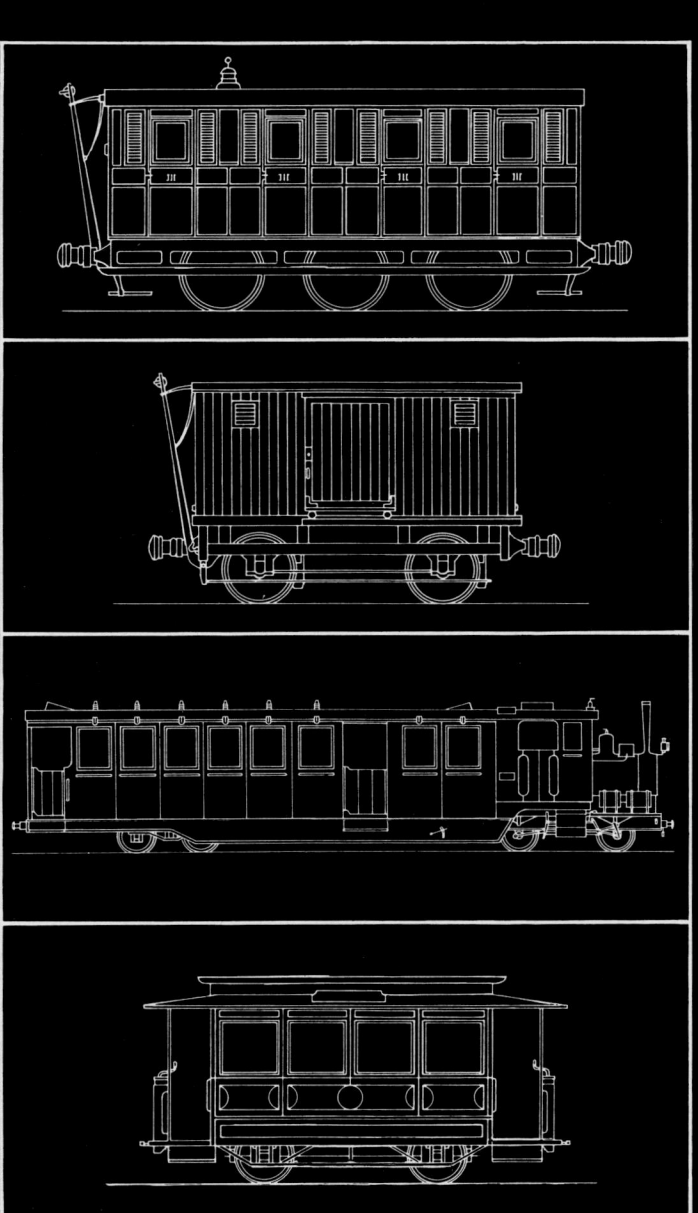

More than 160,000 vehicles for the transport of passengers and goods have been completed in our workshops since our company was founded in 1841. Our customers benefit from the development and manufacturing experience gained worldwide in close collaboration with railway administrations in and outside Germany.

For further information write M.A.N. Dept. Vf
Postfach 44 01 00
D-8500 Nürnberg 44

M.A.N. Rolling Stock

Hitachi rolling stock rolls around the world

In Chile, electric multiple-unit suburban trains are helping to ease transportation problems.

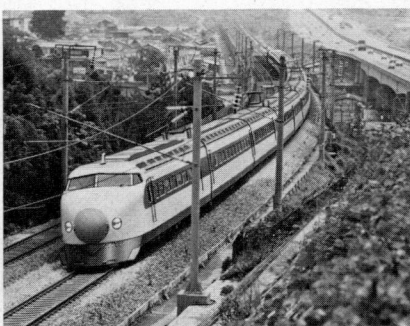

In Japan, the Shinkansen "Bullet Express," a 210 km/h electric train, has set international records for speed and safety.

In Sri Lanka, tourists are riding in comfort on Hitachi's air-conditioned diesel multiple-unit trains.

In Iran, diesel electric locomotives (Bo-Bo, 1050 PS) are being used for shunting and branch line service.

In Morocco, electric locomotives (Co-Co, 3000 kW) are being used to haul phosphate.

In Zaire, electric locomotives (Bo-Bo-Bo, 2400 kW) are helping with industrialization plans.

In Bolivia, diesel electric locomotives (Bo-Bo-Bo, 3020 HP) are providing outstanding service in rugged terrain.

In Nigeria, first class passenger cars supplied by Hitachi are making it more fun to see the country by train.

In Brazil, Hitachi's all stainless steel electric cars are making life easier for commuters on the inter-urban run.

Main Products
- Electric locomotives ● Diesel electric locomotives
- Diesel hydraulic locomotives ● Electric cars
- Diesel railcars ● Monorail cars ● Computerized railway operation and maintenance systems
- Electric equipment for rolling stock and railway substation systems

We keep things rolling

HITACHI

Hitachi, Ltd.
Transportation Equipment Dept. (XL)
6-2, Otemachi 2-chome, Chiyoda-ku, Tokyo 100, Japan
Telephone : Tokyo (03) 270-2111
Cable : "HITACHY" TOKYO
Telex : J22395, J22432, J24491, J26375 (HITACHY)

[26]

We set Standards

Thousands of Krupp locomotives and special rail vehicles stand the test in many countries and also under extreme conditions.

Krupp with their know-how are your partners for all traction tasks, for solving special transportation problems and for questions of rail vehicle fabrication and maintenance.
Krupp are leaders in wheel/rail research and development for tomorrow's railways.

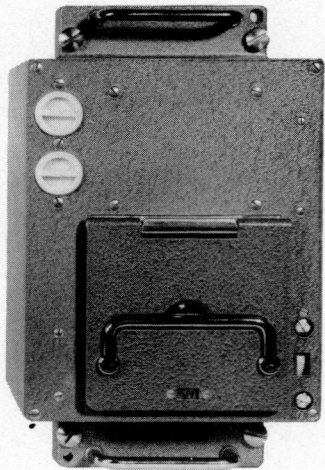
[28]

ISGEC PRESSES

ISGEC, one of the largest manufacturers of Hydraulic Presses, can supply the Wheel & Axle Presses that you need.

With know-how acquired from a world-renowned British firm, ISGEC is capable of producing Wheel & Axle Presses in a wide range presently extending up to 1000 Tonnes.

ISGEC Wheel & Axle presses are suitable for "pressing in" and "pressing off" for all types of wagons and locos. ISGEC also manufactures other types of presses for railway workshops: forging presses, dishing presses, straightening and bending presses, spring buckling and de-buckling presses, lip rolling presses, and other varieties. Already 24 Wheel Presses from ISGEC are in operation.

ISGEC's specialist team of engineers ensures adherence to the highest quality standards. Highly trained welders—the same that help ISGEC match exacting Lloyd's standards of Class I fusion welding—are employed for thick plate welding. While stringent non-destructive testing is diligently enforced.

Finally, all ISGEC presses are incorporated with power packs of such internationally renowned manufacturers as Rexroth, Towlers, Abex Denison and Vickers Sperry. ISGEC's standard range

Superior quality plus low cost produces the cost efficiency that counts

of hydraulic presses includes 9 models varying from 200T to 1000T.

You too can benefit with ISGEC' twin offer—superior quality and low cost. Like so many others hav

Indicative F.O.B. prices are :

● US $ 50,000 for a 400T Press

● US $ 220,000 for a 1000T Pres

THE INDIAN SUGAR & GENERAL ENGINEERING CORPORATION
(The Heavy Engineering Division of Saraswati Industrial Syndicate Ltd.)
Yamunanagar 135 001 (Haryana), India Phone: 1180 to 1184 Telex: DEL 031-3394 Cable: "ISGEC" Yamunanagar
Branches in Bombay, Calcutta, Delhi & Madras

ULKA-IJT-23

Economy and reliability: the far seeing choice for the Thaïland railways.

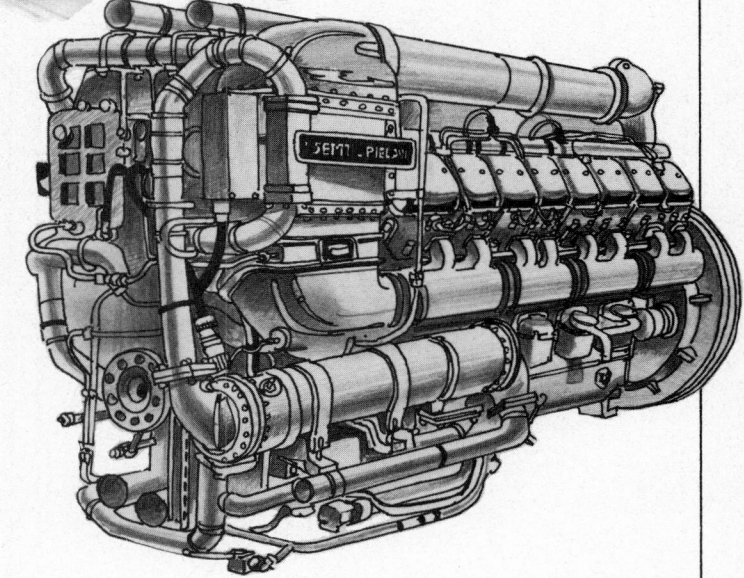

GM experience:
Why more railroads worldwide count on GM locomotives.

We've been delivering locomotives outside the U.S. since 1946. And, to date, we supply more locomotives to railroads than any other manufacturer. In gauges ranging from 3 feet to 5 feet 6 inches. With ratings up to 3900 horsepower. And if you require custom work on your locomotives, we'll build them to your specifications.

But our experience is also based on a lot of other demanding applications. We supply Diesels for ships, oil rigs, power generation systems and standby power units. The result in each case is productivity.

One reason is our engine. EMD engines have supplied over 100 million horsepower—a world record in our horsepower range. And we know a lot about building reliable, economical, easily maintainable Diesels.

The EMD PowerPak, for instance, is a complete cylinder assembly that cuts routine cylinder maintenance time in half.

EMD service engineers are strategically located throughout the world to assist our customers. Our customers also enjoy the advantage of having access to our vast parts distribution system.

So before you invest in your next locomotive, contact your GM representative for information on how GM experience can help make your railroad more productive.

Or write Export Locomotive Sales, Electro-Motive Division of General Motors, La Grange, Illinois 60525. Telex: 270041, Cable: ELMODIV.

ELECTRO-MOTIVE

Division of General Motors Corporation

FFA

Flug- und Fahrzeugwerke AG Telefon 071 43 01 01
Altenrhein Telex: 77230 ffa ch
CH-9423 Altenrhein Telegramm: FFA Rorschach

- Rail passenger and freight carriages
- Steel and light alloy constructions
- Power and passenger carriages for Meter and normal gauge
- Street tram-cars
- More than 25 years experience in light alloy rail-carriage construction

"RIC" coach with folding berths (Type Bcm Z1)

DC TRACTION SPECIALISTS

for both conventional and advanced drive systems

Holec Machines & Systems have wide experience
in traction drives for urban and suburban rolling stock.

Operational:

71 metro trains Rotterdam
37 metro trains (part delivery) Amsterdam
95 trams Rotterdam
25 trams Amsterdam
290 trains suburban services
   Dutch Railways

On order, drives for:

50 metro trains Rotterdam
33 trams (three-phase current) Rotterdam
11 metro trains Amsterdam
53 trams (chopper) The Hague
30 trains Dutch Railways
   Suburban Services
12 trams Amsterdam
27 rapid transit cars Utrecht

All this experience is at your disposal

HOLEC H+H
machines & systems group

smit slikkerveer b.v.
P.O. Box 50
2980 AB Ridderkerk, Holland
Ringdijk 390, Slikkerveer
Telephone: (01804) 136 33
Telex: 20377 wsmit nl

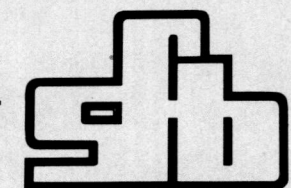

KOLMEX

The sole Polish exporter and importer of rolling-stock offers the following modern and reliable equipment:

- Electric and diesel locomotives
- Electric trains
- Passenger cars and luggage vans
- All types of goods wagons
- Special wagons such as: tank wagons, heavy duty flat wagons and others
- Containers
- Rolling-stock components and spare parts
- Wheel sets, wheels and wheel bands
- Wagon equipment components
- Equipment for railway track maintenance and construction

We export to 44 countries all over the world. Our company is one of the largest rolling-stock exporters in the world. We guarantee competent and reliable service to our customers.

1. A 6D-type, 590 kW diesel locomotive off to Morocco.

2. A 203E-type, two-segment electric locomotive rated at 4,000 kW.

Foreign Trade Enterprise

Mokotowska 49, 00-542 Warszawa

PO Box : 236
Telex : 813270/813714
Phone : 282291
Cables : KOLMEX-WARSZAWA

3. A 408S-type, four-axle special railcar for powdered cargo transport, with load carrying capacity of 47.5 Mg.

KRAUSS MAFFEI

Optimum railway operation with Krauss-Maffei electronics.

Krauss-Maffei railway electronics are the logical response to matters of cost-effectiveness, safety, improvement of adhesion and optimization of performance in railway operations.

With our proven electronic command and monitoring system based on modular technique, any kind of rail vehicle complies with the requirements of better modern technology, safety and economic efficiency by using

– automatic command and control
  including brake control
– wheel-spin and slip protection for
  traction vehicles
– wheel-spin protection for waggons.

The Krauss-Maffei electronic system is ready for installation in any traction vehicle and can be operated in connection with any suitable remote radio control system. Even older locomotives can be modernized with our devices.

Krauss-Maffei has essentially contributed to safety and progress of railway operation in the following areas:

Locomotives
Locomotives of all power ratings and transmissions for domestic and foreign operation in industrial and state railways, including remote control.

Research
Basic research for future rail traction: dynamic simulator for investigating the limits of the wheel/rail system, magnetic levitation technology system TRANSRAPID.

Development
Improvement of riding dynamics and reduction of maintenance costs, main contractors for the development of the mechanical part of the new DB three-phase electric locomotive generation (E 120).

Production
Locomotives, railway electronics, sanding devices, brake discs, rubber buffers, axles, magnetic levitation vehicles, dynamic simulators.

Services
Testing and metrology services, overhaul and modernization, maintenance and spare parts services, licensing and transfer of know-how.

Any request for more detailed information will be promptly responded to. Please do not hesitate to write or phone us.

**Krauss-Maffei Aktiengesellschaft
Transportation
Technology Division
Krauss-Maffei-Strasse 2
D-8000 München 50
Telephone 0 89/8 89 91
Telex 05/23 163**

FUJI HEAVY INDUSTRIES LTD.
all-round specialists in rolling stock

Diesel cars

Passenger coaches

Catenary work cars

Fuji Heavy Industries Ltd. manufactures a full range of top-quality rolling stock. In addition to passenger coaches, diesel motor cars, electric cars and tank cars, our Rolling Stock Division manufactures a wide variety of track and overhead structure construction and maintenance vehicles.

These include small diesel locomotives, railway inspection cars, tower cars, revolving platform cars and maintenance & inspection cars. The wire reel car shown above is part of our Shinkansen task force. We can provide you with our ready designed cars or design rolling stock to meet your requirements. Contact us for further details.

 **FUJI HEAVY INDUSTRIES LTD.**
Rolling Stock Division,
Main Office: Subaru Bldg., 7-2, 1-chome, Nishishinjuku, Shinjuku-ku, Tokyo, 160 Japan
Tel: 03-347-2436/2447   Telex: 232-2268

50 c/s GROUP
GROUPEMENT 50 Hz
50 Hz-ARBEITSGEMEINSCHAFT

**ACEC
AEG-TELEFUNKEN
ALSTHOM-ATLANTIQUE
BROWN BOVERI
MTE
SIEMENS**

E 41/50 Hz 7825

Nineteen months after receiving the order, the first of one hundred 25 kV, 50 Hz Co'Co'-locomotives has been completed and in the meantime handed over to the South African Railways & Harbours.

These new Class 7E-locomotives are thyristor controlled. Each of the two rectifier groups is composed of two semi-controlled bridges in sequence control, and provides facilities for selfcommutation by means of capacitors and

turn-off thyristors-thus reducing reactive power consumption and ensuring high compatibility with the feeding system. The continuous rating of the locomotives is 2925 kW at a speed of 34 km/h.

The mechanical part is built by Union Carriage & Wagon Company (Pty) Ltd. Many other components as rectifiers, equipment frames etc. of the electrical portion are also manufactured in South Africa.

Railway electrification at industrial frequency is economic and efficient. Hence more and more railway companies are adopting this system.

The „50 c/s Group", a group comprising European electrical companies of world repute, caters for all aspects of railway electrification from planning and design to technical co-ordination and the supply of traction rolling stock and stationary installations.

Pooled experience and development enable the very latest techniques to be offered in ideal combinations.

**50 c/s GROUP
POB 433
Löwenstrasse 31
CH 8021 Zürich 1**

50 c/s GROUP
GROUPEMENT 50 Hz
50 Hz-ARBEITSGEMEINSCHAFT

Toshiba is justifiably proud of its "air-conditioning" technology. And no wonder. We've put confortable, refreshing systems into thousands of buildings, factories, and homes. And we scored another "world first" by introducing unit cooling systems for rolling stock. Not only offering top performance, these systems also come in a wide variety of types and capacities to meet every demand.

- A line of unit cooling systems ranging from an underfloor concentration type to a ceiling-mounted, dispersed or concentration type are available in capacities as small as 2,250kcal/h to as large as 42,000kcal/h designed for commuter trains.
- An optimum type of a unit cooling system is selectable according to car size and installation restrictions for both newly built cars as well as for those already in operation.
- The electronic automatic temperature controller constantly maintains car interior temperature at the most comfortable cooling level.
- Toshiba unit cooler systems for about three hundreds of cars have been exported to the Philippines, Australia, Republic of Korea, United Arab, New Zealand, and elsewhere throughout the world.

Toshiba know-how ensures comfortably cool car interiors

Toshiba **TOSHIBA**

TOSHIBA CORPORATION

1-6, UCHISAIWAICHO, 1-CHOME, CHIYODA-KU, TOKYO, 100, JAPAN
TELEX: J22587 TOKYO CABLE: TOSHIBA TOKYO PHONE: TOKYO 501-5411

Ganz-MÁVAG's new 3-unit de luxe Diesel train built for the Tunisian Railways

Top speed: 130 km/h
Engine type: Ganz-MÁVAG/
  S.E.M.T.- Pielstick 8PA4 185
Rated output: 883 kW/1200 HP
Power transmission: hydrodynamic
  with a two-convertor
  transmission type H-122 made by
  Ganz-MÁVAG

Number of seats:
1st Class: 38
2nd Class: 110
Axle-load on standard
gauge: 17,5 metric tons

The train is air-conditioned and is equipped with a multi-purpose bogie developed by Ganz-MÁVAG.

GANZ-MÁVAG
LOCOMOTIVE AND RAILWAY CARRIAGE
MANUFACTURERS, MECHANICAL ENGINEERS

H-1967 BUDAPEST
Telex: 22-5575

POB 136

Phone: 335-950

Cables:
Ganzmávag

Voith perfect the drive systems of modern railcars

Voith have been manufacturing power drive components for railcars for a great many years, earning a worldwide reputation in the process and developing of a highly specialist knowledge of the locomotive industry.

We are thoroughly familiar with the engineering problems posed by difficult operational conditions – in the desert or the tropics, during sub-zero winters, at high attitudes, on high-speed stretches through flat country – as well as the characteristics of narrow-gauge railways. All these factors have been taken into account in the perfecting of the drive system.

Our aim is to achieve compatability between engine, transmission, cardan shafts, axle drive and cooling unit. Voith's comprehensive service embraces all necessary calculation work and assistance in control system design through to advice, training and after-sales service, and is available throughout the world.

In the final analysis Voith's expertise can provide the key to your power drive problems.

1 Transmission
2 Brake
3 Axle gearbox
4 Cardan shaft
5 Cooling unit

G 7835 e/'35

Voith products for railcars:
- Hydrodynamic transmissions
- Hydrodynamic brakes
- Axle gearboxes
- Cardan shafts
- Cooling units
- Cooperation in the design and improvement of drive controls.

Voith Getriebe KG
P.O. Box 1920, D-7920 Heidenheim
Telephone (07321) 3291, Telex 0714888

VOITH

RELIABLE TRACTION ENGINES
even under extrem climate conditions

Output range from 90 to 4420 kW (120 to 6000 hp)

DIESEL POYAUD: 135 and 150 mm bore - **DIESEL SACM:** 175, 195 and 240 mm bore

1	2	3
4	5	6

1. CC type locomotive - 1 × 2945 kW - Peoples' Republic of China
2. CC type locomotive - 1 × 2945 kW - French State Railways
3. 4 B type locomotive - 1 × 2650 kW - Cameroun Railways
4. AD12B type locomotive - 1 × 885 kW - Burma Railways
5. Fast railcar 2 × 773 kW
   One traction unit at each end of the train
   Yugoslavia
6. Y 8000 type shunting locomotive - 220 kW - French State Railways

Photos : SACM · ALSTHOM/ATLANTIQUE · MTE · MOYSE · H+H Conseil

[45]

CIMT

**CIMT LORRAINE
60 YEARS OF TECHNICAL PROGRESS
AND EXPERIENCE IN THE FIELD OF PASSENGER
TRANSPORT AT YOUR SERVICE.**

éditions RC PARIS 748 201 H-M-3

MASS TRANSIT
AND COMMUTER TRAINS

DOUBLE DECK TRAINS

PASSENGER COACHES

DIESEL RAILCARS

CABLE CARS

GANG CARS

PRELIMINARY STUDIES
OF COMPLETE SYSTEMS

MANAGEMENT
OF INDUSTRIAL
CONSORTIUMS

CIMT LORRAINE

COMPAGNIE INDUSTRIELLE DE
MATÉRIEL DE TRANSPORT

42, AV. RAYMOND-POINCARÉ,
75116 PARIS - TÉL. : 505.14.00
TELEX : CIMTRAM 610119 F.

Paris mass transit

Marseilles mass transit

Ivory coast railcar

Mexico City mass transit

Paris suburban double deck coaches

Trolleybus

[47]

DAEWOO ROLLS ON

SOLVE ROLLING STOCK PROBLEMS ECONOMICALLY

Daewoo Heavy Industries' Rolling Stocks Division, a recognized producer of sturdy, dependable, precision made freight cars, deluxe passenger cars, electric subway cars and other rolling stock, successfully built and tested its first locomotive in 1978 and is now able to meet any requirements of the customers to their full satisfaction.

Daewoo's rolling stock have already received wide acclaim for their superior performance in Southeast Asia, Argentina, New Zealand and Bangladesh. Efforts are now expanding to other parts of the globe where Daewoo rolling stock are becoming more and more the economical answer to railway transport problems. For further details, contact us — we'll keep you on the right track.

DAEWOO
DAEWOO HEAVY INDUSTRIES LTD

•HEAD OFFICE & FACTORY 6, Manseog-Dong, Dong-Gu, Incheon, Korea Tel.: Incheon (72) 1011-16, (72) 2011-16 Telex: DHILTD K28473, Cable: DHILTD INCHEON •SEOUL OFFICE KOSAMI Bldg. 5-8th Fl., C.P.O. Box 7955, Seoul, Korea Tel.: (783) 4611—5, (783) 4811—5 Telex: DHILTD K23301 •ANYANG FACTORY 462-2, Samri, Euiwang-Myeon, Shiheung-Gun, Kyeonggi-Do, Korea Tel.: Anyang (2) 6171—4

turbosuperchargers

HISPANO-SUIZA

**Division Turbomachines Industrielles - B.P. 60 - Rue du Capitaine Guynemer
92270 BOIS-COLOMBES - Téléphone: 780.71.70 - Télex: 620131 F**

[51]

HYUNDAI builds tomorrows.

"HYUNDAI Rolling Stock can go every place where railway goes" with broadly experienced and highly skilled manpower and a complete range of modern equipment. HYUNDAI offers to railway around the world finest locomotives and other rolling stock with durable construction, easy maintenance, smooth riding and safety, for every purpose, for every gauge and to every specification at the most reasonable price.

Diesel-electric locomotive
Electric locomotive
Electric rail car
Passenger coach
Freight car
& other railway rolling stock.

 HYUNDAI
ROLLING STOCK CO., LTD.

NEW!

Generating Equipment for Interior Ventilation of Railroad Refrigerator Trucks

This particular generating equipment serves, in connection with four ventilators, the interior ventilation of railroad refrigerator trucks with 2 ice-boxes.

The slipringless generator of the revolving-field type consists of two phases offset 90⁰ spatially and 180⁰ electrically and not interlinked when led to the terminal board. This arrangement has the advantage that the voltage maintains the direction of rotation independently of the generator's direction of rotation.

The efficiency of the generator amounts to 2 x 285 VA, a power sufficient to supply four ventilators arranged inside the truck, each of which is driven by a brushless AC motor. On the generator a crank handle is provided for checking the generator, when the railroad truck is stationary.
If it is not intended to ventilate the goods due for refrigerating during the journey itself, the said generator can be switched off by means of the crank used for checking as mentioned above.

PINTSCH BAMAG
DINSLAKEN

PINTSCH BAMAG Antriebs- und Verkehrstechnik GmbH · D-4220 Dinslaken · Postfach 10 04 20/40 · Tel. (02134) 602-1* · Telex 08551938

The other landmark of Paris will be in aluminium.

Paris has always given technology a chance. This was not only demonstrated by the famous steel tower erected by Mr. Gustave Eiffel, but also by the decision of the Paris Metro to use aluminium for the first time for its new trains.
Everyone knows that aluminium weighs less than steel, but is more expensive. The Alusuisse consulting engineers therefore developed a new technology permitting the 1000 cars to be made from preformed elements – called extruded sections by the experts. These elements, with cross-sections up to 600 mm and each of 15 metres length, are welded together. This simplified assembly saves the French manufacturer, Société Franco-Belge de Matériel de Chemins de Fer, so much labour that the new trains can be produced more economically than conventional designs. Quite apart from the saving in driving power.
When, therefore, the new trains are running beneath the streets of Paris, it will be possible to say that the material has changed but the spirit has remained the same. The spirit which places technology at the service of mankind.

Aluminium is our business.

Swiss Aluminium Ltd.
Buckhauserstr. 11, CH-8048 Zurich, Tel. 01/54 22 41, Telex 52310

[56]

ANSALDO group

In the Public Transport Field

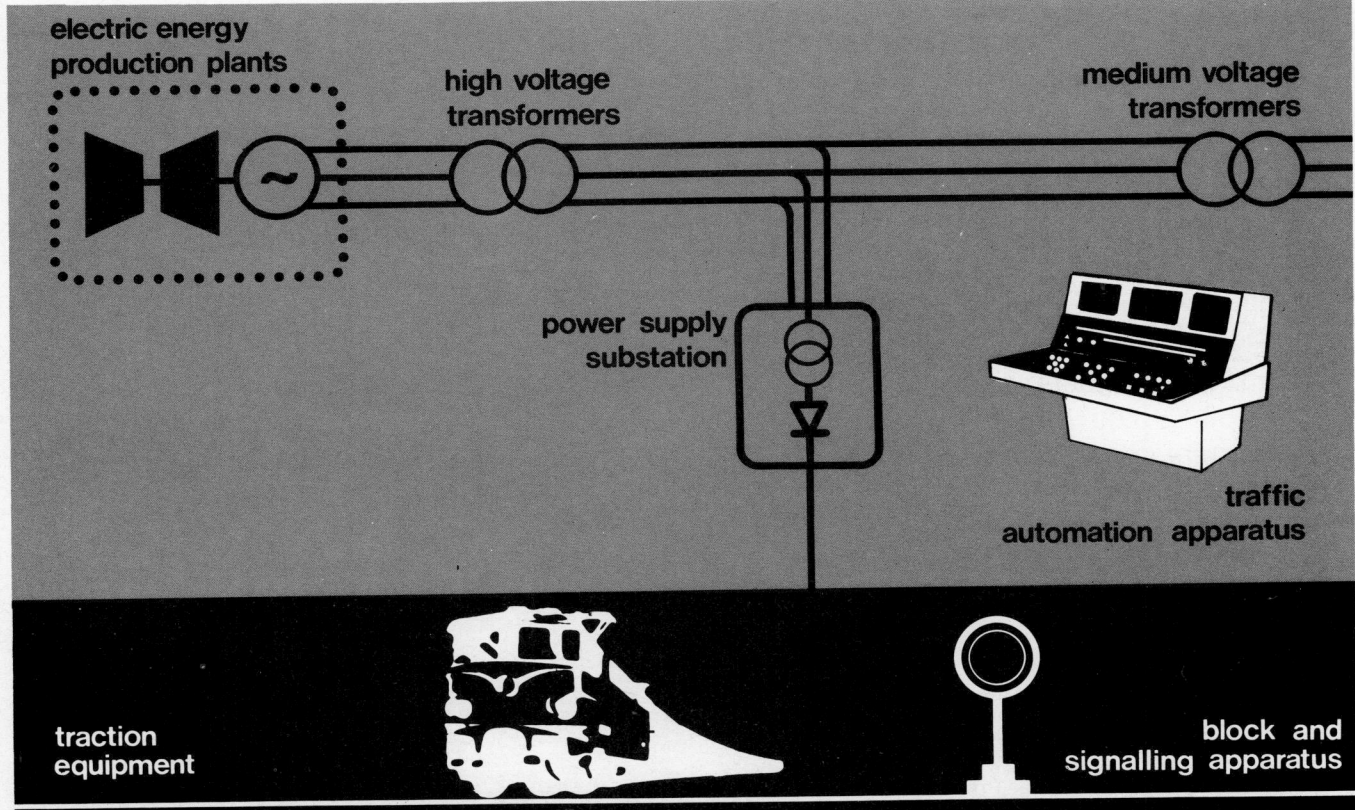

electric energy production plants

high voltage transformers

medium voltage transformers

power supply substation

traffic automation apparatus

traction equipment

block and signalling apparatus

Electrified public transport is one of the most significant exploitation of electric energy.

Efficient electrified public transport is the best answer to collective transportation needs, environmental preservation, energy savings.

Electrified public transport, in order to be a fast, confortable, reliable service, becomes more and more an integrated system of advanced technologies.

The transport and distribution sector of **ANSALDO** group with its human resources, experiences, innovation capabilities in the field of advanced electromechanical and electronic technologies, is in a position to supply:

- electrical equipment both with conventional and thyristor control for:

☐ railway motive power units
☐ urban, suburban and subway vehicles

- railway and rapid transit signalling, traffic control and automation apparatus
- power supply substations for electrified transport systems
- a.c. and d.c. traction motors, electronic converters and regulators, diodes and thyristors, ancillary apparatus and machines
- simulation and operational research methodologies for transport system planning, designing and optimum management
- power transformers and reactors, both normalized and special up to the maximum ratings and voltages
- assembling, installation, service

Furthermore, it masters all the phases of electric energy distribution and exploitation in the field of transport.

The transport and distribution sector includes manufacturing and engineering units in Genoa, Milan, Pomezia and Naples.

The sector's head office is in Naples.

ANSALDO Group
Transport and Distribution Sector

Via Nuova delle Brecce 260
80147 Naples

TWO WAYS MITSUBISHI MAKES RAIL TRAVEL COMFORTABLE.

TOKYO

NAGOYA

KYOTO

SHIN-OSAKA

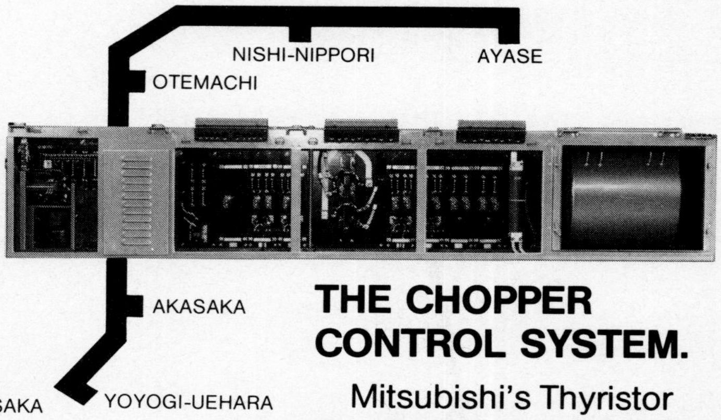

NISHI-NIPPORI

AYASE

OTEMACHI

AKASAKA

YOYOGI-UEHARA

SHIN-KOBE

HIROSHIMA

HAKATA

THE WN DRIVE SYSTEM.

You'll find Mitsubishi's WN Drive System used on JNR's crack 210 km/h Shinkansen bullet trains. This system makes rail travel a quiet, comfortable experience. Mitsubishi's WN Drive System consists of a completely spring-mounted motor, an axle-mounted self-contained gear unit, and a flexible gear coupling. To date, there are well over 25,000 units in daily use. For performance and reliability that's way out front, look to Mitsubishi's well-proven, durable system.

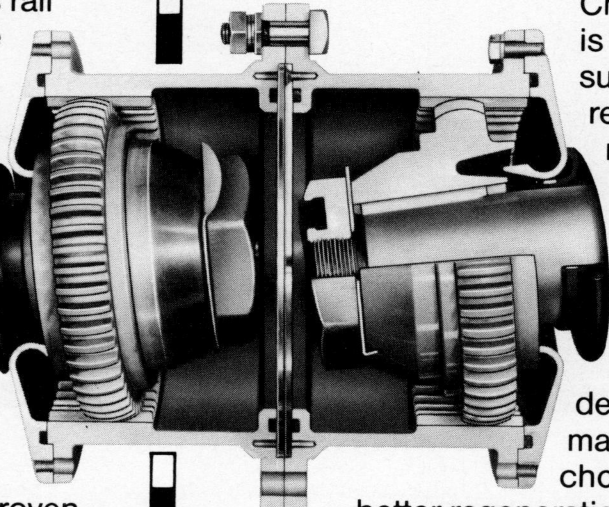

THE CHOPPER CONTROL SYSTEM.

Mitsubishi's Thyristor Chopper Control System is particularly suited for subways because it replaces control-circuit resistors with a virtually maintenance-free electronic control system that dramatically reduces heat build-up in both powering and braking. We have also developed an AVF (Automatic Variable Field) chopper system featuring better regeneration performance and excellent automatic field control. This system is successfully being used by the TRTA, Nankai Electric Railway and Nagoya Municipal Transportation Bureau.

MITSUBISHI ELECTRIC

MITSUBISHI ELECTRIC CORPORATION, 2-3, Marunouchi 2-chome, Chiyoda-ku, Tokyo 100. TELEX: J24532 Cable: MELCO TOKYO

Braking – braking – braking...

We are braking too — since we are specialists in this field. Of course, always with the exact air-pressure resulting in reliability of operation.
With this in mind we know precisely how much depends on our railway braking control systems.

35–77

RAILWAY CONSTRUCTIONS

CONSTRUCTION AND REPAIR OF

- PASSENGER, LUGGAGE AND MAIL CARS
- COOLING AND REFRIGERATING CARS
- COVERED AND UNCOVERED GOODS WAGGONS, FLAT AND SPECIAL WAGGONS AND TANK-CARS

JANE'S
WORLD RAILWAYS

TWENTY-SECOND EDITION

EDITED BY
PAUL GOLDSACK

1980-81

JANE'S

LONDON • NEW YORK • SYDNEY

"Jane's" is a registered trade mark

Copyright © 1980 by Jane's Publishing Company Limited

Published in the United Kingdom by
Jane's Publishing Company Limited, 238 City Road, London EC1V 2PU

ISBN 0 7106 0704 0

Published in the United States of America by
Jane's Publishing Incorporated, 730 Fifth Avenue, New York, NY 10019

ISBN 0 531 03938 2

ALL TYPES OF SLEEPER, ALL TYPES OF RAILWAY, ALL TYPES OF CLIMATE.

ONE MAKE OF RAIL CLIP.

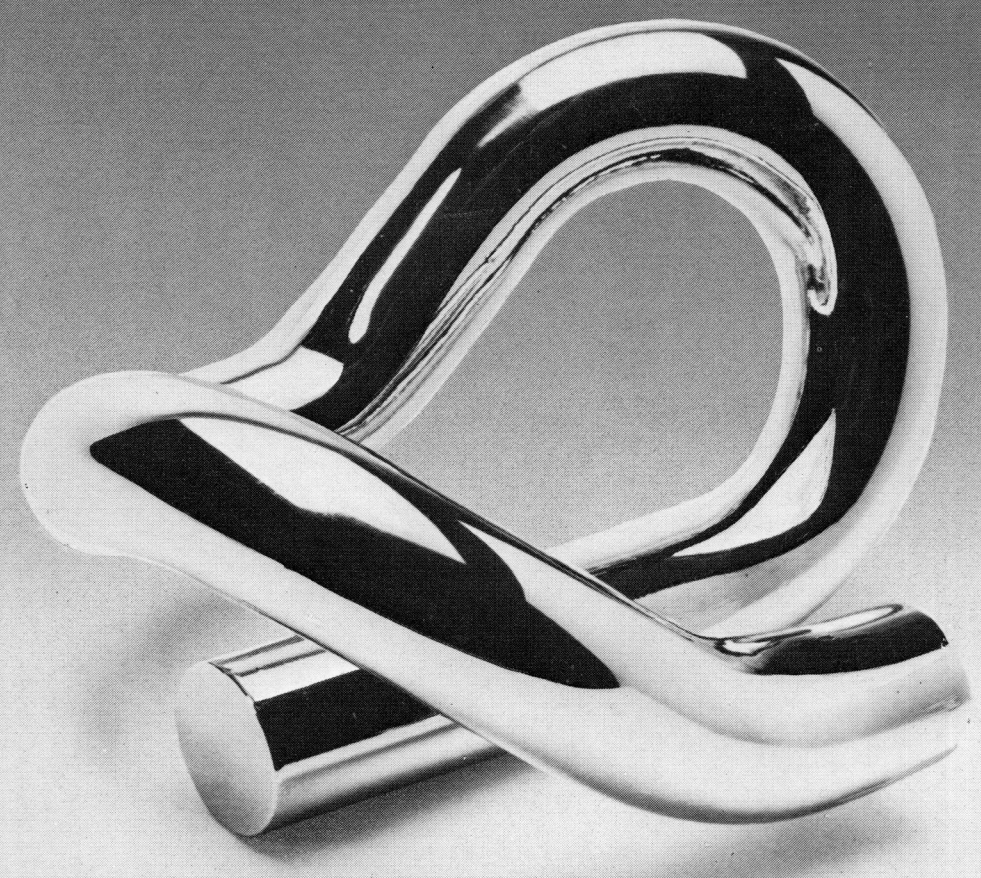

THE CLIP

CONTENTS

FOREWORD

A new railway age is approaching, spurred by the belated acceptance by governments that the world's energy resources are swiftly diminishing. That much, at least, is clear as we enter a new decade. Governments in all continents are spending more now on railways: on modernisation, electrification and new construction, than for generations. And if railways had not been around for so many years, people would be exclaiming at the wonder of this miracle of energy-efficient transport technology. One positive result of the rediscovery of the railway is that the railway supply industry is not being affected quite so badly as other sectors of industry by the economic crisis now afflicting so much of the Western hemisphere. One estimate published earlier this year put the figure for international railway capital expenditure in 1980 (excluding the Eastern bloc) at US $32,000 million, a substantial increase on investment in 1979. But there have been some casualties, notably in the freight car field. The great French company Franco-Belge went into receivership in July; and the chill wind blowing through the freight car market is being generated not only by the general slowdown of freight traffic, but also by the introduction of sophisticated computer technology in the operation and control of freight car fleets. Better utilisation has made it possible for many railways sharply to reduce freight car purchases.

In the United States freight traffic slumped in the second quarter of 1980 to produce a gloomy picture for operators and suppliers alike. On 1 July about 200,000 of a total fleet estimated at 1,700,000 freight cars were standing empty, thousands of locomotives were idle, and thousands of workshop staff had been laid off. Current US estimates are for the manufacture of 70,000 new freight cars this year, compared with 90,000 in 1979, and even this estimate may prove optimistic. One component supplier in the US expects the figure to drop to about 40,000 in 1981. Fortunately most Class 1 railways are in a much better position to ride out the storm than would have been the case two or three years ago. Class 1 railways together earned US $813.9 million in net income in 1979, the best result since 1966. And during the first quarter of 1980, as a result of a mild winter, higher freight tariffs and other factors, net earnings reached $274 million, more than five times that of the comparable period of 1979.

Much, much higher earnings may be expected by the end of the decade if current moves towards merger are approved by the government. By then only three or four giant Class 1 railways may remain and each will have a near-monopoly in its territory. Seven major mergers are now under study: Burlington Northern and Frisco; Santa Fe and Southern Pacific; Norfolk & Western and Southern; Union Pacific and Western Pacific; Chessie System and Seaboard Coastline Industries; Union Pacific and Missouri Pacific; and Grand Trunk Western with Detroit, Toledo & Ironton. Southern Pacific also plans purchase of the Rock Island Tucumcari line. Should all these mergers go through, they will almost certainly produce for the new railroads a sharply increased return on investment. They will also make the whole US railway system more vulnerable to take-over by the Federal Government: a possibility made less improbable by the creation of the federally-funded Amtrak and Conrail corporations.

The increasing price of fuel oil and the energy crisis itself have been contributing factors to the economic downturn in the west. But both factors improve the long-term prospects for railways. For the first time since the early 1950s railways may now start substantially to increase their share of the market, reversing the downward trend of the past 30 years. Far-sighted governments in Europe and other parts of the world, recognising railways as more energy-efficient than other modes of transport, are supporting and extending their railway systems. West Germany, for instance, makes massive compensation payments annually to Deutsche Bundesbahn (DB) for 'social costs' borne by the railway. At the same time DB is continuing with a huge programme of capital investment: almost DM 4600 million this year alone. France, Italy, Spain and Austria, not to mention the Soviet Union and other Comecon countries, are all spending heavily on railway development. Only in Britain does government policy deny the kind of capital investment necessary to extend electrification and improve the railway's competitive position. Belgium, with a railway less than a quarter the extent of British Rail, is spending more on railway modernisation this year than Britain.

Railway growth is a world-wide phenomenon: Brazil, China, Iraq, Algeria, the Soviet Union are all involved in massive construction projects. The remarkable growth of railways in China is likely to be matched by even faster growth to the end of the century. Over the past 30 years China has spent more than 30,000 million yuan (about US $23,000 million) on building new lines. Now six new main lines are to be built, with construction for three lines scheduled to begin this year, next year and 1982. And work is moving fast on a new line which will link Beijing (Peking) with Lhasa, the capital of Tibet. Alongside new construction goes the continued extension of electrification in China and in many other countries. Only in North America is there solid resistance on account of the very high initial capital costs. The energy crisis would need to get very much more serious before any railway in the United States or Canada decided to put really substantial sums into electrification.

Less is likely to be said about super speeds in this decade than in the seventies. Many railroad operators are coming to the conclusion, and rightly, that when you try to make a train ape an aeroplane you lose the best characteristics of both. So we are unlikely to see trains operating at speeds of 250 km/h, except on very short stretches, on either Italy's high-speed Direttissima line or on the new Paris-Sudest line. And Britain's Advanced Passenger Train, scheduled to enter revenue service in October, will operate at a maximum of 200 km/h, though designed for 250 km/h operation. But more will be done to improve comfort, service and reliability: the three factors which attract passengers to the railway.

If the move back to railways can be clearly seen, the move towards city rail transit systems is likely to be more dramatic.

CONCRETE SLEEPERS MADE TO ORDER FOR YOUR KIND OF TRAFFIC.

Monier supplies specially designed prestressed sleepers to private industry and Government authorities and has done since the Company pioneered the development and manufacture of concrete sleepers in Australia more than twenty years ago.

Our special pride is our proven manufacturing systems which are low in capital cost, low in labour content and flexible in capacity to meet varying client demands.

Should you want further information or a copy of our introductory booklet, "Prestressed Concrete Railway Sleepers", 'phone or write to any office of Monier Limited.

MONIER CONCRETE SLEEPERS

For a short period in the seventies there was some hesitation as city and government authorities pondered the very high cost of going underground. Now the pace has quickened again. And many of those cities which, like Paris, have had effective rail transit systems for many years, are expanding those systems under the pressure of congested city streets. Where cost was a major factor in delaying the adoption of transit plans, many cities are now opting for light rail surface systems far removed from the old trundling tramway concept. New underground metro and surface light rail systems are being built all over Europe, in India, Japan, China, Egypt, the United States and other parts of the world.

Those people who, just a few short years ago, were forecasting the early demise of the railway are now strangely quiet. The railway is coming into its own.

The Publisher
July 1980

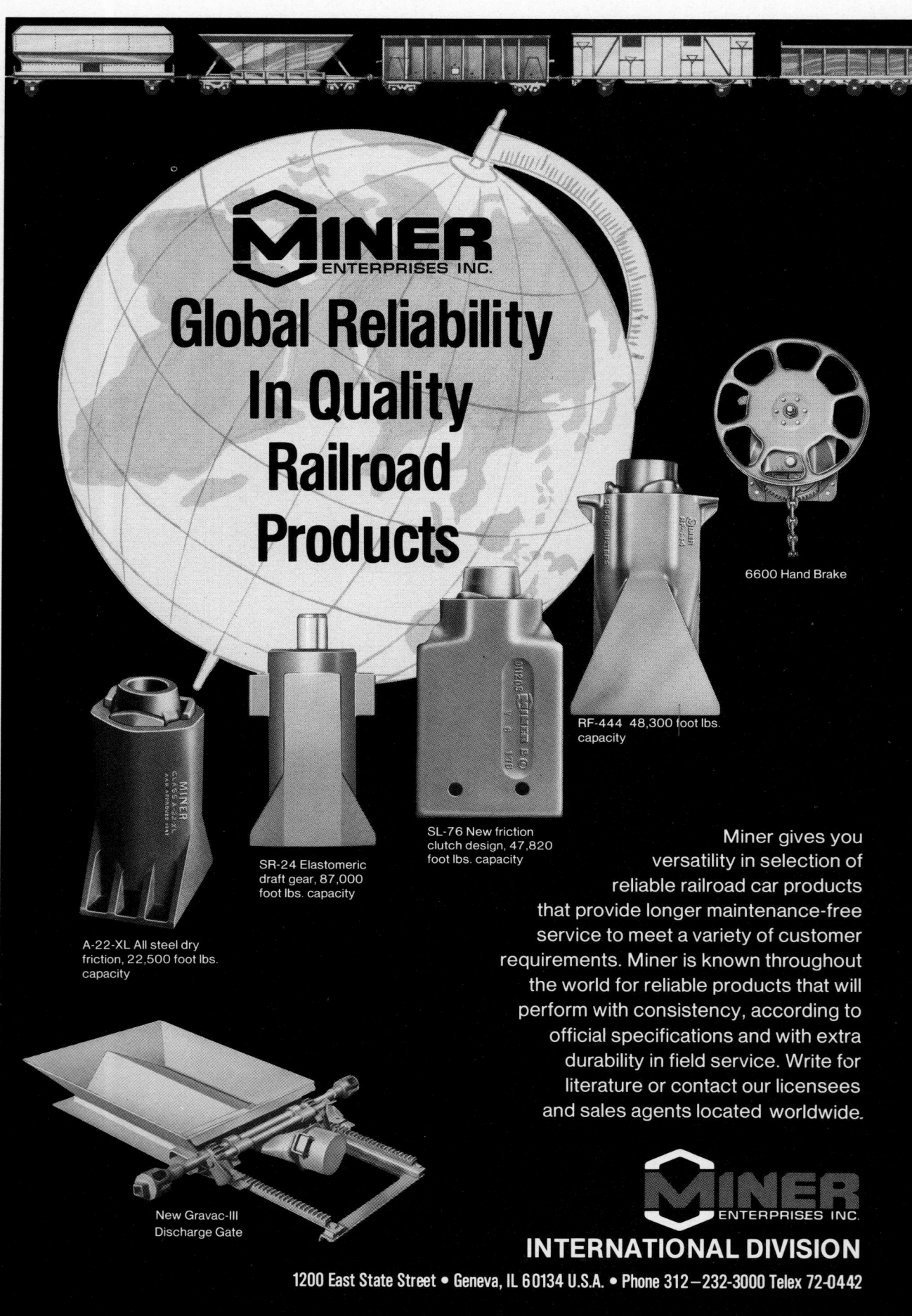

MANUFACTURERS

LOCOMOTIVES AND ROLLING STOCK

ACEC
Ateliers de Constructions Electriques de Charleroi

ACEC BP4, B-6000 Charleroi 1, Belgium

Telephone: 3271 36 20 20
Telegrams: ACEC, Charleroi
Telex: 51.227

Products: Railway, tramway and metro electric equipment for locomotives, railcars and multiple unit stock.

President: A Dubuisson
Managing Director: P Uytden Hoef
Director, Transport Division: G Tanghe
Marketing Director: A Leriche

Constitution: Founded 1904
Turnover: Total BFr. 12 805 million (consolidated BFr. 17 810 million)
Exports: BFr. 4 220 million
Number of employees: 8 506
Major shareholders: Westinghouse World Investment Corp (47.9%); Société Générale de Belgique (6.5%)

ACF
ACF Industries, Incorporated
Amcar Division
Shippers Car Line Division

Head Office: 750 Third Avenue, New York, New York 10017, USA

Amcar Division: Main & Clark Streets, St Charles, Missouri 63301, USA
Telephone: (314) 724 7850

Shippers Car Line Division: 620 N Second Street, St Charles, Missouri 63301, USA
Telephone: (314) 723 9600

Products: Amcar designs and builds freight cars for railroads, industrial shippers, and Shippers Car Line's lease fleet. Amcar also produces railway car parts, piggyback trailer hitches, ingot mould and mine cars, pressure vessels, mixing bowls and storage tanks. Shippers Car Line leases and sells special-purpose railroad freight and tank cars to industrial corporations and provides maintenance for cars in the service lease fleet at seven plants.

President: Henry A Correa
Amcar General Manager: James C O'Hara
Shippers Car Line General Manager: Bruce A Gustafsen

Sales: Freight wagon orders received during 1978 came from the following purchasers: Burlington Northern (200 XL wagons); Chessie (565 covered hopper wagons); Chicago & Illinois Midland (46 gondola wagons); Chicago, Rock Island & Pacific (20 covered hoppers); Elgin, Joliet & Eastern (1 000 gondola wagons); Florida East Coast (200 flat wagons); Grand Trunk Western (172 box wagons); Itel Corporation (1 000 flat wagons, 1 552 box cars); Missouri-Kansas-Texas (100 covered hopper wagons); Missouri Pacific (750 box wagons, 200 covered hopper wagons); Railbox (2 210 box wagons); Seaboard Coast Line (575 covered hopper wagons); Southern Pacific (50 flat wagons, 500 hopper wagons, 700 box wagons); Trailer Train (700 flat wagons); Union Pacific (400 covered hopper wagons); Various industrial companies (11 276 assorted types); Western Pacific (50 covered hopper wagons).

Southern Pacific's new articulated, double-stacked cars
The crane loads six containers on the revolutionary design of car, built in three units over just four sets of wheel bogies. The car is said to reduce the weight of rail equipment needed to carry the containers by 50 per cent, compared to single-level flat wagons.

Coalveyor open wagon is the largest of four sizes offered by ACF
The wagon has a capacity of 1 200 m³ (4 240 cu ft). Elimination of the centre sill, normally a feature of wagons of this type, provides a clean bore interior.

AEBI
Robert Aebi AG

Uraniastrasse 31-33, 8023 Zürich, Switzerland

Telephone: (01) 211 09 70
Telegrams: AEBI, Zürich
Telex: 813 795

Products: Diesel-hydraulic and diesel-mechanical locomotives.

AECKERLE
Hugo Aeckerle

2000 Hamburg 66 (Ohlstedt), Bredenbekstrasse 12, Federal Republic of Germany

Telephone: 6 05 01 69
Telegrams: UNILOK, Hamburg
Telex: 02-12359

Products: Unilok road/rail shunting locomotives.

AEG-TELEFUNKEN
Nachrichten-und Verkehrstechnik AG, Geschäftsbereich Bahnen

Head Office: Hohenzollerndamm 150, D-1000 Berlin 33, Federal Republic of Germany

Works: Gutleutstrasse 82, D-6000 Frankfurt (Main), Federal Republic of Germany

Telephone: (030) 828-1
Telegrams: ELEKTRON BAHNEN, Berlin
Telex: 185 498

Products: Electric equipment for ac/dc locomotives, rail cars, multiple units including diesel-electric vehicles for mainline and branchline services, mining and industrial locomotives, transit stock for suburban and underground railways, trams and trolleybuses.

Constitution: For more than 80 years AEG-Telefunken has been concerned with the development of generation, distribution, and consumption of electric power for all purposes. Manufacture of traction equipment started in 1889, and to date, more than 9 000 locomotives have been equipped by AEG-Telefunken.

Turnover: DM 7 867 million of which transport equipment accounted for 6 per cent of the total.
Exports: DM 4 430 million.
Number of employees: 87 000.
Major shareholders: General Electric Overseas Capital Corporation, New York, USA.

Sales: AEG-Telefunken delivered the electrical equipment for a series of 73 freight locomotives class 151 (16 2/3 Hz, 15 kV) for the German Federal Railways (DB) in co-operation with Krupp, Essen. Class 151 locomotive has a Co Co wheel arrangement, a nominal rating of 6000 kW at 95 km/h and a maximum speed of 120 km/h.
For the delivery of two and four-system locomotives in 1966, AEG-Telefunken pioneered the introduction of power electronics in electric locomotives. The success of this research and development work is demonstrated by the 25 two-frequency locomotives series 181.2 delivered in 1974 to German Federal Railways.
AEG-Telefunken further developed the thyristor rectifiers for the electrical multiple unit trains ET420 of the German Federal Railways and participated in the supply of more than 100 complete electrical equipments for these trains in the period 1970-78.
These three-car units have a continuous output of 2 400 kW and a maximum speed of 120 km/h.
As a member of the 50 c/s GROUP the company participated in deliveries of 90 electric locomotives (60 Hz, 25 kV) for Korean National Railroad (KNR).
In January 1978 the first of the new SAR class 7E locomotives was handed over by the 50 c/s GROUP. A hundred units were delivered in 1978/79. These locomotives, at 3 000 kW continuous rating, are the first ac type locomotives for the South African Railways (SAR).
AEG-Telefunken designed the thyristor converter equipment with LUB Sector Control as well as the traction motors and is delivering a substantial part of the equipment. Thyristor rectifier drives were delivered by AEG-Telefunken for 46 electrical multiple units type JZ 411 of the Yugoslav Railways.
20 LUB sector control thyristor drives for the Austrian Federal Railways were under delivery in 1979. 20 further LUB drives are on order.

AFNE
Astilleros y Fabricas Navales del Estado

Corrientes 672, 1043 Buenos Aires, Argentina

Telephone: 45 7031/39

Products: Diesel-hydraulic locomotives, rolling stock and bogies.

Sales: AFNE is building 100 diesel-hydraulic shunting locomotives for Argentine Railways (KA) under Cockerill (Belgium) licence.

AGEVE
AB Gävle Vagnverkstad

Telephone: (026) 11 58 90
Telegrams: AGEVE, Gävle
Telex: 47106

PO Box 655, S-80127 Gävle, Sweden

Products: Freight wagons and mine locomotives.

New equipment: Range of special-purpose wagons produced by AGV includes: ore unit with loading capacity of 80 tons; Uahs tank wagon, capacity 50 tons, volume 63 m³; Qbo long-loader with capacity of 45 tons on a platform length of 22 m. Mine equipment includes two- and four-axle tipping wagons and 18 types of locomotive. Battery, electric and diesel locomotives are available.

Constitution: AGEVE was founded in 1933. It employs about 300 and reports an annual turnover of around SKr. 75 million.

Sales: AGEVE won an order for 610 freight wagons from Zambian Railways during 1979. The bogies have been contracted out to Gloucester Railway Carriage & Wagon of the UK.

Ore transport wagon
Gauge 1.435 m; volume 28.5 m³; weight 24.8 tonnes; payload 63.2 tonnes; axle load 22.0 tonnes.

Insulated tank wagon for oil transport
Gauge 1.435 m; length 14.340 m; volume 63 m³; weight 22.8 tonnes; axle load 20 tonnes; max speed 100 km/h. The tank is insulated and fitted with interior heating pipes.

ALCAN
Alcan Canada Products

Telephone: 416 366 7211
Telegrams: ALCAN, Canada

Box 269, Toronto-Dominion Centre, Toronto, Ontario, Canada

Products: Aluminium bodies for freight wagons and passenger coaches.

Sales: The LRC (Lightweight Rapid Comfortable) is being developed jointly by Alcan, Dofasco and MLW-Industries. Built with the financial backing of the Federal Department of Industry (Canada) and extensively tested with the assistance of the Federal Transportation Development Agency, the LRC is designed to operate at high speeds as a push pull unit with up to 12 coaches and a locomotive at each end or as a shorter unit with a single locomotive. Lightness, low centre of gravity, diesel-electric traction and a servo-controlled body tilting suspension are the basics of the design.

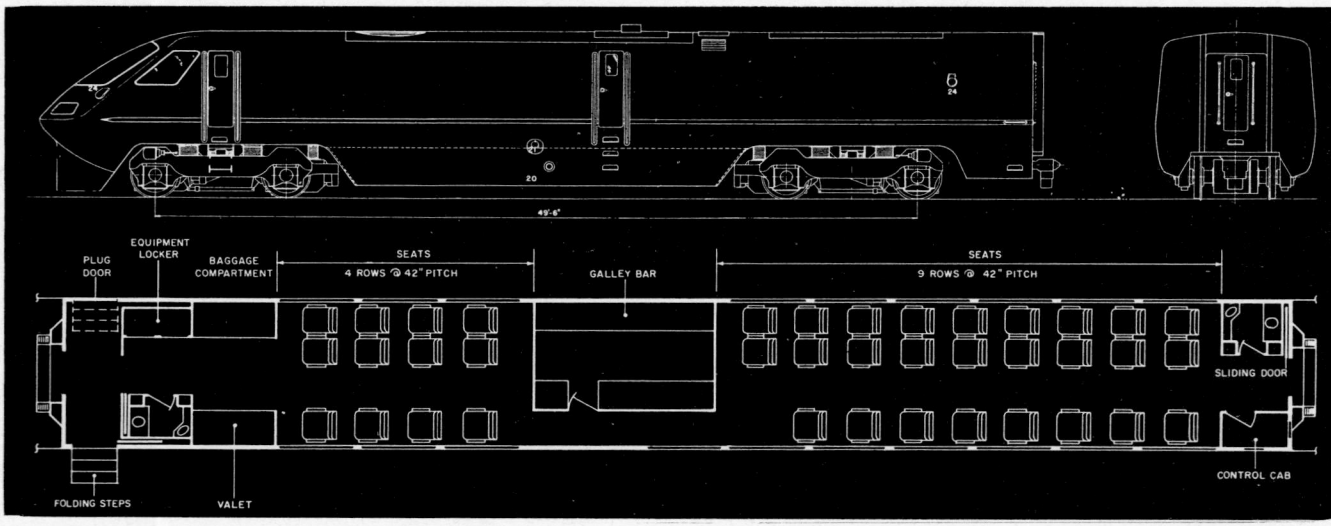

LRC train developed jointly by Alcan, Dofasco and MLW Industries
VIA Rail, Canada's agency responsible for rail passenger services, believes there is a big future for the LRC. President and Chief Executive Officer of VIA Rail, J Frank Roberts, says that the big advantage of the new train is the improved suspension system.

ALSTHOM-ATLANTIQUE
(Member of Traction Export)

Telephone: 502 14 13
Telegrams: ALSTHOM, Paris
Telex: 611 938

Head Office: 38 avenue Kléber, 75784 Paris, France
Railway Transport Materials Division: Tour Neptune, 72086 Paris La Défense, Cedex 20, France

Number of employees: 16 528
Major shareholders: Groupe de la Compagnie Générale d'Electricité (56.65 per cent), Compagnie Financière de Suez (3.72 per cent), Omnium de Participations Financières et Industrielles (3.45 per cent).

Products: Electric, diesel-electric, industrial and mining locomotives; electric, diesel and gas-turbine railcars; electric and diesel multiple units; rail transit cars and rolling stock; passenger coaches; automatic couplers; electrical equipment and transmissions; railway electrification; signalling systems and apparatus.

Chairman: Pierre Loygue
General Director: Roger Chalvon Demersay
Export Sales Director: Paul De Lieven
Railway Division Manager: Franck Vaingnedroye
Counsellor to Management for Railway Matters: Jacques Bedel De Buzareingues

Constitution: Established by Société Alsacienne de Constructions Mécaniques and Cie. Français Thomson-Houston, Alsthom became a public company in 1928. During 1977 Alsthom and Société Franco-Belge de Matériel de Chemins de Fer agreed to co-operate in the optimum utilisation of their manufacturing capacity, technical research and export marketing. In addition, Alsthom has taken a 12.5 per cent holding in the capital of Franco-Belge.

Turnover: Fr 1956.1 million.
Exports: Fr 1041 million.

Sales: SNCF started running tests with the first of two pre-series electric high-speed TGVs in August 1978 following delivery from Alsthom-Francorail-MTE at the end of July. The second trainset was delivered in November 1978.
The first TGV fully equipped for commercial operation in passenger service was presented in early 1979. Full-scale test running over electrified tests were due to begin in Saône et Loire on a 76 km section in June/July 1980. TGVs will begin a revenue service over the existing Paris-Lyon main line as they are delivered from the builders before the link to the new Paris-Sud Est line opens at St Florentin in October 1981.
During 1979 a consortium of French builders, comprising Alsthom, CIMT-Lorraine, Francorail-MTE and Traction CEM-Oerlikon, won an order for 52 three-car sets for Cairo's metro valued at Fr. 410 million ($US93 million at 1979 prices).
The company continues its activities in Africa. In mid-1977 an order was placed by Senegal Railways (Régie de Chemins de Fer du Sénégal) with Alsthom for three type AD 18B diesel-electric locomotives valued at Frs 10 million. During 1977 the company delivered six new diesel-electric locomotives to Gabon State Railways (OCTRA). The locomotives are a B-B design with a nominal (UIC) output of 3 000 hp, although under Gabon's difficult climatic conditions the rating is reduced to 2 800 hp. Westinghouse air

brakes act in conjunction with rheostatic braking. A single AGOV12DSHR diesel engine is installed which drives a three-phase alternator and rectifier set supplying dc to the two traction motors. Each locomotive weighs 92 tonnes and has a maximum speed of 85 km/h. The body is 15.8 m long and has air-conditioned cabs raked forward. Alsthom sales in Africa continued during 1978 with announcement of an order for seven 2 000 hp diesel locomotives, worth $9.8 million, placed by Uganda Railways.

ALTAI
Altai Wagon Works

Head Office: Altai, USSR
Exports: Energomachexport, 127486 Moscow, Deguninskaya, Str. 1, Korp 4, USSR
Products: Freight wagons

Telephone: 1472177
Telex: 7565

New equipment: Recently built by Altai for Soviet Railways (SZD) is a four-axle covered wagon with a capacity of 62 tonnes. Used by SZD for grain transports, the wagon has an inside body length of 12.8 m and an inside body width of 2.76 m. Height of the body over sidewall is 2.791 m.

AMHERST
Amherst Industries, Inc

Port Amherst, Charlestown, West Virginia 25306, USA

Telephone: (304) 925 1171

Products: Freight wagons; interior linings for tank and hopper wagons.

AMMENDORF
VEB Waggonbau
(Member of Maschinen-Export)

Ammendorf, German Democratic Republic

Products: Long-distance passenger coaches and restaurant cars.
Works Manager: Helmut Fritzsche
Chief Designer: Dipl-Ing Rainer Jäke

Telephone: 22050
Telex: 11 26 89

Number of employees: 22 000

Sales: Among export sales recorded during 1979 were 72 passenger coaches ordered by Chinese Railways. During the same fiscal period Ammendorf completed its 18 000th long-distance passenger coach built for the Soviet Union.

ANBEL
The Anbel Group

2323 South Voss Road, Houston, Texas 77057, USA

Products: Diesel-hydraulic locomotives (300 to 1 500 hp; remanufacture only of diesel-electric locos to 3 000 hp); freight wagons.

Telephone: (713) 977-9737
Telex: 910-881-1168 anbel hou

Chairman: Kenneth Roy Nichols
Engineering Director: Alan R Cripe
Chief Sales Director: G A Brichford
Export Sales: R A Huber

Diesel-hydraulic locomotive number RT-18 built for TTC of Canada
One of the DH-700 type diesel-hydraulics delivered by Anbel during 1977 to the Toronto Transit Commission of Canada. The units are rated at 700 hp, are 13 030 mm long over headstocks, 11 353 mm between bogie centres, have a bogie wheelbase of 2 000 mm and are 3 582 mm high above rail and 3 048 mm wide.

ANF-INDUSTRIE
Société ANF-Industrie

Tour Aurore, Place des Reflets, 92080 Paris-Défense (Cedex 5), France

Works: Blanc-Misseron, Marly-les-Valenciennes

Products: Turbotrains, diesel motortrain units, railcars, light alloy trailers for railcars; passenger coaches; underground railway materials for urban and suburban networks; all kinds of wagon; bogies for motor materials and trailers.

Chairman: Jean Pelabon
General Manager: Pierre Vacher

Telephone: 778 62 62
Telex: 610 817

New equipment: The RTG-type turbotrains first went into service with French National Railways in May 1973. The 70 units subsequently delivered are designed to run at 200 km/h. Each power car is propelled by an 850 kW nominal output Turbomeca Turmo IIIF turbo engine. Rate of output to weight is 7.5 kW/ton for a set of five coaches. Transmission is by an L411 or U Voith hydraulic transmission box with torque converter, coupler and reverser. Coupling between drive box and motor axle is through a cardan shaft. Powered bogies are Y223 type; both powered and non-powered bogies are equipped with four braking packages and two electro-magnetic rail-brake skids. In addition, non-powered bogies carry additional disc brakes plus one holding brake on every vehicle. A hydrodynamic brake is mounted on the transmission box. Auxiliary power is delivered by one generating set per powered car, comprising an Astazou A Turbomeca turbo-motor driving a 50 Hz 220)380 V, 210 kVA alternator.
For latest turbotrains ANF-Industrie can supply a more powerful gas turbine: the Turmo XII A from Turboméca.
After trials for more than a year operating an average of 18 000 km a month, the new Turmo XII shows the following improvements over RTG turbotrains equipped with the Turmo III F: a motor power increase of 46 per cent; specific fuel consumption reduction of 17 per cent; power-to-weight ratio increase of 16 per cent.
The number of coaches per train can also be increased and so reduce the cost price per seat/km.

Pocket wagon for road semi-trailer transport

Trains can be equipped with two TURMO XII turbines, one TURMO XII and a TURMO XII operating as a booster, or a single TURMO XII.

In 1978 ANF-Industrie studied and manufactured the first light alloy type XR 6000 passenger coaches for use in commercial service by SNCF. These trailers can be combined according to traffic necessities: one 440 kW railcar with one, two or three trailers, or two 440 kW railcars interconnected by one, two, three or four coaches. New hot drawing techniques of rolled aluminium section were used for the wide sections of these trailers, leading to considerable weight saving, while the price remains approximately the same as for the more conventional type of construction with semi-stainless steel.

Sales: ANF-Industrie has sold 70 gas turbine trains of the ETG or RTG type, four of them to the Iranian State Railways; six RTG trains to AMTRAK in USA and seven RTG trains intended for AMTRAK after being manufactured under licence in the USA by ROHR.
The company also sold in 1974/75 to French National Railways (SNCF) 27 self-propelled elements of 330 and 660 kW making a total of 400 self-propelled elements supplied to the SNCF.
ANF-Industrie has shared orders for French National Railways' new Corail coaches since the first examples went into mainline service in 1976. By March 1979 2 830 Corail coaches had entered service. There are two main Corail series: the VTU open coaches and the VU side-corridor vehicles. Spearheading the Paris-Montparnasse rolling stock and equipment exhibition held by SNCF and the Fédération des Industries Ferroviaires

in June 1979 was the second-class Corail stock with luggage area, six eight-seat compartments and end driving cab for push-pull operation built jointly by ANF and De Dietrich. The firms are building 750 Corail coaches.

Furthermore ANF-Industrie is manufacturing 700 RILS wagons with mechanical sheeting for the SNCF and 1 450 wagons of different types for exportation.
The Iranian State Railways (RAI), which operate RTG Turbotrains, returned to ANF-Industrie in 1978 to order 70 second-class passenger coaches and 25 dining cars.
In co-operation with De Dietrich, ANF-Industrie has already supplied or is now manufacturing a thousand UIC type CORAIL SERIES passenger compartment coaches. These first, second-class or couchette coaches have been ordered by SNCF.
The first hundred XR 6000 light alloy trailers were delivered to SNCF in 1978. At the same time ANF-Industrie has delivered 50 type X 2.100 440 kW railcars which are suitable for operation with these trailers.
The French postal authorities ordered from ANF-Industrie in 1978 eight 440 kW railcars for postal containers, intended for rapid postal connections over medium distances.
The wagon department received in 1978 orders for 3000 wagons of various types (Rils wagons with mechanical sheeting, tube transport wagons, wagons for the transport of semi-trailers, wagons for the transport of liquid gas, flat wagons, bogie tank wagons, bogie cereals wagons, hopper wagons, etc).
An order for 1900 wagons is to be carried out by ANF-Industrie as part of a contract for 4500 wagons negotiated between the German Democratic Republic and French builders, Franco-Belge, Arbel Industrie and ANF-Industrie.

440 kW motortrain units (for French National Post and Telecommunications and SNCF) and 300 kW diesel motortrain unit for Cannes city

Bogie motor for the "Interconnexion" SNCF RATP rolling stock

New type XR 6000 light alloy railcar outside ANF-Industrie's Crespin shops in March 1978
The new X 2.100 railcar, one of 50 built for SNCF specifically for use with the 100 type XR 6000 light alloy trailers built by ANF-Industrie in 1978.

Two coupled 440 kW railcars built for French post office authorities
The eight railcars ordered for French postal services are to be used on new high-speed postal express services.

ANSALDO
Ansaldo Group

Head Office: Via Pacinotti 20, 16151 Genoa, Sampierdarena, Italy

Transportation Division: Via Nuova della Brecce 260, 80147 Naples, Italy

Products: Electrical equipment for electric and diesel-electric locomotives, railcars, mu's, subway cars, trams, trolley buses with conventional or thyristor control.

Chairman and Managing Director: Daniele Luigi Milvio
Managing Director: Giobatta Clavarino
General Manager, Transport Sector: Giancarlo Maimone

Telephone: (081) 266022
Telegrams: ANSALDO CORNIGLIANO LIGURE — ANSALDO MILANO
Telex: 27098 7131 ITRAF NA

Sales: Ansaldo Group is the main contractor for Italian State Railways (FS) supplying in 1979/80 electrical equipment for 15 locomotives type E 656 (3 kV dc, 4 200 kW, Bo-Bo-Bo, 110 metric tons, L60 km/h); electrical equipment for 20 diesel-electric DE 445 locomotives (2120 hp, three-phase/dc transmission, B-B, 64 metric tons, 130 km/h), including auxiliary generator for train heating or air-conditioning at 3 kV dc; 40 3-K chopper four-car trainsets (M + T + T + M, 1900 kW) for suburban service (a pre-series has already been put into service); 55 full-chopper locomotives type E 633 (3 kV dc, 4200 kW, B-B-B; 98 metric tons, 160 km/h); 5 full chopper locomotives type E 844 (3 kV dc; 5600 kW, B-B-B-B, 130 metric tons, 110 km/h). Ansaldo is building a 3 kV dc Bo-Bo locomotive equipped with four inverter-fed asynchronous motors with high modularity electrical equipment for utilisation in single-phase systems, such as that of Sardinia (the first 25 kV network in Italy).

ARAD
Arad Car and Carriage Building Works (Intreprinderea de Vagoane)
(Member of the Industrial Group for Technological Equipment and Rolling Stock)

2900-Arad, Avenue Aurel Vlaicu 41-43, Romania

Products: Passenger coaches, freight wagons (open, covered, flat, self-discharge, ballast) up to 60 tonnes loading capacity. Special-purpose wagons of up to 32 axles.

Chairman: Eng Marin Nedelcu
Managing Director: Eng Nicolae Iosif
Export Sales: Eng Mihai Scorteanu

Telephone: 30411/35020/37020/30520
Telegrams: VAGO ANE ARAD
Telex: 46273/46256

Sales: Exports were completed in 1978 to Egypt (third-class coaches), the Philippines (coaches), Nigeria (wagons) Syria (air-conditioned passenger coaches, electric power vans, vapour generator cars), Greece (air-conditioned and non air-conditioned coaches), Iran (ore transport and flat wagons), Algeria (various types of ore and phosphate wagon). Under manufacture are passenger coaches for Gabon, Angola, Mozambique, Sri Lanka and a wide range of freight wagons for all East-European railway administrations.

ARBEL
Arbel Industrie

194 boulevard Faidherbe, 59506 Douai, France

Products: Freight wagons; mining equipment; rolling stock components.

President and General Manager: Conrad Bernstein
Sales Director: Antoine Azais

Telephone: (27) 88 33 11
Telegrams: INDARBEL, Douai
Telex: Indarbel 130 036

Licensing agreements: *Italy:* Omeca (Reggio Calabria)
Ferrosud (Matera)
Licensing agreements: *Spain:* CAF (Beasain)
Ateinsa (Madrid)

Bogie wagon for the transport of powdered and granulated products
Length of underframe 17 800 mm; length between buffers 19 040 mm; capacity 90 m³; tare 25.5 tonnes; loading capacity 53.5 tonnes.

Tank wagon for soda shipments
Capacity 41 m³; tare 22 tonnes; maximum load 58 tonnes; length overall 12 500 mm; the cylindrical tank is completely welded and coated on the inside with epoxy paint.

Container wagon mounted on three bogies
Length overall 27 100 mm; length between bogies 10 700 mm; bogie wheelbase 1 800 mm; maximum useful payload 88 tonnes; tare (with air and screw brake) 25.8 tonnes; total weight on rails (with screw brake) 113.8 tonnes; weight without screw brake 113.6 tonnes.

Sales: Under construction at Douai during 1979 were the following wagons: 1 800 bogie wagons for scrap-iron (for SNCF); 500 bogie wagons for coils transportation, with sliding roofs (for SNCF); 1 000 covered bogie hopper wagons (66 m³ capacity) for German State Railways (DR); 350 bogie hopper wagons (66 m³ capacity) for German State Railways (DR); 150 bogie tank wagons for the transport of miscellaneous powder and granulated products for German State Railways (DR); 200 bogie wagons of various types for the Ivory Coast (RAN); 60 four-wheeled wagons for phosphate transportation for CTMB of Togo.

ASEA AB

S-721 83 Västerås, Sweden

Telephone: (021) 10 00 00
Telegrams: ASEA, Västeras
Telex: 4720

Products: Electric ac and dc locomotives; commuter and intercity trains with thyristor control; subway cars with thyristor (chopper) control; electrical equipment for railway electrification and rolling stock; rotary and static convertors for ac and dc substations; marshalling yard equipment; mining and industrial equipment.

Chairman: Curt Nicolin
Managing Director: Torsten Lindström
Chief Sales Director: Arne Bennborn
General Manager, Transport Division: Åke Nilsson
Sales Manager: Lars Olof Nilsson

Constitution: The company was founded in 1883 and built its first dc locomotive in 1891 and its first complete railway electrification project for 25 Hz single-phase was carried out in 1907.

Turnover: (Transport) $US 216 million
Number of Employees: 3 100

Sales: Notable orders received during 1979 included a contract for 40 class Rc 4 thyristor locomotives from the Swedish State Railways (SJ) with an option on a further 30 units and a contract to the consortium Walkers-ASEA Pty Ltd for a further 33 passenger cars for the Brisbane rail electrification project.
The first prototype four-car commuter train in a series of four was delivered mid-1979 to the Danish State Railways for trial service in the Greater Copenhagen area. Two of the new trains are provided with ASEA thyristor chopper control equipment. The new four-car trains can carry 240 seated and 550 standing passengers and have a maximum speed of 120 km/h. Each four-car train has a continuous rating of 8 × 200 kW.

The first thyristor-controlled three-car unit in the initial contract for 39 electric cars awarded to Walkers-ASEA Pty Ltd is undergoing tests in the Brisbane area. Electric passenger train services were planned to start in November 1979 on the Ferry Grove-Darra section of the line. Services will be extended to Ipswich in late 1980. A three-car unit comprises a driver motor car, a central motor car and a driver trailer car. The two motor cars are each powered by four 135 kW dc traction motors. The trains are designed for a maximum speed of 120 km/h and operate from a 25 kV, 50 Hz overhead contract wire. A six-car train has a seating capacity of 500.
The first of the 30 high-speed, lightweight electric locomotives, class AEM 7, being built by the Electro-Motive Division (EMD) of General Motors Corp, were delivered to Amtrak in November 1979. These locomotives are used to pull trains at speeds up to 200 km/h in the Northeast Corridor between Boston, New York and Washington. The new locomotives are based on the Rc 4 locomotive built by ASEA, Sweden. EMD, US licensee of ASEA electric locomotive technology, has obtained a licence to build a locomotive similar to the ASEA unit but with more power and higher speed. Special features include a PRESSDUCTOR dynamic slip control system developed by ASEA, which enables the locomotive to make the maximum use of the adhesion under all rail conditions. The new locomotives are capable of operating on three different power supply systems, including the 25 kV, 60 Hz system used in the upgraded Northeast Corridor.
The first production model of British Rail's Advanced Passenger Train (APT) is undergoing its final tests and is being put into regular service in 1980. ASEA has supplied six 3000 kW sets of traction and auxiliary power supply equipment for the first series of power cars. The APT is designed for a maximum speed of 250 km/h.

Six of the new class E1 16 electric locomotives delivered by ASEA to the Norwegian State Railways (NSB) during 1977-79. Another four units are due for delivery in 1980
Main data: max speed, 140 km/h; length over buffers, 15.52 m; weight, 80 tonnes; axle load, 20 tonnes; number of traction motors, 4; continuous rating, 4440 kW; max starting effort, 328 kN.

Three-car passenger train for Brisbane
Deliveries of 72 cars are due to be completed by the ASEA-Walkers consortium in 1983-84 at a cost of $A 250 million. The first three-car unit left the Walkers Ltd works in 1979.

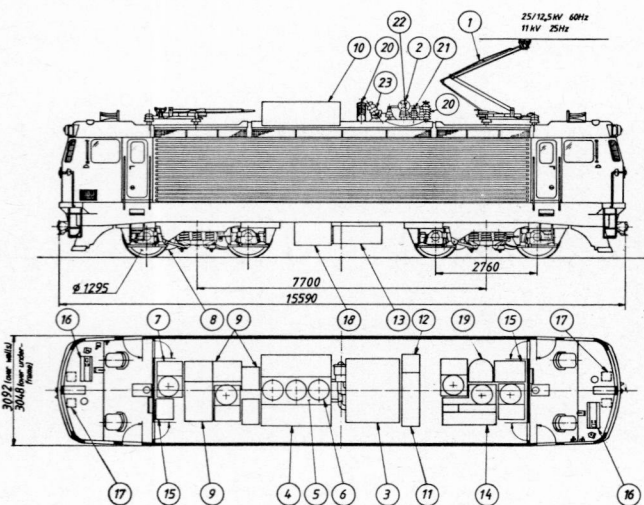

A further result of the licence agreement between General Motors of the USA and ASEA is the AEM 7 locomotive for Amtrak
(1) pantograph **(2)** main circuit breaker **(3)** main transformer with smoothing reactor **(4)** thyristor converter **(5)** oil cooler **(6)** blowers for 4 and 5 **(7)** blowers for 8 **(8)** traction motor **(9)** static converter for head-end power **(10)** braking resistors **(11)** electrical cabinet **(12)** electronic cabinet **(13)** battery box **(14)** main compressor/separator rack **(15)** air brake racks (2) **(16)** engineer's console **(17)** cab heaters **(18)** filter capacitors **(19)** toilet **(20)** lightning arresters **(21)** isolating switch **(22)** power source detector **(23)** high-voltage bushing
Main data: max speed, 201 km/h; length over buffers, 15.59 m; weight, 91 tonnes; axle load, 27.75 tonnes; number of traction motors, 4; max starting effort, 240 kN.

Prototype commuter train for Greater Copenhagen
Trial services began in Spring 1979. The set carries 240 seated and 550 standing passengers at a max speed of 120 km/h.

The 200th thyristor locomotive to be delivered to SJ by ASEA was handed over to the customer in September 1978
Main data: max speed, 135 km/h; length over buffers, 15.520 m; weight, 78 tonnes; axle load, 19.5 tonnes; number of traction motors, 4; continuous rating, 4680 kW; max starting effort, 290 kN; traction motor control, thyristors; transmission, ASEA hollow-shaft motor drive; brakes, disc brakes with tread brakes.

ASTARSA
Astilleros Argentinos Rio de la Plata SA

Head Office: Tucumán 1438, Buenos Aires, Argentina

Works: Solis Y Rio Lujan, (1648) Tigre, Argentina

Associated Company: General Motors Corporation

Products: Diesel-electric locomotives.

Telephone: 40 3425/7014
Telegrams: ASTARSA, Buenos Aires
Telex: 0121692

Licences: MTE and Alsthom (France)

Sales: ASTARSA is responsible for constructing the underframe, cabins and general assembly of 170 GM locomotives for Argentine Railways (FA). In August 1978 the company delivered the first model GT22CU to FA.

AT
Compania Auxiliar de Transportes SA

Avenida José Antonio 20, Apartado 358, Madrid 14, Spain

Products: Diesel-hydraulic locomotives; passenger coaches; freight wagons.

Telephone: 797 91 00
Telegrams: AUTRANS, Madrid

ATEINSA
Aplicaciones Técnicas Industriales SA

Head Office: PO Box 3276, Zurbano 70, Madrid 10, Spain

Works: Factoria de Villaverde, Carretera Villaverde, Vallecas 18, Madrid 21, Spain

Products: Locomotives: electric, diesel/electric; railcars: diesel; rolling stock: passenger carriages, goods wagons, mineral wagons, ballast wagons, special-purpose freight cars for steel works and other industries.

President: Manuel Costales Gómez-Olea

Telephone: 419 95 50
Telegrams: ATEINSA, Madrid
Telex: 22055 ATIE

Constitution: ATEINSA was set up in 1974/75 to take over the railway rolling stock production of ASEA.

Sales: 400 high-sided wagons type XX and 1015 type ORE 1 wagons placed by Spanish National Railways (RENFE); 41 special ingot casting wagons placed by ENSIDESA; 147 iron ore wagons with automatic discharge placed by Vagones Frigorificos SA; 27 type PMM wagons ordered by Altos Hornos de Vizcaya.

AUGUST, 23
"23 August" Works
(Member of Mecanoexportimport)

10 M Eminescu Street, Bucharest, Romania

Products: Diesel-hydraulic and diesel-electric locomotives.

Constitution: The "23 August" Works started production of 150-1 500 hp diesel-hydraulic locomotives to be used for shunting and secondary line duties in 1964, with turnover based on licences purchased from Sulzer, Alco, Maybach-Mercedes-Benz, Voith, Brown Boveri and Knorr-Bremse.

Sales: Apart from series orders carried out for East-Europe railway administrations, the "23 August" plant has completed five new 1 500-hp diesel-electric locomotives for the Hedjaz Railway. Prime movers for the locomotives were supplied by MTU, Friedrichshafen, Federal Republic of Germany and consists of MTU 12 V 652 TD 11 diesel engines with external air-change cooling equipment.
Locomotives produced by the plant include the LDH45 (450 hp BB), the LDH70 (700 hp

Telephone: 12 46 00
Telex: 10269

BB) and the LDH125 (1 250 hp BB). The full range of the company's diesel locomotives forms an interesting example of efficient assembly. In the LDH45 unit, for instance, the MB836Bb six-cylinder turbo-charged 1 450 rpm diesel motor is manufactured under a Maybach-Mercedes licence, the turbo-blower is to a Brown Boveri design, the type TH1 turbo transmission and axle drive gears are built at Hidromechanica, Brasov, under licence from Voith, and brake equipment is to Knorr designs. Top speed of the LDH45 is 60 km/h in secondary freight of passenger line haul operations and 30 km/h in shunting duty. Total length is 11.46 m with bogie centre spaces at 5.64 m and axles spaced at 2.5 m.
A much larger locomotive is the LDH125 designed for heavy shunting, transfer and line duties. The unit features a Sulzer licenced type 6LDS28 direct injection six-cylinder diesel, built at the Resita works, which drives the axles through a TH2 Voith hydraulic transmission and an NE1200/2 Voith reversing reducer. Top speed on line duties is 100 km/h, total length is 13.7 m with a pivot base of 9.7 m and axles spaced at 2.5 m.

BABCOCK & WILCOX ESPAÑOLA
Sociedad Española de Construcciones Babcock & Wilcox

Alameda de Recalde, 27 Bilbao 9, Spain

Products: Electric, diesel-electric, diesel-hydraulic locomotives; electric and diesel railcars; industrial and mining locomotives; special freight wagons.

Chairman and Managing Director: Angel Simon
Chief Sales Director: Julio Larrea
Export Sales Director: D Luis Moreno

Sales: Under construction in 1978/79 were ten diesel-electric locomotives for line and shunting duties in the 650 to 1050 hp range; 54 special wagons for Altos Hornos del Mediterraneo, 100-ton load and 32-ton axle load; 16 C-C wagons for hot ingots for

Telephone: Bilbao 4415700
Telegrams: BABCOCK, Bilbao
Telex: 33776 bw-bil

Empresa Nacional Siderurgica SA 100-ton load, 35-ton axle load; three 200-ton capacity torpedo ladle wagons for Altos Hornos de Vizcaya, SA; 136 double reduction gear units for 140-160 km/h, 3000 V electric locomotives purchased by Red Nacional de Ferrocarriles Espanoles (RENFE); 16 OGI system variable gauge axle and wheel sets for RENFE.

Constitution: Founded 1951
Turnover: 100 wagons per month
Plant area: 35 000 m²

200-tonne capacity torpedo ladle wagon built for Altos Hornos de Vizcaya

Type U10B diesel-electric locomotive built under GE (USA) licence during 1978 for the port of Gijon

650 hp diesel-electric industrial locomotive

BADONI

Antonio Badoni SpA

Corso Matteotti 7, 22053 Lecco, Italy

Products: Diesel-hydraulic shunting locomotives; hydrostatic transmissions.

Chairman: Dott Emilio Walter
Vice Chairman: Dott Ing Dante Weber

Telephone: 341 364306
Telegrams: BADONI, Lecco
Telex: 380086 Badoni I

Managing Director: Ditt Ing Guiseppe Riccardo Kramer Badoni
Sales Director: Dott Angelo Airoldi

BAGULEY-DREWRY

Baguley-Drewry Ltd

Uxbridge Street, Burton-on-Trent, Staffordshire DE14 3JT, England

Products: Diesel-mechanical, diesel-hydraulic, diesel-electric, industrial and mining

Telephone: 0283 66751
Telegrams: BAGULEY, Burton-on-Trent

locomotives (battery and trolley); diesel-mechanical and diesel-hydraulic railcars.

Chairman: W R Souster

BARCLAY

Andrew Barclay, Sons & Co Ltd

Caledonia Works, Kilmarnock, Ayrshire KA1 2QD, Scotland

Products: Diesel hydraulic, diesel-electric locomotives (30 to 1 000 hp); steam, fireless and crane locomotives; boilers and locomotive components; general engineering and fabrications.

Telephone: 0563 23573/4/5/6
Telegrams: BARCLAYSON, Kilmarnock
Telex: 778497

Chairman: C R C Fryers
Managing Director: S E H Kewney

388 hp diesel-hydraulic shunter built for Britain's National Coal Board

252 hp diesel-hydraulic locomotive built for the British Steel Corporation

BARLOWS

Barlows Heavy Engineering Ltd (Rolling Stock Division)

PO Box 183, Benoni 1500, Transvaal, South Africa

Products: Freight wagons; end-of-car and sliding sill hydraulic cushioning; underframes for locomotives and passenger coaches.

Chairman: K C Comins
Managing Director: A L Snell
Sales Manager (Rolling Stock Div): G M Kew

Constitution: Barlows Heavy Engineering Ltd (the major engineering subsidiary of the Barlow Group) is one of the largest companies of its kind in South Africa. The company

Telephone: (011) 54-7511
Telegrams: SWIVEL, Benoni
Telex: 80559 SA

was founded in 1889 when the original company of Wright Boag & Co was established in Johannesburg. In 1946 Wright Boag & Co merged with Head Wrightson & Co. In 1965 Thos Barlow & Sons Ltd bought the share capital of Wright Boag and was renamed Barlow Head Wrightson. This was followed by Barlows taking over the Head Wrightson shareholdings, thus making it a wholly-owned South African subsidiary of the Barlow Group.
In October 1956 the company entered the rolling stock manufacturing field when the Rolling Stock Division was formed. Since 1956 nearly 18 000 wagons of various types have been built.

BATIRUHR

54 rue Santos-Dumont, Paris 15, France

Products: Diesel-hydraulic, diesel-mechanical, mining and industrial locomotives; electric and diesel personnel coaches for industrial and mining operations.

Telephone: 531 87 49
Telegrams: BATIRUHR, Paris

BAUTISTA BURIASCO
Bautista Buriasco E Hijos Ltda SA

Av Bautista Buriasco s/n, 2445 Maria Juana, Province Santa Fe, Argentina

Products: Freight wagons.

Telephone: 35 2103/2335/5580

Sales: During 1977/78 the company delivered 300 hopper wagons to Argentine Railways (FA).

BAUTZEN
VEB Waggonbau Bautzen

DDR 86 Bautzen, Neuesche Promenade, German Democratic Republic

Products: Passenger coaches; freight wagons.

Sales: The first in a new generation of 26.4 m-long dining cars was handed over by Bautzen to Czechoslovak State Railways (CSD) at the end of 1978. Given the floor dimensions laid down for passenger coach type X as per UIC, the new dining car provides 5 m² extra floor space, permitting a new compartment design to be adopted in which the kitchen and equipment area is at the car's centre. A buffet area for 20 passengers at six tables is provided. With the supply of 40 of the cars, Bautzen has delivered 2 800 passenger coaches to CSD.

BBC BROWN BOVERI
BBC Brown, Boveri & Company Ltd

Postfach 85, CH - 5401 Baden, Switzerland

Telephone: (056) 75 11 11
Telegrams: BROWNBOVERI
Telex: 52921, 53203

Associate companies:
Austria
Oesterreichische Brown Boveri-Werke AG
Postfach 184, A - 1101 Vienna
Telephone: (0222) 64 25 48/62 01 27
Telegrams: Brownboveri Wien
Telex: 011 760 Oe BBWA

Brazil
Industria Elétrica Brown Boveri SA
CP 5528, 01000 São Paulo
Telephone: (011) 802 2111
Telegrams: Brownboveri São Paulo
Telex: 33446

Canada
Brown Boveri Canada Ltd
4000 Trans-Canada Highway, Pointe Claire, PQ H9R 1B2
Telephone: (514) 697 6210
Telex: 05 821 542

Federal Republic of Germany
Brown, Boveri & Cie Aktiengesellschaft
Postfach 351, D - 6800 Mannheim 1,
Telephone: (0621) 381-1
Telegrams: Brownboveri Mannheim
Telex: 462411 122 bbd

France
Société de Traction CEM-Oerlikon (TCO)
37, rue du Rocher, F - 75383 Paris (Cedex 08)
Telephone: (01) 522 85 90
Telegrams: Oerlik Paris
Telex: 650 663

Italy
Tecnomasio Italiano Brown Boveri SpA
Casella postale 3392, I - 20100 Milan
Telephone: (02) 5797
Telegrams: Tecnomasio Milano
Telex: 310153

Norway:
A/S Norsk Elektrisk & Brown Boveri
Postboks 1174 Sentrum, N - Oslo 1

Telephone: (02) 55 70 90
Telegrams: NEBB Oslo
Telex: 11268

Spain
Brown Boveri de España SA
Apartado 36127, E-Madrid 16
Telephone: (01) 270 54 04
Telex: 43236/27572 BBCME

USA
Brown Boveri Corporation
1460 Livingston Avenue, North Brunswick, New Jersey 08902
Telephone: (201) 932 6000
Telex: 844 464/5

Products: Electrical equipment for all traction applications (main-line, local and industrial railways, including systems for very high speeds; local transport services, such as fast suburban and underground lines, trams and trolleybuses); rack railways and ropeways; new unconventional transport systems. Supply of components: electrical machines for traction and auxiliary duties for ac, dc and multisystem vehicles, thermo-electric and thermo-hydraulic vehicles as well as battery-fed vehicles. Equipment for conversion and distribution of electrical energy, such as transformers, static convertors, switchgear, resistors, etc. Protective and control systems for the traction and auxiliary circuits. Lighting, heating and air-conditioning equipment for railway coaches. Data transmission and processing systems for continuous train control. Contact-wire systems for all traction applications.

New equipment: Following tentative testing with an experimental three-phase electric locomotive since 1974, Deutsche Bundesbahn (DB) placed orders with Krauss Maffei, Krupp, Thyssen Henschel and BBC Brown Boveri for five new 15 kV 16²/₃ Hz Bo-Bo electric locomotives (designated class E120) with a continuous rating of 4 400 kW and a 20-minute rating of 5 600 kW. Evaluation trials were due to start at the end of 1978 and series production expected to follow before 1980. The advantages of three-phase motors for electric traction appear to be numerous. Those listed by BBC Brown Boveri as the most important are: better use of available adhesion resulting in markedly higher traction forces at maximum speeds; lighter bogies—the two bogies on the E120 unit will weigh only about 15 tonnes compared with 22 tonnes using conventional motors; three-phase locomotives have all the characteristics needed to haul both passenger trains at a top speed of 160 km/h and heavy freight; absence of slip rings, commutator and brushgear will result in lower maintenance costs; electric braking is simplified. BBC Brown Boveri predicts that the three-phase brushless traction motor will prove universally applicable to all traction systems.

BEML
Bharat Earth Movers Ltd (Railcoach Division)

Unity Buildings, J C Road, Bangalore 560 002, India

Products: Integral passenger coaches in steel; welded lightweight stock such as second-class coaches, brake and luggage vans, couchette cars, sleeping coaches.

Managing Director: O M Mani
Chief of Production: M Y Mudabidri
General Manager: K T Sampathgopal
Group Executive (Technical Services): H Sreenivasiah
Senior Design Manager: K S Jagannatha

Constitution: The Railcoach Division of Bharat Earth Movers Ltd was the first factory in India to take up manufacture, in 1947, of all-metal broad-gauge railcoaches, steel, welded, lightweight passenger coaches, postal vans, parcel vans, brake and luggage vans, day-cum-sleeper coaches, motor-cum-parcel coaches.

Sales: The Railcoach Division manufactures about 300 coaches annually for the Indian Railways. So far over 6 650 coaches have been supplied to the railways. As a first step towards export drive, 50 broad-gauge third-class coaches have been delivered to Bangladesh Railways. Diversification of production is on hand and more than 200 twelve twin-wheel low bed tank transporters have been built together with 20 tonne low deck trailers.

BERWICK
Berwick Forge and Fabricating

PO Box 188, West Ninth Street, Berwick, Pennsylvania 18603, USA

Products: Freight wagons.

Telephone: (717) 752 2784

Sales: Deliveries in 1979 totalled 4 977 box wagons (mainly 100-tonne capacity units) and 220 open wagons.

BETHLEHEM STEEL
Bethlehem Steel Corporation

Bethlehem, Pennsylvania 18016, USA

Foreign agents: Brettenham House, Lancaster Place, London WC2E 7EN, England

Products: Freight wagons; components; axles; rails and track accessories.
Chairman: L W Foy
Sales: J D Dougherty

Telephone: (215) 694 2424

Vice-Chairmen: F W West Jr
C W Ritterhoff
R M Smith

Sales: Deliveries during 1979 and early 1980 were: 6 247 hopper wagons (including 2 500 for Conrail); 3 715 flat wagons (including 2 700 for Trailer Train); and 2 184 open wagons.

BN

Constructions Ferroviaires et Métalliques "BN" SA

Rue de la loi 74, B-1040 Brussels, Belgium

Telephone: 02 230 12 25
Telegrams: BRUNAG
Telex: 61 736

Products: Diesel-electric, diesel-hydraulic and electric locomotives, passenger coaches, freight wagons, LRV and metro stock; containers; industrial equipment.

Chairman: A Dubuisson
Managing Director: O J Bronchart
General Manager: M Simonart
Manager, General Transport Division: P Van de Sijpe

Constitution: Present style of the BN company dates from July 1977 when La Brugeoise et Nivelles absorbed Constructions Ferroviaires du Centre.

Sales: Since 1973 the combined companies have won the following contracts: 128 articulated pre-metro cars for Brussels; 54 PCC tramcars for Ghent; 40 PCC tramcars for Antwerp; 70 single unit tramcars for The Hague; 30 metrocar-units for Brussels; 61 double articulated pre-metro cars for Brussels; 105 articulated tramcars for Charleroi and the line alongside the Belgian coast; 68 single articulated pre-metro cars for Rio de Janeiro; 55 two-car commuter trains for Belgian National Railways (SNCB); 40 double articulated tramcars for The Hague.

During 1980 BN is to start deliveries of a second series of 35 metro car sets for Brussels together with a new generation of M4 passenger coaches for SNCB (455 units) which began rolling off the production lines in October 1979. Now under construction is a new type of Bo-Bo electric locomotive (4 150 kW; 3 000 V dc).

7000 hp electric locomotive standing alongside a four-car electric trainset
Both built for Belgian National Railways (SNCB) by BN in collaboration with other Belgian suppliers.

Coil wagon with telescopic roof and sides designed and built by BN for SNCB

Six-axle articulated pre-metro car built for Rio de Janeiro

Type M4 passenger coach
One of 455 units ordered by Belgian National Railways.

Luggage and mail van delivered by BN to SNCB during 1977-78

BOEING

Telephone: (206) 773 2121

Boeing Aerospace Company

PO Box 3999, Seattle, Washington 98124, USA

Products: Automated transportation systems including people movers.

Sales: Associate contractor responsible for equipment and technical integration on Phase II of Personal Rapid Transit system at Morgantown, West Virginia, funded by US Department of Transportation and completed in 1979. Phase II expands present Morgantown system, which has been in public service since October 1975. System manager for Morgantown Phase I, and designer (for Kobe Steel, Ltd) of automated transit system which carried visitors at International Ocean Exposition, Okinawa, Japan, official 1975 World's Fair.

Boeing Aerospace received a $27 million federal contract during 1979 to develop an advanced automated transit system which could reduce gasoline consumption, pollution and traffic congestion in urban areas by offering a convenient alternative to the automobile for commuter travel. The six-year engineering development program, funded by the US Department of Transportation's Urban Mass Transportation Administration (UMTA), will include a demonstration of test hardware at the Boeing Space Center near Seattle. Known as Advanced Group Rapid Transit (AGRT), this system will employ small rubber-tyred vehicles, electrically powered and computer-controlled, operating with headways (time intervals between cars) as short as three seconds. With this capability, a fleet of the driverless 12-passenger vehicles would be able to move 14 000 people an hour on a single 9-ft (2.7-m) wide lane of guideway. The AGRT could be installed in a city's central business district, then expanded into a large network of guideways reaching out to neighbourhoods and suburban communities. It would transport passengers directly to their destinations with no stops at

intermediate stations. Service could be available 24 hours a day with waiting times of less than five minutes.

Under the Boeing concept, vehicle movements would be controlled automatically by onboard digital computers which communicate with computers in passenger stations and a central control facility. Radar sensors mounted on the front of each car would ensure that the three-second interval between vehicles is maintained even if the control system should fail. The radar collision-avoidance system is being developed by Sperry Gyroscope of Great Neck, New York, under subcontract to Boeing.

Boeing's AGRT concept is derived from the Morgantown people mover. The Morgantown system began revenue operation in late 1975 with a fleet of 45 21-passenger vehicles.

Boeing has set aside nearly 45 acres at its Space Center for a one-mile guideway and control center for its AGRT test program. The test track will be designed by ABAM Engineers of Tacoma, Washington. Construction will begin in late 1980. Boeing's program manager is Douglas H Christenson. LaVern E Leistikow is chief engineer.

Boeing Vertol Company

PO Box 16858, Philadelphia, Pennsylvania 19142, USA

Products: Rapid transit stock.

Sales: Production under way on 275 Light Rail Vehicles (streetcars) for Boston and San Francisco.

BOFORS-NOHAB

AB Bofors-Nohab

Telephone: 0520/18000
Telegrams: NOHAB
Telex: 42084

S-46182 Trollhättan, Sweden

Products: Diesel-electric, diesel-hydraulic and electric locomotives; snow-clearing machines.

General Manager: H de Verdier
Division Manager: L B Alin
Sales Director: H Sörsdahl

Sales: Orders for locomotives in 1978 amounted to 88 million kroner. Invoiced sales dropped to 48 million kroner. Among orders reported in 1979 were 15 diesel-electric locomotives (type T44) for Swedish State Railways.

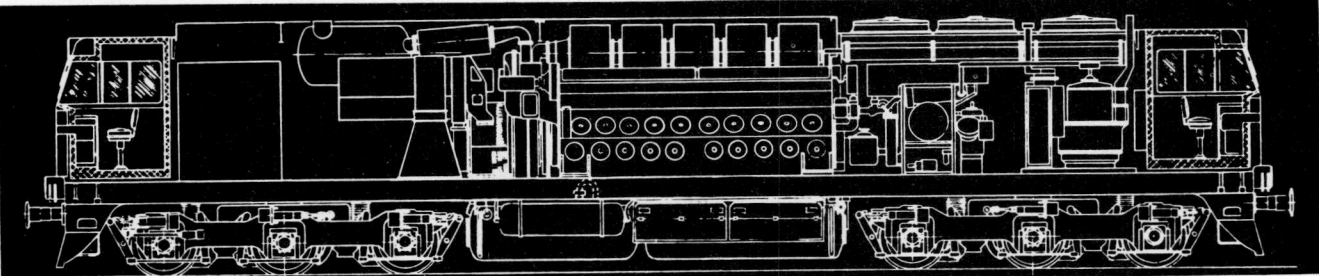

3 900 hp diesel-electric Co Co locomotive type Mz *(above and left below)*
Two-cab, full width, self-supporting on two three-axle motor bogies of flexi-coil type. A total of 46 have been delivered to Danish State Railways.

Type T46 3 900 hp locomotive

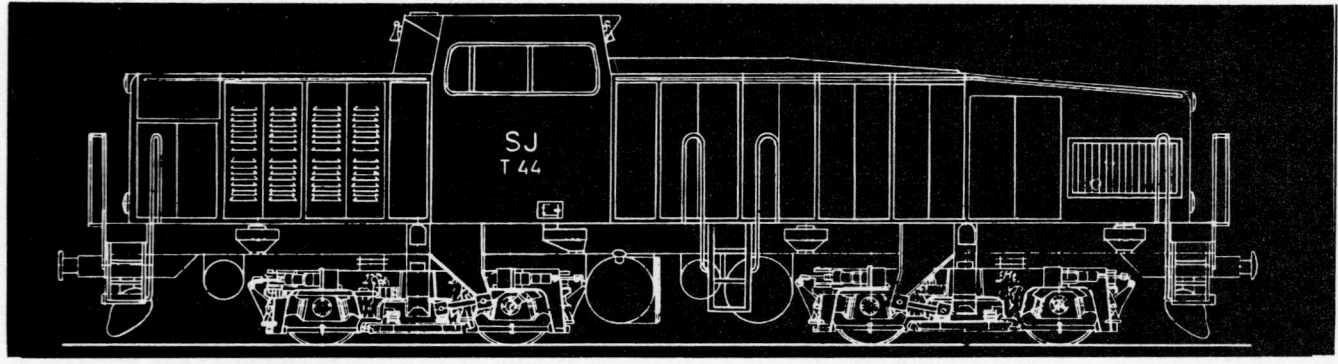

1 650 hp diesel-electric Bo Bo locomotive type T44
Designed for Swedish State Railways heavy shunting and freight haulage. Can be geared for speeds of between 105 and 143 km/h.

BOMBARDIER INC
(Rail and Diesel Power Products Division)

1505 Dickson Street, Montreal, Quebec H1N 2H7, Canada

Products: Diesel-electric locomotives from 900 to 4 500 hp (with single engine), for passenger, freight and switching service; diesel engines; subway cars; freight cars; heat exchangers; pressure vessels; industrial machinery.

President, Rail and Diesel Products Division and Thermal Products Division: Gérard Lepage
President, Mass Transit Division: Raymond Royer
Vice President, Marketing, Rail and Diesel Products Division: John Byrne
Sales Manager, Rail and Diesel Products Division: C M Dathan
Manager, Marketing, Rail and Diesel Products Division: F Lorek
Vice President, Marketing, Mass Transit: Carl Mawby
Sales Manager, Rail Passenger Equipment: W E McLean

Constitution: Bombardier Inc (an all-Canadian company, formerly MLW Division of Bombardier Inc) has manufactured locomotives for 76 years. Since 1948 the company has built diesel electric units for Canadian railroads and for export to countries world wide.

Telephone: (514) 255 3681
Telegrams: MONLOCO, Montreal
Telex: 05 828841 (Marketing)
05 829538 (Engineering and Service)
05 828849 (Spare parts)
05 828759 (Material Control)

A Canadian consortium, comprising Bombardier Inc, Alcan Canada Products and Dominion Foundries and Steel has designed, built and is marketing the LRC (light, rapid, comfortable) high-speed inter-city passenger train. The LRC is designed to operate economically as a basic unit of one locomotive and five coaches which can be twinned as a push-pull train with ten coaches or made up in other configurations. The light weight of the LRC is due in part to the use of aluminium for the structure of the locomotive and coaches. Its low centre of gravity, along with its prime power source, a 3 725 gross hp 16-cylinder diesel engine, provide the train with its responsive performance — high top speed of about 125 mph (200 km/h), rapid acceleration and low power requirement. The banking system is the most significant engineering innovation in the design of the LRC. Power banking is built into the coaches allowing them to tilt as much as ten degrees from the perpendicular. This hydraulic banking system is activated by sensors that nullify the centrifugal forces. Since 1974 the LRC prototype has undergone extensive and rigorous testing, completing some 150 000 miles (240 000 km) on main lines, under a wide variety of operating conditions. The results of the tests

Portuguese Railways diesel-electric locomotive, model MXS-627 (3 000/2 700 hp)
One of 13 units delivered in the first quarter of 1978.

have given proof of the integrity of the design and technology applied to the LRC concept. The LRC is maufactured by the Energy and Transportation Group of Bombardier Inc. By developing the LRC, Bombardier Inc and its partners have taken their share of the challenge of modernising and revitalising intercity passenger transportation by rail.

LRC Locomotive
Technical Data

Engine, net hp for traction	2 700
Carbody	Box, full width
Weight (fully loaded)	225 000 lb (102 000 kg)
Weight variation between trucks, fully loaded, not to exceed	2 000 lb (907 kg)
Max operating speed	125 mph (200 km/h)
Engine gross hp	3 725
Clearance	
a Roof height max	12' 0'' (3.6576 m)
b Max width over grab handles and above 4' 4'' over rail	10' 5⅝'' (3.1751 m)
c Length over couplers	63' 8'' (19.4056 m)
Wheel arrangement (two 2-axle trucks)	B-B
Number of traction motors	4
Type of journal bearings	Roller
Journal bearing diameter	6½'' (165.100 mm)
Minimum curvature, coupled units	23° radius curve
Brakes	Pneumatic, electropneumatic, dynamic and blended
Pneumatic brake schedule	26L
Dynamic brake	Standard range
All compressor capacity	237 cfm @ 1 050 rpm
Couplers	Type H with alignment control
Draftgear	Type NC390 rubber
Wind deflectors	2 with rearview mirrors
Air-conditioning	Provision for
Fuel capacity	Minimum 1 500 Imp gal
Train services power-head end	500 kW, 480 Vac 3 phase, 60 Hz
Type of control	Single station MU

LRC Coach
Technical Data

Length over couplers	85' 4'' (26.0096 m)
Length over corner posts	82' 4'' (25.0952 m)
Height roof (max)	12' 0'' (3.6576 m)
Height floor to window glass line	30'' (0.7620 m)
Width — side door	3' 0'' (0.9144 m)
Ceiling height	7' 0'' (2.1336 m)
Max interior width of car (at waist rail level)	9' 9'' (2.9718 m)
Truck centres	59' 6'' (18.1356 m)
Minimum radius of horizontal track curve with cars coupled	23°
Coach weight	96 700 lb (438 264 kg)
Weight equalisation between trucks	within 2%

Licensing Agreements: Bombardier has agreements with Commonwealth Engineering (NSE) Pty, Ltd, Australia, EMAQ, Brazil and CAF, Spain.

Sales: Bombardier received orders for locomotives from Venezuela, Iraq, Cuba, Jamaica, Greece, Mexico, Sri Lanka, Tunisia, Portugal, Bangladesh, the Canadian domestic market, and re-sales to Tanzania and Malawi. They also received in 1977/78 orders from the Canadian Government and Via Canada for 22 LRC locomotives and 50 coaches along with a lease/buy agreement from Amtrak for two LRC locomotives and ten coaches.

Equipment: Bombardier locomotives, available from 1 000 hp to 4 500 hp, meet most of the world's gauges, from 3 ft upwards and axle loads from 12 tonnes and up and conform to international clearance outlines, including North American and UIC specifications.
Bombardier Inc maintains extensive development facilities to keep abreast of an up to pioneer world railroad technology.

BRAINE-LE-COMTE
Usines de Braine-le-Comte SA

Rue des Frères Dulait, B-7490 Braine-le-Comte, Belgium

Products: Freight wagons.

Telephone: (067) 55 31 07
Telegrams: USINES, Braine-le-Comte
Telex: 57458

Chairman: Pol Boël
Manager: Jaques Preud'homme

BRAITHWAITE
Braithwaite & Co Ltd

Telephone: 45 9901
Telegrams: BROMKIRK, Calcutta
Telex: CA 7910

Head Office: 5 Hide Road, Calcutta 700043, India

Works: Clive Works, 5 Hide Road, Calcutta 700 043, India
Angus Works, Angus PO, Hooghly, West Bengal, India

Products: Freight wagons; pressed steel tanks; containers; cranes; wagon components.

Chairman and Managing Director: R N Sen
Chief Controller (Commercial and Technical): K R Sundaram
General Manager (Clive Works): R L Sengupta
General Manager (Augus Works): A N Sarkar

Constitution: Braithwaite is a Government of India undertaking, specialising in the manufacture of railway wagons, bridges, buildings for factories, power houses and steel plants, overhead electric travelling cranes, wharf cranes, railway breakdown cranes, diesel-electric cranes, trailers, coal and other material handling plants, jute mill machinery, pressed steel tanks, iron castings, steel forgings, etc. Braithwaite has also successfully executed orders for equipment from undertakings abroad in the Republic of Korea, Taiwan, Malaysia, Ghana, Philippines, Kenya, Yugoslavia, Burma, Sri Lanka and New Zealand. In recognition of its performance in the export market, the company received the first Award from the Government of India for outstanding performance in the export field (railway wagons and other engineering items).

Sales: Latest sales in 1977/78/79 include 300-tonne capacity 48-wheel wagons for Indian Railways, tank wagons for Tanzania, all side-door wagons to Uganda, PS wagons to Kuwait, Iraq, Bahrain and United Arab Emirates.

Furnace oil tank wagon for Burma Railways

A rake of open high-sided wagons (EAS) for Yugoslav Railways

Metric-gauge petrol tank wagons for Tanzanian Railways

30-tonne capacity wagon for Taiwan Railway

Special-purpose 300-tonne capacity 48-wheel wagon

All side-door bogie covered CGBW wagon (34 tonnes) for Uganda Railways

BRATSTVO

Preduzece Sinskih Vozila Subotica, Yugoslavia

Products: Freight wagons.

New equipment: The Bratstvo wagon plant is at present producing five types of wagon; a 13 m long flat wagon designed for carrying containers; types 1 and 2 two-axle covered wagons; a two-axle covered wagon ordered for operation over 1 000 mm gauge operation in Greece; and a bogie 1 000 mm gauge wagon also ordered by Greek Railways.

Telephone: 23 762 5
Telegrams: VAGONI, Yugoslavia
Telex: 15138

Sales: Last deliveries for domestic railways were three-axle coupled two-level wagon units for carrying automobiles. The unit accommodates 10 medium-class passenger cars or 20 light cars, or (maximum) 12 medium-class cars or 28 light cars.
The running gear and brake equipment is suited for the speeds of 100 km/h or alternatively for 120 km/h.
For 1 000 mm gauge a number of four-axle covered freight cars have been delivered to the Brazilian Railways. The wagon, with bogies and automatic couplings, sides and roof from thin metal, is designed for carrying 60 tonnes in tropical climate conditions.

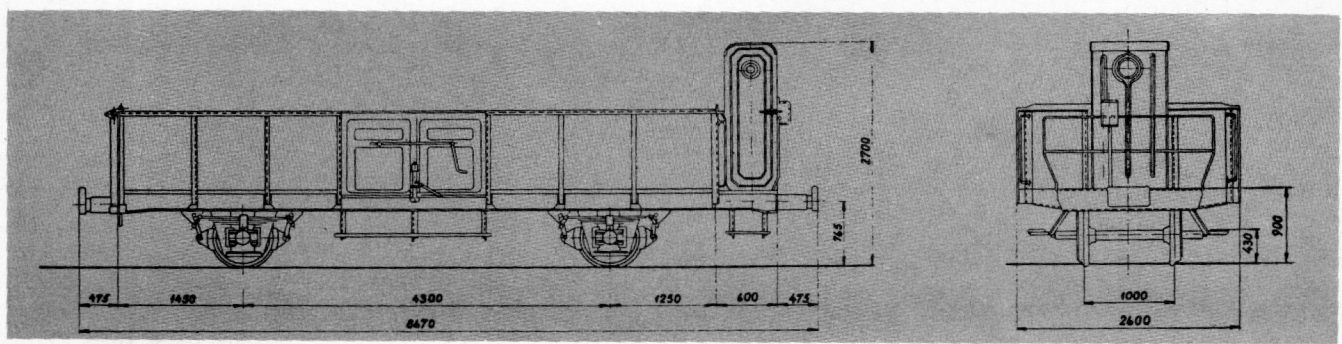

Two-axle open wagon 1 000 mm gauge

Two-axle open wagon for 1 000 mm gauge operation on Greek Railways

BREDA
Breda Costruzioni Ferroviarie SpA

Via Ciliegiole, 51100 Pistoia, Italy

Products: Passenger coaches, light alloy or steel electric trainsets for long distances, for rapid transit of commuters and for underground lines.

Chairman: Dr Eng Giuseppe Capuano
Vice Chairman: Dr Ing Pietro Fattori
General Manager: Dr Ing Corroda Fici
Vice General Manager: Alberto Bracco

Constitution: The San Giorgio Co was founded in 1907 in Pistoia as part of the company of the same name in Genova Sestri engaged in the repair of railway rolling stock. In 1914 this type of manufacturing was replaced by war production for the Army and Air Force. The production for the Air Force was later resumed in 1937. In 1949, after the firm split off from the San Giorgio Co, the trade name was changed into Officine Meccaniche Ferroviarie Pistoiesi SpA. In the post-war period, in addition to the basic activity involving the construction of trailing and trailed railway rolling stock, the company began to manufacture public transportation vehicles like buses and trolley cars. In 1968, as a result of the reorganisation of the State participation firms operating in the railway sector into the EFIM and after the Officine Meccaniche Ferroviarie Pistoiesi was absorbed into the Breda Ferroviaria of Milan, the new company was given the trade name of "Ferroviaria Breda Pistoiesi". This trade name was then finally changed into Breda Costruzioni Ferroviarie with head office and works in Pistoia.

Telephone: (0573) 367801
Telegrams: FERBREDA, Pistoia
Telex: 570186 BCF I

Light rail vehicle for Cleveland (USA) under construction at Breda's Pistoia plant

Sales: Following award of a contract from GCRTA of Cleveland, Ohio, USA in 1978 for 48 light rail vehicles valued at $30 960 000, Breda won another US order in 1979 from WMATA of Washington for the supply of 94 rapid transit cars for subway operation at a cost of $75 372 000.

BREL
British Rail Engineering Ltd
(wholly-owned subsidiary of British Railways Board)

Offices: Railway Technical Centre, London Road, Derby DE2 8UP, England
274/280 Bishopsgate, London EC2M 4XQ, England

Products: Diesel and electric locomotives and multiple units; passenger coaches; freight wagons; bogies; containers; steel, iron and non-ferrous castings; coil and laminated springs; crane machinery.

Chairman: J G Urquhart
Managing Director: I D Gardiner
Engineering Director: M V Casey
Financial Director: C R Wood
Commercial Director: J F Thring

Constitution: The company was formed in January 1970 as a subsidiary of the British Railways Board to manage the thirteen main railway works. It undertakes all types of railway engineering work both for British Rail and private companies. Exports are handled by BRE-Metro Limited, the joint export sales company of British Rail Engineering Ltd and Metro-Cammell Ltd.

Sales: To British Rail: High Speed Trains, comprising diesel electric power cars fitted with Paxman diesel engines giving an output of 1680 kW and Mk III passenger coaches with full air-conditioning, double-glazed windows and automatic internal doors. These trains are currently running at 200 km/h between Bristol/South Wales, London and Edinburgh and London and the West of England.
Advanced Passenger Train consisting of electric power cars and specially-designed aluminium trailer cars, capable of speeds up to 250 km/h on existing track. A unique feature of these trains is their ability to negotiate track curves at speeds up to 40 per cent higher than conventional trains by means of a tilt system.
Mk III coaches, similar in design to those used in HST formations, for use on locomotive-hauled main-line services.
3250 hp diesel-electric locomotives for heavy freight services.
Bogie steel carrying wagons (100-tonnes GLW, 24-tonnes tare).
Two-axle mineral hopper wagons (46-tonnes GLW, 13-tonnes tares).
Two-axle open vans (46-tonnes GLW, 14.5-tonnes tare).
30 ft steel dry freight containers (for Freightliner).

Telephone (Derby): 0332 49211
Telex (Derby): 37367 BRTEK G
Telephone (London): 01 247 5444
Telex (London): 885353 BR LNGHQ LDN G

Private Customers:
Diesel-hydraulic shunting locomotives and five types of wagon for Kenya Railways.
Coaches and four types of wagon for Tanzania Railways Corporation.
Ferry vans for use throughout Europe (80-tonnes GLW, 26-tonnes tare).
Narrow gauge bogies for Kalmar Verkstads AB of Sweden.
Two types of bogie wagon (narrow and broad-gauge) for Bangladesh Railways.

Interior of a second-class APT trailer car

Class 56 diesel electric heavy-duty freight locomotive

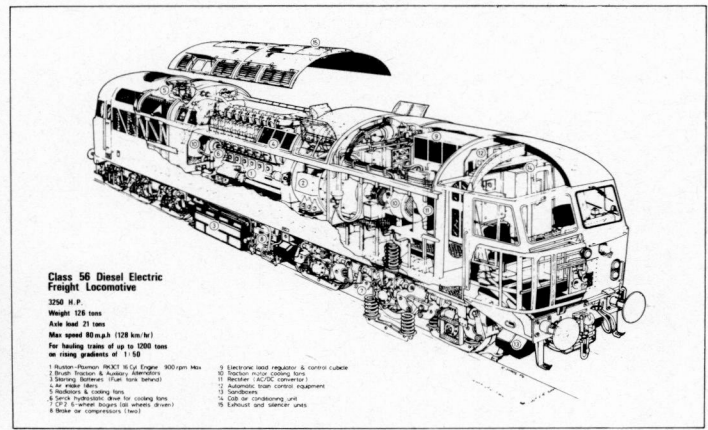
Cut-away view of Class 56 locomotive

High-Speed Train built by BREL at Derby and Crewe

APT undergoing trials on British Rail's West Coast main line

Class 314 electric multiple unit built at BREL's York Works for service in the Glasgow area

BREMER

Bremer Waggonbau GmbH

Postfach 110 109, Pfalzburger Strasse 251, 2800 Bremen 11, Federal Republic of Germany

Products: Passenger coaches; freight wagons, in particular repair and renovation.

Managing Director: Peter Müller
Export Sales: Chr Trahm

Telephone: 45 40 11
Telegrams: BREMER WAGGONBAU Bremen
Telex: 024 4423

Constitution: The company was formed in December 1975. The works occupy the site of the former Hansa Waggon AG.

BRE-METRO

(Export sales company of BRE and Metro-Cammell Ltd)

Offices: 274/280 Bishopsgate, London EC2M 4XQ, England
Railway Technical Centre, London Road, Derby DE2 8UP, England
(Registered Office): PO Box 248, Leigh Road, Washwood Heath,
Birmingham B8 2YJ, England

Products: Diesel and electric locomotives; multiple-unit trains; passenger coaches; freight wagons; rapid transit stock; bogies.

Chairman: J G Urquhart
General Manager: F D Pinto
Senior Sales Engineers: R A Hedge
R W Kelly
T Robson
Contracts Manager: N A Brunt
Senior Contracts Engineer: R J Champion

Sales: Recent sales include diesel-hydraulic shunting locomotives and bogie wagons of five different types (low-sided wagons, covered wagons with sliding roofs, covered

Telephone: (London) 01 247 5444
(Derby) 0332 49211
(Birmingham) 021-3274777
Telex: (London) 885353 BR ENGHQ LDN G
(Derby) 37367 BR TEK G
(Birmingham) 33401 METRO BHAM

wagons with sliding doors, covered wagons with hinged doors and hopper wagons) to Kenya Railways; coaches (first-class, second-class and restaurant cars) and four types of bogie wagon (low-sided wagons, high-sided wagons, covered wagons with sliding doors and brake vans) to the Tanzania Railways Corporation; two types of bogie covered wagon (broad-gauge and narrow-gauge) to Bangladesh Railways; high-capacity ferry vans (80 tonnes GLW, 26 tonnes tare) to Danzas SA of Switzerland; narrow-gauge bogies to Kalmar Verkstads AB of Sweden.
Current projects include the design of a new locomotive and coach specifically for the export market, as well as the continuous development of existing designs of all types of rolling stock and bogies for individual customers.

525 hp diesel-hydraulic shunting locomotive built for Kenya Railways

High-capacity ferry wagon built for Danzas SA of Switzerland

Covered van with sliding roof built for Kenya Railways

440 of these low-sided open wagons have been supplied to Kenya Railways by BRE-Metro Ltd

BRIGGS & TURIVAS
Briggs & Turivas, Inc

Box 270, 310 Grant Street, Dennison, Ohio 44621, USA

Telephone: (614) 922 5994

Products: Freight wagons.

BRISSONNEAU ET LOTZ
SA Des Établissements Brissonneau et Lotz

38 avenue Kleber, 75784 Paris, France

Products: Electric, diesel-electric, diesel-hydraulic, gas-turbine, mining and industrial locomotives; electric, diesel, gas-turbine railcars; electric and diesel multiple units; passenger coaches.

Telephone: (1) 727 35 79
Telegrams: ETABRIS, Paris
Telex: 62719F

Constitution: The railway division was taken over by Alsthom in 1972 and merged with that company's Traction Division. The name of Brissonneau et Lotz is, however, still being used.

BRITANNIA ENGINEERING
Britannia Engineering Works (Wagon Division)

PO Mokameh, Distt. Patna, Bihar 803302, India

Telephone: 51 Mokameh
Telegrams: BRITTANIA, Mokameh

Products: Freight wagons as follows:
CR - 4 wheeler Covered Wagon (BG) Carrying capacity 22 tonnes, Plain Bearing
'O' 4 wheeler Open Wagon (BG) Carrying capacity 24 tonnes, Plain Bearing
MC 4 wheeler Covered Wagon (MG) Carrying capacity 24 tonnes, Plain Bearing
MCM 4 wheeler Covered Cattle Wagon (MG) Carrying capacity 24 tonnes, Plain Bearing

MOX 4 wheeler Open Wagon (MG) Carrying capacity 24 tonnes, Plain Bearing
MBTPX 8 wheeler Tank Wagon (MG) Carrying capacity 24 tonnes, Plain Bearing
BCX 8 wheeler Covered Wagon (BG) Carrying capacity 52 tonnes, Roller Bearing
BOX 8 wheeler Open Wagon (BG) Carrying capacity 55 tonnes, Roller Bearing
CRT 4 wheeler Covered Wagon (BG) Carrying capacity 28 tonnes, Roller Bearing

---

BROOKVILLE
Brookville Locomotive

PO Box 340, Pickering Street, Brookville, Pennsylvania 15825, USA

Vice President (Marketing): Dalph S McNeil
Sales Engineer: Robert R Schreyer

Telephone: (814) 849 7321
Telegrams: BROLOC

Products: Four to 20 tonne diesel or gasoline locomotives with hydraulic torque converter or mechanical transmissions, designed for industrial, plantation, mining or yards.

Examples from Brookville's standard locomotive production line; designed for industrial, plantation, mining or yards

---

BRUSH
Brush Electrical Machines Ltd (Traction Division)
(Member of the Hawker Siddeley Group)

Falcon Works, Loughborough, Leicestershire LE11 1HJ, England

Products: Mainline diesel-electric and electric locomotives. Diesel-electric transfer and shunting locomotives. Power equipments including alternators, generators, motors,

Telephone: 0509 63131
Telegrams: BRUSH, Loughborough
Telex: 341091

and auxiliary machines, transformers, rectifiers, invertors, electronic and conventional control gear equipment for diesel-electric and electric locomotives, diesel rail cars, diesel and electric multiple unit trains; complete electrical propulsion equipment for rapid transit trains.

Thyristor controlled three-car electric multiple unit class 314 operated by British Rail
Brush equipment is installed in the Clyderail Class 314 trainsets, a 25 kV/6.25 kV 50 Hz single-phase system operation; equipment supplied consists of a transformer mounted under the trailer pantograph car, an under-car mounted three-arm assymetric bridge, two-stage control thyristor convertor and four dc series with axle suspended traction motors continuously rated at 410 V, 275 A (75% field), permanently connected in a series parallel configuration. Associated control and protection equipment is included.

Chairman: J M Durber
Managing Director: A R Creswick
Traction Director: G S W Calder
Contracts Manager: R J Gardener
Sales Manager: D R Minkley
Engineering Manager: P Duerden

Constitution: Brush Electrical Engineering Ltd was formed in 1889 with the acquisition of the Falcon Engine and Car Works in Loughborough, and the company has been closely involved in electric traction since that time. Falcon Works' history of rail traction building began in 1875, with the manufacture of steam locomotives. Originally producing tram cars in large numbers, Brush entered the diesel-electric field in 1948 and since that date have built 2 000 diesel locomotives and power equipments and provided electrical equipment for over 2 500 power cars.

Sales: Major sales during 1979 were 30 sets of electric train heating equipment (including alternator and control equipment), 236 sets of auxiliary supply equipment for sleeping coaches, four diesel-electric 350 hp shunting locomotives for Kaduna Oil Refinery, Nigeria.

BUDD

The Budd Company (Railway Division)

Head Office: Red Lion & Verree Roads, Philadelphia, Pennsylvania 19115, USA
Works: Red Lion Plant, Red Lion & Verree Roads, Philadelphia, Pennsylvania 19115, USA

Products: Stainless-steel passenger coaches and components, fabricated passenger coach bogies and components.

Chairman: G F Richards
General Manager (Railway Division): W I Wilson
Marketing Manager (Railway Division): S W Madeira
International Sales Manager (Railway Division): R H Behrend

Foreign Agent Europe: 9 rue de l'Industrie, 92 Courbevoie, France

Constitution: In April 1978 Budd became a US-based operation of Thyssen AG of Federal Republic of Germany.

Export Sales: International Activities, Philadelphia, Pennsylvania 19115, USA

Recent Sales: Deliveries during 1979 include 300 rapid transit cars for Chicago Transit Authority; 208 rapid transit cars for the cities of Baltimore (Mass Transit Administration) and Miami (Metropolitan Dade County); 55 double-decked suburban cars for Chicago Regional Transportation Authority; 13 SPV-200s for Connecticut Department of Transportation, to be operated by Amtrak; one SPV-2000 for the Federal Railroad Administration, US Department of Transportation.

New Equipment: In 1978 Budd introduced the International Rail Car (IRC) designed for worldwide use. It is manufactured in modular units so that it can be easily assembled using local labour and industry or assembled complete. The car can be custom finished to meet local needs and special conditions, but uses standardised components.
The entire structure of the IRC, except for the end underframes which are of high-tensile carbon steel, is made of stainless steel. The interior has been designed for low maintenance and easy adaptability, and numerous optional configurations are available. The coach seats 109 passengers and is equipped with two rest rooms, fluorescent light and moulded fibreglass seats. The IRC is available with centre AAR couplers or UIC hook and side buffers, and in varying lengths, track gauges and wheel sizes. The IRC consists of major subassemblies which are joined together with bolts or resistance welding, depending on the customer's circumstances. It will meet UIC strength requirements. Construction is of stainless type 200 or 300 steel, with collision posts, coupler pocket, end sill bolster and side sills made from a high-strength alloy steel.
The standard gauge bogie is a modified Budd Pioneer design using inboard bearings. It is made of high-strength steels and standard sections whenever possible. A pneumatically-controlled pressure braking system is fitted with a standard handbrake at "B" end of car.
Two toilet facilities are provided at one end of the car. Each includes a stainless-steel hopper, steel wash basin and cold water tap, towel and toilet tissue dispensers, waste bin, coat hook and mirror. A total of 600 litres of water is carried in high-density moulded polyethylene tanks above the vestibule ceiling. Fluorescent fixtures in the ceiling provide sufficent light for reading.
An axle-mounted brushless generator is powered by a belt drive, supplying low-voltage direct current. It charges a lead-acid battery mounted beneath the floor.
Seats are of glassfibre reinforced plastic, mounted back-to-back on painted steel tubular frames, for three and two-seating. Tinted laminated 6.350 mm safety-glass windows can be lowered to provide a 508 mm clear vertical opening. Floor deck is covered with smooth sheet rubber. Four stainless-steel sliding doors are on the sides, two at each end of the compartment. Interior doors for toilet and locker are melamine-faced plywood. Six stainless-steel static exhaust ventilators are in the roof.
The entire exterior of the car is stainless steel. Two steps, each with open risers and stainless-steel anti-skid treads, can be made to match any platform height. Galvanised

Telephone (Office): (215) 673 1020
Telegrams (Office): LIONRED
Telex (Office): 710 670 9970
Telephone (Works): 215-OR 3-1020
Telegrams (Works): LIONRED
Telephone (European Agent): 333 58 60
Telex (European Agent): 842 61061

Basic interior of the IRC with 109 seats

Budd-designed and built International Rail Car
The IRC can be shipped as either a complete car or in kit form (see picture top right).

safety chains are provided to hook across open passages at both ends and at side entrances. Optional equipment includes: hook and buffers in place of couplers, wooden-slatted blinds on windows, curtains on windows, insulation of side frame, end frame and floor. Seating: hard bench seats, vinyl-cushioned seats (three and two or two and two seating), fibreglass (two and two seating), Eastern-style toilets, retention type toilet, electro-mechanical water cooler, six exhaust fans and five recirculating fans in place of static exhaust, increased water capacity, electric heating with power train-lined from locomotive, truck wheel size modification (larger), variation in track gauge, air-conditioning with power trainlined from locomotive.

Length over couplers 22.8 m; height, overall max, incl exhaust 3.8 m; width overall, 2.8 m; height, couplers 0.8 m (options available); height, floor 1.1 m (approx); width, inside clear 2.1 m; height, inside clear 2.2 m; aisle width 0.5 m; bogie centres 16 m (options available); bogie wheelbase 2.1 m; wheel diameter 0.7 m (options available); track gauge 1.4 m (options available); seat spacing 1.6 m (options available); seated capacity 109 (options available); weight (ready to run) 22 tonnes (approx).

Budd said its survey indicates that a market for approximately 14 000 cars of this type exists within the next five years.

In January 1978 the company introduced the SPV-2000, a diesel self-propelled passenger railcar capable of speeds up to 120 mph (193 km/h). The SPV-2000 subsequently completed a successful testing and demonstration tour of several major cities, including Washington, Philadelphia, Boston and Atlantic City.

The Budd Company's new railway vehicle, the SPV-2000 (right)
It moves more people a given distance on one gallon of fuel than any other type of train. Shown is the commuter version which seats 109 passengers. A coach version can seat 86.

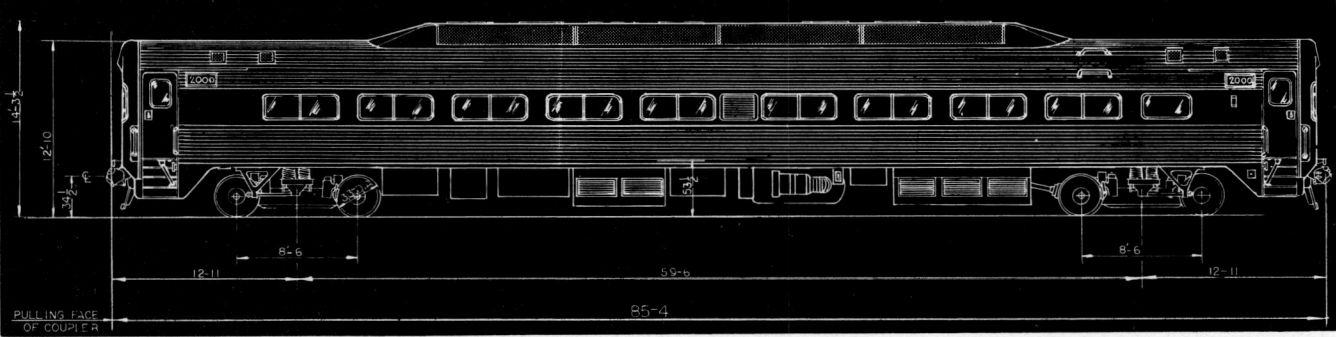

Commuter version of Budd's new SPV-2000

Bodyshell is of ribbed spot-welded stainless steel and meets AAR strength requirements including the 363 200 kg compression test. The prototype SPV-2000 has an aerodynamically-shaped fibreglass nose bolted on to one end. This will become the inter-city version; the commuter version, shown right and above, will operate without the nose. Both versions have Pioneer III bogies featuring coil springing and air suspension.

BURN STANDARD CO LTD

Head Office: Burn Standard Co Ltd, 10-C Hungerford Street, Calcutta-700 017, India

Works: Howrah, Burnpur, Raniganj, Durgapur, Ondal, Gulfarbari, Jabalpur, Niwar & Salem.

Chairman and Managing Director: Lalit Chandra Chib

Products: Railway rolling stock and components; centre buffer couplers and components; points and crossings; crossing sleepers; casting-steel, grey iron, S G iron and alloy steel; forging, stamping and pressing; railway sleepers and fishplates; springs for railway and automotive industry.

Constitution: Burn Standard Company Ltd, a Government of India Undertaking, is successor to Burn and Co Ltd and The Indian Standard Wagon Co, Ltd. The company came into existence following the nationalisation of the undertakings of the two companies by the President of India on 1 April, 1975. The company has two engineering

Telephone: 44-1067, 1762, 1772, 1788
Telegrams: BURNWAGON Calcutta
Telex: BURN CAL CA2795

units located at Howrah and Burnpur in West Bengal and nine refractory and ceramic units spread over different parts of the country.

Established in 1874, the Howrah Works of the company was the first manufacturer of rolling stock in India and pioneers in foundry practice and structural steel fabrications of a wide range including bridge construction. The Works have extensive facilities for manufacture of railroad equipment such as crossing sleepers, switches and crossings. The Burnpur Works manufactures prototype of almost all new types of wagons introduced by the Indian Railways and have guided the Railway Board in design and manufacture of wagons for use in the country and also for export. It specialises in production of springs for coaches, locomotives, wagons and automobiles and for various other uses. The Burnpur Works also specialises in heavy die forgings, material handling structurals and equipment for the mining industry.

CADOUX

Établissements Cadoux

9 rue de Bassano, 75016 Paris, France

Telephone: 53 74 62

Products: Freight wagons.

CAF

Construcciones y Auxiliar de Ferrocarriles SA
(Member of Servicio de Exportacion de Material Ferroviario)

Padilla 17, Madrid 6, Spain

Products: Electric, diesel-electric and diesel-mechanical locomotives; electric and diesel-electric railcars; passenger coaches; rapid transit stock; freight wagons; rolling stock components.

President: José I Cangas
Chairman: Pedro Ardaiz
General Manager: Juan José Anza

Telephone: 225 11 00
Telegrams: CAFAUXILIAR, Madrid
Telex: 23197

Constitution: The present company, Construccones y Auxiliar de Ferrocarriles, SA was formed by the merger of Material Movil y Construcciones, SA (MMC) into Compania Auxiliar de Ferrocarriles, SA (CAF) retaining the initials CAF. It is the largest manufacturer of railway rolling stock in Spain. Established in 1917 when deliveries started for RENFE.

CALLEGARI

José Callegari E Hijos

Rivadavia y Peru, Zarate, Pcia Buenos Aires, Argentina

Products: Freight wagons.

Telephone: 2800 3228

President: Pablo A A Callegari
Director General: Clara Mandelli Vda de Callegari
Sales Director: Ing Eduardo Rivas
Export Director: Ing Eduardo Rivas

CANTON MOTIVE POWER

Canton Motive-Power Machinery Works

Canton, Kwangtung, People's Republic of China

Products: Basically steam locomotives, but a trial 380 hp internal combustion narrow-gauge locomotive was produced in March 1975 and two others have been produced subsequently for local province operation.

CAREL FOUCHE
Carel Fouché SA

Head Office: 55 rue d'Amsterdam, 75366 Paris (Cedex 8), France

Works: Aubevoye; Le Mans

Sales Organisation: FRANCORAIL-MTE

Products: Railway passenger cars of stainless steel and conventional design.

President: R Juchs

Constitution: For nearly a century rolling stock has been the main activity of Carel Fouché. The company has two factories specialising in rail car manufacture, at Le Mans and Aubevoye. From 1935 onwards construction transferred to stainless steel and

Telephone: 874 01 71
Telegrams: CARLANG, Paris 8
Telex: 290985F

since then Carel Fouché has been continuously producing motor trainsets and inter-city passenger coaches.

Among the company's main stainless-steel products in France are all the electrical motor trainsets for the Paris suburban network, trainsets for regional services, main-line coaches for the Trans-Europ-Express and the Mistral. In the export field several countries have opted for stainless steel, including Algeria, Brazil, the Ivory Coast, Congo and Tunisia.

In August 1973, together with the companies Creusot-Loire, De Dietrich, Jeumont-Schneider and MTE, Carel Fouché created a *Groupement d'Intérêt Economique* under the name of Francorail-MTE.

Second-class/baggage car with driver's cab for push-pull working by diesel locomotive in Algeria (SNTF)

CASARALTA
Officine di Casaralta SpA

Via Ferrarese 205, I-40128 Bologna, Italy

Products: Electric locomotives and railcars; single and double-deck passenger coaches; freight wagons.

President: Rag Aldo Farina
Chairman: Dott Ing Giorgio Regazzoni
General Manager: Dott Ing Carlo Farina

Telephone: 35 84 54
Telegrams: ROTABILI, Bologna
Telex: 511068

Model of Italian State Railways E656 electric locomotive hauling double-deck coaches

CAT
Compañia Auxiliar de Transportes SA

Avenida José Antonio 20, Apartado 358, Madrid 14, Spain

Products: Freight wagons.

Telephone: 797 91 00
Telegrams: AUTRANS, Madrid

President: D Miguel Igartua Losa
Sales Director: D José Ma Oteiza

Sales: Under construction at the end of 1979 were bulk powder cars and tank wagons.

CATTANEO
Ferriere Cattaneo SA

6512 Giubiasco, Switzerland

Products: Freight wagons.

Managing Director: Rag Fausto Cattaneo

Constitution: The company was established in 1870.

Sales: Among work in hand or recently delivered are various types of freight car

Telephone: 092 27 31 31/32/33/34
Telegrams: FERRUM
Telex: 79392

including special wagons for carrying cement and grain for Swiss Federal Railways and for private customers.

New equipment: Wagon range now includes a 58 m³ capacity cement tank wagon which consists of two separate tanks (2 × 29 m³). Tare weight is 24.2 tons; length over buffers, 13.2 m. Pneumatic loading and emptying is by the Cattaneo-Streblow system operating at a pressure of 2 atm.

CEGIELSKI
Cegielski Locomotive and Wagon Works
(Member of Kolmex)

Zaklady Przemyslu Metalowego H Cegielski, 61-485 Poznan ul Dzier zynskiego 223/229, Poland

Exports: Mokotowska, 49.00-542, Warsaw, Poland

Telephone: 212 31
Telex: 0415343

Products: Electric locomotives. During 1977, Cegielski's plant at Poznan completed the first 4 000 kW production electric locomotive which entered operation with Polish State Railways (PKP) during 1978 as tandem units hauling primarily heavy freight trains. During 1978 the company also delivered 75 two-class compartment coaches to PKP.

CENTRAL CHINA PLANT
Central China Locomotive and Rolling Stock Plant

Changsha, Hunan, People's Republic of China.

Products: Since 1969 has produced high-powered diesel-electric locomotives; also manufactures passenger coaches and freight wagons.

CESKA LIPA

Vagonka Ceska Lipa
(Member of Strojexport)

Telephone: 248 851
Telex: 171 208

Vaclabske nam 56, Prague 1, Czechoslovakia

Products: Freight wagons.

New equipment: In 1978 Ceská Lipa started to manufacture a new type of two-axle open goods wagon for the transportation of piece, paletised and bulk consignments not requiring covering. Besides the usual ways of loading and unloading, the wagon may be emptied on rotary or end tipplers. The steel body with a wooden floor has a two-leaved door 1 800 mm wide and of equal height with the walls. End walls which are formed as detachable flaps are hinged at the upper edge and secured by a locking shaft on the headstock.

The underframe is welded from rolled and pressed sections. Front parts of the underframe are calculated and designed for additional mounting of automatic couplers according to OSShD/UIC prescriptions. Side walls are welded from rolled sections and flat sheets of 5 mm thickness. There is no upper cant rail at the door openings. Door leafs, pressed from 6 mm sheets, may be opened so that they lie flat on the side walls and may be locked in this position. The end flaps have welded frames from rolled sections and 5 mm flat sheets. After releasing of safety catches the end flaps may be removed. Labyrinth arrangement of the end flaps and door edges ensures tightness against losses of bulk material above 2 mm granulation.

Running gear with double shackle suspension, roller bearings, leaf springs U C type 20,

and monoblock wheels is designed for 20-tonne axle loads. Flat horn guides are riveted to the longitudinal bearer.

Non-continuous drawgear is provided with springs of a peak force of 400 kN and 65 mm hub. Plunger buffers with spring collars of a peak force of 350 kN and 75 mm stroke. Air brake DAKO. Space is provided for additional mounting of an electromagnetic brake and feed piping.

Main specifications:

Gauge (mm)	1 435
Weight of empty wagon (tonnes)	13
Carrying capacity (tonnes)	27
Weight of loaded wagon (tonnes)	40
Loading length (mm)	8 760
Loading width (mm)	2 760
Loading area (m²)	24
Loading space (m³)	36
Height of walls (mm)	1 500
Max speed at 20-tonne axle load (km/h)	100

The wagon complies to S regulations at 20-tonne axle load, but the wagon body is designed to sustain loading corresponding to 22-tonne axle loads.

CFD

Compagnie de Chemins de Fer Départementaux

Telephone: 561 14 30
Telex: 660 955F

10 avenue Friedland, 75008 Paris, France

Products: Diesel-hydraulic locomotives from 200 hp to highest power range and for all track gauges; lightweight diesel-hydraulic railcars.

President: F de Coincy
Director General: M Grau

Two type C 500 H diesel-hydraulic locomotives linked together in a multiple unit at Oujda, Morocco

Type B 400 HSP diesel-hydraulic heavy-oil safety locomotive

Type BB 1500 diesel-hydraulic locomotive (1 500 hp)

Two 2300 railcars in the form of a multiple unit (metric gauge) working in Portugal

---

CFMF

Compagnie Française de Matériel Ferroviaire

Telephone: (1) 574 98 39
Telex: 642 503

36 rue Guersant, 75017 Paris, France

Products: Freight wagons; tank wagons.

CHANGCHOU DIESEL LOCOMOTIVE WORKS

Changchou, Kiangsu, People's Republic of China.

Products: Has produced diesel locomotives ranging from 60 to 120 hp since 1965; larger diesel-hydraulic locomotives up to 500 hp have been produced for mine and industrial service since 1968. Biggest production is devoted to the CZ80 narrow-gauge diesel used mainly in China's forestry, salting plants, power-stations and construction works. The CZ80A is for 762 mm gauge operation and the CZ80B for 600 mm gauge. General characteristics are as follows: axle arrangement: 0-3-0; wheel diameter: 600 mm; weight in working order: 12 tons; axle weight: 4 tons; axle base: 900 mm; full axle base: 1 800 mm; speed, tractive effort and tons hauled (table overleaf):

CZ80 hp diesel locomotive

Gear No	Speed (km/h)	Tractive effort (kg)	Tons hauled on gradients (percentage)						
			0	5	10	15	20	25	30
1	6.06	2 664	254	166	121	95	77	64	55
2	9.88	1 705	159	102	73	56	45	37	30
3	15.96	1 055	94	58	41	30	23	18	14
4	25.61	656	54	32	21	14	10	7	4

Note: resistance is assumed at 10 kg/tonne on average

minimum curve: 20 m; transmission: mechanical type; coupler height: 600 or 320 mm; fuel tank: capacity 180 kg; sander: capacity 50 kg; diesel engine: model 4135 k-1, rated output 80 hp at 2 500 rpm, fuel consumption 175 g/hp/h, starting motor 24V; overall dimensions: with chain coupler, length × width × height = 5 170 × 1 910 × 2 740 mm, with pin coupler, length × width × height = 5 070 × 1 910 × 2 740 mm.

CHANGCHUN LOCOMOTIVE WORKS

Changchun, Jilin, People's Republic of China

Products: Steam locomotives. Changchun has produced steam locomotives, including the Heping (Peace) freight locomotive, since 1959. The locomotive has a top speed of 80 km/h, operates at 21 km/h on 0.6 degrees gradient. Also constructs 234 hp steam locomotives for mine operations.

CHANGCHUN PASSENGER CAR WORKS

Changchun, Jilin, People's Republic of China

Products: Lightweight passenger coaches for high-speed (160 km/h) operations. Latest

equipment manufactured includes (Peking) Beijing Metro sets which first went into operation in October 1969: 19 m long cars designed to operate at a max of 80 km/h, accommodate 186 passengers (60 seated), operate over 750 V dc lines; passenger coaches and sleeping cars. The type YM-22 third-class sleeping coaches, first built in 1959 by Changchun, are still in operation: eight sleeping compartments, max speed 120 km/h.

CHIANGAN ROLLING STOCK
Chiangan Rolling Stock Plant

Chiangan, Wuhan, Hupei, People's Republic of China.

Products: Freight wagons and passenger coaches.

CHICAGO FREIGHT CAR
Chicago Freight Car Co

205 W Touhy Avenue, Park Ridge, Illinois 60068, USA

Products: Special and industrial freight wagons.

CHICHIHAERH CAR PLANT
Chichihaerh Railway Car Plant

Chichihaerh, Heilungkiang, People's Republic of China.

Products: Freight wagons; latest reported product is a 370 tonne flat wagon for transport of complete machines and heavy equipment.

CHISHUYEN ROLLING STOCK
Chishuyen Rolling Stock Plant

Changchou, Kiangsu, People's Republic of China

Products: Diesel-electric and diesel-hydraulic locomotives. Produced a 2 000 hp

locomotive with electric transmission in 1958. In 1975/76 produced the 5 000 hp diesel-hydraulic locomotive, *Dongfanghong 4,* after five years' development. Tests were carried out during 1976 in mountainous territory in north-west China, and in service on the Shanghai—Nanking and Shanghai—Hangchow lines. The unit is reported to have overcome earlier tortional vibrations which occurred when the high-output engine was operated at full load at 1 500 rpm.

CHUCHOU ROLLING STOCK WORKS

Chuchou, Hunan, People's Republic of China

Products: Gondola wagons and all types of freight wagon. More recently development work on electric locomotives has started.

CID
Cid SA

Telephone: 33163/39

Calle 37, No 1005, Rosario, Argentina

Products: Passenger coaches; freight wagons.

CIMMCO INTERNATIONAL

ECE House, 28A Kasturba Gandhi Marg, New Delhi-110001, India

Products: Flat, hopper, box, open high-sided, tank, covered, container, bottom discharge and special-purpose wagons.

General Manager: D K Goyal

Telephone: 44381
Telegrams: CIMWAG New Delhi
Telex: 3618 CIMC IN

Marketing Manager: C S Madharan

Sales: Railway equipment sales in 1978/79 totalled approximately $US 25 million. Orders have been carried out for Nigeria, Sri Lanka, Viet-Nam, Burma, Bangladesh, Sudan and Pakistan.

CIMT-LORRAINE
Compagnie Industrielle de Matériel de Transport

42 avenue Raymond Poincaré, 75116 Paris, France

Products: Diesel-electric and electric trainsets; passenger coaches; freight wagons.

President: Roland Koch
Director General: Jean Collin

Telephone: 505 14 00
Telex: CIMTRAN 610 119F

Commercial Manager: Jacques Smith

Constitution: Founded in 1918.

CKD
CKD Praha
(Member of Czechoslovakia's Pragoinvest diesel locomotive exporting group)

Head Office: U Kolbenky 159, Praha 9, Czechoslovakia

Export sales: Pragoinvest, Ceskomoravská 23 18 056 Praha, Czechoslovakia

Telephone: 83 13 54
Telegrams: CKD, Praha
Telex: 01 1160/01 1229

Products: Diesel-electric locomotives; diesel engines.

Constitution: The company began steam locomotive production in 1900 and diesel locomotive production in 1927.

CLAYTON EQUIPMENT
Clayton Works, Hatton, Derby DE6 5EB, England

Products: Battery, trolley and diesel locomotives with electric, hydraulic or mechanical transmissions; electric and battery driven industrial and mining locomotives; special purpose internal combustion engined or electric rail vehicles.

Telephone: 0283 88 2382
Telegrams: CLAYQUIP, Derby
Telex: 341828

General Manager: R A Boast

Constitution: The Clayton Equipment Co Ltd, now the Clayton Unit of Clarke Chapman Ltd's International Combustion Division, was incorporated in 1931 by S R Devlin to carry on the manufacture of locomotives, rail cars, transfer cars and general engineering products.

In 1957 International Combustion (Holdings) Ltd acquired the whole of the shareholding in the company, but Clayton's continued to operate as an entirely self-contained and self-supporting unit.

In 1969 the company was fully integrated into International Combustion Ltd which merged with Clarke Chapman Ltd in 1974. At this time the present Clayton Unit was formed to operate as an independent manufacturing and marketing organisation for Clayton Locomotives.

CLW

Chittaranjan Locomotive Works

Telephone: Asansol 2021/2022/2023
Telegrams: LOCOWORKS

Chittaranjan, Burdwan District, West Bengal, India

Products: Electric locomotives; diesel shunters; narrow-gauge diesel locomotive.

General Manager: K S Ramaswamy

Constitution: This motive power plant, a production unit of Indian Railways, started production in January 1950 and by the end of March 1977 had built a total of 3 253 locomotives, 2 351 steam, 593 electric, and 309 diesel.

Sales: During 1976/77 a total of 44 electric and 32 diesel locomotives were delivered to Indian Railways.

New equipment: CLW is simultaneously manufacturing five types of locomotive, three types of electric and two types of diesel, all entirely designed and developed in the country by the Design Wing of the Research, Designs and Standards Organisation and the Chittaranjan Locomotive Works.

The first dual voltage (ac/dc) electric locomotive manufactured in India was turned out in January 1975 and series production of this type of locomotive has been commenced. These locomotives are to be used to haul both high speed passenger trains and heavy goods trains between Bombay and Ahmedabad on the Western Railway. The section from Bombay Central to Virar was electrified at 1.5 kV dc during the period 1928-36, whereas electrification from Virar to Ahmedabad, recently completed, is on the modern system of 25 kV, 50 cycle, single-phase ac.

The manufacture of traction motors and traction equipments for electric locomotives was taken up in 1965. The largest traction motors ever built in India, each with 1 580 hp, were manufactured by the CLW for use on ac freight type locomotives. CLW is currently manufacturing type TAO-659 traction motors for ac mixed traffic (WAM-4) and ac/dc dual voltage locomotives (WCAM-1).

Class WCG-2 dc freight locomotive built by CLW for Indian Railways
Co-Co; 4 200 hp; axle load 22 tonnes; voltage supply 1 500 V dc; weight 132 tonnes; max speed 120 km/h; braking, rheostatic.

Class WAM-4 mixed traffic electric locomotive of which 185 have been delivered by CLW to Indian Railways
Co-Co; axle load 18.8 tonnes; supply voltage 23 kV; weight 112.8 tonnes; braking, rheostatic; max service speed 120 km/h; 3 640 hp.

Class WDS-4 diesel-hydraulic shunter for Indian Railways
Axle load, 2 000 kg; max speed, shunting, 27 km/h; max speed, mainline service, 65 km/h; weight 6 000 kg.

CLYDE

The Clyde Engineering Company Pty Ltd

Telephone: 682 2111
Telegrams: CYDEENGCO, Sydney
Telex: 21647

Head Office: Factory Street, Granville, New South Wales 2142, Australia.

Branches (Workshops): Sydney Road, Bathurst, New South Wales, Australia. Neptune Terrace, Rosewater, South Australia. Links Avenue, Eagle Farm, Queensland, Australia.

Products: Diesel-electric and diesel-hydraulic locomotives; rapid transit stock.

Chairman: Maj Gen Sir Denzil MacArthur-Onslow, CBE, DSO, ED
Managing Director: Owen G Edwards
Sales Manager: Kevin C Thomson

Constitution: This company has from the early days built steam locomotives for Australian Railways. In 1951, by arrangement with General Motors Corporation, they started to build diesel-electric locomotives to GM design incorporating Electro-Motive power equipment.

Sales: Contracts completed 1978/79: fourteen 2 200/2 000 hp diesel-electric locomotives and twelve 1 650/1 500 hp diesel-electric locomotives for Queensland Railways; 42 1 650/1 500 hp and twelve 1 425/1 310 hp diesel-electrics for New Zealand Railways (rebuild and modernise).

CNCFSA

Constructora Nacional de Carros de Ferrocarril SA

Telephone: 5 28 80 21/ 5 28 77 11
Telegrams: CONCARRIL, Mexico City

Paseo de la Reforma 369, Mezzanine, Mexico 5, DF, Mexico

Lightweight, all-metal subway car built by SNCFSA for Mexico City

Products: Box car 70- or 100-ton capacity, outside post, nailable steel floor; covered hopper car 70- or 100-ton capacity, without centre sill, with centre discharges, all steel, welded with outside post or open top hopper; open top gondola car with fixed ends solid bottom floor, 70- or 100-ton capacity for general service; 70-ton airside dump car; bulk commodity gondola 100-ton capacity; tank car non-insulated DOT111A100W1 designed to carry 20 000 gallons of non-hazardous materials; flat car 70-ton capacity for general service equipped with hydraulic and pneumatic absorption device; flat car (piggy-back) equipped to carry trailer-bodies or containers; top cupola caboose equipped with oil heaters, toilets, water tanks and standard features; lightweight subway cars for 162/165 passengers with fully automatic controls; and passenger cars equipped with fabricated bogies and all-steel body for 68 persons.

Director-General: Ing Enrique Ollivier Guibaudet
Subdirector, Sales: Ing César Mota Aguilar
Subdirector, Marketing: Lic Sergio Camargo Piñuela

Sales: Deliveries completed during 1979 included: 800 box cars for Chicago, Rock Island & Pacific; 500 open wagons for Missouri Pacific; 300 covered hopper wagons for North American, in addition to completion of domestic orders for Mexican National.

General-purpose tank wagon
During 1979 a number of tank wagons were designed and built for Mexican Railroads.

COBRASMA
Cobrasma SA

Rua da Estacão, 523 Osasco, São Paulo, Brazil

Products: Freight wagons; passenger coaches; 'Ride Control' bogies; rolling stock components.

President: Luis Eulalio de Bueno Vidigal
Vice-President: Luis Eulalio de Bueno Vidigal Filho
Vice President: Marcos Xavier da Silveira

Telephone: 801 8000/227 6711
Telegrams: COBRASMA, São Paulo
Telex: (011) 23145

Managing Director: José Teixeira Beraldo
Export Sales: Eduardo Hubert Kirmaier Monteiro

Constitution: Cobrasma has the largest steel foundry in Latin America with a capacity of 30 000 tonnes of finished products annually. The company has the capacity to produce 3000 freight wagons (1 252 were built in 1978), 300 passenger coaches, emus, metro and pre-metro cars, and 1200 track turnouts annually.

COCKERILL
SA Cockerill-Ougrée-Providence et Espérance-Longdoz

Avenue Adolphe Greiner 1, B-4100 Seraing, Belgium

Products: Diesel-hydraulic locomotives.

Chairman: Baron Clerdent
Managing Director: Julien Charlier
Sales Manager: Roger Wolfers

Constitution: The present company was formed in 1970 by the merger of SA Cockerill-Ougrée-Providence and SA Métallurgique d'Espérance-Longdoz.

Telephone: Liège 34 08 10/34 28 10
Telegrams: COCKERILL-OUGREE, Seraing
Telex: 41225

Sales: Since its inception the company has sold a wide range of industrial locomotives throughout the world. Shunting locomotives built by Cockerill for major railways include: 238 for Belgian National Railways (SNCB) ranging from 320 hp to 750 hp; 13 for the former Chemin de Fer du Bas-Congo au Katanga (320 hp; 30 tonnes); seven for Vicicongo (220 hp; 16 tonnes) and 131 for Argentine Railways (FA) consisting of 81 33-tonne units and 50 29-tonne units all rated at 320 hp. Mainline locos have been sold to Belgium (SNCB), Congo (Otraco), Argentine Railways (FA) and Sudan.

CODER
Établissements Coder

Marseille-Saint-Marcel (Bouches-du-Rhone) 13, France

Products: Freight wagons.

Telephone: 47 68 13
Telegrams: CODER, Marseilles
Telex: 42722

COMENG
Comeng Holdings Ltd

41 Berry Street, Granville, New South Wales 2142, Australia

Products: Electric, diesel-electric, diesel-hydraulic locomotives; railcars; passenger coaches, light rail vehicles, trains; freight wagons; containers, Miner draftgear; track equipment.

Chairman: D A Pratten
Managing Director: K P McInerney.
Export Sales Director: I Silink

Constitution: Comeng Holdings Ltd and its subsidiary companies comprise the largest rolling stock manufacturing group in the southern hemisphere with manufacturing plants in all Australian States, including: Commonwealth Engineering (NSW) Pty Ltd; Commonwealth Engineering (Queensland) Pty Ltd; Commonwealth Engineering (Victoria) Pty Ltd; Comeng Western Australia; Comeng Aresco Pty Ltd, South Australia; Mittagong Engineering Pty Ltd (New South Wales).

Sales: Major sales in 1978/79 include: 300 stainless-steel carriages forming 50 six-carriage trains, each consisting of four power and two trailer carriages for Victorian Railways Suburban Rail System; 30 Intercity Express Passenger units consisting of ten power cars and 20 passenger carriages forming train consists of two power cars and five passenger carriages for PTC-NSW; 374 aluminium bottom discharge coal wagons, ten water rail tank cars and 16 brake vans for Queensland Railways; 20 ballast wagons for Public Transport Commission for NSW; 15 water rail tank cars for ANR; one M636 Comeng-Alco diesel-electric locomotive for Cliffs Robe River.

New Equipment: The 10 Comeng 3000 V dc 2700 kW mainline electric locomotives ordered by PTC-NSW weigh 120 tons and represent the first contract let for electric locomotives designed and manufactured by an Australian company. They have Co-Co wheel arrangement with axle-hung traction motors mounted on roller bearing suspension and the drivers' cabs are fully air-conditioned.
Several of the 30 Comeng-Alco 2 200/2 000 hp diesel-electric locomotives have been delivered to the Public Transport Commission of NSW.
The 18 driving trailer cars being supplied by Comeng to the State Transport Authority represent the first of a new generation of diesel rail cars for the Adelaide Suburban Rail Service and are the first cars ordered by the newly formed STA of SA.
Comeng has introduced its new Inter-City design concept in the luxury express passenger trains for the Public Transport Commission of NSW. This is a development of the well-known British Inter-City 125 Units designed to meet Australian operating conditions.
Delivery of the 50 stainless-steel EMU trains for Victorian Railways is expected to commence during 1980. This will be the first train to operate on Melbourne's Suburban Network to be completely constructed in stainless steel and to incorporate full air-conditioning for the comfort of the commuters. Depending on demand these may run in six or three-car consists; two motors and one trailer make up each three-car consist.

Telephone: 02 682 3677
Telegrams: COMHOLD, Sydney
Telex: AA24572

New freight wagons developed by Comeng include: Stainless-steel coal hopper wagons for Public Transport Commission of NSW with tare weight 22 tons and gross weight 100 tons. All surfaces with which the coal may come into contact are stainless steel to avoid any problems with corrosion, wear; A 76-ton aluminium cement hopper wagon with pressure and gravity discharge, the first of the type to be produced in Australia; Woodchip wagons for Westrail manufactured in 350 grade steel with gross weight of 76 tons with four large longitudinal bottom discharge doors which open in pairs for rapid discharge.

Class 23 tramcar for Melbourne and Metropolitan Tramways Board

Comeng-Alco 80 class 2 200/2 000 hp diesel-electric locomotive for the Public Transport Commission of NSW

Aluminium coal wagons for tippler loading supplied to Queensland Railways

One of 20 ballast wagons built for New South Wales

Comeng 3 000 V dc 2 700 kW mainline electric locomotive

COMETAL

Cometal-Mometal Sarl

PO Box 1401, Maputo, Mozambique

Products: Freight wagons; inspection cars.

Telephone: 752124/5/6/7/8
Telegrams: COMETAL, Maputo
Telex: 6-535 DNIME MO

Sales: Major sales in 1977/78 include 100 tank wagons for South African Railways and 120 drop sided wagons for Mozambique Railways.

Bogie petrol tank wagons built by Cometal for South African Railways

Bogie covered wagons with sliding doors built for the Tanzam Railway

COMETARSA

Cometarsa SA

LN Alem 619, 3°P Buenos Aires, Argentina

Telegrams: COMETARSA, Buenos Aires

Products: Diesel-electric, diesel-hydraulic locomotives; freight wagons.

COSTAMASNAGA

Costamasnaga SpA

22041 Costamasnaga (Como), Italy

Products: Freight wagons.

Chairman: Paolo Angelo Figliodoni
Managing Director: Luciano Trevisan
Sales Director: Ida Magni
Director (Exports): K M Glensy

Double-deck automobile-carrying wagon built for Italian State Railways
Tare 27 tonnes; load capacity 19 tonnes; carrying capacity, 10 large automobiles on 2 platforms.

Telephone: 031 855 192
Telex: 380184
Telegrams: COSTAIAT, Como

Bogie tank wagon for compressed gas transport
Tare 33.5 tonnes; load capacity 46.5 tonnes; carrying capacity 93 m³.

One of 125 4-axle ballast wagons built for Italian State Railways (FS) by Costamasnaga in 1977/78

4-axle covered wagon with sliding roof
One of 100 built by Costamasnaga for private industry in 1977/78.

32-axle special wagon (type UAI)
Tare 202 tonnes; load 500 tonnes; length over buffers 51.765 m; length of loaded wagon 63.990 m.

CREUSOT-LOIRE

Société Creusot-Loire (Traction Division)

31/32 quai National, 92806 Puteaux, France

Products: Diesel-electric, diesel-hydraulic locomotives and railcars, mechanical equipment; freight wagons; bogies.

Telephone: 776 41 62
Telex: 61425

President: M Forgeot
Director: Henry Julien

CZECHOSLOVAK WAGON WORKS

Ceskoslovenské Vagónky Praha
(Member of Pragoinvest, Strojexport and Skoda)

Kartouzska 2, 150 21 Prague 5, Czechoslovakia

Products: Electric and diesel railcars; passenger coaches; types Es, Eas, Fads, Rs, Rmms, Les, Leks and Uah; freight wagon.

Chairman: Ing Jiri Spevák
Managing Director: Ing Oldrich Nepras
Sales Director: Ing Ivo Dolezal

Telephone: 549 251
Telegrams: EVIKAVAGON, Praha
Telex: 122043 VUSLc

2-axle car-carrying wagon Leks for transportation of 13 small passenger cars

Self-discharge hopper wagon Fads with pneumatically-operated discharge doors

2-axle light steel railcar M 152 for secondary lines
Shown in Czechoslovak State Railways' (CSD) livery *right* and in profile *below.*

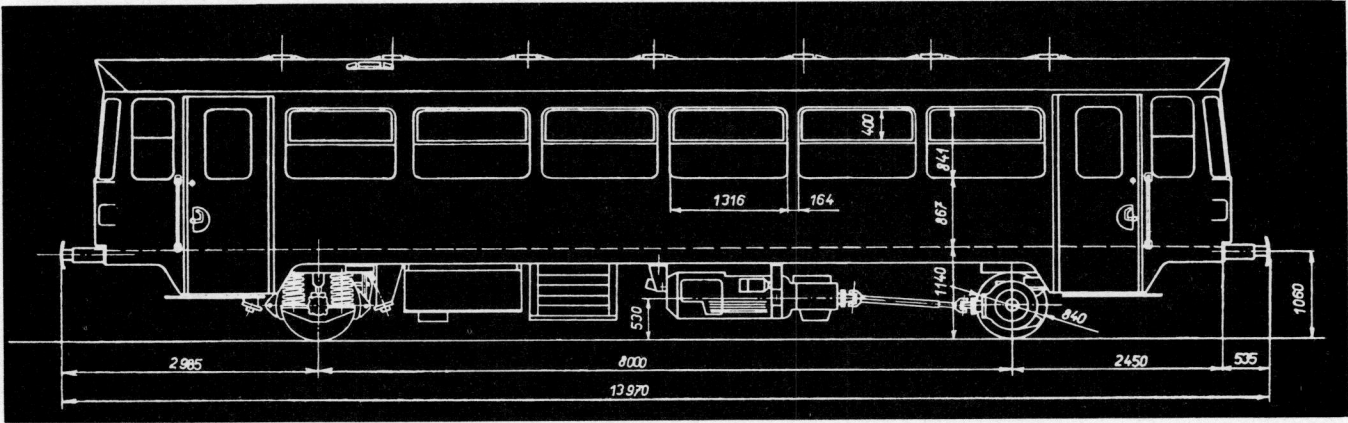

DAEWOO

Daewoo Heavy Industries Ltd

PO Box 7955, Seoul, Republic of Korea

Products: Passenger coaches, freight wagons, locomotives, railcars, electric multiple unit and car components.

Chairman: Woo Choong Kim
Executive Managing Director: Myun Hoo Hong
Rolling Stock Division Director: Jae Ho Kim
Export Sales Manager: Soon Hyuck Park

Affiliated Companies:
Daewoo International [America] Corp
100 Daewoo Place, Carlstadt, New Jersey 07072, USA   Tel: (201) 935 8700

Daewoo International Co [Montreal] Ltd
540 Beauharnios, 2nd Floor, Montreal H2N 1L2, Canada   Tel: (514) 381 4431/3

Daewoo International [Panama] SA
Edificio 25, Colon Free Zone, Colon, Republic of Panama   Tel: (47) 6823/7003, 23 8144

Daewoo Handels GmbH
6000 Frankfurt/M, 71-Niederrad, Saonestrasse 1, Federal Republic of Germany
Tel: 0611 666011/5

Daewoo Industrial Co [UK] Ltd
11th Floor, Bastion House, 140 London Wall, London EC2, England   Tel: 01 588 0081/7

Daewoo France
Centre Seine T41, 23 rue Linois, 75015 Paris, France   Tel: 575 15 30

Daewoo Industrial Co [HK] Ltd
Room 1901-5, Lane Crawford House 19/F, 64-70A Queen's Road Central, Hong Kong
Tel: 5-230825/230589

Telephone: Seoul 28 5231   Anyang 2 6171.
Telegrams: DHILTDINCHEON
Telex: K23301/K28473

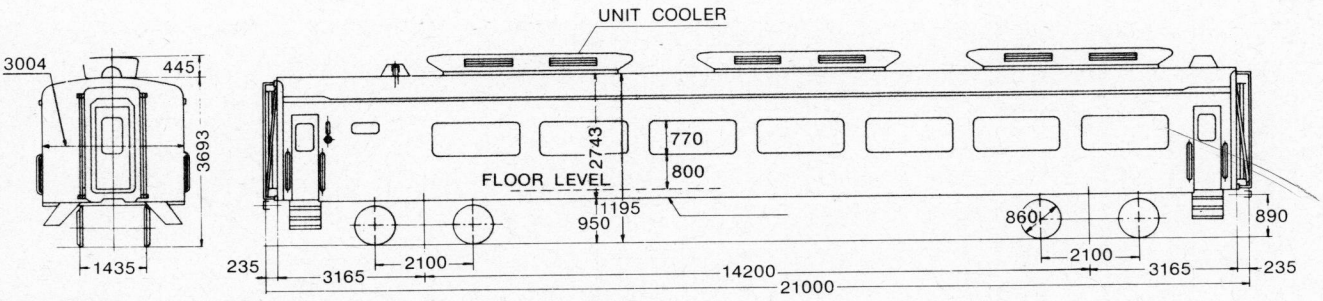

During 1978/79 Daewoo built 30 express passenger coaches for Korean National Railways
Seating capacity is 56 passengers on a floor area of 48 m²; tare weight is approximately 36 tonnes.

Constitution: The company was founded in 1937 as the Chosun Machine Works for the production of industrial machines, mining equipment, and weapons.

After 1945 the company was nationalised and resumed production of industrial machines. In 1963 the government established the company as a corporation under the name of Hankook Machine Ind Co, and in 1968 transferred its shares and management to private hands.

Since 1968, the company has extended business areas and diversified its main products. In 1973 the company merged with the Bugok Rolling Stocks Plant and added railway wagons and coaches to its production line. In 1975 the company established the Diesel Engine Plant and began to produce MAN engines in technical collaboration with the Maschinefabrik Augsburg-Nuernberg Aktiengesellschaft using financial assistance from the Federal German Government.

In 1976 the company merged with Daewoo Machinery Co and enlarged to include four main plants: the Industrial Machine Plant and the Diesel Engine Plant in Inchon, the Rolling Stock Plant in Bugok, and the Precision Machine Plants in both Seoul and the Machine Tools Plant in the Changwon Industrial Complex.

Despite its leading role in Korean industry, the company was in deficit until 1975. However, in 1976 the Daewoo Industrial Co Ltd, together with its affiliates, took over 46.2 per cent of the shares and participated in management, changing deficit into surplus.

It was renamed Daewoo Heavy Industries Ltd in 1976.

Export sales in 1978/79 were as follows:

	Description	Quantity	Customer
1978	M/G third-class passenger coach	59	Bangladesh Railways (BR)
	3-axle bogie	36	Taiwan Machinery Manufacturing Corp (TMMC)
	Coupler	126	TMMC
1979	Carriage bogie underframe	20	Malayan Railway Administration
	3-axle bogie	34	TMMC
	M/G bogie full first-class coach	28	BR
	B/G third-class luggage & brake	10	BR
	B/G Inspection car with air-conditioning	1	BR
	B/G bogie third-class coach	3	BR
	Coupler	200	TMMC

Equipment: Daewoo Heavy Industries Ltd produces ac/dc dual-current commuter type electric trains. The train comprises Trailer Car with control cab (abbreviated as Tc) which has a driving cab but no propulsion equipment and Intermediate Motor Car (abbreviated as M) which has propulsion equipment but no driving cab. The motor car is of two-cars in one unit and its eight-traction motors are controlled as one group. Such cars are abbreviated as M and M'. On the motor car M a main controller is mounted for speed control, and electric power source devices such as main transformer, main rectifier, etc are mounted on the other motor car M'.

The minimum unit to function as a train is a four-car combination of Tc M M' Tc, but this minimum is not considered for revenue service. The usual train is a six-car combination of Tc MM' MM' Tc. However consideration has been given for future extension of car numbers in a train to eight cars, Tc MM' MM' MM' Tc and ten-cars, Tc MM' TMM' TMM' Tc or Tc MM' Tc · Tc MM' MM' Tc.

Sales: As of October 1979 the following major domestic sales were recorded in 1978/79:

	Description	Quantity	Customer
1978	50-tonne bulk cement tank car	40	Privately owned companies
	Electric multiple unit (1 unit comprises 3 cars)	7	Seoul Metropolitan Government (SMG)
	Electric multiple unit	6	Korean National Railroad (KNR)
	Oil tank car	30	Korea Oil Corporation
	18-tonne diesel locomotive	1	Korea Electric Co
	Express coach	24	KNR
	Electric power source car	5	KNR
	Box car	150	KNR
	Cold slab car	2	Pohang Steel Co (POSCO)
	Mould car	6	POSCO
	Ingot car	15	POSCO
1979	Special express coach	4	KNR
	Express coach	6	KNR
	Dining car	6	KNR
	Electric power source car	14	KNR
	Limited express coach	31	KNR
	Box car	385	KNR
	Gondola car	539	KNR
	Ore car	70	KNR
	Sulphuric acid tank car	40	Onsan Copper Refinery Co Ltd
	Electric multiple unit	12	KNR
	Diesel rail car trainset (1 trainset comprises 5 cars)	1	KNR

Air-conditioned diesel rail car trainset built by Daewoo for Korean National Railroad

Daewoo commuter type electric train

Data: Rail gauge, 1 435 mm; electrification system, ac 25 kV 60 Hz and dc 1 500 V; acceleration, 2.5 km/h/s; deceleration, 3.5 km/h/s (service) 4.5 km/h/s (emergency); speed control system, rheostatic control, series-parallel control and field control; brake system, SELD electro-pneumatic brake (with automatic emergency brake), hand brake; car M, 43.5 tons, seating 54, standing 106, total 160; car M', 46.5 tons, seating 54, standing 106, total 160; car Tc, 34.5 tons, seating 48, standing 100, total 148.

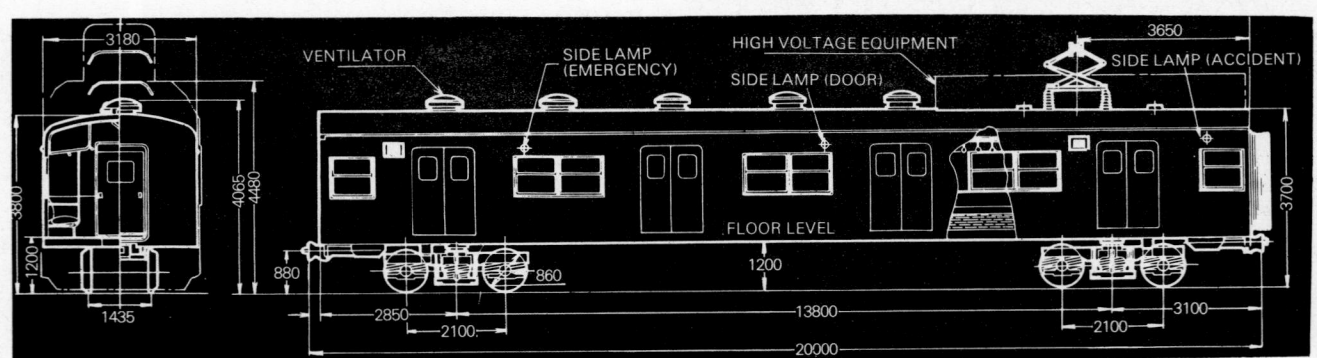

DAVIS
W H Davis & Sons Ltd

Langwith Junction, Mansfield, Nottingham NG20 9RZ, England

Products: Freight wagons; specialised stock for industry.

Chairman: W H T Davis

Telephone: 062 385 2621
Telex: 37657

Sales: D Sharpe
M Burge

Constitution: The company was formed in 1900.

50-tonne special purpose wagon designed and built by Davis for carrying steelworks scrap skip

50-tonne capacity palletised UKF fertiliser wagon
Stainless-steel body, tare weight 24.4 tonnes, maximum speed 96 km/h (60 mph).

Hopper bogie wagon delivered in 1979 to Bangladesh Railways
Gross laden weight 64 tonnes; tare weight 22.5 tonnes; rail gauge 5 ft 6 in (1.676 m).

Two-axle hopper wagon built for operations in the United Kingdom
Gross laden weight 51 tonnes; tare weight 12.45 tonnes; max operating speed 96 km/h (60 mph).

DE DIETRICH
De Dietrich & Cie

67 Reichshoffen, 67110 Niederbronn-les-Bains, France

Products: Passenger coaches; special wagons for steel shipments (torpedo ladle wagons).

Sales Organisation: Francorail-MTE (for railway rolling stock)
De Dietrich & Cie (for other equipment)

President: Gilbert de Dietrich
Director (Rolling Stock Division): Maurice Canioni

Constitution: Established in 1684, the company went into the construction of rolling stock during the middle of the nineteenth century. In 1973 the companies De Dietrich, Carel Fouché Languepin, Creusot-Loire, Jeumont-Schneider and MTE, created the Groupement d'Intérêt Economique 'Francorail-MTE'.
The company deals with contracts covering high-speed bogies, long UIC cars, and cars for the main lines of the French National Railways and other railway companies abroad. Besides rolling stock, the company makes and sells other equipment related to railways such as special wagons for the steel industry and points and crossings for the railways and underground networks.

Sales: Sales in 1979 include UIC mainline coaches, TGV coaches, special conference cars, Y32 bogies and special wagons for the steel industry.

Telephone: (88) 09 16 66
Telegrams: DIETRIWAGONS
Telex: 870850 F

Special conference car for SNCF

B11u second-class air-conditioned Corail coach with 11 compartments and 88 seats

Torpedo ladle car with removable covers
Capacity: 450 tonnes of molten iron.

DESSAU

Veb Waggonbau Dessau

Joliot-Curie-Strasse 48, DDR-45 Dessau, German Democratic Republic

Products: Mechanically-refrigerated wagons and trains; ice-cooled wagons.

Sales: At the 1978 Leipzig Fair Waggonbau Dessau showed a type MK4-432-78, class lags, machine-cooled refrigerator bogie wagon built in 1977 for Romanian State Rail-

ways (CFR). Insulating walls have 115 mm of polyurethane foam sandwiched between 1.5 mm outer steel sheets and 1.5 mm inner sheets of aluminium alloy. This allows interior temperatures from 14 to —20°C to be maintained at outside temperatures varying between 36 and —20°C.

Two cooling units, powered by 21 kVA diesel-electric motor-generator sets work under an electronic control system. Usable storage capacity in the loading room, which is 16 800 mm long and 2550 mm wide, is 86 m³. Doors are 2.7 m wide and 1.9 m high. Length of the wagon is 19 800 mm and it can negotiate curves of 60 m radius. Tare weight is 37.5 tonnes and maximum speed is 100 km/h.

DIEMA

Diepholzer Maschinenfabrik Fritz Schottler GmbH

Diemastrasse 11, Postfach 1170, 2840 Diepholz 1, Federal Republic of Germany

Products: Standard and broad-gauge diesel shunting locomotives, narrow-gauge diesel mine locomotives, narrow-gauge industrial locomotives, hydraulic tippers.

Telephone: 0 54 41 30 41/43
Telegrams: DIEMA DIEPHOLZ
Telex: 0941 222

Managing Director: Ing Peter Benzien
Sales Director: Klaus Fuhrmann

Type DVL 90 diesel locomotive
100 hp; weight 14 tonnes.

Type DVL 150 diesel shunting locomotive
190 hp; weight 24 tonnes; hydraulic power transmission; cardan shafts; bevel gear axle drive.

DIFCO

Difco Inc

PO Box 238, Findlay, Ohio 45840, USA

Products: Airside dump wagons.

Chairman: D F Flowers
Managing Director: Fred F Flowers
Chief Sales Director: Robert J Ward

Telephone: (419) 422 0525
Telegrams: DIFCO, Findlay

Constitution: Founded in 1915 for the production of heavy and light industrial railway rolling stock and mine haulage equipment.

Sales: Recent sales reported in 1979 were: 92 Airside dump wagons for US Steel's Minntac Taconite mining (100 ton capacity); 30 Airside dump wagons for Santa Fe Railway (77 ton); 12 Airside dump wagons for Norfolk & Western.

Difco Airside dump wagon

DORBYL

Dorbyl Limited

PO Box 2997, Johannesburg 2000, South Africa

Products: Diesel-electric locomotives, electric (25 kVA HVAC) locomotives, industrial locomotives, freight wagons, guards' vans, steam heat vehicles, cast steel wheels and axles.

Executive Chairman: C D Ellis
Group Managing Director: T L Roux
Executive Director, Rolling Stock Division: C R L Thorp
Manager, Export and Project Operations: R E Searle

Constitution: The company, a subsidiary of International Pipe and Steel Association (IPSA), was established in South Africa as Wade & Dorman Ltd, Structural Engineers in 1909. The manufacture of rolling stock and railway wagons was begun in 1944. In August 1978 the 100 000th railway wagon built by the Dorbyl Group was handed over to South African Railways.

Sales: In 1978/79 the South African General Electric-Dorman Long locomotive manufacturing consortium completed an order for 100 GE SG10B shunting locomotives for the South African Railways, for marshalling yard hump duty and inter-yard working. A further order was placed with the consortium for 50 GE U15C branch line locomotives to be used on general duties on the South African Railways' Transvaal network.

Telephone: (011) 724 1441
Telegrams: DORLONSA, Johannesburg
Telex: 8-7539

Railway wagon built by Dorbyl
A refrigerator wagon, type LA-3, built for SAR. Dorbyl was due to build a further 300 mechanical refrigerator wagons for SAR for delivery in 1979/80

Dorbyl also built 48 Hitachi-designed and electrically-equipped 25 kVA HVAC locomotives. These were supplied to the South African Railways by the main contractor, Nissho Iwai, during 1978/79.

Seven types of railway wagon were due for completion during 1979/80:

104 double deck automobile transport wagons, type SCL-4, length 19.5 m over headstocks, to carry four vehicles on each deck, fitted with air brakes. 25 of the wagons will possibly be fitted with air and vacuum brakes for greater diversification in traffic.

300 mechanical refrigerator wagons, type LA-3, with a length over headstocks of 17.64 m. A 17 mm layer of polyurethane foam insulation is sandwiched between the outer skin of steel and the inner lining of aluminium. The inner and outer body frame is joined with high-density polypropylene material. Thermo-King refrigerator units, Youngstown sliding plug doors and FreightMaster 254 mm stroke end of car cushion units are fitted. Tare is 32 450 kg with palletised payload of 40 000 kg. 272 meathooks are provided for suspending carcasses.

1100 coal gondola wagons, type CCR-3, bath tub construction. The body and underframe members are of unpainted Corten steel except for the stencilling. Length over end plates is 11.27 m with a payload of 52 800 kg. Volumetric capacity is 67.4 m³. A Type F rotary coupler is fitted at one end and a Type F fixed coupler at the opposite end, for discharging the load by means of a rotary tippler without uncoupling the wagons. Air brakes are used, with a load detector valve for varying the pressure on the brake blocks under tare and load conditions.

1250 pallet wagons, type O-3, made for conveying palletised loads of fruit, with a capacity of 70 m³. The central bulkhead has facing panels which can be pushed up against the load by screw jacks to prevent the loads from toppling. Being an all-sliding plug door wagon, access for loading and unloading by fork lift truck is unrestricted. The grooves in the floor plate permit loads to be moved transversely by Joloda palletveyors which can be retracted and removed after use. Insulation is used in the ceiling, doors and ends. The length of the wagon over headstocks is 13.6 m. Cushioning is by means of a sliding sill.

500 iron ore gondola wagons, type CR-5 for the Sishen-Saldanha line, built of unpainted corten steel for the body and underframe. Except for the stencilling, the wagons have a capacity of 32.3 m³, a tare of 20 000 kg and payload of 80 000 kg. Designed for tippling in pairs on a rotary tippler, each wagon pair is fitted with a Type F rotary coupler at one end, a bar coupler connecting the two wagons, with non-rotary and rotary elements, and a fixed Type F coupler at the other end.

Air brakes are fitted for unit train operation of up to 220 wagons per train, with load detection valves for varying the pressure on the brake blocks under tare and load conditions.

The bogies used are the HS Mk V Cross Anchor type with self-steering, high conicity profile wheels and high-stability characteristics under all conditions. They are an improved version of the HS Mk II bogies, designed and developed by Herbert Scheffel of the South African Railways, in conjunction with the South African Inventions Development Corporation and Dorbyl. With the experience gained in service on the Cross Anchor bogies, it has become the accepted practice to re-turn the wheel tread and flange profiles on the wheels at 300 000 km. The 914 mm-diameter cast steel wheels, rim-quenched, are manufactured by Vecor and assembled locally on forged steel axles made by Steel Wheel and Axle South Africa (Pty) Ltd, both firms being part of the Dorbyl group. Composition brake blocks supplied by Metpro Development Co (Pty) Ltd are used for longer service life, and a more constant co-efficient of friction under variations of braking pressures and temperatures.

An order was received from the South African Railways for 600 ballast wagons, Type AY-12, to be delivered during 1979/80. These wagons are to a new all-welded design and conform to the physical strength and requirements laid down in *Standard Specifications for Design, Fabrication and Construction of Freight Cars* issued by the Association of American Railroads. Length over headstocks is 12.65 m with a capacity of 30 m³, a tare of 23 500 kg and payload of 49 000 kg. The operation of the discharge doors is such as to deposit the ballast on the outside of the rails or between the rails.

550 flat wagons, Type SHL-5, 13.87 m over headstocks and fitted with twistlocks for ISO containers, were due to be built during 1979/80. These wagons were to be fitted with air brakes for unit train operation.

DURO DAKOVIC

Duro Dakovic Industries

Slavonski Brod, Yugoslavia

Products: Diesel-electric, diesel-hydraulic and diesel-mechanical locomotives; electric locomotives; diesel railcars and trainsets; passenger coaches; freight wagons.

Telephone: 41 011
Telegrams: LOKOMOTIVE, Slavonski Brod
Telex: 28 521/102 155

Constitution: Duro Dakovic was founded in 1921 as the first Yugoslavian locomotive and wagon manufacturer. Diesel locomotives have been produced since 1954.

DÜWAG

(A division of Waggonfabrik Uerdingen AG)

Königsberger Strasse 100, 4000 Düsseldorf, Federal Republic of Germany

Products: Street cars; light rail vehicles; pre-metros; subway-cars; bogies of bi- and mono-motor type; car components of fibre glass; people mover system type H-Bahn.

Recent Sales: Light rail vehicles for domestic market (Frankfurt, Kassel, Dortmund, Essen Krefeld, Düsseldorf) and export (Edmonton, Calgary, San Diego, Rotterdam) as well as bogies for Hong Kong Mass Transit Railways and Kowloon Canton Railways.

Telephone: 0211/77071
Telegrams: DÜWAG
Telex: 08582722

Deliveries and work in hand during 1979 included: 21 type ET 420 trainsets for Deutsche Bundesbahn (DB); 450 type Res-687 wagons for DB; 500 type Eaos wagons for DB; 104 sliding-door wagons for private companies; 26 double-unit diesel trains and 19 diesel railcars for Netherlands Railways (NS).

ELECTROEXPORTIMPORT

(Romanian foreign trade company)
Calea Victoriei 133, Sector 1, Bucharest, Romania

Products: Romanian-built electric and diesel-electric locomotives for export.

Telephone: 50 28 70
Telegrams: ELECTROEXPORTIMPORT, Bucharest
Telex: 11388

General Manager: Ing D Suteu
Deputy Manager: Ing D Togui

Major Sales: The following table summarises Electroexportimport's sales since 1960:

	2100 hp DEL	1250 hp DEL	3000 hp DEL	4000 hp DEL	3500 hp DEL	5100 kW EL
Year of manufacture	1960	1975	1977	1976	1976-1977	1967
Licence	Sulzer-SLM-Brown Boveri	Romanian design	Romanian design	Romanian design	Romanian and Brush design	ASEA
Output	2100 hp	1250 hp	3000 hp	4000 hp	3500 hp	5100 kW(UIC)
Engine type	Sulzer type 12LDA 28-2300 hp(UIC)	Sulzer 6LDA28 1256 hp(UIC)	Alco R251 12CIL	Alco R251 16CIL	GEC English Electric 16 RK 3 CT	
Max speed	100-120 km/h	100 km/h	140-160 km/h	140-160 km/h	130 km/h	120 km/h goods trains 160 km/h slow trains
Wheel arrangement	Co-Co	Bo-Bo	Co-Co	Co-Co	Co-Co	Co-Co
Weight of loco	115 tonnes (2/3 Supply)	—	120±2% (Full Supply)	126±2% (Full Supply)	128 tonnes (Full Supply)	—
Weight per axle	—	20 tonnes	20 tonnes	21 tonnes	21·3 tonnes	21 tonnes
Max traction effort on starting	32 000 daN	22 000 daN	40 000 daN	40 000 daN	—	40 000 daN
Continuous traction effort	20 000 daN at 21·25 km/h	13 000 daN at 18·5 km/h	25 000 daN at 24 km/h	25 000 daN at 32 km/h	—	26 500 daN at 69·5 km/h
Transmission	dc-dc	dc-dc	ac-dc	ac-dc	ac-dc	ac-dc
Minimum radius of curves	100 m	100 m	100 m	100 m	70 m	90 m
Line voltage and frequency	—	—	—	—	—	25 kV/50 Hz
Maximum Temperature	+40°C	+40°C	+40°C	+40°C	—	+40°C
Minimum Temperature	−30°C	−30°C	−30°C	−30°C	—	−30°C
Humidity	80%	80%	80%	80%	—	80%
General information	First 2 locos have run over 2 million km in 18 years without major repair. 33% of production exported	Derived from 2100 hp DEL. 6 cylinder engine	Manufactured with 3 gear ratios: 65/19 67/17 76/16	Manufactured with 3 gear ratios: 65/19 67/17 76/16	Built for British Rail	15% of production has been exported

---

ELECTROPUTERE

Electroputere, Craiova

7 Matei Millo St, Bucharest, Romania

Products: Diesel-electric Co-Co locomotives from 2 100 to 2 500 hp; electric Co-Co locomotives of 7 350 hp.

Telephone: 14 94 30
Telegrams: MASEXPORT Bucharest
Telex: 216

EMAQ

Sao Paulo, Brazil

Products: Locomotives; rolling stock.

Sales: The company is sharing a 1977/78 order with Villares placed by RFFSA of Brazil for 140 locomotives. Emaq is to supply 74 units.

ENERGOMACHEXPORT

V/O Energomachexport

127486 Moscow, Deguninskaya, Str 1, Korp 4, USSR

Telephone: 147 21 77
Telegrams: ENERGOEXPORT
Telex: 411926 ENEK SU
411965 ENEK SU

Products: Soviet exports of diesel and electric locomotives; electric trainsets; passenger coaches; freight wagons; railway interlocking equipment; signalling and block systems; subway stock; track machines and mechanisms.

Chairman: V Pavlov
Sales Directors: V Tubin, N Lubin

Constitution: The company was formed to handle all railway equipment exports from the Soviet Union. Principal partners include locomotive works Ludinovo, Novocherkassk, and Voroshilvograd.

Model TE-129, a powerful single-unit locomotive (4000 hp)
Electrical ac-dc transmission equipped with electro-dynamic brakes and electrical train heating, intended for service on 1·524 or 1·435 m railways.

Model TE-109 developed for export to countries with 1·435 m track gauge
The locomotives have the same standardised units and mechanisms as the TE-114.

Model M-62 2000 hp locomotive
Designed for hauling freight trains but can be used for passenger service. It can be operated on main lines in the USSR and abroad.

Model TE-114, a main-line diesel-electric locomotive for tropical climates
A power of 2600 to 2800 hp using alternating and direct current. The model is intended for service on railways with a gauge of 1·52 and 1·435 m in countries with a high dust content in the air.

Model TGM-6A eight-wheel 1 200-hp shunting diesel-hydraulic locomotive
Designed for shunting and transfer service on 1.524- and 1.435-mm railways.

Model TGM-4 750-hp diesel-hydraulic locomotive
Designed for shunting service at railway yards and industrial enterprises with 1 524-mm tracks.

Model TGM-8 800-hp diesel-hydraulic locomotive
Designed for shunting and transfer service.

Model TGM-23B 500-hp diesel-hydraulic locomotive of the bonnet type
Designed for shunting work on 1 524-mm tracks of railways and industrial enterprises.

Model TU7E 400-hp diesel-hydraulic locomotive
Designed for shunting and train service on railway lines, at yards, on the industrial tracks of timber-felling, peat-processing enterprises and quarries having 750-mm tracks.

Model TEM-6 general-purpose 1 500-hp diesel-electric locomotive
Designed for freight, passenger and shunting service on 1 524-mm railways.

Model TEM-2 1200-hp diesel-electric locomotive with dc transmission
Designed for shunting, train and humping service on 1 435- and 1 524-mm railways.

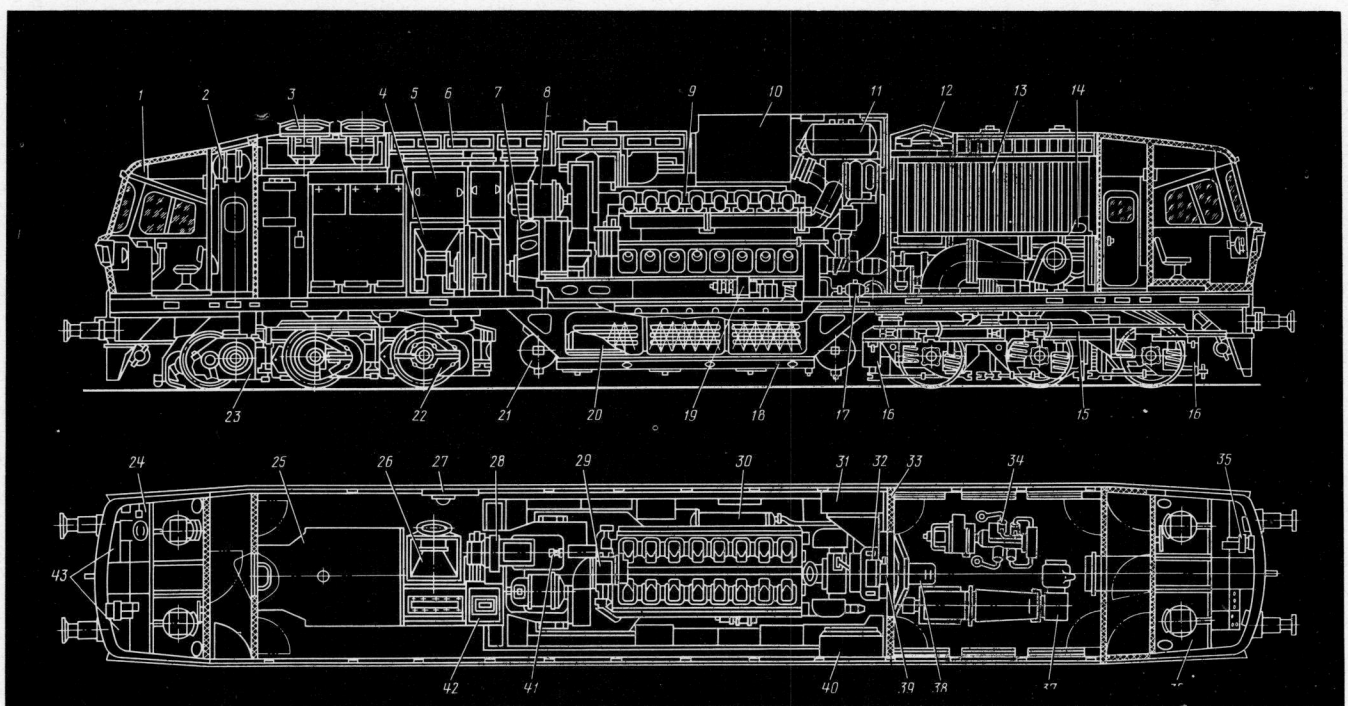

The single unit 3 035 hp ac/dc Model TE 109 diesel-electric is built for heavy freight and passenger service
(1) driver's cab (2) reservoir of control and servicing air piping (3) motor fan of electrodynamic brakes (4) fan cooling rectifier unit (5) rectifier unit (6) train heating generator (7) traction generator (8) starter-generator (9) diesel engine (10) muffler (11) water tank (12) motor fan of cooler chamber (13) cooler chamber (14) reservoir of fire-extinguishing unit (15) bogie (16) bunker of sanders (17) fuel-feed unit (18) fuel tank (19) oil-feed unit (20) accumulator battery (21) main air reservoir (22) housing of traction transmission (23) traction motor (24) control panel (25) high-tension chamber (26) fan cooling front traction motors (27) wash stand (28) fan cooling train heating generator and frequency converter (29) fan cooling traction generator (30) heat exchanger (31) right-hand air filter (32) fuel heater (33) instrument board (34) brake compressor (35) heating and ventilating unit (36) rear driver's cab (37) fan cooling rear traction motors (38) water heating boiler (39) circulation water pump (40) left-hand air filter (41) exciter unit (42) frequency converter (43) windshield wiper

---

ESW

Export Association of Swiss Rolling Stock Manufacturers

Member companies: SIG (Swiss Industrial Company); SWS (Swiss Car & Elevator Manufacturing Corp Ltd); SWP (Schindler Carriage & Wagon Co Ltd).

Products: Electric and diesel railcars; electric multiple units; diesel multiple units; passenger coaches; freight wagons.

EUSKALDUNA DE CONSTRUCTION

Euskalduna de Construction y Reparation de Buques SA Cia

Bilbao, Spain

Products: Electric, steam, diesel-electric, diesel-mechanical, mining locomotives.

Telephone: 41 14 50
Telegrams: EUSKALDUNA, Bilbao
Telex: 33712

FABLOK

Locomotive Works Fablok

32-500 Chrzanow ul, Fabryczna 10, Poland

Export sales: Kolmex, 49 Mokotowska, 00-542 Warsaw, Poland

Telephone: 22 31
Telegrams: FABLOK CHRZANOW
Telex: 032256

Products: Diesel-electric, diesel-hydraulic and diesel-mechanical locomotives; brake equipment.

FABRICACIONES MILITARES

Buenos Aires, Argentina

Sales: The company was awarded a contract in 1978 to build 104 metro cars for Buenos Aires in conjunction with E Fiat Cordoba, under general supervision by Fiat.

FAUVET-GIREL

Établissements Fauvet-Girel

4ter avenue Hoche, 75008 Paris, France

Products: Light rail shunters (300 to 1 600-hp); hopper wagons; tank wagons; special wagons; semi-trailers; containers.

President: Jacques Dambrine
Assistant General Managers: Hubert Foullon and G Reille
Commercial Director: J Martin

Telephone: 766 04 10
Telegrams: FAUVGIR
Telex: 650 337

Constitution: The company was formed in 1918 and has two main wagon-building plants at Arras and Lille.

Sales: Fauvet-Girel builds between 1 000 and 1 500 wagons a year. A large number go for export.

FAVYS SAIC

Fabrica Argentina de Vagones y Silos

Maipo 726, 3er piso, Buenos Aires, Argentina

Telephone: 392 2736

Products: Rolling stock.

FERROSTAAL

Ferrostaal AG

PO Box 10 12 65, Hohenzollernstrasse 24, 4300 Essen, Federal Republic of Germany

Products: Diesel-electric, diesel-hydraulic, diesel-mechanical, diesel mining locomotives; diesel railcars; railbuses; diesel multiple units; passenger coaches; freight wagons; track materials.

Directors: Dr Hans Singer
Wilhelm Haverkamp
Wilhelm Lüttenberg
Dr Klaus von Menges
Gerhard Thulmann
Hans-Ulrich Gruber

Telephone: Essen 20141
Telegrams: FERROSTAAL, Essen
Telex: 0857100

Ferrostaal lightweight three-car diesel trainset
Part of a contract for ten units delivered to Bolivia in April 1978

FERROSUD

Ferrosud SpA

PO Box 94, Via Appia Antica, Km 13, 75100 Matera, Italy

Products: Electric and diesel locomotives; railcars and trailers for electric and diesel trains; passenger coaches; freight wagons; bogies.

Chairman: Dr Ing Renato Piccoli
Vice-Chairman: Dr Ing Giuseppe Capuano
Managing Director: Dr Ing Angelo Mangone

Constitution: Ferrosud was set up in 1963 for the manufacture and marketing of railway and tramway rolling stock. Production began in 1968. Export sales are handled through Fiat and Breda Costruzioni Ferroviarie.

Sales: During 1977/78 major sales included 170 type 402A flat wagons for private companies. Since 1969 the following sales to Italian State Railways have been recorded: 117 couchette coaches; 52 luggage vans; 1 050 box cars; 1 952 flat wagons; 48 three axle diesel-hydraulic locomotives; nine 124 bogies of various types; 35 postal vans; 19 railcars and 11 trailer coaches; and 224 type 402A flat wagons for private companies.

Telephone: PBX 212114
Telegrams: TF 212114 FERROSUD
Telex: 760025 FERSUD I

UIC-X type Dz-X luggage van built for Italian State Railways

FFA

Flug- und Fahrzeugwerke AG Altenrhein

Flug- und Fahrzeugwerke AG, Altenrhein, CH-9423, Switzerland

Products: Complete passenger wagons for all gauges, lightweight steel and aluminium alloy design, normal carriages, traction carriages and pilot carriages, bogies for all types of carriages, street cars and tram bogies, postal, goods and container wagons.
Special constructions for all purposes, designs, understructure, modification and individual components and sub-assemblies.

Chairmen: Dr C Caroni and Dr L Caroni
Managing Director: H Eisenring
Sales Director: H Hutter

Constitution: The FFA were founded in 1925. In the 1930s the container department was added, producing entire systems and installations, transport and storage tanks for

Telephone: (071) 43 01 01
Telegrams: FFA Rorschach
Telex: 77 230 FFA CH

textile, food and chemical industries. At about the same time the department for surface treatment of aluminium and alloys had been set up. In the years 1931-35 the first funiculars and suspension cable cars were built. 1945-47 saw the beginnings of the rail carriage department. Today the FFA supply rolling stock for the SBB (Swiss Federal Railways) as well as for a large number of private and municipal railway undertakings. Since 1947 the FFA production has comprised passenger railway coaches, traction and pilot cars, baggage and goods rail wagons for all gauges as well as street tram cars.

RIC coach with folding berths (type Bcm Z1)

Shuttle service train for the Trogener Bahn
Motor car Bo-Bo + 2-2 with permanently coupled control car. One driver's cab at each end. One hour rating 400 kW; weight 39 tons; length over couplers 30.2 m; seating capacity 74; max speed 65 km/h.

FIAT
Fiat Ferroviaria Savigliano SpA

Head Office: Corso Ferrucci 122, 10141 Turin, Italy
Works: 4 Piazza Galateri, 12038 Savigliano (Cuneo), Italy

Products: Electric, diesel-electric locomotives; electric and diesel railcars; multiple units; passenger coaches; freight wagons; bogies and components.

Chairman: Ing Niccolò Gioia
Managing Director: Ing. Renato Piccoli
Works Director: Ing Franco Bergamasco
Commercial Director: Ing Vincenzo Milanesio

Constitution: The activity of FIAT in the field of railway rolling stock began in 1917 with the manufacture of passenger and freight cars. In 1926 in collaboration with Italian Brown Boveri, the first diesel-electric locomotives were built for Eritrea. In 1960 production of standardised light railcars, powered by petrol engines began, diesel engines having been introduced in 1934.
By the end of 1975 all the activities of FIAT concerning design and manufacture of railway rolling stock were entrusted to FIAT Ferroviaria Savigliano SpA.

Sales: Following almost two decades of continuous production with the standard ALn 668 diesel-hydraulic railcar, Fiat produced a redesigned version specifically to meet the

Telephone (Office): 332033/332133
Telephone (Works): (0172) 366791
Telex (Office): FIATFERS 22515
Telex (Works): FERSAV 21234

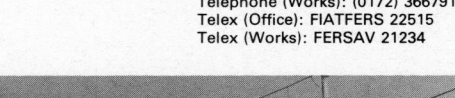

ALn 668 diesel railcar supplied to FS by Fiat
One of Fiat's ALn 668 diesel railcar range of which 1000 units have been delivered since 1960. Main characteristics: power output 2 × 200 hp; weight 38.2 tonnes; max speed 132 km/h; wheel arrangement 1A-A1; seats 12 first class/56 second class.

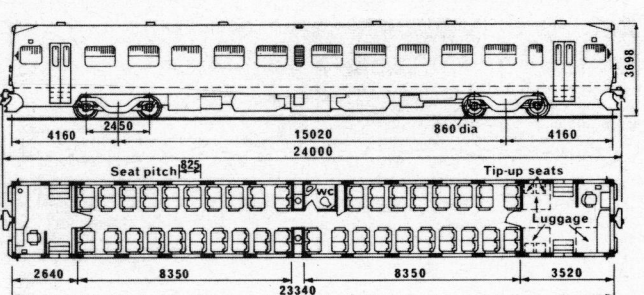

Modified ALn 668 (photo and line drawing) redesigned specifically by Fiat for Swedish State Railways

requirements of Swedish State Railways (SJ). Following trials, SJ placed an order with Fiat in 1977 for 100 railcars based on the ALn 668. The SJ cars are single units with driving cabs at both ends. They are intended for suburban routes in non-electrified territory.

In 1979 RENFE (Red Nacional de los Ferrocarriles Espanoles) ordered 124 railcars type 593 based on the standard model ALn 668. These vehicles will be manufactured by CAF (Construcciones y Auxiliar de Ferrocarriles SA, Beasain) and licenced by Fiat. The engines and mechanical equipment will be supplied by Fiat Ferroviaria Savigliano. The order is valued at about $US 90 million. Fiat Ferroviaria Savigliano planned the chopper electric locomotive E633 for Italian State Railways (FS) and furnished all its mechanical parts, bogies and drives. AMT (Ansaldo-Marelli-Tecnomasio Brown Boveri) supplied other electrical equipment. Fiat Ferroviaria Savigliano manufactured the first five prototypes. In 1979 the Italian State Railways (FS) ordered 80 of these chopper E633 units.

Prototype E633 chopper locomotive built by Fiat for Italian State Railways
Output 4 500 kW; weight 106 tonnes; max speed 160 km/h; wheel arrangement B-B-B.

FIAT-CONCORD

Fiat-Concord Saic (Division Energia y Transporte Ferroviario)

Cerrito 740, Buenos Aires, Argentina

Telephone: 35 3044
Telegrams: CONCORDSA
Telex: 012 1144

Products: Diesel-electric, diesel-hydraulic, diesel-mechanical locomotives (locotractors); railcars; passenger coaches; special wagons; mail vans.

Chairman: Dr Ing Angelo Ridolfo

Constitution: Fiat-Concord began production of railway rolling stock in 1960.

Sales: Contracts signed or completed during 1977/78 include 24 electric passenger railcars, 40 suburban coaches and 42 new diesel engines for Argentine Railways; 40 first-, second-class and dining coaches to Bolivia; and 54 metro cars for Buenos Aires. The company has delivered to Argentine Railways over 2 000 passenger coaches; 339 multiple unit diesel railcars; 41 1 000-hp Bo-Bo diesel-electric locomotives and 70 diesel engines to repower diesel-electric locomotives. Also 280 diesel engines were delivered for 1 050/1 350 hp Co-Co diesel electric locomotives made in Argentina. To Uruguayan National Railways it has delivered 12 suburban passenger coaches; to Chilean Railways, 30 first class passenger coaches. Contracts have been signed to supply to Chilean Railways 20 sets of electric (3 000 V dc) passenger trains and with Cuban Railways to supply 185 first-class, air-conditioned passenger coaches, 15 mail vans and 100 diesel-hydraulic air-conditioned railcars.

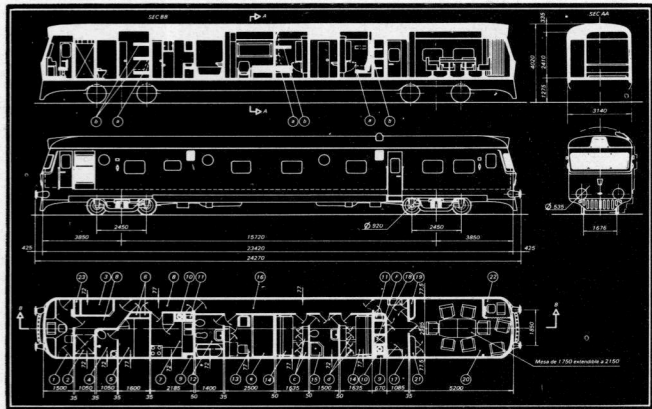

Travelling track gang coach
Specially built for Argentine railways (FA) by Fiat-Concord for long-distance track inspection jobs.
(1) cabin No 1 (2) air-conditioning unit (3) power group room (4) driver's WC (5) driver's bedroom with three beds (6) driver's cupboard (7) kitchen with oven and gas irons (8) service corridor (9) engine air inlet (10) engine gases outlet (11) engine expansion water

tank compartment (12) main WC with bath (13) main living room (14) bedroom with two beds (15) WC and shower bath (16) main corridor (17) hall (18) clean clothes and luggage closet (19) electrical rig case for engine control panel and auxiliary control panel (20) dinner room (21) closet (22) cabin No 2 (23) electrical rig case for engine No 1 only on the upper part.

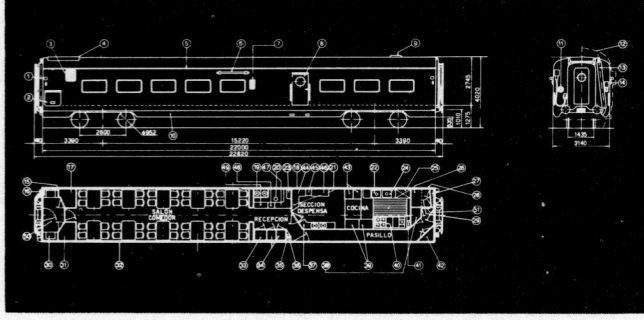

Dining car built for export by Fiat-Concord
The one shown is now working on Cuban Railways (F de C).
(1) electric tail light on both sides of the railroad car (2) doors (on both sides of the car) for passing empty bottles basket: minimum 750 by 700 cms (3) air inlet on both sides (4) roof opening access to air-conditioning unit (5) rain drain (6) destination rack (7) engine air inlet (8) foodstuffs loading-door (9) fumes outlet (10) flat hinged sheet for access to equipment under frame (11) hand brake at one end only (12) rolling stock gauge (13) engine air outlet (14) tail light holder (15) small fire extinguisher (16) hand brake (17) air-conditioning equipment cabinet (18) foodstuffs loading-door 750 by 700 cms (19) bottled gas cylinders cabinet (20) maitre seat (21) sliding window (22) vegetable box (23) display cabinet for drink and cigarettes, etc (24) stainless-steel sinks (25) express-coffee machine table (26) empty containers storage compartment (movable shelves) (27) cupboard with hangers (28) round window (29) wardrobe (30) cupboard, empty

bottles basket underneath (31) electrical appliances cupboard (32) double fixed windows (33) wine cellar (34) refrigerator (reaches the ceiling) for drinks (35) large fire-extinguisher (36) ice water tap and sink (37) used clothes/laundry cabinet (38) clean-clothes cabinet (39) folding-out tables (40) bottled-gas, kitchen (41) bottled-gas water-heater (42) clean-clothes cabinet (43) refrigerators (44) working table (45) cutlery drawer (46) bread bins (47) counter (48) folding-out table (49) empty bottles basket enclosure (50) lobby (51) sliding door

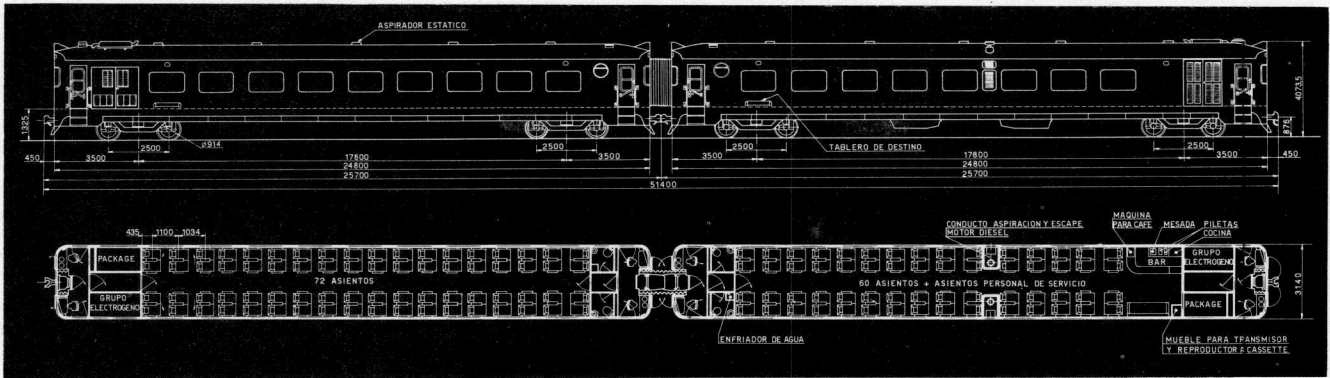

Two-car diesel trainset built for Cuban Railways (F de C) as part of an order for 100 railcar and 20 air-conditioned restaurant cars
The railcars are powered by two Fiat engines of 280 hp. Braking is by Westinghouse.
The motor coach seats 60 passengers: trailers 72.

Sleeping car for FA by Fiat Concord (left and below)
(1) lighted sign (2) tail light (electric) (3) water tank 1500 litres (4) roof opening and access to air-conditioning unit (5) rain drain (6) upwards sliding window blind (7) fixed arm support (8) baggage compartment (9) top folding-out bed (10) seat back; folds out for bed (11) air-conditioning equipment (12) flat hinged sheet for access to equipment located under the frame (13) wardrobe (14) folding out table (15) air renewal filters (16) bottle and glass holders for use at night (17) magazine rack (18) baggage rack (19) baggage rack (20) top folding-out bed (21) seat back, folds out for bed (22) emergency valve (23) mirror (24) hand brake (25) wash basin (26) gentlemen's WC (27) air-conditioning equipment control cabinet (28) fixed bed (29) wardrobe in waiter's room (30) electric equipment control cabinet (31) fixed windows, double glass "Thermopan" type (32) baggage rack (33) wash basin (34) ladies WC (35) wash basin (36) mirror (37) large fire extinguisher (38) wardrobe (39) rooms that may be transformed from two-to four-passenger (40) engine, air inlet duct (41) engine water tank (42) water-cooler equipment (43) generator set control equipment (44) small fire extinguisher (45) cupboard (46) electric equipment control cabinet (47) cupboard in waiter's room (48) bottle and glass holder for use at night (49) magazine rack (50) air-conditioning equipment (51) water cooler

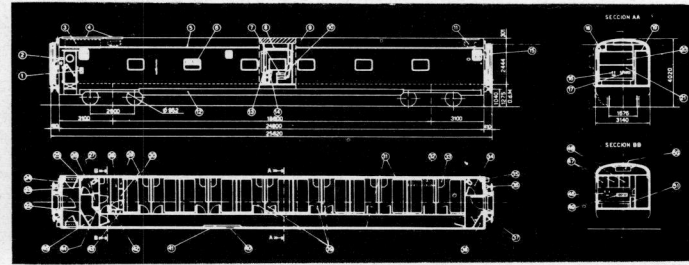

FIVES LILLE-CAIL
Société Fives Lille-Cail

7 rue Montalivet, Paris 8, France

(The company has ceased production of railway equipment)

FMC
FMC Corp (Marine and Rail Equipment Division)

4700 NW Front Avenue, PO Box 3616, Portland, Oregon 97208, USA

Products: Freight wagons.

Telephone: (503) 228 9281
Telex: 36 0672

President: John E Carroll Jr
Chief Engineer: R J Landregan
Chief Sales Officer: William R Galbraith

100-tonne capacity covered hopper wagon designed for a wide range of bulk commodities including grain and mineral products

70-tonne capacity wood products box wagon for a wide variety of lading; features include nailable steel decking, 10-ft sliding doors and cushioned underframe

100-tonne open top gondola wagon designed for unit train operation utilising rotary dump service

---

FNV

Fábrica Nacional de Vagões SA

Avenida Maria Coelho Aguiar no 215, Block A 8th floor, 05804 São Paulo; Brazil

Products: Freight wagons; passenger coaches; electric trainsets; Barber stabilised bogies; draft gears; couplers; wheels and components.

President: Aureliano Pires e Albuquerque

Telephone: 011 545 1122 (Ext 3546)
Telegrams: FABRIVA
Telex: 01121901

Industrial Director: Dr Waldemar Fonseca
Commercial Director: Dr Leon Ravinowich
Constitution: The company was formed in 1943 to manufacture freight wagons. Today the plant covers an area of over 80 000 m².

Box wagons for 1.600 m gauge with stamped sides, doors, ends and roof delivered to RFFSA of Brazil in 1977/78

Drop bottom wagon for metre-gauge operation on FEPASA of Brazil

---

FRANCO-BELGE

Société Franco-Belge de Matériel de Chemins de Fer

49 avenue George V, 75008 Paris, France

Products: Passenger cars for main line, suburban and underground railways; electric multiple unit; standard and special freight cars; standard and special bogies for passenger and freight cars.

President: Francois Herlicq
General Manager: Serge Fauconnet
Assistant General Manager: Pierre Treps
Works Manager: André Rousset
Commercial Manager: Jean Nobilet

Constitution: The company came under the control of the Herlicq Group in 1962.

Telephone: 723 55 24
Telegrams: LOCOMORAM, Paris
Telex: Herlicq No 290 060F

Sales: As part of the newly-formed Gie Norfer, Franco-Belge won a contract worth Frs 1000 million in 1978 for 4500 special freight wagons for the German Democratic Republic.
Advances in aluminium passenger coach production enabled the company to win substantial contracts in recent years. Orders placed include: 120 cars for the Metropolitan Atlanta Rapid Transit Authority of the USA; 1000 cars for the Paris Metro (RATP); 750 cars for interconnection operations between French National Railways (SNCF) and RATP.

First subway car for MARTA is swung aboard ship

"Interconnexion" trainset built for SNCF and RATP of Paris

FRANCORAIL-MTE

Telephone: 292 05 10
Telex: 290638 F

2 rue de Léningrad, 75008 Paris, France

Managing Directors: R Juchs, President of Carel Fouché-Languepin
G de Dietrich, President of De Dietrich & Cie
H Jullien, General Manager of Société MTE
J Lerebours-Pigeonnière, President of Société MTE
Secretary: André Gubi
Commercial Managers: H Dhaussy
S Bartmann

Constitution: The FRANCORAIL-MTE group, established in 1973, pools the technological know-how, research and design capacities and means of production of five companies: Carel Fouché, Creusot Loire, De Dietrich & Cie, Jeumont-Schneider, Société MTE.
FRANCORAIL-MTE co-ordinates the activities of railroad rolling stock manufacturers supplying main line electric and diesel-electric locomotives; shunting locomotives and other hauling stock; electric and diesel motor coach trains, railcars, metro cars; passenger coaches and other rolling stock; bogies; constituent sub-assemblies of the above-mentioned equipment; advanced vehicles and transport systems; metropolitan rapid transit systems; suburban transport systems.

Electric trainset supplied by Francorail-MTE to FEPASA of Brazil

FREIGHTER
Freighter Industries Ltd

Telephone: 03 267 3888
Telegrams: ESCOR, Melbourne
Telex: AA 31148

409 St Kilda Road, Melbourne 3004, Australia

Products: Hy-Rail road-rail conversion vehicle; all-steel containers. Hy-Rail equipment is designed to enable a conventional road vehicle to be converted to run on railway lines with a minimum of effort and time. The basic principle is the use of small flanged rail wheels which come in contact with the rail line and take a percentage of the vehicle weight. These act as guides preventing the road wheels from running off the track. The traction for acceleration and braking is provided in the normal manner by the road tyres being in contact with the line.
Hy-Rail can be fitted to nearly all road vehicles provided tyre track is compatible with or can be safely modified to suit the particular rail gauge required. In Australia gauges of 1 067 mm (3' 6''), 1 435 mm (4' 8½''), 1 600 mm (5' 3'') are the most commonly used by the various railway companies and Governments. Hy-Rail can be built to suit all gauges and uses its patented over-centre principle to lock the rail wheels into their on-rail mode. The same method is used in locking down aircraft under carriages.

Hy-Rail kit for road/rail conversion which is fitted to conventional highway vehicles to enable it to operate over railway lines
The Range Rover inspection unit pictured here is guided by four special partial load bearing rail wheels, with drive and braking provided through the vehicle's road tyres in contact with the track.

FRICHS
A/S Frichs

Telephone: 06 15 85 55
Telegrams: FRICHS, Aarhus
Telex: 64373

PO Box 115, DK-8100 Aarhus C, Denmark

Products: Diesel locomotives and railcars; diesel engines; centrifugally-cast cylinder liners for diesel engines.

Managing Director: B Bigaard Soerensen

Constitution: Founded as a general engineering company in 1854; the manufacture of diesel locomotives started in 1925.

FRUEHAUF
Fruehauf Railcar Division

Telephone: (201) 779 1976

660 Van Houten Avenue, Clifton, New Jersey 07015, USA

Products: Freight wagons.

General Manager: H W Crank
General Sales Manager: R S Warntz

Constitution: The Division, successor to the Magor Corporation, was set up in 1964. Steel open wagons, box wagons, flat wagons, steel and aluminium covered hopper wagons, wood chip wagons, pulpwood wagons and dump wagons comprise the major part of production.

FUCHIN (PU ZHEN)
Fuchin (Pu Zhen) Rolling Stock Works

Nanking, Kiangsu, People's Republic of China

Products: Passenger coaches; roller bearings; axle boxes; brake cylinders.

Constitution: Originally a locomotive repair yard, now a passenger coach repair and manufacturing works.

FUJI
Fuji Heavy Industries Ltd

Telephone: 03 347 2436
Telegrams: FUJIHEAVY, Tokyo
Telex: 0 232 2268

7-2 Nishi-Shinjuku 1-chome, Shinjuku-ku, Tokyo, Japan

Products: Electric and diesel trainsets; passenger coaches; freight wagons; works vehicles.

Chairman: Eiichi Ohara
President: Sadamachi Sasaki
Executive Director: Sukemitsu Irie
Director & General Manager: Yutaka Hasegawa
Manager, Rolling Stock Sales: Masami Suwabe

Constitution: Fuji Heavy Industries stems from the Nakajima Aircraft Company. The Nakajima Company was dissolved in 1945, but in 1953 it was reorganised as Fuji Heavy Industries, specialising in building SUBARU automobiles, buses, rolling stock and aircraft.

Sales: Sales for 1978 include 135 passenger coaches; 50 diesel rail cars; 30 sleeping cars; 90 electric cars; 160 track construction and maintenance machines; 15 tank cars and various freight wagons.
Among 1978/79 exports were 13 passenger cars for Nigeria, four crane cars for New York and one track maintenance car for Cleveland, USA.

FUJI CAR
Fuji Car Manufacturing Co Ltd

Telephone: (Sakai) 0722 (36) 5761
Telegrams: FUJCAR, Sakai
Telex: 05374487 FUJCAR J

383 Sayamacho, Minamikawachigun, Osaka-589, Japan

Products: Passenger coaches; freight wagons; bogies.

Chairman: Kanichi Nakayasu

Managing Director: Takeomi Nishimura
Export Sales: Hisashi Okumura

Constitution: The company was formed in 1924 by the Ishihara Brothers. In 1945 the name was changed in order to specialise in the manufacture of rolling stock.

FUNKEY

C H Funkey & Co (Pty) Ltd

Telephone: 864 2725
Telegrams: FUNKEYCO
Telex: 8 4989

Fuchs Street, Alrode, PO Box 3790, Alberton 1451, Transvaal, South Africa

Products: Diesel-hydraulic shunting locomotives; diesel mining locomotives; battery-operated and trolley wire electric mining locomotives; track inspection railcars.

Chairman: J P Funkey
Managing Director: J J Galloway

GALLINARI

A Gallinari SpA

Telephone: 31 641
Telegrams: GALLINARI, Reggio Emilia
Telex: 53601 Galre I

Viale Ramazzini 37, 42100 Reggio Emilia, Italy

Products: Passenger coaches; flat and covered wagons, tank wagons, baggage and mail cars.

GANZ

Ganz Electric Works

Telephone: 158 210
Telegrams: Alterno, Budapest
Telex: 225363

Budapest 1024, Lövóház utca 39, Hungary

Products: Electric mainline locomotives; railcars and trainsets; trams; railway signalling and interlocking equipments; complete power transmission equipments; complete substations.

General Manager: Eng György Papp

Deputy General Manager: Eng Béla Farkas
Export Sales Manager: Sándor Csernock
Constitution: This enterprise developed from the electrical department started by Ganz and Co in 1878. Since 1892 the plant has supplied more than 1 000 vehicles of various types.

Articulated light rail vehicle

5 100 kW thyristor controlled electric locomotive

Three-car mainline electric multiple unit set

GANZ-MÁVAG

Ganz-Mávag Locomotive and Railway Carriage Manufacturers and Mechanical Engineers

Telephone: 335 950/137 020
Telegrams: GANZMAVAG Budapest
Telex: 22 5576/22 5575

Budapest VIII, PO Box 136, Könyves Kálmán krt., 76, Hungary

Products: Diesel-electric, diesel-hydraulic locomotives (350 to 3 000 hp); diesel railcars and multiple units.

Chairman: Dr András Dunajszki
Managing Director: Dr Antal Fleck
Sales Manager (Railway Stock): Tibor Trompler

Constitution: Ganz Railway Carriage Manufacturers and Mechanical Engineers, and Mávag Locomotive and Machine Works were merged in 1959 to form Ganz-Mávag.

New equipment: The great demand for low-powered diesel-hydraulic locomotives intended for branch-line and light shunting service as well as shunting to be performed in explosive areas has incited Ganz-Mávag to develop a new family of locomotives. Axle load is 10 to 12 tonnes to meet branch-line conditions with poor track superstructure. Running order weight is approximately 35 tonnes for specified hauling duties requiring an output of 300-368 kW (400 to 500 hp). The hydraulic transmission is provided by a pair of torque converters developed by the factory itself. The 300 kW (400 hp) diesel-hydraulic locomotives type DHM 8 manufactured for the petro-chemical industries are flame- and explosion-proof variants of the standard series type DHM 6 light shunter. The design meets the temperature limits of inflammability category G-3 defined in the German Standard DIN applying to the outdoor service. Surface temperature of the loco and exhausts are kept under 160°C while working in hazardous areas. Both variants are characterised by C (0-6-0) axle arrangement, 12-tonne axle load, 60 km/h top speed, 9 800 daN continuous tractive effort on adhesion limit and a hydraulic reversing gear. The latest versions of this family are the types DHM 9 and DHM 10. The DHM 9 was developed for broad-gauge lines, the DHM 10 type for narrow gauge lines. The former has a C (0-6-0) axle arrangement, while the latter is a B-B loco to achieve a lighter axle load. The locomotives are braked by compressed-air brake, the hauled carriages and wagons by vacuum brakes. For design of both loco types, extreme tropical conditions have been taken into account, such as extraordinary high ambient temperature, high dustload of air, heavy rain storms and high relative humidity.

Sales: Fifteen diesel trainsets were manufactured for the Uruguay State Railway Authority (AFE) in 1977. The trains consist of a parcel power car with driver's cabs at both ends, a second-class intermediate trailer and a first-class control trailer with a bar conmpartment. The trainsets can be completed by an additional first-class intermediate trailer. The power cars are fitted with a 690 kW (935 hp) 12 VFE 17/24-T type diesel engine and a Hydro-Ganz type three-speed hydromechanical gearbox of the

factory's own construction. The control system of the engine and transmission is fully automatic through a patented control device of electronic elements. The standard-gauge trainsets have a maximum axle load of 12 tonnes and a top speed of 100 km/h. Construction of the well-known four-unit Ganz suburban diesel trainsets for the Soviet Railways will continue over the next few years. From 1964 to 1979 450 of this type were delivered for the same customer.

The most recent products in the railcar field are 20 diesel trainsets for standard- and metre-gauge operation on Tunisian Railways. These three-car sets are similar to the trains delivered to Greece. The Tunisian sets consist of a power car equipped with an 882 kW (1 200 hp) Ganz-Mávag Pielstick 8PA4-185 engine and Ganz-Mávag two-stage hydro-dynamic transmission type H 122, a second-class intermediate trailer and a first-class control trailer fitted with a bar. All the train cars are air-conditioned. Top speed is 130 km/h; maximum axle load for metre-gauge, 16 tonnes; for standard-gauge, 17.5 tonnes. The trains are equipped with all-round bogies developed by Ganz-Mávag having a combination of rubber springs and coil springs as secondary suspension. One of the compartments is of 'grand comfort' grade. Electric power for the whole train is supplied by two diesel-electric generating sets of 75 kVA each. Voltage of ac network of 50 Hz frequency is 380/220 V. The brake system is of Westinghouse block-type brake for 1 000 mm gauge and disc-type for 1 435 mm gauge.

Ganz-Mávag builds structural parts for the mainline electric locomotives of Hungarian State Railways (MÁV) and also for the 46 three-unit 25 kV ac straight electric thyristor-controlled trainsets ordered by the Yugoslav State Railways Zagreb and Sarajevo divisions.

3-unit de luxe air-conditioned diesel-hydraulic trainset built for the Tunisian Railways

Diesel-hydraulic locomotive type DHM 7 rated at 1 325 kW (1 800 hp) built for Hungarian State Railways (MAV)

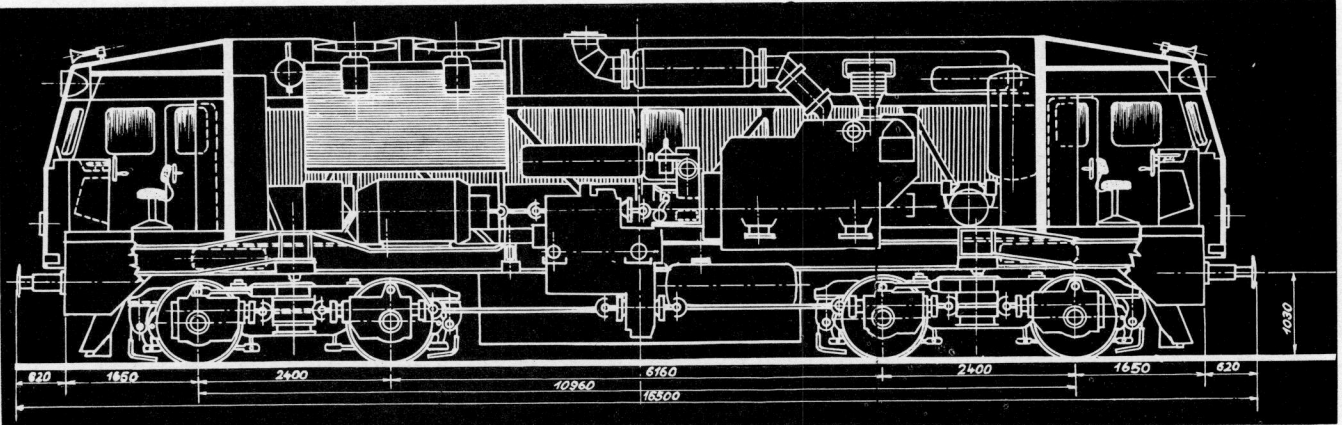

Type DHM7 diesel-hydraulic locomotive rated at 1 800 hp

GARRETT

Garrett-AiResearch

Torrance, California, USA

Products: Rapid transit trainsets.

Constitution: Garrett joined the railway industry in 1974 when Boeing Vertol, acting on behalf of the US Department of Transportation, awarded a contract worth US$ 8 million to Garrett for construction of a two-car prototype Advanced Concept Train.

New equipment: The twin ACT prototype cars left Garrett's Torrance plant in 1977 and are undergoing tests at DOT's Transportation Test Centre at Pueblo, Colorado.

GARRETT RAILROAD

Garrett Railroad Car & Equipment, Inc

PO Box 2208, East Cherry Street, Newcastle, Pennsylvania 16102, USA

Telephone: (412) 658 9061

Products: New and rebuilt freight wagons for interchange and industrial use; reconditioned and used rolling stock parts; complete airbrake repair facility.

GATX

General American Transportation Corp

120 South Riverside Plaza, Chicago, Illinois 60606, USA

Products: Tank wagons.

New equipment: General American Transportation Corporation has designed and developed a proprietary product of interconnected railroad tank cars called the TankTrain system. Significant features which differentiate TankTrain cars from conventional equipment are flexible interconnecting commodity hoses, elbow pipes, protective housings and tank isolation valves which are at the top ends of each car. A maximum string length of 20 cars can be loaded with liquid commodity through a

single connection to the B-end of the first car. Displaced vapours may be easily collected from one connection at the A-end of the strings or vented into the atmosphere.

At the unloading site a reverse procedure can be used to unload an entire string of cars, using compressed air or inert gas, depending upon the flammability of the liquid involved. An unloading pump can be incorporated to increase the unloading flow rate. With the proper equipment, maximum flow rates of 3 000 gallons per minute can be attained.

Characteristics of the DOT111A100W1 23 150-gallon capacity TankTrain car are: approximate lightweight 79 300 lbs; gross weight 263 000 lbs; length over striker 54 ft 9 in; overall height 15 ft 5½ in; AAR plate "C" clearance diagram.

This equipment comes in various size capacities to fit a specific commodity. TankTrain cars are in service carrying such diverse commodities as #2 and #6 fuel oil, petrol, 32 per cent urea ammonia nitrate, sulphuric acid, and 105 per cent super phosphoric acid.

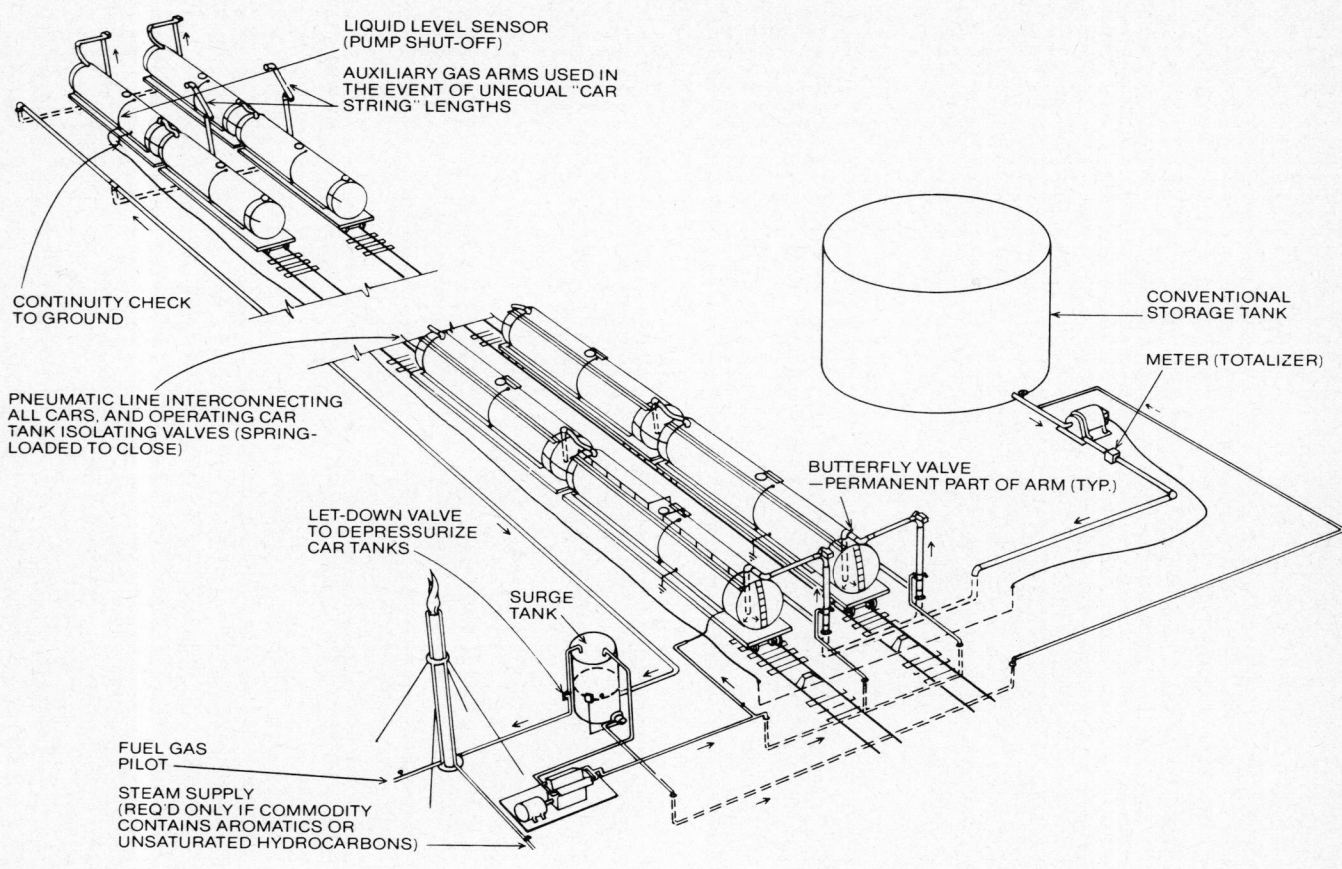

LIQUID LEVEL SENSOR
(PUMP SHUT-OFF)

AUXILIARY GAS ARMS USED IN
THE EVENT OF UNEQUAL "CAR
STRING" LENGTHS

CONTINUITY CHECK
TO GROUND

CONVENTIONAL
STORAGE TANK

METER (TOTALIZER)

PNEUMATIC LINE INTERCONNECTING
ALL CARS, AND OPERATING CAR
TANK ISOLATING VALVES (SPRING-
LOADED TO CLOSE)

BUTTERFLY VALVE
—PERMANENT PART OF ARM (TYP.)

LET-DOWN VALVE
TO DEPRESSURIZE
CAR TANKS

SURGE
TANK

FUEL GAS
PILOT

STEAM SUPPLY
(REQ'D ONLY IF COMMODITY
CONTAINS AROMATICS OR
UNSATURATED HYDROCARBONS)

Loading "closed system"

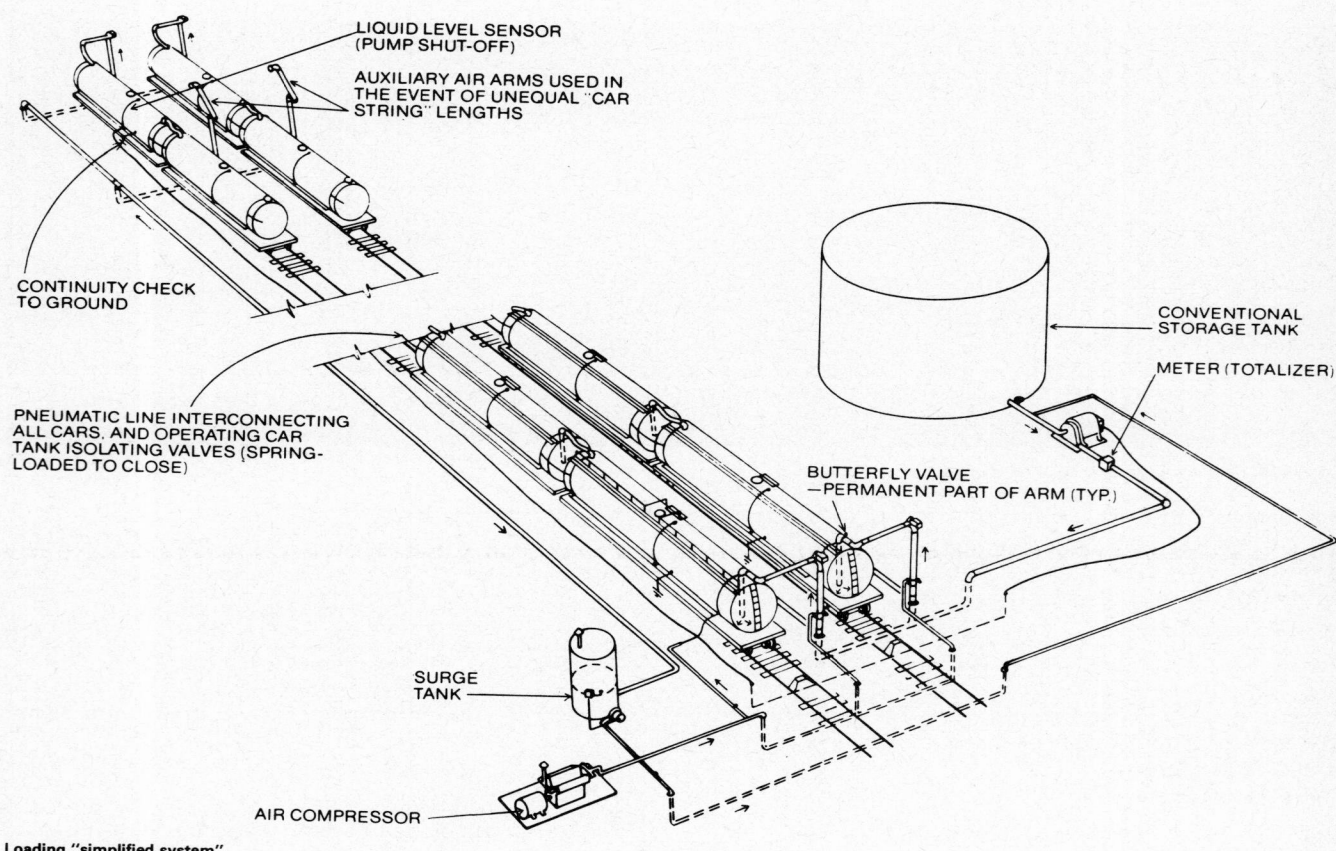

LIQUID LEVEL SENSOR
(PUMP SHUT-OFF)

AUXILIARY AIR ARMS USED IN
THE EVENT OF UNEQUAL "CAR
STRING" LENGTHS

CONTINUITY CHECK
TO GROUND

CONVENTIONAL
STORAGE TANK

METER (TOTALIZER)

PNEUMATIC LINE INTERCONNECTING
ALL CARS, AND OPERATING CAR
TANK ISOLATING VALVES (SPRING-
LOADED TO CLOSE)

BUTTERFLY VALVE
—PERMANENT PART OF ARM (TYP.)

SURGE
TANK

AIR COMPRESSOR

Loading "simplified system"

GEC AUSTRALIA

GEC Australia Ltd

Evans Road, Rocklea, Queensland 4106, Australia

Products: Electric and diesel-electric locomotives; rolling stock; electric and diesel-
electric traction power and control equipment.

Divisional Managing Director: J Brown

Telephone: 07 2771611
Telegrams: GECHED, Brisbane
Telex: AA 40167

Sales Director: R Bennett

Sales: No locomotives have been manufactured in the works since mid-1977 and no
orders were held at November 1978 for future manufacture.

GEC INDUSTRIAL

GEC Industrial Locomotives

Vulcan Works, Newton-le-Willows, Merseyside WA12 8RU, England

Telephone: 09252 5151
Telegrams: ENELECTICO, Newton-le-Willows
Telex: 627131

Products: Diesel-electric and diesel-hydraulic locomotives, line-fed electric locomotives (both trolley and pantograph types), flame-proof battery locomotives and special-purpose locomotives. Locomotive designs are available for most industrial uses and many light railway duties also: weights 12-100 tonne; powers 150-15000 hp; gauges 600-1678 mm; in 2-axle, 3-axle and 4-axle designs with rigid frames or bogies.

Director and General Manager: P A Heron

Constitution: GEC Industrial Locomotives Ltd was set up in 1978 as part of the General Electric Company of England. It has close ties with GEC Traction but is managed separately . GEC Industrial Locomotives Ltd incorporates the industrial loco activities of many well-known companies such as AEI, Bagnall, BTH, EE, Hawthorn Leslie, Metro-Vick, Robert Stephenson, Ruston & Hornsby and Vulcan Foundry. (It can trace its ancestry to the Robert Stephenson Company, formed in 1823). Sales of locomotives from these constituent companies have been made to operators in 68 countries.

GEC TRACTION

GEC Traction Ltd

Head Office: Trafford Park, Manchester M17 1PR, England

UK Works: Manchester, Preston and Sheffield

Telephone: 061 872 2431
Telegrams: ASSOCELECT, Manchester
Telex: 667152

Products: Complete electric and diesel-electric locomotives; multiple unit trains, power cars, power propulsion equipments; traction and auxiliary alternators and auxiliary generators; traction motors; main drive gears, control gear (thyristor, rectifier contactor or camshaft); inverters; speedometers and vigilance; pantographs.

Managing Director: J Legg
Sales Director: D R Love
Contracts Director: K Gunary
Technical Director: A L Fairbrother
Manufacturing Director: C J Salt

Constitution: GEC Traction traces its railway history back to the Robert Stephenson Company which, in 1823, was the first company in the world to be established specifically to build locomotives. The company has been continuously in the railway traction business longer than any other manufacturer in the world. In addition to Robert Stephenson, the company now incorporates the traction activities of many other locomotive and electric traction manufacturers, notably AEI, BTH, Dick Kerr, English Electric, GEC, Metro-Vickers, Siemens (UK) and the Vulcan Foundry.
GEC Traction is the United Kingdom's largest exporter of electric traction propulsion equipment. Sales of 27 000 electric and diesel locomotives and equipments have been made to 70 countries over a period of about 90 years. The locos and equipment have operated in widely differing conditions from tropical heat through desert to the Arctic; in altitudes ranging from below sea level to the world's highest railway (over 15 000 ft); on slow freight and high-speed Inter-City services, and on mass transit systems. The production range includes thyristor control for the world's standard electrification voltages: 25 and 50 kV, 50 and 60 Hz; 3000, 1500, 750 and 600 V dc and battery.

Sales: Recent major sales include: Hong Kong; propulsion equipments for 150 cars for the Tsuen Wan extension of the Mass Transit Railway Corporation. These will be added to the existing orders covering 210 cars for the initial system.
Propulsion equipments for 45 three-car emu suburban trains (both inner and outer suburban) for the Kowloon Canton Railway which is being electrified at 25 kV 50 Hz.
New Zealand: Propulsion equipment for 44 two-car emu trains for the 1 500 kW Wellington suburban services.
Australia (Vicrail): 1 500 V propulsion equipment for 200 power cars and 100 trailers. Delivery for the contract is to be spread over a five-year period and involves some manufacture in Australia.
British Rail: Thyristor controlled propulsion equipment for Class 317 outer-suburban emu trains for the St Pancras-Bedford 25 kV electrification.

Contracts completed in 1979 include:
ISCOR: 50 kV 50 Hz heavy freight locomotives. Consists of three locomotives regularly haul trains exceeding 20 000 tonnes over the 800 km narrow-gauge line from Sishen to Saldanha.

Taiwan: The 20 Bo-Bo locomotives and 13 five-car luxury express trains have all been delivered for this newly electrified system (25 kV 60 Hz).
Denmark: 1 500 V emu with regenerative chopper control.
British Rail: Thyristor controlled emu trains for Trans-Clyde (Class 314, 25 kV 50 Hz) and Southern Region (750 V dc). The latter incorporates GEC's STAR regenerative chopper circuit which reduces both first costs and running costs.
Camshaft controlled 750 V emus have been supplied for Merseyrail (Class 507) and Southern Region (Class 508), generally similar to the Great Northern Class 313 equipments.
London Transport: Camshaft control equipments for the 1973 Tube Stock (Heathrow Line) and C77 surface stock are completed, as is the regenerative chopper control equipment for the Experimental Tube Train (ETT).
Tyne & Wear: Equipments for all 90 of the articulated 1 500 V two-car train have been delivered. The service is expected to start in 1980 on completion of extensive civil engineering works.
Glasgow: The 33 cars for the very small tube line of Greater Glasgow entered service during 1979.

Work in hand during 1979/80 includes:
Portugal: Propulsion equipment for 1 500 V suburban emu trains for the Caiscais Line in Lisbon.
USA: Complete locomotives with dual voltage regenerative chopper control and arranged for multiple or remote control.
Brazil: Traction motors and control gear for 3 000 V multiple unit trains for suburban services in Rio de Janeiro.
South Africa: Equipment for 3 000 V Bo-Bo locomotives (Class 6E1) and multiple unit trains. When current orders are completed GEC will have powered or supplied more than 3 300 electric vehicles for this one railway operator.
British Rail: Work is well advanced on the propulsion equipment for the 25 kV thyristor controlled Class 315 emu trains for the Liverpool Street to Shenfield services. Production of traction motor and gears for the West of England High Speed Trains is well advanced and is due to start on those for the north-east/south-west route.
London Transport: Control equipment for the D78 surface cars.
India: Traction motors, generators and control gear for metre gauge diesel electric locomotives.

Development: Continuing work on regenerative braking choppers, the most recent example being for Denmark and British Rail Southern Region. The Company's STAR circuit offers both reduced capital costs and reduced running costs.
Work is continuing, jointly with British Rail, on non-synchronous three phase traction motors and their power conditioning equipment, as well as a project for a regenerative ac locomotive. There is a development contract for the production (squadron) series of Advanced Passenger Trains.
Work has started on a 150 kVA three-phase auxiliary micro-processor controlled inverter and (in the non-railway field) on development of a new generation of trolley bus equipment.

GENERAL ELECTRIC

General Electric Company
(Transportation Systems Business Division)

2901 East Lake Road, Erie, Pennsylvania 16531, USA

Export Office: Export Sales & Service Division, GE Co, 570 Lexington Avenue, New York, New York 10022, USA

Products: Diesel-electric and electric locomotives; switching and mining locomotives.

Chairman: Reginald H Jones
Managing Director: Marion S Richardson
Sales Director: John C Dwyer
Export Sales: Robert F Vunk (ESSD, New York)

Licence agreements: General Electric (USA) has locomotive licence agreements with the following:
Australia: A Goninan & Co
Brazil: General Electric do Brazil
Federal Republic of Germany: Krupp
South Africa: Dorbyl
Spain: Babcock & Wilcox Espanola CAF

Sales: Recent orders received by General Electric:

Telephone: (814) 455 5466
Telegrams: GECO 14 ERI

Export diesel-electric locomotives

Quantity	Description	Country
10	U20C	Zambia*
18	U20C	Jordan
24	SG10	South Africa

*Licensee manufacture

Domestic type diesel-electric road locomotives (orders from mid-1978 to -1979):

Quantity	Description	Railway
24	C30-7	Santa Fe
15	B23-7	Santa Fe
120	C30-7	Burlington Northern
49	B30-7	Chessie
57	B23-7	Conrail
32	C30-7	Louisville & Nashville
105	C30-7	Mexican Railways
20	B23-7	Missouri Pacific
16	C30-7	Seaboard Coast Line
40	C30-7	Union Pacific

Export Models — Locomotive types

	U10B	U11B	U15C	U22C*	U18C	U26C	28C80	36C80
Gross hp	1 050	1 100	1 650	2 300	1 950	2 750	3 000	3 940
hp for traction	950	1 000	1 550	2 165	1 820	2 600	2 800	3 600
Number of axles	4	4	6	6	6	6	6	6
Track gauge	All gauges from 914 to 1 676 mm						1 435 to 1 676 mm	
Couplers	To suit railway requirements							
Tractive effort at continuous motor rating (kN)	161	161	241	241	241	241	289	289
Max speed km/h	103	103	103	103	103	103	110	110
Minimum weight (kg)	49 700	49 700	80 500	88 900	80 500	96 200	113 000	117 000
Electrical system	dc/dc	dc/dc	dc/dc	dc/dc	ac/dc	ac/dc	ac/dc	ac/dc
Engine	CAT	CAT	GE	GE	GE	GE	GE	GE
	D379	D398	FDL8	FDL12	FDL8	FDL12	FDL12	FDL16
Traction gen/alt	GT 601	GT 601	GT 581	GT 581	GTA11	GTA11	GTA11	GTA11
Traction motors	GE761	GE761	GE761	GE761	GE761	GE761	GE786	GE786

*Streamlined dual cab design available.

Electric Locomotives

	E60CP	E60C	E42	E25B
Rail hp, continuous	5 100	5 100	3 570	2 125
Rail hp, short time	9 800	NA	NA	NA
Voltage, kV	11/12·5/25	25/50	25	25
Frequency	25/60	50/60	60	60
Number of axles	6	6	6	4
Minimum weight				
lbs	350 000	264 000	198 000	240 000
kg	159 100	120 000	90 000	109 100
Maximum speed				
mph	120	70	68	70
km/h	193	113	110	113
Continuous tractive effort				
lbs	34 000	85 200	44 000	55 000
kg	15 455	38 700	20 000	25 000
Track gauges				
in	56·5/66	56·5/66	39·4/42	56·5/66
mm	1435/1676	1435/1676	1000/1067	1435/1676
Major equipment				
Traction motors	GE780	GE780	GE761	GE780
Line breaker	Vacuum circuit breaker			
Transformer	Core-foam, forced oil cooled			
Power converter	Forced air cooled thyristors			
Ventilating system	Single blower, self cleaning filters			

General Electric Model U11B locomotive
Recently delivered on transfer bogies to Fecosa Railways of Costa Rica.

General Electric Model C30-7 domestic locomotive
Over 100 have been ordered by Mexican Railways since 1978. These 3 000 hp (for traction) locomotives are built to North American design standards and used in high-speed freight and mineral service.

General Electric C30-7 locomotive
One of several hundred GE locomotives of that type in service on Burlington Northern and other North American Railroads. Recent deliveries feature significant improvements in full economy and reliability.

General Electric B36-7 locomotive of the type scheduled for service on Southern Pacific and other railroads
The B36-7 locomotive features 900 hp per axle throughout the full operating range and includes GE's new sentry adhesion control system and full parallel motor connections. Other New Series features include a Model 7S1616 turbocharger designed and manufactured by GE.

General Electric 136-tonne switching locomotive in heavy duty service on C&NW Railway
This locomotive is available to adhesive weights of 144 tonnes.

Domestic Models

Builder	GE	GE	GE	GE	GE	GE	GE	GE	GE
Model	B18-7	B23-7	C23-7	B28-7	C28-7	B30-7	C30-7	B36-7	C36-7
Service	General purpose	General purpose	General purpose	General purpose	General-Purpose	General-Purpose	General-Purpose	General-Purpose	General-Purpose
Operating cab & controls	Yes	Yes	Yes	Yes	Yes	Yes	Yes	Yes	Yes
Wheel arrangement	B-B or 0-4-4-0	B-B or 0-4-4-0	C-C or 0-6-6-0	B-B or 0-4-4-0	C-C or 0-6-6-0	B-B or 0-4-4-0	C-C or 0-6-6-0	B-B or 0-4-4-0	C-C or 0-6-6-0
Engine data:									
Number	1	1	1	1	1	1	1	1	1
Horsepower	1800	2250	2250	2750	2750	3000	3000	3600	3600
Total horsepower	1800	2250	2250	2750	2750	3000	3000	3600	3600
Number of cylinders	8	12	12	12	12	16	16	16	16
Model	GE-FDL-8	GE/FDL-12	GE-FDL-12	GE-FDL-12	GE FDL-12	GE FDL-16	GE FDL-16	GE FDL-16	GE FDL-16
Bore and stroke, inches	9 × 10-1/2	9 × 10-1/2	9 × 10-1/2	9 × 10-1/2	9 × 10-1/2	9 × 10-1/2	9 × 10-1/2	9 × 10-1/2	9 × 10-1/2
rpm	1050	1050	1050	1050	1050	1050	1050	1050	1050
Compression ratio	12.7:1	12.7:1	12.7:1	12.7:1	12.7:1	12.7:1	12.7:1	12.7:1	12.7:1
Cycle	4	4	4	4	4	4	4	4	4
Turbo-charged	Yes	Yes	Yes	Yes	Yes	Yes	Yes	Yes	Yes
Engine cooling fans	1	1	1	1	1	1	1	1	1
Engine cooling fan drive	Engine	Engine	Engine	Engine	Engine	Engine	Engine	Engine	Engine
Traction Equipment:									
Main generator	GTA-11	GTA-11	GTA-11	GTA-11	GTA-11	GTA-11	GTA-11	GTA-11	GTA-11
Motor	4 - GE752	4 - GE752	6 - GE752	4 - GE752	6 - GE752	4 - GE752	6 - GE752	4 - GE752	6 - GE752
Motor blowers	1	1	1	1	1	1	1	1	1
Blower drive	Engine	Engine	Engine	Engine	Engine	Engine	Engine	Engine	Engine
Wheelslip correction	auto sanding auto unloading of main alternator	auto sanding auto unloading of main alternator	auto sanding auto unloading of main alternator	auto sanding auto unloading of main alternator	auto sanding auto unloading of main alternator	auto sanding auto unloading of main alternator	auto sanding auto unloading of main alternator	auto sanding auto unloading of main alternator	auto sanding auto unloading of main alternator
Air brake schedule:	26L	26L	26L	26L	26L	26L	26L	26L	26L
Length	56' 8"	62' 2"	67' 3"	62 2"	67' 3"	62' 2"	67' 3"	62' 2"	67' 3"
Height	14' 9-1/4"	14' 9-1/4"	15' 4-1/4"	14' 9-1/4"	15' 4-1/4"	14' 9-1/4"	15' 4-1/4"	14' 9-1/4"	15' 4-1/4"
Width	10' 3-1/4"	10' 3-1/4"	10' 3-1/4"	10' 3-1/4"	10' 3-1/4"	10' 3-1/4"	10' 3-1/4"	10' 3-1/4"	10' 3-1/4"
Bolster centers	30' 8"	36' 2"	40' 11"	36' 2"	40' 11"	36' 2"	40' 11"	36' 2"	40' 11"
Truck wheel base	9' 0"	9' 0"	13' 7"	9' 0"	13' 7"	9' 0"	13' 7"	9' 0"	13' 7"
Minimum track curvature, radius and degree									
For single unit	150' or 39°	150' or 39°	273' or 21°	150' or 39°	273' or 21°	150' or 39°	273' or 21°	150' or 39°	273' or 21°
For MU or coupled to train	250' or 23°	250' or 23°	273' or 21°	250' or 23°	273' or 21°	250' or 23°	273' or 21°	250' or 23°	273' or 21°
Driving wheel diameter:	40"	40"	40"	40"	40"	40"	40"	40"	40"
Weight:									
On drivers, minimum and maximum	230 600/268 000	253 000/280 000	359 000/420 000	253 000/280 000	359 000/420 000	259 000/280 000	366 000/420 000	259 800/280 000	366 000/420 000
Total, minimum and maximum	230 600/268 000	253 000/280 000	359 000/420 000	253 000/280 000	359 000/420 000	259 000/280 000	366 000/420 000	259 800/280 000	366 000/420 000
Tractive effort:									
Starting at 257, adhesion for minimum and maximum weight	5 650/67 000	63 250/70 000	89 750/105 000	63 250/70 000	89 750/105 000	64 750/70 000	91 500/105 000	64 950/70 000	91 500/105 000
Continuous tractive effort & speed mph									
For smallest pinion	60 400/8.6	60 400/10.8	90 600/6.8	60 400/10.7*	90 600/8.5	60 400/10.7*	90 600/9.6	54 100/12.0*	90 600/11.8
For largest pinion	43 480/11.9	43 480/15.0	65 220/9.4	43 480/14.9*	65 220/11.8	43 480/14.9*	65 220/13.4	43 480/14.9*	65 220/16.4
Gear ratio and max speed mph:									
Smallest pinion	74/18 - 70	74/18 - 70	74/18 - 70	74/18 - 70	74/18 - 70	74/18 - 70	74/18 - 70	81/22 - 75	74/18 - 70
Intermediate pinion	80/23 - 79	80/23 - 79	80/23 - 79	80/23 - 79	80/23 - 79	80/23 - 79	80/23 - 79	80/23 - 79	80/23 - 79
Largest pinion	77/26 - 93	77/26 - 93	77/26 - 93	77/26 - 93	77/26 - 93	77/26 - 93	77/26 - 93	77/26 - 93	77/26 - 93
Supplies:									
Fuel - gallons for min & max tank	1 200/2 150	2 150/3 250	3 250/4 000	2 150/3 250	3 250/4 000	2 150/3 250	3 250/4 000	2 150/3 250	3 250/4 000
Coolant - gallon	335	350	350	350	350	365	365	365	365
Lube Oil - gallon	245	300	300	300	300	380	380	380	380
Sand - cubic feet	60	60	60	60	60	60	60	60	60
Compressor, air CFM:									
Max delivery	296	296	296	296	296	296	296	296	296
Delivery idling	127	127	127	127	127	127	127	127	127
Cooling type	Water	Water	Water	Water	Water	Water	Water	Water	Water
Layover protection	Optional	Optional	Optional	Optional	Optional	Optional	Optional	Optional	Optional
Dynamic brakes	Standard	Standard	Standard	Standard	Standard	Standard	Standard	Standard	Standard
Draft gear	MC-391 with Align. Control	MC-391 with Align. Control	MC-391 with Align. Control	MC-391 with Align. Control	MC-391 with Align. Control	MC-391 with Align. Control	MC-391 with Align. Control	MC-391 with Align. Control	MC-391 with Align. Control
Air-filtering Devices:									
Primary	Vortex self clean	Vortex self clean	Vortex self clean	Vortex self clean	Vortex self clean	Vortex self clean	Vortex self clean	Vortex self clean	Vortex self clean
Secondary engine air intake	GE Paper	GE Paper	GE Paper	GE Paper	GE Paper	GE Paper	GE Paper	GE Paper	GE Paper
Engine room pressurised	Yes	Yes	Yes	Yes	Yes	Yes	Yes	Yes	Yes
Main generator pressurised	Yes	Yes	Yes	Yes	Yes	—	—	—	Yes
Head end power supply	—	—	—	—	—	—	—	—	8
Production date	1977	1977	1977	1977	1977	1977	1977	1977	1977

*Power match
NOTE: ALL UNITS EQUIPPED WITH ROLLER-BEARING JOURNALS.

GENERAL ELECTRIC DO BRAZIL
General Electric do Brazil S/A

Head Offices: Rua Antonio de Godoy 88, Sao Paulo, Brazil
Av Almirante Barroso 81, Rio de Janeiro, Brazil

Works: Bairro Boa Vista s/nº, PO Box 1150, 13100 Campinas SP, Brazil

Products: Electric, diesel-electric locomotives

Chairman: G T Smiley
President: T Romanach
Manager, Locomotive Operation: L C Mascarenhas

Telephone (Sao Paulo Office): 222 1177
Telex (Sao Paulo Office): 011 24018

Telephone (Rio de Janeiro Office): 224 3312
Telex (Rio de Janeiro Office): 021 21694

Telephone (Works): 41 1944
Telex (Works): 019 1168-INGENETRIC

Railroad Operation, Enterprise, Transportation and Electrification: Guilhermo Marin

Sales: Locomotive orders completed or in hand at September 1978 include:

Client	Locomotive	Number	hp	Tonne	Gauge (m)	Type of Service	Year completed	Country
Companhia Siderúrgica Paulista (COSIPA)	Diesel-Electric	18	500/670	91	1.6	Shunting	1966/75/78	Brazil
Companhia Paulista de Estrada de Ferro (Fepasa)	Electric-C-C (3 000 V-CC)	10	5 200	144	1.6	Line	1967	Brazil
Estrada de Ferro Sorocabana (Fepasa)	Electric B-B (3 000 V-CC)	30	2 200	73	1.0	Line	1967	Brazil
Companhia Docas de Santos (CDS)	Diesel-Electric 80 Tonne	20	570	73	1.6	Shunting	1970/72	Brazil
Rêde Ferroviária Federal S/A (RFFSA)	Diesel-Electric U10B	80	1 000	60	1.0	Line	1971/72	Brazil
Administracion Nacional de Combustibles, Alcohol Y Portland (ANCAP)	Diesel-Electric 80 Tonne	1	570	73	1.435	Shunting	1971	Uruguay
Usinas Siderúrgicas de Minas Gerais S/A (Usiminas)	Diesel-Electric 80 Tonne	12	570	73	1.0	Shunting	1971/72/74/77	Brazil
Administração do Porto do Rio de Janeiro (APRJ)	Diesel-Electric 100 Tonne	4	670	100	1.6	Shunting	1972/76	Brazil
Rede Ferroviária Federal S/A (RFFSA)	Diesel-Electric U23C	170	2 250	165/180	1.6	Line	1972/74/75/76	Brazil
Companhia Siderurgica Mannesmann (CSM)	Diesel-Electric 80 Tonne	3	570	73	1.6	Shunting	1974/78	Brazil
Companhia Siderurgica Nacional (CSN)	Diesel-Electric 80 Tonne	12	570	73	1.00/1.6	Shunting	1974/75/77/78	Brazil
Aços Anhanguera	Diesel-Electric 25 Tonne	1	145	25	1.6	Shunting	1974	Brazil
Ferrovias Paulista S/A (FEPASA)	Diesel-Electric U20C	136	2 000	108	1.0	Line	1974/80	Brazil
Companhia Siderúrgica Nacional (CSN)	Diesel-Electric UM 10B	11	1 050	100	1.6	Shunting	1975	Brazil
Rêde Ferroviaria Federal S/A (RFFSA)	Diesel-Electric U20C	105	2 150	108	1.0	Line	1975/76/77	Brazil
INACESA-Chile	Diesel-Electric 45 Tonne	1	300	45	1.0	Shunting	1977	Chile
Companhia Siderúgica da Guanabara- (COSIGUA)	Diesel-Electric 100 Tonne	1	91	91	1.6	Shunting	1976	Brazil
Adm. Porto do Recife	Diesel-Electric 25 Tonne	1.0	166	22.5	1.0	Shunting	1977	Brazil
Cia Acero del Pacifico	Diesel-Electric 65 Tonne	2	570	65	1.676	Shunting	1977	Brazil

Client	Locomotive	Number	hp	Tonne	Gauge (m)	Type of Service	Year completed	Country
ENFE-Bolivia	Diesel-Electric U20C	8	2 150	100	1.0	Line	1976/77	Bolivia
ENFE-Bolivia	Diesel-Electric U10B	9	1 050	65	1.0	Shunting	1977	Bolivia
ACESITA	Diesel-Electric 65 Tonne	2		65	1.0	Shunting	1977	Brazil
ACESITA	Diesel-Electric 45 Tonne	4	300	45	1.0	Shunting	1978	Brazil
SOMISA-Soc Mixta Sid Argentina	Diesel-Electric 85 Tonne	2	570	65	1.676	Shunting	1978	Argentina
Enami	Diesel-Electric 25 Tonne	3	166	22.7	1.0	Shunting	1979	Chile
DNPCF-Mozambique	Diesel-Electric U20C	25	2 150	108	1.067	Line	1978/79	Mozambique
AÇOMINAS	Diesel-Electric 80 Tonne	9	570	73	1.6	Shunting	1978/79	Brazil
AÇOMINAS	Diesel-Electric UM10B	3	1 050	127	1.6	Shunting	1979	Brazil

GENERAL MOTORS

Electro-Motive Division, La Grange, Illinois 60525, USA

Head Office: Detroit, Michigan, USA

Export Office: La Grange, Illinois, USA

Products: Diesel-electric locomotives.

Telephone: (312) 387 6000
Telegrams: ELMODIV, La Grange
Telex: 270041

General Manager: Peter K Hoglund
Director of Sales and Service: Warren A Fox
General Sales Manager, Domestic Locomotives and Associates: R E Hill
General Sales Manager, Export Locomotives: F J Babel

Domestic Models

		Road Switchers		B-B Locomotives		C-C Locomotives		
Model number		SW1001	MP15	GP38-2	GP40-2	SD38-2	SD40-2	SD45-2
Engine type		8-645E	12-645E	16-645E	16-645E3B	16-645E	16-645E3B	20-645E3B
Turbo-charged		No	No	No	Yes	No	Yes	Yes
Rated hp		1 100/1 000	1 650/1 500	2 200/2 000	3 300/3 000	2 200/2 000	3 300/3 000	3 900/3 600
Wheel diameter and gear ratio		40 in 62:15	40 in 62:15	40 in 62:15	40 in 62:15	40 in 62:15	40 in 62:16	40 in 62:15
Continuous tractive	lb	41 700	46 800	55 400	55 400	83 400	83 100	83 100
	kg	18 910	21 228	25 130	25 130	37 830	37 690	37 690
Continuous speed	mph	6.7	9.3	10.8	11.3	6.8	11.1	11.3
	km/h	10.8	15.0	10.4	18.2	10.9	17.9	18.2
Max speed	mph	65	65	65	65	65	65	65
	km/h	105	105	105	105	105	105	105
Weight	lb	230 000	248 000	250 000	256 000	368 000	368 000	368 000
	kg	104 330	112 490	113 400	116 120	166 920	166 920	166 920
Overall length	ft in	44 ft 8 in	47 ft 8 in	59 ft 2 in	59 ft 2 in	68 ft 10 in	68 ft 10 in	68 ft 10 in
	m	13.61	14.52	18.03	18.03	20.98	20.98	20.98
Overall height	ft in	14 ft 3 in	15 ft	15 ft 4 in	15 ft 4 in	15 ft 7 in	15 ft 7 in	15 ft 7 in
	m	4.34	4.57	4.67	4.67	4.75	4.75	4.75
Overall width	ft in	10 ft	10 ft	10 ft 4 in	10 ft 4 in	10 ft	10 ft	10 ft
	m	3.05	3.05	3.15	3.15	3.05	3.05	3.05

Export Models

		B-B Locomotives			C-C Locomotives		
Model number		G-18U	G-22U	G-22CW	G-26CW	GT-22CW	GT-26CW-2
Engine type		8-654-E	12-645-E	12-645-E3B	16-645-E3B	12-645-E3	16-645-E3
Turbo-charged		No	No	No	No	Yes	Yes
Rated hp		1 100/1 000	1 650/1 500	1 650/1 500	2 200/2 000	2 475/2 250	3 300/3 000
Wheel diameter and gear ratio		40 in 63:14	40 in 63:14	40 in 62:15	40 in 62:15	40 in 62:15	40 in 62:15
Continuous tractive	lb	33 600	33 360	58 200	57 960	57 840	67 220
	kg	15 240	15 130	26 400	26 290	26 240	30 490
Continuous speed	mph	8.6	13.5	7.2	10.3	12.1	14.1
	km/h	13.8	21.7	11.6	16.6	19.5	22.7
Max speed	mph	60	60	65	65	65	65
	km/h	97	97	105	105	105	105
Weight	lb	143 8001	63 560	196 800	209 400	219 750	255 400
	kg	65 230	74 190	89 270	94 980	99 690	115 850
Overall length	ft in	38 ft	46 ft 6 in	46 ft 6 in	51 ft 9 in	57 ft	64 ft
	m	11.58	14.17	14.17	15.76	17.37	19.51
Overall height	ft in	12 ft 3 in	12 ft 7 in	12 ft 7 in	12 ft 7 in	13 ft 3 in	13 ft 6 in
	m	3.73	3.88	3.83	3.83	4.04	4.11
Overall width	ft in	9 ft 8 in	9 ft 3 in	9 ft 3 in	9 ft 3 in	9 ft 3 in	9 ft 3 in
	m	2.95	2.82	2.82	2.82	2.82	2.82

GENERAL MOTORS OF CANADA

Diesel Division, General Motors of Canada Ltd

PO Box 5160, London, Ontario N6A 4N5, Canada

Products: Diesel-electric locomotives ranging from 1 000 to 3 600 hp in four- and six-axle configurations for track gauges from 1 to 1.68 m.

Telephone: (519) 452 5274
Telegrams: GEMODIESEL
Telex: 064 7231

General Manager: A G Warner
General Sales Manager: P G Brewer
Locomotive Sales Manager: K C Langtry

GT-22 LC, 2 250 hp 6-motor, 6-axle diesel-electric locomotive supplied by Diesel Division to Le Chemin de Fer Abidjan-Niger, Ivory Coast

1 500 hp G-22CU locomotive equipped with two 3-axle, 3 motor trucks, as supplied to Pakistan Railways by Diesel Division

Sales: During 1978/79 Diesel Division delivered locomotives to New Zealand, Togo, Ivory Coast, Pakistan, Egypt and Senegal. Domestic deliveries included hump booster units for Canadian National (CN); and locomotives for Ontario Hydro (20 operated by CN and 16 operated by CP Rail), Toronto Area Transit Operating Authority (Government of Ontario Transit), Canadian Pacific (CP Rail) and Cape Breton Development Corporation, Devco Railway.
Current orders for delivery during 1980 include locomotives for Yugoslavia, CN, CP

Rail, New Zealand and more hump booster units for CN.
Diesel Division is the sole manufacturer of certain components for all General Motors locomotive production and also manufactures city transit coaches, school bus chassis and Terex earth-moving equipment, being the only GM source of the diesel-electric off-highway haulers for open pit mining operations. The year 1980 will also see the division begin production on articulated buses for city transit.

Locomotive models currently available

Model	Engine	Tractive (hp)	Axles	Continuous tractive effort (kg)	Axle weight (kg)	Gauge (mm)	Gear ratio*
G-18U	8-645E	1 000	4	15 240	15 218	1 000-1 676	63:14
G-18W	8-645E	1 000	4	17 600	16 307	1 435-1 676	62:15
G-22U	12-645E	1 500	4	15 132	18 030	1 000-1 676	63:14
G-22W	12-645E	1 500	4	17 600	18 552	1 435-1 676	62:15
G-22CU	12-645E	1 500	6	22 969	14 061	1 000-1 676	63:14
G-22CW	12-645E	1 500	6	26 399	14 878	1 435-1 676	62:15
GL-22C	12-645E	1 500	6	20 194	12 738	1 000-1 676	57:16
G-26CU	16-645E	2 000	6	22 861	15 599	1 000-1 676	63:14
G-26CW	16-645E	2 000	6	26 290	16 310	1 435-1 676	62:15
GL-26C	16-645E	2 000	6	19 976	13 562	1 000-1 676	57:16
GT-22CU	12-645E3	2 250	6	22 793	16 677	1 000-1 676	63:14
GT-22CW	12-645E3	2 250	6	26 237	18 227	1 435-1 676	62:15
GT-22LC	12-645E3	2 250	6	20 047	14 303	1 000-1 676	57:16
GT-26CU	16-645E3	2 700	6	24 900	17 585	1 000-1 676	63:14
GT-26CW	16-645E3	3 000	6	30 490	19 818	1 435-1 676	62:15

NOTE: *Other Gear Ratios Available

GESTESA
Groupo Español Suizo de Trenes Electricos SA

Calle Felipe IV, 10-1° Dcha, Madrid, Spain

Products: Electric multiple units.

Telephone: 28 52 36
Telegrams: GESTREN, Madrid

Constitution: This group comprises La Maquinista Terrestre y Maritima; Material y Construcciones SA; Industrias Aguirena SA.

GESTIONI
Gestioni Industriali SpA Soc

Via Adriano Cecchetti, 62012 Civitanova Marche (Macerata), Italy

Telephone: 72 918/72 787
Telegrams: ROTABILI

Products: Diesel railcars; freight wagons; passenger coaches.

GLOUCESTER
Gloucester Railway Carriage & Wagon Co Ltd

Bristol Road, Gloucester GL1 5RS, England

Products: Freight wagon designs; bogies; suspension systems; Miner door gear.

Chairman: E A Madenski
Managing Director: J S P Phillips
Sales Director: R A Clark
Engineering Director: R S Morris

Telephone: 0452 25104/5
Telegrams: RAILCAR, Gloucester
Telex: 4 37173

Constitution: First known as the Gloucester Wagon Co Ltd, the company was formed in 1860 and two years later built the first iron wagon in the United Kingdom. Since 1969 the company has concentrated on the design of railway wagons and the design and manufacture of bogies and vehicle suspensions.

GONINAN
A Goninan & Co Ltd

PO Box 21, Broadmeadow, New South Wales 2292, Australia

Products: Diesel-electric locomotives; freight wagons; passenger coaches.

Telephone: 049 61 3811
Telegrams: PLATINUM NEWCASTLE
Telex: AA28061

General Manager: E W Eddy
Assistant General Manager: J G Fitzgerald

Two new double-deck cars for Sydney, designed in conjunction with Pullman Standard, USA, awaiting delivery at the Goninan plant
The cars have the following basic dimensions: coupled length, 20 216 mm; overall height, 4368 mm; overall width, 3036 mm; tare weight (trailer) 33 800 kg; (power) 45 000 kg.
The power cars obtain supply from a 1500 V dc overhead catenary and are driven by one traction motor per axle. Maximum service speed will be 115 km/h.
Significant feature of these cars is the ability to carry a large number of passengers in a

relatively short train. The passenger capacity of each car is: (trailer) vestibule, standing 70; upper deck, seated 53; standing 16; lower deck, seated 53; standing 16; end saloons, seated 24; standing 47; total 279; (power) vestibule, standing 70; upper deck, seated 48; standing 14; lower deck, seated 47; standing 14; end saloons, seated 18; standing 38; total 249.

Engineering Manager: A Rice

Sales Manager: K Moss

Constitution: Engaged in the general engineering field for more than 76 years, this company has extended its licence agreement with General Electric, USA for diesel

electric locomotives, and entered a new licence agreement with Pullman Standard Division, USA, for rail passenger coaches.

Sales: Under a contract worth approximately $44 million with the Public Transport Commission of New South Wales, Goninan has built double-deck stainless-steel passenger cars for use on the Sydney suburban network. 70 power cars and 80 trailer cars will be supplied and the first vehicles were delivered in December 1978.

GOODWIN

A E Goodwin Ltd

863-871 Bourke Street, Waterloo, New South Wales 2017, Australia

Products: Freight wagons; draft gear; track construction and equipment.

Telephone: Sydney 698 1163
Telegrams: GOODWINENG
Telex: AA 22656

Chief Executive: D W Chambers

GÖRLITZ

Veb Waggonbau Görlitz

DDR-89 Görlitz, Brunnenstrasse 11, German Democratic Republic

Products: Passenger coaches; sleeping cars; double-deck coaches; bogies.
New equipment: On show at the 1978 Leipzig Fair was a double-deck coach by Görlitz. The company has already manufactured large numbers of double-deck coaches for DR,

Telephone: 690
Telegrams: WAGGONBAU, Görlitz
Telex: 286227

CSD, PKP, BD2 and CFR. The latest product runs on Görlitz VI type bogies with 2 500 mm axle distance and 19 500 mm between centres. Gangway connections at the ends are at the same height as those of standard RIC stock so the coaches can be incorporated in any standard train formation. The coach is 26 800 mm long and 4630 mm high. It weighs 44 tonnes empty and can accommodate 128 seated and 210 standing passengers. Its top speed is 120 km/h.

GOSA

Gosa Wagon and Steel Construction

Head Office: Industrijska 1, 11420 Smederevska Palanka, Yugoslavia
Sales Office: Nemanjina 4, 11 000 Belgrade, Yugoslavia

Products: Passenger coaches; diesel and electric trainsets; tank wagons; refrigerated cars; and special-purpose wagons.

Chairman: Tihoslav Tosić
Managing Director: Srba Trajković
Sales Director: Slavko Djorić
Export Sales: Slavko Ivanović

New equipment: Latest "Y" type passenger coach built by Gosa complies with UIC specification 567 for international services.
The car underframe is constructed of all-welded rolled and pressed sections. The underframe end construction allows the subsequent installation of automatic coupling without need for extensive reconstruction.
The car body is of steel, with posts and other components of pressed sheet metal and sheathing sheet metal. These elements are welded by electric arc. The roof consists of a number of roof arches made of pressed roof sheathing metal sheets joined by arc-welding.
The car is provided with two bogies of Wegmann type, or alternatively of Minden-Deutz type. The wheel assemblies are designed in accordance with UIC Standard specification 813. The axle bearings are IKL or Pretis roller type, in compliance with UIC Standard specification 512. The bogies are made of welded rolled sections and pressed steel sheets which form box-like bolsters.
The draft gear is of end type to UIC 520 and 521 specifications, with a hook of 100 tonne capacity and a screw-type coupling of 85 tonne braking strength.
The buffer gear consists of four sleeve-type buffers all to UIC Standard, of 30 tonne strength as per UIC 528 and 567 specifications.
The car is provided with an automatic air brake of large braking capacity, Oerlikon-Rapid type, in accordance with UIC 546 specifications. The brake leverage is provided with an automatic SAB DRV2 regulator. The brake head supports two brake shoes according to UIC 541 specification. Each compartment is provided with a brake handle to be used in case of emergency.
The hand brake is in one of the end entrances and acts on one of the bogies indepen-

Telephone: 011 831 022
Telegrams: GOSA SMEDEREVSKA PALANKA
Telex: 11 684 yu gosa
Telex (sales): 11568 yu imo

dently of the air brake. Each end of the car is provided with two terminal end tapes of the main line in accordance with UIC 541.
Electric lighting is designed in compliance with UIC standard specification No. 550 and 532. The car compartments are provided with standard light and blue light. The regulator is of Pintsch type. The generator is of 24-30 V, and 7.5 kW. Storage batteries are for 24 V, 2 × 240 Ah.
The car heating may be electric or by steam. The installation for steam heating system is of low pressure, Friedmann type. The temperature of the heating elements must not exceed 95°C. They are located under the seats. Each compartment is provided with a handle for the regulation of temperature. The corridor, washroom and lavatory are each provided with heating elements, but with no temperature control devices.
The electric heating is designed in accordance with UIC specifications 552 and 553. The water supply system in the washroom and lavatory consists of a water tank, pipes, taps, and waste pipe. The water tank is filled through connectors, and is thermally insulated so that freezing is prevented for 12 hours at a temperature of −10°C, provided that the initial temperature in the moment of switching-off of heating was +20°C.
The compartment ventilation is carried out by the Kuckuck system, a device for natural aeration.
The closed-circuit broadcasting installation in the car is designed in compliance with UIC specification 568.

International "Y" type first-class passenger coach for Yugoslav Railways (right and below)
Gauge 1 435 mm; overall length over buffers 24 500 mm; length over underframe end sills 23 200 mm; car body width 2 883 mm; height from top of rails 4 050 mm; bogie pivot centres 17 200 mm; wheel taping line diameter 920 mm; bogie wheel base 2 500 mm; lightweight 40 tonne; maximum speed 160 km/h.

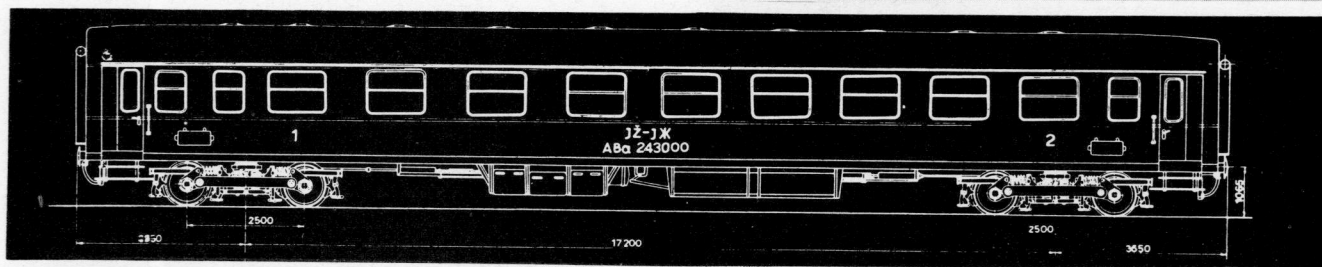

Composite passenger car for PJKA, Indonesia
Third-class, kitchen and restaurant included. Length 20.5 m, track gauge 1067 mm, speed 120 km/h.

Two-axle refrigerated car for CH, Greece
Length 14.1 m, track gauge 1435 mm, speed 120 km/h, regime SS, insulation coefficient 0.24 Kcal/m²h°C, volume (water ice) 57.5 m³, (dry ice) 62.5 m³.

GRAAFF

Graaff Kommanditgesellschaft

320 Elze 1, Postfach 160/180, Federal Republic of Germany

Products: Containers; railroad rolling stock; road vehicles; plywood van bodies; sandwich panels.

Telephone: 05124/20 41
Telegrams: GRAFFWAGGON, Elze
Telex: 09 27168 graaf d.

Managing Director: Dipl Ing Wolfgang Graff

Constitution: The works was founded in 1914.

GREENBAT

Greenbat Ltd

Albion Works, Armley Road, Leeds LS12 2TP, England

Products: Battery, trolley, trolley/battery and pantograph locomotives up to 30 tonnes in weight; coke car locomotives; motor transmission and control units.

Chairman: T H de Monte
Sales Director: E P Hartmann
Sales Manager: K G Wainwright

Telephone: 442933
Telegrams: GREENBAT LEEDS
Telex: 55468

Sales: Battery locomotives to Nigeria; trolley/battery locomotives to Zambia Copper Mines; battery-driven locomotives used for track laying on Hong Kong's Mass Transit Railway.

Licensing Agreement: Mining and Allied Machinery Corporation Ltd, West Bengal, India.

GREENVILLE

Greenville Steel Car Company

Greenville, Pennsylvania 16125, USA

Products: Freight wagons.

Chairman: Edwin Hodge, Jr
President: A F Sarosdy
Executive Vice-President: D F Lewis
Vice-President, Sales: J T Egbert

Constitution: Formed in 1910 as the Greenville Metal Products Co, the present name was adopted in 1914 when the company first undertook repair of freight wagons. In 1916 the first new wagons were built and this has been the major activity since, combined with extensive repair work and supply of replacement parts.

Sales: Major freight car orders completed in 1978: Missouri Pacific 300 100-ton wood-chip hoppers, Bessemer & Lake Erie 600 100-ton quadruple hoppers, Norfolk & Western 363 100-ton 86 ft 6 in high cube box cars, Chicago, Rock Island and Pacific 300 100-ton triple hopper cars, Southern Railway 562 100-ton quadruple hoppers, Consolidated Rail Corporation 312 100-ton 86 ft 6 in high cube box cars, Pittsburgh & Lake Erie RR Co 300 100-ton triple hoppers, Gifford Hill & others 159 100-ton twin aggregate cars, Atchison, Topeka & Santa Fe Railway 100 100-ton triple hoppers, Lake Erie, Franklin & Clarion RR 180 100-ton triple hoppers, Southern Pacific Transportation Co 500 100-ton twin aggregate hoppers, Southern Railway 40 100-ton automatic dump quadruple hoppers.

New equipment: The manufacturer claims that a new coal car from Greenville Steel Car Company is lighter, has more cubic capacity than most coal cars and can be built

Telephone: (412) 588 7000
Telegrams: GREENCAR

from readily-available materials. The car features two transverse tubs, providing greater floor area and lowering the centre of gravity to 79.2 in loaded and 47.2 in empty. Called twin-tub, the car is designed to be rotary-dumped. Twin-tub has the capacity to handle 104 tons, four tons more than conventional 100-ton cars and has a capacity of 4545 cubic feet with a ten inch heap, suiting the car for both low and high density coals.

New Twin-Tub coal car from Greenville handles 104-ton loads

GREGG

Gregg Europe SA

53 avenue Huysmans, B-1660 Beersel (Lot), Belgium

Products: Freight wagons; bogies.

Parent Company: The Gregg Company Ltd, PO Box 430, Hackensack, New Jersey 07602, USA

President: Richard T Gregg
Managing Director: Roger de Groote
Commercial Manager: A Timmerman

Telephone: Brussels 02376 20 10
Telegrams: GREGGCAR, Lot
Telex: GREGG B 21 357

Sales: Major sales in 1977/78 include: 108 aluminium hopper wagons for Saudi Government Railroad Organisation, Saudi Arabia; 130 covered goods wagons and 20 cattle wagons for Uganda Railways, Uganda; 125 sets of Y32 bogies for M4 coaches, for Belgian National Railways. Products ordered in 1978 include: 50 aluminium tank wagons for transport of chemical products for Maschinen-Export, German Democratic Republic; 210 wagons for transport of phosphate for Aqaba Railway Corporation, Jordan.

Covered freight wagons for 1000 mm track gauge with 39 metric ton capacity equipped with side and end hinged doors

Aluminium covered hopper wagon of welded construction for movement of cereals with two hoppers

Air dump car for 914 mm (36 in) track gauge, with 35 metric ton capacity and dumping on both sides

Ballast wagon equipped with Gregg-Morrison-Knudsen discharge doors and sliding roof, capacity 47 m³

GRIVITA ROSIE
CFR Grivita Rosie Works

Telephone: 1494 30
Telex: 216

7 Matei Millo Street, Bucharest, Romania

Exports: Mecanoexport, 10 Mihail Eminescu Street, Bucharest, Romania

Products: Tank wagons up to 90 m³ capacity for oil products and derivatives, liquid and liquefied gas.

GSI
General Steel Industries Inc, Engineering Division

Telephone: (314) 423 6500

PO Box 2396, 8400 Midland Boulevard, St Louis, Missouri 63114, USA
Products: Design of cast steel rapid transit, coach and locomotive bogies.

Vice President and General Manager: Keith L Jackson
Sales Manager: Thomas P Taylor

Manager of Engineering: Eugene L Benner

Constitution: GSI was founded in 1904 by General Steel Castings Corp and became Castings Division, GSI, in 1964, and Engineering Division in 1973.

HÄGGLUNDS
AB Hägglund & Söner

Telephone: 0660 80000
Telegrams: HÄGGLUNDSÖNER
Telex: 6051 haegg s

PO Box 600, S-891 01, Örnsköldsvik, Sweden

Products: Electric locomotives; X10 trains; rapid transit surface and underground cars; street (tram) cars; bogies; mining and construction equipment; heavy trucks; bus bodies; hydraulic motors.

Chairman: Alde Nilsson
Managing Director: Thore Hägglof

Sales Director: Hans Wikstrom

Constitution: Hägglunds was founded in 1899 and is one of the largest engineering companies in northern Sweden. In 1972 it became a subsidiary company of ASEA of Västeras. In 1973 Hägglunds acquired the railcar and locomotive division of ASJ of Linköping and production was transferred to Örnsköldsvik.

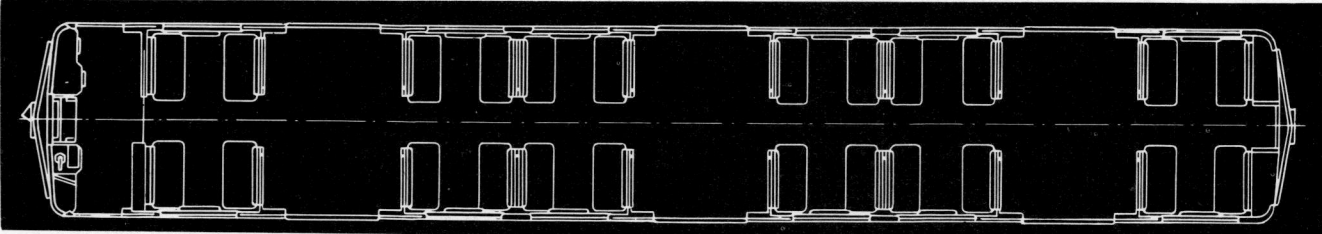

General arrangement drawing of the C8-type cars built for Stockholm by Hägglunds, photographed running into Stockholm *(right)*.

Wheel diameter (new) 864 mm; distance between bogie centres 11 000 mm; bogie wheelbase 2 300 mm; height of floor from top of rail 1 170 mm max; max width over body 2 800 mm; overall length of ten-coach train 174 000 mm; vehicle length over body 17 320 mm; tare weight (two-car set) 47 tonnes; seating capacity 96; standing capacity 216; number of traction motors 8; number of starting steps 19; rating, one-hour (750/2 V) 8×110=880 kW; rating, continuous (750/2 V) 8×100=800 kW; gear ratio 126:20; transmission: bogie-suspended motor and double gear coupling; maximum acceleration on level tangent track (laden) 1.1 m/s².

HAWKER SIDDELEY
Hawker Siddeley Canada Ltd

Telephone: (416) 362 2941
Telegrams: HAWSIDCAN, Toronto
Telex: 06 217711

Head Office: 7 King Street East, Toronto, Ontario M5C 1A3, Canada

Sales Offices: *(Freight Equipment)* Suite 1515, 800 Dorchester Boulevard West, Montreal, Quebec H3B 1X9, Canada. *(Passenger Equipment)* PO Box 67, Station F, Thunder Bay, Ontario P7C 4V6, Canada.

Products: Railway freight cars of all types; subway, commuter and inter-city passenger coaches; light rail vehicles; wheels and axles; bogies; railway castings.

Chairman: Sir Arnold Hall
President and Chief-Executive Officer: E J White
Export Manager (Freight Wagons): R C Frost
Director of Marketing: R L McCallum

Sales Managers:
  Freight Equipment: G W Smith
  Passenger Equipment: K Chapman

Constitution: The Eastern Car Company Ltd, one of the original predecessors of this company, started in the railway freight car business in 1913.
The Canadian Car Division of Hawker Siddeley Canada Ltd pioneered the long, lightweight rail car on the North American continent.

Double-deck commuter cars in GO Transit livery shown entering Union Station, Toronto

Upper deck of the double-deck GO Transit cars

Raised skirts on the double-deck cars give access to brakes and battery box

Sales: Double-deck commuter cars from the Canadian Car Division at Thunder Bay, Ontario are in service on the Toronto Area Transit Operating Authority GO Transit commuter routes. The 80-car order was completed in 1978. Deliveries of 138 rapid transit cars for the Toronto Transit Commission and 200 mainline coaches for Mexican National Railways (N de M) are complete. Contracts underway are for 190 rapid transit cars for Boston and 190 light rail vehilces for operation by the Toronto Transit Commission. At the company's Trenton Works Division freight car plant in Nova Scotia 1 386 freight and tank wagons were turned out in 1978. Production in 1979 included 92 clinker cars and 12 tank wagons for Togo, 30 ballast cars for Malawi, 240 box cars for Cameroon, 800 covered hopper wagons for the Canadian Wheat Board and 285 tank wagons for Canadian General Transit.

New developments: Since 1967 Hawker Siddeley Canada has supplied more than 100 commuter coaches to the Toronto Area Transit Operating Authority (TATOA) for operation on GO Transit rail services in the southern sector of the Province of Ontario. The 85 ft (25.9 m) long, 94-seat single-deck cars have a lightweight body on a steel underframe, a design concept applied by the company to both subway and intercity rail cars. To resolve the problem of increasing passenger demand in the Toronto area, Hawker Siddeley Canada designed and produced 80 double-deck cars in 1978. General features include: light alloy body on a steel underframe; two decks plus mid-level compartments over the bogies seating 162 passengers in an overall length of 85 ft (25.908 m); two double, air-operated doors per side; full air-conditioning, plus electric heating.

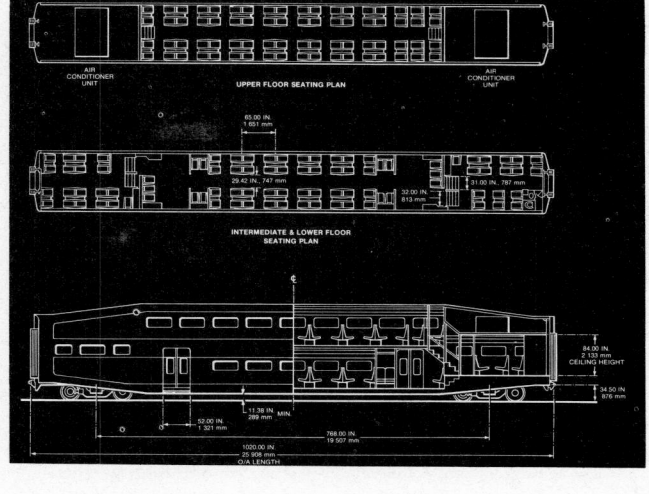

Plans and profile of the GO Transit double-deck cars built by Hawker Siddeley Canada

Canadian Light Rail Vehicles
Designed by the Urban Transportation Development Corp, the new LRVs were under construction during 1979 for deliver to the Toronto Transit Commission.

Blue Line mass transit cars
Delivered to the Massachusetts Bay Transportation Authority (USA) by Hawker Siddeley Canada during 1979.

HEAD WRIGHTSON

Head Wrightson Teesdale Ltd
(Mechanical Engineering and Process Equipment Division)

PO Box 10, Stockton-on-Tees, Cleveland TS17 6AZ, England

Telephone: 0642 62241
Telex: 58533

Managing Director: J N G Mallinson
Divisional Director: G Burns
Sales Manager: B Preece

Products: Rolling stock for ironworks: ore transfer wagons, scale wagons, hot metal transfer wagons, slag ladle wagons, torpedo ladle wagons (100-300 tonnes capacity); for steelworks: hot metal transfer wagons, slag ladle transfer wagons, ingot casting wagons; for non-ferrous works: slag ladle wagons (air/hydraulic tipped).

Constitution: The Mechanical Engineering and Process Equipment Division of Head Wrightson Teesdale designs and manufacturers a wide range of special purpose industrial rolling stock for iron, steel and non-ferrous metalworks.

One of six wagons built by Head Wrightson for the Southern Peru Copper Corporation's Cuajone Project where it is used to haul molten slag at Ilo, Peru
Normally the wagons run in a train of six. The ladles are dumped independently by remote control from the attendant locomotive. Each wagon is fitted with a manually-operated air dumping mechanism for emergency use. Dumping controls are electro-pneumatic, using a 32 V dc electric supply provided by the locomotive. Working in conjunction with the air dump cylinder is a closed-circuit hydraulic system which controls and restrains the speed of dumping. Air brakes and hand-operated parking brakes are fitted as standard.

Hot metal ladle transfer wagon designed and manufactured by Head Wrightson Teesdale for Huachipato steelworks, Chile
The design has several special features including remote control with a rotating platform capable of turning the ladle through 90 degrees, and a wheel gauge of approximately 5 m (16 ft 6 in). The wagon is 8 m long, 6.3 m wide and weighs approximately 60 tonnes.

250 tonne capacity, torpedo ladle type, hot metal wagons destined for Altos Hornos de Mexico SA
Each wagon weighs approximately 100 tonnes without refractory lining.

A road/rail vehicle designed to carry 150 tonne loads by rail from the quayside at Apapa, Nigeria to a railhead at Mokwa for trans-shipment to truck for an 88-km haul by road to the hydro-electric station at Kainji on the River Niger
Head Wrightson designed and built the wagon for the Niger Dams Authority. The highway bogies were provided by Crane Fruehauf and the towing vehicles by Scammell. Balfour Beatty of London and Nedeco of the The Hague were consultants for this vehicle which is provided with alternative sets of rail and highway bogies for interchange without assistance from equipment not carried on the vehicle. Here the wagon is seen in course of final assembly on to rail bogies at Head Wrightson Teesdale Thornaby-on-Tees works.

HENSCHEL

Thyssen Industrie AG, Henschel

D-3500 Kassel 2, Henschelplatz 1, Federal Republic of Germany

Products: Diesel-hydraulic, diesel-electric and electric locomotives; diesel engines for rail traction, marine and stationary duties.

General Manager (Locomotives): Dipl Wirtschaftsingenieur R Jasper
Director, Sales and Service: Ing M Kunis
Chief Engineer: Dipl Ing S Kademann

Constitution: Henschel started manufacturing locomotives in 1848 and more than 32 000 locomotives have been supplied to railways around the world. In 1975 Thyssen Industrie AG became the new group name of the Rheinstahl companies.

Sales: Orders announced in 1979 included 34 diesel-electric locomotives of 2 500 hp for Egypt, 15 for Thailand and 20 for Norway and Denmark; also substantial repeat orders for diesel-hydraulic locomotives from Tanzania, Uganda, Ivory Coast and Indonesia.

New developments: The joint development undertaken by Thyssen Henschel and

Telephone: 0561 8011
Telegrams: HENSCHEL Kassel
Telex: 099793

Brown Boveri & Cie of mainline locomotives with three-phase power transmission met with continuing success. Asynchronous squirrel-cage traction motors (without commutators and brushes) are fed by three-phase current of steplessly controlled frequency from solid-state invertors. This unique system called "Henschel BBC DE 2500" is being used for diesel-electric as well as electric locomotives (dc and ac) and is finding wide application. The prototypes DE 2500 BB and CC are with Deutsche Bundesbahn; Swiss Federal Railways received six diesel-electric CoCo locomotives of 2 500 hp; Eisenbahn & Häfen and Ruhrkohle AG (two major German industrial railways) were each supplied with six heavy BoBo locomotives for 600 V dc + 600 hp diesel-electric equipment and 50 cycles + 16 2/3 cycles 15 kV respectively; the Norwegian and the Danish State Railways placed orders for six (NSB) and 16 (DSB) mainline diesel-electric CoCo locomotives of 3 300 hp. Also Deutsche Bundesbahn received first prototype units of their new class 120, an electrical BoBo locomotive of 5 600 kW which, thanks to the newly developed three-phase power transmission, is equally well suited for high-speed express trains (160 km/h) and heavy goods trains (100 km/h) and will thus constitute the beginning of a new generation in locomotive design. The Norwegian State Railway (NSB) followed suit and ordered six electric locomotives using the same new technique developed by Henschel and BBC.

1 000 hp Henschel diesel-hydraulic locomotive delivered to Tanzania in 1979

HITACHI

Hitachi Ltd

6-2 Nippon Building, Otemachi, 2-chome Chiyoda-ku, Tokyo 100, Japan

Products: Electric, diesel-electric, diesel-hydraulic locomotives; electric and diesel railcars; passenger and freight cars; industrial rolling stock.

President and Representative Director: Hirokichi Yoshiyama
Executive Vice President and Director: Masafumi Misu
Executive Managing Director: Kiyoshi Shimai

Telephone: (03) 270 2111
Telegrams: HITACHY Tokyo
Telex: J22395, J22432, J24491, J26375 (HITACHY)

Constitution: Fabrication and assembly of railcars takes place at the Kasada works while locomotives are assembled at Mito.

Sales: By early 1978 only two minor locomotive orders were in hand: eight 2000 hp Bo-Bo-Bo diesels for Bolivia and four light axle-load class DD51 diesel-hydraulics for Japanese National Railways (JNR). Emu orders underway include a wide range of stock for JNR and transit stock for Nagoya and Osaka.

Hitachi standard diesel-hydraulic locomotives

Model	HG-20/25B	HG-30/35BB	HG-45/50BB	HG-55/60BB
Type	Gear drive	Gear drive	Gear drive	Gear drive
	End cab type	Semi centre-cab type	Centre-cab type	Centre-cab type
Axle arrangement	B	B-B	B-B	B-B
Weight in working order (tonnes)	20/25	30/35	45/50	55/60
Engine	Cummins NH220BI X 1 set	Cummins NRT0-6 X 1 set	Cummins KT1150L X 1 set	Cummins KTA 1150L X 1 set
	190 hp/2 100 rpm	335 hp/2 100 rpm	450 hp/2 100 rpm	550 hp/2 100 rpm
Converter	Nico (twin disc type)	Nico (twin disc type)	Nico (twin disc type)	Nico (twin disc type)
	CB 100	CBS 115	CBS 115	CBS 115-2
Starting tractive effort (kg)	5 000/6 250	7 500/8 750	11 250/12 500	13 750/15 000
Continuous tractive force (kg)	4 600-1 360	7 000-2 800	10 300-3 000	12 900-3 700
Continuous speed (km/h)	5.6-20.0	4.8-19.3	5.9-20.7	5.8-21.2
Max height above rail (mm)	3 620	3 745	3 745	3 745
Max width over all (mm)	2 600	2 700	2 700	2 700
Max length over end frames (mm)	5 800	10 900	10 900	10 900
Wheel diameter (mm)	860	860	860	860
Driving stand	Single	Single	Single	Single
Brake system	Straight air brake (locomotive only)	Straight air brake (locomotive only)	Straight air brake (locomotive only)	Straight air brake (locomotive only)

In Chile electric multiple-unit suburban trains help to ease transportation problems

In Sri Lanka tourists travel in comfort on Hitachi's air-conditioned diesel multiple-unit trains

In Morocco electric locomotives (Co-Co, 3 000 kW) are used to haul phosphate

In Brazil Hitachi's stainless-steel electric cars for commuters on the inter-urban run

In Japan the Shinkansen *Bullet Express*, a 210 km/h electric train, has set international records for speed and safety

In Iran diesel-electric locomotives (Bo-Bo, 1 050 hp) are used for shunting and branch line service

In Zaire electric locomotives (Bo-Bo-Bo, 2 400 kW) help with industrialisation plans

In Bolivia diesel-electric locomotives (Bo-Bo-Bo, 3 020 hp) provide service in rugged terrain

First-class passenger cars supplied by Hitachi for Nigeria

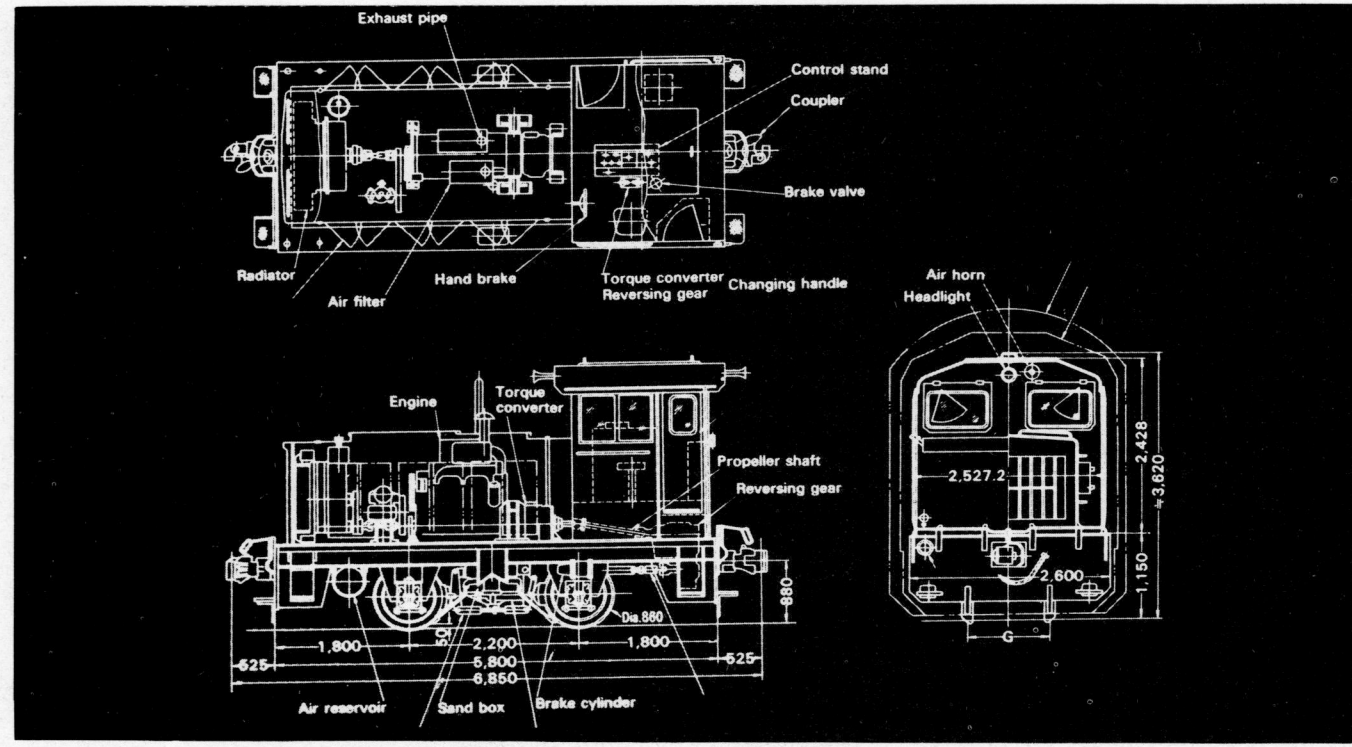

Model HG-20/258 diesel-hydraulic locomotive designed for switching and short-run service

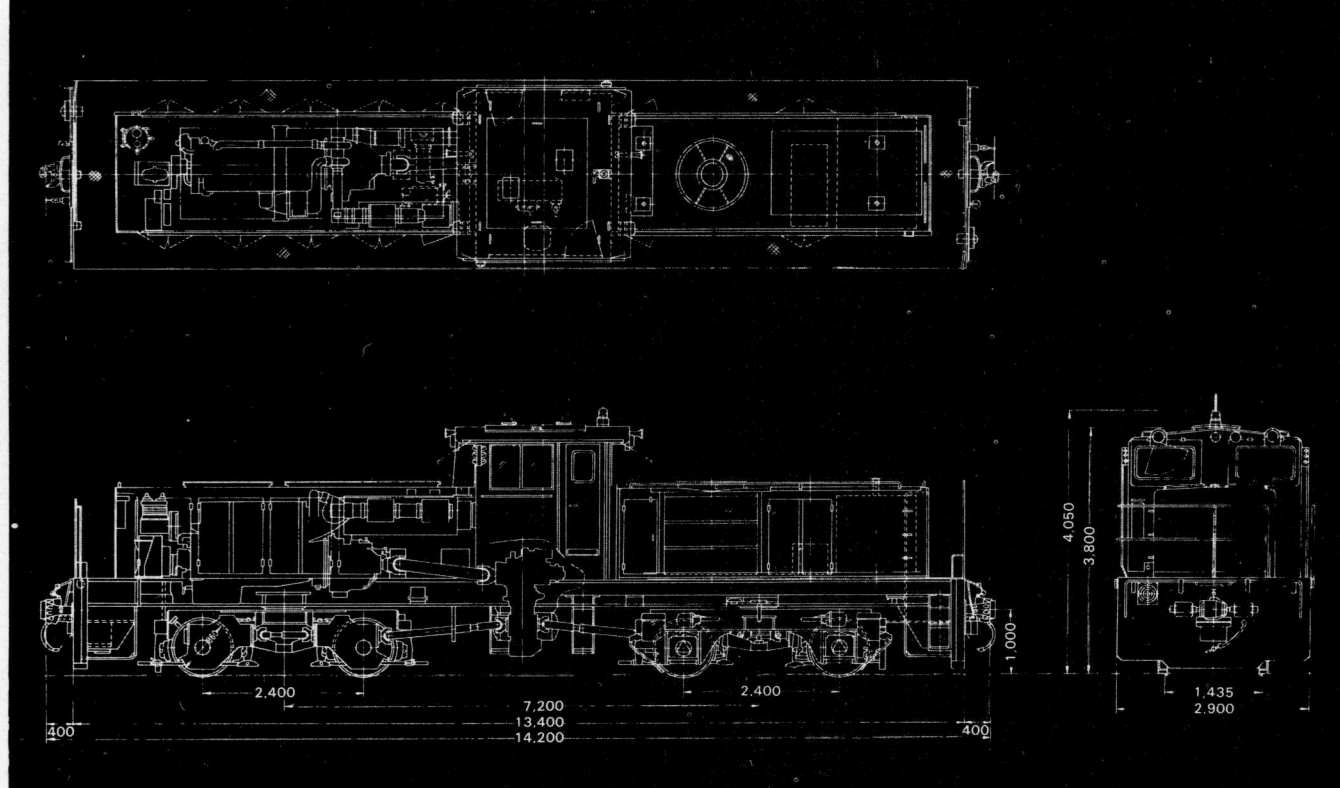

Model HG-70/80BB in operation throughout Japan

HOLEC

Holec Machines & Systems
(Traction Group)

Head Office: PO Box 50, 2980 AB Ridderkerk, Netherlands
Works: Ringdijk 390, Slikkerveer, Netherlands

Products: Electrical equipment for electric vehicles for mainline, inter-urban, urban-rapid-transit, underground and industrial railways; tramways and trolleybus systems; traction power supply equipment.

Telephone: 01804 13633
Telex: 20377 wsmit nl

Chairman: Drs J C Smit
Managing Director: I Hoogeveen
Chief Sales Director: F H Schreve
Production Director: Ir H M van Dantzig
Technical Director: A Verhoef

HSIANGTAN

Hsiangtan Electric Generator Plant

Hunan, People's Republic of China

Products: Electric locomotives. The plant produced China's first electric CC locomotive in the 1950s, a 4 900-hp unit based on the Soviet-designed N-60s; numbered 6-Y-1.

HUDSON (RALETRUX)

Robert Hudson (Raletrux) Limited

PO Box 4, Morley, Leeds LS27 8TG, England

Products: Industrial rolling stock, including special cars for mine main haulages, quarries and estates; complete narrow-gauge railway systems for all applications.

Chairman: M J Bradford

Telephone: 0532 534931
Telegrams: RALETRUX, Morley
Telex: 55133

Managing Director: C R Whyte

Constitution: Manufacturing facilities were established in 1865, and the company exports to hard-rock mining operations throughout the world. Robert Hudson (Raletrux) Ltd is now part of the Firsteel Group of companies.

HUDSON (SOUTH AFRICA)

Robert Hudson & Sons (Pty) Ltd

PO Box 25259, Ferreirasdorp, Transvaal, South Africa

Products: Mainline freight cars, narrow gauge mine and estate cars; electric locomotives for mines.

Chairman: W R Hudson

Telephone: 836 9772/3
Telegrams: RALETRUX
Telex: 43 0250

Managing Director: R H Wardrop

Constitution: Manufacturing facilities were established at Durban in 1927. A further manufacturing plant was established at Benoni in 1948.

HUDSWELL CLARKE

Hudswell Clarke & Co Ltd

125 Jack Lane, Leeds LS10 1BT, England

Products: Industrial, shunting and mine locomotives; track-laying equipment

Chairman: C R C Fryers
Managing Director: P J O Alcock
Sales Director: G Derret-Smith

Telephone: 0532 32261
Telegrams: HUNSLT, Leeds
Telex: 55237

Constitution: Hudswell Clarke was established at Jack Lane, Leeds, by William Hudswell and John Clarke, both of whom had been with Kitson & Co. Locomotives had been built at the Railway Foundry since its founding in 1838, its previous occupants being the pioneer locomotive firm of E B Wilson & Co.

HUNGARIAN

Hungarian Railway Carriage and Machine Works

9002 Györ, PB 50, Hungary

Products: Passenger and freight cars; air-conditioning equipment (Stone licence) for passenger cars.

Telephone: 12 300
Telegrams: Rába Györ
Telex: 02 4253

Constitution: This concern started building railway rolling stock in 1897 and two years later the thousandth wagon was completed, adding self-propelled railcars and motor-cars in the early 1900s. It is commissioned by the Hungarian State Railways to build rolling stock and to supply switches, track construction materials, cranes, etc.

HUNSLET

The Hunslet Engine Company Ltd

Hunslet Engine Works, Leeds LS10 1BT, England

Products: Diesel-mechanical, diesel-hydraulic, diesel-electric and steam locomotives; fully flame-proof surface and underground mine diesel locomotives; electric trolley and battery locomotives; flame-proof diesel power packs and standard flame-proof components; final drive and reverse gearboxes; diesel exhaust gas conditioners; track maintenance equipment.

Chairman: C R C Fryers
Managing Director: P J O Alcock
Sales Director: G S Derrett-Smith

Telephone: 0532 32261
Telegrams: HUNSLT, Leeds
Telex: 55237

Constitution: The Hunslet Engine Company-built locomotives since 1864, introduced diesel shunting locomotives in 1927 and pioneered the first flame-proof diesel locomotive for coal mine working in 1939. The Hunslet Engine Company incorporates Kerr Stuart & Co, The Avonside Engine Company, Manning Wardle & Co, Kitson & Co, and The Hunslet Group includes the Associate Companies Hudswell Clarke & Co Ltd, and Andrew Barclay Sons & Co Ltd.

Sales: Work was in hand during 1978 on 35 diesel-hydraulic locomotives for Kenya Railways. During 1977/78 locomotives were exported to Brunei, Eire, Fiji, Iran, Malaysia, Pakistan, Peru, Sarawak, South Korea, Sudan, Zambia.

Hunslet's new underground rack locomotive designed to work either conventional or rack drive, depending on the gradient

Two 562 hp diesel-hydraulic locomotives designed to work in tandem for a South Korean cement company

HUNSLET TAYLOR
Hunslet Taylor Consolidated

PO Box 178, Germiston 1400, Transvaal, South Africa

Products: Shunting locomotives for surface operations, from ten 80 tonnes; underground locomotives from 2½ to 15 tonnes.

Chairman: P J T Herbert
Managing Director: P G E Fitch

Sales: Hunslet Taylor announced the delivery of the company's 2 500th locomotive. This 20-tonne 0-4-0 diesel-hydraulic locomotive was officially handed over to the South

Telephone: 27 11 825 1212
Telegrams: HUNSLETCO, Germiston
Telex: 8 0899 SA

African Railways in June 1979. Other new orders and deliveries include four 15-tonne diesel-hydraulic locomotives, four 40-tonne diesel-hydraulic locomotives, three 30-tonne diesel-hydraulic locomotives, four 20-tonne diesel-hydraulic locomotives and one 15-tonne battery traction locomotive for surface application. Orders were also received for over 160 Battery Traction Locomotives, of which 130 are 6-tonne mass and the balance 10 and 12-tonne units. In addition, 30 5-tonne diesel underground locomotives were sold.

HYUNDAI
Hyundai Heavy Industries

178 Sejongro, Jongkro-ku, Seoul, Republic of Korea

Telephone: 70 7711/20
Telex: K28361

Products: Diesel-electric, electric locomotives; passenger coaches; freight wagons; rails.

ICF
The Integral Coach Factory

Perambur, Madras 600 038, India

Products: Railway passenger coaches of all types: third-, second-, first- and mixed classes, kitchen cars, dining cars, pantry cars, brake and luggage vans, air-conditioned first-class, chair cars and 2-tier sleepers, oscillograph car, track recording cars, double-deckers, motor coaches and trailers for electric multiple units, diesel rail cars and power cars.

General Manager: L R Gosain
Chief Mechanical Engineer: G S Vittal Rao

Constitution: This is a production unit under the Ministry of Railways, Government of India, and was set up during the first Five Year Plan in collaboration with Messrs Swiss Car & Elevator Manufacturing Corporation Ltd, Switzerland. Commencing production in 1955, the factory has turned out to July 1979 13 593 passenger coaches of 70 different types for the Indian Railways and has an installed capacity of 750 coaches a year.

Sales: Production during 1978/79 included air-conditioned coaches of different types: first-and second-class composite coaches and two-tier sleepers, non-air-conditioned first and second-class coaches, ac electric multiple units and pantry cars. ICF also produced special coaches with upholstered seats for superfast metre-gauge expresses, and coaches with upholstered sleeper berths for the superfast broad-gauge expresses, as well as coaches for India's first double-decker train.

Telephone: 661091
Telegrams: RAILCOACH
Telex: 7390

General view of ICF's main assembly shop

ICF coach for The Philippines being loaded in Madras

Recent deliveries include coaches for Uganda Railways

IGARRETA
Igarreta SA

Avda Amancio Alcorta 2200, Buenos Aires, Argentina

Telephone: 28 3198/2660

Products: Electric subway coaches.

INARCO
Inarco SA

N Videla 666, Quilmes, Buenos Aires, Argentina

Telephone: 253 3788

Products: Freight wagons.

INDEMDET
Industrielle de Matériel de Transport & Cie

42 avenue Raymond Poincaré, 75116 Paris, France

Telephone: 704 51 10
Telegrams: CIMTRANS, Paris
Telex: 61 119 F

Products: Trolley locomotives; electric multiple units; passenger coaches; freight wagons.

INTERNATIONAL COMBUSTION

Clayton Works, Hatton, Derby DE6 5EB, England

Telephone: 0283 88 2382
Telegrams: CLAYQUIP
Telex: 37581

Products: Battery, trolley and diesel locomotives with electric, hydraulic or mechanical transmissions; electric- and battery-driven industrial and mining locomotives; special-purpose internal combustion engine or electric rail vehicles.

General Manager: R A Boast

Constitution: The Clayton Equipment Co Ltd, part of International Combustion Ltd, was incorporated in 1931 by S R Devlin to carry on the manufacture of locomotives, rail cars, transfer cars and general engineering products. Many types of locomotive and other equipment were made for export to various countries, such as Australia, New Zealand, Poland and Korea and a number of diesel-electric locomotives were made for British Railways.

In 1957 International Combustion (Holdings) Ltd acquired the whole shareholding in the Company, but Clayton's continued to operate as an entirely self-contained and self-supporting unit.

In 1969 the company was integrated into International Combustion Ltd and while retaining its original work site, it became absorbed into the Group operation.

ITALSIDER
Italsider SpA

Via Corsica 4, Genova, Italy

Telephone: 010 5999
Telegrams: ITALSIDE, Genova
Telex: 270690 Italsid

Products: Special-purpose freight wagons.

Chairman: Ing Franco Cai
Sales Director, Export Sales: Ing G Cattaneo

Special 12-axle 150 tonne torpedo wagon, capacity 24 m³

Tilting ladle wagon with double pneumatic device for slag transport, capacity 16 m³

4-axle 50 tonne side-tipping wagon, capacity 18 m³

ITALTRAFO

Via Nuova delle Brecce 260, 80147 Naples, Italy

Telephone: 266022
Telegrams: ITALTRAFO, Naples
Telex: 71131 Itraf Na

Products: Electrical equipment for electric and diesel-electric locomotives, electric trains, trolley-buses, trams; distribution, power and special transformers of any size and voltage.

Constitution: ITALTRAFO incorporates four of the largest Italian electro-mechanical concerns: the transformer department of ASGEN, OCREN, ALCE, and Breda Elet-tromeccanica. The company is concerned with research, engineering, manufacturing and servicing transformers of any type and rating, and traction equipments.

Sales: In the traction field OCREN, ALCE and Breda supply electro-mechanical equipments to the Italian State Railways and a number of foreign customers.

JANKO GREDELJ

Zagreb, Yugoslavia

Telephone: 515 266
Telegrams: TEZEV Zagreb

Products: Diesel-electric trainsets.

New equipment: An aluminium four-car diesel-electric trainset, comprising one motor car on each end of the coach, with 40 seats, a luggage compartment, and a power-unit compartment; one trailer with bar and 48 seats; one trailer with 64 seats.

The motor coaches are of streamline design, capable of double-switching. Coach control is possible from either end by remote controls.

The bogies under the motor cars are driving type. Each is provided with two electric traction motors, the power of which is transferred to axles through gears. The cars are coupled by a central draft-buffer gear. For reduced air friction the cars are coupled by a telescopic concertina connection. The ends of the motor cars are provided with standard draft and buffer gear which make connection of the coaches at the end of standard gauge possible. The motor coach is provided with two-winged doors opened and closed pneumatically.

The motor coach is provided with two diesel engines which drive an electric alternator. The electric alternator is manufactured by Raeezjocarof Zagreb, and is of 270 kV rating. The driving electric motor is produced by Rade Koncar and has a continuous rating of 81 kV at 1 530 rpm.

The control desks, accommodating all control instruments for train operation, generator operation, and operation of driving and auxiliary diesel engines, are in the driver's cab. By a special switch the remote control system is switched on for the diesel aggregate on the other end of train, or for an additional diesel train if operated jointly. The air compressors are connected to the engine of the auxiliary aggregate. Capacity is satisfactory for requirements of airbrake, pneumatic opening of doors, horn and other pneumatic equipment. Speedometers are in both driver's cabs; one of them is of registering type.

The deadman's provision is connected with pneumatic drive and electric controls. The driver's cabs are provided with a telephone and the train can be fitted with a closed-circuit broadcasting system used for giving information to passengers.

Heating of cars is by hot air. Each car is provided with independent heating apparatus of Webasto type.

The ventilation of cars is by ventilators built in the car roof, enabling 14 complete exchanges of air in the passenger compartments.

Braking is by automatic airbrake, an electro-magnetic track brake, built on all bogies, and an electric brake through traction motors. Each car is provided with hand and auxiliary brakes.

JARSEA

Japan Rolling Stock Exporters' Association

Telephone: (03) 201 3145

Head Office: 1 Tekko Building, 8-2 Marunouchi 1-chome, Chiyoda-ku, Tokyo, Japan
Information Office: Yaesu 1-chome building, 6-2 Yaesu 1-chome, Chuo-ku, Tokyo, Japan

The Association comprises major Japanese rolling stock manufacturers, relating parts manufacturers and major trading firms, whose combined experience benefits the rolling stock industry world-wide.

JEFFREY

Jeffrey Mining Machinery Division

Telephone: (614) 297 3123
Telegrams: JEFFREY
Telex: 245486

PO Box 1879, Columbus, Ohio 43216, USA

Products: Underground mine electric, battery, trolley locomotives.

Executive Vice-President: Trevor J Jones
Vice-President, Marketing: Paul L Vergamini
Manager, Domestic Sales: William J Loudermilk
Manager, International Sales: Robert E Hess

Constitution: A division of Dresser Industries, Inc.

Sales: 27-ton and 50-ton locomotives for Consolidated Coal Co, 8-ton locos for Monterey Coal Co, 20-ton, 37-ton and 50-ton locos for Bethlehem Mines Corp and 11-ton locos for Island Creek Coal Co.

Four-wheel locomotives—specifications

Model	27C	20A	20B	15A	15B	11A	11B	8A	6A	6B
Nominal weight—tons	27	20	20	15	15	11	11	8	6	6
Actual weight—tons	27	24	23	15	18	12	12	9	7	7
Voltage—dc	250	250	250	250	250	250	250	250	250	250
Total hp	360	300	300	190	190	100	120	80	60	60
Rated drawbar pull—lb	13 500	10 000	10 000	7 500	7 500	5 500	5 500	4 000	3 000	3 000
Speed at rated drawbar pull—mph	10.8	10.2	10.2	8.3	9.4	5.9	6.9	6.5	6.7	6.9
Motor type	MH 2340	MH 2411	MH 2411	MH 2409	MH 2409	MH 2313	MH 2328	MH 2100	MH 2186	MH 288
Gear ratio	15:68	16:76	16:76	14:65	16:63	15:74	14:75	14:74	14:58	13:75
Track gauge—in	42	42-48	42-48	42-44	42	42-48	42	42	42-44	24-30
Width—in	80	82	82	70	78	78	78	66	66	60
Length over end frames—ft	22.8	22.5	23.3	20.0	24.1	18.7	18.7	17.1	14.5	14.5
Height over frame—in	42	34	34	30	30	32	32	30	29	32
Height over locked-down trolley pole or cable reel—in	49	41	41	37	37	39	39	42	36	39
Wheel diameter—in	36	31	31	27	27	28	28	26	20	26

Eight-wheel locomotives—specifications

Model	50A	50B	37A	37B	37C	27A	27B
Nominal weight—tons	50	50	37	37	37	27	27
Actual weight—tons	52	60	44	44	40	33	33
Voltage—dc	250	250	250	250	250	250	250
Traction motors—number	4	4	4	4	4	4	4
Total hp	720	720	600	600	600	380	380
Rated drawbar pull—lb	25 000	25 000	18 500	18 500	18 500	13 500	13 500
Speed at rated drawbar pull—mph	10.5	11.0	10.6	10.2	10.6	9.6	9.6
Track gauge—in	42	42	36	42	42	42-48	42-44
Width—in	88	90	74	74	84	88	80
Length over end frames—ft	37.0	37.3	34.3	34.3	34.5	36.3	31.0
Height over frame—in	42	50	44	44	43½	38	41¾
Height over locked-down trolley pole—in	49	57	50	50	45½	45	48
Wheel diameter—in	34	36	33	31	33	27	27
Motor type	MH 2340	MH 2340	MH 2370	MH 2411	MH 2370	MH 2409	MH 2409
Gear ratio	15:66	15:68	14:66	16:76	14:66	16:63	16:63

JENBACHER

Jenbacher Werke AG

Telephone: 2291-5
Telegrams: Motor Jenbach
Telex: 053756-7

A-6200 Jenbach, Austria

Products: Diesel-mechanical and diesel-hydraulic rail tractors and locomotives; passenger coaches; diesel engines; diesel compressors; diesel generator and pumping sets.

Managing Director: Dr H Wenisch
Technical Director: Dr Söllner
Sales Manager: F Franer

Constitution: The company was started in 1946 for the manufacture of diesel engines and combined units. It builds diesel-powered locomotives up to 1 500 hp.

Developments: The first Schlieren-designed passenger coach, among an order for 40 being built by Jenbacher, completed trials in 1977. All cars were due to be delivered at the end of 1978.

JESSOP

Jessop & Co Ltd, Calcutta

Telephone: 22 5041 22 3426
Telegrams: JESSOPS
Telex: 021-2135/021-7564

63 Netaji Subhas Road, Calcutta 700 001, India

Products: All types of rolling stock including electric multiple unit coaches, passenger coaches.

Chairman and Managing Director: P K Banerji
Director (Finance): P Chakrabarti
Director (Commercial): V R Pappu

Constitution: Jessop and Co was founded in 1788, one of the oldest engineering firms in India. The works at Dum Dum, which cover 80 acres, comprise six separate units: wagon, coach, structural, road roller, mechanical and paper works.
The works at Durgapur, built on 116 acres, manufacture heavy duty iron castings. Annual output is about 480 million rupees (£30 million sterling).

Sales: Sales in 1978/79 netted an income of 350 million rupees (£22 million sterling approx).

JEUMONT-SCHNEIDER
Jeumont-Schneider SA

31-32 quai National, 92806 Puteaux, France

Products: Power equipment for electric locomotives and transit stock.

Telephone: 776 43 23
Telex: 610 425 melec F

Chairman: P Boulin
Managing Director: C Devin

(See Société MTE and FRANCORAIL-MTE.)

JUNG
Arn Jung, Lokomotivfabrik GmbH

D-5242 Jungenthal b, Kirchen a/d Sieg, Federal Republic of Germany

Products: Electric and diesel locomotives.

Telephone: 02741 6831
Telegrams: LOKOMOTIVFABRIK, Kirchen-Sieg
Telex: 08 753 19

Type RC 43 C diesel-hydraulic locomotive developed by Jung for shunting and branch-line duties

Designed as a three-axle rigid-frame locomotive, it is driven by an MTU four-stroke diesel engine and equipped with Voith hydrodynamic forward/reverse transmission. The axles are driven via cardan shafts and axle gear boxes. Axles are sprung by rubber springs and equipped with hydraulic shock absorbers. The driver's cab is designed for good all-round vision. Controls are electro-pneumatic. In service with Deutsche Bundesbahn the locomotive is frequently equipped with radio control equipment.

	405 kW version	580 kW version
Axle arrangement	0-6-0	0-6-0
Gauge (mm)	1 435	1 435
Wheel base (mm)	3 400	3 400
Length over buffer (mm)	8 640	8 640
Smallest curve radius (m)	60	60
Engine make	MTU	MTU
Power (kW)	405	580
Engine rpm	2 100	2 100
Power transmission	hydro-dynamic	hydro-dynamic
Transmission type	Voith-forward reverse transmission L2r3z	Voith-forward reverse transmission L4r4U2
Wheel diameter (mm)	950	950
Weight (tonnes)	48-60	48-60
Speed (normal) (km/h)	0-20; 0-40	0-42

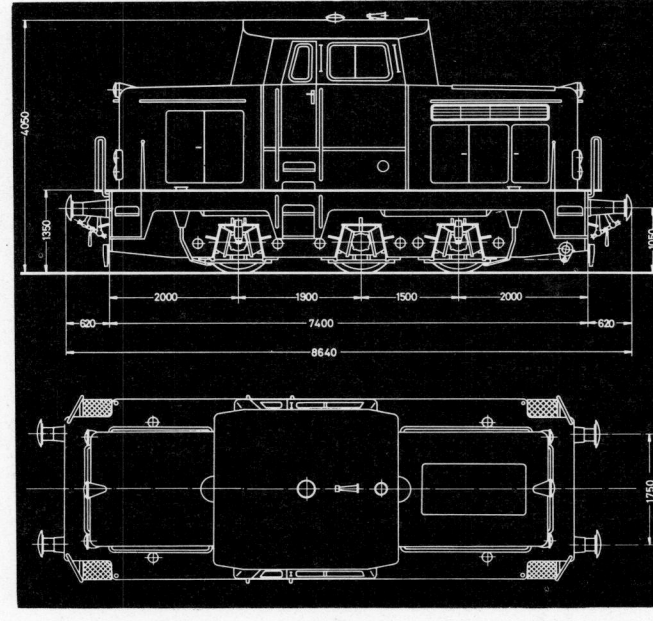

Type RC 43 C locomotive

KAELBLE-GMEINDER
Carl Kaelble U Gmeinder GmbH & Co

Postfach 1260, 6950 Mosbach, Baden, Federal Republic of Germany

Products: Diesel-electric and diesel-hydraulic locomotives up to 1 200 hp; special freight wagons.

Telephone: 06261 4041
Telegrams: GMEINDER, Mosbachbaden
Telex: 04 66111

Managing Directors: Rudolph Zornow
Hans Kärcher
Friedrich Mezger
Export Sales: Friedrich Krone

Type D36B (332 kW) diesel locomotives double heading a Norwegian State Railways (NSB) freight train

---

KALMAR

Kalmar Verkstads AB

PO Box 943, S-391 29 Kalmar, Sweden

Telephone: Kalmar 0480/150 70
Telegrams: KVAB, Kalmar
Telex: 43029

Products: Passenger coaches; freight wagons; railcars; locomotives (diesel).

Chairman: Johan Åkerman
Managing Director: Sven Arnerius
Director, Railway Products: Hans Lönn

Sales: Deliveries in 1977-80 include freight wagons and tank wagons for Zambia Railways, and passenger coaches for Kenya and Tanzania.
New orders include 150 passenger coaches for Swedish State Railways (deliveries started mid-1979) and 30 railcars (subcontractor to Fiat, Italy, for Swedish State Railways) for delivery in 1980.

One of Kalmar's new passenger coaches built for Kenya and Tanzania railways

---

KAWASAKI

Kawasaki Heavy Industries Ltd, Rolling Stock Group

Head office: World Trade Centre Building, 4-1 2-chome, Hamamatsu-cho, Minato-ku, Tokyo, Japan

Telephone (Kobe): 078 671 5021
(Tokyo): 02867 3 0022
(Tochigi Pref): (03) 435-2589
Telegrams: KAWASAKI HEAVY, Tokyo
Telex: J-22672, J-26888, (Domestic) 242-4371

Works: 1/18 Wadayama-Dori 2-chome, Hyogo-ku, Kobe, Japan
2857-2, Naka Okamoto, Kawachi-cho, Kawachi-Gun, Tochigi Pref, Japan

Products: Electric, diesel-electric, diesel-hydraulic locomotives; electric railcars; diesel railcars; freight cars; passenger coaches; containers.

Chairman: Kiyoshi Yotsumoto
President: Zenji Umeda
Executive Vice Presidents: Tsuneo Ando
Toraichi Imai
Managing Director (Rolling Stock): Shigeru Mori
Director (Rolling Stock): Masahiko Ishizawa

Sales: During 1977/79/80 Kawasaki has delivered 338 electric cars, 41 electric and diesel locomotives, and 775 freight cars to JNR. The Group also delivered 209 electric cars of various types, and 83 tank cars to private companies.
Exports include 85 passenger cars and 109 freight cars to Nigeria, 32 electric cars to Brazil, 40 freight cars to Hong Kong, 34 passenger cars to Malaysia, 140 freight cars to Zambia, 8 electric cars to Indonesia, 5 diesel locomotives, 25 passenger cars and 25 freight wagons to Burma.

Constitution: Kawasaki Heavy Industries Ltd was formed in 1969 by the merger of Kawasaki Rolling Stock Manufacturing Co, Kawasaki Aircraft Co and Kawasaki Dockyard Co Ltd. In 1972 Kisha Seizo Kaisha Ltd was taken over and merged into Kawasaki Heavy Industries Ltd.

Diesel electric trainset built by Kawasaki for New Zealand Railways' long-distance services

Manufactured as an ace train for NZR, the main power source is provided by a Caterpillar 1 010 hp engine. The train is formed by two cars (maximum of six) and is used for the Silver Fern express service between Wellington and Auckland (680 km).

Track gauge (mm)		1 067
Tare weight (tonnes)	power car	61
	trailer car	43
Passenger capacity	power car	36
	trailer car	60
Length over coupler face (mm)		23 720
Overall width (mm)		2 743

Height to top of roof (mm)		3 759
Bogie centre distance (mm)	power car	17 374
	trailer car	17 552
Wheel base (mm)	power bogie	1 650 + 1 650
	trailing bogies	2 200
Wheel diameter (mm)		787
Diesel engine output (mm)		940
(at 1 300 rpm) (hp)		1 010
Max speed (km/h)		112

Diesel-hydraulic locomotive delivered to Burma Railways Corp in 1978

Electric subway set handed over to Kobe Municipal Transportation Bureau in 1979

Third-class passenger car built for Nigerian Railway Corp

Refrigeration wagon delivered to Burma Railways

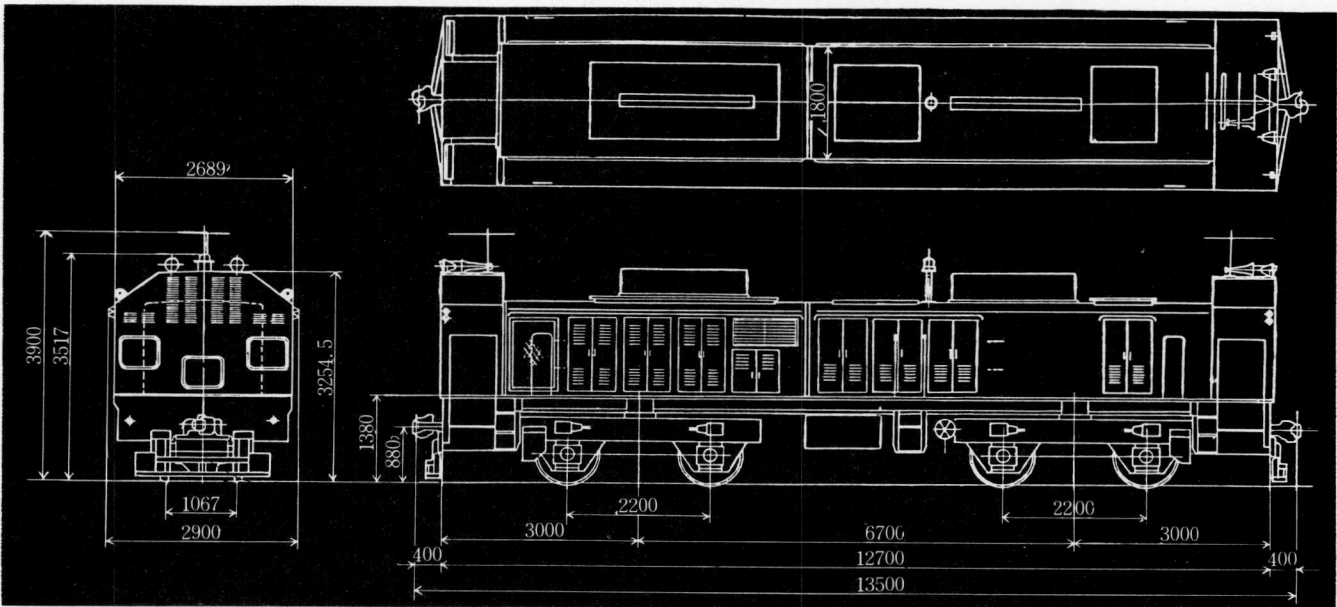

Radio controlled diesel hydraulic locomotive built by Kawasaki for the parent company steel corporation

No operating controls are fitted, in keeping with the main design specification, which creates a purely remote-control locomotive.

Track gauge (mm)	1 067
Weight in working order (tonnes)	70
Max tractive effort (kg)	21 000
Max service speed (km/h)	17.5
Diesel engine	
Model/Quantity	DMF 31SI/1
Standard output (hp)	600 metric
Hydraulic transmission	
Model/Quantity	Shinko DS1.35A/1

Gear ratio	12:287
Control system	Electro-magnetic, electro-pneumatic remote control by radio
Storage battery	
Voltage (V)/capacity (Ah)	dc 24/400 (20 hour rating)
Brake system	Air brake by electro-magnetic control and hand brake
Capacity of fuel tank (litres)	2 000

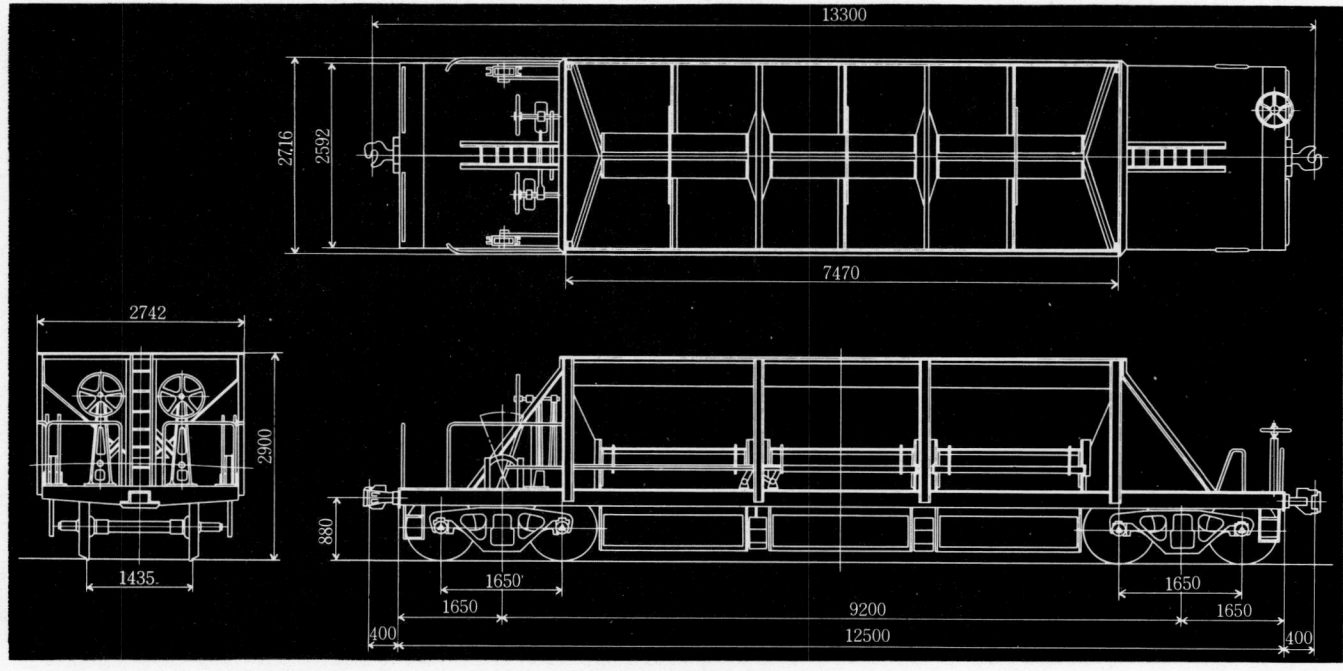

2-axle bogie 30-ton ballast hopper wagon designed to scatter ballast on the track of JNR's Shinkansen

To regulate 3-way scattering over the track bed a special scatter adjusting door is provided, operated by a handle on the deck at the end of each wagon.

Track gauge (mm)	1 435
Loading capacity (tonnes)	30
Tare weight (tonnes)	19
Body capacity (m³)	18

Length over coupler face (mm)	13 300
Overall width (mm)	2 742
Height to top of body (mm)	2 900
Bogie centre distance (mm)	9 200
Wheel base (mm)	1 650
Wheel diameter (mm)	860
Max speed (km/h)	75

Series 500 electric car built by Kawasaki for Keihan Electric Railway

While normal seating is 38 per car, during off peak periods extra seats can be brought down from the ceiling to increase seating capacity to 54. To obtain maximum lightness, aluminium light-alloy construction is used throughout.

Track gauge (mm)	1 435
Electric system (V) dc	600
Tare weight (Motor car) (tonnes)	32
Passenger capacity (Motor car)	
Total	150
Seating	38 or 54

Length over coupler face (mm)	18 700
Overall width (mm)	2 726
Height to top of roof (mm)	3 710
Bogie centre distance (mm)	12 000
Wheel base (mm)	2 100
Wheel diameter (mm)	860
1 h rating output (kW)	
(2 motor cars 1 unit)	1 040
Max speed (km/h)	120

KIDRIC

Boris Kidric

Maribor, Yugoslavia

Products: Passenger coaches.

New equipment: The B-type two-axle passenger coach is of all-welded rolled steel sections. The body sheathing is of 2-mm sheet steel, and the roof is 1.5 mm thick. The car floor is of 1.5 mm trapezoid-shaped corrugated steel, welded by electric arc to the underframe.

The sides and ends are lined with a layer of 4.4 mm lesonite board, and over it a layer of lesomine board of the same thickness. The car ceiling is lined with two glued lesonite boards enamelled white.

The passenger space is divided into three compartments. Seats have soft backs and are upholstered in artificial leather. The car can be manufactured either with an electric heating system or a Friedmann-of-Wien steam-heating system.

Body length (mm)	14 200
Height from top of rails (mm)	4 145
Number of seats	70
Speed permitted (km/h)	80
Light weight (tonnes)	18.5

The A-type coach is all-welded steel-rolled and pressed sections. The car sheathing is of 2-mm pickled sheet steel, and the roof is 1.5 mm thick. The floor is 1.5 mm corrugated steel electrically welded to the underframe. A frame of oak billets is fastened over the floor and lined with waterproof panels. The car is equipped with electric heaters and has five compartments, 1 780 × 2 155 mm, with eight seats in four compartments, and seven seats in the fifth, or a total of 39 seats. The seats and backs are soft. The car is provided with a low-pressure steam heating system of Friedmann type.

Height from top of rails (mm)	4 145
Number of seats	39
Speed permitted (km/h)	100
Light weight (Tonnes)	19.3

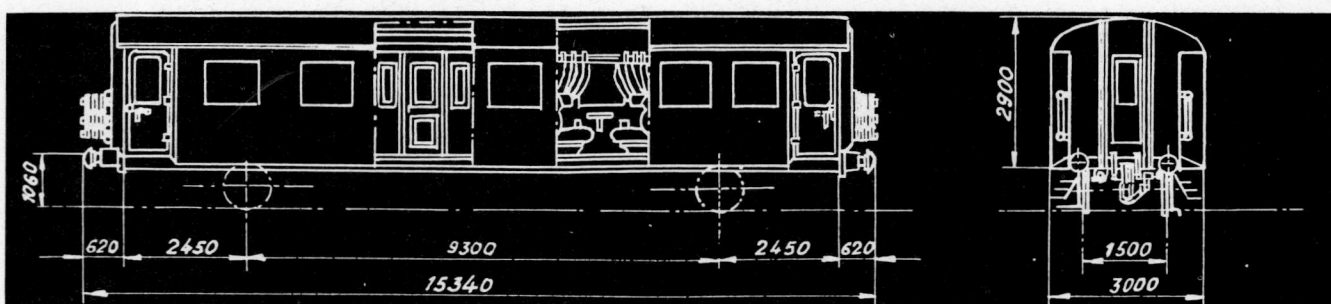

A-type coach—seats 39 passengers in four compartments

KINKI SHARYO

The Kinki Sharyo Co Ltd
(Kinki Rolling Stock Manufacturing Co Ltd)

Head Office: 966-1 Inada, Higashi-Osaka, 577, Japan

Tokyo Office: 527, Nippon Bldg, Ohtemachi, Chiyoda-ku, 100, Japan

Telephone: (Osaka) 745 1231
Telegrams: Kinsha Fuse
Telex: 527 8911 KINSHA J

Telephone: (Tokyo) 270 3431
Telex: 222 3105 KNSTOK J

Products: Electric and diesel railcars; tank cars; refrigerator cars; passenger and freight cars; industrial wagons and equipment.

President: Toshio Muramatsu
Managing Director, General Manager of Tokyo Office: Seihei Katayama

Constitution: In 1920 a factory was started in Osaka for manufacture of rolling stock which in 1936 became the Tanaka Sharyo Co. In 1945 the latter company was taken over by the Kinki Nippon Railways Co, the largest private railway company in Japan, forming the present company.
The company is now one of the largest manufacturers of rolling stock to domestic and overseas railways, and is granting technical assistance to rolling stock manufacturers in Egypt, Mexico, Argentina and others.

Sales: Major sales in recent ten years: 1 321 electric railcars for Japanese National Railways including Shinkansen cars; 914 electric railcars for the Kinki Nippon Railways Co and other private railways; 406 subway cars for Tokyo and Osaka Metros; 572 electric railcars for Egypt; 120 passenger cars for Mexico; 186 passenger cars for Burma; 40 passenger cars for Hong Kong; 33 passenger cars for Nigeria; 24 subway cars for Korea; 20 electric cars for Argentina; 17 diesel railcars for the Philippines; 10 passenger cars for Indonesia; 6 passenger cars for Zambia.

Equipment: The 962 Shinkansen prototype was manufactured in 1978/79 on a test basis incorporating new technology acquired since the early days of the Tokaido Shinkansen. Six cars constitute a train set. This prototype is scheduled to be converted into an electric test-inspection car when the service on the pilot line is over. Arrangement of windows and the interior are based on a design scheme for the layout required of the electric test-inspection car. The main dimensions are the same as those of the Tokaido Shinkansen, but the nose of the front end is about 600 mm longer. The outside colouring has been tentatively changed to the two-tone colour of green and cream from the characteristic colours, ivory white and light blue, of existing Shinkansen stock. The body is of aluminium.
Compared with the Tokaido and Sanyo Shinkansen lines, the Shinkansen in future will have more long tunnels and longer continuous grades. This makes it imperative for the electric car to have a big output. For this reason the output of the traction motor of the new car has been increased to 230 kW, or about 25 per cent over the existing electric cars of the Tokaido and Sanyo Shinkansen.
Kinki Nippon Railway Co presented to traffic service its first double-deck electric car, Vistacar, in 1969. For 20 years Kinki Nippon Railway worked it as the company's representative limited-express electric car. In 1979 Kinki Sharyo built 28 new-model double-deck electric cars, New Vistacars, capitalising on the experience. Working in permanently coupled four-car train sets, the two intermediate cars have a two-deck construction. To make the upper-deck seats of the double-deck cars as spacious as possible, the four cars are coupled at an elevated floor level. At the coupling part of the head-end car and the double-decker, steps are installed on the head-end car, and dressing room and toilet are also installed.

Five diesel-hydraulic locomotives for Burma Railways Corporation were manufactured in 1978. The locomotive is essentially a remodelled DD-907 type for hauling mainline trains. To make it suitable for shunting operation, it is equipped with a special turbo-transmission system which can do away with the mechanical reversing gear rigging usually used in the diesel-hydraulic locomotive. This turbotransmission system is able to function to produce liquid dynamic brake force, so it is a locomotive having particularly superior performance capacity suitable for shunting locomotives for intra-yard use. Upon delivery to BRC, three of these locomotives have been assigned to Rangoon and two to Mandalay, and they are in use for the traction of local branch-line trains as well as the train make-up operation in station yards or shunting at the marshalling yard. The weight of the locomotive is 40 tons and its maximum speed 42 km/h so that the bilateral services for shunting in yard and hauling local trains on branch lines can be met with an engine output of 600 hp. The maximum tractive force at the periphery of driving wheel at starting is about 11 650 kg, meaning that the adhesion coefficient against the locomotive weight is about 28.7 per cent.

Double-deck electric car for Kinki Nippon Railway Co

Electric tramcar for Cairo Transport Authority, Egypt

Tilting electric car for Japanese National Railways

KOLMEX

Mokotowska 49, 00-542 Warsaw, Poland

Products: Electric and diesel locomotives; electric trainsets; passenger coaches; freight wagons.

Chairman: Eng Włodzimierz Rachiborski
Managing Director: Władysław Kostuj
Chief Sales Director: Eng Antoni Łukasiewicz

Constitution: Kolmex acts as the Foreign Trade Enterprise of TASKO and is the sole exporter of railway motive power and passenger and freight stock manufactured in Poland. Its members are Cegielski, Pafawag, Fablok, Konstal, Zastal, and Swidnica.

Sales: Among deliveries in 1979 Kolmex reports the following: 200 self-dumping iron ore wagons to Austrian Federal Railways; 123 various types of wagon to Greek Railways; 60 passenger coaches and 120 tank wagons for Syrian Railways; 100 six-axle flat wagons and 12 brake/crew vans to Iraqi Railways.

KONSTAL

Steel Construction Works Konstal

41-500 Chorzow, ul Metalowcow 7, Poland

Export Sales: Kolmex, 49 Mokotowska, 00-542 Warsaw, Poland

Telephone: 41 10 51
Telegrams: KONSTAL, Chorzow
Telex: 0312451

Products: Electric and storage battery mine locomotives; freight wagons; wheel sets.

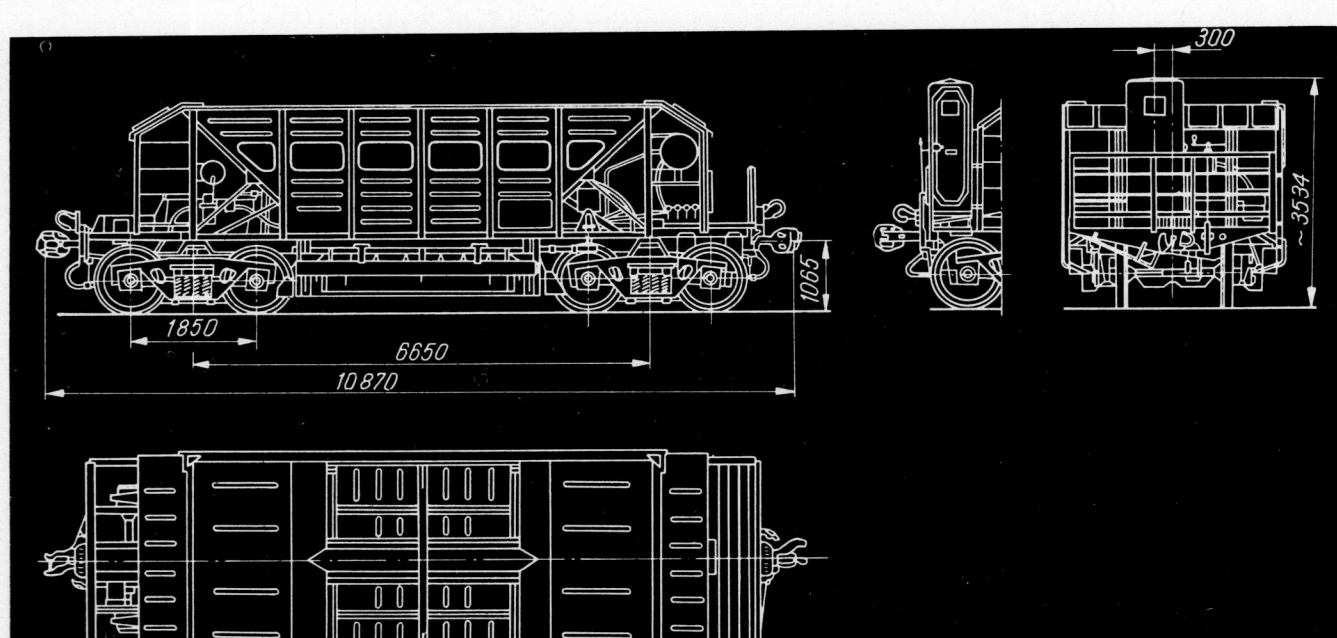

Hopper wagon type 902V designed for hauling ballast		Car width, between farthest protruding parts (mm)	3242
Track gauge (mm)	1524	Car length, between bogie pivots (mm)	6650
Loading capacity (tonnes)	60	Car height, above top of rail (mm)	3167
Car weight (tonnes)		Number of flaps	
with parking brake	23.6	exterior hatches	2
with hand brake	23.7	interior hatches	2
Max axle load (tonnes)	21	Discharge opening dimensions of flaps (mm)	
Capacity (m³)		exterior	2680 × 345
with prism	40	interior	2680 × 330
without prism	32.4	General clearance space of discharge openings (m²)	3.62
Car length, between automatic coupling axes (mm)	10 870	Vehicle gauge	to GOST 9238-59 1-T

KOREA SHIPBUILDING & ENGINEERING

55-4 Sussomun-Dong, Jong-Gu, Seoul, Republic of Korea

Products: Open, tank and container wagons, cast steel bogies, bolsters, couplers and wheels.

Chairman: Nam Kong Ryum

Telephone: 28 4281 5
Telegrams: SHIP YARD, Seoul
Telex: KSEC K2269

Managing Director: Pyun Chai Yung
Chief Sales Director: Shim Dong Shik
Export Sales Director: Choi Joon Kee

Sales:

	Customer	Commodity	Quantity	Rail Gauge (mm)	Coupler	Brake	Loading Capacity	Bogie	Max Speed (km/h)	Wheel Diameter (mm)	Total Length (mm)
1977	Malaysia Railway (MRA)	Ballast Hopper Wagon	50	1000	MCA-DA Type	Automatic Vacuum	37 ton	A-3 Cast Steel, Ride Control	80	851	13 646
1977	Saudi Arabia Railway (SGRRO)	50 tonne flat car	100	1435	AAR E Type Automatic	ABSD Type, Air	50 ton	S-2 Barber, Stabilised	80	838	14 250
1977	Saudi Arabia Railway	50 tonne Tank Car	50	1435	AAR E Type Automatic	ABSD Type, Air	10 000 g/a	S-2 Barber, Stabilised	80	838	13 610
1977	Saudi Arabia Railway	50 tonne Gondola Car	50	1435	AAR E Type Automatic	ABSD Type, Air	50 ton	S-2 Barber, Stabilised	80	838	13 132
1977	Saudi Arabia Railway	50 tonne Box Car	50	1435	AAR E Type Automatic	ABSD Type, Air	50 ton	S-2 Barber, Stabilised	80	838	13 414
1977	Korean National Railroad	50 tonne Gondola Car	300	1435	Shibata Type Automatic	K-C Type, Air	50 ton	Barber	100	860	13 850
1977	Korean National Railroad	Limited Express Coach	2	1435	H Type Tightlock Automatic	Disc Type, Air	72 Passengers	4-Wheel, Pressed Steel	150	860	21 000
1977	Korean National Railroad	Limited Express Power Source Car	1	1435	H Type Tightlock Automatic	Disc Type, Air	72 Passengers	4-Wheel, Pressed Steel	150	860	17 970
1977	Korean National Railroad	Conductor Car	10	1435	Shibata Type Automatic	K-C Type, Air	72 Passengers	Barber	100	860	10 200
1977	Korea Oil Co	11 000 g/a Tank Car	69	1435	Shibata Type Automatic	K-C Type, Air	G/A 11 000	Barber	80	860	11 800
1978	Saudi Arabia Railway	10 000 g/a Tank Car	42	1435	AAR E Type Automatic	ABSD Type, Air	G/A 10 000	S-2 Barber, Stabilised	80	838	13 610
1978	Korean National Railroad	50 tonne Box Car	100	1435	Shibata Type Automatic	K-C Type, Air	50 ton	Barber	100	860	13 950

KRALJEVO

Kraljevo Car Factory

Kraljevo, Yugoslavia

Products: Passenger coaches and freight wagons.

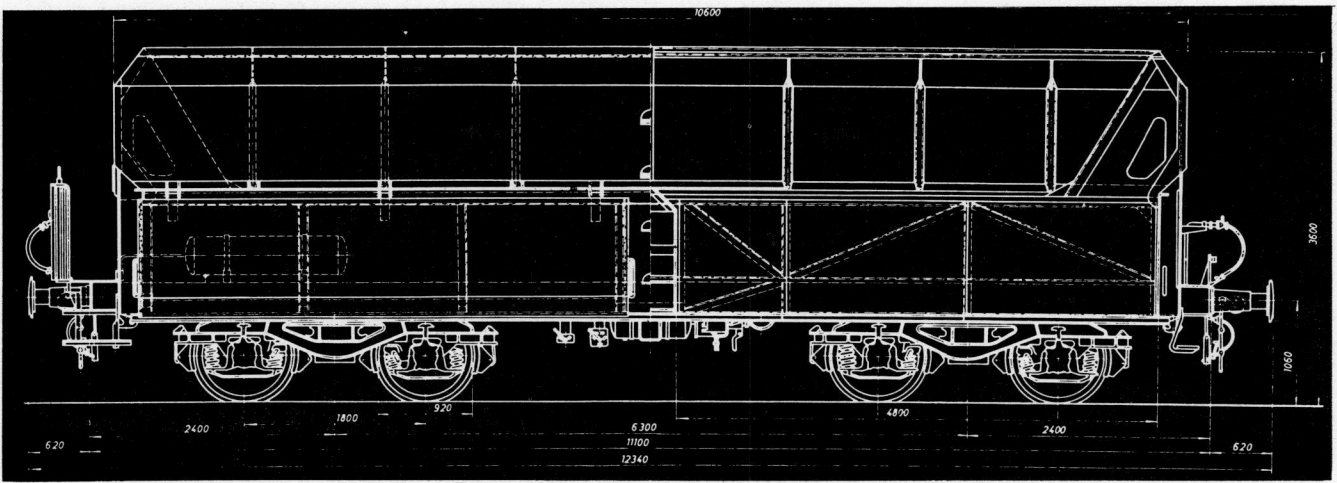

4-axle iron ore hopper wagon

Gauge (mm)	1435	Bogie wheel base (m)	1.8
Overall length (m)	12.3	Hopper volume (m³)	60
Width (m)	2.86	Unladen weight (tonnes)	23
Height, from top of rails (m)	3.6	Load limit (tonnes)	57
Bogie pin centres (m)	6.4	Gross weight (tonnes)	80
		Axle-loading (tonnes)	20

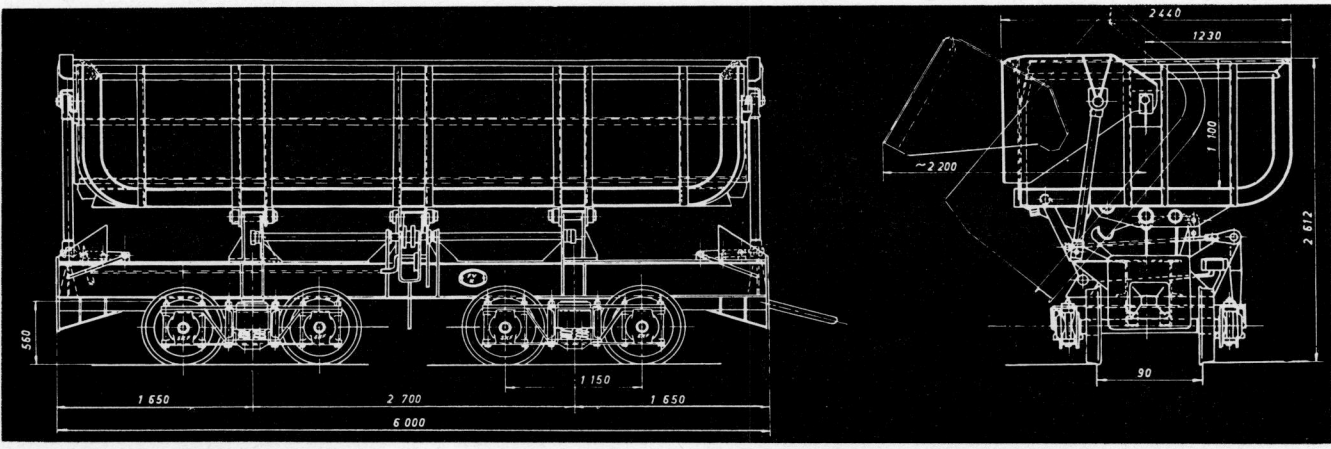

900 mm gauge 4-axle wagon for coal haulage
Unloading can be on both sides directly into bunkers by mechanical devices for door opening. Door control is from the locomotive. Pneumatic and remote-control door systems can also be opened by hand. The wagon is intended primarily for use in mines. Coupling is through a central draft and buffering coupler, with cushioning being provided by worm springs.

KRAUSS-MAFFEI

Krauss-Maffei Aktiengesellschaft

8 München 50, Krauss-Maffei Strasse 2, Federal Republic of Germany

Telephone: 089 88991
Telegrams: KRAUSSMAFFEI Müchenallach
Telex: 05 23 163

Products: Diesel and electric locomotives; track-bound high speed systems with contact-free suspension and guidance.

Board of Directors: Dr rer pol Hans-Heinz Griesmeier
Dipl-Ing H-D v Bernuth
Wolfgang Raether
Managing Director, Transportation Division: Dipl-Ing Hans-Dietrich von Bernuth

Constitution: The present firm of Krauss-Maffei was created by the merger in 1931 of two locomotive builders, J A Maffei AG, founded in 1837, and Krauss & Co KG, founded in 1866. In 1935-37 a factory, replacing the former two plants, was erected at Allach, a suburb of Munich.

Sales: The company supplies mechanical parts for five prototypes of a new three-phase electric locomotive, type E120 being built for Deutsche Bundebahn by a German Consortium.
All five locomotives were to be delivered in 1979 and undergo tests on two 100 km track sections. The locomotives are to be used for high-speed passenger trains, heavy freight trains and express freight trains.

Developments: First tests started in 1977 on Krauss Maffei's new test facility at Munich DB repair shop on which speeds of up to 500 km/h can be simulated. The purpose of the specially-commissioned dynamic test stand is to explore the technical and economic limits of conventional rail technology.

E 111, used for DB long and short-haul passenger trains and high-speed freight services

In the sector of railway electronics, Krauss Maffei has developed new electronic anti-slip and anti-glide equipment for locomotives. An electronic anti-slip device is being developed jointly with DB for use on passenger coaches. Series production was due to begin late in 1978.

Since 1976 Krauss Maffei has supplied two types of electronic equipment for remote control of locomotives. One is for assembling trains from a portable transmitter, the other for automatic humping locomotives operated by a central processing computer. The Transrapid magnetic levitation train with linear motor propulsion continues under development by Krauss Maffei and Messerschmitt Bolkow Blohm. In 1977 the Transrapid 04 test vehicle (see picture) achieved a speed of 206 km/h and is being retro-fitted for speeds over 250 km/h. A speed of 401 km/h was set up by the unmanned test magnetic levitation vehicle Comet.

A public demonstration system in magnetic levitation technology developed by the two companies was operational at the International Transport Exhibition held in Hamburg in 1979.

The Transrapid magnetic levitation train set up a speed of 206 km/h and is being prepared for speeds of over 250 km/h.

KRUPP

Fried Krupp GmbH
Krupp Industrie und Stahlbau, Railway Rolling Stock Division

Helenenstrasse 149, 4300 Essen 1, Federal Republic of Germany

Chairman: Dr Ing Hans-Wilhelm Obrig
General Manager of Products: Dipl Ing Werner Görlitz
Export Sales Manager: Horst Ehlis

Products: Electric locomotives, diesel-electric and diesel-hydraulic locomotives, multiaxle multipurpose heavy-load carriers up to 1000-tonnes capacity, ladle wagons for transporting liquid iron up to 500 tonnes, railway cranes, special rail vehicles to individual specifications, turn-key plants for manufacturing and repairing all types of motive power.

Constitution: Krupp Industrie- und Stahlbau is a company of the Krupp Group originating from the Cast Steel Works of Friedrich Krupp founded in 1811. Since the invention

Telephone: 0201 31901
Telegrams: KRUPP, Essen
Telex: 08 57 9331

of the seamless railway tyre by Alfred Krupp in 1852, the company has been closely connected with almost every aspect of railway engineering. Components for railway products have been manufactured since 1850, general rolling stock since 1865 and complete locomotives since 1919. Combining the know-how of a wide scope of railway engineering with its well-known plant-making experience the company considers the promotion of national railway industries in developing countries its specific objective.

Sales: During 1978 the company built five 32-axle special freight wagons for the Soviet State Railways. The order is worth DM 19 million. The wagons carry up to 500 tonnes. Krupp, together with several German manufacturers, supplied the mechanical parts for five prototypes of a new three-phase electric locomotive for Deutsche Bundesbahn. Currently Krupp, in conjunction with the German Federal Railway's research department in Munich, is developing a three-car trainset test vehicle for Rheine-Freren line.

DD 950 diesel-hydraulic locomotive for Burma Railways Corporation
Delivery of 16 of these locomotives began in late 1978.

32-axle heavy load carrier, one of Krupp's special-purpose wagons

KUIBYSHEV

Kuibyshev Diesel Locomotive Works

Kolomensk, USSR

Products: Diesel locomotives.

New equipment: Locomotives powered by 6 000, 8 000 and 10 000-hp diesel engines were designed for operation on the Baikul-Amur (BAM) Railway.

LEW

VEB Lokomotivbau-Elektrotechnische Werke "Hans Beimler"

1422 Hennigsdorf, German Democratic Republic

Products: Electric, diesel-hydraulic and diesel-electric locomotives; special electric locomotives; multiple unit trains.

Telephone: 510
Telegrams: ELEKTROLOK
Telex: 158 531

Constitution: Member of Transportmaschinen Export-Import.

New series 270 multiple-unit trainset built for the Berlin elevated S-Bahn

Electric trainset delivered in 1978 for Budapest suburban service

Six-axle BR250 electric locomotive designed for operation at 16⅔ cycles on the Deutsche Bundesbahn network

LEW's special EL16 electric towing vehicle with battery drive

Picture and diagram show narrow-profile trainset for East Berlin Metro service

LINKE-HOFMANN-BUSCH

Linke-Hofmann-Busch Waggon-Fahrzeug-Maschinen GmbH

Postfach 411160, D-3320 Salzgitter 41, Federal Republic of Germany

Telephone: 214033
Telegrams: Linkebusch Salzgitter 41
Telex: 954452

Products: Passenger and freight cars; electric and diesel railcars and trainsets; electric and diesel locomotives; underground railway cars; tramcars.

Technical Director: Dipl-Ing Heinz Alten
Commercial Director: Dr Jürgen Isermeyer
Chief Sales Director: Siegfried Albrecht
Export Sales Director: Armin Marwede

Constitution: Established in 1839 at Breslau under the name of Carbuilding Workshops of Gottfried Linke the company amalgamated with Gebruder Hofmann & Co in 1912 to form Linke-Hofmann Werke AG, Breslau. In 1928 the Waggon & Maschinenfabrik AG was formed. Busch joined the company to form Linke-Hofmann-Busch. After World War II the company's works at Breslau had to be abandoned, but in 1949 L-H-B resumed their activities at Salzgitter-Watenstedt, near Braunschweig.

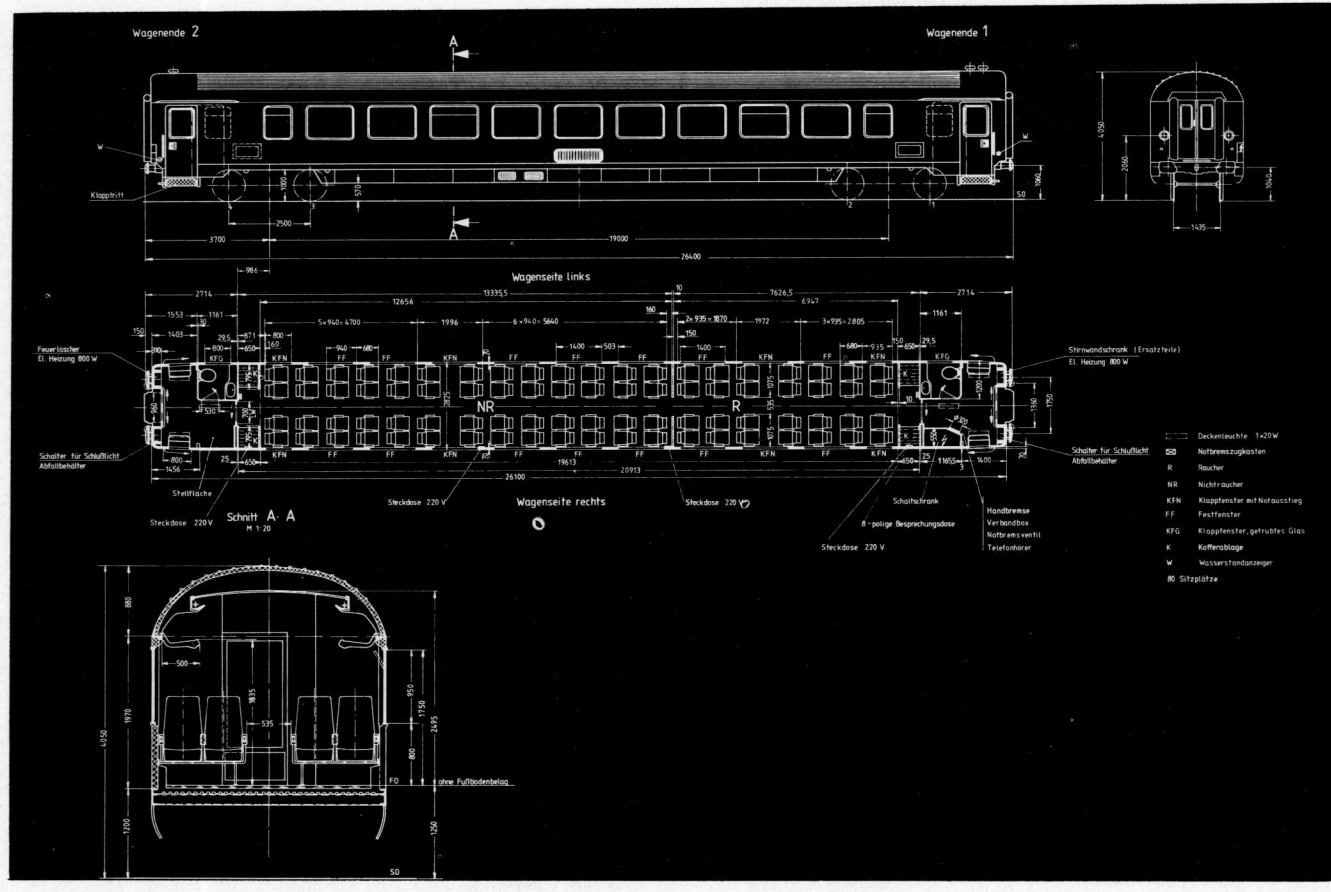

Open saloon passenger coach type Bpmz for Deutsche Bundesbahn (DB)

High-capacity sliding wall wagon for ferry service in Britain, built for VTG

LKM

Lenin Kohászati Müvek

Lenin Metallurgical Works, Miskok-Diósgyör, Hungary

Telephone: 14 731
Telex: 06 2326

Products: Locomotives; passenger carriages; wagons; wheel discs, tyres and axles.

MACOSA

Material y Construcciones, SA

Herreros, 2PN Barcelona -19, Spain

Telephone: 307 05 00
Telegrams: MATERIAL
Telex: 52286 MAYCO-E

Products: Electric, diesel-electric and diesel-hydraulic locomotives; passenger and freight cars.

Chairman: Eugenio Martin Antelo
Managing Director: José Maria Ardevol Vidiella
Chief Sales Director: José Sanz Roca

Constitution: This company was formed in 1947 by the merger of Material para Ferrocarriles y Construcciones, SA of Barcelona and Construcciones Devis, SA of

Valencia. The first was founded in 1895 by Girona Agrafel and made into a limited liability company in 1881. The second was started in Valencia in 1897 by Miguel Devis Pérez as a boiler works, became Construcciones Devis SA in 1929, and in 1941 opened the present factory at Alcázar de San Juan.

Sales: Orders placed by Spanish National Railways (RENFE) include: 50 diesel-electric GM26T 3 345-hp locomotives, 250 grain hopper wagons and 100 box wagons fitted with sliding roofs.
Orders placed by private companies in 1973 include: 350 tank wagons.

MAFERSA
Material Ferroviario SA

Av Raimundo Pereira de Magalhães, 230 São Paulo, Brazil

Products: Freight cars; passenger cars; stainless-steel cars (Budd licence); wrought steel forged wheels; heavy forgings.

Chairman: José Carlos do Couto Vianna

Constitution: Mafersa is divided into three groups: passenger coach division, based in Sao Paulo; freight wagon division, based in Belo Horizonte; and wheel and axle division, based in Cacapava.
Main production items at the 18 500-m² São Paulo passenger coach plant are stainless-steel coaches built under Budd licence.

Sales: For 35 years Mafersa has specialised in transportation equipment and is one of the largest industrial organisations of its kind in Latin America and the largest Brazilian company in sales of railway equipment. For 21 years, up to 1978, it pioneered in Brazil the use of stainless steel in the building of railroad passenger cars, 752 units of which have already been manufactured, with 644 on order.

Telephone: 261-8911-260-4591
Telegrams: Mafersa
Telex: (011) 23862

In its three plants in São Paulo, Cacapava and Contagem Mafersa had manufactured by mid-1979 8 100 freight cars of various types, 830 000 wrought carbon steel wheels and 45 000 railroad axles. In three years (1975—1978) Mafersa's net assets have grown from 320 million cruzeiros to 1 642 million cruzeiros.
The first 22 stainless-steel subway cars for the Rio Metro, of a 270-car order, were delivered ahead of schedule, enabling the Rio Metro to inaugurate the first priority section of their subway system on 5 March 1979. Prior to the Rio Metro order, the first 198 subway cars for the São Paulo Metro were delivered. Now Mafersa is producing 240 additional cars for São Paulo Metro, of which 26 were delivered in time for the inauguration of the first section East/West line on 10 March 1979 and the remaining cars will run on other sections. 150 new cars were ordered by FEPASA — Ferrovia Paulista SA (Railroad System of São Paulo State) in order to meet its suburban network improvement plan. Another 120 suburban cars are being built by Mafersa for the Rede Ferroviária Federal SA (Federal Railroad System). These cars were designed by Mafersa's Brazilian technical personnel.

MAK
MaK Maschinenbau GmbH

Postfach 9009, 2300 Kiel 17, Federal Republic of Germany

Products: Diesel-hydraulic locomotives from 275 hp up to highest power range and for all track gauges; diesel engines for rail traction.

Board of Directors: H Hartung
                     Dr Holtmeier
                     Joseph Kempa
                     Dr Lembcke

Telephone: 0431 3811
Telegrams: MaK Kiel
Telex: mak d 02 99877/78

Constitution: MaK has continued the development of the products of the former Deutsche Werke Kiel AG (DWK) which started designing internal combustion engine railcars in 1920, and has constructed diesel locomotives since 1925.

Type G 761 C standard diesel-hydraulic locomotive
It is radio-controlled, with forward-reverse turbo transmission, 500 kW (680 hp).

V291 built by MAK for German Federal Railway for heavy duty shunting service

Type G 1202 BB standard diesel-hydraulic locomotive
It has radio control; Voith forward-reverse turbo transmission; 1000 kW (1360 hp).

Lightweight diesel-hydraulic railcar type VT 627 built by MAK for German Federal Railway for local and district service

---

MAN
Maschinenfabrik Augsburg-Nürnberg AG
Mechanical and Structural Engineering Division

Head Office: D-8500 Nürnberg, Katzwangerstrasse 101, Federal Republic of Germany
Sales Office: D-8500 Nürnberg 44, Postfach 440 100, Federal Republic of Germany

Products: Light and heavy diesel railcars and multiple unit diesel stock; electric railcars and multiple unit electric stock for ac/dc or ac three-phase supply; underground railway stock; urban railway stock; suspended monorails; passenger stock, luggage and mail vans; freight cars, high-capacity well wagons and bogie trucks for all applications, especially air suspension type.

Chairman: Gerhard Neipp
Directors: Wilhelm Noller
          Heinz Rädeke
          Heinz Hennig

Telephone: 0911/181
Telegrams: Manwerk Nürnberg
Telex: 0622291

Twin-car dc train unit for suburban services in Tunis

Constitution: For over 125 years the railway department of the Nuremburg works has been responsible for pioneering work in the development of railway vehicles. Important developments include the mass production of railway carriages and wagons in 1850, the manufacture of tramcars in 1882, the first steam-operated railcar built for the royal Bavarian state railway in 1906, and the first diesel-operated railcar in 1926.

Sales: Underground railway stock for Nürnberg under repeat order for identical design with dc traction and new ac traction batch production of series Res 687 flat wagons, ET 420 air suspension bogies and prototype EMU trains for Rio.

Type 614 diesel train developed for DB

MARELLI
Ercole Marelli & C SpA

Telephone: 2494
Telegrams: VENTILATOR, Milano
Telex: 31043 MILANO

Viale Edison, 50 Sesto San Giovanni, Milan CAP 20099, Italy

Products: Electric equipment for all types of electric traction and auxiliary equipment.

Managing Director: Umerto Di Capua
Plant and Systems Division, Energy: Giancarlo Lucchini
Traction Department Manager: Ferdinando Gambassi

Constitution: Ercole Marelli & C was founded in 1891 for the production of small electric motors and fans and grew to become a large producer of electric machinery and equipment. Products for the railway industry form an important part of the company's activities.

Sales: Sales include shunt chopper locomotives class E 444 for Italian State Railways (FS), full chopper and traditional electric multiple unit trains for FS suburban services, electronic systems for the tilting body trainsets of both FS and RENFE, diesel-electric locomotives class D 345 for FS; full chopper motor coaches for Milan Metro and light transit system cars for Milan Municipal Transport Authority.

MARINE INDUSTRIES
Marine Industries Ltd
(Railway Car Division)

Telephone: 743 3351
Telegrams: MARINDUS, Quebec
Telex: 055 61081

PO Box 550, Sorel, Quebec J5P 5P5, Canada

Products: Freight wagons.

MARTIN & KING
Martin & King Pty Ltd

Telephone: 305 4160
Telegrams: MARKING, Melbourne

Somerton Road, Campbellfield, Victoria, Australia

Products: Electric, diesel railcars; electric multiple units; passenger coaches; freight wagons.

Constitution: An associate company of Clyde Industries Ltd.

MASCHINEN-EXPORT

Telephone: 2240
Telegrams: MASCHEXPORT, Berlin
Telex: 112461

DDR-108 Berlin, Mohrenstr 53/54, German Democratic Republic

Products: Locomotives; freight wagons, passenger coaches.

Constitution: The exporter of motive power and rolling stock built in the German Democratic Republic.

MBB
Messerschmitt-Bölkow-Blohm GmbH
Helicopter and Transport Systems Division

Telephone: 0906 711
Telegrams: EMBEBE, Donauwörth
Telex: 51843 mbbvd

Industriestrasse, 885 Donauwörth, Federal Republic of Germany

Products: Rail vehicles in lightweight construction for underground and rapid transit commuter services, mainline passenger coaches for short-haul and long-haul services, sleeping cars, dining cars, saloon cars, diesel and electrically powered trainsets, rail service cars, overhead line inspection and maintenance cars, track recording and dynamometer vehicles, ultrasonic inspection vehicles.

Technical Director: Dieter von Hummel
Commercial Director: Dieter Matthies

Constitution: Formerly trading under the name of WMD (Waggon- und Maschinenbau Donauwörth).

Sales: MBB is a leading developer and manufacturer of the electric inter-city express train ET 420/420 for the German Federal Railways, the ET 473 for the rapid transit commuter services of Hamburg, the electric ultra-high-speed ET 403, prototypes of the rapid transit reversible trainset cars for the German Federal Railways, two-car trainsets for the Munich underground railways and the overhead line inspection and maintenance car VT 704.

MECHANOEXPORTIMPORT
10, Mihail Eminescu Street, Bucharest, Romania

Telephone: 12 46 00
Telegrams: MECANEX, Bucharest
Telex: 269

Products: Electric and diesel-electric locomotive railcars; passenger coaches; freight wagons.

Constitution: The Romanian railway rolling stock export/import enterprise.

METALLURGIQUE
Cie Français de Produits Métallurgiques

Telephone: 742 24 50
Telegrams: COMPAWAGON
Telex: 68 444

4 rue de Ventadour, Paris, France

Products: Freight wagons.

METRO-CAMMELL
Metro-Cammell Ltd
(subsidiary of Metropolitan Cammell Ltd)

Telephone: 021-327 4777
Telegrams: METRO, Birmingham
Telex: 337601

PO Box 248, Leigh Road, Washwood Heath, Birmingham B8 2YJ, England

Export Sales: BRE-Metro Ltd, 274/280 Bishopsgate, London EC2M 4XQ, England

Products: Rapid transit cars for surface, sub-surface and underground routes; design and construction of cars for pre-metro and full metro and suburban rapid transit systems.

Chairman: A H Sansome
Director and General Manager: D B Whitehouse
Director and Chief Engineer: F J Bonneres

Production Director: G E Canham
Financial Controller/Secretary: A V Tipper
Sales Manager: W J Wright

Constitution: The company originated from a coach builder's works in London operated by Joseph Wright, who owned most of the stage coaches running between London and Birmingham. He started building railway carriages in 1840, transferred the business to Birmingham in 1845 and within a few years the firm of Joseph Wright & Sons was building rolling stock for railways in Britain, Europe, Egypt, South America, India and Australia. In 1862 the company became Metropolitan Railway Carriage & Wagon Co Ltd and, over the years, having absorbed several other rolling-stock build-

ers, the carriage building interests of Vickers Ltd and Cammell Laird & Co Ltd were merged in 1929 to form Metropolitan-Cammell Carriage & Wagon Co Ltd with the object of concentrating production in the Birmingham area.
In the latter part of 1966 Metropolitan-Cammell absorbed the railway rolling stock business of Cravens of Sheffield. In 1969 Vickers Ltd relinquished their 50 per cent shareholding and a new company was formed for railway matters under the style of Metro-Cammell Ltd.

Sales: Major sales in 1978/79 include 150 further cars for Hong Kong MTRC, making 360 in total, and 75 six-car trains for the District Line (D78 stock) for London Transport.

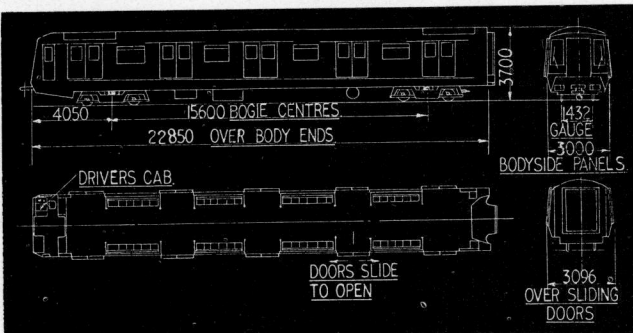

The original order for 140 cars for Hong Kong's MTRC has been increased to 210

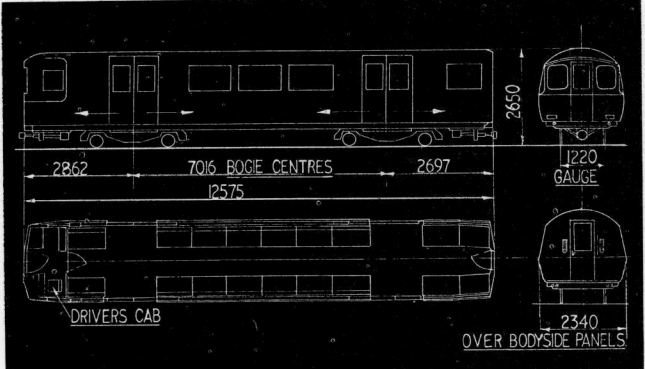

Glasgow Underground has taken delivery of 83 cars from Metro-Cammell

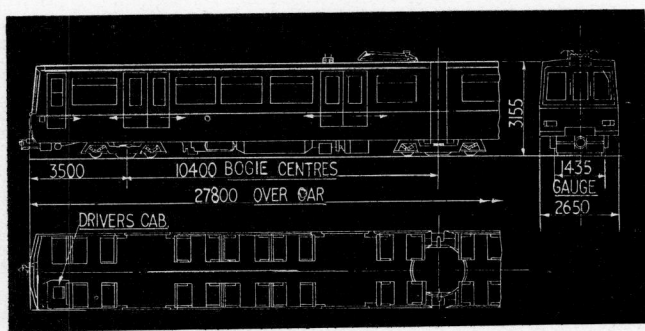

Delivery is in progress on a contract for 88 articulated light rail trainsets for the new Tyne & Wear Metro

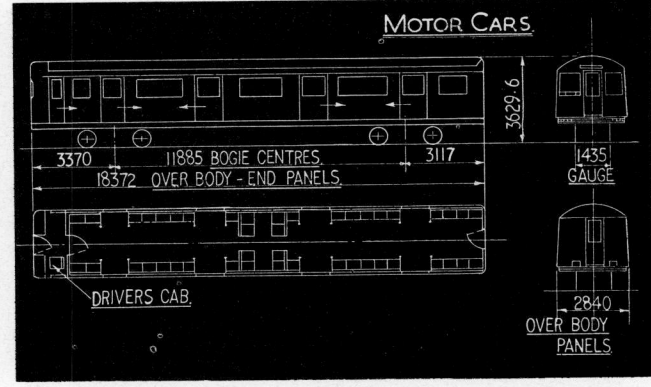

Orders are underway for 450 new-design surface stock cars for London Transport's District line (type D 78 stock)

MEYER
Josef Meyer AG

CH-4310 Rheinfelden, Switzerland

Telephone: 061 88 12 41
Telegrams: JOSEFMEYER, Rheinfelden
Telex: 64894

Products: Freight wagons.

MIN
Masinska Industrija Nis

Sumadijcka 1, Nis, Yugoslavia

Telephone: 65 129
Telegrams: MIN, Nis
Telex: 16187

Products: Diesel-hydraulic locomotives; petrol railcars; electric multiple units; diesel multiple units; freight wagons.

MISKIN CRNI
Vaso Miskin Crni

Industrija Transportnih Sredstava, 1 Masina, Sarajevo, Yugoslavia

Products: Freight wagons; passenger coaches.

Telephone: 41 222/41 234/41 343
Telegrams: MISKIN CRNI, Sarajevo
Telex: 41119

Constitution: Vaso Miskin Crni was founded in 1890 and is ranked among the oldest manufacturers of railway vehicles in Yugoslavia.

MITSUBISHI
Mitsubishi Heavy Industries Ltd
Second Industrial Machinery Department

5-1 Marunouchi 2-chome, Chiyoda-ku, Tokyo, Japan

Products: Electric, diesel-electric, diesel-hydraulic and diesel-mechanical locomotives; freight and tank cars of all types; air-brakes; traction diesel engines.

Telephone: 212 3111
Telegrams: HISHIJU, Tokyo
Telex: J22282

President: Masao Kanamori
Managing Director: Kazuhiko Hamano
Manager, Rolling Stock Section: Eikichi Kojima

Constitution: Founded in 1870, Mitsubishi Heavy Industries Ltd is the largest heavy industry manufacturer in Japan. Annual sales exceed 1 100 000 million Yen (US$ 3 700 million).

Sales: Major sales in 1978/79 include 45 electric locomotives for Spanish National Railways, eight diesel-electric locomotives for Bolivian National Railways, eight electric towing locomotives for Panama Canal Commission, five diesel-hydraulic locomotives for Nippon Kokan KK, 40 freight wagons for Indonesian State Railways and 660 freight wagons for Japanese National Railways.

1 050 hp diesel-electric locomotive for New Zealand
64 diesel-electric locomotives of this type were delivered to New Zealand Government Railways in 1967-69 to be used for general purpose.

80-tonne diesel-hydraulic locomotive built for Nippon Kokan KK (Japan) in 1978

MITSUBISHI ELECTRIC
Mitsubishi Electric Corporation

Telephone: 218 3404
Telegrams: MELCO, Tokyo
Telex: J24532

2-3 Marunouchi 2-chome, Chiyoda-ku, Tokyo, Japan

Products: Electric, diesel-electric, industrial and mining electric battery and trolley locomotives; electric railcars; electric multiple units.

President: Sadakazu Shindo
General Manager (Overseas Marketing Department): Shinichi Yufu
Manager (Transportation Department of Itami Works): Takashi Kitaoka

Capital: Yen 70 064 million (US$ 315 million approx)

Constitution: A member of Mitsubishi Group.

Sales: Major sales in recent years included 207 series 279, 289, 269 electric locomotives, four series 269 chopper electric locomotives, and 216 EMUs for series 432, 440 railcars for RENFE; 262 EMUs for suburban double-decker railcar and 16 EMUs for interurban double-decker railcar, 36 diesel-electric locomotives and ten electric locomotives for PTC NSW; 64 EMUs for General Urquiza, Argentine Railways; 4 978 traction motors, 770 main transformers, 217 silicon rectifiers, 404 tap-changers, 115 ATCs for JNR Shinkansen Line; 110 electric locomotives for JNR (since 1970); 150 chopper controllers for TRTA and other Japanese municipal bureaus.

New equipment: 1 500 V dc, 2 700 kW, 120 000 kg electric locomotive with regenerative braking; 2000 hp, 120 000 kg diesel-electric locomotive including 6-205 kW traction motors and 1 500 kVA ac main alternator; 1 500 V dc EMU including 140 kW continuous traction motors, 85 kVA motor alternator, regenerative braking controllers, for NSW PTC Australia; 3 000 V dc, B-B, 88 000 kg, 3 100 kW, chopper controlled electric locomotive for RENFE; 750 V dc EMU including 130 kW traction motor, two phase chopper controls provided with natural cooling system by means of boiling and condensing heat transfer, for Osaka MTB; 1 500 V dc EMU including 130 kW traction motor, two phase chopper controls provided with natural cooling system by means of boiling and condensing heat transfer, and micro computerised monitoring system for Kyoto MTB; 1 500 V dc EMU including 150 kW traction motor, two phase AVF chopper controls provided with natural cooling system by means of boiling and condensing heat transfer, and micro computerised dynamic testing system for TRTA; newly developed transportation system 6 600/600 V 60 Hz 3-phase, rubber tyre guideway bus system, including four 90 kW dc motor drives per two motor cars and one trailer car, thyristor control, regenerative braking, full automatic operation for KNT.

Series 269 electric locomotive for RENFE
3 000 V dc; rated output 3 100 kW; max speed 140 km/h; weight 88 tonnes; designed by Mitsubishi Electric.

TRTA Yurakucho line ten-car train (6M4T) equipped with Mitsubishi EMU
1 500 V dc catenary; gauge 1 067 mm; max speed 100 km/h; traction motor 150 kW, 1-hour rating with WN gear coupling; two-phase AVF chopper control system with regenerative braking; chopping frequency 660 Hz.

MOËS
Moteurs Moës, SA

Telephone: 019 32 23 52
Telegrams: MOTORMOES
Telex: 41568

62 rue de Huy, 4370 Waremme, Belgium

Products: Narrow-gauge diesel-hydraulic, diesel-mechanical, diesel-mining locomotives.

Chairman: M Wisse
Managing Director: G M G Verschoor
Sales Director: F A C Haegeman

MOUTY
Etablissements Jean Mouty

Telephone: 46 63 20
Telex: 82 178

La Sentinelle (Nord), France

Products: Freight wagons.

MOYSE
Moyse, SA

Telephone: 838 91 06
Telegrams: Locotrol Paris
Telex: Locotro 680765F

7 rue Pascal, 93126 La Courneuve Cedex, France

Products: Diesel-electric and diesel-hydraulic 0-4-0, 0-6-0 and Bo-Bo locomotives from 100 to 1 400 hp and from 18 to 80 tonnes, for all track gauges. These units can be fitted with remote control, flame proof, double traction and low constant speed equipment.

President: G Delille
Directors: A Haffner
A Justafré
J C Gimaray
Sales Manager: M Audra
Export Sales: V Bräunlich

Constitution: Founded by Gaston Moyse in 1922, the company specialises in the manufacture of diesel locomotives. The factory and offices were rebuilt and extended in 1954 and in 1965 additional capital was invested in the company to increase production and extend the product range. At the same time Moyse became a private limited company.

Sales: Major sales in 1977/78 include: Ten locomotives (Bo-Bo) for the National Algerian Steel Corporation. Main characteristics are: weight in working order 90 tonnes; diesel power 900 hp; maximum speed 34 km/h. Ten Bo-Bo locomotives for Cameroon State Railways. Main characteristics are: weight in working order 68 tonnes; diesel power 900 hp; maximum speed 60 km/h. Six Bo-Bo locomotives for the Angola

State Railways.
Main characteristics are: weight in working order 32 tonnes; diesel power 400 hp; maximum speed 40 km/h.

Agents:
Austria:
Firma Büll & Ertel, Industriestrasse B, Nr 12, A 2345 Bruhl-am-Gebirge
Federal Republic of Germany:
Firma Josef Peltzer, Lacombletstrasse 29, D 4 Düsseldorf 1
Italy:
Cark Kälble Italiana Srl, Viale Lazio 6/A, I 20135 Milan
Netherlands:
Rail en Transport Bemo BV, Postbus 435, Oranjelaan 49, 1800 Ak Alkmaar
Switzerland:
Victor Asper Maschinenbau, Seestrasse 205, CH 8700 Kusnacht/Zurich
United Kingdom:
Railway & General Engineering Co Ltd, Midland Works, Meadow Lane, Nottingham NG2 3GN
USA & Canada:
FEDESCO, Federated Equipment and Supply Co Inc, 353 Huntington Way, Bolingbrook, Illinois 60439

Moyse type Y8000 locomotive in French National Railways (SNCF) livery

Moyse type BBF 80 ESA 1400 MGO locomotive built for Régie Départementale des Bouches du Rhône

---

MTE
Société MTE

Telephone: 776 41 62
Telex: 610 425F

Head Office: 32 quai National, 92806 Puteaux, France

Works: Le Creusot, Jeumont, La Plaine St Denis, Champagne-sur-Seine, Lyons, France

Products: Electric, diesel-electric and diesel-hydraulic locomotives and railcars; industrial and mining locomotives; explosion-proof diesel shunting locomotives; railcars; motor coach trainsets; bogies and electrical equipment for high-speed trainsets used on urban and suburban rail transport networks. Design and engineering of any class of traction equipment and motive stock, incorporating the products of the traction divisions of Jeumont-Schneider and Creusot-Loire; planning and implementation of traction policy and commercial strategy of the Francorail-MTE, incorporating; Carel-Fouché, Creusot-Loire, De Dietrich, Jeumont-Schneider and Société MTE.

Chairman: J Lerebours-Pigeonniere
Managing Director: H Jullien

Works at:
Le Creusot, Traction Unit (CL): (power bogies for locomotives and railcar, bogies for fast trainsets and metros).
Jeumont (JS): (traction motors and ac generators).
Plaine St Denis (JS): (traction control equipment for dc-powered locomotive trainsets and railcars, signalling equipment).

Champagne (JS): (ac single-phase current control equipment, auxiliary current converters).
Lyons (JS): (Transformers for ac-powered locomotives, trainsets and railcars).

Sales: One of the main suppliers of the French National Railways (SNCF) and the Paris Metro Transit Authority (RATP), Société MTE, is actively engaged in manufacturing a significant part of the rolling and motive stock for French Railways.
MTE is supplying 400 BB 7200-15000-22000 class electric locomotives; 87 TGV high-speed electric trains; 200 MF 77 Series RATP five-car trainsets; Z 2 class SNCF inter-city electric trains; Marseilles Metro equipment and the interconnection equipment for RATP and SNCF networks in the Paris conurbation.
A major French exporter, MTE has booked substantial orders from abroad in partnership with European and local manufacturers: 50 six-car trainsets for Sao Paulo suburbs; 60 four-car trainsets for Rio de Janeiro suburbs; 68 articulated two-car units for Rio de Janeiro pre-metro; 25 six-car trainsets for Sao Paulo Metro; ten five-car trainsets, repeat order for Santiago Metro; 140 powered cars for Caracas Metro; 40 three-car trainsets for the suburbs of Ankara and Istambul; 30 plus 18 optional BB 4 500 kW electric locomotives, very similar to the SNCF BB 7200 class locomotives for Netherlands Railways; 50 three-car trainsets for Cairo suburbs and 355 1 800-2 400 hp diesel-electric locomotives for Turkey over a ten-year period.
MTE also deals with general network rehabilitation, already well-advanced for the Guinea Railways.

2 400-hp (UIC) diesel-electric Co Co locomotive for Turkish State Railways (TCDD)
200 of this class of locomotive operate on TCDD lines. 150 more are being built in Turkey.

BB 7200 class dc chopper control locomotive supplied to SNCF (4 500 kW)
A closely derived machine is soon to be supplied to the Netherlands.

3 000 V dc chopper control 6-car trainset
In operation on the suburban network for FEPASA (Brazil).

BB 15 000 class locomotive supplied in single phase 25 kV, 50 Hz current, defined for a power of 4 499 kW (6 000 ch) and designed to run at 180 km/h

MTM
La Maquinista Terrestre y Maritima SA

PO Box 94, Calle Fernando Junoy, 2 San Andrés, Barcelona 16, Spain

Products: Electric, diesel-electric, diesel-mechanical and diesel-mining locomotives; marine and stationary diesel engines; railway traction engines; steam generators; electric equipment for railway traction; electric generating units; electric, diesel rail-cars; passenger coaches; freight wagons

Telephone: 345 5700
Telegrams: MAQUINISTA
Telex: 54539

President of the Board of Directors: Alvaro Alvarez Lipkau
Managing Director: Adolfo Ramiro Fernandez
Secretary: Ricardo Fornesa Ribó

MYTISCHY
Mytischy Railway Car Works

Mytischy, USSR

Products: Passenger coaches; subway cars.

Constitution: Member of Energomachexport.

NATIONAL STEEL CAR
National Steel Car Corporation Ltd

Telephone: (514) 866 7461
Telegrams: NASTEEL
Telex: 052 4488 NASTEEL MTL

70 ton air-side dump wagon for the British Columbia Railway, delivered in 1977 by National Steel Car.

Sales Office: Suite 1011, 1155 Dorchester Boulevard West, Montreal, Quebec H3B 2J2, Canada

Products: Freight cars of all types; industrial and speciality cars and car parts.

President and Chief Executive Officer: T F Rahilly, Jr (Hamilton)
Vice President, Engineering: J A Aitken (Hamilton)
Vice President, Finance: R W Cooke (Hamilton)

Vice President, Purchases: L G Dornan (Hamilton)
Vice President, Sales: J W Nelham (Montreal)
Comptroller and Secretary: M G Nichols (Hamilton)
Manager, Special Products: N A Mackay (Hamilton)

Constitution: National Steel Car Corporation was incorporated in 1919 and is a wholly-owned subsidiary of Dominion Foundries and Steel Ltd, Hamilton, Ontario.

NEI

Northern Engineering Industries Ltd
(A merger of Clarke Chapman and Reyrolle Parsons)

Clayton Works, Hatton, Derby DE6 5EB, England

Products: Battery, trolley and diesel locomotives for mining, tunneling and surface applications, including flame-proof locomotives for operation in coal mines.

General Manager: R A Boast

Sales: During 1978/79 major sales went to the National Coal Board (Britain), Yugoslavia, India, Philippines, Mexico and the USA.

Telephone: 0283 812382
Telex: 341 828 Claton G

NEI's 90-hp 15-tonne battery electric locomotive

NIESKY

VEB Waggonbau Niesky

892 Niesky, Federal Republic of Germany

Products: Freight wagons, passenger coaches.

Constitution: Member of Transportmaschinen Export-Import.

Telephone: 661
Telex: 0198 621

2-axle self-discharging wagon for transport of powder and granulate goods, type U-y
The wagon is loaded via a hatch in the upper part of the container. Unloading is done into bunkers between or below the rails.

4-axle well wagon, type Ua-s
The wagon is for transporting bulky goods, especially those with high centre of gravity. The well surface is equipped with fold-down fastening stanchions.

2-axle self-discharging wagon for transport of pig iron slag, type Us-y

---

NIIGATA

Niigata Engineering Co Ltd

4-1 Kasumigaseki 1 chome, Chiyoda-ku, Tokyo 100, Japan

Products: Electric and diesel railcars; diesel-hydraulic locomotives; passenger and freight cars; transit cars.

Chairman: Tomio Nogima
Managing Director: Mitsuaki Ishiyama
Chief Sales Director: Hiroyuki Shono

Constitution: In 1895 Niigata Engineering Co Ltd, was established at Niigata City as Niigata Iron Works of the Nippon Oil Co Ltd. In 1910 Niigata Iron Works separated from the Nippon Oil Co Ltd and became the present Niigata Engineering Co Ltd to manufacture a wide range of heavy industrial machinery. Niigata has expanded to keep pace with increased industrial demand.

Sales: Work delivered or in hand includes diesel railcars for Japanese National Railways, diesel-hydraulic locomotives, railcars, passenger and freight for national and private railways and industrial concerns.

Telephone: 03 504 2111
Telegrams: Nite Tokyo
Telex: 222 7111 NITETOJ

Diesel hydraulic locomotive
Weight 56 tons, engine 600 hp/1 500 rpm × 2 units, max speed 45 km/h, max tractive effort 14 000 kg.

Diesel Railcar
Engine 220 hp/1 600 rpm, max speed 95 km/h, seating capacity 68.

New Niigata transportation system
NTS is a completely automated system for transporting both passengers and cargo by container, pallet etc. The main emphasis of the design is to minimise pollutant emission, material waste, labour requirement, capital and operational costs. The guideway is a U-shaped construction with a refuge line for emergency and a simple quick and accurate switching device. NTS has been adopted by Osaka, Japan for the new Guideway Transportation system.

Electric car
Train formation MC1 M2 TC, passenger capacity 152, max speed 90 km/h, motor capacity MC1 100 kW × 4 sets.

Passenger coach for limited express
Max speed 110 km/h, seating capacity 64, diesel generation 270 hp/1 800 rpm, 210 kVA.

NIPPON SHARYO

Nippon Sharyo Seizo Kaisha Ltd
(Japan Rolling Stock Manufacturing Co Ltd)

Head Office: 1-1 Sanbonmatsu-cho, Atsuta-ku, Nagoya, Japan

Tokyo Office: Kaisei Bldg, 2-33, Nihonbashi-Kabuto-cho, Chuo-ku, Tokyo, Japan

Works: Toyokawa, Nagoya, Narumi, Kinuura, Ohye and Ohtone

Products: Electrical and diesel locomotives and railcars; passenger coaches; freight cars of all types including tank cars; containers; tractors and trailers; steel castings; construction machinery; electrical equipment; steel-structure bridges, chemical plant and vessels.

President: Shunichi Amano
Senior Vice President: Kunio Akahoshi
Chief of Export Division: K Nishimura (Tokyo Office)
K Yamaguchi (Head Office)

Telephone: 882 3311
Telegrams: Nishiya Nagoya
Telex: 447 3411

Telephone: 668 3331
Telegrams: NIPPONSHARYO TOKYO
Telex: 252 2095

Constitution: The founding of this company in 1896 marked the start of railway rolling stock building in Japan. It manufactures all types of motive power and rolling stock and obtains a major share of the home market as well as overseas railways in South-East Asia, Middle East, Africa, America and Australasia.

Sales: Deliveries in 1978/79 to overseas customers include diesel cars and electric cars to Indonesia, passenger cars to Nigeria, freight cars to Zambia and cement tank cars to Indonesia.

Shinkansen electric cars
Type 925 for Tohoku and Joetsu Line, Japanese National Railways. 1 435 mm gauge; max cruising speed 210 km/h.

Electric commuter train for a private railway in Japan
Carbody stainless steel; 1 067 mm gauge.

Diesel-hydraulic locomotive for Steel-Mill Works, wholly controlled with micro-computer
1 067 gauge; weight 60 tons; 200 hp.

High-sided bogie wagon for Zambia Railways
1 067 mm gauge; loading capacity 44.2 tons; Nissha-Barber stabilised bogies.

NOVOCHERKASSK

Telex: 7565

The Novocherkassk Electric Locomotive Works

V/O Energomachexport, 35 Mosfilmovskaya ul, Moscow 117330, USSR

Products: Electric locomotives and railcars.

Constitution: Output at Novocherkassk is due to be trebled between 1978 and 1985 as a result of major investment in production facilities.

New Equipment: Company engines were awarded a USSR State Prize for design of the new VL8VR electric locomotive which has a rated output of 6 520 kW.

Telephone: 0231 17601
Telegrams: ORENKOP, Dortmund
Telex: 0822 222

O & K

Orenstein & Koppel AG

Karl-Funke-Strasse 30, 4600 Dortmund 1, Federal Republic of Germany

Products: Diesel locomotives; railcars; passenger and freight cars; transit stock.

Managing Directors: Walter Borchel
Dr-Ing Helmut Heusler
Dr Heinz-Günter Kohlen
Dr Robert Mann
Dr Bodo Paul
Dr-Ing Alfred Welte

Constitution: The O&K Orenstein & Koppel AG was founded in 1876 at Berlin. The first product of the company was portable and narrow-gauge rail equipment, then the manufacture of robust and inexpensive light railway locomotives. Before the turn of the century O&K began to manufacture standard-gauge locomotives for European and overseas state railways and a whole range of passenger railcars and special wagons for freight traffic. Around 1900 O&K's own construction division was laying railway lines in practically every continent. Between 1903 and 1906, the 600 km long Otavi Railway was planned, built and equipped with rolling stock.
By 1940, 24 000 locomotives had been produced by O&K, 14 000 of these being steam driven and 10 000 being IC-engine powered. Since 1949 the company has manufactured over 8 000 diesel locomotives of all sizes, 10 000 goods wagons, more than 1 000 passenger coaches and about 1 000 railcars for underground and fast suburban services.
O&K employs almost 11 000 people and annually produce and sell products worth more than DM 1 300 million. There are six factories in Germany and three abroad as well as 12 subsidiary companies and more than 200 agencies in Europe and overseas.

Sales: During 1978/79 O & K delivered railcars to Berlin Underground (BVG) and special dining coaches to German Federal Railways (DB) for Quick-Pick services.

Quick-Pick dining coach built for DB by O & K

New Equipment: Includes diesel locomotives: within the power range 60-2 200 hp, service ratings of 6-120 tonnes, equipped with diesel-hydraulic or diesel-electric power transmission, two, three, four or six sets of wheels, for all gauges and for shunting or mainline service.
Railcoaches for passenger traffic; diesel-engined railcars and train sets, electric railcars and multiple unit trains, rapid transit underground trains, passenger coaches, dining cars (in quick pick design), sleeping cars, saloon cars, luggage vans and mail vans.
Wagons for goods traffic: bottom-discharging wagons, large-body tipping wagons, ore wagons, wagons for steel works, tank wagons, bucket cars, tipping wagons, saddle-back wagons, container wagons and side-discharging wagons.

OMS

Officina Meccanica della Stanga

Telephone: 76 04 88
Telegrams: OMS Padova
Telex: 430218

Corso Stati Uniti No. 3, 35100 Padova, Italy

Products: Diesel-electric locomotives, electric and diesel railcars and multiple unit trainsets; passenger cars; freight wagons.

Chairman: Dr Dino Marchiorello
Vice-Chairman: Ing Aldolaial
Managing Director: Ing Ugo Soloni

General Manager: Ing Antonio Romano

Sales: Sales in 1979/80 included: 15 glass-carrying wagons, 150 bogie sliding side wagons for Italian State Railways (FS), 300 bogies (Y25 Cs2 type) for FS, 24 middle distance coaches and 30 suburban coaches.

ORTNER

Ortner Freight Car Co

Telephone: (513) 871 2600

2652 Erie Avenue, Cincinnati, Ohio 45208, USA

Products: Freight cars and components.

President: Robert C Ortner
Vice-President: Henry E Keniston

New equipment: Ortner Freight Car Company engineers and builds standard or special designs of freight cars including gondolas, flat cars, open and covered hopper cars, log cars, as well as the Rapid Discharge self-clearing car. This car is available in various cubic capacities and hopper configurations necessary for handling coal, ores, aggregates, wood chips and other bulk commodities.

The Rapid Discharge car is designed to unload in motion. Its patented electro-pneumatic door mechanism can be operated manually or automatically through a wayside signal. The system utilises an air reservoir mounted on each car and an air line running from the locomotives' compressed air system, independent of the air brake line.
A transverse door design is used on the Rapid Discharge car because this permits use of a full-length centre sill for maximum strength to withstand the forces of train action. All major parts of the door system are readily visible for inspection from wayside. A typical unit train of Rapid Discharge cars can unload in motion in 25 minutes over a trestle. Equipment utilisation is extremely high because of the fast turnaround; labour involvement is minimal, usually one or two men at the dump site and unloading is not

dependent on a single piece of equipment that can break down and disable the terminal.

Unloading in motion is a systematised approach to bulk material handling in which transportation and material handling are isolated from each other. With adequate capacity beneath a dumping trestle, any number of trains can unload quickly and at will, freeing them to return to the point of origin for reloading. One south-eastern US

utility reports unloading nine 70-car trains in a 12-hour period. Materials under the trestle can then be moved or conveyed at a convenient time, and with nominally-sized equipment.

Over 10 000 Rapid Discharge cars are in service world-wide moving coal, ores, aggregates and other bulk materials.

Five-pocket, fully-automated, 100-tonne Rapid Discharge car built for the Santa Fe Railroad

Three-pocket, manually-operated, 100-tonne Rapid Discharge car built for the Georgetown Railroad for construction aggregates

1 500 ft³, 100-tonne covered hopper car for high-density Illmenite ore

100-tonne capacity longwood-log car

Designed to carry full tree-length plywood and pulpwood logs, more than four truck-loads at once. Wood in lengths of 17, 25, 34 and 60 ft can be transported in a variety of different patterns. The log bolsters and posts are specially designed for easy loading and unloading with conventional log handling equipment.

ORVAL
Ateliers de Matériel Ferroviaire d'Orval

53 avenue Paul-Doumer, 75016 Paris, France

Products: Freight wagons.

President: Jacques Marret
General Manager: Jacques Lafin
Commercial Manager: Philippe Gautier

Telephone: 870 82 50
Telex: 62645

Constitution: Founded in 1945, the company designs and builds wagons for the transport and ease of loading and unloading of heavy products, powders and liquids, for the oil, chemical, food, forestry, steel and other industries, hopper and covered hopper cars, tank cars, open cars, flat cars, tippers, special cars. The company holds the licence for the Spitzer system of air discharge of powdered products.

PAFAWAG
PFW Pafawag

Panstwowa Fabryka Wagonow Pafawag, 53-609 Wroclaw ul. Robotnicza 12, Poland

Telephone: 340 61
Telex: 034431

Constitution: Member of Kolmex Foreign Trade Enterprise.

PAKISTAN RAILWAY CARRIAGE
Pakistan Railway Carriage Factory

PO Box 286, Rawalpindi, Islamabad, Pakistan

Products: Passenger coaches; freight wagons.

Chairman: Gulzar Ahmed

Telephone: 67256, 67260
Telegrams: CARFAC, Islamabad

Managing Director: M Rashid
Sales Director: Z I Puri

Sales: In 1978 Bangladesh awarded a contract for 58 broad-gauge passenger coaches, 34 third-class brakes and 24 second/third-class mixed.

PERRY
Perry Engineering Division
(Johns Perry Industries Pty Ltd)

Railway Terrace, Mile End South, 5031 South Australia, Australia

Products: Railway rolling stock.

General Manager: G J Munday

Telephone: 352 1777
Telegrams: SPERRY, Adelaide
Telex: AA 82493

Constitution: In 1966 Perry Engineering Co Ltd merged with Johns and Waygood Holdings Ltd of Melbourne to form the Johns-Perry Group and became part of an Australia-wide structural, mechanical and electrical engineering business with over 3 500 employees.

PETRU GROZA
7, Matei Millo Street, Bucharest, Romania

Products: Mine wagons of 0.75-1 and 1.2 m³ capacity; tipping wagons of 0.36 and 0.4

Telephone: 14 94 30
Telex: 216

m³ capacity; mineral wagons of 1.5 m³ capacity; self-discharge VA-3 wagons of 3 m³ capacity.

PLYMOUTH

Plymouth Locomotive Works
(A Banner Industries Inc Co)

607 Bell Street, Plymouth, Ohio 44865, USA

Products: Diesel-hydraulic locomotives for heavy-duty hauling and switching ranging from 3 to 120 tons; Mine-O-Motive mining locomotive.

Managing Director: William S Sturman

Telephone: (419) 687 4641
Telegrams: Fateco
Telex: 810 491 2552

Sales Manager: Donald Shaver
Sales Director: Beecher Candill
Export Sales: Miles W Christian

Equipment: Mine-O-Motive range of mine locomotive covers: HSD series 1½-10 tons, F series 5-7½ tons, D series 8-16 tons, J series 12-35 tons, M series 25-45 tons.

PRAGOINVEST

(Czechoslovak locomotive export group)

Ceskomoravská, 23 Praha, Czechoslovakia

Products: Locomotives.

PRICE

A & G Price Ltd

Beach Road, Thames, New Zealand

Products: Diesel-hydraulic, diesel-mechanical and battery locomotives; freight wagons.

Managing Director: R S O'Hagan
Resident Manager: J W Wiseman

Constitution: This company stems from a foundry and workshop set up at Onehunga near Auckland in 1868 by two brothers, Alfred and George Price. Their first connection with railways was the supply of undergear and carriage bodies for the new Auckland-

Telephone: 86060
Telegrams: PRICECO, Thames
Telex: NZ 2655

Drury Railway in 1872. The Thames works was opened in 1870 and four years later the Onehunga works was closed down, all operations being concentrated at Thames. The first locomotive, a geared type, was built in 1883 for a gold mine, then in 1903, five years after the railway reached Thames, Price began building locomotives for the New Zealand Railways and continued to do so until 1928 when their last order was completed following a decision by NZR to build all locomotives in Railway workshops.

Sales: The company has produced over 70 diesel-mechanical and diesel-hydraulic locomotives for New Zealand Railways and private users. Production in 1979 included ore cars for the Nauru Phosphate Corp in the Republic of Nauru.

PROCOR

Procor Ltd, Rail Car Division

2001 Speers Road, Oakville, Ontario L6J 5E1, Canada

Products: Freight wagons.

Chairman: S H Bonser
President and Chief Executive Officer: K Jagger
Vice President, Sales: Gordon C Mills
Vice President, Marketing: A Stremecki

Telephone: (416) 827 4111
Telex: 06 98 2241

Constitution: Procor's Rail Car Division designs and manufactures tank cars and freight cars for a great variety of products, for lease to shippers in Canada and the United Kingdom. Procor operates and maintains the largest fleet of railway freight cars (over 14 000) in Canada.

PROCOR (UK) LIMITED

Horbury Wagon Works, Horbury, Wakefield, West Yorkshire WF4 5QH, England

Products: Railway freight rolling stock.

Managing Director: F J Swindell
Financial Controller: N Casson
Director of Sales: J K Jagger

Telephone: 0924 271881
Telex: Procor Horbury 556457

Constitution: Procor (UK) Ltd, a wholly-owned subsidiary of the Trans Union Corporation, Chicago designs, builds, sells, hires, leases, repairs and maintains all types of railway freight rolling stock. With a fleet of over 3 000 wagons, Procor is the largest wagon hiring company in the United Kingdom and has customers in the petroleum, chemical, food and construction industries.

83-ton gross laden weight liquified petroleum gas wagon

50-ton gross laden weight aggregate hopper wagon

50-ton gross laden weight pressure flow pressure discharge wagon

PULLMAN-STANDARD
Division of Pullman Incorporated

200 South Michigan Avenue, Chicago, Illinois 60604, USA

Products: Freight and passenger cars of all types.

President: J A McDivitt
Executive Vice President: E T Ahnquist
Executive Vice President and General Manager, Freight: R A Cumming
Executive Vice President and General Manager, Passenger: C M Parrish
Senior Vice President, Marketing, Freight: Stanley Brown
Vice President, Marketing, Passenger: T W Fenske
International Affairs, Freight: T C Nault

Telephone: (312) 322 7070

Constitution: In 1867 George M Pullman formed Pullman's Palace Car Co to build and operate sleeping cars, the name being changed to the Pullman Co in 1899. In 1921 the Haskell & Barker Car Co, founded in 1852, was acquired and three years later the various car-building activities were consolidated in a new company, Pullman Car & Manufacturing Corporation. In 1927 Pullman Incorporated was formed as the parent company with two main subsidiaries, The Pullman Co operating sleeping cars, and Pullman Car and Manufacturing Corp building cars. In 1934 the latter was merged with Standard Steel Car Co (acquired in 1930) to form Pullman-Standard Car Manufacturing Co. Then in 1959 this company merged into Pullman Incorporated as Pullman-Standard Division. Following a federal court order requiring separation of sleeping car operation and the manufacture of railroad cars, in 1947 Pullman Incorporated sold the Pullman Company to a group of railroads.

RAMON MUGICA
Herederos de Ramon Mugica SA

Barrio de Ventas, s/n Apartado No 14, Irun, Spain

Products: Special wagons to customer's requirements: tank cars, hopper cars, flat cars, bulk powder cars, low-bed type cars, etc.

Telephone: 61 34 45
Telegrams: HEREM
Telex: 36 195 Herem E

Chairman: Juan O Ohlsson
Managing Director: Francisco Mauleón
Chief Mechanical Engineer: José R Jusué
Assistant Manager: Inigo Saldãna

REGGIANE
Officine Meccaniche Italiano SpA

27 Via Vasco Agosti, Reggio Emilia, Italy

Products: Electric, diesel-electric, diesel-hydraulic and diesel-mechanical locomotives, railcars, passenger, pilot, dining, sleeping, saloon cars; freight wagons; rolling stock components.

Chairman: Avv Prof Crisanto Moandrioli

Telephone: 41341, 41741
Telegrams: REGGIANE
Telex: 51265 Reggiane

Managing Director: Dr Ing Pietro Fascione
Administrative Manager: Rag Gino Rovegno
Sales Manager: Dr Ing Edmondo Del Cupolo

Constitution: Founded in 1904 to build rolling stock and, a few years later, steam locomotives. After being largely destroyed during 1943 the works were rebuilt and re-equipped.

REMAFER
Société de Construction et de Réparation de Matériel Ferroviaire

3 rue Christophe Colomb, 75008 Paris, France

Telephone: 723 76 51
Telex: 290471

Products: Rolling stock.

RESITA
Resita Machine Building Works

7 Matei Millo Street, Bucharest, Romania

Telephone: 14 84 30
Telex: 216

Products: Diesel-electric and diesel-hydraulic locomotives.

RIGA
Riga Carriage Building Works
Riga, USSR

Products: Motive power and rolling stock.

Constitution: Member of Energomachexport.

RUHRTHALER
Ruhrthaler Maschinenfabrik, Schwarz & Dyckerhoff KG

Scheffelstrasse 14-28, D-4330 Mülheim/Ruhr, Postfach 01 12 60, Federal Republic of Germany

Hauling capacities and principal details of Ruhrthaler diesel mine locomotives

Telephone: 0208 44131
Telegrams: RUHRTALOKO, Mülheimruhr
Telex: 0856710

Products: Diesel-hydraulic, diesel-mechanical locomotives; suspended monorail.

Type	G 22 H 2	G 30 H 2	G 40 H 2	G 50 H 2	G 50 H/St	G 70 H 2	G 70 HVE	G 100 HVE	G 150 HVE
Throttled capacity (hp) for underground operation (rpm)	23 2 600	28.5 3 000	40 2 800	58 2 550	55 2 400	70 2 550	70 2 400	100 2 000	134 1 800
Continuous capacity (hp) DIN 6270 for surface operation (rpm)	30 3 000	30 3 000	45 3 000	64 2 600	64 2 600	105 2 600	105 2 600	158 1 800	158 1 800
Number of cylinders	2	2	3	4	4	6	6	6	6
Speed infinitely variable (km/h)	0..10.8	0..12.5	0..14	0..17.2	0..17.2	0..15.6	0..14.4	0..14.4	0..14.4
Draw bar pull (kp)	970-395	1 090-440	1 330-515	1 700-555	1 700-550	2 420-760	2 420-880	3 390-1 300	3 890-1 790
Load hauled, in tons — on the level 1:00	121-49	136-55	166-64	212-70	212-69	302-95	302-110	423-162	484-212
¼% 1:400	91-36	103-41	125-48	160-51	160-50	228-70	228-81	320-120	365-165
Rolling resistance 8 kp/ton (against a gradient of) — ½% 1:200	73-29	82-32	100-37	127-40	127-40	182-55	182-64	255-94	291-130
¾% 1:133½	60-23	68-26	83-30	106-32	106-32	151-44	151-52	211-77	242-107
1% 1:100	51-19	58-22	71-25	90-27	90-27	129-37	129-43	180-64	206-90
Length over buffers (mm)	3 200	3 200	3 850	4 000	4 000	4 650	4 950	5 500	5 600
Minimum length for transport approx. (mm)	2 800	2 800	2 450	2 700	2 700	3 200	2 800	3 100	3 115
Width (mm)	850	850	900	900	900	1 000	930	1 050	1 050
Height (mm)	1 400	1 400	1 500	1 600	1 600	1 600	1 650	1 650	1 650
Wheel base (mm)	750	750	900	1 000	1 000	1 100	1 100	1 350	1 350
Radius of smallest curve (m)	8	8	10	10	10	12	12	15	15
Service weight ±5% (kg)	4 000	4 500	5 500	7 000	7 000	10 000	10 000	14 000	16 000
Empty weight ±5% (kg)	3 850	4 350	5 300	6 750	6 750	9 700	9 700	13 700	15 700
Shipping weight ±5% (kg)	3 950	4 450	5 400	6 850	6 850	9 800	9 800	13 800	15 800
Shipping dimensions (m)	3.1 × 0.9 × 1.5	3.1 × 0.9 × 1.5	3.7 × 1 × 1.6	4 × 1 × 1.7	4 × 1 × 1.7	4.4 × 1.1 × 1.7	4.8 × 1 × 1.8	5.1 × 1.1 × 1.8	5.2 × 1.1 × 1.8

Type		D 24 H 2	D 30 H 2	D 45 H 2	D 60 H 2	D 60 H	D 100 H 2	D 150 H	D 175 HL
Continuous capacity		26	30	45	60	60	105	150	175
'B' DIN 6270		3 000	3 000	3 000	3 000	2 250	2 600	1 800	1 800
Number of cylinders		2	2	3	4	4	6	6	10 V
Speed infinitely variable (km/h)		0..12.5	0..12.5	0..15	0..15	0..16.5	0..15.5	0..20	0..20
Draw bar pull (kp)		970-390	1 090-455	1 330-560	1 570-775	1 700-650	2 420-1 230	3 870-1 420	3 870-1650
Loads hauled, in tons	on the level 1:00	121-49	136-57	166-70	196-96	212-82	302-154	484-178	484-206
	½% 1:200	73-28.5	82-33	100-41	118-57	128-48	182-91	292-103	292-121
Rolling resistance 8 kp/ton	1% 1:100	51-19.5	58-23	71-28	83-39	90-32	129-63	206-70	206-83
	2% 1:50	33-11	36-13	43-16	51-23	56-18	79-37	127-39	127-48
	3% 1:33¼	22-7	25-8	30-10	35-15	39-12	56-24	89-25	89-31
Length over buffers (mm)		2 900	3 000	3 600	3 700	3 700	4 500	5 300	5 300
Width (mm)		1 200	1 200	1 200	1 200	1 200	1 700	1 700	1 800
Height (mm)		2 000	2 000	2 200	2 200	2 200	2 800	3 000	3 000
Wheel base (mm)		750	750	1 000	1 000	1 000	1 100	1 350	1 350
Radius of smallest curve (m)		8	8	15	15	15	15	15	15
Service weight ±5% (kg)		4 000	4 500	5 500	6 500	7 000	10 000	16 000	16 000
Empty weight ±5% (kg)		3 800	4 300	5 300	6 250	6 750	9 750	15 750	15 750
Shipping weight ±5% (kg)		3 900	4 400	5 400	6 350	6 850	9 850	15 850	15 850
Shipping dimensions (m)		2.7 × 1.2 × 2.1	2.7 × 1.2 × 2.1	3.3 × 1.2 × 2.3	3.4 × 1.2 × 2.3	3.4 × 1.2 × 2.3	4.3 × 1.7 × 2.9	4.9 × 1.7 × 3.1	4.9 × 1.8 × 3.1

Estimated coefficient of friction between wheel and rail , = 0.25. Details for 600 mm track gauge

SAALASTI OY

Arinatie 4, 00370 Helsinki 37, Finland

Telephone: 90-557 775
Telegrams: 124694 insa sf

Products: Diesel shunting locomotives; road/rail shunting tractor; rail repair locomotives; shunting couplings; snow ploughs.

Chairman: Eng Tapio Saalasti

Range of locomotives produced

Otso shunting locomotives	OTSO 1	OTSO 2	OTSO 3	OTSO 4	Track maintenance truck
Weight (tonnes)	18	26-29	30-40	43	16-36
Power (hp)	115-180	220-240	300-330	430	170
Traction force (tonnes)	5.4	7.8-8.5	11	13	4.3
Speed (km/h)	20-30	20-50	20-25	25	60
Overall length (mm)	6380	7154	7200	7200	10 000
Overall height (mm)	3250	3440	3900	3900	4000
Max width (mm)	3200	3200	3200	3200	3200
Wheel diameter (mm)	960	960	960	960-985	960
Transmission	Hydraulic				
Brakes	Direct action air brake and mechanical parking brake. Train brake if necessary.				
Electrical equipment (V)	24	24	24	24	24

New developments: Latest developments by Saalasti include the Little Bear road/rail shunting vehicle. The basic unit for Little Bear is a rear-wheel driven tractor, the rear wheels of which have been removed and replaced with flanged steel wheels provided with rubber spring action. A drum for the drive of traction-providing rubber wheels has been fixed to the hub of these wheels. The rear rubber wheels for driving over terrain have been mounted on the rear end of tractor chassis. The wheels are hydraulically lowered to the terrain-engaging position or raised to the track-engaging position with the aid of a valve manoeuvred from the driver's cab.

Radio-controlled locomotive, engine power 150-200 hp

Rail repair locomotive
Weighs 15-40 tons, engine power 150-300 hp.

Diesel locomotive Otso, engine power 300-500 hp
These locomotives can be supplied with or without driver's cabin and equipped with radio-control system.

Small locomotive Nalle
It can move from track to track, weighs 16 tons, engine power 150-200 hp. Ordered by Finnish State Railways.

Diesel road/rail Little Bear shunter with a rated output of 110 hp

SANTA MATILDE
Cia Industrial Santa Matilde

Telephone: 252 6090
Telex: 021 21042

Head Office: Rua Espirito Santo, 466-13°. andar, Belo Horizonte, Minas Gerais, Brazil

Export Sales Office: Rua Buenos Aires, 100-7°, CEP 1854, Rio de Janeiro, Brazil

Products: Passenger coaches; freight wagons; containers.

Constitution: Companhia Industrial Santa Matilde, founded in 1916, was initially engaged in mining manganese ore, in Conselheiro Lafaiete, in the State of Minas Gerais where the head office and one of its industrial units are today. Ten years later it began repairing railroad passenger and freight cars and at the same time prepared for the manufacture of rolling stock and electric train units which began in 1946.

The company has a capital of Cr$ 550 million and operates two industrial units. One of these, in Conselheiro Lafaiete (MG), has a covered area of 29 500 m² and a total area of 220 000 m², housing the plants that produce railroad cars of all kinds for every purpose: passenger cars; steel tubing; steel structures and spare parts for railroad cars.
The other plant, in Três Rios (RJ), has a covered area of 50 300 m² and a total area of 300 000 m², and houses the plants that produce electric trains, fibreglass products, naval equipment, harvesters, tractors and hot-dip galvanisation unit. With almost 3 000 employees the company is equipped to produce per year 2 400 freight cars, 60 four-car electric train units, 300 passenger cars, 10 000 hand brake units, 10 000 brake triangles, 7 200 fibreglass hatch covers for cars, a number of fibreglass items intended for passenger cars and electric train units, such as seats, panels, etc.

SCANDIA
Scandia-Randers A/S

Udbyhøjvej 66, PO Box 200, DK-8900 Randers, Denmark

Telephone: 06 42 53 00
Telegrams: SCANDIA, Randers
Telex: 65145 scanas dk

Products: Passenger and freight cars; electric railcars; railbuses.

SCHINDLER
Schindler Carriage & Wagon Co Ltd

CH-4133 Pratteln, near Basle, Switzerland

Products: Electric and diesel railcars; passenger and freight cars.

Managing Director: P Piffaretti
Managers: H Knecht
M Corneille
K Harnisch (Sales)

Telephone: 061 81 55 11
Telegrams: SCHINDLERWAGON
Telex: 62386

Interior of a first-class passenger coach for Saudi Arabia

Passenger train controls for Saudi Arabia

Passenger coach for Jamaica

SCHLIEREN
Swiss Car and Elevator Manufacturing Corp Ltd

CH-8952 Schlieren, Switzerland

Products: Passenger coaches, motor coaches and driving trailers in all-welded steel lightweight and light alloy design; day-cum-sleeper coaches RIC; car transport vehicles, motor luggage cars; wagon bogies for freight liner trains, motor and trailer bogies for all types of rolling stock; streetcars, articulated twin streetcars; lifting jacks for rail and road vehicles as well as for big containers.

Delegate of Board of Directors: Fritz Keller

Telephone: 01 730 70 11
Telegrams: SCHLIECO, Schlieren
Telex: 52961 SWS ch

Director, Rolling Stock: Pierre Matthey
Director, Works: Helmut Agustoni

Constitution: The company was formed in 1899 for the manufacture of rolling stock, an elevator department started in 1917.

Sales: Passenger coaches, driving trailers, luggage vans, tunnel inspection vehicles, articulated twin railcars.

Articulated twin motor coach, type Be 8/8, for the Uetliberg Line of the Sihltal-Zurich-Uetliberg Railway (Switzerland)
Bi-directional unit formed of two close-coupled passenger coaches, second class. Electric traction equipment supplied by Siemens AG.

Articulated twin railcar, type Be 8/8 Forchbahn 2000, for the Forch Railway, Zurich
All-electric vehicle consisting of two close-coupled railcars for passengers; 4 motor bogies supplied by Schindler Carriage and Wagon Co Ltd, Pratteln, and electric traction equipment built by Brown Boveri & Co Ltd.

Shuttle-service train for the Wynental and Suhrental Railway, Aarau (Switzerland)
Consisting of a railcar Be 4/4 and a driving trailer Bt. Electric traction equipment built by
Brown Boveri & Co Ltd.

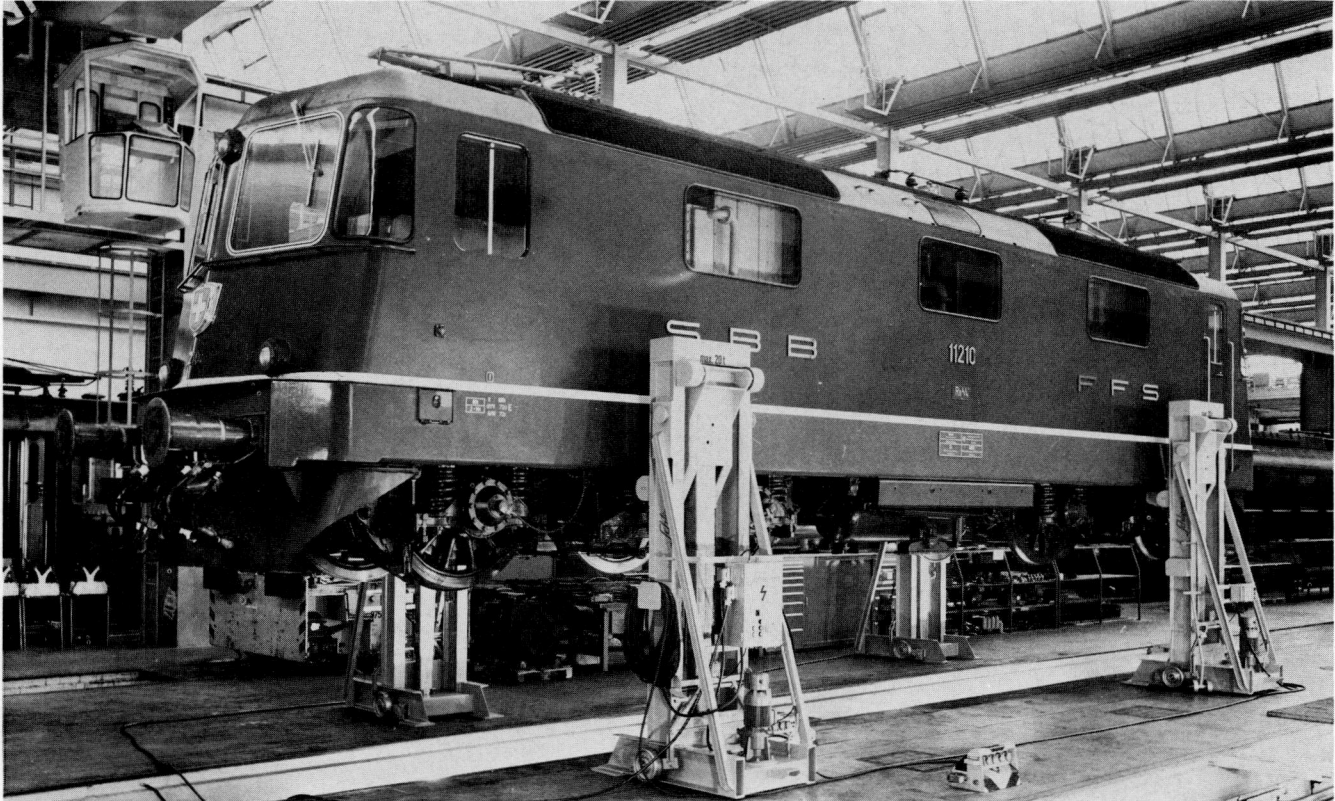

Electric lifting jacks, type Schlieren 20S
Lifting capacity 20 tonnes per jack, with high performance for heavy traction vehicles.

SCHOMA

Christoph Schöttler Maschinenfabrik GmbH

Postfach 1509, D2840 Diepholz 1, Federal Republic of Germany

Products: Shunting, narrow gauge and mining locomotives with hydrodynamic, hydrostatic or mechanical transmission; gang trolleys; trailers and diesel railcars.

Manager: Ing Fritz Schöttler
Sales Manager: Ing L. Niermeyer

Sales: Major sales in 1977/78 include 11 double traction locomotives (250 hp, 22 ton) for MTRC, Hong Kong; 12 flameproof mine locomotives (85 hp, 10 tonnes) for Carbones de Berga, Spain; 20 railcars fitted with hydraulic cranes for German Federal Railways (DB)

Telephone: 05441 2047/2048
Telegrams: SCHÖMA, Diepholz
Telex: 09 41217

Equipment: Schoma locomotives are powered by water or air-cooled diesel engines. Hydrodynamic or hydrostatic transmission is used in most of the locomotives, while mechanical transmission can be supplied optionally for less-powerful narrow-gauge, or mining locomotives. Power is transmitted by propeller-shafts to the axle gears. Final drive consists of cast steel axle boxes with vertical torque supports, bevel gears and pinions with spiral teeth (Gleason or Klingelnberg system) running in anti-friction bearings. Oil seals, mounted on hard ground wear-rings fitted on the axles, or labyrinth packings are used. Lubrication is splash type. Oil levels are checked by sight glasses. The final drive, which is highly efficient, does not need any maintenance apart from oil changing.

Frame is of box type fabricated steel, reinforced with additional cross stays to counteract torsional effects. The front plates are strengthened to take bumping shocks. Inspection holes are cut into side plates to provide accessibility for maintenance and repair purposes. The frame is suspended either by laminated springs or by trapezoidally arranged rubber-metal springs. Mechanically or pneumatically operated sand gear is applied to the leading axle in both directions of travel. The sand boxes are fitted with water-proof covers. All locomotives can be fitted with closed cabins with rubber supported windows of security glass giving a good aspect in both directions. Heat and

noise isolated cab can be provided.
The main controls are dually arranged and all the other instruments are so arranged that they are within easy reach of the driver from any position. Remote controls can be supplied.
Light locomotives are provided with screw type brakes which act on all wheels. In locos with hydrostatic transmission the main braking is through the hydrostatic drive. In heavy locomotives a pressurised direct air brake system is provided. Indirect train air brake can be fitted.

Schoma locomotive, one of eleven ordered for Hong Kong

Schoma rail wagon, one of twenty ordered by German Federal Railways

---

SECHERON

SA des Ateliers de Sécheron

14 avenue de Sécheron, 1202 Geneva 21, Switzerland

Products: Complete electrical equipment for trolleybuses; components for locomotives and rolling stock; wheel flange lubricators; earthing brushes; manual and automatic couplers; dc circuit breakers; complete dc substations.

General Manager: C Rossier
Sales Manager: A Reymond
Manager, Traction Division: R Kratzer
Deputy Manager, Traction Division: H Hintze

Constitution: Member of the Brown Boveri Group. The company was founded as A de Meuron & Cuenod for the manufacture of electrical equipment and in 1883 was

Telephone: 022 32 67 50
Telegrams: Electricité Geneva
Telex: 22130 SAAG CH

awarded a diploma for a two-pole generator shown at the Swiss National Exhibition at Zurich. In 1884 the first power transmission was carried out, and by 1891 35 power transmission installations and 40 power stations had been completed. By this time the name had been changed to Compagnie de l'Industrie Electrique et Mecanique. In the traction field, the electrical equipment for a number of tramways and railways had been supplied when, in 1903, the first application of high voltage to electric traction was given to the metre-gauge St Georges de Commiers-La Mure Railway (2 400 V).

Sales: Sécheron has supplied electrical equipment with power chopper control for trolleybuses in Switzerland, Bergen (Norway), Budapest (Hungary) and Vancouver (Canada).

SEMAF

Société Générale Egyptienne de Matériel des Chemins de Fer

Ein Helwan, Cairo, Egypt

Products: Railcar trailers; passenger coaches; freight wagons.

Chairman: Eng F Abu Zaghla
Technical Director: Eng H F Babyoomy
Commercial Manager: Eng F El-Barkouky

Telephone: 38715
Telegrams: SEMAF, Cairo
Telex: 2364 ORIP UN

SGI

Società Gestioni Industriali SpA

62012 Civitanova Marche, Italy

Products: Freight cars of all types, pressure tank cars for compressed gas and acids; refrigerator cars; special tanks for motor vehicles.

Managers: Dott Giuseppe Manni (Administration and sales)
Dott Ing Giorgio Caputo (Technical and production)

Telephone: (0733) 72 918/72 787/770 493/770 555
Telex: 566 896 SOGESTIN
Telegrams: ROTABILI CIVITANOVA MARCHE

Constitution: In 1957 SGI took over the business of Costruzioni Meccaniche A. Cecchetti, which had been wound up previously, having been operating since 1892.

S-G-P

Simmering-Graz-Pauker AG

Mariahilfer Strasse 32, 1071 Vienna, Austria

Products: Diesel and electric locomotives; diesel and electric railcars; passenger and freight rolling stock; special wagons.

Telephone: 02 22/93 05 21
Telegrams: ESGEPE, Vienna
Telex: 32574/01 32767

Sales: Delivery of two-car sets for Vienna Metro by S-G-P was on schedule in 1978 and several sets have been in regular service since 1973.

SIAM DI TELLA

Siam di Tella Ltda (Division Electromecanica)

Derqui 1868, San Justo, Buenos Aires, Argentina

Telephone: 651 0020/9
Telegrams: SIAMLECTRI
Telex: 012 1046

Products: Electrical equipment for diesel and electric locomotives.

SIDERURGIA

Ferrovias y Siderurgia SA

Cedaceros 4, Madrid 14, Spain

Products: Freight wagons.

Telephone: 222 6490
Telegrams: FERROVIAS, Madrid

President: Don Carlos Roeb Ungeheuer
Director General: Don Luis Rios Sidro

SIEMENS

Siemens Aktiengesellschaft

Power Engineering Group, Railway Department

Telephone: 09 131 71
Telegrams: SIEMENS, erlangen
Telex: 6 29 871

Werner-von-Siemens-Strasse 50, Postfach 32 40, D-8520 Erlangen 2, Federal Republic of Germany

Products: Electric and diesel-electric vehicles and associated electrical equipment for mainline, interurban, urban-rapid-transit, underground, narrow-gauge, industrial and mine railways, also for tramways and trolley bus systems; power transmission and overhead contact wires including accessories and fittings, traction power supply equipment; electrical equipment for railway stations and workshops.

President: Peter von Siemens
Chairman: Bernhard Plettner
Director of Rolling Stock Department: Karl Werner Seibert

Sales: Equipment for 146 Class 111 Locomotives Bo Bo with a continuous rating of

4 040 kW for inter-city and freight services of the German Federal Railways (DB). The electrical equipment of the locomotives with a top speed of 160 km/h has been developed by Siemens AG. The locomotives are based on the well-proven E 110 Series keeping such main components as the traction motors, drives, tap changers etc, but also incorporating improvements resulting from experience gained in service and from technical advances in this field.

As member of the 50 c/s GROLLP, comprising ACEC, AEG, Alsthom, Brown Boveri, MTE and Siemens, Siemens is participating in deliveries for numerous Railways eg South Korea, Portugal, India and Yugoslavia. Of special importance is an order of 100 thyristor-controlled freight traffic Co Co locomotives (Class 7E) for the South African Railways (SAR). Delivery ended in 1979.

Class 7E thyristor-controlled locomotive for South African Railways
With mechanical equipment by Union Carriage, the 50 c/s Group designed and built the electrical equipment.

E111 for German Federal Railways
Based on the proven E110 series, the E111 has a top speed of 160 km/h and is intended for inter-city, commuter and freight services. Mechanical equipment by Krauss Maffei; electrical components by Siemens.

SIG
Schweizerische Industrie-Gesellschaft (Swiss Industrial Company)

CH-8212 Neuhausen Rheine Falls, Switzerland

Telephone: 053·8 15 55
Telegrams: SIG, Neuhausenamrheinfall
Telex: 7 68 02 sig ch

Products: Air-conditioned luxury train units; railcars and pilot cars; rapid transit stock; commuter trains; single and articulated type tramway cars; rack and pinion stock; shunting locomotives; passenger coaches; saloon coaches; mail vans and baggage cars; special transport cars; high-speed air-sprung and other type of power and trailer bogies; all-welded light alloy integral carbody designs; special system of tilting carbody suspension; specific designs of draught-free, dust- and water-proof intercar gangway crossovers for urban, suburban, inter-urban and long distance traffic stock; miscellaneous components for all kind of rail vehicles.

Chairman of the Board: Fritz Halm
Managing Director: Wolfgang Gähwyler
Director, Coach Factory: Peter Gsell

Constitution: Founded in 1853 for the manufacture of railway rolling stock.

Sales: Deliveries and work in hand during 1977/78/79 include: modified air-conditioned TEE-type express trains for long-distance operation on the Ontario-Northland Railway in Canada; air-conditioned light aluminium alloy Swiss express coaches with tilting carbody suspension for the Swiss Federal Railways; standard passenger carriages for domestic and international traffic; various types of power car, pilot car, and coach for Swiss Private Railway Companies, ie Montreux-Oberland-Bernois, Gruyère-Fribourg-Morat, Furka-Oberalp-Railway etc; high power railcars for the South Eastern Railway; commuter train units for the Bernese regional traffic system VBW/SZB, Ferrovie Autolinee Regionali Ticinesi, Ferrovia Lugano-Ponte Tresa; CLRV/four-axle single tramway motor cars for the Toronto Transit Commission TTC/Canada; type Be 4/6 articulated light rail vehicles for NS/NV Verenigd Streekvervoer Westnederland (Utrecht/Nieuwegeinlijn); air-sprung motor bogies for SGM-sprinter-type train units of the Netherlands Railways; power and trailer bogies for diesel-railcars and two-coach diesel-train units of the Netherlands Railways; extra-wide inter-car gangway crossovers for metro-train units of the Hongkong Mass Transit Railway Corporation and for Lyntog-type trains of the Danish State Railways; special inter-car gangway crossovers for type Z-2 railcar units of the French National Railways, generator vans, restaurant cars and passenger coaches of the Saudi Government Railroad, type 7 passenger carriages of the Norwegian State Railways as well as three-car EMU train units of the Kowloon-Canton-Railway.

Two-coach commuter trainset of the Ferrovie Autolinee Regionali Ticinesi, passing over the lattice bridge near Intragna on the famous Locarno-Domodossola (Centovalli) line
Train units designed and built by SIG.

SIKORSKY
Surface Transportation Systems sub-division of Sikorsky Aircraft Division of United Aircraft Corporation

Stratford, Connecticut 06602, USA

Telephone: (378) 6361

(Sikorsky has withdrawn from manufacture of railway equipment including the gas-turbine powered Turbo Trains originally produced for Canadian National.)

SIMPLEX
Simplex Mechanical Handling Ltd
(Subsidiary of The Wemyss Development Co Ltd)

Simplex Works, Elstow Road, Bedford, Bedfordshire MK42 9LB, England

Products: Narrow-gauge diesel-mechanical and diesel-hydraulic locomotives from two to 14 tons.

Chairman: A M J Wemyss
Managing Director: R A Wenham

Telephone: 0234 56422
Telegrams: SIMPLEX, Bedford
Telex: 82254 Simbed g

Sales: In addition to the many units in daily use in the home market, large numbers are in service overseas, particularly in Africa and the Far East, including approximately 1 000 in South Africa, 400 in East Africa and 300 in Malaysia.

Locomotive Range: G Series 2¼-3 tons, 40S Series 2½-4½ tons, 60S Series 4-6 tons, U Series 5-10 tons, T Series 9-12½ tons.

Simplex Series T narrow-gauge locomotive re-designed for use on the Indonesian sugar plantations

SKODA
Skoda, Plzen

31600 Plzen, Námesti Ceskych Bratri 8, Czechoslovakia

Products: Electric locomotives.

Telephone: 211
Telex: 154221
Telegrams: SKODA, Plzen

Constitution: Since production of electric locomotives began in 1927, Skoda has manufactured more than 3 500 units.

Type 77E freight locomotive
Bo-Bo + Bo Bo axle arrangement, built for Polish State Railways and first produced in 1976. Traction current 3 000 V dc; gauge 1.435 m; total weight 2 × 82 tonnes; output 4 080 kW; max speed 100 km/h.

Type 68E universal locomotive
Designed for hauling passenger and freight trains over Bulgarian State Railways' main lines, the 68E operates BDZ lines as class 43R. First produced 1975. Axle arrangement: Bo-Bo; traction current 25 kV 50 Hz; gauge 1.435 m; total weight 87 tonnes; output 3 020 kW; max speed 130 km/h.

Type 66E express locomotive
Used by Soviet Railways for express service, the Bo-Bo + Bo-Bo type 66E has an output of 8 000 kW, total weight of 152 tons and operates SZD lines at max speed of 200 km/h.

Type 51E shunting locomotive
The 51E, built for Czechoslovak State Railways, has a Bo-Bo arrangement and is widely used on CSD's 25 kV 50 Hz electrified lines.

SLM
**Schweizerische Lokomotiv-und Maschinenfabrik
(Swiss Locomotive and Machine Works)**

CH-8401 Winterthur, Switzerland

Products: Electric and thermal mainline and shunting vehicles for adhesion railways; electric and diesel traction units for rack railways, including traction units for combined rack and adhesion operation; special-purpose rail vehicles; industrial gears; gears for special vehicles; light-metal castings.

President, Board of Management: Rudolph Schmid
General Manager: K von Meyenburg
Commercial Department, Deputy Vice President: Dr M Knüsli
Technical Department, Assistant Vice President: E Künzler
Works Department, Assistant Vice President: R Konrad
Sales Department, Assistant Vice President: W Grütter

Telephone: 052 85 41 41
Telegrams: LOCOMOTIVE, Winterthur
Telex: 7 61 31 slm ch

Electric adhesion locomotive Ge 4/4 111 for the Furka-Oberalp Railway

SNAV
Société Nouvelle des Ateliers Vénissieux

4 ter avenue Hoche, 75008 Paris, France

Products: Railway wagons; ISO containers.

President: J Dambrine
Assistant General Managers: H Foullon
G Reille

Telephone: 766 04 16
Telegrams: FAUVGIR
Telex: 650 337

Commercial Director: J Martin

Constitution: Located in the south-east outskirts of Lyons, the works occupy an area of 42 acres (17 hectares) of which 15.5 acres (65 000 m²) are covered.

SNIA
Divisione Ingegneria

20121 Milan, 18 via Montebello, Italy

Telephone: (02) 63321
Telex: 320 503

Products: Electric locomotives; suburban trainsets; passenger coaches; freight wagons; refrigerator wagons; containers.

SOCIMI
Società Costruzioni Industriali Milano SpA

Head Office: 20122 Milan, via S. Calimero 3, Italy
Works: 20082 Binasco, Via Enrico Fermi 25, Italy

Products: Electric trainsets for suburban railways and transit systems, diesel locomotives, passenger coaches, trams, freight wagons to UIC and AAR subsidiaries.

Chairman: Dr Eng Alessandro Marzocco
Managing Director: Dr Eng Pierino Sacchi
Export Sales: Argo Pignedoli

Sales: Orders placed during 1977/78 included: 28 passenger coaches to Ferrovie Nord of Milan, 10 single-motor bogies (five to ATM of Milan, five to ACOTRAL of Rome), 40 motor bogies for motor coaches to Ferrovie Nord of Milan, 10 pilgrinage coaches to FS (Italian State Railway), 150 EAOS cars to FS, and 25 move locomotives to FS.

Telephone: 02 54 65251/5
Telex: 31331

Body shell of a Socimi transit car for Milan with a motor bogie in the foreground

SOFER
SOFER—Officine Ferroviarie, SpA

Via Miliscola 33, Pozzuoli (Naples), Italy

Products: Electric, diesel-electric and diesel-hydraulic locomotives; electric and diesel trainsets; diesel and electric railcars; trailers; passenger coaches of all types and classes; luggage and mail vans; motor and carrying bogies for articulated electric trainsets.

Telephone: 867 1200; 867 2522/3/4; 867 2543
Telegrams: SOFER, Pozzuoli
Telex: 710048 SOFER

Chairman: Dr Ing Giuseppe Capuano
General Manager: Dr Ing Giovanni Alfano

SOMA
Soma Equipamentos Industrias SA

Head Office: Parque Industrial Mariano Ferraz, Avienda Soma, 700 Sumaré, São Paulo, Brazil

São Paulo Office: Avienda Brigadeiro Faria Lima, 1709-7° andar conjumto A CP 2321, São Paulo, Brazil

Products: Freight cars; tank cars; refrigerator cars; ore cars; ingot cars; hopper cars; car building, repairing, maintenance and leasing.

Constitution: The company was founded in 1929 and was the first company in South

Telegrams: SOMAFER
Telephone: 210 2218
210 2925

America to manufacture freight cars. It has specialised in the development of refrigerator cars and tank cars which are leased to various concerns for transportation. In addition to the usual tank cars SOMA developed and built 32 large ones of a capacity of 70 000 litres in 1956, designed and built 18 units of 92 000 litres capacity for 1.6 m gauge in 1973, and one 100 000-litre unit delivered in 1974.
In addition to the Railroad Division, there is an Equipment Division whose products include compressors and blowers, equipment for the cement industry and equipment for mining and processing industries.

SOREFAME
Sociedades Reunidas de Fabricações Metálicas, SARL

Head Office: Rua Vice-Almirante Azevedo Coutinho, Amadora, Portugal

Works: Amadora, Portugal

Products: Passenger and freight cars; locomotives; electric trainsets; special wagons.

Board of Directors: Eng Eduardo Abranches de Magalhães
Dr Dominique M G Vincent Rousseau
Dr Antunes da Silva
Rolling Stock Sales Manager: Eng M Andrade Gomes

Constitution: The company was established in 1943, and has supplied rolling stock for Portugal, Africa, North America and Brazil as well as electromechanical equipment for hydro-electric and thermal power stations (classical and nuclear), equipment for the chemical and petroleum industry, offshore equipment for oil exploration and production.

Sales: Orders placed by Fepasa (Brazil) continued throughout 1979: design of 50 electric stainless-steel three-car trainsets and the supply of related 50 motor coaches which were nearing completion in 1979 in collaboration with ACEC (Belgium), Mafersa and Villares. Deliveries were carried out at the rate of four cars a month; 30 diesel locomotives for the Portuguese National Railways are in full production for delivery during 1980; 58 passenger cars for the Portuguese National Railways (Cascais Line), deliveries to begin in the second quarter of 1980 for completion during the first quarter of 1981; 40 motor coaches for the Lisbon Underground scheduled for delivery during 1982. A new contract was signed in 1979 with the Portuguese National Railways for the supply of 15 electric stainless-steel three-unit trainsets.

Telephone: 97 60 51
Telegrams: SOREFAME, Amadora
Telex: 12 608/16 101 SOREFAM-P

Two new motor cars being shipped out of Lisbon and bound for Fepasa (Brazil) in late 1979

SOULE
Soulé-Fer et Froid

PO Box 1, 65200 Bagnères-de-Bigorre, France

Telephone: (62) 95 07 31
Telegrams: Soulé-Bagneres de Bigorre
Telex: 530 179 SOULÉ bagnb

Products: Diesel railcars and trailers; passenger cars; insulated and mechanically refrigerated wagons.

Chairman: André de Boysson
General Manager: Joseph Anglade
Sales Director: Dominique Outters

Constitution: Founded in 1862, the company has specialised in the manufacture of standard and metre gauge diesel-electric railcars and passenger cars, metre and standard gauge insulated and mechanically refrigerated wagons and standard gauge postal cars for European systems.

Sales: Standard and metric gauge railcars and passenger coaches for African railways; containers and refrigerated wagons for French National Railways; 115 postal vans for Postes Françaises.

Passenger coach for Gabon

Refrigerated wagons for French National Railways

Postal vans for Postes Françaises

SOUTHERN IRON
Southern Iron & Equipment Manufacturing Operations

Telephone: (404) 457 3176

PO Box 81067, 5522 New Peachtree Road, Chamblee, Georgia 30341, USA

Products: Freight cars, freight car leasing.

President (Railcar Division): C Richard Barney

Vice President, Sales: Jack Foster
Director, Manufacturing: J A Wilde

Constitution: Southern Iron was founded by Frank P Kern in 1889 and is now a division of Evans Transportation Co, a wholly-owned subsidiary of Evans Products Co.

STAG
Stag Ltd

Telephone: 085 9 19 02
Telex: 7 42 69

CH-7304 Maienféld, Switzerland

Products: Tank wagons for the transport of dry flowable materials with pneumatic discharge.

STANDARD

The Standard Railway Wagon Co Ltd
A Mercantile Credit Co

Green Lane, Heywood, Lancashire OL10 1NB, England

Products: Freight cars of all types.

Chairman: P R Pollard
Managing Director: L T Reddy

Subsidiary: Railease Ltd (formed to supply wagons on hire throughout the UK).

Telephone: 0706 64135/9
Telegrams: WAGONS, Heywood
Telex: 63327

Constitution: The L & Y Works at Heywood have been building railway wagons for over a century. The company designs and builds all types of four-wheel and bogie freight rolling stock.

Sales: Deliveries include a high-capacity pressure discharge wagon for soda ash. The wagon is of 50 tons GLW and has a capacity of 45 m³

STEELE

E G Steele & Co Ltd

25 Dalziel Street, Hamilton, Lanarkshire ML3 9AU, Scotland

Associated Companies: SA Ateliers de Construction de Jambes-Namur, Belgium

Directors: E G Steele Dipl. R.T.C., J.P.
    M S Steele
    J G Steele, B.Sc.

Telephone: 0698 283765
Telegrams: MOUNTINGS Hamilton
Telex: 77454

Products: Locopulsor shunting machines; wagon mountings.

Constitution: E G Steele & Co are rolling stock contractors, hirers, repairers, and suppliers of wagon mountings. They also supply purpose-built wagons for internal works traffic. They are the British manufacturers of the Locopulsor shunting machines.

STEEL INDUSTRIES

K T Steel Industries Pvt, Ltd

Chattan, 9 SK Barodawalla Marg, PO Box 6517, Bombay 400 026, India

Products: Rolling stock.

Chairman: T K Gupta
Chief Sales Director: N K Gupta
Export Sales Director: S R Gupta

Sales: Principal sales during 1978 were mineral wagons for Iranian State Railways and wagon spares for Sri Lanka Government Railway.

Insulated milk tanker built by KT Steel
The barrel is made of stainless-steel and has a capacity of 40 000 litres

Telephone: 38 24 42
Telegrams: METTICORAIL, Bombay
Telex: 011 2649

STROJEXPORT

(Czechoslovak foreign trade corporation for the export and import of machines and machinery equipment)

PO Box 662, Václavské n 56, Prague 1, Czechoslovakia

Telephone: 2131
Telegrams: STROJEXPORT, Prague
Telex: Prague 121671

Products: Strojexport handles all transactions for the export of passenger and freight rolling stock built by Czechoslovak Wagon Works.

STRÖMBERG

Oy Strömberg Ab

Head Office and Vaasa Works: PO Box 69, SF-65101 Vaasa 10, Finland
Helsinki Works: PO Box 118, SF 00101, Helsinki, Finland

Products: Electric drives, especially traction drives for trains, undergrounds, locomotives, trams and trolley buses.

Chairman: Mika Tiivola
Managing Director: Antti Potila
Chief Sales Director: Lars-Erik Hurriken
Export Sales Director (electric drives): Vesa Kivinen

Sales: The traffic authorities of Rotterdam (Rotterdamse Elektrische Tram-RET) in The Netherlands placed an order in September 1979 for a series of 13 articulated tramcars. The series will be equipped with the traction motor drive based on inverter techniques originally developed for Helsinki metro trams by Oy Strömberg.

Telephone: (901) 258 222 (Vaasa) (90) 550045 (Helsinki)
Telegrams: Dynamo Vaasa
Telex: 74211 strv sf (Vaasa) 124405 strp sf (Helsinki)

New equipment: Oy Strömberg has long had the thyristor-inverter controlled ac induction motor drive under intensive study and development. The traction motor drives of electric vehicles have been the primary objective. After successful prototype test runs it was possible in the beginning of 1974 to offer an ac induction motor drive to the Helsinki City Metro Office for their new metro coaches. In December 1974 the Helsinki City decided to purchase six coaches, which are to be provided with the ac induction motor drive. The following were the most decisive features: a robust ac induction motor as a traction motor requires little maintenance and, above all, the total weight of the drive proves to be extremely favourable. Further mention can be made of the properties of this drive in regard to the avoidance of slide and slip. In the Helsinki Metro this is of special importance, as most of the metro track runs in the open.

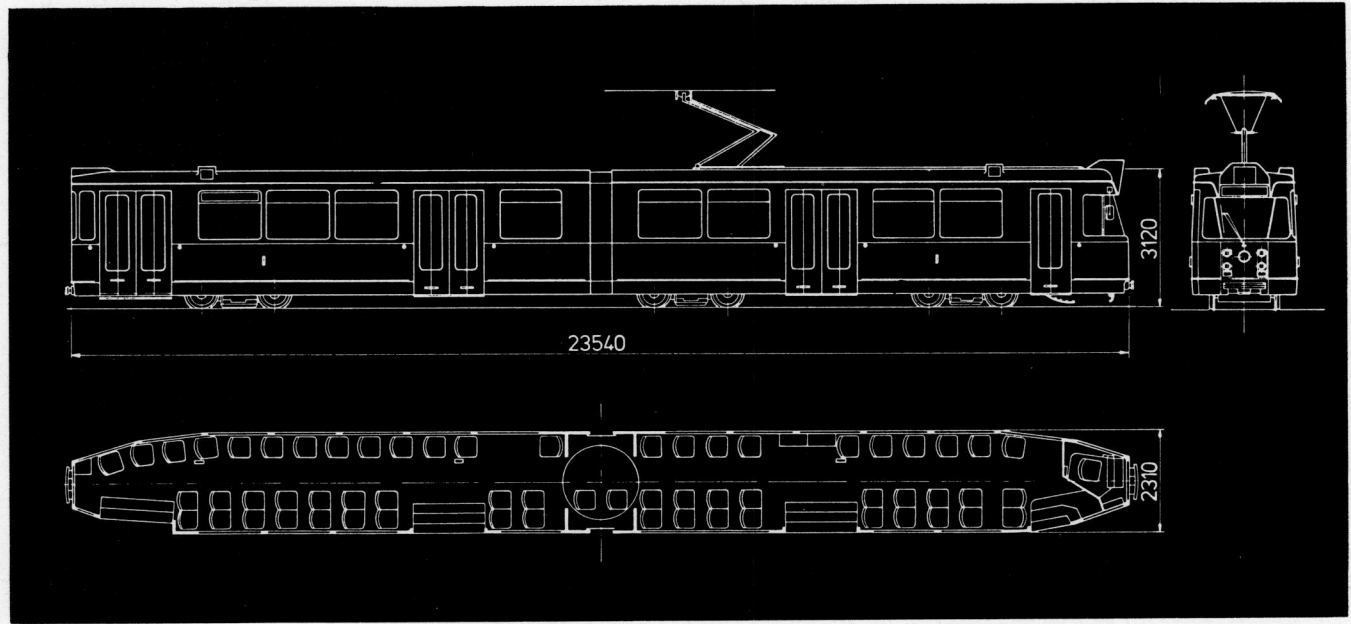

Dimension drawing of the new articulated tramcars order by Rotterdam
Strömberg will equip a series of 13 cars with inverter-controlled traction motor drive.

Strömberg's ac induction motor drives are used as fraction motor drives in the Helsinki metro trains

Strömberg supplied the electric drives and equipment for the two-car electric suburban trainsets built by Valmet for Finnish State Railways (VR)

Sales:

Vehicle	Purchaser	Contractor	Electric drive	Quantity	Delivery time
Electric train	The Finnish State Railways	Valmet Oy (Finland)	Oy Strömberg Ab	100	1968—1981
Metro train	Rapid Transit Office of the City of Helsinki	Oy Strömberg Ab	Oy Strömberg Ab	3	1971—1972
Metro train*	Rapid Transit Office of the City of Helsinki	Metrovaunut Ay (Finland)	Oy Strömberg Ab	42	1977—1984
Electric locomotive	The Finnish State Railways	Energomachexport (USSR)	Oy Strömberg Ab	85	1971—1980
Articulated tramcar	Helsinki City Transport	Valmet Oy	Oy Strömberg Ab	40	1973—1975
Articulated trolleybus	Winterthur Municipal Traffic Authority (Switzerland)	Volvo Lyss & Carrosserie Hess AG (Switzerland)	Oy Strömberg Ab/ Hanel AG	1	1973
Articulated trolleybus	Winterthur Municipal Traffic Authority (Switzerland)	Adolph Saurer AG & Carrosserie Hess AG (Switzerland)	Oy Strömberg Ab/ Hanel AG	1	1977
Electric locomotive	The Finnish State Railways	Oy Strömberg Ab	Oy Strömberg Ab	1	1979
Trolleybus	Helsinki City Transport	Oy Strömberg Ab Oy Wiima Ab Oy Suomen Autoteollisuus Ab	Oy Strömberg Ab	1	1979
Diesel-electric locomotive, power increase	The Finnish State Railways	Oy Wärtsilä Ab	Oy Strömberg Ab	1	1980
Consulting agreement	Holec Machines & Systems (Netherlands)	Oy Strömberg Ab			1979

*with ac traction drive

STRÖMMENS

A/S Strömmens Vaerksted

PO Box 83, N-2011 Strömmen, Norway

Products: Electric trainsets; diesel railcars; passenger and freight cars of all types; tramcars and subway cars; containers.

Managing Director: P Hauan
Technical Director: H S Svendsen

Constitution: The company was established in 1873 for the manufacture of railway

Telephone: 02 71 36 40
Telegrams: VERKSTEDET, Strömmen
Telex: Oslo 11551 SVSTR N

rolling stock and is now the only car builder in Norway. It took over the rolling stock building activities of A/S SKABO in 1960 and A/S HÖKA in 1968.

Sales: On 1 April 1979 Strömmens became a subsidiary company of NEBB, a member of the Brown Boveri Group.
Recent deliveries include passenger coaches and goods wagons for Norwegian State Railways and electric cars for Oslo Underground.

STUDÉNKA

Vagonka Studénka, np, Studénka, Czechoslovakia

Products: Passenger coaches, freight wagons, electrical components and motors.

Telephone: 713 73/714 66
Telegrams: VAGONKA, Studenka

SWIDNCA

Wagony-Swidnca Factory

Ul. Strzdinska 35, Swidnca 58-100, Poland

Telephone: Centrala 29 83/29 89
Telex: 034222

Products: Tank wagons, flat wagons; self-discharging wagons.

TALBOT

Waggonfabrik TALBOT

Jülicherstrasse 213-237, 51 Aachen, Postfach 1410, Federal Republic of Germany

Products: Passenger and freight cars.

Constitution: This is the oldest German railway rolling stock manufacturer, founded in 1938.

Telephone: 0241 4681
Telegrams: Talbot Aachen
Telex: 08 32 845 watal d

In addition to conventional stock, Talbot designs and builds freight cars with special features, including self-discharging wagons able to empty to either side and between the rails, covered hopper wagon with swivelling roof, covered wagon with telescopic sliding-section body and piggyback flat with pocket for wheels of semi-trailer.

TCO

Traction CEM-OERLIKON
(A member of the Brown Boveri Group)

Head Office: 37 rue du Rocher, 75008 Paris, France
Works at: Ornans 25290, Lyon-Villeurbanne 69267
Agencies abroad: Brown Boveri Co International Agencies

Products: Electric and diesel-electric trainsets (railcars and trailers); diesel-electric locomotives 300 to 1 600 hp; metro rolling stock including pneumatic tyred cars; rapid transit and interconnection motor cars; traction motors and alternators; static converters for two, three or four-system line inputs up to 450 kW; choppers, main transformers and auxiliaries; high-voltage contactors, electronic control.

Telephone: 522 85 90
Telex: 650663 Oerlik Paris

President: R Kitten
General Manager: C Alleman
Sales Manager: B Philippe
Technical Manager: JP Jouas

Sales: Deliveries include electrical equipments and/or major parts of it in Europe for the following railway networks: France (SNCF), Netherlands (NS), Switzerland (SBB), Germany (DB), Italy (FS), Belgium (SNCB), Austria (OBB), in America for Brazil (Rede) and (FEPASA), in Africa for the Ivory Coast (RAN) and Congo (CFCO). Furthermore, electrical and electronic equipments were supplied for rapid transit systems and Metros in Paris, Marseilles, Lyons, Lille, Montreal, Mexico City and Santiago.

THOMAS HILL

Thomas Hill (Rotherham) Ltd
(Subsidiary of Rolls-Royce Motors Ltd)

Telephone: 0709 582571
Telegrams: ENGINE, Rotherham
Telex: 54421 HILL RG

Vanguard Works, Hooton Road, Kilnhurst, Nr Rotherham, South Yorkshire, England

Products: Industrial locomotives and railcars; diesel hydraulic, diesel electric and battery-electric.

Chairman: G R Torrance
Managing Director: D A Harper
Marketing Director: J N Capes
Directors: T W Hill
 C A Simpson
 J Moore

Constitution: The company was founded by Thomas A Hill and between 1937 and 1956 collaborated with Sentinel Wagon Works (1936) Ltd (later Sentinel (Shrewsbury) Ltd) in connection with the maintenance and sales of Sentinel steam and diesel road vehicles and steam industrial locomotives. In 1956 Sentinel (Shrewsbury) Ltd was acquired by Rolls-Royce Ltd, to become the Headquarters for their Oil Engine Division. Production of steam locomotives ceased in 1958 and was replaced by Sentinel—Rolls-Royce diesel-hydraulic locomotives in 1959. A complementary range of Rolls-Royce powered locomotives was introduced under the registered trade name VANGUARD, particularly to cater for special applications such as flame-proofed locomotives for use in oil refineries and similar fire hazardous industries.
In 1963 Rolls-Royce Ltd acquired a controlling interest in the company. During 1970/71 the complete transfer of locomotive building from Rolls-Royce Ltd to Thomas Hill (Rotherham) Ltd at Vanguard Works, Kilnhurst took place. A completely new locomotive erection and fabrication shop was commissioned in August 1978, trebling the build capacity available and improving production facilities. First contract in the new shop was four locomotives for Shell UK Ltd.
The standard range of shunting locomotives includes a power range of 100 to 800 hp and weight range of 20 to 75 tons. The company also quotes for smaller locomotives for plantation and similar light duties.

Equipment: Standard types are:
Rigid frame: Diesel-hydraulic or diesel-electric 0-4-0, 0-6-0, 0-8-0.
Bo-Bo: Diesel-electric.
Articulated: Diesel-hydraulic or diesel-electric 0-4-0 + 0-4-0, 0-6-0 + 0-6-0.
Power range: 170 to 1 300 hp gross per locomotive multiple operation of locomotives or locomotives and powered tenders operated from one loco cab.
Weight range: 20 to 100 tons.
Flame-proof locomotive: Full flame-proof equipment including water quenched exhaust systems and electric system to BS 5501 and BA SEFA.

Vanguard UPC battery electric underground personnel carrier certified for use in coal and other mines

Rail gauges: 2 ft 0 in to 5 ft 6 in.
Sound proofing: Noise levels in driving cab can be reduced to 85 dB at full power when required and specified.

New equipment: Battery electric underground personnel carrier. A small railcar designed for transporting up to six people on underground rail systems. Fully certificated for use in coal and other mines.

Vanguard 45-ton 350 hp diesel-hydraulic locomotive

Vanguard 300 hp diesel-hydraulic locomotive with roller chain final drive

THRALL

Thrall Car Manufacturing Co

PO Box 218, Chicago Heights, Illinois 60411, USA

Products: Freight cars.

President: R L Duchossois

Telephone: (312) 757 5900

Executive Vice President: J A Thrall
Executive Vice President: C H Wright
Vice President, Sales: J P Lynch
Vice President, Finance: S D Christianson

Constitution: The company was founded in 1916 by A J Thrall, the present Chairman of the Board.

Coil steel car with removable hoods

Unit train coal car high-side gondola for rotary dump service

Thrall centre beam car

Covered hopper car, 100-tonne, 4 750 ft³ capacity

THUNE
Thune-Eureka A/S

PO Box 38, N-3401 Lierbyen, Norway

(This company ceased manufacture of locomotives in 1978.)

Telephone: 83 80 50
Telegrams: THUNE, Drammen
Telex: 18608 Thune N

TIBB
Tecnomasio Italiano Brown Boveri

Piazzale Lodi 3, 20137 Milan, Italy

Products: Electric, diesel-electric and industrial locomotives; electric trailers; turbo-chargers for traction diesel motors; equipments and bogies for railway and subway

Telephone: (02) 57971
Telegrams: TECNOMASIO, Milan
Telex: 310153 TIBB

cars, trams and trolleybuses; complete electrical plants for all kinds of industrial installations; electrical machinery and apparatus for the production and distribution of electric power.

TOKYU
Tokyu Car Corporation

Head Office: 1 Kamariya-cho, Kanazawa-ku, Yokohama, Japan
Sales and Export Department: 7, 5-cho, Yaesu, Chuo-ku, Tokyo

Products: Electric and diesel railcars; stainless-steel cars with bogie, passenger cars with bogie, bogies of various types, marine and railway use containers of several types and turnouts.

Chairman: Toshiji Yoshitsugu
President: Ihaho Takahashi
Executive Vice-President: Ichiro Kato
Export Manager: Kenichiro Tanimoto

Constitution: This company was formed in 1948, its predecessors being the Yokohama

Telephone: Tokyo 272 8091/3
Telegrams: TOKYUCARCORP TOK
Telex: 0222 2020 TCCTOK J

Plant of the Tokyo Electric Express Railway Co. It has grown rapidly and built the first stainless-steel trainset in Japan following technical agreement with the Budd Company of USA in 1960. Merging Teikoku Car & Manufacturing Co of Osaka into its organisation in 1968, the company is now the largest Japanese supplier of rolling stock to home and overseas railways.

Sales: Major sales in 1978/79 include: 347 electric railcars for Japanese National Railways including 68 SHINKANSEN cars; 250 electric railcars for private railways in Japan including stainless-steel railcars; 70 subway cars for Tokyo Metro; 60 stainless-steel cars for Tokyu Corporation; 36 commuter cars for Selbu, Japan Railways; nine diesel railcars for Philippine National Railways and 50 bogies for MAFERSA SA, Brazil.

Shinkansen car for Japanese National Railways

Stainless-steel car for Tokyu Corporation, Tokyo

Stainless-steel car for Shizuoka Railway

Aluminium alloy car for Tokyo Metro

TOMLINSON
Tomlinson Steel Ltd

PO Box P1223, Perth, Western Australia 6001, Australia

Products: Freight rolling stock.

Chairman: E E Tomlinson
Managing Director: A Moredoundt
Secretary: L K Glasson

Constitution: The company was founded in Perth, Western Australia in 1892 as Tomlinson Bros. and was formed into a public company in 1951 with its present name. Deliveries and work in hand include iron ore trucks for mining companies.

100 000-litre capacity petrol tank car, under frameless design

70-ton capacity iron ore car, bottom discharge type

Tandem pair of 100-tonne iron ore cars, gondola type

TOSHIBA CORPORATION

Telephone: 501 5411
Telegrams: TOSHIBA, Tokyo
Telex: J2 2587 Toshiba

1-6 Uchisaiwai-cho 1 chome, Chiyoda-ku, Tokyo, Japan

Products: Electric, diesel-electric and diesel-hydraulic locomotives; electric and diesel railcars; trolley buses; electric traction equipment; coach air-conditioner.

Constitution: Established in 1875, the company's range of products now covers almost everything electrical and electronic from power stations to electronic computers.

Sales: Railway equipment has been supplied to Algeria, Argentina, Australia, Brazil, Chile, Egypt, India, Morocco, Korea, New Zealand, Philippines, South Africa, Thailand, Zaire and Zambia, as well as Japanese National Railways and Japanese private railways.

Diesel-electric locomotive for AAC, Zambia, 1050-hp power rating

ac electric locomotive, 2400-kW power rating for Indian Railways

Surface Metro cars for Alexandria Passenger Transport Authority, dc 600 V system

TOYO
Toyo Denki Seizo KK
(Toyo Electric Manufacturing Co Ltd)

Telephone: (271) 6372
Telegrams: YOHDEN, Tokyo
Telex: (0) 222 4666/7

Yaesu Mitsui Building, No. 7-2 Yaesu, 2-chome, Chuo-ku, Tokyo, Japan

Products: Electric locomotives; diesel-electric locomotives; traction motors and electric machinery and apparatus for railway vehicles.

President: Atsushi Doi

Constitution: Established in 1918, this company produces traction motors and control equipment for home and export. It was responsible for the axle drive with cardan shaft and steel blade coupling which is used as standard equipment by the Japanese National Railways and by many of the private railways in Japan.

Sales: Railway rolling stock and equipment has been delivered to JNR and Japanese private railways, Korean National Railroad, Soeul Metropolitan Government Railway, Chilian State Railways, Argentine Railways, Panama Canal Co, Indian Railways and Egypt (Cairo Transit Authority, Heliopolis and Alexandria).

Towing locomotive delivered to the Panama Canal Commission

TRACTION—EXPORT
Société Française d'Exportation de Matériel de Traction

Telephone: 500 90 01
Telegrams: Tractionex
Telex: 270105F (ref 594)

3 avenue Victor Hugo, 75116 Paris, France

Products: Electric locomotives, diesel-electric locomotives, diesel-hydraulic locomotives, railcars, motor coaches and trailers for city underground and suburban rapid transit systems.

Constitution: Traction-Export is a subsidiary organisation of Alsthom and MTE, created to develop the export of rail traction equipment manufactured by Alsthom; Brissonneau; Creusot-Loire; and Jeumont-Schneider.

Developments: Companies within the Traction-Export organisation are building 87 TGV turbotrains for operation over the new Paris-Sud Est high-speed line in France at a cost of about FFr 834 million. The production sets are to be based closely on TGV 001 prototype built by Alsthom as main contractor with Brissonneau et Lotz, MTE and Turbomeca as associates. The trains will carry 300 passengers in a three-car set. General characteristics of the TGV 001 are as follows: track gauge 1.435 m; maximum designed speed 300 km/h; installed power (thermal) with TURMO III G (4 turbines of 940 kW each) 3 760 kW, with TURMO X (4 turbines of 1 100 kW each) 4 400 kW; installed power (electric) main alternators (2 X 2 250 kW) 4 500 kW; maximum axle load 16 tonnes; new wheel diameter 0.9 m; total length of trainset 92.9 m; height above rail 3.4 m; width 2.814 m; total weight in working order (with full fuel capacity) 192 tonnes; bogie between centres, power car 14 m, coaches 18.3 m; bogie wheelbase 2.6 m; fuel tank capacity (2 x 4 000 l of fuel oil) 8 000 litres; minimum curve negotiable 100 m. With a total weight of 192 tonnes (including test equipment), a total length of 92.9 m and maximum axle loading of 16 tonnes, the trainset consists of three coaches with a power car at each end. The whole total adhesion assembly is articulated and rests on six "B" type bogies with all axles being driving axles.

The profile of the complete trainset was developed following design study and wind tunnel test results. Each power car supplies the six traction motors on the three bogies of the corresponding half of the trainset. The two end coaches have been fitted out, one as a first class coach, the other in second class, the middle coach being equipped to serve as a mobile laboratory.

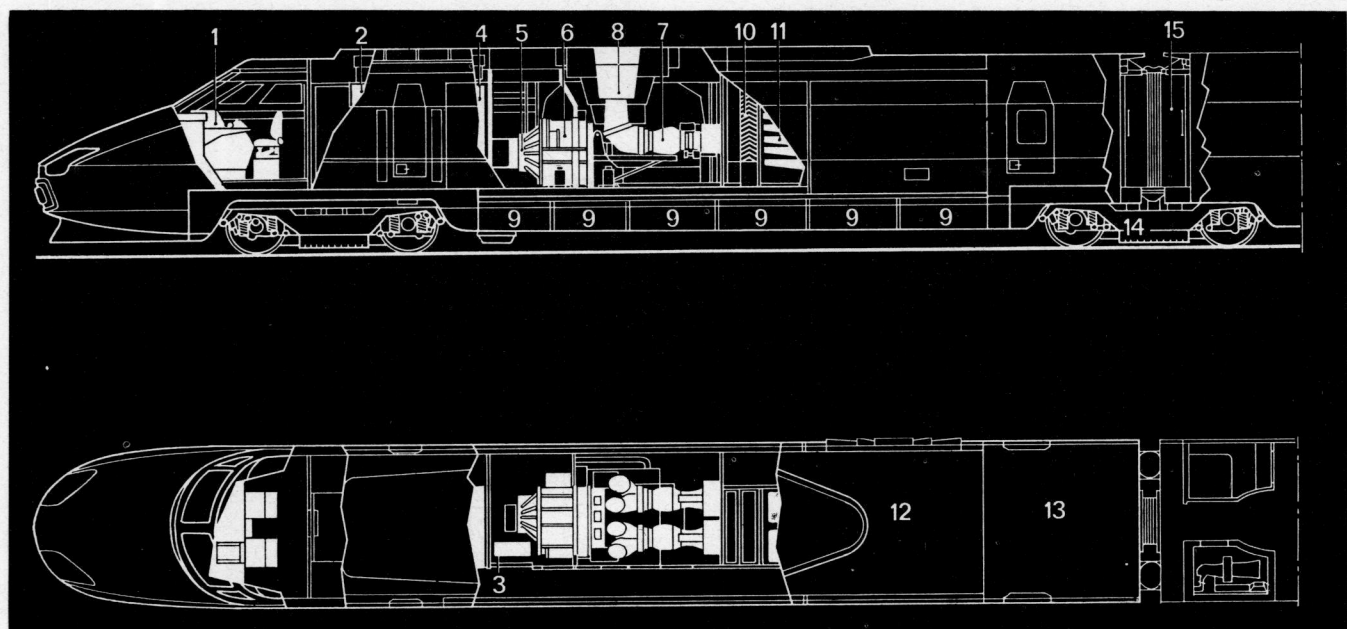

(1) Driver's position **(2)** Electrical equipment block **(3)** Rectifier unit **(4)** Rheostatic breaking unit **(5)** Auxiliary alternator **(6)** Main alternator **(7)** Gas turbine **(8)** Turbine exhaust **(9)** Air reservoir, fuel tanks, thermal and pneumatic auxiliary equipment, air-conditioning equipment **(10)** Sound baffle **(11)** Air filter unit **(12)** Air intake compartment **(13)** Luggage compartment **(14)** Rail brake **(15)** Intercirculation element

---

TRANSPORTMASCHINEN EXPORT-IMPORT
Volkseigener Aussenhandelsbetrieb- der Deutschen Demokratischen Republik

Taubenstrasse 11/13, DDR-108 Berlin, German Democratic Republic

Telephone: 22050
Telegrams: TRANSMASCH
Telex: 11 26 89

Constitution: Transportmaschinen Export-Import is a member of Vereinigter Schienenfahrzeugbau der DDR, eV (United Rolling Stock Manufacturers of the German Democratic Republic) and is the sole exporter for the products of locomotive and coach and wagon factories.

TURNU-SEVERIN
Turnu-Severin Wagon Works

7 Matei Millo Street, Bucharest, Romania

Products: Freight wagons.

UNIKON
Fabryka Urzadzen Wagonowych UNIKON

70-893 Szczecin, Poland

Telephone: 61271
Telex: 042221

Products: Freight wagons.

UNIO
Unio-Satu Mare

7 Matei Millo Street, Bucharest, Romania

Products: Diesel, electric and battery mine locomotives; forestry wagons; mine wagons; freight wagons.

UNION CARRIAGE
Union Carriage & Wagon Co (Pty) Ltd

Marievale Road, Vorsterkroon, Nigel, Transvaal, South Africa

Telephone: 739 2411
Telegrams: UNICARWAG
Telex: 8 6328 SA

Products: Designers and manufacturers of electric and diesel locomotives and passenger coaches.

Chairman: Dr W J de Villiers
Managing Director: J Clarke

Constitution: General Mining and Finance Corp, Anglo-American Corp and Comeng Holdings are the principal shareholders of this company. Less than 25 per cent in value of all the contracts received is spent overseas, mostly on electrical traction equipment which is not obtainable from South African sources. Formed in 1957 to supply South Africa Railways with passenger coaches, Union Carriage has expanded its business to supply the export market and to produce diesel locomotives, both electric and hydraulic.

Sales: Deliveries include such varied types of railway vehicles as three-kV, dc, emu suburban motor and trailer coaches, mainline coaches, both sleepers and open saloons, three-kV, dc mainline electric locomotives, 25 kV ac thyristor-controlled mainline electric locomotives, 50 kV, ac thyristor-controlled mainline electric locomotives, two prestige Blue Trains consisting of 32 luxury coaches, diesel locomotives both electric and hydraulic, various specialised vehicles such as dining cars, kitchen cars, and electrical test cars. The 50 kV, ac electric locomotives are the most powerful electric locomotives in the world on 3 ft 6 in gauge.

UNION TANK
Union Tank Car Co
(An affiliate of Trans Union Corporation)

111 West Jackson Boulevard, Chicago, Illinois 60604, USA

Telephone: (312) 431 3100

Products: Steel, stainless-steel, and aluminium tank cars carrying liquids, compressed gases, and granular solids.

Equipment: Union Tank Car Co developed a number of modern tank car designs to meet the needs of shippers in the chemical, petroleum, food, and fertiliser industries. An innovation was Funnel-Flow sloping tank design for fast, complete unloading of liquids. Union Tank also developed the Sandwich car for superphosphoric acid, polyglycols, and food products. Temperature control is provided by urethane foam insulation with no metal-to-metal contact. For granular solids such as cement, the company's pneumatically-operated Pressure-Flow car unloads quickly. For anhydrous ammonia and liquefied petroleum gas, Union Tank has introduced pressure cars in 30 000 and 33 800-gallon sizes.

The company owns and operates a fleet of 43 000 tank cars which are leased to shippers.

VALMET
Valmet Oy Tampere Works

Telephone: 931 65 3322
Telegrams: VALMET, Tampere
Telex: 22112 vallesf

PO Box 387, SF-33101 Tampere 10, Finland

Products: Diesel-hydraulic locomotives; electric multiple unit trains; rapid transit cars; articulated tramcars; coaches for special purposes.

President: Matti Kankaanpää
General Manager (Tampere Works): Eske Määttänen

Sales: For Finnish State Railways: All-aluminium 720-kW electric two-car trainsets (motor coach and driving trailer) with seats for 200 and maximum speed of 75 mph (120 km/h); 1 400 hp Bo Bo diesel-hydraulic general-purpose locomotives; 355 hp B diesel-hydraulic shunting locomotives. For the Rapid Transit Office of the City of Helsinki: All-aluminium 1 000 kW rapid transit two-car units with seats for 134 and maximum speed of 56 mph (90 km/h). For Finnish and Swedish industry: two and three-axle diesel-hydraulic shunting locomotives.

Valmet two-axle diesel-hydraulic shunting locomotive
The locomotive can be equipped with alternative engines from 250 to 450 hp and alternative transmissions. The gauge can vary from 1000 to 1676 mm, weight from 24 to 40 tons and max speed up to 75 km/h.

VICKERS CANADIAN
Vickers Canadian Ltd

5000 Notre Dame Street East, Montreal, PQ H1V 2B4, Canada

Products: Rapid transit cars, commuter trains, double deck coaches, car bodies, fabricated shells and parts.

Constitution: Vickers' growing involvement in public transportation began with the supply of the first 369 passenger cars for Montreal's Metro. Since then the company has built double-deck commuter trains for CP Rail, supplied stainless-steel car shells for the New Haven Railroad commuter system, and during 1978/79 were producing 46 self-propelled, high-speed commuter cars for the Delaware River Port Authority, Philadelphia, USA.

Transit cars for the Delaware River Port Authority

Double-deck gallery cars for CP Rail

Montreal metro cars

VOROSHILOVGRAD
Voroshilovgrad Diesel Locomotive Works

Voroshilovgrad, USSR

Products: Diesel locomotives.

Constitution: Member of Energomachexport.

New equipment: The Soviet 3 000-hp diesel locomotive can be seen in a number of European countries. Exports of Soviet diesel locomotives started in 1958 with a delivery of 750-hp shunting units. The development of 2 000 hp mainline diesel locomotives for use on European railways was an important milestone in promoting this line. These locomotives, designated M-62 in Hungary, 120 in the German Democratic Republic, T-679.1 and T-679.5 in Czechoslovakia, CT-44 in Poland and K-62 in the Korean People's Democratic Republic, are handling a considerable proportion of the freight and passenger transport there.

WAGGON UNION
Waggon Union GmbH

Telephone: 0271 702 1
Telegrams: WAGGONUNION, Siegen
Telex: 08-72843 wusi d

PO Box 2240, 5902 Netphen 2 and Miraustrasse 30, 1000 Berlin 27, Federal Republic of Germany

Management: Dipl-Phys Karl-Heinz Siepe
Prof Dr-Ing Walter Döpper

Products: Freight cars of all types, covered, open, mineral, tank, refrigerated, and for transport of road vehicles and containers; electric and diesel-powered railcars, railbuses, and multiple-unit trainsets; passenger cars, tramways, underground trains; double deck buses and fabricated bogies for freight cars and passenger coaches.

Constitution: This company was formed in 1971 as a result of the merger between SEAG Waggonbau (of Rheinstahl Transporttechnik) and DWM Deutsche Waggon- und Maschinenfabrik GmbH.

6-axle articulated, high capacity freight car with 4 sliding walls, developed and built for the Volkswagen-Audi Co

4-axle, high capacity freight car with 3 sliding walls, developed and built for the Transwaggon Co

WALKERS

Walkers Ltd

Telephone: 21 2321
Telegrams: ITOLZAK
Telex: 49718

Bowen Street, Maryborough, Queensland 4650, Australia

Products: Diesel-hydraulic locomotives from 250 to 1 200 hp; passenger and freight rolling stock.

Chairman: T Braddock
Managing Director: Dr W L Hughes
Secretary: M F Dittmann

Constitution: The company was started at Ballarat, Victoria, in 1864 by John Walker as

The Union Foundry, to build mining machinery for the newly-opened goldfields, and the works at Maryborough were opened on the present site in 1868. In 1884 a public company was formed with the name John Walker & Co, Ltd, later changed to Walkers Ltd.
In addition to general engineering, sugar mills and ships, Walkers Ltd have been producing steam, diesel-mechanical, diesel-electric and diesel-hydraulic locomotives since 1896. The company has specialised in the production of a standard range of diesel hydraulic locomotives which is available in a power range from 250 to 1 200 hp.

WEGMANN

Wegmann & Co

Telephone: 105 1
Telegrams: WEGMANN, Kassel
Telex: 99 859

Head Office: 35 Kassel, August-Bode-Strasse I, Federal Republic of Germany

Works: Kassel-Rothenditmold (rolling stock construction).
Kassel-Bettenhausen (fittings, frames and castings).

Products: Passenger and freight cars of all types, including lightweight construction; railcars; electric trainsets; air-conditioned units; freight cars of all kinds; tramcars; München-Kassel motor and trailer bogies; containers.

Directors: Dipl Ing F Bode
Dr E Bode

Constitution: This company was established in 1882 and has specialised in passenger and freight car building.

Sales: Deliveries include a Royal train for Iran, saloon coaches for Yugoslavia and Guinea, passenger coaches for Ghana, Denmark, Luxembourg, Spain and Germany; goods wagons with opening roofs for Ghana and German railways, torsionally flexible trucks for Strassenbahn, Bremen, Norwegian Railways, Danish Railways, German Railways and the Chicago Transit Authority.

WESTINGHOUSE SA

(Formerly CENEMESA)

Telephone: 2 31 72 00
Telex: 22430

Avda José Antonio 10, Madrid 14, Spain

Products: Electric locomotives, electric railcars.

President: D Santiago Foncillas Casaus
General Mamager: D Carlos Alvarez de Toledo
Commercial Manager: Angel de Niolás Diaz de Garayo

Constitution: Member of the Westinghouse Electric group of companies.

Sales: Recent sales include 16 Type BB locomotives rated 2 700 kW 1 500-3 000 V dc, 40 type BB locomotives rated 3 100 kW 3 000 V dc, 42 type BB locomotives rated 3 100 kW 3 000 V dc, 50 type BB locomotives rated 3 100 kW 3 000 V dc, 38 type BB locomotives rated 3 100 kW 3 000 V dc, 20 luxury railcars (motor and trailer) rated 1 160 kW 1 500-3 000 V dc, 58 electric trainsets (motor and trailer) rated 1 160 kW 3 000 V dc, 23 electric trainsets (motor and trailer) rated 1 160 kW 3 000 V dc, 60 electric trainsets (motor and trailer) rated 1 160 kW 3 000 V dc and 65 emu's series 5 000 rated 180 × 4 kW 600 V dc for Metro Madrid.

65 emu's series 5000 rated at 180 × 4 kW 600 V dc were delivered by Westinghouse SA to Madrid Metro

WHITEHEAD & KALES

Whitehead & Kales International, Inc

Telephone: (313) 849 1200
Telegrams: ZMV Whitekales
Telex: 23 0732

Fully-enclosed multi-level auto rack installed on a railway flat car

58 Haltiner Street, River Rouge, Michigan 48218, USA

Products: Freight cars of all types; car components and underframes, shipping racks; containers; and special dunnage.

Chairman: Paul A Johnston
President: Walter W Borland
Vice-President: A F Debicki

WHITING
Whiting Corporation

Harvey, Illinois 60426, USA

Products: Speciality railcars; domestic and foreign auto and truck bi- and tri-level rail-cars and superstructures; flat cars, standard and bulk headed.

New equipment: The 4TM trackmobile is a 43-hp diesel-powered switcher (shunter)

Telephone: (312) 8 9400

with a TE of 7 400 lb *(3 368 kg)* at 1.5 mph *(2.4 km/h)* in first gear. Having moved wagons to the desired position, the 4TM is quickly raised clear of the track, driven on its road wheels to another location and lowered to the track in 30 seconds ready for its next task, provided that the road surface is roughly level with the top of the rails as in industrial plants, or can be temporarily built up with planks.
Weight transfer from loaded wagon to Trackmobile is by the two projecting arms of the hydraulic jacking coupler. The Trackmobile can be fitted for operation with automatic couplers or with European-type centre-hook and buffers.

WICKHAM
D Wickham & Co Ltd

Crane Mead, Ware, Hertfordshire SG12 9QA, England

Products: Diesel railcars and rail buses; gang trolleys; inspection cars; overhead line maintenance and inspection cars; crane trolleys; small trailers; self propelled special-purpose vehicles; vehicle washing equipment.

Chairman and Managing Director: James Cooper
Sales Director: J E Atkinson
Chief Designer: K J F Bishop

Constitution: D Wickham & Co, which was incorporated as a private limited company in 1912, has been building railway vehicles since 1922. The company pioneered the use of roller bearing axle boxes, welded steel frames, underslung springs and all steel bodies, using solid drawn square steel tubing to eliminate the conventional underframe and produce cars with a high power/weight ratio for operating under arduous mountain conditions. The company specialiss in track maintennne and inspection vehicles and offers a wide range of equipment for this purpose.

Equipment: The year 1979/80 has seen the further development of the new Type 38 Gang Car, now offered with a semi-enclosed body. The basic 15-seater arrangement with a driving position at one end only is similar to that featured in *Jane's World*

Telephone: 0920 2491/7
Telegrams: WICKHAM, Ware
Telex: 81340

Railways 1978-79. Roll-down side curtains can be fitted for added protection and, as with all Wickham cars, full performance of the petrol or diesel engine is available in either direction of travel. Having controls at one end only allows the car to be fitted with alternative bodies, such as a 2/4 stretcher ambulance or clinic car, a travelling workshop, a drop-side open truck or flat deck transporter with cab accommodation for five. Both of the last two types can be supplied with a hand-pumped hydraulic crane with a lifting capacity of 1 000 kg (2 200 lb).
A revised version of the popular Type 27 trolley has been produced with carden shaft transmission instead of the usual chain drive and specially-designed bodies have been fitted to different versions of the Type 42 Engineers Inspection Car to special orders.
The Type CR2000 crane trolley illustrated is one of a repeat order batch for Egypt. It mounts a Hiab 550 hydraulic crane with a lifting capacity of 3 250 kg (7 160 lb) through 360 degrees. Hydraulic steadying jacks are standard and the deck seats for a gang of 20 are removable to allow the loading of rails along either side of the driving cab. Rollers are fitted at each end of the chassis to facilitate the end loading of rails. A total payload of 2 000 kg (two tonnes) can be carried on the deck. An air-cooled diesel engine with four-speed gearbox and reversing box gives a top speed of 65 km/h (40 mph) in either direction, while standard centre couplings allow the trolley to be operated with a useful trailing load.

Overhead line inspection car with raised observation cabin

Type 38 trolley, semi-enclosed, for Sudan Railways

WINDHOFF
Rheiner Maschinenfabrik Windhoff AG

Hovstraße 10, Postfach 1160, 4440 Rheine, Federal Republic of Germany

Products: Standard types of shunting vehicle; Windhoff Tele-Trac with tractive forces up to 25 000 daN, diesel or electrohydraulically driven, control of shunting course and coupling operations is by radio or by interlinking with the loading programme.

Tele-Trac shunter in operation at a bulk loading station

YALE & TOWNE
Yale & Towne Inc
(A subsidiary of Eaton Yale & Towne Inc)

Trojan Division, Batavia, Illinois, USA

Products: Pneumatic tyred switching tractors; materials handling equipment; earth moving equipment.

Equipment: Although it does not run on rails, the Trojan 254R tractor operates as a yard switching (shunting) locomotive, with the additional facility that, on completion of one

duty, it can quickly and easily travel across intervening tracks to its next duty without having to be switched around the lines. Its low-pressure rubber tyred wheels straddle the rail track and enable it to operate on cross ties and to cross tails, drainage trenches, and uneven surfaces generally.
The tractor is equipped with standard couplers at front and rear; coupling and uncoupling is by the driver operating a lever in the cab. It also has its own 35 cubic feet per minute compressed air system with connecting hoses for operation of the air brakes on the cars being moved.
The Trojan 254R weighs 31 500 lb *(14 300 kg)* and can push or pull up to 1 500 tons of rolling stock.

ZASTAL
ZZPM Zastal Zelona Gora

Zaodrzanskie Zaklady Przemyslu Metalowego Zastal, 65-114 Zielona Gora, ul. Towarowa 10, Poland

Telephone: 4411
Telegrams: ZASTAL, Zielona gora
Telex: 043201

Products: Freight wagons.

ZWEIWEG-FAHRZEUG

Vertriebs KG, Innlände 18, D-8200 Rosenheim, Federal Republic of Germany

Telephone: 08031/15031
Telex: 525 731

Products: Interesting novelties in the field of rail and road operations are manufactured by Zweiweg-Fahrzeug. The track-keeping device, comprising articulated track-keeping rollers, which are adapted to the Daimler-Benz Unimog, has been supplied by Zweiweg for many years. These rollers turn the well-known road vehicle into a valuable rail vehicle, admitted by all railway administrations. Besides its use as a shunting unit (its tractive power equals about that of a 20-ton locomotive) the track-keeping device ZW-82S also permits use of the Unimog on rails as a working unit, equipped with various supplementary equipment.

A Zweiweg Unimog model ZW-82S provided with a steam-jet equipment for points cleaning (in use in Switzerland for example), another unit equipped with a loading crane (and at the same time as a shunting unit) it pulls up to 25 laden wagons. Another one has been equipped as auxiliary vehicle (in operation with the German Federal Railways). For winter operation a rotary snow plough or a drum-type snow plough can be fitted, permitting effective snow removal on rails as well as on the road.

Two special units are available for the construction and maintenance of the aerial lines: a Zweiweg Unimog with hydraulic lifting platform and a new special vehicle, the Zweiweg road-railer with working platform which was initially constructed for the Dutch State Railways. This equipment proved a great success so that several units were ordered subsequently.

The Zweiweg Unimog vehicles are also available for broad-gauge lines.

The Trenkle all-purpose vehicle Model A-52S equipped with track-keeping device ZW-52S is available for demonstrations on narrow gauge lines.

Director: Adolf Löw

Constitution: It is just over ten years since the firm of Zweiweg-Fahrzeug GmbH & Co, Vertriebs-KG in Rosenheim was founded. Adolf Löw was appointed Director and has been in charge of the management up to this day.

The firm's track-holding device enables road vehicles to be operated on the rail.

The bulk of the vehicles supplied during the past decade has been in the following sequence: Daimler-Benz Unimog, the Trenkle all-purpose vehicle A-52S for narrow-gauge lines and the Mercedes-Benz transporter 307D and 308.

Zweiweg Unimog model ZW-82S for points cleaning

DIESEL ENGINES
FOR RAIL TRACTION

ABC

Anglo Belgian Co
43 Wiedauwkaai, Gand, Belgium

Formed in 1912, to take over the SA des Anciens Ateliers Onghena which had been building gas engines since 1904, the company manufactures four-stroke diesel engines for marine, industrial and rail traction services.

DXS and DXC Series

Type: 6 and 8 cylinder vertical in-line, 4-cycle turbo-charged and charge air cooled (DXC), water cooled.
Cylinders: Bore 9.53 in *(242 mm)*. Stroke 12.6 in *(320 mm)*. Swept volume 14.72 litres per cylinder. Compression ratio 12.05:1. Cast iron wet type cylinder liners with two rubber seal rings. Cast iron cylinder heads secured by studs.

Model		DXS		DXC	
Turbo-charged		Yes	Yes	Yes	Yes
No of cylinders		6	8	6	8
bhp continuous		630	840	900	1 200
Max engine speed	rpm	750		750	
Bmep continuous	lb/in²	121.8		170	
	(kg/cm²)	(8.56)		(12.22)	
Bmep max	lb/in²	134.1		187	
	(kg/cm²)	(9.43)		(13.4)	
Weight (dry without flywheel)	lb	16 710	22 490	17 710	22 490
	(kg)	(8 035)	(10 200)	(8 035)	(10 200)
Length	in	130	159	130	159
	(mm)	(3 320)	(4 030)	(3 320)	(4 030)
Width	in	44		44	
	(mm)	(1 120)		(1 120)	
Height	in	74		74	
	(mm)	(1 890)		(1 890)	
Consumption Fuel	lb/hp/hr	0.354		0.354	
	(g/hp/h)	(160)		(160)	
Lube oil		0.5% fuel consumption			

Rated output: DIN specification

Pistons: Aluminium alloy with four compression rings (first ring chrome-plated) and one oil control ring with expander. Fully floating gudgeon pin.
Connecting rods: Heat treated alloy steel drop forged H section. Steel bearing shells lined with copper lead. Phosphor bronze bushes.
Crankshaft: Forged alloy steel crankshaft with copper lead lined steel bearing shells.
Crankcase: Cast iron.
Valve gear: One inlet and one exhaust silichrome steel overhead valve per cylinder. Valve seat insert in cylinder head. Gear-driven camshaft located inside the cylinder block.
Fuel injection: Direct injectors with one pump per cylinder.
Supercharger: Exhaust gas turbo-blower.
Lubrication: Forged feed with one lubricating and one scavenging gear pump.
Cooling system: Panel radiator with one centrifugal pump.
Starting: Electric or compressed air.

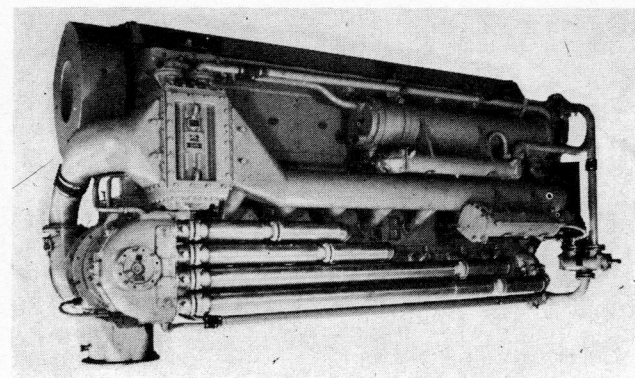

Model 8DXC 8-cylinder turbo-charged and charge air-cooled engine developing 1 200 hp at 750 rpm

ALCO POWER INC

100 Orchard Street, Auburn, New York 13021, USA

Although they have ceased manufacturing diesel-electric locomotives, ALCO continue to manufacture their diesel engines for both stationary and marine applications and for locomotives, and through licensees in various parts of the world including Canada, Argentina, Australia, India and Romania. They also continue to supply renewal parts and rebuilding components on a world-wide basis.
ALCO was the first manufacturer in the USA to introduce turbo-supercharging for a diesel engine. The 12 and 16 cylinder V-type 244 model was introduced in the 1940s. First rated at 1 580 hp at 1 000 rpm, it was developed to give 1 760 hp at the same speed. The V16 model gave 2 360 hp. The 251 series with the same bore and stroke supersedes these with many improvements in design, and research work continues to obtain even higher specific outputs. Engine design approved by international regulating bodies ABS, Lloyds, GL, DNV, BV for stationary and marine service.

251 Series

6 cylinder in-line, 8, 12, 16 and 18 cylinder Vee, 4-cycle high pressure turbo-charged with charge air cooling.
Cylinders: Bore 9 in *(228 mm)*. Stroke 10½ in *(267 mm)*. Swept volume 668 cu in per cylinder. Compression ratio 11.5 : 1. Cast iron water cooled heat treated cylinder liners, chrome plated on inner surface. Cast iron-nickel alloy cylinder heads.
Pistons: Forged aluminium body with steel cap, embodying ring grooves, bolted on. Pistons cooled by pressure-circulated oil, and piston pins are full-floating type.
Connecting rods: Drop-forged steel in an H beam cross-section. Piston-pin end has pressed steel-backed bronze bushing. Crank-pin bearing is grooveless in the load-carrying area.
Crankshaft: Alloy-steel forging, precision machined and heat-treated for hardness. Fully counter-balanced. Rifle-drilled oil passages through crankshafts.

Crankcase: Fabricated steel.
Valve gear: Air and exhaust valves are of wear-resistant alloy and are completely interchangeable. Cast iron valve guides are replaceable, and cylinder-head wear is reduced by use of replaceable stellite valve-seat inserts in the head. Two camshafts, one for each bank, inside engine block gear driven from crankshaft.
Fuel injection: Designed for flat fuel-consumption curves. System is high-pressure, with fuel supplied to cylinders by individual single-acting plunger pumps.
Turbo-charger: High pressure ratio exhaust gas driven turbo-charger. ALCO designed and built with replaceable blades on the turbine wheel. Water cooled charge air cooler.
Fuel: ASTM specification 2-D. Other fuels can be used (heavy oils, natural gas, crudes, etc) with suitable standard modifications to fuel injection equipment and governing apparatus.
Lubrication: Forced feed with one gear driven pump.
Cooling System: Varies with type, locomotive or other installation. One ALCO pump, gear driven from engine.
Starting: Motored main generator, or air.
Mounting: 4-point.

251 Series

No of cylinders		6 in line	8V	12V	16V	18V
Turbo-charged		Yes	Yes	Yes	Yes	Yes
Continuous rating	bhp	1 500	1 820	3 000	3 900	4 500
Engine speed	rpm	1 100	1 000	1 100	1 100	1 100
Bmep max	lb/in²	269	252	269	269	269
	(kg/cm²)	(18.9)	(17.7)	(18.9)	(18.9)	(18.9)
Engine weight (dry)	lb	24 700	26 400	32 300	42 500	49 000
	(kg)	(11 200)	(12 000)	(14 700)	(19 300)	(22 200)

Locomotive ratings

		6F	8V-F	12V-F	16V-F	18V-G
Turbocharger		Yes	Yes	Yes	Yes	Yes
Continuous rating		1 500	1 820	3 000	3 900	4 500
Engine speed	rpm	1 100	1 000	1 100	1 100	1 100
Bmep	lb/in²	269	269	269	263	270
	(kg/cm²)	18.9	18.9	18.9	18.5	19.0
Engine weight	lb	22 500	25 700	33 000	42 000	49 200
	(kg)	10 206	11 658	14 969	19 051	22 317
Loco & stat						
Length	ft in	12 10	11 7	15	17 9	20 7
Width	ft in	4 8	5 1	5 1	5 1	5 1
Height	ft in	7 5	8 5	9 1	9 1	9 5

Shallow base ratings @ 90°F; 28.25"Hg 1500'—19 350 BTU/# D2 fuel (Ref DEMA)

ALSTHOM ATLANTIQUE

2 quai de Seine, 93203 St Denis, France

SEMT-Pielstick PA4-185 Series

Type: 6 cylinder in-line horizontal; 6 and 8 cylinders in-line vertical; 6, 8, 12, 16 and 18 cylinders Vee (90°), 4-cycle, water cooled.
Cylinders: Bore 185 mm *(7.28 in)*. Stroke 210 mm *(8.25 in)*. Swept volume 5.65 litres (345 in³) per cylinder. Wet liners, individual cast iron cylinder heads. Central pre-combustion chamber fitted with pintle type injectors.
Pistons: Cast iron pistons cooled by pressure lubricating oil fed through connecting rod and piston pin into an annular chamber level with top compression ring.
Connecting rods: Identical for both banks of cylinders and arranged side by side on crankpins. Thin wall steel backed copper lead lined bearings for big end.
Crankshaft: Steel alloy with induction hardened journals. Balance weights bolted to circular webs. Power can be taken off from either end of engine.
Crankcase: Tunnel type frame unit, with integral timing gear case, is enclosed by the sump.
Valve gear: 2 inlet and 2 exhaust valves with pressed in valve inserts. Valves operated through roller type followers by a single camshaft between cylinder banks.
Fuel injection: Pintle type injectors fitted to pre-combustion chambers. Monobloc injection pump located inside Vee, controlled by hydraulic governor.

Superchargers: Exhaust gas turbo-chargers, one for 6 and 8 cylinder engines, one or 2 for 12 cylinders and 2 for 16 and 18 cylinders are between cylinder banks. Air coolers arranged on timing gear side.
Lubrication: Pressure feed throughout with pumps in sump below oil level.
Cooling: Water pumps fitted on timing gear end of frame.
Starting: Either electrically or by compressed air.

SEMT-Pielstick PA6-280 Series

Type: 6, 8 and 9 cylinders in line, 12, 14, 16, 18 and 20 cylinder Vee, supercharged, water cooled.
Cylinders: Bore 280 mm *(11 in)*. Stroke 290 mm *(11.40 in)*. Swept volume 17.85 litres *(1 090 in₃)* per cylinder. Wet liners directly mounted in the crankcase, without cooling jackets. Individual cast iron cylinder heads. Single combustion chamber. Direct injection.
Pistons: Pistons made of light alloy, with inserted head, cooled by lubricating oil circulating in an annular chamber; oil is delivered by the connecting rod to the piston pin.
Connecting rods: Identical for both cylinder banks, arranged side by side on the crankpins. Notched connecting rod big end bevel cut. Screwed cap. Cupro-lead shell on thin steel backing for the big end, babbitted steel bushing for the small end.

Crankshaft: Made of alloy steel, high frequency treated. Power can be taken off on either end of the shaft.

Crankcase: One piece, of Mechanite special, iron cast with crankshaft underslung bearings. Inlet air box integrated on top.

Valves: 2 inlet valves and 2 exhaust valves per cylinder head, with inserted seats. Valves operated through rocking levers and cam followers from two camshafts (one per cylinder bank), housed in the crankcase, outside the Vee.

Fuel injection: Direct injection by means of injectors of the multi-hole type. Individual injecting pump housed in the crankcase, directly controlled by the camshafts. Injection controlled by hydraulic speed governor.

Turbo-chargers: 2 per engine, driven by a turbine on the exhaust gas, and housed in the centre line of the engine above each end of the crankcase.
Air cooler at supercharger outlets, housed above the middle of the crankcase, and crossed by a special water line.

Lubrication: 2 pumps of the gear type, driven by a timing gear train sunk into the sump.

Cooling: 2 water pumps of the centrifugal type, driven by the timing train, one for jacket and cylinder head line, the other for air-cooler and lube-oil line.

Starting: Compressed air.

360-hour UIC test

The first 18-cylinder 18PA6V-280 engine has officially run its 360-hour UIC locomotive test in accordance with ORE regulations.

SEMT-Pielstick PA4-200 Series

Type: 8, 12, 16 and 18 cylinders Vee (90°) 4 cycles, water cooled.
3 models:
 DI: Direct Injection
 VG: Variable geometry pre-combustion chamber
 VG, DS VG + 2: stage turbo-charging

Cylinders: Bore 200 mm (7.88 in). Stroke 210 mm (8.25 in). Swept volume 6.6 litres (403 in³) per cylinder. Wet liners, individual cast iron cylinder heads.

Pistons: Cast iron pistons cooled by pressure lubricating oil fed through connecting rod and piston pin into an annular chamber level with top compression ring.

Connecting rods: Identical for both banks of cylinders and arranged side by side on crankpins. Thin wall steel backed copper lead lined bearings for big end.

Crankshaft: Steel alloy with induction hardened journals. Balance weights bolted to circular webs. Power can be taken off from either end of engine.

Crankcase: Tunnel type frame unit, with integral timing gear case, is enclosed by the sump.

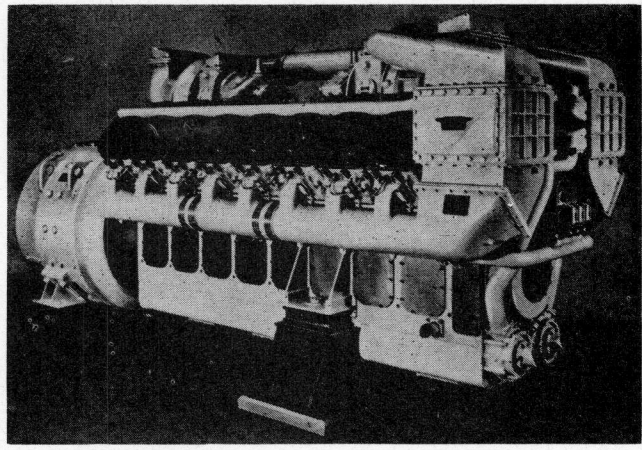

SEMT-Pielstick 16PA4V-185 engine
UIC rating 2 400 hp at 1 500 rpm.

Valve gear: 2 inlet and 2 exhaust valves with pressed in valve inserts. Valves operated through roller type followers by single camshaft between cylinder banks.

Fuel Injection: Monobloc injection pump inside the Vee, controlled by hydraulic governor.
 DI: Direct system, spray type injectors
 VG: Variable geometry pre-combustion
 VG, DS: chamber

Superchargers: Exhaust gas turbo-chargers, one for 8 cylinder engine, 2 for 12, 16 and 18 cylinders are between cylinder banks. Air coolers arranged on timing gear side.

Lubrication: Pressure feed throughout with pumps in sump below oil level.

Cooling: Water pumps fitted on timing gear end of frame.

Starting: Either electrically or by compressed air.

SEMT-Pielstick 18PA4V-200 engine
UIC rating 3 150 hp at 1 500 rpm

SEMT-Pielstick 18PA6V-280 engine
UIC rating 1 200 hp at 1 050 rpm

| | IN-LINE | | | | | VEE | | |
	6 PA6L	8PA6L	9PA6L	12PA6V	14PA6V	16PA6V	18PA6V	20PA6V
No of cylinders	6	8	9	12	14	16	18	20
Supercharged	Yes	Yes	Yes	Yes	Yes	Yes	Yes	Yes
Charge air cooled	Yes	Yes	Yes	Yes	Yes	Yes	Yes	Yes
Power rating (UIC)	2 400	3 200	3 600	4 800	5 600	6 400	7 200	8 000
Engine speed	1 050	1 050	1 050	1 050	1 050	1 050	1 050	1 050
Piston speed	1 015	1 015	1 015	1 015	1 015	1 015	1 015	1 015
Bmep	2 030	2 030	2 030	2 030	2 030	2 030	2 030	2 030
Weight (dry)	11 200	14 400	16 000	18 800	21 500	24 100	26 200	28 500
Length	3 860	4 700	5 120	3 675	4 135	4 595	5 055	5 515
Width	1 425	1 425	1 425	1 780	1 780	1 780	1 780	1 780
Height	2 630	2 670	2 670	2 480	2 480	2 480	2 480	2 480

| | PA4 200 VG | | | | PA4 200 VG DS | | | |
No of cylinders	8	12	16	18	8	12	16	18
Turbo-charged	yes	yes	yes	yes	yes	yes	yes	yes
Charge air cooled	yes	yes	yes	yes	yes	yes	yes	yes
Power rating	1 540	2 310	3 080	3 465	1 920	2 880	3 840	4 320
Bmep	17.3	17.3	17.3	17.3	23	23	23	23
Weight (dry)	4 500	6 200	7 900	8 800	5 300	7 200	9 300	10 200
Length	2 090	2 530	3 130	3 430	1 878	2 975	3 078	3 378
Width	1 580	1 450	1 700	1 700	1 450	1 450	1 850	1 850
Height	1 865	1 800	1 865	1 865	2 226	2 285	2 225	2 225

		6PA4H 185	6PA4L 185	8PA4L 185	6PA4V 185	8PA4V 185	12PA4V 185	16PA4V 185	18PA4V 185	8PV4V 200	PA4 200 Di 12PA4V 200	16PA4V 200	18PA4V 200
No of cylinders		6 horiz	6 line	8 line	6 Vee	8 Vee	12 Vee	16 Vee	18 Vee	8	12	16	18
Turbo-charged		Yes	Yes	Yes	Yes	Yes	Yes	Yes	Yes	Yes	Yes	Yes	Yes
Charge air cooled		Yes	Yes	Yes	Yes	Yes	Yes	Yes	Yes	Yes	Yes	Yes	Yes
Power rating (UIC)	hp	1 000	1 000	1 335	1 000	1 335	2 000	2 670	3 000	1 400	2 100	2 800	3 150
	rpm					1 500					1 500		
Piston speed	ft/min					1 968					1 968		
	(m/s)					(10.5)					(10.5)		
Bmep	lb/in²					227					227		
	(kg/cm²)					(16.0)					(16.0)		
Weight dry	lb	7 500	7 500	9 700	7 100	8 530	12 390	15 700	17 700	9 500	13 200	17 000	19 000
	(kg)	(3 400)	(3 400)	(4 400)	(3 220)	(3 870)	(5 620)	(7 120)	(7 970)	(4 300)	(6 000)	(7 720)	(8 620)
Length	in	117.3	120.2	143.8	63.8	75.8	99.4	123.1	134.9	75.8	99.4	123.1	134.9
	(mm)	(2 980)	(3 054)	(3 654)	(1 626)	(1 926)	(2 526)	(3 126)	(3 426)	(1 926)	(2 526)	(3 126)	(3 426)
Width	in	68.9	33.9	33.9	57.1	57.1	57.1	57.1	57.1	67.0	62.0	57.1	66.9
	(mm)	(1 750)	(860)	(860)	(1 450)	(1 450)	(1 450)	(1 450)	(1 450)	(1 702)	(1 575)	(1 450)	(1 700)
Height	in	33.5	65.4	65.4	73.3	73.3	75.6	73.3	73.3	73.4	75.6	73.4	73.6
	(mm)	(850)	(1 660)	(1 660)	(1 863)	(1 863)	(1 921)	(1 863)	(1 863)	(1 865)	(1 920)	(1 865)	(1 920)

BRITISH LEYLAND

British Leyland (UK) Ltd
(Power Systems Operations)
Leyland, Lancashire PR5 1SN, England

Flat form railcar engines, 138 to 240 bhp models. 4.5 kg per bhp four stroke.

CATERPILLAR

Caterpillar Tractor Co
Industrial Division, Peoria, Illinois 61602, USA

Caterpillar Overseas SA
118 rue du Rhône, 1211 Geneva 3, Switzerland

Caterpillar builds a range of diesel engines with outputs from 85 to 1 300 hp. These engines are designed for a wide range of industrial and railway applications.

Specification for all models
Cylinders: Removable wet type cylinder liners of hardened cast iron. Alloy cast iron cylinder heads with water directors and removable precombustion chambers.
Pistons: Aluminium alloy with cast-in-iron ring band, stainless steel heat plug, and chrome-faced rings.
Connecting rods: Forged of Boron steel and shot peened.
Crankshaft: Total hardened crankshaft, superfinished and dynamically balanced.
Crankcase: Strongly reinforced, one-piece alloy cast iron with large inspection plates.
Fuel injection: Gear-type transfer pumps, replaceable full-flow filter elements, individual fuel injection pumps and single orifice injection valves. Designed and built by Caterpillar.
Fuel: No 2 fuel oil (ASTM Specifications D396-48T). Premium quality diesel fuel can be used, but it is not required.
Lubrication: Full pressure system. Includes gear-type pump, efficient filter elements and water-cooled oil cooler.
Cooling system: Built-in, centrifugal-type circulating pump. Thermostatic water temperature control.
Starting: Air, electric.

Caterpillar Model D399 16-cylinder Vee engine

		D399	D398	D379	D353	D349	D348	3412	3408	3406	3306	3304
Bore & stroke	in	6.25 × 8	6.25 × 8	6.25 × 8	6.25 × 8	5.4 × 6.5	5.4 × 6.5	5.4 × 6	5.4 × 6	5.4 × 6.5	4.75 × 6	4.75 × 6
	(mm)	(159 × 203)	(159 × 203)	(159 × 203)	(159 × 203)	(137 × 165)	(137 × 165)	(137 × 152)	(137 × 152)	(137 × 165)	(121 × 152)	(121 × 152)
No of cylinders		V-16	V-12	V-8	1-6	V-16	V-12	V-12	V-8	1-6	1-6	1-4
Turbo-charged		Yes	Yes	Yes	Yes	Yes	Yes	Yes	Yes	Yes	Yes	Yes
Aftercooled		Yes	Yes	Yes	Yes	Yes	Yes	Yes	Yes	Yes	Yes	No
Locomotive rating		1 300	975	650	490	1 130	850	750	475	375	270	165
bhp*	rpm	1 300	1 300	1 300	1 300	2 000	2 000	2 100	2 100	2 100	2 200	2 200
Weight (dry)	lb	15 000	11 800	9 000	6 180	9 900	8 100	1 955	1 474	2 890	1 960	1 628
	(kg)	(6 800)	(5 350)	(4 080)	(2 800)	(4 490)	(3 675)	(1 955)	(1 474)	(1 323)	(890)	(738)
Length	in	128.34	105.6	83.50	80.4	100.71	85.55	77.05	61.08	64.88	50.62	38.92
	(mm)	(3 260)	(2 682)	(2 120.1)	(2 042)	(2 558)	(2 172.9)	(1 952)	(1 551.4)	(1 647.9)	(1 285.7)	(988.6)
Width	in	59.3	59.3	59.3	46.83	60.12	60.12	58.4	25.62	35.5	29.71	29.71
	(mm)	(1 505.7)	(1 505.7)	(1 505.7)	(1 189.48)	(1 527)	(1 527)	(1 483.4)	(673.6)	(902.2)	(754.6)	(754.6)
Height	in	78.8	78.8	75.36	65.8	65.28	65.28	53.9	54.2	51.6	43.5	39.4
	(mm)	(2 001)	(2 001)	(1 914)	(1 671)	(1 658)	(1 658)	(1 496)	(1 376)	(1 311)	(1 104)	(1 101)

* Consult factory for applicable ratings dependant on service.   Also TA version

COCKERILL

SA Cockerill-Ougrée-Providence et Espérance-Longdoz
Seraing, Belgium

The present firm of SA Cockerill was formed in 1970 by a merger of the two companies SA Cockerill-Ougrée-Providence and SA Métallurgique d'Espérance-Longdoz. Their first diesel engine was built in 1913 with assistance from its inventor Rudolph Diesel.

Series 240CO
Type: 6 and 8 cylinders in-line, 12, 16 and 18 cylinders in Vee, 4 cycle water cooled.
Cylinders: Bore 9.5 in (241.3 mm). Stroke 12.0 in (304.8 mm). Swept volume 13.92 litres per cylinder. Cast iron wet cylinder liners, separate cast iron cylinder heads, direct injection combustion chambers.
Pistons: Oil-cooled pistons made of aluminium alloy.
Connecting rods: Drop forged.
Crankshaft: Cro-Mo steel induction hardened pins and journals.
Crankcase: One piece modular cast iron cylinder block.
Valve gear: Two inlet and two exhaust valves per cylinder.
Fuel injection: Mechanical pumps and nozzles.
Lubrication: One pressure pump.
Cooling system: One centrifugal water pump.

Model			6TR	8TR	240 CO Series V12TR	V16TR
No of cylinders			6	8	12	16
Turbo-charged			Yes	Yes	Yes	Yes
Charge air cooled			Yes	Yes	Yes	Yes
Weight (dry)	lb		18 722	24 230	34 580	45 815
	kg		8 500	11 000	15 700	20 800
Length	in		129.92	156.93	171.77	232.28
	mm		3 300	3 986	4 363	5 900
Width	in		47.64	48.03	86.62	84.25
	mm		1 210	1 220	2 200	2 140
Height	in		104.73	104.73	93.11	105.08
	mm		2 660	2 660	2 365	2 669
Speed				750 rpm		
Continuous power	hp		1 200	1 600	2 400	3 200
Bmep	lb/in²		244	244	244	244
	(kg/cm²)		17.2	17.2	17.2	17.2
Piston speed	ft/min		1 501	1 501	1 501	1 501
	(m/s)		7.63	7.63	7.63	7.63
Fuel consumption	lb/hp/h		0.342	0.346	0.346	0.340
	g/hp/h		153	155	155	152
Speed				1000 rpm		
Continuous power	hp		1 650	2 200	3 300	4 400
Bmep	lb/in²		253	253	253	253
	kg/cm²		17.8	17.8	17.8	17.8
Piston speed	ft/min		1 999	1 999	1 999	1 999
	m/s		10.16	10.16	10.16	10.16
Fuel consumption	lb/hp/h		0.340	0.346	0.350	0.335
	g/hp/h		152	155	156.5	150.0

CREUSOT-LOIRE

Société Creusot-Loire, Traction Division
31-32 quai National, 92806 Puteaux, France

The company has been manufacturing diesel engines for over 50 years. They hold licences to manufacture the designs of several companies including, since 1957, engines for rail traction of Adolf Saurer Ltd, Switzerland. Nearly a thousand diesel units have been built, and a special workshop has been equipped for serial production of the S series engine, developed for mounting beneath the floor of railcars.

Special efforts have been made regarding the design and development of the six-cylinder horizontal versions of this engine to meet the requirements of under-floor-engined railcars.

More than 400 SDHR engines have been mounted in new SNCF railcars. Some of these engines have more than 500 000 miles (800 000 km) of running to their credit.

The SDHR engine, equipped with oil cooled pistons, has passed acceptance tests, in accordance with UIC regulations, at 550 nominal hp at a 1 500 rpm rated speed. It is possible to increase this power output to 600 hp with the SIDHR.

The power ratings, according to UIC regulations, of the S series CL. SAURER engines are as follows:

		Power ratings in metric hp at 1 500 rpm
SD	6 normally aspirated vertical cylinders	315
SDH	6 normally aspirated horizontal cylinders	315
SDL	6 turbo-charged vertical cylinders	450
SDHL	6 turbo-charged horizontal cylinders	450
SDR	6 turbo-charged vertical cylinders with air cooling	550/600
SDHR	6 turbo-charged horizontal cylinders with air cooling	550/600
SEV	12 normally aspirated Vee arranged cylinders	630
SEH	12 normally aspirated horizontal cylinders	630
SEVL	12 turbo-charged Vee arranged cylinders	900
SEHL	12 turbo-charged horizontal cylinders	900
SEVR	12 turbo-charged Vee arranged cylinders with air cooling	1 100/1 200
SFV	16 normally aspirated Vee arranged cylinders	840
SFVL	16 turbo-charged Vee arranged cylinders	1 200
SFVR	16 turbo-charged Vee arranged cylinders with air cooling	1 400/1 600

The normally aspirated SD315 hp 6-cylinder engine is mounted in light rail tractors.

Mention must also be made of developments covering the 16-cylinder Vee engine in the field of stationary power generating sets.

CL. SAURER type SDHR 6-cylinder horizontal engine

CUMMINS

Cummins Engine Co, Inc
Columbus, Indiana 47201, USA

Telephone: (812) 372 7211
Telex: 217 411 Columbus
Telegrams: CUMDIEX, Columbus

Cummins Engine Co manufactures a range of diesel engines from 175 to 1 600 hp for a wide variety of applications. Experience in industrial and railway installations covers a span of 40 years. Over 2 000 sales and service outlets are located throughout the world. Cummins design features are listed below for the K series.

General Specification

Bearings: Precision type, steel backed inserts. 7 main bearings, 6.5-in (165 mm) diameter. Connecting rod, 4.25-in (108 mm) diameter.

Camshaft: Dual camshafts control all valve and injector movement. Induction hardened alloy steel with gear drive.

Camshaft followers: Roller type for long cam and follower life.

Connecting rods: Drop forged 11.4 in (290 mm) centre to centre length. Rifle drilled for pressure lubrication of piston pin. Taper piston pin end reduces unit pressures.

Crankshaft: High tensile strength steel forging. Bearing journals are induction hardened.

Cylinder block: Alloy cast iron with removable, wet liners.

Cylinder heads: Individual cylinder heads. Drilled fuel supply and return lines. Corrosion resistant inserts on intake and exhaust valve seats.

Fuel system: Cummins PT (TM) self-adjusting system with integral flyball type governor. Camshaft actuated injectors.

Gear train: Heavy duty, induction hardened, at front of cylinder block.

Lubrication: Force feed to all bearings, gear type pump. All lubrication lines are drilled passages, except pan to pump suction line.

Pistons: Aluminium, cam ground, with two compression and one oil ring. Oil cooled.

Piston pins: 2.4 in (61 mm) diameter, full floating.

Turbo-charger: Scroll diffuser, top mounted.

Valves: Dual intake and exhaust each cylinder. Each valve 2.22 in (56 mm) diameter. Heat- and corrosion-resistant face on exhaust valves.

Cummins KTA-2300-L engine

Engine	Intermittent Traction rating BS 2953: 1958 hp at rpm		Continuous Traction rating UIC and BS 2953: 1958 hp at rpm		Displacement Cubic Inches (litres)	Bore and Stroke Inches (mm)	Number of Cylinders	Aspiration	Net Weight lb (kg)
Locomotive Engines									
N-855-L3	235	2 100	210	2 100	855 (14.0)	5½×6 (140 × 152)	6	N	2 590 (1 175)
NT-855-L4	335	2 100	285	2 100	855 (14.0)	,,	6	T	2 625 (1 191)
NTA-855-L3	400	2 100	340	2 100	855 (14.0)	,,	6	T/A	2 750 (1 247)
VTA-1710-L1	700	2 100	595	2 100	1 710 (28.0)	,,	12	T/A	5 780 (2 621)
VTA-1710-L2	800	2 100	680	2 100	1 710 (28.0)	,,	12	T/A	5 780 (2 621)
KT-1150-L	450	2 100	380	2 100	1 150 (18.8)	6¼ × 6¼ (159 × 159)	6	T	3 450 (1 565)
KTA-1150-L	600	2 100	510	2 100	1 150 (18.8)	,,	6	T/A	3 500 (1 588)
KT-2300-L	900	2 100	765	2 100	2 300 (37.6)	,,	12	T	7 750 (3 315)
*KTA-2300-L	1 200	2 100	1 020	2 100	2 300 (37.6)	,,	12	T/A	9 250 (4 200)
*KTA-3067-L	1 600	2 100	1 360	2 100	3 067 (50.3)	6¼ × 6¼ (159 × 159)	16	T/A	12 000 5 455
Railcar Engines									
N-855-R2	235	2 100	210	2 100	855 (14.0)	5½ × 6 (140 × 152)	6	N	2 600 (1 185)
NT-855-R4	335	2 100	285	2 100	855 (14.0)	,,	6	T	2 700 (1 200)
NTA-855-R	400	2 100	340	2 100	855 (14.0)	,,	6	T/A	2 800 (1 255)

*Certified to BS 2953: 1958 BSI Certificate No 36791 (KTA-2300-L); Certificate No 50015 (KTA-3067-1)

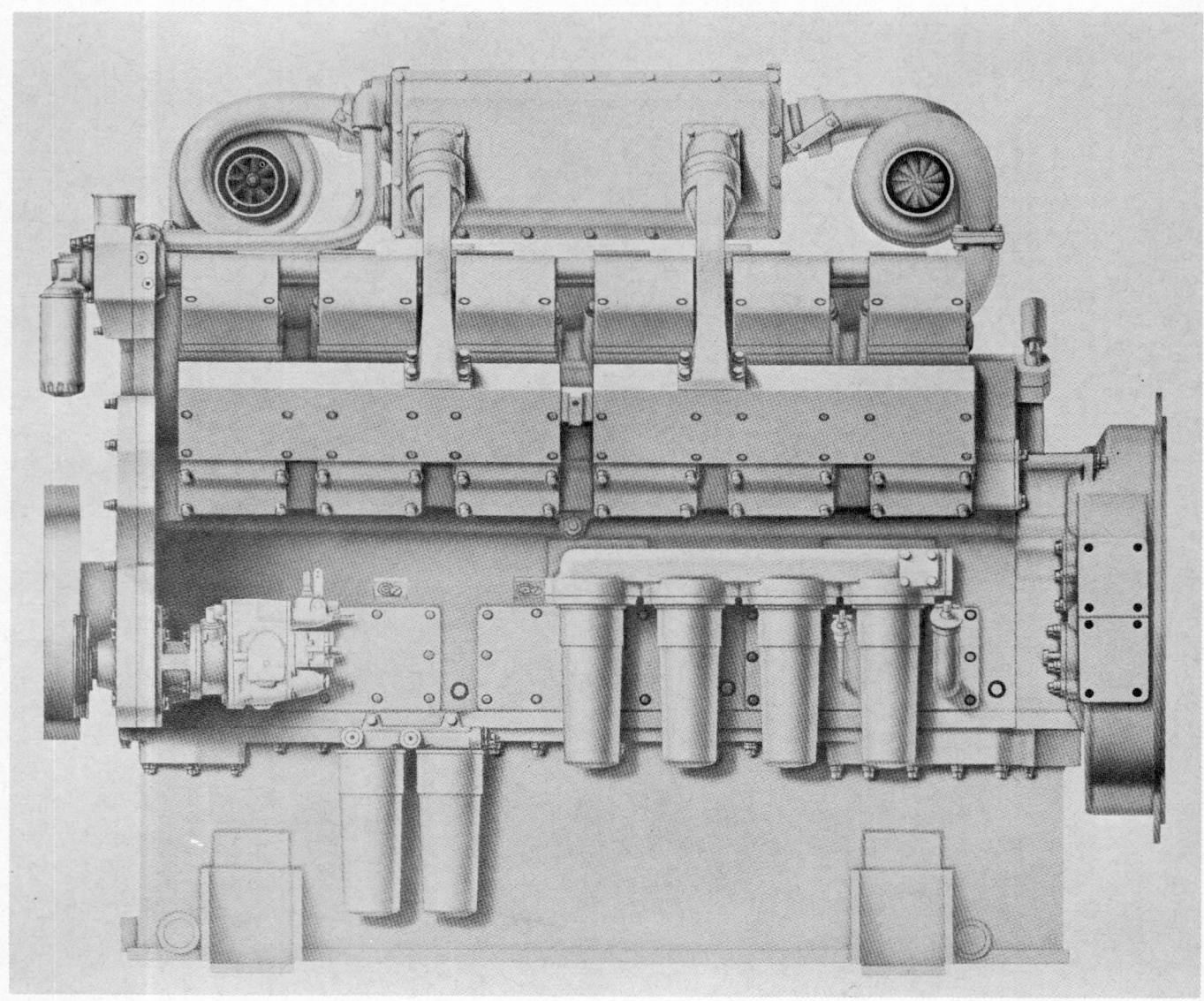

Cummins KTA-3067-L engine

DEUTZ

Klöckner-Humboldt-Deutz AG
D-5000 Köln-Deutz, Postfach 800509, Federal Republic of Germany

The Deutz Engine Works is the oldest internal combustion engine factory in the world. Started in 1864 as N A Otto & Co, it soon became Gasmotorenfabrik Deutz AG. The first engine working on the OTTO or four-stroke cycle, invented by N A Otto, was built in 1876.

Deutz diesel engines range from 3-9 856 hp (2-7 250 kW) for industrial, marine, rail, traction and automotive applications. They are all four-stroke, air-cooled (3-525 hp) or water-cooled (109-9 856 hp). For rail traction series B/FL 413F, BAM 816 and PAGV 280 are used.

Series B/FL 413F
Type: 6, 8, 10 and 12 cylinder Vee 4-stroke, air-cooled, direct injection or 2-stage combustion.
Cylinders: Bore 4.92 in (125 mm), stroke 5.12 (130 mm), swept volume 1.59 litres per cylinder. Compression ratio 18 : 1 (naturally aspirated), 16.5 : 1 (turbo-charged).

Series BAM 816
Type: 6 and 8 cylinder in-line, 12 and 16 cylinder Vee, 4-stroke, water-cooled, two-stage combustion system.
Cylinders: Bore 5.59 in (142 mm), stroke 6.30 in (160 mm). Swept volume 2.53 litres per cylinder. Compression ratio 16.1:1.

Deutz F12L 413F 12-cylinder air-cooled engine
Output (UIC) 246 kW (335 hp) at 2 500 rpm.

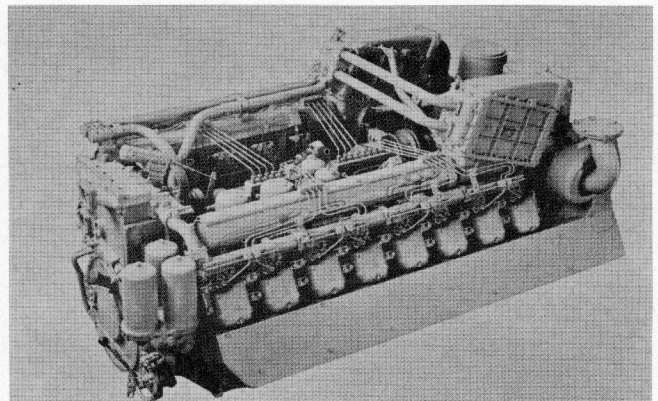

Deutz BA16M 816 16-cylinder water-cooled engine
Output (UIC) up to 830 kW (1 130 hp) at 1 800 rpm.

Series B/FL 413F		F6L	BF6L	F8L	BF8L	F10L	BF10L	F12L	BF12L	BF12L*
No of Cylinders		6V	6V	8V	8V	10V	10V	12V	12V	12V
Turbo-charged			Yes		Yes		Yes		Yes	Yes
Output (UIC)	kW	123	157	165	210	206	262	246	315	349
	hp	167	214	225	286	280	356	335	428	475
Engine speed	rpm	2 500	2 500	2 500	2 500	2 500	2 500	2 500	2 500	2 500
Length	in	41¼	45³/₈	47¹¹/₁₆	49⁵/₈	55⁹/₁₆	56⁵/₁₆	62	61¹⁵/₁₆	62¼
	(mm)	(1 047)	(1 153)	(1 211)	(1 260)	(1 412)	(1 430)	(1 575)	(1 573)	(1 582)
Width	in	40⁷/₈	41⁷/₈	40⁷/₈	42³/₁₆	40⁷/₈	44	40⁷/₈	46¹⁵/₁₆	47¹/₁₆
	(mm)	(1 038)	(1 060)	(1 038)	(1 072)	(1 038)	(1 118)	(1 038)	(1 192)	(1 196)
Height	in	33⁷/₈	34⁷/₈	33⁷/₈	40⁹/₁₆	36⁷/₈	41⁵/₁₆	37⁵/₈	41⁵/₁₆	48¹⁵/₁₆
	(mm)	(860)	(886)	(860)	(1 030)	(937)	(1 050)	(956)	(1 050)	(1 243)
Weight	lb	1 335	1 500	1 700	1 985	2 070	2 425	2 470	2 755	2 945
	(kg)	(605)	(680)	(770)	(900)	(940)	(1 100)	(1 120)	(1 250)	(1 335)

*Charge air cooled.

Series BAM 816		BA6M LLK U	BA6M LLK W	BA8M LLK U	BA8M LLK W	BA12M LLK U	BA12M LLK W	BA16M LLK U	BA16M LLK W
No of cylinders		6	6	8	8	12	12	16	16
Turbo-charged		Yes	Yes	Yes	Yes	Yes	Yes	Yes	Yes
Charge air cooled		Yes	Yes	Yes	Yes	Yes	Yes	Yes	Yes
Output (UIC)	kW	295	335	390	450	590	670	780	900
	hp	400	456	536	612	800	912	1 060	1 224
Engine speed	rpm	1 800	1 800	1 800	1 800	1 800	1 800	1 800	1 800
Length	in		72		84⁷/₈		76¹³/₁₆		97¹/₈
	(mm)		1 829		2 156		1 951		2 467
Width	in		38³/₄		37¹/₂		64		64
	(mm)		984		952		1 626		1 626
Height	in		56¹¹/₁₆		58		52¹⁵/₁₆		52¹⁵/₁₆
	(mm)		1 440		1 473		1 345		1 345
Weight	lb		3 540		4 520		6 395		7 980
	(kg)		1 605		2 050		2 900		3 620

Series PA6V 280		12PA6V	14PA6V	16PA6V	18PA6V
No of cylinders		12V	14V	16V	18V
Turbo-charged		Yes	Yes	Yes	Yes
Charge air cooled		Yes	Yes	Yes	Yes
Output (UIC)	kW	3 533	4 122	4 710	5 299
	hp	4 800	5 600	6 400	7 200
Engine speed	rpm	1 050	1 050	1 050	1 050
Length	in	144³/₄	162³/₄	181	199
	(mm)	3 675	4 135	4 595	5 055
Width	in	70¹/₁₆	70¹/₁₆	70¹/₁₆	70¹/₁₆
	(mm)	1 780	1 780	1 780	1 780
Height	in	97⁵/₈	97⁵/₈	97⁵/₈	97⁵/₈
	(mm)	2 480	2 480	2 480	2 480
Weight	lb	41 360	47 300	53 020	57 640
	(kg)	(18 800)	(21 500)	(24 100)	(26 200)

ENERGOMACHEXPORT
127486 Moscow, Deguninskaya St, 1, Korp 4, USSR

Model D49 16-cylinder vee engine
Turbo-charged and charge air cooled. Output 3 000 hp at 1 000 rpm. Built by Kolomna Diesel Works.

Series		D49				D50			D70				M		1D
Type		4-stroke Vee				4-stroke in line			4-stroke Vee				4-stroke Vee		4-stroke Vee
Bore	in		10.24				12.5			9.45				7.09	5.9
	(mm)		(260)				(318)			(240)				(180)	(150)
Stroke	in		10.24				13.0			10.63				7.88/8.26	7.09/7.35
	(mm)		(260)				(330)			(270)				(200/208.8)	(180/186.7)
Model		4D49	12D49	D49-V16	D49-F	D50	D50M	11D1M	8D70	12D70	D70	D70F	M753	M756	1D12
No of cylinders		6	12	16	16	6	6	6	8	12	16	16	12	12	12
Output	hp	1 200	2 000	3 000	4 000	1 000	1 000	1 200	1 200	2 000	3 000	4 000	750	1 000	400
Engine speed	rpm	1 000	1 000	1 000	1 000	740	740	750	1 000	1 000	1 000	1 000	1 400	1 500	1 600
Piston speed	ft/min	1 713	1 713	1 713	1 713	1 604	1 604	1 624	1 772	1 772	1 772	1 772	1 837/1 929	2 087/2 205	1 890
	(m/s)	(8.7)	(8.7)	(8.7)	(8.7)	(8.15)	(8.15)	(8.25)	(9.0)	(9.0)	(9.0)	(9.0)	(9.3/9.8)	(10.6/11.2)	(9.6)
Bmep	lb/in²	188	156	174	232	110	110	131	196	175	196	262	105	131	82.5
	(kg/cm²)	(13.2)	(11.0)	(12.2)	(16.3)	(7.7)	(7.7)	(9.2)	(13.8)	(12.3)	(13.8)	(18.4)	(7.4)	(9.2)	(5.8)
Weight	lb	14 300	24 200	30 900	30 900	39 700			24 700	31 300	37 500	37 500	35 300	39 700	41 900
	(kg)	(6 500)	(11 000)	(14 000)	(14 000)	(18 000)			(11 200)	(14 200)	(17 000)	(17 000)	(16 000)	(18 000)	(19 000)
Length	in	96	142	170	170	205			157	181	217	220	89.4	95.3	61.4
	(mm)	(2 400)	(3 600)	(4 300)	(4 300)	(5 200)			(4 000)	(4 600)	(5 500)	(5 600)	(2 270)	(2 420)	(1 560)
Width	in	55	63	63	63	59			63	63	63	63	42.7	44.1	33.7
	(mm)	(1 400)	(1 600)	(1 600)	(1 600)	(1 500)			(1 600)	(1 600)	(1 600)	(1 600)	(1 085)	(1 120)	(856)
Height	in	90	102	110	110	98			110	114	118	118	47.3	58.3	42.3
	(mm)	(2 300)	(2 600)	(2 800)	(2 800)	(2 500)			(2 800)	(2 900)	(3 000)	(3 000)	(1 200)	(1 480)	(1 075)

Series		D100				D40	D45
Type		2-stroke, opposed piston				2-stroke Vee	2-stroke Vee
Bore	in		8.15			9.06	9.06
	(mm)		(207)			(230)	(230)
Stroke	in		10.0			11.8/11.98	11.8/11.98
	(mm)		(254)			(300/304.3)	(300/304.3)
Model		6D100	2D100	10D100	9D100-F	1D40	11D45
No of cylinders		8	10	10	12	12	16
Output	hp	2 000	2 000	3 000	4 000	2 000	3 000
Engine speed	rpm	850	850	850	900	750	750
Piston speed	ft/min	1 417	1 417	1 417	1 496	1 476	1 476
	(m/s)	(7.2)	(7.2)	(7.2)	(7.6)	(7.5)	(7.5)
Bmep	lb/in²	111	88	132	108	115	129
	(kg/cm²)	(7.8)	(6.2)	(9.3)	(7.6)	(8.1)	(9.1)
Weight	lb	34 200	42 750	46 300	50 700	23 100	30 400
	(kg)	(15 500)	(19 400)	(21 000)	(23 000)	(10 500)	(13 800)
Length	in	238.3	240.7	243.3	260.6	145.7	158.3
	(mm)	(6 052)	(6 115)	(6 180)	(6 620)	(3 700)	(4 020)
Width	in	66.5	56.7	68.1	59.1	69.7	66.9
	(mm)	(1 690)	(1 440)	(1 730)	(1 500)	(1 770)	(1 700)
Height	in	118.6	127.6	126.4	124.0	95.3	97.2
	(mm)	(3 013)	(3 240)	(3 210)	(3 150)	(2 421)	(2 470)

GANZ-MÁVAG

PO Box 136, Budapest, Könyves Kálmán körut 76, Hungary

Ganz-Mávag Works build various diesel engines, mainly for their own makes of locomotive and railcar. Here is a brief description of two typical engines in these ranges.

Type: SEMT-PIELSTICK 12PA4-V-185 VG made under licence from Alsthom-Atlantique, France
General: 12 cylinders in Vee, 4 stroke with Variable Geometry combustion chamber, turbocharged and intercooled.
Cylinders: Bore 185 mm, stroke 210 mm. Swept volume 5.65 litre per cylinder. Individual cylinder heads and separate cast-iron water jackets with wet liners. Nodular graphite iron pistons with internal oil cooling.
Connecting rods: Side-by-side type.
Crankcase: Tunnel type, with integral oil sump of arc-welded steel castings and steel plates.
Fuel injection: Conventional type injection pump and pintle type injectors.
Valve gear: Single camshaft in the Vee, with push-rods and rockers.
Output: Nominal power rating 1 472 kW/2 000 hp at 1 500 rpm.
Dry weight: About 6 700 kg complete with all accessories.

Type 12 VFE 17/24-T
General: 12 cylinders in Vee, 4 stroke with prechamber, turbo-charged and intercooled.
Cylinders: Bore 170 mm, stroke 240 mm. Swept volume 5.45 litre per cylinder. Individual cylinder heads, wet liners and light metal oil cooled pistons.
Connecting rods: Fork-and-blade type.
Crankcase: Light alloy casting with separate oil sump.
Fuel injection: Jendrassik type spring injection pump and semi-open injectors.
Valve gears: Single camshaft in the Vee, with push-rods and rockers.
Output: Nominal power rating 736 kW/1 000 hp at 1 250 rpm.
Dry weight: About 5 000 kg complete with accessories.

PA4 engine range also comprise 6, 8, 16 and 18 cylinder models. 17/24 range also comprises 6 and 8 cylinder models.

Ganz Mavag 12VFE 17/24 12-cylinder Vee
1 000 hp at 1 250 rpm.

Ganz-Mavag-Pielstick 12 PA4V-185 engine
12-cylinder Vee, turbo-charged and charge-air cooled, developing 2 000 hp at 1 500 rpm (UIC rating).

GARDNER

L Gardner & Sons Ltd
Barton Hall Engine Works, Patricroft, Eccles, Manchester M30 7WA, England

Founded by the Gardner brothers in 1898 as a general engineering works on the present site, employing 80 men, the works to-day cover nearly 20 times the original area and has 2 800 employees. In 1901 a limited company, L Gardner & Sons Ltd, was formed, and this is now the parent company of Gardner Engines (Sales) Ltd. Hot air engines and horizontal gas engines were built at first and development of the compression ignition engine followed. For example, a 6-cylinder Gardner engine which is claimed to be the first diesel rail traction unit in the British Isles; this was a 52-seat railcar built by County Donegal Railways in 1931.

Production comprises automotive, rail traction, marine and industrial engines. For rail traction the main types are L3B, 8LXB, and 6LXB from 180 to 260 hp. They are fitted in locomotives and railcars produced by numerous builders including Barclay, Baguley-Drewry, Hunslet, Hudswell Badger. The National Coal Board (GB) uses LW type engines in flame-proof underground locomotives, and British Rail operates a large number of small diesel mechanical shunting locomotives powered by the larger Gardner engines. Gardner-powered railcars and locomotives are in service in countries throughout the world.

Gardner 6HLXB 6-cylinder horizontal diesel engine

6LXB, (vertical) and 6HLXB (horizontal)

Type: 6 and 8 cylinder, 4-cycle, vertical, in-line, water cooled.
Cylinders: Bore 120.6 mm (4¾ in). Stroke 152.4 mm (6 in). Swept volume 1.7 litres per cylinder. Compression ratio 14 : 1. High tensile cast iron cylinder blocks with dry type renewable liners. Detachable cast iron cylinder heads in two 3-bore units, secured with H.T. studs and nuts with indented steel (corrojoint) cylinder head packing.
Pistons: Medium silicon aluminium alloy with combustion chamber in crown. 2 compression rings and one oil control ring, fully floating hollow gudgeon pin.
Connecting rods: Chrome molybdenum steel H section stampings machined all over. Pre-finished steel shell bearings lined with copper lead overlay plated for big-ends and bronze bushes for small ends.
Crankshaft: Solid one piece chrome molybdenum steel die stamping with hollow main and crankpin journals. Pre-finished steel shell main bearings lined with copper lead overlay plated.
Crankcase: Aluminium alloy with separate detachable cast iron single cylinder block fitted with renewable dry liners.
Valve gear: One exhaust and one inlet alloy steel overhead valve per cylinder. Press fit renewable stellite faced valve seats. Camshaft in crankcase driven by triplex bush roller chain.
Fuel injection: Multi-hole non-adjustable Gardner injectors with twin CAV type BPF (3 Ram) pumps.
Fuel: High-speed diesel fuel oil.
Lubrication: Pressure feed throughout with one gear-type pump. Additional pump and oil cooling radiator as required.
Cooling System: Gardner centrifugal type pump with spherical carbon gland. Gardner multi-tube radiator and fan or proprietary make.
Starting System: 24 V electric starter.
Starting System: 24 V CAV or Simms axial motor.

8L3B

Type: 8 cylinder, 4-cycle, vertical in-line, water cooled.
Cylinders: Bore 140 mm (5½ in). Stroke 197 mm (7¾ in). Swept volume 3.0 litres per cylinder. Compression ratio 12 : 1. Detachable cast iron wet liners with renewable dry type liners. Detachable individual cast iron cylinder heads secured with studs and nuts. Metal to metal joint with no packing.
Pistons: Low expansion medium silicon aluminium alloy with combustion chamber in crown. Two compression rings and one oil control ring, fully floating hollow gudgeon pin.
Connecting rods: Chrome molybdenum steel stampings machined all over. Pre-finished steel shell bearings lined with copper lead overlay plated for big ends and bronze bushes for small ends.
Crankshaft: Solid one piece chrome molybdenum steel die stamping with hollow main and crankpin journals. Pre-finished steel shell main bearings lined with copper lead overlay plated.
Crankcase: Upper and lower half type cast iron crankcase with detachable cast iron cylinder blocks.
Valve gear: One exhaust and one inlet alloy steel overhead valves per cylinder. Press fit renewable hardened alloy iron valve seats. Camshaft in crankcase driven by triplex bush roller chain.
Fuel injection: Multi hole non-adjustable Gardner injectors with CAV type BPF pumps.
Fuel: High-speed diesel oil fuel.
Lubrication: Pressure feed throughout with one gear type pump. Additional pump and oil cooling radiator as required.
Cooling system: Gardner centrifugal type pump with spherical carbon gland. Gardner multi-tube radiator and fan, or proprietary make.
Starting system: 24 or 32 V electric starter.
Mounting: 6 point.

Gardner 8L3B 8-cylinder diesel engine

Model		8 L3B	LXB	HLXB	8LXB
No of cylinders		8	6	6	8
Max bhp		260	180	180	240
Engine speed	rpm	1 300	1 850	1 850	1 850
Weight approx	lb	5 523	1 560	1 707	2 045
	(kg)	(2 505)	(707.6)	(774.3)	(927.6)
Length	in	97¾	55	55	64
	(mm)	(2 483)	(1 397)	(1 397)	(1 626)
Width	in	34½	26¼	55	27
	(mm)	(807)	(667)	(1 397)	(686)
Height	in	50¾	45¼	26	50
	(mm)	(1 276)	(1 149)	(660)	(1 270)

Above engines are normal aspiration. BS AU 141A ratings are: 6LXB HLXB 188 bhp; 8LXB 250 bhp.
Road Vehicles only.

GE

General Electric Co
Transportation Systems Business Division,
2910 East Lake Road, Erie, Pennsylvania 16531, USA

Series FDL (8, 12 and 16 cylinder 45° Vee)

Type: 4 cycle turbo-charged with water cooled charge air cooler.
Cylinders: Bore 9 in (229 mm). Stroke 10½ in (267 mm). Swept volume of 668 cu in per cylinder. Individual unitised cast cylinder with renewable liner and head. Compression ratio 12.7:1.
Pistons: Current-production engines use 2-piece pistons. The steel crown, contoured on the top to form the combustion chamber and on the bottom to form cooling-oil passages, is bolted to an aluminium-alloy skirt.
Pistons used in older engines were one-piece, cast-iron pistons, with 6, and later 4, rings. Current-production engines also use 4 rings, 3 compression rings and one oil-control ring.
Crankcase: Main frame of high strength cast iron.
Valve gear: Roller type cam followers, push rods and rockers, 4 valves per cylinder. Gear driven sectionalised camshaft on each side of engine.
Fuel injection: Individual injectors and fuel pumps.
Turbo-charger: One, exhaust driven (no gear drive to crankshaft).
Lubrication: Forced full flow filtered oil to all bearings and pistons, gear type engine driven pump.
Cooling system: Forced circulation water cooling of cylinders, turbo-charger, and intercoolers. The water passages are external of the crankcase and main frame.

General Electric 3 940 hp (UIC) 16-cylinder Vee engine

Current Design Engine Specifications

Model	7FDL8	7FDL12	7FDL16
No of cylinders	8	12	16
Output (UIC) standard	1 970	2 960	3 940
Stroke cycle	4	4	4
Cylinder arrangement	45-degree V	45-degree V	45-degree V
Bore	9 in (228.6 mm)	9 in (228.6 mm)	9 in (228.6 mm)
Stroke	10½ in (266.7 mm)	10½ in (266.7 mm)	10½ in (266.7 mm)
Compression ratio	12:7-1	12:7-1	12:7-1
Idle speed	450 rpm	450 rpm	450 rpm
Full-rated speed	1 050 rpm	1 050 rpm	1 050 rpm
Firing order	1R-1L-2R-2L-4R-4L-3R-3L	1R-1L-5R-5L-5L-3R-3l-6R 6L-2R-2L-4R-4L	1R-1L-3R-3L-7R-7L-4R-4L 8R-8L-6R-6L-2R-2L-5R-5L
Turbo-charger	Single	Single	Single
Engine Dimensions:			
Height (excluding stack)	86¼ in (2 191 mm)	90⅛ in (2 289 mm)*	9⅛ in (2 289 mm)
Length (over-all)	128½ in (3 264 mm)	159½ in (4 051 mm)	193 in (4 902 mm)
Width (over-all)	68¼ in (1 734 mm)	68⅜ in (1 740 mm)	68⅜ in (1 740 mm)
Weight (dry)	27 000 lb (12 200 kg)	35 000 lb (15 900 kg)	43 500 lb (19 700 kg)

*Note: This dimension is for domestic (USA) type engines. The export model has a lower water header (86¼ in—2 191 mm)

GEC DIESELS

GEC Diesels Ltd
Vulcan Works, Newton-le-Willows, Merseyside WA12 8RU, England

GEC Diesels Ltd is the parent company of Ruston Diesels Ltd, Paxman Diesels Ltd and Dorman Diesels Ltd.

Engine range	Company	Location
Dorman	Dorman Diesels Ltd	Tixall Road, Stafford
English Electric	Ruston Diesels Ltd	Newton-le-Willows, Merseyside
Paxman	Paxman Diesels Ltd	Colchester, Essex
Deltic	Paxman Diesels Ltd	Colchester, Essex
Alco	Alco Power Inc	Auburn, New York 3021, USA

DELTIC ENGINES

The Deltic is an opposed piston engine with the cylinders arranged in three banks, each bank forming one side of an inverted equilateral triangle with a crankshaft at each apex. Power from the three crankshafts is transmitted through phasing gears to a single central output shaft.

Specification
Type: 18 cylinder. Opposed piston. 2-stroke cycle. Compression-ignition, liquid cooled. The cylinders are arranged in 3 banks each forming one side of an inverted equilateral triangle with crankshaft on each apex. Power from the 3 crankshafts is transmitted through phasing gearing to a single output shaft.
Cylinders: Bore 130.17 mm (5.125 in). Stroke 184.15 mm (7.25 in) × 2. Swept volume 4.91 litres (299 m³) per cylinder. Compression 16:1 (13.8:1 *CT18-52B*). Cylinder blocks are identical light alloy castings of monobloc construction. Open ended wet type cylinder liners machined from hollow steel forgings, chromium plated in bore.
Pistons: Aluminium alloy body with copper-alloy crown, oil cooled, with 3 compression rings and 3 oil control rings. Fully floating hardened steel gudgeon pin.
Connecting rods: Each crankpin carries 2 high-tensile, alloy steel, forged connecting rods, one plain and one forked. The forked rod, to which the exhaust piston is attached, is reinforced at the big end by a nitrided steel sleeve which has a thin wall bearing on the inside and, on the outside, provides a journal for the big end of the plain rod to which the inlet piston is attached.
Crankshaft: Nitrided steel with hollow crank pins statically balanced. The top crankshafts are identical and rotate clockwise; the bottom crankshaft has opposite-handed throws and rotates anti-clockwise. Thin-wall, lead-bronze, lead-plated, indium-infused main bearings.
Crankcase: 2 crankcases are arranged between adjacent cylinder blocks to form the triangular engine assembly, the 6 separate castings being secured together by high-tensile bolts. The 2 upper crankcases are identical but the lower one is deepened in section to provide effective oil drainage for the dry sump lubrication system.
Valve gear: None. Inlet and exhaust ports are provided in each cylinder.
Fuel injection: CAV inward opening valve injectors, one per cylinder, with CAV individual jerk type pumps.
Scavenge air blower: Double sided single-stage centrifugal blower, mounted on the free end of the engine. Mechanically driven from top crankshafts. Provides complete scavenging and a degree of supercharge.
Turbo-blower: Exhaust gas driven and mechanically coupled to the engine. The unit consists of a centrifugal air compressor and a single stage axial flow turbine. On the CT 18-528 engine the charge-air coolers are integral with the blower unit.
Fuel: To BS 2869: 1970 Class A1 and A2 diesel fuel.
Lubrication: Dry sump system. Pressure fed to all bearings and gear trains, with one pressure pump and one scavenge pump.
Cooling system: Forced draught radiator with engine driven centrifugal pump. On charge-cooled engines, the coolers are fed by an independent system comprising a radiator and engine-driven pump.
Starting system: Electric or compressed air.
Mounting: 4-point.

The Deltic can be either mechanically blown or turbo-charged, the turbo-charged engines being available with or without charge-air cooling. British Railways 3 300 hp Type 5 diesel electric locomotives in service on Eastern region are powered by two

Deltic 18-25 mechanically blown engine

mechanically blown Deltic engines.
Several of these have now completed 3.2 million km *(2 million miles)* in under 12 years service, and others are approaching this total.

		Type 18-25B Mechanically blown	Type T18-27B Turbo-charged	Type CT18-52B Charge air cooled Turbo-charged
Length	in	94	123	126
	(mm)	(2 388)	(3 124)	(3 200)
Width	in	70	70	70
	(mm)	(1 778)	(1 778)	(1 778)
Height	in	90	90	90
	(mm)	(2 286)	(2 286)	(2 286)
Weight (dry):	lb	10 850	11 600	13 600
	(kg)	(4 920)	(5 260)	(6 170)
Engine speed	rpm	1 500	1 600	1 600
Power ratings:	bhp			
Intermittent		1 825	2 300	2 750
Continuous:		1 750	2 200	2 625
Fuel consumption:	lb/bhp/h			
Intermittent:		0.350	0.365	0.358
Continuous:		0.350	0.368	0.358

Rated output on all Deltic engines is based on BS 2953

DORMAN ENGINES

Special features of the Dorman series of diesel engines are the wide speed range of 800 to 2 600 rpm on the water cooled engines, and 1 000 to 2 500 rpm on the air cooled engines; their compact and robust design and excellent power to weight ratio, standard cylinder sizes, maximum standardisation and parts interchangeability throughout each series. Fuel consumption is economical.

Dorman 12 QTCW engine generator unit
Turbo-charged and air-to-water charge cooled. 572 kW at 1 800 rpm.

DA Series: 4 and 6 cylinders in line, 8 cylinder Vee, air cooled
L   Series: 6 cylinders in-line, water cooled
Q   Series: 6 cylinders in-line, 8 and 12 cylinder Vee, water cooled
J   Series: 8 and 12 cylinder Vee, water cooled
F   Series: 8 cylinder Vee, water cooled

	Bore	Stroke
DA Series:	4.134 in *(105 mm)*	4.724 in *(120 mm)*
L Series:	5.000 in *(127 mm)*	5.118 in *(130 mm)*
Q Series:	6.250 in *(159 mm)*	6.500 in *(165 mm)*
J Series:	5.118 in *(130 mm)*	5.921 in *(125 mm)*
S Series:	6.250 in *(159 mm)*	7.500 in *(190 mm)*
F Series:	4.330 in *(110 mm)*	4.724 in *(120 mm)*

Connecting rods: DA, L and 6Q, alloy steel H section stampings. 8Q, 8J, 12Q, 12S, H and 8F section alloy steel stampings, side by side on common crankpin.
Crankshafts: Dynamically balanced, hardened steel crankshaft.
Bearings: Steel backed lined with reticular tin.
Crankcase: Rigid cast-iron structure, Monobloc in the case of water cooled engines and with separate barrels in the case of air cooled engines.
Cylinder heads: Water cooled engines; high grade iron castings. Air cooled and 8F engines die cast light alloy.
Pistons: Aluminium Alloy with toroidal combustion chamber.
S, Q and DA series have 3 pressure rings and 2 oil control rings
L series have 2 pressure rings and 2 oil control rings
J series have 2 pressure rings and one oil control ring
Starting: Air, electric or hydraulic.

Dorman 8J 8-cylinder Vee engine
234 hp at 2 200 rpm.

		L Series					
Model	6LD	6LDT	6LDTCA	6LDTCW	6LE	6LET	6LETCA
No of cylinders	6	6	6	6	6	6	6
Turbo-charged	No	Yes	Yes	Yes	No	Yes	Yes
Charge air cooled	No	No	Air to air	Air to water	No	No	Air to air
bhp continuous	162	216	227	227	186	224	250
Engine speed rpm	2 400	1 800	1 800	1 800	2 200	1 800	1 800

								Q Series						
Model	6Q	6QT	6QTCA	6QTCW	8Q	8QT	8QTCA	8QTCW	12Q	12QT	12QTCA	12QTCW	12QBTCA	12BQTCW
No of cylinders	6	6	6	6	8	8	8	8	12	12	12	12	12	12
Turbo-charged	No	Yes	Yes	Yes	No	Yes	Yes	Yes	No	Yes	Yes	Yes	Yes	Yes
Charge air cooled	No	No	Air to air	Air to water	No	No	Air to air	Air to water	No	No	Air to air	Air to water	Air to air	Air to water
bhp continuous	250	345	385	414	318	540	575	570	477	691	769	827	825	760
Engine speed rpm	1 800	1 800	1 800	1 800	1 800	1 800	1 800	1 800	1 800	1 800	1 800	1 800	1 800	1 500

		J Series		S Series	DA Series				F Series	
Model	8J	8JT	12JAT	12ST	4DA	6DA	8DA	6DAT	8F	8FT
No of cylinders	8	8	12	12	4	6	8	6	8	8
Turbo-charged	No	Yes	Yes	Yes	No	No	No	Yes	No	Yes
Charge air cooled	No	No	No	No	No	No	No	No	No	Yes
bhp continuous	234	330	450	760	68	103	134	95	161	217
Engine speed rpm	2 200	2 200	2 000	1 500	2 500	2 500	2 500	1 800	2 600	2 600

RUSTON/ENGLISH ELECTRIC ENGINES

Ruston/English Electric RKC series
The RKC engine provides a maximum output of 262 hp (196 kW) per cylinder at 1 000 rpm. The engine is manufactured in 6 cylinder inline and vee 8, 12 and 16 cylinder forms (vee angle 45 degrees). The engine covers a power band of 1 410-4 200 hp over a speed range of 720-1 000 rpm. This is equivalent to an elctrical power band of 1 000-3 000 kW. The RKC medium speed engine with cylinder dimensions of 254 mm (10 in) bore and 305 mm (12 in) stroke throughout the range offer long periods between overhauls with a high degree of interchangeability of components.

Type: 4-stroke, water cooled.
Pistons: Single piece construction each with a cast-in cooling passage behind the top ring. Cooling oil is transferred from the connecting rod through a slipper arrangement. The ring pack includes a chrome faced top ring, taper faced second and third rings and a comfortable oil control ring.
Connecting rods: Alloy steel forging with a shank of I section and integral bearing housings.

Crankshaft: One piece forged in alloy steel. Separate balance weights are fitted to the crankwebs to achieve optimum oil films in the main bearings.
Crankcase: Cast iron construction housing both cylinder lines and camshafts.
Valve gear: Two inlet and two exhaust valves in each cylinder head seated on renewable wear resisting inserts. The camshaft is chain driven from the crankshaft on inline engines but for vee engines a spur gear drive is used.
Fuel injection: Individual pumps and injectors for each cylinder.
Turbocharger: Normally Napier turbochargers are specified but other proprietory makes can be supplied.
Lubrication: Wet sump lubrication with an engine driven oil pump. The system includes full flow filtration, thermostat and oil cooler.
Cooling System: The jacket cooling system is thermostatically controlled using an engine driven water pump.
Starting System: Electric starting from the locomotive battery, either by starting windings in the driven machine or by starter motors mounted on the engine.

Engine type	Speed rpm	No of cylinders	Continuous power output brakepower		Approx Dimensions Length		Width		Height		Approx weight of engine with flywheel	
			kW	hp	mm	in	mm	in	mm	in	kg	lb
6RKC	900	6	1 134	1 520	4 648	183	1 397	55	2 235	88	12 109	26 670
6RKC	1 000	6	1 175	1 575	4 648	183	1 397	55	2 235	88	12 109	26 670
8RKC												
8RKC												
8RKC	900	8	1 492	2 000	4 343	171	1 702	67	2 337	92	14 213	31 340
8RKC	1 000	8	1 567	2 100	4 343	171	1 702	67	2 337	92	14 213	31 340
12RKC	900	12	2 268	3 040	5 207	205	1 829	72	2 235	88	19 293	42 540
12RKC	1 000	12	2 350	3 150	5 207	205	1 829	72	2 235	88	19 293	42 540
16RKC	900	16	2 984	4 000	6 325	249	1 803	71	2 311	91	23 864	52 620
16RKC	1 000	16	3 133	4 200	6 325	249	1 803	71	2 311	91	23 864	52 620

Note: The powers shown are available for traction duty in accordance with BS 5514. These ratings can be developed under the following conditions: Charge air cooler water temperature not exceeding 52°C (125°F) altitude 610 m (2 000 ft).

16 RKC engine, as fitted in British Rail Class 56 locomotive

PAXMAN ENGINES

Paxman engines were first introduced into railway traction in 1930. The Paxman engines in the present range are of compact design while providing maximum accessibility for maintenance. They combine high power-to-weight ratio with the rugged construction necessary for reliable traction service.

British Rail's high-speed train in public service is powered by two 12-cylinder Valenta 12 CL engines. Two years of exhaustive testing proved the performance and reliability of the train wich achieved a speed of 229 km/h (143 mph), a world record for diesel traction. Over 200 engine sets are on order or in service with British Rail.

Recent orders include a further repeat for Valenta 12CL engines from British Rail and 20 8RPHL normally aspirated engines for the Tanzania Railway Corporation.

RPH, YH, and Ventura and Valenta Series

Type: 4-cycle water-cooled 60° Vee (in-line Valenta 6CL) pressure-charged (suffix X to engine type number) or pressure-charged and intercooled (suffix C). All Valenta and Ventura engines are pressure-charged and intercooled.

Housing: Cast iron RPH and YH with cast cylinder blocks mounted on housing. Cast iron, one piece housing, Ventura and Valenta. Fabricated Ventura 8, 12 and 16, Valenta 8, 12, 16 and 18. Housing or blocks carry cast iron cylinder liners, dry (RPH), wet (YH). Ventura and Valenta housing carries steel, wet-type liners chromium plated on waterside and in cylinder bore.

Valenta 12 cylinder engine as used by British Rail to power the High Speed Trains

Engine Type	Turbo charged or Turbo charged/ intercooled	No of Cylinders	Cont Traction Rating kW Brake (bhp)	Engine Speed rpm	Bmep bar (lbf/in2)	Piston Speed m/s (ft/min)	Full Load Fuel Consumption g/bhp/h (lb/bhp/h)	Bore mm (in)	Stroke mm (in)	Displacement litres (in3)	Compression Ratio	Approx dimensions in mm and in				Approx Dry Weight lb (kg)
												Length	Width	Height	Crankcase Centre Line Height	
*6RPHCL	TC/I	6	280 (375)	1 500	7.6 (110)	9.84 (1937)	192 (0.424)	178 (7)	197 (7.75)	29.3 (1 790)	15.5 : 1	1 638 (64.5)	1 245 (49)	1 753 (69)	490 (19.25)	2 469 (5 445)
*8RPHXL	TC	8	303 (406)	1 500	6.2 (90)	9.84 (1 937)	189 (0.417)	178 (7)	197 (7.75)	39 (2 386)	15.5 : 1	1 880 (74)	1 245 (49)	1 575 (62)	490 (19.25)	3 016 (6 650)
*6RPHCL	TC/I	8	373 (500)	1 500	7.6 (110)	9.84 (1 937)	192 (0.424)	178 (7)	197 (7.75)	39 (2 386)	15.5 : 1	1 880 (74)	1 245 (49)	1 755 (69)	490 (19.25)	3 061 (6 750)
12YHXL	TC	12	671 (900)	1 500	9.2 (133)	9.84 (1 937)	170 (0.374)	178 (7)	197 (7.75)	58.7 (3 580)	13.0 : 1	2 540 (100)	1 588 (62.5)	1 905 (75)	686 (27)	4 898 (10 800)
12YHCL	TC/I	12	783 (1 050)	1 500	10.7 (155)	9.84 (1 937)	170 (0.374)	178 (7)	197 (7.75)	58.7 (3 580)	13.0 : 1	2 540 (100)	1 588 (62.5)	1 955 (77)	686 (27)	5 034 (11 100)
Ventura 6CL	TC/I	6	560 (750)	1 500	11.4 (165)	10.8 (2 125)	170 (0.375)	197 (7.75)	210 (8.5)	39.4 (2 405)	13.0 : 1	1 600 (63)	1 420 (56)	1 780 (70)	535 (21)	3 320 (7 320)
Ventura 8CL	TC/I	8	746 (1 000)	1 500	11.4 (165)	10.8 (2 125)	165 (0.363)	197 (7.75)	210 (8.5)	52.6 (3 207)	13.0 : 1	1 700 (67)	1 335 (52.5)	2 110 (83)	585 (23)	3 855 (8 500)
Ventura 12CL	TC/I	12	1 119 (1 500)	1 500	11.4 (165)	10.8 (2 125)	165 (0.363)	197 (7.75)	210 (8.5)	78.9 (4 811)	13.0 : 1	2 060 (81)	1 335 (52.5)	2 010 (79)	585 (23)	5 111 (11 270)
Ventura 16CL	TC/I	16	1 492 (2 000)	1 500	11.4 (165)	10.8 (2 125)	166 (0.365)	197 (7.75)	210 (8.5)	105.1 (6 415)	13.0 : 1	2 670 (105)	1 335 (52.5)	2 060 (81)	505 (23)	6 789 (14 970)
Valenta 6CL	TC/I	6	839 (1 125)	1 500	17 (247)	10.8 (2 125)	170 (0.376)	197 (7.75)	210 (8.5)	39.4 (2 405)	13.0 : 1	2 673 (105.25)	1 073 (42.25)	1 804 (71)	635 (25)	4 730 (10 430)
Valenta 8CL	TC/I	8	1 119 (1 500)	1 500	17 (247)	10.8 (2 125)	170 (0.376)	197 (7.75)	210 (8.5)	52.6 (3 207)	13.0 : 1	1 936 (76.25)	1 460 (57.5)	2 350 (92.5)	740 (29)	5 057 (11 150)
Valenta 12CL	TC/I	12	1 679 (2 250)	1 500	17 (247)	10.8 (2 125)	165 (0.363)	197 (7.75)	210 (8.5)	78.9 (4 811)	13.0 : 1	2 458 (96.75)	1 460 (57.5)	2 305 (90.75)	740 (29)	6 735 (14 850)
Valenta 16CL	TC/I	16	2 238 (3 000)	1 500	17 (247)	10.8 (2 125)	173 (0.382)	197 (7.75)	210 (8.5)	105.1 (6 415)	13.0 : 1	2 980 (117.5)	1 460 (57.5)	2 350 (92.5)	740 (29)	9 010 (19 870)
Valenta 18CL	TC/I	18	2 522 (3 380)	1 500	17 (247)	10.8 (2 125)	166 (0.366)	197 (7.75)	210 (8.5)	118.3 (7 217)	13.0 : 1	3 207 (126.25)	1 460 (57.5)	2 260 (89)	740 (29)	9 873 (21 770)

Engine ratings: Continuous traction rating corrected for altitude of 150 m (500 ft), air temperature of 85°F (30°C) and (C engines and RP 200) water temperature to intercooler 113°F (45°C).

*Engines marked with an asterisk can be offered with an intermittent rating 10 per cent higher for shunting duty. *Dimensions:* These are for engines with standard equipment.

Engine weights: These include fuel and lubricating oil filters, oil cooler (YJ and RP 200), damper and sump, but exclude flywheel, air filters, and mounting. Those for 8, 12 and 16 YJ include fabricated housing.

Crankshaft and main bearings: Underslung forged steel crankshaft drilled for large end lubrication. Ventura and Valenta crankshafts nitride hardened. Steel bearings shells tin aluminium lined.

Connecting rods and bearings: Fork and blade machined steel stampings drilled for small end lubrication and piston cooling. Large end (forked rod) tin aluminium lined, large end (blade rod) steel shells lined with copper-lead (RPH and YH), lead-bronze (Ventura and Valenta) and flashed with lead (RPH and YH), lead-tin (Ventura and Valenta). Small end bushes nickel gunmetal.

Pistons: Aluminium alloy, oil cooled with 3 compression and one oil control ring (except Ventura which has 2 oil control rings). Iron insert for top chrome-faced pressure ring (plain ring Ventura and Valenta).

Governor: Regulators 1100 Series hydraulic servo type for mechanical, electric or pneumatic control (all engines).

Pressure charging: (X and C engines). Exhaust gas driven, air-cooled (RPH, YH and 6YK) water-cooled (YJ, 8 and 12YK and RP200) turbo-blower.

Intercooling: (C engines and RP200). Air to water cooler.

Lubrication: Pressure lubrication to all bearings by engine driven gear type pumps separate pump for cooling system (not YK and RP200). Engine mounted oil filters (RPH and YH), independently mounted (YJ, YK and RP200). Integral oil cooler (YJ and RP200). Cooling by engine jacket water (YJ), radiator-cooled (other engines).

Cooling: Centrifugal, gear-driven pump.

Starting: Electric, air or hydraulic starter motors, motoring by main generator or dynastarter.

Rotation: Anti-clockwise, looking on flywheel.

Fuel: To BS 2869: 1970 Class A1, A2 or B1 (RPH, YH and YK), Class B2 (RPH and YK) or Class A1 or A2 (YJ and RP200), or as may be agreed.

12 cylinder Ventura engine
Available in turbocharged/intercooled versions, 1 350/1 500 bhp at 1 500 rpm.

GENERAL MOTORS CORPORATION

Electro-Motive Division
La Grange, Illinois 60625, USA

The Electro-Motive Division of General Motors first developed the Model 567 diesel engine in 1938 when it began locomotive manufacture at La Grange, Illinois, USA. To provide increased horsepower and greater efficiency, the Model 645 engine was introduced in mid-1965. The major change in the Model 645 over the 567 is the increase in cylinder liner bore from 216 mm (8½ in) to 230 mm (9¹/₁₆ in), the stroke remaining at 254 mm (10 in).

The Model 645 engine, either mechanically supercharged (Roots blown) or turbocharged, is standard for US domestic type locomotives and is also available for export.

Model 645E Series		Roots Blown			Turbocharged	
No of cylinders		8	12	16	16	20
Traction Rating	hp (SAE)	1 000	1 500	2 000	3 000	3 600
Engine rpm		900	900	900	900	900
Max Bmep	lb/sq in	94	94	94	141	133
	(kg/mm)	(69.2)	(69.2)	(69.2)	(99.1)	(93.5)
Max piston speed	ft/min	1 500	1 500	1 500	1 500	1 500
	(m/sec)	(7.63)	(7.63)	(7.63)	(7.63)	(7.63)
Weight (dry)	lb	18 700	25 000	33 400	34 500	41 100
	(kg)	(8 480)	(11 340)	(15 150)	(15 650)	(18 640)
Length	in	142	176	215	215	248
	(mm)	(3 607)	(4 470)	(5 461)	(5 461)	(6 299)
Width	in	63	65	63	67	67
	(mm)	(1 600)	(1 651)	(1 600)	(1 702)	(1 702)
Height	in	89	89	89	98	98
	(mm)	(2 260)	(2 260)	(2 260)	(2 489)	(2 489)

GM model 16-645E

GM model 20-645E3

GMT

Grandi Motori Trieste SpA
(FIAT-ANSALDO-CRDA)
Corso Cavour, 1 Trieste, Italy

Telephone: 040 8991
Telegrams: GRANDIMOTORI, Trieste
Telex: 46274/46275 GMT

Grandi Motori Trieste build diesel engines for railway traction, marine and industrial applications. For rail traction their locomotive engine range includes series A210 and B230 from 612 to 3 700 kW.

Series A210
Type: 4-stroke, turbo-charged, with charge air cooling.
Cylinders: Bore 210 mm (8.27 in). Stroke 230 mm (9.05 in).

Series B230
Type: 4-stroke, turbo-charged with charge air cooling.
Cylinders: Bore 230 mm (9.05 in). Stroke 270 mm (10.62 in).

The other main characteristics, common to the two types of engine are as follows:
Cylinder liners: Wet type removable liners of special cast iron.
Cylinder heads: One per cylinder, in alloyed cast, iron; each has 2 inlet and 2 exhaust valves and the fuel injector in the centre.
Pistons: Aluminium alloy, oil cooled. They have 3 compression rings and one oil scraper ring.
Crankshaft: Of highly alloyed forged steel. The surface of the pins is hardened by electric induction process. Thin walled three metal bearings.

GMT 4-stroke diesel engine type B230.20, turbo-charged with aftercooling; 5 000 bhp at 1 200 rpm

Frame: Cast iron.

Valve gear: One or 2 camshaft for in-line and Vee engines respectively driven at flywheel side. The 2 inlet and 2 exhaust valves are driven by rollers/push rods/rocker arms through a transverse piece.

Turbo-charging: Achieved by means of exhaust gas turbo-blowers operating with pulse systems. The air is then cooled in suitable coolers.

Fuel injection pumps: Of plunger type with a spiral groove. The fuel injection is controlled by rotating the plunger by means of a transversal rack.

Fuel: Gas oil.

Lubrication: Forced fed by directly driven gear pump.

Cooling system: Fresh water fed by two centrifugal pumps, one for the engine, one for the oil and air cooling system.

Engine	Data	Version	Cyl-inder	Output kW (UIC)	Weight kg	Length mm	Width mm	Height mm
A 210								
Output	153 kW/Cyl	A 210.4	4 V	612	4 400	1 700	1 770	1 570
Bore	210 mm	A 210.6	6 V	918	5 500	2 000	1 770	1 570
Stroke	230 mm	A 210.8	8 V	1 224	7 000	2 250	1 820	1 930
Speed	1 500 rpm	A 210.12	12 V	1 836	9 500	2 835	1 820	2 020
MEP	15,67 kg/cm²	A 210.16	16 V	2 448	11 800	3 415	1 820	1 980
MPS	11.5 m/s	A 210.20	20 V	3 060	14 600	4 050	1 820	2 020

Length: at crankshaft *Width:* overall *Height:* from underside of feet

Fuel consumption: 215 g/kW/h

Engine	Data	Version	Cyl-inder	Output kW (UIC)	Weight kg	Length mm	Width mm	Height mm
B 230								
		B 230.4	4 L	740	5 700	2 290	1 200	1 960
Output	185 kW/Cyl	B 230.6	6 L	1 110	7 900	2 960	1 200	1 960
Bore	230 mm	B 230.8	8 V	1 480	9 500	2 670	1 720	2 250
Stroke	270 mm	B 230.12	12 V	2 220	14 500	3 490	1 720	2 200
Speed	1 200 rpm	B 230.16	16 V	2 960	18 000	4 310	1 720	2 250
MEP	16.49 kg/cm²	B 230.18	18 V	3 330	21 000	4 720	1 720	2 270
MPS	10.8 m/s	B 230.20	20 V	3 700	23 500	5 730	1 720	2 380

Length: at crankshaft *Width:* overall *Height:* from underside of feet

Fuel consumption: 217 g/kW/h

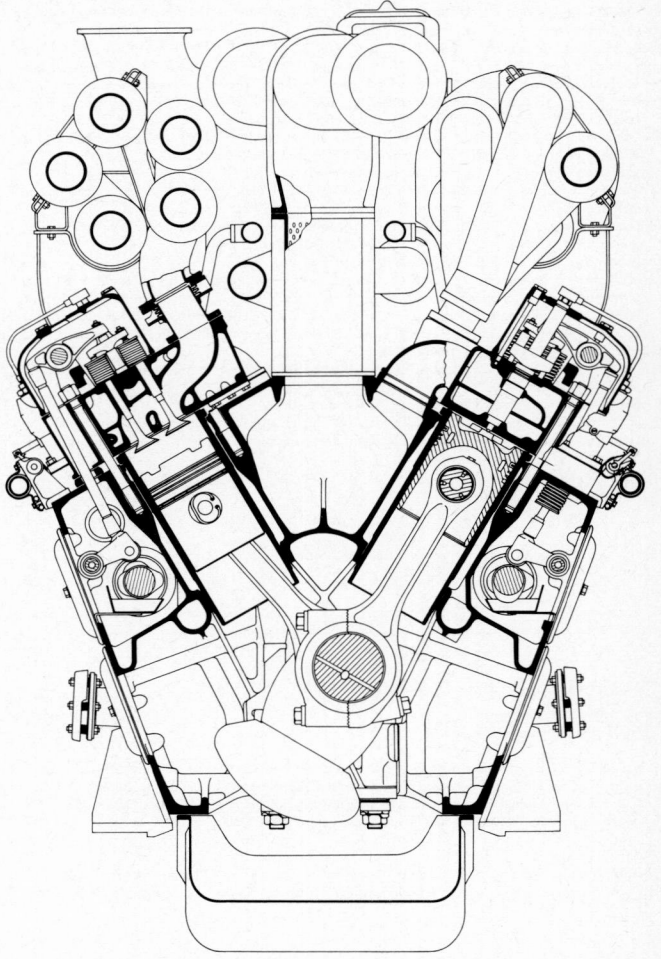

Cross-section of the B230 V form

GROSSOL

Société Grossol
PO Box 104, 14 rue Chaptal, 92303 Levallois-Perret, France
Commercial Division for Poyaud Series

Telephone: 757 82 90
Telex: 620 207F grossol Lvall

After many years' research into the problems of diesel engine design, construction and utilisation, Société Grossol was formed by the two engineers concerned, Grosshans and Ollier, comprising a bureau of continuous study and research as well as a commercial service to users. Manufacture of their designs of engine has been taken up by two famous French engineering firms, Société Surgérienne de Constructions Mécanique (Poyaud series) and Société Alsacienne de Constructions Mécanique (MGO and AGO series).

MGO: The initials of the three people concerned in the original engine design are S N Marep, F Ollier, and J Grosshans.

AGO: Following the success of the MGO engines manufactured under licence by SACM (Société Alsacienne de Constructions Mécanique) that company joined with the Société Grossol to design engines with a higher output. These are the AGO range.

ISOTTA FRASCHINI SpA

Via Milano 7, Saronno 21047, Italy

Telephone: 02 960 3251/2/3
Telex: 332403

Isotta Fraschini build diesel engines for rail and road traction, marine and industrial applications.

Rail and road traction: Locomotives, railcars, special railroad vehicles, earth moving equipments.

For rail traction the locomotive engine range includes: series ID 19 from 450 to 680 hp, series ID 38 from 200 to 330 hp and series ID 36 from 300 to 1 900 hp.

Isotta Fraschini ID 19 series
12 cylinder horizontally opposed, 4-stroke, direct injection, water cooled.
Cylinders: Bore 145 mm (5.71 in). Stroke 180 mm (7.09 in). Swept volume 35.67 litres. The output is based on UIC specification.

Isotta Fraschini ID 38 series
6 cylinders, 90° Vee, 4-stroke, direct injection, water cooled.
Cylinders: Bore 128 mm (5.04 in). Stroke 126 mm (4.96 in). Swept volume 1.62 litres per cylinder. The output is based on UIC specifications.

Isotta Fraschini ID 36 series
6, 8, 12 and 16 cylinders, 90° Vee, 4-stroke, direct injection, water cooled.
Cylinders: Bore 170 mm (6.69 in). Stroke 170 mm (6.69 in). Swept volume 3.858 litres per cylinder. The output is based on UIC specifications. Engine speed maximum 1 800 rpm. Engine type ID 36/8 V can be supplied with cylinders opposed for railcar applications.

Model		ID38 series N6V	SS6V	ID36 series N6V	SS6V	N8V	SS8V	N12V	SS12V	N16V	SS16V
No of cylinders		6	6	6	6	8	8	12	12	16	16
Turbo-charged		—	Yes	—	Yes	—	Yes	—	Yes	—	Yes
Charge air cooled		—	Yes	—	Yes	—	Yes	—	Yes	—	Yes
bhp (UIC)		200	330	300	640	400	850	600	1 285	800	1 710
Engine speed	rpm	2 700	2 700	1 650	1 650	1 650	1 650	1 650	1 650	1 650	1 650
Weight (dry)	lb	1 655	1 766	3 780	4 000	5 115	5 335	7 115	7 445		9 277
	(kg)	(750)	(800)	(1 700)	(1 800)	(2 300)	(2 400)	(3 200)	(3 350)		(4 200)
Length max	in	39.37	42.91	—	53.15	—	63	—	88.55	—	118.11
	(mm)	(1 000)	(1 090)		(1 350)		(1 600)		(2 250)		(3 000)
Width max	in	35.43	35.43	—	47.24	—	47.24	—	47.24	—	51.18
	(mm)	(900)	(900)		(1 200)		(1 200)		(1 200)		(1 300)
Height max	in	37	37	—	51.57	—	49.60	—	58.26	—	70.86
	(mm)	(940)	(940)		(1 310)		(1 260)		(1 480)		(1 800)
Fuel consumption All models		Normally aspirated and turbo-charged = 170 g/hp/h; turbo-charged and intercooled =165 g/hp/h									

N = Naturally aspirated SS = Turbo-charged and intercooled.

ID 36 series diesel engine for railway traction from 300 up to 1 100 bhp at 1 650 rpm

ID 38/6 V series diesel engine for railway traction from 200 up to 330 bhp at 2 700 rpm

JW

Jenbacher Werke AG
A-6200 Jenbach, Austria

Formed in 1946, this company builds diesel locomotives and diesel engines for industrial and marine purposes up to 3 000 hp

LM Series

Type: 6, 8 and 12 cylinder 90° V, 2 stroke, water cooled, direct injection.
Cylinders: Bore 240 mm (9.45 in) stroke 250 mm (9.84 in) swept volume 11.3 litres per cylinder. Cast iron with centrifugally cast wet cylinder liners. Individual cylinder heads.
Pistons: Light alloy, oil cooled. 4 compression rings, and 2 oil control rings.
Connecting rods: Separate side by side drop forged with steel-backed lead-bronze big end bearings, and fixed gudgeon pin.
Crankshaft: Drop forged, carried in steel-backed lead-bronze main bearings.
Fuel injector: Gear-driven from flywheel end of crankshaft.
Scavenge blower: Centrifugal type driven from flywheel end of crankshaft.
Lubrication: Gear pump.
Starting: Electric or compressed air.

Model		LM750	LM1000	LM1500
No of Cylinders		6	8	12
Output	kW	501	735	1 100
Speed	rpm	1 000	1 000	1 000
Weight (dry)	kg	7 400	8 900	11 000
Length	mm	2 400	2 800	3 600
Width	mm	1 720	1 720	1 760
Height	mm	2 150	2 150	2 150
Fuel consumption	g/kWh	235	238	234

Jenbacher LM1500 12-cylinder engine
1 500 hp at 1 000 rpm

MAK

Krupp MaK Maschinenbau GmbH Kiel
PO Box 9009, 2300 Kiel 17, Federal Republic of Germany

Before the 1939-45 war Deutsche Werke Kiel produced diesel locomotives and railcars. MaK was formed after the war to continue this programme, concentrating engine production on the slow running type M 300. The original output was 60 hp per cylinder at 750 rpm which was increased to 125 hp with high-pressure supercharging. By increasing the engine speed to 900 rpm an output of 150 hp per cylinder was attained. The new rail traction engine M282 is a result of continuous search for product improvement, and retains the best features of the previous designs, the M300 and M 301. It is of compact and modern design, a medium-speed unit with high performance and extended overhaul periods.

Series M 282

Type: 6 and 8 cylinders in-line, 12 cylinder Vee, 4-stroke-cycle, water cooled.
Combustion method: All M 282 series engines have direct injection.
Cylinders: Bore 240 mm (9.44 in). Stroke 280 mm (11.02 in). Swept volume 12.66 litres per cylinder. Compression ratio 12.2:1. Removable wet type cast iron liners; individual cast iron cylinder heads bolted to cylinder block.
Pistons: A depression in the crown of the piston in conjunction with the cylinder head forms the combustion chamber. The material used for the piston is a heat-resisting light-metal alloy with the best heat conducting quality. Four self-tightening elastic piston rings are fitted on the piston. One oil control ring is arranged above the gudgeon pin.
Connecting rods: Drop forged steel.
Crankshaft: Solid forged steel.
Constructional features: Closed engine housing with hanging bearings and underhung sump. Main and big-end bearings of the bronze-lined steel shell type, with lead-tin bearing surface. The bearings can be exchanged without removing the crankshaft.
Valve gear: Each cylinder head carries 2 inlet and 2 exhaust valves. Gear train driven camshaft in cylinder block.

MaK model 12 M 282 AK 12-cylinder engine

Fuel injection: Bosch injectors with individual Bosch pumps.
Supercharger: Exhaust gas turbo-blower, Brown Boveri.
Starting: Electric, compressed air alternatively.
Mounting: Elastic suspension by metal bonded rubber elements.

Model		A	6M282 A(k)	A(k)	Ak	A(k)	8M282 A(k)	AK	12M282 A(k)	A(k)	AK
No of cylinders		6	6	6	6	6	8	8	12	12	12
Turbo-charger, BBC		—	VTR 200	VTR 200	VTR 250	VTR 250	VTR 250	VTR 250	2 × VTR 200	2 × VTR 250	2 × VTR 250
Charge air cooled		—	—	single circuit	single circuit	double circuit	single circuit	double circuit	single circuit	single circuit	double circuit
Max bhp (UIC)		530	700	900	1 000	1 200	1 200	1 600	1 800	2 000	2 400
Engine speed	rpm	1 050	1 000	1 000	1 000	1 000	1 000	1 000	1 000	1 000	1 000
Max Bmep	lb/in²	83.9	118.0	150.7	167.8	201.9	150.7	201.9	151.4	168.4	201.9
	(kg/cm²)	(5.9)	(8.3)	(10.6)	(11.8)	(14.2)	(10.6)	(14.2)	(10.65)	(11.84)	(14.2)
Max piston speed	ft/min	1 929	1 840	1 840	1 840	1 840	1 840	1 840	1 840	1 840	1 840
	(m/s)	(9.6)	(9.35)	(9.35)	(9.35)	(9.35)	(9.35)	(9.35)	(9.35)	(9.35)	(9.35)
Weight (dry)	lb	14 770	15 200	15 670	16 000	16 200	20 200	20 300	25 360	26 000	26 000
	(kg)	(6 700)	(6 900)	(7 100)	(7 250)	(7 350)	(9 150)	(9 200)	(11 500)	(11 800)	(11 800)
Length	in	113	113	113	113	115.5	139	139	111.5	111.5	111.5
	(mm)	(2 876)	(2 876)	(2 876)	(2 876)	(2 934)	(3 530)	(3 530)	(2 831)	(2 831)	(2 831)
Width	in	53.5	55	55	61	61	61	61	65	65	65
	(mm)	(1 360)	(1 400)	(1 400)	(1 550)	(1 550)	(1 550)	(1 550)	(1 650)	(1 650)	(1 650)
Height	in	79	79	80	80	80	80	80	86.5	86.5	86.5
	(mm)	(2 006)	(2 006)	(2 035)	(2 035)	(2 035)	(2 035)	(2 035)	(2 196)	(2 196)	(2 196)
Fuel consumption	lb/hp/h	0.372	0.358	0.354	0.349	0.338	0.354	0.352	0.354	0.349	0.338
	g/hp/h	(166)	(160)	(158)	(156)	(151)	(158)	(157)	(158)	(156)	(151)

MAN

Maschinenfabrik Augsburg-Nürnberg AG
8500 Nürnberg, Katzwangerstrasse 101, Federal Republic of Germany

The world's first diesel engine was built at Augsburg between 1893 and 1897 by Maschinenfabrik Augsburg AG established in 1840. Shortly afterwards a merger with Maschinenbau AG, Nürnberg, produced MAN.

The range of diesel engines produced by the Nuremberg Division includes a number of underfloor engines for railway applications. The engines incorporate MAN's M or HM system of combustion which provides controlled diesel combustion for low engine stress levels and low noise level. Dubbed the whisper engine, these units are noted for their flexibility permitting fast load acceptance. Direct injection confers efficient fuel utilisation and fuel economies. High unit ratings and good power weight ratios permit installation in a minimum of space. Little maintenance is needed, and low stress levels throughout the engine ensure reliability in service.

MAN horizontal engines
Model D3256 BTY UE/310

Type: 6 cylinder horizontal, 4-stroke, water cooled, direct injection, turbo-charged
Cylinders: Bore 132 mm (5.197 in), stroke 150 mm (5.906 in), swept volume 12.32 litres (52 in³), compression ratio 15 : 1
Output: UIC rating 228 kW (310 hp) at 2 100 rpm
Torque, max: 1 180 NM at 1 400 rpm
Fuel consumption: 155 g/hp/h (0.348 lb) at 1 600 rpm
Length: 1 363 mm (53.65 in)
Width: 1 237 mm (48.70 in)
Height: 619 mm (24.37 in)
Weight: 1 060 kg (2 340 lb)

Series D 3650

Three (Models D 3650 and HM12U) are railcar underfloor engines, and one (Model D 3650 HM5U) is used as heating generator set.

Type: 12 cylinder horizontally opposed, 4-cycle, water cooled, HM combustion system, normally aspirated.
Cylinders: Bore 136 mm (5.354 in), stroke 155 mm (6.102 in), swept volume 27.02 litres (1 649 in³), compression ratio 16 : 1.
Rated output:
HM5U: 377 kW (512 hp) (UIC), 500 hp (service), at 1 950 rpm
HM12U: 377 kW (512 hp) (UIC), 500 hp (service), at 1 950 rpm
Torque, max:
HM12U: 196 mkgf (1 418 ft lbf) at 1 400 rpm
HM5U: 196 mkgf (1 418 ft lbf) at 1 400 rpm
Fuel consumption:
HM12U: 172 g (0.379 lb)/hp/h at 1 950 rpm
HM5U: 169 g (0.373 lb)/hp/h at 1 950 rpm
Length: HM5U: 2 300 mm (90.55 in); others 2 300 mm (90.55 in)
Width: HM5U: 1 800 mm (70.87 in); others 2 770 mm (109.06 in)
Height: HM5U: 1 650 mm (64.96 in); others 870 mm (34.25 in)
Weight:
HM12U: 2 800 kg (6 170 lb)
HM5U: 3 000 kg (6 600 lb) without generator

Model D3650 HM5U 12-cylinder horizontal engine
Power unit of heating generator set for installation in locomotives.

Model D 3650 HM12U 12-cylinder horizontal engine
For underfloor mounting in railcars.

MITSUBISHI

Mitsubishi Heavy Industries Ltd

Head Office: 5-1, 2-chome, Marunouchi Chiyoda-ku, Tokyo, Japan

Works: 3000 Tana, Sagamihara-City, Kanagawa Prefecture, Japan

54 to 1 400 bhp engines for locomotives (1 000 to 3 600 rpm).

MÖES

Moteurs Möes SA
62 rue de Huy, 4370 Waremme, Belgium

Four-stroke vertical engines up to 380 bhp.

MTU

Motoren- und Turbinen-Union Friedrichshafen GmbH
Postfach 2040, D-7790 Friedrichshafen 1, Federal Republic of Germany

Telephone: 07541 207 1
Telegrams: Motorunion
Telex: 734360

The manufacturing programme of MTU Friedrichshafen for rail traction application includes diesel engines in the power range of 525 to 100 kW.
MTU Friedrichshafen diesel engines are equally suitable for diesel-hydraulic or diesel-electric drive.

MTU model 12V 331

MTU model 12V 396

Rail traction

Application group		Rail traction	
Engine	Speed	ISO 3046/1 (UIC rated power)	
	1/min	kW	hp
6 V 331 TC 12	2 200	525	715
8 V 331 TC 12	2 200	700	950
12 V 331 TC 12	2 200	1 050	1 430
6 V 396 TC 12	1 800	525	715
8 V 396 TC 12	1 800	700	950
12 V 396 TC 12	1 800	1 050	1 430
12 V 652 TB 11	1 500	1 350	1 840
16 V 652 TB 11	1 500	1 800	2 450
12 V 956 TB 12	1 500	2 460	3 350
16 V 956 TB 12	1 500	3 280	4 460
20 V 956 TB 12	1 500	4 100	5 580
12 V 1163 TB 12	1 200	2 460	3 350
16 V 1163 TB 12	1 200	3 280	4 460
20 V 1163 TB 12	1 200	4 100	5 580

Train electric power supply

Application group		Train electric power supply	
Engine	Speed	ISO 3046/1 (UIC rated power)	
	1/min	kW	hp
6 V 331 TC 12	2 200	460	625
8 V 331 TC 12	2 200	610	830
12 V 331 TC 12	2 200	920	1 250
6 V 396 TC 12	1 500	415	565
	1 800	460	625
8 V 396 TC 12	1 500	550	750
	1 800	610	830
12 V 396 TC 12	1 500	830	1 130
	1 800	920	1 250

NIIGATA

Niigata Engineering Co Ltd
4-1 Kasumigaseki 1, Chiyoda-ku, Tokyo, Japan

Founded in 1895, one of Japan's leading engineering manufacturers, Niigata build diesel engines for marine and industrial use up to 20 000 hp and for rail traction up to 2 000 hp.

DMP81Z

16-cylinder Vee, water cooled, 4-stroke, turbo-charged and charge air cooled. Bore 180 mm (7.09 in). Stroke 200 mm (7.87 in). Swept volume 5.09 litres (311 m³) per cylinder.

DMF31ZN

6-cylinder vertical in-line, water cooled, 4-stroke turbo-charged and charge air cooled. Bore 180 mm (7.09 in). Stroke 200 mm (7.87 in). Swept volume 5.09 litres (311 m³) per cylinder.

General specifications for both models

Cylinders: Monobloc cast iron cylinder block and crank case, removable cast iron liners with integral water jacket. Cast iron cylinder heads secured by studs.
Pistons: Oil-cooled 2 piece pistons with 3 compression rings and 2 oil control rings; fully floating gudgeon pins.
Connecting rods: Nickel chrome steel drop forged.
Crankshaft: Alloy steel forging, copper-lead lined steel shell bearing (DMF31ZN), roller bearing (DMP81Z).
Valve: 2 inlet and 2 exhaust steel valves per cylinder.
Fuel injection: Bosch type injectors and Bosch type pump.

Turbo-charger: Niigata-Napier type turbo-blower. Two for DMP81Z, one for DMF31ZN.
Lubrication: Forced feed.
Starting: Electric starter.

Model		DMP81Z	DMF31ZN
Turbo-charged		Yes	Yes
Charge air cooled		Yes	Yes
No of Cylinders		16V	6
Power rating (max)	hp	2 000	700
Engine speed	rpm	1 500	1 500
Bmep (max)	lb/in²	209	167.5
	(kg/cm²)	(14.73)	(13.74)
Piston speed	ft/min	1 970	1 970
	(m/s)	(10.0)	(10.0)
Weight (dry)	lb	19 600	7 280
	(kg)	(8 900)	(3 300)
Length	in	170	129
	(mm)	(4 322)	(3 280)
Width	in	74	51.6
	(mm)	(1 880)	(1 310)
Height	in	78	70.7
	(mm)	(1 978)	(1 795)
Fuel consumption	lb/hp/h	0.370	0.375
	(g/hp/h)	(168)	(170)

Niigata DML 30H SH 12 cylinder engine

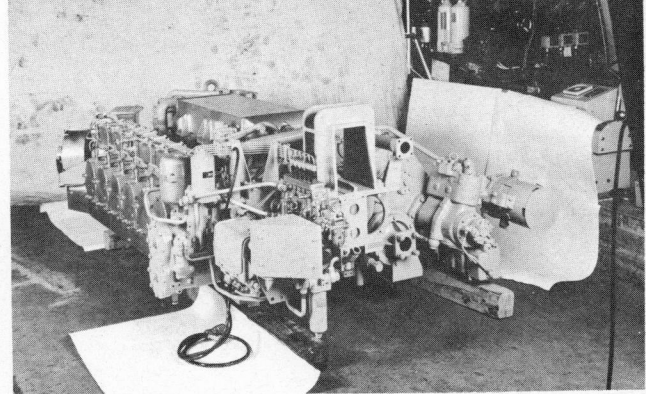

Niigata DMF 15 HSA

OM

OM SpA
Head Office: Piazza San Ambrogio 6, Milan, Italy
Works: Via Fiume 25, Brescia, Italy

Saurer designed four-stroke vertical, Vee and horizontal engines for locomotives and railcars.

Rating: 150 to 1 100 bhp at 1 500 rpm.

PERKINS

Perkins Engines Group Ltd
Perkins Engines Group, Peterborough, Cambridgeshire, England

The Perkins Engines Group has its international headquarters in Peterborough. The main factory at Eastfield, Peterborough, was opened in 1947 and has a production capacity of 1 350 engines a day. The company employs more than 9 000 people. World production of Perkins engines from all sources is approaching 600 000 units a

Telephone: 0733 67474
Telegrams: PERKOIL
Telex: 32501

year, of which more than 40 per cent are built in the UK and nearly 90 per cent of these are exported.
Perkins three, four, six and V-eight cylinder industrial diesels power locomotives, rail cars, cranes, compressor sets, hydraulic test rigs, road rollers, welding sets, excavators, tractor shovels and a wide range of industrial plant.

Perkins D3 152 industrial diesel engine

Perkins V8.540 diesel engine

Engine	Turbo-charged	No of cylinders	Bore in (mm)	Stroke in (mm)	Swept volume in³ (litre)	Compression ratio	Continuous Rating to BS 649 : 1958 bhp (kW)	eng speed rpm	Max Intermittent Rating to BS AU 141a : 1971 bhp (kW)	eng speed rpm	Max Gross Torque lbf ft (kgf)	Engine speed rpm	Length in (mm)	Width in (mm)	Height in (mm)	Bare engine dry weight lb (kg)
D3.152	No	3	3.6 (91.4)	5.0 (127.0)	152.7 (2.50)	18.5:1	39 (29.0)	2 250	49 (36.5)	2 500	118 (160)	1 400	24.0 (610)	20.7 (526)	31.1 (791)	458 (208)
4.108	No	4	3.125 (79.4)	3.5 (88.9)	107.4 (1.76)	22:1	38 (28.0)	3 000	45 (33.5)	3 000	83 (113)	2 300	23.2 (590)	19.1 (485)	25.7 (653)	330 (150)
4.165	No	4	3.622 (92.0)	4.0 (101.6)	164.9 (2.70)	21:1	52 (39.0)	3 000	62 (46.0)	3 000	113 (153)	2 100	25.8 (655)	25.7 (653)	32.7 (830)	442 (201)
D4.203	No	4	3.6 (91.4)	5.0 (127.0)	203.6 (3.34)	17.4:1	50 (37.0)	2 250	61 (45.5)	2 400	152 (206)	1 350	28.2 (715)	19.4 (493)	29.4 (746)	484 (220)
4.2032	No	4	3.6 (91.4)	5.0 (127.0)	203.6 (3.34)	19.1			60 (44.5)	2 600	156 (211)	1 500	28.2 (717)	19.4 (493)	29.4 (746)	485 (220)
4.236	No	4	3.875 (98.4)	5.0 (127.0)	235.9 (3.86)	16:1	64 (48.0)	2 250	81 (60.5)	2 600	197 (267)	1 350	28.8 (721)	20.7 (525)	32.1 (816)	594 (270)
4.248	No	4	3.975 (101.0)	5.0 (127.0)	248.2 (4.07)	16:1	66 (49.0)	2 250	84 (63.0)	2 500	194 (263)	1 400	30.6 (778)	20.4 (519)	28.4 (722)	548 (249)
6.3544	No	6	3.875 (98.4)	5.0 (127.0)	353.8 (5.80)	16:1	94 (70.0)	2 250	122 (91.0)	2 600	283 (384)	1 400	38.0 (965)	25.1 (637)	35.4 (900)	957 (435)
T6.3544	Yes	6	3.875 (98.4)	5.0 (127.0)	353.8 (5.80)	16:1	117 (87.0)	2 250	145 (108.0)	2 600	346 (469)	1 600	36.8 (935)	29.3 (743)	30.7 (780)	979 (445)
V8.540	No	8	4.25 (108.0)	4.75 (120.7)	539.1 (8.83)	16.5:1	148 (110.0)	2 250	192 (143.0)	2 600	410 (556)	1 700	36.7 (933)	32.7 (830)	35.5 (902)	1 338 (608)
V8.640	No	8	4.63 (117.6)	4.75 (120.7)	639.8 (10.48)	16.2:1	165 (123.0)	2 250	215 (160.0)	2 600	485 (658)	1 650	40.6 (1 030)	32.7 (830)	39.1 (992)	1 604 (729)
TV8.640	Yes	8	4.63 (117.6)	4.75 (120.7)	639.8 (10.48)	15.0:1	208 (155.0)	2 250	255 (190.0)	2 600	602 (816)	1 700	41.3 (1 070)	32.8 (832)	38.6 (980)	1 659 (754)

ROLLS-ROYCE

Rolls-Royce Motors Ltd
Diesel Division, Shrewsbury, Salop SY1 4DP, England

Telephone: 0743 52262
Telegrams: 35171/2
Telex: ROYCAR, Shrewsbury

Rolls-Royce manufacture a range of rationalised high-speed diesel engines for rail traction available as vertical or Vee types. The engines are also used in automotive, earth moving, generating, industrial and marine applications.
In rail traction applications complete installations (engines, transmissions and controls) tailored to customers' requirements are supplied and the company deals directly with railway builders and operators in all countries.
Rolls-Royce diesel engines for rail traction can be classified under two headings:

C Range
Comprising 4-stroke, direct injection, normally aspirated, or turbo-charged, vertical, in-line engines with outputs varying from 100 to 400 bhp. For all normally aspirated turbo-charged engines, the engine has two cylinder heads, each covering half the total number of cylinders and having one inlet and one exhaust valve per cylinder.

Rolls-Royce DV8T 90° Vee type 8 cylinder engine

Type: In-line, 4-stroke, water cooled direct injection.

Bore: 130.175 mm (5.125 in) all models.

Stroke: 152.4 mm (6 in) all models.

Capacity: 6 cylinder 12.13 litres (742.64 in³); 8 cylinder 16.2 litres (990.19 in³).

Compression ratio: Normally aspirated 16 : 1. Turbo-charged 14 : 1.

Mean piston speed: 1 800 ft/min at 1 800 rpm.

Crankcase and cylinders: Monobloc integral construction in close grained cast iron with brass push fit core plugs and differentially hardened wet-type cylinder liners.

Crankshaft: Forged chrome molybdenum steel, nitride hardened, dynamically balanced with 7 or 9 main bearings.

Connecting rods: Forged chrome molybdenum steel, drilled for lubrication to gudgeon pins and cross drilled for cylinder lubrication.

Bearings: Pre-finished lead-bronze steel-backed shell-type; lead indium bearing surfaces.

Pistons: Tin plated aluminium alloy with straight sided toroidal cavity combustion chambers. Molybdenum inlayed top compression rings carried in Ni-resist inserts. Spring backed conformable type oil control rings. Fully floating nickel-chrome case-hardened gudgeon pins.

Valve gear: Overhead; in nickel chrome steel with stellited stem-tips and valve seats. Valve rockers are drilled for lubrication, and are operated by pushrods and chilled cast iron tappets.

Camshaft: Forged chrome-molybdenum steel, nitride hardened, 7 or 9 lead-bronze bearings.

Lubrication: Pressure feed to all bearings wheelcase gears, rocker arms and compressor when engine mounted. Engine mounted oil-coolant heat exchanger.

Fuel injection: Jerk-type pump with hydraulic or mechanical governor. Multi-hole injectors and engine mounted filters.

Cooling: Gear driven circulating pump; thermostat control and heat exchanger for lubricating oil. Engine or radiator mounted multi-belt driven fans for vertical engines. Shaft, hydrostatic or electric driven fans for horizontal engines.

Starting: Axial-type electric starter motor.

Mounting: 4-point; engine front and fly-wheel housing.

Output: Fly-wheel and fly-wheel housing to suit hydraulic, electric or mechanical transmission.

	Continuous Traction Rating to BS 2953 : 1958 lb/in² (kg/cm²)	Intermittent Traction Rating to BS 2953 : 1958 lb/in² (kg/cm²)	Maximum rating for yard shunting locomotives lb/in² (kg/cm²)
Max Bmep			
Normally aspirated	101 *(7.1)*	106 *(7.45)*	112 *(7.87)*
Turbo-charged	140 *(9.8)*	156 *(10.97)*	164 *(11.53)*

D Range

Comprising 90 degree V-type, 4-stroke, direct injection, normally aspirated or turbo-charged, with or without charge air cooling, 8-cylinder engines with outputs ranging from 423 to 750 bhp.

Type: 8-cylinder, 90° Vee, 4-stroke, liquid-cooled.

Combustion system: Direct injection with toroidal cavity pistons.

Bore: 168.275 mm (6.625 in).

Stroke: 184.150 mm (7.25 in).

Capacity (swept volume): 32.776 litres (2 000 m³).

Maximum governed rpm: 1 800.

Mean piston speed: 11.11 m/s (2 174 ft/min) at 1 800 rpm

Compression ratio: Naturally aspirated 15.5 : 1. Turbocharged 13.5 : 1.

Rotation: Anti-clockwise viewed on flywheel.

Hydraulic transmission equipment: 3 stage hydro-kinetic torque converter of Lysholm-Smith type, manufactured by Rolls-Royce under licence from Twin Disc Clutch Co. The operating fluid is diesel fuel oil or other approved fluids, cooled by a shell and tube heat exchanger in the engine coolant circuit. Various designs are available to suit all Rolls-Royce engines and rail traction applications.

Reversing gearboxes:

(a) Rolls-Royce type CG 100, air operated, coupled direct to torque converter ratio 1 : 1.

(b) Rolls-Royce type CGF 310, axle mounted final drive air operated, ratios from 2 : 1 to 4.44 : 1.

Model designation	bhp rating (BS 2953) Intermittent rating B	Max governed speed rpm	Engine form	2 or 4 stroke	No. of cylinders	Valves per cylinder	A B	Cylinder bore in (mm)	Piston stroke in (mm)	Full-load Bmep lb/in² (kg/cm²)	Piston speed max rpm ft/min (m/s)	Full-load fuel consumption lb/bhp/h (g/bhp/h)	Starting system	Complete engine weight (dry) lb (kg)	Overall length in (mm)	Overall width in (mm)	Overall height in (mm)
C6NFL	179	1 800	V	4	6	2	—	5.125 (130.175)	6 (152.4)	106 (7.455)	1 800 (9.14)	0.379 (172)	E	2 499 (1 133)	57.07 (1 449)	29.12 (740)	41.30 (1 039)
C6TFL	262	1 800	V	4	6	2	A	5.125 (130.175)	6 (152.4)	155.2 (10.91)	1 800 (9.14)	0.360 (163.3)	E	2 613 (1 185)	61.43 (1 560)	33.80 (858)	50.97 (1 295)
C8NFL	239	1 800	V	4	8	2	—	5.125 (130.175)	6 (152.4)	106.2 (7.466)	1 800 (9.14)	0.390 (177)	E	3 079 (1 396)	70.74 (1 797)	31.00 (787)	41.30 (1 039)
C8TFL	350	1 800	V	4	8	2	A	5.125 (130.175)	6 (152.4)	155.5 (10.93)	1 800 (9.14)	0.370 (168)	E	3 242 (1 470)	70.74 (1 797)	33.30 (836)	49.30 (1 252)
DV8N	445	1 800	90° Vee	4	8	4	—	6.625 (186.275)	7.25 (184.150)	97.92 (6.884)	2 174 (11.11)	0.381 (173)	E	7 700 (3 493)	70.95 (1 802)	60.35 (1 533)	63.20 (1 605)
DV8T	534	1 800	90° Vee	4	8	4	A	6.625 (168.275)	7.25 (184.150)	117.5 (8.261)	2 174 (11.11)	0.410 (186)	E	7 860 (3 565)	75.90 (1 927)	60.35 (1 533)	67.55 (1 716)
DV8TCE	618	1 800	90° Vee	4	8	4	A & B	6 625 (168.275)	7.25 (184.150)	136 (9.562)	2 174 (11.1)	0.380 (172.4)	E	8 060 (1 656)	75.90 (1 927)	60.35 (1 533)	67.55 (1 716)
DV8—TCA	707	1 800	90° Vee	4	8	4	A & B	6.625 (168.275)	7.25 (184.150)	155.6 (10.94)	2 174 (11.11)	0.384 (174.2)	E	8 060 (1 656)	75.90 (1 927)	60.35 (1 533)	67.55 (1 716)

Engine Form:	V	Vertical	Starting:	E	Electrical
	90°	Vee configuration			
	A	Pressure charged			
	B	Charge cooled			

SACM

SACM Diesel Group

Société Alsacienne de Constructions Mécaniques de Mulhouse

1 rue de la Fonderie, 68054 Mulhouse (Cedex), France

Engine type: 175 type (MGO) available in 8, 12 and 16 cylinders in Vee form. 195 and 240 types (AGO) available in 12, 16 and 20 cylinders in Vee form. All series 4 stroke water cooled.

Cylinders: Centrifugal cast iron cylinder liners. Individual cast iron cylinder heads with 4 valves.

Pistons: Aluminium alloy with combustion chamber in the crown. 3 compression rings (one chromium plated) and 1 oil control ring.

Connecting rods: The rods are articulated, giving each bank of cylinders a different piston stroke. The knuckle of the articulated rod is in the big end cap of the master rod.

Crankshaft: Heat treated chrome-molybdenum forged steel. Steel shell bearings lined with copper-lead alloy.

Valve gears: 2 inlet and 2 exhaust valves per cylinder. Separate camshaft for each cylinder bank operating rocker arm.

Fuel injection: Multicylinder injection pumps for 175 and 195 type. Individual injection pumps for 240 type.

Fuel: Normal diesel fuel.

Supercharger: Brown-Boveri, Hispano, KKK or Garrett exhaust gas turbochargers.

Lubrication: Pressure feed with 2 geared pumps. Water cooled heat exchanger.

Cooling: Gear driven centrifugal pump.

Starting: Compressed air or electric starter motor. RVR engines are preheated before starting.

Type 240V12 DSHR railway engine
Electric power transmission.

Type SACM V16 BZSHR railway diesel engine
Electric power transmission.

175 type

Model		V8ASHR	V8BZSHR	V12A	V12ASH	V12ASHR	V12BZSHR	V12RVR	V16BSHR	V16BZSHR	V16RVR
No of cylinders		8	8	12	12	12	12	12	16	16	16
Turbocharged		Yes	Yes	No	Yes	Yes	Yes	Yes	Yes	Yes	Yes
Charged air cooled		Yes	Yes	No	Yes	Yes	Yes	Yes	Yes	Yes	Yes
Continuous rating (UIC)	kW	440	590	440	610	700	885	1 030	1 030	1 175	1 320
	(bhp)	(600)	(800)	(600)	(825)	(950)	(1 200)	(1 400)	(1 400)	(1 600)	(1 800)
Engine speed	rpm	1 500	1 500	1 500	1 500	1 500	1 500	1 500	1 500	1 500	1 500
Mean piston speed	m/s	9	9	9	9	9	9	9	9	9	9
	(ft/min)	(1 772)	(1 772)	(1 772)	(1 772)	(1 772)	(1 772)	(1 772)	(1 772)	(1 772)	(1 772)
Bmep	bar	9.8	13.2	6.5	9.0	10.4	13.2	15.3	11.5	13.2	14.7
	(lb/in²)	(142)	(190)	(95)	(131)	(149)	(190)	(222)	(165)	(190)	(214)
Weight (dry)	kg	3 220	3 500	3 900	4 300	4 500	4 800	4 900	6 100	6 200	6 400
	(lb)	(7 100)	(7 720)	(8 600)	(9 500)	(9 940)	(10 600)	(10 800)	(13 450)	(13 670)	(14 100)
Length	mm	1 870	1 870	1 941	2 220	2 220	2 220	2 220	2 590	2 590	2 590
	(in)	(73.6)	(73.6)	(75)	(87.5)	(87.5)	(87.5)	(87.5)	(102)	(102)	(102)
Width	mm	1 320	1 320	1 280	1 280	1 330	1 330	1 330	1 330	1 330	1 330
	(in)	(52)	(52)	(50.4)	(50.4)	(52.3)	(52.3)	(52.3)	(52.3)	(52.3)	(52.3)
Height	mm	1 774	1 774	1 486	1 755	1 900	1 900	1 900	1 750	1 750	1 750
	(in)	(70)	(70)	(58.5)	(69)	(74)	(74)	(74)	(69)	(69)	(69)
Fuel consumption	g/kW/h	214	214	218	218	214	210	214	210	210	214
	(lb/hp/h)	(0.346)	(0.346)	(0.353)	(0.353)	(0.346)	(0.340)	(0.346)	(0.340)	(0.340)	(0.346)

195 and 240 type

Model		V12CSHR	V12RVR	V16CSHR	V16RVR	V20CSHR	V12DSHR	V12RVR	V16ESHR	V16RVR	V20EZSHR
No of cylinders		12	12	16	16	20	12	12	16	16	20
Continuous rating (UIC)	kW	1 320	1 470	1 900	2 020	2 200	2 420	3 000	3 230	4 000	4 400
	(bhp)	(1 800)	(2 000)	(2 580)	(2 750)	(3 000)	(3 300)	(4 080)	(4 400)	(5 450)	(6 000)
Engine speed	rpm	1 500	1 500	1 500	1 500	1 500	1 350	1 350	1 350	1 350	1 350
Bmep	bar	15.9	17.7	17.1	18.2	15.9	17.8	22	17.8	22	19.4
	(lb/in²)	(232)	(258)	(249)	(265)	(232)	(260)	(321)	(260)	(321)	(283)
Mean piston speed	m/s	9	9	9	9	9	9.9	9.9	9.9	9.9	9.9
		(1 764)	(1 764)	(1 764)	(1 764)	(1 764)	(1 944)	(1 944)	(1 944)	(1 944)	(1 944)
Weight (dry)	kg										
	(lb)	(5 000)	(5 700)	(7 000)	(7 800)	(8 500)	(12 000)	(13 000)	(15 000)	(16 000)	(20 000)
Length	mm	2 500	2 700	4 100	4 100	4 600	3 480	3 580	4 190	4 450	5 588
	(in)	(98.5)	(106)	(161)	(161)	(181)	(137)	(141)	(165)	(175)	(220)
Width	mm	1 460	1 460	1 460	1 460	1 460	1 752	1 803	1 752	1 803	1 803
	(in)	(57.5)	(57.5)	(57.5)	(57.5)	(57.5)	(69)	(71)	(69)	(71)	(71)
Height	mm	1 961	1 961	1 961	1 961	2 020	2 610	2 610	2 490	2 490	2 610
	(in)	(77.2)	(77.2)	(77.2)	(77.2)	(79.5)	(103)	(103)	(98)	(98)	(103)
Fuel cnsumption	g/kW/h	205	215	205	215	205	205	215	205	215	215
	lb/hp/h	(0.332)	(0.348)	(0.332)	(0.348)	(0.332)	(0.332)	(0.348)	(0.332)	(0.348)	(0.348)

SCANIA

Saab-Scania, Scania Division
Industrial Engine Section, Södertälje, Sweden

Telephone: 0755 81000
Telegrams: Scania Söder Tälje
Telex: 13479 SCANMOTS

The company, which produced its first internal combustion engine in 1897 and its first diesel engine in 1936, specialises in high-speed engines.

Types D8, DS8, D11, DS11
6 cylinder in-line, 4-stroke, water cooled.
Cylinders: Bore and stroke. D8 and DS8 115 × 125 mm (4.53 × 4.92 in). D11 and DS11 127 × 145 mm (5.0 × 5.71 in). Wet type centrifugal cast iron cylinder liners, the outer surfaces directly flushed by cooling water. Alloy cast iron cylinder heads, each covering 2 cylinders (D8 and DS8), or 3 cylinders (D11, DS11).

Type DS14
8 cylinder Vee, 4-stroke, water cooled.
Cylinders: Bore and stroke 127 × 140 mm (5.0 × 5.51 in). Alloyed cast iron cylinder heads, one for each cylinder.
Pistons: Light alloy. For the top compression ring there is a cast-iron insert to reduce wear of the ring groove to a minimum. Compression rings and oil control ring of alloy cast iron. Top compression ring chromium-plated. Case hardened chrome nickel steel fully floating gudgeon pins.
Connecting rods: Heat treated special alloy steel H section stampings with steel backed indium-coated thin-wall type big end bearings, and bronze bushes.
Crankshaft: Alloy steel one piece stamping, statically and dynamically balanced, carried in steel backed indium-coated thin-wall type bearings. Individual bearings can be exchanged without dismounting crankshaft.
Crankcase: Cylinder block and crankcase integrally cast of cast iron alloy. The main bearing caps are steel forgings.
Valve gear: One inlet and one exhaust valve per cylinder, of stellite faced heat resisting steel with chromium plated stems. Heat resistant alloy replaceable valve seats. Hardened steel forging camshaft.
Fuel injection: Multi-hole type injectors with special cold starting device. Helical gear driven injection pump.
Turbo-charger: Exhaust gas turbo-charger.
Fuel: Diesel fuel.
Lubrication: Forced feed to all bearings and gear trains with intermittent oil supply to the valve rocker mechanism. One gear-type pump.

Scania DS14 turbo-charged 8-cylinder engine

Cooling system: One centrifugal type water pump driven from the crankshaft through vee-belts (DS14 through gear chain). Thermostatic control for low temperature operation.
Starter: Electric.

Industrial Diesels

Model	D8	DS8	D11	DS11	DS11	DS14
No of cylinders	6	6	6	6	6	V8
Cylinder volume; cm³ (cu in)	7.8 (475)	7.8 (475)	11.0 (673)	11.0 (673)	11.0 (673)	14.2 (866)
Max intermittent output kW (hp)/rpm DIN 6270	123 (167) /2 400	154 (210) /2 400	158 (215) /2 200	213 (290) /2 200	224 (305) /2 200	295 (401) /2 200
Continuous output, gen sets kW (hp) 1 500 rpm	73 (99)	96 (130)	106 (144)	153 (208)	161 (219)	206 (281)
1 800 rpm	86 (117)	114 (155)	123 (167)	173 (235)	182 (247)	237 (322)
2 000 rpm	96 (131)	126 (171)	134 (182)	— (—)	— (—)	— (—)
2 100 rpm	— (—)	— (—)	— (—)	186 (253)*	196 (266)*	257 (350)*
Max torque intermittent	530 (54) 391	700 (71) 514	775 (79) 571	1 130 (115) 832	1 187 (121) 875	1 510 (154) 1 114
Max torque continuous	475 (49) 354	630 (64) 463	697 (71) 514	1 020 (104) 752	1 069 (109) 788	1 399 (139) 1 005
Nm (kpm) Lbf. Ft/rpm	/1 500	/1 400	/1 200	/1 300	/1 300	/1 300
Specific fuel consumption, continuous output g/kWh (g/bph)/1 500 rpm	230 (169)	215 (158)	220 (162)	207 (152)	212 (156)	212 (156)
lb/kWh (lb/bph)/1 500 rpm	0.51 (0.37)	0.47 (0.39)	0.49 (0.36)	0.46 (0.34)	0.47 0.34	0.47 (0.34)
Dry weight, kg (lb)	740 (1 631)	760 (1 676)	905 (1 995)	930 (2 050)	930 (2 050)	1 160 (2 557)

*Only for generating sets with reduction gear.

SEMT

Société d'Etudes de Machines Thermiques
2 quai de Seine, 93203 St Denis, France

The Société d'Etudes de Machines Thermiques (SEMT), formed in 1947 to develop diesel engines, is a subsidiary company of Alsthom Atlantique. It has successfully designed and developed diesel engines in the high-speed range.

SEMT-Pielstick PA series of engines are used for rail traction, generating plants, drilling and pumping sets, and for submarine and fast ship propulsion. More than 2 300 PA engines are in service around the world, manufactured by SEMT licencees.
The PA series includes the following models:
PA4-185 developing 167 hp per cylinder at 1 500 rpm
PA4-200 developing 192, 250 hp per cylinder at 1 500 rpm
PA6-280 developing 400 hp per cylinder at 1 000 rpm

S-G-P

Simmering-Graz-Pauker AG
Mariahilferstrasse 32, Vienna V11, Austria

Four-stroke vertical Vee and horizontal engines for locomotives and railcars.
Rating: 130 to 1 515 bhp at 1 000 to 1 515 rpm.

SHINKO

Shinko Engineering Co Ltd
1682 Motoima-cho, Ogak 503, Japan

Telephone: 0584 89 3121
Telex: 4793 624

This is a subsidiary of Kobe Steel Co Ltd. Manufacture of high-speed diesel engines for rail traction began in 1950 and their present range is from 140 hp to 2 000 hp. They also build hydraulic torque converters capable of up to 1 600 hp.

Vertical in-line watercooled 4-cycle

DMF 13C	6-cylinder normally aspirated
DMH 17C	8-cylinder normally aspirated
DMH 17S	8-cylinder turbo-charged
DMH 17SB	8-cylinder turbo-charged
DMF 31SB	6-cylinder turbo-charged
DMF 31SI	6-cylinder turbo-charged and charge air cooled
DMF 31ZB	6-cylinder turbo-charged and charge air cooled
DMH 41S	8-cylinder turbo-charged
DMH 41Z	8-cylinder turbo-charged and charge air cooled
DMH 41ZB	8-cylinder turbo-charged and charge air cooled

Horizontal in-line watercooled 4-cycle

DMH 17H	8-cylinder normally aspirated
DMH 17HS	8-cylinder turbo-charged
DMF 15HS	8-cylinder turbo-charged
DML 30HS	12-cylinder turbo-charged opposed cylinder

Vee-type watercooled 4-cycle

DML 61S	12-cylinder turbo-charged
DMH 61Z	12-cylinder turbo-charged and charge air cooled
DML 61ZA	12-cylinder turbo-charged and charge air cooled
DML 61ZB	12-cylinder turbo-charged and charge air cooled
DMP 81Z	16-cylinder turbo-charged and charge air cooled

Vertical in-line

Model		DMF13C	DMH17C	DMF31SB	DMF31Z	DMF31S1	DMF31ZB	DMH41S	DMH41Z	DMH41ZB
Bore	in	5.12	5.12	7.09	7.09	7.09	7.09	7.09	7.09	7.09
	(mm)	(130)	(130)	(180)	(180)	(180)	(180)	(180)	(180)	(180)
Stroke	in	6.30	6.30	7.87	7.87	7.87	7.87	7.87	7.87	7.87
	(mm)	(160)	(160)	(200)	(200)	(200)	(200)	(200)	(200)	(200)
No of cylinders		6	8	6	6	6	6	8	8	8
Displacement	in³	777	1 036	1 864	1 864	1 864	1 864	2 483	2 483	2 483
	(litres)	(12.74)	(16.98)	(30.55)	(30.55)	(30.55)	(30.55)	(40.7)	(40.7)	(40.7)
Turbo-charged		—	—	Yes	Yes	Yes	Yes	Yes	Yes	Yes
Charge air cooled		—	—	—	Yes	Yes	Yes	—	Yes	Yes
Power rating continuous	hp	140	180	500	550	600	750	700	800	1 000
Engine speed	rpm	1 500	1 500	1 500	1 500	1 500	1 500	1 500	1 500	1 500
Bmep	lb/in²	93.7	90.5	139.8	153.6	167.8	209.0	146.5	167.8	209.0
	(kg/cm²)	(6.59)	(6.36)	(9.83)	(10.8)	(11.8)	(14.7)	(10.3)	(11.8)	(14.7)
Piston speed	ft/min	1 576	1 576	1 970	1 970	1 970	1 970	1 970	1 970	1 970
	(m/s)	(8.0)	(8.0)	(10.0)	(10.0)	(10.0)	(10.0)	(10.0)	(10.0)	(10.0)
Weight, dry	lb	2 430	3 090	6 830	7 055	7 276	7 716	9 921	9 987	10 031
	(kg)	(1 100)	(1 400)	(3 100)	(3 200)	(3 300)	(3 500)	(4 500)	(4 500)	(4 550)
Length	in	65.4	79.2	105.2	105.4	109.1	105	126.6	126.6	126.6
	(mm)	(1 661)	(2 011)	(2 672)	(2 677)	(2 772.6)	(2 667)	(3 210)	(3 217)	(3 216)
Width	in	44.5	44.5	37.8	49.9	51.2	49.9	42.0	41.9	41.9
	(mm)	(1 131)	(1 131)	(961)	(1 269)	(1 300)	(1 268)	(1 066.5)	(1 066)	(1 066)
Height	in	38.9	38.9	78.6	66.7	66.7	66.7	71.0	70.9	70.9
	(mm)	(987)	(987)	(1 995)	(1 695)	(1 695)	(1 695)	(1 803.5)	(1 803)	(1 803)
Fuel consumption	lb/hp/h	0.419	0.419	0.397	0.397	0.386	0.386	0.397	0.397	0.386
	(g/hp/h)	(190)	(190)	(180)	(180)	(175)	(175)	(180)	(180)	(175)

Horizontal / Vee-type

Model		DMH17H	DMH17HS	DMF15HS	DML30HS	DML61S	DML61Z	DML61ZA	DML61ZB	DMP81Z
Bore	in	5.12	5.12			7.09	7.09	7.09	7.09	7.09
	(mm)	(130)	(130)	(140)	(140)	(180)	(180)	(180)	(180)	(180)
Stroke	in	6.30	6.30			7.87	7.87	7.87	7.87	7.87
	(mm)	(160)	(160)	(160)	(160)	(200)	(200)	(200)	(200)	(200)
No of cylinders		8	8	6	12	12	12	12	12	16
Displacement	in³	1 036	1 036	901	1 803	3 728	3 728	3 728	3 728	4 970
	(litres)	(16.98)	(16.98)	(14.78)	(29.56)	(61.10)	(61.10)	(61.10)	(61.10)	(81.5)
Turbo-charged		—	Yes	Yes	Yes	Yes	Yes	Yes	Yes	Yes
Charge air cooled		—	—	—	—	—	Yes	Yes	Yes	Yes
Power rating continuous	hp	180	250	250	500	1 000	1 100	1 250	1 500	2 000
Engine speed	rpm	1 500	1 500	1 600	1 600	1 500	1 500	1 500	1 550	1 500
Bmep	lb/in²	90.5	125.6	135.1	135.1	139.8	153.6	174.9	203.3	209.0
	(kg/cm²)	(6.36)	(8.83)	(9.5)	(9.5)	(9.83)	(10.8)	(12.3)	(14.3)	(14.7)
Piston speed	ft/min	1 576	1 576	1 674.5	1 674.5	1 970	1 970	1 970	2 035	1 970
	(m/s)	(8.0)	(8.0)	(8.5)	(8.5)	(10.0)	(10.0)	(10.0)	(10.33)	(10.0)
Weight dry	lb	2 420	2 420	3 968	7 495	12 130	12 240	12 346	14 330	19 842
	(kg)	(1 550)	(1 550)	(1 800)	(3 400)	(5 500)	(5 550)	(5 600)	(6 500)	(9 000)
Length	in	93.2	105.9	64.8	97.5	108.1	108.1	108.9	108.9	141
	(mm)	(2 392)	(2 691)	(2 149.5)	(2 477)	(2 746)	(2 746)	(2 768)	(2 768)	(3 582)
Width	in	53.7	48.2	61.4	76.5	65.0	72.4	72.4	74.0	74.0
	(mm)	(1 363)	(1 225)	(1 561)	(1 944)	(1 652)	(1 840)	(1 840)	(1 880)	(1 880)
Height	in	29.6	29.5	28.2	37.6	36.9	36.9	72.2	72.2	72.6
	(mm)	(753)	(750)	(716)	(955)	(936)	(936)	(1 833)	(1 833)	(1 844)
Fuel consumption	lb/hp/h	0.419	0.408	0.397	0.386	0.397	0.397	0.386	0.395	0.395
	(g/hp/h)	(190)	(185)	(180)	(180)	(180)	(180)	(175)	(170)	(170)

SSCM

Société Surgérienne de Constructions Mécanique
(Part of SACM Diesel Group)
1 rue de la Fonderie, 68054 Mulhouse Cedex, France

Poyaud Series

Series PZ: 6-cylinder vertical in-line engines.
Series 150: 6 cylinder in-line, 12-cylinder Vee.

Prefix: A=vertical engine, **C**=horizontal engine.
Suffix: S=supercharged (Turbo-charged), **Sr**=Supercharged with temperature water intercooling (charge air cooling), **SrH**=Supercharged with high temperature water intercooling (Charge air cooling) and piston cooling.
All are water cooled.
Cylinders: Bore 150 mm (5.9 in). Stroke 180 mm (7.1 in). Swept volume 3.18 litres per cylinder. Compression ratio: normally aspirated, 15.1 : 1, supercharged 14.4 : 1. Removable wet type cast iron cylinder liners. Individual cast iron cylinder heads. Special alloy removable valve seats.

Pistons: Aluminium alloy pistons with 3 compression rings (the top one chromium plated) and one oil control ring. Combustion chamber in crown. Case hardened gudgeon pin.

Connecting rods: Die casting of special hardened steel.

Crankshaft: Solid forging of chrome molybdenum steel. Steel bearing shells with lead-copper lining, interchangeable for either crankshaft main bearings or connecting rod bearings.

Crankcase: Monobloc iron casting, strongly ribbed with a crankshaft bearing between each cylinder. Access doors on each side.

Valve gear: 2 admission and 2 exhaust valves per cylinder. Gear driven camshaft.

Fuel injection: Bosch or Sigma multiple hole injectors. Bosch type P fuel pump or SIGMA DM fuel pump.

Supercharger: Holset exhaust gas-driven turbo-charger.

Lubrication: Forced feed throughout by gear-type feed pump.

Cooling system: Centrifugal circulating pump.

Starting: Electric; compressed air; Berger hydraulic.

*Dimensions of horizontal engines as follows:
Length; C6150 1 850 mm (72.8 in), others 2 350 mm (92.5 in)

Width; all engines 1 680 mm (66.1 in)
Height; all engines 765 mm (30.1 in)

Series 520: 6 cylinder vertical in-line, 8 and 12 cylinder Vee 4-stroke cycle, water cooled, combustion chamber in cylinder head.

Suffix: NS=naturally aspirated; SI=turbo-charged; S2=turbo-charged and charge air cooled.

Cylinders: Bore: 135 mm (5.316 in). Stroke 122 mm (4.803 in). Swept volume per cylinder 1.745 litres (106.5 in³).

Poyaud C 6150 SrH 6-cylinder horizontal engine
Turbo-charged and charge air cooled 420 hp at 1 800 rpm

Poyaud V12 SI 12-cylinder Vee engine
Turbo-charged 480 hp at 2 500 rpm.

Series 150		A4150	A6150 C6150	A6150S C6150S	A6150Sr C6150Sr	A6150SR C6150SR	A6150SrH C6150SrH	A8150	A8150S	A8150Sr	A8150SR	A12150	A12150S	A12150Sr	A12150SR	A12150SrH
No of cylinders		4	6	6	6	6	6	8V	8V	8V	8V	12V	12V	12V	12V	12V
Turbo-charged		No	No	Yes	Yes	Yes	Yes	No	Yes	Yes	Yes	No	Yes	Yes	Yes	Yes
Charge air cooled		No	No	No	Yes	Yes	Yes	No	No	Yes	Yes	No	No	Yes	Yes	Yes
bhp continuous		160	240	340	375	420	450	276	400	440	480	480	680	750	840	900
Engine speed	rpm	1 800	1 800	1 800	1 800	1 800	1 800	1 500	1 500	1 500	1 500	1 800	1 800	1 800	1 800	1 800
Mean piston speed	ft/min	2 124	2 124	2 124	2 124	2 124	2 124	1 772	1 772	1 772	1 772	2 124	2 124	2 124	2 124	2 124
	(m/s)	(10.8)	(10.8)	(10.8)	(10.8)	(10.8)	(10.8)	(9.0)	(9.0)	(9.0)	(9.0)	(10.8)	(10.8)	(10.8)	(10.8)	(10.8)
Bmep	lb/in²	92.5	92.5	128	139	154	154	92.5	135	148	161	92.5	128	139	154	154
	(kg/cm²)	(6.5)	(6.5)	(9.0)	(9.8)	(10.8)	(10.8)	(6.5)	(9.5)	(10.4)	(11.3)	(6.5)	(9.0)	(9.8)	(10.8)	(10.8)
Weight (dry)	lb	2 866	3 968	4 409	4 960	4 960	4 960	5 181	6 173	6 283	6 283	6 614	7 275	7 937	7 937	7 937
	(kg)	(1 300)	(1 800)	(2 000)	(2 250)	(2 250)	(2 350)	(2 350)	(2 800)	(2 850)	(2 850)	(3 000)	(3 300)	(3 600)	(3 600)	(3 600)
Length	in	49.6	65.4*	92.5*	92.5*	92.5*	92.5*	61.0	77.6	77.6	77.6	81.1	84.6	84.6	96.9	96.9
	(mm)	(1 260)	(1 600)	(2 350)	(2 350)	(2 350)	(2 350)	(1 548)	(1 969)	(1 969)	(1 969)	(2 056)	(2 151)	(2 151)	(2 459)	(2 459)
Width	in	33.5	33.5*	33.5*	33.5*	33.5*	33.5*	42.9	42.9	42.9	42.9	42.9	42.9	42.9	43.7	43.7
	(mm)	(850)	(850)	(850)	(850)	(850)	(850)	(1 087)	(1 087)	(1 087)	(1 087)	(1 087)	(1 087)	(1 087)	(1 110)	(1 110)
Height	in	57.1	57.1*	58.3*	58.3*	58.3*	58.3*	54.7	66.1	66.1	67.1	54.7	67.3	67.3	67.3	67.3
	(mm)	(1 450)	(1 450)	(1 480)	(1 480)	(1 480)	(1 480)	(1 390)	(1 675)	(1 675)	(1 705)	(1 390)	(1 710)	(1 710)	(1 710)	(1 710)

Series 520		6L NS	6L S1	6L S2	V8 NS	V8 S1	V8 S2	V12 NS	V12 S1	V12 S2
No of cylinders		6	6	6	8V	8V	8V	12V	12V	12V
Turbo-charged		—	Yes	Yes	—	Yes	Yes	—	Yes	Yes
Charge air cooled		—	—	Yes	—	—	Yes	—	—	Yes
bhp continuous		170	230	290	220	310	400	360	480	600
Engine speed	rpm					2 500				
Weight (dry)	lb	2 140	2 195	2 290	2 625	2 690	2 845	3 640	3 725	3 900
	(kg)	(970)	(995)	(1 040)	(1 190)	(1 220)	(1 290)	(1 650)	(1 690)	(1 770)
Length	in	57.5	57.5	57.5	50.4	53.2	53.2	69.8	73.5	73.5
	(mm)	(1 460)	(1 460)	(1 460)	(1 279)	(1 351)	(1 351)	(1 767)	(1 866)	(1 866)
Width	in	28.0	31.9	31.9	43.3	46.5	46.5	40.9	46.2	46.2
	(mm)	(710)	(810)	(810)	(1 098)	(1 181)	(1 181)	(1 038)	(1 174)	(1 174)
Height	in	42.7	45.6	45.9	36.8	36.8	42.7	36.8	36.8	42.7
	(mm)	(1 085)	(1 158)	(1 166)	(935)	(935)	(1 084)	(935)	(935)	(1 084)

TAMPELLA

Oy Tampella Ab Engineering Division
Lapintre 1, 33101 Tampere 10, Finland

Telephone: 931 32400
Telegrams: TAMPELLA, Tampere
Telex: 22117 tamec sf

Formerly known as the Tampere Linen and Iron Co, the company was formed in 1861 by the merger of an engineering works founded in 1842 and a linen mill built in 1856. Later, wood pulp mills, paper mills and a cotton mill were added, and the company has considerable interests in hydro-electric schemes. The company commenced the manufacture of diesel engines in the early 1930s and supplied the first diesel engines to the Finnish State Railways.

From 1955 to 1972 the company made MAN WV 22/30 (subsequently RV 22/30) and VV 22/30 engines, and from 1960, MGO V engines of 175 mm bore.* The engines built to date total about 600 000 hp.

In developing engines special consideration has been given to the requirements imposed on engines by the severe Finnish winters.

*Under licence to SACM Mulhouse.

Tampella-MGO V16BSHR engine
Turbo-charged and charge air cooled, 1 400 bhp at 1 500 rpm

THYSSEN HENSCHEL

HENSCHEL Dieselmotoren, D-3500 Kassel 2, Henschelplatz 1, Federal Republic of Germany

Telephone: 0561 8011
Telegrams: Henschel Kassel
Telex: 099793

Since 1958, HENSCHEL has manufactured high-speed locomotive diesel engines with or without turbo-charging. These engines, operating on the direct injection system, have been developed as a result of more than 35 years' experience in the design and manufacture of diesel engines. Output ranges from 240 to 3 000 hp, 4-stroke, water cooled, for rail traction and industrial and marine applications.

Series 1516
Type: 6 cylinders in-line, 8 and 12 cylinders in Vee form, 4-stroke, watercooled, turbocharged. Bore 145 mm (5.71 in), stroke 155 mm (6.10 in).

Series 2423
Type: 12-cylinder Vee 4-stroke, watercooled, turbo-charged and intercooled. Bore 240 mm (9.45 in), stroke 230 mm (9.06 in).
Cylinder frame and crankcase: A monobloc of cast iron.
Individual cylinder heads: Cast iron, 2 inlet, 2 exhaust valves.
Cylinder liners: Centrifugal cast iron, wet type, easily replaceable.
Pistons: Light alloy with combustion chambers in crown, (series 2423; oil-cooled by annular chamber, shaker effect).

Connecting rods: Die-forged steel, double T-cross section.
Crankshaft: Forged steel with induction-hardened journals.
Bearings: 3-material type.
Valve gear: Gear driven camshaft (series 1516 one per engine; series 2423 one camshaft for each cylinder bank), push rods and rocker arms.
Supercharging: With turbo-charger; series 1516 intercooling possible; series 2423 intercooled.
Fuel injection: Bosch multi-hole nozzles, Bosch block-injector pumps.
Lubricating system: Forced feed by gear pump, water-cooled oil cooler and micro-filters in the main system, centrifugal-filters in the secondary system.
Cooling system: One separate circulation system each for cylinder and charge-air cooling.
Starting: Compressed air.
Mountings: Multi-point suspension using rubber-metal pads.

HENSCHEL model 12V 1516A turbo-charged and intercooled engine

HENSCHEL model 12V 2423A turbo-charged and intercooled engine

Model		6R1516A	8V1516A	12V1516A	12V2423Aa
No of cylinders		6 in-line	8 Vee	12 Vee	12 Vee
Turbo-charged		Yes	Yes	Yes	Yes
Power output range (a)	bhp	330 to 388	440 to 517	660 to 782	2 500 to 3 000
Engine speed	rpm	1 800	1 800	1 800	1 500
Bmep	lb/in²	154 to 179	154 to 179	154 to 180	171 to 205
	(kg/cm²)	(10.8 to 12.6)	(10.8 to 12.6)	(10.8 to 12.7)	(12.0 to 14.4)
Mean piston speed	ft/min	1 836	1 836	1 836	2 264
	(m/s)	(9.3)	(9.3)	(9.3)	(11.5)
Weight	lb	3 645	4 273	5 616	24 230
	(kg)	(1 655)	(1 940)	(2 550)	(11 000)
Length	in	82.64	67.72	83.66	122.24
	(mm)	(2 098)	(1 720)	(2 125)	(3 105)
Width	in	33.39	47.64	48.82	69.29
	(mm)	(848)	(1 210)	(1 240)	(1 760)
Height	in	50.59	51.77	54.13	88.98
	(mm)	(1 285)	(1 315)	(1 375)	(2 260)
Fuel consumption	lb/hp/h	pme62	0.360	0.362	0.358
	(g/hp/h)	(162)	(161)	(162)	(160)

(a) Continuous output B according to DIN 6270 corresponding approx to UIC conditions depending upon applications   without fan

TRANSMISSION SYSTEMS

ACEC
Ateliers de Constructions Électriques de Charleroi

PO Box 4, B-6000 Charleroi, Belgium

Telephone: (07) 44 21 11
Telex: 51 227 ACEC CHARLEROI

Products: Electrical transmission for diesel-electric locomotives and railcars.

Constitution: A member of the Westinghouse Electric Group

ALSTHOM
Société Générale de Constructions Électriques et Mécaniques Alsthom

38 avenue Kleber, 75784 Paris, France

Telephone: 727 77 79
Telex: 27672

Works: Belfort and Tarbes

Telephone (Belfort): (84) 28 12 31
Telephone (Tarbes): (62) 93 02 97

Products: Complete electrical transmissions. The actual production power range with main dc generators is up to 2 800 hp and with alternators up to 5 000 hp.

ASEA
Allmänna Svenska Elektriska AB

S-721 83 Vasteras, Sweden

Telephone: 021 10 00 00
Telex: 40720

Products: Entire electrical transmissions for 150 hp stock and above.

BRISSONNEAU & LOTZ
Brissonneau & Lotz Chaudronnerie, SA

38 avenue Kléber, 75784 Paris, France

Products: Electric transmissions with main generators of up to 2 400 hp.

BROWN BOVERI (BBC)
Brown, Boveri & Cie

Postfach 85, CH-5401 Baden, Switzerland

Telephone: 056 75 11 11
Telex: 52921 and 53 203.

Works: Baden, Birr, Turgi Zurich-Oerlikon, Switzerland

Associated Companies: Brown Boveri & Cie AG, Mannheim, Federal Republic of Germany; Cie, Electro-Mécanique, Paris, France; Tecnomasio Italiano Brown Boveri SA, Milan, Italy; Oesterreichische Brown Boveri-Werke AG, Vienna, Austria; A/S Norsk Elektrisk & Brown Boveri, Oslo, Norway; Industria Eletrica Brown Boveri SA, Osasco, São Paulo, Brazil; Hindustan Brown Boveri Ltd, Bombay, India.

Products: Complete electric transmissions for railcars and locomotives.

BRUSH
Brush Electrical Machines Ltd (Traction Division)

PO Box 18, Loughborough, Leicestershire LE11 1HJ, England

Telephone: 0509 63131
Telegrams: BRUSH, Loughborough
Telex: 341091

Products: Electric transmission systems of up to 6 000 hp

Constitution: A Hawker Siddeley company

CANADIAN GENERAL ELECTRIC
Canadian General Electric Co Ltd

PO Box 417, Toronto, Ontario M5L W2, Canada

Telephone: 416 366 7311
Telex: 022 052

Works: 107 Park Street North, Peterborough, Ontario K9J 7B5, Canada

Telephone: 705 742 7711
Telex: 029 826

Associated Company: General Electric Co Ltd, USA

Products: Diesel-electric traction systems 600 to 4 000 hp per single unit; rapid transit propulsion systems.

ELEKTRO-MECHANIK
Elektro-Mechanik GmbH

Wendenerhütte 596 OLPE, Postfach 40, Federal Republic of Germany

Telephone: 02762 1631
Telex: 0876 616

Products: Hydraulic and hydro-mechanical transmissions 150/600 hɼ (AEG-EMG system), cardan shaft axle drives.

ERCOLE MARELLI
Ercole Marelli & C SpA

Via Borgonuovo 24, Milan 20121, Italy

Telephone: 2494
Telegrams: Ventilator, Milano
Telex: 32 0575/310043 EMDITE I

Works: Viale Edison 50, 20099 Sesto S Giovanni, Italy

Products: Complete electric transmissions for locomotives and railcars.

FIAT
Fiat Ferroviaria Savigliano SpA

Corso Ferrucci 122, 10141 Turin, Italy

Telephone: 33 20 33/33 21 33 (011)
Telex: 220315 FIATSV I

Works: Piazza Galateri 4, 12038 Savigliano (Cuneo), Italy

Telephone: 596784

Products: Hydro-mechanical, hydraulic and mechanical transmissions of up to 500 hp axle drives.

GANZ MAVAG
Ganz Mavag

Könyves Kálmán Krt 76, Budapest VIII, Hungary

Telephone: 137 020

Products: Ganz mechanical transmissions up to 620 hp; in conjunction with co-operating company, electric transmissions of 550 to 3 000 hp per unit; hydraulic and hydro-mechanical transmission 350 to 1 800 hp.

GE
General Electric Co (USA)

570 Lexington Avenue, New York, New York 10022, USA

Telephone: (212) 750 2000

Works: 2901 East Lake Road, Erie, Pennsylvania 16531, USA

Telephone: (814) 455 5466

Products: Complete electric transmissions.

GEC TRACTION
GEC Traction Ltd

Trafford Park, Manchester M17 1PR, England

Telephone: 061 872 2431
Telegrams: ASSOCELECT MANCHESTER
Telex: 667152

Products: Electric propulsion equipment for ac and dc electric locomotives and multiple units as well as for diesel electric and battery vehicles. Suitable for all rail gauges above 914 mm, for axle loads up to 30 tonne, and speeds of more than 200 km/h; new and replacement gears and pinions, straight spur or helical, single or double reduction, parallel or right-angle drives.

GENERAL ELECTRIC (BRAZIL)
General Electric do Brazil SA

Estrada Campinas-Monte Mor km 103-13, 100 Campinas, SP, Brazil

Telephone: 2 1011
Telex: 025819

Associated Company: General Electric Co (USA)

Products: Electrical transmission 1 000 to 2 400 hp axle hung motor

GM

General Motors Corporation
(Detroit Diesel Allison Division)

Detroit Diesel Allison Division International Operations, 252 Telegraph Road, Southfield, Michigan 48075, USA

Telephone: (313) 424 4800

Works: Detroit Diesel Allison Division GMC, J5A, PO Box 894, Indianapolis, Indiana 46206, USA

Telephone: (317) 243 1874

Products: Hydraulic Torqmatic transmissions of 80 to 1 000 hp

GOTHA

Getriebewerk Gotha

58 Gotha, Karl-Liebknecht-Strasse 26, Federal Republic of Germany

Products: Axle drives for diesel powered vehicles.

HITACHI

Hitachi Ltd

6-2, Otemachi 2-chome, Chiyoda-ku, Tokyo 100, Japan

Telephone: (03) 270 2111
Telex: J22395, J22432, J24491, J26375 (HITACHY)

Products: Complete control equipment, electric transmissions and hydraulic transmissions.

HUNSLET

Hunslet Precision Engineering Ltd

Hunslet Engine Works, Leeds LS10 1BT, England

Telephone: 0532 32261
Telegrams: HUNSLT LEEDS
Telex: 55237

Products: Main transmission gears forward and reverse and final drives; axle drive units for diesel-mechanical; mechanical change-speed, hydraulic and hydro-mechanical transmissions of up to 1 000 hp; gearing for electrical transmissions; gears and gear boxes.

HURTH

Carl Hurth Maschinen-und Zahnradfabrik

Holzstrasse 19, D-8000 Munich 5, Federal Republic of Germany

Telephone: (089) 23 70 21
Telex: 05 29322

Products: Jackshaft gears; hollow shaft and bevel gear axle drive units; cardanic axle couplings; mechanical change-speed gears: alternate-speed and reverse-reduction gears of up to 500/600 hp.

ISOTTA

Isotta Fraschini

Via Milano, 7-Saronno (VA), Italy

Products: Hydraulic and mechanical transmissions for locomotives and railcars. Axle drives for electric and diesel-powered vehicles.

KAELBLE-GMEINDER

Carl Kaelble u. Gmeinder GmbH & Co

695 Mosbach/Baden, PO Box 1260, Federal Republic of Germany

Telephone: 06261 4041
Telex: 04 66111

Products: Mechanical gears; axle drives; alternate-speed and reduction gears for hydraulic transmissions with jackshaft, cardan shaft and chain drives.

KAWASAKI

Kawasaki Electric Manufacturing Co Ltd

1-2 chome, Wadayama-dari, Hyogo-ku, Kobe, Japan

Telephone: 581 6291
Telex: 356 28

Products: Complete control equipment and electric transmissions.

MaK

Krupp MaK Maschinenbau GmbH

PO Box 9009, 2300 Kiel 17, Federal Republic of Germany

Telephone: 0431 3811
Telex: 0299877/78 mak d

Products: Axle drives.

MECANOEXPORTIMPORT

Mecanoexportimport

10 Milhail Eminescu Street, Bucharest, Romania

Telephone: 12 46 00
Telex: 269

Works: Hidromecanica Works, 78 Boulevard Lenin, Brasov, Romania.

Telephone: 6153

Products: Hydraulic transmissions.

MONTMIRAIL

Ateliers de Montmirail

10 avenue de Friedland, 75008 Paris, France

Telephone: 561 14 30
Telex: 660 955

Works: Montmirail (Marne).

Telephone: 26 42 21 90

Parent Company: Cie de Chemins de Fer Départementaux.

Products: Asynchro mechanical change-speed transmission with cardan-shaft drive, from 200 to 3 000 hp.

MPM

Meccanica Padana Monteverde SpA

Viale dell 'Industria 46/48, 35100 Padova, Italy

Telephone: 049 655566
Telegrams: INGRANAGGI PADOVA
Telex: 430320 MPM PD I

Products: Traction gears, special gear boxes, special axle drive units. MPM is staffed and equipped to design and manufacture complete transmission for rail vehicles with case hardened ground and profile correction for long life and smooth running.

Sales Director: Vittorio Rasera

MTE

Société MTE

31-32 quai National, 92806 Puteaux, France

Telephone: (33-1) 776 41 62
Telex: 610425 F MELEC C

Works: Société Creusot-Loire, Le Creusot (S & L); Jeumont Schneider—Usines de Jeumont (Nord), La Plaine Saint Denis (Seine); Champagne-sur-Seine (S & M), Lyon (Rhone), France.

Products: Full range of electric transmissions.

MTU

Motoren-und Turbinen-Union Friedrichshafen GmbH

D-7990 Friedrichshafen 1, Federal Republic of Germany

Telephone: 07541 207
Telex: 0734 360

Products: Axle drives; Mekydro hydraulic transmissions 500 to 2 500 hp.

NIIGATA

Niigata Converter Co Ltd

Nambu Building, 27-9 Sendagaya 5-chome, Shibuya-ku, Tokyo 151, Japan

Telephone: 03 354 7111
Telex: 2323105 NICOTO J

Products: Nico transmissions; hydraulic torque converters.

OM

OM SpA

Piazza San Ambrogio 6, Milan, Italy

Telephone: 898351

Works: Via Pompeo Leoni 18, Milan, Italy

Telephone: 53 14 61

Products: Reverse reduction gears; OM/SRM hydraulic and hydro-mechanical transmissions built under licence; axle drives

ROCKWELL INTERNATIONAL
(Supply and Mass Transit Division)

2135 West Maple Road, Troy, Michigan 48084, USA

Products: Gear boxes and couplings for subway stock.

SCG
Self-Changing Gears Ltd

Lythalls Lane, Coventry, West Midlands CV6 6FY, England

Telephone: 0203 88881
Telegrams: Selfchange, Coventry
Telex: 31644

Products: SCG final drives for heavy-duty locomotives and railcars.

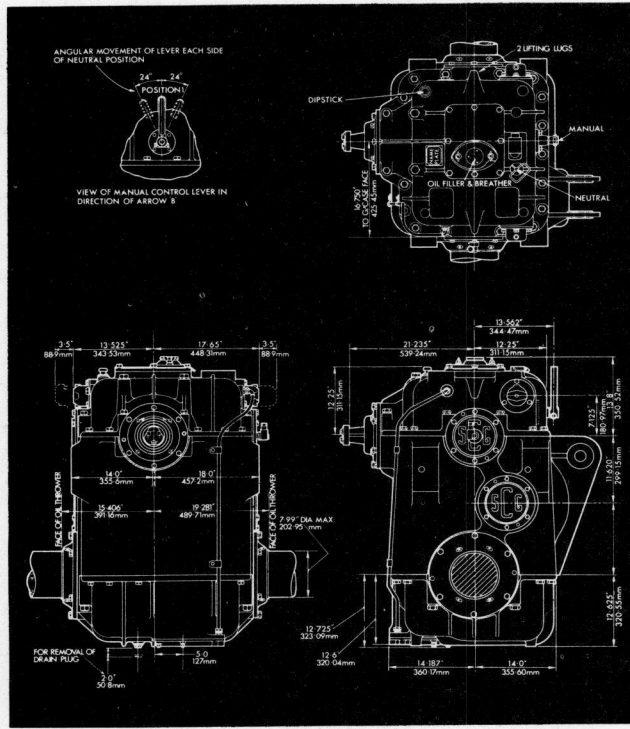

Basic installation details of the SCG type RF11 final drive for locomotives
Data: ratios, 5.03:1 up to 15.32:1 reduction; max input torque variable up to a max
1 300 kgf/m² (9 400 lbf/ft²); operation, pneumatic 3.5-5.6 ATU (50-80 lb); weight with oil
2 000 kg (41.5 cwt); CFD power shift box from 200 to 1 000 hp, axle drives, free wheels
for industrial and railway applications.

SECMAFER
Secmafer SA

Chemin des Meuniers Buchelay, 78203 Mantes, France

Telephone: 092 40 00
Telex: 600815

Products: Axle drives; hydrostatic transmissions for up to 8 000 hp.

SHINKO
Shinko Engineering Co Ltd

1682 Motoima-cho, Ogaki 503, Japan

Telephone: 0584 89 3121
Telex: 4793 624

Products: Cardan shaft drive hydro-mechanical transmissions of up to 1 600 hp;
Shinko torque converters.

SIEMENS
Siemens Aktiengesellschaft

Werner-von-Siemens-Strasse 50, D-8520 Erlangen 2, Federal Republic of Germany

Telephone: 09131 71
Telex: 629871

Products: Entire electric transmissions of up to 4 000 hp.

SRM
SRM Hydromekanik AB

Skattegårdsvägen 120, PO Box 16, 162 11 Vällingby-Stockholm, Sweden

Telephone: (08) 38 02 30
Telegrams: HYDESSAREM
Telex: 17412 HYDESSM

Products: SRM hydraulic transmission of 30 to 2 000 hp. Licensees: Fiat SpA (Italy), Oy
Tampella AB (Finland), Zahnraderfabrik Renk AG (Federal Republic of Germany), and
CKD Praha (Czechoslavakia).

STROMUNGSMASCHINEN
VEB Strömungsmaschinen

83 Pirma Sonnenstein, Postschliebfach 64, Dresden, German Democratic Republic

Works: Otto-Buchwitz-Strasse 96, 806 Dresden, German Democratic Republic

Products: Hydraulic couplings; hydraulic and hydrodynamic transmissions, flow converters.

TWIN DISC
Twin Disc Incorporated

1328 Racine Street, Racine, Wisconsin 53403, USA

Telephone: (414) 634 1981
Telex: 264432

Associated Companies: Twin Disc International SA, Chaussée de Namur 54, 1400
Nivelles, Belgium
Telephone: 067 2249 41
Telex: 57 414

British Twin Disc Ltd, Knight Rd, Rochester, Kent ME2 2AT, England
Telephone: 0634 77855
Telex: 96182

Twin Disc (Pacific) Pty Ltd, Union Road, PO Box 126, Lavington, New South Wales 2641,
Australia
Telephone: (060) 25 2577
Telex: 56973

Twin Disc (South Africa) Ltd, PO Box 75140, 2047 Gardenview, Transvaal, Johannesburg, South Africa
Telephone: 616 5018

Twin Disc (Far East) Ltd, PO Box 155, Jurong Town Post Office, 40 Lokyang Way,
Jurong, Singapore 9161
Telephone: 2618909
Telex: RS 24284

Twin Disc Transmissoes Ltda, Rua Carlos, Seiol, 585 Caju, Cep 20 931, Rio de Janeiro,
Brazil
Telephone: 264 6513
Telex: 212 3329/264 6513

Affiliated Company: Niigata Converter Co Ltd, Nambu Building 27-9, Sendagaya
5-chome, Shibuya-ku, Tokyo 151, Japan
Telephone: 354 7111
Telex: 2323105

Products: Universal joints; gas turbine starting drives; power take-offs; mechanical,
hydraulic and pneumatic clutches; control systems; hydraulic torque converters,
power-shift transmissions.

VOITH
Voith Getriebe KG

Heidenheim/Brenz, Federal Republic of Germany

Telephone: 3291
Telex: 7 14888

Products: Fluid couplings; axle drives; cooling units, hydrodynamic brakes, hydrostatic equipment, mechanical gearboxes, Voith hydraulic transmissions (turbo transmissions); torque converters; DIWA and DIWA-matic hydro-mechanical transmissions.

ZAHNRADFABRIK VELBERT
Zahnradfabrik Velbert

D-562 Velbert, Postfach 926, Federal Republic of Germany

Products: Reining transmissions including flexible steel mainwheel for the transmission of ac electric locomotives; type SWP-CEV multiple transmission supplied to the
Vevey-Bloney-Le Pleiades mountain railway (combination of spur wheel stages with
cyclo-palloid-toothed bevel wheel stage); single motor bogie drive type K520 specially
developed for high-speed suburban and local service trains with a speed reduction
ratio of 5.83:1, a maximum speed of 2 800 rpm and an input torque of 950 Nm, and the
type CC-2400 coupling with spur wheel and hollow shaft for electric locomotives.

BRAKES AND DRAWGEAR

ABEX
Abex Corporation (Railroad Products Group)

Valley Road, Mahwah, New Jersey 07430, USA

Telephone: (201) 529-3450

Products: Metal and composition brake shoes, disc brake pads.

President: N George Belury
Export Sales Director: Edwin R Ambrose

European Works and Sales Office: Frendo-Sud SpA, 83100 Avellino, Italy

Telephone: 825 26 811

AIRESEARCH
AiResearch Manufacturing Co of California

2525 West 190th Street, Torrance, California 90509, USA

Telephone: (213) 323 9500

Products: Brake equipment.

AJAX
Ajax Consolidated Co

4615 West 20th Street, Chicago, Illinois 60650, USA

Telephone: (312) 242 0940

Products: Brake equipment including power hand brakes.

ASF
American Steel Foundries
(A member of Amsted Industries)

1005 Prudential Plaza, Chicago, Illinois 60601, USA

Telephone: (312) 645 1746
Telex: 25 4187

Products: Automatic couplers and yokes. ASF designs the Alliance Coupler System. This knuckle-style coupler system covers a range of styles suitable for applications from small mine cars to the largest freight cars and passenger cars. Alliance couplers can include provision for rotary dumping, interlocking and slack control. A full range of accessories such as yokes, drawbars and transition systems is included. ASF products are also available directly from Amsted licensees in many countries.

AVON
Avon Industrial Polymers (Bradford-on-Avon) Ltd

Bradford-on-Avon, Wiltshire BA15 1AA, England

Telephone: 02216 3911
Telegrams: INDUSTRIAL Bradford-on-Avon
Telex: 44856

Products: Draftgear, drawgear, buffers, air-brake hose, rubber suspension systems and air springs.

AZBEST
Ploce, Yugoslavia

Products: Composition brake linings built under licence from Jurid Werke of the Federal Republic of Germany.

BHARAT
Bharat Brakes and Valves Ltd
(Successors to Gresham & Craven of India (P) Ltd)

22 Gobra Road, Calcutta-700 014, India

Telephone: 44 1754
Telegrams: CYLVAC CALCUTTA
Telex: GNC-021-2545

Products: Vacuum brake equipment; rotary exhausters; air brake valves and reservoirs.

BLAIR
Geo Blair & Co (Sales) Ltd

Pottery Lane, Forth, Newcastle-upon-Tyne, England

Telephone: 610711/6
Telex: 53464

Products: Extensive range of steel castings and assemblies for railway rolling stock including automatic couplers.

Chairman: I L Blair
Managing Director: J V Raine

BRADKEN
Bradken Consolidated Ltd

22 O'Riordan Street, Alexandria, Sydney, New South Wales, Australia

Products: Friction draftgear.

BREMSENWERK
VEB Berliner Bremsenwerk

Hirschberger Strasse 4, 1134 Berlin, German Democratic Republic

Telephone: 55740
Telex: 0112408

Products: Braking equipment.

BRITISH VITA
British Vita Co Ltd

PO Box 7, Porterfield Road, Renfrew, Scotland

Telephone: 041 886 2384
Telex: 777238

Products: Vacuum brake hoses, rubber springs, wide range of standard products and special components.

BSI
Bergische Stahl-Industrie

Papenberger Strasse 38, PO Box 10 07 40, D-5630 Remscheid, Federal Republic of Germany

Telephone: 02191 3641
Telex: 8513858

Products: Brake systems and equipment; disc brakes with high thermal capacity and cooling by self-ventilitation; tread brakes; automatic centre buffer couplers; shunting couplers; steel castings for the railway industry; brake control equipment.

BUFFALO BRAKE BEAM
Buffalo Brake Beam Co

400 Ingham Avenue, Lackawanna, Buffalo, New York 14218, USA

Products: Brake Beams

Chairman: Lester A Crone
Managing Director: Richard Adams
Chief Sales Director: E Vey

Agent: Canada-Davanac Industries Ltd, 155 Montpellier Boulevard, Montreal, Quebec H4N 2G3, Canada.

Telephone: (716) 823 4200

CARDWELL WESTINGHOUSE
Cardwell Westinghouse Company

332 South Michigan Avenue, Chicago, Illinois 60604, USA

Telephone: (312) 427 5051
Telegrams: CARDWELL
Telex: 25 4210

Products: Friction draftgear; hand brakes; automatic slack adjusters, and friction bolster springs (snubbers).

Export Sales: J L Karrigan.

Licence Agreements:
Argentina: Siam Di Tella Ltd, Division Electrodom estica, Tucman 633, Buenos Aires
Australia: Vickers Hadwa Division, 123 Railway Parade, Bassendean, Western Australia 6054
Bradken Consolidated Ltd, 22 O'Riordan Street, Alexandria, Sydney, New South Wales
Belgium: Acieries de Haine-Saint-Pierre & Lesquin, 7160 Haine Saint Pierre
Brazil: Cobrasma SA, PO Box 8225-ZP-1, Sao Paulo
Portugal: Engenharia E Comercio Lda, Rua da Alegria, 61 R/C, Lisbon 2
South Africa: Sturrock (South Africa) Ltd, 91 Commissioner Street, PO Box 2863, Johannesburg

CARRIER KHEOPS
Carrier Khéops SA

12 villa d'Este, 75643 Paris (Cedex 13), France

Telephone: 583 90 01
Telex: KHEOPS 200 800F

Products: Electro-pneumatic braking systems.

COBRA ®
Railroad Friction Products Corporation

Wilmerding, Pennsylvania 15148, USA

Telephone: (412) 273 1106

Products: Composition brake shoes.

Chairman: D J Price
Managing Director: W I Graham
Chief Sales Director: E W Kojsza

Agents: Cobra Friction Products Ltd, Hamilton, Ontario L8N 3T5, Canada

Cobra Disc Brake Linings:

Model no	Wabco Pc no	Disc size (in)	Average weight (lb)	Pad thickness (in)	Pallet qty	Description
V2844	579544	28	4.75	1.00	132	28″ lining metal Toed-4
V2646	579546	26	4.10	1.00	154	26″ lining metal Toed-4
V2852	579552	28	3.45	1.00	132	28″ lining
V2645	579545	26	2.85	1.00	154	26″ lining
V2448	579548	24	3.15	1.00	154	24″ lining
V2449	579549	24	3.55	1.18	126	24″ lining
V2435	581235	24	3.45	1.18	126	24″ lining
V2150	579550	21/19	4.00	1.18	—	21″ lining
V2601	—	25.2	2.76	0.94	250	UIC style-right
V2602	—	25.2	2.76	0.94	250	UIC style-left

COBRASMA
Cobrasma SA

Rua da Estacao, 523 Osasco, São Paulo, Brazil

Telephone: 801 8000/227 6711
Telegrams: COBRASMA, São Paulo
Telex: 23145

Products: Brake equipment and friction draftgear.

COBREQ
Cia Brasileira de Equipamentos

Praia do Flamengo 200-9° andar, Rio de Janeiro, Brazil

Telephone: 285 2233
Telegrams: Calderon
Telex: 021 21632

Products: Non-metallic composition brake shoes and brake pads for railroad vehicles.

Chairman: Nelson Molina
Chief Sales Director: Flávio Simôes Ligabue
Export Sales Director: Rodolfo Luiz Darigo

COMMONWEALTH ENGINEERING
Commonwealth Engineering (NSW) Pty Ltd

11 Berry Street, Granville, New South Wales 2142, Australia

Telephone: (02) 637 0166
Telegrams: COMENG, Sydney
Telex: AA 25283

Products: Miner RF170, RF185, RF361 and RF444 draftgear.

CONBRAKO
Conbrako (Pty) Ltd

PO Box 14010, 167 Tedstone Road, Wadeville 1422, Transvaal, South Africa

Telephone: 34 3431
Telegrams: CONBRAKO
Telex: 8 4721 JH

Products: Vacuum brakes; hand brakes; brake regulators; drawgear.

DAVANAC
Davanac Industries Ltd

155 Montpellier Boulevard, Montreal, Quebec H4N 2G3, Canada

Products: Brake beams under licence to Buffalo Brake Beam Co, USA.

DAVIES AND METCALFE
Davies and Metcalfe (Equipment) Ltd

Injector Works, Romiley, Nr Stockport, Cheshire SK6 3 AE, England

Telephone: 061 430 4272/5
Telegrams: EXHAUST, Romiley
Telex: 668801

Products: Air brakes; electro-pneumatic braking; overspeed protection equipment; automatic couplers; two-stage air compressors; disc brakes; wheel slip detection and correction equipment. The company offers a range of products developed for rapid transit systems, including:
Type EBC/5 electro-pneumatic brake system, supplied with a variable (anologue) or stepped (digital) control;
Two-stage air compressors, with flange-mounted ac or dc electric motors and an integral intercooler with forced air cooling to ensure effective performance;
Metcalfe-BSI Compact coupler, fully automatic with wide coupling capacity in all planes to carry up to 140 electrical connections and two through pneumatic circuits (this device also provides buffing and draft gear functions);
Spring parking brake, a spring applied air released mechanism controlled from any of the driving positions;
Metcalfe-BSI disc brake sets, fully ventilated patented construction (both axle and wheel mounted sets, with actuators and release indicator systems).

Subsidiaries: Davies & Metcalfe Engineering Ltd, 22 George Street, Granville, New South Wales 2142, Australia

An important licence agreement was concluded between Davies & Metcalfe and Bergische Stahl-Industrie of Ramscheld, Federal Republic of Germany, in 1977.
The agreement gives Davies & Metcalfe exclusive rights to a range of railway products developed by Bergische Stahl-Industrie (BSI) comprising railway disc brake systems, multi-function automatic couplers for rail vehicles, electro magnetic rail brakes and other equipment. In addition to the UK market Davies & Metcalfe have exclusive rights for all Commonwealth countries and some other territories.
Davies & Metcalfe (Equipment) Ltd, a subsidiary of the parent company specialise in the BSI range of products in addition to equipment designed for rapid transit applications. Already this has led to important contracts: 190 Compact type automatic couplers and 400 sets of disc brake equipment for the 95 articulated cars being built for the Tyne & Wear Metro. The Metcalfe-BSI couplers are also specified for the 140 rapid transit cars being built by Metro-Cammell for the Hong Kong Metro.
30 sets of electro-pneumatic brake equipment for the New South Wales double-deck inter-urban cars are being supplied by Davies and Metcalfe Engineering Ltd, the Australian subsidiary Co. Davies & Metcalfe brake equipment has also been fitted to coaches being built in India for Tanzania. The company has also received an order for 16 sets of locomotive brakes and vigilance control equipment for locomotives being built in India for Tanzania.

Chairman: Richard Metcalfe
Sales Director: E Mulryan

DAVIS BRAKE BEAM
Davis Brake Beam Co

Johnstown, Pennsylvania, USA

Telephone: (814) 535 1595

Products: Solid-truss brake beams and bogie-mounted braking system manufactured under the trade-name, TRU-PAC.

DIMETAL
Dimetal SA

Km 18 800 de la Antigua Carretera de Madrid a Barcelona, Torrejon de Ardoz, Madrid, Spain

Telephone: 6 75 11 00
Telegrams: WABCO, Madrid
Telex: 22332

Products: Brake equipment built under licences from Westinghouse Air Brake of the USA, Westinghouse Brake & Signal.

DOWSON & DOBSON
Dowson & Dobson Ltd

179 Voortrekker Road, Factoria, Krugersdrop 1740, PO Box 4018, Luipaardsvlei 1743, Transvaal, South Africa

Telephone: 011 684 8100
Telegrams: Downright, Luipaardsvlei
Telex: 8-7956/8-3327 SA

Products: Miner RF-361 draftgear and hand brakes under licence; air brakes under licence to New York Airbrake Co Inc.

DRESSER
Dresser Industries Inc (Transportation Equipment Division)

2 Main Street, Depew, New York 14043, USA

Telephone: (716) 683 6000

Products: Automatic couplers.

ELLCON-NATIONAL
Ellcon-National Inc

30 King Road, Totowa, New Jersey 07512, USA

Telephone: (201) 256 7110
Telex: 130154

Products: Geared hand brakes, automatic double-acting slack adjusters, empty/load devices.

Chairman: Emil P Konda
Chief Sales Director: Ryan M Caulfield

Licensees:
Canada: Beclawat Ltd, 1128 Berlier Street, Laval, Quebec
Mexico: Dinamica SA, Avenida Madero 40, Mexico 1 DF
South Africa: Conbrako Ltd, Tedstone Road, Wadeville, Transvaal

EMILE HENRICOT
Usines Émile Henricot SA

1490 Court-Saint-Etienne, Belgium

Products: Goods wagon bodies, couplers, draftgears, buffers and snubbers.

ENERGOMACHEXPORT
V/O Energomachexport

127486 Moscow, Deguninskaya Str, 1, Korp 4, USSR

Telephone: 1472177
Telegrams: ENERGOEXPORT, Moscow
Telex: 411926 ENEK SU

Products: Matrosov system automatic pneumatic brakes; drawgear including the type SA-3 automatic central buffer couplings.

FABRIKA VAGONA KRALJEVO

Postanski FAH 90, Kraljevo, Yugoslavia

Products: Draftgears; buffers under licence from Miner; brake equipment; automatic couplers.

FERMAT
La Société Fermat

19 quai du Moulin, 92230 De Cage, Gennevilliers, France

Telephone: 793 45 44

Products: Oerlikon braking systems.

FERODO
SA Française du Ferodo

64 avenue de la Grande Armée, 75017 Paris, France

Telephone: 380 56 50
Telegrams: FERODO, Paris
Telex: 20053 IF

Products: Brake shoes.

FIAT
Fiat Ferroviaria Savigliano SpA

Corso Ferrucci, 122, 10141 Turin, Italy

Telephone: 332033/332133 (011)
Telex: 220515 FIATSV I

Works: Piazza Galateri 4, 12038 Savigliano (Cuneo), Italy

Telephone: (0172) 36791
Telex: 210234 FIATSV I

Products: Brake equipment; draftgear; buffers; couplers; snubbers.

FNV
Fabrica Nacional de Vagoes SA

Avenida Maria Coelho Aguiar 215, 05804, São Paulo, Brazil

Telephone: 011 545 1122
Telegrams: FABRIVA, Sao Paulo
Telex: 01121901 FNVA BR

Products: Draftgears and couplers.

FORGES DE FRESNES

80 rue Pasteur, 59970 Fresnes sur Escaut, France

Telephone: (27) 47 42 22

Products: Weldless brake triangles for bogie and wagons; drop forging parts.

FORJA
Forja Argentina SA

Reconquista 661, 6th floor, Buenos Aires, Argentina

Telephone: 37 9833

Works: Calle 1 No 171, Barrio Talleres E, Cordoba, Argentina

Products: Screw and chain couplings.

FREIGHTMASTER
(A Halliburton Company)

8600 Will Rogers Boulevard, Fort Worth, Texas 76140, USA

Telephone: (817) 293 4220
Telex: 75 8284

Products: End-of-car cushioning units; electronic training simulators.

President: O E Seay
Sales Director: P D Howard

FRESINBRA
Fresinbra Industrial SA

Praia do Flamengo 200-9°, PO Box 422, 20 000 Rio de Janeiro, Brazil

Telephone: 021 233 2122
Telegrams: FREINDUS

Works: Rua Lauriano Fernandes Jr 10, Sao Paulo, Brazil

Telephone: 011 260 3122

Products: Automotive brake components under licence of Wabco-Westinghouse GmbH; couplers.

Constitution: The company is a joint venture of Fonseca Almeida of Brazil and Westinghouse Air Brake (Wabco) of the USA. Equipment supplied includes AB and ABD air brakes for locomotives and couplers for mass transit vehicles.

GIRLING
Lucas Girling Ltd

Railway Product Group, Abelson House, 2297 Coventry Road, Sheldon, Birmingham B26 3PR, England

Telephone: 021-742 2323
Telex: 339464

Works: Thermal Road, Bromborough, Cheshire, England
Kings Road, Tyseley, Birmingham, England

Products: Wheel-mounted disc brakes; transmission disc brakes; axle-mounted disc brakes; wheel slide prevention equipment.

Girling wheel-mounted disc brakes consist of air-operated caliper assemblies which operate on discs mounted on both sides of the vehicle wheel. Axle and transmission-mounted disc brakes are identical in operation to wheel-mounted equipment with the exception that the discs are mounted either on the axle or transmission and are capable of operating at speeds in excess of 3000 rpm. Wheelslide prevention equipment marketed by the company consists basically of two individual units: one, the sensing device attached to the axle box, and the other an electro pneumatic valve which, when energised, momentarily releases the brake on the axle from which excessive deceleration has been sensed.

Products Group Manager: P L Quinn
Sales and Service Manager: E A Leason
Export Sales: M D Evans

Agents:
Australia: Westinghouse Brake & Signal Co Ltd, 27-29 George Street, Concord West, NSW 2138
Denmark: Axel Ketner, 23 Frabriksparken, DK 2600, Glostrup
Finland: Oy Elektro Diesel AB, Vanha Kaarelante 28, 01610 Vanta 61
Netherlands: Transmark BV, Handelmaatschappij, PO Box 30, Bussum
Portugal: Conde Barao, Avenida 24 De Julho 62-64, Largo do Conde Barao, Lisbon
Sweden: Helge Meuller AB, Bredgrand 2, 11130 Stockholm

Sales: Since 1958 when Girling first designed railway disc brakes, over 25 000 vehicle sets have been supplied to British Rail.

GODWIN
Godwin Warren Engineering

Emery Road, Bristol BS4 5PW, England

Telephone: 0272 778399
Telex: 449375

Products: Friction stop buffers.

Chairman: H B Derbyshire
Managing Director: D A Ball
Marketing Director: M T Roberts
Export Sales Director: G D Soames

GRAHAM-WHITE
Graham-White Sales Corp

1209 Colorado Street, Salem, Virginia 24153, USA

Telephone: (703) 387 5620

Products: Pneumatic and electro-pneumatic devices for locomotives including air brake system filters and dryers; railroad sanding systems.

GRESHAM & CRAVEN
Gresham and Craven Ltd

Chippenham, Wiltshire SN15 1JD, England

Telephone: 0249 4141 Ext 374
Telegrams: BRAKE, Chippenham
Telex: 449411/12

Products: Complete vacuum brake equipment and systems; exhauster equipment for locomotives together with portable and fixed installation test sets; air control equipment for hopper door, engine speed control.

Chairman: D Pollock
Managing Director: J R C Boulding
Sales Director: S J Pursey

Agents:

Australia & Tasmania: Westinghouse Brake & Signal Co (Australia) Pty Ltd, Railway Brake & Industrial Products Division, PO Box 21, Burwood, New South Wales 2134

Austria; Bulgaria; Czechoslovakia; Hungary; Romania; Yugoslavia: WABCO Westinghouse GmbH, 1205 Vienna 20, Hochstadtplatz 4, Postfach 49, Austria

Bangladesh: Purbachal Commercial Agencies, PO Box 28, 1167 Dacca Trunk Road, Kadamtali, Chittagong

Belgium: Auxicom SPRL, 58 rue des Déportes, 6510 Morlanwelz

Brazil: Norton Megaw & Co Ltd, Avenida Presidente Wilson, 165-30, PO Box 34, Rio de Janeiro

France (North): Auxicom SPRL, 58 rue des Déportes, 6510 Morlanwelz, Belgium

Germany (Federal Republic): WABCO Westinghouse GmbH, 3000 Hannover 91, Postfach 911280

Ghana: Goodwill Associates Ltd, PO Box 10630, Accra North

Iraq: Hakim's Bros Co, Alwiyah Andalus Square, PO Box 2089, Alwiyah, Baghdad

Italy: WABCO Westinghouse, Divisione Equipaggiamenti, Veicoli Ferroviari, Via Pier Carlo Boggio 20, 10138 Turin

Japan: Jardine Matheson (Japan) Ltd, Nissoki Honkan Central, PO Box 282, Tokyo

Nigeria: Nigerian Technical Equipment, Services Ltd, 125A Apapa Road, PO Box 359, Apapa, Lagos

Pakistan: Flecbon Corporation, Lloyds Bank Building, 3rd Floor, Merewether Tower, II Chundrigar Road, Karachi 2

Portugal: Sociedade Victor Limitada, Rua Filipe Folque, 5-1° DTO, Lisbon 1

South Africa; Angola; Botswana; Lesotha; Mauritius; Mozambique; Namibia; Swaziland; Zambia: Westinghouse Bellambi (Pty) Ltd, PO Box 453, Johannesburg 2000

Spain: Dimetal SA, Plomo 10, Madrid 5

Sri Lanka: P Rajagopal, 18A Alfred Place, Colombo 3

Sudan: National Engineering Co Ltd, PO Box 208, Khartoum

Sweden: WABCO Westinghouse, Idunsgatan 26, 21446 Malmo

Switzerland: WABCO Westinghouse AG, 3018 Bern, Freiburgstrasse 384

Thailand: Yip In Tsoi & Jacks Ltd, 523 Mahaprutharam Road, PO Box 2611, Bangkok

Zaire: Auxicom SPRL, 58 rue des Déportes, 6510 Morlanwelz, Belgium

Zimbabwe-Rhodesia: Bellamy & Lambie (Pty) Ltd, PO Box 3101, Hermes Road, Southerton, Salisbury

GREYSHAM
Greysham & Co

7249 Roop Nagar, Delhi 110007, India

Telephone: 22316/225914
Telegrams: GREYSHAMCO
Telex: 031 3872

Products: Brake equipment.

HAINE SAINT PIERRE
Acieries de Haine-Saint-Pierre & Lesquin

7160 Haine-Saint-Pierre, Belgium

Products: Brakes and drawgear equipment.

HURST AIRHEART
Hurst Airheart Products

20235 Bahama Street, Chatsworth, California 91311, USA

Telephone: (213) 882 6600

Products: Disc brakes.

JAY SREE
Jay Sree Supply Agency

14-2 Old China Bazaar Street, Calcutta 1, India

Works: 118 Garfa Main Road, Calcutta 75, India

Telephone: 72 2045/72 4323

Products: Couplers.

JURID
Jurid Werke GmbH

Postfach 1249, 2057 Reinbek/Hamburg, Federal Republic of Germany

Telephone: 72711
Telegrams: JURIDAG, Hamburg
Telex: Jurid hmb 0217834

Products: Composition brake blocks; disc brake linings; friction plates. Main product line is plastic friction linings for block disc brakes made of one piece for friction sizes up to 300 cm² and in two pieces for friction area sizes over 300 cm².

Chairman: Dr Schroiff
Managing Director: Hr Glanz
Sales Director: Dr Ehlers

Licensees: Azbest Ploce, Yugoslavia

KNORR-BREMSE
Knorr-Bremse GmbH

Moosacher Strasse 80, D-8000 Munich 40, Federal Republic of Germany

Telephone: (089) 35051
Telex: 0524228

Products: Air brake systems and equipment; disc brakes; electro-magnetic brake equipment; slip prevention devices; automatic central buffer couplings, type UIC and Willison.

New equipment: New modular brake units developed by Knorr-Bremse provide a simplified method of interconnection, saving on labour costs in the installation of piping, maintenance and overhaul. In the design of the modular units three basic types have been evolved: 1) with bored manifold plate for small basic units: 2) with laminated layer manifold plate for medium-sized units where limited space is available; 3) the panel unit for medium and large units which can be manufactured economically even in small series. In the plate of the bored manifold the air connections are provided for in the form of holes bored in co-ordinated right angles through the plate.
The laminated layer manifold consists of a control plate, in which the air connection channels have been machined, and a mounting plate in which all the necessary tappings and connecting elements have been drilled. The two panels are laminated together and glued, a sealing gasket providing air tightness and mechanical strength. In the panel unit the manifold is a fully sealed off sheet metal cabinet in which copper tubing and adapter nipples are used to form the air connections. The modular units are bolt connected to pre-rivetted nuts on the panel front. The air connections to the piping system are made through the use of sealing rings.
Knorr-Bremse's axle-mounted disc brake consists of a grey cast-iron friction ring and a cast steel hub, connected by radially-arranged elastic resilient sleeves. The friction ring is manufactured as a solid component or in a split version when the two halves are held together by two tight-fit screws. Splitting the disc, Knorr points out, permits easy renewal without the additional expenditure involved in having to press the wheel off the axle.
Among the range of braking equipment manufactured by Knorr-Bremse is the type PK7S pneumatic block brake which has been designed for installation in the generally limited space available on bogies. The unit comprises a CK7S brake cylinder, a hanger, a brake block and brake block insert. Built into the brake block is a single-acting slack adjuster which ensures automatic compensation of the wear on the block. Used in conjuction with a disc brake, the PK7S exerts a cleaning action on the wheel, improving the coefficient of friction between wheel and rail.

KOLMEX
(Foreign Trade Enterprise of the Railway Rolling Stock Industry Union Tasko)

Mokotowska 49, 00-542 Warsaw 1, PO Box 236, Poland

Telephone: 28 22 91/29 92 41
Telegrams: KOLMEX WARSZAWA
Telex: 813270/813714

Products: Brake equipment and components.

LAYCOCK
Laycock Engineering Ltd

Archer Road, Millhouses, Sheffield 8, England

Products: Layrub couplings.

LDA
Engenharia e Comercio LDA

Rua da Alegria, 61 R/C, Lisbon 2, Portugal

Products: Brake equipment and friction draftgear.

LITTON
Litton Connectors

95 High Street, Slough SL1 1DH, England

Telephone: 0753 28267
Telex: 84 7548

Products: Litton LMB connectors.

LLOYD
F H Lloyd & Co Ltd (ABC Coupler Division)

James Bridge Steel Works, Wednesbury, West Midlands WS10 9SD, England

Telephone: 021-526 3121
Telex: 337538

Products: Automatic couplers; semi-rigid bar couplers; draftgear; side buffers; carbon and alloy steel castings for the railway industry.

Chairman: F Clymer
Managing Director: A D Harris
Sales Director: D A Silcox

Agents:
Bangladesh: James Finlay & Co Ltd, Finlay House, PO Box 118, Chittagong
India: James Finlay & Co Ltd, 2 Netaji Subhas Road, PO Box 209, Calcutta 1
Japan: Jardine, Matheson & Co (Japan) Ltd, 3-12 Nisseki Honkan, Nishi Shimbashi 1-Chome, Minato-Ku, PO Box 282, Tokyo 105
South Africa: Conbrako (Pty) Ltd, PO Box 14010, 167 Tedstone Road, Wadeville, Transvaal

MACLEAN FOGG
Maclean Fogg (Railroad Division)

106 Wilmot Road, Deerfield, Illinois 60015, USA

Telephone: (312) 945 4590
Telex: 25-4470

Products: Hand brakes, load securement systems, track bolts and fasteners.

President: Barry L MacLean
Chairman: John A MacLean
Export Sales Manager: E S Steck

MACOSA
Material y Construcciones, SA

Ausias March 26, Barcelona, Spain

Products: Draftgears; buffers; snubbers; hand brakes.

MECANOEXPORTIMPORT

10 Mihail Eminescu Street, Bucharest, Romania

Telephone: 124600
Telegrams: MECANEX
Telex: 269

Products: Brakes built under licence from Knorr-Bremse; drawgear equipment for locomotives and rolling stock.

MINER
Miner Enterprises Inc (International Division)

1200 East State Street, Geneva, Illinois 60134, USA

Telephone: (312) 232 3000
Telegrams: MINER Geneva
Telex: 720442

Products: Draftgears; buffers; snubbers; hand brakes; discharge systems for bulk commodities.

President: G A Withall
Vice President J R Fuenzalida
General Sales Manager: R J Bredin
Sales Engineer: M L McGuigan

Foreign Sales Offices:
Argentina: D G Cormick SRL, Casilla de Correo 5260, Buenos Aires
Bolivia: Mercantil Sudamericana Ltda, Casilla de Correo, 1185 La Paz
Chile: Alfredo Campaña T, Casilla de Correo 2080, Santiago
Colombia: Quinteros Ltda, Apartado Aereo 4308, Bogota
Federal Republic of Germany: Knorr Bremse GmbH, Postfach 40-1060, 800 Munich 40, (For Comecon countries only)
Iran: Metco Consulting Co, Park Avenue, 27th Street 7, Teheran
Mexico: Mexican Railway Appliance Co, Avenida Coyoacan 912, Mexico 12 DF
Thailand: Anglo-Thai Engineering Ltd

MINER Y MENDEZ
Miner y Mendez de Mexico SA

Avenida Coyoacan 912, Mexico 12, DF, Mexico

Products: Miner draftgears; buffers; snubbers; brake equipment built under licence, and Flopak lubricators for freight wagons and passenger stock.

The company represents US and European companies in Mexico, marketing air-conditioning equipment, heating and lighting appliances, roller bearings, bogie levers, stabilisers, rail joints and miscellaneous railway components.

MITSUBISHI
Mitsubishi Heavy Industries Ltd

5-1 Marunouchi 2-chome, Chiyoda-ku, Tokyo, 100 Japan

Telephone: 03 212 3111
Telegrams: HISHIJU, TOKYO
Telex: J22443 HISHIJU

Products: Air brakes.

NEW YORK AIR BRAKE
New York Air Brake Co
(Member of the General Signal group)

Starbuck Avenue, Watertown, New York 13601, USA

Telephone: (315) 782 7000

Products: Pneumatic, electro-pneumatic and hydro-pneumatic air brakes and related hardware.

NIPPON AIR BRAKE
The Nippon Air Brake Co Ltd

Sannomiya Building, Nishikan 1-12, Goko-dori 7-chome, Fukiai-ku, Kobe 651, Japan

Telephone: 078 251 8101
Telegrams: NABCO, Kobe
Telex: 5622-143

Works: Kobe, Seishin, Konan, Yokosuka, Tokyo

Products: Air brakes; NABCO composition brake shoes; automatic slack adjusters.

Chairman: Kenshiro Saito
Managing Director: Tatsuya Shiono

OERLIKON-BURHLE
Machine Tool Works Oerlikon-Burhle Ltd

Birchstrasse 155, CH-8050 Zurich, Switzerland

Telephone: 01 463610
Telegrams: OUTIL, Zurich
Telex: 52147

Products: Air brakes for automatic and manual systems, anti-wheel slip equipment, electro-pneumatic controls.

OHIO BRASS
Ohio Brass Co
(A subsidiary of Harvey Hubbell Inc)

380 North Main Street, Mansfield, Ohio 44902, USA

Telephone: (419) 522 7111
Telegrams: Electric
Telex: 987414

Products: Automatic couplers.

President: William R Cress
Marketing Manager: Alex J Karcic

OLEO
Oleo Pneumatics Ltd

Walcote, Blackdown, Leamington Spa, Warwickshire CV32 6QX, England

Telephone: 0926 21116/8
Telex: 311458 Oleo G

Products: Self-contained hydraulic buffers for railway vehicles of all kinds, including the latest advanced passenger trains, service life of ten years as established by British Railways, robust design utilising steel forgings with integral cylinder ends; specially designed shock absorber units for freight wagon giving protection during marshalling, with strokes of up to 760 mm, widely used in Europe for freight protection during marshalling. All Oleo buffer units provide constant deceleration during impact, achieved by simple orifice and metering pin control of oil flow. Recoil provided by unbreakable air spring. Highly efficient energy absorption and dissipation.

PAULSTRA

61 rue Marius Aufan, 92305 Levallois-Perret, France

Telephone: 757 31 14
Telex: 620 898 Paulval

Products: Buffers; shock absorbers for UIC automatic couplings; primary and secondary suspension springs, bushes and oil seals.

PHOENIX
Phoenix AG

21 Hamburg 90, PO Box 90 11 40, Federal Republic of Germany

Telephone: 040 76 67 1
Telegrams: PHOENIXAG
Telex: 02 17571 pxhh d

Products: Vacuum brake hose.

PURDY
Purdy Co

2400 West 95th Street, Chicago, Illinois 60642, USA

Telephone: (312) 239 4200

Products: Brake equipment.

RESERVOIR, LE
La Société le Réservoir

Rue Jean Henri Fabre, 03103 Montlucon, France

Telephone: 05 39 74

Products: Brake reservoirs and cylinders.

REUNERT & LENZ
Reunert & Lenz Ltd

PO Box 92, Johannesburg 2000, South Africa

Telephone: 011 836 1351
Telegrams: ROCKDRILL
Telex: 8 7426 SA

Products: Brake regulators; disc brakes; parking brake equipment; load brake equipment; weighing valves.

RINGFEDER
Ringfeder GmbH

4150 Krefeld-Uerdingen, Duisburger Strasse 145, Postfach 486, Federal Republic of Germany

Telephone: 4491
Telegrams: RINGFEDER
Telex: 0853846

Products: Side buffers, draw and buffing gear for automatic central coupling, draw gear.

ROCKWELL
Rockwell International
Supply and Mass Transit Division

2135 West Maple Road, Troy, Michigan 48084, USA

Products: Heavy-duty braking systems: wedgem, cam, disc or spring brakes actuated by air or hydraulic pressure.

SAB
SAB Industri AB

Instrumentgatan 15, Landskrona, Fack S-261 02, Landskrona, Sweden

Telephone: 0418 162 80
Telegrams: SAB Landskrona
Telex: 72416 SAB S

Products: Double-acting, rapid working brake regulators for automatic brake slack adjustment; tread brake and disc brake units; hydraulic and spring-applied parking brake equipment with mechanical, quick release device; load brake equipment for automatic adjustment of braking force; weighing valves.

Chairman: Alf Luning
Managing Director: Hans Wallgren
Sales Director (Sweden): Knut Sorensson
International Sales Director: Lennart Nilsson

Subsidiaries:
Belgium: SAB Broms SA, Walenstraat 30, B-3072 Nossegem
Telephone: 02 759 79 12
Brazil: Suecobras Indústria e Comércio SA, Rua Cachambi 713 ZC-16, Rio de Janeiro
Telephone: 201 4552
Telegrams: SUECOBRAS, Riodejaneiro
Telex: 2123702 Suic BR
France: Société SAB, 126 avenue du Général Lelerc, BP No 70, F-92105 Boulogne Billancourt
Telephone: (1) 604 91 01
Telegrams: REGLEURSAB
Telex: SAB 250935F
Italy: SAB Broms SpA, Via Faentina 218, 1-500 10 Caldine
Telephone: 55 58 04 76
Spain: SAB Ibérica SA, Calle Andrés Mellado, 31 Madrid-15
Telephone: 1 449 46 62
Telegrams: SABIBERICA, Madrid
United Kingdom: SAB Brake Regulator Co Ltd, Aycliffe Industrial Estate, Darlington, Co Durham DL5 6HR
Telephone: 02571 2666
Telegrams: BRITSAB, Darlington
Telex: 58416 Britsab Ayclif
USA: SAB Harmon Industries Inc, Grain Valley, Missouri 64029
Telephone: (810) 249 3112
Telex: 426398 HARMON GRNV

SAB BROMS
SAB Broms SA

Walenstraat 30, B-3072 Nossegem, Belgium

Products: SAB brake equipment.

SAMBRE ET MEUSE
Usines et Acieries de Sambre et Meuse

Tour Aurore, 92080 Paris-Défense (Cedex 5), France

Telephone: 788 15 15
Telex: 620 161

Products: Drawgear; disc brakes; shoe insert holders; couplers including UIC type, and Miner RF4-29 drawgear built under licence.

Chairman: Pierre Boissier
Sales Director: Gilbert Labadie

Major sales: Drawgear equipment in 1976/77 was manufactured for French National Railways (SNCF), Iranian State Railways (RAI) and Italian State Railways (FS).

SECHERON
Des Ateliers de Sécheron SA

14 Avenue de Sécheron, 1202 Geneva 21, Switzerland

Telephone: 022 32 67 50
Telegrams: ELECTRICITE
Telex: 22130 SAAG CH

Products: Automatic couplers.

SKF ARGENTINA
Compañia SKF Argentina SA

Casilla de Correo 197, 1068 Buenos Aires, Argentina

Telephone: 33 3061/8
Telegrams: ROULEMENT
Telex: 012 1475

Products: Ball and rolling bearings, axle boxes and mounting tools; SAB brake regulators.

Chairman: Ernesto Bergmann
Managing Director: Raúl Horacio Gaspar
Chief Sales Director: Héctor Montanini

SOCIMI
Societa Costruzioni Industriali Milano SpA

20122 Milan, Via S Calimero 3, Italy

Telephone: 02 54 65 251/5
Telex: 310331

Products: Disc brakes under BSI licence, electro-magnetic track brakes, automatic couplers.

STABEG
Stabeg Apparatengesellschaft GmbH

Reinlgasse 5-9, A-1140 Vienna, Austria

Telephone: 92 23 57
Telex: 01 2466

Products: Brake regulators; disc brakes; load brake equipment; weighing valves; parking brake equipment, air springs.

STONE
Stone Platt Electrical (India) Ltd

16 Taratalla Road, Calcutta 700 053, India

Telephone: 77 3077
Telex: 021 7249

Products: Wabco designed direct and graduated release air brakes; locomotive valves 28 LAV systems (Wabco); SAB designed brake regulators.

STURROCK
Sturrock (South Africa) Ltd

91 Commissioner Street, PO Box 2863, Johannesburg, South Africa

Products: Friction draftgear; brake automatic slack adjusters; friction snubbers; hand brake units.

SUECOBRAS
Suecobras Industria e Comercio SA

Rua Cachambi 713 ZC-16, Rio de Janeiro, Brazil

Products: Brake regulators; disc brakes; parking brake equipment; load brake equipment; weighing valves.

SUMITOMO
Sumitomo Metal Industries Ltd

New Sumitomo Building, 1-3-2 Marunouchi, Chiyoda-ku, Tokyo, Japan

Telephone: 03 282 6111
Telex: J22865 SMI METAL

Products: Couplers; draft gear and steel castings for the railway industry.

TECHNIKA

10 Graf Ignatiev Street, Sofia, Bulgaria

Products: Brake regulators; disc brakes; parking brake equipment; load brake equipment; weighing valves.

THOME
Thomé-Industries

2 rue Alfred-de-Vigny, 75008 Paris, France

Telephone: 227 98 85
Telex: 640 105 F

Products: Steel castings for railways including buffing equipment.

TITO
Oal Metalski Zavod Tito

Postfach 545, Skopje, Yugoslavia

Products: Brake regulators; disc brakes; parking brake equipment; load brake equipment; weighing valves.

TOKYU CAR
Tokyu Car Corporation

1 Kamariya-cho, Kanazawa-ku, Yokohama 236, Japan

Telephone: 045 701 5151
Telex: 3822 392

Products: Disc brakes.

TRIST, DRAPER

Trist, Draper Ltd
(Rail Products Division)

804-818 Bath Road, Bristol BS4 5LH, England

Telephone: 0272 777093
Telex: 44665

Products: TBL 800 composition brake blocks for passenger and freight stock; TBL 600 blocks for rapid transit applications; TBL 700 disc pads.

UNIVERSAL

Universal Railway Devices Co

332 South Michigan Avenue, Chicago, Illinois 60604, USA

Telephone: (312) 427 7775

Products: Automatic slack adjusters.

UZINEXPORTIMPORT

Calea Victoriei 133, Bucharest, Romania

Products: Brake regulators; disc brakes; parking brake equipment; load brake equipment; weighing valves.

VALTIONRAUTATIET

Rautatiehallitus, PO Box 488, SF-00101 Helsinki, Finland

Products: Brake regulators; disc brakes; parking brake equipment; weighing valves.

VOEST-ALPINE

Voest-Alpine AG

A-1040 Vienna, Prinz-Eugen/Strasse 8-10, Austria

Telephone: 65 67 11
Telegrams: VOEST ALPINE, Vienna
Telex: 13 2683

Products: Draftgears; buffers; snubbers; hand brakes; automatic couplers.

WABCO

Westinghouse Air Brake Division, American Standard Inc

Wilmerding, Pennsylvania 15148, USA

Telephone: (412) 273 1000
Telegrams: WESTINGHOUSE, Willmerding
Telex: 866467

Products: Freight wagon air-brake control equipment including control valve (type ABDW), brake cylinder, retaining valve, combined dirt collector and cut-out cock reservoir and angle cocks, Cobra high friction composition brake shoe, bogie mounted WABCOPAC brake assembly; locomotive brake equipment including air brake control equipment with engineer's brake valve, control valve, relay valves, safety control valves and brake cylinders; air compressors; mass transit car brake equipment including control equipment, both pneumatic and electro-pneumatic; bogie mounted brake equipment, and various transit car devices including automatic couplers, air compressor units and air spring levelling valves.

Affiliated Companies:
Austria: WABCO Westinghouse, Hochstadtplatz 4, Postfach 48, 1205 Vienna
Belgium: WABCO Westinghouse, Avenue Van Volxem 164-166, 1190 Brussels
Brazil: Fresinbra Industrial SA, PO Box 8776, 01236 São Paulo, SP
Federal Republic of Germany: WABCO Westinghouse, PO Box 91 12 80, D-3000 Hannover 91
France: WABCO Westinghouse, PO Box 2, 93270 Freinville-Sevran
Italy: WABCO Westinghouse, Via Pier Carlo Boggio, 20 10138 Turin
Netherlands: WABCO Westinghouse, Mient 12-16, PO Box 26, Capelle Ald Ijssel
South Africa: WABCO Westinghouse (Railway Brake) (Pty) Ltd, PO Box 2863, Johannesburg 2000
Sweden: WABCO Westinghouse, NYA Agnes Fridsvagen 190, 213 75 Malmo
Switzerland: WABCO Westinghouse, 384 Freiburgstrasse, Bumplitz, 3018 Berne

International Offices:
Argentina: Westinghouse Air Brake Trade Corp, Tucuari 147-4°, 1071 Buenos Aires
Mexico: Westinghouse Air Brake Trade Corp, EDIFICIO AZTLAN, Desp 506, Avenida Juarez 76, Mexico 1, DF

Wabco Licences:
Argentina: SIAM Di Tella Ltda, Division Electromecanica, Derqui 1868, San Justo, Provincia de Buenos Aires
Australia: Westinghouse Brake & Signal Co (Australia) Ltd Pty, Railway Brake & Industrial Products Co, PO Box 120, Concord West, New South Wales 2138
Japan: Nippon Air Brake Co Ltd, Sannomiya Building, Nishikan 1-12, Goko-Dori, 7-chome, Fukiai-ku, Kobe 651 and Mitsubishi Electric Corp, 2-2-3 Marunouchi, Chiyoda-ku, 2-chome, Tokyo 100

WALTON

Walton Products Inc

868 Sussex Boulevard, Broomall, Pennsylvania 19008, USA

Telephone: (215) 544 8410
Telex: 831765

Products: Automatic couplers, including mechanical coupler assemblies, electro-pneumatic system, designed and manufactured by the wholly-owned subsidiary, Walton Electric Coupler Inc.

Chairman: G Gobrecht
Managing Director: D Murphy
Chief Sales Director: R Dethloff

The company has no licencing agreements abroad but seeks inquiries from foreign suppliers of coupling assemblies and sales agents.

WESTINGHOUSE BRAKE AND SIGNAL

Westinghouse Brake and Signal Co Ltd and Works

Chippenham, Wiltshire, England

Telephone: 0249 4141
Telex: 449411

Products: Air and vacuum brake equipment; electro-pneumatic brake equipment; E Weslake slack adjusters; Westcode brake control system.

WILDE

Wilde, SAICI

Monte 521, Buenos Aires, Argentina

Products: Draftgears; buffers; snubbers; hand brakes built under Miner licence.

BOGIES AND SUSPENSION SYSTEMS, WHEELS AND AXLES

ADIRONDACK
Adirondack Steel Casting Co Inc

Watervliet, New York 12189, USA

Products: One piece, cast steel bogies.

AMMENDORF
VEB Waggonbau
(Member of Maschinen-export)

Ammendorf, German Democratic Republic

Telephone: 22050
Telex: 11 26 89

Products: Bogies (including the type KWS-ZNII) being fitted to latest long-distance coaches for Soviet Railways; primary and secondary suspension systems, wheels, wheelsets.

ANF/INDUSTRIE
Société ANF Frangeco

Tour Aurore, place de Reflets, 75092 Paris-Défense, (Cedex 5), France

Telephone: 788 15 15
Telex: 610 817

Products: Power and trailer bogies for passenger stock, including rubber-tyred bogies for transit vehicles.

Sales: In 1977/78 the company was supplying to SNCF all bogies for 440 kW railcars, XR 6000 trailers, type Z 7.300 self-propelled suburban trainsets, type VB 2N double-deck coaches, and inter-connection coaches for SNCF and RATP. Latest orders include 280 bogies for the Caracas underground.

ARAD
Arad Car and Carriage Building Works

41-43 Avenue Aurel Vlaicu, 2900-Arad, Romania

Telephone: 3 50 20/3 70 20
Telex: 46273/46256

Products: Bogies, types Y22 Cs, H, Minden-Deutz; axles and solid wheels.

ASEA AB

S-721 83 Västerås, Sweden

Telephone: 021 10 00 00
Telegrams: ASEA Vasteras
Telex: 4720 aseava s

Products: Special bogies incorporating rubber suspension.

ASF
American Steel Foundries

1005 Prudential Plaza, Chicago, Illinois 60601, USA

Products: Ride control bogies. The ASF ride control bogie snubbing system is a built-in design that maintains constant control of spring action. The ASF side frames and bolsters exceed AAR strength requirements and can be furnished either as grade B or grade C steel castings. The pressure between the friction shoes and the side frame friction plates provides the necessary loadings to exercise optimum control. This pressure is generated by the ride control springs which force the friction shoes up the inclined ledges and outwardly against the friction plates. These ride control springs are compressed during assembly, and this amount of compression is not changed by varying bolster loads or truck spring movements.

AVON
Avon Industrial Polymers (Bradford-on-Avon) Ltd

Bradford-on-Avon, Wiltshire BA15 1AA, England

Telephone: 02216 3911
Telegrams: INDUSTRIAL Bradford-on-Avon
Telex: 44856

Products: Rubber suspension systems, air springs, draftgear, drawgear, buffers and air brake hose.

Commercial Manager: D A Washbrook
Sales Manager: B O'Meara
Commercial Development Engineer: E J Widdowson

Sales Offices:
Australia: Walker Radial Pty Ltd, PO Box 15, Dulwich Hill, 2203 New South Wales
Belgium: J S Oury, Place Albert Leemans, 1050 Brussels
Canada: Westcode Ltd, 3688 Nashua Drive, Mississauga, Ontario L4V 1M5
Egypt: The Mechanical Tools Co, 62 Gamhouria Street, Cairo
Finland: Oy Interco AB, 00121 Helsinki 12, P1 179 PB
Japan: Matheson & Co Ltd, Matheson House, 142 Minories, London EC3N 1QL
Jardine Maheson S Eng Dept, Central PO Box 282, Tokyo 100-91
Kenya: Avon Rubber Co (East Africa) Ltd, PO Box 18270, Nairobi
Korea: Paterson, Simons & Co Ltd, 67 Upper Thames Street, London EC4V 3AH
Ewkoe Trading Co Ltd, 901 Insurance Building, CPO Box 1162, Seoul
Portugal: Unilock SARL, Aven de Republica 52-8°, Lisbon
South Africa: Conbrako (Pty) Ltd, Tedstone Road, Wadeville , Transvaal
Spain: Promar, SA P1 Duque de Medinaceli, 5 Barcelona (2)
Sudan: National Engineering Co Ltd, PO Box 208, Khartoum

Sweden, Norway and Denmark: Ulinco Industrial Agency AB, Kungsgatan 38-40, S 411 19 Goteborg, Sweden
Zaire: Armand Dutry & Co Ltd, Claridge House, 32 Davies Street, London W1

BETHLEHEM
Bethlehem Steel Corporation

Bethlehem, Pennsylvania 18016, USA

Products: Axles to AAR standards including mounted sets with or without roller bearings.

BRADKEN
Bradken Consco Ltd

22 O'Riordan Street, Alexandria, Sydney, New South Wales, Australia

Telephone: 02 699 3000
Telegrams: BRADKEN
Telex: AA 21512

Products: Passenger and freight bogies.

Chairman: A Trimble
Managing Director: W Kendall
Chief Sales Director: R Hunter
Export Sales Director: D Watson

BRAINE-LE COMTE
Usines de Braine-le Comte SA

Rue des Frères Dulait, B-7490 Braine-le Comte, Belgium

Telephone: 067 553107
Telegrams: USINES BRAINE-LE-COMTE
Telex: 57458

Products: Wagons; 3-axle bogies.

Manager: Jacques Preud'homme

BREL
British Rail Engineering Ltd

Railway Technical Centre, London Road, Derby DE2 8UP, England

Telephone: 0332 49211 Ext 3795
Telex: 37367 BRTEK G

Products: BREL manufactures a wide range of bogies. Recent products include bogies for both power cars and coaches of British Rail's 200 km/h high-speed train, all the bogies for the new 250 km/h advanced passenger train, with bogies for a variety of multiple units, coaches and wagons, both narrow and standard gauge. A new cross-braced freight bogie has also been developed by the company which is suitable for all narrow-gauge applications. The main advantage of this bogie is the reduction in both wheel flange and rail wear. The bogie is being marketed jointly by BREL and the Gloucester Railway Carriage and Wagon Co Ltd.

BRITISH VITA
British Vita Co Ltd

PO Box 7, Porterfield Road, Renfrew, Scotland

Telephone: 041 886 2384
Telegrams: RUBBER, Renfrew
Telex: 777238

Products: Rubber mouldings for locomotive and rolling stock underframe construction including drawbar rubber springs, water hose, door edgings, swing link suspension pads, vacuum brake hose and other standard rubber products.

Chairman: F A Parker
Chief Executive: R McGee
Sales Manager: J Duncan
Export Manager: K Bradshaw

Agent: National Engineering, Khartoum, Sudan

BUCKEYE
Buckeye Steel Castings
(Division of Buckeye International, Inc)

2211 Parsons Avenue, Columbus, Ohio 43207, USA

Telephone: (614) 444 2121

Products: Six, eight, ten and twelve-wheel bogies. Buckeye six-wheel elasto-cushion trucks, with equalised design, introducing controlled lateral movement to cars with modern anti-friction bearings, reducing wear to truck and underframe assemblies. Draft arms attached to eight, ten, and twelve-wheel truck span bolsters have been used with cars of relatively long overhang to enable them to negotiate curves of short radii with standard coupler and draftgear arrangements.

President: J T Hughes
Chief Sales Director: W D Reuter

CANADIAN STEEL WHEEL
Canadian Steel Wheel Division
(Member of Hawker Siddeley Canada Ltd)

1900 Dickson Street, Montreal, Quebec H1N 2H9, Canada

Telephone: (514) 255 3605
Telex: 05 828603

Products: Wrought carbon steel wheels.

CARDWELL WESTINGHOUSE

332 South Michigan Avenue, Chicago, Illinois 60604, USA

Products: AAR standard and alternate standard coil springs.

COMETNA
Companhia Metalúrgica Nacional Sarl

Rua Academica das Ciências 5, Lisbon 2, Portugal

Telephone: 32 00 11
Telegrams: FREDALVES
Telex: 12819 COMENA P

Products: Cast steel bogies; cast steel monobloc wheels.

Chairman: Mario Caldeira
Managing Director: Antonio Taveira Pinto
Sales Manager: Julio Carlos Gaspar

DORBYL LTD
Dorman Long Vanderbijl Corporation Ltd

PO Box 229, Boksburg 1460, South Africa

Telephone: 52 8276
Telegrams: Dorlonsq
Telex: 8 9356

Products: Sambre et Meuse type bogies under licence.

DRESSER
Transportation Equipment Division, Dresser Industries, Inc

2 Main Street, Depew, New York 14043, USA

Telephone: (716) 683 6000
Telex: 91-277

Products: Caboose cushioning and cushion underframe components including Hydra-cushion underframe equipment; couplers; yokes; draftgears and railroad steel castings.

President: M J Franklin
Marketing Director: W F Greenwood

DUNLOP
Dunlop Polymer Engineering Division

PO Box 98, Evington Valley Road, Leicester, Leicestershire LE5 5LY, England

Telephone: 0533 730281
Telegrams: POLYENG, Leicester
Telex: 34397

Products: Rubber-bonded-to-metal springs for primary and secondary suspension systems; anti-vibration mountings; flexible bearings.

Sales Offices:
North America: Metalastik Canada, 11 Curity Avenue, Toronto, Ontario M4B 1X5, Canada (Telephone (416) 755 77871)
Australia: Dunlop Automotive & Industrial Group, Industrial & Aviation Division, 838 Mountain Highway Bayswater, PO Box 41, Victoria 3153 (Telephone 729 6411)
Belgium: Dunlop Ltd, Polymer Engineering Division, 31 rue du Sel, Brussels 1070 (Telephone 02 21 00 10/22 79 21)
Denmark: P Otterstrom's EFTF, Trading & Engineering Company, 64 Tietgensgade, DK 1704 Copenhagen V (Telephone 01 21 67 11)
Federal Republic of Germany: Dunlop Metalastik GmbH, Postfach 2005, 7500 Karlsruhe 1 (Telephone 0721 571034)
Finland: Ab Axel von Knorrings Tekniska Byra, SF-00381 Schliessfach, Helsinki 38 (Telephone 554488)
India: Dunlop India Ltd, Dunlop House, 57B Mirza Ghalib Street, PO Box 9023, Calcutta 700016 (Telephone 24 9641)
Netherlands: Dunlop Nederland BV Polymer Engineering Division, Schiedamsedijk 55a Rotterdam 3001 (Telephone 010 83 28 44)
Norway: Per-Kr Askim A/S, Tollbodgt 28, Oslo 1 (Telephone 41 00 16)
Portugal: Turbomar Comercio E Tecnica De Maquinas Lda, Linda-A-Velha (Telephone PPC 2190006)
Spain: Productos Pirelli SA, Avda Jose Antonio 612-614, Barcelona 7 (Telephone Cornella 277 09 54)
Sweden: Metalastik Sweden Division of Svenska Dunlop AB, Kopmangatan 7, 15136 Sodertalje (Telephone 0755 344 90)
Switzerland: Karl Troxler AC, Pumpwerkstrasse 26, CH 8105 Regensdorf (Telephone 01 840 39 60)
Yugoslavia: Jugohemija Beograd Gen Zdanova 31, PO Box 441 (Telephone 341 141)

ENERGOMACHEXPORT
V/O Energomachexport

127486 Moscow, Deguninskaya Str, 1, Korp 4, USSR

Telephone: 487 31 82
Telegrams: ENERGOEXPORT, Moscow
Telex: 411 926 ENEK SU

Products: Full range of bogies; primary and secondary suspension units; wheels; wheelsets.

FORJA
Forja Argentina SA

Reconquista 661, 6th floor, Buenos Aires, Argentina

Telephone: 37 9833
Telex: 122573AR FORJA

Works: Calle 1 171, Barrio Talleres 3, Cordoba, Argentina

Products: Wheels and wheelsets; tyres and axles.

Chairman: Carlos Alberto Benavides
Managing Director: Jorge Norberto Vilaclara
Sales Director: Jorge Anselmo Garcia

FRANCO/BELGE
Société Franco-Belge de Matériel de Chemins de Fer

49 avenue George V, 75008 Paris, France

Telephone: 723 55 24
Telegrams: LOCOMORAM, Paris
Telex: 290 060F

Products: Standard and special bogies for passenger coaches and freight wagons.

FREIGHTMASTER
(A Halliburton Co)

8600 Will Rogers Boulevard, Fort Worth, Texas 76140, USA

Telephone: (817) 293 4220

Products: Hydraulic cushioning units; electronic training simulators.

President: O E Seay

Agents:
Canada: Hawker Siddeley, Canada Ltd, Montreal
South Africa: Dorbyl Ltd, PO Box 229, Boksburg 1460

GLOUCESTER
Gloucester Railway Carriage & Wagon Co Ltd

Bristol Road, Gloucester, Gloucestershire GL1 5RS, England

Telephone: 0452 25104/5
Telegrams: RAILCAR, Gloucester
Telex: 437173

Products: Freight bogies, suspension systems and Miner doorgear.

Chairman: E A Madenski
Managing Director: J S P Phillips
Sales Director: R A Clark
Engineering Director: R S Morris

GRESHAM & CRAVEN
Gresham & Craven Ltd

Chippenham, Wiltshire SN15 1JD, England

Telephone: 0249 4141 Ext 374
Telegrams: BRAKE, Chippenham
Telex: 449411/12

Products: Air suspension equipment

Sales Director: S J Pursey

GRIFFIN
Griffin Wheel Co

200 West Monroe Street, Chicago, Illinois 60606, USA

Products: Griffin, a subsidiary of Amsted Industries, is believed to be the world's largest producer of steel wheels. These wheels are produced in two plants in Canada and five plants in the USA, with another now under construction. Griffin wheels, fully approved for service in locomotive, freight and passenger applications, are available in all sizes and chemistries in common use and conform to AAR and International Standards.

HANSENS
Hansens Gummi & Packungs-Werke KG

D-3000 Hannover, 89 Hildesheimer Strasse, Postfach 89, Federal Republic of Germany

Telephone: 05 11 87 20 91
Telegrams: gummihansen hannover-Wülfel
Telex: 09 22841 a haha

Products: Rubber shock absorbers for all types of rolling stock and motive power.

Chairman: Jürgen Hansen

HENRICOT
Usines Emile Henricot SA

B-1490 Court-St-Étienne, Belgium

Telephone: 010 6 12205
Telegrams: 59071 COURT-ST-ETIENNE
Telex: HENRICOT

Products: Goods wagon bogies, draftgears, couplers, buffers and snubbers.

Presidents: Paul Henricot
       Jean Henricot
Managing Director: Roger Leclercq
Sales Manager: E De Vos

HIGH DUTY ALLOYS

High Duty Alloys Forgins Ltd
(A Hawker Siddeley Co)

Windsor Road, Redditch, Worcestershire B97 6EF, England

Telephone: 0527 64211
Telegrams: ALLOYS, Redditch
Telex: 337773

Products: Hand and die forged components in aluminium alloys for various railway uses.

HOLLAND

Holland Co, Freight Equipment Division

1470 North Farnsworth Avenue, Aurora, Illinois 60505, USA

Telephone: (312) 851 8200
Telegrams: AURORA, Illinois

Products: Hydraulic and friction snubbers; plastic wear plates; uncoupling levers.

President: J A Liddell
Vice-President: R F Murphy
Sales Director: H B Nordstrom

ICF

Integral Coach Factory

Perambur, Madras 600 038, India

Telephone: 661091
Telegrams: RAILCOACH, Madras
Telex: 7390

Products: Passenger coaches of all types.

General Manager: L R Gosain
Chief Mechanical Engineer: G S Vittal Rao

Sales: ICF has exported 47 MG bogies to Thailand, 68 MG bogies to Burma, 244 MG bogies to Taiwan, six caboose cars of 1 067 mm gauge to Zambia, 50 day coaches and ten sleeper coaches of 1 067 mm gauge to the Philippines, 15 third-class coaches and two first-class coaches to Tanzania, 20 MG third-class coaches to Uganda. ICF is manufacturing 50 MG coaches for Viet-Nam.

ITALSIDER

Italsider SpA

Via Corsica 4, 16128 Genoa, Italy

Telephone: 010 5999
Telex: 270690 Itasid

Products: Freight wagon bogies, wheels and wheelsets.

KNORR-BREMSE

Knorr-Bremse GmbH

Moosacher Strasse 80, D-8000 Munich 40, Federal Republic of Germany

Telephone: (089) 35051
Telex: 0524228

Products: Sambre et Meuse bogies under licence.

KONI

Koni BV

Langeweg 1, PO Box 1014, Oud-Beijerland, Netherlands

Telephone: 01860 2500
Telegrams: KONI, Oudbeijerland
Telex: 21181

Products: Primary and secondary dampers; shock absorber testing equipment. In addition to the normal range of vertical and horizontal dampers Koni has developed the yaw damper which is designed to control small amplitude sinusoidal rotational movements which enables vehicles to operate at higher speeds than ever before. A vehicle's yaw response is dependent on wheel conicity, yaw inertia and plan view stiffnesses, and proper damping reduces wear and the level of input forces to the suspension. The French gas turbine-powered TGV train fitted with Koni yaw dampers attained speeds of up to 340 km/h (212 mph). Other railways using the design include British Rail (HST and APT trains together with classes 86/2 and 87 locomotives), Deutsche Bundesbahn (Types 103, 105, 181.2 and 111 experimental locomotives) and Austrian Federal Railways-ÖBB (Types 1010, 1110 and 2050 locomotives).

Chairman: M de Koning
Managing Director: M de Koning
Chief Sales Director: G E Seckel

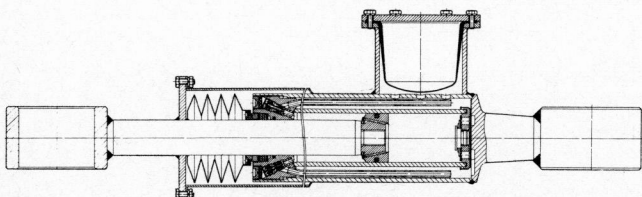

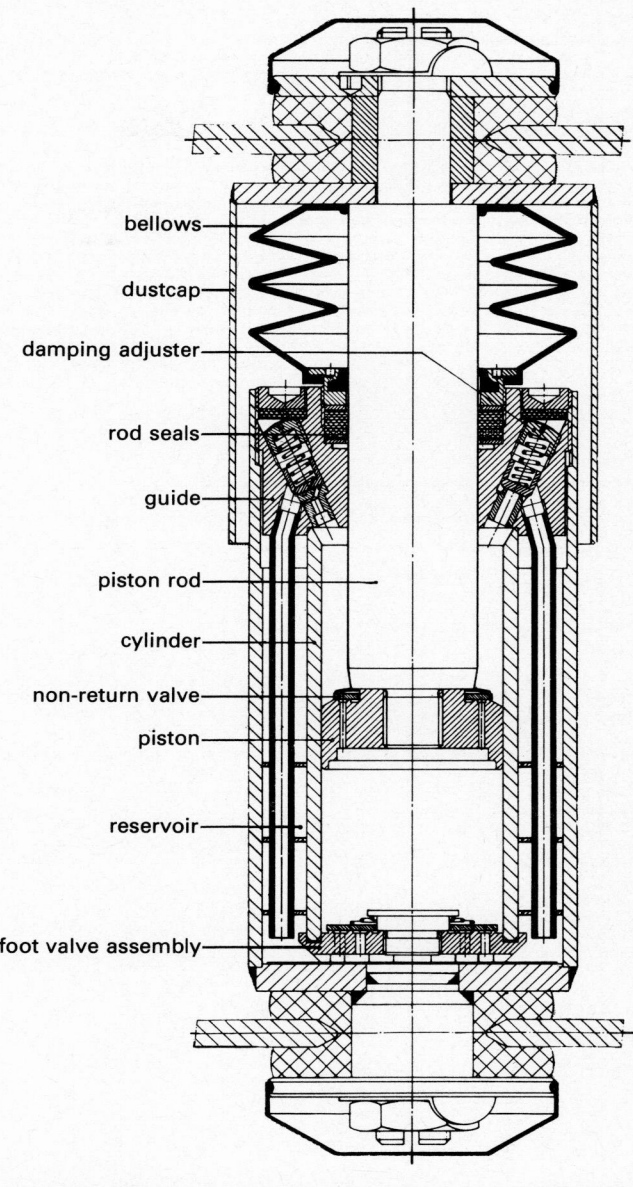

The principle of yaw damper operation is similar to that of the normal Koni railway damper
The same valve controls both extension and compression forces. During extension the one-way valve in the piston is closed, whereas during the compression stroke the one-way base valve is closed. By selecting certain proportions of piston and piston rod diameters, symmetrical damping characteristics can be obtained. By varying the damping valves, seats and springs all practical damping characteristics can be realised. In order to limit the maximum forces that would otherwise occur at high damper velocities additional (cut-off) valves are provided, the number being dependent upon the characteristic required.

Major Agents:
Austria: Siems & Klein KG, Fach 126, 1015 Vienna (Telephone 0222 521 631 Telex: 01 2885)

Federal Republic of Germany: De Koning GmbH, Industriegebiet, 5431 Ebernhahn /Uww (Telephone 02623 5060 Telex 863104)

France: Koni France SARL, 41 rue Bayen, Paris 75017 (Telephone 33 15 740330 Telex 290518)

United Kingdom: B & M Stork, 695A London Road, North Cheam, Surrey (Telephone 13303505, Telex 918778)

LEW

Veb Lokomotivbau-Elektrotechnische Werke Hans Beimler

1422 Henigsdorf, German Democratic Republic

Telephone: 510
Telegrams: ELEKTROLOK, Henigsdorf
Telex: 158 531

Products: Power and trailer bogies for passenger stock and locomotives. Among latest developments by LEW is a Series 277 powered bogie for use with electric multiple units. With slight modifications the same bogie can be used for non-powered applications.

LORD

Lord Kinematics
(Vehicle Products Group)

1635 West 12th Street, PO Box 2051, Erie, Pennsylvania 16512, USA

Telephone: (814) 456 8511
Telex: 914438

Products: Bogie springs and adapter mountings; LC pads for use between adapter and sideframe; V-springs; Lastosphere springs.

MAFERSA
Material Ferroviario SA Mafersa

Ave Raimundo Pereira de Magalhaes 320, CEP 05092, Sao Paulo, SP, Brazil

Telephone: 260 4591
Telegrams: MAFERSA, Sao Paulo

Products: Forged and rolled steel wheels and wheelsets. Mafersa is the only Brazilian company to manufacture wrought carbon steel railroad wheels, using Brazilian methods, developed in the organisation's own laboratories. Its plant at Caçapava in the State of São Paulo is also engaged in the production of wheels for overhead travelling cranes and railroad axles. The plant occupies 20 000 m² in an area of 460 000 m², with an installed capacity for manufacturing 140 000 wheels and 12 000 axles a year, for which the plant processes 70 000 tons of steel. More than 830 000 wheels were delivered up to September 1979 to the Brazilian market and to countries such as Uruguay, Peru, Mexico, Pakistan, Bolivia, Costa Rica and the USA. Mafersa is using steel ingots purchased on the domestic market and is setting up its own steel mill within the plant, with a capacity of 64 000 tons a year. This will enable it to expand its range of products by manufacturing cast steel wheels as well as wrought steel wheels to AAR Standard and customers' own specification and by employing the latest methods of production and quality control.

MAN
Maschinenfabrik Augsburg-Nurnberg AG, Railway Division

Katzwanger Strasse 101, 8500 Nurnberg 1, Federal Republic of Germany

Telephone: 0911 18-1
Telegrams: MANWERK, Nurnberg
Telex: 0622291

Products: Bogies and air suspension equipment.

NIKEX
Nikex Hungarian Trading Co

1016 Budapest, Meszaros utca 48-54, Hungary

Telephone: 851 122/852 111
Telegrams: NIKEXPORT, Budapest
Telex: 224971 nikex H

Products: Tyres and tyred wheelsets

General Manager: J Merath
General Manager (Deputy): H Szucs
Director: I Minya
Export Sales: Z P Szadvary

PAULSTRA
Société Paulstra

61 rue Marius Aufan, PO Box 164, 92305 Levallois-Perret, France

Telephone: 757 31 14
Telex: 620 898 Paulval

Products: Rubber/elastomer suspension systems.

PHOENIX
Phoenix AG

2100 Hamburg 90, Hannoversche Strasse 88, Federal Republic of Germany

Telephone: 040 76 67 1
Telex: 02 17571 pxhh d

Products: Rubber/metal axle springs.

PIONEER
Pioneer Springs (Pioneer Export Division)

23 George Street, Homebush, New South Wales 2140, Australia

Telephone: 73 1361
Telegrams: PIOSPRING, Homebush
Telex: AA22154

Products: Springs for railway suspension units.

Chairman: K H Storey
Managing Director: P C Murray
Sales Manager: F Hemming
Export Manager: W Stephens

Associated Companies:
Ethiopia: Girma W Giorgis, PO Box 577, Addis Ababa
Hong Kong: Fuda & Co, PO Box 1130
Indonesia: E Herman, Jalan Mangga Besat, IV-P 58A Jakarta
Iran: T Sarhang Pour, 3/90 Iranshahr Street, Teheran
Kenya: E Auto Spares Ltd, PO Box 1439, Nairobi
Malaysia: Yew P Ong P/L, 302 Hardware Hse, 400 Jalan
      Tuanku Abdul Rahman, Kuala Lumpur
New Zealand: Fox & Gunn, PO Box 1537, Wellington 1
Pakistan: Overseas Distributing, PO Box 7342, Karachi 3
Philippines: Allenco Steel Corp, PO Box 2266, Manila
Singapore: Yew P Ong & Co, Queen Street, PO Box 3
Sri Lanka: Milhuisen & Hock, 47/19 Galla Road, Colombo 3
Thailand: Kayha Wat Co Ltd, 461 Nakorm Swan Road, Tavakum Bridge, Bangkok

ROCKWELL
Rockwell International
(Supply and Mass Transit Division)

2135 West Maple Road, Troy, Michigan 48084, USA

Products: Complete bogies and components for locomotives, freight wagons, transit and commuter passenger stock.

RUHFUS
A Ruhfus GmbH & Co Kg

Budericher Strasse 7, PO Box 980, D-4040 Neuss, Federal Republic of Germany

Telephone: 02101 26116
Telegrams: RUHFUS, Neuss
Telex: 08 517807

Products: Leaf, buffer and helical springs.

Managing Director: Ulrich Ruhfus

R W MAC
R W Mac Co

525 Craig Avenue, Crete, Illinois 60417, USA

Telephone: (312) 672 6376

Products: Car-safe bogie bolster supports for 50 to 90-tonne wagons.

Principal Officers: R W MacDonnell
              O A Shander

Agent: H S Cooper, Davanac Industries Ltd, 155 Montpellier Boulevard, Montreal, Quebec, Canada

SAB
SAB Industria AB

Instrumentgatan 15, PO Box 515, S-261 24 Landskrona, Sweden

Telephone: 0418 162 80
Telegrams: SAB, Landskrona
Telex: 72416 SAB S

Products: Resilient wheels.

SAMBRE ET MEUSE

Tour Aurore, place des Reflets, 92080 Paris-Défense, (Cedex 5), France

Telephone: 778 63 63
Telex: 620 161F

Products: Design, testing and manufacturing of bogies for all gauges, including the UIC Y25 type and its derivatives; wheels and wheelsets. The Sambre et Meuse design of sprung bolster is made to AAR, British Rail and Crown Agents specifications.

Managing Director: Pierre Boissier
Sales Director: Gilbert Labadie

SCHINDLER
Schindler Carriage & Wagon Co Ltd

CH-4133 Pratteln, Switzerland

Telephone: 061 81 55 11
Telegrams: SCHINDLERWAGON, Pratteln
Telex: 62386

Products: Passenger stock and freight wagon bogies.

SCHLIEREN
Swiss Car and Elevator Manufacturing Corp Ltd

CH-8952 Schlieren, Switzerland

Telephone: 01 730 70 11
Telegrams: SCHLIECO, Schlieren
Telex: 52961 SWS ch

Products: Motor and trailer bogies; trailer bogies for high speeds; 3-axle bogies for heavy traffic wagons.

Delegate of Board of Directors: Fritz Keller

SCULLIN
Scullin Steel Co

6700 Manchester Avenue, St Louis, Missouri 63139, USA

Telephone: (314) 645 0400

Products: Castings for freight wagon bogies.

SOCIMI
Societa Costruzioni Industriali Milano SpA

Via S Calimero 3, 20122 Milan, Italy

Telephone: 02 54 65 251/5
Telex: 31331

Products: Bogies.

Chairman: Dr Eng Alessandro Marzocco
Sales: Argo Pignedoli

STANDARD
Standard Car Truck Co

332 South Michigan Avenue, Chicago, Illinois 60604, USA

Telephone: (312) 427 1466
Telegrams: CARTRUCKS
Telex: 25-6140

Products: Barber stabilised bogies. The Barber load-sensitive variable damping system includes a friction shoe (iron-alloy casting with large bearing areas), hardened steel wear plate bolted and/or welded to the side frame column, and preloaded spring which provides actuating support for the friction casting as well as C-PEP steel and elastomer centre plate extension pads which effectively enlarge the centre-plate bearing surface to ensure stability.

Associated companies: Barber products designed and engineered by Standard are available under licence throughout the world.

STUCKI
A Stucki Company

2600 Neville Road, Pittsburgh, Pennsylvania 15225, USA

Telephone: (412) 771 7300

Products: Hydraulic truck stabilisers, HS-7, designed to control harmonic rocking and vertical bounce in 50, 70 and 100-ton freight cars; single and double roller steel truck side bearings, resilient constant contact side bearings for 50, 70 and 100-ton freight cars.

President: W S Hansen
Executive Vice President: W B Thomas
Vice President, Sales: Thomas E Schofield

SUMITOMO
Sumitomo Metal Industries Ltd

New Sumitomo Building, 1-3-2 Marunouchi, Chiyoda-ku, Tokyo 100, Japan

Telephone: 03 282 6111
Telex: J22865 SMIMETAL

Products: Bogies, suspension systems, wheels and wheelsets

General Manager, Sales: F Saito
Manager, Export Section: H Nakata

UNION SPRING
Union Spring and Manufacturing Co

New Kensington, Pennsylvania 15068, USA

Telephone: (412) 337 4571

Products: Suspension systems including Everlast springs, spring plates, undercushion springs, journal box lids, wear plates and pedestal liners.

UNITY
Unity Railway Supply Co, Inc

805 Golf Lane, Bensenville, Illinois 60106, USA

Telephone: (312) 595 4562

Products: No-sway locomotive stabilisers; wheels; axles.

VALDUNES
Valdunes (Creusot Loire SVI)

12 rue de la Rochefoucauld, 75428 Paris Cedex 09, France

Telephone: 280 65 77
Telex: CLLAR 650 802 F

Products: Wrought solid wheels; straight axles; mounted wheelsets

Managing Director: Pierre Altier
Chief Sales Director: Jean Cambuzat

Constitution: Valdunes represents the combined resources of SVI and Creusot Loire.

VANGUARD
Vanguard Corp

PO Box 525, Highland Park, Illinois 60035, USA

Telephone: (312) 432 2425

Products: Trioid side bearings: model 173 for all types of freight wagon; model 190 for cabooses; model 1002-1 replacement for existing single solid steel roller, model 1002-2 replacement for double solid steel rollers on 90, 100 and 125 tonne wagons.

WOODHEAD
Woodhead Rail Springs

Walbottle Road, Newburn, Newcastle-upon-Tyne NE15 9UD, England

Telephone: 0632 674141/513/142
Telegrams: WOODHEAD RAIL SPRINGS

Products: Laminated springs for locomotives, wagons, mine cars; rolled eye and solid forged main plates; solid and welded type buckles; conventional, featherlite and minimum leaf parabolic tapers; telescopic shock absorbers; coil springs.

Chairman: T S Richardson
General Manager: Gordon Smith

YUSOKI KOGYO
Yusoki Kogyo KK

102 Kamihamacho, Handa, Aichi, 475, Japan

Telephone: 0569 21 3311
Telex: 4563 605

Products: Passenger coach and freight wagon bogies.

BEARING MANUFACTURERS

ABEX

Abex Corporation (Railroad Products Group)

Valley Road, Mahwah, New Jersey 07430, USA

Products: Standard steeple back bearings; alternate standard Hi-Hat bearings; roller bearing adapters, to AAR standards.

President: N George Belury
Export Sales Director: Edwin R Ambrose

AMERICAN KOYO

American Koyo Corp

29570 Clemens Road, PO Box 45028, Westlake, Ohio 44145, USA

Telephone: (216) 835 1000

Products: ABU type journal roller bearings.

BRENCO

Brenco Inc

PO Box 389, Petersburg, Virginia 23803, USA

Telephone: (804) 732 0202
Telex: 828300

Products: Tapered roller bearings, railroad and industrial.

COMET

Comet Industries Inc

4800 Deramus Avenue, Kansas City, Missouri 64120, USA

Telephone: (816) 483 3757

Products: Roller bearings.

FAG

FAG Kugelfischer Georg Schäfer & Co

PO Box 1260, D-8720 Schweinfurt 2, Federal Republic of Germany

Telephone: 0 97 21 911
Telegrams: FAG Schweinfurt
Telex: 06 73 45-21

Products: Journal roller bearings with light metal housings.

FAG

FAG Bearings Corporation

Stamford, Connecticut 06904, USA

Products: Journal roller bearings.

FUJIKOSHI

Fujikoshi Ltd

World Trade Centre Building, 4-1 Hamamatsucho 2 chome, Minato-ku, Tokyo 105, Japan

Telephone: 03 435 5111
Telegrams: NACHI TOKYO
Telex: J 24327

Products: Ball bearings, roller bearings, linear ball bearings.

GARRETT

Garrett Railroad Car and Equipment Inc

PO Box 2208, Newcastle, Pennsylvania 16102, USA

Telephone: (412) 658 9061

Products: Roller bearings.

GRIFFIN

Griffin Wheel Co

200 West Monroe, Chicago, Illinois 60606, USA

Telephone: (312) 346 3300

Products: Journal bearings (brass).

ILLINOIS RAILWAY EQUIPMENT COMPANY

80 East Jackson Boulevard, Chicago, Illinois 60604, USA

Products: Economy journal centring guides; Mobil insert-type journal stops.

KOYO SEIKO

Koyo Seiko Co Ltd

9-2 Sueyoshibashi, 3-chome, Minami-ku, Osaka 542, Japan

Telephone: 06 271 8451
Telegrams: KOYOBRG, Osaka
Telex: J 63040 KAYOOS J

Products: Axle box, grease-sealed journal bearings (ABU type); roller bearings, ball bearings, needle roller bearings, pillow blocks.

Managing Director: Eizo Imura
Chief Sales Director: Yoshitaka Ikeda

KUGELFISCHER

See FAG Kugelfischer Georg Schäfer & Co

MAGNUS PRODUCTS

(NL Industries, Bearings Division)

5461 Southwyck Boulevard, Toledo, Ohio 43614, USA

Telephone: (419) 385 9911

Products: Roller bearings; solid and flat back journal bearings.

MULTI-SERVICE SUPPLY

Multi-Service Supply Inc
(Subsidiary of the Buncher Co)

1080 Third Street, PO Box 149, North Versailles, Pennsylvania 15137, USA

Telephone: (412) 824 3630

Products: Roller bearings.

NIPPON SEIKO

Nippon Seiko KK

Osaka Building, 1-1 Kyobashi 1-chome, Chuo-ku, Tokyo 104, Japan

Telephone: 03 274 5451
Telegrams: NSKBEARING, Tokyo
Telex: 02224280 NSKBRG J

Products: Axle boxes, tapered roller bearings and package units for rolling stock, ball bearings, cylindrical and spherical roller bearings.

Chairman: H Imazato
Managing Director: M Hasegawa
Chief Sales Director: J Banshoya
Export Sales Directors: T Hirano
                       T Nagashima

NL BEARINGS/NL INDUSTRIES INC

PO Box 934, Toledo, Ohio 43694, USA

Telephone: (419) 385 9911

Products: Solid journal bearings; roller bearing adaptors; motor support bearings; internal engine bearings; lubricator pads.

General Manager: R Sabatino
Chief Sales Director: James Doherty

NTN BEARING CORP OF AMERICA

31 East Oakton Street, Des Plaines, Illinois 60018, USA

Telegrams: TOYOBEAR, Des Plaines
Telex: 282 586

Products: Journal roller bearings, including the new NTN Titan, a self-contained, doublerow RCT bearing and housing unit.

NTN TOYO

NTN Toyo Bearing Co Ltd

3-17-chome, Kyomachibori, Nishi-ku, Osaka, Japan

Telephone: 06 443 5001
Telegrams: TOYOBEAR, Osaka

Tokyo Office: 17-22, 7 Nishigoranda, Shinagawa-ku, Tokyo, Japan

Telephone: 03 494 5861
Telegrams: TOYOBEAR, Tokyo

Products: Journal roller bearings.

RAILKO

Railko Ltd
(A BBA Group Co)

Loudwater, High Wycombe, Buckinghamshire HP10 9QU, England

Telephone: 062 85 24901
Telex: 848406

Products: Plastics bearings, including the Railko centre pivot liner developed to replace greased metal on UIC-Y25C type bogies.

SKF

Aktiebolaget SKF

Gothenburg, Sweden

Products: Roller bearings.

TIMKEN

The Timken Co

Canton, Ohio 44706, USA (US sales)
British Timken, Duston, Northampton NN5 6UL, England

Telephone (UK): 0604 52311

Subsidiaries: Manufacturing plants in Australia, Brazil, Canada, United Kingdom, France, South Africa and the USA

Products: Tapered roller bearings.

UNITY

Untiy Railway Supply Co, Inc

805 Golf Lane, Bensenville, Illinois 60106, USA

Telephone: (312) 595 4562

Products: Journal package including: no-sway side-bearing stabiliser; journal box rear seal; journal stop for use in rib or non-rib types; easy-ply lid seal.

VANDERVELL

Vandervell Products Ltd

Norden Road, Maidenhead, Berkshire, England

Telephone: 0628 23456
Telex: 847006

Products: Plain axle bearings for the world's rolling stock based on automative practice. Two series: S is a replacement for brasses; R is a sleeve bearing for use as a superior bearing to roller bearings, and also as an alternative means of improving old rolling stock currently using brasses. Many advantages over rollers particularly in prolonging the life of axles by use of u/s shafts and u/s pre-sized bushes.

Chairman and Managing Director: N E Ratcliffe
Sales Director: D N Pink

PASSENGER COACH EQUIPMENT

ADAMS & WESTLAKE
Adams and Westlake Co

1025 North Michigan Street, Elkhart, Indiana 46514, USA

Telephone: (219) 264 1141
Telegrams: ADLAKE
Telex: 25-8458

Products: Windows and lighting equipment.

AIR INDUSTRIE
(Subsidiary of the Saint-Gobain-Pont A-Mousson Group)

75783 Paris (Cedex 16), France

Products: Air-conditioning equipment.

AIRSCREW HOWDEN
Airscrew Howden Limited

Weybridge, Surrey, England

Telephone: 97 45511
Telex: 929515

Products: Railcar air-conditioning fans, ceiling mounted ventilator fans, main engine cooler groups, braking resistor cooling fans, electronics cooling fans, mixed flow fans, small brushless dc fans.

Chairman: A B R Cheek
Managing Director: M C Beal
Chief Sales Director: J D Stewart

Sales: Major sales for 1978/79 were: British Rail Class 50 engine cooling fans — spares; British Rail Class 37 engine cooling fans; British Rail EMU pressure ventilation fans; British Rail Mk 3 evaporator cooling fans; LTE D78 cabin heater blower spares.

Agents: Airscrew-Plannair Deutschland, Agnes-Bernauer-Strasse 73, 8 Munich 21, Federal Republic of Germany and Airscrew Howden Limited, 1640 Fifth Street, Santa Monica, California 90401, USA

ALNA KOKI
Alna Koki Co Ltd

4-5 Higashi Naniwacho 1-chome, Amagasaki, Hyogo 660, Japan

Telephone: 06 401 7281
Telegrams: ALNA Amagasaki
Telex: 524 2782

Products: Aluminium window sash for electric railcars and passenger coaches.

BBC
Brown Boveri & Cie Aktiengesellschaft

Postfach 351, D-8600 Mannheim, Federal Republic of Germany

Telephone: 0621 381-1
Telegrams: BROWNBOVERI Mannheim
Telex: 462411 120 bbd

Products: Air-conditioning systems.

BECKETT, LAYCOCK & WATKINSON
Beckett, Laycock & Watkinson Ltd

Acton Lane, London NW10, England

Telephone: 01-965 5403
Telegrams: BECLAWAT London
Telex: 261770

Products: Beclawat windows, door systems and route indicators.

Chairman and Managing Director: L W Robins
Chief Sales Director: D E W Albous

Sales: Major sales during 1977/78 were to British Rail, London Transport Executive, Tyne and Wear Metro, Finnish Railways, Oslo Underground and Jamaican Railways.

Agents:
Bangladesh: Elite International Ltd, PO Box 395, Elite House, OR Nizam Road, Chittagong.
Denmark: Gertsen & Olufsen A/S, Radjuspladsen, DK-1550 Copenhagen
Federal Republic of Germany: R Scholz, 19 Muhlenstrasse, 4401 Everswinkel, Bez Munster.
Finland: S Weintraub & Co, Fredrikinkatu 41C, 00120 Helsinki 12.
Netherlands: Auerhaan & Zonen bv, postbus 301, Amsterdam.
Norway: Rodin & Co A/S, PO Box 142, 2020 Skedsmokorset.

Licensing arrangements: Vastberga Mekaniska Verkstad AB, Segersbyvagen 10, S 145 63 Norsborg, Sweden. Beclawat (Australia) Pty Ltd, 83/89 Athol Road, Springvale South, Victoria 3172, Australia. Beclawat Ltd, PO Box 884, 345 Bell Boulevard, Belleville, Ontario K8N 5B5, Canada. Conbrako Ltd, Tedstone Road, Wadeville, Transvaal, South Africa. Sessa Pasquale & Co, CAP 21040 Castronno, Italy.

BELZ
August Belz Apparatebau GmbH

Postfach 12 25, D-7990 Friedrichshafen 1, Federal Republic of Germany

Products: Sapor soap dispensers supplied to nine European railway companies.

CLEMANCON
Société Clemançon

75783 Paris (Cedex 16), France

Products: Heating and regulation equipment; lighting systems.

DEANS AND LIGHTALLOYS
Deans & Lightalloys Ltd

PO Box 8, Grovehill, Beverley, North Humberside HU17 0JL, England

Telephone: 0482 883171

Products: Doors, seats, windows, general fittings and internal assemblies including complete sliding doors and pneumatically-operated equipment.

ELLCON-NATIONAL
Ellcon-National Inc

30 King Road, Totowa, New Jersey 07512, USA

Telephone: (201) 256 7110
Telex: 130154

Products: Transit equipment, window sash, interior trim items, hand rails and windscreen assemblies.

Chairman: Emil P Kondera
Sales Director: Ryan M Caulfield

ERCOLE MARELLI
Ercole Marelli & C SpA

Via Borgonuovo 24, Milan, Italy

Telephone: 2494
Telegrams: VENTILATOR MILANO
Telex: 320575 EMDITE I

Products: Air-conditioning systems and equipment.

FAIVELEY
Faiveley SA

93 rue du Docteur Bauer, BP 151, 93404 Saint-Ouen (Cedex), France

Telephone: 264 12 60
Telex: 290653

Products: Manually operated doors; electro-pneumatic doors and door gear; electric and electro-pneumatic door control fittings, electric and electronic control fittings for heating equipment; miscellaneous electronic equipment. To date about 80 000 door equipments have been supplied to a number of railways, including: Montreal Metro (access door suspension and co-ordinating mechanism); Mexico Metro (automatic access door equipment including door leaves and mechanism); Santiago Metro (automatic access doors); Rio Metro (access door controls); Madrid Metro (access door controls); Barcelona Metro (access door controls) Paris Metro (access door equipment). Mainline railways using Faiveley door equipment include: Danish State Railways, Italian State Railways, French National Railways, Romanian State Railways, South African Railways, Australian Railways, Iranian State Railways.

FINDLAY
Findlay, Irvine Ltd

Bog Road, Penicuik, Midlothian, Edinburgh, Scotland

Telephone: 0968 72111
Telegrams: AUTRONICS Penicuik
Telex: 727502

Products: Heating thermostats and switches.

Chairman: James S Findlay

GRAHAM WHITE
Graham White Sales Corp

1209 Colorado Street, Salem, Virginia 24153, USA

Telephone: (703) 387 5620

Products: Distributors for heated hi-impact windshields in the USA, which are manufactured by the Sierracin/Sylmar Corporation in Sylmar, California.

President: Harvey F Bredlow
Vice President: Stewart Bruce

HITACHI
Hitachi Ltd

Nippon Building, 6-2, 2-chome Otemachi, Chiyoda-ku, Tokyo 100, Japan

Telephone: 03 270 2111
Telegrams: HITACH Tokyo
Telex: J 22395, J 22432, J 24491

Products: Air-conditioning equipment.

Unit cooler	*Roof-mounted Type*
Model	FTUR-550-202
Dimensions	
(length×width×height)	4 030 mm × 1 780 mm × 390 mm
Weight	900 kg
Cooling capacity per coach	40 000 kcal/h
Evaporator inlet air temperature	DB 28°C—WB 22.9°C
Condenser inlet air temperature	DB 33°C
Heating capacity per coach	
Heating device	
Refrigerant	R-22
Power source	
Main power source	ac 3ø 440 V or 220 V 60 Hz
Control power source	ac 2ø 100 V 60 Hz
Compressor	
Type	Hitachi hermetic type
	750FH4
Motor	5.5 kW
Number of units used	2
Condenser	Air-cooled multipath
	fin-and-tube type
Evaporator	Direct expansion multipath
	fin-and-tube type
Blower for condenser	
Type	Centrifugal fan
Air flow rate per coach	170 m³/min × 2
Motor	1.5 kW
Blower for evaporator	
Type	Tandem type double-suction
	multiblade fan
Air flow rate per coach	120 m³/min
Motor	2.2 kW
Throttling	Capillary tubes
Cycle protective device	
Temperature control	Two-stage type thermostat

Unit cooler	*Floor-mounted Type*
Model	FTUF-550-201
Dimensions	
(length×width×height)	1 450 mm × 850 mm × 1 850 mm
Weight	1 515 kg
Cooling capacity per coach	30 300 kcal/h
Evaporator inlet air temperature	DB 26.7°C—WB 19.4°C
Condenser inlet air temperature	DB 36.7°C
Heating capacity per coach	8 600 kcal/h
Heating device	Sheathed wire with fins
Refrigerant	R-12
Power source	
Main power source	ac 3ø 440 V 60 Hz
Control power source	ac 2ø 100 V 60 Hz
Compressor	
Type	Copelametic semi-sealed type
	9RC1-0760-TFD
Motor	5.5 kW
Number of units used	2
Condenser	Air-cooled multipath
	fin-and-tube type
Evaporator	Direct expansion multipath
	fin-and-tube type
Blower for condenser	
Type	Centrifugal fan
Air flow rate per coach	300 m³/min × 3
Motor	1 kW
Blower for evaporator	
Type	Tandem type double-suction
	multiblade fan
Air flow rate per coach	128 m³/min
Motor	1.5 kW
Throttling	Temperature type automatic
	expansion valve
Cycle protective device	High-and low-pressure switches
Temperature control	Thermostat × 3

Unit cooler	*Underfloor-mounted Type*
Model	FTU-750-101
Dimensions	
(length×width×height)	3 290 mm × 1 170 mm × 772 mm
Weight	1 450 kg
Cooling capacity per coach	40 000 kcal/h
Evaporator inlet air temperature	DB 28°C—WB 21.2°C
Condenser inlet air temperature	DB 40°C
Heating capacity per coach	
Heating device	
Refrigerant	R-500
Power source	
Main power source	ac 3ø 220 V 50 Hz
Control power source	ac 2ø 200 V 50 Hz
Compressor	
Type	Hitachi semi-sealed type
	1000FSVW6-A
Motor	7.5 kW
Number of units used	1 × 2
Condenser	Air-cooled multipath
	fin-and-tube type
Evaporator	Direct expansion multipath
	fin-and-tube type
Blower for condenser	
Type	Double suction multiblade fan
Air flow rate per coach	200 m³/min × 2
Motor	3.75 kW
Blower for evaporator	
Type	Single-suction multiblade fan
Air flow rate per coach	120 m³/min
Motor	1.5 kW
Throttling	Temperature type automatic
	expansion valve
Cycle protective device	High-and low-pressure switches
Temperature control	Thermostat

HUTTMANN

Richard Hüttmann GmbH & Co KG

D-3575 Kirchhaim Bez Kassel, Federal Republic of Germany

Telephone: 06422 3013/3014
Telegrams: Hüttman 3575 Kirchhaim
Telex: 04 821 817

Products: 24 V dc special aero fans for roof and wall mounting.

KISMOTOR ÉS-GEPGYAR

Budapest XI, Fehervari ut 44 (RB), Hungary

Telephone: 452-150
Telex: 4 384

Products: Door and window gear.

KLEIN

Etablissements Georges Klein

36 rue Boussingault, 75013 Paris, France

Telephone: 589 58 96
Telegrams: GEOKLEIN Paris
Telex: GEKLEIN 270 507 F

Products: Hera type window balancing and operating devices; all types of aluminium window and automatic access controls.

KUCKUCK

Kuckuck Bau Stromungstechnischer Apparate

Bremen an der Weide 29/40, Federal Republic of Germany

Telephone: 32 43 73
Telex: 02 44479

Products: Exhaust fans.

LUWA

Luwa GmbH

Hanover Landstrasse 200/202, 6 Frankfurt am Main, Federal Republic of Germany

Telephone: 4035-229
Telegrams: LUWA
Telex: 04-11775

Products: Air-conditioning, air-heating systems and air ventilation of all kinds.

Chairman: B W Herr
Managing Director: R Dorn
Chief Sales Director: H Spannagel

Sales: Major sales during 1978/79 included air-conditioning equipment to Federal German Railways and Iranian State Railways.

MEALSTREAM CATERING

Mealstream Catering Systems
(A Henshall Group Company)

38 Woodham Lane, New Haw, Weybridge, Surrey KT15 3NA, England

Telephone: 97 54335
Telegrams: MELSTAM, Weybridge
Telex: 928460

Products: Microwave ovens, coffee-pot warmers supplied to British Rail for use in the catering vehicles of High Speed Trains, the APT Inter-City trains.

Chairman: R MacDonald-Hall
Director: R Humphrey
Sales Manager: W D Francis

Agents: *France:* CLEA, 48 avenue Gabriel Peri, 78630 Montesson; *Germany (Federal):* (a) HO & Technical, Burger Eisenwerke AG, 6348 Herborn, Postfach 1120; (b) Senkingwerk GmbH, 32 Hildesheim 1, Postfach 86; *Norway:* K E Gleditsch, Radhusgt 30, Oslo 1; *Sweden:* Maskinkonstruktioner AB, Klangfargsgatan 8, 421 52 Vastra Frolunda; *Denmark:* Oluf Brønnum & Co A/S, Holbergsgade 8, 1057 Copenhagen K; *Netherlands:* Marja International BV, Koningsweg 4, Utrecht, Postbus 2381; *Switzerland:* CORY AG, CH 8703 Erlenbach, Drusbergstrasse 1; *Australia exc SA:* Luke Equipment, 30 Queens Parade, North Fitzroy, Victoria 3068; *South Australia:* Commonwealth Industrial Gases, PO Box 305, Cowandilla, SA 5033; *Federal Republic of Ireland:* Masser Irish Food Machines Ltd, Precision Works, Kylemore Road, Dublin 10; *Northern Ireland:* GKS Supplies, 100 University Avenue, Belfast BT7 1GY; *Italy:* Solisa snc, Via B Bouzzi 12/2, 40067 Rastignano, Bologna.

MONOGRAM INDUSTRIES

Monogram Industries Inc (Venic Division)

3226 Thatcher Avenue, Venice, California 90291, USA

Telephone: (213) 870 8772
Telegrams: MONOVEN Venice A
Telex: 65-2447

Products: On-board waste handling and sewage treatment systems; self-contained retention toilet equipment. Systems marketed world-wide include: Model 12952-001 Chemical Recirculating System used on French National Railways' (SNCF) RTG/TGV trainsets; Model 28000 On-Board Waste Handling System designed for Amtrak of the United States; Model 20000-001/002 Centralised Waste Treatment System designed for Amtrak and also installed in new bi-level passenger coaches manufactured by Pullman Standard; Models 55000-002 and 15000-001 Self-Contained Flushing Toilets installed as standard production units by Amtrak, Canadian National, Swedish State Railways (SJ), Swiss Federal Railways (SBB), Finnish Railways (VR), Norwegian State Railways (NSB).

European Office: Monogram Industries Inc, BP 20, 6160 Roux, Belgium

Telephone: 571 45 46 66
Telex: 51 310 BRIHAY

Agents: *Federal Republic of Germany:* Gebr Happich GmbH, 56 Wuppertal-Elberfeld, Neuenteich 62-76; *Scandinavia:* Monomatic Sanitation Sys AB, 421 32 V Frolunda, Frotallsgatan 30; *France:* Faiveley SA, 93 rue du Docteur Bauer, 93404 Saint-Ouen; *Belgium, Netherlands, Luxembourg:* I Auerhaan & Zonen, Spuistraat 36-38, NL Amsterdam-C, Netherlands; *Spain:* Ercesa SA, Alcala 29, E-Madrid 14; *South America:* Marcopolo SA, Carrocerias E Onibus, Rua Marcopolo 280, 95100 Caxias do Sul-RS, Brazil; *Thailand, Burma, Malaysia, Singapore, Laos:* Satchawatana, 486-488 Mahajak, (Klong Thom Wattuk), Bangkok, Thailand; *USA, Canada:* Vapor Corporation, 6420 W Howard Street, Chicago, Illinois 60648, USA

PHOENIX
Phoenix AG

21 Hamburg 90, PO Box 90 11 40, Federal Republic of Germany

Telephone: (040) 76 67 1
Telegrams: PHOENIXPARA
Telex: 02 17571 pxhh d

Products: Rubber sealing profiles for windows and doors, rubber floor coverings.

PLC ENGINEERING
PLC Engineering Co Ltd
(Peters Doorgear)

Pasadena Close, Bilton Way, Hayes, Middlesex UB3 3NS, England

Telephone: 01-573 6172
Telex: 934542

Products: Power operated doors and control systems.

RESEARCH PRODUCTS/BLANKENSHIP CORPORATION

2639 Andjon Drive, Dallas, Texas 75220, USA

Telephone: (214) 358 4238
Telegrams: 2639 Andjon Dr Dallas, Tx 75220
Telex: 730161

Products: Electric incinerating toilet for diesel locomotives.

Managing Director: E Bayne Blankenship

SAB
SAB Industri AB

Instrumentgatan 15, Box 515, S-261 24 Landskrona, Sweden

Telephone: 0418 16 280
Telegrams: SAB
Telex: 7241 6 SAB S

Products: Electrolux vacuum-operated train toilets.

SABLE
Sable International

22 rue du Pré St-Gervais, 93507 Pantin, France

Telephone: 843 61 91

Products: Seating for SNCF Corail and TGV stock.

SCHALTBAU

8 München 90, Hohenwaldeckstrasse 1, Federal Republic of Germany

Telephone: (098) 62 32 - 1
Telex: 05 23 156

Products: Heating, control and lighting equipment for passenger coaches.

SOCIMI
Societa Costruzioni Industriali Milano SpA

Via S Calimero 3, 20122 Milan, Italy

Telephone: (02) 54 65 251/5
Telex: 31331

Products: Automatic doors.

Chairman: Dr Eng A Marzocco
Managing Director: Dr Eng P Sacchi
Export Sales: Dr Eng C Landolina

SOFANOR

94 rue Valériani, 59920 Quierrechain, France

Products: All types of passenger coach equipment.

STANRAY CORPORATION
Standard Railway Equipment Division

200 South Michigan Avenue, Chicago, Illinois 60604, USA

Telephone: (312) 922 8480

Products: Cooling and refrigeration units for cold storage.

STONE-PLATT ELECTRICAL
Stone-Platt Electrical Ltd
(Electrical Division of Stone-Platt Industries)

PO Box 5, Gatwick Road, Crawley, West Sussex RH10 2RN, England

Telephone: 0293 27711
Telex: 877481

Products: Air conditioning; pressure ventilation; train lighting equipment; alternators; water equipment.

Chairman: J B McGrath
Marketing Director: P B Happé

Divisional manufacturing and marketing companies: *Argentina:* Stone-Platt Electrical SAI y C, Cassilla Correo Centrale 1197, 1000 Buenos Aires, Tel: 33 5419 and 33 3626, Telex: 121025; *Australia:* Stone-Platt Electrical (McColl) (Pty) Ltd, PO Box 31, Springvale 3171, Victoria, Tel: 546 8622, Telex: 32365; *Canada:* Stone-Platt Electrical (Canada) Ltd, 165 Steelcase Road, Markham, Ontario L3R 1G1, Tel: 416 495 1500, Telex: 219899; *India:* Stone-Platt Electrical (India) Ltd, PO Box 16731, Calcutta 700053, Tel: 45-2891, Telex: 217249; *Pakistan:* Stone-Platt Electrical (Pakistan) Ltd, PO Box 4943 Karachi 2, Tel: Karachi 20 14 86, Telex: 23746; *Republic of South Africa:* Stone-Platt Electrical (Stamcor) (Pty) Ltd, PO Box 50292, Randburg, 2125, Tel: Randburg 48 1150 Telex: 8-0913; *Spain:* Stone Iberica SA, Antonio Maura 8, Madrid 14, Tel: 231 39 07, Telex: 23245; *United Kingdom:* Stone-Platt Crawley Ltd, PO Box 5, Gatwick Road, Crawley, West Sussex RH10 2RN, Tel: 0293 27711, Telex: 87132; *USA:* Safety Electrical Equipment Corporation, PO Box 798, Wallingford, Connecticut 06492, Tel: 203 265 7131 Telex: 963454

STUART TURNER
Stuart Turner Ltd

Henley-on-Thames, Oxon RG9 2AD, England

Products: Pressurised water system for passenger coaches.

TEMPERATURE
Temperature Ltd

192-206 York Road, London SW11 3SS, England

Telephone: 01 223 0511
Telegrams: TEMTUR LONDON
Telex: 28228

Products: Unit air-conditioning for all passenger stock and locomotives; heating and ventilation units for multiple unit stock; refrigeration units.

TOSHIBA
Toshiba Corporation

1-6 Uchisaiwaicho 1 chome, Chiyoda-ku, Tokyo 100, Japan

Telephone: 03 501 5411
Telegrams: TOSHIBA Tokyo
Telex: J 22587, J 24344, J 24576 TOSHIBA

Products: Lighting, air-conditioning, blower and heating equipment and systems.

TOYO DENKI
Toyo Denki Seizo KK

Yaesu Mitsui Building No 7-2, Yaesu 2-chome, Chuo-ku, Tokyo, Japan

Telephone: (271) 6372
Telegrams: YOHDEN Tokyo
Telex: X TOK (0) 222 4666/7

Products: Door operating equipment.

VAPOR
Vapor Corporation (Transportation Systems)

6420 West Howard Street, Chicago, Illinois 60648, USA

Products: Automatic 'Slim-Line' door control units; self-contained Newmatic toilets and a full range of railway accessories.

YOUNG WINDOWS
Young Windows Ltd

Claydon Works, Millbank Road, Wishaw ML2 0JD, Scotland

Telephone: 06983 72557
Telegrams: WINDOWS, Wishaw
Telex: 779150

Products: Constant balance half-drop windows; fixed windows and full drop windows.

Managing Director: S H Magnus BSc

Sales: Major sales during 1977/78 were to Swedish, Italian, Norwegian and Portuguese Railways.

Licensing Agreements: The company has agreements with Macosa (Spain) and Sorefame (Portugal).

YUSOKI KOGYO
Yusoki Kogyo KK

102 Kamihamacho, Handa, Aichi 475, Japan

Telephone: 0569 21 3311
Telex: 4563 605

Products: Door panels.

SIGNALLING, COMPUTER
AND CONTROL EQUIPMENT

ACEC
Ateliers de Constructions Electriques de Charleroi SA

PO Box 4, B-6000 Charleroi, Belgium

Telephone: 071 442111
Telegrams: VENTACEC, Charleroi
Telex: 051.227 ACEC Charleroi

Products: Station interlocking; automatic block signalling; centralised traffic control; level crossing protection (all-relay and static style); automatic stop equipment; automatic train control equipment, etc.

ACI
ACI Systems Corporation

16950 Westview, South Holland, Illinois 60473, USA

Products: Track circuit equipment and accessories; marshalling yard equipment.

AEG-TELEFUNKEN
AEG-Telefunken Nachrichten-und Verkehrstechnik AG

Hohenzollerndamm 150, D-1000 Berlin 33, Federal Republic of Germany

Telephone: (030) 828-1
Telegrams: ELEKTRONBAHNEN Berlin
Telex: 1 85 498

Products: Signalling equipment; automatic block systems; mobile radio equipment; centralised computer controlled traffic control; continuous automatic train control; electronic axle counters; train detection devices; process computer-controlled information display, marshalling yard equipment, control panels and desks, point machines.

Recent Sales: A complete signalling system for Amsterdam Metro, including ATC and computer-controlled train destination indicators.

ALKMAAR
Nederlandse Machinefabriek Alkmaar

PO Box 50, 1800 AB Alkmaar, Netherlands

Telephone: 072 127070
Telegrams: Nemal
Telex: 57213

Products: Level crossing protection; flashing light installations; light signals; electric point machines; electric point detectors; electric point blocks.

Director: A G J Lucassen

ALSTHOM ATLANTIQUE
Société Générale de Constructions Electriques et Mécaniques Alsthom
Signalling Dept
Transport Division, Signalling Department, 25 rue des Bateliers, 93403 Saint-Ouen, France

Telephone: 257 12 34
Telegrams: ALSTHOMSIG
Telex: 290.317

Products: Point machines ac and dc; luminous signals; all types of track circuit, particularly jointless track circuits for railways and metros; manual block system; automatic block system (single or double track) wireless type; electric level crossing equipments with half barriers (2 or 4) and signals; electric signalling systems for all stations (individual or route type); entrance-exit type with or without presetting; remote control for signalling installations; parking electric mechanism.

Managing Director: Francis Hornvilleur
Sales Director: S Dryll

AMF SASIB
Division of CIR SpA

Via Di Corticella 87, 189 40128 Bologna, Italy

Telephone: (051) 36 04 01
Telegrams: SASIB Bologna
Telex: 510020 SASIB

Parent Company: American Machine & Foundry Inc., 777 Westchester Avenue, White Plains, New York 10604, USA

Products: Mechanical and power signalling apparatus; block signalling apparatus; track circuiting equipment and accessories including jointless overlay track circuits, electrical indicating and train describing equipment; level crossing gates, barriers and warning signals, automatic train control equipment and train-stops, centralised traffic control and remote control systems; marshalling yard equipment and retarders (conventionally and computer controlled, process computers for operation control); rapid transit control systems.

General Manager: Ottavio Frisoni
Sales Manager: Antonio Attobelli

ANSALDO
Transport Systems Division

Via Nicola Lorenzi 8, 16152 Genoa Cornigliano, Italy

Telephone: Genoa 010-41051
Telex: 270094 ANSALDO

Products: Power signalling apparatus; block signalling and token type instruments; track circuit equipment and accessories; automatic train control equipment and train stops; centralised traffic control and remote control systems; marshalling yard equipment including retarders.

ASI
Algemene Sein Industrie BV
(GRS—Standard Electric)

Head Office: Croeselaan 28, 3521 CB Utrecht, Netherlands

Works: PO Box 1013, The Hague, Netherlands

Telephone: (030) 94 26 46
Telegrams: GENRASIG Utrecht
Telex: 47455 grasi nl

Parent Companies: General Railway Signal Co, Rochester, New York, USA; Nederlandsche Standard Electric Mij BV, The Hague, Netherlands

Products: Power and block signalling apparatus; electrical indicating and train describing equipment; track circuit apparatus and accessories; level crossing barriers and warning signals; automatic train control and train stops; centralised traffic and remote control systems (including radio control of locomotives); marshalling yard equipment and retarders; computerised traffic control systems, etc.

Manager: P J A van Dÿk

BENDIX
Bendix Corp (Transportation Systems)

3621 South State Road, Ann Arbor, Michigan 48107, USA

Products: Power signalling, block signalling, automatic train control, centralised traffic control.

BROWN BOVERI
Brown, Boveri & Company, Limited

Postfach 85, CH-5401 Baden, Switzerland

Telephone: (056) 75 11 11
Telegrams: BROWNBOVERI Badenschweiz

Products: Linear transmission of information between track and train and vice-versa; radio remote control of shunting locomotives; automatic motoring and braking control of traction vehicles; speed control to set reference value; automatic fixed-point braking; stored running programme, etc.

Agents: *Switzerland:* BBC Brown, Boveri & Co Ltd, Postfach 85, CH - 5401 Baden
Telephone: (056) 75'11'11. Telex: 52921, 53203. Telegrams: Brownboveri
Federal Republic of Germany: Brown, Boveri & Cie AG, Postfach 351, D - 8600 Mannheim
Telephone: (0621) 381-1. Telex: 462411 120 bbd. Telegrams: Brownboveri Mannheim
France: Société de Traction CEM-Oerlikon, 37 rue du rocher, F - 75383 Paris (Cedex 08)
Telephone: (01) 522 8590. Telex: 650 663. Telegrams: Oerlik Paris
Austria: Oesterreichische Brown Boveri-Werke AG, Postfach 184, A - 1101 Vienna
Telephone: (0222) 62810. Telex: 011 760 Oe BBWA. Telegrams: Brownboveri Vienna
Brazil: Industria Elétrica Brown Boveri SA, Caixa Postal 5528, 01000 São Paulo
Telephone: (011) 802 2111. Telex: 33446. Telegrams: Brownboveri São Paulo
Italy: Tecnomasio Italiano Brown Boveri SpA, Casella postale 3392, I - 20100 Milan
Telephone: (02) 5797. Telex: 31153. Telegrams: Tecnomasio Milano
Norway: A/S Norsk Elektrisk & Brown Boveri, Postboks 429 Sentrum, N - Oslo 1
Telephone: (02) 55 70 90. Telex: 11268. Telegrams: NEBB Oslo
Spain: Brown Boveri de Espana SA, Apartado 12120, E - Barcelona 11
Telephone: (03) 321 6900, (03) 321 6950. Telegrams: Brownboveri Barcelona
Other countries: Brown Boveri International, Postfach 85, CH - 5401 Baden, Switzerland
Telephone: (056) 75'11'11. Telex: 54 595 bbci ch, 59 634 bbci ch. Telegrams: Brown-Boveri Baden

Works recently completed: LZB-ORE continuous automatic train control system—installation on the Turgi-Koblenz line of Swiss Federal Railways. Automatic fixed-point braking for multiple-unit trains on Milan Underground Railway.

CANADIAN GENERAL ELECTRIC
Canadian General Electric Co Ltd

Head Office: PO Box 417, Commerce Court North, Toronto, Ontario M5L W2, Canada.

Works: 107 Park Street North, Peterborough, Ontario K9J 7B5, Canada.

International Sales Office: 1900 Eglinton Avenue East, Scarborough, Ontario MIL 2M1, Canada.

Products: Automatic train control and train stops.

CARRIER-KHEOPS
Carrier-Kheops SA

12 villa d'Este, Tour Atlas, 75643 Paris (Cedex 13), France

Telephone: 583 90 61
Telex: 200 800F

Products: Plugs and sockets for signalling equipment.

Managing Director: Mr Delaunay
Export Sales Director: Mr Courtaigne
Sales Director: C Derenemesnil

Sales: Major sales during 1977/78 included equipment to French, Belgian, German, Greek, Spanish and Italian Railways.

CIVEL CONSTRUÇÃO
Civel Construção Industria Viacão e Engenharia SA

Rua de Lapa 180, 11° e 12° Andares, Rio de Janeiro 20000, Brazil

Products: Wireless networks; transmission and distribution lines; installation of fixed and movable stations.

CLAVIER
Clavier Corp

743 Park Avenue, Huntingdon, New York 11743, USA

Telephone: (516) 423 5850

Products: Automatic train controls.

CLYDE ENGINEERING
Clyde Engineering Co Pty Ltd
(A member of Clyde Industries Group)

Factory Street, Granville, PO Box 73, New South Wales, Australia

Telephone: 682-2111
Telegrams: CLYDEENGCO
Telex: 21647

Products: Railway signal equipment (under licence from GRS International, Rochester, New York, USA).

COBRASMA
Cobrasma SA

Rua da Estação 523, Osasco, PO Box 8225, São Paulo, Brazil

Products: All kinds of signalling apparatus.

CONTROL CHIEF
Control Chief Corporation

PO Box 141, Bradford, Pennsylvania 16701, USA

Telephone: (814) 362 6811

Products: Radio remote control equipment; data telemetry link and anti-collision devices for overhead cranes.

President: C L Shields, Jr
Vice President, Sales: A Clark

Sales: Major sales during 1979 were to Burlington Northern, Chicago and North Western, Illinois Central Gulf, MOPAC, Union Pacific, Alco, Bucyrus, Erie, Siemens Allis, Goslin Birmingham and Alcoa.

CSEE
Compagnie de Signaux et d'Entreprises Electriques

Head Office: 17 place Etienne Pernet, 75738 Paris (Cedex 15), France

Works: 15 avenue Archon Despérouses, 63201 Riom, ZI de Périgueux Boulazac, 24000 Périgueux-Boulazac and 2 avenue Descartes, 92350 Le Plessis Robinson

Telephone (Paris): 33 (1) 533 7444
Telephone (Riom): 33 (73) 381766
Telephone (Périgueux): 33 (53) 536426
Telephone (Le Plessis): 33 (1) 630 2224
Telex (Paris): 203926 F
Telex (Riom): 990476 F
Telex (Périgueux): 550755 F
Telex (Le Plessis): 204325 F

Research Centre: Zone d'activités de Caurtabeuf, Avenue des Tropiques, 91400 Orsay (Telephone: 33 (1) 907 7801)

Associated Companies: SAT, 41 rue Cantagrel, 75013 Paris and SAGEM, 6 avenue d'Iéna, 75016 Paris

Products: Mechanical and power signalling; electronic remote control and centralised traffic control systems; automatic block control; jointless track circuits; cab-signalling equipment; level crossing barriers and warning signals; automatic train stops and train control; marshalling yard equipment; hot box detectors; electronic treadles; safety relays.

DIMETAL
Dimetal SA

San Fernando de Henares, Apartado Correos 14.485, Madrid 5, Spain

Telephone: 294 6000

Products: Electric interlockings, electronic CTC; automatic traffic control and marshalling yard control signalling equipment; level crossing protection and radio telephone equipment, as licensees of the WABCO group of Westinghouse Companies.

President: Don Frederico Escario y Nuñez del Pino

Recent Installations: Electric signalling on 134 stations, relay interlocking at 43 stations, automatic block on 372 miles *(600 km)*, electronic single line block on 136 miles *(219 km)*, five CTC installations on 200 miles *(325 km)*.

Work in hand: Vicalvaro marshalling yard control and retarders, and CTC on 304 miles *(490 km)*, as major contract.

DSI
Dansk Signal Industri A/S

Stamholmen 175, Avedore Holme, DK-2650 Hvidovre, Denmark

Products: Relay interlockings; automatic block systems; level crossing signals and lifting gates.

Managing Director: A Wiuff

Work completed: Relay interlockings on approximately 100 stations, including geographical systems for Copenhagen Main, Korsor, Roskilde, and Aalborg stations and 45 stations on Copenhagen suburban lines. 700 level crossings installations for DSB and road authorities in Denmark. Relay interlockings and audio frequency CTC on 55 stations for DSB and private railways.

Work in hand: Geographical systems for interlockings and automatic blocks and an ATC system for Copenhagen suburban lines. CTC for Copenhagen suburban lines based on electronic components in association with L M Ericsson of Stockholm; Computerised system for interlocking plants for DSB.

ELECTRO PNEUMATIC
Electro Pneumatic Corp

2525 Kansas Avenue, Riverside, California 92507, USA

Telephone: (714) 784 0410

Products: Automatic block signalling apparatus.

ERICO
Erico Products Inc

34600 Solon Road, Solon, Ohio 44139, USA

Telephone: (216) 248 0100

Products: Power and signal bonds and track circuit connections.

Vice President: R E Risely
General Manager: E G Acrey
Marketing Manager: E M Cranston

Subsidiary Companies:
Brazil: Ericodo Brasil Com E Ind Ltda, Avienda Santa Marina, Nd 588-LAPA, Sao Paulo SP. Telephone: 263-5929/6097/7734, Telex: (011) 22410 Jose Silveira
Great Britain: Erico Europa (GB) Ltd, 59/61 Milford Road, Reading, Berkshire. Telephone: 734 582154, Telex: 848565, Ernst Groenevelt.
Netherlands: Erico Europa BV, Jules Vernweg 75, 50 15 BG Tilburg. Telephone: 013-320045, Telex: 52182, Tony Kies.

ERICSSON
Telefonaktiebolaget L M Ericsson

S-126 25 Stockholm, Sweden

Telephone: 08 1900 90
Telegrams: Ellemsignal
Telex: 10442 LMEJ S

Associated Companies: Member of the Ericsson group, with representatives in most countries.

Products: Relay and computer based interlockings; automatic train control (ATC); automatic and tokenless block systems; level crossing protection; centralised traffic control with such adjuncts as train describers with or without automatic route setting features based on computer technique; internal train control and marshalling yard equipment.

Chief of Department: H Golteus

Work completed: Centralised traffic control on 4 040 km of Swedish State Railway lines with some 440 field stations and 12 central offices and on a further 3 200 km in Europe and Asia. Interlocking installations with CTC and ATC for about 30 stations for the Taiwan Railway Administration. Earlier installations on Taiwan have been re-signalled and equipped with ATC in connection with installation of electric traction system. A first stage of the computer based interlocking system for the Gothenburg area (Swedish State Railways). Among installations taken into service and continuously extended are electronic CTC for the Stockholm Area (Swedish State Railways), Copenhagen Suburban Network (Danish State Railways). The installations are computer based and include train describer and automatic routeing systems. The Stockholm installation has about 60 stations and 400 km of track and Copenhagen has 50 stations along 125 km in service.

Work in hand: Marshalling Yard Pipri in Pakistan with 48 sorting tracks and reception and departure yards. Electronic CTC and Train Describer System for Karachi-Pipri. Interlocking installation for 16 stations along Ilan Line in Taiwan. Electronic CTC and traingraph installation for 25 stations along 160 km in Bosnia, Yugoslavia. Electronic CTC for Nimba-Buchanan Ore line in Liberia. Electronic CTC for the Pieksimäki-Kuopio line, 89 km (Finnish State Railways). Computer based interlocking system for Malmö area and extension of that in Gothenburg (Swedish State Railways). ATC system for the Swedish State Railways was to be commissioned for the complete Stockholm Area Commuter Service in 1979 and installed on the entire network. ATC equipment for Danish State Railways. Computer based control system for the Oslo Area of the Norwegian State Railways, the Barcelona Area of the Spanish National Railways, the Melbourne underground loop and suburban area in Australia and the Vrpolje-Sarajevo area in Yugoslavia.

FRENOS CALEFACCION Y SENALES
Sociedad Espanola de Frenos, Calefaccion y Senales

Nicolas Fuster 2, Pinto, Madrid, Spain

Telephone: 91 6910054

Products: Manufacturer of railway supplies.

FRESINBRA
Fresinbra Industrial SA

Head Office: Praia do Flamengo 200-9°, 20000 Rio de Janeiro, Brazil

Telephone: (021) 285 2233
Telegrams: FREINDUS

Works: Rua Lauriano Fernandes Jr 10, São Paulo, Brazil

Telephone: (011) 260 3122

Products: Railway signalling and braking systems, under licence of Westinghouse Air Brake Co; electro-pneumatic door operating mechanism; air compressors.

Work in hand: This company, in which the Westinghouse Air Brake Co of Pittsburg, Pennsylvania, USA, is the majority stockholder, is supplying its products to the Brazilian National Railway network, the São Paulo State Railways, the Companhia Vale de Rio Dôce (iron ore railway) and several railway vehicle builders. At present its activities are limited to Brazil.

FUJITSU
Fujitsu Limited

6-1, Marunouchi 2-chome, Chiyodaku, Tokyo, Japan

Telephone: (Tokyo) 216 3211
Telegrams: FUJITSULIMITED TOKYO
Telex: J22 833

Products: Telephone exchange, carrier transmission and radio communication equipment; telegraph and data communication equipment; electronic computers and peripheral equipment (FACOM); remote control and telemetering equipment; electronic components.

President: Taiyu Kobayashi

Works: Kawasaki, Suzaka, Oyama, Nagano, Kobe, Akashi and Aizu of Japan

Related Companies: Fuji Electric Co, Ltd

Work in hand: Fujitsu manufactures all forms of communications and electronics equipment. In the railway field it supplies Japanese National Railways (JNR) with radio communications equipment, telephone exchange equipment, carrier transmission equipment, electronic computer systems and especially group control system of machine tools.

GEC - GENERAL SIGNAL
GEC-General Signal Limited

Elstree Way, Borehamwood, Hertfordshire WD6 1RX, England

Telephone: 01-953 8211
Telegrams: RAILSIGKO Borehamwood
Telex: 22777

Products: Power signalling apparatus (including route-relay interlocking, geographical circuitry and electro-mechanical points machines); electronic control indicating and train describing equipment; track circuit equipment and accessories; level crossing equipment; automatic train control; centralised traffic and remote control systems for mainline and industrial railways; rapid transit and personalised rapid transit systems.

Managing Director: T P Cunningham
Sales Manager: W S Morton

Work recently completed:

Scottish Region—BR	Resignalling on West Coast mainline, including train describer systems at Glasgow and Motherwell.
Southern Region—BR	Train describer system at Feltham, and London Bridge.
London Transport Executive	Computer control system equipment for the Northern and Victoria Lines.
Hoogovens Estel, Holland	Signalling and control system.
Mt Newman Mining Co	Centralised control system for 415 km of track from mine to Port Resig.
Eastern Region—BR	Resignalling of Kings Cross Station and the Great Northern Line as far as Sandy and including the Hertford Loop. Resignalling of East Coast mainline between Kings Cross and Stoke (Grantham), a distance of 122 route miles *(195 km)*.

Work in hand:

Scottish Region—BR	Signalling and control systems for Edinburgh and East Coast mainline modernisation.
Southern Region—BR	Resignalling and modernisation, including a train describer system, for Victoria Station and its approaches.
Eastern Region—BR	Train describer system for Liverpool St-Shenfield.
RFFSA—Brazil	Signalling and control systems for the Central Line and complementary lines includng the steel railroad within the economic triangle Belo Horizonte-Rio de Janeiro-Sao Paulo. Resignalling of the Pombal-Pinheirinho section of the Rio de Janeiro-São Paulo line including centralised control systems.
Netherlands Railways	Hague and Rotterdam train describer systems.

GRS
General Railway Signal Company

PO Box 600, Rochester, New York 14602, USA

Telephone: (716) 436 2020
Telegrams: GENRASIG, Rochester, NY
Telex: 978317 GENRASIG

Products: Centralised traffic control; route-type interlockings; automatic block signalling; level crossing warning signals and gates; overlay track circuits; hot journal detection systems; automatic gravity marshalling yard systems; radio remote control of locomotives; automatic train control; train stops and rapid transit control systems.

President of GRS Company: G E Collins
President of GRS International: A W Gebhardt

Offices of Affiliates and Associates:
GEC-General Signal Ltd, Borehamwood, Hertfordshire, England
Algemeine Sein Industrie BV, Utrecht, Netherlands
General Railway Signal Co de Argentina SAIC, Buenos Aires, Argentina
GRS Trading Corporation, Rochester, New York, USA

GRS (ARGENTINA)
General Railway Signal Co De Argentina SARL

Aréralo 3070, 1426 Buenos Aires, Argentina

Telephone: 772 9542

Products: Automatic signalling; level crossing equipment.

HARMON
SAB Harmon Industries Inc

RRI, Grain Valley, Missouri 64029, USA

Telephone: (816) 249 3112

Products: Power signalling; track circuit equipment; CTC.

HARRIS
Harris Corporation (Controls Division)

PO Box 430, Melbourne, Florida 32901, USA

Telephone: (305) 727 5764

Products: Locotrol remote control train equipment.

HUDSWELL
Hudswell, Clarke & Co Ltd

125 Jack Lane, Hunslet, Leeds LS10 1BT, England

Products: Marshalling yard equipment.

HWD
Henry Williams Limited

Dodsworth Street, Darlington, Co Durham, England

Telephone: 0325 62722
Telegrams: WILLIAMS Darlington
Telex: 58421

Products: Mechanical and electronic signalling equipment; level crossing protection systems; control panels and electro-mechanical rail treadles.

Managing Director: O M Williams
Electrical Division Manager: R A Thompson

IBERICA
Iberica de Construcciones Electricas, Soc

Head Office: Zurbano 14, Madrid, Spain

Works: Poligono Industrial de Coslado, Madrid, Spain

Telephone: 672 15 12
Telex: 45030

Products: Mechanical, power and block signalling apparatus; electrical indicating and train describing equipment; track circuit equipment; level crossing barriers and warning signals; automatic train control and train stops; centralised traffic control and remote control systems.

Chairman: Juan Ignacio Trillo
Managing Director: Ismael Olea
Chief Sales Director: Jaime De Gregorio
Export Sales Director: Mateo Avellan

INTEGRA
Integra Ltd Zürich

Industriestrasse 42, CH-8304 Wallisellen, Switzerland

Telephone: Zürich 830 16 11
Telegrams: INTEGRA Wallisellen
Telex: 56022 tegra CH

Products: Signal lamp unit for railway signals and a special wide/short range asymmetric type for level crossing signals; safety relays for packaged circuits and as individual plug-in units; DOMINO unit construction panels for all railway purposes including marshalling yards and for any application as monitoring and control panels; alphanumerical key-board control electric point motors and trailable type point locks; jointless electronic overlay track circuits for treadle functions; electronic track circuits, electronic axle counting system and last vehicle detection for automatic block purposes; all relay and mixed electronic relay remote control; all electronic 10 000 Baud remote control.

Chairman: Jürg G Oehler

Systems: DOMINO* all-relay signalling schemes incorporating a packaged geographical circuit technique; RAB all-relay block systems with manual control (tokenless block) or automatic control with track circuiting, axle counting or last vehicle detection; automatic level crossing protection with flashing lights and half barriers; centralised traffic control with automatic crossing loops and remote supervision of line; automatic train control, intermittent type multi-aspect ATC with or without speed control, and the AWD (Approach Warning Device) system as a simplified form of ATC; an electronic train describer system for display of train numbers and for automatic train routeing.

ITT BUSINESS SYSTEMS
(Data Systems Division)

Works: Crowhurst Road, Hollingbury, Brighton BN1 8AN, England

Telephone: 0273 507111
Telegrams: Teleprinta Telex Brighton
Telex: 87 169

Products: Remote control systems.

Chief Executive: J Ford
Marketing Director: P Benstead
Export Sales: C Buckton

JEUMONT-SCHNEIDER
Jeumont-Schneider SA
Division Appareillage Traction Signalisation

BP No 51, 93212 La Plaine St-Denis, France

Telephone: 33-1 820 63 73
Telegrams: Apparjeumont Paris
Telex: 620 387 MECALEC Pldni

Products: Automatic block system; CTC and remote control; tokenless block, all-relay interlockings; points and signal machines; safety relays; solid state safety relays; electronic track circuits, mechanical, electromechanical and electronic operation of all safety and signalling equipment; centralised control and monitoring; teletransmissions.

Chairman: P Boulin
Managing Director: C Devin
Export Sales Director: G Tournois
Division Manager: Michel Gillet

Sales: Sales during 1978-79 netted the company Fr 150 million.

KYOSAN
Kyosan Electric Manufacturing Co Ltd

Head Office: 5-4 Ohtemachi 1-chome, Chiyoda-ku, Tokyo, Japan

Telephone: (03) 212 0451
Telegrams: SIGNALKYOSAN, Tokyo
Telex: (222) 3178 KAYOSAN J

Works: Tsurumi Factory, 29, 2-chome, Heiancho, Tsurumi-ku, Yokohama City, Japan
Osaka Factory, 12-8, Nagao kagu-machi, 2-chome, Hirakata-shi, Osaka, Japan

Products: Total traffic control equipment; train describers; programmed train control equipment; relay interlocking equipment; automatic block signalling equipment; tokenless block instruments; power switch machines and relays; cab signal and cab alarm equipment; automatic train control equipment; marshalling yard control equipment; car retarders; automatic route setting; highway crossing signal and crossing gates; automatic control device for diesel engine starter; ac and dc automatic voltage regulators; silicon and selenium rectifiers.

LAMP
Lamp Manufacturing & Railway Supplies Ltd

1 Curtis Road, Industrial Estate, Dorking, Surrey RH4 1XB, England

Telephone: 0306 4411

Products: Railway signalling lamps of all types; electric, oil, propane; acetylene electric switch heaters; electric, natural gas or propane; heavy duty terminal blocks of a wide range.

ML ENGINEERING
ML Engineering (Plymouth) Ltd

Burrington Way, Plymouth, Devon PL5 3NB, England

Telephone: 702541
Telex: 45383

Products: Power signalling apparatus.

Chairman: J G Mobbs
Directors: G D Miller
F G Rayers
E Ware

MODERN INDUSTRIES
Modern Industries Inc

101 Outer Loop, PO Box 14287, Louisville, Kentucky, USA

Telephone: (502) 361 1113

Products: Power signalling, level crossing equipment; CTC; marshalling yard equipment.

NATIONAL ELECTRIC
National Electric Control Co

2931 Higgins Road, Elk Grove Village, Illinois 60007, USA

Products: Level crossing gates and warning signals.

NIPPON SIGNAL
Nippon Signal Co Ltd

Head Office: 3-1, Marunouchi, 3-chome, Chiyoda-ku, Tokyo, Japan

Telephone: (Tokyo) (03) 212 8371
Telegrams: SIGNAL Tokyo
Telex: 222 2178 SIGNAL J

Works: Yono Factory, 13 1-chome, Kamikizaki, Urawa City, Japan
Utsunomiya Factory, 2-11 Hiraide Kougyo Danchi, Utsunomiya City, Japan

Associated Companies: Nisshin Industrial Co Ltd, Nisshin Electrical Installation Co Ltd.

Products: Centralised traffic control (CTC); relay interlocking; automatic block signalling; level crossing signals and automatic gates; overlay track circuits; automatic train control (ATS, ATC); automatic train protection (ATP); remote control equipment (Rc); programmed route control equipment (PRC); automatic announcing system; inductive type wireless remote control equipment; electrical, electro-pneumatic point machine; various kinds of traffic control equipment; various kinds of relays for signalling; integrated traffic control system by computer (ITC).

President: T Hayashi
Chairman: T Akiyama
Chief Sales Director: H Shinohara
Export Sales Manager: K Mapsushind

Sales: The company's products have been supplied to domestic railway markets and to foreign countries.

NORD
Nord Instruments Co Inc

5457 JAE Valley Road, Roanoke, Virginia 24014, USA

Products: Automatic train control equipment, remote control systems.

OMERA
(Subsidiary of TRT)

49 rue Ferdinand-Berthoud, 95101 Argenteuil, France

Telephone: 982 09 42
Telex: 696797 F

Products: Driver's alertness control equipment which ensures the impossibility of accidental or deliberate system disablement; TAR 241 remote control and remote signalling system.

ORLIANS
Orlians & Co, NV

Populierendreef 33-35, 2800 Mechelen, Belgium

Telephone: 015 21 85 85
Telex: 25587 ORLIAN B

Products: Warning signals for crossing gates; signal lanterns for electric railways.

PHILIPS
Philips Telecommunicatie Industrie BV

Anthony Fokkerweg 7, PO Box 32, Hilversum, Netherlands

Telephone: 035 899111
Telegrams: Signal Hilversum
Telex: 43712

Products: Telecommunications (carrier, telephone and telegraph), exchanges, data systems, mobile radio, radio relay, transceivers.

Chairman: E P L van Doveren
Chief Sales Director: J Poot

Other Products in the Philips Group:

Intercommunication and public address systems	N V Philips
Fire alarm and electric clock systems	Gloeilampenfabrieken,
Message repeater system	Eindhoven
High frequency heating	
Interlocking signalling systems	
Automatic block systems	TRT
Centralised traffic control systems	Paris
Wagon and train identification systems	
Telemetering equipment	MBLE, Brussels
Traffic automation systems	Spoorweg Sein Industrie

PINTSCH BAMAG
Pintsch Bamag Antriebs- und Verkehrstechnik GmbH

D-4220 Dinslaken, Postfach 10 04 20, Federal Republic of Germany

Telephone: 0 21 34 602-1
Telegrams: PINTSCHBAMAG-DINSLAKEN
Telex: 8551938

Products: Electrical and electronic power supply, lighting, heating and air-conditioning equipment for rail vehicles; level crossing protection equipment (hand-operated or rail-actuated) with flashlights and luminous signals, with barrier guarding and radar obstacle detection; train approach indicator for gang warning; fibre-optic luminous signal indicators; electric gas-operated infra-red and oil-fuelled circulation, compact-tyre point heating equipment; solid state snow detectors; train pre-heating equipment; test sets for electrical installations on rail vehicles.

Directors: Dr Ing Dieter Böhm
Dr rer pol Gerhard Kummer

PLESSEY
Plessey Controls Ltd

Sopers Lane, Poole, Dorset BH17 7ER, England

Telephone: 02013 5161
Telex: 41272

Products: Train-to-track data systems; positive train identification, wagon identification, monitoring on-train equipment; track-to-train data systems; in-cab displays, automatic control of on-train equipment; on-train data systems; centralised remote control and status monitoring of equipment on multiple unit trains; signal-post telephone systems; automatic revenue collection systems and associated equipments.

Chairman: Dr B F Willetts
Managing Director: E Clark
Chief Sales Manager: A H Taylor

ROBOT
Robot Industries Inc

7041 Orchard Street, Dearborn, Michigan 48126, USA

Telephone: (313) 846 2623

Products: Power signalling apparatus; level crossing gates; barriers and warning signals; centralised traffic control and remote control systems.

SAFETRAN
Safetran Systems Corporation

Head Office: 7721 National Turnpike, Louisville, Kentucky 40214, USA

Telephone: (502) 361 1691

Works: Railroad Accessories Co, Division of Safetran Systems Corporation, 7721 National Turnpike, Louisville, Kentucky 40214; 4650 Main Street, NE, Minneapolis, Minnesota 55421; Marquardt Industrial Products Co, 9271 Arrow Highway, Cucamonga, California 91730.

Products: Power signalling apparatus; track equipment and accessories; level crossing gates and warning equipment; centralised traffic control equipment.

SAXBY

40 rue de l'Orillon, 75011 Paris, France

Telephone: 357 65 30
Telegrams: SAXBY SA PARIS
Telex: 220554F

Products: Route relay interlocking; automatic block systems; centralised traffic control; automatic level crossing barriers; marshalling yard equipment and retarders; passenger information systems.

SCHEIDT
Scheidt & Bachmann GmbH

132 Breite Strasse, D-4070 Rheydt, Rhineland, Federal Republic of Germany

Telephone: Rheydt 4531
Telex: 0852818

Products: Power signalling apparatus; level crossing gates; barriers and warning signals; mechanical signalling equipment and accessories; automatic train control equipment and train-stops; centralised traffic control and remote control systems.

SEL
Standard Elektrik Lorenz AG

Head Office: Hellmuth-Hirth-Strasse 42, 7000 Stuttgart-Zuffenhausen, Federal Republic of Germany

Telephone: (0711) 8211
Telegrams: STANLOR, Stuttgart
Telex: 7 211-0

Works: At 22 locations in Federal Republic of Germany

Associated Companies: SEL has 27 associate companies outside Germany (the name of the majority incorporating the word Standard) and utilises its association with the International Telephone and Telegraph Corporation (ITT) in providing local manufacture in many parts of the world.

Products: Geographic relay interlocking system; computer controlled traffic control systems and continuous train control systems; electronic axle counters; automatic humping control; control panels and desks; relays; signalling equipment; switch machines; train detection devices; centralised traffic control; automatic block equipment, automatic train control; train describers and indicating systems, mobile radio equipment, cables; etc.

SERVO
Servo Corporation of America

111 New South Road, Hicksville, New York 11802, USA

Telephone: (516) 938 9700
Telegrams: SERVOGRAM
Telex: 51022 11872 Servo Corp

Products: Railway signalling grade crossing controls; car identification systems.

Marketing Manager: C A Gallagher
Director of Marketing: W W Weedon Jr

SIEMENS
Siemens Aktiengesellschaft
Railway Signalling Division

3300 Braunschweig, Ackerstrasse 22, Federal Republic of Germany

Telephone: (0531) 706 1
Telegrams: stellwerk braunschweig
Telex: 952 495

Products: Power signalling (all-relay interlocking) and block systems; geographical circuitry Spoorplan interlockings; central operation control by data processing, electrical indicating and train describing equipment; track circuit and axle counter equipment; scanner and indicator equipment for automatic vehicle identification and train control and locating; marshalling yard equipment and retarders; level crossing gates, barriers and warning signals; remote control and supervisory systems; centralised traffic control (CTC); automatic train control (ATC) and train stops; continuous automatic train control (CATC) for high speed transportation and rapid transit; equipment for underground railway signalling systems; data processing equipment for operative scheduling, seat reservation and statistical problems.

President: Peter von Siemens
Chairman: Bernhard Plettner
General Manager of Railway Signalling Division: Horst Girke
Chief Sales Manager: Joachim Rempka

SIGNAUX ET D'ENTERPRISES ELECTRIQUES CIE

2-8 rue Caroline, 75850 Paris (Cedex 17), France

Telephone: 387-39-29
Telex: 650519

Products: Mechanical and power signalling equipment; automatic train control; centralised traffic control; train indicating and describing equipment.

SILEC
Soc Industrielle de Liaisons Electrques (SILEC)

69 rue Ampère, 75017 Paris, France

Telephone: 267.20.60
Telex: 280748 SILECSI

Products: Electro-mechanical treadles, safety relays, punctual data transmission.

Chairman: R. Thibault
Managing Director: P. Loisel
Sales Director: R. Le Bail

TOSHIBA
Toshiba Corporation

Offices: 1-6 Uchisaiwai-cho, 1-chome, Chiyoda-ku, Tokyo, Japan

Works: Fuchu Works, 1, Toshiba-machi, Fuchu-shi, Tokyo

Products: Automatic train control equipment, automatic train stop equipment, electrical indicating and train describing equipment, centralised traffic control and remote control systems, marshalling yard equipment, including retarders, etc.

TOPS ON-LINE
Tops On-Line Services Inc

111 Pine Street, San Francisco, California 94111, USA

Products: Data collection, processing and distribution.

TRANSCONTROL
Transcontrol Corporation
(A wholly owned subsidiary of Siemens)

Head Office: 6 Manhassett Avenue, Port Washington, New York 11050, USA

Telephone: (516) 883 6900

Products: Power signalling apparatus, automatic train control equipment, centralised traffic control equipment, marshalling yard equipment, track circuit equipment and accessories, level crossing gates, barriers and warning signals.

Chairman: Mr Zeiler
Managing Director: John M Pelikan
Chief Sales Director: Gerald Erno
Export sales Director : Edward Riddett

TRANSPORTATION TECHNOLOGY

Head Office: PO Box 7293, Denver, Colorado 80207, USA

Products: Automatic train control equipment.

TRT
Télécommunications Radioélectriques et Téléphoniques

88 rue Brillat-Savarin, Paris 13, France

Telephone: 707 77 79

Products: Electronic railway signalling equipment.

TRW
TRW Inc

One Space Park, Building R4/2128, Redondo Beach, California 90278, USA

Products: Train control system; automatic train control equipment; central traffic control equipment.

WABCO
Union Switch & Signal Division
American Standard Inc

Swissvale, Pittsburgh, Pennsylvania 15218, USA

Telephone: (412) 273 4000
Telex: 86 6648

Products: Electronic car or train detection and identification; automatic train control; mechanical, power, and block signalling and switching; highway crossing barriers and warning signals; automatic train stops; centralised traffic control; track circuit apparatus; classification yard equipment and retarders; computerised dispatching systems for control, indication and information; etc.

Branch Offices: Chicago, Montreal, New York, San Francisco, Philadelphia, St Louis, St Paul, Jacksonville

European Facility: Wabco Westinghouse SpA, Volvera 50, Piossasco (Torino) 10045, Italy

Vice-President and General Manager: G E Stinson
Vice-President, International Organisation: C F Wert

WABCO WESTINGHOUSE
207 boulevard du Souverain, B-1160 Brussels, Belgium

Telephone: 73 60 53

Products: Automatic train control; block signalling; level crossing barriers and warning signals; automatic train stops; remote control systems; centralised traffic control; train describers; track circuit apparatus; cab signalling system of both intermittent and continuous type; two-way railway radio; marshalling yard equipment and retarders, etc.
Complete systems and devices for all aspects of motive power control, locomotive and train braking, and passenger car lighting, heating and air-conditioning.
Grouped under the marketing identity of Wabco Westinghouse, the Westinghouse Air Brake companies have designed and manufactured railway signalling and braking equipment since the turn of the century. Current developments include advanced magnetic track brake systems, air and electric converters for automatic car couplers, motive power control devices for gas turbine powered vehicles, radar for speed assessment and computerised retarder actuation in marshalling yards, etc.
The manufacturing companies in the Wabco Westinghouse group are as follows:—
Austria: Westinghouse Bremsen- und Apparatebau GmbH, Hochstadtplatz 4, 1205 Vienna XX
Belgium: International Brake and Rectifier, SA, rue des Anciens Etangs 6, 1190 Brussels
France: Compagnie des Freins et Signaux Westinghouse, PO Box 2, 93 Freinville-Servan
Federal Republic of Germany: Westinghouse Bremsen- und Apparatebau GmbH, PO Box 21-280, 3 Hannover-Linden
Italy: Compagnia Italiana Westinghouse Freni e Segnali, Via Pier Carlo Boggio 20, 10138 Turin
Netherlands: Westinghouse Remmen en Apparatuur NV, Postbus 29, Capelle a/d ljssel
Spain: Dimetal SA, Apartado de Correos 14.485, Madrid
Sweden: Westinghouse Broms- och Regleteknik AB, Idungsatan 26, 214 46 Malmö
Switzerland: Westinghouse Bremsen- und Signale AG, 384 Freiburgstrasse, 3018 Bern Bumplitz

Vice-President and Group Executive: Richard W Foxen

WESTERN-CULLEN-HAYES INC
Western-Cullen-Division

2700 West 36th Place, Chicago, Illinois 60636, USA

Telephone: (312) 254 9600
Telegrams: WESTRAILSUP
Telex: 25 3206

Products: Track circuiting equipment and accessories; level crossing barriers and warning lights; marshalling yard equipment; including retarders, etc.

Executive Vice President: R L McDaniel
Chief Sales Director: J P Schaeter

WESTERN INDUSTRIES
Western Industries (Pty) Ltd

7th Floor, 192 Hendrik Verwoerd Drive, Randburg, 2194 Transvaal, South Africa

Telephone: 48 9740
Telegrams: SUDAMAT Jhb
Telex: 4 22171 SA

Products: Power signalling apparatus; track circuit equipment and accessories.

Chairman: N C Adams
Managing Director: C Potgieter
Signalling Director: G B Anderson

WESTINGHOUSE
Westinghouse Brake and Signal Co Ltd

Head Office: 3 John Street, London WC1N 2ER, England

Works and Sales Office: Chippenham, Wiltshire, England

Telephone: 0249 4141
Telex: 449411

Products: Signalling equipment; remote control systems; air, electro-pneumatic and vacuum brake equipment, level crossing protection, marshalling yard equipment, traction rectifiers; computer-based train description; automatic train operation; automatic fare collection; railway door equipment; electricity power control supervision systems.

Managing Director: D Pollock
Divisional Manager, Signals: H Duckitt
Divisional Manager, Brakes: J R C Boulding

Work in hand and recently completed: Contracts in Chile, South Africa, Spain, South Korea, Pakistan, Australia, New Zealand, USA, Hong Kong and for British Rail.

Subsidiary Companies:
England: Gresham & Craven Ltd; Douglas (Sales & Service) Ltd; Partridge Wilson Ltd.
Australia: Westinghouse Brake (Australasia) Pty Ltd; Westinghouse Road Brake Co Pty Ltd; Westinghouse—McKenzie—Holland Pty Ltd; Westinghouse Track & Engineering Pty Ltd.
New Zealand: McKenzie & Holland (New Zealand) Ltd.
France: Westingred SA
Canada: Westcode Ltd.
USA: Westcode Inc.

Associated Companies:
England: Bendix Westinghouse Ltd; Partridge Wilson & Co Ltd; Westinghouse Cubic Ltd.
South Africa: Westinghouse Bellambie (Pty) Ltd.

WESTINGHOUSE-BELLAMBIE
Westinghouse Bellambie (Pty) Ltd

Head Office: 112 Clarke Street North, Alrode Alberton, Johannesburg, South Africa

Telephone: 864 2150
Telegrams: Bellambie, Johannesburg
Telex: 8-8223

Works: Clarke Street North, Alrode Alberton, Transvaal, South Africa

Products: General railway signalling equipment and systems design, remote control, centralised traffic control, telecontrol schemes, mechanical hydraulic lifting equipment, rail and road braking equipment.

Associated Companies: Westinghouse Brake & Signal Co Ltd London, Roberts Construction Co Ltd

Chairman: J E Cheetham
Managing Director: H T Jenkins
Divisional Manager (Signals and Telecontrol): M Bayerl
Manager, Export: H F Collom

WILLIAMS
Henry Williams Ltd

Dodsworth Street, Darlington, Co Durham, England

Telephone: 0325 62722
Telegrams: WILLIAMS DARLINGTON
Telex: 58421

Products: Mechanical and electronic signalling equipment, level crossing protection systems; control panels; Silec electro-mechanical rail treadles.

WSF
Westinghouse Saxby Farmer Ltd

Head Office: 17 Convent Road, Calcutta 14, India

Telephone: 24-7161 (7 lines)
Telegrams: Interlock, Calcutta
Telex: SAXBY CA 2348

Products: Mechanical and electrical signalling equipment, point layouts and mechanism, relays, point and signal machines, ball and tablet token instruments, reversers, electric control panels and illuminated diagrams, colour light signals and route indicators, wagon retarders, hump yard equipment, vacuum and air brake equipment for wagons, coaches, locomotives, compressors and slack adjusters.

Works: At above address and at 24 Canal South Road, Calcutta 15, India

Managing Director: D K Chakravorty
Financial Adviser & Chief Accounts Officer: S K Gupta-Roy
Chief Executive (Marketing Electrical): R N Sengupta

Westinghouse Saxby Farmer Ltd is a joint enterprise of Westinghouse Brake & Signal Co Ltd of London, England, and the State Government of West Bengal, India.

ZONE CONTROLS
Zone Controls Ltd

Building 39, Pensnett Trading Estate, Brierley Hill, West Midlands DY6 7PN, England

Telephone: 270171/2/3
Telegrams: CONTROLS BRIHILL
Telex: 338359

Products: Power signalling apparatus including relay interlocking and geographical circuitry; key token instruments; multiple lamp route indicators; circuit controllers; electric safety locks.

Chairman: F V Waller
Managing Director: E Jones
Chief Sales Director: B R Whiting
Export Sales Director: B R Whiting

COMMUNICATIONS SYSTEMS AND EQUIPMENT

AEG/TELEFUNKEN

Head Offices: D-1000 Berlin 33, Hohenzollerndamm 150, Federal Republic of Germany

Telephones: 030 6281/(0611) 6001
Telex: 183581/411076

Products: Telecommunications, radio-telephone and data processing equipment. Due to the increasing overloading of the frequencies available for remote-control AEG-Telefunken has developed a new radio system which enables operation of a large number of remote-control installations upon one high-frequency channel (simplex) independent of the site control and of each other. If the new system is used for control of shunting operations, it can be adapted for at least 10 locomotives on one channel. The system consists of two components arranged in pairs: transmitter unit and mobile installation. Operation is by selective calling and data transmission on one simplex channel in the frequency range of 160-460 MHz at a data transmission speed of 2400 bites/s. Instructions are transmitted by means of short remote-control messages automatically emitted quasi-periodically. An error correction code is used to ensure reliable transmission. 'Due to the reliability of the system,' says the supplier, 'an acknowledgement of the executive signal is not necessary.' A maximum of 16 separate remote-control commands, independent of each other, may be transmitted in one remote-control message.

ANTENNA SPECIALISTS
Antenna Specialists Co

Head Office: 12435 Euclid Avenue, Cleveland, Ohio 44106, USA

Export Sales: 2200 Shames Drive, Westbury, Long Island, New York 11590, USA

Products: Two-way communications systems.

AUTOPHON
Autophon (Sales Management and International Sales Division)

CH-8036 Zurich, Steinstrasse 21, Switzerland

Telephone: 01 35 85 35
Telex: 53838

Products: The Swiss-based Autophon company has supplied radio communication systems over the past 15 years to railways in Switzerland, France, Finland, Norway, The Netherlands and Sweden. The company markets four basic systems: 1) the Suba, designed for branch-line operations; 2) the Palyma—adopted by French National Railways (SNCF)— for mainlines requiring practically total radio coverage: 3) the Safra developed for mainlines with high traffic density; 4) radio communication for shunting operations. In addition, Autophon supplies the Informatic Display System for station platforms.
The Suba system was developed for branch and private lines needing radio communications between operator and trains as well as train-to -train. The system consists of a base station, a remote control unit and mobile transceivers in the trains. By adding portable units to the basic system, Suba can also be adopted for use in shunting operations.
The Palyma system consists of three basic elements: base transceivers, station centres and mobile on-board equipment. All section base stations are connected to a line installed parallel to the track. The system operates on the frequency diversity principle with three successive stations working on different frequencies. It is possible to replace the wire transmission by radio links with the link between base stations controlled from a radio centre.
The Safra system for mainlines is a development of the basic Palyma. With its greater flexibility of communication and control Safra is able to cope with a quick succession of trains, optimally adapted speeds and ensures high traffic safety.

BAYLY ENGINEERING
Bayly Engineering Ltd

167 Hunt Street, Ajax, Ontario L1S 1P6, Canada

Products: 12 channel open wire carrier system (J Carrier); 12 channel open wire carrier system (CCITT); open wire line terminal T3-O; stackable, single channel carrier type 640; wayside radio control type 5260; party line signalling systems; remote radio control type 7772; radio telephone interface, BRT-500; in-band remote control type 5025/5026; radio transfer panel type 7710; DTMF test set TTS-01.

BICC
BICC Ltd (Formerly British Insulated Callender's Cables)

21 Bloomsbury Street, London WC1B 3QN, England

Telephone: 01-637 1300
Telegrams: BICALBEST LONDON
Telex: 23463/28624

Products: Communication cables of all types.

CARRIER KHEOPS

12 Villa d'Este, 23 avenue d'Ivry, Tour Atlas, 75643 Paris (Cedex 13), France

Telephone: 583 90 01
Telex: 200800 F

Products: On-train public address systems.

CGE
Compagnie Generale d'Electricite

54 rue La Boétie, 75382 Paris (Cedex 08), France

Telephone: 266 54 60
Telegrams: ELECTRICITE PARIS 8
Telex: 28.953

Products: Telecommunications equipment and systems.

CIT/ALCATEL
Compagnie Industrielle des Télécommunications

33 rue Emeriau, 75725 Paris (Cedex 15), France

Telephone: 577 10 10
Telex: 250 927

Products: Electronics and telecommunications equipment and systems.

Chairman: Ambroise Roux
Managing Director: Georges Pebereau

DRALLIM TELECOMMUNICATIONS
Drallim Telecommunications Ltd

Brett Drive, Bexhill-on-Sea, East Sussex TN40 2JR, England

Telephone: 0424 221144
Telegrams: DRALLIMIND BEXHILL
Telex: 95285

Products: Pressurisation systems for telephone cables and waneguides; microprocessor alarm monitoring systems for pressurising cables and security.

Group Chairman: A W Millard
Group Managing Director: B Davis
Chief Executive: J R Tickner
Sales Manager: H Cox

Agents abroad
Argentina: Industrias Pirelli SA, Industrial Y Comercial, Maipu 1300, Buenos Aires. Telephone: BA 32-2021/2031; *France:* Technic Servis, 60 avenue de la Timone, 13010 Marseille. Telephone: (91) 79 3810/78 51 55. *Greece:* Reteco Ltd, Skoufa 6, Athens 136. Telephone: 629283 — 616523. Telex: 219250 RETE; *Netherlands:* Van Lessen & Punt BV, Rotterdam PO Box 23010, Scheepstimmermanslaan 25-27. Telephone: 010-365266. Telex: 23564 L & P; *India:* Hirdaynath Bhargava & Co, PO Box 1156, Delhi 110006. Telephone: 526806. Telex: 031-2265; *Iran:* Trident Engineering Group, 13 Karimkham, Zand Avenue, Tehran. Telephone: 62185. Telex: 2464; *Kenya, Tanzania and Uganda:* S A Pegrume & Co Ltd, PO Box 41093, Nairobi, Kenya. Telephone: 25873. Cable address: Pegrume Nairobi; *New Zealand:* S D Mandeno Electronic Equipment Co, 10 Woodhall Road, Auckland 3. Telephone: 600-008. Cables: 'Nucleonic' Auckland; *Pakistan:* Flecbon Corporation, Lloyds Building, 3rd Floor, Mereweather Tower, 1.1 Chundrigar Road, Karachi — 2. Telephone: 230685. Cables: Profession; *South Africa:* R Watt, PO Box 334, Rivonia, Transvaal 2128. *USA:* Jackson Associates, 480 Central Street, Suite 40, Northfield, Illinois 60093. Telephone: (312) 441 7820.

ERICSSON
LME Telefonaktiebolaget LM Ericsson

Telefonplan, S-126 25 Stockholm, Sweden

Telephone: 08-719 00 00
Telegrams: TELEFONBOLAGET STOCKHOLM
Telex: 174 40

Products: Designs, manufactures, markets and installs all kinds of telecommunications systems and products including telephone telex and data communication systems intercom systems, transmission equipment, radio communications equipment, cables and wires.

F & G
Felten & Guilleaume Carlswerke AG

D-5000 Koln-80, Schanzenstrasse 24, Postfach 80 50 01, Federal Republic of Germany

Telephone: 0221 676-1
Telegrams: CARLSWERK KOLN
Telex: 08 873 261 fug d

Products: Wires and cables, switchgear, telecommunications equipment.

FERRANTI
Ferranti Limited

Bridge House, Park Road, Gatley, Cheadle, Cheshire SK8 6HZ, England

Telephone: 061 428 3644
Telex: 666326

Products: Information displays and telecommunications equipment, microwave links.

FUJITSU
Fujitsu Ltd

6-1, Marunouchi 2-chome, Chiyoda-ku, Tokyo, Japan

Telephone: Tokyo 216-3211
Telegrams: FUJITSULIMITED TOKYO
Telex: J22 833

Products: Telephone exchange, carrier transmission and radio communication equipment, telegraph and data communication equipment.

President: Taiyu Kobayashi

GEC TELECOMMUNICATIONS

GEC Telecommunications Ltd
(A management company of the General Electric Co Ltd of England)

PO Box 53, Coventry CV3 1HJ, England

Telephone: 0203 452152
Telegrams: SPRINGJACK COVENTRY
Telex: 31361 GEC TEL

Products: A comprehensive range of frequency division and time division multiplex equipment together with associated co-axial cable, optical-fibre cable and microwave-radio systems, all tailored to railway communication systems requirements; private telephone exchanges; telephone instruments.

Managing Director: W D Morton
Assistant Managing Director: J M Price

Work in hand: Contracts in hand for British Rail include: the supply of 12-circuit carrier-on-cable equipment and 30-channel pcm equipment in preparation for the introduction of thyristor locomotives in the Midland region; an extension to the Reading-Newbury 30-channel pcm system, and a 30-channel pcm system between Plymouth and St Blazey in the Western Region; pcm and fdm equipment for the Victoria re-signalling scheme, and additional carrier-on-cable equipment and the re-arrangement of existing equipment to provide automatic dialling facilities for the Southampton area in the Southern Region; 30-channel pcm equipment with automatic standby protection for Edinburgh and the East of Scotland re-signalling scheme and various 12-circuit carrier-on-cable systems around Glasgow and Motherwell in the Scottish Region.

GRS

General Railway Signal Company

PO Box 600, Rochester, New York 14602, USA

Telephone: (716) 436 2020
Telegrams: GENRASIG ROCHESTER NY
Telex: 978317 Genrasig

Products: Radio remote control systems.

President: G E Collins

GTE LENKURT

GTE Lenkurt Inc

Dept C134, 1105 County Road, San Carlos, California 94070, USA

Telephone: (415) 595 3000
Telegrams: 9103764396
Telex: 348425

Products: Type 79F1 600-channel 2-GHz microwave radio system with choice of 0.25, 5 or 10 W output power, programmable digital AFC and built-in test and meter facilities; type 70F2 72-channel light-route 2-GHz microwave radio system with noise performance of 25 dBrncO or better and receiver noise figure of only 6.5 dB; the new 82B fibre optic transmission system, which provides up to six full duplex circuits over a single fibre optic pair—its non-conductive fibres provide noise-free circuits not affected by lightning, power surges and crosstalk from other communications channels; type 36A2 614-channel radio multiplex system with channel translation and signalling equipment available; type 46A3 radio multiplex system up to 2 700 channels, with standard configurations including directly formed supergroup (DFSG) and direct-to-line (DTL) channel equipment; complete line of data transmission equipment.

President: Herbert K Krengel
Vice President: Kenneth S Durey
General Sales Manager: John A Stockford

HARRIS

Harris Corporation (RF Communications Division)

1680 University Avenue, Rochester, New York 14610, USA

Telephone: (716) 244 5830

Products: Two-way radio systems.

KRAUSS-MAFFEI

Krauss-Maffei Aktiengesellschaft

8000 München 50, Krauss-Maffei-Strasse 2, Federal Republic of Germany

Telephone: 089 8899551
Telegrams: KRAUSSMAFFEI, Munchenallach
Telex: 05-23 163

Products: Two-way radio specially developed for hump locomotives at Deutsche Bundesbahn's Mannheim yard.

KRUPP

Krupp Industrie- und Stahlbau

4100 Duisburg-Rheinhausen, Federal Republic of Germany

Products: Radio communications. Krupp offers a transmitter/receiver capable of 16 function commands for radio remote control of shunting locomotives. The transmitter/receiver weighs 2.5 kg. Commands are given in the form of a remote control telegram which is transmitted quasi-periodically. Faultless transmission is ensured by use of an error detecting code. The electric power unit which serves as an adapter between the receiver and the running and brake control system in the form of a printed circuit card which is protected against shock and vibration by metal-rubber isolators and wired through flat plug connectors. A pneumatic control unit is used as the link to the traction and braking equipment.

LARRY McGEE

Larry McGee Co

4937 Fullerton Avenue, Chicago, Illinois 60639, USA

Telephone: (312) 237 7000

Products: Loudspeaker and telephone communicating systems for yards, shops, freight stations, dispatcher offices, way stations, terminals; radio control systems.

LMT

Le Matériel Téléphonique

46/47 quai Alphonse Le Gallo, 92103 Boulogne-Billancourt (Hauts-de-Seine), France

Telephone: 604 81 00
Telegrams: MICROPHON PARIS
Telex: 20.972

Products: Electro-mechanical and electronic telephone circuit switching equipment.

MOTOROLA

Motorola Communications and Electronics Inc

1303, East Algonquin Road, Schaumburg, Illinois 60172, USA

Telephone: (312) 576 7851

Products: Railway communications equipment including the Micor two-way radio now used by more than 95 US railroads.

Sales Manager: Jack A L M Crantz

NELSON TANSLEY

Nelson Tansley Limited

10 Shepherds Bush Road, London W6 7PJ, England

Telephone: 01-749 1393
Telegrams: Thectron London W6

Products: Communications and control equipment for railway and rapid transit networks; remote-controlled inter-station public address; standard time system (centralised clock); in-train passenger address system; inter-train radio; end-to-end train crew intercommunication; etc. The trade name "ENTEL" covers certain products.

Chief Design Engineer, Rail Division: M Millett
Sales Director, Rail Division: G N Bowling

Work completed: Work in hand and recently completed includes installation of inter-station public address system for British Rail; ENTEL 390 end-to-end driver/guard telephone inter-communication, and ENTEL 378 in-train public address system to all passenger cars (6 loudspeakers per car), radio-telephone communications between driving cabs of two closely-following trains of up to 16 multi-unit cars per train for London Transport.
A development and production contract provides driver/guard and passenger address equipment for the Piccadilly Line stock for London Transport.

NEUMANN

Neumann Elektronik AG

Mulheim-Ruhr, Federal Republic of Germany

British Office: Lea Industrial Estate, 151 Lower Luton Road, Harpenden, Hertfordshire AL5 5EQ, England

Telephone: 67011
Telex: 826638

Products: Radio communications systems, Intercom equipment for direct speech links between control centres and men working in marshalling yards and similar locations. Sealed reed switches are used to ensure high reliability and resistance to corrosion.

Managing Director: A D Cooper
Chief Sales Manager: R J Howard
Export Sales Director: A D Cooper

PHILIPS

N V Philips

Anthony Fokkerweg 7, PO Box 32, Hilversum, Netherlands

Telephone: 035 899111
Telegrams: Signat Hilversum
Telex: 43712

Products: Telecommunications and radio communication systems.

Chairman: C P L van Doveren
Chief Sales Director: J Poot

PIRELLI GENERAL

Pirelli General Cable Works Ltd

PO Box 4, Southampton, Hampshire, England

Telephone: 0703 20381
Telegrams: PIGEKAYBEL
Telex: 47522

Products: Power and telecommunications cables. Pirelli has introduced low-smoke, low-toxicity, non-flame propagating cable designs for signalling and communications purposes. The new cables were named Low-smoke and were specifically designed for railway subway systems. Low-smoke cables were developed in close collaboration with London Transport with full testing carried out on the London underground. During tests, the behaviour of the cables was monitored under artificially-induced fire conditions in a disused section of line.

PLESSEY
The Plessey Company Ltd

2-60 Vicarage Lane, Ilford, Essex IG1 4AQ, England

Telephone: 01-478 3040
Telegrams: PLESSEY ILFORD
Telex: 23166

Products: Telecommunications systems.

RACAL
Racal Electronics Ltd

Western Road, Bracknell, Berkshire RG12 IRG, England

Telephone: 0344 3244
Telegrams: RACAL BRACKNELL
Telex: 848166

Products: Radio communication systems, data communications.

RIPPER
Ripper Systems Ltd

281-283 Bedford Road, Kempston, Bedfordshire MK42 8QB, England

Telephone: 0324 854080
Telegrams: Ripper Bedford
Telex: CITEC 825072

Products: Communications and public address systems for mobile and static railway applications.
The Company designs and builds to customers' specific requirements or can offer a standard range of equipment, for mainline and rapid transit surface and underground rail services. Typical products are:—
  driver to guard telephone links
  conductor to passenger public address systems
  driver to control communications
  information tape broadcasting systems
  emergency talk back systems between passenger and driver
  audible alarms for use in driving cabs
Currently on order or being supplied to British and other railways are: Audio and FM public address, crew communication equipment, emergency passenger to driver communication system and through train engine control systems.
The Company specialises in communications systems using through train wires also used for other functions such as 1 000 V heating wires, lighting and pantograph control etc. Also by using special circuitry several communication links can be achieved by using only one pair of existing wires.

Directors: P B Williams
                 C Quincey
                 R A Ripper

SAFETRAN
Safetran Systems Corp

7721 National Turnpike, Louisville, Kentucky 40214, USA

Telephone: (502) 361 1691

Products: Mobile radio access system; centralised dispatcher radio control system; dispatcher call decoder; communications control console; yard paging systems; intercoms; speakers.

SEL
Standard Elektrik Lorenz AG

D-7000 Stuttgart 40 (Zuffenhausen), Hellmuth-Hirth Strasse 42, Postfach 40 07 49, Federal Republic of Germany

Telephone: 0711 8211
Telegrams: STANLOR STUTTGART
Telex: 72110

Products: Railway signalling and control systems; telecommunications equipment; mobile radio systems, cables.

SIEMENS
Siemens Aktiengesellschaft

D-8000 Munchen 2, Wittelsbacherplatz 2, Postfach 103, Federal Republic of Germany

Telephone: 089 23 41
Telegrams: SIEMENSDIR Munchen
Telex: 523 121

Products: Telecommunications equipment.

SOLAR POWER
Solar Power Corp

Braintree, Massachusetts, USA

Products: Solar electric generator module designed for remote power applications . such as radio repeater stations, microwave links, signalling devices. Following tests with a solar energy unit near Montreal CP Rail has installed an experimental solar unit at Silver Creek in British Columbia. In this application the solar energy is used for communications. A panel of silicon solar cells is mounted in a fixed position on Mount Cotterell. The energy generated by the cells is used to charge a battery housed in an adjacent building. The battery powers a radio repeater for transmission of conversations between CP track maintenance personnel. Until now the Silver Creek radio installation has been powered by electricity supplied from two diesel-powered generators located in a valley. CP Rail hopes that use of solar power will eliminate fuelling of remote generators and allow an important reduction in maintenance requirements.

STC
Standard Telephones and Cables Ltd

STC House, 190 Strand, London WC2R 1DU, England

Telephone: 01 836 8055
Telegrams: RELAY London WC2
Telex: 22385

Related Companies: Many subsidiary and associated companies within the United Kingdom. Associated companies abroad within the International Telephone and Telegraph Corporation (ITT).

Products: Coaxial line and optical cable systems, pulse code modulation equipment and frequency division multiplex equipment for railway communication networks; telephone exchanges and instruments, office intercom systems, public address and loudspeaker systems; telephone instruments, remote control and telemetry systems; teleprinters and message switching systems for teleprinter network, data terminal and modems; control and communication cables.

Chairman and Chief Executive: K G Corfield
Marketing Director: R T Soper

TELEPHONE CABLES
Telephone Cables Limited

Chequers Lane, Dagenham, Essex RM9 6QA, England

Telephone: 01-592 6611
Telegrams: DRYCORE DAGENHAM
Telex: 896216

Products: Cables for telecommunications systems.

Chairman: O S Johnson
Managing Director: J W Baker
Commercial Director: M J Spoor
General Sales Manager: A Circus

THOMSON/CSF

23 rue de Courcelles, 75362 Paris (Cedex 08), France

Telephone: 563 12 12
Telex: TCSF 204 780 F

Products: Telecommunications, audiovisual communications, rail control systems.

President: Jean-Pierre Bouyssonnie

TRT
Télécommunications Radioélectriques et Téléphoniques

88 rue Brillat Savarin, 75640 Paris (Cedex 13), France

Telephone: 589 69 45
Telegrams: TERATEL PARIS
Telex: 25.828 F

Products: Electronic and telecommunications equipment including rail control systems. As one of the first French companies to develop a ground-train radio link in co-operation with SNCF, TRT has created a series of systems which conform with UIC requirements. The company is supplying ground/train communications systems to both the SNCF and Algerian National Railways (SNCFA). Each ground/train link consists of:
1) A mobile transceiver which includes UHF transmission and reception functions, the AF signalling facilities necessary for operating, and an automatic frequency search device. The transceiver is controlled by a synthesiser allowing its use as a service duplex link.
2) A mobile operating desk which includes all the specific operating controls for a mainline network. It can be used for either simple telephone communication or equipped with auxiliary devices, for digital data transmission.
3) A fixed station including a telephone line interconnection device. Where telephone links are not available a two-way amplification repeater equipment is used.
4) Radiation device. Transceiver radiation is accomplished by means of omnidirectional or directional antennae, or by radiating-slot cables, arranged to fit the topographical requirements of the system.
5) Controller's desk with all monitoring and control elements.

WABCO
Union Switch & Signal Division
American Standard Inc

Swissvale, Pennsylvania 15218, USA

Telephone: (412) 273 4000
Telex: 86 6648

Products: Electronic car or train detection and identification; automatic train control; mechanical, power, and block signalling and switching; highway crossing barriers and warning signals; automatic train stops; centralised traffic control; track circuit apparatus; classification yard equipment and retarders; computerised dispatching systems for control, indication and information.

Branch Offices: Chicago, Montreal, New York, San Francisco, Philadelphia, St Louis, St Paul, Jacksonville, Houston, Omaha, Toronto.

European Facility: WABCO Westinghouse SpA, Volvera 50, Piossasco (Torino) 10045, Italy

Vice-President and General Manager: G E Stinson
Vice-President, International Organisation: C F Wert

WESTERN-CULLEN-HAYES
Western-Cullen-Division, Federal Signal Corp

2700 West 36th Place, Chicago, Illinois 60632, USA

Telephone: (312) 254 9600
Telex: 25-3206

Products: Voice Patrol II radio and other railroad equipment for railroad communications.

ELECTRIFICATION EQUIPMENT

ACEC
Ateliers de Construction Electriques de Charleroi

BP4, B-6000 Charleroi, Belgium

Telephone: (071) 44 21 11
Telegrams: Transportation Division Charleroi
Telex: 51227 ACEC CHARLEROI

Products: Railway electrification equipment.

ALSTHOM
Société Générale de Constructions Electriques & Mécaniques

38 avenue Kléber, 75016 Paris, France

Telephone: 727 77 79
Telegrams: ALSTHOM PARIS
Telex: 27672

Products: Generators, alternators and traction motors.

ANSALDO
Ansaldo Group

Via Nicola Lorenzi 8, 16152 Genoa Cornigliano, Italy

Telephone: Genoa 010 41051
Telex: 270098 ANSALDO

Products: Fixed power equipment for electrified railways and sub stations.

Chairman and Managing Director: Daniele Luigi Milvio
General Manager: Giancarlo Maimone

Major work during 1977/78: Several complete substations with conversion to 1.5 or 3 kV dc with or without regeneration; high speed circuit breakers and remote controls for plants and substations.

ASEA AB

Västerås, Sweden

Telephone: Vasteras 021-10-00-00
Telegrams: ASEA VASTERAS
Telex: 40720 aseava s

Products: Railway electrification systems.

BALFOUR BEATTY
Balfour Beatty Power Construction Ltd
Traction and General Division

PO Box 12, Acornfield Road, Kirkby, Liverpool L33 7UG, England

Telephone: 051 548 5000
Telegrams: 627249
Telex: BICALCON KIRKBY TELEX

Products: Design, provision and erection of complete overhead equipment for railway electrification.

Chairman: C G Moss
Managing Director: A Pearson
Commercial and Sales Director: G B Suthers

BBC
Aktiengesellschaft Brown Boverie & Cie

Haselstrasse, CH 5401 Baden, Switzerland

Telephone: (056) 75 11 11
Telegrams: BROWN BOVERIE, BADEN SCHWEIZ
Telex: 52921 and 53203

Products: Generators and traction motors.

BICC
BICC Ltd
(Formerly British Insulated Callender's Cables)

PO Box 5, 21 Bloomsbury Street, London WC1B 3QN, England

Telephone: 01-637 1300
Telegrams: BICALBEST LONDON
Telex: 23463/28624

Products: Electric cables of all types and their associated accessories; civil, mechanical and electrical engineering.

BRECKNELL, WILLIS
Brecknell, Willis & Co Ltd
(A member of the Beyer Peacock Group)

Chard, Somerset TA20 2AA, England

Telephone: 04606 2246
Telegrams: PROGRESS CHARD
Telex: CHARD 46518

Products: Range of overhead line fittings, pantographs, third rail shoe gear and complete current collector systems. The company also offers a consultancy service for current collection requirements.

Chairman: B S Geddes
Managing Director: K B McQueen
Chief Sales Director: L F Durrans

New equipment: The company has pioneered Brecktrack—a new safety covered conductor rail system together with new design of the single arm Highreach pantograph for electrically propelled rapid transit vehicles.

BRISSONNEAU AND LOTZ CHAUDRONNERIE SA

38 avenue Kléber, 75784 Paris, France

Products: Traction and generator motors.

BRUSH
Brush Electrical Machines Co Ltd

Falcon Works, Loughborough, Leicestershire LE11 1HJ, England

Telephone: 0509 63131
Telegrams: BRUSH LOUGHBOROUGH TELEX
Telex: 341091

Products: Complete electrical propulsion systems and traction motors.

CEM/OERLIKON

37 rue du Rocher, 75008 Paris, France

Telephone: 522 85 90/74 61
Telex: 650663

Products: Subway electric and electronic equipment.

CGE
Compagnie Générale d'Electricité

54 rue la Boétie, 75382 Paris (Cedex 08), France

Telephone: 563 14 14
Telegrams: ELECTRICITE PARIS 8
Telex: 280953

Products: Electrical and electronic equipment and construction.

DEARMEDELEC
Dearmedelec SAIC

Juramento 4182/86, 1430 Buenos Aires, Argentina

Telephone: 52-6766/3409/7036

Products: Static exciting systems, traction motor transition systems, battery charge regulator.

DELTA
Delta Enfield Cables Ltd

Millmarsh Lane, Brimsdowne, Enfield, Middlesex, England

Telephone: 01-804 2468
Telex: 261749

Products: Accessories, power cables, rubber cables, plastic cables and specialised equipment.

ELECTRACK
Electrack Inc

1925 K Street NW, Washington, DC 20006, USA

Parent Companies: General Cable (USA), Balfour Beatty Group of BICC Ltd (UK)

Products: Power supply for signalling for railway electrification projects; engineering and project management of catenary systems.

ERCOLE MARELLI
Ercole Marelli & C SpA

Via Borgonuovo 24, Milan, Italy

Telephone: 2494 Milano
Telegrams: Ventilator-Milano
Telex: 320575 EMDITE I

Products: Main traction and auxiliary electric equipment for locomotives, railcars and light vehicles.

Chairman: Luigi Nocivelli
Managing Director: Umberto di Capua

Major Sales 1977/78: Equipment for electric class E656 and diesel-electric class D345 locomotives for Italian Railways (FS), equipment for electric suburban class ALe 801-804 and 644 railcars to FS and FNM (Ferrovie Nord Milano); equipment for underground and tramways for Rome and Milan City Transport.

EVR
Electronique des Véhicules et des Réseaux

11 rue de la Nouvelle, 93301 Aubervillers, France

Telephone: 833 23 45
Telex: 680075

Products: Statodyne equipment.

FUJI ELECTRIC

New Yurakucho Building 12-1, Yurakucho 1 chome, Chiyoda-ku, Tokyo 100, Japan

Telephone: 211-7111
Telex: J22331

Products: Traction motor with chopper control, static convector, brushless motor generating set, pantograph for Shinkansen (250 km/h); power supply equipment: remote supervisory control equipment with computer, freon cooling silicon rectifier, sfb gas circuit brakes and mini high-speed circuit brakes; moulded transformer and automatic station service equipment.

GEC
GEC Rectifiers Ltd

Stafford ST17 4LN, England

Telephone: 0785 51222
Telex: 35206

Products: Rectifiers for dc power supply, power electronics instrumentation and control; power conditioning units for traction vehicles.

Managing Director: N W C Gardner

Major sales 1978/79: Rectifiers, transformers, ac/dc switchgear and auxiliary items for the Hong Kong Mass Transit Railway Corporation Tsuen Wan extension.

GEC TRANSPORTATION PROJECT LIMITED

45 Victoria Street, St Albans, Hertfordshire AL1 3UG, England

Telephone: 0727 33181
Telex: 298782

Products: Main contract for the supply, installation and project management of composite electric railway systems.

GENERAL DI ELECTRICITA

Via Bergognone 34, Milan, Italy

Telephone: Milan 4242
Telegrams: Cogenel, Milan
Telex: 31092

Products: Electric transmissions.

GENERAL ELECTRIC CO (USA)

570 Lexington Avenue, New York, New York 10022, USA

Telephone: (212) 750 2000
Telegrams: Ingeco New York

Products: Locomotives, substation equipment and automation.

GENERAL ELECTRIC SA

Campinas, Sao Paulo, Brazil

Telephone: 31 9144
Telegrams: INGENETRIC CAMPINAS
Telex: 025189

Products: Traction equipment for electric locomotives.

GROUPEMENT 50 HZ
(50 c/s Group)

Löwenstrasse 31, PO Box 433, CH-8021, Zurich 1, Switzerland

Telephone: (01) 221 1744
Telegrams: Coordinat Zurich
Telex: 813 954 sehz ch

Products: Provision and erection of complete railway electrification equipment.

HITACHI
Hitachi Limited

Nippon Building, 6-2, 2-chome, Ohtemachi Chiyoda-ku, Tokyo 100, Japan

Telephone: 270 2111
Telegrams: HITACHY TOKYO
Telex: J22395, J22432

Products: Electrification substation equipment, ac switchgear, transformers, rectifiers, inverters, protective devices, supervisory remote control equipment, control computer for power system managing equipment.

MTE

31-32 quai National, 92806 Puteaux, France

Telephone: 776 41 62
Telex: 61425

Products: Conventional control aparatus, generators, alternators, traction motors, transformers and rectifiers.

OHIO BRASS CO
(A subsidiary of Harvey Hubbell Inc)

380 North Main Street, Mansfield, Ohio 44902, USA

Telephone: (419) 522 7111
Telegrams: Electric
Telex: 987414

Products: Catenary overhead equipment, third rail current collectors and insulators.

PIRELLI
Consruction and Co Ltd

Leigh Road, Eastleigh, Hampshire, England

Telephone: 042 126 2261
Telex: 477525

Products: Railway overhead electrification equipment, provision and erection.

SECHERON
SA des Ateliers de Sécheron

14 avenue de Sécheron, CH-1202 Geneva 21, Switzerland

Telephone: 022 32 67 58
Telex: 22130

Products: Transformers for railway electrification, dc traction substations. Rectifiers and circuit breakers, line protection devices for dc traction networks.

Chairman: E Camponovo
Managing Director: C Rossier
Chief Sales Director: A Reymond

SIEMENS

Werner-von-Siemens Strasse 50, D-8520 Erlangen 2, Federal Republic of Germany

Telephone: 09131 71
Telex: 629871

Products: Railway electrification equipment.

SOCIMI
Societa Costruzioni Industriali, Milano SpA

20122 Milan, Via S Calimero 3, Italy

Telephone: (02) 54 65 251/5
Telex: 31331

Products: Pantographs.

Chairman: Dr Eng Alessandro Marzocco
Managing Director: Dr Eng Pierino Sacchi
Export Sales and Marketing: Dr Eng Corrado Lardolina

STROJEXPORT

PO Box 662 886, Václavské n 56, Praha 1, Czechoslovakia

Telephone: 245 041
Telex: Strojexport Praha

Products: Railway electrification equipment.

TECNOMASIO ITALIANO BROWN BOVERI SpA

PO Box 3392, 20100 Milan, Italy

Telephone: 02 5797
Telegrams: Tecnomasio, Milan
Telex: 31153

Products: Generators and traction motors.

TOSHIBA
Toshiba Corporation

1-6 Uchisaiwaicho 1 chome, Chiyaea-ku, Tokyo 100, Japan

Telephone: 03 501 5411
Telegrams: Toshiba Tokyo
Telex: J22587 J24344 J24576

Products: Electric railcard control equipment.

TOYO DENKI SEIZO KK

Yaesu Mitsui Building, 7-2 Yaesu 2-chome, Chuo-ku, Tokyo 104, Japan

Telephone: 271 6372
Telegrams: YOHDEN TOKYO
Telex: 222/4666/7

Products: Electric locomotives, control equipment, pantograph.

WICKHAM
D Wickham & Co Ltd

Crane Mead, Ware, Hertfordshire SG12 9QA, England

Telephone: 0920 2491/7
Telegrams: WICKHAM, Ware
Telex: 81340

Products: Overhead line inspection cars.

PERMANENT WAY EQUIPMENT

AEBI
Robert Aebi AG

Uraniastrasse 31-33, Postfach 8023, Zürich, Switzerland

Telephone: 01 211 09 70
Telegrams: AEBI, Zürich
Telex: 813 795

Products: Rotary snow ploughs.

AI WELDERS
AI Welders Ltd

Academy Street, Inverness IV1 1LZ, Scotland

Telephone: 0463 39381
Telegrams: Alwelds Invss'.
Telex: 75271

Products: Rail welding machines, rail stripping machines, ancillary equipment for rail welding plants.

Chief Executive: B C Hilton
Sales Director: H L Abbott

Products: AI have alternative designs of rail welding machines available to handle either continuous welded rail or combined programmes of continuous welded rail, switches and crossings. These machines are supplied with either ac or dc welding systems and incorporate special features for de-twist and aligning the rail ends prior to commencement of the welding operation in order to meet the tolerances and specifications demanded by major railway organisations who are designing their track systems for operating at speeds of up to 250 km/h. The machines incorporate control and post heating systems to enable the welding of wear resistant steels to be carried out. In addition to the design and manufacture of rail welding and ancillary machines, AI supply complete rail welding depot installations including rail handling and cranage systems.

A & K
A & K Railroad Materials Inc

PO Box 1276, Building 12, Freeport Center, Clearfield, Utah 84016, USA

Telephone: (801) 773 3236
Telegrams: Building 12 Freeport Center
Telex: 389 406

Products: Complete switches, frogs, anchors, bolts, spikes, lockwashers, gauge rods, sleepers, hand track tools.

President: K W Schumacher
Executive Vice President: M H Kulmer

ALDON
The Aldon Co

3410 Sunset Avenue, Waukegan, Illinois 60085, USA

Telephone: (312) 623 8800

Products: Lightweight straddle-type rerailers.

ALUMINOTHERMIQUE
L'Aluminothermique

15/17 rue de Chabrol, 75480 Paris (Cedex 10), France

Products: Rail welding equipment.

ARNEKE
Arneke & Co, Heinrick

Seelze, Hannover, Federal Republic of Germany

Telephone: 05137 818

Products: Sleeper placing machines and track laying equipment.

ATLANTIC TRACK
Atlantic Track and Turnout Co

270 Broad Street, Bloomfield, New Jersey 07003, USA

Telephone: (201) 748 5885
Telex: 138049 ATTRACK

Products: New or used rail track accessories and switch material.

Chairman: G L Morrow
Chief Sales Director: R H Dreesen
Export Sales Director: W F Oster

ATLAS
Atlas Engineering Co

84 Lillie Road, London SW6 1TN, England

Telephone: 01-385 9323
Telegrams: Fabricants, London SW6
Telex: 895 1847

Products: Jacks, screwing machines, underfloor wheel truing machines, double wheel lathes, hydraulic wheel presses.

Directors: R F Allen, H J Kemp
Sales Director: P J Hines

ATLAS COPCO
Atlas Copco (Great Britain) Ltd

PO Box 79, Swallowdale Lane, Hemel Hempstead, Hertfordshire HP2 7HA, England

Telephone: 0442 61201
Telegrams: Atlascopco

Products: Self-contained power tamper/drill and pneumatic equipment, pumps, tampers.

BEILHACK
Martin Beilhack GmbH

8200 Rosenheim 2, Postfach 160, Federal Republic of Germany

Telephone: 4033
Telex: 05 25840

Products: Light, demountable ploughs with clearing width of 3.15 m; heavy, special snow ploughs, model PB600 with adjustable clearing width of 3 to 6 m; demountable snow blowers with approximately 2.5 tonnes per hour clearing capacity; snow blowers with adjustable clearing head, clearing width of 3-6 m; self-propelled and pushed special snow removal machines, reversible for clearing operations in both directions, with a clearing capacity of up to approximately 14 tonnes per hour.

Beilhack snowploughs for German Federal Railways

BOC
BOC Limited

Hammersmith House, London W6 9DX, England

Telephone: 01-748 2020
Telegrams: Britoxygen, London W6
Telex: 934664

Products: Hand and machine gas cutting equipment, gas and electric welding equipment.

BOFORS
AB Bofors-Nohab

S-461 01, Trollhättan, Sweden

Telephone: 0520 18000
Telegrams: 'Nohab Trollhättan'
Telex: 42084

Products: Snow-clearing equipment.

BOOT
Henry Boot Engineering Limited

Dronfield, Sheffield S18 6XZ, England

Telephone: 0246 414615
Telex: 547079

Products: Railway switches and crossings, lever boxes and ancillary equipment; construction and maintenance of railway track.

Chairman: E H Boot
Managing Director: D H Boot

Henry Boot switches under construction

BRITISH VITA
British Vita Co Ltd

PO Box 7, Porterfield Road, Renfrew, Scotland

Telephone: 041 886 2384
Telex: 777238

Products: Line equipment and components including resilient rubber railpads, oil hoses, heater hoses, rubber plugs, drawbar rubber springs, diesel coolant hoses; wide range of standard products and special components.

BTR
BTR Limited
Rail Fastener Division

Silvertown House, Vincent Square, London SW1P 2PL, England

Telephone: 01-834 3848
Telex: 22524

Products: FIST-BTR and B-TREC elastic rail fasteners for concrete sleepers.

Associated Companies: Rail Track Fasteners Pty Limited, PO Box 72, Bentley, 6102 Western Australia, Australia.
Lesteel Spring Company (Pty) Limited, PO Box 4261, Luipaardsvlei 1743, South Africa.
BTR-TREC Inc, 1800 Peachtree Centre, 230 Peachtree Street NW, Atlanta, Georgia 30303, USA.
Fist do Brazil Ltda, Paulists 1439, 01311 Sao Paulo, Brazil.

CANRON
Canron Railgroup
(Formed by merger of Tamper and Matisa)
(Division of Canron Corp)

2401 Edmund Road, West Columbia, South Carolina 29169, USA

Telephone: (803) 794 9160
Telex: 573423

Products: Canron Railgroup manufactures a complete range of railway track maintenance of way equipment including: ballast cleaning and dressing machines, bolting machines, brush cutters and attachments, track lubricators, frog and switch point grinders, track gauges, mobile generator sets, inspection and recording cars, spike drivers, spike pullers, production tampers, switch tampers, spot tampers, tie inserters and removers, track levelling and lining equipment, rail saws, rail drills, rail bolting machines, snow blowers and a complete contracting service.

Division Headquarters:
Canada: 171 Eastern Avenue, Toronto M5A AH7
Australia: PO Box 150, Niddrie, Victoria 3042
Switzerland: Case Postale, CH-1001 Lausanne
Italy: Matema SpA, Via Quintino sella n.8, 1-00187 Rome
France: 39, rue d'Amsterdam, F-75000 Paris
United Kingdom: 14 Elstow Road, Bedford MK42 9LA
Federal Republic of Germany: Markgrafenstrasse 1, D-48 Bielefeld-BRD
Spain: c/Alcala No 65, Madrid-14
Japan: PO Box 1058, Tokyo 100-91

Parts Depot: St Paul, Minnesota 55104, USA
Telephone: (612) 645 5055

Agents: Argentina, Bolivia, Brazil, Chile, Colombia, Costa Rica, Ecuador, El Salvador, Guatemala, Honduras, Jamaica, Mexico, Peru, Trinidad, Uruguay, Venezuela.
Canron Railgroup is further represented in most other countries. The names of representatives in the above and other countries can be obtained by contacting the head office.

CEMAFER
Cemafer Gleisbaumaschinen und Gerate GmbH

7814 Breisach, Ihringer Landstrasse 3, Postfach 1327, Federal Republic of Germany

Telephone: 07667 585
Telex: 7722524

Products: Power wrenches, coach-screwing machines, rail drills, rail saws, sleeper drills, sleeper adzing and drilling machines, rail grinding equipment, rail benders, light tampers, inspection trolleys, trailers, portal cranes, hand tools, electric generators (portable), gauges, jacks, rail cutting machines, rail stripping machines, sleeper boring machines, sleeper placing machines, spanners, spike drivers and extractors, track laying equipment, wrenches.

CHEMETRON
Chemetron Corporation, Railway Products Division

111 East Wacker Drive, Chicago, Illinois 60601, USA

Telephone: (312) 565 5000
Telegrams: Chemrail
Telex: 25-4383

Products: Contract welding of continuous rail of 25 to 82 ft lengths into quarter-mile lengths; dual rail pusher cars; rail welding units, rail trains and rail handling equipment.
Formerly known as The National Cylinder Gas Division of Chemetron Corporation the present name was taken in 1970 following a reorganisation of operations.

COLES CRANES
Coles Cranes Ltd

Head Office: Crown Works, Sunderland, Tyne and Wear SR4 6TT, England

Sales: Harefield, Uxbridge, Middlesex UB9 6QG, England

Telephone: 089 582 3777
Telex: 21619

Products: Diesel-electric, diesel-hydraulic, mobile truck-mounted, tower cranes, diesel mechanical cranes.

COSTAIN
Costain Concrete Co Ltd

Duncan House, Dolphin Square, London SW1V 3PR, England

Telephone: 01-821 1581
Telex: 919858 G

Products: Prestressed concrete sleepers.

Managing Director: David B Scott

DEHE
Société des Entreprises A Dehe et Cie

40 quai de l'Ecluse, 78290 Croissy-sur-Seine, France

Products: Track construction and maintenance equipment.

DELACHAUX
C Delachaux SA

119 avenue Louis-Roche, 92231 Gennevilliers, France

Telephone: 790 61 20
Telex: DECHO 620 118F

Products: Aluminothermique rail welding equipment.

DESQUENNE ET GIRAIL
Société Desquenne et Girail

26 rue Lalo, 75016 Paris, France

Products: Track maintenance equipment.

DONELLI
Donelli, SpA

Via Romana 69, 42028 Poviglio, Reggio Emilia, Italy

Telephone: (0522) 689046
Telegrams: Donelli Poviglio
Telex: 530320

Products: Ballast regulators, hydraulic cranes, jacks, sleeper placing machines, track aligners, track laying equipment, track lining machines.
Donelli offers gantry equipment as part of a complete package of track relaying machinery: gantries, rail threaders, sleeper positioners, hydraulic track lifters and slewers. The two motorised gantries combine with a lifting beam to form a 36-m track panel lifter and sleeper laying unit. Straddling the track on which it is working, the equipment is capable of renewing 300 mph. Auxiliary rails used for operation of the unit are later turned onto the new sleepers to provide the final track rail. The gantries are hydraulically operated.
The rail-threader and sleeper positioner works in conjunction with the gantry. It automatically spaces and aligns sleepers as it threads on the new rail. The unit is diesel powered and all operations are hydraulic. With outputs of up to 2 000 mph, the supplier claims big savings in time and manpower.
For lifting the track during new construction and relaying, Donelli markets a hydraulic track lifter and slewer which jacks the track out of the ballast. Hydraulic rail clamps grip the rail while the lifting jacks are extended onto the ballast. After lifting the machine and track, jack cylinders are tilted to displace or slew the track laterally.

DOW MAC
Dow Mac Concrete

Head Office: Tallington, Stamford, Lincolnshire, England
Telephone: 0778 342301

Works: Eaglescliffe, Cleveland, England
Telephone: 0642 781811

London Office: 110/112 The Strand, London WC2, England
Telephone: 01-836 8918

Products: Dow Mac prestressed concrete sleepers.

Chairman: I C Parkins
Managing Director: A S Darroch
Chief Sales Director: P B Burgin

DROUARD
Société Drouard Frères

153 rue de la Pompe, 75782 Paris (Cedex 16), France

ELEKTRO-THERMIT
Elektro-Thermit GmbH

4300 Essen, Federal Republic of Germany

Telephone: 0201 1731
Telegrams: Elektrothermit
Telex: 0857 727/728

Products: Thermit rail welding equipment and materials, rail de-stressers, rail grinding machines, glued insulated rail joints.

Managing Directors: Dr Hans Guntermann
Johann Hugo Wirtz

ENERGOMACHEXPORT
V/O Energomachexport
(Export company for all Soviet-built railway products)

127486 Moscow, Deguninskaya Strasse, 1, Korp 4, USSR

Telephone: 147 21 77
Telegrams: Moscow Energoexport
Telex: 411926 ENEK SU

Products: Ballast cleaning machines; tamper-leveller-liner machines; track laying cranes and gantries; snow ploughs; snow clearing and removal equipment; rail welding equipment; portable powered machines for tamping, rail cutting-drilling-grinding and spike driving-pulling; electronic and ultrasonic fault finding equipment; inspection cars; gang and maintenance railcars and trailers.

ERNEST HOLMES
(A Dover Corporation Division)

2505 East 43rd Street, Chattanooga, Tennessee 37407, USA

Telephone: (615) 867 2142
Telegrams: WRECKER, New York
Telex: 235203 Wreck, New York

Products: Wrecking cranes.

Chairman: Thomas C Sutton
Managing Director: Donald W Humphreys
Vice President: Robert L Freeman
President, Export: Donald H Baldwin

FAIRMONT
Fairmont Railway Motors
A division of Harsco Corporation Mississauga

Head Office: Fairmont, Minnesota 56031, USA

Works: Fairmont, Minnesota 56031, USA and 6230 NW Drive, Mississauga, Ontario, Canada

Telephone: (507) 235 3361
Telegrams: Fairmotor
Telex: 910 565-2122

Products: Inspection cars; section and gang cars; hy-rail equipment for road or rail movement; motor car engines; push cars and trailers; wheels, axles and bearings; derrick cars; ballast maintenance cars; weed control equipment; track liners; tie sprayers, tie and rail renewal equipment and rail grinding systems.
The company was founded in 1909 and has been a manufacturer of railway track machinery during this time. Its products are used around the world by the railways of 70 countries.
Latest product from Fairmont is the W119-B tie inserter which inserts, levels and squares new sleepers tight under the rail at the rate of 3 sleepers/minute. No respotting or additional handling of the units are required, says the supplier. All functions, including the inserting force of 4 020 kg, are hydraulically powered and electronically controlled with very little operator effort. A three-section telescoping boom provides a reach of 4.25 m from track centre-line, with a lift of 450 kg when fully extended. The machine will handle both timber and concrete sleepers.

Export Manager: K J Nelson

FAMATEX
Famatex SRL

Aviendia San Martin 7910, San Martin, Province of Buenos Aires, Argentina

Telephone: 755 0352

Products: Inspection cars, light and heavy gangers' trollies.

FINDLAY, IRVINE
Findlay, Irvine Ltd

Bog Road, Penicuik, Midlothian, Scotland

Telephone: 0968 72111
Telegrams: AUTRONICS PENICUIK
Telex: 727502

Products: Points heating controller; thermostats. The Icelert Model 162 points heating controller is suitable for controlling electric or gas points heating and a special temperature and moisture probe assembly has been designed for this particular application. It controls on a temperature and moisture detection basis and only when the temperature set point (usually 1°C) is reached and moisture is detected at the probes will a relay be activated. This gives a better degree of control than the normal thermostat working on a temperature basis only. Another control knob is provided to enable the selection of a second operating point at a number of degrees below the normal operating level. The heaters will be switched on when the ambient temperature falls to this level and moisture and snow is not detected.

Chairman: James S Findlay
Managing Directors: John A Irvine and James S Findlay
Industrial Division Manager: W C Taylor

FOSTER
L B Foster Co

Foster Building, 415 Holiday Drive, Pittsburgh, Pennsylvania 15220, USA

Telephone: (412) 928 3400

Products: Rail track accessories, frog and switch material crossings, railroad ties, steel mine ties and track tools.

President: Milton Porter

FRAMAFER
Société Française de Construction de Matériel Ferroviaire

90 rue de la Gare, 57801 Bening-les-Saint-Avold, France

Telephone: (87) 04 54 54
Telex: 860243

Products: Automatic track levelling, tamping and lining machines, ballast cleaners and ballast regulators.

FRUEHAUF
Fruehauf Division, Fruehauf Corporation

10900 Harper Avenue, Detroit, Michigan 48232, USA

Telephone: (313) 267 1000
Telegrams: Fruco Detroit

Products: On-track/off-track service vehicles; highway trailers; containers.

FSSA
Ferrovias y Siderurgia SA

Cedaceros 4, Madrid-14, Spain

Telephone: 231 97 52/39 49
Telegrams: FERROVIAS

Products: Railway track materials, turnouts, expanding joints, single and double slips, turntables.

President: Carlos Roeb Urqeheuer
General Manager: Luis Rios Sidro

GEISMAR
Société des Anciens Etablissements L Geismar

113 bis avenue Charles de Gaulle, 92200 Neuilly sur Seine, France

Telephone: (1) 747 55 00
Telex: Fermar NLLSN 620700

Works: 5 rue d'Altkirch, 68006 Colmar, France.
Telephone: (89) 41 48 83. Telex: Fermar NLLSN 620700

Products: Rail saws; rail drills; coachscrewing machines; fishbolt fastening machines; rail profile grinding machines; rail butt grinding machines; sleeper drilling machines; chamfering machines; sleeper adzing machines; lightweight ballast tampers; illumination plants; track warning devices; hydraulic rail benders; hydraulic rail joint straighteners; rail lubricators; trolleys (1 to 200 tons); inspection trolleys; rail loaders; rail pullers; rail changers; sleeper loading machines; tamping and slewing jacks; complete range of hand tools; self propelled track laying gantries; thermit weld shears; hydraulic rail tensors; heavy-duty sleeper changing machine; spike drivers and pullers; combination track gauge and level; in-plant sleeper adzing-drilling-sawing machine; track-slewing and lining machines; electronic train warning device for gangs working on the track; electronic train loading gauge control device, etc.
Geismar markets a comprehensive range of track relaying equipment, which includes hydraulic portal cranes with hoisting capacities of 16, 24 and 30 tons. These machines lay or relay track at a rate of about 1 000 ft (304.8 m)/h. A recent addition to Geismar equipment is a self-propelled hydraulic rail threader designed to move rail lengths to and from the track position. The machine is able to remove old rails before threading new rails into fixing and welding. Operation is by one man and all lifting and transferring movements are made hydraulically. Rail and sleeper positioner; ballast regulators; ballast compactors; light and heavy duty traction rail cars; rail heaters (4, 8 and 16 burners); turnkey installations (machining and reclaiming of sleepers, and rail welding and reprofiling).

GEMCO
George Moss Pty Ltd

10-14 Woolwich Street, Leederville, Perth, Western Australia, Australia

Telephone: 81 2033
Telegrams: ROCKDRILL PERTH
Telex: 92645

Products: Hydraulic controlled track machines for sleeper extraction and replacement, track lifting, levelling, ballast scarifying, sleeper boring, spike pulling and bolt renewal. Also Australian agents for Geismar rail maintenance machines.

GEORGE COOPER
George Cooper (Sheffield) Ltd
Glynwed Screws and Fastenings Ltd

Templeborough Works, Sheffield Road, Sheffield S9 1RS, England

Telephone: (0742) 449011
Telex: 547092

Products: Fish bolts, track bolts, screw spikes, crossing bolts, frog bolts.

Marketing Manager: S F Johnson
Managing Director: P C Beardsley
Sales Manager: R M Saxton

GRANT LYON EAGRE
Grant Lyon Eagre Ltd

80A Scotter Road, Scunthorpe, South Humberside DN15 8EF, England

Telephone: 0724 62131
Telex: 527215

Products: Switches and crossings, cast iron baseplates, blocks, collector shoes.

Managing Director: D W Schafer
Directors: J W Woodford
R F M Grant

GRINAKER PRECAST
Grinaker Precast (Pty) Ltd

PO Box 365, Brakpan 1540, South Africa

Telephone: 011 813 2340
Telex: 82322

Products: Prestressed concrete sleepers.

Chairman: O W Grinaker
Managing Director: E J Sadie
Chief Sales Director: J F Cairns

Grinaker Precast's concrete sleepers

GRUNDY
Grundy and Partners Ltd

Bond's Mill, Stonehouse, Gloucestershire GL10 3RG, England

Telephone: 045 382 3611
Telex: 43484

Products: Traklink mobile stud and pin brazing equipment.

Chairman: S W Grundy
Managing Director: C G Burcher
Product Manager: H R Stocken

GTG
Greenside Hydraulics Ltd

Greenside, Chapeltown, Sheffield S30 4RY, England

Telephone: 07415 4971
Telex: 54118

Products: Rail tensors for tensioning continuous welded rail; rail support arms and rollers; rail welding jigs; track lifting machines; rail joint straightening machines; rail manipulators; rail lifting bars; lightweight trolleys; rail curving machines.

Chairman: J W Thompson
Directors: Guy Lees Thompson
Margaret Thompson

HENRY BOOT
Henry Boot Engineering Ltd

Dronfield, Sheffield S18 6XZ, England

Telephone: 0246 414615
Telex: 547079

Products: Railway switches and crossings; lever boxes and ancillary equipment; construction and maintenance of railway track.

Chairman: E H Boot
Managing Director: D H Boot
General Manager, Contracting Division: G A Jarrett
General Manager, General Engineering Division: J M Stevenson
Marketing and Sales Manager: J Newby

HOLLAND
Holland Co (Railweld Division)

1020 Washington Avenue, Chicago Hts, Illinois 60411, USA

Telephone: (312) 756 0650

Products: Rail welding equipment and services.

President: J A Liddell
Vice President: R F Murphy
Sales Engineer: Jonathan Margules
Sales Director: H B Nordstrom

HRS
Hoesch Rothe Erde-Schmiedag AG

D-4600 Dortmund 1, Tremoniastrasse 5-11, Federal Republic of Germany

Telephone: 0231 1961
Telex: 8 22 245

Products: Elastic rail fasteners, permanent way material for all types of sleeper, ribbed base plates for tracks and switches, coach screws, hook bolts and clip plates.

HUNSLET
The Hunslet Engine Company Ltd

Hunslet Engine Works, Leeds LS10 1BT, England

Telephone: 0532 32261 (10 lines)
Telegrams: Hunslt Leeds
Telex: 55237

Products: Self-propelled six-foot and shoulder ballast cleaning machines; rail mounted drainage trenchers.

IRVINE
J E Irvine & Co Ltd

Knoll Road, Camberley, Surrey, England

Telephone: 0276 5069/21419

Products: Sleeper placing machines and track laying equipments including wagon-mounted cranes for rail handling (in association with Heinrick Arneke & Co, Hanover).

ITALSIDER
Italsider SpA

Via Corsica 4, Genova, Italy

Telephone: 010 5999
Telegrams: ITALSIDER GENOVA
Telex: 270690 Itasid

Products: Permanent way equipment including baseplates, fishplates, clips, switches and crossings.

ITS
International Track Systems, Inc

620 West 32nd Street, Ashtabula, Ohio 44004, USA

Telephone: (216) 992-9206 (216) 993-8076

Products: Rubber products for railway track such as butyl rubber shock barriers for use between the base of rails and steel tie plates and between the plates and sleepers.

Managing Director: Alfred E Carey
Sales Director: L L Chung

JACKSON
Jackson Vibrators Inc

General Sales Office: 1905 Bernice Road, Lansing, Illinois 60438, USA

Telephone: (312) 895 0100
Telegrams: Jaktamp

Factory: Ludington, Michigan

Products: Complete line of tie tampers, automatic with or without liners (curve and tangent one unit); non-automatic switch tampers; surfacing light beam fits all manufacturers' tampers; hand tampers; Jackson/Jordon spreader-ditcher-snow plough.

Vice-President, Sales: J H Bush
Marketing Manager: Allan McCarthy

JAMBES-NAMUR
Jambes-Namur, SA Des Ateliers de Construction

B-5100 Jambes, Belgium

Telephone: 081 30 18 51
Telegrams: Jamur, Jambes
Telex: 59127

Products: Vibrators for testing of sleepers and rail fixing devices; vibrators for ballast car unloading.

JARRAH
Jarrah & Karri Export Marketing Ltd

Vistec House, 185 London Road, Croydon, Surrey CR0 1QE, England

Telephone: 01-681 1271
Telex: 946195

Products: Sleepers.

KANGO
Kango Electric Hammers Ltd

Lombard Road, South Wimbledon, London SW19 3XA, England

Telephone: 01-542 8544
Telegrams: Kangolim London SW19
Telex: 261789 Kango G

Depots: Leyton, London E10 7JQ; East Dulwich, London SE22 9AN; Prestwich, Manchester; East Kilbride, Scotland.
Kango Ballast Tamping Equipment is in use in Australia, Belgium, Brazil, Canada, Chile, France, Greece, Netherlands, Hong Kong, Hungary, India, Malaysia, Norway, South Africa, South Korea, Sweden, Thailand, Yugoslavia and the United Kingdom.

Products: Kango electric ballast tampers and power generators.

Chairman: J Francis
Marketing Director: R F D Riber
Export Sales Director: M C Brailey

KERSHAW
The Kershaw Companies, Inc

PO Box 9238, 2205 West Fairview Avenue, Montgomery, Alabama 36108, USA

Telephone: (205) 263 5581
Telex: 59-3416

Products: Complete range of self-propelled machines for mechanised track, switch and yard maintenance: ballast regulator and ballast broom—snow switch cleaner—brush cutter attachment; track patrol with attachments; brush type kribber; track broom; yard cleaner; dual tie saw and end remover; tie bed scarifier and tie inserter; tie end remover; tie injector; tie, bridge and bundle cranes; crawler adzer; snow switch cleaner; track and switch liner; clear way brush cutter and snow blower; super jack all; Railroader trailer; undercutter and ballast cleaner; portable set off.

Managing Director, International Operations: Peter H Deckert

Affiliated Companies:
Kershaw Manufacturing Canada Ltd, 2062 Chartier Avenue Dorval, Quebec, Canada
Royce Kershaw Company, Inc, Montgomery, Alabama 36108, USA
Evans Deakin Industries Ltd, 12 Boundary Street, South Brisbane, Queensland 4101, Australia

KOEHRING
Koehring GmbH—Bomag Division

Postfach 180, 5407 Boppard/Rhein, Federal Republic of Germany

Telephone: 06742 2051
Telegrams: Bomag Boppard
Telex: 04 263 16

Products: Tamping compactors, reversing vibratory plate compactors, trench compactors, double vibratory rollers, single drum vibratory rollers, double vibratory slope compactors, tandem vibratory rollers, single drum vibratory rollers, towed vibratory rollers, sheepsfoot rollers, pneumatic tyred rollers, soil stabilisers, refuse compactors.

KRAUTKRAMER
Krautkrämer GmbH

5 Köln-Klettenberg, Luxemburger Strasse 449, Federal Republic of Germany

Telephone: 44 60 61
Telegrams: Impulsschall, Koeln

Products: Stationary rail testing installations, rail testers, rail test cars. This equipment is in use in Belgium, France, Federal Republic of Germany, United Kingdom, Greece, Hungary, Republic of Ireland, Italy, Japan, Luxembourg, Sweden, Switzerland, USA.

Affiliated Company: Wells Krautkramer Ltd, Blackhorse, Letchworth, Hertfordshire, England

LORAM
Loram Maintenance of Way, Inc

3900 Arrowhead Drive, Hamel, Minnesota 55340, USA

Telephone: (612) (478) 6014
Telex: 29 0391

Products: Autotrack, single track ploughs, double track ploughs, ballast sleds, winch carts, multi-purpose machines (undercutters), autosleds, rail grinders, shoulder ballast cleaners, sleeper inserters, sleeper extractors, rail corrigation analysers, undertrack fabric applicators.

Marketing Manager: G A Harris

MATEMA
Matema Materiali Meccanici SpA

Via Ardeatina Km 21, 00040 S Palomba, Rome, Italy

Telephone: 919112
Telegrams: Matistal Pomezia
Telex: 68150

Products: Track recording trolleys; automatic track levelling, tamping, and lining machines; ballast cleaners; ballast regulators; heavy and light gang cars; sleeper boring machines; rail power saws; wrenches and drills; continuous-rail welding machines and grinding machines; electric generators (portable); gauges; handfacing equipment; jacks; screwing machines; sleeper placing machines; spike drivers and extractors; track laying equipment.

Chairman: R Blomqwist
Managing Director: R Naggar
Chief Sales Director: F Vittori
Export Sales Director: G Uccelli

MATISA
Matériel Industriel SA

Head Office: MATISA Matériel Industriel SA, Case Postale, CH-1001 Lausanne, Switzerland

Works: Renens and Crissier (Lausanne), Santa Palomba (Rome)

Associated Companies:
Federal Republic of Germany: Matisa Maschinen GmbH, Markgrafenstrasse 1, D-4800 Bielefeld.
United Kingdom: Matisa (UK) Ltd, 14 Elstow Road, Bedford MK42 9LA.
Spain: Matisa Española, C/Alcalá 65, Madrid-1.
Italy: Matema Materiali, Meccanici SpA, Via Ardeatina Km 21, 1-00040 S. Palomba, Rome.
Japan: Matisa Japan, Co Ltd, Inose Building 6th floor, 16-6 Chiba 5-chome, Minato-ku, Tokyo.
France: Matisa, Agence en France, rue d'Amsterdam 39, F-75009 Paris.

Products: Automatic tamper-leveller-liners; universal switch tamper-leveller-liners; medium tamper-leveller-liners; light tampers; ballast cleaners; ballast regulators; and hopper wagons; ballast crusher wagons; ballast compactors; track recording trolleys; rail cars and coaches; track measuring and analysing equipment; curve calculators and curve correctors; track renewal train; power wrenches; rail saws and rail drills; sleeper drills; sleeper adzing; and drilling machines; portable rail grinders; rail scooters; and length gang trolleys.

Latest equipment:

B 200

Tamper-leveller-liners

Modular design providing a choice of nine models:
single workhead for tamping in open track
double workheads for tamping in open track
single workhead for tamping in open track with check rail where obstacles are present.
Each type can be fitted with:
2 axles: 3-point suspension, UIC standard
3 axles: front axle and rear bogie, 3-point suspension UIC standard
4 axles: 2 railway type bogies with primary steel coil spring suspension, anti-yaw dampeners.

B 133

Universal Tamper-leveller-liner
"Regelfahrzeug" train formation for switches and plain track
80 km/h self-propelled
100km/h in train formation
Production speed on plain track: 500 mph
Complete treatment of:
simple switch: 20 min.
double switch: 30 min.
cross-over: 40 min.
cross-over/junction: 60 min.

B 85

Tamper-leveller-liner
of proven reliability.
easy to use and maintain.
model M with double tools: 1 000 mph
model N with single tools: 600 mph
New lining device on the axle.

LCR 04

Tamper-liner
for all gauges from 700 mm, restricted structure gauges, special adaptations for mine railways, steelworks, urban and metro lines.

BL 09

Light Ballast Tamper
Single head and double head.
Single or double head, motorised, for gradients up to 60 per cent, for loop lines, sidings, etc.

C 330

Ballast Cleaner
Very high output.
for worksites where advance is extra rapid
Production: 600 m³/h

C 311

Universal Ballast Cleaner
with lifting and track holding device, for difficult, sinuous, uneven tracks of restricted gauge with various fixed obstacles.
Production: 350 m³/h

12 CB 8

Ballast Cleaner
High output, proven reliability
Production: 450 m³/h

R 7 D + WB 1

Ballast Regulator with Ballast Hopper
for all transfers
Working speed:
from 2 to 20 km/h in either direction
Travel speed: 80 km/h
Optional equipment: excavator-loader arm

D 912

Crib and Shoulder Compactors-Production Speed 900 mph
Optional equipment: ploughs and brush for finishing in one pass

P 811

Track Renewal Train Valditerra System
for all types of rails and sleepers
Length: 67 m
Length of cut: 4 m
Personnel: 14
Production speed: 600 mph
Worksite start-up time: 18 min.
Worksite clearance time: 12 min.
Economic operation even during very short track occupations.

Further Development:

Track Renewal Train or New Track-Laying Train
For all types of rail and sleeper.
Gauge: from 1 000-1 675 mm
Length: 44.6 m
Production speed: 600 mph
Economic operation even during very short track occupations.
Operating Posts: 4

PV 7

Track Recording Trolley
with Matisa analyser AV 521 for numerical values of the 7 parameters
Recording speed: 30 km/h

M 422

Track Recording Railcar
with Matisa analyser AV 522 for numerical values of the 7 parameters
Recording speed: 80 km/h

A 461

Track Recording Coach
with Matisa analyses AV 522 for the numerical value of 10 parameters.
Recording speed: 160 km/h
Coach layout including a recording compartment, a conference room, a two-berth sleeping compartment, kitchen and toilets, as well as small workshop with generator for independent power supply of the coach and its equipment.

MATIX-INDUSTRIES
Société Matix Industries

59 rue Saint-Lazare, 75009 Paris, France

Products: Track maintenance machinery including inspection cars.

McGREGOR
McGregor Paving Ltd

Turnoaks Lane, Birdholme, Chesterfield, Derbyshire S40 2HB, England

Telephone: 0246 76971
Telegrams: McGREGORS CHESTERFIELD
Telex: 547467

Directors: F D Lebish
F Haniewicz

Products: In collaboration with British Rail's Research and Development Division, Robert McGregor developed PACT—the Paved Concrete Track system. PACT was developed as an alternative to classical track of steel rails, sleepers and ballast to reduce expenditure involved in maintenance. The system consists essentially of continuously welded rails laid on a continuously reinforced concrete slab, designed to ensure that the track geometry remains within tolerance over long periods, with negligible maintenance. Resilient rail fastenings locate the rails on the slab and resilient pads are interposed between the rail foot and slab surface.
Several versions of PACT have been constructed, both in Britain and overseas.
An essential feature of PACT is the provision of custom-made slip form pavers, which can be used to construct the concrete track bed on a single width right-of-way. Associated with the pavers is machinery which dispenses and places the slab reinforcement, and carried the concrete into the paver—ensuring a continuous progress of slab construction.

MONIER
Monier Limited

The Monier Building, 6-8 Thomas Street, Chatswood, New South Wales 2067, Australia

Telephone: 02 411 1122
Telegrams: Monier, Sydney
Telex: AA 26673

Products: Concrete sleepers; plant and equipment for manufacture of prestressed concrete sleepers.
Monier have developed and operate a highly efficient and economical method of producing prestressed concrete sleepers adaptable to a wide range of plant capacity requirements and have licensed this system in countries overseas.

Chairman: E S Owens
Managing Director: J N Davenport
General Manager: R S H Duncan
Marketing Manager: B G Dive

NCM
Nederlandse Constructiebdrijven en Machinefabrieken NV

Schieweg 2, Delft, PO Box 10, Netherlands

Telephone: 015 569244
Telegrams: NECEM, Delft
Telex: 31031

Products: Rails and accessories, switches, crossings and turntables, trackmobiles.

NEI CLARKE CHAPMAN
NEI Clarke Chapman Cranes Ltd

Woodeson House, Rodley, Leeds LS13 1HN, England

Telephone: 0532 579001
Telegrams: Cranes Rodley
Telex: 55159

Products: Heavy diesel breakdown cranes, turntables, track laying machines, hydraulic railway equipment.

ORTON
Orton McCullough Crane Company

Oakbrook Executive Plaza, 1211 West 22nd Street, Oakbrook, Illinois 60521, USA

Telephone: (312) 654 1695
Telegrams: ORCRANE

Products: Cranes and heavy lifting gear.

PANDROL
Pandrol Ltd

9 Holborn, London EC1N 2NE, England

Telephone: 01-242 5252
Telegrams: PANDROL LONDON
Telex: 21474 PANERS G

Products: Resilient rail fastenings, lock spikes, elastic rail spikes and screw spikes.

Managing Director: B Clough
Sales Director: G G Leeves

PERSONER
Personer Spårteknik AB

S-27100 Ystad, Sweden

Telephone: 0411 13800
Telex: 33235 pst s

Products: Heavy-duty point lock.

PINTSCH BAMAG
Pintsch Bamag Antriebs-und Verkehrstechnik GmbH

Postfach 10 04 20, D-4220 Dinslaken, Federal Republic of Germany

Telephone: 02134 602-1
Telex: 08551938

Products: Automatic propane-fuelled infra-red point heating equipment and solid state snow detectors.

PLASSER
Plasser & Theurer

Head Office: Johannesgasse 3, 1010 Vienna, Austria

Telephone: 52 66 01
Telegrams: Bahnbau Vienna
Telex: 132117

Factory: Pummererstraße 5, 4020 Linz, Austria

Plasser Dromatic 08-32

Companies of the Plasser & Theurer Group:
Australia: Plasser Australia, Pty Ltd, PO Box 53, St Marys, New South Wales 2760
Brazil: Plasser do Brasil Ltda, Comercio, Industria e Representycoes, Avenida Marechal Camara, 271/1.201, 20.000 Rio de Janeiro
Canada: Plasser Canada Ltd, 2705 Marcel Street, Montreal 9, Quebec
France: Framafer, 90 rue de la Gare, 57801 Bening-les-St Avold
Federal Republic of Germany: Deutsche Plasser Bahnbaumaschinen GmbH, Works: D-8228 Freilassing, Industriestraße 31—Spare Parts Depot and Customer Service: D-8 München 81, Friedr Eckart-Straße 35
Great Britain: Plasser Railway Machinery (GB) Ltd, Manor Road, West Ealing, London W13
India: Plasser (India) Private Ltd, B/52 Greater Kailash, New Delhi-110048
Italy: Plasser Italiana S.r.l., Sales Department, Service, Workshop, Spare Parts: Piazzale Stazione F.S., 00049 Velletri (Rome)
Japan: Nippon Plasser K K, 26—11, Kasuga, 2-chome Bunkyoku, Tokyo
South Africa: Plasser Railway Machinery (South Africa), Pty Ltd, PO Box 10494, Johannesburg
Spain: Plasser Espanola SA, Posterior Occidental 8, Madrid
USA: Plasser American Corporation, 2001 Myers Road, Chesapeake, Virginia 23324

Products: Automatic track tamping, surfacing and lining machines; universal points and crossing tamping machines; ballast consolidating machines; ballast regulators; ballast cleaning machines; rail rectification machines; track recording cars, railway motor vehicles; railway cranes and lightweight equipment for track maintenance.

Latest equipment: The Plasser & Theurer 07 and 08 Series of tamping machines covers a range of machines for the most different conditions and demands. The latest equipment is the 08-Quatromatic which tamps, levels and lines 4 sleepers at a time, which guarantees highest output.
Outstanding features of the 08-275 points and crossing tamping machines are the lateral moveable tamping heads, the sidewards tiltable tamping tools and the operator's cabin which is situated immediately in front of the working units.
The ballast regulators SSP 103 and SSP 100 have an x-shaped centre plough which enlarges their working capability.
The dynamic track stabiliser DGS applies lateral vibration and horizontal pressure to the track, thus stabilising it immediately after the tamping operation.
The RM 76 U is the first undercutter cleaner, which as well as plain track can also undercut and clean switches and crossings.
The assembly line principle was applied to track relaying by Plasser & Theurer in 1968 with the development of the track relaying train SUZ 2000. Today the series SUZ 350, SUZ 500 and SUM 800 are manufactured, which can be adapted for any railway conditions.
The self propelled track recording and analysing car EM 80 works with electronic track measuring systems which have proven their reliability under most severe conditions from extreme cold weather to tropic and desert conditions.
With the K 355 PT the flash butt welding principle—which up to now had been used stationary only—became mobile and flash butt welding can be carried out on track now.
The range of rail rectification machines is designed for the complete process of rail treatment, reprofiling of outside or inside of rail edge, reprofiling of the rail running service and rail grinding. For the demands of customers additionally a wide range of special machines for track maintenance and track works is supplied, including all kinds of motor vehicles and one- or twin-jib heavy railway cranes as well as lightweight track maintenance equipment.

PLASTICA

Plastica Kunststoffwerk GmbH

Ambrosius-Brand Strasse 20, Postfach 2165, 5828 Ennepetal 1, Federal Republic of Germany

Telephone: 02333 7821/92
Telegrams: Plastica Ennepetal
Telex: 0823 382

Products: Resilient rail fastenings and insulating elements.

Managing Director: Dr Hucke

PLUTO

Société d'Exploitation des Poutres de Levage Universelles et Travelleuses Oleopneumatiques

BP 63, 78000 Les Mureaux, France

Telephone: 097 881 34 42
Telegrams: Tracman-Wrexham

Products: Track laying and replacement wagon.

PORTEC INC

300 Windsor Drive, Oak Brook, Illinois 60521, USA

Telephone: (312) 325 6300

Products: Rail anchors, insulated rail joints, rail and flange lubricators, rail joint heater, sleepers, track machines, tampers, snow blowers, rail laying equipment.

Chairman: James A Miller
Vice-President: Robert Wollberg

PORTEC (UK)

Portec (UK) Ltd

Vauxhall Industrial Estate, Ruabon, Wrexham, Clwyd LL14 6UY, Wales

Telephone: 0978 820820
Telegrams: TRACMAN WREXHAM
Telex: 61369 PORTEC G

Products: Rail anchors, rail and flange lubricators, maxi-mu adhesion fluid applicators, track switch protectors and two way rail benders.
Rail and flange lubrication as a method of saving rail wear is becoming more and more important as the cost of materials and labour spirals upwards. The Portec range of track-mounted lubricators—marketed under the old company name of P&M—includes the well-tried Model C4, which bolts to the rail, and the Pammek series which clamps to the rail. Latest additions to the range are the Tramway Lubricator for lubrication of tramway grooved rails and the PL150 model for normal tracks which has a very large capacity of 150 kg.

Portec PL150 rail and flange lubricator

Chairman: James A Miller
Managing Director: Derek J Joy
Technical Director: John A Hill

POUGET

Pouget, Etablissements SA

190 bis avenue de Stalingrad, 93240 Stains, France

Telephone: 826 62 12
Telegrams: Motovoi Pouget/Stains
Telex: Pouget 630574F

Products: Track laying gantries, coach screwing machines, sleeper drills, rail saws, rail drills, portable vibrating tampers, rail grinding machines, rail loaders, sleeper adzing and drilling machines, jacks, hand tools, light ballast cleaner, rail cutting machines with disc.

PRORAIL

(Group consisting of Stedef, Freyssinet International and Sateba)

16/18 boulevard de la République, 92100 Boulogne-Billancourt, France

Telephone: 620 54 00
Telex: 200 888

Products: Prestressed and two block sleepers; rail fastenings.

RACINE

Racine Railroad Products Inc

PO Box 4003, 1524 Frederick Street, Racine, Wisconsin 53404, USA

Telephone: (414) 637 9681

Products: Portable rail saws; drills and cut-off machines; rail clip applicators and adjusters; electronic gaugers; cribbers; brooms; vibrators; hydraulic power packages; wrenches; spike drivers; spike hole filling material and applicators.

Chairman/Chief Executive Officer: G W Christiansen, Sr
President & Treasurer: Robert C Schrimpf
Executive Vice President & Secretary: George W Christiansen, Jr
Service Engineer: R L Turner

RAILS CO

The Rails Company

101 Newark Way, Maplewood, New Jersey 07040, USA

Telephone: (201) 763 4320
Telex: 138 206

Products: Rail anchors, switch point locks, switch heaters (propane and natural gas), snow detectors.

President: G N Burwell
Export Sales Director: E A Judge

REXNORD

Railway Equipment Division

Export Sales Head Office: 3073 South Chase Avenue, Milwaukee, Wisconsin 53201, USA

Licensee: Noyes Bros Pty Ltd, Frederick Street, St Leonard's, New South Wales, Australia.

Products: Trackliners, switchliners, self-propelled adzers, rail drills, surf-rail grinders, heavy duty rail grinders, utility grinders, spike hammers, hydraulic spike pullers, spike straighteners, tie drills, self-propelled spike pullers, hydraulic power jacks, dun-rite gauging machines, hydra-spikers, line indicators, E-Z lifts, tie spacers, rail gang spikers, X-level indicators, track-inspectors, one-man scanifier inserters and tie removers.

Nordberg Model B Hydra-Spiker featuring dual control system

RMC

Portec Inc, RMC Division

Head Office: PO Box 1888, Pittsburgh, Pennsylvania 15230, USA

Telephone: (412) 782 6000
Telegrams: Ramaco Pittsburg
Telex: 86-6145

Export Sales Office: Portec International, 300 Windsor Drive, Oak Brook, Illinois 60521, USA

General Sales: E J Powell (Pittsburgh)

Products: RMC Hydramatic 16-tool tamper, 8-tool tamper, 4-tool switch/spot tamper, tie master, line master, tie spacer, spike master, auto-spiker, bolt master, rail and joint straightener, anchor master, tie unloader, surfacing and lining devices, ballast distributor and ballast distributor/cleaner, brush cutter, snow blowers typhoon model (delivers 165 mph wind blast—Hurricane Jet Engine Model delivers 650 mph blast), concrete tie clip machine, anchor distributing cart, spike distributing cart, equipment for laying rail and welded rail, tie plate broom, track broom, rail end-hardening machine, rail and fastener spray machine, spot car repair systems and components for freight car and locomotive repair, anchor adjuster, zapper railgang spiker, zapper tie gang spiker, RMC sand blower, RMC line measuring device.

ROBEL

Robel GmbH & Co

Thalkirchnerstrasse 210, 8000 München 75, Federal Republic of Germany

Telephone: 7233011
Telegrams: robelco munchen
Telex: 05-23012

Products: Powered ganger's trolleys with hydraulic tipping platform and crane, trailers, stationary and mobile machines for processing sleepers and rails, equipment for loading and unloading long-welded rails, rail drilling machines, rail saws, power wrenches, rail grinders, hydraulic rail benders, ratchet track jacks and spanners, gauges, automatic track lining machines, portal cranes and so on.

ROLBA

Rolba Co Ltd

Barengasse 29, CH-8039, Zurich, Switzerland

Products: Rotary snowploughs from 10 to 1 000 hp.

RS

Roger P Sonneville

Tour Maine-Montparnasse, 75755 Paris (Cedex 15), France

Telephone: 538 73 20
Telex: Sonevil 260 881 F

Products: Steel and reinforced two block sleepers, elastic insulated fastenings.

RT-W

The Railway Track-Work Company

2381 Philmont Avenue, Bethayres, Pennsylvania, USA

Telephone: (215) 947 7100

Products: Tie handlers, cross grinders, rail drills.
Equipment has been supplied to practically all the railways in the United States and Canada, to The Danish Railways and to the US Government.

SATEBA

262 boulevard St-Germain, 75007 Paris, France

Telephone: 551 59 19/551 67 51
Telex: 200 800 F

Products: Vagneux type prestressed concrete sleepers.

SCHLATTER

Schlatter AG HA

Bandstrasse, CH-8952 Schlieren, Switzerland

Telephone: 01 730 0951
Telegrams: Elektropunkt Schlieren
Telex: 53054

Products: Rail welding equipment, rectifier rail welding and burr-removing plant GAas 80.

Automatic rail-welding and burr-removing plant GAas 80

SECEMM

Société d'Etudes et de Constructions Electriques, Mécaniques et Métallurgiques

15/17 rue Chabrol, 75480 Paris (Cedex 10), France

Products: Track maintenance and inspection equipment.

Road rail locotractor

SECMAFER

Secmafer SA

Chemin des Meuniers, Buchelay, 78203 Nantes, France

Telephone: 092 40 00
Telex: 600815

Products: Complete track relaying trains for mechanised track maintenance and construction; fully automatic relaying gantries; ballast regulators; track assembly and lining machines; fully automatic ballast cleaning and levelling machines; shunting locomotives, etc.
For 20 years Secmafer has been marketing beam and gantry systems for mechanised track maintenance and rehabilitation, consisting of two mobile gantries connected by a longitudinal beam. Power is supplied by 80 hp diesel engines. The gantries are telescopic, allowing work to be carried out beneath overhead wires and in confined areas such as tunnels. The machines can position new track (prefabricated panels or single ties) at a rate of 350 mph.
In 1975 Secmafer built a new type of gantry/beam system which—sold to Iran and Scandinavia—increases track relaying speeds to 600 mph. The 216 M10 gantries and 401 BR beam form a monoblock assembly about 18 m long. As in previous models, they simultaneously dismantle two old track panels of 18 to 24 m in length, and on a second pass relay the corresponding number of new sleepers.
Main differences between the new and old models is that motive power consisting of two diesel-air engines rated at 250 hp each, is installed on the beam instead of the gantry. This, says the maker, leaves two solid but streamlined gantries with all wheels driven—"giving increased adherence to the running rails and a firm guarantee against derailment".

Managing Director: Jean-Jacques Boyer

Agents Abroad: Agents and after sales service throughout the world.

SOCADER

2 rue de Leningrad, 75008 Paris, France

Telephone: 293 56 10
Telex: 641217 SOCADER

Products: Points and crossings.

SOLA

Ing Guido Scheyer

A-6840 Gotzis, Postfach 36, Austria

Products: Track measuring equipment.

SPENO

Speno International SA

22-24 parc Chateau-Banquet, 1211 Geneva, Switzerland

Telephone: 022 31 81 41
            32 04 48
            32 84 07
Telex: 23 921

Products: In-track rail rectification and reprofiling units; wave formation recording car.

SPERRY

Sperry Rail Service
Division of Automation Industries Inc

Head Office: Shelter Rock Road, Danbury, Connecticut 06810, USA

Telephone: (203) 748 9243
Telegrams: SPERRY PRO
Telex: 710/456 6372

President: W J Gallagher
Managing Director: P B Simpson
Vice-President: K E Ault

Australian Office: Automation Sperry Ltd, Rydalmere, New South Wales, Australia

Sperry started rail testing in 1928 and since then have inspected more than 6 400 000 miles of track and detected over 3 500 000 rail defects.
They own and operate a fleet of 26 Induction-Ultrasonic Cars and two All Ultrasonic Cars.
Sperry services has been used by more than 100 North American Railroads as well as many in Europe and Australia.

SPIE BATIGNOLLES
Société SPIE Batignolles (Service Voies Ferrées)

6-8 rue du Quatre Septembre, 92130 Issy-les-Moulineux, France

Products: Track construction and maintenance equipment.

SRS
Swedish Rail System AB SRS

Framnäsbacken 18, PO Box 1031, S-171 21 Solna, Sweden

Telephone: 08-830660
Telegrams: RAILSYSTEM STOCKHOLM
Telex: 104 06 rail s

Products: Concrete sleepers; Hambo rail fastenings; FIST rail fastenings; machines developed for the mechanical mounting of sleepers and Hambo fastenings; gantry cranes; rail threaders; hydraulic track lifters.

Managing Director: Ingvar Svensson

STEDEF

16/18 rue de la République, 92100 Boulogne, France

Telephone: 620 54 00
Telex: Rail 200 888 F

Products: Track materials and equipment including elastic fastenings.

TAMPER
Canron Railgroup
(Division of Canron Group)

2401 Edmund Road, West Columbia, South Carolina 29169, USA

Telephone: (803) 794 9160
Telex: 573423

Division Headquarters:
Australia: 15-19 Marshall Road, Airport West, Melbourne, Victoria 3042
Canada: 171 Eastern Avenue, Toronto, Ontario M5A 1H7
United Kingdom: 14 Elstow Road, Bedford MK42 9LA

Tamper is also represented by Matisa in the following locations:

Federal Republic of Germany: Markgrafenstrasse 1, D-48 Bielefeld
France: 39 rue d'Amsterdam, F-75008 Paris
Italy: Matema SpA, Via Quintino sella 8, 00187 Rome
Japan: PO Box 22, Tokyo 100-91
Spain: c/Aleala No 65, Madrid-14
Switzerland: Case Postale, CH-1001 Lausanne

Agents: Argentina, Brazil, Chile, Columbia, Ecuador, France, India, Mexico, Mozambique, Peru, Uruguay, Venezuela, Spain, Sweden, Indonesia, Japan, Pakistan, Philippines, Turkey.
Tamper Inc., is further represented in most other countries. The names of representatives in the above and other countries can be obtained by contacting the head office.

Products: Tamper (Canron Railgroup) manufactures a complete range of railway track maintenance of way equipment including ballast cleaning and dressing machines, bolting machines, brush cutters and attachments, track lubricators, frog and switch point grinders, track gauges, mobile generator sets, inspection and recording cars, spike drivers, spike pullers, production tampers, switch tampers, spot tampers, tie inserters and removers, track levelling and lining equipment, rail saws, rail drills, rail bolting machines, rail change-out units, track renewal units, snow blowers and a complete contracting service.

Road/rail tamper (manufactured at Matisa (UK) Ltd)

TEMPLETON
Templeton, Kenlya Co

16th and Gardner Road, Broadview, Illinois 60153, USA

Telephone: (312) 865 1500
Telegrams: TEMKENCO, Broadview, Illinois
Telex: 72 1434

Products: Mechanical trip/track jacks, hydraulic rail puller and expanders, hydraulic rerailing system.

Managing Director: Tom Bowden
Chief Sales Director: Byron McBride
Export Sales Director: E A Zimmerman

THERMIT WELDING
Thermit Welding (GB) Ltd

Ferry Lane, Rainham, Essex RM13 9DP, England

Telephone: 76 53322
Telegrams: THERMIT DAGENHAM
Telex: 896296/7

Products: Portable rail welding equipment; welding consumables; insulated rail joints.

Directors: D H Guntermann
M Geiger
D Peters

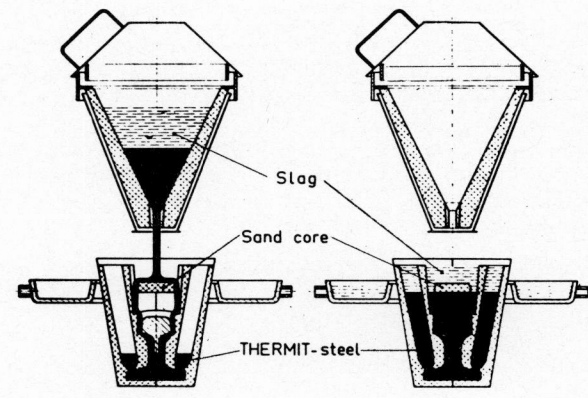

Casting method SKV process

THOS W WARD
Thos W Ward (Railway Engineers) Ltd

Midland Foundry, Osmaston Street, Sandiacre, Nottingham NG10 5AN, England

Telephone: 0602 395252

Products: Switches and crossings in all rail weights and associated fittings.

Chairman and Managing Director: W M Tomlinson
Directors: Eric W Marwood
D V Adams
P B Dodson
D B Knapton

TREC
Tempered Railway Equipment Co

PO Box 20, Park Works, Foley Street, Sheffield S4 7YU, England

Telephone: 0742 20031
Telex: 54103

Products: KTG resilient rail clips.

UNIT RAIL ANCHOR
Unit Rail Anchor Company

2 N Riverside Plaza 2336, Chicago, Illinois 60606, USA

Telephone: (312) 454 1813
Telex: 28-3407

Products: Rail anchors, spring washers.

President: J C Cosgrove

VÖEST-ALPINE AG

A-1040 Vienna, Prinz-Eugen-Strasse 8-10, Austria

Telephone: 656711
Telex: 1 32683

Products: Rails, switches, fishplates, soleplates, steel and plastic sleepers.

VON ROLL

Von Roll Ltd
Machines and Handling Systems Division

CH-3001 Berne, Switzerland

Products: Rail fastenings, points, crossings.

VOSSLOH-WERKE

Vossloh-Werke GmbH

Postfach 1860, 5980 Werdohl 1, Federal Republic of Germany

Telephone: 02392 521
Telegrams: VOSSLOHWERKE
Telex: 08 26 444 vauwe d

Products: Resilient rail fastenings including: Tension Clamp Skl 1 on concrete sleepers with lateral angled guide plates; Tension Clamp Skl 3 on timber sleepers with ribbed plates.

WESTERN-CULLEN-HAYES INC

Western-Cullen Division
Federal Sign and Signal Corporation

2700 West 36th Place, Chicago, Illinois 60632, USA

Telephone: (312) 254 9600
Telegrams: Wesrailsup Chicago
Telex: 25 3206

Products: "Burro" locomotive cranes, rail tongs and threaders, panel track lifters; multiple rail lifters, derails, track liners, rail benders, power drills, hand drills; "Western" (formerly Buda) hydraulic, journal and mechanical jacks, 100 models from 3 to 100 tons capacity; bumping posts, derails, vehicle warning lights.
Western-Cullen-Hayes is a consolidation of the Western Railroad Supply Co, the Cullen-Friestedt Co and the Hayes Track Appliance Co.

Executive Vice President: R L McDaniel
Chief Sales Director: J P Schaefer

WICKHAM

D Wickham & Company Ltd

Crane Mead, Ware, Hertfordshire SG12 9QA, England

Telephone: 0920 2491-7
Telegrams: WICKHAM, Ware
Telex: 81340

Products: A range of self-propelled railway track and overhead line inspection cars, maintenance gang trolleys, and other special-purpose vehicles; also hand and push cars and track tools.

Agencies Abroad: World-wide; addresses available from the company.

Countries Supplied: Angola, Argentina, Australia, Bolivia, Brazil, Burma, Kampuchea, Cameroon, Canada, Chile, China, Colombia, Congo, Republic Costa Rica, Egypt, Guyana, Honduras, India, Indonesia, Iran, Ivory Coast, Jamaica, Kenya, Lebanon, Malawi, New Zealand, Nigeria, Pakistan, Paraguay, Peru, Portugal, Mozambique, Sabah, South Africa, Sudan, Swaziland, Taiwan, Thailand, Trinidad, Uruguay, United Kingdom, Venezuela, Zimbabwe.

WINDHOFF

Rheiner Maschinenfabrik Windhoff AG

Hovestrasse 10, Postfach 1160, 4440 Rheine, Federal Republic of Germany

Products: Overhead line inspection and maintenance car.

ZWICKY

Zwicky Engineering Limited
Sky Hi Division
(A member of Electrical and Industrial Securities Ltd)

Molly Millars Lane, Wokingham, Berkshire RG11 2RY, England

Telephone: 0734 782500
Telegrams: C. F. Taylor, Wokingham
Telex: 848478

Works: Wokingham

Products: Track and wagon hydraulic jacks; jack test rigs; rail benders; rail hole broach units (hand or power operated); air-draulic power packs.

Directors: R F D Reed
P F Drewitt
J J Hobbs
B H Wormsley
Sales Manager: F E Bing

AUTOMATIC FARE SYSTEMS

ALMEX
AB Almex

Sankt Goransgatan 160B, S-112 51 Stockholm, Sweden

Telephone: Domestic— (08) 54 02 20
International— 468 5402 20
Telegrams: MEXAL STOCKHOLM
Telex: 10646 Almex S

Products: Systems and machinery for fare collection and ticket issuing; systems for passenger counting and vehicle location monitoring.

Chairman: Arne Blomgren
Managing Director: Per Wejke
Manager, Sales: Jan-Patrik Reutersward
Sales Administration Manager: Dan Erik Goransson

AUTOMATIC SYSTEMS
Automatic Sytems Ltd

Brussels, Belgium

Products: Full range of gates, turnstiles and special electro-mechanical barriers, card readers, ticket dispensers.

CGA
Compagnie Générale d'Automatisme
(Consortium including Camp, Crouzet, Klein)

9 rue de la Croix-Faubin, 75011 Paris, France

Products: Automatic fare equipment based on the use of microprocessors and using multimode magnetically coded tickets; turnstile gates; automatic ticket vendors.

CONTROL SYSTEMS
Control Systems Ltd

The Island, Uxbridge, Middlesex UBB 2UT, England

Telephone: 89 51255
Telegrams: CONTROL SYSTEMS
Telex: 22225

Products: Electronically-controlled ticket issuing systems assembled from standard modules in configurations designed for individual requirements.

Chairman: F D Penny
Managing Director: E H Mude
Chief Sales Manager: M C S Moore
Export Sales Manager: J B C de Jager

CUBIC TILTMAN LANGLEY
Cubic Tiltman Langley Ltd

177 Nutfield Road, Merstham, Surrey RH1 3HH, England

Telephone: 649 4021
Telex: 946678

Products: Automatic turnstile gates and associated equipment.

CUBIC WESTERN
Cubic Western Data

PO Box 80787, 5650 Kearny Mesa Road, San Diego, California 92111, USA

Telephone: (714) 268 3100
Telegrams: Cubic Ind SDG
Telex: 01 335 1550

Products: Automatic fare collection equipment including entry and exit only barriers, reversible barriers, ticket vendors, change makers, addfare machines (excess fares), ticket analysers, sorter/encoders, coin sorter/counters, control/monitor units, central audit units.

Chairman: Walter J Zable
Managing Director: Walter J Zable
SRVP Marketing: Raymond L de Kozan

Major sales during 1978/79: Hong Kong Mass Transit Corp; Metropolitan Atlanta Rapid Transit Authority; Public Transport Commission of New South Wales; and London Transport.

FIRTH CLEVELAND
Firth Cleveland Limited

GKN House, 22 Kingsway, London WC2B 6LG, England

Telephone: 01-404 5861
Telegrams: Fircleve London
Telex: 24911

HASLER
Hasler Ltd

Belpstrasse 23, CH-3000 Berne 14, Switzerland

Telephone: 031 652111
Telex: 32413 hawe ch

Products: Automatic ticket and money changing machines.

LAAKMANN
H Laakmann K G Kartonfabrik

5620 Velbert-11-Langenberg, Bonsfelderstrasse 1-4, Federal Republic of Germany

Telephone: 02127 3016
Telegrams: LAAKMANN LANGENBERGRHEINLAND
Telex: 08516863

Products: Tickets for automatic machines

Chairman: H W Laakmann
Managing Director: Dr W R Roloff
Chief Sales Director: E Junkersfeld
Export Sales: R Mollenkott

LANDIS & GYR
Landis & Gyr Ltd

Victoria Road, North Acton, London W3 6XS, England

Telephone: 01-992 5311
Telex: 21486

Products: Bank note acceptors, escrow and storage system, coin verifier, recirculatory change systems, etc.

Chairman: G Straub
Managing Director: G E Robertson
Sales Director: L J Croston

NIPPON SIGNAL
Nippon Signal Co Ltd

Head Office: 3-1, Marunouchi 3-chome, Chiyoda-ku, Tokyo, Japan

Telephone: (03) 212 8371
Telegrams: SIGNAL TOKYO
Telex: 222 2178 SIGNAL J

Works: Yono Factory, 13-8, Kamikizaki 1-chome, Urawa City, Japan
Utsunomiya Factory, 11-2, Hiraide Kougyo Danchi, Utsunomiya City, Japan

Associated Companies: Nisshin Industrial Co, Ltd
Nisshin Electrical Installation Co, Ltd

Products: Automatic fare collection equipments such as bill changer, ticket vending machine, gate controller, passenger gate, automatic fare adjusting machine, ticket issuing machine for station staff, data processing machine.

President: Y Hayashi
Chairman: T Akiyama
Chief Sales Director: H Shinohara
Export Sales Manager: K Matsushima

OMRON
Omron Tateisi Electronics Co

Osaka Centre Building, 9F, 68, 4-chome, Kita-Kyutaro-cho Higashi-ku, Osaka, Japan

Telephone: 06 282 2631
Telex: 522 143

Products: Automatic fare collection system including money changers, ticket vendors, ticket checking and collecting gates, ticket issuing machines, automatic fare adjuster, season ticket issuing machines.

TOSHIBA
Toshiba Corporation

1-6, Uchisaiwaicho 1 chome, Chiyoda-ku, Tokyo 100, Japan

Telephone: 03 501 5411
Telex: J 22587, J24344, J 24576 TOSHIBA

Products: Automatic fare collection systems.

TOYO DENKI
Toyo Denki Seizo

7-2, Yaesu 2-chome, Chuo-ku, Tokyo 104, Japan

Telephone: (271) 6372
Telegrams: YOHDEN TOKYO
Telex: YOK (0) 222-4666/7

Products: Season ticket issuing machine, automatic ticket gate equipment.

YARD AND TERMINAL EQUIPMENT

AABACAS
Aabacas Engineering Co Ltd

Kelvin Road, Wallasey, Merseyside L44 7DN, England

Telephone: 051-638 5932
Telegrams: Aabacas Wallasey

Products: Double girder four point lift cranes, suitable for container terminals, manufactured in spans ranging from 25 to 80 ft and in safe working load capacities from 10 to 20 tons.

ABEX
Abex Corporation (Railroad Products Group)

Valley Road, Mahwah, New Jersey 07430, USA

Telephone: (201) 529 3450
Telex: 642415

Products: Yard control systems.

ACEC
Ateliers de Constructions Electriques de Charleroi SA

PO Box 4, B-6000 Charleroi, Belgium

Telephone: 071 44 21 11
Telegrams: VENTACEC CHARLEROI
Telex: 051.227—ACEC Charleroi

Products: Yard control systems.

ACI
ACI Systems Corporation

16950 Westview, South Holland, Illinois 60473, USA

Products: Yard control systems including retarders.

AEG/TELEFUNKEN
AEG/Telefunken Nachrichten und Verkehrstechnik AG Geschaftsbereich Bahnen

Hohenzollerndamm 150, D-1000 Berlin 33, Federal Republic of Germany

Telephone: 030 828-1
Telegrams: ELEKTRONBAHNEN BERLIN
Telex: 1 85 498

Products: Marshalling yard equipment; automatic humping control; control panels and desks; point machines.

AIP
American Identification Products Inc

143-145 58th Street, Brooklyn, New York 11220, USA

Products: Nameplates, signs, card and label holders.

ALLEN
Allen Cranes (Northampton) Ltd

Spencer Bridge Works, Salthouse Road, Northampton NN5 7DT, England

Telephone: 0604 52242
Telex: 311264

Products: Goliath type rail mounted container cranes. Capacity up to 40 tonnes for road to rail transfer operations. Electric overhead travelling container cranes associated with refuse, disposal compaction stations.

ALLIS CHALMERS

Industrial Truck Division, 218000 South Cicero Avenue, Matteson, Illinois 60443, USA

Telephone: (312) 747 5151

Products: Heavy duty sideloaders and front loading forklift trucks suitable for container handling.

AMERICAN HOIST
American Hoist and Derrick Co

63 South Robert Street, St Paul, Minnesota 55107, USA

Telephone: (612) 228 4321

Products: Yard mobile wagon cranes.

AMF-SASIB
AMF-Sasib SpA

Via Di Corticella 87/89, 40128 Bologna, Italy

Products: Yard control equipment and retarders (conventional and computer controlled).

ANSALDO
Transport Systems Division

Via Nicola Lorenzi 8, 16152 Genoa Cornigliano, Italy

Telephone: Genoa 010-41051
Telex: 270098 Ansaldo Genoa

Products: Yard control equipment including retarders.

ASCHE

Botany Estate, Soverign Way, Tonbridge, Kent, England

Telephone: 63377/8/9
Telegrams: CONJACK TONBRIDGE
Telex: 95516

Products: Terminal tractors trailer systems, container handling equipment for lifting and transporting of containers and stuffing of containers.

ASEA
ASEA Mechanical Products Division

Fack S-251 01, Helsingborg, Sweden

Telephone: 042 13 93 00
Telegrams: ASEA Helsingborg
Telex: 72330 (ASEAHA)

Products: Railway terminal gantry cranes for container handling and yard conveyance systems. Together with the Swedish State Railways, ASEA has developed a hydraulic retarder with self-regulating braking power for use in railway marshalling yards. The spiral-type retarder consists essentially of a steel cylinder bolted to the rail. As each wagon wheel passes the retarder it runs on a spiral cam, which under hydraulic resistance, forces the cylinder to rotate one revolution, thus braking the wheel. Each time the cylinder rotates it starts an internal hydraulic pump, which yields an oil flow proportional to the wheel speed. At a preset value the oil flow is shut off and is not released again until the oil pressure corresponds to a braking force of 10 kNm. The wagons will therefore be braked smoothly and precisely. Retarders working according to this principle do not require any measuring device or computer control.
ASEA's hydraulic retarders have aroused considerable international interest and deliveries have been made to the following marshalling yards, among others:

Canada	Vancouver	12
Denmark	Copenhagen	385
German Democratic Republic	Dresden	850
	Halle	280
	Seddin (Potsdam)	135
Italy	Milan	500
Sweden	Helsingborg	725
	Gothenburg	800
	Malmö	750
	Sundsvall	350
Switzerland	Basle	21

The Helsingborg marshalling yard in Sweden is equipped with ASEA hydraulic retarders

ASI
Algemene Sein Industrie BV

Croeselaan 28, 3521 CB Utrecht, Netherlands

Telephone: 030 94 26 46
Telegrams: GENRASIG UTRECHT
Telex: 47455 grasi nl

Products: Yard control equipment and retarders.

BABCOCK & WILCOX
Babcock & Wilcox Espanola

Alda de Recalde 27, Bilbao 9, Spain

Telephone: 415700
Telex: 33776

Products: Container handling cranes with 50 tonnes lift capacity above the spreader.

BASF WYANDOTTE

BASF Wyandotte Corporation (Chemical Specialities Div)

1532 Biddle Avenue, Wyandotte, Michigan 48192, USA

Telephone: (313) 282 3300

Products: General maintenance and overhaul cleaning compounds; degreasers; rust removers; paint strippers; locomotive and car-washing products.

BATTIONI & PAGANI

BP—Battioni & Pagani SpA

Localita Croce, 43058 Sorbolo, Parma, Italy

Telephone: 69157
Telex: 53081

Products: A complete range of side loaders including container handling machines up to 45 ton capacity equipped with telescopic spreaders.

BROWN BOVERI

Brown, Boveri & Company Ltd

Postfach 85, CH-5401 Baden, Switzerland

Telephone: 056 75 11 11
Telegrams: BROWNBOVERI BADENSCHWEIZ

Products: Radio remote control of shunting locomotives.

CLYDE

Clyde Engineering Co Pty Ltd

Factory Street, Granville, PO Box 73, New South Wales 2142, Australia

Telephone: 682 2111
Telex: 21647

Products: Yard control equipment, including retarders.

COLES

Coles Cranes Ltd

Harefield, Uxbridge, Middlesex UB9 6QG, England

Telephone: 420 3777
Telex: 21619

Products: Coles mobile port tower and mobile port cranes equipped with appropriate spreaders for handling freight containers in ports, rail yards and inland container terminals.

CONRAD-STORK

Conrad-Stork BV

(Member of VMF-Stork Group)

Waaderweg 80, PO Box 134, Haarlem, Netherlands

Telephone: 023 319170
Telex: 41048

Products: Ship-shore container cranes, bridge type container stacking cranes and multi-purpose cranes.

COSTAMASNAGA

Costamasnaga SpA

22041 Costamasnaga (Como), Italy

Telephone: 855 192
Telex: 380184

Products: Container handling crane for rail and sea terminals.

COVENTRY CLIMAX

Coventry Climax Ltd

Sandy Lane, Coventry CV1 4DX, England

Telephone: 0203 555355
Telex: 31632

Products: Fork-lift trucks and side loaders.

DICKERTMANN

Gebr Dickertmann Hebezeugfabrik AG

PO Box 2109, Hakenort 47, 4800 Bielefeld 1, Federal Republic of Germany

Telephone: 0521 323021
Telegrams: GEDI D
Telex: 09 32 750 gedi d

Products: Gedi shunting winch type 289; screw jacks type 370 for lifting locomotives, wagons and other heavy loads; lifting equipment for complete trains.

DIMETAL

Dimetal SA

San Fernando de Henares, Apartado Correos 14.485, Madrid 5, Spain

Telephone: 294 6000

Products: Yard control signalling equipment.

ERICSSON

Telefonaktiebolaget L M Ericsson

PO Box 42015, S-126 25 Stockholm, Sweden

Telephone: 08 1900 90
Telegrams: ELLEMSIGNAL
Telex: 10442 LMEJ S

Products: Yard communications and signalling control equipment.

ERNEST HOLMES

Ernest Holmes Division (Dover Corporation)

Railroad Crane Dept, 2505 East 43rd Street, Chattanooga, Tennessee 37407, USA

Telephone: (615) 867 2142

Products: Yard cranes.

FERGUSSON

Alex C Fergusson Company

Spring Mill Drive, Frazer, Pennsylvania 19355, USA

Telephone: (215) 647 3300

Products: Cleaners, sanitisers and lubricants.

GRAEMROSS

Graemross Plant and Equipment Ltd

Automation House, Rosebery Road, Anstey, Leicester LE7 7EJ, England

Telephone: 053 721 4248
Telex: 36183

Products: Equipment for wagon handling including wagon controllers, Hydrabrakes, automatic wheel and buffer stops and squeezer retarders.

GODWIN WARREN

Godwin Warren Engineering Ltd

Emery Road, Bristol BS4 5PN, England

Telephone: 0272 778399
Telex: 449375

Products: Level crossing barrier systems; friction buffers.

Managing Director: A D Parsons

GRS

General Railway Signal Co

PO Box 600, Rochester, New York 14602, USA

Telephone: (716) 436 2020
Telegrams: Genrasig, Rochester, New York
Telex: 978317 GENRASIG

Products: Yard control systems.

President: G E Collins
President, GRS International: A W Gebhardt

HAACON

Josef Haamann Hebe- und Transporttechnik

Josef Haamann Straße 3, D-6982 Freudenberg, Federal Republic of Germany

Telephone: 09375 571
Telex: 689224

Products: Stationary container lifting systems; jacks and winches.

HAUHINCO

Hauhinco Maschinenfabrik G Hausherr Jochums GmbH & Co KG

Zweigertstrasse 28/30, PO Box 10 16 61, D-4300 Essen 1, Federal Republic of Germany

Telephone: 0201 771071
Telegrams: HAUHINCO ESSEN
Telex: 857 834 hinco d

Products: Wagon shunting equipment for classification and sorting tracks at marshalling yards and industrial sites; railway weighing systems.

Buffer-action transport car

HUDSWELL

Hudswell, Clarke & Co Ltd

125 Jack Lane, Leeds LS10 1BT, England

Telephone: 0532 32261
Telegrams: HUNSLT, Leeds
Telex: 55237

Products: Yard control equipment.

HUNGARIAN/CRANE

Hungarian Shipyards and Crane Factory

Budapest, XIII, Vaci ut 202, Hungary

Telephone: 496 370
Telex: 22 5047

Products: Container gantry cranes.

HYSTER

Hyster Europe Ltd

PO Box 54, Berk House, Basing View, Basingstoke, Hampshire RG21 2HQ, England

Telephone: 0256 61171
Telex: Basingstoke 858384

Products: Lift trucks for handling loads from 1 to 37 tonnes, including 20, 30 and 40 ft ISO containers.

IHI

Ishikawajima-Harima Heavy Industries Co Ltd

New Ohtemachi Building, 2-chome 2-1 Ohtemachi, Chiyoda-ku, Tokyo 100, Japan

Telephone: 03 244 6496
Telegrams: IHICO TOKYO
Telex: J22232

Products: Standard dockside container crane; multi-purpose dockside container crane (IHI's Universe); Speed Tainer System.

INTEGRA

Integra Ltd Zurich

Industriestrasse 42, CH-8304 Wallisellen, Switzerland

Telephone: Zurich 830 16 11
Telegrams: INTEGRA WALLISELLEN
Telex: 56022 tegra CH

Products: DOMINO unit construction panels for marshalling yard control systems; alpha-numerical key-board control.

JAMBES/NAMUR

Ateliers de Construction de Jambes-Namur SA

B-5100 Jambes, Belgium

Telephone: 30 18 51
Telegrams: Jamur-Jambes
Telex: 59127 Jamur-Jambes

Products: Shunting machine "Locopulseur Pulso"; transporters; elevators; trucks.

Managing Director: Ma Jean
Chief of sales: André Riquette

Recent sales: During the last two years, Locopulseur Pulso machines were sold to Spanish National Railways (RENFE), French National Railways (SNCF), Kolmex, Poland, Algerian steel companies, Jeumont Schneider, Belgian National Railways (SNCB), Italian State Railways (FS).

Equipment: The Locopulseur Pulso shunting machine is a single-wheel vehicle capable of moving freight cars weighing 160-200 tons on straight level track. It can also move cars in curves, split a line of cars and handle a car on a turntable. Power is supplied by a 490 cc (29.9 in³) Lombardini single-cylinder 4-stroke petrol engine (tyres 602 L and 602 LH) or by a 510 cc Lombardini single-cylinder 4-stroke diesel engine (types 602 LD, 602 LDex, 602 LHD, 602 LHDex). The types LDex and LHDex are explosion proof. The engine is controlled with automatic throttle regulator. The driving wheel has a special profile high-pressure pneumatic tyre to fit over and grip the rail. The 4-speed gearbox is pre-selective; a Fr:1:27 planetry reduction gear is fitted in the wheel hub. Two small side-wheels allow easy handling. The machine is designed to provide, through the driving wheel, the grip and power necessary for propulsion.
On the types 602 L, LD and LDex, the "pushing head" is raised into position by a hand-operated mechanical device. The types 602 LH, LHD and LHDex, incorporate a hydraulic system for raising the head, involving no operator effort.

JONES

Jones Cranes Limited

PO Box 13, Letchworth, Hertfordshire SG6 1LU, England

Telephone: 04626 2360
Telegrams: Jones, Letchworth
Telex: 82112

Products: Mobile, crawler tracked and truck-mounted cranes with lifting capacities up to 45 tons.

KONE

Kone Oy Crane Division

PO Box 6, SF-05801 Hyrinkáá, Finland

Telephone: Hyvinkáä 271
Telegrams: Kone
Telex: 15-122 or 15-175

Products: Container handling dockside cranes, multipurpose cranes, twin container cranes, railway terminal gantry cranes, cargo and container handling gantry cranes, container storage cranes, overhead travelling cranes for containers and other loads.

Kone type CT4 container crane loading for Finnish State Railways
The CT4 has a hoisting capacity of 40 tonnes, lifting height of 9.1 m, hoisting speed of 9 m/min, trolley traversing speed of 20 m/min, crane travelling speed of 90 m/min and slewing speed of 1.5 rpm.

KYOSAN

Kyosan Electric Manufacturing Co Ltd

5-4 Ohtemachi, 1-chome, Chiyoda-ku, Tokyo, Japan

Products: Yard control equipment.

LETOURNEAU

Marathon Letourneau Company
(Subsidiary of Marathon Manufacturing Company, Longview Division)

PO Box 2307, Longview, Texas 75601, USA

Telephone: (214) 753 4411
Telex: MARLET LGV 730 371

Products: Gantry Cranes and the 'Letro Porter' handling equipment for containers and piggyback trailers.

LIEBHERR
Liebherr Container Cranes Ltd

Head Office: Killarney, Co Kerry, Republic of Ireland

Telephone: 064 31511
Telex: 6946

UK Sales Office: Liebherr Great Britain Ltd, Travellers Lane, Welham Green, Hatfield, Hertfordshire, England

Telephone: 3065381
Telex: 261271

Products: Liebherr Container Cranes Ltd manufacture and sell rail mounted container handling cranes for ship-to-shore terminals, railway and trucking terminals and storage yards. Sizes, speeds and safe working loads to meet all international tenders and specific customers' requirements.
Liebherr owns sales and service companies in Austria, France, Federal Republic of Germany, Great Britain, Republic of Ireland, Switzerland, Brazil, Canada, USA and South Africa.

Agents: World-wide on agent and project agreements.

Directors: K Noeke
R Geiler
P Bickel
Secretary: H Brunner

Trackmobile road/rail shunting unit

MARINE ELECTRIC
Marine Electric Railway Products Div, Inc

166 National Road, Edison, New Jersey 08817, USA

Telephone: (201) 287 2810
Telex: 833351

Products: Marshalling yard communication systems.

MITSUBISHI
Mitsubishi Heavy Industries Ltd

5-1 Marunouchi 2-chome, Chiyoda-ku, Tokyo, Japan

Telephone: 03 212 3111
Telex: J22282

Products: Straddle carrier and gantry cranes.

MODERN INDUSTRIES
Modern Industries Inc

101 Outer Loop, PO Box 14287, Louisville, Kentucky, USA

Products: Yard control equipment.

NEI CLARKE CHAPMAN
NEI Clarke Chapman Cranes Ltd

Woodeson House, Rodley, Leeds LS13 1HN, England

Telephone: 0532 579001
Telegrams: Cranes Rodley
Telex: 55159 Cranes Rodley

Products: Container transporter cranes, Goliath transporter cranes, all types of bridge crane and other cranes.

NIPPON SIGNAL
Nippon Signal Co Ltd

Head Office: 3-1 Marunouchi, 3-chome, Chiyoda-ku, Tokyo, Japan

Telephone: 03 212 8371
Telegrams: SIGNAL TOKYO
Telex: 222 2178 SIGNAL J

Works: Yono Factory, 13-8, Kamikizaki 1-chome, Urawa City, Japan
Utsunomiya Factory, 11-2, Hiraide Kougyo Danchi, Utsunomiya City, Japan

Associated Companies: Nisshin Industrial Co, Ltd
Nisshin Electrical Installation Co, Ltd

Products: Automatic freight car control system for marshalling yards, automatic self gravity car-retarder equipment and various indication control boards for passengers.

President: T Hayashi
Chairman: T Akiyama
Chief Sales Director: H Shinohara
Export Sales Manager: R Matsushima

NOORD-NEDERLANDSCHE
Noord-Nederlandsche Machinefabriek BV

ST Vitusstraat 81, PO Box 171, Winschoten, Netherlands

Telephone: 05970 15225
Telex: 53096

Products: Road/rail range of Trackmobile shunting units.

PACECO
Paceco Inc
Subsidiary of Fruehauf Corp

2320 Blanding Avenue, Alameda, California 94501, USA

Telephone: (415) 522 6100
Telex: 335-399

Products: Rubber-tyred and railmounted Transtainers for handling loads up to 50 tons; Universal lifting spreaders; Shiptainer cranes; Portainer pierside handling crane.

PEINER
Peiner Maschinen-und Schraubenwerke AG

3150 Peine, PO Box 1649, Federal Republic of Germany

Telephone: 05171 501
Telegrams: Peinerag Peiner
Telex: 09 2662/63 peined

Products: Peiner container cranes; PPH 32D and 33D straddle carriers; spreaders, harbour and wharf cranes, grabs, scaffolding equipment, nuts and bolts.

PENETONE
Penetone Corporation

74 Hudson Avenue, Tenafly, New Jersey 07670, USA

Telephone: (201) 567 3000

Products: Rolling stock cleaners and equipment.

ROSS AND WHITE
The Ross and White Company

50 West Dundee Road, Wheeling, Illinois 60090, USA

Telephone: (312) 537 0060

Products: Railway sand handling equipment including cleaning, drying, storage and delivery of sand to locomotives; Buck Cyclone Cleaners for rail passenger coach interiors incorporating high-pressure, high volume hand guns; brush scrubbing systems for passenger coach exteriors; pressure washing equipment for locomotives.

SAALASTI
Saalasti Oy

Arinatie 4, 00370 Helsinki 37, Finland

Telephone: 90 557 775
Telex: 124 694

Products: Shunting road/rail tractor.

SAFETRAN
Safetran Systems Corporation

7721 National Turnpike, Louisville, Kentucky 40214, USA

Telephone: (502) 361 1691

Products: Marshalling yard communication systems.

SAXBY

40 rue de l'Orillon, 75011 Paris, France

Telephone: 357 65 30
Telex: 220554F

Products: Route relay interlocking, automatic block systems, centralised traffic control, automatic level-crossing barriers, marshalling yard equipments and retarders, passenger information systems.

SEL
Standard Elektrik Lorenz AG

Hellmuth-Hirth-Strasse 42, 7000 Stuttgart-Zuffenhausen, Federal Republic of Germany

Telephone: 0711 8211
Telex: 7 211-0

Products: Mobile radio equipment; automatic humping control; yard control equipment.

SIEMENS
Siemens Aktiengesellschaft

PO Box 433, Ackerstrasse 22, 33 Brunswick, Federal Republic of Germany

Telephone: 706-1
Telex: 9 52 858

Products: Yard control equipment and retarders.

SMITH BROS & WEBB
Smith Bros & Webb Ltd

Brittannia Works, Arden Forest, Industrial Estate, Alcester, Warwickshire, England

Telephone: 0789 763222
Telex: 338212 CHAMCOM G BRITANNIA

Products: Train washing systems including the Britannia fully-automatic train washer.

British Rail High Speed Train going through a Britannia washer

SOCIMI
Società Costruzioni Industriali Milano SpA

Via S Calimero 3, 20122 Milan, Italy

Telephone: 54 65 251/5
Telex: 310331

Products: Electro-magnetic track brakes.

STEELE
E G Steele & Co Ltd

25 Dalziel Street, Hamilton, Lanarkshire ML3 9AU, Scotland

Telephone: 0698 283765
Telegrams: MOUNTINGS HAMILTON
Telex: 77454

Associated Company: SA Ateliers de Construction de Jambes-Namur, Belgium

Products: Locopulsor shunting machines; wagon mountings.

STOTHERT & PITT LTD

PO Box 25, Bath, Avon BA2 3DJ, England

Telephone: 0225 63401
Telegrams: Stothert, Bath, England
Telex: 44311

Products: Telescopic spreader beams, twin lift spreader beams, automatic or manual fixed length spreader beams; Goliath cranes for container marshalling and for loading on road/rail transport; quayside transporter cranes for loading container vessels; jib cranes for container handling.

STRACHAN & HENSHAW

PO Box 103, Ashton Works, Ashton Vale Road, Bristol BS99 7TJ, England

Telephone: 0272 664677
Telex: 44170

Products: Rotary couplers to enable wagons to be rotated in the dumper for discharging without being uncoupled.

TAKRAF
VVB Takraf

701 Leipzig, German Democratic Republic

Telephone: 7 92 20
Telex: 051577

Products: Container transporters and stackers; side-loading inter transport transfer devices; railway wrecking and general-purpose cranes.

TOSHIBA
Toshiba Corporation

1-6 Uchisaiwai-cho, 1-chome Chiyoda-ku, 1-chome, Tokyo, Japan

Products: Yard control equipment including retarders.

TRANSCONTROL CORPORATION
A subsidiary of Siemens

6 Manhassett Avenue, Port Washington, New York 11050, USA

Telephone: (516) 883 6900

Products: Yard control systems.

Chairman: M Zeiler
Managing Director: John M Pelikan
Chief Sales Director: Gerald Erno
Export Sales Director: Edward Riddett

TYSOL
Tysol Products Inc

919 N Michigan Avenue, Chicago, Illinois 60611, USA

Telephone: (312) 642 4823

Products: Rolling stock cleaning equipment.

UNILOKOMOTIVE
Unilokomotive Ltd (International Division)

46-49 Upper O'Connell Street, Dublin 1, Republic of Ireland

Telephone: 744953, 744958, 743576
Telegrams: LOCOMOTIVE DUBLIN
Telex: 31128, 30559

Production and international sales were taken over from the Hugo Aeckerle Co of Hamburg in 1976 and all sales and production are now controlled from Dublin.

Products: Unilok road/rail switching locomotives for industrial and railway siding work: 17 sizes with tractive effort beginning at 5000 kg and rising to 15 000 kg for loads ranging from 400 to 2 500 tonnes. Uniloks are built for all gauges and all coupler systems. The machines are now in rail service with 55 countries.

UNION SWITCH
Union Switch & Signal Division
American Standard Inc

Swissvale, Pennsylvania 15218, USA

Telephone: (412) 273 4000
Telex: 86 6648

Products: Yard control systems and retarders.

VALMET
Valmet Oy

Tampere Works, PO Box 387, SF-33101 Tampere 10, Finland

Telephone: 931 653 322
Telex: 22-112 valle sf

Products: Straddle carriers of standard and special design and forklift trucks suitable for container handling.

VOLLERT
Hermann Vollert KG Maschinenfabrik

7102 Weinsberg/Wurtt, Federal Republic of Germany

Telephone: 0728 736

Products: Shunting robot offering radio control and high tractive power.

WABCO WESTINGHOUSE

207 boulevard de Souverain, B-1160 Brussels, Belgium

Telephone: 73 60 53

Products: Two-way radio equipment; yard control systems and retarders.

WESTERN-CULLEN-HAYES INC

2700 West 36th Place, Chicago, Illinois 60632, USA

Telephone: (312) 254 9600
Telegrams: WESTRAILSUP
Telex: 25 3206

Products: Yard control equipment including retarders.

Executive Vice-President: R L McDaniel
Sales Director: J D Schaefer

WESTERN INDUSTRIES
Western Industries (Pty) Ltd

PO Box 50857, Randburg 2194, Transvaal, South Africa

Telephone: 48 9740
Telegrams: SUDAMAT Jhb
Telex: 4 22171 SA

Products: Yard control equipment, including retarders.

Chairman: N C Adams
Managing Director: C Potgieter

WESTINGHOUSE
Westinghouse Brake and Signal Co Ltd

Chippenham, Wiltshire, England

Telephone: 0249 4141
Telex: 44941

Products: Yard control equipment.

WHITING
Whiting Corporation

15700 Lathrop Avenue, Harvey, Illinois 60426, USA

Telephone: (312) 468 9400
Telex: 2 53274

Products: Yard control systems; jacks; Hydrabrake car speed retarder; train washing systems; Trackmobile wagon movers; transfer table with remote car movers; rip jacks; interior hopper and tank car washers.

Chairman: T L Hammond
Managing Director: T R E Imblad
Chief Sales Director: H K Waters
Export Sales Director: R E Florine

WINDHOFF
Rheiner Maschinenfabrik Windhoff AG

Hovestrasse 10, Postfach 1160, 4440 Rheine, Federal Republic of Germany

Products: Tele-Tac shunting vehicle with tractive forces up to 25.000 daN, diesel or electrohydraulically driven, control of shunting course and coupling operations by radio or by interlinking with loading programme; marshalling yard equipment; turntables and traversers; screw jacks for lifting locomotives, wagons and other heavy loads; lifting equipment for complete trains.

ZAGRO
Zagro Bahn und Baumaschinen GmbH

D-6927 Bad Rappenau-Grombach, Muhlstrasse 13, Federal Republic of Germany

Telephone: 07266 458
Telegrams: ZAGRO
Telex: 782381

Products: Yard shunting system incorporating special rail mounted chassis powered by an unmodified fork lift truck.

ZONE CONTROLS
Zone Controls Ltd

Building 39, Pensnett Trading Estate, Brierley Hill, West Midlands DY6 7PN, England

Telephone: Kingswinford 270171/2/3
Telegrams: Controls Brihill
Telex: 338359

Products: Railway signalling equipment.

Chairman: F V Walter
Managing Director: E Jones
Export Sales Director: B R Whiting

WORKSHOP EQUIPMENT

ALZMETALL
Machine Tool Factory and Foundry Friedrich & Co

D-8226 Altenmarkt/Alz, Federal Republic of Germany

Telephone: 08621 881
Telex: 05 63124

Products: Drilling machines, boring mills.

ATLAS
Atlas Engineering Company

84 Lillie Road, London SW6 1TN, England

Telephone: 01-385 9323
Telegrams: FABRICANTS LONDON SW6
Telex: 8951847

Products: Mobile railway lifting jack (up to 35 tons capacity); wheel profile truing machines; crank axle turning machines.

Chairman: H J Kemp
Sales Director: P J Hines

During 1978/79 railway machinery was sold to: British Railways, Sudan, Malawi, Sri Lanka, Republic of Ireland, Saudi Arabia, Sweden, Taiwan, Kenya, Tanzania, Canada, Bolivia and Hong Kong.

BAHCO VENTILATION
Bahco Ventilation Ltd

Bahco House, Beaumont Road, Banbury, Oxon OX16 7TB, England

Telephone: 0295 57461
Telex: 837567

Products: Workshop heating systems.

CAM INDUSTRIES
Cam Industries Inc
(Peerless Tool Division)

215 Philadelphia Street, PO Box 227, Hanover, Pennsylvania 17331, USA

Telephone: (717) 637 5988
Telegrams: CAM
Telex: 840-470 (CAM HNVR)

Products: Specialists in direct current electric motor equipment for manufacturing and repair workshops.

Managing Director: Charles A McGough

DICKERTMANN
Gebr Dickertmann Hebzeugfabrik AG

48 Bielefeld, Federal Republic of Germany

Telephone: 6 80 05
Telex: 09 32 750

Products: Spindle lifting jacks, underfloor elevators, bogie lifting platforms, various types of hoist.

HEGENSCHEIDT
W Hegenscheidt

514 Erkelenz/Brd, Postfach 2109, 4800 Bielefeld 1, Federal Republic of Germany

Telephone: 02431 6011

Products: Wheelset reconditioning and wheel boring machinery including a full wheelset reconditioning line.

PROBAT
Probat-Werke

Emmerich/Rhein, Federal Republic of Germany

Telephone: 25 61
Telegrams: PROBAT EMMERICH
Telex: 8 125 154

Products: Spring testing machines.

WAGNER
Gustav Wagner Maschinenfabrik

Postfach 113, 741 Reutlingen, Federal Republic of Germany

Telephone: 07121 2081
Telex: 0729846

Products: Rail sawing and drilling machines.

WINDHOFF
Rheiner Maschinenfabrik Windhoff AG

Hovestrasse 10, Postfach 1160, 4440 Rheine, Federal Republic of Germany

Products: Spindle lifting jacks; hydraulic wheelset and bogie lifts.

YVAC
Yvac Company Inc

Suite 1713, 1 World Trade Center, New York, New York 10048, USA

Telephone: (212) 432 0192
Telegrams: YVACCOMP

Products: Designers and builders of railroad shop facilities.

CONTAINER MANUFACTURERS

ACKERMAN/FRUEHAUF CORP & CO

5600 Wuppertal-Vohwinkel, Ludwig-Richter-Strasse 1-9, Federal Republic of Germany

Telephone: 0202 73 20 81
Telex: 859 1754

Products: Containers for the transport of standard European railway pallets; part of a demountable body system known as Eurotainers.

Chairman: Willi Back
Managing Director: Dietrich Hellmann
Sales Director: Friedhelm Bernhardt
Export Sales Director: Klaus Offermann

ADAMSON CONTAINERS LTD

Station Road, Reddish, Stockport, Cheshire, England

Telephone: 061 432 0211
Telex: 668174

Products: All-steel, all-welded freight containers constructed to ISO standards and conforming to UIC regulations.

Deputy Managing Director: J B Corcoran
General Sales Manager: R A Walker

Agents and licensing agreement: The Company has licensing agreement with Equimental, Portugal.

BEHALTER
Behalter und Apparatebau Erich Wolff GmbH & Co

7100 Heilbronn/Neckar, Lichtenberger Strasse 24, Federal Republic of Germany

Telephone: 07131 10981

Products: ISO tank containers.

BRAIDESI
Costruzioni Meccaniche Braidesi SpA

Via XXIV, Maggio 10, 12042 Cuneo, Italy

Telephone: 43611
Telex: 21366

Products: Open and tilt-type steel dry freight containers.

BREMER
Bremer Waggonbau

Pfalzburger Strasse 251, PO Box 110 109, 2800 Bremen, Federal Republic of Germany

Telephone: 0421 454011

Products: Dry freight and insulated ISO containers.

BRUGEOISE
SA La Brugeoise et Nivelles

B-8201 Saint-Michiels, Belgium

Telephone: 050 330721-51
Telex: 811.22 BNBRGE

Products: General-purpose, insulated and refrigerated containers.

BUDD
The Budd Company

Trailer Division Headquarters, Dowington, Pennsylvania 19335, USA

Telephone: (215) 458 5301

Products: Aluminium, plastic/plywood, refrigerated and insulated containers.

BUTTERFIELD
W P Butterfield Engineers Ltd

PO Box 38, Shipley, West Yorkshire BD17 7HA, England

Telephone: 0274 52244
Telegrams: TANKS SHIPLEY
Telex: 51583

Products: 20 × 8 × 8 ft module size, ISO tank containers for carriage of bulk liquids and gases.

Chairman: M J Bradford
Managing Director: R J Brook
Chief Sales Director: C O Farmer

BSL
Bignier Schmid-Laurent

25 quai Marcel Boyer, BP 205, 94201 Ivry S/Seine, France

Telephone: (1) 680 85 00
Telex: 270615 F

Products: 20, 30 and 40 ft stainless-steel tank containers supplied for all the major leasing companies, operating and shipping lines.

COMET
Comet Corporation

3808 North Sullivan Road, Spokane, Washington 99216, USA

Telephone: (509) 924 4800
Telegrams: Spokane WA
Telex: 32-6358

Products: Dry freight and refrigerated containers supplied to Alaska Railroad.

Chairman: Thoburn C Brown
Executive Vice-President: Bruce G Dykes
Director of Sales: Gene M Stone
Plant Manager: Richard G Webster

CONTAINER SAFE
Container Safe AB

PO Box 5031, S 42105 Vastra Frolunda, Gothenburg, Sweden

Telephone: 292 130
Telex: 21085

Products: 20 and 40 ft ISO containers supplied to Swedish State Railways.

CONTAINERTECHNIK
Containertechnik Hamburg GmbH & Co

2000 Hamburg 20, Heilwigstrasse 75, Federal Republic of Germany

Telephone: 4 60 20 31
Telex: 213571 cthh

Products: Tank containers, standard and non-standard dry freight containers.

CRANE FRUEHAUF
Crane Fruehauf Containers Ltd

Cromer Road, North Walsham, Norfolk, England

Telephone: 06924 3411
Telex: 97366 FRUENWG

Products: Dry freight, insulated and refrigerated containers; Tilt-tainers, container tanks, hopper container tanks to ISO, TIR, Lloyds, ABS and UIC standards.

Chairman: George Malley
Managing Director: Philip Croft
Chief Sales Director: Barry J Fiske

DAVIS
W H Davis & Sons Ltd

St Annes Building, 349 Clifton Drive North, St Annes-on-Sea, Lancashire FY8 2NA, England

Telephone: 0253 729912
Telex: 67641

Products: Multistack 20, 30 and 40 ft dry freight containers.

DORSEY
Dorsey Trailers

Hichman Avenue, Elba, Alabama 36323, USA

Telephone: (205) 897 5711
Telegrams: Elba, Alabama 36323
Telex: 810 744 3110

Products: Piggy-back trailers, vans, chassis.

President: G L Collier
Vice-President, Sales: Joe B DeVane

DURAMIN
Duramin Engineering Co Ltd

Harbour Road, Lydney, Gloucestershire GL15 4EN, England

Telephone: 05944 2371-8
Telex: 43289 DURAMN G

Products: Insulated, refrigerated, temperature controlled, semi-insulated dry freight containers; principal users include British Rail and ACT.

Chairman: P A Bown
Deputy Chairman and General Manager: P B Conolly

EIMAR
Constructora de Equipos Industriales y Marinos, SA

Poligono Industrial de Malpica, Calles A-D, Zaragoza, Spain

Telephone: 299350
Telex: 58163

Products: ISO steel dry freight containers.

FINSAM
Finsam A/S

PO Box 3064, Elinesberg, Oslo 2, Norway

Telephone: 02 441860
Telex: 18050

Products: Containers and refrigerating systems.

FREIGHTER
Freighter Industries Ltd

409 St Kilda Road, Melbourne 3004, Victoria 3004, Australia

Telephone: 03 267 3888
Telex: Escor AA 31148

Products: 20 and 40 ft all-steel containers designed for Australian inter-road/rail transport; operated by Australian National Railways.

FRUEHAUF
Fruehauf Division

10900 Harper Avenue, Detroit, Michigan 48232, USA

Telephone: (313) 267 1000
Telex: 23 5351

Products: All sizes and types of dry freight, insulated and refrigerated tank, platform and open top containers.

FRUEHAUF FRANCE

2 avenue de L'Aunette, 91130 Ris-Orangis, France

Telephone: 943 30 00
Telex: 690 967/691 381

Products: Steel, aluminium GRP plywood dry cargo and refrigerated containers; ventilated bulk flat containers.

Chairman: J Gaschard
International Sales Director: J Richard

GRAAFF
Graaff Kommanditgesellschaft

Postfach 160-180, 3210 Elze 1, Federal Republic of Germany

Telephone: 05124 2041
Telex: 09 27 251

Products: Dry freight, insulated, refrigerated, top loading and tank containers.

GRÄNGES GRAVER
SA Gränges Graver NV

Molenweg 107, B-2660 Willebroek, Belgium

Telephone: (031) 86 71 11
Telex: 31 293

Products: 20, 30 and 40 ft aluminium tilt containers for transporting dry chemicals.

HANSA
Hansa Waggonbau GmbH

2800 Bremen 11, Pfalzburger Strasse 251, Postfach 110 109, Federal Republic of Germany

Telephone: 45 40 11
Telex: 0244423

Products: Dry freight plastics/plywood ISO containers.

HUNGARIAN SHIPYARDS
Hungarian Shipyards and Crane Factory

Budapest XIII, Vaci ut 202, Hungary

Telephone: 200-800
Telex: 22-5047

Products: 20 ft all-steel containers and 20 ft tank containers built to ISO, UIC and TIR standards; production is approved by the Hungarian State Railways (MAV).

LUCHAIRE
Luchaire SA

Département Conteneurs, 180 boulevard Haussmann, 75008 Paris, France.

Telephone: 766 51 44
Telegrams: CHAIRELU - Paris
Telex: 650372

Products: 20 and 40 ft ISO containers as well as special units for road and rail use; French National Railways (SNCF) are among the principal users.

Chairman: J J Wilmot-Roussel
Director: J L Quilhot
Manager: P Giraud

McARDLE
Thomas McArdle Ltd

Industrial Estate, Coe's Road, Dundalk, Louth, Republic of Ireland

Telephone: 042 35533
Telex: 4572

Products: Full range of containers to ISO standards and conforming to UIC requirements.

MITSUBISHI
Mitsubishi Heavy Industries Ltd

5-1 Marunouchi 2-chome, Chiyoda-ku, Tokyo, Japan

Telephone: 03 213 3111
Telex: J22443

Products: Aluminium and plywood dry freight and refrigerated containers.

MORTEO SOPREFIN
Morteo Soprefin SpA

Corso Andrea Podesta 8, 16128 Genoa, Italy

Telephone: 593261
Telex: 27570 Morteo

Products: Dry freight and refrigerated all-steel containers to ISO and UIC standards.

NORFRIG A/S

Hvam, DK-8620 Kjellerup, Denmark

Telephone: 06 66 73 00
Telex: 66 299 nfrig

Products: Insulated and refrigerated containers.

PACTON
Pacton BV

PO Box 50, Strangeweg 1, Ommen, Netherlands

Telephone: 05 291 15 0 0
Telex: 42199

Products: Dry freight, tank and special-purpose containers.

SNAV
Société Nouvelle des Ateliers de Vénissieux

4ter avenue Hoche, 75008 Paris, France

Telephone: 766 04 10
Telex: 650337

Products: Steel, aluminium, plywood containers to ISO, UIC and TIR standards.

SOUTH AFRICAN RAILWAYS
South African Railways and Harbours Administration

Paul Kruger Building, Wolmarans Street, Johannesburg, South Africa

Telephone: 713 2100
Telegrams: SAR Johannesburg
Telex: 8 6537

Products: ISO type three and six-metre containers for dry freight for own use only.

Director General: Dr J G H Loubser

STEADMAN
Steadman Containers Ltd

150 Glidden Road, Brampton, Ontario L6W 3L2, Canada

Telephone: (416) 457 9700
Telex: 06-97536

Products: Containers, side lift container handlers.

Director: W L Serenbetz
President: P Schwartz
Vice-President: D McGuire
Controller: C D Cowley

STRICK
Strick Corporation

260 New York Drive, Fort Washington, Pennsylvania 19034, USA

Telephone: (215) 628 8000
Telex: 84-3412 Strick FTWN

Products: Full range of dry freight containers together with insulated and refrigerated units.

Chairman: Sol Katz
Managing Director: Martin Baehman
Chief Sales Director: William T Meyrick
Export Sales Director: Frank Katz

THYSSEN

Thyssen Behalter und Logertechnik

Postfach 20, 5758 Frondenberg-Langschede, Federal Republic of Germany

Telephone: 02378 3031 821
Telex: 0 858 7965

Products: Full range of dry freight, refrigerated and insulated containers conforming to ISA, ASA, UIC, TIR and DIN standards.

TOKYU

Tokyu Car Corporation

Container Sales, Yaesu-Mitsui Building, 7-5 chome, Yaesu, Chuo-ku, Tokyo, Japan

Telephone: 272 7061
Telex: 0222 2020 TCCTdk J

Products: Steel and GRP/plywood dry freight and refrigerated containers.

TRAILOR

Trailor SA

3 Route No 10, Coignières, BP49, 78311 Maurepas Cédex, France

Telephone: 050 61 26
Telex: 69.896f

Products: Bulk containers.

WEW

Westerwälder Eisenwerk Gerhard GmbH

5241 Weitefeld/Sieg, Federal Republic of Germany

Telephone: 02743 1071
Telex: 0875323

Products: Tank containers for the transport of hazardous and non-hazardous liquids, granular bulk solids and gases.

YORK

York Trailer Co Ltd

Northallerton, North Yorkshire DL7 8UE, England

Telephone: 0609 3155
Telex: 58600

Products: All-steel containers, kangaroo TIR trailers.

Chairman: F W Davies
Managing Director: W Driscoll
Chief Sales Director: J T Peck
Export Sales Director: G J Brant

Range:

	EG10	EG20		EG30	
Length (nominal) ft in	10 0	20 0	20 0	30 0	30 0
Height (nominal) ft in	8 0	8 0	8 6	8 0	8 6
Weight-gross rated lb (kg)	22400 (10160)	44800 (20320)	44800 (20320)	56000 (25400)	56000 (25400)
Weight-standard container lb (kg)	2940 (1340)	4274 (1936)	4513 (2045)	6640 (3012)	7065 (3200)
By weight lb (kg)	19460 (8820)	40526 (18384)	40287 (18275)	49360 (22388)	48935 (22200)
By cube ft³ (m³)	525 (15)	1092 (31)	1166 (33)	1658 (47)	1772 (50)
Overall length ft in (mm)	9 9¾ (2991)	19 10½ (6058)	19 10½ (6058)	29 11¼ (9126)	29 11¼ (9126)
Inside length ft in (mm)	9 9¼ (2826)	19 4 (5893)	19 4 (5893)	29 5 (8966)	29 5 (8966)
Overall height ft in (mm)	8 0 (2438)	8 0 (2438)	8 6 (2590)	8 0 (2438)	8 6 (2590)
Inside height* ft in (mm)	7 3½ (2223)	7 3½ (2223)	7 9½ (2375)	7 3½ (2223)	7 9½ (2375)

Range:

	EG40	EG40GN	EG40H
Length (nominal) ft in	40 0	40 0	40 0	40 0
Height (nominal) ft in	8 0	8 6	8 6	9 6
Weight-gross rated lb (kg)	67200 (30480)	67200 (30480)	67200 (30480)	67200 (30480)
Weight-standard container lb (kg)	7635 (3458)	7815 (3545)	8288 (3759)	8932 (4050)
By weight lb (kg)	59565 (27022)	59185 (26935)	58912 (26721)	58268 (26430)
By cube ft³ (m³)	2225 (63)	2377 (67)	2377 (67)	2680 (76)
Overall length ft in (mm)	40 0 (12192)	40 0 (12192)	40 0 (12192)	40 0 (12192)
Inside length ft in (mm)	39 5⅜ (12024)	39 5⅜ (12024)	39 5⅜ (12024)	39 5⅜ (12024)
Overall height ft in (mm)	8 0 (2438)	8 6 (2590)	8 6 (2590)	9 6 (2895)
Inside height* ft in (mm)	7 3½ (2223)	7 9½ (2375)	7 9 (2362)	8 9½ (2680)

Dimensions apply to units built to ISO standards.
*Dimensions with standard corrugated self-drain roof.
Width: All models 8' 0'' (2438 mm) overall, 7' 8'' (2337 mm) inside.
Door opening: 7' 8'' (2337 mm) wide x container overall height minus 1' (305 mm).

Agents
Netherlands: York Trailer Europa BV, Maxwellstraat 27, 3316 GP Dordrecht, Rotterdam. Telephone: 078 179500. Telex: 29210.
Canada: York Transport Equipment Ltd, 10 Kelfield Street, Rexdale, Ontario M9W 5A2. Telephone: (416) 245 8980. Telex: (807) 21 06 989358.
USA: Anthony York Co, 1807 North Bloomington Avenue, Illinois 61364. Telephone: (230) 404 391.

Licensees: Container Manufacturer Licensees: Interaco Industrias, Metallicas SARL, Rua Jose Estevao, 83 E 1 DTO, Lisbon, Portugal. Telex: 18471. Jindo Industrial Co Ltd, 371-36 Garibong-Dong, Youngdeungpo-ku, Seoul, Republic of Korea. Telex: K 26541.

INTERNATIONAL
RAILWAY ASSOCIATIONS AND AGENCIES

INTERNATIONAL

INTERNATIONAL UNION OF RAILWAYS (UIC)

Union Internationale des Chemins de Fer

Offices: 14-16 Rue Jean-Rey, 75015 Paris, France

Telephone: 273 01 20
Telex: 270835 Unionfer

Directors and Officers
President (Vice-Minister German State Railways): M. G. de Bruin
Secretary General: B. H. de Fontgalland
Chief Executive Officers: P. Ballet, M. K. Ebeling

The UIC was founded in 1922. The object is the standardisation and improvement of railway equipment and operating methods, in particular international traffic. All principal European railways are members and also a considerable number of non-European countries. The UIC has a number of specialist agencies: the Office for Research and Experiments (ORE) for the pooling of technical research; a publicity centre for preparing publicity campaigns; the Public Relations Centre, for ensuring that the railways' interests are maintained; the Documentation Bureau, for the exchange of information between railways (publishes ten times a year *A Selection of International Railway Documentation* in English, French, German and Spanish, jointly with the International Railway Congress Association); the Statistics Bureau, which publishes *Annual Summary of Monthly Statistics*; the Railway Film Bureau, enabling information to be exchanged in this field and the Central Clearing House in Brussels, which is responsible for settling accounts between railways.

Office de Recherches et d'Essais—ORE
Oudenaard 60, 3513 EV Utrecht, Netherlands (Tel: 314646)

Bureau Central de Compensation—BCC
B-1060 Brussels, 49A ave Fonsny, Section 31, Belgium

Bureau International du Film du Chemin de Fer—BFC
F-75009 Paris, 88 rue Saint-Lazare, France

Bureau de Documentation—BD
Bureau de Statistiques—BS
14 rue Jean-Rey, 75015 Paris, France

INTERNATIONAL RAILWAY CONGRESS ASSOCIATION

(Association Internationale du Congrès des Chemins de Fer)

Offices: 85 rue de France, 1070 Brussels, Belgium

Telephone: 522 62 83

Management Committee
President: G. Vanhee, Director General Belgian National Railways Company
Vice-Presidents: P. Lazarus, Deputy Secretary, Transport Industries and International Policy, Department of Transport; A. D. Karetnikov, Director of the Railway Scientific Research Institute of the USSR
Secretary General: R. Squilbin, Deputy Director of Belgian National Railways Company

Established in 1885 the IRCA exists to promote the development of railway transport by all possible means. It holds periodic congresses and general or specialised meetings, supplying information on specific problems to members and publishing technical reviews.
The Association bulletins are published in English, French, German, Russian and Spanish.

INTERNATIONAL UNION OF PUBLIC TRANSPORT (UITP)

Head Office: 19 avenue de l'Uruguay, B-1050 Brussels, Belgium

Telephone: 673 33 25 and 673 04 66

President: R. Belin, Paris
Vice-Presidents: K. N. Andersen, Copenhagen
R. Bennett, London
H. L. Fisher, New York
M. Hansen, Brussels
K. Klopotov, Moscow
R. Gutknecht, Aachen
C. G. Leeuwen, Rotterdam
General Secretary: Andre J. Jacobs

This association established in 1885 pools information and experience of urban and interurban public transport undertakings, operating buses, tramways, trolleybuses, metropolitan and light railways for joint study and research and promotes the technical and economic development of the industry.
Publications include the reports of congresses, technical papers, and a periodic review and a bibliographical card index. They are published in English, French and German.

CENTRAL OFFICE FOR INTERNATIONAL RAILWAY TRANSPORT (OCTI)

Office: Gryphenhübeliweg 30, 3000 Berne, Switzerland

Telephone: (031) 43.17.62
Telegrams: 'OCTI Berne'

Chairman of Administrative Committee: Peter Trachsel
Director: Hans P Amberg
Vice-Director: Pierre Baudry

INTERCONTAINER

Company for International Transport by Transcontainers
(Société Internationale pour le Transport par Transcontainers)

Margarethenstrasse 38, CH-4008 Basle, Switzerland

Telephone: 22 25 25
Telegrams: Transcofer Basle
Telex: 62 298

General Manager: G. Fléchon
Manager, Operating Dept.: R. Bouvry
Manager, Finance and General Affairs: M. Bussy
Manager, Commercial Service: W. Nitsche
Manager, Technical Service: G. Sempio
Manager, Marketing Services: G. L. E. M. Koopman
Manager, Organisation and Data Processing Department: L. Février

The national railway administrations of the following 24 European countries participate in the Company for International Transport by Transcontainers known as INTERCONTAINER:
Austria, Belgium, Bulgaria, Czechoslovakia, Denmark, Finland, France, Germany (DB), Germany (DR), Greece, Hungary, Republic of Ireland, Italy, Luxembourg, Netherlands, Norway, Poland, Portugal, Romania (through a co-operation agreement), Spain, Sweden, Switzerland, United Kingdom, Yugoslavia.

SCOPE OF OPERATIONS
As common commercial agency of its member railways, Intercontainer's task is to market international container transportation. Essentially, this consists of grouping consignments to form large, regular traffic flows. Individual railways can then reduce their unit costs, which in turn results in keener prices for Intercontainer. The price advantage is passed on by Intercontainer to its customers in proportion to the scale and regularity of their traffic.
For the first time in their history, the European railways have granted a jointly-owned subsidiary far-reaching commercial powers. A first step has thus been achieved towards a "European Railway".
Intercontainer is represented in each country, either by the relevant railway itself or through a firm appointed by it.

RAIL CONTAINER SERVICES
The transportation services provided by Intercontainer fall into two categories:
1. Movement of containers individually, or in small groups by TEEM- and TEC-Services.
2. Specialised container trains; TECE services.
3. Company trains for individual customers.

Individual container movements
The facilities provided are extremely diverse. All the specialised container terminals, of which nearly 700 are already operational throughout the European rail network, can be served, the concentration of traffic upon these terminals being the key to the improvement of service quality. So, while the majority of freight stations and private sidings throughout Europe are open to Intercontainer consignments, preference is naturally given to development of the flows between the natural centres of concentration.
Within the catchment area of each terminal, Intercontainer can usually provide a range of road collection and delivery services, either with vehicles of its local representative or of the national railway concerned. Customers, too, have direct access to the terminals with their own road vehicles.
To obtain the best possible transit times, individual container consignments and small groups are normally carried on the widely developed network of TEEM (Trans-Europ-Express Marchandises) and TEC (Transports Européens Combinés) trains.

SPECIALISED CONTAINER TRAINS (TECE):
These services operate along routes with a regular large scale volume of traffic. They offer the following advantages:
rapid, regular and reliable transit, by direct terminal—terminal container trains
no shunting, the transit-time being therefore considerably reduced
often no formalities at frontiers
mainly customs clearance at the terminals
movement between well equipped terminals where Intercontainer road-services are available, when required
competitive rates

At present, the following trains of this type are regularly in operation:
Amsterdam/Rotterdam/Basle/Milan and vice versa.
Zeebrugge/Antwerp-Basle and vice versa.
Antwerp/Zeebrugge-Turin-Novara-Rivalta Scrivia-Milan and vice versa.
Dunkirk-Turin-Milan-Rivalta Scrivia and vice versa, 5 times a week.
Paris-Novara-Milan and vice versa.
Amsterdam-Rotterdam-Antwerp-Zeebrugge and vice versa.
Paris-Madrid and vice versa.
Paris-Barcelona and vice versa.
Hamburg-Copenhagen and vice versa.
Hamburg-Jutland and vice versa.
Paris-Köln-Düsseldorf and vice versa, connections to Düsseldorf, Hannover, Bielefeld, Hamburg etc on the German side, on the French side to Nantes, Bordeaux, Toulouse, Marseilles, Lyons etc.
Paris-Antwerp/Rotterdam and vice versa, both services with connections to Nantes, Bordeaux, Toulouse, Marseilles, Lyons etc.
Paris-Turin-Novara-Milan and vice versa, 5 times a week.
Göteborg-Oslo and vice versa, with connections to Western Norway.
Rotterdam-Le Havre, and vice versa.

These services form a basic network of special container trains, connecting the most important industrial centres in Europe.

COMPANY TRAINS
In addition, trains for single customers operate regularly on different routes under similar conditions to TECE trains and at particularly favourable rates. If regularity and traffic volume are suitable, anybody can profit from this possibility. For special traffics of sufficient volume, extra trains can be arranged on demand.

TERMINALS
Intercontainer does not operate its own terminals, but uses those run by railways or private companies, of which over 400 are now in operation.

CONTAINERS AND WAGONS
Intercontainer does not own any containers at the moment, but on some routes for example, Western Germany-Spain, it places a number of hired containers at the disposal of its customers in order to develop its traffic in the pure continental market. Also some of its representatives have containers available, under interchange agreements for international traffic.
Intercontainer owns 1 352 specialised 60 ft (18.5 m) wagons built for its own use and 100 80 ft articulated wagons of a completely new type.

TRAFFIC

The Intercontainer traffic has increased progressively since the Company began operations in May 1968, as is shown by the following table:

Year	Number of containers in TEU (20 ft equivalent units)	Compared to the year before
1972	327 969	+ 28%
1973	435 865	+ 23%
1974	456 511	+ 5%
1975	414 753	− 9%
1976	493 022	+ 19%
1977	577 641	+ 17%

Intercontainer transports all ISO standard containers (20, 30, 40 ft); in addition containers diverting slightly from the norms (European inland containers, swap bodies, 35 ft maritime containers) are also carried.

REPRESENTATIVES

Austria
Generaldirektion der Oesterreichischen Bundesbahnen (OeBB)
Kommerzielle Direktion, Abteilung IV/5, Gauermanngasse 4, A-1010 Vienna
Telephone: (222) 5650 ext 5823, 5329
Telex: 12104

Belgium
Société Anonyme Interferry
Zomerweg 26, B-2030 Antwerp
Telephone: (31) 416950
Telex: 32529

Bulgaria
Bulgarische Staatseisenbahnen (BDZ)
ul. Iwan Wazow 3, BG-Sofia
Telephone: 843 43 34, 843 44 34
Telex: 22423

Czechoslovakia
SKD-Intrans
Krisilova 2
CS 18686 Prague
Telephone: 21 24
Telex: 121738

Denmark
Danske Statsbaner (DSB)
Generaldirektoratet Godssalgskontoret, Sølvgade 40, DK-1349 Copenhagen K
Telephone: 14 04 00 Ext 3429
Telex: 22225

Finland
Valtionrautatiet Rautatiehallitus (VR)
Betriebsabeilung, Vilhonkatu 13, SF-00101 Helsinki 10
Telephone: 717711
Telex: 1230151

France
Compagnie Nouvelle de Cadres (CNC)
BP No. 55, 20, rue Hector Malot, F-75560 Paris Cédex 12
Telephone: (1) 345 32 20 — (1) 346 12 05
Telex: 22500 — 21494

Germany (DB)
Transfracht GmbH
Gutleutstrasse 160/164, D-6 Frankfurt (Main)
Telephone: (611) 23 03 51
Telex: 41 45 45

Germany (DR)
Deutsche Reichsbahn DDR-Cont
Otto-Grotewohl-Strasse 25, DDR-108 Berlin
Telephone: (31) 220 01 21
Telex: 173 096

Greece
Organisation des Chemins de Fer Hélléniques SA(CH), Direction Commerciale
Bureau de Représentation Intercontainer, 1 rue Karolou GR-Athens 107
Telephone: (21) 524 4822
Telex: 215 187

Hungary
Mavtrans-MAV
Szàllitmànyozasi Iroda, Deak Fernc-ùtca, 23, H/Budapest V
Telephone: 38 23 24
Telex: 225343

Ireland, Republic
Coras Iompair Eireann (CIE)
Office of the Commercial Manager,
Transport House, EIR-Dublin 1
Telephone: 741857
Telex: 5695

Iran
Perse Transport Bar (PTB)
International Forwarding Co Ltd
165 Takhte Tavous Ave, PO Box 1197
Telephone: 859 050 51 52
Telex: 212 626

Italy
INT
Via Savoia 19, I-00198 Rome
Telephone: (6) 861 851

Luxembourg
Société Nationale des Chemins de Fer Luxembourgeois (CFL)
Service Commercial, Place de la Gare 9, L-Luxembourg
Telephone: (352) 49901
Telex: 288

Netherlands
NV Nederlandse Spoorwegen (NS)
Dienst van Commerciele Zaken
Ie Afdeling, Sectie Containers, Moreelsepark 1, NL-Utrecht
Telephone: (30) 35 45 52
Telex: 70 131

Norway
Norges Statsbaner (NSB)
Hovedadministrasjonen, Salsavdelingen, Storgaten, 33, N-Oslo 1
Telephone: (2) 20 95 50 ext 2147
Telex: 11168

Poland
Przedsiebiorstwo Spedycji Krajowej Zarzad (PSK)
ul. Ordona 2a, PL-01237 Warsaw
Telephone: 36 69 23

Portugal
Companhia dos Caminhos de Ferro Portugueses (CP)
Commercial Department, Gabinete do Trafego de Contentores,
Rua Vitor Cordon 45, P-Lisbon 2
Telephone: 366935, 367236
Telex: 12382

Spain
RENFE
Trafico Intermodales
Direccion Comercial, Paseo del Rey 32, E-Madrid 8
Telephone: 247 67 52, 248 02 71
Telex: 27632

Sweden
Statens Järnvägar
Commercial Dept., Mäster Samuelsgatan 70, S-10550 Stockholm C
Telephone: (8) 226420 ext. 4316
Telex: 1410

Switzerland
Chemins de fer Fédéraux Suisses
Service Commercial, Trafic Marchandises, Mittelstrasse 43, CH-3000 Bern
Telephone: (31) 60 11 11
Telex: 32500

United Kingdom
(Harwich Terminal)
British Railways Board
Shipping & Int. Services Division
163-203 Eversholt Street, London NW1 1BG
Telephone: 01-387 4776, ext 2029
Telex: 269 295

(Freightliner Terminal)
Freightliners Limited
43 Cardington Street, London NW1
Telephone: 01-388 0611, ext 3324
Telex: 24743

Yugoslavia
Zajednica Jugoslovenskih Zeleznica (JZ)
Zastupnistvo Intercontainera, Nemanjina 6/II YU-11000 Belgrade

INTERFRIGO

(International railway-owned company for refrigerated transport)

General Management: Wettsteinplatz 1, PO Box 341, CH-4005 Basle, Switzerland
Registered Office: 85 rue de France, Brussels, Belgium

Telegrams: Interfroid Basle
Telephone: 26 33 33
Telex: 62 231 and 63 372

Board of Directors:
Chairman, Deputy General Manager, French National Railways: Mr. Dupuy
Director General, Italian State Railways: Mr. Talamanca
Commercial Manager of The Netherlands Railways Company: Mr. Boender
General Manager, Swiss Federal Railways: Mr. Wellinger
Members
  Manager of the Economic Department of Danish State Railways: Mr. Jenstrup
  General be vollmächtigter des Vorstands, German Federal Railways: Mr. Scotland
  General Manager, Swiss Federal Railways: Mr. Wellinger
  Chief Freight Manager, British Railways Board: Mr. Sanderson
  Manager, Belgium State Railways: Mr. Gatez
Secretary
  Legal Adviser to Belgian State Railways: Mr. Demanche
Auditors
  Financial Manager of Swiss Federal Railways: Mr. Diemant
  Ministerial Adviser to the General Management of German Federal Railways: Mr. Eiermann
  Chief Financial Inspector of Belgian State Railways: Mr. Duchêne
  Manager of the Construction Department of Italian State Railways: Mr. Monopoli
General Management
  General Manager: Mr. Gritz
  Organisation and Methods Manager: Mr. Carlier
  Technical Manager: Mr. Cresti
  Commercial Manager: Mr. Klaassen
  Operating Manager: Mr. Schick
  General Studies Manager: Mr. Bombois
  Data Processing Manager: Mr. Gatez

Registered Office: 85, rue de France—Brussels
General Management: 1, Wettsteinplatz—Basle

In 1978 the total number of ton-kms of traffic was 3 950 million. This figure is 8.5 per cent lower than in 1977.
After having achieved highly satisfactory results with a steady upward trend in the first 24 years of its existence, followed by a slight drop in traffic for three years and a considerable increase in 1977, INTERFRIGO, which was founded on 24 October 1949, again experienced a decline in its total traffic which fell in 1978 to its 1970 level.

Year	Ton-kms loaded (in millions)	Percentage change in relation to preceding year	Index (1974 = 100)
1970	3 967	+12.8%	92.0
1971	4 209	+6.1%	97.7
1972	4 294	+2.0%	99.6
1973	4 468	+ 4.1%	103.7
1974	4 310	− 3.5%	100.0
1975	4 266	− 1.0%	99.0
1976	4 054	− 5.0%	94.1
1977	4 318	+ 6.5%	100.2
1978	3 950	− 8.5%	91.6

This decrease is attributable mainly to refrigerator wagon traffic, the mainstay of the Company's activity. The other areas of activity, in mechanically refrigerated wagons and containers, showed a marked expansion. The decline in refrigerator wagon traffic is principally due to the increasingly keen competition over both long and medium distances: exports of fruit and fresh vegetables were impaired by poor weather conditions, principally in Italy and Hungary. The market difficulties resulting from currency fluctuations also adversely affected many traditional traffics. The reforms introduced on 1 July 1975 in agreement with the member administrations have had favourable effects, although these have been somewhat impaired by the persistent monetary upheavals that took place during 1978.

Traffic in refrigerated wagons

General remarks

The number of ton-kms loaded, which in 1978 was 3 794 million as against 4 185 million in 1977, showed a decline of 9.3 per cent in actual traffic. There were further diminutions in the number of refrigerator wagons loaded, which fell from 244 217 in 1977 to 225 843 in 1978, and in the number of tons carried, which fell by 8.1 per cent from 3 056 995 in 1977 to 2 809 802 in 1978.

The average load per wagon was virtually the same, with 12.4 tons in 1978 compared with 12.5 tons in 1977.

Finally the average distance travelled per ton decreased slightly from 1 369 km in 1977 to 1 350 km in 1978.

When evaluating the results, allowance should be made for the productive activity of the wagons on long-term rental for seasonal domestic transport (which amounted to 69 950 days of use as against 70 350 in 1977) and is not apparent in the statistics.

	1975	1976	1977	1978
Number of shipments	253 228	235 649	244 217	225 843
Total number of tons carried (thousands)	3 077	2 973	3 057	
Average load carried per wagon (tons)	12.2	12.6	12.5	12.4
Total number of ton-kms (million)	4 203	3 968	4 185	3 794

Variations in traffic at point of departure

a. Traffic on the increase (number of tons carried)

Germany (GFR)	+ 17 173 = + 6.4%	(Bananas, apples and pears, dairy products)
Spain	+ 12 461 = + 33.3%	(Citrus fruit, peaches)
Norway	+ 3 139 = + 34.0%	(Fresh fish)
France	+ 2 138 = + 0.8%	(Peaches, apples and pears, fruit, cauliflowers, tomatoes)

There were also increases in traffic from Luxembourg with + 1 165 tons (potatoes), Germany (GDR) with + 831 tons (citrus fruit, beverages) and Great Britain with + 201 tons (potatoes).

b. Traffic on the decrease (number of tons carried)

Italy	− 141 865 = − 12.1%	(Apricots, citrus fruit, bananas, apples, pears, plums, carrots, cabbages, tomatoes, potatoes, industrial products)
Greece	− 29 765 = − 20.0%	(Peaches)
Netherlands	− 23 246 = − 17.3%	(Fresh meat products, frozen meat)
Bulgaria	− 22 206 = − 9.3%	(Apples and pears, beverages)
Belgium	− 21 604 = − 28.9%	(Bananas, frozen meat)
Romania	− 18 672 = − 7.7%	(Vegetables, preserves, foodstuffs)
Denmark	− 8 651 = − 10.8%	(Potatoes, fresh and frozen fish, foodstuffs, frozen meat)
Sweden	− 3 906 = − 25.2%	(Apples and pears, frozen meat and fish)
Yugoslavia	− 3 624 = − 9.5%	(Grapes, fresh vegetables, potatoes)
Switzerland	− 3 424 = − 14.5%	(Apples and pears, cheese)
Austria	− 3 250 = − 21.0%	(Potatoes)
Hungary	− 2 601 = − 1.2%	(Apricots, apples and pears, cabbages, salad, fresh meat, foodstuffs)

A decrease was also recorded in traffic from Poland with −1 564 tons (foodstuffs).

Variations in traffic at the point of arrival

a Traffic on the increase (number of tons carried)

Hungary	+ 21 471 = + 51.5%	(Citrus fruit and pineapples foodstuffs, beverages)
Austria	+ 14 951 = + 10.1%	(Bananas, peaches, apples and pears, grapes, misc. fruit, cauliflowers, frozen meat and poultry)
Czechoslovakia	+ 10 388 = + 4.2%	(Bananas, peaches, meat products, beverages)
Yugoslavia	+ 7 632 = + 21.8%	(Citrus fruit and pineapples, fresh and frozen poultry and game)

There was also an increase in traffic to Spain with +2 104 tons (apples and pears, frozen products) and to Greece with +1 297 tons (bananas).

b. Traffic on the decrease (number of tons carried)

France	− 141 869 = − 33.5%	(Citrus fruit and pineapples, peaches, apples and pears, potatoes, industrial products)
Italy	− 39 250 = − 17.5%	(Bananas, fresh vegetables, potatoes, fresh and frozen meat)
Poland	− 31 332 = − 21.1%	(Citrus fruit and pineapples, butter, fresh and frozen poultry and game, foodstuffs, frozen meat)
Germany (GDR)	− 28 080 = − 10.6%	(Apples and pears, carrots, tomatoes, preserves, frozen meat)
Germany (GFR)	− 23 576 = − 3.5%	(Citrus fruit and pineapples, peaches, cabbages fresh vegetables, preserves)
USSR	− 15 961 = − 8.5%	(Beverages)
Sweden	− 7 059 = − 6.2%	(Citrus fruit and pineapples, apples and pears, cabbages)
Belgium	− 4 839 = − 5.4%	(Peaches, apples and pears, fresh fruit)
Switzerland	− 3 719 = − 1.5%	(Citrus fruit and pineapples, bananas, peaches, apples and pears, grapes, carrots, frsh vegetables, potatoes)
Romania	− 3 481 = − 20.4%	(Citrus fruit and pineapples, foodstuffs)
Norway	− 2 668 = − 11.0%	(Peaches, apples and pears)
Netherlands	− 1 063 = − 2.8%	(Citrus fruit and pineapples)

There was also a fall in traffic to Iran with −688 tons (apples and pears), Luxembourg with −433 tons (citrus fruit and pineapples, peaches and fresh fruit), Bulgaria with −287 tons (fresh vegetables, frozen meat), Denmark with −287 tons (citrus fruit, peaches, foodstuffs) and Great Britain with −177 tons (apples and pears, tomatoes, fresh vegetables).

Variations in the nature of goods carried

a The main increases were observed in the following types of goods (number of tons carried):

Dairy products	+ 5 347 = + 9.4%	(Butter, eggs, cheese)
Sea products	+ 2 537 = + 5.7%	(Fresh fish)

b The main decreases were the following (number of tons carried):

Fresh fruit	− 91 444 = − 6.7%	(Citrus fruit and pineapples, peaches, apples and pears)
Potatoes	− 60 772 = − 34.6%	
Frozen products	− 56 794 = − 28.4%	(Meat, poultry and fish)
Foodstuffs	− 26 103 = − 27.5%	(Chocolate, foodstuffs)
Misc products	− 12 564 = − 3.6%	(Beverages, industrial products)
Fresh vegetables	− 5 339 = − 0.8%	(Carrots, cabbages, vegetables)
Meat products	− 2 111 = − 3.5%	(Fresh meat)

Traffic in mechanically refrigerated wagons

Total traffic in mechanically refrigerated wagons showed an increase of 27.9 per cent over 1977. Traffic in Interfrigo mechanically refrigerated wagons increased by 27.1 per cent. The number of ton-kms carried was 117 million in 1978 compared with 106 million in 1977, representing an increase of 10.3 per cent.

The number of shipments increased from 3 363 in 1977 to 4 300 in 1978. The average distance travelled per ton diminished from 1 311 km in 1977 to 1 086 km in 1978 due to the loss of traffic to Iran. The average load per wagon was 25.1 tons in 1978 as against 24.1 tons in 1977.

	1975	1976	1977	1978
Number of shipments	1 567	1 832	3 363	4 300
Total number of ton-kms loaded (million)	40	63	106	117
Total number of tons carried (thousands)	31	40	81	108
Average distance travelled per ton carried (km)	1 290	1 574	1 311	1 086
Average load carried per wagon (tons)	20.1	21.9	24.1	25.1

Traffic in mechanically refrigerated transcontainers

Traffic "per journey"

The rail transport of privately-owned mechanically refrigerated containers in Europe (including Interfrigo containers on long-term rental), particularly in overseas traffic, showed an increase of 21.2 per cent over 1977.

	1975	1976	1977	1978
Number of units carried:				
Private containers (P), including IF containers on long-term rental	2 126	3 726	5 616	6 807
Interfrigo (IF) containers "per journey"	4 071	3 087	1 516	1 691
Total (P + IF)	6 197	6 813	7 132	8 498
Total number of ton-kms loaded (million)	23	23	26	38
Total number of tons carried (thousands)	36	45	48	60
Average distance travelled per ton carried (km)	638	499	545	632
Average load carried per unit (tons)	12.4	13.2	13.8	13.7

Traffic in containers on long-term rental

37.1 per cent of the Interfrigo mechanically refrigerated container stock was rented on the basis of long-term agreements in 1978, compared with 67.3 per cent in 1977.

Number of INTERFRIGO-owned mechanically refrigerated transcontainers	20'	40'	TEU (equiv to 20')
A = total	240	159	558
B = "on long-term rental"	98	54	207
Percentage $\frac{100\,B}{A}$	40.8%	34.0%	37.1%

General

Despite the maintenance of vigorous sales promotion efforts together with increased vigilance with respect to competition from road transport, the expansion in the total Interfrigo traffic in terms of ton-kms observed in 1977 did not continue. On the contrary, in 1978 it was followed by a drop in traffic of 8.5 per cent in relation to 1977. In the field of publicity a large-scale press advertising campaign was conducted in a wide variety of trade journals. In 1978 Interfrigo also participated in the following functions:
"Grüne Woche 1978" in Berlin
International Spring Fair in Budapest
4th International Port Exhibition in Antwerp
4th International Transport Fair in Belgrade
"Transport 78" in Munich

Traffic "per journey"

The decline in traffic "per journey" in refrigerator wagons, in terms of ton-kms, amounted to 9.3 per cent in 1978. In particular there were substantial drops in traffic from France and Italy. In this connection the most important contributing factors were unfavourable weather conditions, the continuing sluggishness of the European economy and increased competition from road transport.

It is also increasingly apparent that the complexity of the railway's traditional offering in the international transport of fruit and vegetables—for which, either directly or through his forwarding agent, the shipper must apply to the railway for actual transport, to Interfrigo for specialised rolling stock, and to the ice factories for the supply of ice—is more and more out of keeping with the demands of the market. In comparison with road haulage, the unclarity of the complete price of railway transport is aggravated by the complex structure of many railway tariffs.

"Complete transport service"

The adverse effects of the complexity of rail transport "per journey" are probably best demonstrated by the fact that by contrast, traffic in the "Interfrigo complete transport service" is steadily increasing. In this service Interfrigo has the position of "sole railway negotiating partner" and quotes all-in prices to customers which comprise rail transport, the provision of rolling stock, and refrigeration with surveillance.

This "complete transport service" is particularly intended for specialised forwarding agents, with whom Interfrigo works in close co-operation and who provide additional services (customs clearance, transfer to consignee's address, intermediate storage, etc).

On its introduction in 1969, this service was restricted to traffic in mechanically refrigerated wagons, where it still has a predominant position. However, in view of customers' growing demand for this type of transport, refrigerator wagons also came to be provided under the "complete transport service", particularly in shortages of mechanically refrigerated stock and for large shipments of frozen or fresh products. In addition to the traditional traffics, the following new contracts have been concluded:
—Hungary—Yugoslavia: poultry, meat and eggs
—Germany (GFR)/Belgium—Greece: Bananas
—Yugoslavia—USSR: meat
—Netherlands/Germany (GFR)/Denmark—USSR: frozen chickens and preserves.
Traffic to the Middle East was interrupted in 1978 for political reasons. However, Interfrigo was able to conclude a tariff agreement with the Turkish State Railways allowing it to make competitive offers. Furthermore, the maximum axle load for traffic to Iran has been increased from 17 to 20 tons.

Refrigerated containers

The number of shipments in privately-owned mechanically refrigerated containers increased by more than 20 per cent in 1978.

This traffic involves principally the continental section of transport to and from the major seaports. The first series of Interfrigo mechanically refrigerated containers, which came into service from 1969 onwards and have now reached the end of their useful life, are being progressively withdrawn from service. This accounts for the decline in their share of the stock on long-term rental.

Interfrigo rolling stock in service
The company's total rolling stock decreased from 7 659 units at the end of 1977 to 7 647 units at the end of 1978 as a result of:

7 refrigerator wagons, 2 insulated wagons and 11 mechanically refrigerated containers were scrapped
of the eight old postal wagons purchased for conversion into crew dormitory cars, three were brought into service in 1978, two will come into use at the beginning of 1979, and three still have to be converted
2 refrigerator wagons and 1 mechanically refrigerated wagon were converted into insulated wagons
36 refrigerator wagons were converted into mechanically refrigerated wagons
150 refrigerator wagons: removal of meat hooks and supporting rails
21 mechanically refrigerated wagons were equipped with an electric heating system.

Annual average stock available diminished from 7 660 units in 1977 to 7 652 units in 1978.
104 319 journeys were made with the total stock (102 628 in wagons, 1 691 in containers) in 1978, compared with 106 123 (104 607 in wagons, 1 516 in containers) in the preceding year, a decline of 1.7 per cent.
The share of total wagon traffic accounted for by Interfrigo wagons increased from 42.3 per cent in 1977 to 44.6 per cent in 1978.

Type of stock	In service on 31.12.78
1. **Refrigerator wagons**	
GC (Continental loading gauge)	1 843
GC (British loading gauge)	1 321
TGC	3 741
SC	121
Total	7 026
2. **Insulated wagons**	
GC (Continental loading gauge)	20
GC (British loading gauge)	9
TGC	2
SC	1
Total	32
3. **Liquid nitrogen wagons**	
GC (Continental loading guage)	1
GC (British loading gauge)	5
Total	6
4. **Mechanically refrigerated wagons**	
2-axle	121
Bogie	50
Total	171
5. **Mechanically refrigerated containers**	
20-foot	240
40-foot	159
Total	399
6. **Crew dormitory cars**	13
Grand Total	7 647

The suspension of new construction due to the present decline in traffic provided the Company with an opportunity to give close attention to the optimisation of its rolling stock. This has been effected principally by means of the following measures:
Increased technical adaptations to improve commercial performance.
For this purpose the following principal steps have been taken:

Over the past two years meat hooks and supports have been removed from 886 large capacity refrigerator wagons to adapt them to the requirements of fruit and vegetables in the best possible way.
The marking of 3 300 GC and TGC refrigerator wagons was begun in 1978, enabling their payload to be increased to 4 tons and optimalising their loading possibilities.
The preparation, on the basis of known and expected commercial requirements, of a veritable catalogue of technical characteristics allowing rapid selection in conformity with the service required.
The creation of suitable administrative instruments.

All these measures are part of an overall plan which has been elaborated by the Company in order to adjust its general policy to the altered requirements of its customers and to present future railway transport conditions, particularly with regard to investments and the use of rolling stock.

Rolling stock owned by the Railway Administrations and specialised companies
The insulated, refrigerator and mechanically refrigerated wagons hired by Interfrigo in international traffic decreased from 18 368 units at the end of 1977 to 18 029 units at the end of 1978.
Rolling stock hired by Interfrigo from member administrations and specialised companies completed 127 515 journeys in 1978 compared with 142 973 in 1977; this corresponds to 55.4 per cent of the total wagon traffic, compared with 57.7 per cent in 1977.
With regards to a long-term investment policy, the Company reiterates its wish for the scrapping of old wagons. With this in view, a joint plan for the attainment of this objective and for effecting a synthesis of administrative and investment problems with the aim of optimalising community policy has been submitted to these administrations.

Traffic conditions
During 1976 the operating conditions of refrigerator wagon traffic were characterised principally by the following factors:

Reduction in the average turn-round time from 13.57 days in 1977 to 13.44 days.
A decline in the overall productivity of the jointly owned rolling stock, whose utilisation decline by 2.5 per cent.

Operational development
In the traffic sector too, in 1978 Interfrigo continued its efforts to improve the jointly offered services with a view to maintaining and if possible expanding traffic for which it is responsible.
In this connection:

It has stepped up its activities within UIC and CEM by increased participation in the study of matters which relate principally to its own traffic.
It has oriented the efforts of the Community, in its own committees and by means of bilateral contacts with the railway administrations, towards the rapid and effective improvement of the offering in the operational domain, this being the principal objective at the present time.
It has continued the indispensable studies and preparatory work for the application of the "Centralised Control of Goods Traffic" (GCTM) to the distribution of the refrigerator wagons under its administration.
It has studied the further application of electronic data processing in the operational domain with a view to the still more effective utilisation of this modern technique.

An analysis of the trends observed during 1978 in Interfrigo's transport market revealed two outstanding factors which will increasingly influence transport in the near future:

The gradual transfer of traffic in various major exporting countries from smaller-capacity refrigerator wagons (PC, N, GC) mainly to TGC refrigerator wagons, this development being attributable mainly to:
an increase in the size of the trading units of certain types of goods (potatoes, bananas) in terms of weight (and therefore also of volume), and
the development of railway tariffs.

The increasing importance of palletised shipments, for whose transport TGC wagons are generally required.
In these two domains, the Interfrigo community will have to adapt to the new conditions with all their consequences. A general working programme has been established in order to successfully meet this development.
1978 was devoted to the improvement of services offered, and in particular was dominated by the introduction and phased development of the "transport service for perishable foodstuffs with programmed routings" ("IF-AP Service").
Considerable efforts have been made in this field, and have in particular led to the following results:

The introduction of a method for the checking of transport conditions on the routes suitable for the introduction of the "IF-AP Service". This involves the checking by data processing methods of the actual transit times over the complete journey, and their comparison with the intended transport plans.
The institution of the second phase of the geographical extension of the "IF-AP" study, which now covers connections between 135 Italian and 8 Greek "Principal Departure Stations" (GEP) and 61 "Principal Destination Stations" (GDP) distributed between ten railway administrations.
The putting into effect of a first package of concrete measures enabling one day to be gained on the transit time of certain international shipments from Italy.

In this connection, however, it should be borne in mind that these measures, which are essentially of an operational nature, are necessary but not sufficient for the maintenance and promotion of the traffic in question. At the appropriate time Interfrigo will take such commercial measures as appear desirable in order to strengthen the competitive position of rail transport.

Appropriation of profits
The profit and loss account for the 1978 business year showed a profit of FrB 4 112 849, plus FrB 80 474 carried forward from the preceding year.
The profit distributed to the owners of the Company as dividends represented 12 per cent of the value of the shares forming the Company's registered capital. After deduction at source of taxes by shareholders, the net dividend received by them was approximately ten per cent.

Assets
On 31 December 1978 the gross fixed assets showed an increase of FrB 12.4 million in relation to 31 December 1977; this increase is due in particular to the renewal and enlargement of the mechanically refrigerated wagon stock.
The other fixed assets showed a diminution of FrB 8.8 million due to security issue expenses (—FrB 8.8 million depreciation).
Operating assets, which are accounted for by spare parts and stocks of material, show an increase of FrB 11.6 million.
The increase of FrB 239.5 million in liquid or easy realisable assets is due principally to accounts payable, which showed a rise of FrB 220.1 million.

Liabilities
Capital and reserves showed no change in relation to the preceding year.
The increase of FrB 215.2 million in the provisions for risks and charges is due principally to the making of a provision for exchange-rate losses on loans (FrB 211.9 million). Long-term debts diminished by FrB 137.5 million. The increase of FrB 33.3 million in short-term debts is accounted for by an increase in the long-term debts falling due in the course of the year (+ FrB 0.7 million) and an increase in other debts (+ FrB 32.6 million).
Equalisation accounts, which represent interest accrued on loans, showed an increase of FrB 2.1 million.

Supercapacity bogie mechanically refrigerated wagons crossing Lake Van (Eastern)

Non-balance sheet items
On 31 December 1978 the amount of guarantees secured by the founding railway administrations in application of Article 30 of the Statutes was FrB 2 800.9 million (FrB130.9 million less than on 31 December 1977). This corresponds in effect to the items *Non-convertible bonded loans* and *Debts with a term of more than one year falling due in the course of the year.*
The ceiling for guarantees which the founding organisations are able to provide is at present FrB 4 000 million.

Profit and loss account
Sales and services provided amount to FrB 1 759.9 million compared with FrB 1 692.5 million in 1977 (+ FrB 67.4 million).
The costs of sales and services, including depreciation of FrB 151.7 million (FrB 287.7 million in 1977), amounted to FrB 1 459.5 million (FrB 1 447.4 million in 1977). Depreciation was effected at the following rates on the acquisition value:
    1 per cent on buildings; an average of 3.8 per cent for wagons and containers; 10 per cent on furnishings, equipment, machinery and tools.
The operating profit of FrB 300.4 million, as against FrB 245.1 million in 1977, showed an increase of FrB 55.3 million. The financial result showed charges of FrB 296.6 million as against FrB 237.1 million in 1977. Tax payable amounted to FrB 4.2 million as against FrB 4.4 million in 1977. The net profit for the business year was FrB 4.1 million.

INTERFRIGO REPRESENTATIVES
Austria
Oesterreichische Bundesbahnen (OeBB)
Verkaufsdirektion—Abt IV/3, A-1010 Vienna, Gauermanngasse 4
Tel: (0222) 5650/5329
Telex: 112104

Belgium
NV Interferry
B-2030 Antwerp, Zomerweg 26
Tel: 41 69 50
Telex: 32529

Bulgaria
UEE—"BDZ"—Eisenbahnkühltransporte INTERFRIGO-Zentralbüro
Sofia, Gavril Genov-Strasse 1
Tel: 87 72 02
Telex: 22423

Czechoslovakia
"CSKD Intrans"/Oddĕleni INTERFRIGO
CS-18686 Prague 8, Karlin Kŕižikova 2
Tel: 2124 (ext 4953)
Telex: 121 486

Denmark
Danske Statsbaner (DSB)
DK-1560 København V, Kalvebod Brygge 32
Tel: (01) 140400
Telex: 27054

Finland
Valtionrautatiet (VR)
Rautatiehallitus, PB 488, SF-00101 Helsinki 10
Tel: 90 717 711
Telex: 12-30151 VRSF

France
Stef, 93 bd Malesherbes, F-75008 Paris
Tel: 522 8894
Telex: 280969

Germany (GDR)
Deutsche Reichsbahn—Ministerium für Verkehrswesen
INTERFRIGO-Büro DDR-1086 Berlin 8, Voss-Strasse 33
Tel: 530201
Telex: 112250

Germany (GFR)
Operating representation:
Deutsche Bundesbahn, Zentrale Transportleitung—Abteilung VW
D-65 Mainz 1, Kaiserstrasse 3
Tel: (06131) 15 58 47 or 15 58 25
Telex: 04187732

Commercial representation:
Transthermos GmbH, D-28 Bremen 1, Parkstrasse 123, Postfach 100929
Tel: (0421) 340 21
Telex: 244457 or 245518

Greece
Hellenic Railways Organisation Ltd
Athens (107), Karolou Street 1/3
Tel: 54 25 84
Telex: 215187

Hungary
Magyar Allamvasutak (MAV), Vezérigazgatósága 8B,
INTERFRIGO-Vezérkepviselet, H-1940 Budapest VI, Népköztársaság Utja 73
Tel: 428-575 or 220-660/183
Telex: 224342

Iran
Iranian State Railways (RAI)
49 West Takhte Jamshid Avenue, Teheran
Tel: 525121-28
Telex: 213103

Ireland, Federal Republic
Coras Iompair Eireann (CIE)
Office of the Commercial Manager, Transport House, Bachelor's Walk, EIR-Dublin 1
Tel: 741851
Telex: 5695

Italy
Ferrovie Italiane dello Stato
Direzione Generale (for transports in refrigerator wagons)
1-00161 Rome, Piazza della Croce Rossa
Servizio Movimento
Tel: 8490/2136
Telex: 61089
Servizio Commerciale e del Traffico
Tel: 8490/2329-33625

Telex: 61089
Istituto Nazionale Trasporti
(for transports in mechanically refrigerated wagons and containers)
1-00198 Rome, Via Savoia 19
Tel: 861 851
Telex: 68504 FERRINT

Luxembourg
Chemins de Fer Luxembourgeois
Service commercial
9 place de la Gare, Luxembourg
Tel: 49901
Telex: 2288

Netherlands
NV Nederlandse Spoorwegen (NS)
Dienst van Commerciële Zaken, 1e Afdeling
3500 HA Utrecht, Katreinetoren
Tel: (030) 35 45 52
Telex: 70131

Norway
Norges Statsbaner (NSB)
Hovedadministrasjonen, N-Oslo 1, Storgaten 33
Tel: 20 95 50
Telex: 11168

Portugal
Companhia dos Caminhos de Ferro Portugueses (CP)
Departamento Comercial
Largo dos Caminhos de Ferro, Lisbon-2
Tel: 86 41 81-86 61 01/8
Telex: 12382

Romania
Caile Ferate Române (CFR)
Service INTERFRIGO
Bucharest 7, Bulevardul Dinicu Golescu 38
Tel: 17 20 60
Telex: 11553

Spain
Transfesa
Madrid (3), Bravo Murillo No 38-2°, Apartado 3225
Tel: 448 89 00
Telex: 27745 or 22632

Sweden
Statens Järnvägar (SJ)
Centralförvaltningen-Kammersiella avdelningen, S-105 50 Stockholm
Tel: 22 64 20
Telex: 19410

Switzerland
Frigosuisse (National Representation)—Schweizerische Bundesbahnen
—Kommerzieller Dienst Güterverkehr
CH-3000 Bern, Mittelstrasse 43
Tel: (031) 60 32 81
Telex: 691212

Betriebsabteilung-Sektion 6
CH-3000 Bern, Schwarztorstrasse 57
Tel: (031) 60 39 71
Telex: 69121 2

Bahnhofkühlhaus AG, Münchensteinerstrasse 93
CH-4002 Basel, Postfach 111
Tel: (061) 50 44 11
Telex: 622712

Société de Gares Frigorifiques et Ports Francs de Genève
CH-1227 Carouge, rue Blavignac 5, Case postale 88
Tel: (022) 43 87 60
Telex: 28177

Marco Celoria SA
Fabrique de glace, CH-6830 Chiasso
Tel: (091) 44 26 02

Turkey
Türkiye Cumhuriyeti Devlet Demiryollari (TCDD)
Hareket Dairesi Baskanligi, Ankara
Tel: 24 12 20 (ext. 205)
Telex: 42571

United Kingdom
General Operating Representation (wagons):
British Railways Board
Executive Director, Systems and Operations, Freight Rolling Stock Officer, 222 Marylebone Road, London NW1 6JJ
Tel: 01-262-3232 (ext. 5619)
Telex: 24678

General Commercial Representation:
British Rail European Rail Traffic Office
(for all traffic in refrigerator wagons, mechanically refrigerated wagons and transcontainers originating from or destined for Harwich)
163-203, Eversholt St, London NW1 1BG
Tel: 01-387-1234
Telex: 269295

Operating and Commercial Representation:
Freightliners Ltd
(for international transports in mechanically refrigerated transcontainers originating from or destined for the inland Freightliner terminals other than Harwich)
43 Cardington Street, London NW1 2LR
Tel: 01-387-9400 (ext 3326)
Telex: 24743

Yugoslavia
Zajednica Jugoslovenskih Zeleznica (JZ)
Zastupnistvo INTERFRIGA i Intercontainera (1-4)
YU-11000 Belgrade, Nemanjina 6/11
Tel: 682-525
Telex: 11166

INTERNATIONAL ASSOCIATION OF ROLLING STOCK BUILDERS
(Association Internationale des Constructeurs de Matériel Roulant—AICMR)

Offices: 12 rue Bixio, 75007 Paris, France

Telegrams: 'Interwagon, Paris'
Telephone: 705 36 62

President: Baron P. van der Rest (Belgian)
Delegate General: J-L. Burckhardt (Swiss)

INTERNATIONAL CONTAINER BUREAU (BIC)

Offices: 38 cours Albert 1, Paris 8, France

Telephone: 261 85 97
Telex: INCOMERC PARIS 650770

President: J. Martial

INTERNATIONAL FEDERATION OF RAILWAY ADVERTISING COMPANIES

Offices: Orell Füssli Expo AG, Bähnhof-u, Aussenwerbung, Bühlstrasse 1, 8125 Zollikerberg, Switzerland

Telephone: 63 96 40

Secretary: H. Menti

INTERNATIONAL ORGANIZATION FOR STANDARDIZATION (ISO)
(Organisation Internationale de Normalisation)

Postal address: Case postale 56,1 rue de Varembé, 1211, Geneva 20, Switzerland

Telephone: 34 12 40
Telex: 23887

President: M. Henri-Durant (France)
Vice-President: R. L. Henessy (Canada)
Treasurer: Gérard Fatio
Secretary General: Olle Sturen

INTERNATIONAL SLEEPING CAR COMPANY (CIWLT)
(Cie Internationale des Wagons-lits et du Tourisme)

Head Office: 40 rue de l'Arcade, Paris, France

Telephone: 266 24 00
Telegrams: 'Wagolits' PARIS
Telex: 650 233 Wagocia-Paris

Administrator Director General: Jacques Bernard Dupont
Director General (Joint): François Boyaux
Financial Director: André Frandeboeuf
Director of Railways: Wilhelm Scheiff
Director of Hotels: Guy Trarieux
Secretary General: Claude de Crecy
Representative of the Director General (Brussels): Jacques de Meeus d'Argenteuil
Personnel Director: Jean-Pierre Mayet
Director of Tourism: Michel Tondeur

Founded in 1876 in Brussels the company's vehicles and trains were known all over Europe by 1914 and further extended in 1919.
Since 1971, most of CIWLT sleeping cars and dining cars have been taken over by various national and international railway systems under the "Trains Euro Nuit" (TEN). CIWLT staffs, caters and maintains the sleeping and dining cars on behalf of the various railways.

INTERNATIONAL RAIL TRANSPORT COMMITTEE (CIT)

Offices: Managing Railway: General Management of the Swiss Federal Railways, Wildhainweg 9, CH-3030 Bern, Switzerland

Telephone: 60 25 65 or 60 27 94

President and Chairman: M. Desponds
Secretary: M. Bertherin

INTERNATIONAL UNION OF PRIVATE RAILWAY TRUCK OWNERS' ASSOCIATIONS

Offices: General Secretary, 21 Via Calprino, CH-6900 Lugano-Paradiso, Switzerland

Telephone: (091) 54 16 21/54 52 14
Telex: 73 774 misu ch

Secretary General: Walter Suter

INTERNATIONAL UNION OF RAILWAY MEDICAL SERVICES (UIMC)

Offices: 85 rue de France, 1060 Brussels, Belgium

Telephone: 02/23.80.80-2503/4

Treasurer: Dr J. Dufaux SNCB

CONTINENTS

LATIN AMERICAN RAILWAY ASSOCIATION

Head Office: Florida 783, ler Piso, 1005 Buenos Aires, Argentina

Telephones: 31 9463 and 32 5151

Officers:
General Secretary: Emiliano A. S. Flouret
Administrative Secretary: Felipe Muniain

The Association was founded at a meeting of Latin-American Railway representatives in Argentina in 1964. Principal objectives are the creation of transcontinental routes; settling of traffic interchange problems; development and integration of Latin-American railways; elimination of frontier and customs difficulties; the exchange of technical information and the sale, loan or exchange of railway material between members; co-ordination of railway industries in Latin America and the creation of a code of standards for Latin-American built railway equipment and the formation of a Latin-American Railway Bank.

PAN AMERICAN RAILWAY CONGRESS ASSOCIATION

Offices: Av. 9 de Julio 1925, Piso 13,1332 Buenos Aires, Argentina

Telephone: 38 4625

Officers:
President: Juan Carlos De Marchi
Vice Presidents: Roberto Agostini Centeno and Miguel A. Basagoitia Pando
General Secretary: Cayetano Marletta Rainieri
Treasurer: José Luis de Pabón

Inaugurated in 1907 at the celebrations of the 50th anniversary of the first Argentinian railway, the Association was originally made up of Latin American countries. Originally the USA was limited to sending observers to congresses but now all the American Republics are members and the main aim of the Association is to promote the development and progress of railways in the Western hemisphere.

UNION OF AFRICAN RAILWAYS (UAR)

Offices: Avenue Tombalbaye, 869, PO Box 687, Kinshasa, Zaire

Foundation: The Constituent Conference of the UAR took place in Addis Ababa in September 1972 under the aegis of the United Nations Economic Commission for Africa (ECA) with the financial co-operation of the German Development Foundation. The Constitution of the Union was adopted at this Conference and submitted to the Council of Ministers of the ECA in Accra in March 1973, to the Ministers of the Organisation of African Unity (OAU) in May and to the Tenth Assembly of Heads of State and Government of the OAU in Addis Ababa in June 1973.

Objectives: At the First General Assembly held in Addis Ababa in June 1973 an inter-subregional Committee was set up to draw up a programme of action for the UAR. In October 1974 in Kinshasa, the Second General Assembly adopted this programme, the main features of which are the unification of African Railways, the improvement of railway services, the interconnection of African railways, the co-ordination of rail

transport with other modes of transport and the normalisation and standardisation of equipment.

Establishment of sub-regional training centres: The UAR envisaged the establishment of four training centres for railway engineers in each of the sub-regions of Africa: Brazzaville (Congo) for Central Africa, Lusaka (Zambia) for East Africa, Zaria (Nigeria) for West Africa and Wardan (Egypt) for North Africa.

Status with the OAU: The Thirteenth Assembly of Heads of State and Government of the Organisation of African Unity (OAU) held in Port Louis, Mauritius from 2-4 July 1978 adopted Resolution CM/Res 507 (XXVIII) granting UAR the status of Specialised Agency of the OAU in the field of rail transport in Africa.

Organs of the UAR: The General Assembly, made up of delegates of member railways; The Executive Board, comprising the president and four vice-presidents elected for two years renewable only once and representing each of the sub-regions of Africa (Centre, West, North, East); The General Secretariat; Technical Committees, covering materials and equipment, permanent way and interconnections, traffic, supplies, finance and investment, personnel and training, documentation and information, signalling and telecommunications, and data processing.

Master plan: The Fourth General Assembly held in Accra in 1976 adopted a draft master plan providing for the following interconnections (none of these projected linkages are final):
Bamako (Mali)—Bobo Dioulasso (Upper Volta)
Ouagadougou, Dori (Upper Volta)—Niamey (Niger)
Niamey, Dosso (Niger)—Kaura Namoda (Nigeria)
Gaya (Niger)—Zaria (Nigeria)
Maiduguri (Nigeria)—Ndjamena (Chad)—Nyala (Sudan)
Dimbokro (Ivory Coast)—Nzerekore (Guinea)
Tambacounda (Senegal)—Nouakchott (Mauritania)
Nouakchott, Nouadhibou (Mauritania)—Marrakesh (Morocco)
Karoussa (Guinea)—Bamako (Mali)
Sunyani (Ghana)—Ouagadougou (Upper Volta)
Takoradi (Ghana)—Abidjan (Ivory Coast)
Tema (Ghana)—Lomé (Togo)
Parakou (Benin)—Dosso—Niamey (Niger)
Niamey (Niger)—Gao (Mali)
Anecho (Togo)—Segbrone (Benin)
Pobe (Benin)—Ilaro (Nigeria)
Yaoundé (Cameroon)—Bangui (Central African Republic)
Bangui (Central African Republic)—Belinga (Gabon)
Belinga (Gabon) Yaoundé (Cameroon)
Aswan (Egypt)—Wadi Halfa (Sudan)
Wau (Sudan)—Gulu (Uganda)
Juba (Sudan)—Mugbere (Zaire)
El Sallom (Egypt)—Tripoli (Libya)—gabès (Tunisia)
Mchinda (Malawi)—Mpika (Zambia)
Argodat—Tessenei (Ethiopia)
Addis Ababa (Ethiopia)—Nairobi (Kenya)
Ilebo-Kinshasa (Zaire) Brazzaville (Congo)
Serpa-Pinto (Angola)—Kataba (Zambia)
Namibia (Gobabis)—Frencistown (Botswana)
Isumed (Namibia)—Serpa-Pinto (Angola)
Kinshasa (Zaire)—Brazzaville (Congo)—Mbinda
Franceville (Gabon) in the very long term
Gao (Mali)—Abadla (Algeria) in the very long term

EUROPEAN

EUROPEAN COMPANY FOR THE FINANCING OF RAILROAD ROLLING STOCK (EUROFIMA)

Offices: Rittergasse 20, CH-4001 Basel, Switzerland

Telephone: 22.33.40

General Manager: Heinz Weber

EUROPEAN CONFERENCE OF MINISTERS OF TRANSPORT (ECMT)

Offices: 19 rue de Franqueville, 75775 Paris Cedex 16, France

Telephone: 524-82 00
Telegrams: 'Comitrans, Paris'
Telex: 20.999 Paris

Chairman: M. A. Zelic, President of the Federal Committee of Transport and Communications (Yugoslavia)
First Vice-Chairman: M. K. Gscheidle, Federal Minister of Transport (Federal Republic of Germany)
Second Vice-Chairman: M. V. Saarto, Minister of Communications (Finland)

EUROPEAN DIESEL AND ELECTRIC LOCOMOTIVE MANUFACTURERS' ASSOCIATION

(Constructeurs Européens de Locomotives Thermiques et Electriques—CELTE)

Offices: 12 rue Bixio, Paris 75007, France

Telephone: 705 36 62
Telegrams: Interwagon, Paris

President: Dip. Ing Eric Kocher (Federal Republic of Germany)
Delegate General: J-L. Burckhardt (Swiss)

TEE
TRANS-EUROP-EXPRESS

Administration: Netherlands Railways, 3500 HA Utrecht, Moreelsepark 1, Netherlands

It was in 1954, following a proposition put forward by Mr. Den Hollender, then President of the Netherlands Railways, that the railway administration of Belgium, France, Federal Republic of · Germany, Italy, Luxembourg, Netherlands and Switzerland decided to form the Trans-Europ-Express Group, with the object of connecting the major European centres of population and industry by a network of very fast and very comfortable trains. Two more countries, Austria and Spain, have since joined.
The Managing Administration of the TEE-Group, with offices at the Headquarters of the Netherlands Railways in Utrecht, is charged with coordinating the TEE activities of the member administrations, and with studying the possibilities of improving existing services and developing others. The TEE group is not a railway system as such; it is an organisation of studies and direction.
All the motive power units and rolling stock are owned and operated by the various railway administrations in the Group. However all the trains carry the emblem "TEE" and have to satisfy certain minimum specifications as to speed and comfort.
For accountancy purposes, because each country has its own currency, the money basis adopted is the UIC franc. The tariff applicable to TEE trains consists of the first class fare in force in each of the countries in which they operate, plus a supplement in proportion to the distance.
In order to reduce the length of, or to eliminate, stops at frontiers, arrangements are made for customs and security controls to be effected during the journey; and the use of multi-current electric locomotives and trainsets gives smooth change-over, without stopping, from one system of electrification to another, irrespective of country.
Since it commenced on 2 June 1957, the Trans-Europ-Express train-service has gone

EUROPEAN GOODS TIMETABLE CONFERENCE

Offices: Czechoslovak State Railways, Na Prikopé 33, 110 05 Praha, Czechoslovakia

Telegrams: 'Domini Praha CEM/EGK'
Telephone: Praha 2122/3029
Telex: 121096

President: Ing Ladislav Stros
Secretary: Josef Basta

EUROPEAN PASSENGER TIMETABLE CONFERENCE

Conférence Européenne Des Horaires des Trains de Voyageurs (CEH)

Offices: c/o Direction Générale des Chemins de Fer Fédéraux Suisses, Hochschulstrasse 6, CH-3030 Berne, Switzerland

Telephone: (031) 60 11 11
Telex: 32500

President: K. Wellinger *(General Manager, Swiss Federal Railways)*

EUROPEAN WAGON POOL (EUROP AGREEMENT)

Communauté d'Exploitation des Wagons Europ (Convention Europ)

Offices: Société Nationale des Chemins de Fer Belges, 17-21 rue de Louvain, 1000 Brussels, Belgium

Telephone: (02) 513 18 70
Telex: 24607

from strength to strength. Today it covers nine countries (Austria, Belgium, France, Germany, Italy, Luxembourg, Netherlands, Spain and Switzerland) and is served by 37 trains stopping at over 190 stations, carrying some 5 million passengers annually. TEE-trains are first-class only. Seat reservation (supplementary charge) is not essential but is strongly recommended. Seats can be reserved up to three months in advance and can be reserved for both outward and homeward journeys at the same time.
TEE-trains provide maximum comfort such as individual reclining seats, fluorescent lighting, cloakrooms, luggage-racks, air-conditioning and soundproofing. Amongst normal facilities a loudspeaker-system can be mentioned, used for announcing stations, passport-control or other relevant messages. Paris-bound trains offer an extra facility which avoids delay on arrival; during the journey passengers are able to reserve taxis by paying an amount which covers the first kilometre plus a small reservation-fee. These reserved taxis wait at a special lane near the station exit.
The first TEE-trains were diesel multiple-unit trainsets with a maximum speed of 87 mph *(140 km/h)*. Capacity varied from 81 to 163 seats. In 1961 the Swiss Federal Railways introduced four five-coach multi-current electric trainsets (still running) on the Brussels-Zurich and Milan-Zurich routes. In 1967 the capacity was adjusted to the increased demand by adding a sixth coach to the units which brought capacity up to 168 seats, apart from the restaurant capacity.
In 1964 France and Belgium formed a pool of 36 stainless steel coaches hauled by multi-current electric locomotives. This made it possible to vary the seating capacity to adjust for the peaks of the day and of the week. On Monday mornings and Friday nights TEE trains composed of 15 coaches carrying 550 passengers are no exception.
In 1965 the *Helvetia* was electrified with air-conditioned rolling stock of German type. Other German locomotive-hauled trains followed and replaced the diesel-stock.
The Italian diesel trainsets have been replaced by electric locomotive-hauled coaches of special Fiat design. *Lemano, Ligure* and *Mediolanum* run with this stock, as well as the TEE trains in Italian internal traffic.
The *Catalan-Talgo* tightens Spain to the TEE-network by means of a special design of

Name of Train	Route	Distance miles	km	Booked time h	min	Intermediate stops	Average speed mph	km/h
Adriatico	Milan-Bari	540	869	9	10	14	59	95
Ambrosiano	Milan-Rome	393	632	5	53	2	67	107
Aquitaine	Paris Austerlitz-Bordeaux	361	581	3	50	2	94	151
Bacchus	Dortmund-Munich	465	749	7	13	12	65	104
Brabant	Paris Nord-Brussels Midi	194	312	2	24	—	81	130
Le Capitole du Matin	Paris Austerlitz-Toulouse	443	713	6	04	5	67	118
Le Capitole du Soir	Paris Austerlitz-Toulouse	443	713	6	02	4	67	118
Le Catalan Talgo	Barcelona-Geneva	541	870	9	22	12	58	93
Cisalpin	Paris Lyon-Milan	510	821	8	20	7	61	99
Diamant	Hamburg Altona-Munich	524	844	7	50	8	64	103
Erasmus	Amsterdam-Frankfurt (Main)	299	481	4	56	9	60	97
Etendard	Paris Austerlitz-Bordeaux	361	581	3	50	2	94	151
Etoile du Nord	Paris Nord-Amsterdam	344	554	5	01	6	68	110
Faidherbe	Paris Nord-Tourcoing	168	271	2	19	5	73	117
Friedrich Schiller	Dortmund-Stuttgart	253	407	4	57	9	51	82
Gambrinus	Hamburg Altona-Munich	683	1 100	10	13	17	67	108
Gayant	Paris Nord-Tourcoing	168	271	2	25	5	70	112
Goethe	Dortmund-Frankfurt (Main)	211	340	3	17	8	64	103
Gottardo	Basel SBB-Milan-Zurich	237	381	5	02	3	47	76
Heinrich Heine	Dortmund-Frankfurt (Main)	211	340	3	23	8	62	100
Ile de France	Paris Nord-Amsterdam	344	554	5	08	6	67	108
Iris	Brussels Midi-Zurich	424	683	7	02	11	60	97
Kleber	Paris Est-Strasbourg	313	504	3	56	1	80	128
Lemano	Geneva-Milan	232	373	3	58	3	58	94
Ligure	Avignon-Milan	424	682	7	20	12	57	91
Mediolanum	Munich-Milan	370	595	7	00	8	53	85
Memling	Paris Nord-Brussels Midi	194	312	2	21	—	83	133
Le Mistral	Paris Lyon-Nice	676	1 088	9	06	9	75	120
Oiseau Bleu	Brussels Nord-Paris Nord	198	318	2	37	3	76	122
Rembrandt	Munich-Amsterdam	552	889	8	57	15	62	100
Rheingold	Geneva-Amsterdam	644	1 037	10	39	17	61	98
Roland	Bremen-Stuttgart	423	681	6	39	6	63	102
Rubens	Paris Nord-Brussels Midi	194	312	2	21	—	83	133
Settebello	Milan-Rome	393	632	5	35	2	70	113
Stanislas	Paris Est-Strasbourg	313	504	3	52	1	81	130
Vesuvio	Milan-Naples Mergellina	524	843	7	55	3	66	106
Watteau	Paris Nord-Tourcoing	168	271	2	22	5	72	115

wheel-adjustment, to compensate for gauge difference, which came into operation in 1969. Today it is the only diesel-hauled train. In general, speeds have increased in the 1957-1979 period; for example the average speed of the TEE trains between Brussels and Paris is now 83 mph *(133 km/h)*. In Federal Republic of Germany and France some trains are run at a top speed of 124 mph *(200 km/h)*, where the track has been upgraded and special modifications of signals have been arranged.

The *Dramant* does so on the Munich-Augsburg and Hanover-Hamburg sections, as do the *Etendard* and *Aquitaine* on the Paris-Bordeaux 581 km route of which roughly half is available for this speed. The *Aquitaine* has the highest average speed of 93 mph *(151 km/h)* and the longest non-stop journey of all the TEE trains.

London is on the TEE-teleprinter network, but the nearest connection is Hook of Holland—Utrect or Ostend-Brussels. The linking of British Rail with the TEE-network, should the Channel tunnel be built, is on the planning-table. Timings of 4½ hours from London to Paris (city centre to city centre) would be possible. The night-ferry—once called "The only train leaving the country"—may someday be one of a series of common (market) daily practice.

TEEM

TRANS-EUROP-EXPRESS-MARCHANDISES

The importance of the creation of fast timings, particularly with transit traffic, between the large centres of production and consumption, led to the eventual creation of TEEM by the European railway administrations.

The timings had originally been decided by bilateral agreements between the administrations concerned. In 1961 the idea of creating a network of fast goods trains arose which, by analogy with what had been done for passengers with the TEE trains, received the designation of Trans-Europ-Express-Marchandises or, in brief, TEEM. The first TEEM trains were introduced in May 1961. The reductions in transit times they made possible from the moment of their introduction were quite considerable; for example, the Bologna to London time fell from 60 to 38 hours.

Since 1961, however, the network of TEEM connections has steadily been improved and extended. There now exist 126 connections between 20 countries. Apart from the normal TEEM trains operating during the whole year there are several season connections assuring the transport of perishable goods between the agricultural areas and the regions of consumption.

TEEM routes have been established for Spanish fruit to the other countries of Western Europe, for French vegetables from Brittany to Belgium, Netherlands and Federal Republic of Germany, and most of the transport of fruit in refrigerator wagons from the Balkans is executed by TEEM trains. The rapidity and the regularity of the transits provided by them make it possible to present a solid front against road competition and to promote international trade between the centres of production and consumption. The development of the Common Market has contributed to accelerate the traffic by simplifying the customs formalities. The stops at the frontiers have been reduced to a minimum.

Another significant factor of TEEM is that its network reaches into eastern Europe, for its advantages are apparent to all European countries.

Co-ordinated by the Czechoslovakian Railways, the managing administration of TEEM, the European railways are continually aiming at improvements to this system.

Stops of minimum duration are made at all frontier stations for customs and other formalities. A certain number of stops are also made at intermediate stations, some of which provide rail connections to and from other destinations.

TEEM trains operate at maximum speeds of 53-62 mph *(85-100 km/h)*, and are restricted to wagons carrying the international marking S which indicates that they are capable of safe operation at 100 km/h. The only other restrictions are (a) wagons to and from Spain must be fitted for interchangeable axles because of the difference in gauge, and (b) only ferry-boat wagons can be used for through traffic by train-ferry to and from England. The TEEM network provides the essential long-distance international routes linking the railway systems of all European countries west of the USSR and Finland. It is intended for the rapid transport of perishables and other products requiring speedy transit, excluding very heavy freight such as coal, stone, metals etc. There are no supplementary charges for transport by TEEM trains.

Representative TEEM trains

Train No.		Route	Distance miles	km	Intermediate stops	Time hours	Average speed mph	km/h
102	Alicante (Spain)	Dunkirk (France)	1 397	2 248	1	53	26	42
112	Marseille (France)	Brussels (Belgium)	756	1 216	4	26	29	46
129	St. Pol-de-Léon (France)	Munich Ost (Federal Germany)	949	1 527	6	29	32	52
153	Sagunto (Spain)	Geneva (Switzerland)	751	1 209	2	32	23	37
300	Bologna (Italy)	Zeebrugge (Belgium)	900	1 448	6	31	29	46
303	Antwerpen (Belgium)	Chiasso (Switzerland)	659	1 060	3	25	26	42
333(a)	Stockholm (Sweden)	Salzburg (Federal Germany)	1 246	2 005	10	51	24	39
363	Rotterdam (Netherlands)	Vienna (Austria)	756	1 216	5	26	29	46
423	Cheb (Czechoslovakia)	Budapest (Hungary)	525	845	2	18	29	47
412(b)	Budapest (Hungary)	København (Denmark)	944	1 520	7	44	21	35
630	Thessaloniki (Greece)	Munich (Federal Germany)	1 051	1 692	7	41	25	41
740	Warsaw (Poland)	Hannover (Federal Germany)	569	915	6	23	24	39
781(c)	Hamburg (Federal Germany)	Stockholm (Sweden)	689	1 108	6	32	21	34

(a) via 2 train ferries:— Hälsingborg (Sweden)-Helsingør (Denmark) and Rødby F. (Denmark)-Puttgarden (Federal Germany)
(b) via 1 train ferry:— Warnemünde (GDR)-Gedser (Denmark).
(c) via 1 train ferry:— Sassnitz Hafen (GDR)-Trelleborg (Sweden)

UNION OF EUROPEAN RAILWAY INDUSTRIES

(Union des Industries Ferroviaires Européennes—UNIFE)

Offices: 12 rue Bixio, 75007 Paris, France

Telephone: 705-36-62
Telegrams: 'Interwagon, Paris'

President: Baron P. Van der Rest (Belgian)
Delegate General: J-L. Burckhardt (Swiss)

UNITED NATIONS ECONOMIC COMMISSION FOR EUROPE

Offices: Palais des Nations, Geneva, Switzerland

Telephone: 34 60 11

Officers:
Executive Secretary: J. Stanovnik
Deputy Executive Secretary: A. I. Alexandrov
Director Transport Division: H. G. Halbertsma

Established in 1947 to advise and help with the reconstruction of Europe. It has three main working parties for rail, road and inland water transport.

In the rail transport field it deals with customs, frontier formalities for passengers and goods; the exchange of transport equipment; the introduction of automatic coupling; the unification and standardisation of rolling stock; the adoption of a standard type of electro-pneumatic brake and measures for achieving high speed in rail transport.

NATIONAL

CANADA

DEPARTMENT OF TRANSPORT

Tower C, Place de Ville, Ottawa, Ontario K1A ON5

Telephone: (613) 996 5861

Minister: Don Mazankowski
Deputy Minister: Arthur Kroeger
Sr Asst Deputy Minister: S. D. Cameron
Asst Deputy Minister, Strategic Planning: N. Mulder
Asst Deputy Minister, Co-ordination: J. L. Charron
Administrator, Canadian Surface Transportation Administration: R. Y. J. Giroux
President, Canadian Transport Commission: E. J. Benson

Railway Transportation Directorate:
Director General: K. Henderson
Freight Capacity Development: E. Gilliatt
Railway Relocation & Crossing: J. H. Galvin
Railway Planning: R. Kennedy
Railway Passenger Development: R. Taborek

Transportation and Handling Grains Group Directorate:
Director General: A. W. Burges

CANADIAN TRANSPORT COMMISSION (RAILWAY TRANSPORT COMMITTEE)

Les Terrasses de la Chaudière, Ottawa, Ontario K1A ON9
Telephone: (819) 997 6567

Chairman: J. T. Gray, QC
Commissioners: M. D. Armstrong, J. D. Drainville, D. H. Jones, E. H. LaBorde, R. M. March, J. A. D. Magee, J. M. McDonough, J. B. G. Thomson, J. F. Walker, B. R. Wolfe
Executive Director Railway Transport Committee: A. G. Hibbard
Acting Director Safety & Standards: D. H. Dunphy
Director Rail Systems Development: E. W. Eastman
Director Rail Economic Analysis: M. C. Tosh

UNITED KINGDOM

DEPARTMENT OF TRANSPORT

2 Marsham St, London SW1P 3EB

Telephone: 01-212 3434

Minister of Transport: Rt. Hon. Norman Fowler MP
Parliamentary Secretary: Kenneth Clark MP

Railways:
Under-Secretary: J. Palmer
Assistant Secretaries: J. A. Page, A. T. Baker

Railway Inspectorate:
Chief Inspecting Officer: Lt Col I. K. A. McNaughton
Inspecting Officers: Major P. M. Oliver, Major A. G. B. King, Major C. F. Rose, Lt Col A. G. Townsend Rose
Senior Railway Employment Inspector: G. F. W. Sincock

CROWN AGENTS FOR OVERSEA GOVERNMENT AND ADMINISTRATIONS
4 Millbank, London SW1P 3JD

Telephone: 01-222 7730
Telegrams: CROWN LONDON SW1
Telex: 916205

Senior Crown Agent and Chairman: S. A. W. Eburne, MC
Crown Agent and Deputy Chairman: J. F. Goble
Crown Agents: Sir Leslie Kirkley, CBE
              P. W. Bulfield
              J. L. Jones, CH, MBE
              D. Williams, CB, CVD
Board of Management:
Managing Director and Chairman: A. C. Frood
Financial and Administration Controller: A. H. N. Molesworth
Director of Supplies and Recruitment Services: H. T. Eaton
Director of Marketing Development: A. J. D. Simpson
Director of Financial Services: H. Dale
Director of Engineering: G. T. Fitch
Head of Personnel: K. A. Goldsmith
Head of Railway Division: L. N. Ludlow

Representative Offices:
Bahrain: Suite 102, 10th Floor, National Bank of Bahrain Building, PO Box 531, Manama. Telephone: 254672. Telegrams: Crown Bahrain. Telex: 8307 Crown BN
Barbados: Barclays Bank Building, Roebuck Street, PO Box 82, Bridgetown. Telephone: 60458. Telegrams: Crownagents Barbados. Telex: Barbados 311.
Indonesia: PO Box 2169, Jakarta. Telephone: 584493/4. Telex: Pexmn IA 46170.
Kenya: 2nd Floor, IPS Building, Kimathi Street, PO Box 47246, Nairobi. Telephone: 25524/26917. Telegrams: Millbank, Nairobi. Telex: 22536.
Malaysia: 7th Floor, Angkasa Raya, 123 Jalan Ampang, Kuala Lumpur. Telephone: 483915/483927/4832600. Telegrams: Crogen Kualalumpur. Telex: MA 30924.
Nigeria: Western House, 8/10 Broad Street, PO Box 583, Lagos. Telephone: 630476/635889. Telegrams: Crownagents Lagos. Telex: 21416 Crown NG and 2 Mundubawa Avenue, PO Box 978, Kano. Telegrams: Crownagent Kano.
Papua New Guinea: PO Box 5790, Boroko. Telephone: 259777. Telegrams: Crownag Port Moresby. Telex: NE 22370a/b Crownag.
Saudi Arabia: PO Box 6094, Riyadh. Telephone: 66631. Telex: 202407 CAFOGA SJ
Singapore: Suite 609, Cathay Building, Mount Sophia, Singapore 0922. Telephone: 3211678. Telegrams: Millbank Singapore. Telex: RS 22171
Tanzania: PO Box 4190, Dar-es-Salaam. Telephone: 25650/29244. Telex: 41179
USA: 3100 Massachusetts Avenue NW, Washington, DC 20008. Telephone: (202) 462 1340. Telegrams: Crown Washington. Telex: Prowsh 64224

Supplies and Inspection Offices:
Bangladesh: c/o Hotel Purbani, International Suite 704/11, Dilkusha Comm Area, Dacca 2. Telephone: 254081/256081. Telegrams: Crown Dacca
Hong Kong: Room 728, Tung Ying Building, 100 Nathan Road, Kowloon. Telephone: K683528. Telegrams: Crownagents Hong Kong
India: Kada Building, 2nd Floor, 22 Richmond Road, Bangalore 560025. Telephone: 55141/579167. Telegrams: Crown Bangalore. Telex: 845 454 A B CABA IN
Japan: 6th Floor Shin Fuyo Building, 2-26 Isobe-Dori, 4-chome, Fukiai-ku, Kobe 651. Telephone: 232-3083/4. Telegrams: Agents Crown Kobe. Telex: 05622-872 AGCRWNJ

The regional offices in Singapore, Malaysia and the USA also deal with purchasing. There are also inspection offices in the industrial regions of the UK and in Federal Republic of Germany and Singapore.

ASSOCIATED SOCIETY OF LOCOMOTIVE ENGINEERS AND FIREMEN
9 Arkwright Rd, London NW3 6AB

Telephone: 01-435 6300/2160

General Secretary: R. W. Buckton

ASSOCIATION OF BRITISH RAILWAY CARRIAGE & WAGON MANUFACTURERS
7 Ludgate, Broadway, London EC4V 6DX

Chairman: T. Roland Bell
Secretaries: Peat, Marwick, Mitchell & Co.

ASSOCIATION OF CONSULTING ENGINEERS
Alliance House, 12 Caxton Street, Westminster, London SW1H 0QL

Telephone: 01-222 6557

Chairman: D. J. Coats
Secretary: Major-General P. J. M. Pellereau
Deputy Secretary: Cdr. G. D. Palmer

ASSOCIATION OF MINOR RAILWAY COMPANIES
Offices of Derwent Valley Railway, Layerthorpe Station, York YO3 7XS

Telephone: 0904 58981

Chairman: A. G. W. Garraway (Festiniog Rly)
Vice-Chairman: D. Ferreira (Ravenglass & Eskdale Rly)
Secretary: J. Acklam

ASSOCIATION OF PRIVATE RAILWAY-WAGON OWNERS LTD
18 Great Marlborough St, London W1V 2NJ

Telephone: 01-629 8434

Secretary: J. M. B. Gotch

BRITISH TRANSPORT OFFICERS' GUILD
Room 307, West Side Offices, King's Cross Station, London N1 9AX

Telephone: 01-837 0782

CHARTERED INSTITUTE OF TRANSPORT
80 Portland Place, London W1N 4DP

Telephone: 01-580 5216

President: Dr. L. St John Devlin
Director General: Brig. D. N. Locke OBE
Secretary: L. F. Aldridge

COUNCIL OF ENGINEERING INSTITUTIONS
2 Little Smith St, London SW1 P3DL

Telephone: 01-799 3912

Secretary: M. W. Leonard

DIESEL ENGINEERS AND USERS ASSOCIATION
18 London Street, London EC3R 7JR

Telephone: 01-481 2393

Secretary: J. W. Nairn

FEDERATION OF CIVIL ENGINEERING CONTRACTORS
Cowdray House, 6 Portugal Street, London WC2A 2HH

Telephone: 01-404 4020
Telex: 8955101

INSTITUTION OF BRITISH ENGINEERS
Regency House, 3 Marlborough Place, Brighton BN1 1UB

Telephone: 0273 61399

Secretary: Dorothy Henry

INSTITUTION OF CIVIL ENGINEERS
Great George St, London SW1P 3AA

Telephone: 01-222 7722
Telegrams: Institution London SW1

President: W. G. N. Geddes CBE
Secretary: R. Campbell

INSTITUTION OF ELECTRICAL ENGINEERS
Savoy Place, London WC2R 0BL

Telephone: 01-240 1871

President: Prof. J. Brown
Secretary: Dr. G. F. Gainsborough

INSTITUTION OF MECHANICAL ENGINEERS RAILWAY DIVISION
1 Birdcage Walk, London SW1H GJJ

Telephone: 01-222 7899
Telex: 917944

Chairman: K. Taylor
Secretary: J. M. Johnson MBE

INSTITUTION OF RAILWAY SIGNAL ENGINEERS
Hon General Secretary: R. L. Weedon, 21 Avalon Rd, Earley, Reading, Berkshire

LOCOMOTIVE & CARRIAGE INSTITUTION
General Secretary: D. Kirkland, 208A Chapter Rd, Willesden, London NW2 5NB

Telephone: 01-459 5326

NATIONAL COUNCIL OF INLAND TRANSPORT
5 Pembridge Crescent, London W11 3DT

Telephone: 01-727 4689

Hon Chairman: A. W. T. Daniel
Hon Secretary and Acting Treasurer: K. Meyer

NATIONAL UNION OF RAILWAYMEN
Unity House, Euston Rd, London NW1 2BL

Telephone: 01-387 4771

General Secretary: S. Weighell

PERMANENT WAY INSTITUTION
27 Lea Wood Rd, Fleet, Hampshire GU13 8AN

Hon General Secretary: L. J. Harris

RAILWAY DEVELOPMENT SOCIETY
BM-RDS, London WC1V 6XX

Telephone: 01-405 0463

Acting Secretary: J. M. Stanley MA, 12 Westcombe Park Road, London SE3

RAILWAY INDUSTRY ASSOCIATION OF GREAT BRITAIN
9 Catherine Place, London SW1E 6DX

Telephone: 01-834 1426

Director: G. R. Curry

TRANSPORT & GENERAL WORKERS UNION
Transport House, Smith Square, London SW1P 3JB

Telephone: 01-828 7788

TRANSPORT SALARIED STAFFS' ASSOCIATION
Walkden House, 10 Melton St, London NW1 2EJ

Telephone: 01-387 2101

General Secreatry: Tom Jenkins

UNITED STATES OF AMERICA

ASSOCIATION OF AMERICAN RAILROADS
American Railroads Building, 1920 "L" St, NW, Washington, DC 20036

Telephone: (202) 293 4000

Chicago Office: 59 East Van Buren St., Chicago, Illinois 60605. Telephone: (312) 939 0770
New Jersey Office: Gateway 1, Suite 2610, 7-45 Raymond Plaza West, Newark, New Jersey 07102. Telephone: (201) 623 0703
Research Centre: 3140 South Federal St., Chicago, Illinois 60616. Telephone: 312-567 3575

President and Chief Executive Officer: W. H. Dempsey
Executive Vice President: R. E. Briggs
Vice President: J. P. Marshall
Vice President—Assistant to President: J. E. Murray
Vice President (Law): C. H. Johns
Vice President and General Counsel: H. J. Breithaupt, Jr
General Counsel: P. F. Welsh
General Solicitor: J. T. Tidd
Vice President (Economics and Finance): H. A. Levine
Vice President (Operations and Maintenance): A. W. Johnston
Vice President (Research & Test): W. J. Harris, Jr
Vice President (Legislative): E. F. Waldrop, Jr
Vice President (Management Systems): H. W. Meetze
Vice President (Information and Public Affairs): L. H. Kaufman
General Attorney and Secretary: H. G. Duensing
Treasurer: C. P. Safrit

THE AMERICAN SHORT LINE RAILROAD ASSOCIATION
2000 Massachusetts Ave NW, Washington, DC 20036

Telephone: (202) 785 2250

President and Treasurer: P. H. Croft
Vice-President and General Counsel: Thomas C. Dorsey
Traffic Department:
  Vice President: K. G. Ozburn (Atlanta)
  Vice President: J. C. Johnson (Chicago)
  Vice President: J. S. Dow (Washington)
Regional Vice-Presidents:
  Pittsburgh, Pa: R. R. Firestone
  Yreka, Ca: W. B. Kyle
  Moultrie, Ga: W. L. Pippin
  Camden, Ar: D. Chandler
  Minneapolis, Minn: D. J. Boyer

AMERICAN PUBLIC TRANSIT ASSOCIATION (APTA)
1225 Connecticut Avenue NW, Washington, DC

Telephone: (202) 331 1100

Chairman: Harold I. Fisher
President: Houston P. Ishmael
Executive Vice President: B. R. Stokes
Secretary-Treasurer: James R. Maloney

APTA is the organisation which represents transit operators in the USA and Canada, including all systems operating rail facilities. In addition to more than 300 operating members, APTA also has more than 300 associate members including contractors, consultants, manufacturers and suppliers.

DEPARTMENT OF TRANSPORTATION
400 7th Street, SW Washington, DC 20590

Secretary: N. E. Goldschmidt
Under Secretary: Vacant
Deputy Under Secretary: Vacant
Executive Secretary: E. G. Lewis
General Councillor: Linda Heller Kamm
Assistant Secretary for Policy and International Affairs: Vacant
Assistant Secretary for Budget and Programmes: M. L. Downey
Assistant Secretary for Governmental Affairs: S. J. Williams, Acting
Assistant Secretary for Administration: E. W. Scott
Director of Public Affairs, Office of Secretary: R. A. Holland
Administrator of Federal Aviation Administration: L. M. Bond
Administrator of Federal Highway Administration: Karl S. Bowers
Federal Railroad Administrator: J. M. Sullivan
Administrator of Urban Mass Transportation: Vacant

Administrator of Research and Special Programmes Administration: M. J. Dvgoff
Administrator of National Highway Traffic Safety Administration: Joan Claybrook

INTERSTATE COMMERCE COMMISSION
12th & Constitution Ave NW, Washington, DC 20423

Telephone: (202) 275 7252

Chairman: A. Daniel O'Neal
Vice Chairman: Betty Jo Christian
Commissioners: Virginia Mae Brown
            Robert C. Gresham
            G. M. Stafford
            Charles L. Clapp
Rail Services Planning Officer: Alan M. Fitzwater
Dir Bar of Investigations & Enforcement: P. M. Shannon
Secretary: H. Gordon Homme
Managing Director: Pierce A. Quinlan
General Counsel: M. L. Evans
Director Bureau of Accounts: James B. Thomas Jr.
Director Bureau of Economics: Ernest R. Olson
Director Bureau of Operations: J. E. Burns
Director Bureau of Traffic: M. Foley
Director of Communications: D. Baldwin
Chief Administrative Law Judge: Robert M. Glennon
Director Office of Proceedings: Robert J. Brooks
Director Small Business Assistance Office: Bernard Gaillard
Director Policy Review Office: George M. Chandler
Congressional Relations Officer: Bruce N. Hatton
Rail Public Counsel: Howard A. Heffron (quasi-independent)

FEDERAL RAILROAD ADMINISTRATION
400 7th Street SW, Washington, DC 20590

Telephone: (202) 426 4000

Eastern Office: 434 Walnut St, Rm 1020, Philadelphia, Pennsylvania 19106. Telephone: (215) 597 0750
Southern Office: 1568 Willingham Dr, Suite 216B, College Park, Georgia 30337. Telephone: (404) 763 7801
Southwestern Office: 819 Taylor St, Rm 11A23, Ft Worth, Texas 76102. Telephone: (817) 334 3601
Western Office: Two Embarcadero Center, Suite 630, San Francisco, California 94111. Telephone: (415) 556 6411

Administrator: J. M. Sullivan
Chief Counsel: R. K. James
Associate Administrator for Administration: F. G. Bremer
Associate Administrator, Office of Safety: J. W. Walsh
General Manager, Alaska RR: Vacant
Associate Administrator for Research and Development: R. E. Parsons
Public Affairs Officer: R. Michael Avenenti
Acting Associate Administrator, Federal Assistance: W. E. Loftus

NATIONAL MEDIATION BOARD
1425 K St NW, Suite 910, Washington DC 20572

Chairman: Robert O. Harris
Members: G. S. Ives, Robert J. Brown
Executive Secretary: Rowland K. Quinn, Jr
Staff Mediation Director: E. B. Meredith
General Counsel: Wm. E. Fredenberger, Jr
Hearing Officer: Ronald M. Etters

NATIONAL TRANSPORTATION SAFETY BOARD
800 Independence Avenue SW, Washington DC 20594

Chairman: James B. King
Member: Elwood T. Driver
Member: Patricia A. Goldman
Member: G. H. Patrick Bursley
Member: F. H. McAdams
General Counsel: F. L. Puls
Managing Director: James Shepard
Chief Administrative Law Judge: William E. Fowler Jr.
Director of Public Affairs: E. E. Slattery Jr.

URBAN MASS TRANSPORTATION ADMINISTRATION
Department of Transportation, 400 7th Street, SW Washington, DC 20590

Administrator: R. S. Page
Deputy Administrator: C. F. Bingman
Special Assistant: R. Falknor
Director of Civil Rights: H. B. Williams
Associate Administrator for Administration: W. H. Boswell
Chief Counsel of Office of Chief Counsel: M. M. Ayres
Associate Administrator for Technology Development and Deployment: G. J. Pastor
Associate Administrator of Office of Transportation Management and Demonstrations: R. J. McManus
Associate Administrator, Office of Transit Assistance: J. K. Taylor
Director, Office of Public Affairs: F. D. Trecker
Associate Administrator Office for Policy & Programme Development: L. C. Liburdi
Associate Administrator for Transportation Planning: R. Gallamore

RAILROAD RETIREMENT BOARD
844 Rush Street, Chicago, Illinois 60611

Telephone: (312) 751 4500

Chairman: William P. Adams
Members: Earl Oliver
         C. J. Chamberlain
Secretary of the Board: R. F. Butler
Chief Executive Officer: Eugene Koch

AMERICAN ASSOCIATION OF RAILROAD SUPERINTENDENTS
18154 Harwood Ave, Homewood, Illinois 60430

Telephone: (312) 799 4650

President: C. W. Powers
Secretary: A. Wilson

AMERICAN RAILROAD TRUCK LINES ASSOCIATION
516 West Jackson Blvd, Chicago, Illinois 60606

Telephone: (312) 236 7600

President: D. H. Bergmann (Manager, Intermodal Ops, N&W Rly)

AMERICAN RAILWAY CAR INSTITUTE
11E 44th St, New York, NY 10017

Telephone: (212) 867 6577

Chairman: E. T. Ahnquist (Pullman-Standard)
President, Secretary and Treasurer: W. A. Renz
Vice-Presidents: W. T. Anthony (Bethlehem Steel Corp, Railroad Products)
    R. C. Ortner (Ortner Freight Car Co)

AMERICAN RAILWAY DEVELOPMENT ASSOCIATION
c/o Conrail, 1528 Walnut Street, Philadelphia, Pennsylvania 19104

President: W. J. Rettie
Secretary: J. R. Hyland

AMERICAN RAILWAY ENGINEERING ASSOCIATION
2000 L Street NW, Washington, DC 20036

Telephone: (202) 293 3692

President: Mike Rougas
Executive Director: L. T. Cerney

AMERICAN SOCIETY OF MECHANICAL ENGINEERS — RAIL TRANSPORTATION DIVISION
1000 West Shore Dr, Culver, Indiana 46511

Telephone: (219) 842 3989

Chairman: W. H. Chidley
Secretary: N. E. Bateson

ASSOCIATION OF RAILROAD ADVERTISING MANAGERS

President: R. G. Nelson (East Adv Manager, Union Pacific)
Executive Secretary: J. D. Singer

ASSOCIATION OF RAILROAD EDITORS
American Railroads Building 413, Washington, DC 20036

President: Ruben Levin, Labor Newspaper, 400 First Street, NW, Washington, DC 20001
First Vice-President: James H. Beck, Union Pacific Railroad, 1416 Dodge Street, Omaha, Nebraska 68179
Second Vice-President: Duncan Haimerl, Canadian National Railways, PO Box 8100, Montreal H3C 3N4, Canada
Secretary-Treasurer: W. W. (Woody) Thompson, Association of American Railroads, American Railroads Building 413, Washington, DC 20036

Membership: 70 organisations in the USA, Canada, Mexico.
    120 individual members.

Annual Conference: 1980; Ottawa, Canada
    1981; San Diego, California

ASSOCIATION OF SOUTHEASTERN RAILROADS
1920 L St NW, Washington, DC 20036

Telephone: (202) 293 3140

Chairman: P. F. Osborn
Assoc Secretary: H. W. Hird

CENTRAL RAILWAY CLUB OF BUFFALO
39 Paul Place, Buffalo, NY 14210

President: C. R. Shero
Executive Secretary: C. M. Voll

LOCOMOTIVE MAINTENANCE OFFICERS' ASSOCIATION
3144 Brereton Ct, Huntington, West Virginia 25705

Telephone: (304) 523 7276

President: T. A. Tennyson
Secretary: J. J. T. Koerner

NATIONAL RAILROAD ADJUSTMENT BOARD
220 South State St, Chicago, Illinois 60604

Chairman: G. L. Naylor

NATIONAL RAILROAD INTERMODAL ASSOCIATION
2 North Charles Street, Balto, Maryland 21201

President: G. A. Volkers (Dir Operations and Equipment, TOFC/COFC, Chessie)
Vice-President: E. W. Frey (General Manager TOFC, Santa Fe)
Secretary: W. C. Noble

NATIONAL RAILWAY LABOR CONFERENCE
1225 Connecticut Ave, 1901 L Street, Washington, DC 20036

Telephone: (202) 862 7200

Chairman: C. I. Hopkins

NATIONAL RAILROAD CONSTRUCTION AND MAINTENANCE ASSOCIATION INC
9331 Waymond Avenue, Highland, Indiana 46322

Telephone: (219) 924 1709

President: R. Deprizio
Secretary: Randy Poggemiller
Executive Director: I. shields

RAILROAD PERSONNEL ASSOCIATION
American Railroads Bldg, Washington, DC 20036

Telephone: (202) 293 4137

President: L. M. Frye
Secretary: H. S. Dewhurst

RAILROAD PUBLIC RELATIONS ASSOCIATION
American Railroads Bldg, Washington, DC 20036

Telephone: (202) 293 4191

President: Barry B. Combs
Secretary: J. N. Ragsdale

RAILWAY ENGINEERING—MAINTENANCE SUPPLIERS ASSOCIATION INC
5600 Marina Drive, Holmes Beach, Florida 33510

Telephone: (813) 778 4121

President: R. C. Crosby (Marmon/Transmotive)
Secretary: W. J. Gallagher (Sperry Rail)
Executive Secretary: L. D. McGuan

RAILWAY PROGRESS INSTITUTE
700 No Fairfax St, Alexandria, Virginia 22314

Telephone: (703) 836 2332

President: R. W. Smith
Chairman: C. B. Ramsdell
Vice-President: R. A. Matthews
Treasurer: R. F. Griffin

RAILWAY SUPPLY ASSOCIATION
332 S Michigan Ave, Suite 1540, Chicago, Illinois 60604

Telephone: (312) 939 4478

President: W. J. Burrows (Vapor Co)
Vice President: P. O. Williams (New York Air Brake Co)
Executive Secretary: A. Schiffers, Jr

RAILWAY SYSTEMS SUPPLIERS, INC
Rm 120 A, 401 Seventh Ave, New York, NY 10001

Telephone: (212) 239 7038

Chairman and President: E. H. Cole
Executive Vice President: G. Harmon
Executive Director and Secretary: F. Aikman, Jr

ROADMASTERS AND MAINTENANCE OF WAY ASSOCIATION OF AMERICA
Cary Bldg, 18154 Harwood Ave, Homewood, Illinois 60430

Telephone: (312) 799 4650

President: D. J. Gale
Secretary: A. Wilson

TRAFFIC CLUBS INTERNATIONAL
1040 Woodcock Rd, Orlando, Florida 32803

Chairman of Board: J. M. Beaupre
Secretary: Althea B. Erikson
Executive Director: C. T. Harper

CONSULTANCY SERVICES

AMERICAN TRANSIT CORPORATION

120 South Central Ave, St Louis, Missouri 63105, USA

Telephone: (314) 726 9200
Telex: 442 466 ATC STL

Vice-President: Paul J. Ballord

AMMANN & WHITNEY

Two World Trade Center, Ste 1700, New York, NY 10048, USA

Telephone: (212) 938 8200

Partner: Allen M. Custen

PROJECTS
Reconstruction of trackage, one swing bridge, eleven fixed bridges and Providence Union Station for the Northeast Corridor Improvement Project (three projects, $40 million); Inspection and analysis of 70 miles (112 km) of elevated mass transit structures for the New York City Transit Authority; Programme to study noise and vibration problems on elevated mass transit systems in the USA for the Department of Transportation; inspection, analysis and contract documents for the rehabilitation of Boston's subway tunnels totalling 15 miles (24 km) for the MBTA; detailed analysis and programme development of rail transit alternatives in the Queens-Midtown corridor in New York City for the New York City DOT; Construction Management for signal enclosures, relay room and signal tower for the New York City Transit Authority.

ANGUS McDONALD & ASSOCIATES INC

2150 Shattuck Avenue, Berkeley, California 94704, USA

Telephone: (415) 548 5831

President: Angus N. McDonald

PROJECTS
Financial planning for California Transportation Commission ($100 000); Economics and finance project BART impact Programme ($190 000) for Metropolitan Transportation Authority (MTC), Berkeley, California.

ARTHUR ANDERSEN & CO

1666K St NW, Washington, DC 20006, USA

Telephone: (202) 862 3100

Partner: Michael E. Simon

One Market Plaza, San Francisco, California 94105, USA

Telephone: (415) 546 8200

Partner: William T. VanLieshout

One Surrey Street, London WC2R 2PS, England

Telephone: 01-836 1200

Partner: David R. Kaye

PROJECTS
Management information systems planning, design and installation for variety of transit and railroad clients in the USA and UK; performance audits of transit operations for regional and state oversight agencies.

WS ATKINS & PARTNERS

Woodcote Grove, Ashley Road, Epsom, Surrey KT18 5BW, England

Telephone: 78 26140
Telegrams: Kinsopar Epsom
Telex: 23497

Principal officers
Director, Transportation Engineering Division F. L. Johnson
R. A. Long
H. Ormiston

CAPABILITIES
As a major subsidiary of the WS Atkins Group of planning, engineering and management consultants, WS Atkins & Partners have experience in railway projects in various parts of the world. Their overall capability includes feasibility studies, traffic forecasts, cost estimates, detailed design of trackwork, civil engineering, signalling/communications and systems engineering and supervision of construction. Studies devoted to the socio-economic aspects of a project, route assessment, environmental impact analysis, rationalisation of services, operating methods, future strategy, inventories of facilities and asset valuations are also undertaken. WS Atkins & Partners frequently work with Henderson Busby Partnership.

PROJECTS
Industrial railways associated with major steelworks complexes including studies of linking railways to main systems in Venezuela and Morocco; upgradings in Algeria; similar works in the UK for the power generation, coal and steel industries; design of mainline railway in Saudia Arabia. Other projects include:

Suburban modal interchanges in Melbourne.
Land use and traffic forecast in East Sussex, UK.
Rapid transit in Cardiff-Llantrisant, UK.
Container terminal feasibility, Melbourne.
Multi-modal facilities in Tasmania.
Route selection and environmental impact analyses for Channel Tunnel rail link.
Signal and telecommunication, services maintenance rationalisation for British Rail.
Suburban rail service feasibility in Venezuela.
Railway workshop modernisation in New South Wales.
Valuation of entire steelworks railway system in Sweden.

MICHAEL BAKER JR INC

4301 Dutch Ridge Rd, Beaver, Pennsylvania 15009, USA

Telephone: (412) 495 7711

Principal: Edgar C. Richardson

PROJECTS
East Busway ($65 million) for Port Authority of Allegheny County (PAT); Section EHB of Northeast Corridor Improvement project; and terminal bulk storage facility near Pittsburg for Chessie system.

R L BANKS & ASSOCIATES INC

900 17th St NW, Washington, DC 20006, USA

Telephone: (202) 296 6700

President: Robert L. Banks

PROJECTS
Rail planning studies for Colorado, Minnesota, North Dakota, Delaware, Maryland, New Hampshire and the District of Columbia; Line acquisition assessments for Genessee & Wyoming Railroad, Grand Trunk Western Railroad and Southeastern Pennsylvania Transportation Authority; Operations analysis of Chicago, Milwaukee, St Paul and Pacific Railroad, Consolidated Rail Corp, Canton Railroad and British Columbia Railway; Analysis of rail terminal operations at St Louis; Traffic and economic forecasting for Chicago, Rock Island & Pacific Railroad, Southern Railway and Western Pacific Railroad; Costing study for Michigan Northern Railway.

HAROLD BARTHOLOMEW AND ASSOCIATES

188 Jefferson Ave, Memphis, Tennessee 38103, USA

Telephone: (901) 527 3521

PROJECTS
Transit technical study at Savannah Ga, for Chatham County Metropolitan Planning Commission; Southeast Florida transit corridor study (Miami region) for Florida Department of Transportation (DOT).

BARTON-ASCHMAN ASSOCIATES, INC

820 Davis St, Evanston, Illinois 60201, USA

Telephone: (312) 491 1000

Senior Vice-President: Michael A. Powills Jr

PROJECTS
Feasibility study of intermodal terminal roadway in Chicago, Illinois for the Federal Railroad Administration ($190 000).

BECHTEL INCORPORATED
(Hydro & Community Facilities Division)

50 Beale Street, San Francisco, California 94119, USA

Telephone: (415) 768/6945
Telegrams: WATEKA- SF, CA
Int'l Telex: 470195
Dom Telex: 34783

Associated companies:
Bechtel Power Corporation (same address).

CAPABILITIES
Started in 1898, Bechtel's headquarters are located in San Francisco, California, with worldwide regional offices. The staff totals nearly 30 000 permanent employees, over half of which are graduate engineers and technical personnel.
Rail projects are the responsibility of Bechtel's Hydro and Community Facilities Division, headquartered in San Francisco, California, USA. The Rail Projects Department in this division is staffed with railway specialists, planners, engineers, and project managers covering all principal railroad disciplines. Bechtel performs railway services in terms of techno-economic feasibility studies, master planning, preliminary and final engineering, procurement services, construction engineering, and construction, or a combination of these. When called upon to handle complete packages Bechtel also offers assistance in securing required financing.
Bechtel's experience in railroad projects dates back to 1898 when the founder of the company, Warren A. Bechtel, started building railroads in what is now Oklahoma. Bechtel's comprehensive railroad construction activities started in 1920, with work on the realignment of Southern Pacific's Overland Route and the building of other parts of that system, as well as the original construction of the Western Pacific and the Northwestern Pacific. Experience increased worldwide over the following five decades.

PROJECTS

Assignment	Completion Date
Northeast Corridor Improvement Project—for high-speed rail service Boston to Washington. Technical support for all phases of this 730 km project.	1981
Coronado Railroad—engineering, procurement and construction management of a 75 km coal hauling railroad for unit train operation.	1978
Springerville Railroad—engineering design of a 40 km railroad for unit train operation by AT & SF Railway.	1978
Electrification Study—feasibility and cost effectiveness of electrifying some main lines of the Union Pacific, AT & SF, and Conrail systems as a basis for installing large energy storage units was studied	1978
Concrete Tie Programme—installation and test of concrete ties on mainline railroads in the USA and analysis of the resulting experience.	1978
Coal Haul Railroads—analysis and cost estimates of the factors involved in building and operating coal haul railroads to serve power generating stations in comparison with other modes of transportation.	1978

Assignment	Completion Date
Boardman Railroad—engineering, procurement and construction management of a 20 km spur line of the Union Pacific Railroad to serve a generating station.	1977
Venezuela Railroad—technical analysis of turnkey tenders for proposed 600 km railroad including rolling stock, equipment and personnel training.	1977
Railroad Track and Land Use study for proposed port development.	1977
Regional Railroad Inventory—co-ordinate and perform inventory and costs of rehabilitation of bankrupt railroads in the northeast and midwest USA—over 30 000 km of routes.	1975
Big Stone Plant—assistance in arranging unit coal transportation, including freight rates, tariffs, design of 13 km of mine and plant trackage and development of fliptop covered gondola cars.	1974
St Louis Area Rail/barge Terminal—assistance in evaluating railroad capabilities and track capacities, unloading options and terminal facilities.	1974
Navajo Mine—design of 16 km railroad from mine to power plant; prepared car and locomotive specifications.	1973
MBR 644 km railroad to handle iron ore—consultation on expansion and modernisation of existing line to increase capacity.	1973
Maryland and Pennsylvania Railroad—final design of physical improvements to rehabilitate a 56 km section of line to carry 153 metric ton nuclear fuel cars; includes 35 bridges.	1973
Muskogee Station—assistance in arranging unit coal transportation from Wyoming, including freight rates, tariffs, and freight car specifications.	1973
Amarillo Copper Refinery—analysis of plant switching of rail cars for yard layout and design of access spur.	1973
Robe River 167 km railroad to handle iron ore; design, construction management, procurement and operating procedures including selection of rolling stock and maintenance facilities.	1970
Mt Newman 432 km railroad to handle iron ore; construction management and procurement of rolling stock and other items.	1970
Centralia Power Plant—design, engineering and construction management of 8 km access railroad.	1970
Cerro Bolivar Mine—field engineering and construction management for 145 km heavy duty iron ore railway including terminal and support facilities.	1952

BLAUVELT ENGINEERING CO

1 Park Ave, New York, NY 10016, USA

Telephone: (212) 481 1600

Partner: Francis M. Fuerst

PROJECTS
Vienna Line ($40 million) for Washington Metropolitan Area Transit Authority (WMATA); Oakland Station, South Line ($12.5 million) for Metropolitan Atlanta Rapid Transit Authority (MARTA).

BOGEN JENAL ENGINEERS PC

983 Willis Ave, Albertson, New York 11507, USA

Telephone: (516) 747-4220

President: Samuel A. Bogen, PE
Vice-President: Joseph R. Jenal, PE

PROJECTS
Final M/E design for the following Washington Metro sections: D-6 ($45 million); E-1 ($85 million); F-3 ($50 million).

BOGEN, JOHNSTON, LAU & JENAL PC
(A Minority Business Enterprise)

983 Willis Avenue, Albertson, New York 11507, USA

Telephone: (516) 747 4220/(212) 895 3358

President: Wallace O Johnston, PE
Vice-President: Samuel A Bogen, PE

PROJECTS
Design of following work on the Northeast Corridor (Washington to Boston) Railroad Improvement Programme for Federal Railroad Administration: Connecticut River Bridge, movable bridge control house, power, bridge controls, utilities ($6 million); Portal Bridge, movable bridge power and bridge controls ($7.5 million); Track Improvements, Bush River, Maryland to Perryville, Maryland ($10 million); Interim Signals, Washington, District of Columbia to Hudson, New Jersey ($5 million); Signal System renovation, Massachusetts Bay Transportation Authority ($2.5 million).

BOLT BERANEK AND NEWMAN INC

50 Moulton St, Cambridge, Massachusetts 02138, USA

Telephone: (617) 491 1850

Department Manager: David N. Keast

PROJECTS
Vehicle noise control consulting engineering for New York City Transit Authority (NYCTA); environmental analysis and preliminary engineering on the Boston southwest corridor for Massachusetts Bay Transportation Authority (MBTA). Additional projects: noise and vibration accessment and control for AMTRAK. Northeast Corridor improvement project; locomotive quieting project for US Department of Transportation.

CAM INDUSTRIES INC

215 Philadelphia St, PO Box 227, Hanover, Pennsylvania 17331, USA

Telephone: (717) 637 5988
Telex: 840-470 (CAM Hnvr)

CAPABILITIES
Planning and equipping of railway electric shops.

CANAC CONSULTANTS LTD
(A subsidiary of Canadian National Railways)

935 Lagauchetiere St W, PO Box 8100, Montreal, Quebec H3C 3N4, Canada

Telephone: (514) 877 4816
Telegrams: CONDIV MONTREAL
Telex: 055 60753

President: V. R. Cox

CAPABILITIES
This multimodal arm of Canadian National Railways and Air Canada has carried out transportation consultancy projects in Africa, Asia, the Caribbean and North and South America. Services offered include: market and economic surveys; organisation and management studies; management and personnel training and development programmes; route reconnaissance and construction supervision; motive power and rolling stock evaluation; signal system studies.

CANADIAN PACIFIC CONSULTING SERVICES LTD

Room 171, Windsor Station, Montreal, Quebec H3C 3E4, Canada

Telephone: (514) 395 7002
Telex: 055-60147

Subsidiary: Servicosde Constructoria Pacifico Canadaiense SA, PO Box 248, Centro Colon, SA Jose, Costa Rica

Associated Company: Transource Inc, One World Trade Centre, Suite 5075, New York, NY 10048, USA

Telephone: (212) 466 1391

Parent Company: Canadian Pacific Limited

OFFICERS
Chairman of the Board: J. A. McDonald
President and Chief Executive Officer: H. M. Romoff
Vice-President & General Manager: G. T. Fisher
Vice-President Business Development: J. Denis Bélisle
Assistant General Managers: R. H. Ballantyne
      R. A. Shea
Secretary: R. L. Partridge
Directors: J. Fox
    R. Klein
    R. T. Riley
    L. M. Riopel
    W. W. Stinson
    G. A. Worden
    J. P. T. Clough
    A. F. Joplin

CAPABILITIES
Canadian Pacific Consulting Services is the international consulting arm of Canadian Pacific. Canadian Pacific was incorporated in 1881 and today has assets of over $9 000 million Canadian with extensive interests in railroad, water, road, and air transport, real estate development, oil and gas, mining, metals, chemicals, and timberlands.
CP Rail operates 26 600 km of track across Canada and controls another 7 600 km in the USA. Its equipment includes approximately 70 000 freight cars, 1 300 locomotives and five coastal vessels and barges. The railway has played a pioneer role in the development of sophisticated unit train systems and pricing techniques for transporting bulk commodities such as coal, sulphur, and grain.
Canadian Pacific group CPCS is able to call upon the professional, technical and latest methods of interfacing rail, truck and ship traffic, and the ability to provide cost-benefit studies using computer-oriented financial analysis programmes for any given present and foreseeable traffic requirements places it in a unique position to optimise any conceivable transportation investment. Through its affiliation with the Canadian Pacific group, CPCS is able to call upon the professional, technical and operating personnel of any of the group's member companies to meet specific engineering, research, economic, marketing or supervisory requirements of individual projects anywhere in the world.

PROJECTS
Railway clients served by Canadian Pacific Consulting Services Ltd include the following:
Turkish State Railways; Korean National Railroad; Tunisian National Railways; Congo-Ocean Railway; Egyptian Railways; Mozambique Railways; Honduran National Railways; Venezuelan National Railways; Rede Ferroviaria Federal S.A. of Brazil; Malayan State Railways; Bangladesh Railway; Indonesian State Railways; Western Australian Government Railways; Quebec North Shore and Labrador Railway; British Columbia Railway; Togo Railway.
Ghana Railway; East African Railways Corp; State Railway of Thailand; Mt. Newman Railway (Australia); Hamersley Iron Ore Railway (Australia); Quebec Cartier Mining Railway (Canada); Peruvian National Railways; Sri Lanka Railway; Nicaraguan Pacific Railway; Cameroon National Railways; South African Railways; Panama Railroad; Jamaican Railway Corporation; La Société Nationale des Transports Ferroviaires of Algeria; Caminhos de Ferro Portuguese; White Pass and Yukon Railway; Costa Rican National Railways.

CAN DEUB FLEISSIG AND ASSOCIATES

11 Hill St, Newark, New Jersey 07102, USA

Telephone: (201) 643 3919

Vice-President: Burton R. Cohen

PROJECTS
Environmental Impact Statement ($975 000) for New Jersey Department of Transportation (DOT).

CAPITAL CONSULTANTS

5508 Wilson Lane, Bethesda, Maryland 20014, USA

Telephone: (301) 656 1180

Principal Partner: Edwin L. Mueller

PROJECTS
Automated transit guideway survey (under $10 000).

C-E MAGUIRE INC

31 Canal St, Providence, Rhode Island 02903, USA

Telephone: (401) 272 6000

Executive Vice-President: Vincent M. Cangiano

PROJECTS
Red Line extension tunnel design ($110 million) for Massachusetts Bay Transportation Authority (MBTA); Section 2 tunnel design ($38 million) for Washington Metropolitan Area Transit Authority (AMATA); Orange Line Transport study ($40 million) for Massachusetts Bay Transportation Authority (MBTA); Northeast Corridor rail improvement, New Howley to Guilford ($22 million) for Federal Rail Administration.

CENTURY ENGINEERING INC

32 West Rd, Towson, Maryland 21204, USA

Telephone: (301) 823 8070

Assistant Vice-President: Robert G. James

PROJECTS
Glebe Road station section design ($31 million) for Washington Metropolitan Area Transit Authority (WMATA).

CHASE, ROSEN & WALLACE, INC

901 North Washington St, Alexandria, Virginia 22134, USA

Telephone: (703) 836 7120

Vice-President: Stanley B. Rosen

PROJECTS
Improved services for handicapped and demonstration development based on survey for Urban Mass Transportation Administration (UMTA); Microfiche-based information system for transit information agents for Chicago Transit Authority (CTA).

CITIES CORPORATION

102 Mount Auburn St, Cambridge, Massachusetts 02138, USA

Telephone: (617) 491 8007

Director of Transit Mapping: Barbara Petersen

PROJECTS
System map design projects for Rhode Island Public Transit Authority (RIPTA) and Metro Regional Transit Authority, Akron, Ohio.

TERENCE J COLLINS ASSOCIATES, INC

Suite 101, Woodfield Grove Business Center, 830 East Higgins Road, Schaumburg, Illinois 66195, USA

Telephone: (312) 843 7300

President: Terry Collins

PROJECTS
Project management of the Chicago Transit Authority's radio and data communications system, including location function for Emergency Vehicle Location (EVL), for their entire bus fleet of 2400, and supervisory system for 100 vehicles; Responsibility extends to construction and consolidation of the control centre facilities to accommodate the rail, bus, supervisory and power supervisor (rapid); Also responsible for the review/co-ordination and implementation of the diagnostic computer system; Contract value: $5 million.
Retained by the Gary Public Transportation Corporation, for the preparation of the final specification for their proposed radio and data communications system, together with the subsequent co-ordination of the implementation of the entire system through to final system acceptance; Contract value: $350 000.
Retained by the Chicago Transit Authority to prepare a comprehensive performance specification for a Consolidated Radio Communications System and Train Supervision System for the entire rail system, both above ground and in the subways, which allows for the interface of both the Chicago Police and Fire Departments. In addition, the specification covers the integration of the existing bus and associated supervisory systems, with the rail communications system. Contract value: $14 million.
Preparation of a comprehensive radio communications system for the Suburban Bus Systems of northeastern Illinois, operated by the Regional Transportation Authority. Contract value: $1.3 million.

COMSUL LTD

417 Montgomery St, San Francisco, California 94104, USA

Telephone: (415) 989 6700

Vice-President: Colin W. Halford

PROJECTS
Providing engineering services in the planning, design, testing and review of the combined communications network for San Francisco Municipal Railway.

CRS DESIGN ASSOCIATES INC

1100 Milam Building, Suite 500, Houston, Texas 77002, USA

Member companies: STRAAM Engineers, Inc; Clark, Dietz & Associates-Engineers, Inc

Telephone: (713) 658 9511

President: C Herbert Paseur

PROJECTS
Engineering consultants for Washington Metropolitan Area Transit Authority (WMATA) and Metropolitan Area Rapid Transit Authority (MARTA); Claims consultant for Bay Area Rapid Transit District, San Francisco (BARTD); Engineering consultant for the Chessie System; Construction Manager for Denver Regional Transit District (RTD) Transit Mall; Bridge Designer for Chicago & Eastern Illinois Railroad, Chicago & Northwestern Railroad, Gulf, Mobile & Ohio Railroad, Illinois Central Gulf Railroad, Saint Louis-San Francisco Railroad and Norfolk & Western Railroad; Marshalling Yard Designer for Louisville-Nashville Railroad; Bridge Designer for Southern Railroad Company.

DALTON-DALTON-NEWPORT, INC

3605 Warrensville Center Rd, Cleveland, Ohio 44122, USA

Telephone: (216) 283-4000

Vice-President: Frederick J. Richardson

PROJECTS
Northeast Corridor high-speed passenger programme design sections (three); high-speed rail passenger study, Ohio Rail Transportation Authority; classification yard, Ames, Iowa, Chicago and Northwestern Railroad.

DANIEL, MANN, JOHNSON & MENDENHALL

3250 Wilshire Blvd, Los Angeles, California 90010, USA (other offices world-wide)

Telephone: (213) 381 3663

Vice-President/Transportation: Richard J. Bouchard

PROJECTS
Design of Baltimore rapid transit system ($850 million) for Maryland Mass Transit Administration (MTA); San Bernardino busway ($90 million) for Southern California Rapid Transit District.

DAY & ZIMMERMANN, INC

1818 Market St, Philadelphia, Pennsylvania 19103, USA

Telephone: (215) 299 8000

President, Consulting Services Division: Charles A. Graves

PROJECTS
Systems design for Niagara Frontier Transportation Authority's light rail rapid transit system ($439 million); electrification design, 12th Street Station design and construction management for Southeastern Pennsylvania Transportation Authority's centre city commuter rail tunnel ($300 million); design and construction management of modernisation of electrification for Connecticut Department of Transportation's New Haven commuter rail line ($5 million); programme monitoring and review for Federal Railroad Administration's Northeast Corridor rail improvement project.

DECONSULT
Deutsche Eisenbahn Consulting GmbH

Postfach 700 476, 6000 Frankfurt/Main 70, Federal Republic of Germany

Telephone: (0611) 6050-1
Telex: 4 14 516 decond
Telegrams: DECONSULT FRANKFURTMAIN

Supervisory Board: Dr jur. E. Schneider
    Dip-Ing. P. Koch
    Dr rer. pol. S. Eichler
General Manager: Dr-Ing. R. Janousch
    F. W. Möller
Manager, Personnel Administration, Economics: Hr. Liese
Manager Transport, Engineering: Hr. Scheller
Project Division Managers: General—Hr. Wendt
    Germany—Hr. Wendt
    Africa and Iran—Dr Ing. Haucke
    Middle and Far East: Hr. Kabisch
    America—Hr. Grossmann
    Europe, Iraq, Turkey—Hr. Müller-Hande

CAPABILITIES
DECONSULT—an international consulting enterprise—carries out planning and consultancy work in the transportation sector all over the world. The main accents in such activities are placed upon national and municipal railway networks. The firm was founded in 1966 by the Federal German Railways and the Deutsche Bank AG, which are today still the only shareholders.
At present, DECONSULT employs about 200 engineers and economists. As DECONSULT operates a staff exchange scheme with the Federal German Railways, both the home office staff and the expert teams working abroad can be quickly supplemented to meet current requirements.

Associated Offices: DECONSULT has offices in:
Algiers, Algeria; Aqaba, Jordan; Baghdad, Iraq; Jakarta/Bandung, Indonesia; Lisbon, Portugal; Sao Paulo, Brazil; Taipei, Taiwan; Tehran/Esfahan, Iran.

PROJECTS
DECONSULT has executed or is at present executing projects in the following countries:
Algeria, Argentina, Brazil, Burma, Cameroon, Costa Rica, Federal Republic of Germany, Ivory Coast, Ghana, Greece, Guinea, India, Indonesia, Iran, Iraq, Jordan, Malaysia, Pakistan, Paraguay, Peru, Portugal, South Korea, Sudan, Taiwan, Thailand, Togo, Upper Volta, Venezuela, Viet-Nam, Zaire.

PROJECTS (CIVIL ENGINEERING)

Country	Client	Description of Project	Date of Completion
Algeria	SNTF	Preliminary project for the construction of the station of Oran	1977
Algeria	SNTF	Preparation for supervision of construction of new line Touggourt-Ghardaia	1977
Algeria	SNTF	Preliminary and final design, tendering for track-doubling of the El Harrach/Thenia railway line incl. structures, signalling and telecommunications systems	1977
Algeria	SNTF	Study, improvements and extensions of the railway and mass-transit network of the Metropolitan Area of Algiers	1978
Brazil	Ferrovia Paulista SA (FEPASA)	Advisory services, organisation and instruction of the FEPASA in the field of tracks	1978
Brazil	Ferrovia Paulista SA (FEPASA)	Continuation of supervision of construction as regards the new line of the FEPASA in the Vale do Ribeira	1976
Brazil	Companhia Metropolitana Rio de Janeiro	Advisory services in the fields of construction, direct rail support, power supply, operation, signalling	1977
Germany (FDR)	Deutsche Bundesbahn Research Office Minden	Draught for regulation "structure gauge"	1977
Germany (FDR)	Bundesbahn Frankfurt	Assistance when planning new lines and extending existing ones	1977
Iran	Iranian State Railways (RAI)	Detailed project for both track doubling and electrification of the lines Qom-Isfahan-Riz and Sagzi-Kerman	1978
Portugal	Portuguese State Railways (CP)	Modernisation of the suburban service in the region of Lisbon	1976
Portugal	Metropolitano de Lisboa, Empresa Nacionalizada	Metro Lisbon Underground railway junction Rotunda	1977
Venezuela	Deutsche Gesellschaft für technische Zusammenarbeit (GTZ)	Assistance to the Venezuelan State Railways (IAAFE) when elaborating tender documents for a new railway line	1976

PROJECTS (MECHANICAL)

Country	Client	Description of Project	Date of Completion
Brazil	Ferrovia Paulista SA (FEPASA)	Final acceptance of 155 saddle wagons and 75 sliding door wagons at Waggonunion in Siegen	1976
Germany (FDR)	Osthannoversche Eisenbahnen AG, Celle	Expertise for improvement of the maintenance system	1977
Germany (FDR)	Bergbau-Forschung GmbH Essen	New design of special freight wagons for pit coal underground working	1977
Indonesia	Department of Transport, Communication and Tourism	Consulting services for rehabilitation of maintenance of diesel locomotives	1977
Iran	Iranian State Railways (RAI)	Assistance when wagons were based by DB to RAI	1976
Liberia	Bong Mining Comp.	Acceptance of tank wagons, hopper wagons and bogies	1976

PROJECTS (SIGNALLING/ELECTROTECHNIQUES)

Country	Client	Description of Project	Date of Completion
Germany (FDR)	Deutsche Bundesbahn München	Planning of signalling systems	1978
Germany (FDR)	Deutsche Bundesbahn (DB)—ZTL	Investigations for new high speed railway lines comprising tele control engineering, power supply, and standardised substations	1977
Indonesia	Department of Transport, Communication and Tourism	Supervision of construction of the telecommunication system	1978
Korea	Korean National Railroad (KNR)	Supervision of assembly of signalling equipment within the main area of Seoul	1977

TRANSPORTATION STUDIES

Country	Client	Description of Project	Date of Completion
Brazil	RFFSA	Economic studies on the construction of a 170 km long railway line connecting the cement works at Barroso	1976
Germany (FDR)	Transnuklear GmbH, Hanau	Transportation study on heavy traffic container "Kalkar"	1976
Indonesia	Deutsche Gesellschaft für Technische Zusammenarbeit (GTZ)	Completion project "Train dispatching". Advisory services to the Indonesian State Railways (PJKA) on technical and economic fields	1977
Iraq	Ministry of Transport, Baghdad	Baghdad Rapid Transit System (BRTS) (Study on preliminary project)	1977

MISCELLANEOUS PROJECTS

Country	Client	Description of Project	Date of Completion
Iran	Ministry of Roads	Trainings project for Iranian State Railways (RAI)	1978
Iran	Ministry of Roads	Training of Iranian Railwaymen at schools of the German Federal Railway (DB)	1978
Iran	Knight Wegenstein Consultants	Reorganisation of the Iranian State Railways (RAI)	1976
Zaïre	Office des Routes	Preparation of tender documents for ferries including economic evaluations	1976

DE LEUW, CATHER & COMPANY (DCCO)

165 West Wacker Drive, Chicago, Illinois 60601, USA

Telephone: (312) 346 0424
Telegrams: DELCAC CHICAGO, USA
Telex: 9102215842

Offices: Chicago, Atlanta, Boston, Buffalo, Denver, Houston, Los Angeles, New York City, Philadelphia, San Francisco, Seattle, and District of Columbia.

Associate Companies: De Leuw, Cather International Inc. (Chicago); De Leuw, Cather of Australia Pty. Ltd. (North Sydney, NSW and Canberra, ACT); De Leuw, Cather & Company of New York, Inc; De Leuw, Cather & Company of Michigan; De Leuw, Cather & Company of Virginia; and De Leuw, Cather Professional Corporation.

President and General Manager: J. A. Caywood
Executive Vice President: J. E. Linden
Vice President, Acting Manager, Western Region: L. D. Hazzard
Senior Vice President, Manager, Eastern Region: R. S. O'Neil
Senior Vice President, Manager, Central Region: G. M. Randich
Senior Vice President, Special Assignments: L. A. Dondanville
Senior Vice President, Manager, International Region: V. P. Lamb
Vice President: T. Langford
Treasurer/Financial Manager: C. J. Blase
Vice President, Marketing and Sales: J. S. Collins
Vice President, Corporate Services, Assistant Secretary: D. W. Harig
Controller and Assistant Treasurer: L. Alvarez
Secretary: D. K. Jorgensen
Assistant Secretary/Assistant Treasurer: L. E. Luberda
Assistant Secretary: H. Webber

CAPABILITIES
Services undertaken by DCCO include: feasibility studies, preliminary and final design, site development, surveys, soils investigations, specifications and cost estimates, contract documents, construction supervision, construction management.

PROJECTS
DCCO, in a joint venture with The Ralph M. Parsons Company, is currently responsible for the management of the Northeast Corridor Improvement Project. This Federal Railroad Administration programme to rehabilitate the 744 km (456 mile) rail line and facilities between Washington DC, and Boston will allow Amtrak passenger and Con-Rail service to operate at speeds up to 120 mph.

Main Line Relocations, Extensions, Consolidations, and Improvements: Major projects have been completed in California, Georgia, Illinois, Indiana, Iowa, Massachusetts, Michigan, Minnesota, Nebraska, Nevada, New Jersey, Pennsylvania, Texas, and Wisconsin as well as Canada, Indonesia, and Turkey.

Railroad Grade Separations and Related Studies: Assignments involving a variety of disciplines have been completed in 15 states, Australia, and Jordan.

Railroad Appraisals, Inventories, and Operational Studies: Engineering and economic analyses; revenue studies; operational studies; valuation appraisals; and condition reports for major railroad facilities in the United States, Canada, and the Philippines.

Railroad Signalling and Communications: Projects have included automatic interlocking circuits; remote control interlocking; electrification; design of signal and communication systems or modifications to existing facilities; and automatic crossing protection.

Yards, Shops, and Terminal Facilities: Modernisation of existing facilities or construction of new facilities in 13 states, Thailand, and Venezuela.

C H DOBBIE AND PARTNERS

Francis House, Francis Street, London SW1P 1DQ, England

Telephone: 01-834 2923
Telex: 917220 a/b Dobbie G

PROJECTS
Station buildings including Birmingham International Station serving National Exhibition Centre; Harecastle tunnel and line diversions; sidings; carriage washing plants; wagon repair shops, maintenance depots including 300 m depot for Kowloon-Canton Railway Co, Hong Kong; signal boxes, computer centre and telephone exchanges; over 300 bridges in British Rail electrification programme; survey and design for new railways in Guinea and Liberia.

DUBIN, DUBIN, BLACK AND MOUTOUSSAMY

55 West Wacker Dr, Chicago, Illinois 60601, USA

Telephone: (312) 641 0700

Architect: Arthur D. Dubin

PROJECTS
Modernisation of Loyola station ($2.1 million) for Chicago Transit Authority (CTA); Modernisation of Granville Station ($860 000) for Chicago Transit Authority (CTA); Modernisation of Davis Station ($300 000) for Chicago Transit Authority (CTA); New stations and ancillary facilities with 10 750 ft (533 m) of tunnel, track and platform work ($55 million) in association with Harza Engineering Co: Zoological Park Station, Cleveland Park Station, Van Ness Station, (1) Chiller Plant, (3) Transformer Sub-stations, for Washington Metropolitan Area Transit Authority (WMATA).

THOMAS K DYER, INC

1762 Massachusetts Ave, Lexington, Massachusetts 02173, USA

Telephone: (617) 862 2075

Executive Vice-President: W. K. Hale

PROJECTS
Upgrading track and signals Dorchester Branch ($16 million) and Red Line extension to South Braintree for Massachusetts Bay Transportation Authority (MBTA).

EDWARDS AND KELCEY/WYER, DICK & CO

70 South Orange Avenue, Livingston, New Jersey 07039, USA

PROJECTS
Planning, environmental studies, evaluations, operations, management, design and construction management for railways, terminals, tunnels and bridges.

ENVIRODYNE ENGINEERS, INC

222 West Adams Street, Chicago, Illinois 60606, USA

Telephone: (312) 263 0114

Senior Vice President: Marshall Suloway
Vice Presidents: Charles F. May
Edward D. Ripple

PROJECTS
Design of Riverside maintenance and repair facility; study of St Louis gateway yards; design of track and structure, NEC; study of locomotive power and use trends; design of rail commuter facilities in Chicago.

W A FAIRHURST & PARTNERS

Cragside House, Heaton Road, Newcastle-upon-Tyne NE6 1SN, England

Telephone: 0632 657112
Telex: 53440 Chamco G for Fairhurst

PROJECTS
Fairhursts are responsible to the Tyne and Wear Passenger Transport Executive for the following projects which are part of the new Tyne and Wear Metro: 350 m long steel truss bridge across the Tyne between Newcastle and Gateshead; Installation of overhead line equipment throughout the 56 km length of Metro, including design of all structural elements, procurement of components and supervision of installation; Design of the depot for all equipment to be installed in Metro.

FORD, BACON & DAVIS

2 Broadway, New York, New York 10004, USA

Telephone: (212) 344 3200

Manager: C. N. Peterman

PROJECTS
Southern Pacific Transportation co-evaluation of equipment; training programmes for Union Pacific, Southern Pacific, Bessemer and Lake Erie, Providence of Worcester Railroad.

FOSTER ENGINEERING, INC

120 Howard St, Suite 670, San Francisco, California 94105, USA

Telephone: (415) 543 1193

President: H. A. Foster

PROJECTS
Design, management, construction administration for various rail transit projects for Bay Area Rapid Transit District (BART), City of San Francisco Municipal Railway, and Niagara Frontier Transportation Authority, Buffalo, New York.

FREEMAN FOX & PARTNERS

25 Victoria Street (South Block), Westminster, London SW1H 0EX, England

Telephone: (01) 222 8050
Telegrams: Traction London SW1
Telex: 916018 FOXVIC G

Partners: J. T. Edwards
W. T. F. Austin
B. P. Wex
W. C. Brown
M. F. Parsons
D. A. Meyers
N. J. Dallard
D. R. Wolstenholme

Consultants: Sir Ralph Freeman
O. A. Kerensky
C. D. Crosthwaite
Anthony Bull
J. C. A. Roseveare

Transportation Engineer: G. W. Wallwork
Railway Engineer: A. J. S. Blanchfield

Associated Firms (in respect of railway work):

Freeman Fox (Far East), 42-46 Gloucester Road, Hong Kong

Telephone: 5-272127
Telex: 73868 FRFOX HX

Partners: J. T. Edwards
B. P. Wex
C. R. Coulson
N. J. Dallard
J. Webb
R. A. Chaning-Pearce

Freeman Fox International Ltd, 42-46 Gloucester Road, Hong Kong

Telephone: 5-272127
Telex: 73868 FRFOX HX

Directors: Sir Ralph Freeman
J. T. Edwards
W. T. F. Austin
B. P. Wex
M. F. Parsons
N. J. Dallard
D. R. Wolstenholme
D. R. Culverwell
C. R. Coulson
W. K. Chan
R. A. Chaning-Pearce
J. H. Earp
K. J. James
D. G. Morton
J. F. Webb
M. J. Taylor
C. L. Warren-Smith

Halcrow Fox & Associates

Directors: F. A. Sharman
J. O. Tresidder
B. K. Hartshorne
J. T. Edwards
A. N. Muir Wood
D. A. Meyers
D. S. Kennedy

CAPABILITIES
Freeman Fox & Partners was founded in 1857 by Sir Charles Fox who established an international engineering consultancy practice primarily concerned with railway work. In the early years, the firm was responsible for railways in the United Kingdom, the Americas, Africa and India. In Southern Africa, the firm was responsible for over 8 000 km of railway and continued as consulting engineers for the Rhodesian and Benguela Railways to within the last decade. This work for the African railways included, in addition to civil engineering, specification and inspection during manufacture of all kinds of rolling stock, signalling and communication equipment etc.
During the 1950s, following World War II, the firm designed three major bridges that were rebuilt for the Royal Thailand State Railway and, for the Indian Ministry of Railways, designed two major road/rail bridges for crossings of the Rivers Ganga and Brahmaputra.
During the 1960s the firm entered the field of traffic and transportation engineering, this work being undertaken by Freeman Fox and Associates. A large number of national and regional studies have been completed, many of them related to railway operations. From 1 May 1977 this part of the Freeman Fox Group became jointly owned by Freeman Fox & Partners and Sir William Halcrow & Partners, and was re-named Halcrow Fox and Associates.
In earlier days, Freeman Fox & Partners had been concerned with sections of the London Underground system (particularly the Charing Cross-Hampstead section of the present Northern Line) and, in the 1960s, the firm returned to this field when it commenced studies for the Hong Kong Mass Transit Railway now being built at a cost of £500 million.
During the last decade the firm's work for main line railways, in addition to the projects listed below, has been principally concerned with the design, specification and inspection during manufacture of rolling stock, including double-deck motor car transporter wagons, refrigerator wagons, freight wagon bogies and the development of a new large-capacity hopper wagon for carrying ores.

PROJECTS
Principal railway projects undertaken by the Freeman Fox Group during the last ten years are as follows:

Hong Kong Mass Transit Railway: This is the major railway project for which the firm is currently responsible. Work commenced in 1966 with the Hong Kong Transport Study which required:
a) study of all forms of transport and an evaluation of their potential in the changing conditions of Hong Kong;
b) evaluation of alternative routes for the potentially most attractive systems;
c) estimates of short-term and long-term travel demands;
d) proposals for long-term public transport development.

The firm then undertook further studies which led to the recommendation of a mass transit railway consisting of 4 separate lines with a combined route length of 64 km and 50 stations. Associated with Freeman Fox in this work were a number of specialist consultants including Kennedy & Donkin, Design Research Unit, Charles Haswell & Partners and Per Hall Associates. The firm were also required to specify the Initial System which should be put in hand first in order to provide maximum benefit to the community.
In 1972 Freeman Fox & Partners (Far East) began detailed design for the Initial System and have been responsible for evaluation of tenders and programming of contract activities. Construction on a multi-contract basis began in November 1975 and the first trains commenced operation on a limited section in 1979 and the Initial System will be completed in 1980 before programme date and within budget. In August 1977 authorisation was given for a start to be made on design of the second part of the full system so that construction could continue as resources became available on completion of the Initial System. By the mid-1980s when the whole system is in operation, the Hong Kong Metro will be carrying 2.7 million passengers daily with an average trip length of 5 km, making it possibly the most heavily used system in the world.

Taiwan Railway Electrification: In association with Kennedy & Donkin and China Engineering Consultants Inc the firm worked on an electrification study of the 500 km of double-track narrow gauge line from Keelung in the north, through the capital Taipei, to Kaohsiung in the south. The study required a forecast of future traffic; engineering plans for handling the traffic by either electrical or diesel traction; and estimates of the capital and operating costs of electrical and diesel traction, with cost benefit comparisons of the alternatives. The report was submitted in 1971.

Metropolitan Rapid Transit System for Guadalajara: This study, which was undertaken in association with Kennedy & Donkin, was commissioned to prepare an outline plan for the first stage of a metropolitan underground railway for the City of Guadalajara.

The consultants were required to recommend the type of metropolitan railway to be adopted and to provide layouts showing provisional alignments, type of construction, station locations, depots etc. The report was submitted in 1970.

Elevated Railway in Taipei City: The purpose of this study was to evaluate the economic and technical aspects of alternative schemes for improving the railway and road transport of the Taipei-Keelung metropolitan area. In particular, the study called for evaluation of elevating the railway through the urban area of Taipei (to eliminate the numerous level crossings existing) and build a new high-level ten-track station. The report was submitted in 1969.

Hovertrain Studies: The firm was retained in 1971 by the UK Department of Trade and Industry to assess the feasibility and cost of constructing and operating two high-speed Hovertrain routes, one operating at 240 km/h, the other at 400 km/h. A detailed engineering study was also made to ascertain an economic overhead structure able to accommodate the forces and speeds involved.

Railway yards for British power stations: Freeman Fox & Partners were consulting engineers to the Central Electricity Generating Board for civil engineering for three major coal-fired power stations in Britain: Castle Donington (600 MW), High Marnhan (1 000 MW) and Aberthaw B (1 500 MW). Each of these power stations required extensive rail sidings to main-line standards. The largest, for High Marnham, included 65 turnouts with a comprehensive electrical control and signalling system. At Aberthaw, the trains operate on a 'merry-go-round' principle, handling over 3 million tons of coal annually.

Istanbul Metro: Completed during 1978, a feasibility study in association with Kennedy & Donkin, for a 12 km line mainly underground, to carry 400 000 passengers daily. The line will have 12 stations including an interchange with the suburban railway.

Amsterdam Metro: Traffic and economic studies conducted during 1976-78.
Studies of rail and mass transit systems by Halcrow Fox and Associates, additional to their participation in above projects, for Kuwait, Manila, Surabaya, Bogota, East Africa and West Yorkshire, England.

GANNETT FLEMING CORDDRY AND CARPENTER INC

PO Box 1963, Harrisburg, Pennsylvania 17105, USA

Telephone: (717) 763 7211

Chief, Mass Transit: Robert J. Dietz PE

PROJECTS
Final Design and Construction Services for Lindenwold Line (PATCO) expansion programme ($35 million), Buffalo, New York, Light Rail Rapid Transit System ($60 million), and rail maintenance facilities ($12 and $10 million) for Massachusetts Bay Transportation Authority, Boston, Massachusetts, and Southeastern Pennsylvania Transportation Authority, Philadelphia, Pennsylvania; Detroit regional transit alternatives analysis ($1.6 million) for Southeastern Michigan Transportation Authority (SEMTA); feasibility and preliminary engineering for DPM systems ($90 and $80 million) for Georgia Department of Transportation (DOT) and SEMTA; economic and transportation feasibility study ($125 000) for the City of Norfolk, Virginia; Phase 1 preliminary engineering and design ($1 million) for the Miami Downtown People Mover for the Metropolitan Dade County, Florida.

GEC TRANSPORTATION PROJECTS LTD

45 Victoria Street, St Albans, Hertfordshire AL1 3UG, England

Telephone: 0727 33181
Telex: 298782

Chairman: H. A. Codd
Managing Director: H. Kline
Chief Sales Director: J. Rose

CAPABILITIES
Main contractor for the supply, installation and project management of composite electric railway systems.

GIBBS & HILL INC

393 Seventh Avenue, New York, NY 10001, USA

Telephone: (212) 760-4000
Telegrams: GIBBSHILL NEW YORK
Telex: 127636

Branch and Subsidiary Offices:
Gibbs & Hill, Inc., 8420 West Dodge Road, Omaha, Nebraska 68114 (Telephone: (402) 391 0330 Telex: 9106220294)

Gibbs and Hill Inc., 1754 Technology Drive, San Jose, California 95110 (Telephone (408) 293 16909)

Gibbs Hill Lockwood Greene, 1776 Peachtree Road NW, Atlanta, Georgia 30309 (Telephone: (404) 873 3261)

Gibbs & Hill, Inc., 1801 K Street NW, Washington, DC 20006 (Telephone: (202) 785 1901)

Gibbs & Hill Espanola, SA, Magallanes, 3 Planta 9, Madrid 15, Spain (Telephone: 447 4800 Telegrams: GANDHESA MADRID)

Gibsin Engineering Limited, Chia-hsim, Second Building, 96 Chung Shan North Road, Section 2, Taipei, Taiwan (Telephone: 561 2035 Telegrams: GIBSIN Taipei, Taiwan Telex: 785 26350)

Parent Company:
Dravo Corporation, Pittsburgh, Pennsylvania, USA

President and Chief Executive Officer: A. Matiuk
Executive Vice President and Chief Engineer: F. Mele
Senior Vice President, Power and Energy Division: R. H. Gordon
Vice President, Power and Energy Division: F. D. Hutchinson
Vice President, Power Engineering: F. W. Gettler
Vice President, Power Projects: K. L. Schepple
Vice President, Power Projects: T. R. Cuerou
Vice President, Consulting Engineering: P. P. DeRienzo
Vice President, International: D. P. Davis
Vice President, Transportation and Transmission Division: E. P. Foley
Vice President, Arch/Urban Development Division: R. W. Yokom
Manager (Omaha): M. S. Blair
Vice President, Manager (Dallas): J. C. Bridgefarmer
Manager (San Jose): Peter Cartright
Managing Director (Madrid): R. Safier
Vice President (Far East): S. M. Loo
Senior Vice President, Corporate Operations: R. Breach

CAPABILITIES
Gibbs & Hill was founded in 1911 to provide engineering and design services for the then new field of railway electrification. The company has designed the electrification systems for over 70 per cent of all ac rail systems in the United States.
Following incorporation in 1923, the firm began diversifying into a number of related fields, including power engineering, now the major source of company business.
In 1965, Gibbs & Hill became a wholly owned subsidiary of Dravo Corporation, expanding the capabilities of both companies.
Overall, the company has a staff of more than 2 700 professional and support personnel, providing a variety of vital services.
The Transportation and Transmission Division operates as an integrated group with a permanent technical staff of over 100, together with all necessary supporting personnel. Assignments in the transportation field have comprised: engineering and economic feasibility reports; system planning studies; alternative transportation mode studies (bus, rail, private car); preliminary design and cost estimates; environmental impact studies and reports; preparation of project loan applications; site and right-of-way investigations; comprehensive investigations and appraisals of available hardware and rolling stock. Additionally, actual detailed engineering and design services have been furnished for: railroad and rapid transit electrification, including traction power supply and transmission facilities, substations, and overhead catenary or third rail distribution systems; signaling and train control; communications; automation; operations analysis and computer simulation; shops, yards and terminals; waste treatment and disposal facilities; steam generation; and all ancillary and supporting facilities.

PROJECTS
Texas Utilities Services, Inc Dallas, Texas: Engineering and design services for a complete 25-kV, 60-Hz catenary-type distribution system including several configurations of wood and steel supporting structures, together with all necessary catenary arrangements, insulator assemblies and hardware. This system has been developed for the electrification of two lignite haulage railroads in eastern Texas. The first project, for the Martin Lake Electric Station near Tatum, involves the electrification of approximately 17.6 km (11 single-track miles) including two loading stations, a central shop and storage yard, and the unloading facilities for two lignite consists, at the powerplant. In addition to the electrification facilities, a three-phase, 25 kV distribution line was engineered and designed. This line parallels the railroad and is supported from the electrification structures, and provides power to the loading stations, the drag-line erection site, as well as for the ctc signal system.
The second project, for the Monticello Electric Station near Mount Pleasant, involves the electrification of approximately 10 single-track miles *(16.0 km)* and includes one loading station, a central shop, and the dumping facilities at the powerplant.
Extensions of approximately 10 single-track miles *(16.0 km)* are planned for both projects as the demand for lignite increases.

Port Authority of Allegheny County, Pittsburgh, Pennsylvania: General architectural and engineering services for design of all facilities required for implementation of the Authority's Transportation Implementation Programme, Stage I—Light Rail Transit System. A major portion of the work will be applied to the development of the Final System Design Specification (FSDS), the master document on which all subsequent design will be based. The FSDS will include appropriate treatment of the following: system description; overall system requirements; passenger vehicles; right-of-way and support structures; switches and transfer mechanisms; platforms and stations; maintenance, storage, and shop and yard areas; control system; communications system; traction power and distribution system; maintenance provisions.
Gibbs & Hill's participation will be principally with respect to system definition, electrification, traction power, signals and train control, communications, and value capture analysis. Work performed in Joint Venture with Parsons, Brinckerhoff, Quade & Douglas.

New Jersey Department of Transportation, Trenton, New Jersey: A major project comprising the comprehensive physical rehabilitation and electrification of the New York and Long Branch Railroad between South Amboy and Red Bank, a distance of about 15 miles *(24 km)* Gibbs & Hill's portion of the work includes the design of all electrification facilities, as well as all signals, communications and controls. The work is being done under subcontract to Edwards & Kelcey.

Maryland Mass Transit Administration, Baltimore, Maryland: Engineering services as electric utility rate consultant to the Administration in connection with the Baltimore Subway Project. Gibbs & Hill will perform research, analyse and prepare data and presentation materials for a power rate schedule to be used by the Administration in their negotiations with the local utility company.

New Jersey Department of Transportation, Trenton, New Jersey: Engineering and design services for a major modernisation and rehabilitation programme of the Erie-Lackawanna Railway, an important link in the New York suburban area commuter network. The project includes the following assignments: (1) Conversion of the existing 3 kV, dc traction power system to 25 kV, 60 Hz; (2) Rehabilitation and reconstruction, where necessary, of 58 route miles *(92.8 km)* of overhead catenary system; (3) Extension of electrification system from Dover to Netcong, a distance of 10 route miles *(16 km)*; (4) Modifications to signal and communication systems to ensure compatibility with the ac traction power system; (5) Modification of existing heavy repair shops to accommodate new self-propelled rolling stock; (6) Provision of substantial additions to car storage facilities; (7) Siting and architectural design of three new passenger stations; (8) All necessary related modifications to existing facilities, auxiliary apparatus and systems.

Metropolitan Transportation Authority, New York: Engineering services for studies, design and supervision of construction in connection with the $200 million plus rehabilitation programme of the Long Island Rail Road which has the highest density commuter traffic of any railroad in the world. The plan involves extension of the electrification system, purchase of new rolling stock, design of 60 new traction-power substations, new central supervisory control system, increase of wayside electric traction system to permit train operation at speeds of up to 100 mph *(160 km/h)*, improved track alignment, and potential connections with New York City's rapid transit systems. Preparation of preliminary plans, long-lead item specifications and cost estimates for the proposed extension of third-rail electrification and necessary improvements on the Main Line from Hicksville to Ronkonkoma, and on the Port Jefferson Branch from Huntington to Port Jefferson. New electrification facilities, including substations, will be required for 46.2 additional track miles *(74.4 km)*. This work performed by Parsons, Brinkerhoff-Gibbs & Hill, with Gibbs & Hill responsible for all electrical engineering.

Washington Metropolitan Area Transit Authority (WMATA), Washington, DC: Engineering and design of automatic computerised train control, signal, and communications system for the fully automated transit system being built in Washington DC. This system provides for 90-sec headway with top speeds of 75 mph and features automatic schedule maintenance by a central computer system. A second computer functions as a backup, which at the central operator's option, performs dynamic changes to operating schedules. These are then implemented by the online control computer. A computer simulation programme has been prepared for use in optimising the system design and will be extended for use in determining operating strategies to be automatically used by the system under a large number of modes for transit system failures.

Consolidated Rail Corporation, Philadelphia, Pennsylvania: Engineering services to evaluate the technical and economic feasibility of providing electrified freight service from Pittsburgh (Conway) to the Eastern markets between Alexandria, Virginia (Potomac Yard) and Newark, New Jersey, and to estimate the improvements which can be achieved by improving the existing signalling and communication system are being provided. The study is especially complex in that it entails the evaluation of both presently electrified and non-electrified rail lines totalling more than 615 route miles. Both commercial frequency and 11 kV, 25 Hz systems require study. A complete operations analysis is being performed to arrive at representative train consists and schedules for all route segments. Optimum diesel and electric locomotive sizes are developed along with fleet size, fleet management and dispatching policy, power change points and maintenance shop locations. Energy requirements for both modes are defined. Track lines, sidings, yards, spurs, etc, were evaluated to assess adequacy for future traffic projections. Maintenance costs for each mode of operation are detailed.

Delaware River Port Authority, Camden, New Jersey: Gibbs & Hill, Inc played an important role in the implementation of America's first 75 mph completely automated rapid transit line, PATCO (Port Authority Transit Corporation). Owned by the Delaware River Port Authority, the 14.5 mile connection runs from downtown Philadelphia across Benjamin Franklin Bridge to Camden, New Jersey, and on to suburban Lindenwold. Revenue service began early in 1969. Gibbs & Hill, Inc designed the traction-power system, and specified the communications, signalling and control systems. Subsequently, Gibbs & Hill, Inc supervised the installation of the systems in the field. The power distribution features solid-state apparatus for conversion of the commercial frequency alternating current to 688-V direct current in the third rail. Voice communications between trains and control points utilise carrier-frequency transmission over the direct-current traction-power system.

GREINER ENGINEERING SCIENCES INC

PO Box 23646, Tampa, Florida 33623, USA (Principal Offices)

Telephone: (813) 879 1711

Vice-President: N. William Bryan

One Villiage Square, Baltimore, Maryland 21210, USA

Telephone: (301) 323 8100

Vice-President: Charles B. Mudd

PROJECTS

North Shore Rapid Transit studies and design ($100 million) for Massachusetts Bay Transportation Authority—Phase 1; Environmental analysis for North Shore Rapid Transit improvements ($250 million)—Phase II; Northeast Corridor railroad line study and design, including Niantic River Bridge, for Federal Railroad Administration ($5 million); Subconsultant on two additional line sections of the Northeast Corridor railroad system; Selected for design of a 3-mile elevated line section for the Dade County Rapid Transit System.

GUTTERIDGE HASKINS & DAVEY PTY LTD

Principal Offices: 20 Young Street, Sydney, Neutral Bay, NSW 2089, Australia

Telephone: (02) 9082399
Telex: AA 25648

380 Lonsdale Street, Melbourne, Victoria 3000, Australia

Telephone: (03) 679341
Telex: AA 33262

87 Wickham Terrace, Brisbane, Queensland 4000, Australia

Telephone: (07) 2217955
Telex: AA 41276

PROJECTS

Location	Length (km)	Scope
Moura-Moura Mine	15	Survey/Design/Supervision
Moura-Gladstone	225	Preliminary location and estimates
Blackwater South	40	Survey/Design
Mackay bypass	32	Study
Cairns (cane haulage)	65	Survey/Design
Moura-Kianga	24	Study
Greenvale-Townsville	230	Survey/Design/Supervision
Hail Creek-Nebo-Mackay	265	Study
Hail Creek-Dudgeon Point	150	Study
Yarrabee	40	Survey/Design
Peak Downs-Saraji-Norwich Park	170	Study
Gin Gin-Bingarra	25	Study
Mingela-Fanning River	25	Study
Stuart Cement Works	In yard	Study
Erakala-Mackay	12	Study/Survey/Design
Stuart Cement Works	5	Study
Tolmies-Gregory	67	Design/Documentation/Estimates

HAMBURG-CONSULT
Gesellschaft für Verkehrsberatung und Verfahrenstechniken mbH

Steinstrasse 20, 2000 Hamburg 1, Federal Republic of Germany

Telephone: (040) 32104 2131
Telegrams: HOCHBAHN HC
Telex: 02-161 858 hha-d

Parent company: Hamburger Hochbahn Aktiengesellschaft (Hamburg Public Transport Company)

Managing Directors: Dipl.-Volksw. Josef Hoffstadt
Dr.-Ing. Fritz Pampel
Dr.-Ing. Martin Runkel
Vice Directors: Dipl.-Ing. Peter Lenke
Dipl.-Ing Peter Kirchhoff
Dipl.-Ing. Arnold Mies

CAPABILITIES
HAMBURG-CONSULT is a subsidiary of the public transport company, the Hamburger Hochbahn, and works in close connection with the management of the parent company as well as other affiliated local railroad companies.
Activities comprise consultancy services and advice in all fields of public short distance transport systems: electric suburban railways, underground railways (RTS), modern light railways and streetcars, unconventional public transport: (such as automated cabin taxis and monorails), bus and ferry services.

PROJECTS
Projected Amsterdam underground railway (1970-75): Preparation of timetables with the simulation of various operating conditions; selection of rail section and types of switch and crossing; design of track layouts; selection of train safety devices and operating control; ventilation of tunnel sections; acoustic measures; protective measures for foreign ducts and cables in the vicinity of tunnels; fire precaution measures. Siting, formation and design of stations; criteria for escalators at station entry and exit points; set-up of the electrical power supply; insurance cover during underground railway construction; suggestions for rolling stock construction; preparing and carrying through running-in operations; basic principles of rolling stock maintenance; designs for the workshops.

Projected Helsinki underground railway (1970-81): Preparation of basic technical and economic principles for rolling stock and operations: investigations into rolling stock/route layout systems up to and including the draft timetable using an analogue data processing unit: basic planning principles for operational layouts, tracks and stations as well as workshops and sidings; management techniques for operations and operating control, models for decentralised and centralised operating control and for automatic operations; technical components of the automation system, continuous train-running control equipment, passenger information, passenger handling and ticket machines; results of automatic trial operations; suggestions for draft tender specifications; recommendations for track current supply and live rail feed control; expert opinion on trial driving car, preparation of tender specifications for purchasing rolling stock in series production. Planning of the subway workshop; expert opinion on a test motor train unit; functional and economical proving of the capacity of the track configuration of two stations.

Other rapid transit studies: Radiotelephone system for Berlin in conjunction with AEG-Telefunken; planning Dusseldorf U-Bahn; optimum routing for Munich tunnel sections; construction advice on Vienna Metro; wheel rail investigations for Lisbon Metro; fire investigations on the rubber-tyred Montreal Metro. Transit system reliability study for Denver, Colorado, USA; several investigations of rail transit operation without personnel; automatic train operation by data processing techniques; development of the failure monitoring system BEFUND to detect and evaluate vehicle defects and to store failure data (the system is controlled by a microprocessor and data from this unit are transmitted to an operational central control); investigations of an integrated transportation system rail transit-taxi (INTAX); investigations of subway vehicles with small profile and of different sizes.

DELON HAMPTON & ASSOCIATES

8701 Georgia Ave, Ste 800, Silver Spring, Maryland 20910, USA

Telephone: (301) 589 5555

President: Delon Hampton

PROJECTS
Design of catenary support structures for a 170 mile (274 km) section of the NECIP; design of approximately 1.5 miles (2.4 km) of rapid rail aerial structure to support portions of the Dade Area Rapid Transit (DART) System.

HARBRIDGE HOUSE INC

11 Arlington St, Boston, Massachusetts 02116, USA

Telephone: (617) 267 6410

Chairman: Charles D. Baker

CAPABILITIES
International management consulting; specialisation in economic analyses and senior executive development.

HARZA ENGINEERING COMPANY

150 South Wacker Dr, Chicago, Illinois 60606, USA

Telephone: (312) 855 7000

Vice-President: Dr Ramon S. La Russo

PROJECTS
Section A-6 Rockville route, two miles rock tunnels and three stations ($100 million) for WMATA.

HENDERSON HUGHES AND BUSBY
(Member of The Henderson Busby Partnership)

16 St. John Street, London EC1M 4AY, England

Telephone: (01) 251 2051
Telegrams: Engecon London EC1
Telex: 28726 a/b ENGCON G

Partners: Andrew B. Henderson MA CEng FICE FIMechE MConsE
Robert H. Busby ERD CEng FICE MInstHE MConsE
C. W. H. Hay CEng FICE FIStructE
T. H. Rosbotham BSc (Eng)
Associates: M. G. Howard BSc MRAES MACM (USA)
J. G. Jackson BSc MICE
Consultants: G. A. Hughes BA FCIT
D. McClure-Fisher FRICS FIArb
E. T. Williams CMG CEng MICE
G. A. Wilmot BA FCIT
W. G. Rhodes CEng MIMechE FIMarE
H. G. Kidner CEng FIEE
C. Scott CEng FIMechE
R. Tildesley AMechE FCIT

CAPABILITIES & PROJECTS

The firm was founded for Railway Consultancy work in 1862. Some of the projects recently carried out are as follows:
—Design of modernisation and electrification of the Tehran-Tabriz line, Iran.
—Management and technical advice on rehabilitation and realignment of Ma'an—El Hassa Railway, Jordan.
—Design and operation of large sugar cane wagon yard, Mozambique.
—Survey and detailed report with advice on rehabilitation on Guayaquil—Quito Railway, Ecuador.
—Supervision railway rehabilitation in Zaire.
—Feasibility Study and outline design of Baghdad-Kut-Um Qasr standard gauge railway, Iraq.
—Technical survey and design of alignment with economic study of Tanzam Railway, Tanzania and Zambia.
—Coal transportation by rail, Colombia.
—Advisers on all railway technical work, Benguela Railways, Angola; Malawi Railways, Malawi; Antofagasta (Chili) and Bolivia Railway, Chile.
—Advising on diesel locomotives and rolling stock, 22 railways throughout the world.
—Survey study and design on strengthening for 500 railway bridges in Thailand.
—Design and supervision of construction of Eccleston Bridge, UK.
—Rail Investment Study for Irish Republic Railways and Northern Ireland Railways.
—Design and supervision Jubail-Dammam Railroad, Saudi Arabia.
—Electrification and signalling of Steelworks Railway, Algeria.
—Advise on modernisation and electrification, Brazil.
—Feasibility Study on new railway, Costa Rica.
—Design of layouts and components, Hong Kong Mass Transit Railway.
—Rates and tariff implementation, Ghana.
—Economic investment study, Bangladesh.
—Signalling and telecommunication study, Bangladesh.
—Economic study for electrification of railway, Pakistan.

HENNINGSON, DURHAM AND RICHARDSON INC

8404 Indian Hills Dr, Omaha, Nebraska 68114, USA

Telephone: (402) 399 1000

Vice-President: Robert A. Rohling

PROJECTS

Plans and specifications for 8 500 ft of line and one station ($25 million), for Metropolitan Atlanta Rapid Transit Authority (MARTA); Plans and specifications, 2.5 miles of line; two stations ($30 million) for Washington Metropolitan Rapid Transit Authority (WMATA).

IBI GROUP/TELERIDE CORPORATION

156 Front Street West, Toronto M5J 2L6, Canada

Telephone: (416) 596 1930

Managing Director: N. A. Irwin

PROJECTS

Automatic vehicle monitoring systems for Toronto surface bus system and for the Go Transit commuter rail system; Automatic passanger information for Mississauga (Ontario) bus system.

INSTITUTION OF PUBLIC ADMINISTRATION

1717 Massachusetts Ave NW, Washington, DC 20036, USA

Telephone: (202) 667 6551

Dir Transport-Technology: Sumner Myers

PROJECTS

Technical assistance to service and method demonstration programme ($184 000); study of alternative means of financing mass transportation systems ($135 000) for Urban Mass Transportation Administration (UMTA).

JARTS
Japan Railway Technical Service

No 3 Marunouchi-Nomura Building, 2-1-2 Otemachi, Chiyoda-ku, Tokyo, Japan

Telephone: (03) 241 6731
Telegrams: RAILWAYTECHS TOKYO
Telex: J25254

Jarts was set up to co-operate with overseas countries in the development of mainline, suburban and transit railways, operating under the guidance of Japan's Ministry of Transport and in co-operation with Japanese National Railways. Fields of activity include: studies, surveys and projects relating to land transportation (railway, subway, monorail), construction of new lines, modernisation and improvement of railway track, electrification, dieselisation, modernisation of rolling stock, automatic train control and centralised traffic control, seat reservation systems, marshalling yard automation.

KAISER ENGINEERS INC

PO Box 23210, Oakland, California 94623, USA

Telephone: (415) 271 4355

Vice-President/Transportation: Zoltan A. Stacho

PROJECTS

Design and systems construction management, 28-mile (61 km) Baltimore region rapid transit project, $735 million, in joint venture, for Maryland Mass Transit Administration; Design, 20-mile (32 km) Miami rapid transit system, $867 million, in joint venture, for Metropolitan Dade County, Florida; Final design and construction consultation, 4.7-mile (7.8 km) transit, rail and highway, Boston Southwest Corridor, in joint venture, for Massachusetts Bay Transportation Authority; Economic and technical feasibility, 35-mile (58 km) subway lines 3 & 4, Seoul, $680 000, for Daewoo Engineering Co Ltd, Korea.

KAMPSAX INTERNATIONAL A/S

Dagmarhus, Raadhuspladsen, DK-1553 Copenhagen V., Denmark

Telephone: (01) 14 14 90
Telegrams: KAMPSAX COPENHAGEN
Telex: 15508 kmpsx dk

Subsidiary and Associate Companies:
IRAN-KAMPSAX Ltd, PO Box 11, Tehran, Iran.
KAMPSAX (Nigeria) Ltd, PO Box 5810, Lagos, Nigeria.
Geoplan A/S (Aerial photography and mapping), Dagmarhus, DK-1553 Copenhagen V, Denmark.
Geodan (Soils survey, geotechnical engineering), Gribskovvej 2, DK-2100 Copenhagen Ø, Denmark.
Geodata A/S, (Computer services), Dagmarhus, DK-1553 Copenhagen V, Denmark.

Parent Company:
KAMPSAX A/S, Dagmarhus, DK-1553 Copenhagen V., Denmark

OFFICERS
Managing Directors: Mogens Kierulff
Niels Brockenhuus-Schack
Erik Norsk
Svend Østrup
Chief Railway Engineer: A. Carlsen
Chief Engineer, in charge of overseas acquisition: E. Gejel-Hansen

CAPABILITIES & PROJECTS

KAMPSAX was founded in 1917 as a general Danish civil engineering firm by the three civil engineers Per Kampmann, Otto Kierulff and Jørgen Saxild. Ten years later, the firm entered the international market as consulting engineers. In Denmark, the firm still provides complete engineering services including construction, and through this activity the company has been able to apply much practical experience on its consulting activities abroad.

As Consultants, the company has the capacity and experience to undertake a wide range of projects, a range which continually expands. Transport and communications have been the most important KAMPSAX activity, and the company has undertaken major projects within all modes of transport. One of the earliest tasks was the consulting services related to the Trans-Iranian Railway, a major international engineering undertaking between the World Wars.

The company undertakes design and supervision, and covers planning, maintenance, and training activities as well. In recent years KAMPSAX has done preliminary investigations, preparation of country-wide and regional long-term transport development and investment programmes, and project feasibility studies, and has provided technical assistance for improvement of maintenance, and for administration and management of public sector transport agencies.

In 1966 Malawi entrusted KAMPSAX with the detailed planning and design of a new 100 km railway line linking an existing line with the railway system of neighbouring Mozambique. The firm subsequently supervised the construction of this new railway during 1968-70. In 1970, the firm was retained to carry out further railway studies in Malawi: rehabilitation of some 160 km of existing line, and appraisal of alternative alignments for a 120 km extension to the new capital, Lilongwe.

In 1972 the firm conducted a pre-feasibility study for a new railway in Iran between the port of Bandar Abbas and Kerman and Bafq on the existing railway, as well as for a line between Kerman and Zahedan. In 1974, the local subsidiary company IRAN-KAMPSAX was awarded a contract for final studies, complete design, and construction supervision of the 900 km Bandar Abbas—Kerman/Bafq electrified double-track railway. Rising from the coast 2 500 m above sea level, it crosses very difficult terrain. The design was completed in mid-1972, and this modern railway has a total of 26 km of bridges, 17 km of tunnels, 60 000 m² of station buildings and 800 staff dwellings.

Late in 1974 KAMPSAX was further called upon by the Iranian Government to furnish railway expertise for evaluating projects to increase the capacity of the existing line between Tehran and Bandar Shahpour on the Gulf. This 1 000 km section of the Trans-Iranian Railway was to be provided with a second track, to be electrified and modernised to handle 21 million tons of cargo yearly by the end of 1978. Subsequently KAMPSAX was awarded the assignment of establishing the necessary specifications, design criteria and terms of reference for this huge task, and eventually also of undertaking a selection study of a new alignment for 250 km of the railway through mountainous country to replace a part of the existing line.

The firm has been entrusted with the preparation of a new complete design manual, to be used for future railway construction in Iran. The manual deals with the principles of electrification of new and existing lines, and signalling and telecommunications systems in order to achieve uniformity in the entire network.

KAMPSAX has been engaged by the Iranian Government to draw up technical specifications and establish a procurement programme for electric locomotives for the entire 6 000 km rail network in Iran.

In 1979 the firm was entrusted with the study, design and construction supervision of a single-track 143-km line joining Chachoengsao on the existing State Railway of Thailand to Port Saltship on the Gulf of Thailand.

A T KEARNEY INC

100, South Wacker Dr, Chicago, Illinois, USA

Telephone: (312) 782 2868

Vice-President Transportation: Lester K. Kloss
Principal: Lee Eshelman

PROJECTS

Organisational and planning studies for rail carriers; rail technology assessment studies, intermodal project feasibility studies, rail industry economic analysis and projection for US Department of Transportation, Federal Railroad Administration (DOT/FRA); unit train implementation planning and cost estimating, rail service qualilty assessments, and marketing studies for various rail related firms.

KENNEDY & DONKIN
(Consulting Engineers)

Premier House, Woking, Surrey GU21 1DG, England

Telephone: (048) 62 5900
Telegrams: KINEMATIC WOKING
Telex: 859123

The firm's head office is in Woking and district offices and representatives are situated in Manchester (Generation Department and Inspection Department), and many countries throughout the world.

Kennedy & Donkin is an independent partnership founded in 1889 from which date it has provided engineering services on electrical and mechanical engineering continuously. The firm is a member of the Association of Consulting Engineers. The current staff level exceeds 750 of whom 450 are professionally qualified. Activities cover generation, transmission, distribution and utilisation of electric power.

J. Alexander Kennedy BSc, MIMechE, FIEE is the partner in charge of transportation work and is supported by consultants who have held senior posts in transport undertakings such as British Rail and London Transport.

These include:
E. G. Brentnall OBE MEng, MICE, MIMechE, FIEE, FIRSE
A. Bull CBE, CStJ, MA, FCIT
A. H. Cantrell OBE, ERD, BSc (Eng), FICE
A. R. Dunbar CBE, FCIT, FRSA
Brigadier C. A. Langley CB, CBE, MC, FCIT
E. A. Rogers MBE, MIEE, FIRSE

The transportation department of the firm is staffed with engineers who have wide experience, either of railway organisations or with manufacturers.

Transportation engineers include:
Chief Engineer: H. B. Calverley BSc (Eng), FIMechE, FIEE
Rolling Stock: N. D. Ball MIMechE, MIEE
Power Supply: M. J. Woodmore MIEE
Overhead Power Supply: J. W. Butler MIEE
Partner (Kennedy & Donkin International): Dr R. K. Edgley MSc (Eng), PhD, FIEE
Project Engineer Hong Kong Mass Transit: J. Cantwell, MA, MIMechE, MHKIE, AMBIM

PROJECTS

The engineering services provided include the preparation of feasibility and economic reports, project reports with preliminary designs and cost estimates; the preparation and issue of technical specifications, conditions of contract and enquiry documents; tendering procedures and the subsequent preparation of contract documents; the supervision of engineering design, plant manufacture, installation and the control of contract accounts. The firm in addition can provide comprehensive progressing and works inspection throughout the world, and site staff for the supervision of plant installation and of final commissioning tests.

Services for railway adminstrations and rapid transit authorities cover railway organisation, motive power, rolling stock, signalling and train control, power supply, telecommunications, permanent way, ventilation, escalators, ticketing machines and all other related mechanical and electrical equipment.

Major projects with which the firm has recently, or is currently, concerned include the following:

Hong Kong Mass Transit Railway: Kennedy & Donkin collaborated with Freeman Fox & Partners for work in connection with rolling stock, permanent way, signalling, telecommunications and train control, station equipment, power supplies, maintenance facilities, station, tunnel and vehicle ventilation. This commenced in 1966 with preliminary studies and in 1970 in the Final Report on Further Studies. In 1972 Kennedy & Donkin in collaboration with Freeman Fox & Partners were retained for the complete engineering design of the Hong Kong Underground Mass Transit System. Kennedy & Donkin had responsibility for all electrical and mechanical equipment for the system. The final system will have 50 route-km of double track. Electric multiple unit trains were designed by Kennedy & Donkin to provide a track capacity of 60 000 passengers per hour in each direction with trains operating on a two-minute headway.

This was followed in 1975 by preparation of detailed specifications for all electrical and mechanical equipment for the Modified Initial System under eleven contracts for international tendering. The tenders for this System were evaluated and the contracts were awarded with full engineering advisory activities throughout all stages of design completion, manufacture, delivery and commissioning. Inspection in manufacturer's works on much of the equipment was also undertaken by Kennedy & Donkin. The trains commenced running on 1 October 1979 over the first part of this System and the full Modified Initial System was to have been completed in February 1980.

Guadalajara rapid transits: 1970: Sponsored by the UK Ministry of Overseas Development, Kennedy & Donkin reported to the Mexican Government on the projected rail rapid transit system for the city of Guadalajara. The firm was responsible for the complete study and arranged for the civil engineering costs to be assessed by a Mexican firm to general designs prepared by Freeman Fox & Partners, and for the traffic analysis and proposals for fare structures to be prepared by Freeman Fox & Associates. The report recommended a three line system of 33 route km for completion by 1978. Further work, including a detailed investigation of the capabilities of Mexican industry in the rapid transit field was undertaken in 1971.

Taiwan Railway electrification: 1970: Financed by the International Bank for Reconstruction and Development (IBRD), Kennedy & Donkin carried out an economic feasibility study for the Taiwan Railway Administration of the electrification of the trunk lines of the Taiwan Railway. Various development programmes and associated traffic forecasts for the next 20 years were prepared based on the alternative use of electric and diesel traction on the trunk lines in order to determine the programme most beneficial to the Taiwan economy. In this study Kennedy & Donkin led a team assisted by China Engineering Consultants, Freeman Fox & Partners and Freeman Fox & Associates.

Australia: 1973: Perth Central City Railway feasibility study: Kennedy & Donkin collaborated with Wilbur Smith and Associates, MacDonald, Wagner & Priddle Pty Ltd, and other consultants in the feasibility study to electrify and place underground the urban railway in Perth, Australia. The firm was responsible for advising on electrification aspects such as traction system, power supplies, signalling and telecommunications.

1973: Tasmanian Government Railways-Signalling: In response to a request from Maunsell & Partners, Kennedy & Donkin prepared a report with recommendations on the rehabilitation of signalling for the Tasmanian Government Railways.

1974: Australia Urban Passenger Train: Also in association with Maunsell & Partners, Kennedy & Donkin were appointed by the Department of Transport, Canberra, to undertake a feasibility study to determine the viability and consequential advantages of constructing a standardised Urban Passenger Train for all urban rail systems in Australia.

The recommendations of this study were accepted by the Department of Transport and the firm was then later retained to carry out the complete design study and full detailed specifications of such a vehicle.

Brazil: Railway Electrification: 1975: In collaboration with the Brazilian consulting engineering firm, Hidroservice, Kennedy & Donkin were responsible to Rede Ferroviaria Federal SA for determining all technical parameters associated with the proposed electrification of the main line railway between Rio de Janeiro and Sao Paulo (Barra Mansa—Manoel Feio). This responsibility included the preparation of all detailed technical specifications associated with the project.

This project was of special interest since the suburban sections at both ends of the main line were already electrified at 3 000 V dc and compatibility of these systems with the eventual main line electrification parameters was obviously one of the principal considerations.

Canada: Urban Rail Vehicle Design: 1974: Kennedy & Donkin took part in a design study of metro vehicle construction by Canadair Ltd, Montreal.

East African Railways Study: 1972: Kennedy & Donkin (Africa) were appointed by the East African Railways in association with Freeman Fox & Associates and Cooper Brothers and Co, to study and make recommendations to the Railway and the three

Governments concerned in the future operation of passenger services over the whole system and freight and passenger services on some branch lines.

This study provided information on the effect of closing certain branch lines found to be uneconomical and of curtailing passenger traffic, and devised procedures for recovering costs of such lines required to remain open for social or communication purposes.

Taiwan: Interference Aspects of Electrified Railways: 1975: Kennedy & Donkin were appointed to advise Taiwan Telecommunications Authority on the levels of interference to be expected in their communication systems due to the electrification being carried out on the Taiwan Railway network. They were also responsible for recommending methods to reduce this interference to a safe and acceptable level.

Underground Amenity Study: 1972: Kennedy & Donkin carried out a detailed investigation into the noise and vibration caused by tube railways and their effect upon the structure and amenities of buildings within the immediate vicinity of a proposed extension to the London Underground network.

UK: Personal Rapid Transit Power Distribution Study: 1974: Kennedy & Donkin were appointed to advise Hawker Siddeley Dynamics Ltd, in connection with power supplies distribution for a project definition study of a minitram system which they were carrying out for the Department of the Environment with particular reference to the City of Sheffield.

Mexico: Kennedy & Donkin advised a consortium on the supply of power to a proposed high-density 60 Hz rail system in Mexico.

Turkey-Istanbul Metro: In 1978 Kennedy & Donkin provided the input as regards rolling stock, power supply and train control systems for a feasibility study undertaken by Freeman Fox & Partners and Botek SA of a 12-km new metro line in Istanbul.

Hong Kong: 1978: Kennedy & Donkin International were retained as electrical and mechanical consultants for the Tsuen Wan Extension, to assist in initial planning, particularly in respect of route alignment; calculation of predicted train performance and energy consumption; preparation of conditions of contract and general technical specifications; assessment of tenders; approval of completion of designs; and supervision of the contract up to commissioning of the completed installations.

UK 1979: Kennedy & Donkin undertook for a client a study of control equipment for battery-operated vehicles.

Yugoslavia 1979: Kennedy & Donkin were assisting as regards train performance and other aspects in a study for a proposed long railway tunnel. Freeman Fox & Partners were principal consultants.

KUTTNER, COLLINS AND PARTNERS
(with affiliated offices)

46 Alfred Street, Milsons Point, New South Wales 2061, Australia **Telephone:** 92 6034 (Head Office)
276 The Avenue, Parkville, Victoria 3052, Australia **Telephone:** 387 2622
171 Queen Street, Brisbane, Queensland 4000, Australia **Telephone:** 229 3322
PO Box 230, Canberra, Australian Capital Territory 2608, Australia **Telephone:** 49 1055
26 Broome Street, Nedlands, Western Australia 6009, Australia **Telephone:** 86 6572
PO Box 783, Bandar Seri Begawan, Brunei **Telephone:** 3370
175B Goldhill Shopping Centre, Thomson/Newton Road, Singapore 11 **Telephone:** 25 22611
UDA/KCP Project Office, Special Project 1196, 4th Floor, 126 Jalan Bukit Bintang, Kuala Lumpur **Telephone:** 421257
KC-Romaho, PO Box 4483, Jakarta, Indonesia

Telegrams (all offices): Calculus
Telex: ANTENG AA 24432

Principals: W. L. Kuttner, G. A. Collins
Additional Directors (Victoria): M. J. Smyth, J. G. Flather, J. Colquhoun
Associate Directors: P. R. Brown, A. Weiss

PROJECTS
1956-62: Supervision of construction of Circular Quay Railway Loop, Sydney; Deviation of main southern line near Bethungra; Railway engineering aspects of the Study of the Movement of Goods into, from and within the State of Tasmania for the Tasmanian Government; Specialist consultant for resignalling of the Brisbane suburban railway system.
1962-67: Responsible for design and construction of Standard Gauge line from Albury (NSW) to Melbourne including ancillary works; Responsible for design and construction of Melbourne Yard including design of automatic yard, truckwork, bridge-work and other associated facilities; Responsible for maintenance and safety of tracks, bridges and buildings in Metropolitan area.
1972: Glen Waverley Line "Before" Study—Victorian Railways.
1975: Urban Development Authority, Kuala Lumpur, Malaysia: Phase 1; Pre-feasibility studies for new marshalling facility for Kuala Lumpur.
1977: Phase 2; Final selection of site and determination of inter-connecting links; Preliminary considerations for associated traffic control systems; Organisation and management of the proposed new facility.
1978: Preliminary consideration of air space development over railway properties.
1978-79: Phase 2B; Preparation of detailed report for cabinet on engineering and fiscal considerations and preparation of preliminary details for upgraded existing marshalling facilities of Kuala Lumpur, and associated works.

LARAMORE, DOUGLASS AND POPHAM

332 South Michigan Ave, Chicago, Illinois 60604, USA

Telephone: (312) 427 8486

Vice-President: Richard T. Spada

PROJECTS
Power supply and substation improvements ($60 million) for Massachusetts Bay Transportation Authority (MBTA); substation modernisation ($100 million) for Chicago Transit Authority (CTA); power supply and catenary system ($25 million) for Niagara Frontier Transportation Authority (NFTA).

J W LEAS AND ASSOCIATES INC

910 Potts Lane, Bryn Mawr, Pennsylvania 19010, USA

Telephone: (215) 525-1952

President: J. Wesley Leas

PROJECTS
Specifications for fare collection equipment for Parsons Brinckerhoff/Metropolitan Atlanta Rapid Transit Authority (MARTA); system study for future fare collection and revenue control system for Toronto Transit Commission (TTC); system study for fare collection for rapid transit system, Kaiser Transit Group/OTA Dade County; fare collection system for Day and Zimmermann/Niagara Frontier Transportation Authority; LRRT System determination for DMJM/KE/MTA, Baltimore Rapid Transit system; fare system analysis for LT Klander Associates/Metro Potitan Transportation Authority, Long Island Railroad.

ARTHUR D LITTLE INC

1 Maritime Plaza, San Francisco, California 94111, USA

Telephone: (415) 981 2500

Manager San Francisco Office: David Hurley

LONDON TRANSPORT INTERNATIONAL SERVICES LIMITED

55 Broadway, Westminster, London SW1H 0BD, England

Telephone: (01) 222 5600
Telegrams: Passengers London
Telex: 8812227 Intran

London Transport International is a wholly owned subsidiary of London Transport Executive.

Chairman: Ralph Bennett, CEng, FIMechE, FCIT
Managing Director: A. O. Knight, FCIT
Board Members: R. M. Robbins, CBE, FCIT
J. G. Glendinning, OBE, FCIT
W. W. Maxwell MA, CEng, FIMechE, FIEE, FCIT, FIRSE
J. C. F. Cameron, CEng, MICE, FIPM, FCIT
Dr. D. A. Quarmby, BA, PhD, FCIT
Secretary: E. R. Ellen, BA, FCIT
Consultancy Manager: D. H. Coombs, MCIT
Assistant Consultancy Manager: L. W. Rowe, FCIT

PROJECTS
Bombay (1972): A short term study was carried out in Bombay to identify the most suitable and economic corridors for a mass transit system for Bombay and to suggest a basis for a subsequent techno-economic feasibility study.

Cairo (1972): A report was prepared for the Governor of Cairo and the Cairo Public Transport Authority on the possible construction of an underground railway for Cairo.

Caracas (1977 and subsequently): A team of senior London Transport officials is resident in Caracas to advise the authorities on the formation of a proposed Metropolitan Transit Authority which will include the operation of the new Metro within its overall responsibilities for public transport in Caracas. The advice given by London Transport International includes staff training in advance of the commissioning of the new line.

Caracas (1971): An evaluation of rolling stock and signalling specifications for the Caracas Metro was carried out on behalf of the International Bank for Reconstruction and Development.

Chicago (1974): Advice was given to the Illinois Department of Transportation on the railway implications for a Preliminary Regional Operations Plan for Chicago. This required a study to be made of the existing commuter railroad operations in the Chicago area with suggestions for rationalisation of the terminal facilities, revised timetables with through running via Union Station, improvement of passenger facilities and maintenance arrangements.

Glasgow (1974 and subsequently): Assessments were made of both rolling stock and signalling specifications for the modernisation of the Glasgow Subway, and assistance was given in staff training. Substantial recent help has been given covering signalling design and equipment installation, rolling stock commissioning, training of signalling and maintenance staff and a number of other areas.

Helsinki (1971 and subsequently): Advice was given to Helsinki Rapid Transit Office on system layout, traffic estimates and rolling stock design for the Helsinki Metro.

Hong Kong: London Transport International has been associated with the Hong Kong Mass Transit Railway project since the planning days and has formed part of a consortium lead by Freeman Fox and Partners which has served as adviser to the Hong Kong Government and the Mass Transit Railway Corporation. Apart from general operating and planning advice, London Transport International has undertaken training for the Mass Transit Railway staff and also for technical inspection work in respect of rolling stock, signalling and power supply equipment and lifts and escalators being manufactured in the United Kingdom and in Federal Republic of Germany. London Transport International has also provided expertise to the Mass Transit Railway Corporation by seconding serving London Transport staff to work in Hong Kong during the commissioning period for the new railway.

Isle of Man (1976-78): Work has been undertaken for the Isle of Man Railways (formerly the Manx Electric Railway Board) on the modernisation of the Snaefell Mountain Railway trams, utilising equipment from second-hand tramway vehicles from Federal Republic of Germany.

Johannesburg (1971): A report was submitted on the feasibility of a rapid transit system for the City of Johannesburg.

Madrid (1975): An appreciation was carried out of the project for a new maintenance and overhaul workshop for the Cia Metropolitano de Madrid.

Melbourne (1971): Advice was given to the Melbourne Underground Railway Loop Authority on operational and signalling aspects of the Melbourne Loop scheme.

Rio de Janeiro (1977-78): A senior training consultant was assigned to advise the Rio Metro on all aspects of staff training in readiness for completion of the new Metro line.

San Francisco (1974): Advice was given to the Bechtel Corporation on concrete tunnel lining development work being undertaken by Bechtel for the United States Federal Department of Transportation.

Sao Paulo (1976-77): A senior railway operating official of London Transport International was seconded to the Cia Metropolitano de Sao Paulo for a period of one year to assist with operating advice following the opening of the new Metro system.

Singapore (1979-80): Advice is currently being given to the Singapore Public Works Department as part of a preliminary engineering design study for the planning of a proposed rapid transit railway system for the city state of Singapore.

Toronto (1971): Advice was given to Toronto Transit Commission on alignment problems faced on the northern extension of the Yonge Street Subway.

Tunis (1972 and subsequently): An evaluation was carried out for the International Bank for Reconstruction and Development of proposals made to the Bank for improvements in the Tunis—La Marsa railway.

Tyneside (1973): Assistance was given to Tyneside PTE in regard to legal aspects of land acquisition, estates matters and operational features for the new Tyneside rapid transit system.

United States of America (1975): Advice was given to US Consulting firms on certain aspects of the Disruptive Effects of Tunnelling, on subway maintenance procedures and on station design and construction.

Washington (1972): Assistance was given to Control Data Corporation, Rockville, Maryland, with technical advice for the automatic fare collection system for the proposed Washington Subway.

New York (1978-79): London Transport International participated in a management study of New York Mass Transit Authority, being particularly involved in railway operating and maintenance aspects.

LOUIS T KLAUDER AND ASSOCIATES

2000 Philadelphia National Bank Building, Philadelphia, Pennsylvania 19107, USA

Telephone: (215) 563 2570
Telegrams: LTKlauder PHA
Telex: 83-4783

OFFICERS:
Partners: Louis T. Klauder, Sr.
Paul D. Dohan
John R. Vollmar
J. Richard Tomlinson
John A. Bailey
David H. Cushwa
Louis T. Klauder, Jr
Robert G. Stacy
Albert N. Ferrari
John W. Irvin
Associates: Robert B. Price
Richard F. Miller
Henry T. Raudenbush
Robert G. Schwab
Rush D. Touton, Jr.
Robert B. Watson
John J. Wilkins

CAPABILITIES
Louis T. Klauder and Associates, Consulting Engineers, offers a wide variety of engineering, managerial and planning services designed specifically for the transportation field. Based in Philadelphia, Pennsylvania, since its founding on 15 March, 1921, the firm has provided professional and technical assistance to numerous clients throughout the United States and Canada, as well as in Australia, Brazil, Japan, New Zealand and Spain.
The firm was established by Louis Tobias Klauder, former Construction Engineer of the Philadelphia Rapid Transit Company. During its early years, the firm concentrated its energies almost entirely in the field of electric utilities, providing engineering services for reports, appraisals, economic feasibility studies, and design and supervision of construction.
In 1935 Mr Klauder was named electrical engineer for the design of the rapid transit line over the Benjamin Franklin Bridge between Philadelphia, Pennsylvania and Camden, New Jersey. The firm's activities in the transit and railroad field have steadily increased since that time. In recent years, the firm's clients have been composed predominantly of public agencies operating bus, light rail, rapid transit, railroad and people mover systems, both domestically and overseas.
At the death of its founder in 1945, the firm was changed from sole proprietorship to a partnership headed by his son, Louis Thornton Klauder. In addition to Partners and Associates, there are 75 men and women on the professional and technical staff, of whom 45 hold at least one degree in engineering or other allied fields. Including supporting staff, the total number of personnel is approximately 150.

PROJECTS
Latest assignments undertaken by Louis T. Klauder since 1976 include assistance of the following electric rolling stock purchases:

Year	No of Cars	Car Type*	Owner
1976	46	Transit	Delaware River Port Authority (Lindenwold High Speed Line).
1977	190	Transit	Massachusetts Bay Transportation Authority (70 No. 4 Blue Line Cars and 120 No. 12 Orange Line Cars).
1977	—	Transit	Urban Mass Transportation Administration US DOT (Member of Consultant Team Development Standards for Urban Rapid Transit cars).
1978	48	Light rail	Greater Cleveland Regional Transit Authority (for Shaker Heights Rapid Transit).
1978	27	Light rail	City of Calgary, Alberta, Canada, (for South Corridor Line).
1978	60	Rapid transit	Greater Cleveland Regional Transit Authority.
1978	130	Commuter	Metropolitan Transportation Authority of the State of New York (for Conrail and LIRR service).
1979	251	Rapid transit	New York City Transit Authority.
1979	35	Commuter	Northern Indiana Commuter Transportation District.
1979	94	Rapid transit	Washington Metropolitan Transportation Authority.

Advice on purchase of non-electric commuter cars during 1976/79 includes:

Year	Number	Type	Owner
1976	8	Push-Pull	Metropolitan Transportation Authority of the State of New York (for Erie Lackawanna push-pull trains).
1978	42	Gallery	Chicago Regional Transit Authority.
1979	65	Push-Pull	New Jersey Department of Transportation.
1979	60	Locomotive hauled	Metropolitan Transportation Authority of the State of New York (rehabilitation engineering for 4 400 series for Harlem & Hudson — to be used again later as MU).

The firm has assisted in the purchase of 776 locomotive-hauled passenger cars, 65 multiple-unit electric cars and 2 three-unit articulated gas turbine trains for inter-city passenger services since 1965:

Year	No of Cars	Car Type	Owner
1965	50	Metro	United States Department of Commerce (for New York-Washington service).
1965	2	Turbo	(United States Department of Commerce (for New York-Boston service).
1965	4	Test	United States Department of Commerce (for Trenton-New Brunswick high speed test track).
1966	11	Metro	Pennsylvania Department of Commerce and Southerneastern Pennsylvania Transportation Authority.
1973	492	Locomotive hauled	National Railroad Passenger Corporation
(Amtrak's			
1974	284	Locomotive hauled	National Railroad Passenger Corporation (Amtrak's Bi-level cars).

Latest experience of Louis T. Klauder with electric and diesel-electric locomotives is as follows:

Federal Railroad Administration 1976: As subcontractor to Unified Industries, Incorporated, technical assistance in the evaluation of domestic and foreign locomotives as part of the FRA's Improved Passenger Equipment Evaluation Programme (IPEEP).

Federal Railroad Administration 1976: As subcontractor to DeLeuw Cather/Parsons Associates, engineering and technical support in the modification of existing electric locomotives (both freight and passenger) as part of the Northeast Corridor Railroad Improvement Programme (NECIP) to permit their operation at 25 000 V, 60 Hz, as well as at the present 11 000 V, 25 Hz catenary supply.

Metropolitan Transportation Authority of the State of New York 1977: Preparation of plans and specifications for the rehabilitation and equipping for push-pull service of approximately 40 FL-9 type diesel-electric/straight electric locomotives used on the Harlem and Hudson lines in commuter service operated by the Consolidated Rail Corporation (ConRail) for the MTA.

New Jersey Department of Transportation 1979: Engineering services in connection with preparation of specifications, assistance during bid period, design approval and acceptance testing of ten locomotives for push-pull operation.

Southeastern Michigan Transportation Authority (SEMTA) 1976: Evaluation of available diesel-electric locomotives for use in the Detroit-area commuter service, including locomotive characteristics and design feature comparisons, train performance simulation, energy and fuel consumption, etc.

Miscellaneous projects undertaken by the firm include the following assignments:

Brisbane Metropolitan Transit Project Board, Queensland, Australia 1977: As subcontractor to P. G. Pak-Poy and Associates, Pty, Ltd, assistance with the Brisbane-to-Gold Coast Corridor Transit Study.

City and County of Honolulu, Hawaii 1977: Assistance to the Director of Transportation Services concerning the Honolulu fixed guideway rapid transit system.

City of Calgary, Alberta 1976: As a subcontractor to DeLeuw Cather, Canada, Ltd, provide engineering services in the areas of light rail vehicles, signal systems, and electrification in connection with a study of transit improvements for the City of Calgary.

County of Los Angeles, California 1976: Preliminary Operations feasibility study of the proposed Sunset Coast Line rail rapid transit system.

Delaware River Port Authority (Camden) 1979: Development of software and installation of a computerised reporting system for the PATCO line.

Federal Railroad Administration 1976: As subcontractors to Dalton, Dalton, Little, Newport, assistance in assessing the preliminary environmental impact of proposed railroad improvements in the Northeast Corridor.

Florida Department of Transportation 1976: As subcontractor to Harland Bartholomew and Associates, assistance in a study of alternatives for improving public transportation between Miami and North Palm Beach as part of the Southeast Florida Transit Corridor Study.

Florida Department of Transportation 1978: Railroad safety and speed study, optimising railroad speeds and grade crossing safety for two railroads in Broward County (Miami suburb).

Florida Department of Transportation 1979: Systems and programming services in connection with a work programme administration system.

Kansas City Area Transportation Authority 1979: Inspection and follow-on engineering services during manufacture of 62 advanced design transit coaches.

E J Lavino and Company 1979: Inspection and follow-on engineering services for construction of 158 hopper cars by the Chessie System.

Massachusetts Bay Transportation Authority 1976: As subcontractors to Sverdrup & Parcel and Associates, preliminary engineering for signals and communication, on the Red Line Extension from Davis Square to Alewife Brook Parkway, including information collection, signal and communication analysis and preliminary engineering, cost estimates, review of special problems and project management.

Massachusetts Bay Transportation Authority 1979: Design engineering services and bid evaluation for new work cars, ballast cars, flat cars, skid generators, car moving vehicles, power cars.

Memphis Area Transit Authority 1977: Pre-aware evaluation of a recording fare collection system designed for use on buses.

Metropolitan Suburban Bus Authority 1976: Computation of revenue yield from alternative possible revisions of fares.

Metropolitan Transportation Authority of the State of New York 1977: Technical study of a fully-automated fare collection system for passenger stations of the Long Island Rail Road.

Metropolitan Transportation Authority of the State of New York 1978: Evaluation of alternative stationary fare collection systems for the Long Island Rail Road.

Metropolitan Transportation Authority of the State of New York 1979: Transit Co-ordination study for railroad, high-speed transit and buses on Long Island east of New York City.

Michigan State Department of Highways and Transportation 1977: Preliminary engineering investigation of the feasibility and cost of retrofitting commuter rail coaches of the Southeastern Michigan Transportation Authority to accommodate elderly and handicapped passengers.

Ministry of Transport, South Australia 1979: Services in connection with the preliminary design of the northeast LRT project from preliminary design requirements and design standards to capital and O and M costs and some generalised car specifications and preliminary fare collection policies and systems.

New York City Transit Authority 1976: Implementation of Transit Police Major Crime Information System (MCIS).

New York City Transit Authority 1977: Systems analysis and programming services in connection with the Inventory Control System and allied applications.

Pioneer Valley Transit Authority (NA) 1978: Develop and install programmes for computerising, accounting, information and reporting system.

Port Authority of Allegheny County 1977: As subcontractor to Parsons Brinckerhoff-Gibbs & Hill, evaluate vehicle alternatives, estimate cost of fleet and prepare draft specifications and bidding documents for light rail vehicles required for Stage I of the Pittsburgh Light Rail Transit (LRT) Programme. In addition, analyse and evaluate fare collection systems for above with special emphasis on interface with proposed vehicles and stations and impact upon existing bus/streetcar system.

Port Authority Transit Corporation of Pennsylvania and New Jersey (PATCO) 1976: Assistance in meeting Project FARE accounting system reporting requirements.

Regional Transportation Authority of Chicago 1979: Inspection and follow-on engineering services for 34 gallery push-pull commuter cars.

Regional Transportation District in Colorado 1976: Pre-award survey of the production capabilities and ability to make promised delivery of a manufacturer of recording fare collection equipment designed for use on buses.

Regional Transportation District in Colorado 1977: Engineering and Quality Assurance services during the manufacture and installation of wheelchair lifts of 18 transit coaches being built by the Flexible Company.

San Mateo County Transit District 1977: Engineering and Quality Assurance services during the manufacture by Transportation Design and Technology of wheelchair lifts to be installed in 24 transit coaches being built by AM General Corporation.

Southeastern Michigan Transportation Authority 1976: Operations planning and other engineering services in connection with the evaluation of proposed commuter railroad service improvements for six transportation corridors serving Detroit and its suburbs.

Southeastern Michigan Transportation Authority 1979: Inspection services during the manufacture of 54 small buses.

Southern California Rapid Transit District 1976: Technical analysis and evaluation of wheelchair lifts being manufactured by Transportation Design and Technology for installation on 200 transit coaches being built by AM General Corporation.

Trustees of the Penn Central Transportation Company 1977: Systems and programming services in support of operating cost model and related studies.

Trustees of the Penn Central Transportation Company 1976: Assist in the identification of Penn Central branch lines that would have value as public transportation routes.

Unified Industries, Inc. 1976: Assistance to the Federal Railroad Administration in railroad passenger systems and equipment research.

City of Edmonton, Alberta 1977: Analise and evaluate alternative fare structures, levels and collection methods; recommend an interim immediate action plan with emphasis on total co-ordination and compatibility between bus and rail services.

Metropolitan Transportation Authority of the State of New York 1978: Analise and evaluate alternative automatic station fare collection systems for the Long Island Rail Road.

Tri-County Metropolitan Transportation District, Portland, Oregon 1978: Determine feasibility of implementing light rail transit in the Banfield Corridor and evaluate the use of articulated buses in the same corridor.

Various private clients 1978-79: Preparation of specifications for remanufacturing diesel-electric locomotives, assessment of potential of available locomotive repair shops for rebuilding of same, estimates of manpower and parts for remanufactured locomotives, studies of plant modifications for such work.

MARTIN AND VOORHEES

Martin and Voorhees Associates Transportation and Planning Consultants.

112 Strand, London WC2R 0AA, England

Telephone: (01) 836 9381
Telegrams: Martinvor London WC2
Telex: 298648 MARVOR G

Directors: Brian Martin BSc (Chairman)
Martin Richards MSc (Managing Director)
Alan Powell MSc
Simon Coventry MSc
Brian Large MSc
Hugh Neffendorf BSc
Mick Roberts MSc

CAPABILITIES

The company has been commissioned for over 85 projects either exclusively or partially concerned with railways. These cover a wide range including rail investment, planning, operation and marketing.

The Consultancy is a British company concerned with transportation and planning. The company undertakes a comprehensive range of projects concerned with the planning of transport systems covering urban, regional, national, corridor and rural areas. These projects are concerned with the short term issues of marketing, operation and management as well as the larger term issues of investment policy. The consultancy was originally formed in 1968 as a subsidiary of AMV Inc with whom it still continues to have an association.

Clients for rail and rail related studies in United Kingdom have included: British Rail; Northern Ireland Railways; London Transport; Greater Manchester Passenger Transport Executive; Tyne and Wear Passenger Transport Executive; West Midlands Passenger Transport Executive; Mid and South Glamorgan County Council; South Yorkshire County Council; Tyne and Wear County Council; West Yorkshire County Council; Highlands and Islands Development Board; Peak Park Planning Board; Redditch Development Corporation; Transport and Road Research Laboratory.

International clients include: Union Internationale des Chemins de Fer (UIC); Coras Iompair Eireann (Ireland); Public Works Authority, Hong Kong; Mass Transit Corporation, Hong Kong; Urbanisticki Zavod Grada Beograda (Yugoslavia); West Pakistan Government; Ministry of Communications, Libya; Ministry of Transport, Victoria, Australia; EYSER (Madrid) for Commission for Planning, Valencia Region (Spain); National Railroad Passenger Corporation (AMTRAK).

Project Experience

The Consultancy undertakes railway projects at many different levels including strategic studies (investment, operating and marketing), transport planning and co-ordination, and studies concerned with short term issues in respect of facilities such as catering and reservations or pricing and promotion.

Set out below are some short project descriptions together with listings of similar or related projects.

Investment Studies

In Greater Manchester, the Consultancy developed a strategy for the rail network, to replace previous proposals which were based on a central area tunnel. Short-term trip demand forecasts were made, and social research techniques used to explore likely public reaction to system changes. Alternatives were compared, using cost-effectiveness techniques developed for the project. Study recommendations included a short central area surface link, together with a series of measures aimed at improving ridership.

The National Rail Investment Study involved a detailed evaluation of the investment programme for CIE's passenger services, over the period 1981-2005. The effect of maintaining the system at its current level, the base system, was compared with the effects of several investment options. Statistical techniques were developed to derive revenue and trip forecasts for both base and options throughout the period. The study concluded with recommendations for investment, involving speed and frequency increases, which could be implemented in stages, in line with a phased programme for track upgrading and for stock purchase.

Local Rail or Area Studies

The Consultancy has undertaken a number of planning studies concerned with optimisation or rationalisation of urban railway networks.

In Wales, the Counties of Mid and South Glamorgan commissioned a study to assess how the rail infrastructure could contribute to planning objectives and overall transport responsibilities. Within the project a wide range of options were costed and evaluated for technical feasibility, financial return, and economic and social value. The options included network extensions or rationalisation, the opening, re-siting and closing of stations, alternative forms of traction and changes in speed and frequency. Mathematical modelling techniques were developed to forecast future traffic and indicate the loadings on the various parts of the network in many different circumstances.

Rail Rapid Transit Studies

In its original Land Use and Transportation Study for the Tyne-Wear Region it was concluded that a rail rapid transit system should be included in the recommended plan. This was followed by a detailed study of alignments and an evaluation of the forms of the system concluding with a recommendation for an LRT version. Finally a cost benefit analysis was conducted comparing the rail rapid transit with all bus and 'busway' alternatives. This last study supported the successful application for Parliamentary Authority to proceed with construction. The first phase is scheduled for opening during 1980.

In Hong Kong, the Consultancy provided advice and assistance, to a Government team, on the development of a transport strategy for the densely populated urban corridor on Hong Kong Island. A comparative evaluation of five alternatives was achieved within a cost benefit framework, over a 30 year investment period. The phased development of a tramway system to an LRT route was recommended, complemented by an express bus network. The company is currently engaged in the preparation of a preliminary design of the system.

Other rapid transit studies have included: Rapid transit feasibility study for Urbanisticki Zavod Grada Beograda (Belgrade); Dublin rapid transit study for Coras Iompair Eireann (Ireland).

Special Projects

Many studies have been concerned with the design orientation of railway stock, stations and facilities towards rail user requirements. One study recently completed was designed to determine the scale of priorities as perceived by commuters which could be incorporated into objective standards to cover the provision and operation of all British Rail's commuter services to Central London. The research concentrated on the quality of service features under the control of British Rail in the short to medium term, while recognising the distinction between inner and outer suburban services and the demographic variations between catchment areas.

Another major study for British Rail utilised extensive engineering, physiological and psychological research to evaluate, and demonstrate conclusively, the economic case for new inter-city rolling stock and for air-conditioning. The results of a study which examined the modernisation of main line stations, using a combination of economic and attitudinal research techniques in conjunction with observational studies of passengers at stations, were incorporated into British Rail's station investment programme.

Many studies have been conducted concerned with pricing and fares structures covering short and medium timescales. Commuter and main line fares elasticities have been analysed. Projects for British Rail have ranged from the evaluation of the national fares policy through detailed studies for individual routes to the evaluation of many different forms of low fare offers. A series of studies have been undertaken to monitor the effects of successive promotions, sponsored by British Rail in conjunction with the manufac-

turers of consumer products, in which tokens from the products are exchanged for rail vouchers and, ultimately, free rail tickets for children. In each study, social research techniques have been combined with sophisticated statistical methods to prove that the offers have consistently generated additional rail revenue.

Studies have been conducted in Britain, Ireland, and Australia for rail and other transport clients of various forms of rail inter-change facilities. Forecasts have been produced of car parking requirements for commuters and main line travellers. Economic justifications for such facilities have been assessed and advice given on user charges.

Reservations systems have been studied in respect of different categories of rail passengers and the costs involved.

Booking and information system studies conducted for British Rail have covered a wide range of issues ranging from the best method of disseminating information about late or irregular running through to the provision of preferential booking systems for business travellers. The role of Travel Agents has also been assessed.

Numerous studies have analysed the relationship between railway staff and the public and many recommendations have been formulated and adopted.

Marketing Railway Services

The Consultancy has frequently undertaken marketing studies in support of British Rail and its advertising agents. There have been specific studies for local services in 17 locations and a comparable number conducted at different times over the inter-city network. The studies normally consist of the objective analysis of catchment area data, a comparative evaluation of rail and competing modes, and surveys to determine user profiles and market segmentation. This is supported by attitudinal studies to establish knowledge, awareness and motivations towards rail and the attractions it services. Advice is given to the rail operator in respect of possible service changes, pricing variations and potential innovations in respect of facilities. Additionally, promotional recommendations are formulated concerning target markets and advertising themes.

MAUNSELL CONSULTANTS

277 William Street, Melbourne, Victoria 3000, Australia

Telephone: 60 1135
Telegrams: MAUNCIVIL MELBOURNE
Telex: 31067

Senior Partner: J. W. Baxter, CBE, BSc, FCGI, FICE, FIEAust, FInstPet, MSocCEF, FIHE, MConsE, MConsEAust.
Managing Partner: J. B. Laurie BE, FICE, FIEAust, MConsEAust.
Partners: L. M. Ramage, BSc, FICE, FIStructE, MIHE, MConsE, MConsEAust.
D. J. Lee, BScTech, DIC, FICE, FIStructE, FIHE, MConsE, PrEng, PEng.
P. G. Sands, BSc, ACGI, FICE, FIEAust, MConsE, MConsEAust.
P. H. F. Andrews, BSc, ACGI, DIC, FICE, FIE Aust
G. N. Fernie, BE, FICE, MIEAust, MConsEAust.
D. M. A. Hook, MA, FICE, FIStructE, FIHE, MConsE.
J. W. Downer, BE, FICE, FIEAust, MIES, MConsE, MConsEAust.
J. G. Clayton, BE, MICE, MIEAust, MConsEAust.
J. A. Leslie, BE, FICE, FIEAust, MConsEAust.
C. J. Price, MBE, BE, FIEAust, MConsEAust
P. H. N. Norman, FACQS
B. Richmond, BSc, ACGI, PhD, DIC, FICE
T. F. D. Sewell, BSc, FICE
H. B. James, BSc, ACGI, FICE
R. A. Cochrane, MA, MICE
P. H. Gray, MA, FIE Aust, MS, FICE, MITE, MIHE

ASSOCIATED COMPANIES:
G Maunsell & Partners
London, England
Contact:
Managing Director: D. J. Lee
Yeoman House, 63 Croydon Road, Penge, London SE20 7TP, England
Also: Offices in Birmingham, Swansea and Manchester
Telephone: 01-778 6060
Telegrams: Mauncivil, London, SE20
Telex: 946171

Maunsell & Partners Pty Ltd
Melbourne, Australia
Contact:
Managing Director: J. B. Laurie
277, William Street, Melbourne, Victoria 3000, Australia
Also at: Perth, Sydney, Canberra, Hobart and Brisbane
Telephone: 60 1135
Telex: 31067
Telegrams: Mauncivil, Melbourne

Maunsell Consultants Asia
Kowloon, Hong Kong
Contact:
Managing Partner: J. W. Downer
14th Floor, 1, Kowloon Park Drive, Kowloon, Hong Kong
Also at: Singapore, Kuala Lumpur, Jakarta and Bangkok.
Telephone: 3-695251
Telex: HX 74458
Telegrams: Mauncivil, Hong Kong

Al-Kubaisi and Partner
Baghdad, Iraq
Contact:
Resident Partner: S.I. Al-Kubaisi
PO Box 615 Baghdad, Iraq
Telephone: 93734
Telegrams PL 615 Baghdad

Maunsell Ibironke Consultants Ltd.
Lagos, Nigeria
Contact:
Managing Director: E. V. Jenkins
13/17 Breadfruit Street, PO Box 5382, Lagos, Nigeria
Telephone: 27023 27443
Telegrams: Com Eng Cons Lagos

Waad Maunsell Associates
Kuala Lumpur, Malaysia
Contact:
Resident Partner: R. K. Grieve
Wisma Perdana, Jalan Dungan, Damansara Heights, Kuala Lumpur 23-05, Malaysia
Telephone: 945811, 945866
Telegrams: Mauncivil Kuala Lumpur

Sindhu Maunsell Consultants
Bangkok, Thailand
Contact:
Partner: Sindhu Pulsirivong
Chongkolee Building, 56 Suriwong Road, Bangkok, Thailand
Telephone: 233-7950
Telex: Wepress TH 2549

Ingentra Maunsell Consultants
Munich, Federal Republic of Germany
Contact:
Managing Director: Josef Jares
8000 Munchen 21, Maria-Birnbaum-Strasse 12, Federal Republic of Germany˙
Telephone: (0.89) 575460/576833
Telex: 525281

Maunsell P.N.G. Pty Ltd
Port Moresby, Papua New Guinea
PO Box 809, Port Moresby, Papua New Guinea
Telephone: Port Moresby 211627

Chan Chee Wah Maunsell & Partners
Singapore
Contact:
Managing Partner: Chan Chee Wah
3216 International Plaza, 16 Anson Road, Singapore 2
Telephone: 2227288
Telex: RS 24297
Telegrams: Mauncivil Singapore

CAPABILITIES

The firm of G. Maunsell & Partners was established in London by the late Mr G. A. Maunsell to provide civil engineering consultancy services both in the British Isles and overseas. A branch office was established in Melbourne and this later became the head office of a separate Australian firm named Maunsell and Partners, which was incorporated as a propriety Company in 1970 and practices under the name Maunsell and Partners Pty Ltd.
The British firm is based in London with branch offices in Birmingham, Glasgow and Swansea.
The Australian firm is based in Melbourne with branch offices in Canberra, Sydney, Perth, Adelaide, Hobart, Brisbane and Albury.
Following a re-organisation of the activities of the firms designed to improve world-wide operations, the international partnership of Maunsell Consultants was formed. This international partnership comprises the partners of G. Maunsell & Partners and the directors of Maunsell & Partners Pty Ltd, and normally undertakes assignments in all parts of the world other than the British Isles and Australia, which are served by the appropriate constituent firms.
Al-Kubaisi and Partner was formed to undertake the assignments in Iraq.
Maunsell Ibironke Consultants Limited was formed to undertake assignments in Nigeria and other West African countries.
Waad Maunsell Associates was formed to operate as a local partnership in Malaysia with a prime interest in those areas of engineering concerned with the improvement and protection of the environment.
The group is operating in many parts of the world and is registered with bodies concerned with world-wide developments, such as the International Bank for Reconstruction and Development, the United Nations Industrial Development Organisation, the Asian Development Bank, etc.
Some of the wide range of services offered are:

Engineering
The group can provide co-ordinated planning and control of a project from its inception to final completion. Particular aspects of this work are:
Feasibility studies and report estimates.
Detailed design, preparation of working drawings, contract documents, etc.
Evaluation of tenders and placing of contracts.
Supervision of construction and certification of interim and final payments to contractors.
Full Contract Management Services, with computer back up for major multi-discipline engineering contracts.

Land Survey
A comprehensive and fully experienced land survey section, employing the latest techniques and equipment is available to undertake work anywhere in the world. Electronic equipment is available to facilitate accurate linear measurement over any terrain.

Ground Exploration
The group employs qualified personnel fully experienced in soil mechanics, foundation engineering and geology and it arranges and supervises contracts for ground exploration.

Transportation Studies
A traffic engineering department was established in 1963 and is able to undertake transportation studies of all kinds together with the associated economic and cost benefit analyses, route location, traffic management and studies of environmental effects.

Town and Regional Planning
One of the international consultants in the group is a past president of the Town Planning Institute and additionally, there are strong links with architects, landscape architects, building quantity surveyors and others so that the group is able to handle assignments involving town or regional planning.

Environmental and Health Engineering
The Health Engineering section designs and supervises the construction and installation of water supply systems, sewage treatment plants and solid waste disposal facilities. The group has been particularly active in the field of solid waste disposal and undertakes comprehensive studies which cover economic appraisal and management aspects. The group is well equipped to advise on liquid waste disposal problems. Expansion of the Group's activities in the fields of irrigation and major water supply schemes has been recently accomplished.
The organisation is active in the field of environmental engineering and carries out surveys to evaluate and appraise pollution of all forms including noise and gaseous emissions.

Economic Studies
When the scope of the work so demands, the group associates with various specialist firms or individuals who are experts in the field of economics.

Computing
Comprehensive computer facilities are available for the solution of problems in engineering design, traffic engineering, and land and marine surveying while specialised programmes for use with the foregoing have been developed by the group's engineers and applied mathematicians.
The Maunsell firms which employ over 850 staff, have dealt with outstanding engineering projects in many parts of the world.

PROJECTS SINCE 1975

Completion Date	Project	Country	Client	Value $US (When Built)
in hand	Mass Transit Railway Tsuen Wan Extension (4 stations and 400 m tunnel)	Hong Kong	Mass Transit Railway Corporation Hong Kong	90 000 000
1978	Mass Transit Railway (2 stations and 1 100 m tunnel)	Hong Kong	Paul Y Construction Ltd.	55 000 000
1977	Mount Newman Railway (31 km new route and duplication of 65 km railway and sidings)	Australia	Mount Newman Mining Company	50 000 000
1975	Railway Crossing Accidents Study	Australia	Commonwealth Department of Transport	
1975	Australian Urban Passenger Train Studies	Australia	Commonwealth Department of Transport	
1976	Survey of rail passenger movements, CBD, Melbourne	Australia	With Transmark for Ministry of Transport, Victoria	
1976	Kowloon—Canton Railway	Hong Kong	With Transmark	
1976	State Railway System— Tasmania Master Plan	Australia	Tasmanian Government Railways	

Upgrading of Tasmanian Government Railways: Client: Transport Commission of Tasmania; work started in 1973. The advent of considerable increased traffic both from wood chipping operations, general industrial expansion and from the rising importance of the port of Bell Bay made necessary the complete upgrading of the Tasmanian Railway System. This system consisting of some 788 km of railway was very run down as a result of years of under-expenditure on maintenance and no capital works.
A complete appraisal of the system and recommendations for upgrading was prepared in 1973 and an eight year programme of work was proposed. The total cost was estimated (at 1973 prices) to be some $US 88 million.
The work of design, contract preparation, supervision and co-ordination with all parties proceeded but due to financial restrictions work was stopped after the first 70 km.

Mount Newman Railway, Western Australia: Client: Mount Newman Mining Co Pty Ltd; Work started in 1976. Expansion of heavy iron ore railway currently handling in excess of 30 million tonnes per year. Maunsell carried out engineering investigation design and documentation for the regrading of 31 km of the route, and the duplication of a further 65 km in scattered localities.
Total estimated value of work around $US 50 million.

Mass Transit Railway, Hong Kong: The Mass Transit Railway Corporation is to provide and then run the colony's first underground railway and the modified initial system covers a length of 15.6 km at an estimated cost of $US 160 million including land acquisition. Maunsell's, in conjunction with a local firm of contractors, have won four of the major contracts against international competition for the design and construction of two stations and two lengths of tunnels linking them.

Choi Hung Station: This station comprises a two tier underground structure with a passenger concourse at the upper level and two platforms served by three tracks at the lower level. The plan dimensions are approximately 300 × 30 m and the depth to track level is 8.50 m below ground level. The ground, in which the station is constructed, is decomposed granite rock. The construction includes main walls built by the diaphragm method and a combination of king plates and jack arches.

Diamond Hill Station: This is generally similar to Choi Hung Station but has a central platform serving two tracks. A particular feature includes provision for later widening by removal and reconstruction of the main outer walls to permit five tracks to be served by four platforms.

Tunnels: One length of tunnel serving two and three tracks will be constructed by cut and cover methods in decomposed granite rock with extensive use of sheet piling. The length of tunnel included in this contract is approximately 800 m and the depth of track slab level is 8.50 m below ground. A wide variation of cross sections is necessary to accommodate track turnouts and connections. The second length of tunnel comprises four separate bored tunnels passing through solid granite and decomposed granite rock for a net length of 300 m. The tunnels serve both running lines and lines leading to the main depot.

Tsuen Wan Extension: Following their feasibility study into preferred methods of construction for the eleven stations on the proposed extension, Maunsells were appointed to undertake the full design of the first four underground stations on the Tsuen Wan Extension. All are double storeyed boxes constructed by the cut and cover method and each serves two tracks. The upper storey is an underground concourse located with one exception under existing main thoroughfares. The concourses are connected to the platforms by escalators and to ground level by further escalators, passageways and fixed staircases. All the stations and running tunnels will be air conditioned. In addition to the stations Maunsells are responsible for a length of cut and cover tunnel, crossing land reclaimed from the sea.

Ermelo Marshalling Yard, South Africa: Client: South African Railways; Work started in 1972 on the design of a new servicing and control centre. Stage 1 provides facilities for operation of block coal trains and a local traffic goods yard and consists of 50 km of track and 175 turnouts, maintenance depot, CTC complex and ancillary services with a construction cost of US$ 4 million. Completion to final stage comprises the main marshalling yard with automatic hump sorting and expanding servicing and maintenance facilities.

Main line Railway, Venezuela: The first phase of construction of a standard gauge railway network for Venezuela is a 700 km line between Cuidad Guyana and San Juan de los Morros, including a spur line through difficult mountainous country to Tuy Medio. Maunsells were retained by a consortium of contractors preparing a tender for the construction work. Visits were made to investigate ground conditions along the route and to asses the availability of suitable construction materials. Outline designs were prepared for significant structures including a range of standard designs. Construction methods were established so that costs could be estimated.

MODJESKI & MASTERS

PO Box 2345, Harrisburg, Pennsylvania 17105, USA

Telephone: (717) 761 1891

Partner: R. E. Felsburg

PROJECTS
Project JBA—Northeast Corridor Improvement Programme ($18 million) for DeLeuw, Cather/Parsons; Tennessee—Tombigbee Waterway (Columbus) Bridge ($11 million) for Illinois Central Gulf Railroad; Gulf Intracoastal Waterway (Houma) Bridge ($11 million) for Southern Pacific Transportation Co; Napa River Bridge ($5.6 million) for Southern Pacific Transportation Co; Sterling, Illinois grade separation and track relocation ($3 million), Chicago and Northwestern Transportation Company, for Illinois Department of Transportation; regularly scheduled maintenance inspection of structures for Denver and Rio Grande Western Railroad; Norfolk and Western Railway Company; New Orleans Public Belt Railroad.

MORRISON/KNUDSEN COMPANY INC

Two Morrison-Knudsen Plaza, PO Box 7808, Boise, Idaho 83729, USA

Telephone: (208) 345-5000
Telex: 368439

Consultancy subsidiary company: International Engineering Company Inc (IECO)

220 Montgomery St, San Francisco, California 94104, USA

Vice President and General Manager, Railroad Division: Joseph G. Fearon

CAPABILITIES
Morrison-Knudsen ranks as one of the largest and most widely experienced railroad construction operations in the world. Since the Company's first railroad project in 1915, Morrison-Knudsen forces have built thousands of miles of new railroad grade; erected bridges; bored tunnels, crushed countless carloads of ballast; performed emergency repairs after storms, floods and earthquakes; and laid many miles of new track.
Design/engineering work for the railroad industry is performed by International Engineering Company Inc (IECO), Morrison-Knudsen's San Francisco-based subsidiary. International Engineering Company has been engaged in the design of various heavy civil engineering projects, including railroads and their associated facilities for over 60 years. Comprehensive programmes for increasing the safety, speed and economy of railroad services are a result of extensive studies and economic evaluations determining the size, capacity, location and disposition of various elements making up a railroad system.
In the design of railroads and maintenance facilities, M-K's staff is qualified and experienced, having conducted field reconnaissance, site and route surveys, prepared economic studies, quantity and cost estimates, yard trackage layouts and facilities design on dozens of projects. A partial inventory of M-K's railroad engineering accomplishments totals well over 21 000 km of overland railways.
The following provides a summary of a few of the more recent railroad engineering projects undertaken by Morrison-Knudsen's subsidiaries and divisions:

Union Pacific Railroad Diesel Running Repair Facilities: The Union Pacific Railroad began operating a newly constructed Diesel Running Repair Facility at North Platte, Nebraska. This facility was designed and constructed by Morrison-Knudsen. The UP facility is the largest and most modern running repair facility in the United States, capable of maintaining a fleet of over 600 locomotives. Scheduled repair and inspections are completed on over 400 locomotives per month by handling forty locomotives simultaneously inside the shop building. The facility requires a total staff of over 300 for around-the-clock operations. An adjacent washing facility is capable of washing 200 locomotives per day in temperatures ranging from 20° F to plus 110° F.

Locomotive Repair Shop–Tubarao, Brazil: IECO/M-K has recently completed engineering designs for a Locomotive Repair Shop Complex at Tubarao, Espirito Santo, Brazil for Companhia Vale Do Rio Doce. This complex, now under construction, is designed to maintain a fleet of 200 locomotives with provisions in the facility for expansion to a fleet of 300 locomotives. Fuelling, sanding and washing facilities were provided for in the design. IECO also prepared the engineering design for an earlier maintenance shop at Tubarao, as part of an overall terminal complex for CVRD.

Locomotive Running Repair and Service Facilities–Pocatello, Idaho: IECO/M-K prepared the preliminary engineering designs, quantity and cost estimates for a locomotive running repair and servicing facility for the Union Pacific Railroad at Pocatello, Idaho. This installation now services 60 assigned switch locomotives and road locomotives as the need arises.

Muni Metro Rail Center–San Francisco, California: Presently under construction, this facility was designed by IECO for the maintenance, storage and terminal facilities of a new fleet of 110 standard light-weight rail vehicles being acquired by the San Francisco Municipal Railway. Washing and sanding facilities are provided for in the design.

Study for Rolling Stock Maintenance–RFFSA, Brazil: This current project involves managing a study team to review, update, and, as necessary, supplement the design of the Maintenance Shop Plans as these items relate to the system-wide "Five Year Plan of Action and Investment" of Rede Ferroviaria Federal SA (RFFSA), the national railroad of Brazil.

Remanufacturing Facilities–Morrison-Knudsen Co Inc: M-K also performed the mechanical design for the Morrison-Knudsen Company locomotive remanufacturing facilities in Boise, Idaho. This specially equipped facility for major locomotive rebuilding and overhaul is capable of accommodating 16 locomotives simultaneously.
In addition to these specific shop facilities, M-K/IECO has had considerable experience in the field of railroad alignment design and design of yards and terminal facilities.

RMC Railcar Maintenance Facility – Alliance, Nebraska: Morrison-Knudsen designed and completed the construction of a railcar preventive maintenance facility at Alliance, Nebraska for Railcar Maintenance Company. This facility is capable of handling 3 000 unit-train coal cars a year on a double shift basis. Appurtenances include a truck shop and a semi-automated wheel shop for reconditioning wheel/axle assemblies. A primary feature of this shop is a car body rotator, designed and manufactured by M-K. The rotator is designed to lift the car body from the trucks, rotate it 90 degrees, lower it onto two transfer carts and move it to either side of the main shop track. This provides easier access for repair of centre plates and underframe structure. On completion of the necessary repairs, the process is reversed. The car body is returned to the upright position, lowered onto reconditioned trucks and moved to the next station. The facility was designed to allow for future expansion of the preventive maintenance shop to double its present capacity and for the addition of a paint shop and heavy repair shop as the need develops.

ITEL Corporation Railcar Maintenance Facility – Pueblo, Colorado: Preliminary engineering was performed for ITEL Corporation. Included was the development of conceptual design and construction and operating cost estimates for a railcar maintenance facility near Pueblo, Colorado. The facility was designed to serve a 2 000-car fleet initially, with future expansion to 5 000 cars. The site is between two railroad lines with service provided to both. The proposed facility ultimately includes a main shop building with four through tracks for inspection and preventive maintenance and two tracks for heavy repair. Support facilities include a truck shop for reconditioning and repairing railcar trucks, an automated wheel/axle shop, a bearing reconditioning facility, a paint shop and supporting yard tracks and storage areas. In addition to capital and operating cost estimates, an operating plan was developed, which included equipment and manpower requirements.

Commuter Car Assembly Plant – Erie, Pennsylvania: Another facility for the railway industry was a 350 000-ft² commuter car assembly plant constructed by Morrison-Knudsen near Erie, Pennsylvania, for the General Electric Company. The first production from the plant of high-speed rapid transit cars was delivered to agencies of New York and Connecticut for use on the New Haven Line.
The following examples are representative of the type and complexity of railroad construction projects performed by Morrison-Knudsen in recent years.

Great Salt Lake Causeway: One of the most significant railroad projects Morrison-Knudsen has completed was the design and construction of the Great Salt Lake Causeway in Utah. The causeway rises from a dredged foundation trench ranging from 175 to 600 ft (54 to 182 m) in width and rises to a maximum height of 97 ft (30 m). Over 45 000 000 yds³ (41 000 000 m³) of fill material was handled in three and a half years of earthmoving. The causeway, which replaced an old wooden trestle, was completed nine months ahead of schedule.

Australian Port-to-Mine Railroads: Another significant railroad project completed in 1973 was the construction of pioneer port-to-mine railroads to transport iron ore from deposits in the outback of Western Australia to the coast along the Indian Ocean. A total of 699 miles (1124 km) of track was constructed from the four roads using continuous-welded rail. Track laying operations included a record day in which 4.35 miles (7 km) of track were laid, spiked and anchored in 11 hrs 40 mins, and a top month in which 49.7 miles (80 km) of track were completed.

Black Mesa and Lake Powell Railroad: The world's first 50 kV electrified railway was designed, built and equipped by Morrison-Knudsen and IECO, under a "turnkey" programme. Known as the Black Mesa and Lake Powell Railroad, the all new line is an automated coal transportation route reaching 78 miles (124 km) across Navajo Indian lands in northern Arizona. Train loading and unloading are all automatically regulated by an extensive "Rail-safe" automation system which stops the train in the event of any malfunction in the train or control system.

Railroad Switch Yard—Union Pacific Railroad Company: In October 1977 Morrison—Knudsen completed a $3 million project for Union Pacific in Oregon. This work required the development of a ballast pit, grading, sub-ballast and placement for a major UP switch yard facility.

Surinam Railroad—$50 526 000, Ministry of Development, Surinam: This is the first contract awarded by the Surinam government in the plan to develop the resources in the western portion of the country. The rail route will link a new bauxite mine deep in the Bakhuis Mountains with a port to be established at Apoera, a village on the Corantijn River. M-K's construction programme, in addition to clearing the 72-km long jungle corridor, involves excavation, grading, structure erection, supply of track, track-laying, and ballasting of the standard-gauge rail. Other work encompasses a service road 12 m wide that parallels the railroad its entire length, and erection of 14 permanent dwellings, engineering offices, a quay and a rail maintenance shop at Apoera port. The project on completion will require an estimated six million cubic metres of excavation. Track laying will involve nearly 88 km of rail (with siding), 430 000 cubic metres of lateritic sub-base material, and 210 000 cubic metres of track ballast. In addition the railroad builders will erect a seven-span steel girder bridge approximately 100 m long over the Nickerie River, and install 4 300 m of culvert ranging in diameter from 6 cms to 3 m from stream crossings.

Operations and Maintenance: Congruent with railroad design/engineering and construction, Morrison-Knudsen is also experienced in railroad operations. The Wabash Valley Railroad Co, a subsidiary of Morrison-Knudsen, is one of the newest short line railroads in the USA, and operates between Decatur and Paris, Illinois. Part of M-K's work here includes an extensive programme of renovation and reconstruction to FRA Class I Standards.
M-K has operated and maintained other new railroads in the USA and overseas. These include the Black Mesa-Lake Powell Railroad in Arizona; the Hamersley Iron Railroad, the Mount Newman Railroad and the Robe River Railroad, all in Australia; the Quebec North Shore and Labrador Railroad in Canada; the Orinoco Railroad in Venezuela; the Southern Peru Copper Railroad in Peru; and the Burlington Northern Railroad at Libby, Montana.
M-K's work with these and other railroads have included maintenance of trackage, signal systems, rolling stock and locomotive remanufacturing, and a comprehensive programme of personnel training.

PROCUREMENT
Morrison-Knudsen also offers a capable and experienced organisation for the procurement of railroad materials, equipment, supplies, subcontracting and the appropriate expediting services to complement the procurement. These services have been singularly effective in supporting overseas operations in remote areas of the world where manufacturing, repair, or service facilities are severely limited. This service is the responsibility of M-K's Railroad Division and supported by the Procurement Department. Specialised buyers in the Railroad Division assist in the procurement of equipment for the overall project. This staff also solicits bids and carries out the analysis and evaluation of equipment and materials bids, including contractor bids on the various construction services. Analyses and evaluations are carried to the point of recommending award of the contract. Depending on the size of the project, key buyers are assigned as part of the project task force.

MANUFACTURING AND REMANUFACTURING
Locomotive manufacturing and remanufacturing is a products speciality of Morrison-Knudsen who maintain one of the largest non-railroad-owned-locomotive remanufacturing facilities in the USA.
Within M-K's specially-equipped remanufacturing complex at Boise, Idaho, M-K performs a full-scale programme of mechanical and electrical locomotive restoration. Services include complete engine rebuild, complete rewiring, electrical cabinet update and modification, truck rebuilding, cab and hood fabrication, fuel tank fabrication, repainting, load testing, wheel truing, airbrake rebuild and frame fabrication.
The main shop can house as many as 16 locomotives simultaneously, with a combined shop complex in excess of 200 000 ft² (48 000 m³) of working space.
In 1978 Morrison-Knudsen introduced the first new locomotive ever designed, constructed, and manufactured in the USA for many years, the TE 70-4S (tractive effort 70 000 lbs, four drive axles, Sulzer engine). The TE 70-4S incorporates a Swiss-made, 3 240 hp, 12 ASV 25/30 diesel engine with M-K's innovative design Behr cooling system, and a Brown-Boveri turbocharger to produce a power unit which will require low-down time and maintenance and maximum power output efficiency. Morrison-Knudsen also is completely remanufacturing 30 locomotives for Conrail. This portion of Conrail's fleet consists of GP7 and GP9 class locomotives. For Amtrak, four FA9's will be remanufactured and for Southern Pacific Railroad Co, M-K forces are currently restoring 33 GP-35 class locomotives.
The repair and fabrication of railroad ballast doors is another M-K speciality. Since 1973 M-K has provided over $18 million in ballast door products to the railroad industry. M-K's control flow doors are a patented system employing a unique adjustable friction control device which permits absolute accuracy in dumping either inside or outside the rail. A new arming device completely eliminates material compaction and waste/spillage.

MOTT, HAY & ANDERSON

Head Office Address: 20/26 Wellesley Road, Croydon, Surrey CR9 2UL, England

Telephone: 01-686 5041
Telegrams: LYDONIST-CROYDON
Telex: 917241

Associated Companies: Mott, Hay and Anderson International Limited, Consulting Engineers, Croydon, England.
Mott, Hay, Preece Cardew, Railway and Rapid Transit Consultants, Croydon and Brighton, England.
John Connell-Mott, Hay and Anderson Pty. Limited, Consulting Engineers, 60 Albert Road, South Melbourne 3205, Victoria, Australia.
Girec SA, 430 Avenue Louise, Boite No. 5, 1050 Brussels, Belgium.
Transit and Tunnel Consultants Inc., Suite 811, The Rand Building, 14 Lafayette Square, Buffalo, New York 14203, USA

CAPABILITIES

The Mott, Hay & Anderson group operates throughout the world as engineering and project management consultants.
Mott, Hay & Anderson was founded in 1902. Since 1970 the group has operated in over 40 countries and, in order to give their clients the best service, taking into account the need to consider local problems, a number of permanent links have been established with consulting engineering practices in other countries.
The group is linked by a degree of common ownership. Each member of the group is independent and controlled by its own board of directors.
The group deploys a staff of about 1 200 professional and technical personnel.

DIRECTORS

J. R. Prosser BSc FICE
J. V. Bartlett CBE MA FICE FIEAust FASCE
C. D. Brown BSC FICE
A. J. Holland FCA
S. G. Tough BSc FICE FGS
B. L. Bubbers BSc FICE
E. M. T. Powell BSc FIMechE FIEE FIHVE
T. D. Wilson BSc FICE FIStructE FIMunE FIHE
F. P. D. Stables FICE MSAICE
J. A. Turnbull FICE MIMunE FIHE
R. Beresford BEng MICE
J. M. Whitefield BSc MICE FIHE MASCE
E. A. Cruddas BSc FICE MIStructE FIHE
A. A. Cairncross BSc FICE (Melbourne)
K. W. Torpey BSc FICE MIStructE FIHE
J. K. C. Henderson BA (Cantab) FCIT
T. J. Thirlwall BSc MICE MIES MIStructE MCONSE PEng
R. A. Vickers FICE
R. Hodges BSc FICE MIStructE FIArb
J. E. D. Lord BEng FICE FIHE

PROJECTS 1976-78

Name of Project	Year Completed	Approx. Const. Cost	Details of Project
Caracas Metro	1976	£50.0m	Advice on section of underground railway
Mersey Railway Extensions	1977	£23.0m	Design and supervision of civil engineering works
Toronto Subway Extensions	1977	£21.5m	Design and supervision of tunnelling lengths
Baltimore Regional Rapid Transit Scheme	1977	£450.0m	Advice on tunnelling and construction
Caracas Metro	1977	£40.0m	Design assistance and advice
Melbourne Underground— Rail Loop, Australia		£188m	Design and supervision of construction
Antwerp Metro, Belgium	—	£5.6m	Design and supervision of construction of new section
Brussels Metro, Belgium	—	£8m	Design of section F4 of underground railway
Brussels Metro, Belgium	—	£5.1m	Design of Troncon G6 extension of railway
Rio de Janeiro Metro, Brazil	—	£30m	Study and preliminary design of new section
Helsinki Metro, Finland	1978	£8.4m	Design and supervision of running tunnels for section of railway
Tehran-Tabriz Railway, Iran	—	£1 400m	Design of new electrified railway
Dublin Suburban Railway, Ireland	1977	£35m	Design for electrification of existing line
Rapid Transit to Tallaght, Ireland	—	over £50m	Re-assessment of the Central Dublin to Tallaght railway line
Tripoli—Misurata Railway and Tripoli Central Station, Libya	—	Not yet known	Study and design
Bilbao Metro, Spain	—	Not yet known	Re-appraisal of proposed scheme
Tyne & Wear Metro, UK	—	£60m	Design and supervision of light rapid transit railway for Tyneside
Manchester Urban Railway, UK	—	£50m	Study of alternative rail links
Jubilee Line, UK	—	£40m	Advice on new section of London underground from Fenchurch Street to Thamesmead
Buffalo Light Rail Rapid Transit System, USA	—	£197.6m	Design of new system
Caracas Metro, Venezuela	—	£580m	Advice on the design and construction of a new rail rapid transit system

Tehran (Shahyad)-Tabriz Project, Iran

In 1976 Mott, Hay & Anderson International Ltd were appointed to assist Transmark Ltd (British Rail's export consultancy) in the design of a new electrified railway between Tehran and Tabriz. The existing diesel operated single line railway follows a route of some 740 km. The prime requirement for the new railway is a main-line twintrack 630 km railway between the Iranian capital and its principal links to the Soviet and Turkish frontiers. This railway will provide a high speed passenger service between Tehran and Tabriz as well as a major freight connection to deal with the increasing import/export requirement.

For the initial 440 km from Tehran westwards as far as Mianeh, the route generally follows the existing line and about two-thirds of this length will be constructed by widening the existing embankment. The remainder will be realigned to give improved running speeds. From Mianeh to Tabriz a completely new direct route through mountainous terrain is being planned. This line will be more than 100 km shorter than the existing route via Maragheh. Many major structures will be required including bridges, tunnels, viaducts and earthworks. In addition the existing 300 km route (Mianeh-Maragheh-Tabriz) will be upgraded. The project involves track length in excess of 1 500 km in total.

Mott, Hay & Anderson under the directions of the Chief Civil Engineer, British Railways Board are preparing the design of all earthworks, drainage, river training works, bridge works and tunnels together with the associated contract documents required for the civil engineering construction of the entire project.

This has required close collaboration with British Rail engineers to determine railway criteria to be adopted in design and consultation with others engaged on route selection and the geometric layout of the railway.

Fieldwork as part of the Transmark engineering team in Iran includes the supervision of soil investigations carried out by the client, geotechnical studies, structure surveys and hydrological studies to assist in the determination of the design criteria to be adopted.

Client: Transmark Ltd for the Ministry of Roads and Transportation, Iran
Capital cost of engineering works: £1 000 m

PETER MULLER-MUNK ASSOCIATES

(Division of Wilbur Smith & Associates)

Room 717, Four Gateway Center, Pittsburgh, Pennsylvania 15222, USA

Telephone: (412) 261 5161

Director: Paul R. Wiedmann

PROJECTS

Advanced concept train (ACT-1) for AiResearch/Urban Mass Transit administration (UMTA); Australian Urban Passenger Train (AUPT) for Ministry of Transport, Australia; Station signage system for greater Cleveland Regional Transit Authority.

NATIONAL CITY MANAGEMENT RAPID TRANSIT LINES

9720 Town Park Dr, Ste 109, Houston, Texas, USA

Telephone: (713) 772 1272

President/General Manager: Stan Gates Jr.

PROJECTS

Management contracts with Rhode Island Public Transit Authority; Connecticut Department of Transportation; West Palm Beach, Fla; Central Ohio Transit Authority; Central Arkansas Transit, Little Rock; Shreveport, La; Colorado Springs, Colo; Spokane Transit System, Spokane, Wash.

NATIONAL INSTITUTE FOR COMMUNITY DEVELOPMENT INC

1815 North Lynn Street, Suite 1000, Arlington, Virginia 22209, USA

Telephone: (703) 522 1461

Senior Associate: Edward T. Herlihy

PROJECTS

Census data processing for the urban planning system for Urban Mass Transportation Administration (UMTA).

PARSONS BRINCKERHOFF CENTEC INC

Parsons Brinckerhoff CENTEC International Inc

8301 Greenboro Drive, Suite 220, McLean, Virginia 22102, USA

Telephone: (703) 790 8040
Telex: 89 9493 CENTEC MCLN

President: R. K. Pattison
Executive Vice-President: R. A. Symons

PROJECTS

Consultant in joint venture with others for preliminary and final location and design of 850-km new railway line in Morocco; Consultant for study of rehabilitation and upgrading of the Sudan Railways system; Advisors to Government of Colombia for the design of a coal haul railroad; consultant for the design of the track signal and bridge rehabilitation programme for the Massachusetts Bay Transportation Authority; Design of track work for new Buffalo, New York light rail rapid transit system.

THE RALPH M PARSONS COMPANY

100 West Walnut, Pasadena, California 91124, USA

Telephone: (213) 440 2000

Vice-President: Forrest C. Six

PROJECTS

Northeast Corridor High Speed Rail Improvement Project for US Department of Transportation: a $1 750 000 million Washington, DC to Boston, Massachusetts programme to rehabilitate track, electrification, bridges, stations, signalling, communications and introduce automated track laying system (TLS) for first-time installation of concrete ties in USA; Washington Metropolitan Area Transit Authority (WMATA): five contracts totalling approximately $200 million for design of lines and stations in the District of Columbia and surrounding metropolitan areas in Virginia and Maryland; Metropolitan Atlanta Rapid Transit Authority (MARTA): Atlanta, Georgia station, line design and construction field engineering, approximately $25 million; Baltimore Region Rapid Transit System for the Baltimore (Maryland) Metropolitan Transit Authority, consists of underground and elevated rails, stations and auxiliary support systems, $750 million project, construction management services. Additional railroad project information listed under De Leuw, Cather and Company, an operating subsidiary of the The Parsons Corporation.

PEAT, MARWICK, MITCHELL & CO

1025 Connecticut Ave NW, Washington, DC 20036, USA

Telephone: (202) 223 9525

Principals: D. M. Hill, C. Macdorman

PROJECTS
Alternatives analysis restudy for Metropolitan Washington Council; alternatives analysis study for Southeastern Michigan Transportation Authority (SEMTA).

PEREGRINE AND PARTNERS

PO Box 3, Royston, Hertfordshire SG8 7BU, England

Telephone: (0763) 42384
Telex: 817178 PERIN G

US Associates: H. K. Friedland and Associates, PO Box 893, Solana Beach, Cal 92075, USA
Telephone: (714) 481 9339

Established in 1950, the firm has an international practice in mechanical engineering design, manufacture and commissioning of prototypes and working machinery for Governments, Universities, Consulting Firms and major industry; Invention; Arbitration.

PICKERING-WOOTEN-SMITH-WEISS INC

5909 Shelby Oaks Dr, Memphis, Tennessee 38134, USA

Telephone: (901) 382 2350

Vice-President: Robert L. Haynie

PROJECTS
Transit planning southern corridor for Shelby County, Tennessee.

WM S POLLARD CONSULTING INC

1395 Madison Ave, Memphis, Tennessee 38104, USA

Telephone: (901) 726 6300

President: William S. Pollard

PROJECTS
Environmental impact assessment, Wilmington Outer Loop (approx $167 000) for North Carolina Department of Transportation (DOT).

PORTER AND RIPA ASSOCIATES INC

200 Madison Ave, Morristown, New Jersey 07960, USA

Telephone: (201) 267 8800

Senior Vice-President: Michael J. Dillon

PROJECTS
State airport system plan report for New Jersey Department of Transportation (DOT); Transportation centre (multi-modal)—$60 million—for Essex County (NJ).

R H PRATT ASSOCIATES INC

10400 Connecticut Ave, Kensington, Maryland 20795, USA

Telephone: (301) 942 0332

President: Richard H. Pratt

PROJECTS
Transportation control strategy implementation ($100.258) for Metropolitan Washington Council; Western Prince George's County transportation alternatives study ($91 000) for Maryland Department of Transportation.

PRC RAILWAY SYSTEMS

7798 Old Springhouse Road, McLean, Virginia 22101, USA

Telephone: (703) 893 4310
Telegrams: AMVOR, McLean
Telex: 899105

Associated Companies:
Alan M. Voorhees & Associates, Inc.
Martin and Voorhees Associates
PRC Harris, Inc.
Economic Research Associates
H. B. Maynard International
Logica

Parent Company
Planning Research Corporation
1850 K Street NW, Washington, DC 20036, USA

Principal: Richard H. Wiersema

Services Offered:
Consultancy services in railroad management planning and engineering.

CAPABILITIES
Planning Research Corporation is a diversified consulting firm working in many areas of transportation. PRC Railway Systems is the unit of Planning Research Corporation responsible for coordinating PRC services involving railroads.

PROJECTS
US Agency for International Development: Feasibility study of railway passenger car production plant.

Delaware River Port Authority: Design and construction supervision of a rapid transit line (Lindenwold line).

Association of American Railroads: Feasibility study of a centralised car location message system.

United States Railway Association: Development of techniques for projecting rolling stock requirements.

Federal Railway Administration: Development of an intermodal management information system.

Danish Railways: Design of workshops for emu cars.

Spanish Railways: Design of locomotive workshop.

RAIL INDIA TECHNICAL & ECONOMIC SERVICES LTD (RITES)

27 Barakhamba Road, New Delhi House, New Delhi 110001, India

Telephones: 44915/45362/42903
Telex: 031-4143 and 031-3996
Telegrams: RITESRAIL NEW DELHI (INDIA)

Parent Company: Wholly owned by the Government of India.

OFFICERS
Chairman: G. P. Warrier
Managing Director: A. B. Ribeiro
Director Technical: C. M. Malik
Manager (Engineering): K. Rangachari
Chief Engineer: R. M. Raina
Manager (Finance): G. C. Sharman
Chief Manager (Mechanical): S Kasy Aiyar

PROJECTS COMPLETED
Up to 1978 RITES had completed 14 assignments — one in Bangladesh, two in Ghana, four in India, three in Iran, one in Malaysia, one in Nigeria, one in Sri Lanka and one in Syria.
During 1979 the following projects were completed:
Consultancy to Bangladesh Railways for rationalising the scheduling of trains.
Consultancy to the State Trading Corporation, India regarding storage and bulk transportation of edible oils.
Consultancy regarding bulk handling and transportation of 10.5 m tonnes of sand per annum from river sources to colliery sites, India.
Preliminary cost-cum-feasibility study for a rail link to a proposed cement plant in Nepal.
Investment planning study for rehabilitation of rolling stock, bridges and track, Viet-Nam.

PROJECTS UNDER WAY
Loaning the services of experts from different railway disciplines and providing necessary back-up services to the Zairean Railways.
Consultancy to the Philippine National Railway for rehabilitation of the Manila-Legaspi section and overall improvement to the entire railway system.
Consultancy to the Ghana Railways regarding new facilities for maintenance of rolling stock and training of personnel.
Consultancy to National Thermal Projects Corporation (India) for a Merry-Go-Round Railway Transport System, for moving coal from pitheads to the four super-thermal power stations at Singrauli, Korba, Ramagundam and Farakka.
Macro transport optimisation study for the Planning Commission at all India level.
Investment planning studies in connection with the Bangladesh Railway Development Planning Project — an Asian Development Bank sponsored project.
Techno-economic feasibility studies for location of major road bridges across the rivers Ganges and Kosi in India.
River survey and model studies for planning bridge protection works for Almaru bridge in the State of Andhra Pradesh, India.
Preliminary engineering and traffic studies for a new line between Koraput and Parvathipuram, India.
General engineering and resident engineering services to the Ministry of Transport in respect of the Baghdad-Hsaibah and Al Qaim-Akashat new line construction project, Iraq.
Integrated technical and economic services to the Organisation for Designs and Studies of Major Projects, Ministry of Transport for Iraq.
Contract management of the Nigerian Railway Corporation for a period of three years.

REAL ESTATE RESEARCH CORP

1101 17th St NW, Washington, DC 20036, USA

Telephone: (202) 223 4500

Vice-President: C. H. Broley

PROJECTS
People movers for US Department of Transportation.

RENDEL PALMER & TRITTON

61 Southwark Street, London SE1 1SA, England

Telephone: 01 928 8999
Telex: 919553 a/b RENDEL G.
Telegrams: RENDELS LONDON SE1

Associate Firms:—
RPT Economic Studies Group
28 Maiden Lane, London WC2 7JS, England
Telephone: (01)-240 2054. Telex: 919553
Bush & Rennie Associates
Bush & Rennie International Ltd,
53 Bishopric, Horsham, Sussex, England
Telephone: 0403 50694
Telex: 877542 Bushren G
Rendel & Partners
PO Box 62, 166 Albert Road, South Melbourne, Victoria 3205, Australia
PO Box 288, Toowong, Brisbane, 4066 Queensland, Australia
43 Ventnor Avenue, West Perth, 6005 Western Australia, Australia
118-122 Queen Street, Woollahra 2025, New South Wales, Australia
Irendco
PO Box 2588, Tehran, Iran
RPL Engenharia e Consultoria Ltda.,
Rua Costa Ferreira 106, Rio de Janeiro, Brazil.

Partners: P. A. Cox, FICE
J. C. Munro, FICE
D. M. S. Fairweather, FIMechE
R. Downham, FRINA, FIMarE
J. A. N. Dennis, FICE
F. A. Fisher, FICE
B. J. Luxton, FICE
P. J. Clark, FICE
L. W. Hinch, FICE
D. W. Hookway, FICE
E. T. Haws, FICE
Consultant: J. L. Koffman, DipIng, FIMechE

PROJECTS:
Railway Consultancy projects completed since 1970 or at present under way include:
Northern Ireland Railways
Redevelopment of York Road terminal and Workshops, Belfast.
New freight yard at Adelaide, Belfast.
Reconstruction of Belfast Central railway and new Central Station.
Review of motive power and rolling stock.

British Rail
Channel Tunnel rail link—preliminary plans for 27 kms of route.
Design of 23 bridges and erection schemes for Eastern Region.
Reports and preliminary design of 11 bridges.

Australia
Investigation and report on Burragorong-Scarborough railway (60 kms.)
Goldsworthy-Kennedy Gap railway—design of 96 km of new railway.
Mt. Newman Mining Co.—reporting and advising on locomotives and track maintenance problems.

Malaysia
Investigation, report and outline relocation plan for Port Dickson railway.

Jordan
Survey, design and construction of El Hasa-Manzil extension (25 kms).
Report and preparation of tender documents for new rolling stock.
Transport study for carriage by road and rail of imports and exports; feasibility study for railway extension from Aqaba to Wadi 2.

Sudan
Comparative study of road and rail transport for agricultural products.

Iran
Transportation study, rail-road-sea for oil and gas fields development.

India
Report to Indian Railways Board on riding qualities of locomotives.

KENNETH R ROBERTS & ASSOCIATES INC

10560 Main Street, Suite 515, Fairfax, Virginia 22030, USA

Telephone: (703) 591 6008

President: Kenneth R. Roberts

PROJECTS
Transit operations and maintenance systems; planning and scheduling integration; RVCUS, SIMS, UTPS and Section 15 implementations; Automatic passenger counting and vehicle monitoring. Current Projects in Santa Clara and Orange Counties, California; Rochester and Syracuse, New York; Salt Lake City, Utah; San Francisco, California; Winnipeg and Manitoba, Canada.

RUMMEL, KLEPPER & KAHL

1035 North Calvert St, Baltimore, Maryland 21202, USA

Telephone: (301) 685 3105

Partner: A. L. Deen Jr

PROJECTS
Shady Grove extension of Rockville route, 2.7 miles ($35 m) for Washington Metropolitan Area Transit Authority (WMATA); Phase I Section B of the Baltimore Region Rapid Transit System, 6.2 miles ($53 m).

S & S SYSTEMS INC

8585 North Stemmons Fwy, Dallas, Texas 75247, USA

Telephone: (214) 630 2287

President: J. G. Srygley

PROJECTS
Control system simulation for Metropolitan Atlanta Rapid Transit Authority (MARTA).

STV ENGINEERS

Griffith Towers Building, Pottstown, Pennsylvania 19464, USA

Telephone: (215) 326 4600
Telex: 84-6430

Chairman and President: F. Wm Heilman, PE
Executive Vice President: C. E. Defendorf, PE RA

Key Rail Staff: C. E. Defendorf, PE, RA
F. G. Fisher, PE
S. F. Taylor, JD
D. M. Servedio
I. P. Yatzkan, PE
W. E. True, PE

CONSTRUCTION PROJECTS
Northeast Corridor High Speed Rail Passenger Service Improvement Study (construction cost $4 000 million) for Federal Railroad Administration (FRA).
Railroad Track Maintenance Inspection Programme in Northeastern and Midwestern

USA (construction cost $160 million) for US Railway Association (USRA).
Freight Car and Locomotive Rehabilitation Programme Loan Application Analysis (construction cost $60 million) for FRA.
Flatbush Avenue Terminal and Community Development Project (construction cost $27 million) for Metropolitan Transportation Authority and Triborough Bridge Authority.
New York Dock Railway Waterfront Modernisation Project (construction cost $30 million) for New York State Department of Transportation and FRA.
Commuter Rail Rolling Stock Upgrade Study and Engineering (construction cost $26 million) for Massachusetts Bay Transportation Authority.
Woonasquatucket River Railroad Bridge Replacement (construction cost $3.5 million) for National Railroad Passenger Corp (Amtrak).
Hightower Road Rapid Transit Station and Elevated Track Structures (construction cost $9 million) for Metropolitan Atlanta Rapid Transit Authority.
Philadelphia Center City Commuter Rail Connection Sections (construction cost $360 million) for City of Philadelphia.
Rapid Rail Transit Station, Tunnel and Bridge (construction cost $24 million) for Washington, DC Metropolitan Area Transit Authority.
Cold Spring Lane Rapid Rail Transit Station and Track Structures (construction cost $18.5 million) for Baltimore Region Rapid Transit Authority.

STUDY CONTRACTS
Evaluation of Train Signal/Control System Equipment and Technology (engineering fee $550 000) for FRA.
Northeast Regional Railroad Inventory (engineering fee $750 000) for USRA.
Storage Yard and Maintenance Facilities Modernisation and Expansion Study (engineering fee $250 000) for New York City Transit Authority.

SCHIMPELER CORRADINO ASSOCIATES

1429 South Third St, Louisville, Kentucky 40208, USA

Telephone: (502) 636 3555

Principal: Joseph C. Corradino

PROJECTS
Rapid transit implementation for Metropolitan Dade County Transit Agency, Miami; Transit alternatives analysis in Houston, Texas; Dallas, Texas; and Detroit, Michigan; Environmental Impact Assessment Guidelines for US Department of Transportation, Urban Mass Transportation Administration.

SHERIDAN ASSOCIATES

575 Lexington Ave, New York, NY 10022, USA

Telephone: (212) 750 6960

President: James J. Sheridan

PROJECTS
ACT-1 vehicle design for General Electric Corp.

SIMPSON AND CURTIN

Division of Booz, Allen & Hamilton, Inc

1346 Chestnut St, Philadelphia, Pennsylvania 19107, USA

Telephone: (215) 545 8000

President: Michael G. Ferreri
Vice-President: John T. Doolittle, Jr

PROJECTS
Statewide organisation and finance of public transportation for New Jersey Department of Transportation (DOT); Litigation assistance in Conrail reorganisation for US DOT, Office of the Secretary.

FRANK C SMITH & ASSOCIATES

8585 Stemmons Freeway, Dallas, Texas 75247, USA

Telephone: (214) 630 4716

Principal: Frank C. Smith PE

PROJECTS
System availability studies in support of UMTA programme for Urban Mass Transportation Administration (UMTA).

SMITH AND LOCKE ASSOCIATES INC

500 12th St SW, Ste 808, Washington, DC 20024, USA

Telephone: (202) 554 2040

President: Irving P. Smith

PROJECTS
Study of transportation for the elderly and handicapped ($60 000) for Urban Mass Transportation Administration (UMTA); also National mass transit marketing project for UMTA; DOT sponsored study on transit productivity.

WILBUR SMITH AND ASSOCIATES

155 Whitney Ave, New Haven, Connecticut 06507, USA

Telephone: (203) 865 2191

Chairman: Wilbur S. Smith

PROJECTS
Corridor environmental impact study for State of Rhode Island; Transportation programme management for Tri-County Metropolitan Transportation District of Oregon (Tri-Met).

SOFRERAIL
(Société Française d'Etudes et de Réalisations Ferroviaires)

3 avenue Hoche, 75008 Paris, France

Telephone: (755) 97 08
Telegrams: SOFRERAIL Paris
Telex: SOFRAIL 280084 Paris

President: Marcel Tessier
Managing Director: Bernard Broca
Commercial Director: Jean Gastine
Deputy: Dominique Boblet
Technical Director: Hubert Autruffe
Deputy: Jean-Bernard Bergouignan

Société Française d'Etudes et de Réalisations Ferroviaires is a private company, founded in 1957, first of its kind to supply consultancy services for all fields of railway activity.
Overall studies involve: reorganisation of rail networks, preparation of investment plans, construction of new lines and electrification projects. Special studies cover very diverse sectors: analysis of transport costs, tariff reform, containerisation, maintenance of rolling stock, modern track maintenance, signalling and telecommunications systems and adaptation to traffic and town planning projects. Technical assistance is carried out by teams of specialists and technicians for the application, down to working level, of the resulting recommendations.
Sofrerail is backed up by the important knowledge and know-how potential of high-level engineers, economists and managers, as well as technicians of the French National Railways (SNCF) who can supply quickly, depending on needs.
For over 20 years Sofrerail has continued to carry out numerous railway and transport studies in more than 80 countries on behalf of governments, international agencies and railway administrations.

SOFRETU
(Société Française d'Etudes et de Réalisations de Transports Urbains)

Tour Gamma D, 195 rue de Bercy, 75012 Paris, France

Sofretu was set up specifically to deal with transit consultancy projects.

SUNDBERG-FERAR INC

1548 American Center, Southfield, Michigan 48034, USA

Telephone: (313) 356 8600

President: Richard A. Heck

PROJECTS
Follow-up vehicle designs for Metropolitan Atlanta Rapid Transit Authority (MARTA) and Washington Metropolitan Area Transit Authority (WMATA).

SVERDRUP CORPORATION

801 North 11th Blvd, St Louis, Missouri 63101, USA

Telephone: (314) 436 7600

Vice-President: George H. Andrews

PROJECTS
Red line extension cut-and-cover tunnel and two stations ($100 million) for Massachusetts Bay Transportation Authority (MB.TA); Railway relocations for Burlington Northern in Montana; Railway relocation for Frisco Railway in Alabama; Track evaluation studies for Norfolk and Western; Northeast Corridor Improvement Project between Washington DC and Boston; Railroad rehabilitation studies for US Railway Association East St Louis railyard reconstruction project for Illinois Department of Transportation.

SYNERGY CONSULTING SERVICES

PO Box 199, Northridge, California 91328, USA

Telephone: (213) 993 0926

Project Co-ordinator: Dennis Cannon

PROJECTS
Planned fully accessible transit system and district headquarters for Southern California Rapid Transit District (SCRTD).

SYSTEMS CONSULTANTS INC

1054 31st St NW, Washington, DC 20007, USA

Telephone: (202) 342 4000

Senior Programme Engineer: William V. Garvey

PROJECTS
Analysis and specification for automated telephone transit information system ($80 000) for Washington Metropolitan Area Transit Authority (WMATA); Designed/implemented automated information dissemination system ($95 000) for Southeastern Pennsylvania Transit Authority (SEPTA).

TIPPETTS-ABBETT-McCARTHY-STRATTON

The Tams Building, 655 Third Avenue, New York, New York 10017, USA

Telephone: (212) 867 1777

Partners: Austin E. Brant, Jr
Raymond J. Hodge
Robert F. Heins

PROJECTS
Trans-Gabon Railway; Mass Transit projects: Atlanta, Georgia; Washington DC; Baltimore, Maryland; New York.

TRANSIT AND TUNNEL CONSULTANTS INC

14 Lafayette Sq, Suite 8II, Rand Building, Buffalo, NY 14203, USA

Telephone: (716) 853 7800

President: Richard W. Wilson

PROJECTS
Design and construction management of Buffalo light rail rapid transit 3.5 mile (5.6 km) twin rock tunnel including five stations ($150 million) for Niagara Frontier Transportation Authority.

TRANSMARK
Transportation Systems & Market Research Limited

International House, 62/72 Chiltern Street, London W1M 2EN, England

Telephone: 01-486 0331
Telegrams: Transmark London W1
Telex: 8953218

Parent Company: British Railways Board, 222 Marylebone Road, London NW1 6JJ, England

Directors and Consultants
Managing Director: K. V. Smith
Deputy Managing Director: D. L. Bartlett
Director: J. E. Todd
Principal Consultants: J. A. Houlder
Dr. A. E. Metcalf
Associate Directors: A. B. Englert
N. J. B. Alexander
Special Consultants: A. W. McMurdo
A. E. Robson
R. A. Long
Senior Consultants: A. Buckoke
B. G. Nukley
P. J. Symes
P. B. Kettle
I. C. Cowe
W. A. C. Trethewey

PROJECTS AT PRESENT UNDERWAY

Country	Client	Project Description
Argentina	Ministry of Economics	Major management study of Argentinian Railways
Australia	Queensland Railways	i) Brisbane Suburban Electrification Design Contract ii) Rockhampton/Toowoomba Main Line Electrification and and Upgrading Study
Australia	Westrail	Rationalisation of Workshops
Australia	Comeng	HST Licence Agreement
Bangladesh	Asian Development Bank	Technical assistance to Bangladesh Railways (including enconomic and planning study for future investment)
Bangladesh	Overseas Development Administration	Maintenance assistance to Bangladesh Railways at Saidpur and Pahartali
Botswana	Overseas Development Administration	Provision of advisory team and back-up services to Botswana Government
Botswana/ Namibia	Bertline (for the Commonwealth Secretariat)	Feasibility Study for a Trans-Kalahari Transport Link
Brazil	GEC	Belo Horizonte Railway i) Technical Consultancy ii) Staff Training
Brazil	Ptel/Electra (Rio de Janeiro)	Amza Electrification
Denmark	Danish State Railways	Assistance with development of new trainsets
Hong Kong	Hong Kong Government	i) Kowloon-Canton Railway Implementation Phase ii) Kowloon Tong Interchange Station: Detailed Design
India	Overseas Development Administration	Heavy Gradient Technical Advice, Central Railway
Kuwait	Municipality of Kuwait	Advice on Railway Development
Libya	Mott Hay Anderson (for National Consultants Bureau, Libya)	Tripoli-Misurata (Urban) and Brak-Sebha
Northern Ireland	Northern Ireland Railways	Northern Ireland Railways Electrification Feasibility Study
Portugal	Charter CJB Mineral Services Ltd	Aljustrel to Sinez Mineral Project
Saudi Arabia	Granges International Mining (Stockholm)	Thaniyat Phosphate Railway
Sudan	Overseas Development Administration	Livestock Transportation Adviser
Swaziland/ Botswana	European Association for Co-operation	Regional Training Programme

County	Client	Project Description
USA	Federal Railroad Administration	i) Sale of BR CROWS Programme and supporting consultancy ii) Establishment of Train Planning Unit for NE Corridor iii) General Motors Locomotive Design and Development iv) BR/Leyland Railcar — New Hampshire Demonstration
Venezuela	London Transport International	Caracas Metro Civil Engineering Assistance
Yugoslavia	Freeman Fox & Partners	Operating Study for Long Tunnel Project

PROJECTS COMPLETED IN 1978

Country	Client	Project Description
Australia	Hammersley Iron	i) Testing of S & T Relays ii) S & T Interference Protection Study
	New South Wales Public Transport Commission	Picton-Port Kembla — Advice on Electrification of a new Mineral Railway
	Brisbane Metropolitan Transit Authority	Optimisation of Suburban Schedules
Costa Rica	Overseas Development Administration	i) Rail Transportation Study For Banana Industry ii) Cement Line Feasibility Study
Czecho-slovakia	Regnencentralen	Marshalling Yard Symposium
Egypt	Egyptian Ministry of Transport	Bahayira Sand Study
Guinea/ Liberia	Mifergui-Nimba	Railway Facilities for Transport of Iron Ore
Hong Kong	Yuncken and Freeman	Sha Tin Town Centre Planning Study
Jamaica	Jamaica Railway Corporation	Civil Engineering Advice
Northern Ireland	Northern Ireland Railways	i) Centralised Traffic Control System ii) Computer Software Requirements iii) TV Control Level Crossing Design
Pakistan	PRACS	Advice on Stores
Spain	RENFE	Introduction of TOPS to Renfe Operations
Swaziland	Swaziland Railways	General Transport Study
Thailand	BCEOM (Paris)	Transport Planning Study
USA	Federal Railroad Administration	i) Investment Plan Analysis ii) Various consultancy assignments in connection with the North East Corridor Project iii) Study of Amtrak Catering and Sleeping Car Services
	AMSTED DCP	Bogie Dynamic Evaluation i) ASEA/GM Locomotive Evaluation ii) Specialised Advice on High Speed Track iii) Commuter Timetabling Passenger Train Operations

THE TRANSPO GROUP, INC

23-148th Avenue SE, Bellevue, Washington 98007, USA

Principal: Daniel I. Riley

PROJECTS
Transit, transportation and traffic engineering/planning consultants.

TRANSPORTATION DEVELOPMENT ASSOCIATES INC

316 Second Ave South, Seattle, Washington 98104, USA

Telephone: (206) 682 4750

President: William R. Eager

PROJECTS
Transportation centres in Portland, Oregon and Denver and Boulder, Colorado; industrial market research (transit) for North America; transportation in recreational areas; transportation requirements of energy development in Western Colorado; parking and traffic analyses for hospitals, hotels and other developments.

TREVOR CROCKER & PARTNERS

Drive House, 323/339 London Road, Mitcham, Surrey CR4 4BE, England

Telephone: (01) 640 1981
Telex: 942153 Expert G

CAPABILITIES
Trevor Crocker & Partners carry out feasibility and economic studies for new railway facilities, transportation and traffic studies, route location studies, bridges, railways, workshops and ancillary facilities, preparation of specifications and tender documents, supervision of construction.

PROJECTS
Australia
Tom Price-Paraburdoo Railway
Hamersley Railway

Iraq
Baghdad-Erbil-Mosul High-Speed Railway
Assessment of alternative sleeper designs

UK
Feasibility studies for British Rail on Reconstruction of Liverpool Street Station
Reconstruction of London Bridge Station
Gatwick Airport Station
Railway Workshops
15 Rail over Motorway bridges
Bridgeworks for London-Bedford Electrification
40 Underline and Overline bridges.
Bridgeworks for Preston-Blackpool Electrification

TUDOR ENGINEERING CO

149 New Montgomerey St, San Francisco, California 94105, USA

Telephone: (415) 982 8338

President: Louis W. Riggs

PROJECTS
Rapid transit system ($1 100 million) for MARTA; rapid transit system planning for Metro de Caracas, Venezuela ($1 000 million).

UNIMARK INTERNATIONAL CORP

2 North Riverside Plaza, Chicago, Illinois 60606, USA

Telephone: (312) 782 5850

General Manager: Anthony Spadaro

PROJECTS
Northeast Corridor rail improvement programme in a joint venture with De Leuw Cather/Parsons for the Federal Railroad Administration.

URBAN ENGINEERS INC

19th St and Delancey Place, Philadelphia, Pennsylvania 19103, USA

Telephone: (215) 546 3222

Vice-President: K. Yervant Terzian

PROJECTS
Surface section, light rail transit line ($12 million) for Niagara Frontier Transportation Authority; airport high speed rail line ($70 million) for the City of Philadelphia.

URBITRAN ASSOCIATES

15 Park Row, Suite 2610, New York, NY 10038, USA

Telephone: (212) 267 6310

Partner: Dr. Edmund J. Cantilli

PROJECTS
Design of railroad for Ismailia, Egypt ($5 000 000); Evaluation of automated guideway transit alternative analyses ($83 000) for UMTA; Subcontract: Detroit DPM Phase I Preliminary Engineering and Environmental Impact Analysis ($26 000); Application of Transportation System Safety Methodology for rail rapid transit and rail facilities.

URS/MADIGAN-PRAEGER INC

150 East 42nd St, New York, NY 10017, USA

Telephone: (212) 953 8600

President: Elmer B. Isaak

PROJECTS
Glenmont Section for WMATA; Mondawin Station for Baltimore.

Past projects undertaken are as follows:

Client	Project	Length (ft)	Special Features	Estimated cost ($US)
MBTA	Haymarket Square—Charlestown	600	Sunken tube line	4 612 528
WMATA	New Carrollton Route—Section D4a	4 372	Earth tunnels	23 037 115
WMATA	New Carrollton Route—Section D4b	1 065	1 station & cut & cover line	18 518 085
WMATA	New Carrollton Route—Section D4c	698	1 station	11 090 923
WMATA	New Carrollton Route—Section FD4b	3 450	Finish work	3 363 632
WMATA	New Carrollton Route—Section FD4c	2 685	Finish work	2 479 870
NYCTA	Utica Avenue Subway—Section 1	2 791	A typical transition	23 171 800
NYCTA	Utica Avenue Subway—Section 2	4 630	2 stations	58 302 932
NYCTA	Utica Avenue Subway—Section 3	2 410	Cut & cover line	20 410 490
NYCTA	Utica Avenue Subway—Section 4	2 420	Cut & cover line	20 170 810
NYCTA	Utica Avenue Subway—Section 5	2 685	1 station	39 194 305
NYCTA	Utica Avenue Subway—	2 515	1 station	33 627 558

Client	Project	Length (ft)	Special Features	Estimated cost ($US)
	Section 6			
NYCTA	Utica Avenue Subway—Section 7	2 370	Cut & cover line	18 608 649
NYCTA	Utica Avenue Subway—Section 8	2 515	1 terminal station	35 407 468
NYCTA	Utica Avenue Subway—Section 9	1 853	Maintenance & storage yard	25 104 514
WMATA	L'Enfant-Pentagon Route-Section L1	3 263	Sunken tube & cut & cover line	37 040 548
WMATA	L'Enfant-Pentagon Route-Section FL1	9 335	Finish work	424 600
WMATA	Glenmont Route—Section B11 (4 contracts)	10 500	7 700 LF twin rock tunnels, 2 000 LF cut and cover box section, 800 LF Glenmont Station & 1 800 car parking garage	85 000 000
WMATA	Glenmont Route—Section FB11	9 340	Finish contract	5 000 000
MARTA-PBTB	Proctor Creek Branch Section DP 23	5 625	Cut & cover and at grade line + station	15 200 000
Baltimore Rapid Transit-DMJM/KE	Mondawmin Station—Section NW-06	645	Deep cut & cover	13 400 000

VTN CONSOLIDATED INC

PO Box C-19529, 2301 Campus Drive, Irvine, California 92713, USA

Telephone: (714) 833 2450

Direction Transportation: J. Peter Cunliffe

WALLACE, McHARG, ROBERTS AND TODD

1737 Chestnut St, Philadelphia, Pennsylvania 19103, USA

Telephone: (215) 564-2611

Partner: David A. Wallace

PROJECTS
Baltimore Metro Phase II transportation plan and systemwide environmental impact and route selection studies ($1.7 million) for the Washington Metropolitan Area Transit Authority.

HARRY WEESE & ASSOCIATES

600 Fifth St NW, Washington, DC 20001, USA

Telephone: (202) 637 1761

Vice-President: Robert J. Karn

PROJECTS
Washington Rapid Rail Transit System: General Architectural Consultant for 100-mile (160 km), 86-station system; Metropolitan Dade County Aerial Transit System: General Architectural Consultant for 21-mile (33 km) 20-station system; Buffalo, New York, Light Rail Transit System: General Architectural Consultant for 6.4-mile (10 km), 14-station system.

RAILWAY SYSTEMS

ALBANIA
ALBANIAN STATE RAILWAYS
Hekurudhaeä Shqiperisë, Tirana

Gauge: 1.435 m
Route length: 292 km

The railways of Albania have no physical connection with the European railway network and for many years will remain isolated from the major railways of the continent. In 1979, however, an agreement was reached for construction of a new rail link with Yugoslavia (see under *Civil Engineering*). "Hekurudhae ë Shqiperisë"—Albanian Railways—have now 292 route-km of standard gauge single track lines, fanning out from the port of Durrës (Durazzo) to the country's capital of Tirana, the important city of Elbasan and newly-built industrial centres. The line runs north via Lac to the railroad at Shkoder, about 40 km south of the northwest border with Yugoslavia.

The first lines built in Albania were the 168 km 600 mm and 336 km 700 mm gauge military lines constructed by Austrian army engineers in the final stage of World War I. These were, however, completely destroyed by the retreating Austrian troops in 1918. It was a 12-km industrial railway of 950 mm gauge, built around 1930 by an Italian firm exploiting the asphalt mines of Selenicë and Mavrovë near the port of Vlorë (Valona), which formed the country's first lasting railway.

During the Italian occupation of Albania the first plans for a public railway from Durrës to Tirana were drawn up and some minor construction work carried out. But full construction was not completed until after World War II when the new Communist Party government of Albania undertook a vast industrialisation programme, calling for extensive railway building. The first section of Albanian Railways from Durrës to Peqin (41 km) was opened on 7 November 1946 and this line was extended 30 km to Elbasan on 22 December 1950. In the meantime, another line from Durrës to Tirana, 38 km long, was completed on 23 February 1949. Building then continued at a much slower pace. In 1964 a 29 km spur from Vorë on the Tirana line to the superphosphate fertiliser plant at Laç was opened for traffic and one year later an industrial spur line east of Elbasan was completed.

A 54 km line from Rrogozhina on the Elbasan branch to a second fertiliser factory at Fier was completed in 1969.

There is a short length of narrow gauge industrial line which is not operated by the Albanian State Railways. This 950 mm gauge runs from Vlorë, on the Adriatic, 5 miles *(8 km)* to the bitumen mine at Selenicë with a 2.5 mile *(4 km)* branch to Mavrove.

TRAFFIC
After completion of the present Sixth Five-Year National Plan in 1980, railway traffic in Albania should be about 62 per cent above the 1979 level, Prime Minister Shehu told the 7th Party Congress meeting in Tirana. Railway share of total freight transport in Albania will then be about 38 per cent, Congress was told.

Freight traffic is mainly bulk transport with nickel and chrome ore, asphalt, wood coal and cement being the main commodities. Passenger traffic shows the same rising trend as freight traffic: the mere 30 million passenger-km in 1950 went up to 110 million in 1964, whereas the 8.5 million km-tonnes in 1950 augmented to 90 million in 1964. Train-km in the same years were 0.7 million and 2.9 million. Since 1964 no more traffic details have been released.

CIVIL ENGINEERING
At a ceremony in Tirana in April 1979 an agreement was signed between the Albanian Deputy Minister of Communications, L. Leka, and the Yugoslav Vice President of the Federal Committee for Transport, A. Zvonic, under which a 40 km standard-gauge line is to be built connecting the Albanian railhead at Shkoder with Yugoslav Railways' recently completed Belgrade—Bar line at Titograd. This will be Albania's first rail link with a foreign railway. The line will carry chromite and nickel ore mined in Albania into East Europe while Yugoslav raw materials and finished goods are expected to flow south into the terminal at Tirana.

Most lines are laid with rails weighing 86.7 lb per yd *(43 kg/m)* imported from Czechoslovakia. Maximum axle load is 21 tonnes.

There are six tunnels varying in length from 761 ft *(232 m)* to 2 460 ft *(750 m)*; and ten concrete bridges from 200 ft *(60 m)* to 720 ft *(220 m)*.

LOCOMOTIVES AND ROLLING STOCK
Albania has no railway industry, therefore all equipment, especially rolling stock and motive power, must be imported. A first batch of steam locomotives came from Chrzanow works in Poland, whose engines were similar to PKP's Tkt-48 class standard general-purpose superheated 1D1 (2-8-2) tank type. Some second-hand engines seem to have found their way from Poland to Albania too. In 1958, Albanian Railways followed the world-wide trend to dieselisation and bought their first two diesel-mechanical class BN 150 shunting locomotives from CKD Praha, followed by two more of the same type and two 750 hp BoBo diesel-electric road locomotives of CSD's T 435.0 class in the next year. Two other T 435.0 went to Albania in 1961 and three of the same class in 1962. Four more diesel-electrics of the slightly heavier T 458.1 class were delivered in 1967.

Passenger cars are mostly two-axled from the railways of the German Democratic Republic, Hungary and Czechoslovakia, but an increasing number of bogie coaches are being put into service.

Freight cars generally are older 15-tonne 2-axle types; the latest are modern bogie cars with a capacity of 45 tonnes, built in Czechoslovakia, Hungary, and China.

ALGERIA
ALGERIAN NATIONAL RAILWAYS (SNTF)
Société Nationale des Transports Ferroviaires, 21-23 boulevard Mohamed V, Algiers

Telephone: 61 1510
Telegrams: CEFAFER, Algiers
Telex: 52 455

Director General: Saddek Benmehdjouba
Commercial Director: Bouifrou Tahar
Transport Director: Rabhi Rachid
Director of Technical/Economic Studies and Planning: Budin Karim
Director of Personnel and General Administration: Ahmed Merouani
Director of Material: Mustapha Aris
Director of General Installations: Ali Touri
Director of Equipment: Abdenour Hadji
Director of Finances: Mohamed Smaala

Gauge: 1.435 m; 1.055 m; 1.00 m
Route length: 265.7 km; 1 129 km; 120 km (total: 3 908 km)

Since Algeria gained independence in 1962, the economic importance of the railways has gradually increased in accordance with the country's industrialisation programme. From 1976 two organisations replaced the former Société Nationale des Chemins de Fer: the Société Nationale des Transports Ferroviaires (SNTF) in charge of day-to-day operations and the Société Nationale d'Etudes et de Réalisation de l'Infrastructure Ferroviaire in charge of track renewals and new works planning.

During 1979 the Algerian government and the SNTF administration took positive steps to improve the rail system which is in need of modernisation and rehabilitation in order to cope with traffic demand. Consultancy teams from Austria, Belgium and India signed agreements to aid SNTF improvements. In February and March 1979 delegations from the Belgian Ministry of Communications and Austrian Federal Railways completed negotiations to finance and advise on railway improvements and construction of a new personnel centre. Cost ceilings of $US 2 755 million for 1 140 km and about $US 800 million for modernisation were established.

An agreement signed in India in May 1979 by Smail Kerdjoudi of the Algerian Transport Ministry and India's Railway Minister, Madhu Dandevate, provided for technical assistance in a number of projects. Included is assistance by Rail India Technical and Economic Services (RITES) in setting up a new organisation to improve operations on the existing network. Extending passing loops and remodelling marshalling yards to increase the length of trains will be given early priority.

Civil engineers will asess the need to strengthen bridges to cope with heavier trains. Ways to increase single-track capacity will also be examined. The agreement provides for India to receive favourable consideration when bids are called for construction work as a result of the investigations by RITES.

Also undertaking consultancy work for SNTF during 1979-81 is Deutsche Eisenbahn Consult (DEC) which is carrying out a survey on restructuring all railway lines and services in the heavily-congested Algiers commuter area by the year 2000. The survey is likely to combine closely with RITES studies into a possible metro for Algiers that will link suburban lines with a tunnel under the city centre.

FREIGHT TRAFFIC
After a climb from 1962 to 1968, general traffic (other than minerals and phosphate) increased sharply in 1971 and has shown since then a further rise in tonnage. SNTF believe the future of freight growth lies in long-distance haulage of large quantities of basic raw materials and semi-products. Main increases are expected to be in iron ore and phosphate rock, steel products and cereals. Some forecasts calculate that freight traffic will double between 1977 and 1982.

	1977	1978	1982*
Tonne-km (millions):	1 699	2 151	2 798
Train-km (freight and passengers) (thousands):	12 569	13 843	—

*Estimated

On 1.435 m gauge lines SNTF operates a fleet of 9 800 freight wagons; on 1.055 m gauge lines, a total of 1 413 wagons. There are in addition 989 convertible-gauge wagons. The railway owns and operates a pool of 730 containers, although no container trains are operated, movements being carried out by mixed freight trains. Container traffic averages about 280 tonnes a month.

In reply to SNTF's call for additional wagons the state-owned Société Algérienne de Constructions Métalliques awarded a $US 35 million contract to Pullman of the USA during 1979 to expand its rolling stock production plant. Production capacity will be boosted from 1 000 to 3 000 freight wagons a year.

Multiple-traction for freight trains are being operated using the Locotrol system in which a slave locomotive in the middle of the train is controlled by radio from the lead locomotive. The system is being used primarily to increase the length and carrying capacity of unit phosphate trains.

PASSENGER TRAFFIC
Following steady growth of passenger traffic since 1960 (3 489 073 passengers in 1963; 16 million by 1977) SNTF would like to shed some of its short and middle-distance traffic and concentrate on long-distance intercity services. The system, however, intends to retain commuter traffic.

	1977	1978	1979*
Passenger-km (millions)	1 369	1 644	1 932

*Estimated

On the 1.435 m gauge network the railway operates 386 passenger coaches and 33 railcars; on 1.055 m gauge lines, eight railcars and 33 passenger coaches. There are, in addition, three railcars operated on the 120 km metre-gauge lines.

FINANCIAL	1975	1976
		(Dinar 'millions)
Revenues	306	405.3
Expenditure	379	428.5

MOTIVE POWER
The railway operates 30 electric and 250 diesel-electric locomotives, 87 locotractors and 44 railcars.

Between 1971 and 1978 SNTF has bought 146 locomotives and 33 diesel railcars: 69 General Motors type GT26 locomotives rated at 3300 hp for standard-gauge freight operations; 25 General Motors type GT22 rated at 2500 hp for mainline passenger operations; 32 electric locomotives type 6CE from LEW of the German Democratic Republic for ore and phosphate hauls on the Tébessa—Annaba line; 33 diesel railcars, type ZZN 200 from Fiat of Italy; and 20 diesel-hydraulic shunters rated at 600 hp from LEW. Latest purchases include 25 locomotives (1500 hp) from General Electric (USA) and 30 narrow-gauge (760 hp) locomotives from General Motors (USA and Canada).

CIVIL ENGINEERING
At the beginning of April 1979 it was announced that Cogeffar of Italy is to double and upgrade the 85 km Ramdane—Djamal—El Gourzi line. The line was built as a single-track in 1870 and can no longer handle the increased volume of freight traffic which by 1990 is expected to exceed seven million tonnes annually. Track doubling and modernisation is expected to increase the capacity for iron and steel products from the El-Hadjar and Jijel works and iron ore from the Bou-Khadra mine. The line passes through Constantine where a revised track layout will provide for fast-growing passenger traffic and a new passenger station is to be built between 1980 and 1982. A new freight station is to be constructed in the Oued-Hamimine area. Civil engineering work on the line will be heavy with three tunnels, 16 bridges and one viaduct to be constructed. Level crossings will be eliminated. Seven stations will be rebuilt and modern signalling installed along the whole route. The project will take four years to complete at a cost of 681 million dinars.

Canadian Pacific Consulting Services began work during 1978 on a two-year engineering study of a projected 1500 km iron ore railway planned to run from Gara Djebilet in the west to La Macta on the Mediterranean. The line is to be built to move 40 million tonnes of iron ore, coal and dolomite annually. It is to be designed for trains of 15 000 to 20 000 gross tonnes carried in up to 200 wagons.

Two other line studies were carried out during 1978: one by Transcon Consultora Tecnia, Brazil on the southeast route between Touggourt and Hassi-Messaoud running westward to Ouargla (construction of the 420 km line is estimated at $US 450 million) and the second on the new east—west Rocade Railway running inland from the coastal strip between Tébessa and Sid Bel Abbès.

The Rocade Railway will be a considerable project. At the end of 1978 Italconsult won the contract to design the first 200 km stage from Tébessa to Sid Bel Abbès. It will eventually replace the existing line to Khenchela as part of an overall plan to eliminate narrow-gauge tracks in Algeria. Once the first stage is completed, the Rocade line will expand 1000 km westwards via Batna, M'Sila, Ain-Oussara and Tiaret to Sidi Bel Abbès. North—south connections will link the railway with the existing network between Bordj-Bou-Arréridj and M'Sila, the Algiers region, Ain-Oussara and south to Djelfa, replacing the existing 280 km narrow-gauge line between Blida and Djelfa. A connection between Relizane and Tiaret (140 km) will replace the existing narrow-gauge line between these two centres. Also likely to be extended in the future is the Djelfa line, to Laghouat and Ghardaia, to form a link with the oil-producing complex at Hassi-Messaoud.

Under study by Transion Consult of Belgium is a railway to connect Constantine and Jijel, designed to link a new iron and steel producing plant at Jijel. Construction is planned during the 1980s. Also planned is a line joining Thenia with the existing Tixi-Ouzou line. Construction of a link between Oran-Es Senia, Mers El Hadjadj and Mostaganem is also planned to handle freight traffic originating at new industrial centres along the Oran—Arzew—Mostganem axis. As part of a new line construction, SNTF is setting up two new concrete sleeper plants during 1978-81 to supplement present production at Annaba where capacity is to be increased.

ELECTRIFICATION
Algeria has only one electrified line running 298 km between Tébessa and Annaba at 3 000 V dc.

SIGNALLING
Electrically-operated mechanical signals are gradually being replaced by colour light signal displays throughout the system while on new lines and upgraded tracks automatic signalling as being installed.

STAFF PRODUCTIVITY
To cope with increasing traffic demand the number of SNTF personnel was increased from 12 523 in 1976 to 12 523 in 1978, while train-km in 1976 was stepped up from 12 569 to 13 843 in 1978.

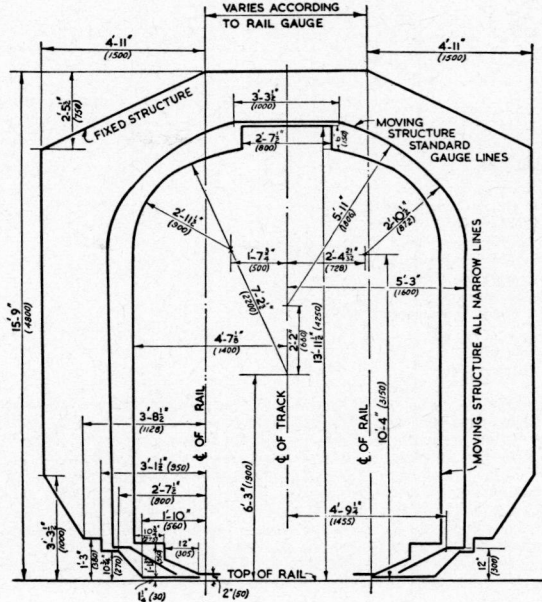

DIESEL LOCOMOTIVES

Class	Axle Arrangement	Transmission	Rated Power hp	Max. kg	Tractive Effort Continuous at kg	kmlh	Max Speed kmlh	Wheel Dia. mm	Axle Load Tons	Total Weight Tons	Length mm	No. Built	Year first Built	Mechanical Parts	Engine	Transmission
Standard Gauge:																
040DA	A1AA1A	Elec.	1 520	24 700	19 414	16.9	96	1 066	21.3	124.6	17 700	15	1946	Baldwin	Baldwin	Westinghouse
040DB	A1AA1A	Elec.	1 520	25 200	14 060	23.3	130	1 066	21.3	124.6	17 700	25	1947	Baldwin	Baldwin	Westinghouse
040DC	A1AA1A	Elec.	1014	22 800	14 700	15.2	85	1 066	17.4	103.1	16 175	20	1948	Baldwin	Baldwin	Westinghouse
040DD	A1AA1A	Elec.	1 520	21 400	17 000	20.0	120	1 016	19.5	110.7	16 896	5	1950	Alco	Alco	GE
040DG	A1AA1A	Elec.	1 622	21 500			120	1 016	19.8	113.8	17 050	5	1951	Alco	Alco	GE
060DB	CoCo	Elec.	1 315	16 800	12 600	15.0	120	950	14.5	87.0	17 200	10	1956	Schneider	Baldwin	Schneider
060DC	CoCo	Elec.	1 840	30 000	15 500		120	1 050	18.9	113.4	19 814	37	1957	Alsthom	SACM	Alsthom
060DD	CoCo	Elec.	3 300		26 020	26.6	124	1 016	20.0	120.0	20 745	29	1971	GM	GM	GM
060DF	CoCo	Elec.	3 300		26 020	26.6	124	1 016	20.0	120.0	20 745	25	1973	GM	GM	GM
40EA	B	Mech.	40				12	900	5.3	10.6	5 610	3	1955	Moyse	Renault	
80DA	B	Mech.	80				17	950	10.4	20.8	6 770	23	1955	Moyse	Renault	
150DEA	B	Elec.	150				25	950	15.9	31.8	6 770	5	1952	Moyse	Ricardo	
150DEB	B	Elec.	150				60	1 050	16.9	33.8	8 900	8	1956	Decauville	Poyaud	Oerlikon
200DA	C	Mech.	200				29	1 016	11.0	32.5	7 930	14	1948	Hunslet	Gardner	
200DB	B	Mech.	200				29	1 050	16.0	32.0	8 180	5	1955	Billard	Willème	
200DC	B	Mech.	200				29	1 050	16.0	32.0	8 170	1	1957	Billard	Willème	
400DA	B	Hydr.	400				55	1 050	17.3	34.6	9 360	16	1956	ANF	Saurer	Voith
400DB	B	Hydr.	400				55	1 050	18.4	36.7	9 360	8	1960	Billard	Saurer	Voith
400DC	B	Hydr.	400				50	1 050	17.3	34.6	9 360	4	1962	DeDietrich	Saurer	Voith
600DA	D	Hydr.	600				60	1 100	15.4	61.4	10 920	10	1971	LEW	LEW	LEW
600DB	D	Hydr.	600				60	1 100	15.4	61.4	10 920	10	1972	LEW	LEW	LEW
1 055 mm Gauge																
060YDA	CoCo	Elec.	960		14 800	20.0	85	914	12.0	72.0	18 550	10	1953	DeDietrich	Sulzer	Oerlikon
060YDB	BoBoBo	Elec.	920	16 000	9 200	18.0	80	920	10.0	59.0	13 360	10	1958	Alsthom	SACM	Alsthom
060YDC	BoBoBo	Elec.	935	18 500	10 000	19.0	80	920	12.0	72.0	14 396	6	1961	Alsthom	SACM	Alsthom
Y80DA	B	Mech.	80				17	950	10.1	20.2	7 060	2	1959	Moyse	Berliet	
Y150DA	C	Hydr.	150		6 160	4.8	22	860	9.9	29.6	7 340	10	1951	LLD	Willème	
Y200DA	B	Mech.	200				29	1 050	12.0	24.0	8 070	1	1957	Billard	Willème	
1 000 mm Gauge																
XZZDN	BoBo	Elec.	600				90	860	9.6	38.4	16 200	5	1938	DeDietrich	Saurer	Oerlikon
X200DA	B	Mech.	200				29	1 050	12.0	24.0	8 290	4	1957	Billard	Willème	

ELECTRIC LOCOMOTIVES

Class	Axle Arrangement	Line Current kV Type	Rated Power hp	Max kg	Tractive Effort Continuous at kg	kmlh	Max Speed kmlh	Wheel dia. mm	Weight tonnes	Length mm	No. Built	First Built	Mechanical Parts	Electrical Equipment
6BE	CoCo	3 dc	3 120		22 500	37.5	80	1 250	134.1	18 922	8	1958	Alsthom	Alsthom
6CE	CoCo	3 dc	2 700		24 600	30.0	80	1 350	130.0	18 640	32	1972	LEW	Skoda

ANGOLA
BENGUELA RAILWAY

Caminho de Ferro de Benguela, CP 32, Lobito

Telephone: 2645
Telex: 8253

General Manager: Eng. L. Lamas de Oliveira
Deputy General Manager: Eng. F. Melo Sampaio
Assistant General Manager: Dr. F. Fuso
Personnel Manager: J. Rocha
Operations Manager: Dr. J. Teixeira de Sousa
Track and Civil Engineering Manager: Eng. Tec. M. Monteiro
Administrative Manager: Dr. G. Pratas
Commercial Manager: J. Avelar
Planning and Organisation Manager: A. Guedes

Gauge: 1.067 m
Route length: 1 304 km

Due to continued hostilities in Angola, numerous railway services were severely disrupted between 1973 and 1979, but through services on the Benguela Railway between Zaire and the port at Lobito were reported to be back in operation in September 1979. The Benguela Railway virtually ceased transit operations to Zaire and Zambia during 1975 while the 968 km Caminho de Ferro de Moçâmedes in the south suspended all services between Entroncamento (east of Sade Bandeira) and Serpa Pinto by mid-1977 due to damage to track and bridges on the line. The Benguela Railway managed to maintain, virtually without interruption, internal traffic operating between Lobito and the end of the line at Luan.

The Benguela Railway, 810 miles *(1 304 km)* route length of 3 ft 6 in *(1.067 m)* gauge, serves an extensive area of the Angola territory and connects the port of Lobito with Zaire and Zambia.

The traffic carried is mainly of minerals and ores from Zaire and Zambia, for shipping from Lobito. In the upward direction, the traffic consists essentially of machinery, petrol and oils, coal, coke and general merchandise.

Construction of a 163 km alternative alignment known as the Cubal Variant has reduced the distance between Lobito and Cubal by 22 miles *(35 km)* on a minimum radius of curvature of 1 017 ft *(310 m)* with gradients not exceeding 1.25 per cent.

FINANCIAL RESULTS	1972	1973	1974	1975	1976
		(Thousands of Escudos)			
Revenue	873 080	1 211 862	1 273 361	805 294	122 109
Expenses	612 352	683 120	968 753	1 247 045	890 344
Operating ratio (%)	70.1	—	—	—	—

OPERATIONS

Freight tonne-kms	1 772 805	2 309 209	2 427 738	—	—
Total tonnes carried	1 900 600	2 566 700	2 383 700	1 207 300	239 000
Tonnes originating	—	—	—	—	—
Tonnes in transit	—	—	—	—	—
Passenger kms	—	152 047.8	205 721	—	—
Total passengers carried	1 412 600	1 587 700	1 983 000	1 635 200	1 309 400

MOTIVE POWER

Motive power and rolling stock includes 101 steam locomotives, six diesel-hydraulic shunters, 22 mainline diesel-electric locomotives, 58 passenger coaches, four dining cars, 79 baggage and brake vans, 1 900 freight wagons.

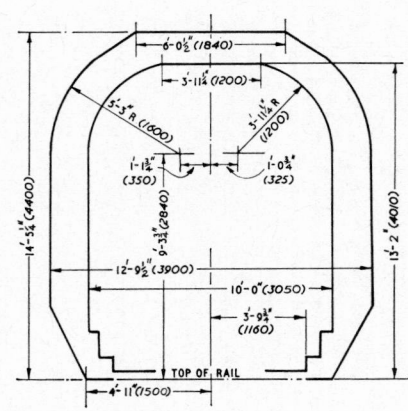

Caminho de Ferro de Benguela

BENGUELA RAILWAY DIESEL LOCOMOTIVES

Loco number	Axle arrangement	Transmission	Rated power hp	Tractive effort Maximum lbs (kg)	Continuous at lbs (kg)	mph (km/h)	Maximum Speed mph (km/h)	Wheel diameter in (mm)	Total Weight tonnes	Length ft in (mm)	No Built	Year first built	Builders: Mechanical parts	Engine & type
D1-D4	C	Hydraulic	425	24 000 *(10 890)*	9 000 *(4 080)*	12 *(19)*	17 *(27)*	40 *(1 016)*	40	28' 5½'' *(8 680)*	4	1960	North British	Paxman 8RPHXL
580-81	C	Hydraulic	425	24 000 *(10 890)*	9 000 *(4 080)*	12 *(19)*	17 *(27)*	40 *(1 016)*	41	28' 5½'' *(8 680)*	2	1972	Andrew Barclay	Paxman 8RPHXL
D101-D122	Co-Co	Electric	2 150	59 520 *(27 000)*	50 400 *(22 800)*	12 *(19)*	64 *(103)*	36 *(914)*	90	55' 00'' *(16 764)*	22	1972	General Electric	General Electric

ARGENTINA
ARGENTINE RAILWAYS

Ferrocarriles Argentinos EFA Avienda Ramos, Meijia 1302, Buenos Aires

President: Hugo Carassai
General Co-ordinator: Alberto B. Abadia
Director of Traffic: Ing. Emilio B. Nastri
Commercial Director (freight): Ing. Cayetano Marletta Rainieri
Inspector General: Ing. Angel Ceci
Director of Economic Studies: Ctdor. Horacio M. Allemand
Financial Director: Ctdor. Carlos F. Martin
Mechanical Director: Ing. Jorge A. Bilotti
Director, Way and Works: Ing Victor Gilardoni
Director, Planning: Ing. Alfredo Fernández
Director, Special Studies: Ing. Antonio P. Estévez
Chief of Public Relations: Mayor (R.E.) D. Jorge A.V. Mastropietro
Regional Directors: F.C. Gral. Roca: Ing. Roberto Pedernera
F.C. Gral. Belgrano: Ing. Osvaldo Garau
F.C. Gral. Urquiza: Ing. Angel S. Butti
F.C. Gral. San Martin: Ing. Luis Donzelli
F.C. Gral. Mitre: Sr. Natalio D. Viola
F.C. D.F. Sarmiento: Ing. Hugo Berro

Gauges: 1.00; 1.435; 1.676 m
Route length: 34 117 km

Regions	Gauge (metres)	Length of lines In service 1973	In service 1975
Roca	1.676	8 159	8 159
	0.750	403	403
		8 562	8 562
Mitre	1.676	6 241	6 174
San Martin	1.676	4 625	4 625
Sarmiento	1.676	3 830	3 830
Urquiza	1.435	3 086	3 086
Belgrano	1.000	13 461	13 461
Total Empresa		39 805	39 738

The military administration which took over control of FA in April 1976 passed the railway back to a civil administration in April 1979 when Hugo Carassai took over as president from General Tomás Caballero. During the first six months of operations of military administration (April-September 1976) the railway's fortunes—which had fallen to a very low level in 1975—improved substantially. By 1977 it looked as though FA

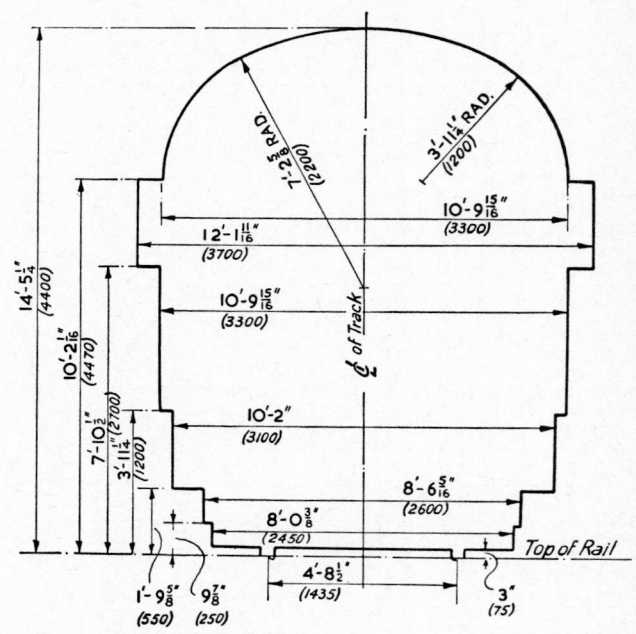

Northwest Region—standard gauge

had begun to turn the corner: freight traffic was up from 17.8 million tonnes (11 000 million tonne/km) in 1976 to 20.174 million tonnes (11 600 million tonne/km) in 1977. At the same time passenger journeys dropped from 445 million (14.6 million passenger/km) to 407 million (12.5 million passenger/km) over the same period, providing substantial savings in operating costs. The military's main solution to FA's problems was to trim the network size down from a total length of 39 779 km in 1976 to 34 293 km by 1978. As a result, several uneconomic passenger services were cut, subsidies reduced (the deficit was cut from $US 2 million a day in 1976 to only half-a-million US dollars a day in 1978) and there has been a big reduction in labour, with 115 000 on FA's payroll by the end of 1978, compared with 126 000 at the end of 1977.

A major programme of modernisation, including major projects outlined in the earlier, medium-term plan is being financed by a World Bank loan of $US 96 million; credit worth $US 33 million to cover purchase of 250 diesel locomotives and spares and a $US 270 million finance agreement under which the Japanese will start work on the long-awaited Roca suburban electrification. Investment during the 1978-80 period is expected to have exceeded $US 1000 million.

FREIGHT

	1975	1976	1977
Freight tonne-km	10 676 190 000	11 000 000 000	11 600 000 000
Freight tonnage	16 337 700	17 800 000	20 174 000

During 1977/78 FA took delivery of 761 new freight wagons, scrapped 5 000 old wagons and ended 1978 with a total of 47 439 wagons in operation. Delivered during 1977/78 were: 300 hopper wagons for Dautista Buriasco; 62 covered grain hoppers from CID; 160 container flat wagons from Gabricaciones Militares; 160 bulk cement hopper wagons from FAVYS; 10 double-deck automobile carriers; 530 dry-cargo containers from FAVYS.

PASSENGERS

	1975	1976	1977
Passenger-km	14 366 749 000	14 600 000 000	12 500 000 000
Passengers carried	436 459 000	445 000 000	407 000 000

Following withdrawal of numerous non-profitable passenger trains (among the withdrawals in 1979 was the luxury Buenos Aires—San Carlos de Bariloche 1 740-km 29-hour express), FA has made successive tariff reductions in a bid to attract business. Discounts of up to 50 per cent of the normal fare were offered in mid-1979.
Only 27 new passenger coaches were put into service during 1978 while 500 were withdrawn, bringing the total passenger and baggage car fleet to 2 363 vehicles by the end of that year.

MOTIVE POWER
By the end of 1978, FA had taken delivery of 63 type GT22CU metre-gauge diesel-electric locomotives from General Motors (output 2475 hp) and 27 type G22CW also from GM (2475 hp). The deliveries were part of FA's order for 170 units from GM of Argentina: 20 broad-gauge (1.676 m) type GT22CW units; 34 metre-gauge type GT22CU; 76 metre-gauge type G22CU (1650 hp); and 40 standard-gauge rated at 1650 hp. Through a programme of retirements, the railway ended 1978 with a diesel motive power park totalling 1157 compared with 1171 at the end of 1977.
Using two World Bank loans of $40 million, FA is to purchase 250 diesel-electrics from General Motors, 80 of which will be supplied complete while the remainder will be erected locally by GM from imported components. The remainder of the money will fund purchase of spares for the existing locomotive fleet.
For the Roca electrification project (see under *Electrification*) FA is to purchase 52 sets of three-car multiple units expected to go into service by 1983. 40 of the sets will be built in Japan with the remaining 12 built locally under licence. Cars will be 25 m long with three double-leaf doors on each side. Motor cars will have seats for 64 and weigh 50 tonnes while the trailers seat 68 and weigh 49 tonnes. Formation will be motor-trailer-motor capable of nine-car rakes. All axles of the motor car will be powered with each motor rated at 220 kW producing 1 760 kW per set and maximum acceleration of 0.8 m/s^2 up to 54 km/h. By running six-car formations FA will be able to move 18 000 passengers an hour in each direction, an 80 per cent increase on the current service. Later FA plans to order additional sets to strengthen peak-hour services.
Improvement of marshalling facilities resulted in a steady withdrawal of the system's remaining steam locomotives. At the end of 1977 there were 681 steam units still operating; 138 broad-gauge, 123 on standard-gauge and 420 working narrow-gauge tracks. By the end of 1978 300 of them had been retired. Replacing steam throughout the system's marshalling yard network are a series of new 130 diesel-hydraulic shunters ordered in 1977 from Cockerill of Belgium.

INVESTMENTS
Including expenditure of 297 786 million pesos in 1979 FA is preparing to invest the equivalent of $US 1 000 million during 1978-80. Purchases during 1979 included 44 mainline diesel-electric locomotives, 32 diesel-hydraulic shunters and 45 passenger coaches. Other spending included work on new line construction over 3.5 km, track improvements over 650 km and general signalling and civil engineering improvements

CIVIL ENGINEERING
Most urgent of the problems facing new FA administrators is track renewal. Plans for upgrading and renewing 4 109 km of track were, in fact, unveiled in 1974, but were inevitably delayed following FA's worsening operating situation. Now the plans are in hand.
Track improvements planned are aimed at raising maximum speeds to 160 km/h on broad and standard-gauge tracks, and to 100 km/h on narrow-gauge lines. Work to be undertaken during the 1979/82 period includes:
Renewal of 412 km during 1979, together with major improvements to 425 km and

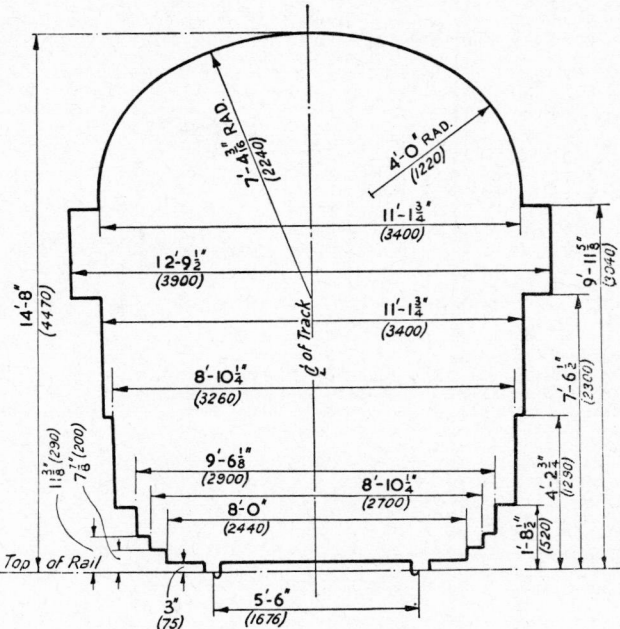

Central and Southwest Regions—5 ft 6 in (1·676 m) gauge

Cereal wagon designed to transport 65 tons

Class 10 000 diesel-hydraulic shunter built by Cockerill for yard service

mechanised maintenance of 18 000 km;
Renewal of 468 km during 1980, major improvements to 356 km and 24 000 km mechanised maintenance;
Renewal of 490 km, major improvements to 441 km and 29 000 km mechanised maintenance;
Renewal of 436 km, major improvements to 399 km and 29 000 km mechanised maintenance.

ELECTRIFICATION
The total electrified route at the end of 1977 was 259 km. Lines now under electrification include the 130-km urban network of the Urquiza and the Roca suburban system.
Exchange of contracts between FA and a consortium of Japanese companies for electrification of the former Roca Railway suburban lines out of Plaza Constitucion station in Buenos Aires signals the go-ahead at last for complete upgrading and energising of the 130 route-km of 1.676-m gauge track. Work comprising the lines to Glew and Ezeiza, and to La Plata by two routes, is expected to be completed by 1984/85.

Fiat-type 7164 diesel-electric in FA livery

Fiat diesel railcar

The Japanese consortium comprises Marubeni, Toshiba, Hitachi and Mitsubishi Electric. Nine Argentinian companies are involved: Marubeni, Techint, SADE, Ecofisa, Impresit de Sideco, Fabricaciones Militares, Fiat-Concord, Siam di Tella and Desaci. Work will be carried out in two stages: firstly two of the four tracks between Plaza Constitucion, Avellaneda and Temperley and the double track lines running on to Glew and Ezeiza (47 km); secondly, the line from Avellaneda to La Plata together with the orbital link from Temperley to Villa Elisa and the short connection between Barazategui

and Bosques. Traction power will be single phase ac at 25 kV 50 Hz.
Signalling will be by colour light automatic block combined with inductive automatic train stop (ATS).

STAFF
115 000 were employed at the end of 1978, a big reduction on the 126 000 at the end of 1977.

AUSTRALIA

AUSTRALIAN NATIONAL RAILWAYS

Norwich Centre, 55 King William Road, North Adelaide, South Australia 5006

Telephone: 2674300
Telegrams: AUSrail Adelaide
Telex: 88445

Chairman: K. A. Smith O.B.E.
General Manager: Dr. D. G. Williams
Assistant General Manager, Engineering and Planning: M. L. Nayda
Assistant General Manager, Administration: T. M. Williams
Assistant General Manager, Tasmania: A. F. Maddock
Executive Officer: W. E. May
Chief Planner: Vacant
Operations Manager: A. R. Polmear
Marketing Manager: T. A. Snigg
Finance and Supply Manager: N. B. Walkom
Sales Manager: J. D. Harris
Chief Mechanical Engineer: J. Dudley
Chief Civil Engineer: D. P. Smith
Signals/Communications Engineer: D. J. Both

Gauges: 1.435 m; 1.067 m; 1.600 m
Route length: 2 140 km; 869 km; 511 km

ANR is responsible for the management and operation of railways owned by the Commonwealth Government and provides a key link in the chain of inter-system rail transport operating round Australia. It is a statutory authority under the Australian National Railways Act operating as a commercially-oriented business enterprise on behalf of the people of Australia.
The network comprises the former Commonwealth Railways, the non-metropolitan South Australian network and the former Tasmanian Government Railways.
In the three regions ANR operates 330 locomotives, 12 619 goods and livestock wagons, 376 passenger coaches and 1 156 service stock vehicles.
The combined railway carries approximately 11·58 million tonnes of freight and 960 000 passengers a year. Headed by a six-man commission, ANR employs 12 000 people and has net fixed assets totalling about $390 million.

Operating Offices
Adelaide, South Australia; Port Augusta, South Australia; Launceston, Tasmania.

Commercial Offices
Sydney, New South Wales; Melbourne, Victoria; Perth, Western Australia.

ANR comprises:
Northern Region: (formerly Commonwealth Railways) comprising the Trans-Australian Railway (1 435 mm gauge) from Port Pirie (South Australia) to Kalgoorlie (Western Australia), a distance of 1 782 km; the 1 435 mm gauge Port Augusta—Whyalla branch, 75 km long; the Central Australia Railway (1 435 mm gauge) from Stirling North to Marree (350 km) and the 1 067 mm gauge section from Marree to Alice Springs (869 km); the North Australian Railway in the Northern Territory (1 067 mm gauge) Larrimah (502 km) (not operating); and the Australian Capital Territory Railway (1 435 mm gauge) connecting Canberra, the Federal Capital, with the New South Wales Government System at Queanbeyan (8 km). A new 831 km 1 435 mm gauge line is being constructed between Tarcoola (South Australia) on the Trans-Australian Railway and Alice Springs; scheduled for completion in October 1980 it will allow closure of the flood-prone 1 067 mm gauge line between Marree and Alice Springs (see under *Civil Engineering*).
Length and gauge: 2 215 km, 1 435 mm; 1 380 km, 1 067 mm; total 3 595 km.
Locomotives and rolling stock: standard-gauge: 72 diesel-electric mainline locomotives, two diesel-electric shunting locomotives, one diesel-mechanical locomotive, three diesel-hydraulic railcars, 165 cars, 3 006 goods and service stock. Narrow-gauge: 30 diesel-electric mainline locomotives, three diesel-hydraulic shunting locomotives, 23 cars, 947 goods and service stock.

Central Region: (formerly non-metropolitan South Australian Railways).
Length and gauge: 2 391 km, 1 600 mm; 398 km, 1 435 mm; 963 km, 1 067 mm; total, 3 752 km.
Locomotives and rolling stock: broad-gauge: 107 diesel-electric locomotives, 14 diesel rail cars, seven diesel rail car trailers, 110 passenger carriages (includes 51 Victorian and Australian National Railways joint stock passenger cars), 5 056 freight vehicles, 312 service vehicles. Standard-gauge: 28 diesel-electric locomotives, three passenger carriages, 838 freight vehicles, 75 service vehicles. Also 60 vehicles (Indian Pacific) jointly operated by Western Australian and Australian National Railways and the Public Transport Commission of New South Wales. Narrow-gauge: 14 diesel-electric locomotives, 1 115 freight vehicles, 143 service vehicles.

Tasmanian Region: (formerly Tasmanian Government Railways).
Length and gauge: 851 km, 1 067 mm.
Locomotives and rolling stock: 50 diesel-electric locomotives, 19 diesel locomotives, two diesel-hydraulic locomotives, 13 diesel rail cars, 5 diesel railcar trailers, 34 passenger carriages, 2 054 goods wagons, 56 vans.

FREIGHT TRAFFIC
The Trans-Australian Railway carries just over 700 000 tonnes a year with most movements occuring westbound. Westbound inter-system freight increased 7.2 per cent during 1976/77 to 662 423 tonnes compared with the previous year. Eastbound inter-system freight increased by 39 563 tonnes (17.5 per cent) due primarily to continued growth in van load traffic, forwarding agents' truckloads and, to a lesser degree, container traffic.
On the Central Australia Railway northbound freight in 1976/77 decreased by 6 228 tonnes compared with the previous year. Actual tonnages involved were 101 901 tonnes for 1975-76 and 95 673 for the previous year. The main reason for the loss of traffic, to highway hauliers, was the cumulative effect of the closure of the line for 12 weeks during the year. Southbound traffic increased by 3 721 tonnes to 22 557 tonnes due to increased movements of copper concentrates and cattle.
With the withdrawal of rail services on the North Australia Railway from June 1976, approval was given for co-ordinated rail/road traffic to and from Darwin. Loading and unloading at Darwin of all through booked rail/road traffic is undertaken by NAR while the transport of goods from Alice Springs and Darwin to intermediate road locations is carried out under contract. Refrigerated containers are made available to clients for the carriage of perishables beyond Alice Springs.

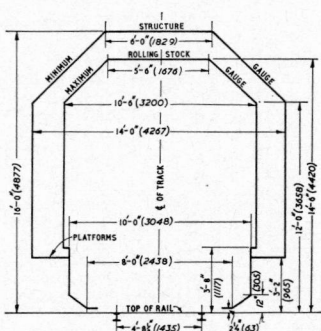

ANR 1.435 m gauge (the former Commonwealth Railways)

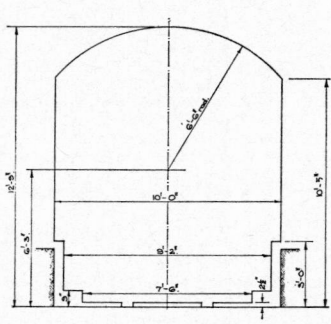

ANR 1.067 m gauge lines in the Tasmanian region (former Tasmanian Government Railways)

Freight over the Australian Capital Territory Railway increased slightly in 1976/77 to 210 424 tonnes compared with 210 071 tonnes the previous year. Freight revenue on the line was $A229 802, an increase of $A36 999. Petroleum products (154 615 tonnes) comprised the bulk of freight carried by rail into Canberra.

	1976	1977
Tonnes carried (thousands)	3 758	3 630
Tonne-km (thousands)	2 729 340.9	2 609 030.6
Train-km (thousands)	3 788.4	4 040.6
Average haul (km)	728.78	718.665
Revenue per train-km ($)	12.48	9.92

Freight rolling stock
Following the deliveries of new rolling stock in 1976/77, ANR now operates a freight fleet totalling 12 261 vehicles (5 025 for 1.600 m gauge, 3 292 over 1.435 m gauge routes and 3 944 over 1.067 m): 112 covered wagons; 118 open wagons; 41 flat wagons.

Intermodal services
ANR operates regular container services between Adelaide and Darwin, Alice Springs and Tennant Creek while piggyback is operated over both the Trans-Australian Railway and the Central Australia Railway by semi-trailers and pantechnicons.
The Railways of Australia Container Express (RACE) operates containerised freight by high-speed block trains throughout Australia. RACE operates between Sydney and Brisbane, Sydney and Welbourne.

PASSENGER TRAFFIC
The number of through passengers on the Trans-Australian Railway declined from 124 000 in 1975-76 to 101 000 the following year. To reduce heavy losses in passenger train operations the service was rationalised in 1977 when the westbound *Trans-Australian* was cancelled on Sundays, Tuesdays, Thursdays and Fridays (running on alternate days) and eastbound on Tuesdays, Thursdays, Saturdays and Sundays. Services on these days have been taken over by the *Indian Pacific*.
The number of passengers on the Central Australian Railways has declined owing mainly to a reduction in the twice-weekly service to once a week. Passenger traffic on the Australian Capital Territory Railway has increased slightly over the past two years.

Motorail services
The only region operating Motorail services is the Trans-Australian where a new service between Port Pirie and Kewdale was introduced, carrying a total of 1 319 motor vehicles during 1976/77.

Passenger rolling stock
The ANR passenger fleet includes 14 power cars, seven railcar trailers (all working the 1.600 m gauge lines), 102 coaches on 1.600 m gauge, 169 coaches on 1.435 m gauge and 113 on 1.067 m lines. A total of 111 of the coaches are owned jointly on the *Overland* and Trans-Australian *Indian Pacific* services.

	1976	1977
Passenger journeys	181 949	212 891
Train-km	1 346 102	1 543 008
Revenue per train-km ($)	4.86	4.19

FINANCES

	1976	1977
	(thousands)	
Earnings	63 318.8	54 455.5
Expenditure	68 517.3	65 120.1
Operating deficit	5 198.5	10 664.6
Percentage of expenditure to earnings	108.21%	119.58%

MOTIVE POWER

Following deliveries of five 1.435 m gauge 2 460/2 240 kW diesel-electric locomotives in 1976/77 the total ANR locomotive fleet reached 326 units. Based on an effective strength of 45 GM class and 16 CL class locomotives the average daily distance per locomotive is an estimated 366 km for the GMs and 561 km for the CLs. The new AL class locomotives from Clyde Engineering are being used on general freight services, completing about 242 333 km a year. Narrow-gauge NSU, NT and NJ locomotives operate on the Central Australia Railway.

ANR locomotive Fleet

Class	Region	Intro- duced	Power (kW)	Type	Gauge 1 600 mm (Broad)	1 435 mm (Stan- dard)	1 067 mm (Narrow)	No Units
350	Central	1949	260	D/E	2	—	—	2
500	Central/ North	1964/69	373	D/E	27	7	—	34
600	North	1965/70	1 340	D/E	—	7	—	7
700	Central/ North	1971/72	1 490	D/E	3	3	—	6
800	Central	1956/57	490	D/E	10	—	—	10
830	Central/ North	1959/70	670	D/E	16	11	14	41
900	Central	1951/53	1 190	D/E	9	—	—	9
930	Central	1955/67	1 190	D/E	37	—	—	37
AL	North	1976/77	2 240	D/E	—	8	—	8
CL	North	1970/72	2 240	D/E	—	17	—	17
DE	North	1948	260	D/E	—	2	—	2
DR	North	1964	112	D/H	—	1	—	1
GM1	North	1951/52	1 120	D/E	—	11	—	11
GM12	North	1955/67	1 300	D/E	—	36	—	36
NB	North	1957	105	D/H	—	—	1	1
NC	North	1966	186	D/H	—	—	2	2
NJ	North	1971	1 120	D/E	—	—	6	6
NSU	North	1954/56	635	D/E	—	—	13	13
NT	North	1965/68	970	D/E	—	—	10	10
U	Tasmania	1958/60	76	D/M	—	—	6	6
V	Tasmania	1948/64	152	D/M	—	—	11	11
VA	Tasmania	1948	114	D/M	—	—	2	2
W	Tasmania	1959	250	D/H	—	—	2	2
X	Tasmania	1950/52	450	D/E	—	—	27	27
XA	Tasmania	1951/52	450	D/E	—	—	5	5
Y	Tasmania	1961/71	595	D/E	—	—	8	8
Z	Tasmania	1972/73	1 340	D/E	—	—	4	4
ZA	Tasmania	1973/76	1 750	D/E	—	—	6	6

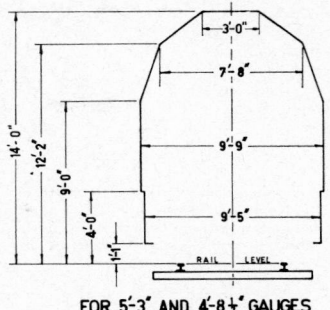

FOR 5'-3" AND 4'-8½" GAUGES

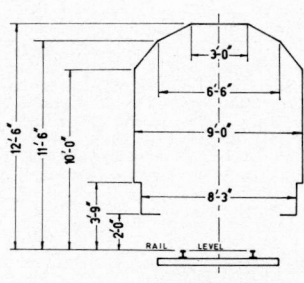

FOR 3'-6" GAUGE

ANR loading gauge for former South Australian Railways 1.6 m and 1.435 m lines (*above*) and 1.067 m lines (*below*)

INVESTMENTS

During 1979 ANR budgetted for a capital expenditure programme costing $A 22 million. Major purchases were freight wagons costing $A 923 500, major track improvements valued at $A 14.9 million, signalling ($A 400 800) and communications ($A 890 000).

CIVIL ENGINEERING

Construction of the standard-gauge line from Tarcoola to Alice Springs is planned for October 1980 which is opening about twelve months ahead of schedule. Being built at a cost of $A 145 million, the new line runs about 150 km west of the present narrow-gauge Marree—Alice Springs section of the existing Central Australia Railway. Track-laying had reached a point some 260 km north of Tarcoola at the beginning of 1980. Completion of infrastructure to the outskirts of Alice was scheduled for July 1980.

Track details

Standard rail: Flat bottom throughout, weighing 53, 46.8, 39.7 31.2, 29.8, 24.8, 29.8 to 20.3 kg/m
Joints: Fishplates, bolts and welding.
Rail fastening: Dog spikes, elastic rail spikes, with or without plates.
Cross ties (sleepers): Impregnated hardwood 8 ft 0 in × 9 in × 4½ in *(2 438 × 228 × 114 mm)* (4 ft 8½ in *(1.434 m)* gauge), 6 ft 0 in × 8 in × 4½ in *(1 828 × 203 × 114 mm)* (3 ft 6 in *(1.066 m)* gauge).
Spacing: 1 600 to 690 per km.
Filling: Crushed stone and gravel ballast.
Minimum radius of curves: 4.4° curvature.
Maximum gradient: 1.25%.

STAFF/PRODUCTIVITY

A total of 3 695 full-time and 80 part-time staff were employed during 1977 while train-km operated (passengers and freight) totalled 5.1 million compared with 5.5 million in 1976. Total number of staff in 1976 was 4 140.

Loading of road transports at ANR's Northern Region operational centre of Port Augusta for piggyback rail transport across the Trans-Australian Railway to Western Australia

The Geismar Sleeper-Laying Gentry working on ANR's new 831 km Tarcoola—Alice Springs Railway
It lifts 40 concrete sleepers at a time and into position, perfectly spaced and aligned, in two drops.

STATE RAILWAY AUTHORITY/SRA (NEW SOUTH WALES)
Transport House, 11-31 York Street, Sydney, NSW 2000

Telephone: 219 8888

Commissioner: Alan S. Reiher

Gauge: 1.435 m
Route length: 9 756 km

Under major reorganisation of public transport services, the former Public Transport Commission was replaced by two new bodies during 1979: the State Rail Authority (SRA) and the Urban Transit Authority. SRA now operates all rail passenger and freight services in New South Wales and UTA handles bus and ferry services in Sydney, Wollongong and Newcastle.

FREIGHT TRAFFIC
Total freight tonne/km in 1977/78 was 9 243 331 compared with 9 320 153 tonne/km in 1976/77. Tonnage carried was 33.4 million tonnes in 1977/78 compared with 33.7 million tonnes in 1976/77. Revenue for freight services during 1977/78 increased by $14.6 million to $268.8 million.

The freight wagon fleet continued to be modernised during 1979 with a further 260 bogie wagons added to the existing 15 614 freight wagons. Most of the new acquisitions were coal hoppers. With continued growth of coal movements confidently expected (export coal traffic accounts for half SRA's annual tonnage) further expansion of export coal capacity is being undertaken. Following completion of a new rail terminal and port loading facilities at Newcastle (giving it a capacity of up to 20 million tonnes of coal annually) work began during 1979 on expansion of coal loading facilities at Port Kembla where capacity is to be increased to 14 million tonnes a year. Among Port Kembla's new facilities will be a new ship-loader (capacity 5 000 tonnes/hour) and terminal rail loop with capacity to receive, unload and despatch trains of 3 000 tonnes per hour.

The Commission operates the following containers:

40	Side loading (SL)
500	Modified side loading (MSL)
4	ISO containers for dry cargo
500	General Cargo (GC)
500	Ventilated Cargo (VC)
160	Refrigerated (LRC)

Intermodal services
Two maritime container terminals, served by rail, are located at Sydney. The Balmain or White Bay Terminal which, owned by the Maritime Services Board, is operated under lease by Seatainer Terminals Ltd, and the Glebe Island Terminal also owned by the Maritime Service Board, is operated as a "common user" terminal under lease by a consortium—Glebe Island Terminals Pty Ltd. Each is also served by road.

At Newcastle, container ships call at No. 1 Throsby Wharf and No. 4 Western Basin Wharf, each of which is serviced by rail.

Container consolidation depots in the Sydney are located at Chullora and Leightonfield, 18 km and 24 km res-ectively from the Balmain/Glebe Island Terminals. These depots are served by captive container trains on a 24-hour, seven days a week, basis.

Further rail served container complexes are located at Homebush 26 km and Yennora 29 km from Balmain/Glebe Island specialising mainly in containerisation of export wool.

Approximately 75 000 (TEU) containers are handled per annum on the captive container trains operating between the terminals and depots.

	1976/77	1977/78	1978/79
Total freight tonne/km	9 320 153 191	9 243 330 500	
Total freight tonnes	33 776 588	33 434 453	33 300 000

PASSENGER TRAFFIC
A high-speed train system is to be introduced by 1981 to provide passenger services between Sydney and the major rural towns in New South Wales. The new trains, to cost

a total of $A 45 million, will be designated Intercity XPT (express passenger train) and will be derived from the British High Speed Train using the same power equipment. The Australian-built vehicles, however, will be of stainless-steel construction. The SRA intends to buy a total of 100 XPT vehicles made up of 26 power cars, 32 coaches, 25 coaches with guard's compartment, nine buffet vehicles and eight driving trailer cars. The trains will be marshalled with two power cars and either five, seven or eight passenger vehicles giving seating capacities of about 270, 376 or 500. Intercity XPT services will operate between Sydney and Wollongong, Nowra, Kempsey-Grafton, Tamworth-Armidale, Bathurst-Orange, Wagga Wagga and Canberra.

A highlight of 1979 was the opening of Sydney's Eastern Suburbs Railway, a 10 km underground extension which provides a rapid-transit service to the densely populated Eastern Suburbs of Sydney. The ESR connects with the existing metropolitan network at Erskineville and follows a route, completely underground (except for two viaducts and one short section) via Redfern, Central, Town Hall, Martin Place, Kings Cross, Edgecliff to Bondi Junction. New underground stations have been built at all these locations, except Town Hall, which was extended to accommodate additional platforms.

The Eastern Suburbs Railway is double-track and uses the same 1 500 V overhead wiring method as the present electric network.

SRA's suburban electric multiple-unit fleet was further increased during 1979 by the addition of 74 double-deck cars to the existing 1 211 suburban and inter-urban electric coaches (440 of which are double-deck). A further 148 double-deck cars were on order in 1980 and it is planned to re-equip all services with a further 800 double-deckers by 1985.

	1976/77	1977/78	1978/79
Total passenger journeys	184 421 382	183 539 855	138 000 000

FINANCIAL
Rail earnings during 1978-79 amounted to $A 381 million. The result was disappointing primarily because freight loadings fell short of expectations. During the year expenditure increased by six per cent to $A 751 million, resulting in a total government subsidy of $A 370 million for maintenance of rail services. Operating costs increased by only five per cent.

	1976/77	1977/78	1978/79
Revenues	358 286	389 139	381 000
Expenses	567 844	638 126	751 000
Operating loss	209 558	248 987	370 000

(Figures in thousands, Australian dollars)

MOTIVE POWER
The SRA is constantly upgrading its passenger and freight vehicle and locomotive fleets.

Deliveries were under way during 1980 of 30 diesel-electric locomotives rated at 1 600 kW and ten electrics rated at 2 700 kW. Studies at the same time were being made of a lightweight diesel-electric rated at 2 200 kW for hauling export coal. Following deivery of the first of the COMENG-ALCO diesel-electric 80 class locomotives by Commonwealth Engineering Pty Ltd on 9 August 1978, the motive power fleet at the end of 1979 consisted of 447 diesel-electric locos, 60 diesel-hydraulic locos, 20 diesel rail tractors, 49 electric locos, 105 diesel railcars.

INVESTMENTS
SRA is engaged in a billion dollar modernisation programme involving heavy expenditure on freight and passenger rolling stock and facilities, signalling and workshops and an extensive track upgrading programme. During 1979 $A 199 million was made available by the New South Wales government for capital investments on rail. During 1980 SRA is budgeting for a $A 207.5 million programme involving purchase of rolling stock ($A 52.6 million), track works ($A 37.5 million) and miscellaneous items.

ELECTRIFICATION
Electrification of the Metropolitan network has been extended to Waterfall from Loftus on the Illawara Line at a cost of about $6 million.

High speed unit grain train
5.3 million tonnes of grain was hauled in NSW during 1976/77.

When present orders are completed, more than 50% of Sydney's electric trains will be double-deck

This work was expected to be completed by April 1980 and includes the provision of a new substation, installation of overhead wiring structures with catenary wires, signalling relays and cables. With this section electrified the Commission will operate electric trains over a 460 route kilometre network.

Preliminary planning has started for the extension of electrification from Gosford to Newcastle on the main Northern Line.

CIVIL ENGINEERING

Work started in May 1976 on the Western Line between Blacktown and Lithgow where track is progressively being upgraded by ballast cleaning and other sophisticated machinery. The cost of upgrading the Western Line is estimated at $28.5 million.

Another major job recently completed was the upgrading of the track bed and the widening of the Zig Zag tunnels, thereby enabling double-deck inter-urban trains to travel through to Lithgow.

Major track upgrading was extended to the Northern Line in February 1978 when a programme was commenced to completely improve the track between Hornsby and Gosford at a cost of about $12 million.

Track upgrading is being carried out in various parts of the State, including sections in the suburban area.

When completed, the upgrading programme will result in better riding qualities for passengers, freight and livestock; faster speeds and considerable economies in maintenance costs for carriages, wagons and the track itself.

Machinery used for track upgrading work is costly, but time-saving, and the Commission is using the most modern and sophisticated machines available. The newest and largest ballast cleaners can clean an average 150 metres of track each hour.

Another current major track project is the building of additional tracks between Seven Hills and St Marys at a cost of about $20 million; construction of a new $10.4 million bridge over the Parramatta River at Meadowbank, and the building of additional tracks (Stage 1) between Strathfield and Epping at a cost of $4.2 million.

TRACK

Minimum curvature:
  Main Lines: Generally 8.7° = minimum radius of 201 m, but at two locations curvature is 10.85° = minimim radius of 161 m.
  Branch Lines: 10.85° = minimum radius of 161 m, but there are two lines in difficult terrain where curvature is 17.4° = minimum radius of 101 m.

Max gradient, compensated:
  Main Line: 3.3% = 1 in 30 (electric traction on City Railway). 1.5% = 1 in 66 elsewhere.
  Branch Line: 4.4% = 1 in 25 and 3.3% = 1 in 30.

Max gradient, uncompensated:
  Main Line: 2.5% = 1 in 40, but there is a 30.5 km electrified length of 1 in 30 to 1 in 33 on the Blue Mountains.
  Branch Lines: 3.3% = 1 in 30 and 2.5% = 1 in 40.

Longest continuous uniform gradient: Werris Creek to Binnaway Branch, 13 kms of 1% grade, 75% curved with radii varying from 282 m to 1 207 m (6.2° to 1.45°) with average of 503 m (3.5°). Compensated grade, single track, no tunnels.

Worst combination of curvature and gradient: On Batlow Line: radius of 90 m (19.3° curve) on 4% (1 in 25) compensated grade.

Max altitude: 377 m on main Northern Line, 645 kms from Sydney.

Standard rail: Rolled steel, flat bottom; 60, 71½, 80, 90, 94, 100, 103, 107 and 109 lb per yd (29.8, 35.5, 39.7, 44.6, 46.6, 49.6, 51.1, 53.1, 54.1 kg/m). All rails are flash-butt welded at depot before laying.
  Main Lines: Adopted 1963: 107 and 94 lb per yd (53.2 and 46.7 kg/m) in 45 ft lengths. All rails are flash-butt welded at depot before laying. Older sections, 90 and 100 lb (44.6 and 49.6 kg/m) exist in 30 and 45 ft lengths; being replaced.
  Branch Lines: 60, 71½, 80, 90 and 94 lb per yd (29.8, 35.5, 39.7 44.6 and 46.7 kg/m).

Rail joints: 4-hole bar type fishplate on some lines, General Main Line standard 6-hole bar type.
  Cross ties (sleepers): Australian hardwood, 9 in × 4½ in × 8 ft 0 in (228 × 114 × 2 438 mm) (larger size 230 × 130 × 2 440 mm recently introduced), spaced 24 in (160 mm) centre to centre, except at rail joints 18 to 20 in. Where track is being reconstructed a closer spacing of 20 to 22 in is being introduced.
  Concrete 12 in × 8 in × 8 ft 0 in (305 × 203 × 2 438 m). Test section only.

Rail fastenings: Dog spikes with double shouldered rolled steel sleeper plates secured to wood sleepers with "Lockspikes".

Pads under rails: 9 in × 5¾ in (299 × 146 mm) Neoprene ³/₁₆ in (5 mm) thick and composition pads locally manufactured to departmental specification on concrete sleeper test section only.

Filling (ballast):
  Main Lines: Broken basalt 65.40 mm, 270 mm below sleepers.
  Branch Lines: Basalt, ashes, gravel, sand, earth, or quarry dust, 5½ in (140 mm) below sleeper.

Air-conditioned double-deck inter-urban trains operate on the scenic Blue Mountains and Central Coast routes

8001-class leader of 30 diesel-electric locomotives being manufactured by Comeng for the PTC of NSW

PTC double-decked suburban train on the approaches to the famous Sydney harbour bridge

DIESEL LOCOMOTIVES

Class	Axle Arrangement	Transmission	Rated Power hp	Max. lb (kg)	Tractive Effort Continuous at lb (kg)	mph (km/h)	Max. Speed mph (km/h)	Wheel Dia. in (mm)	Total Weight Tons	Length ft ins (mm)	No. Built	Year first Built	Builders: Mechanical Parts	Engine & Type	Transmission
42	Co-Co	Elec.	1 900	80 500 (36 500)	61 250 (27 780)	9 (14.5)	71 (113)	40 (1 016)	120	60' 10" (18 542)	6	1955	Clyde Eng. Co.	GM 16-567C	Clyde
421	"	"	1 950	72 576 (32 209)	70 920 (32 170)	6.9 (11.1)	"	"	108	62' 0¾" (18 911)	10	1965	"	"	"
422	Co-Co	"	2 200	72 760 (33 000)	70 920 (31 170)	77 (124)				60' 6" (18 440)	20	1969/ 70	Clyde Eng. Co.	GM645E EMD	"
44 see note (a)	"	"	1 950	75 300 (34 150)	47 000 (21 300)	11.5 (18.5)	80 (129)		112	58' 5" (17 805)	11	1957	Goodwin	Alco 251B	G.E.
44 see note (b)	"	"	1 950	71 500 (32 400)	40 200 (18 200)	13.7 (22)	75 (121)		106	"	47	1957	"		G.E. & A.E.I.
44 see note (c)	"	"	1 950	74 021 (33 575)	44 000 (20 000)	12.9 (20.8)	80 (129)		110	"	42	1965/ 67	"	Alco 251C	A.E.I.
442	"	"	2 150	75 900 (34 400)	52 000 (23 600)		70 (113)	40 (1 067)	113	61' 3" (13 669)	24	1971/ 72	"	Alco 251B	A.E.I.
45	"	"	1 950	74 250 (33 780)	68 000 (30 800)	7.4 (11.9)	75 (120)		110.5	58' 8" (17 881)	40	1962	"	Alco 251C	G.E. & A.E.I.
47	"	"	1 125	56 400 (25 580)	38 460 (17 540)		70 (113)		84	50' 0¾" (15 260)	12	1972	Hitachi	Caterpillar D 299	Hitachi
48 see note (d)	"	"	975	49 700 (22 500)	40 200 (18 200)	5.8 (9.2)	"	"	74	48' 5" (14 757)	45	1959		Alco 251B	G.E.
48 see note (d)	"	"	1 050	"	"	"	"	"	"	"	40	1964	"	"	G.E. & A.E.I.
48 see note (b)	"	"	1 050	51 500 (23 360)	42 500 (19 300)	6.5 (10.5)	"	"	76.6	"	80	1966/ 71	"	"	A.E.I.
49	"	"	950	53 760 (24 385)	37 200 (16 875)	6.3 (10)	77 (124)	"	80	50' 4¼" (15 348)	18	1960	Clyde Eng. Co.	G.M.8/567C	Clyde
70	C	Hyd.	580	32 200 (14 600)	25 600 (11 600)	6 (9.6)	45 (72)	48 (1 219)	48	33' 4" (10 160)	10	1960	Com. Eng. Ltd.	Caterpillar D397	Voith L37zUC Deutsche-Getribe GmbH
73	B-B	Hyd.	700/670	33 000 (15 000)	25 000 (11 340)	5.4 (8.7)	40 (64)	40 (1 016)	49	39' 4" (11 989)	45	1970/ 72	Walkers Ltd.	Caterpillar D379 Series B	Voith L4r4U2

Notes: (a) Fitted with G.E. 731 Traction Motors. (b) Fitted with A.E.I. 253 Traction Motors. (c) Fitted with A.E.I. 254 Traction Motors. (d) Fitted with G.E. 761 Traction Motors.

NEW SOUTH WALES RAILWAYS—MAIN LINE ELECTRIC LOCOMOTIVES

Class	Axle Arrangement	Line Current	Rated Output hp	Max. lb (kg)	Tractive Effort (Full Field) Continuous at lb (kg)	mph (km/h)	Max. Speed mph (km/h)	Wheel dia. in (mm)	Weight tonnes	Length ft in (mm)	No. Built	Year Built	Builders Mechanical Parts	Electrical Equipment
46	Co+Co	1 500 V. d.c.	3 780	60 500 (27 450)	40 800 (18 500)	34.5 (55.5)	70 (112)	45 (1 143)	108	53' 11¼" (16 440)	40	1956	Beyer Peacock	Metropolitan-Vickers

DIESEL RAILCARS

Class	Axle arrangement	Transmission	Rated power hp	Max lb	Tractive effort continuous at lb	mph	Max speed mph	Wheel diameter in	Total weight tons	Length ft in	No. built	Year first built	Builders Mechanical parts	Engine & type	Transmission
Rail Motor	2-A1	Hydraulic	145	4 280	2 900	10.5	54	32	20	44 8	33	1923	PTC	GM 6057	Twin Disc torque converter
100	1A-A1	Hydraulic	1 000	17 900	12 300	17	75	37	63	64 10	4	1937	PTC	GM62 400RA	GMTCLA 965 converter
600	1A-A1	Hydraulic	320	6 600	4 500	17.5	63	33	29	63	5	1948	PTC	GM 6081	Allison converter Model 655
620	1A-A1	Hydraulic	450	9 300	6 000	17	70	33	37	63	18	1961	PTC	GM 62808	Allison converter Model 850
900	1A-A1	Hydraulic	500	9 120	5 500	17	70	33	39	63	18	1951	PTC	GM 62808	Allison converter Model 850
1 100	1A-A1	Hydraulic	500	8 140	5 500	17	70	37	51	78 3	4	1960	Comm Eng	GM 62806	Allison converter Model 850
1 200	1A-A1	Hydraulic	600	11 000	7 700	17	71.5	37	60	78 10	8	1970	Tulloch	Cummins NT855	Voith T1135

ELECTRIC RAILCARS

Class	Axle arrangement	Line Volts	Rated output hp	Max lb	Tractive Effort (full field) continuous at mph	mph	Max speed mph	Wheel dia-meter in	Weight tonnes	Length ft in	No built	Year first parts built	Builders Mechanical equipment	Electrical
3200*	2-B	1500DC		16 000	8 000	26	50	42	50	63 8	350	1927	Various	MV 172
3500*	2-B	1500DC		16 000	8 000	26	50	42	50	64 10	72	1940	Tullochs	MV 172
3700	B-B	1500DC	660	16 000	9 000	27	70	37	52	65 2	40	1957	Comm Eng	MV 222
5000	B-B	1500DC	660	16 000	9 000	27	70	37	49	67 6	40	1957	Comm Eng	MV 222
8000	B-B	1500DC	750	17 000	10 000	25	70	37	53	78 7	24	1970	Comm Eng	Mitsubishi 471
3800	B-B	1500DC	720	22 000	12 200	21	70	36	45	66 4	172	1972	Comm Eng	Mitsubishi 3179-A

*Being scrapped as double-decked 3800 class enter service

QUEENSLAND GOVERNMENT RAILWAYS

305 Edward St, Brisbane, Queensland 4000

Telephone: 225 0211

Commissioner for Railways: P. J. Goldston
Deputy Commissioner and Secretary: A. J. Neeson
Assistant Commissioner (Electrification): D. V. Mendoza
Chief Engineer (Civil): H. N. Walker
Chief Mechanical Engineer and Workshops Superintendent: J. F. Jeffcoat
Chief Accountant: R. T. Sheehy
General Manager, Brisbane: C. J. Kelso
General Manager, Toowoomba: W. L. Fraser
General Manager, Rockhampton: T. K. Keating
General Manager, Townsville: C. V. Walton

Gauge: 1.435 m; 1.067 m
Route length: 111 km; 9 796 km

1979 was of major importance to QR, marking the introduction of electric services in metropolitan Brisbane and gains in coal and commodity traffic. Rising operating costs, however, remained a constant problem.

FREIGHT TRAFFIC

For the first time since 1960/61, QR failed in 1977/78 to record an increase in freight tonnage transported. The decline was 82 000 tonnes on the 34 million tonnes railed the previous year with reduced hauls recorded for all commodities except coal, coke, minerals, timber, cotton and livestock. Traffic, however, increased in 1978/79 to around 35 million tonnes thanks largely to increased shipments of coal from the expanding export mining industry.
1980 is expected to see a marked rise in coal train traffic as new mines at Gregory and Norwich Park begin production. Coal tonnage is expected to rise by five million tonnes a year to about 26 million tonnes during 1980/81.

Intermodal services

There has been a general expansion in container movements and further emphasis is being placed on this form of traffic during 1980. Overseas container movements are reported at a high level while RACE (Railways of Australia Container Express) is being used in increasing numbers between Queensland and southern states for both general and fruit traffic. During 1979 the demand for refrigerated containers encouraged QR in conjunction with neighbouring SRA to acquire 100 new refrigerated containers for interstate operations. In 1977/78, 9 577 containers were forwarded to Queensland destinations and 8 965 units to interstate destinations. A total of 21 544 were received. The railway owns 821 containers and operates terminals at Toowoomba, Townsville, Roma Street, South Brisbane, Clapham, Acacia Ridge and Dalby. All are equipped with gantry cranes.
Approximately three trains a week operate from Townsville to Brisbane and four weekly from Rockhampton to Brisbane.
The freight fleet in 1978/79 included 23 150 wagons.

	1975/76	*1976/77*
Freight tonne-km	10 101 201 389	10 286 000 000
Freight tonnage	33 117 597	34 200 000

PASSENGER TRAFFIC

There was a further decline during 1977/78 in total passenger journeys, from 31 to 29.2 million. The third successive drop in suburban journeys represents a loss of 20 per cent of patronage over three fiscal years.
Passenger stock in 1978/79 included 979 coaches.

	1975/76	*1976/77*
Passenger journeys	34 278 244	31 000 000 000

FINANCIAL RESULTS

Freight tonnage in 1977/78 produced revenue of $A 249.7 million, more than $A 9 million up on the previous year. Passenger revenue in the same period rose by $A 71 000 to $A 12.6 million. The increased total revenue of $A 273.5 million was largely accounted for by the rise in mineral and livestock traffic. Expenditure rose by 13 per cent to $ 337 million. After payment of interest and other charges there was a deficit of $A 121.5 million, some $A 30 million up on the 1976/77 figure.

	1973 $A	*1974* $A	*1975* $A	*1976* $A	*1977* $A	*1977/78* $A
Revenue (thousands)	134 258	149 843	183 686	230 491	263 000	273 500
Expenses (thousands)	129 285	161 922	227 924	265 661	299 000	337 000

DIESEL LOCOMOTIVES

Class	*Axle Arrange-ment*	*Trans-mission*	*Rated Power hp*	*Max. lb (kg)*	*Tractive Effort Continuous at lb (kg)*	*mph (km/h)*	*Max. Speed mph (km/h)*	*Wheel Dia. in (mm)*	*Total Weight Tons*	*Length ft in (mm)*	*No. Built*	*Year first Built*	*Builders: Mechanical Parts*	*Engine & Type*	*Transmission*
1150	Co-Co	Elec.	1 100	59,200 *(26 850)*	31 000 *(14 100)*	10.5 *(16.9)*	50 *(80)*	36 *(914)*	89	56' 0⅞" *(17 091*	13	1952	General Electric (U.S.A.) and Australian Electrical Industries	Cooper Bessemer (U.S.A.) FVL-12T	General Electric (U.S.A.) and Australian Electrical Industries
1170	A-1-A+ A-1-A	,,	640	26 880 *(12 200)*	19 750 *(8 960)*	9.6 *(15.4)*	,,	,,	60	41' 6" *(12 649)*	12	1956	Walkers (Aust.)	Cooper Bessemer (U.S.A.) FWA-6T	Australian Electrical Industries
1200	Co-Co	,,	1 280	60 000 *(27 200)*	30 500 *(13 850)*	12.7 *(20.4)*	,,	37.5 *(952)*	90	54' 10⅜" *(16 722)*	10	1953	Vulcan Foundry (Gt. Britain)	English Electric (Gt. Britain) 12-SVT	English Electric (Gt. Britain)
1250 (Locos 1250-54	Co-Co	,,	1 440	,,	41 500 *(18 800)*	10.3 *(16.6)*	,,	,,	85.7	52' 11" *(16 129)*	5	1959	English Electric (Aust.)	,,	,,
1250 (Locos 1255-66)	Co-Co	,,	1 440	,,	,,	,,	,,	,,	87.3	,,	12	1960	,,	,,	English Electric (Aust.) and Gt. Britain
1270 (1270-81)	Co-Co	,,	1 440	,,	,,	,,	,,	,,	84.9	,,	16	1964	,,	,,	,,
(1282-99)	,,	,,	,,	,,	47 500 *(21 500)*	8.7 *(14)*	,,	,,	,,	,,	14	1966	,,	,,	,,
1300	Co-Co	,,	1 795	,,	50 400 *(22 860)*	10.8 *(17.4)*	,,	,,	88	51' 5" *(15 672)*	42	1967/ 71	English Electric (Aust.)	English Electric 12-CSVT	English Electric
1400	A-1-A+ A-1-A	,,	1 310	36 288 *(16 400)*	28 000 *(12 700)*	14.7 *(23.7)*	,,	Drivers 40 *(1 016)* Idlers 30 *(762)*	76 (Fab Bogie) 78.8 (C.S. Bogie)	47' 10⅜" *(14 590)*	13	1955	Clyde Eng. (Aust.)	General Motors EMD (U.S.A.) 12-567C	General Motors EMD (U.S.A.)
1450	Co-Co	,,	1 310	54 432 *(24 700)*	42 000 *(19 050)*	9.5 *(15.3)*	,,	40 *(1 016)*	90	52' 8⅜" *(16 062)*	10	1957	,,	,,	,,
1460 (1460-1501)	Co-Co	,,	1 310	,,	50 820 *(23 050)*	7.5 *(12.1)*	,,	,,	,,	53' 4" *(16 256)*	42	1964	Commonwealth Eng. (under sub-contract to Clyde Eng.)	,,	General Motors EMD (U.S.A.) & Clyde Eng. (Aust.)
(1502 on)	,,	,,	1 500	,,	,,	8.8 *(14.1)*	,,	,,	,,	,,	23 6	1967 1969	,,	General Motors 12-645 E	,,
	Co-Co	,,	1 500	60 480	50 820 *(27 430)*	8.8 *(23 050)*	,,	,,	90	59' 2¼"	9	1972	,,	,,	,,
1 550	Co-Co	Electric	1 500	269	226	50 *(80)*	40 *(1 016)*	28	90	59' 2¼" *(18 040)*	32 (To 30th June '77)	1972	Commonwealth Engineering under Sub-Contract to Clyde Engineering	General Motors EMD (USA) 12-645 E	General Motors EMD-Clyde Engineering Australia
1600	Co-Co	,,	838	41 500 *(18 800)*	30 000 *(13 600)*	7.8 *(12.6)*	,,	37.5 *(952)*	61.5	44' 2" *(13 462)*	18	1963	English Electric (Aust.)	English Electric (Gt. Britain) 6-CSRKT	English Electric (Aust.) and Gt. Britain)
1620	,,	,,	862	,,	,,	,,	,,	,,	62.5	45' 5" *(13 843)*	28 6	1967 1969	,,	,,	,,
1700	Co-Co	,,	875	39 650 *(18 000)*	33 600 *(15 250)*	7.1 *(11.4)*	,,	,,	59	43' 10" *(13 360)*	12	1963	Commonwealth Eng. (under sub-contract to Clyde Eng.)	General Motors EMD (U.S.A.) 8-567CR	General Motors EMD (U.S.A.) Clyde Eng. (Aust.)
1720	Co-Co	,,	1 000	,,	,,	8.4 *(13.5)*	,,	,,	62.5	43' 11⅜" *(13 395)*	56	1966/ 1970	,,	General Motors EMD (U.S.A.) 8-645E	Clyde Eng. (Aust)

Class	Axle Arrangement	Transmission	Rated Power hp	Max. lbs (kg)	Tractive Effort Continuous at lbs (kg)	mph (km/h)	Max. Speed mph (km/h)	Wheel Dia. ins (mm)	Total Weight Tons	Length ft ins (mm)	No. Built	Year first Built	Builders: Mechanical Parts	Engine & Type	Transmission
2100	Co-Co	,,	2 000	58 060 (26 390)	50 820 (23 050)	11.5 (18.5)	,,	40 (1 016)	96	59' 2¼" (18 040)	30	1970/ 72	,,	General Motors EMD (U.S.A.) 16-645E	General Motors EMD (U.S.A.) Clyde Eng. (Aust.)
2 370	Co-Co	Electric	2 500	224	224	50 (80)	36.5 (952)	90		56' 2" (17 120)	4	1975	English Electric Australia	English Electric 12 CSVT. Mk III	English Electric
2 130	Co-Co	Electric	2 000	58 060 (26 390)	50 820 (23 050)		50 (80)	40 (1 016)	96	59' 2¼" (18 040)	11	1974	English Electric Australia	General Motors EMD (USA) 16-645 E	General Motors EMD (USA)— Clyde Engineering Australia
Dh	B-B	Hyd.	465	25 000 (11 350)	18 000 (8 150)	6 (9.7)	,,	36 (914)	40	36' 5" (11,100)	70	1968 1970	Walkers Ltd. (Aust.)	Caterpillar D355 Series E	Voith L42 or U2 (Germany)
2 150	Co-Co	Elec.	2 000	58 060 (26 390)	—	—	50 (80)	40 (1 016)	97.5	59' 2¼" (18 040)	14 On order		Commonwealth Eng. sub-contract to Clyde Eng.	General Motors EMD (USA) 16-654E	General Motors EMD (USA) Clyde Eng.

Note: 1250 Class locomotives numbered 1250 to 1254 have been upgraded from original 1 290 hp to 1 440 hp.
2 400 (1 550 Class) details included in 1 550 Class above.

MOTIVE POWER

The fleet in 1979 included 429 diesel-electric locos, 13 diesel-mechanical locos, 73 diesel-hydraulic units. New acquisitions included 72 new electric cars from a consortium formed by Walkers and ASEA.

INVESTMENTS

In 1980 QR is spending $A 171 million on capital improvements and new purchases. Investments include $A 5 million on six new mainline diesel-electric locomotives, $A 12.25 million on eight new electric mainline locomotives, ten passenger coaches at $A 600 000 and 18 electric cars at $A 13 million (part of the $ A45 million contract for 72 emu sets for the Brisbane electrification). Other major investments include $A 48 million for 172 km of new line construction and $A 22 million for major track improvements.

ELECTRIFICATION

Feasibility studies were carried out during 1979 into electrification throughout the QR system in an attempt to make use of Queensland's large and accessible coal reserves which could be harnessed to provide electric rail power. Following studies by PG Pak-Roy & Associates of Adelaide together with Transmark and Elrail, the federal cabinet of Canberra approved in principle at the end of 1979 electrification of Australia's busiest interstate trunk line running 960 km from Sydney to Melbourne. The cabinet also decided in principle that all major QR lines could eventually be converted to electric traction. QR inaugurated its first electrified suburban line at 25 kV ac from Darra to Ferny Grove in November 1979 and hope to complete the Darra-Ipswich conversion by the end of 1980. Conversion of the Kingston line, authorised during 1979, should be completed by 1982.
The projected Sydney—Melbourne electrification scheme will be converted at 25 kV ac. The first stage will cover 443 route-km. The second stage will run from Brisbane to Gladstone. Cost is estimated at $A 274 million. About 70 electric locomotives will be needed.

CIVIL ENGINEERING

An extensive track upgrading programme is continuing on the Townsville—Mount Isa line. The five-year programme, which will cost about $A 20 million, involves replacement of all timber bridges, and general improvement and realignment of the track.

SIGNALLING

Single-line working by staff-and-ticket or electric staff is being replaced by CTC. Major coal routes have been CTC-operated since 1975. To improve train movements on other busy lines CTC installation is being expanded as part of a $A 25 million programme. Installation of CTC over 700 km between Brisbane and the Central Queensland coalmines (via Gladstone, Rockhampton and Blackwater) is planned to be completed in 1982 following a November 1979 start.

TRACK

Standard rail: Flat bottom 94, 82, 80, 63, 61 and 60 lb per yd *(47, 41, 40, 31 and 30 kg/m)*, in lengths of 40 ft *(12.2 m)*. On certain branch lines, 42 lb *(20 kg)*.
107 lb *(53 kg)* rail was used on the Goonyella Line, secured by 19 mm dog spikes in lieu of the normal 16 mm spike.
Joints: 4- and 6-hole angle and bar fishplates.
Welding: See "Welded Rail".
Cross ties (sleepers): Mostly unimpregnated local timber 9 in × 4½ in × 7 ft 0 in *(230 × 115 × 2 150 mm)*, 6 in *(150 mm)* thick on mineral lines.
Spacing: 2 640 per mile *(1 650 per km)* on main lines.
Rail fastening: Normal standard was 16 mm and 14 mm dog spikes, but in recent years Elastic Rail Spikes have been used, mainly with welded track. 19 mm dogspikes used on the Goonyella Line. The use of elastic spikes has now been discontinued.
Ballast: Mainly broken stone. River gravel is used on many branch lines.
Max curvature: Generally 17.3° = radius of 330 ft *(100 m)*, with a few curves down to 21.8° = 264 ft *(80 m)*.
Max gradient: 3% = 1 in 33 uncompensated, but generally does not exceed 2.0% (1 in 50).
Longest continuous gradient: Between Brisbane and Gympie, ruling grade is 1 in 75 with 2 sections (one being 3.2 km long) of 1 in 50.
Max altitude: 3 035 ft *(925 m)* near Cairns.
Max permitted speed:
Freight: 35 mph *(60 km/h)*
Passenger: 45 mph *(70 km/h)* but on certain selected sections where track conditions, alignments, etc. are favourable, speed boards indicate speeds up to 50 mph *(80 km/h)* maximum for passenger trains and express freight trains.
Max axle load: 19.8 tonnes.
Bridge loading: All bridges on important lines can carry loading equivalent to Coopers E25-E30. Many are equivalent to Coopers E35 and most new construction is to this standard. New mineral lines eg, to Moura, Goonyella, Greenvale and Phosphate Hill have their bridges built to carry Cooper's E50 loading.
Welded rail: The total length of track laid with welded rail is 4 064 km. Normal future programme is to be between 80 and 100 miles *(130-160 km)* per year.
Rail used weighs 53, 47, 41 and 31 kg/m in 22.2 m bars, which are flashbutt welded at depot into 61 and 110 m lengths. The longest lengths of welded rail in track are 110 m (depot welded) and 244 m (4 × 61 m) thermit welded at site; but consideration is being given to increase rail length by site welding to form CWR (continuous welded rail).
Sleepers are wood 2 150 × 230 × 150 or 115 m thick to which the rails are secured by elastic spikes or dogspikes.
Standard method of laying is by mechanised gang using a Pettibone Mullken crane. Because of the increasing shortage of timber, the adoption of concrete sleepers is being considered.
Rail fastenings: Elastic spikes or dogspikes, depending on conditions, are standard but the use of elastic spikes has now been discontinued.

VICTORIAN RAILWAYS (VicRail)

67 Spencer Street, Melbourne, Victoria 3000

Telephone: 6 1001
Telegrams: Railways, Melbourne
Telex: 358 01 VRail AA

Victorian Railways Board
Chairman: A. G. Gibbs
General Manager: I. G. Hodges
Members: J. J. Brown
　　　　　R. W. Ellis
　　　　　L. M. Perrott
　　　　　F. R. G. Strickland
　　　　　J. G. W. Urbahns
　　　　　N. G. Wilson
Assistant General Manager (Technical) and Deputy General Manager: L. A. McCallum
Assistant General Manager (Operations): A. J. Nicholson
Assistant General Manager (Finance & Administration): N. H. Rashleigh
Secretary for Railways: A. Augustine
Heads and Assistant Heads of Branches:
　Chief Traffic Manager: M. W. B. Ronald
　Chief Freight Manager: L. A. Krausgrill
　Chief Civil Engineer: D. D. Wade
　Chief Mechanical Engineer: S. F. Keane
　Chief Electrical Engineer: A. Firth
　Director of Personnel: V. A. Winter
　Comptroller of Accounts: J. K. McGowan
　Chief Marketing Manager: A. W. Weeks

Gauge: 1.6 m; 1.435 m; 0.762 mm
Route length: 6 645 km; 332 km; 13 km

With responsibility for operating the busy Melbourne suburban network VR is recognised as primarily a passenger railway. The government sets a financial target which includes a substantial subsidy or "revenue supplement" to compensate for provision of this community service.

FREIGHT TRAFFIC

VR has been steadily rationalising freight services and in mid-1979 opened a network of 35 regional freight centres served from Melbourne by fast overnight freight trains. Highway trucks deliver and collect freight from the centres privately under contract. Freight is palletised or otherwise used as much as possible.
Grain comprises around 25 per cent of annual tonnage and freight revenue, as VR is one of the few Australian railways which lacks large bulk coal or mineral traffic. During 1978 the railway moved 4.2 million tonnes of grain. Other important freights include industrial raw materials and finished goods railed over the interstate trunk routes linking Melbourne with Sydney and Adelaide. Moving in trainloads over relatively long hauls, this traffic represents 46 per cent of VR's annual freight totalling around 3 100 million tonne-km. It is subject to fierce road competition and over the 1980-90 period VR intends to substantially upgrade track, terminal and operating facilities.

	1975	1976	1978
Total freight ton-km	3 091 439 393	3 071 373 278	3 100 000 000
Total freight tonnage	11 056 834	10 802 692	11 100 000

Intermodal services

The railway operates four special container services: Melbourne-Sydney (nightly), Melbourne-Brisbane (daily), Melbourne-Adelaide (nightly), Melbourne-Perth (every five days). Container traffic in 1978 totalled 53 000 units carrying 635 000 tonnes (260 million tonne-km).

PASSENGER TRAFFIC

The biggest of VR's passenger movements takes place in Melbourne over a major suburban commuter network (nearly all electrified at 1 500 V dc) where the railway handles more than 100 million passengers a year over an average journey of 16 km.

	1975	1976	1978
Total passenger-km	2 400 411 699	2 327 852 262	2 390 000 000
Total passengers carried (Railways)	117 719 511	109 669 067	112 000 000

FINANCIAL

VR not only met its financial subsidy target in 1977/78 of $A 152.6 million but, in fact, slightly bettered it. The annual revenue supplement paid to VR by the government has fallen (in constant money values) since 1975/76 and it was expected that the railway's financial target would again be met in 1978/79.

	1975	1976	1977
Revenues	130 087 339	147 449 945	162 677 500
Expenses	256 373 369	286 770 710	301 754 700
(Includes Interest Charges)			

MOTIVE POWER AND ROLLING STOCK

Over standard-gauge tracks the railway operates 13 diesel-electric locomotives, one diesel-hydraulic loco, 65 passenger and special coaches and 853 freight wagons. On broad gauge the fleet includes 13 steam locos, 35 electric locos, 245 diesel-electric locos, 29 diesel-hydraulic locos, 46 diesel railcars, 16 railcar trailers, 1 087 electric coaches, 406 passenger coaches and 17 851 freight vehicles. Narrow-gauge stock includes four steam locos, 13 passenger coaches, three luggage vans and 24 freight wagons. Of the freight vehicles operating, 2 753 are suitable for operation on either broad (1.6 m) or standard (1.435 m) gauge tracks through bogie exchange.

During 1977/78 ten Class C 3 300 hp diesel locomotives were delivered to VicRail. The class, a turbo-charged 16-cylinder design, is the most powerful on the system. Clyde Engineering built the locos using General Motors equipment. High-adhesion bogies on the new class are the result of re-arranged traction motors facing one direction only. This redistributes axleload during motoring and therefore increases adhesion. It means that the locos can haul loads up to 1 800 tonnes on services from the New South Wales border to Melbourne. Before introduction of the new turbo-charged engine, two Class X locos would have been needed to do the same job.

CIVIL ENGINEERING

Over the next ten years up to 1990 VR plans to improve track standards between Melbourne, Albury and Serviceton (about 750 km) by replacing the existing 94 lb/yd rail with new 60 kg/m section. Concrete sleepers will also be installed.

Track details

During 1977/78, 45 km of track was relaid with new rail, and a further 26 km with serviceable rail. Further progress was made with the programme of mechanised track maintenance, and mobile gangs were introduced over four additional sections of line. A total of 1 288 km of track was maintained by mechanical means, and 193 000 sleepers, representing 63 per cent of the total number of sleepers replaced during the year, were installed by fully-mechanised gangs. A contract was placed for purchase of a Plasser & Theurer 74 UHR ballast cleaner. Reconstruction of bridges at five sites was completed, and major bridge works are in hand at a further five locations.

Standard rail: Flat bottomed 94 lb and 107 lb per yard *(46.6 kg and 53.1 kg per m)* in 45 ft rolled lengths.

Cross Ties (Sleepers): Non-impregnated Australian hardwood 254 × 127 mm cross section in 2 743 mm lengths for 1.60 m gauge and 2 591 mm lengths for 1.435 m gauge. At insulated joints, sleepers of 304 × 153 mm are used. There is a current contract for the pressure treatment of 50 000 hardwood sleepers with creosote and oil.

First of VicRail's ten new class C locomotives built by Clyde-GM

Spacing: 2 420 per mile *(1 513 per km)*.

Rail Fastening: Dogspikes; double shoulder sleeper plates 4-hole angle and bar type fishplates; Fair rail anchors. No pads are used in conjunction with sleeper plates. A 6-hole bar fishplate is now used as the standard for 94 and 107 lb per yard rail rolled by BHP Australia.

Ballast: Generally broken stone or gravel 12 in thick under sleepers for track with welded rail in lengths over 180 ft; 10 in thick for all other first class track; 6 in thick on second class track and non-welded rail.

Max curvature: 11 ft = radius of 28 ft *(161 m)* × *(150 m)* 492R.

Max gradient:
Main line: 2.08% = 1 in 48
Branch line: 3.33% = 1 in 30.

Longest continuous gradient: 16.7 miles of 1 in 42 (0.24%) grade with 0.72% curves = radius of 7 920 ft *(2 414 m)* 9.24 miles of 1 in 40 (2.08%) grade with 2.48° curves = radius of 2 310 ft *(704 m)*.

Max altitude: 2 562 ft *(781 m)* near Shelley on Wodonga-Cudgewa line.

Max axle load: (standard and broad gauges) 18.75 tons.

Welded Rail: Standard 45 ft new rail and serviceable rails are welded into lengths between 90 ft and 270 ft at the central Flash Butt Welding Depot.
Rails in the track are welded into continuous lengths between insulated joints or crossing work and distressed to be stress-free between rail temperatures of 32°C and 36°C.

SIGNALLING

Urgent priority has been given to installation of CTC on the Ararat-Serviceton section (251 km) of the Melbourne-Adelaide freight line.

VICTORIA RAILWAYS—MAIN LINE DIESEL LOCOMOTIVES

Class	Axle Arrange-ment	Trans-mission	Rated Power hp	Max. lb (kg)	Tractive Effort Continuous at lb (kg)	Tractive Effort Continuous at mph (km/h)	Max. Speed mph (km/h)	Wheel Dia. in (mm)	Total Weight Tons	Length ft in (mm)	No. Built	Year first Built	Builders: Mechanical Parts	Builders: Engine & Type	Builders: Transmission
B	Co-Co	Elec.	1 500	60 000 *(27 200)*	40 000 *(18 150)*	11.0 *(17.7)*	83 *(134)*	40 *(1 016)*	111.6	60' 10'' *(18 542)*	26	1952	Clyde—G.M.	G.M. 567B	G.M.
F	C	,,	350	33 000 *(15 000)*	11 000 *(5 000)*	7.25 *(11.7)*	20 *(32)*	48½ *(1 232)*	49.5	29' 3'' *(8 915)*	16	1951	English Electric	English Electric 6 KT	E.E.
H	Bo-Bo	,,	1 050	44 800 *(20 320)*	33 380 *(15 140)*		60 *(97)*	40 *(1 016)*	80	43' 11'' *(13 386)*	5	1969	Clyde—G.M.	G.M. 8-645	G.M.
L	Co-Co	,,	2 400	47 000 *(21 300)*	25 200 *(11 400)*	30.0 *(48.3)*	75 *(120)*	40 *(1 016)*	93	59' 0'' *(17 983)*	25	1952			,,
S	Co-Co	,,	1 800	63 800 *(28 940)*	53 500 *(24 270)*	9.5 *(15.3)*	83 *(134)*	,,	114	60' 11'' *(18 567)*	16	1957	Clyde—G.M.	G.M. 567C	G.M.
T	Bo-Bo	,,	950	38 080 *(17 275)*	28 000 *(12 700)*	,,	62 *(100)*	,,	68	47' 9'' *(14 554)*	28	1955	,,	,,	,,
			950	,,	33 880 *(15 370)*	7.5 *(12.1)*	,,	,,	,,	43' 11'' *(13 386)*	52	1959	,,	G.M. 8-567CR	,,
			1 050	,,	,,	8.8 *(14.1)*	,,	,,	,,	,,	2	1966	,,	G.M. 8-645	,,
											12	1968	,,	,,	,,
W	C	Hyd.	650	32 250 *(14 630)*	29 200 *(13 240)*		40 *(64)*	48½ *(1 232)*	48	30' 1'' *(9 169)*	27	1959	Tulloch	Mercedes-Benz MB82OB	Krupp
X	Co-Co	Elec.	1 800	64 000 *(29 030)*	53 700 *(24 360)*	9.5 *(15.3)*	83 *(134)*	40 *(1 016)*	112	60' 3'' *(18 364)*	20	1966	Clyde—G.M.	G.M. 16-567E	G.M.
			2 000									1970	,,	G.M. 16-645E	Clyde-G.M.
Y	Bo-Bo	,,	750	35 800 *(16 240)*	17 550 *(7 960)*	10 *(16.1)*	40 *(64)*	42 *(1 067)*	64	43' 7'' *(13 284)*	50	1963	,,	G.M. 567	G.M.
											25	1968	,,	G.M. 645E	
C	Co-Co	,,	3 000	85 000 *(38 548)*			83 *(134)*	40 *(1 016)*	132	66' *(20 117)*	12	1977	,,	G.M. (645E3)	G.M.

STATE TRANSPORT AUTHORITY (SOUTH AUSTRALIA)
GPO Box 2351, Adelaide, South Australia 5001

Telephone: 51 0231

General Manager: J. R. Harris
Traffic Manager (Rail): J. R. Renshaw
Chief Engineer: C. R. Stewien
Administration Manager: R. J. Heath
Personnel Manager: C. R. Lindsay

Management Services Officer: D. F. Callow
Development Manager: K. W. Drew

Gauge: 1.6 m
Route length: 142.38 km

The former non-metropolitan section of South Australian Railways was fully amalgamated into the Australian National Railways Commission on 1 March, 1978. The Metropolitan Railways have been merged with the Bus and Tram Division of the State Transport Authority under a new management structure.

WESTERN AUSTRALIAN GOVERNMENT RAILWAYS (WESTRAIL)
Westrail Centre, West Parade, East Perth, Western Australia

Telephone: 326 2811
Telex: WARAIL 92879

Commissioner: W. I. McCullough
Secretary for Railways: A. E. Williams
Chief Traffic Manager: R. A. Hunter

Chief Civil Engineer: A. B. Holm
Chief Mechanical Engineer: L. Pitsikas
Commercial Manager: B. W. E. Copley
Comptroller of Accounts and Audit: R. L. Denison
Comptroller of Stores: R. B. Martin
Director, Management Services Bureau: D. G. Stevenson

Gauge: 1.067 m; 1.435 m; Dual gauge
Route length: 4 393 km; 1 229 km; 148 km

The Western Australian Government operates all railways running through the state with the exception of the Trans-Australian line between Kalgoorlie and the South Australian border and four iron ore railways in the northern region.

Despite varying demands for minerals and irregular arrivals of grain ships in the 1978/79 financial year Westrail exceeded the record haulage it achieved three years ago and moved a total of 19.29 million tonnes, compared with 19 million tonnes in 1977. A major feature of the year's operation was the increased haulage of bauxite.

However 1978/79 was a disappointing year in terms of financial results and the $A 24.14 million loss represented a regression of $A 8.07 million on the previous year.

There are a number of reasons for the increased deficit. However one basic reason needs special emphasis. Westrail has not been able to adjust rail charges regularly to compensate for cost inflation and there has been a progressive widening of the gap between income and expenditure.

TRAFFIC

A record harvest for the last grain season enabled Westrail to haul 3.2 million tonnes of wheat, barley and oats despite a cut-back in grain services caused by the irregular arrival of ships. During one particular week in January Westrail handled 133 122 tonnes, its largest ever weekly tonnage.

Following the record harvest there was a rise of 36 000 tonnes in the haulage of fertiliser to country centres.

Plans were also set in motion to handle an anticipated 3.5 million tonnes of grain during the 1979/80 season and an additional 16 narrow-gauge hopper wagons were built at Westrail's Midland Workshops to augment the fleet for the coming harvest. Bauxite was Westrail's most important mineral traffic. For 1978/79 the amount hauled from Alcoa's mines at Jarrahdale to their refinery at Kwinana rose by one million to 5.4 million tonnes. It was a record movement for both Alcoa and Westrail and was the largest single contributing factor in maintaining rail tonnage figures during that year.

However, there was a setback in the haulage of nickel products and mineral sands, while movement of interstate freight, wool, oil and cement maintained a level similar to previous years. Despite the depressed conditions of the iron and steel industry there was improvement in demand for iron ore in the later part of the financial year. This resulted in a slight rise in haulage between Koolyanobbing and Kwinana of 30 000 to 1.2 million tonnes. Also on the credit side were increases in coal by 150 000 to 1.3 million tonnes, woodchips by 82 000 to 600 000 tonnes, and alumina by 56 000 to 2.3 million tonnes.

Unfortunately interstate operations were disrupted by industrial action in other states. One prolonged strike in South Australia during June and July effectively stopped all interstate passenger and freight trains for 25 days.

Since the start of interstate standard-gauge freight train operations during 1970-71, east/west traffic through Kewdale Freight Terminal has more than trebled, topping one million tonnes for the third year in succession. A third of Westrail's tonnage is carried on the 500-km section of the standard-gauge railway between Kwinana and Koolyanobbing emphasising the line's importance to local as well as interstate operations.

	1977	1978	1979
Total freight tonne-km	4 532 551 992	4 273 064 133	4 178 845 840
Total freight tonnage	19 003 276	18 624 824	19 288 450

PASSENGER TRAFFIC

Interstate passenger rail service to Bunbury and Kalgoorlie showed an overall increase in patronage during 1978/79. The rise on the Perth-Bunbury Australind service was due, in part, to the promotion of educational tours. However, patronage on the interstate passenger trains Indian Pacific and Trans Australian showed a slight decline of five per cent in 1978/79 compared to the previous year. The Albany Progress train was withdrawn on 1 December 1978 because of declining passenger numbers and the deteriorating condition of carriages. It was no longer possible to provide a service of an acceptable standard without large expenditure on construction of new rolling stock. The train has been replaced by five additional return motor coach services each week, including an express coach with limited stops. There are now 15 weekly motor coach services to Albany.

New N Class locomotive hauling a bauxite train on the narrow-gauge line from Jarrahdale to Kwinana
It is travelling over a 260-m test area using dual-gauge concrete sleepers and 60 kg/m rail.

Semi-trailers being loaded on flat top wagons for the journey across Australia at Westrail's Piggyback area at Kewdale Freight Terminal

Interstate passenger train, Indian-Pacific, on the Woodbridge Triangle en route to Forrestfield for re-victualling

Patronage on Westrail's country motor coach services improved by 11 000 passengers during 1978/79 with principal increases recorded on the Albany, Bunbury and Geraldton routes. Motor coaches ran a total of 2.8 million km. To maintain the service the last of 12 new air-conditioned vehicles were introduced into the fleet, enabling 17 older models to be withdrawn.

Work is proceeding on several new projects to attract more passengers to rail public transport along the Armadale and Midland lines, following cessation of the Perth-Fremantle services on 1 September 1979.

A major project is a new bus/rail interchange station at Kelmscott. Here buses from four routes will feed into the new facility which will provide for direct transfer of passengers as buses will drive onto the platform.

City Station, and the area adjacent to it, is being progressively upgraded as part of the planned urban renewal programme. The forecourt of City Station is being converted into a pedestrian plaza in conjunction with the Perth City Council.

	1977	1978	1979
Total passenger-km, rail	108 470 217	97 322 913	98 328 727
Total passenger-km, road	37 380 676	36 815 848	44 411 838
Total passengers carried, rail	247 543	230 737	233 688
Total passengers carried, road	166 507	159 418	168 584

FINANCES

	1977	1978	1979
Income (A$)	138 310 547	150 588 042	155 966 391
Expenses (A$)	149 403 923	166 644 470	180 048 047

Intermodal services

Westrail operates a comprehensive network of road freight services in conjunction with its rail programme. In 1978/79 just over two million km were run by Westrail trucks to areas not serviced by rail or as ancillary to existing train services. Weekly road truck services were also introduced as replacement for overnight freight trains on the Albany and Mullewa routes which were withdrawn on weekends. Facilities for handling containers are available at Kewdale, Forrestfield, Avon Yard, West Merredin, West Kalgoorlie and Robb jetty.

CIVIL ENGINEERING

The five-year rehabilitation of the standard-gauge line between Kwinana and Koolyanobbing was officially launched at Northam on 18 May 1979 by the Premier of Western Australia, Sir Charles Court. Roberts Constructions Pacific Pty Ltd, awarded the contract for renewal of the main track, is using the P811 machine imported from Italy. This machine simultaneously removes rails and sleepers, reshapes the ballast and places new sleepers and rails in position in one continuous operation. It is the first machine of its type to operate in Australia.

On-track equipment, designed by SRS of Sweden, is being used for the replacement of 160 turnouts between Kwinana and Koolyanobbing. This is also the first time that equipment of this type has been used in Australia.

During 1978/79 the concrete sleeper factory at Meckering, operated by John Holland (Constructions) Pty Ltd, produced 160 000 sleepers and over 150 000 tonnes of ballast for the project. A new flashbutt welding depot at Midland has been built to weld the 60 kg/m rail into 274-m lengths for despatch to the resleepering and rerailing site between Northam and Grass Valley. The welding depot was officially opened by the State Minister for Transport, E. C. Rushton, on 23 November 1979.

During Westrail's scheduled track maintenance programme in 1979 two mechanised contract teams renewed 180 000 timber sleepers and completed 560 km of maintenance. A Westrail resleepering team replaced 98 000 sleepers over 300 km of narrow-gauge track.

To improve train operations associated with the Agnew nickel project and other mining developments in the area, a two-year contract to upgrade the 260 km standard-gauge line between Kalgoorlie and Leonora is under way. The contract includes resleepering and replacement of gravel ballast with crushed rock. This line is also to be progressively replaced with recovered 47 kg/m rail which will allow heavier axle loading.

Fieldwork has started on the installation of a new 120 channel cable carrier communication system between Perth and Northam. It is due for completion late 1980.

Work on the Picton/Coolup CTC project has also commenced. When completed, signalling on this 82 km stretch of line will be electronically controlled from a new centre at Picton, using microprocessor based equipment.

Track Details

Standard Rail: Flat bottom in 13.72 m length, weighing 46.6 kg/m and 40.61 kg/m (94 lb/yd and 82 lb/yd) and older rail of varying weights. New rail is 60 kg/m.

Joints: Fishplates; but in relaying the lengths are flashbutt welded to 109.75 m then Thermit Welded at into 439 m lengths or into continuous rail.

Rail fastenings: Dogspikes.

Cross ties (sleepers): Local hardwood, Jarrah, Wandoo etc. Standard & Dual Gauge: 2.5 m × 225 mm × 130 mm. Narrow Gauge: 2.1 m × 225 mm × 115 mm

Spacing: Standard Gauge: 1 640 km. Narrow Gauge: 1 310 km.

Ballast: 38 mm granite ballast on main lines. Iron stone gravel on branch lines.

Curves, min radius: Main lines: 242 m = 7.25° curve. Branch lines: 141 m = 12.5° curve

Max gradient: 1 in 40 × 2½%

Max altitude: 520 m Meekatharra

Axle Loading: 1 067 mm gauge; Main lines 19 tonnes, Branch lines 11 tonnes. 1 435 mm gauge; Main lines 24 tonnes, Branch lines 16 tonnes

Sleepers: track rehabilitation of the standard-gauge line between Kwinana and Koolyanobbing (490 km) using 60 kg/m rail and concrete sleepers has commenced.

New Rail Laid (1978)

47 kg	52.3 km
41 kg	5.2 km

Grain train hauled by an L Class locomotive ready for departure from Merredin and bound for coastal silos

P811 tracklaying machine renewing the standard-gauge line between Koolyanobbing and Kwinana with 60 kg/m rail on concrete sleepers between Grass Valley and Northam

Type XW narrow-gauge wheat hopper wagon used to transport grain from country silos to transfer depots at major centres for onward haulage to coast-based silos

A three-tier automobile carrier built at Westrail's workshops

Class L 2 386—2 162 kW Co-Co diesel-electric main line locomotive

Rail Fastenings: 19 mm square dogspikes, Pandrol clips and lockspikes.
Pads under rails: Double shoulder sleeper plates 13 mm thick made by BHP

SIGNAL & TRAIN CONTROL
New Signalling Installations (1978)

Description	Route Length	Location	Position of Control	Installed by
Mechanical lever operated route setting system Brunswick junction	19.95 km	Benger-Brunswick junction-Beela	Brunswick Junction	Westrail
Remote interlocking route setting system	12.6 km	Forrestfield-Kenwick East-Canning Vale	Forrestfield	Westrail
Remote interlocking route setting system	3.2 km	Welshpool	Cannington	Westrail

Flashlight & Boomgate Installations

Description	Supplier	Installed by
5 level crossings with half boom barrier protection	WB&S (Aust)	Westrail
8 level crossings with flashlight protection	WB&S (Aust)	Westrail

Class RA 1 454—1 342 kW Co-Co diesel-electric main line locomotive

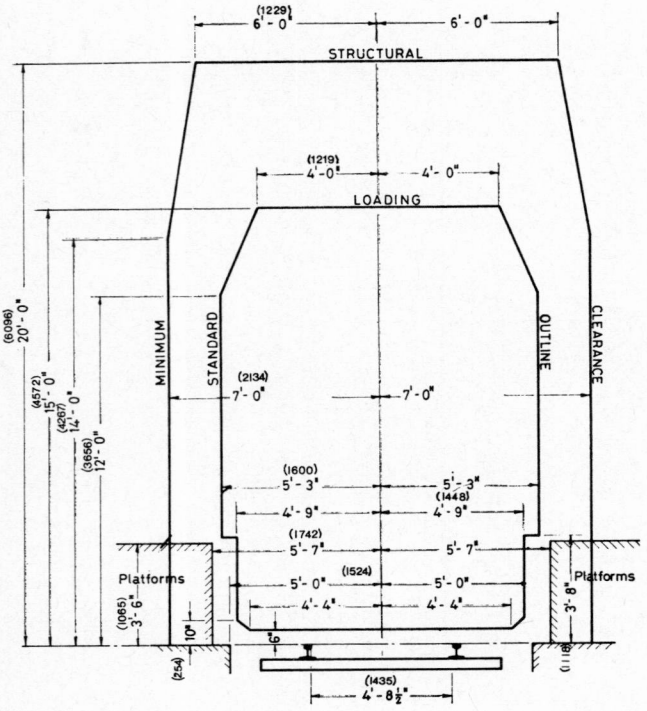

Westrail's 1.435 m loading and structural gauge

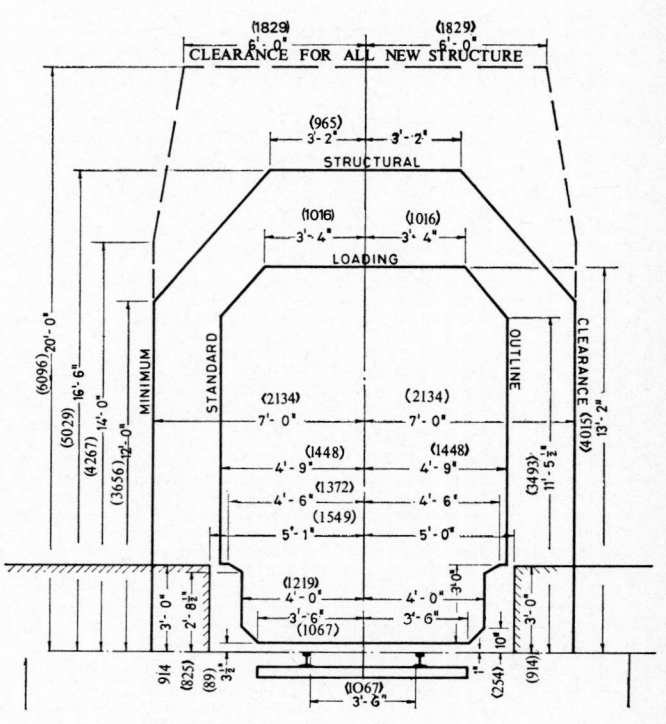

Westrail's 1.067 m loading and structural gauge

MAIN LINE DIESEL LOCOMOTIVES

Gauge mm	Class	Axle Arrangement	Transmission	Rated Power kW	Max. kN	Tractive Effort Continuous at kN	kmlh	Max Speed kmlh	Wheel dia. mm	Total Mass tonnes	Length mm	No. Built	Year First Built	Builders Mechanical Parts	Engine & Type	Transmission
1.067	A	Co-Co	Elec.	1 063/977	240	226	12	100	1 016	89.16	15 036	12	1960	Clyde. Eng. Co.	EMD 12-567C	EMD D25-D29
,,	AA	,,	,,	1 230/1 120	240	226	14	100	1 016	90.51	15 036	5	1967	Clyde Eng. Co.	EMD 12-645E	EMD D25-D29
,,	AB	,,	,,	1 230/1 120	240	226	14	100	1 016	96.00	15 494	6	1969	Clyde Eng. Co.	EMD 12-645E	EMD D32-D29
,,	C	,,	,,	1 145/1 035	240	200	14.5	96	1 016	90.42	15 033	3	1962	English Electric	English Electric 12 SVT	EE 822 6C-548
,,	D	,,	,,	1 640/1 490	310	245.3	18	90	1 016	107.85	17 044	5	1971	Clyde Eng. Co.	EMD 16-645E	EMD D32-D29
,,	DA	,,	,,	1 640/1 490	310	245.3	18	90	1 016	96.72	17 044	7	1972	Clyde Eng. Co.	EMD 16-645E	EMD D32-D29
,,	F	AIA-AIA	,,	560/510	163.7	99.6	15.3	80	952	64.92	12 800	7	1958	English Electric	English Electric 6 SRKT	EE 827/4C-525
,,	G	Co-Co	,,	768/708	240	191.2	9.5	90	952	76.20	12 496	2	1963	,,	English Electric 8 SVT	EE 819/7E-548
,,	R	,,	,,	1 454/1 338	275	226.9	17.5	96	952	94.05	15 240	5	1968	,,	English Electric 12 CSVT	EE 822/16J-548
,,	RA	,,	,,	1 454/1 342	298	226.9	17.5	96	952	96.00	16 306	10	1969	,,	,,	EE 822/16J-548
,,	X, XA, XB	2-DO-2	,,	824/779	124.5	53.3	39	88	800	79.00	14 630	46	1954	Metro-Vickers	Crossley HST V8	MV TG 4203-136

Gauge mm	Class	Axle Arrangement	Transmission	Rated Power kW	Max. kN	Tractive Effort Continuous at kN	Tractive Effort Continuous at km/h	Max Speed km/h	Wheel dia. mm	Total Mass tonnes	Length mm	No. Built	Year First Built	Builders Mechanical Parts	Builders Engine & Type	Builders Transmission
„	B	0-6-0	Hyd.	396/353	102.3	80	10	42	1 016	38.96	7 785	10	1962	Comm. Eng. Co.	Cummins VT-12-B	Twin Disc-Wiseman
„	E	0-6-0	„	186	80	—	—	40	915	26.42	5 588	1	1957	Comm. Eng. Co.	Rolls Royce C6SFL	Twin Disc-DF 11 500
„	M	B-B	„	522/484	—	109	9.6	53	1 016	49.66	10 961	2	1972	Walkers Ltd.	Cummins VTA 1710-L	Voith L4r4U2-G
„	MA	B-B	„	522/484	—	109	9.6	53	1 016	44.8	10 955	3	1973	Walkers Ltd.	Caterpiller D379B	Voith L4r4U2-G
„	T	0-6-0	Elec.	492/447	111.2	69	18.6	65	1 016	37.35	75.69	5	1967	Tulloch	Cummins VT-12-825	Brush TG 78-43 TM 68-46
„	TA	0-6-0	„	492/447	111.2	69	18.6	65	1 016	38.10	7 569	10	1970	„	Cummins VTA-1710-L	Brush TG-43 TM 68-46
„	Y	Bo-Bo	„	306/280	102.3	40	18.5	72	915	38.80	10 020	18	1953	British Thompson Houston	Paxman 12 RPHI	RTB 8944-B.T.H. 124 PV
„	Z	0-6-0	Mech.	106/96	37.8	—	—	28	800	15.14	5 752	3	1953	Drewry Car Co.	Gardner 8 LW	Wilson Epicyclic
1.435	K	Co-Co	Elec.	1 454/1 388	298	189	19	130	1 016	117.3	16 764	9	1966	English Electric	English Electric 12 CSVT	EE 822/16L-538
*1.435	KA	Co-Co	Elec.	1 454/1 342	293	226.9	17.5	96	952	99	16 306	3	1969	English Electric	English Electric 12 CSVT	EE 822/161 548
„	L	„	„	2 386/2 162	337.2	311.4	21	135	1 016	137.16	19 355	25	1967	Clyde Eng. Co.	EMD 16-645E3	EMD AR1O-D77
„	H	Bo-Bo	„	708/641	240	167.7	10	100	1 016	72.38	12 952	5	1965	English Electric	English Electric 6 CSRKT	EE 819/8F-538
„	J	„	„	485/447	159.2	117.8	11.2	100	1 016	66.64	13 004	5	1966	Clyde Eng. Co.	EMD 6-567C	EMD D25-D29
„	N	Co-Co	Elec.	1 940/1 800	371	241	21	103	952	103.46	17 000	11	1977	Comm. Eng. Co.	Alco type 251E	SGTA11B4
DIESEL RAILCARS																
1 067	ADG	1A-A1	Hyd.	90				80	800	30.99	19 050	18	1954	Cravens	AEC A 219	Voith DIWA 501
1 067	ADX	1A-A1	Mech.	112				80	800	33.53	19 050	10	1960	Westrail	AEC A 220	B.U.T. R 14
1 067	ADH	1A-A1	Hyd.	90				80	800	30.99	19 050	4	1963	Cravens	A.E.C. A 219	Voith DIWA 501
1 067	ADK	1A-A1	„	195				85	800	33.28	20 254	10	1968	Comm. Eng. Co.	Cummins NHHTO-6-B1	Voith DIWA 501
1 435	WCA	1A-A1	„	283				144	940	68.22	27 076	5	1972	Comm. Eng. Co.	M.A.N. D 3650 HM6U	Voith T113R

*Locomotive converted from 1.067 m gauge class RA unit in 1974.

AUSTRIA

AUSTRIAN FEDERAL RAILWAYS (ÖBB)

Österreichische Bundesbahnen (ÖBB), Elisabethstrasse 9, A-1010 Vienna

Telephone: 56500
Telegrams: Genbandion
Telex: 3103 obbgs A

General Manager: Dr. Wolfgang Pycha
Deputy General Manager: Dr. Otto Seidelmann
Director, Managing Board: Dr. Friedrich Herzog
Director, Managing Board: Dipl. Ing. Dr. techn. Roman Jaworski
Board of Directors:
  President: Dkfm. Dr. Alfred Weiser
  Vice-President: Karl Novak
Staff Office, Data Processing and Cybernetics: Seilerstätte 1, 1010 Vienna
  Manager: Dipl. Ing. Rudolf Waitzer
Staff Office, Management and Audit: Hegelgasse 7, 1010 Vienna
  Manager: Dr. Heinz Berger
General Secretariat:
  Secretary General: Dr. Johann Pregant
Administrative Directorate:
  Administrative Manager: Dr. Helmut M. Hencker
Personnel Directorate:
  Personnel Manager: Dr. Herbert Schartl
Financial Directorate:
  Financial Manager: Dipl.Ing. Johann Mlinek
Operational Directorate:
  Operational Manager: Dr. Josef Pucher
Sales Directorate: Gauermanngasse 2-4, 1010 Vienna
  Sales Manager: Dr. Karl Zach
Machinery Directorate: Langauergasse 1, 1150 Vienna
  Machinery Directorate: Dipl. Ing. Viktor Köttner
Building Directorate: Elisabethstrasse 18, 1010 Vienna
  Building Manager: Dipl. Ing. Franz Pröll
Purchasing Directorate: Operngasse 24, 1010 Vienna
  Purchasing Manager: Dr. Max Pasch
Electronics Directorate: Daffingerstrasse 4, 1030 Vienna
  Electronics Manager: Dipl.Ing. Gunther Winkler

Gauge: 1 435 m; 760 mm/1 m
Route length: 5 409 km; 454 km

At the head of ÖBB affairs is an 18-member Administrative Council and a four-man directorate for day-to-day management. The Council, which has a three-year term, comprises 12 members appointed by the Government. The directorate has a five-year mandate from the Government.

FREIGHT TRAFFIC

During the financial year 1976 Austrian Federal Railways (ÖBB) enjoyed the first fruits of the post-recession upturn in Europe's industrial activity. Total freight tonnage rose to 49.9 million tonnes with tonne-km reaching 10 548 million, which was 1 169 million more than in 1975. However, ÖBB ended 1977 with freight tonnage barely higher than the 46 million tonnes carried in 1975. Freight tonnage in 1977 fell by 3.4 million over 1976 figures to 46.5 million tonnes, while tonne-km was down by 670 million to 9 879 million. Poor loadings in the first half of 1978 resulted in freight traffic sinking to 9 498 million tonne-km, only just above the figure for 1975. Tonnes carried amounted to 44.9 million. At the end of 1978 the railway freight park totalled 35 858 standard-gauge wagons, 1 397 special vehicles and 692 narrow-gauge wagons.

PASSENGER TRAFFIC

ÖBB carried 169 million passengers in 1978, slightly less than the 171.3 million in the previous year. Passenger-km amounted to 7 108.7 million which represented a five per cent increase. The railway attributes the passenger-km improvement to the introduction of regular-interval intercity services and wider use of refurbished and new rolling stock. Average journey length in 1978 was 42.1 km compared with 39.5 km in 1977. Passenger stock operating in 1979 included 3 670 coaches, 95 diesel railcars and 97 electric motor coaches.

FINANCES

Revenues in 1976 totalled 14 942 million schillings while expenses were 18 734 million schillings. (1975: Revenue 13 114 million schillings, expenses 20 138 million schillings). Income from all sources in 1977 increased by 1 373 to 16 315 million schillings.

Operating expenditure was only slightly higher at 10 888 million schillings. After all charges were taken into account, ÖBB ended the year with a deficit of 3 795 million schillings. Operating revenue for 1978 was 11 760.4 million schillings and after government compensation, total revenue was 17 741 million schillings. Although expenditure at 21 520 million schillings was higher than in 1977, the deficit was reduced by 16.5 million schillings to 3 779 million schillings.

MOTIVE POWER

The motive power fleet in 1978 included 111 standard-gauge steam locomotives, 24 narrow-gauge steam locos, 643 standard-gauge electric locos, 16 narrow-gauge locos, 192 standard-gauge diesel locos and 35 narrow-gauge diesel locos.
After trials with one of Ruhrkohle AG's six electric locomotives with three-phase motors during 1979, ÖBB ordered an initial batch of five units. Rated at 1 200 kW, the Bo-Bo 15 kV 16²/3 Hz locomotives have electrical equipment supplied by Brown Boveri & Cie.

INVESTMENTS

In 1978 OBB spent nearly 5 000 million schillings on capital improvements, including 6 075 million schillings on purchase of 25 new mainline electric locomotives, 612.4 million schillings on passenger coaches, 659.2 million schillings on nine new trainsets, 500 million schillings on purchase of 879 freight wagons and 690 million schillings on track improvements and various miscellaneous expenditures. During 1980 the railway plans to invest 6 011 million schillings with the highest single sum allocated for track improvements.

ELECTRIFICATION

In order to remain independent of coal supplies from abroad, ÖBB has in recent years increased the rate of conversion to electrified tracks. By the end of 1976 the electrified route length totalled 2 727 km on standard-gauge (1 435 mm) and 91 km on narrow-gauge track, all at single phase. At the end of 1977 the total electrified route length was 2 859 km, accounting for about 90 per cent of ÖBB's total traffic. Electrification works completed during 1978 brought the total route length converted to 2 929 km.
A total of 2 838 km are electrified at 15 000 V single phase ac, 16²/3 Hz. Minor Austrian railways account for a further 13 km electrified on this system. The remainder of ÖBB's electrified lines operate on 6 500 V single phase ac, 25 Hz.

CIVIL ENGINEERING

Rail Laid (end 1976):
Type S 64 rail weighing 129.6 lb/yd *(64.29 kg/km)* laid on 30.07 km
Type B rail weighing 99.7 lb/yd *(49.43 kg/km)* laid on 4 361.81 km
Type C rail weighing 108.5 lb/yd *(53.81 kg/km)* laid on 587.75 km

TRACK CONSTRUCTION DETAILS
Standard Rail:
  Standard gauge: 108.5, 99.7 89.5 lb/yd *(53.81, 49.43, 44.35 kg/m)*
  Narrow gauge: 50.7 lb/yd *(26.15 kg/m)*
Length:
  Standard Gauge: 98.4 ft and 196.8 ft *(30m and 60m)*
  Narrow Gauge: 65.6 ft *(20 m)*
Cross Ties (sleepers):
  Standard Gauge: Impregnated wood 8 ft 6⅜ in × 10¼ in × 6¼ in *(2 600 × 260 × 160 mm)*
  also steel and concrete
  Narrow gauge: Impregnated wood 5 ft 3 in × 7 in × 5⅛ in *(1 600 × 200 × 130 mm)*
Cross ties spacing:
  Standard gauge: 600—700 mm *(1 540 per km)* 2 480 per mile
  Narrow gauge: 810 mm *(1 235 per km)* 1 970 per mile
Rail fastening:
  Standard gauge: Resilient fastening, ribbed slabs, clips and bolts, keyed plates and bolts, Pandrol (spring U-bolt) and Macbeth (spring grip spike)
  Narrow gauge: base plates and spikes
Filling:
  Standard gauge: broken stone ballast
  Narrow gauge: broken stone ballast
Thickness under sleepers:
  Standard gauge: 8 to 12 in *(200-300 mm)*
  Narrow gauge: 6 in *(150 mm)*
Minimum or sharpest curvature:
  Standard gauge: 9.7 = min rad of 590 ft *(180 m)*
  Narrow gauge: 29.1 = min rad of 197 ft *(60 m)*

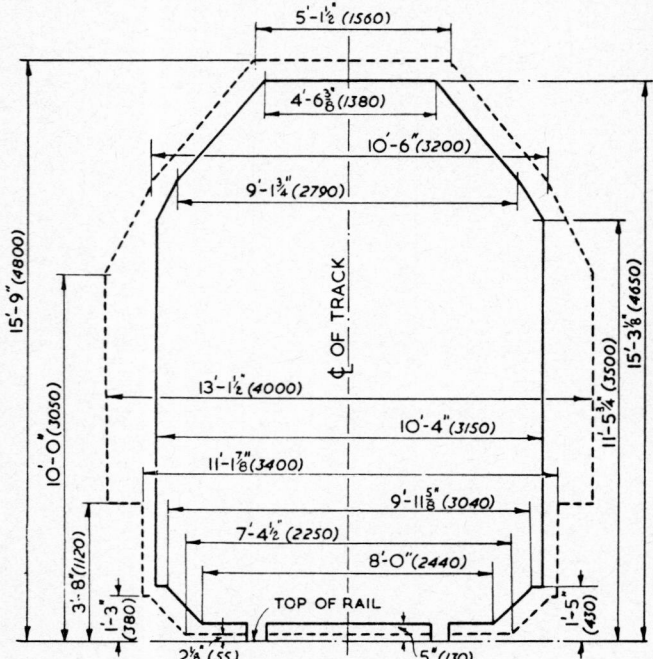

OBB structure and clearance gauge

Electric locomotive class 1044 of the Austrian Federal Railways
Thyristor control and rippled dc traction motors; one hour rating 5 240 kW at 82 km/h; top speed 160 km/h; feeding system: single phase 15 kV/16²/3 Hz; electrical equipment developed by Oesterreichische Brown Boveri-Werke AG and supplied in close cooperation with other Austrian manufacturers of such equipment.

Maximum gradient compensated:
Standard gauge: 1 in 22 *(4.6%)*
Narrow gauge: 1 in 40 *(2.5%)*
Maximum gradient uncompensated:
Standard gauge: 7.4%
Maximum combination of gradient and curvature:
Standard gauge: 1:46 with 125 m curve radius
Narrow gauge: 1:40 with 100m radius
Gauge width with maximum curvature:
Standard gauge: 20 mm
Narrow gauge: 20 mm
Maximum super elevation:
Standard gauge: 160 mm
Narrow gauge: 60 mm
Maximum axle load:
Standard gauge: 20 tonnes
Narrow gauge: 12 tonnes

Maximum permitted speeds:
Passenger trains on standard gauge: 140 km/h
Narrow gauge: 50 km/h
Freight trains on standard gauge: 120 km/h
Narrow gauge: 40 km/h

Unbroken welded rail: At the end of 1976 the total length of welded track was 3 779 km of which 392 km had been laid during the year. The longest individual length of continuous welded rail is 18.3 km.
Rail types most used are Form B *(49.43 kg/m)* and Form C *(53.81 kg/m)* in 30m or 60 m lengths. Sleepers are wood, steel or concrete. Ribbed slabs, Pandrol or Macbeth fastenings are used.

ELECTRIC LOCOMOTIVES

Class	Axle Arrangement	Line Current	Rated Output hp	Max. lb (kg)	Continuous lb (kg)	at mph (km/h)	Max. Speed mph (km/h)	Wheel dia. in (mm)	Weight tonnes	Length ft in (mm)	No. Built	Year Built	Mechanical Parts	Electrical Equipment
1010	Co-Co	15 kV. 1/16⅔	5 400	57 300 (26 000)	26 500 (12 000)	62 (99)	81 (130)	51⅛ (1 300)	110	58' 7'' (17 860)	20	1955	S.G.P.	A.B.E.S.
1110	Co-Co	15 kV. 1/16⅔	5 400	61 700 (28 000)	30 900 (14 000)	53 (85)	68 (110)	51⅛ (1 300)	110	58' 7'' (17 860)	30	1956	S.G.P.	A.B.E.S.
1020	Co-Co	15 kV. 1/16⅔	4 350	65 300 (29 600)	33 000 (15 000)	44 (71)	56 (90)	49¼ (1 250)	120	61' 0'' (18 600)	47	1941	Krauss/Lofag	A.E.G./Ö.S.S.W.
1040	Bo-Bo	15 kV. 1/16⅔	3 200	44 000 (20 000)	22 500 (10 200)	44 (71)	50 (80)	53⅛ (1 350)	80	42' 5'' (12 920)	16	1950	Lofag	A.B.E.S.
1041	Bo-Bo	15 kV. 1/16⅔	3 200	57 300 (20 600)	22 500 (10 200)	44 (71)	50 (80)	53⅛ (1 350)	83	50' 3'' (15 320)	25	1952	S.G.P.	A.B.E.S.
1042	Bo-Bo	15 kV. 1/16⅔	4 770	46 296 (21 000)	26 455 (12 000)	57 (91)	80 (130)	49¼ (1 250)	84	53' 2'' (16 220)	58	1963	S.G.P.	B.E.S.
1042-500	Bo-Bo	15 kV. 1/16⅔	5 360	46 296 (21 000)	24 900 (11 300)	63 (102)	93 (150)	49¼ (1 250)	84	53' 2'' (16 220)	176	1967	S.G.P.	B.E.S.
1043	Bo-Bo	15 kV. 1/16⅔	4 830	66 100 (30 000)	37 000 (16 800)	48 (78)	84 (135)	49⅛ (1 260)	77.4 ‡	51' 1½'' (15 580)	10	1971/72	ASEA	ASEA
1044	Bo-Bo	15 kV. 1/16⅔	5 400	—	—		160 (160)	(1 300)	83	(16 000)	2	1974	S.G.P.	B.E.S.
1141	Bo-Bo	15 kV. 1/16⅔	3 400	48 500 (22 000)	20 000 (9 040)	53 (85)	68 (110)	51⅛ (1 300)	80	46' 9½'' (14 260)	30	1955	S.G.P.	A.B.E.S.
1046	Bo-Bo	15 kV. 1/16⅔	2 200	26 500 (12 000)	11 350 (5 150)	58.7 (94.5)	78 (125)	41 (1 040)	67	53' 7'' (16 330)	25	1956	Lofag	A.B.E.S.
1062	D	15 kV. 1/16⅔	870	41 900 (19 000)	11 900 (5 400)	30 (49)	31 (50)	44⅞ (1 140)	68	35' 6'' (10 820)	12	1955	Lofag	A.B.E.S.
1018	1-D-1	15 kV. 1/16⅔	4 400	42 900 (19 450)	24 900 (11 300)	65 (105)	80 (130)	63 (1 600)	110	55' 6'' (16 920)	8	1939	Lofag	A.E.G.; Siemens
1161	D	15 kV. 1/16⅔	980	30 900 (14 000)	12 300 (5 570)	22 (36)	25 (40)	44⅞ (1 140)	56	34' 5½'' (10 500)	21	1928	Lofag	A.E.G.
1245	Bo-Bo	15 kV. 1/16⅔	2 400	45 750 (20 750)	22 900 (10 400)	36 (58)	50 (80)	53 (1 350)	82	42' 8'' (12 920)	38	1934	Lofag	A.B.E.S.
1670	1A-B-A1	15 kV. 1/16⅔	3 100	40 800 (18 500)	22 500 (10 200)	47 (75)	62 (100)	53 (1 350)	107	47' 5½'' (14 460)	26	1928	Lofag/Krauss	Siemens

‡Nos. 1043-01, 02, 03 (1971) = 77 tonnes
No 1043-04 (1972) = 82 tonnes.

DIESEL LOCOMOTIVES

Class	Axle Arrangement	Transmission	Rated Power hp	Max. lb (kg)	Continuous lb (kg)	at mph (km/h)	Max. Speed mph (km/h)	Wheel Dia. in (mm)	Total Weight Tons	Length ft ins (mm)	No. Built	Year first Built	Mechanical Parts	Engine & Type	Transmission
2020	B-B	Hyd.	2 200	52 150 (23 640)	37 300 (16 950)	12.5 (20)	68 (110)	39⅜ (1 000)	75.4	59' 10'' (18 240)	1	1960	S.G.P.	2×SGP T 12b	Voith
2043	B-B	Hyd.	1 500	45 182 (20 500)	30 636 (13 900)	30.5 (19)	62 (100)	37⅜ (950)	67.2 / 67.7	48' 5'' (14 760) / 51' 8½'' (15 760)	76	1964	Jenbach	JW 1500	Voith
2045	Bo-Bo	Elec.	1 000	34 200 (15 500)	13 450 (6 100)	20.6 (33.2)	56 (90)	39⅜ (1 000)	71	48' 6¾'' (14 800)	18	1952	S.G.P.	2×S.G.P. S 12a	ELIN/ÖBBW
2050	Bo-Bo	Elec.	1 520	40 100 (18 200)	32 700 (14 850)	13.1 (21.1)	62 (100)	41 (1 040)	75.5	58' 2½'' (17 740)	18	1958	Henschel	G.M. 12-567C	G.M.
2060	B	Hyd.	196	22 500/ 11 300 (10 200/ 5 130)	15 200/ 7 700 (6 900/ 3 500)	2.2/4.3 (3.5/6.9)	19/37 (30/60)	37 (940)	27.4	22' 0'' (6 700)	100	1954	Jenbach	Jenbach JW200	Voith
2062	B	Hyd.	390	27 000/ 18 400 (12 270/ 8 350)	17 600/ 12 000 (8 000/ 5 450)	4.7/7.0 (7.6/ 11.2)	25/37 (40/60)	37 (940)	32	26' 3'' (8 000)	45 / 20	1958 / 1965	Jenbach	JW 400	Voith
2067	C	Hyd.	600	33 070 (15 000)	26 500 (12 000)	4.3 (7.0)	40 (65)	44⅞ (1 140)	49.1	33' 11'' (10 340)	63	1959/ 64	S.G.P.	S.G.P. S 12a	Voith
2095	B-B	Hyd.	600	21 200 (9 600)	16 700 (7 600)	7.5 (12.0)	37 (60)	35½ (900)	32	34' 1½'' (40 400)	10 / 5	1961 / 1962	S.G.P.	S.G.P. S 12a	Voith
2143	B-B	Hyd.	1 500	42 757 (19 400)	29 754 (13 500)	11 (18)	62 (100)	37⅜ (950)	65.4	51' 6'' (15 760)	33	1965	S.G.P.	T12c	Voith

BANGLADESH
BANGLADESH RAILWAY (BR)
Railway Building, Chittagong

Telephone: Chittagong 86011
Telegrams: Eprail

Chairman, Railway Board: Maqbul Ahmad
Member, Administration, Planning and Engineering: M. Asjad Ali
Member, Mechanical and Procurement: M. M. Haque
Member, Operation and Commercial: Mahmud Hasan
Member, Finance: Hamed Shafiul Islam
Chief Electrical Engineer: M. N. Karim
Chief Planning Officer: M. Nazmul Haque
Chief Operating Superintendent: M. A. Chowdhury
Chief Mechanical Engineer: Raisuddin Ahmed
Chief Signal and Telecommunication Engineer: S. A. B. M. Karimushan
Chief Operating Superintendent: Md Mostaque Ahmed Chowdhury
Chief Engineer: A. H. M. R. Islam Bhuiyan
Engineer-in-Chief: M. A. Matin
Divisional Superintendent, Chittagong: A. K. M. Amanul Islam Chowdhury
Divisional Superintendent, Dacca: A. M. Z. Mahmud
Divisional Superintendent, Paksey: A. H. Khan
Divisional Superintendent, Lalmonirhat: A. B. M. Shamsuddain Ahmed

Gauge: 1.676 m; 1.0 m
Total route length: 1 786.22 miles *(2 874 km)*
Total track length: 2 797.49 miles *(4 510 km)*

Bangladesh Railway is the principal transportation organisation of the country. It serves a population of about 80 million living in an area of 88 715 km² *(55 126 miles²)*. The railway has always played a vital role in the development of the country and in the expansion of trade, commerce and industry. Bulk of the export and import traffic is still rail-borne, with the railway feeding industry with raw materials and subsequently shipping finished products at an economical cost. The railway moves food grains, fertilisers and consumer goods to all parts of the country at reasonably high speed and at comparatively low cost.
At the end of 1976-77, Bangladesh Railway had a total of 483 stations spread over 2 874 km (1 786.02 route miles) consisting of two gauges, broad (1.676 m) and metre gauge (1.0 m).

FREIGHT TRAFFIC
During the financial year 1977-78 freight tonnes carried, as well as freight tonne-miles, increased by 12.9 per cent and 10.3 per cent respectively, as compared to those of 1976-77. Freight tonnes carried in 1977-78 were 3.51 million against 3.11 million tonnes in 1976-77 and tonne-miles were 481 million in 1977-78 against 436 million in 1976-77. Freight revenue in 1977-78 was Taka 29.25 crores as compared to Taka 24.64 crores of the previous year which is an increase of 18.7 per cent.
The number of freight wagons owned by Bangladesh Railway at the end of 1977-78 was 16 656, comprising 13 257 covered wagons, 1 670 open wagons, 1 192 special type stock (for carriage of liquids, explosives, machinery, livestock, timber, rails, etc) and the rest departmental wagons. 14 588 of these wagons are four-wheelers and 2 068 bogie wagons. However, availability of freight wagons for effective use were 3 814 BG and 12 952 MG.
The gauge breakdown of the wagons in terms of units and four-wheelers since 1964-65 is given below:

	Broad gauge		Metre gauge		Narrow gauge		Total	
	Units	Four-wheelers	Units	Four-wheelers	Units	Four-wheelers	Units	Four-wheelers
June—July								
1964-65	4 801	4 883	14 696	17 787	12	12	19 509	22 582
1965-66	4 791	4 873	14 500	17 596	12	12	19 303	22 481
1966-67	4 612	4 682	14 168	17 213	12	12	18 792	21 907
1967-68	4 538	4 602	13 756	16 782	12	12	18 306	21 396
1968-69	4 567	4 716	13 003	15 795	12	12	17 582	20 523
1969-70	4 464	4 632	12 359	14 984	12	12	16 835	19 628
1970-71	4 418	4 585	11 860	14 382	12	12	16 290	18 979
1971-72	4 387	4 553	11 672	14 155	12	12	16 071	18 720
1972-73	4 274	4 437	11 826	14 230	—	—	16 100	18 667
1973-74	4 237	4 400	11 844	14 173	—	—	16 081	18 573
1974-75	4 152	4 314	11 474	13 428	—	—	15 626	17 742
1975-76	4 483	4 645	12 319	14 258	—	—	16 802	18 903
1976-77	4 624	4 786	12 301	14 219	—	—	16 925	19 005
1977-78*	4 484	4 645	12 172	14 079	—	—	16 656	18 724

*Out of freight wagons owned as shown above the stock actually available for effective use was 3 814 broad-gauge and 12 952 metre-gauge (in 4-wheelers), including 16 = 32 molasses tank wagons manufactured locally.

Canadian MLU-14 diesel-electric locomotive received in 1978

PASSENGER TRAFFIC
In the passenger traffic sector, the steady growth continued during 1977-78. The number of passengers totalled 96.2 million, as compared to 94.4 million in 1976-77. Passenger-miles also increased in 1977-78 by 8.02 per cent as compared to that of the previous year, in that passenger-miles went up from 2 879 million to 3 110 million in 1977-78. Passenger revenue in 1977-78 was Taka 23.80 crores, an increase of 8.37 per cent, as against Taka 21.96 crores of the previous year. In 1969-70, the last normal operating year before liberation of the country, the number of passengers carried was 73 million, with passenger-miles totalling 2 061 million.
Coaching (parcel) earnings in 1977-78 were Taka 7.44 crores, as against Taka 6.55 crores in 1976-77.
At the end of 1977-78 Bangladesh Railway had a total of 1 168 vehicles for passengers, and 344 vehicles for luggage, parcels, mail, automobiles, horses, etc, as well as departmental vehicles. However, availability of passenger vehicles for effective use were 224 BG and 840 MG. In addition there were four diesel railcars and eight trailer coaches.
The breakdown of the vehicles (in terms of units) is given below:

	Broad gauge		Metre gauge		Narrow gauge		Total	
	Passenger carriages	Other coaching vehicles	Passenger carriages	Other coaching vehicles	Passenger carriages	Other coaching vehicles	Passenger carriages	Other coaching vehicles
June—July								
1964-65	302	183	961	310	32	2	1 295	495
1965-66	309	180	1 005	303	32	2	1 346	485
1966-67	313	174	933	303	32	2	1 278	479
1967-68	295	163	917	293	28	1	1 240	457
1968-69	287	150	894	332	27	1	1 208	483
1969-70	275	143	890	335	27	1	1 192	479
1970-71	276	140	886	327	27	1	1 189	468
1971-72	271	137	881	322	27	1	1 179	460
1972-73	300	142	895	337	—	—	1 195	479
1973-74	312	142	935	311	—	—	1 247	453
1974-75	323	115	884	293	—	—	1 207	408
1975-76	296	87	872	276	—	—	1 168	363
1976-77	284	85	908	273	—	—	1 192	358
1977-78*	267	85	901	259	—	—	1 168	344

*Out of passenger carriages owned as shown above, the stock actually available for effective service was 224 broad-gauge and 840 metre-gauge carriages, including 7 manufactured locally by 30 June 1978.

Traffic statistics:

	1977/78	1978/79
Total train-km (millions)	13.65	14.92
Percentage of train-km by steam	19.99	19.80
by diesel	80.01	80.20
by electric	—	—
Total freight tonnage (millions)	3.51	3.18
Average haul (km)	220.37	259.45

	BG	MG	BG	MG
Average net train load (tonnes)	456	356	502	399
Average wagon load (tonnes)	18.43	11.88	17.44	12.67

	1977/78	1978/79
Total passenger-km (millions)	5 004.68	4 832.32
Total passengers carried (millions)	96.21	89.76
Passengers carried,		
air-conditioned (millions)	0.03	0.02
First-class (millions)	0.39	0.26
Second-class (millions)	7.58	7.04
Third-class (millions)	88.21	82.44
Average length of passenger journey (km)	52.02	53.84

FINANCES
Average revenue per passenger as well as per passenger-mile increased during 1977-78 as compared to 1976-77. Revenue per passenger increased from Taka 2.32 to Taka 2.47 or by 6.46 per cent and revenue per passenger-mile increased from 7.32 poisha to 7.46 poisha (1.91 per cent) which could be attributed to greater increase in the movement of higher-class passengers. The increase in revenue per passenger (6.46 per cent) was higher than the increase in revenue per passenger-mile (1.91 per cent) and this was due to the telescopic effect of the rise in the average distance travelled by a passenger from 30.5 to 32.3 miles.
In the case of freight traffic, there were increases in revenue per tonne and revenue per tonne-mile. Average revenue per tonne increased by 7.69 per cent from Taka 75.25 in 1976-77 to Taka 81.04 in 1977-78 and revenue per tonne-mile showed an increase of 9.56 per cent from 52.3 poisha in 1976-77 to 57.3 poisha in 1977-78. These increases were brought about by the increased movement of high-rated commodities like jute, sugar, wheat, petrol and kerosene oil.

The railway at present operates 337 steam locomotives

Operating revenue for the year 1977-78 amounted to Taka 62.38 crores as compared to Taka 54.30 crores in 1976-77 representing an increase of 14.9 per cent. Passenger earnings in 1977-78 amounted to Taka 23.80 crores which represent an increase of 8.37 per cent over the amount for 1976-77. Other coaching (parcel) earnings in 1977-78 were Taka 7.44 crores compared to Taka 6.55 crores for the previous year, representing an increase of 13.6 per cent. The freight earnings during 1977-78 amounted to Taka 29.25 crores compared to Taka 24.64 crores for 1976-77, registering an increase of 18.7 per cent. Miscellaneous earnings showed an increase of 64.3 per cent from Taka 1.15 crores in 1976-77 to Taka 1.89 crores in 1977-78.
The operating expenses for the railway for the year 1977-78 were estimated to be Taka

65.72 crores, an increase of 14.8 per cent, compared with the expenditure for 1976-77 which amounted to Taka 57.25 crores. Net operating income showed a deficit of 3.33 crores in 1977-78 as against the deficit of Taka 2.96 crores in 1976-77. The percentage of earnings to expenses was almost the same in both years (105.3 in 1977-78 against 105.4 in 1976-77).

	1974	1975	1976	1977
Revenue (thousands)	278 300	403 000	505 000	624 000
Expenses	354 000	410 000	494 000	657 000

Operating revenue

	Passenger earnings		Other coaching earnings		Freight earnings		Miscellaneous earnings		Total
	Taka	(%)	Taka	(%)	Taka	(%)	Taka	(%)	Taka
1977-78	238 168	38.0	74 352	11.9	292 492	46.6	22 202	3.54	627 214
1978-79	304 460	36.8	85 608	10.3	422 768	51.1	14 898	1.80	827 734

Operating expenses

	Admini-stration	Repairs and main-tenance	Operation staff	Operation fuel	Operation other than staff and fuel	Miscell-aneous expenses	Depreci-ation	Total
1977-78	103 085	245 517	90 531	161 407	36 931	19 792	3 057	660 320
1978-79	125 153	277 500	117 887	160 194	38 066	30 616	6 585	756 001

MOTIVE POWER AND ROLLING STOCK
Number of locomotives in service (1978) included:
(1) Steam—155 broad-gauge line haul; 92 broad-gauge shunters; 192 metre-gauge line haul; 181 metre-gauge shunters.
(2) diesel-electric—32 broad-gauge line haul; 32 broad-gauge shunters; 151 metre-gauge line haul; 141 metre-gauge shunters.
Rail buses in service include four diesel metre-gauge and eight trailers.

CIVIL ENGINEERING
Work is already underway on extensive track upgrading plans to be carried out under a loan of $US 24.4 million from the Asian Development Bank. Most of the money is expected to be spent on upgrading the track and bridges along the metre-gauge Dacca-Chittagong line—the country's principal rail artery. Generally, existing 30 kg/m rail on all metre-gauge lines is to be replaced with 37 kg/m welded rails laid on new semi-hard Gojou timber sleepers which are expected to last up to 20 years. Studies are now underway into the economics of concrete sleepers. Broad-gauge lines are laid with 45 kg/m rails and it is proposed to keep the same weight rail on newly-welded broad-gauge sections.
Under the improvement programme, five lines have been selected for extensive upgrading at a total cost of £10 million: Akhaura-Chhatak; Bhairab Bazar-Bahadurabad; Khulna-Darsana; Dacca-Mymensingh; Sirajganj-Ishuradi-Abdulpur-Amnura.
A new line is planned from Faridpur to Barisal at a cost of Taka 44.2 million. So far 16 km has been completed linking Faridpur with Talma and work is underway on the next 16 km section as far as Bhanga.
Following completion of track doubling between Pahartali and Mirsarai, embankments and bridges between Laksam and Hasanpur have been constructed.
Work is continuing on track doubling between Chittagong and Sholashahar. This is due for completion when yard remodelling is concluded at Sholashahar and Jhaytala.
Meanwhile, preliminary engineering and detailed traffic surveys have been carried out on proposed new lines from Laksam to Dacca, Bagerhat to Perojpur, Jessore to Kamarkhali, Kishoreganj to Tangail, and Madaripur to Khulna.
In addition a proposal for construction of a new line from Khulna to Mongla—to include a major new bridge over the Rupsa river—has been submitted to the government for approval.

Track details:
Rail types and weights: 75 lbs 'A' 90 lbs 'A' FF BSS rails, 50 lbs 'R' 60 lbs 'R' 90 lbs 'R' FF BSS rails, 50 NS, 50 ISR & 80 lbs.
Sleepers (cross ties) type:
Thickness: (a) wooden sleeper BG 5", (b) steel through sleeper BG ½", (c) cast iron CST/9 block, (d) wooden sleeper MG 4½", (e) steel through sleeper MG $^{11}/_{32}$", (f) cast iron sleeper CST/9 (block).
Spacing: N+1, N+2, N+3, N+4, and N+5.
Rail fastenings (types used): Fish Plates, Fish Boxes, Dog Spikes, Bearing Plates, Anchor Bearing Plates, Round Spikes, Steel Keys and Steel Jaws and Rail Anchors of different sizes.
Signal and train control installations
Type: (i) Relay interlocking (ii) Mechanical interlocking

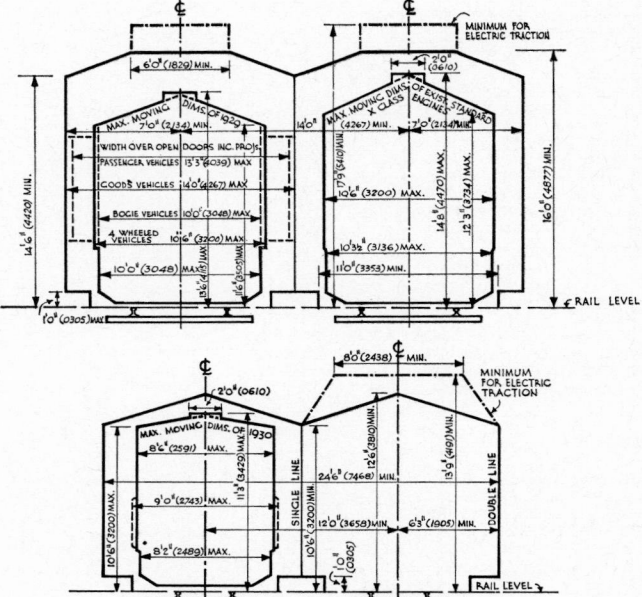

Loading and structure-gauge diagrams for Bangladesh Railways showing (top) for broad-gauge tracks and (bottom) for metre gauge

RAILWAY-OWNER SHIPPING SERVICES, TRAIN AND ROAD VEHICLE FERRIES
Routes served:
(i) Jagannathganj-Serajganj ghat (passenger ferry services)
(ii) Bahadurabad-Tistamukh ghat (passenger and wagon ferry services)
Description of vessels: 1 Steamer, 6 Tugs, 9 Barges.
Type and volume of traffic: 1973: Passengers carried 519 979. Tons carried 185 720.
1974: Passengers carried 536 749. Tons carried 158 652.

DIESEL LOCOMOTIVES

					Tractive Effort Continuous at		Max. Speed	Wheel Dia.	Total Weight	Length	No. Built	Year first Built	Builders:		
Class	Axle Arrange-ment	Trans-mission	Rated Power hp	Max. lb (kg)	lb (kg)	mph (km/h)	mph (km/h)	in (mm)	Tons	ft ins (mm)			Mechanical Parts	Engine & Type	Transmission
METRE GAUGE															
GEU-14	Co-Co	Elec.	1 300		42 900		71	3' 4"	70.5	48' 4¾"	10	1964	M/s International Gen Co, USA	7F-DL 8 AG	
ELU-6	Bo-Bo	Elec.	500		13 500		35	3' 0"	40.4	28' 0"	26	1971	M/s English Elec. AE-1 England	Model No. 4 SRKT	
BROAD GAUGE															
MLU-20	00-00	Elec.	2 000		42 540		66	3' 4"	106.5	58' 4½"	16	1970	M/s MLW Worthing Ton/Canada	Model No. 251-C	
DIESEL RAILCARS (METRE GAUGE)															
	Bogie	Hyd.	180				50	2' 4½"	32.98	68' 7⅝"	4	1963	M/s LHB	Bussing Diesel Engine-U.11/200	

BELGIUM

SOCIÉTÉ NATIONALE DES CHEMINS DE FER BELGES (SNCB)

17-21 rue de Louvain, Brussels 1

Telephone: 523 80 80
Telegrams: Railbel

General Manager: G. Vanhee
Assistant General Manager: R. Weber
General Manager's Office:
Manager: R. Squilbin
Chief Engineer, Assistant to Manager: J. Neruez
Chief Legal Adviser, Assistant to Manager: M. Demanche
Chief Engineer: L. Verberckt
Press and Public Relations Officer; W. Van Gestel
Operating department:
Manager: A. Soete
Chief Engineers: P. Fransen
    D. Demonie
    L. Gueret
    A. Guillaume
Chief Inspector: F. De Mesel
Equipment department:
Assistant General Manager: G. Deprez
Chief Engineer, Assistant to Manager: K. Suls
Chief Engineers: M. De Wulf
    R. Verboven
    H. Malengreau
    H. Van Poucke
Chief Inspector: J. Van den Torren
Permanent Way Department:
Manager: O. Debaize
Chief Engineer, Assistant to Manager: P. Stordiau
Chief Engineers: L. Dogniez
    L. Franssen
    T. Bibauw
    A. Couvreur
    G. Gunst
    E. Lallemand
Financial directorate:
Manager: L. De Smet
Chief Inspectors: A. Duchene
    M. Hendrickx
Commercial department:
Manager: F. De Haeck
Chief Inspectors: C. Lokker
    R. Boonen
    E. Marnef
Personnel and Social Services Department:
Manager: E. Arys
Chief Medical Officer, Assistant to Manager: J. Bouckaert
Chief Inspector, Assistant to Manager: J. Roolant
Chief Medical Officer: J. Dufaux, G. David, F. Javaux, R. Van Roy
Chief Inspectors: M. Mahu
    L. Rigaux
Gauge: 1.435 m
Route length: 4 003 km

All standard-gauge lines in the country are operated by the Société Nationale des Chemins de Fer Belges (SNCB), and all metre-gauge light railways by the Société Nationale des Chemins de Fer Vicinaux (SNCV).

At the end of 1977, SNCB operated a route length of 4 003 km of which about 1 300 km are electrified at 3 kV dc with diesel traction on the remainder. Freight traffic is carried over the whole system; passenger traffic on 2 926 km.

TRAFFIC

Although there was a small decline (1.2 per cent) in passenger traffic during 1978, freight traffic showed a recovery, a major contribution being made by an increase of 8.3 per cent in wagonload traffic. Train-km totalled 91.8 million, 3.8 per cent up on 1977, partly because of increased goods traffic but also because of augmented services. Electric traction accounted for 54.8 per cent of the movement.

At 31 December 1978 the number of passenger coaches in internal service was 1 959, of which 1 041 were built between 1933 and 1937, and 918 between 1953 and 1960. Recent construction has concentrated on electric multiple-unit stock in order to meet the requirements of an extended electrified system. A five-year renewals plan is in hand to provide 580 Class M4 vehicles by the end of 1985, comprising 50 first-class, 430 second-class, 65 first-class brakes, and 35 second-class with luggage compartment and snack bar. Orders for 30 first-class and 245 second-class coaches were placed in 1978. The freight wagon fleet at the end of 1978 totalled 46 602 while passenger stock consisted of 2 327 coaches and 66 baggage cars.

FINANCES

Total revenues in 1978 were BFr 39 526 million compared with BFr 37 138 million in 1977. Expenses totalled BFr 39 698 million in 1978 compared with 38 455 million in 1977.

MOTIVE POWER

By the end of 1978 SNCB was operating a fleet of 249 electric locomotives, 936 diesel locomotives, 466 electric railcars and 87 gas/oil railcars.

INVESTMENTS

During 1980 SNCB is planning capital expenditure totalling BFr 24 149 million with major investments allocated for track improvements (BFr 5 794 million), civil engineering works (BFr 6 848 million) and electrification (BFr 3 227 million).

ELECTRIFICATION

During 1979 SNCB will complete the first part of a programme to electrify about 700 km of secondary lines. The programme was first announced in 1976 as a major revision to SNCB's 1970-80 ten-year plan, and electrification work will continue until 1984. First lines to be energised were Hasselt—Genk (15 km) and Braine-LeComte—Manage (28 km). At the end of the year electric traction started on the 42-km line between Ghent and Kortrijk. Wires on the Luttre—Manage section will be energised in 1980, together with the following routes: Manage—La Louvière—Mons; Antwerp—Lier—Aarschot—Louvain; Lier—Herentals.

PERMANENT WAY AND INSTALLATIONS

	1976	1977
Length of line (km) non-electrified	2 701.6	2 701.4
electrified	1 296.2	1 301.5
Number of stations	360	354
Number of branchlines	1 192	1 119
Number of level crossings	4 726	4 623
Lines equipped with automatic block signalling (km)	3 998	4 003
Renewed track (km) (rails and sleepers)	38	61
(rails only)	147	153

TRACK DETAILS

Standard rail: Flat bottom, 100.8 lb per yd *(50 kg/m).*
Length: 88.68 ft *(27.028 m).*
Joints: 4-hole and 6-hole fishplates.
Rail fastenings: Soleplates and screws for wood sleepers. Type RN flexible fastenings on RS concrete sleepers; rigid clips on FB concrete sleepers. Pads are inserted under the rail when concrete sleepers are used. "Pandrol" fastenings are used in tunnels.
Sleeper (crossties): Generally oak, 11 in × 5½ in × 8 ft 6⅜ in *(280 × 140 × 2 600 mm).* Two types of concrete sleeper are used:— Type RS (two blocks joined by a steel bar) with Type RN flexible rail fastenings, and Type F.B. pre-stressed concrete with rigid fastenings.
Rail fastenings: Soleplates and screws. "Pandrol" fastening is used in tunnels.
Cross ties (sleepers): Generally oak, 11 in × 5½ in × 8 ft 6⅜ in *(280 × 140 × 2 600 mm).* Sections of welded-rail track have been laid with two types of concrete sleeper: Type RS (two blocks joined by a steel bar) with Type RN flexible rail fastenings, and Type F.F. (two blocks and a tie) with rigid fastenings.
Spacing: 2 670 to 2 190 per mile *(1 665 to 1 370 per km).*
Filling: Broken stone or slag.
Max curvature:
    Main line: 2.18° = radius of 2 625 ft *(800 m).*
    Secondary line 3.5° = radius of 1 64h nt *(500 m).*
    Running lines 8.75° = radius of 656 ft *(200 m).*
    Sidings 11.7° = radius of 492 ft *(150 m).*
Max gradient: 1.8% = 1 in 55½; except 2 sections of 3.5% = 1 in 28½.
Max altitude: 1 759 ft *(536 m)* at Hockai on the Pepinster-Trois Ponts line.
Max permitted speed: 87 mph *(140 km/h)* on major main lines. 75 mph *(120 km/h)* on all other main lines.
Max axle load: Certain locomotives have axle load of 24 tons. Except for certain bridges they can operate anywhere on the system, subject to speed restriction.

Welded rail: On 1 Jan 1974 the total length of track with welded rail was 1 621 km of which 57 km had been laid in 1973. Rail used (type 50R) weighs 101 lb/yd *(50 kg/m)* in bars 88 ft 7 in *(27 m)* long. These are flash-butt welded at depot into 708 ft 8 in *(8 × 27 m)* lengths and, after laying, the joints are thermit welded to form continuous rail. The longest individual length is 3.5 miles *(5.7 km).*

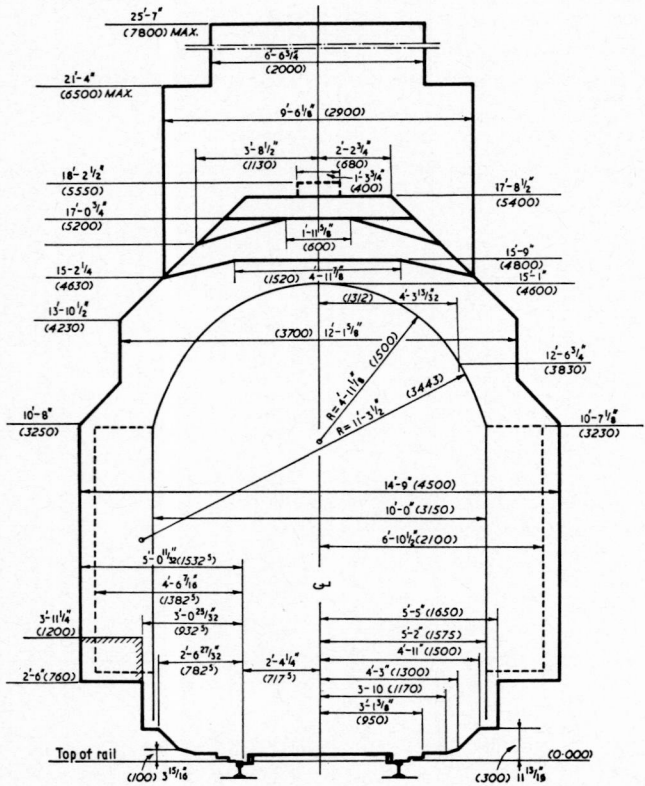

SNCB loading and structure gauge diagram

DIESEL LOCOMOTIVES

Class	Axle Arrangement	Transmission	Rated Power hp	Max. lb (kg)	Tractive Effort Continuous at lb (kg)	mph (km/h)	Max. Speed mph (km/h)	Wheel Dia. in (mm)	Total Weight Tons	Length ft ins (mm)	No. Built	Year first Built	Builders: Mechanical Parts	Engine & Type	Transmission
51	Co-Co	Elec.	2 150	61 200 (27 750)	37 250 (16 900)		75 (120)	39¾ (1 010)	117	66' 1¾" (20 160)	93	1961	Cockerill-Ougrée	Cockerill-Ougrée	ACEC-SEM
59	Bo-Bo	Elec.	1 750	44 000 (20 000)	37 500 (17 000)		75 (120)	44 (1 118)	87	53' 1" (16 180)	55	1955	Cockerill; Baume et Marp.	Cockerill (licence Baldwin)	ACEC (licence Westinghouse)
52-53	Co-Co	Elec.	1 720	55 000 (25 000)	35 500 (16 100)		75 (120)	39¾ (1 010)	108	61' 10" (18 850)	13 19	1955	Anglo-Franco-Belge	GM (USA)	GM (USA) Smit
54	Co-Co	Elec.	1 900	55 000 (25 000)	27 500 (12 500)		87 (140)	,,	108	,,	8	1957	Anglo-Franco-Belge	GM (USA)	GM (USA); Smit
55	Co-Co	Elec.	1 950	61 200 (27 750)	38 000 (17 250)		75 (120)	,,	110	64' 2⅜" (19 550)	42	1961	Brugeoise et Nivelles	GM (USA)	ACEC-SEM licence GM
60	Bo-Bo	Elec.	1 400	44 000 (20 000)	24 250 (11 000)		75 (120)	,,	85.4	56' 11" (17 350)	106	1961	Cockerill-Ougrée	Cockerill (licence Baldwin)	ACEC
64	Bo-Bo	Hyd.	1 400	45 200 (20 500)	(P)25 350 (11 500) (F)37 500 (17 000)	(P)75 (120) (F)51 (82)		44 (1 118)	82	57' 5" (17 500)	6	1962	Ateliers Belges Réunis; A.B.R.	Cockerill-Ougrée	Voith
62 Bogie Flexicoil	Bo-Bo	Elec.	1 425	47 600 (21 600)	24 250 (11 000)		75 (120)	39¾ (1 010)	80	55' 1" (16 790)	136	1961	Brugeoise et Nivelles	GM (USA)	GM (USA)
62 Bogie BN	Bo-Bo	Elec.	1 425	47 600 (21 600)	24 250 (11 000)		75 (120)	,,	81.6	,,	3	1961	Brugeoise et Nivelles	,,	ACEC lic. GM
62 Bogie BN	Bo-Bo	Elec.	1 425	47 600 (21 600)	24 250 (11 000)		75 (120)	,,		,,	35	1962	Brugeoise et Nivelles	,,	ACEC lic. GM
65	B-B	Hyd.	1 460	42 978 (19 500)	(P)25 350 (11 500) (p)27 500 (17 000)	(P)75 (120) (F)51 (82)		44 (1 118)	76 79	,, ,,	6 6	1963 1965/6	Brugeoise et Nivelles	GMC 2-speed Type 12-567DI	Voith
66	B-B	Hyd.	950	39 700 (18 000)	(P)27 500 (12 500) (F)46 300 (21 000)	(P)50 (80) (F)31 (50)		39¾ (1 010)	72	43' 9½" (13 350)	3	1962	A.B.R.	ACEC (licence MAN)	Voith L.217
90	B	Hyd.	245	21 800 (9 900)	16 000 (7 250) 7 500 (3 400)		(1g)13 (21) (2g)28 (45)	36¼ (920)	35.4	21' 9" (6 625)	60	1961	Cockerill-Ougrée	Cockerill-Ougrée	Cockerill-Ougrée
91	B	Hyd.	335	22 000 (10 000)	(S)21 560 (9 800) (L)10 340 (4 700)	13 (21) 28 (45)		49⅝ (1 262)	36	21' 9" (6 625)	60	1961	Cockerill Brugeoise et Nivelles ABC	GM HM	Twin-Disc + Cockerill
92	C	Hyd.	350	(S)33 000 (15 000) (L)20 700 (9 400)		(S)17 (28) (L)28 (45)		49⅝ (1 262)	50.55	34' 1½" (10 400)	24	1960	Brugeoise et Nivelles	S.E.M.	Voith
84	C	Hyd.	550	(S)35 300 (16 000) (L)33 000 (15 000)		(S)20 (33) (L)31 (50)		,,	55.8	34' 11¼" (10 650) 33' 3½" (10 150)	35 25 10	1963 1955 1959	A.B.R.; Baume et Marpent	Anglo-Belgian Company	Voith L 37U
85	C	Hyd.	550	,,		,,		,,	58.5	32' 10" (10 000)	25	1956	Forges, Usines et Fonderies Haine St. Pierre	S.E.M.	Turbo-transmission Voith L37U Inverseur-réduct SEMt.B.122
83	C	Hyd.	550	,,		,,		,,	57	35' 3¼" (10 750)	25	1956	Cockerill-Ougrée	Cockerill-Ougrée (lic. Hamilton) 695 SA	Turbo-transmission Voith L37U Invers.-reduct.
80	C	Hyd.	650	(S)38 800 (17 600) (L)28 400 (12 900)		(lg)24 (38) (2g)49 (78)		49¼ (1 250)	52.1	34' 0" (10 360)	69	1960	Brugeoise et Nivelles; A.B.R.	Maybach	Voith
70	Bo-Bo	Elec.	700	44 000 (20 000)	34 000 (15 400)		31 (50)	42⅛ (1 070)	83	39' 10¼" (12 150)	6	1954	Baume et Marpent	Anglo-Belgian Company	ACEC (licence Westinghouse)
71	D	Hyd.	750	52 900 (24 000)			31 (50)	49⅝ (1 262)	90	37' 8" (11 480)	5	1956	Baume et Marpent	S.E.M.	Turbo-transmission Voith L217A Invers.-reduct.
72	D	Hyd.	750	(S)48 500 (22 000) (L)43 600 (19 800)		(S)20 (33) (L)31 (50)		,,	80	39' 7½" (12 080)	15	1956	Brugeoise et Nivelles	S.E.M.	Voith L37Z
82	C	Hyd.	650	42 978 (19 500)			37 (60)	49⅝ (1 262)	57	36' 7¾" (11 170)	75	1965/6	Brugeoise et Nivelles; Atel Belges Réunis	Anglo-Belgian Company Type DXS 6 cyl	Voith L217U
73	C	Hyd.	750	47 386 (21 500)			37 (60)	49⅝ (1 262)	56	36' 7¾" (11 170)	75	1965/8		Cockerill-Ougrée Type T695A 6-cyl	Voith L217U
74	C	Hyd.	750	47 386 (21 000)			37 (60)	49⅝" (1 262)	59	36' 7¾" (11 170)	10	1977	Brugeoise et Nivelles	Anglo Belgian Company 6 DXC	Voith L217V

ELECTRIC LOCOMOTIVES

Class	Axle Arrangement	Line Current	Rated Output hp	Max. lb (kg)	Tractive Effort (Full Field) Continuous at lb (kg)	Tractive Effort (Full Field) Continuous at mph (km/h)	Max. Speed mph (km/h)	Wheel dia. in (mm)	Weight tonnes	Length ft in (mm)	No. Built	Year Built	Builders: Mechanical Parts	Builders: Electrical Equipment
20	Bo-Bo	3 000 V dc	2 200	44 000 *(20 000)*	21 600 *(9 800)*	30 *(49)*	62 *(100)*	53⅛ *(1 350)*	81.5	42′ 3½″ *(12 890)*	20	1949	Baume-Marpent	ACEC Charleroi et SEM Gand.
20	Co-Co	3 000 V dc	7 000	70 100 *(32 000)*	52 100 *(23 600)*	50 *(80)*	100 *(160)*	49¼ *(1 250)*	111	63′ 11¾″ *(19 500)*	15	1975	Brugeoise et Nivelles	ACEC Charleroi
22	Bo-Bo dual-current	3 000/ 1 500 V dc	2 560	44 000 *(20 000)*	27 600 *(11 500)*	32 *(51)*	81 *(130)*	49⅝ *(1 262)*	87	59′ 0¾″ *(18 000)*	50	1954	Brugeoise et Nivelles	ACEC Charleroi et SEM Gand.
23	Bo-Bo	3 000 V dc	2 560	44 000 *(20 000)*	27 600 *(12 000)*	32 *(51)*	81 *(130)*	,,	93.3	59′ 0¾″ *(18 000)*	82	1955	Atel Metallurgiques de Nivelles	ACEC Charleroi et SEM Gand.
24	Bo-Bo	3 000 V dc	2 560	44 000 *(20 000)*	27 600 *(12 500)*	32 *(51)*	81 *(130)*	,,	93.3	59′ 0¾″ *(18 000)*	1	1955	Atel Metallurgiques de Nivelles	ACEC Charleroi et SEM Gand.
25	Bo-Bo	3 000 V dc	2 560	44 000 *(20 000)*	27 600 *(12 500)*	32 *(51)*	81 *(130)*	,,	83.9	59′ 0¾″ *(18 000)*	22	1960	Brugeoise et Nivelles	ACEC Charleroi et SEM Gand.
25.5	Bo-Bo dual current	3 000 V 1 500 dc	2 560	44 000 *(20 000)*	21 600 *(12 500)*	32 *(51)*	81 *(130)*	49⅝ *(1 262)*	83.9	59′ 0¾″ *(1 800)*	8	modified 1973	Brugeoise et Nivelles	ACEC Charleroi and SEM Gent
26	B-B Mono motor Bogies	3 000 V dc	3 070	58 200 *(26 400)*	34 400 *(15 600)*	30.7 *(49.5)*	100 *(160)*	45¼ *(1 150)*	82.4	56′ 5″ *(17 280)*	48	1963/73	Brugeoise et Nivelles	ACEC Charleroi
28	Bo-Bo	3 000 V d.c.	2 700	44 000 *(20 000)*	25 600 *(11 600)*	32 *(51)*	81 *(130)*	49⅝ *(1 262)*	85	56′ 4½″ *(17 180)*	3	1949	Baume-Marpent	ACEC Charleroi and SEM Gent
15	Bo-Bo triple-current	25 kV 1/50 3 000 V. dc 1 500 V dc	3 600	38 400 *(17 400)*	22 000 *(10 000)*	56 *(91)*	93 *(150)*	49¼ *(1 250)*	77.7	58′ 3″ *(17 750)*	5	1962	Brugeoise et *Nivelles*	ACEC Charleroi
16	Bo-Bo quadri current	25 000 V 50 Hz 15 000 V 16 Hz. 3 000 V dc 1 500V	3 780	44 000 *(20 000)*			100 *(160)*		84	54′ 7¾″ *(16 650)*	8	1966	Brugeoise et	ACEC Charleroi Siemens
18	C-C quadri current	R 5 000 V-50 HZ 15 000 V-16 ⅝ HZ 3 000 V dc 1 500 V dc	6 050	37 300 *(17 000)*	26 500 *(12 000)*	81 *(130)*	112 *(180)*	43⅓ *(1 100)*	113	72′ 5⅓″ *(22 080)*	6	1973	Brugeoise et Nivelles	Alsthom

BENIN

ORGANISATION COMMUNE BENIN-NIGER DES CHEMINS DE FER ET DES TRANSPORTS (OCBN)

Boite Postale 16, Cotonou

Telephone: 31 33 80
Telegrams: Orcobeni Cotonou
Telex: 5210

Director General: Boukary Alidou
Chief of Planning: K. Romeuf

Gauge: 1.00 m.
Route length: 578 km.

OCBN operates, on behalf of Niger and Benin, a total route length of 359 miles *(578 km)* of single track metre gauge railway consisting of:—

Northern Line	fom Cotonou to Parakou via Pahou	272 miles	*438 km*
Eastern Line	from Cotonou to Pobè	66 miles	*107 km*
Western Line	from Pahou to Ségboroué	21 miles	*33 km*

From Parakou freight traffic is transported by road.

A future project is the extension of the Northern Line from Parakou to Dosso a distance of 300 miles *(480 km)*. An agreement was signed in 1976 between Niger and Benin for the construction of a rail link between Parakou and Niamey to give Niger access to the sea at Cotonou. Finance remains the major problem; cost of the 622 km route is estimated at CFA Fr 50 000 million.

FREIGHT TRAFFIC

Freight traffic made a recovery in 1978 from the decline experienced in 1976 when tonne-km fell from 127 million to just over 120 million. An upsurge in 1978 pushed the figure to 137 million and the tonne-km for 1979 was almost 140 million.
The present freight park includes 341 wagons.

PASSENGER TRAFFIC

An increase in passenger traffic is causing problems for OCBN. Passenger-km rose to 130 million in 1978 and was expected to rise a further ten per cent in 1979. With only 33 passenger vehicles available, the railway has experienced difficulties in handling the traffic. However delivery in 1979 of four 950 hp railcars and 24 trailers from Soulé of France should ease the situation.

MOTIVE POWER

Number of locomotives in operation at the end of 1979 totalled 13 diesel-electrics, nine shunting tractors. Railcars totalled nine diesel-electric and six diesel.

INVESTMENTS

Spending of more than CFA Fr 3 200 million (about $US 13.5 million) is being made by Benin Railways during the 1978-80 period for the purchase of rolling stock and track equipment. In addition work began in 1978 on a 650 km northern extension from Parakou to Gaya and Niamey in Niger at a cost of CFA Fr 50 000 million.

CIVIL ENGINEERING

From Parakou the new 650 km northern metre-gauge extension will run almost due north through the province of Borgon to Kandi. It will then veer slightly to the east before descending to cross the Niger river at Bodjecali to reach Gaya, Niger. The work is expected to be completed in six years.

TRACK

Within the limits of the OCDN budget and with aid from FAC subventions, track is being upgraded. Work in progress includes the complete renewal of track using rail weighing 60.5 lb per yard *(30 kg/m)* in place of the existing 42.4 lb *(22 kg)* rail; closer sleeper spacing under 22 kg rail, 1 770 sleepers per km in place of the existing 1 330; and ballast renewals.
Rail used weighs 60.5 lb per yd *(30 kg/m)* in 46 ft *(14 m)* bars, Thermit welded into 505 ft *(154 m)* lengths. After laying in track the joints are Thermit welded in situ from station to station.
The rails are secured by clips and bolts to "Cameroun" type metal sleepers 5 ft 9 in *(1 750 mm)* long and 9⅛ in *(232 mm)* wide.

CONTAINER OPERATION

Present stock consists of 15 of 3 m³ and 20 of 8.8 m³ for domestic use and 8 independently owned transcontainers 35 ft × 8 ft × 8 ft 6 in for service between France and Niger via OCDN.

Containers

Type	3m³	8.8 m³
Number	6	10
Length	6 ft 5 in *(1.96 m)*	6 ft 11 in *(2.10 m)*
Width	3 ft 9 in *(1.14 m)*	6 ft 11 in *(2.10 m)*
Height	5 ft 10 in *(1.78 m)*	8 ft 2½ in *(2.50 m)*
Capacity	106 ft³ *(3.0 m³)*	282 ft³ *(8.8 m³)*
Load	1.104 tonnes	4.25 tonnes
Tare	0.396 tonnes	0.75 tonnes
Total weight	1.5 tonnes	5.00 tonnes
Method of lifting	2 rings at the top	4 rings, one at each top corner
Access	1 side door	2 side doors
Owned by	OCDN	OCDN

The 8 large containers owned by the Société de Transit SO.CO.PAO of Cotonou, for shipment to and from France and carried through Benin into Niger by rail and road, are 35 ft 0 in *(10 668 mm)* long, 8 ft 0 in *(2 435 mm)* wide, 8 ft 6 in *(2 590 mm)* high; capacity 2 040 ft³ *(57.75 m³)*; load 23 tonnes, tare 2.84 tonnes.

Lifting equipment

1 20 tonne fixed crane which can lift 26 tonnes (at Parakou)
3 Hyster 5 tonne cranes
1 Pinguelly 10 tonne crane
1 Weitz 10 tonne mobile crane on pneumatic tyres
1 5 tonne fork lift truck
2 1.5 tonne fork lift trucks

BOLIVIA

BOLIVIAN NATIONAL RAILWAYS

Empresa Nacional de Ferrocarriles, Casilla 428, La Paz

Telephone: 27401 54756
Telegrams: ENFE, La Paz

Director General: Ing. Carlos Azurduy Trigo
Director, Operations: Ing. Rolando Suarez Montoya
Director, Administration: Valentin Quiroga Sarmiento
Heads of Departments
Financing: Lic. Rodolfo Morales Ugarte
Traffic and Operations: Sr. Juan Herrera P.
Traction: Ing. Hugo Urquila M.

Gauge: 1.00 m.
Route length: 3 628 km.

As Bolivia is a landlocked country the railways are of major importance, because they constitute the principal means of access to ports on the Pacific and Atlantic Oceans via the neighbouring countries. These essential international railway connections are as follows:—
   with Chile to the Pacific ports of Arica and Antofagasta;
   with Argentina to the Atlantic ports of Rosario and Buenos Aires;
   with Brazil to the Atlantic port of Santos;
   with Peru (by ship across Lake Titicaca to Puno) to the Pacific port of Matarani.
The Empresa Nacional de Ferrocarriles (ENFE) consists of two separate rail systems:—Western, operating 2 202 km of route; and Eastern, operating 1 426 miles *(1 222 km)* of route. There is no connection between them as yet, but a link line is planned between Aiquile—Santa Cruz and Zudañez—Santa Cruz. In 1978 work continued on the Santa Cruz—Trinidadi line with operations beginning in 1978 over the 100 km first stage of the 204 km line.
With the aid of World Bank loans and other financial assistance, ENFE has been carrying out a modernisation plan since 1973. Second phase of the programme was launched in 1975, backed by a World Bank loan of $US 32 million—although this was subsequently reduced to $US 28.7 million when the railway failed to take up an allocation of $US 3.3 million for the purchase of diesel locomotives.
The most important single construction project to be carried out is the linking of the Eastern and Western networks. Following completion of final engineering studies the link will run from Aiquile, passing through Saipina, Quiñe, Mataral, Panpa Grande, Mairana, San Juan del Rosario, Angostura and Santa Cruz. The scheme will also include a branch line between Mataral and Valle Grande. Once the link is completed the transcontinental railway will run 3 952 km from Santos in Brazil to Arica in Chile. The Brazilian sector will cover 1 883 km, the Bolivian sector 1 864 km and the Chilean section 205 km.
ENFE plans to improve 810 km of track over the Andes route up to 1981. The programme called for 151 km to be completed in 1978, a further 254 km in 1979, followed by 204 km in 1980 and 210 km in 1981.

TRAFFIC

	1977	%	1978	%
Total train-km	64 536	100	66 874	100
Percentage of train km				
by steam:	4 098	6.4	2 133	3.2
by diesel:	60 438	93.6	64 741	96.8
by electric:	—		—	
Total freight				
tonnage (miles)	1 178		1 186	
Average haul (km)				
Average net	492		495	
train load	430		501	
Average wagon load				
Total passenger-km	25		26	
(miles)	396		397	
Total passengers				
(miles)	1 289		1 236	

FINANCES

	1977	1978
	($B million)	
Revenues from passengers and baggage	77.9	102.1
Average receipt per passenger-km	0.221	0.205
Revenues from freight and mail	538.7	609.6
Average receipt per freight tonne-km	1.007	1.039
Miscellaneous	81.8	57.4
Total revenues	698.4	769.0
Expenditure		
Staff/personnel expenses	291.7	399.8
Materials and services	160.1	217.7
Operating costs	72.6	61.4
Depreciation	108.9	131.5
Financial charges	58.9	85.0
Total expenditure	692.2	895.4

MOTIVE POWER AND ROLLING STOCK
(At the end of 1978)

	Line haul	Shunting
Locomotives in service		
Diesel-electric	54	—
Diesel-hydraulic	5	4
Railcars, diesel	14	

ENFE is mid-way through the third phase of a rehabilitation programme (1977-81) which began in 1973. Emphasis at present is on track modernisation and telecommunications costing $US 14.8 million and new motive power and rolling stock ($US 7.9 million). Total expenditure during the third phase is expected to reach $US 35 million.

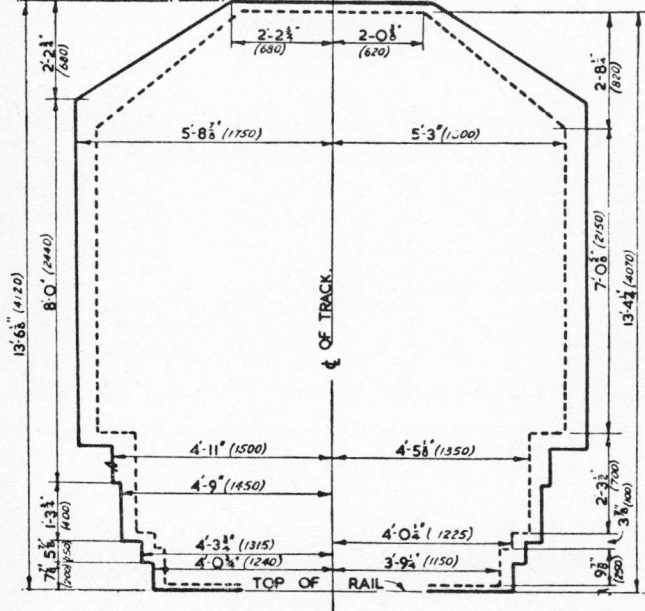

ENFE loading and structure gauge

One of the eight Mitsubishi-built diesel locomotives delivered to ENFE in 1978

Diesel railcar delivered in 1968

New trainsets delivered by Ferrostal in 1978

BRAZIL

REDE FERROVIARIA FEDERAL SA (RFFSA)
Praca Duque de Caxias 86, Rio de Janeiro

President: Colonel Stanley Fortes Baptista
Assistants: Eng. Fernando Limeira França
　　　　　　Col. João Monteiro de Lima Melo
Chief of Cabinet: Eng. Geraldo Costa Guimarães
Public Relations: Enio Amaral
Directors:　Eng. Geraldo Soares Berford
　　　　　　Cel. Eng. Carlos Aloysio Weber
Admistrative and Financial Director: Eng. Paulo M. H. Andrade
Director of Engineering: Eng. Domingos Daré
Director of Personnel: Dr. Geraldo Jose de Oliveira
Director of Special Projects: Eng. José Himério da Silva Oliveira
Director of Planning: Eng. Fernando L. de Franca
Director of Operations: Eng. Napoleão Goretti
Commercial Director: Eng. René Fernandes Schoppa
Regional Superintendents:
Rio de Janeiro: Eng. Antonio Geral Soares Berford—Ed. D. Pedro 11-10° andar—Rio de Janeiro
São Paulo: Eng. José Teófilo dos Santos—Praça da Luz n° 1-São Paulo
Belo Horizonte: Eng. Clovis Vaz da Costa—Rua Sapucai 571-Belo Horizonte—Minas Gerais
Curitiba: Eng. Renato Meister—Rua João Negrão 940-Curitiba-Paraná
Recife: Eng. Emerson Loureiro Jatobá—Praça da Central s/n°-Recife-Pernambuco
Porto Alegre: Eng. Plauto Adroaldo dos Santos—Facin Largo Visconde de Cairu 17-3° andar-Porto Alegre-RS

Gauge: 1.60 m; 1.00 m; 0.762 m.
Route length: 23 649 km.

In addition to the 13 Federal-owned lines there are several other railways in operation, some owned by autonomous Federal departments, some by State governments, and some privately. RFFSA is now administered by six regional authorities and one commuter railway division (Rio de Janeiro). Brief descriptions of each region follow:
Recife Region (SR-1) serves the provinces of Maranhão, Piaui, Rio Grande do Norte, Ceará, Paraiba, Pernambuco, Alagoas, Sergipe and Northern Minas, Bahia. Length and gauge of the region is 7 004 km operating on 1.0 m gauge. Motive power and rolling stock includes 181 diesel locomotives, five electric locomotives, nine electric motor coaches, 215 passenger coaches and 3 770 freight wagons. The region is sub-divided into three divisions: Pertaleza (SP1-1) with head offices at Praço Castro Carreira, Fortaleza, Ceará; Recife Division based at Av Rio Capibariba 147 (PO Box 1943), 10° Andar, 50 000 Recife, Pe; and the Salvador Division at Praça de Inglaterra, Salvador, Bahia.
Belo Horizonte Region (SR-2), serving the provinces of Minas Gerais, Goiás, Brasilia (DF), São Paulo and Estado do Rio. Length of track operating in the region is 4 262 km running on 1.0 m gauge, 202 km on 760 mm gauge track, 13 km on 1.6 m, and 136 km over mixed 1.6 and 1.0 m gauges. A total of 5 450 km of Belo Horizonte line is electrified at 3 000 V dc. Motive power and rolling stock totals 51 narrow-gauge steam locomotives, 299 diesel-electric locomotives, 23 electric locomotives, nine electric motor coaches, 332 passenger coaches and 6 691 freight wagons.
Rio de Janeiro Region (SR-3) serves the provinces of Rio de Janeiro, Minas Gerais, São Paulo and Espirito Santo. Length of line operated by the region is 1 258 km over 1.6 m

gauge track and 1 889 km over 1.0 m gauge. There are two divisions within the Rio de Janeiro Region: the Broad Gauge Division (SP3-1) and the Narrow Gauge Division (SP3-2) both based in Rio de Janeiro.
São Paulo Region (SR-4) serves the provinces of São Paulo and Mato Grosso, operating 251 km of 1.6 m gauge track (190 km electrified at 3 000 V dc) and 1 613 km of 1.0 m gauge. Two divisions operate within the Region: São Paulo Division (SP4-1) and the Bauru Division (SP4-2).
Curitiba Region (SR-5) serving the provinces of Parana and Santa Catarina over 3 356 km of track all on 1.0 m gauge.
Porto Alegre Region (SR-6) serving the provinces of Santa Caterina and Rio Grande do Sul. Length of line is 3 384 km operating on 1.0 m gauge.
Greater Rio Suburban Special Division, the special autonomous division created for Greater Rio de Janeiro which operates 22 km over 1.6 m gauge (177 km electrified) and 158 km over 1.0 m gauge.

FREIGHT TRAFFIC
Increases in freight traffic during 1978 were more modest than expected. Stagnation of the world's steel industry resulted in a 1.7 per cent drop in iron ore carryings, offset to a large extent by a further rise in movement of finished steel products as the country's own steel industry recovered. Poor harvests of wheat, soya and rice cut into agricultural traffic. RFFSA, however, achieved a two per cent rise in tonne-km to 25 670 million, representing 55.5 million tonnes carried. Number of wagons in service in 1978 totalled 42 992.

PASSENGER TRAFFIC
Reflecting policies to slim down long-distance passenger traffic, a decline of 30 per cent in passenger-journeys in 1978 followed the drop of 12 per cent in 1977. This contrasted sharply with the boom in suburban traffic as investments continued in rolling stock and infrastructure in Rio de Janeiro and Sao Paulo. In particular, Sao Paulo saw passenger-journeys rise by 25 per cent to 144 million. Passenger coaches during 1978 totalled 1 704.

FINANCES
Operating expenditure, excluding interest and depreciation, rose by 32 per cent between 1975-76. Since then RFFSA has taken stringent measures to keep costs within bounds, expecting operating expenditure in 1978 to have been 11 800 million Cruzeiros, only 180 million above the 1976 figure. In fact the overall deficit was reduced from 9 300 million Cruzeiros in 1976 to only 8 200 million in 1977 and the administration budgetted for a further decrease to 7 200 million Cruzeiros in 1978. A programme of staff reduction, bringing the number of employees down to 92 000, helped to raise productivity, and this contributed to a reduction in expenditure of 792 million Cruzeiros at 1978 prices. Income rose by three per cent in real terms to 5 380 million Cruzeiros.

MOTIVE POWER
Locomotives in traffic during 1978 were 26 steam, 1 337 diesel and 53 electric. Multiple unit trains totalled 368, railcars 34. During 1978 orders were placed with several manufacturers for locomotives and electric multiple units. Altogether 176 diesel and electric locomotives were on order during 1978. Of these 140 are being built in Brazil by Equipamentos Villares and Engenhariae Maquinas. The remaining 36 locomotives are under construction by Macosa of Spain.

CIVIL ENGINEERING
The new President of Brazil, General J. Baptista Figueiredo, announced in 1979 that the 400 km Steel Railway (Ferrovia do Aco) between Jeceaba near Belo Horizonte and Volta Redonda is to go ahead as a priority project. The cost of completing the line is likely to exceed $US1 200 million. Civil works had already been carried out when financial problems caused the project to be postponed in 1978.

General Electric diesel electric locomotive, 60 tonne, 900/810 hp

One of the 120 electric railcars (3 000 V dc) built mainly for commuter services around Rio de Janeiro

All stainless steel passenger/buffet self-propelled rail diesel car unloading from a Brazilian freighter for operation with RFFSA

3 000 V dc 2 820 kW electric locomotive used on RFFSA rack-adhesion section with 10 per cent gradient

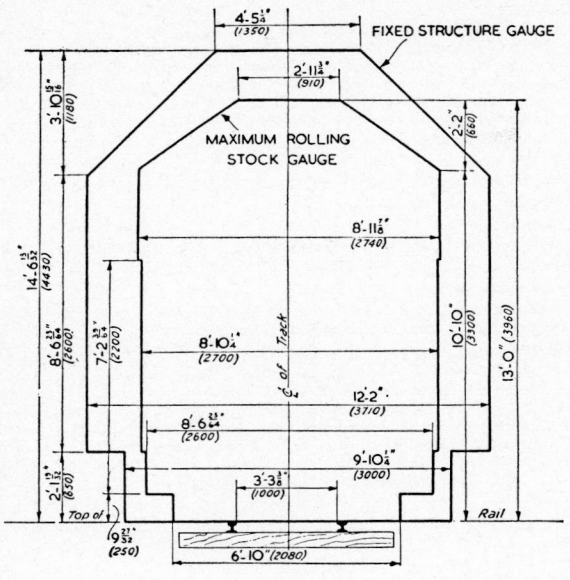

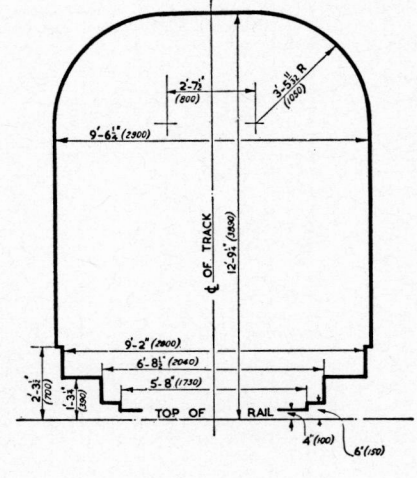

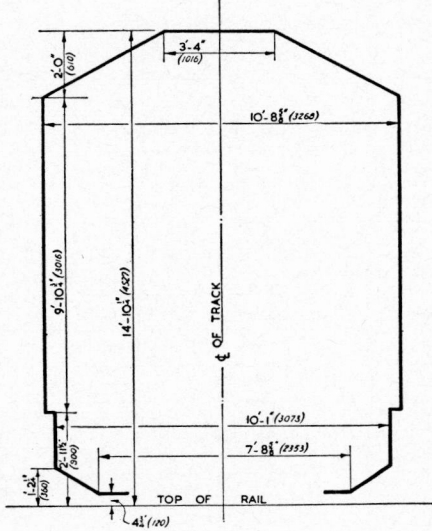

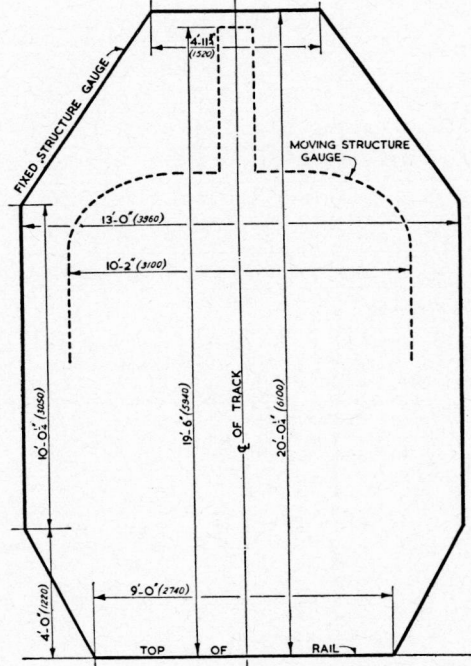

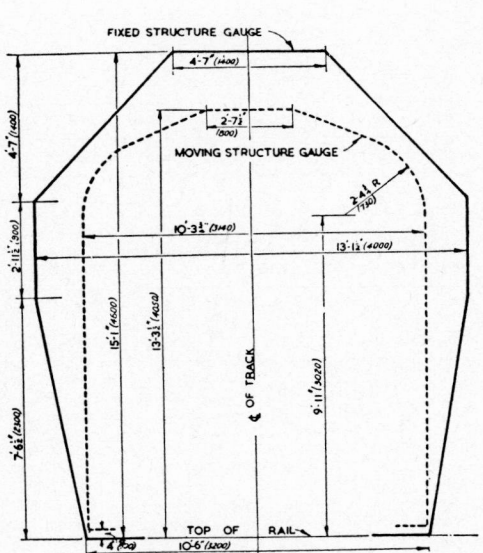

Six types of loading and structural gauge are encountered over Brazil's railway lines

FERROVIA PAULISTA SA (FEPASA)
Rua Libera Badaró 39, São Paulo

President: Walter Pedro Bodoni
Director, Administrative: Walfrido de Carvalho
Director, Commercial: Calim Eid
Director, Financial: Econ, Jarbas Maranhão
Director, Operations: Eng. Chafic Jacob
Director, Public Relations: Claudio de Asumpção Cardoso
Director, Technical: Eng. Oliver H. Salles de Lima
Director, Assistant to President: Eng. Ascelino Lopes de Morais
Director, Personnel: Prof. Ary Baddini Tavares

Departmental Heads:
Planning: Sergio de Azevedo Marques
Mechanical Engineering: Eng. Carlos Augusto Bandeiro de Mello
Civil Engineering: Eng. Guido Luciano A. Toselo
Permanent Way: Eng. Antonio Carlos C. de Camargo
Electrical Engineering: Eng. Cassio Penteado Serro
Systems: Eng. Mariano H. Aranho Domingues
Operations: Eng. Francisco de Paula R. Pesso Neto
Traction: Eng. Carlos Adolpho Mariante
Stations: Eng. Wilson De Bello
Supplies: Eng. José Carlos A. Fusaro
Commercial: Eng. Reynaldo José B. Nunes Sumares

Finance: Econ. Oscar Fernando S. Villas Boas
Economics: Econ. Carlos Alberto Lüders.

Gauge: 1.60 m; 1.00 m.
Route length: 1 647 km; 3 649 km.

FEPASA was formed in 1970 to consolidate the operation of five railways owned by the State of São Paulo. There are three divisions: First (the former Paulista and Araraquara); Second (the former Sorocabana); Third (the former Morgiana and São Paulo—Minas).

TRAFFIC

Late in 1975 FEPASA dropped movement of all small consignments through pricing railway-hauled less-than-wagonload freight and express goods out of the market. The railway raised its rates by 100 per cent. Not surprisingly almost all small consignments left the railway, enabling FEPASA to concentrate on expanding block train services between bulk loading and unloading depots. As a result the first quarter figures for 1977 showed a 20 per cent increase in tonnage.
Passenger services in country areas have been cut dramatically. By early 1977 100 of FEPASA's 155 daily long-distance trains had been withdrawn.

	1976/77	1977/78
Total freight ton-km	4 454 437 000	4 607 290 000
Total freight tonnage	12 448 575	12 884 492
Total passenger-km	2 594 991 000	2 412 260 000
Total passenger journeys	45 051 699	46 057 772

FINANCIAL

Although revenue rose from 521 million Cruzeiros in 1973 to 1 033 million Cruzeiros in 1976, expenditure increased by a much greater rate, from 722 million to 2 133 million Cruzeiros. Drastic action by FEPASA's President, Walter Pedro Badoni, has rid the railway of almost all long-distance passenger trains and general freight; as a result by fiscal year 1976/77 FEPASA was in a much better financial position: revenues totalled 2 266 336 000 Cruzeiros, expenses 2 853 153 000 Cruzeiros. By fiscal year 1977/78 expenses began once again to outstrip revenue growth rate: expenses totalled 4 126 012 000 Cruzeiros against revenues of 2 787 432 000.

INVESTMENTS

Under the government's five-year plan, 1975-79, FEPASA spent 12 000 million Cruzeiros on wagon repairs, the purchase of 2 000 new wagons, the acquisition of 138 new diesel locomotives and track improvements over 2 500 km. During 1979 alone the railway invested $US407.4 million on major improvements, including $US85.8 million on the purchase of 1 327 freight wagons, $US30.1 million on major track improvements, $US17.5 million on new line construction over 118 km and $US119.9 million on improving suburban services.

MOTIVE POWER

Number of locomotives in service in 1978 (with 1973 figures in brackets) was: 147 (165) electrics; 351 diesel-electrics (329).

ROLLING STOCK

Passenger coaches in service in 1978 totalled 702 compared with 1 001 in 1973. Freight wagon totals have gone down from 16 738 in 1973 to 15 823 in 1978.

ELECTRIFICATION

Total electrified route length at the end of 1977 was 657 km over metre-gauge track and 493 km over 1.60 m track; all electrified at 3000 V dc.

PERMANENT WAY AND INSTALLATIONS

By mid-1978 FEPASA had seven new lines either under construction or recently completed. Opened in 1978 was the 23 km Piaeaguerra—Paraitinga branch carrying metre-gauge trains to the big new Cosipa steel plant. Also opened during the year was the 44 km Hirapina—Sta. Gertrudes section and the new 65 km Bauru-Garca line. New lines under construction include the 62 km Guedes (near Campinas)—Mato Seco section and the 170 km Ribeiro—Uberaba variant. Also under construction is an extension from Juquia to the gypsum centre of Jacupiranga.

TRACK

Rail, types and weights: TR 50—50 kg/m (principal lines), TR 45—45 kg/m (secondary lines)
Sleepers (cross ties)
  Type: RS/SL—conrete, and wooden
  Thickness: RS/SL: 1 750 × 280 × 220 × 680 mm: wooden: 2 000 × 220 × 160 mm
  Spacing: 1 500 sleepers/km; 1 600 sleepers/km
Rail fastenings (types used): RN (concrete) and direct (wooden).

DIESEL LOCOMOTIVES

Class	Axle arrangement	Transmission	Rated power (hp)	Tractive effort continuous at (kg)	(km/h)	Max speed (km/h)	Wheel diameter (mm)	Total weight (tonnes)	Length (mm)	No built	Year first built	Builders
3 000	B + B	gear unit	330	6 640		80	838	43.2	10 706	2	1948	General Eléctric/Caterpillar
3 100	B + B	gear unit	600	9 934	14.0	80	838	64.0	11 785	25	1948	General Eléctric/Cooper Bessemer
3 200	B − B	gear unit	1 200	15 422	17.0	138	910	71.2	14 970	22	1957	General Eléctric
3 500	C − C	gear unit	900	11 200	18.0	95	1 050	68.1	14 232	10	1958	General Eléctric/ALCO
3 600	B − B	gear unit	875	15 370	13.0	100	1 016	56.7	12 344	15	1961	General Motors
3 600	B − B	gear unit	875	15 370	13.0	100	1 016	60.5	11 300	23	1960	General Motors
3 650	B − B	gear unit	1 310	16 300	18.0	100	1 016	74.9	14 429	30	1957	General Motors
3 700	B − B	gear unit	770	12 650	14.0	90	1 050	70.0	14 500	27	1969	Lew Hennigsdorf
3 750	B − B	gear unit	1 120	12 650	20.5	100	1 050	74.0	14 500	16	1968	Lew Hennigsdorf
3 800	C − C	gear unit	2 000	22 800	19.6	103	914	108.0	16 846	76	1974	General Eléctric do Brasil
7 000	B − B	gear unit	1 750	19 600	20.0	105	1 016	110.7	17 120	17	1961	General Motors
7 050	B − B	gear unit	1 310	18 160	16.0	124	1 016	80.0	14 589	18	1958	General Motors
7 600	A1A − A1A	gear unit	2 238	18 600	27.0	128	1 016	140.6	20 014	1	1953	General Eléctric/ALCO
7 650	A1A − A1A	gear unit	1 601	26 300	14.0	104	1 016	116.0	17 062	10	1951	General Eléctric/ALCO
7 740	B − B	gear unit	912	13 835	13.0	106	914	68.0	15 143	9	1959	General Eléctric
7 760	B − B	gear unit	770	12 650	14.0	90	1 050	74.0	14 500	36	1967	Lew Hennigsdorf
7 800	C − C	gear unit	2 000	22 800	19.6	103	914	108.0	16 846	26	1977	General Eléctric do Brasil

ELECTRIC LOCOMOTIVES

Class	Axle arrangement	Line current	Rated output hp	Tractive effort continuous at (kg)	(km/h)	Max speed (km/h)	Wheel diameter (mm)	Weight (tonnes)	Length (mm)	No built	Year first built	Builders
2 000	1 − c + c − 1	3 000 V dc	2 320	12 450	12.0	90	1 118	130.0	18 590	25	1943	General Electric
2 050	1 − c + c − 1	3 000 V dc	2 320	12 750	17.0	90	1 118	130.0	18 590	21	1943	Westinghouse
2 100	B − B	3 000 V dc	1 840	11 800	22.0	90	1 117	72.7	13 942	30	1968	General Electric
6 350	c − c	3 000 V dc	4 386	22 800	20.0	134	1 168	144.0	18 339	10	1967	General Electric
6 370	2 − c + c − 2	3 000 V dc	3 818	14 600	22.0	145	1 168	165.1	23 101	22	1940	General Electric
6 400	B + B	3 000 V dc	1 428	12 000	16.5	65	1 066	88.9	11 938	5	1921	General Electric
6 410	c + c	3 000 V dc	1 521	13 600	9.0	65	1 015	107.0	15 291	7	1927	Westinghouse
6 420	1 − c + c − 1	3 000 V dc	2 172	16 620	11.0	80	1 168	133.3	18 212	5	1928	General Electric
6 450	2 − D + D − 2	3 000 V dc	4 656	35 000	9.0	110	1 200	242.6	27 076	5	1951	General Electric
6 500	B − B	3 000 V dc	458	6 890	8.5	64	1 016	55.5	12 649	9	1924	General Electric
6 510	B − B	3 000 V dc	458	6 890	8.5	65	1 016	55.5	12 649	8	1947	General Electric

DIESEL RAILCARS

Class	Axle arrangement	Transmission	Rated power (hp)	Max speed (km/h)	Wheel diameter (mm)	Total weight (tonnes)	Length (mm)	No built	Year first built	Builders
5 000	B − B	gear unit	218	105	838	41.1	18 745	2	1962	Budd
5 010	B − B	gear unit	218	105	838	42.9	18 745	2	1962	Budd

BULGARIA

BULGARIAN STATE RAILWAYS (BDZ)
Ministry of Transport, Sofia

General Manager: Ing. Iosiff Smilov

Gauge: 1.435 m; 760 mm
Route length: 4 045 km; 245 km

Structurally, the railway network is basically complete. In recent years, only a few sections of lines have been built which rationalise the transport system and create transport facilities for some new industrial objectives and sources of raw materials: Dulovo-Silistra, Zlataritza—Elena, Tscherven brajag—Zlatna Panega, etc. The systematic development of the different modes of transport, including railway transport, and the rational distribution of goods between these modes is the responsibility of the national Transport Authority which combines all the modes, including road transport; this ensures a high degree of efficiency in railway transport.

The rapid economic development of the country during the last 25 to 30 years has led to a considerable increase in the volume of goods and passenger traffic. In 1975, goods traffic had increased by 40 per cent and passenger traffic by 17.8 per cent compared with 1965 or, expressed in absolute figures, by 22.8 million tonnes of goods and more than 16 million passengers.

To enable the railway to cope with the offered volume of goods and passenger traffic, a technical reconstruction and modernisation of all the railway equipment (locomotives, vehicles, permanent way, stations, remote control installations, etc.) has been carried out in recent years. Priority is being given to highly effective measures which ensure a rapid increase in line and processing capacity.

TRAFFIC

It is predicted that the railways will have to carry 110 million tonnes of goods and 118 million passengers in 1980, and 180 million tonnes of goods and 155 million passengers in 1990.

Total tonnage carried in 1975 was 79 000 000 tons (17 500 000 ton-km).

Number of passenger journeys in 1975 was 104 000 000. Number of passenger-km: 7 500 million.

Co-operation between Bulgaria and Greece on rail transit traffic under the 1964 agreements is making good progress. Transit freight traffic in 1976 was 30 per cent up on the previous year, and there are good prospects for increasing passenger traffic. The Kulata-Promahon line is to be rebuilt to increase its capacity allowing more traffic from Greece to be handled. Passenger services will be improved with a daily diesel railcar service between Sofia and Salonika and more of these units will be used on the Sofia-Athens line.

INVESTMENTS

BDZ is spending 1 381.5 million Leva during the seventh (1976-80) five year plan on capital improvements, more than double the investments in the sixth five-year plan period.

MOTIVE POWER AND ROLLING STOCK

The accelerated introduction of diesel traction enabled BDZ in 1977, to increase the share of electric and diesel traction in the total traction programme to more than 85 per cent—an increase that has taken place within a period of 12 to 14 years.

BDZ began taking delivery during 1977 of 70 class ER25 ac electric trainsets from the Soviet Union works at Riga.

The structure of the wagon fleet has been greatly improved by the modernisation of existing wagons and the introduction of heavy-duty and specialised goods wagons for carrying a variety of goods at speeds of 100 to 120 km/h.

The exacting demands for a better passenger service have led to a rapid renewal of the fleet of passenger coaches and to the additional introduction of coaches offering a higher level of travelling comfort and suitable for speeds ranging from 140 to 160 km/h.

ELECTRIFICATION

By the end of 1970, steam still accounted for 39 per cent of all BDZ traction. At the end of 1975, electric traction and diesel units were hauling 86.6 per cent of tonne-km—reducing steam traction to 13.4 per cent of the total.

Electrification of most of the principal railway lines has now been completed, using single-phase ac with voltage of 25 kV and 50 Hz frequency; 1 326 km of 1.435 m gauge track is electrified.

For the first electrified sections, 3 000 kW, four-axle series 41.0 electric locomotives were supplied by Skoda, Czechoslovakia. First batch of diesel locomotives were purchased from Simmering-Graz-Pauker, Austria.

Included in the new locomotives taken into service during the present plan period are: mainline electrics from Skoda; 3 000-hp diesels from the Soviet Union; 2 200-hp diesels from Romania.

Under the seventh plan (1976-80) about 900 km is being electrified: included sections Sofia-Mezdra; Plovdiv-Simnitsa; Gorna Orehovitza-Sindel; Sofia-Dimitrovgrad South; Tulovo-Stara Zagora; Plovdiv-Svilengrad.

Proportion of electrified lines are planned to reach about 50 per cent of the total network by 1980. This will permit a 40 per cent increase of throughput and carrying capacity. At the same time the speed of freight and passenger trains will increase and there will be a sharp reduction in environmental pollution.

Introduction of new electric services will enable the railway to increase the gross weight of freight and passenger trains over lines at present restricted to low weights by nature of Bulgaria's terrain.

PERMANENT WAY AND INSTALLATIONS

Measures have been taken for continuous improvement of track. Over 36 per cent of the network has now been equipped with 49 kg/m rails. The proportion of continuous welded rails is now 24.3 per cent of the total length of running track. These measures have permitted train speeds to be increased to 100-120 km/h on some sections of line. Until now track doubling has been carried out relatively slowly. By 1973, only 253 km had been doubled—less than 6 per cent of the total length. Doubling is now planned during the seventh plan over 800 km: from Sofia to Plovdiv; Plovdiv to Zimnitsa; Mezdra via Gorna Orehovitza to Ruse; and Gorna Orehovitza to Sindel. In 1976 a total of 35 km was doubled and 120 km electrified. During 1977 track doubling and electrification was authorised for two routes totalling 725 km: Gorna Oryakhovitza to Sindel and Plovdiv to Zimnitsa via Stara Zagora.

Growing traffic is to be met, together with the increase in running speeds on individual railway lines, by double-tracking the single-track main lines and reconstructing them to a standard permitting a speed of 160 km/h. It is planned to introduce speeds ranging from 140 to 160 km/h for passenger trains and from 100 to 120 km/h for freight trains by perfecting vehicle design, permanent way and signalling techniques.

Associated with the double-tracking of the main lines is an extensive programme for improving the horizontal and vertical alignment of the permanent way and increasing its capacity through the introduction of rails with a metre weight of 54 and 60 kg. Also associated with the double-tracking of the lines is the reconstruction of stations with a view to lengthening tracks.

As a result of the double-tracking of about 780 route kilometres during the years 1976-1980, the share of double-track sections in the total route mileage will be raised to about 25 per cent.

Two marshalling yards have been equipped with automatic humps, and 89 stations have been fitted with route re-lay centralisation.

As part of plans to speed delivery of freight and coordinate the operations of rail and road transport, loading and unloading will be concentrated at 100 to 150 terminals. This will help create conditions for full mechanisation of freight handling operations, with more efficient use of containers, pallets and packages.

BDZ's target is to mechanise 92 per cent of all freight handling operations by 1980. This will mean total elimination of manual labour, considerable qualitative changes in the material/technical base of the whole freight industry, and significant improvement in the organisation and management of rail transport.

SIGNALLING

There is to be increased application of automation and telemechanisation. Route-relay centralisation is to be installed at 65 stations and all electrified lines and mainline electric locomotives are to be equipped with semi-automatic cab signalling. By 1980, a total of 621 km will be equipped with semi-automatic relay blocking, and 400 level crossings will be fitted with automatic crossing devices.

Up to 1980, some 1 000 route kms of open lines will be equipped for central traffic control, and some 70 per cent of all locomotives will be equipped for automatic train control. All stations on the principal lines are being equipped with modern relay-type signal cabins.

Marshalling operations are being concentrated at the major marshalling yards which are equipped for the remote control of the marshalling process, making the most of the facilities provided by electronic data processing plants and other automatic equipment. The development of these key yards, capable of dealing with 500 to 600 wagons in 24 hours, is accompanied by that of auxiliary yards of lower capacity which handle the traffic of a number of minor yards in the same area.

3 200 kW diesel-electric locomotive built by Skoda

BURMA
UNION OF BURMA RAILWAYS
PO Box 118, Bogyoke Aung San Street, Rangoon

Telephone: 14455
Telegrams: Rheostat

Chairman, Management Board; Colonel Seng Ya
Managing Director: Colonel Seng Ya
General Manager: U Aye Pe
Deputy General Manager: U Kyaw Myint
Chief Traffic Manager: U Tun Aung
Chief Mechanical and Electrical Engineer: U Saw Clyde
Chief Engineer: U Tin Ohn

Gauge: 1.00 m
Route length: 3 130 km

Burma has a metre-gauge network comprising a main section and two short isolated sections of railway. The most important line connects the two principal cities, Rangoon the capital, and Mandalay 619 km to the north. Three passenger trains daily run in each direction, the fastest taking a scheduled 12 hours to cover the journey. Two classes of travel—upper and lower class—are offered..

A crash programme was announced in 1976 to upgrade services and track. Aim was to improve train speeds and frequencies by early 1977. A total of 34 additional freight trains were due to go into service together with 12 extra passenger services.

TRAFFIC	1975/76	1976/77
Total freight tonne-miles	237 251 365	242 492 812
Total freight tonnage	1 619 888	1 675 369
Total passenger-miles	21 554 302 320	17 282 439 937
Total passenger journeys	49 055 360	32 053 102

FINANCES	1975/76	1976/77
		(Kyats/thousand)
Revenues	181 066.96	198 813.07
Expenses	196 204.37	223 650.17

MOTIVE POWER AND ROLLING STOCK
Alsthom, of France, signed a new contract with Burma Railways in 1977 for the supply of 21 new locomotives valued-together with spares—at Frs 73 million. Delivery of the locomotives, all rated at 1 600 hp, will bring the number of Alsthom-built motive power units in operation by the railway to 127.

Also during 1977, the railway awarded contracts worth Yen 4 070 million to a Japanese consortium for locomotives, coaches and wagons. The group, comprising Sumitomo Shoji, Kawasaki and Kinki Sharyo, is to supply five diesel-hydraulic locos of 500 hp, 12 first and 60 second-class passenger coaches, 20 tank wagons for petroleum products and five refrigerated wagons.

Number of locomotives in service	Line haul	Shunting (switching)
Steam	179	50
Diesel electric	79	15
Diesel hydraulic	72	—
Number of diesel trainsets	21 sets (3 car sets)	
	2 sets (4 car sets)	
Number of passenger train coaches	1 228	
Freight train wagons	9 527	

TRACK CONSTRUCTION DETAILS
Standard rail: Flat bottom B.S.
  Main line: 75 and 60 lb *(37.2* and *29.8 kg)* in 39 ft lengths.
  Main branches: 60 lb *(29.8 kg).*
  Other branches and sidings: 50 lb *(24.9 kg).*
Joints: Suspended; joint sleepers 14 in centres. Rails are joined by fishplates and bolts.
Welded track: 117 ft *(35.7 m)* lengths. Thermit welded in situ.
Cross ties (sleepers): Hardwood (Xylia Dolabriformis) and creosoted soft wood, 8 in × 4½ in × 6 ft *(203 × 115 × 1 829 mm).*
Spacing:
  Main line: N + 3.
  Branch line: N + 2.
  (N = length of rail in linear yards).
Rail fastening: Dog spikes. Elastic Rail Spikes (Elastic Rail Spike Co, Ltd, London). Macbeth Rail Spikes (Exors. of James Mills Ltd, Cheshire, England) are under experimental use.
Filling (ballast): Broken stone, 2 to ¾ in *(50.8 to 19.1 mm),* shingle on branch lines.
Thickness under sleeper: 6 in *(150 mm).*
Max. curvature:
  Main line: 6° = radius of 955 ft *(291 m).*
  Branch line: 17° = radius of 338 ft *(103 mm).*
Max. gradient:
  Main line: 0.5% = in 200 compensated.
  Branch line: 4.0% = 1 in 25 compensated.
Max permitted speed:
  Main line: 30 mph *(48 km/h).*
  Branch line: 20 mph *(32 km/h).*
Max axle load: 12 tons on 75 and 60 lb rail.
Bridge loading: Indian Railway Standard ML.

Class DD 900 diesel-hydraulic locomotive, rated at 960 hp, built for Burma in 1969; a total of six are still in service with the railway

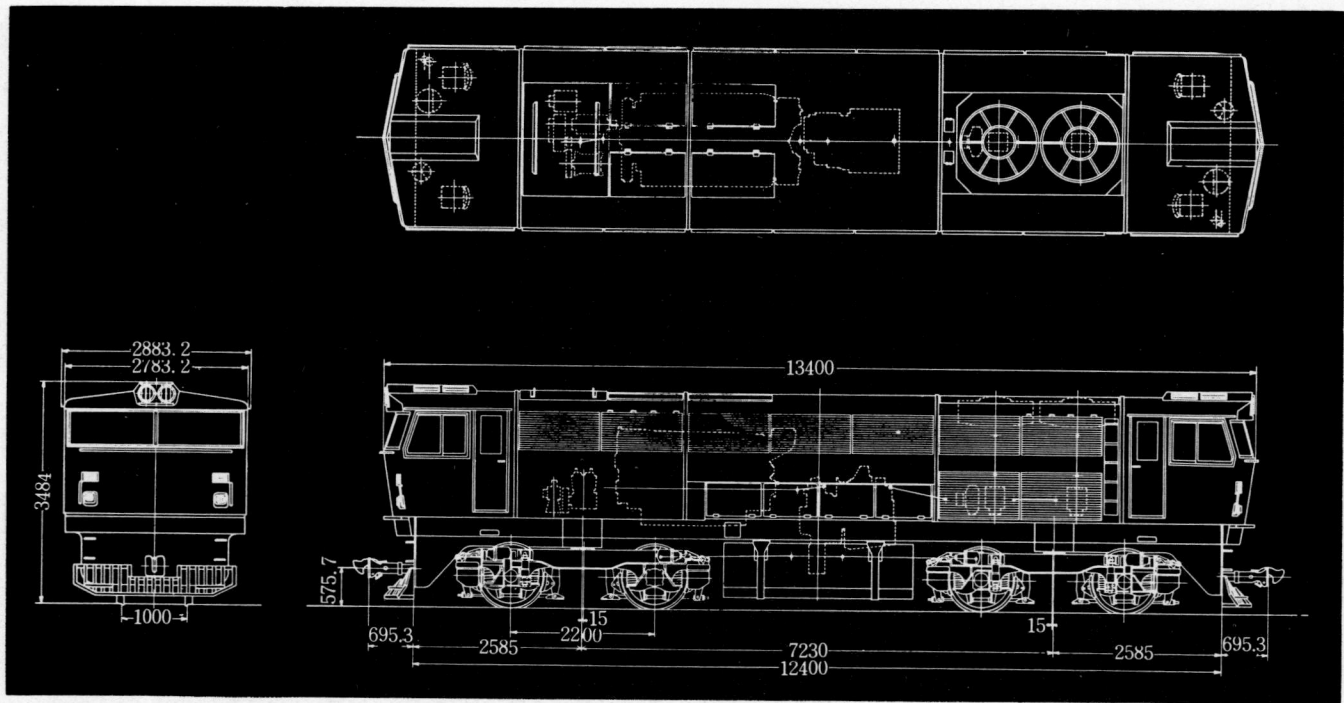

Type DD 1500 diesel-hydraulic locomotive built for Burma by Kawasaki for steep grade mainline service

CAMEROON

REGIE DES CHEMINS DE FER DU CAMEROUN (REGIFERCAM)
PO Box 304, Douala

Telephone: 42-60-45
Telegrams: REGIFERCAM-DOUALA
Telex: 5607

President and General Manager: Gilbert Ntang
Technical Adviser: Samuel Minko
Assistant General Manager—Management: René Kamo
Assistant General Manager—Studies: Henri Leyrat
Administrative Manager: Eitel Ndedi-Mpacho
Assistant Administrative Manager: Jean Marie Omog-Samnick
Information Service: Samuel Evengue-Nsomoto
Financial Manager: Alfred Tamfu-Nchoko
Assistant Financial Manager: Jean Calvin Nana
Operations Department: Justin Teulale
Motive power and Rolling Stock Department: Paul Djoko Moyo
Track and Building Department: Gaston Monayong

Gauge: 1.00 m
Total track length: 1 168 km

The Regifercam system consists of two lines: West line running 172 km from Bonaneri to Nkongsamba and the Transcamerounian line opened in 1974 between Douala-Nyaoundéré (935 km), Otele-Mbalmayo (37 km), and Mbanga-Kumba (29 km).

FREIGHT TRAFFIC

Freight traffic carried by Cameroon National Railways Authority in the financial year 1975-76 totalled 437·3 million tonne-km compared with 400·2 million tonne-km in the previous year.

PASSENGER TRAFFIC

A drop in passenger traffic was 3 per cent more than forecast with passenger-km totalling 260·8 million compared with 282·0 million in 1974-75. The average journey of the 1·86 million passengers carried was 140·4 km.

FINANCIAL

Total receipts for 1976 were FrCFA 6 425.6 m, about 26 per cent more than in the previous year. Expenditure rose to FrCFA 6 085.2 m, leaving an operating profit of FrCFA 340.4 m.

MOTIVE POWER

Type	Weight (tons)	Power (kw)	Number
Locomotives			
CEM AGO 4B 3 600	127	2 650	9
Alsthom AGO CC 2 400	86	1 250	5
Alsthom MGO BB 1 200	56	720	12
Alsthom MGO BB 300/500	54	415	17
Alsthom Sulzer BB 200	52	380	2
Total			45
Railcars			
Billard/Soulé/MGO ZE 10	45	315	7
Soulé/CEM/Poyaud ZE 100	47	500	4
Total			11
Locotractors			
CEM/MGO YE	30	215	32
Total			32

CIVIL ENGINEERING

Work began in November 1978 on reconstruction of the Eeda-Douala section of the Transcamerounian line. In mid-1978 Canada granted a loan of $C31.2 million to Cameroon for re-alignment of the section.
Re-alignment of the Youandé to Maloume section of the Transcamerounian was completed and commissioned in mid-May 1978.

CANADA

BRITISH COLUMBIA RAILWAY
1095 West Pender Street, Vancouver, British Columbia V6E 2N6

Telephone: 681 3131

Vice-President: M. C. Norris
Public Relations Manager: H. D. Armstrong
Administration Manager: G. L. Ritchie
Chief Mechanical Officer: G. L. Kelly
Operations and Maintenance Manager: N. A. McPherson
Controller: J. Pasowysty
Chief Engineer, Maintenance-of-way: A. G. Richmond
Chief of Engineering Services: V. W. Shtenko
Manager, Sales and Marketing: A. C. Sturgeon
Chief Financial Officer: J. R. Clarke
Chief of Communications: C. D. Marlatt
Chief of Transportation: A. T. Shannon

Gauge: 1.435 m.
Route length: 2 017 km.

The British Columbia Railway's main track is geographically segregated into two operating divisions; the Cariboo and Peace River—Omineca Division. Within each of these lie the following subdivisions.
Cariboo Division: The Squamish subdivision is the southernmost on the railway, running from Mile 0.0 at North Vancouver, to Mile 157.5 (Lillooet). It is followed by the Lillooet sub-division which runs from Mile 157.5 to Mile 312.7, (Williams Lake) and the Prince George subdivision, which extends from Mile 312.7 to Mile 462.5 (Prince George).

Peace River—Omineca Division: The Peace River portion runs from Prince George, over the Chetwynd Subdivision from Mile 462.5 to Mile 659.3 (Chetwynd). The Fort St John subdivision is next, running from Mile 659.3 to Mile 816.5 (Beatton). The railway's northernmost subdivision, the Fort Nelson, follows, extending from Mile 816.5 to Mile 979.4 (Fort Nelson). It should be noted that the 21.1 Mile Mackenzie Industrial Lead and the 61.1 Mile Dawson Creek subdivision are also included in the Peace River Division. The Omineca portion begins at Odell, which lies in the Chetwynd subdivision. It is composed of the Stuart subdivision, which runs from Mile 0.0 at Odel to Mile 151.5, and the Takla subdivision, which extends from Mile 151.5 to Mile 336.0. Beyond Driftwood, which is situated at Mile 220.0, construction work on the extension was suspended in April 1977.

TRAFFIC

The railway hauled a record volume of carloadings in 1977. Total loadings, at 152 597, were 20 per cent above the previous record achieved in 1973 and 28 per cent higher than loadings in 1976. Net tonnage hauled, also at a record level, totalled 8 283 169, up from 6 800 934 in 1976.
Factors contributing to 1977's record traffic performance were improved market conditions for forest industry products, a virtual absence of work stoppages on the railway, improved track conditions, an adequate supply of locomotives and rail cars and especially the effort by the railway's employees.
The British Columbia Railway's operating performance during the first six months of 1978 showed a marked improvement over the same period in 1977. Operating revenues were up from $48 million to $54.7 million. An operating profit of $1.5 million, before interest charges, was recorded in the first half of 1978 compared with operating losses of $3.1 million and $11.3 million during the first six months of 1977 and 1976 respectively. After interest charges, net loss for the first six months of 1978 was $25.4 million compared with $25.7 million during the first six months of 1977.
Reflecting the substantial impact of the debt carried in the railway's accounts, interest on long-term debt totalled $27.1 million for the first six months of 1978 compared with

MLW type M420 diesel locomotive built for British Columbia Railway; rated at 2 000 hp and used in road service

$23.2 million for the same period in 1977.

Operating results for the first half of 1978 reflected a continuing strong demand for BC's forest products. Despite rail car shortages in the first half of the year, carloading levels closely parallelled those of the previous year. Total loadings to the end of August 1978 were 105 291 compared with 103 836 during the same period in 1977. For all of 1977 loadings at 152 597 were the highest in the railway's history.

Freight traffic accounts for 77 per cent of the railway's revenues and 58.2 per cent of the freight revenue is derived from forest products. Of annual carloadings, 69.8 per cent are derived from forest products (excluding pulp and paper), and 14.1 per cent from manufacturing.

	1976	1977
Total freight ton-km	3 504 100 120	4 373 436 701
Total freight tonnage	6 800 934	8 283 169
Total passenger-km	749 202	903 518
Total passenger journeys	66 143	78 770

FINANCES

1977 was eventful for the company. Early that year the Provincial Government appointed a Royal Commission to inquire into all aspects of the railway's operations. Hearings concluded in January 1978 and the final report became available later that year. In March 1977 the Provincial Government concluded arrangements with the Federal Government on the development of railways in the northwest region of the Province. As a result BCR received a grant of $81 million toward the construction of the Dease Lake extension. Subsequently construction work was halted on the extension pending the report of the Royal Commission on BCR. In August 1977 the railwest rail-car manufacturing plant was closed due to lack of demand for rail-cars in Canada in the foreseeable future and current excess capacity in the Canadian rail-car industry. The company's operating loss in 1977 was reduced by $12.6 million compared with the previous year. The improvement can be attributed to record traffic, strike-free operations and improved cost controls.

INVESTMENTS

In 1979 the BCR spent $C33 831 400 on major improvements, a slight increase on the 1978 spending which totalled $C31 million. Expenditure during 1979 was allocated towards: track improvements ($C22.7 million); track maintenance ($C877 400); bridges and buildings ($C7.1 million) and miscellaneous items.

	Fiscal year ended			
	1974	1975	1976	1977
	$C (thousands)			
Operating revenues	48 983	57 765	66 998	100 639
Operating expenses				
Transportation	29 323	33 548	37 008	41 972
Road maintenance	12 091	19 772	20 172	25 018
Equipment maintenance	8 760	10 007	11 529	19 337
Depreciation	9 467	10 237	11 860	12 783
Other	3 160	6 507	7 485	10 081
	62 801	80 071	88 054	109 091
Operating loss	13 818	22 306	21 056	8 452
Other expenses				
Interest and dept expense	19 531	25 126	33 726	7 983
Less other income	1 107	1 561	1 379	1 034
	18 424	23 565	32 347	49 839*
Net loss	32 242	45 871	53 403	58 291

*Includes $C 2 890 000 loss on discontinued car manufacturing plant.

MOTIVE POWER AND ROLLING STOCK

At year end 1979, the railway utilised the following equipment in revenue freight service:

FREIGHT CARS
Box	3 518
Flat	3 850
Gondola	1 491
Hopper—Open top	234
Covered	59
Refrigerator	24
Stock	14
Tank	43
	9 233

CANADIAN NATIONAL RAILWAYS (CN)
PO Box 8100, Montreal, Quebec H3C 3N4

Telephone: 877 5430
Telegrams: CANANATIONAL MONTREAL

Chairman of the Board: J. A. Bextraze
President & Chief Executive Officer: Dr. R. A. Bandeen
Corporate Vice-President: J. M. Duncan
Corporate Vice-President: J. H. Spicer
Senior Vice-President: A. H. Hart, Q.C.
Vice-President and Senior Executive Officer, CN Rail: R. R. Latimer
Vice-President, CN Marine: J. Gratwick
Vice-President, Operations: J. L. Cann
Vice-President, Public Relations: J. G. Cormier
Vice-President, Industrial Relations & Organisation: K. E. Hunt
Vice-President, Freight Marketing: R. E. Lawless
Vice-President: T. Cedraschi
Chief of Motive Power and Car Equipment: W. H. Cyr
Chief Engineer: G. A. van de Water

Gauge	4' 8½" (1.435 m)	3' 6" (1.067 m)	
	miles	miles	Total miles
Route length: 1st Main Track	22 784.07	711.88	23 495.95
Track length:			
Main Tracks	23 718.68	711.88	24 430.56
Sidings	8 768.08	121.41	8 889.49
Total	32 486.76	833.29	33 320.05
	(38 962 km)	(1 146 km)	(58 173 km)

Major CN rail routes link Halifax-Montreal, Toronto and Montreal-Vancouver, via Winnipeg, Saskatoon, Edmonton and Jasper. While CN Rail accounts for about 63 per cent of revenues, the company owns a chain of hotels, a telecommunications company, an express company, highway freight lines, steamships, ferry services and an airline. It also owns three railroads in the USA: Grand Trunk Western, Central Vermont and Duluth, Winnipeg and Pacific. The three railroads are encompassed within the Grand Trunk Corporation which in 1977 reported an income of $28.6 million, up $14 million on 1976.

TRAFFIC

Freight tonnage and inter-city passenger traffic increased substantially in 1977/78. The number of inter-city passengers carried (4.2 million) was the highest number since 1972. During 1978 CN Rail signed a series of contracts with Via Rail Canada Inc, which is now responsible for the subsidised rail passenger services provided by CN and CP Rail. All CN Rail passenger services (with the exception of commuter operations) became the responsibility of Via Rail by mid-1979.

	1974	1975	1976	1977
Freight (million ton miles)	74 142	72 729	76 240	77 781
Freight tonnage	119 074 989	108 154 572	119 796 965	123 311 457
Passenger miles (millions)	1 340.1	1 329.1	1 369.9	1 358.1
Passengers carried (thousands)	11 984	10 286	9 765	9 862

FINANCIAL

CN Rail income for 1977 was $199.4 million, $42.3 million more than in 1976. Revenues at $1 872.8 million were 8.2 per cent higher than in 1976. Expenses during the year totalled $1 673.4 million, an increase of only 6.3 per cent. Savings resulting from selective station closings, carload centre consolidations and administrative and manpower controls helped to hold the increase in basic operating costs to less than 0.5 per cent. The balance of the rise in costs resulted from inflationary increases in wages, materials and fuel. At a time of indifferent economic growth, increased emphasis was made on selective development of marketing concepts. For example piggyback revenues increased to $78.3 million or 14 per cent more than 1976, mainly because of further market penetration and optimisation of round-trip/back haul pricing. Import/export container revenues climbed 35.2 per cent from 1976 to $55.3 million.

	1976	1977
	$C (thousands)	
Revenues	2 454 501	2 656 725
Expenses	2 321 573	2 492 828

INVESTMENTS

In efforts to build a foundation for greater productivity CN Rail continues to invest heavily in new equipment and major improvements. Spending in 1979 totalled $300.6 million with major investments allocated for: track improvements ($125 833 000); 360 new freight wagons ($18.2 million); new line construction ($9 372 000); track maintenance machinery ($14 156 000); shops or repair facilities ($20 016 000); yards and terminals ($6 852 000); signalling ($3 710 000); communications ($1 460 000); and bridges and buildings ($14 960 000).

MOTIVE POWER AND ROLLING STOCK

CN's locomotive fleet on 1.435 m tracks in 1979 totalled 1 774 units: 14 electric locomotives; 1 760 diesel-electrics (1 473 road haul and 287 switching units). Rolling stock included 95 571 freight wagons; 1 120 passenger cars (including six multiple units and 44 diesel mechanical railcars); and 8 365 miscellaneous cars.
Stock working 1.067 m gauge lines include 51 diesel-electric road haul locomotives, 1 672 freight wagons, 41 passenger cars and 261 miscellaneous cars.
New locomotives delivered in 1977 were: 50 diesel-electric road freight (3 000 hp); 20 diesel-electric road switchers (2 000 hp).

ELECTRIFICATION

Total electrified route length (1979) was 27 miles (43.5 km). Following several studies CN Rail told the Ontario Royal Commission on Electric Power in January 1979 that it sees no major or clear advantages in railway electrification at present, and probably not for several decades. Instead CN expects developments in the future use of fossil fuels; the railway has been using synthetic crude oil produced from the Athabaska tar sands for about ten years.

PERMANENT WAY

New lines projected (length, location): Total of 480 miles between 1975 and 1985. Line north from Terrace, British Columbia, will be about 270 miles; lines to carry iron ore are projected in northern Quebec (100 miles) and northern Ontario (80 miles); a 10 mile line is projected in northern Ontario to serve proposed pulp and paper mill; in northern Manitoba a 20 mile line is projected to serve a Nelson River power development.
Rail, types and weights: Current sections being bought are 132 RE (2 564 miles in track); 115 RE (4 055 miles in track); and 100 ARA-A (7 556 miles in track). Balance is 31 different older sections 130 to 50 lbs/yard.
Sleepers cross ties type:

	Wood		Concrete (CN 60A)
	Main lines	Branch lines	Main lines
Thickness:	7" or 6"	6"	8" at rail seat
Spacing:	3 110 per mile	2 840 per mile	2 640 per mile
Rail fastenings types used:	6" or 5½" × ⅝" track spikes		Pandrol fastenings

Welded rail:
Total length of track laid 31 December 1975: 4 324.42 CWR*; 1 752.47 SWR†; total 6 076.89.
Length laid in 1975 during year: 660.45 mi CWR, 3.68 mi SWR, total 664.13.
Notes: *CWR Continuous Welded Rail (over 400 ft long).
†SWR Short Welded Rail (sections less than 400 ft long).
Standard method of welding: Rails are electric pressure flash butt welded into lengths of about 1 170 ft in central plants, and after laying are field welded into longer lengths by alumino thermic process.

VIA RAIL

Via Rail Canada Ltd
1801 McGill College Avenue, Suite 1300, Montreal, Quebec

Telephone: (514) 286 2311

President and chairman: J. F. Roberts
Vice-President, Marketing: G. C. Campbell
Vice-President, Development and Planning: R. Bechamp
Vice-President, Operations: E. H. Shute
Vice-President, Via Atlantic: A. W. Raftus
Vice-President, Via Quebec: J. L. Moisan
Vice-President, Via Ontario: A. R. Campbell
Vice-President, Via West: H. F. Murray

Via Rail took over all Canadian passenger operations on 1 April 1978. The new company was incorporated on 12 January 1977 as a subsidiary of Canadian National, although it is neither comprised in CN's railway operation nor consolidated in its accounts. To meet Government objectives under the new railway passenger policy announced by Transport Minister Otto Lang on 29 January 1976, Via Rail Canada was set up to manage all railway passenger services in Canada including services operated "over railway lines and services substituting for an ancillary to passenger services operating over railway lines but excluding commuter rail services and the carriage of goods." Via Rail contracts with the Government of Canada for the provision of railway passenger services specified by the minister. It contracts with any railway company for the operation of such services and agrees with non-railway entities for goods and services incidental to the provision of railway passenger services and with non-railway transportation firms for the provision of services such as bus services which substitute rail passenger services. It manages all railway passenger services and related facilities and activities within plans and budgets approved by the Government, including but not necessarily limited to management and performance of customer services (on-board services, information, reservations, fares and baggage handling), store functions, handling claims, complaints and accounting.
Via Rail is acquiring or leasing rolling stock and facilities required to provide passenger services and is to prepare programmes for the modification or acquisition of new equipment and facilities.
It will be their responsibility to develop recommendations for new or revised routes, schedules and services to meet the Government of Canada objectives, to recommend a pricing programme for transportation and on-board services, arrange for the transfer to Via Rail of such employees of CN and CP as may be required for the performance by Via Rail of its obligations.

TRAFFIC

In Canada during 1978 there were about 180 passenger trains a day, about 16 mixed trains and about 30 chartered buses. In 1977 CN and CP carried a total of about seven million passengers, about 19 200 passengers a day.
Via Rail believes the market for Canadian passenger services is 100 to 400 miles (161 to 644 km). With new LRC (light, rapid, comfortable) trainsets on the way, President J. Frank Roberts hopes that the distance can be increased to 400 to 500 miles (644 to 805 km). At present almost 92 per cent of all Canadian inter-city passenger journeys of 500 miles (805 km) or less are made by private car: 4.2 per cent travel by bus, 2.7 per cent by air and 1.2 per cent by rail.

FINANCES

Losses in the railway passenger business in 1976 in Canada were $260 million. Under the 1967 National Transportation Act, the government picks up 80 per cent of that loss. In 1976 railways had to absorb a $55 million loss. Via Rail expects the loss to reach $400 million by 1980 and $500 million by 1982 if nothing is changed. But with the institution of Via Rail and the government picking up 100 per cent of the loss, Via Rail officers forecast the loss in 1982 as $238 million.
Via Rail's estimated operating revenues for 1978 are about $115 million.

INVESTMENTS

Via Rail forecasts about $250 million in capital spending over 1979-83, about $30 million a year for equipment and about $20 million a year for other needs.

MOTIVE POWER AND ROLLING STOCK

By mid-1978 Via Rail had ordered ten trainsets of LRC (light, rapid, comfortable) equipment for delivery by November 1979. The system has 96 self-propelled Budd RDC cars built during 1954/56; some are being rebuilt as prototypes.

CP RAIL

Canadian Pacific Limited
Windsor Station, Montreal, Quebec H3C 3E4

Telephone: 395 5151
Telegrams: CANPACRY

Chairman and Chief Executive Officer: I. D. Sinclair
President: F. S. Burbridge
Vice-President, Special Projects: K. Campbell
Vice-President and Secretary: J. C. Ames
Vice-President, Adminstration: R. T. Riley
Vice-President, Corporate Development: J. A. McDonald

Law Department
Vice-President and General Counsel: D. S. Maxwell, Q.C.

Finance and Accounting
Vice-President, Finance and Accounting: J. P. T. Clough

CP Rail
Executive Vice-President: W. W. Stinson
Vice-President, Operations and Maintenance: C. R. Pike
Vice-President, Industrial Relations: J. C. Anderson
Vice-President, Purchases and Stores: J. M. Bentham
Vice-President, Marketing and Sales: R. C. Gilmore
Vice-President, Pacific Region: J. D. Bromley
Vice-President, Prairie Region: J. W. Malcolm
Vice-President, Eastern Region: R. S. Allison
Vice-President, Atlantic Region: G. E. Benoit
Assistant Vice-President, Marketing: D. C. Coleman
Assistant Vice-President, Sales: C. C. Watson
General Manager, Coastal Marine Operations: R. L. Purdy
General Manager, Intermodal Services: R. A. Teoli
General Manager, Pricing: J. L. Difruscia
General Manager, Grain and Passenger Services: W. H. Somerville
General Manager, Overseas Trade: G. H. Creighton
Chief of Transportation: J. H. Geddis
Chief Engineer: J. Fox
Chief Mechanical Officer: W. Mummery

The title "Canadian Pacific Limited" is used to identify an integrated multimodal transportation enterprise which includes operation of trains, trucks, ships, aeroplanes and telecommunications, as well as hotels and resource development undertakings through Canadian Pacific Investments Ltd.
CP Rail operates 17 000 miles of track extending from the Maritimes to the Pacific coast and controls another 4 700 miles in the USA. Its equipment includes more than 65 000 freight cars, 1 300 diesel locomotives and 40 pieces of passenger equipment.
The railway has developed sophisticated unit train systems for moving bulk commodities such as coal and sulphur; has one of North America's most advanced automated freight classification yards at Calgary to handle rapidly-increasing freight shipments to and from the Pacific coast; provides piggyback service (the movement of highway trailers on railway flatcars) and domestic container service across the country and operates commuter passenger train services in the provinces of Quebec and Ontario.
CP Rail has played a leading role in the development of container traffic in Canada. The railway is a joint owner of Brunterm Limited, a $4 million container terminal at Saint John, NB. CP Rail's network of lines stretches from coast to coast with important extensions in the USA in the states of Vermont, New York, Illinois, Wisconsin, Minnesota and North Dakota.

TRAFFIC AND FINANCIAL

Net income from CP Rail in 1978 was $C63.5 million, an increase of $8.7 million from $51.1 million in 1976. The increase was primarily due to an increase in freight charges, more remunerative traffic carried, improved operating efficiency and productivity gains in equipment and track maintenance. Canadian economic growth and a moderation in the rate of inflation also contributed to improved earnings. Wage rates were up 7 per cent in 1978, diesel fuel went up by more than ten per cent and prices of other railway materials increased by more than ten per cent.
During 1979 and the latter half of 1978, CP Rail made a number of service and operating improvements designed to increase the efficiency of the railway.
CP Rail has embarked on a major programme of transcontinental domestic containerisation using new 44 ft 3 in *(14.2 m)* containers designed to provide the same cubic capacity as highway trailers. Equipment ordered for the $11 million first phase of the operation includes 375 new containers, 100 new flatcars and 100 new highway chassis. The first phase of the operation began in October 1979 from Montreal and Toronto to Calgary, Edmonton and Vancouver and back. The second phase of the operation will begin in 1980 when a new order for $23 million worth of similar equipment is delivered.
In November 1979 CP Rail opened two new double-tracking projects in the Rocky Mountains of British Columbia designed to substantially increase mainline capacity to the west coast. One runs 4.5 miles *(7.2 km)* between Revelstoke and Clanwilliam and cost $10.9 million. The other runs 11 miles *(17.7 km)* between Salmon Arm and Notch Hill and cost $13.9 million. A third section of 5.5 miles *(8.9 km)* from Lake Louise to Stephen costing $12 million will open in late 1980, while a fourth section of 19 miles *(30.6 km)* is being surveyed just east of the Rodgers pass for the construction of new track and an eight-mile *(12.9 km)* tunnel. This project is estimated to cost $200 million.
In 1979 the railway established in Montreal a new system car management centre designed to monitor the movement and allocation of cars. By co-ordinating car requirements and routing patterns the railway expects to achieve a five per cent improvement in car utilisation during the first year of operation. One manifestation of the new car management approach is the development of special high-priority empty car trains. These trains are designed to ensure that high-demand cars are returned as quickly as possible from western Canada to eastern Canada where they are needed for westbound shipments.
As an expansion of CP Rail's car management policy, the company is introducing solid trains for the transport of potash from western Canada to the mid-west USA. In mid-1979 CP Rail's solid trains of automobiles from Ontario to the West carried their 300 000th vehicle.
During 1979 CP Rail also introduced a new high-speed rail change-out machine. It was one feature of a capital expenditure programme of approximately $190 million. Of this, approximately $50 million was for 25 new locomotives and 485 new cars and approximately $140 million was for fixed plant improvements. Under the programme, some 500 miles *(804.7 km)* of track was upgraded with new rail, ties and ballast.
The company's automated repetitive way-billing system, "Fastway", was fully implemented in 1979 and handled its 1 000 000th way-bill.
Also of significance in 1979 was the signing of a negotiated, three-year labour contract with all railway employees which provides for a 26 per cent salary increase over three years. The settlement also allows the railway to gradually introduce the reduction of freight train crews on most of its routes in Canada.
VIA Rail Canada took over all inter-city rail passenger services from CP Rail during 1979, thereby eliminating one non-compensatory company service. The company still loses up to $5 million annually providing suburban commuter services in the Montreal area.
CP Rail also incurred uncompensated losses exceeding $90 million transporting grain. While no action has been taken by government to relieve the railway of this burden, there is growing recognition that some way must be found to ensure that the full cost of transporting grain by rail be paid.

RAIL REVENUE

	1977	*1978*
	(in thousands)	
Freight revenue	$C1 112 099	$C1 235 376
Passenger service	21 541	28 873
Other railway	35 878	41 097
Coastal steamships	14 763	22 109
Government payments	102 111	100 980
	$C1 286 392	$C1 428 435

TRAFFIC

	1978
Total freight ton-km	84 654 539 000
Total freight tonnage	82 802 411
Total passenger-km	432 738 955
Total passengers carried	3 403 745

MOTIVE POWER AND ROLLING STOCK

CP Rail's fleet of diesel-electric locomotives comprise 1 047 road units and 224 switchers. The road units range from 1 500 hp to 4 000 hp, built by MLW-Worthington and General Motors. The railroad operates approximately 40 pieces of passenger equipment. The freight car fleet comprises approximately 65 000 cars.
In early 1979, CP Rail ordered 24 new 3 000 hp locomotives from the diesel division of General Motors of Canada Ltd for delivery in 1979.
The SD40-2 six-axle diesel electric units are valued at more than half a million dollars each, and have become the backbone of CP Rail's motive power fleet. The 70-ft, 197-ton locomotives have been instrumental in increasing the railway's freight handling capacity.
CP Rail's fleet of 65 000 (Aug 1977) freight cars includes more than 30 different types of specialised equipment. There are two and three-level auto transporters with longitudinally cushioned ("floating") superstructures; slurry cars for mineral concentrates in semi-liquid form; container and piggyback flatcars; insulated boxcars for the protection of cargo from Canada's harsh climate; bulkhead-end flatcars for durable goods such as building products; covered hopper cars for weather-sensitive dry bulk commodities; and gondola cars for unit trains which load and unload on the move.

INTERMODAL SERVICES

One of the familiar names in Canadian transportation circles, CP Rail Piggyback Services has become known as CP Rail Intermodal Services, combining the railway's piggyback and container handling operations.

In addition to the line haul movement of highway trailers, the railway's Intermodal Services group has responsibility for the handling of containers between Canada's east and west coast ports and a network of inland terminals across the country, as well as responsibility for the development and operation of the inland terminals themselves.

Upon arrival at any of CP Rail's 52 TOFC (piggyback) or 17 container handling facilities, containers are transferred to local delivery trucks which make final deliveries to customers and pick up new traffic.

Intermodal Services handled approximately 130 000 trailers and 180 000 TEU containers in 1976.

The movement of import and export containers grew from 74 283 TEUs in 1972, when Intermodal Services took over, to approximately 190 000 TEUs in 1977—an increase of more than 130 per cent.

Domestic containerisation, a natural outgrowth of trailer-on-flatcar movements within Canada, is a comparatively new aspect of Intermodal Services.

CP Rail has also developed 81 ft container flatcars with cushioned couplers that can carry four 20 ft or two 40 ft containers, all loaded to maximum weight.

TOFC (Piggyback)

Intermodal Services has established a coast-to-coast network of 52 TOFC terminals from which it is possible to serve any location in Canada with highway access and, via connections with US railways, to virtually any point in North America.

Terminal to terminal TOFC service is provided for motor common carriers and private industry semi-trailers. Door-to-door trailer service is provided in railway-owned semi-trailers. The most-used TOFC service, one which involves shipping goods in railway-owned trailers, has grown 700 per cent since 1967.

The TOFC side of Intermodal Services has five basic plans:

Plan 1: CP Rail supplies the flatcar and handles a trailer of a "for-hire" common motor carrier containing truck-billed traffic. The rail movement is on a ramp-to-ramp basis, confined to points between which the motor carrier has authority to operate by highway.

Plan 2: The railway handles traffic directly from the shipper to the consignee on rail billing and uses railway-owned trailers and flatcars.

Plan 3: The railway supplies the flatcars for movement of trailers owned by private shippers, not common motor carriers.

Plan 4: The shipper supplies the trailer and flatcar. The railway provides only the motive power.

Plan 5: A system of joint rail/truck rates. The rates serve to extend the territory of each carrier into that of the other and permit them to handle shipments originating in, or destined to, the territory of the other.

Another type of piggyback movement, to which no plan number has been assigned, is the handling of new or used empty semi-trailers on piggyback flatcars. These are mostly new trailers being shipped by the trailer manufacturers to the purchaser.

CONSULTING SERVICES

Canadian Pacific Consulting Services Limited is a broadly-based engineering, transportation and economic consultant to governments and business around the world. The company can call on professional, technical and operating personnel in the Canadian Pacific group to meet the specific engineering, research, economic, marketing or supervisory requirements of projects anywhere in the world.

Since its formation in 1969, CPCS has carried out major projects in Canada, Australia, Indonesia, Malaysia, Tunisia, the Congo, Cameroon, Venezuela, Ghana, Togo, Panama, Costa Rica, Nicaragua, Zambia, Nigeria, Turkey, Egypt, Brazil, Algeria and Thailand.

CARTIER RAILWAY

(Cie de chemin de fer Cartier)
Port Cartier, Quebec G58 2H3

President: L. J. Patterson
Vice-President: L. S. Heyborne
General Manager: R. L. Boudreau
General Superintendant, Transport: J. R. Robertson
Divisional Superintendant, Railway Operations: H. R. McKay
Divisional Superintendant, Railway Maintenance: J. L. Leblanc
Chief Engineer, Transport: P. D. Giacomin
Director of Purchases: G. S. Peniston
Superintendant, Signalling and Communications: L. R. Martin

Gauge: 1.435 m
Route length: 449 km

On 10 December 1960 the 191 mile (307.4 km) long railroad that carried an anticipated volume of eight MM NLT per year of iron ore concentrate from Lac Jeannine (mine and concentrator site) to Port Cartier, (harbour site) was completed. On 11 April 1961 the first ore train left Lac Jeannine for Port Cartier with 31 ore cars. In 1972 an 86 mile (138.4 km) long railroad extension was built to Mt Wright where a second concentrator was being built for another iron ore mine exploitation. This increased anticipated iron ore concentrate transportation by 18 MM NLT per year.

In 1975/76 a 3 mile (4.8 km) long bypass was constructed to transport crude ore from Fire Lake (mine site) (which was opened to compensate for the closing of the Lac Jeannine mine) to Lac Jeannine (concentrator site). Also in 1975/76 13 additional sidings were built for these late mining developments.

The anticipated volume to be transported on the railroad at full production level forecast (ie by 1980) is as follows: 18.4 MM NLT of iron ore concentrate between Mt Wright and Port Cartier (260 miles, 418.4 km); 14.5 MM NLT of crude ore between Fire Lake and Lac Jeannine (60 miles, 96.6 km); 6.0 MM NLT of iron ore concentrate between Lac Jeannine and Port Cartier (191 miles, 307.4 km).

TRAFFIC

	1976	1977	1978*
		(thousands)	
Freight tonne-km	8 152 875	9 445 464	3 963 595
Freight tonnage	15 588	16 828	8 184

*Figures for the first nine months.

MOTIVE POWER AND ROLLING STOCK

Total fleet consists of 54 diesel-electric live haul locomotives and 2 000 freight wagons.

DIESEL LOCOMOTIVES

Class	Axle Arrangement	Transmission	Rated power hp	Tractive effort continuous at lb (kg)	mph (km/h)	Max. speed mph (km/h)	Wheel dia. in (mm)	Total Weight Tons	Length ft in (mm)	No. built	Year first built	Builders: Mechanical parts	Engine & Type	Transmission
RS	2-2	Elec	1 750	60 000 (27 216)		65 (104.6)	40 (1 016)	130	56' 2" (17 120)	7	1960	GM (London)	GM Diesel & V-16	GM
RS	2-2	Elec	1 800	64 900 (29 439)		65 (104.6)	40 (1 016)	129	56' 11¾" (17 367)	7	1960	MLW (Montreal)	251- & V-12	MLW
RS	3-3	Elec	2 400	96 530 (43 786)		65 (104.6)	40 (1 016)	193	67' 1" (20 447)	6	—	Alco (New York)	251-B & V-16	Alco
RS	3-3	Elec	3 000	103 000 (46 721)		65 (104.6)	40 (1 016)	195	69' 6" (21 298)	10	1966	Alco (New York)	251-E & V-16	Alco
RS	3-3	Elec	3 600	104 000 (47 174)		65 (1 016)	40	186 (21 298)	69' 10"	16	1970-3	MLW (Montreal)	251-F & V-16	MLW
RS	3-3	Elec	3 600	108 000 (48 989)		65 (104.6)	40 (1 016)	194.2	69' 6" (21 184)	3	1968	Alco (New York)	251- & V-16	Alco
RS	3-3	Elec	3 600	108 000 (48 989)		65 (104.6)	40 (1 016)	200	69' 10" (21 285)	5	1975	MLW (Montreal)	251-F & V-16	MLW

QUEBEC NORTH SHORE AND LABRADOR RAILWAY

PO Box 1000, Sept-Iles, Quebec G4R 4L5

Chairman: R. F. Anderson
President: M. B. Mulroney
Executive Vice-President: R. Geren
Senior Vice-President: J. B. Galligan
Senior Vice-President: W. F. Miller
Assistant Secretary: L. A. Halsey
Manager: G. A. Dolliver

Gauge: 1.435 m
Route length: 638.77 km

Construction of the 356 miles (572.9 km) of main track between the port of Sept-Iles and Schefferville commenced in September 1950 and was completed February 1954. This construction required the operation of the largest civilian airlift in history. A branchline of 38 miles (61.2 km) between mileage 224 and Carol Lake was completed in May 1960. 40 per cent of the mileage is curved track. The first trains from Schefferville in 1954 consisted of 105 cars with three GP-9 locomotives. The size of trains were gradually increased to their present length of 240 car locotrol trains with four SD-40 locomotives.

TRAFFIC

	1976	1977
	(thousands)	
Freight tonne-km	16 000 000	16 000 000
Freight-tonnage	32 800	36 080
Passenger-km	8 120	8 800
Passenger journeys	19.3	21.2

FINANCIAL

	1976	1977
	($C)	
Revenues	64 000 000	71 000 000
Operating expenses	58 000 000	63 000 000

MOTIVE POWER AND ROLLING STOCK

The fleet at the end of 1978 consisted of 65 diesel-electric line haul and 16 diesel-electric switching locomotives, 572 freight wagons, 3 600 ore cars and 191 miscellaneous freight train cars.

DIESEL LOCOMOTIVES

Class	Axle arrange-ment	Trans-mission	Rated power (hp)	Max lb (kg)	Tractive effort Continuous at lb (kg)	mph (km/h)	Max speed mph (km/h)	Wheel diameter in (mm)	Total weight (tons)	Length ft in (mm)	Year first built	Builders Mechanical parts	Engine & type	Transmission
SD-40	C-C (0660)	Elec	3 000	84 000 (38 000)	84 000 (38 000)	11.1 (17.86)	71 (114.26)	40 (1 016)	185	65' 8" (20 015)	(1966-71)	GM	GM	GM
SD40-2	C/C (0660)	Elec	3 000	84 000 (38 000)	84 000 (38 000)	11.1 (17.86)	71 (114.26)	40 (1 016)	185	68' 10" (20 980)	1972	GM	GM	GM
GP-9	B-B (0440)	Elec	1 750	48 000 (22 000)	48 000 (22 000)	11.1 (17.86)	71 (114.26)	40 (1 016)	120	56' 7" (17 247)	(1954-60)	GM	GM	GM

WHITE PASS AND YUKON ROUTE
PO Box 4070, Whitehorse, Yukon Territory YIA 3TI

President and Executive Officer: J. F. Fraser
General Manager, Railroad: W. A. Hisman

Gauge: 915 mm
Route length: 178 km

The White Pass & Yukon Route railway, consisting of British Columbia-Yukon Railway, British Yukon Railway, Pacific & Arctic Railway & Navigation Co, was built during 1898-1900 to transport men and supplies to the goldfields of the Klondike. The 110.7 mile (178 km) narrow-gauge railway operates all year round between Skagway, Alaska and Whitehorse, Yukon. Originally financed by British interests and constructed under the supervision of Canadian contractor Michael Heney, the railway, part of The White Pass & Yukon Corporation Ltd is totally Canadian owned.
The White Pass railway carried general freight for a declining Yukon population until

1942 when the US Army leased the railway for the duration of World War II to haul material for the construction of the Alaska Highway. At the end of the war new mines came into operation in the Yukon, the railway became part of the White Pass world-leading innovator of integrated ship, train, truck and freight service. The railway underwent major upgrading in 1969 and the general upgrading programme has continued.

TRAFFIC

	1976/77
Freight tonne	271 235 476
Freight tonnage	750 644
Passenger journeys	75 630

MOTIVE POWER AND ROLLING STOCK
The White Pass has 19 line haul and two switching diesel-electric locomotives on the fleet roster although four are at present in storage. Rolling stock consists of 378 freight train wagons and 30 passenger coaches.

LINE HAUL DIESEL LOCOMOTIVES

Class	Axle arrange-ment	Trans-mission	Rated power (hp)	Max lb (kg)	Tractive effort continuous at lb (kg)	mph (km/h)	Max speed mph (km/h)	Wheel diameter in (mm)	Total weight (tons)	No. built	Year first built	Builders Mechanical parts	Engine & type	Transmission
90	C-C	Diesel-electric	900	50 000	24 000		40	34	85	11	1954	General Electric	Alco Power 251B	General Electric
01	C-C	Diesel-electric	1 200	53 590	35 000		65	36	105	8	1969	MIW	Alco Power 251D	General Electric

CHILE
CHILEAN STATE RAILWAYS
Empresa de Los Ferrocarriles Del Estado de Chile
Alameda Libertador Bernardo O'Higgins, 924 Santiago

Telephone: 382577

Director General: Ing. Juan E. Ossa Gatica
Subdirector (operations): Ing. Juan E. Ortiz Navarro
Subdirector (administration and personnel): Abogado Santiago Santa Cruz Fernández
Department Heads:
Planning: Ing. Victor Celis Celis
Finances: Ing. Antun Domic Bezic
Traction (maintenance and production): Ing. Anibal Gajardo Prieto
Traffic: Ing. Guido Fregonara Costa
Chief Engineer: Ing. Guillermo Zenteno Peyrin
Personnel: Sr. Pedro Javier Moreno G.

Gauge:	1.676 m	1.435 m	1.00 m
Route length:	4 274 km	235.5 km	3 443 km

The complete system consists of:—
Red Norte (Northern Network): Extends 1 527 km from La Calera, near Valparaiso, change-of-gauge junction with Southern section, northward to Pueblo Hundido. It is completely dieselised.

Red Sur (Southern Network): Extends 4 601 km from Puerto Montt northward through Santiago to Valparaiso. The main line is electrified between Santiago and Concepcion, north from Santiago and west to Valparaiso and east to Los Andes. All branch lines on this section are diesel-operated.

FC Arica: Extends 227 km from Arica, on the coast close to Peruvian border, to Visvir where it connects with Bolivian section to La Paz. A 24 mile (39 km) section is operated by rack system.

FC Iquique-Pueblo Hundido: Extends southwards from Iquique on the coast to connection with Red Norte at Pueblo Hundido. All metre-gauge except for 155 miles (250 km) of 4 ft 8½ in (1.435 m) gauge, and a 3-rail combined gauge section of 79 miles (126 km).

FC Transandino: Extends from Los Andes at the foot of the Andes Mountains to Caracoles on the Chile-Argentina border, connecting with Argentine State Railways (Northwest Region). Electrified; part rack rail.

Augusta Victoria-Socompa Line: Connects at Socompa with Argentine State Railways (Northwest Region), giving through service to Buenos Aires. Operated by FC Iquique-Hundido.

PERMANENT WAY
A number of proposals for line renewal have been put to the Government for approval. These include:— line renewal in the North and South networks involving a total of 281 km with rail type K (119 RE) over 190 km; type Z (100 RA) over 66 km and type Y (80 AS) over 25 km; and line renewal over 155 km of the international railway from Arica to La Paz including renewal of signalling and communications over the whole of the Chilean section (206 km) and the acquisition of locomotives.
Several new lines are projected for future construction, including: Santiago—Valparaiso (108 km); Angol—Pidina (38 km); Hualqui—Cabrero (53 km); Curanilahue—Los Alamos (21 km); Nos—Puente Alto (17 km).

Suburban electric trainset, built in Argentina for FFCEE for service between Valparaiso

New electric switch board panel at Curico, 180 km south of Santiago

Petroleum block train awaiting unloading in the Concepción region, 600 km south of Santiago

Standard rail: Type K, 119 lb/yd *(59 kg/m);* Type Z, 100.9 lb *(50 kg);* Type Y, 80.7 lb *(40 kg);* Type U, 64.5 lb *(32 kg/m);* Type F, 60.5 lb *(30 kg);* Type P, 51.4 lb *(25.5 kg);* Type L, 50.4 lb *(25 kg);* and older rail of varying weights.
1.676 m gauge: Types K, Z, Y; 76.6 lb *(38 kg).*
1.435 m gauge: Type F; also 85 lb *(42.16 kg).*
1.000 m gauge: Types Y, U, L, P; also 70.6 lb *(35 kg),* 55.7 lb *(27.5 kg),* and 54.4 lb *(27 kg).*
0.600 m gauge: 50.4 lb *(25 kg)* and 30.3 lb *(15 kg).*
Sleepers (cross ties): Wood, 5.9 in *(15 cm)* deep × 7.9 in *(20 cm)* wide; except on rack rail section of FC Transandino:—metal.
Spacing, main lines: 3 025 per mile *(1 880 per km).*
Spacing, branch lines: 2 415 per mile *(1 500 per km).*
Spacing, rack rail: 1 835 to 3 100 per mile *(1 140-1 930 per km).*

ELECTRIFICATION
Route length of electrification at December 31, 1977: 1 103 km.
Lines planned for electrification include: Laja—Temuco (189 km); Alameda—Cartagena (117.7 km).

TRAFFIC
(figures in thousands)

Year	No. of passengers	Passenger km	Goods carried (tonnes)	Tonnes/ km
1961	20 158	1 738 567	8 280	1 506 590
1968	20 879	2 071 193	13 478	2 186 789
1969	21 684	2 209 600	13 522	2 173 000
1971	20 750	2 706 000	14 128	2 250 000
1972	24 900	3 028 000	12 381	2 167 000
1973	28 193	3 467 190	12 485	2 175 030
1974	26 877	2 815 596	12 873	1 929 068
1975	20 554	2 095 588	11 086	1 472 562
1976	21 800	2 356 100	10 700	1 650 900
1977	18 845	2 350 100	9 800	1 622 200

FINANCIAL

	1975	1976 (Pesos)	1977
Revenues (thousands)	369 919 970	2 075 700	2 018 800
Expenses (thousands)	526 082 377	2 577 200	2 697 900

MOTIVE POWER AND ROLLING STOCK
Locomotives in service (1977)

steam	305
electric	133
diesel electric	231
electric railcars	52
diesel railcars	16
passenger coaches	764
freight wagons	9 980

SIGNAL AND TRAIN CONTROL INSTALLATIONS
Existing signalling between Valparaiso and Talca is being changed to electric block and colour light signals. Total route length is 273 miles *(440 km).*
Supplier: Union Switch and Signal, USA.
Centralised Traffic Control (CTC) has been installed between Talca and Puerta Montt. The line is divided into 5 sections. The first 3 sections, Talca-Chillán, Chillán-Concepcion, and San Rosendo-Temuco, are controlled from Concepcion. The other 2 sections, Temuco-Valdivia and Antilhue-Puerto Moutt, are controlled from Valdivia. Total route length is 510 miles *(820 km).*
Supplier: Westinghouse Brake & Signal Co. Ltd., England.

One of 24 new electric locomotives built under licence from Fiat of Italy in 1976. The locomotives are rated at 1 715 hp

Santiago's Mapocho station—new point of departure for rapid trainset service between the Chilean capital and Concepción

Suburban electric trainset running since 1972 in and around Santiago

ARICA—LA PAZ RAILWAY (FCALP)

Ferrocarril de Arica a la Paz
Casilla 9-D, Arica

Director General: Jorge Correa G.
Administrator (delegate): Fernando Ipinza M.
Secretary: Manuel Avendaño L.
Chief of Traction and Workshops: Gustavo Moya R.
Chief of Way and Works: Roberto Vergara T.
Chief of Transport: Sergio Leal L.
Chief of Accounting: Mario Hidalgo M.
Chief of Personnel: Victor Cisternas Z.

Gauge: 1.00 m.
Route length: 206 km (Chile section).

For more than half a century the Arica to La Paz Railway, belonging to the Chilean State Railways, has been railing freight and passengers between Chile and Bolivia. Its origin goes back to the years following the end of the War of the Pacific (1883) and its building was provided in the Peace and Friendship Treaty subscribed by the Chilean and Bolivian governments in 1904. The Chilean government financed the construction of the complete network of the line.
Because of its difficult mounting route, FCALP reflects one of the most remarkable examples of railway engineering. In turn, it represents "the shortest route from the Pacific to Bolivia", (its own slogan), covering 440 km between the port of Arica in Chile to the Bolivian capital city of La Paz. The difficulties arising out of its ascending layout to the Bolivian plateau and its high operational and maintenance costs are the main reasons for its low profitability.
A plan to streamline operations contemplates the up-dating of infrastructure, particularly a full renewal of the railtrack. About 70 km of the former 27.5 kg/plm rail on a 206 km section of the Chilean section have been replaced to date with Japanese 39.82 kg/plm Y track. Financing is being procured to purchase 3 new up-to-date saloon motorcoaches of a greater capacity to cover the passenger-tourist traffic in place of the existing stock which has already outrun its useful life.
The final studies entrusted to the Brazilian GEIPOT transport organisation with a view to completing the inter-continental rail network link between Arica (Chile) on the Pacific and Santos (Brazil) on the Atlantic, are now underway. The Government of Brazil has allocated the sum of $US 6 000 000 as its contribution to complete studies on the railroad layout connecting Aiguile and Santa Cruz. This represents approximately 300 km of track in Bolivian territory, which is the only missing connection in the Atlantic—Pacific intercontinental railway link. Work has been started by a Brazilian consulting firm with the co-operation of the Ministry of Transport of Bolivia. It is estimated that this new route will be completed and inaugurated by late 1980.

TRAFFIC	*1975*	*1976*	*1977*
Total freight tonne-km	24 511 879	17 404 645	18 773 937
Total freight tonnage	120 063	85 679	90 959
Total passenger-km	8 505 573	9 219 433	8 839 759
Total passenger journeys	43 363	41 781	42 563

MOTIVE POWER AND ROLLING STOCK

The Arica to La Paz Railway operates 8 General Electric diesel-electric, 1 320 hp locomotives; 3 General Electric 600 hp locomotives and 3 General Electric—3 000, 270 hp locomotives.
For its passenger service, FCALP operates 2 Schindler 360 hp saloon motor-coaches and 1 Schindler 360 hp first class motor-coach.
In 1969, the old rack-rail steam locomotives used up and down the line between Central and Puquios stations were replaced by the GE locomotives. The haulage capacity in this difficult sector is of 300 tonnes per train pulled by two locomotives.
Freight stock consists of 411 wagons: 313 BCt and DGt boxcars; 113 LMt, P5Ct and PCt flatcars; 10 double-deck motor vehicle carrying cars; 17 CCt container cars.

CHINA, PEOPLE'S REPUBLIC

CHINESE PEOPLE'S REPUBLIC RAILWAYS

Ministry of Railways, Peking

Minister of Railways: Tuan Chun-yi

Gauge: mainly 1.435 m
Route length: 50 000 km

ORGANISATION

The Ministry of Railways at present administers 20 railway bureaus and 16 sub-bureaus throughout China, as well as most of China's 33 locomotive and rolling stock factories via the Locomotive and Rolling Stock Factories Department.
The Chinese People's Republic Railways (CPRR) consists of six major regions or routes:
Northeast Region made up of three main lines, Harbin-Suiching, Harbin-Manchouli and Harbin-Talien, together with about 60 secondary lines.
Peking-Paotou and **Paotou-Lanchow lines** linking Peking with Inner Mongolia, Shansi, Hopei, Ningsia and Kansu.
Tientsin-Shanghai Railway which runs along the eastern seaboard through the North China Plain to Nanking (via the Yellow and Huai river basins) and Shanghai.
Lung-Hai and **Lanchow-Sinkiang lines** which link the Yellow Sea coast with the north-east frontier over 3 600 km.
Peking-Kwangchow running north-south through the Peking region and five provinces.
Southwestern Region, including Paochi-Chengtu, Chengtu-Chungking, Chengtu-Kunming, Yunau-Kwangsi and Hunan-Kweichow lines.
Following successful completion of the 1971-75 and 1975-79 Five Year Plans, major objectives completed include construction of new railway lines in the far west provinces of Tibet and Xinjiang which have so far been untapped by rail because of difficulty of access. In April 1978 China's Minister of Railways, Tuan Chun-yi, outlined the planned development of the rail network over 1979-87. The plan is basically aimed at increasing railway capacity, extending lines to remote regions and modernising existing facilities. The main features are construction of six new trunk lines; upgrading of nine existing trunk routes, including Peking-Canton and Tientsin-Shanghai; doubling of the 1 300 km line from Tientsin to Pukou and the 2 300 km Peking-Kwangchow line; increased use of electric and diesel motive power together with electrification of four trunk lines and lines converging on Peking; development of high-capacity wagons and lightweight passenger coaches; installation of heavy-duty rail on selected routes together with strengthening of bridges to take heavier axleloads; and doubling of railway capacity between 1979-81.

FREIGHT TRAFFIC

By the end of the first Five Year Plan (1953-57) the railway accounted for 63 per cent of all freight hauled, 77·8 per cent of tonne-km and 73 per cent of passenger-km. The railway now carries a slightly lesser proportion, hauling 945 million tonnes in 1975—59 per cent of the 1 598 million tonnes of freight moved by all modes. In 1978 an estimated 960 million tonnes were carried.
According to the last available official figures, in 1958 the average daily run per freight locomotive was 391 km; the average gross weight hauled per freight locomotive was 1 704 tonnes; the average daily efficiency per freight locomotive was 600 000 tonne-km; the average turn-round distance per freight wagon was 703·6 km; the average daily run per freight wagon was 255·6 km; the average stopping time per freight wagon per run was 10·4 hours; the average speed per freight train, including halts, was 25·7 km/h; average load per freight wagon was 37·5 tonnes; and the average daily efficiency per freight wagon was 6 596 tonne-km.
The efficiency of the Chinese railway system has almost certainly improved significantly since then.
Railways are still the dominant mode of freight transport in China. Even a light-traffic frontier line like the Kweiyang-Kunming carries an annual traffic of more than 3 million tonne-km per route-km. On such key lines as the Peking-Shenyang and the Peking-Wuhan, traffic densities have reportedly exceeded 25 million tonne-km per route-km.
The average wagon turnaround time in 1977 was reported as 3.4 days.
A major boost to freight transport was given in August 1978 with the introduction of a new national timetable when 1 000 new freight train services were introduced.

PASSENGER TRAFFIC

China's railways are critical links for passenger transport between major cities. The volume of passengers handled is immense. Even in 1958, the last year for which official data is available, approximately 346 million Chinese paid to travel by train. Between 1949 and 1958, the number of rail passengers increased by 236 per cent. Observers calculate that at present the railway is annually carrying between 450 and 500 million passengers, and the figure of 100 000 million passenger-km is expected to double by 1987.
The new timetable introduced in 1978 lists 87 new passenger services. All China's mainland provincial and autonomous regional capitals, with the exception of Lhasa, are now linked with Peking by express train. Faster and more frequent services are rapidly being introduced. Peking-Shanghai takes only 19 hours instead of the pre-1978 time of 20 hours 51 minutes, thanks to the introduction of expresses and fewer stops. Prime aim is to get average speeds up from 70 to 110 km/h.

MOTIVE POWER

China's modern locomotive park was originally based on Soviet-built stock, delivered between 1956 and 1959. Among the most significant of Soviet deliveries were about 1 000 of second-hand FD 2-102 class steam units. These relatively new and powerful locomotives represented a considerable upgrading of China's fleet of aging pre-war Consolidations, Mikados and so on. They were converted to Chinese gauge at Changchun and dubbed the 'Friendship' class. Soviet specialists also helped the Chinese to build the Heping ('Peace') steam locomotive—a more powerful 2-10-2 very similar to the Soviet LV 1-5-1 which was then just going out of production in the Soviet Union. The first prototype was assembled at Talien in 1956 and the Heping was in serial production by 1959.
European and Japanese locomotive builders entered the Chinese railway scene after 1960.
The first Chinese-built locomotive was a 2-8-2 constructed at Tsingtao in 1952. A 4-6-2 for passenger service and the Heping 2-10-2 for freight followed soon after. It was a practical move for the Chinese to build steam locomotives at a time when much of the rest of the world was moving over to diesel, bearing in mind the plentiful coal supplies available. In the late 1950s and early 1960s, however, a few prototypes of electric, diesel-electric and diesel-hydraulic designs were built. By the mid-1960s the Chinese had set up production line facilities for the 'Giant Dragon' and 'East Wind' series of locomotives. By 1975 China was producing about 530 locomotives annually—about 275 of which were diesel and 250 steam.
By 1975 it is thought China was producing about 530 locomotives a year, about 275 of which were diesel and 250 steam. Inventory was about 8 300 units. Production of locomotives increased about 16 per cent during the Fourth Five-Year Plan (1971-1975) while rail-freight turnover rose by 30 per cent to 458 000 million ton-kms. At the same rate, the PRC's production will be about 610-620 units by late 1980, when steam output should be minimal, and turnover will be about 595 000 million ton-kms.
In early 1978, Minister Tuan reported that only 13 per cent of trains were hauled by diesel or electric locomotives. By 1985, he said, the proportion should have increased to 60 per cent, with steam being gradually phased out.
Output of freight cars rose from 14 000 in 1971 to 18 500 in 1975, according to US Government estimates, a rise of 32 per cent Inventory in 1975 was about 237 000 units. By 1980 annual production should be about 24 000 units.
During the 1971-75 plan China's laid track increased by 12 per cent to 52 280 km; at the same rate China's total track should reach 58 000 km by late 1980.
To serve newly-electrified lines, Chinese builders have supplied new Shaoshan-type electric locomotives and orders were placed in 1974 with the Hans Beimler works of the German Democratic Republic for 30 type EL2 electric locomotives.
There are at present five Chinese plants building locomotives: at Dalian in Liaoning province; Datong in Shanxi province, building exclusively steam locomotives; in Sichuan and Guizhou provinces where new factories were set up in 1973.
At the start of the fourth plan, CPRR was operating a motive power fleet consisting of 12 per cent diesel-electric and diesel-hydraulic locomotives and 88 per cent of steam locomotives. Of the system's 1977 total of 10 000 locomotives, 80 per cent are steam and the remainder diesel-hydraulic, diesel-electric or electric. Since 1971 a total of 50 diesel locomotives have been purchased from Alsthom, France, each rated at 4 000 hp. In addition, six 24 ton diesel shunters were purchased from Japan in 1975 at a cost of $US 500 000 per unit.

Sales of foreign locomotives to China:
1968-72 Henschel
30 diesel-hydraulic CC 138 ton locos; max speed 120 km/h; length 23 610 mm; width 3 120 mm; height 4 570 mm; tractive effort (starting) 45 500 kg; Voith L820 hydrodynamic drives; gauge 1 435 mm; comprise ten NY6 4 600 hp (UIC), site rating 4 300 hp; with two MB16V652 diesel engines by MTU, and twenty NY7 5 400 hp. (UIC), site

A Henschel diesel-hydraulic locomotive for the Chinese railways

rating 5 000 hp, with two MA 12V 956 engines by MTU; bodies and cabs acoustically and thermally insulated, plus comprehensive heating system with Henschel WK200 boiler to keep engine, transmission oils and fuels warm; Behr cooling system; tank capacity 10 000 litres for 2 000 km range due to limited fuelling points.

1970-73 Alsthom—MTE
40 Co-Co, 7 300 hp electric locos for 5 400 km dc op. with silicon semi-conductors; for 25 kV/50Hz system; hauling capacity exceeding 36 tons at 4.5 km/h; energy recovery when braking 4 300 kW; numbered 6G 51-90; 138 tons; max speed 112 km/h; rated tractive effort of 353 kN at 55 km/h continuous; provision for multiple working on very heavy freight trains; gauge 1 435 mm.

1971-74 Alsthom—MTE
50 Co-Co, 4 000 hp diesel-electric 138 ton locos with single-C motor trucks; 3-phase continuous ac/dc transmission; max speed 100 km/h single; AGO V-16 ESHR motor by SACM; supplying 3 650 hp at 30°C, towing at 1 350 rpm; withstand —40°C without anti-freeze; able to maintain traction performance at 30 km/h with two engines coupled in multiple units tracking in one-way 5-km tunnels; freight use; numbered ND 4 1-50 by Chinese; tractive effort (starting) 48 000 kg; 23 020 mm long; width 3 290 mm; height 4 500 mm; gauge 1 435 mm; separate heating system; fuel capacity of 10 000 litres gives range of 2 000 km, two days normal use; large resistance banks provide dynamic braking at 4 000 hp; designed, when double-headed, to haul 5 000 ton freight train at 80 km/h on level, maintain 24 km/h hp and 25 km/h down 1.0 per cent gradient; also to haul 2 000 tons up 2.5 per cent grade and maintain 30-40 km/h down 2.5 per cent incline.

Early 70s East Germany
Heavy industrial electric locos 150 ton EL-1, 1 500 V dc overhead line op; 100-ton EL-2, with alternative 1 200-2 400 V dc rating; used in opencast mines, number unknown.

1973 Henschel
36 diesel locos, 5 500 hp, valued at $8 million.

1974 Nippon Sharyo Seizo Kaisha, Japan
Six 24 ton diesel locos valued at about $500 000; deal arranged via Nichimen.

1975 Electroputere, Romania
20 diesel-electric locos, 2 100 hp.

1978 Veb Hennigsdorf
90 electric locomotives for use in opencast lignite mines; to be standard machines series EL1 and EL2.

China: Estimated production of locomotives and freight cars 1970-75:

	Mainline Locomotives (Units)				Freight Cars (Units)
	Total	Steam	Diesel	Electric	
1970	435	250	180	5	12 000
1971	455	250	200	5	14 000
1972	475	250	220	5	15 000
1973	495	250	240	5	16 000
1974	505	250	250	5	16 800
1975	530	250	275	5	18 500

Chinese-made locomotives:
Aiming to the Sun, (Shang Yan) (SY), Tangshan. Construction, **(Jian She) (JS),** Tsingtao/Peking 2-7. 2-8-2 steam loco, trip and branch line work. 1952, 1958 steam 2-8-2 2 270 hp; 56 175 lbs TE; 54'' WD; 54 mph; Cyls: 22.8'' × 28''; BP: 220 psi; wgt: 201 317 lbs; TW: 70 600*.

East is Red, (Dong Hang Fong) (DFH), Tsingtao. **(Dong Fang Hong 4),** Chishuyen. 1968, 2 000 hp diesel hydraulic. 1976, 3 000 hp diesel hydraulic. 102 1 000 hp and 2 000 hp diesels shipped to Tanzania/Zambia.

East Wind, (Dong Feng W), Talien. 1 800 hp diesel loco remodeled in "design of a foreign diesel locomotive," used in Chengchow south locomotive section. According to NCNA "Most diesel locos used on major railways are of the "Dongfeng W" type for passenger services." In 1966, 2 000, 3 000 and 4 000 hp diesel electric versions noted.

(Dong Feng 4), Talien. Spring 1974, model at Canton Fair, with ac/dc electric transmission; 4 000 hp, 1 hr rating of diesel; 3 600 hp continuous rating.

Forward, (Qian Jin) (QJ), Tatung. 1965 (?), 2 .10 .2, 2 980 hp; 73 405 lbs TE; 59'' WD; 50 mph; Cyls: 25.6'' × 31.5''; BP: 220 psi; wft: 262 400 lbs; TW: 65 000.

Giant Dragon, (Ju Lung) (JL), Talien. 1963, series production 1965, 278 000 lbs, CC unit. Two 2 000 hp opposed piston diesel engines operate 1 350 kw dc generator. Traction capacity said to be 3 500 mt at 100 kW/h.

Liberation, (Jie Fang) (JF), 2-8-2, 1 545 hp, 52 985 lbs TE; 54'' WD; 54 mph; Cyls: 22.8'' × 28''; BP: 206 psi; wgt: 207 500 lbs; TW: 63 900.

Mao Tse-tung, Tsingtao. 2-8-0 or 2-8-2. Single steam loco rebuilt from foreign loco in 1946, had done 3 million miles by 1976.

Peace, (Heping) (HP), Changchun. Talien. 1956, 2-10-2 prototype 2 780 hp. 1959, max. 3 154 hp, 80 km/h. Total prod: 100 pa thru 1971. "Chinese designers borrowed heavily from the blueprints of the Soviet L-class 2-10-2 and threw in the best features of locomotives from other countries. The cylinder cocks were an American design; the blower was adapted from a Belgian design; and the self-adjusting wedges were Japanese. The Heping was given a mechanical stoker and lubricator, pneumatic rocking grates, and any other modern labour-saving device the Chinese could design. Crew comfort was a primary consideration. Inside the all-weather cabs are a small stove for tea and snacks, small changing room with a mirror and even a heater

for keeping the engineer's feet warm. The Heping allegedly can haul 80 per cent more than the Construction 2-8-2 on an 0.4 per cent grade at 25 mph, while burning 12 per cent less coal. No thought was given to making the Heping an oil burner because China had massive coal deposits. (Sizable petroleum reserves were not discovered and exploited until fairly recently). The Heping is estimated to weigh between 330 000 and 485 000 lbs." (Trains 11.72).**Peking (Beijing) (BJ),** Peking. 1958, steam loco. Also 3 000 hp diesels trial produced 1969.

Peking (Subway), (Beijing), Changchun. 1969, electric 750-V dc, 19 m cars; max speed: 80 km/h.

People, (Renmin) (RM), Pre-1956, 4-6-2 steam loco, 1 900 hp, 39 800 lbs TE; 70'' WD; 68 mph; Cyls: 22.4'' × 26''; BP: 220 psi; wgt: 198 000 lbs; TW: 70 600 lbs.

Red Flag (Hungqi) (HQ);, Talien. 1958, steam, freight.

Rocket, Changchun. 1960, small steam loco, 234 hp, wgt 54 426 lbs; rural and small mine use.

Satellite, (Wei Xing) (WX), Tsingtao. 1959, 1960, 1 000 hp diesel hydraulic, 2 000 hp version, wgt; 188 000 lbs; BB, speed to 85 mph.

Shaoshan, (Shaoshan) (SS), Tienhsin. 1969, 5 200 hp electric for 25 000 V 50 cycle, single phase ac system.

Victory, (Shengli) (SL), ?. 4-6-2 steam passenger loco, 1 600 hp, 37 220 lbs TE; 70'' WB; 68 mph; Cyls: 22.4'' × 26''; BP: 206 psi; wgt: 195 600 lbs; TW: 61 500 lbs.

Others:
NA, Canton. 1975, 380 hp steam loco, narrow-gauge.
NA, Tsingtao. 1959, 2 000 hp hydraulic transmission internal combustion loco.
T-6, Tsingtao. 1960, 1 500 hp steam passenger loco.
288, Tsingtao. Steam loco.
NA, Chuchou. Electric locos.
NA, Hsiangtan. 150 ton electric locos.
NA, Peking Feb. 7. 3 000 and 6 000 hp diesel hydraulic locos.
"2-8-2", Talien. 1956, 1 544 hp steam freight loco.
NA, Talien. 1959, 4 000 hp freight diesel; 2 000 hp diesel electric with electric transmission.
NA, Tatung. Gas turbine loco.
NA, Tientsin. Internal Combustion loco.
NA, Shenyang. Internal Combustion loco.

Chinese locomotive weights and lengths:

Locomotive Type	Total Weight of Locomotive With Coal and Water Cars (Tons)	Length of Locomotive With Coal and Water Cars (Metres)
XK₂	48	11.0
MG₄, ₅, ₆	66	17.6
DB₁	66	14.3
JF₈	69	19.8
KD₅	71	18.7
ET₁, ₈	74	14.3
DB₂	78	14.3
Dong-Fang-Hong (East is Red)	82	17.6
PL₂, ₉	86	20.9
KD₆, ₉	89	20.9
SL₉	95	22.0
KD₂	98	23.1
JF₃, ₅, ₇, ₁₂	99	22.0
JF₆, ₉, ₁₀, ₁₁, ₁₃	102	23.1
DK₁	102	23.1
SL₃	104	23.1
DK₂	105	23.1
Dong-Feng₂ (East Wind)	106	16.5
SL₁₂, ₁₃, ₁₄, ₁₅	109	24.2
KD₇	111	22.0
Dong-Feng (DF) (East Wind)	118	16.5
Sheng-Li (SL) (Victory)	120	25.3
Ren-Min (RM) (People's)	122	24.2
SL₅	123	25.3
Jien-She (JS) (Construction)	126	24.2
Jie-Fang (JF) (Liberation)	127	24.2
Shao-Shan	138	17.6
6Y₂	138	23.1
SL₇, ₈	140	27.2
JF₂, ₄	140	25.3
KF₁	144	30.8
Qian-Jin (QJ) (Forward)	154	29.7
FD	178	29.7

Alsthom 7 300-hp electric locomotive

Source: Table in *Railroad Yards,* Prepared by the North China College of Communications, Transportation Division; Published by the People's Communications Press, Peking, September 1973. 18 000 copies known printed in two separate printings. Second in October 1974.

ROLLING STOCK

At the end of the 1971-75 plan a total of 200 000 freight wagons were in operation. Of these, 100 000 are hopper or open type and 40 000 are tank wagons. Practically all the wagon fleet have a bogie capacity of 50 tonnes. Annual wagon production in China is 140 000 units.

CPRR appears to be stepping up purchases of passenger equipment from abroad. From Japan, Nippon Sharyo announced in 1978 that it had received an enquiry for 100 air-conditioned passenger coaches from China's Railway Technology and Equipment Corporation. And other Japanese builders, including Hitachi, Kawasaki and Tokyu Car, say they have also received enquiries from China for rolling stock. China has also asked companies from Japan, France, Federal Republic of Germany, Canada and Sweden to assist in the modernisation of the Changchun carriage works where production is scheduled to increase from 600 coaches a year at present to 2 000 by 1981.

The German Democratic Republic's rolling stock export group Maschinenexport, won an order in late 1978 from CPRR for 72 passenger coaches to be built by VEB Ammendorf and delivered in 1981.

ELECTRIFICATION

Two lines have now been electrified: Paochi-Chengtu energised in 1975 and Yangpingkuan-Ankang (356 km) completed early in 1977. A third is being electrified at CPRR's standard 25 kV 50 Hz: Chungking-Hsingfan (916 km) which is being converted together with other routes in Szechwan, Hupeh and Shensi; they all connect with the Paochi-Chengtu line and together will form a core network of high-capacity electrified lines in the western part of central China. Work is simultaneously proceeding on lines running in the west and southwest from Peking to link with the core network. In 1978 the east-west line from Taiyuan, capital of Shansi province, to Shihchiachuang (capital of Hopei province) was being electrified. Preliminary work was also in progress on the line from Taiyuan to Chining where it connects with the cut-off route under construction from Chang Chia Kou. The Chining-Paotou line is also being electrified.

The system employed is 25 000 V, single phase, 50-cycles, with overhead conductor. The French electrical industry has assisted in the development of 50-cycle electrification in China and technical assistance has also been made available by the USSR.

LINE PROJECTS

Most important of new trunk lines projected is the 2 200 km link between Lhasa, capital of Tibet, and the existing network in the province of Tsinghai. Construction started in about 1974 and more than 400 km of rail had been laid by mid-1978. Also under construction is a new trunk line running 474 km from Tulufan to Kuerhlo in China's far west. The first section was opened in 1979. Leaving the main Lanchow-Wulumuchi line at Tulufan (about 150 km southeast of Wulumuchi), the line runs across the Tulufan depression before veering west after Toksun to penetrate a spur of the Tienshan mountain range. The route emerges at Hoshuo before dropping to the Yenchi basin. The line will terminate at Kuerhle.

Other trunk lines to be completed by 1985 include the Taian (in Shantung province eastern China) to Chingyuan in Kansu province in the north west. The section from Hantan (Hopei province) to Changchih (Shansi province) was nearing completion at the end of 1978.

The 853 km Chih-Liu line and the Hunan-Kwangsi line were both near completion during 1978, as was the 870 km Sha-Tung line where experimental operation began in 1977.

A Japanese National Railways mission to Peking in 1978 reported that China is seeking co-operation for the design and construction of a high-speed line between Peking and Tientsin. It would use the existing route and would be electrified. Top speed would be 160 km/h.

PERMANENT WAY

Length of the Chinese People's Republic Railways in 1975 was 46 500 km—double the length reported in 1949. About 1 000 km of new track is being added, on average, every year; in 1970 more than 2 700 km was laid. Present track length is about 100 000 km. Standard rails are 50 kg/m.

For the first few years after 1949, the new government of China concentrated on restoring the existing network to a more serviceable condition, although the construction of new lines also began rather quickly. The remote but populous interior province of Szechwan saw its first railroad in 1952, when the Chengtu-Chungking was completed. The mid-1950s brought the completion of the Yingtan-Amoy on the coast opposite Taiwan, the mountainous Paoki-Chengtu, and the trans-Mongolian railway which shortened the train trip from Peking to Moscow by about 700 miles. Also, 1956 saw the building of the first railway bridge across the Yangtze River, at Wuhan. In the late 1950s the desert line from Paotow to Lanchow was completed, and then carried in two directions to Sining and Urumchi. Another bridge across the Yangtze, at Chungking, was also built at the close of the decade.

During the 1960s, despite the severe economic difficulties of the early years, several additional lines were opened to traffic. Among these were the Chungking-Kweiyang (1965) and the Kweiyang-Kunming (1966). A third bridge across the Yangtze, at Nanking, was finished in 1968—its double tracks greatly expediting traffic between Shanghai and Peking. In 1976, officials indicated 120 trains used this bridge daily.

The 1970s have been a period of substantial further construction, beginning with the Chiaotso-Chihkiang and the Chengtu-Kunming lines in 1970. The Hunan-Kweichow was finished in 1972 and the Nenlin Railway through Manchuria's frigid Greater Khingan Mountains was opened to traffic in 1974.

Supplementing China's standard-gauge railroads is a system of lightweight, narrow-gauge lines. Information on this system is scanty, but the pattern in Honan province is revealing. In 1973 the Honan network was about 600 miles in length and reached into thirty counties. The gauge is described as half that of an ordinary railroad, and is therefore probably 750 mm.

A supplementary Shanghai-Nanking railway line was opened to traffic on June 29, 1976. It is 291.5 km long and required the expansion and building of 41 railway stations, the laying of more than 300 km of rails on the main line and more than 270 km of rails on branch lines. Natural difficulties meant slow progress in construction. There are many lakes and rivers and streams along the route. There is quick sand present and the geological structure is complex. This posed difficulties for the design and construction of bridges.

The 1 805-km Chengtu-Kunming railway line which passes through three of China's richest southwest provinces—Szechwan, Kweichow and Yunnan—had also been successfully completed. Reportedly with 427 tunnels and 653 bridges, the link passes through extremely rugged terrain typical of the area. It was expected to alter the industrial deployment of the area it serves.

Expansion of border trade, particularly with Pakistan, is difficult without rail links. Plans to build a line from Urumchi in Sinkiang to join the feeder service to the Soviet and Mongolia collapsed along with the Sino-Soviet dispute. But despite political and border differences of opinion, there was more emphasis on Sino-Soviet rail links, with two-way trade, mostly carried by rail, expected to pass $US 330 million in 1979.

DOUBLE TRACKING

The 1 300 km Tientsin-Shanghai Railway, a trunk line in east China running from Tientsin in the north to Shanghai in the south through Hopei, Shantung, Anhwei and Kiangsu Provinces, has been double-tracked. Joined with the double-tracked Peking-Tientsin line, it forms an important link between the capital and east China. Double-tracking the line will help greatly to develop industry and agriculture in the coastal areas, facilitate construction in China's hinterland and consolidate its national defence.

The old Tientsin-Shanghai line was of poor quality and its installations and equipment were obsolete. Construction of the second track began in 1958. The project, however, virtually stopped in 1960. Work was resumed during the cultural revolution.

Apart from professional builders, local people along the line turned out in large numbers to help. Progress quickened in the second half of 1975. A year's hard work since then included the moving of 9 140 000 m³ of earth and stone for the roadbed and the building of more than 400 large and small bridges including a 5.7 km long bridge with 163 arches which spans the Yellow River at Tsinan. The double-tracking was completed ahead of schedule recently.

COLOMBIA

NATIONAL RAILWAYS OF COLOMBIA (FNdeC)

Ferrocarriles Nacionales de Colombia (FNdeC), Calle 13, No 18-24 Bogotá

Telephone: 2775577
Telegrams: FERROCARRILES

President: Enrique Vargas Ramirez
Principal Members of the Board: Alfonso Davila Ortiz
Jaime Salazar Gomez
Salvador Otero Ospina
Jose Maria Castro
Director General: Sofia Medina de Lopez Villa
Deputy-Director: Ary Martinez Cortazar
Secretary General: Miguel Viana Patiño
Administrative Director: German Hernandez
Commercial Director: Fabio Roldan
Technical Director: Hernan Garcia
Financial Director: Herbert Cabrera

Gauge: 914 mm
Route length: 3 403 km

	miles	*km*
Division Pacifico		
Buenaventura to: Popoyan, A. Lopez, Manizales	561	903
Division Central		
Bogota to: Neiva, Ibague, Grecia, Barbosa, Belencito	850	1 368
Division Magdalena		
Santa Marta to: Garmarra	264	425
Division Santander		
Gamarra to: Grecia, Bucaramanga, Puerto Wilches	249	400
Division Antioquia		
Grecia to: A. Lopez	211	340
Total route length	2 135	3 436

Colombia's latest four-year railway plan was launched in 1978 under a $US 72 million improvement programme. Major investments will include:
$US 44.778 million for updating the infrastructure and fixed installations; $US 18.727 million for new motive power, passenger coaches, freight wagons and containers, and towards modernisation of existing stock together with new workshop equipment; $US six million for yard and station improvements; $US 2 503 000 for training and consultancy fees.

TRAFFIC	*1974*	*1976*	*1977*	*1978*
Freight ton-km	2 124 000 000	1 221 000 000	1 215 400 000	1 232 000 000
Freight tons	2 899 000	2 990 000	2 518 000	2 680 000
Passenger-km	482 502 000	510 000 000	319 000 000	342 000 000
Passenger journeys	4 552 000	4 050 000	2 967 000	2 560 000

FINANCES	*1973*	*1974*	*1977*	*1978*
			$'000s	
Revenue	658 023	892 601	1 527 500	1 961 000
Expenses	857 621	1 314 378	2 185 400	2 824 000

Operating deficit in 1976 reached Pesos 426 936 950 on a total income of Pesos 1 230 327 138.

INVESTMENTS

Spending on capital equipment and works in 1978 totalled $Colombian 608 000 000, with principal purchases as follows: track improvements ($70 000 000); communications ($14 000 000); signalling ($5 000 000); bridges and buildings ($7 000 000); shop equipment and contingencies ($512 000 000). Spending in 1979 was increased to $988 534 000 with the bulk going towards track improvements ($415 195 000) and track maintenance machinery ($230 889 000).

MOTIVE POWER

Number of locomotives in service at the end of 1979 was: 10 mainline steam units and 169 diesel-hydraulic units.
Number of petrol-powered railcars in service was 23.

ROLLING STOCK

Total number of passenger train coaches: 282; freight wagons, 5 406.

LINE PROJECTS

The most important proposed new link is likely to be between Barbosa and Puerto Berrio, designed to replace the uneconomic service between La Dorada and Facatativa. Steep gradients and narrow curves mean that trains travelling between the coast and the Mexican border have to be split up. From preliminary investigations it seems likely that the possible variant will run from a point located between Saboya and Garavito at approximately 182 km from Bogota. It would continue through easy mountainous terrain over 90 km to Landazuri where the line would descend to the plains before reaching Las Mulas (42 km north of Puerto Berrio). Mountainous sections would have a maximum gradient of two per cent and the cost would be approximately $360 million.

A line between Bogota and the port of Buenaventura was started in 1913 and abandoned in 1930 when the railhead had reached midway point on the Ibague—Armenia section of the line. Now an alternative route is under consideration which would replace the entire 109 682-m Ibague—Armenia section with a 11 600 m tunnel cut-off.

Other lines under study would provide direct rail connections to the regions of the Carribean, Barranquilla and Cartenga at an estimated cost of $660 million.

CONGO

CHEMIN DE FER CONGO-OCÉAN (CFCO)

PO Box 651, Pointe Noire

Telephone: 94-05-63
Telegrams: CONGO OCEAN

General Manager: Nazaire Niambi
Motive Power and Rolling Stock: M. Mazaleyrat
Chief Civil Engineer: Jean Allot
Operations: Jean Parc

Gauge: 1.067 m
Route length: 515 km—running from the port of Pointe Noire to Brazzaville.

Congo is served by the Congo-Ocean Railway which extends from Pointe Noire to Brazzaville; a 285 km branch line, built by the Compagnie Miniere de i'Ogooue (Comilog) connects Mont-Belo station (200 km from Pointe Noire) with M'Binda and public service over this line is now provided by the Congo-Ocean Railway. A major realignment of 100 km between Holle and Monte Belo was started in late 1976. When completed in 1980 CFCO's capacity will be increased by 20 per cent.

TRAFFIC

With timber traffic increasing, CSCO's total freight tonnage grew to 1 460 000 tonnes in 1977, representing 508 million tonne-km. Comilog's manganese traffic over the Mout Belo branch (where CFCO runs Comilog trains) amounted to 1 853 000 tonnes in 1977 compared with 2 255 000 tonnes the previous year. Logs represented 38 per cent of CFCO's traffic in 1977 and hydrocarbons 14 per cent. Potash was another important traffic (accounting for 400 000 tonnes in 1976) but the former potash mine closed in

June 1977. In 1980 CFCO expects to handle 622 million tonne-km of freight, in addition to 1 900 000 tonnes of manganese, rising to 2 000 000 tonnes by 1982.
The railway's passenger traffic has grown steadily in recent years. In 1970 CFCO carried 1 256 000 passengers (144 million passenger-km). This rose to 1 608 000 passengers and 249 million passenger-km in 1975 and to 1 903 000 passengers and 260 million passenger-km in 1977. The railway forecast 2 266 000 passengers in 1980 and a substantial 460 million passenger-km by 1986.

FINANCES

During 1976 revenues totalled Frs CFA 589 566 000 million compared with Frs CFA 5 118 million in 1974. Expenses in 1975 totalled 4 743 million.

MOTIVE POWER AND ROLLING STOCK

CFCO's traction park in 1978 consisted of ten B-B-B-B diesel-electric locomotives of 3 600 hp built by MTE of France, 20 B-B diesel-electrics of 1 800 hp also built by MTE, and six C-C diesel-electric locomotives of 2 400 hp built by Alsthom of France. Rolling stock included 24 coaches, 42 railcar trailers, 82 baggage vans, 534 covered wagons (27 of which have sliding sides), 219 open wagons, 65 flat wagons, 596 log wagons and 113 track wagons. Wagons have an axle load of 17 and 18 tonnes; average load is: timber traffic; 15 m wagons, 30 tonnes; 22 m wagons, 60 tonnes; hydrocarbons traffic; 15 m wagons, 43 tonnes; manganese ore; 8.8 m wagons, 46 tonnes. Braking: vacuum, train of maximum 600 m. Can be improved by accelerating valves; Coupling: Willison automatic. The permitted effort is 115 tonnes for 35 per cent of the stock, and 37 tonnes for 65 per cent of the stock.

CIVIL ENGINEERING

Upgrading of the 510 km line between Pointe Noire and Brazzaville continued on schedule in 1979, when work on the 43 km section to the potash mines at Makola was completed. Work is continuing on upgrading other sections providing financing can be arranged following reported refusal by some backers to increase allocations.

COSTA RICA

FERROCARRILES DE COSTA RICA (FECOSA)

Apartado 543, San Jose

Telephone: 26-11-53/26-11-86

General Manager: J. Vargas
Railway Division Manager: Stanley Peralta Arias
Secretary: Julieta Casal B.
Chief Engineer: Ing. A. Rodriquez S.
Departmental Heads:
  Maintenance: Ing. C. Voljo
  Electromechanical Design: Ing. Alvaro A. Rodriguez Salazar
  Traffic: M. T. Alvarado
    I. Solano
  Maintenance of way: A. Cruz

Gauge: 1.067 m
Route length: 116 km—running from the port of Puntarenas inland to San José with a branch from Ciruelas to Alajuela.

The country's two principal railways, the National Atlantic and the Pacific were merged under the title of Ferrocarriles de Costa Rica in 1977.

TRAFFIC

Bananas form a substantial part of the traffic on FECOSA's Atlantic route with about 715 000 tonnes (40 million crates) exported annually through the port of Limón. Following government plans to double banana output in the next few years the railway is hoping to upgrade and electrify the main banana rail route from Rio Frio to Limón. In 1976, freight traffic on the Pacific Railway totalled 393 905 tonnes. A total of 967 781 passenger journeys were recorded. The National Railway carried 1 234 822 tonnes of freight in 1976 and 1 177 771 passengers.

FINANCES

Total revenue on the Pacific Railway in 1976 was Colons 22 333 503. Income on the National Railway was Colons 89 250 851.

INVESTMENTS

Capital expenditure totalled $US 34 392 591 in 1978, increasing to $US45.6 million in 1979. Spending in 1979 was allocated as follows: electric locomotives ($US9.6 million);

new line construction over 110 km ($US 18 million); track maintenance ($US1.5 million); bridges and buildings ($US4.5 million); electrification over 135 km ($US12 million).

MOTIVE POWER

Fde CR purchased in 1977 all locomotives and rolling stock of the defunct Central Newfoundland Railway.
Most recent new purchases of locomotives was made with Faur of Romania for a total of four 1 000-hp diesel hydraulic locomotives. With the equivalent of $US 9.6 million set aside for electric locomotive purchases in 1979, FECOSA hopes to increase its present fleet by 1980/81.

Number of electric locomotives:	14
Number of diesel locomotives:	77
Number of railcars:	57

ROLLING STOCK

In an attempt to solve the problem of wagon shortages, the Costa Rican Government was negotiating with the Agency for International Development in 1977 for financing for 50 covered wagons, 25 flat wagons and 25 dump wagons.

Number of passenger coaches:	108
Number of freight wagons:	1 716

ELECTRIFICATION

The former Pacific Railway was electrified over 156 km in 1929/30 at single-phase 20 cycles/s, 15 000 V overhead. Electrification has been proposed for two other routes: the 100 km Limón—Rio Frio banana line; and a 58 km line from a new cement works at Colorado. The banana line would be electrified at 25 kV 60 Hz and the cement line at 15 kV 20 Hz initially, and ultimately at 25 kV 60 Hz. Work began in 1979 on electrification of the Limón—Rio Frio line when the European 50 Hz Group was awarded the contract worth DM 52 million.

CIVIL ENGINEERING

F de CR called for tenders in 1977 upgrading the 106 km line between Limon and Rio Frio. A group of Canadian companies headed by Canadian Pacific Consulting won the contract for the job in June 1978. Work began the same year and will be completed in 1980. Key item in the contract is the construction of a 430 m bridge across the River Chirripó near Rio Frio. The bridge is to be constructed by Western Bridge Division of Canron. Other companies participating are Pandrol Canada, Canron Railgroup, Sydney Steel Corporation and Abex. The contracts are worth $C30 million.
A project is under study for total modernisation of the railway based on studies carried out by Firm Electroproyectos of Brazil. Construction of a 50 km branch line to serve a new cement factory at Colorado de Abangares has been proposed. Production of the plant will total 1 500 tons daily.

COMPANIA BANANERA DE COSTA RICA

(Ferrocarril del Sur)
Golfito

President and Chief Executive: W. W. Booth

General Manager: V. C. Heyl
General Passenger Agent: R. Ortega

Gauge: 1.067 m
Route length: 317 km

CUBA

CUBAN NATIONAL RAILWAYS (FdeC)

Ferrocarriles de Cuba
Ave Independencia y Tulipan, Havana

Vice-Minister for Railways: Manuel Alepuz Llansana
Director Western Division: Pedro Madruga Bello
Director Central Division: Pablo Figueroa Campos
Director East-Central Division: Alvaro Mentero Pasamonde
Director Eastern Division: Ramón López Vázquez
Director of Locomotives: Julio Fernandez Moreno
Director of Track and Bridges: Otto González Peniché
Director of Track Construction: Emilio Lluveras Martinez
Director of Safety: Michel Deverceaux Czaby
Director of Movements: Manuel Ferradas Acosta

Gauge: 1.435 m
Route length: 5 201.5 km

All the public service railways in the country are operated by the FF.CC. Nacionales. The system is being progressively rationalised, uneconomic lines being closed down and replaced by road transport.
The Cuban Government is investing Pesos 650 million in railway modernisation during the present Five-Year Plan (1976-80) under an integrated development programme for railway, highway and maritime transport.

ELECTRIFICATION

Route-km of electrified lines at the end of 1978 totalled 150.1 km.

TRAFFIC

Improvements to the network have helped increase both freight and passenger traffic. The railway expected to increase freight haulage to 18 million tonnes (2 860 million tonne-km) by 1980. It is expected that sugar cane and its derivatives will form 43 per cent of tonnage and 22 per cent of tonne-km while general freight will contribute 42.5 per cent of tonnage and 67 per cent of tonne-km.

	1975	1976
Freight tonne-km	1 762 800 000	1 847 900 000
Freight tonnes carried	10 862 400	11 277 200
Passenger-km	667 900 000	766 000 000
Passenger journeys	11 216 700	12 610 500

FINANCES	1975	1976
	('000 Pesos)	
Income	61 628.0	66 795.0
Expenses	45 512.3	53 926.0

MOTIVE POWER AND ROLLING STOCK

During the 1976-80 plan F de C is purchasing 90 high-power locomotives. At present Soviet-built M-62-K locomotives with an output of 1 100 hp and top speed of 1 600 hp are used in passenger service.
Orders were placed in 1975 with MLW-Worthington for 20 diesel locomotives valued at $C 10 million. Deliveries were completed in 1976.

Following delivery of first-class coaches and mail vans to Cuban Railways in 1975, Fiat Concord Argentina delivered the first of 100 diesel railcars and trailers, and 20 air-conditioned restaurant cars to Havana in 1976.

Each of the diesel railcars is powered by two Fiat 6-cylinder (in-line) diesel engines developing 280 hp at 2 000 rpm. Engines are mounted between the bogies. For auxiliary circuits a 24 V generator is coupled to the traction motor. Braking is Westinghouse type SM.2 air-brake self-regulated and automatic for multiple-unit operation. Compressors are Marelli type AC.77.A, one for each diesel engine. A cab and control desk is provided at each end of the car. All controls are illuminated by ultra-violet light. Each motor coach is equipped with a bar and small kitchen for snacks. Distance between couplers (for both motor coaches and trailers) is 25 700 mm; between bogie centres 17 800 mm; between rail and roof 4 073.5 mm. oweight of the motor coach is 50 tonnes, of the tailer 42.3 tonnes. The moto noach seats 6h hassengers, the trailer 72.

Each of the restaurant coaches is fitted with 25 tables. The service kitchen is provided with two cookers, refrigerator and other equipment. In addition there is a bar section with refrigerator, soft-drinks machine and coffee machine. The cars are fitted with Westinghouse U-type air brakes with an emergency valve in each car. Length between coupler heads is 25 560 mm; distance between bogie centres 18 300 mm; height from railhead to roof 407.3 mm; and width 3 140 mm. Diesel sets and restaurant cars are built of sheet steel treated to prevent corrosion. Bogies are Fiat, with helical spring suspension and hydraulic shock absorbers. Bogie frame is H-type. Automatic couplers are Alliance AAR 10, supplied by Miner Argentina. All cars have taped music with roof-mounted loudspeakers.

Number of locomotives in service:

	1975	1976
Steam	1	—
Electric	12	12
Diesel electric	234	300
Diesel hydraulic	74	74

Number of two-axle railcars:

Electric	15	15
Diesel	69	65
Diesel trailers	62	62

Number of passenger coaches: 209

Number of freight wagons: 6 256   6 315

Sugar Railways

The railways serving the sugar plantations and factories total about 6 200 miles (10 000 km) of which some 65 per cent are standard gauge.

The rolling stock on the sugar industry railway is only used during the sugar cane harvest (100 days). Cuba intends to increase its sugar production to 10 million tons in the next few years and modernise the railway network simultaneously, as well as using it for the transport of other agricultural products and minerals.

PERMANENT WAY

Main emphasis for railway improvements will be on renewing the 880-km mainline between Havana and Santiago. Reconstruction of the line began in 1975 and by the end of 1977, 350 km of new rail had been laid and extensive renewal of the railbed carried out. Upgrading on the route is due for completion in 1980 when traffic capacity will be substantially increased and operating speeds increased to 140 km for passenger trains and 100 km/h for freight.

Cuba, the largest island in the West Indies, with an area of 44 210 miles² (114 425 km²) is roughly 780 miles (1 255 km) long and 55 miles (88 km) wide, and lies about 100 miles (161 km) south of Florida. Cuba's economy is mainly based on agriculture, sugar and tobacco being the principal products.

At present the tracks are being renewed with Soviet rails, wooden bridges are being replaced by concrete ones and some unprofitable branch lines are being closed down and replaced by road transport. For the first time Cuba has introduced an express inter-city service (imported and air-conditioned Pullman restaurant and entertainment cars).

CZECHOSLOVAKIA

CZECHOSLOVAK STATE RAILWAYS (CSD)
Ceskoslovenské Státni Dráhy (CSD), Na prikopy 33, Prague 1
Ministry of Transport 110 05 Praha, Na prikope 33

Telephone: 2122
Telex: 121096 Domi C
Telegrams: DOMINI PRAHA

Minister of Transport: Ing V. Blazek
First Vice-Minister: Ing J. Lajciak
Vice-Minister: Ing L. Blazek
         Ing J. Filinsky
         Ing. S. Houska
         J. Dykast
General Manager: Ing Matej Tichy
Department Directors:
Finance: Ing Z. Slezak
International: Ing J. Sir
Movement and Traffic: Ing L. Stros
Traction: Ing V. Farbula
Track: Ing J. Simůnek
Telecommunications and signalling: R. Farbula
Material: Ing J. Hlavác

Gauge: 1.435 m
Route km: 13 180

Overall responsibility for all forms of transport throughout the country—railways, road, urban, waterways, internal airlines—is vested in the Ministry of Transport.

The CSD system is divided into four administrative regions each of which is largely autonomous being responsible for traffic and for management and control of all installations and equipment in its area:—

Name of Railway	Headquarters
Eastern	Bratislava
Midland	Olomouc
North-Eastern	Prague
South-Western	Pilsen

During the last 20 years the Czechoslovak railways have been in a state of technical reconstruction including the construction and reconstruction of railway stations and border stations as well as the reconstruction of important railway junctions (Praha, Brno, Bratislava).

For 20 years the Czechoslovak state invested more than 75 million Koruna in the development of the railway traffic (including the planned expenses for the current year).

Basically the principle is followed to ensure a sufficient capacity and quality of railway transport for inland and foreign carriers including the increased transit service.

TRAFFIC

Czechoslovakia's national economic plan anticipated relatively small annual increases in freight traffic volume for the remainder of the 1970s. In 1973, for instance, CSD carried a volume of 258 500 000—only 2.5 million tons more than in 1972, a modest rise of less than one per cent. For most of the past decade, freight volume has increased by about 6 per cent a year. Total freight carried by CSD was 57 million tonnes more than in 1977.

	1976
Freight tonne-km	64 335 000 000
Passenger-km	17 908 000 000

MOTIVE POWER

In 1978 CSD took delivery of 240 new locomotives, including 50 from the Soviet Union, and 5 300 freight wagons.

ELECTRIFICATION

The change-over from steam to electric and diesel traction proceeded rapidly and by 1975 steam accounted for less than 2 per cent, compared with 11 per cent of the total in 1973 and 96.9 per cent in 1950. Electrification is scheduled for 795 miles (1 280 km) of 25 000 V ac and 1 243 miles (1 840 km) of 3 000 V dc, a total of 2 038 miles (3 280 km) which is 25 per cent of the present route length.

Considerable extension of the ac system was scheduled with plans for electrifying a further 600 km of track between 1978-80. More than 2 000 km is at present electrified. In 1975 the position was:—

	miles	km
3 000 V dc	1 243	31 840
25 000 V ac	795	1 280
	2 038	3 120

CSD Class E4990 universal electric loco built by Skoda after World War II

The Bo Bo Class 4580 electric was first built in 1972 and is still used at major junctions and stations

Class ES 4990 is used for express service over CSD's two current electrified systems

The increase in ore traffic has necessitated the electrification of the Vrutky-Cierna to Tisou line, which connects with the Soviet railway network at Cop. A new broad gauge line, 55 miles *(88 km)*, was opened from Uzhgorod (USSR) to the VSZ iron works near Barca in Czechoslovakia.

Main electrification work underway in 1977 was continuation of the Haniska—Soviet border conversion project. For the past eleven years the line has carried iron ore from the Soviet Union to the East Slovak Iron and Steel Works. CSD officers estimate that electric locomotives will haul 4 200 tonne gross trains, compared with existing 3 200 tonne trainloads now hauled by diesel stock.

PERMANENT WAY
In order to meet the demands of the increasing freight traffic and the heavier and faster trains being put into service, a programme of track strengthening and additional track laying is in hand.

SIGNALLING AND TRAIN CONTROL INSTALLATIONS
Automatic block system is installed on 524 miles *(843 km)* of line. Automatic train warning/stop system is in service on 258 miles *(415 km)* of line with cab signalling apparatus on about 715 locomotives. Remote control of switch points and signals by all-relay installations in operation at 45 major centres.

A contract was signed in 1977 with the Soviet Union for delivery of new signalling installations including a central control desk at the Bratislava railway centre and a central control panel for the Bratislava—Sturovo and Bratislava—Brelav lines.

CONTAINERS
CSD aims to invest heavily in containers, wagons and terminals during the next 12 years. With preliminary planning completed, the first major works are being carried out. Containerisation has been planned in three overlapping stages— 1973-78, 1976-82 and 1980-85. Construction of 21 terminals by 1985 will cost 19 000 million Koruna (at present values). CSD spent 6 000 million Koruna by 1976 on equipment—containers,

Special Skoda-built mine locomotive

cranes, and other terminals machinery, and special container wagons. Containers will carry about 30 per cent of total freight volume. Savings could average about 100 Koruna a ton.

DENMARK
DANISH STATE RAILWAYS (DSB)
Danske Statsbaner (DSB), 40 Sølvgade, 1349-Copenhagen K

General Manager: Povl Hjelt
Directors:
Way and Works: K. A. H. Gulstad
Mechanical Engineering: Verner Adelkvist
Commercial and Transport: E. Rolsted Jensen

Gauge: 1 435 mm
Total route length: 1 999.1 km
Total track length: 4 640.4 km

DSB is almost absolute in Denmark as far as rail transport is concerned, accounting for 97 per cent of the total passenger rail traffic and 99 per cent of the total freight rail traffic. The remainder is carried out by a number of smaller private railway companies. DSB's rail network is nation-wide and has a total length of 2 000 km with about 200 manned stations.

The geography of the country makes ferries a necessity; DSB operate ten routes with a total of some 50 ferries and other vessels either alone or in conjunction with the Swedish and West German state railways. Five of the ferry routes are served by rail ferries that transport rail wagons.

TRAFFIC	1974/75	1975/76	1976/77	1977/78
Freight ton-km	1 765 394 000	1 591 806 000	1 783 000 000	1 800 000 000
Freight tonnage	7 981 000	7 209 000	7 980 000	8 100 000
Passenger-km	3 333 440 000	3 299 664 000	3 639 000 000	3 400 000 000
Passengers carried	106 366 000	99 703 000	110 000 000	100 000 000

FINANCES	1973/74	1974/75	1975/76
	(Kroner)	(Kroner)	(Kroner)
Revenues	1 445 030 000	1 661 997 000	1 865 752 000
Expenses	2 040 241 000	2 468 357 000	2 689 706 000

MOTIVE POWER AND ROLLING STOCK
Motive power and rolling stock operated by DSB in 1979 were: eight steam locomotives; 288 diesel-electric locomotives; 93 shunting tractors; 78 diesel-electric railcars, including 11 high-speed trains; 287 electric rail cars; 1 165 passenger coaches and 8 308 wagons. The railway also owns and operates 460 buses, 21 train ferries and seven diesel motorcar ferries.

Total DSB annual running expenses (rail, ferries and bus network) amount to about DKr 3 000 million and the corresponding turnover amounts also to some DKr 3 000 million. DSB's investments, which in constant prices have been almost stable for the last four or five years, amount to DKr 800 million per annum.

DSB's planned investments for the period 1978-1989 allocated to product groups:
(DKr million in 1977 prices)

Passenger traffic (excluding local traffic, S trains in Copenhagen)	2 400
S trains (local traffic in Copenhagen)	1 400
Freight	1 000
Ferry services (ferries as well as other vessels and port infrastructure)	1 150
Common infrastructure (infrastructure that cannot be allocated to product groups)	1 000
Rolling stock (cannot be allocated to product groups)	1 000
Other investments	250
Overhead charges	700
Total	**8 950**

ELECTRIFICATION
Total electrified route length on 31 December 1976: 103 km.
Total electrified track length on 31 December 1976: 243 km.
System of electrification: 1 500 V dc
Copenhagen suburban services are the only electrified services in Denmark, operating on 1 500 V dc overhead supply. DSB has set up an organisation charged with the task of carrying out a programme of mainline electrification which could see as much as half of the 2 000 km network energised by the mid-1990s. Following agreement in principle by parliament in 1978, the Electrification Law received its third reading on May 17 1979. This brought to a formal conclusion six years of study and negotiation between DSB and government departments, and cleared the way for work to begin, although funds to cover major construction contracts will not become available until 1982.
Since the mid-1950s all new overline structures have been designed with electrification in mind, but the clearance specified was only adequate for 1.5 kV dc, of which DSB already had 103 route-km in the form of a suburban network around Copenhagen. Despite the existence of these S-Bane services (largely on segregated tracks), DSB has decided to electrify the main lines at 25 kV 50 Hz because the higher voltage is cheaper. 1980 will see a start on detailed design of the first route from Copenhagen to Helsingor.

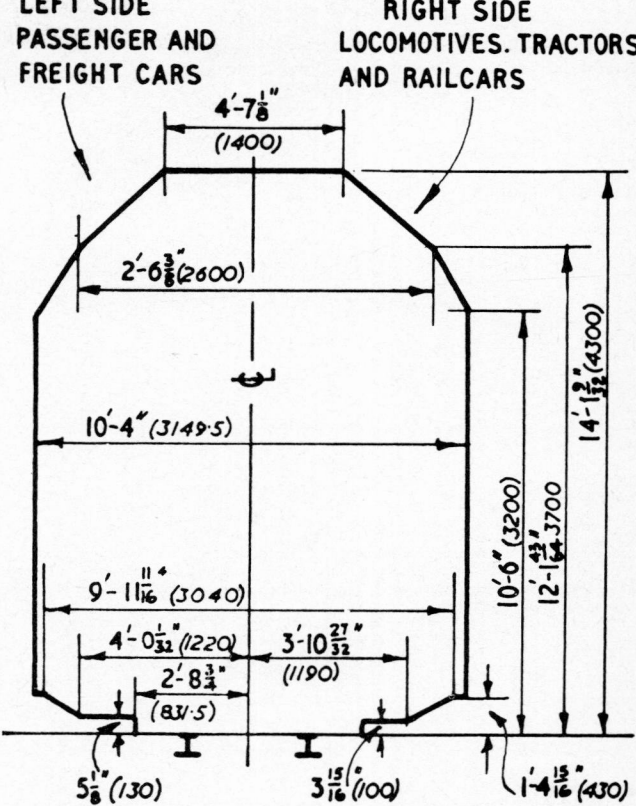

DSB load clearance diagram

LEFT SIDE PASSENGER AND FREIGHT CARS

RIGHT SIDE LOCOMOTIVES. TRACTORS AND RAILCARS

DSB operates three hydrofoil services for passengers

By the end of 1981 erection of masts on the Kokkedal—Helsingor section should have started, but work will not be in full swing until 1982. The first section should be energised early in 1983. Electric trains will start running from Copenhagen to Helsingor late in 1984.

Electrification west of Copenhagen towards Korsor and Rodby will begin in 1982, starting with the 14 km Borup—Ringsted segment, but electric trains will not be running in this area until 1987.

Type MZ diesel-electric locomotives, of which 150 units went into service in 1975

New MV Dronning Margrethe II rail ferry

Gradients: Max gradients are 0.5%, 0.67%, 1% and 1.25%. Approximately 26% of lines are level.
Gauge widening on sharpest curve: 0.59 in *(15 mm)*
Super-elevation: 6.3 in *(160 mm)* on 902 ft *(275 m)* curve.
Rate of slope of super-elevation: Between 0.083 and 0.25% (1 in 1 200 and 1 in 400).
Max. permitted speed: 87 mph *(140 km/h)*
Max axle loading:
On 45 and 60 kg rail: 20 metric tonne.
On 37 kg rail: 16-18 metric tonne.
On 32 kg rail: 14 metric tonne.
Snow fences: Protection is given each year to 348 miles *(560 km)* of line.

FERRY SERVICES
DSB is Denmark's largest passenger-carrying ferry operator and under a 685 million Kroner ferry plan three new broad-beamed Great Belt ferries are under construction. They are due in service by 1981. Following completion of the Great Belt bridge in 1987 the ferries will be transferred to the Baltic crossing between Denmark and West Germany.

		Miles	km
Korsør-Nyborg	rail and car ferries	16	26
Halsskov-Knudshoved	passenger and car ferries	12	19
Kalundborg-Århus	passenger and car ferries	58	94
Bøjden-Fynshav	passenger and car ferries	9	14
Helsingø-Helsingborg (Sweden)	rail and car ferries	3	5
København-Malmö (Sweden)	rail and car ferries	19	30
Rødby Faerge-Puttgarden (W. Germany)	rail and car ferries	12	19
Gedser-Warnemünde (E. Germany)	rail and car ferries	30	48
København-Malmö (Sweden)	passenger and car ferries	22	36
Dragør-Limhamn	passenger and car ferries	11	17

The services are operated by 29 DSB ferries, 1 ship, 4 hydrofoils, and 8 foreign ferries or ships.

REPRESENTATIVE DSB FERRIES

Vessel	Engines max. hp	Routes	Service	Length of rail tracks	Number of Auto-mobiles	Number of Passen-gers
MV Romsø (1973) (5 603 tons, 17 knots)	2 diesel 12 000	Halsskov-Knudshoved	B		440 on 3 decks	1 500
MV Dronning Margrete II (1973) (5 623 tons, 17 knots)	2 diesel 12 000	Korsør-Nyborg	A	320.7 m in 3 tracks		1 500
MV Prins Henrik (1974) (5 623 tons, 17 knots)	4 diesel 11 500	Korsør-Nyborg	A	320.7 m in 3 tracks		1 500
MV Holger Danske (1976) (1 667 tons, 11 knots)	4 diesel 3 200	Helsingør-Helsingborg	A+B	80 m in one track or 70 cars		800
MV Danmark (1968) 6 352 tons, 16 knots)	2 diesel 12 000	Rodby Faerge-Puttgarden	A	1 22 ft *(342 m)* in 3 tracks		1 500
			B		310 on 2 decks	1 500

Notes: A—as train ferry
B—as passenger and car ferry

PERMANENT WAY
A start was made in 1979 on the 18 km Great Belt bridge linking Jutland and Zealand, with 1987 as completion date. The bridge will carry both road and rail traffic. Cost of construction is an estimated 5 800 million Kroner.
Standard rail: Flat bottom, 121 to 45.4 lb/yd *(60 to 22.5 kg/m)*.
Joints: 4-hole flat or angle fishplates and bolts.
Rail fastenings: The rail is secured to wood sleepers by type RN and to concrete sleepers by type RS double flexible fastenings. In both cases a 4.5 mm thick chevron-grooved rubber pad is inserted between rail and sleeper. In switch points and sharp curves the rail sits on 16 mm steel sole plates on wood sleepers and is secured by "K" type fastenings.
Cross ties (sleepers): Creosoted beech or pine.
6 ft 8 in × 6¼ in × 10¼ in *(2 600 × 160 × 260 mm)* on all main tracks.
6 ft 8 in × 5½ in × 9½ in *(2 600 × 140 × 240 mm)* on branch lines.
Filling: Generally broken stone 1⅛-2¾ in *(30-70 mm)*.
Curves: Min. radius varies from 787 to 3 281 ft *(240 to 1 000 m)* = max. curvature of 7.3° to 1.75° except between Aarhus H and Aarhus Ö where min. radius is 328 ft *(100 m)* = max curvature of 17.6°.

DIESEL LOCOMOTIVES

Class	Axle Arrange-ment	Trans-mission	Rated Power hp	Max. lb (kg)	Tractive Effort Continuous at lb (kg)	mph (km/h)	Max. Speed mph (km/h)	Wheel Dia. in (mm)	Total Weight Tons	Length ft ins (mm)	No. Built	Year first Built	Builders: Mechanical Parts	Engine & Type	Transmission
MZ 1401-1426	Co-Co	Elec.	3 300	66 000 (27 480)	44 000 (20 000)	15 (24)	89 (143)	40 (1 015)	120	68' 3'' (20 800)	26	1967	Nydqvist & Holm; Firchs	GM 16-645-E3	A/S Thrige
1427-1446	Co-Co	Elec.	3 900				103 (165)		121-126		20	1972	,,	,,	GM
MX 1001-1045	A1A-A1A	Elec.	1 425	35 300 (16 000)	28 700 (13 000)	13.7 (22)	83 (133)	40 (1 015) and 37½ (950)	89.0	60' 0½'' (18 300)	45	1960	Nydqvist & Holm, Frichs	GM-567C and D, 12 cyl.	A/S Thrige, Odense, Denmark
MV 1101-1105	A1A-A1A	Elec.	1 700	39 700 (18 000)	32 000 (14 500)	14.6 (23.5)	83 (133)	40 (1 015)	98.6	62' 0'' (18 900)	5	1954	Nydqvist & Holm, Frichs	GM-657B 16 cyl.	GM
MY 1106-1159	A1A-A1A	Elec.	1 950	39 700 (18 000)	35 500 (16 100)	14.6 (23.5)	83 (133)	40 (1 015)	101.6	62' 0'' (18 900)	54	1956	Nydqvist & Holm, Frichs	GM-567C 16 cyl.	GM & Thrige
MT 151-157	B-B	Elec.	400	26 500 (12 000)	13 250 (6 000)	7.5 (12)	43 (70)	39⅜ (1 000)	52.1	41' 0'' (12 490)	17	1958	A/S Frichs	MTU MB12V 493 AZ 10	A/S TITAN
MH 301-420	C	Hyd.	440	26 900 (12 200) and 29 750 (13 500)	25 800 (11 700)	2.5 (4)	37/18.5 (60/30)	45¼ (1 150)	40.5 and 45.0	31' 0'' (9 440)	117	1960	A/S Frichs	MAN 8 cyl.	Voith
MH 201-203	C	Hyd.	440	26 900 (12 200)	25 800 (11 700)	2.5 (4)	37/18.5 (60/30)	45¼ (1 150)	40.5	31' 0'' (9 440)	3	1957	Henschel	MAN 8 cyl.	Voith

ECUADOR

STATE RAILWAYS OF ECUADOR (ENFdeE)
Empresa de los Ferrocarriles del Estado, Bolivar 443, Quito

General Manager: Ing V. Pace Merizalda
Traffic Manager: René Cevallos
Workshop Manager: Ing Luis Barragán
Motive Power Superintendent: Eduardo Alban
Permanent Way Engineer: Ing Jorge Cifuentes
Chief Technical Dept: Ing H. Remache

Gauge: 1.067 m; 0.750 m
Route length: 697 km

Ecuador, 106 178 miles² in area, is bordered by the Pacific Ocean on the west, Colombia on the north, and Peru on the south and east. There are three public service railways including the Ferrocarril Guayaquil-Quito, the Ferrocarril Quito-Ibarra-San Lorenzo and the Ramal Austral Sibambe-Cuenca all owned and operated by the Government, and several industrial railways.
The Quito plateau is about 9 375 ft (2 867 m) above sea level. In 49 miles (79 km) the F.C. de Guayaquil á Quito climbs 9 650 ft (2 942 m).
The railways comprising the State system are:—

Railway	Gauge	Route length miles	km
F.C. Guayaquil-Quito	3 ft 6 in (1.067 m)	281	452
*F.C. Quito-San Lorenzo	,,	232	373
F.C. Sibambe-Azogues	,,	72	116
F.C. Puerto Bolivar-Pasaje	,,	16	25
F.C. Puerto Bolivar-Piedras	2 ft 5½ in (0.750 m)	46	75
F.C. Bahia-Chone	,,	50	80
		697	1 121

*The F.C. Quito-San Lorenzo is operated as a separate railway.

The major railway system in Ecuador is laid to 1.067 m (3 ft 6 in) gauge, and is operated by the Empresa de los Ferrocarriles del Estado, whose headquarters are in the capital, Quito.
The principal line, 452 km long, connects Guayaquil, the main port and largest city of the country, with Quito, which lies at some 2 800 m altitude in the Sierra of the Andes. From Duran, the terminus for Guayaquil, the line runs across low lying plains for 87 km to Bucay, at the foot of the western slopes of the Andes. Over the next 79 km the line climbs no less than 2 944 m, an average grade over the whole section of 3.7 per cent (1 in 27). The line contains many sharp curves, and several stretches are laid on a grade of 5.5 per cent (1 in 18), including a double reversing zig-zag which was required to negotiate a particularly awkward mountain outcrop known as the Nariz del Diablo (Devil's Nose). Once the summit of this section is reached at Palmira, 3 238 m in altitude and 166 km from Durán, the line remains in the high Sierra, never falling below 2 500 m, and rising to 3 609 m at the overall summit of Urbina, 264 km from Durán.
Riobamba, 230 km from Durán, is the major intermediate station on the line, and the terminus of the daily mixed train from Durán. Between Durán and Bucay, on the coastal section, mixed trains are operated by both steam locomotives and diesels of a fleet of Spanish built Eskalduna Alco type Co-Co general purpose locomotives, which have been introduced in recent years. In addition, there is a supplementary service of small passenger railcars which operate from Durán to intermediate stations on this section. Beyond Bucay freight is handled mainly by Baldwin built 2-8-0 steam locomotives, the most recent of which date from the 1950s. Trains worked over this steeply graded section have to be split into very short sections, and there is an additional operating

problem due to landslides and river flood damage caused during the rainy seasons. Between Riobamba and Quito there is a diesel hauled service of freight trains, and in addition a service of modern railcars operates three times a week in each direction between Durán and Quito, taking some 12 hours over the journey.
The two remaining lines of the system are Quito with San Lorenzo, on the northwest coast of Ecuador near the Colombian border; and Sibambe, 131 km from Durán on the main line, with Cuenca, an important provincial capital in the southern part of the country. The San Lorenzo line is 373 km long and was finally completed, with the aid of French backing, in 1957. Regrettably, San Lorenzo has failed to show the promise as a thriving port that was originally expected of it. Freight services are operated on this line by diesel locomotives, with the Cuenca line small railcars providing a passenger service. The Cuenca line is operated mainly by steam locomotives and small railcars, and is 148 km long.
The Guayaquil to Quito line was built in sections between 1873 and 1908, the major work on the western slopes of the Andes being carried out at the turn of the century. Originally operated by a private company with capital from the United States and England, the railway was taken into State control in 1944. Road competition is keenly flat, particularly between Riobamba and Quito where line is paralleled by the Pan American Highway, and much of the equipment in operation shows signs of considerable age.
Several studies of the railway system have been carried out by overseas consultants and a French team was in the country during 1975 making a further report on the economics and viability of the whole system, which is subsidised at present to the order of 50 million Sucres annually, according to the local press.
In 1966 it was announced that the State Railways were to be rehabilitated and 102 million Sucres would be spent during the next six years with authorisation to obtain loans up to 20.2 million Sucres from abroad for railway modernisation. The project, however, was largely abandoned.
The poor condition of rolling stock and of the permanent way, left without renewal during the past twenty years, gives rise to a permanent national problem. To remedy the situation a programme of rehabilitation and reorganisation of the State Railways is long overdue.
Studies have been carried out by Parsons, Brickerhoff, Quade Douglas of USA in 1963 on behalf of the World Bank. These were used as a basis for the development policy adopted in the Plan of Development.
Studies by Livesey Henderson of Great Britain on behalf of the Ecuador government in 1964 recommended, as the first step, the rehabilitation of the railway from Guayaquil-Quito-Cuenca, showing that it is essential to maintain rail services on this line in order to assist the commercial, industrial, agricultural, social and cultural development of the country. The closure of this railway would cost the Government more than rehabilitation.
Under Decree No. 180 on Railway Rehabilitation, work should have begun immediately on the modernisation and rehabilitation of the Guayaquil-Quito-Cuenca line. A first allocation of 10 million Sucres was made in 1966 for the Quito-Ibarra-San Lorenzo railway.

MOTIVE POWER AND ROLLING STOCK
It was announced in 1978 that ENFdeE would purchase a number of heavy-duty motive power units.

Number of locomotives in service (diesel-electric):	13
(steam):	9
Number of railcars in service:	31
Number of passenger coaches:	50
Number of freight wagons:	160

INVESTMENTS
During 1980 the railway is to spend 195.6 million Sucres on capital improvements including purchase of four mainline diesel-electric locomotives, 30 freight wagons and ten passenger coaches.

EGYPT

EGYPTIAN RAILWAYS (ER)
Ramses Square, Cairo

Chairman: Eng. Abd el Moniem Hashmat Gado
Deputy Chairmen: Eng. Zoul Hemma el Sharkaway
  Eng. Mohmoud Adel Bahget
Heads of Departments:
  Finance: Hassan Louty El-Boureiny
  Administration: Eng. Abu El-Ela Gaballa
  Fixed structures: Eng. Mohammed Anwar Yousef
  Central Region: Eng. Aly Hassein Abboud
  Planning: Eng. Mohammed Refaat Shafik
  Operations: Eng. Zo El-Hemma
  Mechanical and Electrical: Eng. Aly El-Nakib

Gauge: 1.435 m; 0.750 m
Route length: 4 510 km; 347 km

The railways in Egypt are mainly confined to the more fertile area of the Nile Delta, with a line following the course of the Nile southward to Shâllal, just below Assuan.
The Egyptian Republic Railways, which forms the largest system in the country, extends from the Mediterranean down the Nile Valley, serving the Nile Delta, Cairo, Alexandria, Port Said, Ismailia, Suez and connecting at Shâllal, its southernmost point, with the river steamers of Sudan Railways. From El Quantara, on the Port Said-Ismailia line, a branch runs east following the coast and connects with Israeli Railways.
The first section was between Alexandria and Cairo, opened to traffic in 1854. This was the first railway in Africa.
Under the 1976-80 plan ER is carrying out the system's biggest investment plan ever (£E400 million, excluding a number of new lines).

TRAFFIC
There was a sudden drop in ER's freight traffic in 1973/74, caused mainly by increased importation of highway trucks. Most of the traffic taken by the truckers consisted of less-than-carload short-haul traffic. ER still has a lot of less-than-carload traffic—about 30 per cent of total traffic.
Main aims of the 1976-80 plan are to increase freight traffic from 7.3 million tonnes in 1976 to 13 million tonnes by 1980 and passengers from 300 million to 355 million over the same period. Targets set in the plan were the movement of 11.4 million tonnes in 1979 and 13 million tonnes in 1980.

	1976	1977	1978
		(millions)	
Freight tonne-km	2 021	2 036	2 789
Freight tonnage	7.3	8.3	10.2
Passenger-km	8 748	9 191	10 363
Passenger journeys	293	318	366

FINANCES
Deficits have grown since the £E2.6 million recorded in 1975 to £E12.9 million in 1976 and £E20.4 million in 1977. A deficit of £E33.6 million was reported in 1978.

INVESTMENTS
Capital expenditure in 1979 topped £E233 million with spending allocated on: 1 650 hp and 2 500 hp diesel-electric locomotives (£E43.9 million), 502 passenger coaches (£E60.5 million), 52 electric trainsets (£E33.3 million; 40 per cent of the probable total), 115 freight wagons (£E4.2 million), 200 km of new line construction (£E19.2 million), major track improvements (£E34.6 million), track maintenance machinery (£E1.5 million), bridges and buildings (£E11.9 million), signalling (£E12.4 million), communications (£E2.6 million) and shops or repair facilities (£E8.6 million).

MOTIVE POWER
During the 1976-80 plan period ER is expecting 220 locomotives to become obsolete. Emphasis is therefore being put on acquisition of new motive power. Purchases under the plan include 80 diesel locomotives rated at 2 000 and 2 500 hp which will supplement 15 type G26 CW 2 200 hp diesels from General Motors, Canada, delivered between 1975 and 1977. Also planned are purchases of 45 (1 000 hp) and 20 (1 400 hp) locomotives. Henschel is delivering 65 locomotives of 2 475 hp. Henschel locomotives type AA22T first went into Egyptian service in 1975.
ER also operates 23 Soviet locomotives type TE-114 specially designed for operation in hot climates.
The 97 B-B 1 600 hp locomotives to be purchased during the plan period will come from General Motors. 82 had been delivered by the end of 1978.
To supplement the existing fleet of 45 electric three-car sets operating between Cairo

Henschel-built 2 510 hp diesel locomotive in ER livery

and Helwan, ER has placed orders with LEW Hennigsdorf, German Democratic Republic, for 52 three-car electric trainsets.

Number of locomotives (diesel-electric): 434
Number of locomotives (steam): 39
Number of locomotives (electric): 50

ROLLING STOCK

A lot of equipment has reached Egypt from the GDR in recent years, and more are already on the way. In 1974 Waggonbau Bautzen supplied 125 third-class coaches and 45 second-class. During 1977 ER took delivery of 110 air-conditioned passenger coaches built by East German suppliers. Freight equipment has also been imported from the German Democratic Republic, particularly from Waggonbau Niesky. Now Egypt's own SEMAF plant, at Helwan, is able to supply most of ER's needs—though braking equipment has been delivered in quantity to SEMAF from VEB Berliner Bremsenwerk in the GDR.

During 1979/80 540 new passenger coaches are being purchased. Local builder, SEMAF, will build 120 a year and the remaining 300 will be imported from Romania. The plan provides provision for 1 700 freight wagons of various capacity and 100 brake vans of 25 tonnes. However, by the end of 1978 only 15 refrigerated wagons had been called for tender. The present fleet includes 1 709 bogie box wagons of 40 tonnes, 1 560 tank wagons of 12, 35 and 40 tonnes, 1 112 open 40 tonne wagons, 4 302 two-axle box wagons and 3 370 two-axle open wagons.

Number of passenger coaches: 1 362
Number of freight wagons: 17 216

ELECTRIFICATION

Total length of electrified line is 25 km.

PERMANENT WAY

Two lines were under construction in 1978: a 120 km cut-off running from new port facilities at Alexandria to Itai Baroud being built exclusively for freight with UIC54 rails and steel sleepers, and a 95 km line between Port Said and Mansurah.

Two more line projects are under study. One is a 525 km railway running from the phosphate mines at Tartour in the western desert to a new port at Safaga on the Red Sea. UIC 60 rails will be used to meet axle loadings of 29 tonnes. Bigger and stronger concrete sleepers have been specified. The second project is a 450 km line linking Egypt with Sudan, running from El-Sadd El-Aali to Wadi Halfa on the Egyptian section.

Welded rail: Total length of track with welded rail is 792 km, of which 56 km was laid in 1975. The longest individual length of continuous welded rail is 1.0 mile *(1.6 km)*. Standard rail used weighs 105 lb per yard *(52 kg/m)* in 59 ft *(18 m)* lengths. Prefabricated track panels are carried to site, the rail joints being Thermit welded in position. Three types of fastening are used with 52 kg rail:

(a) to steel sleepers with standard clips and bolts;
(b) to concrete sleepers with resilient clips and bolts;
(c) to concrete sleepers with rigid clips and screw spikes.

For the future, it is intended to extend the use of welded rail, using resilient fastenings on both wood, steel and concrete sleepers.

SIGNALLING

Signal projects: Improvements to signalling, particularly on lines to and from Cairo, are considered vitally important if increased traffic is to be kept moving. In 1978 ER signed a number of contracts for supply of signalling equipment. A DM22 million order was placed with Siemens of the Federal Republic of Germany for an inductive automatic train control system to be installed between Cairo and Alexandria. Siemens is also to supply electronic train control equipment for the Menashi-Itai Baroud line and a semi-electronic traffic control system for the Qalyub-Benha line under separate contracts valued at DM58 million.

Other contracts have been awarded to the French companies, Saxby, CSEE and Alsthom-Atlantique.

Three-car diesel trainset from Hitachi
One of 36 sets delivered to ER for inter-urban operation in 1964.

EL SALVADOR

EL SALVADOR NATIONAL RAILWAYS
Ferrocarriles Nacionales de El Salvador (FENADESAL)
Comision Ejecutiva Portuaria Autonoma (CEPA), Boulevard de los Heroes, San Salvador

Telex: 20-194 Area 301

President (CEPA): Ing. José Luis Andreu Ruiz
General Manager (CEPA): Ing. Heriberto Reyes V
General Manager (FENADESAL): Lic Juan Agustin Nunez-Barillas
Head of Operations (FENADESAL): Lic Francisco Javier Zepeda
Head of Planning (FENADESAL): Ing Héctor Romero Paz
Chief Transportation: U. Escobar
Chief Traffic: A. Escoto
Chief Equipment: R. Fratti
Chief Maintenance of Way: S. Huids

Gauge: 0.914 m
Route length: 602 km

Ferrocarriles Nacionales de El Salvador (FENADESAL) was formed from two railways which were formerly the property of overseas companies: The Salvador Railway, which passed to the state on 11 October 1965 under the name of Ferrocarril de El Salvador (FES); and the International Railway of Central America—a railway undertaking which includes the railway system and port at Cutuco—which was nationalised on 3 October 1974 under the name of Ferrocarril Nacional de El Salvador (FENASAL).

The two undertakings were merged under state control on 22 May 1975, and renamed Ferrocarriles Nacionales de El Salvador. The railway is now administered by Commision Ejecutiva Portuaria Autonoma (CEPA).

The track of the railways (FES and FENASAL) has a gauge of 0.914 m and a length of 602 km, distributed in three districts:

District No. 1 which comprises San Salvador (Capital of the Republic) to the port of Cutuco, Department of La Union, (East Zone of the country) (252 km).

District No. 2 which runs from San Salvador to the frontier of El Salvador with Guatemala (West Zone) comprising 146 km and a Texis Juntion branch to Ahuachapan, in the West of the country with 60 km.

District No. 3 which leaves from San Salvador to the port of Acajutia, on the Pacific Ocean, comprising 104 km, and a branch from Sitio del Nino to Santa Ana in the west of the Republic with 40 km.

Studies began in 1978 on the renewal and rehabilitation of the 620 km three-line system. Aimed at increasing freight and passenger capacity to meet growing demand following El Salvador's social and economic growth, the studies will include a master plan for the port of Cutuco, owned and managed by FENADESAL. Timetables, personnel allocation and the number of trains in operation are being revised and changes will be introduced to improve the railway's financial situation.

Several renewal and improvement projects were underway in 1978/79: renewal of 94 km of track due for completion by 1979; programme of reconstruction and reinforcing of bridges to meet increasing freight tonnage loadings; improvements to the telecommunications system started in 1977; reconstruction of the docks at Cutuco begun at the end of 1978; reconstruction of 21 stations; and two line interconnections planned for 1980 and 1981. Next in the pipeline is a plan to replace the existing 53 steam locomotives with a smaller diesel-electric locomotive fleet—although it is intended to retain some steam on lines popular with tourists.

TRAFFIC

	1976	1977	1978
Freight tonne-km	46 578 371	56 041 718	75 000 000
Freight tonnage	480 765	511 322	600 000
Passenger-km	26 186 835	30 664 075	31 000 000
Passenger journeys	1 745 789	1 980 453	2 000 000

FINANCES

An improvement in the annual deficit position (down 28 per cent in 1977 on the previous year) and a reduction in the operating ratio (down to 125 from 139 in 1977) were features of the 1977 results of FENADESAL's operations.

	1975	1976	1977
		(Colons)	
Revenue	8 268 300	8 674 081	9 782 093
Expenses	9 967 600	12 076 937	12 243 292

INVESTMENTS

Following capital expenditure totalling 4 268 785 Colons in 1978, FENADESAL is to invest over 9 155 000 Colons during 1980 on the purchase of two passenger coaches, track improvements and repair facilities.

MOTIVE POWER AND ROLLING STOCK

Number of diesel-electric locomotives: 20
Number of diesel railcars: 4
Number of passenger coaches: 64
Number of freight wagons: 559

PERMANENT WAY

At present, renovation of the principal line on District 3 is under way, where mainly rails of 44 and 54 lb/yd are laid.

Rails of 65 and 70 lbs/yd are now being relaid for future diesel operations. Complete renovation of 94 km was planned during 1978/79 for which orders are being programmed for rails and accessories.

ETHIOPIA

JIBUTI-ADDIS ABABA RAILWAY (CFE)

Compagnie du Chemin de Fer Franco-Ethiopian de Jibuti a Addis Ababa
PO Box 1051, Addis Ababa

Director General: M. Bekele Geleta
Assistant Director General: Ato Guerma Weldeyes
Technical Director: M. Max Rosso
Chief of Material and Traction Division: M. Wolde Guiorguis Assefa
Chief of Track Division: Ato Techome Wolde Guiorguis
Chief of Commercial Transport Division: M. Tchiane Tamerou
Chief of Financial Division: Mme Frehiwet Asrat
Chief of Administrative Division: M. Engueda Guebre Medhin
Chief of Planning and Research Division: M. Yohannes Kassa

Gauge: 1.00 m
Route length: 781 km

There are two separate railways:—the larger is the metre gauge CFE Railway running from the port of Jibuti to Addis Ababa, a route length of 485 miles *(781 km)* of which 62 miles *(100 km)* are in Jibuti; the other is the 3 ft 1⅜ in *(0.95 m)* gauge Northern Ethiopia Railway, 191 miles *(306 km)* long, running from the Red Sea port of Massawa inland to Agordat.

TRAFFIC

	1972/73	1973/74	1974/75	1975/76
Total freight ton-km ('000)	223 217	243 611	243 697	260 075
Total freight tonnage ('000)	405	444	453	470.6
Total passenger-km ('000)	78 733	95 164	107 681	131 955
Total passenger journeys ('000)	367	502.9	613.3	770.5

FINANCIAL

	1969/70	1970/71	1971/72	1972/73	1973/74	1975/76
			Thousands of Birr			
Revenue	15 614	17 416	16 704	17 209	21 406	25 298.3
Expenses	12 731	14 064	14 807	15 861	22 970	20 978.6

MOTIVE POWER AND ROLLING STOCK
Diesel Locomotives:

No. of units	Type	Builder year	Engine type	Rated Power CV	Trans-mission	Total weight Tonnes	Max speed mph (km/h)
9	Bo-Bo	SLM 1950/51	SLM 6VO25	580	Elec	48	43 (70)
6	Bo-Bo	Alsthom 1955	MGO V12SHR	675	Elec	48	43 (70)
3	Bo-Bo	Alsthom 1963	MGO V12BSHR	840	Elec	50	43 (70)
2	Co-Co	Alsthom 1965	Pielstick 16PA4	1 850	Elec	78	37 (60)
2	Co-Co	Alsthom 1968	Pielstick 16PA4	1 850	Elec	78	56 (90)
6	C	Coferna 1955	Poyand 6PX1	180	Hyd	26	16 (25)
4	C	Billard 1955	Poyaud 6VPX1	205	Hyd	33	19 (30)
4	Bo-Bo	Alsthom 1973		1 200	Elec	52	50 (70)

Rolling Stock
Number of passenger coaches   56
Number of freight wagons   872

PERMANENT WAY

Improved methods of maintenance are being adopted. Track rebuilding and strengthening is proceeding. Following reconstruction of 24 bridges between Dire Dawa and the border at Daouente, the Jibuti-Addis Ababa railway was reopened to traffic in June 1978.

Rail type	20 kg, 25 kg, 30 kg
Sleepers	Metalbloc
Fastenings	Clips and bolts

Rail Laying: On average, depending on Planning and Investment programmes, 17 miles *(13 km)* of track is relaid with 60.5 lb/yd *(30 kg/m)* rail per year.

Welded rail: About 160 miles *(200 km)* of Thermit welded track has been laid, of which 10 miles *(16 km)* was laid in 1972/73. The longest continuous length is 5.40 miles *(8 687 m)*. Rail used weighs 60.5 lb per yd *(30 kg/m)* in bars 49 ft 3 in *(15 m)* long, and is laid on steel sleepers 5 ft 11 in *(1 800 mm)* long, secured by clips.

FINLAND

FINNISH STATE RAILWAYS (VR)

Valtionrautatiet (VR), Helsinki

Director General: Paul Paavela
Director in Chief and Director of Traffic: Herbert Römer
Director of Adminstration: Eero Jaakkola
Director of Economy: Panu Haapala
Director of Way & Works: Pertti Lattunen
Director of Rolling Stock: Jaakko Toivanen

Gauge: 1.524 m
Route length: 6 057 km

The railway network was shaped for a large part in the last century, when the railways were the most important form of transport in long-distance traffic. Only a few lines have been built since the Second World War, during the period of rapid changes in the economy and the social structure of the country. In the last few decades, the railway network has been considerably improved, so that traffic with 20-ton axle loads is now permissible almost on the whole of it. The maximum admissible speed for passenger trains is 120 km/h and the average speed approx. 80 km/h.

With the population concentrating in large centres, the number of railway stations in the thinly populated areas has diminished in recent years and various operations connected with traffic are being centred at the larger stations. For that reason, the main purpose in improving the railway network in recent years has been to renew the present system and to complete it with new lines, creating fast connections between large population centres and improving mass transport around them.

Despite the economic recession, continuous construction and further development of the railway system has been in progress. The emphasis has been on continuous electrification of the mainline network. This conversion project is probably the most important investment of the entire traffic sector in the 1970s. An important inter-mediary stage was achieved in June 1977 with the completion of electrification to Kouvola. When electrification reached the border between Finland and the Soviet Union at Vainikkala in the summer of 1978, the Finnish State Railways had converted all important north-south and east-west branches to electric traction.

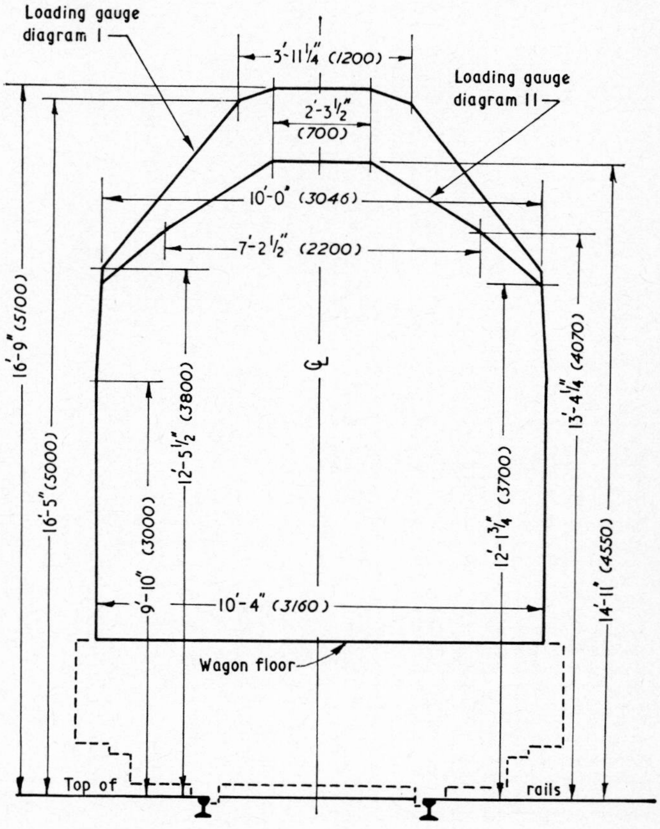

TRAFFIC

Wagonload service is the dominant factor in all goods services provided by the Finnish State Railways. In 1978 it accounted for nearly 98 per cent of the total number of ton-km in commercial goods traffic. The full effect of the world-wide economic recession was reflected in the Finnish economy in 1975. The heavy increase in freight traffic on the railways during the first years of this decade stopped. In 1976 the demand for transport increased again by 3.6 per cent, but a new downward trend began in 1977. In 1978 the demand for freight traffic services increased again by 2.5 per cent, amounting to 22.6 million tons. The total volume of wagonload traffic amounted to 22.0 million tons.

Part-load service plays a minor role in total goods traffic. Since 1973 the amount of part-load transports has been decreasing at an average annual rate of 13 per cent. The part-load tonnage totalled 422 000 tons in 1978. The decrease from the previous year was 6.6 per cent. Thus the heavily decreasing trend in part-load service since 1973 clearly slackened.

	1977	1978
	(thousands)	
Freight tonne-km	6 399 000	6 327 900
Freight tonnage	22 079	22 629

Long-distance passenger services clearly account for most of the total number of passenger-km, amounting to 77 per cent in 1978. However, long-distance journeys account for only a fifth of total journeys. The effects of the economic recession were seen in passenger traffic for the first time in 1977. In 1978 an increase was again registered. The total number of journeys 1978 increased by 1.4 per cent compared with the previous year. The number of long-distance journeys was 8.6 million, which is 1.5 per cent more than in 1977. The number of passenger-km was 3.0 thousand million, which meant a decrease of 0.2 per cent compared with the previous year. The average length of journey in long-distance passenger traffic is about 270 km. It is the length of the journey that makes this traffic suitable for the railway. The railways also aim at continuous improvement of passenger traffic by shortening the travelling time and increasing comfort.

Local traffic in the Helsinki area includes journeys made by local trains on the lines

Loading gauge diagram I
Loading gauge diagram II
3'-11¼" (1200)
2'-3½" (700)
10'-0" (3046)
7'-2½" (2200)
16'-9" (5100)
16'-5" (5000)
12'-5½" (3800)
9'-10" (3000)
10'-4" (3160)
13'-4¼" (4070)
12'-1¾" (3700)
14'-11" (4550)
Wagon floor
Top of ... rails

between Helsinki and Riihimäki (71 km to the north), Helsinki and Kirkkonummi (38 km to the west) and Helsinki and Martinlaakso (14 km to the northwest). This traffic is separated from other local traffic as it involves heavy passenger flows, and thus differs essentially from other local traffic. Local traffic in the Helsinki area accounted for 69 per cent of total journeys in 1978. Since the beginning of this decade, local traffic in the Helsinki area has grown rapidly: 15 per cent per year on average. This growth has been possible due to electrification and the acquisition of new electric railcars. In 1977 however, the growth slackened. In 1978 the number of journeys totalled 25.7 million. This indicated an increase of 3.2 per cent compared with the year before. Because of heavy passenger flows, local traffic in the Helsinki area is well suited to the railway. The railways have therefore concentrated on improving this traffic. In addition to investment in building projects, efforts are being made to raise passenger comfort by adjusting supply to demand by means of acquiring new rolling stock.

Other local traffic consists of journeys made by railcar units outside the Helsinki area. This traffic plays only a minor part in total passenger traffic. In 1978 it accounted for four per cent of the total number of passenger-km. The number of local journeys has been decreasing. 310 million journeys were made in 1977, which meant a decrease of 12 per cent compared with the previous year.

	1977	1978
	(thousands)	
Passenger-km	2 977 000	2 983 133
Passenger journeys	36 762	37 262

Coupled three-car trainsets running over the newly-completed line from Jämsäkoski to Jyväskylä

DIESEL LOCOMOTIVES

Class	Axle Arrange-ment	Trans-mission	Rated Power hp	Max. lb (kg)	Tractive Effort Continuous at lb (kg)	at mph (km/h)	Max. Speed mph (km/h)	Wheel Dia. in (mm)	Total Weight Tons	Length ft ins (mm)	No. Built	Year first Built	Builders: Mechanical Parts	Engine & Type	Transmission
Dr 12	Co-Co	Elec.	1 900	28 000	12 800	30	120	1 180	121.8	18 560	39	1959-1963	Lokomo Oy, Valmet Oy	Tampella-MAN V8V 22/30 m.A.u.L.	Strömberg-BBC
Dr 13	Co-Co	Elec.	2 800	28 300	19 400	30	140	950	98.1	18 576	50	1962-1966	Alsthom, Lokomo Oy, Valmet Oy under licence by Alsthom	Tampella-MGO V 16 BSHR (two engines)	Strömberg-Alsthom
Dv 12	B-B	Hyd	1 360	17 000	12 600	20	125	1 000	60.8	14 000	} 178	1964-1966	Lokomo Oy, Valmet Oy	Tampella-MGO V 16 BSHR	Voith L 216 rs
Dv 12	B-B	Hyd	1 360	17 000	12 000	20	125	1 000	69.0	14 000		1974-1978	Valmet Oy	Tampella-MGO V 16 BSHR	Voith L 216 rs
Dv 12	B-B	Hyd	1 360	18 700	12 600	20	125	1 000	65.6	14 000		1965-1968, 1971-1972	Lokomo Oy, Valmet Oy	Tampella-MGO V 16 BSHR	Voith L 216 rs
Dv 15	D	Hyd.	840	18 800	14 300	10	75	1 180	60.0	11 930	58	1958-1961	Lokomo Oy, Valmet Oy	Tampella-MAN W8V 22/30 AmA	Voith L 217 U
Dv 16	D	Hyd.	950	18 800	14 850	10	85	1 270	60.0	11 930	28	1962-1963	Lokomo Oy, Valmet Oy	Tampella-MAN W8V 22/30 AmAuL	Voith L 217 U
Dv 11	D	Hyd./Mec.	840	16 500	12 000	10	75	1 180	56.0	11 930	16	1958-1959	Lokomo Oy, Valmet Oy	Tampella-MAN W8V 22/30 AmA	Tampella-SRM D S 1,2
Dr 14	B-B	Hyd.	1 190	24 100	21 900	5	75	1 050	86.0	14 000	24	1969-1972	Lokomo Oy	Tampella-MAN R8V 22/30 ATL	Voith L 206 rsb

Class Dr 12 diesel-electric passenger and freight locomotive
Axle arrangement Co-Co; Transmission electric; Rated power 1 900 hp, Tractive effort Max 28 000 kg; Continuous 12 800 kg at 30 km/h; Maximum speed 120 km/h; Wheel dia. 1 180 mm; Axle load max 20.3 tons; Total weight 121.8 tons; Length 18 560 mm; Number of units in VR service 39; Builders mechanical parts Lokorno Oy, Valmet Oy, Engine Tampella-MAN (VBV 22/30), Transmission Stromberg-BBC.

Dr 14 diesel-hydraulic shunting locomotive
Axle arrangement B-B; Rated power 1 190 hp; Max speed 75 km/h; Weight 86 tonnes; Length 14 000 mm; Number of units in service 24; Builders Lokomo Oy.

Class Sr 1 electric passenger and freight locomotive
Axle arrangement Bo-Bo; Transmission electric, Rated power 4 460 hp; 3 100 kW; Max speed 140 km/h; Wheel dia. 1 250 mm; Axle load max 21.5 tons; Total weight 84.0 tons; Length 18 960 mm; Number of units 62; Builders mechanical parts Novocherkassk Works, USSR, Electrical equipment Stromberg; System of electrification 25 kV, 50 Hz, 37 locomotives being built by Novocherkassk Works, USSR.

Dv 12 all purpose diesel-hydraulic locomotive
Axle arrangement B-B; Rated power 1 360 hp; Max speed 125 km/h; Weight 60.7 tonnes; Length 14 000 mm; Number of units in service 178; Builders Lokomo Oy (64), Valmet Oy (84).

Sm2 electric multiple unit

FINANCES

At the beginning of 1978 railway tariffs were raised. The rise was applied from January 1978, except for the timber tariffs which were raised from March 1978. The general rise of charges in goods traffic was 7.3 per cent and was lowest in part-load charges, that is some four per cent. In passenger traffic, the prices of single and return tickets went up by 6.7 per cent and the prices of monthly tickets by 10.4 per cent. The part-load and passenger tariffs stayed at the level of the beginning of October 1976 for the year. Receipts amounted to 1 343 million Marks in 1978, 3.6 per cent more than in 1977. The main part of the receipts came from goods traffic services; the share of wagonload traffic alone accounted for nearly 60 per cent of the receipts.

The operating expenditure of the railways totalled 1 809 million Marks in 1977, 8 per cent more than the year before. The growth in costs varied considerably according to cost group. Wage and other personnel expenditure only increased by six per cent. The growth of costs was almost entirely due to the increase in the wage and price level.

	1976	1977	1978
		(thousands)	
Revenues	1 176 968	1 296 702	1 343 235
Expenses	1 529 305	1 677 206	1 809 464

INVESTMENTS

Investment expenditure amounted to 713.5 million Marks in 1978. Compared with the year before, the decrease was 55.7 million Marks, or 7.2 per cent. The reduction affected railway constructions, track renewals and acquisition of traction equipment and working machines. For other investment projects more funds were used than in the previous year.

PRODUCTIVITY

The total traffic product of the railways (the number of unit-km) diminished by 0.7 per cent during 1978. As the growth of the operation staff was 0.8 per cent, the productivity of labour diminished by nearly two per cent. However, in the long run the productivity of railway operation has increased annually by nearly three per cent.

MOTIVE POWER AND ROLLING STOCK

The rolling stock of the Finnish State Railways has undergone a thorough renewal in recent years. With the advancement of electrification, diesel traction has been replaced by electric traction, which is gradually gaining ground as the main tractive power on the Finnish State Railways. The carrying stock has been renewed at the same time. New wagons with higher carrying capacity have been acquired. Wooden passenger coaches have gradually been withdrawn from service and replaced by modern all-steel coaches. During 1978 nine new Dv 12 diesel locomotives were placed in service. These locomotives were built in Finland. The number of electric locomotives built in the Soviet Union increased at the rate of one unit per month. Furthermore, ten more domestic electric railcars were placed in service in local traffic in the Helsinki area during the year.

The number of passenger coaches in commercial traffic was 1 107. Two new sleeping cars and 29 second-class day coaches were built in Pasila workshop.

Among the new freight wagons taken in service were 46 peat-transport wagons (Fat) and 51 bulk wagons (Tad). The Pasila workshop has built a total of 391 new wagons, 327 less than in the previous year. In addition 70 high-sided open wagons were delivered by the Soviet Union.

The output of rolling stock increased in 1978. At the end of the year, the railways had the following tractive stock:

Type of locomotive	Number	Output MW
Diesel locomotives	393	421
Electric locomotives	62	192
Diesel railcars	24	18
Electric railcars	86	66
Railbuses	148	19
Light tractive stock	136	19
Total	873	735

At the end of 1978, the number of wagons in commercial traffic totalled 21 017, of which more than half were open wagons.

Type of wagon	Number	Capacity 1 000 tons
Covered wagons	7 618	193
Open wagons	13 026	387
Tank wagons	987	51
High-capacity wagons	6	1
Total	21 017	633

ELECTRIFICATION

Electrification proceeded on the sections of line Kouvola—Pieksämäki and Seinäjoki—Kokkola. The Kouvola—Vainikkala line section was electrified by the spring of 1978 and electric traffic started at the end of May 1978.

System of electrification is 25 kV 50 Hz. On 31 December 1978 the total route length of electrified lines was 672 km.

Electrified lines	km	completion
Helsinki—Kirkkonummi	38	1969
Helsinki—Kerava	29	1970
Kerava—Riihimäki	42	1972
Riihimäki—Iittala	58	1973
Iittala—Toijala	18	1974
Toijala—Seinäjoki	199	1975
Huopalahti—Martinlaakso	9	1975
Riihimäki—Kouvola	121	1977
Kuovola—Vainikkala	91	1978
Luumäki—Imatra	67	1978
Total	672	
Work in progress		
Kouvola—Kuusankoski	10	1979
Kuovola—Kotka	49	1979
Kouvola—Pieksämäki	275	1980
Seinäjoki—Kokkola	132	1981
Kokkola—Oulu	202	1983
Future electrification		
Pieksämäki—Iisalmi	174	1983
Imatra—Joensuu	191	1985
Pieksämäki—Jyväskylä—Tampere	234	1985

SIGNAL & TRAIN CONTROL

At the end of 1978 the Finnish State Railways had 124 all-relay interlocking boxes, of which one box was installed during that year. (Supplier: Siemens, WSSB and USSR). Automatic block signalling is in operation on the following lines:

	km
Pasila—Kirkkonummi	35
Huopalahti—Martinlaakso	9
Helsinki—Tampere	186
Riihimäki—Lappeenranta	206
Kouvola—Pieksämäki	184
Tampere—Lielahti	6
Parikkala—Joensuu	130
Lielahti—Seinäjoki	155
Total	911

CTC is in service on the following lines:

	km
Kouvola—Pieksämäki	184
Luumäki—Lappeentanta	27
Parikkala—Joensuu	130
Lielahti—Seinäjoki	155
Huopalahti—Martinlaakso	9
Tampere—Lielahti	6
Total	511

CTC is under construction on the following lines:

Oulunkylä—Tikkurika	9
Pieksämäki—Kuopio	89
Orivesi—Jyväskylä	113
Total	211

Plans for future conversion into CTC:

Seinäjoki—Oulu	334

The central control plant in Helsinki, for the traffic area Helsinki—Oulunkylä was completed in 1975. The central control plant for Seinäjiki was completed in 1978. Tampere, Seinäjoki, Kouvola and Pieksämäki will have similar equipment in the future. On the line Tampere—Parkano—Seinäjoki, all the necessary interstation connections (including axle counting) as well as the circuits between the stations and the CTC-centre are arranged with radio links. For communication to and from the traction units there is a line radio system.

Line radio systems are in operation on the following main lines:

	km
Helsinki—Turku	200
Turku—Uusikaupunki	65
Turku—Naantali	15
Hyvinkää—Hanko	149
Helsinki—Parkano—Tornio—Kolari	994
Kemi—Misi	162
Tampere—Haapamäki—Seinäjoki	232
Tampere—Rauma	144
Peipohja—Pori	38
Riihimäki—Kouvola—Parikkala—Joensuu	437
Hamina—Inkeroinen	26
Kotka—Kouvola—Kontiomäki—Oulu	684
Kontiomäki—Vartius	94
Ylivieska—Iisalmi	154
Pieksämäki—Haapamäki	158
Jyväskylä—Jämsänkoski	53
Total	3 605

Line radio system under construction:

Orivesi—Jämsänkoski	59

Marshalling yard radio systems comprise 168 relaying base stations and several hundred portable radios. All diesel and electric locomotives are equipped with radio telephones, which are able to use both line radio and marshalling yard radio systems.

PERMANENT WAY
At the end of 1976 the total length of track laid with continuous welded rail was 2 363 km of which 265 km were laid during the year. The longest individual section of continuous welded rail is 19 miles *(31 km)*.
UIC rail weighing 54.45 kg/m is electric resistance welded in workshops into 492 ft *(150 m)* lengths. After laying at site these are Thermit welded into continuous lengths. Both wood and concrete sleepers are used, the latter being either German prestressed type or Swedish two-piece type.
Rails are secured to wood sleepers by Hey-Back fastenings, and to concrete sleepers by Pandrol and RN.
Future programme is to lay continuous welded rail at a rate of about 163 miles *(250 km)* of track per year.

FERRY SERVICE
A ferry service is run between Helsinki and Lübeck, West Germany, but rail wagons are not carried on this route, which provides an international container service to central and southern Europe.
There is also a train ferry service between Hanko, Finland, and Travemünde, West

VR's new Tad wagon, designed for economical bulk freight carrying

New tank wagon (Uac) series for hauling bulk powdered freight

Germany, operated by a company Oy Railship Ab. The route was opened in February 1975.
The Hanko—Travemünde route is operated with a three-deck train ferry. For rail transports the company has a number of flat wagons and covered wagons with changeable wheelsets (gauges 1 435 mm and 1 524 mm).

CONTAINERS
The railway system has 50 cranes of 20-40 ton lifting capacity. The number of rail terminals equipped with cranes capable of handling containers is 20. With few exceptions these cranes are stationary installations. The frontier station of Vainikkala on the border with the USSR and the rail terminal between Finland and Sweden at Tornio are equipped with mobile gantry cranes for container handling.
The Finnish State Railways has no purpose-built container-carrying wagons. Containers are carried on four-axled bogie wagons capable of carrying three 20 ft (6.1 m) containers. The two-axled type of wagon can take either two 20 ft (6.1 m) or one 40 ft (12.2 m) container.
In 1978 the Finnish State Railways handled 18 760 containers.
A subsidiary of Finnish State Railways, Oy Pohjolan Liikenne Ab, has ten small containers which can be loaded transversely on to railway wagons.
These units, which have been designed and constructed in co-operation with Finnish State Railways, are operated on the service between Helsinki and Oulu. An order for 30 more small containers is under construction.

FRANCE

FRENCH NATIONAL RAILWAYS (SNCF)
Société Nationale des Chemins de Fer Français, 88 rue Saint-Lazare, Paris

Chairman of the Board: Jacques Pelissier
General Manager: Paul Gentil
Assistant General Managers: Jean Dupuy
Louis Lacoste
Marc Pieffort
Secretary General: Jean Jacques Burgard
Press Officer: Jean-Philippe Bernard

Personnel Department
Personnel Manager: Pierre Descoutures
Assistant Manager: Pierre Blancher

Operations Department
Operating Manager: Roger Gérin
Assistant Manager: Guy Carenco
 Passenger Operating: Jean Toubeau
 Freight Operating: Marc Cauty
 Safety: Jean Guéraud
 Transport Studies: Marcel Biot
 Traction and Circulation: Robert Vagner

Commercial Goods Department
Director Commercial Goods: Jean Luc Flinois
Assistant Director Commercial Goods: Jean Querleux
Marketing Department: Claude Boutté
Sales Department: Maurice Auroy

Commercial Travel Department
Director of Travel: Jean Ravel
International Fares: Andre Poupardin
Marketing: Maurice Poinsignon
Traffic: Yves Chenel
Publicity: Daniel Courtois
Personnel Department: Paul Perche

Rolling Stock and Traction Department
Manager, Rolling Stock and Traction: Jean Bouley
Assistant Manager: Roger Forray
 Administration: Rene Perraud
 Traction Equipment Maintenance: André Coste
 Rolling Stock Maintenance: Yves Roussier
 Department of Construction: Raymond Garde
 Department of Testing: André Révillon

Department of Investment: Maurice Gaide
Laboratories: Yves Deraud

Way and Works Department
Manager, Way and Works: Jean Alias
Assistant Manager: Henri Lecronier
 Administration: Robert Flauw
 Maintenance: Maxime Cexus
Track Design and Research: Georges Janin
Signalling: Philippe Roumeguere
Electrical Installations: Rene Delavergne
Works: Andre Guilmard
 Buildings: Gilbert Renault
 Bridges and Tunnels: Jean-Louis Picquand
 New Lines: Guy Verrier

Gauge : 1.437 m
Route length: 34 522 km

Several factors have contributed to a renewal of confidence in the future of French National Railways (SNCF): 1) a renewed flow of traffic back to the railway; 2) Vast sums are being poured into capital investments with the substantial Fr 6 685 million allocated in 1978 increased to Fr 7 019 million in 1979 and 6 516 in 1980; 3) Financing has been guaranteed for the new high-speed passenger line between Paris and the South-east, and construction is in full swing preparing for the opening of the first section in 1981 and traffic running in 1983.

FREIGHT TRAFFIC
SNCF traffic in the years 1975-77 fluctuated following the high level of business recorded in 1974. Freight movements suffered most, falling in 1975 from the previous year's 72 400 million to 59 790 million tonne-km. The recovery was encouraging in 1976 when freight movements totalled 63 970 million tonne-km, but disappointed SNCF officers in 1977 when it fell to 66 210 million tonne-km. 67 320 million tonne-km were recorded in 1978. Only 214 million tonnes of freight were carried in both 1977 and 1978, compared with 227 million tonnes in 1976. Steel production in France dropped from 27 million tonnes in 1974 to 22 million in 1977; as a result SNCF was among the first to suffer. Over the period the railway lost traffic amounting to 4·3 million tonne-km of iron ore and steel products. Construction materials dropped by 2.2 million tonne-km as public works projects were cut back.

PASSENGER TRAFFIC
There has been no fall in passenger traffic which continued to grow from 42 850 million passenger-km (606 million journeys) in 1972 to 53 500 million passenger-km (684 million journeys) in 1978. Traffic on mainline routes went up by 3.4 per cent (46 040 million passenger-km in 1978 compared with 44 520 million in the previous year) and Paris suburban traffic grew by 2.2 per cent (7 460 million passenger-km in 1978 compared with 7 300 million in 1977).

TGV-001 prototype turbotrain which will form the basic design for new trainsets to operate planned high-speed service over the new Paris-Lyon line

	1975	1976	1977	1978
Freight ton-km (million)	59 790	63 970	61 770	67 320
Freight tons carried (million)	217	225	214	214
Passenger-km (million)	50 700	51 500	52 300	53 500
Passenger journeys (million)	658	675	694	684

FINANCES

Under EEC regulations SNCF receives about Fr 16 000 million compensation annually paid by the central government and local authorities, the largest item being Fr 4 800 million for the pension fund.

	1974	1975	1976	1977	1978
			(Frs millions)		
Revenues	20 849	22 959	24 138·8	27 142·19	32 363
Expenses	20 929	24 142	25 254·6	28 094·81	33 482

INVESTMENTS

SNCF capital spending in recent years has been substantial. The figure for 1978 was Fr 6 685 million, growing to a planned record of Fr 7 019 million in 1979. An estimated Fr 6 516 million is being invested during 1980. The biggest single investment in 1979 was Fr 1 198 million allocated for the construction of the Paris-Sud Est line. Paris suburban services are receiving generous treatment, with Fr 640 million set aside in 1979 for new infrastructure and Fr 323 million spent on Paris suburban passenger coaches. Fr 816 million was budgetted for rapid and express coaches which is below the Fr 1 161 million invested in inter-city passenger stock in 1976, when 700 coaches (mainly Conrail) were turned out by French builders.

MOTIVE POWER AND ROLLING STOCK

SNCF locomotives in service include:

	1976	1978
Electric	2 306	2 379
Diesel	2 217	2 191
Locotractors	1 358	1 384
Passenger stock in operation includes:		
Railcars (diesel)	886	888
Railcar trailers (diesel)	1 027	1 084
Turbotrains (four-car ETG sets)	14	14
(five-car RTG sets)	39	38
Railcars (electric)	670	606
Railcar trailers (electric)	1 254	1 232
Passenger coaches (express stock)	8 114	8 517
(buses)	1 874	1 599
(Paris suburban stock)	1 256	1 444
Wagons in operation	273 900	257 000

ELECTRIFICATION

There are two main systems of electrification in France: 25 000 V, 50 cycles ac and 1 500 V dc. There are however shorter lengths of different voltages, the total electrified route length at the end of 1978 being made up as follows:

	km
25 000 V single phase, 50 cycles	4 477
1 500,V, dc	5 100
850 V, dc	63
650/700 V, dc	34
750 V, dc	36

SNCF has adopted a programme of electrification to cost Fr 400 million annually (at 1977 prices) by about 1988. Under the programme, the bypass route leading north to south around Paris is to be electrified, followed by conversion of the line southwest from Amiens to Rouen, providing a bypass route just north of Rouen to ensure free access to Le Havre. Also due for early electrification is the major freight route from Nantes through Anvers, Tours, Clermond-Ferrand and Lyon.

At present 1259 additional kilometres are planned for future electrification. The entire right bank route along the Rhône from Givors (Lyon) to Nimes and Avignon was commissioned by the end of 1979, completing a relief route to the Paris — Marseille trunk line. By July 1980 the link between Bordeaux and Montauban (near Toulouse) was to have been completed, followed in November by the important route into Spain from Narbonne to Cerbère. All these lines will be electrified at 1.5 kV and mainline diesel traction will be eliminated by the end of 1981. Of the 2316 electric locomotives in service with SNCF early 1978, 1140 were 1.5 kV only, 795 were 25 kV only and 380 were able to run over both systems.

The only 25 kV electrification in progress at present is the conversion of the remaining 650V dc third-rail suburban lines to the west of Paris. By the 1990s SNCF hopes to bring the total electrified route to 13 500 km, with about 7 700 km on 25 kV and 5 700 km on 1.5 kV. By then electric traction will be handling 85 per cent of mainline passengers, 88 per cent of freight, and all Paris suburban travel.

TRACK

Annually, SNCF is renewing about 1 000 km of track at a cost of Fr 478 000/km. Complete renewals are being carried out mainly on high capacity, UIC classes 1 to 5, tracks. These groups comprise about 30 000 track-km of SNCF's 58 000 km of mainline tracks. Standards adopted for all track renewals includes adoption of 60 kg/m rails where the track carried at least 25 000 gross tonnes daily, and 50 kg/m in other cases. Rails are continuous welded, mounted on RS-type sleepers.

Work on the 388 km new high-speed line between Paris and Lyon has been in hand since mid-1976. Opening date of the Paris-Sud Est southern section from Lyon to St Florentin is set for October 1981. Basic characteristics of the line, which is being built for 270 km/h operations initially and 300 km/h eventually, are: UIC 60 kg/m rail welded end-to-end including points on twin-block sleepers with 840 mm blocks; prestressed monobloc sleepers installed over some sections for test purposes; curve radius 4 000 m, except for three curves of 3 250 m radius near Bois-Clair; cant calclated so that a

Series BB 17 000 25kV electric locomotive

Series BB 15 000 locomotive

Series BB 9 200 V dc electric locomotive

minimum of work will be necessary to increase line speed from 270 to 300 km/h in the future; parabolic transitions with cant variation of less than 0.6 mm/m, and a 40 m entry at either end; maximum gradient of 3.5 per cent for lengths of up to 4 km; vertical curve radius of 25 000 m wherever possible (giving 0·03 g at 300 km/h), and in no case less than 14 000 m (0·05 g at 300 km/h); distance measured between track centres is 4.2 m.

SIGNALLING

SNCF now has a total of more than 6 780 km of automatic block—6 600 km on the Block Automatique Lumineux-permissif (BAL) system and the remainder on Block Automatique à Permissivité Restreinte. During 1976-78 a total of 463 km of double track was fitted with automatic block signalling—401 km with BAL and 62 km with BAPR. Now, BAL is being installed at the rate of about 220 route-km annually. During 1976/77, a total of 37 PRS (poste tout relais a transit souple) boxes have been installed to control a total of 1 277 routes—including 690 sets of motorised points and 616 signals. In addition, SNCF has installed one new PRMI box (all relay interlocking installation with individual locks), one PELI power signal box, four PMV all relay boxes with track locks, and two PEMU electro mechanical unified signal boxes as well as one PM 45 mechanical signal box. The railway now has 430 electric signal boxes in operation, of which 284 are of the PRS type.

The signal box opened at Versailles-Chantiers in February 1977 replaced seven existing boxes on the 17 km section between Sevres RG and St. Quentin-en-Yve lines. Later the control area of the box is to be extended to Ram-bouillet in the south, to Plaisir-Grignon and Noisy le Roi and Argenteuil. The computer-controlled box incorporates the first large-scale automatic train describer taken into operation by SBCF. A similar system may now be developed for control of the Paris-Southeast line, with all signalling controlled over the double track route between Paris and Lyon from a single box. The line will also be equipped with a track to train cab signalling system with automatic override if speed control commands are not obeyed.

For the Paris suburban network and as part of the Paris SNCF-Metro interconnection scheme, studies are being made for introduction of automatic train operation. The system could be put into operation by 1982.

Series BB 67 000 diesel-electric locomotive

Series CC 6 500 locomotive rated at 5 900 kW—SNCF's most powerful

DIESEL LOCOMOTIVES

Class	Axle Arrangement	Transmission	Rated Power hp	Max. lb (kg)	Tractive Effort Continuous at lb (kg)	mph (km/h)	Max. Speed mph (km/h)	Wheel Dia. in (mm)	Total Weight Tons	Length ft ins (mm)	No. Built	Year first Built	Mechanical Parts	Engine & Type	Transmission
AIA-AIA 62000	AIA-AIA	Elec.	510	32 200 (14 600)	27 800 (12 600)		60 (96)	42⅛ (1 070)	110	58′ 1″ (17 700)	100	1946	Baldwin	Baldwin 606 HA	Westinghouse
AIA-AIA 68000 et 68500	AIA-AIA	Elec.	2 230	67 000 (30 400)	39 700 (18 000)	19 (30.6)	81 (130)	49⁷/₃₂ (1 250)	106	58′ 8½″ (17 920)	108	1963	C.A.F.L. Fives-Lille	Sulzer 12LVA 24 or SAMC-AGO V12-DSHR	C.E.M.
CC65500	Co-Co	Elec.	1 600	80 700 (36 600)	47 800 (21 700)		50 (80)	47¼ (1 200)	123	63′ 8½″ (19 420)	35	1955	C.A.F.L.	Sulzer 12LDA28	C.E.M.
CC65000	Co-Co	Elec.	1 300	56 200 (25 000) 37 500 (17 000)	32 800 (14 900) 19 000 (8 600)		75 (120)	41¼ (1 050)	112	65′ 0″ (19 814)	20	1956	Alsthom C.A.F.L.	SACM MGO V12SHR	Alsthom
CC72000 mono-motor bogies (2 gears)	C-C	Elec.	3 000	19 300 (36 400) 81 600 (37 000)	30 900 at 34.7 (12 400 at 65) 51 800 at 21.5 (23 500 at 34.5)		160 (140) 53 (85)	44⅞ (1 140)	114	66′ 3¼″ (20 190)	92	1967	Alsthom	SACM-AGO V16 ESHR	Alsthom
CC72075 mono-motor bogies (2 gears)	CC	Elec.	4 000	19 300 (36 400)	11 000 at 99) (21 000 at 52)		99 (160) 53 (85)	44⅞ (1 140)	118	66′ 3¼″ (20 190)	1	1973	Alsthom	SEMT-Pielstick PA6-280	Alsthom
BB63000	Bo-Bo	Elec.	475	37 500 (17 000)	23 100 (10 500)	6 (10)	50 (80)	41¼ (1 050)	68	48′ 2″ (14 680)	108	1953	Brissonneau et Lotz	Sulzer 6LDA22C	Brissonneau et Lotz
			580	37 500 (17 000)	24 200 (11 000)	8 (13)	50 (80)	41¼ (1 050)	68	48′ 2″ (14 680)	142	1957	Brissonneau et Lotz	Sulzer 6LDA22D	Brissonneau et Lotz
BB63500	Bo-Bo	Elec.	600	37 700 (17 100)	28 400 (12 900)	7.5 (12)	50 (80)	41¼ (1 050)	68	48′ 2″ (14 680)	603	1956	Brissonneau et Lotz	SACM MGO V12 SH	Brissonneau et Lotz
BB66000	Bo-Bo	Elec.	1 110	44 000 (20 000)	28 700 (13 000)	13.7 (22)	75 (120)	43¼ (1 100)	70	48′ 10½″ (14 898)	434	1959	Alsthom, CAFL, Fives-Lille, SACM	SACM MGO V16BSHR	Alsthom, C.E.M.
BB67000 mono-motor bogies (2 gears)	B-B	Elec.	1 930	45 400 (20 600) 68 300 (31 000)	26 500 at 26 (12 000 at 42) 39 700 at 17.4 (18 000 at 28)		87 (140)	45¼ (1 150)	80	56′ 1″ (17 090)	192	1963	Brissonneau et Lotz M.T.E.	SEMT-Pielstick 16PA4	M.T.E. Oerlikon
BB67400	B-B	Elec.	2 045	(29 000)	(14 400 at 37)		(140)	49⁷/₃₂ (1 250)	83	56′ 1″ (17 090)	232	1969	Brissoneau et Lotz M.T.E.	SEMT-Pielstick 16PA4	M.T.E. Oerlikon
BB71000	B-B	Mech.	540	37 500 (17 000)			50 (80)	34 (860)	55	38′ 10½″ (11 850)	30	1965	Fives-Lille	Poyaud	Asynchro
C61000	C	Elec.	380	35 250 (16 500)	18 300 (8 500)		37 (60)	55⅛ (1 400)	53	31′ 2″ (9 500)	48	1950	C.F.M.H.	Sulzer 6LDA22A	C.E.M.
Y 7100	B	Hyd.	175	16 300 (7 400)			34 (54)	41¼ (1 050)	32	29′ 4″ (8,940)	209	1958	Billiard Decauville	Poyaud 6PYT	Voith
Y 7400	B	Mech.	175				(60)	(1 050)	32	(8 940)	488	1963	Decauville De Dierich	Moyse/Polyaud 6 PYT	BV Asynchro
Y 8000 (2 gears)	B	Hyd.	290	13 600 (6 750)	2 750 at 20		(60)	(1 050)	36	(10 140)	62 (138 on order)	1977	Moyse Fauvet Girel	Poyaud Y12-52ONS	Voith

ELECTRIC LOCOMOTIVES

Class	Axle Arrangement	Line Current	Rated Output hp	Tractive Effort (Full Field) Max. lbs (kg)	Continuous at lb (kg)	mph (km/h)	Max. Speed mph (km/h)	Wheel dia. in (mm)	Weight tonnes	Length ft in (mm)	No. Built	Year Built	Builders Mechanical Parts	Electrical Equipment
2D2-9100	2-Do-2	1 500 V dc	5 010	61 700 (28 000)	41 200 (18 700)	44 (70.5)	87 (140)	39⅜ (1 000) 68⅞ (1 750)	144	59' 4" (18 080)	35	1950	Fives-Lille-Cail	Cie. Electro-Mécanique
BB-8100	Bo-Bo	,,	2 850	67 000 (30 400)	36 000 (16 300)	25.8 (41.5)	65 (105)	55⅛ (1 400)	92	42' 5" (12 930)	171	1949	Alsthom	Alsthom
BB-8500 (2 gear ratios)	B-B	,,	4 000	44 300 (20 100) 73 850 (33 000)	28 200 (12 800) 46 700 (21 200)	51.3 (82.5) 30.6 (49.2)	93 (150) 56 (90)	43¼" (1 100)	79	48' 3" (14 700)	146	1965	Alsthom	Alsthom
BB-7200	B-B	1 500 V dc	5 600		30 400 (13 800)	60 (97)	112 (180)	49⁷/₃₂ (1 250)	84	57' 4⁷/₃₂" (17 480)	66 (44 on order)	1973	Francorail-MTE-Alsthom	Francorail-MTE-Alsthom
BB-9200 BB-9300	Bo-Bo	,,	5 230	58 500 (26 500)	32 600 (14 800)	58 (93)	100 (160)	49¼ (1 250)	82	53' 2" (16 200)	131	1958	M.T.E.	M.T.E.-C.E.M.
BB-9400	B-B	,,	3 000	60 600 (27 500)	34 800 (15 800)	31 (50)	81 (130)	40⅛ (1 020)	60	47' 3" (14 400)	132	1959	Fives-Lille-Cail	M.T.E.
CC 6500 (2 gear ratios)	C-C	,,	7 900				62 (100) 137 (220)	45" (1 140)	116	66' 3" (20.190)	74	1969		
CC-7100	Co-Co	,,	4 740	58 500 (26 500)	34 600 (15 700)	49.5 (79.5)	93 (150)	49¼ (1 250)	107	62' 1" (18 922)	58	1950	Alsthom	Alsthom
BB-12000	Bo-Bo	25 kV 1/50	3 350	79 400 (36 000)	41 900 (19 000)	29.5 (47.5)	75 (120)	49¼ (1 250)	83	49' 10½" (15 200)	146	1954	M.T.E.	M.T.E.
BB-13000	Bo-Bo	,,	2 720	55 100 (25 000)	26 000 (11 800)	40.5 (65)	75 (120)	49¼ (1 250)	84	49' 10½" (15 200)	49	1954	M.T.E.	M.T.E.
BB-16000	Bo-Bo	,,	5 540	69 500 (31 500)	33 500 (15 200)	53 (85)	100 (160)	49¼ (1 250)	84	53' 2" (16 200)	61	1958	M.T.E.	M.T.E.
BB-15000	B-B	,,	5 600	64 000 (29 000)	33 000 (15 000)	62 (100)	112 (180)	49⁷/₃₂ (1 250)	88	57' 4¼" (17 480)	63	1971	Alsthom	Alsthom
BB-16500 (2 gear ratios)	B-B	,,	3 500	72 700 (33 000)	24 900 (11 300) 42 300 (19 200)	51 (82) 30 (48)	93 (150) 56 (90)	43¼ (1 100)	74	47' 3" (14 400)	291	1958	Alsthom	Alsthom
BB-17000 (2 gear ratios)	B-B	,,	4 000	44 300 (20 100) 73 850 (33 000)	28 200 (12 800) 46 700 (21 200)	51.3 (82.5) 30.6 (49.2)	93 (150) 56 (90)	43¼" (1 100)	78	48' 3" (14 700)	105	1965	Alsthom	Alsthom
CC-14000	Co-Co	,,	3 590	99 200 (45 000)	51 100 (23 200)	17.7 (28.5)	37 (60)	43¼ (1 100)	122	62' 0" (18 890)	11	1955	Batignolles-Chatillon	Oerlikon
CC-14100	Co-Co	,,	2 520	94 700 (43 000)	51 200 (23 200)	17.7 (28.5)	37 (60)	43¼ (1 100)	126	62' 0" (18 890)	96	1954	Alsthom	Alsthom
BB-20200 (2-current) (2 gear ratios)	B-B	25 kV 1/50 15 kV 16⅔	3 900 2 220				93 (150) 56 (90)		80	49' ⁷/₃₂" (14 940)	13	1971	Alsthom	Alsthom
CC-21000 (2-current) (2-gear ratios)	C-C	25 kV/50 1.5 kV dc	7 900				62 (100) 137 (220)	45" (1 140)	122	66' 3" (20 190)	4	1969	Alsthom-M.T.E.	
BB-22200 (2-current)	B-B	25 kV/50 and 1 500 V dc	5 600 5 600		30 400 (13 800)	60 (97)	112 (180)	49⁷/₃₂" (1 250)	89	57' 4⁷/₃₂" (17 480)	75 (75 on order)	1973	Francorail-MTE-Alsthom	Francorail-MTE-Alsthom
BB-25100 (2-current)	Bo-Bo	25 kV/50 and 1 500 V dc	5 600 4 600	81 600 (37 000)	39 000 (17 700)	52 (83.5)	81 (130)	49¼ (1 250)	83	53' 3" (16 200)	69	1964	M.T.E.	M.T.E.
BB-25200 (2-current)	Bo-Bo	25 kV/50 and 1 500 V dc	5 600 4 600	68 300 (31 000)	32 600 (14 800)	62 (99.5)	99 (160)	49¼ (1 250)	83	53' 2" (16 200)	51	1964	M.T.E.	M.T.E.
BB-25500 (2-current) (2 gear ratios)	B-B	25 kV/50 and 1 500 V dc	3 900 3 900	44 300 (20 100) 73 850 (33 600)	25 100 (11 400) 41 900 (19 000)	51 (82) 30 (48)	93 (150) 56 (90)	43¼" (1 100)	78	53' 3" (14 700)	194	1964	Alsthom	Alsthom
CC-40100 (4-current) (2 gear ratios)	C-C	25 kV/50 15 kV/16⅔ 3 000 V dc 1 500 V dc	6 000 6 000 6 000 6 000	32 000 (14 500) 8 600 44 500 (20 200)	19 000 (12 000) 27 000 (12 000)	95.4 (153.5) 68 (110)	149 (240) 99 (160)	42½" (1 080)	108	72' 3¼" (22 030)	10	1964	Alsthom	Alsthom

DOOR-TO-DOOR SERVICES

In addition to palletised freight carried in covered rail wagons, French Railways deal with the transport of unitised freight by (a) the use of containers and (b) the long-distance conveyance of highway semi-trailers.

CONTAINER OPERATIONS

Compagnie Nouvelle de Cadres (CNC)

20 boulevard Diderot, Paris 12e
Telephone: 345-32-20
Telegrams: Cadroferdir Paris
Telex: 22500-Cadrofer Paris

Chairman and General Manager: Jean Daudemard-Gregnac
Operating Manager: Henri Megoeuil
Chief Rolling Stock Manager: Gilbert Braud

In France CNC operates in more than 50 towns, arranges road collection and delivery, and offers assistance to provide the most suitable transport facilities at the best rates.

Series CC 72 000 diesel locomotive

SNAV double-deck automobile-carrying wagon

SNCF central computer room now handling freight management throughout the network

GABON

GABON STATE RAILWAYS

Le Chemin De Fer Du Gabon
Office Du Chemin De Fer Transgabonais (OCTRA)
PO Box 2198, Libreville

Telephone: 244 78/209 74
Telex: 5307

Director General: L. Vion
Secretary: Paul Moukambi

The Gabonese Government announced the decision to construct the first section of the Transgabonese Railways (gauge: 1.435 m) from Libreville/Owendo to Booué (328 km) in 1972. Construction work started in 1974. Estimated traffic capacity of the line is 1 200 000 tons annually, mainly timber. The line between Owendo and N'Djole (185 km) opened to traffic in January 1979.
Estimated cost of construction is Fr CFA 36 million, raised through international loans.

CONSTRUCTION

Some civil engineering work was completed in 1974/75 and track laid at Owendo docks, plus a 10-km length of trackbed on the plains section. Other work included construction of offices and workshops at Owendo for OCTRA, the Trans Gabon Railway Authority.
A major change has been announced in the OCTRA plans, which originally called for construction first of the main Owendo-Booué section, and later extensions south to Franceville and north to iron ore fields at Belinga. However, the economic case for simultaneous construction of the Booué-Franceville line was found to be overwhelming, as there are large deposits of manganese at Moanda in the Haut-Ogooué as well as extensive reserves of timber. The present manganese output of only two million tonnes a year is transported from Moanda by a 75-km aerial ropeway across the border into the Congo at M'Binda, and thence by the Comilog and Congo-Ocean railways to Pointe-Noire for export. The Franceville extension will enable production to be expanded over 10 or 15 years to five million tonnes.
The 230-km branch northwards to Belinga, where vast iron ore deposits are awaiting exploitation will be financed by the Somifer (a consortium formed by Bethlehem Steel and several European mining companies). There seems little doubt that the branch will be built eventually, but the present world recession in the steel industry makes development of the Belinga ore fields less urgent.
Similar track standards have been devised for both sections of the Trans-Gabon. Rail will be 50 kg/m throughout, laid on 1 670 wood sleepers per km in 25 cm of ballast; maximum axle-load will be 23 tonnes. Steepest gradient against coast-bound trains will be 1 per cent between Franceville and Booué, and 0.5 per cent onwards to Owendo. Eastbound, the maximum grade is 1.5 per cent throughout. Several major river crossings are required, and standard steel spans are being designed for these. There is only one tunnel on the line—of 280 m at Junckville.

80-tonne Bo Bo diesel-electric locomotive delivered to Gabon by Traction Export

TRAFFIC

When the line is completed OCTRA expects an annual traffic of 2 200 000 tonnes of logs; 12 million tonnes of iron ore (eventually rising to 25 million tonnes), and five million tonnes of manganese ore. The line will also carry about 400 000 passengers a year.

MOTIVE POWER AND ROLLING STOCK

OCTRA's first 12 locomotives (six built by Alsthom-Atlantique and six by General Electric) were delivered during 1977. The Alsthom units are B-B design with a nominal (UIC) rating of 3 000 hp, although under Gabon's severe climatic conditions the rating is reduced to 2 800 hp. A single AGOV12DSHR diesel engine is fitted which drives a three-phase alternator and rectifier set supplying dc to the two traction motors. Each locomotive weighs 92 tonnes and has a top speed of 85 km/h. The body is 15.8 m long. In contrast the UM22C General Electric locomotives have a Co-Co wheel arrangement. They are rated at 2 200 hp and are powered by a 7FDL12D25 series 265777 diesel engine. Weight is 108 tonnes.
In addition OCTRA operates four 450 hp Moyse locomotives. Deliveries of wagons to date include 260 bogie vehicles for timber transport, 30 ballast wagons, 55 flat wagons and 35 covered hoppers.

GERMANY
(Democratic Republic)
GERMAN STATE RAILWAY (DR)

Deutsche Reichsbahn, Voss Strasse 33, DDR 1086 Berlin

Telephone: 43 002 16
Telex: 112 250

Minister of Transport and General Manager of the German State Railway: Ing. O. Arndt
Deputy Minister and Assistant General Manager: Dipl. jur. H. Gerber
Secretary of State and Assistant General Manager: Dr. rer. oec. V. Winkler
Deputy Minister and 1st Assistant General Manager: Dr. Ing. H. Schmidt
Deputy Minister and Assistant General Manager: Dipl. Ing. D. Wöstenfeld
Assistant General Manager: Dipl. Ing. oec. G. Knobloch
Assistant General Manager: Dipl. Ing. D. Weiss
Assistant General Manager: Dipl. rer. oec. E. Grahl
Chief Departmental Manager of the International Department: Dr. oec. H. Meissner
Department Manager of International Affairs: Dipl. Ing. W. Wricke
Chief Finance Officer: Dr. rer. oec. D. Schwarzer
Chief Operating and Traffic Manager: Ing. oec. R. Becker
Chief Rolling Stock Manager: Ing. G. Klotz
Chief Mechanical and Electrical Engineer: Ing. R. Wagner
Chief of Railway Installations: Dr. Ing. G. Arnhold
Chief Safety and Telecommunications Engineer: Dipl. Ing. H. Klemm
Chief Management and Operations Officer: Dipl. Ing. oec. H. Krüger

Gauge: 1.435 m.
Route length: 14 215 km.

TRAFFIC

The rapid and constant growth of the state economy of the DDR is making increased demands on the transport system. In 1977 DDR public transport carried a total of 1 079 million tonnes of freight, and freight transport output comprised 150 million tonne-km. Compared to 1970 the amount of freight transported increased by 315 million tonnes (29 per cent), and freight transport output increased by 22 million tonne-km (15 per cent). DR's share in this transport output of 1977 was 299 million tonnes of the total amount and 52 million tonne-km of the output. Compared to 1970 DR's share of the amount of freight carried was increased by 36 million tonnes (12 per cent), and the freight transport output increased by 11 million tonne-km (26 per cent). This means that in 1977 the State Railways transported on average over 800 000 tonnes of freight daily. Of the freight carried in 1977, 29 per cent comprised coke and coal, 22 per cent building materials and cement and nine per cent metals.
In addition to the growing volume of freight transported considerable increases were also recorded in the transport of transit goods. The amount of freight carried in transit transport increased from nine million tonnes in 1970 to 13 million tonnes in 1977.
The number of passengers in 1977 was 4 051 million (14 per cent more than in 1970). In the same period the volume of rail passengers increased from 43 million passenger-km to 54 million passenger-km. Despite the increasing use of individual transport in the DDR since 1970, the DR also carried more passengers. In 1977 a total of 631 million passengers were carried by rail, i.e. seven million more than in 1970. This means an increase in the output of passenger transport from 18 million to 22 million passenger-km.
According to the specific transport requirements of the DDR the DR has concentrated during the last few years on safe, timely and qualitatively better accomplishment of trade, student and long-distance travel. Thus, in addition to the S-Bahn (fast local/suburban) system already operating in Berlin, similar fast local/suburban train connections have been established in several main district cities such as Rostock, Magdeburg, Halle, Dresden, Leipzig and Erfurt.
To improve long-distance traffic a system of express train connections have been established in addition to the existing fast inter-city trains between district capitals and the capital of the DDR, Berlin. These express trains, which provide a high degree of travel comfort, operate on the following lines: Dresden-Berlin-Dresden, the Elbflorenz (Elbe Florence); Zwickau-Karl-Marx- Stadt-Berlin- Karl Marx-Stadt-Zwickau, the Sachsenring (Saxon Ring); Gera-Berlin-Gera, Elstertal (Elster Valley); Berlin-Leipzig-Berlin, the Lipsia; Meiningen-Suhl-Erfurt-Halle-Berlin-Meiningen, the Rennsteig (Race track platform); Magdeburg-Berlin-Magdeburg, the Börde; Schwerin-Berlin-Schwerin, the Petermännchen; Rostock-Berlin-Rostock, the Stolteraa.

MOTIVE POWER AND ROLLING STOCK

Major additions to the motive power fleet in the 1970-75 plan included purchase of 1 433 new locomotives—many of them Soviet-built series 120 and 130 to 132 series

diesel locomotives, and series 211 and 242 electric built in the German Democratic Republic.
The introduction of over 50 000 freight wagons and taking out of service of obsolete, mainly 2-axle freight carriages, has also resulted in an increase in transport volume. The long-term plan of the rationalising programme of the DR is to improve output and make more efficient use of the available carriage park.

ELECTRIFICATION

Following electrification of the Berlin—Leipzig and Berlin—Dresden lines which was programmed for the early 1980s, other lines (in particular Rostock—Berlin, Berlin—Frankfurt/Oder and Rostock—Magdeburg) are also to be electrified. The DR plans to cease operation of steam locomotives on its network during the same period. About 1 123 km are at present electrified. The proportion of modern traction methods (electric and diesel traction) in the train haulage volume comprised 87 per cent in 1977. In detail, this amounted to 70 per cent for diesel traction, 17 per cent for electric traction and 13 per cent for steam traction.

CIVIL ENGINEERING

In 1978 the DR comprised a track network of 14 215 km in length, of which 3 700 km were double or multiple-track lines. To increase line permeability and travelling speed it was planned to double more than 800 km in the period 1976-80. Of this, 351 km were completed by the end of 1977. (A total of 732 km of track was doubled in the period 1971-75).
The track consists of Type S49 and R65 rails, flash-butt welded in the workshops in 82 ft (25 m) lengths and then thermit-welded after laying in continuous lengths. The rails are laid on 0.24 in (6 mm) thick rubber pads or 0.2 in (5 mm) thick wooden (poplar) pads, secured by Type K fasteners either on 6.3 in (160 mm) thick wooden or 7.9 in (200 mm) thick concrete sleepers.
The equipment of the DR has been further improved with rational safety and telecommunications technology by the introduction of more efficient push-button signal boxes and relay interlocking systems, modern track crossing safety installations, as well as the construction of automatic train stopping devices and an automatic block system. The rolling stock of the DR has been brought into line with the most modern standard of railway technology.

3 000 hp Co-Co BR132 diesel locomotive built by the Soviet Union

1 000 hp B-B diesel-hydraulic general-purpose locomotive Type 110, built by VEB LEW Hans Beimler, Hennigsdorf

FERRIES

In 1979 the Königslinie ferryboat line between Sassnitz and Trelleborg, operated by the German State Railway and Swedish State Railways, celebrated its 70th anniversary. It has provided an important link in the rail passenger and freight transport system between Scandinavia and the continent since it was opened and has carried road vehicles as well.

In 1979, total freight carried by rail alone over this route since the service was started reached 50 million tonnes. The German State Railway and Swedish State Railways are making efforts to improve the capacity and productivity of the service by introducing modern ferry boats and improving handling facilities on land. Although in the initial years of its existence this line only carried some 100 000 tonnes of freight a year, the average figure has risen to three million tonnes (rail and heavy lorry traffic) in the last five years.

BR 250 Co-Co, 15 kV 16²/₃ Hz electric locomotive
Built by LEW Hennigsdorf and rated at 5 400 kW for 120 km/h operation.

Double-deck passenger cars for suburban service

ELECTRIC LOCOMOTIVES

Class	Axle Arrangement	Line Current	Rated Output hp	Max. lb (kg)	Tractive Effort (Full Field) Continuous at lb (kg)	mph (km/h)	Max. Speed mph (km/h)	Wheel dia. in (mm)	Weight tonnes	Length ft in (mm)	No. Built	Year Built	Builders Mechanical Parts	Electrical Equipment
211 (E 11)	Bo-Bo	15 kV 16²/₃ Hz	2 290	49 383 (22 400)	20 276 (9 200)	—	74.5 (120)	53.0 (1 350)	83	53' 4'' (16 260)	—	1960	VEB Lokomotivbau-Elektrotechnische Werke 'Hans Beimler' Hennigsdorf, Berlin	
218 (E 18)	1—Do—1	,,	3 040	46 284 (21 000)	25 346 (11 500)	—	93.2 (150)	62.9 (1 600)	109	55' 6'' (16 920)	—	1935	AEG; Krupp	AEG
242 (E 42)	Bo-Bo	,,	2 920	67 883 (30 800)	27 990 (12 700)	—	62 (100)	53.0 (1 350)	83	53' 4'' (16 260)	—	1963	VEB Lokomotivbau-Elektrotechnische Werke 'Hans Beimler' Hennigsdorf, Berlin	
244 (E 44)	Bo-Bo	,,	2 200	44 080 (20 000)	26 007 (11 800)	—	56 (90)	49.1 (1 250)	77	50' 2'' (15 290)	—	1933	Henschel; Krauss-Maffei	SSW
254 (E 94)	Co-Co	,,	3 300	81 548 (37 000)	56 863 (25 800)	—	56 (90)	49.1 (1 250)	119	61' 0¼'' (18 600)	—	1940	AEG; Krupp; Henschel; Krauss-Maffei	AEG; SSW; BBC
251 (E251)	Co-Co	25 kV 50 Hz	3 660	85 074 (38 600)	3 967 (27 600)	—	49 (80)	53.0 (1 350)	126	61' 2'' (18 640)	—	1965	VEB Lokomotivbau-Elektrotechnische Werke 'Hans Beimler' Hennigsdorf, Berlin	
250	Co-Co	15 kV 16²/₃ Hz	7 241	35 074 (38 600)	(18 100)	—	745 (120)	49.1 (1 250)	123	(19 500)	—	1977	VEB Lokomotivbau-Elektrotechnische Werke 'Hans Beimler' Hennigsdorf, Berlin	

DIESEL LOCOMOTIVES

Class	Axle Arrangement	Transmission	Rated Power hp	Max. lb (kg)	Tractive Effort Continuous at lb (kg)	mph (km/h)	Max. Speed mph (km/h)	Wheel Dia. in (mm)	Total Weight Tons	Length ft ins (mm)	No. Built	Year first Built	Builders: Mechanical Parts	Engine & Type	Transmission
106 (V 60)	D	Hyd.	650	38 570 (17 500) 27 770 (12 600)	36 145 (16 400) 20 280 (9 200)	7 (4.5) 14 (9.0)	19 (30) 38 (60)	43.2 (1 100) (60)	60	35' 8½'' (10 880)		1960	VEB Lokomotivbau-Elektrotechnische Werke "Hans Beimler" Hennigsdorf Berlin	12 kV D 18/21	VEB Strömungsmaschinen Pirna
107 (V 75)	B-B	Elec.	750	45 400 (20 600)	22 920 (10 400)	9 (14)	38 (60)	39.3 (1 000)	63	41' 2½'' (12 560)		1962	CKD Praha	6 S 310 DR	
110 (V 100)	B-B	Hyd.	1 000	46 300 (21 000) 33 060 (15 000)	33 060 (15 000) 20 720 (9 400)	7 (11) 11 (17)	63 (100)	39.3 (1 000)	64	45' 9'' (13 940)		1966	VEB Lokomotivbau-Elektrotechnische Werke "Hans Beimler" Hennigsdorf, Berlin	12 kV D 18/21 A-II	VEB Strömungsmaschinen Pirna
118 (V 180)	B-B	Hyd.	1 800 2 000	47 400 (21 500) 57 300 (26 000)	27 330 (12 400) 35 700 (16 200)	13 (21)	75 (120)	39.3 (1 000)	78	63' 10'' (19 460)		1962	VEB-Lokomotivbau "Karl Marx" Babelsberg	12 kV D 18/21 A-1 12 kV D 18/21 A-II	VEB Strömungsmaschinen Pirna; Voith
118 (V 180)	C-C	Hyd.	2 000	57 300 (26 000)	35 700 (16 200)	13 (21)	75 (120)	39.3 (1 000)	90	63' 10'' (19 460)		1966	VEB Lokomotivbau "Karl Marx" Babelsberg	12 kV D 18/21 A-II	VEB Strömungsmaschinen Pirna; Voith
120 (V 200)	Co-Co	Elec.	2 000	84 440 (38 300)	54 900 (24 900)	9.5 (15.1)	63 (100)	41.3 (1 050)	116	57' 7'' (17 550)		1966	Vorovshilovgrad USSR	14 D40	Charkov Works USSR
130 (V 300)	Co-Co	Elec.	3 000	66 100 (30 200)	38 800 (17 600)	21.4 (34.5)	87 (140)	41.3 (1 050)	120	67' 8'' (20 620)		1969	Vorovshilovgrad USSR	6 D49	Charkov Works USSR
131	Co-Co	Elec	3 000	(35 000)	(27 000)	(21.5)	(100)	41.3 (1 050)	122.5	67' 8'' (20 620)		1973	Vorovshilograd USSR	6 D49	Charkov Works USSR
132	Co-Co	Elec	3 000	(30 000)	(20 200)	(32.5)	(120)	41.3 (1 050)	123.6	67' 8'' (20 620)		1973	Vorovshilograd USSR	6 D49	Charkov Works USSR

GERMANY (Federal Republic)

GERMAN FEDERAL RAILWAY

Deutsche Bundesbahn (DB), Friedrich-Ebert-Anlage 43-45, Frankfurt (Main)

Telephone: 26 51
Telex: 04 414 087

Chairman of the Board: Dr. Hermann J. Abs
President: Dr. Wolfgang Vaerst
Members: Franz Eichinger
        Peter Koch
        Hans Hermann Reschke
Personnel: Hans Joachim Gröben
Traction and Rolling Stock: Prof. Dr.-Ing. Alfred Kniffler
Operating: Dipl.-Ing. Walter Völker
Civil Engineering: Dipl.-Ing. Karl Freidrich Kümmell
Traffic and Tariffs: Kurt Samtleben
Finance: Alois Meyer
Planning: Hans Kalb
Operating Economics: Dr.Ing. Willi Effmert
Federal Railway Central Office, Minden (Westphalia): Dr.-Ing. Heinrich Lehmann
Federal Railway Central Office, Munich: Dr.-Ing. Heinrich Lehmann

Gauge: 1.435 m
Route length: 28 564 km

Legislation passed by the Federal Republic of Germany, on 27 April 1977 charged German Federal Railway with the task of progressively reducing the annual operating loss so that it is eliminated by 1985. A wide range of rationalisation measures including line closures is specified in a programme *(Leistungsauftrag)* drawn up by the Ministry of Transport. Subsidies at present totalling DM8 000 million, which include compensation for lossmaking suburban passenger traffic as well as pension payments, will continue to be paid from the Federal budget under EEC rules. The main points of the rationalisation programme are:

1 Rural passenger traffic on 6 000 km of the present passenger network of 23 500 km is to be replaced by bus services by 1981. The Federal Government and the *Länder* will decide jointly which routes are affected.
2 Freight traffic will be withdrawn from 3 000 km by 1981. This will effectively reduce the total network size to 25 500 km.
3 Staff numbers are to be reduced from the present figure of 370 000 to 315 000 by 1981; this is to be achieved by natural wastage and by increasing job mobility.
4 Inter-city passenger traffic is to be more market-orientated and must cover its own cost.
5 Wagonload freight traffic must cover its own costs, but subsidies will be paid on loss-making access lines which the Ministry requires to remain open because of their economic importance as feeder routes and because they will minimise the need to construct new roads.
6 Suburban passenger traffic is to be operated to standards set by the Ministry of Transport with costs being covered as far as possible from fares.
7 DB organisation is to be restructured so that it can be run more on the lines of private industry; this will necessitate a change in the basic railway law *(Bundesbahngesetz)*. In future members of the four-man Directorate *(Vorstand)* will be responsible for specific areas, and an additional position will be created at Directorate level to handle personnel matters.
8 Sales and marketing to be intensified with special attention paid to staff motivation and modern business methods.
9 Priority to be given to rationalisation measures which do not require capital investment.
10 Only those investments showing a good rate of return will be approved, but orders will be placed as far as possible as a rolling programme to give an even workload.

TRAFFIC

	1977	1978	1979
Freight tonne-km	61 000 000	62 500 000	67 000 000
Freight tonnes	3 125 000	3 180 000	3 500 000
Passenger-km	37 400 000	37 540 000	38 600 000
Passenger journeys	960 000	990 000	1 010 000

FINANCES

In 1978 DB's total operating loss in S-Bahn and other local traffic reached DM 4 085 million (without interest). The Federal Government paid a subsidy of DM 2 875 million, leaving DB with a residual deficit on local traffic of DM 1 210 million. In 1979 operating costs rose again and the deficit was expected to be even greater. DB is negotiating with the Federal Government for a more effective subsidy and is hoping to be given more freedom to adjust prices and services to produce a more rational result. Medium and long-distance traffic is expected to operate without deficit. But at the end of 1978 there was an accumulated deficit of DM 400 million. By further rationalisations and better marketing, DB aims to eliminate that deficit as soon as possible.

INVESTMENTS

During 1979 DB invested over DM 1000 million on new equipment and facilities. Spending included DM 68 million on 19 new electric locomotives and DM 216 million on passenger coaches. Also scheduled was new line construction costing DM 660 million for work over 100 km. In 1980 the railway listed investments totalling DM 4 590 million.
A major investment programme to 1985 was first outlined by DB in 1971. It called for investment of DM 31 000 million over 15 years, with the Federal Government putting up more than 50 per cent of the cost.
Major proposals included:
—Construction of 950 km of new 300 km/h lines
—Upgrading of 1 250 km of existing track for speeds of up to 200 km/h
—Electrification of 3 000 km
—Construction of four new marshalling yards
—Elimination of grade crossings throughout the system
Federal investment in all forms of transport was DM 15 600 million in 1970.
Given the money for overall system development, DB planners forecast a surge of new traffic towards the railways. By 1985, they say, total passenger-km could reach 79 000 million—more than twice the 1972 total of 37 000 million. And of the 1985 total, more than 47 000 million passenger/km are likely to be on the longer distance routes.
Anticipated increase in wagonload freight traffic is from 60 700 million ton/km in 1972 to around 97 500 million ton/km by 1985.
So by 1985 traffic revenues should yield DM 19 610 million. Federal subsidies for loss-making passenger services, track equalisation costs claimed by DB could yield DM 4 900 million. Operating costs are estimated at DM 21 470 million. Net result: operating surplus of DM 3 040 million.
If the programme is not developed DB believes there could then be a traffic growth across the board of just about 10 per cent. Receipts would rise only marginally, from the 1972 figure of DM 12 260 million to DM 13 370 million. Expenditures would go up from DM 18 590 million to DM 20 570 million. Subsidies would be at about the same level—DM 3 963 million. Result of DM 3 237 million.

MOTIVE POWER

Since scrapping its final steam locomotive on 26 October 1977, DB has been investing heavily in new electric and diesel traction following the trend set up in 1974/75. The railway purchased its last diesel locomotive in 1978. A big future is forecast for three-phase traction motors, but meanwhile DB is buying class 111 electric locomotives. In 1980 19 mainline electric locomotives (at a cost of DM 550 million) are to be purchased.
Electric locomotives now on order, in addition to the five prototype class E120s, include 95 class BR 111 units and 34 class BR 151 locomotives. The BR 111 is comparatively new, having first entered service in 1976. It has proved itself a worthy successor to the class E110 which it will eventually replace on long-distance and suburban passenger services. Principal specifications of the Bo-Bo class E111 are: hourly output, 3 700 kW; starting tractive force, 28 tonnes; braking force of the electric resistance brake at 150 to 160 km/h, 9 tonnes; maximum speed, 150 km/h; service weight (with automatic central buffer coupling) 84 tonnes; length over buffers, 16 750 mm; minimum negotiable curve radius, 100 m; axle load 20 tonnes.
The class E151 locomotive, designed to haul freight trains of 1 000 tonnes at 120 km/h is gradually helping DB to phase out existing class 150 locomotives which are proving inadequate for present-day requirements. The E151 weighs 181 tonnes for a continuous rating of 6 000 kW and a top speed of 120 km/h—compared with 198.6 tonnes, continuous rating of 4 400 kW and maximum speed of 100 km/h for class 150.
With the delivery during 1975/76 of 24 class ET 420 and 27 class ET 472 units, DB's fleet of electric trainsets now totals 1 124. In 1977 the railway decided to halt further purchases of the three-car ET 472—at least for the present—and concentrate trainset investments on purchases of 121 class ET 420s. Designed for S-Bahn services, the 420 has each axle powered, giving a total output of 3 700 kW for a four-car set. Speeds of up to 120 km/h can be reached in 37 seconds.
At the end of 1978 DB was operating 2 688 electric locomotives, 3 117 diesel locos, 1 234 emus, 237 battery railcars, 253 diesel railcars and 493 rail buses.

Four-axle thyristor locomotive class 181.2
Hauls passenger trains at speeds of up to 160 km/h and freight trains up to 2 000 tonnes   on border traffic between West Germany, France and Luxembourg on 16⅔ Hz 15 kV and 50 Hz 25 kV systems.

PERMANENT WAY

Important improvements in passenger train speeds will come when DB has been able to construct its planned high-speed links, suitable for operation to 300 km/h. Seven new links are planned including Mannheim—Stuttgart (105 km) at a cost of DM 900 million; Hanover—Gemunden (280 km), at a cost of DM 4200, Aschaffenburg—Wurzburg (65 km) at a cost of DM 1 200 million, and Cologne—Cross Gerau (180 km) at a cost of about DM 3 000 million.

The other three high-speed lines DB would like to build are Stuttgart—Munich (220 km; cost, DM 2 900 million); Rastatt—Offenburg (50 km; cost DM 330 million); and Kaiserslautern—Ludwigshafen (50 km; cost DM 670 million).

Work started on construction of the Hanover—Kassel—Gemunden line during 1973. At the start of the 1979/80 timetable a 12 km section of line between Hanover—Bismarckstrasse and Rethen on the Hanover—Würzburg line went into service. During 1979-84 the length of line passed for 200 km/h (125 mph) will total about 500 km (310 miles). The present figure is around 175 km (109 miles) comprising the following four sections: Lochausen to Augsburg—Hochzoll (Munich—Augsburg line); Augsburg—Oberhausen to Donauwörth, and Langenhangen to Uelzen (Hanover—Hamburg line); and Sprötze to Lauenbrück (Hamburg—Bremen line). Sections to be upgraded in 1980 are Hamm (Westfalen) to Brackwede and Rotenburg to Sagehorn, 79.5 km (49.4 miles) in all. Among later work, a major programme covering 200 km (124 miles) is planned for 1983.

Track details:

Standard rail: Type S49, weighing 99 lb/yd *(49.5 kg/m)*, type S54, 109.8 lb/yd *(54.5 kg/m)* and type S64, 130.3 lb/yd *(64.9 kg/m)*. Lengths are generally 30 to 120 m.

Type of rail joints: 4- and 6-hole fishplates.

Welded rail joints: See paragraph below

Cross ties (sleepers): Wood; steel; reinforced concrete.
Wood sleepers are impregnated beech, fir or oak, 8 ft 6⅜ in × 10¼ in × 6¼ in *(2,600 × 260 × 160 mm)*
Steel, 8 ft 6⅜ in long of 9 mm thickness, weighing 190 lb *(86.3 kg)*
The latest type of RC sleeper (Spannbetonschwelle B58) weighs 518 lb *(235 kg)*, is 7 ft 11 in *(2,400 mm)* long, 7½ in *(190 mm)* thick under rails, 11 in *(280 mm)* wide at bottom and 5⅜ in *(136 mm)* at top.

Spacing: 25 in *(650 mm)* to 31½ in *(800 mm)*

Rail fastenings: Baseplates and bolts, clips and spring washers with thin rubber or wood (poplar) pad between rail and plate; resilient rail spikes with wood and concrete sleepers and resilient rail clips with steel sleepers.

Max gradient: Main lines: 2.5% = 1 in 40.
Secondary lines: 6.6% = 1 in 16.5.

Max curvature: Main lines: 9.7° = min rad of 590 ft *(180 m)*
Secondary lines: 17.5° = min rad of 328 ft *(100 m)*

Gauge widening on curves: Radius over 984 ft *(300 m)* widening is *0 mm*
Radius 984-656 ft *(300-200 m)* widening is *5 mm*
Radius 656-492 ft *(200-150 m)* widening is *10 mm*
Radius 492-394 ft *(150-120 m)* widening is *15 mm*
Radius 394-328 ft *(120-100 m)* widening is *20 mm*

Max super-elevation: 5.9 in *(150 mm)* on curves of 590 ft *(180 m)* radius and under.

Rate of slope of super elevation: Generally 1: 10V (V = speed in *mph*). On occasion this may be increased to 1: 8V up to 1 in 400. On reverse curves the permissible limit is 1: 4V up to 1 in 400.

Max altitude: Main Line: 3 172 ft *(967 m)* between Klais and Mittenwald. Highest station is Klais, 3 061 ft *(933 m)*
Secondary Line: 3 179 ft, *(969 m)* between Bärenthal and Aha on the Titisee-Seebrugg Line.

Max axle loading: 20 metric tons.

Welded rail: At the end of 1974 the total length of track laid with welded rails was 32 311 miles *(53 000 km.)*

Track Work: Considerable work was carried out on track renewal and maintenance, involving the extensive use both of wood and concrete sleepers, and UIC-60 rail (weighing 60.3 kg/m), provision having been made for the laying of this rail in the proportion of 45 per cent The complete mechanisation of this work was facilitated by the use of the new track-renewal train UP 2.

The length of continuously welded rail increased to 79.3 per cent of the total rail laid on all tracks, and the number of welded points to 79.2 per cent of the total number. Research was carried out into the laying of track without sleepers, and track simplification continued, with the result that the number of points has been reduced, since 1960, by some 42 700.

The heating of points, principally by electricity, continued and now covers more than 15 000 sets.

SIGNALLING AND INSTALLATIONS

Automatic train control: A total of some 7 087 motive-power units has now been equipped for automatic train control.

Telecommunications: After extensive studies, radio communication with trains was introduced on the DB, for the first time, between Lübeck and Puttgarden. Communication is maintained between the operating staff on the ground and 50 locomotives already equipped with radio, and the results have proved to be satisfactory.

In general, DB has made use of radio for a long time, and the number of sets employed was further increased by an additional 3 000 two-way radio, and other transmitting and receiving sets, to give a total of some 14 000.

Use of Computers: The "Electronic Seat Reservation Centre" in Frankfurt (Main) deals with the reservation of all accommodation in TEE, Intercity and through trains. It is the largest in Europe using real-time data-processing methods and is connected with the Austrian, Belgian, Luxembourg and Danish Railways.

Work is continuing on the development of computer programmes for the preparation of timetables, the economic turn-round of coaches used for holiday traffic, and duty rosters.

Local Transport: Some 25 per cent of DB's total building investments were in local transport in conurbations, including the Munich S-Bahn system and the airport line at Frankfurt (Main), although work on other S-Bahn projects, at Frankfurt (Main), Hamburg, and in the Ruhr, was delayed, largely because of increasing costs. S-Bahn projects in Stuttgart and Cologne were begun in 1971 and 1972, respectively.

Marshalling Yards: Work on the future Maschen marshalling yard, to the South of Hamburg, continued actively in order to complete the planning of the North-South system, and the preparation of the Jesteburg-Maschen arrival line, having a length of some 8 miles *(13 km)*. 46 bridges are to be built over the lines, and 19 miles *(30 km)* of track and 60 sets of points were laid.

Having regard to the satisfactory experience obtained with the first fully-automatic hump used in Seelze marshalling yard, a commencement was made in the Mannheim marshalling yard with the provision, in an East-West direction, of installations for the automatic adjustment of the speed of shunted wagons.

Work on the Marshalling yards in Hamm (Westph.), Hagen-Vorhalle, Kornwestheim and Saarbrücken is proceeding according to plan.

Class 103 six-axle high-speed locomotive
Built for 16⅔ Hz 15 kV operation at a max of 200 km/h; one hour rating 6 400 kW; weight in working order 116 tonnes.

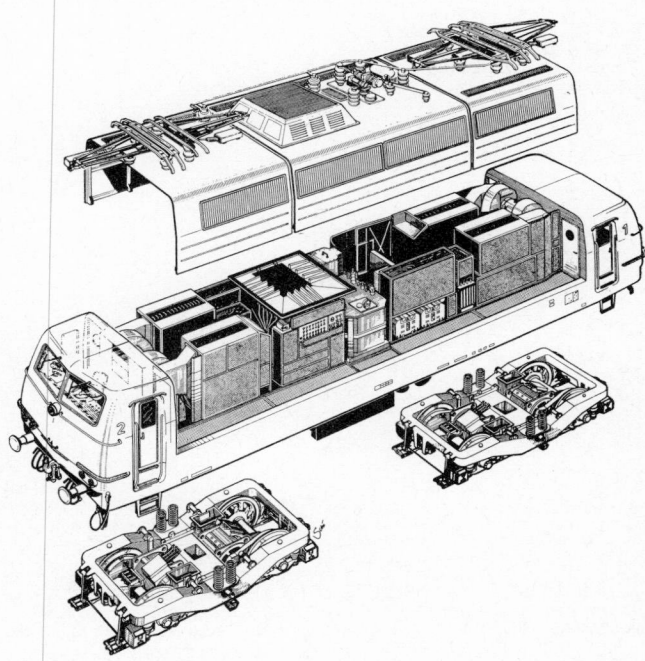

Class 184 (formerly E410)
Built for four-system multi-electric system service. One hour rating 3 200 kW; weight 84 tonnes; speed 150 km/h.

Class 120 with three-phase propulsion
Synchronous squirrel cage traction motors fed by static converters. Continuous rating 5 600 kW at all speeds between 80 and 160 km/h. Feeding system single phase 15 kV 16⅔ Hz.

Containers: The new container transhipment depot in Göttingen came into operation, the existing depots in Mannheim, Basle, and Wuppertal-Langerfeld were extended, and a second container crane was installed in the depot at Ludwigsburg.

Bridges and other structures: 160 new railway bridges, and 121 new road bridges, were opened together with 25 new, and 11 re-built, rail underpasses.
Joint work on structures in Hanover, Munich and Frankfurt (Main) continued actively, under the reorganisation of the DB, as did work on the railway buildings in Hanover, Frankfurt (Main), and Munich, and on S-Bahn buildings in the Hamburg, Rhine-Ruhr, Rhine-Main and Munich conurbations.

Signalling and Telecommunications: 137 old-type signal boxes were replaced by 45 signal boxes with push-button geographical circuitry, to which 1 290 sets of points are connected. The DB has built a total of 1 061 signal boxes with geographical circuitry (of which 1 033 are in operation), to which 27 302 sets of points and derailers are connected, and which enabled 2 551 old-type mechanical and electro-mechanical signal boxes to be removed. The largest-signal boxes with geographical circuitry are those at the stations in Fürth (Bavaria), Buchholz (Kr. Harburg), Kirchweyhe, and Lauda.
The network of single and double track lines equipped with automatic block now covers a distance of 3 362 miles *(5 410 km)* including, installed recently, Bassum-Sagehorn, Altenbeken-Warburg (Westph.), Gemünden (Main)-Waigolshausen-Schweinfurt and Gauting-Starnberg.

Level Crossings: 187 flashing-light and colour-light installations, with and without half-barriers, 38 other barriers, and 81 colour-light signals on barriers, were installed, and connections between barriers and protective railway signals were provided at 77 level crossings.

CONTAINER OPERATIONS: Container operations, domestic and international, are operated on behalf of the DB by:
TRANSFRACHT GmbH
Gutleutstrasse 160-164, 6 Frankfurt (Main)
Telephone: (611) 23 03 51
Telex: 41.45.45

General: The DB owns and operates some 23 700 containers of approximately 5.5 tonnes load capacity for domestic door-to-door service including collection and delivery by road. There are 12 main types, suitable for a variety of products.

Large DB-Containers for European International Service: These new 20 ft and 40 ft DB-containers, larger in width and height than Transcontainers, are intended for inland service in West Germany and certain other European countries whose loading gauge permits. They conform to ISO standards in every other respect, including type and location of corner castings.

GHANA

GHANA RAILWAY CORPORATION (GR)
PO Box 251, Takoradi

Telephone: 2181

General Manager, Ghana Railway & Ports Authority: Edward Moore
Training & Manpower Planning Manager: J. B. Yorke
Administrative Officer: J. R. Holdbrooke
Engineering:
  Chief Engineer: S. Oduro
  Deputy Chief Engineers: J. Owusu
                      A. Ababio
Traffic:
  Deputy Traffic Manager: G. L. Yamuah
  Assistant Traffic Manager: J. M. W. Aggrey
Locomotive:
  Chief Mechanical Engineer: F. G. Asamoah
Deputy Chief Mechanical Engineers: K. M. Amuah, J. A. K. Baidoo
  Senior Mechanical Engineer: J. J. Thompson
Port Management:
  Chief Ports Manager, Tema: D. A. Minta
  Port Manager, Takoradi: J. B. Kofie
  Port Manager, Tema: L. C. O. Cobblah
  Senior Port Superintendents: E. E. Thompson
                          H. C. Ogoe
Electrical:
  Senior Electrical Engineer: J. K. Ankomah

Gauge: 1.067 m
Route length: 953 km

The Ghana Railway and Ports Authority was replaced by two separate bodies, the Ghana Railway Corporation being formed in July 1977. A multi-million pound facelift for Ghana Railways was announced by the Commissioner for Transport and Communications at the end of 1976. Under the programme priority is being given to the realignment of the Takoradi-Hunt Valley line including double tracking.
During 1977 it was announced that Rail India Technical and Economic Services is to carry out consultancy and feasibility studies for the railway under a $US 1.7 million agreement.
Under the railway's Five-Year Development Plan (1975-79) rail services were extended 153 km from Awaso to Sunyani, capital of the Brong Ahafo region and from Bosuso to Kibi in the eastern region. The railway is also considering the extension of rail facilities from the existing Shai Hills network to link with lake transport at Akosombo to provide an alternative means of cheap bulk transport for the heavy rice and livestock traffic originating in the north.

MOTIVE POWER AND ROLLING STOCK

	Line haul	Shunting (Switching)
Locomotives in steam	37	55
Locomotives in diesel-electric	66	12
Locomotives in diesel-hydraulic	—	22
Number of railcars, diesel	4	
Number of passenger train coaches	182	
Number of freight train cars	3 289	

PERMANENT WAY
The proposal to extend the railway from Awaso to Sunyani has never yet got off the ground, mainly because inflation has increased investment costs and interest charges. Now, however, the Ministry of Communications has allocated funds to meet the cost of feasibility studies—expected to reach Cedis 300 000. Actual construction cost is estimated at Cedis 35 million.
Ghana's railway network has excessive curvature in several sections, and this tends to increase line occupation and reduce line capacity. For example, between Kumasi and Takoradi there are 504 curves in a section of 270.48 km. Also there are several areas with excessively sharp curves—on the 12.88-km section between Kasi and Eduadin, for instance, there are 24 sharp curves, about two curves per km. Realignment of the permanent way on these sections will be aimed at increasing minimum curve radius to 335 m, improving train speeds and lessening the risk of derailments and damage to property.
One major realignment project involving nine sharp curves has already been completed on the Nsawam-Pakro section of the Eastern Line, and work on realignment of the section between Insu and Kuranti on the Western Line is also in hand. Total cost of

all the realignment projects, covering the entire system, is expected to reach Cedis 25 833 500.
Track renewal, some track relaying, and installation of many new switches and crossings. Also included in the plan is: existing 39.7 kg/m rail to be replaced by 45 kg/m rail. A ballasting programme to provide for a depth of 15.7 cm of ballast on existing track and 23.6 cm on track which is to be relaid; this will involve laying 63,000 tonnes of ballast a year, and should result in a minimum of 15.7 cm beneath sleepers on all tracks after 12 years.

TRACK CONSTRUCTION
Standard rail, type and weight:
  Sekondi-Nsuta—RBS 81 lb/yd *(40.2 kg/m)*
  Nsuta-Obuasi—ARA 80 lb/yd *(39.7 kg/m)*
  Obuasi-Kumasi—RBS 80 lb/yd *(39.7 kg/m)*
  Kumasi-Tafo—BS 60 lb/yd *(29.8 kg/m)*
  Tafo-Accra—RBS 60 lb/yd *(29.8 kg/m)*
  Prestea branch—RBS 60 lb/yd *(29.8 kg/m)*
  Cen. Prov. Rly.—BS 60 lb/yd *(29.8 kg/m)*
  Awaso Branch—ASCE 75 lb/yd *(37.2 kg/m)*
Joints: 4-hole fishplates.
Cross ties (sleepers): Standard steel; and wood 5 in × 10 in × 6 ft 6 in *(127 × 254 × 1 981 mm)*
Spacing: 2 200 per mile *(1 365 per km)*
Rail fastenings:
  wood sleepers: Dog spikes, Macbeth spike anchors, Elastic rail spikes. Tests are being made with Lockspikes (England) and single shank spring spikes (West Germany).
  steel sleepers: Keys, 1 and 0 clips, ARA clips, ABK clips.
Filling: Mainly crushed granite, some gravel.
Max Curvature: Sekondi-Kumasi 8° 40'=rad of 663 ft *(202 m)*
  Kumasi-Accra 8° 40'= rad of 663 ft *(202 m)*
  Cent. Prov. Rly. 8° 40'=rad of 663 ft *(202 m)*
  Prestea Branch 17° = rad of 338 ft *(103 m)*
  Awaso Branch 6° = rad of 955 ft *(291 m)*
Max gradient: 1.25% = 1 in 80; except Prestea Branch 2.5% = 1 in 40.
Longest continuous gradient: 6.2 miles with ruling grade of 1.25% and max curves of 8° 40'.
Max altitude: 938 ft *(286 m)* near Kumasi.
Permitted speeds:
  Freight trains 35 mph *(56 km/h)*
  Passenger trains 40 mph *(64 km/h)*
  Except Prestea branch:
  Freight trains 18 mph *(29 km/h)*
  Passenger trains 25 mph *(40 km/h)*
Axle loading:
  Sekondi-Kumasi-Accra 16 tons
  Central Province Railway 12½ tons
  Prestea Branch 13½ tons
  Awaso Branch 16 tons
Gauge widening on sharpest curve: 1 in
Super-elevation on sharpest curve: 3½ in
Rate of slope of super-elevation: ½ in per rail length.

SIGNALLING
A separate project aimed at providing a centralised traffic and telecommunications system which will rely heavily on radio-telephone links is underway. The cost is estimated at Cedis 5 million. Most important features of the project are:
1. Extension of the trunk dialling telephone system.
2. Radio-telephone communication between control post and cab.
3. Automatic train reporting.
4. Centralised message centre, with telegraph/teleprinter system.
5. Takoradi region traffic control.
6. Centralised traffic control feasibility studies.

OTHER IMPROVEMENTS
Railway electrification, especially in such traffic intensive areas as the Western Line route and from Huni Valley to Takoradi where traffic density is highest, is believed to be vital. Feasibility studies into an electrification programme are to be carried out, with detailed examination of the engineering and economic aspects of the proposal.
Technical and feasibility studies are also to be made into track doubling on the Western Line. The studies will examine:
a) The present and anticipated future passenger and freight traffic volume, to determine when saturation would make it essential to double certain sections.
b) The comparative costs of equipment to improve train safety, improve performance and increase line capacity, as an alternative to track doubling.
c) A cost-benefit study of the project as a whole.

GREECE

HELLENIC RAILWAYS ORGANISATION

Organisme Des Chemins De Fer Héllénique SA,
1-3 Karolou Street, Athens 107

Telephone: 541 510
Telex: 215187

Governor and Chairman: John Lambros
Vice-Governor: J. Arzimanogion
General Directors: M. Bardis
        A. Dimoulas
        A. Apergis
Central Administration:
  Personnel: F. Petalas
  Operation: A. Papanicolaou
  Traction: G. Efstathiadis
  Track: N. Karagiorgas
  Organisation Design and Planning: C. Kochilas
  Commercial: K. Marinakos
  Finance: N. Diamantopoulos
  Workshops Manager: G. Charamis
Regional Management:
  Athens: Th. Kounoupis
  Thessaloniki: A. Tsamourtzis
  Peloponnesus: G. Sakellarion

Gauge: 1.435 m; 1.00 m; 0.75 m
Route length: 1 565 km; 892 km; 22 km

The Hellenic Railways Organisation (GR) operates a 2 479 km long railway network, which consists mainly of single track line, with the exception of a 119 km long section consisting of double track line. 63 per cent of the total track length consists of normal gauge line (1.435 m) and the remainder is narrow-gauged (36 per cent 1.00 m and one per cent 0.75 m).

The authorised weight per axle is 20 tonnes for nearly all the standard-gauge tracks; 14 tonnes for nearly the whole of the metric gauge of the Peloponnesus, and 11 tonnes for the metric gauge of Thessaly. The network is linked to certain large ports of the country (Piraeus, Thessalonica, Volos, Alexandroupolis, Kalamata and Patras) and with industrial complexes, but of limited number.

Greek Railways (CH) are investing 6 200 million Drachmas (about 800 million French Francs) between 1977 and 1982 to modernise the railway network. Aspects of modernisation stressed by the new plan include:

1. Renewal of all old rails and sleepers on the lines linking Athens with Thessaloniki and on to Idomeni, and from Thessaloniki to Alexandroupolis.
2. Important realignments to permit higher commercial speeds, particularly on the Athens-Thessaloniki and Thessaloniki-Alexandroupolis lines.
3. Signalling improvements and resignalling throughout the network and installation of CTC on the Tithorea-Domokos line.

4. Construction of more industrial sidings, extension of sidings at stations and improvements to station buildings.
5. Modernisation of the railway's telecommunication system.
6. Purchase of new locomotives and rolling stock.

In addition to the railway's direct investments, Dr.1100 million is being allocated for various works from the Public Investment Budget. These investments will be controlled by the Ministry of Public Works.

A new international service between Paris and Athens was introduced in 1977, which shortens the journey between the two capitals from 57 to 50 hours. The route followed is: Lausanne, Milan, Ancona, Bari, Brindisi, and by ferry to Patras.

The Governments of Greece and Syria signed an important agreement in Damascus on the development of shipping links between their two countries. This document gives special priority to setting up a wagon ferry service between the ports of Volos or Salonica and Latakia or Tartus, a distance of about 1 500 km. This will provide an alternative route to the present single-track railway line via Istanbul for traffic towards the Middle East.

TRAFFIC
In 1978 Hellenic Railways carried the following traffic:

Passenger journeys	10 661 000
Passengers-km	1 567 781 000
Freight tonnes	3 594 000
Tonnes-km	854 342 000

FINANCES

	1976	1979
	(Drachmas-millions)	
Revenues	3 611*	4 154**
Expenses	4 278	4 948

*Including Dr 787 million from the state as subsidy.
**Including state subsidy of Dr 849 million.

MOTIVE POWER AND ROLLING STOCK
After delivery of new rolling stock in 1977, fleet figures are as follows:

Diesel-locomotives	Standard gauge	145
	Narrow gauge	43
Rail-cars	Standard gauge	63
	Narrow gauge	57
Passenger coaches	Standard gauge	321
	Narrow gauge	159
Freight wagons	Standard gauge	8 608
	Narrow gauge	1 952
Containers-tank wagons	Standard gauge	329

SIGNALLING AND TRAIN CONTROL
New signalling installations included automatic signalling over the Athens-Inoi and Thessaloniki-Plati routes which operates by colour lights through short isolated sections of track. Supplier was Spoorweg Sein Industrie.
A total of 330 grade crossings have been selected for automatic barriers by Westinghouse.

Alsthom CC diesel electric rated at 2 100 hp for a top speed of 105 km/h; fitted with SEMT 16 PA 4 diesel engine

Standard-gauge railcar set built by Ganz-Mavag

Three-car Esslingen diesel trainset built by Ferrostaal

2 150-hp Co-Co Alco diesel-electric heading the Hellas-Balkan express

GUINEA

CHEMIN DE FER DE LA GUINÉE

PO Box 581, Conakry

Director: Diane Pierre

Gauge: 1.00 m
Route length: 662 km

The railway from Conakry to the River Niger joins the limits of navigability of the Upper Niger (Kouroussa) with the sea port of Conakry on the coast of Guinea. The railway was opened from Conakry as far as Kouroussa in 1910. In 1914, it was extended as far as Kankan, on the River Milo, a tributary of the Niger.

Studies have been completed and initial earthworks started on a new 1 400 km Trans-Guinea line which will link new bauxite deposits at Tongue and Dabola and the agricultural region of Nimba with the port of Conakry.

The new line, to be built to metre-gauge standards, will partly replace the existing Conakry-Kouroussa railway, as much of the present track is too lightly laid and gradients are too steep to handle growing traffic. Maximum gradient at present is 15 per cent compensated and maximum axle loading 13 tonnes. Existing 20 kg/m rails are to be replaced by 30 kg/m sections.

The Trans-Guinea (as it is to be called) will in part replace the lightly-laid 600 km metre-gauge track built in 1900-14 to link navigable parts of the Niger river system with the sea at Conakry. Its basic function is to link bauxite deposits at Tougue and Dabola and iron ore mines at Simondou as well as Nimba with Conakry, but as the main line and branches will penetrate large tracts of the country hitherto unexploited, it will also boost agricultural, forestry and industrial development.

MOTIVE POWER AND ROLLING STOCK

The present motive power fleet includes 27 mainline diesel locomotives, five diesel shunters and eight diesel railcars. Rolling stock includes 23 passenger coaches and 483 freight wagons.

Latest purchases include two model GL 22C diesel-electric 1 500-hp main-line diesels from General Motors which went into service in 1978.

INDUSTRIAL RAILWAYS

There are three other lines in operation, all serving mineral deposits.

The CF de Fria, opened in 1960, carries the products of the bauxite mine and aluminium plant at Fria to the port of Conakry. It is of metre gauge, 89 miles (143 km) long single track, laid with 92.7 lb/yd (46 kg/m) continuous welded rail on metal sleepers. Three Alsthom 1 100 hp diesel-electric locomotives hauling 50-tonne load wagons transport some 500 000 tonnes of export per year.

The CF de la Compagnie Minière de Conakry is a 4 ft 8½ in × 3 (1.435 m) gauge line 9 miles (14 km) long, running between an iron ore mine on the outskirts of Conakry and the port. About 800 000 tonnes per year are carried to the port using two Alsthom 700 hp diesel-electric locomotives.

The Boke Railway is a mineral ore line, running 145 km inland from Port Kamsar on the coast of Guinea. Built by a consortium of European contractors, the line was inaugurated in mid-1973 and has, since then, been operated by Canac Consultants on behalf of the Guinea government and the railway administration, Office d'Aménagement de Boke. Canac was initially contracted to manage the operation of the line and to train Guinean staff for self management.

The first half of the line runs through the coastal sea plain while the upper half reaches into the foothills of the Fouta Djalon mountains. The line is standard gauge with 60 kg/m continuously welded UIC profile rail laid entirely on steel sleepers. The line has a capacity of 12 million tonnes annually with ore moving in European built wagons hauled by US-built rolling stock. In 1975 a passenger operation was started up.

HONG KONG

KOWLOON-CANTON RAILWAY (BRITISH SECTION KCR)

Hung Hom, Kowloon

Telephone: 3-646321

General Manager: D. M. Howes
Assistant General Manager (Planning/Administration): U. L. Wong
Assistant General Manager (Traffic): Y. H. Choi
Assistant General Manager (Technical): J. B. Manson
Project Manager: S. S. Choi
Departmental Secretary: K. C. Cheng
Operations Manager: T. L. Ma
Terminals Manager: K. Y. Ngan
Railway Chief, Civil Engineer: K. S. Chung
Permanent Way Engineer: M. R. Elvy
Railway Chief, Electrical & Mechanical Engineer: B. T. Chiu
Rolling Stock Manager: Chang Yu-hong

Gauge: 1.435 m
Route length: 33.5 km

The Kowloon-Canton Railway (British Section), which has been in existence since 1910, is a single line railway 33.51 km long. During 1978-81 the whole railway is being rebuilt in situ. The route between Kowloon and Lo Wu is being provided with two tracks. Full electrification and modernisation programme at a cost of $2 billion is in hand. Target date for full electrification of the railway is the end of 1982.

A new loop line and station near the Railway workshops at Ho Tung Lau (Sha Tin) to service the new racecourse was completed in October 1978. Work on constructing a new double track tunnel through Beacon Hill to replace the present single bore tunnel began early in 1978. The new tunnel which is 2.3 km long will be completed by early 1981. All the existing stations are to be rebuilt.

TRAFFIC	1976/77	1977/78	1978/79
Total freight ton-km	46 142 100	51 200 113	63 595 838
Total freight tonnage	1 386 865	1 505 941	1 870 506
Total passenger-km	244 732 600	296 114 929	336 859 300
Total passengers carried	12 210 985	14 490 912	16 401 335

FINANCES	1976/77	1977/78	1978/79
Revenue	HK$34 845 185	45 274 362	51 573 213
Expenses	HK$30 818 614	41 050 042	50 778 318

(Note: KCR's financial year ends on 31 March.)

INVESTMENTS

During 1979/80 the KCR is spending $HK 550 million on capital improvements including $HK 70 million on resignalling the entire line. Total capital expenditure in 1978/79 was $HK 120 million.

MOTIVE POWER

KCR operates 12 line-haul diesel electric locomotives.

ELECTRIFICATION

In January, 1977, Transportation System and Market Research Ltd (Transmark), a subsidiary of British Railways, was appointed to carry out a study of the electrification of the line and the viability of the following extensions: from Hung Hom to Tsim Sha Tsui, Tai Wai to Kwai Chung, Beacon Hill Tunnel (North Portal) to Sha Tin Racecourse Station via Yuen Chau Kok, Tai Po Market to Tai Po Industrial Estate and from a connecting point near Tai Po Market to Tuen Mun via Yuen Long. A report on their findings was submitted to Hong Kong Government in September 1977 and a final agreement was signed in 1979.

Three new 2 000 hp locomotives delivered by General Electric between 1974 and 1977

The new Kowloon station in Hung Hom

PERMANENT WAY AND INSTALLATIONS

Work on double tracking the line from Hung Hom to Sha Tin (excluding the Beacon Hill tunnel) which commenced in October 1975 and was completed at the end of 1977, gives an additional daily capacity of 16 000 passengers in each direction.

The double tracking of the second third of the line from Sha Tin to Tai Po Market has recently been approved by the Hong Kong Government and work commenced in January 1978. It is expected to be completed in the middle of 1982.

Two sidings at Fo Tan (near Sha Tin) were completed in July 1977. One, an oil siding, was opened to traffic in May 1977 for unloading rail-borne petroleum products from China.

A marshalling Yard at Lo Wu, which will consist of 7 tracks with an overall trackage of 3 139.44 m (10 300 ft), was partially in use in September 1977 and was completed at the end of 1979.

Heavier UIC 54 rails with concrete sleepers and long welded sections are being introduced progressively to replace 95 lb/yard rail on wooden sleepers.

SIGNALLING

Existing semaphore signals are being replaced by modern colour light signalling. A central train control room is to be provided at Hung Hom to monitor train movements along the whole line.

DIESEL LOCOMOTIVES

Class	Axle Arrange-ment	Trans-mission	Rated Power hp	Max. lbs (kg)	Tractive Effort Continuous at lbs (kg)	mph (km/h)	Max. Speed mph (km/h)	Wheel Dia. in (mm)	Total Weight Tons	Length ft in (m)	No. Built	Year first Built	Builders: Mechanical Parts	Engine & Type	Transmission
G-12	Bo-Bo	Electric	1 125		28 000 (12 700.576)		62 (99.8)	40 (1 016)	71T	44' 6'' (13.6)	2	1954	The Clyde Engineering Co Pty Ltd, Australia		
G-12	Bo-Bo	Electric	1 310		32 600 (14 787.099)		62 (99.8)	40 (1 016)	72T	44' 6'' (13.6)	3	1954	The Clyde Engineering Co Pty Ltd, Australia		
G-16	Co-Co	Electric	1 800		50 520 (22 915.468)		62 (99.8)	40 (1 016)	98T	56' 8'' (17.4)	3	1961	Electro-motive Division, General Motors Corporation, USA		
G-26	Co-Co	Electric	2 000		50 400 (22 861.037)		62 (99.8)	40 (1 016)	98T	56' 8'' (17.4)	1	1965	The Clyde Engineering Co Pty Ltd, Australia		

HUNGARY
HUNGARIAN STATE RAILWAYS (MAV)
Magyar Allamvasutak, Népköztársaság Utja 73-75, 1940 Budapest VI

General Manager: Zoltán Szücs
Assistant General Managers: Dr. János Telek
       János Gulyás
       Béla Szabó
       Alajos Mester
Chief of Secretariat: Jenó Toppantó
Chief of International Section: Dr. Lászlo Várkonyi
Departmental Managers:
  Planning and Development: Béla Maráz
  Construction and Track Maintenance: István Kummer
  Engineering and Traction: Imre Tongori
  Operations: Jotvàn Egri
  Automation and Signalling: Sándor Urbán
  Workshops: Tibor Kardos
  Commercial: Miklòs Juhász
  Control of Materials: Alajos Horváth

Gauge: 1.435 m
Total route length: 7 483 km

More than 40 000 million forints are being spent on railway modernisation in Hungary under the present 1976-80 Five-Year Plan. The programme includes upgrading of over 1 600 km of track and the installation of 800 light-protected or half-barrier level-crossings. A further 270 km of track will be electrified, including the 155-km line from Budapest to Kelebia. This will bring the total electrified length of track to 1 450 km or 60 per cent of the mainline system. Electrified trackage at present carries 50 per cent of traffic on MAV.
More than 70 railway yards are to be fitted with Integra-Domino safety equipment.
By 1980 an estimated 96 per cent of all trains will have been electric or diesel hauled and 88.7 per cent of shunting carried out by diesel locomotives.
Rolling stock is to be increased by the purchase of 750 new passenger coaches and 10 000 large-capacity freight wagons.

ELECTRIFICATION
To accelerate work on the Budapest-Kelebia electrification project, MAV has signed a 5-million rouble ($US 6 700 000) credit agreement with the Comecon international investment bank. Cost of electrification will be 1 000 million forints. The new loan made it possible for MAV to switch over to electric haulage on the line by July 1979.

Total electrified route length: 1 280 km.
Total electrified track length: 3 254 km.
System of electrification: 25 000 V, 50 Hz.

TRAFFIC

	1977/78	1978/79
Total train-km	106 551 000	106 872 000
Percentage of train km		
by steam	7.1%	5.5%
by diesel	44.0%	44.9%
by electric	48.9%	49.6%
Total freight tonnage	133 800 000	134 114 000
Average haul	1 166	1 159
Average net train load	593	589
Average wagon load	26.5	27.5
Total passenger-km	14 190 000 000	13 751 000 000
Total passengers carried	320 100 000	304 450 000
Passengers carried		
1st class	19 500 000	19 700 000
2nd class	300 700 000	284 800 000
Average length of passenger journey: 63 km		

FINANCES

	1977/78	1978/79
	(Forints)	
Revenues from passengers and baggage	7 984 000 000	8 300 000 000
Revenues from freight and mail	16 714 000 000	16 450 000 000

DIESEL LOCOMOTIVES

Class	Axle Arrangement	Transmission	Rated Power hp	Max kg	Tractive Effort Continuous at kg	km/h	Max Speed km/h	Wheel Dia. mm	Axle Load Tons	Total Weight Tons	Length mm	No. Built	Year first Built	Builders: Mechanical Parts	Engine	Transmission
M28	B	Mech.	135	5 490	5 250	5.0	30	950	10.0	20.0	7 390		1955	MVG	Ganz	MVG
M31	C	Hyd.	450	15 700	9 600	7.0	60	1 232	15.0	45.0	9 830		1958	MAVAG	Ganz	Voith
M32	C	Hyd.	350				60	920	12.0	36.0	9 510		1973	MAVAG	Ganz	Ganz
M38	C	Hyd.	350	11 000	7 000	5.0	60	920	10.6	32.0	8 850		1960	MVG	MVG	UVA
M40	BoBo	Elec.	1 000	24 300	13 600	13.7	100	1 040	18.9	75.6	13 590		1966	MAVAG	Ganz	Ganz
M41.20	BB	Hyd.	1 800	19 740	12 700	20.0	100	1 100	16.5	66.0	16 500		1973	MAVAG	Pielstick	Voith
M41.21	BB	Hyd.	1 200	25 400	15 200	14.00	100	920	15.7	62.6	13 940		1969	MAVAG	Pielstick	
M44	BoBo	Elec.	600	18 600	12 030	8.3	80	1 040	15.5	62.0	11 290		1956	MAVAG	Ganz	MVG
M46.0	BB	Hyd.	610	11 400	7 400	12.0	60	920	11.9	47.6	12 090		1964	MAVAG	Ganz	Ganz
M46.2	BB	Hyd.	760	13 050	7 900	13.0	65	920	12.0	48.0	11 840		1964	MAVAG	Ganz	Ganz
Mk48	BB	Mech.	135	4 740	4 480	5.0	50	700	4.4	17.6	8 965		1960	MVG	Ganz	MVG
Mk49	BB	Hyd.	270	8 000	7 800	5.0	50	700	6.8	27.0	11 060		1968	MVG	MVG	UVA
M61	CoCo	Elec.	1 950		21 000	19.2	100	1 040	18.5	108.0	18 900		1963	NOHAB	GM	GM
M62	CoCo	Elec.	2 000		20 000	20.0	100	1 050	20.0	120.0	17 560		1965	Lugansk	Kolomna	Charkow
M63	CoCo	Elec.	2 700	40 000	21 700		130	1 250	20.0	120.0	19 540		1971	MAVAG	Pielstick	MVG
MDa	BB	Hyd.	800				100		10.5	41.0	15 520			Mavag	Pielstick	Ganz
M43	BB	Hyd.	450	14 000	11 000	5.0	60	920	12	48.0	11 460		1974	Aug 23	Aug 23	
M47	BB	Hyd.	700	15 000	11 500	5.0	70	920	12	48.0	11 460		1974	Aug 23	Aug 23	

Mk48, Mk49: 760 mm Gauge.

ELECTRIC LOCOMOTIVES

Class	Axle Arrangement	Line Current kV	Type	Rated Power hp	Max kg	Tractive Effort Continuous at kg	km/h	Max Speed km/h	Wheel Dia. mm	Weight tonnes	Length mm	No. Built	Year First Built	Builders Mechanical Parts	Electrical Equipment
V41	BoBo	25	50 ac	1 390		14 600	65.0	80	1 040	73.0	12 290	30	1958	MAVAG	Ganz
V42	BoBo	25	50 ac	1 650		15 500	70.0	80	1 040	74.0	12 290	42	1960	MAVAG	Ganz
V43	B B	25	50 ac	3 000		15 000	52.5	130	1 180	78.0	15 700	205	1963	MAVAG	Ganz
V63	CoCo	25	50 ac	5 000				120		116.0	19 540	2	1975	MAVAG	Ganz

INDIA

INDIAN GOVERNMENT RAILWAYS (IR)
MINISTRY OF RAILWAYS (RAILWAY BOARD)
Rail Bhavan, New Delhi 110001

Minister for Railways: Kamalapati Tripathi
Minister of State for Railways: C. K. Jaffer Sharief
Railway Board
  Chairman: M. Menezes
  Financial Commissioner: P. N. Jain
  Member, Traffic: S. N. Sachdev
  Member, Mechanical: K. S. Ramaswamy
  Member, Engineering: V. C. A. Padmanabhan
General Managers
  Central Railway: Krishan Chandra
  Eastern Railway: Prabhinder Singh
  Northern Railway: R. K. Natesan
  North Eastern Railway: Laljee Singh
  Northeast Frontier Railway: B. Vankataramani
  Southern Railway: T. M. Thomas
  South Central Railway: N. N. Sarma
  South Eastern Railway: J. S. D. David
  Western Railway: M. S. Gujral
Manufacturing Units
  Chittaranjan Locomotive Works: K. Raman
  Diesel Locomotive Works: K. P. Jayaram
  Integral Coach Factory: (Vacant)
  Wheel and Axle Plant: B. B. Lal
Research, Design and Standards Organisation
  Director General: B. Mohanty

Gauge: 1.676 m (30 909 km); 1.00 m (25 503 km); 0.762 m and 0.610 m (4 281 km)
Route length: 60 693 km

Indian Railways organised under one management as a Central Government Undertaking is the main artery of the nation's inland transport. Extending over 60 693 route km, of which 4 719 km are electrified, the rail network operates on three gauges: broad gauge (1.676 m), metre gauge (1.000 m) and narrow gauge (0.762 m and 0.610 m). With an investment of more than 5 896 rupee crores (1977/78) and staff strength of over 1.5 million (excluding about 0.23 million casual labour), IR is Asia's largest and the world's second largest state-owned railway system under unitary management. There is a fleet of about 11 100 locomotives, 36 800 coaching vehicles and 397 800 freight wagons. Over nine million passengers and 655 000 tonnes of freight are carried daily in about 11 000 trains serving 7 100 stations. The daily average loading is 25 318 wagons on the broad gauge, 6 136 on the metre gauge and 558 on the narrow gauge.

TRAFFIC

In 1977-78 IR moved 237.3 million tonnes of revenue-earning freight traffic (212.6 million tonnes in 1976/77). The average lead slightly declined during the year to 677 km from 685 km in 1975-76. Revenue freight traffic in terms of both tonnage and tonne kilometres increased at a fast rate during IR's first three Plans, from 1950-51 to 1965-66, but the rate of growth slowed down thereafter. In the First Plan the traffic increased by 5 per cent per annum in terms of tonnes originating and 7 per cent in terms of tonne-km; in the Second Plan the increase was 6 per cent and 8.7 per cent respectively and in the Third Plan 7 per cent and 7.4 per cent respectively. From 1966-67, the tonnage hovered around the level reached in 1965-66. However, in 1975-76 and 1976-77 there was an increase in the traffic, and by the end of 1976-77 the tonnage lifted was a record 212.6 million tonnes. But in 1977-78, the tonnage showed a drop of 1.8 millions or 0.85 per cent as compared to the previous year.

The upward trend in passenger traffic continued in 1977-78, the number of passengers carried during the year being 3,504 million, an all time high and 6 per cent more than in 1976-77. Passenger kilometres increased by 7.9 per cent to 176 700 million. While the increase in passenger traffic in terms of passenger-km was more significant in non-suburban travel (8.3 per cent as against 6.3 per cent for suburban travel) the number of passengers increased more on suburban section: 7 per cent against only 5.2 per cent for non-suburban traffic.

	1975-76	1976-77	1977-78
		(millions)	
Total freight tonne-km	148 219	156 756	162 687
Freight tonnage	223.3	239.1	237.3
Total passenger-km	148 761	163 836	176 704
Passenger journeys	2 945	3 300	3 504

FINANCES

The gross traffic receipts of the Indian Railways for the year 1977-78 amounted to 2 123.42 rupee crores. After meeting working expenses of 1 750.12 rupee crores, the net traffic receipts for the year came to 373.30 rupee crores. The net revenue for the year was 352.9 rupee crores, yielding a rate of return of 7.35 per cent of the capital-at-charge of 4 797.12 rupee crores. After payment of the obligatory dividend of 226.56 rupee crores, the year ended with a surplus of 126.23 rupee crores, a record.

	(Crores of Rupees)	
	1976-77	1977-78
Gross traffic receipts	2 036.11	2 123.42
Working expenses	1 718.56	1 750.12
Net traffic receipts	317.55	373.30
Miscellaneous transactions	(—) 21.26	20.51
Net revenue	296.29	352.79
Dividend	209.05	226.56
Surplus for the year	87.24	(+) 126.23
Working expenses to gross traffic receipts (Operating Ratio)	84.40	83.0
Net revenue to capital-at-charge	6.54	7.35

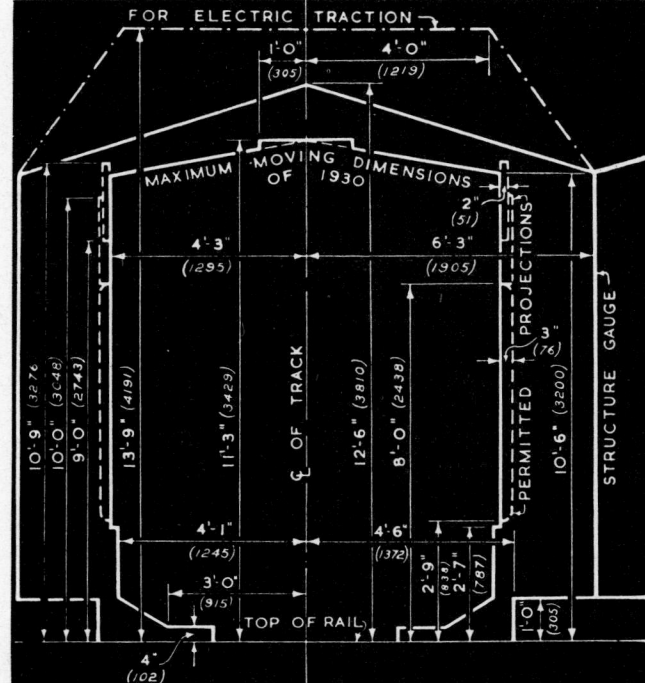

Medium Gauge

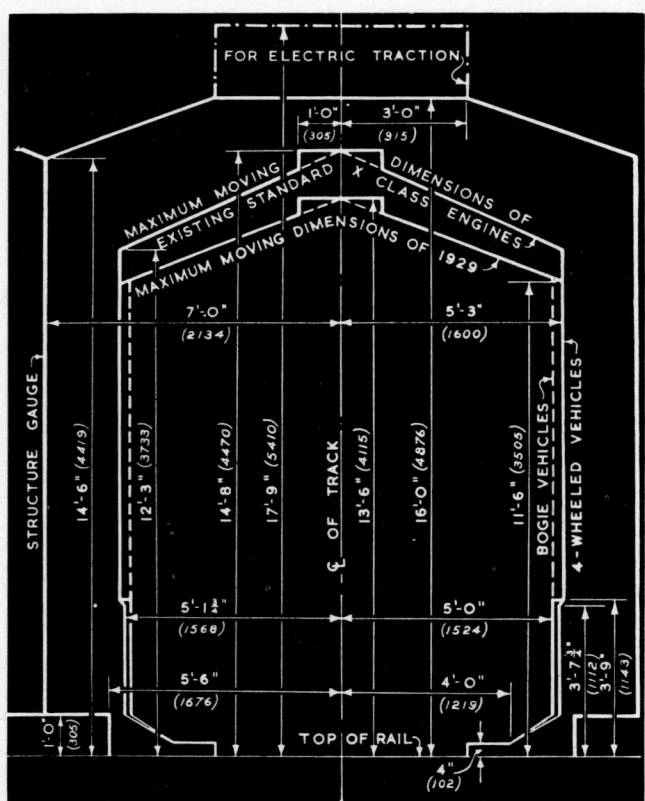

Broad Gauge

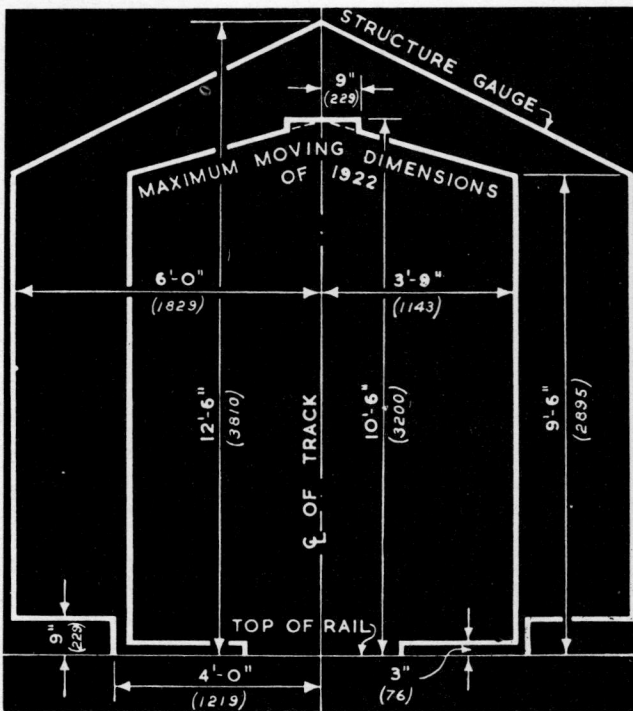

Narrow Gauge

MOTIVE POWER AND ROLLING STOCK

Diesel and electric traction in 1978 accounted for 71 per cent of IR's total freight train-km while 17 per cent of passenger train-km was handled by diesel power. To a large extent the use of steam is restricted to passenger trains, assistance services, shunting, work trains and stand-by duties. Diesel locomotives make up ten per cent of the shunting fleet.

Number of locomotives in service at the end of 1978:

	Broad gauge	Metre gauge	Narrow gauge
Steam	4 921	2 977	365
Electric	1 063	47	58
Diesel electric	1 198	381	—

Number of two-axle railcars:

	Broad gauge	Metre gauge	Narrow gauge
Electric power cars	684	45	—
Diesel power cars	25	30	14
Electric trailers	1 474	129	1 603
Passenger coaches	14 681	10 082	1 352
Freight wagons	30 337	89 336	5 080

The total electric locomotive fleet on IR by mid-1978 was 743 ac, 106 dc and 30 ac-dc units. In addition, extensive suburban electrification on the cities of Bombay, Madras and Calcutta is served by a fleet of 748 motor coaches and 1 615 trailer coaches, running in 8/9 car rakes.

So far 77 dc and 555 ac and ac-dc electric locomotives of freight and mixed traffic types have been built. The current series under production are WAM/4 (a 3 600 hp, 6-axle locomotive for mixed traffic duty) and WCAMI (a 25 kV ac/1 500 V dc mixed traffic locomotive for dual voltage operation). A heavier freight version of WAM/4 locomotive, as well as a higher speed version expected to be capable of 130 km/h plus speed, is also under design/manufacture.

The electrical multiple units are built by the state-owned Integral Coach Factory at Perambur, and M/s Jessops and Co, Calcutta. The electric traction equipments are supplied by IR production shops at CLW and Bharat Heavy Electricals Ltd, Bhopal, for suburban stock.

With further electrification from Virar to Ahmedabad over the Western region of the Indian Railways, (25 kV, 50 Hz ac system) and techno-economic justification for retaining the existing adjoining electrified section under 1 500 V dc system from Bombay Central to Virar, it became essential to develop a dual voltage locomotive.

The first prototype was turned out of Chittaranjan Locomotive Works in February 1975 to a design developed by Research Designs and Standards Organisation.

On ac section, with a line voltage of 22.5 kV and half-worn wheels, the locomotive is capable of the following performance characteristics:-
(a) Starting a trailing load of 3 660 tonnes box wagons on a gradient of 1 in 350 and hauling at a balancing speed of 100 km/h on level.
(b) Starting a trailing load of 2 340 tonnes four-wheeler wagons on a gradient of 1 in 350 and hauling at a speed of 72 km/h on level (limited by the maximum permissible speed of four-wheeler wagons).
(c) Hauling a passenger train of 800 tonnes at a balancing speed of 120 km/h on level. Though the 19.5 tonne axle-load version of the locomotive has been cleared for an operating speed of only 100 km/h, it is expected that 18.9 tonne axle-load version, provided with modified bogies with resilient thrust pad, will be suitable for operation at 120 km/h.

ELECTRIFICATION

Total electrified route length by mid-1978 was 4 719 km, consisting of 4 553 km over broad-gauge and 166 km metre-gauge. Total track length was 9 152 km. System of electrification is 25 kV 50 Hz ac although a short section on Central Railway's suburban lines is electrified at 1 500 V dc.

PERMANENT WAY

The following table shows the route-kilometrage of railways by States in 1977/78. Uttar Pradesh heads the list with 8 759 route-km, followed by Madhya Pradesh with 5 716 route-km.

	Route-km
Andhra Pradesh	4 714
Assam	2 193
Bihar	5 303
Gujarat	5 670
Haryana	1 445
Himachal Pradesh	256
Jammu & Kashmir	77
Karnataka	2 960
Kerala	887
Madhya Pradesh	5 716
Maharashtra	5 233
Nagaland	9
Orissa	1 948
Punjab	2 137
Rajasthan	5 608
Tamil Nadu	3 765
Tripura	12
Uttar Pradesh	8 759
West Bengal	3 716
Union Territories	
Chandigarh	11
Delhi	168
Goa, Daman & Diu	79
Pondicherry	27
TOTAL	60 693

During 1978 about 73 km of new broad gauge lines were added to the network: Gohana-Panipat B.G. restoration (40 km) and construction of a new line Shahadara-Baghpat Road (33 km) which is a part of Shahadara-Saharanpur section. Two new lines, namely Karaila Road-Jayant and Bhadrachallam Road-Manuguru covering collectively 87 km, were approved during the year bringing the total of approved new line construction including restorations to 1,204 km at the end of 1978.

Although 21 per cent of trunk routes have so far been doubled, there are patches on the lines between Delhi-Bombay, Delhi-Madras, Madras-Trivandrum, Bombay-Madras and other important sections where double tracking is becoming necessary. During the 1977-78 fiscal year, 122 km of high density single line sections were doubled and the work on another 717 km was in various stages of progress.

25 kV ac/1 500 dc type WCAM1 electric locomotive

At the beginning of 1978, there were 10 approved projects for conversion from metre gauge to broad gauge, covering 2 276 kilometres of railway lines. Two more projects were added during the year, making the route kilometrage 3 364. The conversion projects of Suratgarh-Bhatinda (142 km), Barabanki-Samastipur (587 km), Veeramgam-Okha (557 km), Guntakal-Bangalore (267 km) and New Bongaigaon-Gauhati (157 km) progressed significantly during the year.

Rail, types and weight:

	Type/specification	Weight per metre
Flat bottom 65 kg steel rails	Gost 8160 & 8161-56	65 kg
Wear resistant rails 60 kg/metre	UIC 860/0 grade 'C'	60 kg
Wear resistant rails 52 kg/metre	UIC 860/0 grade 'B'	52 kg
Medium Manganese Flat bottom	IRS speen T 12	52 kg
Rails 52 kg/metre		
,, BS90R	,,	44.61 kg
,, BS75R	,,	37.13 kg
,, BS60R	,,	29.76 kg
,, BS50R	,,	24.80 kg

Sleepers: Wooden, cast iron and steel sleepers. A start has also been made with the use of concrete sleepers.

Thickness (dimensions):
Concrete sleepers: Mono block concrete sleepers, thickness at rail level 196.25 mm, length 2 750 mm. With Pandrol Rail clips, thickness at rail level 210.00 mm, length 2 750 mm. Two block concrete sleepers, thickness at rail level 215.50 mm, length 722 mm each with MS angle iron tie bar of 75 × 75 × 10 mm.

Wooden sleepers:
Broad Gauge 2 750 mm × 250 mm × 130 mm
Metre Gauge 1 800 mm × 200 mm × 115 mm
Narrow Gauge 1 500 mm × 180 mm × 115 mm

Spacing: 1 540 sleepers are provided per km.
Rail fastenings:
1. Fish plates and bolts and nuts to suit the type of rails viz. 65 kg, 60 kg, 52 kg, 44.61 kg, 37.13 kg, 27.76 kg and 24.80 kg rails.
2. Fittings for concrete sleepers:
   (a) For monoblock concrete sleepers

	Drawing No.
Pandrol clips	PR 401
Nylon liners	RDSO/T-383
Grooved Rubber pads	RDSO/T-382
Inserts	RDSO/T-381

   (b) For twin—block concrete sleepers:

Grooved Rubber pads	RDSO/T-476
Clips and clamps	IRN 202 RDSO/T-465
Liners	RDSO/T-466
Bolts and nuts	RDSO/T-477
Rubber Heel Pads	RDSO/T-479

3. Fillings for steel trough sleepers:

Spring steel loose jaws	IRS spn. T.12
M.S. keys	Drg. No. T. 405 (m), IRS spn. T-8
(For high speed tracks)	
Modified loose jaws	RDSO/T-1801
Grooved Rubber pads	RDSO/T-382
Pandrol clips	PR/401

Fittings for wooden sleepers:

Mild steel or cast iron bearing plates	IRS Spen T.7
Screw spikes, Round spikes or Dog spikes or Rail screws	IRS Spen T.4.66
Keys	B.G. Drg. No. T405 (M) & MG T413(M)
Rail Anchors	
(For high speed tracks)	
C.I. Bearing plates	RDSO/T-646
Screw spikes	RDSO/T-650
Pandrol clips	PR-401
Grooved Rubber pads	RDSO/647

Fittings for cast iron sleepers:
Tie bars, B.G. Drg. No. T.404(M), M.G. Drg. No. T.433(M).
Standard method of welding:
New rail is flash butt welded in workshops into 3 or 5 rail bar lengths, carried to site on specially designed wagons then alumino-thermic welded into LWR lengths after laying in position.

DIESEL LOCOMOTIVES

Class	Axle arrangement	Transmission	Rated power hp	Max. TE (kg)	Continuous rating TE (kg)	Speed (km/h)	Max speed (km/h)	Wheel dia. (mm)	Total weight tonnes	Length over head stock (mm)	No. of locos built	Year first built	Mechanical parts	Builders: Engine & Type	Transmission
1 676 mm gauge WDM1	Co-Co	Elec	1 977	27 900	19 300	19	104	1 016	112	16 777	100	1958	Alco, USA	Alco 251-B-12 cyl	GE, USA
WDM2	Co-Co	Elec	2 636	30 450	24 600	18	120	1 092	113	15 850	1 000	1962	DLW, India	DLW 251-B-16 cyl	Bhel, India
WDM3	B'-B'	Hyd Hyd-Mech	2 500	High-speed 22 000 Low-speed 25 080	High-speed 14 000 20 000	28 18.5	High-speed 120	1 092	76	14 800	2 6	1970	Henschel, West Germany	MD-108 oz 20 cyl	Myu, West Germany
WDM4	Co-Co	Elec	2 636	28 200	20 600	24	120	1 092	113	17 270	72	1962	GM, USA	GM567D3 16-cyl	GM, USA
WDS1	Bo-Bo	Elec	193	11 550	5 000	10	56	965	46	9 061	16	1945	GE, USA	Caterpiller D-17000-8 cyl	GE, USA
WDS2	O-C-O	Hyd	440	High-speed 9 200 Low-speed 15 420	High-speed 7 300 14 750	7.55 3.86	High-speed 54 Low-speed 27.6	1 092	51	7 265	30	1945	Krauss Maffei, West Germany	MAN W 8V-17-5/ 22A 8 cyl	Voith, West Germany
WDS3	O-C-O	Hyd	618	High-speed 10 400 Low-speed 1 700	High-speed 7 500 18 000	12 4	High-speed 65	1 092	57	9 430	7	1961	MAK, West Germany	Maybach MD-435 8 cyl	MAK, West Germany
WDS4	O-C-O	Hyd or Hyd-Mech	700	High-speed 11 500 Slow-speed 18 000	High-speed 8 500 16 900	13 Low-speed 5.5	High-speed 65 27	1 092	60	9 730	179	1969	CLW, India 6M28A(k) 6 cyl	MAK/CLW India	Kirloskar,
WDS4A	O-C-O	Hyd	660	High-speed 16 700 Slow-speed 18 000	High-speed 12 400 17 000	8 5	High-speed 65	1 092	60	9 730	5	1968	CLW, India 6M282A(k) 6 cyl	MAK	Voith, West Germany
WDS5	Co-Co	Elec	1 065	31 500	32 300	3.2	109	1 092	126	1 540	21	1967	ALCO 251-B-6 cyl		GE, USA
1 000 mm gauge YDM1	B'-B	Hyd	634	10 920	8 230	12	88	864	44	10 630	20	1955	North British, UK	Paxman 12 rph XL	Voith UK
YDM3	IB-B' 1	Elec	1 390	14 300	10 300	24.5	80	Driving 865 Carry-ing 762	58	12 350	30	1962	GM, USA	12 cyl 12-567 c 12 cyl	GM GM, USA
YDM4	Co-Co	Elec	1 400	18 935	19 200	15.65	96	965	72	1 318	233	1962	DLW, India	DLW/251-D 6 cyl	Bhel, India
YDM4A	Co-Co	Elec	1 400	18 935	19 200	11.6	96	965	72	13 818	99	1964	MLW, Canada	MLW/251-D 6 cyl	GE, Canada
YDM5	C'-C'	Elec	1 390	21 792	11 250	22.35	80	865	69	13 260	25	1964	GM, USA	GM 12 567c 12 cyl	GM, USA
N/ZDM1	B'-B'	Hyd	145	8 790	7 500	5	33	700	29	8 400	ZDM1-5 NDM1-3	1955	Arn Jung West Germany	MWM TRHS 518 S 6 cyl	Voith, West Germany
ZDM2	B'-B'	Hyd-Mech	700	10 560	8 500	12.5	50	700	32	9 120	25	1964	Mak, West Germany	Maybach MD 435 8 cyl	Mak, West Germany
ZDM3	B'-B'	Hyd-Mech	700	10 500	9 800	6.4	32	700	35	10 300	20	1971	CLW, India	CLW/Mak 6M 282A (k) 6 cyl	Kirloskar, India

ELECTRIC LOCOMOTIVES

Class	Axle arrangement	Line current	Rated output (hp)	Max. (kg)	Tractive Effort (Full Field) Continuous (kg)	at Rating (km/h)	Max. speed (km/h)	Wheel dia. (mm)	Weight (tonnes)	Length (mm)	No. built	Year built	Builders Mechanical Parts	Electrical Equipment
25 kV ac locomotives WAM1	Bo-Bo	25 kV ac	2 830	25 000	14 900	52.0	112.5	1 140	74.0	15 892	100	1960	Group	
WAM2	Bo-Bo	25 kV ac	2 790	25 242	14 500	52.0	112.5	1 090	76.03	15 000	10	1961	Mitsubishi	
WAM3	Bo-Bo	25 kV ac	2 790	25 242	14 500	52.0	112.6	1 090	76.0	15 000	2	1964	Mitsubishi	
WAM4	Co-Co	25 kV ac	3 640	33 840	17 600	56.0	120	1 092	112.8	18 974	232	1971	CLW	CLW & Bhel

ELECTRIC LOCOMOTIVES

Class	Axle arrangement	Line current	Rated output (hp)	Max. (kg)	Tractive Effort (Full Field) Continuous at (kg)	Rating (km/h)	Max. speed (km/h)	Wheel dia. (mm)	Weight (tonnes)	Length (mm)	No. built	Year built	Builders Mechanical Parts	Builders Electrical Equipment
WAG1	B-B	25 kV ac	2 900	30 000	23 700	33.0	80	1 140	85.2	17 092	112	1963	Group & CLW	
WAG2	B-B	25 kV ac	3 120	30 000	22 600	38.0	80	1 140	85.2	16 882	45	1964	Hitachi	
WAG3	B-B	25 kV ac	3 150	30 000	23 200	36.5	80	1 140	87.32	17 092	10	1965	Group	
WAG4	B-B	25 kV ac	3 150	30 000	23 200	36.5	80	1 140	87.6	17 216	186	1967	CLW	
WCAM1	Co-Co	25 kV ac/ 1 500 V dc	2 640 2 930	33 840 28 200	16 000 22 600	60.0 35.0	120	1 092	112.8	20 950	36	1975	CLW	CLW & Bhel
YAM1	B-B	25 kV ac	1 630	19 500	12 300	34.5	80	865	52.0	13 150	20	1965	Mitsubishi	
1 500 V dc electric locomotives WCM1	Co-Co	1 500 V dc	3 170	31 000	17 690	48.3	120.5	1 220	123.98	20 834	7	1955	EE Co Ltd & Vulcan Foundry	
WCM2	Co-Co	1 500 V dc	2 810	31 298	12 300	61.7	120.5	1 092	112.8	20 066	12	1957	EE Co Ltd & Vulcan Foundry	
WCM3	Co-Co	1 500 V dc	2 460	28 200	10 220	65.0	120.7	1 220	113.0	19 583	3	1961	Hitachi	
WCM4	Co-Co	1 500 V dc	3 290	31 250	18 700	47.5	120.5	1 220	125.0	20 000	7	1961	Hitachi	
WCM5	Co-Co	1 500 V dc	3 170	31 000	17 690	48.3	120.5	1 220	124.0	20 168	10	1961	CLW	
WCG2	Co-Co	1 500 V dc	4 200	35 600	21 900	52.5	80	1 092	135.0	19 974	57	1971	CLW	Bhel & CLW

DIESEL RAILCARS

Class	Axle arrangement	Transmission	Rated power (hp)	Max TE (kg)	Continuous TE (kg)	Rating speed (km/h)	Max speed	Wheel dia. (mm)	Total weight (tonnes)	Length over head stock (mm)	No of built	Year first built	Builders Mechanical parts	Engines & type	Transmission
1 676 mm gauge WRD1	1A-1A1	Mech	400	—	—	—	110	915	47.4 (tare) 82.10 (a)	22 241 (buffer to buffer)	24	1958	Commonwealth Eng Co Ltd, Australia	Leyland EN-900H	SCG Epicylic SE4
1 000 mm gauge YRD1	B'-2	Mech Hyd-Mech	— 225	—	—	—	88	724	28.5 (tare) 37.5 (loaded)	18 700	6 6	1956	M/s Fiat Co, Italy	Fiat 700-110/3	Fiat Fiat/Twin Di, Italy
YRD2	1A-2	Hyd-Mech	180	—	—	—	88	724	30 (tare) 39 (loaded)	18 440	12	1956	M/s Nippon Sharyo, Japan	Shinko 1MH-17h	Shinko, Japan
YRD3	1A-2	Mech	200	—	—	—	72	724	31 (tare) 40 (loaded)	19 500	2	1956	ICF, India	Leyland 0.680(H)	Wilson SC 2G
YRD4	1A-2	Hyd	285	—	—	—	93	724	31 (tare) 40 (loaded)	19 500	10	1967	ICF, India	Kirloskar Cummins NHHR TO-6	Kirloskar Twin Disc, India

ELECTRIC RAILCARS

Class	Axle Arrangement	Line Current	Rated Output hp	Max. (kg)	Tractive Effort (Full Field) Continuous at (kg)	Rating at (km/h)	Max. Speed (km/h)	Wheel dia. (mm)	Weight (tonnes)	Length (mm)	No. Built	Year Built	Builders Mechanical Parts	Builders Electrical Equipment
1 500 dc BG EMUs WCU3	Bo-Bo	1 500 V dc	1 200	7 400	6 980	52.2	104	915	160.88	85 344	12	1951	M/s British Thompson Houston	M/s Metro Cammell
WCU4	Bo-Bo	1 500 V dc	1 080	7 000	5 816	49.9	104	914.4	161.49	85 344	16	1951	M/s Metro Cammel	M/s English Electric Co
WCU5	Bo-Bo	1 500 V dc	1 080	7 000	5 816	49.9	104	914.4	170.8	82 904	12	1956	M/s Breda Ferroviaria SpA Milomo Hitachi	M/s English Electric Co
WCU6	Bo-Bo	1 500 V dc	1 120	7 200	6 465	48.15	104	914.4	177.86	82 904	6	1957	Hitachi	Hitachi
WCU7	Bo-Bo	1 500 V dc	1 120	7 200	6 465	48.15	104	914.4	174.9	82 904	12	1958/59	NSSK	NSSK
WCU8	Bo-Bo	1 500 V dc	732	10 000	3 846	54.5	104	952	120.90	62 178	16	1958/59	MAN	AEG

ELECTRIC RAILCARS

Class	Axle Arrange-ment	Line Current	Rated Output hp	Max. (kg)	Tractive Effort (Full Field) Continuous at (kg)	(km/h)	Max. Speed (km/h)	Wheel dia. (mm)	Weight (tonnes)	Length (mm)	No. Built	Year Built	Builders Mechanical Parts	Builders Electrical Equipment
WCU10	Bo-Bo	1 500 V dc	1 096	7 500	6 100	49.2	104	914.4	166.20	82 904	12	1959	M/s Breda Ferroviana	M/s Ansaldo-Sangeorgic
WCU12	Bo-Bo	1 500 V dc	840	11 000	4 592	49.75	104	952	141.23	62 178	34	1961	Jessop	AEI
WCU13	Bo-Bo	1 500 V dc	744	13 320	4 200	48.6	105	952	116.11	64 722	352 + 19S PMC	1970 1960	ICF Jessop	Bhel Bhel
WCU14	Bo-Bo	1 500 V dc	744	13 320	4 200	48.6	105	952	116.11	64 722	352 + 19S PMC	1970 1960	ICF Jessop	Bhel Bhel
WCU15	Bo-Bo	1 500 V dc	744	13 320	4 200	48.6	105	952	116.11	64 722	352 + 19S PMC	1970 1960	ICF Jessop	Bhel Bhel
25 kV ac/dc BG EMUs WAU-1 SIG (conv)	Bo-Bo	3 000 V dc/ 25 kV ac	848	8 900	4 400	50	104	952.5	117	64 312	16	1958/59	SIG	Secheron
WAU-2 Jessops (conv)	Bo-Bo	3 000 V dc/ 25 kV ac	840	11 600	4 592	49.75	104	952	141.23	62 178	16	1959/60	Jessop	AEI
25 kV ac BG EMUs WAU-3 (Hitachi)	Bo-Bo	25 kV ac	900	12 600	4 240	58.2	96	915	151.58	82 904	31	1966	ICF	Hitachi
WAU-4	Bo-Bo	25 kV ac	896	13 100	4 900	49.5	105	952	148.3	86 243	225 + 4 SPMC	1964	ICF	Bhel
25 kV ac MG EMUs YAU-1	Bo-Bo	25 kV ac	688	9 000	2 550	70.7	90	MC838 TC725	112	81 134	43 + 2 SPMC	1966	ICF	M/s Nichoman, Japan

INDONESIA

INDONESIAN STATE RAILWAYS
Perusahaan Jawatan Kereta Api (PJKA)
Jalan Geraja, 1, Bandung

Principal Officers:
  Chief Director: R. Soemali
  Director Personnel: Aswasmarmo
  Director Finance: Imam Rustadi
  Director Civil Engineering: R. Moerhadi
  Director Mechanical Engineering: Pantiarso
  Director Transportation: Chaidir Nien Latief
  Managing Secretary: Hersubno
  Chief Planning: Sandjojo
  Chief Research & Development: Partosiswojo
  Chief Audit: Soedharmoen Pintodihardjo
Regional Managers:
  East Java Region, Surabaya: Soeparto
  Central Java Region, Semarang: Soeharso
  West Java Region, Jakarta: Soetarno
  South Sumatra Region, Palembang: Sugiarto
  West Sumatra Region, Padang: Soekirian
  North Sumatra Region, Medan: Asmanu

Gauge: 1.067 m; 0.75 m; 0.60 m.
Route length: 6 389 km; 497 km; 78 km.

The railway network in Indonesia is confined to the islands of Java (including Madura) with about 4 900 km and Sumatra with about 2 000 km of route length. The system was built up to its present size during the 70 years prior to World War II, at which time 40 per cent of the network was owned privately. Nationalisation took place in the 1940s and 1950s.
Organisationally, the railway is divided into six regional divisions (three in Java and three in Sumatra), and 17 departmental sub-divisions (11 in Java and six in Sumatra).

TRAFFIC
The total tonnage of freight carried by PJKA in 1977 was registered at 2 398 000 tonnes and 854 million tonne-km, an increase of 28 000 and 150 million over the 1976 figures. This resulted in an increase of freight revenue from Rp 4 144 million in 1976 to Rp 5 537 million in 1977. The commodities which effected a substantial increase in carload shipment were oil, fertiliser, coal estate products and cement.
The volume of passenger traffic for 1977 increased in comparison to the 1976 figures. Its revenue totalled Rp 14 234 million, or Rp 2 047 million higher than the previous year's figures. It still remained the bigger portion of PJKA total revenue, (53.1 per cent). The total number of passengers carried in 1977 (not including ferry services) was 20 634 million, showing an increase of 151 000. Passenger-km registered 3 642 million, an increase of 254 million over 1976. The increase of passenger traffic was mainly attributable to the new city commuter system in Jakarta. An average distance per journey in 1977 was 176.5 km, about 6.3 km longer than in 1976.

FINANCES
The operating revenue of the PJKA for the budget year 1977 amounted to Rp 26 781 million, showing an increase of Rp 4 043 million (17.7 per cent) from the previous year. Operating expenses increased from Rp 23 961 million to Rp 32 152 million, or 34.2 per cent higher than the previous year. The operating ratio for 1977 was 120 per cent.

MOTIVE POWER

	Mainline	Shunting	Side line	Total	In service	Percentage in service
Locomotives						
Steam	225	87	80	392	173	44.1
Diesel	219	131	26	376	292	77.7
Electric	9	—	—	9	1	11.1
Diesel railcars	10 + 12 set	—	—	10 + 12 set	5 + 11 set	72.7
Electric railcars	5 set	—	—	5 set	5 set	100.0
Passenger cars in units	—	—	—	2 020	883	43.7
Freight cars in units	—	—	—	15 468	10 244	77.5
In terms of four wheelers (2 axles)	—	—	—	17 660	11 853	77.9

INVESTMENTS
During 1980 the railway intends to spend 24 248 million Rp as part cost on two mainline diesel-electric locomotives, 24 passenger coaches, 187 freight wagons, track improvements, signalling, etc.

ELECTRIFICATION
The electrified system in Java covers a distance of 60 km between Jakarta and Bogor and some sections around the city of Jakarta. Electric locomotives and electric railcars are running on these lines serving the suburban transportation system of the Jakarta Metropolitan City.
Further modernisation and expansion are contemplated in this system for the coming years. Developments include replacement of rectifiers, procurements of rolling stock, electric railcars and eventually extension of the electric system itself.

	Single track	Gauge 1.067 m Double track	Total
Total electrified route length on 31 December 1976	45 km	32 km	77 km
Total electrified track length on 31 December 1976	45 km	56 km	101 km

System of electrification=Catenary system, 1 500 V dc, with four sub-stations

CIVIL ENGINEERING
Approval has been granted for relaying the North line from Jakarta to Surabaya, totalling 725 km, with R14A rail weighing 42 kg/m on wooden sleepers. Additional ballast is to be provided to make the entire route suitable for speeds up to 100 km/h. Bridges are also to be strengthened. Part of the scheme, between Jakarta and Cirebon (207 km), has already been completed. The plan also provides for rehabilitation of the following sections of the main line in Java: Cirebon-Yogjakarta-Surabaya; Bandung-Kroya; Jakarta-Merak; Kalisat-Banyuwangi; and Malang-Blitar.
Beginning with the Five Year Development Plan year of 1977/78, PJKA is engaged in constructing a new line connecting Bukitputus and the Cement Factory of Indarung in

West Sumatra. The track length is about 17 km, with construction work comprising new tracks, four bridges, two viaducts, sidings and shunting yards. The estimated cost for this new construction is about Rp 2 600 million.

Replacement of unserviceable sleepers and track fittings on main lines in Java, and North and South Sumatra will continue. Broadly, the plan provides for renewal of about 102 km of rail, 1.35 million sleepers, provision of new fastenings for 1 670 km of track, laying of 2.8 million m³ of ballast, and reconstruction of 262 turnouts.

Besides equipping track gangs with a full complement of tools for mechanised maintenance of permanent way, a track repair workshop is to be set up at Mediun, equipped with plant for carrying out repairs to points and crossings; cropping, strengthening and welding of rail; and repairs to steel sleepers.

TRACK CONSTRUCTION DETAILS

Standard rail:
1.067 m gauge: R14A 86 lb/yd *(43.59 kg/m)*; R3 67 lb/yd *(33.4 kg/m)*; R2 52 lb/yd *(25.75 kg/m)*.
0.750 m gauge: R10 33 lb/yd *(16.4 kg/m)*.   *0.600 m gauge* ID 25 lb/yd *(12.38 kg/m)*.
Type of joints: Fishplates and bolts; welding is also used.
Cross ties (sleepers): Mainly untreated teak, 6 ft 6¾ in × 8⅝ in × 4¾ in *(2 000 × 220 × 120 mm)*; some metal. Cross ties spacing: Main line, 27 in *(690 mm)*; Branch line, 31½ in *(800 mm)*.
Rail fastening: Base plates, spikes and screws, elastic fastenings.
Filling (ballast): Stone ballast, 2-2¾ in *(50-70 mm)*
Thickness under sleeper:
  Main line: 8.75° = min rad of 656 ft *(200 m)*
  Branch line: 11.6° = min rad of 492 ft *(150 m)*
Max gradient: 4% = 1 in 25.
Gauge widening on sharpest curve: 0.787 in *(20 mm)*
Super elevation on sharpest curve: 4.33 in *(110 mm)*

Rate of slope of super-elevation: 1 in 450 to 1 in 1 200.
Max altitude: 4 088 ft *(1 246 m)* near Garut, Java.
Max axle loading:
  Main line: 13½ tons.
  Branch line: 8 to 10 tons.
Max bridge loading:
  Main line: 8.75 T. per metre.
  Branch line: 5.56 T. per metre.
Max permitted speed:
  Main line:
    Passenger trains, 62 mph *(100 km/h)*
    Freight trains, 43½ mph *(70 km/h)*
  Branch line:
    Passenger trains, 37 mph *(59 km/h)*
    Freight trains, 37 mph *(45 km/h)*

SIGNALLING

Except for the Jakarta-Bogor, Cikampek-Bandung, and Surabaya-Malang routes and the Jakarta area, where train services are frequent, PJKA's main lines are equipped with obsolete signalling. The plan provides for installing Siemens-Halske mechanical tokenless block system on the main lines of Java and some sections in Sumatra. Much of the equipment for this can be manufactured locally using imported materials. Improved signalling will be provided at 157 stations on Java main lines and at 33 stations in Sumatra.

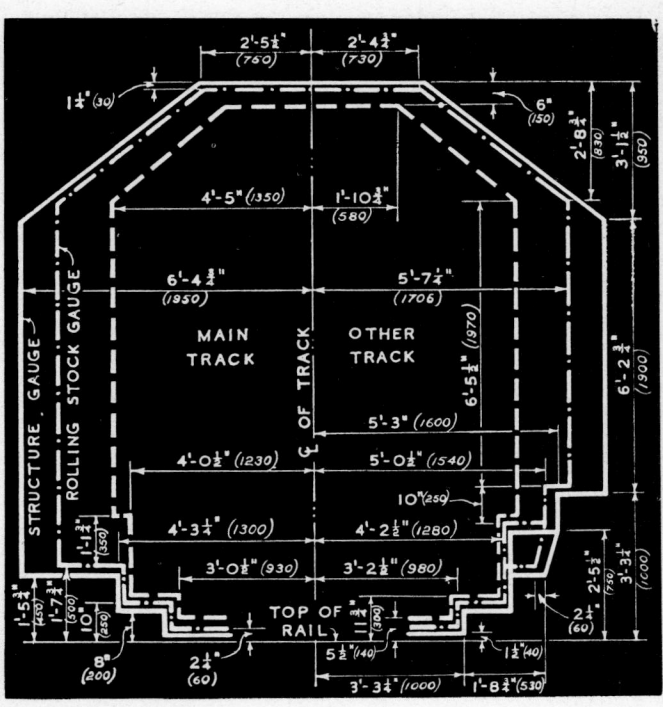

Loading gauge: main lines

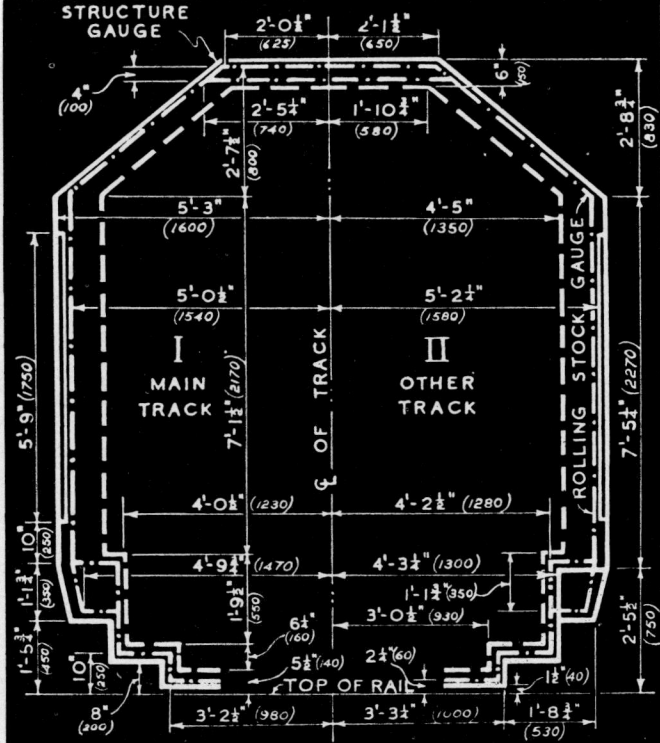

Loading gauge: secondary lines

DIESEL LOCOMOTIVES

Class	Axle Arrangement	Transmission	Rated Power hp	Max. (kg)	Tractive Effort Continuous at (kg)	(km/h)	Max. Speed (km/h)	Wheel Dia. (mm)	Total Weight Tons	Length (mm)	No. Built	Year first Built	Mechanical Parts	Engine & Type	Transmission
CC200	C-2-C	DE	1 600	21 623	4 074	—	99.68	908	96	17 070	01-27	1951		12V.244E GE	
BB200	AIA-AIA	DE	875				120	1 016	74.8	14 006	01-35	1956		B.567CR GM	
BB201	AIA-AIA	DE	1 310	21 810		15	120	1 016	78	14 026	01-11	1964		G12,567C GM	
BB202	AIA-AIA	DE	1 100	21 810		12.7	100	1 016	65	12 900	01-08	1968		GL8 645E GM	
BB300	B-B	DH	680	10 100			75	909	36	11 890	01-30	1956		MB820B	
BB301	B-B	DH	1 500	15 800	11 700	19	120	904	52	13 380	01-45 51-55	1962/ 63		MD655/MD12V 538TB10	L630 VU2
BB302	B-B	DH	1 100	14 520	12 500	15	80	904	44	12 810	01-06	1969		MB820	L520 rU 2
BB303	B-B	DH	1 150	14 100	11 500	15	90	904	42.8	12 320	01-21	1971		MB12V,493TZ	L520rU 2
BB304	B-B	DH	1 500			20	120	904	52	13 380	01-11	1974		MTU12U652TB11	L720 rU 2
CC201	C-C	DE	1 950		1 825			952	848	14 133	01-28	1976		7FDL8	
C300	C	DH	350	9 800	9 250	4,5	30	904	30	8 020	01-20	1964		MB.836B	L203U
C301	C	DH	260		5 750	6.5	30	877	14.5	5 240	01-8	1969		BV71 N60	DBG115
D300	D	DH	340	10 200		5	50	904	34	9 279	01-30	1956		MB836B	2WIL1.15
D301	D	DH	340	8 400		5	50	904	28	8980	01-80	1960		MB8368/2	2WIL1.15 Krupp

ELECTRIC LOCOMOTIVES

Class	Axle Arrangement	Line Current	Rated Output hp	Max. (kg)	Tractive Effort (Full Field) (kg)	Continuous at (km/h)	Max. Speed (km/h)	Wheel dia. (mm)	Weight (tonnes)	Length (mm)	No. Built	Year Built	Builders Mechanical Parts	Electrical Equipment
BBC	IAA-AAI		1 130		300 000	25	90	1 500	69.2	12 530	1-4	1924		
WH	IAA-AAI		880		300 000	59	75	1 350	72	15 050	1-5	1924		
AEG	IB-IB		1 200		300 000	70.5	90	1 350	79	14 100	101; 102; 301	1923		

DIESEL RAILCARS

Class	Axle Arrangement	Transmission	Rated Power hp	Max. (kg)	Tractive Effort Continuous at (kg)	(km/h)	Max. Speed (km/h)	Wheel Dia. (mm)	Total Weight Tons	Length ft ins (mm)	No. Built	Year first Built	Builders: Mechanical Parts	Engine & Type	Transmission
MBW/ MADW	D	DH	215	200			90	784	36	19 640	01-071 01-03	1964		BV-71	DIWABUS U + S
MCW	IA-2	DH	180				90	774	42	20 000	01-24	1976		DMH 17	TC-2A

ELECTRIC RAILCARS

Class	Axle Arrangement	Line Current	Rated Output hp	Max. (kg)	Tractive Effort (Full Field) (kg)	Continuous at (km/h)	Max. Speed (km/h)	Wheel dia. (mm)	Weight tonnes	Length (mm)	No. Built	Year Built	Builders Mechanical Parts	Electrical Equipment
MCW	AA-AA		160				100	860	49.4	20 000	501-510	1976		HS-836
VCW											801-810			

IRAN

IRANIAN STATE RAILWAYS
49 West Takhte-Djamshid Ave, Tehran

Minister of Roads and Transportation: M. Salehi
President: F. Mahmoodian
Technical Vice-President: M. Badii
Financial Vice-President: N. Nakhai
Planning and Studies Vice-President: E. Nurzad
Administrative Vice-President: A. H. Guiti
Director, Administration: A. H. Guiti
Director, Confidential Affairs: D. J. Vaziri Nejad
Director, Traction Department: T. Bolandhemmat
Director, Track Department: M. Zandjany Nassab
Director, Operating: A. Assadi
Director, Electric Department: S. Hamed
Director, Telecommunications and Electrical Signalling: A. Sepahi
Director, Accounting Department: Tahbaz
Director, Personnel Department: M. Mousavi
Director, Legal Office: A. Fardaad
Deputy Director, Purchase Department: K. H. Zarandarz
Director, Assets Department: T. Afrashteh
Superintendent, Buffet and Restaurant Services: A. Aslanian
Director, Training Department: H. Rezapur
Chief, Railway Police Department: M. Parivar
Director, Planning and Studies Department: M. Behzadi
Director, Public Relations and Social Services Office: Hadj Alilu
LORESTAN DIVISION
Head Office: Andimeshk
Director of Division: Rezai
ARAK DIVISION
Head Office: Arak
Director of Division: M. Yahyavi
ESFAHAN DIVISION
Head Office: Esfahan
Director of Division: A. Tahmassebi
TEHRAN DIVISION
Head Office: Tehran
Deputy Director of Division: A. Niruzad
NORTH DIVISION
Head Office: Saari
Director of Division: G. H. Malek
SOUTH DIVISION
Head Office: Ahwaz
Director of Division: G. H. Hendizadeh
YAZD DIVISION
Head Office: Yazd
Director of Division: Aramesh
NORTH-EAST DIVISION
Head Office: Shahrood
Director of Division: G. H. Malek
KHORASSAN DIVISION
Head Office: Mashad
Director of Division: K. H. Bozorgmehr
NORTH-WEST DIVISION
Head Office: Zandjan
Director of Division: R. Anoshirvani
AZARBAYJAN DIVISION
Head Office: Tabriz
Director of Division: M. Khorrami

Gauge: 1.435 m.
Route length: 4 525 km.

The Iran State Railways is working on one of the world's largest expansion programmes to modernise and extend the country's rail network to link all major urban and industrial centres. The multi-billion rail programme provides for the creation of 10 000 km of new tracks and the electrification of existing lines and changing them from single to double tracks.

The first phase provides for improvement of the existing facilities and services. Iran's existing rail network is generally out-dated and cannot answer the country's requirements. The Tehran-Gorgan, Tehran-Abadan and Tehran-Tabriz tracks are old and full of technical problems while the Tehran-Mashad roadbed has not been constructed to accommodate the high-speed turbotrains that run on the route. The increase in the number of passengers and cargo handled by the state railways during 1976, and the need for faster freight and passenger trains has placed the country's railwork under great pressure. In order to ease this pressure and boost the railway's capacity the state railways recently started work on electrification of most of the existing lines.

The first project provides for the electrification of the Bandar Shahpur-Andimeshk-Tehran line and the construction of a double set of tracks along this route. Due to the expansion of port facilities at Bandar Shapur, which will become Iran's largest port over the next few years, the Tehran-Andimeshk-Bandar Shahpur project has been given top priority and construction work is to begin as soon as the necessary funds, already approved by the Government, are allocated.

The western tracks, connecting Tehran with Turkey via Tabriz are also being electrified and transformed from single to double tracks. New tracks are also to be laid between Mianeh and Tabriz to shorten the Tehran-Tabriz line by 110 km. A similar project is planned for the Tehran-Isfahan-Zarand line and construction work on the 80 km stretch between Zarand and Kerman was completed in 1978.

The existing Tehran-Mashad line will be modified to handle electric trains at speeds of up to 240 km/h. Another set of rails will be established alongside the existing tracks to enable two-way traffic.

Railway experts have also been working on another set of plans, studies on which have already begun, to extend the existing network. These projects provide for construction of 700 km of track to connect Bandar Abbas with Baft via Gol Gowhar linking the Persian Gulf port with the nation-wide network. Pakdaman said that the project has already been offered to tenders and construction work would begin as soon as the necessary funds are allocated.

The next project will connect the railway network to Pakistan by construction of 560 km of track from Kerman to the border.

Other projects provide for the creation of lines from Isfahan to the Soviet border, a line along the Caspian coast, an Isfahan-Shiraz-Bushehr line and a Bandar Pahlavi-Qazvin, Qom-Qasr-e-Shirin (Iraq border), Andimeshk-Kermanshah-Sanandaj-Maragheh, Mashad-Zahedan-Chahbahar and Persian Gulf coastal tracks to connect Bandar Abbas with Bandar Shahpour.

With the completion of these projects the country's total track will be increased from 4 500 to more than 14 000 km, connecting all major Iranian urban and industrial centres and linking the country's rail network to the Soviet Union, Pakistan, Afghanistan, Turkey and Iraq.

Meanwhile the State Railways is working on the creation of a number of railway stations, three in Tehran, Shahyad Square, Aramghah, south Tehran and Qasre Firuz in east Tehran, and other stations in various cities.

The railways have also been working to improve the ticket sales and reservation system. Mechanisation of ticket sales and reservations, the creation of ticket stalls throughout Tehran and arrangements for the sale of tickets at travel agencies are other projects underway.

TRAFFIC

	1975	1976
Freight ton-km	4 916 679 276	5 309 188 849
Tonnage	8 829 163	7,950 514
Passenger-km	2 266 458 233	3 484 646 317
Passenger journeys	4 535 313	6 457 502

FINANCES

	1975 Rials	1976 Rials	1977 Rials
Revenue	8 251 456 328	10 249 129 385	11 055 986 222
Expenses	6 253 432 460	10 700 568 897	11 600 000 000

DEVELOPMENT PLANS
The present plan involves only the first stage in Iran's railway development programme. A 20-year plan calls for the construction of several completely new lines and new links with several neighbouring countries. Following the doubling and electrification projects for existing lines, a 550-km line is to be built between Kerman and Zahedan, terminus of the existing Pakistan Railways line projecting into Iran. A bogie-changing station will also be built at Zahedan.

During the Seventh and Eighth Plan periods the network will be extended from Shahrud to Bandar Shah and along the Caspian coastal strip to form a tourist route right up to the Soviet border at Astara.

During the Sixth and Seventh Plan periods the network will be extended 366 km up from Tehran to Bandar Pahlavi on the Caspian coast and up to Astara on the Soviet border. Then the railway will be continued eastwards along the Caspian coast through Lahijan, Rudsar, Shahsavar, Nowshahr, Amol and Sari, a distance of about 430 km. Also during the Seventh Plan (beginning in 1988), the programme provides for the existing Tehran-Mashad line to be extended up to Gorgan, from Shahrud. The line will also be extended from Mashad to provide another link with Soviet Railways at Sarakhs—giving RAI a much closer connection with the Trans-Siberian railway—and to Kal-Kaleh on the Afghanistan border. RAI also plans to offer technical and economic assistance to Afghanistan to construct a railway through to Kabul.

The line to Isfahan is to be extended 500 km to Shiraz, and then on for a further 140 km to Firuzabad. From there the line will continue 580 km to Bandar Abbas. About 330 km of new track will link Isfahan with Bebahan, in the southwest. The line will then turn northwest to Aghajari (88 km) and a further 150 km to Ahvaz. A connecting line will be built along the 410-km route from Firuzabad to Behbahan.

Other projected lines will run from Isfahan to Azna, on the existing south line, and from Qom, on the south line, to link with Iraqi Railways at Qasr-e-Shirin.

MOTIVE POWER
At the end of 1978 RAI's motive power fleet consisted of: 344 diesel-electric line haul units; 99 diesel-electric shunters.

Standard diesel locomotives operated by RAI were provided by General Motors. 134 GM 3 300-hp locomotives have been delivered and orders were placed for 54 type GT 26 CW 3 000-hp units and 20 type G22 1 500-hp units with General Motors.

Introduction of four turbotrains from ANF Frangeco, at a cost of 500 million rials each, have substantially reduced transit time between Tehran, Mashad and Isfahan. However, it was reported that RAI had dropped its option on 18 other turbotrains.

For heavy shunting, RAI has taken delivery of 28 Hitachi locomotives with an output of 1 050 hp, continuous tractive effort of 12 420 kg, Bo-Bo axle arrangement and top speed of 100 km/h.

ROLLING STOCK
At the end of 1978 RAI had a fleet of 13 872 freight wagons. A total of 577 passenger coaches and four turbotrain sets were in operation during 1978. In 1978 orders were placed with ANF Industrie, France, for 70 passenger coaches and 25 restaurant cars for delivery in 1979-80.

ELECTRIFICATION
Lines are to be electrified in stages under the Sixth Development Plan (1978-83). These include Tehran-Bandarshahpour-Khorramshahr, and Julfa-Tabriz which were due for completion by 1980.

TRACK CONSTRUCTION DETAILS
Standard rail:
  Main line:
  Type U33, 92.8 lb/yd *(46 kg/m)*
  Type IIA, 77 lb/yd *(38.4 kg/m)* in *12.5 m* lengths.
  Type III, 67 lb/yd *(33.5 kg/m)* in *12.0 m* lengths.
  Branch line:
  Type IV, 62 lb/yd *(30.9 kg/m)* in *12.8 m* lengths.
  American, 70 lb/yd *(34.7 kg/m)* in *10.0 m* lengths.
Rail joints: 4 and 6-hole fishplates; and welding (see below).
Cross ties (sleepers): Creosote impregnated hardwood, steel and concrete. Wood, 8 ft 6¾ in × 9⅞ in × 6 in *(2 600 × 250 × 150 mm)*. Steel 7 ft 10½ in × 11⅞ in × 2¾ in *(2 400 × 300 × 70 mm)*. Concrete sleepers under welded rail.
Cross ties spacing: Wood sleepers, 2 180 per mile *(1 360 per km)*. Steel sleepers: 2 320 per mile *(1 450 per km)*.
Rail fastenings: Wood sleepers: Sole plates, screws and bolts. Steel sleepers: Clips and bolts.
Filling: Part broken stone, and part river ballast; min of 7⅞ in *(200 mm)* under sleepers.
Max curvature: 7.9° = min rad of 722 ft *(220 m)*.
Longest continuous gradient: 10 miles *(16 km)* of 2.8% (1 in 36) grade between Firouzkouh and Gadouk.
Max gauge widening: 0.95 in *(24 mm)* on 7.9° curves.
Max super-elevation: 3.94 in *(100 mm)* on 7.9° curves.
Max altitude: 7 273 ft *(2 177 m)* near Nourabad station.
Max axle loading: 25 tons.
Max permitted speed:
  Freight trains: 28 mph *(55 km/h)*.
  Passenger trains: 40 mph *(80 km/h)*.

Tehran station with Hitachi Bo-Bo locomotive on station pilot duties

First-class passenger coach delivered to RAI in 1976 by Linke-Hofmann-Busch

G16 diesel electric locomotive

General Motors Co-Co No 90-802

IRAQ
IRAQI REPUBLICAN RAILWAYS (IRR)
Baghdad

Telex: 2272 railway ik

President: Khalid Abdul Halim
Director General: Khalid Saleh Ammar
Director General (central region): Ibrahim Mahmoud Abdul Rahman
Director General (southern region): Hashim Abdullah Ibrahim
Director General (northern region): Rajih Jassim Mohammed
Director General (western region): Ahmed Jwad Moussa
Planning: Khalid Hassan Bakir
Finances and Operating: Hisham Abdul Latif
Construction: Zuhair Raouf Suleiman
Studies: Hashim Habib Sarsam
Director of International Affairs: Aziz Thomas Djardis

Gauge: 1.435 m; 1.00 m.
Route length: 1 235 km; 1 294 km.

Model MXS620, 2 000 hp, 1.43 m gauge locomotive built by MLW for Iraqi Republican Railways service

TRAFFIC

The aim in 1978 was to increase passenger traffic by 30 per cent and freight traffic by 7 per cent. Emphasis was laid on increasing train speeds and extending transport facilities. Traffic on the Baghdad-Maqal-Umm Qasr line was raised from three million tonnes in 1977 to six million tonnes; by 1980 it was hoped the line would carry 11 million tonnes of freight a year. Most important traffics are oil products (about 940 000 tons last year), cement (600 000 tons), sugar (225 000), wheat and barley (113 000 tons). Total ton/km handled in 1972 was nearly 1 123 215 000—compared with about 1 032 140 000 in the previous year. By 1975 tonne-km carried had risen to 1 853 million, while passenger-km had gone up from 444 million in 1965 to 643 million in 1975. Already, increased sulphur production in Iraq is testing IRR facilities to the full. One extraction plant near Kirkuk is now railing nearly 200 000 tons/year of sulphur to Basra.

FINANCIAL RESULTS

	1970	1972
	(000's of Dinars)	
Revenue	6 633.4	6 821.3
Expenses	7 320.6	8 961.2
Operating ratio	110.5	—

INVESTMENTS

Railway improvement projects cost IRR just over 90 million Dinars in 1978.

MOTIVE POWER

New locomotives delivered in 1976 included 31 diesel-electrics rated at 2 000 hp built by MLW at a cost of $C 19.8 million.
The new locomotives supplement earlier MLW units and 20 diesel-electric locomotives purchased in 1972 from Traction-Export, France.

ROLLING STOCK

During 1977, the railway took delivery of the first 50 of an order for 84 passenger coaches supplied by Maschinen-Export of the German Democratic Republic. In March 1977, Maschinen-Export won an IRR order for 250 freight wagons.

PERMANENT WAY

A contract was signed in October 1978 for construction of a standard-gauge line running 404 km from Baghdad to Husaiba and a 155 km branch line from Al Qaim to Akashat. Contractor is Mendes Junior of Brazil. The lines are to be built by 1982 at a cost of $US 1 210 million. Construction began in January 1979. Meanwhile, the government has been studying IRR plans for a new 250 km line linking Mosul with Nusaybin in Turkey; this would bypass the existing route through Syrian territory.
Also under study is a line from Basra to Kuwait.

TRACK CONSTRUCTION DETAILS

Standard rail:
   Standard gauge: 90 lb. *(44.6 kg.)* on new line. 75 lb. *(37.2 kg.)* BSR, and German type.
   Metre, main: 75 lb. *(38.8 kg.)* USA, 75 lb. BS, BSR, RBS, USA.
   Metre, branch: 75 lb. BS and BSR, 60 lb. R, and 50 lb. BS and RBS.

SIGNALLING

A semi-automatic block system was installed in 1974 on the 585-km Baghdad-Mosul-Rabia line, using materials and technical assistance supplied by the German Democratic Republic.

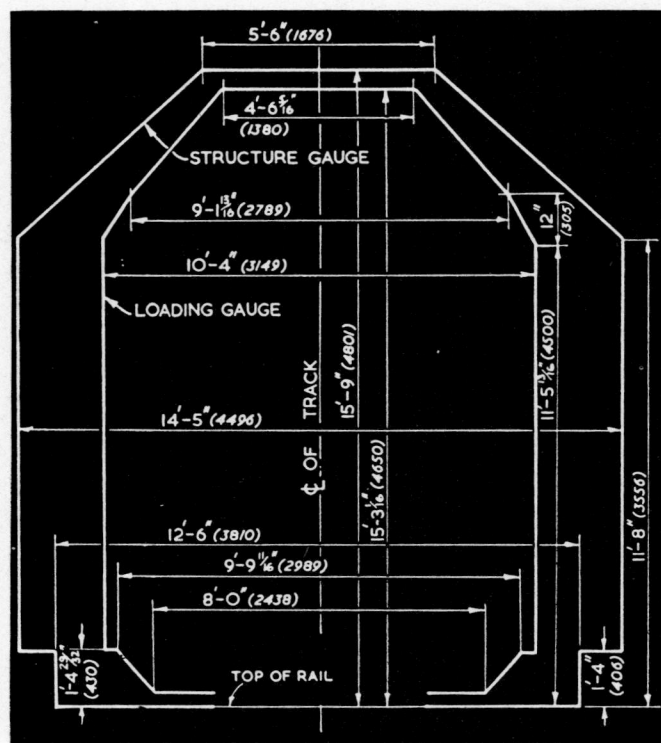

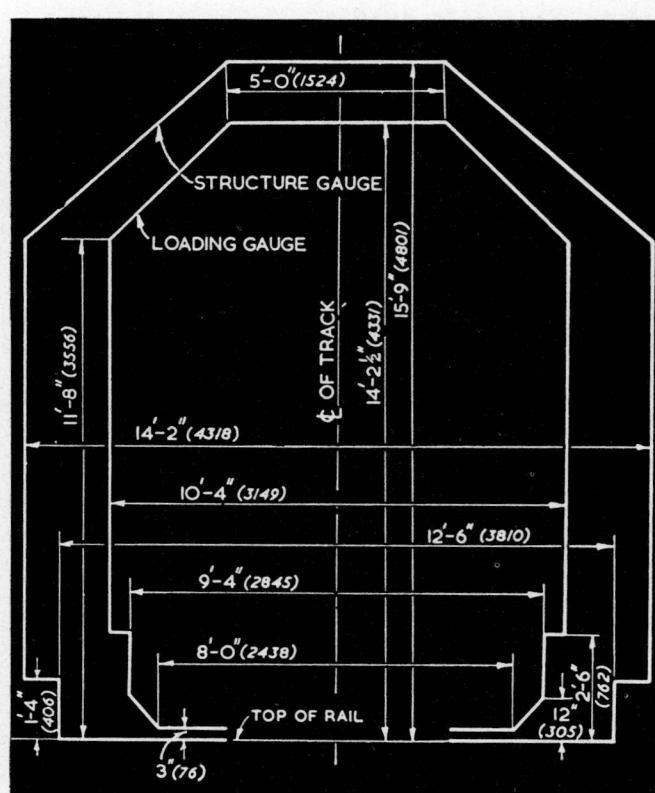

IRELAND

CORAS IOMPAIR EIREANN (CIE)

Irish Transport Company, Heuston Station, Dublin 8

Telephone: 771871
Telex: 5153

Chairman of the Board: Dr. Liam St. John Devlin
Members: B. Connaughton
          E. Farrell
          W. J. Fitzpatrick
          E. Larkin
          E. Markey
General Manager: J. F. Higgins
Assistant General Manager, (Marketing): C. Finegan
Assistant General Manager, (Railways): M. J. Devereux
Assistant General Manager, (Personnel): P. Murphy
Assistant General Manager, (Finance): M. Grace
Assistant General Manager, (Operations): P. J. Darmody
Director of Information: P. G. Byrne
Secretary: M. J. Hayes
Solicitor: M. J. Kenny
Purchasing Officer: D. Stephens
Mechanical Engineer (Rail): R. P. Grainger
Chief Civil Engineer: T. C. Yates
Area Manager:
  Dublin: E. O'Connor
  Cork: C. F. Clune
  Galway: C. MacGiolla Ri
  Limerick: E. B. Kehoe
  Waterford: J. A. O'Connor
Computer Services Manager: F. J. Curtin
Manager, Road Passenger Planning Group: J. Browne
Manager, Road Freight Planning Group: M. Flannery
Manager, Dublin City Services: B. J. Fitzgerald

Gauge: 1.600 m.
Route length: 2 189 km.

Development plans for the Irish Railways, adopted in 1971, have made steady progress and it was anticipated that they would be fully implemented by 1980.
Developments on the passenger side call for the provision of a total fleet of air-conditioned rolling stock, and this with the recent purchase of 18 class 071 locomotives will provide more comfortable service and faster journey times between all major locations.
The Railways Development Plan is a precise blue-print for the development of the railways up to 1980. Aimed at containing the rising railway deficit, the plan involved modernisation of stations and depots, introduction of new equipment and handling methods and redeployment of manpower. The plan has taken six years to implement. Progress was also made during 1973/74 in the preparation of plans for improving Dublin City transportation. The Government approved in principle the recommendations in the Dublin Transportation Study in relation to the suburban rail system. CIE personnel are now at work on the detailed designs. CIE has also employed Alan M. Voorhess and Company as consultants to examine the feasibility of building an underground rail system in Dublin. This also follows one of the recommendations of the Dublin Transportation Study.
Freight operations are being concentrated on a lesser number of highly utilised depots, the conventional loose coupled train being replaced by high speed vacuumed braked liner or block trains, with all loading and discharge being effected by mechanical means.
Track improvements and upgrading to permit higher speeds and loads, and the modernisation of the signalling and communications networks provide a highly efficient rail system to meet the challenges of the future.

TRAFFIC

Total revenue for 1977 was £25.603 million, which was an increase of ten per cent on the figure of £23.262 million for 1976. Expenditure at £52.969 million exceeded the costs for 1976 by £5.552 million. The deficit for the year was £27.365 million, which was £3.211 million higher than the previous year. An encouraging feature was the reversal of the trend in previous years of diminishing passenger journeys. Although there was no change in basic mainline passenger fares, revenue from passenger train operations increased by 15.4 per cent and passenger journeys by eight per cent, an additional 600 000 on the mainline railway and 489 000 on the Dublin suburban line.
Although freight rates were increased in April 1977, goods trains revenue only improved by 3.3 per cent to £10.285 million. Freight tonnage at 3.509 million tons was only one per cent higher than the previous year. The major loss was in the sundries operation.

	1975	1976	1977
Freight ton kms (incl livestock)	559 081 571	585 189 257	586 865 281
Freight tonnage (incl livestock)	3 385 266	3 477 899	3 509 268
Passenger kms	898 620 547	787 626 256	812 542 773
Passengers carried	13 891 145	13 607 724	14 696 912

FINANCES	1975 £	1976 £	1977 £
Revenues	20 270 940	23 262 004	25 603 662
Expenses (operating)	38 412 539	44 960 231	49 927 912

Sundries (less than wagonload traffic) is now handled by a new system which was fully implemented in CIE throughout 1977
Goods are loaded in order of delivery point in 10 ft ISO containers which are carried by liner trains to 40 railhead depots where they are transferred by gantry to specially-designed Bedford lorries fitted with hydraulic tail lifts. Goods are not handled from the time they are loaded at the forwarding depot until the cage pallets are wheeled from the containers to the consignees' premises. Picture shows transfer of container of sundries from rail to road at Longford station.

The modern freight terminal at North Esk, four miles outside Cork on the Cork-Cobh line
The terminal handles contract trains of ISO containers and trainloads of palletised fertilisers from the Nitrigin Eireann factory at Arklow. Transfer of containers between rail and road vehicles is by high-capacity gantry.

Bogie wagon for mineral ores in bulk
With automatic loading and unloading and top lid to prevent pollution by ore dust during transit. These wagons carry 54 tonnes each, running in block trains from Nevinstown, near Navan to Dublin port, under contract to Tara Mines.

Container for chemicals traffic from Dublin Port to Ballina for Asahi Ltd
These containers are carried on specially-modified flat wagons (22 ft (6·7 m) conflats) and run in block trains under special precautions for dangerous chemicals traffic. The chemicals carried are acrylonitrile and methyl acrylate. Capacity is 16 tonnes on a tare weight of 3.9 tonnes.

Standard wagon for CIE rail freight operations is the 12.8 m (42 ft) bogie conflat
Designed to accommodate varying combinations of 10, 20, 30 and 40 ft containers.

MOTIVE POWER AND ROLLING STOCK
Following delivery of 18 class 071 diesel-electric 2 250 hp locomotives from General Motors (USA) in 1976/77, CIE's motive power fleet consists of 186 line haul diesel-electric locomotives and 27 diesel-hydraulic shunters. Number of freight wagons totals 5 659 (including 120 brake vans); passenger coaches total 491.

TRACK DETAILS
Standard rail:
 Main line: Flat bottom; 113 lb/yd *(50 kg/m)*, 95 and 92 lb/yd Bullhead; 90 and 87 lb/yd.
 Branch line: Flat bottom; 85, 83, 80 and 74 lb/yd Bullhead; 85 lb/yd.
Length of rail:
 Main line: 60 ft and 45 ft
 Branch line: 45 ft and 30 ft
Joints: 4-hole fishplates, some welding.
Cross ties (sleepers), broad gauge: Wood, 8 ft 6 in × 10 in × 5 in *(2 600 × 260 × 130 mm)* Prestressed concrete.
Spacing: 1 970 per mile *(1 230 per km)* 2 112 per mile (timber), 2 146 per mile (concrete).

Rail fastenings: Wood sleepers—bolts: Concrete sleepers—H-M & Pandrol fastenings.
Filling: Stone ballast, min of 100 mm under sleeper.
Max curvature:
 Main line (Dublin to Cork): 9° 40'.
 Principal lines: 12° 25'.
 Secondary lines: 21° 44'.
Max gradient:
 Main line: 1.66% (1 in 60) for 1⅜ miles.
 Other lines: 2.0% (1 in 50) for 2 miles.
Longest continuous gradient: 5¼ miles, with 1% (1 in 100) ruling gradient.
Max altitude: 630 ft. *(192 m)* at Barnagh, Co. Kerry.
Max permitted speed: 75 mph *(120 km/h)*.
Max axle loads:
 Principal lines: 16½ tons for locomotives, 15½ tons for wagons.
 Secondary lines: 16½ tons for locomotives, 15½ tons for wagons.
 Branch lines: 16½ tons for locomotives, 15½ tons for wagons
Bridge loading: 20 b.s. units for all renewals.

DIESEL LOCOMOTIVES

Class	Axle Arrange-ment	Trans-mission	Rated Power hp	Max. lb (kg)	Tractive Effort Continuous at lb (kg)	Tractive Effort Continuous at mph (kmlh)	Max. Speed mph (kmlh)	Wheel Dia. in (mm)	Total Weight Tons	Length ft ins (mm)	No. Built	Year first Built	Builders: Mechanical Parts	Builders: Engine & Type	Builders: Transmission
071	Co-Co	Elec.	2 475/ 2 250	65 000 (29 484)	43 264 (19 625)	16.4 (26.39)	89 (143.2)	40'' (1 016)	99 (100.6)	51' 0'' (15 545)	18	1976	GM	GM12-645 E3	Elec
AR (01)	Co-Co	,,	1 325/ 1 250	54 000 (24 494)	18 000 (8 165)	21.5 (34.6)	75 (120.7)	38'' (965.2)	82 (83.3)	51' 0'' (15 545)	50	1955/ 56	Metro-Cammell	GM12-645 E	Elec
AR (01)	Co-Co	,,	1 650/ 1 500	43 300 (19 656)	22 415 (10 166)	21.5 (34.6)	75 (120.7)	38'' (965.2)	82 (83.3)	51' 0'' (15 545)	9	1956	Metro-Cammell	GM 12-645	Elec
B (101)	AIA-AIA	,,	960/ 890	41 800 (18 960)	16 900 (7 666)	17.0 (27.4)	75 (120.7)	37½'' (952.5)	75 (76.2)	45' 0'' (13 716)	12	1956/ 57	BC & W Co	Sulzer 6LDA 28	Elec
B (121)	Bo-Bo	,,	950/ 875	36 000 (16 330)	30 400 (13 789)	8.0 (12.9)	77 (123.9)	40'' (1 016)	64 (65)	39' 10'' (12 141)	15	1961	GM	GM 567 CA	Elec
B (141)	Bo-Bo	,,	950/ 875	36 000 (16 330)	27 500 (34 304)	9.0 (14.5)	77 (123.9)	40'' (1 016)	67 (68)	44' 0½'' (13 424)	37	1962/ 63	GM	GM 567 CR	Elec
B (181)	Bo-Bo	,,	1 100/ 1 000	37 500 (17 010)	26 400 (11 975)	11.0 (17.7)	89 (143.2)	40'' (1 016)	67 (68)	44' 0½'' (13 424)	12	1966	GM	GM B-645 E	Elec
CR (201)	Bo-Bo	,,	1 100/ 1 040	34 200 (15 513)	14 200 (6 441)	22.2 (35.7)	75 (120.7)	38'' (965.2)	61½ (62.5)	42' 0'' (12 802)	31	1957/ 58	Metro-Cammell	GM B-645 E	Elec
CR (201)	Bo-Bo	,,	950/	29 500 (13 378)	12 250 (5 556)	22.2 (35.7)	75 (120.7)	38 (965.2)	61½ (62.5)	42' 0'' (12 802)	2	1958	Metro-Cammell	Maybach	Elec
E (401)	0-6-0	Hyd	400/	25 300 (11 476)	—	—	—	38'' (965.2)	42¾ (43.4)	31' 4¼'' (9 557)	27	1962/ 63	CIE	Maybach MD 650	Hyd

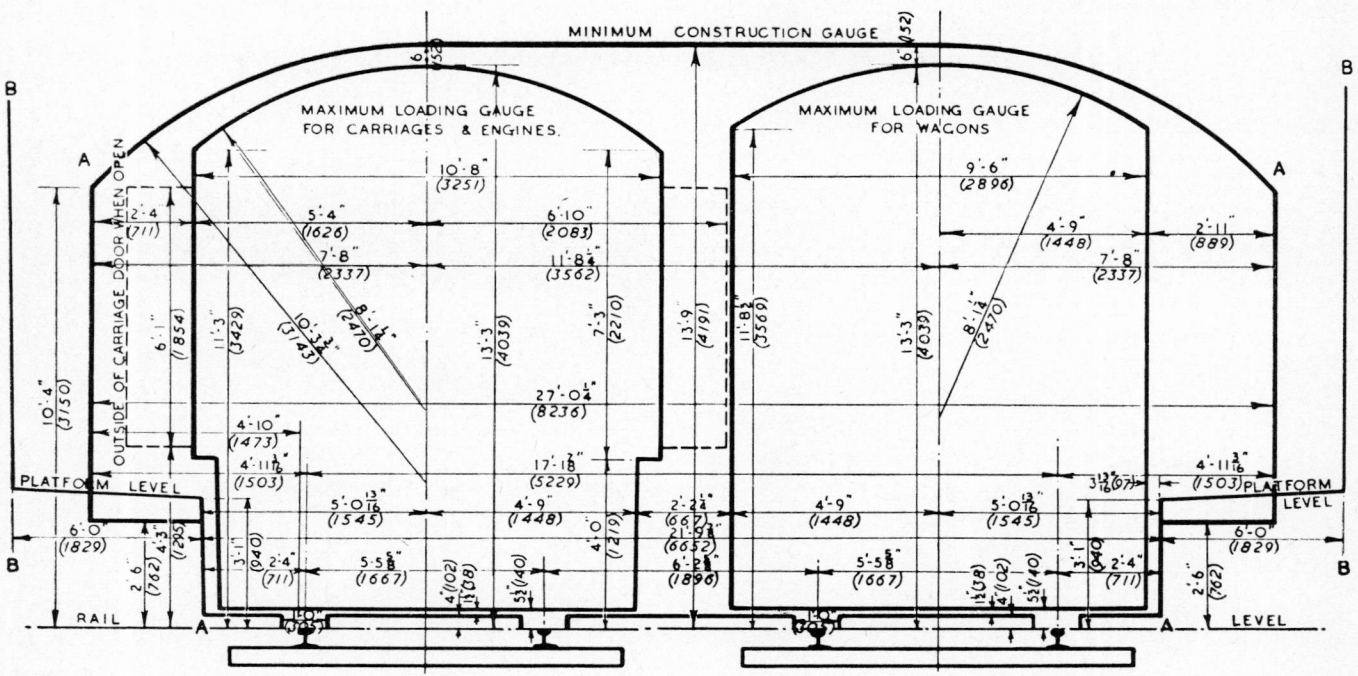

NOTE

AA Minimum distance for all works along line including signal boxes, signal posts, lamps etc.

BB Minimum distance for all station works above platform level. Level of passenger platforms only may be inside the construction gauge.

ISRAEL

ISRAEL RAILWAYS (IR)
Central Station, PO Box 44, Haifa

Telephone: 04 641 761
Telex: 46570 IRAIL IL

General Manager: Zvi Tsafriri
Deputy General Manager: I. Bar-Ilan
Deputy General Manager (Admin): L. Heyman
Traffic and Commercial Manager: E. Inbal
Deputy Chief Mechanical Engineer: A. Micsel
Assistant General Manager and Public Relations: D. Guy
Chief Engineer: K. Slutzker
Chief Accountant: S. Klayer
Head, Supply and Stores Department: O. Trichter
Chief Signalling and Telecommunications Engineer: M. Lozar
Personnel Manager: Ch. Shadmi
Legal Adviser: H. Cassel
Management Secretary: B. Z. Balila
Chief Economist: I. Falkov
Head of Planning and Development: A. Golan

Gauge: 1.435 m.
Route length: 552 km.

Israel Railways operate a total route length of 552 km, including the reconnected Yad Mordekhay-Gaza line opened to El-Arish in Sinai, 58 miles (98 km). The railways are entirely diesel powered. Most of the country's rail network taken over from the Mandatory government in 1948, was in a run-down condition and unsuited to the geographic and economic needs of that period and future development. The first step was to recondition the network and to add new lines to provide a rail link to the closely settled coastal belt and to the development areas and mining sites in the Negev. The length of the main lines today is 519 km with secondary lines and sidings forming

another 200 km, all single track. The southern line (Beersheba—Oron) has been extended to Har Tsin, site of the new phosphate mine in the process of development. This 34 km long section was opened at the end of 1977 and forms part of the trans-Negev and Arava line to Eilat. Also the Government has approved a budget for the detailed planning of the line from Hatseva to Eilat.

TRAFFIC
IR carries less than ten per cent of all inland freight and only three per cent of passenger traffic. Passenger trains on the busiest route, between Tel Aviv and Haifa, carry only 30 per cent of total traffic between the cities. The growing demand for bulk transport, especially containers, grains and minerals, has led the government to consider seeking foreign investment capital for developing the railways as the nation's major transport facility. In 1978/79 IR carried about 2.8 million passengers and 4.5 million tonnes of freight, mainly phosphates, potash, grains, building materials and containers.

	1977	1978
Freight tonnage	4 200 000	4 500 000
Tonne-km	558 600 000	620 000 000
Passenger journeys	3 000 000	3 000 000
Passenger km	266 000 000	216 000 000

FINANCES
The 1977 state subsidy of £Israeli 121 million was reduced to £Israeli 80 million in 1978/79 due to IR's improved financial situation. In 1978/79 the turnover of IR was £Israeli 440 million, not including a development budget of about £Israeli 131 million.

INVESTMENTS
Total allocation for development projects in 1979 was £Israeli 100 million. Over half that sum was spent on four new type GM 26 diesel-electric locomotives from General Motors (USA), 156 freight wagons and eight passenger coaches.

MOTIVE POWER
Number of diesel locomotives in mainline service totals 36; number in shunting duties, 22. The railway took delivery of four G 26 locomotives from General Motors in 1978.

ROLLING STOCK

Number of freight wagons in operation at the end of 1977 totalled 2 044, including 475 flat wagons, 403 grain hopper wagons, 254 for mineral transport, 174 for liquid transport and 843 miscellaneous general duty wagons. Number of passenger coaches in service (including buffet cars) totalled 114.

Arbel of France supplied a batch of 60 tonne capacity freight wagons during 1978. Eight second-hand 62-seat modern passenger coaches were bought in Britain by Israel Railways during 1977.

CIVIL ENGINEERING

The standard of services is limited because of the inadequate track network and the priority accorded to the speedy development of the roads. Since 1948 only 250 km of main lines have been built: from Remez Junction (near Hadera) to Tel Aviv Central Station (in Arlosorov street), from Na'an to Beersheba (1956), from Beersheba to Dimona (1965), and from Dimona to Oron (1970). The Negev lines serve mainly the phosphate mines and the potash works on the Dead Sea whose output is carried to the chemical plants in Haifa and to Ashdod for export. Potash is carried to Dimona by truck and there loaded into freight wagons. The increasing world demand for potash and phosphates has in recent years resulted in a growth of export shipments of these minerals.

A new line between Oron and Har-Zin was officially opened in December 1977. This line in fact constitutes a section of the Trans-Israelian which extends as far as Eilat, near the Gulf of Akaba, 180 km to the south of Hor Hahar. Scheduled completion date is 1982. During 1977, the Transport Minister announced plans for construction of a direct line between Jerusalem, Lod and Tel Aviv, by-passing the present circuitous route. Construction started during 1979 on a 210 km link line from the present terminal at Har Zin to the Red Sea port at Eilat. Cost of the line has been calculated at $US 100 million. At the end of 1978 IR decided to build the long-planned chord line between Qiryat Gat in the Negev desert and Ashqelon on the existing coastal route. Construction began in April 1979. The line will be 22 km long and used mainly for hauling phosphates from the Negev to the port of Ashrod. Cost will be about £Israeli ten million.

Awaiting investment capital is doubling of the single-track line between the northern railhead at Nahariya and Tel Aviv. The 125 km line carries both passengers and freight and badly needs additional capacity.

Structure and loading gauge for 1.435 m standard-gauge track

ITALY

ITALIAN STATE RAILWAYS

(Ferrovie dello Stato Italia) (FS)
**Direzione Generale delle Ferrovie dello Stato,
Piazza della Croce Rossa, 00100 Rome**

Telephone: 8490
Telex: Min Trasp 61089

Director General: Dott. Ercole Semenza
Heads of Departments:
  Operations: Ing. Antonio Piciocchi

Commercial and Traffic: Dott. Mauro Ferretti
Motive Power and Rolling Stock: Ing. Paolino Camposano
Personnel: Dott. Aldo Bonforti
Electrical Installations: Ing. Enrico Bianco
Maintenance and Construction: Ing. Arnaldo d'Alessio
General Business: Ing. Francesco Monopole
Financial: Prof. Carlo Rolandi
Supplies and Stores: D. H. Piener Haggi
Medical: Prof. Mario Monti
Research Institute: Ing. Giulio Giovanardi
Divisional Managers:
  Ancona: Ing. Aristide Loria
  Bari: Ing. Gerardo Sangineto
  Bologna: Ing. Domenico Muzzioli

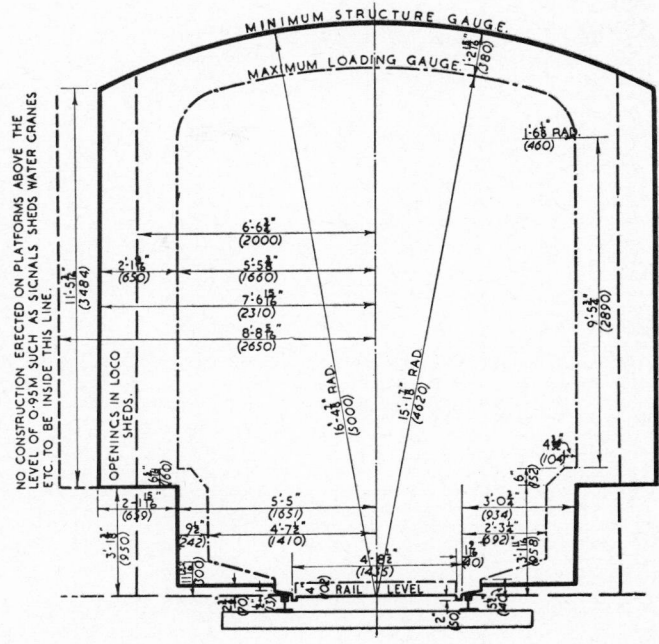

Electric locomotive class E 633
One hour rating 4 905 kW at 75 km/h (gear ratio 27/64) or 92 km/h (gear ratio 33/64), top speed 130 or 160 km/h. Feeding system 3 000 V dc. Locomotives of this class equipped with chopper control. Electrical equipment supplied by Tecnomasio Italiano Brown Boveri SpA.

Cagliari: Ing. Ferdinando Salvatori
Florence: Ing. Tullio Grimaldi
Genoa: Ing. Francesco Melis
Milan: Ing. Armando Sottile
Naples: Ing. Luigi Frunzio
Palermo: Ing. Armando Colombo
Reggio Calibria: Ing. Antonino Bitto
Rome: Ing. Alberto Allegra
Turin: Ing. Eduardo Oliva
Trieste: Ing. Francesco Ricciardo
Venice: Ing. Quirido Castellani
Verona: Ing. Salvatore Puccio
Public Relations: Dott. Alberto Ciambricco

Gauge: 1.435 m.
Route length: 16 086 km.

FREIGHT TRAFFIC

During 1978 total traffic fell two per cent over the previous year although income rose 14 per cent as the effect of tariff increases introduced in 1977 was felt. Freight traffic declined slightly to 52 million tonnes but tonne-km increased by about five per cent to 17 200 million. Average length of haul per tonne was 330 km. Freight income was up by 17 per cent at Lire 426 000 million.

As well as modernisation of freight terminals and marshalling yards, and the provision of computer-based wagon control, FS is expanding its intermodal business. FS carried 128 898 containers in 1973, and this total had risen to 216 056 in 1978. Together with other intermodal traffic, this represented 221 million tonne-km in 1978. Containers are normally carried in block trains between specialised depots, and this traffic is developing to such an extent that in 1978 the railway carried 26 per cent of wagonload traffic in block trains.

PASSENGER TRAFFIC

Passenger-km in 1978 fell by two per cent to 37 900 million and passenger journeys totalled 389 million. Average journey length remained virtually unchanged at 97.5 km. Revenue from passengers increased by 13 per cent to Lire 626 000 million.

	1975	1976	1977	1978
Freight ton-km (million)	14 667	16 375	16 300	17 200
Freight tonnage (thousands)	42 666	48 433	52 600	52 000
Passenger-km (million)	36 332	39 118	40 000	39 700
Passenger journeys (thousands)	370 115	390 070	895 000	389 000

FINANCIAL	1975 (Lire)	1976 (Lire)	1978 (Lire)
Revenues (millions)	1 465 526	1 864 638	1 108 968
Expenses (millions)	2 278 239	2 740 420	3 793 379

INVESTMENTS

Present annual investments are covered by an Integrated Plan for 1979-83. In addition the Government has allocated specific sums for rolling stock, track improvements and signalling. The Lire 1 655 000 million for motive power and rolling stock approved in 1979 is expected to cover the 1979-81 period.

MOTIVE POWER AND ROLLING STOCK

The Integrated Plan calls for deliveries of 120 mainline electric locomotives, 60 four-car emus and 910 coaches. Present motive power and rolling stock consists of 270 steam locos, 1 840 electric locos, 396 mainline diesel locos, 968 diesel shunters, 534 electric motor coaches and trainsets, 1 079 diesel railcars, 13 856 coaching stock vehicles, 113 427 freight wagons and 15 137 private-owner wagons.

ELECTRIFICATION

Electrified route length rose to 8 383 km in 1978, electrified at 3 kV dc.
Electrification absorbed Lire 96 000 million under the 1975-79 programme, a quarter spent on strengthening the catenary and providing new or remodelled substations to allow heavier and faster trains.

CIVIL ENGINEERING

The Italian Minister of Transport, Mr. Attilio Ruffini opened the first section (Rome-Città della Pieve, 122 km) of the new Rome-Florence highspeed rail link in 1977. The southern 122 km of this line were opened in 1977. The main purpose of the *direttissima* is to provide 260 km of quadruple track within the Milan—Florence—Rome—Naples axis, which carries 30 per cent of all traffic. From Figline to Rovezzano (near Florence) a further 20 km of the infrastructure will be completed in 1981, as will the 52 km from the northern end of the section now open to Arezzo Sud. For the 43 km from Arezzo Sud to Figline the Integrated Plan provides Lire 315 000 million, a sum which includes track,

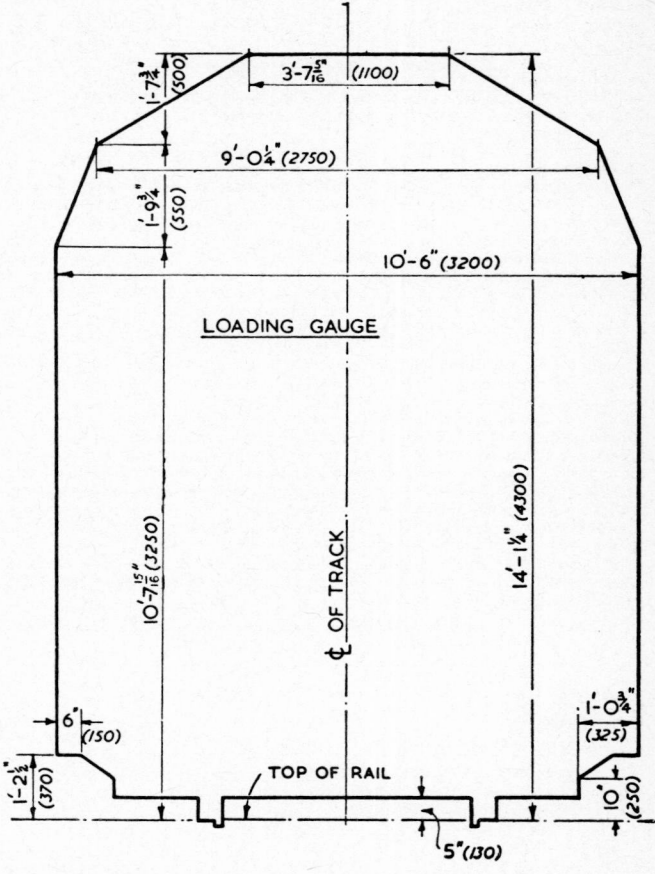

LOADING GAUGE

The minimum lateral clearance between Loading Gauge (diagram above) and Fixed Gauge varies according to the radius of curvature, e.g.:

Radius of curve		inside of curve		Clearance outside of curve	
feet	metres	ins	mm	ins	mm
820	250	5.9	150	5.9	150
656	200	7.9	200	8.3	210
492	150	11.1	283	12.2	310
328	100	26.6	676	27.8	706
230	70	44.0	1 177	47.7	1 211

signalling and electrification of the other sections under construction as well as additional expenditure caused by inflation.

Out of 20 700 track-km of running lines, principal routes account for 13 000 track-km; all are now laid with 50 or 60 kg/m rail for axle loads of 20 or 22 tonnes. For other routes 46 or 49 kg/m rail is used with the exception of 1 500 track-km laid with 36 kg/m section. The Integrated Plan forces the expenditure of 1 490 000 million Lire on track renewal and new line construction. FS aims at renewing 1 200 track-km annually.
Switches are being renewed at a rate of 4 500 a year.

SIGNALLING

Between 1975 and 1979 Lire 300 000 million was spent on signalling improvements. The Integrated Plan is allocating Lire 700 000 for signalling between 1979 and 1983. Plans include extension of block working, provision of route-relay signalling centres and computer-based traffic control centres.

Ale electric power car and Le 803 trailer

Class D445 diesel locomotive

ELECTRIC LOCOMOTIVES

Class	Axle Arrangement	Line Current	Rated Output hp	Max lbs (kg)	Tractive Effort (Full Field) Continuous at		Max Speed mph (km/h)	Wheel Dia. ins (mm)	Weight tons tonnes	Length ft in (mm)	No. Built	Year First Built	Builders Mechanical Parts	Electrical Equipment
					lb (kg)	mph (km/h)								
E.432	1-D-1 (1-4-1)	3 600 V 3/16⅔	2 200	31 000 (14 000)	18 300 (8 300)	23.3 (37.5)	62 (100)	64⅛ (1 630)	93	45' 8'' (13 910)	40	1929	Breda	Breda
					31 000 (14 000)	31 (50)								
					22 000 (10 000)	44.6 (75)								
					15 400 (7 000)	62 (100)								

ELECTRIC LOCOMOTIVES

Class	Axle Arrangement	Line Current	Rated Output hp	Max lbs (kg)	Tractive Effort (Full Field) Continuous at: lb (kg)	mph (km/h)	Max Speed mph (km/h)	Wheel Dia. ins (mm)	Weight tons tonnes	Length ft in (mm)	No. Built	Year First Built	Builders: Mechanical Parts	Electrical Equipment
E.554	E (0-10-0)	,,	2 000	31 000 (14 000)	23 000 (10 500) 31 000 (14 000)	15.5 (25) 31 (50)	31 (50)	42⅛ (1 070)	76	35' 5" (10 800)	183	1928	Meccaniche Navali Napoli; Brown Boveri; Terni; Savigliano; OM; CENSA Saronno; Ansaldo; Reggiane	Meccaniche Navali Napoli; Brown Boveri; Terni; Savigliano; OM; CENSA Saronno; Ansaldo; Reggiane
E.626	Bo-Bo-Bo	3 000 V dc	2 100	50 300 (22 800) 57 800 (26 200)	26 000 (11 800) 30 200 (13 700)	32 (52) 28 (45)	59 (95)	49¼ (1 250)	93	49' 1" (14 950)	448	1928	Savigliano; CGE; Brown Boveri; Elettromeccaniche; Saronno; Breda; OM; Ansaldo; CENSA Saronno; Reggiane; FIAT	Marelli; Savigliano; CGE; Brown Boveri; Elettromeccaniche Saronno; Breda; OM; Ansaldo; CENSA Saronno
E.428	2-Bo-Bo-2	,,	2 800	44 000 (20 000) 48 500 (22 000)	23 000 (10 500) 25 300 (11 500)	48 (77) 44 (71)	80 (130)	74 (1 880)	135	62' 4" (19 000)	241	1934	Breda; Ansaldo; Reggiane; FIAT; Brown Boveri	Breda; Ansaldo; Marelli; Brown Boveri
E.424	Bo-Bo	,,	1 660	43 000 (19 500)	20 900 (9 500)	34 (55)	62 (100)	49¼ (1 250)	72.4	50' 10" (15 500)	158	1943	Breda; Savigliano; Ansaldo; Reggiane; Brown Boveri; OM	Breda; Savigliano; Ansaldo; Marelli; Brown Boveri; CGE
E.444	Bo-Bo	,,	4 020	44 500 (20 200)	25 400 (11 500)	56 (91)	112 (180)	49¼ (1 250)	79	55' 3" (16 840)	44	1967	Savigliano; Breda; Casaralta; Fiat	OCREN; Asgen; Savigliano
E.636	Bo-Bo-Bo	,,	2 100	48 500 (22 000)	25 300 (11 500)	32.3 (52)	75 (120)	49¼ (1 250)	101	59' 10½" (18 250)	469	1940	Breda; Brown Boveri; Savigliano; OM; Reggiane; Pistoiesi	Breda; Brown Boveri; Savigliano; CGE; Ansaldo S. Giorgio
E.645	Bo-Bo-Bo	,,	4 320	64 400 (29 200)	37 000 (16 800)	44.7 (72)	75 (120)	49¼ (1 250)	112	60' 0" (18 290)	93	1964	Breda; Brown Boveri; Savigliano; OM; Reggiane; Pistoiesi; IMAM	Breda; Brown Boveri; Savigliano; CGE; Marelli; Ansaldo S. Giorgio; OCREN
E.646	Bo-Bo-Bo	,,	4 320	52 500 (23 800)	29 750 (13 500)	57 (92)	93 (150)	49¼ (1 250)	110	59' 10½" (18 250)	203	1958	Breda; Brown Boveri; Savigliano; OM; Reggiane; Pistoiesi; IMAM	Breda; Brown Boveri; Savigliano; CGE; Marelli; Ansaldo S. Giorgio; OCREN
E.321	C(0-3-0)	,,	325	19 850 (9 000)	11 000 (5 000)	12.7 (20.5)	31 (50)	51½	36	30' 5½" (9 280)	50	1960	FS; Verona	Brown Boveri
E.444	Bo-Bo	3 000 V		23 600	12 800	105	200		82		117	1967	Savigliano; Breda; Casaralta; Fiat	OCREM Asgen; Savigliano
E321	C	3 000 V	190	9 000	5 000	20, 5	50	1 310	36	9 280	40	1961	Officine FS Verona (Transformte de loc)	TIBB
E.322	C	3 000 V	190	9 000	5 000	20, 5	50	1 310	36	9 280	20	1961	835	
E.323	C	3 000 V	190	11 700	8 400	11	65	1 040	46	9 240	30	1966	TIBB	TIBB
E.324	C	3 000 V	190	11 700	8 400	11	65	1 040	45	9 240	10	1966	TIBB	TIBB
E.656	Bo-Bo-Bo	3 000 V	4 200	24 900	13 100	103	160	1 250	120	18 290	61	1975	TIBB	TIBB

DIESEL LOCOMOTIVES

Class	Axle Arrangement	Transmission	Rated Power hp	Max. lb (kg)	Tractive Effort Continuous at: lb (kg)	mph (km/h)	Max. Speed mph (km/h)	Wheel Dia. in (mm)	Total Weight Tons	Length ft ins (mm)	No. Built	Year first Built	Builders: Mechanical Parts	Engine & Type	Transmission
D.341	Bo-Bo	Elec.	1 400	40 800 (18 500)	17 300 (7 850)	16 (26)	68 (110)	41 (1 040)	64	47' 6" (14 480)	68	1957	Fiat	Fiat 3212.SF or Breda-Paxman 12 YLX	Brown Boveri; OCREN
D.342	B-B	Hyd.	1 600	45 850 (20 800)	32 000 (14 500)	11.8 (19)	87 (140)	41 (1 040)	63	47' 7" (14 500)	20	1957	Ansaldo	2 Ansaldo-Maybach MD435	Maybach Mekydro C 32
D.343	B-B (monomotor bogies)	Elec.	1 500	41 900 (19 000)	24 250 (11 000)		81 (130)		59.5	43' 5¾" (13 240)	75		Fiat; OM	Fiat 218 SSF or Breda-Paxman 12YJC	TIBB generator; 2 traction motors Breda-Elettromeccanica; OCREN
D.443	B-B (monomotor bogies)	Elec.	2 000	48 500 (22 000)	30 900 (14 000)		81 (130)		69.5	47' 3" (14 400)	50	1967	Fiat; OM	Fiat 2312 SSF or Breda-Paxman 12 YLC	ASG generator; 2 traction motors Breda-Elettromeccanica; OCREN
D.235	C	Hyd.	350	32 200 (14 600)	19 800 (9 000)	4.6 (7.4)	25 Sw. (40) 34 Line (55)	42⅛ (1 070)	39	31' 4½" (9 540)	45	1961	Badoni; Jenbach; OM	Carraro; Jenbach; OM	Hydrotitan; Voith; OM
D.234	C	Hyd.	400	29 750 (13 500)	15 650 (7 100)	5.6 (9)	25 Sw. (40) 37 Line (60)	51½ (1 310)	36	30' 8" (9 340)	37	1961	Breda; OM	Breda; OM	OM
D.225	B	Hyd.	250	21 600 (9 800)	15 400 (7 000)	2.6 (4.2)	19 Sw. (30) 34 Line (55)	35½ (900)	28	27' 4½" (8 322)	97	1956	Breda; Jenbach; Greco	Breda; Jenbach; Deutz	Breda; Voith
D.141	Bo-Bo	Elec.	700	41 900 (19 000)	26 500 (12 000)	6.2 (10)	50 (80)	41 (1 040)	62	43' 5¼" (13 240)	3	1962	T.I.B.B.; Reggiane	Fiat MB	Brown Boveri

DIESEL LOCOMOTIVES

Class	Axle Arrangement	Trans-mission	Rated Power hp	Max. lb (kg)	Tractive Effort Continuous at lb (kg)	mph (km/h)	Max. Speed mph (km/h)	Wheel Dia. in (mm)	Total Weight Tons	Length ft ins (mm)	No. Built	Year first Built	Builders: Mechanical Parts	Engine & Type	Transmission
D.345	B-B	Elec.	1 350	19 000	11 270	25, 1	130	1 040	61	13 240	145	1970	Breda Pist; Sofer Savigliano	218SSF G.M.T.	TIBB; Marelli Italtrofo
D.445	B-B	Elec.	2 120	22 000	14 500	23, 5	130	1 040	72	14 100	35	1970	Savigliano	2112SSF G.M.T.	Asgen
2435	C	Hyd.	500	14 000	11 000	6, 5	60	1 040	48	9 240	312	1962	Reggione OM CNTR	MB820- Frot Gas D26N12V BRIF JW 600 CNTR	OM-SRM BRIF-Voith L24
214	B	Hyd.	130	5 700	4 000	4	35	910	22	7 158	175	1963	Badoni; Greco; Simm CNTR	8217-02,001 Fiat	BRIF-Voith L33

IVORY COAST — UPPER VOLTA

REGIE DES CHEMINS DE FER ABIDJAN-NIGER (RAN)
PO Box 1394, Abidjan, Ivory Coast

Telephone: 32 02 45
Telex: 564 CCP

General Manager: Lancina Konate
Assistant General Manager: Delchan Ouedraogo
Inspector General for Technical Affairs: Bony Aboh
Administrative Director: Ibrahima Coulibaly
Director Rolling Stock and Traction: Ousseyni Diarra
Director Track and Structure: Noël Privat
Director Studies and New Projects: N'Da Ezoa
Financial Director: Christopher Yesso
Commercial Director: Gbon Coulibaly
Improvements Director: André Balma
Head of Personnel and Social Affairs Service: Média Kone
Head of the Supplies and Shops Service: Mélindji Kacou
Head of the Sleeping Car and Tourism Service: Pierre Mariotti
Head of the Professional Services: Auguste Pruvost
Head of the Information Service: Aby Abagnilin
Head of the Telecommunication and Signalling Service: Nabilébié Bazie
Head of the Documentation Service: Bahi Kohirime
Head of the Press and External Affairs Office: Bernard Combes

Gauge: 1.00 m.
Route length: 1 173 km.

The railway comprises a principal line of 713 miles *(1 147 km)* which connects Abidjan, capital of Ivory Coast, with Ouagadougou, capital of Upper Volta, and two branches, one of 7.5 miles *(12 km)* from Abidjan to the oil port of Vridi and the other of 9 miles *(14 km)* from Azaguie *(41 km)* to Ake-Befiat. Two additional lines are planned: San Pedro-Mout Klahoyo (325 km) and Ouagadougou-Tambao (350 km).

TRAFFIC
After setbacks in 1974-75, freight traffic began to recover in 1976 continuing to the 630 million tonne-km carried in 1978. RAN estimates continuing growth at the rate of 6.5 per cent over the next few years.
Passenger traffic provides 50 per cent of commercial revenues. Traffic reached 1 200 million passenger-km in 1978 and is expected to increase at the rate of at least five per cent a year up to 1985.

	1975	1976	1977	1978
Freight ton-km	443 218 305	559 000 000	550 473 952	630 000 000
Freight tonnage	725 370	866 000	797 819	899 000
Passenger-km	945 736 974	1 040 000 000	1 172 778 275	1 200 000 000
Passenger journeys	3 006 736	3 254 000	3 555 642	3 700 000

FINANCES	1974	1975	1976	1977
		(Fr CFA million)		
Revenue	7 473	8 423	11 751	11 776
Expenses	7 470	8 960	9 968	12 035

INVESTMENTS
RAN's $US 334.6 million development plans for 1978/82 calls for major track reconstruction.

MOTIVE POWER AND ROLLING STOCK
At present RAN operates 193 passenger coaches, .6 vans and 662 freight wagons, including 93 tankers owned by oil shippers. Motive power includes 68 locomotives for mainline operation, 90 rail cars and 25 shunters.
During 1978 the railway placed orders with Arbel of France for 200 freight wagons of various types.

PERMANENT WAY
A major programme of track improvement is being pushed through. The swift growth of traffic has caused a number of operating problems, because of the relatively light structure, steep gradients and narrow curves. From Abidjan to Tafire (488 km) the track had gradients of up to 25 per cent and many curve radii as low as 200 m. Rails were only 25 kg/m. Beyond Tafire and up to Ougadougou the track was laid with 30 kg/m rails, with a maximum gradient of 10 per cent and minimum curve radius of 500 m. Modernisation began as soon as it was realised that the line would be unable to cope with the increased traffic.
Between 1970 and 1973 track was realigned between Agboville and Dimbokro (183 km) and 36 kg/m rail, welded from station to station, was laid. As a part of this work, track was doubled between Cechi and Anoumaba.
During the same period re-ballasting of the line was begun and a major programme of rail welding was launched. By the end of 1977 length of welded track totalled 901 km, while track reballasted with granite was 1 065 km.
Realignment is being carried out north of Dimbokro, and was completed as far as Tafire by 1978.
RAN announced in 1974 that it was to spend a further FrCFA15 000 million on track-doubling and other infrastructure works between 1977 and 1980. Four more sections of double track are now to be laid between Abidjan and Bouaké at a cost of FrCFA10 000 million. These will bring considerable operating benefits and a further cut in journey time from Ouagadougou to the coast.
FrCFA 4 000 million have been allocated to several small realignment and bridge construction schemes on the line northwards from Tafire to Ouagadougou, and to miscellaneous rerailing with 36 kg/m rail. Total expenditure on infrastructure by RAN during the 1977-80 period was FrCFA 26 000 million.
Meanwhile, feasibility studies are being carried out for a 325-km railway to link iron ore deposits at Mt. Klahoyo near Man with the port of San Pedro.

SIGNALLING AND COMMUNICATIONS
Modernisation of RAN's signalling and telecommunications is also going ahead. Negotiations are in progress with the African Development Bank for a grant to cover part of the FrCFA3 000 million cost of installing CTC throughout the main line and Sofrerail is providing consultancy assistance. There is already a 15-km double-track section between Checi and Anoumaba, just south of Dimbokro, which has considerably eased operation.

JAMAICA

JAMAICA RAILWAY CORPORATION (JRC)
PO Box 489, 142 Barry Street, Kingston

Chairman: John Allgrove
General Manager: Whilston Taylor
Chief of Transportation: E. Shirley
Chief Civil Engineer: Kerrith Foster
Chief Mechanical Engineer: G. Mitchell

Gauge: 1.435 m
Route length: 330 km

TRAFFIC
	1975	1977
Total freight tonnage	4 009 531	4 500 000
Total passengers carried	1 106 002	1 121 000

FINANCIAL DETAILS
	1972 J$	1973 J$	1974 J$	1975 J$	1977 J$
Revenue	3 148 000	3 712 000	5 237 000	6 262 000	6 378 000
Expenses	3 488 000	4 514 000	6 352 000	7 296 000	10 000 000

MOTIVE POWER AND ROLLING STOCK (1978)
Number of locomotives in service
Diesel-electric: Line haul 28; shunting 3
Number of railcars, diesel: 6
Number of trailers: 3 Wickham; 14 Rolls-Royce
Number of passenger train coaches: 23
Number of freight train cars (JRC): 266; (ALCAN) 113; (ALCOA) 40; (REVERE) 21

KAISER BAUXITE COMPANY RAILROAD
Discovery Bay

Vice-President and General Manager: E. J. Coyne

Gauge: 1.435 m
Route length: 25.74 km

The company is engaged in bauxite mining and the railway transports some 5 million short tons per year.

JAPAN

JAPANESE NATIONAL RAILWAYS

6-5, Marunouchi 1-chome, Chiyoda-ku, Tokyo

Board of Directors:
Chairman: Fumio Takagi
Vice-Chairman: Masaji Amasaka
Members: Seiji Kaya   Hideaki Suzuki
Kiyoshi Kawarabayashi Nobuto Takeda
Takei Tojo   Tatsuo Okabe
Dalzo Nakamura   Yasuhiro Tanaka
Shigeo Yamaguchi   Yoshindo Fujita
Koji Takahashi   Tadamasa Yamazaki
Kazumasa Mawatari   Tomoo Kagayama
Hideo Yoshitake   Hiroshi Yoshii

President: Fumio Takagi
Vice-President, Executive: Masaji Amasaka
Vice-President, Engineering: Koji Takahashi
General Manager, Affiliated Enterprises: Shigeo Yamaguchi
Advisory Directors:
Shinkansen Administration: Yasuhiro Tanaka
Hokkaido Region: Hideaki Suzuki
Osaka Region: Tatsuo Okabe
Tokyo Metropolitan Sphere HQ: Tadamasa Yamazaki
Head Office: Kazumasa Mawatari
Head Office, Staff Relations: Hiroshi Yoshii
Kyushu Region: Nobuto Takeda
Sendai Region: Hideo Yoshitake
Head Office: Yoshindo Fujita
Head Office: Tomoo Kagayama
Directors of Departments:
Director, Public Relations Dept: Mistunobu Mastue
Director, International Dept: Toshiyo Nobusawa
Director, Inspection & Audit Dept: Shigeru Nagai
Director, Corporate Planning Dept: Makoto Kagayama
Director, Local Line Countermeasures Dept: Tomoo Kagayama
Directors, Technical Development Dept: Yoshihiro Kyotani
Hisomu Katase
Testuo Mastuo
Keisuke Ishida
Hiroshi Sugiura

	1977
Railway Route Length (km)	21 307
Double- and Multi-tracked Sections	5 479
	(25.7%)
Electrified Sections	8 032
	(37.7%)
Narrow Gauge Lines	
dc	4 822
ac	3 210
Shinkansen	
ac	1 177

PASSENGER TRAFFIC

The passenger-km in 1977 was 199 700 million, a decline of five per cent from the preceding year. Of this 121 900 million passenger-km was for ordinary passenger service, a decrease of eight per cent, and 77 800 million passenger-km for season-ticket passenger service, a decrease of one per cent as compared with the preceding year. Narrow-gauge lines accounted for 79 700 million passenger-km and the Shinkansen 42 200 million passenger-km for ordinary passenger service, a decrease of five and twelve per cent, respectively, as compared with the preceding year.
This was due to the competition put up by airlines and other modes of transport after JNR's tariff rise, as well as to the slower pace of business recovery and sluggish consumer spending.

Type EF 66 dc electric locomotive
JNR planned and carried out successive speed-ups of the passenger trains of conventional narrow-gauge lines other than Shinkansen. Within described schedule, high-speed freight train operation was also planned, to include more powerful locomotive to operate freight trains of more than 1 000 tonnes at continuous speed of 100 km/h, resulting in development of the EF 66 in 1966: the locomotive is of six axles, Bo-Bo-Bo arrangement with axle load of 16.8 tonnes, one hour rating power of 3 900 kW, it is the largest locomotive for narrow-gauge (1 067 mm) lines in Japan.
It produces high-gradient balanced speed (75 km/h at 10 per cent gradient with 1 000 tonne trains) and provides very wide speed selection range for, gradient load.

Type ED 65 ac 20 kV 50 Hz, 1 900 kW silicon rectifier system electric locomotive

Further improvement was made in major city sphere services, especially for commuters, and the ticket reservation system expanded with new features introduced for sales promotion.

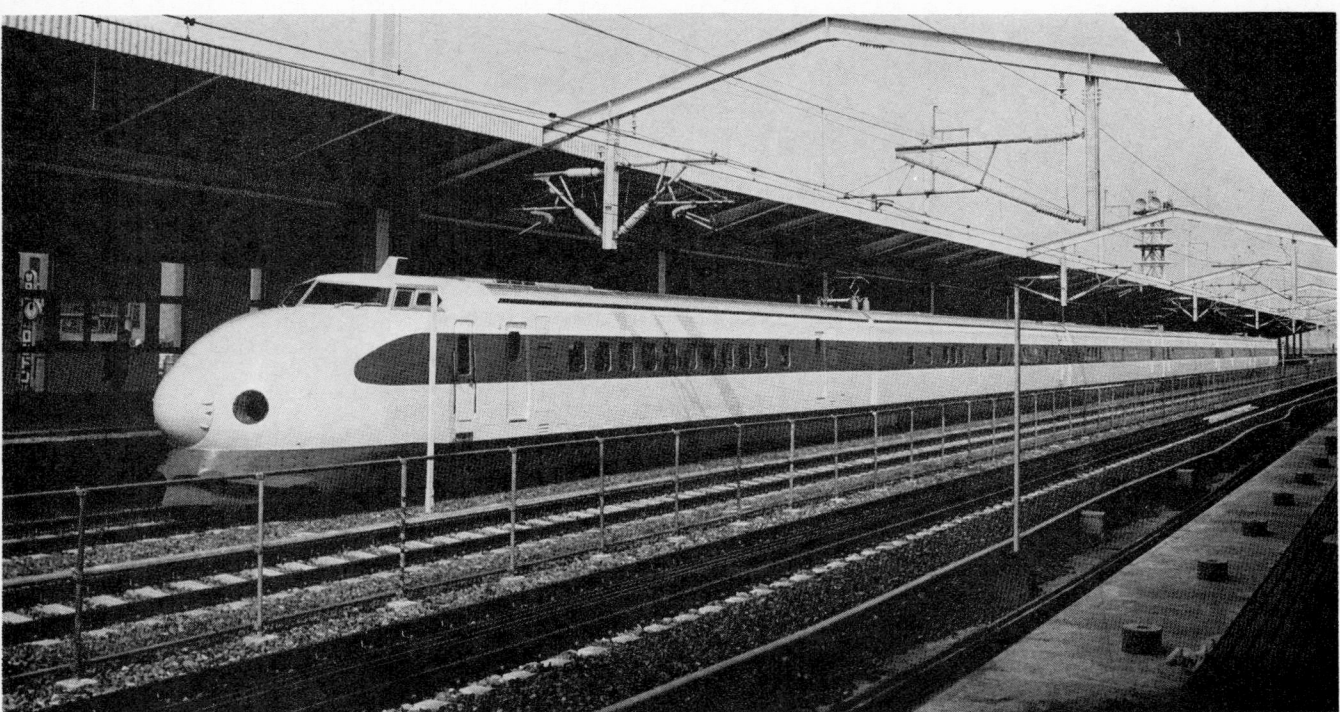

Shinkansen electric railcar prototype 962
Six cars constitute a train set. This prototype is scheduled to be converted into an electric test-inspection car when service on the pilot line is over. Therefore arrangement of windows and interior are based on a design scheme for the layout required for the electric test-inspection car. Main dimensions are same as those of Tokaido Shinkansen, but nose of the front end is about 600 mm longer. Outside colouring has been tentatively changed to two-tone colour of green and cream from characteristic colours,

ivory white and light blue, of existing Shinkansen cars. For research purposes cars #1 and #4 are fitted with various chairs test-manufactured, and their spacings changed. Interior finishing wall and curtains also given two kinds of colouring for trial application. To prevent falling snow from sticking to carbody, underfloor electric equipment is completely covered by members of body structure in body-mount fitting. Body is built of aluminium.

Shinkansen: The Shinkansen carried 126.8 million passengers, 11.6 per cent less than in 1976, and the passenger-km went down to 42 187 million, 12.4 per cent less. On Sundays and holidays, as many as 275 trains were operated a day, 132 Hikari's and 143 Kodama's.

Narrow gauge lines: In 1977 an average of 1 618 limited express and ordinary express trains and 16 572 local trains, totalling 18 190, were scheduled per day.
The passenger-km by limited express was 29 566 million, seven per cent less than in 1976. Limited express trains continued to enjoy popularity, although the number of passengers carried went down slightly. On the other hand ordinary express trains saw a large drop in patronage, particularly after fares and charges had been raised.
Only a small-scale improvement took place in passenger service, such as the strengthening of the transport capacities of the Sobu, Joban and Narita lines in connection with the opening of the New Tokyo International Airport.
The Tohoku and Takasaki lines have reached the limit of their capacities, making it urgent to complete the Tohoku and Joetsu Shinkansen lines which are presently under construction.

Passenger-kilometres

| | Shinkansen | Narrow-gauge lines | | |
		Express train	Local train	Total
1973	38 989	61 105	108 003	208 097
1974	40 671	63 921	110 972	215 564
1975	53 318	52 990	108 981	215 289
1976	48 147	50 815	111 778	210 740
1977	42 187	46 655	110 810	199 653

Note: Express train denotes limited express and ordinary express trains.

FREIGHT TRAFFIC
Freight traffic in 1977 amounted to 132 million tonnes, six per cent less than in the preceding year. The tonne-km decreased by 11 per cent to 40 600 million. Although there were fewer service interruptions than in the preceding year, freight traffic decreased under the impact of the tariff rise effected in November 1976 and sluggish business conditions. The decrease in tonne-km in relation to tonnage was particularly notable due to the decline in the demand for long-distance carload freight transport.

| | Tonnes carried | Tonne-kilometres | Average distance of haul/tonne (km) |
	(millions)	(thousand millions)	
1973	176	57.4	326.8
1974	158	51.6	327.1
1975	142	46.6	328.7
1976	141	45.5	323.1
1977	132	40.6	307.6

Of the tonnage carried, mineral oil and limestone ranked first, each accounting for 13 per cent, followed by cement 11 per cent, and container goods, 8 per cent.
The tonnage of container traffic diminished by 13 per cent to 10 017 000 tonnes and the tonne-km to 8 035 million.
The tonnage by freightliners which accounted for over a half of the total container traffic went down by 15 per cent from the preceding year. The drop in the tonnage carried in co-ordination with freight companies was especially large.
Sea-borne container goods fell from 20 000 tonnes in 1976 to 13 000 tonnes, a decline of 34 per cent.

Number of kinds of freight cars:

Box cars	67 320
Refrigerated cars	1 717
Ventilated cars	198
Tank cars	32
Gondola cars	22 615
Flat cars	1 616
Container cars	6 887
Hopper cars	5 757
Others	3 581
Total	109 723

ELECTRIFICATION
As of October 1978 37.7 per cent or 8 032 km of the total route length of JNR was electrified. Steam locomotives were all withdrawn from service in March 1976.

	Route length ac/dc electrified (km)	Percentage to total route length
1973	6 961.4 (2 629.1)	33.0
1974	7 374.8 (2 829.3)	34.9
1975	7 628.1 (3 036.1)	35.9
1976	7 813.0 (3 210.2)	36.7
1977	7 813.0 (3 210.2)	36.7
1978 (Oct)	8 032.2 (3 210.2)	37.7

Notes: 1. The figures in parentheses indicate the route length ac electrified. 2. Route length electrified does not include the Shinkansen (Tokyo—Hakata), 1 176.5 km.

SHINKANSEN
The Shinkansen carried 1 300 million passengers between its opening in October 1964 and 31 March 1978 without a single casualty. Passengers carried in 1978 numbered 126.8 million (a daily average of 347 000), 11.7 per cent less than in the preceding year; passenger-km 42 187 million, 12.4 per cent less; and the distance travelled per passenger 333 km, three km less.
Two trains are presently scheduled every hour for through operation between Tokyo and Hakata, and up to nine trains per hour between Tokyo and Shin Osaka.

Revenue and expense

| | | | | | *(thousand millions of yen)* |
	1973	1974	1975	1976	1977
Revenue	290.3	325.6	477.9	547.2	615.1
Expense	135.0	168.9	296.0	330.7	370.5
Operating ratio (%)	46	52	62	60	60

Dual-gauge (ac 20 kV 50 Hz/60 Hz and dc 1 500 V) 2 550 kW type EF 81 electric locomotive

Pendulum emu limited express series 381
Series 381 is a high-speed electric railcar of natural pendulum type, light in weight, low in centre of gravity, with pendulum structure of body and running capacity of bogie improved. A train of Series 381 cars runs at top speed of 120 km/h on the Chuo line and the Kisei line which abound with curves.

Main features of Shinkansen

	Tokyo—Shin Osaka	Shin Osaka—Hakata
Route length	515.4 km	562.0 km
Time required	3 h 10 min	3 h 44 min
Maximum speed	210 km/h	210 km/h
Scheduled speed	162.8 km/h	148.3 km/h
Gauge	1 435 mm	1 435 mm
Grade	Max 20/1 000	Max 15/1 000
Curve radius	Min 2 500 m	Min 4 000 m
Rail	53.3 kg/m	60.8 kg/m
	1 500-m long welded rails	1 500-m long welded rails
Train control	Automatic Train Control (ATC)	
	Centralised Traffic Control (CTC)	
	Computer-aided Traffic Control (COMTRAC)	
Power system	ac 25 kV 60 Hz, single-phase	
	Centralised Substation Control (CSC)	
	Booster-transformer feeding system	Auto-transformer feeding system
Construction period	5½ years	5 years (Shin Osaka—Okayama)
		5 years (Okayama—Hakata)
Construction cost (millions of yen)	380 000	224 000 (Shin Osaka—Okayama)
		718 000 (Okayama—Hakata)
Opening date	1 Oct 1964	15 Mar 1972 (Shin Osaka—Okayama)
		10 Mar 1975 (Okayama—Hakata)
Seating capacity of Hikari train	1 342 passengers	
Seating capacity of Kodama train	1 483 passengers	

FINANCES
The 1977 operating revenues showed a gain of only 19 per cent compared with the preceding year in spite of the steep upward revision of tariff effected in November 1976 and increased subsidies from the State. This was largely due to suspension of the proposed tariff revision in 1977, stiffer competition with other modes of transport and the slow pace of recovery in the nation's economy. As a result the revenue fell short of the targeted amount by 453 800 million yen. The operating expenses increased by ten per cent over the preceding year, although there was a saving of 118 400 million yen in the targeted amount in spite of rising personnel costs.

TECHNICAL DEVELOPMENT PLAN
In JNR overall plans for technical development are drafted, in line with the Long-term Management Plan, by the Technical Development Department in the Head Office, which also studies and works out measures for current technical problems of importance. Technical themes for research and development are decided each year. For 1977 emphasis was put on:

Higher safety and reliability of service

For the prevention of freight car derailment, a computer-aided simulator for bogie freight cars was being developed, using the data obtained from the test track laid especially for the purpose; and with test apparatus, the effects of various factors on running stability were studied.

For the prevention of train collisions and accidents due to overspeeding on turnouts, research was under way to develop a speed-check type ATS, under which the train speed is detected before the train comes up to a signal or a turnout and, in case of overspeeding, the brake automatically goes into action, be it an electric, diesel, multiple unit or loco-hauled train.

To minimise disorders with the overhead wire and the pantograph, a study on the various results caused by the interaction between wire and pantograph, improvement of the pantograph and wire fittings and testing of newly developed ones was under way.

Labour and cost saving

For the mechanisation of ticket selling and examining, development and testing of automatic medium-and-long-distance ticket vending machines and automatic Shinkansen ticket examining machines was in progress.

For the mechanisation of flat yard operations, a newly developed freight car decelerating device was being tested.

To reduce the construction cost, safer and more economical ways to construct underground railways in city areas and a way to speed up slab track laying was under study.

Noise abatement

For the abatement of train noise JNR experts have been at work from the outset of Shinkansen construction, using long welded rails, double elastic fastening, pneumatic spring bogie structure and body-side skirts. In progress for further improvement are:
(1) Analysis of the noise source and other elements.
(2) Noise abatement for rolling stock:
   Control of the tread surface of wheels.
   Development of vibration-proof wheels and resilient wheels.
   Development of vibration-proof supports for the axle spring liner, sound-absorbing materials under the car floor and sound-insulating plates for bogies. New shapes for the pantograph and insulator, better materials for the slider and improvement of the spring.
(3) Noise abatement for track:
   Control of rail tread surface, such as rail corrugation.
   Development of non-vibratory rails and vibration-proof materials for rail.
   Development of slab mats and ballast mats.
   Development of elastic fastening.
(4) Noise abatement for structures:
   Development of sound-barrier walls, sound-barrier walls with overhang, higher sound-barrier walls, viaduct undercover, sound-insulating materials and various sound-barrier structures.
   Augmentation of massiveness for structures, elasticisation of girder supports, sound-proof girders, etc.
(5) Abatement of overhead wire noise:

Electric ac locomotive Type ED75

ED75 is the standard type of ac electric locomotive. Of all types, ED75 locomotives are produced in the greatest number and used all over Japan, in Hokkaido in the North, with cold proofing, and in Kyushu in the South.

Higher elasticity of the overhead wire, change of distance between supporting structures.

As a result of these studies, the noise level even on the viaduct has been reduced to around 80 dB(A) by the combined use of sound barrier walls with overhang and mats. At this value the noise of running part and power collector, the swishing sound of carbody and the secondary noise of structure vibrations are seen to contribute an equivalent degree of noise as the sound sources. Therefore the noise-abating work is being conducted with all these factors taken into consideration.

Comprehensive tests for improvement of Shinkansen operation

For the testing of newly developed noise-abating and vibration-damping devices and for the development of safety measures and technology for Shinkansen operation in the future, it is planned to use a completed part of the Tohoku Shinkansen as a test track. Rolling stock, track, structures and electric facilities are being prepared for test runs on this track.

Magnetic-levitation linear-motor railway

Development of a Maglev railway is at the stage where a near-actual-scale model can be tested within high-speed ranges, as a result of the data obtained from the various basic experiments and low-speed running tests conducted at the Railway Technical Research Institute.

To ascertain the running capacity, a 7-km long test track, almost straight and level, capable of testing up to the target speed of 500 km/h, is under construction. On the completed 3.1 km section, all sorts of running tests are being conducted.

This will make it possible to test the magnetic support, guiding device, linear synchronous motor, emergency brake, guideway and power supply facilities within high-speed ranges.

ELECTRIC LOCOMOTIVES

Class	Axle Arrangement	Line Current	Rated Output kW	Max lb (kg)	Tractive Effort (Full Field) Continuous at lb (kg)	mph (km/h)	Max Speed mph (km/h)	Wheel Dia. in (mm)	Weight tonnes	Length ft in (mm)	No. Built as of 31/3/78	Year Built	Builders (abbreviations) M: (Mitsubishi Electric Co, Mitsubishi Heavy Industries). T: Tokyo Shibaura Elec. Co. H: Hitachi Mfg Co. K: Kawasaki Heavy Industries. To: Toyo Elec. Co. N: Nippon Sharyo Seizo Ltd.
ED 71	B-B	20 kV 1/50	1 900	35 270 (16 00)	26.5 (42.4)		59 (95)	44 (1 120)	67	47' 3'' (14 400)	52	1959	M. T. H.
ED 72	B-2-B	20 kV 1/60	1 900	31 100 (14 100)	30.5 (49.1)		62 (100)	44 (1 120)	87	57' 1'' (17 400)	20	1961	T.
ED 73	B-B	20 kV 1/60	1 900	31 100 (14 100)	30.5 (49.1)		62 (100)	44 (1 120)	67.2	47' 3'' (14 400)	22	1962	T.
ED 74	B-B	20 kV 1/60	1 900	31 100 (14 100)	30.5 (49.1)		62 (100)	44 (1 120)	67.2	46' 11'' (14 300)	6	1962	M.
ED 75	B-B	20 kV 1/50	1 900	31 100 (14 100)	30.5 (49.1)		62 (100)	44 (1 120)	67.2	60' 4½'' (18 300)	301	1963	M. H. T.
ED 76	B-2-B	20 kV 1/50 or 60	1 900	31 100 (14 100)	30.5 (49.1)		62 (100)	44 (1 120)	90.5	60' 4½'' (18 400)	130	1965	H. M. T.
ED 77	B-2-B	20 kV 1/50	1 900	31 100 (14 100)	30.5 (49.1)		62 (100)	44 (1 200)	75	51' 10'' (15 800)	16	1965	H. M .T.
ED 78	B-2-B	20 kV 1/50	1 900	31 100 (14 100)	30.5 (49.1)		62 (100)	44 (1 120)	81.5	58' 9'' (17 900)	12	1968	H.
EF 59	2C + C2	1 500 V dc	1 350	26 000 (11 800)	26 (42)		56 (90)	49¼ (1 250)	106.6	65' 4¼'' (19 920)	24	1963	JNR. (R. B)
EF 62	C-C	1 500 V dc	2 550	51 600 (23 400)	24.2 (39)		62 (100)	44 (1 120)	96	59' 1'' (18 000)	52	1962	K. T. To.
EF 63	B-B-B	1 500 V dc	2 550	51 600 (23 400)	24.2 (39)		62 (100)	44 (1 120)	108	59' 3'' (18 050)	23	1962	T. M. K.
EF 64	B-B-B	1 500 V dc	2 550	44 850 (20 350)	28 (45)		71 (115)	44 (1 120)	96	58' 9'' (17 900)	79	1964	T. K. To.
EF 65	B-B-B	1 500 V dc	2 550	44 850 (2 350)	28 (45)		71 (115)	44 (1 120)	96	54' 2'' (16 500)	260	1964	K. To. T. N.
EF 66	B-B-B	1 500 V dc	3 900	43 200 (19 590)	44.9 (72.2)		75 (120)	44 (1 120)	100	59' 8½'' (18 200)	56	1968	K. To.
EF 70	B-B-B	20 kV 1/60	2 300	42 990 (19 500)	26.1 (42.0)		62 (105)	44 (1 120)	96	54' 11½'' (16 750)	81	1961	H. M.
EF 71	B-B-B	20 kV 1/50	2 700	46 500 (21 100)	28.6 (46.1)		62 (100)	44 (1 120)	100.8	60' 8'' (18 500)	15	1968	M. T.
EF 30 Dual current	B+B+B	1.5 Vdc 20 kV 1/60	1 800	30 420 (13 800)	29.0 (46.7)		53 (85)	39⅜ (1 000)	96	54' 4'' (16 560)	22	1960	H. M. T.
EF 81 Dual current	B--B-B	1.5 kVdc 20 kV 1/50, 1/00	2 550	44 050 (19 980)	28.4 (45.7)		62 (115)	44 (1 120)	100.8	61' 0'' (18 600)	140	1968	H. M.
EF 80 Dual current	B-B-B	1.5 kVdc 20 kV 1/50	1 950	31 970 (14 500)	29.8 (48)		62 (105)	44 (1 120)	96	57' 5'' (17 500)	63	1962	H. M.

DIESEL LOCOMOTIVES

Class	Axle Arrangement	Transmission	Rated Power hp	Max lb (kg)	Tractive Effort Continuous at lb (kg)	mph (km/h)	Max Speed mph (km/h)	Wheel Dia. in (mm)	Total Weight Tons	Length ft in (mm)	No. Built as of 31/3/78	Year first Built	Builders	Engine & Type	Transmission Type
DD 51	B-2-B	Hyd.	2 200		39 680 (18 00)		59 (95)	33¹³/₁₆ (860)	84	59' 1" (18 000)	626	1962	H. M. K.	2×1 100 hp DML 61Z	DW2A DW 2A
DD 53	B-2-B	Hyd.	2 200		39 680 (18 000)		59 (95)	,,	81	53' 2" (16 200)	3	1964	K.	2×1 100 hp DML 6182	DW 2AR DW 2AR
DD 54	B-1-B	Hyd.	1 820		37 040 (16 800)		59 (95)	,,	70	50' 2½" (15 300)	18	1966	M.	DMP 86Z	DW 5
DD 13	B-B	Hyd.	1 000		37 040 (16 800)		44 (70)	33¹³/₁₆ (860)	56	44' 7½" (13 600)	395	1957	K. M. N. H.	2 × 500 hp DMF 31SB	DS 12/135
DD 14	B-B	Hyd.	1 000		(18 540)		44 (70)	33¹³/₁₅ (860)	58	47' 0" (14 325)	36	1960	K.	2 × 500 hp DMF 31 SBR	,,
DD 15	B-B	Hyd.	1 000		36 380 (16 500)		44 (70)	33¹³/₁₆ (860)	55	44' 7½" (13 600)	50	1961	N.	,,	,,
DD 16	B-B	Hyd.	800		31 750 (14 400)		47 (75)	,,	49	38' 10" (11 840)	65	1972	J. N. R. N. K.	DML 61Z	DW 2A
DE 10	AAA-B	Hyd.	1 350		43 000 (19 500)		53 (85)	33¹³/₁₆ (860)	65	46' 5" (14 150)	692	1966	K. N. H.	DML61ZA, B	DWA
DE 11	,,	,,	,,		46 300 (21 000)		,,	,,	70	,,	112	1968	K. N.	,,	,,
DE 15	,,	,,	,,		43 000 (19 500)		,,	,,	65	,,	44	1967	N.	,,	,,
DF 50	B-B-B	Elec.	1 200		27 550 (12 500)	(17.5)	56 (90)	39⅜ (1 000) (85.7)	109	53' 10" (16 400)		1965	K. N. T. H.	MANV6V22/30mA Sulzer 8LDA25	
Shinkansen 911	B-B-B	Hyd.	2 200	100	59 500 (27 000)		35⅞ (160)	90 (910)	63' 8" (19 400)	3		1964	N.	2 × 1 100 hp DWZB DML61Z	
Shinkansen 912	B-B	Hyd.	740		(14 000)		44 (70)	33¹³/₁₆ (860)	56	44' 7¼" (13 600)	20	1959	N.	2 × 370 hp DMF 31S	DS 12/135

JORDAN

HEDJAZ JORDAN RAILWAY (HJR)
AQABA RAILWAY CORPORATION (ARC)
PO Box 582, Amman

General Manager (HJR): M. R. Qoseini
General Manager (ARC): Eng. A. Hijazi
Assistant to General Manager: Walid Dahdees
Departmental Heads:
　Finance: Ibrhim Qanah
　Operating and Mechanical: H. Haddadeen
　Traffic: Fauzi Rasheed
　Permanent Way: M. Molla
　Engineering: M. K. Emad Eldein
　Stores and Supplies: I. Abu Taha
General Inspector: B. S. Nuseir
Administration: Shaher Majali

Gauge: 1.050 m.
Route length: 271 km (16 tonnes axle load)
　　　　　　237 km (10 tonnes axle load)

A separate directorate for the newly-formed Aqaba Railway Corp (ARC) was set up in May 1978. Jordan began carting rock phosphate from its mines at Al-Hassa to the Port of Aqaba in 1976 over 161 miles (260km) of new and rebuilt rail lines. The line should not only speed up the export of Jordan's phosphates—its most important foreign exchange earner—but it might also signal the start of a new effort to revive the Hedjaz railway.
About 74 miles (120 km) of the new route—Hettiya west to Aqaba, which was never before connected to the line—is completely new; the rest, from Hettiya north to Al-Hassa, is the original Hedjaz line, newly strengthened and repaired.
The entire project, carried out by the West German contractors Held & Francke, cost JD 25 million ($US80.6 million). As part of the improvement scheme, the Jordanians have also purchased ten new 1 800 hp locomotives, built by General Electric, and 140 new hoppers. According to officials at the Jordanian Ministry of Transport, the new system will be able to handle 1.6 million tons of phosphate a year—equal to Jordan's phosphate exports in 1974.
The Hedjaz Jordan Railway called for pre-qualification bids in 1977 from contractors to reconstruct the railway from Al-Hasa to Menzil. In addition to reconstruction of 21 km of existing track, contractors have been asked to bid on construction of 3.5 km of new track to the phosphate mine at Al-Hasa and erection of a new station at Menzil.
Meanwhile, Jordanian and Syrian Transport Ministries have asked an international consultant to conduct economic and feasibility studies to standardise the existing narrow-gauge railway between Amman and Damascus. It will form part of the reconstruction of the 1 300 m Hedjaz railway linking Medina in Saudi Arabia with Western Europe. Cost of the Amman-Damascus section is estimated at $200 million. Sofrerail of France has completed studies for standardisation of the line between Amman and the Syrian border.

TRAFFIC	1973	1974	1975	1976	1977
Freight km	28 210 815	7 693 539	14 299 948	89 934 096	—
Freight tonnage	56 067	89 488	95 475	352 541	164 038 458
Passenger-km	1 521 930	5 714 885	7 718 796	6 920 047	7 510 561
Passenger journeys	7 021	80 125	94 815	96 649	64 949

FINANCIAL	1973	1974	1975 (JDI)	1976	1977
Revenues	JD368 881	421 363	465 000	661 881	1 254 500
Expenses	JD369 745	409 787	465 000	811 454	1 273 000

MOTIVE POWER AND ROLLING STOCK
Present stock consists of 9 steam line locomotives, 18 line haul diesel-electrics, five steam shunters, six diesel-electric shunters, 5 passenger cars and 411 freight cars. An additional 210 hopper wagons were under manufacture in 1978 when tender documents for 65 freight wagons were under preparation.

SIGNALLING AND TRAIN CONTROL INSTALLATIONS
Type: semi automatic; Route length: 265 km; Location: Aqaba-El Hasa; Supplier: ML Engineering (Plymouth) England.
Originally designed to meet the need for a railway signalling tokenless block system for operation over a radio link where the environment is potentially noisy, the new system style 20, developed by ML Engineering of Britain, has been installed on the El Hasa-Aqaba Railway. Ultra high-frequency radio is being used in Jordan to provide communications links between drivers and to control block sections. In addition to the System, ML has equipped the 17 stations between El Hasa and Aqaba with local control consoles for conventional point operation through route-relay interlocking. Passing loop switches are power operated, and through train movements are supervised from the main traffic control room. Station areas are fully track-circuited, and ML colour-light signals are used throughout, equipped with filament changeover relays arranged to indicate main filament failures.
The fail-safe Style 20 FDM equipment, which forms the heart of the system, allows block signalling from station to station, using UHF radio, and if speech is required over the same circuit, 16 individual channels are available within the carrier frequency 2000 Hz to 3400 Hz for speech, allowing up to 2000 Hz for speech. The system operates on a frequency shift principle with both carrier frequencies being detected independently. Each channel can transmit one out of six bits of information at any given time.

KAMPUCHEA

Phnom Penh

Telephone: 25156
Telegrams: FERCAM Phnom Penh

President and Managing Director: In Nhel
Deputy Managing Director: Seng Kim Chun
Technical Director: Bou Saman
Chief, Mechanical Engineering: Khlaut Thol
Chief, Permanent Way: Youg Sokhon
Chief, Operating: Em Thoul

Gauge: 1.00 m.
Route length: 649 km.

The 385-km line from Phnom-Penh, the capital, to Poipet where connection is made with the State Railway of Thailand, was built in two sections in 1930/32 and 1939/40 when the entire area was known as French Indo-China. The first section, to Mongkolborey, was built and worked by the Compagnie des Chemins de Fer du Sud de l'Indochine. This was purchased in 1936 by the Chemin de Fer Non Concedes de l'Indochine. In July 1952, all lines within Kampuchea (then Cambodia) were formed into the Chemins de Fer du Cambodge.

The metre gauge Cambodian Railways has a total route length of 649 km of which only 33 per cent is in operation. The newest line on the system, between Phnom Penh and Kompong Som (264 km), opened in 1969, and has been closed to traffic since 1970 owing to damage caused during hostilities in the region. This is the country's only rail outlet to the sea, other than via Thailand to Bangkok. The Phnom Penh—Poipet line is at present cut off between Phnom Penh and Pyrsat.

TRAFFIC

	1972	1973
Total freight ton-km	9 769 343	11 512 900
Total freight tonnage	89 911	117 460
Total passenger-km	50 555 046	55 064 745
Total passenger journeys	902 813	1 027 317

MOTIVE POWER

Majority of the railway's present traction requirements are being met by 13 diesel-electric locomotives and a large number of steam locomotives. Backbone of the diesel electric fleet are the Alsthom-built BB 1 200 hp units fitted with MGO-V12 BZSHR which were delivered in 1966/67. Due to lack of spares, however, the workshops department experienced difficulties over the 1975/76 period in keeping these locomotives in operation.

PERMANENT WAY AND INSTALLATIONS

A line linking Phnom-Penh and Saigon has been projected for a number of years but consistently cancelled owing to hostilities. The line would fill one of the missing links in the Transasian Railway Project.

Following Chinese assistance during 1977/78 Kampuchea began work on repairing and upgrading the line running from the port of Kompong Som to Phnom-Penh. Following outbreak of hostilities with Viet-Nam, work was halted in early 1979. It was announced in mid-1978 that a new line was to be built between Samrong and Kompong Speu City following a study by Chinese engineers.

KENYA

KENYA RAILWAYS (KR)
PO Box 30121, Nairobi

Telephone: 21211
Telex: 22254

Chairman: James King'ang'i Njoroge
Managing Director: Davidson Karundi Ngini
Directors: Dr Morris N. Ndangana
    John Gituma
    Dr R. J. Onyango
    Kabere M'mbijjiwe
    Jackson Tengwer
    Charles Ngari Kebuchi
Chief Traffic Manager: Brown Waweru
Chief Civil Engineer: Joel Mudhune
Chief Mechanical Engineer: Julius Mimano
Chief Administrative Secretary: Benjamin Edward Ombuoro
Chief Personnel Manager: Charles Muthee
Chief Accountant: Zadock Baraza Kambogo Shimba
Chief Supplies Officer: James Karanja

Gauge: 1.0 m
Route length: 2 084 km

The break up of the East African Railways Corporation in 1976 gave rise to the creation of three separate railway systems and the birth of Kenya Railways in 1977 with its headquarters in Nairobi.

Kenya Railways is a State Corporation run by a Board of Directors.

The Kenya Railways operates a total of 2 084 route-km of metre gauge line consisting of the main line from Mombasa through Nairobi, Nakuru and Eldoret to the border of Kenya with Uganda and the branch line joining the Lake Victoria town of Kisumu to the farming centre of Nakuru. The rest are branch lines linking Nairobi to Nanyuki near Mt Kenya, Gilgil to Nyahururu, Voi to Taveta, Kisumu to Butere, Konza to Magadi and Rongai to Solai.

The Kenya Railways submitted a draft development plan to the Government for inclusion in the 1979/83 National Development Plan of the Republic. It is hoped that the Government will provide funds either from its own resources or through external loans to finance some of the projects.

Emphasis in the development plan has been placed on improvement of the track, provision of locomotives and wagons (the whole requirement of which is now on order by the Kenya Government) and coaching stock either to replace worn out stock or to cater for anticipated growth both in the goods and passenger traffic.

TRAFFIC

The former East African Railways when originally developed had no other competitive modes of transport. Today Kenya Railways is not only faced with severe road competition parallel to its routes, but also the white oil pipeline which from February 1978 took all its white petroleum products. Despite the competition, the railway remains the main transportation mode for the bulk goods most of which are agricultural inputs, industrial and mining products. In 1978 freight tonnage fell to 3.7 million tonnes but this was expected to be a temporary decline. Passenger journeys rose by over 100 000 in 1978 to reach 1.4 million.

	1976	1977
Freight tonne-km	2 270 394 684	2 211 328 192
Freight tonnage	3 793 996	3 844 986
Passenger-km	309 022 190	326 509 800
Passenger journeys	1 358 545	1 373 100

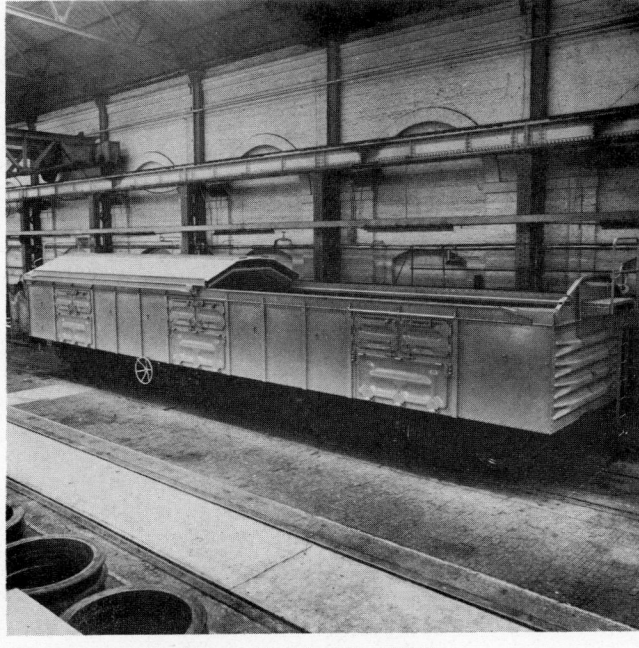

Covered wagon with sliding roof built for KR in 1977/78
Part of an order placed with BRE-Metro of the UK for 1 200 wagons and 20 shunters.

Freight operations earned Shs 581 865 million in 1978 compared with Shs 554 032 million the previous year. Earnings from passenger traffic reached Shs 32 411 million in 1978 (Shs 26.84 million in 1977).

FINANCES

	1977	1978
	(Shs)	
Revenues	567 241 000	614 276 000
Expenses	559 336 000	638 000 000

MOTIVE POWER AND ROLLING STOCK

The 130-strong diesel fleet was augmented by two batches of mainline units in 1978: 56 diesel-hydraulics by Thyssen-Henschel (Class 62) and 26 diesel-electrics (Class 93) from General Electric (USA). An order placed with Hunslet of the UK for 35 diesel shunters (Class 47) was also completed by the end of 1978. Also delivered during the year were 29 passenger coaches from Kalmar Verkstad of Sweden and 1 200 freight wagons (in knocked-down condition) from British Rail Engineering. Fleet numbers at the end of 1978: 103 steam locos; 191 diesel locos; 542 passenger coaches; 7 937 freight wagons.

DIESEL LOCOMOTIVES

Class	Axle Arrange-ment	Trans-mission	Rated Power hp	Max. lb (kg)	Tractive Effort Continuous at lb (kg)	mph (km/h)	Max. Speed mph (km/h)	Wheel Dia. in (mm)	Total Weight Tons	Length ft ins (mm)	No. Built	Year first Built	Builders: Mechanical Parts	Engine & Type	Transmission
92	1Co-Co1	Elec.	2 550	77 000 (35 000)	43 500 (19 730)	16.5 (26.4)	45 (72)	37½ (953)	114	59' 1¼" (18 015)	15	1971	MLW Ind	Alco 251F	GE Canada
87 (90)	1Co-Co1	Elec.	1 840	51 600 (23 300)	44 500 (20 180)	11.7 (18.8)	45 (72)	37½ (953)	101.5 (79.3) (Adhe-sive)	55' 7¼" (16 948)	10 14 20	1960 1964 1967/8	English Electric	E.E. 12 CSVT	E.E.
72	1Bo-Bo1	Elec.	1 240	40 000 (18 150)	32 500 (14 750)	10.7 (17.2)	45 (72)	37½ (953)	70.1	43' 9¼" (13 341)	10	1972	GEC Traction	EE 8CSVT	GEC
71 (91)	1Bo-Bo1	Elec.	1 240	40 000 (18 150)	32 000 (14 400)	10.5	45 (72)	37½ (953)	69 (13 341)	43' 9¼"	10	1967	English Electric	EE 8CSVT	EE
62	B-B	Hyd.	760	27 750 (12 500)	21 825 (9 900)	7.8 (12.3)	45 (72)	37½ (953)	38	37' 5" (11 404)	20	1972	Rheinstahl AG	MTU 493TZ(10) MTU 396TC(10)	Voith L520-U2
46 (86)	D	Hyd.	606 (2×203)	32 900 (14 900)			20 (32)	39½ (1 003)	48	36' 1¼" (11 007)	22	1967	Andrew Barclay	2 × Cummins	British Twin Disc CF 11500
45 (85)	D	Hyd.	855	35 000 (15 880)			22 (35)	45 (1 156)	52	34' 11" (10 643)	10	1957	N.B.L.	M.A.N. WBV 22/30A	N.B.L./Voith L 37zV
44 (84)	D	Hyd.	510	33 300 (15 102)			High 35 (56) Low 20 (32)	39½ (1 003)	52	33' 0¼" (10 065)	3	1956	N.B.L.	Davey Paxman 12PRHXL Ser. 2	N.B.L.-Voith L24V

DIESEL LOCOMOTIVES

Class	Axle Arrangement	Trans- mission	Rated Power hp	Max. lb (kg)	Continuous at lb (kg)	mph (km/h)	Max. Speed mph (km/h)	Wheel Dia. in (mm)	Total Weight Tons	Length ft ins (mm)	No. Built	Year first Built	Mechanical Parts	Engine & Type	Transmission
43 (83)	D	Hyd.	312	20 000 (9 070)			High 35 (56) Low 20 (32)	39½ (1 003)	42	31' 11¼" (9 734)	14	1955	N.B.L.	Davey Paxman 8 RPHL Ser. S	N.B.L.-Voith L24V
35	C	Hyd.	300	24 460 (11 100)	20 000 (9 070)	3.8 (6.1)	17 (27)	39½ (1 003)	36	29' 7¼" (9 023)	15	1972	Andrew Barclay	Paxman 8 RPHL	Voith L320V
33 (81)	C	Mech-Hyd.	194	15 800 (7 166)			26.2 (42.2)	39½ (1 003)	29.4	26' 5¾" (8 071)	6	1950	Drewry Car Co.	Norris Henty & Gardner Gardner 8L3	Type 23 Vulcan Sinclair Hyd. C CAJ Wilson-Drewry-Gearbox
32 (80)	C	Mech.	80	6 850 (3 107)			15 (24)	28 (711)	18.5	23' 5½" (7 150)	6	1950	John Fowler	J. & H. McLaren McLaren Kk. 3	Fowler
93	Co-Co	Elec	2 610	66 138 (30 000)	52 114 (23 638)	—	45 (72)	37½ (953)	100.2	—	26	1976	GE (USA)		
62	B-B	Hyd.	660	—	—	—	—	—	—	—	56	1977	Thyssen	—	—

KOREA

KOREAN NATIONAL RAILROAD (KNR)

168 Bongrae-dong, Jung-ku, Seoul

Administrator: Lee, Yong Shik
Deputy Director General, Business Management: Hwang Sung Yeun
Director General, Material Management Office: Shin, Young Kook
Director General, Engineering Bureau: Ham, Kiel
Director General, Rolling Stock Bureau: Im, Young Tack
Director General, Electrical Bureau: Oh, Hwa Suk
Deputy Administrator: Hwang, Hae Joong
Director General, Planning & Co-ordinating Office: Kim, Yong Kwan
Director General, Finance & Accounting: Lee, Yong Seoung
Director General, Transportation Bureau: Ahn, Chang Hwa
Director, Overseas Co-operation Division: Bang, Suk Ki

Gauge: 1.435 m; 0.762 m.
Route length: 3 099.4 km; 47 km.

The backbone of the system is the 444-km double track Kyongbu Line, running between the nation's two principal cities, Pusan on the southeast coast across the Tsushima Straits from Japan and the capital city of Seoul in the northwest. Principal intermediate cities reached by this route include Taegu and Taejon. While it constitutes less than 15 per cent of total KNR route-km, the Kyongbu Line accounts for nearly half of the system's operating revenues. A second north-south route, and a revenue source second only to the Kyongbu Line, is afforded by the Chungang (Central) and Tonghaenambu lines. Diverging to the southwest from the Kyongbu Line at Taejon, the Honam Line reaches into the rich agricultural plain of North and South Cholla provinces and the important southwestern port of Mokpo. Branching from the Honam Line at Iri is the Cholla Line, which extends southward to Yosu, an important southern port and the site of a major oil refinery.
Linking these two lines across the south coast of Korea with the Kyongbu Line near Pusan is the Kyongchon Line. The Yongdong Line, which links the east coast with the Chngang Line at Yongju, was extended northward to the major east coast city of Kangnung. KNR's second route to the east coast was completed through the heart of the Taebaek mountain range late in 1973.

TRAFFIC
KNR continues to experience high growth rate parellelling steady expansion of the national economy. In the five-year period from 1974 to 1978 KNR's annual passenger-km nearly doubled while freight tonne-km grew by nearly 20 per cent. Passenger-km exceeded 20 000 million in 1978 and 31 000 million passenger-km is expected by 1981. Freight traffic in 1978 reached a level of 10 926 million tonne-km and the railway is forecasting a further increase to 13 000 million tonne-km by 1981.

	1978 (thousands)
Freight tonne-km	10 926 000
Freight tonnage	46 000
Passenger-km	20 000 000
Passengers journeys	401 000

FINANCES
Revenue

	1977	1978
		(Won million)
Passenger Revenue	55 604	78 059
Freight Revenue	66 256	75 680
Other Operating Revenue	6 895	10 317
TOTAL	249 077*	289 438*

Expenditure

Wages and Salaries	58 585	72 266
Fuel Expense	16 260	17 530
Maintenance	28 346	33 825
TOTAL	249 077**	289 438**

* Including non-operating revenue and loans
** Including interest and repayments from capital account

INVESTMENTS
A $US 120 million World Bank loan to finance part of KNR's 1977-81 investment programme was approved in 1978. The railway has earmarked $US 406 million to finance double-tracking, electrification, purchase of diesel-electrics, passenger coaches and wagons, installation of CTC, track upgrading and construction of a new passenger coach workshop.

MOTIVE POWER AND ROLLING STOCK
Under KNR's 1977-81 programme the motive power and rolling stock fleets are being increased by the purchase of 30 diesel-electric locomotives, 211 passenger coaches and 1 400 wagons. Number of locomotives in operation includes 386 diesel-electrics, 89 electrics, 210 electric railcars, 120 diesel railcars, 68 steam locomotives and two preserved diesels. Latest motive power purchases were 20 GT 26CW diesel-electric locomotives delivered by General Motors (USA) in October 1978 and 40 electric railcars from Daewoo of Korea, which went into service in June 1979.
Passenger stock in operation during 1979 consisted of 83 first-class coaches, 836 ordinary-class coaches and 232 dining and baggage cars. The freight fleet includes 4 794 box cars, 6 697 gondola cars, 2 623 tank wagons and 1 586 miscellaneous types including flat wagons and cabooses.

ELECTRIFICATION
Total electrified route at the end of 1979 was over 500 km. Booster transformers are used on 542.9 track-km over the 25 kV 60 Hz ac system and auto-transformers over 286.4 track-km. Under the 1978-84 seven-year-plan a total of 1 600 km of route is being put under the wires, when over 85 per cent of freight will be hauled by electric motive power.

PERMANENT WAY
Apart from track-doubling over Seoul suburban lines during the 1977-81 period, 330 km of route is due to be relayed and 150 000 concrete sleepers installed over reballasted mainlines. Re-alignment and grade separation is to be carried out at a number of locations. New lines were laid during 1978 on two sections (5.7 and 12.2 km) of the

GM built 3 000 hp diesel loco hauling limited express coaches at the east coast near Gangreung

European 50 C/S Group locomotive near Chiag station on Jungang Line

Daejon—Iri line, over the 4.7 km junction lines leading north from Jochiwon and over a 10 km re-alignment just outside of Ma San. Scheduled for new construction is a 148.1 km line between Bong Varg and Jochiwon and a 32.3 km line between Yeong DeungPo and Su Won.

Improvements in 1979 included the addition of third and fourth tracks on the heavily-used 32 km segment of the Gyeongbu line south of Seoul between Guro and Suweon. Also advanced is doubling of the 127 km Chungbug line between Jochiweon and Bongyang, with completion scheduled for 1983.

A plan is under study for construction of a new high-speed line to relieve the heavily burdened Seoul—Busan—Gyeongbu line. This new line would be exclusively for passenger traffic, while the existing route would be devoted to freight. The line would cost an estimated 800 000 million won.

Track

	km
Total trackage	5 618.8
Service	3 144.2
Main Line (double track)	4 149.8
Sidings	1 469

Rail

Type of Rail	Length	Percentage
50 kg/m	3 117.0 km	53
37 kg/m	2 049.9 km	37
30 kg/m	451.9 km	10

Sleepers

Type	Number	Percentage
Wooden Ties	7 000	80
Pre-stressed Concrete Ties	1 700	20
Total	8 700	100

Tunnel and Bridge

Tunnel	Number	–
	Longest Tunnel	4 505 m
Bridge	Number	2 388
	Longest Bridge	1 112m

Curvature

Main line/Radius	Tangent	400 m	Under 600 m	Over 600 m
(100%)	(66)	(8)	(13)	(13)
4 149	2 697 km	350 km	546 km	556 km

Gradient

Total	Level	Less than 10/1 000	Less than 20/1 000	More than 20/1 000
(100%)	(37)	(32)	(25)	(6)
4 149 km	1 543 km	1 346 km	1 019 km	241 km

SIGNALLING

548 km of CTC on five sections of heavily-used single track is being installed together with automatic block signals on the 88 km of double track recently completed between Daejon and Iri. All of this work is scheduled for completion in 1981.

Type	Line	Location	Route Length	Number of Station	Supplier
CTC	Jung Ang Line	Mangu-Bongyang	48.1 km	32	Westinghouse (British)
	Seoul Metropolitan Area	Seoul-Incheon	38.9 km	11	Siemens (W. Germany)
		Yeongdeungpo-Suwon	32.3 km	6	,,
		Yongsan-Seongbug	18.2 km	4	,,
		Seoul-Susaeg	8.5 km	3	,,
	Total		246.5 km	56	
Relay	Tae Baeg Line	Jecheon-Baegsan		18	50 C/S Group (Europe)
Inter-locking System	Yeong Dong Line	Cheolam-Bogpyeong		14	,,
	Gyeong Bu Line	Saeryu-Sojeongri		9	Local
	Total			41	
ABS	Gyeong Bu Line	Seoul-Busan	444.5 km	Local	

Type	Line	Location	Route Length	Supplier
ATS	Jung Ang Line	Cheongryangri-Gyeongju	382.7 km	Local
	Ho Nam Line	Daejeon-Mogpu	260.4 km	,,
	Jeon Ra Line	Iri-Yeosu	198.3 km	,,
	Tae Baeg Line	Jecheon-Baegsan	103.7 km	,,
	Yeong Dong Line	Cheolam-Bugpyeong	61.8 km	,,
	Jang Hang Line	Cheonan-Janghand	143.5 km	,,
	Gyeong Weon Line	Yongsan-Seongbug	18.2 km	,,
	Gyeong In Line	Seoul-Incheon	38.9 km	,,
	Gyeong Eui Line	Seoul-Susaeg	8.5 km	,,
	Ham Baeg Line	Yemi-Jodong	9.7 km	,,
	Gyeong Bu Line	Seoul-Busan	444.5 km	,,
	Gyeong Bug Line	Gimcheon-Yeongju	115.2 km	,,
	Yeong Dong Line	Yeongju-Cheolam	86.4 km	,,
	Total		1 829.1 km	

DIESEL LOCOMOTIVES

Class (Series)	Axle Arrange-ment	Rated power (hp)	Max Speed (km/h)	Wheel Dia. (mm)	Total Weight (Tons)	Length (mm)	No Built	Year First Built	Mechanical parts	Engine & Type
SW 8 (2000)	Bo-Bo	800	105	1 016	94.5	13 420	13	1957	GMC (USA)	8-567 BC
SW 1001 (2100)	Bo-Bo	1 000	105	1 016	87.0	13 610	28	1969	,,	8-645 E
G8 (3000)	Bo-Bo	875	105	1 016	75.0	14 325	51	1959	,,	8-567 CR
ALCO (3100)	Bo-Bo	950	105	914	71.5	14 650	48	1967	ALCO (USA)	6-251 B
G12 (4000)	Bo-Bo	1 310	105	1 016	78.5	14 325	15	1963	GMC (USA)	12-567 C
G12 (4100)	Bo-Bo	1 310	105	1 016	85.0	14 325	10	1966	,,	12-567 C
G22 (4200)	Bo-Bo	1 310	105	1 016	88.0	14 170	22	1967	,,	12-567 E
SD9 (5000)	Co-Co	1 750	105	1 016	141.0	18 500	29	1957	,,	16-567 C
SD18 (6000)	Co-Co	1 800	105	1 016	147.0	18 500	14	1963	,,	16-567 D
SDP28 (6100)	Co-Co	1 800	105	1 016	147.0	18 500	6	1966	,,	16-567 E
SDP38 (6200)	Co-Co	1 800	105	1 016	147.0	18 500	16	1967	,,	16.567 E
SDP38 (6300)	Co-Co	1 800	105	1 016	148.0	18 500	22	1967	,,	16.567 E
G26CW (7000)	Co-Co	2 000	105	1 016	99.0	15 765	10	1969	,,	16-645 E
GT26CW (7500)	Co-Co	3 000	105	1 016	132.0	19 650	80	1971	,,	16-645 E3
GT26CW (7100)	Co-Co	3 000	120	1 016	132.0	19 650	20	1975	,,	16-645 E3

ELECTRIC LOCOMOTIVES

KNR Series	Axle Arrange-ment	Line Current	Rated Out-put (hp)	Tractive Effort Continuous Tons	Tractive Effort Continuous at (km/h)	Max speed (km/h)	Wheel Dia. (mm)	Weight (tons)	Length (mm)	No Built	Year First Built	Builders Mechanical parts	Builders Electrical parts
8 000	Bo-Bo-Bo	ac, 1ø, 25 kV (60 Hz)	5 300	31.3	46	85	1 250	132	20 730	90	1972	Alstom MTE	AEG ACEC

DIESEL RAILCAR

KNR Series	Axle Arrange-ment	Trans-Mission	Rated Power (hp)	Max Speed (km/h)	Wheel Dia. (mm)	Total Weight (tons)	Length (mm)	No. Built	Year Built	Builders Mechanical part	Builders Engine Type
600	Bo-Bo	Hydraulic Converter	420	105	864	51	21 500	11	1962	Nigata (Japan)	N-855-R (Cummins USA)
,,	,,	,,	,,	,,	,,	,,	,,	32	1963	Kinki (Japan)	,,
,,	,,	,,	,,	,,	,,	,,	,,	36	1966	Kawasaki (Japan)	,,

DIESEL RAILCAR

KNR Series	Axle Arrange-ment	Trans-Mission	Rated Power (hp)	Max Speed (km/h)	Wheel Dia. (mm)	Total Weight (tons)	Length (mm)	No. Built	Year Built	Builders Mechanical part	Engine Type
7-12	,,	,,	360	,,	,,	,,	,,	9	1963	Nigata (Japan)	DMH 17 (Japan)
700	,,	,,	420	,,	,,	,,	,,	12	1966	,,	N-855-R (Cummins)
,,	,,	,,	360	,,	,,	,,	,,	8	1966	,,	DMH 17 H (Japan)
550	,,	,,	680	,,	914	76	25 690	2	1969	,,	VTA1710 (Japan)
160	,,	,,	210	,,	711	25	14 750	6	1965	KNR	N-855-R (Cummins)
100	,,	,,	360	,,	914	33.9	10 400	2	1969	Nigata (Japan)	DMH17C (Japan)
510	,,	,,	210	,,	,,	51	21 500	2	1975	,,	N-855-R (Cummins)

ELECTRIC RAILCAR

Axle Arrange-ment	Line Current	Rated Out-put (hp)	Max Speed (km/h)	Wheel Dia. (mm)	Weight (tons)	Length (mm)	No. Built	Year Built	Builders Mechanical Part	Electrical parts
Bo-Bo	ac, 1ø, 25 kv (60 Hz)	1287 (120 kwx 8)	110	860	TC: 33.3 M: 42.1 M: 46.1	20 000	126	1974	Hitachi (Japan)	Hitachi (Japan)
,,	,,	,,	,,	,,	,,	,,	84	1977	Daewoo (Korea)	Hitachi (Japan)

LEBANON
CHEMINS DE FER DE L'ETAT LIBANAIS (CEL)
Transport en commun de Beyrouth et de sa Banlieue CEL/TCB, PO Box 109, Beirut

Telephone: 220760/62
Telex: ASSIKAAT

Director General: Antoine Barouki

Gauge: 1.435 m; 1.050 m
Route length: 335 km; 82 km

The state took over the railways in January 1961. They constitute 208 miles *(335 km)* standard track and 51 miles *(82 km)* 3 ft 5½ in *(1.050 m)* track of which 20 miles *(32 km)* are ABT system rack rail, on seven per cent gradient. A modernisation programme for the Sidon-Beirut-Tripoli route was being drawn up in 1978 to provide capacity for 2 000 passengers and 3 000 tonnes of freight daily. Track-doubling and re-alignment form part of the scheme.

MOTIVE POWER TREND
Proportion total train-km operated by:

		1970	1977
Steam traction	%	39	50
Diesel traction	%	61	50

TRACK DETAILS
Max axle load: 15 tonnes on standard gauge lines; 13 tonnes on narrow gauge lines.
Rail types:

	Weight lb per yd	kg/m	Length laid miles	km
USA	75.0	37.2	51	82
BH	85.0	42.2	70	112
BD	55.7	27.62	51	82
RA	60.6	30.0	56	90
HT	60.6	30.0	29	47

Sleepers (cross ties):

Wood	79	127
Concrete (RS type)	39	63
Metal	139	223

Sleeper spacing: 28 to 35½ in *(710 to 900 mm)*
Curves, min radius: 4 ft 8½ in *(1.435 m)* gauge—715 ft *(218 m)*; 3 ft 5½ in *(1.050 m)* gauge—328 ft *(100 m)*
Gradient, max: 2.0% uncompensated. 7.0% on rack rail section.
Altitude, max: 4 879 ft *(1 487 m)*

Welded rail: At the end of 1973, the total length of track laid with welded rail was 21.3 miles *(34.2 km)*, the longest length being some 165 ft *(50 m)*.
Rail used is 75 lb *(37.2 kg)* USA in 33 ft *(10.06 m)* lengths welded by Alumino-thermic process. Rails are laid on RS type concrete sleepers and secured by RS type fastenings.

LIBERIA
BONG MINING COMPANY
PO Box 538, Monrovia

General Manager: C. H. Enneker
Technical Manager: J. Lauthaler
Maintenance Mechanic Superintendent: J. Bothur
Railroad Engineer: R. Burner
Chief Workshop Engineer: B. Dietsche
Locos and Rolling Stock: R. Knaut
Trackmaster: I. Woods

Gauge: 1.435 m
Route length: 78 km

LAMCO JV OPERATING COMPANY
PO Box 69, Monrovia

Telephone: 397/398
Telegrams: LAMCO

Manager, Lamco Railroad: H. N. Bas. Koenen
Chief, Railroad Operations: Brian Hughes
Chief, Track Maintenance: Björn Ekren

Gauge: 1.435 m
Route length: 330 km

LAMCO, the Liberian American Swedish Minerals Co, is an iron ore mining company with mines at Nimba and Tokadeh. The railroad is operational between mines at Nimba and the deep water port in Buchanan, and carries more than 250 million gross tonnes over its 30 tonne axle load route. Rating gradients for loaded and empty trains are 5 and 17 per cent respectively. The whole line is CTC and atc controlled.

MOTIVE POWER AND ROLLING STOCK
At the end of 1978 motive power consisted of 14 diesel-electric locos, five diesel-electric shunters, six shunting locos and five rail buses. The number of ore wagons totals 512.

LUXEMBOURG
LUXEMBOURG RAILWAYS (CFL)
Société Nationale Des Chemins De Fer Luxembourgeois, Place De La Gare

Telephone: 4 99 01
Telex: 2288 CFL

President: René Logelin
General Manager: Justin Kohl
Secretary General, Finance and Personnel: M. Emile Schlesser
General Technical Inspector, General Technical Department: M. Marcel Conter
Chief of Traction: Theó Molling
Chief Officer, Claims and International Relations: M. Georges Thorn
Chief Officer, Commercial Department: Emile Kamphaus
Chief Officer, Fixed Installations: Ernest Junck
Chief Officer, Personnel: Romain Kugener
Chief Officer, Development: Gilbert Schmit

Gauge: 1.435 m
Route length: 274 km

TRAFFIC

	1973	1974	1977
Total freight ton-km	786 100 000	865 993 000	567 000 000
Total freight tonnage	22 534 000	23 098 000	—
Total passenger-km	269 964 836	288 888 000	277 000 000
Total passengers carried	13 391 646	13 768 000	—

FINANCES

	1974 (Frs)	1975 (Frs)	1977 (Frs)
Revenues	3 668 359 544	4 220 220 500	5 136 506 524
Expenses	3 756 362 573	4 377 325 783	5 212 897 682

MOTIVE POWER
During 1978 CFL operated 19 electric and 55 diesel-electric locomotives. Number of railcars in service totalled 11.

ROLLING STOCK
In service at the end of 1978 were 80 passenger coaches and 3 491 freight wagons.

ELECTRIFICATION
A total of 137 route-km is electrified and operated by 25 electric locomotives over a mixed 3 000 V dc and 25 000 V 50 Hz overhead system.

PERMANENT WAY
Renewal of track in UIC 54 rail laid on wooden sleepers was completed over the Belval-Pétange line in 1974 together with renewal over the Berchem to Oetrange line (total length renewed: 19.9 km).
Rails, types and weights: UIC 60, 54 and S33.
Sleepers: wood.
  Thickness: 15 cm
  Spacing: 1 435 mm
Rail fastenings: 'K' fastenings.
Welded rail: Total length of track laid up to 1975 was 216.2 km. Length of cwr laid in 1974 was 11.6 km.

Signal and train control installations: All-relay interlocking signal boxes with illuminated diagram and push button control on 72 miles *(116 km)* route length. Supplied by Siemens and Integra.

	miles	km
Luxembourg—Wasserbillig	23.0	37
Berchem—Oetrange	7.5	12
Luxembourg—Kleinbettingen	11.2	18
Bettembourg—Rodange	18.0	29
Luxembourg—Pétange	12.4	20

Hybrid installations consisting of electronic circuits and relay switching, frequency control, automatic colour light signalling for two-way working. Suppliers: Jeumont Schneider, Siemens, Integra.

	miles	km
Luxembourg—Wasserbillig	23.0	37
Berchem—Oetrange	7.5	12
Bettembourg—Berchem	2.5	4

MADAGASCAR
RESEAU NATIONAL DES CHEMINS DE FER MALAGASY (RNCFM)
Avenue de l'Indépendance, Antananarivo

Telephone: 205-21
Telex: 222-33

General Manager: Adolphe Rakotoarivony
Rolling Stock Department: Jeannot Rakotondranaivo
Track and Building Department: Gilbert Rananjason M.
Operating Department: Jean Jacques Rakotomanga
Planning Department: André Andriamampianina
Administration: Jean Pierre Rakotomalala
Warehousing and Victualling Department: Nicola Rakotoniaina

Gauge: 1.00 m.
Route length: 883 km.

The Malagasy metre gauge system consists of:

	miles	km
Line Antananarivo-Alarobia (TWS)	3	5
Line Tamatave-Antananarivo (TCE)	231	371
Line Moramanga-Ambatosoratra (MLA)	104	167
Branch Vohidiala-Morarano	12	19
Line Antananarivo-Antisrabe (TA)	98	158
Line Fianarantsoa-Manakara (FCE)	101	163

TRAFFIC	1977/78	1978/79
Total train-km	3 814 440	3 618 162
Total freight tonnage (thousand tonnes)	839	935
Average haul	—	265.8 km
Average net train load	—	121 tonnes
Average wagon load	—	28.4 tonnes
Total passenger-km (thousands)	276 539	290 390
Total passengers carried (thousands)	3 975	4 251

FINANCES	1972	1973	1974	1975	1976	1977
Operating revenues	2 666	2 683	3 470	2 980	3 073	3 505
Operating expenses	2 647	2 675	2 900	2 331	2 713	3 311

INVESTMENTS
During the Five-Year Plan (1978-1982) RNCFM is purchasing nine line-haul diesel-electric locomotives of which two were received in February 1979 and three from Alsthom (France) in January and February 1980 costing FMG 1 222 million, one diesel railcar costing FMG 190 million, ten passenger coaches costing FMG 700 million, 78 freight wagons costing FMG 984 million, 57 ballast wagons of which 12 were received in July 1979 and 45 in December 1979, track renewals over 180 km and track improvements over 140 km costing FMG 3 028 million and 136 points and crossings costing FMG 534 million. These purchases are financed by the International Development Association (USA) and Caisse Centrale de Coopération Économique (France).

Number of line locomotives
Three diesel-electric Alsthom, type BBB 625 hp.
Six diesel-electric Alsthom, type BB 200, 1 050 hp.
Two diesel Brissonneau & Lotz, 130 hp.
Nine diesel-electric Alsthom, type BB 220 AD 12 B, 1 200 hp.
12 diesel-electric Alsthom, type BB 120 850 hp.
One diesel-electric CEM, type BBBB 3 600 hp.

Number of shunting locomotives
Four diesel Whitcomb Locomotive Co, type B 160 hp.
14 diesel De Dietrich, type B 150 hp.
One diesel CEM Fauvet-Girel, type B 400 hp.
Three diesel-electric Alsthom, type BBB 575 hp (unclassed).

Number of railcars
Two Micheline Carel-Fouché, diesel 80 hp.
Six diesel-electric De Dietrich, 2-bogie 500 hp.
Five diesel-electric D Soulé, 2-bogie 580 hp.

MOTIVE POWER AND ROLLING STOCK
RNCFM operates 31 line-haul diesel-electric locomotives, 22 diesel-electric shunters, 13 diesel railcars, 56 diesel trailer cars, 42 passenger coaches and 974 freight train wagons.

MALAWI
MALAWI RAILWAYS LTD (MR)
PO Box 5144, Limbe

Telephone: 652244
Telex: 4116

Executive Chairman: D. R. Katengeza
Deputy Executive Chairman: M. L. Y. Kwengwere
Deputy Chairman: S. B. Somanje
Directors: J. A. A. Henderson
  R. G. Zanda
  Chief Timbili
  E. F. W. MacPherson
  A. W. Mwafulirwa
General Manager: G. G. Geddes
Deputy General Manager: G. Ellis
Secretary: P. B. Galafa
Chief Civil Engineer: R. F. MacLean
Management Accountant: G. H. Woodcock
Works Manager: W. W. Gordon
Chief Traffic Manager: P. T. K. Nyasulu
Chief Diesel Engineer: J. R. P. McCrindle
Chief Personnel Officer: G. L. Lungu

Internal Auditor: P. K. Hounsham
Stores Superintendent: P. A. Ridgeway
Data Processing Manager: A. F. Morgan

Gauge: 1.067 m
Route length: 677 km

In addition to the railway, the administration also operates passenger and cargo services on Lake Malawi and trunk road haulage services throughout the Central and Northern Region of the country.

TRAFFIC	1977/78	1978/79
Total train-km	1 037 196	987 748
Total freight tonnage (tonnes)	1 115 800	1 101 800
Average haul (km)	180.19	182.32
Average net train load (tonnes)	193.85	203.37
Average wagon load (tonnes)	23.36	23.57
Total passenger-km	58 717 000	67 774 000
Total passengers carried	964 155	1 083 789
Passengers carried		
1st class	773	850
2nd class	2 943	4 715
3rd class	960 439	1 078 224
Average length of passenger journey (km)	61.0	62.5

Class	Axle Arrangement	Transmission	Rated Power hp	Tractive Effort Max kg	Tractive Effort Continuous at lb	Tractive Effort mph	Max Speed kmlh	Wheel Dia. in	Total Weight Tons	Length ft in	No. Built	Year First Built	Builders Mechanical Parts	Builders Engine and Type	Builders Transmission
DIESEL LOCOMOTIVES															
Shunter	0-6-0	Hyd.	340	20 200			24	40	40.5	25' 6"	2	1962	Bagnall	R.R. C8-Tel-IV	Twin Disc
Shunter	0-6-0	Hyd.	355	21 800			25	41	43.0	24' 0"	2	1967	A. Barclay	Cummins NT 400	Twin Disc
Shunter	0-6-0	Hyd.	388	33 800			16	43	40.0	25' 4"	4	1975	Hunslet (UK)	Cummins NT 400	Twin Disc
Transfer	Bo-Bo	Hyd.	525	23 000			35	33	38.0	32' 4"	7	1969	Hunslet (SA)	Cummins VT 12	Niigata
Main Line	Bo-Bo	Hyd.	492	20 350			35	34	38.0	34' 6"	4	1968	N. Sharyo	Cummins NTA 380	Niigata
Main Line	Co-Co	Elec.	1 200	50 000	40 000	8	50	36	81.0	46' 3"	14	1963	M. Cammell	Sulzer	AEI
Main Line	Co-Co	Elec.	1 500	72 000	60 500	10	64	36	86.0	57' 7"	4	1973	MLW	Alco 8-251-E	GE
DIESEL RAILCARS															
PRC	Ao-Io	Hyd.	200	33 000			50	34	33		2	1952	Drewry	Leyland Re-902	V. Sinclair 550

The total tonnage of goods traffic carried in 1976 and 1977 dropped following the closure of the Rhodesia/Mozambique border in 1976 which in turn closed the direct all rail route for imports and exports between Malawi and Southern Africa.

FINANCES

Revenues (Malawi Kwacha)		
Passengers and baggage	542 564	633 394
Average receipt per passenger-km	0.00924	0.00935
Freight and mail	7 502 220	7 494 878
Average receipt per freight tonne-km	0.03731	0.03731
Total	11 850 000	11 860 000

Expenditure (Malawi Kwacha)		
Staff/personnel	3 817 000	4 449 000
Materials and services	5 113 000	5 807 000
Depreciation	902 000	956 000
Financial charges	1 024 000	1 018 000
Total	10 856 000	12 230 000

MOTIVE POWER AND ROLLING STOCK

The diesel fleet consists of 18 mainline diesel-electrics (including four on hire), 11 diesel-hydraulic mainline locomotives, eight diesel-hydraulic shunters and two diesel rail cars.
The 11 diesel-hydraulic locomotives now used on the mainline will eventually revert to shunting duties when the track improvements on the Northern Extension now in hand are completed and additional diesel-electric locomotives are received. At the end of 1979 a batch of 16 diesel-electric Co-Co locomotives were on order from Bombardier Inc of Canada.
The fleet consisted of 714 goods wagons (including tank cars), 35 passenger coaches, 55 service vehicles and 21 vans.

PERMANENT WAY

Work on the new 111 km extension from Salima to Lilongwe was completed in 1978 under the direction of a team of Canadian engineers. Now the railway is building a 113 km new link from Lilongwe to Mchinji using BS 80 'A' flat bottomed rail and prestressed concrete sleepers. Completion date is 1981.

Standard rail: 80 lb and 60 lb per yd
Cross ties (sleepers): Steel trough, 5 ft 8½ in *(1 750 mm)* long and hardwood 6 ft 6 in × 5 in × 10 in. Concrete 6 ft 6 in *(1 980 mm)* × 9 in *(226 mm)* base
Spacing: 12 per 33 ft rail
15 per 39 ft rail
Rail fastening: Clip and steel key, elastic spikes, Pandrol clips with concrete sleepers.
Filling: Broken stone and earth
Max curvature: 15.8° = radius of 363 ft *(111 m)*
Max gradient: 2.27% = 1 in 44
Max axle load: 16½ tons (of 2 000 lb)
Max permitted speed: 35 mph, restricted in hill section to 15 mph
Max altitude: 3 840 ft *(1 107 m)*

MALAYSIA

MALAYAN RAILWAY ADMINISTRATION

Pertadbiran Keretapi Tanah Melayu (PKTM)
PO Box 1, Kuala Lumpur

General Manager: Datuk Ishak Tadin
Deputy General Manager:
Finance and Commerce: Abdul Hai bin Abdul Hadi KMN
Operating and Engineering: K. Kularatnam KMN
Staff: Mohd. Noor bin Abu Osman
Chief Civil Engineer: J. Patrick Lowe AMN
Traffic Manager: G. L. Rodrigo
Chief Accountant: Zahar bin Mohd Shariff
Stores Superintendent: Abdul Hamid bin Mohd. Shariff
Chief Mechanical Engineer: Tang Ying Woun

Gauge: 1.00 m.
Route length: 1 643 km.

Principal route is the 787 km mainline from Singapore north through the capital of Kuala Lumpur to Butterworth, one of Malaysia's principal sea ports on the west coast of the peninsular. Short branches reach sea ports at Port Weld, Telok Anson, Port Kelang and Port Dickson. The other major route is the 528 km east-coast line running northwards from a junction with the Singapore—Butterworth mainline at Gemas to Kota Baaru and Tum Pat. Both lines are linked with the State Railway of Thailand.
At present only 70 per cent of the system's 1 659 km of track is being used; plans are in hand to increase this to 90 per cent by 1982. The railway is also seeking financing to provide faster services and to increase freight movements.

FREIGHT TRAFFIC

While PKTM carried record freight tonne-km in 1978 the railway's market share of business remains only 11 per cent. Plans are being made for PKTM to handle 1 760 million tonne-km by 1990.

	1971	*1973*	*1974*	*1977*	*1978*
Freight tons carried (000's)	3 328	3 416	3 251	3 787	6 502
Ton miles (millions)	—	665.3	602.7	—	1 293

PASSENGER TRAFFIC

KTM operates a comprehensive network of passenger services over almost every one of its lines. In addition to ordinary train services, the system operates day and night express trains on Singapore—Kuala Lumpur and Kuala Lumpur—Butterworth routes, and a single daily express between Gemas and Tum Pat on the east coast line. In conjunction with the State Railway of Thailand, KTM operates the tri-weekly International Express between Butterworth and Bangkok.
The Ekspres Rakyat (Peoples Express) introduced in 1976 is KTM's most popular express service. Operating daily between Singapore and Butterworth via Kuala Lumpur, the train is equipped with both air-conditioned and non-air-conditioned coaches offering a high standard of comfort. Operating over the 787 km run in slightly more than 13 hours, the Ekspres Rakyat service has proved extremely successful. In its first two months of operation, the train averaged a daily total of almost 800 passengers in each direction; by mid-1978 this had increased to a daily average of almost a thousand passengers each way.

	1971	*1973*	*1974*	*1977*	*1978*
Passengers carried (000's)	5 272.9	5 449.9	5 967	6 389	11 924
Passenger miles (millions)	—	495.6	592.6	—	1 300

FINANCES

	1977 ($M)
Revenue	115 991 442
Expenses	118 752 604

INVESTMENTS

A loan of $US 1.8 million is being used by Malayan Railways to finance purchase of a new telecommunications and signalling equipment, as part of a $US 80 million, five-year (1976-81) programme to modernise railways in Malaysia. During the plan period about 40 per cent of passenger coaches are being replaced by 34 air-conditioned luxury class coaches and 53 economy-class (non-air-conditioned) coaches, to improve passenger services and reduce operating costs. Passenger terminal facilities at major stations are being rebuilt or modernised. Freight stock purchases include 341 bogie oil tank wagons, 117 latex tank wagons, 139 bulk hopper wagons, 122 palm oil tank wagons, 100 container flat wagons, 50 cattle wagons and 150 bogie underframes. About $US 12.153 million is being spent on track renewals and realignments, $US 6.382 million on new diesel mainline locomotives, $US 4 million on diesel shunters, and nearly $US 6 million on signalling and telecommunications.
PKTM spent $M 66 million in 1979 with expenditure allocated for ten diesel-electric locomotives ($M 9 370 000), 15 passenger coaches ($M 4 600 000) and $M 22 430 000 spent on line construction and track improvements.

MOTIVE POWER AND ROLLING STOCK

The fleet now includes: 91 mainline diesel-electric locomotives; 23 diesel-electric shunters; 25 diesel-hydraulic shunting units; and 22 diesel railcars.
Three diesel locomotive types now handle all freight and passenger road service. The oldest are a group of 26 Class 20 1 500 hp, Co-Co diesel-electrics delivered by English Electric since 1956. Another 25 are Class 21 1 200 hp, B-B diesel-hydraulic units supplied by Kisha Seizo Kaisha (KSK) and Hitachi since 1956. The most recent are 39 Class 22 Co-Co diesel-electrics rated at 1 700 hp, which were built by English Electric-AEI and Metro-Cammell during the early 1970s. A total of 51 shunting units of several types complete the KTM locomotive roster. A single Class 56 steam locomotive has been retained.
KTM is rapidly phasing out its railcar fleet. More than 20 major investment projects are included in the $M 250 million railway 1976-81 plan. A $M 23 million project will add a total of 20 diesel locomotives to the KTM fleet: ten shunting locomotives and ten main line diesel-electric units of about 1 700 hp capacity.
An additional $M 31 million is going for the purchase of 49 new passenger coaches including 29 air-conditioned, and 20 non-air-conditioned coaches.
Other rolling stock purchases will include a new breakdown crane, and bogies and underframes for 264 wagons which can be used in log, container, or tank wagon service. Existing freight wagons will be upgraded through a conversion of the entire KTM fleet to roller bearings by 1982.
The passenger fleet at the end of 1974 totalled 325 coaches. Freight wagons totalled 5 479 units.

CIVIL ENGINEERING

The railway's present track rehabilitation programme calls for complete renewal of 196 km of track at a cost of $M 46 million. All 30 kg/m rail on the east coast line is being replaced to complete an upgrading programme of all mainline track to 40 kg/m standards. Latest permanent way improvement plans call for increasing the system's maximum operating speeds from 72 to 97 km/h entailing extensive realignments.
The railway is building a new line that will link the Singapore—Kuala Lumpur mainline with a major new port and shipyard now under construction at Pasir Gudang, opposite Singapore in the state of Johore. Design work for the 32 km line started in 1974, and construction is now underway, with completion scheduled for the end of 1980. Estimated total cost for the project is $M 36 million ($US 17 million).

TRACK STANDARDS

Standard rail: Flat bottom in 30 ft and 40 ft lengths.
Main line: 80 lb/yd *(39.7 kg/m)*
Branch lines: 60 lb *(29.8 kg/m)*
Joints: 4-hole flat or angle fishplates and welding.
Rail fastening: Elastic Spikes used on main lines. Dog spikes on other lines and sidings.
Cross ties (sleepers): Malayan secondary hardwoods impregnated with 50/50 mixture of creosote and diesel fuel oil; primary hardwoods on bridges. 10 in × 5 in × 6 ft 6 in *(254 × 127 × 1 981 mm)*. In accordance with ECAFE recommendations for SE Asia, all new supplies are 9 in × 4½ in × 6 ft 6 in-7 ft 0 in *(229 × 114 × 1 981-2 134 mm)*
Spacing: 2 ft 6 in *(762 mm)*
Filling: 2¼ in limestone ballast to a depth of 6 in under sleepers.
Max curvature: 3° = radius of 1 910 ft *(582 m)*; except in the hill sections where there are some curves of 9° = radius of 637 ft *(194 m)* and 12.25° = radius of 467 ft *(142 m)*
Ruling gradient: 1% = 1 in 100; except Taiping Pass 1.25% = 1 in 80.
Longest cont. gradient: 5.1 miles *(8.2 km)* on Prai-Singapore mainline, with 1.25% (1 in 80) grade, the sharpest curve being 12.25° (467 ft radius) for a length of 1 050 ft *(320 m)*
Gauge widening on curves: Nil down to 6.5° curve = radius of 880 ft *(268 m)*
¼ in *(6.4 mm)*: 6.5° to 9° curve = radius of 880 ft *(268 m)* to 636 ft *(194 m)*
⅜ in *(9.5 mm)*; 9° to 13° curve = radius of 636 ft *(194 m)* to 440 ft *(134 m)*
½ in *(12.7 mm)*: below 13°.
Super-elevation on sharpest curve: 3½ in *(89 mm)*
Rate of slope of super-elevation: Steepest permissible gradient 1 : 300 or 11 times max permissible speed of section in mph.
Max altitude: 450 ft *(137 m)* near Taiping.
Max axle load: 16 tons.
Max permitted speed: Passenger trains, mainline and Kedah line: 45 mph *(72 km/h)* East Coast Line and other branch lines: 40 mph *(64 km/h)*. Diesel railcars 50 mph *(80 km/h)*. Freight trains 35 to 40 mph *(56 to 64 km/h)*.

Welded rail: Total length of track laid with welded rail is 625 miles *(1 005 km)*. Rails used are 80 lb in 40 ft lengths flashbutt welded at depot into 480 ft lengths. After laying these are sometimes Thermit welded into 960 ft continuous lengths.
Welded rails are secured by Elastic Rail Spikes to wood sleepers.

MALI

CHEMINS DE FER DU MALI

BP 260, Bamako

Director: Djibril Diallo
Deputy Director: Noumoucounda Savane
Finance: Almany Saounera
Operations: Mamadou Sidibe
Way and Works: Mamadou Bah
Commercial: Kader Diallo

Gauge: 1.00 m
Route length: 641 km

The former Dakar—Niger Railway starts at Dakar in Senegal and runs inland via Kayes to the River Niger. The present C.F. du Mali is that portion of the line inside its territory, the remainder being the C.F. du Sénégal. A new line linking Bamako, capital of Mali, with Conakry, capital of Guinea is planned to give Mali an alternative outlet to the Atlantic route length of 500 miles *(800 km)*, of which 373 miles *(600 km)* will be in Guinea.
Approval for a World Bank loan of $10.5 million to Mali Railways to help finance a $28 million rehabilitation project was granted in June, 1977.
$7.3 million has been allocated for bridge repairs and $3.8 million is to be spent on track upgrading, including relaying of points and crossings.

Rolling stock is another major item with $6.2 million allowed for purchase of mainline locomotives, shunters and railcars, $1.6 million for passenger coaches and $1.9 million for freight wagons, including some rebuilding of existing vehicles. Also included in the project is installation of telecommunications equipment, as well as staff training. Track renewals and ballasting are to be in the hands of Mali Railways' own staff, but bridgework is to be carried out by an outside firm supervised by the French consultants Sofrérail.

TRAFFIC	1974	1976	1977
Total tonnage	373 840	324 420	332 250
Tonne-km	162 180 000	147 990 000	148 630 000
Passenger journeys	500 683	564 724	612 181
Passenger-km	98 260 000	120 128 000	129 228 000

FINANCES	1976	1977
	FISCFA ('000)	
Revenues	4 095 655	4 512 902
Expenses	4 680 140	4 623 066

MOTIVE POWER

CFM operated during 1978 a total of 21 line-haul diesel locomotives, seven loco-tractors, four diesel-electric railcars, six diesel trainsets, 52 passenger coaches (including 16 railcar trailers) and 360 freight wagons. Two locomotives were on order in 1978 from Alsthom (1 000 hp with a top speed of 80 km/h) together with a 950 hp railcar from Soulé of France.

950 hp diesel-electric railcar delivered by Soulé in 1977

MAURITANIA

CHEMINS DE FER MAURITANIA (SNIM-COMINOR)

SA des Mines de Fer de Mauritanie
PO Box 42, Nouadhibou

Telephone: 22-74
Telex: 551 SNIM NKC

General Manager (SNIM): Ismael Ould Amar
Managing Director (COMINOR): R. Guittard
Director of Railway and Port: H. Serres
Assistant General Manager: A. Nicolas *(Paris)*
Deputy Manager: R. Hervouet *(Nouadhibou)*
Director Railway and Harbour: R. Guittard *(Nouadhibou)*

Gauge: 1.435 m
Route length: 650 km

This 4 ft 8½ in *(1.435 m)* line, 404 miles *(650 km)* long, completed in 1963, runs from Nouadhibou (ex-Port Etienne) to Akjoujit for the transport of iron ore from the mines at F'Derik (ex-Fort Gouraud). The maximum gradient against loaded trains is 0.5 per cent and against empty trains 1.0 per cent. The minimum radius of curves is 3 280 ft *(1 000 m)*.
Built and originally operated by Miferma, the line was nationalised in 1974 and is now operated by Société Nationale Industrielle et Minière (SNIM) through a subsidiary department known as Complex Minier du Nord (COMINOR).

TRAFFIC

Principal traffic is iron ore shipments totalling 15.3 million tonnes in 1978. Passengers are carried daily in a single coach running between Nouadhibou and Zouèrate.

MOTIVE POWER AND ROLLING STOCK

Equipment listed in 1977 consisted of 26 mainline diesel-electric locomotives, 11 shunting diesel-electrics, 1 084 ore wagons and 14 passenger-carrying cars.

PERMANENT WAY

Standard rail: 108.9 lb per yd *(54 kg/m)* UIC
Welded joints: Practically the whole line was laid with long-welded rail. 8 × 18 m railbars were flash-butt welded at the depot into 472 ft *(144 m)* lengths, which after laying were Thermit welded into continuous rail. The longest individual length of welded rail is 50 miles *(80 km)*.
Sleepers (cross ties): Type U28 steel weighing 165 lb *(75 kg)*.
Spacing: 23⅝ in *(60 cm)*.
Rail fastening: Clips and bolts to metal sleepers.
Max curvature: 1.75° = min. radius of 3 280 ft *(1 000 m)*.
Max gradient: 0.5% (1 in 200) against loaded trains.
1.0% (1 in 100) against empty trains.
Max altitude: 1 148 ft *(350 m)*.
Max axle load: 25 tonnes.
Max speed: Loaded trains 31 mph *(50 km/h)*; empty 37 mph *(60 km/h)*.

MEXICO

FERROCARRILES NACIONALES DE MEXICO (FNdeM)
Avenida Central 140, Colonia Guerrero, Mexico 3, DF

President: Emilio Múgica Montoya
General Manager: Luis Gómez Zepeda
Assistant to General Manager: Alfredo Suarez Rábago
Assistant to General Manager—MP and RS: Luis Garcia Barrientos
Assistant to General Manager—Traffic: Eduardo A. Cota
Assistant to General Manager—Finances: Pedro C. Garcia Treviño
Assistant to General Manager—Purchases: Guillermo Hernández Tapia
Assistant to General Manager—Administration: Jorge Sanchez Curiel
Assistant to General Manager—Telecommunications: Salvador Rosales Hireso
General Controller: Adolfo González Arellano

Gauge: 1.435 m; 0.914 m
Route length: 13 807 km; 401.8 km

On 17 January 1977, Lic Jose Lopez Portillo, Constitutional President of Mexico, ordered the merger of all Mexican railway enterprises—Pacific Railway, SA de CV; Chihuahua-Pacific Railway, SA de CV; Sonora-Baja California Railway, SA de CV; Southeastern United Railways, SA de CV—with the National Railways of Mexico, under the Management of Luis Gomez Z.

The merger will be fully effective in 1980 when FNdeM will consist of:

	Track km	No. of Employees	(Millions) Ton-km Net-1974	Percentage Total Freight Traffic
Nation Rys of Mexico	14 151.3	60 125	26 303	82.4
Pacific Ry	2 314.6	7 267	3 776	11.9
Chihuahua-Pacific Railway	1 515.5	2 836	903	2.8
Southwestern United Railways	1 359.8	3 051	601	1.9
Sonora-Baja California Ry	607.0	1 558	303	1.0
	19 948.2	74 837	31 736	100.0

FERROCARRILES NACIONALES DE MEXICO
Ferrocarriles Nacionales de Mexico (FNdeM) was constituted as a decentralised firm by presidential decree in 1948. It extends from the northern border with the USA from the cities of Matamoros and Nuevo Laredo, Tamaulipas, from Piedras Negras and Ciudad Acuña, Coahuila and from Ciudad Juarez, Chihuahua to the southern border with Guatemala at Ciudad Hidalgo, Chiapas.
On the Gulf of Mexico, it connects with the ports of Coatzacoalcos, Veracruz, and Tampico. On the Pacific Ocean, it connects with the ports of Puerto Madero, Salina Cruz, and with Manzanillo.
In the interior, it connects the important cities of Mexico City, Queretaro, Leon, Aguascalientes, Zacatecas, Durango, Torreon, Chihuahua, San Luis Potosi, Saltillo, Monterrey, Ciudad Frontera (Coahuila), Morelia, Guadalajara, Colima, Pueblo, Oaxaco, Jalapa and Orizaba.
It interchanges in Coatzacoalcos with the Ferrocarriles Unidos del Sureste, in Guadalajara with the Ferrocarril del Pacifico and in Chihuahua and Ciudad Juarez with the Ferrocarril Chihuahua al Pacifico.
This railroad began in 1873 with the former Ferrocarril Mexicano (presently called the Mexican Division), which went from Mexico City to Veracruz via Orizaba and Córdoba. Afterwards, and through the construction of various lines, of which the most important were the Ferrocarril Central, the Ferrocarril Nacional, the Internacional, the Interoceanico, the Nacional de Tehuantepec, and the Panamericano, the current rail network was formed.
The railroad has 70 000 employees, distributed among 17 divisions with 107 operating districts. The main shop for locomotive repair is in San Luis Potosi and for rolling stock is in Aguascalientes. There are also 47 secondary shops, of which the most important are in Valle de Mexico (Pantaco, DF), Torreon, Monterrey, Ciudad Frontera (Coahuila), Puebla, Tierra Blanca (Veracruz) and Matias Romero (Oaxaca). The office of the General Manager and his deputy, as well as the Assistant Managers of Track and Structures, of Motor Power and Rolling Stock, of Operations, of Planning and Organisation, of Administration, of Finances, of Purchasing, and of Telecommunications, Signals and Electricity are all in Mexico City. Personnel of these departments and personnel in charge of programmed track maintenance are located in smaller offices along the line.
The 17 divisions with the number of operating districts within them are as follows:

Division	Districts
Cárdenas	5
Centro	8
Golfo	4
Guadalajara	6
Jalapa	4
Mexicano	3
México	9
Monclova	8
Monterrey	4
Pacifico	6
Pueblo	10
Querétaro	10
San Luis	6
Sureste V.C.I.	8
Sureste N.T.	3
Sureste P.A.	3
Torreón	10

TRAFFIC
The railroad carries more than 50 million tons of cargo annually, principally: mineral, industrial, agricultural, petroleum and petroleum derivatives and inorganic products.

	1975	1976	1977
Total freight tonne-km (millions)	27 046.5	26 838.8	38 734.6
Total freight tonnage	52 250 412	51 322 262	54 877 364
Total passenger-km (millions)	2 612.7	2 507.6	3 112
Total passenger journeys	19 513 511	19 107 092	22 304 501

FINANCES
Total operating revenue in 1977 amounted to $6 617.8 million (pesos). Total operating expenses amounted to $11 602 million (pesos), resulting in a deficit of $4 984.2 million (pesos).

MOTIVE POWER AND ROLLING STOCK
On 31 December 1978 the National Railways of Mexico's motive power and rolling stock was as follows:

	Units
Diesel-electric line-haul locomotives	913
Diesel-electric shunters	156
Freight cars	32 551
Passenger train cars	1 093

FNdeM DIESEL LOCOMOTIVES

Series	Class	Builder	hp	Year of construction	Number in service	Wheel arrangement
801	DE-28	EMD	800	1971	3	B-B
5001	DE- 1	ALCO	600	1944	1	B-B
5100	DE- 2	GE	600	1962	3	B-B
5300	DE- 3	ALCO	900	1956	1	B-B
5400	DE-28	EMD	800	1964	16	B-B
5504	DE- 5	ALCO	1 000	1944	7	B-B
5602	DE- 6	ALCO	1 000	1950	45	B-B
5800	DE-18	EMD	1 310	1956	76	B-B
5900	DE- 4	ALCO-MLW	1 200	1963	5	C-C
6201-A	DE-10	EMD	1 300	1946	4	B-B
6203-B	DE-10	EMD	1 300	1950	3	B-B
6300-A	DE-11	EMD	1 500	1952	15	B-B
6319-B	DE-11	EMD	1 500	1951	3	B-B
6507-A	DE-13	ALCO-MLW	1 600	1951	4	B-B
6516-B	DE-13	CONV	1 600	1951	1	B-B
6600	DE-14	EMD	1 500	1952	2	B-B
6701	DE-15	ALCO	1 600	1952	4	B-B
6801	DE-16	BLH	1 600	1954	15	C-C
6901	DE-19	ALCO	1 600	1955	1	C-C
7000-A	DE-17	EMD	1 750	1954	26	B-B
7001-B	DE-17	EMD	1 750	1954	8	B-B
7100	DE-21	EMD	1 750	1956	7	B-B
7108	DE-21	SLP-6	1 750	1965	1	B-B
7200	DE-22	ALCO	1 800	1957	14	B-B
7219	DE-22	MLW	1 800	1963	65	B-B
7294	DE-22	SLP-2	1 800	1963	1	B-B
7300	DE-23	EMD	1 800	1958	22	C-C
7400	DE-24	ALCO	1 800	1958	69	C-C
7473	DE-24	SLP-5	1 800	1964	1	C-C
7500	DE-25	EMD	1 800	1961	36	B-B
8100	DE-26	ALCO	2 400	1964	44	B-B
8200	DE-27	EMD	2 500	1964	54	B-B
8300	DE-29	ALCO	2 750	1967	32	C-C
8400	DE-30	EMD	3 000	1967	10	B-B
8500	DE-31	EMD	3 000	1968	83	C-C
8522	DE-31	EMD	3 000	1972	2	C-C
8600	DE-32	MLW	3 000	1972	20	C-C
8700	DE-33	EMD	3 000	1972	56 + 12	C-C
8800	DE-34	EMD	1 500	1973	60	B-B
8900	DE-35	GE	3 500	1973	87	C-C
9000	DE-36	GE	1 800	1974	45	B-B
9100	DE-37	GE	2 250	1975	30	B-B
9200	DE-38	EMD	2 000	1975	20	B-B
9300	DE-35	GE	3 600	1975	17	C-C
9400	DE-38	EMD	2 000		81	B-B

(104 of them switcher units)

FERROCARRIL DEL PACIFICO SA de CV
The Ferrocarril del Pacifico SA de CV, was formed as such by presidential decree on 8 March 1952. It runs through the states of Sonora, Sinaloa, Nayarit and Jalisco. Leaving from Nogales it crosses the state of Sonora headed south, passing through the cities of Hermosillo, Guaymas, Ciudad Obregón and Navojoa. In the state of Sinaloa it follows the Pacific coast connecting the cities of Sufragio, Culiacán and Mazatlán. In the state of Nayarit it touches the city of Tepic and terminates in Guadalajara. From Nogales to the west the railroad has a branch that connects with the towns of Cananea, Naco, Agua Prieta and Nacozari. There are also branches from Orendain to Ameca and to Etzatlán, Jalisco; Quila el Torito, Sinaloa and Navajoa Huatabampo, Sonora.
In the station at Benjamin Hill it interchanges with the Sonora-Baja California Railroad and at Sufragio, Sinoloa, it interchanges with the Chihuahua al Pacifico Railroad.
Upon becoming a separate corporation, the Federal Government acquired the majority of shares and the states of Sonora and Sinaloa the rest. It operates under the control of a board of directors of which the Secretary of Communications and Transportation is the president with members being representatives of the Secretariats of Treasury, National Patrimony, Industry and Commerce, and of the Director General of Operating Railroads, the Union of Railroad Workers of the Mexican Republic and the governments of the states of Sonora and Sinaloa.
The railroad has approximately 7 000 employees. The main repair and maintenance shops for locomotives and rolling stock are in Empalme, Sonora. Secondary shops are in Nogales, Mazatlán, Tepic and Guadalajara. The general offices are in Guadalajara, as are the departments of transportation, motor power, track, administration and accounting. Personnel of these departments and personnel in charge of programmed track maintenance are located in smaller offices along the line.
In this railroad there are two divisions—Sonora and Sinaloa. The Sonora division is divided into five operating districts and the Sinaloa has six. The trains operate on a flat plain, except on the Roseta slope, which is 53 km to Tepic and has a grade of 2.4 per cent. In Empalme Oredain there is also a slope of 2 per cent over a 22 km stretch. Towards the north between the stations of Agua Sarca and Encinas there is a grade of 2 per cent for 9 km, and between Guadalajara and La Venta there is a governing grade of 1.56 per cent for 19 km.
The railway has the following equipment: 93 diesel electric locomotives with a total capacity of 195 000 hp to operate four daily passenger trains, 46 freight trains and 6 mixed passenger/freight trains.
It has 3 700 freight cars: boxcars, gondolas, flatcars, Piggyback flat cars, tank cars, trailers with and without refrigeration, refrigeration cars, etc. Furthermore, it has 155 passenger cars: coaches of first and second class, express cars and mail cars.
The Ferrocarril del Pacifico carries annually an average of five million tonnes of various products, of which the main ones are: a very high percentage of agricultural products, industrial, petroleum and its derivatives as well as mineral products. Passenger traffic has averaged one million annually, a figure which has been maintained for four years.

FERROCARRIL SONORA—BAJA CALIFORNIA, SA de CV

The Ferrocarril Sonora-Baja California, SA de CV was formed by presidential decree on 24 June 1972 and covers the desert area of the states of Sonora and Baja California Norte with 684 km of main and secondary track between the towns of Benjamin Hill, Sonora, and Mexicali, BC with a branch between Tijuana and Tecate, BC.

The railway began operating in 1938 and functioned as a part of the Secretariat of Communications and Transportation until 1972, when it was constituted as a corporation with the Federal Government as sole owner.

The Ferrocarril Sonora-Baja California operated under the control of a board of directors of which the Secretary of Communications and Transportation is the president with members being representatives of the Secretariats of Treasury, National Patrimony, Industry and Commerce, the Union of Railroad Workers of the Mexican Republic and the Director General of Operating Railroads.

The operation is on level terrain except for two short grades of 1.29 per cent and 1.31 per cent of 32 km in length between López Collada and Torres B.

It has the following equipment: 16 diesel electric locomotives with a total output of 36 200 hp to operate four daily scheduled passenger trains and four daily scheduled freight trains, with necessary switching yards at Mexicali and Benjamin Hill.

Also, it has 309 freight cars: boxcars, gondolas, flatcars, open freight cars; and 87 passenger cars.

The system carries annually more than 600 000 tonnes of various products, of which the main ones are: industrial, agricultural, petroleum and derivatives, forest products, animals and animal products. Passenger traffic averaged 450 000 per year.

FERROCARRILES UNIDOS DEL SURESTE SA de CV

The Ferrocarriles Unidos del Sureste, SA de CV, was formed by presidential decree on 29 August 1968 by combining the Ferrocarriles Unidos de Yucatán, which was privately owned, with the Ferrocarril del Sureste, operated by the Secretariat of Communications and Transportation. As its name indicates, it covers the southeastern region of Mexico, beginning in the port of Coatzacoalcos, Veracruz, crossing the same river and proceeding to Tancochapa, Tabasco; Pichucalco, Chiapas; Teapa, Tabasco; Tenosique, Tabasco; Escárcega, Campeche; Campeche, Campeche; Mérida, Yucatán; and Progreso, Yucatán, with 1 043 km of broad gauge (1.435 m) track. There is also 455 km of narrow gauge (0.915 m) track which connects Mérida with Tizimin, Valladolid, Sotuta and Peto.

The Ferrocarriles Unidos de Yucatán began operating with the Mérida-Progresso section in 1881. The Ferrocarril del Sureste began operating as a unit in 1950, but some sections had existed prior to this time such as Campeche-Tenosique and Allende-Teapa.

In 1968 one corporation was formed out of both railroads with the Federal Government as majority stockholder.

The operation is on level terrain, with short compensated grades of 1 per cent, throughout its system.

The railway has the following equipment: 35 diesel electric locomotives with a capacity of 52 700 hp to operate 22 trains: four are passenger and six are freight between Coatzacoalcos-Mérida-Progreso; and 12 are mixed in the narrow-gauge branches.

Also, it has 827 freight cars: boxcars, gondolas, flatcars, open freight cars; and 69 passenger cars: coaches of first and second class, express cars and mail cars.

Ferrocarriles Unidos del Sureste carried annually more than 1.0 million tons of various products, of which the main ones are: industrial, petroleum and derivatives, agricultural, inorganic and mineral.

FERROCARRIL CHIHUAHUA AL PACIFICO, SA de CV

Ferrocarril Chihuahua al Pacifico, SA de CV was formed by the merger of the former Kansas City, Mexico and East and the Northwest Mexico rail systems through the section of new construction which linked the present system in 1960. The Federal Government acquired the Kansas City, Mexico and East Railroad in 1940 and the Northwest Mexico in 1952 and they were administered until 1955 by the Secretariat of Communications and Transportation. In that year the Ferrocarril Chihuahua al Pacifico was created by presidential decree.

The railroad is located in the states of Chihuahua and Sinaloa, uniting the northern border in the terminal at Ojinaga with the capital of the state of Chihuahua and continuing to La Junta. From there, after crossing the Sierre Madre Occidental it descends until it crosses the El Fuerte river where the level part of the state of Sinaloa begins. It continues to the town of Sufragio where it crosses the Ferrocarril del Pacifico and it terminates in the port of Topolobampo. A branch from La Junta, Chihuahua to the north connects the towns of Madera, Mata Ortiz, and Casas Grandes, terminating at the border at Ciudad Juarez. Its lines extend for 1 762 km using broad gauge of 1.435 m.

The line between Ojinaga, La Junta and Topolobampo is called Line A and is 941 km long. The portion between the stations of Agua Caliente and Creel has a continuous

Piggyback trailers still carrying Ferrocarril Chihuahua al Pacifico insignia

General Motors 3 000 hp diesel-electric

grade of 2.5 per cent for 214 km which makes operation costly and difficult. The branch between La Junta and Ciudad Juarez is called Line B and is 570 km long. It has grades of 2 per cent between the stations of Rincón and Las Varas for a distance of 12 km, and between the stations of Chico and Cumbre for a distance of 9 km. Between Caballo and Cumbre there is a 3 per cent grade for 11 km.

The railway has the following equipment: 44 diesel electric locomotives with a capacity of 87 400 hp to operate daily 10 passenger trains, 22 freight trains and 6 mixed. It has 2 354 freight cars: boxcars, gondolas, flatcars, open freight cars; and 62 passenger cars: coaches of first and second class, express cars and mail cars, as well as 13 self-propelled cars (autovias).

The railroad annually carries more than 2 000 000 tonnes of various products, of which the main ones are: forest, industrial, agricultural, mineral and petroleum and petroleum derivatives. Passenger traffic has averaged 500 000 per year.

MOROCCO

MOROCCAN RAILWAYS

Office National des Chemins de Fer du Maroc (ONCFM)
19 ave Allal Ben Abdallah, Rabat

Telephone: 208-51/57
Telex: 31907 FERRABAT

General Manager: Moussa Moussaoui
Chief Engineers: A. Benjelloun
      M. Temri
      D. Kanouni
Heads of Departments:
Operations: Zine-El-Abidne Achour
Motive Power and Rolling Stock: A. Bouamri
Permanent Way and Works: M. El Aichaoui
Administration: A. Benali

Gauge: 1.435 m
Route length: 1 756 km

Under a Dirhams 4 907 million five-year (1978-82) programme, ONCFM is carrying out an ambitious improvement programme.

Of a total railway route length of 1 091 miles (1 756 km) of standard gauge, 440 miles (708 km) is electrified at 3 000 V dc with overhead wire conductor. The electrified lines run from Casablanca eastwards to Fes, south to Marrakech, and southeast to Oued-Zem and Beni Idir.

TRAFFIC

Freight traffic increased about ten per cent in 1978 compared with the previous year. Phosphates are the railway's most important traffic, accounting for 80 per cent of all ONCFM freight. In 1977 the railway carried 18.2 million tonnes of phosphates (2 438 million tonne-km). Passenger traffic is growing by eight per cent a year and the network expects to transport 8.3 million passengers by 1982.

	1976	1977	1978
Total freight tonne-km ('000)	3 143 175	3 410 000	3 749 000
Total freight tonnage ('000)	20 198	4 700	5 100
Total passenger-km ('000)	827 818	835 000	840 000
Total passenger journeys ('000)	5 786	5 891	5 910

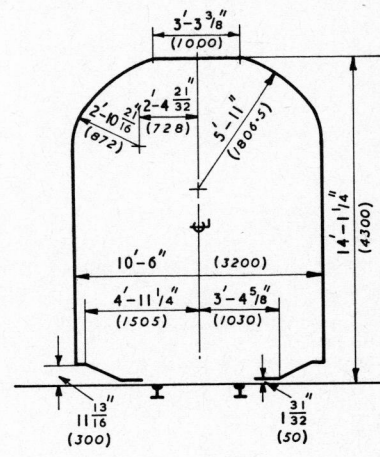

Cie des CF du Maroc

FINANCES	1975	1976
		(DH millions)
Revenues	352.83	302.52
Expenses	293.83	349.15

INVESTMENTS

Under the 1978-82 national economic development plan ONCFM is spending Dirhams 4 907 million on major improvements. The plan includes purchase of new motive power and rolling stock, new line construction, track doubling, construction of sub-stations and extension of rolling stock repair sheds at Casablanca and Meknes.

MOTIVE POWER AND ROLLING STOCK

The existing fleet consists of 102 electric locomotives, 119 diesel locomotives, 415 passenger coaches and 9 483 freight wagons. Latest locomotive acquisitions include 43 electric locomotives purchased between 1973 and 1977 together with 13 line-haul diesel-electrics and 15 shunters. The electric locomotives came from Kolmex of Poland

(23 units; 3 000 kV; 120 tonnes) and Mitsui/Hitachi (22 units; 2 850 kW; 120 tonnes). Newest of the mainline diesels operated by ONCFM were supplied by General Motors. Under the 1978-82 programme the railway is spending 76 per cent of the Dirhams 4 907 million allocated on 28 electric locomotives, nine shunters, 12 road-rail tractors, 218 passenger coaches and 2 143 freight wagons.

ELECTRIFICATION

A total of 708 route-km is electrified on 3 000 V dc overhead. Under the 1978-82 plan additional electrification is planned on a projected line between the phosphate deposits at Sidi-Azzouz and the port of Jorf Lasfar and on the newly-doubled track between Casablanca and Rabat (861 km).

CIVIL ENGINEERING

New track projects listed under the 1978-82 plan include:
Soviet-built rail line from a new phosphate mine at Meskala to Essaouria on the Atlantic coast.
850 km link from Marrakesh to Laayoun.
Doubling of the line between Benguerir and Safi to be completed by the end of 1979.
Doubling of the 816 km Casablanca—Rabat line.
Construction of a cut-off near Matmata on the Fez-Oujda line.
125 km line linking Beni—Ensar with the Taourirt region.
Extensive track renewals throughout the system and construction of 14 new branch lines for ONCFM customers.

MOZAMBIQUE
MOZAMBIQUE STATE RAILWAYS
(Caminhos de Ferro de Moçambique)
PO Box 276, Maputo

Telex: 6438

General Manager: Eng. Fernando Assis Camilo Teixera

Gauge: 1.067 m
Route length: 2 999 km

Mozambique's Minister of Development and Economic Planning, Dr Marcelino dos Santos, announced in 1977 that the 31 km section of line between Moambo and Machava is to be doubled to increase capacity for export traffic from South Africa. South African exports through the Mozambique port of Maputo doubled by mid-1978. The Minister's decision to double the Moambo—Machava section means that a major bottleneck on the 600 km Witwatersrand to Maputo route will be eliminated. It results from a study carried out earlier by a team of South African railway experts led by SAR's General Manager, Mr K Loubser. Concrete sleepers for the line will be supplied from South Africa.
Mozambique Railways consists of three main and two small lines, not connected to each other, running inland from ports on the Indian Ocean. From north to south of the country these are:

Mozambique Division
Gauge: 1.067 m
Route length: 979 km

This line runs from the port of Nacala, with a branch to Mozambique, westward to Nova Freixa and Vila Cabral. From Nova Freixa a new line has been built connecting at the border with Malawi Railways new link line giving Malawi rail access to the port of Nacala.

Quelimane Division
Gauge: 1.067 m
Route length: 950 km

From the port of Beira the line runs eastwards to connect with Rhodesia Railways at Machipanda. From Dondo Junction 18 miles (29 km), from Beira, a line runs northward to connect with Malawi Railways with an extension from D. Ana to Moatize. The section from Dondo to Sena, 181 miles (291 km) is owned by the Trans-Zambesia Railway Co Ltd. A new line 52 miles (83 km) long was built from Inhamitango to Marromeu to replace the old 0.915 m (3 ft) gauge length.

Inhambane and Gaza Division
This consists of an isolated line: Joao Belo to Máuéle, with a branch from Manjacaze to Chicomo, 0.750 m (2 ft 5½ in) gauge, 96 mile (154 km) route length.

Maputo
Gauge: 1.067 m
Route length: 771 km

From the port of Maputo lines run west to connect with South African Railways at Kamatipoort; north to Malvernia and southwest to connect with Swaziland Railways at Goba. A new line 47 miles (75 km) is being built from Umpala, on the Goba line to Salamanga.
In the South, having the port of Maputo (ex-Lourenço Marques) as railhead, there are four railway lines totalling 844 km:

Goba Line (to the border of Swaziland)	64 km
Ressano Garcia Line (to the border of South Africa)	88 km
Limpopo Line (to the border of Zimbabwe, at Chicualacuala)	528 km
Xinavane Line (domestic service)	93 km
Branch Lines (domestic service)	71 km

The first joins up at the border of Swaziland with the Swaziland Railway which connects the Umbovu Ridge iron-ore complex at Kadake with the port of Maputo. The second continues into the Republic of South Africa and carries a considerable portion of traffic from the Witwatersrand in the South Africa to this port—its natural outlet. In the upward direction liquid fuels and general cargo reach the highest figures, and in the downward direction, coal, maize, citrus and mineral ores predominate.
The third goes through Zimbabwe-Rhodesia to Zambia, Botswana and south-east Zaire and conveys hundreds of thousands of tons of cargo per annum. Motor vehicles, chemicals, fertilisers and general cargo comprise the main upward traffic. Copper, mineral ores, and maize are the biggest commodities of the downward traffic. This line also, in effect, serves the Limpopo Valley. The fourth is the natural outlet for the sugar-cane producing region of Xinavane and cattle and dairy products of the Gaza province.
In the centre, with the port of Beira as railhead, there are four lines totalling 995 km in length:

The Beira line (from Beira to Machipanda, on the Zimbabwean border)	318 km
The Trans-Zambesia Railway (from Dondo to Sena)	291 km
The line from Sena to Vila Nova da Fronteira, on the Malawi border, including the branch line from Inhamitanga to Marromeu	132 km
Tete Line (from Dona Ana to Moatize)	254 km

The first continues through Zimbabwe and serves Zimbabwe, Botswana, Zambia and south-east Zaire. It handles a considerable amount of traffic because it is the traditional gateway to these countries. In the downward direction it conveys mainly copper, minerals, tobacco, tea, refrigerated beef, etc. and in the upward traffic, machinery, fertilisers, timber and general cargo, etc.
The second which meets the above at Donda, 33 kms from Beira, is, one of the gateways to Malawi. Therefore it conveys the export and import traffic of that country in addition to the forest and sugar producing regions served specifically the Inhamitanga-Marromeu branchline.
The third meets the second at Dona Ana, on the left bank of the Zambezi River, and carries domestic traffic, made up mainly of coal and agricultural products bound for the coast. Liquid fuels and general cargo are conveyed in the upward traffic, to Cahora Bassa and to Zambia by road.
In the North, having the port of Nacala as railhead, there is a railway network which is 920 km long and comprises:

Mozambique Line to Lichinga (Vila Cabral) and the Eastern regions of Lake Nyasa	800 km
Branchline from Cuamba (Nova Freixo) to the Malawi frontier	78 km
Branchline from Lumbo to Monapo	42 km

NEPAL

NEPAL GOVERNMENT RAILWAY (NR)
Birganj

Ministry of Works & Transport: Babar Mahul, Katmandu
Minister: Hon Beleran G. Mager
Acting Manager: Devendra Singh
Acting Traffic Officer: Pratap Bahadur

Gauge: 750 mm
Route length: 10 km

There are only two short railways within Nepal, operating in the Terai, a fertile and level strip adjacent to the border with India. The Janakpur Railway (JR) runs from Jaynagar in Bihar State, India, across the Nepal border north and west to Janakpurdam (32 km) and on to Bizulpra (21 km).
The Nepal Government Railway (NR) runs from Raxaul in Bihar State across the Nepal border to Birganj (9 km). The line was originally built as a key link in the railway-road-ropeway transport system that supplied the mountain-locked valley of Katmandu—closed to the outside world until the early 1950s.
The line, now terminating at Birganj, formerly continued north to the base of the Siwalik Hills at Amlekhganj.

DEVELOPMENT

The Government is now undertaking to develop Hetauda into a new industrial centre. As part of the scheme, preliminary feasibility studies are being made for the construction of a new rail line from Raxaul to Hetauda.
At the request of the Nepal Government, Indian Railways has made two studies of possible railway extensions from Raxaul to Hetauda. The first was for a metre-gauge line which would essentially follow the existing rail route. The second calls for an entirely new alignment for a broad-gauge line which would pass to the east of Birganj. The first scheme, in fact, has been virtually abandoned due to curvatures and grades necessary. The second, which includes extensive tunnelling through the Siwalik Hills, is now under study.
The broad-gauge scheme could be undertaken in three stages: 1) construction of metre-gauge line—built to broad-gauge engineering standards—to a terminal either on the north side of Birganj or the newly-completed east-west highway further north; 2) extension to Hetauda which would involve difficult mountain work; and 3) conversion to broad gauge when India extends broad-gauge operations to the border.

JANAKPUR RAILWAY (JR)
Khajuri

Manager: D. Singh Khatry
Operations Engineer: Dr. Pratish Chandra Bandopadhyay
Traffic Assistant: Krishna Shresth

Gauge: 750 mm
Route length: 53 km

The Janakpur Railway (JR) was originally built as a timber line designed to open the virgin jungle to the north of Janakpurdam. As the forest has long since been cut, the railway now operates primarily to provide access in an area with few roads. Passengers are the main source of revenue with pilgrims to the temples of Janakpurdam forming the bulk of traffic.
In recent years JR officers have been upgrading track by laying new sleepers and second-hand 16 kg/m rail to replace existing 12.5 kg/m profile. Locomotives (including two Garrats) and wagons released from the Nepal Railway have been rebuilt and pressed into service.
A recent railway mission to Nepal from the Economic Commission for Asia and the Far East (ECAFE) suggested the possible use of diesel rail buses in place of existing steam-hauled trains.

NETHERLANDS

NETHERLANDS RAILWAYS (NS)

NV Nederlandse Spoorwegen (NS),
Moreelsepark 1, 3500 HA Utrecht

Telephone: 030-359111
Telex: 47257 nsut nl

President and Chief Executive: L. F. Ploeger
Chief Executive M. C. de Bruin
Directors and Members of the Management Committee: D. C. Hasselman
J. Walter
L. W. Wansink
J. C. W. Jong

Chief Public Relations Officer: C. P. van Strien

Gauge: 1.435 m
Route length: 1 754 km

FREIGHT TRAFFIC

The situation on the freight transport market remained practically unchanged in 1978; in general a matter of stagnating economic growth. The overcapacity on the goods transport market continued, and was even unfavourably influenced by penetration of foreign road-transport companies in this market. Consequently, the sharp competition between the different kinds of transport increased further, the inequality of the conditions of competition being a disadvantage to transport by train. Nevertheless the volume of goods transport was 18.2 million tonnes, 3.4 per cent more than in 1977. The revenues from goods transport went up from Hfl 240 million to Hfl 253 million. Tariffs were scaled up with 7.5 per cent from 1 January 1978. The average revenue per tonne however increased only slightly.
A considerable increase took place in the transport of lime-products, coal and coke to the blast furnace company of Hoogovens. The transport of salt to Belgium showed an increase, as well as the export of artificial fertilisers to France and Belgium. In wagon load traffic a decline took place in inland transport, especially with regard to chemical products.
The international wagon load traffic remained below the level of 1977, a result of the cancelled coke-export to France. Although the volume of container transport increased only slightly (measured in tonnes) the number of transported containers in 1978 was about ten per cent higher than the year before (16 000 containers).
During the ten years 1968-78 the number of containers transported by NS increased from 19,000 (1968) to 172 000 (1978).
After the recession in 1977 there was a recovery of transport of trailers by rail in 1978. The volume increased from 6 300 trailers in 1977 to 8 800 in 1978. In particular the Huckepack transport between Rotterdam, West Germany, Switzerland and Italy showed considerable growth.

PASSENGER TRAFFIC

After the decrease in passenger traffic (partly caused by the hijacks near Wijster and De Punt) 1978 showed a slight increase to more than 8 100 million passenger-km.
In November 1978 the NS annual ticket was introduced. This ticket, which attracted much publicity, offers unlimited travel for a whole year at reduced prices. At the end of 1978, 8 600 tickets had already been sold.
On 1 October 1978 the tariffs of passenger transport were increased by an average of five per cent. As a result of this increase and the development of the volume of transport, total revenues (excluding government grant for passenger services) increased by Hfl 33 million to Hfl 707 million.

	1977/78	1978/79
Total train-km per day	258 000	257 800
Percentage of train-km		
by diesel	17	17
by electric	83	83
Total freight tonnage (thousands)	17 672	18 209
Total freight tonne-km (millions)	2 805	2 882
Average net train load (tonnes)	285	292
Total passenger-km (millions)	8 013	8 146
Total passengers carried (millions)	170.8	176.3
Passengers carried (thousands)		
1st class	8 833	9 621
2nd class	161 937	166 705
Average length of passenger journey (km)	46.9	46.2

FINANCES

In 1978 total revenues amounted to Hfl 1 987 million (Hfl 89 million more than in 1977). An amount of Hfl 767 million was included as a grant for the continuation of passenger services under EEC regulations. The government's grant in goods transport amounted to Hfl 138 million. In 1978 total costs increased to Hfl 1 971 million (Hfl 1 899 million in 1977). Staff costs increased by almost six per cent to Hfl 1 342 million (Hfl 1 268 million in 1977). This increase is a result of the average increase in labour costs per head of 6.6 per cent and a small decrease of the average number of staff of less than one per cent. Total costs were 3.8 per cent more than in 1977 and were less than the proportional increase of costs and prices which confronted NS in 1978. So in real terms costs were lower than in previous years.

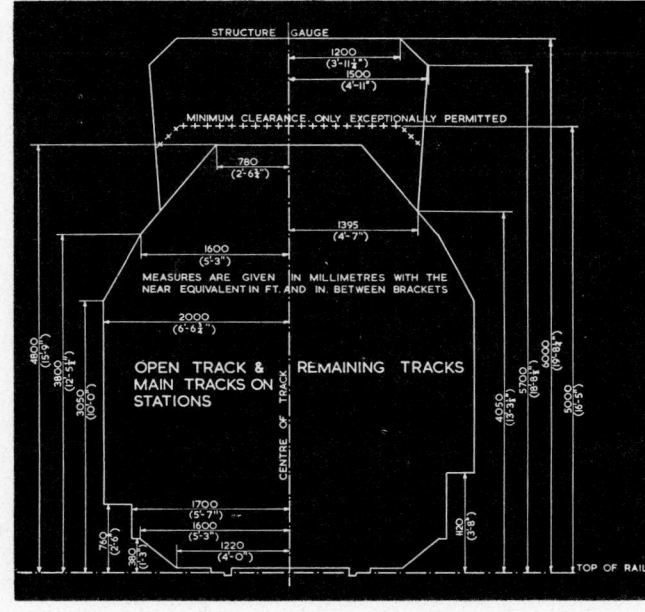

Ex-BR EM2 class 2 490-hp Co-Co locomotive hauling train out of Rotterdam for Mönchengladbach and Cologne

The investments were Hfl 447 million in 1978, ie Hfl 40 million less than in 1977. Hfl 218 million was spent on the existing railway lines and Hfl 229 million on the construction of new lines.

Revenues

	1977/78	1978/79
Passengers and baggage (millions)	675.8	709.7
Average receipt per passenger-km	0.084	0.087
Freight and mail (millions)	264.4	279.4
Average receipt per freight tonne-km	0.082	0.085
Total revenues (millions)	1 899	1 969

Expenditure (millions)		
Staff/personnel	1 268	1 342
Materials and services	353	353
Depreciation	258	261
Financial charges	20	15
Total expenditure	1 899	1 971

MOTIVE POWER

Number of locomotives in service during 1979 totalled 559, of which 112 were electric mainline, 249 diesel electric line, and 218 electric shunters. Number of railcars totalled 30 diesel; number of emu's 549; diesel trainsets 86.

Motive power and rolling stock under order (1979/80)

	Electric loco	Diesel-hydraulic motor cars	2-railcars	Light rail vehicles	Traincoaches for IC-service
Class	1 600	DH 801	DH 802	2-railcars	ICR
Number	30 (48)	19	26	27	226
Axle arrangement	B'-B'	2'B'	(2'B') (2'B')	Bo-B'-Bo	2-2
Max speed (km/h)	160	100	100	80	160
Power (kW)	4 200	212	2 x 212	2 x 228	—
Weight (tonnes)	85	32.4	62.35	35.6	42
Length (mm)	17 640	22 210	43 270	29 800	26 400
Delivery	1980-82	1981-82		1981-82	1980-82
Builders					
Mechanical	Alsthom	Waggonfabrik Uerdingen		SIG	Talbot
Bogies	Creusot	Klöckner		SIG	Soc Franco Belge
Engines	Alsthom	Cummins		BBC	De Dietrich
Electrical install.	Jeumont-Schneider	EMG		Holec	Holec

PERMANENT WAY

In May 1977 NS opened the 11 km first-stage section of the Zoetermee line running from Den Haag Centraal to Zoetermee and Meerzicht/Palenstein. Stage two of the line opened 5 km in May 1979.
Phase one of the Schiphol—Amsterdam-Zuid (11 km) line opened at the end of 1978. Phase two Schiphol—Leiden is due to open May 1981. Other lines under construction include a branchline to Veenendaal and Rhenen (14 km) to open May 1981 and a light-rail line (Utrecht—Nieuwegein/Ijsselstein, 17.5 km) to open mid-1982.

Planned lines include: Connection Schiphol-line—Amsterdam CS via Westelijke Ringbaan; completion between 1986 and 1990; government decision is awaited.
Extension Schiphol-line from Amsterdam Zuid to the RAI (congress and exhibition centre) ± 1 km; to open May 1981.
Flevo-line (Weesp—Almere—Lelystad, 40 km); completion between 1986 and 1990.

Crude oil train from Schoomebeck oilfield hauled by double Alsthom diesel-electric locomotives with total output of 1 700 hp

'Sprinter' two-car electric trainset for high density traffic in urban area

Four-car electric trainset nicknamed 'Hondekap' (Dogshead) used for intercity services

New three-car inter-city trainset—one of seven prototypes delivered by Talbot in 1976

Dutch-Belgian push-pull unit for passenger-service Amsterdam-Brussels vv, suited for 1 500 and 3 000 V dc

Two-car electric trainset type 'plan V' used for stopping trains in densely populated areas, max speed 140 km/h

Important works under construction include:
Hemtunnel: three-track tunnel under Noordzee-Kanaal, substituting Hem-bridge between Amsterdam and Zaandam; completion 1983.
Zaandam—Purmerend; double track; 13 km; completion 1983.
Oss—Wijchen; double track; 15 km; completion 1980.
Zwolle—Dalfsen; double track; 12 km; completion 1980.
Deventer; new bridge (double track) across the river Ijssel; completion 1982.
Westervoort; new bridge (single track) across the river Ijssel; completion 1982.
Utrecht; new bridge (double track) for light-rail system across the Amsterdam—Rhine Canal; completion 1981.
Kijfhoek; new shunting yard between Rotterdam and Dordrecht; in full operation mid-1980.

Standard rail, weights:
Main lines: 94 and 127 lb/yd *(46.9 and 63 kg/m)*
Branch lines: 76.6 and 92.7 lb/yd *(38 and 46 kg/m)*
Standard rail, lengths:
Main lines: 24 and 30 m
Branch lines: 15 and 18 m
Rail joints: 4-hole fishplates and bolts; and some welding.
Cross ties (sleepers): Hard and soft wood, 10 × 6 × 8 ft 6½ in *(250 × 150 × 2 600 mm)*
Cross ties spacing:
Main lines: 2 680 per mile *(1 666 per km)*
Branch lines: 2 145 per mile *(1 333 per km)*

Rail fastenings: Coach screws (on hard wood), coach screws and soleplates (on soft wood), ribbed soleplates and bolts, ribbed soleplates and curved stirrups of spring steel. Elastic fastening with curved stirrups for both wood and concrete sleepers, the clips fitting into a cast iron housing having two pins glued into concrete sleeper or pressed into wood. Cast iron chairs and bolts. Pads under rails are grooved rubber 4 mm thick or wooden wearing plates 4 mm thick.
Experimental sections laid with "Zig-zag" concrete block and steel tube track construction.
Filling: Gravel or broken stone, ⅜ in to 3⅛ in *(10 to 80 mm)*
Minimum thickness under sleeper: 7⅛ in *(200 mm)*
Max curvature: 5.8° = min rad of 984 ft *(300 m)*
Max gradient, compensated: 2% = 1 in 50 (on Sittard-Hertzogenrath line)
Max gradient, uncompensated: 1.43% = 1 in 70 (on Sittard-Hertzogenrath line)
Longest continuous gradient: 5.5 miles *(8.85 km)* of 1 in 300 grade with three curves of 4 921 ft *(1 500 m)* radius.
Worst combination of gradient and curvature: 1 in 175 (0.57%) gradient with curves of 984 ft *(300 m)* radius.
Gauge widening on sharpest curve: 7 mm
Super elevation on sharpest curve: 4.72 in *(120 mm)* on track in gravel. 5.90 in *(150 mm)* on track in broken stone.
Rate of slope of super elevation:
Speed higher than V 105 km/h: 1 in 8V.
Speed 105 km/h or less: 1 in 1 100 with minimum of 1 in 600.
Altitude, max: 596 ft *(181.7 m)* on Simpelveld-German Frontier section.
Max axle loading: 21 tons.
Max permitted speed:
Passenger trains: 87 mph *(140 km/h)*.
Freight trains: 37 mph *(60 km/h)*.
Fast freight trains: 56 mph *(90 km/h)*.

DIESEL LOCOMOTIVES

Class	Axle Arrangement	Transmission	Rated Power hp	Max. lb (kg)	Tractive Effort Continuous at lb (kg)	mph (km/h)	Max. Speed mph (km/h)	Wheel Dia. in (mm)	Total Weight Tons	Length ft ins (mm)	No. Built	Year first Built	Builders: Mechanical Parts	Engine & Type	Transmission
2400 2500	Bo-Bo	Elec.	850	36 400 *(16 500)*	12 830 *(8 090)*	12 *(20)*	50 *(80)*	39⅜ *(1 000)*	60	41' 1'' *(12 520)*	129	1954	Alsthom	SACM, V 12 SHR	Alsthom
2200 2300	Bo-Bo	Elec.	900	40 800 *(18 500)*	27 000 *(12 250)*	8.7 *(14)*	62 *(100)*	37⅜ *(950)*	74	45' 11½'' *(14 010)*	150	1955	Allan Schneider	Stork, Schneider (lic Superior) 40 C-LX-8	Heemaf Westinghouse

DIESEL LOCOMOTIVES

Class	Axle Arrangement	Transmission	Rated Power hp	Max. lb (kg)	Tractive Effort Continuous at lb (kg)	mph (km/h)	Max. Speed mph (km/h)	Wheel Dia. in (mm)	Total Weight Tons	Length ft ins (mm)	No. Built	Year first Built	Builders: Mechanical Parts	Engine & Type	Transmission
511-545 601-665	C	Elec.	400	32 100 (14 600)	14 436 (6 550)	6 (10)	(30)	48⅜ (1 230)	47	29' 9'' (9 070)	35	1949	English Electric	EEC, 6 KT	EEC
200-300	Bo	Elec.	72				60 (98)	39⅓ (1 000)	21	23' 7⅝'' (7 220)	148	1934- 1951	Schneider-Werkspoor	Stork, Hengelo	Heemaf: E.T.I.; Hengelo or Slikkerveer

ELECTRIC LOCOMOTIVES AND RAILCARS

Class	Axle Arrangement	Line Current	Rated Output hp	Max. lb (kg)	Tractive Effort (Full Field) Continuous at lb (kg)	mph (km/h)	Max. Speed mph (km/h)	Wheel dia. in (mm)	Weight tonnes	Length ft in (mm)	No. Built	Year Built	Builders Mechanical Parts	Electrical Equipment
1500	Co-Co	1 500 V dc OH	3 220	45 000 (20 400)	20 000 (9 100)	44.2 (78)	84 (135)	43 (1 092)	69	59' 0'' (17 983)	6	1954	BR	
1300	Co-Co	1 500 V dc OH	3 870	51 000 (23 100)	28 600 (13 000)	31 (50)	84 (135)	49¼ (1 250)	111	62' 2'' (18 950)	15	1952	Alsthom	Alsthom
1200	Co-Co	1 500 V dc OH	3 000	43 500 (19 700)	22 400 (10 200)	31 (50)	84 (135)	43¼ (1 100)	108	59' 4'' (18 080)	25	1951	Werkspoor-Baldwin	Heemaf-Westinghouse
1100	Bo-Bo	1 500 V dc OH	2 580	34 200 (15 500)	14 300 (6 500)	31 (50)	84 (135)	49¼ (1 250)	80	42' 7½'' (12 980)	58	1950	Alsthom	Alsthom
1000	(IA) -Bo (AI)	1 500 V dc OH	3 800	36 500 (16 600)	22 600 (19 300)	31 (50)	84 (135)	61 (1 550)	100	52' 2½'' (16 220)	9	1948	S.L.M.; Werkspoor	Oerlikon; Heemaf; Smit
3001/3035 (MP)	Bo-Bo	1 500 V dc OH					87 (140)	(950)	52	86' 4'' (26 400)	35	1965	Werkspoor	Werkspoor
Electric Railcars														
401-438 441-483 801-965 (EL2)	(2-Bo)+ (Bo-2)	1 500 V dc OH					86 (140)	(950)	85	170' 3'' (52 140)	244	1966/76	Werkspoor Talbot	Heemaf/Smit
502/531 (ELD4)	(2-2)+ (Bo-Bo)+ (Bo-Bo)	1 500 V dc OH					86 (140)	(950)	168	331' 7'' (101 240)	30	1964/65	Werkspoor	Heemaf/Smit
SGM (EL2) 2001-2015 2021-2080	Bo-Bo Bo-Bo	1 500 V dc OH	1 720				80 (125)	(950)	106	(52 200)	75	1975/80	Talbot SIG	Oerlikon Holec
JCIII 4001-4007	Bo-Bo (2-2)+ (2-2)	1 500 V dc OH					(160)	(950)	114	80 600	7	1977	Talbot Wegmann	Heemaf/Smit TCO

NEW ZEALAND

NEW ZEALAND GOVERNMENT RAILWAYS (NZR)
Bunny Street, Wellington

Telephone: 725 599

General Manager: T. M. Hayward
Deputy General Manager, Engineering and Development: I. C. McGregor
Assistant General Manager, Finance and Administration: A. E. McQueen
Assistant General Manager, Personnel: H. G. Purdy
Chief Mechanical Engineer: K. M. Frederic
Chief Civil Engineer: M. R. H. Henare
Chief Traffic Manager: B. B. McKeown
Director, Finance and Accounts Branch: A. J. Whitburn
Director, Management Services: J. S. Beckett
Director, Stores Branch: D. Drummond
Director, Road Services Branch: F. H. Marvelly
Commercial Manager: A. E. McInnes
Publicity and Advertising Manager: I. G. Holland
Director, Land Division: L. S. Harding

Gauge: 1.067 m
Route length: 4 536 km

TRAFFIC
Long-distance passenger journeys remained relatively steady at 1 007 643 in 1978, while suburban journeys increased by 2.2 per cent to 15 741 575. Long-distance passenger revenue increased from $5 852 239 to $6 087 146. Suburban passenger revenue increased from $4 694 704 to 5 519 072.
Freight revenue for the year increased by $23 132 639 to $221 771 161, despite a fall in tonnage carried.

	1976	1977	1978
Total freight			
Gross tonne-km	8 638 392 000	8 922 137 000	8 386 095 000
Total freight tonnage	13 193 019	13 601 372	12 577 236
Total passenger-km	1 089 042 000	1 000 948 000	921 002 000

FINANCES
This increase in expenditure during 1978 was mainly due to wage increases and the escalating price of materials including fuel and electricity on which $17 637 075 was spent. The operating deficit for 1978-79 was $47 273 399. After adding interest charges of $23 534 526 on loans and overseas credits, the net loss for the year on the whole undertaking was $70 807 925.

	1976	1977	1978
Revenues	$170 206 584	$248 068 785	$266 403 905
Expenses	$233 160 088	$260 072 954	$304 183 392

MOTIVE POWER AND ROLLING STOCK
Number of locomotives in service at the end of the 1978/79 fiscal year:

Dx locomotive at the head of a mixed freight train

	Line-haul	Shunting
Steam	2	—
Electric	13	—
Diesel-electric	313	96
Diesel-hydraulic	—	64
Diesel-mechanical	—	36

(Diesel tractors under 200 hp are not included in the above list).

Number of railcars, electric: 49 (multiple units).
Number of railcars, diesel: 16 (12 being converted to passenger cars).
Number of trailer cars, electric: 78 (multiple units).
Number of passenger train coaches: 375.
Number of freight cars: 30 151 (also 3 mail vans, 4 generator vans, and 327 brake vans).
Number of containers (in service and on order)
    Bulk liquid: 35
    Thermal liquid: 30
    General box: 65
    Bulk flour: 56
    General open: 2
    Thermal box: 722
    Bulk line: 90

During 1978/79 333 new goods wagons were placed in service. These comprised five Bkc Class four-wheel wagons for containerised coal, five Na Class and 31 Nh Class four-wheel flat-top wagons, 207 Uk and ten Uka Class bogie container wagons, 32 Us Class bogie flat-top wagons, 34 Yh Class ballast wagons and nine Za Class bogie box wagons.

Twenty new 1 100 kW mainline diesel-electric locomotives were purchased from General Motors of Canada and have been classified as Df locomotives. 1978/79 also saw the rebuilding of NZR's 'Da' locomotives by Clyde Engineering Company of South Australia. By 31 March 1979, 42 locomotives had been shipped to Australia and 27 have since returned to New Zealand as Dc Class. Clyde Engineering Company has also supplied new cab equipment to enable some Da locomotives to be rebuilt in NZR workshops in the same body style as the Australian rebuilds. During 1978/79, six Dh heavy shunting locomotives were bought from General Electric Company of the USA while 30 Dsc shunting locomotives were fitted with new Cummins diesel engine power packages and other modifications to boost their performance.

World-wide tenders were called in 1978 for new passenger rolling stock for the Wellington suburban area. The successful tender for the supply of 44 two-coach electric multiple units was submitted by the Hungarian firm of Ganz-Mavag in association with the General Electric Company of the UK which will provide the traction motors and other major electrical components. The new multiple units are expected to arrive in 1981 when they will replace the aged carriage stock now in use.

The Government has deferred purchasing new commuter carriages for South Auckland to enable a reassessment to be made of local passenger requirements.

During 1978/79 all Vulcan and Drewry built twin-car railcars were withdrawn from service after increasing mechanical unreliability made it impractical to continue using them. 14 twin-car sets have since been converted into articulated carriages hauled by diesel-electric locomotives and now run on several routes where the railcars formerly operated.

NZR's old Da Class locomotive
By 31 March 1979, 42 Da locomotives had been shipped to Australia to be rebuilt as class Dc *(below)*

Dj and Dg locomotive combination hauls a freight train on the North Island main trunk line between Wellington and Auckland

Da Class locomotive hauls a container train out of the Kaimai tunnel
The Kaimai deviation gives direct access for the Bay of Plenty and the important export port of Mount Maunganui to the prosperous Waikato region

One of NZR's new Dc Class locomotive hauls a goods train out of the newly-opened 8.9 km Kaimai tunnel, the longest on the NZR system

NZR's Dj Class locomotive in new livery

SIGNAL AND TRAIN CONTROL INSTALLATIONS

The centralised traffic control area controlled from Hamilton was extended to Tauranga with the opening of the Kaimai deviation. In the South Island centralised traffic control from Christchurch was extended to Timaru.

A nation-wide computerised Traffic Monitoring System (TMS) was introduced in February 1979 with the switching on of the central computer in Wellington. This brought the Napier TMS centre into operation, the first of eight centres to be brought into service. When fully operative the system will provide increased wagon utilisation with improved speed and efficiency.

ELECTRIFICATION

Plans for the electrification of NZR's North Island main trunk line were revived in 1977. Electrification was previously considered in the 1950s but advocates of dieselisation won the argument for the best replacement for steam traction. Now, because of problems caused by the oil crisis, a committee has been formed to reconsider electrifying the 685 km line. Cost is expected to be about $NZ 100 million. NZR is known to want to electrify the Taumarunui to Taihape section as soon as possible. It is the most tortuous section of the line and includes the well-known Raurimu Spiral.

CIVIL ENGINEERING

The 8.9 km Kaimai tunnel was opened on 12 September 1978 making it the longest tunnel on the NZR system. The Kaimai deviation gives direct access for the Bay of Plenty and the important export port of Mount Maunganui to the prosperous Waikato region. The tunnel and associated deviation works totalling 24.2 km cost $56 million while the cost of the tunnel alone was $43 million.

NEW RAIL LAID

Rail Weights:

Main line	50 kg/m; 91 lb/yd, 85 lb/yd
Provincial line	91 lb/yd, 85 lb/yd, 75 lb/yd, 70 lb/yd
Branch lines	70 lb/yd, 55 lb/yd

Rail Laid:

Total length	4 786 km
Total welded	2 160 km
Total CWR	63.2 km
Longest length CWR (through Kaimai tunnel)	8.9 km
Relaid in new rail (50 kg) 1976-77	107 km

Welding Method:
Flash Butt in Depot; Thermit in Field.
New rails are flash butt welded in depots into lengths of 76.8 m and transported to site for laying.
Short Rail in track may be Thermit welded into similar lengths.
Continuous welded rail is now being formed on straight track by Thermit process with lapped expansion joints at extremities and epoxy glued insulated joints.

Sleepers:
Types and Use:
Australian hardwoods: All Lines (superseded by Pine)
NZ pinus softwood: All Lines
Concrete: Main lines only
Spacing:
Main line: Timber 600 mm, concrete 750 mm
Other lines: Timber 650 mm
Fastenings:
Main lines:
Timber: Pandrol Spring fastenings on bed plates with rubber pads and nylon insulators. Clips, screw spikes, spring washers on double shoulder bedplates. Spring clips and screw spikes without bedplates.
Concrete: Pandrol Spring fastenings with rubber pads and nylon insulators.
Branch Lines:
Timber: Elastic Spikes, screws and dog spikes cascaded from higher ranking lines.
Laying Method:
Concrete: By NZR designed and built sleeper laying machine.
Timber: Laid manually either in face or by spotting.

Sleepers (cross ties):
Type: Australian hardwood, 9 in by 4½ in. NZ pinus softwood, 8 in by 6 in. Prestressed concrete 10 in base × 7½ in high all 7 ft (2 134 mm) long.
Sleeper spacing:
Main lines: Timber 600 mm. Concrete: 750 mm.
Branch lines: Timber 675 mm.

Rail fastenings (types used): Pandrol spring fastenings on rolled Pandrol steel bedplates are the new construction standard for the North Island main trunk line. On new deviations and where face resleepering can be justified, concrete sleepers with Pandrol spring fastenings, rubber pads and nylon insulators are being used. Other current types of fastening include double shoulder bed-plates with clips, screw spikes and spring washers, and spring clips and screw spikes without bed-plates. Light traffic lines are generally laid with elastic spikes, screws or dog spikes cascaded down from higher ranking lines.

NZR's Silver Star sleeper express hauled by a Dx Class locomotive arriving in Wellington at the end of its overnight journey from Auckland

NZRs' UKX Class multi-purpose flat-top bogie wagon, 100 of which were brought into use in 1978

Wellington-Napier Endeavour daylight express train, headed by a 1 425-hp Da Class A1A-A1A General Motors diesel-electric locomotive, at Eaipukuran

Welded Rail

Total length of track laid at 31 March 1977	2 100 km
Length laid during 1976-77	75 km
Longest individual length of welded rail	8.9 km through Kaimai tunnel

Standard method of laying: Rails are flash-butt welded at depots into lengths of up to 252 ft *(76.8 m)* (6 × 42 ft) and after laying in open track the ends are fishplated. Joints permit partial expansion and contraction related to a mean temperature of 80°F. In tunnels the ends are Thermit welded to form continuous rail, apart from insulated joints. In the Otira Tunnel a length of 5.2 km is in use. Continuous welded rail is now being adopted on open track by the same method, with lapped expansion joints at the extremities, and epoxy glued insulated track joints.

Rail in use is mostly 91 lb/yd, but small quantities of 100, 90, 85 and 72 lb/yd, have also been laid. 50 kg/m rail is being ordered for future relaying on main lines.

Rails are secured to softwood sleepers, 7 ft × 8 in × 6 in, with double-shoulder bedplates, screw spikes, spring washers, and clips on heavy traffic lines, and screw spikes, with spring clips without bedplates on other lines. Pandrol bedplates and fastenings on softwood sleepers have been adopted for new main line relaying with continuous welded rail. 5 mm synthetic rubber pads are being added between rail and bedplate.

Wellington-Auckland express freight of Zp Class covered wagons and containers travels north near Te Kuiti headed by a 2 750-hp Dx Class Co-Co General Electric diesel-electric locomotive

Auckland—Wellington Silver Star sleeping car express train, headed by a 2 750 hp Dx Class Co-Co locomotive, arriving at Wellington station at the end of its 423 mile journey

DIESEL LOCOMOTIVES

Class	Axle Arrangement	Transmission	Rated Power hp	Max. lb (kg)	Tractive Effort Continuous at lb (kg)	mph (km/h)	Max. Speed mph (km/h)	Wheel Dia. in (mm)	Total Weight Tons	Length ft ins (mm)	No. Built	Year first Built	Builders: Mechanical Parts	Engine & Type	Transmission
Dx	Co-Co	Elec	2 750/ 2 600		46 500 (21 090)	17 (27.4)	75 (120)	37 (940)	96	55' 6'' (16 916)	15 34	1972 1975	GE (USA)	GE 7FDL12 D3	GE (USA)
Da	AIA-AIA	,,	1 425/ 1 310	32 480 (14 730)	28 000 (12 700)	14.7 (23.6)	60 (96)	Driver 40 (1 016) Idler 30 (762)	76	43' 0'' (13 106)	30	1955	GM	GM567C	GM
				''	''	''	''	''	78	44' 6'' (13 564)	10	1957	Clyde-GM	,,	,,
''	''	,,	,,	33 460 (15 180)	30 600 (15 180)	12.0 (19.3)	,,	Driver 40 (1 016) Idler 33 (838)	76	43' 0'' (13 106)	72 34	1961/6GM 1967			
Db	AIA-AIA	,,	950/875		22 050 (10 227)	12.0 (19.3)	60 (96)	Driver 40 (1 016) Idler 30 (762)	67.5	43' 0'' (13 100)	17	1965	,,	GM567CR	,,
Dc	AIA-AIA	,,	1 650/ 1 500	82 tonnes	14 000	21	55 (90)	—	82.5	43' 0'' (13 100)	42	1977	Clyde GM	GM 645E	,,
De	Bo-Bo	,,	660/630	28 600 (12 970)	12 700 (5 760)	15.4 (24.8)	55 (88)	36½ (927)	51	35' 0'' (10 668)	15	1951	English Electric	English Electric 6SRKT	English Electric
Dg	AIA-AIA	,,	750/682	25 600 (11 600)	20 200 (9 160)	10.1 (16.2)	,,	Driver 37 (950) Idler 37 (940)	69	45' 0'' (13 716)	42	1955	,,	English Electric 6SRKT	,,
Dh	Bo-Bo	,,	840	54 tonnes	—	—	—		54	37' 7'' (11 395)	6	1978	GE	Cat 3983	GE

DIESEL LOCOMOTIVES

Class	Axle Arrangement	Transmission	Rated Power hp	Max. lb (kg)	Tractive Effort Continuous at lb (kg)	Tractive Effort Continuous at mph (km/h)	Max. Speed mph (km/h)	Wheel Dia. in (mm)	Total Weight Tons	Length ft ins (mm)	No. Built	Year first Built	Builders: Mechanical Parts	Builders: Engine & Type	Builders: Transmission
Di	Co-Co	,,	1 012/ 923	40 000 (18 200)	29 500 (13 400)	9.0 (14.5)	60 (96)	37 (940)	63	45' 3" (13 792)	5	1967	English Electric Australia	English Electric 6CSRKT/Mk 2	,,
Dj	Bo-Bo-Bo	,,	1 050/ 990		28 900 (13 100)	10 (16)	62 (100)	37 (940)	63	46' 3" (14 100)	62	1967	Mitsubishi Heavy Ind.	Caterpillar D 398 TA	Mitsubishi
Ds	C (0-6-0)	Mech	204	14 300 (6 500)	14 300 (6 490)	4.0 (6.4)	30 (48)	39¾ (1 010)	26	22' 0½" (6 718)	16	1949/ 1955	Drewry Car Co	Gardner 8L3	Hyd coupling Type 23 Epycyclic gearbox CA5 Final Drive gearbox RF11.
Dsa	C (0-6-0)	Mech	,,	16 500 (7 500)	16 500 (7 500)	3.47 (5.6)	26.42 (42)	. ,,	29.5	25' 1" (7 645)	20	1953	,,	,,	,,
,,	,,	Hyd*	304	28 500 (13 000)	13 200 (6 000)	7.2 (11.6)	20 (32)	,,	30	23' 11¼" (7 296)	10	1956	W. G. Bagnall Ltd.	Caterpillar D343	Twin Disc
,,	,,	Mech	250	16 800 (7 620)	16 800 (7 620)	4.75 (7.6)	25.65 (41)	,,	,,	23' 6½" (7 175)	9	1954	Hunslet	National M4AA6	Hunslet clutch and gearbox
,,	,,	Hyd	,,	21 550 (9 770)	12 490 (5 670)	6.38 (10.3)	25.65 (41)	,,	,,	,,	6	1957	,,	,,	Hunslet torque converter & gearbox
,,	,,	,,	315	20 000 (9 100)	17 000 (7 700)	4 (6.4)	35 (56)	39¾" (1 010)	30	27' 10¼" (8 490)	12	1967	Mitsubishi Heavy Ind.	Caterpillar D 343 T	Niigata torque conv DBS 115; Mitsubishi final drive
Dsb	C (0-6-0)	Hyd*	335	26 300 (11 900)	13 200 (6 000)	6.7 (10.8)	20 (32)	,,	36.6	25' 4⅞" (7 744)	25	1954	Drewry Car Co	Caterpillar D343	Twin Disc
,,	v	,,	375	23 000 (10 400)	18 000 (8 200)	4.5 (7.2)	35 (56)	39¾ (1 010)	37.5	27' 10¼" (8 490)	3	1967	Mitsubishi Heavy Ind.	Caterpillar D 343 TA	Niigata torque converter DBS 115
Dsc	Bo-Bo	Elec	420/370	22 700 (10 300)	10 400 (4 720)	8.5 (13.6)	40 (64)	37 (940)	40.5	35' 0" (10 668)	18	1959	A.E.I.	Rolls Royce C6SFL	A.E.I.
,,	,,	,,	,,	,,	,,	,,	,,	,,	,,	,,	52	1963/7NZR†		Leyland 902/903	,,

* Originally provided with National Engines, hydraulic couplings and Self Changing Gear Co's epicyclic gearboxes. They were re-equipped in 1964-66.
† 35 locos re-equipped with Cummins NT-855-L3 engines in 1976.

ELECTRIC LOCOMOTIVES

Class	Axle Arrangement	Line Current	Rated Output hp	Max. lb (kg)	Tractive Effort (Full Field) Continuous at lb (kg)	Tractive Effort (Full Field) Continuous at mph (km/h)	Max. Speed mph (km/h)	Wheel dia. in (mm)	Weight tonnes	Length ft in (mm)	No. Built	Year Built	Builders Mechanical Parts	Builders Electrical Equipment
Ea	Bo-Bo	1 500 V dc	1 285	23 000 (10 460)	18 000 (8 200)	22.5 (36)	45 (72)	40 (1 016)	54	38' 0" (11 582)	5	1968	Tokyo Shibaura	Tokyo Shibaura
Ed	2-D-1	,,	1 240	34 300 (15 560)	11 600 (5 260)	29 (46.6)	55 (88)	,,	86	43' 2" (13 157)	2	1937	Eng Elec & NZR	,,
Ew	Bo-Bo-Bo	,,	1 800	42 000 (19 050)	18 600 (8 440)	30 (48.2)	60 (96)	36½ (927)	75	59' 0" (17 983)	7	1952	,,	,,

NIGERIA

NIGERIAN RAILWAY CORPORATION (NRC)
Ebute Metta

Telephone: Lagos 44302

Chairman: Col J. T. Useni
Director General: K. C. Bansal

Gauge: 1.067 m
Route length: 3 523 km

As a result of the catalogue of operational deficiencies in the Nigerian Railway Corporation (NRC), the Federal Military Government entered into an agreement with the Rail India Technical and Economic Services Ltd (RITES) in October 1978 to provide management and technical support for NRC. The agreement provides for RITES to hand over to the Nigerian Government after a period not exceeding three years an effective and efficiently managed railway system manned fully by Nigerian personnel.
The government commissioned consultants in 1972, 1975 and 1977 to study the NRC and identify the reasons for its deterioration and decay. The combined findings and reports showed that the top management personnel of the corporation did not appear to be competent enough to manage and operate a modern railway system and it was for this reason that the agreement with RITES was drawn up.
Work began during 1979 on conversion of the entire 3 523 km narrow-gauge network to standard-gauge. The first two sections underway (Port Harcourt to Makurdi and Oturkpo to Ajaokuta) will cost about Naira 2 000 million for the 500 km route. For further details see under Civil Engineering.

TRAFFIC
There has been a continuous fall in freight traffic haulage for the past few years. In 1973/74 NRC handled 1.7 million tonnes (1 307 million tonne-km) falling to 335 000 tonnes (274 million tonne-km) in 1977/78. During 1978/79 a rise in traffic was detected, with total tonnage reaching 369 000 tonnes (302 million tonne-km). By 1983 the railway expects to be hauling about 550 000 tonnes a year.
Passenger traffic is also growing again following a continuing reduction in journeys recorded between 1973 and 1978 when traffic fell to an all-time low of 2.2 million journeys and 383 million passenger-km. A slight improvement was expected in 1979 when about 2.6 million passengers were carried (459 million passenger-km) and by 1982/83 NRC hopes to handle 5.5 million journeys a year.

	1973	1978/79
Ton-km ('000s)	1 349 796	302 000
Passenger-km ('000s)	1 024 168	383 000

FINANCES
Although NRC was able to liquidate all bank overdrafts and pay outstanding debts in 1979 following the release of Government funds, there is still a wide gap between

One of 162 passenger coaches built for NRC by Japanese manufacturers in 1978

operating expenditure and revenue. An operating deficit of Naira 28 million was reported for 1979/80 when revenues totalled Naira 72 million (Naira 35 million in the previous year) compared with expenditures of Naira 100 million.

INVESTMENTS
The capital improvement programme in 1979/80 was Naira 60 million.

MOTIVE POWER AND ROLLING STOCK
Orders have been placed for 55 mainline diesel-electric locomotives, 500 freight wagons, 150 passenger coaches and 20 shunters.
By the end of 1978 the motive power fleet included 133 mainline steam locomotives (43 shunting); 130 mainline diesel electrics (39 shunting); eight mainline diesel-hydraulic locomotives. The rolling stock park included 5 738 freight wagons and 55 passenger coaches.

CIVIL ENGINEERING
The Port Harcourt—Makurdi standard-gauge conversion project (first stage of a plan to convert the entire network) will follow a new alignment for 160 km/h operation. The new standard-gauge railway will be designed to UIC standards with UIC 60 rails used on mainlines and UIC 54 or UIC 50 rails at station and marshalling yards. Maximum gradient will be one per cent and minimum curve radius 1 200 m. Rails will be laid on concrete sleepers and ballast with a depth of at least 30 cm.
In addition to construction of a new railway which will broadly follow the lines of the existing 1 067 mm system, NRC also has plans for 1 315 km of new lines. Implementation, however, will be subject to approval by the Federal Military Government. The lines are: Ajaokuta—Ibadan, via Akure (375 km); Minna—Abuja (new federal capital)—Lafia (315 km); Gusau—Sokoto (225 km); Warri—Benin—Okone (250 km); and Umuahia—Calabar (150 km).

NORWAY

NORWEGIAN STATE RAILWAYS

Norges Statsbaner (NSB), Storgt 33 Oslo

Telephone: 20 95 50

Central Administration
  Chairman of the Board: Ole Haugum
  General Manager: Robert F. Nordén
  Public Relations: Odd Kjell Skjegstad
Administration and Finance:
  Director, Administration: B. Egeland-Eriksen
  Director, Personnel: Odd Wessel Larsen
  Director, Purchase and Stores: Oddvar Bø
  Director, Finance: Helge Skudal
Operation and Commerce:
  Chief Director: Knut Skuland
  Director, Operations: Kaare Kristiansen
  Director, Commerce: Martin Killi
Engineering:
  Chief Director: Eivinn Lovseth
  Director, Rolling Stock: A. Øhrn
  Director, Electrification: Kjell Moi

Gauge: 1.435 m
Route length: 4 241 km

TRAFFIC	1975	1976	1977	1978
Total freight ton-km (million)	2 560.8	2 709.4	2 566.7	2 650
Total freight tonnage (1 000)	25 061.5	28 755.7	23 500	26 600
Total passenger-km (million)	1 948.2	1 997.1	2 003.7	2 058.3
Total passengers carried (million)	33.5	32.7	33.6	34.1

FINANCES	1975	1976	1977	1978
Revenues (million Norw crowns)	1 251.9	1 443.5	1 535.4	1 670.2
Expenses (million Norw crowns)	1 570.7	1 895.8	2 187.8	2 334.6

MOTIVE POWER

At the end of 1978 NSB's motive power park consisted of 164 electric train locomotives, 89 diesel train locomotives, 133 electric motor coaches, 45 diesel motor coaches, and 183 shunting engines and maintenance tractors.

ROLLING STOCK

Passenger coaches in service total: 843, freight wagons: 8 758.

ELECTRIFICATION

Total electrified route length on 31 December 1978: 1 516 miles *(2 440 km)*
Total electrified track length on 31 December 1978: 1 954 miles *(3 144 km)*.
System of electrification: 15 kV 1/16 2/3.

TRACK

Extensive construction and building work is in progress at the railway tunnel beneath Oslo, scheduled for opening in 1980, and at Oslo new central station.
Rail, types and weights: s. 54 kg/m, s. 49 kg/m, 41 kg/m.
Sleepers (cross ties) type: Concrete 270 000, wood 50 000.
  Thickness: 6.7 in *(17 cm);*5.5 in *(14 cm)*
  Spacing: 25.6 in *(65 cm);* 23.6 in.-25.6 in *(60 and 65 cm)*.
Rail fastenings (types used): Pandrol; Hey-Back.

Rail fastenings: On main lines the principal fastenings to wood sleepers are Hey-Back and Deenik. Pandrol fastenings have been adopted as standard fastenings on concrete sleepers. On the new Bergen-Tunestveit line, and in long tunnels where UIC54 and S64 rails are used, the fastening is elastic double-shaft railspikes on hardwood sleepers-without baseplates.
On branch lines the fastenings consist mainly of dog spikes, wedge plates and Hey-Back.

Pads under rails: With Hey-Back fastenings a thin, 0.05 in *(1.25 mm)* rubber pad is inserted between rail and baseplate.
With "Pandrol" fastenings a 0.19 in *(5 mm)* thick plastic pad is inserted between rail and concrete sleeper.
As a general rule pads are not used under rails except with Hey-Back fastenings.

Welded rail: By 31 December 1978 the total length of track laid with welded rail was 2 228 km, the length laid during the year being 218 km. The programme for welding track in 1979 was 250 km.
Rails are pre-welded at depot or site by flash-butt method. Site welding into continuous length is generally thermit.
Several continuous welded rails in the open are more than 100 km long and the longest continuous welded rail is more than-200 km.
Sleepers used in welded track are:—

Under rail types	Material	Thickness	Width	Length
S35, S49	Soft Wood (fir)	5.5 in	9.84 in	8 ft 2.4 in
		(140 mm)	*(250 mm)*	*(2 500 mm)*
UIC54, S64	Hardwood (beech)	6.3 in	10.24 in	8 ft 6.4 in
		(160 mm)	*(260 mm)*	*(2 600 mm)*
UIC54, S54, S49, S41	Concrete	6.3 in	11.0 in	7 ft 6.6 in
		(170 mm)	*(280 mm)*	*(2 400 mm)*

It is intended to continue the laying of long continuous welded rail in main line track.

SIGNAL AND TRAIN CONTROL INSTALLATIONS

New signal installations (1974):
  Type: NSI 63.
  Route length: 44 miles *(71 km)*.
  Location: Vikersund-Hønefoss and Fredrikstad-Halden.
  Supplier: a/s Elektrisk Bureau, Oslo.

3 600-hp Bo-Bo electric locomotive built in Norway under licence from Brown Boveri

Class El 16 locomotive delivered in 1977/78 by Strommen and ASEA

6 930-hp electric locomotive built in Norway by Thunes under SLM licence

ELECTRIC LOCOMOTIVES

Class	Axle Arrange-ment	Line Current	Rated Output hp	Tractive Effort (Full Field) Max. lb *(kg)*	Tractive Effort Continuous at lb *(kg)*	mph *(km/h)*	Max. Speed mph *(km/h)*	Wheel dia. in *(mm)*	Weight tonnes	Length ft in *(mm)*	No. Built	Year Built	Builders: Mechanical Parts	Builders: Electrical Equipment
El-8	1-Do-1	15 kV 1/16⅔ ac	2 830	35 700 *(16 200)*	19 000 *(8 650)*	52 *(83)*	68 *(110)*	43⅞ *(1 350)*	83	45′ 3¼″ *(13 800)*	16	1940- 1949	Thunes	Norsk Electrisk; Brown Boveri
El-9	Bo-Bo	15 kV 1/16⅔ ac	970	22 700 *(10 300)*	13 700 *(6 200)*	22 *(36)*	37 *(60)*	39⅜ *(1 000)*	48	33′ 5½″ *(10 200)*	3	1947	Thunes	Norsk Electrisk; Brown Boveri
El-10	C	15 kV 1/16⅔ ac	700	23 400 *(10 600)*	11 700 *(5 300)*	17 *(27)*	28 *(45)*	43¼ *(1 100)*	47	31′ 6″ *(9 600)*	17	1949- 1952	A.S.J.	A.S.E.A.
El-11	Bo-Bo	15 kV 1/16⅔ ac	2 280	35 280 *(14 300)*	17 640 *(7 800)*	44 *(71)*	62 *(105)*	40⅜ *(1 060)*	62	47′ 5″ *(14 450)*	40	1951- 1964	Thunes	Norsk Electrisk; Brown Boveri
El-12	1-D+D-1	15 kV 1/16⅔ ac	6 520	99 200 *(45 000)*	8 157 *(3 700)*	31 *(60)*	47 *(75)*	53⅛ *(1 530)*	180	82′ 4″ *(26 490)*	4	1954- 1957	Motala	A.S.E.A.
El-13	Bo-Bo	15 kV 1/16⅔ ac	3 600	41 900 *(19 000)*	28 700 *(13 000)*	43 *(69)*	62 *(100)*	53⅛ *(1 350)*	72	49′ 2½″ *(15 000)*	37	1957- 1966	Thunes	Norsk Electrisk; Brown Boveri
El-14	Co-Co	15 kV 1/16⅔ ac	6 900	77 200 *(35 000)*	47 619 *(21 700)*	41 *(76)*	75 *(120)*	50 *(1 270)*	105	58′ 5″ *(17 740)*	31	1968- 1973	Thunes	Norsk Electrisk; Brown Boveri
El-15	2 (Co-Co)	15 kV 1/16⅔ ac	14 700	171 600 *(78 000)*	111 480 *(53 400)*	44 *(71)*	75 *(120)*	49¼ *(1 250)*	132	130′ 4″ *(19 900 +19 900)*	3	1967	Thunes	A.S.E.A.-Per Kure
El-16	Bo-Bo	15 kV *1/16⅔* ac	6 040	72 311 (32 800)	45 194 (20 500)	48 (78)	81 (140)	51 (1 300)	80	(15 520)	6	1977- 1978	Strømmen	A.S.E.A.

DIESEL LOCOMOTIVES

Class	Axle Arrange-ment	Trans-mission	Rated Power hp	Max. lb *(kg)*	Tractive Effort Continuous at lb *(kg)*	mph *(km/h)*	Max. Speed mph *(km/h)*	Wheel Dia. in *(mm)*	Total Weight Tons	Length ft in *(mm)*	No. Built	Year first Built	Builders: Mechanical Parts	Builders: Engine & Type	Builders: Transmission
Di 2	C	Hyd	575 600	30 600 *(13 900)*	26 500 *(12 000)*	3.7 *(6)*	50 *(80)*	49¼ *(1 250)*	45	32′ 10″ *(10 000)*	6 48	1954 1958	MaK Thunes	MaK MS301A BMV-LT6	Voith
Di 3a	Co-Co	Elec	1 775	48 500 *(23 000)*	37 900 *(17 200)*	14 *(23)*	65 *(105)*	40 *(1 016)*	102	61′ 0″ *(18 590)*	32	1954- 1969	NOHAB	GM 16-567C	GM-ASEA
Di 3b	(A1A)-	Elec	1 775	37 478 *(17 000)*	30 864 *(14 000)*	11 *(26)*	81 *(143)*	40 *(1 016)*	104	62′ 0″ *(18 900)*	3	1959	NOHAB	GM 16-567C	GM-ASEA

PAKISTAN

PAKISTAN RAILWAY (PR)

Shara-E-Sheikh Abdul Hameed Bin Badees, Lahore

Chairman, Railway Board: Gulzar Ahmad
Chief Engineer (Survey and Constructions): S. S. A. Wahidi
Chief Mechanical Engineer: Z. I. Puri
Chief Mechanical Engineer (Carriage Factory Project): M. Rashid
Chief Operating Superintendent: G. M. Khan
Chief Commercial Manager: A. B. Khan
Chief Controller of Stores: S. A. Hussain
Chief Controller of Purchase: S. M. Danial
Chief Personnel Officer: G. Abdullah
Chief Medical and Health Officer: Dr. A. H. Saeed
Chief Electrical Engineer: S. H. Nawab
Chief Officer (Administration and Budget): M. Siddique
Chief Officer (Research): S. A. Sasheed
Chief Superintendent (Watch and Ward): Rauf Ali
Chief Officer (Organisation and Research): M. A. Kahn
Chief Officer (Traffic): Muhammad Asghar
Financial Adviser and Chief Accounts Officer: A. Ahmed

Gauge: 1.675 m; 0.762 mm; 1 m
Route length: 7 754 km; 610 km; 444 km

A new five-year Rs 6 773 million development plan was announced in December 1977 for the period 1978/82. Major items of expenditure include: purchase of 133 diesel-electric locomotives; rebuilding of 60 locos and 25 diesel railcars; construction of 750 passenger coaches; and extension of the Lahore—Khanewal electrification to Samasatta (117 km). Emphasis has been laid on permanent way upgrading and renewal—some 1 200 km of track is to be relaid with heavier section rail and sleeper renewal carried out over 1 800 km. Five concrete sleeper plants are to be set up to reduce dependence on imported timber.

Construction of two important links is to be undertaken: the connection from Rawalpindi to Islamabad was to have been completed by March 1979 at a cost of Rs 40 million. Major task, however, will be a 99 km line connecting Chishtian, on the Samasatta—Bahawalnagar branch, with both the Lodhran—Raiwaind line at Mandi Burewala, and the Karachi—Lahore main line at Chichawatni Road. Cost of construction is put at Rs 240 million. Final location surveys have been completed and the line could open in 1983.

Another essential project is provision of modern telecommunications to replace the existing open-line network. Core of the system will be a microwave link between Karachi and Rawalpindi, with branches to Quetta, Multan and Lahore. Outlying areas will be served by UHF links, while VHF radio will be provided at about 200 base stations and in 500 locomotives, giving voice communication between controllers and moving trains. Automatic block signalling will be installed between Hyderabad and Lodhran and tokenless block between Lodhran and Wazirabad. Total cost will be Rs 372 million.

Other important works will include strengthening or renewal of bridges; further expansion of marshalling yard capacity; and modernisation of rolling stock works and maintenance procedures.

The total expenditure of Rs 8 000 million is more than double the figure originally budgetted for the period up to 1982-83. Foreign exchange element of the total is Rs 4 800 million, for which further loans will have to be sought.

TRAFFIC

Major problem for PR is lack of capacity through rolling stock shortages, bottlenecks and increasing demand. Passenger traffic rose by 17 per cent in 1977/78 from the 12 872 million passenger-km recorded in the previous year. This was followed by a further seven per cent rise in the first half of 1978/79. Freight demand also rose with tonne-km hauled in 1978/79 about 15 per cent up on the previous year's record.

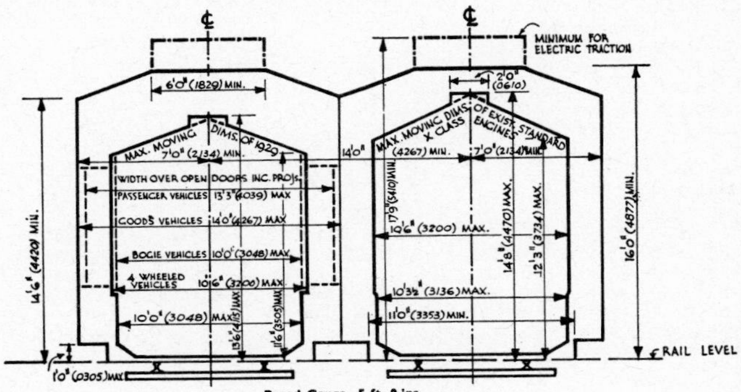

Broad Gauge—5 ft. 0 ins.

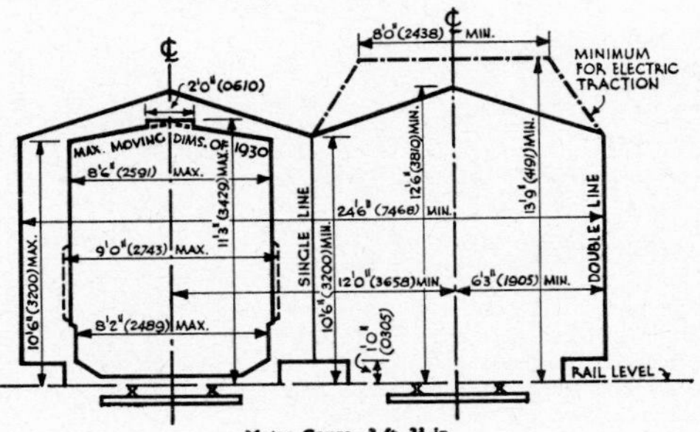

Metre Gauge—3 ft. 3⅜ in.

FINANCIAL

The highest operating ratio recorded was 87 per cent in 1974/75. By 1977/78 the figure was down to 72 per cent. Of the Rs 2 119 million earned in 1977/78, 30 per cent came from passengers, 65 per cent from freight and four per cent from parcels.

INVESTMENTS

Capital investment planned by PR up to 1982/83 is as follows:

	Foreign exchange Rs million	*Total investment Rs million*
Rolling stock (including improvements to braking systems)	1 037	2 104
Workshops	100	253
Track renewal	1 206	1 963
Electrification	76	160
New lines	7	112
Extra tracks and terminals	68	324
Bridge renewal	37	366
Marshalling yards	42	102
Signalling	48	119
Telecommunications	152	305
Miscellaneous and contingency including R & D	468	965
Totals	3 241	6 773

MOTIVE POWER AND ROLLING STOCK

Pakistan Railways is to recondition 47 life-expired diesel locomotives following a pilot project in which four locomotives were reconditioned for half the cost of equivalent new units. The work will be carried out in 1979/81 and will provide the locomotives with a further 20 years of useful life.

An ambitious programme for the building of 750 passenger coaches in the Islamabad coach factory has been outlined by Pakistan Railways. Of the total, 58 will be supplied to Bangladesh under a recently-signed contract. The scheme would involve building 150 coaches a year for five years, at a cost of Rs 1 120 million with a foreign exchange component of Rs 300 million. Major imports would include steel sheet, train lighting equipment, axle boxes, roller bearings and other components. Pakistan Railways expects to require 1 032 new coaches during the next five years if traffic projections prove correct.

In 1978 PR ordered 30 broad-gauge 1500 hp diesel-electric locomotives from Canada at a cost of Rs185 million. During the year it was announced that the railway is to spend a total of Rs 347 million on modernising the freight wagon fleet. Four-wheeled wagons are to be converted to bogie stock and air brakes and central couplings are to be fitted.

ELECTRIFICATION

The go-ahead was given by the government in 1978 for extension of electrification by 118 km from Khanewal to Samasata. Cost is put at Rs 170 million. PR's first electrification project was completed in 1970 when the 286 route-km Lahore-Khanewal line was electrified at 25 kV 50 Hz.

CIVIL ENGINEERING

Engineering surveys and traffic forecasts for a Pakistan Railways' link between Fort Sandeman and Manzai were completed by the end of 1977. The link will allow through running of narrow-gauge services from Boston along the Zhob river valley to Tank and Lakki Marwat. Pakistan Railways is also planning in the long term to convert the whole of the route to broad gauge to allow an alternative link from Baluchistan province to Northwest Frontier province other than the existing main line up the Indus valley. Economic viability of the scheme rests on opening up of magnesite and other mineral deposits along the route.

A new railway line is to be built between Dadu and Larkana, Prime Minister Mr Zulfikar Ali Bhutto announced in 1977. The line will run via Johi, Khairpur, Nathan Shah, Mehar, Nasirabad and Kambar.

Work began in May 1977 on a new railway passenger terminal in Karachi, Pakistan. Cost is estimated at Rs 60 million ($US 6 100 000). The terminal will have nine new passenger platforms, a terminal building with modern facilities, and an administrative block. Once the terminal comes into operation, the existing cantonment and city station will handle only freight trains and suburban passenger traffic.

The Federal Communications Ministry has proposed a double-track rapid transit system costing Rs 1 300 000 as the solution to Karachi's transport problems. Called the Integrated Mass Rapid Transit System, the underground line will link Mereweather Tower with North Karachi via Saddar, Liaquatabad and North Nazimabad— the route with the highest traffic density. It will also be linked with the Karachi Circular Railway which will be improved and extended to North Kårachi. According to the Ministry study, the present population of Karachi (4.5 million) will increase to 6.9 million by 1985 and 12.6 million by 2000. Peak hour traffic is expected to rise to between 30 000 and 40 000 an hour each way, on the route of the proposed rapid transit railway alone, by 1985. The annual recurring losses resulting from the lack of such a system are estimated at Rs 86 million in 1985. The study recommended against increasing the number of buses in the city on the grounds that this would aggravate air pollution and result in more accidents.

Work started in 1978 on construction of a new rail link between Chichawatni—Mandi Burewala—Chishtian at an estimated cost of Rs 234 million.

In 1979 PR was also building two additional railway links: Bahawalpur—Yazman (29.9 km) and the aforementioned Chichawatni—Burewala—Chishtian (99.4 km). Conversion of the 144 km Mari Indus—Bannu line from narrow-gauge to broad-gauge at a cost of Rs 130 million also began in 1979. PR launched a Rs 1 620 million six-year programme in 1977 to renew 1 223 km of track. In 1978 rails were renewed over 136 km of track using 50 kg/m rails and sleepers renewed over 32 km. Total cost was Rs 230 million. Branch lines over 72 km were also renewed using 45 kg/m rails.

PARAGUAY

FERROCARRIL PRESIDENTE CARLOS ANTONIO LOPEZ
Mejico 145, CC 453 Asuncion

Chairman of the Board of Directors of the Railway: Ricardo Garay
Director: Dr. Bader Rachid Lichi
Director: Arq. Miguel Angel Barrios Arce
Manager: Dr. Modesto Alí
Chief Accountant: Juan Manuel Arnella
Director of Planning: Dr. Héctor Benítez P.
Chief of the Statistic & Costing Dept.: Dr. Wildo Netto M.
Chief of the Warehouse Dept.: Eduardo Perinetti
Chief of the Traffic Dept.: Palmiro Rojas
Chief of the Workshop & Traction Dept.: Nemecio Encina
Chief of the Track & Work Dept.: Eng. Julio C. Zucchini
General Superintendent: Felipe Matianda
General Secretary: Aníbal Maidana
Chief of the Personnel Dept.: Lic. Ramon Ayala A.
Chief of Public Relations: Cap. Carlos Royg F.
Supervisor Bridges Buildings: Genero León
Treasurer: Jorge R. Esquivel

Gauge: 1.435 m
Route length: 440 km

Paraguay has four separate railways, only one being a passenger carrier, the F.C. Presidente Carlos Antonio Lopez, the others being industrial lines in western Paraguay and the Chaco.

The F.C. Presidente C.A. Lopez is the longest in the country, extending from Asuncion southeast to Encarnacion and Pacú-Cua, 234 miles *(376 km)* with a branch from San Salvador to Abai 40 miles *(65 km)* long. At Encarnacion a train ferry across the River

Alto Parana connects at Posadas with the Argentine State Railways (F.C. General Urquiza).

The present name was adopted when the former F.C. Central was acquired by the Paraguan Government at the end of 1961.

Plans were announced in 1977 to modernise the railway at a cost of about $US 70 million, covering electrification, track renewal, replacement of motive power and rolling stock. The plan would be carried out in two stages: 1) track renewal—rail and sleeper changing, realignment of some gradients and ballasting over the 376 km between Asunción and Pacúa Cúa on the Argentinian border. The first stage would also include purchase of new locomotives, freight wagons and passenger coaches, as well as new signalling and communications; 2) electrification.

TRAFFIC	1974	1975	1976	1977
Total freight ton-km	32 503 998	20 382 000	16 123 000	23 866 624
Total freight tonnage	144 367	—	—	95 488
Total passenger-km	26 980 764	23 550 000	16 086 000	17 581 899
Total passengers carried	207 619	—	—	155 053

FINANCES	1974	1976	1977
		(Guaranies)	
Revenues	247 669 357	259 874 000	250 373 924
Expenses	209 056 949	268 356 000	286 946 940

MOTIVE POWER AND ROLLING STOCK

Last motive power and rolling stock purchases were made in 1971 which increased the railway's locomotive fleet to 22 steam locomotives. Passenger coaches in service total 28; freight wagons 170.

ELECTRIFICATION

Electrification is projected on the 376 km Asunción-Encarnación line for completion by 1983. A Brazilian financial group made a loan of $US 70 million to Paraguay in 1978 to help finance the project. At the same time Argentina has agreed to provide technical assistance to improve the line at an estimated cost of $US 80 million.

PERU

ENAFER-PERU

Empresa Nacional de Ferrocarriles del Peru, Ancash 207, Lima

Telephone: 28-9440
Telex: 25068 PE ENAFER

General Manager: J. Acosta
Chief, Technical Division: Ing. Carlos Meneses
Technical Adviser: C. I. Mercer
Chief, Economic Commercial Division: C. Torres
Chief, Internal Control Office: F. Davila
Chief, Systems Department: C. Peña
Legal Adviser: A. Sierralta
Public Relations Officer: A. Santisteban
Budgets: G. Sifuentes
Office Supervisor: G. Rosenthal
Treasurer: V. Dianderas
Purchasing: A. Celis

Enafer-Perú was formed in 1972 with the nationalisation of The Peruvian Corporation railways, a private company who ran most of Perú's railways and the Lake Titicaca services. The system now comprises the Central and Southern Railways with headquarters in Lima and Arequipa respectively.

TRAFFIC	1977
Freight tonne-km	633 500 000
Freight tonnage	2 271 800
Passenger-km	551 039 575
Passenger journeys	3 442 124

The Central Railway hauled 1.4 million tonnes of freight (492 million tonne-km) in 1977 and made 1.2 million passenger journeys. Income was Soles 1 209 million and expenses Soles 1 230 million.

The Southern Railway hauled 942 300 tonnes of freight (939.5 million tonne-km) and made 2.5 million passenger journeys.

Income totalled Soles 1 373 million and expenditure Soles 1 449 million.

MLW DL 560 about to leave Desamparados station, Lima

FINANCES	1977
	(Soles Oro)
Revenues	2 369 254 000
Expenses	2 575 690 000

CENTRAL RAILWAY

ENAFER—Ferrocarril del Centro
Ferrocarril del Centro del Perú
Ancash 201, Lima

Acting Manager: G. Corrales
Operations: W. Medina
Traffic: P. O'Brien
Mechanical: J. Wright
Purchasing: A. Celis

Gauge: 1.435 m, 0.914 m
Route length: 384 km, 129 km

ROLLING STOCK

40 locomotives (7 oil, 31 diesel-electric, 3 diesel-mechanical). 1 279 freight cars, 54 passenger cars, 10 rail motor, 124 miscellaneous.

The total route length with branches is 240 miles *(384 km)* of standard gauge and 80 miles *(129 km)* of narrow gauge. The standard gauge main line runs 216 miles *(346 km)* from Callao to Huancayo where it connects with the 80 mile *(129 km)* 3 ft 0 in *(0.914 m)* gauge line to Huancavelica.
There are 66 tunnels with aggregate length of 5.3 miles *(8.9 km)*, 59 bridges and 9 zig-zags (reversing stations) on the standard gauge section and 38 tunnels on the narrow gauge line.
The main line climbs from sea level to its highest point 15 688 ft *(4 782 m)* in the Galera Tunnel in 106 miles *(171 km)* from Callao on an average gradient of 1 in 25 (4 per cent).
The highest point on the system is 15 844 ft *(4 829 m)* at a siding at La Cima on the Ticlio-Morococha branch. This makes it the highest standard gauge line in the world.
The steepest gradients occur in the first 138 miles *(222 km)* from Callao, at sea level to Oroya at 12 222 ft *(3 726 m)* above sea level.

SOUTHERN RAILWAY

ENAFER—Ferrocarril del Sur
Ferrocarril del Sur
Casilla 194, Arequipa

Acting Manager: V. C. Foulkes
Traffic: A. Vizcarra
Mechanical: D. Russell
Operations: V. Foulkes
Chief Engineer: R. Ricketts

Gauge: 1.435 m, 0.914 m
Route length: 923 km, 172 km

ROLLING STOCK

52 locos (6 oil, 43 diesel-electric, 3 diesel-mechanical), 900 freight cars, 122 passenger cars, 30 rail motor cars, 133 miscellaneous.

STEAMSHIP SERVICE

Lake Titicaca 204 kms from Puno, Perú to Guaqui, Bolivia.
Ships comprise of 1 train ferry, 3 passenger-freight vessels, 1 dredger and 2 launches.
The total route length with branches is 576 miles *(923 km)* of standard gauge and 107 miles *(172 km)* of narrow gauge. The standard gauge main line runs from Mollendo to Juliaca 297 miles *(476 km)* where the line divides, to the right to Puno 29 miles *(47 km)* for connection with the Lake Titicaca steamer service to Bolivia and to the left to Cuzco 211 miles *(338 km)* where it connects with the 107 mile *(172 km)* 3 ft 0 in *(0.914 m)* gauge line to Quillabamba.
The main line climbs from sea level to its highest point at Crucero Alto 14 688 ft *(4 477 m)* in 224 miles *(359 km)* from Mollendo on an average gradient of 1 in 33 (3 per cent).
The steamer service on Lake Titicaca at 12 526 ft *(3 818 m)* is the highest in the world.

The Cuzco-Quillabamba narrow gauge passes Machupicchu, site of an Inca township, discovered in 1911 and which thousands of tourists visit yearly.

TACNA-ARICA RAILWAY

(Administered by Southern Railway)
A Aldarracin 484, Tacna

Gauge: 1.435 m
Route length: 62 km

ROLLING STOCK

1 steam locomotive, 40 freight cars, 1 passenger car, 9 rail motor cars.

PERMANENT WAY

The military government has recently made several announcements on new lines to be built in the near future such as Chimbote-Lima-Nazca; a coastal line that would link the iron ore deposits of Nazca with the steel making complex in Chimbote. The joining of the Central and Southern Railways by standard gauge track between Huancayo and Cuzco which would then give, via the Lake Titicaca service, rail connection from Lima to the capitals of Bolivia, Chile, Argentina and Brazil. Also a line from La Oroya on the Central Railway to Pucallpa on the River Ucayali which would give access to the unexploited rich agricultural and forest lands on the eastern slopes of the Andes and the upper Amazon basin.
Plans for the development of the railways is in the hands of the Ministry of Transport; Enafer-Peru acts solely in an operational role.

Standard rail:
80 lb/yd *(39.7 kg/m)* BS(R)
75 lb/yd *(37.2 kg/m)* BSS
75 lb/yd *(37.2 kg/m)* ASCE
70 lb/yd *(34.7 kg/m)* ASCE
70 lb/yd *(34.7 kg/m)* Livesey
Lengths: 24, 30, 33, 39 and 46 ft
Joints: 4-hole angle fishplates and bolts.
Cross ties (sleepers): Peruvian hardwood, 8 in × 6 in × 8 ft 0 in—1 435 mm track, 8 in × 6 in × 6 ft—914 mm track.
Made-up sleepers consisting of 2 blocks of reinforced concrete joined by a piece of used rail have been used in sidings and on straight stretches of main line.
Spacing:
Main line: 2 575-2 735 per mile *(1 600-1 700 per km)*
Branch line: 2 195-2 735 per mile *(1 365-1 700 per km)*
Rail fastenings:
Soleplates and ⅞ in coachscrews.
Soleplates and ⅝ in dogspikes.
Pandrol fastenings are being fitted where new 80 lb/yd rail is being laid.
Filling: 2 in to 4 in broken stone ballast; 6 in under tie on main lines and 3 in on branch lines.
Max curvature: 17.5° = min rad of 328 ft *(100 m)*
Max gradient: 4.4% = 1 in 22.7 uncompensated.
Worst combination of curve and grade: 512 ft *(156 m)* curve on 4.22% (1 in 23.7) grade for 771 ft *(235 m)*
Gauge widening on sharpest curve: ½ in *(12.7 mm)*
Super-elevation on sharpest curve: 4 in *(101.6 mm)* speed limited.
Rate of slope of super-elevation: 1 in 360.
Max altitude: 15 844 ft *(4 829 m)*. On the Central Railway at La Cima siding on Ticlio-Morococha Branch, 107 miles *(173 km)* from Callao. On main line; 15 690 ft *(4 782 m)* inside Galera Tunnel, 107 miles *(172 km)* from Callao.
Max axle loading: 18.52 tons.
Bridge loading: Coopers E-40.
Max permitted speed:
Standard gauge: 50 mph (80 km/h) on level and low gradient section.
31 mph (50 km/h) on high gradient sections.
Narrow gauge: 37 mph (60 kph).

DIESEL LOCOMOTIVES

Class	Axle Arrangement	Transmission	Rated Power hp	Max. lbs (kg)	Tractive Effort Continuous at lbs (kg)	mph (km/h)	Max. Speed mph (km/h)	Wheel Dia. ins (mm)	Total Weight Tons	Length ft ins (mm)	No. Built	Year first Built	Builders: Mechanical Parts	Engine & Type	Transmission
DL 531	Co-Co	Electric	675		(18 000)	—		40	71.6	46' 7''	1	1958	ALCO	6 cyl 251 B	Electric
DL 532	Bo-Bo	Electric	950		(14 736)	(14.5)	(80)	40	69.4	(14 390)	5	1974	MLW	6 cyl 251 B	Electric
DL 535A	Co-Co	Electric	1 200		(23 760)	(8.1)	(80)	40	69.7	(15 420)	2	1967	ALCO	6 cyl 251 B	Electric
DL 535B	Co-Co	Electric	1 200		(23 760)	(8.1)	(80)	40	81.4	(1 5410)	14	1963	ALCO	6 cyl 251 B	Electric
DL 535B	Co-Co	Electric	1 200		(22 068)	(8.1)	(80)	40	81.0	(15 410)	5	1974	MLW	6 cyl 251 D	Electric
DL 500	Co-Co	Electric	1 340		(20 863)	(19.5)	(100)	40	163,7	(17 958)	6	1956	ALCO	12 cyl 251 B	Electric
DL 543	Co-Co	Electric	1 800		(23 818)	(19.2)	(100)	40	110	(17 794)	11	1962	ALCO	12 cyl 251 B	Electric
DL 560	Co-Co	Electric	2 400		(32 600)	(14.8)	(105)	43	110	(17 272)	14	1964	ALCO	16 cyl 251 B	Electric
DL 560	Co-Co	Electric	2 400		(32 600)	(14.8)	(105)	43	110	(17 120)	15	1974	MLW	16 cyl 251 E	Electric

PHILIPPINES

PHILIPPINE NATIONAL RAILWAYS (PNR)

943 Claro M. Recto Avenue, Manila

Telephone: 210011

Chairman: Col. Salvador T. Villa
Vice-Chairman: Col. Nicanor T. Jimenez
Members: Roberto V. Reyes
Alfredo Pio de Roda, Jr
Aber P. Canlas
Victor G. Nituda
Antonio M. Locsin
General Manager: Nicanor T. Jimenez
Asst. Gen. Manager on Admin.: Benjamin C. Garcia
AGM on Civil Engineering: Pio G. Valle
AGM on Finance: Benito P. Isip
AGM on Development: Dionisio Figueroa

AGM on Rolling Stock: Jesus Remotigue
AGM on Trans-Mark: Juan N. de Castro Jr
Corporation Auditor: Amancio Garcia
Corporate Secretary: Rodolfo G. Flores
Director, PEG: Cesar Poblete
Chief, Executive Dept.: Salvacion Bundoc
Personnel Manager: Dominador F. Macaranas
Chief, Corp. Legal Counsel: Jose B. Calimlim
Chief, Actg. Dept.: Francisco V. Silva
Chief, Const. Engineer: Jose Bonuel
Chief, Engineer Dept.: Ramon Mariano
Mech. Supt.: Jacinto Oller
Medical Director: Felicisimo Manalese
Purchasing Agent: Simeon dela Cruz
Real Estate Manager: Recaredo Lagula
Manager, Motor Service: Cesar Diaz
Supt. Transport: Jose G. Nuguid
Marketing Manager: Delfin E. Reyes
Treasurer: Julita G. Vida
Manager Commuter, Service Management Body: Ramon Jimenez

Traction fleet includes

Particulars	901-905	1001-1010	2001-2020	1501-1510	2501-2513	3001-3010	4001-4010
Class	Streamliner	Streamliner	Streamliner	Streamliner	Streamliner	Road Switcher	Road Switcher
Type (Road No.)	900 type	1000 type	2000 type	1500 type	2500 type	3000 type	4000 type
Wheel (or axle) arrangement	C-C	C-C	C-C	B-B-B	B-B	B-B	B-B
Max speed	82 mph	60 mph	60 mph	60 mph	60 mph	60 mph	40 mph
Dimension							
Width	2 717 mm	2 821 mm	2 821 mm	2 749 mm	2 749 mm	2 743 mm	2 921 mm
Height	3 732 mm	3 683 mm	3 683 mm	3 372 mm	3 687 mm	3 687 mm	3 687 mm
Weight	180 000 lb	182 000 lb	192 000 lb	60.5 tons	120 000 lb	120 000 lb	104 000 lb
Number of units	5	10	20	10	13	10	10
Builders	General Electric	General Electric	General Electric	Alsthom	General Electric	General Electric	General Electric
Tractive effort	54 000 lb	37 400 lb	37 400 lb	38 000 lb	26 400 lb	32 200 lb	16 500 lb

Gauge: 1.00 m
Route length: 1 060 km

PNR is carrying out extensive modernisation and track upgrading with the aid of Asian Development Bank loans. During 1977 a consultancy contract valued at $US 1 million was awarded to Rail India Technical and Economic Services using proceeds of the loan.

TRAFFIC
Passenger traffic fell from 12.9 million journeys in 1977 to 9.6 million in 1978 while passenger revenues dropped from $US 6.6 million to $US5.8 million. During 1978 PNR carried 158 700 tonnes of general freight compared with 194 263 tonnes in 1977 and 347 000 tonnes in 1974. General freight contributed $US 700 000 in revenues in 1978 compared with $1.2 million in 1975. Express freight totalling 37 168 tonnes in 1978 contributed $500 000 to revenues.

PERMANENT WAY
A major project for the total rehabilitation of Philippine National Railways 474 km Southern Lines, from Manila to Legaspi, got underway in May 1979 following the granting of the $US 24 million loan from the Asian Development Bank. Work should be completed within by 1981. The work will involve spreading 367 000 m³ of new ballast and 383 000 m³ of earthworks; and laying 604 800 new sleepers. New and recovered steel rails will be welded to 60 m lengths. New rail fastenings will also be used between Manila and Naga City—a distance of 378 km. In addition, PNR will continue its track doubling on the Manila suburban network. Track is to be doubled out to San Pedro, Laguna, a distance of 35 km, to make it possible to improve commuter train frequencies. Cost is estimated at $162 000 per km.
The Philippines government has approved in principle a proposal to establish a 1 321 million pesos ($US 178 million) railway system in Mindanao to link productive areas in the south with coastal towns in the north. Implementation, however, will depend on whether Philippine National Railways officers give the project priority over the previously approved railway extension to Cagayan Valley. PNR cannot undertake both projects simultaneously because of the huge financial requirement. The proposed Mindanao system would have two main routes. The first would run 330 km from Koronadal, South Cotabato, through Carmen and Malaybalay to Cagayan de Oro City. Cost of the line would be about 620 million pesos. The second line would run 232 km from Magonoy, North Cotabato, to Iligan City passing through Datu Piang, Pigawayan and Molundo.
A new 344 km railway system on Panay Island in the Philippines has also been proposed by General Salvador Abcede, manager of Philippine National Railway services on Panay. The new system, now being studied by the Negros Occidental provincial government, calls for construction of new rail lines between Hinobaan in the south and San Carlos in the north.
A track doubling programme has progressed 11.5 km from Paco to Food Terminal, Inc. junction. The project will reach San Pedro, Laguna, covering 35 km to speed up movement of trains to and from the south and to maximise commuter train frequencies between Manila and Laguna.

TRACK
Standard rail:
  Main line:
    65 lb/yd *(32.2 kg/m)* in 30 and 33 ft lengths.
    75 lb/yd *(37.2 kg/m)* in 33 ft lengths.
  Branch lines:
    65 lb/yd *(32.2 kg/m)* in 30 ft lengths.
    54 lb/yd *(26.8 kg/m)* in 30 ft lengths.
    45 lb/yd *(22.3 kg/m)* in 23 ft lengths.
Type of rail joints: Angle bars with slots for spikes.
Cross ties (sleepers):
  Main line: "Molave" wood, 5 in × 8 in × 7 ft *(127 × 203 × 2 133 mm)*, spaced at 22 in *(558 mm)*
  Branch line: "Molave"wood, 5 in × 8 in × 7 ft *(127 × 203 × 2 133 mm)*, spaced at 24 in *(610 mm)*
  Bridge ties: "Yacal" wood, 8 in × 8 in × 8 ft *(203 × 203 × 2 438 mm)*, spaced at 16 in *(406 mm)*
  A limited number of steel ties are also used.
Rail fastenings: Track spikes; bolts with square nuts; "Hipower" nutlock washer; "elastic rail spikes".
Filling: Volcanic slag; river gravel with 15% sand; some crushed rock.
Max curvature:
  Main line: 9.2° = min rad of 623 ft *(190 m)*
  Branch line: 11½° = min rad of 492 ft *(150 m)*
Max gradient: Compensated, 2.6% = 1 in 38½.
Max gradient: Uncompensated, 1.2% = 1 in 38.
Max axle load: 35 000 lb.
Max permitted speed: 37.5 mph *(60 km/h)*
Signalling: In the Manila terminal area 13.6 km of double track line with semaphore signals controlled from interlocker cabins. On single track lines elsewhere trains operated on English "Staff" system or by telegraph or telephone communication from station to station.

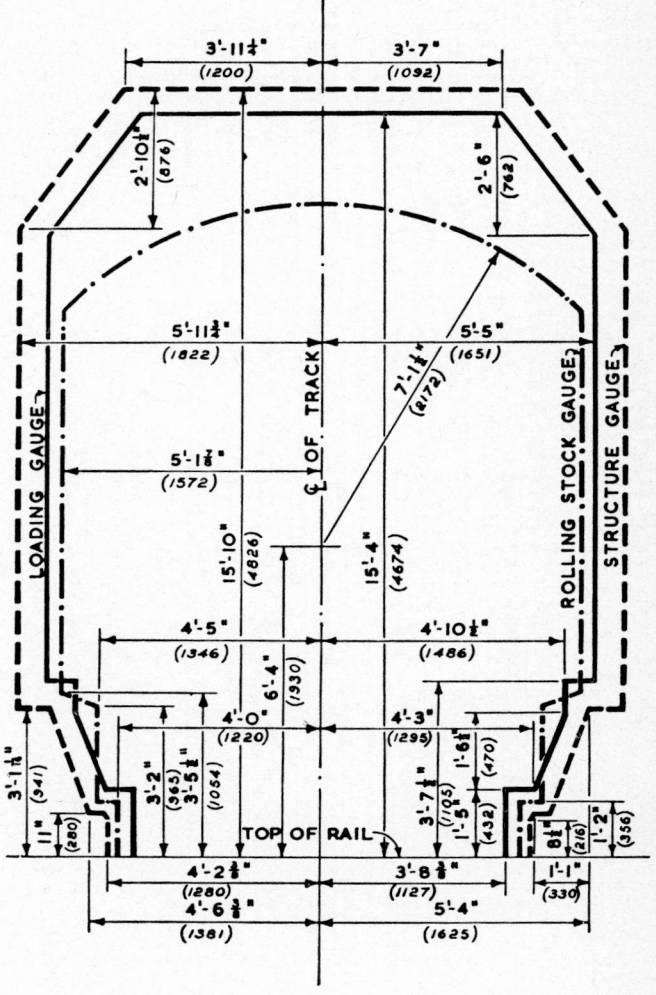

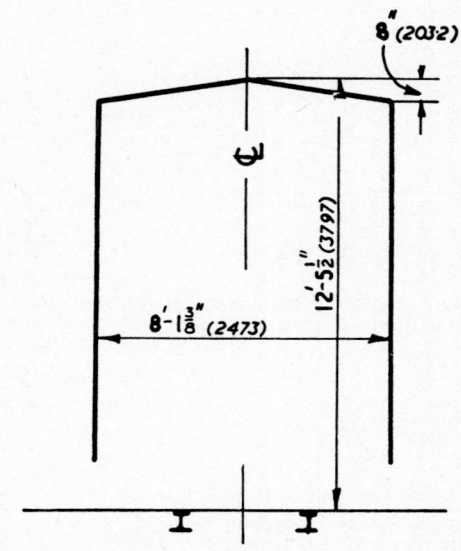

POLAND

POLISH STATE RAILWAYS
Polskie Koleje Panstwowe (PKP) ul Chalubinskiego 4, 00-928 Warsaw

Telephone: Warsaw 24-43-00

Under-Secretaries of State: J. Glowacki, Cz. Gościłowicz, K. Jacukowicz, J. Kamiński, W. Konikowski, A. Markowski, J. Raczkowski
Director, Press Service: K. Pierzyński
Director, Economic Co-operation: W. August
Director, Economic Department: K. Ratajczak
Director, Financial Department: Cz. Gierałtowski
Director, Chief of Investments: E. Kopciński

Gauge: 1.435 m
Route length: 23 953 km

The development of industrial production and the turnover of foreign trade have resulted in PKP being unable to meet demand. There is a shortage of open coal wagons which in addition to coal are used for other bulk loads such as stone, sand, gravel, ore, sugar beet and potatoes.
The greatest share of freight traffic is handled by the Silesian Railway Directorate in Katowice. In 1977 that share amounted to 46.1 per cent. The large part of freight is coal which accounted for 151 million tonnes in 1977. The average daily loadings of coal in week days were 430 000 tonnes and 490 000 tonnes on peak days. The overbalance in export movements results in a large number of empty coal wagons moving into the Silesian region.
Upper Silesia is a highly industrialised region. Besides coal mines there are a number of steel works, one of which is the huge Katowice plant operational from 1976.
To provide regular deliveries to Katowice a 400 km railway line has been built from the Soviet border to the steel mill. The first ore trains on the 1.520 m gauge new line were put in operation in 1979.

TRAFFIC
In freight traffic movements the share of automobile transport is increasing, especially over short distances. In 1970 automobiles accounted for 862.6 million tonnes, increasing to 1 750 million tonnes in 1975 and 2 039 million tonnes in 1977 (40.3 million tonne-km).
In 1977 freight traffic carried on normal gauge lines totalled 18.7 per cent in tonnes and 77 per cent in tonne-km of total freight transportation.
In 1977 the railway carried nearly 1 143 million passengers (44.2 million passenger-km).
In the same year the buses of the State Automobile Transport carried 2 328 million passengers (48 200 million) passenger-km).

	1976	1977	1978*
Freight tonne-km (millions)	130 857	137 000	144 300
Freight tonnage ('000)	465 200	470 000	496 000
Passenger-km ('000)	42 799	44 312	46 600
Passenger journeys (millions)	1 109	1 142.9	1 110

*Estimated

	1977	1978
Total train-km	429 171	430 404
Percentage of train km by steam	21.39	17.62
by diesel	33.70	35.82
by electric	44.91	46.56
Total freight tonnage	481 056	489 385
Average haul	287.1	287.8
Average net train load	702	711
Average wagon load	30.33	31.14
Total passenger-km	44 312	46 716
Total passengers carried	1 151 703	1 131 986

FINANCES

	1977	1978
	(Zlotys)	
Revenues from passengers and baggage	10 353 678	10 460 057
Average receipt per passenger-km	22.1124	21.1961
Revenues from freight and mail	56 739 733	58 794 245
Average receipt per freight tonne-km	35.8889	36.3500
Total revenues	67 093 411	69 254 302

MOTIVE POWER AND ROLLING STOCK
Deliveries in 1977 included 93 electrical locomotives, 349 diesel locomotives, 12 421 freight wagons, 585 passenger cars and 80 three-car electrical trainsets for suburban and local passenger traffic. 330 steam locomotives were outserviced. The plan for 1980 provides for the purchase of 14 000 freight wagons, 180 electric locomotives, 220 diesel locomotives, 80 electric trainsets and 485 passenger cars.

ELECTRIFICATION
Electrification of about 1 700 km during the 1971-75 plan brought the length of electrified lines to about 5 588 route-km, 24 per cent of the PKP network.
The electrification programme plans for electric traction over 10 000 to 11 000 km (40 per cent of the network) by 1985. 2 500 km are being electrified as part of the 1976-1980 Five-Year Plan; at the same time, the PKP is continuing the work of providing the network with electric locomotives.
By the end of 1977 electrified route length totalled 6 308 km at 3 000 V dc and 45 km at 600 V dc. Electrically-hauled trains began service between Poznan Stargard in early 1978, completing the penultimate stage of the Poznan—Szczecin electrification. Energisation was completed to Szczecin by the end of 1978.

PERMANENT WAY
Investment has doubled since 1969 and more than 1 200 km of new line is being built between 1976-80. Most important project is the metal and sulphur line from Hrubieszow and the Katowice steelworks. The first section from Zawiercie to Radzice has already been completed. The second section from Idzikowice to Warsaw is being built and electrified and the third section to Plock with a branch line to Modlin will be completed later. PKP plans to specialise more in long-haul bulk transport with shuttle services carrying coal, building materials, ore and farm produce. Electrification was to be increased from 6 000 to 8 000 km by 1980. Main problems at the moment seem to be inadequate capacity of track and stations, shortage of rolling stock and a slow turn-round of wagons.
In the five years up to 1971 only 160 km of new line was laid. During the last plan (1971-75) about 1 200 km was laid. Most important new line was the central trunk line from Silesia to Warsaw with the first 143 km section between Zawiercie and Radzice entering service in 1974. At the end of 1978 route length was expected to total 24 001 km. During 1978 reports were received that tracklaying on the 1.524 m gauge steelworks line from Hrubieszow to Katowice (200 km) was completed, the 222 km new north-south line from Grodzisk on the outskirts of Warsaw to Zawiercie (Silesia) was in

Six axle type 601 freight wagon

New type Wars dining car

Class SP-47 locomotive delivered in 1977/78 by Cegielski: rated output 3 000 hp

Emu EW-58n which first entered service in 1976

operation, with track doubling to be completed over the route during 1978; also track doubling on the Gniezno-Tzew line was underway.

Sleepers: These are of both wood type INBK4 and concrete type INBK3 5¾ in (15 cm) and 7⁷/₁₆ in (19 cm) in thickness respectively. Wooden pads 7 mm thick are used under the rails.

Welded rail: At the end of 1973 the total length of track with welded rail was 2 548 miles (4 874.5 km) of which 491 miles (790 km) were laid during the year. The longest length of continuous welded rail was 4.3 miles (7.0 km.)
Rails used are Type S 49, Type S 42, and Type S 60 in 98 ft 5 in (30 m) lengths, flash butt welded in workshop and thermit welded at site. Rails are secured to either wood or concrete sleepers (cross ties) by "K" type fastenings, and are laid by means of mobile cranes.

ELECTRIC LOCOMOTIVES

Class	Axle Arrangement	Line Current V Type	Rated Power hp	Max kg	Tractive Effort Continuous at kg	kmlh	Max Speed kmlh	Wheel Dia mm	Total Weight tonnes	Length mm	No. built	Year First Built	Builders Mechanical Parts	Electrical Equipment
EP02	BoBo	3 000 dc	1 840				100	1 220	81.0	15 000		1953	Pafawag	Pafawag
EP03	BoBo	3 000 dc	2 500				100	1 220	81.2	14 170		1951	AS	ASEA
EU04	BoBo	3 000 dc	2 900	23 000	1 700	45.5	110	1 350	86.0	16 370		1954	LEW	LEW
EU05	BoBo	3 000 dc	2 820	24 800	11 400	63.0	125	1 250	82.5	16 140		1960	Skoda Pilzno	Skoda Pilzno
EU06	BoBo	3 000 dc	2 720	26 500	14 400	49.0	125	1 250	80.0	15 915		1961	Vulcan Fdry.	AEI/EE
EU07	BoBo	3 000 dc	2 720	26 500	14 400	49.0	125	1 250	80.0	15 915		1963	Pafawag	Dolmel
EP05	Bo-Bo	3 000 dc	2 820	24 800	8 820	82.7	140/160	1 250	80.0	16 140		1973	Skoda Pilzno	Skoda Pilzno
EP08	BoBo	3 000 dc	2 720	25 500	10 600	63.0	140/160	1 250	82.0	15 915		1973	Pafawag	Dolmel
EU20	CoCo	3 000 dc	4 340	32 000	2 300	50.0	110	1 350	120.0	18 500		1955	LEW	LEW
ET21	CoCo	3 000 dc	3 270	32 000	14 900	49.6	100	1 250	121.0	16 500		1957	Pafawag	Dolmel
EU22	CoCo	3 000 dc	4 080	35 000	21 600	50.0	125	1 250	120.0	19 240		1971	Pafawag	Dolmel
ET40	BoBo + BoBo	3 000 dc	5 660	50 000	31 500	46.4	100	1 250	1 640	34 420		1975	Skoda Pilzno	Skoda Pilzno
ET41	BoBo + BoBo	3 000 dc	5 440	50 000	28 300	50.6	100	1 250	166.0	31 880		1977	Cegielski	Dolmel
ET42	BoBo + BoBo	3 000 dc	5 830	50 000	29 360	52.1	125	1 250	164.0	31 000		1978	Nowoczerkask	Nowoczerkask

DIESEL LOCOMOTIVES

Class	Axle Arrangement	Transmission	Rated Power hp	Max kg	Tractive Effort Continuous at kg	kmlh	Max Speed kmlh	Wheel Dia mm	Axle Load Tons	Total Weight Tons	Length mm	No. Built	Year first Built	Builders Mechanical Parts	Engine	Transmission
SM02	B	Mech	44	4 000			12	850	8.0	16.0	6 000		1955	Chrzanow	Nowotko	Dolmel
SM03	B	Mech	150	5 043			45	950	12.0	24.0	7 000		1960	Chrzanow	Nowotko	Dolmel
SM25	C	Hyd	350	12 700			60	1 100	12.5	37.4	8 600		1961	Chrzanow	Nowotko	Voith
SM30	BoBo	Elec	300	7 500	3 200	15.0	60	850	9.0	36.0	9 440		1956	Chrzanow	Nowotko	Dolmel
SM31	CoCo	Elec	1 200	36 000	16 500	12.3	80	1 100	20.0	120.0	17 000		1976	Chrzanow	Cegielski	Dolmel
SM40	BoBo	Elec	600	18 600	10 400	9.6	80	1 040	15.44	61.76	11 290		1958	Ganz-Mavag	Ganz-Mavag	Ganz
SM41	BoBo	Elec	600	18 600	10 400	9.6	80	1 040	15.44	61.76	11 290		1958	Ganz-Mavag	Ganz-Mavag	Ganz
SM42	BoBo	Elec	800	22 300	11 460	12.5	90	1 100	18.0	72.0	14 240		1967	Chrzanow	Cegielski	Dolmel
SP42	BoBo	Elec	800	23 500	11 400	12.5	90	1 100	17.0	68.0	14 240		1971	Chrzanow	Cegielski	Dolmel
ST43	CoCo	Elec	2 100	32 000	20 000	21.5	100	1 100	19.4	116.4	17 000		1965	EpCr	Resica	EpCr
ST44	CoCo	Elec	2 000	35 000	20 000	20.0	100	1 050	19.4	116.5	17 550		1966	Novoszytowgrad	Kolomna	Charków
SP45	CoCo	Elec	1 700	30 800	13 350	24.8	120	1 100	17.0	102.0	18 990		1968	Cegielski	Cegielski	Dolmel
SU46	CoCo	Elec	2 250	31 700	16 350	28.75	120	1 100	17.5	105.0	18 990		1976	Cegielski	Cegielski	Dolmel
SP47	CoCo	Elec	3 000	38 130/3 597	18 580/15 930	31.8/37.3	120/140	1 100	19.0		20 180		1978	Cegielski	Cegielski	Domel

PORTUGAL

PORTUGUESE RAILWAYS

Companhia dos Caminhos de Ferro Portugueses (CP),
Calçada do Duque 20, 1294 Lisbon

Telephone: 36 31 81
Telex: 12382 Ferpol P

New Alsthom railcar built for CP

Management Council:
Chairman: Eng. Amilcar Marques
Members: Eng. Almeida e Castro
Eng. Gonçalves Ferreira
Dr. Pestana Bastos
Dr. Manuel Moura
Dr. Monteiro Pais

Administration Main Officers:
Master Plan: Eng Belém Ferreira
Planning: Dr. José Aleluia
Information: Dr. Figueiredo e Sousa
Legal Office: Dr. Tinoco de Faria
Public Relations and Press: Dr. Américo Ramalho
Design: Scp. Santa Bárbara
Administration Secretary: Dr. Chaves Brilhante

Operations
Director: Eng. Abilio Rodrigues
Assistant Director: Eng. Victor Biscaia
Commercial Department: Eng. Álvaro Campelo
Fixed Installations Department: Eng. Martins Pinheiro
Northern Region: Eng. Fernando Ávila
Central Region: Eng. Feio Borges
Southern Region: A. M. Coelho Rodrigues
Cascais Line: Eng. Felizardo Brazão
Sintra Line: Vilaca e Moura

Equipment
Director: Eng. Moreira de Andrade
Assistant Directors: Eng. Moreira Andrade
Eng. Fernando Salvado

Financial
Director: Dr. Leal Rosa

Personnel
Director: Eng. Luis Areias

Purchasing & Supplying Division
Manager: Eng. Camarate de Campos
Assistant Manager: Eng. Abilio Lopes

Gauge: 1.665 m; 1.00 m.
Route length: 2 807 km; 759 km

TRAFFIC
In 1977 CP carried 885 million tonne-km of freight and 4 454 million passenger-km.

FINANCES

Revenues	1978 (Contos)
Passengers and baggage	2 826 667
Freight and mail	921 874
Total	10 598 697
Expenditure	
Staff/Personnel	5 196 753
Materials and services	1 678 447
Depreciation	382 247
Financial charges	2 286 152
Total	10 241 240

INVESTMENTS
In 1978 CP spent 1 410 million escudos on infrastructure investments, mainly on track renewal and new line construction (Sines), and 1 559 million escudos on rolling stock acquisition and improvement.
Plans for 1979 envisaged a capital investment of 3 415 million escudos of which 1 538 million were to be capital investments on rolling stock acquisition.

MOTIVE POWER AND ROLLING STOCK
By the beginning of 1979 the railway owned 225 diesel locomotives (208 broad-gauge and 17 narrow-gauge), 46 broad-gauge electric locomotives, 36 narrow-gauge steam, 95 motor coaches and trailers, 98 diesel railcars and 45 trailers, 12 petrol railcars, 564 passenger coaches and 5 318 freight wagons for broad-gauge and 593 for narrow-gauge.

DIESEL LOCOMOTIVES

Class	Axle Arrangement	Transmission	Rated Power hp	Max. kg	Tractive Effort: Continus at kg	kmlh	Max. Speed kmlh	Wheel Dia. mm	Total Weight Tonnes	Length mm	No. Built	Year first Built	Builders: Mechanical Parts	Engine & Type	Transmission
9001/ 003	Bo-Bo	Elec	572	11 500	11 000	15	70	950	46.00	11 174	3	1959	Alsthom	SACM	Alsthom
9004/ 006	Bo-Bo	Elec	590	11 500	9 000	17.5	70	950	46.00	11 174	3	1959	Alsthom	SACM	Alsthom
9021/ 031	Bo-Bo	Elec	715	11 500	10 600	21.5	70	950	46.65	11 360	11	1976	Alsthom	SACM	Alsthom
1001/ 1006	C	Mech	160	7 600	—	—	41.5	991	30.40	7 815	6	1948	Drewry	Gardner	Sinclair
1021/ 1025	B	Elec	425	9 720	9 720	12	65	1 050	36.00	9 090	5	1968	Moyse	Deutz	Moyse
1051/ 1068	B	Elec	120	7 000	7 000	4	38	1 050	28.30	7 280	13	1955	Moyse	Moyse	Moyse
1101/ 1112	Bo-Bo	Elec	255	10 000	4 258	10	56	965	41.20	10 210	11	1946	GE	Caterpillar	GE
1151/ 1186	C	Hyd	250	11 400	—	—	58	1 090	42.00	8 517	36	1966	Sorefame	Rolls-Royce	Rolls-Royce
1201/ 1225	Bo-Bo	Elec	600	16 000	12 200	13	80	1 100	64.70	14 680	25	1961	Sorefame	Ste Alsacienne	Brissoneau & Lotz
1301/ 1312	(A1A)(A1A)	Elec	1 020	15 900	11 140	27	120	1 016	95.40	17 060	12	1952	Whitcomb	Superior	Westinghouse
1401/ 1467	Bo-Bo	Elec	1 025	16 100	14 200	19	105	950	64.40	12 720	65	1967	Sorefame	EE	EE
1501/ 1521	(A1A)(A1A)	Elec	1 730	—	2 100	21	120	1 016	111.00	16 988	17	1948	ALCO	ALCO	GE
1551/ 1570	Co-Co	Elec	1 700	24 300	19 300	22.5	120	1 016	89.70	17 905	20	1973	MLW	MLW/ALCO	Canadian-GE
1801/ 1810	Co-Co	Elec	2 050	26 000	17 750	31	140	1 100	110.30	18 680	10	1968	EE	EE	EE
1961/ 1973	Co-Co	Elec	2 251	45 000	28 200	18.75	120	1 016	120.00	19 895	13	1979	MLW	MLW	Canadian-GE

DIESEL RAILCARS

Series	Axle Arrangement	Transmission	Rated Power hp	Max. kg	Tractive Effort: Continus at kg	kmlh	Max. Speed kmlh	Wheel Dia. mm	Total Weight Tonnes	Length mm	No. built	Year first Built	Builders: Mechanical Parts	Engine & Type	Transmission
9101/103 (NG)	B-B	Hyd	240	4 100	—	—	70	700	22.00	15 500	3	1949	Nohab	Scania Vabis	Lisholm-Smith
9301/310 (NG)	Bo-Bo	Elec	320	9 000	—	—	70	820	23.00	19 510	10	1954	Allan	AEC	
9601/622 (NG)	BO 2' + 2'2'	Hyd	383	4 500	2 850	36	90	880	64.36	38 550	22	1976	Alsthom	SFAC	Alsthom
0051/056 (BG)	(1A) (A1)	Hyd	240	3 750	—	—	80	700	26.10	15 560	6	1947	Nohab	Scania Vabis	Lisholm-Smith
0101/115 (BG)	(1A) (A1)	Hyd	240	3 000	—	—	100	700	27.50	22 490	15	1948	Nohab	Scania Vabis	Lisholm-Smith

DIESEL RAILCARS

Series	Axle Arrange-ment	Trans-mission	Rated Power hp	Tractive Effort: Max. kg	Continus at kg	kmlh	Max. Speed kmlh	Wheel Dia. mm	Total Weight Tonnes	Length mm	No. built	Year first Built	Builders: Mechanical Parts	Engine & Type	Transmission
0301/325 (BG)	Bo-Bo	Elec	360	—	—	—	100	920	51.50	23 630	25	1954	Allan	AEC	
0501/506 (BG)	B' 2'	Mech	384	—	—	—	120	910	56.50	27 780	6	1953	Fiat	Fiat	Fiat
0401/419 (BG)	(1A) (A1) + 2' 2'	Hyd	560	6 200	—	—	110	850	94.10	51 960	19	1965	Soreframe	Rolls-Royce	Rolls-Royce
0601/0640 (BG)	2' B' + B' 2'	Hyd	775	11 400	7 600	22	120	920	110.00	53 480	20	1979	Soreframe	SFAC	Voith
0751/0766 (BG)	AA + 11	Mech	277	2 900	—	—	90	900	32.00	27 500	16	1968	RENFE	Pegaso	Pegaso-Z1

Motive power under order or delivery 1977 to 1979/80

	Supplier	Transmission	Rated power hp	Max speed kmlh	Axle arrangement	Gauge	No. built	Wheel Dia. mm	Weight tonnes
Diesel locomotive:									
9027/9031	Alsthom	Elec	715	70	Bo-Bo	Narrow	5	950	46.65
1901/1913	Soreframe	Elec	2 200	100	Co-Co	Broad	13	1 100	120.00
1931/1947	Soreframe	Elec	2 200	120	Co-Co	Broad	17	1 100	120.00
1961/1973	MLW	Elec	2 251	120	Co-Co	Broad	13	1 016	120.00
Diesel railcars:									
9601/9622	Alsthom	Hyd	383	90	BO2 + 22	Narrow	22	880	64.36
0601/0620	Soreframe	Hyd	775	120	2B + B2	Broad	20	920	110.00
0751/0766	Renfe	Mech	277	90	AA + 11	Broad	16	900	32.00
9701/9740	JZ	Mech	594	60	2B + B2 + 2B + B2	Narrow	10	750	92.00

Couplers: Type used UIC; height above rail 1 040 mm.
Buffers: Centre 2 000 mm; height above rail 1 060 mm.
Bogies: Type used y 21 csem; y 21 cssem.
Braking: Type used vacuum; air.

CIVIL ENGINEERING

CP is constructing an 80 km cut-off route to cater for industrial expansion at the port of Sines in southern Portugal. Plans for the scheme were finalised and bridge and earth-works contracts let in 1977. The route leaves the existing CP southern main line at Poceirão and runs south on a double-track alignment to cross the Setúbal-Alcacer do Sal line north of the river Sado at Pinheiro. A spur will be provided as a link to Aguas de Moura. The line then becomes single track and continues south following the coast, passing just to the west of the Grandola hills. It finally sweeps round to cross the existing line to Sines a short distance east of the port.

The line will include four major civil engineering projects: a 450 m long viaduct at Melides, an 840 m long bridge across the Marateca river, a viaduct almost 2 km long crossing the Sado river and a 550 m bridge at Cascalheira. All four are to be constructed in prestressed reinforced concrete.

Track will be laid with 54 kg/m welded rail on concrete sleepers with profile and curve radii suitable for running. Modern signalling and telecommunications will allow max-imum operating flexibility and high throughput.

Main traffic on the line will be fuel and other oil products from the new refinery at Sines; a tender for manufacture of 80-tonne tank wagons has been awarded to Metalsines. Other freight traffic will build up as industrial development as Sines progresses.

CP's plans call for eventual future extension of the route further south to serve the Algarve.

A plan for renewing track on 497 miles *(800 km)* of route with 54 kg rail has been initiated.

Routes affected are:
    Lisbon—Campanhã
    Campolide—Braço de Prata
    Campolide—Sintra
    Ermezinde—Marco
    Contumil—Nine
    Alfarelos—Figueirada Foz
    Cacéin—Caldas da Rainha

248 miles *(400 km)* of track will be reballasted so average train speeds should increase.

ELECTRIFICATION

50 cycles, 25 000 V OH electrification has been completed between Sintra and Porto and is in process of completion between Esmoriz and Villa Norade Gala in the north. Modern block signalling and signal cabin installations have been constructed on this route. The 406 km Lisbon—Oporto line is electrified as 25 kV 50 Hz.

TRACK DETAILS

Standard rail:
  Broad gauge: 60.5 to 111 lb/yd *(30-55 kg/m)* in 8 to 18 m lengths.
  Narrow gauge: 40.4 to 72.6 lb/yd *(20-36 kg/m)* in 8 and 12 m lengths.

Cross ties (sleepers):
  Broad gauge: 10¼ in × 5⅛ in × 8 ft 6⅜ in *(260 × 130 × 2 600 mm)*, spacing 23⅞ in *(605 mm)*.
  Narrow gauge: 9 in × 4½ in × 5 ft 11 in *(230 × 120 × 1 800 mm)*, spacing 32¼ to 32½ in *(820-850 mm)*.
Rail fastening: Screw spikes or bolts. "RN" flexible fastenings used with welded rail.
Filling: Broken stone gravel or earth.
Max curvature:
  Broad gauge: 5.9° = min rad of 984 ft *(300 m)*
  Narrow gauge: 29° = min rad of 197 ft *(60 m)*
Max gradient:
  Broad gauge: 1.8% = 1 in 55½.
  Narrow gauge: 2.5% = 1 in 40.
Longest continuous gradient:
  Broad gauge: 5.2 miles *(8.3 km)* of 1.4% grade with curves varying from 1 936 to 4 924 ft *(590 to 1 501 m)* in radius.
  Narrow gauge: 4.4 miles *(7.2 km)* of 2.5% grade with curves varying from 246 to 1 640 ft *(75 to 500 m)* in radius.
Gauge widening on sharpest curve: 0.984 in *(25 mm)* for both gauges.
Super-elevation on sharpest curve:
  Broad gauge: 7.874 in *(200 mm)*
  Narrow gauge: 4.724 in *(120 mm)*
Rate of slope of super-elevation: 1 in 2 000 to 1 in 333.
Max altitude:
  Broad gauge: 2 666 ft *(812.7 m)*
  Narrow gauge: 2 878 ft *(849.7 m)*
Max axle loading:
  Broad gauge: 19 tons.
  Narrow gauge: 11 tons.
Max permitted speed:
  Broad gauge: 62 mph *(100 kmlh)*
  Narrow gauge: 50 mph *(80 kmlh)*

Welded rail: The total length of track laid with welded rail is 282 miles *(455 km)*. Thermit process is used. Rail used weighs 109, 101, 90, 80 lb/yd *(54, 50, 45, 40 kg/m)* in 18 m and 24 m lengths. The length of continuous welded rail is usually 2 756 ft *(840 m)* but occasionally 3 150 ft *(960 m)*. Rails are secured to sleepers by RN flexible clips.

RHODESIA—See ZIMBABWE

SAUDI ARABIA
SAUDI GOVERNMENT RAILROAD
PO Box 92, Dhahran

Telephone: 22 042
Telex: 601050 Sagrail SJ

Director General: Faysal M. Shehail
Vice President: Abdul Mohsin Bashawri
Assistant Presidents
  Personnel and Administration: Fahad Zamil Al-Hazmi
  Transportation: Mohammed A. Bubshait
  Engineering: Ahmed Saeed Afandi
  Finance: Burhan Hamdi
Directors
  Planning, Budget and Statistics: Assad Salim Shatara

Operations: Salah Salih
Motive Power and Equipment: Abd Al-Latif Ali
Permanent Way: Abdulla S. Al-Wabil
Finance Controller: Khalil Al-Nammari
Accounts: Saud A. Al-Tobayyeb
Technical Advisor: Saud I. Al-Gehairan
Planning Consultant: C. A. Vali

Gauge: 1.435 m
Route length: 577 km

The Saudi Government Railroad Organisation's track is standard gauge with a route length of 577 km.

There is a daily passenger train service to and from Riyadh. A daily freight train is also scheduled as required, and certain trains are run daily between intermediate points to serve the needs of private business companies.

TRAFFIC

	1977/78	1978/79
Total tonne-km	310 893 616	396 871 544
Percentage of train-km by diesel	100	100
Total freight tonnage	1 321 036	1 402 932
Total passenger-km	96 524 998	85 927 000
Total passengers carried	303 798	264 007

Revenues	1977/78	1978/79
		(Saudi Riyals)
Passengers and baggage (millions)	4 735	3 603
Average receipt per passenger-km	20	24
Freight and mail (millions)	12 867	13 333
Average receipt per freight tonne-km	24	30
Total revenues (millions)	17 602	16 933

Expenditure	1977/78	1978/79
Staff/personnel (millions)	54 284	63 720
Materials and services (millions)	17 025	14 364
Depreciation (millions)	16 661	17 760
Financial charges (millions)	39 153	31 981
Total expenditure (millions)	127 123	127 825

INVESTMENTS

The railway spent Riyals 300 million on track renewals over 245 km during 1979 following a 1978 capital improvement plan costing Riyals 13 million for six line haul diesel-electrics, Riyals 32.5 million for 18 passenger coaches, Riyals eight million for 48 grain wagons and Riyals 157.5 million for track improvements over 105 km.

MOTIVE POWER AND ROLLING STOCK

Number of diesel-electric locomotives 31. Number of passenger coaches 36. Number of freight wagons 1 542.

PERMANENT WAY

The government signed a contract in 1978 with Technital of Italy for a study into upgrading the Dammam Riyadh line to 200 km/h operations. During the same year a contract for feasibility studies and design of a 100 km line from eastern terminus at Dammam to Jubail was signed by Atkins Henderson Consultants. Both lines are scheduled for completion by 1983.

Rail, types and weights: 80 lb ASCE, UIC-54, AREA 100 lbs and AREA 115 lb.
Sleepers (cross ties) type: Wooden Length 8 ft, Width 8 in.
  Thickness: 6 in.
  Spacing: 1 850 mm/km.
Rail fastenings (types used): Base plate and spikes and elastic spikes.

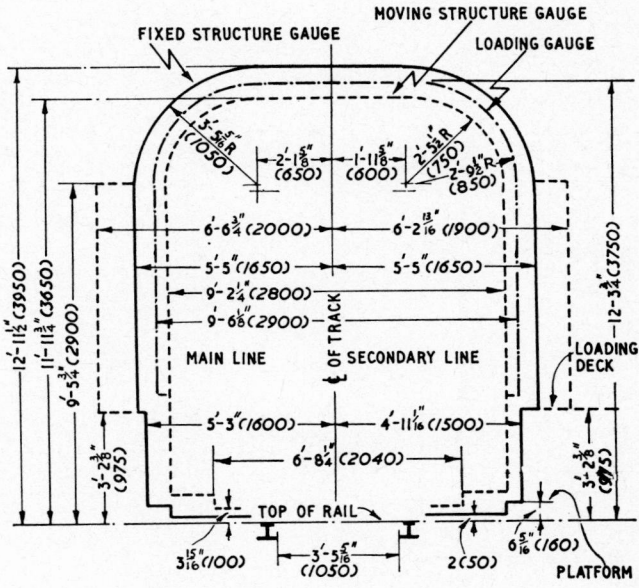

Saudi Government Railway   Reconstructed Hedjaz Railway

SENEGAL

REGIE DES CHEMINS DE FER DU SENEGAL
Cité Ballabey, Thies
Telephone: 317.46

Director General: Papa Malick Mbengue
Deputy General Manager: Gérard Passebosc
Heads of Departments:
  Operations: Mademba Sy
  Motive Power and Rolling Stock: Babacar Ndao
  Way and Works: Cheikh Toure
  Purchases and Supplies: Raymond Alaux

Gauge: 1.00 m
Route length: 1 034 km

The 800 mile principal line formerly known as C.F. Dakar-Niger, runs through Senegal into Mali. It extends 1 286 km from Dakar in Senegal to Koulikoro, the terminus of the railway in Mali. Fortunately the frontier station of Kildiri is exactly halfway along this line, at 643 km.
In Senegal the rail system is administered by the Regie des Chemins de Fer Sénégal. It has a total route length of 642 miles (1 033 km) and consists of:—

	miles	km
Dakar to Kidiri	400	643
Dioubel-Touba branch	29	47
Guinguinéo-Koalack branch	13	21
Thiès to St. Louis du Sénégal	120	193
Louga to Linguère	80	129
	642	1 033

SOUTH AFRICA

SOUTH AFRICAN RAILWAYS (SAR)
South African Railways and Harbours Administration
Paul Kruger Building, Wolmarans Street, Johannesburg

Telephone: 713-2100

Administration:
Minister of Transport Affairs: The Hon. J. C. Heunis, MP
Administrative Secretary to the Ministry of Transport: J. N. Potgieter
Private Secretary to the Ministry of Transport: R. Willemse
Railway Commissioners: C. V. de Villiers
  A. S. D. Erasmus
  P. L. S. Aucamp

Management (Johannesburg):
Director General: Dr. J. G. H. Loubser
Deputy General Manager: Dr. D. J. Coetsee
Deputy General Manager: H. J. L. du Toit
Assistant General Manager (Harbours): B. J. Groenewald
Assistant General Manager (Staff): J. F. M. Venter
Assistant General Manager (Technical): E. A. Fenske
Assistant General Manager (Operating): H. A. Loots
Assistant General Manager (Commercial): C. P. van Coller
Assistant General Manager (Planning): J. C. de Waal
Financial Manager: Dr. E. L. Grove
Assistant General Manager (Manpower): J. P. Verster
Assistant General Manager (Airways): M. E. Smuts

Chief Engineers:
Chief Civil Engineer (Johannesburg): R. D. Hill
Chief Electrical Engineer (Johannesburg): G. B. Jack
Chief Mechanical Engineer (Pretoria): P. A. Marais
Chief Engineer (Signals and Telecommunication) (Johannesburg): R. A. Groves

Gauge: 1.065 m; 0.610 mm
Route length: 22 622 km; 705 km

As part of the South African Railways and Harbours Administration, SAR is divided into ten systems, each under a system manager. The 21 641 route-km railway includes 2 340 route-km in the mandated territory of South-West Africa. In 1957/58 the railways' market share was estimated at approximately 62 per cent of the total ton-km produced. In 1971/72 the railways' share became 56 per cent, and while it is 48 per cent at present, it is expected to decrease to approximately 44 per cent in 1987/88.

FREIGHT TRAFFIC

SAR growth continued during 1978, with freight tonnage up ten per cent over the previous year and freight revenue rising by 22 per cent. Freight results were substantially helped by an increase of over 500 per cent in iron ore tonnage and 71 per cent in coal movements. High-rated traffic suffered a decline (by ten per cent), repeating the trend of the previous year, while low-rated commodities rose by 17 per cent to 87 million tonnes. Most principal traffics showed a decline, but mineral traffic was up by 28 per cent to 51 million tonnes (80 174 million tonne-km, a rise of 15 per cent).

	1976	1977	1978
Total freight tonne-km (millions)	72 076.5	81 603.4	82 000.0
Total freight tonnage ('000)	137 788	153 207	154 200

PASSENGER TRAFFIC

Following the one per cent fall in passenger traffic in 1977 there was a four per cent decline in 1978. Long-distance journeys were down four per cent to 37.2 million, as were suburban passengers at 573 million.

	1976	1977	1978
Total passenger journeys	644 130 688	634 000 000	610 000 000
Passenger-km (millions)			3 233

FINANCIAL

The exploitation of the railways, harbours, airways and pipelines during 1978/79 yielded a surplus of R102 040 363, representing an improvement of R63 936 370 on the net surplus of R38 103 993 recorded the previous year. Revenue derived from the operation of all services reached a new record of R3 199 048 580, compared with the figure of R2 757 360 435 attained during 1977-78, which is an improvement of R441 688 145, or 16 per cent. The improvement in the earnings can be ascribed to the adjustments in rates and fares operative from 1 April 1978, higher volumes of traffic conveyed by the main transportation services, as well as increased tonnages of bulk and general cargo handled at the harbours.

The total expenditure incurred during the year advanced to a new record level of R3 097 008 217; an increase of R337 751 775, or 13.9 per cent, over the previous year's figure. The increase is due mainly to the salary and wage adjustments introduced with effect from January 1978, the sustained high rate of inflation, the increased volumes of traffic conveyed, the increase of 20 per cent in respect of depreciation contributions, as well as higher interest payments on capital.

The working results of the four main services for the past three financial years are reflected in the table below:

	1976/77	1977/78	1978/79
Revenue	R	R	R
Railways	1 695 162 565	2 070 308 101	2 370 923 208
Harbours	132 978 982	165 862 537	198 304 268
Airways	318 668 727	391 375 271	469 194 089
Pipelines	110 736 311	129 814 526	160 627 015
	2 257 546 585	2 757 360 435	3 199 048 580
Expenditure			
Railways	1 774 877 663	2 043 800 879	2 325 940 483
Harbours	82 987 993	119 809 780	137 250 782
Airways	332 650 095	385 311 866	426 846 520
Pipelines	15 384 070	22 659 550	34 897 432
	2 205 899 821	2 571 582 075	2 924 935 217
Surplus			
Railways	(79 715 098)	26 507 222	44 982 725
Harbours	49 990 989	46 052 757	61 053 486
Airways	(13 981 368)	6 036 405	42 347 569
Pipelines	95 352 241	107 154 976	125 729 583
	51 646 764	185 778 360	274 113 363
All Services			
Less			
Net revenue appropriations—			
Contribution to reduce deficiency in Pension Funds	290 927	376 367	
Contribution to Level Crossings Elimination Fund	2 500 000	2 500 000	2 500 000
Contribution to Betterment Fund	55 000 000	80 000 000	60 000 000
Contribution to Sinking Fund—			
Redemption Account	6 422 852	6 438 000	6 789 000
Reserve Account	883 333	58 360 000	102 784 000
Total appropriations	65 097 112	147 674 367	172 073 000
Net surplus	(13 450 348)	38 103 993	102 040 363

Total railway expenditure for 1978/79 amounted to R2 325 940 483 and reflected an increase of R282 139 604 or 13.80 per cent, compared with the figure of R2 043 800 879 for 1977/78:

	1977/78	1978/79
	R	R
Transportation services		
Administrative and general charges	79 784 619	92 451 622
Maintenance of permanent way and works	289 864 527	327 538 883
Maintenance of rolling stock	248 225 447	270 873 958
Motive power operating expenses	298 264 088	330 516 514
Traffic and vehicle running expenses	389 954 741	423 845 118
Cartage services	31 872 656	39 777 416
Ordinary working expenditure	1 337 966 078	1 485 003 511
Depreciation	196 120 990	248 293 215
Total	1 534 087 068	1 733 296 726
Subsidiary services		
Catering and bedding services	17 458 766	18 279 953
Publicity and advertising	276 171	283 233
Grain elevators	2 484 831	2 991 645
Pre-cooling services	11 834 450	14 220 601
Road transport service	60 229 201	68 735 779
Tourist service	16 831 400	18 730 843
Net revenue account		
Interest on funds	1 958 660	2 218 726
Interest on capital	343 824 860	405 321 314
Miscellaneous expenditure	54 815 472	61 861 663
Total	2 043 800 879	2 325 940 483

INVESTMENTS

During 1979 SAR spent R1 385.5 million on capital investments compared with R606.9 million in 1978. Investments in 1980 are anticipated at R1 407.5 million with R62 million set aside for locomotive purchases, R26.8 million for new passenger coaches, R60.6 million for freight wagons, R152 million for track, R12.6 million for signalling improvements and R14.5 million for electrification projects.

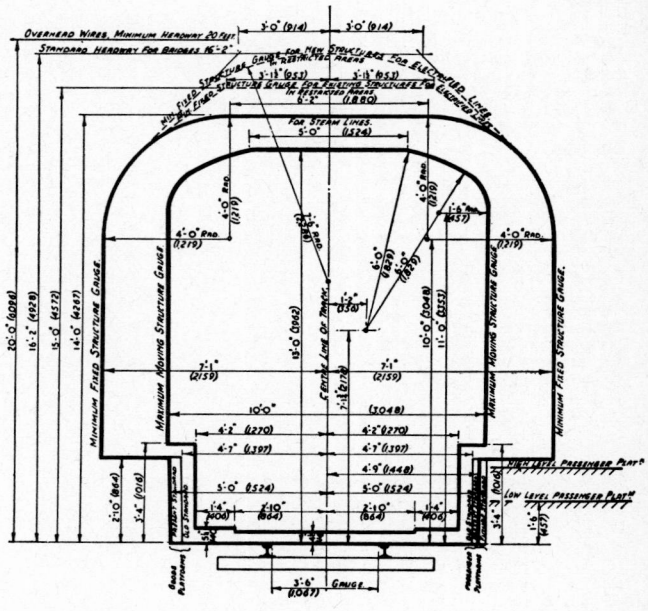

MOTIVE POWER AND ROLLING STOCK

At the end of 1979 SAR was operating 1 659 steam locomotives in mainline service, 140 steam shunters, 1 766 line haul electric locomotives, 24 electric shunters, 1 121 diesel-electrics on line haul service, 100 diesel-electric shunters, nine diesel-mechanical shunters and 20 mainline 610 mm gauge diesel-electric locomotives. Number of rail-cars totalled 1 261 electric and 3 165 trailers. Passenger coaches totalled 6 096; freight wagons 187 956.

CIVIL ENGINEERING

SAR has taken over control of the 880 km Sishen-Saldanha line built by South African Iron and Steel Corporation (Iscor) and brought into operation in May 1976. SAR's ownership of the line—bought from Iscor at a cost of R 650 million—became effective in 1977. The line was built to transport iron ore from the mines at Sishen in the Northern Cape down to the port of Saldanha on the west coast. At present, three ore trains a day run down to Saldanha, giving the line an annual haul of 16.5 million tonnes. When a fourth train comes into operation soon, capacity will reach an annual 22 million tonnes. In just under a year since the line has been operating—at first experimentally—about 4 million tonnes of ore has been railed, 2.5 million tonnes for export.

Following the SAR take-over, iron ore will continue to be the basic-traffic. But other mining commodities are also to be carried, and SAR expects to develop other types of traffic to take up spare capacity.

In two phases, SAR's forward planning policy is aimed first at increasing the annual load of the line to 40 million tonnes. This means that more crossings will have to be built. At the moment there are nine in all: SAR plans to lay ten more. Seven are already under construction. So far no date has been set for phase two of the plan—aimed at raising the annual load to 68 million tonnes.

For the first two years SAR required subsidy of R 15 million. For the third year, R 5 million should be sufficient. After that cost and operating figures should break even. Already operating on the line are 2 170 gondola ore wagons and 300 more are on order. Trains are made up with 210 wagons , headed by 3 × 9E electric locomotives, to give a total length of more than 2 km. Maximum axle loading is 26 tonnes (104 tonnes gross). A total of 24 × 9E electric locomotives are at present in use.

The traffic was at first hauled by diesel locomotives but since mid 1978 three 50 kV 50 Hz GEC-Union Carriage Co-Co locomotives working in multiple have been used to haul the 210-wagon trains carrying about 18 000 tonnes of ore at speeds of up to 72 km/h. A loaded train weight ±22 000 tonnes and this demands an hourly rating for the three locomotives of 11 300 kW.

At the design stage Iscor considered several voltage levels before it became apparent that the advantages of a 50 kV system made it the optimum choice for such a sparsely-populated region without convenient electrical transmission systems.

ELECTRIFICATION

The energy crisis speeded up electrification. By the end of March 1976 no less than 10 634 track-km had already been electrified (approximately 32 per cent of the total rail network). By the end of 1977 11 656 track-km (5 398 route-km) were electrified.

An additional 874.99 km of track were electrified in 1978, bringing the total length of electrified track in South Africa to 11 844.16 km which means that 44.8 per cent of the total track network is now energised. This affected the route distance which increased by 428.09 km and brought the total distance to 5 507.19 route-km. In 1979 3 231 track-km (1 601 route-km) were still under construction or authorised.

Lines under electrification (sanctioned):

	Route-km
Belle Ombre: New station and connecting lines Golf and Bantule	9.00
Brits—Thabazimbi and Brits—Beestekraal— Atlanta	311.00
Kensington—Bellville	14.12
Table Bay Harbour to point on Kensington— Chempet line	8.45
Kensington—Chempet	8.13
Nyanga—Strandfontein	17.70
Winternest—Mabopane new double line	20.00
Houtheuwel—Potchefstroom doubling	86.03
Pretoria North—Pyramid	10.42
Connecting lines to serve Central Yard Bapsfontein Stage 1	23.00
Connecting lines to serve Central Yard Bapsfontein Stage 2	23.00
Connecting lines to serve Central Yard Bapsfontein Stage 3	112.00
De Wildt—Brits doubling	11.20
Central Yard Bapsfontein Stage 1	23.00

Three-door suburban coach designed to speed passenger movement at stations

SAR class 9E electric locomotive

Lines projected for future electrification:
In so far as the future electrification schemes are concerned, the following lines are now to be electrified with alternating current and the anticipated dates of completion are shown in the tables.

Beaufort West—De Aar (late 1982)
Pyramid—Pietersburg (mid-1983)
De Aar—Port Elizabeth (mid-1984)
Springfontein—East London(mid-1985)
Bloemfontein—Novport (mid-1985)

SIGNALLING
Centralised traffic control (CTC) has been introduced on certain sections and is being installed on an additional number of sections and mainline routes. This system greatly increases carrying capacity and the efficiency of operation. The total distance of line already under CTC is 2 742 km.

Computers are used to assist the control of large complex stations and CTC sections carrying heavy traffic. Modern signalling systems also provide such facilities as automatic train routing; automatic train-time printing; automatic train-graph recorders recording the trains' progress on a time-versus-distance chart; automatic train control; and automatic train operation.

New Signalling Installations
POWER SIGNALLING INSTALLATION
Individual Geographic unit interlocking or route relay interlockings.

Location	System	Engineers
Minaar	Western Transvaal	SAR
Springfontein	Orange Free State	Siemens
Jan de Boers	Cape Western	SAR
Vleifontein	Cape Western	SAR
New Brighton	Cape Midlands	SAR
Sydenham	Cape Midlands	SAR

CENTRALISED TRAFFIC CONTROL

Length (km)	Location	System	Engineers
100	Waterval Boven—Nelspruit	Eastern Transvaal	Westinghouse

REMOTE CONTROLLED STATIONS

Location	System	Engineers
Raathsvlei—Enselspruit	Western Transvaal	Siemens
Residensia	Western Transvaal	GEC
Valleydora	Cape Eastern	Siemens
New Brighton	Cape Midlands	SAR
Sydenham	Cape Midlands	SAR

In all cases the equipment was supplied as follows:
(a) Westinghouse Bellambie: Supervisory equipment and points machine.
(b) Siemens: Interlocking equipment, axle counters and control panels.
(c) Western Industries: Track circuit equipment, axle counters and control panels.
(d) GEC Engineering: Colourlight Signals, points machines and Reed equipment.

A 2.54 km train on a test run. The train comprised a class 7E locomotive, a test car, three class 7E locomotives, three class 7E locomotives running dead, 120 CCR loaded coal wagons, seven class 34 diesel locomotives, 64 CCR loaded coal wagons, a staff saloon and a guards van

ELECTRIC LOCOMOTIVES

Class	Axle arrange-ment	Line current kV	Rated output kW	Max load kg	Tractive effort (full field) continuous kN	at km/h	Max speed km/h	Wheel dia mm	Total mass kg	Length mm	No. built	Year first built	Builders Mechanical parts	Electrical equipment
Es	Bo-Bo	3	896	17 018.75	73	19	40	1 219	68 075	13 310	24	1936	SAR—4, Werkspoor Holland—10, Metro Vickers—10	
														4-Metro Vickers 182R traction motors
1E 1ES	Bo-Bo	3	896	17 018.75	73	39	70	1 219	68 075	13 310	39 38	1936	Metro Vickers	
														4-Metro Vickers 182R traction motors
3E	Co-Co	3 kV	2 016/ 1 704	18 796.75	119	51	100	1 219	113 797	17 199	28	1948	Metro Vickers	
														6-Metro Vickers 187 traction motors
4E	Co-Co	3	2 262/ 1 878	13 209/ 21 845	141	46	100	762/ 1 295	157 488	21 844	40	1952	North British	
														6-GEC WT 580 traction motors
5E	Bo-Bo	3	1 508/ 1 300	21 591	104	44	100	1 219	86 364	15 494	160	1955	English Electric	
														4-EE 529 traction motors
5E1	Bo-Bo	3	1940/ 1 456	21 591	122	43	100	1 219	86 364	15 494	690	1959	Metro Vickers—135 Union Carriage and wagon Co Ltd—555	
														4-MV 281 or 4-AEI 281 AZX or 4-AEI 281 AX or 4-AEI 281 X traction motors

DIESEL LOCOMOTIVES

Class	Axle arrange-ment	Rated power kW	Max axle load kg	Tractive Effort continuous kN	km/h	Max speed km/h	Wheel dia mm	Total mass kg	Length mm	No built	Year first built	Builders Mechanical parts	Engine and type	Transmission (all electric)
31	Bo-Bo	985/ 895	18 900	145	18	90	915	74 000	15 150	45	1958	GE	Cooper Bessemer	General Electric
												GE	1 4-stroke V-8 turbocharged and aftercooled C-B type FVBL-8	4 dc 4 pole axle hung 5E type 5GE 761 A4
32-000	Co-Co	1 475/ 1 340	10 160/ 12 700	146	27	100	762/ 915	93 000	16 866	115	1959	GE	Cooper Bessemer	General Electric
												GE	1 4-stroke V-12 turbo-charged and aftercooled C-B type FVBL-12	6 dc 4 pole axle hung GE type 5GE 761A3
32-200	Co-Co	1 475/ 1 340	10 160/ 12 700	146	27	100	767/ 915	93 000	16 866	10	1966	GE	Cooper Bessemer	General Electric
												GE	1 4-stroke V-12 turbo-charged and aftercooled C-B type FVBL-12	6 dc 4 pole axle hung GE type 5 GE 761A9
33-000	Co-Co	1 605/ 1 490	15 749	178	24	100	915	91 000	16 866	65	1965	GE	General Electric	General Electric
												GE	1 4-stroke V-12 turbo-charged and aftercooled GE type 7FDL-12	6 dc 4 pole axle hung GE type 761 A6
33-200	Co-Co	1 640/ 1 490	15 749	178	24	100	915	91 000	17 474	20	1966		EMD General Motors	
												EMD	1 2-stroke V16 Blower Scavengud EMD type 16-645-E	6 dc 4 pole axle hung EMD EMD type D 29CC-7
33-400	Co-Co	1 605/ 1 490	15 749	178	24	100	915	91 000	16 866	115	1968		General Electric	
												GE	1 4-stroke turbo-charged and aftercooled GE type 7 FDL-12	6 dc 4 pole axle hung GE type 5 GE-761 A 6
34-000	Co-Co	2 050/ 1 940	18 850	218	26	100	915	111 000	17 982	125	1971		General Electric	
												GE	1 4-stroke V-12 turbo-charged and aftercooled GE type 7 FDL-12	6 dc 4 pole axle hung GE type 5 GE 761 A 13
34-200	Co-Co	2 145/ 1 940	18 850	218	26	100	1 016	111 000	19 242	50	1971		EMD General Motors	
												EMD	1 2-stroke V-16 turbo-charged and aftercooled EMD type 16-645 E 3	6 dc 4 pole axle hung EMD type D 2 B
34-400	Co-Co	2 050/ 1 940	18 850	218	26	100	915	111 000	17 928	139	1973		South African GE-DC Locomotive Group South Africa	
												GE	1 4-stroke V-12 turbo-charged and aftercooled GE type 7 FDL-12	6 dc 4 pole axle hung GE type 5 GE-761 A 13

ELECTRIC LOCOMOTIVES

Class	Axle arrange- ment	Line current kV	Rated output kW	Max load kg	Tractive effort (full field) continuous kN	at km/h	Max speed km/h	Wheel dia mm	Total mass kg	Length mm	No. built	Year first built	Builders Mechanical parts	Electrical equipment
6E	B-Bo	3	2 492/ 2 252	22 226	193	41	110	1 219	88 904	15 494	80	1970	Union Carriage and Wagon Co Ltd	
														4-AEI 283 AZ traction motors
6E1	Bo-Bo	3	2 492/ 2 252	22 226	193	41	110	1 219	88 904	15 494		1969	Union Carriage and Wagon Co Ltd	
														4-AEI 283 AZ traction motors
EXP/ AC	Bo-Bo	25	2 492/ 2 252	22 226	190	41	110	1 219	85 500	15 494	1	1975	Union Carriage and Wagon Co Ltd 50 C/S group	
													Union Carriage and Wagon Co Ltd	4-AEI 283 AZ traction motors
7E	Co-Co	25	3 240/ 3 000	21 000	300	35	100	1 220	123 500	18 465	100	1978	50 C/S Group (Siemens Ltd)	
													Union Carriage and Wagon Co Ltd	6-MG 680 traction motors
7E1	Co-Co	25	NA 3 000	21 000	300	35	100	1 220	123 115	18 430	2	1979	Nissho Iwai	
													Dorman Long	6-Hitachi HS-1054-GR traction motors
9E	Co-Co	50	4 068/ 3 780	28 000	388	34.5	90	1 220	166 300	21 132	24	1979 (Ex-ISCOR 1978)	GEC Engineering (Pty Ltd)	
													Union Carriage and Wagon Co Ltd	GEC traction 6-GEC G415AZ traction motors

DIESEL LOCOMOTIVES

Class	Axle arrange- ment	Rated power kW	Max axle load kg	Tractive Effort continuous kN	km/h	Max speed km/h	Wheel dia mm	Total mass kg	Length mm	No built	Year first built	Builders Mechanical parts	Engine and type	Transmission (all electric)
34-600	Co-Co	2 145/ 1 940	18 850	218	26	100	1 016	111 000	19 202	100	1974	General Motors South African (Pty) Ltd South Africa		
												GM SA	1 2-stroke V-16 turbo- charged and aftercooled EMD type 16-645-E3	6 dc 4 pole axle hung EMD type D 29B
35-000	Co-Co	1 230/ 1 160	13 720	161	21	100	915	82 000	15 152	70	1972	General Electric		
												GE	1 4-stroke V-8 turbo- charged and aftercooled GE type 7 FDL-8	6 dc 4 pole axle hung GE type 5GE-764-C
35-200	Co-Co	1 195/ 1 065	13 720	161	19	100	915	82 000	16 485	150	1974	EMD General Motors—25 General Motors South Africa (Pty) Ltd—125		
												EMD	1 2-stroke V-8 turbo- charged and aftercooled EMD type 8-645E3	6 dc 4 pole axle hung EMD type D 29CCBT
35-400	Co-Co	1 230/ 1 160	13 720	161	21	100	915	82 000	15 152	50	1976	South African— DC Locomotive Group South Africa		
												GE	1 4-stroke V-8 turbo- charged and aftercooled GE type 7FDL-8	6 dc 4 pole GE type 5GE 764-C1
35-600	Co-Co	1 195/ 1 065	13 720	161	19	100	915	82 000	16 485	100	1976	General Motors South African (Pty) Ltd South Africa		
												GM SA	EMD type 8-645 E3	6 dc axle hung Electric Motors
36-000	Bo-Bo	875/ 800	18 500	141	14	100	915	72 000	15 151	100	1975	South African GE— DC Locomotive Group South Africa		
												GE	GE type 7 FDL-8	4 dc axle hung Electric Motors
91-000	Bo-Bo	52/ 480	12 000	86	15	50	838	44 000	10 580	20	1973 GE	Caterpillar	General Electric	
												GE	1 4-stroke V-8 turbo- charged and aftercooled CAT type D 379	4 dc 4 pole GE type 5GE 778 A1 gear case axle mounted
34-800	Co-Co	2 140/ 1 940	18 850	218	26	100	1 016	111 000	19 202	45	1978	General Motors South African (Pty) Ltd		
												GM SA	EMD type 16-645 E3	6 dc axle hung Electric Motors
34-900	Co-Co	2 050/ 1 940	18 850	218	26	100	915	111 000	17 982	1	1979	South African GE—DC Locomotive Group		
												GE	GE type 7 FDL-12	6 dc axle hung Electric Motors

SPAIN

SPANISH NATIONAL RAILWAYS (RENFE)
Red National de Los Ferrocarriles Españoles (RENFE),
Plaza Sagrados Corazones 7, Madrid (16)

Telephone: 4.57.14.00
Telex: 23420

President: Ignacio Bayon
Vice-president: Alfredo Moreno
Counsellor-Director: Antonio Carbonell
Counsellors: Vicente Diez
Alberto Oliart
Enrique de Aldama
Francisco Mendivil
Carlos Roa
Miguel Herrero
Jaime Badillo
Jorge Hernando
Luis Llubia
Secretary: Jesus de Ledesma

Administration
Director General: Enrique de Aldama
Director of Operations: Antonio Debesa
Inspector General: Emilio Magdalena
Director Way and Works: Jose Escolano
Director of Material: Angel Gomez
Director of Transport: Pelayo Martinez-Regidor
Commercial Director: Jose Augustin Dominguez
Director of Planning: Antonio Dionis
Director of Finances: Francisco Donate
Social Director: Antonio Pinazo
Director of Strategy: Antonio Dionis
Director of Information: Miguel Angel Eced

Gauge: 1.676 m
Route length: 13 509 km

TRAFFIC

RENFE's freight traffic continued to fall in 1978 following the trend started during the 1974/75 recession. In fact rail freight did increase slightly in 1977 to 11 425 million tonne-km but this figure was still below the 1974 results of 11 577 million. Traffic fell away again in 1978 and it seems unlikely that RENFE was able to meet the forecasted six per cent rise in tonne-km and four per cent in total tonnage in 1979. The railway was only 12.13 per cent of Spain's total freight market. One area showing growth is container traffic. In 1975 a total of 79 934 containers were railed. The total rose to 188 818 by 1978.

	1975	1976	1977
	Total figures—millions		
Freight tonne-km	10 693	10 766	11 425
Freight tonnage	37.7	36.0	37.5
Passenger-km	16 146	16 686	17 163
Passenger journeys	199.6	206.3	212.2

FINANCES

	1975	1976	1977
	(Pesetas' millions)		
Revenues	38 156	47 689	56 549
Expenses	44 227	57 095	74 749

INVESTMENTS

RENFE has planned to invest 50 840 million pesetas in 980 on capital improvements including 1.4 million pesetas on new locomotives, 6.6 million pesetas on passenger coaches, 5.1 million pesetas on new line construction (664 km) and 18.5 million on track upgrading and line improvements.

MOTIVE POWER AND ROLLING STOCK

RENFE's locomotive fleet in 1979 consisted of 451 mainline electric locomotives, 361 diesel-electric line haul units, 315 diesel-electric shunters, 41 diesel-hydraulic mainline locos, nine diesel-hydraulic shunters and 46 diesel-mechanical shunters. Additional motive-power included 178 two-axle railbuses, 179 trailers, 385 emus and 80 diesel trainsets. Passenger coaches totalled 1 890; freight wagons, 33 240.
Deliveries in 1978 included 26 electric locomotives with a rating of 3 100 kW, 39 three-car sets rated at 1 160 kW for 3000 Vdc operation, and six two-car sets rated at 600 kW for operation at 1 500 Vdc. Deliveries in 1979 included seven electric locomotives of 3 100 kW, 21 three-car electric trainsets (3000 V) rated at 1 160 kW, two two-car electric trainsets (3 000 V) rated at 1 160 kW, two two-car electric trainsets rated at 524 kW for 1 500 V operation and six additional trailers for 3 000 V sets.
Equipment on order at the end of 1979 included 20 BBB locomotives rated at 4 650 kW, 20 locomotives rated at 3 100 kW, 30 at 4 552 kW, 35 three-car sets rated at 1 160 kW, eight two-car sets rated at 1 160 kW, two two-car sets rated at 524 kW, and 132 three-car diesel trainsets rated at 852 kW.

ELECTRIFICATION

At the end of 1978 RENFE had a total electrified route length of 4 921 km.
Since 1975 major electrification projects have been completed between Cordoba and Seville (137 km) and along the Miranda-Zaragoza-Lerida-Roda-Reus line (543 km). An impressive list of lines now being converted includes:
—Guadalajara-Baides-Torralba (99 km)
—Zaragoza-Ricla-Calatayud (96 km)
—Espeluy-Jaen (32 km)
—Valencia-Jativa (56 km)
—Seville-Cadiz (153 km)
—Seville-Huelva (110 km)
—Cordoba-Malaga (193 km)
—Zaragoza-Mora (191 km)
—Alcazar-Chinchilla (149 km)

TRACK STANDARDS

Standard rail main lines: 109 lb/yd *(54.4 kg/m)* for all relaying. 90.8 lb/yd *(45 kg/m)* and U.I.C. 91 lb/yd *(54.1 kg/m)* in 12 and 18 m lengths.
Branch lines: 85.6 lb/yd *(42.5 kg/m)* in 12.4 m lengths.
Rails weighing 57 lb to 81.7 lb *(28.3 to 40.5 kg)* are being replaced on secondary lines, and 91.8 lb *(45.5 kg)* rail on main lines is also being replaced.
Rail joints: Suspended; 4- or 6-hole fishplates and welding.
Wooden sleepers: Mainly creosoted oak, pine, and sometimes beech. *Sizes:* 2.60 × 0.24 × 0.14 for ordinary track. For points, crossings etc. 3.00, 3.50, 4.00 and 4.50 m of the same width and thickness (the centre crossing sleeper being 4.50 × 0.30 × 0.14), and for expansion joints, 2.60 × 0.35 × 0.14 m. Special sleepers of up to 6.20 m are used for diagonals on double track.
Reinforced concrete sleepers: Type R.S. for 54 and 45 kg rail with a thickness of 22 cms. They are made in Torrejón, Venta de Baños and Alcázar de San Juan.

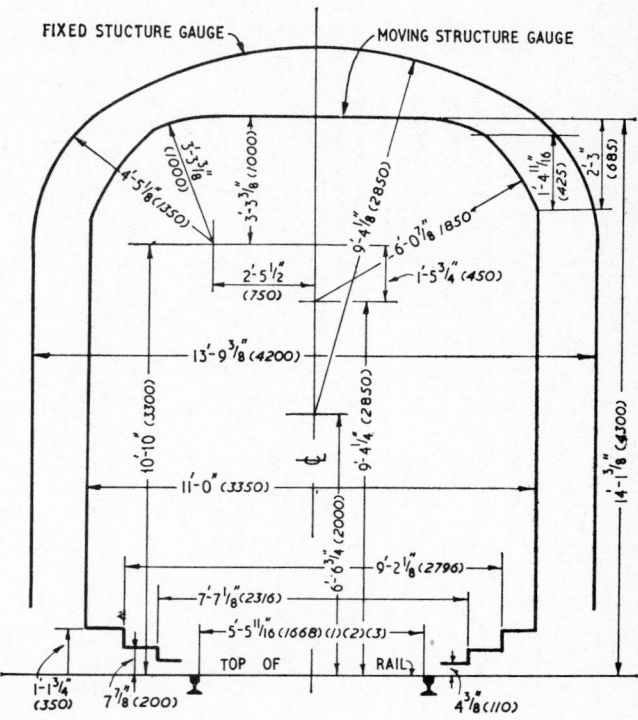

General Motors/Macos-built diesel electric locomotive hauls a mainline passenger train over the Tortosa bridge

Spacing for 45 kg rail: 20 for 12 m lengths; giving 25⅛ in *(640 mm)* spacing for inner sleepers.
   30 for 18 m lengths; 24½ in *(620 mm)*
Rail fastenings: Screw spikes on wood sleepers and elastic clamps on reinforced concrete sleepers. Elastic fastenings for wood sleepers are also being tested.
Filling: Crushed limestone or quartz ore: 1½ to 3 in *(40-80 mm)*
   11⅞ in *(300 mm)* under sleepers on main lines.
   7⅞ in *(200 mm)* under sleepers on secondary lines.
Max curvature: Generally 5.85° = min rad of 984 ft *(300 m)* except 7.6° = min rad of 754 ft *(230 m)* on Ripoll-Puigcerdá line and 8.75° = min rad of 656 ft *(200 m)* on Cordoba-Almorchón line.
Max gradient: 4.1% = 1 in 24½ on Ripoll-Puigcerdá line.
Longest continuous gradient: 5.15 miles *(8.27 m)* of 2% (1 in 50) grade, with 5.85° curves (984 ft *(300 m)* radius) on 3 miles *(4.84 km)*.
Gauge widening on curves:

Radius of curve	Widening
Larger than 1 312 ft *(400 m)*	None
1 230-1 312 ft *(375-400 m)*	0.20 in *(5 mm)*
984-1 230 ft *(300-375 m)*	0.40 in *(10 mm)*
656-984 ft *(200-300 m)*	0.79 in *(20 mm)*

Super-elevation on sharpest curve (8.75°): 6.89 in *(175 mm)*
Max altitude: 4 901 ft *(1 494 m)* on Ripoll-Puigcerdá line.
Max axle load: 22 tons
Max permitted speed:

Talgo trains	87 mph *(140 km/h)*
Diesel trainsets (TAF)	68 mph *(110 km/h)*
Other trains	62 mph *(100 km/h)*

Class 440 electric trainset
Rated at 3 000 hp, the set was built for long-distance service.

Class 269 electric locomotive
Rated at 3 100 kW/3 000 V dc, this CAF-built unit has a top speed of 140 km/h. Electrics are by Westinghouse.

DIESEL LOCOMOTIVES

Class	Axle Arrangement	Transmission	Rated Power hp	Max. (kg)	Tractive Effort Continuous at (kg)	(km/h)	Max. Speed (km/h)	Wheel Dia. (mm)	Total Weight Tons	Length (mm)	No. Built	Year first Built	Builders: Mechanical Parts	Engine & Type	Transmission
313	Co-Co	Elec	1 370	18 480	19 300	14.0	120	1 016	83.9	16 237	50	1965	Euskalduna Alco	Alco Products 251-D	General Electric GEE
314	Co-Co	Elec	1 445	18 450	18 625	16.4	120	1 067	86	15 526	1	1967	Macosa	General Motors 567-C	General Motors
316	Co-Co	Elec	2 180	24 090	18 200	21.7	120	1 016	110	17 872	11	1955	Alco	Alco 251-C-3	General Eléctrica
318	Co-Co	Elec	1 980	24 090	18 200	21.7	120	1 016	110	17 872	24	1958	Alco	Alco 251-B	General Electric
319	Co-Co	Elec	1 977	23 100	18 450	21.6	120	1 067	105	18 472	100	1965	END General Motors Macosa	END General Motors 567-C	END General Motors
321	Co-Co	Elec	2 180	24 640	19 325	22.5	120	1 016	111	18 567	79	1967 1970	Alco, Caf, Naval Euskalduna	Alco	General Electric GEE
333	Co-Co	Elec	3 345	31 710	28 100	23.5	151	1 067	120	20 700	93	1974	Macosa	General Motors 645 E 3	General Motors
340	B' B'	Hyd	2 × 2 000	25 500	17 093	30	130	1 016	88	19 750	26	1966	Krauss-Maffei Babcock & Wilcox	Maybach-Mercedes MD 870/1	Maybach-Mercedes
352	B' B'	Hyd	2 × 1 200	22 100	16 400	20.5	140	950	76.3	17 450	10	1964	Krauss-Maffei Babcock-Wilcox	Maybach-Mercedes MD 650/18	Maybach-Mercedes
353	B' B'	Hyd	2 × 1 500	25 500	19 000	20	180	1 150	88	19 000	5	1969	Krauss-Maffei	Maybach-Mercedes MD6552	Maybach-Mercedes

ELECTRIC LOCOMOTIVES

Class	Axle Arrangement	Line Current	Rated Output hp	Max. (kg)	Tractive Effort (Full Field) Continuous at (kg)	(km/h)	Max. Speed (km/h)	Wheel dia. (mm)	Weight tonnes	Length (mm)	No. Built	Year Built	Builders Mechanical Parts	Electrical Equipment
Bo-Bo	Bo-Bo	3 000 V 1 000 cc	20 944			65		1 400	74.8	11 912	6		1929	CAF	CE Francia
282	Bo-Bo	1 500 V cc	1 120	18 900	12 200		70	1 270	67.5	12 600	5	1932	Babcock-Wilcox	General Electric
276	Co-Co	3 000 V cc	3 000	33 600	16 500	495	110	1 250	120	18 932	136		Alsthom-Macosa CAF-MTM Eusk Babcock-Wilcox	Alsthom-Sice, Gee-Oerlikon Exp Ind Westinghouse
277	Co-Co	3 000 V cc	3 000	31 300	13 850	58	110	1 220	120	20 657	75		Vulcan-Foundry	English Electric
278	Bo Bo-Bo	3 000 V cc	3 000	31 710	16 800	48	110	1 118	120	20 193	28		Wesa-SE Construc Naval	Westinghouse
279	B' B'	1 500/ 3 000 V	3 670	31 200	14 000/ 22 500	69/ 43	130/ 80	1 250 (1 120)	80	17 270	16		Mitsubishi-CAF	Mitsubishi-Cenemesa
280	B' B'	1 500/ 3 000 V	3 000	22 400	12 100 20 700		120/ 70	1 250	80	17 600	4		Alsthom	Alsthom
289	B' B'	1 500/ 3 000 V	4 200	34 300	17 000/ 27 200	67.7/ 40.8	130/ 80	1 250	84	17 270	40	1969	Mitsubishi-CAF	Mitsubishi-Cenemesa
269	B' B'	3 000 V	4 210	34 200	16 700/	63/	140/	1 250	88	17 270	102	1973	CAF	Westinghouse

DIESEL RAILCARS

Class	Axle Arrangement	Trans-mission	Rated Power hp	Max. (kg)	Tractive Effort Continuous at (kg)	(km/h)	Max. Speed (km/h)	Wheel Dia. (mm)	Total Weight Tons	Length (mm)	No. Built	Year first Built	Builders: Mechanical Parts	Engine & Type	Transmission
591	B + 2	Mech	300	5 936	2 900	15	90	910	21	13 750	178 M 161 Rc	1961/ 66/69	Vaggon Fabrik Uerdingen y Construt Españoles Mat M/Macosa CAF/MMC	Pegaso	Pegaso-ZF
595	2' B' + 2' 2' + B' 2		1 050	8 500	3 500	25	120	910	150	83 340	22 M 11 R		Fiat	Fiat	Fiat
597	2' B' + 2' 2'	Hyd	775	12 500	7 000	12	120	910	96.8	53 200	50 M 58 R	1967	CAF/Fiat	Fiat	Fiat OM-(SRM)

ELECTRIC RAILCARS

Class	Axle Arrangement	Rated Output hp	Max. (kg)	Tractive Effort (Full Field) Continuous at (kg)	(km/h)	Max. Speed (km/h)	Wheel dia. (mm)	Weight (tonnes)	Length (mm)	No. Built	Year Built	Builders Mechanical Parts	Electrical Equipment
431	B' B' + 2' 2	1 500	390	10 920	27	40	920	48 300	32 280	3	1923	CAF	Mitsubishi-Westinghouse
432	Bo-Bo + 2' 2' + 2' 2'	3 000/ 1 500	1 578	18 000	83	140	1 000	150 400	79 870	19	1971	Naval	Westinghouse
433	Bo-Bo + 2' 2'	1 500	816	16 800	41	100	996/ 1 006	106 000	41 236	61	1956/ 57	Naval	Cenemesa
434	Bo-B' + 2' 2' + 2' 2'	1 500	816	14 560	32	70	1 006	132 000	66 790	11	1960/ 61/1966/ 67	Naval	Metro Vickers Westinghouse Exp Indust
435	Bo-Bo	1 500	700	15 960	34	70	996	57 000	18 200	6	1932	MTM-Macosa	Brom-Boveri-Secheron
436/437/ 438	B' B' + 2' 2' + 2' 2'	3 000 V cc	1 200	16 240	65	110	1 000	122 000	76 360	157	1958/ 66	Schindler/ Schlieren	Industrias Aguirena
439	Bo-Bo + 2' 2	3 000/ 1 500	1 370	18 144	66	130	1 000	96 800	51 910	28	1967/ 68	Metropolitan Cammell	Acec-Itchneider Cenemesa
440	Bo-Bo + 2' 2' + 2' 2	3 000	1 578	17 730	83	140	940	133 300	79 590	95	1974	CAF	Westinghouse-Meleo
441	Bo-Bo + 2' 2'	1 500	816	13 164	50	90	940	70 360	37 470	3	1977	CAF	Westinghouse
442	Bo-Bo + 2' 2'	1 500	712	10 680	365	60	840	63 200	36 140	3	1976	MTM	Brown Boveri

DIESEL LOCOMOTIVES (SHUNTING)

Class	Axle Arrangement	Trans-mission	Rated Power hp	Max. (kg)	Tractive Effort Continuous at (kg)	(km/h)	Max. Speed (km/h)	Wheel Dia. (mm)	Total Weight Tons	Length (mm)	No. Built	Year first Built	Builders: Mechanical Parts	Engine & Type	Transmission
301	B	Mech	130	5 490	3 150	6.38	50/ 20	860	25	6 780	46	1960	MTM Euskalduna-Macosa	Pegaso III Enasa	
303	C	Elec	350	10 560	6 500	11	45	1 200	48	9 800	201	1953/ 61	MTM-Babcock & Wilcox	MTM-Babcock & Wilcox 6LD-22A 6LD-22B
304	C	Elec	400	10 560	7 000	11	45	1 200	48	8 400	63	1967	MTM	MTM
305	D	Hyd	550	13 200		—	60/ 30	1 150	60	9 560	8	1954	Henshel	Sulzer 6LDA-22
307	Bo-Bo	Elec	725	15 795	10 606	12.74	80	1 100	66	14 700	10	1962	Briddoneau et Leta	MTM Sulzer 6LDA-22E
308	Bo-Bo	Elec	900	12 800	12 900	16.50	120	1 016	64	12 935	41	1866	General Electric Co Babcock & Wilcox	Caterpillar D-398 General Electric GEE

SRI LANKA

SRI LANKA GOVERNMENT RAILWAYS (SLGR)

PO Box No 355, Colombo 10

General Manager: V. T. Navaratne, C.A.S.
Additional General Manager (Technical): P. Rajagopal
Additional General Manager (Administration): B. Polwatta, C.A.S.
Office Assistant to General Manager: M. Supramaniam, C.A.S.
Transportation Superintendents:—
  Operating: A. Chanmugarajah
  Motive Power: B. D. A. J. Fernando
  Administrative: A. G. L. Serpanchy
Commercial Superintendent: S. J. V. Weeraratne
Chief Engineer, Way and Works: J. P. Senaratne
Deputy Chief Engineer, Way and Works: C. Kalidasan
Chief Engineer, Construction: L. S. de Silva
Assistant Chief Engineer, Way and Works: S. Amarasuriya
Superintending Engineer (South): A. B. E. Seneviratne
Superintending Engineer (North): R. Ratnasingham
Signal Engineer, Way and Works: T. W. U. Seneviratne
Chief Mechanical Engineer: E. Rasakulasurier
Deputy Mechanical Engineer: H. M. Jayawardham
Chief Accountant: E. S. P. Seneviratne
Deputy Chief Accountant: S. Nagamani

Gauge: 1.435 m
Route length: 1 496 km

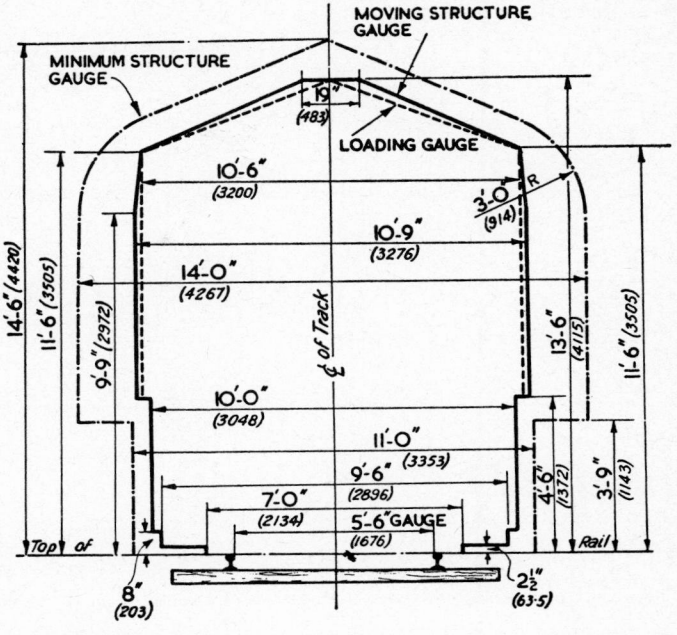

SLGR is based at Colombo where lines radiate north along the coast to Illarankulam, south to Matara and east to the central highlands. From the central highlands the mainline runs to Talaimannar where a ferry provides links with India's Southern Railway. Branch lines run to Trincomalee and Batticalo ports on the Bay of Bengal. A narrow-gauge railway runs from Colombo inland to Ratnapura.

TRAFFIC
Traffic rose five per cent in 1978 following the 390 461 000 tonne-km carried in 1977.

MOTIVE POWER AND ROLLING STOCK
Main motive power problem has been the shortage of spares, necessitating withdrawal from service of a high percentage of the system's 142 diesel locomotives. To supplement the fleet of diesels still in service, a number of the railway's 39 broad-gauge steam locomotives—originally withdrawn entirely from service—have been converted to oil firing and put back to work.

The average age of the present motive power stock is more than 25 years, and if a satisfactory service is to be maintained new stocks of vehicles will have to be ordered soon, says SLGR.

The same is true of passenger coaches and freight wagons. SLGR at present operates 823 broad-gauge coaches. Out of this total, 528 coaches are over 20 years old while nearly 400 are not far short of fifty years old. The railway estimates that more than 50 per cent of the present stock is ready for replacement. A limited programme to rebuild coaches was started in 1973 and up to the end of 1975 about 100 rehabilitated coaches had been returned to service.

Average ages of the wagon fleet are not so critical as those of the coaching stock. Of the 3703 broad-gauge wagons in operation at present nearly 2500 are less than 30 years old. Biggest wagon problem is the high percentage of four-wheelers still in operation—77 per cent of the park, all of which have a very short wheel base of only 2.8194 m. Permissible speed for these units is only 64 km/h; a handicap for speedy operation. SLGR hopes to increase production of locally-built wagons under a three-phase programme for development of a new wagon plant. Under stage one of the programme—put in hand during 1977—a total of 100 wagons are to be built using imported components. Under stage two, certain types of components would be manufactured locally either by SLGR workshops or by local manufacturers. Under stage three, 100 wagons annually, using 100 per cent locally-built components, would be turned out. The railway calculates that local freight wagon manufacture will result in a saving of foreign exchange on 100 wagons of Rs 2.6 million (at 1974 prices).

Once the wagon building project is fully underway it is hoped to expand construction activities to production of passenger coaches. Plans are even being laid for eventual manufacture of both wagons and coaches for export.

CIVIL ENGINEERING
The United Kingdom made a grant of £8.75 million sterling to Sri Lanka in 1978 to fund part of a five-year track renewal programme. Total cost of the programme is £13 million sterling.

Up to 1975 the railway was operating a 1496 route-km broad-gauge system and a 140 route-km narrow-gauge system. Following mounting losses from narrow-gauge operations the Government agreed to close down all 762-mm gauge services—with the exception of commuter operations over a short section between Maradana and Homagama—as from early 1976.

SLGR is still faced with the generally poor condition of remaining broad-gauge lines which have not been kept in a good state of repair due to the inadequate supply of essential track materials.

Railway builders in Ceylon used mainly 32.6 kg/m section rails, with sleepers 9 144 mm apart and an additional two sleepers on the incline for every 6.4 m of rail. With experience it was later found that closer spacing of the sleepers had little effect in reducing stresses on the rail, but that an increase of the weight of rail permitted a higher load-carrying capacity. Since 1957, therefore, the railway has been gradually replacing existing track with 36 kg/m and 40 kg/m rail sections with sleepers spaced at 6 604 mm. Under the last three-year programme the railway purchased and installed 154 km of 40 kg/m rail and 233 km of 36 kg/m sections. Cost of the rail was Rs 10.6 million.

Recent improvement and strengthening of the track with the introduction of steel sole plates has been very successful, reports the railway. It has not only increased the life of the sleepers by transmitting the load through an increased area, but has also provided a better seat for the rail bottom. Provision of additional dog spikes and introduction of elastic spikes has also helped improve the permanent way.

At present imported sleepers mainly of keruing and kempas timber varieties are used on the track along with local varieties of timber. Normal annual replacement requirement is in the region of 150 000 to 200 000 sleepers. With the shortfall in supplies by 1975 the railway needed 400 000 sleepers for normal maintenance work.

The sole local supplier—the State Timber Corporation—is able to supply SLGR with about 100 000 timber sleepers annually. The remainder will have to be purchased from abroad and to supplement these a new concrete sleeper plant is planned to produce about 200 000 units annually.

DIESEL LOCOMOTIVES

Class	Axle Arrangement	Transmission	Rated Power hp	Max. lb (kg)	Tractive Effort Continuous at lb (kg)	at mph (km/h)	Max. Speed mph (km/h)	Wheel Dia. in (mm)	Total Weight Tons	Length ft ins (mm)	No. Built	Year first Built	Builders: Mechanical Parts	Builders: Engine & Type	Builders: Transmission
M1	A1A-A1A	Elec	1 000	33 700 (15 300)	24 600 (11 160)	11.7 (18.8)	55	43	88	50' 9'' (15 469)	25	1953	Brush	Mirrlees JS12VT	Brush
M2	A1A-A1A	Elec	1 425	35 840 (16 250)			55	40	79	46' 9'' (14 250)	10	1954	GM	GM 567C	GM
M2C	A1A-A1A	Elec	1 425	44 240 (20 070)			55	40	79	43' 0'' (13 106)	2	1961	GM	GM	GM
G2	Bo-Bo	Elec	625	35 000 (15 875)	15 000 (6 800)		20	43	54	37' 9'' (11 506)	8	1951	North British Loco Co	Paxman 12RPHXL	GEC
S2	Bo-Bo	Hyd	789				56	43	55	55' 0'' (16 764)	15	1959		Maybach MD 435	Maybach Mekydro K104U
S3 S4	Bo-Bo	Hyd	880				56	36	47	55' 0¾'' (16 780)	30	1959		MAN L12V 18/21	Maybach Mekydro K104U
N1	1-C-1	Hyd	492	20 150 (9 040)			30	36	41	28' 0¾'' (8 550)	5	1953		Deutz T8 M233	Krupp
P1	C (0-6-0)	Jack Shaft & Coupling Rod Drive	132	9 000 (4 080)			19.5	33	20	20' 2¾'' (6 165)	4	1950	Hunslet	Ruston Hornsby	Hunslet Patent
T1	Bo	Elec	180					34	37	61' 0'' (18 593)	24	1947		English Electric Type 6H	English Electric
Y	C (0-6-0)	Hyd	550	29 900	1 900 (5 700)	6.0 (20)	26 (42)				28	1967	Hunslet	Rolls-Royce DV8T	Twin Disc CF 12800
W1		Hyd					50 (80)							Henschel	
W2		Hyd					50 (80)							VEB	

The length of rail sections used has been increased from 6.4 m to 13.7, reducing the number of rail joints needed. Thermit welding has been introduced to weld rails, applied at site for welded panels of about 68.5 m.
A long-term plan has been drawn up to carry out a number of major improvements throughout the system. These projects include:
Expansion of the principal carriage yard at Colombo to accommodate the increased passenger stock;
Remodelling of the former steam shed at Dematagoda to accommodate multiple-units;
Extension and provision of additional lines to the main marshalling yard at Colombo;
Construction of additional platforms at key stations;
Provision of additional crossing facilities at Taple on the coast line and Gatambe on the main line.

SIGNALLING
Although the list and morse system of interlocking is still in operation in the northern parts of Sri Lanka, majority of the SLGR network is signalled by type A6 equipment. Work started during the 1975-77 programme on installation of a route interlocking panel and Centralised Traffic Control system. The route interlocking is at Maradana and Fort, connecting the yards in Colombo. Buttons are mounted on a geographically laid out panel and all points are moved by electrical motors. Miniature light indications on the panel give necessary information on train movements and position of switches and signals. The CTC system at present covers south of Colombo as far as Kalutara (40.2 km), north up to Alawwa (64.3 km), and northwest to Katunayaka (28.9 km). Double line tracks operated by CTC are signalled with automatic block signals with a minimum headway of three minutes at an average speed of 48 km/h.
Projects planned for improvement include:
Extension of Centralised Traffic Control to Chilaw, Polgahawela and Alutgama, and other improvements to signalling;
Provision of a radio communication network between main stations on the island, and the extension of the telephone links to the terminal stations of Badulla and Matale;
Public address systems; installed at all junctions and terminals, together with inter-communication systems at Colombo marshalling yard and Anuradhapura Junction to facilitate better train and traffic control;
Proposals for the electrification of suburban lines and construction of a central work-shop to manufacture spare parts, components and accessories.
Action has already been taken to place orders for 14 main line locomotives and 10 multiple-unit sets and these were expected to arrive on the island in 1978. It was also proposed to purchase 140 carriages for main line passenger service during 1978.

SUDAN

SUDAN RAILWAYS

Atbara

General Manager: Mohamed Abdel Rahman Wasfi
Deputy General Manager for Traffic, Civil, Mechanical & Electric Engineering: Abbas Ali Ragi
Deputy General Manager for Training, Personnel, Financial & Economic Affairs: Ibrahim Hag Ali
Director of Civil Engineering: Yahiya Shams El Deen
Director of Traffic: Abdel Ghafour Tewfik
Director of Mechanical & Electric Engineering: Saleh Mohamed El Tayeb
Director of Personnel: El Sir A Alla
Director of Supplies and Stores: Khawad Ibrahim
Director of Accounts and Finance: Mohamed El Hassan Osman
Assistant Director of Planning and Economic Research: Abdel Rahman Mohamed Fahmi

Route length: 4 780.8 km

The railway is the main transport mode in Sudan, carrying nearly 75 per cent of the nation's passenger and freight traffic. The railway freight traffic is characterised by a very intense seasonal peak extending from December to June and reaching its height during March. Beside the transport of agricultural products the railway is the main mode for the transport of consumer goods, development materials, agricultural inputs, such as fertilisers, from the port to the interior of the country. Petroleum products also form some of the major import commodities. The railway also caters for a considerable volume of internal traffic which is mainly composed of food crops, firewood, cement, flour etc. The railway is also the only means for long-distance passenger traffic and provides a regular link between all urban centres throughout the year.
The International Development Association, two Arab investment banks, and the European Development Fund are lending $US68 million to Sudan for modernisation and development of Sudan Railways during the country's current six-year plan. Principal items of expenditure will be a batch of new diesel-electrics and track-doubling between Port Sudan and Haiya Junction (203 km). Other work will include track upgrading and relating with heavier rail, improvements to signalling and telecommunications, and establishment of a staff training college at Atbara.

TRAFFIC
Rail freight declined through the 1970s with freight hauled in 1977/78 amounting to 2.2 million tonnes (2 004 million tonne-km), a drop of 0.4 million tonnes on the previous year's figures and almost a million tonnes less than the freight moved in 1970/71.
Passenger traffic has not been so badly affected with 1976/77 producing the decades best figures, almost 3.9 million journeys for 1 305 million passenger-km. But journeys fell to three million and passenger-km to 1 192 million in 1977/78.
Sudan's single-track rail network is currently under strain. It was designed to carry 3 million tonnes of goods and 2.5 million passengers a year but at the moment it is having to cope with about 4.5 million tonnes of freight and an increasing number of passengers. Wagon turnround time has declined from 17.3 to 21.9 days recorded in 1978.

	1973/74	*1974/75*	*1975/76*	*1976/77*
Exports (thousands tonnes)	687	644	815	892
Imports (thousand tonnes)	1 379	1 312	1 494	1 433
Local traffic (thousand tonnes)	477	434	346	379
Net tonne-km (millions)	2 426	2 275	2 703	2 479
Wagon-km (thousands)	104 086	102 635	113 014	106 504
Mainline diesel locomotive-km (thousands)	4 253	4 495	5 673	6 245
Number of passengers (thousands)	2 807	2 947	3 069	3 854
Passenger-km (millions)	1 048	1 102	1 167	1 305
Coaching-km (thousands)	29 740	28 589	28 249	35 052

On the basis of increased traffic during the present 1978-83 Six-year Plan SR expects to be railing 6.6 millions tonnes of freight by the end of the plan period.

FINANCES
Freight revenue for 1977/78 fell by £S 2 million to £S 24 million, while passenger income was up by £S 1.4 million to £S 9 million. Operating revenue, at £S 33 million, was very slightly ahead of costs, which amounted to £S 32.6 million.

MOTIVE POWER AND ROLLING STOCK
Mainline locomotives at the end of 1978 included 96 steam and 153 diesels with shunting carried out by 31 steam and 79 diesels. Coaching stock totalled 467; freight wagons, 5 811.
The 1978/1983 plan has allocated the sum of £S 35 million for the procurement of rolling stock: £S 15 million for new locomotives and £S 20 million for passenger coaches and service vehicles. Additional requirements of rolling stock are assessed on the basis of the improved performance or operational targets to be attained during the plan period.
The Six-year Plan aims at reducing the turnround time of freight wagons to ten days at the end of the plan period, and to increase the average run per diesel locomotive to 85 000. The plan aims at increasing the availability of mainline locomotives to 75 per cent.

Under the 1978-83 plan £S 28 million has been set aside for track, signalling and station projects:

	Total cost	*Plan allocation*
	(£S million)	
Doubling of Port Sudan—Haiya line	26.00	15.00
Relaying of Sennar—Damazine line	13.00	5.00
Resleepering of Kassala line	3.00	3.00
Signalling and communications	3.00	2.00
Crossing stations	2.80	2.00
Conversion of halts into stations	0.65	0.65
Buildings and artificial installations	2.00	1.00

The expected increase in the volume of exports and imports will greatly increase the volume of traffic on the Haiya—Port Sudan line. To eliminate congestion on this line and to increase its traffic capacity, the railway has already introduced new crossing stations to eliminate the leading or longest block sections, improved signalling and communication systems, relaid the line with 90-lb/yd rails to increase train loads and speeds and introduced diesel locomotives. Doubling of the line is to proceed under the plan as an alternative to further major improvement works.
The relaying of the Khartoum—Sennar line, which serves the Gezira region, with 90-lb/yd rails, is necessary to meet expected expansion in agricultural production. This line will also serve live-stock traffic coming from the south and west to Khartoum for internal consumption and to Port Sudan for export.
The expected increase in the volume of traffic calls for the relaying of the Rahad—Babanousa line with 75-lb/yd rails. This project will allow heavy locomotives to operate on this section, which links the western and southern extensions with the rest of the railway system.
The Haiya—Kassala—Sennar—El Obied line is formed of fairly new 75-lb/yd rails. However, due to the bad condition of the sleepers, which are more than 20 years old, various sections of the line are put under speed restrictions. The re-sleepering of this line will speed the movement of trains and increase traffic capacity. This line will assume greater importance in the future as it will serve the traffic coming from the western and southern extensions and from the Blue Nile region. The line will also serve the sugar exports, the Rahad project and the cement factory that will be constructed near Durudeib Station.
The Blue Nile Province will see great expansion in agricultural production in the future. This calls for the relaying of Sennar—Damazine line with 90-lb/yd rails. To avoid line obstructions during the rainy season, the project includes also the heightening and widening of banks.

Standard rail: Flat bottom, weighing 50 lb/yd *(24.7 kg/m)* in lengths of 30 ft *(9.14 m)*; and 75 lb/yd *(37.2 kg/m)* in lengths of 36 ft *(10.97 m)*; joined by fishplates and bolts. 90 lb B.S. rail for relaying Khartoum-Port Sudan Line.
Sleepers (ties): Steel; and wood impregnated under pressure in mixture of creosote and oil (½ and ½), 9 in × 5 in × 6 ft 6 in. Concrete has been used in a few cases as an experiment.
Spacing: 1 275/km under 36 ft long 75 lb rail, and 1 311/km under 30 ft long 50 lb rail. This is 12 per rail.
Rail fastenings: 50 and 75 lb rails: screw spikes and elastic spikes. 90 lb rail: clips and screw spikes. Pandrol fastenings are in service under test. Steel sleepers: steel keys are being replaced by clips with bolts and nuts.
Filling: Generally earth is used, but in some stretches of line quarry spoil and ballast.
Max curvature: (Main line) 4.5° except few at 5.0°.
Max gradient: 0.66% (1 in 150) except on section in Red Sea Hills between Summit and Port Sudan, where 1% (1 in 100) occurs. Gradient compensation for curves is 0.04% per 1° curvature.
Longest continuous gradient: The overall gradient from Port Sudan to Summit, a distance of 80 miles *(3.75 129 km)*, is 0.7%, with a continuous 2.3 miles *(3.75 km)* of 0.98%. There are only five short level sections, three of which are stations, in the whole 80 miles.
Worst combination of gradient and curvature: 1% grade with 4½° curve-radius of 1 274 ft *(388 m)*.
Gauge widening on curves: ¼ in *(6.4 mm)* on curves of 4° and over.
Super-elevation on sharpest-curve: 3 in *(76 mm)* max.
Rate of slope of super-elevation:
⅙ in *(4.2 mm)* per rail length for curves under 3° = radius of 1 910 ft *(582 m)*.
⅓ in *(8.4 mm)* per rail length for curves of 3° and over.
Max axle loading:
16½ tons for 75 lb track.
12½ tons for 50 lb track.
Max bridge loading: 17 units B.S.
Max speed:
31 mph *(50 km/h)* on 50 lb track.
37 mph *(60 km/h)* on 75 lb track.
Max altitude: 3 013 ft *(918.5 m)* at Summit Station on Port Sudan line.

By virtue of its location and extent, Sudan Railways forms an important part of the master plan for linking the African railway systems. The extension of the railway line from Nyala, the terminus of the western extension, to Geneina, near the border of Chad, will provide a future link with the railways of West Africa. The extension of the line from Dein, on the Western Extension, to Hofrat Elnahas, near the border of the Central African Republic will achieve the same purpose.
By extending the railway line from Wau to Juba and then to Nimuli, near the border of Uganda, a link will be made with the railways of East Africa.
Sudan and Egypt have made great progress in connecting their railway systems. Engineering and economic surveys have been completed and a loan application made to the African Development Bank. The Egyptian Railways will be extended to Wadi Halfa Station at the northern part of the country. A transhipment station will be constructed to facilitate the movement of traffic between the two systems.

DIESEL LOCOMOTIVES

Engine Class	Axle ArjanE$ ment	Trans- MUSSIOF ment	Rated hp	Total tons	Tractive Effort Max (kg)	Continuous (kg)	(km/h)	Max Speed (km/h)	Length (mm)	Wheel Dia (mm)	No.	Year Built	Builders: Parts		and Type
100	B (0-4-0)	Hyd	340	32					23' 8'' (7 213)	40 (1 016)	6	1962	Robert Stephenson&Hawthorns Ltd. & W. G. Bagnall Ltd. Also Clayton Dewandre-England	Rolls Royce C8TEL	Robert Stephenson Torque convertor-twin disc, 11 500. Final drive gearbox-Wiseman 15 RLBG.
403	C (0-6-0)	Elec	350	43½					30' 1⅛'' (9 173)	48 (1 219)	5	1952	English Electric	English Electric type 6 KT	English Electric
450	C (0-6-0)	Hyd	350	46.26	30 852 (13 770)				32' 5³/₁₆'' (9 885)	48 (1 219)	4	1958	Henschel & Sohn-Kassel	English Electric type 6 KT	Voith; Turbo-transmission
460-466 467-480	C (0-6-0)	Hyd	500	46.5	34 400 (15 360) at 33% adhesion			37.5-18.7 (60-30)	28' 11¼'' (8 820)	45 (1 143)	21	1962 /63	Henschel Werke-GMBH	Rheinstahl Henschel AG 12-cylinder 4-stroke type 12 V1416A	Voith Turbo-Transmission Type L37Vb
1000	Co-Co	Elec	1 850	99	55 000 (24 900)	48 000 (21 770)		45 (72)	55' 0'' (16 764)	36 (914)	25 30	1960 1963 1969	English Electric	English Electric 12 CSVT	English Electric
1200	Co-Co	Elec	1 850	99	55 440 (25 146) at 25% adhesion 66 528 (30 175) at 30% adhesion	35 700 (16 200)		52.8 (85)	57' 7¾'' (17 570)	36 (914)	15	1961	Gregg Cockerill Ougree	Cockerill Ougree-BLH model 608A	A.C.E.C.
1400	AIA-AIA	Elec	1 500	75	33 600 (15 230) at 30% adhesion			50 (80)	48' 6⅝'' (14 800)	36 (914)	2 20	1964 1969	Hitachi	Hitachi-M.A.N. Model V6V 22/30 Maul	Hitachi
1600	B-B	Hyd	1 500	52.8	38 976 (17 400)	35 168 (15 700)	9 375 (15)	56.25 (90)	43' 6¹/₁₆'' (13 260)	36 (914)	1	1965	Henschel Werke AG	Maybach MD 654	Voith L 630 r U2 with hydro dynamic brake and built in reverse gear.

SWAZILAND

SWAZILAND RAILWAY (SR)

Swaziland Railway Building, Johnston Street, PO Box 475, Mbabane

Telephone: 42486/7
Telex: 2053 WD

Chairman: R. V. Diamini
Chief Executive Officer: A. L. Weidemann
Financial Controller: P. Barnes
Chief Operating Executive: C. J. Hubinger
Commercial Manager: G. H. Moore
Chief Civil Engineer: D. I. Cowie
Chief Mechanical Engineer: C. G. Aitkenhead
Acting Chief of Administrative Services: Prince Nqaba Dlamini
Management Services Officer: C. R. Carter
Chief of Personnel and Labour Relations: B. N. Fakudze

Gauge: 1.067 m
Route length: 317 km

TRAFFIC	1979
Freight tonne-km	336 111
Freight tonnage	2 012 637

FINANCES	1976	1977	1979
Revenue	5 429 000	5 709 000	6 522 000
Expenses	5 561 000	5 864 000	6 693 000

MOTIVE POWER & ROLLING STOCK
All locomotives are hired from South African Railways. No passenger coaches are operated; the railway owns 713 freight wagons.

TRACK
A new 192 km line was built from Phuzumoya to Golela in 1978/79 laid on concrete sleepers using 40 kg/m rail. The route leaves Swaziland Railway's Ka Dake-Mlawula (Mozambique) line at Phuzumoya and runs almost due south past the Mtambama mountain range to Lavumisa and the border at Golela, linking up with South African Railways.

Rail—types and weights:
40 kg/m FB mainline
30 kg/m FB sidings
Sleepers (Cross ties) type: Hardwood
Thickness: 127 mm
Spacing: up to 814 mm
Rail Fastenings (types used): Soleplates and coachscrews
Welded Rail: Total length of track laid in 1975: 126 km

SWEDEN

SWEDISH STATE RAILWAYS

Statens Järnvägar (SJ), S-105 50 Stockholm C

General Manager: Bengt Furbäck
Chief Officers:
Operating Department: G. Rosqvist
Commercial Department: E. Sunden
Fixed Installations Department: R. Enberg
Mechanical and Workshops Dept.: B. Larsson
Department of Finance and Economics: M. J. G. Högberg
Administrative Department: B. L. Ulf
Department of Development and Research: P. G. Andersson
Planning Department: P. Jönsson
Legal Department: C. Nordström

Gauge: 1.435 m; 1.067 m; 0.891 m
Route length: 11 195 km; 188 km

Policy control of the SJ is exercised by a Board consisting of eight members under the chairmanship of the Director General. Seven members are appointed by the Government.
The heads of the eight departments and the Director General constitute the Directorate (consultative function).
Operating and Fixed Installations regions coincide with regional centres at Malmö, Göteborg, Norrköping, Stockholm, Örebro, Gävle, Sundsvall and Lulea.

	miles	km	miles	km	miles	km
Route length	6 961	11 200	113	182	7 074	11 382
Electrified route length	4 390	7 063	—	—	4 390	7 063
System of electrification	16 kV 16⅔ Hz		—	—		

The line from Trelleborg, the ferry port on the south coast, northward to Narvik, Norway, is one of the longest continuous electrified lines in the world. It is 1 373 miles (2 210 km) long, of which the last 24 mile (39 km) section is in Norway.
A new line is planned between Getinge and Halmstad on the west coast (25 km) and a new line is at present under construction between Älvsbyn and Bergträsk in the north (12 km).

TRAFFIC
SJ freight transports are to a great extent influenced by the development of mining, iron industry and forestry. SJ freight transport for 1978/79 were still affected by the economic recession, but towards the end of 1978 the volume of transport began to increase. A large part of the rise was due to iron ore transports on the ore railway Kiruna—Narvik. The transport volume of forestry products also increased. Freight services by train in 1978/79 totalled 54.4 million tonnes (compared with 46.1 million tonnes the previous year) and 15 600 million tonne-km (up 15 per cent). The average haul was 287 km and the number of freight train-km totalled 39.4 million (down one per cent).
The direct traffic to and from foreign countries accounted for 51 per cent of transport tonnage and 46 per cent of transport performance (ton-km).
Passenger service by train comprised 23.5 million journeys (down one per cent) and 4 415 million passenger-km (down three per cent). The average distance carried was 188 km. The number of passenger train-km was 54.8 million. (Local traffic in Stockholm area is excluded. It is estimated at about 40 million journeys, but the exact figure cannot be stated.)

FINANCES
The total proceeds of SJ (exclusive of financial and extraordinary items) amounted to 5 373 million Kroner (4 927 million Kroner in 1977/78), of which 49 per cent (48 per cent in 1977/78) referred to freight traffic, 32 per cent (33 per cent in 1977/78) to passenger traffic, 14 per cent (13 per cent in 1977/78) to State compensation for non-profitable rail traffic and five per cent (six per cent in 1977/78) to other proceeds.
Costs increased by 280 million Kroner (up five per cent). Staff costs increased on an average by six per cent (12 per cent in 1977/78) per employee.

SJ's economic result of 1978/79 (after depreciation) was a deficit of 113 million Kroner exclusive of interest on the State capital. The deficit was covered by a reduction in the depreciation. Interest on the capital invested by the State amounted to 191 million Kroner.

INVESTMENTS
The total investments in 1978/79 amounted to 765 million Kroner of which 297 million was for fixed installations and 397 million for rolling stock.

MOTIVE POWER AND ROLLING STOCK
Motive power on order and delivered in 1978/79 included 40 class Rc4 ordered from ASEA in 1979 following 16 class Rc4 delivered in 1978/79. The first diesel railcars class Y1 of 100 units were ordered from Fiat and the first passenger train coaches of 150 units were ordered from KVAB and delivered in 1979.

Number of locomotives in service	Line haul	Shunting
Electric locomotives	618	133
Diesel-electric locomotives	157	—
Diesel-hydraulic locomotives	58	393
Diesel-mechanical locomotives	—	11
Electric railcars	40	
Diesel railcars	160	
Electric trailer cars	38	
Diesel trailer cars	58	
Electric multicar trains	128	
Diesel multicar trains	5	
Number of passenger train coaches	1 592	
Freight train cars	44 803	

ELECTRIFICATION
Total electrified route length on 31 December 1979: 7 063 km
Total electrified track length on 31 December 1979: 11 038 km

In 1979 about 220 km of track were renewed and about 50 km relaid with reconditioned rails. The length of continuous welded rails is about 4 100 km. Track maintenance is highly mechanised. Conventional machinery (Matisa, Plasser & Theurer) and domestic machines are used.

Due to the fact that Swedish State Railways is a merger of former state and privately-owned railways, existing track rails are of many different patterns and weights, varying between 25 and 50 kg/m (50-100 lb/yd). During the last 25 years, however, the number of rail sections has been systematically reduced. While the total network 25 years ago had an average rail weight of about 35 kg/m (70 lb/yd) the corresponding figure today is about 43 kg/m (86 lb/yd). SJ is now purchasing solely 50 kg rails. The joints are suspended.

The normal rail renewal programme amounts to 260 km track per year which corresponds to a total life of 58 years. The new rails will be used on principal mainlines over about 30 years, corresponding to 150-200 million gross tonnes hauled on average. After renewal the released rails are reconditioned and relaid on secondary lines and sidings where they have a second (sometimes a third) life until they are scrapped. The rails are delivered from the mill in standard lengths of 40 m. About 75 per cent of the total length of the mainlines now have rails longer than 20 m and more than 30 per cent have continuous welded rails.

Fastenings
For continuous welded track on wooden sleepers the Hey-Back fastening is used. It is of Norwegian origin and consists of a tie plate fastened to the sleeper by four screw spikes plus two spring clips which are driven into grooves in the plate. The two clips, which are self-securing, exert a total hold-down pressure on the base of the rail of about 1 400 kg (3 100 lb). A resiliant rubber pad is used between the base of the rail and tie plate. This fastening was introduced in 1957 and has behaved excellently on principal main tracks. About 1 500 km of continuous welded track is equipped with this fastening.

The first concrete ties had a unique elastic fastening called the Fist-fastening and about 1 450 km of continuous welded track are equipped with this. The Fist-fastening has now

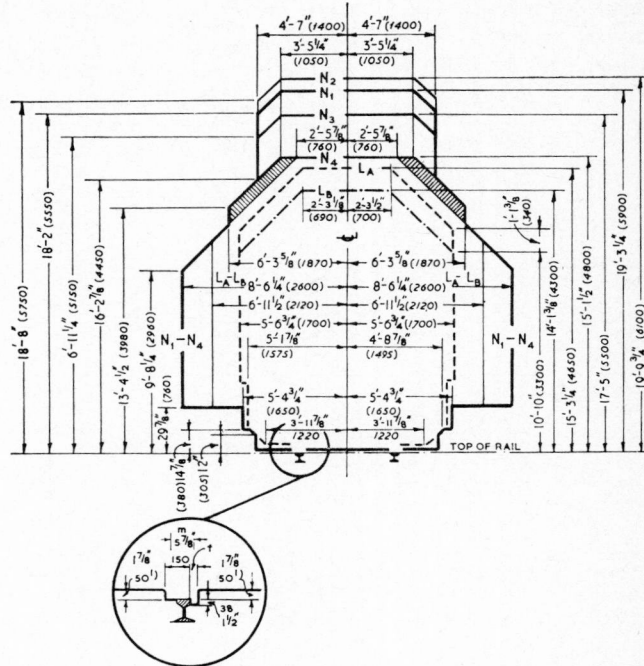

been replaced by two other types of fastening for concrete ties: the Pandrol- and the Hambo-fastenings. Both use elastic steel components of the "fit and forget" type. The Pandrol-fastening has a hold-down pressure on the rail of about 1 300 kg (2 900 lb) and the Hambo-fastening a pressure of about 2 100 kg (4 600 lb).

Sleepers
Normal sleeper spacing on SJ main tracks is 65 cm, sufficient for a 20 tonnes axle-load. The spacing is 60 cm on curves with a radius below 1 000 m and 55 cm if the radius is less than 500 m. An even smaller sleeper spacing of 50 cm is used on the heaviest loaded freight line where the axle-load is 25 tonnes and the annual gross tonnage is up to 50 million.

More than 90 per cent of SJ sleepers are creosoted soft wood ties, $2.6 \times 0.22 \times 0.16$ m. The average life is about 25 years. Two types of concrete tie are also used, both 2·3 m long. The first, known as the 101 tie, consists of two 800 mm blocks of concrete joined together by a steel tube filled with concrete. The sleeper is reinforced with a single steel bar passing through the steel tube and anchored at the outside ends of the concrete blocks by means of washers and nuts. The bar is given a coating of plastic and is post-tensioned to a tensile force of 13·5 tonnes after the concrete has hardened. The rails rest on rubber pads fitted into slots on top of the tie, and attached to the tie by the Fist-fastening.

The second type of tie is a monoblock sleeper reinforced with 12 wires 6.35 mm in diameter. Before casting the wires are pretensioned to a tensile force of 36 tonnes. As in the case of the 101 tie, there are slots for the rails on top of the tie and the Fist-fastening is used.

In 1979 SJ had more than three million concrete ties on the main tracks. About 324 000 concrete ties are annually delivered to the SJ.

Class Rc4 locomotives are being built by ASEA, Nohab and KVAB
Rated output 4 900 hp, max speed 135 km/h, weight 78 tonnes.

Class T44 diesel-electric locomotives, built by Nohab
Rated at 1 670 hp, a total of 73 units are now in service. More are being delivered.

Wagon class H bis

Passenger coach A7/B7

TRACK

Standard rail: The only rail sections now being bought and installed are:
Type SJ 43: 87 lb/yd *(43.2 kg/m)*
Type SJ 50: 101 lb/yd *(50.0 kg/m)*

Sleepers (cross ties):
Wooden sleepers:
Type 1: 9½ in × 6⅛ in × 8 ft 6¾ in *(240 × 155 × 2 600 mm)*
Type 2: 8⅝ in × 6⅛ in × 8 ft 6¾ in *(220 × 155 × 2 600 mm)*
Concrete sleepers:
Type B10: 12½ in × 8¾ in × 8 ft ⅜ in *(320 × 222 × 2 500 mm)*
Type S3: 12½ in × 8¾ in × 8 ft ⅜ in *(320 × 220 × 2 500 mm)*

Rail fastenings: With wooden sleepers the Hey-Back fastening is used. With concrete sleepers the Fist, Pandrol and Hambo types are used with a rubber or plastic pad under the rail.

Sleeper spacing:
Main lines: 25½ in *(650 mm)*
Secondary lines: 29½ in *(750 mm)*
On the ore line Kiruna-Riksgränsen spacing being reduced to 19⅝ in *(500 mm)*.

Welded rail: Total length of track 31 December, 1976: 3 700 km. The rail bars are flash butt welded in workshop into 360 m lengths which are carried on a train of flat cars to site. After laying in position, the rails lengths are Thermit welded to form continuous rail.

SIGNALLING

SJ's first CTC route went into operation in 1955 and the present length of CTC is 4 000 km. Installation of a new ATC system began in 1979. All mainlines will be equipped with this system over the next six years. The first computer based interlocking plant has just been taken into service in Gothenburg. The main supplier of signal material is L M Ericsson.

FERRIES

The Swedish State Railways is linked to the continental railway network by four ferry routes: Helsingborg-Helsingör (DSB), Malmö-Copenhagen (DSB), Trelleborg-Sassnitz (DR) and Ystad-Swinoujscie (PKP). Two of these are freight only, the Copenhagen and the Swinoujscie crossings. Swedish ferries operate on the Copenhagen (one ferry) and Sassnitz routes (three ferries). For the Trelleborg-Sassnitz route a new ferry has recently been contracted for delivery in 1981/82. It will probably become the greatest combined passenger/car/trainferry in the world, with a length of 170 m, width 23 m, track capacity 700 m, lorries 15 × 18 m, about 30 private cars (additional) and 800 passengers.

Class V5 diesel locomotives are being built by Henschel
Hydraulic transmission, rated output 265 hp.

Class Tb is a special diesel-electric snowplough locomotive built by Nohab

ELECTRIC LOCOMOTIVES

Class	Axle Arrange-ment	Line Current	Rated Output hp	Max. lb *(kg)*	Tractive Effort (Full Field) Continuous at lb *(kg)*	mph *(km/h)*	Max. Speed mph *(km/h)*	Wheel dia. in *(mm)*	Weight tonnes	Length ft in *(mm)*	No. Built	Year Built	Builders: Mechanical Parts	Builders: Electrical Equipment
Da	1-C-1	15 kV 1/16⅔	2 500	45 200 *(20 500)*	21 200 *(9 600)*	43.2 *(69.5)*	62 *(100)*	60¼ *(1 530)*	75	42′ 8″ *(13 000)*	92	1952	Nohab; ASJ; Motala	ASEA
Du	1-C-1	15 kV 1/16⅔	2 500	34 600 *(15 700)*	21 100 *(9 600)*	43.2 *(69.5)*	62 *(100)*	60¼ *(1 530)*	80.4	42′ 8″ *(13 000)*	237	1925	Nohab; ASJ; Motala	ASEA
Dm	1-D+D-1	15 kV 1/16⅔	5 600 6 500	137 000 *(62 000)* 137 000 *(62 000)*	63 500 *(28 800)* 63 500 *(28 800)*	32.4 *(51.8)* 37.0 *(59)*	47 *(75)* 47 *(75)*	60¼ *(1 530)* 60¼ *(1 530)*	180.0-186.4 190.0	82′ 3¾″ *(25 100)*	19 (1)	1953 1971	Nohab; ASJ; Motala	ASEA
Dm3	1-D+D+D-1	15 kV 1/16⅔	8 400	205 000 *(93 000)*	96 000 *(43 500)*	32.4 *(51.8)*	47 *(75)*	60¼ *(1 530)*	258.4	115′ 8″ *(32 250)*	3	1960	Nohab; ASJ; Motala	ASEA
Dm3	1-D+D+D-1	15 kV 1/16⅔	9 750	205 000 *(93 000)*	96 000 *(43 500)*	37.0 *(59)*	47 *(75)*	60¼ *(1 530)*	273.2	115′ 8″ *(35 250)*	15(1)	1967	Nohab; ASJ; Motala	ASEA
F	1-Do-1	15 kV 1/16⅔	3 500	44 500 *(20 200)*	20 000 *(9 100)*	58.7 *(94.5)*	84 *(135)*	60¼ *(1 530)*	102	49′ 11¾″ *(15 230)*	23	1942	Nohab; ASJ; Motala	ASEA
Hc	Bo-Bo	15 kV 1/16⅔	1 600	37 400 *(17 000)*	17 200 *(7 800)*	33.6 *(54.1)*	50 *(80)*	43¼ *(1 100)*	59.8	41′ 0″ *(12 500)*	13	1942	Nohab; ASJ Motala	ASEA
Hg	Bo-Bo	15 kV 1/16⅔	1 760	40 200 *(18 300)*	18 500 *(8 400)*	34.1 *(54.9)*	50 *(80)*	43¼ *(1 100)*	64.8	41′ 0″ *(12 500)*	55	1942	Nohab; ASJ; Motala	ASEA
Ma	Co-Co	15 kV 1/16⅔	4 500	82 500 *(37 400)*	36 800 *(16 700)*	44.4 *(71.5)*	63 *(100)*	51⅛ *(1 300)*	105	55′ 1½″ *(16 800)*	32	1953	Nohab: ASJ; Motala	ASEA
Mg	Co-Co	15 kV 1/16⅔	3 600	65 200 *(39 600)*	32 400 *(14 700)*	36 *(58)*	50 *(80)*	43¼ *(1 100)*	102	55′ 1½″ *(16 800)*	16	1944	Nohab; ASJ; Motala	ASEA
Ra	Bo-Bo	15 kV 1/16⅔	3 600	43 200 *(19 600)*	20 000 *(9 100)*	65.5 *(104.5)*	93 *(150)*	51⅛ *(1 300)*	64.0	49′ 6½″ *(15 100)*	10	1955	Nohab; ASJ; Motala	ASEA
Rc1	Bo-Bo	15 kV 1/16⅔	4 900	61 700 *(28 000)*	34 600 *(15 700)*	49 *(78.8)*	84 *(135)*	51⅛ *(1 300)*	80	50′ 9″ *(15 470)*	20	1967	Nohab; ASJ; Motala	ASEA
Rc2	Bo-Bo	15 kV 1/16⅔	4 900	61 700 *(28 000)*	34 600 *(15 700)*	49 *(78.8)*	84 *(135)*	51⅛ *(1 300)*	77	50′ 11″ *(15 520)*	100	1969	Nohab; ASJ; Motala	ASEA
Rc3	Bo-Bo	15 kV 1/16⅔	4 900	52 900 *(24 000)*	31 900 *(14 500)*	57 *(91.8)*	100 *(160)*	51⅛ *1 300*	77	50′ 11″ *15 520*	10	1970	Nohab; ASJ; Motala	ASEA
Rc4	Bo-Bo	15 kV 1/16⅔	4 900	61 700 *(28 000)*	34 600 *(15 700)*	48.5 *(78)*	84 *(135)*	51⅛ *(1 300)*	78.0	50′ 9″ *(15 470)*	85	1975	Nohab; KVAB	ASEA
Rm	Bo-Bo	15 kV 1/16⅔	3 600 kW	65 000 *(31 400)*	50 600 *(23 000)*	34.2 *(55)*	63 *(100)*	49¼ *(1 250)*	92	50′ 11″ *(15 570)*	6	1977	Nohab	ASEA
Ub	C	15 kV 1/16⅔	700	29 800 *(13 500)*	16 700 *(7 600)*	15.5 *(25)*	28 *(45)*	43¼ *(1 100)*	47.4	31′ 6″ *(9 600)*	90	1930	Nohab; Motala	ASEA
Uc	C	15 kV 1/16⅔	700	29 800 *(13 500)*	16 700 *(7 600)*	15.5 *(25)*	28 *(45)*	43¼ *(1 100)*	49.2	31′ 6″ *(9 600)*	1	1933	Nohab	ASEA
Ud	C	15 kV 1/16⅔	840	28 600 *(13 000)*	15 200 *(6 900)*	20 *(32)*	37 *(60)*	43¼ *(1 100)*	50.4	31′ 6″ *(9 600)*	25	1955	Nohab; ASJ; Motala	ASEA

Notes: Class Du, rebuilt from Dg, Dk and Ds.
Class Rc, thyristor control.
(1) Rebuilt from Class Dm to Dm3

DIESEL LOCOMOTIVES

Class	Axle Arrangement	Transmission	Rated Power hp	Max lb (kg)	Tractive Effort Continuous at lb (kg)	mph (km/h)	Max. Speed mph (km/h)	Wheel Dia max (mm)	Axle load tonnes	Total Weight Tons	Length ft in (mm)	No. Built	Year first Built	Mechanical Parts	Engine & Type	Transmission
T21	D	Hyd	800	41 200 (18 700)	26 500 (12 000)	7.5 (12)	50 (80)	49⅜ (1 255)	14.2	57	37' 1" (11 300)	51 3	1955 1956	MAK ASJ	MAK MA 301A	Voith and MAK
T23	D	Hyd	750	26 000 (11 800)			47 (75)	40 (1 015)	13.0	52	35' 9" (10 900)	11 4	1954 1954	MAK AJS	MAK MA301A	Voith and MAK
T41	(A1A)-(A1A)	Elec	1 445	42 300 (19 200)	25 300 (11 500)	14.3 (23)	62 (100)	40 (1 015)	16.0	84	50' 6¼" (15 400)	5	1956	Nohab	GM 12-567C	Asea (GM licence) and GM
T42	Bo-Bo	Elec	1 445	47 600 (21 600)	25 300 (11 500)	14.3 (23)	62 (100)	40 (1 015)	18.0	72	47' 3" (14 400)	1	1954	GM	GM 12-567C	GM
T43	Bo-Bo	Elec	1 445	47 600 (21 600)	28 200 (12 800)	14.3 (23)	59 (95)	40 (1 015)	18.0	72	46' 8¾" (14 240)	50	1961	Nohab	GM 12-567 D1	Asea (GM licence)
T44	Bo-Bo	Elec	1 670	48 600 (22 100)	36 000 (16 500)	11 (17)	56 (90)	40½ (1 030)	19	76	50' 6¼" (15 400)	75	1968-70	Nohab	GM 12-645E	GM
Tb snow-plough	Bo-Bo	Elec	1 670	48 600 (22 100)	36 000 (16 500)	11 (17)	59 (95)	40½ (1 030)	18	72	50' 6½" (15 400)	10	1969	Nohab	GM 12-645E	GM
Tc snow-plough	B	Hyd	625	19 400 (8 800)	13 700 (6 200)	8 (13)	56 (90)	38¾ (985)	16	32	46' 8¾" (14 200)	20	1969	Nohab	KHD BF 12M 716	Voith and Gmeinder
Tp	1-C-1	Hyd	750	23 800 (10 800)	18 700 (8 500)	7.5 (12)	40 (65)	43¼ (1 100)	10.0	46	35' 1¼" (10 700)	10	1954	MAK	MAK MA 301A	Voith and MAK
V3	C	Hyd	450	36 400 (16 500)	15 400 (7 000)	6.8 (11)	31 (50)	43¼ (1 100)	16.7	50	31' 10" (9 700)	50	1952	Esslingen	Deutz V6M536	Voith
V4	C	Hyd	265	34 800 (15 800)	30 400 (13 800)	3.1 (5)	43 (70)	38¾ (985)	16	48	33' 9½" (10 300)	10	1972	Henschel	Deutz BF12M717	Voith and Gmeinder
V5	C	Hyd	265	34 800 (15 800)	30 400 (13 800)	3.1 (5)	43 (70)	38¾ (985)	16	48	34' 11" (10 640)	40	1975	Henschel	Deutz BF12M717	Voith and Gmeinder
Z3	B	Hyd	130	14 500 (6 600)			34 (55)	33½ (850)	10	20	24' 10" (7 570)	10	1953	Klöckner Humboldt Deutz AG, Köln	Deutz A8L 614	Voith and Klöckner Humboldt Deutz
Z4p	B	Hyd	160	10 300 (4 700)			25 (40)	30 (760)	7	14	21' 0" (6 400)	25 14	1950 1956	Kalmar Verkstads	Scania Vabis D812	Atlas Diesel and Kalmar Verkstads AB
Z43	B	Hyd	160	14 500 (6 600)			34 (55)	38⅛ (970)	10	20	28' 10½" (8 800)	52 64	1951 1958	Kockums Mek Kalmar Verkstads	Scania Vabis D812	Atlas Diesel and Kalmar Verkstads AB
Z49	B	Hyd	160	14 500 (6 600)			28 (45)	38⅛ (970)	10	20	28' 10½" (8 800)	22	1944	Kockums Mek	Scania Vabis D802/812	Atlas Diesel and Kockum
Z61	B	Hyd	295	20 500 (9 300)			37 (60)	38¾ (985)	14	28	28' 6½" (8 700)	10	1957	Kockums Mek	M.A.N. AG W6V 17.5/22A	Krupp
Z62	B	Hyd	295	20 500 (9 300)			37 (60)	38½ (980)	14	28	28' 10½" (8 800)	10	1957	AB Hägglund & Söner	Scania Vabis D643/632	Ulvsunda Verkstads AB and Hägglund & Söner
Z63	B	Hyd	295	20 500 (9 300)			37 (60)	38¾ (985)	14	28	27' 2¾" (8 300)	12	1956	Nydqvist & Holm	General Motors Twin Six	General Motors and Deutsche Getriebe Gesellschaft
Z64	B	Hyd	240	20 500 (9 300)			33 (53)	33½ (850)	14	28	24' 2¼" (7 370)	35	1953	Klöckner Humboldt Deutz	Deutz T4M 625	Voith and KHD
Z65	B	Hyd	295	20 500 (9 300)			37 (60)	38¾ (985)	14	28	30' 3¾" (9 240)	102	1962	Kalmar Verkstads	Rolls-Royce C8TFL MK IV	Twin Disc and Deutsche Getriebe Gesellschaft
Z66	B	Hyd	295	21 160 (9 600)			43 (70)	38¾ (985)	16	32	33' 9½" (10 300)	30	1971	Kalmar Verkstads	KHD F12 M 716	Voith and Gmeinder
Z67B	B	Hyd	381	18 900 (8 600)			43 (70)	38¾ (985)	15	30	30' 6" (9 300)	3	1978	Gmeinder	Cummins KT-1150-L	Voith and Gmeinder

Note: Class Tp, Z4p 2 ft 11 in *(0.891 m)* gauge. Class T23 rebuilt from Tp.
Class Z67 rebuilt from Z61, Z62 and Z63 locomotives.

SWITZERLAND

SWISS FEDERAL RAILWAYS

Schweizerische Bundesbahnen (SBB)
Chemins de Fer Fédéraux Suisses (CFF)
Ferrovie Federali Svizzere (FFS)
Hochschulstrasse 6, CH-3030 Bern

Telephone: Bern 60 11 11

Railways Board of Administration:
Chairman: Carlos Grosjean
Members: Werner Meier   Jakob Stucki
Franco Robbiani   Jean-Pascal Delamuraz
Jean Babel   Ernst von Roten
Franz Muheim   Dr Gion Willi
Pierre Arnold   Dr Roger Perret
Hans Munz   Kurt Schweizer
Max Rüegg   Arthur Schmid
Alfred E. Sarasin
Secretary: Dr Arnold Schärer
President and Manager of Financial and Staff Dept.: Ing. Roger Desponds
Departmental Managers:
Traffic Department: Dr Karl Wellinger
Technical Department: Dr Werner Latscha
Heads of Divisions:
Secretariat: Dr Arnold Schärer
Organisation and Planning: Hans Walter
Financial: Heinz Diemant
Personnel: Karl Hartmann
Medical: Dr Antonio Serati
Legal: Dr Eric Bertherin
Passenger Traffic: Samuel Ed. Berthoud
Freight Traffic: Dr Franz Hegner
Traffic control: Jean-P. Berthouzoz
Stores (at Basle): René Auberson
Operating: Max Rietmann
Traction and Workshops: Ing Jacques Bonny
Electric power stations: Jörg Stöcklin

Gauge: 1.435 m; 1.00 m
Route length: 2 853 km; 74 km

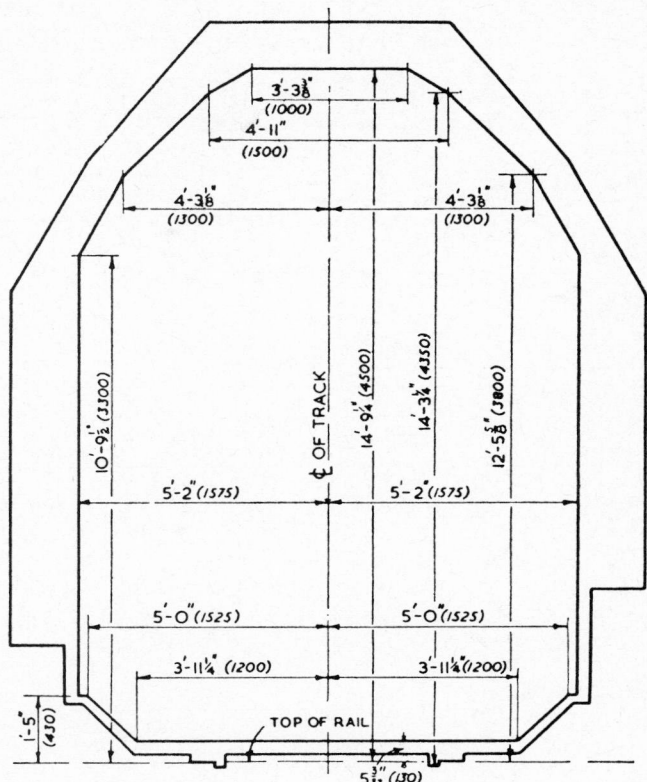

TRAFFIC	1977/78	1978/79
Total train-km	93 728 000	94 221 000
Percentage of train km by steam		
by diesel	0·5	0·5
by electric	99·5	99·5
Total freight tonnage	38 887 000	39 896 000
Average haul (km)	152·6	155·9
Average net train load	204	216
Average wagon load (tonnes)	13·9	14·2
Total passenger-km	8 028	8 094
Total passengers carried	205 452 000	203 443 000
Passengers carried 1st class	15 982 000	15 724 000
2nd class	189 470 000	187 719 000
Average length of passenger journey (km)	39·1 km	39·8 km

FINANCES	1977/78	1978/79
Revenues		(SFr millions)
Passengers and baggage	842·2	833·1
Average receipt per passenger-km	10·1	10·3
Freight and mail	986·5	974·3
Average receipt per freight tonne-km	16·6	15·7
Total	2341·1	2400·8
Expenditure		
Staff/personnel	1865·6	1868·6
Materials and services	493·6	483·5
Depreciation	340·3	344·9
Financial charges	329·9	326·4
Total	3029·4	3023·4

Electric locomotive class Ee 6/6 II for heavy shunting service
Equipped with three phase propulsion, ie with asynchronous squirrel cage traction motors fed by static converters (four quadrant controllers and inverters). Continuous rating 900 kW at all speeds between 8·5 and 85 km/h, top speed 85 km/h, max tractive effort 355 kN (continuously applicable between 0 and 8·5 km/h). Feeding system: single phase 15 kV/162/3 Hz. Electrical equipment supplied by BBC Baden.

PERMANENT WAY

Early in 1977, the SBB Board allocated SFr 69.5 million for the construction of a 4.5 km direct line between Olten and Rothrist; this line will enable the Basle-Olten-Lucerne and Zurich-Olten-Berne traffic flows to be kept separate. At present there are 250 traffic movements a day over the Olten-Aarburg section. The construction of this line will increase the Swiss network's capacity considerably and cut running times appreciably. Work was also underway on a 6.4 km air terminal line between Kloten and Zurich.

MOTIVE POWER AND ROLLING STOCK

Locomotives in service in 1978 included 716 broad-gauge mainline electrics plus two metre-gauge electrics and 164 electric shunters; two diesel electric line-haul units and 107 shunters; six combined electric/diesel-electric shunters and 436 locotractors. Passenger motive power included 147 mainline electric railcars for 1.435 m operation, 16 over the metre-gauge Brünig line and 30 emus. Passenger coaches totalled 3 899; freight wagons, 32 678.

DIESEL LOCOMOTIVES

Class	Axle Arrangement	Trans-mission	Rated Power hp	Max. lb (kg)	Tractive Effort Continuous at lb (kg)	mph (km/h)	Max. Speed mph (km/h)	Wheel Dia. in (mm)	Total Weight Tons	Length ft ins (mm)	No. Built	Year first Built	Builders: Mechanical Parts	Engine & Type	Transmission
Bm 4/4 II (18451-52)	Bo-Bo	Elec	830	22 000 (10 000)	9 700 (4 400)	31.4 (50.6)	68 (110)	41 (1 040)	65	48' 10¾" (14 900)	2	1939	SLM	Sulzer	Brown Boveri
Bm 4/4 (18401-26) (18427-46)	Bo-Bo ,,	Elec ,,	842 ,,	48 500 ,,	28 700 ,,	10.9 (17.5) ,,	47 (75) ,,	41 (1 040) ,,	72 ,,	41' 6" (12 650) 43' 1¾" (13 150)	26 20	1960-65 1968-70	SLM ,,	SLM ,,	Secheron ,,
Bm 6/6 (18501-14)	Co-Co	Elec	1 300	75 000 (34 000)	41 900 (19 000)	11.5 (18.5)	46 (75)	41 (1 040)	106	55' 9½" (17 000)	4 10	1954-55 1960-61	SLM	Sulzer	Brown Boveri Secheron
Em 3/3 (18801-06) (18807-41)	C	Elec Elec	440 ,,	26 500 (12 000) 27 800 (12 600)	15 400 (7 000) 15 400 (7 000)	10.5 (17)	40 (65) 40 (65)	41 (1 040) 41 (1 040)	50.5 50.5	32' 7¾" (9 950) 32' 10½" (10 020)	6 35	1959-60 1963-64	SLM SLM	SLM SLM	Secheron Brown Boveri Secheron
Am 6/6 (18521-26)	Co-Co	Elec	1 950	(40 000)	(40 000)	(13.2)	(85)	(1 260)	111	(17 400)	6	1976	Thyssen-Industrie AG Henschel	Chantiers de l'Atlantique	Brown Boveri

ELECTRIC LOCOMOTIVES

Class	Axle Arrangement	Line Current	Rated Output hp	Max. lb (kg)	Tractive Effort (Full Field) Continuous at lb (kg)	mph (km/h)	Max. Speed mph (km/h)	Wheel dia. in (mm)	Weight tonnes	Length ft in (mm)	No. Built	Year Built	Builders Mechanical Parts	Electrical Equipment
Re 4/4 I (10001-26) (10027-50)	Bo-Bo	15 000 V 1/16⅔	2 480 2 520	31 000 (14 000) 31 000 (14 000)	17 800 (8 100) 18 000 (8 200)	51.5 (83) 51.5 (83)	78 (125) ,,	41 (1 040) ,,	57 58	48' 2¾" (14 700) 48' 10¾" (14 900)	26 24	1946-48 1950-51	SLM	Brown-Boveri; Oerlikon; Secheron
Re 4/4 II (11101-106) (11107-155) (11156-304) (11305-349) (11351-11370)	Bo-Bo ,, ,, ,, Re 4/4 III	,, ,, ,, ,,	5 450 6 320 ,, ,, ,,	,, 57 300 (26 000) ,, ,, (20 000)	32 400 (14 700) 37 500 (17 000) ,, ,, ,,	,, 62 (100) ,, ,, ,,	,, 87 (140) ,, 78 (125) ,,	,, 49⅝ (1 260) ,, ,, ,,	,, 80 ,, ,, ,,	48' 6¾" (14 800) 48' 10¾" (14 900) 50' 6¾" (15 410) ,, ,,	6 49 149 20	1964 1967-68 1969-74 1971	SLM ,, ,, ,,	Brown Boveri; Oerlikon; Secheron ,, ,,
Re 6/6 (11601-689) (11690-724)	Bo-Bo-Bo	,,	10 600	88 600 (40 200)			87 (140)		120		36(+53 on order)	1972-78	SLM	Brown Boveri
Ae 3/5 (10201-24) (10225-26)	1-Co-1	,,	1 800 ,,	31 000 (14 000) ,,	17 000 (7 700) ,,	39 (63) ,,	56 (90) ,,	63⅜ (1 610) ,,	81 85	40' 5" (12 320) ,,	24 2	1922-25 1925	SLM	Secheron
Ae 3/6 III (10261-71)	2-Co-1	,,	1 800	31 000 (14 000)	17 000 (7 700)	39 (63)	56 (90)	63⅜ (1 610)	89	45' 1¾" (13 760)	11	1925-26	SLM	Secheron
Ae 3/6 II (10401-20) (10421-60) (10439 = historical locomotive, other scrapped)	2-C-1	,,	2 000 ,,	33 000 (15 000) ,,	18 300 (8 300) ,,	40 (65) ,,	62 (100) ,,	63⅜ (1 610) ,,	99 97	46' 5" (14 150) ,,	20 40	1924 1925-26	SLM	Oerlikon
Ae 3/6 I (10601-36) (10637-86) (10687-712) (10713-14)	2-Co-1	,,	1 920 2 100 ,, ,,	31 000 (14 000) 33 000 (15 000) ,, ,,	18 500 (8 400) 19 400 (8 800) ,, ,,	38.5 (62) 40 (65) ,, ,,	62 (100) 68 (110) ,, ,,	63⅜ (1 610) ,, ,, ,,	92 95 94 95	48' 5" (14 760) ,, ,, ,,	36 50 26 2	1921-25 1925-27 1927-28 1929	SLM ,, ,,	Brown Boveri Oerlikon Secheron
Ae 4/6 (10801-12)	IA+Bo+AI	,,	5 540	49 000 (22 200)	38 800 (17 600)	53 (85)	78 (125)	53⅛ (1 350)	105	56' 7" (17 250)	12	1941-45 rebuilt 1961-63	SLM	Brown Boveri; Oerlikon; Secheron
Ae 4/6 III (10851)	IA+Bo+AI	,,	2 300	32 600 (14 800)	17 400 (7 900)	49 (79)	68 (110)	49⅝ (1 260)	80	53' 7¾" (16 350)	1	1941 (1961)	SLM; Swiss Fed Rlys	Brown Boveri
Ae 4/7 (10901-72) (10973-002) (11003-27)	2-Do-1	,,	3 120 ,, ,,	44 000 (20 000) ,, ,,	28 700 (13 000) ,, ,,	40 (65) ,, ,,	62 (100) ,, ,,	63⅜ (1 610) ,, ,,	118 123 118	54' 11½" (16 750) 56' 1¼" (17 100) 54' 11½" (16 750)	72 30 25	1927-31 1931-34 1931-34	SLM	Brown Boveri (53); Oerlikon (52); Secheron (22)
Ae 6/6 (11401-02) (11403-50) (11451-11520)	Co-Co	,,	6 000 ,, ,,	80 160 (40 000) ,, ,,	48 400 (22 000) ,, ,,	46 (74) ,, ,,	78 (125) ,, ,,	49⅝ (1 260) ,, ,,	124 120	60' 4½" (18 400) ,, ,,	2 48 70	1952-53 1955-60 1962-66	SLM ,,	Brown Boveri Oerlikon ,,
Ae 8/14 (11801)	IA-AIA-AI+ IA-AIA-AI	,,	7 000	110 000 (50 000)	57 300 (26 000)	40 (65)	62 (100)	63⅜ (1 610)	240	111' 7" (34 000)	1	1931	SLM	Brown Boveri historical locomotive
Re 4/4 IV (10101-104)	Bo-Bo	,,	5 070	300 kN	—		53 (85)	100 (160)	49⅝ (1 260)	80	50' 11" (15 800)	4	1981	SLM	Brown Boveri
Be 4/6 (12303-12) (12313-42) (12320 = historical locomotive, other scrapped)	IB-BI	,,	1 760 2 040	39 700 (18 000) 39 700 (18 000)	20 300 (9 200) 23 400 (10 600)	32 (52) 32 (52)	47 (75) ,,	60¼ (1 530) ,,	107 110	54' 4" (16 260) ,,	30 30	1920 1921-23	SLM	Brown Boveri
Be 4/7 (12501-06) (12504 = historical locomotive, other scrapped)	(1-Bo-1)- (Bo-1)	,,	2 400	44 000 (20 000)	25 600 (11 600)	35 (56)	50 (80)	63⅜ (1 610)	111	53' 5¾" (16 300)	6	1922	SLM	Secheron

ELECTRIC LOCOMOTIVES

Class	Axle Arrangement	Line Current	Rated Output hp	Max. lb (kg)	Tractive Effort (Full Field) Continuous at lb (kg)	mph (km/h)	Max. Speed mph (km/h)	Wheel dia. in (mm)	Weight tonnes	Length ft in (mm)	No. Built	Year Built	Builders Mechanical Parts	Electrical Equipment
Be 6/8 II (13251-59, 61, 63-65) (13253 = historical locomotive, Ce 6/8 II 14253)	IC-CI		3 640	66 000 (30 000)	48 000 (21 800)	28 (45)	47 (75)	53⅛ (1 350)	126	63' 9¾" (19 450)	13	1920-21 (1942-47)	SLM	Oerlikon
Be 6/8 III (13301-18)	IC-CI	,,	2 460	66 000 (30 000)	41 900 (19 000)	22 (35)	47 (75)	53⅛ (1 350)	131	65' 9¾" (20 060)	11	1926-27	SLM	Oerlikon
Ce 6/8 1 (14201)	IC-CI	,,	2 370	57 300 (26 000)	34 400 (15 600)	25 (41)	40 (65)	53⅛ (1 350)	118	63' 2" (19 250)	1	1920	SLM	Brown Boveri historical locomotive
Ce 6/8 II (14266-85)	IC-CI	,,	2 240	57 300 (26 000)	37 000 (16 800)	22 (36)	40 (65)	53⅛ (1 350)	128	63' 9¾" (19 450)	20	1920-22	SLM	Oerlikon
De 6/6 (15301-03)	C+C	,,	1 170	39 700 (18 000)	25 400 (11 500)	17 (27.5)	31 (50)	41 (1 040)	73	45' 11" (14 000)	3	1926	SLM	Brown Boveri
Ee 3/4 (16301-02)	I-C	,,	585	19 900 (9 000)	12 800 (5 800)	17 (27.5)	25 (40)	41 (1 040)	49	32' 2" (9 800)	2	1923	SLM	Brown Boveri
Ee 3/3 (16311-26)	C	,,	585	19 900 (9 000)	12 800 (5 800)	17 (27.5)	25 (40)	41 (1 040)	45	29' 6¼" (9 000)	16	1928		
(16331-50)		,,	,,	,,	,,	,,	,,	,,		29' 10½" (9 100)	20	1930-31	SLM	Brown Boveri
16351-76		,,	,,	,,	,,	,,	,,	,,	11	31' 10" (9 700)	26	1932-42		
16381-414			680	22 000 (10 000)	14 330 (6 200)	18.4 (29.6)	31 (50)	,,	39	31' 2" (9 500)	34	1944-47		
(16421-24)		,,		26 500 (12 000)	15 400 (7 000)	16.5 (26.5)	28 (45)	,,	45	,,	4	1951	SLM	Brown Boveri
(16425-30)											6	1956		Oerlikon;
(16431-36)		,,	,,	,,	,,	,,	,,	,,	,,	,,	6	1961		Secheron
(16437-40)											4	1962		
(16441-60)		,,	,,	,,	,,	,,	,,	,,	44	,,	20	1966	SLM	,,
Ee 3/3 II (16501-02)	C	2-current	685	29 800 (13 500)	15 400 (7 000)	16.5 (26.5)	28 (45)	41 (1 040)	46	31' 2" (9 500)	2	1957	SLM	Brown Boveri
(16503-04)			730	28 700 (13 000)	15 650 (7 100)	16.8 (27)	28 (45)	,,	46	,,	2	1957	,,	Oerlikon
(16505-16511-1)			685	29 800 (13 500)	15 400 (7 000)	16.5 (26.5)	28 (45)	,,	46	,,	11	1958, 1962-63	SLM	Secheron
Ee 3/3 IV (16551-60)	C	4-current	529	26 500 (12 000)	13 250 (6 000)	14.8 (23.8)	37 (60)	41 (1 040)	48	32' 8" (10 020)	10	1962-63	SLM	Secheron
Ee 6/6 (16801-803)	C+C	15 000 V 1/16⅔	1 370	53 000 (24 000)	30 900 (14 000)	16.5 (26.5)	28 (45)	41 (1 040)	90	48' 8¾" (14 850)	2	1952	SLM	Brown Boveri; Secheron
Eem 6/6 (17001-17006)	C+C	2-current	1 045	53 000 (24 000)	26 500 (12 000)	14.8 (23.8)	40 (65)	41 (1 040)	104	58' 7" (17 850)	5	1970-71	SLM	Secheron
			533	,,	,,	7.5 (12.0)								
Ee 6/6 II (16811-820)	C+C	2-current	980	340 kN	340 kN	6 (10.0)	52 (85)	52 (1 260)	104	58' 6" (17 400)	10	1979	SLM	Brown Boveri

Note— Series Ae 4/7. Nos. 10939-51 and 11009/17 weight 120 T.
Series Ee 3/3 II operate on 15 kV 1/16⅔ and 25 kV, 1/50.
Series Ee 3/3 IV operate on 15 kV 1/16⅔ and 25 kV, 1/50 and on 1 500 V and 3 000 V dc.

SYRIA

CHEMINS DE FER SYRIENS

BP 182, Aleppo

Telephone: 13900/2030

Members: Ing. Abdulkader Moulayess
Ing. Vartkès Mardirossian
Ing. Farès Sahhar
Ing. Omar Sultan
Ing. Khaled Dada

Officials
President General Manager: Abdeljabber Koundakji
Assistant General Manager: Abdulhamid El-Hassan
Assistant General Manager: Abdulkader Moulayess
Director, Development Division: Ing Vartkès Mardirossian
Director, Construction Division: Ing Farès Sahhar

Directors
Technical Development Division: Ing Naoufal Kassouha
Goods and Traction: Ing Mourhaf Sabouni
Movement and Traffic: Ing. Zafer Attar
Fixed Installations: Dr. Ing. Adnan Elias
Returns: Fouad Attar
Communications and Signalling: Ing. Tarek Bourhan
Judicial Affairs: Dhémil Sayem El-Dahr
Financial Affairs: Omar Sultan
Stores and Purchasing: Adib Meymeh
Medical: Dr. Sabet Issa
Planning and Statistics: Ing. Laurent Khayat
Technical and Construction Division: Ing. Jean Didos
Tracklaying: Ing. Abdulaziz Koundakji
Steamworks: Ing. Safouan Rihaoui
Bridging works: Ing. Bechir Nasser
Engines and Vehicles: Ing. Abdulghafour Nached
Signalling and Electrification: Ing. Abdulrahman Abou-Saleh

All standard gauge lines in Syria are operated by the Chemins de Fer Syriens, and comprise the lines from the Lebanese border via Homs and Aleppo to the Turkish border and in the northeast, the connecting line between the Turkish and Iraqi borders. A 26 mile (42 km) line between Tartous and Akkari has been completed.
A new standard gauge line of 461 miles (742 km) is under construction from the port of Latakia to Aleppo and then following roughly the line of the River Euphrates to Kamechli.
Two sectic.is of this line, Aleppo-Ragga and Aleppo-Sisr El Choughour, 176 miles (283 km), were completed and opened to traffic in 1972. The whole line is laid with Soviet rails 25 km long on prestressed concrete sleepers.

The 750 km service between Lattaquié and Kamychly became fully operational in 1974, providing a direct outlet to the Mediterranean for the oilfields of Central Syria. This line was built with the technical and financial support of the Soviet Union.
Work on the final section of the 750 km line from the port of Latakia to the oil centre of Kamyshly is now completed. The line was built with Soviet technical and financial assistance, and Soviet diesel locomotives are operating.
Syria was laying 6 000 km of new lines during its 1976-80 development plan. The target—more than four times that set under the Third Five-Year Plan—stresses Syria's continuing emphasis on the development of its railway network.
Two important new lines, between Qamishli and Latakia (750 km) and Damascus and Homs (208 km) are now under construction. Both lines will carry a total of about 5.5 million tonnes of freight annually.

TRAFFIC	1975	1976
Freight tonne-km ('000)	149 505	303 229
Freight tonnage ('000)	992.6	1 315
Passenger-km ('000)	127 500	150 000
Passenger journeys ('000)	841	772

CHEMIN DE FER DU HEDJAZ

BP 134, Damascus

General Manager: Fahmi Kosara
Chief Engineer: Mohamad el Bizen
Manager, Traffic Department: Fayez Hafez
Manager, Accounts Department: Tayssir Kari

Gauge: 1.05 m
Route length operated: 192 miles (307 km)

In addition to its own 150 mile (240 km) route length, the CF du Hedjaz also operates the 42 mile (67 km) long narrow gauge Damascus-Zerghaya line on behalf of the Syrian Government.
The Hedjaz Railway originally extended 809 miles (1 303 km) from Damascus to Medina to carry pilgrims to the Holy Cities of Mecca and Medina. During the 1914-18 war the southern portion was severely damaged and the 524 miles (844 km) section from Maan in Jordan to Medina in Saudi Arabia was left derelict.
In October 1977 the Syrian and Jordanian transport ministers met in Amman to decide in principle to make a second attempt to revive the Hedjaz Railway. The portion of the line passing through Saudi Arabia has not operated since 1917 and a scheme to reopen the section collapsed during the 1960s. Under latest proposals it is hoped to reconstruct the 1 300 km line as a high-quality standard-gauge freight line with 60 kg/m rail and an axle loading of 25 or 30 tonnes.
Because the Hedjaz at present is 1 050 mm gauge the project will entail extensive gauge conversion including the new branch line to Aqaba (116 km) opened in 1975.
Construction teams are already approaching Damascus from the north laying new standard gauge track.

TAIWAN

TAIWAN RAILWAY ADMINISTRATION (TRA)

2 Yen-Ping North Road, Section 1, Taipei

Telephone: 5511131
Telex: 21837

Managing Director: J. Fan
Deputy Managing Directors: W. J. Shan
    Y. L. Po
    J. Wang
Chief Engineering: Y. C. Loh
Chief Secretary: Y. L. Po
Superintendents:
  Transportation Department: T. L. Tao
  Civil Engineering Department: S. F. Chen
  Mechanical Engineering Department: K. M. Lee
  Electrical Engineering: P. T. Lee
  Purchase and Stores Department: I. C. Chen
  Planning Department: C. Y. Liu
  Hualien Office: C. C. Huang
  General Affairs Department: K. C. Ten
  Accounting Department: J. C. Shen
Chief, Finance Control Office: H. Chiang
Chief, Personnel Office: Henry Lei
Chief, Electronic Data Processing Department: M. T. Yang
Gauge: 1.067 m (West); 0.762 m (East)
Route length: 1 926 km; 240 km

The Taiwan Railway is the principal artery of transportation on the island of Taiwan. It consists of three lines—the West Line with its branches, the East Line totalling 1 007.5 km and the new 82.3 km North Link Line from Nanshenghu to Trenpu.
The West Line, a double-tracked railway system, 831.8 km in length, and 1.067 mm in gauge, stretches from north to south along the West Plain Area of the Island, linking the two big seaports of Keelung, and Kaohsiung with the intermediate cities of Taipei, Hsinchu, Tai-chung, Chang-hua, Chia-i and Tai-nan. In the middle section of the system there are two routes from Chu-nan to Chang-hua: The Coast Line runs along the West Coast while the Mountain Line, 91.4 km in length, runs through the cities of Miao-li, Feng-yuan, and Tai-chung joining again with the Coast Line at Chang-hua.
Construction work on the North Link Line commenced in 1973: 5 km at the northern end and 26 km at the southern end (including 5.8 km branch to Hualien Harbour). Construction of the middle section which amounts to 57 km was started in 1974. The 82.3 km line was finally completed at the end of 1978. Tunnel construction forms the most important works on the North Link Line, the expenses of which amount to some 70 per cent of the total cost of the whole project.
Along a narrow valley area of the East Coast, the single-tracked 0.762 m gauge East Line (Hualien-Taitung) runs for 175.7 km in length and is responsible for passenger and freight transportation.

TRAFFIC

The daily averages of passenger and freight traffic are 400 000 persons and 45 000 tons respectively. With the existing route and equipment, the transportation capacity has already reached saturation point.
The total number of passenger journeys in 1978 was 122 239 988. The total number of passenger-km in 1978 was 7 949 million.
The total tonnage in 1978 was 16.4 million tons. The total number of ton-km was 2 496 million.

	1976	1977	1978
Total freight ton-km	2 700 080 323	2 461 926 654	2 495 066 149
Total freight tonnage	17 000 403	16 176 248	16 357 830
Total passenger-km	8 411 660 857	8 070 087 396	7 949 851 007
Total passengers carried	140 032 528	128 883 581	122 239 999

Passenger coaches on the Tze Chiang express

First of TR's EMU vehicles from BRE-Metro of the UK being shipped

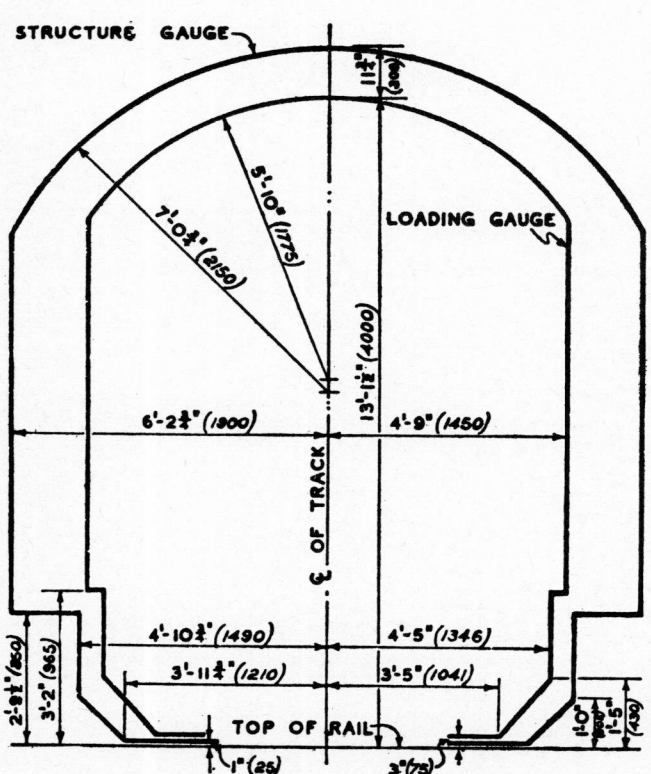

STRUCTURE GAUGE
LOADING GAUGE
7'-0⅞" (2150)
5'-10⅝" (1775)
11⅞" (300)
6'-2¼" (1900)
13'-1½" (4000)
4'-9" (1450)
℄ OF TRACK
4'-10¾" (1490)
4'-5" (1346)
3'-11¾" (1210)
3'-5" (1041)
2'-9½" (850)
3'-2" (965)
TOP OF RAIL
1'-0" (300)
1'-5" (430)
1" (25)
3" (75)

FINANCES

	1976	1977	1978
		$US	
Revenues	171 280 736.08	181 061 366	189 244 786
Expenses	151 287 868.42	174 611 880	214 330 457

INVESTMENTS

Spending in 1978 totalled $NT 7 087 million with allocations for electric locomotives ($NT 1 968 million), 20 passenger coaches ($NT 96 million), 13 railcars ($NT 1 566 million) and 87 freight wagons ($NT 61 million). Major track improvements in 1978 cost $NT 806 million while $NT 1.8 million went towards signalling and communications equipment.

MOTIVE POWER AND ROLLING STOCK

Motive power and rolling stock in service:

Locomotives in steam	43
Electric locomotives	117
Locomotives in diesel-electric	169
Railcars, diesel	71
Trailer cars, diesel	10
Emus	20
Passenger train coaches	1 180
Freight train cars	6 898

ELECTRIFICATION

As part of the national economic development programme, TRA is at present engaged in electrification of the West Trunk Line.
The project covers the electrification of the 495.4 km between Keelung and Kaohsiung and was approved by the Executive Yuan in 1971. The planning stage was concluded when the supply contracts and foreign loan agreements were signed in 1974. An Electrification Unit was established in 1974 to carry out all necessary planning and engineering studies and construction work. Actual work on site was started in 1975. Electrification, at 25 kV 60 Hz, over the initial 107-km Keelung—Hsinchu section was switched in 1977 and the entire line was completed by 1979.

PERMANENT WAY

To meet the requirements of economic development it is planned to build another superspeed railway within ten to 15 years following completion of the Trunk Line Electrification. This railway will be separated from the existing trunk line (there are two alternatives, along the mountain or the coast). Highest speed will be 250 km/h, average about 170 km/h (two hours from Taipei to Kaohsiung). Through and non-through expresses will replace existing multiple kinds of train. Track gauge will be of standard 1.435 m. Maximum gradient will be 1.5 per cent and the minimum radius of curve over 2.500 m.

DIESEL LOCOMOTIVES

Class	Axle Arrange-ment	Trans-mission	Rated Power hp	Tractive Effort Continuous at (kg)	(km/h)	Max. Speed (km/h)	Wheel Dia. (mm)	Total Weight Tons	Length (mm)	Year first Built	Builders: Mechanical Parts	Engine & Type	Transmission
R	AIA	Elec	1 650	15 180	19.2	100	1 016	78	14 266	1960	EMD of GM		
S	Bo-Bo	Elec Mech	950	12 860	14	75	838	54	11 230	1966		EMD of GM	

ELECTRIC LOCOMOTIVES

Class	Axle Arrange-ment	Line Current (kV)	Rated Output hp	Tractive Effort (Full Field) Continuous at (kg)	(km/h)	Max. Speed (km/h)	Wheel dia. (mm)	Weight tonnes	Length (mm)	No. Built	Year Built	Builders Mechanical Parts	Electrical Equipment
E100	Bo-Bo	25	2 752	18 500		110	1 220	72	14 050		1977	GEC of UK	
E200	Co-Co	25	3 758	20 100		110	914	96	16 459		1977	GE of USA	

ELECTRIC RAILCARS

Class	Axle Arrange-ment	Line Current (kV)	Rated Output hp	Tractive Effort (Full Field) Continuous at (kg)	(km/h)	Max. Speed (km/h)	Wheel dia. (mm)	Weight tonnes	Length (mm)	No. Built	Year Built	Builders Mechanical Parts	Electrical Equipment
EM	Bo-Bo	25	1 711	6 180		120	860	55	20 350		1978	GEC of UK	

TANZANIA
TANZANIA RAILWAY CORPORATION (TRC)
PO Box 2834, Dar es Salaam

General Manager: A. Janguo

Gauge: 1.0 m
Route length: 1 442 km

Since the formal break up of the East African Railways Corporation, Tanzania has set up a separate railway administration to operate all railways in the country.
During 1977, Canada agreed to grant Tanzania Shs 110 million towards the first phase of its five-year railway development plan. Under the first part of an agreement Canada will supply 205 petrol tanks, cold storage and cattle wagons worth about Shs 96 million. In the second part the Canadian International Development Agency (CIDA) will provide locomotive spares worth about Shs 12 million for maintenance of the 120 locomotives bought from Canada in 1972. Future agreements will cover construction and equipin OF A LOCOMOTIVE OVERHAUL FACILITY AT Morogoro; provision of additional motive power and rolling stock and expansion of railway training facilities at Tabora. In 1978 British Rail Engineering won a £24 million sterling order from TRC for the supply of wagons and passenger coaches. The contract is for 510 freight wagons and 50 passenger coaches.

TANZANIA-ZAMBIA RAILWAY AUTHORITY (TAZARA)
PO Box 2834, Dar-es-Salaam

Telephone: 68661
Telex: 41059

Chairman: A. C. Mwingira
General Manager: N. B. Nyoni
Deputy General Manager: A. G. I. Shayo
Regional Manager, Zambia, Mpika: J. Kasono
Regional Manager, Tanzania: R. S. Seme

Gauge: 1.067 m
Route length: 1 860 km

The Tanzania-Zambia Railway (TAZARA) was constructed following an agreement signed in September 1967 between the Governments of Tanzania and Zambia, and of the People's Republic of China. Under the agreement, China accepted to provide finance and technical services for a rail link of approximately 1 860 km from Dar es Salaam in Tanzania to Kapiri Mposhi in Zambia, together with equipment, two work-shops and other auxiliary facilities, at an estimated cost of Shs 2 866 200 million. The loan repayment is to commence in 1983 and to be spread over 30 years.
Construction began officially in 1970 and tracklaying was completed in 1975. Of the total length, 970 km is in Tanzania and 890 km in Zambia. The line has 147 stations of which 93 were opened at the initial stage of operations. Trial running of freight and passenger services began in 1975 and the hand-over of the railway and full transporta-tion operations commenced in 1976.
The Tanzania-Zambia Railway is designed with a gauge that permits through goods traffic operations with contiguous railways in Central Africa, in particular Zambia Railways. During the first two years of public operations between July 1976 and June 1978, the new railway provided the main outlet for Zambia's import and export traffic through the Port of Dar es Salaam. From July 1976 to June 1978 the railway conveyed approximately 2 407 400 tonnes of goods and 2 062 920 passengers, earning Shs 685 400 million. There are regular passenger services between Dar es Salaam and Kapiri Mposhi every day except Sunday. The railway crosses areas of scenic beauty and varied fauna, including the world-famous Selous Game Reserve in Tanzania.
The Council of Ministers consisting of three Ministers each from Zambia and Tanzania is the organ established by the two Governments to exercise overall control on the railway. All the railway assets are vested in TAZARA, a corporate body whose principal organ is the Board of Directors consisting of five members each appointed by the two Governments. For operational purposes, the whole railway is divided into two regions for Tanzania and Zambia, with respective regional headquarters at Dar es Salaam and Mpika.

TRAFFIC
During the period of trial operations between October 1975 and June 1976, the Tanzania-Zambia Railway moved 335 081 tonnes of goods, equivalent to an average rate of 502 621 tonnes per annum.

Traffic performance grew in the subsequent two years as follows:-

	1976/77	1977/78 (tonnes)	Total 1976-78
Imports			
Fertiliser	119 449	70 262	189 711
Wheat	104 222	89 838	194 061
Coke	41 837	45 157	86 994
General cargo	125 038	182 938	307 977
Others	39 071	31 746	70 817
Sub-total	429 619	419 942	849 562
Exports			
Copper	434 264	448 107	882 371
Lead	5 138	5 298	10 436
Zinc	27 654	44 995	72 649
Others	32 856	48 110	80 966
Sub-total	499 856	546 510	1 046 422
Local traffic	305 801	305 654	611 455
Total	1 135 333	1 272 107	2 507 440

This performance represents a growth of 12 per cent in the tonnage moved between the first and second year of full operations.
Passenger traffic (in number of journeys recorded):

	Within Tanzania	Tanzania to Zambia	Zambia to Tanzania	Within Zambia	Total
1976/77	467 404	6 638	4 429	350 312	828 783
1977/78	573 442	7 911	7 161	545 634	1 134 148
Total	1 040 846	14 549	11 580	895 946	1 962 931

Chinese-built diesel-hydraulic locomotive under inspection in TAZARA's locomotive sheds near Dar es Salaam
In all, China supplied 102 locomotives for the line; some 1 000 hp and others 2 000 hp
(Courtesy National Council for US-China)

FINANCES

During 1976/77 TAZARA reported revenues of Shs 287.7 million against expenses of Shs 286.1 million. In 1977 revenues grew to Shs 344 million, Shs 2.6 million more than operating expenses.

Goods traffic revenue performance:

	Goods revenue collected (millions)		Operating expenditure (millions)		Revenue per 1 000 tonne-km		Operating cost per 1 000 tonne-km	
	K	Shs	K	Shs	K	Shs	K	Shs
1976/77	27.45	287.73	27.30	286.11	14.32	150.05	13.66	143.15
1977/78	36.48	344.04	36.20	341.40	16.34	154.10	15.97	150.61
Total	63.93	631.77	63.50	627.51	15.33	152.07	14.87	147.88

Passenger traffic revenue performance:

	Revenue (millions)		Revenue per 1 000 passenger-km	
	K	Shs	K	Shs
1976/77	1.66	17.36	7.43	77.86
1977/78	2.69	25.33	9.01	85.00
Total	4.35	42.69	8.22	81.43

Note: July 1976—19 March 1978: K1.00 = Shs 10.48
March 1978—31 July 1978: K1.00 = Shs 9.43

MOTIVE POWER AND ROLLING STOCK

At the beginning of 1978 TAZARA owned and operated 85 mainline diesel-electric locomotives, 17 diesel-electric shunters, 13 diesel railcars, 100 passenger coaches and 2 100 freight wagons. An order for 12 DFH2 mainline diesel-hydraulic locomotives of 2 000 hp was to be completed by People's Republic of China during 1979.

PERMANENT WAY

Rails:
Weight (kg/m): 45 kg/m

Sleepers:
Type: prestressed concrete sleepers
Number per km: 1 520 sleepers per km

Track:
Minimum curvature: mainly 300 m, in some places even 250 and 200 m
Maximum gradient: 20 per 1 000 but ruling gradient is 10 per 1 000
Maximum altitude: Uyole near Mbeya, altitude 1 789.43 m

Axle load:
Maximum: 20 tonnes.

THAILAND

STATE RAILWAY OF THAILAND (RSR)
Krung Kassem Road, Bangkok

BOARD OF COMMISSIONERS
Chairman: Air Chief Marshal Prasong Kunadilok
Members: Lt. Gen. Vasin Isarangkura Na Ayudhya
Dr. Sirilak Chandrangsu
Dr. Panas Simasathien
Major General Pat Urailert
Col. Chawal Kanchanakool
MANAGEMENT
General Manager: Dhawat Sangpradab
Deputy General Managers:
Administrative: Hiran Radeesri
Operating: Banyong Saralamp
Chief of Department attached to the General Manager: Smer Sakhakorn
Chief, Administration Department: Ploen Sootarsukorn
Chief Mechanical Engineer: Somsak Prabhavasit

Gauge: 1.00 m
Route length: 3 830 km

TRAFFIC

	1977/78	1978/79
Total train-km	29 015 169	28 957 487
Percentage of train km by diesel	100	100
Total freight tonnage	6 096 463	6 373 728
Average haul	445·35	428·61
Average net train load	313·93	355·61
Average wagon load	14·20	13·95
Total passenger-km	6 038 578 930	6 873 927 404
Total passengers carried	59 034 542	64 164 041
Passengers carried 1st class	64 529	70 479
2nd class	1 141 464	1 248 142
3rd class	57 828 549	62 845 420
Average length of passenger journey	102·3	107·13

FINANCES

Revenues	1977/78	1978/79
	(Bahts)	
Passengers and baggage	900 056	1 036 463
Average receipt per passenger-km	15 Stang	15 Stang
Freight and mail	588 279	691 050
Average receipt per freight tonne-km	22 Stang	25 Stang
Total	1 608 181	1 853 500
Expenditure		
Staff/personnel	765 678	1 010 100
Materials and services	560 547	726 400
Depreciation	166 702	167 600
Financial charges	75 494	70 000
Total	1 568 421	1 974 100

INVESTMENTS

Following capital expenditure of $US 12.3 million in 1978, RSR spent the equivalent of $US 15 million in 1979. Biggest expenditure was for 49 passenger coaches and 30 freight wagons costing $US 4.6 million. Track improvements received $US 2.4 million and signalling $US 1.2 million.

MOTIVE POWER AND ROLLING STOCK
Locomotives in service (1979):

	Line Haul	Shunting
Steam	33	6
Diesel-electric	146	30
Diesel-hydraulic	57	10

Railbuses, 2-axle (1979):

Railcars, diesel	62
Trailer cars, diesel	63

Rolling stock in service (1979):

	4-wheeled bogie	8-wheeled bogie
Passenger train coaches	6	1 059
Freight train cars	6 363	2 793

A contract for 30 units of diesel-electric locomotives was awarded to the Consortium of Thyssen Industrie AG, Henschel and Fried Krupp GmbH. The first diesel-electric locomotive will be shipped in July 1980 and thereafter at the rate of three-five diesel-electric locomotives per month. The final lot will be shipped in February 1981. General particulars of the diesel-electric locomotives are as follows: wheel arrangement, Co-Co; transmission, electric; rated power (hp), 2 250 (site in Thailand); maximum tractive effort starting (with half-worn wheel), 26 000 kg; continuous rated tractive effort (with half-worn wheel), 20 600 kg; maximum safe service speed in either running direction (with half-worn wheel), 100 km/h; wheel diameter new/worn, 914/844 mm; length over body, 15 000 mm; guage, 1 000 mm; total locomotive weight (full laden), 80·8 ± 2% tonnes.

PERMANENT WAY
The construction of a new line from Chachoengsao to Laem Cha Bang and Sattahip was scheduled to begin in early 1980 and to be completed by October 1982.

Rail, types and weights: Flat-bottom 50 (BS), 60 (BS, ASCE), 70 (BS, ASCE), 80 (BS) lb/yd.

Sleepers (cross ties) type:

	Untreated hardwood	Creosote-treated softwood	2-block concrete (R.S. type)
Thickness:	15 cm	12.5-15 cm	20 cm
Spacing:	65-70 cm	65-70 cm	65 cm
Rail fastenings (types used):	Dog spikes	Dog spikes	R.N. elastic clips

Dörken elastic spikes
Welded rail:
Total length of track laid 31 December 1974: 2 244 km
Length laid during 1974 (standard method of welding): 55 km

DIESEL LOCOMOTIVES

Class	Wheel Arrangement	Transmission	Rated Power (hp)	Max Tractive Effort at wheel rim kgs @ % Adhesion Weight	Minimum Continuous Tractive Effort kgs @ km/h	Max Speed (km/h)	Wheel Dia (mm)	Service Weight (tons)	Length (mm)	No on book	Year in service	Builders Mechanical Parts	Builders Engine & Type	Builders Transmission
Davenport	Bo-Bo	Elec	500	14 770 @ 30%	5 700 @ 16	82	914	48.12	9 893.2	30	1952	Davenport, USA	Caterpillar D.397	Westinghouse, USA
Davenport	Co-Co	Elec	1 000	24 000 @ 30%	11 370 @ 16	92	914	80	16 954.4	15	1955	Davenport, USA	Caterpillar D.397	Westinghouse, USA
Hitachi	Co-Co	Elec	1 040	21 600 @ 30%	13 140 @ 12.76	70	914	72	14 300	27	1961-1962	Hitachi, Japan	M.A.N., W 8 V 22/ 30 m A.U.L.	Hitachi, Japan
GE	Co-Co	Elec	1 320	22 500 @ 30%	17 963 @ 13	103	914	75	16 288	50	1965-1966	General Electric, USA	Cummins, VT 12-825 B1, VTA-1710-L	General Electric, USA
Alsthom	Co-Co	Elec	2 400	24 800 @ 30%	20 600 @ 21	95	914	82.5	16 258	54	1975	Alsthom, France	S.E.M.T. PIELSTICK, 16PA 4V.185	Alsthom, France
Kraus-Maffei	C	Hydr	440	12 000 @ 33.33%	7 450 @ 7.55	27	1 106	36	8 350	5	1955	Krauss-Maffei, West	M.A.N. W 8 V 17.5/ 22A	Voith, West Germany

DIESEL LOCOMOTIVES

Class	Wheel Arrangement	Transmission	Rated Power (hp)	Max Tractive Effort at wheel rim kgs @ % Adhesion Weight	Minimum Continuous Tractive Effort kgs @ kmlh	Max Speed (kmlh)	Wheel Dia (mm)	Service Weight (tons)	Length (mm)	No on book	Year in service	Builders		
												Mechanical Parts	Engine & Type	Transmission
Hunslet	C	Hydr	1 240	19 100 @ 33%	2 430 @ 12.1	19.5	1 106	30	7 658	5	Germany 1964	Hunslet, England	GARDNER, 8L 3B	Voith, West Germany
Henschel	B'-B'	Hydr	1 200	17 160 @ 33%	14 900 @ 11	90	914	52	12 800	27	1965	Henschel, West Germany	MAYBACH, MB.12V 493 TY 10	Voith, West Germany
Krupp	B'-B'	Hydr	1 500	18 150 @ 33%	15 250 @ 14.5	90	914	55	12 800	30	1969	Krupp, West Germany	MAYBACH, MB.12V 652 TB 10	Voith, West Germany

DIESEL RAILCARS

Class	Wheel Arrangement	Transmission	Rated Power (hp)	Max Tractive Effort at wheel rim kgs @ % Adhesion Weight	Minimum Continuous Tractive Effort kgs @ kmlh	Max Speed (kmlh)	Wheel Dia (mm)	Service Weight (tons)	Length (mm)	No on book	Year in service	Builders		
												Mechanical Parts	Engine & Type	Transmission
Niigata	2-4 wheel bogie Driving Trailer	Hydr-mech	320	4 460		85	851	Power Type A. 31.0 Type B. 31.0 Trailer 33.75	20 800	3	1962	Niigata Japan	Cummins NHHRS-6-B	Niigata Japan
Tokyu	2-4 wheel bogie Driving Trailer	Hydr-mech	440	4 560	2 260 @ 25	85	851	Power Type A. 36.8 Type B. 37.0 Trailer 26.9	20 800	7	1965	Tokyu Japan	Cummins NHH-220-B-1	Niigata Japan
Hitachi	2-4 wheel bogie Driving Trailer	Hydr-mech	440	4 560	2 310 @ 27	85	851	Power Type A 37.5 Type B. 37.3 Trailer 27.5	20 800	10	1967	Hitachi Japan	Cummins NHH-220-B-1	Niigata Japan
Hitachi	2-4 wheel bogie Driving Trailer	Hydr-mech	440	4 380	2 340 @ 25	90	851	Power Type A. 38.5 Type B. 38.3 Trailer 28.6	20 800	28	1971	Nippon Sharyo & Hitachi Japan	Cummins NHH-220-B-1	Niigata Japan
Tokyu (stainless)	2-4 wheel bogie Driving Trailer	Hydr-mech	220	5 400	2 175 @ 30	70	851	Power Type A. 33.6 Type B. 32.2 Trailer 27.8	20 800	4	1971	Tokyu Japan	Cummins NHH-220-B-1	Niigata Japan

TUNISIA

TUNISIAN NATIONAL RAILWAYS

Société Nationale des Chemins de Fer Tunisiens (SNCFT)
67 Avenue Farhat Hached, Tunis

President/Managing Director: M. A. Souissi
Assistant Managing Director: N. Fékih
Administrative Director: A. Bellil
Financial Director: L. Soussi
Operations Director: M. Mehiri
Equipment and Rolling Stock Director: M. Chéour
Permanent Way and Works Director: H. Tounsi

Gauge: 1.435 m; 1.00 m
Route length: 5 489 km; 1 516 km

The railway includes 5 489 km of standard gauge lines in the north and 1 516 km of metre-gauge lines in the centre and south.

TRAFFIC

Passenger traffic, which had been declining steadily since 1945 has, since 1965, resumed its progress; in 1975 the SNCFT carried 20 million passengers for 558 million passenger-kms while the lines served by the "Blue Arrows" have increased their traffic by 50 per cent in a single year. SNCFT expects the number of travellers using its services to increase from the present 21.6 million annually to 30.6 million in 1981. The economic development of the last fifteen years and the industrialisation of the country have considerably increased freight traffic without noticeably changing its general pattern; 70 per cent for ore transports, 30 per cent for sundry goods.

	1973	1974	1977
Total freight ton-km	1 391 678 564	1 521 783 960	1 315 000 000
Total freight tonnage	6 852 758	7 367 485	*
Total passenger-km	526 412 954	534 096 461	713 000 000
Total passengers carried	17 986 932	18 783 558	21 610 000
*Figures not available.			

FINANCES

	1973	1974
	(Dinars)	
Revenues	13 406 915	16 541 570
Expenses	15 003 734	17 964 955

INVESTMENTS

Tunisia's fifth Five-Year Economic Plan (1977-81) includes Dinars 570 million for transport developments. SNCFT hopes to complete four projects under the plan: (1) extension and modernisation of tracks (Drs 25 million); (2) purchase of locomotives, passenger coaches and phosphate wagons (Drs 14 million); (3) track rehabilitation on the Tunis-Sfax and Goulette-Kasba lines (Drs 10 million); (4) renewal of the freight wagon fleet (Drs 21 million).
In 1977 investments totalled Drs 3 million for infrastructure and Drs 7 million for motive power and rolling stock. In 1978 Drs 5 million was allocated for infrastructure and Drs 3.5 million on various equipment purchases.

MOTIVE POWER AND ROLLING STOCK

A total of 28 new electric railcars were delivered by MAN and Siemens during 1977 for operation over the electrified (750 V continuous, third rail) line between Tunis and La Marsa. At the end of 1977 Ganz-Mavag won an order worth $US 23.3 million for 20 diesel trainsets consisting of three-car sets for delivery end of 1978/early 1980.
SNCFT plans to purchase 20 locomotives at a cost of Drs 4 million ($9.5 million) and 40 passenger carriages at a cost of Drs 6 million ($14.3 million) over the period of the fifth Five-Year Plan (1977-81).
Dieselisation, which had begun as early as 1922, was completed in 1965. Locomotive-hauled trains have been replaced by railcars and self-propelled multiple-unit trains, particularly the 1 050 hp "Blue Arrows" built by Alsthom and introduced in 1975. This modern rolling stock has a top speed of 130 km/h and has made possible an increase in train occupation on the Tunis-Algeria, Tunis-Bizerte and Tunis-Sfax lines. The diesel-electric locomotives which haul freight trains are more and more powerful; those supplied in 1973-75 by Canada and the USA have 2 000 hp engines.
Carriages and wagons have also been modernised in recent years; modern stair.iess steel carriages built by Francorail-MTE have been introduced on the "Atlas" Transmaghreb service which connects Tunis and Algiers in eighteen hours instead of thirty-three previously. Over thirty metal carriages have recently been ordered from Macosa in Spain.
As regards freight rolling stock, the SNCFT has purchased in Belgium and Spain prefabricated elements for 950 wagons which are being assembled in the Sidi Fath Allah workshops, near Tunis. These workshops are to be reorganised so as to become able to undertake the full construction of wagons. Moreover, 60 containers have been ordered from SNAV. Diesel locomotives in service in 1977 totalled 110, diesel railcars 36, passenger coaches 159 and freight wagons 5 478.

PERMANENT WAY

The Hungarian consultancy Uvaterv has completed initial proposals for a 300-mile rail link between Sfax and Tripoli. The $1.1 million cost of the proposals is being met by the Tunisian government with assistance from Libya. If the proposals are accepted by both governments they will be expanded into firm engineering plans. Uvaterv is also undertaking the planning of signal safety devices, stations and bridges in connection with the track. If approved by the Tunisian and Libyan Governments, the plan is to be elaborated into the 1977-81 construction plan.

Plans under the 1977-81 plan call for construction of a 15 km branch from M'dhilla to Sehib for phoshate traffic together with opening of a section between Kasserine and Haidra and reopening of the Kasserine-Moulares line.

Standard rail:
Standard gauge: Flat bottom, 72.6 to 92.8 lb/yd *(36 to 46 kg/m)* in lengths of 39.4 to 59 ft *(12 to 18 m)*.
Metre gauge: Flat bottom, 50.3 to 72.6 lb/yd *(25 to 36 kg/m)* in lengths of 25.6 to 39.4 ft *(7.8 to 12 m)*.
Welded joints: Thermit welding of rail joints (see below).
Cross ties (sleepers): Oak impregnated with creosote; metal; concrete R.S. type.
Standard gauge: 4¾ in × 8⅝ × 8 ft 4⅜ in *(120 × 220 × 2 600 mm)*.
Metre gauge: 4¾ in × 8⅝ × 6 ft 6¾ in *(120 × 220 × 2 000 mm)*.
Spacing: 2 400 per mile *(1 500 mm)*.
Rail fastenings: To wood sleepers: spikes. To metal sleepers: clips and bolts. To concrete sleepers: special resilient fittings.
Filling: Broken stone.
Gauge widening:
1.435 m gauge: 1⅜ in *(35 mm)*.
1.000 m gauge: 1 in *(25 mm)*.

Max curvature:
1.435 m gauge: 7° = min. radius of 820 ft *(250 m)*.
1.000 m gauge: 11.6° = min. radius of 492 ft *(150 m)*.
Max gradient: 2% = 1 in 50.
Gradients:

	1.435 m	1.000 m
Level	29%	22%
Up to 0.5% (1 in 200)	37%	26%
0.5 to 1.0% (1 in 200 to 1 in 100)	20%	26%
1.0 to 2.5% (1 in 100 to 1 in 40)	14%	26%
	100%	100%

Max altitude: 3 124 ft *(952 m)* on line Haidra to Kasserine.
Max speed:
Standard gauge:
Railcars: 62 mph *(100 km/h)*.
Diesel trains: 56 mph *(90 km/h)*.
Metre gauge:
Railcars: 62 mph *(100 km/h)*.
Diesel trains: 43 mph *(70 km/h)*.
Max. axle load:
Standard gauge: 21 tonnes.
Metre gauge: 18 tonnes.

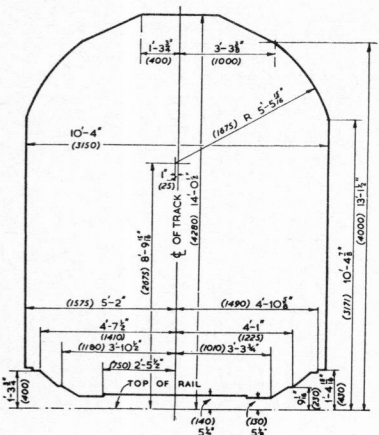

Standard gauge
All vehicles

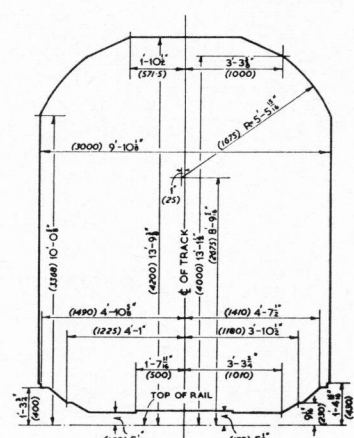

Metre gauge
Locomotives and passenger cars

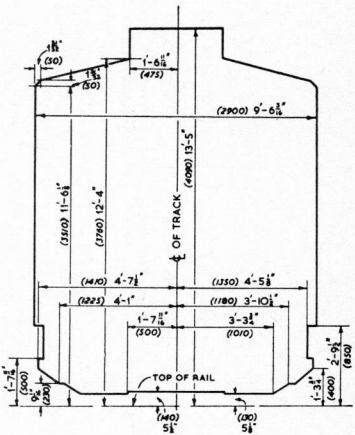

Metre gauge
Freight cars

TURKEY

TURKISH STATE RAILWAYS (TCDD)

Türkiye Cumhuriyeti Devlet Demiryolları
TCDD Isletmesi, Genel Müoürlüğü, Ankara

General Director: Zühtü Oral
Members of Board of Management: Necdet Kalfa
Zühtü Oral
Rifat Serdaroglu
Niyazi Sahin
Department Director, General Inspection: Veli Gültekin
Presidents:
Track Department: Şükrü Karaçali
Traction Department: Haşim Saltik
Commercial Department: Ihsan Kunday
Accounting Department: Vacant
Operating Department: Hayri Ipekeşen
Health Department: Ismet Ülgen
Exterior Relations and Administrative Affairs Department: Hüsnü Kayaoglu
Staff Department: Ziya Seval
Supply Department: Ismail Hakki Akyüz
Ports Department: Ziya Ülkü
Construction Department: Ibrahim Çubukçu
Research, Planning and Coordination Department: Erdal Dikmen
Installation Department: Demirhan Genez

Gauge: 1.435 m
Route length: 5 128 km

TRAFFIC	1975	1976	1977
Ton/km ('000)	7 354 745	7 932 271	7 633 600
Tonnage ('000)	14 676	14 726	16 400
Passenger/km ('000)	4 735 723	4 615 344	5 087 200
Passengers carried ('000)	109 710	107 267	112 600

FINANCES	1975	1976	1977
	TL ('000)		
Revenues	4 931 788	7 004 039	8 412 000
Expenses	6 004 950	7 197 462	9 402 000

INVESTMENTS
Following extensive investment of TL 3 790 million on track renewal, infrastructure improvements and rolling stock in 1978, TCDD has embarked on a TL80 000 million from 1979 to 1983. Under the programme the following improvements are planned: electrification over 1 100 route-km; signalling modernisation; telecommunications installation over the entire system; track upgrading over 2 392 track-km; construction of 330 mainline diesel locomotives, 60 electrics and 30 shunters; construction of 100 three-car emus, 20 three-car diesel railcars and 190 passenger coaches; construction of 10 400 wagons.

MOTIVE POWER AND ROLLING STOCK
Number of locomotives in service:

	Line	Shunting
Steam	315	—
Electric	17	
Diesel-electric	258	72
Diesel-hydraulic	2	—

Number of railcars in service:

Diesel	51
Emu's	30
Dmu's	27

In addition during 1978 the railway operated 1 063 passenger coaches and 17 743 freight wagons.

2 400-hp Co-Co mainline diesel-electric locomotive
Powered by a Pielstick 16PA4-185 engine: weight 112.8 tonnes; max speed 119 km/h supplied by TCDD's own Eskisehir Locomotive and Motor Plant.

A 2 400-hp locomotive under construction at the Eskisehir plant

ELECTRIFICATION

Total electrified route length in 1978 was 204 km on 25 kV, 50 Hz.

CIVIL ENGINEERING

The Turkish Government has approved the construction of the new 279-km line to connect Adapazari with Ankara via Arifiye and Esenkent, thus eliminating the detour by Bilecik-Eskisehir; this new line, which is expected to cost 11 600 million Turkish lira, will be double-tracked, electrified, and will run through 56 km of tunnels. Contract for engineering design went to Hoffmeier of the Federal Republic of Germany during 1977. Construction work is underway on a new line between Tecer and Kengal on the main Sives-Malatya route. Work Total cost is expected to reach about 375 million Turkish lira. The new line will replace the old line which is considered unsafe for the much greater loads now being carried on the section by TCDD. Further development of iron ore transports between the central and eastern parts of Anatolia will be possible.
Total lengths of the new line will be about 47.5 km (69 km with sidings). Grades will be kept to a maximum of 11 per cent, compared with a 22 per cent maximum on the old line. Minimum curve radius has been raised to 1 000 m, so that much higher speeds will be possible.
Rails on the new line will be 49.05 kg/m. They will be laid mainly on reinforced concrete sleepers (though timber sleepers may be used on some sections) manufactured at TCDD's own sleeper plant at Afyon.
Work will include construction of many long bridge sections and 7 500 m of tunnel.
The Turkish Government is considering establishing a rail link across the Bosphorus. Either a railway line across the new Bosphorous road bridge or a tunnel is envisaged.

SIGNAL AND TRAIN CONTROL INSTALLATIONS

Work is in hand on the installation of Centralised Traffic Control (CTC) on the 365 mile (585 km) Haydar Pasa-Adapazari- Arifiye-Ankara line, with control units located at Haydar Pasa, Eskisehir, and Ankara. Equipment is being supplied by the Westinghouse Air Brake Co.
Automatic telephone communications are also being provided on this route.

Dispatching and Telecommunication Works (1973-77)

Location:	Length of route	
	miles	km
Malatya-Elazig-Tatvan	441	459
Yolcati-Diyarbakir-Kurtalan	198	318
Afyon-Konya-Adana	213	643
Izmir-Balikesir-Eskisehir, Balikesir-Bandirma	514	672
Narli-Karkamiş-Nusaybin	326	500
Total	1 692	2 592

Electrical Signalisation Works (1973-77)

Kalin-Sivas-Divrigi	124	200
Basmane-Çigli	11	17
Toprakkale-Fevzipaşa-Narli	81	132
Hisarönü-Zonguldak	17	25
Total	233	374

Renewal of Track Works (1973-77)

Yenice-Mersin	27	43
Toprakkale-Yeşilkent	15	11
Toprakkale-Narli	79	132
Sivas-Çetinkaya	69	112
Yolçati-Erhani	58	103
Malatya-Çetinkaya	87	140
Alayunt-Balikesir	163	262
Adana-Taşkale	49	78
Kayseri-Sivas	139	222
Total	686	1 103

ELECTRIC LOCOMOTIVES

Class	Axle Arrangement	Line Current	Rated Output hp	Max. lb (kg)	Tractive Effort (Full Field) Continuous at		Max. Speed mph (km/h)	Wheel dia. in (mm)	Weight tonnes	Length ft in (mm)	No. Built	Year Built	Builders	
					lb (kg)	mph (km/h)							Mechanical Parts	Electrical Equipment
4001-4003	Bo-Bo	25 kV 1/50	2 200	41 900 (19 000)	23 150 (10 500)	39 (62.5)	56 (90)	51⅛ (1 300)	80	52' 11⅜'' (16 138)		1955	SFAC Alsthom	Alsthom-Jeumont-SW
40001-40008	B-B	,,		4 000	69 500 (31 500)	47 130 (21 350)	30.6 (49.0)	81 (130)	43¼ (1 100)	77	49' 3'' (15 010)	8	1971	Groupement 50 Hz	

DIESEL LOCOMOTIVES

Class	Axle Arrangement	Transmission	Rated Power hp	Max. lb (kg)	Tractive Effort Continuous at		Max. Speed mph (km/h)	Wheel Dia. in (mm)	Total Weight Tons	Length ft in (mm)	No. Built	Year first Built	Builders:		
					lb (kg)	mph (km/h)							Mechanical Parts	Engine & Type	Transmission
U18C	Co-Co	Elec	1 980	60 900 (27 620)	51 000 (23 134)	18 (29)	60 (97)	38 (965)	102	56' 6'' (17 220)	4	1957	GE (USA)	Cooper-Bessemer FV-12	GE
ML2700	C-C	Hyd	2 700	73 400 (33 300)	65 150 (29 550)	10.5 (17)	62 (100)	39⅜ (1 000)	111	64' 6½'' (19 670)	3	1961	Krauss-Maffei	Maybach MD655	Voith
DH 33100	C	Hyd	360	18 200 (8 250) 29 300 (13 300)	2 650 (1 200) 5 950 (2 700)	2.5 (4)	31 (50) 25 (40)	43¼ (1 100)	40.5	30' 4¼'' (9 250)	38	1953	Mak	Mak MS-304	Voith
DH 44100	D	Hyd	800	24 900 (11 300) 40 560 (18 400)	4 000 (1 800) 7 300 (3 300)	3.7 (6)	50 (80) 30 (48)	49¼ (1 250)	58	37' 1'' (11 300)	6	1953-54	Mak	Mak MA-301 A	Voith
DH6500	C	Hyd	650	29 000 (13 150) 35 500 (16 100)	4 400 (2 000) 8 800 (4 000)	5 (8)	37 (60) 18 (30)	49¼ (1 250)	48.8	34' 5¾'' (10 510)	13	1960	Krupp-Eslingen	Maybach GTO 6 A	Voith
Dh4101	C	Hyd	400	15 750 (7 150) 30 650 (13 900)	1 870 (850) 4 630 (2 100)	5 (8) 2.5 (4)	37 (60) 18 (30)	37⅜ (950)	42	30' 5¼'' (9 280)	1	1960	Jenbach	Jenbach Werke JW 400	Voith
DH6001	C	Hyd	600	24 800 (11 250) 35 000 (15 900)	3 850 (1 750) 7 780 (3 500)	5 (8) 2.5 (4)	37 (60) 18 (30)	97⅜ (950)	48	30' 8'' (9 350)	1	1959	Jenbach	Jenbach Werke JW 600	Voith
U20C	Co-Co	Elec	2 150	82 700 (37 500)	76 100 (34 500)	10 (16)	71 (114)	40 (1 016)	111	56' 6'' (17 220)	40	1956	GE (USA)	GE FDL12	GE
DE 24000	Co-Co	Elec	2 400	86 650 (39 300)	46 300 (21 000)	14.6 (24.2)	74 (119)	43¼ (1 100)	112.8	62' 6'' (19 040)	14	1971	ELMS	Pielstick 16PA4-185	Jeumont-Schneider
DE 18000	Bo-Bo	Elec	1 800	57 760 (26 200)	30 850 (14 000)	44.5 (27.8)	74 (119)	43¼ (1 100)	80	54' 0'' (16 440)	3	1971	ELMS	Pielstick 12PA4-185	Jeumont-Schneider
DH 3600	C	Hyd	360	18 210 (8 260) 29 300 (13 300)	2 650 (1 200) 5 950 (2 700)	2.5 (4.0)	15.5 (25) 31 (50)	43¼ (1 100)	40.5	30' 4¼'' (9 250)	8	1971	ELMS	ELMS 360	Voith

UNION OF SOVIET SOCIALIST REPUBLICS

SOVIET UNION RAILWAYS

Ministry of Communications, Novo Basmannaya, 2, Moscow 107174

Administration
Minister of Communications: Ivan Grigoryvich Pavlovsky
First Assistant of the Minister of Communications: Fedor Iosfovich Shuleshko
Department for International Communications: Anatoli Porfireyvich Korotky

Gauge: 1.520 m; 0.60 to 1.10 m; 1.435 m.
Route length: 137 674 km; 2 718 km; 75 km.

The general management of railways and underground (Metro) rail transport throughout the whole of the Soviet Union is vested in the Ministry of Communications, which has its headquarters in Moscow. The Ministry has several directories (departments), including the main operating department in charge of corresponding branches of railway industry (traction, freight, passenger, locomotive economy, electrification and energy economy, track, signalling and communications, industrial railway transport and Metro/underground railways, as well as main departments of material-technical supplies, capital construction, plants for the repair of rolling stock and production of spare parts, and others) and functional directorates (planning-economical, financial, statistical and accounting, computing technology, etc).
The whole railway network is divided into 31 railways each of which has an administrative structure similar to that of the Ministry.
The 31 railways are as follows:—

Azerbaidhanian	Trans-Caucassian	Volga
Alma-Atinsk	Krasnoyarsk	Dniepr
White Russian (Bielorussian)	Kemerovsk	Sverdlosk
Eastern Siberia	Kuybishev	Northern
Gorkovsk	Lvovsk	North Caucassian
Far Eastern	Moldavian	Central Asian
Donetsk	Moscow	Tselinn
Trans-Baikal	Odessa	South Eastern
West Kazakhstan	Oktyabraskaya	South Western
West Siberian	Baltic	Southern
		South Ural

ELECTRIFICATION
By the end of 1978 the length of electrified lines amounted to 41 100 km comprising 29.3 per cent of the total length of railway lines in use. Of these, 16 000 km of electrified lines use industrial ac current.
Power system: 3 kV dc, 25 kV 50 Hz ac.
A total of 543 km of track were electrified in 1978, increasing the traffic capacity of the lines between Leningrad-Ekibastuz, Vyazma-Orsha and several sections of the Far Eastern railway, Donetsk, Oktyabrskaya, Southern and other lines.
At present there are several electrified main lines of considerable length in the USSR: Moscow-Trans-Baikal (6 500 km); Leningrad-Leninakan (3 400 km); Moscow-Chop and Moscow-Sverdlovsk, each of approximately 2 000 km in length. All larger railway junctions are electrified, and electric traction occupies the leading place in inter-town traffic.

TRAFFIC

	1975	1977	1978
Freight turnover (mill ton/km)	3 236.5	3 330.9	3 429.5
Dispatched freight (million tons)	3 621.1	3 723.4	3 776.4
Passenger turnover (mill passenger/km)	312.5	322.2	332.1
Dispatched passengers (million people)	3 470.5	3 544.5	3 603.1

MOTIVE POWER AND ROLLING STOCK
During 1978 the locomotive park of Soviet railways was supplemented by new electric and diesel locomotives intended for mainline and shunting work. Electrified lines using ac current have been supplied, mainly with the 8-axle VL80T freight locomotives developing 6 520 kW and with a designed speed of 110 km/h. Electrified lines using dc current have been provided with the 8-axle VL10u locomotives developing 5200 kW, with a designed speed of 100 km/h, equipped with recuperating braking devices, while the VL11 type electric locomotives, which can be used in multiples (twins-, triples- and quadruples-) are 5200, 7800 and 10 400 kW respectively.
The mainline diesel locomotive park used for freight movement has been supplemented mainly by the 2TE10V and 2TE116 multiple (twin-section) units developing 6 000hp. The shunting park has been augmented mainly by the 6-axle ChME3 series locomotives of 1 350 hp and the TEM2. Passenger traffic has been augmented with the 6-axle ac current ChS4T, and the TEP60 diesels.
On the electrified suburban lines of larger Soviet towns use is made of the ER2, ER22, ER22M (3 kV dc systems), and ER9P (25 kV ac 50 Hz systems) electric trains.
Principal technical characteristics of the ER22 electric passenger train:
Number of carriages:

Motor coaches	4
Coupled trailers	4

Number and power of electric traction motors:

Of each motor coach	4 × 220 kW
Of the complete train	16 c 220 kW
Designed speed	130 km/h
Seating capacity	988
Length overall	200.5 m
Empty (tare) weight	420 tonnes

At present the freight stock park consists mainly of 4-axle wagons of 62-66 tonnes capacity, and a growing number of 8-axle semi-wagons and tank wagons of 125 and 120 tonnes capacity are joining service. Changes are also taking place in the structure of the Soviet freight rolling stock park which is being augmented with specialised wagons for the transportation of cement, grain, chemical fertilisers, motor vehicles, containers and other cargoes. For the transport of perishable goods use is made of refrigerated wagons with self-contained refrigerating equipment, as well as refrigerated trains and (train) sections.

TRACKWORK
In 1978 an additional 638 km of new railway track was introduced into service, of great importance to the development of larger economic areas and improvement of transport connections in the country.
Rails:
Standard type R75, R65 and R50 weighing respectively 74.4, 64.6 and 51.6 kg/m.
Sleepers:
Of impregnated wood, length 2 750 mm; thickness 150-180 mm; width of lower bed (on main tracks) 250 mm; on station tracks 230 mm. Ferro-concrete type: prestressed, length 2 700 mm; width 300 mm; thickness (under rails) 193 mm
Number of sleepers per 1 km:
1 840-2 000
During 1978 the tracks were made stronger mainly by laying new heavy rails of R65 and R75 type, largely thermically strengthened, continuous welded rail and ferro-concrete sleepers, as well as by changing over to stone chipping and asbestos ballast. By the end of 1978 the length of mainline tracks of heavyweight category rails comprised approximately 90 per cent of the total. The length of tracks on ferro-concrete sleepers was increased by 3 000 km, continuous welded rail by 2 800 km.

SIGNAL AND COMMUNICATIONS SYSTEMS
In 1978 3 300 km of track was equipped with automatic block signalling and centralised traffic controls. Communications cables were laid along many sections of line, and the length of track equipped with inter-station radio communications has been increased by 2 000 km.

MARSHALLING YARDS
In marshalling yards extensive use is made of modern mechanisation devices and automatic processes for the division and formation of trains. Marshalling humps are equipped with complex systems: automatic centralised hump release controls (GATs-KR), also providing registration of the actual release programme from the humps and the entering of carriages on each track of the marshalling yard; automatic controls regulating the rolling speed of rakes from the humps (ARS); automatic assignment of release speeds depending on the coupling length (AZSR).
These systems are functionally connected to each other. Of important significance are automatic hump locomotive signalling devices (ALS) which respond to the specific working conditions of locomotives approaching humps and during division of the trains. For spaced and accurate braking of wagon 'cuts' on marshalling yard humps use is made of pneumatically-operated retarders of the following types:
Pincer-weight: KV-72
Pincer-pressure-lifting: KNP-5-73 which has the following characteristics:
Braking power 1.25 m of suppressing energy weight
Time lag of braking action 0.6 s
Time to release brakes 1.0 s.
The KV-72 and KNP-5-73 retarders are intended for installation on the launching tracks of more powerful and medium-power humps. Special single rail hydraulic weight retarders TsNII-3V are used in yard braking positions of automatic marshalling humps, launching tracks of lower capacity humps and profiled manoeuvring tracks. Up to four linked retarders of this type are fitted in one braking position.
Marshalling yards are equipped with a pneumatic mail system for the despatch of transportation documents from the arrival yard to the central technical office (TsTK) and from there to the despatch yard. Advance train information communications system is used to receive details of the composition of arriving trains.
All information regarding trains, preparation of marshalling sheets, numerical calculation of carriages accumulated on the tracks of marshalling yards and the formulation of practical lists of trains to be formed is carried out by EVM (electronic calculators).

DEVELOPMENTS
Under the present Five-Year Plan (1976-80) development of the national economy of the USSR, it is intended to further improve freight capacity and increase efficiency, as well as better use of marshalling yard and goods station technology, and reduced goods turn-over time. Apart from that, it is intended to speed up the movement of freight and passenger trains, increase the amount of freight carried along regular routes and average weight of freight trains. During this five-year plan 3 400 km of new railway track will come into use and work will continue on the Baikal-Amur mainline and its approach lines. During this period it is also intended to supply the Soviet railways with 2 200 electric, 6 400 mainline and 2 500 marshalling diesel locomotives; 400 000 freight and 16 000 passenger carriages.
This five-year period will also see improvement in the organisation of passenger transport, and the continuation of electrification of main rail centres, particularly in suburban traffic movement.

Shunting-trip diesel locomotive TEM7 (2 000 hp)

Passenger diesel locomotive TEP75 (6 000 hp)

Electric locomotive VL-80T

ELECTRIC LOCOMOTIVES

Class	Axle Arrangement	Line Current	Rated Output hp	Max. lb (kg)	Tractive Effort (Full Field) Continuous at lb (kg)	at mph (km/h)	Max. Speed mph (km/h)	Wheel dia. in (mm)	Weight tonnes	Length ft in (mm)	No. Built	Year Built	Mechanical Parts	Electrical Equipment
VL 8	Bo+Bo+Bo+Bo	3 000 V dc	4 200	77 800 (35 300)	66 800 (30 300)	27.5 (44.3)	62 (100)	47¼ (1 200)	184	90' 3½" (27 520)		1955	Novocherkassk Works	Novocherkassk Works
VL 10	Bo-Bo-Bo-Bo	3 000 V dc	5 200	88 000 (40 000)	72 750 (33 000)	32.3 (52.0)	62 (100)	49¼ (1 250)	184	99' 10½" (30 440)		1961	Tiflis Works	Tiflis Works
VL 60	Co-Co	25 kV 1/50	4 140	70 100 (31 800)	58 000 (26 300)	34.2 (55.1)	62 (100)	49¼ (1 250)	138	68' 3" (20 800)		1963	Novocherkassk Works	Novocherkassk Works
VL 60k	Co-Co	25 kV 1/50	4 650	70 500 (32 000)	58 200 (26 400)	34.5 (55.6)	62 (100)	49¼ (1 250)	138	68' 3" (20 800)		1962	Novocherkassk Works	Novocherkassk Works
VL 80k	2(Bo-Bo)	25 kV 1/50	6 520	99 400 (45 100)	90 200 (40 900)	33.3 (53.6)	68 (110)	49¼ (1 250)	184	107' 9" (32 840)		1963	Novocherkassk Works	Novocherkassk Works
VL 80T	2(Bo-Bo)	25 kV 1/50	6 520	99 400 (45 100)	90 200 (40 900)	33.3 (53.6)	68 (110)	49¼ (1 250)	184	107' 9" (32 840)		1966	Novocherkassk Works	Novocherkassk Works
VL 82M Dual-current	2(Bo-Bo)	25 kV and 3 kV dc	6 040	93 476 (42 400)	88 185 (40 000)	31.7 (51.6)	68 (110)	49½ (1 250)	192	107' 9" (32 840)		1972	Novocherkassk Works	Novocherkassk Works
ChS 2T	Co-Co	3 000 V dc	4 620	41 888 (19 000)	35 274 (16 000)	199 (320)	99 (160)	49¼ (1 250)	126	61' 1" (18 920)		1972	Skoda Works Czechoslovakia	Skoda Works Czechoslovakia
Ch S4T	Co-Co	25 kV 1/50	5 100	38 360 (17 400)	37 038 (16 800)	67 (107)	112 (180)	49¼ (1 250)	126	65' 7" (19 880)		1971	Skoda Works Czechoslavakia	Skoda Works Czechoslovakia

DIESEL LOCOMOTIVES

Class	Axle Arrangement	Transmission	Rated Power hp	Max. lb (kg)	Tractive Effort Continuous at lb (kg)	at mph (km/h)	Max. Speed mph (km/h)	Wheel Dia. in (mm)	Total Weight Tons	Length ft ins (mm)	No. Built	Year first Built	Mechanical Parts	Engine & Type	Transmission
TE-3	2 (Co-Co)	Elec	4 000	128 000 (58 200)	95 200 (43 200)	12.4 (20)	62 (100)	41⅜ (1 050)	252	111' 4" (33 940)		1953	Voroshilovgrad	2 × 2D 100	Elektrotyazh-masch
TE-7	2 (Co-Co)	Elec	4 000	73 800 (33 500)	34 000 (15 400)	34.8 (56)	87 (140)	41⅜ (1 050)	252	111' 4" (33 940)		1957	Transmasch Works	2 × 2D 100	Elektrotyazh-masch
TE-10	Co-Co	Elec	3 000	92 600 (42 000)	59 500 (27 000)	14.3 (23)	62 (100)	41⅜ (1 050)	129	61' 1" (18 610)		1958	Transmasch Works	10 D 100	Elektrotyazh-masch
2TE-10	2 (Co-Co)	Elec	6 000	185 200 (84 000)	119 000 (54 000)	14.3 (23)	62 (100)	41⅜ (1 050)	258	122' 2" (37 220)		1960		2 × 10 D 100	Elektrotyazh-masch
2TE-10L	2 (Co-Co)	Elec	6 000	185 200 (84 000)	114 600 (52 000)	14.9 (24)	62 (100)	41⅜ (1 050)	258.6	111' 4" (33 940)		1961	Voroshilovgrad	10 D 100	CKD Prague
TEP-10	Co-Co	Elec	3 000	66 350 (30 100)	38 100 (17 300)	22.4 (36)	87 (140)	41⅜ (1 050)	129	61' 1" (18 610)		1960	Transmasch Works	10 D 100	Elektrotyazh-masch
TEP-60	Co-Co	Elec	3 000	55 750 (25 300)	27 500 (12 500)	31.1 (50)	100 (160)	41⅜ (1 050)	127	63' 2" (19 250)		1960	Kolomna Works	D 45 A	Elektrotyazh-masch
TEM-1	Co-Co	Elec	1 000	79 400 (36 000)	44 000 (20 000)	5.6 (9)	56 (90)	41⅜ (1 050)	123	55' 8" (16 970)		1959	Bryansk Works	2 D 50	Elektrotyazh-masch
TEM-2	Co-Co	Elec	1 200	79 400 (36 000)	46 300 (21 000)	8.7 (14)	62 (100)	41⅜ (1 050)	120	55' 8" (16 970)		1960	Bryansk Works	PD-IM	Elektrotyazh-masch
VME-1	Bo-Bo	Elec	600	39 700 (18 000)	20 300 (9 300)	7.1 (11.5)	50 (80)	41⅜ (1 050)	69	42' 2" (12 850)		1958	Ganz Mavag	XVIIV 170/240	Ganz Mavag
ChME-2	Bo-Bo	Elec	750	48 500 (22 000)	22 900 (10 400)	8.7 (14)	43 (70)	41⅜ (1 050)	64	40' 10½" (12 460)		1959	CKD Prague	6S310-DE	CKD Prague
ChME-3	Co-Co	Elec	1 350	81 350 (36 900)	50 700 (23 000)	7.1 (11.4)	59 (95)	41⅜ (1 050)	123	56' 9" (17 000)		1964	CKD Prague	K6S310 DK	CKD Prague
TG 16	2 (B-B)	Hyd	3 280	99 200 (45 000)	83 800 (38 000)	12.4 (20)	53 (85)	41⅜ (1 050)	136	101' 4½" (30 900)		1966	Lyudinovsk Works	M 756AC	
TG-102	2 (B-B)	Hyd	4 000	119 300 (54 100)	72 000 (39 400)	12.2 (19.5)	75 (120)	41⅜ (1 050)	160	96' 8" (29 460)		1960	Leningrad Works	4 × M 756A	
TGM-1	C	Hyd	400	30 800 (14 000)	24 700 (11 200) / 12 350 (5 600)	3.1 (5) / 6.2 (10)	19 (30) / 37 (60)	41⅜ (1 050)	48	32' 8½" (9 970)		1956	Murom Works	ID12-400	Murom Works
TGM-3	B-B	Hyd*	750	49 470 (22 440)	43 000 (19 500) / 19 850 (9 000)	4.3 (7) / 9.3 (15)	19 (30) / 37 (60)	41⅜ (1 050)	68	41' 4" (12 600)		1958	Lyudinovsk Works	M 753B	Lyudinovsk Works
TGM-6	B-B	Hyd	1 200	52 470 (23 800)	30 860 (14 000)	9.3 (15)	25 (40) / 50 (80)	41⅜ (1 050)	80	46' 11" (14 300)					
TGM-10	C/C	Hyd	1 200	79 400 (36 000)	67 000 (30 400) / 33 500 (15 200)	4.2 (6.8) / 8.4 (13.6)	25 (40) / 50 (80)	41⅜ (1 050)	121	55' 8" (16 970)		1961	Bryansk Works	PD-2	Kaluga Works
2TE116	2(Co-Co)	Elec	2 × 3 000	—	(2 × 26 000)	(23.5)	(120)	(1 050)	2 × 138	(33 938)		1971	Voroshilovgrad	5D49 (2D70)	Elektro-tyazhmasch
M62	Co-Co	Elec	2 000	—	(20 000)	(20)	(100)	(1 050)	116.5	(17 550)		1965	Voroshilovgrad	14D40	Elektro-tyazhmasch
TEP75	Co-Co	Elec	6 000	—	(18 000)	(70)	(160)	(1 220)	138	(21 700)		1976	Kolomensk Works	I/D40	Elektro-tyazhmasch
TEP70	Co-Co	Elec	4 000	—	(17 000)	(50)	(160)	(1 220)	126	(20 470)		1973	Kolomensk Works	5D49	Elektro-tyazhmasch
TEM7	Do-Do	Elec	2 000	55 400 (59 400)	32 000 (35 000)	10.3 (11.7)	(100)	(1 050)	180	(21 500)		1976	Lyudinovsk Works	2D49	Elektro-tyazhmasch
GAS TURBINE G-1	Co-Co	Elec	3 300	92 600 (42 000)	55 100 (25 000)	15.5 (25)	62 (100)	41⅜ (1 050)	140	65' 7" (19 980)		1959	Kolomna Works	GTU-4	Elektrotyazh-masch

* Class TGM-3 has fluid-mechanical transmission.

Mainline diesel locomotive 2TE116 (2 × 3 000 hp)

Passenger diesel locomotive TEP70 (4 000 hp)

UNITED KINGDOM

BRITISH RAIL

British Railways Board, 222 Marylebone Road, London NW1

Telephone: 01-262 3232

MEMBERS OF THE BOARD
Chairman: Sir Peter Parker, MVO
Vice Chairman (Rail): David Bowick, CBE
Vice Chairman: R. L. E. Lawrence, CBE, ERD
Chief Executive (Railways): I. M. Campbell, CVO
Members: T. R. Barron
          Derek Fowler, CBE
          Lord Caldecote, DSC
          Michael Posner
          Sir David Serpell, KCB, CMG, OBE
          Lord Taylor of Gryfe, DL
          J. G. Urquhart
          C. A. Rose
          R. B. Reid

BRITISH RAIL REGIONS
Eastern Region General Manager: F. Paterson
London Midland Region General Manager: D. S. Binnie
Scottish Region General Manager: L. J. Soane
Southern Region General Manager: J. Palette
Western Region General Manager: L. Lloyd

1978 was described as a year of success and strain for British Rail, in which there was an operating surplus before interest of £58.3 million (£68.4 million in 1977). British Rail improved on the financial objectives agreed with the Government for the third year running. After interest and other charges the British Railways Board had a net surplus of £6.4 million compared with £27 million for 1977. Marketing attracted an increase of nearly 8 per cent in passenger-km over two years, and also achieved a small surplus in the non-passenger sector after three years of losses. There was a further growth of 34 per cent in the profits from ships and harbours to total over £12 million, and property increased its operating surplus by nearly 12 per cent to £23.2 million. In addition British Rail Engineering Ltd won overseas orders worth £50 million, and there was a 22 per cent growth in the foreign tourist traffic by British Transport Hotels.

FREIGHT TRAFFIC
In 1978 British Rail carried a total of 170.5 million tonnes of freight (20 000 million tonne-km) which earned £384.5 million in revenue; the first year since 1975 when freight business broke even. In 1975 £66 million of Government support was needed to pay for rail freight losses. Freight lost £27.5 million on revenue of £307 million in 1976 and £5.5 million in 1977 on revenue of £348 million.
In 1979 British Rail hauled about 170.3 million tonnes despite first half year problems when freight volume fell by 3.5 million tonnes (4.5 per cent). During the first six months

British Rail's 125 mph (200 km/h) passenger service began on 4 October 1976 when the first of 27 Inter-City 125 trains entered daily service between London—Bristol/South Wales
The first of a second build of 32 trains for London—Edinburgh, via the East Coast route, came into use in 1978 and when all these trains are in service a further 14 will follow for the London—West of England line. The trains, built by BREL, comprise 2 power cars, each containing a 2 250 hp diesel engine, and 7 or 8 intermediate coaches, including catering vehicles. The prototype train holds the world speed record for diesel trains at 143 mph (229 km/h).

First of British Rail's 3 pre-production Advanced Passenger Trains, designed for running at speeds up to 150 mph (241.4 km/h) on Britain's Inter-City network
The first train was due to be ready for commissioning towards the end of 1979. The 3 trains are for experimental passenger service on the electrified route London—Glasgow. Picture is the sleek line of the driving car.

of 1979 haulage of coal and coke fell by 2.4 million tonnes, minerals by 0.6 million, petroleum and chemicals by 0.2 per cent and other traffic by 0.3 million tonnes.
Long-term plans for substantial changes in British Rail's freight business were under consideration by the Government and the British Railways Board in late 1979. Options open include closing most of the 458 rail freight terminals and the 38 marshalling yards, and investment in specialised aspects of the business. A restructured rail freight business would concentrate on materials, fuel and containers and transport of heavy raw materials. These make up about 70 per cent of British Rail's activities: coal and coke (93.3 million tonnes) account for 54 per cent of all traffic; iron and steel (26.1 million tonnes) for 15 per cent; minerals and construction materials (19 million tonnes) for 11 per cent; oil and chemicals (20.9 million tonnes) for 12 per cent. Low-volume freight traffic accounts for less than 30 per cent of British Rail freight although movements are expected to grow over the next 25 years; British Rail's share, however, may remain marginal unless there are significant changes to the structural and competitive frameworks.
An increase in freight charges of between 18 and 20 per cent was introduced in September 1979 in order to take account of the steep rise in fuel. The Railway's fuel bill in 1979 was about £132.5 million compared with an estimated £85 million.
The Freightliner container freight company was reunited with British Rail in 1978 following three successive years of trading profits on sales revenues up from £31.2 million in 1975 to £51 million in 1978. Freightliner was launched in 1965 essentially as an inland transportation exercise, a trunk conveyor-belt between road-rail transfer centres in the country's principal production areas.

Class 47 diesel locomotive and Speedlink train
The new British Rail service for freight in less-than-trainload quantities under the brand name Speedlink has the slogan: "Speedlink; the freight name for reliability". The Speedlink wagonload services, using new high capacity vehicles running to a strict timetable at up to 75 mph, were developed from a pilot scheme in 1972 between Bristol and Glasgow. Now a national network linking main centres of industry in Britain, with European connections through the Ferry Train ports of Dover and Harwich, is being expanded. Speedlink is complementary to Railfreight's main business of bulk freight traffics in trainloads and the Freightliner system of door-to-door movements for containers.

PASSENGER TRAFFIC

Despite a rise in fares during 1978 passenger journeys rose by three per cent, giving passenger revenues of £702 million. The railway again increased fares in January 1980 by up to 20 per cent, admitting that the higher fares might turn travellers away. When fares rose by 62 per cent during 1975 and 1976 the number of passenger journeys fell by four per cent. The 1980 increases are designed to help meet rising fuel prices and to counter cuts in Government subsidies for rail passenger services. The cash limit imposed by the Government for subsidies for passenger services will be cut by £40 million between 1977 and 1981. The subsidy would fall by £22 million to £460 million by 1980/81 compared with the 1979 financial year.

High speeds and high comfort standards provided on British Rail's intercity services are making an impact on the railway's passenger figures. In 1978 intercity passenger volume rose by six per cent over 1977, with revenues up 19 per cent to £250 million. In 1979 British Rail operated 160 High-Speed Train services a day on the normal Monday to Friday timetable.

At the end of 1979 the Government gave the go-ahead for construction of four more High-Speed Trains costing about £9.3 million. The new trains will give British Rail a high speed fleet of 95.

Meanwhile the Advanced Passenger Train (APT) has been in the development stage since 1966 but British Rail was confident that the first of the high speed tilting trains would be in service by May 1980. It is the Railway's plan to ask the Government for permission to spend £150 million on a fleet of APTs.

FINANCES (1978)

Expenditure	£million
Rail infrastructure costs:	
Track maintenance	294
Signalling, operating and maintenance	138
Associated administration and general expenses	43
	475
Rail operating costs:	
Train services	687
Terminals and miscellaneous	226
Administration and general expenses	208
Provision for replacement of passenger assets	50
	1 171
Corporate expenses	6
Interest	49
Net surplus	6
	1 707

Income	£million
Rail fares and charges:	
Passenger	702
Freight	384
Parcels	119
Miscellaneous	18
	1 223
Payments by government and other agencies:	
PSO payment	434
Payments for level crossings	11
Grants for rail non-passenger sector	—
	445
Exchange loss	−2
Other income (net) from subsidiary activities	41
	1 707

British Railways Board net operating results

	1977 £million	1978 £million
Operating results:		
Railways	44.8	37.8
Freightliner	0.3	0.8
Rail workshops	0.6	0.1
Ship	6.5	9.1
Hovercraft	−0.6	−2.2
Harbours	2.7	3.1
Hotels	1.5	1.0
Non-operational property	7.0	7.0
Net surplus on operations	62.8	56.7
Other income	9.7	7.4
	72.5	64.1
Corporate expenses	4.1	5.8
Net surplus before:	68.4	58.3
Interest	43.0	47.5
Other financing charges		1.6
Taxation	0.2	0.2
Exchange gain/loss	4.5	−2.5
Surplus for year before Grant for rail non-passenger sector	29.7	6.5
Grant for rail non-passenger sector	2.7*	0.1
	27.0	6.4

*Net repayment

MOTIVE POWER

In 1976 Britain became the third country in the world to operate 125 mph (200 km/h) passenger services when the first of 27 High Speed Trains (HSTs) started carrying passengers from London to South Wales and the important commercial and industrial area around the city of Bristol. In early 1980 British Rail asked the government for permission to spend £150 million on a fleet of 60 APTs. This followed a government go-ahead in December 1979 to build four more HSTs costing about £9.3 million. The new HSTs will give the railway a high speed fleet of 95 and will go into service on east-coast mainline services from London's King's Cross station. The railway was operating 160 HST service's a day in 1979 on the normal Monday to Friday timetable. Since services started to Bristol and South Wales there has been a 40 per cent growth in passenger business.

The trains have been designed to provide top quality service on Britain's non-electrified Inter-City routes and attract more customers by considerably reducing journey times. Most important, as far as British Rail's marketing policy is concerned, is that the trains are standard Inter-City trains available to all passengers with first or second class tickets or any of the wide range of special excursion or cut-price tickets which British Rail offers.

Intermediate Trailer Car on British Rail's pre-production APTs

Interior of the APT pre-production first-class saloon

An interesting structural feature of the APT is the driving cab
It consists of a strong aluminium inner frame with a deep buffer beam to withstand buffing and accident loads. Glass reinforced plastic is used to form the windscreen surround and the hinged nose cone.

Passengers in both second and first class sections enjoy air conditioning, wall-to-wall carpeting, individual seats, double glazing to cut down noise and automatic draught free sliding doors at the end of each saloon. New catering vehicles have been designed and built to provide freshly cooked meals which can be ordered by and served to passengers at their seats, or simple hot dishes which passengers may collect from the buffet and take back to their seats.

The High Speed Trains are powered by two 2 250 hp diesel engines located behind a driving cab at each end of the train. The design of the train has been developed from the highly successful prototype train which, on 12 June 1973, became the fastest diesel train in the world when it ran at 143 mph (230 km/h) during engineering trials. Each of the Western Region trains consists of two power cars and seven passenger coaches, and each train on the East Coast route has eight coaches between the two power cars. Advanced technology and design has enabled the weight of each seven-coach train to be reduced from the 466 tonnes of a conventional train to 383 tonnes. Each train can carry 318 passengers and consumes about 3.75 litres of fuel per kilometre at the 125 mph (200 km/h) cruising speed, an important factor when energy costs are continually rising.

Particularly important is the High Speed Train's ability to stop within the same distances as conventional trains thus eliminating the need to modify signalling systems. A wheel slide protection device has been specially developed to ensure that the wheels do not lock during braking, eliminating the risk of skidding.

INVESTMENTS

In 1980 British Rail is scheduled to spend £316 million on capital improvements: 12 mainline diesel-electric locomotives (£8.5 million), 13 HSTs and 48 EMU's (£56.3 million), 1,330 freight wagons (£22.6 million), major track improvements (£77.1 million), track maintenance machines (£10.4 million), electrification (£11.3 million), signalling (£53.1 million), communications (£9.2 million), marshalling yards (£17.5 million), bridges and buildings (£12.2 million), other (£27.8 million).

ELECTRIFICATION

A review of the case for mainline electrification was published in September 1979. The report, prepared by British Rail and the government, quotes substantial cost benefits and improvements in speed, quality of service and reliability from large-scale electrification. British Rail has 21 per cent of route electrified compared with 48 per cent in

Latest generation of electric multiple unit trains to be built for service on British Rail, the Class 312

They are specifically designed to provide fast comfortable travel on long-distance commuter services. Picture shows one of 4 Class 312 Units running between Birmingham and Coventry serving the new railway station at the National Exhibition Centre.

Train of loaded wagons hauled by 2 class 25 diesel-electric locomotives on the new line

The bulk movement of aggregates is an expanding part of British Rail's freight business and several firms have taken advantage of the grants available to provide private sidings for this traffic. Redland Aggregates have developed an existing site near Radlett into a distribution centre for south-east England by constructing a loop from the Midland mainline to allow merry-go-round delivery of crushed granite from its quarry at Budden Wood, Loughborough.

Merry-go-round train with coal from the East Midlands at Didcot power station, one of the largest in Europe

Introduced in 1965 merry-go-round trains carry around 1 million tons of coal per week to 15 power stations in Britain.

The trains operate in a continuous circuit between collieries and power stations where loading and unloading is automatic while the train moves at a steady speed. Although developed for coal traffic, the merry-go-round system has also been adopted to convey other commodities such as gypsum to cement manufacturers.

Italy, 40 per cent in Japan, 35 per cent in the Federal Republic of Germany, 29 per cent in the Soviet Union and 27 per cent in France. Britain's electrified lines handle 45 per cent of total train-kilometres.

The 1979 review made its cost estimates by comparing a base case of electrification with four options incorporating increasing amounts of electrification. The base option includes the St. Pancras (London)—Bedford scheme now in hand plus projects in East Anglia, Strathclyde (Scotland) and the West Coast mainline. The second option, which would increase the electrified network to 31 per cent of total route-kilometres, includes electrification of the East Coast mainline to Newcastle; the Midland mainline to Leeds; Birmingham to York; Edinburgh to Glasgow and Edinburgh to Carstairs. The third option is a medium proposal with emphasis on electrifying passenger services including all main Inter-City routes. Option four is similar to the third choice, but with the emphasis on freight. The last option would increase the amount of electrified lines to just over half the total.

The various options would cost between £230 million and £750 million at 1978 prices. These, however, would be partly offset by lower rolling stock costs bringing net additional investment down to between £160 million and £500 million. Operating cost advantages over the base option ranged between £3 million and £12 million a year, rising to between £11 million and £34 million a year when energy price forecasts are included. And, if escalation in staff costs is also taken into account, the financial benefit increases still further to between £15 million and £47 million a year. If the largest option were implemented British Rail's oil consumption would fall by 545 million litres a year. Work on the £114.9 million scheme to resignal, rationalise and electrify the Moorgate—St Pancras—Bedford line started just over three years ago and is on schedule for completion by early 1982. About 80 km of route is involved. Electric services should be running to Moorgate (London) in January 1982 and to St Pancras (London) in May 1982.

TRACK

Major results of the railway's policy to continuously improve track are one steady spread of continuous welded rail (9 000 miles by mid-1977) which gives passengers a quieter ride, and reduces maintenance costs, rolling stock wear and risks of rail breaks, and replacement of traditional timber sleepers by prestressed concrete sleepers.

Periodic measurement of track geometry and assessment of its ride quality is the key to the optimum economic use of maintenance resources. British Rail has developed a track recording vehicle capable of much more accurate measurements than previously possible and at the same time able to operate at speeds up to 125 mph (200 km/h). The vehicle, known as the High Speed Track Recording Coach, runs behind any scheduled passenger train and measures the quality of the track during the journey. It will run over 80 000 miles each year checking most of British Rail's 21 000 miles of track, and can even be used with the 125 mph High Speed Trains—probably the only test coach of its kind in the world capable of working at these speeds.

Designed to supplement the regular patrolling of track by trained inspection staff, the coach's high speed capability overcomes the problems experienced when trying to fit existing recording vehicles, some of which can only run at 20 mph, in between normal passenger and freight trains.

The on-board electronic systems measure and record during the journey twelve different factors which indicate the condition of the track.

If the computer system detects any major irregularity, it fires a paint gun which marks the location on the track for attention by the local maintenance team.

At the end of each run, the measurements recorded are analysed so that the quality of the track can be assessed and maintenance programmes planned to ensure that the best possible use is made of the maintenance resources available.

The High Speed Track Recording Coach, together with its sister vehicle, the Ultrasonic Test Train, demonstrate British Rail's expertise in the field of automated track inspection systems.

In parallel with the development of the Track Recording Coach, the performance of the Ultrasonic Test Train is being greatly enhanced by the addition of automatic analysis equipment.

The train uses ultrasonic techniques to examine rails for hidden defects, with data from the sensors being recorded on photographic film for subsequent development and analysis. Until recently, this analysis has been carried out by trained evaluators visually scanning the processed film. A joint programme of work with the Nondestructive Testing Centre of the Harwell Laboratory of the United Kingdom Atomic Energy Authority has resulted in the development of an automated defect analysis system which exploits Harwell's expertise in computerised data analysis.

Further technical improvement and economies are expected to be made in the defect inspection system by placing the analysis computer actually on board the Ultrasonic Test Train to provide an automatic real time film-free system which will not only record and process data directly from the ultrasonic probes, but will also operate a track-marking system to pinpoint certain defects. Work on this is proceeding.

Following joint research between British Rail, the British Steel Corporation and two specialist companies, a technique has been developed to enable rails made from the most wear-resistant steel to be welded into continuous lengths, to cut maintenance costs and produce smoother, quieter riding. The work has involved producing a weldable version of Hadfield's austenitic manganese steel, and developing the techniques to make reliable joints.

The first installation using the new development has been made in the tunnels of London's Great Northern Suburban Line. Examination of the installation after several months of intensive use has shown the rail material and the welds to be standing up well to the wear and tear.

Previously the austenitic rail could not be welded satisfactorily, partly because the heat applied during the welding process gave the metal more brittle characteristics, and partly because the material's much higher coefficient of expansion created excessive stresses as the rail expanded or contracted with changes in temperature. This is not a problem, however, in locations where ambient temperature change is small, as in many tunnels. This latest development has promise of considerable application in similar locations at home and abroad, particularly on underground railways.

Advanced passenger trains

The APT project is designed to provide a cost effective solution to the problem of providing fast inter-urban transport on existing tracks, in both financial and energy consumption terms.

APTs have developed from a programme of research into the dynamics of rail vehicles—passenger and freight—which was started in 1964 at the then newly established Railway Technical Centre, Derby.

The cost of the research and development phase of the programme, including building and running the experimental train APT-E has been £10 million.

During the development phase, the experimental train not only became the fastest train ever to run in Britain, running at 152 mph (243 km/h) on 10 August 1975, but even more significantly, two months later it covered the 99 miles (159 km) between London and Leicester in 58½ minutes. It was this demonstration which showed just how effectively APTs can improve on the performance of present day trains. The fastest scheduled Inter-City trains are timed to cover the London-Leicester distance in 1 hour 24 minutes, an average speed of 70.7 mph (112 km/h). APT-E cut the journey time by nearly one-third, averaging just over 100 mph (160 km/h).

The project has now moved from the experimental stage. In October 1974, with Government approval, British Railways Board authorised the building of three prototype electrically propelled passenger carrying APTs at a cost of £9.9 million.

The total cost of the APT prototype programme is about £25 million, including the three trains, production line and other development costs which will not recur, and major items such as maintenance depots which will be required for subsequent trains. £11.6 million has been loaned to the project by the European Investment Bank.

When APT-Ps enter experimental commercial service, the maximum speed will be limited to 125 mph (200 km/h) giving a possible journey time of 3 hours 57 mins from

London to Glasgow with one intermediate stop. This compares with the best present day timing for the 401 mile *(640 km)* journey of 5 hours. Each train will have accommodation for 592 passengers.

Tests with the first of the electric APT-P vehicles formed into a test rake began in 1978, and the testing continues at the present time, combined with a crew training programme. For these trials, the train is based at Shields Depot, Glasgow.

Locomotives and rolling stock in service during 1978 included 76 High Speed Train power cars, 3 290 diesel locomotives, 320 electric locomotives, 302 High Speed coaches, 21 553 passenger coaches, 1979 diesel power cars, 1 346 diesel trailers, 2 732 emu power cars, 4 726 emu trailers, 166 935 freight wagon and 3 787 brake vans.

SIGNALLING

There has been much care and expenditure by British Rail to improve control of traffic and promote maximum safety and efficiency. A major feature of the policy is extension of colour-light signalling with control concentrated in large centres.

The National Signalling Plan envisages that the majority of Inter-City, commuter and important freight routes will ultimately be controlled from about 75 major signalling centres. So far 43 centres have been established, with the remainder of the system controlled from about 2 945 manual signal boxes.

By the end of 1976 about 10 100 single track miles *(16 400 km)* had been equipped with continuous colour-light signalling.

Automatic Warning System– More than 4 138 route miles *(6 650 km)* have now been equipped with AWS. High speed equipment has been developed and is now undergoing service trials.

National Telecommunication Plan– Provides extension-to-extension dialling between approximately 200 railway telephone exchanges; planning is proceeding to connect remaining exchanges to the network. Provision has also been made for a National Radio Plan to be integrated into the network. The network carries the equivalent of £60 000 worth of trunk telephone calls each working day and provides the base system for TOPS, MANIS and many other data transmission systems, effecting large savings on Post Office leased lines.

National Radio Plan– Plan aims to provide two-way radio contact between lineside and traffic staff and a control base. National scheme will have 32 control centres and about 250 static transmitting points. Pilot schemes now cover routes between London-High Wycombe, Northampton and Bedford also Carlisle-Glasgow including Greater Glasgow area. Authority is being sought for Liverpool Street scheme, which would include Fenchurch Street-Southend and Liverpool Street-Clacton and Bishops Stortford. Scheme in progress providing signalbox to train communication on GN inner suburban lines.

One of the first Class 56 locomotives to be built undergoing trials with a train of 'Merry-go-Round' hoppers

Rated at 3 250 hp, the Class 56 locomotives are the most powerful freight only diesel engines working on British Rail. Designed to cope with heavy freight trains up to a maximum speed of around 70 mph *(130 km/h)*, the locomotives also have special control systems to enable them to haul 'Merry-go-Round' trains at a constant speed of about ½ mph (1 km/*h*) whilst they are being automatically loaded or unloaded. The locomotives are 63 ft long *(19.3 m)* and weight 85 tonnes. 60 Class 56 locomotives were ordered in September 1974, 30 from Brush Electrical Machines Limited and 30 from British Rail Engineering Limited. An additional 30 locomotives were ordered from British Rail Engineering in 1975.

Electrification test train with only one pantograph raised running under the dynamically scaled length of Mk IIIA catenary modelled on an actual section in Lancashire

Conventional diesel locomotives hauling ordinary rolling stock and laboratory coaches at 75 mph *(120 km/h)* under a specially-designed overhead wire system are reproducing the conditions produced by an electric train travelling at 150 mph *(240 km/h)* on existing electrified lines. The overhead system, designed by scientists and engineers of British Rail's Research Division and erected on the Midlands test track, is thought to be the only one of its kind in the world. The facility permits the design and testing of the train mounted equipment which will be required to give efficient and reliable current collection for the very high-speed trains of the future while they are being designed and built.

One of 64 three-car units for operation on the inner suburban services of the Great Northern Suburban Electrification

Specifically designed to provide smooth comfortable travel for passengers on the shorter distance inner suburban commuter services are a new generation of trains designed by the Chief Mechanical & Electrical Engineer of British Railways Board. The train design is based on experience gained after extensive passenger and engineering evaluation trials with prototype units.

A Leyland National bus body fitted with a driving cab module at each end and mounted on a modified rail chassis

Trials of this vehicle both as a passive and as a motored unit, will, it is hoped, yield useful information to make possible the design and construction of passenger rail vehicles of lighter weight with cheaper building and maintenance costs.

FREIGHTLINERS LIMITED

National Freight Corporation
43 Cardington Street, London NW1 2LR

Chairman: P. A. Thompson
Managing Director: C. Bleasdale
Assistant Managing Director: G. V. Burks
Directors: D. D. Kirby   D. H. White
        A. D. Mundy   H. R. Wilkinson
        F. Paterson

OFFICERS AND HEADQUARTERS STAFF

Secretary: I. R. C. Johnson
General Sales Manager: I. J. James
Director of Marketing: J. R. Burnham
Chief Engineer: M. K. Filsell
Personnel Manager: D. Watson
Chief Accountant: G. F. E. Mitchell
Chief Officer (Development): S. G. Howard
Operations Manager (Rail and Terminals): M. B. Marsden
Road Services Manager: A. C. Dust
Regional Operations Manager (South): K. F. Bonwick
Regional Operations Manager (North): R. W. Hall
Communications Manager: J. M. Meara

Freightliners Limited operate a network of road/rail container services. Containers are carried on the trunk haul by high-speed rail, with road vehicles on hand at either end of the journey to provide a complete door-to-door capability. From 4 August 1978 full control of Freightliners passed back to British Rail which, since 1969, owned 49 per cent of the company with the National Freight Corporation owning 51 per cent.

Main principle of the Freightliner operation is that the trains run direct and in fixed formation between specially equipped road/rail transfer terminals. The wagons are designed specifically for containers and are capable of high-speed (75 mph) movement; trains run to a laid-down timetable and space is reservable in advance, as with a passenger service. The Company has a fleet of 8 000 containers for customers to load their products into, and it also carries on its trains containers belonging to other organisations. Shipping companies come into this category; indeed, with the recent spread of maritime containerisation, this has been a rapidly increasing facet of the business and now accounts for something like 40 per cent of the total carryings.

The Freightliner service came into being in 1965 and since then the picture has been one of steady expansion. Currently, Freightliner owns 26 terminals and serves a further 11 belonging to other organisations—chiefly port authorities. Some 190 train services operate each day and last year the company carried almost 720 000 containers with a turnover of almost £40 million. The road fleet numbers 600 vehicles and 1 600 trailers, and staff total 2 350.

In addition to regular services between main centres in this country, services operate daily to the ports of Felixstowe, Greenock, Harwich, Southampton and Tilbury for the short sea routes to Europe and deep sea to all parts of the world. The container port at Holyhead has a number of services connecting inland centres with British Railways container ships for Belfast and Dublin and there are also links with Ireland through other terminals.

Terminal	Name of Manager	Address and Telephone Number
Aberdeen	T. Burke	120 Market Street, Aberdeen AB9 2EZ Telephone: (0224) 54817/8
Barking	S. F. C. Smith	Box Lane, Renwick Rd, Barking, Essex IG11 0SE Telephone: (01) 595 1131
Birmingham (Landor St.)	R. W. Howlett	Landor Street, Birmingham B8 1BT Telephone: (021) 359 1985
Bristol	R. A. Hatton	South Liberty Lane, Bedminster, Bristol 3 Telephone: (0272) 632762
Cardiff	S. Jones	Rover Way, Pengam, Cardiff CF2 2YS Telephone: (0222) 497314
Coatbridge	J. H. McCall	Gartsherrie Rd., Coatbridge, Lanarkshire ML5 2DS Telephone: (0698) 69116
Coventry	A. Dawson	46 Binley Rd, Gosford Green, Coventry, West Midlands CV3 1JQ Telephone: (0203) 21330
Dudley	W. Banks	Castle Hill Road, Dudley, Worcs. DY1 4QG Telephone: (0384) 53754.
Dundee	T. Burke	88 Marketgait, Dundee, Angus Telephone: (0382) 23935
Edinburgh	W. H. Nicol	St. Marks Place, Edinburgh EH15 2QA Telephone: (031) 557 2646
Glasgow	A. McFadyen	100 Cathcart Road, Glasgow G42 7BG Telephone: (041) 332 9876. Extension 2018
Hull	W. A. Reed	Clyde Terrace, Brighton Street, Hessle Road, Hull, Humberside HU3 4UW Telephone: (0482) 561121/4
Leeds	H. N. Hall	Wakefield Road, Stourton, Leeds LS10 1SD Telephone: (0532) 31137
Liverpool (Garston)	F. G. Plumb	Dock Road, Garston, Liverpool L19 2JN Telephone: (051) 427 7941
London (Kings Cross)	C. MacDonald	Goods Way, London NW1 1UR Telephone: (01) 837 4200. Extension 4417
London (Stratford)	A. Chapman	Temple Mills Lane, London E15 2EN Telephone: (01) 534 4500
London (Willesden)	W. G. Lapham	Stephenson Street, Willesden, London NW10 6TY Telephone: (01) 965 8541.
Manchester (Longsight)	R. T. Dunn	New Bank Street, Manchester M12 4HD Telephone: (061) 273 2631
Manchester (Trafford Park)	R. Smith	Westinghouse Road, Trafford Park, Manchester M17 1FA Telephone: (061) 872 3072
Newcastle	A. MacDonald	Follingsby Lane, Wardley, Gateshead, Tyne & Wear NE10 8YA Telephone: (0632) 693741
Nottingham	H. W. Cross	Beacon Road, Beeston, Notts NG9 2FP Telephone: (0602) 48531 Extension 2400
Sheffield	E. Earnshaw	The Ickles, Sheffield Road, Rotherham S60 1DN Telephone: (0709) 63294

Terminal	Name of Manager	Address and Telephone Number
Southampton (Millbrook)	S. E. Scarley	Millbrook Road, Southampton, Hampshire SO1 0ST Telephone: (0703) 30223 Extension 2487
Southampton (Maritime)	S. E. Scarley	Weston Docks Extension Telephone: (0703) 30223 Extension 2251
Stockton	D. M. Carter	Haverton Hill Road, Stockton-on-Tees, Cleveland TS18 2NX Telephone: (0642) 612731
Swansea	M. H. Rees	Crymlyn Burrows, Swansea, West Glamorgan SA1 8SH Telephone: (0792) 41704

OTHER TERMINALS SERVED BY FREIGHTLINER SERVICES

BRB TERMINALS

Harwich (Shipping Division)	Telephone: (02555) 4670
Freightliner Agent:	R. W. Meredith
Holyhead (Shipping Division)	Telephone: (0407) 2852

FELIXSTOWE DOCKS & RAILWAY CO

Felixstowe	Telephone: (03942) 70551
Freightliner Agent:	R. Riddell

IPSWICH PORT AUTHORITY

Ipswich West Bank Terminal	Telephone: (0473) 3165
Freightliner Agent:	D. A. Spiller

PORT OF LONDON AUTHORITY

Tilbury Rail Container Terminal

Freightliner Agent:	N. L. Thompson

CLYDE PORT AUTHORITY

Greenock Container Terminal	Telephone: (0475) 26484

CONTROL OF CONTAINER MOVEMENT

The immediate control and allocation of containers is exercised at the terminals, with overall balancing throughout the system directed from Headquarters.

A reservation system operates on all Freightliner services, and space is booked very simply by contacting the originating terminal for the service it is desired to use. Full 'consist' details of all trains are telexed through from originating to destination terminal as they depart, ensuring that resources will be promptly available at the other end to meet the workload.

Charges on the Freightliner system are generally on a per container basis.

FREIGHTLINER/CONTAINER CODE NUMBERS

Numbering system is alpha-numeric using two digits, one letter and two digits in that order, eg 01G00. The four digits make up the fleet number as such within the overall range 0100. The letter denotes the type of container and is interposed so as to ensure accurate reporting and transcription of container stock and movement data.

During 1978 a full real-time computer control system went into operation covering all Freightliner containers as well as those of other operators which may be in the network at any one time.

UNITED STATES
OF AMERICA

NATIONAL RAILROAD PASSENGER CORPORATION (AMTRAK)

400 North Capitol St, Washington, DC 20001

President and Chief Executive Officer: Alan S Boyd
Executive Vice-President and Chief Operating Officer: Martin Garelick
Assistant Vice-President, Finance and Controller: Melvin H Baker
Vice-President, Finance and Treasurer: Don R Brazier
Vice-President, Corporate Planning: William N Daly
Vice-President, Labour Relations and Personnel: George F Daniels
Vice-President, Public Affairs: Edwin E Edel
Vice-President, General Counsel: Nathaniel H Goodrich
Vice-President, Operations: Robert A Herman
Vice-President, Computer Services: Donald L Larson
Vice-President, Chief Engineer: Robert F Lawson
Vice-President, Marketing: Alfred A Michaud
Vice-President: Albert M Schofield
Vice-President, Government Affairs: M L Clark Tyler
Secretary: Elyse G Wander
Assistant Secretaries: W Scott Armentrout, T Page Sharp

Amtrak was created when the Rail Passenger Service Act was enacted on 30 October 1970. The underlying thrust of Amtrak's first efforts was to gradually revitalise public confidence in rail passenger service through service improvements and thereby attract the travelling public back to the trains. Amtrak viewed its first few years as a building period.

The Corporation began with some specific goals: To increase the consideration with which railroad employees served the public; to offer reliable performance and well maintained equipment, and to issue accurate information to travellers.

Most of all, Amtrak developed positive programmes to entice an increasing share of the travel market to train travel. The principal target: the 87 per cent of intercity travellers who use private cars.

MEMBER RAILROADS

Beginning 1 May 1971, Amtrak assumed the responsibility of managing the operation of 23 000 route-miles of intercity passenger trains between the 21 city-pairs designated by the Secretary of Transportation.

The 13 railroads that signed contracts with Amtrak and immediately began operating Amtrak service were: The Santa Fe; Burlington Northern; Baltimore & Ohio-Chesapeake & Ohio (now Chessie System); Milwaukee Road; Louisville & Nashville and Seaboard Coast Line (now The Family Lines). Also included were: Missouri Pacific; Penn Central (now part of Conrail); Richmond, Fredericksburg & Potomac; Southern Pacific; Union Pacific; Gulf, Mobile & Ohio and Illinois Central (now the Illinois Central Gulf).

Because of route expansions, Amtrak later signed contracts with the Boston & Maine; Central of Vermont; Canadian National; Grand Trunk Western; Norfolk & Western; and Delaware & Hudson.

Three railroads—the Denver & Rio Grande Western, the Rock Island, and the Southern—were offered contracts by the Amtrak Incorporators in 1971, but they chose not to operate under the Amtrak system. Since 1 January 1975, these companies have been free to petition appropriate regulatory bodies to discontinue service, and this has been done in some instances.

SERVICES

By law, Amtrak is permitted to experiment with service outside the Basic System at any time. An amendment in 1973 authorised the Secretary of Transportation to designate at least one experimental route each year to be added to the Amtrak system. After two years of operation, the Secretary would determine if the route is to be operated permanently or discontinued. The Act was further amended in 1975 shifting the responsibility for selection of new services to Amtrak's Board of Directors. Under current law, Amtrak is no longer required to start one new experimental route per year, but may do so if resources permit.

Experimental services instituted include:

North Coast Hiawatha—Chicago-Seattle via Billings, Montana, 1971.

Blue Ridge—Washington, DC-Parkersburg, West Virginia, 1971. Modified to Washington-Cumberland, Maryland, 1973, because of poor patronage. Modified to Washington-Martinsburg, West Virginia, 1976, when the Shenandoah began operating between Washington, Cumberland and Cincinnati.

San Joaquin—San Francisco/Oakland-Fresno-Bakersfield, California, 1974.

Inter-American—St. Louis-Dallas-Laredo, 1974. (Extension of Fort Worth-Laredo International service that began 1973.)

Mountaineer—Norfolk-Roanoke-Cincinnati, 1975. Route discontinued 1977, per direction of the Secretary of Transportation.

Lake Shore Limited—Boston-Buffalo-Cleveland-Chicago with a New York section joined at Albany, 1975.

Shenandoah—Washington, DC-Cumberland, Md.-Cincinnati, 1976.

Pioneer—Salt Lake City-Boise-Portland-Seattle, 1977.

The Secretary of Transportation had designated the Lake Shore Limited and Mountaineer routes, both 1974.

Helping rehabilitate Amtrak's Northeast Corridor is a track-laying machine built by Canron Rail Group
About 400 miles (644 km) of Corridor track will be rehabilitated with the Track Laying System (TLS) throughout 1979-81.

1972, Congress authorised International services to Canada at Vancouver and Montreal, and to Mexico via Nuevo Laredo. Such service was inaugurated as follows:
Pacific International—Seattle-Vancouver, BC, 1972.
Montrealer—Washington, DC-Montreal, PQ via Vermont, 1972.
Inter-American—Fort Worth-Laredo, 1973.
Two trains operate with state assistance and serve Canadian points: the Adirondack, New York-Albany-Montreal, and the Niagara Rainbow, Buffalo-Detroit through Southern Ontario.
The Act provides for states or regional agencies to obtain service not included in the Basic System. To do so the local unit must assume 50 per cent of the solely related losses of operating the service, plus capital expenses for equipment, facilities or track repair. Prior to 1 October 1976, other formulas were in effect at different times, depending upon the language of the Act. Such service in operation are:
Illinois Zephyr—Chicago-Quincy, Illinois, 1971.
Philadelphia-Harrisburg—Additional frequency, 1972.
State House—Additional train, Chicago-Springfield, Illinois, 1973.
Illini—Additional frequency, Chicago-Champaign/Urbana, Illinois, 1973.
Black Hawk—Chicago-Dubuque via Rockford, 1974.
Adirondack—New York City-Montreal via Albany, 1974.
Blue Water Limited—Chicago-Lansing-Port Huron, Michigan, 1974.
Empire Service—Additional frequency, New York-Albany, 1974.
Niagara Rainbow—Detroit-Buffalo with through cars to New York City, 1974.
Michigan Executive—Additional frequency, Detroit-Jackson, Michigan, 1975.
Arrowhead—Minneapolis-Duluth/Superior, 1975.
San Diegan Service—Additional frequency, Los Angeles-San Diego, 1976. Second state-assisted frequency, 1977, bringing route total to five daily trains in each direction.
Amtrak has increased frequency on some of its routes, bringing about increased passenger usage. Added trains on the New York-Washington, Chicago-Detroit and Los Angeles-San Diego routes has brought about significant increases in revenues and passengers.
A gain in passenger numbers was also experienced on a long-distance route with added frequency. In 1976, Amtrak began operating its first daytime train in the Carolinas on the heavily travelled New York-Florida route. This New York-Savannah train, the Palmetto, immediately began carrying large numbers of passengers while patronage continued at high levels on the New York-Florida trains. Amtrak will continue to evaluate frequency increases in an attempt to strengthen route ridership.
The Rail Passenger Service Act, enacted on 30 October 1970, created Amtrak to manage the basic national passenger network and be responsible for the operation of all intercity passenger trains under contracts with the railroads.
The legislation identifies three underlying purposes and objectives of the Corporation: (1) Provide modern, efficient intercity rail passenger service within the basic rail system of the nation; (2) Employ innovative operating and marketing concepts to develop fully the potential of modern rail service in meeting intercity transportation needs; and (3) Strive for operation on a "for profit" basis.
This fundamental philosophy has remained, but the Act has been amended in several respects since. The Amtrak Improvement Act of 1973 continued Amtrak's authority beyond the original two-year experimental stage and locked into law for a minimum of one year all of the routes which Amtrak was operating at the end of 1973. The new Act also stated that quality of service should be a major factor in determining compensation to the railroads for the services they provide.
The Amtrak Improvement Act of 1974 expanded Amtrak's scope of responsibilities. It required the Corporation to directly perform its own maintenance and repairs, and directed Amtrak, the US Railway Association and the Secretary of Transportation to cooperate in a project to improve service in the Northeast Corridor.
The Amtrak Improvement Act of 1978 locked into law until 1 October 1979 all routes currently in the system. The "for profit" clause was modified by the Act, and Amtrak is to be "operated and managed" as a for-profit corporation. Additionally, the Department of Transportation was directed to evaluate the common stock ownership of Amtrak and present recommendations on retaining, retiring or converting common stock held by the railroads. The Act also authorised Amtrak to operate commuter services under agreements with a state, regional or local transportation agency.

FUNDING
The Corporation is financed by a combination of earned revenues from passenger service operations and Federal Government assistance. The one exception is a $197 million "entry fee" paid by the railroads over a three year period as compensation for Amtrak assumption of rail passenger service. The fee was equivalent to one half of the participating railroads' passenger service operating losses for 1969. These funds were used by Amtrak to cover operating expenses.
Government assistance has been provided in terms of cash appropriations to cover operating expenses and a mixture of guaranteed loan authority and direct grants for capital improvements.
Supportsprovided up to Fiscal Years(FY) 1977swas:

		($ millions)	
	Operating Grants	*Guaranteed Loan Authority*	*Direct Capital Grants*
Initial Funding FY 1971	40.0	100.0	—
FY 1972-73	179.1	100.0	—
FY 1974	140.0	300.0	—
FY 1975	278.0	400.0	—
FY 1976	357.0	—	114.2
Transition Quarter	105.0	—	25.0
FY 1977	482.6	—	93.1
	$1 581.7	$900.0	$232.3

Federal funding to Amtrak is a multi-step process. Funds must be authorised by legislation ojiginating in both House and Senate by Commerce Committees. Funds must also be appropriated by legislation from House and Senate Appropriations Committees. After the bills have been signed into law by the President, the money is then released to the Department of Transportation. These funds are apportioned to Amtrak on a quarterly basis for operating and capital purposes.
Amtrak funding should be viewed in the context of government assistance to other forms of transportation. From 1921 to 1976, all levels of government provided $457 000 million to build and maintain the nation's highways and streets. About $302 000 million was covered by receipts of Federal, state and local highway user imposts and toll receipts and $155 000 million from general fund revenues.

BOARD ORGANISATION
The Rail Passenger Service Act, as amended, states that the Board of Directors shall consist of 17 members, as follows:
8 Appointed by the President of the USA
2 Ex-officio members
3 Representing Common Stockholders
4 Representing Preferred Stockholders (vacant)

The President of the USA nominates and the Senate confirms eight members of the Board, of whom not more than five shall be from the same political party. Of these eight, not less than three shall be designated consumer representatives; further, not more than two consumer representatives shall be from the same political party.
The two ex-officio Board members are the Secretary of Transportation and the President of Amtrak.
Three Board members are elected annually by the common stockholders of the Corporation. Shareholders were created by a provision of the Act that permitted railroads to take stock instead of tax write-offs when Amtrak was organised. Four railroads are shareholders— Burlington Northern, Milwaukee Road, Grand Trunk Western, and Trustees of the former Penn Central.
Four Board members to be elected by preferred shareholders. To date, no preferred shares have been issued and these seats remain vacant.

CORPORATE ORGANISATION
A large and complex corporation, Amtrak is organised into a dozen departments, each charged with specific objectives as follows:
Executive (overall direction); Computer Systems (Computer and telecommunication support services); Finance (financial management and reporting); Government Affairs (liaison with government agencies and elected officials); Labour Relations and Personnel (employment, benefits, labour relations, equal employment opportunities, security, training, general administration); Law (representation before courts and regulatory bodies, claims); Marketing (advertising, sales, tour development, market research); National Operations (monitors and evaluates train operations over private railroads, plans train operations, directly controls on-board and station services, and performs some maintenance); Northeast Corridor Operations (operates Amtrak-owned lines in the northeast area only); Operations Support (engineering, safety, procurement, real estate and heavy overhaul of equipment); Planning (planning and evaluation); and Public Affairs (communications with public, media and employees).

THE AMTRAK FLEET
By 1977, more than three out of every four passengers on short-distance trains and about half of all passengers were travelling in new equipment purchased by Amtrak within the last three and a half years.
Amtrak started operations with 286 diesel and 40 electric locomotives, and 1 275 cars, all purchased or leased from the railroads. As passenger numbers increased, Amtrak bought more equipment from the railroads. The last major addition to the fleet of old cars was precipitated by the energy crisis in the winter and spring of 1973-74 when Amtrak found 113 usable cars after an extensive nationwide search. Slightly over $114 million was spent in the first three years to purchase and repair this equipment.
The advanced age of the fleet made the need for new equipment quite obvious. Amtrak developed a capital programme to purchase turbine trains for short-distance routes, Amfleet cars for corridor and medium-distance routes and newly designed bi-level cars for long-distance routes.
Amtrak began operating French Turboliners beginning in the summer of 1973 from Chicago to St Louis, and later to Detroit and Milwaukee. In each instance the new equipment brought an increase in passengers. Amtrak began service with two of the French trains, but ultimately purchased four more. Amtrak also ordered seven Americanised versions of the Turboliners and placed them in service on the New York-Albany-Buffalo line in the autumn of 1976, and on the Adirondack route to Montreal in the spring of 1977, once again sparking increases in patronage.
Beginning in October, 1973, Amtrak placed a series of orders, totalling 492 Amfleet cars, with the Budd Company at a total cost of $206.3 million. The cars have an improved suspension system, public address system, attractive and carpeted interiors and seating that may be increased or decreased depending on the market served. The first Amfleet train operated in test revenue service on 7 August 1975, from Washington DC to Boston. Amfleet equipment now operates on a dozen routes throughout the nation, often with modification for long-distance use.
Amtrak placed an order in April 1975 with the Pullman Standard Company for bi-level cars, named Superliners, for long-distance service in the west. Originally fixed at 235 cars, the number has been increased to 284 and the total cost, including escalation payments, is expected to reach $250 million. The first train fully equipped with these cars was expected to begin operation in January 1979, illustrating the long lead times involved in new equipment purchases.
The Superliners' stairways, double-levels and generous lounge and dining areas will provide a spacious and varied train. Improved air-cushioned suspension systems will give passengers a smoother ride. Standardisation of components will make the cars considerably easier to maintain than Amtrak's existing fleet of aged long-distance cars.
The Corporation will lease two LRC (Light, Rapid, Comfortable) trains being built in Canada. These trains incorporate a new suspension system to provide higher speeds around curves and were to be tested in early 1979 between Vancouver, Seattle and Portland.
Amtrak has spent or committed $658.1 million in capital funds over seven years to buy a variety of new equipment, as follows:
150 diesel 3 000 hp locomotives (SDP40F) from General Motors; $68 million; ordered in 1972 and 1973.
26 electric 6 000 hp locomotives (E60CP) from General Electric; $18.4 million; ordered in 1973.
492 Amfleet cars from Budd Company; $206.3 million; ordered in 1973, 1974 and 1975.
6 five-car Turboliners from ANF-Frangeco; $18 million; 1974.
25 diesel 3 000 hp locomotives (P30CH) from General Electric; $12.2 million; 1974.
7 five-car Turboliners from Rohr Company; $30.3 million; 1974.

Amtrak's newest Turboliner
A blend of US and French design with modern lines and comfortable, all-electric interiors. Seven of the red, white and blue turbos, built by Rohr Industries in California, are operating Amtrak intercity rail services.

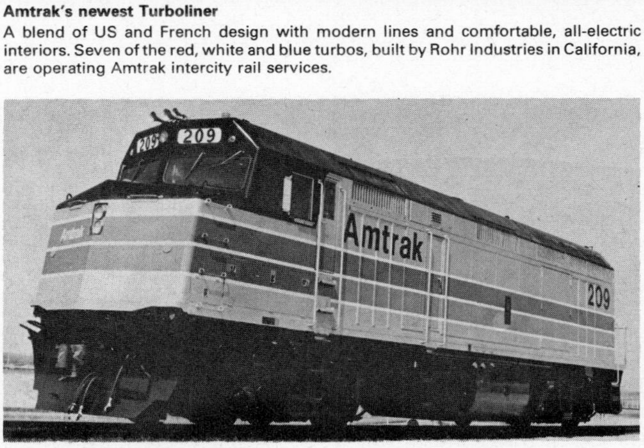

New F40PH four-axle diesel locomotive
A total of 30 of the lightweight 3 000 hp F40PH were ordered from General Motors in 1975 at a cost of $16.3 million; a further 10 were ordered in 1977.

284 bi-level Superliner cars from Pullman Standard Company; $250 million with escalation; ordered in 1975 and 1976.
40 lightweight 3 000 hp diesel locomotives (F40PH) from General Motors; $23.3 million; 1975.
8 lightweight 6 100 hp electric locomotives from General Motors; $21.6 million; 1978. (Amtrak's programme calls for 30 of these locomotives at a cost of $77.9 million.)
Amtrak's Board of Directors approved in September 1978 spending an additional $41.5 million to expand a Metroliner upgrading programme and to buy seven more high-speed electric locomotives to pull Amfleet trains in the Boston-Washington Northeast Corridor. Funding of $19.5 million will add 18 Metroliners to the 16 already being completely rebuilt and upgraded by the General Electric Company at their Erie, Pennsylvania plant.
Funding has been authorised for 15 lightweight locomotives, part of a 30 unit order with a projected cost of $77.9 million. The locomotives, as well as the upgraded Metroliners, provide a 120 mph service on the electrified line when the Corridor upgrading has been completed. By law, in 1981 trains must be able to travel between New York and Washington in two hours 40 minutes and between New York and Boston in three hours 40 minutes.
The locomotives are based on specifications developed after testing the Swedish ASEA Rc4a locomotive in 1977 and are built under licence by the Electro-Motive Division of General Motors at their McCook, Illinois plant. The new locomotives are equipped to operate over the several different power systems that are expected to exist in the Corridor until the Improvement Programme is completed. The locomotive programme is on schedule and the first completed unit is expected to be delivered for testing by 31 December 1979, with all 15 delivered by October 1980.
The 40-year-old GG-1 locomotives that Amtrak uses to haul its Amfleet cars in the Corridor cannot be converted to operate on the newer power frequencies.
In autumn 1977, the Amtrak Board of Directors authorised the beginning of the Metroliner refurbishment programme with $20 million funded for the first 16 cars. The new funding authorisation brings the total to 34 cars at a cost of $39.5 million. Four of the 18 cars funded have had some of the modification work performed previously under a research and development project funded by the Federal Railroad Administration in 1974.
The Metroliner work is performed at General Electric's Erie, Pennsylvania, plant. It includes the complete overhaul of wheel assemblies, traction motors, air-conditioning and heating systems, brakes, couplers, signals and other systems. In addition, the cars are rewired and modifications made to allow compatibility with future Corridor power systems.
The Metroliner interiors are completely refurbished using new carpeting and newly-designed seats with tray tables.
Operating experience since 1969 when the Metroliners began service under the former Penn Central Railroad has revealed some design deficiencies that have contributed to high maintenance costs and poor mechanical reliability. The FRA modifications to four Metroliners solved some of the problems by relocating air intake and brake resistor equipment from underneath the cars to the roofs. As a result, maintenance costs of those four cars were reduced by 40 per cent. The current overhaul programme incorporates those modifications.
The first four refurbished Metroliner cars were expected to be ready for pre-service testing in November, 1978 and should have been in revenue service by the end of that year. The remainder of the programme was to be completed by mid-1979.

MAINTENANCE
Amtrak has assumed many servicing and repair functions formerly performed by the railroads and is now the owner and operator of facilities in Beech Grove (Indianapolis), Boston, Buffalo, Chicago, Dallas, Detroit, Harrisburg, Houston, Jacksonville, Kansas City, Long Island City, Los Angeles, New Haven, New York, Newark, Philadelphia, Rensselaer (Albany), New York, Savannah, St Louis and Wilmington, Delaware.
Amtrak has built one new maintenance base, Brighton Park, in Chicago, for repair and servicing the Midwest Turboliners, and a $14.8 million Turboliner maintenance facility north of the Albany-Rensselaer, NY station which was completed in 1977. Located there is a new 113 000 ft^2 building with two turbo service tracks, a diesel repair track, an all-weather car washer, auxiliary shops and employee facilities.
Improvements are underway at facilities purchased from the railroads. Amtrak is undertaking a $6.8 million programme to begin modernising the 12th Street maintenance yard and 16th Street locomotive shop in Chicago. It is the first phase of a $38 million modernisation programme scheduled for completion by 1981.
On 1 April 1975, Amtrak purchased from Penn Central the rail car overhaul and repair shops at Beech Grove for $3.8 million. It is Amtrak's primary heavy overhaul and car modernisation facility and it, too, is undergoing extensive upgrading in a $29 million programme.

NORTHEAST CORRIDOR
With the acquisition of the Northeast Corridor from the Consolidated Railroad Corp. (Conrail) on 1 April 1976, Amtrak became a full-fledged operating railroad. The property acquired comprised 456 route-miles from Boston to Washington, 62 miles from New Haven to Springfield, Massachusetts, and 103 miles from Philadelphia to Harrisburg, for a total of 621 route-miles.
The properties, along with selected equipment, were conveyed to Amtrak from bankrupt railroads through Conrail under terms of the Regional Rail Reorganisation Act of 1973, as amended by the Railroad Revitalisation and Regulatory Reform Act of 1975.
Operating on Northeast Corridor lines is an average of 960 trains a day, including over 120 Amtrak trains, nearly 660 commuter trains under contract with transportation authorities, and more than 170 Conrail freight trains.
Amtrak has negotiated labour agreements in the region, and by 31 December 1976, an estimated 7 600 people were employed by Amtrak in the Northeast Corridor.
In addition to trackage, Amtrak purchased 107 railroad stations and numerous maintenance shops and yards at key points along the route. The purchase price for Northeast Corridor facilities was about $86 million, the net liquidation value certified by the United States Railway Association. The purchase agreement between Amtrak and Conrail calls for payment over an eight-year period, with an option for accelerated payment.
The Boston-Washington route will undergo improvements in a programme enacted into law on 5 February 1976. The $1 600 000 000 programme calls for upgrading of the Corridor within five years. An additional $150 million in federal money, to be matched by state funds, has been authorised for improvements to non-operational aspects of stations and installation of right-of-way fences.
Track improvements, curve realignments, and bridge and tunnel work account for more than half the total programme cost. New welded rail will be laid; crossties replaced; roadbeds reworked; curves modified; tunnels improved; and bridges reinforced or replaced as needed. New electrification will be installed where none exists from Boston to New Haven, and the existing electrical system between New York and Washington will be modernised.
When completed, electric-powered trains will run at speeds up to 120 mph, and will move travellers between New York and Washington in 2 hours 40 minutes, including intermediate stops, and between Boston and New York in 3 hours 40 minutes also with stops. The programme is funded and administered by the US Department of Transportation, Federal Railroad Administration, in co-operation with Amtrak.
The laws that authorised the Northeast Corridor purchase also permitted Amtrak to buy properties elsewhere. Included are 83 miles of line between Kalamazoo, Michigan, and Michigan City, Indiana; stations at selected points such as Battle Creek, Michigan, Syracuse, NY, Lima, Ohio and Johnstown, Pennsylvania; several maintenance facilities, and 50 per cent stock ownership in both Chicago Union Station and Washington Terminal Company. The purchase price for off-corridor properties was nearly $3.9 million.

Electric type E60CP locomotive on the Northeast Corridor
A total of 11 electric 6000 hp locomotives were purchased from General Electric in 1973 at a cost of $7.3 million.

TRACK IMPROVEMENTS
Outside of the Northeast Corridor, Amtrak routes depend on track improvement on privately owned railroads. Amtrak has upgraded track in a few instances through a contract arrangement that protects the public's interest in the improved property. In several instances, Amtrak has purchased land and built its own new track.
Amtrak plans to construct 12.6 miles of track between Post Road and Rensselaer to eliminate a complicated backup move on the Boston-Albany section of the Lake Shore Limited, allowing a 32-minute faster schedule. This stretch was abandoned in 1972 by the Penn Central and the track removed. The Congress earmarked $4.1 million in Amtrak capital funds for the project.
In 1978 Amtrak completed construction of a $1 million track project in Richmond, Virginia. The connection and improved signalling allowed the Colonial, operating between Boston and Newport News, to bypass a congested freight yard, save schedule time, and reduce operating expenses by over $100 000 a year.
A time-consuming back-up operation in Fort Worth for the Inter-American was eliminated in 1976 after tracks were improved in a $350 000 project. Another round-about routing for this train was eliminated the same year upon completion of a $1.8 million track upgrading project between Temple and Taylor, Texas. In May 1975, before Amtrak purchased the Northeast Corridor, it began a $15 million programme to improve track conditions between New York and Boston. The project was completed on time and within the budget.
A time-consuming back-up operation in Fort Worth for the Inter-American was eliminated in 1976 after certain tracks were improved in a $350 000 project. This train also benefited that year from a $1.8 million track improvement project between Temple and Taylor, Texas, that eliminated a round-about routing.
In a joint programme with Michigan, the Chicago-Detroit line has been improved in a $5.9 million project. In New York, Amtrak financed equipment purchases while a state bond issue is funding improvements on the New York-Buffalo route. A state-sponsored track programme will also permit Amtrak to extend service to Niagara Falls for the first time.
Amtrak has also funded track improvements in terminal areas or when required in conjuction with new services. Included is work in St Paul, Miami, Sacramento, Chicago Union Station, Little Rock, Kenova, Kentucky, Cincinnati, and between Springfield, Massachusetts, and White River Jct, Vermont, after inauguration of the Montrealer.

STATIONS AND TERMINALS
Since Amtrak's inception, 17 new stations have been constructed where previous stations were unavailable, unacceptable for passenger use or presented serious operational problems. More than 300 stations have received some degree of repair or improvement.
Work has been completed and new stations are in use in Cincinnati (1973); Jacksonville (1974); Port Huron, Michigan, Catlettsburg, Kentucky, Richmond, Virginia, Roanoke, Virginia, and Bluefield, West Virginia (all 1975); Worcester, Massachusetts, Cumberland, Maryland (1976); Cleveland, Duluth, and Parkersburg, West Virginia (1977); Rochester, Miami, St Paul, Canton, Ohio, and Richmond, California (1978). Amtrak operates out of a new station in Louisville as a result of a 1976 contract with the Auto-Train Corporation. New stations are under construction in Dearborn, Michigan, and at the Baltimore-Washington International Airport in Maryland. Planning is underway for new terminals in St Louis, Schenectady, Cheektowaga, New York and in New Carrollton, Maryland, which will be a joint Amtrak-subway station in the Washington metropolitan area. Amtrak's station programme generally falls into the following categories:
General Improvements— Major rehabilitation has been completed in Nashville, Laredo, New York, Houston, Chicago and Springfield, Mass., and is underway in Oakland, Cal., Detroit and North Philadelphia. In many instances, station efforts have coincided with inauguration of service over a new route. For example, Amtrak has spent nearly $500 000 to upgrade 13 stations in Utah, Idaho and Oregon in preparation for the Salt Lake City-Boise-Seattle train, the Pioneer.
Northeast Corridor Improvement Plan— Under this project, $115 million in federal funds is available to improve the operationally essential parts of the primary intercity passenger stations between Boston and Washington. This includes some structural work, new or lengthened high-level platforms, and utilities necessary for passenger safety, train operations and train information systems. The major stations are: Boston, Providence, New Haven, Stamford, New York, Newark, Philadelphia, Wilmington, Baltimore and Washington DC. Not included in that sum is $150 million authorised for 50/50 state/federal programmes to improve certain portions of stations such as waiting rooms and ticket offices.
State & Local Government Participation— Amtrak co-operates with various levels of government to share station modernisation costs. In joint programmes with Michigan, a new station was built in Port Huron and seven other stations were upgraded. Amtrak and New York have renovated nine stations and the new Rochester station is being built in conjunction with the city and state. In Texas, Dallas purchased and modernised the station for Amtrak use; Lima, Ohio, helped to refurbish and landscape its station; and Bridgeport, Connecticut, served by many commuter and Amtrak trains, built an entirely new station. Duluth, Minnesota, constructed a new station and leases it to Amtrak, and a joint project is also underway in Minneapolis/St. Paul.
Amtrak has also participated in the construction or remodeling of facilities to be used jointly with transit authorities. Included are the Back Bay Station in Boston, a new station in New Carrollton, Maryland, and another in Richmond, California.
In a programme announced on 29 November 1976, Amtrak committed $1 million to be used as matching funds in a one-year project aimed at encouraging a broad upgrading of stations in smaller communites where current passenger numbers do not permit early improvements by Amtrak acting on its own.

Railroad Contracts— New passenger stations were built in Catlettsburg, Kentucky, and Cumberland, Maryland, as a result of Amtrak's contract with the operating railroads that requires station construction when the old station property is sold, converted to other uses or otherwise unavailable for Amtrak use.

Private Developers— Because of urban renewal concerns and opportunities, private developers saved and completely renewed the historic station in New London, Connecticut, and another developer is building a new station as part of a convention centre in Columbus, Ohio. Similar plans have been formulated to varying degrees in Indianapolis, Kansas City and San Diego.

RESERVATIONS

Amtrak's new nationwide, computerised reservation system has brought order to the previously fragmented railroad information and ticketing procedures. Now, reservation and information clerks at five major locations—Bensalem, Pennsylvania, New York City, Chicago, Los Angeles and Jacksonville— give schedule and fare information and take reservations for Amtrak and Southern Railway trains.

Incoming call volume during 1976 averaged 50 000 calls daily, significantly higher than the average of 32 000 calls per day handled during the peak summer months of 1973. This computerised reservations system is also used by station agents to automatically print tickets. The automatic ticket printing devices are located in busy stations and 65 per cent of all Amtrak ticketing is now done in such a manner. A new reservations service was installed in 1976 that permits deaf persons who have access to teletypewriters to communicate with specially trained Amtrak agents using similar machines. "Talking" is done through the keyboard.

AMTRAK PROFILE

General	1974	1975	1976	1977
System Route Miles (thousands)	24	26	26	27
Stations Served	473	484	512	545
Train Miles Operated (millions)	29	30	31	32
No. of Employees (thousands)	8.3	8.7	18.4	20.5
Passengers				
Passengers (millions)	18.8	17.4	18.6	19.2

	1974	1975	1976	1977
Passenger Miles (millions)	4 258	3 939	4 221	4 333
Total Revenue (millions)	$256.9	$252.7	$287.2	$311.3
On-Time Performance (per cent)				
Systemwide	75	77	73	63
Short-Distance	80	80	75	68
Long-Distance	63	72	67	49
Revenue Cars				
Operating Fleet (thousands)	1 881	1 882	1 932	2 048
Out of Service (daily avg.)				
(per cent)	18.0	17.5	15.4	17.0
Average Age (years)	24.3	24.7	20.3	20.4
Number Overhauled	458	490	496	369
New Deliveries	0	115	241	33
Locomotive Units				
Operating Fleet (Dec 31)	442	362	353	330
Out of Service (daily avg.)				
(per cent)	23.5	13.0	17.1	19.5
Average Age (years)	13.6	14.4	10.7	9.9
Number Rebuilt	24	11	38	26
New Deliveries	110	30	51	0
Turbo-Powered Trains/Units				
Operating Fleet (Dec 31)	5	9	13	
Out of Service (daily avg.)				
(per cent)	9.0	10.0	14.0	
Average Age (years)	5.8	3.7	1.3	
New Deliveries	0	4	7	
Metroliners				
Operating Fleet (Dec 31)	61	61	61	
Out of Service (daily avg.)				
(per cent)	28.7	27.3	25.6	
Average Age (years)	8	9	10	

THE ALASKA RAILROAD

US Department of Transportation,
Federal Railroad Administration,
PO Box No 7-2111 Anchorage, Alaska 99510

Acting General Manager: Steven R. Ditmeyer
Assistant General Manager: Arnold T. Polanchek
Comptroller: E. E. Callihan
Supply Officer: L. D. Parmenter
Chief Counsel: David R. Roderick

LINES AND TERRITORIES

The Alaska Railroad runs from the ports of Seward on the Gulf of Alaska, and Whittier, on Prince William Sound, northward through Anchorage and McKinley National Park to Fairbanks, and eastward to Eielson, with branches serving Palmer and Suntrana. Total route length with branches, 522 miles *(840 km)*.

DEVELOPMENTS

During the mid-1970s, construction of the Trans-Alaska Pipeline brought heavy traffic to The Alaska Railroad. Profits derived from that period of service have been invested in upgrading equipment, track and roadbed; as a result, The Alaska Railroad is well prepared to carry new loads anticipated from construction of the proposed natural gas pipeline and from other anticipated energy development.

Some specific improvements include 15 new 3 000 hp locomotives that enhance the railroad's capabilities to pull loads up some of the three per cent grades along its route. To facilitate transportation of coal cars in these days of energy crises, the Railroad has reconstructed its Healy yard; work includes subgrade build-up, construction of 12 700 ft of new tracks and a new wye track, installation of pollution control equipment and relocation of turnouts and fuelling facilities. This reconstruction prepares the Railroad for new, heavier haulage of coal as Oriental markets materialise and industry converts to coal as fuel.

On the south end of the line, the Railroad has installed four permanent concrete block tunnel portals between the Port of Whittier and Portage. Replacing the original wood construction, these portals, with solar-powered doors, will eliminate severe icing conditions, greatly reduce high maintenance costs in the tunnels, and eliminate winter restrictions on high loads formerly required by overhead tunnel icing.

Congressional appropriations of $5 million are being used to reconstruct the docks at Seward and Whittier. At Seward the piling is being repaired and a protective cathodic system installed. At Whittier the Railroad is completely reconstructing the understructure of the dock, installing a protective cathodic system and modifying the configuration of the dock to accept 8-track barges at Slip 1.

Reduced activity following the high pitch of transporation development during pipeline construction has intensified competition in Alaska. In response, the Railroad has embarked upon a progressive market thrust to develop additional rail traffic. Customer intermodal options have been expanded: shippers can now take advantage of ramp-to-ramp service available to all trucking companies, rail-barge trailer-container service and full service wherein goods hauled by the Railroad are delivered by Railroad trucks from the rail to areas not serviced by the Railroad.

Alaska's wealth of energy resources is fast becoming competitive on the world market as politics and realities affect supply and demand. First construction permits for the natural gas pipeline are expected in 1980; in terms of potential pipe, drilling equipment, and supplies, the Railroad will haul a large proportion of this traffic over the next few years. Interest in another rich Alaska resource (coal) has also accelerated, both from the Orient and from within Alaska.

The Alaska Railroad will no doubt be affected by several transportation studies being conducted by the State of Alaska to assess the transportation needs of the state and develop a transportation plan. Among potential projects are various extensions of the Railroad, including a link extending to the border of Alaska, through the Yukon Territory to join with the British Columbia Railway at Watson Lake. Such a link would fundamentally change The Alaska Railroad from being the end of a transportation line to being a flow-through line joining Oriental markets with the mid-west USA and points throughout Canada and Alaska.

PIGGYBACK AND CONTAINER OPERATIONS

There are 288 containers for door-to-door service. Terminal handling equipment used by the Alaska Railroad includes gantry cranes at Seward for train to ship movement, and an 'American' bridge-type gantry crane at Anchorage and crawler-cranes at Moose Pass and Fairbanks for train to road transport movements.

LOCOMOTIVES AND CARS

In service with the Alaska Railroad are 63 diesel electric locomotives (41 road haul and 22 switcher units); 1 765 freight train cars, 38 of them passenger coaches.

ATCHISON, TOPEKA AND SANTA FE RAILWAY COMPANY

80 East Jackson Boulevard, Chicago, Illinois 60604

Chairman, President and Chief Executive Officer: John S. Reed

Executive Department:
Vice-President, Chicago: John C. Davis
Vice-President, Executive Representative, (San Francisco): R. W. Walker
Vice-President, Washington: F. N. Grossman

Operating Department:
Vice-President: D. G. Regg
Chief Mechanical Officer: M. B. Adams
Assistant Chief Mechanical Officer Administrations: K. A. Wolfe
Assistant General Manager, Mechanical Department, Topeka, Kansas: H. L. Hawkins
Assistant General Manager, Mechanical Department, Amarillo: V. G. Nail
Assistant General Manager, Mechanical Department, Los Angeles: R. T. Dennisen
Assistant Chief Engineer—Signals: B. J. Hutton
Assistant Chief Engineer—Communications: C. A. Crouch
Superintendent of Safety, System: R. D. Shaver
Director, Technical Research and Development, Topeka: C. R. Kaelin
General Manager, Topeka, Eastern Lines: H. J. Briscoe
General Manager, Amarillo, Western Lines: J. R. Fitzgerald
General Manager, Los Angeles, Coast Lines: H. D. Fish
Chief Engineer, System: W. S. Autrey
Assistant Chief Engineer: H. G. Webb
Assistant General Manager, Engineering, Topeka: C. L. Holman
Assistant General Manager, Engineering, Amarillo: E. C. Honath
Assistant General Manager, Engineering, Los Angeles: W. W. Toliver

Finance Department:
Vice-President: R. W. Harper

Traffic Department:
Vice-President: F. J. Wright
Assistant Vice-President, Sales: A. A. Moser
Assistant Vice-President, Pricing: J. A. G. Rygiel

Freight:
Assistant Vice-President—Sales: A. A. Moser
Assistant Vice-President—Pricing: J. A. Grygiel

LINES AND TERRITORIES

Santa Fe operates 12 569 route-miles *(20 228 route-km)* extending from Chicago to the Gulf of Mexico and the Pacific Coast. Authority was granted 31 December 1972 to abandon 369 miles *(594 km)* of uneconomic branch lines and applications have been made to abandon additional lines totalling about 446 miles *(718 km)*.

Santa Fe railway loaded autoveyors leaving the General Motors plant at Oklahoma City

FINANCIAL

Santa Fe's rail operations revenues increased $182 million during 1978. Included in this was $91 million due to freight rail increases. Expenses for rail operations was $140 million of which $88 million was due to wage and payroll tax rate increases.

FREIGHT TRAFFIC

During 1978 freight revenues of $1 490 million accounted for approximately 97 per cent of total railway revenues and were up 13 per cent on the previous year. Of the $173 million increase in freight revenues, $91 million, or 53 per cent, was attributed to freight rate increase. The remainder in revenue tonne miles.

Contribution to gross freight revenues (per cent)

Commodity	1978	1977	1976
Merchandise	19.5	17.8	15.0
Chemicals	13.9	14.3	15.0
Food products	11.9	11.8	12.9
Vehicles and parts	9.3	9.8	8.3
Wheat	6.7	6.5	7.0

	1978	1977	1976
Farm products (other than wheat)	5.4	7.2	7.9
Petroleum products	5.0	5.6	5.4
Paper products	4.0	4.0	4.2
Building material	3.8	3.7	3.5
Metal products	3.5	3.5	3.0
Coal	3.3	1.7	1.6
Forest products	3.2	3.3	3.2
Non-metallic minerals	3.1	2.9	3.2
All other	7.4	7.9	9.8

IMPROVEMENT PROGRAMME

In 1979 $309 million was spent on capital improvements. This included 141 new diesel locomotive units; 1 190 new freight cars, 207 bi-level and tri-level racks for flat cars, 98 rebuilt locomotives, 1 229 rebuilt and converted freight cars, heavy repairs to an additional 400 cars and 456 miles (734 km) of new and reconditioned welded rail. Total rewelded rail is 6 480 miles (10 429 km).

BOSTON AND MAINE CORPORATION

Iron Horse Park, North Billerica, Massachusetts 01862

Trustees: R. W. Meserve, B. H. Lacy
President and Chief Executive Officer: A. G. Dustin
Assistant to President: W. J. Rennicke
Vice-President and Gen. Counsellor: J. J. Nee
Vice-President and Gen. Manager, Transportation: S. B. Culliford
Vice-President, Personnel, Labour Relations: B. E. Rice
Director, Information Services: M. M. Sutin
Claims Agent: J. E. O'Keefe
Treasurer: W. N. Reid

Accounting:
Vice-President and Comptroller: P. W. Carr
Assistant Comptrollers: T. J. Reilly
E. B. Teague
Chief Engineer, Maintenance of Way and Structures: V. R. Terrill
Vice-President, Engineering: D. J. Hughes
Chief Design Engineer: L. B. Boyd

Chief Engineer-Communications and Signals: T. Trovato
Manager-Engineering Systems: V. V. Mudholkar

LINES AND TERRITORIES

The principal lines of the Boston & Maine run north and west from Boston through the states of Maine, New Hampshire, Vermont, Massachusetts, and in eastern New York State where it makes connections at Albany and Schenectady with other lines. Essentially a freight operating railway, the company is under contract with the Massachusetts Bay Transportation Authority to continue passenger service within a 20 mile (32 km) radius of Boston, with some reimbursement of excess expenses by the Authority.
Total length of the B&M network is 970 miles (1 561 km).

FINANCIAL

The 1978 revenue figures were $86.2 million. Expenses during the year stood at $93.5 million.

LOCOMOTIVES AND CARS

B&M's rolling stock and motive power fleet stands at 186 diesel-electric locomotives (119 load haul units and 67 switchers); 3 464 freight train cars.

BURLINGTON NORTHERN

176, East Fifth Street, St Paul, Minnesota 55101

OFFICERS

Chairman of the Board: Louis W. Menk
President and Chief Executive Officer: Norman M. Lorentzsen
President, Transportation Division: Thomas J. Lamphier
President, Resources Division: C. Robert Binger
Executive Vice-President, Finance and Administration: Frank H. Coyne
Vice-President, Law: Frank S. Farrell
Vice-President and Secretary: John C. Ashton
Regional Vice-President, Twin Cities: Robert H. Shober
Regional Vice-President, Seattle: Richard A. Beulke
Vice-President and Regional Counsel, Seattle: Roger J. Crosby
Regional Vice-President, Billings: John O. Davies
Vice-President, Labour Relations: Alvin E. Egbers
Vice-President, Portland: Thomas C. DeButts
Vice-President, Sales & Service: John D. Rezner
Vice-President, Purchasing and Material: Guy M. deLambert
Vice-President—Eastern Counsel Washington, DC: Lloyd L. Duxbury, Jr.
Vice-President and Controller: Robert F. Garland
Senior Vice-President Marketing: Ivan C. Ethington

Senior Vice-President, Operations: John H. Hertog
Vice-President, Industrial Development and Property Management: James C. Kenady
Regional Vice-President, Chicago: Eugene R. Craven
Regional Vice-President, Denver: Wayne L. Arntzen

LINES AND TERRITORIES

Burlington Northern is the largest railroad system in the USA in terms of total miles of road operated and the second largest in terms of 1978 rail transportation revenues. The territory it serves covers 19 states and two Canadian provinces and reaches from the Great Lakes and the Ohio river to California and the seaports of the Pacific Northwest. In addition, it owns the Colorado and Southern Railway Co, and the Fort Worth and Denver Railway Co, which extends its territory via Denver to the Gulf of Mexico at Houston and Galveston, Texas.
As of 31 December 1978, the rail network consisted of 26 398 miles (42 628 km) of track, which included 14 352 miles (23 156 km) of main lines, 10 197 miles (16 495 km) of branch lines and 1 849 miles (2 976 km) of secondary main and branch lines. Operations and services on the system are directly supervised from five regional headquarters: Chicago, Minneapolis, Denver, Billings and Seattle.
The Railroad was formed on 2 March 1970 by a merger of the Chicago, Burlington & Quincy Railroad, Great Northern Railway, Northern Pacific Railway and the Pacific Coast Railroad.

BN 100-car unit coal train being loaded in motion at Peabody Company's Big Sky mine in Montana for Midwest destination
(Burlington Northern photo courtesy Pullman-Standard)

RESULTS OF OPERATIONS

	(In thousands of dollars)		
	1978	1977	1976
Operating revenues and sales			
Railroad	2 110 293	1 801 702	1 642 207
Trucking	46 089	30 524	24 668
Air freight forwarder	154 745	103 410	72 214
Forest products	135 851	103 814	85 471
Oil and gas	35 488	26 925	30 445
Coal and minerals	6 287	7 148	7 358
Land and real estate	34 845	30 987	24 992
Other operations	8 541	4 932	8 777
Total	2 532 139	2 109 442	1 896 132
Operating expenses and cost of sales			
Railroad	2 026 818	1 741 471	1 565 759
Trucking	43 656	28 298	23 384
Air freight forwarder	146 079	98 860	68 779
Forest products	88 513	69 937	57 824
Oil and gas	18 454	15 038	16 215
Coal and minerals	1 352	1 367	1 568
Land and real estate	7 434	5 402	4 826
Other operations	7 892	4 276	8 226
Total	2 340 198	1 964 649	1 746 581
Operating income (loss)			
Railroad	83 475	60 231	76 448
Trucking	2 433	2 226	1 284
Air freight forwarder	8 666	4 550	3 435
Forest products	47 338	33 877	27 647
Oil and gas	17 034	11 887	14 230
Coal and minerals	4 935	5 781	5 790
Land and real estate	27 411	25 585	20 166
Other operations	649	656	551
Total	191 941	144 793	149 551

FREIGHT TRAFFIC

Rail revenues rose for the eigth consecutive year, with a total of 2 100 million, 17 per cent above the $1 800 million reported in 1977. Rail operating expenses totalled $2 000 million, versus $1 700 million in 1977. The result was operating income of $83.5 million, 39 per cent above the previous year. Both operating income and rail pre-tax income of $9.1 million were unsatisfactory, largely due to the costs of BN's rebuilding programme.

Significant revenue increases were achieved in coal, grain, lumber and metallic ore traffic in 1977.

Coal has been BN's largest revenue producer since 1976 and in 1978 brought in $499.2 million, or 24 per cent of BN's gross rail freight revenues. This was 34 per cent higher than the $372.9 million reported a year earlier. Coal traffic originating on the system in 1978 totalled 63.1 million tonnes, 25 per cent greater than the 50.6 million in 1977. Coal accounted for 52 700 million tonne miles, or nearly half the system total, increasing 24 per cent above 1977. Coal carloadings increased 17 per cent to 655 000 or 30 per cent of the company's rail traffic. Tonnage carried by unit trains increased from 47.2 million tonnes in 1977 to 57.2 million tonnes in 1978, or 21 per cent. Of 1978's tonnage, 87 per cent travelled in unit trains. At the end of 1978 BN was operating 118 sets of unit train equipment, including 73 with shipper-owned cars. Of the 14 329 cars in unit coal train service, 9 225 or 64 per cent are shipper-owned.

Some of the growth was produced by nine unit coal train movements that were inaugurated in 1978 between mines in the Powder River Basin and utilities in Arkansas, Iowa, Missouri, Nebraska, Texas and Wisconsin. Eight additional movements scheduled to begin in 1979 to destinations in Iowa, Kansas, Missouri, Oklahoma, Texas, Wisconsin and Wyoming.

The rapid growth of coal traffic, in some instances, has outpaced construction of new and longer segments of double track and servicing facilities. Consequently, some unit coal train movements have been experiencing delays dueto traffic congestion and interference from actual construction and maintenance activities. These delays, which are expected to continue until new track and facilities are completed in 1980, are also resulting in increased expenses, primarily for equipment, wages and fuel.

Three new coal mines were opened on BN lines last year, two in Wyoming and one in Montana. Another new mine is scheduled to open in Campbell County, Wyoming, bringing the number of BN-served mines in the West to 15. Included is the AMAX Belle Ayr mine, near Gillette, Wyoming which is the largest in the USA and in 1978 produced 18.1 million tonnes of coal.

In 1978 the company continued its programme to raise depressed coal rates to compensatory levels.

LOCOMOTIVES AND CARS

In 1978 BN equipment expense was $478.7 million, 14 per cent above the $418.5 million reported in 1977. A significant part of this increase can be attributed to inflated costs for wages and material. There was also an improved effort to make more cars available for grain, lumber and other traffic. BN authorised the addition of more than 1 200 employees during 1978 for locomotive and car maintenance work.

In 1978 BN made a significant reduction in the number of freight cars out of service awaiting repair. By the year end, the bad order ratio declined to 5.4 per cent of BNs 101 223-car fleet from 10.1 per cent in 1977. For covered hoppers and unit coal cars, the year-end bad order ratios were 2.7 per cent and 4.1 per cent, respectively.

Another factor contributing to equipment expense was compliance with a Federal Railroad Administration (FRA) order that all freight cars had to be thoroughly inspected to be permitted to continue in service. Although the FRA announced, in December, a one-year extension for this, 97 per cent of the BN fleet had been completed by the end of the year, which entailed removing from service 21 589 freight cars of BN ownership.

In December 1977 the last of six older wheel shops was closed and during 1978, all wheels for BN, the Colorado & Southern and the Fort Worth & Denver, were supplied from the company's new facility at Havelock, Nebraska, and at a much lower unit cost. In 1978 this facility produced 72 598 wheel sets.

Low-sulphur western coal silo, near Gillette, Wyoming, fills a 110-car BN unit coal train as it inches through the towering structure
It takes approx 4 hours to load the train, which never stops during loading. BN expected to originate 78 million tonnes of coal in 1979 and about 115 to 140 million tonnes by 1983.

OTHER DEVELOPMENTS

Burlington Northern invested a record $313.4 million in capital improvements and additions to its rail plant and fleet in 1977. This brought the total investment for capital improvements for road and equipment since the merger to $1 721.7 million. These capital expenditures are in addition to heavy maintenance expenses incurred for construction and roadway improvement programmes. Likewise equipment maintenance programmes emphasised both regular and preventive maintenance.

In 1977 these maintenance expenditures amounted to $679.3 million, raising the total expended since the merger to more than $360 million.

Of the approximately 546 miles of new rail installed during 1977, 21 were new construction in the Powder River Basin of Wyoming, where Burlington Northern is building a 116-mile line between Gillette and Orin Junction to serve new coal mines. Construction costs have been exceeding $1 million a mile and 47 miles of track were in operation at the end of 1977.

Burlington Northern piggyback/container lifting equipment comprises:—

Location	Equipment	Used for
Chicago, Illinois	2 Side-porters	Containers and trailers
	2 Straddle-port cranes	Piggyback trailers and containers
	1 Overhead crane	Containers and trailers
Kansas City, Missouri	1 Piggypacker	Piggyback trailers and containers
Seattle, Washington	2 Piggypackers	Piggyback trailers and containers
Denver, Colorado	1 Piggypacker	Piggyback trailers and containers
Lincoln, Nebraska	1 Piggpacker	Piggyback trailers and containers
Minneapolis, Minnesota	1 Piggypacker	Piggyback trailers and containers
Portland, Oregon	1 Piggypacker	Piggyback trailers and containers
Spokane, Washington	1 Piggypacker	Piggyback trailers and containers

Through its wholly-owned subsidiary, BN Transport Inc and other various truck line common carriers, Burlington Northern provides direct TOFC/COFC service from the Great Lakes to the Pacific Northwest, from the Canadian Border to the Gulf Coast. TOFC/COFC service is provided through the use of the following owned or leased equipment: 3 761 semi-trailers and 293 railroad flats designed for TOFC/COFC service. Ramp facilities exist in 111 towns of which the following are the largest:

Colorado: Boulder; Brush; Colorado Springs; Denver; Fort Collins; Golden; Greeley; Longmont; Loveland; Pueblo; Sterling; Windsor.
Idaho:
Illinois: Aurora; Chicago; Galesburg; Moline; Mt Morris; Peoria; Quincy; Rochelle; Rock Falls; Rockford; Streator.
Iowa: Burlington; Creston; Des Moines; Dubuque; Ft Madison; Keokuk; Ottumwa; Sioux City.
Kentucky: Paducah.
Minnesota: Brainerd; Cloquet; Crookston; Duluth; Fergus Falls; Hutchinson; Minneapolis; St Cloud; St Paul; Thief River Falls; Willmar; Winona.
Missouri: Carrollton; Hannibal; Kansas City; St Louis.
Montana: Billings; Bozeman; Butte; Glendive; Great Falls; Havre; Helena; Missoula; Shelby; Whitefish.
Nebraska: Alliance; Beatrice; Columbus; Fremont; Grand Island; Hastings; Lincoln; McCook; Omaha; Scottsbluff; Seward.
North Dakota: Devils Lake; Dickinson; Fargo; Grand Forks; Jamestown; Lisbon; Mandan; Minot; Cheyenne; Valley City; Williston.
Oregon: Albany; Eugene; Klamath Falls; Portland; Salem.
South Dakota: Sioux Falls.
Texas: Abilene; Amarillo; Corsicana; Dallas; Fort Worth; Galveston; Houston; Lubbock; Plainview; Teague; Wichita Falls.
Washington: Aberdeen; Bellingham; Everett; Omak; Oroville; Pasco; Seattle; Spokane; Tacoma; Wenatchee; Yakima.
Wisconsin: LaCrosse; Prairie du Chien; Superior.
Wyoming: Casper; Cheyenne; Gillette; Newcastle; Wheatland.
British Columbia: Vancouver.
Manitoba: Winnipeg.

CHESSIE SYSTEM

(Affiliated Chesapeake and Ohio and Baltimore and Ohio Railways and Western Maryland Railroads)
Terminal Tower, Cleveland, Ohio 44101

Chairman of the Board and President: Hays T. Watkins
Executive Vice-President, Operations: John T. Collinson
Executive Vice-President, Commercial: John T. Ford
Senior Vice-President: Norman G. Halpern
Senior Vice-President, Finance: Robert L. Hintz
Senior Vice-President, Merchandise: James B. McCahey Jr
Vice-President, Law and General Counsel: Roland W. Donnem
Vice-President, Taxes: John P. Ganley
Vice-President, Coal Traffic: Jerry E. Gobrecht
Vice-President, Merchandise Pricing: Charles J. Henry Jr

Senior Vice-President, Casualty Prevention: William F. Howes Jr
Vice-President, Marketing Services: Jerome D. Krassenstein
Vice-President, Administration: Robert C. McGowan
Vice-President, Transportation: Richard G. Rayburn
Vice-President, Government Relations: John W. Snow

LINES AND TERRITORIES

In 1972 the affiliated Chesapeake and Ohio Railway and the Baltimore and Ohio Railroad renamed the 11 000-mile *(17 700-km)* transportation network "Chessie System". The two carriers continue to publish separate annual financial and statistical reports. While the C&O company controls the B&O company through stock ownership, the two railroads have unified management in all major areas.

C & O total mileage owned: 3 978 miles (6 402 km); total mileage leased: 224 miles (361 km); used jointly: 682 miles (1 098 km) total 4 884 miles (7 860 km). Territories: Canada, 331 miles (533 km); District of Columbia, 3 miles (4.8 km); Illinois, 44 miles (71 km);

Indiana, 309 miles (497 km); Kentucky, 694 miles (1 117 km); Michigan, 1 391 miles (2 238 km); New York, 34 miles (55 km); Ohio 413 miles (665 km); Virginia, 651 miles (1 048 km); West Virginia, 1 013 miles (1 630 km).

B & O total mileage owned: 3 559 miles (5 728 km); total mileage leased: 1 597 miles (2 570 km); used jointly: 255 miles (410 km); total 5 411 miles (8 708 km), territories: New York, 170 miles (274 km); Delaware, 34 miles (55 km); Pennsylvania, 877 miles (1 411 km); Maryland, 317 miles (510 km); District of Columbia, 21 miles (32 km); Virginia, 34 miles (54 km); West Virginia, 1 223 miles (1 968 km); Ohio, 1 669 miles (2 686 km); Indiana, 533 miles (858 km); Illinois, 519 miles (835 km); Kentucky, 4 miles (6 km); Missouri, 4 miles (6 km).

The Chessie System also owns majority stock in the Western Maryland Railway, and Chicago South Shore and South Bend Railroad.

FINANCE
Chessie System, Inc and Subsidiaries

EARNINGS

Income	1977	1976	1975	1974	1973
Merchandise revenue	840 231	779 540	711 205	768 391	710 147
Coal, coke and iron ore	560 992	552 841	500 665	475 663	349 148
Other freight and passenger	91 393	82 235	77 159	76 888	65 122
Total operating revenue	1 492 616	1 414 616	1 289 027	1 329 943	1 124 417
Other income—net	46 175	39 130	42 776	41 168	31 680
Total income	1 538 791	1 453 746	1 331 803	1 362 211	1 156 097

(Thousands of Dollars)

Expenses

	1977	1976	1975	1974	1973
Payroll	644 792	590 382	544 016	505 331	485 628
Materials, supplies and other	445 710	411 244	385 261	373 006	301 995
Depreciation and retirements	70 309	65 314	72 210	78 650	66 741
Total operating expenses	1 160 811	1 066 940	1 001 487	956 987	854 364
Property & other taxes	131 327	121 200	110 502	115 428	90 483
Equipment and joint facility rents	82 528	87 195	77 384	84 713	64 558
Interest	67 335	60 770	49 617	51 438	52 723
Total expenses	1 443 001	1 336 063	1 238 990	1 208 566	1 062 128
Earnings before taxes	76 790	117 683	94 813	153 645	95 969
Current US and Canadian Inc taxes	1 927	10 188	10 117	34 377	16 507
Deferred US and Canadian Inc taxes	17 287	5 370	2 689	28 929	18 835
Earnings before extraordinary item	77 576	102 125	85 385	90 339	58 627
Extraordinary item	9 614	—	6 027	4 910	8 040
Earnings for the year	87 190	102 125	91 412	95 249	66 667

Earnings per share *(dollars)*

	1977	1976	1975	1974	1973
Primary:					
Before extraordinary item	4.01	5.38	4.59	5.06	3.39
Extraordinary item	0.50	—	0.32	0.27	0.46
Earnings for the year	4.51	5.38	4.91	5.83	3.85
Fully diluted:					
Before extraordinary item	3.77	5.19	4.39	4.45	2.93
Extraordinary item	0.50	—	0.32	0.26	0.42
Earnings for the year	4.27	5.19	4.71	4.71	3.35

(Thousands of Dollars)

Operating Revenues	1977	1976	1975	1974	1973
Merchandise	312 044	295 977	266 004	277 868	267 687
Coal, coke and iron ore—US and Canada	231 283	226 553	190 973	194 799	164 805
Coal and coke—overseas export	46 448	71 823	85 762	68 578	35 375
Other freight services	29 805	27 999	26 471	25 080	20 011
Passenger services	2 431	2 301	2 290	2 505	2 184
Total Operating Revenues	622 011	624 653	571 600	568 830	490 062

Operating Expenses	1977	1976	1975	1974	1973
Maintenance of way and structures	94 787	83 426	71 568	61 618	56 886
Maintenance of equipment	123 315	107 811	103 244	96 263	87 641
Traffic	9 369	9 611	9 153	10 145	10 057
Transportation	262 649	236 141	222 149	212 306	190 667
Miscellaneous and general	35 868	36 820	34 692	35 318	32 024
Total Operating Expenses	525 988	473 809	440 806	415 650	377 275
Net Revenue from Railway Operations	96 023	150 844	130 794	153 180	112 787
Other Income—Net	46 424	12 655	22 212	10 216	9 409
Total	142 447	163 499	153 006	163 396	122 196

Chessie Traffic	1977	1976	1975	1974	1973
Freight revenue (thousands)	1 401 223	1 332 380	1 211 867	1 244 409	1 059 648
Per cent of total operating revenues	95.4	95.6	95.3	95.4	95.3
Revenue ton miles (millions)	53 703	53 896	54 166	63 083	61 612
Average revenue per	.0269	.0247	.0224	.0197	.0172
Tons of coal exported at tidewater (thousands)	12 464	14 950	17 890	15 979	10 527
Per cent of US exports	34.3	35.3	36.5	34.6	27.1
Tons of coal originated (thousands)	77 615	77 520	78 903	82 752	81 096
Percent of national production	11.5	11.7	12.3	14.0	13.8

(Thousands of Dollars)

Chessie Operations	1977	1976	1975	1974	1973
Freight revenue per mile of road	126 911	120 360	109 661	110 770	94 109
Freight train miles per mile of road	2 161	2 165	2 112	2 378	2 565
Average number of cars per train					
Loaded	39.0	40.7	42.1	43.6	40.2
Empty	29.2	31.0	33.5	33.1	31.1
Total	68.2	71.7	75.6	76.7	71.3
Average revenue tons per loaded car	62.9	61.4	59.9	58.3	56.6
Average revenue tons per train	2 182	2 251	2 304	2 345	2 119
Average revenue tons hauled per locomotive unit	827	811	824	846	782

FREIGHT TRAFFIC—C & O	1977	1976
Total miles of road operated	4 884	4 885
Total miles of track operated	9 734	9 763
Freight revenue (thousands)	589 775	594 353
Per cent of total operating revenues	94 890	95.1%
Revenue tons carried (thousands)—		
Coal and coke—		
Tidewater	6 903	11 439
Lake	91 701	10 656
Other	40 523	37 455
Total	57 127	59 550
Merchandise freight	40 335	41 224
Total	97 462	100 774
Tons of coal originated (thousands)	45 540	48 150
Per cent of national production	6.8%	7.1%
Tons of coal exported at tidewater (thousands)	5 324	8 564
Per cent of US exports	14.7%	20.1%
Revenue ton miles (millions)	23 985	26 227
Average miles each revenue ton was carried	246.1	260.3
Revenue tons carried per mile of road	19 956	20 630
Revenue ton miles per mile of road (thousands)	4 911	5 369
Freight revenue per mile of road	120 759	121 676

FREIGHT	1977	1976
Average revenue per ton—		
Coal and coke	4.66	4.75
Merchandise freight	8.02	7.55
All freight	6.05	5.90
Average revenue per ton mile—		
Coal and coke	.0195	.0181
Merchandise freight	.0314	.0295
All freight	.0246	.0227
	63.7	63.3
Average revenue tons per train	2 420	2 472
Average tons per train, including company's freight	2 448	2 500
Average revenue tons hauled per locomotive unit	967	988
including company's freight	978	1 000
Average number of cars per train—		
Loaded	39.7	40.4
Empty	33.0	33.7
Total	72.7	74.1
Freight train mileage per mile of road	2 029	2 172
Freight revenue per freight train mile	59.51	56.02

PASSENGER OPERATIONS
In 1971 all C&O long-distance passenger trains were discontinued, except for the train between Washington and Newport News in the East and Cincinnati in the West which is operated under contract for Amtrak. C&O continues to transport passengers and cars on Lake Michigan trainferries.

EQUIPMENT (Excluding Service Equipment)

Locomotives	Multiple Purpose	Switching	Total
Number owned and used	652	89	741
Number leased from others	191	—	191
Average age—years	16.8	28.4	17.9

Freight Train Cars	Box	Flat	Gondola	Hopper	Cov. Hopper	Other	Total
Number owned and used	10 548	1 101b	5 839c	39 817d	2 357e	463	60 125
Number leased from others	1 521	—	778	6 430	283	222	9 234
Average age—years	16.1	29.7	14.5	18.1	12.2	23.2	17.4

Floating Equipment	Tugboats	Lake Michigan Carferries	Car Floats	Other	Total
Number owned and used	5	3	5	1	14
Average age—years	18.2	26.3	36.0	49.0	28.5

a Includes 2 units held awaiting disposition
b Does not include 1 car leased to Nuclear Fuel
c Does not include 50 cars leased to B&O
d Does not include 1 982 cars leased to B&O
e Does not include 2 cars leased to National Bureau of Standards

CAPITAL EXPENDITURES

(Thousands of Dollars)

Expenditures—Road	1968-1977	1977	1976
Additions and betterments to existing track and roadbed	54 726	10 612	9 315
Erecting and modernising stations and offices	6 362	666	329
Constructing and improving shop buildings, enginehouses and fuel stations	4 494	495	682
Building and improving, wharves and docks	2 109	1 539	17
Erecting and strengthening bridges	7 314	666	1 771
Installing centralised traffic control and modernising interlockers and communication systems	9 653	1 235	1 063
Installing modern roadway and shop machinery	15 565	3 058	2 242
Other additions and improvements to the roadway	1 265	187	368
Total road expenditures	101 468	17 858	15 785

Expenditures—Equipment

Locomotives	54 768	211	98
Freight-train cars	452 444	60 025	86 263
Trainferries and other floating equipment	1 754	69	3
Other equipment	7 249	2 045	(14)
Total equipment expenditures	516 215	62 350	86 350
Total Capital Expenditures	617 683	80 208	102 135

Baltimore and Ohio Railroad Company

EARNINGS (Thousands of Dollars)

Operating Revenues	1977	1976	1975	1974	1973
Merchandise	487 575	437 755	400 162	441 444	400 913
Coal, coke and iron ore	203 427	186 848	158 740	153 418	114 869
Coal and coke—overseas export	45 093	37 261	34 816	29 600	17 340
Other freight services	26 351	22 363	20 290	23 315	21 562
Passenger services	414	570	398	606	747
Total Operating Revenues	763 860	684 737	614 406	648 383	555 426

Operating Expenses					
Maintenance of way and structures	119 376	103 357	94 605	73 765	69 020
Maintenance of equipment	118 031	102 142	90 326	83 766	76 500
Traffic	11 634	11 393	10 702	10 770	11 866
Transportation	269 883	253 860	232 160	236 634	210 161
Miscellaneous and general	38 374	37 671	35 767	39 726	34 590
Total Operating Expenses	548 298	508 423	463 560	444 661	402 137
Net Revenue from from Railway Operations	214 562	176 314	150 846	203 722	153 289

TRAFFIC AND OPERATING STATISTICS—B&O

FREIGHT	1977	1976	1975	1974	1973
Total miles of road operated	5 405	5 412	5 412	5 417	5 433
Total miles of track operated	10 140	10 156	10 146	10 183	10 229
Freight revenue (thousands)	$736 095	$661 864	$593 718	$624 462	$553 117
Per cent of total operating revenues	96.5	96.7	96.6	96.3	96.0
Revenue tons carried (thousands)—					
Coal and coke—					
Tidewater	8 407	7 476	8 164	7 278	5 215
Lake	3 104	3 147	3 076	3 835	5 717
Other	37 175	35 204	34 611	35 105	32 214
Total	48 684	45 827	45 851	46 218	43 146
Merchandise freight	53 419	64 980	52 407	66 886	67 632
Total	102 103	100 807	98 258	113 104	110 778
Tons of coal originated (thousands)	25 566	23 203	25 397	26 954	26 677
Per cent of national production	3.8	4.6	3.4	3.9	4.6
Tons of coal exported at tidewater (thousands)	7 140	6 376	6 423	5 557	4 195
Per cent of US exports	19.7	15.1	13.1	12.0	11.0
Revenue ton miles (millions)	25 559	24 941	24 708	29 179	28 896
Average miles each revenue ton was carried	250.3	247.4	251.5	262.9	260.8
Revenue tons carried per mile of road	18 889	18 627	18 156	20 879	20 390
Revenue ton miles per mile of road (thousands)	4 728	4 609	4 565	5 488	5 319
Freight revenue per mile of road	$136 176	$122 296	$109 704	$115 178	$98 126
Average revenue per ton—					
Coal and coke	$4.72	$4.34	$3.78	$3.48	$2.71
Merchandise freight	$9.48	$8.42	$8.02	$6.93	$6.15
All freight	$7.21	$6.56	$6.04	$5.52	$4.81
Average revenue per ton mile—					
Coal and coke	$.0231	$.0212	$.0183	$.0163	$.0131
Merchandise freight	$.0325	$.0297	$.0276	$.0233	$.0208
All freight	$.0288	$.0265	$.0240	$.0210	$.0184
Average revenue tons per loaded car	61.0	59.4	57.9	55.5	54.0
Average revenue tons per train	2 004	2 076	2 076	2 206	1 940
Average tons per train, including company's freight	2 025	2 229	2 098	2 098	2 073
Average revenue tons hauled per locomotive unit	730	691	689	759	691
Average tons hauled per locomotive unit, including company's freight	737	697	719	759	735
Average number of cars per train—					
Loaded	39.2	41.8	42.1	45.7	41.8
Empty	27.2	30.0	31.7	33.1	31.3
Total	66.4	71.8	73.8	78.8	73.1
Freight train mileage per mile of road	2 360	2 219	2 199	2 488	2 731
Freight revenue per freight train mile	$57.70	$55.10	$49.88	$46.34	$35.94

PASSENGER OPERATIONS

In 1971, all B&O long-distance passenger trains were discontinued. Subsequently, under a contract with Amtrak, a train was added which now operates between Washington DC and Martinsburg, West Virginia. A second train operated for Amtrak started in 1976 providing service between Washington DC and Cincinnati, Ohio. The company continues operation of a limited commuter service at Washington and Pittsburgh.

EQUIPMENT (Excluding Service Equipment)

Locomotives	Multiple Purpose	Switching	Total
Number owned and used	403a	122b	525
Number leased from others	413	8	427
Average age—years	15.5	27.9	17.5

a Does not include 12 units leased to Milwaukee Railroad
b Does not include 32 units leased to B & OCT or 18 units held awaiting disposition

Freight Train Cars	Box	Flat	Gondola	Hopper	Hopper	Other	Total
Number owned and used	5 490c	670	4 610d	19 289e	2 107	407	32 573
Number leased from others	4 840	83g	5 997f	6 636	1 885	209	19 650
Average age—years	14.3	22.0	10.9	14.6	10.7	17.3	13.8

Floating Equipment	Deck Scows	Other	Total
Number owned and used	5	1	6h
Average age—years	21.6	22.0	22.0

c Does not include 1 car leased to C & O
d Does not include 6 cars leased to Dearborn Leasing Co
e Does not include 83 cars leased to Conrail
f Does not include 146 cars subleased to Dearborn Leasing Co
g Includes 17 bi-level flats
h Does not include 1 tug, 11 car floats and 1 floating machine shop leased to New York Dock Railway Co

CAPITAL EXPENDITURES (Thousands of Dollars)

Expenditures—Road	1968-77	1977	1976
Additions and betterments to existing track and roadbed	$55 770	$11 481	$8 720
Construction new branch lines	524	—	—
Erecting and modernising stations and offices	8 737	1 075	710
Constructing and improving shop buildings, enginehouses and fuel stations	4 841	703	125
Building and improving, wharves and docks	2 839	360	48
Erecting and strengthening bridges	8 192	945	1 073
Installing centralised traffic control and modernising interlockers and communication systems	18 602	1 952	2 819
Installing modern roadway and shop machinery	13 355	2 778	2 411
Other additions and improvements to the roadway	524	(5)	40
Total road expenditures	115 389	19 290	15 946

Expenditures—Equipment			
Locomotives	99 526	16 086	71
Freight-train cars	403 910	14 699	114 158
Passenger-train cars	73	—	—
Trainferries and other floating equipment	12	—	—
Other equipment	9 735	3 418	175
Total equipment expenditures	513 256	34 203	114 404
Total capital expenditures	628 645	53 493	130 350

Western Maryland Railway Company (Thousands of Dollars)

EARNINGS	1977	1976	1975	1974	1973
Operating Revenues					
Merchandise	$36 593	$41 709	$41 074	$44 900	$37 315
Coal, coke and iron ore	27 951	25 085	24 748	24 659	13 558
Other freight services	4 665	4 123	5 028	4 606	3 494
Total operating revenues	69 209	70 917	70 850	74 165	54 367

Operating Expenses					
Maintenance of way and structures	7 550	8 090	9 047	6 589	6 495
Maintenance of equipment	14 578	14 164	12 015	11 167	10 304
Traffic	1 852	1 815	1 725	1 660	1 705
Transportation	23 659	24 168	25 509	25 612	21 215
Miscellaneous and general	5 280	4 825	4 580	4 523	3 558
Total operating expenses	52 919	53 062	52 876	49 551	43 277
Net Revenue from railway operations	16 290	17 855	17 974	24 614	11 090
Other income net	7 089	2 502	3 141	4 373	817
Total	23 379	20 357	21 115	28 987	11 907

LINES AND TERRITORIES

The Milwaukee Road has approximately 9 475 miles (15 610 km) of route and 12 200 miles (20 117 km) of track in 16 states. The railroad serves the Midwest and the northern tier of states to the Pacific Northwest, extending both east and west of Chicago while serving the city. Among many other points, the Milwaukee Road serves Tacoma, Seattle, Billings, Kansas City, Omaha, Des Moines, Minneapolis-St Paul, Milwaukee and Louisville. It also serves international shippers directly at Great Lakes and Pacific Northwest ports, through interchange to Gulf and Eastern ports, and through connections with Canadian railroads.

The Milwaukee Road employs approximately 10 556 people and operates approximately 695 locomotives and a fleet of about 25 000 freight cars of various types.

The Railroad has two principal subsidiaries: The Milwaukee Motor Transportation Co and Milwaukee Land Co. Milwaukee Motor provides piggyback and container terminal services at 60 locations for the railroad. It also operates over-the-road trucks under common carrier rights in several states served by the railroad. Milwaukee Land Co is a property-development, timber-producing and land-sales company whose operations span the railroad's territory.

FINANCIAL RESULTS

Consolidated operating revenues in 1978 were $439 200 893 compared with $444 502 636 in 1977. Operating expenses and costs were $513 600 830 in 1978 ($500 405 683 in 1977).

On 19 December 1977 the Milwaukee Road filed a voluntary petition for re-organisation under Section 77 of the Federal Bankruptcy Act. Subsequently, the court appointed a Trustee of the properties of the Milwaukee Road to operate the railroad, including its subsidiaries, and to develop a plan of financial re-organisation.

FREIGHT TRAFFIC

During 1978 grain and soya beans were the prime commodities for which the Milwaukee Road provided transportation service and accounted for 14.4 per cent of the railroad's total revenue. Other profit-making groups include: coal 9.5 per cent; lumber and plywood 9.1 per cent; chemicals 7 per cent; motor vehicles 6.8 per cent; freight forwarder traffic 5.8 per cent; metal products 5.3 per cent and grain mill products 5.1 per cent.

PASSENGER TRAFFIC

Under contract with the Regional Transportation Authority, the Milwaukee Road operates a commuter service to and from suburbs to the west and north of Chicago which serves approximately 30 000 passengers a day with about 80 trains. Amtrak inter-city passenger trains operate over the Milwaukee Road between Chicago, Milwaukee and Minneapolis.

OTHER DEVELOPMENTS

In 1976 the Milwaukee Road was the first railroad to apply for repayable financial assistance for track and equipment rehabilitation made available under the provisions of the Railroad Revitalisation and Regulatory Reform Act (4R) of 1976. In 1977 the railroad received and applied about $9·3 million in 4R funds to the rehabilitation of its mainline route between Milwaukee and St Paul. An additional $45 million in 4R assistance was received in mid-1978 to permit the railroad to continue the Milwaukee-St Paul rehabilitation over a two-year period and to rehabilitate and return to service 111 locomotives and 950 freight cars of various types.

Also under the provisions of the 4R legislation, the Milwaukee Road is actively engaged in a programme to eliminate non-profitable light-density lines and routes from its system. Over a third of the railroad's lines have been identified as either definite or potential candidates for abandonment.

The Milwaukee is working closely with state governments, shipper associations and individual shippers to develop cost sharing programmes for the rehabilitation of potentially-viable lines. Programmes of this type are in progress in several states served by the railroad.

PIGGYBACK AND CONTAINER HANDLING FACILITIES

The Milwaukee Road has Piggyback facilities at 78 locations in various parts of the USA. Container handling facilities only are at: Chicago (Franklin Park), Illinois; Twin Cities, Minnesota (Minneapolis & St. Paul); and Seattle, Washington.

CONSOLIDATED RAIL CORPORATION (CONRAIL)

Transportation Center, Six Penn Center Plaza, Philadelphia, Pennsylvania 19104

Chairman and Chief Executive Officer: Edward G. Jordan
President and Chief Operating Officer: Stuart M. Reed
Executive Vice-President, Finance and Administration: Robert H. Platt
Senior Vice-President, Marketing and Sales: James A. Hagen
Senior Vice-President, Operations: Richard B. Hasselman
Senior Vice-President: John L. Sweeney
Senior Vice-President, Strategic Planning: Leo F. Mullin
Vice-President, Sales: Alfred A. Michaud
Vice-President and Treasurer: H. William Brown
Vice-President, Law: Charles P. Northrop
Vice President, Materials and Purchasing: Jeremy T. Whatmough
Vice-President, Marketing: Richard H. Steiner
Vice-President and Secretary: Richard C. Sullivan
Vice-President, Transportation: Donald A. Swanson

Consolidated Rail Corporation (Conrail) is a private, for-profit corporation chartered in the Commonwealth of Pennsylvania. It was created by an Act of Congress (Regional Rail Reorganisation Act of 1973, as amended) to acquire and revitalise most of the freight operations previously provided by six bankrupt carriers: Central of New Jersey; Erie Lackawanna; Lehigh and Hudson River; Lehigh Valley; Penn Central; and Reading. Conrail began operations on 1 April 1976. It is primarily a freight-carrying railroad. Of its $3 506 million of operating revenues in 1978, almost 87 per cent ($3 049 million) were derived from freight transportation, and about 13 per cent from passenger operations (performed under contract with commuter agencies and Amtrak). Conrail employs approximately 87 000 people.

FREIGHT TRAFFIC

Conrail's 17 000 route-mile system (with 34 000 track miles), 27 358 route-km and 54 717 track-km, stretches from Boston to Chicago, and from St Louis to Washington, DC. Conrail operates in 16 states in the Northeast quadrant of the USA and two Canadian provinces (Ontario and Quebec). Running an average of 1 250 freight trains daily, Conrail utilises an owned and/or leased fleet which includes more than 125 000 freight cars and approximately 4 400 locomotives. Freight operations are conducted in a region which contains more than 50 per cent of the nation's manufacturing plants and employees.

Conrail transported 258 million tons of freight in 1978. Most revenue was derived from movements of coal, coke and ore; farm and food products; automotive products; iron and steel; construction materials; chemicals and allied products; and pulp, paper and allied products. Trailer-on-flatcar operations also accounted for a significant portion of freight tonnage and revenues.

PASSENGER TRAFFIC

Conrail operates certain rail commuter services under contract with local, regional or state authorities. More than 1 800 commuter trains transport 400 000 passengers daily in the metropolitan areas of New York, Northern New Jersey, Philadelphia and Baltimore.

REHABILITATION PROGRESS

In the first 42 months of operations between April 1976 and the end of September 1979, Conrail acquired 561 new locomotives. Another 2 897 were overhauled, rebuilt or converted. About three-fourths of the 4 400-unit locomotive fleet has been upgraded or replaced. Heavy repairs were completed on nearly 64 000 freight cars and 6 304 new freight cars were acquired.

In the same period, Conrail installed nearly 18 million cross ties and over 3 600 track miles of steel rail.

New Conrail diesels
One of 44 locomotives delivered to Conrail as part of the 217 locomotive ($113 million) order placed in 1978.

FINANCIAL RESULTS

The US government has invested money in Conrail in the form of loans. By the end of September 1979, the cumulative investment totalled approximately $2 500 million, more than 88 per cent of which has been spent on improvements to physical assets. In addition Conrail has raised more than $627 million in private financing to acquire new equipment.

Although losses are still being incurred, Conrail's financial performance has shown an upward trend: Conrail lost $413 million in its first full year of operations (April 1976-March 1977), $375 million in its second year and $297 million in the third year (up to March 1979). In the period April-September 1979, Contrail's loss improved by $98.8 million over the losses incurred in the same period in 1978.

FUTURE PROGRAMMES

Capital programmes in 1980 will be structured to balance the needs of staying within the existing federal funding authorisation while continuing to protect and improve the railroad's key physical assets. 1980 will see a short-term reduction in the physical upgrading programmes that Conrail has had under way for more than three years, which is possible because of the upgrading achievements to date.

In addition Contrail announced plans to acquire 126 diesel-electric locomotives for delivery in 1980 and to construct 2 000 100-tonne gondolas at its Samuel Rea car shop at Hollidaysburg, Pennsylvania, beginning in April 1980. The remainder of Conrail's equipment programme in 1980 will be dependent on the availability of private sector financing, as well as the level of economic activity.

THE DENVER AND RIO GRANDE WESTERN RAILROAD COMPANY

1515 Arapahoe St, Denver, Colorado 80202
PO Box 5482, Denver, Colorado 80217

Chairman of the Board: G. B. Aydelott
President and Chief Executive Officer: W. J. Holtman
Vice-President, Traffic: J. D. Key
Vice-President, Finance: H. W. Bushacher
Vice-President and General Counsel: S. R. Freeman
General Manager: A. H. Nance
Purchasing Agent: S. A. Silverman
Chief Mechanical Officer: J. E. Clancy
Chief Engineer: E. H. Waring
Chief Transportation Officer: D. J. Butters

The Denver and Rio Grande Western Railroad Company is now 107 years old. The Rio Grande Railroad operates over 1 850 miles of mainline track from Denver and Pueblo, Colorado, on the east, to Salt Lake City and Ogden, Utah, on the west. The company has over 266 locomotives and 10 330 freight cars of various types. Virtually all its revenue is derived from hauling freight with major items being coal, food products, lumber, steel, and autos and auto parts. Approximately 65.7 per cent of its revenue comes from originating, terminating and local traffic, while 35.1 per cent results from being an intermediate carrier between other railroads.

Rio Grande Industries, Inc (Denver) was established in 1969 as a holding company to control Denver and Rio Grande Western Railroad, and to permit diversification. Although the railroad continues to be its most important activity, diversification has been made into real estate development (Leavell Development Co, Denver, Colorado); people-moving systems (Arrow Development Co); information industries (Computer Sharing Services); and Rio Grande Motor Way.

TRAFFIC RESULTS

In 1978, for the eleventh consecutive year, the Rio Grande Railroad achieved record freight revenues. Freight revenues were 13 per cent above those of 1977. Freight ton-miles increased four per cent, and average revenue per ton mile increased nine per cent. Coal represented 26 per cent of total freight revenues in 1976 which was up 19 per cent over 1975, accounting for about one-third of the year-to-year increase. Passenger revenues were up slightly in 1976 with almost all of the increase coming from the Durango-Silverton narrow gauge tourist train.

FINANCIAL RESULTS

During 1978 the railroad reported an operating revenue of $218 016 000 and total investment of $404 520 000. During the first nine months of the 1979 calendar year, operating expenses were $160 134 000 against an operating revenue of $160 203 000.

LOCOMOTIVES AND CARS

The present fleet of diesel electric locomotives totals 254 units, of which 246 are road units and 20 are switchers.
The passenger fleet comprises 40 cars. Total freight car fleet as of December 1978 was 10 330.

DEVELOPMENT

Installation of Centralised Traffic Control system on the Craig Branch in Northwestern Colorado was completed during 1976, as was the installation of CTC between Springville and Gilluly in Utah.

Additional expenditures involved expansion of fuel handling facilities, terminal expansion and modernisation, machines for roadway and track maintenance, safety and security improvements, including hot box detectors, dragging equipment detectors, rock slide detector fences, etc.

Rio Grande also initiated an extensive programme for modernisation of bridges, installation of new equipment for repair facilities, and construction of industrial spur tracks.

Seventy-six track miles of new and heavier rail, and 329 000 cross ties were installed in 1978.

ILLINOIS CENTRAL GULF RAILROAD

An IC Industries Company
233 N Michigan Avenue, Chicago, Illinois 60601

President and Chief Executive Officer: William J. Taylor
Senior Vice-President, Operations: James E. Martin
Vice-President: G. C. Stuckey
Vice-President and Chief Mechanical Officer: E. L. Pearson
Senior Vice-President and Chief Financial Officer: G. K. Konker
Senior Vice-President—Marketing: Harry J. Bruce
Vice-President—Materials Management: Harry C. Miller
Vice-President & Chief Engineer: Lee F. Fox
Vice-President and Chief Transportation Officer: Ivan B. Hall
Vice-President, Financial Planning and Treasurer: Dennis N. Melin
Secretary: John B. Goodrich
Vice-President Communications & Computer Services: Paul F. Deady
Vice-President, Market Development: Douglas D. Hagestad
Vice-President, Sales: Richard L. Rushing
Vice-President, Pricing: Elias Lyman
Director Corporation Relations: Robert W. O'Brien

The Illinois Central Railroad was founded in 1851. For the first 16 years, it operated entirely within Illinois. Following the Civil War, it entered an era of expansion as more than 200 separate railroads were combined into its system. In 1867 the IC crossed the Mississippi River into Iowa. In the next few years its trackage grew southward into Kentucky, Tennessee, Arkansas, Alabama, and Mississippi, eventually reaching Louisiana and the Gulf ports of New Orleans and Gulfport, Mississippi. There was also movement in other directions: into South Dakota, Minnesota, Wisconsin, Indiana, Missouri and Nebraska.

The Gulf, Mobile & Ohio Railroad, incorporated in 1940, was itself a combination of predecessor lines dating back to the late nineteenth century. Principal predecessor lines were the Gulf, Mobile and Northern, the Mobile and Ohio, and the Chicago and

Alton railroads. GM&O's territory roughly paralleled that of the larger Illinois Central, with the exception of important lines to Mobile, Alabama and Kansas City, Missouri. Through merger and acquisition, the GM&O adhered to its "expand or expire" policy to become a strong, profitable railroad, growing from 400 miles (643 km) in 1929 to a 2 700-mile (4 345 km) carrier at the time of the merger.

ICG service in the state of Arkansas ceased in early 1973 when the 1.78 miles (approx 3 km) operated in that state were transferred to another railroad.

FINANCIAL

Revenues and sales for the first nine months of 1979 were $649 263 000 against operating expenses of $617 600 000. Pre-tax income in 1979 was $28 002 000.

LINES & TERRITORIES

The Illinois Central Gulf is a strong line operating in 13 states in the centre of America and runs from the Great Lakes to the Gulf of Mexico, providing a vital rail connection between about 2 000 communities including Chicago, St Louis, Memphis, New Orleans, Birmingham, Louisville, Omaha, Kansas City, Montgomery and Mobile. It operates 8 948 miles (14 400 km) of line and at the end of 1977 owned or leased 46 483 cars and 1 061 diesel-electric locomotives.

LOCOMOTIVES & ROLLING STOCK

Since 1973, 3 579 new cars have been added to ICG's fleet, 2 562 of which were built at the railroad's Centralia, Illinois, car shop. During the same period, 38 484 freight cars have been given major repairs while 515 others were completely rehabilitated.

ICG has one of the youngest and most reliable locomotive fleets in the industry. Through purchases of new locomotives and the remanufacture of older locomotives at its Paducah, Kentucky, facility, ICG has decreased the average age of its fleet. Since 1975 the average age of the locomotive fleet has dropped from 12.8 years in 1973 to 10.2 by the end of 1978.

PIGGYBACK

The piggyback service Slingshot, between Chicago and St. Louis, continues. The railroad operates three trains a day with a fourth added on demand.

KANSAS CITY SOUTHERN RAILWAY COMPANY
114 West 11th Street, Kansas City, Missouri, 64105

President: Thomas S. Carter
Chairman of the Board and Chief Executive Officer: W. N. Deramus
Senior Vice-President Marketing: M. F. McClain
Secretary: E. F. James
Vice-President and Comptroller: T. A. Giltner
General Manager: J. E. Gregg

Operating Department:
General Manager: J. E. Gregg

Freight Traffic:
Vice-President: L. J. Tamisiea

Kansas City Southern Railway is a member of the Kansas City Southern Industries group of companies. In addition to road and rail transportation, KCSI owns television and radio stations, a plant manufacturing specialised industrial vehicles, coal mines and financial services companies. While transport services continued to contribute the largest share of KCSI's earnings in 1972, transport share fell from 77.6 per cent in 1971

to 61.4 per cent in 1972, whereas contributions from other sources increased to 38.6 per cent in 1972 compared with 22.4 per cent in 1971.

The Louisianna and Arkansas Railway is controlled by KCS but is separately operated.

LINES AND TERRITORY

The main line runs direct from Kansas City to the Gulf ports of New Orleans, Louisiana and Port Arthur, Texas. A line runs west from Shreveport to Dallas.

Total route: Approximately 1 600 miles (2 575 km).

Woodpulp, paper, and petroleum and port expansion are activities which are expanding in the KCS territories.

All passenger train operation has ceased.

Expenditure for the rail operations of Kansas City Southern were $38 344 million during 1978 ($24 713 000 in 1977).

FREIGHT TRAFFIC	1977	1978
Gross tonne-miles	15 080 800	16 156 586
Net tonne-miles		
Revenue	7 690 645	9 497 899
Non-revenue	127 754	141 751

CAPITAL IMPROVEMENTS

Equipment purchased during 1979 included six road diesel locomotives and 600 freight cars, costing $28 800 million.

LONG ISLAND RAILROAD COMPANY
93-02 Sutphin Boulevard, Jamaica Station, Jamaica, New York 11435

President: Francis S. Gabreski
Vice-President, General Counsel and Secretary: Thomas M. Taranto
Senior Executive, Administration: Thomas P. Moore
Senior Executive, Operations: A. Norman Gandia
Superintendent, Transportation: Lawrence W. Dixon
Chief Engineer: John D. Woodward
Chief Mechanical Officer: James W. Yaeger
Director Operations and Service Planning: Donald O. Eisele
Director Public Affairs: Rand A. Burgner

LINES AND TERRITORIES
LIRR is the third oldest railroad in the world still operating under its original name. It is the busiest railroad in the USA, providing the nation's most concentrated rail service to one of its fastest growing areas.
The LIRR operates the whole 100 mile length of Long Island, New York with the inner suburban lines electrified (103 route miles and 294 single track miles) and operated by electric multiple unit stock, and the outer, sparser traffic operated by diesel electric locomotives. Total mileage including electrified lines is 321.
The LIRR operates both diesel and electric trains. Electric territory (third rail) adds up to 266 miles.
The LIRR is a wholly-owned subsidiary of the Metropolitan Transportation Authority, and agency of the State of New York, whose members constitute the railroad's Board of Directors.

FINANCIAL RESULTS
1978/79 revenues from passenger and baggage were $140 million. Compared with $135 million the previous year. Expenses for 1977/78 were $231 million.

FREIGHT TRAFFIC
Total freight ton-km for 1977 were 2 179 434. In sharp contrast to other US railroads, freight accounts for less than one-sixth of gross revenue on the LIRR. Freight volume is about 3.8 million tons a year. Three-quarters of freight is inbound to Long Island; only one quarter is moved westward off the island. LIRR has direct interchange with all trunk line railroads serving the New York area.
Several freight improvements have been put in hand to streamline and improve service provided by the LIRR. A computer record-keeping service, for instance, has been installed to provide greater effectiveness and more efficient means of keeping track of the nearly 100 000 wagons handled each year.

Total car miles during 1978/79 were 55.7 million. This was down on the 1977/78 figure of 56 million.

PASSENGER TRAFFIC
Passengers carried during 1978/79 were 2 616 million. LIRR operates about 800 scheduled trains a day—670 passenger trains and 130 deadheads (empties moving to terminals to begin runs or to yards after runs). About 425 scheduled trains are run on Saturdays and Sundays.
Equipment for the diesel-hauled service continues to be improved. With the conversion to all-Metropolitan service in the electrified zone in 1973, a programme was begun to convert late-model electric cars of older design into coaches for use in diesel service. By the end of 1974, 90 coaches and 19 power cars had been adapted for "push-pull" trains. An additional 33 coaches (including 4 generator cars) have been authorised for conversion and funds from the 1974 Transportation Bond Issue were being sought for the remaining 38 coaches (including 5 generator cars) to be converted for use in diesel service.

One of the 22 new General Motors class GP-38 Type 2 diesel-electric locomotives Long Island has in service

The system is in fact the nation's busiest passenger railroad. Total annual journeys are approximately 69.6 million passengers a year. An average of 260 000 passengers a day are carried, which breaks down to 90 000 commuters who make two trips a day and 80 000 single-fare passengers.
There are 147 stations for the railroad, plus 26 "road-and-rail" bus-stops in Suffolk County. The average distance between stations is slightly over one mile.

ROLLING STOCK
Passenger cars operated by LIRR number 1 067. The Company has 60 line haul diesel electric locomotives and 23 switching locomotives. Electric railcars number 766 and 301 diesel trailer cars.

TRACK IMPROVEMENTS
With the arrival of the 770 new high performance M-1 electric multiple-unit cars and the upgrading of the electric power system which will permit these cars to operate at their designed capability, it was determined that the condition of the Long Island Rail Road's track required improvement to standards consistent with 100 mph operation of this new equipment.
The improvement programme involves the installation on 50 miles of track of all new heavier weight (119 lb) continuous welded rail, new ties and stone ballast, and new heavier weight switches, many of which will have improved turnout angles for higher train speeds and greater riding comfort. Highway grade crossings in the improvement programme areas will be surfaced with modern rubber crossing panels to eliminate the traditional noise and shock normally experienced by vehicles passing over railroad tracks. All salvageable material removed during the programme will be rehabilitated and utilised to upgrade other portions of the railroad.

DIESEL-ELECTRIC LOCOMOTIVES

Class	Axle Arrange-ment	Trans-mission	Rated Power hp	Max lb	Tractive Effort Continuous at lb	mph	Max Speed mph	Wheel Dia in	Total Weight tons	Length ft in	No. built	Year first built	Builders: Mechanical parts	Engine & type	Transmission
E-10			1 000	235 000				40		40' 6''	8	1977	EMD		
E-15			1 500	248 000				40		50' 2''	23	1977	EMD		
L-2			2 000	270 490	45 580	12.8	65	40		60' 3''	8	1968	ALCO		
E-20			2 000	268 500	44 000		82	40		59' 2''	28	1976	EMD		

ELECTRIC RAILCARS

Class	Axle Arrange-ment	Current	Rated Output hp	Max lb	Max Speed mph	Wheel Dia in	Weight tons	Length ft in	No. built	Year first built	Builders: Mechanical Parts	Electrical Equipment
M-1		650 V dc	640	90 750	100	32		85'	764	1968	Budd Co	General Electric

MAINE CENTRAL RAILROAD COMPANY
242, St. John St, Portland, Maine 04102

President: John F. Gerity
Chairman: E. Spencer Miller
Clerk of the Corporation: Stanley W. Watson
Vice-President, Operating and Engineering: Bradley L. Peters
Mechanical and Labour Relations Department:
Executive Vice-President: Arnold J. Travis
Operating:
General Superintendent: A. N. Tupper
Chief Mechanical Officer: S. P. Park Jr
Chief Engineer: J. O. Born
Accounting and Finance Department:
Comptroller: John Michaels
Treasurer: S. W. Watson

LINES AND TERRITORIES
Maine Central Railroad Company is a freight-only railroad and operates 834 miles (1 342 km) of road; 749 miles (1 205 km) in Maine, 58 miles (93 km) in New Hampshire, 22 miles (35 km) in Vermont and 5 miles (8 km) in New Brunswick. Maine Central serves all of the large population centres and with two exceptions the industrial centres of the State of Maine. The primary commodities carried are the raw materials and finished products of the pulp and paper industry with over 50 per cent of Maine Central's traffic

General Motors Bo-Bo 253 on the turntable ready for stabling in the roundhouse at Bangor Maine, Maine Central RR

Two GE U18B 1800 hp Independence Class diesel electrics of Maine Central RR run light into Bangor station yard after uncoupling from a freight brought from Vanceboro, N0400 "General Henry Knox" and No 408" Battle of the Bagaduce"

Bangor, Maine, USA line-up of snowploughs in Maine Central yard MWS75, MWS80, MWS72

generated by this industry. Other major sources of freight revenue are: petroleum products, feed and mill products, corn, clay, chemicals fibreboard and pulpboard, canned food, cement and potatoes.

FINANCIAL RESULTS
Operating expenses increased in 1978 in approximately the same ratio as operating revenues amounting to $47.6 million from $43.7 million in 1977.

LOCOMOTIVE AND CARS
At the end of 1978 Maine Central accepted delivery of 150 new boxcars built in Portland, Oregon. The railroad placed an order with the same builder for 150 100-tonne capacity boxcars for delivery in 1979.
The 1977 programme to upgrade 26 boxcars for crumb pulp service was completed during 1978. Improvements include new steel floors and modified interior linings. Twelve cars were completed in 1978. Six locomotives received major repairs in 1978, including one switcher and five load units. Forty-eight rack cars were modified to permit transportation of either 4 or 8 ft (1.2 or 2.4 m) pulpwood.
As of December 31, 1976, Maine Central held under lease 1 961 units having an aggregate value when new of about $35 000 000. Rental payments for these leased cars are charged against income and accounted for under equipment rents on the income statement.

OPERATING AND FREIGHT TRAFFIC

Mileage:	1978	1977
Train mileage		
Freight service (with locomotives)	780 622	748 430
Work service	22 057	22 532
Total train miles	802 679	770 962
Locomotive mileage		
Freight service	794 730	761 669
Train switching	203 070	193 368
Yard switching	249 960	252 102
Work service	37 353	37 187
Total locomotive miles	1 285 113	1 244 326
Freight train car miles		
Loaded	17 158 699	16 250 748
Empty	15 535 216	15 114 501
Caboose	791 134	758 960
Total freight train car miles	33 485 049	32 124 209

Averages		
Per mile of road		
Operating revenues	$54 612.96	$48 303.61
Operating expenses	$51 906.82	$46 222.57*
Net railway operating income	$3 154.97	$2 201.24*
Per train mile		
Operating revenues	$59.42	$55.52
Operating expenses	$56.47	$53.12*
Net railway operating income	$3.43	$2.53*
Per revenue train mile		
Total freight cars	41.88	41.91
Loaded freight cars	21.98	21.71
Empty freight cars	19.90	20.20
Freight revenue	$45 295 377	$40 450 778

Revenue		
Tonnes of freight carried		
Revenue	8 134 002	7 659 292
Company	120 941	114 348
Total tonnes of freight carried	8 254 943	7 773 640
Tonnes of freight carried one mile		
Revenue	919 788 672	866 249 645
Company	7 478 548	6 845 275
Total tonnes of freight carried one mile	927 267 220	873 094 920

Averages		
Miles of road operated	849.28	860.29
Miles hauled—revenue freight	113.08	113.10
Tonnes of revenue freight per train mile	1 178.28	1 157.42
Tonnes of revenue freight per loaded car mile	53.60	53.31
Revenue per tonne of freight	$5.57	$5.28
Revenue per ton mile (cents)	4.925	4.670
Revenue per revenue train mile	$58.0247	$54.0475
Freight revenue per loaded car mile (cents)	263.9791	248.9164

*Restated to conform to new ICC accounting regulations.

MISSOURI PACIFIC RAILROAD
210 N 13th St, St. Louis, Missouri 63103

Executive Department (St. Louis)
Chairman of the Board: D. B. Jenks
Vice-Chairman: J. H. Lloyd
Vice-President, Executive Department: J. E. Angst
Senior Vice-President, Law: M. M. Hennelly
Senior Vice-President, Traffic: J. A. Austin
Vice-President, Operations: R. K. Davidson
Vice-President, Engineering: J. G. German
Vice-President, Transportation: J. M. Toler
Vice-President, Administration: D. L. Manion
Vice-President, Finance: L. White Matthews III
Vice-President, Information and Control Systems: G. S. Sines

In January 1980 Missouri Pacific and Union Pacific (MoPac), the USA's sixth and ninth largest railroads, announced terms for an agreed merger. The Union Missouri Company would be the third largest, with 21 200 miles (34 118 km) of track.

Gondola car, one of 500 built for Missouri Pacific by Constructora Nacional de Carros de Ferrocarril of Mexico

LINES AND TERRITORIES
Total length of the MoPac system is 11 679 miles (18 788 km). Supplementing the rail lines is a network of approximately 17 000 miles (27 400 km) of truck routes operated by Missouri Pacific Truck Lines. Most of the highway mileage parallels the rail lines but many routes provide scheduled freight service to places not reached by the railroads. The highway subsidiary also performs all terminal and piggy back ramp loading and unloading for Missouri Pacific Railroad traffic and over-the-highway service for piggyback traffic.

FREIGHT TRAFFIC
Revenues from freight during 1979 were $1 260 218 000. Expenses were $1 074 million.

ROADWAY AND EQUIPMENT
MoPac continues to broaden its Transportation Control System (TCS). Using a large computer complex and modern electronic communications, TCS provides control of individual car movements, issues switching instructions and handles car order requirements. During 1978 TCS was expanded to include a car scheduling system which was installed as a pilot project over a major traffic corridor. This programme was designed as a prototype for use by the entire railroad industry. The programme permits precise scheduling and monitoring of each freight car in transit which will provide operating personnel with an early warning of potential congestion or other exceptional conditions.

MOTIVE POWER
Motive power delivered 1977 (55 locomotives):

Model	Supplier	Power (hp)	Max Speed (mph)	Wheel Arrangement	Gauge (ft in)	No. of Units
GP-15-1	EMD/GMC	1 500	65	B-B	4 8½	25
GP-38-2	EMD/GMC	2 000	65	B-B	4 8½	20
U-23-B	GE	2 250	65	B-B	4 8½	10

Motive power delivered 1978 (80 locomotives):

Model	Supplier	Power (hp)	Max Speed (mph)	Wheel Arrangement	Gauge (ft in)	No. of Units
SD-40-2	EMD-GMC	3 000	65	C-C	4 8½	50
B23-7	GE	2 250	65	B-B	4 8½	30

Motive power delivered 1979 (130 locomotives):

Model	Supplier	Power (hp)	Max Speed (mph)	Wheel Arrangement	Gauge (ft in)	No. of Units
GP-15-1	EMD-GMC	1 500	65	B-B	4 8½	30
SD-40-2	EMD-GMC	3 000	65	C-C	4 8½	80
B23-7	GE	2 250	65	B-B	4 8½	20

Motive power on order 1980 (140 locomotives):

Model	Supplier	Power (hp)	Max Speed (mph)	Wheel Arrangement	Gauge (ft in)	No. of Units
GP-38-2	EMD-GMC	2 000	65	B-B	4 8½	80
SD-40-2	EMD-GMC	3 000	65	C-C	4 8½	30
GP-50	EMD-GMC	3 500	65	B-B	4 8½	10
B23-7	GE	2 250	65	B-B	4 8½	20

DIESEL LOCOMOTIVES

Class	Axle Arrange-ment	Trans-mission	Rated Power (hp)	Max (lb)	Tractive Effort Continuous at (lb)	(mph)	Max Speed (mph)	Wheel Diameter (ins)	Total Weight (Tons)	Length (ft in)	No. built	Year first built	Builders: Mechanical Parts	Engine & Type	Transmission
SW-7 Switch	B-B	Elec	1 200	61 650	36 000	9	55	40	123	44 5	6	1950	Electro-motive	EMD 12-567	EMD
SW-9 Switch	B-B	Elec	1 200	61 650	36 000	9	55	40	123	44 5	36	1951	Electro-motive	EMD 12-567	EMD
SW-12 Switch	B-B	Elec	1 200	61 650	36 000	9	55	40	123	44 5	139	1954	Electro-motive	EMD 12-567	EMD
SW1500 Switch	B-B	Elec	1 500	65 290	43 000	10.7	55	40	133	44 8	4	1972	Electro-motive	EMD 12-645	EMD
SL-1 Switch	B-B	Elec	None	63 500	40 870	4.8	55	40	127	44 5	1	1978	Electro-motive	MoPac	EMD
GP-7 RD-SW	B-B	Elec	1 600	62 530	41 000	12	65	40	125	55 11	105	1950	Electro-motive	EMD 16-567	EMD
GP-9 RD-SW	B-B	Elec	1 800	62 530	46 200	12	65	40	125	56 2	52	1955	Electro-motive	EMD 16-567	EMD
GP-18 RD-SW	B-B	Elec	1 800	63 500	46 200	12	65	40	127	56 2	136	1960	Electro-motive	EMD 16-567	EMD
GP-15-1 RD-SW	B-B	Elec	1 500	65 500	46 800	9.3	65	40	131	54 11	90	1976	Electro-motive	EMD 12-645	EMD
MP-15 RD-SW	B-B	Elec	1 500	66 000	46 800	9.6	65	40	133	47 8	25	1974	Electro-motive	EMD 12-645	EMD
GP-28 RD-SW	B-B	Elec	2 000	65 000	51 300	12	65	40	131	56 2	2	1964	Electro-motive	EMD 16-645	EMD
GP-38 RD-SW	B-B	Elec	2 000	65 000	51 300	12	65	40	132	59 2	6	1966	Electro-motive	EMD 16-645	EMD
GP-38-2 RD-SW	B-B	Elec	2 000	66 500	51 300	12	65	40	133	59 2	149	1972	Electro-motive	EMD 16-645	EMD
U-23-B RD-SW	B-B	Elec	2 250	67 000	60 400	10.8	65	40	134	60 2	38	1973	General Electric	GE FDL-12	GE
B-23-7 RD-SW	B-B	Elec	2 250	66 500	60 400	10.8	65	40	133	62 2	30	1978	General Electric	GE FDL-12	GE
GP-35M RD-SW	B-B	Elec	2 000	64 700	51 300	12	65	40	129	56 2	17	1964	EMD	EMD 16-645	EMD
GP-35 RD-SW	B-B	Elec	2 500	64 700	51 300	12	65	40	129	56 2	48	1964	EMD	EMD 16-567	EMD
U30-C RD-SW	C-C	Elec	3 000	98 500	90 600	9.6	65	40	197	67 3	35	1968	EMD	GE FDL-16	GE
SD-40 RD-SW	C-C	Elec	3 000	98 000	77 000	12	65	40	195	65 8	90	1967	EMD	EMD 16-645	EMD
SD-40-2 RD-SW	C-C	Elec	3 000	98 300	77 000	12	65	40	196	68 10	212	1973	EMD	EMD 16-645	EMD
SD-40-2C RD-SW	C-C	Elec	3 000	104 300	90 400	8.5	65	40	208	68 10	54	1976	EMD	EMD 16-645	EMD
SW-8 Switch	B-B	Elec	900	58 500	24 640	9	55	40	117	44 5	5	1952	EMD	EMD 12-567	EMD

MISSOURI-KANSAS-TEXAS RAILROAD COMPANY

Katy Building, 101 East Main Street, Denison, Dallas, Texas 75202

Chairman of Board and Chief Executive Officer: R. N. Whitman
Vice-President and Executive Representative: B. R. Bishop
Vice-President, Traffic: H. T. Dimmerman
Vice-President, Secretary and Treasurer: K. R. Ziebarth
Vice-President, and Chief Operating Officer: H. L. Gastler
Vice-President, Marketing: T. F. Steiniger
Vice-President, Administration: W. H. Zeidel
Comptroller: R. A. Douglas
Vice-President, Operations: T. G. Todd
Operating Department:
General Manager: T. G. Todd
Assistant General Manager: M. L. Janovec
Superintendent Transportation: D. D. Doyle
General Supertendent, Transportation: O. C. Putsche
Chief Engineer: R. N. Wogan
Piggyback and Highway Services
(Co-ordinated & Katy Transportation Companies)
Assistant Vice-President and General Manager: G. B. Bleakney
Traffic Department:
Vice President, Traffic: H. T. Dimmerman
Assistant Vice-President: J. M. Sheridan
Assistant Vice-President: G. J. Elking
Manager TOFC Sales: J. E. Warren
Finance Department:
Executive Vice-President, Secretary & Financial: K. R. Ziebarth

LINES AND TERRITORY

The Missouri-Kansas-Texas Railroad—familiarly known as the "Katy"—operates 2 168 miles of route from Kansas City and St. Louis in the north, to Altus in western Oklahoma, and south to San Antonio and Galveston in Texas.
Principal traffic is in the movement south to port of wheat, lumber, steel products, coal, crushed stone, automobiles and trucks.

FINANCIAL RESULTS

Revenue for 1978 was $135.7 million. Revenue from freight sources totalled $129.3 million.
The M-K-T's freight revenue rose 15 per cent in 1978 compared with 1977. The M-K-T also experienced an increase of four per cent in carloading and eight per cent in ton miles. By way of comparison, the nation's Class I railroads reported increases of only nine per cent in revenue and five per cent in ton miles, and an increase of one per cent in carloads. This increase in revenue is attributed to the M-K-T's efforts to solicit more profitable traffic, to obtain the long haul on the traffic which the Katy is already handling, and to the effects of service improvements resulting from the continuing programme of permanent way rehabilitation.
Several commodities showed substantial gains during 1978. Some of the more prominent categories were petroleum local products, coal, wheat and freight of all kinds. The M-K-T enjoyed a 47 per cent increase. The M-K-T, in 1978, witnessed the initiation of several volume export wheat movements to the Houston and Galveston elevators. This operation consisted of multiple-car shipments which provided better equipment control and turnaround, thereby increasing both revenue and car availability. The 1979 export volume was expected to be as great as 1978 and multiple-car shipments have been expanded to include other customers. Long-term USDA projections up to 2000 indicate a very significant rise in export levels of agricultural products such as wheat, corn, milo and soybeans. The M-K-T, with its short-line mileage from Kansas City to the Ports of Houston and Galveston, will become more important in future movements of these commodities.
The substantial increase in coal traffic is attributed primarily to increased lodgings from on-line points in Oklahoma and Missouri. M-K-T are now moving unit coal trains to the Lower Colorado River Authority power generating station at Halsted, Texas.
Anhydrous ammonia carloadings, part of the chemical classification, rose 82 per cent. Another major revenue increase was derived from petroleum coke, producing 1978 M-K-T gross revenues, before absorptions, of $1 024 000 compared to $157 000 in 1977; this is a component of the petroleum/coal products commodity classification. The coke commenced moving mid-year in heavy volume and improved 1979 revenue from this continuing movement were anticipated. This increase is attributable to publication of annual volume rates from Coffeyville, Kansas to various off-line points. Movements of soda ash from the Wyoming Green River area to destinations on the M-K-T continued to be firm.

TOFC PIGGYBACK

TOFC traffic handled by the M-K-T increased 46.7 per cent in 1978. With the average revenue per trailer up 4.4 per cent, net piggyback revenue rose 69.8 per cent. This gain is substantially higher than the national average of 11.7 per cent.

Line up of MoPac diesel locomotives

LOCOMOTIVES AND CARS

Total locomotive fleet in 1978 consisted of 179 road freight units including 37 switching units.

DIESEL-ELECTRIC LOCOMOTIVE FLEET

Builder	Class	No. Units	hp	Total hp
EMD	Freight F-3 & F-7	3	1 500	4 500
EMD	Freight FP-7	1	1 500	1 500
EMD	Freight F-9	2	1 750	3 500
EMD	Road Switch GP-40	61	3 000	183 000
EMD	Road Switch GP-38	4	2 000	8 000
EMD	Road Switch GP-38-2	18	2 000	36 000
EMD	Road Switch GP-7	33	1 500	49 500
EMD	Switch	19	1 200	22 800
EMD	Switch	6	1 500	9 000
EMD	Switch (Slug)	1	—	—
	Total	148		317 800
GE	Road Switch U23B	3	2 250	6 750
	Total	3		6 750
Baldwin	Switch (Repowered)	8	1 200	9 600
Baldwin	Switch (Repowered)	3	1 200	3 600
	Total	11		13 200
Alco	Road Switch	6	1 500	9 000
	Total	6		9 000
	Grand Total All	168		346 750

DIESEL LOCOMOTIVES

Class	Axle Arrangement	Transmission	Rated Power hp	Max lb (kg)	Continuous at lb (kg)	mph (km/h)	Max Speed mph (km/h)	Wheel Dia in (mm)	Total Weight Tons*	Length ft in (mm)	No. Built	Year first Built	Mechanical Parts	Engine & Type	Transmission
GP-7	Bo-Bo	Elec	1 600	63 750 (28 920)	41 000 (18 600)	12.0 (19.3)	65 (105)	40 (1 016)	127.5	55' 11" (17 040)	174	1950	EMD	EMD 16-567-B	EMD
GP-9	"	"	1 800	62 710 (28 450)	46 200 (20 960)	12.0 (19.3)	"	"	125.4	56' 2" (17 200)	54	1955	"	END 16-567-C	"
GP15-1	"	"	1 500	65 270 (29 610)	46 800 (21 230)	9.3 (14.9)	"	"	130.5	54' 11" (16 740)	60	1976	"	END 12-645-E	"
MP-15	"	"	1 500	66 700 (30 260)	46 800 (21 230)	9.6 (15.4)	"	"	133.4	47' 8" (14 530)	25	1974	"	"	"
GP-18	"	"	1 800	64 235 (29 140)	46 200 (20 960)	12.0 (19.3)	"	"	128.5	56' 2" (17 200)	138	1960	"	EMD 16-567D1	"
GP-28	"	"	2 000	65 825 (29 860)	51 300 (23 270)	12.0 (19.3)	"	"	131.6	56' 2" (17 200)	2	1964	"	EMD 16-645-E	"
GP-35	"	"	2 500	64 700 (29 350)	51 300 (23 270)	12.0 (19.3)	"	"	129.4	56' 2" (17 200)	64	1964	"	EMD 16-567D3A	"
GP-38	"	"	2 000	65 780 (29 840)	51 300 (23 270)	12.0 (19.3)	"	"	131.5	59' 2" (18 100)	7	1965	"	EMD 16-645-E	"
GP38-2	"	"	2 000	67 240 (30 500)	51 300 (23 270)	12.0 (19.3)	"	"	134.5	59' 2" (18 100)	149	1975	"	"	"
U23B	"	"	2 250	67 400 (30 570)	60 400 (27 400)	10.8 (17.3)	"	"	134.8	60' 2" (18 340)	39	1973	G.E.	G.E.7 FDL-12	G.E.
U30C	Co-Co	"	3 000	98 510 (44 680)	90 600 (41 100)	9.6 (15.4)	"	"	197.0	67' 3" (20 500)	35	1968	G.E.	G.E.7 FDL-16	G.E.
SD40	"	"	3 000	98 130 (44 510)	77 000 (34 930)	12.0 (19.3)	"	"	196.2	65' 8" (20 050)	90	1967	EMD	EMD16-645E3	EMD
SD40-2	"	"	3 000	98 100 (44 500)	77 000 (34 930)	12.0 (19.3)	"	"	196.2	68' 10" (20 980)	146	1973	"	"	"
SW7	Bo-Bo	"	1 200	62 025 (28 130)	36 000 (16 330)	9.0 (14.5)	55 (88.5)	"	124.0	44' 5" (13 540)	9	1950	"	EMD12-567-A	"
SW8	"	"	900	58 500 (26 540)	24 640 (11 180)	9.0 (14.5)	"	"	117.0	"	8	1952	"	EMD8-567-B	"
SW9	"	"	1 200	62 390 (28 300)	36 000 (16 330)	9.0 (14.5)	"	"	124.8	"	36	1951	"	EMD12-567-B	"
SW12	"	"	1 200	62 390 (28 300)	36 000 (16 330)	9.0 (14.5)	"	"	124.8	"	139	1954	"	EMD12-567-E	"
SW15	"	"	1 500	65 290 (29 620)	43 000 (19 500)	10.7 (17.2)	"	"	130.6	44' 8" (13 700)	4	1972	"	EMD12-645-E	"

*Weight shown in Short Tons

NORFOLK AND WESTERN RAILWAY COMPANY
8 North Jefferson Street, Roanoke, Virginia 24042

President and Chief Executive Officer: John P. Fishwick
Executive Vice-President: Robert B. Claytor
Senior Vice-President: Richard F. Dunlap
Vice-President, Finance: John R. Turbyfill
Vice-President, Merchandise Traffic: John R. McMichael
Vice-President, Coal and Ore Traffic: T. C. Hamill
Vice-President, Administration: Joseph R. Neikirk
Vice-President, Material Management: R. Alan Brogan
Secretary: Donald A. Middleton
Director, Public Relations and Advertising: Lewis M. Phelps
Chief Engineer: L. A. Durham, Jr
General Manager, Transportation: Leon Atkinson, Jr
General Manager, Motive Power and Equipment: H. L. Scott, Jr

The Norfolk and Western Railway, with a predecessor dating back to 1838, was organised under its present name in 1896, after another predecessor had opened the rich coal fields of western Virginia and southern West Virginia. By the early 1900s, it was a six-state system with a main line connecting Norfolk, Virginia and Cincinnati-Columbus, Ohio. The road has paid dividends on its common stock each year since 1901.

The first of all modern mergers between independent rail lines was effected 1 December 1959, when the Virginian Railway, also connecting the coal fields with Norfolk, became part of the NW.

A project which took over four years was realised on 16 October 1964, when the largest completed railroad consolidation in history became operative. The new 7 800 mile (12 550 km) 14-state NW system was created through merger with the Nickel Plate Road, lease and planned purchase of the Wabash Railroad, purchase of the Columbus-Sandusky line of the Pennsylvania Railroad, and acquisition of the Akron, Canton and Youngstown and the Pittsburgh and West Virginia roads. Operation of the NW system was integrated with headquarters in Roanoke, Virginia.

The new Jersey, Indiana and Illinois Railroad and the Lake Erie and Fort Wayne Railroad are also part of the NW System.

LINES AND TERRITORIES
The Norfolk and Western operates from Norfolk, Virginia and Buffalo, New York, in the east, through 14 states and one province of Canada, to St. Louis, Kansas City and Omaha, Nebraska, in the west. The NW system, which spans 7 659 miles (12 325 km) with a route length of 14 858 miles (23 910 km) serves the rich coal fields of West Virginia, southern Ohio and eastern Kentucky, as well as the industrial centres of Cleveland, Pittsburg, Chicago, Detroit, Columbus and Cincinnati.

FINANCIAL RESULTS
Railway operating revenues for 1977 totalled $1.2 million. Railway operating expenses grew to $919 million from the 1976 level of $845 million.

FREIGHT TRAFFIC
Revenue from hauling merchandise traffic in 1977 increased 7.2 per cent to $645.1 million from $601.6 million in 1976, despite a 3.2 per cent decline in merchandise tonnage during the year.

NW's major hauling merchandise, coal, is found in huge amounts throughout the region and the railroad is well equipped to move coal from mine to market. The NW's track structure is being constantly upgraded for coal traffic. From 1974-77 approximately $55 million has been invested to build 11 major spurs totalling 70.5 miles (approx 113 km) to reach new coal mines. Three additional lines are being built and others upgraded.

Rolling stock, as well as track, is needed to move coal. The company owns 53 000 open-top hopper cars and in 1977 improved its fleet by producing five new hoppers a day. Plans were announced in 1977 to acquire 200 new diesel locomotives over the next four years to keep the railroad fleet in top condition.

TOFC/COFC Ramps

Illinois	Iowa	Ohio	Virginia
Chicago (Calumet)	Des Moines	Bellevue	Bristol
Danville	**Michigan**	Brewster	Norfolk
Decatur	Adrian	Cincinnati	Roanoke
Peoria	Detroit	Cleveland	**Canada**
Indiana	**Missouri**	Columbus	Welland, Ont.
Fort Wayne	Kansas City	Lima	**North Carolina**
Lafayette	Moberly	Montpelier	Winston-Salem
Marion	St. Louis	Toledo	
Muncie	**New York**		
	Buffalo		

RICHMOND, FREDERICKSBURG AND POTOMAC
Broad Street Station, Richmond, Virginia 23220

President: Stuart Shumate
Vice-President, Administration: John J. Newbauer, Jr
General Superintendent Transportation: James D. Doswell
Chief Engineer: James C. Hobbs
Chief Mechanical Officer: Hartwell T. Rainey, Jr
General Traffic Manager: Rupert H. Rose

LINES AND TERRITORIES
The RF & P is an important "bridge", 113 miles *(182 km)* long from Washington DC in the north to Richmond, Virginia in the south.
At Washington it connects to the B & O and Penn Central (now part of Conrail), and at Richmond to the Seaboard Coast Line.

LOCOMOTIVES AND CARS
The Company has 40 diesel-electric locomotives—26 line haul and 14 shunting. Freight train car total is 1 708.

SEABOARD COAST LINE INDUSTRIES INC
The Family Lines System
500 Water Street, Jacksonville, Florida 32202

Chairman of the Board and Chief Executive Officer, Jacksonville, Fla: Prime F. Osborn
President Jacksonville, Fla: A. Paul Funkhouser
Executive Vice-President, Jacksonville, Fla: David C. Hastings
Vice-President, Management Information Services: James A. Bailey
Executive Vice-President, Law, Administration, Jacksonville, Fla: Philip M. Lanier
Vice-President and Treasurer, Richmond, Va: Leonard G. Anderson
Vice-President, Sales, Jacksonville, Fla: James D. Bozard
Vice-President, Operations, Jacksonville, Fla: James L. Williams
Assistant Vice-President, Passenger Traffic, Richmond, Va: R. L. Progner
Vice-President, Marketing, Jacksonville, Fla: James W. Hoeland
Senior Vice-President, Sales and Marketing, Jacksonville, Fla: Welborn E. Alexander Jr

1968 was the first full year of operation of this railroad, formed by merger of the Seaboard Air Line Railroad Company (with head office at Richmond, Virginia) and the Atlantic Coast Line Railroad Company (with head office at Jacksonville, Florida).
SCL maintains two general offices, with the Chairman of the Board at 3600 West Broad Street, Richmond, Virginia 23213 and the President at 500 Water Street, Jacksonville, Florida 32202.
SCL owns the Louisville and Nashville Railroad (into which the Monon was merged in July 1971); has a holding in the RF & P, and leases, equally with L & N, the Clinchfield and Georgia Railroads.
L & N continues to operate as a separate company. Operating results are consolidated, and reproduced under Seaboard Coast Line Railroad Company, including subsidiaries Clinchfield Railroad Company and Georgia Railroad Company.
Combining the SCL and L & N, with their subsidiary Rail Carriers, has created a system of some 16 300 miles (26 232 km), serving 13 states. Together they are known as The Family Lines.

LINES AND TERRITORIES
With 9 300 miles (14 966 km) of route, SCL constitutes the major railway system in Florida and in the coastal states to the north of Florida ie. Georgia, South and North Carolina, as well as Virginia and Alabama; and through the L & N lines to Tennessee, Kentucky, Indiana and Illinois (Chicago).
The Northern headquarters at Richmond, Virginia connect to the RF & P and the North East Corridor to Washington and New York.

FINANCIAL RESULTS
Total operating revenues for 1978 were $1 903 710 000 compared with $1 751 095 000 for 1977, an increase of 8.7 per cent. Net income for 1978 dropped to $676 700 000 from $162 356 000.

FREIGHT TRAFFIC
Revenue
(millions of dollars)

	1974	1975	1976	1977	1978
Coal	205.1	234.5	269.2	320.5	326.7
Phosphate and fertilisers	151.8	149.3	169.5	202.7	216.7
Chemicals	117.2	116.2	137.3	147.2	163.3
Paper and allied products	123.0	113.3	135.6	142.3	159.0
Forest products	101.3	89.3	114.5	128.3	142.5
Construction materials	115.8	101.7	112.6	127.7	140.0
Food, processed	108.5	110.8	120.0	128.1	130.8
Steel, metals and ores	94.5	78.3	83.4	89.1	102.7
Automotive	58.8	53.4	68.7	85.3	95.0
Grain and grain products	53.3	58.8	72.2	69.2	82.5

LOCOMOTIVES AND CARS
1980 capital expenditure of $329 million includes 183 new diesel locomotives costing $119 million of which 130 will be acquired for L & N and placed into service in the coal producing territory. Another $79 million will be used to buy 2 177 new freight cars for delivery during 1980.

TOFC/COFC PIGGYBACK
TOFC continued to achieve growth in both revenue and volume, topping the figures for 1977. Seaboard is the second largest mover of piggyback trailers and containers in the USA. This traffic increased 13.7 per cent to 651 000, while revenue grew 15.7 per cent to $141.4 million.

SCL Ramps
Alabama. Birmingham, Dothan, Elba, Enterprise, Montgomery.
Florida. Arcadia, Auburndale, Avon Park, Bartow, Bell, Bradenton, Brooksville, Clearwater, Clewiston, Dade City, Duda, Fort Lauderdale, Forest City, Fort Myers, Gainesville, Groveland, Haines City, High Springs, Homestead, Immokalee, Jacksonville, Jasper, Lakeland, Lake Wales, Leesburg, Live Oak, Miami, Ocala, Orlando, Oviedo, Palatka, Plant City, Plymouth, Pompano Beach, St. Petersburg, Sanford, Sarasota, Tallahassee, Tampa, Trenton, Umatilla, West Palm Beach, Winter Garden, Winter Haven, Yulee.
Georgia. Albany, Americus, Athens, Atlanta, Augusta, Bainbridge, Brunswick, Cedartown, Columbus, Cordele, Fitzgerald, Gainsville, Jesup, LaGrange, Macon, Manchester, Moultrie, Oglethorpe, Savannah, Thomasville, Tifton, Tucker, Valdosta, Vidalia, Waycross, Woodbine.
North Carolina. Aberdeen, Ahoskie, Charlotte, Durham, Fayetteville, Goldsboro, Greenville, Hamlet, Henderson, Jacksonville, Lumberton, Maxton, Raleigh, Rocky Mount, Roanoke Rapids, Smithfield, Wilmington, Wilson.
South Carolina. Anderson, Barnwell, Camden, Charleston, Chester, Columbia, Conway, Denmark, Estill, Florence, Georgetown, Greenville, Greenwood, Hampton, Inness, Lobeco, Orangeburg, Port Royal, Spartanburg, Stono, Sumter.
Virginia. Franklin, Jarratt, Portsmouth (Norfolk), Petersburg, Richmond, Suffolk.

L & N Ramps
Alabama. Anniston, Birmingham Bridgeport, Florence, Gadsden, Decatur, Huntsville, Mobile, Montgomery, Bylacanga, Tuscaloosa.
Florida. Chipley, Pensacola.
Georgia. Atlanta, Cartersville, Dalton, Ringgold, Tate.
Illinois. Chicago, Danville, Dalton, E. St. Louis.
Indiana. Bloomington, Crawfordsville, Evansville, Hammond (Chicago and District), Indianapolis, Lafayette, Terre Haute.
Kentucky. Bardstown, Bowling Green, Frankfort, Franklin, Glasgow, Hawesville (Stillman Yard), Hopkinsville, Lexington, Louisville, Owensboro, Paducah, Richmond, Williamsburg.
Louisianna. New Orleans.
Mississippi. Gulfport, Pascagoula.
Ohio. Cincinnati.
Tennessee. Alcoa, Athens, Bruceton, Calhoun, Chattanooga, Clarkesville, Columbia, Cookeville, Crossville, Fayetteville, Humboldt, Jackson, Knoxville, Lawrenceburg, Lebanon, Lewisburg, Lexington, Memphis, Morrison, Murfreesburg, Nashville, New Johnsonville, Oak Ridge, Old Hickory, Paris, Pulaski, Sparta, Springfield, Tallahoma.

SOO LINE RAILROAD
500 Line Building, PO Box 530, Minneapolis, Minnesota 55440

Executive:
President: Leonard H. Murray
Executive Vice-President: Charles H. Clay
Vice-President, Staff: Thomas M. Beckley
Vice-President and General Counsel: Fordyce W. Crouch
Vice-President, Traffic: Ray H. Smith
Vice-President, Accounting: Richard L. Murlowski

Operations and Maintenance:
General Manager, Transportation and Maintenance: Dennis M. Cavanaugh
Assistant Vice-President, Transportation Group: Gilbert A. Gillette
Assistant Vice-President, Maintenance Group: Lloyd L. Wasnick

Transportation Department:
General Superintendent: Clifford C. Leary
Director of Transportation, Budgets and Costs: Gerald F. O'Keefe
Director of Transportation Operations: Donald G. Foote

Director of Transportation Administration: F. Godin
Director of Transportation Equipment: Joseph D. Darling

Mechanical Department:
Chief Mechanical Officer: Thomas F. Kearney
Assistant to Chief Mechanical Officer: Wayne O. Ayers

Engineering Department:
Chief Engineer: Bert E. Pearson
Assistant Chief Engineer: Warren B. Peterson
Assistant Chief Engineer, Staff: Bernard R. Prusak
Assistant Chief Engineer, Bridges and Structures: Donald I. Kjellman
Assistant Chief Engineer, Signals and Communications: James H. Tone

FINANCIAL RESULTS
1977 was a record year both for revenues and net income. Revenues reached $217.3 million, a rise of 15 per cent, and net income rose to $18.8 million.
Revenues increased in most major groups of commodities transported. The greatest increase was in the chemical group where the increase was $9.6 million or 25 per cent. Revenues from farm products were higher by $7.1 million or 22 per cent.

Potash produced more revenues than any other commodity, amounting to 32.4 million, up 16 per cent on 1976. Lumber revenues increased 4.3 million reflecting a high level of home construction. Revenue derived from pulpwood and woodchips decreased one per cent while those from scrap iron declined 27 per cent.
Total railway operating expenses increased $19 million due to increased traffic volume and an expanded maintenance programme.

MAINTENANCE OF TRACK AND EQUIPMENT
A substantial programme of track maintenance and improvement was accomplished during 1977. Improvements included the installation of 60 miles (96 km) of new and 38 miles (61 km) of second-hand continuous welded rail; 516 000 yds³ of crushed rock ballast and 315 000 new sleepers. Total expenditures for maintenance of equipment increased $4.4, an increase of 19 per cent over the previous year.

CAPITAL AND OTHER IMPROVEMENT PROGRAMMES
Soo added 400 new freight cars and seven new locomotives to its fleet during 1977 at a cost of approximately $15 million. Equipment acquired during 1978 totalled around $17 million. This included 560 freight cars and three new locomotives. In the 1978 deliveries were 350 100-ton covered hopper cars for bulk commodity shipments.

During 1978 Soo took delivery of nine type GP-38-2 diesel-electric locomotives from General Motors rated at 2 000hp

SOUTHERN RAILWAY SYSTEM
920 15th Street, NW, Washington, DC 20013

Chairman of the Board and Chief Executive: L. S. Crane
Senior Vice-President, Marketing: G. G. Kreyling
Executive Vice-President, Administration: G. S. Paul
President: H. H. Hall
Executive Vice-President, Law and Accounting: A. B. McKinnon

Marketing and Planning:
Assistant Vice-President, Market Management: E. A. Evers
Vice-President, Sales: E. L. Dearhart
Assistant Vice-President, Agri-Business Service: J. P. Duncan, Jr
Assistant Vice-President, Industrial Development: R. S. Geer
Assistant Vice-President, Corporate Planning: P. D. Dieffenbach
General Manager, Services Industries: N. G. Heller

The consolidated figures for Southern Railway Company include many subsidiaries. There are four class 1 subsidiary railroads: Alabama Great Southern; Cincinnati, New Orleans and Texas Pacific; Norfolk Southern; Georgia Southern and Florida; and Central of Georgia. There are several Class II railroads and terminals and other companies—railroads, terminals, motor transport, pipelines and real estates.

LINES AND TERRITORY
The Southern Railways operates 10 259 miles (16 510 km) of route and a total track length of 17 282 miles (27 813 km).
Northern limits are St. Louis, Cincinnati, and Washington, and operation is mainly in the States of Kentucky, Tennessee, Virginia, North Carolina, South Carolina, Alabama and Georgia.

COMPOSITION OF THE SYSTEM
The Southejn Railway system comprises the following companies:—
Class I
  The Alabama Great Southern Railroad Company
  Central of Georgia Railroad Company
  The Cincinnati, New Orleans and Texas Pacific Railway Company
  Georgia Southern and Florida Railway Company
  Norfolk Southern Railway Company

Class II
  Atlantic and East Carolina Railway Company
  Birmingham Terminal Company (67%)
  Camp Lejeune Railroad Company
  The Georgia Northern Railway Company
  Interstate Railroad Company
  Live Oak, Perry and South Georgia Railway Company
  Louisiana Southern Railway Company
  New Orleans Terminal Company
  St. Johns River Terminal Company
  State University Railroad Company (54%)
  Tennessee, Alabama & Georgia Railway Company
  Tennessee Railway Company

FINANCIAL RESULTS
Income for 1978 reached $127.3 million. Railroad expenses were $88.5 million.

CAPITAL EXPENDITURE
Southern spent $252 million on new freight cars and locomotives in 1978. During 1979 $285 was budgeted for capital expenditure, of which $200 million will be spent on new locomotives and cars.

LOCOMOTIVES AND CARS
Total Southern System locomotive fleet at the end of 1977 consisted of 1 159 line haul diesel-electric locomotives and 191 switchers: a total of 1 350 units. The railroad placed in service 71 new diesel locomotives in 1977, and has 75 762 freight train cars and 129 passenger cars.

TOFC/COFC
Intermodal showed a sharp increase in 1978. Volume was up by almost 10 per cent and reserves by 19 per cent. Piggyback share of total freight revenues increased from 6.3 to 6.8 per cent.
During 1978 seven new tracks were added to the piggyback yard at Inman Yard in Atlanta; the tracks now number 19. Some 1 202 new trailers were added to Southern's intermodal equipment fleet, bringing the total number owned and leased to 7 850.

SOUTHERN PACIFIC COMPANY
Southern Pacific Building
One Market Plaza, San Francisco, California 94105

Chairman, President and Chief Executive Officer: B. F. Biaggini
***President, Southern Pacific Transportation Co:** A. C. Furth
Executive Vice-President F. E. Kriebel
Executive Vice-President-Finance: R. J. McLean
***Vice-President: Traffic:** R. L. King
***Vice-President, Operations:** A. D. DeMoss
***Vice-President, Management Services:** J. W. Germany
Vice-President and Controller: D. L. Praeger

*Officers of Southern Pacific Transportation Company only.

LINES AND TERRITORY
Southern Pacific operates 13 209 miles *(21 547 km)* of railway route in the west and southwest and is one of the largest systems in the USA. Additional main track is 1 057 miles *(1 690 km)*; yards and sidings 6 641 miles *(10 674 km)* for a total of 20 988 miles *(33 921 km)* of single track.
Western Lines run from San Francisco north to Portland, Oregon, east to Ogden, Utah, and south to Los Angeles.
From Los Angeles the line runs east, roughly parallel to the Mexican border, through Phoenix and El Paso where it connects to a line northeast to Tucumcari in New Mexico making connections to Kansas City and Chicago. East from El Paso the line—known as the Sunset Route—continues to Galveston, New Orleans and to Fort Worth and Dallas—which are also important traffic feed points.
The Northwestern Pacific Railroad Company is operated as part of the overall Southern Pacific Organisation.
SP's trucking subsidiaries provude common carrier services to 1 800 western and southwestern communities over a 28 392-mile *(45 692 km)*, 10-state route system.
Southern Pacific Pipe Lines, Inc distributes refined petroleum products over 2 480 miles *(3 991 km)* of pipeline in Oregon, Nevada, Central and Northern California, and along the southwestern border of the USA from California to Texas.

DIVERSIFICATION
Southern Pacific Company has pursued a policy of diversification for many years. In addition to holdings in other railways, it owns trucking companies, and a marine transport company which handles containerised freight shipments at the many ports it serves; is active as an air freight forwarder; owns pipelines distributing petroleum products in California, Nevada and Arizona from sources in Texas and California. SP owns land (over 3 million acres); extensive mineral and oil rights; timber lands; and real estate including terminal buildings, and plans to intensify development of its non-railway real-estate.

Southern Pacific rail gang laying track
The railroad operates 13 389 miles (21 547 km) of route in west and southwest USA.

It is active in leasing through its wholly-owned subsidiary Banker's Leasing Corporation, and operates a 275 mile *(443 km)* coal slurry pipeline to bring coal from Arizona to a steam-powered electric plant in Nevada.

FINANCIAL

Total Southern Pacific 1978 operating revenues were $228 million, up from $2.09 million in 1977. Net income during 1978 was $116.2 million compared with the 1973 figure of $118.1 million.

FREIGHT TRAFFIC

Freight revenue-tonnes handled were 125 460 000, down from 126 108 000 in 1977; tonne-miles totalled 78 686 779 000, up from 76 410 280 000. Freight revenues of Southern Pacific Transportation Company and its railroad subsidiaries totalled $1 918 million in 1978 compared with $1 795 million the previous year. Transportation equipment, metal products, miscellaneous manufactures and processed food products shipments showed revenue gains in 1978. Paper product shipments also rose despite an extended strike, which closed many of the mills served by SP. Farm product shipments registered a steep decline for the year, the result of reduced sugar beet production and the continued loss of fresh fruit and vegetable freight business to unregulated operators. In May 1979 the Interstate Commerce Commission deregulated the rail transportation of fresh fruit and vegetables. During the first three months of deregulation SP carried 6 000 carloads of fresh produce, an increase of 30 per cent over the same period in 1978.

PASSENGER TRAFFIC

Amtrak operates all inter-city passenger services in Southern Pacific territory. SP maintains commuter service between San Francisco and San Jose, California.

LOCOMOTIVES AND CARS

Railway equipment owned or leased at 31 December 1978 consisted of 2 422 diesel locomotives, 82 932 freight cars; 84 passenger train cars and 2 323 company service units and cabooses.

New equipment acquired during 1978—
Freight cars

Box	300
Flat	100
Gondola	88
Open top hoppers	294
Auto rack	70
Diesel locmotive units	118

TOFC/COFC PIGGYBACK

Southern Pacific's piggyback volume in 1978 increased to a record level of 380 000 units. Increases came from both domestic and minibridge traffic.

LOADING RAMPS

Loading ramps are located at the following points on the Southern Pacific:
Austin, Tex.; Avondale, La.; Bakersfield, Ca.; Beaumont, Tex.; Brooklyn, Ore.; Brownsville, Tex.; Chico, Ca.; Corpus Christi, Tex.; Dallas, Tex.; Edinburg, Tex.; El Centro, Ca.; El Paso, Tex.; Eugene, Ore.; Ft. Worth, Tex.; Fresno, Ca.; Gregory, Tex.; Guadalupe, Ca.; Hearne, Tex.; Houston, Tex.; Lafayette, La.; Lake Charles, La.; Los Angeles, Ca.; Lufkin, Tex.; Nogales, Ariz.; Oakland, Ca.; Ogden, Utah; Oxnard, Ca.; Phoenix, Ariz.; Redding, Ca.; Roseville, Ca.; Salem, Ore.; Salinas, Ca.; San Antonio, Ca.; San Diego, Ca.; San Francisco, Ca.; San Jose, Ca.; Shreveport, La.; Sparks, Nev.; Stockton, Ca.; Tuscon, Ariz.; Victoria, Tex.; Waco, Tex.; Yuma, Ariz.
Additional loading ramps are located on SP subsidiary, St. Louis Southwestern Railway Co:
Arkansas: Brinkley, Camden, Jonesboro, North Little Rock, Pine Bluff.
Illinois: East St. Louis.
Louisiana: Shreveport.
Tennessee: Memphis.
Texas: Corsicana, Dallas, Fort Worth, Lufkin, Texarkana, Tyler, Waco.

LIFTING EQUIPMENT

Piggypacker units are located at San Francisco (1), Oakland (1), Los Angeles (3), Phoenix (1), Houston (3), and St. Louis (2). Overhead cranes are in use at Oakland (2), Los Angeles (2), Dallas (1), New Orleans (2), Houston (2).

CONTAINERS

Containers move daily in expedited Piggyback trains and trans-continental manifest trains on 85 ft *(25.9 m)* and 89 ft *(27.1 m)* cars.
The great majority of containers in rail-water carrier intermodal service, to and from points in the USA, are furnished by water carriers or container leasing companies on a per diem charge basis.

CONTAINER TERMINALS

Oakland, Ca.; San Francisco, Ca.; Los Angeles, Ca.; Houston, Texas; New Orleans, La.; Dallas, Texas; St. Louis, Mo.; Phoenix, Ariz.
These connect with all US and foreign flag ocean carriers calling at Pacific Coast and Gulf Ports. They participate in routes with all transcontinental rail carriers.

SCHEDULED NATIONAL SERVICES

Between USA and Hawaii through Pacific Coast ports.

SCHEDULED INTERNATIONAL SERVICES

Between USA and Japan, Hong Kong, Australia, Singapore and other Far Eastern ports as well as Europe.
Land-bridge movement—From Far East ports to Pacific Coast thence rail to Atlantic Coast and by ship to Europe as well as to Gulf points for destination delivery or further ship movement to Europe.

Southern Pacific freight train at Ogden, Utah; interchange with Union Pacific for east-bound traffic

Piggy Packers off-loading Southern Pacific trailers

Southern Pacific's TOFC/COFC -iggyback operations at Oakland, California

ST. LOUIS—SAN FRANCISCO RAILWAY COMPANY
906 Olive Street, St. Louis, Missouri 63101

Chairman of Board and President: R. C. Grayson
Senior Vice-President, Marketing: E. D. Grinnell
Senior Vice-President, Operations: W. F. Thompson
Vice-President, Administration: P. E. Odom
Assistant Vice-President, Intermodal Services: L. A. Thomas
General Manager: B. A. Davidson
Chief Engineer: G. E. Warfel
Chief Mechanical Officer, Equipment: R. L. Coulter
Chief Mechanical Officer, Motive Power: O. H. Summers

LINES AND TERRITORIES

The "Frisco" operates 4 657 miles *(7 800 km)* of route in the midwestern and southern states, from Kansas City and St. Louis in the north to Dallas, Texas; Mobile, Alabama; and Pensacola, Florida in the south.
Its central, in-between location makes it an important link in trans-continental and north-south routing.

FINANCIAL RESULTS

1978 total operating revenues increased to $395 521 177 from $356 848 336 in 1977.

FREIGHT TRAFFIC

Average ton-miles for 1978 was 1 688 up on the previous year's figure of 1 558.
Revenue ton-miles were 16 463 236 000 for 1978 (15 025 018 000 1977).

LOCOMOTIVES

At 31 December 1978, Frisco owned 302 road locomotive units and 92 switchers for a total of 394 units.

FREIGHT CARS

At 31 December 1978 Frisco owned or leased 18 395 freight cars.

CAPITAL EXPENDITURE

Since 1973, the Frisco has been spending in the neighbourhood of $36.4 million annually on capital improvements, including major leasing. In 1977, capital expenditures with major leasing totalled $59.2 million, reflecting not only the need for modern equipment and facilities but also the continued inflationary effect of constantly escalating unit costs.
Included in Frisco's 1977 capital spending programme was the acquisition of 29 locomotives and 1 100 freight cars. All of the locomotives were purchased under Conditional Sale Agreements.
Frisco's 1977 capital expenditures included $13.2 million for roadway and structures and $2.2 million for other additions and improvements to its property.

OTHER DEVELOPMENTS

To meet the expanding Company demand for electronic technology, the Frisco has completed a 1 210-mile microwave system to replace the telephone circuits it previously leased from the Bell System. As greater capacity becomes necessary, the present 300-voice channel capacity can be expanded to as many as 600 channels.

Presently, the microwave system consists of 56 sites, with towers ranging in height from 70 ft *(21.3 m)* at Valley Park, Missouri, to a 460-ft *(140.2 m)* tower at Turrell,

Arkansas. Microwave signals are received and transmitted from tower to tower via an electromagnetic beam. Apart from voice transmission, the system also transmits important data to and from the Frisco's computer center at Springfield, Missouri, and is an important adjunct to the Centralised Traffic Control system used in monitoring and directing the movement of trains over the railroad. The microwave system also permits direct dialling to many of its more important wayside stations and affords two-way radio communications between dispatchers and train crews.

UNION PACIFIC CORPORATION
345 Park Avenue, New York, NY 10022

Chairman, Board of Directors, and Chief Executive Officer: Frank E. Barnett
President: James H. Evans
Chairman of the Executive Committee: E. T. Gerry
Executive Vice-President: W. S. Cook
Vice-President-Finance: William F. Surette

In 1969 a new holding company was formed, the Union Pacific Corporation. The Union Pacific Railroad Company is now a corporate subsidiary of the Corporation.

In 1971 the basic business activities of the parent Corporation were realigned into operating groups;

Transportation
Union Pacific Railroad Company, 1416 Dodge Street, Omaha, Nebraska 68179

Oil and Gas
Champlin Petroleum Company, 5301 Camp Bowie Blvd., Fort Worth, Texas 76107.

Land
Upland Industries Corporation, 110 North Fourteenth St., Omaha, Nebraska 68102.

Coal and other minerals
Rocky Mountain Energy Company, 4704 Harlan Street, Denver, Colorado 80212.

UNION PACIFIC RAILROAD COMPANY
1416 Dodge Street, Omaha, Nebr 68179

President: John C. Kenefick
Vice-President, Operation: Robert L. Richmond
Vice-President, Traffic: Walter P. Barrett
Vice-President, Executive Department: C. Howard Burnett
Controller: John P. Deasey
Vice-President, Finance and Administration: T. B. Graves Jr

LINES AND TERRITORIES
The Union Pacific operates an average 9 700 miles *(15 253 km)* of route.
The system extends from Council Bluffs, Iowa and Kansas City, Missouri in the east, to the Pacific Coast ports including Portland, Oregon, Vancouver, Longview, Tacoma and Seattle, Washington, Los Angeles Harbor and Long Beach, California.
The Union Pacific has a reciprocal arrangement with other railroads to avoid breaking up trains and switching at intermediate points.
Union Pacific owns 1 500 dry trailers of various types plus several hundred of various types under lease. Flat cars of 89 ft (27.1 m) are used for transportation of these vehicles.

FINANCIAL
Union Pacific Railroad's 1978 income increased 21 per cent to $140.1 million, which is higher than that for 1977.

FREIGHT OPERATIONS
Union Pacific's revenue tonne-miles reached 68.2, up 12 per cent over 1977. The length of Union Pacific's average haul increased to 689 miles (1108.8 km), compared to 659 miles (1060.6 km) in 1977. The railload's operating ratio was 83.1 compared to 83.4 in 1977.

LOCOMOTIVES AND CARS
During 1978 Union Pacific continued to upgrade its rail fleet, allocating $179.2 for new equipment. Of this $74.9 million was spent on high-speed locomotives. The rail load also purchased 1 566 freight cars of which 1 400 are covered hoppers designed to carry grain, soda ash and other bulk commodities. In addition Union Pacific constructed 619 and rebuilt 785 cars in its shops in Omaha and Albina, Oregon.

OTHER DEVELOPMENTS
The railroad programmed $246.7 million for capital improvements in 1977, up more than $91 million from the 1976 figure of $155.1 million.
The programme includes a previously announced $160 million for new rolling stock consisting of 90 locomotives, 3 079 freight cars, 200 ballast cars and 315 auto racks; plus another $10 million for miscellaneous work equipment and $76 million for road and fixed plant improvements.
Major items in UP's road and fixed plant schedule for 1977 included laying 350 miles *(563.2 km)* of new continuous welded rail, installation of 875 000 cross ties, construction of 115 miles *(185 km)* of centralised traffic control signalling on mainline trackage and continued construction of a major new 32-track automated freight classification yard at Hinkle, Oregon.

TOFC/COFC PIGGYBACK
In 1976, Union Pacific ran through-trains, connecting with nine different railroads, and completed more than 7 000 separate trips to points throughout the country. The Railroad scheduled additional daily, high-speed, all-van trains between Midwest gateway cities and West Coast points.
The Railroad was successful in increasing its trailer and container traffic to an all-time high in 1976. It began to handle an estimated 40 000 trailer-loads of mail a year for the US Postal Service under a four-year agreement. This traffic is being hauled between bulk mail centres in Chicago, Denver, Oakland, Seattle and Los Angeles.
Union Pacific continued to increase its shipments of United Parcel Service trailers throughout its territory. During 1976, the Railroad handled several thousand United Parcel trailers by special high-speed service from Chicago to Denver, Salt Lake City and Portland; and from Los Angeles and Salt Lake City to Denver.

3 000 hp GE 430-C, UP 2852 and two helpers with westbound trains 25 miles (40.2 km) west of Salina, Kansas

Union Pacific bay window caboose, and the first to go into service

WESTERN PACIFIC RAILROAD
526 Mission Street, San Francisco, California 94105

President: R. G. Flannery
Chairman of the Board: Alfred E. Perlman
Chairman of the Executive Committee: Howard E. Newman
Vice-President, Operations: Robert C. Marquis
Vice-President, Marketing: R. G. Meldahl
Vice-President, Finance: Richard W. Stumbo, Jr
Vice-President, Administration: F. A. Tegeler

LINES AND TERRITORIES
Twenty-five track miles *(40.2 km)* of rail have been renewed with heavier rail. A programme of upgrading bridges to handle heavier loadings, was continued. Work also progressed on reinforcing of steel bridges.
Western Pacific is a wholly owned subsidiary of Western Pacific Industries Inc. It operates in the Western portion of the USA, providing freight service from the San Francisco Bay area through California and Nevada to Salt Lake City, Utah. The railroad also provides service North and South between Bay Area and the Oregon Line.
During 1977/78 the Company acquired 200 box cars and 20 diesel-electric locomotive units.

LOCOMOTIVES AND CARS
WP locomotive fleet consists of 141 units of road power (EMD and GE) and 17 switchers.
Delivery was taken during 1975 on 200 new insulated box cars equipped with air bag bulkheads for damage free movement of canned goods, beverages and other packaged products; 65 new 100-ton open hopper cars for crude barites; 35 100-ton covered hopper cars for ground barites, potash, rice and grain; 17 high cube damage free box cars for appliances and 10 enclosed tri-level "safe pak" cars for automobiles.

OTHER DEVELOPMENTS
Arrangements were concluded with Burlington Northern and Canadian Pacific for establishment early in 1976 of new routes via Bieber to and from Western Canada which will open up significant new traffic potenzials for Western Pacific. A sales programme aimed at hauling materials used in constructing the Alaska Pipeline was implemented and produced new reenue. Market development and planning efforts were continued to promote future movements of bulk commodities.
The Safety Programme in 1975 showed further improvements. Total personal injuries were 398, down 25 per cent from 533 in 1974.
Cathode Ray Tubes were placed in service in the Customer Service Center in San Francisco in December 1975 providing instantaneous car and train inquiry response from the newly implemented Advanced Transportation System. Twenty-one track

miles of new and reconditioned rail and 85 000 new mainline hardwood ties were installed in continuance of our improvement programme. Street and highway grade crossing protection was newly installed or improved at 18 locations.

A "one-spot" car repair facility was constructed at Stockton. This facility features a roof over two tracks, three "in floor" hydraulic jacks, two sets of jib cranes for truck repairs and centrally located material racks, all of which will double the productivity of the repair facility. New office facilities were built at the Milpitas repair track facilities along with a new wheel storage area. An air compressor was also installed for the yard air system. A new wheel crane was built at the Sacramento Shops including four new wheel storage tracks, improving handling and efficiency.

TOFC/COFC PIGGYBACK

TOFC/COFC revenue increased by seven per cent.

Intermodal (COFC and TOFC) services were expanded and improved. The Intermodal and International Sales Group was restructured to provide the resources for specific concentration on this important growing segment of the business.

New Western Pacific U23B diesel locomotive

A WP freight heads east behind a new GE U23B diesel locomotive as a Bay Area Rapid Transit (BART) commuter train crosses WP's mainline on elevated tracks near San Leandro, California.

ABERDEEN & ROCKFISH RAILROAD CO

PO Box 917, Aberdeen, North Carolina 28315

President: W. Formyduval
Vice-President: R. Veasey
Secretary: D. C. Russell
Vice-President, Traffic: W. F. Hilliard
Vice-President, Engineering, Construction, Roadway & Equipment: Charles Monroe

47 route miles *(75.6 km)*; 3 locomotives; 1 freight car.

THE AKRON, CANTON AND YOUNGSTOWN RAILROAD COMPANY

8 N. Jefferson St, Roanoke, Virginia 24011

President and Chief Executive Officer: J. L. Cowan
Comptroller and Secretary: D. K. Heidish
Traffic Manager: C. Engelo

171 route miles *(275.2 km)*; 16 locomotives.

ALIQUIPPA AND SOUTHERN RAILROAD CO

PO Box 280, Aliquippa, Pennsylvania 15001

General Superintendent: T. T. Deyak
Superintendent, Transportation: P. O. Wynkoop
Superintendent, M/W & Engineering: R. F. Duffy

48 route miles *(77.2 km)*; 19 locomotives; 891 freight cars.

ANN ARBOR RAILROAD CO

One Parkland Blvd, Dearborn, Michigan 48126

Chairman, President: V. M. Malanaphy
Vice-President and General Counsel: C. W. Chapman
Vice-President, Operations: A. C. Robinson
Vice-President and General Manager: A. J. Hogg

393 route miles *(632.5 km)*; 15 locomotives; 496 freight cars and 69 miscellaneous.

THE APACHE RAILWAY COMPANY

PO Box E, Snowflake, Arizona 85937

President and Chief Executive: Flake Willis
Vice-President: P. C. Gaffney
Manager-Purchases and Equipment: D. M. Ramsey

84 route miles *(135.2 km)*; 8 locomotives; 613 freight cars.

APALACHICOLA NORTHERN RAILROAD CO

803 Florida National Bank Building, Jacksonville, Florida 32201

President: E. Ball
Vice-President: B. R. Gibson
Superintendent and General Traffic Manager: R. H. Ellzey

96 route miles *(154.5 km)*; 11 locomotives; 106 freight cars.

ASHLEY, DREW AND NORTHERN RAILWAY COMPANY

PO Box 757, Crossett, Arkansas 71635

President: S. R. Tedder
Vice-President, Operations: P. H. Schueth
Controller and Auditor: D. W. Smith
Superintendent: J. H. Richards

41 route miles *(66.1 km)*; 7 locomotives.

ATLANTA AND ST. ANDREWS BAY

514 E. Main St, Dothan, Alabama 36302

Chairman and President: A. V. Hooks
Vice-President Operations: J. W. Cunningham
Chief Traffic Officer: Q. D. Bruner
General Superintendant Chief Engineer: D. R. Davis
Chief Mechanical Officer: T. L. Edwards

88 route miles *(141.6 km)*; 13 locomotives; 734 freight cars.

BALTIMORE & EASTERN RAILROAD CO

6 Penn Center, Philadelphia, Pennsylvania 19104

President: A. M. Schofield
Vice-President: E. L. Claypole
Vice-President: F. J. Gasparini

73 route miles *(117.5 km)*.

BALTIMORE & OHIO CHICAGO TERMINAL RAILROAD

2 N Charles St, Baltimore, Maryland 21201

President: H. T. Watkins
Executive Vice-Presidents: J. T. Ford
                                          J. T. Collinson
Vice-Presidents: R. W. Donnem
                          J. P. Ganley
                          R. C. McGowan
Chief Engineer: J. W. Brent.

62 route miles *(100.1 km)*.

BANGOR AND AROOSTOOK RAILROAD COMPANY

Northern Maine Junction Park, R.R.2, Bangor, Maine 04401

Chairman of the Executive Committee and Chief Executive Officer:
   Frederick C. Dumaine
Chairman: Frederick C. Dumaine
President: W. E. Travis
Vice-President, Operations: L. W. Littlefield
Vice-President and General Counsel: W. M. Houston
Vice-President, Marketing: H. L. Cousins, Jr
Vice-President Finance: O. H. Bridgham
Assistant Vice-President, Operating Transportation: R. P. Groves
Manager, Highway Division: S. F. Corey
General Freight Traffic Manager: H. G. Goodness
Chief Mechanical Officer: H. W. Hanson
Chief Engineer: V. J. Welch

503 route miles *(810 km)*; 45 locomotives; 3 865 freight cars; 19 containers.

BELFAST AND MOOSEHEAD LAKE RAILROAD
11 Water St, Belfast, Maine 04915

President: H. H. Hutchings Jr
Vice-President: James F. Murphy
Master Mechanic: Gerard Simoneau

33 route miles *(53.1 km)*; 4 locomotives; 4 freight cars; 1 snow plough.

BELT RAILWAY COMPANY OF CHICAGO
6900 South Central Ave, Chicago, Illinois 60638

President and General Manager: R. E. Dowdy
Vice-President and Controller: R. G. Rubino
Chief Engineer: A. B. Hillman
Superintendent of Transportation Department: J. Overbey
Chief of Motive Power and Purchasing Agent: K. H. Smith

The Belt Railway Company of Chicago was built by the Chicago and Western Indiana Railroad as the Belt Division of the C & WI under a separate charter. The purpose of the Belt Line was to intersect and connect all Chicago trunk lines for interchange of traffic. Construction of the Belt Division was completed in 1883.
The Belt Railway Company at Clearing built and utilises one of the largest hump yards in the world for classification of freight traffic. Clearing Yard has a working capacity of 12 600 cars and has the ability to hump four trains simultaneously during classification. The principle functions of the Belt Railway are to:
1. Provide classification and interchange of freight cars for its twelve owners and for other non-owner roads. In connection with this classification the Belt provides blocked train service for the benefit of many of its owners in connection with their run through train operations.
2. Provide excellent location and switching service for over 325 industries, giving industries access to all Chicago truck lines for movement of their freight.

27 route miles *(43.5 km)*; 48 diesel-electric locomotives; 29 cabooses, maintenance and work equipment cars.

BESSEMER AND LAKE ERIE RAILROAD COMPANY
Gateway 4, 600 Grant St, PO Box 536, Pittsburgh, Pennsylvania 15230

President: M. S. Toon
Vice-President: R. D. Lake
Vice-President, Finance: V. W. Kraetsch
Superintendent, Transportation: J. A. Magner, Jr
Chief Engineer: M. Rougas

221 route miles *(356.1 km)*; 66 locomotives; 8 579 freight cars.

BIRMINGHAM SOUTHERN RAILROAD CO
PO Box 579, Fairfield, Alabama 35064

President: C. D. Cotten
Vice-President: G. W. Parker
Superintendent, Transportation: J. W. Greene

89 route miles *(143.2 km)*; 17 locomotives; 1 003 freight cars.

BUTTE, ANACONDA AND PACIFIC RAILROAD COMPANY
Box 1421, 300 West Commercial Ave, Anaconda, Montana 59711

President: L. V. Kelly
Vice-President: G. W. Parker
Superintendent of M.W. & S.: J. F. Young
Superintendent of Transportation: J. W. Greene
Material Controls Supervisor: E. J. Hamill

56 route miles *(90.1 km)*; 8 locomotives; 750 freight cars.

CALIFORNIA WESTERN RAILROAD
Foot of Laurel St, Fort Bragg, California 95437

President: R. H. Schwarz
Vice-President, and General Manager: F. H. Sturges Jr
Assistant General Manager and Auditor: R. A. Regalia
Roadmaster: Vernon Petrick
Superintendent, Transportation: L. M. Weller
Traffic Manager: Henry A. Foltz

40 route miles *(64.4 km)*; 6 locomotives; 2 railcars-diesel; 8 passenger train coaches.

CAMAS PRAIRIE RAILROAD CO
13th & Main Streets, PO Box 1166, Lewiston, Idaho 83501

President: T. P. Rogers
Vice-President: J. W. Wicks
Manager: J. H. Harwood

256.7 route miles *(413.6 km)*; 20 locomotives.

The Camas Prairie railroad is solely an operating company for the Union Pacific and Burlington Northern railroads.

CEDAR RAPIDS AND IOWA CITY RAILWAY CO
PO Box 351, Cedar Rapids, Iowa 52406

President and General Manager: Duane Arnold
Vice-President and Secretary: J. B. Rehnstrom
General Superintendent: O. R. Woods

27 route miles *(43.5 km)*; 7 locomotives; 47 freight cars.

CENTRAL OF GEORGIA RAILROAD CO
99 Spring Street, Atlanta, Georgia 30303

Chairman and Chief Executive Officer: W. G. Claytor, Jr
President: R. E. Franklin
Vice-President, Operating: L. S. Crane

2 207 route miles *(3 551.8 km)*; 132 locomotives; 5 606 freight cars.

THE CENTRAL RAILROAD COMPANY OF NEW JERSEY
1100 Raymond Blvd, Newark, New Jersey 07102

Trustee: R. D. Timpany

CENTRAL ROMANA RAILROAD
Central Romana, La Romana, Dominican Republic

President: A. L. Carta
President and General Manager: Dr. T. Rossell

233 route miles *(375.1 km)*; 17 locomotives; 1 005 freight cars.

CHICAGO AND ILLINOIS MIDLAND RAILWAY CO
PO Box 139, Springfield, Illinois 62705

President: Carl D. Forth
Vice-President and General Manager: William G. Harvey
Assistant Secretary: Robert Bresemann
Superintendent: A. S. Alstott
Chief Engineer: R. E. Pearson

121 route miles *(194.7 km)*; 21 locomotives; 837 freight cars.

CHICAGO AND NORTH WESTERN TRANSPORTATION CO
400 West Madison Street, Chicago, Illinois 60606

President and Chief Executive Officer: J. R. Wolfe
Vice-President, Administration: R. W. Russell
Vice-President, Operations: J. A. Zito

9 184 route miles *(14 780 km)*; 915 diesel locomotives; 33 657 freight cars.

CHICAGO ROCK ISLAND AND PACIFIC RAILROAD
332 South Michigan Avenue, Chicago, Illinois 60604

Trustee: William M. Gibbons

7 361 route miles *(11 846.4 km)*; 631 diesel-electric locomotives; 25 293 freight cars.

CHICAGO SOUTH SHORE AND SOUTH BEND RAILROAD (ELECTRIC)
Carroll Avenue, Michigan City, Indiana 46360

President and General Manager: A. W. Dudley
Director Freight Sales and Services: G. F. Woods
Comptroller: B. G. Lawler
Superintendent of Transportation: R. D. Shipley
Chief Engineer: C. F. Mulrenan

75 route miles *(121 km)*; 3 electric locomotives; 8 diesel locomotives; 48 electric motor cars; 60 freight cars.

CINCINNATI UNION TERMINAL

President: T. L. Hintz
Vice-President: R. B. Hasselmann
Manager: G. S. Gray

45 route miles *(72.4 km)*; 2 locomotives.

CLINCHFIELD RAILROAD CO
229 Nolichucky Ave, Erwin, Tennessee 37650

General Manager: J. W. Thomas
Assistant General Manager: H. J. May
Chief Mechanical Officer: P. O. Likens
Chief Engineer: J. A. Goforth

275 route miles *(442.5 km)*; 96 locomotives; 6 134 freight cars.

COLORADO AND SOUTHERN RAILWAY CO
1405 Curtis St, Denver, Colorado 80202

President: George F. Difiel
Vice-President, Operations: John H. Hertog

695 route miles *(1 118.5 km)*; 95 locomotives; 2 910 freight cars.

THE CORINTH AND COUNCE RAILROAD CO
Highway 57, PO Box 128, Counce, Tennessee 38326

President: C. W. Byrd
Vice-President: W. C. Wells, III
Transportation Co-ordinator: A. A. Mann

26 route miles *(41.8 km)*; 3 diesel-electric locomotives; 437 freight cars.
Connects at Corinth, Mississippi with ICG and SR.

COLUMBIA, NEWBERRY & LAURENS RAILROAD CO
500 Water St, Jacksonville, Florida 32202

President: P. F. Osborn
Chairman: W. T. Rice
Executive Vice-President: D. C. Hastings
Vice-President and General Manager: James L. Williams

75 route miles (120.7 km); 5 locomotives.

COLUMBUS AND GREENVILLE RAILWAY CO
PO Box 591, Columbus, Mississippi 39701

President: H. L. Morrison
Vice-President and General Counsel: R. C. Stovall, Jr.
Vice-President, Traffic and Assistant to the President: J. B. Swanzey
Traffic Manager: Donald Z. Woolbright
General Manager: C. A. Arnett
Superintendent, Motive Power and Equipment: W. A. Trayler, Jr

168 route miles (270.4 km); 10 locomotives; 229 freight cars.

DETROIT, TOLEDO AND IRONTON RAILROAD CO
One Parkland Blvd, Dearborn, Michigan 48126

President: K. P. Shoemaker
Vice-President, Marketing: M. J. Barron
Vice-President, Operations: A. C. Robinson
Vice-President, Finance: R. Guregian
Director, Multi-Level and Trailerferry Service: M. J. Newbourne
Superintendent: J. E. Schlosser

476 route miles (766 km); 74 locomotives; 4 130 freight cars.

DULUTH, MISSABE AND IRON RANGE RAILWAY COMPANY
Missabe Building, Duluth, Minnesota 55802

President: M. S. Toon
Vice-President and General Manager: D. B. Shank
General Superintendent: M. G. Alderink
Vice-President, Finance: V. W. Kraetsch
Manager, Freight Revenue and Car Accounting: R. W. Haver
Chief Engineer: R. B. Rhode

Locomotives 98; freight cars 9 736.

This railway of 462 miles (743 km) connects the Mesabi Range iron ore deposits with the ports of Duluth and Two Harbours on Lake Superior from where the ore is shipped to the steel centres throughout the Midwest.

DURHAM AND SOUTHERN RAILWAY CO
500 Water Street, Jacksonville, Florida 32202

Chairman: Prime F. Osborn
President: A. Paul Fun Khouser
Executive Vice-President: D. C. Hastings
Vice-President and General Manager: J. L. Williams

59 route miles (94.9 km).

EAST CAMDEN & HIGHLAND RAILROAD CO
PO Box 3180, East Camden, Arkansas 71701

President: R. S. O'Connor
Vice-President and General Manager: D. E. Ghent
Superintendent: J. T. Wagnon

43 route miles (69.2 km); 3 locomotives.

ELGIN JOLIET AND EASTERN RAILWAY
208 S Lasalle St, Chicago, Illinois 60690

President: M. S. Toon
Vice-President, Operating: F. A. Fitzpatrick
General Operating Superintendent: V. M. Christensen

199 route miles (320.2 km); 110 locomotives; 10 442 freight cars.

ESCANABA AND LAKE SUPERIOR RAILROAD
Wells, Michigan 49894

President: N. A. Lemke
Vice-President and General Manager: L. L. Hamilton
Traffic Manager: H. C. Pierson

64 route miles (102.9 km); 4 locomotives; 12 freight cars.

FLORIDA EAST COAST RAILWAY COMPANY
1 Malaga St, St. Augustine, Florida 32084

Chairman: E. Ball
President: W. L. Thornton
Vice-President, Traffic: J. E. Corbett
Vice-President, Transportation: R. W. Wyckoff
General Superintendent: B. D. Vlasin

499 route miles (803 km); 60 locomotives; 1 977 freight cars.

FORDYCE AND PRINCETON RAILROAD COMPANY
Fordyce, Arkansas 71742

President: E. A. Temple
Director and Secretary: W. E. Hastings
Superintendent (Fordyce, Arkansas): Tom Branch

FORT WORTH AND DENVER RAILWAY CO
Union Station Building, Denver, Colorado 80217

President: P. F. Cruikshank
Vice-President, Operating: L. C. Ethington
General Superintendent: A. D. Powers
Superintendent, Transportation: C. N. Parker

1 343 route miles (2 161.3 km); 20 locomotives; 1 505 freight cars.

GAINESVILLE MIDLAND RAILROAD CO
500 Water Street, Jacksonville, Florida 32202

President: W. T. Rice
Vice-President: P. F. Osborn
Vice-President, Operations: D. C. Hastings

40 route miles (64.4 km); 1 locomotive; 1 freight car.

GALVESTON WHARVES
PO Box 328, Galveston, Texas 77553

Chairman, Board of Trustees: Sam G. Tramonte
Executive Director and General Manager: C. S. Devoy
Deputy Executive Director: O. L. Selig
Director of Engineering: Ron Surovik
Traffic Manager: Carl S. Parker, Jr

44 route miles (70.8 km); 6 shunting diesel-electric.

GENESEE AND WYOMING RAILROAD COMPANY
3846 Retsof Rd, Retsof, New York 14539

Chairman of the Board: M. B. Fuller III
President: G. G. Johnson
Vice-President: W. B. Putney, IV
Chief Engineer: F. R. Matthews
Traffic Manager: P. J. Crowley
Vice-President: J. M. Fuller

12 route miles (19.3 km); 6 locomotives; 208 freight cars; 1 passenger train coach.

GEORGIA NORTHERN RAILWAY CO
PO Box 152, Moultrie, Georgia 31768

Chairman: W. G. Claytor
President and General Manager: W. L. Pippin

68 route miles (109.4 km); 1 locomotive.

GEORGIA RAILROAD
1590 Marietta Blvd, NW Atlanta, Georgia 30318

General Manager: M. S. Jones Jr
Chief Traffic Officer: H. M. Emmerson
Chief Engineer: Jack Cherry Jr

331 route miles (532.7 km); 35 locomotives; 1 251 freight cars.

GRAND TRUNK WESTERN RAILROAD CO
131 West Lafayette Boulevard, Detroit, Michigan 48226

President: J. H. Burdakin
Executive Assistant and Corporate Secretary: E. G. Fontaine
General Manager: W. Glavin

1 235 route miles (1 987.5 km); 184 locomotives; 9 344 freight cars; 640 piggyback trailers.

GREAT WESTERN RAILWAY CO
Loveland Depot, PO Box 537, Loveland, Colorado 80537

President (Fort Lee, New Jersey): Emil Ramat
Vice-President (Fairfield, New Jersey): J. Carmine
Executive Vice-President and General Manager (Loveland, Colorado): Byron F. Andrews

52 route miles (83.7 km); 4 line haul diesel electric locomotives; 44 freight cars.

GREEN BAY AND WESTERN RAILROAD
PO Box 2507, Green Bay, Wisconsin 54306

President: Joseph R. Galassi
Vice-President, Traffic: V. J. Maloney
Vice-President, Operations: Robert P. Selby
Treasurer: J. M. Van Oss
Superintendent: J. J. Bruley

256 route miles (411.9 km); 15 locomotives and 11 330 freight cars.

GREEN MOUNTAIN RAILROAD CORP
PO Box 468, Bellows Falls, Vermont 05101

President and Superintendent: R. W. Adams
Vice-President: R. Ashcroft
Supervisor, Maintenance of Way: R. Pingrey

52 route miles *(83.7 km)*; 6 locomotives; 114 freight cars.

HELENA SOUTHWESTERN RAILROAD COMPANY
PO Box 2517, West Helena, Arkansas 72390

President: J. B. Wiseman
Vice-President and General Manager: R. Rich

4 route miles *(6.4 km)*; 1 locomotive.

HOUSTON BELT & TERMINAL RAILWAY CO
202 Union Station Building, Houston, Texas 77002

President and General Manager: L. B. Griffin
Vice-President: J. G. Sheppard
Chief Engineer: J. H. Robertson

53 route miles *(85.3 km)*; 23 locomotives

ILLINOIS TERMINAL RAILROAD CO.
PO Box 72821, 710N 12th Blvd, St. Louis, Missouri 63177

President: Walter J. Cassin
Vice-President and General Manager: D. E. Visney
Chief Engineer: W. O. Pearson

448 route miles *(720.9 km)*; 37 locomotives; 2 602 freight cars.

INDIANA HARBOR BELT RAILROAD CO
Union Station, Chicago, Illinois 60606

President: J. B. Addington
Vice-President, Operations: R. B. Hasselmann

114 route miles *(183.5 km)*; 109 locomotives; 143 freight cars.

KENTUCKY & INDIANA TERMINAL RAILROAD
2910 North Western Parkway, Louisville, Kentucky 40212

President and General Manager: J. J. Gaynor

131 route miles *(210.8 km)*; 21 locomotives.

LAKE ERIE, FRANKLIN AND CLARION RAILROAD
1062 Wood St, Clarion, Pennsylvania 16214

President and Chairman of the Board: J. F. Miller
Vice-President, Operations: J. L. Hartle

15 route miles *(24.1 km)*; 3 locomotives.

LAKE SUPERIOR TERMINAL
AND TRANSFER RAILWAY COMPANY
17 Washington Ave, North, Minneapolis, Minnesota 55401

Superintendent (Highpost Operating Office): K. V. Marthe
President and Director: W. S. Byrne

Owns and operates depot at Superior, Wisconsin.

LAURINBURG AND SOUTHERN RAILROAD CO
PO Box 546, Laurinburg, North Carolina 28352

President: Murphy Evans
Vice-President and General Manager: W. S. Jones

28 route miles *(45.1 km)*; 7 locomotives; 31 freight cars.

LEHIGH VALLEY RAILROAD COMPANY
415 Brighton St, Bethlehem, Pennsylvania 18015

Trustee: Robert C. Haldeman
Vice-President and Special Assistant to the Trustee: S. P. Adik
Vice-President, Finance: M. Dobes

506 route miles *(814.3 km)*; 147 locomotives; 3 966 freight cars.

MANITOU AND PIKE'S PEAK RAILWAY COMPANY
PO Box 1329, Colorado Springs, Colorado 80901

Vice-President and General Manager: Martin R. Frick
President: Wm. Thayer Tutt

9 route miles *(14.5 km)*; 4 diesel-electric cars; 2 diesel-hydraulic twin-cars; 3 diesel-electric locomotives; 3 passenger coaches; 1 freight car; 1 diesel-hydraulic rotary snow plough.

MANUFACTURERS RAILWAY CO
2850 South Broadway, St. Louis, Missouri 63118

President: R. W. Schmidt

42 route miles *(67.6 km)*; 9 locomotives.

MARYLAND AND PENNSYLVANIA RAILROAD CO.
490, East Market St, York, Pennsylvania 17403

Chairman of the Board: Harold Grossman
President: H. Lazarus
General Manager: William Partington

90 route miles *(144.8 km)*; 6 locomotives.

McCLOUD RIVER RAILROAD COMPANY
PO Box A, McCloud, California 96057

President: C. T. Hester
Vice-President, Operations: S. Muma
Traffic Manager: G. Holmquist
Chief Mechanical Officer: Ken Bogard

78 route miles *(125.5 km)*; 4 locomotives; 7 freight train cars.

MINNESOTA TRANSFER RAILWAY COMPANY
2071 University Ave, St. Paul, Minnesota 55104

President: C. R. Grogan
Vice-President and General Manager: J. A. Lehn
Superintendent: W. S. Hammond

13 route miles *(20.9 km)*; 5 locomotives.

MONONGAHELA RAILWAY COMPANY
53 Market St, Brownsville, Pennsylvania 15417

President: H. G. Allyn, Jr
Vice-President: C. W. Owens
Vice-President: H. P. Henshaw, Jr
Superintendent: D. E. Gratz
Supervisor, Freight Transport: A. J. Yuhas
Chief Mechanical Officer: F. H. McHenry
Chief Engineer: W. M. McCracken

171 route miles *(275.2 km)*; 11 locomotives.

MONTANA WESTERN RAILWAY COMPANY
Valier, Montana 59486

President: W. Duncan MacMillan
General Manager, Secretary and Treasurer: H. E. Lovcik
Vice-President: Art Jardine

Associated with BN.

MORRISTOWN AND ERIE RAILROAD COMPANY
PO Box 2206R, Morristown, New Jersey 07960

General Manager: Thomas G. Peterson

11 route miles *(17.7 km)*; 2 locomotives. Connects ConRail. This branch is controlled by Midland Holding Corporation of Washington, DC. It also operates the Caldwell branch of sthesformer Erie Lackawanna railroad.

NEVADA NORTHERN RAILWAY CO
East Ely, Nevada 89315

President: J. C. Kinnear Jr
Vice-President and General Superintendent: H. M. Peterson
Traffic Manager: J. Piccinini

162 route miles *(260.7 km)*; 2 locomotives.

NEW YORK & LONG BRANCH RR CO
1100 Raymond Blvd, Newark, New Jersey 07102

President and General Counsel: R. B. Wachenfeld
Vice-President: R. F. Lawson
Vice-President and General Manager: M. C. Jacobs

40 route miles *(64.4 km)*: No equipment owned. Associated with Central RR of New Jersey.

NEW YORK, SUSQUEHANNA AND WESTERN
RAILROAD
One River Road, Edgewater, New Jersey 07020

Trustee: W. Scott
President: I. Maidman

65 route miles *(104.6 km)*; 15 locomotives and 75 freight train cars.

NORFOLK FRANKLIN AND DANVILLE RAILWAY CO
181 S. Main St, Suffolk, Virginia 23434

President: Richard F. Dunlap
General Manager: L. G. Grace
Chief Engineer: L. A. Durham, Jr
Superintendent: L. C. Capps, Jr

205 route miles *(329.9 km)*; 6 locomotives; 247 freight cars.
Associated with Norfolk & Western.

OREGON & NORTHWESTERN RAILROAD CO
PO Box 557, Hines, Oregon 97738

President: H. H. Howard
Executive Vice-President: J. J. Fitzgerald
Superintendent: R. L. Roy

51 route miles *(82 km)*; 4 locomotives; 395 freight cars.

PENNSYLVANIA-READING SEASHORE LINES
Camden, New Jersey 08103

President: J. B. Abbington
General Manager and Traffic Manager: R. E. Blosser
Superintendent, Transportation: C. L. Ryan
Chief Engineer: C. E. Diefendorf

318 miles *(511.7 km)*; 26 locomotives. Associated with ConRail.

PITTSBURG AND SHAWMUT RAILROAD
R.D. 2 Middle St, Brookville, Pennsylvania 15825

President: W. R. Weaver
Vice-President, Traffic: John Reale

100 route miles *(160.9 km)*; 10 locomotives; 1 400 freight cars.

PORTLAND TERMINAL RAILROAD CO
242 St. John St, Portland, Maine 04102

Chairman: E. Spencer Miller
President: John F. Gerity

23 route miles *(37 km)*. The Company is wholly-owned by Maine Central as one of its subsidiaries.

ROSCOE, SNYDER & PACIFIC RAILWAY CO
PO Box 68, Roscoe, Texas 79545

President: Wm. L. Bailey
Chairman of the Board: D. Wooten

30 route miles *(48.3 km)*; 2 locomotives; 766 freight cars.

ST. JOHNSBURY AND LAMOILLE COUNTY RAILROAD
Stafford Street, Morrisville, Vermont 05661

President: Bruno A. Loati
General Manager: Robert H. Vincelette
Vice-President and General Manager: B. S. Sloboda

98 route miles *(157.7 km)*; 2 locomotives; 4 freight cars.

THE ST. PAUL UNION DEPOT COMPANY
2071 University Ave, St. Paul, Minnesota 55104

President: C. R. Hussey
Chief Engineer: John L. Jensen

1.54 route miles *(2.4 km)*.

SAN FRANCISCO BELT RAILROAD
Ferry Building, San Francisco, California 94111

Superintendent: J. B. Silva
Traffic Manager: T. Grinstead
Chief Engineer: E. L. Sembler

58 route miles *(98.3 km)*; 4 locomotives. Operated by City of San Francisco.

SANTA MARIA VALLEY RAILROAD COMPANY
PO Box 340, Santa Maria, California 93456

President: Marian Hancock Barry
Vice-President and Manager: Sue J. Sword

18 route miles *(28.9 km)*; 8 locomotives.

SIERRA RAILROAD COMPANY
781 S. Washington St, Sonora, California 95370

President: Charles Crocker
General Manager: D. J. Franco

57 route miles *(91.7 km)*; 5 locomotives.

SIOUX CITY TERMINAL RAILWAY COMPANY
Exchange Building, Sioux City, Iowa 51107

President and General Manager: L. V. Kuhl

Loading and unloading rail-borne livestock only. Roadbed leased. No rolling stock.

SOUTH CAROLINA STATE PORTS AUTHORITY
Charleston, Georgetown, Port Royal, South Carolina

Executive Director: W. Don Welch
Director of Operations: Joseph P. D'Amaral

UPPER MERION AND PLYMOUTH RAILROAD CO
PO Box 112, Conshohocken, Pennsylvania 19428

President and Treasurer: Joseph I. Hallman
General Superintendent: V. P. Perone

16 route miles *(25.7 km)*; 8 locomotives; 174 freight cars.

VENTURA COUNTY RAILWAY COMPANY
PO Box 432, Oxnard, California 93032

President: M. V. Smith
Vice-President: R. G. Barnard

11 route miles *(17.7 km)*; 2 locomotives.

VIRGINIA BLUE RIDGE RAILWAY
Piney River, Virginia 22964

Chairman of the Board: Roy C. Lytle
President: John W. Cobb
General Superintendent: E. T. Drumheller

10 route miles *(16 km)*; 2 locomotives; 3 freight cars.

VIRGINIA CENTRAL RAILWAY
PO Box 239, Fredericksburg, Virginia 22401

General Manager: F. Freeman Funk
Connects with R F & P. 1 route mile *(1.6 km)*; 2 locomotives.

WARREN AND OUACHITA VALLEY RAILWAY COMPANY
PO Box 150, Warren, Arkansas 71671

President: R. J. Lane
Vice-President: C. R. Grogan
General Manager: L. Williams, Jr

16 route miles *(25.7 km)*; 1 locomotive. Associated with CRI & P.

WINCHESTER & WESTERN RAILROAD CO
PO Box 264, Winchester, Virginia 22601

President, and Treasurer: Betty L. Hughes
Vice-President, Secretary: Lanny J. Hughes

18 route miles *(28.9 km)*; 1 locomotive. Connects to B & O.

YAKIMA VALLEY TRANSPORTATION CO
Yakima, Washington 98902

President: G. H. Baker
Vice-President and Secretary: J. W. Jack
Manager: J. L. Price
Superintendent, Operating and Traffic: R. B. Hardin

21 route miles *(33.8 km)*; 2 electric locomotives.

URUGUAY

STATE RAILWAYS ADMINISTRATION

Administración de Ferrocarriles del Estado (AFE),
La Paz 1095, Montevideo

President: Cnel. Oscar Maciá
Vice-President: Cnel. Juan C. Reissig
Director: Cnel. Leonel Melgar
Secretary General: Sr. Carlos Baldomir
General Manager: Cr. Carlos M. Lázaro
Office Manager: Cr. Máximo Dellacasa
Manager, Developments: Ing. Martin Zorrilla
Manager, Traction: Ing. Humberto Preziosi
Manager, Works: Ing. José Rinaldi
Chief Signalling and Communications: Ing. Francisco Puppo

Gauge: 1.435 m
Route length: 3 238 km

New rail links with Argentina are major features of a five-year (1977-81) railway
modernisation and expansion plan in Uruguay. The plan includes development of the
Litoral line and continued extension of the central line northwards from km 329. A new
27 km-section between Mercedes and Ombucito was completed in 1979, providing a
cut-off for the existing Chamberlain-Duraznolink with Argentina. Also under construction is a new railway bridge across the Rio Negro river and extension of the present line
running from Sarandi del Yi to 329 km and subsequently to 347 km.

One of 15 diesel trainsets built for AFE during 1977/78 by Ganz-Mavag

TRAFFIC	1977	1978
Total train-km	7 635 105	8 157 363
Percentage of train-km		
by steam	1.14	0.61
by diesel	98.86	99.39
Total freight tonnage	1 538 870	1 474 562
Total passenger-km	388 520 942	493 971 735
Total passengers carried	6 356 944	7 183 382
Passengers carried		
1st class	1 074 328	1 222 279
2nd class	5 282 116	5 961 003
Average length of		
passenger journey (km)	17 416	19 680

FINANCES		
Revenues (N$000s)	1977	1978
Passengers	16.566	29.211
Average receipt per passenger-km	0.042	0.059
Freight and mail	51.975	70.298
Average receipt per freight tonne-km	0.142	0.175
Total	68.541	99.509
Expenditure (N$000s)		
Staff/personnel	81.156	123.463
Miscellaneous	39.879	60.582
Total	121.035	184.045

Motive power and rolling stock
Number of locomotives in service:

	Line haul		Shunting	
	1977	1978	1977	1978
Steam	10	11	1	2
Diesel-electric	43	43	16	17
Railcars, diesel	8	9		
Passenger train coaches	86	102		
Freight train cars	2 380	2 400		

TRACK
(1) Litorial line, running from Bellaco to Paysandú, and forming the first section of a
new projected link with Argentine State Railways (FA) and Ferrocarril Presidente
Carlos Antonio Lopez of Paraguay;
(2) Construction of a new rail bridge across the Rio Negro river and extension of the
present line running from Sarandí del Yi to 329 km, and subsequently to 347 km;
(3) 13-km ore line from Valentines on the Florida-Melo line as far as new mine
deposits.

DIESEL LOCOMOTIVES

Class	Axle Arrangement	Transmission	Rated Power hp	Max. kg	Tractive Effort Continuous at kg	kmlh	Max. Speed kmlh	Wheel Dia. mm	Total Weight tons	Length mm	No. Built	Year first Built	Builders: Mechanical Parts	Engine & Type	Transmission
GE	C-C	Elec	1 500	25 500	21 100	15	95	1 041	102	16 986	30 925	1952	Gardner-Denver Westinghouse	Alco 250 and 244	G Electric
Alsthom	B-B	Elec	825	16 000	9 800	16	90	1 000	56	13 496	en 4 256	1963	Alsthom	MGO 12 VASH	Alsthom
Ganz-Mavag	B-B	Hyd-Mech	925	8 200	5 500	20	100	920	48	16 330	900 AFE	1977	Ganz-Mavag	GM 12 VFE 17/24	GM HM 912

VENEZUELA

VENEZUELA STATE RAILWAYS

Instituto Autónomo, Administración de Ferrocarriles Del Estado, ave Principal los
Ruices, Edif Stemo Pisos 1, 2, 3, Apartado 146, Caracas

General Manager: Manuel Vásquez Moya
General Secretariate: Jesús López Planchart
  Celia Benchimol
  General Nicolás Tesorero
  Gustavo Corredor
  Angel O. Matheus
  José Venegas Carrillo
Planning Manager: Igor José Colmenares Guevara
Operations Manager: Freddy Castejón
Projects Manager: Francisco Urdaneta Alcalá

Gauge: 1.435 m
Route length: 173 km

TRAFFIC	1978
Total train-km	565 044
Percentage of train-km by steam	
by diesel	565 044
by electric	
Total freight tonnage	163 309
Average haul	119.38
Total passenger-km	40 486 873
Total passengers carried	364 820
Average length of passenger journey-km	109.50 km

FINANCES	1978
Revenues (Bolivars)	
Passengers and baggage	1 173 773
Average receipt per passenger-km	0.03
Freight and mail	2 099 462
Average receipt per freight tonne-km	0.09
Total	3 273 235

Shunting operations at Cabello-Barquisimeto, centre of much of the railway's new
plans for massive railway development

Expenditure	
Staff/personnel	4 665 000
Materials and services	2 774 000
Depreciation	1 914 000
Total	9 353 000

MOTIVE POWER
Number of locomotives in service (1978): 11 diesel-electric 1 500/1 750/700 hp.

ROLLING STOCK
In operation: 274 freight wagons; 9 passenger coaches.

TRACK WORK
A plan recommends construction of a rail system measuring 3 700 km by 1990. Work was to commence on the existing line from Puerto Cabello to Barquisimeto line at Yaritagua and proceed towards Acarigua, Villa Bruzual, Guanare and Barinas. Extensions were then to be constructed to San Juan de los Morros, Valle La Pascua, Anaco, El Tigre, Ciudad Bolivar and Ciudad Bolivar. A branchline to Tuy Medio was under consideration.
In addition to these lines which were due for completion by 1979, new sections between Moron, Yaracol and Riecito which will carry a million tons of phosphates annually from the mines of Riecito for processing at the petrochemical plant at Moron are being constructed.
By 1979, therefore, a total of 1 160 km under the plan was to have been completed and 90 km under construction. Cost of construction by 1979 was 2 403 million Bolivars. The lines will give rail access to the Altos Llanos Occidentales area of the Andina region, connecting with the central-western region and uniting the two with the sea and providing outlets for petrochemical plants which will supply fertilisers to agricultural regions under development.
Finally, the planned network will establish a freight corridor by late 1980 able to serve the north-eastern and Guayana regions. In particular the railway will provide a new transport mode for the region of Sidor which is planned to generate 2.65 million tons of freight annually.
Second stage of the plan is to be carried out up to 1985. The following lines will be built:
—North-eastern region: Anaco—Barcelona—Cumana; Anaco—Maturin—Carupano
—Central region: San Juan de Los Morros—Calabozo—San Fernando de Apure; Vaijencia—Puerto Cabello
—Andean region: Barinas—San Antonio de Caparo; San Christobal—La Fria.
By the end of phase two, 1 088 new km of railway lines will have been built, bringing the total in operation to 2 513 km. Investments by 1985 will have totalled 4 055 million Bolivars.
Third and final stage of the mainline network will be completed between the years 1985 and 1990 with completion of the following lines: Barquisimeto—Carora—Sabana de Mendoza—Mene Grande—Santa Rita—Maracalbo—Machiques—Orope; La Fria—El Vigia—Sabana de Mendoza; Yaracal—Coro—Punto Pijo.
Infrastructure investment during the third stage of the plan will total 1 920 million Bolivars and track constructed will total 1 114 km. So, by the end of the plan, 5 593 million Bolivars will have been spent on construction and it is forecast that 1 473 million Bolivars will have been invested in rolling stock.

VIET-NAM

VIET-NAM RAILWAYS SYSTEM

The VRS metre-gauge system has an owned route length of 873 miles *(1 405 km).* During 1977 Vietnamese government officials in Hanoi requested the World Bank for assistance to construct a railway passenger coach and freight wagon factory together with workshop facilities for maintenance of railway equipment. The request was made during a visit by a World Bank mission to Viet-Nam. Government officials who met the Bank economists stressed the nation's need to integrate the northern and southern regions by 1980, the end of the Five-Year Plan period.

TRACK
The last metre of track on the 1 730 km trans-Viet-Nam railway, linking Hanoi with Ho Chi Minh City (formerly Saigon) was laid on 4 December 1976 and two trains started on experimental runs, one from Hanoi and the other from Ho Chi Minh City. The final track was laid on the Vinh Cith to Minh Cam portion, between Chu Le and Minh Cam. In the preceding month the Da Nang—Tien An section of the Thong Nhat railway, over 190 km long, had been opened to traffic, as had the 169 km Hoi-Hue section crossing the Bne Hai river.
But the key development was completion of the 11 km Chau Lau bridge on the Phu My—Da Nang railway section in Quang Nam-Da Nang Province. Because of its remoteness it was necessary to built a 30 km road to bring materials and equipment to the construction site and, despite flooding in October 1977, the workers and cadres strengthened the old piers by means of 460 m³ of ferroconcentrate before assembling the main 180-ton girder bridge.
A total of 725 bridges with an aggregate length of 20 000 m have been built or repaired on the Thong Nhat railway. Among the 475 new bridges are the Yen Xuan bridge across the Lam river in Hghe Tinh Province, 420 m; the Ky Lam bridge over the Thu Bon river in Quang Nam-Da Nang Province, 500 m; and the Tra Khuc bridge spanning the Tra Khuc river in Nghia Binh Province, 550 m. To ensure the success of this bridge-building programme, dozens of engineering works, in co-operation with many mechanical co-operatives of various provinces, manufactured 20 000 tons of girders and tens of thousands of other bridge sections.
VR also completed in 1977 an 80 km link between Kep, north of Hanoi, and coal mines at Uong Bi.

YUGOSLAVIA

YUGOSLAV RAILWAYS
ZAJEDNICA JUGOSLOVENSKIH ZELEZNICA (JZ)
(Community of Yugoslav Railways)
Nemanjina 6, Belgrade 11000

General Manager: Nicola Filipovic
Director Generals:
Belgrade: Miodrag Parlicevic
Sarajevo: Dipl. ing. Dane Maljković
Zagreb: Joakim Crnosija
Skopje: Risto Petrovski
Ljubljana: Dipl. ing. Joze Slokar
Novi Sad: Tima Ilin
Pristina: Zenon Beća
Titograd: Milivoje Lavsevic

Gauge: 1.435 m
Route length: 9 993 km

A number of project guidelines have been drawn up for rail development up to 1985. These include:
—after the completion of the programme in hand, and after the completion of the new line from Belgrade to Bar, the modernisation programme in the narrower sense and the reconstruction of the principal main lines should be concluded;
—electric traction should be extended to another 1 200 km of key sections so that, by 1985, a total of 3 500 km will be electrified, and steam traction will have completely disappeared by 1980;
—modern signalling and telecommunication installations are to be introduced, in keeping with the traffic demands on the different lines;
—the axle loads will be increased so that all principal main lines will be able to take axle loads of at least 20 tonnes; at the same time, these lines are to be remodelled for higher speeds (up to 160 km/h during the first phase);
—where necessary, the capacity of existing lines is to be increased through reconstruction or the addition of another track; these works should, by 1985, cover some 600 route km;
—the railway junctions are to be re-modelled for automatic operation, and the automatic coupling will be introduced;
—motive power units and rolling stock as well as the equipment for integral transport, mechanical handling of goods, cybernetics and automatic data processing are to be modernised;
—the fleet of goods wagons is to be modernised with the aim of increasing the share of modern four-axled wagons, suitable for speeds above 100 km/h, to 80 per cent of the fleet; similarly, there will be a substantial increase in the number of modern passenger vehicles with greatly improved technical and technological characteristics.

DIESEL LOCOMOTIVES

Class	Axle Arrangement	Trans-Mission	Rated Power hp	Max kg	Tractive Effort Continuous at kg	Tractive Effort Continuous at kmlh	Max Speed kmlh	Wheel Dia mm	Axle Load Tons	Total Weight Tons	Length mm	No Built	Year First Built	Builders: Mechanical Parts	Builders: Engine	Builders: Transmission
644	BoBo	Elec	600	16 650	12 030	8.5	80	1 040	15.4	61.7	12 290	80	1960	MAVAG	Ganz	Ganz
642	BoBo	Elec	825	16 000	10 950	14.5	80	1 100	16.8	67.2	14 740	104	1961	Dj. Djakovic	MGO/Dj.Dj.	Br&L/RK
643	BoBo	Elec	925	16 800	10 800	16.5	80	1 100	16.8	67.2	14 740	22	1967	Br&L/Dj.Dj.	MGO/Dj.Dj.	Br&L
644	A1AA1A	Elec	1 650		26 400		100	1 016	14.9	96.0	14 173		1975	Macosa	GM	GM
661	CoCo	Elec	1 950	21 200			120	1 016	18.0	108.0	17 272	218	1960	GM	GM	GM
662	CoCo	Elec	1 650	22 000	10 600	28.4	120	1 100	16.0	96.0	17 740	17	1965	Dj. Djakovic	MGO/Dj.Dj.	RK/Sever
663	CoCo	Elec	3 300		30 490		124	1 016	19.8	118.0	19 520	14	1972	GM	GM	GM
664	CoCo	Elec	2 200		26 290		124	1 016	16.3	108.0	15 764	58	1972	GM	GM	GM
665	CoCo	Elec	2 750				127			127.0		20	1972	MLW	MLW/Alco	GE
731	C	Hyd	400	12 500	3 600	17.0	60	950	14.0	42.0	10 500	44	1958	Jenbach/Dj.Dj.	Jenbach	Voith
732	C	Hyd	600	13 100	6 000	17.0	80	950	14.5	43.5	10 500	77	1969	Dj.Djakovic	Jenbach	Voith
733	C	Hyd	600	15 800	5 000	18.0	60	1 250	16.0	48.0	10 180	37	1968	Dj. Djakovic	MGO/Dj.Dj.	Voith
740	B B	Hyd	600	10 900	3 100	33.0	50	850	8.0	32.0	11 600	40	1968	Dj. Djakovic	MGO/Dj.Dj.	Voith
741	BB	Hyd	1 500	21 300	17 750	14.0	120	920	16.0	64.0	14 000	3	1966	MIN	Maybach	Maybach
742	BB	Hyd	1 650	19 200	16 800	12.0	120	1 000	17.0	68.0	14 400	60	1972	MIN	Pielstick	CKD-SRM
743	BB	Hyd	1 600				120	950	16.0	65.0	15 340	1	1975	Dj. Djakovic	MGO/Dj.Dj.	Voith
761	CC	Hyd	1 950	24 000			120	950	16.5	97.8	20 270	3	1957	Krauss-Maffei	Maybach	Maybach

740: 0.76 m Gauge. RK: Rade Koncar Zagreb. Br&L: Brissonneau & Lotz

ELECTRIC LOCOMOTIVES

Class	Axle Arrange-ment	Line Current kV Type	Rated Power hp	Max kg	Tractive Effort Continuous at kg	kmlh	Max Speed kmlh	Wheel Dia mm	Total Weight tonnes	Length mm	No built	Year First built	Builders Mechanical Parts	Electrical Equipment
341	BoBo	3 dc	2 130	19 000	13 800	53.0	95	1 250	78.0	16 024	1	1954	Alsthom	Alsthom
342	BoBo	3 dc	3 060		14 700		120	1 250	76.0	15 800	40	1968	ASGEN	OMFP
362	BoBoBo	3 dc	4 550	33 000	26 400	45.0	120	1 250	110.0	18 400	40	1960	ASGEN	OMFP
363	Coco	3 dc	3 750	25 000	15 400	63.0	125	1 100	114.0	20 190	40	1976	Alsthom	Alsthom
441	BoBo	25 5oac Hz	5 550	28 000	17 700	65.0	120	1 250	78.0	15 470	190	1967	SGP/RK	Traction Union
461	CoCo	50 5oac Hz	6 840	42 000	26 500	69.5	120	1 250	126.0	19 800	45	1972	Electroputere	Electroputere

TRAFFIC

	1975	1976	1977
Total freight ton-km (millions)	21 638	21 017	22 225
Total freight tonnage (millions)	78	74	77
Total passenger-km (millions)	10 284	9 941	10 459
Total passengers carried (millions)	129	126	124

MOTIVE POWER AND ROLLING STOCK

Total fleet now comprises 1 341 line haul and 217 shunting locomotives.

TRACK WORK

Following completion of the new Belgrade-Bar mainline, Yugoslav Railways (JZ) is building seven new lines during the period 1975-85.

During the same period three lines are being double-tracked: Tabanovci-Skopje-Titov Veles; Zagreb-Novska; and Karlovac-Zagreb.
JZ started double-tracking part of its Ploce line between Doboj Novi and Zenica *(93 km)* to raise capacity. Completion was scheduled for November 1978.

SIGNALLING AND COMMUNICATIONS

JZ is to equip the main lines between Jesenice, Ljubljana, Belgrade and Skopje with high-frequency train radio.

Model DHL-1 600 diesel-hydraulic locomotive for Yugoslav Railways and export
Track gauges from 1.067 to 1.676 m, diesel-engine 1.600 hp, hydraulic transmission Voith, max axle load 16 tonnes, max speed 120 km/h.

4-axle freight car, type Tads-2, capacity 66 m³
A special freight car with sliding roof designed for transport of bulk goods. The loading is performed through the roof along the whole length of the car body and unloading by gravitation on both sides through 8 holes (4 on either side).

ZAÏRE

SOCIETE NATIONALE DES CHEMINS DE FER ZAIROIS (SNCZ)

PO Box 297, Lubumbashi, Shaba Region

Director General: Gaston Goor
Director of Administration: Citoyen Kasongo Ngamvie
Director of Operations: Robert Baudour
Technical Director: Jean de Wergifosse

Gauge: 1.067 m; 1.00 m; 0.60 m
Route length: 3 573 km; 125 km; 1 025 km

SNCZ was created in 1974 with the merger of three former railways: La Compagnie des Chemins de Fer Kinshasa—Dilolo—Lubumbashi (KDL); Les Chemins de Fer des Grands Lacs (CFL); Les Chemins de Fer Vicinaux (CVZ). SNCZ is state owned. A total of 858 km are electrified.
The former KDL railway serves the important mining centres of the Shaba—Lubumbashi, Likasi, Kolwezi and Mososhi—and other important mining and industrial areas such as the manganese mine at Kisenge, cement works at Lubudi, collieries at Luena, diamond mines at Mbuji-Mayi, etc. Expanding agricultural and forest product industries have developed along the line of its route.
It connects at Ilebo (ex-Port Francqui) with the ONATRA inland waterway services; and at Kabongo with the CF des Grands Lacs (CFL).
Internationally, KDL has through connections at Dilolo with the CF du Benguela (CFB) in Angola to the Atlantic port of Lobito; and at Sakania with Zambia Railways and, further on, Rhodesian Railways, CF du Moçambique, and South African Railways.

TRAFFIC

	1977	1978
Total freight tonnes (000's)	4 595	4 164
Freight tonne-kms (000's)	1 842 400	1 683 488
Total passengers carried (000's)	1 078	1 199
Passenger-kms (000's)	390 400	476 000

FINANCES

	1977	1978
	(Zaires)	
Revenues	86 782 540	92 971 388
Expenses	104 527 203	120 833 594

MOTIVE POWER AND ROLLING STOCK

Number of locomotives in service 1976:

	Line	Shunting
Steam	—	3
Electric	56	5
Diesel electric	56	—
Diesel hydraulic	32	65

Number of diesel railcars: 17
Number of passenger coaches: 213
Number of freight wagons: 5 381

ELECTRIFICATION

The heaviest traffic lines, in the Lubumbashi area, have been electrified at 25 000 V, single phase, 50 cycles.

TRACK CONSTRUCTION DETAILS

Standard rail: Vignole 59 and 80.6 lb/yd *(29.3 and 40 kg/m)* in length of *10 m* and *12 m*.
Joints: Fishplates and bolts.
Cross ties (sleepers): Steel. T.2243 (MI) weighing 112 lb *(51 kg)* each, under *37* and *40 kg* rail. T.3376C weighing 93 lb *(42 kg)* each, under *29.3 kg* rail. RS type prestressed concrete sleepers and T.3401A wooden sleepers under long welded rail.
Spacing: 2 400 per mile *(1 500 per km)*.
Rail fastening: By lugs or clips and bolts to steel sleepers. RN flexible fastenings to concrete sleepers.
Filling: Broken stone.
Gauge widening:
  Nil: Tangent to 2.9° curve; rad. of 1 968 ft *(600 m)*.
  0.35 in *(9mm)*: 2.9°-4.3° curvature; min. rad. of 1 968-1 312 ft *(600-400 m)*.
  0.7 in *(18 mm)*: Curves sharper than 4.3°; min. rad. of 1 312 ft *(400 m)*.
Max curvature: 8.75° = radius of 656 ft *(200 m)*.
Max gradient: 1.25% (1 in 80) except between Tenke and Bukama 2% (1 in 50).
Max altitude: 5 295 ft *(1 614 m)* at Dilongo-Yulu near Tenke on Bukama line.
Max permitted speed:
  Electrified lines: 32 mph *(52 km/h)*.
  All other lines: 28 mph *(45 km/h)*.
Max axle load: 15 tons nominal: 20 tons in special cases.

SIGNALLING AND TRAIN CONTROL

Traffic in the industrial zone is increasing so rapidly that the Likasi-Tenke section in particular could become saturated. Accordingly, centralised Traffic Control (CTC) is installed over the line (105 km).

DIESEL LOCOMOTIVES

Class	Axle Arrangement	Trans-mission	Rated Power hp	Max. lb (kg)	Tractive Effort Continuous at			Max. Speed mph (km/h)	Wheel Dia. in (mm)	Total Weight Tons	Length ft ins (mm)	No. Built	Year first Built	Builders: Mechanical Parts	Engine & Type	Transmission
					lb (kg)	mph (km/h)										
1300	Co-Co	Elec	1 650	48 000* (21 750) 57 750† (26 190)	55 500 (25 200)	6.8 (11.0)		37 (60)	36 (914)	87.3	46′ 4½″ (14 134)	38	1971-72	GE (USA)	GE FDL8	GE 76/A.10
1260	Co-Co	Elec	1 500	33 000* (15 000) 39 700† (18 000)	29 750 (13 400)	13.6 (21.8)		45 (72)	42 (1 067)	80	51′ 6″ (15 700)	12	1969 70	Hitachi	MAN V22/30ATL	
1200 v	B-B	Hyd	550	24 800* (11 250)n 29 800† (13 500)	22 300 (10 120)	4.0		20.5	36.6	45	37′ 9″	25	1968	Hitachi	Cummins	Twin-Disc
1160	B (0-4-0)	Hyd	320	19 800 (8 970)	16 500 (7 500)	3.1 (5)		19 (30)	33 (840)	30	17′ 1¾″ (5 225)	13	1965	Cockerill	Cummins NHRS-6	Twin-Disc
1530/40	B-B	Hyd	1 310	28 700 (13 000)				44 (70)	37.6 (950)	52	38′ 6″ (11.722)	8	1967	Krupp	MTU 12V 538 TB 10	Voith
60	0-6-0	Hyd	250	7 425 (3 375)					30.6 (774)	13.5	—	2	1955	Tubize	Cummins NTA	Twin-Disc
70	0-4-0	Hyd	335	8 800 (4 000)					30.6 (774)	16	—	7	1958	Cockerill	Cummins NTA	Voith
80	B-B	Hyd	510	17 600 (8 000)					30.6 (774)	32	—	12	1969	Nippon Sharyo	Cummins VT 1710 L	Niigata
1050	B-B	Hyd	515	22 000 (10 000)					37.6 (953)	40	—	8	1973	Henschel	Henschel 12 V 1516 A	Voith
1010	2-8-0	Hyd	800	29 700 (13 500)					50.0 (1 270)	58	—	2	1959	FUF/HSP	MTU MD 440	Voith
20	0-6-0	Hyd	185	8 800 (4 000)					30.6 (774)	16	33′ 0″ (10 000)	4	1958	Moes	Leyland 0680	Twin-Disc

* 25% adhesion.   † 30% adhesion, using sand.

ELECTRIC LOCOMOTIVES

Class	Axle Arrangement	Line Current	Rated Output hp	Max. lb (kg)	Tractive Effort (Full Field) Continuous at		Max. Speed mph (km/h)	Wheel dia. in (mm)	Weight tonnes	Length ft in (mm)	No. Built	Year Built	Builders Mechanical Parts	Electrical Equipment
					lb (kg)	mph (km/h)								
2200	Bo-Bo	25 kV 1/50 ac OH	2 200	41 900 (19 000)	28 200 (12 800)	28.3 (45.5)	40 (65)	51⅛ (1 300)	76	50′ 1″ (15 260)	9	1956	Brugecise et Nivelles	ACEC
2300	Bo-Bo	,,	2 040	48 500 (22 000)	36 800 (16 700)	19.5 (31.5)	40 (65)	43⅜ (1 100)	75	53′ 4″ (16 260)	11	1958	,,	,,
2400	Bo-Bo	,,	2 000	39 700 (18 000)	26 500 (12 000)	28 (45)	43 (70)	40 (1 016)	60	44′ 8¾″ (13 630)	2 9	1960 1964	,,	,,
2 600	Bo-Bo-Bo		3 250	69 300 (31 500)	50 550 (22 980)	23 (37)	43 (70)	40 (1 016)	93	56′ 0″ (1 700)	10	1974	Hitachi	
200	Bo-Bo	,,	640	46 300 (21 000)	17 200 (7 800)	13.7 (22)	28 (45)	36 (914)	62	45′ 9½″ (13 960)	5	1970	Hitachi	

ZAMBIA
ZAMBIA RAILWAYS
PO Box 935, Kabwe

RAILWAY BOARD
Chairman: B. M. Monze
Members: Senior Chief Mushili
D. A. R. Phiri
A. B. Munyama
A. M. Misiya
M. Nalilungwe
A. M. Mtopa
F. M. Walusiku
C. Masonga
Chief B. Nalubamba
MANAGEMENT
General Manager: A. K. Mazoka
Manager Administration & Company Secretary: L. Y. Kalumba
Commercial Manager: P. C. Nkonkomalimba
Operations Manager: B. C. Chewe
Chief Civil Engineer: N. K. Sikka
Chief Mechanical Engineer: J. Zulu
Chief Signal and Telecommunication Engineer: C. D. Garg
Chief of Transportation: D. Mwape

Gauge: 1.067 m
Route length: 1 104 km

TRAFFIC

	1976	1977
Total freight ton-km	919 401 000	1 294
Total freight tonnage	26 486 000	5 259
Total passenger-km	200 000 000	251
Total passengers carried	10 140 000	1 053

1 200-hp Zambesi class diesel-electric locomotive, supplied by General Electric Traction

FINANCES

	1976/1977	1977/1978
Revenues	39 989 633	41 778 743
Expenses	36 555 730	38 556 084

ROLLING STOCK
Rolling stock in service comprises 64 line haul diesel-electric locomotives and 12 shunting locomotives, plus 16 diesel-hydraulic shunter locomotives.
Deliveries in 1976-77 were six U20C-GEC (USA) locomotives.

ZIMBABWE

RHODESIA RAILWAYS (RR)

Metcalfe Square, PO Box 596, Bulawayo

Telephone: Bulawayo 72211

Chairman, Railway Board: W. N. Wells
Deputy Chairman: J. R. Hedley
Members: A. T. Mills
         J. A. Mcdonald
         R. G. Pascoe
         W. F. Sievwright
Secretary: P. J. Murray
General Manager: W. F. Seinwright
Assistant General Managers: F. C. Viljoen
                    N. Lea-Cox
Chief Medical Officer: Dr. L. B. Thompson
Chief Mechanical Engineer: G. H. Patterson
Chief Civil Engineer: R. F. Maclean
Chief Personnel Officer: J. Henderson
Chief Accountant: J. E. Bolton
Chief Superintendent Operating: N. Lea-Cox
Chief Electrical Engineer: P. L. Overbury
Chief Signal Engineer: A. L. Rutherford-Jones
Chief Commercial Manager: B. Dardagan
Chief Planning Officer: J. F. Carlisle

Gauge: 1.673 m.
Route length: 3 394 km.

TRAFFIC

Despite continuing difficulties in Rhodesia (Now Zimbabwe), total movement capacity in 1978 was sufficient to meet all traffic on offer, both in Rhodesia and Botswana. For most of that year, wagon availability was fluid but, towards the end, a shortage of wagons developed through an upsurge in traffic combined with increased motive power problems. A serious outbreak of foot and mouth disease in Botswana heavily restricted livestock movements for a major portion of the year. Traffic to and from Zaire continued, hampered at times only by certain difficulties north of the border.

A noticeable reduction in passenger patronage on the international trains to and from South Africa resulted in the curtailment of the service to one train each way per week to Cape Town and Johannesburg.

	1978	1977
Revenue earning tonnes (thousands)	11 191	12 108
Free haul tonnes (thousands)	764	725
Total tonnes hauled (thousands)	11 955	12 833
Train engine-km (thousands)	18 017	19 427
Operating revenue per train engine-km ($)	4.514	4.287
Operating expenditure per train engine-km ($)	4.483	4.230
Gross tonne-km (millions)	12 792	13 957
Net tonne-km (millions)	5 588	6 104
Steam locomotive-km (thousands)	3 435	4 442
Diesel locomotive-km (thousands)	16 742	17 641
1st class passengers carried (thousands)	27	36
2nd class passengers carried (thousands)	179	212
3rd class passengers carried (thousands)	174	199
4th class passengers carried (thousands)	1 847	2 166
Total passengers (thousands)	2 227	2 613

FINANCES

Gross revenue for 1978 decreased to $86 706 000, from the previous year's figure of $88 738 000. On the other hand gross expenditure was reduced by a greater margin from $125 650 000 in 1976/77 to $122 403 000. The net deficit of $35 697 000 represents a reduction of 3.29 per cent on the previous year's deficit ($36 912 000). Salaries and

DE2 Loco hauling BR trucks in Botswana

15A class Garrett steam locomotive leaving Bulawayo with a mixed train

wages represented 59.55 per cent of total expenditure, and amounted to $76 714 000, a reduction of $1 150 000 compared with 1976/77.

Revenue earning tonnage dropped to 11 191 000 tonnes from 12 108 000 tonnes in 1976/77, and passenger patronage also reduced to 2 227 000 from a previous total of 2 613 000.

MOTIVE POWER AND ROLLING STOCK

At the end of 1978 RR was operating 165 steam locomotives, 81 diesel locomotives, 466 passenger coaches and 12 641 freight wagons.

The track relaying programme, involving main lines (45 kg continuously welded rail on concrete sleepers) and branch lines continued and the deviation of the main line at Que Que was brought to near completion.

The extension of Centralised Train Control on the South-East Railway was well advanced, with intended completion of the 220 km from Somabula to Rutenga in October 1978.

Triple-headed DE6 locomotives hauling an RR liner train

DIESEL LOCOMOTIVES

Class	Axle Arrangement	Transmission	Rated Power hp	Max. lb (kg)	Tractive Effort Continuous lb (kg)	at mph (kmlh)	Max. Speed mph (kmlh)	Wheel Dia. in (mm)	Total Weight Tons	Length ft ins (mm)	No. Built	Year first Built	Builders: Mechanical Parts	Engine & Type	Transmission
DEl	Co-Co	Elec	920	51 000 (23 150)	17 500 (7 940)	15 (24)	60 (96)	36 (914)	75.8	46' 8" (14 224)	6	1952	Davenport Bessler Corporation	Caterpillar D 397 (2 per Loco)	Westinghouse
DE2	1 Co-Co 1	Elec	1 710	60 500 (27 440)	36 000 (16 330)	13.6 (22.0)	55 (88)	Driven 37½ (952) Carrier 28½ (724)	113	56' 0" (17 069)	35	1955	English Electric	English Electric 16 SVT	English Electric
DE3	1 Co-Co 1	Elec	1 850	59 000 (26 760)	40 000 (18 140)	13 (20.9)	66 (106)	Driven 37½ (952) Carrier 28½ (724)	110	51' 1" (15 570)	16	1962	English Electric	English Electric 12 CSVT	English Electric
DE4	Co-Co	Elec	1 730	50 000 (22 680)	37 500 (17 010)	13.5 (21.9)	60 (96)	40 (1 016)	92	51' 1" (15 570)	14	1963	Brush Electric	Mirrlees JVSST12	Brush Electric
DE6	Co-Co	Elec	2 090	—	47 300 (21 450)	12 (19.3)	72 (116)	36 (514)	89	52' 0" (15 850)	10	1966	GE (USA)	GE FDL-12	GE

PRESERVED RAILWAYS

AUSTRALIA

AUSTRALIAN RAILWAY HISTORICAL SOCIETY
Hon National Secretary: M H Thomson, 24 Flora Street, Stepney, South Australia 5069

Telephone: 425144

Founded in 1933 as the Australian Railway and Locomotive Historical Society. The name was changed in 1951.

EMERALD TOURIST RAILWAY BOARD AND PUFFING BILLY RAILWAY
Narrow Gauge Station, Belgrave, Victoria 3160

Chairman: A P Wymond
Vice-Chairman: P D A Vard
Secretary: R J Bugg

Gauge: 0.762 m
Route length: 13.5 km

The Puffing Billy Preservation Society acts as the management body for Emerald Tourist Railway operating the Belgrave Lakeside (Emerald Lake) Puffing Billy Railway. It is eventually hoped to extend the railway 11 km to Gembrook, the original terminus. In 1978 the line carried 305 608 passengers.

MOTIVE POWER AND STOCK
The railway operates four mainline steam locomotives (plus two under restoration) and 22 passenger coaches.

NEW SOUTH WALES RAIL TRANSPORT MUSEUM
Thirlmere, New South Wales

Situated about 90 km from Sydney, the museum provides steam-hauled services over a 40 km tourist railway, although regular services do not operate over the full length of the line. Principal exhibits at the Thirlmere museum include 50 locomotives, rolling stock and miscellaneous equipment from the government and private railways in New South Wales.

PICHI RICHI RAILWAY PRESERVATION SOCIETY INC (PRRPS)
PO Box 504, Port Augusta, South Australia 5700

Secretary: K H Gray

Gauge: 1.60 m
Route length: 45 km

The Pichi Richi Railway Preservation Society was formed at a public meeting in Port Augusta in 1973 with the aim of preserving the railway through the Pichi Richi Pass and operating it as a tourist attraction. The preserved route carries passenger trains through South Australia's Flinders Ranges over a 19.3 km line from Quorn (located on the main Port Augusta—Quorn road, about 30 km north-east of Port Augusta) to Woolshed Flat.

ROUTE
The journey into the Pichi Richi Pass begins at the Quorn Railway station where the Richman Valley opens out on to the Willochra Plain. Immediately beyond the 1.5 km mark the line begins to curve into the hills on the first of fifteen curves from there to the summit. The gradient rises at 1 in 60 towards Devil's Peak and on to the summit. From here the track falls towards sea level, on to Pichi Richi station, and runs a further 3 km to the terminus at Woolshed Flat.

OPERATIONS
In 1979 the society carried 8 642 passengers, compared with 5 880 in 1978.

MOTIVE POWER
The Pichi Richi Railway operates four steam locomotives and a steam-powered motor coach in addition to a diesel-hydraulic shunter.

The three green liveried W class locomotives haul most of the passenger trains running over the route. They were originally designed for operation on the Western Australian Government Railways' system of light lines laid with 45 lb rail. Built by Beyer Peacock and Company of Manchester, England, they first entered WAGR service in April 1951, less than three months before the first Clyde GM diesel began operations on the Commonwealth Railways' Trans-Australian line. The 60 W class locos originally constructed were designed for both passenger and freight haulage. Another four, with minor alterations were built for the Silverton Tramway Company. The class is a light 4-8-2, or 'Mountain' type incorporating seal cleaning smokebox, roller bearings and Hadfield steam-operated reversing gear. The class was withdrawn from WAGR service in 1971 after only 20 years. Ws 916, 933 and 934 were stored at Collie until purchased by the PRRPS: 933 and 934 arrived at Port Augusta in March 1974, fitted with Westinghouse brake compressors, and 916 was brought to Quorn in December 1975.

The society's T.186 loco is the sole representative of the once-numerous T class locomotives operating in South Australia. The Ts were used extensively over the narrow-gauge system working passenger and freight trains both singly and double-headed or as shunters. Between 1903-17 78 T class locomotives were built. The prototype, T.180, was designed and built at South Australian Railways' Islington workshops, but the majority were turned out by Walkers of Queensland (40) and James Martin & Co of Gawler (34). PRRPS's T.186 entered service in December 1909, and was condemned in May 1970 after 2 060 000 km (1 284 739 miles). It was eventually saved from the scrapyard by the Australian Railway Historical Society and the newly-formed PRRPS. In September 1976 a restored T.186 made its delivery run to Quorn.

The most unique vehicle at Quorn is the NJAB.1, labelled the 'Coffee Pot' by PRRPS members. The engine unit was built by Kitson & Co of Leeds, England in 1905 and the coach by Metropolitan Amalgamated Railway Carriage and Wagon Co Ltd of Birmingham, England. It was introduced by the South Australian Railways in August 1906. Under the original ownership it was classified as Steam Motor Coach No 1 and stabled at Quorn to operate regular connections with trains to Adelaide via Terowie. After purchase by the Commonwealth Railways in June 1921 it was reclassified at NJAB.1 and was used from 1906-31 at the Quorn Depot. From there it went to Alice Springs as a static display until 1975 when it was relinquished by the National Trust for restoration by PRRPS back to working order. The vehicle consists of two main parts, an engine unit and a passenger coach. The rear section pivots on a point beneath the firebox on the engine frame and the cab floor is part of the coach frame. The engine unit consists of a small saturated locomotive type boiler and cab fitted on a four-wheel underframe. Two outside cylinders, with Walshchaerts gear actuating sliding valves, drive the rear axle only. The coal supply is carried in a bunker inside the cab. The coach is finished in dark oak-stained and varnished timber. Interior features include elaborate pressed ceiling patterns, seating framed in stained timber and upholstered in mock leather and linoleum floor covering. Seating is provided for nine passengers in each of two compartments.

PRRPS's 'Coffee Pot' in front of the original Quorn Railway station after delivery to South Australian Railways *(Photo: SAR Archives)*

W class 934 locomotive built in 1951 by Beyer Peacock of England
Main dimensions: cylinder diameter 0.381 × 0.609 m (16 × 24 in); driving wheel diameter 1.219 m (48 in); boiler pressure 200 psi; tractive effort 21 760 lb; length over couplers 18.872 m (61 ft 11 in); total weight 101.11 tonnes. *(Photo: PRRPS)*

PASSENGER COACHES

Nine coaches are leased or owned by the society. Wandana was the first carriage to be completely restored by the society, rebuilt from an original South Australian Railway coach which entered service in 1911 as an observation car for the PRRPS and repainted in the green and cream livery of the SAR's Port Lincoln division cars. Sturt, Light and Flinders were all originally built at Islington in 1909, each containing two compartments with longitudinal seating for 28 passengers. They were converted during 1929/30 to provide accommodation for the SAR Commissioner and his officers while on inspection tours. Flinders was the Commissioner's carriage, with observation lounges at each end. Light was converted to a dining/sleeping car but at a later date the berths were removed and kitchen facilities substituted. It now serves PRRPS as a souvenir and refreshment car. Sturt is a sleeping car but is not generally used on the society's trains. Nilpena is a sleeping car built at the Islington Workshops in 1915 and was used almost exclusively on the Broken Hill Express until 1970. It was one of the largest and most luxurious carriages on the SAR narrow-gauge system. With nine compartments the car has sleeping capacity for 18 passengers and accommodates 40 during the day.

SOUTH PACIFIC ELECTRIC RAILWAY CO-OPERATIVE SOC LTD
Tramway Museum, Royal National Park, Loftus, New South Wales
Postal Address: PO Box 103, Sydney, New South Wales

Trams from the museum's 28 exhibits (22 from Sydney, four from Brisbane, two from Ballarat) are operated over a 0.5 km track. The museum is 27 km south of Sydney on the Princes Highway.

VAN DIEMAN LIGHT RAILWAY SOCIETY
Devonport, Tasmania

Gauge: 0.60/1.067 m
Route length: 3 km

This tourist railway is operated at weekends along the banks of the River Don.

VICTORIAN RAILWAYS
67 Spencer Street, Melbourne, Victoria 3000

The Steam Preservation Co-ordinating Committee, representing Australia's three major enthusiast societies, run Victorian Railway's four retained steam locomotives on the Vintage Steam Train to country destinations. The train is hauled by either a D3, K or R locomotive pulling end-platform and vestibuled side corridor stock.

T.186, only representative of the T class locomotives on South Australia's narrow-gauge lines
Main dimensions: cylinder diameter 0.381 × 0.558 m (16 × 22 in); driving wheel diameter 1.092 m (43 in); boiler pressure 185 psi; tractive weight 21 904 lb; total weight 78.4 tonnes. *(Photo: Peter Mere)*

BELGIUM
CHEMIN DE FER A VAPEUR DES TROIS VALLÉES (CFV3V)
Maison Communale, Grand Place, 6370 Mariembourg

Chief of Operations: Jean-Marie Warzee, 1 rue de Gembloux, 5002 St-Servais

Telephone: (081) 71 11 22

Gauge: 1.435 m
Route length: 28 km

In May 1975 the officers of the Chemin de Fer à Vapeur des Trois Vallées (CFV3V) agreed to take over the Belgian National Railways (SNCB) line between Nismes and Treignes for operation of steam trains. The first tourist trains ran on 27 March 1976 hauled by three locomotives: MF 73, 82 and 91. In 1978 the agreement with SNCB was extended to include an additional section from Nismes to Mariembourg, giving CFV3V a 14 km line running through the picturesque valleys of Eau Blanche, Eau Noire and Viroin. Conveniently, the line has a direct link with SNCB trains from Charleroi to Mariembourg. Access is also possible by highway from Namur, Givet and Rochroi. The line was built in 1848 by the Chemin de Fer de l'Entre-Sambre et Meuse and was taken over by SNCB in 1926, after passing through the administration of the Grand Central Belge to become part of the direct Brussels—Vireux trunk route. The last SNCB passenger train ran on 28 September 1963 and freight trains in the following year.

OPERATIONS
Timetabled steam trains recorded 2 233 km in 1979; specials, 476 km. Diesel-hauled trains ran 4 388 km in timetable service. Number of passengers carried: 20 973.

MOTIVE POWER
The steam locomotive fleet consists of the following units:

Type HL MFL3:
Builder: UMH (Usines Métallurgiques du Hainaut); Year of construction: 1922; Class number: 5279; Axle arrangement: 0-3-0; Weight: 36.5 tonnes.

Type HL SA01:
Builder: SA Anglo-Franco-Belge des Ateliers; Year of construction: 1945; Class number: 2596; Axle arrangement: 0-3-0; Weight: 36 tonnes.

Type HL AD07:
Builder: La Meuse; Year of construction: 1942; Class number: 4672 (1951—originally 4123 in 1942); Axle arrangement: 0-4-0; Weight: 52 tonnes.

Type HL AD08:
Builder: La Meuse; Class number: 4057 (1953); Axle arrangement: 0-4-0; Weight: 55 tonnes.

Type HL SA02:
Builder: SA Anglo-Franco-Belge; Year of construction: 1945; Class number: 2590; Axle arrangement: 0-3-0; Weight: 36 tonnes.

Type HL SA03:
Builder: Ateliers Métallurgiques; Year of construction: 1929; Class number: 2002; Axle arrangement: 0-3-0.

Type HL CA04:
Builder: SA Anglo-Franco-Belge; Year of construction: 1951; Class number: 2681; Axle arrangement: 0-3-0; Weight: 36 tonnes.

Type HL AD05:
Builder: Ateliers Métallurgiques; Year of construction: 1926; Class number: 2442 (1958); Axle arrangement: 0-3-0.

Type HL MF91:
Builder: UMH; Year of construction: 1930; Class number: 5713; Axle arrangement: 0-4-0; Weight: 43.5 tonnes.

Type HL MF82:
Builder: UMH; Year of construction: 1913; Class number: 5313 (1923, 5231 in 1913); Axle arrangement: 0-3-0; Weight: tonnes.

Type HL MF62:
Builder: Baldwin; Year of construction: 1916; Axle arrangement: 0-2-0; Weight: 32 tonnes.

Type HL MF33:
Builder: HSP (Haine-Saint-Pierre); Year of construction: 1911; Class number: 1204; Axle arrangement: 0-2-0; Weight: 20 tonnes.

Type HL MF32:
Builder: HSP (Haine-Saint-Pierre); Year of construction: 1904; Class number: 792; Axle arrangement: 0-2-0; Weight: 19.7 tonnes.

Type HL "Cockerill" type III:
Builder: Cockerill à Seraing; Axle arrangement: 0-2-0; Weight: 18 tonnes.

LI TRIMBLEU
Domaine touristique de comte de Dalhem et environs, Rue de Hervé 91, B-4651 Battice

Telephone: 87 66 43 40

Gauge: 1.00 m
Route length: 11 km

This tourist line operates diesel trains over the scenic route between Trembleur and Warsage via Mortroux. Access to the line is by bus leaving Liege or by car using Autoroute E5.

RAIL DE REBECQ ROGNON (RRR)
Blocu 20, B-1380 Rebecq

Telephone: (67) 63 69 95

Secretary: Andre Fagnard

Gauge: 0.60 m
Route length: 3.1 km

The line was inaugurated between Rebecq and Rognon on 28 May 1978 using two steam locomotives and one diesel-mechanical shunter. The section once formed part of SNCB's line running from Braine-le-Comte to Tubize. The station at Rebecq can be reached by road via Mons or Nivelles.

OPERATIONS
A total of 15 200 passenger journeys was recorded in 1979.

TRAMWAY TOURISTIQUE DE L'AISNE (TTA)
Rue Auguste-Lambiotte 79-81, B-1030 Brussels

Telephone: (23) 45 76 07/(27) 36 19 80

Secretary: F Girardi-Corne

Gauge: 1.00 m
Route length: 12 km

The railway operates 8 km between Pont d'Erezee and Bergister, running steam trains and railcars. The line can be reached by SNCB trains stopping at Melreux station on the Marloie (between Namur and Arlon) to the Liege line. From Melreux station an SNCB bus takes passengers to Pont d'Erezee.

VICINAL DES GROTTES DE HAN
1 rue Joseph-Lamotte, B-5432 Han-sur-Lesse

Telephone: (84) 37 72 13

Gauge: 1.00 m
Route length: 10 km

The 5-km line operates tourist railcars from Han-sur-Lesse (about 50 km south-east of Namur) to the Han Grotto every summer.

CANADA

CAPE BRETON STEAM RAILWAY
Cape Breton Development Corp, PO Box 84, Glace Bay, Nova Scotia

Operations Manager: K MacKenzie

Gauge: 1.435 m
Route length: 19 km

Using two steam locos and 11 coaches, special excursion trains run between June and September.

NATIONAL MUSEUM OF SCIENCE & TECHNOLOGY
1867 St Laurent Boulevard, Ottawa, Ontario K1A 0M8

Telephone: (998) 4566

Director: David M Baird

Apart from 12 steam locomotives on exhibition, the museum operates two steam locos on special trains in July and August.

ONTARIO RAIL FOUNDATION MUSEUM
PO Box 64, Brampton, Ontario

Telephone: (519) 855 4009

Gauge: 1.435 m
Route length: 13 km

Trains are to operate for the first time in the summer of 1980 or 1981 at weekends and holidays from Cheltenham to Georgetown. Meanwhile special steam-hauled excursions have been operating annually over CP Rail trackage and a new building has been set up in Cheltenham to house several locomotives and rolling stock.

PRAIRIE DOG CENTRAL RAILWAY
The Vintage Locomotive Society Inc, PO Box 217, Winnipeg, Manitoba R3J 3R4

Telephone: (284) 2690

Gauge: 1.435 m
Route length: 58 km

The Prairie Dog Central operates on the Canadian National Oak Point Sub-division providing a 58 km round steam trip every summer from Winnipeg to Grosse Isle, Manitoba. Trains depart from Canadian National's St James station, Portage Avenue.

OPERATIONS
In 1979 the Prairie Dog carried 8 769 passengers.

MOTIVE POWER AND ROLLING STOCK
The City of Winnipeg 4-4-0 steam locos haul excursion trains on the Prairie Dog run. An American Standard 4-4-0 built in Scotland by Dubs & Co in 1882 for the CPR operated between Fort William and Kenora, Ontario as Number 22. It was purchased by the City of Winnipeg Hydro in 1918 for their own line between Lac du Bonnet and Pointe du Bois, Manitoba, was retired from service in 1962 and stored, and brought to Winnipeg in 1967 by low-bed trailer.
A combination coach, no 103, was built in 1908 by the Pullman Company of Chicago, Illinois for the Keweenaw Central Railway of Calumet, Michigan and was purchased by the Hydro in 1920 from a used equipment dealer in Duluth, Minnesota. Other coaches include:
Coach 104: Built in 1906 by Crossen of Coburg. Ontario for Canadian Northern. Ex-CN 3402.
Coach 105: Built in 1901 by Barney & Smith of Dayton, Ohio for Canadian Northern. Ex-CN 3422
Coach 106: Built in 1913 by Canadian Pacific Angus Shops. Ex-CP 751
Coach 107: Built in 1911 by Canadian Pacific Angus Shops. Ex-CP 181
Caboose 100: Built in 1912 by Canadian Pacific Angus Shops. Ex-CP 436192

Locomotive No 3, which originally operated in 1882 on the Canadian Pacific Railway line between Fort William and Kenora

DENMARK

DANSK JERNBANE-KLUB (DANISH RAILWAY CLUB)
Baunevej 129, DK-2630 Tastrup

Secretary: Finn Beyer Paulsen

Gauge: 1.435 m
Route length: 12 km

The club provides summer weekend passenger services on the Maribo-Bandholm branch of the Lollandsbanen (Lolland Railway), the Mariager-Handest branch and a siding at Aalborg station.

HELSINGOR JERNBANEKLUB (HELSINGOR RAILWAY CLUB)
Commercial Dept, V/Arne Christensen, Fredericiavej 36, DK-3000 Helsingor

Public Relations: P Moe

Gauge: 1.435 m
Route length: 48 km

The club operates steam trains every Sunday from May to September between Elsinore and Gilleleje, via Hornback.

MUSEUMSTOGET MARIBO-BANDHOLM, LOLLAND
Vesterbrogade 179, 1800 Copenhagen

Telephone: 01 319816

Gauge: 1.435 m
Route length: 7 km

The museum operates enthusiasts' trains through the summer weekends on a branch of the Lolland Railway. Stock operates ten steam and one diesel loco, three railcars and 17 passenger coaches.

FINLAND

JOKIOISTEN MUSEORAUTATIE OY
31600 Jokioinen

Chairman of rail operations: Olavi Kilpiö

Gauge: 0.750 m
Route length: 6.4 km

The museum of Jokioinen (where seven steam, 14 diesel and one electric locomotives are on display) operates two steam and three diesel locos over the 6.4 km museum narrow-gauge line. About 70 per cent of trains are diesel-hauled, carrying 8 900 passengers a year.

FRANCE

CHEMIN DE FER FORESTIER D'ABRESCHVILLER
Association du Chemin de Fer Forestier d'Abreschviller (ACFA), Hôtel des Cigognes, 57560 Abreschviller

Telephone: (87) 03 70 09

Gauge: 0.70 m
Route length: 6 km

Built at the turn of the century as a logging railway, the Abreschviller tourist line offers picturesque steam trips through woods and mountains. Closed by its former owner in 1966, the ACFA logging railway was founded to restore this unique European railway. The line is reached by SNCF railcars from Sarrebourg to Abreschviller or by car on the Sarrebourg—Donon highway.

OPERATIONS
In 1979 the railway carried 36 950 passengers.

MOTIVE POWER
Three steam locomotives haul timetabled trains: a Mallet 020 + 020 T built by Heilbronn in 1906; a Decauville 060 T built in 1927 and a Jung 060 built in 1944. On static display is a Mallet steam loco built by Henschel in 1911 for the Chemin de Fer Avricourt-Blamont Cirey and named Cirey No 2. Diesel loco C built by Coferna in 1953 also hauls passenger trains.

Jung-built 030 loco originally built for Austria's StmLB railway

CHEMIN DE FER FROISSY DOMPIERRE
Association Picarde pour la Préservation et l'Entretien des Véhicules Anciens (APPEVA), PO Box 106, 80001 Amiens Cedex

Telephone: (22) 46 33 81

Operating manager: J Pradayrol

Gauge: 0.60 m
Route length: 7 km

This tourist line operates in the summer along the banks of the Upper Somme in Northern France. The line lies 12 km from French National Railways Albert station (on the Paris—Lille line) and is also reached via Autoroute A1 running from Peronne, then along RN 336 towards Amiens before turning off on the RN 329 towards Bray-sur-Somme.
From Froissy station the line runs along the right bank of the Somme, curving into the Cailloux woods and climbing on a 30 o/oo gradient up to the Plateau station and dropping down into Dompierre along the D164 motorway.

OPERATIONS
In 1979 15 000 passengers travelled over the line. Sixty per cent of trains were hauled by diesel traction and 40 per cent by steam locomotive.

MOTIVE POWER
The association operates three steam locos (an additional five are being restored) and four diesels. Working steam units are an 040 T (No 4) built by Krauss in 1918 when it entered service between Sucrerie Say and Saponay, an 020 T (No 2) built by Neumeyer (1922) for the Rohmer works in Charente and an 020 T (No 1) built by Henschel.

Froissy-Dompierre's 040 (No 4) in 1979

Mallet 020 + 020 built in 1906

CHEMIN DE FER DE LA BAIE DE SOMME
PO Box 9, 80550 Le Crotoy

Telephone: (22) 27 84 15

Secretary: M Moriame, Villa Na-Ni, 2 rue des Tamaris, 80550 Le Crotoy

Gauge: 1.00 m
Route length: 27 km

Serving the seaside resorts of Le Crotoy and Cayeux-sur-Mer as well as the old fortified town of St Valéry-sur-Somme, this small network was one of the last of the narrow-gauge minor railway lines criss-crossing France. The railway originated as two metre-gauge branch lines fanning out from the station at Noyelles-sur-Mer on the Paris-Calais mainline to both sides of the estuary where the river Somme flows into the channel. Services were withdrawn as late as 1969 on the Crotoy line and 1972 between Noyelles and Cayeux. The network was completely reactivated in 1978 when steam trains again began operating around the bay between Le Crotoy and Cayeux. Access to the line is by SNCF trains running into Noyelles mainline station and by road from Abbeville via the D940.

OPERATIONS
A total of 11 500 passengers were carried in 1979; steam locomotives hauled 65 per cent of trains and diesels the remainder.

MOTIVE POWER
The railway operates three steam and two diesel locomotives. The steam park consists of 020 T No 21 built by Corpet-Louvet in 1927 for Entreprise Frot à Troytes, 020 T No 25 from the same works and 030 T No 101 built by Pinguely in 1905 for Forges de Gueugnon (Saône-et-Loire).

030 T No 101 alongside an SNCF 230 G 353

020 T No 21 hauling an early morning train out of Noyelles

CHEMIN DE FER DE LA LOGE DES GARDES
Arcon, 42370 Renaison

Gauge: 0.70 m
Route length: 2.5 km

This steam-only line operates trains in the Loire between Le Gué and La Loge des Gardes. Only access to the line is by route from Vichy, Roanne or Thiers.

MOTIVE POWER
An interesting 0.70 m gauge line for steam enthusiasts, as the locomotive used to haul tourist trains over the route was built in 1971 on the lines of an original 1875 American Standard. A second steam loco is to be built in France.

CHEMIN DE FER DE SAINT-EUTROPE
Société Etudes et Equipements, 5 square Montsouris, 75014 Paris

Telephone: 589 76 49

Gauge: 0.60 m
Route length: 2.5 km

Steam locos and diesel railcars haul tourist trains over a short line running south of Évry (Essonne). Nearest SNCF access point is Évry-Courcouronnes and buses leave Paris for Évry on RATP route 403.

CHEMIN DE FER DU VIVARAIS
CFTM, 8 rue d'Algérie, 69001 Lyon

Telephone: (78) 28 83 34

Route length: 33 km

A mountain line running from Tournon to Lamastre, it is reached via the SNCF station at Tain-L'Hermitage (on the Lyon—Marseille line) which lies about 1 km from Tournon, and by road via the A7, RN 7 or RN 86.

MOTIVE POWER
Most trains are hauled by one of three Mallets in steam: 030 + 030 Ts number 403, 404 and 414. Occasionally a 230 T No E 327 and an 040 T No 24 are used. Oldest locos are the class 403 and 404 Mallets built in 1903 for the original Vivarais railway by SLM at Winterthur. The No 414 Mallet was built by SACM in 1932.

CHEMIN DE FER TOURISTIQUE DES ALPILLES
Ajecta-Provence, 11 boulevard de Briançon, 13003 Marseille

Secretary: P Roche

Gauge: 1.435 m
Route length: 9 km

The association runs steam trains through the summer between Arles and Fontvieille along the Rhône. Arles is reached by SNCF or by road from Tarascon.

MOTIVE POWER AND ROLLING STOCK
One 060 steam loco; one vintage diesel locotractor and five passenger coaches, built between 1900 and 1910.

Steam-hauled train pulls out of Arles with a full rake of five coaches

CHEMIN DE FER TOURISTIQUE DU BREDA
Association des Modélismes Ferroviaires de Grenoble (AMEG), Gare SNCF Voyageurs, place de la Gare, 38026 Grenoble

Administration: Jean Maurice, 38330 St Ismier Cédex 618

Gauge: 1.435 m
Route length: 14 km

The association operates tourist trains every summer weekend over a 14 km line owned by a private company and used during the week for hauling paper products from a pulp plant to the SNCF network. First tourist train was run in October 1979. The line is reached by SNCF train running into Pont-charra-sur-Breda on the Grenoble—Chambéry line or by the A41, D523 or D923 motorways.

MOTIVE POWER
040 T no 17 (60 tonnes), which originally worked a coal line in St Etienne (built 1927); 020 (18 tonnes); four two-axle railcars built in Germany 1917 to 1922.

040 T 17 at the head of a tourist special in mid-1979 *(photo: Caremantrant)*

Ex-SNCF railbus X 5815 *(photo: Caremantrant)*

CHEMIN DE FER TOURISTIQUE CHINON-RICHELIEU
Association de Jeunes pour l'Entretien et la Conservation des Trains d'Autrefois, 41 rue Godot de Mauroy, 75009 Paris

Telephone: 742 26 52

Gauge: 1.435 m
Route length: 21 km

Steam hauled trains and diesel railcars share duties over this 21 km line between Chinon and Richelieu. Access is via the SNCF station at Chinon on the Tours-Chinon line or by the Tours-Chinon D751.

MOTIVE POWER
Four locomotives are in steam: 130 No 30476 built sometime between 1883 and 1922 at the Épernay works of CF de l'Est; 020 T No 2 built by Decauville in 1922 and originally operated at the Sucrerie de Saint-Just-en-Chaussée; 040 TA 137 and 141 TB 407 both once in SNCF service and built by ANF between 1913 and 1922.

CHEMIN DE FER TOURISTIQUE DES LANDES DE GASCOGNE
ABAC, PO Box 01, 33034 Bordeaux Cedex

Telephone: (58) 07 52 99

Gauge: 1.435 m
Route length: 4 km

Running between Sabres and Marquèze in south-west France, the line is reached by motorways RN 10 and RN 134.

MOTIVE POWER
Two type 030 T steam locomotives, one built by Corpet-Louvet in 1932 and another which went into operation in 1979 by La Meuse at Liège in 1903.

CHEMIN DE FER TOURISTIQUE DE LA SARTHE
Transvap, 86 avenue de Choisy, 94380 Bonneuil

Gauge: 1.435 m
Route length: 7 km

One of two preserved tourist railways in Britanny, the Sarthe was opened in September 1979 between Connerre-Beillé and Tuffé. SNCF trains call at Connerre-Beillé station on the Paris—Mans line. Cars reach the line by the RN 23.

MOTIVE POWER
Two steam locos work the line, both 030 T types. A 141-C steam locomotive is on static display at Bonnétable. In addition an ex-100 DM2-PLM locotractor constructed by SPMR in 1934 works the line and two Billard diesel railcars.

CHEMIN DE FER TOURISTIQUE DE LA VALLEE DE LA DOLLER (CFTVD)
3 chemins des Peupliers, Geishouse, 68960 Moosch

Telephone: (89) 82 31 01

President: René Schneider
Director: Michel Latscha

Gauge: 1.435 m (a new 5.1 km, 0.60 m gauge line is to be opened 1981/82)
Route length: 14 km

Founded in 1971 the CFTVD operates between Cernay and Sentheim in eastern France on what was once (1869) a branch line joining the Belfort—Colmar trunk line. It is reached by French National Railways' trains from Mulhouse which call at Cernay and by RN 66 from Mulhouse to Epinal joining the RN 83 to Cernay. From the main station at Cernay trains cross the Benelux—Basle axis before climbing out of the Thur Valley on a gradient of 17 o/oo up to a maximum altitude of 360 m. An easy run down takes passengers over two magnificent metal bridges into Dollar, through a heavily forested region and into the terminus at Sentheim.

OPERATIONS
In 1979 passenger journeys totalled 23 000 with steam trains running 5 700 km and diesel hauled trains 1 300 km. In addition the line carried 4 800 tonnes of freight using diesel power.

MOTIVE POWER
In operation during 1979 were the following:

STEAM LOCOMOTIVES

	Type	Year built	Axles	Weight (tonnes)	Power (hp)	Origin
Meuse	030T	1914	3	32	350	Chemin de Fer Robert-Espagne—Haironville (Meuse)
Couillet	030T	1912	3	31	350	Société Usinor-Montataire, works (Oise)
Franco-Belge	KDL 11	1945	4	23	300	Société Verreries de Blanc-Misseron, works (Oise)
Henschel	020T	1901	2	21	200	Société Carrières de Luzy, works (Nièvre)
Henschel	Mallet	1911	4	36	600	Chemin de fer d'Avricourt à Cirey, later CFA (Meuse)
North British Atlas	140C	1917	5	77	1 200	Later EST, finally SNCF (WE)
Winterthur		1917	2	15	150	Poudrerie Nationale de Vonges, works (Hte Saône)

DIESEL LOCOMOTIVES

	Type	Year built	Axles	Weight (tonnes)	Power (hp)	Origin
Hoffmann	DT 34	1925	2	14	84	East Germany, later Citroën (Bas-Rhin)
Campagne	D 020	1953	2	11	90	Société Boucheny de St-Satur, works (Cher)
Campagne	B. à sel	1915	2	8	76	Société Boucheny de Pithiviers, works (Loiret)
Moyse	20 TDE	1929	2	20	80	Société Dolfuss-Mieg de Mulhouse, works (Haut-Rhin)
Valermi	020	1951	2	20	125	Société de Papéterie de la Haye-Descartes (Indre et Loire)
LLD	200 BN	1953	2	36	200	Usines Peugeot de Montbéliard (Doubs)
Fauvet-Girel	DE 20	1957	2	46	330	EDF, later Centrale nucléaire de Fessenheim (Haut-Rhin)
Moyse		1920	2	5	30	Société Méniel à Meru (Oise)

RAILCARS

	Type	Year built	Axles	Weight (tonnes)	Power (hp)	Origin
De Dion Bouton	M.105	1938	2	17	180	CFTA Réseaux de Franche-comté, later Hérault, finally Gironde
Billard	9132	1948	2	9	90	CFD Réseau affermé de Saône et Loire
De Dietrich	X 3700	1949	4	42	320	SNCF Réseau Est (Haut-Rhin)
Renault U 150	X 5800	1954	4	17	160	SNCF Réseau Centre, later Savoie, finally CFD
Billard	D 693	1932	2	2	40	CFTA Hérault, line Béziers-St-Chinian (Hérault)
Métro Thomson	M 1110	1928	4	40	600	RATP Métropolitain de Paris

ROLLING STOCK

PASSENGER COACHES

Number	Type	Year built	Axles	Weight (tonnes)	Origin
1	Bb 389	1920	4	20	RATP Réseau métropolitain de Paris (Seine)
1	XR 9100	1950	2	6	CFTA Réseau de Gironde (Gironde)
1	C7tf	1901	3	15	SNCF Réseau de l'Est (Haute-Saône)
1	C6tf	1919	3	20	SNCF Réseau de l'Est
4	Bf	1892	2	8	SE later CFTA Réseau de L'Hérault, line from Montpellier to Palavas (Hérault)
1	Bf C 23	1872	2	7	CFMSC (Mamers — St-Calais)
4	B7	1929	2	20	DR then SNCF Réseau de l'Est
1	B4D	1904-50	3	20	PLM then SNCF Réseau de l'Est
3	B6	1904-50	3	21	PLM then SNCF Réseau de l'Est
5	C3, 7, 10, 12, 13	1907	2	10	HBL Réseau de Moselle
1	C 72	1907-50	2	10	HBL Réseau de Moselle Métallisée
1	3349	1927	4	54	CIWL Orient-Express and PLM

BRAKE VANS

Number	Type	Year built	Axles	Weight (tonnes)	Origin
1	Df 809	1884	2	10	CFTA Réseau de Gironde
1	Est	1930	2	20	EST then SNCF réseau EST
1	Dd2	1927	2	19	NORD then SNCF région Nord and Est (1977)
2	Df	1890	2	8	EST then CFTA (Robert-Espagne—Haironville)
1	34X	1946	4	73	

FREIGHT WAGONS

Number	Type	Year built	Axles	Weight (tonnes)	Origin
1	Est (flat)	1890	2	7	EST then CFTA (Robert-Espagne—Haironville)
1	Est (tipping)	1882	2	8	EST later SNCF working at Port d'Atelier
1	— (covered)	1865	2	4	Origin unknown but later Société Japy (Doubs)
2	PLM (covered)	1892	2	7	PLM later Poudrerie Nationale de Vonges (Hte Saône)
1	AL (covered)	1895	2	9	AL later Poudrerie Nationale de Vonges (Hte Saône)
1	— (tank)	1920	2	11	EPC, works (Haut-Rhin)

CFTVD's North British Atlas, built in 1917 at Glasgow (140 C 27)

A trio: left, Meuse No 51, right, Mallet ABC No 2, and behind, Henschel No 3

Locomotive KDL type 040 built in 1945

Billard two-axle railcar powered by a Panhard four-cylinder diesel (90 hp built in 1946)

CHEMIN DE FER TOURISTIQUE DU VERMANDOIS
Cercle Ferroviaire et Touristique du Vermandois (CFTV), PO Box 262, 02104 Saint-Quentin Cedex

Telephone: (22) 84 14 20

Gauge: 1.535 m
Route length: 22 km

Following the opening of the tourist line in September 1979 the CFTV hopes to operate diesel-powered trains every summer. Access is via the SNCF station at Saint-Quentin or by car over the RN 44 motorway. July to September first departure Saint-Quentin.

Operations
During the first month of operation the line carried 430 passengers.

MOTIVE POWER
In addition to a Fives-Lille steam loco under restoration the line owns two diesel railcars: a type SNCF U150 and SNCF ABJ4

CFTV diesel railcars showing an ex-SNCF ABJ4 in the foreground and a U150 behind

CHEMIN DE FER A VAPEUR DU RABODEAU
17 place Turenne, 57100 Thionville

Gauge: 1.435 m
Route length: 10 km

This all-steam tourist railway runs trains every summer on the line from Senones to Étival through the Rabodeau valley. The line is accessible via the SNCF station d'Étival-Clairefontaine (on the Nancy—Sainte-Dié line) or by the RN 59 motorway.

OPERATIONS
During 1979 a total of 6 000 passengers travelled on the line.

MOTIVE POWER
Three are in steam: two 040 types and one 060.

MUSÉE DES TRANSPORTS DE LA VALLÉE DU SAUSSERON
Marie de Butry/oise, 95430 Fluvers/oise

Gauge: 1.00 m; 0.60 m
Route length: 400 m; 450 m

The museum railway in the north of Ile de France works steam trains over two short lengths of track and is spending Fr 600 000 on construction of a 6 km metre-gauge extension.

MOTIVE POWER
One 12.8 tonne 030 steam locomotive (La Ferté Bernard) built in 1898 by Blanc Misseron for the Tramways de la Sarthe (metre-gauge); one 11.7 tonne 030 steam loco (No 16 St Denis d'Orques) built 1887 for Sarthe by Tubize (metre-gauge); one Billard 7.5 tonne 020 diesel (metre-gauge); one 020 electric locotractor (metre-gauge); one motor car from the Tramways de Neufchatel (metre-gauge); an 020 Decauville seven tonner built for 0.60 m gauge operation in 1911; an 020 Orenstein & Koppel 150 hp locotractor (0.60 m gauge).

MUSÉE DES TRANSPORTS DE PITHIVIERS (LOIRET)
Association du Musée des Transports Pithiviers (AMTP), Gare SNCF Pithiviers (Loiret), 7 rue Lacuee, 75012 Paris

Telephone: 628 23 47

Director: M Geiger

Gauge: 0.60 m
Route length: 4 km

In addition to several locomotives (one dating back to 1870), two tramcars, two railcars and one saloon coach on display in the museum hall, a 4 km railing line is operated. The line is the last remnant of the 0.60 m gauge link between Pithiviers and Toury (32 km). Access is made by rail from Paris Sud-Ouest to Pithiviers or by road by motorways RN51 and 721.

OPERATIONS
A total of 18 870 passengers were carried over the line in 1978/79.

MOTIVE POWER
Five locomotives are steam: 030 T named Minihic built by ANF in 1902; 130 T No 9 (Les Fontenelles) built by La Meuse in 1938; 030 T No 2 built by Hainaut in 1910; 040 T No 4 built by Henschel in 1917; 020 T (Colette) built at the Decauville works in 1914. Two diesel locomotives also haul passenger trains during peak periods.

RÉSEAU DE GUERLEDAN
La Gare, 22530 Mur-de-Bretagne

Telephone: (96) 28 59 18

Gauge: 0.31 m
Route length: 5 km

Steam trains run tourist services on this Bretagne line every summer, operating between Mur-de-Bretagne and Caurel. Nearest SNCF stations are at Pontivy (16 km away) and Loudéac (21 km). The Rennes-Brest motorway runs right past the Gueriedan line.

TRAIN FOLKLORIQUE ROSHEIM-OTTROTT
Société des Carrières de Saint-Nabor, 67530 Ottrott

Telephone: (88) 95 81 14

Gauge: 1.435 m
Route length: 8 km

Using steam only the railway, located in the east of France, operates in summer carrying tourists between Ottrott and Rosheim (Bas-Rhin). The line is accessible by SNCF trains calling at Rosheim on the Strasbourg—Sélestat line, via Molsheim, or direct to Ottrott by Autobus des Trasports Strasbourgeois de Strasbourg.

MOTIVE POWER
Two steam locomotives haul trains, the major one being an 030 T No 3 built by Borsig in Berlin (1906) for Carrières de Saint Nabor. On special occasions a North British Atlas 140 C 27 is put into service.

TRAIN TOURISTIQUE GUITRES-MARCENAIS (TTGM)
Association des amis du Chemin de Fer de la Vallée de l'Isle Nord Libournais

Administration: Jean-Louis Marron, 2 place E Barraud, 33230 Coutras

Telephone: (56) 49 03 66

Gauge: 1.435 m
Route length: 13 km

The TTGM operates on the now defunct Saintes—Coutras line opened in 1874. Trains run between Guitres and Marcenais hauled by diesel locos and (from 1980) a Meuse 020 T steam. Guitres station is 5 km from the SNCF station of Coutras, and 15 km from Libourne.

Ex-SNCF diesel railbus before restoration for tourist service over the TTGM

NORWAY
FORENINGEN SETESDALSBANEN
Postboks 81, N-4601 Kristiansand S

General Manager: Carl Fr Thorsager
Secretary: Hans C Sørensen

Gauge: 1.067 m
Route length: 5.0 km

The Setesdal Railway was originally a narrow-gauge line running from Kristiansand to Byglandsfjord and opened in 1896. The present society took over its operation after closure in 1962. The line runs from Grovane station past the Steinsfossen power station and over the Otra river via the Paulen bridge before pulling into Kringsjå. After a ten-minute halt trains continue through a 123 m tunnel on the way to the existing terminal at Løyning. Plans are in hand to extend the line about 3 km to Røyknes.

OPERATIONS
In 1979 the railway carried 5 324 passengers, with steam locomotives hauling 86 per cent of total train-km.

Hauling 1930s stock, locomotive number 2 heads out of the Setesdal Valley on a 1 in 50 gradient

MOTIVE POWER

Class	Loco no	Manufacturer	Year built	Wheel arrangement	Maximum speed (km/h) Forward	Reverse	Full load (tonnes) Water	Coal	Weight (tonnes)	No	Cylinder Diameter (mm)	Stroke (mm)	Boiler pressure (kg/cm²)	Diameter of driving wheels (mm)	Cylinder traction power (kg)
XXI	1*	Dubs	1894	2-6-2	40	40	2.1	0.8	18.7	2	279	457	10	914	2 300
XXI	2	Dubs	1894	2-6-2	40	40	2.1	0.8	18.7	2	279	457	10	914	2 300
XXI	5	Thune	1901	2-6-2	40	40	2.1	0.8	18.7	2	279	457	10	914	2 300
XXII	6	Thune	1902	2-4-2	55	55	1.8	0.8	17.4	2	279	457	10	1 146	1 850

*Stationary exhibit at Grovane station since 1963.

No 81 is on loan from NSB Railway Museum. It arrived in 1978, after 23 years at the museum and worked on the Røros line between Langlete and Rugldalen (together with No 80) as a banker (1914-42). It was then transferred to the Vestfold line and worked there until 1949. It joined the museum on 4 April 1955. Main data: maximum speed 60 km/h; boiler pressure 12 kg/cm² (super heated); cylinder traction power 4 700 kg; service weight 33.4 tonnes; heated area: 45.76 m²; wheel arrangement 2-6-4; axle load 6.3 tonnes.
No 307 was bought from SJ in 1976. Main data: four wheeled; weight 14 tonnes; axle load 7.0 tonnes; restricted to 20 km/h (max 40 km/h); diesel-hydraulic; built by Kalmar (1952).
The diesel railcar, Sulitjelma, was delivered from the Sulitjelma Railway in January 1973. Main data: built by Strømmens Verksted, Oslo (1957); max speed 65 km/h; diesel-mechanical 2 × 200 hp, Leyland 680 EU; weight 20 500 kg; seating 60.
The petrol railcar Cmbo 2672 was built by Strømmens Verksted, Oslo (1932); max speed 65 km/h; transmission mechanical 2 × 125 hp (1 600 rpm), Herkules HXB; weight 18 700 kg; seating 56.

A/L URSKOG-HØLANDSBANEN
Postboks 31, Vinderen, Oslo 3

Principal officer: O Wiegels

Gauge: 0.750 m
Route length: 3 km

The Høland Railway runs from Sörumsand to Fossum. Access is by NSB trains on the Oslo-Kongsvinger line 38 km east of Oslo.

Locos 1, 2 and 5 on the Setesdal Railway were all originally class XXI units and differ only in the date and origin of manufacture

OPERATIONS
In 1979 the line carried 6 450 passengers on steam-hauled trains.

MOTIVE POWER
Locomotives in service are three steam linehaul and one steam shunter. Two diesel-mechanical shunters are also available for station working.

SWEDEN
ANTEN-GRÄFSNÄS JÄRNVÄG (AGJ)
PO Box 300, S-441 26 Alingsås

General Manager: Lennart Nordh

Gauge: 0.891 m
Route length: 11 km

The volunteer society running the AGJ was founded in 1965 when it began to run limited excursion trains on the narrow-gauge line from Gothenburg to Forshem (now closed). It owns its own railway running alongside a lake amid mountainous scenery from Anten to Gräfsnäs Slottspark. A journey on the line usually includes a change of engine at Qvarnabo. Access is via the E3 from Gothenburg towards Alingsas/Stockholm.

BLJ 6's boiler under repair in 1979 (Photo: L Nordh)

Workhorse on the AGJ line, the 1910 Nydqvist & Holm ROJ 3 steam loco (Photo: L Nordh)

Railcar set running alongside the lake of Anten (Photo: A Jansson)

Diesel railcar and ROJ 5 steam loco pass at Kvarnabo station *(Photo: L Nordh)*

Work train hauled by diesel HBA 2 *(Photo: L Nordh)*

OPERATIONS
The number of passengers carried every year totals about 40 000, hauled by steam (87 per cent of train-km) and diesel locomotives (13 per cent).

MOTIVE POWER
Two line-haul locos in steam (six awaiting repairs) and two diesel-hydraulic locos; one railbus and two diesel railcars.

STEAM LOCOMOTIVES

	Built by	Year built
ROJ 3	Nydqvist & Holm, Sweden	1910
ROJ 5	Henschel & Sohn, Germany	1920
KBJ 5 Nanna	Nydqvist & Holm, Sweden	1897
BLJ 6	Motala, Sweden	1915
VGJ 24	Nydqvist & Holm, Sweden	1911
VGJ 31	Henschel & Sohn, Germany	1941
GÖTA 2	Orenstein & Koppel, Germany	1906
HBA 8	Orenstein & Koppel, Germany	1920

DIESEL LOCOMOTIVES

Z4	Kalmar Verkstads AB, Sweden	1951
HBA 2	Krupp, West Germany	1957
HBA 1	Krupp, West Germany	1956

JÄDRAÅS-TALLÅS JÄRNVÄG (JTJ)
PO Box 405, S-801 05 Gävle

Gauge: 0.891 m
Route length: 5 km

This is Sweden's northernmost preserved railway, based at Jädraås, which was once the operating centre of the Dala-Ockel-bo-Norrsundet Railway (DON) until the line closed in 1970. The JTJ was founded in 1968 and operates steam trains over all that is left of the original 86 km DON railway. Trains start at Jädraås at the station building, a big engine shed with turntable, carriage shops and workshop. The line runs north-west through varied woodland along the Jädraån stream. At Pallanite (2 km from Jädraås) there is a passing loop. Locomotives are turned at the terminal at Tallås before the return trip.

MOTIVE POWER
Four steam locomotives: three tank engines, an unusual 0-6-6-0 Mallet, a steam railcar built in 1888 and a steam trolley from 1897. In addition there is a battery locomotive and two small diesel engines.

MUSEISPÅRKVÄGEN MALMKÖPING
Svenska Spårvägssällskapet, PO Box 5024, S-102 41, Stockholm

Gauge: 1.435 m
Route length: 2.8 km

The Malmköping Museum Tramway at Järnvägsgatan 4 in Malmköping is the only one of its kind in Sweden. It is devoted to recreating an old-time Swedish tramway in an authentic setting. The 2.8 km line runs between Malmköping and Hosjo. The enterprise is run on a non-profit-making basis by Svenska Spårvägssällskapet.

STOCK
33 trams plus 23 trailer units representing 11 of the 13 towns in Sweden which once had tramways.

OHS BRUKS JÄRNVÄG (OBJ)
PO Box 179, S-351 04 Växjö

Gauge: 0.60 m
Route length: 15 km

The Ohs Bruks railway (OBJ) is a former narrow-gauge industrial railway constructed in 1907/10 to connect the Ohs pulpwood mill with Bor near the town of Värnamo in Sweden's Småland Province. The present OBJ line runs through an area of forest, lakes, rivers and swamps. The steepest gradient is 1 in 30 and the minimum curvature 100 m. Access to the line is from Motorway E4 via route 27 to Bors and on to Ohs Bruk. On weekdays the Linjebuss bus company operates from Värnamo to Ohs Bruk. SJ trains stop at Bor on the Värnamo-Alvesta line.

OPERATIONS
Total train-km operated in 1979 was 1 366.

MOTIVE POWER
Three steam locos, four diesel-mechanical and one petrol-mechanical locos.

Loco number 4 hauling a logging train
The locomotive was built by Maschinenbau und Bahnbedarf (now O & K) in 1944 before going to Polish State Railways after World War II. It was sold to OBJ in 1975. *(Photo: Rolf Gimle)*

Loco number 2 at Ohs Bruk
Built in 1919 by Saechsische Maschinenfabrik in Chemnitz has a tractive effort of 2 360 kg, enabling it to haul 45 tonne trains up OBJ's 33.3% grades. The loco weighs 13 tonnes in service. *(Photo: Rolf Gimle)*

Early morning starter train arrives at Ohs Bruk hauled by loco number 2 *(Photo: Rolf Gimle)*

Installation of a turntable outside the new Ohs Bruk loco depot
Simplex and Jenbacher Werke diesels are in the background with steam locos Nos 1 (Zobel 1910, Bromberg) and 2. *(Photo: Rolf Gimle)*

ÖSTRA SÖDERMANLANDS JÄRNVÄG (ÖSIJ)

PO Box 53, S-150 30 Mariefred

Chairman: B Sundberg
Traffic Manager: C Malm

Gauge: 0.60 m
Route length: 4 km

When Swedish State Railways (SJ) closed the branch from Läggesta to Mariefred, the ÖSIJ was authorised by parliament to take it over in 1965. The standard-gauge track was removed and replaced by 0.60 m trackwork. During 1973 a new approach to Läggesta was built with sharp curves and steep gradients (1:35) which lead to a bridge over SJ's lines. The new terminus at Läggesta Södra is close to both the SJ stations and the E3 main road. The railway has a total length of 3.4 km on the main Mariefred Läggesta Södra section and 0.4 km over a branch from Mariefred to the harbour station. Situated to the west of Stockholm, the line runs alongside Lake Malaren. ÖSIJ services connect with steamship departures and arrivals at Mariefreds Angbatsstation. SS *Mariefred* sails from Stockholm to Mariefred and back each day during the summer. At Läggestra ÖSIJ trains connect with SJ services on the Stockholm-Eskilstuna line.

OPERATIONS

Passengers carried in 1978 totalled 49 863 with steam locos hauling all trains operated.

LOCOMOTIVES IN STEAM:

Lotta: Typical German industrial loco. Used by Swedish State Railways (SJ) at railway construction sites; later in service at a felspar mine. Arrived at ÖSIJ in 1959.

Virå: Standard engine for Swedish public 0.60 m gauge railways. In later years, in service at a mine in Norway far north of the arctic circle. In service on ÖSIJ since 1967.

Dylta: A bigger sister of Lotta. Used at lime industries in central Sweden. Introduced by ÖSIJ in 1960. Rebuilt at Mariefred with rear carrying axle and large coalbox in 1972.

K M Nelsson: Final stage and the highlight of Swedish 0.60 m design, fitted with superheater and steambrake (Nos 3, 5 and 8 fitted with steambrake at ÖSIJ). At present ÖSIJ's most popular engine, running approx 2 500 miles *(4 123.4 km)* a year. In service since 1975.

Hamra: Articulated, four cylinder compound Mallet. Earlier in service on agricultural and limestone railways. In service with ÖSIJ since 1964. Original boiler is currently being replaced.

Christina Hjelm: Latest delivery to ÖSIJ in 1977, former Polish State Railways (PKP) T4 559. As the strongest and heaviest 0.60 m engine ever operated in Sweden, it takes maximum loads of 12 coaches over the 1:35 grades of ÖSIJ.

The railway's biggest locomotive No 6 Christina Hjelm heading the smaller No 2 Virå into Mariefred station *(Photo: H Gärdvall)*

Mallet locomotive No 5 Hamra *(Photo: H Gärdvall)*

Engine No 8 Emsfors outside Mariefred sheds

The loco was originally built in World War I for transport behind the trenches. *(Photo: H Gärdvall)*

Helgenäs: A small but typical British saddle tank of 1889 vintage. As the smallest engine in the fleet and still retaining the original boiler it has seen limited service since 1970 on special events.

Emsfors: A German Austerity of the First World War. After the war it was sold to a Swedish pulp industry. In service since 1970.
ÖSIJ also has four motor engines, one battery loco and one motorcoach.

Number	1	2	3	4	5	6	7	8
Name	Lotta	Virå	Dylta	K M Nelsson	Hamra	Christina Hjelm	Helgenäs	Emsfors
Builder	O & K†	MV*	O & K	MV	O & K	Hanomag	Hudswell Clark	Sächsische MF
Works number	6620	272	7443	520	930	10194	346	4290
Year	1913	1901	1919	1914	1902	1923	1889	1919
Wheel arrangement	0-4-0	2-4-2	0-4-2	2-6-2	0-4-4-0	0-8-0	0-4-2	0-8-0
Cylinder (in)	5¾	7½	7¼	10¼	7⅝, 11⅝	11½	7½	9½
Stroke (in)	10¼	11	11¾	11	10¼	13¾	12	9½
Wheel, driver (in)	20½	23⅝	23⅝	23⅝	22⅞	26⅜	24	22½
Wheel carrying (in)	—	17¾	16⅛	17¾	—	—	16	—
Wheelbase, rigid (ft in)	3 11¼	3 7¼	4 7⅛	4 11	2 7½	5 3	4 0	2 7
Wheelbase, total (ft in)	3 11¼	10 11⅞	8 4	12 11½	9 6⅛	9 2¼	7 8½	7 6
Weight, empty (tonnes)	4.5	9.8	6.9	14.3	11.8	15.8	4	9.5
Weight, working (tonnes)	5.4	12	8.4	16.4	14.8	19	5	11.8
Weight, adhesion (tonnes)	5.4	7.9	7.6	11.8	14.8	19	4	11.8
Grate area (sq ft)	2.7	3.9	3.8	5.3	5.7	8.2	1.9	4.5
Heating surface (sq ft)	78.5	254	129	243	310	358	69	176
Superheater (sq ft)	—	—	—	72	—	—	—	—
Boiler pressure (hp)	140	155	140	155	185	155	100	170
Tractive effort (at 75% pressure) (lb)	1 700	3 060	2 820	5 730	6 440	7 980	2 094	4 810
Water capacity (galls)	84	220	120	375	340	350	75	240
Coal capacity (lb)	440	660	1 100	1 000	1 500	2 200	265	660
Length over bufferbeams (ft in)	11 6	15 6	14 9	18 2	17 2	19 6	11 10	18 0

* MV: Motala Verkstad, Motala, Sweden
† O & K: Orenstein & Koppel, Berlin, Germany

PASSENGER COACHES

Originating railway	*Class*	*Number*	*No of seats in class 2*	*3*	*Weight empty (tonnes)*	*Length over bufferbeams (m)*	*Builder*	*Year*	*Overhauled at ÖSIJ*	
AOJ	Co	1	—	30	4.0	9.0	Decauville Ainé, Paris	1898	1969	
HRRJ	CFo	7	—	22	4.5	9.0	Decauville Ainé, Paris	1898	1969	
HRRJ	Co	6	—	48	3.8	8.7	Helsingborg Mek Verkstad	1891	1971	
JGJ	Co	2	—	28		10.0	Vabis	1893	—	
JGJ	CNo	62	—	24	4.0	8.0	Hjo Mek Verkstad	1899	1962	
KLJ	C	102	—	12	1.2	4.0	KLJ Verkstad	1888	1975	
KLJ	BCFo	103	8	16	6.3	10.0	R Dohlberg, Rostock	1893	1971	(1)
MJ	Co	1	—	20	4.0	7.0	Vabis	1894	1959	
MJ	Clo	21	—	24	4.2	7.0	Vabis	1894	1967	
NAEJ	BCo	3	8	20	6.0	10.0	Kosta Mek Verkstad	1907	1968	
NAEJ	BCo	4	10	20		10.0	Vabis	1910	—	(2)
StJ	BCo	2	10	20	5.4	10.0	Vabis	1901	1967	

(1) In service since 1959
(2) In service 1979

UPSALA-LENNA-JERNVÄG (ULJ)
PO Box 3076, S-750 03 Uppsala

Telephone: 018 13 05 00

Gauge: 0.891 m
Route length: 20 km

ULJ is a 20 km stretch of the former Stockholm-Roslagens Järnvägar running eastward from Uppsala to Lenna Bruk (former ironworks and sawmill). Opened in 1876, the single track line crosses the Uppsala plain before winding its way through lake and forest scenery of the Roslagen district, north-east of Stockholm. From Selknä Halt the Swedish Tramway Society runs a bus service to Uppsala City park at Fjällnora. From Länna the line continues a further 13 km to Faringe, SRJmf's rolling stock depot. At present, SRJmf has 13 locomotives (six of them steam), 12 veteran passenger coaches, 69 other wagons, two diesel railcars and a variety of other items.

SWITZERLAND
APPENZELLER-BAHN AB
Eastern Switzerland

Steam engine G 3/4 No 14 and two passenger carriages, built 1886, and renovated; plus one renovated summer passenger carriage.

ROUTE
Gossau-Herisau-Urnaesch-Appenzell-Wasserauen.

BERNER-OBERLAND-BAHNEN BOB
Bernese Oberland

Steam engine BOB/MEFEZ G 3/4 No 11 (built 1902 for Rhaetian Railway); rack-and-pinion steam engine to Schynige Platte.

ROUTES
Interlaken Ost-Luetschental-Interlaken Ost, Wilderswil-Schynige Platte-Wilderswil.

BLONAY-CHAMBY BC
Lake Geneva

Museum Railway Line run by enthusiasts.

ROUTES
Blonay-Chamby-Blonay, Chamby-Chaulin (Depot/Museum)-Chamby.

BODENSEE-TOGGENBURG-BAHN BT
Eastern Switzerland

Amor Express, including Maffei steam engine Eb3/5 and four to five special carriages (capacity approximately 200).

ROUTE
Herisau-Nesslau-Neu St Johann-Herisau (journey time 1¼ hours each way).

BRIENZ-ROTHORN-BAHN BRB
Bernese Oberland

Rack-and-pinion mountain railway, the only steam-powered public line which runs daily to a set timetable.

ROUTE
Brienz-Rothorn-Kulm.Brienz.

CHEMIN DE FER FRIBOURGEOIS GFM
Fribourg Region

Excursions run by the Blonay-Chamby Museum Railway Line.

ROUTE
Palezieux-Chatel-St Denis-Bulle-Gruyères-Montsovon and Bulle-Broc.

DAMPFBAHN-VEREIN ZUERCHER OBERLAND DVZO
Zurich

New Museum Railway run by enthusiasts.

ROUTE
Bauma-Baeretswil-Hinwil.

EMMENTAL-BURGDORF-THUN-BAHN EBT
Emmental Region

Steam engine Ed 3/4 No 11 and period carriages (Eurovapor); steam engine Ed 4/5 No 8 and period carriages (Verein Dampf-Bahn Bern).

ROUTE
Burgdorf-Ramsei-Willisau.

OENSINGEN-BALSTHAL-BAHN OeBB
Jura Region/Basel

Chluser Schnaegg steam train.

ROUTE
Balsthal-Oensingen-Balsthal (approx 1 hour).

MOTIVE POWER AND ROLLING STOCK
Krauss Maffei steam locos E3/3 and 3/3; steam loco one Eh2, Baur 50, tender two 2T26, formerly DB (in collaboration with Eurovapor); two B2's of Gotthard Line; bar carriage (music/dance); historic dining car of Simplon-Orient-Express; saloon carriage with bar/saloon; Louis XV salon with bay.

SCHINZNACHER BAUMSCHULBAHN SchBB
Basel/Zurich

0.60 m gauge works railway along track in tree and plant nursery, three steam engines (2/2, 3/3, 4/4), track length 3 km.

SCHWEIZERISCHE BUNDESBAHNEN SBB/CFF/FFS

Swiss Federal Railways organises a few public excursions every year, using one or more of the following steam engines: A3/5 No 705, B3/4 No 1367, C5/6 No 2978, Eb2/4 No 5469 and Eb3/5 No 5819.

SIHLTAL-ZURICH-UETLIBERG-BAHN SZU
Zurich

Schnaaggi-Schaaggi steam train. Le Boeuf, SNCF Steam Engine 4/7, type 241-A-65 can be viewed at Sihlwald.

ROUTE
Zurich Selnau-Sihlwald-Zurich Selnau including one hour stop-over at Sihlwald.

SURSEE-TRIENGEN-BAHN ST
Central Switzerland

Two E3/3 steam engines and three passenger carriages.

ROUTE
Sursee-Triengen (9 km).

VEREIN MIKADO 1244
Zurich

Steam engine Liberation 141 R 1244 (1 D 1), formerly SNCF renovated by the Society Mikado 1244.

ROUTE
Winterthur-Romanshorn-Rorschach return.

WALDENBURGERBAHN WB
Basel Region

Steam train WB, steam engine Gedeon Thommen No 5; steam train Eurovapor; steam engine ex Steyertalbahn.
Narrow-gauge line (0.750 m), 13.5 km.

ROUTE
Liestal-Waldenburg-Liestal.

UNITED KINGDOM
THE BLUEBELL RAILWAY LTD
Sheffield Park Station, Nr Uckfield, East Sussex, England

Line Superintendent: B J Holden
Secretary: J E Potter

Gauge: 1.435 m
Route length: 8 km

Established in 1960 with two locomotives and two coaches, the Bluebell Railway is the home of the largest and most comprehensive collection of vintage railway locomotives, carriages and wagons that operate in the south of England. Situated in the heart of the Sussex Weald the line operates vintage steam trains through the summer. Trains leave Sheffield Park on a 1:75 climb alongside the River Ouse before leaving the valley at Horsted Keynes. Much of the pre-1923 atmosphere of the former London-Brighton and South-Coast Railway has been restored at Sheffield Park while at Horsted Keynes, at the northerly end of the line, the emphasis is on the period immediately following 1923 when the Southern Railway took over. The Bluebell Extension Railway has recently acquired the station site at West Hoathly, north of Horsted Keynes, and hopes to reinstate the line a further 9 km as far as East Grinstead where connections will be possible with British Rail trains. It is possible to reach the railway by rail/express bus services offering bus connections with British Rail Southern region trains at Haywards Heath. Sheffield Park station is exactly 14.5 km from both Lewes and East Grinstead on the A275 road, 3.2 km north of its junction with the A272.

OPERATIONS
In 1979 a total of 291 236 passenger journeys were recorded.

MOTIVE POWER

Loco	*Builder*	*Year*	*Originating Railway*	*Type*
230T	Brighton	1875	LBSCR/Stepney	Stroudley type A1 X
030T		1872	LBSCR/Fenchurch	Stroudley type A1 X
031T		1898	LBSCR/Birch Grove	Billington type E4
030T		1910	SECR	
030T		1910	SECR/Bluebell	Wainright type P
030T		1910	SECR/Pioneer II	Adams type 0415
221T	Neilson	1885	LSWR	Adams type 0415
030T		1880	NLR	
220	Swindon	1938	GWR/Earl of Berkely	
230		1954	British Rail	
020T		1893	LSWR/Normandy	Adams type B4
030T		1901	SECR	
231	Brighton	1946	Southern/Blackmore Vale	Battle of Britain type
030T		1942	Southern	Bulled type Q1
030T	Vulcan, USA	1943	Southern	US identification 030 TU
030T	Avonside	1927	Industrial/Stamford	
110T	Aveling-Potter	1926	Industrial/Blue Linde	
020T	Fletcher	1877	Industrial/Baxter	
Diesel	Howard	1926	Industrial	
150			British Rail (Purchased Oct. 1978)	
132T			British Rail (Purchased Oct. 1978)	
130	Brighton	1928	Southern	

COLNE VALLEY RAILWAY CO LTD

Railway Station, Yeldham Road, Castle Headingham, Halstead, Essex CO9 3DZ, England

Telephone: 0787 61174

Gauge: 1.435 m
Route length: 1.2 km

MOTIVE POWER

Five steam locos.

DART VALLEY LIGHT RAILWAY LTD

(Dart Valley and Torbay and Dartmouth Railways)
The Station, Buckfastleigh, South Devon TQ11 0DZ, England

Telephone: 03644 3536 (office), 2338 (enquiries)

Gauge: 1.435 m

The Dart Valley Light Railway operates two steam lines, the Dart Valley Railway from Buckfastleigh, and the Torbay and Dartmouth Railway between Paignton and Kingswear. Both capture the days of the Great Western Railway. Between them the two railways take passengers down stretches of the River Dart from its middle reaches around Buckfastleigh, passing through the valleys of the Dartmoor foothills on the way to Totnes. Downstream the Torbay and Dartmouth Railway suddenly emerges high on the slopes overlooking the River Dart, a tidal estuary surrounded by steep wooded hills, as it approaches Kingswear and Dartmouth.

When the building of the railways in South Devon was under discussion in the late 1830s/early 1840s, today's British Rail route (via Teignmouth, Newton Abbot, Totnes and South Brent to Plymouth) was eventually chosen.

The seaside resort of Torquay found itself not on a through route but on a branch from the mainline at Newton Abbot. The first section of the Torquay line was opened from Newton Abbot to what is today Torre station in 1848; another 11 years passed before the railway was extended from Torre to Paignton and a further five years were needed to complete the line from Paignton onwards through Churston Ferrers to Kingswear, finally opened to passenger traffic in August 1864. Although the Kingswear branch eventually had double track between Newton Abbot and Paignton it has always remained single line between Paignton and Kingswear with a passing loop at Churston, which was also the junction station for the short branch to Brixham.

The Ashburton branch was built during the 1870s and opened to traffic in May 1872, worked originally by the South Devon Railway. Although original plans for a line to Ashburton envisaged the branch leaving the mainline at Newton Abbot and approaching Ashburton from the east, the branch that was actually built after more than 25 years of discussion left the mainline at Totnes and followed the valley of the River Dart through Staverton and Buckfastleigh to reach Ashburton.

Although independent companies promoted and built the various sections of the railway which today form part of the Dart Valley Light Railway system, working arrangements and takeovers meant that effectively the South Devon Railway operated both the Kingswear and Ashburton lines. The South Devon Railway itself worked very closely with the Bristol & Exeter Railway and both effectively were under the influence of the Great Western Railway which operated the London-Bristol line. The South Devon Railway was amalgamated with the Great Western Railway in 1878 and the GWR remained in charge for the next 70 years until nationalisation of the main railway companies in 1948.

The Dart Valley's Buckfastleigh line running from Totnes to Ashburton was a typical GWR branch, operated by small tank engines and one or two-coach passenger trains, shuttling back and forth to connect at Totnes with the mainline trains between London, Plymouth and Penzance. The line also carried one or two goods trains every day, carrying general freight, with animal feeding stuffs, fertilisers and coal coming into the small country market town and horticultural produce and woollen goods going out. There was also a lively traffic in cattle and sheep.

In contrast, the Paignton-Kingswear line, although having a local service from Newton Abbot or Exeter, was nevertheless regarded as an important mainline since it carried express trains both to London and the Midlands. Highlights of each day were its named expresses, the Torbay Express from London and the Devonian from Leeds.

Although the two lines carried some of the heaviest traffic ever carried on the South Devon railways, the expansion of private motoring took its toll of rail passenger traffic. Little more than a decade after British Railways had taken over from the GWR the beginning of the end of the great steam age was in sight as diesel locomotives and diesel powered railcars gradually took over services in the West of England.

Passenger services on the Totnes-Ashburton branch were among the first on Britain's branchlines to be withdrawn under the 1958 programme of service reductions. Freight traffic continued to trickle along the line until the branch was closed completely in September 1962.

A group of businessmen then published outline details of a scheme for saving the line and restoring passenger services as a tourist attraction with steam engines, following the 1951 restoration of the narrow-gauge Talylln Railway in West Wales and the rescue of the derelict Festiniog Railway in 1954. Encouraging South Devon enthusiasts to save the lines was also the Bluebell Line in Sussex, England, which reopened in 1960 as the first standard-gauge preservation venture for passenger trains and the first to take over a closed section of British Rail.

The Dart Valley Railway was eventually opened on 21 May 1969 although it has never been possible for trains of the privately-owned railway to reach British Rail's Totnes station. Although there is a connection, this is used only for stock transfer or for occasional through-excursions of British Rail trains to Buckfastleigh. From the start of preservation, plans have existed for a new station at Totnes Riverside, near the east bank of the river Dart, with, hopefully, passenger access across the Dart to connect with the British Rail line to Plymouth.

The Dart Valley Light Railway took over the running of the Paignton-Kingswear line late in 1972 under the title Torbay Steam Railway (now known as the Torbay and Dartmouth Railway). The two lines are totally dissimilar in character, both in location and the types of traffic. The original Dart Valley line from Buckfastleigh is purely a branch line, while the Paignton-Kingswear, although single track, was in fact fully up to mainline standards and able to carry the largest and heaviest locomotives ever to run on British Rail. In 1973, for instance, the world-famous London North-Eastern Region Flying Scotsman worked on the Torbay and Dartmouth Railway (TDR). The TDR line, moreover, is situated right in the heart of the important Torbay holiday area, starting at Paignton's town centre. A crossover connection between British Rail's tracks and the TDR at Paignton makes it possible to run through-excursions from British Rail starting points to Kingswear with steam locos taking over from British Rail's diesel units in Paignton station.

The Buckfastleigh line is just off the Exeter-Plymouth A38 dual-carriageway and is reached by British Rail to Newton Abbot, then service 188/9 bus. Other buses run from Torbay and Totnes (service 115) and from Exeter/Plymouth (service 129).

OPERATIONS

Traffic receipts in 1978 for the TDR totalled £135 666, leaving a line profit of £64 303 compared with a profit of £46 808 in 1977. The DVR receipts were £70 287 in 1978 leaving a line profit of £28 276.

MOTIVE POWER

Steam locomotives

Class	*Type*	*No.*	*Name*	*Details*	*Year*
78XX (Manor)	4-6-0	7827	Lydham Manor	Built Swindon WR	1951
5205	2-8-0T	5239		Built Swindon GWR	1924
45XX	2-6-2T	4555		Built Swindon GWR	1924
4575	2-6-2T	4588*a*		Built Swindon GWR	1927
64XX	0-6-0PT	6430		Built Swindon GWR	1937
	0-6-0PT	6435		Built Swindon GWR	1937
16XX	0-6-0PT	1638		Built Swindon WR	1951
1366	0-6-0PT	1369		Built Swindon GWR	1934
14XX	0-4-2T	1420	Bulliver	Built Swindon GWR	1934
	0-4-2T	1450	Ashburton	Built Swindon GWR	1934
BR 4MT	2-6-4T	80064*b*		Built Brighton BR	1953
MOS	0-6-0ST		Maureen*c*	Built Leeds Hunslet	
MOS	0-6-0ST	2766*c*		Built Bagnall	
MOS	0-6-0ST		Glendower*c*	Built Leeds Hunslet	1954
Hall	4-6-0	4920*d*	Dumbleton Hall	Built Swindon GWR	1929
M5	0-4-0ST	1*a*	Ashley	Built Bristol Peckett	1942
R4	0-4-0ST	1690	Lady Angela	Built Bristol Peckett	1926
0398	2-4-0WT	30587*e*		Built Nine Elms LSWR	1874

a Owned by Dart Valley Railway Association.
b Owned by 80064 Group.
c Owned by Glendower Group.
d Owned by Dumbleton Hall Society.
e On loan from National Railway Museum.

4-6-0 No 7827, Lydham Manor: Biggest of the locomotives in services is the Great Western Manor class 4-6-0 No 7827, Lydham Manor. The class was intended for lines with a light axle limit, largely used in Central Wales but also on other cross-country services. No 7827 was bought in 1970 by the Dart Valley Railway Association for restoration, completed at the end of 1972. Apart from use on heaviest trains on the Paignton line it is also employed on British Rail through excursions to Kingswear.

5205 Class 2-8-0T No 5239: The most powerful preserved tank engine in Britain, a development of Churchward's 42XX class of 1910 used mainly on heavy South Wales coal trains. Swindon-built in 1924, 5239 was withdrawn by British Rail in 1963, and bought by the Dart Valley Railway in 1973. After extensive restoration she entered service on the Torbay and Dartmouth line in 1978.

45XX Class 2-6-2Ts Nos 4555 and 4588: Built respectively in 1924 and 1927, basically to the same class but differing in details.

0-6-0 Pannier tanks: There are a number of these engines of various classes on both lines originally built for branch passenger work, short freight trains and empty stock duties. They are fairly powerful machines although the heaviest loads on the Kingswear line are just outside their limits single-handed.

14XX 0-4-2Ts Nos 1420 and 1450: These small tank engines were originally built by the Great Western in the 1930s specifically for branch passenger work, usually in conjunction with one or two push-pull fitted coaches. Used on many of the services on the Buckfastleigh line.

Engines undergoing restoration at present include a British Rail Class 4 2-6-4T, Ministry of Supply Austerity 0-6-0STs, Dumbleton Hall, etc.

Although several of the coaches are British Rail standard types bought for Dart Valley and TDR services almost straight from everyday work on British Rail, and therefore needing little major attention, quite a number of the coaching vehicles, particularly actual Great Western types, had been taken out of service and were stored awaiting disposal or scrapping for some time before rescue. In some cases, because of their historical interest, coaches had been rescued from such uses as engineer's department mess vehicles or engineer's saloons. Bodywork had often been altered, patched up or had rotted away, since practically all of the older coaches had timber bodies.

Apart from the everyday coaches formed from the British Rail open-type vehicles and the former Great Western push-pull saloons, the passenger fleet covers a representative selection of types stretching back for almost 100 years: 1. The Victoria saloon, one of the Royal train vehicles of the Great Western 1894 Royal train, a WR first and second class brake composite coach was used. 2. The wide body super saloons named *King George* and *Duchess of York* which were built by the Great Western in 1932 for the London-Plymouth Ocean Liner boat trains. These were the Great Western's answer to the Pullman cars of the Southern Railway. 3. The *Devon Belle* observation car, another vehicle with an interesting history. It was originally built in 1917 as an ambulance coach for the London & North Western Railway but was converted with a new body in 1921 into a Pullman car. After the second World War it was again rebuilt, this time with an observation end for the Southern Railway's short-lived *Devon Belle* Pullman train between Waterloo and Ilfracombe. After that service was discontinued the observation car was later transferred to routes in the Scottish Highlands where it was attached to ordinary trains as an observation vehicle to give passengers a superb view of Highland scenery; it spent much of its time on the line between Inverness and Kyle of Lochalsh. The railway was fortunate in being able to rescue it after withdrawal from that service and bring it to Buckfastleigh. The Southern had two of these observation cars for the *Devon Belle*; the other car went to the USA with the *Flying Scotsman* tour train in 1969.

Coaches of interest

Type	No.	Name	details	Year
Super Saloon	9111	King George	from GWR Plymouth-London boat train	1932
Super Saloon	9116	Duchess of York	from GWR Plymouth-London boat train	1932
Observation Car	281	Devon Belle	SR Pullman Train Devon Belle	1917*a*
Victoria Saloon	249	Queen Victoria	ex 1894 Royal Train	1894
Hawksworth Brake 1st/2nd	7377		used on Western Region Royal Train	—
Buffet Car	W7		ex GWR Dynamometer car	—

a Originally built as an ambulance coach; converted into Pullman car in 1921; rebuilt after second World War for Devon Belle Pullman running between Waterloo and Ilfracombe.

No 4555 climbs away from Greenway Tunnel towards Churston with a Kingswear-Paignton train *(Photo: Tim Stephens)*

Lydham Manor No 7827 with a train for Kingswear crossing the Hookhills viaduct near Paignton *(Photo: P Cocks)*

Link-up of tanks (left to right): No 1450 Ashburton, No 4555, No 1638, No 1420 Bulliver, and No 1 Lady Angela *(Photo: J R Besley)*

Dart Valley's most powerful tank loco 2-8-0T No 5239 on the Paignton-Kingswear run *(Photo: P Cocks)*

DERWENT VALLEY RAILWAY COMPANY
Layerthorpe State, York, England

Telephone: 0904 58981

Gauge: 1.435 m
Route length: 6 km (York to Dunnington)

MOTIVE POWER
One steam loco and two diesels.

FAIRBOURNE RAILWAY LTD
Beach Road, Fairbourne, Gwynedd LL38 2EX, Wales

Telephone: 034 16 250362

Secretary: J N Murray

Gauge: 0.381 m
Route length: 3.1 km

Although the track gauge of the Fairbourne Railway is only 15 in (381 mm), it is not solely a tourist attraction. It is a useful local passenger route, descended from a nineteenth century horse-drawn freight tramway, which later introduced passenger cars. These ran between the then new resort of Fairbourne and Penrhyn Point where there is a ferry across the narrow channel to Barmouth. In 1916 the track was converted to 15 in (381 mm) gauge and steam traction was introduced, the new system being based on pioneer freight and passenger lines built to this small but practical gauge. The Line runs through dunes and along one of the Cardigan Bay beaches. The views inland include the renowned mountain ringed Mawddach Estuary, and seawards extend over Barmouth Bay northwards to the Lleyn Peninsula.
Access is from Barmouth Quay ferries, connecting with trains at Barmouth Ferry terminus. There are four stops before the other terminus at Fairbourne is reached after a journey of about 3.0 km. This is alongside the British Rail Fairbourne Station and close to the A 493 Dolgellau—Tywyn road.

MOTIVE POWER
Prince Edward of Wales:
Type: 4-4-2 Class 20
Builder: Bassett Lowke
No & Date: 22/1915
Designer: H Greenly
Driving Wheels: 1 ft 6 in
Cylinders: $3^9/_{16}$ × 6 in
Pres: 125 lb. Grid Sup'r Len 14 ft 9 in O'All W.W.O. 1¾ tons
Prince Charles:
(ex Dudley Zoo Railway)
Type: 4-6-0 scale model of LMS Stanier Class 5, Livery—Midland Red.
Builder: G & S Light Eng & Maint Co Ltd, Stourbridge.
No & Date: 9/46
Designer: Maskelyn & Twining
Driving Wheels: 20 in diameter
Cylinders: Two $5^1/_{16}$ dia × 8 in stroke. Piston valves.
Brakes: Steam on engine—Hand brake—Tender
On loan from H T Guest, Stourbridge. Returned to Stourbridge 1962
Katie (original):
Type: 0-4-0-T
Builder: Heywood
No & Date: Duffield Bank 4/1896
Designer: Heywood
Driving Wheels: 1 ft 3 in
Cylinders: $4^5/_8$ × 7 in
Pres: 160 lb. Heywood valve gear. Len 8 ft O'All W.W.O. 3¼ tons.
Count Louis:
Type: 4-4-2 Class 30
Builder: Bassett Lowke
No & Date: ?/1924
Designer: H Greenly
Driving Wheels: 1 ft 8 in
Cylinders: $4^1/_8$ × 6¾ in
Pres: 130 lb. Sup'r (removed) Len 16 ft 4 in W.W.O. 2¼ tons
New tender—1956. Overhauled—1961; steam brakes, two safety valves.
"No 1":
Type: 4-2-2
Builder: Regent St Polytechnic, London
No & Date: 1425/1893
Designer: W G Bagnall, Stafford
Driving Wheels: 2 ft 0 in
Cylinders: 4 × 6½ in
Pres: 150 lb (new) Rigid wheel base 2 ft 9 in
Ernest W. Twining:
(ex Dudley Zoo Railway)
Type: 4-6-2 free-lance Pacific
Builder: G & S Light Eng & Maint Co Ltd, Stourbridge
No & Date: 10/1949
Designer: E W Twining
Driving Wheels: 20 in diameter
Cylinders: Two $5^1/_{16}$ dia × 8 in stroke. Piston valves
Livery: Caledonian blue
Brakes: Engine—steam—Tender, hand
On loan from H T Guest, Stourbridge
Bogie tender, air brakes and new boiler 1966
Siân:
Type: 2-4-2 free-lance—Outside frames
Builder: Guest Eng & Maint Co Ltd, Stourbridge
No & Date: 18/1963
Designer: E W Twining

Driving Wheels: 20 in diameter
Cylinders: Two 5¹/₁₆ dia × 8 in stroke. Piston valves
Livery: Mid-Brunswick green
Brakes: Engine—steam—Tender, Westinghouse air and hand
Katie:
Type: 2-4-2 Free-lance—outside frames
Builder: Guest Eng and Maint Co Ltd, Stourbridge
Date: 1950
Designer: E W Twining
Built for Dudley Zoo and sold to the late Capt Hewett and thence to Fairbourne Railway in 1965. Similar to Siân for which this locomotive could be said to be the prototype.
Dingo:
Type: Bo + Bo Petrol
New Body fitted 1952
Withdrawn
Whippet Quick:
Type: 0-4-4 Petrol
1955—Enclosed cab
Motive Power: Converted 1962 to Diesel. 3 Cylinder aircooled
Withdrawn
Gwril:
Type: 0-4-0 Petrol
Body removed about six years ago
Withdrawn
Rachel:
Type: 0-6-0 Shunter
Builder: G & S Light Eng & Maint Co Ltd, Stourbridge
No & Date: 15/1959
Designer: H T Guest
Motive Power: 2½ litre Daimler engine, with fluid flywheel and pre-selector gears
Brakes: Air-operated and hand transmission
Livery: Mid-Brunswick green
Sylvia:
Type: Bo + Bo
Builder: Guest Eng & Maint Co Ltd, Stourbridge
No & Date: 14/1961
Designer: H T Guest
Motive Power: 3½ litre Daimler Majestic engine, driving through Borg-Warner auto gear box and hydraulic drive to each bogie
This locomotive is unique, in that it is equipped with disc brakes, operated through the Westinghouse system of air brake equipment
Hand transmission brake
Livery: Mid-Brunswick green

Katie 2-4-2, built 1954, standing at the Ferry Terminus

FESTINIOG RAILWAY
Porthmadog, Gwynedd, Wales

Telephone: 0766 2384

Chief Executive: P R Wollan
General Manager: A G W Garraway

Gauge: 0.60 m
Route length: 19.7 km

The views from the Festiniog train are rarely equalled anywhere in the UK. Starting on a journey from Porthmadog, the panorama of Snowdonia on the one hand and Harlech Castle, Borth y Gest and the sea on the other, gradually gives way to the forested valley of the River Dwyryd as the train climbs out of the valley. Tan-y-Bwlch station (12 km from Porthmadog) rests in a bowl in the mountains, where the trains pause for the engine to take water. Above Tan-y-Bwlch the scenery is more open with views south and east to Trawsfynydd and Llan Ffestiniog. Beyond Ddaullt part of the original railway route was compulsorarily purchased some years ago and a completely new route has been built. This includes a complete spiral (the only one in the UK) so the train can gain height and a new tunnel through a spur of the Moelwyn Mountains to the shores of Llyn Ystradau. The line was opened by the present Festiniog Railway Company in 1836; one of the few railway companies formed at that time which are still in existence. The line was engineered with a continuous gradient so that loaded wagons of slate from the quarries in the mountains to Porthmadog could run down on gravity trains. Horses pulled the empties up again. The first steam locomotives arrived in 1863.

The line was closed in 1946 and re-opened for steam-hauled passenger services in 1955.
Porthmadog is reached by road from Caernarvon (A487), Beddgelert (A498), Betws-y-Coed (A470), Harlech (A496) or Dolgellau (A470). British Rail trains from Harlech or Caernarvon connect with the Festiniog at Minffordd station just outside Porthmadog.

OPERATIONS
A total of 410 000 passenger journeys was made in 1978.

MOTIVE POWER AND ROLLING STOCK
The Festiniog maintains 11 locomotives in steam; five for hauling passenger trains and six used for shunting and work train duties. In addition there is a diesel-mechanical loco available for emergency line-haul service. The railway retains 27 first and third-class coaches in addition to 100 freight wagons.

Double Fairlie locomotive passes through Rhiwgoch
Originally used for passing slate trains in the days when they ran down by gravity and returned behind horses.

Linda (right), on push-pull service passes the double Fairlie, Merddin Emrys

GREAT ORME RAILWAY
Victoria Station, Church Walks, Llandudno, Wales

Telephone: 0492 76749

Gauge: 1.067 m
Route length: 1.5 km

A two section railway, changing over to cable haulage at halfway station. Operates from May until October.

ISLE OF MAN STEAM RAILWAY
Terminus Building, Strathallan Crescent, Douglas, Isle of Man

Telephone: 0624 4549/4540

Chief Executive: W Jackson

Gauge: 0.914 m
Route length: 24.75 km

The preserved Victorian/Edwardian steam and Manx Electric Railway, once the 'work horses' of the Island's community, are now operated purely as tourist services. The two railway systems travel through rural and coastal scenery and link up with the Snaefell Mountain Railway.
The vintage steam railway, the longest narrow-gauge steam system in the UK, operates between the southern-most tip of the island at Port Erin and Douglas Bank Hill station.

OPERATIONS
In 1979 the railway carried 106 106 passengers, providing revenue of £55 000.

MOTIVE POWER
Up to recent years the Isle of Man Railway Co owned 16 steam engines, of which two (Nos 14 and 15) were built for the Manx Northern Railway. All carried brass numerals on their chimneys as well as names associated with the Island. The Manx Northern's locomotive stock was four strong, but two did little work for the IOM Railway after takeover and were soon scrapped. They were named Northern and Ramsey.
All the surviving engines were built by Beyer Peacock & Co Ltd of Gorton, Manchester, except No 15 which was supplied by Dubs & Co of Glasgow; all are of 2-4-0 wheel

arrangement except for No 15 which is six-coupled of 0-6-0 type. No tender engines have ever worked on the Island.

The two railcars were purchased by the Company from the Co Donegal Railways' Joint Committee in Ireland, in 1961; they work by running back-to-back, but are not employed on passenger runs. They are driven by diesel motors but have connecting rods on the driving wheels like a steam engine.

Running no.		Built	Maker's no	
1	Sutherland	1873	1253	In store
2	Derby	1873	1254	Dismantled
3	Pender	1873	1255	In store
4	Loch	1874	1416	In traffic
5	Mona	1874	1417	In store
6	Peveril	1875	1524	In store
7	Tynwald	1880	2038	Dismantled
8	Fenella	1894	3610	In store
9	Douglas	1896	3815	In store
10	G H Wood	1905	4662	In traffic
11	Maitland	1905	4663	In traffic
12	Hutchinson	1908	5126	In traffic
13	Kissack	1910	5382	In traffic
14	Thornhill	1880	2028	In store
15	Caledonia	1885	2178	In store
16	Mannin	1926	6296	In store

The two railcars were by Walker Bros Ltd of Wigan, built in 1950 and 1951, together with the ex-Great Northern Railway of Ireland (Dundalk Works) which built the carriage portions. They were CDJC Nos 19 and 20.

No 11, Maitland, simmers gently at Castletown

No 3, Pender, built in 1873, takes on water at Peel

KEIGHLEY AND WORTH LIGHT RAILWAY LTD
Haworth Station, Haworth, Keighley, West Yorkshire, England

Chairman: R S Greenwood
Secretary: J G Bradley

Gauge: 1.435 m
Route length: 8 km

Ex BR (No 75078 built in 1956) hauls a holiday rake on the up line

Re-opened for steam operations in 1968, this 8 km line between Keighley and Oxenhope was originally constructed in 1867 by the Midland Railway. Running through the outskirts of Bradford, it comprises two tunnels, a viaduct and five intermediate stations. Steam provides the principal form of motive power, hauling 72.5 per cent of train-km in 1979. Diesel locos and railcars are primarily used during the morning operating periods.

MOTIVE POWER

	Builder	Year	Number		Origin and name
231	Brighton	1949	34092	BR	West Country Type City of Wells
131T		1949	41241	BR	Ivatt type 2 MT
230		1956	75078	BR	Type 4 MT
132T			80002	BR	Based on type 4 MT-LMS
130		1953	78022	BR	Type 2 MT
030	Beyer Peacock	1887	957	LYR	Originally 030T type 2F
030T		1881	752	LYR	
020T	Horwich	1901	68	LYR	
230		1935	45212	LMS	Type 5MT
140		1944	8431	LMS	
140	Lima, USA	1945	5820	US Army S 160	Ex PKP: imported from Poland in 1977 Tr 203-474
030	Vulcan, USA	1943	72	SR	Type USA
030		1927	L89	GWR/LT	Type 57XX
031T		1899	85	TVR	Type 02; mine loco until 1969
030		1920	3924	MR	Type 4F purchased from WB in 1968
221	Doncaster	1898	990	GNR	Ivatt, first English Atlantic Henry Oakley
020T	Horwich	1901	51218	LYR	
030T	Hudswell C	1903	31	MSCR	Ex Manchester Ship Canal
020T	Horwich	1910	19	LYR	
030T	Hudswell C	1919	67	MSCR	
030T	Peckett	1920	3	NCB	Ex National Coal Board
020T	Peckett	1941	1999	NWGB	Ex North Western Gas Board
030T	Hudswell C	1945	118	Armée	
140	Vulcan		1931	WD	Purchased from Switzerland

Ex 1944 LMS loco (No 8431) leading a double-headed express through England's Brontë country (Photo: Steve Le Chemirant)

Keighley and Worth's ex PKP (US built, originally for the army) purchased from Poland in 1977 (Photo: D J Fowler)

KENT & EAST SUSSEX RAILWAY
(Tenterden Railway Company Ltd)
Town Station, Tenterden, Kent TN30 6HE, England

Operating Managers: D H Wilson, D T Dunlavey

Gauge: 1.435 m
Route length: 15 km (only 6 km in passenger service)

The Kent and East Sussex re-opened in 1974 as a living steam line running 6 km between Tenterden and Wittersham, 20 years after the line was closed for passengers. A total of 37 000 passengers were carried in the first year of tourist operation, rising to 45 000 in 1979. Access is by car or train to Ashford in mid-Kent, then along the secondary road towards Hastings.

MOTIVE POWER

	Builder	Year		Origin and name
030T	Brighton	1872	LBSCR Bodiam	Stroudley type A1x (no 3)
030T	Brighton	1876	LBSCR Sutton	Stroudley type A1 (no 10)
030T		1904	SECR	Wainwright type P (no 11)
			Pride of Sussex	
130	Nohab	1914	NSB (Norway)	(No 19)
030T	Vulcan, USA	1943	SR Wainwright	ex 30070 BR, type USA (no 21)
030T	Vulcan, USA		SR Maunsell	ex 30065 BR, type USA (no 22)
030T			Industrial	11 locos
020T			Industrial	3 locos

LAKESIDE AND HAVERTHWAITE RAILWAY
Lakeside Railway Society, Haverthwaite Station, Ulverston, Cumbria, England

Secretary: A Middleton

Gauge: 1.435 m
Route length: 5 km

This railway is all that is left of the Furness Railway in England's Lake District which was opened in 1869 and closed in 1965. Trains run over continuous gradient along the edges of Lake Windermere.

MOTIVE POWER
The steam park consists of nine locomotives; two 132 Ts (42073 built at the Brighton works and 42085, both for British Rail), five 030T industrial locos and two British Rail 020Ts. There are also two diesel locos used for shunting and occasional train haulage.

LEIGHTON BUZZARD NARROW-GAUGE RAILWAY SOCIETY LTD
Pages Park Station, Billington Road, Leighton Buzzard, Bedfordshire LU7 8TN, England

Traffic Manager: R W Hughes

Gauge: 0.600 m
Route length: 5.6 km

The Light Railway owes its existence mainly to World War I, when cheap supplies of sand from Belgium were no longer obtainable, which brought about a tremendous increase in the demand for Leighton Buzzard sand, particularly for industrial use. In 1919, therefore, pre-war plans for a rail link were introduced and a company formed to build and operate the 0.600 m gauge light railway. Initially as much as 3 000 tonnes of sand were carried along the line each week, but the national rail strike in 1955 hastened the diversion of goods traffic to road, a trend which was reflected in the gradual

decrease in tonnage carried by the Light Railway Company. This continued until the end of the 1960s, when British Rail closed its interchange sidings entirely. Since then the line has been used purely for tourist traffic running from Pages Park over gradients as steep as 1 in 25 to Vandyke Road. Services beyond to Bryans Loop and Stonehenge are suspended due to engineering work. Access to Pages Park is by road, following signs on the A5 for Leighton Buzzard. The railway lies on the east side of Billington Road, the A4146 to Hemel Hempstead. Nearest rail station is at Leighton Buzzard on the London Midland Region, about 20 minutes from the Light Railway.

Operations
10 162 passengers were carried in 1978/79 providing revenue of £4 254. Total expenditure was £12 384.

MOTIVE POWER
No 1 Chaloner 0-4-0VBT de Winton built 1877*
No 2 Pixie 0-4-0ST Wren class Kerr Stuart built 1922
No 3 Rishra 0-4-0T Baguley built 1921
No 4 The Doll 0-6-0T Barclay built 1919
No 5 Elf 0-6-0WT Orenstein & Koppel built 1936
No 6 Caravan 4wD Motor Rail Simplex built 1938
(No 7) (Falcon) 4wD Orenstein & Koppel built 1939
No 8 (Gollum) 4wD Ruston built 1942
No 10 Haydn Taylor 4wD Motor Rail Simplex built 1945
No 11 P C Allen 0-4-0WT Orenstein & Koppel built 1912
No 12 Carbon 4wP Motor Rail Simplex built 1930
(No 14) 4wD Hunslet built 1946
No 15 Tom Bombadil 4wD Hibberd built c1935
No 16 Thorin Oakenshield 4wD Lister built 1939
(No 43) 4wD Motor Rail Simplex built 1954
No 44 4wD Motor Rail Simplex built 1941
*Chaloner is on show at the National Railway Museum, York until early 1981.
Names/numbers shown in parentheses are not carried on the locomotives.

4wD Simplex No 44, built 1941 (Photo: David H Smith)

4wD Lister 11221, built 1939 (Photo: David H Smith)

LINCOLNSHIRE COAST LIGHT RAILWAY
North Sea Lane Station, St Anthony's Bank, Humberston, Grimsby DN36 4EP, England

Chairman: J R Durdett
Secretary: W Woolhouse

Gauge: 0.600 m
Route length: 1.0 km

The Lincolnshire operates along the North Sea coast near the sea port of Grimsby. The diesel-hauled trains carried 29 000 passengers in 1979.

LLANBERIS LAKE RAILWAY
Gilfach Ddu Station, Llanberis, Gwynedd LL55 4TY, Wales

Telephone: 028 682 549

Gauge: 0.600 m
Route length: 3 km

MOTIVE POWER
Five steam locos, three diesels.

Kerr Stuart Wren class 0-4-0ST Pixie, built 1922 (Photo: J Horsley)

THE MAIN LINE STEAM TRUST (GREAT CENTRAL)
13 New Street, Leicester LE5 1NR, England

Telephone: 0533 21443

Secretary: G J Oliver

Gauge: 1.435 m
Route length: 16 km

In 1969 a group of amateurs decided to restore a section of the Great Central Railway system, adopting speeds which were practical for steam operation in the 1950s. A section of track running from Loughborough to Birstall was purchased from British Rail in 1976 for £135 000. Following successful operation over this section, the Association purchased additional lines: Loughborough to Quorn including a branch to Rothley. Steam-hauled trains operate every day from Spring until the end of Summer.

MOTIVE POWER

	Builder	Year	Original number	Originating railway and name
220		1919	506	GCR Butler Henderson
031T	North British	1921	4744	LNER Type N2
020T		1923	985	NER LNER Type Y7
230	Armstrong Whitworth	1936	5231	LMS Type 5MT
150			92212	BR
231		1946	34039	SR Boscastle Bulleid, West Country type
230		1947	61264	LNER Type B1
230		1948	6990	GWR Witherslock Hall
231	Crewe	1954	71000	BR Duke of Gloucester
230	Glasgow	1948	1306	LNER Mayflower Thompson B1
130	Nohab	1919	377	NSB King Haakon VII Ex-Norway
030T				4 locos
020T				2 locos

Ultimate evolution of the standard British 4-4-0 express engine
Director class, built for the Great Central Railway. Number 506, Butler Henderson, is preserved by the Main Line Steam Trust.

THE MANX ELECTRIC RAILWAY
Terminus Building, Strathallan Crescent, Douglas, Isle of Man

Gauge: 0.914 m; 1.067 m
Route length: 28.58 km; 7.65 km

The Manx Electric Railway had its origin in 1892 and the first section of line was completed a year later between the Derby Castle terminus at the northern end of Douglas Promenade and Groudle Glen. The line was extended to Laxey in 1894 and by 1899 the cars were in operation from Douglas to Ramsey, a distance of about 17 miles (27 km). In 1902 King Edward VII and Queen Alexandra travelled on the tramway between Douglas and Ramsey in a special saloon, now trailer No 59.

The first car travelled on the Snaefell Mountain Railway in August 1895, a remarkable achievement of line construction between Laxey and the mountain summit because the venture was only launched eight months earlier by the original syndicate. This line established the first, and to this day the only, electrically worked mountain railway in the British Isles. The electric cars are the only vehicles that can take you to the Snaefell summit (2036 ft, 620 m).

The Manx Electric Railway came into the ownership of the Government of the Isle of Man in 1957, and is maintained in summer on the sections Douglas—Laxey—Ramsey and Laxey—Snaefell.

ROLLING STOCK

Motor Cars Car No	Type	Seats	Built	Builder	Trucks (2)	Motors (4)	hp
1, 2	Unvestibuled saloon	38	1893	Milnes	Brush (a)	WE	25
5, 6, 7, 9	Vestibuled saloon	36 (b)	1894	Milnes	Brush (a)	WE	25
14, 15, 17, 18	Cross-bench (c)	56	1898	Milnes	Milnes	ECC	20
16	Cross-bench (c)	56	1898	Milnes	Brush (a)	WE	25
19-22	Winter saloons	48	1899	Milnes	Brill (a)	WE	25
23	Locomotive (body only)	—	1925	MER	—	—	—
25-27	Cross-bench (c)	56	1898 (d)	Milnes	Brush (a)	WE	25
28-31	Cross-bench (c)	56	1904	UEC	Milnes	ECC	20
32, 33	Cross-bench (c)	56	1906	UEC	Brill (a)	GE60	27½
Trailers							
36, 37	Cross-bench	44	1894	Milnes	Milnes	—	—
40, 41	Cross-bench (c)	44	1930	EE	Milnes	—	—
42, 43	Cross-bench (c)	44	1903	Milnes	Milnes	—	—
44	Cross-bench (c)	44	1930	EE	Milnes	—	—
45-48	Cross-bench (c)	44	1899	Milnes	Milnes	—	—
49-54	Cross-bench	44	1893	Milnes	Milnes	—	—
55, 56	Cross-bench (c)	44	1904	UEC	Brill	—	—
57, 58	Saloon	32	1904	UEC	Brill (a)	—	—
59	Short saloon	18	1895	Milnes	Milnes	—	—
60	Cross-bench (c)	44	1896	Milnes	Milnes	—	—
61, 62	Cross-bench (c)	44	1906	UEC	Brill	—	—

(a) Fitted with Christensen air brakes (supplied by R W Blackwell & Co)
(b) No 5 has transverse seats for 32 instead of longitudinal.
(c) These cars are fitted with roller shutters.
(d) Nos 25-27 ran as trailers until 1903.
All cars have K11C or K12 controllers, and those not fitted with air brakes are referred to by the staff as 'ratchet' cars.

MIDDLETON RAILWAY (MR)
Garnet Road, Leeds LS11 5JY, England

Chairman: J K Lee
Secretary: J D Edwards

Gauge: 1.435 m
Route length: 5 km

Taken over by the Middleton Railway Association in 1960, the MR is publicised as the UK's first standard-gauge railway to be run by enthusiasts. It is the only line of its kind in the country that carries freight for local firms during the week and on week-ends and public holidays a steam-hauled visitors' service.

The Middleton carried coal 200 years ago from pits at Belle Isle and Middleton to the growing town of Leeds. Originally horses were used to pull wagons over level sections of the line with a stationary steam engine hauling them up the gradients. Early in the nineteenth century, the high cost of horse feed forced the company to seek other means of haulage. By 1812 steam locomotives began working the line. The railway continued carrying coals to Leeds until 1947 when the line was cut back to Hunslet Moor. In 1960 it was threatened with complete closure, and the MR Association stepped in to take the line over.

Access to the line is at Hunslet station via the M1 motorway.

MOTIVE POWER

Name/Number	Year	Builder	Type
1310	1891	NER	0-4-0T
385	1893	Danish State Rly	0-4-0WT
Windle	1909	Borrows	0-4-0WT
Henry de Lacy II	1917	Hudswell Clarke	0-4-0ST
John Alcock	1932	Hunslet	0-6-0DM
54	1933	Sentinel	4w VB
Courage	1935	Hudson-Hunslet	4w DM
6	1935	Hawthorn Leslie	0-4-0ST
	1941	Peckett	0-4-0ST
Matthew Murray	1943	Bagnall	0-4-0ST
	1945	Fowler	0-4-0DM
Carroll	1946	Hudswell Clarke	0-4-0DM

Steam: T: Tank engine. WT: Well tank. ST: Saddle tank. VB: Vertical boiler.
Diesel: DM: Diesel-mechanical.

NENE VALLEY RAILWAY
Wansford Station, Old North Road, Stibbington, Peterborough, England

Telephone: 0780 782854

Gauge: 1.435 m
Route length: 8 km

The British Rail route through the Nene Valley in England's East Midlands was taken over for tourist operation in 1977. Steam-hauled trains now operate throughout the summer months between Wansford and Orton Mere.

MOTIVE POWER

	Builder	Year	Original number		Originating railway and name
230	Derby	1954	73050	BR City of Peterborough	Type 5MT standard
230	Henschel	1911	3628	Cie du Nord	Ex 230 D 116 SNCF
132T	Nohab	1953	1928	SJ	Type A20 ex-Swedish
131T	Motala	1914	11787	SJ	Ex-Swedish
030T	Fricks	1949	656	DSB	Type F
131T	Krauss Maffei	1935	64305	DR	
230T				SJ	Ex-Swedish
131				DB	
140				FS	Ex-Italian
231	SR-Brighton	1948	21C92	SR	Type Battle of Britain
030T				Industrial	10 locos
020T				11	2 locos 3 diesel tractors

NORTH NORFOLK RAILWAY CO LTD
Sheringham Station, Sheringham, Norfolk, England

Secretary: D P Madden

Gauge: 1.435 km
Route length: 4 km

Steam trains over this ex-Midland & Great Northern line are operated throughout the summer with permission of British Rail along 4 km of the Norfolk coastal route.

MOTIVE POWER
Ten locomotives are in steam, including a Beyer Peacock 230 built in 1928 for the LNER (original number 8572) and a 1912 GER type J15.

THE NORTH YORK MOORS RAILWAY (MOORSRAIL)
North York Moors National Park Offices, Old Vicarage, Bendgate, Helmsley, North Yorkshire, England

Telephone: 043 92 657

Commercial Manager: Royd Scurrah, Pickering Station, Pickering, North Yorkshire YO18 7AY

Telephone: 07512 72508

Gauge: 1.435 m
Route length: 29 km

This is a steam/diesel-operated tourist railway, which runs through the North York Moors National Park. Moorsrail was originally part of a route engineered by George Stephenson and opened to steam in 1865. British Rail closed the line exactly one hundred years later. It was re-opened in May 1973; now a privately-owned line, it is funded by the Countryside Commission, the park and the Railway Trust. The complete preserved route, between Grosmont and Pickering, is operated by diesel locos (because of fire risk in the park) while steam traction is restricted to the Grosmont—Goatland section. Nearly 300 000 passengers travel on the line every year.

MOTIVE POWER

	Builder	Year	Original number		Originating railway and name
140	Stephenson	1925	89	S & D	Fowler
132T		1956	80135	BR	Riddles type 4MT
030T	Shaip Stewart	1899	1247	GNR	Type J52 Ivatt
031T		1928	6619	GNR	Type 56XX
230	Armstrong Whitworth	1937	5428	LMS Eric Tracy	Type 5MT Stanier
040		1918	2238	NER	Type T2 (on exhibition in York museum)
130	North British	1949	62005	BR	Type K1
031T	Stephenson Crewe	1909	5	LR	
230		1947	4767	LMS George Stephenson	
031T	Kitson	1904	29	LR	
030T				Industrial	5 locos
20T				Industrial	2 locos
230		1936	841	SR Greene King	Type S15

RAVENGLASS AND ESKDALE RAILWAY CO LTD
Ravenglass, Cumbria CA18 1SW, England

Telephone: 06577 226

General Manager: Douglas Ferreira
Chief Engineer: Ian Smith

Gauge: 0.381 m
Route length: 11 km

The Ravenglass & Eskdale Railway was originally opened in 1875 to bring iron ore and, later, passengers from Eskdale to Ravenglass. The line was, in fact, originally built to

0.910 m gauge and later converted to the present 0.380 m after Bassett-Lowke promoted the virtues of the conversion in 1915. A very chequered existence, during which the line was almost closed twice, brought it to the present day when traffic consists entirely of passengers. Always a private company, the railway is supported by a Preservation Society which took over its operation in 1961. The line runs in Western Lakeland from Eskdale at Dalegarth station to Ravenglass on the coast. Most train services to Eskdale connect with British Rail at Ravenglass via the scenic coastal route from Lancashire and south, west and north Cumbria. Easiest access is by road over the Wrynose and Hardnott pass.

OPERATIONS
In 1978/79 the railway carried 302 000 passengers paying £138 000 for the journeys.

MOTIVE POWER
Line haul locos in service:

	Builder	Year		Original owner and name
141	Charkoon	1966	R & ER River Mite	
131	R & ER	1976	R & ER Northern Rock	
141	Davey Paymond	1923	R & ER River Esk	
041T	Ravenglass	1927	R & ER River Irt	Converted from a 040T of 1894
021	Bassett Lowke	1912	Prince Charles	On display only
020	—	1928/29		Diesel
021	—	1933		Diesel
2C2	Severn autorail	1969	R & ER	Diesel
		1977	R & ER	Diesel

RHEILFFORDD LLYN TELID CYF (BALA LAKE RAILWAY)
Yr Orsaf Llanuwchllyn Bala, Gwynedd, Wales

Telephone: 067 84 666

Chairman: T Jones

Gauge: 0.600 m
Route length: 7.2 km

The railway is operated by enthusiasts along the shores of Lake Bala in North Wales. A 1 km extension to the main Bala-Dolgellau road is contemplated for 1981. About 70 per cent of trains are hauled by diesel traction. Between 1972-79 the railway carried 270 835 passengers. Motive power consists of two steam locos, one diesel-hydraulic and four diesel-mechanical.

ROMNEY, HYTHE & DYMCHURCH RAILWAY (RH&DR)
New Romney, Kent, England

Telephone: 067 93 2353

Managing Director: J B Snell
Operating Manager: G A Barlow
Chief Engineer: A R W Crowhurst

Gauge: 0.384 m
Route length: 22.21 km

Since it was opened in 1927, the Romney, Hythe and Dymchurch Railway has been a major holiday attraction in southern England. Its founder had the ambition of building, in miniature, a working reproduction of a fully-equipped, up-to-date mainline railway. Trains carry up to 200 passengers and travel at up to 40 km/h on a track about a quarter the size of standard. The ten steam locomotives are one-third size versions of mainline express power of the 1920s and 1930s; nine of them were built specifically for the RH&DR. The main terminus at Hythe stands alongside the Royal Military Canal, built as part of the coastal defence system during the Napoleonic Wars. Farmland on either side of the line is studded with concrete defence posts, waterlogged bomb craters and other military relics.

Access by road is via the A20 from London, either to Ashford (and then B2070 to New Romney) or to Newingreen and then A261 to Hythe. The A259 brings car travellers from Folkestone, Dover, Rye, Hastings or the South Coast. Nearest British Rail station is at Folkestone Central where buses on routes 94 and 95 connect with Hythe station.

In the foreground is Hurricane, a 4-6-2 built in 1926 which is also identical to the railway's Green Goddess, Northern Chief, Southern Maid and Typhoon locos; on the right is Winston Churchill, another 4-6-2 but this time designed on the North American style

Engine driver/fireman coals up on Black Prince at New Romney station
This was the last of RH&DR's locos to be built, coming into service in 1937 when it was one of three constructed by Krupp of Germany. Design closely follows the large 4-6-2s of Bavarian origin then working many of the fast trains on German railways.

OPERATIONS
In 1979 the railway carried 345 066 passenger journeys, all by steam-hauled trains. Revenue from passengers added up to £175 837.

MOTIVE POWER AND ROLLING STOCK
All passenger trains on the RH&DR are hauled by steam locomotives, most of which were designed and built specially for the railway. The fleet consists of:

No 1 Green Goddess, (4-6-2) LNER green, built 1925.
No 2 Northern Chief, (4-6-2) GWR green, built 1925.
No 3 Southern Maid, (4-6-2) LNER green, built 1926.
No 4 The Bug, (0-4-0) SR green, built 1926.
No 5 Hercules, (4-8-2) maroon, built 1926.
No 6 Samson, (4-8-2) black, built 1926.
No 7 Typhoon, (4-6-2) SR green, built 1926.
No 8 Hurricane, (4-6-2) Caledonian blue, built 1926.
No 9 Winston Churchill, (4-6-2) red, built 1931.
No 10 Doctor Syn, (4-6-2) black, built 1931.
No 11 Black Prince, (4-6-2) black and red, built 1937.

Nos 1, 2, 3, 7 and 8 are modelled on the LNER A3 class 4-6-2s, of which the famous Flying Scotsman is now the last survivor, and nos 5 and 6 are variations of the same design originally intended for freight traffic. No 4 is a modified version of a standard contractor's or industrial light locomotive, full-size, and was used for construction of the railway. Nos 9 and 10 are modelled on typical North American types of the 1920s. No 11, the only locomotive not originally built for the RH&DR, is modelled on a class of locomotive used on fast trains in southern West Germany in the 1930s. Three petrol or diesel locomotives are used for shunting and maintenance work.

SEVERN VALLEY RAILWAY
Severn Valley Railway (Holdings) Ltd
The Railway Station, Bewdley, Hereford and Worcester DY12 1BE, England

Telephone: 0299 403816

Chairman: W B Broadbent
Deputy Chairman: J Earth
Finance Director and General Manager: M J Draper

Gauge: 1.435 m
Route length: 22.5 km

The Severn Valley Railway is a full-sized, standard-gauge line running regular steam-hauled passenger trains for tourists and enthusiasts, from Bridgnorth, Salop, to Bewdley in Hereford and Worcester. The railway was in the transport business as a commercial passenger route for 101 years, from 1862 to 1963. The present Severn Valley

GWR 4-6-0 No 7819 Hinton Manor, near Northwood, approaches Bewdley with the non-stop Severn Valley Limited, a restaurant car train (Photo: J B Hicks)

British Rail standard 2-6-4 tank No 80079 at Bewdley Station about to leave for Bridgnorth shortly after the locomotive's return to service in 1977 (Photo: R H Marrows)

Shoppers at Northwood Halt await the arrival of the 1200 Bridgnorth to Bewdley hauled by an LMSR Jinty 0-6-0 tank (Photo: D C Williams)

LMR Ivatt class 2 2-6-0 No 46443 heads an afternoon train composed of LMSR stock over the Victoria Bridge designed by John Fowler and completed in 1861 (Photo: the late P Riley)

Army 2-10-0 No 600 Gordon at Hampton Loade, on loan to the railway from the Army and Transport Trust *(Photo: D C Williams)*

Steam in sunshine at Bridgnorth station with Ivatt class 2 2-6-0 No 46521 alongside Manning Wardle 0-6-0 saddle tank No 2047 Warwickshire *(Photo: D N Cooke)*

Railway Company began operations in 1970 from Bridgnorth to Hampton Loade, extending services southwards to Bewdley in 1974. The journey over the line provides passengers with views of the Severn Valley. From Bridgnorth the line emerges from the shadow of Castle Hill and for about 200 m runs along an embankment high above the River Severn. About 1.5 km north of Bridgnorth the summit is reached before the line descends through mixed-farming country, punctuated by sandstone cuttings at each side of Eardington Halt. Curving southwards the line enters woodland country and steams up a steep summit at Alveley before dropping down to Highley station. Next stop, Arley, is probably the most picturesque station on the line. Southwards again the line runs through severe curves on the journey to Northwood Halt. Still in woodland, the line leaves Northwood before Bewdley appears, the railway occupying a commanding position above the historic town.

OPERATIONS

In 1979 a total of 130 352 passengers were carried, providing a revenue of £366 840.

MOTIVE POWER AND ROLLING STOCK

There are currently 32 steam locomotives on the railway, together with four diesel shunting locomotives. The majority are on load.

STEAM LOCOMOTIVES ON THE SVR

Ex-Great Western Railway (one built by British Rail)

			Builder	Year	Tonnes
813	PTR	0-6-0ST	Hudswell Clarke, Leeds	1901	44
1501	15XX	0-6-0PT	Hawksworth, Swindon	1949	58
2857	28XX	2-8-0	Churchward, Swindon	1918	115
3205*	2251	0-6-0	Collett, Swindon	1946	80
4141	51XX	2-6-2T	Churchward, Swindon	1946	78
4150	51XX	2-6-2T	Churchward, Swindon	1947	78
4566*	45XX	2-6-2T	Churchward, Swindon	1924	57
4930 **(1)**	Hall	4-6-0	Collett, Swindon	1929	121
5164	51XX	2-6-2T	Churchward, Swindon	1930	78
5764*	57XX	0-6-0PT	Collett, Swindon	1929	47
6960* **(2)**	Modified Hall	4-6-0	Hawksworth, Swindon	1944	122
7714	57XX	0-6-0PT	Collet, Stoke-on-Trent	1930	47
7812 **(3)**	Manor	4-6-0	Collett, Swindon	1938	109
7819* **(4)**	Manor	4-6-0	Collett, Swindon	1939	109
9303	43XX	2-6-0	Collett, Swindon	1932	105

Ex-London Midland & Scottish Railway (some built by British Rail)

2968	6P5F	2-6-0	Stanier, Crewe	1934	111
43106*	4MT	2-6-0	Ivatt, Darlington	1951	99
4500	5MT	4-6-0	Stanier, Crewe	1935	124
45110* **(5)**	5MT	4-6-0	Stanier, Vulcan	1935	124
46443*	2MT	2-6-0	Ivatt, Crewe	1950	84
46521*	2MT	2-6-0	Ivatt, Swindon	1953	84
47383*	3F	0-6-0T	Fowler, Vulcan	1926	49
8233*	8F	2-8-0	Stanier, Glasgow	1940	126

Ex-London and North Eastern Railway

3442* **(6)**	K4	2-6-0	Gresley, Darlington	1938	112

Ex-British Rail

			Builder	Year	Tonnes
70000 **(7)**	7P6F	4-6-2	Riddles, Crewe	1951	143
75069	4MT	4-6-0	Riddles, Swindon	1955	119
78019	2MT	2-6-0	Riddles, Darlington	1954	86
80079*	4MT	2-6-4T	Riddles, Brighton	1954	86

Ex-Army

193* **(8)**	J94	0-6-0ST	Riddles, Leeds	1953	48
600* **(9)**	WD	2-10-0	Riddles, Glasgow	1943	134

Ex-industrial locos

686* **(10)**		0-6-0T	Leeds	1898	35
1738*		0-4-0ST	Bristol	1928	29
2047* **(11)**		0-6-0ST	Leeds	1926	30

Names: **(1)** Hagley Hall **(2)** Raveningham Hall **(3)** Erlestoke Manor **(4)** Hinton Manor **(5)** RAF Biggin Hill **(6)** The Great Marquess **(7)** Britannia **(8)** Shropshire **(9)** Gordon **(10)** The Lady Armaghdale **(11)** Warwickshire
*These locomotives have actually worked on the Railway; the remainder are undergoing restoration for future use.

ROLLING STOCK

SVR passenger trains are usually made up into sets of four or five coaches, with two trains in the Great Western Railway chocolate-and-cream livery, one in the crimson lake of the London & Midland Scottish Railway and another in the armine (red)-and-cream of British Rail in the 1950s. There are nearly 60 coaches on the railway and over 60 goods wagons.

THE SHANES CASTLE RAILWAY
Shanes Castle, Antrim, Northern Ireland

Telephone: 023 841 2216

Gauge: 0.914 m
Route length: 2 km

A tourist railway running in the grounds of Shanes Castle, the line carries about 27 000 people a year on steam-hauled trains. The railway operates two steam locos and one diesel-mechanical.

SITTINGBOURNE & KEMSLEY LIGHT RAILWAY LTD (S & KLR)
The Wall, Milton Regis, Sittingbourne, Kent, England

Telephone: 0795 24899

General Manager: M Burton

Gauge: 0.762 m
Route length: 3.2 km

Until October 1969 the S & KLR was owned and operated by Bowater's UK Pulp and Paper Mills Ltd for carrying freight and company employees from Sittingbourne to the Kemsley Mill. The line was taken over by the Locomotive Club of Great Britain and the first tourist/enthusiast trains ran in 1970. Access to the Sittingbourne terminus can be made by British Rail trains calling at Sittingbourne mainline station or by car branching off to the town from the M3 motorway.

MOTIVE POWER

Premier, built 1905, works number 886, and *Leader*, built 1905, works number 926, (0-4-2ST) were built for the opening of the railway at Edward Lloyd's Sittingbourne Mill and were of Kerr Stuart's Brazil class. A third engine, *Excelsior*, was delivered in 1908 and all three originally carried the numbers 1-3 in addition to their names, a practice later discontinued. *Premier* was rebuilt to its present form in 1909 and the other two were similarly treated in 1912. Main data:
Cylinders: 9 × 15 in; *Driving wheel diameter:* 2 ft 6 in; *Weight in working order:* 14.5 tonnes; *Boiler pressure:* 160 lb/sq in; *Tractive effort:* 5508 lb; *Fixed wheel base:* 3 ft 9 in.
Unique, built 1923, works number 2216 (2-4-0F): This fireless W G Bagnall Ltd locomotive normally worked at Kemsley Mill and the steam reservoir was charged at a specially reinforced charging point connected to the mill steam supply. It could run for eight hours without recharging but was normally recharged every four hours. It remained in use right to the end of operation and was included in the stock transferred to the S & KLR. It is likely to remain a static exhibit as there is no access to a supply of high pressure steam. Main data:
Cylinders: 18½ × 18 in; *Driving wheel diameter:* 2 ft 9¼ in; *Weight in working order:* 26 tonnes; *Reservoir/working pressure:* 220/80 lb/sq in; *Tractive effort:* 12 600 lb; *Fixed wheel base:* 5 ft 0 in.
Melior, built 1924, works number 4219 (0-4-2ST) was another engine of Kerr Stuart's Brazil class but was most unusually fitted with Hackworth valve gear. *Melior* remained in service to the end of Bowater operation but was in poor condition and required heavy repairs. Main data:
Cylinders: 9 × 15 in; *Driving wheel diameter:* 2 ft 6 in; *Weight in working order:* 13.75 tonnes; *Boiler pressure:* 160 lb/sq in; *Tractive effort:* 5508 lb; *Fixed wheel base:* 3 ft 9 in.
Alpha, built 1932, works number 2472, *Triumph*, built 1934, works number 2511 and *Superb*, built 1940, works number 2624:
The design of these three outside framed 0-6-2 side tanks built by W G Bagnall Ltd, owes much to that of the Kerr Stuart's Baretto class 0-6-2T Superior supplied to Lloyds in 1920. Many parts, including the cylinders but not boiler, were interchangeable between the two types. Main data:
Cylinders: 10 × 15 in; *Driving wheel diameter:* 2 ft 3 in; *Weight in working order:* 19.75 tonnes; *Boiler pressure:* 160 lb/sq in; *Tractive effort:* 7554 lb; *Fixed wheel base:* 5 ft 6 in.
No. 4, built 1928, works number 3718, was purchased by six members of the S & KLR in January 1973 from The Associated Portland Cement Manufacturers Ltd, for whom it had worked all its life at their Swanscombe Works, Kent. It was built by R & W Hawthorn Leslie & Co Ltd. Main data:
Cylinders: 15 × 22 in; *Driving wheel diameter:* 3 ft 5 in; *Boiler pressure:* 160 lb/sq in; *Wheelbase:* 6 ft 0 in.
No. 3, Bear, built 1896, works number 614:
This 0-4-0ST locomotive is now the oldest surviving standard-gauge Peckett in England. It is of their type W4. It was presented to the LCGB in February 1967 by Messrs Colvilles Ltd, of Mossend, Scotland. It was stored at the Scottish Railway Preservation Society depot at Falkirk Grahamston until moved to Kemsley Down in August 1971. Main data:
Cylinders: 14 × 20 in; *Driving wheel diameter:* 3 ft 2 in; *Boiler pressure:* 140 lb/sq in; *Wheelbase:* 5 ft 6 in.
S G Fireless AB (0-4-0f), No 1876 of 1925, was purchased from Bowaters of Northfleet in Kent during 1979.
Hudson-Hunslet, four-wheeled diesel-mechanical. Main data:
Driving wheel diameter: 2 ft 0 in; *Overall length:* 11 ft 4 in; *Weight in working order:* 8 tonnes; *Wheelbase:* 6 ft 5 in; *Power unit:* Perkins P6 six-cylinder diesel engine rated at 70 bhp at 2200 rpm; *Gearbox:* Hunslet patented gearbox, 2 forward and 2 reverse gears, chain final drive to each axle.

Victor, built 1953, works number 4182, was given to this engine in 1972, the nameplate having previously been carried by the 0-4-0 fireless locomotive built by Bagnall in 1929 and scrapped in 1967.

Ruston & Hornsby, 0-4-0 diesel-mechanical. Main data:

Driving wheel diameter: 1 ft 6 in; *Overall length:* 13 ft 10½ in; *Weight in working order:* 10 tonnes; *Wheelbase:* 4 ft 0 in; *Power unit:* Ruston four-cylinder YEF engine rated at 75 bhp, drive to gearbox through a Vulcan-Sinclair fluid coupling; *Gearbox:* Constant mesh, oil operated, 4 forward and 4 reverse gears, jackshaft drive to coupled wheels; *Brakes:* Westinghouse straight air brakes working a single shoe on each wheel.

ROLLING STOCK
Butterley Bogie Coaches:

Bowater No	S & KLR No	Wagon built	Converted to coach	Type	Seats	Notes
641	1	1953	1957	Closed	21	1.2
660	2	1953	1957	Closed	20	1
659	3	1953	1957	Closed	20	1
658	4	1953	1957	Closed	20	1
657	5	1953	1957	Closed	20	1
655	6	1953	1971	Open	24	3
633	7	1951	1972	Standee	—	3
626	8	1951	1972	Standee	—	3
647	9	1953	1974	Tourist	28	3

Notes: 1. Converted from a 14 tonne Butterley Pulp Wagon by Bowaters.
2. Staff works coach.
3. Converted by S & KLR.

Leader (0-4-2ST) on train at Milton with **Chattenden** and **Upnor** coaches

SNOWDON MOUNTAIN RAILWAY
Llanberis, Gwynedd, Wales

Gauge: 0.800 m
Route length: 7.4 km

The Snowdon Mountain Railway is the only rack railway in the UK. The line begins at Llanberis and climbs up the north-western slopes of Snowdon, the highest mountain in England and Wales. Summit Station is 1075 m above sea level. Nowhere is the line level, and the easiest gradient is 1 in 50 just outside Llanberis Station. The steepest gradient is 1 in 5.5 occurring near the summit. Nearly half the route is on curved track, the smallest radius being 22°. The line is single track throughout apart from the termini and at three double tracked passing stations at Hebron, Halfway and Clogwyn.

The original Snowdon Mountain Tramroad and Hotels Company Ltd was formed in 1893. Consulting engineers were appointed and they recommended the Abt system powered by steam locomotives; they advised that these should be built in Switzerland. Accordingly a contract for five locomotives was placed with the Swiss Locomotive and Machine Company while the first sod for the railway was cut in December 1894. The 7.4 km track to the summit was completed in 72 working days and the railway opened on Easter Monday 1896.

Today's Mountain Railway trains are composed of a locomotive and bogie coach. Normal practice is that the locomotive always runs chimney first up the mountain pushing the coach in front of it. The coach is not coupled to the locomotive. Trains are timed to cover the journey in one hour; normally the up trains take a few minutes longer than this as their locomotives must take water en route. Maximum speed in either direction is 8 km/h.

Llanberis station is reached by road or train to Caernarvon (on the London Midland line from Chester), then by bus.

MOTIVE POWER
Seven locomotives of two different designs work the railway; all of them standard rack tanks built at Winterthur by the Swiss Locomotive and Machine Works (SLM). The first Snowdon locos arrived at Llanberis in 1895: No 1 (Ladas), No 2 (Enid) and No 3 (Wyddfa). Two more followed in 1896: No 4 (Snowdon) and No 5 (Moel Siabod). The most recent were built in 1922/23: No 6 (Sir Harmood/Padarn), No 7 (Aylwin) and No 8 (Eryri). All still survive with the exception of Ladas which was destroyed on the day the railway opened when it left the track and plunged down the steep side of a ravine. Ladas has never been replaced.

The remaining seven locos are six-wheeled tanks in which the drive is only to the rack pinion shafts and not to the carrying wheels. The cranks drive the extremities of the shafts, the drive being to the second shaft in the earlier designs and to the first in the three youngest locomotives. The two rack pinions are coupled by means of coupling rods outside the frame. The first two pairs of carrying wheels are connected by the

pinion shafts which act as axles. The wheels, however, are able to revolve freely and individually on the shafts. The carrying wheels are flanged.

The trailing pair of carrying wheels is carried in a bissel truck which swivels on a fixed pivot behind the second driving axle.

Both series of Snowdon locomotives have locomotive-type fire-tube boilers which burn coal. In 1972, however, numbers 3 and 8 were converted to burn oil fuel.

It is interesting to note that the original Snowdon locomotives each cost £1 400; less than today's cost for one boiler.

ROLLING STOCK
The Snowdon Mountain Tramroad started work with six coaches built by the Lancaster Carriage and Wagon Co, to Swiss design. The coaches were each carried on two four-wheel bogies, one of which had a double rack pinion on one axle with corrugated brake drum attached to it. Two brake shoes clasp the drum and a centrifugal governor is driven by the axle. Should speeds of 8 km/h be exceeded in the down direction the brake is automatically applied. All these coaches were open above the waist, five were roofed and had canvas wind dodgers which, when they were drawn, gave some protection against wind and rain. The remaining coach had no roof or other protection.

In the early days of the railway, two-coach trains were worked during busy periods, and the roofless coach was always marshalled in the lead of such trains.

The coaches all had seven compartments, each capable of carrying eight passengers. At the leading end of the coach was a half compartment for the use of the conductor and from which the hand brake was operated.

In 1921-22, three further coaches were supplied to the railway by the Société Industrielle Suisse of Neuhausen, and were brought to England loaded on flat wagons of the Swiss Federal Railways by way of the Zeebrugge-Harwich train ferry.

There were now nine coaches on the railway, but the roofless vehicle of the first batch was converted at Llanberis into a caboose. The original frames and bogies were retained, but on the leading (or upper) half, a totally enclosed caboose, or guard's van was constructed with a fuel bunker capable of carrying one tonne of coal or coke. A 700-gallon water tank is carried on the other part of the frames. This most useful vehicle carries fuel and water to the Summit Hotel and as it always forms part of the first train up in the morning, the block-men and other essential railwaymen travel in it.

In 1951 in the railway workshops at Llanberis, a start was made to reconstruct all the coaches with enclosed bodies. Above the waists, plate glass windows at front, sides and rear, protect the passengers from the weather and pull-up windows are fitted to all doors. The superstructures are built up of Miranti hardwood, and the last coach rebuilt has extra small windows for ventilation. Seven coaches were dealt with at the rate of one each year. The remaining old coach was scrapped.

The seven coaches are now all painted bright red below the waist with cream above. The earlier livery was chocolate brown and white.

The capacity of the coaches is officially 56 passengers in the seven compartments. It is, however, quite usual for the conductor to allow three or four passengers to ride with him in his leading half-compartment from which the best views are obtained. This can, therefore, bring the total of fare-paying passengers in the train up to 60.

STRATHSPEY RAILWAY
The Station, Boat of Garten, Inverness-shire PH24 3BH, Scotland

Telephone: 047 983 692

Managing Director: Douglas P Barclay
Traffic Superintendent: Roy Hamilton

Gauge: 1.435 m
Route length: 8 km

The railway runs through a picturesque area of the Scottish Highlands, with the Monadhliaths to the west and the Cairngorms to the east. Unlike many other sections of the Highland Railway there are no steep gradients, only a gentle rise between the terminals at Aviemore and Boat of Garten. Both stations are reached via the A9 Perth to Inverness road. British Rail main line services link Inverness, Carr Bridge, Kingussie, Pitlochry, Perth, Stirling, Glasgow, Edinburgh, Carlisle and many other stations with Aviemore. Highland Omnibuses service links Nethybridge and Grantown-on-Spey with Boat of Garten.

OPERATIONS
In 1979 the line carried 43 074 passengers operating 100 per cent steam haulage.

MOTIVE POWER
The Strathspey Railway's three tender locomotives were all built to London, Midland and Scottish Railway designs. Two were, however, constructed during British Railways days. 46464 (1950) and 46512 (1952) are both lightweight 2-6-0s built for secondary and branch line work. 46464 is known as the Carmyllie Pilot because it worked on the Carmyllie Light Railway in Angus. 46512 spent most of its life on the lines of the former Cambrian Railways which radiated from Oswestry.

The largest of the Strathspey's locomotives is Black Five 5025, one of a class which hauled most trains on the Highland main line for a quarter of a century. 5025 itself worked on the Highland when it was built in 1934, but afterwards spent most of its life on the former London and North Western Railways in England, surviving till the very end of steam on British Railways in 1968.

All five tank locomotives were built by Andrew Barclay of Kilmarnock for industrial service, although they were used in widely differing industries. Balmenach (1936) and Dailuaine (1939) worked traffic between the distilleries they were named after and the Speyside branch. Clyde (1951) came from Braehead (Glasgow) power station and Forth (1926) from Granton gas works in Edinburgh. These four engines are all 0-4-0 saddle tanks. The odd-man-out among the Barclays is an 0-6-0 side tank (1935) which worked colliery traffic on the Wemyss Private Railway in Fife.

There are three diesels, all 0-4-0s, but by different makers. Inverdon was built by Simplex in 1957 for the Scottish Gas Company and arrived in Strathspey from Aberdeen. Inverkeith was constructed by Hudswell Clarke for the RAF in 1939, but like Inveresk, built by Ruston & Hornsby in 1950, worked at the Inveresk Paper Mills at Inverkeithing before going north.

ROLLING STOCK
The carriages on the Strathspey fall into two main groups. The first are British Rail carriages of the 1950s which form the backbone of the passenger stock. There are four corridor coaches, including the buffet car, Glenfiddich, and two non-corridor coaches. These vehicles have been repainted in the Strathspey livery, an adaptation of the Great North of Scotland Railway livery of purple lake and off-white. The second group comprise carriages built to London, Midland and Scottish Railway designs; most of these have been repainted in the LMSR maroon, a livery which was also used for a time by British Rail. There are various other coaches not in passenger use including a London and North Eastern Railway sleeping car and GNSR and North British Railway vehicles which are in departmental stock. The departmental stock also includes a diesel crane from Cupar Sugar Beet Factory and two tank wagons from Dailuaine distillery. Appropriately enough the last surviving Highland Railway carriages, which have been restored, have joined the Aviemore park, although they are only used on special occasions. They are a four-wheeled brakevan of the 1870s and a six-wheeled coach of 1909.

Ivatt class 2 (No 46464) at Boat of Garten station
Hauling ex-British Rail coaches repainted in adaptation of the former Great North of
Scotland Railway's purple lake and off-white livery. *(Photo: Bill Roberton)*

TALYLLYN RAILWAY
Wharf Station, Tywyn, Gwynedd LL36 9EY, Wales

Telephone: 0654 710472

Managing Director: W Faulkner
Chief Engineer: J Bate
Traffic Manager: D Woodhouse

Gauge: 0.686 m
Route length: 11.6 km

The Talyllyn is Britain's only surviving 0.686 m gauge railway; the Corris Railway at
Machynlleth (Wales) and the Campbeltown and Machrihanish Railway (Scotland) were
the only others and both have long been closed. The Talyllyn Railway was born out of

the need to find an economical way of carrying large quantities of finished slates from
Bryn Eglwys quarries (152 m above Abergynolwyn village) for the new roof-tops of the
industrial Midlands in England. The line was surveyed by James Swinton Spooner, an
engineer and member of a Portmadoc family responsible for the construction of the
Festiniog Railway. The railway runs down the Afon Valley to Tywyn, site of the Wharf
station and near the British Rail station of Tywyn on the shores of Cardigan bay. The
quarry declined over the years and finally closed in 1946. The railway continued
working for two or three days a week until its closure in 1950, when the Welsh
narrow-gauge appeared to be at an end. The Festiniog Railway had closed in 1946, and
British Rail then looked on the Vale of Rheidol Railway at Aberystwyth as an unre-
munerative line while the Welshpool & Llanfair was reduced to a freight-only branch.
The Talyllyn Railway Preservation Society was formed at the end of 1950 and operated
the first passenger service between Wharf station and Rhydyronen in June 1951.
Services started with just one locomotive (No 2, Dolgoch) and the five original coaches,
all of which dated back to 1866. Since then, track has been renewed, new station

Loco No 2, Dolgoch, pulling out of Rhydyronen station

No 6, Douglas, hauling an up train near Dolgoch Falls

Loco No 4, Edward Thomas, built by Kerr Stuart in 1921 and overhauled by the company's successor, Hunslet Engine Co Ltd

Bright sunshine for the morning up train running into Dolgoch Falls station pulled by No 3, Sir Haydn

buildings provided and the line extended (in 1976) from Abergynolwyn to Nant Gwernol. The 50-minute journey runs from Tywyn Wharf via Pendre, Rhydyronen, Brynglas, Dolgoch Falls, Abergynolwyn to Nant Gwernol.

Tywyn is on the Cambrian coast between Aberdovey and Barmouth. Nearest British Rail station is at Tywyn on the London Midland Region line or access is by road on the A493 Aberdovey-Dolgellau.

OPERATIONS
In 1979 the line reported 179 831 passenger journeys.

MOTIVE POWER
There are five team locos in regular service, one diesel-hydraulic and two diesel-mechanical:

No 1, Talyllyn, is an 0-4-2 saddle tank built in 1864 by Fletcher, Jennings of Whitehaven, Cumbria specifically for the Talyllyn Railway and delivered in 1865. Weight in working order is 11 tonnes; tractive effort is 4 496 lb at 85 per cent boiler pressure.

No 2, Dolgoch, although long due for a major overhaul, was still in traffic in 1979. An 0-4-0 well tank loco, like Talyllyn, it was built for the railway by Fletcher, Jennings and first went into service in 1866. During the Boer War it carried the name Pretoria. Weight in working order is 9.5 tonnes; tractive effort is 4 090 lb at 85 per cent boiler pressure.

No 3, Sir Haydn, was named after Sir Henry Haydn Jones who gave financial support to the line during 1946-51. This 0-4-2 saddle tank was delivered by Hughes of Loughborough as an 0-4-0 to the Corris Railway in 1878 where it was the last surviving engine when the line closed in 1948. Trailing wheels were added in 1900. Weight in working order is 8.5 tonnes; tractive effort is 2 800 lb at 85 per cent boiler pressure. It is currently Talyllyn's hardest-worked locomotive, running about 8 000 km annually.

No 4, Edward Thomas, was also built originally with the Corris Railway. This 0-4-2 saddle tank of 1921 was built by Kerr Stuart of Stoke on Trent to an adaptation of their standard Tattoo design. It was purchased by the Preservation Society from British Rail and named after the manager of the Talyllyn in 1951. An experimental Giesl Ejector fitted in 1958 has since been replaced with the original chimney.

No 6, Douglas, an 0-4-0 well tank, was built in 1918 as a batch of six locomotives by Andrew Barclay of Kilmarnock, Ayrshire, for Air Service Construction Corps. It entered Talyllyn service in 1954, was rebuilt in 1973 at Pendre and returned to traffic in 1975.

No 7, Irish Pete, was originally sold by Andrew Barclay as an 0-4-2 side tank loco to the 0.914 m gauge Bord na Mona (Irish Turf Board) in Ireland where it was intended to burn peat or turf but was little used. It was purchased by the Talyllyn Railway to be used as the basis for the construction of a new steam locomotive in 1969.

Diesel locos currently used for engineering and works traffic include No 5, Midlander, (built by Ruston and Hornsby in 1940), No 8, Merseysider, (same builder; year 1964), and No 9, Alf (a mine locomotive originally owned by the National Coal Board and built by Hunslet in 1950).

VOLKS ELECTRIC RAILWAY
285 Madeira Drive, Brighton, Sussex, England

Engineer/Manager: M G Wright
Director: A J Hewison

Gauge: 0.820 m
Route length: 2.0 km

When the Volk's Electric Railway opened on 4 August 1883, it became the UK's first regular service electric line and the first in the world. It was essentially a light railway, and remains so today. Its originator was Magnus Volk, born in 1851. Following permission to build a short electric line along Brighton's seafront, Volk joined forces with another Brighton resident, J T Chappell, who laid the light 0.609 m gauge track on a shingle embankment extending about 400 m. The 50 V output of the power plant was fed to the two running rails, which were flat-bottomed and spiked to well-tarred longitudinal sleepers. Volk equipped a simple double-ended four-wheel car with his own motor, using a belt to drive the axles, the current reaching the motor through the wheels via wires running the tyres, and returning through wooden-centred wheels to the opposite running rail. Small brushes were fitted before each wheel to sweep the rails clear of seawood and other seashore debris. The sides of the car were decorated with the flowery capitals, VER.

The ten-passenger car did a great trade and shuttled up and down at 9.6 km/h for 11 hours, effectively demonstrating the tireless efficiency of electric traction. Encouraged by this success, Volk closed the line for reconstruction and extension. The gauge was converted to 0.838 m and the eastern end extended to Kemp Town. The line was then about 800 m with a loop and stopping place about half-way. A new four-wheeled, double-ended car was provided to work it, with a 10 hp motor placed under the centre of the floor and controllers above the driver's head, on the ceiling. Six passengers sat on each platform, and the little saloon, which seated 18, had embossed plate-glass windows and a panelled ceiling decorated with hand-painted flowers and gold beading. Tare weight was two tonnes, and the bodywork was French-polished solid mahogany. Power was later produced by a 12 hp Crossley gas engine, driving a Siemens dynamo in a cave opposite the eastern terminus. The new track was supplied by Kerr, Stuart & Co of London and Glasgow.

The rebuilt line was opened on 4 April 1884, and the first car was so loaded that the sprung frame grounded on the timber of a level crossing. A second car, identical with the first, was delivered later in 1884; from then on a regular 5-6 minute basic service was operated summer and winter until 1940 with few interruptions except those caused by gale-force winds.

An off-centre third rail was installed about 1886 and the track raised on a timber viaduct above the shingle. About the same time the gauge became 0.820 m.

During the 1890s the Brighton Corporation allowed Volk to extend the original railway eastwards, bringing the length to 3.0 km with an extension to a new terminal at Black Rock. At this time the return fare was 4d (about 1¾p in today's currency); speed rarely exceeded 13 km/h, although Volk had claimed in his publicity leaflet that the cars could reach 48 km/h.

In 1937 the Corporation opened a new Bathing Pool at Black Rock and the railway was shortened to the present length. Volk died the same year.

After World War II the track was renewed from end to end in 30 kg/m rails and the reconstructed line was re-opened in 1948. Today the service is worked by two pairs of coupled cars passing at the centre station and the loops. Operation is regulated by a signal light and bell system, operated by a master electrical timing control in the running sheds. There are signal lights at all three stations and an emergency push switch at each end of the line. All cars are painted in yellow and very dark brown with the initials VR and the Brighton coat of arms on the sides and dashes. Access to the line is by British Rail train leaving London's Victoria station for Brighton. The Volk Railway is on the front about 25 minutes away from the British Rail terminal.

OPERATIONS
During recent years an average of 465 000 passengers have been carried annually (459 837 in 1978/79), with a peak figure of 570 000 in 1966. The railway is self-supporting financially, the annual profit formerly passing to the relief of rates now being placed in a renewals and repairs fund.

MOTIVE POWER

No	Built	Type	Capacity as built	Present capacity	Remarks
1	1884	Saloon	30	—	Scrapped 1948
2	1884	Saloon	30	—	Scrapped 1948
3	1892	Semi-open	?	40	Still in use
4	1892	Semi-open	?	40	Still in use
1 (II)	1897	Saloon	32?	—	Scrapped 1928
6	1901	Semi-open	32	40	Still in use
7	1901	Semi-open	32	40	Still in use
8	1901	Semi-open	32	40	Now No 5 (III)
9	1910?	Cross-bench with bulkheads	40	40	Now No 2 (II)
10	1926	Cross-bench	40	40	Now No 1 (III)
5 (II)	1930	Winter saloon	24	—	Scrapped 1948
8 (III)	1898?	Cross-bench with bulkheads	40	40/48	Ex-Southend Pier
9 (II)	1898?	Cross-bench with bulkheads	40	40/48	Ex-Southend Pier

For the present cars 1, 2 and 5, see under 10, 9 and 8 respectively. From 1897 to 1928, No 1 of 1884 was renumbered 5.

Volk cars running over track now laid on concrete sleepers (Photo: J H Price)

WELSH HIGHLAND LIGHT RAILWAY (1964) LTD
Gelert's Fard, Madoc Street West, Porthmadog, Gwynedd, Wales

Chairman and General Manager: K Dicks
Secretary: C C Lodge

Gauge: 0.60 m
Route length: 0.844 km

From 1923 to 1937 the Welsh Highland Railway was the longest narrow-gauge railway in Wales running 34.6 km from Porthmadog (where it connected through the town with the Festiniog Railway) to Dinas Junction, some 2 km south-west of Caernarvon on the London, Midland & Scottish Railway line to Afon Wen. In 1961 the Welsh Highland Railway Society was formed with the intention of re-opening as much as possible of the original railway with steam traction.
The route runs through the scenic Aberglaslyn Pass with a series of tunnels to Beddgelert, then climbs up to Rhyd-Ddu and the western slopes of Snowdon, past Lyn Quellyn to Bettws Garmon, Waenfawr and Tryfan Junction and then on a further 1.2 km into Dinas. The society hopes to run steam trains on the 0.844 km section in summer, 1980. Meanwhile feasibility studies are under way on the 16 km from Porthmadog to Rhyd Ddu.

MOTIVE POWER
First locomotive acquired was the 2-6-2T Russell which has since been restored. At present under overhaul are an Orenstein & Koppel 0-6-0 Pedemoura built in 1924 and a Peckett 0-4-2 Karen tank.

ROLLING STOCK
A passenger coach from The German Democratic Republic is being restored, while a former Vale of Rheidol brake van is undergoing overhaul.

WELSHPOOL AND LLANFAIR LIGHT RAILWAY
Llanfair Caereinion, Powys, Wales

Telephone: 0938 82 441

General Manager: R T Russell
Secretary: C Walker

Gauge: 0.762 m
Route length: 8.8 km

Headquarters of the Welshpool and Llanfair Light Railway lie in the centre of a wide, thinly-populated hill-farming area. Llanfair Caereinion station lies on the northern side of the River Banwy not far from the centre of the town on the A458 road from Welshpool. About 200 m from the station the line starts to head downhill around the Tanllan curve where sidings have been built by the Railway Preservation Company for storing carriages. The line continues alongside the Banwy before climbing out of the valley up a 1 in 24 gradient towards Cyfronydd station (3.77 km). The line climbs steadily on a 1 in 32 incline to Castle Caereinion where the view stretches back towards Llanfair across the Vale of Meifod. Finally the line continues up a steep cutting and through several sharp curves before reaching 176 m above sea level and gradually losing height on the run through open countryside to Sylfaen Halt, present terminal of the railway.
Extension work is underway on a 4 km extension to Welshpool (Raven Square station) which is due to open for passengers in 1981.
The line from Welshpool to Llanfair was opened in 1903, operated by the Cambrian Railways. Following change of ownership to the Great Western Railways, passenger services ended in 1931. The last goods train ran under British Railways' colours in October 1956. In April 1963 the section between Llanfair Caereinion and Castle Caereinion was re-opened to passenger traffic by the non-profit making Preservation Company followed by services all the way to Sylfaen in 1972.

OPERATIONS
In 1979 the railway carried 22 450 passengers, primarily by steam train.

MOTIVE POWER AND ROLLING STOCK
The Preservation Company succeeded in rescuing two of the original locomotives, The Earl and The Countess, together with some of the original freight vehicles. The original passenger coaches had been scrapped in 1936. Coaches from a Royal Naval Armaments depot made possible the new passenger services and since then an all-Austrian rake has been acquired, followed by a set of modern coaches from West Africa.
No 1 The Earl and No 2 The Countess were built in 1902 by Beyer Peacock & Co Ltd, of Gorton Foundry, Manchester, and have a tractive effort of 8 175 lb at 85 per cent boiler pressure. Both locomotives are fitted with a modified form of Walschaerts valve gear and have both vacuum and hand brakes. In 1929/30 the Great Western Railway fitted each loco with a new boiler and extended cab. The copper-capped chimney, large steam dome and brass safety valve cover which surmounted the new boilers were typical Swindon features.
No 6 Monarch was built in 1953 by WG Bagnall Ltd of Stafford (No 3024) and is likely to be the last steam narrow-gauge loco built for industrial service in the UK. In addition to being a four-cylinder articulated engine it features a circular (marine) firebox and an

At Castle Caereinion station the former Austrian 0-8-0 tank, Sir Drefaldwyn, heads a passenger train

eight-element superheater, the latter being rare on narrow-gauge locos in the UK. The loco was new to Messrs Bowater Lloyd's paper mills at Sittingbourne, Kent, England.
No 8 Dougal was constructed by Andrew Barclay Sons & Co Ltd of Kilmarnock in 1946 (No 2207) for the then extensive 0.762 m-gauge system in the Provan Gasworks of Glasgow Corporation which closed in 1958. At Llanfair, it has proved useful as yard shunter.
No 10 Sir Drefaldwyn was built in 1944 by Franco-Belge at Raismes, France, as one of a once-numerous class of 0-8-0 superheated tank/tender engines used by the German Military Field Railways in World War II. After the war it was transferred to Austria. In 1957 the Styrian Local Government Railways, near Graz, Austria, acquired it and rebuilt it into its present form without a tender. With a tractive effort of 13 535 lb, it arrived in Wales in 1969.
No 12 Joan, this far-travelled locomotive spent its working life on the tropical island of Antigua in the West Indies hauling trains of sugar cane until it went to Llanfair in 1971. Built at Stoke-on-Trent by Kerr, Stuart & Co Ltd in 1927, Joan was originally equipped as an oil-burner. During World War II it was converted to burn coal and sugar cane waste. In 1949 a new boiler, firebox and water tanks were supplied by the Hunslet Engine Co, Leeds.
No 14 was rescued from the scrap merchants and this 2-6-2 tank locomotive was shipped back to the UK from West Africa in 1975. Built by the Hunslet Engine Co Ltd, Leeds in 1954, it was the last of a line of 32 similar locomotive supplied to the Sierra Leone Railway where it worked on banking and freight duties.

WEST SOMERSET RAILWAY CO LTD
Railway Station, Minehead, Somerset TA24 5BG, England

Telephone: 0643 4996

Administrative Director: C N M van den Arend

Gauge: 1.435 m
Route length: 34 km

The West Somerset carries an average of 152 000 passengers every year on diesel and steam-hauled tourist and enthusiast trains. Locomotives in service consist of three steam line haul, one steam shunter and two diesel locos. A pair of two-car diesel railcars completes the motive power park.

WINCHESTER AND ALTON RAILWAY
(The Mid-Hants 'Watercress' line)
Mid-Hants Railway Preservation Society Ltd, Alresford Station, Alresford, Hampshire SO24 9JG, England

Chairman: John Taylor
Deputy Chairman: Simon A F Davies
General Manager: David Vidler
Secretary: F Clifton Sherriff

Gauge: 1.435 m
Route length: 5 km

On 30 April 1977 the former British Rail Alresford to Ropley section of the Mid-Hants 'Watercress' line was re-opened for steam traffic following closure by British Rail in 1973. New owners/operators were the parent Winchester & Alton Railway and its supporting body the Mid-Hants Railway Preservation Society Ltd. Originally opened in 1865 by the Mid-Hants Railway, which built the line, and the London & South Western Railway which worked it, the line was one of the many British branch lines lopped by the Beeching axe. It had always been known as the 'Watercress' line because Alresford has been the main source of watercress in southern England for about a century. It was not unusual for eight or nine tonnes of cress to be railed daily during the season and loads of 14 tonnes were recorded on one occasion. All that is left of the line once running busy freight and passenger traffic between Winchester Junction and Alton is the 5 km section linking Alresford and Ropley, although track is to be relaid over the 11 km section to Alton. Between Ropley and Alresford the line meanders between corn fields and watercress beds before crossing the main A31 road into a deep chalk cutting before running into Alresford station. This station, always the busiest and now the line's headquarters, has retained nearly all its buildings and is a perfect example of a Victorian country station.

OPERATIONS
A total of 64 747 tickets were sold in 1978/79 when the railway recorded 128 375 passenger journeys.

MOTIVE POWER
Steam Locomotives

30506, S15 class
Designed by Robert Urie, 506 was one of 20 built at Eastleigh for the London & South Western Railway delivered in October 1920. Most of its life was spent based at Feltham, Middlesex, where it was used to haul heavy freight trains from London to Hampshire,

0-6-2T Joan originally handled sugar cane trains in the Caribbean until ousted by diesels

First train of the Mid-Hants 'Watercress' line's 1979 season
The 1330 hours Alresford-Ropley seen emerging from the chalk cutting just outside Alresford as the N class 2-6-0 No 31874 gets up steam for the 1 in 80 climb to Ropley.

34016 Bodmin, West Country class
One of 110 pacific locomotives built to Southern Railway design after the last war which received West Country and Battle of Britain names. 34016 was built at Brighton and entered traffic at Exmouth Junction, near Exeter, in November 1945. Early duties included the hauling of the Devon Belle during 1948 between Exeter and Ilfracombe. After being rebuilt to its current form in April 1958, it was transferred to Ramsgate from where it regularly worked to London via Chatham. In June 1964 the locomotive was condemned, and after being used for safety-valve setting at Eastleigh for a while, was despatched to the scrapyard having covered 811 674 miles in active service. The 5 500 gallon tender has been paired with Bodmin since April 1958, having previously been attached to Battle of Britain class pacific 34088. On 29 July 1972 the locomotive completed a move by road from the scrapyard to Quainton Road, near Aylesbury, where restoration work commenced. Bodmin was transferred to Alresford in November 1976 and, following a complete overhaul re-entered traffic in 1979. Wheel arrangement 4-6-2; weight, engine 90 tonnes 1 cwt, tender 47 tonnes 15 cwt; boiler pressure 250 lb/sq in; tractive effort 27 720 lb. Previous numbers: 21C116 (to March 1948), s21C116 (to July 1948).

34105 Swanage, West Country class
A further example of the famous Southern Railway pacifics, although this example was not contructed until March 1950 at Brighton, Swanage remained in its original form until condemned in October 1964 having covered 623 405 miles in 14½ years. In April 1976 it was purchased by a group of Mid-Hants supporters. The large, 6 000 gallon tender was rebuilt in February 1962 when it was fitted to a Merchant Navy pacific 35008, although the tender was sent to Barry for scrap attached to pacific 35018. Restoration work is expected to be completed in 1981/82. Wheel arrangement 4-6-2; cylinders (3) 16⅜ × 24 in; driving wheels 6 ft 2 in; weight, engine 86 tonnes, tender 53 tonnes 8 cwt; boiler pressure 250 lb/sq in; tractive effort 27 715 lb.

47324, class 3F
Between 1924 and 1931 a total of 482 0-6-0 tank engines known as Jinties were built for the London Midland and Scottish group. No 47324 was built at the North British Locomotive Co Ltd at Glasgow in 1926. After being purchased by two Mid-Hants members early in 1977, a small amount of restoration work was carried out at Barry scrapyard where the locomotive had been dumped since December 1966. Just over a year later, the move to Hampshire took place and a complete overhaul started in 1979. Wheel arrangement 0-6-0; weight 49 tonnes 10 cwt; boiler pressure 160 lb/sq in; tractive effort 20 835 lb. Previous number: 7324 (to 1948).

76017, BR standard class 4
Following nationalisation in 1948, several types of 'standard' British Rail locomotive designs were produced. Of these, the Standard Class 4 2-6-0 was based on a successful LMS design and production started in 1953. Several were allocated to the Southern Region and of these, 76017 was built by British Rail at their Horwich works in Lancashire during June 1953. During July 1965, after a very short active life, it was condemned. But, in 1972, a small band of enthusiasts based at Slough formed the Standard 4 Locomotive Group, and a year later moved the locomotive to Quainton Road, near Aylesbury, arriving there in January 1974. The long job of restoration commenced, and continued following the move to the Mid-Hants Railway in March 1978. Wheel arrangement 2-6-0; weight, engine 59 tonnes 2 cwt, tender 42 tonnes 3 cwt; boiler pressure 225 lb/sq in; tractive effort 24 170 lb.

2, industrial saddle tank
Built by W G Bagnall at Stafford in 1946, works number 2842, this small tank locomotive was purchased in 1973 by a group of Mid-Hants supporters from the CEGB Croydon Power Station. No 2 will eventually be used on light shunting duties, but in the meantime is normally on display at Alresford. Wheel arrangement 0-4-0; weight 27 tonnes; boiler pressure 160 lb/sq in; tractive effort 13 798 lb.

3, industrial saddle tank
Built by Hudswell Clark at Leeds in 1924, works number 1544, this locomotive worked for 49 years at the Slough Trading Estate, hauling freight around the extensive system there. The last run of No 3 took place on 27 April 1973. Restoration to full working order, including the fitting of a new firebox, is currently in the hands of the Way & Works Dept. who have adopted this locomotive for their own use. Wheel arrangement 0-6-0; cylinders (2) 15 × 22 in; driving wheels 3 ft 7 in; weight 32 tonnes 5 cwt; boiler pressure 160 lb/sq in; tractive effort 15 655 lb.

196, Errol Lonsdale, Austerity saddle tank
A fine example of a popular class of 0-6-0 saddle tank locomotives built in large quantities during and after the second World War. 196 was included in a batch of 14, the last to be ordered by the War Dept., constructed by the Hunslet Engine Company of Leeds in 1952/53. On 8 January 1968, 196 was named Errol Lonsdale: 196 was sold, minus nameplates, and transferred to Rolvenden, on the Kent & East Sussex Railway, arriving there on 20 June 1970. 196 was bought by Mid-Hants supporters in 1976, completely retubed and entered traffic on 30 April 1977. Wheel arrangement 0-6-0; cylinders (2) 18 × 26 in; driving wheels 4 ft 3 in; weight 48 tonnes 4 cwt; boiler pressure 170 lb/sq in; tractive effort 23 870 lb.

although it occasionally worked boat trains to Southampton Docks and other passenger services at holiday times. In January 1964, 30506 was condemned, having run 1 227 897 miles, and was sold for scrap. It remained in the scrapyard until purchased by the Urie S15 Locomotive Preservation Group in 1973 and moved to the 'Watercress' line where it is currently undergoing restoration at Ropley. Prior to September 1956, the tender ran with King Arthur class locomotive 30745 Tintagel. Wheel arrangement 4-6-0; weight, engine 79 tonnes 16 cwts, tender 57 tonnes 16 cwt; boiler pressure 180 lb/sq in; tractive effort 28 200 lb. Previous number 506 (to 1948).

31806, U class
Originally built at Brighton in October 1926 as a K class tank locomotive named River Torridge. Rebuilt June 1928 as a U class tender engine. It was condemned in 1963 and sold to the scrapyard until purchased by two MHRPS directors in July 1975. The tender to be used with 31806 in future worked until 1960 with King Arthur class locomotive 30797 Sir Blamor de Ganis and later with S15 class locomotive 30847. A complete overhaul commenced during 1979. Wheel arrangement 2-6-0; weight, engine 63 tonnes, tender 39 tonnes 5 cwt; boiler pressure 200 lb/sq in; tractive effort 23 865 lb. Previous numbers: A806 (to 1931), 1806 (to 1948).

31874, N class
Only survivor of the mixed-traffic locomotives built from parts made at Woolwich Arsenal to relieve unemployment after the first World War. Upon completion the locomotive was towed to Ashford, Kent for acceptance by the Southern Railway, in September 1925. On 30 April 1977, 31874 hauled the 'Watercress' line's re-opening trains. Wheel arrangement 2-6-0; weight, engine 59 tonnes 8 cwt, tender 39 tonnes 5 cwt; boiler pressure 200 lb/sq in; tractive effort 26 035 lb. Previous numbers: A874 (to 1931), 1874 (to 1948).

UNITED STATES OF AMERICA

ALASKA
ALASKA YUKON CHAPTER
National Railway Historical Society, PO Box 2248, Anchorage, Alaska 99501

Gauge: 1.435 m
Route length: 6.4 km

Type of traction: Steam

ARIZONA
ARIZONA, LEGEND CITY AMUSEMENT PARK
56th and Washington Streets, Tempe, Arizona 85281

Gauge: 0.914 m
Route length: 1.5 km

Type of traction: Steam

CALIFORNIA
ALTON AND PACIFIC RAILROAD
Route 1, PO Box 477, Fortuna, California 95540

Gauge: 0.600 m
Route length: 2 km

Type of traction: Steam

BAY AREA ELECTRIC RAILFAN ASSOCIATION
2119 Marin Avenue, Berkeley, California 94707

Gauge: 1.435 m
Route length: 3 km

Type of traction: Electric

CALIFORNIA WESTERN RAILROAD
Fort Bragg, California 95437

Gauge: 1.435 m
Route length: 64 km

Type of traction: Steam

CASTRO POINT RAILWAY
54 Hancock Street, San Francisco, California 94114

Gauge: 1.435 m
Route length: 5 km

Type of traction: Steam

GHOST TOWN AND CALICO RAILWAY
Knotts Berry Farm, 8039 Beach Boulevard, Buena Park, California 90620

Gauge: 0.914 m
Route length: 2 km

Type of traction: Steam

McCLOUD RIVER RAILROAD
McCloud, California 96057

Gauge: 1.435 m
Route length: 129 km

Type of traction: Steam

ROARING CAMP AND BIG TREES RAILROAD
PO Box 338, Felton, California 95018

Gauge: 0.914 m
Route length: 8 km

Type of traction: Steam

SIERRA RAILROAD
781 Washington Street, Sonora, California 95370

Gauge: 1.435 m
Route length: 61 km

Type of traction: Electric

YOSEMITE MOUNTAIN, SUGAR PINE RAILROAD
Fish Camp, California 93623

Gauge: 0.914 m
Route length: 6 km

Type of traction: Steam

COLORADO
COLORADO CENTRAL RAILWAY
PO Box 721, Golden, Colorado 80401

Gauge: 0.914 m
Route length: 1.5 km

Type of traction: Steam

CRIPPLE CREEK AND VICTOR RAILROAD
PO Box 459, Cripple Creek, Colorado 80813

Gauge: 0.600 m
Route length: 6 km

Type of traction: Steam

DENVER AND RIO GRANDE WESTERN RAILROAD
Rio Grande Depot, Durango, Colorado 81301

Gauge: 0.914 m
Route length: 145 km

Type of traction: Steam

GEORGETOWN LOOP RAILROAD
PO Box 721, Golden, Colorado 80401

Gauge: 0.914 m
Route length: 5 km

Type of traction: Steam

CONNECTICUT
BRANFORD ELECTRIC RAILWAY ASSOCIATION
17 River Street, East Haven, Connecticut 06088

Gauge: 1.435 m
Route length: 5 km

Type of traction: Electric

VALLEY RAILROAD COMPANY
PO Box 172, Essex, Connecticut 06426

Gauge: 1.435 m
Route length: 13 km

Type of traction: Steam

DELAWARE
WILMINGTON AND WESTERN RAILROAD
PO Box 1374, Wilmington, Delaware 19899

Gauge: 1.435 m
Route length: 13 km

Type of traction: Steam

FLORIDA
GOLD COAST RAILROAD
811 SW 6th Street, Fort Lauderdale, Florida 33315

Gauge: 1.435 m
Route length: 6 km

Type of traction: Steam

GEORGIA
SIX FLAGS OVER GEORGIA
PO Box 43135, Atlanta, Georgia 30336

Gauge: 0.914 m
Route length: 1.5 km

Type of traction: Steam

STONE MOUNTAIN SCENIC RAILROAD
PO Box 447, Stone Mountain, Georgia 30083

Gauge: 1.435 m
Route length: 8 km

Type of traction: Steam

HAWAII
LAHAINA, KAANAPALI AND PACIFIC RAILROAD
PO Box 816, Lahaina, Hawaii 96761

Gauge: 0.914 m
Route length: 19 km

Type of traction: Steam

ILLINOIS
CRAB ORCHARD AND EGYPTIAN RAILROAD
PO Box 351, Marion, Illinois 62959

Gauge: 1.435 m
Route length: 25 km

Type of traction: Steam

MONTICELLO AND SANGAMON VALLEY RAILWAY
PO Box 185, Monticello, Illinois 61856

Gauge: 1.435 m
Route length: 5 km

Type of traction: Steam

RAILWAY EQUIPMENT LEASING AND INVESTMENT CORPORATION
PO Box 752, South Elgin, Illinois 60177

Gauge: 1.435 m
Route length: 4 km

Type of traction: Electric

SAUK TRAIL LINE
c/o Thompson Farms, Monee, Illinois 60449

Gauge: 1.435 m
Route length: 0.8 km

Type of traction: Steam

INDIANA
LA PORTE COUNTY STEAM SOCIETY
2940 Mount Clare Way, Michigan City, Indiana 46360

Gauge: 0.600 m/0.914 m
Route length: 4 km

Type of traction: Steam

IOWA
MIDWEST CENTRAL RAILROAD
PO Box 102, Mount Pleasant, Iowa 52641

Gauge: 0.914 m
Route length: 1.5 km

Type of traction: Steam

KANSAS
SMOKY HILL RAILWAY AND HISTORICAL SOCIETY
PO Box 124, Shawnee Mission, Kansas 66201

KENTUCKY
TOMBSTONE JUNCTION RAILROAD
Rural Route, Parkers Lake, Kentucky 42634

Gauge: 1.435 m
Route length: 4 km

Type of traction: Steam

MASSACHUSETTS
EDAVILLE RAILROAD
PO Box 7, South Carver, Massachusetts 02566

Gauge: 0.600 m
Route length: 9 km

Type of traction: Steam

NEW HAMPSHIRE
CONWAY SCENIC RAILROAD INC
PO Box 434, New Hampshire 03818

Gauge: 1.435 m
Route length: 18 km

Type of traction: Steam

MOUNT WASHINGTON RAILWAY COMPANY
Mount Washington, New Hampshire 03589

Gauge: 1.435 m
Route length: 5.6 km

Type of traction: Steam cog

WHIPPANY TOONERVILLE RAILROAD
PO Box 2206, Morristown, New Jersey 07960

Gauge: 1.435 m
Route length: 14.5 km

Type of traction: Steam

WHITE MOUNTAIN CENTRAL RAILROAD
PO Box 1, North Woodstock, New Hampshire 03262

Gauge: 1.435 m
Route length: 3 km
Type of traction: Steam

WOLFEBORO RAIL ROAD COMPANY
Wolfeboro, New Hampshire 03894

Gauge: 1.435 m
Route length: 19 km

Type of traction: Steam

NEW MEXICO
CUMBRES AND TOLTEC SCENIC RAILROAD
PO Box 789, Chama, New Mexico 87520

Gauge: 0.914 m
Route length: 103 km

Type of traction: Steam

NEW YORK
ARCADE AND ATTICA RAILROAD
278 Main Street, Arcade, New York, 14009

Gauge: 1.435 m
Route length: 24 km

Type of traction: Steam

COOPERSTOWN AND CHARLOTTE VALLEY RAILWAY
1 Railroad Avenue, Cooperstown, New York 13326

Gauge: 1.435 m
Route length: 26 km

Type of traction: Steam

LIVONIA, AVON AND LAKEVILLE RAILROAD
Livonia, New York 14487

Gauge: 1.435 m
Route length: 37 km

Type of traction: Steam

NORTH CAROLINA
BEAR CREEK SCENIC RAILROAD
PO Box 377, Robbinsville, North Carolina 28771

Gauge: 1.435 m
Route length: 8 km

Type of traction: Steam

TWEETSIE RAILROAD
PO Box 277, Blowing Rock, North Carolina 28605

Gauge: 0.914 m
Route length: 5 km

Type of traction: Steam

OHIO
CEDAR POINT AND LAKE ERIE RAILROAD
PO Box 759, Sandusky, Ohio 44870

Gauge: 0.914 m
Route length: 1 km

Type of traction: Steam

HOCKING VALLEY SCENIC RAILWAY
2366 Shrewsbury Road, Columbus, Ohio 43221

Gauge: 1.435 m
Route length: 23 km
Type of traction: Steam

OHIO RAILWAY MUSEUM
PO Box 171, Worthington, Ohio 43085

Gauge: 1.435 m
Route length: 16 km

Type of traction: Steam and electric

TOLEDO LAKE ERIE AND WESTERN RAILROAD
1008 Eton Road, Toledo, Ohio 43615

Gauge: 1.435 m
Route length: 26 km

Type of traction: Steam

TROLLEYVILLE USA
7100-B Columbia Road, Olmstead Falls, Ohio 44138

Gauge: 1.435 m
Route length: 4 km

Type of traction: Electric

OKLAHOMA
NORTHWESTERN OKLAHOMA RAILROAD
PO Box 1131, Woodward, Oklahoma 73801

Gauge: 1.435 m
Route length: 6 km

Type of traction: Diesel

OREGON
OREGON ELECTRIC RAILWAY HISTORICAL SOCIETY
Star Route, PO Box 1318, Glenwood, Oregon 97120

Gauge: 1.435 m
Route length: 1.5 km

Type of traction: Electric

OREGON PACIFIC AND EASTERN RAILWAY
101 South 10th Street, Cottage Grove, Oregon 97424

Gauge: 1.435 m
Route length: 29 km

Type of traction: Steam and diesel

PORTLAND ZOO RAILWAY
4001 SW Canyon Road, Portland, Oregon 97221

Gauge: 0.762 m
Route length: 6 km

Type of traction: Steam and petrol

PENNSYLVANIA
ARDEN TROLLEY MUSEUM
PO Box 832, Pittsburgh, Pennsylvania 15230

Gauge: 1.435 m; 1.715 m
Route length: 1.5 km

Type of traction: Steam, diesel and electric

BLAIRSVILLE AND INDIANA RAILROAD
RD No 1, Blairsville, Pennsylvania 15717

Gauge: 1.435 m
Route length: 21 km

Type of traction: Steam

CARROLL PARK AND WESTERN RAILROAD
Carroll Park, Bloomsburg, Pennsylvania 17815

Gauge: 1.219 m
Route length: 3 km

Type of traction: Steam

EAST BROADTOP RAILROAD
Rockhill Furnace, Pennsylvania 17249

Gauge: 0.914 m
Route length: 16 km

Type of traction: Steam

NEW HOPE AND IVYLAND RAILROAD
32 West Bridge Street, New Hope, Pennsylvania 18938

Gauge: 1.435 m
Route length: 23 km

Type of traction: Steam

PIONEER COALMINE TUNNEL RAILROAD
19th and Oak Street, Ashland, Pennsylvania 17921

Gauge: 1.067 m
Route length: 2.4 km

Type of traction: Steam

SHADE GAP ELECTRIC RAILWAY
328 North 28th Street, Allentown, Pennsylvania 18104

Gauge: 1.435 m
Route length: 3 km

Type of traction: Electric

STRASBURG RAIL ROAD
PO Box 96, Strasburg, Pennsylvania 17579

Gauge: 1.435 m
Route length: 14 km

Type of traction: Steam

WANNAMAKER, KEMPTON AND SOUTHERN RAILROAD
PO Box 24, Kempton, Pennsylvania 19529

Gauge: 1.435 m
Route length: 10 km

Type of traction: Steam

SOUTH CAROLINA
LANCASTER AND CHESTER PARK RAILROAD
Springe Park, Lancaster, South Carolina 29720

Gauge: 0.457 m
Route length: 0.3 km

Type of traction: Steam

SOUTH DAKOTA
BLACK HILLS CENTRAL RAILROAD
PO Box 1880, Hill City, South Dakota 57745

Gauge: 1.435 m
Route length: 52 km

Type of traction: Steam

UTAH
WASATCH MOUNTAIN RAILWAY
PO Box 69, Heber City, Utah 84032

Gauge: 1.435 m
Route length: 35 km

Type of traction: Steam

VERMONT
STEAM TOWN FOUNDATION
PO Box 71, Bellows Falls, Vermont 05101

Gauge: 1.435 m
Route length: 35 km

Type of traction: Steam

VIRGINIA
DRY GULF JUNCTION RAILROAD
Star Route Delivery, Wytheville, Virginia 24382

Gauge: 1.435 m
Route length: 3 km

Type of traction: Steam

WASHINGTON
LAKE WATCOM RAILWAY
Wickersham Station, Sedro, Wooley, Washington 98285

Gauge: 1.435 m
Route length: 14 km

Type of traction: Steam

WEST VIRGINIA
CASS SCENIC RAILROAD
Cass, West Virginia 24927

Gauge: 1.435 m
Route length: 35 km

Type of traction: Steam

WISCONSIN
LAONA NORTHERN RAILWAY
Laona, Wisconsin 54541

Gauge: 1.435 m
Route length: 27 km

Type of traction: Steam

RIVERSIDE AND GREAT NORTHERN RAILROAD
Sandley Light Railway Equipment Works, PO Box 164, Wisconsin Dells, Wisconsin 53965

Gauge: 0.381 m
Route length: 6 km

Type of traction: Steam

RAPID TRANSIT, UNDERGROUND
AND SURFACE RAILWAYS

ABIDJAN

Authority:
Abidjan Transport Authority
Abidjan, Ivory Coast

Type of system: 1.00 m gauge metro.

General: Studies were carried out in 1978 on a north-south 36 km metro. Line 1 will run 19 km between Treichville and Anoukonakouté. 3.5 km will be underground. Line 2 will form the second phase, running 17 km east-west from Deux Plateau to Plateau du Banco. Cost is estimated at Fr CFA 7 000 million.

ADELAIDE

Authority:
State Transport Authority
PO Box 2351, Adelaide, South Australia 5001, Australia

Chairman: A. G. Flint
General Manager: F. R. Harris
Traffic Manager: R. J. Renshaw
Chief Engineer: C. R. Stewien

Type of system: Full metro.

General: Under the terms of an agreement between the Commonwealth of Australia and the State of South Australia, responsibility for the non-metropolitan services was transferred to the Commonwealth. The transfer of the financial responsibility under the re-arrangement became effective on 1 July 1975, but the Authority continued to manage the whole of the South Australian Railway systems until 1 March 1978 when the management for the non-metropolitan railways was transferred to the Australian National Railways Commission.
On 1 March 1978 the Authority's Rail Division and Bus and Tram Division were integrated and all administrative staff were transferred to the same location in the Adelaide Railway Station Building. Since that time, all of the metropolitan rail, tram and bus passenger services have been under the control of the one management.

Route: Adelaide—Belair, Adelaide—Noarlunga Centre, Adelaide—Outer Harbor and Grange and Adelaide—North Gawler and Northfield are the four major routes.

Urban structure:
Population of city area: 931 900 (1978)
Land area: 1 854.2 km²

Primary road network within city boundary: no motorways
Number of automobiles registered in city: 308 118 (1972), 397 303 (1978)

Technical data:
Gauge: 5 ft 3 in (Broad) 0.160 m.
Route length: 142.38 km
Track length: 337.86 km
In tunnel: 1.8 km
Number of lines in operation: 4 major and 6 branch lines
Number of stations (total): 102
Average distance between stations: 1.41 km
Max length of station platforms: 410 m
Gradient (max): 1 in 45
Curvature (min): 200 m
Speed (design max): 110 km/h
(average commercial): 40 km/h
Type of rails: 40-53 kg/m
Type of tunnel: Hand excavated and brick or concrete lined.

Traffic and finances:
Max line capacities (one way): 3 minute headways
Max number of trains per hour (one way): Nine (one way-planned): Future 12
Frequency of train services in minutes (currently): 30 minutes off peak, 20 minutes peak
(planned): 30 minutes off peak, 20 minutes peak
Passenger journeys per annum: 11 950 000 (1977/78), 11 368 330 (1978/79)

Revenues: $3 290 220 (1977/78), $3 373 867 (1978/79)
Finances: (Financial Charges) $2 467 404 (1977/78), $2 808 318 (1978/79)

Rolling stock:
Car types: Motor cars 300/400 class and 2 000 class; Trailers 860 class and 2 100 class.
Number of units: (Diesel-hydraulic) 110, 12, 24, 18.
Car dimensions:
Length (m) 20.015, 25.5, 16.98, 25.5
Width (m) 3.045, 3.188, 3.060, 3.188
Height (m) 4.27, 4.27, 3.96, 4 27
Total floor area: 52.6 m², 71.9 m², 46.7 m², 71.9 m²
Number of doors per side: 3, 2, 7, 2
Door width (m): 0.9, 1.3, 6 = 0.65 1 = 1.22, 1.3
Number of passengers per car (total): 100, 80, 100, 110
(seated) 91, 72, 56, 106
Motors per car: 2, 2 traction 1 auxiliary.
Motor rating (kW) 156.7, 375 traction, 130 kW/161 kVa auxiliary.
Power per train (minimum): 4.21 kW/tonne, 3.87 kW/tonne.
(max) 5.62 kW/tonne, 5.14 kW/tonne.
Acceleration (max): N-A, 0.9 m/s², N-A, N-A.
Deceleration (normal service): N-A, 0.9 m/s², N-A, 0.9 m/s²
(emergency): N-A, 1.2 m/s², N-A, 1.2 m/s²
Max design speed: 88 km/h, 120 km/h, 88 km/h, 120 km/h
Bogies (type and manufacturer): Elliptical & coil springs, H Frame with air bags, Elliptical & coil springs, H Frame with air bags.
Distance between bogie pivot: 13.435, 17.500, 10.970, 17.500
Brakes (type): Tread, Disc plus tread, Tread, Disc.
Weight (empty in tonnes): 42.6, 62, 30.2, 42

AMSTERDAM

Authority:
Gemeentevervoerbedrijf Amsterdam (GVBA)
Julianaplein 6, Amsterdam, Netherlands
Telephone: (20) 16 01 28
Telegrams: TRAMWAYS/AMSTERDAM

Type of system: Full-metro.

History: Amsterdam began operation on Line 1 in October 1977. A decision to proceed with the project, taken by the City Council in 1968, was endorsed by the Government in 1970, when financial support of 195 million guilders (approximately £23 million in 1969) was promised, contributing about half the construction cost of an 11 miles (18 km) line that will be the initial line of a planned 48.5 mile (78 km) network. This first line will start at Central Station, Netherlands Railways, and run south-east for about 4.4 miles (7 km) before dividing into two, one route of 3.7 miles (6 km) to East Bijlmer and the other route of 3.1 miles (5 km) to Bijlmermeer. The growing Bijlmermeer community was expected to develop into a new town with 100 000 inhabitants by 1978. Section one of the first line opened in 1977. Opening of the full line is expected in 1981.
The decision to provide Amsterdam with a Metro system was motivated by the need for sophisticated mass transportation between Amsterdam's centre and its suburbs. The bicycle, once predominant as a commuting conveyance, is disappearing as peripheral development increases commuter distances to roughly three times that of the pre-war average of 2.5 miles (4 km).

Technical Data:
Gauge: 1.435 m
Parts of the Eastline (in construction): 2 km (underground): 1 km elevated
Number of lines: one under construction
Number of stations (total): 19
(in tunnel): 5
Average distance between stations: 0.8 km
Stations: platform length (minimum): 150 m

Type of tunnel: In order to keep out ground-water, sections of the underground portions have been built by the pneumatic caisson method, which involved building pre-fabricated rectangular tunnel segments on the surface and sinking them into their final positions (with the tunnel roof 14 ft 9 in (4.5 m) below surface level). Some 820 ft (250 m) will be of cut and cover construction. The outer stretches of the initial line will all be built on viaduct or embankment. The tunnels, 13 ft 6 in (4.10 m) high above rail level and 27 ft 3 in (8.30 m) wide, carry two tracks.

Amsterdam metro-train from the series 33 double units, which came into service in October 1977

Gradient (max): 3.2%
Curvature (max): 300 m
Speed (design max): 80 km/h
(average commercial): 35 km/h
Electric system: Third rail; 750 V
Type of rails: 49 kg/m

Rolling stock: Rolling Stock, built by Linke-Hofmann-Busch, is made up of twin-coupled car units resting on four bogies.

Car type:	MI.1	MI.2
Number of units:		
11 units are being delivered during 1980		
Car dimensions (length):	18.27 m	18.67 m
(width):	3.01 m	3.01 m
(height):	3.54 m	3.54 m

Passenger capacity:		
per car (total):	150	153
(seated):	49	—
Rating:	180 kWh	—
Brakes (type):	Rheostatic	
Weight (tonnes): Motorcar:	26	26

Traffic Data:
Trains/track/hour: 12 (Bijlmer-South)
16 (Bijlmer-East)
Train capacity maximum; usual 600 (2 couples); peak 900 (3 couples)
Total passengers/track/hour: 25 200
Train headways design: 2 minutes

Signalling: ATO is planned together with two-way radio communications.

ANKARA

Authority:
Ankara City Transit
Mayor's Office, Ankara City Administration, Ankara, Turkey

Type of system: Full-metro.

History: New City Transit Authority was set up to plan and design an 11.4 km transit system.

Technical Data:
Gauge: 1.435 m
Projected new lines (in design): 11.4 km
Number of lines: 2
Number of stations (total): 18
Speed (design max): 80 km/h
Electric system: Third rail; 750 dc

Rolling Stock:
Car type: proposed
Number of units: 130
Car dimensions (length): 15 m
(width): 2.6 m

ANTIOQUIA
Colombia

General: Colombia's first rapid transit system will be a 23 km double-track line along the Aburra Valley in Antioquia province. It will serve the provincial capital of Medellin and the municipalities of Bello, Copacabana, Envigado, Itagui, La Estrella and Sabenata. A \$US 60 million contract was finalised in 1978 with Francorail-MTE of France for supply of the first batch of 20 three-car trainsets and fixed installations. Gauge will be 914 mm.

ANTWERP
Authority:
Maatschappij Voor Het Intercommunaal Vervoer te Antwerpen (MIVA)
Grote Hondstraat 58, 2 000 Antwerp, Belgium
Telephone: (031) 30 99 15

General: Antwerp operates a 79.9 km light rail tram system; total length of the ten-line system is 160 km; at present 2.6 km are operated in tunnel.
The pre-metro programme consists of building tunnels within the city boundaries and the improvement of the tracks on own right of way in the suburbs.
To avoid any effects of the work on local traffic and business, only subterranean methods are being applied: drum digger shield (hydro shield) for tunnelling and pressing of reinforced concrete tubes for assembling the station roofs; further construction of the station continues entirely under this roof. The most important project being developed at the moment is a tunnel between the city and Linker Oever (left bank) under the river Schelde.
Length of the final system has still to be decided: up to now the planned length is about 15 km, with 19 stations.

Construction:
First section: Groenplaats—Centraal Station (operative):
The construction of this section started on January 5, 1970. It became officially operative on March 25, 1975. The present route length in use is 1 300 m, or 2 600 m of single track.

Second pre-metro section: Centraal Station—Belgiëlei—Mercatorstraat:
This section consists of two stations (Diamant—Plantijn).
Construction started in October 1973 at Station Diamant. It includes a total length of 3 070 m single track and a route length of 1 570 m.
The section was expected to be in full operation by early 1980.

Third section: Centraal Station—St. Elisabethstraat—Schijnpoort:
Construction of the first part between Astrid and Elisabeth started on 26 March 1979. Test drilling and soil research are in progress for the second part.

Second Axis: Frankrijklei—Stenenbrug:
Construction of the important interchange Station Astrid is nearing completion. Five other stations are being built by subterranean methods. Route length of this axis will be 4 520 m (5 040 m single track). The greater part of the tunnels will be carried out by a hydro-shield: of five sections, two are already completed, and a third section is nearing completion.

Provisional pre-metro access ramp at De Keyzerlei

Interior view of the new Meir pre-metro station

Future planning: Planning includes engineering studies for the tunnel to the left bank of the city, two small extensions near Schijnpoort and the last section of the second axis. A project is ready in hand for the extension of one line on own right of way and several others are being considered. Finally, preparatory studies have started for the future purchase of larger cars.

ATHENS
Authority:
Athens/Piraeus Electric Railway Co Ltd (ISAP)
67 Athenas St, Athens, Greece
Telephone: (21) 3248 311
Telegrams: HSAP Athens

History: The line between Athens and its port of Piraeus was the first railway to be built in Greece. It was electrified in 1904 and in 1930 its northern end was carried under the centre of Athens by means of a tunnel, of "cut-and-cover" construction, extending from the south end of Athenas Street to Attiki Station, and from there to Kifissia in open way track.

General: Piraeus being the principal port of Greece, there is naturally a heavy passenger traffic between it and Athens; much of this traffic is carried by the railway line. There are two lines of buses between Athens and Piraeus and three lines of buses within Piraeus. Further underground lines in Athens have been proposed and work on a 27 km two line system is expected to start in 1981.

Technical Data:
Gauge: 1.435 m
Route length: 25.7 km
Track length: 61 km
In tunnel: 2.9 km
Projected new lines (in design): 21 km
Number of lines: 1
Number of stations (total): 20
(in tunnel): 2
Average distance between stations: 1.35 km
Stations:
platform length (max): 110 m

Type of tunnel: Double track, cut-and-cover, tunnel of rectangular section, 24 ft 1 in *(7.34 m)* wide by 13 ft 9 in *(4.2 m)* high, with centre supports.
Gradient (max): 29‰
Curvature (max): 160 m
Speed (design max): 80 km/h
(average commercial): 30 km/h
Electric system: Third rail; 600 V
Type of rails: Flat bottomed

Traffic and finances:
Max line capacities (one way): 9 300 per hour
Max number of trains per hour (one way): 14
Frequency of train services in minutes (currently): 4.3
Capacity per train (passengers seated): 166 (old types), 222 (new types)
(passengers standing): 439, 472
Passenger journeys per annum: 85 900 000 (1977), 85 300 000 (1978)

Car type (year introduced):	1925	1952-58-68
Number of units:	61	74
Car dimensions (length):	13.8 m	17.8 m
(width):	2.70 m	2.86 m
(height):	3.66 m	3.60 m
Passenger capacity:		
per car (total):	120	180
(seated):	36	56
Motors per car	4	4
Train composition (minimum):	2	2
(max):	5	4
Brakes (type):	Air	Regenerative and Air

Body material:	wood	steel
Motor rating:	95 k/wh	120 k/wh

Power per train (minimum): 4 kW/tonne
(max): 8.5 kW/tonne
Acceleration (max): 0.7 m/s²
Deceleration (normal service): 0.6 m/s²
(emergency): 1.1 m/s²
Max design speed: 80 kW/h
Bogies (type and manufacturer): MAN with two motors for motor car and without motors for trailers (for metallic wagon).
Distance between bogie pivot: 10.5 × 10.9 m in metal, 7.5 × 8.0 m in wood.
Brakes (type): Air for wooden car and rheostatic for metallic.
Weight (empty in tonnes):
Motor cars: 37.2 metallic, 31.54 wooden.
Trailers: 25.8 metallic, 17 wooden.

Traffic Data:
Trains/track/hour: 16
Train capacity (passengers): 900
Total passengers/track/hour (peak): 14 400
Train headways
design: 3.5 minutes
existing: 3.5 minutes
Passengers carried (weekday): 235 000
(annually): 86 010 000
Average journey length: 7.6 km
Vehicle-km operated annually: 13 150 000 km

Signalling: Wayside signals incorporated with non-computerised central traffic control office.

ATLANTA
Authority:
Metropolitan Atlanta Rapid Transit Authority (MARTA)
2200 Peachtree Summit, 401 West Peachtree St NE, Atlanta, Georgia 30308, USA
Telephone: (404) 586 5000

Board Chairman: John E. Wright
Board Vice-Chairman: William R. Probst
General Manager: Alan F. Kiepper
AGM Transit Operations: Donald Valtman
Transit System Development AGM: William D. Alexander
AGM Planning and Public Affairs: Morris J. Dillard
AGM Finance and Administration: Robert Duvall

History: From 1962 onward the Atlanta authorities put forward successive proposals for a massive rail rapid transit system to serve the city and metropolitan area. In 1971, after a public referendum, the go-ahead was finally approved.

General: Atlanta's rapid transit system and its development are based on the Metropolitan Atlanta Rapid Transit Plan adopted by the Board of Directors on 9 August 1971. Three amendments to the plan have been approved. A fourth amendment to the plan, which relates to the Hartsfield Atlanta International Airport, has been proposed and other amendments may be adopted from time to time. The major components of the system are a fixed rail system and a bus system providing both local and express services.

Short-range programme: Implementation of a short range transit improvement programme began with the acquisition of the Atlanta Transit System. Inc, a privately-owned bus company, in February 1972. Since then, the Authority has purchased 540 new air-conditioned buses; constructed a new heavy maintenance facility, two new bus operating facilities and three park and ride lots; expanded and improved service on existing bus routes; initiated new bus routes; improved informational services; and installed passenger shelters. The Authority renders extensive bus service throughout Fulton and DeKalb Counties and also provides limited extended route service into Cobb and Clayton Counties.

Long-range programme: The fixed rail system portion of the system will consist of 52.8 miles (84 km) of double track, of which 16.3 miles (26 km) will be aerial structure, 26.5 miles (42 km) grade structure, and 10 miles (16 km) subway. The fixed rail system will also include 7 aerial stations, 19 grade stations and 13 underground stations. An amendment would extend the fixed rail system by 0.6 miles and add one station, at the new midfield terminal of the Hartsfield Atlanta International Airport. The fixed rail system is designed for steel-wheel trains operating at speeds up to 70 mph (113 km/h) on steel rails using an electrified third rail as the power source. The rail transit vehicles will consist of a fleet of 338 air-conditioned cars operating as single vehicle trains, married-pair trains, or any combination up to a maximum of eight vehicle sets. The fixed rail system will have main trunk lines running in an east-west and north-south direction. The main trunk lines will intersect at the Five Points station in Atlanta's central business district. Service on the main trunk lines will be supplemented with four branch lines and two busways.
The design and construction of the fixed rail system is

divided into phases. Phase A constitutes the initial design and construction stage of the fixed rail system and is designed to be a fully operable system regardless of the construction of subsequent phases. The purpose of Phase B and each subsequent phase will be to extend the operational capabilities of Phase A up to the full 52.8 miles (84 km) presently contemplated under the plan.

Phase A: Initial passenger service on the Phase A East Line from the Avondale station to the Georgia State station began on 1 July 1979 over 10.7 km. On completion Phase A will consist of 13.7 miles (21 km) of double track and 17 stations, the design of 8.1 additional miles (13 km) of track and 7 stations and the preparation for construction of a 2.5 mile (4 km) extension to the Phase A North-South Line. The preparation for construction of this extension was added to Phase A after 1976 and resulted in a $34 million increase in the then estimated cost of Phase A. Phase A will include all 10 miles (16 km) of subway structure, which is the most costly portion of the fixed rail system, and the central storage, repair and communications facilities adjacent to the Avondale station. Phase A will also include the purchase of approximately 100 rail transit vehicles, equipment, land and rights in land.

Phase B: Phase B contemplates the construction of extensions of the North and South Lines to be constructed under Phase A. An additional 5.7 miles (9 km) of track will be added to the North Line, and four

stations will be constructed at Midtown, Arts Center, Lindbergh Center and Lenox. An additional 4 miles (6 km) of track will be added to the South Line, and three stations will be constructed at West End, Oakland and Lakewood.

The remainder of the System contemplates the following extensions beyond Phase B: addition of 8.1 miles (12 km) of track and 4 stations to the East Line, addition of 8.3 miles (12 km) of track and 5 stations to the North Line, addition of 2.2 miles (3 km) of track and one station to the West Line, addition of 5.8 miles (9 km) of track and 3 stations to the South Line and construction of 8 miles (13 km) of rapid busway and two bus stations. In addition, an amendment to the Plan currently under consideration would add 0.6 miles of track, and one station, at the new midfield terminal of the Hartsfield Atlanta International Airport.

Financing: The Authority estimates that Phase A will be completed in 1981 at a cost of $1 051 000 million and Phase B by 1984 at a cost of $542 million. Remainder of the fixed rail system can be completed by 1989 at a cost of $1 680 000 million. Based on such estimates, the Authority's estimate of the total cost of the fixed rail system is $3 273 000 million.

Technical Data:
Number of lines: 4
Number of stations (total): 38

Gauge: 1 435 m
Total route length (Planned): 85.3 km
Total track length (Planned): 170.6 km
Average speed: 0.89 km/sec (Designed)
Max acceleration: 1.88 km/sec (Designed)
Couplers: Ohio Brass Transit Coupler with Walton Electric Heads.
Height above rail (mm): 10 couplers centre line, 558.8 mm *(22")*
Braking: Pneumatic over hydraulic tread brakes; Westinghouse Air Brake Servotrol
Rails: 119 RE
  Weight: 52.12 kg/m (119 lb/yd)
Sleepers:
  Type: Concrete
  Thickness (mm): 152.40 min/194.45 max
  Number per km: 1 312
Track:
  Minimum curvature: 228.60 m (main line); 106.68 m (yard and secondary)
  Max gradient: ±3%
  Maximum altitude: 333.19 m present design

Axle load:
  Max 13 834.8 kg (Standard)
  $$0 \frac{122\,000\#}{4} = 30\,500\#/\text{axle}$$

AUCKLAND
Authority:
Passenger Transport Division
Auckland Regional Authority, 121 Hobson Street, Auckland 1, New Zealand
Telephone: 364 420
Telegrams: TRANSBOARD/AUCKLAND

General: A report on the city's comprehensive transportation needs was released by the regional authority in 1976 after a three-year study. This report indicates that an original scheme—consisting of a 9-km underground inner city loop and a 26-km surface line from Auckland central to Papakura in the south—will no longer provide sufficient benefits to

justify its costs. The latest transit proposals recommend scrapping the underground inner city loop scheme and achieving cost effectiveness through upgrading services on the existing rail line between Auckland and Papakura and supplementing them with a feeder bus service.

BAKU
Authority:
Bakinski Metropolten
Baku City Soviet, Baku, USSR

Type of System: Full metro

History: Construction has been in progress for some time on an underground railway for the city. During excavation for the tunnels and station structures, variations in the ground from rock to water-bearing subsoil were encountered. Tunnel lining methods made use of concrete rather than iron segments, and take the form of ring elements of ferro-concrete blocks, which are said to have had a considerable saving effect on construction costs.

Prior to the recent line extensions the annual total of passengers carried on the Baku Metro was approximately 42 million, including 62.9 million in 1972.

In late 1967 the first section 6.3 miles *(10.1 km)* was opened, with six stations: Narimanov, Gyandzhlyk, 28 April, Shaumyan, 26 Baky Commisars, Baku Sovety, four of which lie at deep level and are served by high-speed escalators. This line connects three main districts, the western administrative, the eastern residential, and the central industrial. Ulduz station was opened in 1970. A further 8.5 km of route

serving 4 more stations is nearing completion. During 1973 extensions to the east and west were opened, to Neftchila and Nizami respectively.

Technical Data:
Gauge: 1.524 m
Route length: 10.5 km
In tunnel: 10.5 km
Projected new lines (in construction): 8.1 km
Number of lines: 2
Number of stations (total): 7
  (in tunnel): 6
Average distance between stations: 1.4 km
Stations
  platform length (max): 100 m

Type of tunnel:
Speed (design max): 75 km/h
  (average commercial): 42 km/h
Electric system: Third rail; 825 Volts
Type of rails: 50 kg/m
Welded joints: 320 m

Rolling Stock:
Car type (year introduced): 1960
Car dimensions (length): 18.8 m
  (width): 2.7 m

Passenger capacity:
  per car (total): 170
  (seated): 40
Motors per car: 4
Train composition (minimum): 5
  (max): 5
Brakes (type): Regenerative and electro/magnetic
Body material: Steel
Weight (tonnes) motorcar: 32
Motor rating: 68 kW/h

Traffic Data:
Trains/track/hour: 20
Train capacity (passengers): 850
Total passengers/track/hour (peak): 17 000
Train headways:
  design: 3 minutes
  existing: 3 minutes
Passengers carried (weekday): 172 000
  (annually): 40 800 000
Average journey length: 4.9 km
Vehicle-km operated annually: 5 500 000

Signalling: Cab signals with non-computerised central traffic control office; ATS and ATC systems are utilised.

BALTIMORE
Authority:
Maryland Mass Transit Administration
109 East Redwood Street, Baltimore, Maryland 21202, USA
Telephone: (301) 383 5506

Principal officers:
  Administrator: L. A. Kimball
  Project Manager: R. J. Murray

Type of system: Full metro

Section A of the Baltimore Region Rapid Transit System, a distance of 12.8 km, is scheduled to be operating in 1982. Cost of construction is calculated at $768 million including purchase of 72 cars.

Initial funding of Section A was approved by the Maryland General Assembly in 1976. Construction began in late 1976 on the Bolton Hill Tunnel segment. Work is now under way on 100 per cent of the route mileage, including six subway stations (Charles Center, Lexington Market, Bolton Hill, Laurens Street, North Avenue, Mondawmin), three aerial stations (Cold Spring Lane, Rogers Avenue and Reisterstown Plaza) and all subway tunnel and aerial lines.

Section A extends from the Charles Center Station in the retail-business district of Baltimore City to the Baltimore City-Baltimore County line at Reisterstown Plaza. It includes nine stations, six subway and three aerial; 4.5 miles in subway, less than one mile at grade, and 2.5 miles of aerial structure.

Design engineering is also under way for Phase I, Section B, a 9.6 km extension of the Section A line from Reisterstown Plaza to Owings Mills. Construction is contingent on receipt of federal and state funds.

Under Phase II planning by the Maryland Department of Transportation, several other lines are being evaluated for future expansion. The primary considerations are a North Central line to Cockeysville, and South, West and Northeast lines.

A feeder bus system, now being designed, will integrate the city's bus network with the rapid transit system, providing fast and efficient access to the outlying stations. The three aerial stations will also be serviced by parking lots and Kiss N' Ride facilities (special lanes for dropping off people by car).

Section A is a dual-track system, high-speed (up to 70 mph) line, with steel-on-steel trains propelled by 700 V dc collected from a third rail. Trains of up to six cars will be composed of married pairs. The Urban Mass Transportation Administration gave approval for Baltimore and Miami to proceed with a joint procurement of rapid transit vehicles of a type generally known and tested throughout the industry. Baltimore purchased 72 vehicles.

The Baltimore system will have a computer-equipped operations centre at the Lexington Market Station, but it is not a computerised central command system. The Baltimore command centre will have information on train performance and scheduling, but it will be up to dispatchers to handle irregularities. This system has the capability for manual operation but could be upgraded to full computerised control if desired in the future.

Automatic fare collection, using encoded cards similar to credit cards, is planned in the Baltimore system. Fares are expected to be compatible with MTA bus fares.

The cost of Section A is estimated to be $768 million, with 80 per cent coming from the Urban Mass Transportation Administration, and 20 per cent from the State of Maryland through its Consolidated Transportation Trust Fund.

It is expected that approximately 83 000 persons will use the system daily.

Urban structure:
  Population of city area: 818 000
  Land area: 78.3 sq miles
  Primary road network within city boundary: 1 486 miles of paved streets
  Number of automobiles registered in city: 260 754 (1970), 274 660 (1979)

Technical data:
Gauge: 4 ft 8½ in
Route length: Section A = 12.8 km
Track length: 26 km
In tunnel: 7.2 km
New lines (planned): Section B = 9.6 km extension of Section A
  (under construction): Section A = 12.8 km
Number of lines in operation: None
Number of stations (total): Section A = 9
  Section B = 3
Number of stations in tunnel: Section A = 6
Average distance between stations: 2 km
Max length of station platforms: All platforms 450 ft
Gradient (max): 1 in 25
Curvature (max): 250 ft (yards) 611 ft (mainline)
Speed (design max): 70 mph
  (average commercial): 30 mph
Type of rails: 115 #RE continuous welded
Type of tunnel: Horseshoe in rock (44%) Shield-driven in soft earth (56%)
Method and voltage of current supply: 700 V dc Third rail

Traffic and finances:
Max number of trains per hour (one way): 30
  (one way-planned): 15
Frequency of train services in minutes (planned): 4 (rush hours), 10 (other)

Max capacity per train (passengers seated): 444
  (passengers standing): 1 200

Rolling stock characteristics:
  Car types: Motor cars, married pairs
  Number of units: 72 cars
  Car dimensions:
    Length (m) 30 m
    Width (m) 3 m
    Height (m) 3.5 m

Number of doors per side: 3 sets biparting doors
Door width (m): 50
Number of passengers per car (total): 160
(seated): 74
Motors per car: 4

Motor rating (kW): 130
Power per train: All axles powered
Acceleration (max): 3.0 mph/s
Deceleration (normal service): 2.1 mph/s
(emergency): 3.1 mph/s

Max design speed: 70 mph
Bogies (type and manufacturer): Budd Co Pioneer
Distance between bogie pivot: 54 ft
Brakes (type): Tread air brakes—WABCO
Weight (empty in tonnes): 76 000 lb (motor cars)

BANGKOK

Authority:
Expressway and Rapid Transit Authority of Thailand
Bangkok, Thailand

Type of system: Full-metro

General: The Expressway and Rapid Transit Authority of
Thailand, formed in 1975, has proposed a three-line
initial mass transit rail system for Bangkok for projected opening by 1986. The lines include: Pra
Kanong-Bangsue (23 km); Wong Wiang Yai-Lard Prao
(16 km); Dao Kanong-Makkasan (13 km). The estimated cost is $US 150 million.

Technical Data:
Gauge: 1.435 m
Route length: 59 km approx
Track length: 117.7 km
In Tunnel: 1.155 km
Number of stations: 59
Number of stations in tunnel: 1
Average distance between stations: 900 m
Maximum length of station platforms: 120 m
Speed: 80 km/h

Rolling Stock:
Car type: 2 car unit
Number of units: 2
Car dimensions: length (m) 18.00
width (m) 2.90
Height (m) 3.50
Total floor area: 47.85 m²/car
Number of doors per side: 3 per car
Door width (m) : 1 300
Number of passengers per car: 189-216
seated: 42-48

BARCELONA

Authority:
FC Metropolitano de Barcelona SA (SPM)
PO Box 83, Ronda de San Pablo, 41, Barcelona 15, Spain
Telephone: (03) 241 00 07

Chief Executive: D. Roberto Cortadas Arbat
Director of Reserves and Development: D. José Piñol
Vidal
Director of Administration: D. Joaquin Buguñá Forcat
Sub-Director, Chief of Operations: D. Juan Maria Mas-
cort Corominas
Director: D. Fernando Coello Goyri

Type of system: Full-metro

History: First sections of each line were opened:—
Line No. 1: June, 1926.
Line No. 2: July, 1959.
Line No. 3: December, 1924.
Line No. 4: February, 1973.
Line No. 5: November, 1969.
General: There are now six underground railway lines in
Barcelona, five are operated by FC Metropolitano de
Barcelona SA, and the other by FC de Sarria a Bar-
celona SA. The lines operated by FCMBSA were once
named but are now numbered.
The whole system is underground, except the
Mercado-Sta. Eulalia section of Line 1 and a section in
Buxeres station.
Extensions now under construction are: Line I (6.46
km), Line II (4.30 km), Line III (3.18 km), Line IV (6.99
km), Line V (5.43 km). 28 new motor cars were delivered in 1978 and 12 were under construction. The
final projected system is 121 route-km with 155 stations.

Technical Data:
Gauge: 1.674 m (Line 1 only)/1.435 m.
Route length: 48.3 km with 41.2 km in tunnel.
Projected new lines (in construction or projected):
72.8 km
Number of lines: 5, all double track.
Passengers per annum (1977): 266 786 595
Number of cars per train: 4 motor cars, or 2 motor cars
with 1 or 2 trailers.
Track gauge:
Line 1: 5 ft 6 in *(1.674 m).*
Lines 2, 3, 4, 5: 4 ft 8½ in *(1.435 m).*
Weight and type of rails:
Lines 1, 2, 4 and 5: 54 kg/m.
Line 3: 50 kg/m.
All flat bottom rail.
Type of tunnel:
Line 1: Double track tunnel 26 ft 3 in *(8 m)* wide and
18 ft 0 in *(5.5 m)* high above rail level.
Line 2: Double track tunnel 23 ft *(7 m)* wide and 19 ft 3
in *(5.85 m)* high above rail level.
Line 3: All as Line 2.
Line 3-B: Similar to Line 4.
Line 4: Double track tunnel 24 ft 1 in *(7.35 m)* wide
and 18 ft 3 in *(5.55 m)* high above rail level.
Line 5: As Line 2, except height 18 ft 5 in *(5.65 m)*
above rail level.
Method and voltage of current supply:
Line 1: Third rail; 37 kg/m; 1 500 V dc Sub-stations
situated at tunnel mouth (Bordeta) and near the
stations Triumfo Norte and Sagrera.
Line 2: Overhead line, 1 200 V dc Sub-station
situated near Sagrera common to this line and to
remainder of Line 1.
Line 3: Overhead line, 1 200 V dc Sub-station
situated near Lesseps.
Lines 3-B and 4: Aluminium steel third rail 6.75 kg/m.
1 200 V dc sub-station at Verdaguer.
Line 5: As Line 2 with extra sub-station at Roma.

Rolling Stock:
Line 1: Class "100": Built 1926-29. Body length 21.7
m, width 3.2 m. Three sets of sliding passenger
doors on each side. Weight per car 55.7 tonnes.
Number of cars: 10 (all motor cars). Class "200-A".
Built 1944. Body length 16.5 m, width 3.2 m. Three
sets of sliding doors on each side. Weight per car 34
tonnes. Number of cars: 4 (all motor cars). Up to
date: out of service. Class "200 B". Four sets of
doors on each side. Built 1953-54-55. Number of

Train leaving Pueblo Seco station, Barcelona, on line 3

cars: 20 (10 motor cars, 10 trailers). Class "400".
Number of cars: 80 (60 motor cars, 20 trailers).
Weight per car 40 tonnes (motor), 28.2 tonnes (trailers). Built 1958-59-62-65-66-67-68. Body length 16.5
m, width 3.14 m. Four sets of doors on each side.
Line 2: Included in Line 5.
Line 3: Class 300-R: Built 1924. Body length 13.7 m.
Width 2.52 m. Weight 27.2 tonnes (motor cars), 22
tonnes (trailer). Number of cars: 12 motor cars and 8
trailers. Three sets of sliding doors on each side.
Class 300-S: Built 1944. Body length 14.3 m. Width
2.35 m. Weight 29.2 tonnes. Number of cars: 2. Four
sets of sliding doors on each side. Class 300-B: Built
1949-50-59. Body length 14.30 m. Width 2.51 m.
Weight 30.1 tonnes (motor car), 19 tonnes (trailer).
Number of cars: 6 motor and 4 trailers. Four sets of
sliding doors on each side. Class 300-C: Built 1962-
63-66-67-68-70. Body length 14.3 m. Width 2.49 m.
Weight 31.4 tonnes (motor car), 20.3 tonnes (trailer).
Number of cars: 2 motor cars and 10 trailers. Four
sets of sliding doors on each side.
Line 3-B: Class 1100: Built 1975-76-77. Body length
16.5 m. Width 2.75 m. Weight 29.9 tonnes. Number
of motor cars: 44 composed of 22 double units (cars
class S.1100 must go coupled in pair-forming units).
Four sets of sliding doors on each side.
Line 4: Class 300-C: Similar characteristics to those
of line 3. Number of cars: 16 motor cars and 5 trailers. Class 1100: Similar characteristics to those of
line 3-B. Number of cars: 34, forming 17 double
units.
Line 5: Class 300-C: Similar characteristics to those
of line 3. Number of cars: 11 trailers. Up to date: out
of service. Class 600: Built 1959. Body length 16.5 m.
Width 2.72 m. Weight 37 tonnes. Number of motor
cars: 12. Four sets of sliding doors on each side.
Class 1100: Similar characteristics to those of line
3-B. Number of cars: 16 forming 8 double units.
Class 1000: Built from 1970-74. Similar characteristics to those of class 1100 from line 3-B. Number of
cars: 100 forming 50 double units.
Signalling: Automatic block, with ac track circuits, and
colour-light signals. Central Traffic Control on Line
4.
Station layout: Station platform lengths vary from 88 m
on Lines 1 and 2, to 96 m on Line 5, (75 to 90 m on
Line 3). Their arrangements are various, adapted as

the system grew (from formerly individual lines) for
interconnection. Cataluna and Triunfo stations are
common with the Spanish National Railways, which
parallel the Metro Transversal on that section.

Authority:
FC de Sarria a Barcelona SA
1, Plaza de Cataluna, Barcelona, Spain
Telephone: (03) 221 14 90

Type of system: Full-metro

General: This line was originally wholly on the surface,
and steam-operated. It has since been electrified, and
its intown section (under the Calle de Balmes) has
been rebuilt in tunnel. The Tibidabo line was opened
in 1954. The line runs underground from Cataluna to
Tibidabo and to Sarria. At the latter point it connects
with the surface system of the associated Cataluna
Railway Company, which has the same gauge, running on to Tarrasa and Sabadell.

Technical Data:
Gauge: 1.435 m
Route length: 7.1 km to Sarria and Tibidabo.
In tunnel: 4.4 km
Projected new lines (in construction): 0.9 km
Number of lines: 2 (radial)
Number of stations (total): 12
(in tunnel): 11
Average distance between stations: 0.790 km
Stations:
platform length (max): 85 m
(minimum): 68 m

Gradient (max): 4%
Curvature (max): 150 m
Speed (design max): 60 km/h
(average commercial): 30 km/h
Electric system: Catenary; 1 300 V
Type of rails: Flat-bottomed

Rolling Stock:
Car type (year introduced): 1959
Number of units: 26 (all motor cars)
Car dimensions (length): 19.0 m
(width): 2.70 m

Passenger capacity:
per car (total): 116
(seated): 56
Motors per car: 4
Ratings: 92 kWh
Train composition (minimum): 1
(max): 2

Traffic Data:
Trains/hour/track: 24
Trains capacity (passenger): 232
Total passengers/track/hour (peak): 5 570
Train headways: 2.5 minutes
Passengers carried (annually): 26 500 000

Line	Route	Length km	Stations
1	Sta. Eulalia—Torras y Bages	12.2	20
2	Sagrada Familia—Horta	5.3	8
3	Lesseps-Pueblo Seco	4.9	8
3-B	Pueblo Seco-Zona Universitaria	6.0	9
4	Selva de Mar-Guinardó	10.2	14
5	San Ildefonso-Sagrada Familia	9.7	13
	Total in service	48.3	72

Construction work underway at present:

Line	Route	Length km.	Stations	Date scheduled for completion
1	Sta. Eulalia—Hospitalet RENFE	3.2	4	1981
1	Torras y Bages—Sta. Coloma	2.4	3	1982
3	Lesseps—Montbau	3.2	4	1980
4	Hospitalet RENFE—Hospitalet-Catalanes	0.9	1	1981
5	San Ildefonso—Cornella Centro	1.5	2	1983
5	La Paz—Pep Ventura	3.9	5	1982
	Total	26.4	32	

Estimated costs in million Pts.

Line	Route	Infrastructure	Superstructure	Total route
1	Sta. Eulalia—Hospitalet RENFE	650	575	1.225
1	Torras y Bages—Sta. Coloma	480	373	853
2	Pueblo Seco—Sagrada Familia	1 069	498	1.567
3	Lesseps—Montbau	890	573	1.463
4	Barceloneta—Selva de Mar	956	519	1.475
4	Selva de Mar—La Paz	557	500	1.057
4	Guinardó—Les Roquetes	599	473	1.072
5	San Ildefonso—Cornella Centro	420	301	721
5	La Paz—Pep Ventura	1 080	765	1.845
	Total	5 943	4 227	10 170

Rolling Stock

Series	Year introduced	Number of cars Motors	Trailers	Total	Gauge (metres)	Weight (kg) Motor	Trailers	Length (metres)	Capacity Seated passengers	Standing	Current	Power
Series 300-R	1924	12	8	20	1.435	37 200	22 000	13.70	18	100	1 200 V catenary	4 × 120 = 480 hp
Series 100	1926	10	—	10	1.674	55 700	—	21.69	54	184	1 500 V conductor	4 × 130 = 520 hp
Series 100	1929	2	—	2	1.674	55 700	—	21.69	54	184	1 500 V conductor	4 × 130 = 520 hp
Series 200-AX	1944	4	—	4	1.674	34 000	—	16.50	44	150	1 500 V conductor	4 × 90 = 360 hp
Series 300-S	1944	2	2	4	1.435	29 200	18 000	14.30	12	90	1 200 V catenary	4 × 120 = 480 hp
Series 300-B	1949	3	1	4	1.435	30 100	19 000	14.30	18	100	1 200 V catenary	4 × 125 = 500 hp
Series 300-B	1950	—	1	1	1.435	—	19 000	14.30	18	100	—	—
Series 200-B	1953	6	5	11	1.674	43 000	28 700	16.50	33	160	1 500 V conductor	4 × 170 = 680 hp
Series 200-B	1954	4	—	4	1.674	43 000	—	16.50	33	160	1 500 V conductor	4 × 170 = 680 hp
Series 200-B	1955	—	5	5	1.674	—	28 700	16.50	33	160	—	—
Series 400-1°	1958	2	1	3	1.674	40 000	28 200	16.50	33	160	1 500 V conductor	4 × 130 = 520 hp
Series 400-1°	1959	12	6	18	1.674	40 000	28 200	16.50	33	160	1 500 V conductor	4 × 130 = 520 hp
Series 600	1959	12	—	12	1.435	37 000	—	16.50	30	140	1 200 V catenary	4 × 105 = 420 hp
Series 300-B	1959	3	2	5	1.435	30 100	19 000	14.30	18	100	1 200 V catenary	4 × 125 = 500 hp
Series 300-C	1962	—	2	2	1.435	—	20 360	14.30	18	100	—	—
Series 400-2°	1962	6	3	9	1.674	40 000	28 200	16.50	33	160	1 500 V conductor	4 × 130 = 520 hp
Series 300-C	1963	—	3	3	1.435	—	20 360	14.30	18	100	—	—
Series 400-3°	1965	6	2	8	1.674	40 000	28 200	16.50	33	160	1 500 V conductor	4 × 130 = 520 hp
Series 400-3°	1966	14	2	16	1.674	40 000	28 200	16.50	30	160	1 500 V conductor	4 × 130 = 520 hp
Series 300-C	1966	2	—	2	1.435	31 490	—	14.30	18	100	1 200 V catenary & conductor	4 × 125 = 500 hp
Series 300-C	1967	4	—	4	1.435	31 490	—	14.30	18	100	1 200 V catenary & conductor	4 × 125 = 500 hp
Series 400-3°	1967	10	1	11	1.674	40 000	28 200	16.50	33	160	1 500 V conductor	4 × 130 = 520 hp
Series 400-3°	1968	10	5	15	1.674	40 000	28 200	16.50	33	160	1 500 V conductor	4 × 130 = 520 hp
Series 300-C	1969	11	12	23	1.435	31 490	20 360	14.30	18	100	1 200 V catenary & conductor	4 × 125 = 500 hp
Series 300-C	1970	1	7	8	1.435	31 490	20 360	14.30	18	100	1 200 V catenary & conductor	4 × 125 = 500 hp
Series 1000-1°	1970	30	—	30	1.435	29 900	—	16.50	36	200	1 200 V catenary	4 × 136 = 544 hp
Series 1000-1°	1971	33	—	33	1.435	29 900	—	16.50	36	200	1 200 V catenary	4 × 136 = 544 hp
Series 1000-1°	1972	27	—	27	1.435	29 900	—	16.50	36	200	1 200 V catenary	4 × 136 = 544 hp
Series 1000-1°	1973	4	—	4	1.435	29 900	—	16.50	36	200	1 200 V catenary	4 × 136 = 544 hp
Series 1000-1°	1974	6	—	6	1.435	29 900	—	16.50	36	200	1 200 V catenary	4 × 136 = 544 hp
Series 1000-2°	1974	32	—	32	1.435	29 900	—	16.50	36	200	1 200 V conductor	4 × 136 = 544 hp
Series 1000-2°	1975	22	—	22	1.435	29 900	—	16.50	36	200	1 200 V conductor	4 × 136 = 544 hp
Series 1000-2°	1976	14	—	14	1.435	29 900	—	16.50	36	200	1 200 V conductor	4 × 136 = 544 hp
Series 1000-2°	1977	28	—	28	1.435	29 900	—	16.50	36	200	1 200 V conductor	4 × 136 = 544 hp
Series 1000-2°	1978	4	—	4	1.435	29 900	—	16.50	36	200	1 200 V conductor	4 × 136 = 544 hp

BELGRADE

Authority:
Metro Belgrade
Belgrade, Yugoslavia

General: Construction began in 1977 on a projected five-line 68 km metro for completion by the year 2000. The first three lines, totalling 14.2 km, with 11.8 km underground, will be completed by 1985.

BERLIN (EAST)

Authority:
VE Kombinat Berliner Verkehrs-Betriebe (VEB)
Rosa-Luxemburg-Str 2, 102 Berlin, German Democratic Republic
Telephone: (02) 51 03 11

Type of system: Full-metro

General: Line A, Pankow-Thalmannplatz, small profile, 4.66 miles *(7.49 km)*, including 3.32 miles *(5.32 km)* in tunnel. Line E, Alexanderplatz-Friedrichfeld, large profile, 4.41 miles *(7.095 km)* all in tunnel.

Technical Data:
Gauge: 1.435 m
Route length: 14.6 km
In tunnel: 12.4 km
Projected new lines (in design): 56 km by 1995
Number of lines: 2
Number of stations (total): 22

Average distance between stations: 0.772 km

Gradient (max): 4%
Curvature (max): 74 m
Speed (design max): 50 km/h
(average commercial): 25 km/h
Electric system: Third rail; 750 V

Rolling Stock:

Car type	A1	A2	E3
Number of units:	165[1]	89[2]	52[3]
Car dimensions			
(length):	12.1 m	12.4 m	18 m
(width):	2.3 m	2.3 m	2.6 m
(height):	3.2 m	3.2 m	3.4 m
Passenger capacity			
per car (total):	129	122	163
(seated):	27	26 motor cars	38
		34 trailers	
Motors per car:	4	4	4

Rating: 60 kWh 60 kWh 60 kWh
Train composition
(minimum): 4 4 4
(max): 8 8 8
Acceleration (max): 1.2 m/s²
Deceleration (emergency): 1.2 m/s²
Brakes (type): Electro-pneumatic

[1] 92 motor cars; 73 trailers
[2] 45 motor cars; 44 trailers
[3] 26 motor cars; 26 trailers

Traffic Data:
Trains/track/hour: 30
Train capacity (passengers): 1 200
Total passengers/track/hour (peak): 36 000
Train headways: 2 minutes
Passengers carried (annually): 61 000 000
Vehicle-km operated (annually): 11 200 000

BERLIN (WEST)

Authority:
Berliner Verkehrs-Betriebe (BVG)
Berlin (West) Eigenbetrieb von Berlin,
Potsdamer Str 188, 1000 Berlin 30, Federal Republic of
Germany
Telephone: (0311) 2561
Telegrams: BEVAUGE BERLIN WEST

Type of system: Full-metro.

History: Before the political division of Berlin in 1961, its U Bahn system, one of the oldest on the Continent, served the whole city. Today there are two systems (that part in the German Democratic Republic is referred to in the Berlin (East) entry) operating under their own organisations. The BVG Authority operates bus services in the western sector of Berlin in addition to its U Bahn.

The first section of the present systems was opened in 1902, an 11.2 km stretch of line (now Line 1), of which most was on viaduct and only 2.3 km in tunnel, from Warschauer Brücke westward through central Berlin. There has been progressive building of new lines and extensions to existing lines in Berlin's western sector since World War II, the last extension being on Line 8, Osloer Str.—Gesundbrunnen.

The BVG transport network covers 8 underground lines of a total length of 93.0 km of track and 100 stations, 15 of them interchange stations, as well as 83 bus lines having a total length of 1 046 km and 4 317 stops.

The West Berlin Underground handles about 45 per cent of the City's public transport needs and it is expected that this proportion will rise to 55 per cent by 1985. Some 315 million passenger journeys a year are now handled by the U-Bahn.

New construction includes a 4.8 km extension of the U-Bahn's longest line, Line 7. On completion, work will continue for a further 5.3 km to Spandau. This section is due to open in 1984. A 6 km extension to Line 8 is also under construction and a completely new Line 10 is planned. Construction costs are estimated in the region of DM 80 million per km, excluding cars.
Route length: 93 km, including 75.8 km in tunnel.

Number of lines: 9 all double track.
Number of stations served: 100, including 15 interchange stations.
Average station spacing: 0.48 miles *(0.77 km)*.
Passengers per annum: 315 million (1979)
Passengers carried per annum on the whole of the BVG system (Bus, U Bahn) (1977): 685 650 000.
Max number of cars per train: "Large profile" lines 6; "small profile" 8.
Max line density: about 40 000 passengers per hour (Line 7).
Average scheduled speed (including stops): "Large profile" lines 33.5 km/h.
Average scheduled speed (including stops): "Small profile" lines: 28.8 km/h.
Track gauge: 4 ft 8½ in *(1.435 m)*.
Weight and type of rails: 82.8 lb/yd *(41 kg/m)*, flat-bottomed, laid in *18 m* lengths.
Max gradient: 1 in 25 (4%).
Minimum radius of curves: 285 ft *(74 m)* on running lines; 164 ft *(50 m)* on sidings.
Type of tunnel: There are two sizes of tunnel—"large profile", on the former North-South Company lines (now lines 6, 7, 8, 9 and E), and "small profile" on the former Elevated and Underground Company lines (now lines 1, 2, 3, 4 and 5). All are double-track rectangular tunnels, with and without centre supports; the large profile tunnels are 22 ft 8 in *(6.9 m)* wide and 11 ft 10 in *(3.6 m)* high from rail level, while the small profile tunnels are 20 ft 6 in *(6.24 m)* wide and 11 ft 2 in *(3.4 m)* high. Construction was mostly by cut-and-cover method, the tunnels being generally just below surface level. Tunnel linings are of concrete.
Method and voltage of current supply: Third rail; 780 V dc. Bottom contact current collection on large profile lines.
Rolling Stock: Number of cars owned: 914 coupled 2-car sets, 570 for the broad profile lines 6, 7, 8 and 9 and 344 for the narrow profile lines 1, 2, 3, 4 and 5, 25 trailer cars (in three western sectors of Berlin only).
Details: Cars on the large-profile lines are 50 ft 10 in *(15.5 m)* long and 8 ft 8 in *(2.65 m)* wide, with 3 double-leaf doors on each side, and are made up in 2-car units. The latest (1960-66) small profile cars are 12.5 m long (body) and 2.30 m wide, with Scharfenberg coupling.

Two-car trains of Berlin Underground manufactured by O & K

They are made up in 2-car units.
Signalling: Automatic block, with colour-light signals and train stops.
Station layouts: Stations on the older sections of line were built with platforms 262 ft 6 in *(80 m)* long. Later stations had platforms 360 ft 10 in and 393 ft 8 in *(110 and 120 m)* long.
With the exception of stations on the oldest sections of the small profile lines, which have separate side-platforms, the standard station layout is of island type. There are additional platforms at some of the terminal stations. There is a variety of ticket hall layouts, many being sub-surface, with stairwells from the street. Interchange passages are provided at stations where lines intersect, and where connection is made with the electric suburban system of the main line railways (the "Stadtbahn").

BILBAO

Authority:
Bilbao Metropolitan
Bilbao, Spain

Type of system: Full-metro

General: Work started in April 1978 on construction of a planned 47.85 km metro system. The first section, running 6 km from Moyua to Basauri is due to open in early 1983 and will cost 3 900 million pesetas to build.

In 1984 the second section will open 5.9 km between Santurce and Baracaldo followed in 1985 by the 6.3 km section from Moyua to Baracaldo. The final network, to include 45 km underground, will be opened by 1996.

BIRMINGHAM

Authority:
West Midlands Passenger Transport Executive
Operator: British Railways Board, Rail House, Euston Square, PO Box 100, London NW1 2D2

Type of system: Suburban

General: Birmingham's new 30.5 km Cross-City line began revenue service in 1978. The line runs from south-west to north-east and has 16 stations. 76 three-car sets operate all local services including the Cross-City Line.

BOCHUM

Authority:
Bochum-Gelsenkirchener Strassenbahnen AG
Universitatsstrasse 50/54—Postfach 100349, 4630 Bochum 1, Federal Republic of Germany
Telephone: (0234) 374818

Type of system: Pre-metro and tramway

General: Bochum began construction in 1970 on a planned 43-km network with 1.6 km of tunnel from Bochum to Hattingen. The first 1.6 km section was opened in 1979. Future pre-U-Bahn lines are planned

and constructed to Herne/Witten, Castrop-Rauxel and Wattenschied. Some of the existing 138 km of tramway lines are to be incorporated. Details listed below record facts on the existing tramway system.

Technical Data:
Gauge: 1.00 m
Route length: 106.1 km of which 61 km is over exclusive right-of-way
Projected new lines (in construction): 2.1 km (in design): 42 km
Number of lines: 10
Speed: 19.2 km/h

Rolling Stock:
6-axle tramway, 6-axle pre-metro, type M6

Number of units:
97 6-axle tramway
33 6-axle pre-metro

Car dimensions (length):
20.1 m, 19.7 m
(width): 2.2 m, 2.3 m

Passengers carried (1978): 33 280 700
Passenger-km (1978): 144 000 000

BOMBAY

Authority:
Metropolitan Transport Project (Railways)
Churchgate Station Bldg, (Annexe) 2nd Floor, Bombay 400 020, India

General: The HTP, working under the Ministry of Railways, has recommended construction of two rail transit corridors: 6 and 7. Proposed corridor 6 would comprise a 33.7 km double-track line costing Rs 1 590 million (at 1972 values). The line would be mainly surface except at the Fort Market south end terminal.

Corridor 7 would run 26.4 km and cost an estimated Rs 4 484 million; the line would run 1 km on the surface; 7 km elevated and 18 km underground.
In addition to corridors 6 and 7, the organisation has also carried out a traffic-cum-engineering survey for West-East Connector between Bandra and Kurla linking Western Railway with Central Railway at an estimated cost of Rs51.43 crores. The line is mostly elevated and joins the existing Harbour Branch lines on the surface between Kurla and Chembur. The length of the track will be 6.82 km. There will be four stations on this link and both Bandra and Kurla will be elevated

stations. The construction will be to suburban standards and the period of construction would be six years.
A techno-economic feasibility survey was taken for a surface rail connector between the island of Bombay and the main land across the Thane creek where twin city is being developed to decongest the overcrowded South Bombay island. The survey was expected to be completed by March 1980. This link, along with Bandra-Kurla connector, would form the future West-East Corridor between Greater Bombay and New Bombay.

BOSTON

Authority:
Massachusetts Bay Transportation Authority (MBTA)
50 High St, Boston, Massachusetts 02110, USA
Telephone: (617) 722 5000

Type of system: Full-metro

General: The Massachusetts Bay Transportation Authority is seeking federal approval of a plan to reconstruct 8 km of existing railway line at a total cost of $476 million. The federal share would be $380.8 million. The project involves relocation of the existing elevated Orange Line as well as improvements to the

railroad line, which is used for MBTA-sponsored commuter service and is also part of Amtrak's intercity network. Eight new rapid-transit stations will be constructed; three of them—Back Bay, Massachusetts Avenue and Ruggles Street—will accommodate intercity passengers as well as Orange Line travellers.
The system is at present constructing 11 km of new metro lines. Orders were placed in 1978 with Pullman-Standard for 25 aluminium commuter cars.

Technical Data:
Gauge: 1.435 m
Route length: 48 km
In tunnel: 15 km
Projected new lines: 15 km

Number of lines: 4
Number of stations (total): 72
(in tunnel): 21
Average distance between stations: 1.2 km
Stations:
platform length (max): 146 m
(minimum): 76 m

Gradient (max): 5%
Curvature (max): 122 m
Speed (design max): 80 km/h
(average commercial): 31 km/h
Electric system: 6.5 km operated with catenary; all remaining is third rail, 600 V dc
Type of rails: 42-57 kg/m

Rolling Stock:

Car type (year introduced)*:	1957	1963	1968
Number of units:	50 × 2	46 × 2	76
Car dimensions:			
(length):	16.77 m	21.18 m	21.18 m
(width):	2.84 m	3.15 m	3.05 m
(height):	3.63 m	3.80 m	3.77 m
Passenger capacity			
per car (total):	240	308	228 (motors)/ 239 (trailers)
(seated):	48	54	60/64
Motors per car:	4	4	4
Rating:	75 kWh	75 kWh	75 kWh
Train composition			
(minimum): 1			
(max): 8			
Acceleration			
(max):	1.12	1.12	1.12
Deceleration			
(emergency):	1.56	1.55	1.45
Brakes (type):		Regenerative	
Weight (tonnes)			
Motorcar:	26.3	32.0	29.1
Trailer:			27.6

* Additionally pre-metro operated on five lines using 230 PCC vehicles, and 38 light rail vehicles.

Traffic Data:
Trains/track/hour: 27
Train capacity (passengers): 1 060
Total passengers/track/hour (peak): 29 000
Train headways: 2.5 minutes
Passengers carried (weekday): 580 000
(annually): 145 740 000
Annual vehicle operation: 11 037 765 revenue miles

New Orange Line car built by Hawker Siddeley on test track

Signalling: One line is operated via cab signal and the other two by ATS, ATC and Train/Car Identification.

BRATISLAVA
Authority:
Bratislava Metropolitan
Bratislava, Czechoslovakia

General: Government approval was given in 1977 for construction of a full-metro system.

BRISBANE
Authority:
Queensland Railways
Brisbane, Queensland, Australia
Telephone: 225 0211

Type of system: Suburban

General: During early 1979 electric train commuter services were begun over the 1.2 km cross-river link between South Brisbane and the city centre. First full stage of the rail programme provides for electric services on a 34 km route between Darra and Ferry Grove. Electrification is at 25 kV single-phase ac. An initial order for 39 electric cars was won by Walkers-ASEA at a value of $20 million. A further 180 cars are planned.

BRUSSELS
Authority:
Société Des Transports Intercommunaux de Bruxelles (STIB)
Avenue de la Toison d'Or 15, 1060 Brussels, Belgium
Telephone: (02) 512 17 90
Telegrams: STIB-Bruxelles

Engineer in Chief: Jacques Devroye

Type of system: Full-metro/Pre-metro

General: Public urban transport in Brussels includes buses, trams and metro. Over the 252 km of bus route, the 153 km of tram double track length and the 11.7 km of metro double track length, some 208 million passengers were carried in 1978.

Compared to other European cities, Brussels tram services suffer increasingly from delays wherever they operate in traffic-congested streets. To obviate such delays it was decided to segregate trams from other traffic in affected areas.

22.3 km of a metro-standard substructure have been constructed. Running tunnels are rectangular (apart from a short section of circular tunnel) internally 24 ft (8 m) wide and 13 ft (4 m) high from rail level. Station platforms are 13 ft (4 m) wide and 311 ft (95 m) long, sufficient to accommodate conventional metro-trains of five cars.

The first station of tunnel, 3.5 km long (De Brouckere—Schumann) on the Est-Ouest axis, became operative in 1969, with six stations. The same line with its extensions at one end to Tomberg and Beaulieu (7.3 km) and at the other to Sainte-Catherine (0.9 km) has operated with a full-metro since September 1976.

By 1985 full-metro operations on this axis are planned over 15 more km.

The axis Nord-Sud, Petite et Grande Ceinture (on the whole 10.6 km) are operated with trams in single and articulated units according to a system named "prémétro" (17 stations); a system of automatic signalling and braking permits service frequencies of 50 s.

The tramcars offer from 100 to 180 seats.

The substructures are realised according to metro-standards, but a light rail system will be used at medium-term.

Technical Data:
Year of introduction: 1976
Total number of cars: 90 (+ 70 ordered)
Route length: 11.7 km
New extensions: 10 km (being constructed)
5 km (planned till 1985)
Number of lines: 1
Number of stations: 13 underground stations
5 surface stations
Average distance between stations: 600 m
Min platform length of the stations: 95 m
Max gradient: 6.2%
Min curvature: 100 m (50 in the workshop)

Train Data:
Basic operating unit: set of two permanently-coupled cars

Usual operating train: basic unit × 2 (4 cars)
Max train composition: 5 cars

Car Data:
Overall length: 18.2 m
Overall width: 2.7 m
Overall height: 3.42 m
Tare weight: 31 tonnes
Acceleration (max): 1.16 m/s²
Deceleration (emergency): 1.70 m/s²
Average commercial speed: 30 km/h
Max running speed: 72 km/h
Number of seated passengers: 40
Total number of passengers: 210
Body material: framework in light alloy
Gauge: 1.435 m
Number of motors: 2
Motor rating: 266.2 kW/h
Brake system (service): electrical, regenerative or rheostatic
(emergency): pneumatic (on the axles), electromagnetic (on the rails), hydraulically controlled axle disc brakes for long immobilisation of the car.

Traffic Data:
Trains/track/hour: 20 on the common stump (peak hours)
10 on the branches (peak hours)
12 on the common stump (off-peak)
6 on the branches (off-peak)
Total passengers/track/hour (peak): 12 250
Train capacity (4 cars): 840 passengers

BUDAPEST
Authority:
Budapesti Közeledesi Vallat (BKV)
Budapest, Hungary

Type of system: Full-metro.

General: First 3.7 km subway line opened in 1896. It was subsequently lengthened by 1.2 km, modernised and capacity increased to 9 000 passengers hourly in 1973. First of the modern Metro lines (running 10.1 km east-west) was opened in 1972 and at present operates five-car trainsets carrying about 530 000 passengers daily on headways of 135 s in peak periods. Now under construction is the 14.7-km north-south line, with the first 3.7 km section between Nagyvarad Square and Deak Square opened at the end of 1976. The complete line is scheduled to go into operation by the end of 1985.

Construction is to start on a planned southwest-northeast 15.6-km line in 1985 and should be completed between 1990 and 2000 at a cost of Fr 28 000 million. The line will run from Obuda and Kelenföld.

Technical Data:
Gauge: 1.435 m
Route length: 4.9 km
In tunnel: 3.28 km
Number of lines: 1
Number of stations (total): 11
(in tunnel): 9
Average distance between stations: 360 m
Stations:
platform length (minimum): 24 m

Gradient (max): 3%
Curvature (max): 40 m
Speed (design max): 40 km/h
(average commercial): 19 km/h
Electric system: catenary; 550 V

Rolling Stock:

Car type	OLD	OLD	Ganz-Mavag
Number of units:	17 (motors)	16 (trailers)	21 sets

Car dimensions (m):			
(length):	11.1	9.6	30.4
(width):	2.35	2.30	—
(height):	2.67	2.62	—
Passenger capacity			
per car (total):	60	64	171
(seated):	14	12	48
Motors per car:	2	—	4
Rating:	44 kWh	—	61 kWh
Body material:	steel/wood		
Weight (tonnes) Motorcar:	16.5		

Traffic Data:
Trains/track/hour: 30
Train capacity (passengers): 171
Total passengers/track/hour (peak): 5 130
Train headways
existing: two minutes
Passengers carried (annually): 21 000 000
Average journey length: 3.3 km
Vehicle-km operated annually: 2 200 000

BUENOS AIRES

Authority:
Subterraneos de Buenos Aires (SBA)
Bartolomé Mitre 3342, Buenos Aires 1201 DF, Argentina

Type of system: Full-metro

History: The present day Buenos Aires Subway system is not more than 30 years old, but its earliest line (Plaza Mayo-Primera Junta) has been running since 1914. It was operated by the Anglo-Argentine Tramways Company; it is now known as Line A.
The second line (Leandro N. Alem-Federico Lacroze) was opened in October 1930, and was operated by the Buenos Aires Central Terminal Railway; it is now Line B. The remaining three lines (Retiro-Plaza Constitucion Catedral-Palermo, and Plaza Constitucion-Boedo) were opened between 1930 and 1944, and were operated by a Spanish Company with interests in Argentina (CHADOPYF); they are now respectively Lines C, D and E. The Buenos Aires Transport Corporation was formed by law in October 1939 for the co-ordination of passenger transport (including the underground railways) in Greater Buenos Aires. A consortium ran the principal services until 1952 when the Corporation was dissolved and its authority transferred to the Ministry of Transport. In June 1963 a new State entity, the "Subterráneos de Buenos Aires" was formed under Government decree to operate the City's underground system.
Plans have been approved for a new east-west line and two of the five lines are being extended.
The new cross-city Line F will run to the north and almost parallel to the existing Line C, starting at Constitucion and on to Santa Fe in the east, intersecting Lines A, B, D and E. The 3.867 km line is to have eight stations.
Line D is being extended 1.255 km from the terminal at Palermo to the Mitre Railway where a new underground rail complex, General Manuel Savio is to be built, along with an extention to the line from Cabildo and Avenue General Paz. A 0.564 km tunnel into the complex is being driven.
Line E is being extended by 2.5 km from the terminal at JM Moreno to La Fuente.

Technical Data:
Gauge: 1.435 m

Route length: 64.9 km
In tunnel: 34.7 km
Projected new lines (in construction): 10.2 km
(in design): 5 km
Number of lines: 5
Number of stations (total): 58
(in tunnel): 58
Average distance between stations: 600 m
Stations:
platform length (minimum): 106 m

Type of tunnel: The tunnels are double track, of cut-and-cover construction only in Line A and some of the stations in Lines B, C and D. The other lines and stations were constructed by tunneling. The Line A tunnel is 25 ft 3 in (7.7 m) wide, and 14 ft 7 in (4.45 m) high from rail level; it is of rectangular section without centre supports. Line B runs partly in tunnel of rectangular section. 27 ft 9 in (8.45 m) wide by 15 ft 3 in (4.65 m) high, with centre supports, and partly in tunnel with arches over each track.

Gradient (max): 4%
Curvature (max): 80 m
Speed (design max): 10 km/h
(average commercial): 18.26 km/h

Electric system: On Line A, overhead wire distribution; 1 100 V dc. On Line B, third rail distribution; 550/600 V dc. On Lines C, D and E, overhead wire distribution: 1 600 V dc.

Type of rails: Track is chaired, (except on Line B, which has spiked flat-bottom rails), with timber sleepers and stone ballast; rails weigh 88 lb/yd (49.6 kg/m) on Line B, and 91 lb/yard (45.93 kg/m) on other lines. Heavier rail at 50.5 kg/m is laid on concrete sleepers on new sections of Line E.

Traffic Data: Fabricaciones Militares is building 20 cars for Line B. Twelve have been delivered. Ninety bogies, with Siemens traction motors, on stock in service on Lines C and E, are being renovated.
Work started in 1979 on the renewal of signalling on Line B. Escalators and booking offices are being modernised throughout the system. Work is in hand on the installation of a train telephone system.
During 1979 SBA handled 198 million passenger journeys. The 1980 figure is expected to be around 200 million.

Rolling Stock:

Car type:	CDE/67	CDE/33	A/26	B/30	B/77
Number of units:	80	108	124	90	12
Car dimensions					
(length): (m)	17	17	15	17	17
(width): (m)	2.6	2.6	2.6	3.2	3.2
(height): (m)	2.52	2.34	3.41	2.6	2.6
Passenger capacity					
per car (total):	160	160	150	170	170
(seated):	42	40	42	42	42
Motors per car:	4		2	2	2
Rating:	116 kWh	115 kWh	115 kWh	109 hp	109 hp
Train composition (minimum): 2					
(max): 6					
Body material:	steel	steel	steel/wood	steel	steel
Weight (tonnes):					
Motorcar:	30	32	28	32.5	32.5
Trailer:	25	21	—	—	—

BUFFALO

Authority:
Niagara Frontier Transportation Authority
181 Ellicott St, Buffalo, NY 14205, USA
Telephone: (716) 856 6524

Chairman of the Board: Chester R. Hardt
Executive Director: James E. Kelly
Authority Engineer: Col. Loren W. Olmstead
General Manager, Marine Division: Arthur Lancaster
Trade Development Manager: Richard H. Van Derzee
Executive Vice-President, Metro Bus: Robert G. Decker
Urban Transportation Planner: David A. Casciotti

Metro Construction Division
(Light Rail Rapid Transit Project)
General Manager: Kenneth G. Knight
Office of Systems Development: Eugene C. Lepp
Director, Office of Contracts & Programme Control:
Theodore Beck

Type of system: Light rail

Technical Data:
Projected new lines (in design): 17.7 km with 13.5 km in tunnel
Number of Stations (total): 15
(in tunnel): 11

Type of tunnel:
Gradient (max): 3%
Curvature (max): 305 m
Speed (design max): 89 km/h
Electric system: third rail/650 V

Rolling Stock:
Car type: Proposed
Car dimensions (length): 20.4 m
(width): 2.9 m
(height): 3.4 m
Passenger capacity
per car (total): 200
(seated): 60

CAIRO

Authority:
Transport Planning Authority
Ministry of Transport, Cairo, Egypt

General: Egypt's Ministries of Economy and Planning approved plans in 1978 for work to begin on a projected Metro. First phase of the scheme includes construction of the Bab Allouk and Kopri Allaymoun lines.

CALCUTTA

Authority:
Metropolitan Transport Project (Railways)
Calcutta City Government, 14-16 Government Place East, Calcutta, India

Type of system: Full-metro

General: Target date for completion of stage one of the 4.5 km Dum Dum-Shyambazar section and the 8 km Esplanade-Tollyganj section is 1984. Phase 2 running 5 km between Chittaranjan Avenue is due by 1986. Cost of the planned initial 16.45 km double-track system is Rs 2 500 million.
Work on 1.9-km of Calcutta's planned 16.3-km first Metro line between Dum Dum and Tollyganj in the city's north-south corridor is nearing completion.
The first section includes an elevated line running alongside the existing suburban railway line and the initial tunnel section between surface and underground construction.

Work has also begun on the second, 1.8-km section while feasibility studies are underway on expanding the system by construction of an east-west line and a second north-south link, the final Metro programme of highway and commuter railway improvements in the area.
Metro authorities have drawn up a plan calling for completion of a 139-km system by 1990. This would entail construction of three additional lines and a short extension to Tucuruvi on the north-south line.
Orders have been made for 144 cars for Calcutta, first sections due open in 1984. The cars are being built at the Integral Coach Factory, Madras and electrics are being supplied by BHEL, Bhopal and NGEF, Bangalore.
Construction is under way on the 3.68 km section between Dum Dum and Shyambazar and the Southern section between Esplanade and Tollyganj (7.51 km). It is expected that the 5.13 km linking section will open in 1986.
Total cost of the line, including Rolling stock is estimated at Rs 2 500 million at 1973 prices.

Technical Data:
Gauge: 1.676 m
Projected new lines (in construction): 3.7 km
(in design): 139 km
Number of lines: 1 (under construction)
Number of Stations (total): 17
(in tunnel): 16
Speed (design max): 80 km/h
Electric system: third rail; 750 V

Traffic Data (estimated):
Trains/track/hour: 24
Train capacity (passengers): 2 560
Total passengers/track/hour (peak): 61 440
Train headways design: 2 minutes
Passengers carried (weekday): 1 320 000 (1979)
(annually): 442 000 000
Vehicle-km operated annually: 27 300 000

CALGARY

Authority:
The City of Calgary Transportation Department
PO Box 2100 Calgary, Alberta T2P 2M5, Canada

Director: W. C. Kuyt
General Manager: E. C. Orford
LRT Manager: O. Bowen

General: A network of almost 13 km of partially grade-separated routes has been devised in an attempt to incorporate a standard of rapid service which is the highest prospective transit development for the area. Consideration is given to the provision of exclusive grade-separated rights-of-way for high-speed vehicles.
A route to the south provides the opportunity to serve the stampede grounds (which includes potential for a major park-ride facility, 11 months of the year), Chinook Center and the rapidly expanding residential section south of 82nd Avenue. The Killarney-26th Avenue area south and west of the centre is a third sector for consideration of grade-separated transit. Major traffic flows to the centre are generated along

Center Street in the north sector—consideration must be given to this dense area for improved transit facilities.
The Calgary area is laced with a number of existing rail rights-of-way. Careful consideration has been given to these in the development of possible routings for high-speed service to the corridors mentioned above. However, comparison with the locations of these rights-of-way and the locations of population (and, therefore, travel demand) indicate a disparity between available right-of-way and convenient travel for workers and shoppers. Canadian Pacific tracks to the west

of the centre follow the Bow River and are relatively inaccessible. The north line crossing the Bow River at Nose Creek and following the valley past the airport is also circuitous and inaccessible. The CPR line running south from the CBD is better situated than other routes but still bypasses most of the major travel generators to the south.

Service is due to start in June 1981.

Construction of the 13.7 km line linking the central area with Anderson Road will cost $146.3 million.

A second line to the northwest was approved in February 1979 and the project for this 10 km line has reached the functional design stage.

Calgary has ordered 27 two-directional articulated cars from Siemens Electric Canada. They will be built in co-operation with Wagon Fabrik Vendingen of West Germany, where body shells will be manufactured. For assembly in Calgary. The cost is $19.75 million, plus import duty.

The cars are 23 m long and run in consists of up to five vehicles.

Top speed is 80 km/h. Two Traction motors, each with a one-hour rating of 150 kW, provide starting acceleration of up to 1.32 m/s².

Traction supply is 600 V dc.

Each car can accommodate 64 seated and 98 standing passengers.

Technical Data:
Gauge: 1.435 m
Route length (under construction): 13 km

CARACAS
Authority:
Oficina Ministerial Del Transporte (OMT)
Ministerio de Obras Publicas, Edificio Camejo 5 Piso, Esquina de Camejo, Caracas, Venezuela
Telephone: 426651
Telegrams: METROMOP-CARACAS

Type of system: Full-metro

General: Following approval of a 2 000 million bolivars loan in 1975, work has started on tunnelling and station construction over the projected 16-km first line of the city underground rail system. The line is to run east-west from Pro-Patria in the west to Chacaito and will include 14 stations. First section of the line is due to go into operation in 1980 and the entire line is expected to be in service by 1983. Cost will be about 3 200 million bolivars.

Generally, the line is located under the most important urban arterials; from west to east: Avenidas España and Sucre in Catia, Avenida Universidad in the centre, Calle Real de Sabana Grande (Avenida Lincoln) and Aven da Miranda in the eastern part of the city.

Storage yard and maintenance shops will be located at the extreme western end of the line, north of the first station in Pro-Patria. The yard will occupy land presently being used by the "Cuartel Urdaneta" (armoury) and a part of that being used by "Banco Obrero" (public housing). The underground line starts at the Pro-Patria Station and runs east a short distance before curving northward underneath Avenida España. The line then curves to the east, continues under Avenida Sucre, and surfaces near Manicomio Station after passing over "Quebrada Caroata" (drainage ravine). The line then proceeds towards Avenida Universidad, passing through Caño Amarillo on an aerial structure over the block presently occupied by "Los Bultos Postales" (Customs Warehouse) and continues below Avenida Universidad to La Hoyada Station.

The Catia-Petare line crosses the Central Business District of the city from the west to east underneath Avenida Universidad until it reaches the end of Avenida Mexico, where it turns toward Avenida Libertador. It continues below Avenida Libertador, turning south towards Plaza Venezuela, and then proceeds under Avenida Lincoln in Sabana Grande, until Chacaito.

The line follows the alignment of existing major arteries for most of its route except in the following places: in Catia where the two curves pass under residential development, to the south of Avenida Sucre, where the line is at grade alongside the channelised Quebrada Caroata (drainage ravine), in Caño Amarillo where it runs on aerial structure, between Santa Rosa and Plaza Venezuela, and at the end of the line at Petare. Since the streets of Caracas are fairly narrow in many parts of the city (the Avenidas España, Universidad and Lincoln are only 18.5 to 20 m wide on the average), the edges of the stations and the line sections often encroach upon existing buildings, and it will be frequently necessary to expropriate or underpin structures in these areas of the city.

In general the line descends from the west to the east. The top of rail elevations in the Pro-Patria and Petare terminals are at 971 and 838 m above sea level, respectively—a difference in elevation of 133 m in 20 km. As could be expected, the profile does not descend uniformly but adapts itself to the topography and fixed obstacles that cross the line in numerous places. These obstacles are generally drainage ravines, avenues and overpasses. Among the major drainage ravines affecting the profile of the Catia-Petare Line are: Caroata in the west and in the centre of the city, Catuche and Anauco in the centre, La Florida and Chacaito in Sabana Grande and Seca and Tócome in the east. The major overpasses and crossings are: the Caracas-La Guaira Autopista under Avenida Sucre, Avenida Fuerzas Armadas under Avenida Universidad, and the Avenida Libertador under Avenida Miranda.

Nowhere does the resulting depth of the line exceed reasonable limits. The maximum depth of 20 m occurs in the centre of the city but the average depth of the line varies between 14 and 15 m. Similarly, the grades achieved are moderate, never exceeding 3.8 per cent. At present, 31 per cent of the total population and 44 per cent of the total employment of Caracas is located within walking distance of the line; even though the area so defined by this distance constitutes only 25 per cent of the total developed area. It is estimated that because of the expansion of the city by 1990, the area within walking distance of the line will constitute only

Cut-and-cover works under way in Caracas

14 per cent of the total developed area, but it will still contain 24 per cent of the total population and 40 per cent of the total employment for that year.

According to the results of the 1975 patronage demand study, 34.8 per cent of the total daily trips made by potential bus users and 38.0 per cent of potential "jitney" taxi users will be diverted to the Catia-Petare Line for at least a part of their trip. That is, 36 per cent of the estimated 1 785 000 total daily trips to be made by public transportation in 1975 will use the Metro for all or part of the trip.

It is hoped to have a total of 49.7 km of underground rail transit lines in service by the year 2000, serving approximately 50 stations. Other lines planned include: Antimano-Morelos (together with a branch to El Silencio), 15 km; La Rinconada-Panteon, 11.8 km; La Bandera-Plaza Venezuela, 3.2 km.

Fourteen French companies led by SGTE and CIMT will supply air-conditioned cars, signalling and train control systems, electrical systems and steel rails. The contract includes provision of 140 cars, 50 with driving cabs.

Principal Characteristics of the Metro System Lines (1990)

Line	Operating Length (km)	Number of Stations	Passenger Volumes (1000s)	Cost (Millions of Bolivars)
1 Catia-Petare	19.7	22	1 151.4	1 260
2 Caricuao-Center	13.9	11*	505.2	700**
3 La Rinconada-El Valle Center-Panteón	11.6	12*	446.2	750**
4 El Valle-Plaza Venezuela	3.0	3*	56.5	120**
Totals	48.2	48	2 159.3	2 830

* Assumed for the purposes of estimating patronage.
** Derived by an extension of the costs estimated for the Catia-Petare Line.

General Characteristics of the Catia-Petare Line

Stage	Operating Length (km)	Number of Stations	Volume of Passengers (Daily)*
Catia-Silencio	6.7	8	245 150 (1973)
Catia-Chacaito	11.9	14	465 200 (1974)
Catia-Petare	19.7	22	642 700 (1975)

* For the first year of operation.

Technical Data:
Gauge: 1.435 m
Projected new lines (in construction): 16 km
(in design): 49.7 km (2000)
Number of lines: 4
Number of stations: 4 (first line)
Average distance between stations: 0.9 km
Stations:
  platform length (minimum): 150 m

Gradient (max): 3.5%
Curvature (max): 225 m
Speed (design max): 80 km/h
  (average commercial): 37 km/h
Electric system: Third rail; 750 V

Rolling Stock:
Car type: Proposed
Number of units: 210
Car dimensions (length): 21.35 m
  (width): 3.05 m
  (height): 3.20 m
Passenger capacity per car (total): 180
  (seated): 60
Motors per car: 4
  Rating: 75 kWh
Train composition (max): 7
Acceleration (max): 1.48
Deceleration (emergency): 1.35
Weight (tonnes) Motorcar: 33

Traffic Data (estimated):
Train/track/hour: 40
Train capacity (passengers): 1 260
Total passengers/track/hour (peak): 40 000
Train headways
  design: 1.5 minutes
Passengers carried (weekday): 650 000
  (annually): 200 000 000

CHARLEROI

Authority:
Société des Transports Intercommunaux (STIC)
Chaussée de Namur 28 Montignies sur Sambre, 6080, Charleroi, Belgium
Telephone: (071) 32 05 70

Type of system: Pre-metro

General: At Charleroi—a large area but with a relatively low density of population—the first section of a new pre-metro system was opened for operation in 1976.

Existing tramway routes were diverted into tunnels or over viaducts. The system will consist of a circular central section with a series of branches on their own right of way. By 1985 the central section plus five branches should be in operation. Branches will be short but designed for intensive exploitation. There will be a network of bus feeder routes.
A new series of wide articulated cars with capacity for 160 passengers and all doors at the sides were to be delivered for Charleroi in 1979 and 1980. Builders are Constructions Ferroviaires et Métallique.s and Brugeoise et Nivelles.

Technical Data (Existing system):
Gauge: 1.00 m
Route length: 19.4 km
Number of lines: 3
Rolling Stock:
Car type: 2x
Number of units: 23
Car dimensions (length): 10.2 m
(width): 2.2 m
Passenger capacity
per car: (total): 75
(seated): 22

CHICAGO

Authority:
Chicago Transit Authority
Merchandise Mart Plaza, PO Box 3555 Chicago, Illinois 60654, USA
Telephone: (312) 664 7200

Chairman: E. M. Barnes
Vice-Chairman: J. P. Gallagher
Board Members:
  J. J. McDonough
  J. Hoellen
  H. C. Medley Snr.
  N. Ruggiero
Executive Director: G. Krambles
General Attourney: E. J. Egan
First Assistant General Attorney: R. F. Bartkowicz
Secretary: W. Mansker

Division Managers:
  Operations: H. H. Geissenheimer
  Finance: P. J. Kole

Type of system: Metro

History: Prior to 1943 Chicago had a system of urban elevated railways (including the famous "loop"), but no underground passenger railways. In that year, the first passenger "subway" line—The State Street Line—was opened: 4.6 miles (7.4 km) long. It provides an in-town underground link between the North Side Elevated Lines near Armitage Avenue and the South Side Elevated Lines near Sixteenth Street. The second passenger "subway" line—the Milwaukee-Dearborn-Congress Line—was opened in 1951.
In April, 1964, CTA began operating a rail rapid transit service on the Skokie Swift line, non-stop between the terminals at Howard Street, Chicago and Dempster Street, Skokie. The five-mile line was purchased from the former North Shore Line. Standard CTA cars were equipped with remote-control overhead current collection devices for this line.
Completed in September, 1969, the Dan Ryan extension connects with the elevated structure at 18th Street and operates south via expressway median between 26th and 95th Streets. Average travel to and from the 9 new stations is 120 000 passengers daily. Lake-Dan Ryan trains operate a distance of 20.75 miles between the Harlem and 95th terminals.
An extension of the Milwaukee branch of the West-Northwest route completed in February, 1970, operates through a 1.2 mile subway and then for 3.9 miles in the median of the Kennedy Expressway to Jefferson Park terminal. About 63 000 passengers use the 6 new stations daily.
Urban Structure:
Population of city area: 3 002 500
Land area: 260 square miles in service area
Number of automobiles registered in city:
1970—954 426, 1978—998 664

Technical Data:
Gauge: 4 ft 8½ in (1.498 m)
Route length: 89.4 miles (143 km) (right-of-way)
Track length: 321.1 miles (517 km)
In tunnel: 10.1 miles (16 km) (right-of-way)
New lines (planned): Rapid transit to O'Hare. This important eight-mile rapid transit extension linking O'Hare International Airport with the CTA's Jefferson Park Transit Center to provide fast trips to and from Chicago's town centre is expected to be completed by the spring of 1982. This two-track extension is being constructed mostly in the median strip of the Kennedy Expressway and the airport access road. It will reach the airport's terminal area in a 3 500-ft tunnel, with a station beneath the main parking garage. Total length of the extension from Jefferson Park is 7.9 miles (12.8 km).
Between the airport and Jefferson Park, there will be stations at Harlem Avenue and Cumberland Road and a third station known as Rosemont at DesPlaines River Road. The Cumberland and Rosemont stations will have parking facilities for 1 400 cars. The running time of CTA's trains between the airport and the Dearborn Street Subway stations will be about 35 minutes. It is estimated that 36 500 journeys will be made on the extension daily.

New Boeing-Vertol trainset for Chicago

The extension is estimated to cost $150 million. The US Urban Mass Transportation Administration is providing 80 per cent of the funds, with the remainder coming from the Illinois Department of Transportation and the City of Chicago.

New lines (under construction): Construction on the extension to O'Hare Airport began in the spring of 1980.
Number of lines in operation: six: North-South, West-Northwest, West-South, Ravenswood, Evanston, Skokie
Number of stations (total): 140
Number of stations in tunnel: 20
Average distance between stations: 0.7 miles (1.1 km)
Maximum length of station platforms: Generally up to 528 ft (161 m), though a few stations have longer platforms in order to accommodate multiple entrances.
Gradient (max): 1 in 28.6 (3.5%)
Curvature (max): 90 ft (27.4 m)
Speed (design max): 70 mph (113 km/h)
  (average commercial): system—25 mph (40 km/h)
  (averages by route range from 19 to 38 mph)
Type of rails: 90 lb/yd flat-bottomed, 50% of rail system
100 lb/yd flat-bottomed, 25% of rail system
115 lb/yd flat-bottomed, 25% of rail system
All new rail will be 115 lb/yd
Type of tunnel: The underground sections are generally about 40-50 ft (12.2-15.3 m) below surface level. Some portions of the lines are in tube tunnels, others are of cut-and-cover construction. The tube tunnels have an internal diameter of 20 ft 5 in (6.2 m), the top of the tunnel being 16 ft 10½ in (5.1 m) from sleeper level.
Method and voltage of current supply: Third rail systemwide, except trolley wire on two miles of the Skokie line, 600 V dc.
Traffic and Finances:
Max line capacities (one way): Theoretical capacity is a train every 90 s.
Max number of trains per hour (one way):
  24 on one route (West-Northwest)
  30 on Loop L (two routes sharing same track)
Max number of trains per hour (one way planned): Train

congestion should be reduced when eight-car train operations begin on West-Northwest, and when different town centre routing options are available.
Frequency of train services in minutes (currently): Varies by route from 2½ to 5 in rush hours, and 3¾ to 15 midday.
(planned): Changes will be based on passenger changes.
Capacity per train (passengers seated): up to 400
(passengers standing): up to 800
Passenger journeys per annum and fleet size:

	(unlinked trips)	fleet size)
Rail, 1977:	148 860 410	1 100
1978:	156 314 991	1 100
Bus, 1977:	513 686 634	2 400
1978:	533 097 489	2 400

	(1977)	(1978)
Operating expenses:	$330.1	$365.1
System generated revenue:	206.9	215.8
Public funding required for operations:	123.2	149.3
Retirement of 1947 revenue bonds—net:	—	13.7
Interest on revenue bonds:	1.6	1.2
Unanticipated capital expenditures:	—	.1
Total public funding required:	$124.8	$164.3

Rolling Stock Characteristics:
Total floor area: 17.64 m²
Number of doors per side: All rail cars, except 2 400 series, have two sets per side of 2-leaf blinker panel doors separated by a post. The 2 400 series have two sets per side of bi-parting pocket doors.
Door width (m):
(car series)
1-50: 20½ in per blinker panel
6 000: 20¾ in per blinker panel
2 000: 20¼ in per blinker panel
2 200: 20¹⁄₁₆ in per blinker panel
2 400: 50 in
Number of passengers per car (total): approx 150
(seated): average 50

CLEVELAND

Authority:
Greater Cleveland Regional Transit Authority
1404 East 9th St, Cleveland, Ohio 44114, USA
Manager of Operations: Thomas A. Nooner
Comptroller: William E. Deckman
General Manager: Leonard Ronis
Manager of Marketing and Communications: Gregory N. Fern

History: The most important event on this rapid transit railway since its opening in 1955, was the line's extension in 1968 to the city's airport. As this airport-city direct rapid transit link is the first in the USA, keen interest is being shown in the future of Cleveland's air-rapid transit traffic trend.
General: Cleveland operates two rail systems, a 21.3 km light rail route with 29 stations and a 30.6 km rapid transit route with 18 stations.

The Authority began complete reconstruction of the light rail system in 1979. Work should be completed in 1981. Also a complete rehabilitation programme is planned on the Rapid Transit line. Estimated construction cost for these projects is £122 million.
In 1978 Cleveland ordered 48 light rail vehicles from Breda Costruzioni Ferroviarie, at a cost of $30.96 million. Each car will seat 84 passengers.

Greater Cleveland Rapid Transit line also has an order for 70 high-platform railcars.
Route length: 19 miles *(30.6 km)*.
Number of Stations: 18.
Passengers per annum: (1972): 12 702 206. (1974): 11 348 244. (1975): 14 496 698.
Number of cars: 116 heavy high platform cars and 55 PCC cars. Bids have been taken for 60 new light rail cars for Shaker and it is planned to purchase 20 high platform cars for the RTA high platform system.
Car details: Length of 87 older-type cars is 48 ft 6 in *(14.7*

m). Length of 30 newer-type cars is 70 ft *(21.3 m)*. All have two double sliding doors on each side.
Capacity per car: Seats for 52 passengers in single units (older-type cars), 54 per car in the double units (older-type) and 80 per car in the newer-type cars. Three new transit cars, on test in service on the airport line, features a new WABCO power system with pulse width modulation (PWM) propulsion. The effect of this system is to convert the dc traction current to variable voltage, variable frequency 3-phase power for delivery to the induction motors. Advantages claimed for

the new system include improved propulsion control and lower maintenance.
Average scheduled speed: 30 mph *(48 km/h)*.
Station details: Platforms of 300 ft minimum length are of island type at all but two stations. Escalators at eight stations.
Type of rail: Continuous welded rail on wood sleepers.
Current supply: 600 V dc with overhead equipment.
Signalling: Automatic block with train stops, three colour light signals. The new four-mile extension has an audio frequency "in-cab" signal system.

COLOGNE
Federal Republic of Germany

On 11 October 1968, the first 0.9 mile *(1.4 km)* east-west section of the new underground tramway (street-car) system for Cologne opened, between Cathedral-Hauptbahnhof and Friesenplatz. The ultimate object of this large project is to provide segregated rights of way for some 75 miles *(120 km)* of Cologne's tramway system, by the construction of cutting and embankment, and by tunnelling. The work is divided into phases and sub-divided into stages. The new town of Chorweiler on the northern outskirts will typically be served by tram route partly in tunnel, partly in cutting and partly on embankment. There are now 4.1 miles *(6.6 km)* of underground route operative served by sub-surface stations. The most recently operative stretches of tunnel-line are those extending north from Hauptbahnhof U Bahn stations and south from Zeughaus U Bahn station, the latter tunnel dividing into two just beyond Postrasse station.
The project will accelerate travel by tramcar and relieve congestion in the city centre. Main north-south thoroughfares in Cologne are semi-circular following

the course of the River Rhine. The Underground network will first be built along a north-south axis across the city centre, with radiating spurs. These will link with inner radial thoroughfares and in three instances will project to outer radial thoroughfares. Long-term planning envisages some outer stretches of tram-route being in part placed in tunnel, or where remaining at surface level, being made crossing-free of other traffic. Of the 93 miles *(150 km)* (approximate) of Cologne's tram-route, some 25 per cent may additionally be replaced by bus services.
The double-track tunnel of rectangular section is internally 15 ft 3 in *(4.65 m)* high and 23 ft 11 in *(7.30 m)* wide. Tunnel height above rail level *(4.09 m)* allows clearance for the cars' overhead pantograph system. There are no centre supports. The tunnels are sufficiently large to accommodate conventional underground trains should this system be required later.
Stations, with platforms 80 m long, accommodate two trains of twin-articulated tramcars (or later one conventional underground train). They are spaced in inner areas 600 m apart on average, and 800 m apart on average in the outer areas, allowing for average service

speeds, including stops, of 24 km/h and 30 km/h respectively. The passage of trams automatically actuates fixed visual signals.
Since 1968 a total of 20.4 km with 21 stations—with 11.1 km and 15 stations in tunnel—have been opened on the four-track Ebertplatz-Hauptbahnhof-Appelhof cross-city line and on an unconnected 1 km stretch in the north-west from Longerich to Chorweiler where a later connection with the S-Bahn is planned.
Plans have been made up to 1990, with total system of 120 km expected to take 70 to 80 years. Public transport demand was expected to be 2.65 million passengers yearly by 1980. Park-and-ride facilities with space for 12 500 automobiles are planned for 35 stations.
Construction costs since 1963 have totalled around DM 500 million.
Cologne is hoping to expand the system by an additional 7.5 km within four years. Under construction at present are 5.53 km from Kalk to Vingst, expected to be in service by 1980/81, and the 2.94 km Deutz section due to be operational by 1983. Costs are expected to total around DM 500 million with DM 162 million scheduled to be spent over the next two years.

DORTMUND
Authority:
Stadtbahn Dortmund
Stadtverwaltung Dortmund—Stadtbahnbauamt—Viktoriastrasse 15, 4600 Dortmund 1, Federal Republic of Germany

General: On 22 September 1969 the Dortmund City Council decided to go ahead on the Inner City underground extension. The new section begins at the pres-

ent terminus Mallinckrodt-Str or Münsterstr, crosses the Inner City and ends at the Ruhr High Speed Railway (B1) with branches to Hörde and Hacheney. The overall length is 10.5 km.
Dortmund has invested DM 330 million on the construction of 6.73 km of pre-V-Bahn Line 1 in tunnel running north to south beneath the city. Construction work on the final 3.1 km section is under way and should go into service in 1983. Twenty eight-axle cars

were delivered in 1979 for trials over the completed sections. A further 23 cars were due for delivery in 1980 to be followed by 12 six-axle units by 1982/83. By 1990 the city plans a three-line network totalling 11 km. Construction on the 6.1 km Line II should begin in 1981. Its estimated cost is DM 375 million. The cost of Line III's first section is estimated at DM 150 million. Eventually Dortmund hopes to operate a 30 km network over five lines.

DUSSELDORF
Authority:
Stadt Düsseldorf
Düsseldorf, Federal Republic of Germany

General: The first 1.5 km of Düsseldorf's pre-U-Bahn is planned to start operations in 1981. The first line will

run in tunnel from Kennedydamm to Heinrich-Heine-Allee (Opernhaus). Total cost of construction is estimated at DM 160 million.
Thirty-four vehicles will run over the initial system, 12 special B80 articulated light rail vehicles on order and 22 GT8S tramcars converted for use through 900 m high station platforms.

EDMONTON
Authority:
Edmonton Transit
10426 81 Avenue, Edmonton, Alberta T6E 1X5, Canada

General Manager: E. V. Miller

Type of system: LRT

General: The city's first 7 km light rail line was opened in 1978, serving five stations (two underground). Three new cars have been delivered and are in course of assembly.

Urban structure:
Population of city area: 478 000
Land area: 320 km²
Primary road network within city boundary: 350 km
Number of automobiles registered in city: 167 661 (1972), 380 535 (1979)

Technical Data:
Gauge: 1.435 m
Route length: 7.2 km
Track length: 16 km
In tunnel: 1.6 km

New lines (planned): West to 109 Street, 0.9 km (under construction): Northeast to Clareview, 1.7 km
Number of lines in operation: One
Number of stations (total): Five
Number of stations in tunnel: Two
Average distance between stations: 1.8 km
Max length of station platforms: 122 m
Gradient (max): 3%
Curvature (max): main line 140 m, yard 25 m
Speed (design max): 80 km/h
(average commercial): 28.8 km/h
Type of rails: 100# ARA
Type of tunnel: Tangent pile/Cut & cover/Bored
Method and voltage of current supply: Simple Catenary, 600 V dc

Traffic and Finances:
Max line capacities (one way): 5 400
Max number of trains per hour (one way): 12 (one way-planned): 30
Frequency of train services in minutes (currently): 12 (planned): 30
Capacity per train (passengers seated): 128 (passengers standing): 322
Passenger journeys per annum: 4 312 876 (part year,

1977/78), 6 077 679 (Sept/Sept, 1978/79)

Rolling Stock Characteristics:
Car types: 6-axle articulated motor cars
Number of units: 14
Car dimensions:
Length (m): 24.3
Width (m): 2.65
Height (m): 3.66
Total floor area: 50 m²
Number of doors per side: 4 Double
Door width (m): 1.6
Number of passengers per car (total): 225
(seated): 64
Motors per car: 2
Motor rating (kWh): 150
Power per train (minimum): single car, 300 kW (max): 5-car train, 1 500 kW
Acceleration (max): 1.32 m/s²
Deceleration (normal service): 1.0 m/s² (emergency): 3.0 m/s²
Max design speed: 80 km/h
Bogies (type and manufacturer): Duwag Monomotor
Distance between bogie pivot: 7.72 m
Brakes (type): Dynamic/Disc/Magnetic
Weight (empty in tonnes): 31

ESSEN
Authority:
Essener Verkehrs AG
43 Essen 1, Zweigerstrasse 34, Postfach 470, Federal Republic of Germany

General: Essen has a 5 km U-Bahn line in service, as part of a 15-km system, due by 1985. Total planned network is 58 km with 20 km underground. The first line, opened in 1977, runs from the new Wiener Platz station to Essen Hauptbahnhof and Bismarck Platz.

FRANKFURT AM MAIN
Authority:
Stadtwerke Frankfurt am Main
Börneplatz 36000, Frankfurt-am-Main 1, Federal Republic of Germany.

Managing Director: Hans-Joachim Krull
Operating Manager: Helmut Oesterling

Type of system: Metro

General: The U Bahn system being developed in Frankfurt am Main is part of a 5-year road-rail redevelopment project for the city and its environs. Segregation of the city's street-car traffic from general road traffic became necessary in certain busy thoroughfares and at junctions in order to relieve street congestion, and this is being accomplished by diverting street cars into sub-surface tunnels under the thoroughfares. A newly-developed, conventional

underground type of vehicle operates in tunnel and at street surface. Trains of this type of vehicle comprise four twin-car articulated units, with greater acceleration and overall capacity than the ordinary street cars, which themselves are normally coupled to form trains of cars. The latter will be phased out over a period of years as the system develops and more conventional underground-type cars come into service.
U-Bahn trainsets, built by Duwag, now share rights-of-way over 38.13 km of rapid transit tracks. Line U has

9.75 km and 16 stations in operation between the suburb of Nordwestzentrum and Theaterplatz. The line is due to be extended across the Main river to Sachsenhausen by 1985.

Line B (5.22 km) runs from Theaterplatz to Giessner Strasse with an extension to the thickly-populated Bornheim district in the northeast which was due for completion by 1980.

The U Bahn was extended southward from Hauptwache to Theaterplatz in 1974. Future development plans include: (1) Continued construction of the S Bahn (Federal Railway), in a four track tunnel which will be common to both S Bahn and U Bahn trains, between Hauptwache and Konstabler Wache. (2) Construction of a new U Bahn line in tunnel running from North-East (Bornheim) to Central Station (Hauptbahnhof) with 8 stations including a junction station with the existing North-South-U Bahn line at Theaterplatz and one cross-station with the S Bahn (Hauptbahnhof). The ultimate U Bahn network extending north and south of the River Main will comprise 123 km of tunnel and segregated surface route.

Stations: Tunnel stations have side platforms minimally 640 ft (195 m) long. On the segregated stretch of surface line, halts have raised platforms and are approached by pedestrian tunnels from the pavement.

Tunnels: Depth below street level varies between 39 ft and 46 ft (12-14 m) of box section, they are double-tracked (track gauge 1.435 m), 23 ft 4 in (7.10 m) wide internally and 15 ft 9 in (4.80 m) high, providing clearance for current-collecting pantographs, with which U Bahn cars are equipped.

Rolling Stock: Type U 2 articulated units, 75 ft 5½ in (23.0 m) long and 8 ft 8½ in (2.65 m) wide, are powered by two 150 kW motors. Doors: Four double-leafed, automatically operated. Passenger capacity: 230 per unit (including 64 seats). Max speed: 80 km/h. 127 articulated units are at present operative.

Urban Structure:
Population of city area: 640 000

Technical Data:
Gauge: 1.435 m
Route length: 52.91 km
Track length: 38.13 km

Type U2 light rail trainset, built by Uerdlingen (under licence from Duwag) for Frankfurt with electrical control and switching equipment from Siemens

Number of lines in operation: 4
Number of stations (total): 58
Average distance between stations: 700 m
Max length of station platforms: 100 m
Speed (design max): 80 km/h
(average commercial): 28 km/h
Type of rails: S41, S49
Method and voltage of current supply: 600 V dc

Traffic and Finances:
Max number of trains per hour (one way): 30

Frequency of train services in minutes (currently): 120 s
Capacity per train (passengers seated): 180
(passengers standing): 420
Passenger journeys per annum: 33 (1978/79)

Rolling Sotck Characteristics:
Car types: US P8 motor cars
Number of units: 127
Car dimensions:
Length (m): 25 and 28 m
Width (m): 2.65 and 2.35 m

GLASGOW

Authority:
Greater Glasgow Passenger Transport Executive
Bus and Underground Division, 46 Bath Street, Glasgow G2 1HN, Scotland.

Underground Operations Superintendent: W. Rodger
Chief Engineer: M. Lockheed
Underground Engineer: J. Wright

History: The line was opened in December 1896 as a cable railway. From 1923 to 1973 it was owned by the Glasgow Corporation, but in June of that year it was transferred to the Greater Glasgow Passenger Transport Executive. It was converted to electric traction in 1935.

General: In 1974, the Secretary of State for Scotland announced approval of a 75 per cent Government Grant towards the £12 million project by the Greater Glasgow Passenger Transport Executive for the modernisation of the Glasgow Underground.

The project, work on which began in 1974 and will be completed in 1980, involves the rebuilding of stations with the provision of escalators; the complete replacement of rolling stock and new facilities for its repair and maintenance; and new signalling and track. The permanent way and signalling will be replaced and the first of the new rolling stock was delivered in 1977.

Thirty-three new cars being run as two or three-aar trains were built by Metro-Cammell Ltd of Birmingham and delivered between January 1978 and May 1979. Each car is capable of carrying 36 seated pas-

sengers and 54 standing. Circuit time has been reduced from 30 to 24 minutes. The trains are equipped for one-man operation with Automatic Train Operation between stations.

Two-aspect colour light signalling operated by conventional track circuits and incorporating trainstops has been used. The track-to-train control signals are by passive transponders laid in the track. There is a radio communication link between all trains and the Central Control.

The system was completely closed in May 1977 for modernisation and was due to re-open in the first half of 1980.

Route length: 6.6 miles (10.4 km)
Number of lines: 1 (circular line); double track.
Number of stations served: 15. Average station spacing: 0.44 miles (0.71 km).
Trains/track/hour: 17 with potential for 27.
Max number of cars per train: 2 with potential for 3.
Estimated capacity per car: 90 (of which 36 are seated seated).
Average schedule speed (including stops): 16.37 mph (26.0 km/h).
Track gauge: 4 ft 0 in (1.219 m).
Weight and type of rails: 80 lb/yd (39.7 kg/m), flat-bottomed, continuously welded.
Max gradient: 1 in 16 (6.25%).
Minimum radius of curves: 104 m (343 ft) on main line, 50 in depot yard.
Type of tunnel: Double tubes, each of 11 ft (3.35 m) nominal diameter. Tunnelling was by means of shields. Depth of the tunnel top ranges from 7 ft to 115

ft (2 to 35 m) below surface; average depth is 29 ft (8.84 m).

Method and voltage of current supply: Third rail; 600 V dc.

Rolling Stock: Number of cars: 33 identical driving motor cars, all axles motored. Each car is 12.6 m long and 2.6 m high from rail level. Two pairs of air-worked double sliding doors per side, all longitudinal seating, fluorescent lighting. Full width cab at one end. Automatic couplers at both ends of car.

Signalling: Track circuit operated automatic two-aspect colour-light acting in conjunction with train stops for safety signalling. Automatic Train Operation command system using passive transponsers superimposed.

Station lay-out: Nine stations have island platforms, eight of which are about 2.7 m wide and one about 4.0 m wide. Three stations have two flank platforms and three stations one flank and one island. There are a total of 28 escalators and two passenger conveyors at nine of these stations. Two stations have underground concourses and the remainder surface ticket halls.

Workshops: Maintenance building constructed in 1976-78 consists of three pitted roads, two long-term maintenance roads, bench area, lifting shop, machine shop, battery loco charging area, stores, etc.
Stabling shed converted from original workshop has five stabling roads capable of accommodating 14 two-car trains and a wash bay.

GORKY

Authority:
Gorky City Soviet
Gorky, USSR

General: Construction work on the city's first 10 km line began in 1977. The line will have eight stations.

GOTHENBURG

Authority:
Gothenburg Transit Authority
PO Box 424, 401 26 Gothenburg, Sweden

Type of system: Light rail.

General: A 1.3 km extension of the city's 10.3 km light rail transit system opened at the end of 1978 at a cost of SKr 17 million. In 1979 the line was extended 0.5 km to Drottningtorget at a cost of SKr 4.5 million. Reconstruction work commences in 1981-84 when the single track will be replaced with double track. The estimated cost is SKr 30 000 000. The rolling stock will be

exchanged from 1985 onwards. Following that, plans are to exchange vehicles on the light rail rapid transit line. Estimated cost for 300 vehicles is SKr 600 000 000.
Also planned for construction in 1981-84 is a new workshop and repair facility. Estimated cost is SKr 50 000 000.

GUADALAJARA

Authority:
Commision Inter-Departmental Para El Estudio del Transporte Masivo en la Cuidad de Guadalajara
Guadalajara, Mexico

Type of system: Projected full-metro

History: The transit authority was set up in 1967 and work has begun on construction of the first line.

Technical Data:
Gauge: 1.435 m
Projected new lines (in design): 33 km
Number of lines: 3
Number of stations: (total): 34 planned
Speed (design max): 35 km/h
Electric system: Third rail; 1 500 V
Type of rails: 48 kg/m

Rolling Stock:
Car type: Proposed
Passenger capacity
per car: (total): 210
(seated): 76
Rating: 500 hp
Train composition (minimum): 4
(max): 6

Traffic Data:
Trains/track/hour: 20
Train capacity (passengers): 1 260
Total passengers/track/hour (peak): 15 000
Train headways design: 1.5 minutes
Passengers carried (weekday): 1 000 000 estimated

Tunnelling complete on the first section of the north-south line

Cut and cover work in progress on the first line section

HAGUE, THE

Authority:
The Hague Transit Authority (HTM)
Dynamostraat 10, The Hague, Netherlands
Telephone: (070) 889280

Type of system: Tram system, partly pre-metro.

General: A new 5.2 km standard-gauge, double-track line is planned as an extension of the existing tramway system. Cost of the scheme, to begin in 1980, is estimated at Dfl 60 million, excluding rolling stock. Completion is planned for 1981. The existing tramway is 71 km operating 234 four-axle cars. An additional 60 eight-axle articulated light rail vehicles are planned.

Urban Structure:
Population of city area: 600 000
Land area: 12 858 ha (The Hague, Voorburg, Rijswijk, Leidschendam)

Technical Data:
Route length: 98.7 km

Track length: 70.9 km
New lines (planned): Number 21 from Laan van Nieuw Oust Indie to Kraaijenstein. Expansion of 3 km in both directions (one side to Beethovenplantsoen, other side to Voorburg/Leidschendam.
Number of lines in operation: 10
Number of stops (total): 474
Average distance between stations: 420 m
Gradient (max): 4½ %
Curvature (max): minimal 22 m
Speed (design max): 70 km/h
(average commercial): 20.4 km/h
Type of rails: RI60 and S41
Method and voltage of current supply 600 V dc
Frequency of train services in minutes (currently): 3-15
Capacity per train (passengers seated): 76
(passengers standing): 135
Passenger journey per annum:
75 670 000 (1977/78), 75 705 000 (1978/79)
Revenues: Dfl 44.1 million
Expenses: Dfl 158.6 million

Rolling Stock Characteristics:
Car types: PCC motor cars, PCC trailers
Number of units: 234
Car dimensions:
Length (m): 13.4 (13.2) m
Width (m): 2.35 m
Height (m): 3.13 m
Total floor area: 24 m²
Number of doors per side: 5
Door width (m): 75 cm
Number of passengers per car (total): 101
(seated): 36
Motors per car: 4
Motor rating (kW): 40.5
Acceleration (max): 1.9 m/s²
Deceleration (normal service): 1.8 m/s²
(emergency): 4.5 m/s²
Max design speed: 70 km/h
Distance between bogie pivot: 6.21 m
Brakes (type): Electrical, drum and track
Weight (empty in tonnes): 17.5 for motorcars; 16.5 for trailers

HAIFA

Authority:
Municipal Corporation of Haifa
City Engineers Dept
122 Hanassi Ave, Haifa, Israel
Telephone: (4) 83765

Type of system: Funicular subway.

General: An underground railway has been in operation since 1959. It commences about ¼ mile from the harbour at Paris station, in the town-centre district, and runs in a straight line for 1.12 miles *(1 800 m)* to its other terminus, Gan Haem, in the Carmel district. It ascends nearly 900 ft *(274 m)*. Before its inception there was increasing traffic on the steep winding roads between the business district, the shopping and entertainment district on the lower slopes of Mount Carmel, and the large residential area higher up the mountain. To provide a better public transport system between the districts a tunnel railway was constructed, but because of the steep gradient it was necessary for the trains to be cable hauled.
This funicular railway is built wholly in rock tunnel. The roof is of concrete bearing directly on the rock sides, except where the rock is unsound. At these points reinforced concrete walls have been constructed. The tunnel depth below surface varies from 112 ft *(35 m)* to 20 ft *(6 m)*. It was designed by the French Société d'Etudes des Transports et de Communications and built by the Municipality jointly with the Cie. Dunkerquoise d'Entreprises and a local building firm, Solel Boneh. The cars also were built by the

Cie. Dunkerquoise.
The railway is single track throughout except for a passing point where two trains cross. The track is of concrete strips on which the pneumatic tyred cars run, guided by steel rails. At intermediate stations, "up" passengers use one platform and "down" passengers the other. All platforms are 100 ft long, conforming to the train's length, but because of the slope of the tunnel and track they are built as a series of level sections stepped to follow the line of the slope. When a train stops, its doors are opposite a platform section. The cars, 49 ft long and 7 ft 9 in wide, coupled two to a train have multi-level floors like the platforms. A stepped gangway with seats either side connects the level floor vestibules. There are four sets of air-operated doors on each side of each car, and a cab at each end for the train attendant who operates the doors and, if necessary, can apply a service brake or emergency brake on the train.
The trains normally are braked by the cable, which is wound by two 675 hp electric motors in the machine room, situated at the highest station. The motors are geared to an 8 ft diameter cable pulley. This railway, which was opened in 1959, has six stations and a train every six minutes. It has a capacity of 4 000 passengers per hour. The normal capacity per car is 160 passengers, but a maximum of 200 can be carried. Escalators working in the upward direction are provided at five stations. Fares are paid for tokens that operate mechanical turnstiles.

Technical Data:
Gauge: 1.980 m

Route length: 1.75 km
In tunnel: 1.75 km
Number of lines: 1
Number of stations (total): 6
(in tunnel): 6
Average distance between stations: 350 m
Stations:
platform length (minimum): 30.5 m
Gradient (max): 15.5%
Curvature (max): 0
Speed (average commercial): 30 km/h
Electric system: 1 200 V

Rolling Stock:
Car type (year introduced): 1959
Number of units: 4
Car dimensions (length): 15 m
(width): 2.4 m
(height): 3.8 m
Passenger capacity
per car (total): 160
(seated): 24
Train composition (minimum): 2
(max): 2
Brakes (type): Cable

Traffic Data:
Total passengers/track/hour (peak): 2 000
Train headways existing: 6 minutes
Passengers carried (weekday): 45 000
(annually): 6 000 000
Vehicle-km operated annually: 250 000

HAMBURG

Authority:
Hamburger Hochbahn Aktiengesellschaft
Steinstr 20, Postfach 6146, 2000 Hamburg, Federal Republic of Germany
Telephone: (0411) 321041
Telegrams: HOCHBAHN-HAMBURG

Type of system: Full metro

History: The Hamburger Hochbahn AG, a public company 90 per cent of whose shares are held by the city and state, has since 1918 operated the city's underground, street-car, bus and water-borne public transport. Of the present U Bahn system, the first operative line was the circular line running beneath the inner city. Work on it began in 1906 and it was opened in stages, fully operating in 1912. By 1914 two spur lines, to Hellkamp and Ohlsdorf, were opened, and between 1921-27 the Wolddorfer Railway's two lines to Ohlstedt and Gross Hansdorf had been incorporated.
Work started in 1978 on extension of the existing line U2 from Hagenbecks Tierpark to Nordalbinger Weg—a 6 route-km extension. Construction will cost an estimated DM 286 million. Work began in mid-1979 on a 6 km extension of the existing U2 U-Bahn Line running from Hagenbeck Zoo to Nienforf. Completion date is 1983. The extension is to have five stations and estimated cost is DM 300 million.

Technical Data:
Gauge: 1.435 m
Route length: 89.5 km
In tunnel: 32 km

Number of lines: 3
Number of stations (total): 80
(in tunnel): 36
Average distance between stations: 1.052 km
Stations:
platform length (max): 125 m
(minimum): 90 m

Type of tunnel: Rectangular section. Construction in town was by cut and cover method. On the Ochsenzoll line extension, apart from a short section of twin circular tunnel, prefabricated "concrete box" sections of tunnel, each 6 ft 6 in long, 24 ft wide and 13 ft 9 in high, supported by centre columns, were lowered into open cut. This method speeded the work and minimised the period during which streets along the railway route were rendered unusable. The new transverse line is in part in shield-driven tunnel under the city centre (Schlump-Hauptbahnhof).

Gradient (max): 5%
Curvature (max): 68 m
Speed (design max): 70-80 km/h
(average commercial): 31 km/h
Electric system: Third rail; 750 V
Type of rails: 37 kg/m

Rolling Stock:

Car type:	DT 1	DT 2	DT 3
Number of Units:	50 × 2	184 × 2	127 × 3
Car dimensions:			
(length):	28.44 m	28.44 m	39.52 m
(width):	2.50 m	2.56 m	2.56 m
(height):	3.34 m	3.37 m	3.35 m

Passenger capacity			
per car (total):	260	256	364
(seated):	82	82	116
Motors per car:	8	4	8
Rating:	74 kWh	80 kWh	80 kWh
Train composition (minimum): 2			
(max): 9			
Acceleration			
(max):	1.0	0.9	1.2
Deceleration			
(emergency):	1.25	1.3	
Brakes (types): Regenerative			
Weight (tonnes):			
Motorcar:	50.5	39.1	45.5

Traffic Data:
Trains/track/hour: 24
Train capacity (passengers): 1 092
Total passengers/track/hour (peak): 25 000
Train headways existing: 2 minutes
Passengers carried (weekday): 540 000
(annually): 178 300 000
Average journey length: 5.6 km
Vehicle-km operated annually: 55 100 000

Signalling: Automatic block, with colour-light signals. An automatic train guidance system was introduced during 1972 to a passenger carrying section of line. In 1974, the Hamburger Hochbahn began to install train telephones linking U-Bahn train drivers with a central control room. By mid-year, twelve power cars had been fitted with cab telephones. During the year track cables for the system were laid on the 33 km Wandsbek Markt-Ohlsdorf line (UI).

HANOVER

Authority:
Hannoversche Verkehrsbetriebe (USTRA) AG
Hanover Am Hohen Ufer 6, Federal Republic of Germany

Type of system: Pre-metro.

General: The first 7 km of Hanover's projected 90-km pre-U-Bahn system opened to traffic between Oberricklingen and the Hauptbahnhof on Line A in September 1975. By spring 1976 construction had been completed over a further 7 km and trains are now operating the full 14 km (3.9 km in tunnel; 10.1 km at grade) on Line A between Oberricklingen in the southwest and Lahe in the northeast.

The newly completed 25 km Line B goes into operation between Largenhager/Sahlhamp and Empelde. Construction costs have been DM 360 million for the 6 km tunnel section and DM 140 for the remainder.

Another step forward in the city's rapid transit plan is the conversion of the existing tram lines between Largenhager-Kropcke and Alte Heide-Empelde to pre-U-bahn operation.

Work is continuing on Line C. A tunnel extension

Pre-metro trainset shown operating on the underground section of Line A and on the surface.

South from Line B is due to go into operation in 1982. The first Line C tunnel section running west beneath

the city is due to open in 1983, followed by the Eastern tunnel section in 1985.

HELSINKI

Authority:
Helsingin Kaupungin Metrotoimisto
PO Box 53242
Toinen Linja 7, 00531 Helsinki 53, Finland
Telephone: 71 83 21

Managing Director: Unto Valtanen

Type of system: Full-metro.

General: The local traffic in the metropolitan area is handled by the State Railways lines, namely the northbound main line and Martinlaakso line as well as the westbound coast line. The planned metro network forming a part of the basic network of rail traffic for the metropolitan area consists of an east-west coast line and a U-line serving the inner city. The coast line of the metro connects the eastern suburbs and regional centres with the city centre and the State Railways lines. The U-line serves the traffic in the inner city. Helsinki's first metro line from Kamppi to Puotinharju is scheduled for opening in 1982 as the first stage in the plan to build about 35 km of new rapid transit rail lines within the city by the year 2000.

Length of the Kamppi-Puotinharju line will be 11.5 km including 4 km double tunnels. Five of the nine stations shall be underground, all the others surface stations. A small section of the tunnel will be built below the ground water level using a freezing method. By the end of 1977 all the tunnels and platforms of the underground stations were blasted but the ticket halls are still under construction. The active freezing of the soil is now completed and the installation of cast iron lining is under work.

Total cost of the line including stations, bridges, viaducts, 7.5 km surface and 4 km underground double track, depot, electrical supply system, ATO and ATC systems, relay interlocking system and rolling stock

will work out at about FM 1040 million. Tunnel stations are expected to take about FM 300 million; surface stations about FM 70 million; track FM 110 million; yard and workshop about FM 80 million; rolling stock FM 310 million and miscellaneous equipment (such as power supply, safety equipment) about FM 170 million.

Trials have been carried out with a six-car prototype train since 1972 on a 2.8 km track section.

The rolling stock—42 two-car sets—for the first line are now under construction.

Urban Structure:
Population of city area: 485 000
Land area: 18 178 hectares
Primary road network within city boundary: 192 km
Number of automobiles registered in city: 103 000 (1970), 122 000 (1978)

Technical Data:
Gauge: 1.524 m
Route length: 11 km
Track length: 31 km
In tunnel: 4 km double
New lines (planned): 4 km (under construction): 11 km
Number of stations (total): 9
Number of stations in tunnel: 5
Average distance between stations: 1.1 km
Max length of station platforms: 135 m
Gradient (min): 35 o/oo
Curvature (min): main track 300 m, depot area 100 m
Speed (design max): 80 km/h
(average commercial): 43 km/h
Type of rails: UIC 54 kg/m
Type of tunnel: douple roch
Method and voltage of current supply: third rail 750 V dc

Traffic and Finances:
Max line capacities (one way): 36 000 h (2 min interval)
Max number of trains per hour (one way-planned): 30
Frequency of train services in minutes: 2.5 during rush hour, 5 at other times, 10 at night
Capacity per train (passengers seated): 420 (train consisting of six cars)
(passengers standing): 780

Rolling Stock Characteristics:
Car types: M 100 (preserial 3 two-car sets, serial 39 two-car sets), altogether 42 two-car sets.
Car dimensions:
Length (m): 22.1 × 2
Width (m): 3.20
Height (m): 3.7
Total floor area: 66 m², standing area 30 m²
Number of doors per side: 3
Door width (m): 1.4
Number of passengers per car (total): 200
(seated): 67
Motors per car: 4 (3-phase asynchronous motor fed by PWM-inverters)
Motor rating (kW): 125 kW/motor
Power per train (minimum): 1 000 kW (two-car set)
(max): 3 000 kW (3 two-car sets)
Acceleration (max): 0-27 km/h, 1.2 m/s²; 0-80 km/h, 0.9 m/s²
Deceleration (normal service): 80-0 km/h, 1.2 m/s²
(emergency): 80-0 km/h, 1.2 m/s²
Max design speed: 90 km/h
Bogies (type and manufacturer): Air springs two motor bogies by Valmet
Distance between bogie pivot: 15 m
Brakes (type): RHEOSTATIC/disc/magnetic track
Weight (empty in tonnes): 31.6

HONG KONG

Authority:
Hong Kong Mass Transit Railway Corporation
PO Box 9916, General Post Office, Hong Kong

Type of system: Full-Metro

Chairman: N. S. Thompson
Managing Director: Dr T. M. Ridley
Project Director: R. J. Mead
Engineering Director: P. H. F. Andrew
Operations Director: A. R. Cotton

Following ten years of planning, Hong Kong started work on a 15 station, 15.6 km Metro line in September 1975.

The cost estimate for completion of the line by 1979-80 was $5 800 million (HK). The line will run from Chater Station in the Central District of Hong Kong Island via immersed tube beneath Hong Kong Harbour through Kowloon to Kwun Tong in the north-east. The line will run in twin-tunnels, partly bored and partly constructed using cut-and-cover.

Trains, to be built by Metro Camell, will be equipped with conventional steel wheels running on standard-gauge steel track. Four-car trains are planned initially. There will be standing room for 327 people with 48 seated in each car. The number of cars will be increased to six and by the mid-1980s, eight cars.

In July 1977, the Government gave the Corporation approval to construct a line extension to Tsuen Wan. Work on the 10.7 km extension began during the middle of 1978 and will be completed in 1982. There will be 11 stations on the extension. The estimated construction cost of the extension is HK$4 100.

Technical Data:
Construction Period: November 1975—December 1979
Number of Lines: 1
Length of Line:
Total: 15.6 km
Overhead: 2.8 km
Underground: 12.8 km
Including a Cross Harbour Tunnel of: 1.4 km
Stations:
Total: 15

Overhead: 3
Underground: 12
Depth: 17-25 m
Length: Chater: 380 m
Others: up to 270 m
Platform length: 182 m
Mean Spacing between stations: 1.1 km
Facilities: Escalators, Automatic Fare Collection, Public Address, CCTV, No Smoking, Air Conditioned (underground only)

Trains:
Car Builder: Metro-Cammell Ltd, Birmingham, England
Car length over headstock:
A cars: 22 750 mm (including cab)
C cars: 22 000 mm (no driving cab)
Car width: 3 096 mm
Car height: 3 700 mm
Height of floor above rail: 1 110 mm
Car Weight: Tare—A car: 39 tonnes
C car: 39 tonnes
Gross—A car: 60.5 tonnes
C car: 60.5 tonnes
Headroom, floor to ceiling: 2 060 mm
Number of doors per side: 5
Doorway width: 1 400 mm
Doorway height: 1 800 mm
Bogie centres: 15 600 mm
Wheel base: 2 500 mm
Wheel dia (new): 850 mm
(Fully worn): 775 mm
Motors: 4 per car 90 kW GEC
Motor Suspension: Nose suspended, axle hung
Motor voltage: 350V dc
Gear ratio: 82 : 15
Gear drive: Parallel Helical
Brake system (service): Rheostatic/air
(emergency): Air
No of passengers:
Total (Max load): 375
Seated: 48
Standing: 327
Train Configuration:
4 car: A – C + C – A
6 car*: A – C + B – C + C – A
8 car*: A – C + B – C + B – C + C – A

Facilities: Load control acceleration and braking rates, Public address, Air conditioning, automatic train operation and protection, No smoking, Air operated doors, vestibules between cars
Operation:
Frequency of trains: 2 mins at peak
Journey time overall: 28 min
Station dwell time: 30s
Mean speed including stops: 33 km/h
Max service speed: 80 km/h
Passenger volume per day: 1 million by mid-1980s

Vehicle Performance & Data:
Design speed: 90 km/h
Service speed (max): 80 km/h
Service acceleration rate: 1.3 m/s²
Service retardation rate: 1.0 m/s²—1.35 m/s²
Emergency retardation rate: 1.4 m/s²
Max jerk rate: 0.8 m/s³

Electrical & Control System:
Line voltage: 1 500V dc
Current collection: Pantograph on C car
Exterior lights: Incandescent heavy duty head lamp
Saloon lights: Fluorescent
Train control: Automatic Train Operation (Manual Control Available)

Body Specification:
Frame: Aluminium extrusion—monocoque
Exterior cladding: Rivetted aluminium alloy panels
Interior cladding: Epoxy powder aluminium alloy
Ceiling cladding: Nylon faced aluminium alloy
Floor: Vinyl faced plywood on aluminium troughing
Windows: Tinted high strength safety glass
Air-conditioning: 80 kW heat load per car 2 roof mounted package units
Air-conditioning drive: 1 package driven from own car, other from adjacent car, 440 V 60 Hz
Noise—Inside: 75 dBA max

* B Cars will be identical with C cars in structure, but have identical equipment to A cars, and no driving cab.

ROLLING STOCK

	Car type A	Car type C
Year of manufacture	1977-78	1977-78
Dimensions:		
Length, m	22 750	22 000
width, m	3 096	3 096
height, m	3 700	3 700
(powered cars with and without driver's cab)	Powered cars with driver's cab	Powered cars without driver's cab
Tare weight (powered and trailer cars), tonnes	39	39
Body material	Aluminium	Same as for Car type A
Bogie material	Steel	"
Materials for interior trim	Melamine faced aluminium	"
Total carrying capacity, persons	375	"
including seating capacity, persons	48	"
Arrangements of seats: longitudinal, transverse, mixed	Longitudinal	"
Number and dimensions of doors	10@ 1 400 mm × 1 800 mm	"
Method of door operation	Electropneumatic	"
Noise level in driver's cab	75 dBA max	"
passenger compartment	75 dBA	"
Ventilation	AC driven A/C Units	"
Lighting	Fluorescent 250 lux	"
Specific electric power consumption, kWh/1 000 tonne-km	50	"
Design speed, km/h	90	"
Operating speed, km/h	Max 80 km/h.	"
	Overall mean including 30s station dwell time 33 km/h	
Type of body suspension	Primary suspension rubber chevron; secondary air springs	
	Nose suspended, axle hung	"
Bogie wheelbase, mm	2 500 mm	"
Distance between bogie centres	15 600 mm	"
Type of automatic coupling	BSI Automatic and BSI Semi-Permanent Splittable type	
Wheel dia, mm, and type	ø850 mm new, ø775 mm fully worn; Steel monobloc type	
Number and power of motors	4 × 90 kW	Same as for Car type A
Weight of one motor (without gear train), kg	1 020 kg	"
Armature rotating speed, rpm	2 900 rpm	"
Commutator dia, mm	ø235 mm	"
Braking—service	Rheostatic/Air	"
—emergency	Air	"
Time required for an empty car to accelerate on level track to 80 km/h	54.2s	"
Ditto to 50 km/h	17s	"
Time required for braking an empty car on level track from 80 km/h	22s	"
Ditto from 50 km/h	14s	"
Time required for emergency braking of an empty car on level track from 80 km/h	16s	"
Ditto from 50 km/h	10s	"
Degree of automation (automatic train operation, automatic speed control, train radio communication, etc).	Automatic Train, Operation and Protection, Communication channels, Driver to Control, Driver to Passengers, Control to passengers	

HONOLULU

Authority:
Honolulu Rapid Transit
Honolulu, Hawaii, USA

General: Construction of Honolulu's planned rail transit system was due to start in 1980. The first section will be 22.4 km long with 16 stations. Completion is due by 1986/87 at a cost of about $800 million. Rolling stock will total 120 cars initially.

ISTANBUL

Authority:
Istanbul Elektrik, Tramvay re Tünel Isletmeleri (IETT)
BP 2175, Umum Müdürlügü, Istanbul, Turkey

Type of system: Underground electric incline railway

History: Prior to 1970 the cable-operated subterranean incline line was steam powered but has since been converted to electric operation. The line first began operating in 1875. Preparatory works for construction of a metro system was put in hand in 1978.

Technical Data:
Gauge: 1.510 m

Route length: 570 m
In tunnel: 570 m
Number of lines: 1
Number of stations (total): 2
(in tunnel): 2
Average distance between stations: 570 m
Stations:
platform length (minimum): 30 m

Gradient (max): 14.9%
Speed (design max): 30 km/h
(average commercial): 30 km/h
Electric system: 440 V

Rolling Stock:
Car type (year introduced): 1970
Number of units: 2
Car dimensions (length): 16.0 m
(width): 2.5 m
Passenger capacity per car (total): 200

Traffic Data:
Train capacity (passengers): 200
Total passengers/track/hour (peak): 6 000
Train headways, existing: 2 minutes
Passengers carried (1976): 6 672 838
Vehicle-km operated (1976): 67 980

JAKARTA

Authority:
Municipal Authorities
Jakarta, Indonesia

General: A new rapid transit rail system is being planned for Indonesia's capital city. Basically, the scheme consists of four cross-city routes and a central area circle line.
The proposals are being based on recommendations made by engineers from Orge Intertraffic-Lenzconsult of the Federal Republic of Germany which prepared a study on future city transport needs in 1974.
Motive power and vehicles to be used are expected to consist of five sets of four-car electric trainsets and 12 sets of two-car diesel trains. Maximum speeds will be limited to 40 km/h and trains are expected to operate at 20 minute intervals.

KHARKOV

Authority:
Kharkov City Transport
Kharkov, USSR

Type of system: Full-metro

General: The first stage of an underground railway system is under construction in Kharkov. The city's extensive bus, tram and trolleybus services are inadequate to meet demands and an urban underground railway system is projected.
The underground tunnels are to be built 18 ft in diameter to accommodate Soviet underground rolling stock. The Riga coach building works are building the cars. They will be capable of speeds of 56 mph (90 km/h). Car seats will be arranged transversely and the car capacity will be 240-250 passengers.
The underground lines will be transverse, crossing the city east-west and north-south via the Southern Railway Terminal. The first underground line will be 6.2 miles (9.8 km) long and have two deep-level stations and six of cut and cover type. Stations will be from 0.9 km to 1.7 km apart, and will have platforms 328 ft (100 m) long. They will be: Sverdlova Street, Yuzhny Vokzal, Rynok (Market), Centre, Levada Stadium, Zavod Malysheva, Turbinni Zavod. During peak hours it is expected that 15 trains each made up of two pairs of 4-car units will serve the line initially. Construction of the second stage will add 11¾ miles (7.3 km).

Technical Data:
Gauge: 1.524 m
Projected new lines (in construction): 10.6 km with 8.9 km in tunnel
(in design): 27 km
Number of lines: 2
Number of stations (total): 14
(in tunnel): 6
Average distance between stations: 13 km
Stations:
Platform length (minimum): 100 m
Gradient (max): 4%
Speed (design max): 90-120 km/h
Electric system: Catenary; 3 000 V

Rolling Stock:
Car type: proposed
Car dimensions (length): 19.60 m
(width): 2.70 m
(height): 3.70 m
Passenger capacity per car (total): 260
(seated): 40
Motors per car: 4
Rating: 68 kWh
Train composition (max): 8
Acceleration (max): 1.0
Deceleration (emergency): 1.2
Brakes (type): Rheostatic
Body material: Steel
Weight (tonnes) Motorcar: 30

Traffic Data:
Trains/track/hour: 30 (estimated)
Train capacity (passengers): 2 080
Total passengers/track/hour (peak): 62 400
Train headways
design: 2 minutes

KIEV

Authority:
Kievski Metropolitan Railway
Kievski City Soviet, Brest Litovsku Prospect 37A, Kiev 55, USSR

Type of system: Full-metro

General: The third metropolitan railway in the USSR came into operation in 1960 in Kiev. The first section of 3.2 miles *(5.2 km)* served 5 stations: Terminus, University, Kretschatik (also the city's principal street), Arsenal and Dnieper.
In 1963 the line was extended 2.1 miles *(3.3 km)* to Zavod Bolshevik, in 1965 a further 2.7 miles *(4.4 km)* to Darnitsa, and in 1968 to Konsomolskaya via the Metro bridge crossing of the Dnieper River. In the north-west two further stations, Oktyabrskaya and Zavodskaya, were opened in 1973.
A new transverse line from Priorka, south east, south and south-west to Teremky, crossing the existing line at Kreshchatic, now also under construction, will add 16 more stations to the system.

Technical Data:
Gauge: 1.524 m
Route length: 18.2 km
In tunnel: 14.0
Projected new lines (in construction): 10.7 km
Number of lines: 1
Number of stations (total): 15
(in tunnel): 10
Average distance between stations: 1.4 km
Stations:
platform length (minimum): 100 m

Gradient (max): 4%
Curvature (max): 400 m
Speed (design max): 75 km/h
(average commercial): 38 km/h
Electric system: Third rail; 825 V
Type of rails: 50 kg/m

Rolling Stock:

Car type	Diesel	Electric
Number of units:		194
Car dimensions (length):	18.8 m	18.8 m
(width):	2.7 m	2.7 m
(height):	3.7 m	3.7 m

Passenger capacity		
per car: (total):	210	220
(seated):	44	40
Motors per car:	4	4
Rating:	73 kWh	68 kWh

Train composition:
(minimum): 3
(max): 3
Acceleration (max): 1.3
Brakes (type): Rheostatic / Electro-pneumatic
Body material: Steel
Weight (tonnes) Motorcar: 32

Traffic Data:
Trains/track/hour: 30
Train capacity (passengers): 750
Total passengers/track/hour (peak): 22 500
Train headways
existing: 2 minutes
Passengers carried (weekday): 486 900
(annually): 177 700 000
Average journey length: 5.6 km
Vehicle-km operated annually: 23 200 000

KOBE

Authority:
Railway Dept, Transportation Bureau
Kobe City Office, Kobe, Japan

General: This important port has four surface railways (besides the Japanese National Railway) whose terminal stations were until 1968 unconnected by rail with each other. The underground-elevated Kobe Rapid Railway provides this rail connection and permits interworking of three of the surface railways' services. The linking railway begins in the west at the Sanyo Electric Railway's Nishidai station and runs for 3.5 km to Kosoku-kobe central station. There it forks, one branch running for 2.2 km to the Hankyu Electric Railway's Sannomiya station and the other for 1.5 km to the Hanshin Electric Railway's Motomachi station, both in the east. Additionally, from an intermediate underground Shinkaichi station, a short 0.4 km spur runs north to the Kobe Electric Railway's Minatogawa station.

This heavily used railway, built by the Kobe Rapid Railway Co Ltd at a cost of Yen 16 000 000 000 (about £16m at that time) carries 1 500 trains daily. The first 5.6 km section of an east-west transverse line from Naya to Shin-Nagata has been under construction by the Municipal Authority since 25 November 1972, and was opened in December 1975. It will be extended from the city centre eastward to Nunobiki to complete a total route length of 13.4 km.
A new guideway system is planned to run on elevated tracks 6.4 km from Sannomiya Station to Port Island via a new bridge. A total of nine stations is planned. Completion of the 7.7 km Yamat Line in Kobe is scheduled for completion in 1982 at a cost of about Yen 100 000 million. The line starts at the Shinnagata terminal of the 5.7 km Sheishin Line which opened in March 1977. Kobe has plans to build another 22 km of subway line but no detailed decisions have yet been released. Twenty-four trains equipped with automatic train control (ATC) and automatic train and automatic train operation (ATO) are in operation. Plans are to buy

eight more. Kawasaki cars, which are in operation on Kobe's Western Line have automatic variable filed chopper control with regenerative braking. Each car has seating for 56 and standing room for 94 passengers.

Tunnels: Double-tracked sub-surface Box-Rahmen type.
Gauge: 1.435 m (standard) east-west line, 1.067 m north-south line.
Station lengths: 120-160 m.
Motive power: Current is collected from overhead compound catenary wires (part rigid type) at 1 500 V dc, supplied initially at 33 000 V.
Signalling: Automatic block with lineside signals and train stops. A control centre is equipped with a train position indicator and train classifying equipment.
Rolling Stock: The Kobe Rapid Railway owns no stock. The Sanyo, Hankyu and Hanshin Electric Railways interwork their own stock over the east-west line, and the Kobe Electric Railway over the narrow-gauge north-south line.

KYOTO

Authority:
Municipal Transportation Bureau
Kyoto, Japan

Type of system: Full-metro

General: Kyoto is connected to Osaka and Tokyo by the Japanese National Railway's Tokaido trunk line, and with Osaka also by the Keihan and Keihanshin Kyuko private electric railways. The latter railway approaches the city from the west and continues underground to terminate at its centre.
In 1963 the original underground portion of this line, opened in 1931, was extended to its present length of 2.2 miles *(3.6 km)*. It runs beneath a main thorough-

fare, in rectangular tunnel for the most part, with sufficient headroom for overhead current collection by pantograph. A sub-surface continuous concourse provides connection with the railway below, and entry from street level is by stairways situated at a number of points along the main thoroughfare. There are four stations.
Studies for a rapid transit alternative were completed in 1979 and work began on an initial route of the planned 45 km two-line system in 1974. The route runs 15 km under Karasumadori. A 12 km section under construction will extend from a northern terminal at Kitayama to Takeda in the south. The entire line will be in tunnel. The section from Kitaoja station to Kyoto is due to start operation in March 1981.
Takeda's 3.6 km extension on the Southern Line will cost Yen 80 000 million and is due in service in 1983.

When completed the Karasuma Line will cover 15 km and have a projected capacity of 250 000 passengers daily.

Technical Data:
Projected new lines (in design): 21 km system
Speed (design max): 30 km/h

Rolling Stock:
Car type: proposed
Number of units: 112
Passenger capacity per car (total): 130

Traffic Data:
Passengers carried (weekday): 430 000 (estimated for 1985)

LAHORE

Lahore, Pakistan

General: A preliminary plan for construction of a 6.5 km metro line was proposed in 1977. Preliminary cost is Rs 900 million. The line would link up with a 16 km light rail or electric trolley-bus system now under study.

LENINGRAD

Authority:
Leningradski Metropoliten Imeni V.I. Lenina
Moskovskit Prospekt 28, Leningrad LI3, USSR

Type of system: Full-metro.

General: Over a million use the Metro every working day. Its two busiest stations are Park Pobedy and Moscovskaya in the southern residential districts.
The Leningrad Metro was the second underground system in the USSR. The first line 6.7 miles *(10.8 km)* long from Avtovo in the south to Ploshchad Vosstania was opened in November 1955, and extended to Ploshchad Lenina in June 1958. It connected five main-line stations.
In 1961 the first 3.5 mile *(5.6 km)* section of the Moscovsko-Petrogradskaya was opened, crossing the existing line at Technical Institute and connecting the city's southern district with the right side of the River Neva. In 1963 it was extended north four stations to Petrogradskaya.

Construction began also in 1963 of the Nevsko-Vasiliostrovskaya line and four stations of this line were opened in 1967, in which year the Avtovo-Ploshchad Lenina was extended south to Dachnoe. In 1969 the Moscovsko-Petrogradskaya line was extended south to Moskovskaya Station.
The original underground line, last extended to Ploshchad Lenina in 1958, is being extended considerably in the north and also extended southward. Completed during 1978 was a 5 km section of the Kirov-Vyborg line.
Plans call for an eventual network totalling 240 km. By 1980 a system of 116 km and 72 stations was planned.

Technical Data:
Gauge: 1.524 m
Route length: 45 km
In tunnel: 44.4 km
Projected new lines (in construction): 10+km
(in design): 71 km

Number of lines: 3
Number of stations (total): 29
(in tunnel): 28
Average distance between stations: 1.44 km
Stations:
platform length (minimum): 80 m

Type of tunnel: The line is of deep-level tube construction, and depending on the cambresian clay formation, is at places nearly 200 ft (over *60 m)* below surface level. Each single-track tunnel is of metal and ferro-concrete tube construction and has an internal diameter of 5.1 m.

Gradient (max): 4%
Curvature (max): 400 m
Speed (design max): 65 km/h
(average commercial): 40 km/h
Electric system: Third rail; 825 V

Rolling Stock:

	Diesel	Electric
Car type:		
Car dimensions (length):	18.77 m	18.77 m
(width):	2.70 m	2.70 m
(height):	3.70 m	3.70 m
Passenger capacity		
per car (total):	250	250
(seated):	44	40
Motors per car:	4	4
Rating:	73 kWh	68 kWh
Train composition		
(minimum): 2		
(max): 6		

Acceleration (max):	1.2	1.3
Deceleration (emergency):	1.1	
Brakes (type): Rheostatic/Electro magnetic		
Body material: steel		
Weight (tonnes)		
Motorcar:	36.2	32

Traffic Data:
Trains/track/hour: 30
Train capacity (passengers): 1 500
Total passengers/track/hour (peak): 45 000
Train headways
existing: 2 minutes

Passengers carried (weekday): 1 321 000
(annually): 399 000 000
Average journey length: 6.8 km
Vehicle-km operated annually: 70 100 000

Signalling: Automatic operation of trains is being introduced progressively on the system. On the first line, full automatic control in operation includes programmed traffic interlocking control and automatic train operation.

LILLE

Authority:
Lille Rapid Transit
Lille, France

Type of system: Automated light-rail

General: The French Government finally gave its approval to the construction of the Lille light-rail automated Metro (VAL) system in June 1975. The first line will be 11.5-km long, comprising cut-and-cover and bored tunnel sections in the town centre and viaduct sections east of Helemmes and on the approach to the terminal at the Regional Hospital. Total cost of the project—which is scheduled for completion by 1980/81—will be about Frs 1 200 million.

The VAL system, developed for Lille by Matra, has undergone a number of modifications since trials started on a 1.6-km oval test track at Lille-Est. While it was initially planned to use two-car sets, the system is now to be adapted for eventual introduction of four-car consists made up of two articulated units. Designed to run at 60 s intervals, capacity will be 15 000 passengers an hour.

To meet this requirement, station platforms are to be just over 50 m long and it has been decided to provide three wide double doors on the side of each car instead of four narrow doors. Also modified is the automatic control system which was to have been supervised from a central control cabin. Now that the length of the line is to be increased from the original 8.5 km to 11.5 km, separate control desks are to be located at approximately every 4 km.

Construction on the line has now begun and a preliminary order for six two-car trainsets has been placed with Matra. It is eventually intended to operate up to 50 two-car units on the line.

LISBON

Authority:
Metropolitano de Lisboa SARL (ML)
28 Av Fontes Pereira de Melo, Lisbon 1098, Portugal
Telephone: 57 5457
Telegrams: METROPOLITANO-LISBOA

Type of system: Full-metro

General: The building, owning and operating authority of the Lisbon Metro was a private company, the majority of whose shares were held by the Municipality. The Metro was built between 1955 and 1972 to provide a fast mass transit facility between Lisbon's northern districts and the centre. The first section was opened on 30 December 1959, the extension to the city's commercial centre at Rossio in January 1963 and two extensions, to Anjos and then to Alvalade, in 1966 and 1972 respectively. The metro was nationalised in 1975.

Technical Data:
Gauge: 1.435 m
Route length: 12.0 km
In tunnel: 12.0 km
Projected new lines:
(in design): 7 km
Number of lines: 1 with one branch

Number of stations (total): 20
(in tunnel): 20
Average distance between stations: 630 m
Stations:
platform length (minimum): 40 m (to be lengthened)

Type of tunnel: Arched roof on vertical side walls, and straight or arched inverts. Minimum dimensions on alignments are:—double track 16 ft 3 in *(4.95 m)* high, 24 ft 1½ in *(7.35 m)* wide; single track 14 ft 3 in *(4.35 m)* high, 14 ft 9 in *(4.5 m)* wide.
Built by the cut and cover method, except on a few short sections tunnelled or built by the Belgian method, and on part of the central area where both underpinning of 18th Century buildings and temporary decking under roadways was necessary. Linings are of concrete and, at stations, of reinforced concrete.

Gradient: (max): 4%
Curvature (max): 150 m (100 m exceptionally)
Speed (design max): 60 km/h
(average commercial): 28 km/h
Electric system: Third rail; 750 V dc
Type of rails: 50 kg/m
Welded joints: 18 m lengths

Rolling Stock:

	1959	1970
Car type (year introduced):		
Number of units:	38	32
Car dimensions: (length):	16.4 m	16.5 m
(width):	2.7 m	2.7 m
(height):	3.45 m	—
Passenger capacity		
per car: (total):	200	200
(seated):	36	36
Motors per car:	4	4
Rating:	90 kWh	100 kWh
Train composition:		
(minimum): 2 (weekends)		
(max): 4 (on weekdays)		
Acceleration (max):	0.9	
Deceleration (emergency):	1.2	
Brakes (types): Rheostatic/Pneumatic electro-magnetic		
Body material: Steel		
Weight (tonnes)		
Motorcar:	36.5	—

Traffic Data (1977):
Trains/track/hour: 18.4
Train headways existing: 3 minutes 15 s
Passengers carried (annually): 924 400 000
Average journey length: 3.3 km
Vehicle-km operated annually: 6 800 000

LIVERPOOL

Authority:
British Railways (London Midland Region)
Euston House, London NW1, England

General: The Mersey Railway Company was incorporated in June 1866 to construct a railway tunnel under the river Mersey, but it was not until January 1886 that the line was opened, with steam operation. Electrification was introduced in May 1903. In March 1938, the local Wirral (surface) lines of the London Midland and Scottish Railway were electrified, and through-running between them and the Mersey Railway began. Since 1948, the Mersey Railway has been incorporated in the London Midland Region of the nationalised British Rail system. Through trains to the Wirral run from Liverpool to New Brighton and West Kirby via Birkenhead Park and to Rock Ferry via Birkenhead Central.

The length of the under-river section of the Mersey Railway tunnel between James Street and Hamilton Square is 1 mile 350 yards *(1 930 m)*. The total length of the tunnels, extending from Liverpool Central to Birkenhead Central and Park is 3¼ miles. The line runs from Liverpool (Central) southwestwards under the river to Hamilton Square, on the Birkenhead side, where it splits, one branch running northwestwards to Park, and the other southwards to Rock Ferry. The line is double track throughout.

Current supply on the Mersey Railway is at 650 V dc, and until 1955 (when it was converted to third-rail, as on the Wirral lines), four-rail distribution was used. Trains consist of multiple unit stock. Before its incorporation into British Rail, the Mersey Railway Company owned about 80 cars. The last rolling stock replacement programme was completed in 1957. The Company's system had a route length of 4.8 miles *(7.7 km)*.

On 5 March 1970 the recently-formed Merseyside Passenger Transport Executive agreed that detailed drawings should be made, at a cost of about £240 000, for a new underground railway line for Liverpool. This would form a 2-mile terminal loop running beneath the city centre, connecting at James Street station with the Mersey Railway, and extending the latter to link with Exchange, Lime Street and Central Stations and back to James Street.
Construction work on the Loop scheme started in January 1972, with completion estimated at a cost of approximately £23·6 million. The 5.6 km extension from Walton Junction to Kirkby was completed in 1977 and the 8.8 km extension from Liverpool Central to Garston was completed in 1978. Platforms are designed to accommodate six-car trains. Lime Street underground station is sited under St. George's Plateau with a subway connection to the mainline station.

Including station tunnels, the single track has been formed using Dosco Roadheader machines which are crawler mounted and have a cylindrical cutting head. On the Liverpool side of the Mersey it is between 55 and 124 ft *(16.8 and 37.8 m)* in depth. As part of the project a new burrowing junction at Hamilton Square station, which will eliminate the present double-line junction and allow for greater train frequencies, is approximately 113 ft deep.

A further proposal was for another underground line (the Link scheme) 1⅛ miles long, to extend the Southport and Ormskirk lines from Exchange to Central Station. Trains would then use Moorfields Station enabling Exchange Station to be closed.

As presently envisaged, the system will continue to be operated by British Rail, but the Passenger Transport Executive will be responsible for service frequency and fare structure.

Rail Types and Weights:
In new tunnel section: 113A (56 kg/m) Flat Bottom UIC Class B
In other sections: 113A Flat bottom or as existing

Conductor Rail:
In new tunnel section: 150 lb/yd (74 kg/m)
Elsewhere: 106 lb/150 lb mixture

Sleepers:
In new single bore tunnels: Short lengths, 2 m long concrete. 152 mm thick spaced at 750 centres
Outside tunnels: Standard timber or concrete sleepers for third rail electrified lines
Slab Track: There are 7 130 m lengths of slab track situated in station platform areas, with rail laid in modified cast iron base plates.

Rail Fastenings:
In single bore tunnel: Malleable cast iron shoulders with pandrol clips or pandrol clips in modified base plate

Elsewhere: Timber sleepers with chairs on base plates or concrete sleeper with built-in shoulder.

Signalling: The proposed signalling between Exchange Junction and Brunswick is three aspect colour light with continuous track circuiting and is arranged for a two minute headway service with 30 second station stops. Train stops are to be provided at all running stop signals in the tunnel section.

This signalling, together with the existing signalling, installed in the Sandhills area in December 1973, and at present controlled by Liverpool Exchange No 1 signal box, is to be controlled from a new power signal box at James Street.

Four digit train describers will be provided working to fringe boxes at Kirkdale East, Bootle Junction and Hunts Cross. Telephone services, public address and train indicators will be provided at Sandhills, Moorfields and Central stations and telephones for communications will be provided at all running stop signals.

The proposed signalling for the Liverpool loop section is two aspect colour light, with train stops fitted at all running signals and continuous track circuiting. The signals are designed to cater for a headway of 95 seconds, allowing a station stop of 30 seconds duration.

The scheme will be controlled from the new station box at James Street. Four figure train describers will be provided, working to fringe signal boxes at Birkenhead Park and Birkenhead Central.

Telephone services, public address and train indicators will be provided at all stations.

An emergency telephone circuit will be provided in the tunnels which will enable the train driver to isolate the section of track he is occupying and/or communicate with the Electrical Controller. Telephones for communication to the signalbox will be provided at all running signals.

James Street PSB

	Loop	Link
Route miles	4¾	4
Track miles	7¼	8
Controlled running signals	16	22
Repeater signals	9	11
Automatic signals	15	5
Position light ground signals	4	3
Number of routes	40	41
Number of point ends	12	24

The following "Fringe" signalboxes work to James Street PSB:

Loop	*Link*
Birkenhead Park	Kirkdale East
Birkenhead Central	Bootle Junction
James St (Link)	James St (Loop)
	Hunts Cross West

Main Contractors

	Loop	*Link*
Signalling	ML Engineering (Plymouth) Ltd	(Work to be carried out by BRLM Region)
Telecommunications		
Cables	BICC (Telephone Cables Division) Prescot	BICC (Telephone Cables Division) Prescot
Public Address Equipment	Planned Equipment Ltd, Northolt	Planned Equipment Ltd, Northolt
CCTV	Rediffusion Ltd, Surbiton	Rediffusion Ltd, Surbiton
Train describers	AP Electronics Ltd, Wembley	AP Electronics Ltd, Wembley
Platform Indicators	Telesign Ltd, London	Telesign Ltd, London

LONDON

Authority:
London Transport Executive
55 Broadway, London SW1H 0BD, England
Telephone: 01-222 5600
Telegrams: PASSENGERS-LONDON

Chairman: Ralph Bennett
Deputy Chairman: John Stansby
Managing Director (Railways): W. W. Maxwell

History: On 1 January 1970, the Greater London Council became the statutory planning authority for London, with responsibilities which include the effective integration of its transport, including that of London Transport. The London Transport Executive is responsible for the operation of London Buses and the Underground. During 37 years previous to 1970, all London urban public transport services were under the control of a single Authority, known successively over the period as the London Passenger Transport Board, the London Transport Executive, and latterly the London Transport Board.

The first sub-surface steam railway, opened by the Metropolitan Railway Company on 10 January 1863, was a development of an idea of Charles Pearson, a London City solicitor, who foresaw the possibility of underground travel to overcome the increasing street congestion in the mid-19th Century. The first section of the line opened was nearly four miles in length between Paddington (Bishops Road) and Farringdon Street.

The opening of this railway was followed by another sub-surface enterprise, the Metropolitan District Railway Company which, by the end of 1868, had opened a length of line between Gloucester Road and Westminster, joining up with the Metropolitan Railway which by then had been extended from Edgware Road to South Kensington. By 1871, the Metropolitan District had been extended to Mansion House and by 1876 the Metropolitan to Aldgate. A line joining these stations was opened in 1884 thus completing the railway which became known as the Inner Circle and is today the Circle Line.

These lines were mainly built by the 'cut and cover' method.

The first 'tube' railway in the world was a subway between Tower Hill and Bermondsey through which passengers were carried by a cable-operated car. It was opened in August 1870 but was not a success and after only a few months, the car was withdrawn and the subway converted for pedestrian use until 1896 by which time Tower Bridge was opened.

The first tube railway proper, the City and South London Railway, was opened on 18 December 1890 running from King William Street in the City of London to Stockwell, south of Thames, a distance of three and a quarter miles. This railway employed electricity as its motive power.

The next tube railway, the Central London, popularly known as the "Twopenny Tube", was opened from Shepherd's Bush to the Bank in the centre of the City of London, a distance of nearly six miles, on July 30, 1900. It derived its popular title from the fact that when it first opened a uniform fare of 2d was charged whatever the distance travelled. By 1907, the Baker Street and Waterloo, the Great Northern, Piccadilly and Brompton and the Hampstead tube railways had been added to the map so that in a matter of less than fifty years there had grown from the embryo of the Metropolitan Railway a network of underground railways reaching out to many parts of London and its suburbs.

All these railways were started by individual companies and—except for the Metropolitan—became amalgamated into the Underground group in 1915. The Metropolitan remained a separate company until 1933 when the London Passenger Transport Board was formed.

In 1949, far-reaching plans for the improvement of railway facilities in the London area were put forward which at that time were estimated to cost some £340 million. They proposed the construction of several new tube lines as well as further electrification and improvement works on certain suburban lines of British Railways. However, owing to economic conditions, it was only in the summer of 1955 that powers were sought by the British Transport Commission for the carrying out of the first and most urgently needed of these works. This was a tube known to the planners as "Route C" since named the Victoria Line. Government approval for the construction of the first ten-mile section of this line—linking Victoria and the West End with the main line railway termini at Euston, King's Cross and St. Pancras and with the densely populated north east suburbs of Tottenham and Walthamstow—was given in August, 1962. Within a few weeks construction work had been started and on September 1, 1968 the first section of the line—between Walthamstow Central and Highbury & Islington—was opened for passenger traffic. The second section—from Highbury & Islington to Warren Street came into operation

Royal opening of the Jubilee Line by the Prince of Wales, April 1979

on 1 December, and the third section—through the West End to Victoria—was officially opened by Her Majesty the Queen on 7 March 1969.

The 3½-mile southern extension of the Victoria Line from Victoria to Brixton, on which work started in August 1967, was officially opened by HRH Princess Alexandra on July 23, 1971. Except for Pimlico station, which was opened by the Lord Mayor of Westminster on 14 September 1972, this extension marked the completion of the Victoria Line between Walthamstow and Brixton.

As well as opening up new cross-town and cross-river links, the Victoria Line relieves the heavy strain placed on other Underground lines and eases street congestion. Of the sixteen stations on the Victoria Line—all of which are in tube—fifteen provide interchange facilities with other underground or British Railways lines. Incorporating automatic train operation, automatic ticket issue and control and closed circuit television, the Victoria Line is one of the most highly-automated and technically advanced underground railways in the world.

Work commenced in April 1971 on the construction of the first section of the extension of the Piccadilly Line beyond Hounslow West to Heathrow Airport (for which Parliamentary Powers were obtained in 1967). The first section from Hounslow West to Hatton Cross was opened on 19 July 1975, and the extension to Heathrow Central was opened by Her Majesty the Queen on 16 December 1977. Work commenced in 1972 on the construction of London's new Underground railway, Stage 1 of the Jubilee Line, which was opened by the Prince of Wales on 30 April 1979. The new line takes over the former Stanmore branch of the Bakerloo Line and continues through new tunnels from Baker Street via Bond Street and Green Park to Charing Cross. At Charing Cross the new Underground station embraces the former Strand and Trafalgar Square stations. Parliamentary powers have been obtained for the construction of the second stage from Charing Cross to Fenchurch Street and powers will be sought shortly for a proposed extension through Docklands to Thamesmead.

There are today nine lines making up the London Transport system of Underground railways, these are:

Metropolitan: Covering 55 route miles and serving 61 stations, the Metropolitan is the longest line in the system and is operated in three sections:
Main section: Baker Street (Aldgate in peak hours) to Amersham, with branches to Chesham, Watford and Uxbridge.
Hammersmith and City section: Hammersmith to Whitechapel, with a peak hour extension to Barking.
East London Line: Whitechapel (Shoreditch in peak hours) to New Cross or New Cross Gate.

District: Between Upminster and Ealing Broadway with branches to Richmond, Wimbledon, Edgware Road and Olympia, covers 40 route miles and serves 60 stations.

Circle: The Circle Line is basically a combination of the central sections of the Metropolitan and District lines. Thirteen miles in length and serving 27 stations, it connects most of London's main line railway termini.

Bakerloo: From Elephant & Castle to Stanmore, or Queens Park, with a peak hour extension to Stonebridge Park and Watford Junction, covers 7 miles (21 in peak hours) and serves 16 stations (31 in peak hours).

Central: Ealing or West Ruislip to Hainault or Epping with a branch to Ongar and a loop from Woodford to Hainault. It covers 52 miles and serves 52 stations.

Northern: Morden to Edgware, Mill Hill East or High Barnet via Bank or Charing Cross; serves 40 stations. Within its 36 route miles is the longest continuous railway tunnel in the world—the 17¼ miles from East Finchley to Morden via Bank.

Piccadilly: Cockfosters to Heathrow Central or Uxbridge, with a peak hour shuttle branch from Holborn to Aldwych, covers 40 miles and serves 51 stations.

Victoria: Walthamstow Central to Brixton; serves sixteen stations and is fourteen miles in length.

Jubilee: Stanmore to Charing Cross; serves 17 stations and covers 14 miles.

The first three lines listed above are of the 'cut and cover' or sub-surface type, the other six being tube lines. A seventh tube is the Waterloo & City Line which runs from Waterloo main line station to Bank. This line is owned and operated by The Southern Region of British Rail and has never been part of the London Transport Underground system.

Route length: (January 1979): Served by London Transport trains 255 miles of which 238 miles are administrated by London Transport, the remainder being British Rail lines over which London Transport trains run. Of the whole system, 98 route miles are underground, 77 miles in small-diameter deep-level tube tunnels, and 21 miles in sub-surface tunnels of larger section.

Rolling Stock: Broadly speaking there are two types of Underground rolling stock—'surface' and 'tube', the first identifying the stock on the Metropolitan, District and Circle lines (the tunnels on which are of the 'cut and cover' type) which is larger than the stock on the 'tube' lines. All Underground cars are of the saloon type with seating for 32-40 passengers (54-58 in the Metropolitan Line stock) and standing room for about 100. The length of trains is mainly six, seven or eight cars, although shorter units of four cars are used in off-peak hours on the Metropolitan Main Line and all day on certain sections. In the peak hours so intense is the service that trains run at intervals as short as 90-120 seconds in the central area and the average length of time a train stops at a station is only 20-25 seconds. High speed trains are not generally practicable because of the frequency of the service and the short distance between stations, but acceleration is high; 20 mph is reached in about 15 seconds (10 seconds on the Victoria Line and slightly less on the H & C and Circle Stock) and 40 mph in the open in about one minute. On the Metropolitan Main Line, some trains cover quite long distances between stops, and speeds of 60 mph are sustained over a number of sections.

All cars are fitted with air-operated sliding doors, which, except on automatically-driven trains, are under the control of the guard. A 'pilot light' is illuminated when all doors are closed and not until he gets this light can the guard give the bell signal for the driver to start. On the automatically-driven trains of the Victoria Line and the Woodford-Hainault section of the Central Line, which have no guard, the pilot light is situated in the driving cab and the starting and door circuits are inter-locked to ensure that a train cannot start unless the doors are closed.

Railway cars with light alloys instead of steel in body construction have been in use since 1952, the reduced weight affecting a substantial saving in running costs. The first of these trains, on the District Line, was painted red to match the rest of the fleet, but subsequent light alloy stock has been left unpainted and, for uniformity, those which were painted red have now been painted silver. All the Metropolitan, Central, Circle, Piccadilly, Victoria, Northern Line and Jubliee trains are composed of unpainted aluminium stock although some types have painted doors or panels to provide a splash of colour.

Although the Victoria Line trains were the first to be designed and built for automatic operation on the Underground, four trains, specially converted, have been driven automatically on the Woodford-Hainault branch of the Central Line since 1964. Delivery was completed in 1971 of new unpainted aluminium 'surface' stock for the Circle and Hammersmith and City Lines. Although the stock is initially for two-man operation, conversion to one-man operation can be undertaken by means of minor modifications. Thirty new trains ordered for the Northern Line entered service in the summer of 1972 and delivery was completed in the first part of 1973. These are similar to those on the Victoria Line, but have a two-man crew, as the layout of stations on the Northern Line makes the future conversion of the line to ATO (with consequential one-man operation) difficult. A second batch of 33 similar trains (known as 1972 Mk 11 Stock) originally ran on the Northern Line but now operate on Stage 1 of the new Jubilee Line. New Stock (1973 Stock) is now operating on the Piccadilly Line and the displaced stock has been transferred to the Northern Line. The new 6-car Piccadilly line trains feature a new electrical braking system and more space for luggage.

New trains, designated D78 stock, were ordered for the District line. They feature passenger-activated doors; the crew retains overall control, but doors only open on demand. This helps to keep trains warm in outlying sections where passenger traffic is small.

Maintenance: Repairs and day-to-day maintenance of Underground trains are carried out at rolling stock depots and car sheds. There are twelve passenger depots, basically two per line except that Hammersmith Depot caters for the Hammersmith and City and Circle Lines and Neasden deals with two lines—the Metropolitan and The Jubilee. A new depot for Bakerloo trains has recently been built at Stonebridge Park. There is one depot—at Northumberland Park—for the Victoria Line. There are also a number of minor depots at some of which minor repairs and inspections are carried out—for example New Cross for the East London Line.

All major overhauls are carried out at Acton Works, the older rolling stock being overhauled every five years and the newer at varying periods up to 10 years.

Trains operate daily from 05.00 to 01.00 hours and it is only during the intervening four hours that maintenance of tracks and signals can be carried out. In this comparatively short period every yard of tunnel is inspected.

Signalling: The signalling on the Underground has two vital functions to perform: to ensure complete safety of operation and to enable maximum possible use to be made of the available line capacity. It is based on a system of track circuiting whereby individual sections of track are isolated from each other electrically. The passage of each train over one section automatically sets the coloured light signals behind it at danger, the signals clearing automatically once the train has proceeded a safe distance. All sections of the Underground which are free of junctions are automatically signalled in this way. A safety device, known as the 'trainstop', is installed to halt a train automatically should it pass a signal at danger.

The signalling of junctions is semi-automatic but under the supervision of a signalman; again special safety interlocking devices are fitted to guard against any element of human error. The gradual development of a system of 'route control signalling'—under which one manual act in the signal cabin clears the signals and sets the points for a complete route—and remote control have enabled cabins to control train movements over much wider areas.

On London Transport railways, 'programme machines' are employed—a system pioneered by London Transport in the fifties which automatically signals a complete day's train service. This is done by means of a plastic roll, with coded information about each train's origin, destination, route and time, passing through a machine which sets the signals and points for each train in the timetable.

Programme machine signalling, which needs no human intervention unless the service is seriously dislocated, is now installed on the Northern and parts of other Underground lines and is the basis of junction signalling on the Victoria Line, where the safety signalling is otherwise carried out by a system of coded impulses in the rail.

Automatic Train Operation: The system of automatic train operation employed on the Victoria Line was designed and developed by London Transport. Following initial tests on a short section of the District Line in 1962, full-scale trials were started in 1964 on the Woodford-Hainault branch of the Central Line using four specially converted trains, the branch being worked as a self-contained automatic railway.

Each train responds to safety codes which are transmitted through the running rails and high frequency driving commands that are injected at predetermined intervals on short sections of the track, these signals are picked up by coils mounted in front of the leading wheels. The train cannot run unless safety code is being picked up and these codes ensure that the speed of the train is being controlled to keep it a safe distance from the train in front. If this safety factor is infringed for any reason, the safety codes will automatically stop the train.

The driving commands control the motors and brakes so that the train, once the Train Operator has pressed the twin starting buttons, will accelerate, coast and brake to a stop in the right position at the next station without further intervention from the Operator. They will also cause the train to observe any speed restrictions and to stop and restart as required by the traffic conditions on the way.

The Victoria Line employs no signalmen, all junctions are set automatically by a programme machine and the whole line is supervised from one central control point at Euston.

Power Supply: The electric power for operating the Underground services today comes mainly from London Transport's own generating stations at Lots Road (Chelsea), and Greenwich. In addition, a bulk supply is taken from the Central Electricity Generating Board at Neasden, Heathway and Old Oak Common to feed sections of the surface lines in those areas, leaving Lots Road and Greenwich generating stations to supply power to the deep level tubes, and certain other areas.

The modernisation and re-equipment of Lots Road Generating station, to convert it from coal-fired to oil-fired boilers was completed at the end of 1968, and modernisation of Greenwich, the smaller of the two stations, was completed in December 1972; the coal-fired boilers, and steam driven turbo-alternators previously installed have now been replaced by eight turbo-alternators each driven by the exhaust gas of a Rolls Royce 'Avon' jet engine, to produce the electrical power. Greenwich is remotely-controlled from Lots Road and operates in parallel with Lots Road through a 22 kV cable distribution network. Only 20 to 25 staff are needed to operate the station compared with about 350 staff previously employed. The two generating stations, which have a total installed capacity of 298 megawatts, have been converted to use natural gas as an alternative to oil if desired. It is intended that natural gas will normally be used as it should be cheaper and reduce atmospheric pollution, but the ability to use either fuel will give greater flexibility and enable the electricity supply for about 70 per cent of the Underground system to be maintained even if the supply of one of these fuels is interrupted.

Lifts and Escalators: 270 escalators with capacities to move 9 000 passengers an hour in either direction and travelling speeds of 90 to 145 ft a minute are installed at 71 stations. The longest is at Leicester Square and has a vertical rise of 80 ft 9 in.

There are 68 station passenger lifts in service at 25 stations, the average rise being 68 ft and the longest 181 ft at Hampstead. The majority of these lifts travel at 180 ft per minute with a maximum load of 50 passengers in the car, but in more recent years a number of high speed lifts with modern equipment have been installed at Goodge Street, Hampstead and Queensway. These travel at speeds varying between 300 ft and 800 ft per minute according to the rise and are arranged for completely automatic control, no lift operator being required, although provision is made for operator control if traffic conditions require this. Automatic control has also been added to some of the older lifts.

Fare Collection: Modern 'self-service' coin operated machines which print, cut and issue a ticket in three seconds are provided for the convenience of passengers.

On the Victoria Line a system of automatic fare collection operates.

The system has been developed as a deterrent to fraudulent travel and to reduce costs. Passengers entering Underground stations have their tickets checked by automatic gates in the booking halls. Two types are being used—the four-door and the tripod gates. They are operated by yellow tickets with magnetic oxide backing—like that of a recording tape—on which journey details are magnetically encoded. When a passenger inserts his ticket into a slot in the gate these details are "read" by electronic equipment, and the doors open or the tripod arm is released if the ticket is valid. Both types of gate return tickets to ingoing passengers. All passengers leaving stations at present use ticket collectors' barriers, but London Transport has proposed a completely closed system, with a check on all tickets both entering and leaving the system. The proposed system will be able to handle all tickets, including seasons, and will be compatible with a system being developed by British Rail, so that through tickets will also be accepted.

Station Car Parks: At a number of suburban stations, London Transport provides car parking facilities for its railway passengers and has been engaged on a programme of expansion in this field by providing completely new parks at certain stations and by extending existing ones. At present nearly 11 500 car spaces are provided at 66 stations.

Tunnel Cooling and Draught Relief: More than 100 fans handling nearly 2 400 m/s of air per second, are in operation on the system. This means the temperature underground is kept at an annual average in the region of 23°C. (73°F).

To reduce draughts created by movement of trains in the tube tunnels, special relief shafts are provided at some 31 stations to bypass some of the 'train-moved' air from the escalator shafts and passageways, directly to the open air.

The Victoria Line is equipped with 16 fans handling 531 m^3 of air per second with draught relief at every station. The average annual temperature on this line does not exceed 21°C. (70°F).

Radio and Television Communications: A closed-circuit television system is installed throughout the Victoria Line. Cameras located on platforms and at other key points in stations transmit pictures to station operations rooms and to the line's control centre at Cobourg Street, Euston, enabling the control staff to see what conditions are like at any time and to take any action that may be necessary. A two-way sound system enables the staff to hear as well as see what is going on and to make announcements over the public address systems. Coupled with this equipment at certain stations, are push-button enquiry booths, provided to enable passengers to obtain travel information from the operations room.

Closed-circuit television has been introduced at a number of other stations to combat hooliganism.

By means of a carrier wave system fed through the current rails the staff at Cobourg Street can speak to any train operator, whether or not the train is moving. Similar systems, using radio, are being developed on other lines. On all modern rolling stock, the train operator can make announcements to passengers on the train through loudspeakers in each car.

Urban structure:
Population of city area: 6 970 000
Land area: 630 square miles
Number of automobiles registered in city: 1 660 000 (1970); 1 794 000 (1978)

Technical Data:
Gauge: Standard
Route length: 255 miles (run over); 238 miles (owned)
Track length: 662 (track milegage owned)
In tunnel: Cut and cover 21 miles, tube 77 miles, total 98 miles
Number of lines in operation: Nine
Number of stations (total): 278 (served), 249 (managed)
Speed (design max): 60 mph (100 km/h)
(average commercial): 20.4 mph (32.8 km/h)
Type of rails: *Running rail:* 47 kg/m BH, 54 kg/m FB. *Conductor rail:* Open and sub surface: 74 kg/m FB, 53 kg/m FB. Tube tunnel: 64 kg/m rectangular
Type of tunnel: Tube, cut and cover
Method and voltage of current supply: 600V dc, 4 rail

Traffic and finances:
Max number of trains per hour (one way): 33
Passenger journeys per annum: 569 000 000 (1978)

Rolling stock characteristics:
Number of units: 2 843 motor cars, 1 380 trailers
Number of doors per side: Conventional: 2 double & 1 single on cars with driving positions; 2 double & 2 single on others. A stock: 3 double; C stock: 4 double; D stock: 4 single
Door width (m): Single 0.7 m, double 1.4 m, single 1.1 m (D stock)
Motor rating (kWh): 1978 tube and D78: 50
C69/77: 68
1967 and 1972 tube: 53
A stock: 52
1938 tube: 72
Power per train (minimum): 723 kW: 7 cars, 1938 tube stock.
(max): 847 kW: 7 cars, 1972 tube stock
Acceleration (max): 1.16 m/s^2, 1973 tube stock
Deceleration (normal service): 1.0 m/s^2
(emergency): 1.34 m/s^2
Max design speed: 60 mph (96.6 km/h)
Bogies: Riveted steel plate frame with aluminium headstocks from 1967 tube stock onwards. D78 has welded box section H configuration
Distance between bogie pivot: Conventional tube 33 ft. 1973 tube: 11.12 m. Conventional surface 36 ft. D78: 11.88 m
Brakes (type): Friction tread using two composite blocks per wheel controlled by electro-pneumatic valves with mercury switch retardation control. From 1967 onwards additional rheostatic braking on motor cars and brake blocks reduced to one per wheel on all cars. All with Westinghouse pneumatic emergency brake.
1973 tube stock and D78 has Westcode air brake and rheostatic braking with load weighting. Emergency brake is electrically controlled 'energised to release'. All brake blocks are operated by individual brake units without rigging.

LOS ANGELES
Southern California Rapid Transit District
Los Angeles, California, USA

In December 1976, UMTA committed funds for the Southern California Rapid Transit District to proceed with refinement of plans for a 246 km rapid transit starter segment. A decision was awaited at the end of 1978 on a planned Starter transit rail line from central Los Angeles

to North Hollywood. Alternative routes vary from 12.8 to 25.6 km.

The District is committed to the development of a high-capacity modern rapid transit system while improving and expanding existing bus services—the backbone for a future rapid transit feeder network.

On 23 July 1973, the RTD Board of Directors received the Consultants' Recommendations for a rapid transit system in the Los Angeles Basin. At that time, the Board

directed District staff to take the report to the field and elicit public response.

The aforementioned effort is exclusive of the El Monte Busway Project, the first seven miles of which went into operation in January 1973. The 11-mile route, which takes railroad rights of way as well as central and side strips of the highway route, will permit a trip of 18 minutes, less than half that of the corresponding automobile trip.

LYON
Authority:
Société d'Economie Mixte du Metropolitain de l'Agglomération Lyonnaise (SEMALY)
25 cours Emile Zola, 69100 Villeurbanne, France

Director General: René Waldman

Type of system: Full-metro.

General: The city of Lyon is completing construction of a new 11.4 km Metro system and extending the existing rack railway. SEMALY was set up to prepare a city transport programme for the years up to 1985. SEMALY's plan, first published in 1970 and given Government backing in 1971, calls for immediate construction of two rubber-tyred Metro routes—Lines A and B—and an 0.3 km extension to the existing 0.6 km rack railway. By April 1975 a 1.6 km section of line A between the new workshop depot and Cusset was completed and tests had begun with a prototype two-car trainset built by Alsthom. The complete initial system opened for commercial operation in 1978.

First line section (9.4 km—with 8 km running underground) from Perrache station (the interchange with French National suburban and intercity trains) to the city outskirts in the east opened in 1978. There are 13 stations, with Charpennes providing interchange with Line B. The entire 1.4 km Line B (with three stations) is constructed underground.

Cut-and-cover construction is being used for both lines—a method made necessary by the poor soil conditions and exceptionally high water table, says SEMALY.

Phase two of the Metro programme called for construction to start on a 2.5 km extension of Line B at a cost of Fr 295 million. Phase three is to be started with work on projected Line D which will connect with Line B. Completion of this line is due in 1985. No date has yet been given for commencement of the final stage of construction which calls for a 9 km extension to Line D and 3 km extension to line A, giving a complete system totalling 50 km with 57 stations.

Technical Data:
Gauge: 1.995/1.435 m (rubber/steel)
Projected new lines:
(in construction): 9.2 all in tunnel
(in design): 30.8 all in tunnel
Number of lines: 4
Number of stations:
(total): 16
(in tunnel): 15
Stations:
platform length (minimum): 70 m
(max): 100 m
Gradient (max): 7%
Curvature (max): 150 m

Alsthom trainset standing at Foch station

Speed (design max): 90 km/h
(average commercial): 30 km/h
Electric system: Two-side guide bar; 750 V
Welded joints: Yes

Rolling Stock:
Car type (year introduced):

	1975 (proto-type)	1977 (motor cars)	(trailers)
Number of units:	—	42	21
Car dimensions:			
(length):	16.5 m	17.9 m	18.6 m
(width):	2.9 m	2.9 m	2.9 m
(height):	3.2 m	3.4 m	3.4 m

		M	R
Passenger capacity			
per car (total):	—	126	132
(seated):	50	52	56
Rating:	—	2	4
Train composition			
(minimum):	3	2	2
Acceleration			
(max):	1.3	1.2	—
Deceleration			
(emergency):	2.6	1.6	—

Traffic Data:
Trains/track/hour (planned): 20
Total passengers/track/hour (peak): 7 700
Train headways design: 1.5 minutes

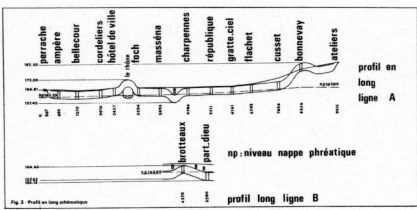

Profiles of Lines A and B

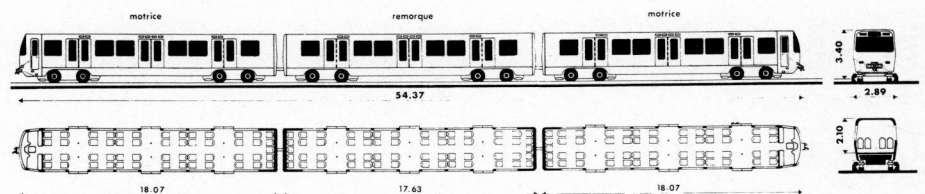

Line drawing of the new Alsthom trainset

MADRID
Authority:
Cia. Metropolitano de Madrid
Cavanilles, 58, Madrid 7, Spain
Telephone: (01) 252 49 00

Type of system: Full-metro

Chairman: Carlos Mendoza
Delegate Director: Juan Torres Piñon
Manager: Adolfo Pool
Schemes and Planning: Javier Valero
Rolling Stock: Ricardo Tejero

History: Madrid's growth in recent years has been largely due to a consistently planned expansion of its Metro network, facilitating urban travel and encouraging the growth of industry. To meet transportation needs the city expects then to be served by a 100 km network of Metro lines (besides suburban lines). The Metro was first opened in 1919 with a line from Sol at the centre northwards to Caminos. There have been regular additions and extensions to the system since

Exterior of new type 5000 two-car trainset built by CAF-Wesa equipped with MTE-supplied Sumiride air suspension bogies, Krupp-Bochum resilient wheels and 210 kW fully-suspended Jeumont motors. Electrical power regulator is by AEG; air brakes by Knorr

Interior of the new type 5000 car able to seat 80 passengers; crush capacity is 360 standing plus 80 seated

then, and at the time of writing, known extensions under construction total 12.3 miles *(19.8 km)* of route.
General: Two new line extensions were opened in 1977, extending the 60 km system length by 5 km. Now under construction is a 2-km extension to existing Line 4 and a 3-km extension to Line 5. First section of the new Line 6 between C. Caminos and Pacifico was opened in 1977 and the entire line to Oporto was in operation by 1978. Line 9 between Herrera Oria and Pavones was opened in 1978 and line 8 between Fuencarral and Ministerios in 1979.
Construction of 35 km of new lines and extensions is expected. Completion of a total network comprising 130 km was authorised by the government for construction by 1985.

Route length: Metro: 66 km with 54.9 km in tunnel.
Number of lines: 5 Metro, 1 Suburban (4 transverse and 2 radial), double track.
Number of stations served: 90; 85 underground.
Average station spacing: 550 m.
Passengers per annum: 547 000 000.

Average length of journey: 5.2 km.
Car km per annum: 60 800 000.
Number of cars per train: 6 on Lines 1 and 6; 4 on Lines 2, 3 and 4; 3 on Suburban.
Track gauge: 4 ft 8⅞ in *(1.445 m).*
Weight and type of rails: 90.9 lb per yd *(45 kg/m),* flat-bottomed; laid in 18 m lengths on oak sleepers, with quartz ballast.
Max gradient: 1 in 20 (5%).
Minimum radius of curves: 295 ft *(90 m).*
Type of tunnel: Double track tunnel 22 ft 6 in *(6.86 m)* wide. The height above rail level is 14 ft 7 in *(4.45 m)* on sections of cut-and-cover construction and 15 ft 5 in *(4.70 m)* on sections tunnelled by the Belgian (gallery) method. Tunnel linings are of concrete, masonry or brick.
Method and voltage of current supply: Overhead wire, with collection trolleys on the car roofs. 600 V dc (transformed by 9 sub-stations from the three-phase 15 000-V supply of the public grid).
Signalling: Automatic block, with ac track circuits and colour-light signals. There are electric interlocking

installations at Goya, Sol, and Cuatro Caminos stations. Lines 3 and 5 have centralised traffic control (CTC) and Line 5 automatic train control (ATC) with cab signals.

Station layout: Some stations have separate side platforms, 197 ft *(60 m)* long, in a single elliptical station tunnel 45 ft 11 in *(14 m)* wide. The platforms themselves are 13 ft 1 in *(4 m)* wide at main stations, and 9 ft 10 in *(3 m)* wide at others. Terminal and junction stations have additional platforms.
Sub-surface ticket halls are favoured, with stairwell entrances at street corners. The most important individual station is Sol (Puerto del Sol), where three lines cross. There is a large central sub-surface ticket-hall and concourse, with pedestrian subways to and between the three lines.

Workshops: The main workshops and depot facilities are at Cuatro Caminos. At Ventas, Aluche and P. de Castilla there are smaller workshops and depot facilities, and at Arguelles and Moncloa there are underground depots.

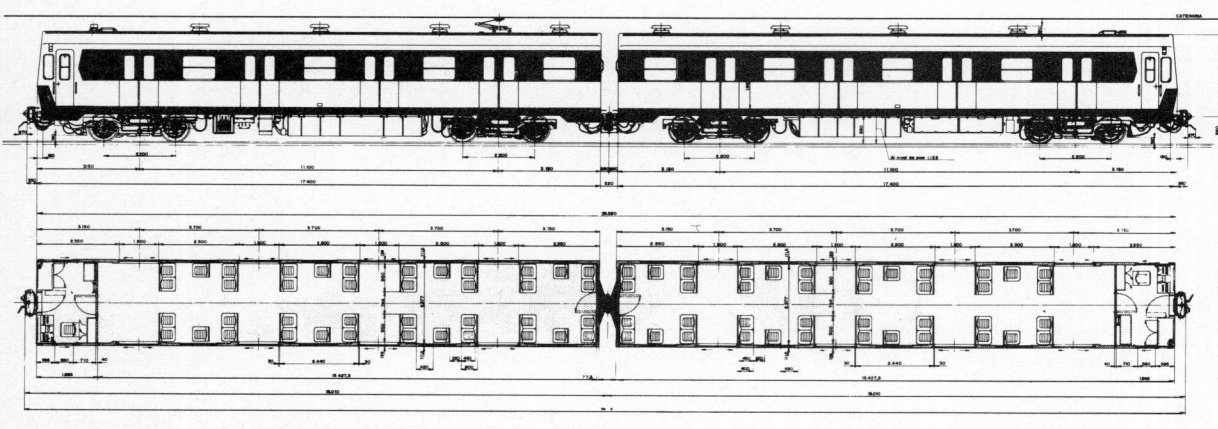

General arrangement drawing of the type 5000 trainset

Length over carbody 35 320 mm; Width 2 800 mm; Height rail to floor 1 125 mm; Empty weight 64 000 kg; Gross weight 100 000 kg; Inside width 2 577 mm; Headroom, centre aisle 2 182 mm; Width, centre aisle 724 mm; Doorway width 1 200 mm; Doorway height 1 900 mm.

MANCHESTER
Authority:
Greater Manchester Passenger Transport Executive
PTE Peterhouse, Oxford Street, Manchester M1 5AW, England
Telephone: 061-236 4707
Telegrams: CIVICBUSES-MANCHESTER

Type of system: Metro link line

General: Greater Manchester Passenger Transport Executive is responsible on behalf of the Metropolitan County of Greater Manchester for promotion and operation of an efficient public passenger transport service within the county.
GMPTE's Long Term Plan for Transport in the conurbation has as its objective development of an integrated bus/rail public transport system which will be able to compete with the private car.
The Picc/Vic Tunnel Scheme is Stage 1 of the Long Term Plan. It provides a tunnel with five central area stations to bring people into the commercial heart of the City. Associated works involve up-grading the rail network to link four services in the south of the city with two in the north.
In December 1974 the DoE indicated that at the time the scheme could not be financed and would have to be deferred. It was, therefore, decided that Greater Manchester Council, DoE and BR should co-operate in

developing a package of rail up-gradings compatible with future provision of a tunnel. The package which was developed concentrated on up-grading the Northern Radial Lines, being those routes in the conurbation in most urgent need of attention. The object was to provide a cross-conurbation electric service affecting three main radial routes centring on two northern Manchester stations, Victoria and Salford. Bus/rail interchange was planned at several locations. However, further announcements indicated that there is no prospect of investment on the scale required for Picc/Vic for some years.
The PTE assisted by BR have, therefore, developed a package of rail improvements to be carried out. The aim has been to spread the investment to give benefits to each area of the conurbation. DoE are encouraging the provision of park-and-ride and bus/rail interchange facilities at selected locations; the main objective being to significantly increase rail passengers over the next five years. It has been accepted that the provision of new stations and track and signalling alterations to improve capacity is compatible with the overall policy.
Greater Manchester have not abandoned their Long Term Plan for Transport although it now appears that major investment may not be forthcoming for up to ten years. All works being carried out to suburban railways within the conurbation have the long term plan in mind and, as far as possible, are compatible with eventual implementation of the Picc/Vic scheme.

Technical Data:
Gauge: 1.435 m
Projected new lines (in design): 17.7 km
Number of lines: 1
Number of stations (total): 15
Electric system: Third rail; 750 V
Type of rails: 113 lb/yd

Rolling Stock:
Car type: Proposed
Number of units: two-car sets
Car dimensions (length): 23.3 m
(width): 3.05 m
(height): 3.66 m
Passenger capacity per car:
(total): 200
(seated): 80
Motors per car: 4
Train composition (minimum): 2
(max): 6
Acceleration (max): 1.3
Deceleration (emergency): 1.6
Weight (tonnes) Motorcar: 29.0

Traffic Data:
Train capacity (passengers): 800 (planned)
Total passengers/track/hour (peak): 24 000 (planned)
Train headways design: 1.5 minutes

MARSEILLE
Authority:
Ville de Marseille RATVM
6 rue Sénac, 13001 Marseille, France

President, Administration: Mr Lauga, Mr Perrot

Type of system: Rubber-tyred metro.

General: Operations began in November 1977 on Marseille's first 6 km section of the new 9 km Metro line on a route running beneath the city centre to the north-east suburbs. Construction comprised 6 km of tunnelling, a 690 m viaduct at the north-east terminal of the line, 1 300 m of track running on the median strip of a new motorway, and 800 m of open cutting. A prototype three-car trainset was delivered in July 1976 with bodies by CIMT, bogies by ANF, motors by STCO and electrical equipment by MTE. Capacity of the set under normal load will be 352 passengers, with 136 seated. By the addition of a fourth car the capacity could be increased to 472 passengers with 184 seated. Overall length of the three car set is 49.070 m, width 2.6 m,

height above rail 3.55m, tare weight about 70 tonnes. Installed power for the three-car set is 1 400 kW giving a top speed of 80 km/h and an acceleration on the level of 1.3 m/s². At the start of operations, 21 three-car sets had been delivered.

Urban structure:
Population of city area: 1 100 000
Land area: 299 km²

Technical Data:
New lines (under construction): 1
Number of lines in operation: 1
Number of stations (total): 12
Number of stations in tunnel: 9
Average distance between stations: 820 m
Max length of station platform: 70 m
Gradient (max): 5.5%
Curvature (min): 150 m
Speed (design max): 65 km/h
(average commercial): 32 km/h
Method and voltage of current supply: 750 V

Two Marseille trainsets from CIMT of France

Traffic and Finances:
Max number of trains per hour (one way): 16
Frequency of train services in minutes (currently): 3/7 (11 in evening)
Capacity per train (passengers seated): 136 (passengers standing): 216
Passenger journeys per annum: 57 000 (1978), 74 400 (1979)

Rolling Stock Characteristics:

	Motor cars Type A	Trailers Type A
Car types:		
Number of units:	42	21
Car dimensions:		
Length (m):	16.20	15.3
Width (m):	2.60	2.60
Height (m):	27.6	20.5
Total floor area:	29 m²	30 m²
Number of doors per side:	3	3
Door width (m):	1.30	1.30
Number of passengers per car		
(total):	116	120
(seated):	44	48
Motors per car:	4	

Acceleration (max): 1.3 m/s²
Deceleration (normal service): 1 m/s²
(emergency): 1.2 to 1.5 m/s²
Max design speed:
Bogies: Motored with pneumatic suspension.
Distance between bogie pivot: 11 m
Brakes (type): Air brakes, electric brakes
Weight (empty in tonnes): 7.5 (motor cars);
4.5 (trailers)

MELBOURNE

Authority:
City Transit Office
Melbourne, Australia

General: Melbourne (Victoria) transport facilities comprise an electric railway system and a network of roads on which trams, buses, private cars and commercial vehicles compete with one another for right of way. The railway system makes a major contribution to the transportation needs of the commuters of this metropolis

Planning provides for duplication of existing single track sections, the construction of a third track or double track sections and the provision of four tracks on the inner sections of heavy traffic lines, together with improved signalling throughout the system.

The increased route capacity resulting from these works will mean an increase in the number of peak hour trains arriving and departing the central terminal, Flinders Street Station, where additional capacity must likewise be provided. Provision must also be made to relieve the increasing commuter congestion at Flinders Street Station.

This will be relieved by the building of the Underground Loop and dispensing the city's work force through a number of stations around the central business district instead of concentrating them at one. Linking these stations to the existing rail tracks to form a loop will improve the train capacity of Flinders Street Station.

The underground will comprise four single track tunnels connecting with the four major groups of suburban lines as follows:
1. The Eastern group, passing through Burnley;
2. The South-eastern group, passing through Caulfield;
3. The North-eastern group, passing through Clifton Hill;
4. The Northern and Western groups, passing through North Melbourne.

There will be three new city stations on the underground part of the system and all the trains passing round the loops will also pass through Flinders and Spencer Street stations, so that passengers will have the choice of five stations in the city area. In order to operate the loop trains in the direction of the predominant traffic flow in each peak period, signalling will be reversible. Each of the loops will have an effective capacity of 24 trains an hour and, in addition to the loop trains, at least another 60 trains an hour will, as a result of overall improvements to the suburban system, be able to operate to and from Flinders Street station. It is estimated that a total comfortable capacity of 130 000 passengers an hour will be reached. The modern seven-car suburban train has a comfortable capacity of 850 and a peak load capacity of 1 300 passengers.

The Metropolitan Planning Authority estimates that when the city's population reaches 3 700 000 in 1985, from its present figure of just over 2 250 000, planned improvements to the rail system will be adequate to meet the maximum forseeable demands made upon them. It is also anticipated that the new underground loop will attract more passengers to the suburban railway system and so reduce road congestion.

Work under way at Parliament underground station

In 1970, the Melbourne Underground Rail Loop Authority was constituted by Act of Parliament to finance and build the Underground Rail Loop. The first 'sod' of this multi-million project was turned by the Minister of Transport, the Honorable Vernon Wilcox, on 22 June 1971, and work on building access tunnels, under-passes and ramps for the four line tunnels is progressing.

By 1980 the loop was expected to link up with Victorian Railway's urban electric rail system through the two central terminal stations at Spencer Street and Flinders Street.

MEXICO CITY

Authority:
Sistema de Transporte Colectivo (STC)
Delicias 67, Mexico 1, DF, Mexico
Telephone: 521 86 20

Type of system: Rubber-tyred metro

General: The Mexico City Metro system is closely modelled on the Paris Metro, its architecture and pneumatic-tyred rolling stock particularly reflecting French influence. The latter country's interest extended to a 15-year loan to assist construction, besides consultancy as to its construction. The Metro operates under a computerised electronic system of traffic control.

While work continues on extending the Mexico City Metro, the Mexican National Railways has completed studies on a new suburban rapid transit system calling for construction of six new lines. The aim of the plan is to encourage development of nearby towns and relieve the population strain on the metropolitan area. Line 1 would run from San Lazaro in the eastern part of the city southeast to Los Reyes (17 km), and could eventually be extended north to Texcoco and south to Chalco. Line 2 would connect Tacuda with Tlanepantla (9 km), and could be continued on to Zumpango—proposed future site for a new international airport. Line 3 would run from La Villa de Guadalupe east to Ecatepec (19 km), and could be extended to Teotihuacan. Line 4 would run along the Periferico (95 km), using two lanes of the existing freeway for the double-track line. Line 5 is planned as a suburban link between the Benito Juarez international airport and the projected new one at Zumpango (45 km). Line 6 would run from Calzada Ignacio Zaragoza to Texcoco (26 km).

Technical Data:
Gauge: 1.995/1.435 m (rubber/steel)
Route length: 40 km
In tunnel: 30.9 km
Projected new lines (in design): 45 km
Number of lines: 3
Number of stations (total): 48
(in tunnel): 37
Average distance between stations: 830 m
Stations:
platform length (minimum): 150 m
Gradient (max): 7%
Curvature (max): 105 m
Speed (design max): 80 km/h
(average commercial): 34.6 km/h
Electric system: Two-side guide bar; 750 V
Type of rails: 35 kg/m

Rolling Stock:	Motors	Trailers
Car dimensions (length):	17.2 m	16.2 m
(width):	2.5 m	2.5 m
(height):	3.7 m	3.7 m
Passenger capacity per car		
(total):	162	165
(seated):	38	39
Motors per car:	4	
Rating:	110 kW	
Train composition (minimum):	6	
(max): 9		
Acceleration (max): 1.35		
Deceleration (emergency): 2.25		
Brakes (type): Rheostatic/pneumatic		
Weight (tonnes) Motorcar: 24.6		
Trailer: 16.9		

Traffic Data:
Trains/track/hour: 20
Train capacity (passengers): 1 530
Total passengers/track/hour (peak): 30 600
Train headways
design: 1.5 minutes
existing: 3 minutes
Passengers carried (weekday): 1 200 000
(annually): 390 000 000
Average journey length: 7.6 km
Vehicle-km operated annually: 60 800 000

MILAN

Authority:
Azienda Trasporti Municipali
Foro Buonaparte 61, 20121 Milan, Italy

General: The system is designed for operation by one man for each train (driver) and one man for each station, who controls the entry barriers of passengers and, by means of TV, the platforms at the lower floor. Four extensions of the two existing lines are under construction:
Line 1 (red line): QT8 to S Leonardo (3.3 km, 4 stations), crossing a large residential neighbourhood (Gallaratese).

Line 2 (green line): Cascina Gobba to Bettolino (3.4 km, 3 stations), reaching large residential areas outside Milan and crossing the eastern motorway by-pass; Gorgonzola to Villa Fornaci (2.9 km, 2 stations) reaching an important road junction in the east of Milan; Cadorna to Stazione Genova of the National Railways (1.9 km, 3 stations).

In 1979 the Milan Municipal Administration passed the new Transport Plan for the city, envisaging a further development of the underground network.

New extensions of the two existing lines are envisaged:

Line 1: S Leonardo to Molino Dorino, at the north-western end of the line (0.9 km, 1 station); Inganni to

Line 2: Stazione Genova FS to Romolo (1.2 km, 1 station) to realise a multi-mode interchange area (railways, bus lines, cars) to serve the main lines entering Milan from the south-east.

The Transport Plan also envisages the construction of the third underground line (yellow line) (8.1 km, 13 stations), running north-south from Rogoredo to the Central Station FS, and a system of interchange parking areas along every line. These parking areas are to

Bisceglie, at the south-western end of the line (0.8 km, 1 station); Sesto Marelli to Sesto S Giovanni, FS station (2.2 km, 2 stations) to realise an interchange point with the railway main lines from Chiasso, Sondrio and Bergamo.

be built chiefly in peripheral areas, near to the terminal stations.

Metro route length: Line 1, 8.8 miles *(16.9 km)* all in tunnel; Line 2, 13.85 miles *(22.3 km)* of which 4.85 miles *(7.8 km)* is in tunnel.
Number of lines: 2 transverse, double track, with branch.
Number of stations: 50.
Average station spacing: 0.38 miles *(0.61 km)*, (Line 1). 0.52 miles *(0.83 km)* (Line 2).
Passengers per annum: (1976) 151 500 000; (1977) 153 000 000; (1978): 174 400 000.
Passengers per annum carried by the whole system of Azienda Trasporti Municipali (includes metro, trams, buses, trolleybuses and ATM suburban services): (1978): 528 000 000.
Max number of cars per train: 6.
Average total places: 206 in motor cars, 228 in trailers, seats vary from 27 to 46.
Average schedule speed: 18.6 mph *(30 km/h)* including stops. Over the suburban section it rises to 24.8 mph *(40 km/h)*.
Journey time on line: (Marelli-QT8) 27 minutes, (Marelli-Inganni) 29 minutes. (Gadorna-Gorgonzola) 35 minutes.
Type of tunnel: Large profile, double track tunnels 24 ft 7 in *(7.50 m)* in width and 12 ft 9½ in *(3.9 m)* in height (above rail level).
Tunnelling was by the "Milan" method of cut and cover which permitted the resumption of surface wheeled traffic, after a minimum period of interruption, over temporary surfaces while excavation proceeded below ground. Tunnel roofs are generally 10 ft *(3 m)* below street level, allowing space between tunnel extrados and street level for pedestrian subways and public utility services. The actual tunnel is of rectangular section in cast concrete. Part of Line 2 has been built in shield-driven tunnel to minimise surface traffic interference.
Method and voltage of current supply: 750 V dc on Line 1. Traction current is collected by shoes contracting 3rd outside rail on a vertical plane, and returns via 4th rail. 1 500 V dc on Line 2, via overhead wire system, with current return through insulated track rail. Line 1 has 9 sub-stations and Line 2, 8. All are unmanned.
Rolling Stock: Number of cars owned in 1979: 255 motor cars and 99 trailers, total 354. The motor cars, each with single control cab are 17.50 m long, 3.50 m high and 2.85 m wide. Weight 33 tons. Each car has four sets of air operated doors on each side. Motive power is supplied by four 90 kW *(120 hp)* motors to each car. Braking is electro-regenerative and pneumatic, incorporating electro-magnetic and mechanical standby braking equipment. Trailer cars, unladen weight 27.5 tons, are of the same dimensions as motor cars. Delivery continued through 1972 of a batch of 54 motor cars and 27 trailer cars, in light alloy, for Line 2. Details are:
Car dimensions (length): 17.5 m
(width): 2.85 m
(height): 3.47 m
Doors: 3 per side (line 2), 4 per side (line 1).
Passenger capacity: 200, including 46 seated
Motors: 4
Max speed: 90 km/h
Train make up: 3-car units (M-T-M)
Signalling: Automatic block, with signal aspects repeated in control cabs and automatic speed control. Automatic train stops. Differing colour signals indicate permissive train speeds; green 50 mph *(80 km/h)*; yellow 31 mph *(50 km/h)*; red-yellow 18.6 mph *(30 km/h)*; permissive red 9.3 mph *(15 km/h)*; red stop. Train movement is under remote central control with monitoring installations for each switch.
Station lay-out: All stations have side platforms 347 ft 9 in *(106 m)* long. Stations have ticket halls which are located between railway and street level and are equipped with escalators, of which there are 80 on Line 1 and 59 on Line 2. Admission to platform is via ticket-actuated electronic turnstiles (with magnetic checking of ticket) placed across ticket halls. Closed circuit television equipment is installed.

MONTREAL

Authority:
Montreal Urban Community Transit Commission
159 St. Antoine Street West, Montreal 126, Quebec, Canada
Telephone: (514) 877 6300

Chairman and General Manager: Yvon Deschamps
Commissioners: Robert Hainault, M.C.
Armand Lambert, C.A.
Secretary: Urqel Bourgie
Director of Transportation: Guy Blain, Eng.
Director of Engineering: Georges Donato, Eng.
Director of Vehicle Maintenance: Gaston Beauchamp, Eng.
Director of Planning: Henri Bessette, Eng.

General: Montreal's Metro system is a comparatively modern concept, as reflected in its enlightened architecture and operational performance. Serving as it does the second largest French-speaking city, the Metro understandably reflects French influence in both its stations and rolling stock. It was originally planned, constructed and financed by the City of Montreal. Actual construction began on 23 May 1962.
On 6 August 1963, the City Council approved extensions of Line 2 at both ends and construction of Line 4 to serve the communities on the south shore of the St. Lawrence river, and also the 1967 World Exhibition. The major portions of Lines 1 and 2 were put into operation on 14 October 1966, and all three lines were in full operation on 1 April 1967.
On 12 February 1971, the Montreal Urban Community Council voted a loan Bye-law for the borrowing of $430 m to be used to extend the Metro system a further 28.5 miles. Lines 1 and 2 would be extended east, west, and north-west. A new north-east line would be built and connected midway by a cross-city line to lines 1 and 2, the whole being served by an additional 50 stations. Extension work eastward on line No 1, started on 14 October 1971.
In mid-June 1976 Montreal opened a 7.6-km extension to the existing 6.1-km line one—in time to cope with big traffic increases expected in conjunction with the Olympic Games in the city. When completed sometime in 1984, the entire Metro system will total 74.3 km and include 85 stations.

Technical Data:
Route length: 38.2 km
Number of lines: 3.
Number of stations: 43.
Average Station spacing: 0.91 km.
Passengers per annum (Rapid Transit): Annual figures approximately 150 million passengers. Approx. 550 000 revenue and transfer passengers use RT on typical weekday.
Total passengers per annum (Bus and Rapid Transit): 300 000 000 approx.
Car km per annum, estimate: 50 000 000.
Max number of trains per hour: Line 1: 20; Line 2: 24; Line 4: 12.
Number of cars per train: 9.
Passenger capacity per car: 160.
Average schedule speed: Line 1: 20 mph *(32.2 km/h)* Line 2: 23 mph *(37.1 km/h)*; Line 4: 32 mph *(51.1 km/h)*.
Track gauge and weight and type of rails: Pneumatic tyred traction system is used, requiring standard gauge, 4 ft 8½ in *(1.435 m)* steel security rails (70 lb/yd), flanked by 10 in wide concrete running tracks, and lateral guide bars.
Max gradient: 6.3%.
Minimum radius of curves: Main line 460 ft *(140 m)*.
Type of tunnel: All lines in single tunnel 23 ft 4 in wide, containing both tracks. Generally through rock, they are concrete lined, with vertical walls and arched roof 16 ft high at centre. About 30 per cent of tunnels were constructed by cut and cover method using single rectangular concrete section. Depth of tunnels varies from 20 ft to 180 ft below ground level. In the downtown area the lines are located beneath streets closely paralleling those carrying heavy traffic.
Method and voltage of current supply: Traction current is at 750 V dc delivered to the guide bars from 26 rectifying stations. Primary supply is at 12 000 V ac from Quebec Hydro power distribution system.
Rolling Stock: 506 motor cars, 56 ft 5 in *(17.2 m)* long. 253 trailer cars, 53 ft 10 in *(16.5 m)* long. All cars are 8 ft 3 in *(2.5 m)* wide.
The cars were manufactured by Vickers Canada Montreal and Bombardier (for the new rolling stock). They are semi-permanently coupled in three-car sets, comprising two motor cars with trailer in the centre. Each of the car's two bogies rest on four pneumatic-tyred wheels, each doubled by an auxiliary flanged steel wheel mounted on the same axle. The latter wheels in normal service conditions do not touch the steel security rail, but act as standbys in the event of a pneumatic tyre failure. There are also four horizontally-mounted pneumatic-tyred guide wheels

Rubber-tyred trainset, supplied by Vickers Canada, enters Bonaventure terminal station

per bogie. Maximum length of train, comprising three 3-car sets (9 cars) is 500 ft. Each motor car has four 150 hp motors. Braking is electro-pneumatic, with wood shoes acting on the steel security wheels. Each car has four double doors on each side. Maximum speed is 47 mph *(75.2 km/h)*.
Signalling: Conventional block system with line-side indications.
Station layout: All stations are of the side platform type with concourse above. Platforms are 500 ft long and 13 ft wide. Except in three cases the entire two-level station structures are below street level. At Berri-de-Montigny station where the three lines intersect there are four levels below ground. There are no sidewalk entrances to stations. Accesses are through small off-street structures and through commercial buildings. Escalators are provided wherever the difference in level is 12 ft or more.

MORGANTOWN

Morgantown, West Virginia, USA

General: The only automated system operating in an urban environment in the USA is the Personal Rapid Transit (PRT) system at Morgantown, West Virginia, developed by Boeing Aerospace Company for the US Department of Transportation's Urban Mass Transportation Administration (UMTA).
The Morgantown people mover employs driverless vehicles which operate entirely under computer control on exclusive guideways. The cars cruise at speeds up to 48.3 km/h, with headways of only 15 seconds between vehicles. Rubber-tired and electrically powered, the cars are virtually noiseless and produce no exhaust pollutants. They operate on a fixed schedule or upon the summons of individual passengers and carry passengers direct to their destinations without stopping.
The system was developed as a national demonstration project of UMTA, intended to demonstrate and evaluate this type of transit in a real-world environment. Undertaken in 1970 as little more than a far-sighted concept, it began passenger service on 3 October 1975.
Used principally by the student body and staff of West Virginia University, it had carried 4½ million passengers by mid-1978 and is being expanded to serve a larger area of the city (30 000 permanent residents plus a university population of about 22 000).
Though Morgantown is the prototype of this form of automated transit, it was preceded into public service by a similar system developed by Boeing and Kobe Steel Ltd of Japan for the International Ocean Exposition on the Japanese island of Okinawa, the 1975 World's Fair. The Okinawa system, derived from Morgantown technology, linked major exhibits at the exposition. During the fair's six-month run, ending in January 1976, the 16 vehicles carried four million passengers over a 2.8 km stretch of two-way guideway. For the final six weeks of operation, the system maintained a reliability rate of 99½ per cent.
Operating statistics compiled so far at Morgantown indicate that such a system can achieve a lower cost per passenger-mile than today's urban bus systems. Its vehicles operate under the control of computers rather than drivers, and their movement is dictated strictly by passenger needs. This eliminates one of the principal causes of today's mounting transit deficits: manned buses or trolleys travelling their routes nearly empty during off-peak hours.
When UMTA chose Morgantown as the site for its people-mover experiment in 1970, its objective was to determine the concept's feasibility in public operation rather than in a test laboratory. It also wanted to place the system where it would meet a real need. Morgantown was ideal from both standpoints. Although it has a relatively small community, it contains, in capsule form, the same degree of traffic congestion found in America's largest cities. West Virginia University has three separate campuses, and traffic between them

One of Morgantown's driverless vehicles

peaks at least five times a day. Narrow arterials form traffic bottlenecks, making it impossible for students to schedule successive classes on different campuses. Snow and ice often compound the problem.

Boeing Aerospace Co, as system manager for UMTA, brought the Morgantown system through its research and development phase and an extensive testing programme, and delivered it to UMTA in September 1975 at a cost of $59.8 million. The first year of operation constituted the public demonstration phase of the UMTA programme, testing out the system in actual service.

The original Morgantown system consisted of a fleet of 45 vehicles, a central control and maintainence facility, three passenger stations and 5.3 miles (8.5 km) of single-lane guideway connecting the city's business district with two university campuses.

The system expansion now under way, funded by UMTA and administered by the West Virginia Board of Regents, will extend the guideway to student dormitories and the university's Medical Center. The larger system is expected to increase vehicle fleet mileage 2½ times while raising operating and maintainence costs by only 50 per cent.

Overall length of the completed system will be 5.3 km but it will include 14 km of single-lane guideway. The present end-of-the-line engineering station is being expanded to off-line configuration, two new stations are being built and the vehicle fleet is being increased to 73.

As associate contractor for this phase of the project, Boeing is building the 28 new cars, supplying the automated computer control system, installing a new heated power rail, and integrating all technical elements. The Morgantown vehicles, sized for the city's needs, carry no more than 21 passengers each, but the computerised control system can also handle larger cars. During periods of heavy traffic the computer dispatches cars on a schedule tailored to changing passenger requirements. At other times it functions in what is known as the demand mode, with passengers summoning cars and selecting destinations by pushing a button.

The heart of the system is its central control room, from which only two operators conduct the entire operation. Closed-circuit television monitors and a large display panel with a moving light for each vehicle enable them to monitor all parts of the system, and they can assume direct control if abnormal conditions arise. Two-way radio provides direct communication with vehicle passengers and each station platform. The system is designed for all-weather operation. In cold weather, a heated mixture of water and glycol is

Driverless vehicle approaches station on West Virginia University Campus

pumped through pipes embedded in the concrete guideways, preventing the accumulation of snow and ice.

Although the Morgantown system is still generally referred to by its original designation of PRT (Personal Rapid Transit) this may change with the new terminology now evolving for the entire field of auto-

mated guideway transit. The name Group Rapid Transit (GRT) is increasingly being applied to sophisticated systems whose vehicles, like those of Morgantown, carry ten or more passengers. Simpler systems whose guideways employ a few switches, such as those at airports, are now usually categorised as Shuttle-Loop Transit.

MOSCOW

Authority:

Moskovski Metropolitenv Imeni V.I. Lenina
5 Kolokolnikov Street, Moscow 103045, USSR
Telephone: 222 10 01

History: Soviet theory and practice in underground railway engineering has changed radically since Moscow's first underground line was built (1933-35). Excavation then was accomplished partly with pneumatic tools, but largely with pick and shovel, and the spoil removed by light railways much implemented by wheelbarrows. Slow progress then can be compared with a recently reported 440 yard tunnel excavation in a day, accomplished by massive mechanical excavators and earth movers.

Moscow's urban street transport at the end of the 19th century consisted of tramways and thousands of cabs. River ferries, tramway extensions and bus services developed from the 1920s, and trolleybuses in 1935. An expansion of the city boundaries and siting of large projects away from the centre, besides a concentration of railway terminals in the north and commercial and social activities at the centre, involved increasingly long journeys for the Muscovites which were expedited by the construction of Moscow's Metro system. It serves a population (1978) of 8 million.

The first 7.2 mile (11.6 km) section between Sokolniki and Park Cultury, crossing the city, was opened on 15 May 1935. The second section of underground completed in 1938 was from Smolenskaya to Kiev Station, and two other lines were built at the time to Kursk Station and towards Sokol in the north-west, thus developing a small network of radial lines about 16 miles (26 km) in route length. Underground building continued during the World War (1941-1945) for economic and cultural reasons and to provide shelters from enemy air raids. By the war's end 25 miles (40 km) of Metro linked the city's area with 7 radial stations, and by 1954 all main railway stations were connected by Metro. The first major stage of Metro building concluded with the merging of the several radial lines with the circular underground route.

New sections were added to the system as large-scale building projects were launched in 1954 in areas of new developments.

Arbat underground section was originally built at shallow depth in 1933-38, crossing the Moscow river by bridge. Closed down in 1953 and retubed under the river, the Arbat-Fili line six years later was linked to a newly-built Kutusovskaya-Kiev Railway Station line, which was extended in stages westward to the

developing areas reaching to Molodezhnaya in 1966. In 1966 a further addition to the system, the eastern rapid Zhdanovskaya line, became operative. There are seven stations, with the inner terminus at Taganskaya (for interconnection with the Ring Line). The line at its inner end is at deep level in twin tube, and afterwards runs at sub-surface and surface levels.

In August 1969 the extension of the line from Avtozavodskaya to Kakhovskaya with 4 stations came into operation. This line will have a spur from Kashirskaya to Lenino. On 5 January 1972, a new 1.9 mile (3 km) north-south tube across central Moscow was opened, linking existing north and south lines between Prospect Mira and Ploshchad Nogina, enabling the through north-south Moscow run to be reduced to 31.5 minutes.

New lines in operation are Taganskaya-Novogireevo towards the east, and Krasnopresnenskaya-Planernaya, a large new development area to the west of the capital. The latter extension, from Tanganskaya in east-central Moscow, westward across the city to Planernaya, will be 14.2 miles (22.8 km) in length.

Moscow's Kaluga-Riga line from the VDNCh station to Medvedkovo (8.2 km) with four new stations is now in operation.

Also operational is the Kalinin radial line from Marksistskaya to Novogireyevo—a distance of 11.1 km.

Future plans call for completion of a new Serpukhov radial line from Dobryninskaya to Dniepropetrovskaya (12.8 km with eight stations).

Cost of construction work is at present estimated at between 10 and 17 million Roubles per km.

In the more distant future there is to be a Timiryazev line from Novoslobodskaya to the Academy of Agriculture, via the Savyolovo Railway Station. There is the choice either of building a new large circular underground route to include new areas, or of linking up the radial lines' terminal stations, in elliptical loops, to ease the congestion of passengers on the central stations while improving communications in the outlying areas. Running towards the centre and bypassing the Kremlin area in semi-circles these new radial lines would become diametrical and greatly ease passenger traffic in the old central area.

A network of 196 route-km and 113 stations is planned.

Route length: (1979): 184 km.
Number of lines: 7 (6 transverse and 1 circular); all double track.
Number of stations served: 114 (1979).
Average station spacing: 1.69 km.
Average daily passenger total: (1979): 6.2 million.
Passengers per annum: (1978): 2 173 million.

Max line capacity (one way): 88 600 passengers.
Max number of trains per hour each way: 45.
Max number of cars per train: 7.
Estimated capacity per car: 170 (including 40 seated).
Average schedule speed (peak periods, including stops): 25.2 mph (40.55 km/h).
Track gauge: 5 ft (1.524 m).
Type of rails: 101 lb per yard (50 kg/m). Flat-bottomed: welded up to 1 066 ft (325 m).
Max gradient: 4 %.
Minimum radius of curves: 655 ft (200 m).
Type of tunnel: The earlier sections were partly of cut-and-cover construction, the tunnels being double-track and of rectangular section, 25 ft 0 in (7.6 m) wide by 12 ft 10 in (3.9 m) high from rail level. Subsequent lines (including the ring line recently built) have been largely of deep-level tube construction, each single-track tube tunnel having an internal diameter of 17 ft 11 in (5.46 m). Tube lines are as much as 131 ft (40 m) below surface level (for example, at Dynamo Station).
Method and voltage of current supply: Third rail; 825 V dc; contact on underside of current rail. Centrally controlled unmanned transformer substation system.
Rolling Stock: Length of car over couplers 61 ft 5 in (18.7 m); external width 8 ft 10 in (2.7 m): tare weight 31.7 metric tons. Each car has four sets of automatic double doors on each side. Seating is longitudinal. Automatic centre buffer couplers. All motored axles. The cars are manufactured at the Mytishchi Engineering Plant, near Moscow.
Signalling: Automatic block, with colour-light signals, speed control, and train stops. Over the next six years it is planned that all rolling stock will be converted to an automatic driving system with automatic speed control.
Station layouts: Stations are of island type, often embodying a vast circulating concourse between the two platforms. The surface buildings of the Moscow Metro are palatial and the whole system has the reputation of a show-piece. As an example of station dimensions, the concourse of Komsomolskaya Station is 538 ft (164 m) long, 59 ft (18 m) wide, and 37 ft 9 in (11.5 m) high. Escalators are widely used. The ring line alone has 82 escalators out of a system total of 376 (1979). Reversing at termini is carried out on sidings beyond the stations. Platforms are 510 ft (155 m) long. The busiest stations include Ploshchad Sverdlova, Prospekt Marksa, Belorusskaya and Sokol. Experiments being carried out on the shunting of trains at terminal stations using automatic control equipment are reducing the number of teams of shunters now employed.

MUNICH

Authority:
Stadtwerke Verkehrsbetriebe München (MVB)
Einsteinstr 28, 8000 München 80, Postfach 801860, Federal Republic of Germany
Telephone: (089) 2 19 11

Type of system: Full-metro

General: Since construction began on the Munich U Bahn 12 years ago, a total of 35 km of lines have been put into operation.

Under the city's medium-term plan further new lines totalling 15.5 km are to be built by 1985: the 3.3-km west line from Hauptbahnhof to Rotkreuzplatz, and the 10.2-km Laim-Bogenhausen line, to run via Ostbahnhof.

Construction costs since work began on the system in 1965 have totalled DM 1 200 million. To complete the medium-term programme U Bahn authorities estimate that a further DM 1 000 million will be needed.

On 19 October 1971, 6½ years after the start of construction, the first 12 km of the north-south subway line were opened, running from the service depot at Freimann to Goetheplatz in the south-west of the city centre. This was followed soon afterwards, on 8 May 1972, by the opening of another 4 km section. The volume of traffic was unexpectedly high from the very beginning and has increased steadily since then. The total of some 230,000 passengers on working days is about 27 per cent above the altogether optimistic forecasts made before service started. The fact that the subway is used by such large numbers in the central urban area guarantees a relatively favourable cost-benefit ratio (figures for 1973: at 38 million DM operating costs and 60 million passengers carried, 0.63 DM per passenger). The priority given to the inner network in the city's development and transportation policies is thus justified from the point of view of business economics also.

Construction of the route section between Goetheplatz and Harras—the southern branch of line U 6—began in August 1971. The section is about 2.7 km long and runs from the previous terminus at Goetheplatz, under Lindwurmstrasse and Implerstrasse to Implerplatz, and from there in a wide curve in a westerly direction to the new terminus at Harras. The construction work was divided into four project sections and cost some 208 million DM.

The construction work was accompanied by a number of problems which made exceptional demands upon all people involved. Engineers, geologists and tunnellers were repeatedly forced by extremely unfavourable geological and hydrogeological conditions to find solutions and make decisions that were not in any "textbooks". The tunnels were driven under the protection of a very carefully planned pre-drainage system which, in the interests of safety, was always given trial runs to check its efficiency. Whenever there was an adequate covering of marl above the apex of the tunnel, the tunnel was driven below the upper ground water stratum, so that it was possible for the groundwater lowering activities to be directed at the lower ground water strata only. Over long sections, considerable difficulties were caused by an unusually thick "Flinz" marl with a tendency to cave in, which, in conjunction with the driving conditions, initially led to surface subsidence and caused the shield to deviate from its course.

The subway station at Harras was the first station building in the Munich subway system to be constructed entirely of waterproof concrete. This is cheaper than the conventional method (no bituminous insulation) and, above all, safer (no fire risk). On the other hand, it requires experience in the difficult process of making large concrete areas.

Munich's U 3 Line

The platform hall and service rooms in the subway station at Poccistrasse were built by underground means between the tunnels which had already been driven. The underground hall was made by driving 31 cross tunnels, about 10 m long, between the main tubes, and by subsequent step-by-step construction of floors, columns, and vaults in exposed concrete and waterproof concrete.

The next line to be tackled in the Munich subway network was the line 8/1, in June 1971. This line is 16 km long and runs from the existing junction station at Scheidplatz (U 3), via Schwabing-West through Augustenstrasse and Luisenstrasse, to Munich Central station and on to Sendlinger Tor Platz. From the station at Sendlinger Tor (intersection with line U /3) it runs via the Isarvorstadt, Au, Giesing, Ramersdorf and Perlach districts to the planned joint station on the Kreuzstrasse rapid-transit route.

The overall project is divided into 29 sections.

Since 1974, the construction of subway line 8/1 has involved some impressive new developments which have already achieved cost reductions in comparison with conventional methods. In this way it has been possible to keep the overall subway costs at a stable level in the last few years, in spite of the general rise in prices.

For project section 7.1 (Isar underpassing) a subway tunnel in a water-bearing foundation was, for the first time in Germany, lined with a single shell of rubber-sealed precast reinforced-concrete segments. The tunnel was driven with a fully-mechanical shield driving machine using compressed air, without sheet piling at the working face. This type of tunnel lining has proven more economical than the cast-iron segmental lining often used. There is considerable interest in this new development, both at home and abroad.

Plans: Munich's U-Bahn development programme has been extended from 1985 to 1992 and the projected system expanded from a planned 52 km to around 70 km. Under construction is a 16 km section of the U8/1 line from Scheidplatz to Neupersach Süd which is due to come into operation in time for the 1980/81 Winter timetable. A 3.3 km section between the Hauptbahnhof and Rotkreuzplatz is expected to be completed by late 1982 and a 13.3 km east-west connection on line U5/9 is due to be completed in 1984/85.

By mid-1980 35 km of new tracks will have been in operation. By 1995 a further 25 km of extensions to the outskirts of the city should be opened. Construction work on three sections is planned to start between 1983-85. Since construction began in 1965, a total of DM 1 850 million has been invested in the system.

Munich has placed an order for 53 articulated rail cars to be used on the U8 Perfach-Süd-Scheidplatz line and the Rotkreuzplatz-Insbrucker line on line U1.

Route length: 11.9 miles *(18.5 km)*.
Number of stations: 17.
Passengers carried: 180 000 per working week average.
Max line capacity: 40 000 passengers per hour in each direction.
Max Number of cars per train: 3 twin-car units.
Capacity per 6-car train: Max 1 158 persons, including 294 seated.
Average scheduled speed: 22 mph *(35 km/h)*.
Max speed: 50 mph *(80 km/h)*.
Track gauge: 4 ft 4½ in *(1 432 mm)*.
Type of tunnel: Shield-driven circular tunnel 18 ft 10 in *(5.74 m)* diameter; rectangular cross-section cut and cover tunnel, and vaulted cross-section where built by tunnelling method.
Method and voltage of current supply: 3rd rail underside contact, 750 V dc.
Rolling Stock: No of cars owned: 54 double motor coaches (built by a consortium of German manufacturers), powered by four 180 kW traction motors. Car width 9 ft 6 in *(2.90 m)*, single car length 59 ft 1 in *(18.00 m)*. Three sets of sliding doors on each side. Aluminium-alloy carbodies.
Signalling: The continuous automatic train control system, incorporating line control cables carrying variable-speed, braking and stopping instructions, permits minimum headways of 90 seconds. Train starting is by driver-push-button control.

NAGOYA

Authority:
Nagoya Municipal Transportation Bureau
1-1 Sannomaru 3-chome, Naka-ku, Nagoya, Japan

General Manager: Shigeyuki Tani
R.T. Construction Manager: Sunao Miura
R.T. Division Manager: Tomoji Shimogaki
Engineering Manager: Yukihiko Kawai

General: In order to cope with increasing population, and travel demands which could no longer be met by private railway, street-car and bus services, the city embarked on an extensive municipal Subway system programme, which began soon after World War II. Line 1 from Nagoya main-line station east to Sakaemachi was opened for passenger traffic in 1957. The north-south Line 2 was initially opened in 1967, and the Subway network has developed in regular stages of extensions or new lines since 1965.

A network of 77.4 km in 5 lines was planned for 1980. Nagoya's 1972 population of 2 million is expected to increase to 3½ million by 1985. Based on this assumption Nagoya plans a rail rapid transit network totalling 5 lines and 48.1 miles *(77.4 km)* route length, all within the city limits.

Construction work on No. 4 line proceeding at a cost of approx. Yen 25 200 million (£38 million), is that from Kanayama to Aratamabashi 3.5 miles *(5.6 km)*. Together with No. 2 line, No. 4 line will eventually form a 16 mile *(26 km)* circular line. The 8.2 mile *(13.6 km)* section between Fushimi and Akaike on Line No. 3 is now under construction at a cost of Yen 73 000 million (£110 million).

Public transportation within the city area includes three JNR trunk lines and two private railways, the Nagoya Electric and the Kinki Nippon, totalling 53.5 miles *(86 km)*.

Operative route length: 32.4 km.
Number of lines: 2 Transverse.
Number of stations served: 36 (33 in tunnel).
Average station spacing: 0.59 miles *(0.95 km)*.

Passengers per annum:
(1971): approx 143 million.
(1972): approx 179 million.
(1975): approx 235 million.
Max number of trains per hour each way: 30.
Number of cars per train: 4 to 5.
Estimated capacity per car: 115.
Average scheduled speed: 20.4 mph *(32.8 km/h)*.

Track gauge: 4 ft 8½ in *(1.435 m)*.
Weight and type of rails: 101 lb/yd *(50 kg/m)*; flat-bottomed.
Max gradient: 1in 28 (3.5%).
Minimum radius of curves: 410 ft *(125 m)*.
Type of tunnel: Double track rectangular tunnel, of cut-and-cover construction, with centre supports except where the tunnel is circular, shield driven.
Method and voltage of current supply: Third rail; 600 V dc.
Rolling Stock: The cars are all motored, with each axle motor driven. They are 51 ft 1½ in *(15.58 m)* long overall, 8 ft 3 in *(2.50 m)* wide and 11 ft 3 in *(3.43 m)* high from rail level. The wheels are resilient to reduce noise in tunnels. There are three double-leaf doors on each side of each car. Weight of cars, 24 tonnes.
Signalling: Automatic block, with colour-light signals. On Line 2 a system of cab signalling and Automatic Train Control is employed.
Station layouts: Stations have an extensive sub-surface (mezzanine) concourse, flanked by shops, from which stairs lead down to side or island type platforms 341-656 ft *(104-200 m)* long and 11 ft 6 in-37 ft 0 in *(3.5-11.3 m)* wide.
Workshops: At Fujigaoko, Meijo and Meiko, with capacity for 330 cars, 28 cars and 96 cars respectively.

NAPLES

Authority:
Naples Rapid Transit
Direzione Comple FS, Campania, Naples, Italy

General: In 1925, while the original Rome-Naples "Direttissima" line was under construction, an underground railway was opened in Naples, running westwards from the Central Station to Mergellina, a suburb four miles away. This underground section was intended to provide an alternative approach for the "Diretissima" into Naples from the west, and at the same time form the nucleus of a local underground system for Naples itself. The actual length of the tunnel between Mergellina and Naples Central is 3.4 miles *(5.5 km)*. Mergellina is an open station, but there are three intermediate stations on the tunnel section—Piazza Amedeo, Montesanto, and Piazza Cavour—connected with the surface by escalators. The tunnel is at places 98 ft 6 in *(30 m)* below street level. Both main line (non-stop) and local (stopping) trains operate electrically through the tunnel section.

Plans have been put in hand for a new 8-km underground line with 15 stations; 1 500 V dc overhead electrification.

Naples is also served by the 140 km long Circumvesuviana Railway, which is being up-graded and equipped with new rolling stock. The line's gauge is only 2 ft 5½ in, but the new stock is being built wider than the old (2.7 m as against 2.35 m). The vehicles will be formed into 3-car articulated units resting on 4 bogies. The modernised railway has been described as a metropolitan-suburban line.

NEWCASTLE-UPON-TYNE

Authority:
Tyne and Wear Passenger Transport Executive
Cuthbert House, All Saints, Newcastle-Upon-Tyne
NE1 2DA, England
Telephone: (0632) 610431

Type of system: Full-metro

Director General: D. P. C. Fletcher
Director of Engineering: D. F. Howard
Project Director (Metro):
Director of Integrated Operations: G. E. Hutchinson

General: Britain's first light-rail rapid transit in the Newcastle area of north-east England will be ready for operation in 1980. The Tyneside Rapid Transit system will consist of a 55.6-km network comprising 14.8-km of new line construction and 40.8-km of existing railway at present operated by British Rail who continue to operate limited freight services over parts of the route.

The transit system first got official approval in 1973, following announcement of a 75 per cent grant towards the project cost of £143 million by the Government.

By late 1979 a large amount of new construction was virtually completed and conversion of existing lines well in hand.

Two prototype trainsets built by Metro Cammell are still running on the 2.5 km Test Track in North Tyneside but are now used largely for showing visitors, the concept of the system.

Route-kilometres of new underground construction will total 5·5 and length of new or substantially new surface routes about 9·3 km. New construction work includes twin north/south tunnels under Newcastle town centre and neighbouring Gateshead. There are to be seven new underground stations at Jesmond, Haymarket, Monument, Central Station, St. James Park and Gateshead. The first section to be opened will connect Haymarket with Kenton Bank Foot in the north-west, and Tynemouth on the coast. This will be followed by an extension southwards over the Tyne to Heworth and from Tynemouth along the north bank of the river to St. James. These sections will open in 1981 but completion to South Shields will not be achieved until 1983. Four services will provide peak-hour frequencies of 2½ minutes through the Central Area and the system is expected to carry up to 300 million passengers annually as compared with the six million a year who previously used the British Rail commuter service in the area.

Metro will form the backbone of the country's first fully integrated system of rail/road/ferry public transport in which all routes are planned as a network and over which through-ticketing will be available.

Possible extensions to the basic system are being examined as part of the County Council's Structure Plan. These include lines south through Washington New Town to Sunderland; west from St. James and from Kenton Bank Foot to the Airport; and from Benton to Killingworth.

Rolling Sotck: The two prototype articulated sets have been tested since June 1975 and over 40 of the production order for 88 units have been completed. These are supplied by Metropolitan Cammell. All electrical equipment is by GEC Traction; Duwag mono-motor bogies and articulation; Westinghouse plug doors and Westcode braking system; BSI automatic couplers and Brecknell Willis pantograph.

Technical Data:
Gauge: 1.435 m
Route length: 55.6 km
Track length: 130 km approx
In tunnel: 5.5 km
New lines (planned and authorised): 6.4 km (under construction): 49.2 km
Number of stations (total): 41
Number of stations in tunnel: 7
Average distance between stations: 1.35 km
Max length of station platforms: 65 m (extension to 95 m allowed for)
Gradient (max): 1 in 30
Curvature (max): 50 m (service line) 210 m (main line)
Speed (design max): 80 km/h (average commercial): 34.3 km/h
Type of rail: BS.113AFB
Type of tunnel: Various, including bored, segmental lined tube, in-situ lined inverted U, cut and cover.
Method and voltage of current supply: 1 500 V dc overhead

Traffic and finances:
Max line capacities (one way): 30 trains per hour
Max number of trains per hour (one way): 24 (one way-planned): 24
Frequency of train services in minutes (planned): 2½ minutes (max)

First Metro production car for Newcastle

Capacity per train (passengers seated): 168 (two cars) (passengers standing): 376

Rolling stock characteristics:
Car types: Twin articulated unit motor cars
Number of units: 90
Car dimensions:
  Length (m): 27.800
  Width (m): 2.650
  Height (m) (overall): 3.445
Total floor area: 68 m² (available standing area = 33 m²)
Number of doors per side: 4
Door width (m): 1.3
Number of passengers per car (total): 272 (crush load) (seated): 84
Motors per car: 2
Motor rating (kW): 180 kW continuous/205 kW 1 h
Power per train (minimum): 360 kW (max): 720 kW
Acceleration (max): 1 m/s²
Deceleration (normal service): 1 m/s² (emergency): 2.3 m/s²
Max design speed: 80 km/h
Bogies (type and manufacturer): DUWAG—box section modified H-frame. Rubber primary suspension, air secondary
Distance between bogie pivot: 10.4 + 10.4 m
Brakes (type): Rheostatic, spring operated/air released disc, emergency only
Weight (empty in tonnes): 39 motor cars

NEW YORK

Authority:
Staten Island Rapid Transit Operating Authority
25 Hyatt Street, Staten Island, NY 10301, USA
Telephone: (212) 447 1581

Type of system: Transit line

Chairman: Richard Ravitch
Senior Executive Officer: Steven K. Kaufmann
Executive Officer: Charles Kalkhof
General Superintendent: G. A. Duszak
Superintendent: C. H. Bergman

Urban Structure:
Population of city area: 300 000
Land area: 60.9 sq miles

Technical Data:
Gauge: 4 ft 8½ in

Route length: 14.3 miles
Track length: 28.6 miles
Number of stations (total): 22
Average distance between stations: 0.65 miles
Max length of station platforms: 428 ft
Gradient (max): 1.9%
Curvature (max): minimum radius of curvature (trucks) 145 ft
Speed (design max): 40 mph (passenger), 30 mph (freight) 30 mph (average commercial)
Type of rail: 49.6 kg/m
Method and voltage of current supply: Third rail 600 V

Traffic and finances:
Max number of trains per hour (one way): 7
Frequency of train services in minutes (currently): 12
Capacity per train (passengers seated): 74 (passengers standing): 300
Passenger journeys per annum: 5 000 000
Revenues: $2 250 000

Finances: $6 500 000

Rolling stock characteristics:
Car types: R44 motor cars
Number of units: 52
Car dimensions:
  Length: 71 ft 6 in
  Width: 10 ft
  Height: 12 ft
Number of doors per side: 2
Door width: 3 ft 10 in
Number of passengers per car (total): 300 (seated): 74
Motors per car: 4
Motor rating (kW): 86
Power per train (max): 55 mph
Bogies (type and manufacturer): BoBo—General Steel Industries, St. Louis Car Division
Distance between bogie pivot: 4 ft 6 in
Brakes (type): WABCO RT-5-C

NEW YORK—NYCTA

Authority:
New York City Transit Authority
370 Jay Street, Brooklyn NY 11201, USA
Telephone: (212) 330 3140

Chairman (MTA):
  Richard Ravitch
Chief Executive Officer (MTA):
  John D. Simpson
Senior Executive Officer/General Manager (NYCTA):
  Steven K. Kauffman
Executive Officer—Rapid Transit:
  Charles Kalkhof
Executive Officer—Surface:
  Andrew Schiavone
Executive Officer—Construction & Engineering:
  George Ziegler
Executive Officer—Controller:
  Andrew T. O'Rourke
History: The history of New York's rapid transit railways began in the 1870s with the first of what was to become a network of elevated railways. The "Elevated" has all disappeared (except for the subway extensions in outlying areas) and the ubiquitous Subway, dating from 1904, now covers the New York and district areas with a dense network of lines. Until recent years the network was subdivided into three groups of lines, the Interborough Rapid Transit, the Brooklyn-Manhattan Transit and the Independent (IRT; BMT; IND), which developed historically in that order. The first two were Company concerns and the last was owned by the City from the outset. In the year 1940 and those immediately following, the New York City Board of Transportation, already controlling the IND group, acquired the undertakings of the first two, together with several street-car, bus and trolley-bus systems. In 1953 the New York City Transit Authority was created, empowered to lease, operate, improve and extend the city's passenger facilities.

In March 1968, the NYCTA came under the jurisdiction of the Metropolitan Transportation Authority, which is an agency created by the New York State Legislature.

General: Construction work is now underway to add 24.6 km of new lines to that basic system. The following projects are now under construction: East 63rd Street line (4.8 km; cost $750 million); Remodified super-express line (9.3 km; cost $450 million); Southeast Queens line (7.3 km; cost $650 million).

The New York subway system carries more passengers per annum than any other underground railway system in the world. On the other hand, the total number of passengers on all public transport (underground and road services) is less in New York than London, a much larger proportion of the total in London using buses.

Many of the New York City Transit lines have parallel fast (limited-stop) and local (all-stations) services in each direction. Such services are worked either on four tracks (with one fast and one slow track in each direction) or on three tracks (with one slow track in each direction) and the third track is used for fast trains in the direction of passenger traffic during peak hours. A flat-rate fare operates over most of the NYCTA System.

In addition to the Port Authority Trans Hudson System (dealt with separately) two railway systems in the vicinity of New Yok are designated as self-contained Rapid Transit railways.

One is the Newark Subway which acts in part as a feeder to the HMUDSON Bey Tube. It runs south for three miles on the surface and one mile underground to terminate in Newark City beneath the Pennsylvania Railroad Station and the Hudson Bay Terminal. It operates with 30 PCC-type cars drawing power at 600 V dc from overhead wires.

The Staten Island Rapid Transit Railway Company was turned over to the Metropolitan Transportation Authority on 1 July 1971 and is now operated by the Staten Island Rapid Transit Operating Authority, a subsidiary of the MTA. The line runs the length of an island that is politically the Richmond Borough of New York. Its multiple-unit stock matches the latest equipment of the BMT Division of the NYCTA, but a contemplated connection with that System never materialised. Power is at 600 V dc through third rail top contact.

Work was completed in 1974 on the $69 480 000 contract for the East River Tunnel, which was started in November 1969. Construction began in 1971 of the tunnel under part of Central Park which will connect the existing lines in Manhattan with those in Queens. The tunnel will be double-decked with two tracks being built for Subway use and two tracks for Long Island Railroad trains. Construction began also in 1972 on the 14 mile Second Avenue Subway in Manhattan and the Jamaica Line Subway extension on Archer Avenue, Queens. This work is being done with the assistance of a $2 500 million transportation bond issue approved by the governor, the legislature and the voters of New York State, which will finance the biggest expansion in the history of the New York City Subway system.

During 1974 1.13 miles of the Culver Shuttle line was closed.

Route length: 231.73 miles *(372.2 km),* including 137.05 miles *(220.1 km)* in tunnel and 71.80 miles *(114.8 km)* on elevated structures.

Number of lines: 3 major systems (IND, IRT and BMT), and comprising a total of 30 lines and branches. The lines are all of a transverse or radial type. The whole system is double-, treble-, quadrupled-tracked.
Number of stations served: 462.
Average station spacing: Approx ½ mile between local stations and 1-4 miles between "Express stop" stations.
Passengers per annum: 1 096 006 529.
Passengers per annum carried by New York City Transit system (including road services as well as railways): 1 559 030 395.
Max number of trains per hour each way: 34.
Max number of cars per train: 10 local, 11 express.
Estimated capacity per car: 54 seated, 146 standing.
Average schedule speed (including stops): Express trains 22 mph *(35 km/h)*; Local trains 20 mph *(32 km/h)*.
Track gauge: 4 ft 8½ in *(1.435 m)*.
Weight and type of rails: 100 lb/yd *(49.6 kg/m)*, flat-bottomed.

Minimum radius of curves: 52 m.
Type of tunnel: Many of the underground railway tunnels in New York are of "cut-and-cover" construction, being of rectangular section and double or multiple-track width. The double-track tunnels of the first subway line, opened in 1904, were 25 ft 3 in *(7.96 m)* wide and 12 ft 9 in *(3.886 m)* high (from rail level), and had centre supports. There are, however, several sections of tube construction (particularly under the East River) where concrete tunnel linings were used.
Method and voltage of current supply: Third rail; 600 V dc, The New York City Transit Authority has sold its 3 power generating stations to the Consolidated Edison Co, from whom power is now being purchased. There are about 150 sub-stations, which are being retained by the Transit Authority. Modernisation of the power distribution system to meet requirements of high-acceleration cars, and an increase in the total number of cars, includes the building of additional sub-stations, and replacement of some now manually operated by centrally-operated sub-stations.
Rolling Stock: Number of cars owned: about 6 800. This includes 1 000 cars manufactured by the Pullman Car Company for service on the former BMT and IND Divisions and for the Staten Island Railroad, mentioned subsequently. These cars are being used to replace older equipment and are of an entirely new design with an overall length of 75 ft.
Details: Cars introduced since the war on the BMT and IND Divisions are 60 ft *(18.3 m)* long, 10 ft *(3.05 m)* wide and 12 ft *(3.66 m)* high. The latest model (R-44) is 75 ft long in four-car units, made of low alloy, high tensile steel and fibreglass with stainless steel exteriors and aluminium roofs. They are capable of increased acceleration and of reaching a speed of 70 mph.
Signalling: Automatic block, with colour light signals and train stops. An "Indentra" train operating system, similar to the electronic "programmes" train operating system used on London Transport, is in use on the IRT-Flushing line.

NEW YORK—NEW JERSEY—PATH

Authority:
Port Authority Trans-Hudson Corporation
One World Trade Center, New York, NY 10048, USA

New York
President: P. C. Goldmark
Vice President and General Manager:
F. A. Gorman
Supv. Passenger and Community Programmes:
M. L. Hurwitz
Claims Agent: W. Coupland
Purchasing Agent: A. Robertson

Jersey City
General Superintendent: T. C. Rutmayer
Superintendent Transportation: C. Ryan
Superintendent Car Equipment: W. H. Miller
Acting Superintendent Power, Signals & Communications: E. Nicholson
Superintendent Track and Structures: L. Pelton

General: In 1962, following passage of legislation by the States of New Jersey and New York, the Port Authority Trans-Hudson Corporation (PATH) was created to acquire, operate and modernise the bankrupt inter-state rapid transit system, which faced the prospect of abandonment.
PATH began operations on 1 September 1962, and initiated a long range, multi-million dollar rehabilitation and modernisation programme. PATH has now invested over $262 million in acquisition, rehabilitation and modernisation of the 14-mile rail system. The PATH modernisation programme includes the design and purchase of a fleet of 250 new air-conditioned cars, completed in 1972; completion of a new World Trade Center terminal in lower Manhattan in 1971; and completion and dedication of a new PATH Journal Square Transportation Center in Jersey City, New Jersey, in October 1975. Other modernisation work includes the rehabilitation and rebuilding of the signal system and replacement of the electric traction power system, and rehabilitation of track, tunnel drainage, station, communications systems and operations control.

Passengers per annum:
(1976): 40 667 590
(1977): 40 476 670
(1978): 41 750 000
(1979): 44 000 000
(estimated).

Method and voltage of current supply: Third rail, 650 V dc. A new traction power system employing ultra-modern silicon rectifiers, has been installed at PATH's New York and New Jersey sub-stations, at cost of over $8 million, to replace the old rotary converter system.
Rolling Stock: Number of cars owned 291. At present, the fully air-conditioned passenger car fleet consists of 42 cars acquired in 1958 and 203 cars acquired in 1965-67, all of which were manufactured by the St. Louis Car Division of General Steel Industries, Inc. There are also 40 various pieces of work equipment. The 1965-67 stock comprises 121 driving cars and 82 motored trailer cars. Bodies are aluminium with capacities of about 140 (41 seated and 42 seated respectively). Two automatic double doors on both sides of each car. All the cars are 51 ft 3 in *(15.62 m)* long, 9 ft 4½ in *(2.86 m)* wide, 11 ft 8½ in *(3.56 m)* high. The cars were supplied with dynamic braking down to 10 mph *(16 km/h)* and then electro-pneumatic. They can be in trains of from 2 to 10 cars. During 1972, 46 air-conditioned cars, type PA-3 manufactured by Hawker Siddeley Canada, Ltd. were delivered. They permit longer trains to be operated on PATH's services between Newark, Harrison, Jersey City, Hoboken and the World Trade Center terminal in lower Manhattan. Other aspects of PATH's extensive modernisation programme includes improvement of stations, rebuilding of the signal system; rehabilitation of track; tunnel drainage, and utility systems, installation of a two-way train-to-wayside radio communication system, and the implementation of exact change fare collection system.
At the heart of PATH is Operations Control at the Journal Square Transportation Center, one of the most advanced installations of its kind. There, key operating personnel monitor the system and rapidly respond to any crisis or problems that arise.
It opened in stages from late 1973, with completion of the entire project in October 1975. Also at Operations Control is a bank of video monitors connected to a closed-circuit television system to oversee passenger flow and provide around-the-clock surveillance of stations and facilities. Closed-circuit television is also a vital part of PATH's modernised fare collection programme. The monitors observe the fare-control areas, where exact-change turnstiles and change-vending machines have replaced the old token system and eliminated the need for station agents.
A major addition to the PATH system is the World Trade Center terminal which opened in 1971 replacing the obsolete Hudson Terminal in downtown Manhattan. It lies beneath the twin 110-storey office and Trade Center towers. Both the World Trade Center terminal and the PATH Journal Square Transportation Center will better equip PATH to meet the increased peak hour traffic demands which are expected in the years ahead.

Technical Data:
Speed (design max): 70 mph (112.7 km/h)
(average commercial): 19.2 (30.9 km/h)
Type of rail: 110 lb
Type of tunnel: Ring
Method and voltage of current supply: 3rd Rail 650 V dc

Traffic and finances:
Max line capacities (one way): 400 cars/h
Max number of trains per hour (one way): 40 (38 actual operation)
(one way-planned): 40
Frequency of train services in minutes (currently): 3
(planned): 3
Capacity per train (passengers seated): 42
(passengers standing): ±80
Passenger journeys per annum: 41 750 000 (1977/78),
Estimated—44 000 000 (1978/79)
Revenues: $14.05 million (1978)
Finances: $50.37 million

Rolling stock characteristics:
Car types: K PAI, PAII, PAIII
Number of units: 291
Car dimensions:
Length (m): 15.62
Width (m): 2.86
Height (m): 3.56
Total floor area: Average 41½ m²
Door width (m): 1.27 for Ks (entire door opening)
1.36 for PA I, PA II/III (entire door opening)
Number of passengers per car (total): 120
(seated): 42
Motors per car: 4
Motor rating (kW): 298
Power per train (minimum): 400 hp
(max): 400 hp
Acceleration (max): 2½ miles/h/s (4.02 km/h/s)
Deceleration (normal service): 3.0 mph/s (4.82 km/h/s)

Interior of a PA-3 car

One of the air-conditioned PA-3 cars delivered to PATH in 1972

One of the platforms at PATH's new World Trade Center Terminal

(emergency): 3.0 mph/s (4.82 km/h/s)
Max design speed: 70 mph (115 km/h)
Bogies (type and manufacturer): GSI General #70
Distance between bogie pivot: 33 ft (10.06 m)
Brakes (type): Westinghouse Air
Weight (empty in tonnes): ±5 900 lb (motor cars);
57 500 lb (trailers).

NUREMBERG

VAG Verkehrs Aktiengesellschaft
Hochhaus am Plärrer, 85 Nürnberg, Federal Republic of Germany
Telephone: (0911) 2711
Telegrams: VAG-NURNBERG

General: By early 1978 a total of 9.3 km of the city's new U Bahn system had been opened with the completion of Line 1 as far as Bahnhof Turm. The complete line should be finished not before 1982 when trains will be running from Langwasser in the south to Furth in the north. A final U Bahn system of 43.9 km is planned at a cost of around DM 1 700 million with annual construction costs amounting to about DM 70 million.

Technical Data:
Gauge: 1.435 m
Route length: 8.5 km
In tunnel: 6.2 km
Projected new lines (in construction): 2.0 km
(in design): 5.4 km
Number of stations (total): 14 existing; 13 planned
(in tunnel): 10; 10
Stations:
platform length (minimum): 90 m
Gradient (max): 4%
Curvature (max): 100 m
Speed (design max): 80 km/h

(average commercial): 30.9 km/h
Electric systems: Third rail; 750 V

Rolling Stock:
Car type (year introduced): 1971
Number of units: 24 Doppeltriebwagen
Car dimensions (length): 18.6 m
(width): 2.90 m
(height): 3.55 m
Passenger capacity per car (total): 290
(seated): 98
Motors per car: 4
Rating: 180 kW

Train composition (minimum): 2 cars = 1 unit
(max): 4 cars = 2 units
Brakes (type): Rheostatic
Body material: Aluminium
Weight (car): 26 tons unloaded

Traffic Data:
  Trains/track/hour: 16
  Train capacity (passengers): 580
  Total passengers/track/hour (peak): 9 280
  Train headways existing: 3¾ minutes

A MAN-built trainset at Langwasser Sud terminal station

OSAKA

Authority:
Osaka Municipal Transportation Bureau
Kujo Minami-I, Nishi-ku, Osaka 550, Japan
General Manager: Maseya Nishio
Superintendents:
  Management & Planning: Megumu Yamamoto
  General Management: Tomio Morita
  Subway Transportation: Masataka Sawaoka
  Automobile: Junichi Michiba
  Engineering: Yoshio Akamatsu
  Rapid Transit: Yasunori Hayaki
  R.T. Planning: Tsunehisa Miura
  R.T. Construction: Takeshi Oura

General: Japanese commerce centres largely on Osaka, Japan's second city. The city proper has 2.79 million inhabitants but its day-time population is 1.21 million more. Numerous rapid transit lines of both national railways and 5 private railways bring incoming passengers from the suburbs and other cities, to be distributed by Osaka's municipal public transport and the 13.5 mile (21.7 km) Osaka Loop Line.
The efforts being made to improve travel conditions include reserved bus lanes and implementation of suburban and subway extensions, recommended by the Ministry of Transport, to deal with an expected daily inflow of 1.8 million in 1990.
Osaka's first underground railway opened in May 1933 with two miles of line. Extensions were made in subsequent years and resumed after World War II despite financial difficulties. Expansion has been particularly rapid since 1964, when Line 1 was extended to provide interconnection with the JNR New Tokaido Line at Shin Osaka.
Osaka's Emergency Subway Construction Project was completed in 1970, but rapid expansion has continued, with a 2.8 km extension of Line 3 in 1972, and a 3.1 km extension of Line 2 in 1973.
With a present route length of 75.6 km the Osaka

Municipal Transportation Bureau intends to construct a total of 20 km new subway lines by 1985.
Already under construction are two new sections: Tennoji to Yao-Minami (10.4 km; estimated cost Yen 135 336 million); Shin-Fukae to Minamitatsumi (3 km; estimated cost Yen 39 252 million).
In 1977 work started on other two lines; Fukaebashi to Nagata (3 km; estimated cost Yen 45 675 million) and Moriguchi to Dainichi (0.6 km; estimated cost Yen 12 530 million).
A new 6.9 km elevated guideway system is under construction from Suminoe Park to Nakafuto in Port Town.
The Transportation Bureau also operates the city's buses. With the considerable increase in Subway patronage, and in general surface traffic, the city's trams were withdrawn in 1969, and the trolley-buses in June 1970.
The metropolitan transport area of Osaka is served by a network of electrified lines, comprising the JNR Osaka Loop Line and 9 private railways, 5 of which have their terminals in the city centre. Between Lines 1 and 6, and the Hanku and Osaka North Express railways, there is reciprocal working of lines.
The extension on Line 2, 5.4 km from Miyakojima northeast to Moriguchi was opened to traffic on 6 April 1977 and 10.4 km from Tennoji to Yao-Minami is being completed in 1980.

Route length: 75.6 km, mostly in tunnel, partly on elevated track.
Number of lines: 6 (5 transverse, 1 radial); double track.
Number of stations served: 61.
Average station spacing: 0.70 miles (1.10 km).
Average length of journey: 4.15 km.
Total passengers per annum carried by Osaka Municipal Transit System (including road services): (1976): 715 million passengers.
Car km per annum on underground system:
58 167 647.

Number of cars per train: Line 1, 8; Line 2, 6; Lines 3 and, 6, 5; Lines 4 and 5, 4.
Max number of trains per hour each way: 27 (Line 1).
Track gauge: 4 ft 8½ in (1.435 m).
Type of rail: Flat-bottomed, 100.8 lb/yd (50 kg/m).
Max gradient: 1 in 28.6 (3.5%).
Minimum radius of curves: 393 ft (120 m).

Type of tunnel: Generally double-track, cut and cover tunnel, rectangular section, mostly in re-inforced concrete with centre supports. At the city centre, parts of Lines 2 and 4 are at deep level in twin, single-track tube, internal diameter 18 ft 8 in (5.7 m). The depth of rectangular tunnel below surface varies from 75 ft (23 m) to 25 ft (7.5 m).
Method and voltage of current supply: Third rail, at 750 V dc and on Line 6, overhead wire at 1 500 V dc.
Rolling Stock: Number of cars owned: 692.

Details of latest cars: Series 30 (1973): Length 18.70 m 4 double-leaf doors on each side. Passenger capacity 130-140. Designed for short in-town passenger journeys, with rapid acceleration and deceleration characteristics.
Series 10 (1973): Length 18.9 m 4 double-leaf doors on either side. Aluminium construction. Provided with current chopper.
Most trains carry inductive radio equipment.

Signalling: Automatic block, with colour-light signals and train stops. In addition, protection is afforded by continuous Automatic Train Control (ATC) and Centralised Traffic Control (CTC).

Station layout: Some stations have an island platform (eg Shinsaibashi), others have separate side platforms (eg Showacho). Platform lengths vary from 120 m to 180 m (10-car train length).
Daikokucho Station's two island platforms permit cross-platform interchange between Line 1 and Line 3 in each direction.
Most stations have mezzanine space for ticket halls and passenger circulation.

OSLO

Authority:
A/S Oslo Sporveier
PO Box 2857 Kampen, Oslo 5, Norway
Administrative Director: Ove Skaug

General: Prior to 1966, Oslo's rapid transit system comprised a group of electrified light railway or tramway lines serving its western outskirts, and inter-urban tramways serving the east and south-east suburbs. The western groups, until 1928, had a common terminal at Majorstua, but a double-track underground line 1.25 miles (2.0 km) long, opened in that year, extended the group's services to the city centre at National Theatre.
There was no such facility for the east and south-east Oslo suburbs, where there has been considerable industrial and residential development since 1950. A new "Tunnelbane" system has therefore been constructed to link this area with the business centre. The whole scheme, the "Oslo Eastern Rapid Transit System", will include 21.75 miles (35.0 km), double-track line. Of this 18.1 miles (29.2 km) is now operative.
As part of the scheme, two new lines, the Grorud and Lambertseter Lines, have been constructed, and, together with the newly constructed common line (Tøyen-Jernbanetorget) linking them with the city centre, they were opened for traffic in 1966. The old tramway line, the Ostensjø line to Oppsal Station, has been re-constructed to rapid transit standards and extended to Skullerud. A fourth line, the Furuset, was opened for traffic in November, 1970, for a distance of 2.4 km serving two new stations. This line includes five stations, and work is proceeding with a further extension. The length of this new tunnel section is approximately 1 km. The completion date is estimated to be mid-1981.
The town centre tunnel project, running 0.74 km between Jernbanetorget station and National Theatre is now completed. This section includes a new station at Stentrum. Opened three years ago, all the trains on the Eastern system turn at this station. The Authority has decided Stentrum will also be the terminus for western system trains.

The next phase 2, which includes running-through for all trains, is being considered.
It is planned to eventually extend the section as far as Slottsparken, enabling interconnection with the western suburban branchline service. The alignment to Slottsparken passes mainly through rock, but as the rockroof has proved too weak cut-and-cover construction is to be adopted. Work on this section was started in 1977 and due to be completed in 1980 at a cost of Nkr 90 million.
Biggest project at present under construction is the 2.28 km Furuset branchline being built through clay and rock using open cut methods. Estimated cost of the line is Nkr 65 million.
A future extension is planned at a cost of Nkr 45 million from Furuset to Ellingsrud, via Ellingsrudasen—a length of approximately 1 km, with half in tunnel and half on the surface.
Details of the system in operation are as follows:

Number of stations: 43.
Average station spacing: 0.51 miles (815 m).
Minimum radius of curves: 656 ft (200 m).
Gauge: 1 435 mm
Main line curves (radius minimum): 200 m
  In the workshop area (radius minimum): 50 m
Max gradient, stations: 3%
Platform length: 110 m
Platform width: 4—8 m
Platform level above rail: 1.00—1.07 m
Ballast, main line: 0.45 m
Ballast, concrete tunnels: 0.35 m
Switches, main line: 1 : 9
Switches, workshop area and sidings: 1 : 7
Number of cars per train: 6.
Estimated capacity per car: 150 (incl. 63 seats).
Average scheduled speed: 19.8 mph (32 km/h).
Method and voltage of current supply: 3rd rail, underside contact, from Oslo Electricity Supply Commission at 5 000 V ac transformed to 750 V dc through 14 rectifier stations. Total installation 55 000 kW.
Signalling: Cab signal system, actuated by coded signal impulses through track, controls the following speeds: 70-50-30-15 km/h. Train services operate under Central Traffic Control at Traffic Centre building

at Tøyen. Trains' communication equipment includes radio and telephone.
Power Supply: 14 Rectifier stations 750 V dc. Third rail, weight 40 kg/m. Underside contact. Total installation 71 900 A.
Signal and security equipment:
  Cab-signals based on: Max speed on level straight line: 70 km/h
  Train interval: Joint tunnel 90 s
  Branches 120 s
Following speeds are controlled:
  H—70 km/h: High
  M—50 km/h: Middle
  L—30 km/h: Low
  K—15 km/h: Crawl
  In the joint tunnel 50—30—15 km/h are controlled, on the branch lines 70—50—15 km/h.
Telecommunications:
  A Two-way telephone communications, incl. Oslo Telephone and special internal lines.
  B One-way telecommunication installations, loudspeaker and amplifier, alarm for fire and assault clocks, thermometers and indicators for ground water levels.
  C Radio communication between traffic control centre and trains.
  D Miscellaneous installations for tunnel lighting, tunnel ventilation, tunnel gates and electric heating of switches.
Stations: Five inner stations are underground. Grønland station is built on two levels, with circulating area, ticket offices and shops over platforms and tracks. Side platforms, 110 m long, are sufficient for 6-car trains.
Rolling Stock: 62 cars, all motored and of steel construction, are 17.0 m long overall, 3.20 m wide, and have 3 double doors, opening to 1.25 m on each side. Four 98 kW motors per car. Dynamic, air and handbraking equipment is installed.
Distance between couplings: 17.50 m
Length of body: 17.00 m
Max external width: 3.20 m
Max height above rail: 3.67 m
Floor level above rail: 1.14 m

Dia. of wheels, new tyres: 0.82 m
Max wear on tyres: 60 mm
Distance between bogie centres: 11.00 m
Weight, unladen type 1$_1$: 28.8 tonnes
    type 1$_2$: 29.8 tonnes
Weight, laden, 170 pass. type 1$_1$: 40.8 tonnes
    type 1$_2$: 41.8 tonnes
Number of motors in each car: 4
Capacity of motor, 1 hour, 1 540 R/M: 98 kW
Capacity of motor, lasting: 86 kW

Voltage: 375 V dc
Gear ratio: 6.73 : 1
Double sliding doors on each side: 3
Clearance of door openings: 1.25 m
Seats for passengers, type 1$_1$ = 60
    type 1$_2$ = 63
Standing passengers (allowed): 107
Max speed: 70 km/h
Acceleration (0-40 km/h): 1.0 m/s^2
Middle retardation from 50 km/h to standstill:

emergency brakes 0.9 m/s^2
dynamic brakes max 1.35 m/s^2
Load dependent dynamic brakes and compressed air brakes. Hand-brake
Current collectors, on each bogie: 2
Car Dept: Near Ryen station on Lambertseter line. Capacity 120 cars, but equipped for maintenance of 150 cars. Extra capacity of workshop is used for tram-car bogie maintenance during winding-up period of Oslo's tramway system.

PARIS

Authority:
Régie Autonome des Transports Parisiens (RATP)
53ter quai des Grands Augustins, Paris (6e), France

Chairman: Roger Belin
General Manager: Jacques Deschamps
Railways Manager: Philippe Essig

General: The present Paris Metro system originated as a short cross-city line of some 6¼ miles serving 18 stations, which were opened for passenger traffic in 1900. Over subsequent years it developed rapidly into a closely-meshed urban underground railway system, confined until 1934 within the Paris city boundaries. It extended into the suburbs and now operates over 275.5 miles of route (including the 92.1 km Regional Express system) serving 333 named stations corresponding to 412 stopping stations.
The main characteristics of the Paris Metro system (with the exception of the Regional Express system) are the close proximity of its stations one with the other and the general shallowness of its tunnels and stations. It has in consequence the advantages both of accessibility and convenience which, coupled with most intensive train service, accounts for the fact that the Metro carries more than half of all the passengers conveyed by the Paris Transport Authority. Like most other extensive urban systems the present Metro is a product of formerly separate transport undertakings. In 1942 it was joined with the Paris bus organisation, and in 1949 the present Authority, the Régie Autonome des Transports Parisiens (a public corporation) came into being.
The Paris Metro system carries much short-distance traffic, and although the number of passengers carried exceeds that on the London Transport rail system, the average distance travelled is much less. Of the 15 urban lines, 9 are wholly underground, the remaining 6 having short sections on the surface or on viaduct. Unlike the French main-line railways, the urban system (but not the Regional Express system) has right-hand running throughout its urban system.
Already operating 183.4 km of Urban Metro Lines (1) and 92.2 km of Regional Express System (RER), RATP has a number of lines under construction and several projected up to 1990.
With the opening on 4 October 1979 of an extension of line 7, between Porte de la Villette and Fort d'Aubervilliers, the total route length of the urban metro now reaches 185.8 km (about 116 miles).

Route length (1978): 171 miles *(275.6 km)* including Line A (Saint-Germain-en-Laye—Boissy-Saint-Léger) 33.8 miles *(54.5 km)* and Line B (Sceaux Line) 23.4 miles *(37.7 km)*.
Number of lines: 13 radial, 2 circumferential, and the Regional Express System (Lines A and B).
Number of stations served: Urban system 353: Lines A28, B31.
Average station spacing: Urban system 0.34 miles *(0.54 km)*; Line A 1.24 miles, Line B 0.74 miles.
Passengers per annum (1978):
    Urban system 1 103 500 000
    Line A 119 300 000
    Line B 58 900 000
Total passengers per annum carried by Paris Transport Authority (including road services and Montmartre cable-railway as well as Metro and RER (1978): 2 003 400 000
Car-km per annum (1978): Urban system 189 100 000
    Line A 33 400 000
    Line B 15 500 000
Number of trains operated on each line at peak hours: 4 (Line 3 bis) to 66 (Line 9)
Number of cars per train: Metro 4, 5 or 6; RER 3, 6 or 9
Average scheduled speed (including stops): Metro 23.6 km/h (14.8 mph)
RER Line A
    Omnibus 48.1 km/h (30 mph)
    Semi-direct 51.4 km/h (32.1 mph)

Line B
    Omnibus 31.3 km/h (19.5 mph)
    Semi-direct 40.7 km/h (25.3 mph)
Track gauge: 4 ft 8^{11}/$_{16}$ in (1.44 m).
Method and voltage of current supply: Motive power is supplied to the Metro at 750 V dc through 109 automatic rectifier stations. Initially the power for traction, lighting and signalling is received at 63 000 V ac and 225 000 V ac and then stepped down to 15 000 V through 11 main transformers (and exceptionally received at 20 000 V).
Power distribution to conventional trains is via third rail and on lines with pneumatic-tyred stock through insulated lateral guide bars and laterally-operating shoes returning through the running rails
For the RER system the method of current supply is the same as for the urban system, but motive power is supplied at 1 500 V dc through 36 automatic transformer-rectifier stations and distributed through overhead line and pantograph. The RER rectifier stations distant from the centre of Paris are fed directly from l'Electricité de France at 20 000 V ac
Rolling Stock:
Urban system: 1 979 motor cars including 613 pneumatic-tyred cars, 935 new conventional cars on lines 3, 5, 7, 8, 9, 10, 12 and 13 (31 are of the latest type, called MF 77) and 60 motor units of the articulated sets operating on line 10; 1 455 trailers including 315 pneumatic-tyred cars, 599 new conventional cars (20 are of the latest type called MF 77) and 40 trailers of the articulated sets operating on line 10
RER: 384 motored cars, 148 of which are of older type (Z type) on line B (former Sceaux line). The remaining motored cars are of MS 61 type, 118 trailers of MS 61 type
The new motored cars (MF 77) on the urban system. are 51 ft 8 in (15.50 m) long with driving cab and 51 ft

New Paris RATP/SNCF "interconnexion"

7 in (15.47 m) long without driving cab. The overall length of a Regional Express train 3-car unit is 239 ft 2 in (72.900 m).
Signalling: Generally automatic block, with ac track circuits, and three-aspect colour-light signals. No train stops are used. Line B: 4-aspect colour-light signals with instantaneous repetition of overrun signal inside drivers cab. Line A: French National Railways signalling- signals repeated in cab on console showing aspect which train passes and of signal approaching.
Revenues (1978): Urban system Fr2 414 500 000, RER Fr826 000 000. Road services Fr1 957 800 000

Lines recently completed or under construction

Lines	Sections	Completion
RER		
A (Saint-Germain-en-Laye—Boissy-Saint-Léger and Noisy-le-Grand-Mont d'Est)	Auber—Nation	Dec 1977
	Vincennes—Noisy-le-Grand-Mont d'Est	Dec 1977
B (Châtelet—Saint-Rémy-lès-Chevreuse and Robinson) (former Sceaux Line)	Châtelet-Les Halles—Luxembourg	Dec 1977

Lines	Sections	Planned opening
A	Noisy-le-Grand-Mont d'Est—Torcy	1980
B	Châtelet-Les Halles Gare du Nord	1981
	This junction will be the first stage of the interconnection between the RER lines (Paris Transport Authority) and the SNCF suburban railway lines	

METRO Lines	Extensions under construction Sections	Opened/planned opening
7	Porte de la Villette—Fort d'Aubervilliers	1979
10	Porte d'Auteuil—Boulogne Jean Jaurès	1980
	Boulogne Jean Jaurès—Boulogne Rhin et Danube	1981
13 bis	Porte de Clichy—Asnières—Gennevilliers I	1980
7	Porte d'Italie—Kremlin-Bicêtre	1982

Planned extensions at short term Lines	Sections	Planned opening
7	Kremlin-Bicêtre—Villejuif III	1984
5	Eglise de Pantin—Bobigny Préfecture	1984
7	Fort d'Aubervilliers—La Courneuve Quatre Routes	
4	Porte d'Orléans—Bagneux	
13	Châtillon-Montrouge—Châtillon II	after 1984
1	Pont de Neuilly—La Défense	
RER (Line B)	Construction of the Saint-Michel station	
RER (Line A)	Interconnection of Line A at Nanterre Préfecture with the Cergy-Pontoise line of the French National Railways	1984

Eventual extensions at long term Lines	Sections	
9	Mairie de Montreuil—Rosny-sous-Bois	
11	Mairie des Lilas—Romainville	
13	Saint-Denis Basilique—Stains	
13	Châtillon II—Vélizy	
8	Créteil Préfecture—Créteil Parc Régional	

PEKING

Authority:
Metropolitan Railway Department
Peking Municipal Council City Administration Building, Peking, People's Republic of China

Type of system: Full-metro.

General: Peking Underground Railway is the first Chinese-built underground railway. The last construction project was to build a circle line and two radial lines with a total track length of about 57 km, completed in 3 phases.
First phase: from Peking station to Apple Farm Station. Second phase: comprising two sections, one from Peking station starting north before turning west

through the city farm areas and then south to complete the semi-circle at Fu-xin Gate station. The other from Peking station to the Thermoelectric Plant station.
Third phase: from western Straight Gate station to Yi-he station.
The first phase project covered a total length of 23.6 km. Construction started in July 1965 and was completed in September 1969.
There are now 17 stations along this route, with one above-ground section where the carriage depot is. The average distance between stations is 1.47 km, the longest distance is 2.56 km and the shortest is 0.85 km.
The 17 stations are categorised into three types, A, B and C, in accordance with their position importance and expected passenger flows. Type A is the largest

station and type C the smallest.
The following are the 17 stations grouped under the three types:
A type: Peking station.   B type: Chong-wen Gate, Xuan-wu Gate, South Li-Shi Road, Mu-xi-di, Military Museum, Li-xin, Five Pines and Yu-quan Road.
C type: Xin-hua Street, Zhang-chun Street, Wan-shou Road, Ba-bao Hill, Ba-jiao Village, Old Town Road and Apple Farm.
The effective length of the station platform is 118 m, available for six carriages to stop, but the actual length of the platform is 120 to 150 m. The decorative surface materials for the station include raw marble, grinding stone and tiles.
The Peking Underground Railway electric carriages were jointly built by Zhang-chun plant and Xiang-tan

electric machinery factory.
The first phase project employed BJ-2 and BJ-3 types electric carriages which are 19 m long, 3.509 m high and 2.65 m wide. Each carriage carries 186 passengers including 60 seated and 126 standing.
Each carriage has three doors either side 1.2 m wide. Each electric carriage is self-powered, with a construction speed of 80 km/h. Every section comprises two carriages and every 2, 4 or 6 carriages can be hooked together as one train. The electric carriage traction uses direct current at 750 V with the third rail supplying the electricity.
The communication system includes automatic telephone, scheduling telephone, station announcing devices and electric clocks.
The signal system includes electric interlocking, automatic block, concentration of scheduling, locomotive signal and automatic stopping devices.
Longitudinal ventilation installations are used for tunnel ventilation and ventilation equipment and chambers are used for every station and track section.
The track gauge is 1.435 mm and the radius of the track's flat curve is generally over 300 m, while some are only 200 m.
At present four carriages are used per train, giving a top speed of 70 km/h. The minimum time between each train is four minutes. In 1979 the total number of passengers was 46 million.
The 2nd phase circle line project is still under construction.

PHILADELPHIA

Authority:
Southeastern Pennsylvania Transportation Authority
200, W. Wyoming Avenue, Philadelphia, USA

Chairman: James C. McConnon
General Manager: William R. Eaton

General: Philadelphia and District present another example of large-scale co-ordination of different transport concerns serving a region, integrated under a single Authority. In 1963 the Southeastern Pennsylvania Transportation Authority was created by legislature to co-ordinate and improve transportation in the five-county area of Philadelphia, Bucks, Chester, Delaware and Montgomery Counties. Previously these services were operated separately by public and privately owned concerns.
Progressive amalgamation or acquisition over the years culminated in the creation of SEPTA, which variously owns and operates, leases (or renders financial aid to) the services formerly individually operated. The last acquisition was the Norristown rapid transit railway and a suburban bus system from the Philadelphia Suburban Transportation Company in January 1970.
The oldest underground-elevated line in Philadelphia is the east-west Market Street Line, completed in 1908. Alongside its in-town tunnel tracks for part of their length run also the tracks of local street cars. The "Frankford Elevated" to Bridge in the north-east followed in 1922; the wholly-underground north-south Broad Street Line in 1928, and a spur off this line to the 8th Avenue shopping district in 1932. The Camden Line from 16th Street to Camden, across the Benjamin Franklin Bridge over the Delaware River, was opened initially in 1936. It now forms part of the Lindenwold Line mentioned below.
Interworking of the Market Street-Frankford Line on one hand and the Broad Street, and Ridge-Eighth, on the other hand, is impossible because of the different gauges. In addition to its underground system, the Authority subsidises suburban Penn-Central and Reading Railroads' Philadelphia commuter services through annual purchase of service contracts. It also operates an extensive network of bus, trolleybus, and tramway services.
Planned is a 6.4 mile *(10.3 km)* extension of the same line at its northern end, branching out north-east from Erie Station. The extensions form part of a $1 400 m Capital Programme announced under a comprehensive Plan for the whole of Philadelphia and its Regions' mass transit systems.
A basic cash fare system operates on any of the Transportation Company's vehicles for any distance within the City limits, plus a small charge for first and for subsequent transfers.
Route length: 29 miles *(47 km)* including 18 miles *(29 km)* in tunnel.
Number of lines: 4 (2 transverse, 1 radial, and 1 in-town); all double or quadruple track.
Number of stations served: 52.
Average station spacing: 0.58 miles *(0.93 km)*.
Passengers per annum (subway-elevated system only): (1975): 58 000 000. The authority now records only revenue passengers. The stated total thus excludes transferees from other services.
Average journey (subway elevated system): 3.5 miles.
Max number of trains per hour each way: Broad St. Line 25, Market St. Line 26.
Max number of cars per train: 6.
Estimated capacity per car: Broad Street cars: 190 (including 67 seats). Market-Frankford: 150 (including 56 seats).
Average schedule speed (including stops): Broad St. Line, local: 17.2 mph *(27.7 km/h)*. bmarket St. Line: 20.2 mph *(32.5 km/h)*. (Broad St. Line carries both local and express trains).
Track gauge: Market Street-Frankford Line 5 ft 2¼ in *(1.581 m)*; Broad Street, Ridge-Eighth and Camden Lines 4 ft 8½ in *(1.435 m)*.
Weight and type of rails: 100 lb/yd *(49.6 kg/m)*. All flat-bottomed.
Max gradient: 1 in 20 (5%).
Minimum radius of curves: Market Street-Frankford Line, 105 ft *(32 m)*: Broad Street and Ridge-Eighth Lines, 160 ft *(49 m)*.
Type of tunnel: Double or multiple track tunnel, of rectangular section.
Method and voltage of current supply: Third rail (top and bottom contact, according to line); 600 V dc
Rolling Stock: Number of cars owned: 466. Stainless steel cars have now replaced the older stock on the Market-Frankford Line. They were manufactured by the Budd Company of Philadelphia and are 55 ft long and 9 ft 1 in wide. 46 single cars seat 54 passengers per car; 112 coupled pairs seat 56 passengers per car. There are four driving motors per car. The single cars have controls at each end and can be operated in combination with the coupled cars. On the latter there is only one control position, and these cars cannot be operated singly. Braking is dynamic and/or pneumatic.
Signalling: Automatic block, with colour-light signals.
Station layout: Many of the stations have direct entrance from buildings and shops. Around the City Hall, there is a vast complex of passageways and concourses, providing undercover connection between eight underground stations, the Pennsylvania and Reading Railroad terminals, and numerous offices and shops.
Other railways: Philadelphia is also served by a system of suburban lines including a self-contained rapid transit railway, the Norristown High-speed Line, also operated by SEPTA. This electrified line runs from 69th Street Terminus of the Market Street Line northwest for 13½ miles *(8.4 km)* to Norristown. Track gauge is 4 ft 8½ in *(1.435 m)* and current supply is by top contact third rail. There are 19 cars run as single units or 2-car sets, and two former "Electroliner" trains.

Authority:
Port Authority Transit Corporation (PATCO)
Benjamin Franklin Bridge Plaza, Camden, NJ 08101, USA
General: Additional to the SEPTA networks, a Rapid Transit surface-underground railway to serve Philadelphia was opened on 15 February 1969 to passenger traffic. The surface portion together with the former Locust Street Subway and Delaware Bridge line comprises the new Lindenwold Line whose in-town end is at 16th Street. It is operated by PATCO a subsidiary of the Delaware River Port Authority. The services are operated by 6-car commuter type trains, the stock of 75 cars, built by the Budd Company, being powered by four dc traction motors giving train speeds of up to 75 mph *(121 km/h)*. The Westinghouse system of signalling includes cab signalling devices automatically governing train speeds from start to stop.
A renewal of interest in expanding the PATCO system has arisen since the encouraging growth in passenger numbers, from 6.1 million in 1969 to 8.6 million in 1970, and approximately 10.5 million in 1972. The expansion plan endorsed by the Delaware Valley Regional Planning Commission proposed that first priority be given to a four-station extension east from Broadway (Camden) to Moorestown Mall, and further expansion is planned.
Present route length of the Philadelphia rapid transit line operated by PATCO is 22.6 km. Of that length about 18 per cent is in subway and the remainder either depressed below grade in open cut or elevated on embankments or viaducts.
Since it opened in 1969 the line has carried over 70 million passengers and present daily average is about 42 000. There are 14 passenger stations, each equipped with television surveillance and automatic fare dispensing equipment.
While there is no construction work under way at present, approval and funds have been provided for residual requirements and a new station on the existing line.
Future line projects are in the planning stage and an extensive study for expanding the system is now nearing completion. Projects under study include:
—extension of the existing line from Lindenwold, 11.1 km to Atco at an estimated cost of $95 million.
—construction of a new branchline extending south from Camden, 29.7 km to Glassboro at an estimated cost of $308 million.
—construction of a branchline from Camden, 22.9 km to Mount Laurel at an estimated cost of $267 million.

Technical Data:
Gauge: 1.435 m
Route length: 22.6 km
In tunnel: 4.6 km
Number of lines: 1
Number of stations (total): 12
(in tunnel): 6
Average distance between stations: 2.12 km
Electric system: Third rail; 600 V

Rolling Stock:

Car type (year introduced):	1968(1)	1968(2)
Number of units:	25	50
Car dimensions (length):	20.57 m	20.57 m
(width):	3.05 m	3.05 m
(height):	3.76 m	3.76 m
Passenger capacity per car		
(total):	120	120
(seated):	72	80
Motors per car:	4	4
Rating:	116 kW	116 kW
Train composition (minimum): 1 (max): 8		
Acceleration (max):	1.34	1.34
Deceleration (emergency):	1.43	1.43
Brakes (type): Rheostatic		
Body material: Steel		
Weight (tonnes) Motorcar:	36.1	33.9

Traffic Data:
Trains/track/hour: 12
Train capacity (passengers): 960
Total passengers/track/hour (peak): 11 520
Train headways
existing: 5 minutes
Passengers carried (weekday): 38 000
(annually): 9 500 000

PITTSBURGH

Authority:
Port Authority of Allegheny County (PAT)
Beaver and Island Avenues, Pittsburgh, Pennsylvania 15233, USA

Chairman, Board of Directors: Donald H. Hoffman
Executive Director: James R. Maloney

Type of system: Proposed PTS.

General: The Port Authority's Mon Valley commuter rail system is 18.2 miles long, starting in Pittsburgh near the Monongahela River. It follows the Monongahela River through Hazelwood, Braddock and McKeesport where the route follows the Youghiogheny River to Versailles Boro. The commuter rail operation uses Chessie and P&LE Railways trackage.
The Pittsburgh trolley system consists of 22.5 miles of right-of-way used by President's Conference Committee (PCC) trolleys. This system services the South Hills corridor of the Pittsburgh area. The Stage I LRT system consists of the reconstruction of 10.5 miles of the existing system plus electrical rehabilitation of the remaining 12 miles. It is a line-haul system over which new light rail vehicles (LRV) and the existing PCCs will operate.
The Stage I LRT system will rebuild the present 42/38 (Mt Lebanon via Beechview) trolley line and a section of the Shannon Library and Shannon Drake Routes (35 and 36) south of Castle Shannon; construct an extension to the South Hills shopping centre in Upper St Clair, a new LRT tunnel under Washington Road in Mt Lebanon, an express entry into Pittsburgh town centre via the Panhandle railroad bridge, and a town centre distribution system consisting of a subway alignment; and purchase of approximately 55 new light rail vehicles. Stage IA is anticipated by the end of 1984.

Urban structure:
Population of city area: 1 800 000
Land area: 55 sq miles
Primary road network within city boundary: Parkways, inter-state, route I-76

Technical Data:
Gauge: 5 ft 2½ in (Light Rail System); 4 ft 8½ in (Commuter Rail System)
Route length: 25 miles; 14 miles
Track length: 25 miles; 18.2 miles
New lines (planned): Reconstruction of 10.5 miles (double track); —
Number of routes in operation: 4; 1
Number of stations (total): 85 stops; 4 stations
Average distance between stations: 0.33 miles; 4.5 miles
Max length of station platforms: 210 ft; 200 ft
Gradient (max): 9.2%
Curvature (max): 32 ft minimum radius
Speed (design max): 55 mph; 55 mph
Method and voltage of current supply: 600 V dc
Frequency of train services in minutes (currently): min 2/h, max 12/h; 2 trips/peak hour
(planned): 1/minute; 2 trips/peak hour
Capacity per train (passengers seated): 52; 360
(passengers standing): 50; 150

Rolling stock characteristics: (Commuter Rail System)
Car types: Motor cars; Trailers; LRT
Number of units: (proposed) 2F9 locos, push-pull type; remanufactured 1600 Series Pullman coaches; PCCs
Car dimensions: 2 units consisting of 1 loco + 4 coaches each unit
Number of doors per side: 1/side/coach, 2/side/RDC; 2/car, one side only
Number of passengers per car (total): 130 (RDC); 80 (Coaches); 80 (LRT)
(seated): 90; 52; 52
Motors per car: 1; 2
Motor rating (kW): 1 750 hp; 600 V dc

PRAGUE

Authority:
Dopravni Podnik Hlavniho Mesta Prahy (DP)
Bubenska 1, Praha 7, Czechoslovakia
Telephone: 37 25 41

Type of system: Full-metro.

General: With 6.5 km of subway in operation since 1974 Prague authorities completed construction of 11 km of new lines in 1978. Total length of the planned underground rail system is 90 km.
The ultimate underground network will consist of three transverse lines A, B, C laid with 4 ft 8½ in *(1.435 m)* gauge track, which will form a triangle of lines at the centre supplemented by Line D. The first stage until 1983-85 comprises a network of three surface and underground lines of a total projected length of 21 miles *(34 km)*. The ultimate network will be about 58 miles *(93 km)* in total route length, serving 104 stations.
The work completed in 1978 is that on the first 4.2 miles *(6.8 km)* of Line C, which is all in tunnel except for the Botic River and valley crossing by the 480 m Klement-Gottwald Bridge. 2.9 km of this section is being built in rectangular tunnel by the cut and cover method, which employs the 'Milan' method of wall construction. The remaining 3.4 km will be in circular tunnel 18 ft 8 in *(5.10 m)* internal diameter, lined with concrete segments except where iron lining is assumed necessary in water-bearing or disturbed soil. Excavation is by Soviet-built shield.
In 1959, the first full year of operation, the metro had an 8.8 per cent share of the city's transport traffic. The authorities predicted that by 1980 the metro would have a 9.2 per cent share.
The third section of Line C from Sokolovská to Vvben Ského is due to start operations by the end of 1982. Prague's metro cars are built at the Mytyshchinsky plant in the Soviet Union. Each vehicle is an independent motor car with driver's cab, and trainsets of up to five cars can be operated.

Technical Data:
Gauge: 1.435 m
Route length: 6.5 km
In tunnel: 6.5 km
Projected new lines (in construction): 11 km
(in design): 78.2 km
Number of lines: 1
Number of stations (total): 9
(in tunnel): 8
Average distance between stations: 850 m
Stations:
platform length (minimum): 100 m
Gradient (max): 4%
Curvature (max): 300 m
Speed (average commercial): 35 km/h

Electric system: Third rail; 750 V

Rolling Stock:

Car type (year introduced):	Proposed	Type Ecs Production
Number of units:	8	50
Car dimensions (length):	15.84 m	19.21 m
(width):	2.90 m	2.71 m
(height):	3.70 m	3.70 m
Passenger capacity		
per car (total):	192	220
(seated):	44	42
Motors per car:	4	4
Rating:	84 kW	84 kW

Train composition (minimum): 3
(max): 6

Acceleration (max):	1.0	1.15
Deceleration (emergency):	1.2	1.2

Brakes (type): Rheostatic/Electro pneumatic
Body material: Steel

Weight (tonnes) Motorcar:	23.0	32.5

Traffic Data:
Trains/track/hour: 40 (planned)
Train capacity (passengers): 1 000
Total passengers/track/hour (peak): 40 000 (planned)
Train headways
design: 1.5 minutes
existing: 3 minutes

RIO DE JANEIRO

Authority:
Companhia do Metropolitano do Rio de Janeiro Metro
Avenue N.S. de Copacabana 493, Rio de Janeiro, Brazil

Type of system: Full-metro.

General: Following a slow start on Rio de Janeiro's first 12.8 km subway line—with only 1.4 km completed between 1969 and 1975—work is now being stepped up and the section between Botafogo and Anterode Quental came into operation in 1979.

Technical Data:
Gauge: 1.60 m
Route length: 37 km (5.1 presently operating)
Track length: 88 km
In tunnel: 13.5 km
New lines (planned): 133.5 km, (under construction): 33.8 km
Number of lines in operation: 1 (practically)
Number of stations (total): 31 (15 in line 1; 5 in line 2; 11 in pre-metro).
Number of stations in tunnel: 15
Average distance between stations: 860 m
Max length of station platforms: 136 m (line 1); 180 m (line 2)
Gradient (max): 4%
Curvature (max): 500 m
Speed (design max): 100 km/h (metro car) and 80 km/h (pre-metro car).
(average commercial): 35 km/h (both)
Type of rail: 56.9 km/h
Type of tunnel: Rectangular section in cut and cover; Bernold System for 550 m; and Copacabana—New Aystrian tunnelling method (NATM).

Traffic and finances:
Max number of trains per hour (one way): 4
Frequency of services in minutes:
(currently): 7
(planned): 2
Capacity per train (passengers seated): metro car (40) pre-metro car (58)
(passengers standing): metro car (271)
pre-metro car (258)
Passenger journeys per annum: In December 1979 about 50 000 passengers were registered.

Rolling stock characteristics:
Car type: Rio Metro has only motor cars; A with cabin and B without cabin.
Number of units: 106 (A); 164 (B); 68 (PM)
Car dimensions:
Length (m): 21.885; 21.75; 25.476
Width (m): 3.17 ; 3.17; 2.7
Height (m): 3.65; 3.65; 5.75
Total floor area (m^2): 69.38; 68.95; 55
Number of doors per side: 3; 3; 4
Door width (m): 1.90; 1.90; 1.30
Number of passengers per car:
(total): 350; 377; 317
(seated): 40; 48; 58
Motors per car: 4; 4; 2
Motor rating (kW): 143; 143; 200
Power per train (minimum): 3.432; 3.432; 8
Acceleration (max): 1.12; 1.12; 1
Deceleration (normal service): 1.2; 1.2; 1.2
(emergency): 1.2; 1.2; 1.5
Max design speed (km/h): 100; 100; 80
Bogies (type): regenerative/rheostatic/pneumatic; rheostatic/pneumatic/magnetic
Weight (empty in tonnes): 40; 38; 38

ROME

Authority:
Societa delle Tramvie e Ferrovie Elettriche di Roma (STEFER)
Piazzale Ostrense 6, 00154 Rome, Italy
Telephone: (06) 57 98
Telegrams: STEFER-ROMA

General: Construction of Line A continues. The line's infrastructure has been completed from Termini eastward to Ostaria del Curato *(10.3 km)* and from Termini westward to Piazzale Flamingo *(2.2 km)*. Line A, when complete, will extend from Via Ottaviano in the west for some 9 miles *(15 km)* to Ostaria del Curato.
The existing Metro serves a less populated area than will the proposed new lines. The whole line was opened to public traffic on 10 February 1955. The Metro was built wholly at State expense, but is at present being operated (with its own rolling stock) by STEFER, a private company also operating the Rome-Ostia line, over whose tracks some Metro trains operate via a connection at Magliana.
Route length: 6.8 miles *(11.03 km)*, including 3.7 miles *(6.1 km)* in tunnel.
Number of lines: 1 (radial); double track.
Number of stations served: 11.
Average station spacing: 0.6 miles *(1.1 km)*.
Passengers per annum: 25 300 000.
Passengers per annum on whole Rome Public Transport (including buses, trams, trolley buses): 718 177 700.
Average length of journey: 3.9 miles *(6.2 km)*.
Number of cars per train: 6 (Termini-Lido); 3 (Termini-Laurentina).
Estimated capacity per car: 240 (including 48 seated).
Track gauge: 4 ft 8½ in *(1.435 m)*.
Weight and type of rails: 93.8 lb/yd *(46.5 kg/m)*, flat-bottomed.
Minimum radius of curves: 640 ft *(195 m)*.
Max gradient: 1 in 28.6 *(3.5%)*.
Type of tunnel: Double-track, elliptical tunnel, 26 ft 4 in *(8.02 m)* wide and 18 ft 1 in *(5.5 m)* high from rail level.
Method and voltage of current supply: Overhead wire; 1 500 V dc. There are four sub-stations, drawing their power from the public electricity supply.

Rolling Stock:

Car type:	1954	1956
Number of units	18	22
Car dimensions (length):	19.10 m	19.10 m
(width):	3.04 m	3.04 m
(height):	3.61 m	3.61 m
Total floor area (m^2):	57	57
Doors per side;	4	4
Door (width):	1.25 m	1.25 m
Passages per side:	8	8
Passengers		
per car: (total):	243	247
(seated):	48	52
Motors per car:	4	4
Motor rating:	117 kW 161 hp	117 kW 161 hp
Power per train		
(minimum):	1 404	1 404
(max):	1 404	1 404
Acceleration (max):	—	1.25
Deceleration		
(normal service):	—	0.84
Speed (max):	100 km/h	—
Bogie truck rigid base:	2.8 m	—
Distance between bogie Pivot:	11.0 m	—

Brakes (type): Rheostatic/Electro-magnetic
Body material: Aluminium
Weight-empty (tons): 40.5
Tare/floor area (kg/m^2): 711
Tare/length (kg/m): 2 120
Tare/passenger (kg/pass): 167
Signalling: Automatic block, with track circuiting. Cab signalling is contemplated, with a signalling capacity of 40 trains per hour.
Station layout: Stations have side platforms. Some ticket offices are underground, others on the surface.

ROTTERDAM

Authority:
Rotterdam Electric Tramways
Kleiweg 244, Rotterdam 12, Netherlands

General: The Rotterdam Metro follows a main traffic route connecting southern dock and residential areas with the city centre north of the River Maas. The Metro took 8 years to build, from 1960 to its opening for traffic in February 1968.
It connects at Central station with the Netherlands Railways, and along the Metro route with more than 30 bus and tram routes, including an express tram route. To the south-west the line has been extended from Slinge to Hoogvliet.
The Metro's relatively long construction period was due to the complexities of projecting a railway under a wide river, and building it partly within a city that lies below river level. Prefabricated tunnel sections, built in excavated dry dock and excavated trenches, were sealed, the dock or trench flooded, and the sections floated wholly or partially submerged to their respective sites and sunk into position.
Construction work is underway to add a new 13-km centre-east city line (5-km in tunnel) by 1981. In 1979 it was decided to build two possible extensions: a 1.5-km underground extension to the existing line, and a new branchline to Marconiplein (1 km).
Operative route length: Approx 10.5 miles *(17 km)* of which 2.7 miles *(4.3 km)* is on viaduct, 3 km underground or underwater tunnel.
Number of lines: 1 transverse, double track.
Number of stations served: 12.
Passengers per annum: 35 million.
Passengers per annum on the whole Rotterdam public transport system, including buses, trams and Metro, (all operated by RET): 131 million.
Number of coach-units per train: 4 (articulated) maximum.
Estimated capacity per articulated unit: 230 passengers, included 80 seated.
Max number of trains per hour: 20 in each direction.
Line capacity: 35 000 passengers per hour.
Track gauge: 4 ft 8½ in *(1.435 m)*.
Track detail: Welded rail is fixed by spring clamps direct on to longitudinal concrete supports. There are no cross-ties.
Minimum radius of curves: 650 ft 6 in *(192.7 m)*.
Max gradient: 1 in 26.
Type of tunnel and viaduct: Rectangular twin-track underground tunnel with supporting web, 32 ft 2 in by 18 ft 4½ in externally, lies at maximum depth of 31 ft 6 in (underwater tunnel's maximum depth is 58 ft 1 in). The viaduct, carrying tracks approximately 30 ft above ground, is basically longitudinal concrete beams resting on recessed transverse beams, carried on single piers at 150 ft intervals.
Current supply: Third rail underside contact, 750 V dc, rectified from 10 000 V main supply through 7 substations.
Rolling Stock: Number of coach-units owned: 71. The articulated units 95 ft 3 in long overall and 8 ft 9⅝ in wide, rest on three bogies, each of the unit's six axles being motored. Braking is electro-dynamic with electro-pneumatic disc wheel brakes.
Signalling: A visual signals system in the driving cab operates under Automatic Train Control from the control centre at Hilledijk car depot.
Station lay-out: Mostly side platforms, 393 ft 8 in *(120 m)* long, equipped with close-circuit television for surveillance. Below-ground concourses at underground stations and intermediate level concourses at elevated stations are reached by escalators, further escalators at latter stations rising to platform levels.

SAN FRANCISCO

Authority:
Bay Area Rapid Transit District
800 Madison St, Oakland, Cal 94607, USA
Telephone: 465 4100

Type of system: Full-metro.

BART construction officially began on 19 June 1964. Completed 10 months later, the test track was used to develop and evaluate new and sophisticated design concepts for BART's transit cars and automatic train control system.
A joint venture enterprise formed to manage all technical, as well as construction aspects of the BART project, PB-T-B was comprised of three well-known engineering consultant firms: Parsons-Brinckerhoff-Quade & Douglas of New York (who had done the original BART transportation plan); Tudor Engineering Company of San Francisco; and Bechtel Corporation of San Francisco.
Construction began on the Oakland subway in January 1966.
The 3.2-mile bore through the hard rock of the Berkeley hills was completed in February, 1967, after 466 work days.
In July 1967 work began on the Market Street subway and stations. Carried out 80-100 ft below heavy downtown traffic, against the combined pressure of mud and Bay water, the work required one of the greatest concentrations of tunneling crews and equipment in construction history. Construction of the giant five-storey-high stations beneath Market Street, and the tunnels themselves, was accomplished under extremely difficult conditions imposed by the high water table in San Francisco, plus a maze of underground utilities installed over the last 100 years.
The San Francisco line between Montgomery Street and Daly City stations was opened for revenue service on 5 November 1973. Service remained a shuttle operation on that eight-mile, eight-station line, however, until the District obtained State approval of its operating procedures to open the seven-and-a-half mile transbay line. Daily patronage (which had quickly recovered to 35 000 after the summer strike) doubled with San Francisco service. Four trains were operating on the line, in addition to the 18 trains on the three East Bay lines. Train lengths ranged from five to seven cars.
In technical areas, meanwhile, major programmes were going forward to improve the overall reliability of the vehicle fleet and also improve margins of train safety under automatic train operation, as desired by both the District and the California Public Utilities Commission (CPUC).
In December 1973, Westinghouse was directed to install a new train detection system, called SOR (for Sequential Occupancy Release), as an added safety back-up to the basic ATC detection system.
On 16 September 1974 passenger-bearing BART trains began travelling at 80 mph through the tube. Opening at the same time was the Oakland West Station, at the tube's eastern end, leaving only the Embarcadero Station to open in mid-1976.
Patronage, which had been 73 000 prior to opening of the tube, jumped to 118 000 within the first week. The number of trains operating increased from 22 to 30. Having linked its East Bay and West Bay lines, the District's next objective was to improve the reliability of both the cars and the train control system. Once this was accomplished, the District could address the question of extending service hours to nights and weekends—an issue of increasing concern to the public.
The District has worked out BART-to-bus transfer systems with both ac Transit (which operates buses in the East Bay) and the San Francisco Municipal Railway (which operates buses in that city). The District is also working to help get local bus service to all on-line communities where none yet exists.
The initial contract for the production and delivery of the revolutionary BART electric transit car was signed with Rohr Industries, Inc, of Chula Vista, California, in July, 1969. The contract called for delivery of 250 cars, with the first 10 vehicles to serve as test prototypes. The first prototype car was delivered at the Hayward Shop in August, 1970. The prototype cars were run many thousands of miles day and night over the next 16 months to ferret out as many design and manufacturing problems as possible before Rohr began full-scale work on the production cars.
The taxpayers' suits which literally halted the project before it could begin cost the District $12 million in lost time. Moreover, it presaged a decade of many such costly delays. These delays, plus improvements or changes made to the system, substantially increased the cost, or value, of the system.
While delay and inflation factors were sapping capital reserves, pressures from public and governmental groups resulted in the relocation of 15 miles of right-of-way and 15 stations, as well as a general upgrading of station plans. Stations were also substantially altered after construction to include elevators and other facilities for the handicapped and elderly at an added cost of $10 million. The cost of the transbay tube rose to $180 million from the originally estimated $133 million.
Shortage of funds also held up ordering transit cars. When the first 250 cars were finally ordered from low bidder Rohr Industries, Inc, of Chula Vista, California, the cost was $80 million—$8 million more than the original cost estimate for the entire 450-car fleet. (Subsequently, 200 more transit cars were ordered for another $80 million. Delivery of the total 450-car fleet was completed by 30 July 1975).
Included in the construction contract for the lower Market Street subway was the basic "box" structure for the Embarcadero Station. Not in the original plans, the system's 34th station was added as a result of increasing development of the lower Market Street area. Station funding was co-operative, with the San Francisco business community raising money for design, and BART spending $25 million on construction. (Of the latter figure, $16 million was raised by curtailing construction of the Muni subway at the west portal station instead of St. Francis Circle as originally planned.) It serves as the turnaround terminal for the Muni streetcar subway, as well as the first BART train stop west of the transbay tube.

Technical Data:
Gauge: 1.676 m
Route length: 121 km
In tunnel: 32.5 km
Number of lines: 1
Number of stations (total): 34
(in tunnel): 14
Average distance between stations: 3.7 km
Stations:
platform length (minimum): 244 m
Gradient (max): 4%
Curvature (max): 150 m
Speed (design max): 128 km/h
(average commercial): 80 km/h
Electric system: Third rail; 1 000 V

Rolling Stock:

Car type:	1969A	1969B
Units:	150	100
Car dimensions (length):	22.84 m	21.36 m
(width):	3.20 m	3.20 m
(height):	3.20 m	3.20 m
Total floor area (m²):	71.3	66.6
Doors per side:	2	2
Door (width):	1.37 m	1.37 m
Passages per side:	4	4
Passengers		
per car: (total):	216	228
(seated):	72	72
Motors per car:	4	4
Motor rating:	112 kW 150 hp	112 kW 150 hp
Power per train:		
(minimum):	896	896
(max):	4 480	4 480
Acceleration (max):	1.34	1.34
Deceleration:		
(normal service):	1.34	1.34
(emergency):	1.34	1.34
Speed (max):	80	80
Bogie truck rigid base:	2.13	2.13
Distance between bogie pivot:	15.2	15.2
Brakes (type): Rheostatic/Electro-magnetic		
Equipment used:		
air conditioning		
cushion seats		
Body material: Aluminium		
Weight-empty (tons):	25.6	25.0
Tare/floor area (kg/m²):	359	375
Tare/length (kg/m):	1 121	1 170
Tare/passenger (kg/pass):	119	110

SAN JUAN

Authority:
Department of Transport and Public Works
San Juan, Puerto Rico

Type of system: Proposed metro.

General: Still in the planning stage according to the 1979 proposed schedule, construction of the initial 23.8 km system is expected to begin in 1983 with completion date 1989. Estimated cost is $8 million.

SANTIAGO

Authority:
Ministry of Works
Morande 71, Santiago, Chile

Type of system: Full-metro (rubber-tyred).

General: Santiago, Chilean capital with a population exceeding two million, is now operating the first section of Line 1 of an eventual 5-line Metro system (La Red de Transporte Colectivo Independiento do Metro de Santiago). The decision to construct a Metro is welcomed by city authorities, who estimate that average vehicle speeds in the Santiago central area are down to 7½ mph *(12 km/h)* during busy periods owing to street congestion.
The total length of the proposed 5-line system will be approximately 37 miles *(59.3 km)*, consisting of Line 1, 14.5 km; Line 2, 11.5 km; Line 3, 8.3 km; Line 4, 17.0 km; Line 5, 8.0 km. The main characteristic of the system is its division into urban and suburban portions, using two different types of rolling stock. The urban portion will carry fast and frequent services over a network of 1.435 m gauge track. The suburban portion will carry less frequent services, linking existing State Railway stations but running on independent tracks; which will be of the same wide gauge *(1.676 m)* as the State Railways. The passenger, however, will not be affected by the Metro's two physical divisions as he will be offered interchange facilities over the whole system. The main features of the east-west Line 1 are as follows: double tracks in vaulted reinforced concrete tunnel, approx 7-9 m below street level, throughout, (except the westernmost portion which temporarily is in open cut); straight tunnels are 32.5 m section (slightly larger at curves).

Technical Data:
Gauge: 1.995 m/1.435 m
Projected new lines (in construction): 26.3 km (20.5 km in tunnel)
(in design): 31.2 km
Number of lines: 1/5
Number of stations (total): 35
(in tunnel): 26
Average distance between stations: 740 m
Stations:
platform length (minimum): 135 m
Gradient (max): 4.5%
Curvature (max): 260 m
Speed (design max): 80 km/h
(average commercial): 30 km/h
Electric system: 2 side guide bars

Rolling Stock:
Car type: Motorcars
Units: 137 (ordered)
Car dimensions (length): 17.18 m
(width): 2.60 m
(height): 3.62 m
Total floor area (m²): 43.6
Doors per side: 4
Doors (width): 1.3 m
Passages per side: 8
Passengers
per car (total): 169
(seated): 38
Motors per car: 2
Motor rating: 120 kW; 165 hp
Power per train
(minimum): 720
(max): 720
Distance between bogie pivot: 11.0
Brakes (type): Rheostatic
Weight-empty (tons): 25
Tare/length (kg/m): 1 455
Tare/passenger (kg/pass): 148

SÃO PAULO

Authority:
Companhia Do Metropolitano de São Paulo
Rua Augusta 1626, São Paulo, Brazil.

Type of system: Full-metro

General: Construction work under way since 1969 on a Metro system for São Paulo, had by 1974 reached completion of the entire 17.2 km which went into revenue service in September 1975. São Paulo's population of approximately 10 million is expected to increase to 15 million by the year 2000.

To provide mass urban transit commensurate with a city of this size and potential, it aims to have a conventional Metro system of four lines, totalling 66.2 km, to which extensions may later be made. Line 1, cross-city, links the northern suburb of Santana with Jabaquara in the south, with a branch to Moema, totals 21 km. Line 2, crossing the city east-westward from Vila Maria for 13.3 km to Casa Verde; Line 3, crossing the city from the south-west to the south-east, from Pinheiros to Via Anchieta, with a branch to Vila Bertioga (total 23.8 km), and Line 4, running from Madalena in the north-west, southeast for 8 km to join Line 1 at Paraiso, will complete the primary network.

The outer stretches of Line 1 leading to Santana and Meoma is at elevated level. Nearly all the remainder of this line, that is the main north-south line to Jabaquara, is in cut and cover tunnel. The exceptions are short inner stretches of the main and branch lines totalling 920 m, which are in driven tunnel excavated by the shield method. In cut and cover the tunnels are double-tracked, 29 ft 10 in *(9.1 m)* wide and 11 ft 6 in *(3.5 m)* high. The single-track driven tunnel is 18 ft 8 in *(5.7 m)* in diameter. These larger than normal dimensions allow for more generously proportioned rolling stock running on wide gauge track, in this case 5 ft 3 in *(1.60 m)*.

Line 2, east-west, will link all districts between Itaquera and Lapa. The east segment of this line begins at Sé Station, then crosses Parque Dom Pedro II, passes over the railway tracks at Brás Station, and then continues parallel to the railway line until Artur Alvim in the Itaquera District, after crossing the districts Brás, Belezinho, Tatuapé, Vila Matilde, Vila Guilhermina and Patriarca. After Artur Alvim the Line will leave the railway and run towards the yard in Itaquera.

The east segment will be constructed prevailingly on surface, with some minor sections in aerial structure or underground. Between Arouche and Sé it will be in tunnels to be bored by the shield method. From Arouche Square, already at the west side, the Line will follow to the districts Santa Cecilia, Pacaembu, Perdizes, Pompéia up to Lapa.

Late in December 1975 a contract was awarded for the first work phase of the Yard and Repair Shops of Line 2, east-west, which will be located in a 780 000 m² area, including an area reserved for Metró's future Technological Training Center. In size and capacity, the Yard of Line 2 will be three times as large as that of Line 1, north-south. The Itaquera yard will have a road access system through a large avenue. To provide possibility for future extension of Line 2, farther to east towards Moji das Cruzes, the location chosen is parallel to the Metró line and not at its end.

Sao Paulo's east-west metro line is scheduled to open by 1981. It runs between Santa Cecilia and Taluapé.

The first section between Sé and Brás opened in 1979. During 1980 the line is being extended to Belém in the east. Future developments include completion of the east-west line from Barra Funds to Itaquera. Cobrasina is building 150 new cars and Mafersa 132. Deliveries are due between late 1980 and early 1983.

Technical Data:
Gauge: 1.60 m
Route length: 17.2 km
In tunnel: 17.2 km
Projected new lines (in construction): 4.2 km
   (in design): 44.8 km
Number of lines: 1
Number of stations (total): 23
   (in tunnel): 16
Average distance between stations: 900 m
Stations:
   platform length (minimum): 136 km
Gradient (max): 4%
Curvature (max): 300 m
Speed (design max): 100 km/h
   (average commercial): 35 km/h
Electric system: Third rail; 750 V
Type of rails: 57 kg/m

Rolling Stock:
   Number of units: 99 × 2

Car dimensions (length): 21.20 m
   (width): 3.17 m
   (height): 3.55 m
Total floor area (m²): 65.5
Doors per side: 4
Door (width): 1.30 m
Passages per side: 8
Passengers per car (total): 354
   (seated): 34
Motors per car: 4
Motor rating: 75 kW
   103 hp
Power per train
   (max): 1 800
Acceleration (max): 1.35
Deceleration
   (normal service): 1.20
Bogie truck rigid base: 2.1
Distance between bogie pivot: 15.6
Brakes (type): Rheostatic
Weight-empty (tons)
   (Motors): 32.4

Traffic Data:
   Trains/track/hour: 40
   Train capacity (passengers): 2 000
   Total passengers/track/hour (peak): 80 000
   Train headways existing: 1.5 minutes

SAPPORO

Authority:
Sapporo Municipal Transportation Bureau
Sapporo, Japan

History: The Sapporo Municipal Transportation Bureau embarked an improvement plan of the city transit network in 1962. The city council introduced a demand on realisation of the new rapid transit plan, and the test line of centre-guide pneumatic-tyred system and car were prepared in 1964.

The third test car, propelled by two gasoline engines, was completed in 1965.

The fourth test car, twin-coupled and propelled by electric motors, succeeded its test run in 1967.

The first line, so called Nan-boku (south-north) line, between Kita 24 Jo (North 24th Street) and Makomanai, distance of 12.625 km was prepared as one of the major projects for the 1972's Sapporo Olympic Winter Games to transport visitors, and its construction work was started on 7 February 1969. This line was opened on 16 December 1971, and a train run in 23 minutes to cover whole line.

In order to serve a densely populated area in the northern part of Sapporo city, the northern extension of Line 1 between Kits 24 Jo and Azabu-cho, distance of 2.500 km was constructed in 1977.

The construction work of Line 2, so called To-zai (east-west) line, between Shiroishi and Kotoni, distance of 10.670 km, was started in 1973, and completed in 1977.

Work began at the end of 1978 on extension of the east-west line from Shiroishi to Atsubetsu (7.5 km). Completion is due 1981 at an estimated cost of Yen 105 000 million.

Route length: Line 1: 12.625 km (underground 7.950 km; elevated 4.675 km)
   Line 1 extension: 2.500 km (underground)
   Line 2: 10.670 km (underground)
   Total: 25.795 km, including 21.120 km tunnel
Number of lines: 2 transverse lines
Number of stations served: Line 1: 14, Line 1 extension: 2
   Line 2: 11
   Total: 27
Average station spacing: Line 1: 0.92 km, Line 1 extension: 1.10 km
   Line 2: 0.97 km

Passengers per annum (1973): Line 1: 70 996 000
Average length of journey: Line 1: 3.6 km
Number of cars per train: Line 1: 6, Line 2: 8
Max number of trains per hour: Line 1: 11
Track gauge and type of rails: Line 1: pneumatic-tyred car 2.180 mm in width. Centre-guide rail steel I-beam (310 × 446 mm). Running tracks paved with epoxy-resin plastics.
   Line 2: pneumatic-tyred car 2.190 mm in width. Centre-guide rail steel I-beam. Running tracks paved with steel plates.
Passenger capacity per car: Line 1: 96 and 90
   Line 2: 126 and 116
Average schedule speed: Line 1: 31.6 km/h
   Line 2: 38.0 km/h
Max gradient: Line 1: 4.3%
   Line 2: 3.5%
Minimum radius of curve: Line 1: 205 m
   Line 2: 205 m
Type of tunnel: Generally double-tracks, cut and cover tunnel, rectangular section, mostly reinforced concrete with centre supports. Under the Toyohira-river, the sections were constructed by caisson-method. Elevated section has circular aluminium shelter to avoid heavy snowfalls.
Method and voltage of current supply: Line 1: Third rail 750 V dc
   Line 2: Overhead rigid body rail 1 500 V dc

Rolling Stock:
Number of cars
   Line 1: 84
   Line 2: 80
   These cars were manufactured by the Kawasaki Heavy Industry Co Ltd. Kobe
Class 1 000: Passenger capacity 96 (44 seats, 52 standings)
   90 (38 seats, 52 standings)
Length overall: 27 m
Width: 3.05 m
Height: 3.7 m
Motors per car: Four 90 kW 375 V dc
   Fluorescent lighting. Cars have four sets of double leaf sliding doors in each side.
Car Type (year introduced): 1971
Units: 56
Car dimensions (length): 27.6 m
   (width): 3.08 m
   (height): 3.7 m

Doors per side: 4
Door (width): 1.40 m
Passages per side: 8
Passengers per car (total): 180
   (seated): 60
Motors per car: 4
Motor rating: 90 kW
   125 hp
Acceleration (max): 1.1
Deceleration (normal service): 1.1
   (emergency): 1.4
Speed (max): 75
Bogie truck rigid base: 1.15
Distance between bogie pivot: 5.5
Brakes (type): E1Pn
Equipment used:
   dead man control
   air conditioning
   cushion seats
Body material: Aluminium
Weight-empty (tons): 33.0
Tare/length (kg/m): 1 100

Signalling: Full Automatic Train Control (ATC) and Centralised Traffic Control (CTC) devices were installed, moreover, tyre-puncture detecting device and automatic announcement system were synchronised in Line 1, and Automatic Train Operating (ATO) system will be introduced in Line 2.

Station layout:
Island platform stations : Line 1: 5
   Line 1 extension: 1
   Line 2: 5
Separate side stations: Line 1: 9, Line 1 extension 1
   Line 2: 6
Platform length; Line 1 extension : 120 m (to take 8-car train)
   Line 2: 170 m (to take 9-car train)

Workshops:
   Line 1: There is a train depot and workshop at Jieitaimae, elevated level.
   Line 2: There is a train depot and workshop at 24 Ken, underground.

SEOUL

Authority:
Seoul Metropolitan Rapid Transit Bureau
Seoul Metropolitan Government
Seoul, Korea

Type of system: Full-metro.

General: In 1972 after a decade of expansion at the expense of the rural areas, the population of Seoul's metropolitan area had reached six million, and there are now proposals for a decentralisation programme. The need for a city mass transit rail system has been met by the construction of a 10.31 km line initially, and by a proposed extensive regional network in the long term. Korean manufacture of equipment using Japanese technology, plus Japanese financial aid, are enabling features.

Future subway construction will be on a radial alignment in ten directions from the central area of Seoul, taking into consideration current transport conditions, prospective regional development, and linking with other transport facilities. Total length of the five subways to be constructed is 133 km, of which the underground portion will be 61 km: in the direction of Suyuri, Bulgwangdong, Seoul Station, Cheonhodong, Gurodong, Cheongryangri, Jamsilri, Yeongdong, Yeoyido and Yonhidong

Work was started on the 48.8 km loop line linking the town centre business district with residential areas,

south of the Han River. First section will be opened 1981 followed by the remainder by 1985.

Technical Data:
Gauge: 1.435 m
Route length: 10.31 km
In tunnel: 8.60 km
Projected new lines (in design): 18 km
Number of lines: 1
Number of stations (total): 9
   (in tunnel): 9
Average distance between stations: 975 m
Stations:
   platform length (minimum): 120 m
Gradient (max): 3.5%
Curvature (max): 120 m
Speed (design max): 80 km/h
   (average commercial): 35 km/h
Electric system: Catenary; 1 500 V dc
Type of rails: 50 kg/m

Rolling Stock:

Car type:	Motorcars	Trailers
Units:	124	62
Car dimensions (length):	20.1 m	20.1 m
(width):	3.18 m	3.18 m
(height):	3.8 m	3.8 m
Total floor area (m²):	60.5	55.2
Doors per side:	4	4
Door (width):	1.3 m	1.3 m
Passages per side:	8	8
Passengers per car: (total):	160*	148*
(seated):	54	48
Motors per car:	4	—
Motor rating:	120 kW	
	165 hp	
Power per train		
(minimum):	1 920	—
(max):	2 880	—
Acceleration (max):	0.7	—
Deceleration		
(normal service):	1.0	—
(emergency):	1.2	—
Speed (max):	111	—
Bogie truck rigid base:	2.1	2.1
Distance between bogie pivot:	13.8	13.8
Brakes (type): Electro-pneumatic		
Equipment used:		
dead man control:		
cushion seats:		
Body material:	Steel	Steel
Weight-empty (tons):	43.5	34.5
Tare/Floor area (kg/m²):		
Tare/length (kg/m):	2 164	—
Tare/passenger (kg/pass):	272	—

*peak crush load equals 360 persons

Traffic Data:
Trains/track/hour: 12
Train headways existing: 5 minutes
Passengers carried (weekday): 560 000 (1974)

STOCKHOLM

Authority:
AB Storstockholms Lokaltrafik
Tegnérgaten 2A, Stockholm, Sweden

General Manager: Ingemar Bäckström
Vice General Manager: Olaf Hultman
Operating Manager: Karl-Erik Rapp

Type of system: Full-metro.

General: Greater Stockholm's public transport organisation has since 1971 been fully established under the administration of Storstockholms Lokaltrafik, a company whose shares are held by the County Council and whose responsibilities include the operation of the Underground, buses, and commuter train services of the State Railways. The Stockholm T-Bana (tunnel railway) system is modern, all construction (including conversion in 1949-50 of about 1 mile of tunnel tramway south of Slussen to conventional Underground standards) having taken place since World War II. The T-Bana was built to meet the transportation needs of a fast expanding city, Stockholm having more than doubled its population since 1920.
Nearly one-half of the system is in tunnel, but construction posed problems, including underwater crossings involving new methods of tunnelling, since about one-half of the area within the boundaries of Greater Stockholm is open water. Extensions and new T-Bana lines have periodically added to the system since 1951, and the process is continuing as Stockholm's suburban areas develop. The third line was Vårberg over Vårby Gård-Masmo to Fittja was opened in October 1972, inaugurated in August 1975.

Urban structure:
Population of Greater Stockholm area: 1.4 millions
Land area: 3.461 km²
Number of automobiles registered in Stockholm county: 415 000 (1970); 475 000 (1979)

Technical Data:
Gauge: 1.435 m
Route length: 104 km
In tunnel: 56 km

New lines (planned): Mörby Centrum—Täby Centrum, 6.2 km
(under construction): Västra Skogen—Rinkeby, 6.3 km
Number of lines in operation: 3 with branches
Number of stations (total): 94
Number of stations in tunnel: 48
Average distance between stations: 1 000 m
Max length of station platforms: 180 m
Gradient (max): 40‰ (exceptional 48‰)
Curvature (min): 200 m (exceptional 120 m)
Speed (design max): 80-90 km/h
(average commercial): 30-40 km/h
Type of rail: flat-bottomed, 50 kg/m
Type of tunnel: concrete, rock and steel
Method and voltage of current supply: third rail, 650-750 V

Traffic and finances:
Max line capacities (one way): 90 s
Max number of trains per hour (one way): 30
Frequency of train services (currently): 120 s
Capacity per car (passengers seated): 48
(passengers standing): 110 (train: 4-10 cars)
Passenger journeys per annum: 189 million (1978)
Revenues: Kr814 million
Finances: Kr1 118 million

Rolling stock characteristics:
Car types: C1-C12
Number of units: 873
Car dimensions:
Length (m): 17
Width (m): 2.7-2.8
Height (m): 3.7
Total floor area: 45 m²
Number of doors per side: 3 × 2
Door width (m): 1.2
Number of passengers per car (total): 158
(seated): 48
Motors per car: 4
Motor rating (kW): 4 × 87 kW-4 × 100 kW
Power per 8-car train (minimum): 175 kN
(max): 415 kN
Acceleration (max): 1.0-1.3 m/s²

Deceleration (normal service): 1.1 m/s²
(emergency): 1.0 m/s²
Max design speed: 80-90 km/h
Bogies (type and manufacturer): two motor air-rubber-suspended, ASEA
Distance between bogie pivot: 11 m
Brakes (type): electrodynamic and compressed air
Weight (empty in tonnes): 23.6-30 (motor cars)

Rolling Stock (1971): Number of cars owned 873. Details: The cars were built by the Svenska Järnvägverkstäderna of Linköping, in collaboration with ASEA. Each car has an overall length of 57 ft 1 in (17.4 m), a body length of 55 ft 10 in (17.0 m), and a width of 9 ft 2 in (2.8 m). Each car has three double-leaf automatic sliding doors on each side, and is equipped with centre-buffer couplers. The latest types C4, C5 and C6 have rubber suspension, and have driving and guard's cab at one end only. Type C5 were built by Hägglund Söner; Type C6 by ASJ, ASEA and Hägglund
Signalling: The signalling provides for 1½-minute train intervals, and 30-second station stops. Cab-signalling is employed, with two speed ranges, up to 9.3 and 31 mph (15 and 50 km/h) and a third for higher speed. Fixed lineside signals are installed only at junctions. Central Control office is linked to all trains through radio-communication.
Planned expansion of the system includes the following extensions: T-Bana 3 in the northwest, from Hallonbergen to Akalla (4 stations, length 6.2 km) and in the City from T-Centralen to Kungsträdgården (1 station, length 0.7 km) opening 1977. T-Bana 2 from Universitetet to Mörby Centrum (3 stations, length 4.2 km) opening 1978. T-Bana 3 Västra Skogen-Rinkeby, (5 stations, length 7.0 km) opening 1982-1985 and T-Bana 2 Mörby Centrum-Täby Centrum (3 stations, length 6.2 km) also opening 1982-1985.
Fare structure: A common fare system operates over all undertakings controlled by the Stockholm County Council. These include underground, buses, tramways and railways within the county region. The fare system is zonal, the region being divided into 43 zones. Payment is for travel coupons, minimally two for travel within one zone adding one coupon for each additional zone, maximum 10 for unlimited travel within a time limit.

STUTTGART

Authority:
Stuttgarter Strassenbahnen AG
Schockenriedstrasse 50, 7000 Stuttgart 80, Federal Republic of Germany

General: Stuttgart, with a population of about 580 000, is engaged on projects similar to those being undertaken in Frankfurt and in other German cities. Much of Stuttgart's tramway (street-car) system will be diverted into tunnel beneath the central area, in order to relieve street congestion and to accelerate services. The work is being completed in sections. Section 1, comprising 0.75 miles (1.2 km) of tunnel line crossing beneath the busy road junction at Charlottenstrasse, together with an underground tram station, has been in operation since 1966. Section 2, 1.6 miles (2.5 km) of

tunnel line from Charlottenplatz south-west to Marienplatz, became operative in September 1971, and Section 3, 0.9 miles (1.5 km) of tunnel line north-east from Charlottenplatz to Neckartor, became operative in May 1972. The first part of section 4, 2.8 km of tunnel line from Schillerstraße beneath Hauptbahnhof to Universität and to Türlenstraße was finished in April 1976. The second part of section 4, a tunnel line running south from Hauptbahnhof beneath Schloßplatz to Charlottenplatz was completed in November 1978. Section 5, 0.8 km of tunnel line from Wilhelmsbau to Fritz-Elsass-Straße, is in course of construction.
The tunnels of cut-and-cover construction, are approximately 4.7 m high, and 7.5 m wide, in rectangular section. The tramcars will be equipped with pantographs for overhead power supply and sufficient tunnel headroom has been allowed for these. The overall dimensions are also sufficient to allow for possible

future adaption for larger-profile, conventional subway cars. The tramway system has been named the Stadtbahn.

Technical Data:
Gauge: 1.000 m
Route length: 484 km
Track length: 743.6 km
In tunnel: 20 km
Number of lines in operation: 10
Averge distance between stations: 533 m
Speed (design max): 60 km/h
(average commercial): 20 km/h
Frequency of train services in minutes (currently): 6-12
Passenger journeys per annum: 146.8 million (1977); 146.3 million (1978)

SYDNEY

Authority:
Public Transport Commission of New South Wales
11-31 York St, Sydney, Australia

General: The Public Transport Commission of NSW operates all NSW rail and government bus services and the Sydney Harbour ferry services.
The urban and suburban electrified rail system in the Sydney area includes an underground City Railway in the form of a loop that is linked with the suburban railway systems at Central and Wynyard. The length of the loop is 3½ miles (5.6 km) approximately three-quarters of it being underground. Four of the six stations (Town Hall, Wynyard, St James and Museum) are underground. Central is at ground level and Circular Quay is elevated and forms an open break in the

tunnel loop. The City railway is all double-track with trains operating in both directions. As with the suburban railway system the City railway is electrified with power being supplied through single overhead wiring at 1 500 V dc.
Automatic block signalling (with five aspect colour-light signals, and a system of speed signalling with electro-pneumatic train stops) is provided.
Extensions: Work is nearing completion on the Eastern Suburbs Railway, a 10 km underground extension which will provide a rapid transit service to the densely populated eastern suburbs of Sydney. The ESR will connect with the existing metropolitan network at Erskineville and will follow a route, completely underground (except for two viaducts) via Redfern, Central, Town Hall, Martin Place, Kings Cross, Edgecliff to Bondi Junction. New underground stations are being built at all these locations except Town Hall

which is being extended to accommodate additional platforms.
The Eastern Suburbs Railway will be double-track and will use the same 1 500 V overhead wiring method as the present electric network.

Trains: Sydney urban and suburban electric trains comprise double-deck and single-deck rolling stock. In 1977 364 of the total of 1 195 suburban and interurban electric carriages, were double-deck and a further 230 double-deck cars were being manufactured. The Sydney suburban and Outer Metropolitan (interurban) electrified route distance is 446 km and extends West to Lithgow 154 km and North to Gosford 80 km from Sydney. On an average weekday over 1 400 'train runs' operate on this network and during one year electric trains travel over 16 million km—passenger journeys total over 500 000 each working day.

TASHKENT

Authority:
Tashkent Metropolitan Railways Authority
Tashkent, USSR

Type of system: Full-metro.

General: Tashkent, capital city of the Uzbek Soviet Socialist Republic, announced plans for a new 'Metro' system in 1967. In 1973 it had a population of 1 504 000, and as the centre of the Tashkent region. The project for a metropolitan railway for Tashkent was begun in 1968. The first line, now completed, is transverse, from the south-west to the city centre and

then to the north-east to serve a region of mass housing construction. It was 12.5 miles (20.2 km) of route with 14 stations and runs from Dustlik in the south-west to Lenin Square in central Tashkent.

Technical Data:
Gauge: 1.524 m
Route length: 20.1 km
(in design): 28 km
Number of lines: 1
Number of stations (total): 14
Average distance between stations: 1.5 km
Stations:
platform length (minimum): 100 m
Gradient (max): 4.0%

Speed (design max): 90
Electric system: 825 V

Rolling Stock:
Car type: proposed
Car dimensions (length): 19.2 m
(width): 2.7 m
Doors per side: 4
Passages per side: 8
Passengers
per car: (total): 170
(seated): 44
Motors per car: 4
Motor rating: 66 kW
Brakes (type): Rheostatic

TBILISI

Authority:
Tbilisski Metropolitena
Tbilisi, USSR

Type of system: Full-metro.

General: Tbilisi is the capital of the Georgian republic, with a population in 1973 of 946 000. Public transport in Tbilisi includes trains, buses and trolleybuses. In 1946 design work for an underground railway was carried out by the Caucasus Design and Survey Institute, for an underground railway that would provide means of mass rapid transit between the city's large industrial and residential areas and its centre. The lines' geography was dictated by the lay-out of Tbilisi along the River Kura, with the industrial and residential areas at either end. The planned lay-out of the railway system centres on the city's main throughfare, Rustaveli Prospekt.
Construction of tunnels, and excavation for station structures, was undertaken from the surface. Both solid rock and ground impregnated with water from mineral springs were encountered, the latter neces-sitating heavy machinery to pump out subsoil waters. The first 3.9 mile *(6.3 km)* section of the underground came into operation in 1966. The line then had six stations, two of which, Didube and Electrodepovskaya were surface stations. In 1967 the line was extended eastwards 2.4 miles *(3.9 km)* to 300 Aragvintsev and further extended in 1971 for 1.5 miles *(2.4 km)* to Samgory. A further westward extension with two more stations is under construction.
Planned for the second construction phase is a ring line with four stations; Saburtalo, Vokzalnaya, Rustaveli. The name for the fourth station has not yet been decided.

Technical Data:
Gauge: 1.524 m
Route length: 12.9 km
In tunnel: 11.4 km
Projected new lines (in construction): 6.0 km
Number of lines: 1
Number of stations (total): 11
  (in tunnel): 9
Average distance between stations: 1.17 km
Speed (average commercial): 38.1 km/h

Electric system: Third rail; 825 V

Rolling Stock:
Car type: E-1960
Car dimensions: (length): 18.8 m
  (width): 2.70 m
  (height): 3.70 m
Doors per side: 4
Door (width): 1.28 m
Passages per side: 8
Passengers
per car: (total): 170
  (seated): 40
Motors per car: 4
Motor rating: 68 kW (94 hp)
Power per train:
  (max): 816
Brakes (type): rheostatic/electro-pneumatic

Traffic Data:
Passengers carried (weekday): 256 000
  (annually): 68 000 000
Average journey length: 3.7 km
Vehicle-km operated annually: 9 300 000

TOKYO

Tokyo, Japan

The metropolis of Tokyo covers an area of 2 145 km², including 23 wards (581 km²), 26 cities (724 km²), one county (437 km²) and some small islands (403 km²). The population of Tokyo is about 11.7 million, of which 8.5 million live in the ward area.
Tokyo's public transport system is composed of Japanese National Railways, subways, private railways, streetcars and buses.
The Transportation Bureau of Tokyo Metropolitan Government operates 47.6 km of subway lines, 12.2 km of streetcar lines and 779.5 km of bus lines mainly within the inner part of the city.
The present subway network in Tokyo consists of ten lines with a total length of 176.4 km of which seven lines, 127.6 km, are operated by the Teito Rapid Transit Authority.
The outer part of the city proper and its suburbs are served by seven major private railway companies.

Line	Name	Gauge	Route km	Total km
1	—	4' 8½''	19.5	*20.0
2	Hibiya	3' 6''	20.3	21.1
3	Ginza	4' 8½''	14.3	17.5
4	Marunouchi	4' 8½''	27.4	28.2
5	Tozai	3' 6''	30.8	31.7
6	—	3' 6''	13.1	30.5
7	—	—	—	20.7
8	Narimasu	—	—	33.2
9	Chiyoda	3' 6''	14.7	32.7
10	—	—	—	31.2
11	—	—	—	19.4

*Of which 1.2 km from Sengakuji to Shinagawas is operated by the Keihinkyuko Railway Co.

Authority:
Teito Rapid Transit Authority (TRTA)
19-6, Higashi Ueno 3-Chome, Teito Ku, Tokyo, Japan
Telephone: (03) 832 2111

Type of system: Full-metro.

History: The first section of Line 1 from Oshiage southward to Asakusa was opened in 1960, and extended in stages southward to its present terminus at Nishimagome. The TBTMG subsequently assumed operation of Line 6 Nishitakashimadaira to Mita.

General: Line 1 connects with private railways at each end, and thus provides the latter's suburban trains access to the city centre. At present (1976) Lines 1 and 6 are carrying about 810 000 passengers daily on average.

Technical Data:
Gauge: 1.067/1.435 m
Route length: 40.8 km
In tunnel: 35.7 km
Projected new lines (in construction): 14.5 km
Number of lines: 2
Number of stations (total): 44
  (in tunnel): 38
Stations:
  platform length (max): 165 km
Gradient (max): 3.5%
Curvature (max): 164 m
Speed (design max): 100 km/h
  (average commercial): 30.9-31.4 km/h
Electric system: Overhead; 1 500 V

Rolling Stock:

Car type:	Line 1	Line 6
Units:	164*	168*
Car dimensions: (length):	18.0 m	20.0 m
(width):	2.80 m	2.79 m
(height):	3.65 m	3.65 m
Total floor area (m²):	44.6	49.8
Doors per side:	3	4
Door (width):	1.3 m	1.3 m
Passages per side	6	8
Passengers per car:		
(total):	145	160
(seated):	50	54
Motors per car:	4	4
Motor rating:	85 kW	100 kW
	117 hp	137 hp
Power per train:		
(max):	2 040	2 400
Brakes (type):	Rheostatic	

*Motorcars

Authority:
Transportation Bureau of the Tokyo Metropolitan Government (TBTMG)
109-1 2-Chome, Yurakucho, Chiyoda-Ku, Tokyo, Japan
Telephone: (03) 216 1411

Type of system: Full-metro.

History: Operations began on the 14.3 km Ginza line (now Line 3) in 1927.

General: Teito operates 4 lines (Hibiya—20.3 km; Ginza 14.3 km; Maranouchi 27.4 km; Tozai 30.8 km) and is constructing two others: the 20.9 km Chiyodaline and the 10.2 km Yurakucholine.

Technical Data:
Gauge: 1.067/1.435 m
Route length: 123.9
Projected new lines (in construction): 31.1 km
Number of lines: 4
Number of stations (total): 115
Average distance between stations: 1.1 km
Gradient max): 4%
Curvature (max): 200 m
Speed (average commercial): 44.9 km/h
Electric system: Third rail and overhead
Type of rails: 50/60 kg/m

Rolling Stock:

Car type:	Line 2	Line 5	Line 9
Units:	304	246	178
Car dimensions:			
(length):	18.0 m	20.0 m	20.0 m
(width):	2.79 m	2.80 m	2.80 m
(height):	3.65 m	3.90 m	3.69 m
Total floor area (m²):	49.0	54.6	54.6
Doors per side:	3	4	4
Passengers per car:			
(total):	124	140	140
(seated):	52	54	51
Motors per car:	4	4	4
Motor rating:	75 kW	100 kW	145 kW
	103 hp	137 hp	200 hp
Power			
per train: (minimum):	600	800	—
(max):	3 000	—	—
Acceleration (max):	0.98	—	1.4
Deceleration:			
(normal service):	0.98	—	1.6
(emergency):	—	—	2.1
Bogie truck rigid base:	2.1	—	2.2
Distance between bogie pivot	13.8	—	13.6
Brakes (type):	Rh/Pn	Rh/Pn	Rh/Pn
Weight-empty (tons):			
M:	31.5	32.0	30.2
R:	—	—	34.5
Tare/floor area (kg/m²):	643	586	553
Tare/length (kg/m):	1 750	1 600	1 510
Tare/passenger (kg/pas):	254	229	216

Traffic Data:
Passengers carried (weekday): 3 896 000
Average journey length: 7.2 km

TORONTO

Authority:
Toronto Transit Commission
1900 Yonge Street, Toronto, Ontario, M4S 1Z2 Canada

Type of System: Full-metro

Chairman: Julian Porter
Manager: Michael Warren

History: This urban underground railway was the first subway to be built in Canada, to relieve surface congestion on the streets of Toronto. The first line, on a north-south axis (opened in 1954) and the second line on an east-west axis (opened fully in 1968) follow the course of the two main traffic arteries, Yonge Street, and Bloor Street and Danforth Avenue. A 2.68 mile section of the Yonge northerly extension opened 31 March 1973 and a further 2.73 miles opened on 30 March 1974.
Construction has been completed on a total of 8.65 miles of new subway. The Spadina subway runs 6.17 miles from a terminal station at Wilson Avenue to St. George Station. The line includes eight stations at an estimated cost of $220 million with the Province of Ontario and Metropolitan Toronto sharing the cost 75 per cent and 25 per cent respectively.
Construction is also in progress on a one-mile westerly extension and a 1.6 mile easterly extension of the Bloor-Danforth subway. Target date for opening 1980. The Commission also operates the City's 690-mile surface transit system of street cars, electric trolley buses and diesel buses.
Approval has been given to build a 4.3-mile light rail line, exclusive right-of-way, to connect the Scarborough Town Centre, a large Metro sub-centre, to the Bloor—Danforth subway at Kennedy subway station. Target date for opening is 1982.
A total of 134 new subway cars worth $C65.7 million, the largest subway car purchase in the history of the Toronto Transit Commission, have been delivered from Hawker-Siddeley Canada for operation on the Spadina line and to meet additional service demands on the existing 50-km subway system.

General: Total cost of the 8 miles of new Bloor-Danforth Line was $C160 million. A further $77 million was expended on the recent east and west extensions. The western extension from Keele to Islington, 3.49 miles *(5.6 km)*, includes 5 intermediate stations. The eastern extension from Woodbine to Warden, 2.77 miles *(4.8 km)* includes two intermediate stations. Total cost of the Yonge subway extension $140 million.

Technical Data:

Route length: 32.72 miles (52.66 km) including 5.38 miles in shield-driven tunnel. Remainder in cut-and-cover or open cut construction.

Number of cars per train: old stock: 2-car units coupled to form 4, 6, or 8-car trains. New stock: 2 to 6 cars.
Rolling stock: number of cars owned 632. Old stock: 134 cars built by the Gloucester Carriage and Wagon Co, England. Overall length 57 ft 1½ in (17.4 m) and external body width 10 ft 4 in (3.15 m).
Gauge: 4 ft 10⅞ in (1.5 m)
Route length: 32.72 miles (52.657 km)
Track length (single track): 95.9 miles (153.44 km)
In tunnel (double track): 5.38 miles (8.657 km)
New lines (Scarborough Light Rail Transit): 4.35 miles (7.00 km)
  (under construction): Kennedy extension—1.72 miles (2.768 km)
  Kipling extension—0.92 miles (1.481 km)
Number of lines in operation: 2
Number of stations (total): 56
Number of stations in tunnel: 2
Average distance between stations: 2 524 ft (757.20 m)
Max length of station platforms: 500 ft (150 m)
Gradient (max): 1 in 29 (3.45%)
Speed (average commercial): 20 mph (32 km/h)
Type of rail: flat-bottomed 115 lb/yd (57 kg/m)
Type of tunnel: Steel reinforced poured concrete box structures 13 ft 9 in high (4.12 m)
  Between stations: 28 ft 6 in wide (8.55 m)
  At stations: 48 ft 4 in wide (14.49 m)
  Shield driver precast concrete or cast iron tunnels
  Between stations: 16 ft (4.8 m)
  At stations: 24 ft (7.2 m)

Method and voltage of current supply: Third rail, 600 V dc

Traffic and finances:
Max line capacities (one way): 40 000 passengers
Max number of trains per hour (one way): 26-27 (one way-planned): Scarborough Light Rail Transit, 10
Frequency of train services in minutes (currently):

	Min	Max
Yonge-University-Spadina	2.15	4.40
Bloor-Danforth	2.43	5.05
Scarborough Light Rail Transit—(planned)	6.00	10.00

Capacity per train (passengers seated): 496-498 (passengers standing): 1 368-1 416
Passenger journeys per annum: 203 800 000 (1977); 196 500 000 (1978)
Revenues: $137 729 000 (1977); $146 000 000 (1978)
Deficit: $42 252 000 (1977); $50 400 000 (1978
Subsidised by: Metropolitan Toronto and Province of Ontario

Rolling stock characteristics:
Car types: 632 motor cars
Number of units per train: 4, 6, or 8

Car dimensions:
length (m): 57 ft ¼ in or 74 ft 5⅝ in
width (m): 10 ft 3⅜ in or 10 ft 4 in
height (m): 11 ft 11½ in
Total floor area: 27.3 m² or 34.5 m²
Number of doors per side: 3 or 4
Door width (m): 3 ft 9 in (1.143 m)
Number of passengers per car (total): 233 to 319 (seated): 62 to 84
Motors per car: 4
Motor rating (kW): 51, 90, 90/86, 86½ or 94 kW

	G1, 2, 3, 4	M1	H1, H2	H3	H4	H5
Car type (all cars motored)	134	36	230	6	88	138
Number of units per train	4.6	6.8	6.8	6.8	6.8	6.8
Car dimensions						
Length (m)	17.4	22.8	22.8	22.8	22.8	22.8
Width (m)	3.1	3.1	3.1	3.1	3.1	3.1
Height (m)	3.65	3.65	3.65	3.65	3.65	3.65
Total floor area, excluding seating area (m²)	27.3	34.5	34.5	34.5	34.5	34.5
Number of doors per side	3	4	4	4	4	4
Door width (m)	1.14	1.14	1.14	1.14	1.14	1.14
Number of passengers per car (total)	233	319	319	319	319	319
(seated)	62	83	83	83	77	76
Motors per car	4	4	4	4	4	4
Motor rating (kW) (1h rating)	51	90	90/86	86½	86½	94
Power per train (kW) while accelerating	192	153	180	NA	180	NA
		(low-rate)	(high-rate)	(choppers)	(high-rate)	(choppers)
Acceleration (max) m/s/s	1.25	1.25	1.25	1.25	1.25	1.25
Deceleration (normal service) m/s/s	1.25	1.25	1.25	1.25	1.25	1.25
(emergency) m/s/s	1.35	1.35	1.35	1.35	1.35	1.35
Bogies (type and manufacturer)	GRCW	Dofasco	Dofasco	Dofasco	Dofasco	Dofasco
Distance between bogie pivot (m)	11.6	16.5	16.5	16.5	16.5	16.5
Brakes (type): rheostatic, electro-pneumatic, pneumatic service, pneumatic emergency brake	No rheostatic	All	All	also regenerative	All	No rheostatic, has regenerative
Weight (empty in tonnes) approx	85 to 73	60	56½	66/68	58	66/68 (H5 has air conditioning)

VIENNA

Authority:
Wiener Stadtwerke-Verkehrsbetriebe
Favoritenstrasse 9, 1041 Vienna, Austria

Director: Rudolf Cabana

Vice Directors: Arnulf Maier
Friedrich Wilhelm

History: The Stadtbahn system was opened, with steam traction, in June 1898. Electric traction was introduced between June and October 1925.

General: Vienna's tramway system is the most extensive and the largest of Vienna's carriers, with 296.0 km (55 per cent) of the city's total 541 km of bus, tram and Stadtbahn route, and 67 per cent of the passenger total. As part of the declared policy to separate public transport from other traffic, some central tram routes are being diverted underground. In 1966 a semi-circular tunnel line was put into operation near the Ring (city centre) and in January 1969, additional tunnels for 4 tram routes, comprising 2 tunnel branches with 6 underground halts, became operational. Designated Phase Two in the tram-tunnel project, this section is situated on the South Belt, near the Süd-bahnhof. The tram tunnels are suitable for, and may form part of a 3-line U Bahn network, U1, U2, U4 for Vienna. In November, 1969, work commenced on Line 1 of this network and first section of the line was completed at the end of 1973.
Line 1 begins at Praterstern near the North Schnell-bahn station and runs for about 6 km southward, under the city centre and via Favoritenstrasse to Reumannplatz, just beyhond the Gürtel (outer Ring Road). Tunnel construction is by the cut and cover method and shield-driven tunnel. Conventional underground trains will carry approximately 382 passengers per two-car unit. Line 1 was partly operational by 1977 for completion by 1980. It is proposed that Line 2 will incorporate the tram tunnels mentioned earlier, and Line 4 part of the existing Stadtbahn.
Another separate, but later, project is the proposed spur for the existing Stadtbahn, to link Vienna's growing north-eastern suburbs by rail with the city centre. This link would take the form of a tunnel beneath the river Danube, joining the present Stadtbahn at Nuss-dorferstrasse.
Vienna is also served by a surface rapid transit railway, the Austrian Federal Railway's "Schnellbahn". This line has recently been extended and now runs from Strebersdorf and Sussenbrunn, south-west to Liesing, a total route length of about 20.0 miles (32 km). A common fare tariff applies to Vienna's Stadtbahn and Schnellbahn system.
Stadtbahn route length: 16.65 miles (26.8 km) (including 3.9 miles (6.3 km) in tunnels).
Number of lines: 4 lines (DG, GD, WD, G), which are physically connected to form a single operating system; all double track.
Number of stations served: 25.
Average station spacing: 0.6 miles (1 km).
Stadtbahn passengers per annum: (1973) 73 500 000; (1974) 70 000 000. (1975): 75 000 000.

Number of cars per train: 3-9 cars.
Estimated capacity per car: Driving car, 20 seated, 52 standing; trailing car, 20 seated, 62 standing.
Track gauge: 4 ft 8½ in (1.435 m).
Weight and type of rails: 35.8, 48.3 and 59.7 kg/m; flat-bottomed.
Max gradient: 1 in 35.
Minimum radius of curves: 426½ ft (130 m), on running lines.
Type of tunnel: Tunnels are double track. On some sections they are 33 ft (10 m) wide, with vertical walls and an elliptical roof with a maximum height of 19½ ft (5.93 m). On other stretches of line, they have a circular cross-section with a diameter of 29 ft 6 in (9 m).
Method and voltage of current supply: Overhead; 750 V dc. Power is supplied by the Vienna Electricity Works partly at 5 000 V ac and partly at 10 000 V ac and is transformed to 750 V dc at seven substations:— Hut-teldorf; Unter St. Veit; Sechshaus; Thury; Kaunitz; Hauptzollamt; and Heilgenstadt.
Rolling Stock: Cars are two-axled. Simmering-Graz-Pauker have in recent years delivered 128 motor cars and 200 trailer cars with a length over buffers of 39 ft 1 in (11.9 m), width 7 ft 4 in (2.24 m) and height 10 ft 6 in (3.2 m). Motor cars weigh 17.25 tonnes, trailer cars 10.25 tonnes. Each car has two sets of doors on each side. Motor cars are equipped with single panto-graphs. All cars fitted with automatic central buffer-couplers.
Signalling: Automatic block, with ac track circuits and two-aspect colour-light signals.
Station layout: Mostly side-platforms.

WARSAW

Authority:
Biuro Planowainia Rozwoju
ul. Batorego 16, Warsaw, Poland

Telephone: 25 47 60

Type of system: Full-metro.

General: The electrified suburban lines of the Polish State Railways in the Warsaw area include an underground section running through the centre of the city in an east-west direction. The tunnel which is 2.8 miles (4.5 km) long, four-tracked, and of "cut-and-cover" construction, lies on the so-called "Warsaw Through Line" between Warszawa Sródmiescie and the River Vistula, and passes for most of its length beneath main roads. Power is supplied at 3 000 V dc by overhead conductor wires. Electrification was carried out between 1936 and 1938 by British contractors, and the multiple-unit rolling stock supplied consisted of 3-car trainsets (one motor car and two articulated trailers), with automatic air-worked doors and Scharfenberg couplers. Severe damage was done to the Warsaw electrified lines during the second World War, but reconstruction took place after 1945, and the electrification has since been further extended outwards from Warsaw along the main lines. New multiple-unit stock purchased from Sweden or built in Poland since the war for the Warsaw suburban lines is similar to the pre-war stock; the new cars have automatic doors (3 double-leaf doors on each side) and automatic centre-buffer couplers, and are coupled to form 3-car trainsets.
At present the Greater Warsaw area, about 188 m² (486 km²) is served by about 43 miles (70 km) of conventional railways with more than 20 stations linked with the countrywide Polish Railways network. These lines are used for suburban traffic and also link the outskirts with the town centre. Detail includes: 3-car traction units produced by PAFAWAG Wroclaw. Continuous hp of traction motors type Lkc-450 is 580 kW; dead load 125 tons; maximum speed 68 mph (110 km/h), number of seats 228, standing room for 372 passengers; Knorr braking system. The economic speed of trains of 3-car units in the Warsaw district is 27 mph (45 km/h).
There is also a separated segment about 5 miles (8 km) long of normal track line to Grodzisk Mazowiecki handled by different rolling stock, 600 V dc, produced by PAFAWAG Wroclaw. The electrification of the Warsaw railway and all its suburban sections was completed in 1972. At present the electrified lines carry suburban passenger traffic in seven directions radially from Warsaw.
Final design studies are being completed on Warsaw's first rapid transit line to run 24 km between the southern and northern districts via the city centre. The entire line will run in tunnel at an average depth of 10 m below the surface. At present 23 stations are planned to be spaced at approximately 600 to 700 m intervals through the centre of the city and at 1 200 m intervals on the outskirts. Track gauge is to be 1.435 m and planned power supply, third rail 825 V dc. The line is expected to operate with six-car trainsets on a 90 second headway. The line is to form the first stage of a projected subway system of 100 km, comprising four lines with 102 stations.

Technical Data:
Gauge: 1.435 m
Projected new lines (in design): 23 km
Number of lines: 1
Number of stations (total): 23
Average distance between stations: 989 m
Electric system: Third rail; 825 V dc

WASHINGTON

Authority:
Washington Metropolitan Area Transit Authority
600 Fifth Street NW, Washington, DC 20001, USA

General: Following the opening of the metro in March 1976 the system now covers 33.8 km following the opening of a 17.7 km section in 1977 and an 8.8 km section in 1978. Construction of a further 30.5 km is underway at a cost of $2 400 million. The final planned network is 160 km. Deliveries of 425 transit cars were made by Rohr Industries in 1977/78.

WUPPERTAL

Authority:
Wuppertal Stadtwerke AG
Bromberger St 39-41, 5600 Wuppertal 2, Federal Republic of Germany

Telephone: (0202) 5691
Telegrams: STADTWERKE-WPT

Type of system: Suspended monorail.

History: Operations commenced 1901.

Technical Data:
  Gauge: Monorail
  Route length: 13.3 km
  Number of lines: 1
  Number of stations (total): 18
  Speed (design max): 80 km/h
    (average commercial): 25.1 km/h

Electric system: Third rail; 600 V

Average distance between stations: 782 m
Max length of station platforms: 40 m approx
Gradient (max): 40‰
Curvature (max): r = 75 m
Speed (design max): 60 km/h
  (average commercial): 26.6 km/h
Type of rail: 800 mm
Method and voltage of current supply: 600 V dc

Traffic and finances:
  Max number of trains per hour (one way): 21
  Frequency of train services in minutes (currently): 3
    (planned): 1.5
  Capacity per train (passengers seated): 48
    (passengers standing): 156
  Passenger journeys per annum: 28.7 million
    (1977/78); 14.3 million (1978/79)
  Revenues: Pf12.5/Pass-km (1977/78); Pf20.7/Pass-km
    (1978/79)

Rolling stock characteristics:
  Car types: GTW motor cars
  Number of units: 28
  Car dimensions:
    Length (m): 24.1
    Width (m): 2.2
    Height (m): 2.9
  Total floor area: 53.00 m²
  Number of doors per side: 4
  Door width (m): 1.3 m
  Number of passengers per car (total): 204
    (seated): 48
  Motors per car: 4
  Motor rating (kW): 50
  Power per train (Max): 200 kW
  Acceleration (max): 1.1 m/s²
  Deceleration (normal service): 0.8 m/s²
    (emergency): 1.2 m/s²
  Max design speed: 1 700 rpm
  Bogies (type and manufacturer): Aluminium, MAN
  Distance between bogie pivot: 7.65 m
  Brakes (type): E1 Disc
  Weight (empty in tonnes): 22.175

YOKOHAMA

Authority:
Municipal Transportation Bureau
3-31 Chome Honmachi, Nakaku 231, Yokohama, Japan

Type of system: Full Metro.

General: Construction work on Yokohama's new underground railway system has been in progress since 1970.

The recent population increase in Yokohama has caused excessive congestion of road traffic as well as transportation facilities. In order to modernise the latter to cope with the aggravated traffic situation, the City of Yokohama decided to discontinue street car services and construct rapid transit railways instead. In 1966, a plan for the construction of an extensive rapid transit system including subway lines linking the suburban and downtown areas was approved by the Municipal Transportation Council. It was agreed that the subway system should be completed by 1985.

This rapid transit project calls for the construction of four lines with a total length of 46.3 miles (64.5 km) costing Y155 000 million which will be raised by floating bonds.

The following four lines are planned:
Line 1: Shonandai (Fufisawa City) — Totsuka — Kamiooka — Isezaki-cho; 11.4 miles (18.6 km).
Line 2: Byobugaura — Yoshinocho — Yokohama Station — Kanagawa Shinmachi; 7 miles (11.4 km).

Line 3: Honmoku — Yamashitacho — Isezakicho — Yokohama Station — Shin Yokohama Station — Katsuda; 11.8 miles (19.2 km).
Line 4: Tsurumi — Sueyoshibashi — Katsuda — Moto Ishikawa; 9.4 miles (15.3 km).

Priority is being given to the important rapid transit routes 1 and 3 passing through the city's central area. The section of Line 1 from Kami-Ohoka to Isezakichoja-machi (5.3 km) was opened to traffic on December 16, 1972, and a 2.7 km southward extension to Kami-Nagaya was due to open in 1974.

On Line 3, construction work from Yokohama Central, south to Onoe-Cho 1.71 miles (2.75 km), was started in February 1972.

The network will consist of sub-surface lines in box-type tunnel under urban Yokohama, rising to elevated tracks in the suburbs. The trains, drawing power at 750 V dc from a current rail, will initially comprise three-car units, increasing to six-car units ultimately. They will operate under a system of automatic train control. The track gauge of 14 ft 8½ in (1.435 m) will be similar to that adopted in most of the recent Japanese rapid transit railway construction.

Technical Data:
  Gauge: 1.435 m
  Route length: 5.7 km
  In tunnel: 5.7 km
  Projected new lines (in construction): 8.5 km
    (in design): 50.3 km
  Number of lines: 1

Number of stations (total): 6
  (in tunnel): 6
Stations:
  platform length (minimum): 120 m
  Speed (design maximum): 90 km/h
  Electric system: Third rail; 750 V

Rolling stock:
  Car type (year introduced): 1971
  Units: 21
  Car dimensions:
    (length): 18.0 m
    (width): 2.78 m
    (height): 3.54 m
  Total floor area (m²): 50.0
  Door per side: 3
  Door (width): 1.30 m
  Passages per side: 6
  Passengers per car:
    (total): 145
    (seated): 52
  Motors per car: 4
  Motor rating: 120 kW
    165 hp
  Power per train:
    (maximum): 1 440

Traffic Data:
  Train/hours/track: 12
  Train capacity (passengers): 435
  Total passengers/track/hour (peak): 5 220
  Train headways existing: 5 minutes

TABULATED DATA

ALBANIA	456	LEBANON	490
ALGERIA	456	LIBERIA	490
ANGOLA	456	LUXEMBOURG	490
ARGENTINA	456		
AUSTRALIA	456	MADAGASCAR	490
AUSTRIA	458	MALAWI	492
		MALAYSIA	492
BANGLADESH	460	MALI	492
BELGIUM	460	MAURITANIA	492
BENIN	460	MEXICO	492
BOLIVIA	460	MONGOLIA	492
BRAZIL	460	MOROCCO	492
BULGARIA	462	MOZAMBIQUE	492
BURMA	462		
		NEPAL	494
CAMEROON	462	NETHERLANDS	494
CANADA	462	NEW ZEALAND	494
CHILE	464	NICARAGUA	494
CHINA	466	NIGERIA	494
COLOMBIA	466	NORWAY	494
CONGO	466		
COSTA RICA	466	PAKISTAN	494
CUBA	466	PANAMA	494
CZECHOSLOVAKIA	468	PARAGUAY	496
		PERU	496
DENMARK	468	PHILIPPINES	496
DOMINICAN REPUBLIC	468	POLAND	496
		PORTUGAL	498
ECUADOR	468	PUERTO RICO	498
EGYPT	468		
EL SALVADOR	470	ROMANIA	498
ETHIOPIA	470		
		SABAH	498
FIJI	470	SAUDIA ARABIA	498
FINLAND	470	SENEGAL	498
FRANCE	470	SIERRA LEONE	498
		SOUTH AFRICA	498
GERMANY, Democratic Republic	470	SPAIN	498
Federal Republic	470	SRI LANKA	502
GHANA	480	SUDAN	502
GREECE	480	SURINAM	502
GUATEMALA	480	SWAZILAND	502
GUINEA	480	SWEDEN	502
GUYANA	482	SWITZERLAND	502
		SYRIA	508
HAITI	482		
HONDURAS	482	TAIWAN	510
HONG KONG	482	TANZANIA	510
HUNGARY	482	THAILAND	510
		TOGO	510
INDIA	484	TUNISIA	510
INDONESIA	484	TURKEY	510
IRAN	484		
IRAQ	484	UNION OF SOVIET SOCIALIST REPUBLICS	510
IRELAND	484	UNITED KINGDOM	510
ISRAEL	484	UNITED STATES OF AMERICA	518
ITALY	484	URUGUAY	546
IVORY COAST	488		
		VENEZUELA	546
JAMAICA	488	VIET-NAM	546
JAPAN	488		
JORDAN	490	YUGOSLAVIA	546
KAMPUCHEA	490	ZAÏRE	548
KOREA	490	ZAMBIA	548
		ZIMBABWE	548

NAME OF COMPANY ADDRESS	Gauge ft. in. (metres)	Route length incl. E=Electrified miles (km.)	Track length incl. E=Electrified miles (km.)	Elect. system and type of conductor	Loco-motives L=Line S=Shunt / Steam Electric Diesel De=elec. Dh=hyd.		Rail-cars Electric Diesel Trailer Railbus Multiple Unit set		Pass. train cars	Freight train cars	Freight movement Total Volume carried. Con-tainers Thousands of tonnes	Av'ge haul per ton miles (km.)	Av'ge net train load tonnes	Max. trailing load tonnes	Passengers Total number carried in 1000s	Aver-age jour-ney miles (km.)

ALBANIA
*Albanian State Railways
Hekurudha e Shqiërisë, Tirana

ALGERIA
*Société Nationale des Transports Ferroviaires (SNTF)
21-23 blvd Mohamed V, Algiers
— Gauge 4' 8½" (1·435); Route 2 429 E 185 (3 912) (299); Elect. 3 000 V dc; Loco E 47, De 172; Railcars D 41, T 73; Passengers 10 220

ANGOLA
*Caminho de Ferro de Benguela (Benguela Railway Company)
C.P. 32, Lobito
— Gauge 3' 6" (1·067); Route 810 (1 304); Track (1 664); Loco SL 95, DeL 10, SS 12, DhS 6; Pass. train cars 54; Freight train cars 1 838; Average journey 1·9

Caminho de Ferro do Amboim
Avenido Infante Santo, Lisbon, Portugal
Local office: Porto Amboim
— Gauge 1' 11⅝" (0·600); Route 77 (123); Track 78 (126); Loco SL 5, DS 2; Railcars D 4; Pass. train cars 6; Freight train cars 73; Total Volume 8·0; Av'ge haul 598 218 383 ton-km; Average journey 34·2

Caminhos de Ferro de Luanda
Caixa Postal 1229
Luanda
— Gauge 3' 6" (1·067) 263 (424), Track 324 (521); 1' 11⅝" (0·600) 19 (31); Loco SL 21, DeS 9, DhS 11; Railcars D 6, DT 3; Pass. train cars 38; Freight train cars 569; Max. trailing load 1 100; Passengers 728·3

Caminho de Ferro de Moçamedes
Caixa Postal 130, Sá da Bandeira
— Gauge 3' 6" (1·067); Route 536 (863); Track 623 (1 003); Loco De 37, Dh 17, Dm 9; Railcars D 5; Pass. train cars 16; Freight train cars 1 377; Total Volume 6 818·3; Av'ge haul 325·6 (524·1); Max. trailing load 3 316; Passengers 272·1; Average journey 83·3 (134·1)

Direcção dos Servicos de Portos, Caminhos de Ferro e Transportes
— Gauge 3' 6" (1·067) 558 (899), 1' 11⅝" (0·600); Loco DeL 37, DhL 19, DhS 10; Railcars D 5; Pass. train cars 18; Freight train cars 25; Total Volume 6 219·4; Av'ge haul 563 343 824 ton-km; Passengers 394·1

ARGENTINA
*Ferrocarriles Argentinos
Argentine Railways
Avenida Ramos Mejia 1302, Buenos Aires
The former 6 separate railways have been re-formed into 4 regional systems

Región Centro (Central)
Avenida Ramos Mejia 1302, Buenos Aires
Formerly: FC Gen. Mitre and FC Gen. San Martin
— Gauge 5' 6" (1·676); Route 6 774 (10 902) E 36 (58); Track 7 331 (11 798) E 94 (115); Elect. 800 V dc 3 R; Loco S 306, D 516; Railcars E 386, D 167, T 126; Pass. train cars 1 372; Freight train cars 23 166

Región Noreste (North-East)
Rivadavia 456, Concordia, Entre Rios
Formerly: FC Gen. Urquiza
— Gauge 4' 8½" (1·435); Route 1 920 (3 091) E 14 (23); Track 2 238 (3 603) E 28 (45); Elect. 600 V dc OH; Loco SL 108, SS 32, DeL 45, E 10; Railcars E 88, D 53, EMU 16; Pass. train cars 181; Freight train cars 3 646; Max. trailing load 346; Passengers 650
— Gauge 1' 11⅝" (0·60); Route 130 (209); Track 137 (221)

Región Noroweste (Northwest)
Avenida Maipu No. 4, Buenos Aires
Formerly: FC Gen. Belgrano
— Gauge 2' 5½" (0·75) 48 (77), Track 377 (607); 3' 3⅜" (1·00) 8 358 (13 451), 9 870 (15 885); Loco S 124, D 45; Railcars D 107, E 95; Pass. train cars 349; Freight train cars 3 592; Max. trailing load 291; Passengers 630

Región Suroeste (South-West)
Plaza Constitución, Buenos Aires
Formerly: FC Gen. Roca and FC Gen. Sarmienta
— Gauge 5' 6" (1·676) 7 808 (12 656) E 26 (42), Track 8 219 (13 228) E 82 (132); 2' 5½" (0·75) 250 (403), 250 (403); Elect. 800 V dc 3R; Loco S 450, D 630, E 4; Railcars E 312, D 219; Pass. train cars 1 387; Freight train cars 18 895; Max. trailing load 390

AUSTRALIA
*Australian National Railways
55 King William Road, North Adelaide, SA 5006

NEW SOUTH WALES
State Railway Authority/SRA (New South Wales)
11-31 York St, Sydney, NSW 2000
— Gauge 4' 8½" (1·435); Elect. 1 500 V dc OH; Loco EL 41, DeL 428, DhS 79; Railcars E 629, ET 647, D 89, DT 68; Pass. train cars 628; Freight train cars 12 997; Total Volume 33 800; Av'ge haul 106, 6 170; Passengers 842 389

QUEENSLAND
*Queensland Government Railways
305 Edward St, Brisbane, Queensland 4000
— Gauge 3' 6" (1·067) 6 054 — (10 091); 4' 8½" (1·435) 66 — (111); Loco SL 4†, DeL 464, DhS 73, Dm 4; Railcars RE 12, RD 51, ET 6, DT 14; Pass. train cars 8·99; Freight train cars 23 025, C 157; Total Volume —; Av'ge haul —; Passengers 29 231·4

SOUTH AUSTRALIA
State Transport Authority
PO Box 2351, Adelaide, SA 5001
— Gauge 5' 3" (1·60) 1 572 (2 531), Track 2 010 (3 235); 3' 6" (1·067) 598 (963), 671 (1 035); 4' 8½" (1·435) 245 (395), 290 (470); Loco SL 4, DeL 2; Railcars D 116, DT 24; Pass. train cars 33; Freight train cars 12; Passengers 11 368·3

The Emu Bay Railway Co Ltd
PO Box 82, Burnie, Tas 7320
— Gauge 3' 6" (1·067); Route 83 (133); Track 89 (143); Loco DhL 11, DS 1, DhS 1; Pass. train cars 2; Freight train cars 123; Total Volume 536·7; Av'ge haul 63 881 957 ton-km; Average journey 1·3

VICTORIA
*Victorian Railways
67 Spencer St, Melbourne, Vic 3000

* See main entry
† Reserved for excursions

Average Speeds			Financial Data		Couplers	Buffers	Rails	Sleepers (crossties)		Curvature max.	Gradient max. (U=not compensated)	Axle load max.	Altitude max.	Staff employed. Total no. (inclu. workshop)	Names of officials. Extended lists can be found at the end of the individual country in the report section immediately following
Freight Train	Pass. Train	Speed max.	Revenue Expenses	Braking (continuous)	Type and Height above rail	Centres and Height above rail	Weight	Type and thickness	Spacing Number per mile (per km) or centres						
mph (km/hr)	mph (km/hr)	mph (km/hr)	in 1 000s		ins (mm)	ins (mm)	lb. per yd (kg/m)	ins (mm)	ins (mm)			tonnes	feet (m)		
							86 (43)					21			
		74 (120)			Screw Semi-Auto	Air	91/110 (45/54)	Wood Conc. & Steel		218 ft (200 m)	3·0%	22		12 380	Dir. Gen: Benmechdjonba
21 (34)	25 (40)	43 (70)	Escudos 1 273·4 978·7	Vac. Gresham & Craven	Auto Henricot 34⅝ (880)		90/60 (45/30)	Wood and steel	2 655 (1 650)	1 020 ft (310 m)	2·5% 2·0% U	15·0	5 413 (1 650)	12 800 (1 312)	Gen. Man: Eng. L. Lama de Oliveira
12·5 (20)	22 (36)	Freight 16 (25)	Escudos 1 429·3 4 621·0	Vac. Jourd. Monn; Davies & Metcalfe	Chain 20 (510)	Central 20 (510)	40/35 (20/17)	Wood 4¾ (120)	18" (460)	246 ft (75 m)	3·8% U	7	3 358 (1 054)	400 (65)	Director: Gabriel Aguiar dos Santos
25 (40)	37 (60)	50 (80)		Vac. Gresham	Atlas Auto 35¼ (896)		130/30 (65/15)	Metal	2 260 (1 450)	361 ft (110 m)	3·1% U	14	3 806 (1 160)	2 158 (470)	Eng. Luis H. E. Abreu Eng. B. L. Almeida Eng. J. P. Duarte
23·9 (38·5)	24·8 (40·0)	40 (65)	Escudos 563 378·7 279 540·0	Vac. Gresham	Atlas IR & 2 38·7 (983)		90/60 (43/30)	Metal & wood 5½ (140)	Metal 2 250 (1 400) Wood 2 575 (1 600)	377 ft (115 m)	2·8%	16	6 266 (1 910)	4 591 (877)	Eng. Maria Augosto de Paiva Neto
			$ 679 161·0 333 513·8												Director: Eng. Agostinho A. S. de Almeida
															President: Gen. Emiliano A. S. Flouret
				Air W'hse	Screw (1 065/950)	Crs. 77 (1 950) Ht. (1 065/ 950)	100/60 (50/30)	Wood 4¾ (120) Some Steel	2 160 (1 350)	656 ft (200 m)	2·4%	10·4		55 000	
				Air W'hse			80/50 (40/25)	Wood 4¾ (120)	2 240 (1 400)	5·8°	1·31%	15		11 562 (1 541)	
	56 (90)			Air W'hse	Auto 31¼ (795)		80/50 (40/25)	Wood 4¾ (120) and Metal	2 320 (1 450)	295 ft (90 m)	3·19% Rack 6·0%	6·8	2 780 (4 475)	50 009 (7 977)	
							90/70 (45/35)	Wood 4¾ (120)	2 240 (1 400)	5·0°	2·5% 1·5%	10 (8·52)		31 131	
							100/60 (50/30)	Wood 4¾ (120)	2 160 (1 350)	7·0°	3·8%	9·69		12 528	
15 (23)	25 (40)	70 (115)	$A 388 382 759 727	Air W'hse	Auto 34½ (880)	Crs 69 (1 750) Ht 40 (1 031)				792 ft (240 m)	3%	21	4 526 (1 377)		Chf. Comm: A. S. Reiher
															Chf Comm: P. J. Goldston
			$A 3 373·9 24 877·3											7 949	Gen. Man: J. M. Doyle
18 (29)	28 (45)			Vac G & C	Screw 30½ (775)	57 (1 448) 30½ (775)	82/63 (31/41)	Wood 5 (127)	24" (610)	330 ft (100 m)	3·0% 2·5% U	14·25	2 201 (671)	160	Ast. Man: D. H. Beath

NAME OF COMPANY ADDRESS	Gauge ft. in. (metres)	Route length incl. E=Electrified miles (km.)	Track length incl. E=Electrified miles (km.)	Elect. system and type of conductor	Loco-motives L=Line S=Shunt Steam Electric Diesel De=elec. Dh=hyd.	Rail-cars Electric Diesel Trailer Railbus Multiple Unit set	Pass. train cars	Freight train cars Con-tainers	Total Volume carried. Thous-ands of tonnes	Av'ge haul per ton miles (km.)	Av'ge net train load tonnes	Max. trailing load tonnes	Total number carried in 1 000s	Aver-age jour-ney miles (km.)

AUSTRALIA (contd.)

WESTERN AUSTRALIA
***Westrail**
Westrail Centre,
West Parade,
East Perth, WA 6000

Colonial Sugar Refining Co Ltd 55 Clarence Street, Sydney, NSW *Operates seven sugar mills in Queensland*	2' 0'' (0·610)		466 (750)		DhS 8 DhL 46			14 000	5 700·0	10 (16)	555 500 000 train-km	300		
Goldsworthy Railway Goldsworthy Mining Ltd. Box 84, Port Hedland, WA 6721	4' 8½'' (1·435)	113 (179)	121 (195)		DeL 6 DeS 2			257	6 062·5					
Hammersley Railways Hamersley Iron Pty Ltd Box 21, Dampier, WA 6713	4' 8½'' (1·435)	240 (382)	365 (588)		DeL 40 DeS 1		1	2 237	34 821		11 509 000 000 ton-km			
Mt Newman Railroad Mt Newman Mining Co Pty Ltd 200 St Georges Terrace, Perth, WA 6001	4' 8½'' (1·435)	265 (426)	324 (521)		De 51		1	2 083	20 120		12 575 000 000 tonne-km			

AUSTRIA

***Austrian Federal Railways OBB** (Österreichische Bundesbahnen) Elisabethstrasse 9, A-1010 Vienna	4' 8½' (1·435) E 1 702 (2 744)	3 361 (5 418)	6 062 (9 756) E 3 678 (5 913)	15 000 V 16⅔ OH	SL 111 EL 597 DeL 51 DhL 165 DhS 276 ES 43 DeS 2	D 51 DT 266 EMU 97	3 404	35 858	46 358·0		10 547 877 ton-km		168 172·0	24·8 (39·7)
	3' 3⅜'' (1·00) 2' 6'' (0·76)	9 (15) 273 (439) E 57 91	319 (513) E 60 (97)	6 500 V 25 OH										
Achenseebahn AG Jenbach, Tirol	3' 3⅜'' (1·0)	4·3 (6·8)	4·6 (7·4)		S 3		6	3					77·000	
Graz-Köflacher Eisenbahn und Bergbau-gesellschaft Grazbachstrasse 39, A-8010 Graz	4' 8½'' (1·435)	59 (95)	90 (145)		DS 2 DhL 5 DeL 3 DhS 6	D 12 DT 21	39	514	1 700·0	31 (50)	800	1 600	3 041·0	16 (26)
Montafonerbahn AG A-6780 Schruns (Vorariberg)	4' 8½'' (1·435) E 8 (13)		E 9 (14)	15 kV 16⅔ OH	S 1 De 1	R 2 E 3 DT 1 ET 1	6	4	153·1	3·5 (5)		500	825·2	5·6 (9)
Reisseck-Kreuzeck Höhenbahnen Österr. Draukraftwerke AG A 9020 Klagenfurt, Anzengruberstr. 50	1' 11⅝'' (0·60)	2·0 (3·3)	2·2 (3·6)		D 2 Dh 1**		2	7	1·2	2·0 (3·3)		13	121·9	2·0 (3·3)
Raab-Oedenburg-Ebenfurter Eisenbahn† Vienna 1	4' 8½'' (1·435)	39‡ (64)	50 (81)		S 27 D 4	D 12	104	540	1 680·1	15·5 (25)			315·4	14 (22)
Salzburger Stadtwerke Verkehrsbetriebe-Lokalbahn A-5020 Salzburg, Kaiserschützenstr 26	4' 8½'' (1·435) E 15 (25)		E 20 (32)	1 000 V dc OH	EL 2 ES 2	E 10	15	16	319·5				1 318·6	8 (13)
Steiermärkische Landesbahnen A-8011 Radetzkystrasse 31, Graz, Postfach 553 *(Operates following 8 lines):*	4' 8½'' (1·435) 2' 6'' (0·76)	121 590 (195 681) E 19 349 (31 279)	140 106 (225 479) E 20 191 (32 497)		DhS 2 DmS 2	SL 9 EL 1 DeL 8 DhL 3	E 5 ET 1	35	388	471·4		6 660·5 ton-km		819·2	
Feldbach-Bad Gleichenberg A-8330 Feldbach	4' 8½'' (1·435) E 13 (21)		E 14 (22)	1 800 V dc OH	E 1	E 2	1	8	129·6		684 927 tonne-km	120	40·8	10·5 (17·0)
Gleisdorf-Weiz *Local office:* A-8160 Weiz	4' 8½'' (1·435)	9 (15)	11 (18)		S 1 De 2		5	6	47·0		1 819·4 tonne-km	172·5	436·3	8·2 (13·1)
Kapfenberg-Seebach-Turnau *Local office:* A-8605 Kapfenberg	2' 6'' (0·76)	12 (20)	15 (25)		Dh 1 SL 1 De 1			134	128·6		1 514 402 tonne-km	160		
Lokalbahn Mixnitz Lokalbahn Mixnitz-St. Erhard AG *Local office:* A-8131 Mixnitz	2' 6'' (0·76) E 6·2 (10)		E 7·4 (12)	800 V dc OH	ES 2 EL 2 DeS 1 DhS 1			42	54·7		601 161 tonne-km			5·4 (8·6)
Peggau-Übelbach A-8124 Ubelbach	4' 8½'' (1·435) E 7 (11)		E 8 (13)	15 kV 1/16⅔ OH		E 3 T 1		1	6·1		46 892 tonne-km	214·0	203·8	
Preding-Wieselsdorf-Stainz A-8510, Stainz	2' 6'' (0·76)	7 (11)	7·5 (12)		S 1 DhS 2		4	23	7·5		89 376 tonne-km	170		13·7 (22·0)
Murtalbahn-Unzmarkt-Mauterndorf A-8850 Murau	2' 6'' (0·76)	48 (76)	53 (85)		SL 4 DeL 3 DmS 1		17	132	135·1		1 879·9 tonne-km	240	160·7	17·5 (25)
Feistritztalbahn Weiz-Ratten A-8160 Weiz	2' 6'' (0·76)	27 (43)	31 (50)		S 2 De 2 DhS 1		8	84	44·4		886·6 tonne-km	240	12·6	6·2 (10·0)

Stern & Hafferl Lokalbahn Betriebe
Postfach 3, A-4810, Gmunden
(Operates 7 railways, 6 of which it owns):

* See main entry
** Snow-clearing locomotive
† Details for Austrian section only. Extends into Hungary as Györ-Sopron Ebenfurt
‡ Includes figures referring to Neusiedlerseebahn AG

Average Speeds			Financial Data	Braking (continuous)	Couplers	Buffers	Rails	Sleepers (crossties)		Curvature max.	Gradient max. (U=not compensated)	Axle load max.	Altitude max.	Staff employed. Total no. (inclu. workshop)	Names of officials. Extended lists can be found at the end of the individual country in the report section immediately following
Freight Train	Pass. Train	Speed max.	Revenue Expenses		Type and Height above rail	Centres and Height above rail	Weight	Type and thickness	Spacing Number per mile (per km) or centres						
mph (km/hr)	mph (km/hr)	mph (km/hr)	in 1 000s		ins (mm)	ins (mm)	lb. per yd (kg/m)	ins (mm)	ins (mm)			tonnes	feet (m)		
10 (16)							60/45 (30/22)	Wood 4 (102) & Conc.	24" (610)	100 ft (30·5 m)	2·0% U	6	200 (61)		Gen. Man: Dr. A. M. Hertzberg
	26 (42)	35 (56)		Air W'hse	Alliance 35 (889)		101 (50)	Wood 5 (127)	24 (610)	1 900 ft (579 m)	1·0% U 1·04%	23·5	442 (135)	161 (50)	Supt: J. G. Fitzgerald
	30 (48)	40 (64)	$A 28 497·0	Air W'hse ABD/W	Type F 35½ (902)		136/119 (67/59)	Wood Conc. 6 (152)	19½" (495)	1 300 ft (396 m)	2·0% U 1·92%	30	2 500 (762)	955	Man: M. S. Purcell
	Loaded 35 (56) Empty 40 (64)			Vac W'hse	Type F 34½ (876)		132 (65·5)	Jarrah 6 (152)	21" (533)	1 900 ft (579 m)	1·5%	30	1 680 (512)	924	RR Man: R. S. Murphy
	Main 87 (140) Second 37 (60) Narrow 25 (40)		Schillings 13 487 000 17 399 000	Air Oerlikon (under licence) (940)	Standard Screw Max 41¾ (1 065) Min F.37 P 38½ (980)	68⅞ (1 750) Height as for Coupler	130/99 (64·3/ 49·4) 5⅛ (130)	Wood Standard gauge 6½ (160) Narrow (650/700) Conc 8 (200) 7 (180)	25½ (650) 25½/27½ 18·2	6·5° N: 25·5% N.	Std: Main 2·97% Other 4·0% Rack Narrow 4·0%	Std: 20 12	Std: 5 773 (1 796)	71 274 (9 182)	Gen. Dir.: Dr. Wolfgang Pycha
	9 (14)	13 (20)			Central 29½ (750)		46 (23)	Iron & Wood 5½ (140)	33½ (850)	13·0°	16% (rack)	10	3 182 (970)	19	Dir. Engelbert Hackel
19 (30)	30 (50)	56 (90)		Air Hardy; Knorr	Standard Railcar Scharff	Standard	98/53 (49/26)	Form I, II & III	2 400 (1 500)	7·3°	1·57%	16	1 476 (450)	1 060	Dr. Edward Prochaska
19 (30)	30 (50)	47 (75)	S.32 163·9 31 816	Air Oerlikon	Standard Railbus Scharff	Stand-ard	67 (33)	Wood 6 (152)	25½ (650)	10·0°	2·5%	20	2 231 (680)	58	Ing: H. Rabitsch
3 (5)	9 (14)	10 (15)			Buffer coupler		36·5 (18·3)	Wood	2 010 (1 250)	38·0°	3·9%	2	7 375 (2 248)	7	
										5·8°	0·8%			175	
20 (33)	22 (35)	37 (60)		Vac Hardy	Auto 23⅝ (600)		67 (33)			7·5°	2·1%	18		121	Man.: Dipl. Ing B. Robenhaupt
			Schillings 34 926·6 86 355·9											269	Gen. Man.: Dr. Jur. W. Zauhar
19 (30)	25 (40)	28 (45)	Schillings 5 144·8 7 949·5							11·7°	4·1%	16	1 280 (390)	26	
19 (30)	28 (45)	37 (50)	Schillings 8 769·7 15 333·6							8·7°	1·5%	18	1 499 (457)	56	
		15·5 (25)	Schillings 6 583·4 10 713·4							22·0°	3·0%	10	2 352 (717)	31	
12·5 (20)		12·5 (20)	Schillings 2 827·8							29·0°	3·0%	10	2 031 (619)	12	
				Standard Air Oerlikon Narrow Vac.	Standard European Narrow Buffer-	Standard European Narrow 22½	Standard 72/52 (36/26) Narrow 52/36	Wood 5½ (140)	28 (710)						
19 (30)	19 (30)	25 (40)	Schillings 2 325·7 3 070·8							9·7°	3·2%	16	1 673 (510)	11	
9 (14)		9·5 (15)	Schillings 688·1 1 948·6	Hardy	Coupler	(570)	(26/18)			17·5°	1·1%	12	1 070 (326)	8	
19 (30)		28 (45)	Schillings 9 293·9 34 035·6							22·0°	2·0%	6·5	3 652 (739)	105	
15·5 (25)	19 (30)	19 (30)	Schillings 3 523·3 12 760·2							29·0°	2·5%	6·5	2 424 (739)	32	

Dipl. Ing Ingobert Stern

NAME OF COMPANY ADDRESS	Gauge ft. in. (metres)	Route length incl. E=Electrified miles (km.)	Track length incl. E=Electrified miles (km.)	Elect. system and type of conductor	Loco-motives L=Line S=Shunt Steam Electric De=elec. Dh=hyd.		Rail-cars Electric Diesel Trailer Railbus Multiple Unit set		Pass. train cars	Freight train cars Con-tainers	Total Volume carried. Thous-ands of tonnes	Av'ge haul per ton miles (km.)	Av'ge net train load tonnes	Max. trailing load tonnes	Total number carried in 1 000s	Aver-age jour-ney miles (km.)
AUSTRIA *(contd.)*																
Burmoos-Trimmelkam Trimmelkam, Upper Austria	4' 8½'' (1·435)	E 6 (9)	E 8 (13)	1 000 V dc OH	EL	2	E	2		0		5·3 (8·5)		450		4·3 (7)
Lokalbahn Gmunden-Vorchdorf AG Postfach 2, 4810 Gmunden	3' 3⅜'' (1·00)	E 9 (15)	E 10 (16)	750 V dc OH			E	4	6	5	2·7	30 116 ton-km			597	5 (8)
Lokalbahn Lambach-Vorchdorf-Eggenberg Lambach	4' 8½'' (1·435)	E 7 (12)	E 8 (13)	750 V dc OH	E-D	1	E	2	3	7		8·4 (13·5)	35	180		
Linzer Localbahn AG (Linz-Eferding-Waizenkirchen) A-4020 Linz	4' 8½'' (1·435)	E 27 (43)	E 29 (47)	750 V dc OH	EL ES	5 1	E	7	10	10		9·3 (15)	260			9·3 (15)
Lokalbahn Neumarkt-Waizen-kirchen-Peuerbach AG *Local office:* Waizenkirchen	4' 8½'' (1·435)	E 10 (16)	E 11 (18)	750 V dc OH			E	3	3	3	324·9	4 448 400 ton-km			2 322·2	5 (8)
Lambach-Haaga/Hausruck	4' 8½'' (1·435)	E 17 (27)	E 20 (32)	750 V dc OH	EL	1	E	2	2	3		6·2 (10)				8 (13)
Lokalbahn Volkermarkt-Attesee AG Postfach 2, 4810 Gmunden	3' 3⅜'' (1·00)	E 8 (13)	E 9 (15)	750 V dc OH			E	5	6	24	7					5 (8)
Stubaitalbahn AG Klostergasse 2, A-6010 Innsbruck	3' 3⅜'' (1·00)	E 11 (18)	E 12 (20)	3 000 V ac			E	4	7	12	6·0	6 (10)			700·0	6 (9)
Wiener Lokalbahn AG Eichenstrasse 1, Vienna XII	4' 8½'' (1·435)	19 (29) E 16 (26)	38 (62) E 33 (54)	850 V dc OH	ES DhL	1 2	E T	26 6	35	31	103·1	3 113 200 ton-km	1 000	4 232·6	6·8 (11)	
Zillertalbahn Zillertaler Verkehrsbetriebe AG Austrasse 1, A-6200 Jenbach	2' 6'' (0·760)	20 (32)	24 (38)		SL DeS DhL DhS	4 1 2 3	D	2	19	74	81·4	15·5 (25)	120	394	842·7	10 (16)
BANGLADESH																
***Bangladesh Railways** Central Railway Buildings Chittagong	B.G.† M.G.†	598 (964) 1 187 (1 910)	994 (1 589) 1 810 (2 932)		BG SL81 SS 74 DeL 32 DeS 32 MG SL 172 SS 156 DeL 135 DeS 148		R DT	4 8		BG318 BG4 317 MG975 MG11 676						
BELGIUM																
***Soc. Nat des C. F. Belges (S.N.C.B.)** 21 Rue de Louvain, 1000 Brussels	4' 8½'' (1 435)	2 735 (4 045) E 807 (1 307)			EL DL	249 936	E D	466 87	2 344	47 252	63 187	6 888 000 000 tonne-km			170 757	
Soc. Nat. des C.F. Vicinaux (SNCV) 14 Rue de la Science, 1040 Brussels	3' 3⅜'' (1·00)	127 (205) E 124 (200)	(334) (329)	600 V dc OH	SL	5	E D	174 9	129						312 219	4·5 (7·3)
BENIN																
***Organisation Commune Benin-Niger des Chemins de Fer et des Transports (O.C.B.N.)** B.P. 16, Cotonou, République du Benin	3' 3⅜'' (1·00)	359 (579)	395 (635)		DeL	14	D T	6 5	31	387 C 23	388·4	152 253 043 ton-km			1 651·7	49 (80)
BOLIVIA																
***Empresa Nacional de Ferrocarriles** Casilla 428, La Paz	3' 3⅜'' (1·00)	2 191 (3 538)	2 125 (3 427)		DeL DhL DhS	54 5 4	DMU	14	121	2 151	1 186	586 710 000 ton-km			397 193 000 pass-km	147 (237)
Guaqui-La Paz Railway Casilla 280, La Paz	3' 3⅜'' (1·00)	54 (87) E 5½ (9)	61 (98) E 8 (13)													
F.C. Machacamarca-Uncia Corporacion Minera de Bolivia Machacamarca	3' 3⅜'' (1·00)	65 (105)	74 (119)		SL SS DeL DS	1 1 4 2	D R	2 5	12	84	765·6				17·8	31 (50)
F.C. Uyuni—Pulacayo Pulacayo	2' 6'' (0·762)	20 (32)	24 (39) E 8 (13)		S E D	5 11 1				47						
BRAZIL																
***Rede Ferroviaria Federal SA (RFFSA)** Praça Duque de Caixas 86, Rio de Janeiro *Formed into 6 Regions*	2' 6'' (0·762) 3' 3⅜'' (1·00) 5' 3'' (1·60)	125 (202) 14 088 (22 671) 1 039 (1 673) E 678 (1 092)														
Regional Rio de Janeiro Otoni	3' 3⅜'' (1·00) 5' 3'' (1·60)	1 012 (1 664) 687 (1 145)	E 120 (186)		EL DeL	11 321			8 022	26 363 C 48	24 112	336 (551)	971 1 619	—	1 392·0	

* See main entry
† BG = Broad Gauge, MG = Metre Gauge

Average Speeds			Financial Data		Couplers	Buffers	Rails	Sleepers (crossties)		Curvature max.	Gradient max. (U=not compensated)	Axle load max.	Altitude max.	Staff employed. Total no. (inclu. workshop)	Names of officials. Extended lists can be found at the end of the individual country in the report section immediately following
Freight Train	Pass. Train	Speed max.	Revenue Expenses	Braking (con-tinuous)	Type and Height above rail	Centres and Height above rail	Weight	Type and thick-ness	Spacing Number per mile (per km) or centres ins						
mph (km/hr)	mph (km/hr)	mph (km/hr)	in 1 000s		ins (mm)	ins (mm)	lb. per yd (kg/m)	ins (mm)	(mm)			tonnes	feet (m)		
25 (40)	25 (40)	31 (50)					66 (33)	Wood 6 (150)		6·7°	1·5%	18			Dipl. Ing Ingobert Stern
	25 (40)	31 (50)	S.461 900 448 600	Vac			48/36 (24/18)	Wood 5 (140)		11·5°	4·0%	8·5	1 763 (557·5)	35	Dipl. Ing Ingobert Stern
25 (40)	25 (40)	31 (50)					61 (30)	Wood 6 (150)		6·0°	1·5%	16	1 381 (421)		Dipl. Ing Ingobert Stern
19 (30)	28 (45)	31 (50)								7·6°	2·7%	20	1 283 (391)		Dipl. Ing Ingobert Stern
19 (30)	25 (40)	31 (50)	S.46 624 50 987	Freight W'hse Air Pass. Hardy Vac	Standard	Standard (33)	66 5 (140)	Wood		6·0°	1·6%	16 (384)	1 260	190	Dipl. Ing Ingobert Stern
19 (30)	25 (40)	31 (50)					61 (31)	Wood 6 (150)		7·6°	2·8%	18			Dipl. Ing Ingobert Stern
22 (35)	22 (35)	31 (50)		Vac			44/36 (22/18)	Wood 5 (140)		28·0°	4·7%	7·5	1 866 (569)		Dipl. Ing Ingobert Stern
		16 (25)	Revenue S.3 600·0	Air	Buffer Coupler	21⅞ (555)	53/38 (26·5/ 18·7)	Wood	1 930 (1 200)	44·0°	4·5%	6·0	3 304 (1 007)	46	
12 (20)	21 (33·8)	31 (50)	S.34·685 46 552	Vac Hardy	B.S.I. Compakt 20⅝ (525)	Centre Buffer Coupler	66·6 (33)	Wood 6¼ (160)	26 (650)	57·0°	5·0%U	18	755 (230)	296 (91)	Gen. Man.: Dipl. Ing E. Hübner
16 (25)	28 (45)	31 (50)	S.13 685·0 14 450·0	Vac Hardy Air W'hse	Centre Buffer Coupler 22⅜ (570)	Centre Buffer Coupler	53/36 (26·2/ 17·9)	Wood 5½ (140)	28⅜″-31⅞″ (700-810)	0·25°	1·6%U 1·5%	12·5	2 058 (627)	102 (30)	Dir.: Dipl. Ing Erich Heiss
BG40 (6·8) MG40 (6·8)	10 (16) 9 (15)	34 (55) 28 (45)	Taka 827 730 756 000												
			Fr 395 258 838 39 698 162											59 330	
Steam 19 (30)	Town 12 (19) Coun-try 14 (23)	*	FR. 4 297 171 9 665 549	Air and Vac W'hse Oil Pieper	18⅛ (460)	Crs. 26⅜ (671) Ht. 25⅝ (650)	64·5 (32)	Wood 7¾ (200) 4¾ (120)	1 780-2 220 (1 110-1 390)	58°F 95°P	Diesel 6% Steam lines 3%				Dir. Gen: M. C. Henrard
20 (33)	33 (53)	50 (80)	CFA 1 175 628·4 1 168 957·6	Vac Wh'se Jourdain Monn	Willison Auto & unified type 55/70 tons 30 (760)	Crs. 15¾ (400) Ht. 30 (760)	60/40 (30/22)	Metal	2 400 (1 500)	525 ft (160 m)	2·3%	13	1 276 (389)	1 588 (418)	Gen. Man: M. A. Boittiaux
15 (25)	22 (35)	37 (60)	$b 28 550 25 800	Air W'hse	Henricot Auto 342 (792)		80/50 (40/25)	Wood 4¾ (120)	2 400 (1 500)	Rad 252 ft (76·6 m)	3·09%	15	15 702 (4 787)	6 457 (502)	Gen. Man: Ing. Carlos Azurday T.
19 (30)				Air W'hse	"Visco" Alliance Engl: St:		60 (30)	Wood 6 (150) Conc. 5½ (140)	23⅝ (600)	17·5°	6% U	11	13 416 (4 069)	679 (100)	Gen. Man: J. G. Lances
	25 (40)			Air W'hse	Centre Buffer Coupler	29½ (750)	60/50 (30/25)	Wood 4¾ (120)	31·5″ (800)	14·5°	2·5% 3·5% U	12	14 436 (4 400)	234 (67)	Gen. Man: Ricardo M. Bayá B
							35 (17·3)	Wood 6 (150)	3 200 (2 000)	17·0°	3·28%	14			Gen. Man: Samuel Fernandez C.
			$Cr 2 933 094 4 160 412											21 973	Supt: V. Vanni Nardelli

NAME OF COMPANY ADDRESS	Gauge ft. in. (metres)	Route length incl. E=Elec- trified miles (km.)	Track length incl. E=Elec- trified miles (km.)	Elect. system and type of con- ductor	Loco- motives L=Line S=Shunt Steam Electric Diesel De=elec. Dh=hyd.	Rail- cars Electric Diesel Trailer Railbus Multiple Unit set	Pass. train cars	Freight train cars Con- tainers	Total Volume carried. Thous- ands of tonnes	Av'ge haul per ton miles (km.)	Av'ge net train load tonnes	Max. trailing load tonnes	Total number carried in 1 000s	Aver- age jour- ney miles (km.)
									Freight movement				Passengers	

BRAZIL *(contd.)*

NAME OF COMPANY ADDRESS	Gauge	Route length	Track length	Elect.	Loco-motives	Rail-cars	Pass. cars	Freight cars	Total Volume	Av'ge haul	Av'ge train load	Max. load	Total carried	Journey
Regional Recife	3' 3⅜" (1·00)	4 060 (6 768)	E 30 (50)		EL 4 DeL 150 DeS 32	E 7 ET 21	44 182	16 205	2 410·0	330 (563)			11 942·0	
Regional Curitiba	3' 3⅜" (1·00)	2 022 (3 370)	—		DeL 148 DeS 30	R 6 D 6	5 615	25 545	5 889·0	235 (392)			1 429·0	
Regional Sao Paulo	3' 3⅜" (1·00) 5' 3" (1·60)	968 (1 613) 156 (251)	E 114 (191)		EL 18 DeL 110 DeS 27	R 4 E 4 ET 378	167 166	25 677 C 37	6 146	189 (316)			150 124	
Regional Porto Alegre	3' 3⅜" (1·00)	2 406 (4 002)	—		SL 14 SS 2 DeL 129 DeS 27	DT 18 MU 6	3 945	31 037	7 316	189 (316)			1 423	
Regional Belo Horizonte	2' 5½" (0·76) 3' 3⅜" (1·00) 5' 3" (1·60)	121 (202) 2 565 (4 276) 70 (118)	E 269 (449)		SL 8 EL 16 DeL 201 SS 2 DeS 44	ET 24 MU 8	22 583	76 251	8 343	287 (479)			4 880	
***Ferrovia Paulista SA (FEPASA)** Rua Libera Badaró 39, 01009 São Paulo, SP *Formed into 3 divisions*	5' 3" (1·60) E 306 (492) 3' 3⅜" (1·00) E 498 (802)	1 030 (1 657) 2 234 (3 595)	4 206 (6 769)	3 000 V dc	EL 165 DeL 329 DhS 20 DS 4	*Metre* E 34 ET 68 D 8 DT 16	*Broad* 418 *Metre* 661	*Broad* 5 727 *Metre* 11 689	10 564·0	198·0 (318·6)		1 500	45 698·5	44·2 (71·1)
1a Divisão Rua Libero Baderó 39, São Paulo, SP *(Formerly Paulista and Araraquara)*	5' 3" (1·60) E 306 (492)	1 030 (1 657)												
2a Divisão Praça Julio Prestes 148, São Paulo, SP *(Formerly Sorocabana)*	3' 3⅜" (1·00) E 498 (802)	1 253 (2 016)												
3a Divasão Rua Visconde do Rio Branca 148, Campinas, SP *(Formerly Mogiana and São Paulo-Minas)*	3' 3⅝" (1·00)	981 (1 579)												
Estrado de Ferro do Amapá Box 396, 66000 Belem, Para, SP	4' 8½" (1·435)	121 (194)	129 (207)		De 5		6	139	1 338·8	158·9 (225·8)		2 900	130·3	106·9 (172·0)
Estrado de Ferro Campos do Jordão Pindamonhangaba, SP	3' 3⅜" (1·00)	E 29 (47)	E 30 (49)	1 500 V dc OH		E 13	7	5	7·0	23·1 (37·2)			533·9	8·5 (13·7)
Estrado de Ferro Vitória a Minas (EFVM) Ave Governador Bley 236 Vitória, Espirito Santo, Brazil	3' 3⅜" (1·00)	438 (705)	807 (1 300)		DeL 136 DeL 25 DhL 16		49	9 000	66 385·7	35 244 873 044 ton-km			1 871·6	83 (134)
Estrado de Ferro Votorantim Votorantim, SP	3' 3⅜" (1·00)	E 9 (14)		600 V dc OH					520·4	9 (14)		*Suburb* 2 480		9 (14)

BULGARIA
***Bulgarian State Railways (BDZ)** Ministry of Transport, Sofia

BURMA

***Union of Burma Railways** PO Box 118, Rangoon	3' 3⅜" (1·00)	1 949·25 (3 127)	2 701 (4 347)		SL 179 SS 50 DeL 79 DeS 15 DhL 72	D 23	1 228	9 527	1 675·3	242 492 812 ton-miles				

CAMEROON

***Régie des C.F. du Cameroon (RÉGIFERCAM)** Boite Postale 304, Douala	3' 3⅜" (1·00)	521 (839)	727 (1 172)		DeL 49 DeS 32	D 11	80	1 243	1 168·8	400 163 798 tonne-km		750	1 956·3	64 (103)

Office du F.C. Trancameronnais Yaoundé, PO Box 625 *(To take charge of Trans-Cameroon Railway—Yaoundé to Ngaounderé)*

CANADA
***Canadian National Railways** 935 Lagauchetiere St West, (PO Box 8100) Montreal H3C 3N4, Que

***CP Rail** Canadian Pacific Limited Windsor Station, Montreal, Que H3C 3E4

Algoma Central Railway PO Box 7000, Sault Ste. Marie, Ont P6A5P6	4' 8½" (1·435)	322 (518)	422 (680)		DeL 32 DeS 2		55	1 806	3 662·0	1 038 510 000 ton-km			216·0	108·6 (174·8)
Alma and Jonquiere Rly Co Alma, Lac St. Jean, Que.	4' 8½" (1·435)	10 (16·0)	27 (43)		DeLS 2			6	1 200·0	10 (16)	600	1 800		
BCH Railway British Columbia and Power Authority 260-12th Street New West- minster, BC V39 4H3	4' 8½" (1·435)	103 (166)	193 (311)		DeL 21 DeS 4			14	2 558·0		1 500	4 500		
***British Columbia Railway** 1095 W. Pender St, Vancouver 1, B.C., V6E 2N6 *(Formerly Pacific Great Eastern Railway)*	4' 8½" (1·435)	1 248 (1 845)	1 616 (2 607)		DeL 117 DeS 3	D 6		9 957	6 173·0	4 101 950 000 ton-km			75·9	

* See main entry

Average Speeds			Financial Data	Braking (continuous)	Couplers	Buffers	Rails	Sleepers (crossties)		Curvature max.	Gradient max. (U=not compensated)	Axle load max.	Altitude max.	Staff employed. Total no. (inclu. workshop)	Names of officials. Extended lists can be found at the end of the individual country in the report section immediately following
Freight Train	Pass. Train	Speed max.	Revenue Expenses		Type and Height above rail	Centres and Height above rail	Weight	Type and thickness	Spacing Number per mile or centres						
mph (km/hr)	mph (km/hr)	mph (km/hr)	in 1 000s		ins (mm)	ins (mm)	lb. per yd (kg/m)	ins (mm)	ins (mm)			tonnes	feet (m)		
			$Cr 641 249 2 306 527												Supt: C. Luiz Alves
			$Cr 973 087 1 723 344												Supt: R. Meister
			$Cr 1 956 222 2 363 830												Supt: J. Teó Filo dos Santo
			$Cr 975 716 1 683 515												Supt: P. Nunes Leal
			$Cr 1 369 265 2 538 369												Supt: J. Riberio Gontijo
Broad 18 (29) Metre 14 (23)	Broad 37 (60) Metre 30 (48)	75 (120)	$Cr 288 914·8 472 131·7	Air	Alliance Cobrasma 29½ (750)		115/60 (57/30)	Wood 6¾ (170) Conc Steel	Wood 2 575 (1 600) Conc 2 414 (1 500)	492 ft (150 m)	2·0%	25	4 068 (1 240)	29 104 (4 642)	President: Sr. J. Pires de Castro
		34 (55)	$Cr. 45·1 5 367·1	Air W'hse	Type E		129/88 (64/44)	Wood 6¾ (170)		1 066 ft (325 m)	0·35% 1·5% U		400 (122)	128	Gen. Man: Antonio José de Castro Lyra Porto
8·6 (14)	27 (44)	38 (62)	$Crt 358 774 871 228	Air W'hse	Interlock F 29½ (750)	29½ (750)	115 (57)	Wood 6¼ (160)	2 640 (1 640)	8·7° up 12·2° down	1·0% up 0·5% down	24	2 723 (830)	5 593 (1 093)	Gen. Man: Eng. Joao Christostomo Belesa
			Kyats 198 813·6 223 650·1											29 223	
18 (30)	25 (40)	37 (60)	Fr CFA 5 339 007·3 6 498 345·9	Vac W'hse (Jourdain Monn- eret)	Willison Auto 33½ (850)		72/40 (36/20)	Metal Metal & conc	2 400- 2 800 (1 500- 1 750)	394 ft (120 m)	2·1% U 1·7%	13	2 625 (860)	3 094 (1 000)	Pres; Gen. Man.: Gilbert Ntang
20 (32)	21 (34)	P 50 (80) F 45 (72)	$ 21 211·0 18 541·0	W'hse AB	Type E 34½ (876)		100/80 (50/40)	Wood 7 (178)	22" (559)	13·5°	Sth. 2·5% Nth. 1·5%		1 511 (461)	690	Gen. Man (Rail): S. A. Black
20 (32)		55 (40)		W'hse AB	AAR 27 (686)		100/85 (50/43)	Wood 6 (153)	2 900 (1 800)	5·0°		110 Per car	400 (122)	25 (2)	Gen. Supt.: J. R. Gosselin
20 (32)		35 (56)		W'hse Air	AAR 34½ (876)		115/60 (57/30)	Wood 6 (153)	22" (559)	Mn. 15° Sid. 23°	3·0% 3·0% U	33	433 (132)	320	Man.: G. I. Stevenson
17 (27)	32 (51)	F 40 (64) P 50 (80)	$C 114 309·0 168 196·6	W'hse Air	AAR. 34 (880)		85/115 (42/57)	Wood 7 (178)	1970/km	Rad. 145 m	2·2%	33	433 (132)	3 000	Pres: M. C. Norris

† Excludes iron ore receipts credited to the Cie Vale Rio Doce, owner of EFVM

NAME OF COMPANY ADDRESS	Gauge ft. in. (metres)	Route length incl. E=Electrified miles (km.)	Track length incl. E=Electrified miles (km.)	Elect. system and type of conductor	Locomotives L=Line S=Shunt Steam Electric Diesel De=elec. Dh=hyd.		Rail-cars Electric Diesel Trailer Railbus Multiple Unit set		Pass. train cars	Freight train cars Containers	Total Volume carried. Thousands of tonnes	Av'ge haul per ton miles (km.)	Av'ge net train load tonnes	Max. trailing load tonnes	Total number carried in 1000s	Average journey miles (km.)
CANADA (contd.)																
Burlington Northern (Manitoba) Ltd. 963, Lindsay St., Winnepeg, Man R3N IX6 (Formerly Midland Railway Co of Manitoba)	4' 8½" (1·435)	73·3 (117·4)	95·74 (159)		DeS	1				1	850 000	83 (134)				
Canada and Gulf Terminal Rly. PO Box 578, Mont Joli, Que G5H 3LB	4' 8½" (1·435)	36 (58)	41 (67)		DeS	2				**	242·5	4 709 803 ton-miles			32	(51·4)
Cumberland Railway Sydney & Louisburg Division PO Box 2500 Sydney, NS	4' 8½" (1·435)	39 (63)	101 (162)		DeS	15				1 100	3 258·9	10·0 (16)	1 641	2 500		
Esquimalt and Nanaimo Railway Co Cordova & Granville St, Vancouver 2, BC (Division of CP Rail)	4' 8½" (1·435)	196 (316)	253 (407)		DeL DeS (all CPR)	11 1	D	1			†			1 200	3 200	
Essex Terminal Railway Co. 1070 University Ave, Windsor Ontario N9A 5S4	4' 8½" (1·435)	23 (37)	54 (85)		De	6				4	11 384 000 ton-miles					
Greater Winnipeg Water District Rly. 598 Plinquet St., St. Boniface, Man	4' 8½" (1·435)	92 (148)	120 (193)		DeL De	4 1	D De	1 1	3	118	724·1	50 912 ton-km			4·4	75 (121)
Napierville Junction Railway Co. 1117 St. Catherine St. West, Montreal 2	4' 8½" (1·435)	42 (68)	82 (132)		D	2					1 988·8	27·0 (43·4)			218·5	40·0 (64·3)
Northern Alberta Railways Co 13025 St. Albert Trail, Edmonton, Alta T5L 4L4 (Jointly owned by CNR and CPR)	4' 8½" (1·435)	922 (1 484)	1 064 (1 701)		DeL	21			2	279	2 695·0	1 092 000 000 ton-km			7·9	
Ontario Northland Railway 195 Regina St., North Bay, Ont P1B 8L3	4' 8½" (1·435)	753 (1 212)			DeL	34	DMU	4	300	950	6 000·0				127·8 22 059·0	17
***Quebec Cartier Mining Co., Ltd** Port Cartier, Quebec G5B 2H3	4' 8½" (1·435)	193 (310)	226 (364)		Dh	54			12	1 779	24 657·6	2 750 197 ton-km	13 000	16 400 (306)	7 776	190
Quebec Central Railway Sherbrooke, Que.	4' 8½" (1·435)	355 (571)	426 (686)		De	9			8	341						
***Quebec North Shore and Labrador Railway Company** PO Box 1000, Sept-Iles, Que, G4R 4L5	4' 8½" (1·435)	391 (629)	422 (680)		DeL	83			26	4 500	30 626	38 339 094 000 ton-km			20·8 (325)	202
Roberval and Saguenay Rly Co PO Box 277, Arvida, Que G75 4K8	4' 8½" (1·435)	35 (56)	102 (164)		DhL DhS	12 2				453	4 270					
Toronto, Hamilton and Buffalo Rly Co 36 Hunter St E, Hamilton, Ont L8N IMI	4' 8½" (1·435)	106 (170)	158 (250)		DeL DeS	10 8				1 162	2 491·6	37 (60)			14·0	37·6 (60·7)
***White Pass & Yukon Route** PO Box 4070, Whitehorse, Yukon Territory Y1A 3T1 Comprises: Pacific and Artic Rly and Nav Co British Columbia-Yukon Rly Co The British Yukon Rly Co The British Yukon Nav Co Ltd																

CHILE
***Ferrocarriles del Estado (FFCCE)** (Chilean State Railways) Avenida Bernardo O'Higgins, No. 924 Casilla 134-D, Santiago Comprising:*

NAME OF COMPANY ADDRESS	Gauge ft. in. (metres)	Route length incl. E=Electrified miles (km.)	Track length incl. E=Electrified miles (km.)	Elect. system and type of conductor	Locomotives		Rail-cars		Pass. train cars	Freight train cars Containers	Total Volume carried.	Av'ge haul per ton miles (km.)	Av'ge net train load tonnes	Max. trailing load tonnes	Total number carried in 1000s	Average journey miles (km.)
F.C. Arica-La Paz (Chilean Section)	3' 3⅜" (1·00)	129 (207)	152 (244)													
Red Norte (Northern Network)	3' 3⅜" (1·00)	920 (1 481)	1 210 (1 630)													
Red Sur (Southern Network)	5' 6" (1·676) 3' 3⅜" (1·00) 1' 11⅝" (0·600)	2 086 (3 357) E 499 (803) 177 (285) 22 (35)	2 711 (4 363) E 795 (1 280) 203 (327) 24 (38)													
F.C. Iquique (See footnote)	Combined (1·00/ 1·435) 4' 8½" (1·435) 3' 3⅜" (1·00)	70 (113) 84 (135) 657 (1 057)	78 (126) 155 (250) 710 (1 143)													
F.C. Transandino por Los Andes (Chilean Transandine)	3' 3⅜" (1·00)	E 44 (71)	52 (83)	3 000 V dc OH												
Antofagasta (Chile) and Bolivia Rly Co Ltd Head office: 1 Broad St. Place, London, E.C.2 Local office: Antofagasta	3' 3⅜" (1·00)	438 (704)	449 (722)		DeL DeS	16 4			92	2 692 1 385	407 921 000 tonne-km		24·0	131 (211)		

* See main entry
** All freight cars on hire basis from CP Rail
† All operational data embodied in CP Rail figures

Average Speeds Freight Train mph (km/hr)	Pass. Train mph (km/hr)	Speed max. mph (km/hr)	Financial Data Revenue Expenses in 1 000s	Braking (continuous)	Couplers Type and Height above rail ins (mm)	Buffers Centres and Height above rail ins (mm)	Rails Weight lb. per yd (kg/m)	Sleepers Type and thickness ins (mm)	Sleepers Spacing Number per km (per mile) or centres ins (mm)	Curvature max.	Gradient max. (U=not compensated)	Axle load max. tonnes	Altitude max. feet (m)	Staff employed. Total no. (inclu. workshop)	Names of officials. Extended lists can be found at the end of the individual country in the report section immediately following
		50 (80)					90/68 (45/34)	Wood (7 178)						24 (1)	Pres.: N. M. Lorentzsen Supt.: J. A. Lowry
30 (48)	30 (48)	35 (56)	$ 705·1 641·5	Clasp	Type E 34 (864)		80 (40)	Wood 7 (178)	20″	5·0°	1·5	39	60 (18)	29	Gen. Man.: J. B. Quimper
15·0 (24)		25 (40)		W'hse AB	Type E 34½ (876)		100/85 (50/42)	Wood 6 (153)	30″ (762)	4·40°	1·5% U	30	140 (43)	345 (43)	Gen. Man.: H. S. Haslam
13 (20·9)		F 52 P 45		W'hse	E 50		85/65 (42/32)	Wood 8 (203)	20″ (508)	14·0°	2·2% 1·74% U		1 285 (392)	266 (59)	Pres.O oj. N. Fraine
10 (16)		35 (65)	$3 400·0 2 500·0	K-1 W'hse	Type E 34½ (876)		100/85 (50/42)	Wood 6 (153)	3 000 (1 864)	18·0°	1·00%U	31		90	Gen. Man M. A. Elder
25 (40)	35 (56)	50 (80)		W'hse Air	Type K		85/60 (42/30)	Wood 6 (153)	3 500 (2 174)	6°	4·5% U	20	1 060 (322)	24 (15)	Dir.: A. Penman Supt: J. Nielsen
30 (48)	55 (88)						132/127 (65/63)	Wood 7 (178)	2 970 (1 845)	7°	0·58%				
19 (30)	38 (61)	P 50 (80) F 35 (56)		W'hse Air	Type E and D 34½ (876)		100/60 (50/30)	Pine 7 (178) and 6 (153)	2 111 (534)	12°	2·4%	32·8	2 660 (811)	572	Gen. Man.: J. O. Pitts
30 (48)	35 (56)	60 (97)	$81 000·0 78 000·0	W'hse Air	Type E 34½ (986)		115/80 (57/40)	Wood 7 (178)	22″ (559)	M. 6·5° B. 12°	1·5%U	32·8	1 289	1 683 (350)	Chairman: W. J. Matthews Gen. Man: F. S. Clifford
25 (40·2)	35 (56)	F. 40 (64) P. 50 (80)		W'hse Air	33½ (851) E& F Nat. Mall. Steel Co.		132 (66)	Wood 7 (178)		7°	loaded 0·4% empty 1·35%	32·5	1 970 (600)		Pres.: L. J. Patterson
							100/75 (50/37)	Wood 7 (178)	20″ (508)	10·0°	2·67%	62·5			
34·5 (55)	34 (59·5)	F. 30 (55) P. 60 (97)	$ 58 400 61 500	W'hse AB	Nat. Mall. Can Car. Type F		132 (65/5)	Wood 7 (178)	20″ (508)	8·0°	1·32%	32	2 066 (628)	1 084 (309)	Pres.: W. J. Bennett
30 (48)		No limit	$ 10 400 9 200	W'hse AB	Standard		100 (49·6)	Wood 6 (153)	2 900 (1 800)	10·0°	1·25%	32·5	400 (122)	275	Supt. of Railway Operations: Raymond J. Girard
40 (64)	50 (80)	F. 60 (96) P. 65 (104)	$7 697·9 7 755·1	W'hse	AAR 34½ (876)	105/80		Wood 19·5″ 6 (153)	(495)	6°	1·04% U	31	525 482 (100)	320	Gen. Man.: J. A. Hill
		31 (50)		W'hse Air	Henricot Auto 30 (762)		75/65 (37/32)	Wood		246 ft (75 m)	3·0%	15	14 396 (4 388)	1 558	Gen. Man: L. D. Sutherland Ops. Man: H. Jeria

NAME OF COMPANY ADDRESS	Gauge ft. in. (metres)	Route length incl. E=Electrified miles (km.)	Track length incl. E=Electrified miles (km.)	Elect. system and type of conductor	Loco-motives L=Line S=Shunt Steam Electric Diesel De=elec. Dh=hyd.		Rail-cars Electric Diesel Trailer Railbus Multiple Unit set		Pass. train cars	Freight train cars Con-tainers	Total Volume carried. Thous-ands of tonnes	Av'ge haul per ton miles (km.)	Av'ge net train load tonnes	Max. trailing load tonnes	Total number carried in 1 000s	Average journey miles (km.)

CHILE *(contd.)*

NAME OF COMPANY ADDRESS	Gauge	Route length	Track length	Elect.	Locomotives		Rail-cars		Pass.	Freight	Total Vol.	Av'ge haul	Av'ge net	Max. trail.	Total no.	Av. jrny
F.C. Rancagua al Teniente *Sociedad Minera El Teniente SA* Milan 1040, Rancagua	2' 6" (0·762)	42 (68)	61 (98·7)		DeS 1 DeL 13	R 11 D 3			37	297		33 (53)	60	170	960·2	43 (65)
F.C. de Concepcion a Curanilahue Apart 141, Coronel	5' 6" (1·676)	80 (128)			30				43	807						
F.C. Potrerillos Potrerillos *(Owned by Andes Copper Mining Co.)*	3' 3⅜" (1·00)	61 (98)	64 (103)		SS 3 DeL 6 DeS 2				4	175	557·5	43·5 (70)	320	Up 750 Down 1 150	1·5	43·5 (70)
F.C. Militar de Puente Alto a El Volcan Regimento de Ingenieros de Ferrocarriles No. 7, Puento Alto	1' 11⅝" (0·600)	37 (60)	43 (70)		DL 6	D 5			10	52 C 2	21·4	155 (250)	90	120	113·0	18 (29)
F.C. Tocopilla al Toco (Soc Quimica y Minera de Chile SA) Casilla 2098, Tocopilla *Also operates:*	3' 6" (1·067) E 35 (57)	73 (117)	106 (170) E 50 (80)	1 500 V dc OH	EL 7 DeL 5 DeS 7				8	853	889·7	59·8 (96·2)	400		3·1	30·4 (48·9)
Maria Elena Mine Railway *(Industrial Line)*	3' 6" (1·067)		E 68 (109)	550 V dc	B 22 E 13				8	506						
Pedro de Valdivia Mine Railway *(Industrial Line)*	3' 6" (1·067)		E 88 (141)	550 V dc	B 28 E 13				14	533						
F.C. Salitrero de Taltal (Soc. Quimica y Minera de Chile SA) O' Higgins Station, PO Box E, Taltal	3' 6" (1·067)	65 (104)	79 (127)		D 5				3	350						

CHINA
*Chinese People's Republic Railways
Ministry of Railways, Peking

*COLOMBIA

NAME OF COMPANY ADDRESS	Gauge	Route length	Track length	Elect.	Locomotives		Rail-cars		Pass.	Freight	Total Vol.	Av'ge haul	Av'ge net	Max. trail.	Total no.	Av. jrny
Ferrocarriles Nacionales de Colombia Edif, Estacion de la Sabena calle 13, No. 18-24, Bogotá	3' 0" (0·914)	2 135 (3 436)			S 10 De 169	D 23			282	5 400 C 2	2 680·0		1 232 000 000 tonne-km		2 560·0	58·0 (93·3)

Consists of the following lines:
Division Central		850 (1 368)													
División Santander		249 (400)													
División Magdalena		264 (425)													
División Pacifico		551 (889)													
División Antioquia		211 (340)													

CONGO

NAME OF COMPANY ADDRESS	Gauge	Route length	Track length	Elect.	Locomotives		Rail-cars		Pass.	Freight	Total Vol.	Av'ge haul	Av'ge net	Max. trail.	Total no.	Av. jrny
*C.F. Congo-Océan B. P. 651, Pointe-Niore	3' 6" (1·067)	320 (515)	392 (640)		DeL 34 DeS 7 DhS 16	D 7			58	1 165 C 62	3 612·0	207 (333)	631	1 250	1 220·5	71 (114)
C.F. Comilog Compagnie, Miniére de l'Ogooué, Moando, Gabon *Local office:* Makabana	3' 6" (1·067)	177 (285)	193 (311)		DeL 16 DS 4	R 9				374	1 511·6	302 (485)	2 000	3 600	0	

COSTA RICA

NAME OF COMPANY ADDRESS	Gauge	Route length	Track length	Elect.	Locomotives		Rail-cars		Pass.	Freight	Total Vol.	Av'ge haul	Av'ge net	Max. trail.	Total no.	Av. jrny
Ferrocarril Nacional Al Atlántic Apartado 10096, San José	3' 6" (1·067) E 98 (158)	309 (499)	379 (610)	20 Hz single phase 15 kV	ES 1 EL 13 DeL 47 DeS 13 DhL 10 DhS 2 DS 2	R 1			108	2 272	1 560·0		Level 400 5% gr. 200		1 900·0	
Chiriqui Land Company *(Extensions only of United Fruit Co's lines in Panama)*	3' 0" (0·914)	30 (48)														
Ferrocarril del Sur Cia, Bananero de Costa Rica, Golfito Costa Rica, Provincia de Puntavenas	3' 6" (1·067)	155 (249)	184 (297) 155 (249)		DeL 13	D 6			12	559	367 028	56 (90)	1 000	1 440	150 097	30 (48)

CUBA
Cuba Nacional Railways
FF.CC. Nacionales de Cuba
Ministry of Transportation
Havana

NAME OF COMPANY ADDRESS	Gauge	Route length	Track length	Elect.	Locomotives		Rail-cars		Pass.	Freight	Total Vol.	Av'ge haul	Av'ge net	Max. trail.	Total no.	Av. jrny
Western Region	4' 8½" (1·435) E 11 (17)	1 220 (1 963)														
(Narrow gauges are 3' 0" (1·067 m) and 2' 6" (0·762 m)	Narrow	70 (113)														
Camaguey Region	4' 8½" (1·435)	1 270 (2 044)								10 765·9					17 912·2	
Guantanamo Region	4' 8½" (1·435)	81 (130)														
Camilo Cienfuegos Region	4' 8½" (1·435) 3' 0" (0·914)	208 (335)														

* See main entry

Average Speeds			Financial Data	Braking (continuous)	Couplers	Buffers	Rails	Sleepers (crossties)		Curvature max.	Gradient max. (U=not compensated)	Axle load max.	Altitude max.	Staff employed. Total no. (inclu. workshop)	Names of officials. Extended lists can be found at the end of the individual country in the report section immediately following
Freight Train	Pass. Train	Speed max.	Revenue Expenses		Type and Height above rail	Centres and Height above rail	Weight	Type and thickness	Spacing Number per mile (per km) or centres						
mph (km/hr)	mph (km/hr)	mph (km/hr)	in 1 000s		ins (mm)	ins (mm)	lb. per yd (kg/m)	ins (mm)	ins (mm)			tonnes	feet (m)		
8·6 (14)	8·6 (14)	18·6 (30)	$ 10·2 4 428·4	W'hse Air	Alliance ACF 27 (686)		75/60 (37/30)	Wood 6 (152)	3 200 (1 987)		4·39% 5·36% U	16	6 933 (2 113)	800 (300)	Supt: R. T. Patton
							50 (25)	Oak		476 ft (145 m)	1·62%				
16 (26)	18 (30)	37 (60)		W'hse	Type E 30 (762)		70 (35)	Oak 7 (175)	2 720 (1 690)	279 ft (85 m)	3·5% U	13·5	9 449 (2 880)	350 (62)	Gen. Man: L. O. Fines
18·6 (30)	21·8 (35)	25 (40)		Air W'hse	Hook & Chain 19⅝ (500)	Crs. 15¾ (400) Ht. 19⅝ (500)	82 (37)	Oak 6 (150)	19⅝ (500)	197 ft (60 m)	5·5% 1·2% U		4 593 (1 400)	84	
22 (35)	22 (35)	25 (40)		Air W'hse	Alliance 30 (762)		80/60 (40/30)	Oak 6 (150)	24½" (620)	180 ft (55 m)	1·51% 4·1% U	18·2	4 900 (1 493)	389 (284)	Gen. Man: Miguel Alvarez A.
9 (15)		16 (25)		Manual	Chain 32½ (825)	Central 32½" (825)	Steel 56/40 (28/20)	Wood 8 (200)	2 414 (1 500)	230 ft (70 m)	4·19% 3·25% U	10	7 169 (2 185)	147 (69)	Gen. Man: P. S. Dias Martinez
12·6 (20·3)	12·6 (20·3)	47 (75)	1 961 000 2 824 000	Air W'hse	Auto 24 (610)		75/50 (37/25)	Wood 6 (153)	2 720 (1 700)	262 ft (80 m)	3·8%	10	9 512 (2 900)	11 291 (2 300)	Gen. Man.: Mario Romero Ospina
23 (37)	34 (60)	50 (80)	Francs C.F.A. 3 347 718·3 3 109 743·9	Vac Jourdain Monneret	Willison auto. 34¼ (870)	Buffer-coupler	72/60 (36/30)	Metal 4¾ (120)	2 816 (1 750)	492 ft (150 m)	2·2%	16	1 578 (481)	3 086 (1 172)	Gen. Man.: S. R. Tchichelle
14 (23)		34 (55)	Francs C.F.A. No revenue	Vac J.M.R. & Gresham	Willison auto. 34¼ (870)	Crs 34¾ (884) Ht. 34¾ (870)	60·4 (30)	Metal 7 (178)	22½" (570)		2·5% 2·3% U	16	2 142 (653)	1 234 (242)	Gen. Man.: M. Lauraint (Moanda) A. Brittiaux (Makaban)
10 (16)	18 (29)	30 (48)	$41 843·0 50 599·8	Air W'hse & Lee Neville	Tower 29 (737)		70/50 (35/25)	Wood (Some steel) 6 (153)	2 640 (1 620)	Rad. 164 ft (40 m)	5·0% U	13	5 074 (1 547)	2 200 (455)	Pres. and Gen. Man.: Ing. Luis D. Bolanós
20 (32)	18 (29)	30 (48)	$101 400 604 300	Air W'hse	Magor & Pullman 25 (635)		70 (35)	Pine Wood 6 (153)	2 900 (1 800)	Rad. 470 ft (143 m)	Loaded 0·65% Empty 1·0%	Coopers E. 40	265 (81)	138 (21)	Supt: Alvero Arias Gutiérrez
				W'hse Air	Auto		100/200 (99/120)	Wood 6 (153) 7 (178)		459 ft (195 m)	2·0%	20			

NAME OF COMPANY ADDRESS	Gauge ft. in. (metres)	Route length incl. E=Electrified miles (km.)	Track length incl. E=Electrified miles (km.)	Elect. system and type of conductor	Loco-motives L=Line S=Shunt / Steam Electric Diesel De=elec. Dh=hyd.	Rail-cars Electric Diesel Trailer Railbus Multiple Unit set	Pass. train cars / Containers	Freight train cars	Total Volume carried. Thousands of tonnes	Av'ge haul per ton miles (km.)	Av'ge net train load tonnes	Max. trailing load tonnes	Total number carried in 1 000s	Average journey miles (km.)

CZECHOSLOVAKIA
*Czechoslovak State Railways CSD
Prague

DENMARK
*Danish State Railways DSB
Sølvgade 40, DK-1349 Copenhagen K

NAME OF COMPANY ADDRESS	Gauge	Route length	Track length	Elect. system	Loco-motives	Rail-cars	Pass. cars / Cont.	Freight cars	Total Volume	Av'ge haul	Av'ge net train load	Max. trailing load	Total no. carried	Avg journey
Amagerbanen (AB) DK-2770, Kastrup	4' 8½'' (1·435)	3 (5)	6 (7)		Dh 1				118·9					
Gribskovbanen (GDS) DK-3400 Hilleröd, Sjaelland	4' 8½'' (1·435)	26 (42)		DeL1	DMU 5 DhL 1 D 1	6		6·1			106 545 ton-km		899·3	11·6 (18·4)
Hads-Ning Herreders Jernbane (HHJ) DK-8300 Ödder, Jutland	4' 8½'' (1·435)	16·7 (26·5)	23 (36)		DeL 3	R 5	6	5	92 634		795 540 ton-km		542 771	
Helsingoer-Hornbaek-Gilleleje Jernbane (HHGB) DK-3000 Helsingoer	4' 8½'' (1·435)	15 (25)	19 (31)		DeL 1	R 3 RT 3 DMU 4		2	2·2	8·6 (13·8)			683·9	8·1 (13·0)
Hilleroed-Frederiksvaerk-Hundested Jernbane (HFHJ) DK-3400 Hilleröd, Sjaelland	4' 8½'' (1·435)	24 (39)	29 (47)		DeL 1 DhL 2 DS 3	DMU 6 R 1	8	10	153·9		3 972 954 ton-km		1 325·3	13·7 (22·0)
Hjørring Privatbaner (HP) Banegardspladsen 6[1], DK 9800 Hjørring	4' 8½'' (1·435)	11 (18)	12 (20)		DeL 1 DhL 2	DMU 3	7	1	41·7		739 047 ton-km		170·9	9·5 (15·3)
Høng-Tølløse Jernbane (HTJ) Holbaek, Sjaelland	4' 8½'' (1·435)	32 (51)			SL 2 DeL 1	D 1 R 3 RT 2	7 / 5	28	7·7	14·4 (23·1)			277·9	8·6 (13·9)
A/S Lollandsbanen 4930 Maribo Lollandske Jernbane (LJ) DK-4930, Maribo	4' 8½'' (1·435)	49 (77·5)	31·5 (50·7)		DeS 1 DeL 5 DhL 6 DhS 1 D 3		9	27	4 829·6		751 245 train-km		658·1	16 (25)
Lyngby-Naerum Jernbane (LNJ) Firskovvej 28, 2800 Lyngby, Sjölland	4' 8½'' (1·435)	5 (8)	5 (8)			D 4	2						1 278·1	3·7 (5·9)
Odsherreds Jernbane (OHJ) DK-4300 Holbaek, Sjaelland	4' 8½'' (1·435)	31 (50)	35 (56)		SL 2 D 8	D 2 RT 6 R 5	9	20	31·1	18·8 (30·4)			498·2	13·4 (21·6)
Ostsjaellandske Østbanen 4652 Haarlev, Sjaelland	4' 8½'' (1·435)	29 (46)	37 (59)		DeL 2 D 1	D 3 R 7 RT 8		20	54·9	16·5 (26·8)			269·4	12·0 (19·3)
Skagensbanen (SB) DK-9990 Skagen, Jutland	4' 8½'' (1·435)	25 (40)	28 (46)		DeL 3	DMU 4	2	8	15·6		192 700 train-km	500	374·1	16·2 (26·0)
Varde-Nörre Nebel Jernbane (VNJ) Varde, Jutland	4' 8½'' (1·435)	24 (38)	31 (50)		S 2 DeL 2	R 3 RT 3	7	6	43·7	11·7 (18·8)			181·4	11·6 (18·7)
Vemb-Lemvig-Thyboron Jernbane (VLTJ) 7620 Lemvig, Jutland	4' 8½'' (1·435)	37 (60)	42 (68)		DeL 1 DS 2	D 11 R 6 RT 5	2	1	44·2		1 322 528 ton-km	180	307·6	27·4 (44·1)

DOMINICAN REPUBLIC

NAME OF COMPANY ADDRESS	Gauge	Route length	Track length	Elect. system	Loco-motives	Rail-cars	Pass. cars / Cont.	Freight cars	Total Volume	Av'ge haul	Av'ge net train load	Max. trailing load	Total no. carried	Avg journey
F.C. Central Rio Haina Apartado 1258, Haina	4' 8½'' (1·435)	70 (113)	128 (206)		D 13			800						
F.C. de Central Romana La Romana	4' 8½'' (1·435)		220 (354)		DeL 11 S¶ 1 DL 3 DS 1		None	970	3 000	20 (32)		1 200	2 000	
F.C. Unidos Dominicanos (Ceased operation)	2' 6'' (0·76)	65 (105)												
	3' 6'' (1·067)	72 (116)												

ECUADOR
*Empresa de Ferrocarriles del Estado

NAME OF COMPANY ADDRESS	Gauge	Route length	Track length	Elect. system	Loco-motives	Rail-cars	Pass. cars / Cont.	Freight cars	Total Volume	Av'ge haul	Av'ge net train load	Max. trailing load	Total no. carried	Avg journey
*Empresa de Ferrocarriles del Estado Bolivar 443, Quito Operates following railways:	3' 6'' (1·067) / 2' 5½'' (0·750)	600 (966) / 96 (155)	726 (1 169)		S 53 DeL 14	D 10	46	430	589·0	140 (225)		1 000	1 687·0	38·5 (62)
F.C. de Bahia a Chone	2' 5½'' (0·750)	50 (80)												
F.C. de Guayaquil a Quito	3' 6'' (1·067)	281 (452)												
F.C. de Puerto Bolivar a Pasaje	3' 6'' (1·067)	15 (25)												
F.C. de Puerto Bolivar a Piedras	2' 5½'' (0·750)	46 (75)												
F.C. Quito a San Lorenzo	3' 6'' (1·067)	232 (373)												
F.C. de Sibamba a Azogues	3' 6'' (1·067)	72 (116)												

EGYPT
*Egyptian Railways
Ramses Square, Cairo

* See main entry

Average Speeds			Financial Data		Couplers	Buffers	Rails	Sleepers (crossties)							
Freight Train	Pass. Train	Speed max.	Revenue Expenses	Braking (continuous)	Type and Height above rail	Centres and Height above rail	Weight	Type and thickness	Spacing Number per mile (per km) or centres	Curvature max.	Gradient max. (U=not compensated)	Axle load max.	Altitude max.	Staff employed. Total no. (inclu. workshop)	Names of officials. Extended lists can be found at the end of the individual country in the report section immediately following
mph (km/hr)	mph (km/hr)	mph (km/hr)	in 1 000s		ins (mm)	ins (mm)	lb. per yd (kg/m)	ins (mm)	ins (mm)			tonnes	feet (m)		
				Knorr Air			90/74 (45/37)								Min. of Tpt: Ing. V. Blažek
37 (60)	43 (70)	43 (70)	Kr 5 534·0 9 633·6	Knorr Air	Standard	Standard	74 (37)	Wood 6 (150)	2 400 (1 500)	7·0°	1·4%	15·4		80	Dir: M. Krusen-stjerna-Hafstrøm
		43 (70)	Kr 6 723 912 11 568 900	Air	Standard	Standard (37/22)	74/45 6 (150)	Wood (1 250)	2 000	4·7°	1·25%	14		61	Dir: Aagard Frandsen
		47 (75)	Kr 2 793 207 7 987 097	Knorr Air	Scharff (760)	Buffer Coupler	74 (37)	Wood 6 (150)		3·5°		10		57	Man. Dir: K. Sørensen
44 (70)	47 (75)	47 (75)	Kr 9 896·4 11 514·4	Knorr Air	Standard †	Standard	74/67 (37/33·4)	Wood 6 (150)	2 400 (1 500)	7·25°	1·25%	20		124	Gen. Man: K. Hafstrom
37 (60)	47 (75)	47 (75)	Kr 5 621 6 382	Knorr Air	Standard (1 060)	Standard (1 750)	74 (37)	Wood		3·7°	5·0%	20		73	Gen. Man: Aage Velling
		43 (70)		Knorr Air	Standard	Standard	90/74 (45/37)	Wood 4¾ (120)	29½" (750)	4·1°	1·0%	16·3	161 (49)	20	Gen. Man:: N. D. Andersen
50 (80)	62 (100)	62 (100)	Kr 12 962·9 20 876·8		Standard	Standard (32/24½)	64/49 5 (125)	Pine	2 500 (1 560)	2·8°	0·5%	14·3		158	Dir: S. D. Brandt
			Kr 3 047·6 5 579·1	BSI 29½ (750)	69/42 (1 750)	81 (37)	Wood 6 (125)	(790)		7·0°	1·25%	18		38	Dir: H. Grundsøe
		43 (70)		Knorr Air	Standard †	Standard	55·5/ 74 (27·6/ 37)	Beech 5⅛ (130)	27½/29½" (700/750)	3·7°	1·25%	16·3	164 (50)	69	
					Standard	Standard	56 (28)	Wood 5½ (140)		7·0°	1·0%	14·3			Dir: F. E. Nielsen
37 (60)	47 (75)	47 (75)	Kr 3 700·0 4 900·0	Knorr Air	Standard	Standard	74 (37)	Wood 5½ (140)	25¾" (650)	2·5°	4·5%U	20		49	Gen. Man: J. V. Petersen
				Air	Standard	Standard (27·5)	55 5½ (140)	Pine	2 150 (1 335)	5·8°	1·25%	16			
37 (60)	47 (75)	47 (75)	Kr 4 769·5 7 526·5	Knorr Air	Standard	Standard	110/90 (55/45)	Pine 6 (150)		4·6°	0·67%	16·5			Gen Man: J. Frandsen
				W'hse			80/60 (40/30)	Wood 8 (203)	20" (510)	640 ft (140)	1·5% U				
40 (40)	50 (80)			W'hse Air	Type E 28½ (725)		80/60 (40/30)	Wood 7-8" (610)	24" (610)	476 ft (145 m)	1·5%	17·5	300 (91)	425 (30)	Gen. Man: Dr. T. Rosell
15·5 (25)	18·6 (30)			Air W'hse	Gould X-E 31 (788)		70/45 ASCE 6 (150)	Wood 6 (150)	24" (610)	197 ft (60 m)	5·5%	15·4			
							70/55 (35/27)				5·5%				
							60/35 (30/17)				3·0%				
							43/35 (21/17)				2·5%				

† Railcars have Scharffenburg couplers; no buffers

NAME OF COMPANY ADDRESS	Gauge ft. in. (metres)	Route length incl. E=Electrified miles (km.)	Track length incl. E=Electrified miles (km.)	Elect. system and type of conductor	Loco-motives L=Line S=Shunt / Steam Electric Diesel De=elec. Dh=hyd.	Rail-cars / Electric Diesel Trailer Railbus Multiple Unit set	Pass. train cars	Freight train cars / Containers	Total Volume carried. Thousands of tonnes	Av'ge haul per ton miles (km.)	Av'ge net train load tonnes	Max. trailing load tonnes	Total number carried in 1 000s	Average journey miles (km.)
EGYPT *(contd.)*														
Basse Egypt Railway Mansura	3' 3⅜'' *(1·000)*	157 *(253)*			S 23	20	54	371						
EL SALVADOR **International Railways of Central America** *Head office:* 15 Exchange Place, Jersey City, New Jersey, USA *Local office:* San Salvador *(Connects with the I.R.C.A. lines in Guatemala)*	3' 0'' *(0·914)*	285 *(459)*	316 *(509)*		S 36 D 2		57	513	560·1	96·6 *(160)*	70	1 200	2 216·5	27 *(43·4)*
***FC de El Salvador** San Salvador *(Owned by Government of El Salvador; operated by Comison Ejecutivo Portuaria Autonoma)*	3' 0'' *(0·914)*	100 *(161)*	116 *(187)*		S 17	D 11	28	234						
ETHIOPIA ***Cie du C.F. Franco-Éthiopien de Djibouti a Addis Ababa** PO Box 1051, Addis Ababa														
Northern Ethiopia Railway PO Box 218, Asmara	3' 1⅜'' *(0·95)*	191 *(306)*	221 *(355)*		DhL 3 SL 8 SS 10 DS 3	D 5	19	565	109·0	82·1 *(132·1)*			215·0	33·7 *(54·3)*
FIJI **The Fuji Sugar Corporation Ltd** PO Box 283, Suva	2' 0'' *(0·610)*	400 *(644)*	420 *(676)*		S 7 Dm 41		5	† 7 000	1 750·0	15 *(24)*	200	360	N.A. Free travel	15 *(24)*
FINLAND ***Valtionrautatiet VR** Finnish State Railways Vilhonkatu 13, 00100 Helsinki	5' 0'' *(1 524)*	3 730 *(6 057)* E 420 *(672)*	5 673 *(9 132)*	50 Hz single phase 25 kV	E 62 D 393	D 24 E 86 R 148	696	12 830	22 600 41 604 000 train-km	170 *(282)*			37 300	
Jokioisten Museorautatie 31600 Jokioinen	2' 5½'' *(0·75)*	43 *(0·5)*	4·9 *(8·0)*		SL 2 DL 3			30				3·0		3·7 *(6)*
Karhulan-Sunilan Rautatie Oy 48600 Karhula	5' 0'' *(1·524)*	4·1 *(6·4)*	6·5 *(10·7)*		DhL 2			751	4 806 000 ton-km		1 800			
FRANCE ***Société Nationale des Chemins de fer Française (SNCF)** 88 rue Saint-Lazare, 75436 Paris, Cedex 09	4' 8½'' *(1 435)*	21 170 *(34 522)* E 6033 *(9 710)*	25 000 V *(4 477)* 1 500 V *(5 100)* 850 V *(63 km)* 750 V *(34 km)* 650/700 3rd rail *(36 km)*		E 2379 D 2191	R 888 T 1084 TT‡ 246 E 606	11 560 C 6 100	257 000	214 000	673 000 tonne-km			684 000	
Cie C.F. Départementaux 10 avenue de Friedland, Paris	4' 8¹¹/₁₆'' *(1·440)* 3' 3⅜'' *(1·00)*	77 *(124)* 189 *(304)*												
Soc. Gen. de Chemins de Fer et de Transport Automobiles (CFTA) Cité de Londres 4, Paris, 9e	4' 8½'' *(1·435)* 3' 3⅜'' *(1·00)*	488 *(746)* 323 *(520)*			S 38 D 16 S 29 D 7	D 24 D 26	78 95	1 427 1 178						
C.F. de Chamonix au Montenvers Mer de Glace, Chamonix, Ht. Savoie *(Rack railway)*	3' 3⅜'' *(1·00)*	E 3·7 *(6)*	E 4·3 *(7)*	11 000 V 1/50 OH	SL 3 Dh 1	E 5	7	3		3·7 *(6)*			200·0	3·7 *(6)*
C.F. de L'est de Lyon 86 rue du Dauphiné, Lyon	4' 8½'' *(1·435)*	45 *(70)*			D 11			300	1 100·0		1 100			
Regie du C.F. de Mamers à St. Calais 1 rue Hauréau, 72000 Le Mans, Sarthe *(Ceased operations 1 January, 1978)*	4' 8½'' *(1·435)*	62 *(100)*			Dd 1 DeL 1 Dm 3	R¶ 3		· 31			73 341 ton-km	450		
Chemin de Fer de la Provence 52 rue Dabray, Nice 06003	3' 3⅜'' *(1·00)*	94 *(151)*	104 *(168)*		D 5	D 12 T 6		11					220	80
Embanchement Ferroviaire Desserte Industrielle (EFPI) 1 Ave. des Chenevières, 51370 Saint Bruce	4' 8¹¹/₁₆'' *(1·440)*	8 *(13)*			DeS 4				864·0	1·2 *(2)*	2 143 157 ton-km	800		
C.F. d'Anzin 97 rue Pierre Matthieu, 5900 Anzin	4' 8¹¹/₁₆'' *(1·440)*	(320) *(199)* E 0·5 *(0·9)*	144 *(233)*	25 000 V dc 1/50 OH	De 17 Dh 6			2 045	5 438 252	5·5 *(8·9)*	1 000	1 700		
C.F. de Super Lagnères Luchon, Hte. Garonne	3' 3⅜'' *(1·00)*	E 3·5 *(5·6)*	3·8 *(6·1)* E 3·7 *(5·9)*	3 000 V ac 3-phase	EL 4	EMU 4	8	6				10		7·0 *(11·2)*

***GERMANY, Democratic Republic**
Deutsche Reichsbahn
Ministerium für Verkehrswesen
DDR-1086 Berlin, Voss Strasse 33

GERMANY, Federal Republic
***Deutsche Bundesbahn**, German Federal Railway, Central Administration, Friedrich-Ebert-Anlage 43-45, 6 Frankfurt (Main)

* See main entry
† Container capacity is 2.5 to 3 tons of sugar cane
‡ Turbo-train cars

Average Speeds: Freight Train mph (km/hr)	Average Speeds: Pass. Train mph (km/hr)	Speed max. mph (km/hr)	Financial Data: Revenue Expenses in 1 000s	Braking (continuous)	Couplers: Type and Height above rail ins (mm)	Buffers: Centres and Height above rail ins (mm)	Rails: Weight lb. per yd (kg/m)	Sleepers (crossties): Type and thickness ins (mm)	Sleepers (crossties): Spacing Number per mile (per km) or centres ins (mm)	Curvature max.	Gradient max. (U=not compensated)	Axle load max. tonnes	Altitude max. feet (m)	Staff employed. Total no. (inclu. workshop)	Names of officials. Extended lists can be found at the end of the individual country in the report section immediately following
				Triple K-KI- KII-F- H. W'hse	Auto: Tower; Sheran; Alliance Atlas 26 *(660)*		70/54 *(35/27)*	Wood 6 *(150)*	Average 2 900 *(1 800)*	361 ft *(110 m)*	3·9% 4·0% **U**	15			
							60/54 *(30/27)*	Wbbd 6 *(150)*		377 ft *(115 m)*	4·5%				
			E.$1 980·7 2 557·2	Nil	Buffer- coupler 32⅞ *(605)*		56/50 *(28/25)*	Metal	1 955- 2 310 *(1 222- 1 444)*	230 ft *(70 m)*	3·5%	12·5			
7-10 *(11-16)*	7-10 *(11-16)*			Air and manual			61/35 *(31/17)*	Steel, conc. 4 *(102)*	28″ *(711)*	Rad. 460 ft *(140 m)*	0·33%	7	400 *(122)*	700 *(100)*	Ch'man: A.S. Hermes Gen. Man: G. M. R. Day
			Fmk 1 343 235·0 1 809 464·0												
12·4 *(20)*	12·4 *(20)*	18·6 *(30)*			23⅝″ *(600)*	Buffer Couplers	44 *(22)*	6 *(150)*	27½ *(700)*	394 ft *(120 m)*	1·6%	8	328 *(100)*	20 *(2)*	Ch'man: Vesa Venho
15·5 *(25)*		25 *(40)*	Kr. 1 686·1 1 802·3	W'hse Air	Auto Vapit	Crs 72″ *(1 830)* Ht 41·3″ *(1 060)*	60 *(30)*	Pine 6½ *(165)*	27½ *(700)*	541 ft *(165 m)*	1·0%	7		38	Gen. Man: Jouko Punnonen
			Francs 32 363 000 33 482 000												
							1·44 g *(46/24)* 1·0 g *(30/20)*	Oak 4¾/5½ *(120/140)*	*(700/ 850)*	1·44 g 5·8° 1·0 g 8·7°	3·3%	1·44 g 18 1·0 g 11	1 575 *(480)*		
9 *(15)*	9 *(15)*	12 *(20)*				Centre buffer- coupler	40 *(20)*	Metal		17·5°	20%		6 276 *(1 913)*	50	Dir: P. Bayle
		28 *(45)*		W'hse Air	Standard	Standard	93/61 *(46/30)*	Oak 5½ *(140)*	26″ *(660)*	11·0°	1·6% **U**	15	1 112 *(339)*	43 *(2)*	Pres: R. Baratier
15·5 *(25)*		43 *(70)*	Francs 980·1 1 707·9	Air W'hse	Screw and Automatic 39⅜″ *(1 000)*	68⅞″ *(1 750)* 39⅜″ *(1 000)*	84/60 *(42/30)*	Oak 4⅜ *(120)* Metal	31½″ *(800)*	3·8°	1·5%	19	577 *(176·5)*	40	Gen. Man: G. Dauxerre
	25 *(40)*	53 *(85)*		W'hse Air	Buffer- coupler	31½ *(800)*	50·5 *(25)*	Oak 4¾ *(120)*	31½ *(800)*	11·6°	3·0%	11	3 340 *(1 018)*	140	Dir: P. Saracino
7 *(10)*		16 *(25)*	1 991·5	Air W'hse	Standard		92/82 *(46/41)*	Wood 6 *(150)*	2 400 *(1 500)*	7·5°	2·0%	21	262 *(80)*	20 *(2)*	Dir: Lucien Beauchard
19 *(30)*		25 *(40)*		W'hse Air	Type V *(940-* 1 065)	68⅞″ *(1 750)* Ht. 40¾″ *(1 035)*	100/70 *(50/35)*	Wood 5⅜ *(135)*	2 400 *(1 500)*	5·8°	1·3% **U**	18·4			Tfc. Supt: N. Brunot Op. Supt: M. Cochoise
5·1 *(8·2)*	5·1 *(8·2)*						40 *(20)*	Metal	31½″ *(800)*	25·0°	25·5%	9	5 906 *(1 800)*	24 *(5)*	Gen. Man: A. Nérou
														181 535	Gen. Dir.: Ing. O. Arndt

GERMANY, FEDERAL REPUBLIC (contd.)

NAME OF COMPANY / ADDRESS	Gauge ft. in. (metres)	Route length incl. E=Electrified miles (km.)	Track length incl. E=Electrified miles (km.)	Elect. system and type of conductor	Locomotives L=Line S=Shunt; Steam/Electric/Diesel De=elec. Dh=hyd.	Rail-cars Electric/Diesel/Trailer/Railbus/Multiple Unit set	Pass. train cars	Freight train cars	Con-tainers	Total Volume carried. Thous-ands of tonnes	Av'ge haul per ton miles (km.)	Av'ge net train load tonnes	Max. trailing load tonnes	Total number carried in 1 000s	Average journey miles (km.)
Nebenbahn Achern-Ottenhöfen (Operated by Sudwestdeutsche Eb.AG)	4' 8½'' (1·435)	6 (10)	9 (14)		SL 1; DL 1	D 1; T 3	5	1		69·0	4·5 (7·2)			458·6	4·1 (6·6)
Ahaus-Enscheder Eisenbahn 4442 Bentheim Bahnhofstr 24 (Operated by Bentheimer Eb.AG)	4' 8½'' (1·435)	6 (9)	8 (12)							16·1	3·4 (5·5)				
Albtalbahn Albtal-Verkehrs GmbH, Tullastrasse 71, 7500 Karlsruhe	4' 8½'' (1·435)	E 27 (43)	E 39 (63)	720 V dc OH	DhS 2	E 26				64·0		353 000 ton-km		7 377·0	3·9 (6·2)
Alsternordbahn (ANB) 2 Hamburg 1, Steinstrasse 20	4' 8½'' (1·435)	6 (10)	8 (13)			D 4; T 3								1 169·5	3·7 (5·9)
Altona-Kaltenkirchen-Neumünster Eisenbahn-Ges D-2000 Hamburg 1, Steinstrasse 20 (Also operates Alsternordbahn; and Elmshorn-Barmstedt-Odelsloer)	4' 8½'' (1·435)	60 (97)	115 (185)		DhL 4; DhS 10	D 12; T 9; M 9				1 036·2		10 289 700 ton-km		3 761·3	8·2 (13·2)
Nebenbahn Amstetten-Gerstetten Württembergische Eisenbahn GmbH, 7 Stuttgart 1, Konigstr 1B	4' 8½'' (1·435)	12·5 (20)	13·5 (22)			D 1	2			22·8	9·6 (15·5)		500	110·2	4·8 (7·7)
Nebenbahn Amstetten-Laichingen Württembergische Eisenbahn GmbH, 7 Stuttgart 1, Konigstrasse 1B	3' 3⅜'' (1·00)	12 (19)	14 (22·5)			D 3; T 4	2	3		18·2	9·5 (15·4)		165	220·0	5·9 (9·4)
Ankum-Bersenbrücker Eisenbahn 4559 Ankum, Bersenbrücker str (Operated by Bentheimer Eisenbahn)	4' 8½'' (1·435)	3 (5)	4 (6)							2·0	3·1 (5·0)				
Augsburger Localbahn 8900 Augsburg, Friedburger str 41	4' 8½'' (1·435)	18 (29)	53 (75)		DS 5					443·0		5 761 600 ton-km			
Bad Orber Kleinbahn Kreiswerke Gelnhausen GmbH, 646 Gelnhausen, Barbarossastr 28	4' 8½'' (1·435)	4 (7)	5 (8)		D 2			1	2	3·4	4·3 (7·0)			491·5	4·3 (7·0)
Bayerische Zugspitzbahn AG D 8100 Garmisch-Partenkirchen, Olympiastr 27, Bavaria. Part adhesion (A); Part rack (R)	3' 3⅜'' (1·00)	(A) E 4·7 (7·5); (R) E 6·9 (11·1)	14·2 (22·8)	1 650 V dc OH	(A) E 4; (R) E 4	E 6 (R)	17	6		14 800		2 260 000 ton-km		773 876	10 (16)
Bentheimer Eisenbahn AG Bentheim, Bahnhofstr 24. Operates other lines: Ahaus-Enscheder, Ankum-Bersenbrücker, Wittlager-Kreisbahn	4' 8½'' (1·435)	47 (76)	58 (94)		Dh 8	R 45	1	6		433·3	20·1 (32·4)	13 865 600 ton-km		3 523·0	
Nebenbahn Biberach-Oberharmersbach (Operated by Sudwestdeutsche Eb. AG)	4' 8½'' (1·435)	7 (11)	8 (13)			D 2	2			11·3	2·9 (4·6)			323·6	5·0 (8·1)
Birkenfelder Eisenbahn GmbH 6588 Birkenfeld (Nahe)	4' 8½'' (1·435)	3 (5)	4 (7)		D 1			1		30·2	3·7 (6·0)				
Borkumer Kleinbahn und Dampfschiffahrt GmbH Am Georg Schutte Platz, 2972 Borkum	2' 11½'' (0·90)	4 (7·4)	9 (15·7)		DeL 1; DhL 2	D 1	17					245 572 train-km	70	522 291	4·5 (7·3)
Hafenbetriebsges Braunschweig GmbH 33 Braunschweig-Veltenhof, Hafenstr. 14	4' 8½'' (1·435)	2·2 (3·5)	9 (15)		SL 1; D 2			7		263·1	2·2 (3·5)				
Bregtalbahn (Operated by Südwestdeutsche Eb. AG)	4' 8½'' (1·435)	19 (30)	22 (36)		SL 1; DhL 1	D 2	9	2		33·3	10·7 (17·2)			283·0	7·7 (12·4)
Bremervörde-Osterholzer Eisenbahn GmbH Am Bahnof Süd 3, Bremervörde (Operated by Osthannoversche Eisenbahn)	4' 8½'' (1·435)	30 (48)	37 (59)		DhL 2; DhS 2	R 2; RD 2	5	4		92·2	17 (27·0)	47 200 train-km		491·4	8·7 (14·0)
Brohltal Eisenbahn GmbH 5474 Brohl-Lützing 1, Bahnhofstr 11	3' 3⅜'' (1·00)	16 (26)	19 (31)		Dh 4				135	167·5	7·4 (11·9)		450		
Nebenbahn Bruschsal-Hilsbach-Menzingen (Operated by Sudwestdeutsche Eb.AG)	4' 8½'' (1·435)	21 (34)	24 (39)			D 6; T 1	6	1		38·4	9·0 (14·5)			977·4	6·3 (10·1)
Buxtehude-Harsefelder Eisenbahn 215 Buxtehude, Kleinbahnhof (Operated by Osthannoversche Eisenbahn)	4' 8½'' (1·435)	9 (15)	12 (19)		DhL 2; DS 2	D 1; T 1		*		73·0	6·1 (9·9)	13 400 train-km	900		
Delmenhorst-Harpstedter Eisenbahn GmbH Bahnof, 2833 Harpstedt Bez Bremen	4' 8½'' (1·435)	14 (23)	15 (24)		DL 2; DS 2	D 1	2			85·3	7·1 (11·4)				

Deutsche Eisenbahn-Ges
Frankfurt/Main Mainzerlandstr 41
Operates 11 lines:
Farge-Vegesacker
Frankfurt (M)-Konigstein
Geilenkirchener Kb.
Jülicher Kreisbahn
Kassel-Naumberg
Kiel-Schönberg
Moselbahn
Neheim-Hüsten-Sundern
Reinheim-Gross Bieberau
Rinteln-Stadthangener
Teutoburger Wald Eb

* Freight cars supplied by Deutsche Bundesbahn

Average Speeds			Financial Data		Couplers	Buffers	Rails	Sleepers (crossties)		Curvature max.	Gradient max. (U=not compensated)	Axle load max.	Altitude max.	Staff employed. Total no. (inclu. workshop)	Names of officials. Extended lists can be found at the end of the individual country in the report section immediately following
Freight Train	Pass. Train	Speed max.	Revenue Expenses	Braking (continuous)	Type and Height above rail	Centres and Height above rail	Weight	Type and thickness	Spacing Number per mile (per km) or centres ins (mm)						
mph (km/hr)	mph (km/hr)	mph (km/hr)	in 1 000s		ins (mm)	ins (mm)	lb. per yd (kg/m)	ins (mm)				tonnes	feet (m)		
		31 (50)		Knorr Air	Standard	Standard	66 (33)	Wood 5½ (140)	(700-800)	7·3°	3·3%U	18	978 (298)	24 (2)	Gen. Man: A. Deissler
														2	Man: Heinrich Heijnk
19 (30)	25 (40)	31 (50)	DM 14 350·3 11 900·0	Knorr S 75/0	Compakt		70/82·6	Wood Conc	(1 500)	Rad 80 m.	3·50%	20	1 155 (352)	251	Gen. Man: Dipl. Ing. Kurt Stengel
20 (32)	31 (50)			Knorr Air	Standard	Standard	110/108 (55/54)	Wood 6 (150)	25½ (650)	7·0°	1·0%	20	125 (38)	23	Gen. Man: Dipl. Ing. H. Wittenbecher
15 (25)	25 (40)	37 (60)	DM 19 082 26 275	Knorr Air	Standard Draw-hook Scharffenberg	Standard 68⅞	100 (50)	Wood	(1 539)	7·0°	2·1%	20	138 (42)	376	Gen. Man: Dipl. Ing. Hans Wittenbecher
		31 (50)		W'hse Knorr			67·4 (33·4)	Wood 6 (150)	25½" (650)	8·7°	2·5%	18	2 257 (688)	17	Gen. Man: Franz Grossrubatscher
		25 (40)		W'hse Knorr			49·2 (24·4)	Wood 5½ (140)	26¼" (666)	12·5°	2·86%	18	2 427 (740)	23	Gen. Man: Werner Morlok
16 (25)	19 (30)		DM. 150·3 143·9		Standard	Standard		Wood 5½ (140)	937 (1 500)	2·5°	1·6%			2	Man: Heinrich Wübben
9·3 (15)	12·5 (20)			Standard	Standard	Standard	98/66 (49/33)	Wood St. conc.	24⅝" (625)	9·7°	0·98% 2·2% U	20	1 621 (494)	63 (17)	Gen. Man: Dr. Max Keller
														25	Gen. Man: Ing. Hans Malkmes
A. 25 (40) R. 6 (9)	A. 25 (40) R. 11 (18)	A. 25 (40) R. 13 (20)	DM. 4 806 727 3 600 695	Locos. A.E.G. Railcar S.L.M.	Scharffenberg 19¼-20 (490-508)		A. 68 (34) R. 61 (30·2)	A. Wood 5½ (140) R. Metal	31½" (800)	22·0°	A. 3·7% R. 25·0%	15	8 694 (2 650)	92	Gen. Man: Dipl. Ing. P. Hirt
21 (35)	31 (50)	37 (60)		Knorr W'hse. Air	Standard	Standard	82·6 (41)	Wood 6 (150)	2 400 (1 500)	5·7°	1·33%	20		182	Gen. Man: Peter Hoffmann
		25 (40)		Knorr Air	Standard	Standard	66/48 (33/24)	Wood 5½ (140)	(650-850) 850	8·7°	2·0% U	18	1 027 (313)	16	Gen. Man: Edmund Lutz
														17	Gen. Man: Walter Kunz
15·5 (25)	15·5 (25)	19 (30)			23·6 (600)		48 (24)	Wood 6·2 (16)	27½" (700)	251 ft (80 m)	0·6%	8·0	2 (0·9)	39	Gen. Man: M. Graff von Spee
		25 (40)		Air	Standard	Standard	67/49 (33/24)	Wood 5½ (140)	25 (650)	5·8°	1·6% U	20	164 (50)	54 (4)	Gen. Man: Arthur Kraatz
22 (35·4)	25·1 (40·5)	31 (50)		Knorr Air	Standard 39⅜ (1 000)	Standard	67/49 (33/24)	Wood 6 (150) Steel	23½" (600)	9·2°	1·0%U	18	2 812 (857)	37	Gen. Man: Wilhelm Lust
			DM 1 069·8 1 713·5											55	Gen. Man: Dr. zum Felde
12 (20)			DM. 1 146 1 310	Hardy W'hse	Standard	Standard					1·2	12		39	Gen. Man: J. Annen
12·4 (20·0)	16·0 (26·0)	31 (50)		Knorr Air	Standard	Standard	66/48 (33/24)	Wood 5½ (140)	(650-850)	9·7°	2·5%U	18	801 (244)	49	Gen Man: Werner Lehmann
19 (30)	30 (50)		DM 638·0 611·1	Knorr Air	Screw	Standard	56 (27·5)	Wood 6 (160)	(580-680)	9·0°	1·4% 1·4%U	20	60 (18)	7	Gen. Man: Geerdts

GERMANY, FEDERAL REPUBLIC (contd.)

NAME OF COMPANY / ADDRESS	Gauge ft. in. (metres)	Route length incl. E=Electrified miles (km.)	Track length incl. E=Electrified miles (km.)	Elect. system and type of conductor	Locomotives L=Line S=Shunt (Steam, Electric, Diesel, De=elec., Dh=hyd.)	Railcars (Electric, Diesel, Trailer, Railbus, Multiple Unit set)	Pass. train cars	Freight train cars / Containers	Total Volume carried. Thousands of tonnes	Av'ge haul per ton miles (km.)	Av'ge net train load tonnes	Max. trailing load tonnes	Total number carried in 1 000s	Average journey miles (km.)
Dortmunder Eisenbahn Dortmunder Hafen und Eisenbahn AG 46 Dortmund, Speichstr. 23	4' 8½" (1·435)	11 (18)	43 (69)		DhL 10 DhS 5			369	13 094·6	7·6 (12·3)	900	1 500		
Nebenbahn Ebingen-Onstmettingen Tailfingen Würtembergische Eisenbahn GmbH 7000 Stuttgart 1, Konigstrasse 1B	4' 8½" (1·435)	5 (8)	7 (11)			D 1 T 2	2	2	28·5	4·0 (6·5)		500	83·0	3·5 (5·7)
Elmshorn-Barmstedt-Oldesloer Eisenbahn (Eis.-Ges. Altona-Kaltenkirchen-Neumunster)	4' 8½" (1·435)	32 (52)	37 (59)		D 1	D 6 T 4	1		168·4	21·7 (35·0)			1 025·9	5·6 (9·1)
Industriebahn der Stadt Zulpich Postfach 1180, 5352 Zulpich	4' 8½" (1·435)	2 (3)	3 (5)						115·0	3 (5)	602 000 ton-km			
Extertalbahn AG 4923 Extertal Am Bahnhof 1	4' 8½" (1·435)	E 15 (24)	E 17 (28)	1 500 V dc OH	EL 2			2	46·4	9·4 (15·1)	238 000 train-km	350		
Farge-Vegesacker Eisenbanh (Operated by Deutsche Eb.G)	4' 8½" (1·535)	6 (10)	9 (15)		SL 2 DhL 1		1	8	788·4	5·8 (9·4)				
Filderbahn Hauptstätterstrasse 153, 7 Stuttgart	3' 3⅜" (1·00)	E 17* (48)	E 30 (49)	OH	E 2	E 15		9	102·0	2·8 (4·5)			5 654·1	3·4 (5·4)
Kleinbahn AG Frankfurt (M)-Königstein (Operated by Deutsche Eb.G)	4' 8½" (1·435)	10 (16)	14 (22)		DL 1	D 6 DT 5	6	3	19·6	5·5 (8·8)			2 114·6	5·5 (8·9)
Nebenbahn Gaildorf-Untergröningen Untergröningen (Operated by Württembergische Eb.G)	4' 8½" (1·435)	12 (19)	13 (21)			D 1 T 1	3	1	49·0	4·7 (7·6)			185·9	5·2 (8·3)
Geilenkirchener Kreisbahnen (Operated by Deutsche Eb.G)	3' 3⅜" (1·00)	7 (11)	7·5 (12)		DhS 2	D 1		7	25·2	6·3 (10·1)				
Kreiswerke Gelnhausen 646 Gelnhausen, Barbarossastr. 28 Operates bus services and one rail line:– Bad-Orber Kleinbahn														
Georgsmarienhütten Eisenbahn Georgsmarienhütte bei Osnabrück	4' 8½" (1·435)	8 (13)	39 (63)		DL 3 DS 7	D 2 T 2	1	104	1 200·0	4·5 (7·3)			76·0	4·0 (6·5)
Gross Bieberau-Reinheimer Eisenbahn (Operated by Deutsche Eb. GmbH)	4' 8½" (1·435)	2·5 (4)	3 (5)		D 1				42·3	2·5 (4)				
Eisenbahn Gross Ilsede-Broistedt	4' 8½" (1·435)	8 (13)	11 (18)		D 3			57	1 615·7	8·6 (13·9)				
Nebenbahn Haltingen-Kandern (Operated by Sudwestdeutsche Eb.AG)	4' 8½" (1·435)	8 (13)	9 (15)			D 2 T 1		1	21·5	6·5 (10·5)			190·7	3 (7·0)
Hersfelder Kreisbahn 643 Bad Hersfeld Heinrich Börnerstr 10	4' 8½" (1·435)	16 (26)	22 (36)		Dh 3	D 4	6	1	931·8	3·6 (10·2)			613·2	8·1 (13·8)
Hildesheim-Peiner Kreiseisenbahn (Ceased railway operations)	4' 8½" (1·435)	3·4 (5·5)												
Hohenlimburger Kleinbahn AG D5300 Wagen, 5-Hohenlimburg, Mühlenteichstrasse 8	3' 3⅜" (1·00)	2 (3·3)	7 (11·5)		Dh 5			114 074	161·7	1·5 (2·4)	242 900 ton-km			
Hohenzollerische Landesbahn AG Hofgartenstr 39, Hechingen	4' 8½" (1·435)	67 (107)	71 (115)		D 6	D 7 T 2 R 1	15	13	415·6	4·1 (6·6)			1 196·0	7·7 (12·4)
VB Grafschaft Hoya GmbH 3092 Hoya/Weser	4' 8½" (1·435) / 3' 3⅜" (1·00)	4 (6) / 25 (40)	5 (9) / 30 (49)		D 5	D 4 T 2			94·2	13·7 (22·1)			329·1	11·6 (18·6)
Hummlinger Kreisbahn 4476 Werlte	4' 8½" (1·435)	16 (25)	19 (30)		D 3	D 2	2	5	74·6	12 (20)				
Kb Ihrhove-Westrhauderfehn 2953 Westrhauderfehn, Bahnofstr 4 (Bentheimer Eb. AG)	4' 8½" (1·435)	7 (11)	8 (12)						27·3	4·5 (7·2)				
Ilmebahn Ges. AG 3352 Einbeck, Langer Wall 14	4' 8½" (1·435)	8 (13)	10 (16)		S 1 D 2		3	5	136·6	2·4 (3·8)			417·3	2·5 (4·0)
Nebenbahn Jagstfeld-Ohrnberg (Operated by Württembergische Eb.G)	4' 8½" (1·435)	14 (22)	16 (26)			D 1		1	28·9	6·6 (10·7)		400	109·1	3·8 (6·1)
Jülicher Kreisbahn (Operated by Deutsche Eb. G)	4' 8½" (1·435)	9 (15)	11 (18)		D 1	D 1	1	2	91·6	4·7 (7·5)			53·7	5·5 (8·9)
Juister Inselbahn 2981 Norddeich Reederei Norden-Frisa	3' 3⅜" (1·00)	2 (3)	3 (4)		D 2	D 4	8	24 C 60	21·1	1·9 (3·0)			230·8	1·9 (3·0)
Kahlgrund Eisenbahn Schöllkrippen Landkreis Alzenau	4' 8½" (1·435)	14 (23)	16 (26)			D 5	10		25·2	7·5 (12·1)			744·3	7·4 (11·9)
Kaiserstuhlbahn (Operated by Südwestdeutsche Eb.AG)	4' 8½" (1·435)	25 (40)	30 (49)		DhL 1	D 5 T 2	10	4	68·4	10·9 (17·6)			754·4	5·2 (8·3)

* Of which 6.6 miles has a third rail for standard gauge operation

Average Speeds			Financial Data	Braking (continuous)	Couplers	Buffers	Rails	Sleepers (crossties)		Curvature max.	Gradient max. (U=not compensated)	Axle load max.	Altitude max.	Staff employed. Total no. (inclu. workshop)	Names of officials. Extended lists can be found at the end of the individual country in the report section immediately following
Freight Train	Pass. Train	Speed max.	Revenue Expenses		Type and Height above rail	Centres and Height above rail	Weight	Type and thickness	Spacing Number per mile (per km) or centres						
mph (km/hr)	mph (km/hr)	mph (km/hr)	in 1 000s		ins (mm)	ins (mm)	lb. per yd (kg/m)	ins (mm)	ins (mm)			tonnes	feet (m)		
19 (30)		25 (40)		Knorr Air	Standard	Standard	98/83 (49/41)	Wood Types I & II	25½" (650)	9·25°	1·60%	30	417 (127)	304	Dir: W. Schürmann
		31 (50)		W'hse Knorr			67·4 (33·4)	Wood 6 (150)	25½" (650)	11·6°	2·5%	18	2 627 (801)	19	Gen. Man: Adolf Weiss
12 (20)	20 (33)	31 (50)		Knorr Air	Screw	Standard	(92/108) (45/54)	Wood 5½ (140)	25½" (650)	8·8°	1·0%	20	164 (50)	58	Man: Dipl. Ing. H. Wittenbecher
			DM 120·0 120·0	Kunze-Knorr	21 (530)	480 (750)	66/44 (33/22)	Wood 5½ (140)	27½" (700)	35·0°	3·0%	9		5	Man: Wolfram Linnartz
4·7 (7·6)		25 (40)		Bosch air/elec	Albert (450)	Buffer-coupler	117/60 (58/30)	Wood 8½ (220)	25½" (650)	8·7°	2·5%	20	840 (256)	40 (15)	Dir: B. Rehm
		25 (40)		Knorr Air	Standard	Standard	99/83 (49/41)	Wood 6¼ (160)	25½" (650)	6·5°	1·1% U	20	8 621 (2 625)	46 (10)	Dr: jur. Frank Niethammer Dipl. Ing: Herbert Güldner
														132	Man: Otto Neef
7 (11)	22 (35)	37 (60)		Air	Standard	Standard	99/67 (49/33)	Wood 5½ (140)	27/28 (670/700)	8·7°	1·4% U	20	11·5 (340)	37	Dir: Dr. E. Paul
		25 (40)		W'hse Knorr			67·4 (33·4)	Wood 6 (150)	25½" (650)	9·7°	1·0%	18	1 158 (353)	15	Man: Willi Kunz
		19 (30)		Air	Buffer-coupler (750)		49·2 (24·4)	Wood 5½ (140)	2 360 (1 470)	17·5°	2·0% U	16	567 (173)	7	Dr: jur. Frank Niethammer Dipl. Ing. Herbert Güldner
25 (40)	25 (40)			Air Knorr	Screw 41½ (1 060)	Crs. 68⅞ (1 750) Ht. 41½ (1 060)	99 (49)	Wood 6¼ (160)	27½" (700)	2·50	0·9%	20	407 (407)	201 (3)	Gen. Man: F. Beier Frt. Man: C. Suendorf
														7	Man: Dr. Karlheinz Geuckler
														29	Dir: D. Werner Jurisch
	17·4 (28)	31 (50)		W'hse Knorr Air	Standard	Standard	66/48 (33/24)	Wood 5½ (140)	(650-850)	13·5°	1·50% U	16	1 135 (346)	53	Gen. Man: Karl Fischer
				Knorr Air	Screw 17¾ (450)	(1 750) (940)	83·5 (41·4)	Wood 6 (150)	24¾" (630)	8·75°	2·0%	18	1 169 (357)	63	Man: Hans Stuckhardt
			DM 775 084 989 071											10	Dipl. Ing. Hans Joachim Slaz
				W'hse & Knorr Air	39⅜ (1 000)	(1 750) (1 000)	67/51 (33·4/25)	Wood 6 (150)		11·0°	2·8%	18	2 398 (731)	224	Dir: Stirsel
														33	Dir: Wilhelm Leder
25 (40)				Knorr Air	Standard	Standard	99/67 (49/33)	Wood 6 (150)	30¾" (680)	5·7°	1·0%	20	112 (34)	16	Dir: Joseph Kimmann
															Dir: Peter Elster
														29	Dir: Heinrich Dietrich
		31 (50)		W'hse Knorr			67·4 (33·4)	Wood 6 (150)	25½" (650)	9·7°	1·11%	18	584 (178)	22	Gen. Man: Karl Volz
		25 (40)		Air	Standard	Standard	67/49 (33/24)	Wood 5½ (140)	28" (700)	8·7°	1·18% U	16		12	Dir: Dr. Innecken
														25	Dir: Carl-Ulfert Stegmann
				Kunze-Knorr Air	Standard	Standard	67·4 (33·4)	Wood 5½ (140)	30" (760)	8·8°	1·0%	16	668 (204)	38	Man: Hans Lux
18·6 (29·9)	22·7 (36·6)	31 (50)	DM 786·3 823·5	Knorr Air	Standard 39⅜ (1 000)	Standard 39⅜ (1 000)	67 (33·4)	Steel ⁵/₁₆ (9)	23½" (600)	8·70	1·1%	18	627 (191)	51	Man: Richard Riesch

NAME OF COMPANY ADDRESS	Gauge ft. in. (metres)	Route length incl. E=Electrified miles (km.)	Track length incl. E=Electrified miles (km.)	Elect. system and type of conductor	Locomotives L=Line S=Shunt Steam Electric Diesel De=elec. Dh=hyd.	Rail-cars Electric Diesel Trailer Railbus Multiple Unit set	Pass. train cars	Freight train cars Containers	Total Volume carried. Thousands of tonnes	Av'ge haul per ton miles (km.)	Av'ge net train load tonnes	Max. trailing load tonnes	Total number carried in 1 000s	Average journey miles (km.)
GERMANY, FEDERAL REPUBLIC *(contd.)*														
Kleinbahn Kassel-Naumberg AG *(Operated by Deutsche Eb.G)*	4' 8½'' (1·435)	21 (33)	25 (41)		DL 3	D 1, T 1	8	5	911·2	5·0 (8·1)			219·1	8·8 (14·2)
Kerkerbachbahn AG 6251 Runkel/Kerkerbach	4' 8½'' (1·435)	2·4 (3·8)	4·3 (7·0)		D 2			1	204·2	1·9 (3·1)				
Kiel-Schonberger Eisenbahn *(Operated by Deutsche Eb.G)*	4' 8½'' (1·435)	15 (24)	18 (29)		D 2	D 2	5	4	270·4	4·8 (7·7)		600	463·4	8·3 (13·3)
Kleinbahn Köln Deutz-Porz-Zündorf Bayenstr 2, Koln	4' 8½'' (1·435)	10 (16)	13 (21)		Dh 3			10	640·4	3·1 (5·0)				
Köln-Frechen-Benzelrather Eisenbahn Kölner Verkehrs-Betriebe AG Scheidtweilerstr 38, 5000 Köln 41	4' 8½'' (1·435)	23·8 (38·1) E 8 (13)	63 (102) E 9·3 (15)	800 V dc OH	DeL 14		12	54	3 839·0		38 010 000 ton-km		3 234	5·6 (9)
Nebenbahn Korntal-Weissach *(Operated by Württembergische Nb.AG)*	4' 8½'' (1·435)	14 (22)	16 (26)			D 5, T 2	8		38·9	7·9 (12·7)		160	449·2	6·9 (11·2)
Städtische Eisenbahn Krefeld 4150 Krefeld-Uerdingen, Oberstrasse 13	4' 8½'' (1·435)	12 (19)	28 (45)		Dl 5, DhS 5			52	1 027·6	1·9 (3·0)	8 108 739 ton-km			
Krefelder Eisenbahn-Gesellschaft 4150 Krefeld, St. Töniser Str. 270 *(Dissolved Aug. 1978)*														
Nebenbahn Krozingen-Münstertal-Sulzburg *(operated by Sudwestdeutsche Eb.AG)*	4' 8½'' (1·435)	10 (17)	12 (19)		D 2		1	1	31·7	3·0 (4·8)			414·8	4·2 (6·7)
AG Lokalbahn Lam-Kötzting 8496 Lam, Eisenbahnweg 1	4' 8½'' (1·435)	11 (18)	13 (20)		DhL 2, DhS 2	D 4, T 6		1	17·5	6·7 (10·8)		300	356·9	6·3 (10·2)
Langenfeld-Monheim-Hitdorf (See Bahnen de Stadt Monheim GmbH)														
Inselbahn Langeoog Schiffahrt der Inselgemeinde Langeoog 2941 Langeoog	3' 3⅜'' (1·00)	1·6 (2·6)	2·4 (3·8)		DhL 2, DmL 1	D 2, TD 2	7	1	23·0				358·2	1·6 (2·6)
Marburger Kreisbahn *(Operated by Deutsche Eb.)*	4' 8½'' (1·435)	10 (17)	14 (22)		D 2			23	126·7	7·8 (12·5)				
Meppen-Haselunner Eisenbahn Bahnhofstr 24, Bentheim *(Operated by Bentheimer Eisenbahn)*	4' 8½'' (1·435)	19 (31)	22 (35)		D 4			2	121·6	8·0 (12·9)				
Merzig-Büschfelder Eisenbahn Losheimerstr 1, 664 Merzig	4' 8½'' (1·435)	11·8 (19)	16·1 (24)		D 2			8	100·5	3·0 (4·8)				
Mindener Kreisbahnen 495 Minden (Westfalen)	4' 8½'' (1·435)	55 (88)	69 (111)		D 12	D 3	13	28	1 147·0	5·3 (8·5)		1 253	231	7·0 (11·2)
Mittelbadische Eisenbahnen AG Friedrichstr 59, Lahr (Schwarzwald) *(Operated by Südwestdeutsche Eb.AG)*	3' 3⅜'' (1·00) 4' 8½'' (1·435)	25 (41)	31 (50)		D 2	D 2	2	46	139·2	6·2 (10·0)			372·7	5·6 (9·1)
Nebenbahn Möckmühl-Dörzbach *(Operated by Sudwestdeutsche Eb.AG)*	2' 5½'' (750)	24 (39)	27 (43)		D 3	D 2	6	30	42·9	15 (25)			76·8	6·2 (9·9)
Bahnen der Stadt Monheim Heinsetr 2, 4019 Monheim	4' 8½'' (1·435)	E 8 (12)	E 10 (17)	E	E 3			2	175·4	3·7 (5·9)				
Moselbahn *(Operated by Deutsche Eb.G)*	4' 8½'' (1·435)	2·4 (4)	6 (10)		D 2			1	113·2	2·5 (4·0)				15 (25)
Nebenbahn Neckarbischofsheim-Hüffenhardt *(Operated by Sudwestdeutsch Eb.AG)*	4' 8½'' (1·435)	10 (17)	13 (20)			D 3	3	1	32·2	8·5 (13·6)			348·5	3·9 (6·3)
Kleinbahn Niebüll-Dagebüll Nordfriesische Verehrsbetriebe AG Bahnhofstr 6, 2260 Niebüll	4' 8½'' (1·435)	9 (14)	11 (17)			D 2	2	6	5·7	8·4 (13·5)			206·0	7·5 (12·1)
Eb. Neheim Hüsten-Sundern *(Operated by Deutsche Eb.)*	4' 8½'' (1·435)	9 (14)	13 (21)		D 1	D 1, T 2	3		79·0	5·8 (9·3)			65·6	5·5 (8·8)
Neukölln Mittenwalder Eb-Ges Gottlieb Dunkelstr 47, Berlin 42	4' 8½'' (1·435)	10 (16)	22 (36)		D 5			9	569·1	4·2 (6·8)				
Neusser Eisenbahn Hammer Landstr 3a, 404 Neuss/Rh	4' 8½'' (1·435)	7	30 (49)		DhS 5, Dm 1			7	1 472·4		7 734 200 ton-km	1 200		
Nebenbahn Nürtingen-Neuffen Neuffen *(Operated by Württembergische Eb.G)*	4' 8½'' (1·435)	5·5 (9)	6·2 (10)			D 5, T 1	8	12	570·7	5·4 (8·7)		800	762·0	4 (6·4)
Niederrheinische Verkehrsbetriebe AG (NIAG) Homberger Strasse 113, 4130 Moers	4' 8½'' (1·435)	22 (36)	33 (54)		DhL 4	RD 1, TD 2, MU 1		106	2 370		20 022 979 ton-km		2·1	7·7 (12·4)
Oberrheinische Eisenbahn-Gesellschaft AG 68 Mannheim, Käfertalerstr 9-11	3' 3⅜'' (1·00)	37 (60·9)	61·7 (99·4) E 76 (129)	7 500 V dc OH	EL 2, DmS 1	E 38, T 19	57	1	18·0		210 900 ton-km	150	12 786	5·6 (9·1)
Osterwieck Wasserlebener-Eisenbahn Brannlage Harz Bahnhof	4' 8½'' (1·435)	3·7 (6)	5 (8)		Dh 1	D 4, T 3	1		3·5	3·2 (5·1)			77·0	3·1 (5·0)

Average Speeds: Freight Train mph (km/hr)	Average Speeds: Pass. Train mph (km/hr)	Speed max. mph (km/hr)	Financial Data: Revenue Expenses in 1 000s	Braking (continuous)	Couplers: Type and Height above rail ins (mm)	Buffers: Centres and Height above rail ins (mm)	Rails: Weight lb. per yd (kg/m)	Sleepers (crossties): Type and thickness ins (mm)	Sleepers (crossties): Spacing Number per mile (per km) or centres ins (mm)	Curvature max.	Gradient max. (U=not compensated)	Axle load max. tonnes	Altitude max. feet (m)	Staff employed. Total no. (inclu. workshop)	Names of officials. Extended lists can be found at the end of the individual country in the report section immediately following
25 (40)	25 (40)	37 (60)		Air	Standard	Standard	67/55 (33/27)	Wood 5½ (140)	27/28″ (680/700)	8·7°	1·3%	20	1 322 (403)	70 (9)	Dir: Dr. Edgar Paul
				Knorr	Joch Kuppl 22½ (570)	19⅝ (500) 29½ (750)	68·6 (34)	Wood 5½ (140)	23″ (580)	22·0°	2·0%	18		35	Dir: Richard Kuhn
15 (25)	23 (37)	31 (50)		W'hse Air	Standard	Standard	67/49 (33/24)	Wood 5½ (140)	2 110 (1 320)	8·25°	1·6%	20	1 575 (480)	18 (7)	Dr. Oskar Sommer
			DM 675·0 1 203·0											37	Dir: A. Causemann
18·6 (30)	14·8 (23·8)	Pass 37 (60) Frt 25 (40)	DM 16 428·0 28 633·0	Knorr Air	Standard	Standard	99 (49)	Oak 6-6¼ (150-160)	25½″ (650)	9·7°	1·66%	20	322	485	Dir: Dipl. Ing. J. Prinz
		31 (50)		Knorr W'hse	42 (1 065)	68⅞ (1 750) 41⅞ (1 065)	67·4 (33·4)	Wood 6 (150)	25½″ (650)	8·7°	2·0%	18	1 312 (400)	19	Gen. Man: Hans Schweizer
9 (5)					Screw	Standard	95/66 (47/33)	Wood 6 (150)	26⅜″ (670)	11·3°	2·0%	20	111 (34)	87	Man: Oskar Märkisch
9·3 (15·0)	16·2 (26·0)	31 (50)		Knorr Air	Standard	Standard	66/48 (33/24)	Wood 5½ (140)	(650- 850)	8·7°	2·2%**U**	18	1 217 (371)	35	Man: Bruno Weber
15·5 (25)	22 (35)	31 (50)	DM 717·5 773·5	Knorr Air	Standard	Standard	66·8 (33·4)	Wood 5½/6 (140/150) and concrete	23½ (600)	9·7°	1·2% **U**	16		38 (10)	Dir: Dipl. Ing. Max Janker
		16 (25)	DM 1 016·5 1 077·5	Knorr Air	Scharf- enberg	Central	80 (40)	Wood	23½″ (600)	11·3°		6		17	Gen. Man: A. Schmidt
				Knorr W'hse	Standard	Standard	67·2 (33·3)	Steel Wood	23¾″ (620)	9·0°	2·13%	18	902 (275)	25	Man: Gotthard Dinter
15·5 (25)	22 (35)	25 (40)		Knorr W'hse	Standard	Standard	67·4 (33·4)	Wood 6 (150)	25½″ (650)	5·7°	1·0%			30	Man: Ewald Schómaker
														17	Man: Franz Schneider
18 (30)		31 (50)		Knorr	Standard	Standard (1 750)	82/67 (33/41)	Wood 5½ (140)	25½-30¾″ (650-780)	12·5°	2·78%	18/20	15 (4·6)	153	Gen. Man: Pfefferkorn
														54	Gen. Man: Klaus Helbling
6·8 (11)		16 (25)		Knorr Air	Chain	Central (630)	48/40 (24/20)	Wood 5½ (140)	(650- 850)	22·0°	1·0% **U**	16	784 (239)	34	
														16	
		25 (40)		Air W'hse	Standard	Standard	170/67 (84/33)	Wood 5½ (140)	25½ (650)	9·7°	1·09%	20	449 (137)	8 (1)	
		22 (35)		Knorr Air	Standard	Standard	66/48 (33/24)	Wood 5½ (140)	(700- 850)	8·7°	1·67% **U**	18	974 (297)	22	Man: Anton Bott
														34	
				Knorr W'hse	Standard	Standard								14	Dr. jur: Frank Niethammer
														54	Dir: Werner Britze
9 (15)		12 (20)	DM 4 201·5 5 766·8	Knorr Air	Standard	Standard	100 (49·4)	Wood (5 150)	26 (660)	11·5°	2·22%	20		84	Dir: Ludwig von Hartz
		31 (50)		W'hse Knorr			100 (49·4)	Wood 6 (150)	23⅝″ (600)	8·7°	2·0%	18	1 293 (394)	18	Gen. Man: Horst Bell
10 (16)	20 (32)	32 (50)	DM 8 322 6 524	Knorr Kunze	Standard	Standard	108/92 (54/46)	Oak 6½ (160)	25½″ (650)	1·1°	1·47%**U**	20		75	Gen. Man: Josef Fenger
15·5 (25)	28 (45)	43·5 (70)	DM. 14 981 18 870	W'hse Knorr	Scharff- enberg 18¾ (475)	Central 24¼ (615)	192/76 (95/38)	Steel Sl 9 (250) Wood 6 (150)	27½″ (700)	17·5° Tram track 44·0°	1·7% 3·3% **U**	11	374 (114)	351 (164)	Dir. A. Simon Carl Hartwig
				Air W'hse Knorr	Standard	Standard	130/90 (54/44)	Wood 6 (150)		3·5°	0·3%	20		19	Ewald Weishof

NAME OF COMPANY ADDRESS	Gauge ft. in. (metres)	Route length incl. E=Electrified miles (km.)	Track length incl. E=Electrified miles (km.)	Elect. system and type of conductor	Loco-motives L=Line S=Shunt Steam Electric Diesel De=elec. Dh=hyd.		Rail-cars Electric Diesel Trailer Railbus Multiple Unit set		Pass. train cars	Freight train cars Con-tainers	Total Volume carried. Thous-ands of tonnes	Av'ge haul per ton miles (km.)	Av'ge net train load tonnes	Max. trailing load tonnes	Total number carried in 1 000s	Aver-age jour-ney miles (km.)
GERMANY, FEDERAL REPUBLIC (contd.)																
Kreisbahn Osterode am Harz-Kreniesen Am Bahnhof 6, Osterode (Harz) 336	4' 8½'' (1·435)	5 (8)			DhL	1					18·3	5·0 (8·0)				
Osthannoversche Eisenbahnen AG Biermannstr 33, 3100 Celle 1 Also operates: Bremervörde-Osterholzer Eb Buxtehude-Hansefelder Eb Gittelde-Bad Grund Eb Steinhuder Meer-Bahn Wilstedt-Zeven-Tostedter Eb	4' 8½'' (1·435)	202 (326)	247 (399)		DL 2 DhL 30		D 10 R 1		17	39	2 547·4	141 440 026 tonne-km		1 800	244·5	
Osthavelländische Eisenbahn Bahnhof, Johahnesstift, Berlin, Spandau	4' 8½'' (1·435)	9 (15)	14 (22)		D	4			2	10	804·0	5·3 (8·6)				
Peiner Eisenbahn Am Hillenholz 28	4' 8½'' (1·435)	33 (54)	84 (136)		D 74 Dm 10		D 1			1 500	39 232	274 354 000 ton-km		1 400	612	4 (6·4)
Hafenbahn Regensburg Linzer Str 6 D-8400 Regensburg	4' 8½'' (1·435)	2·4 (3·5)	32 (52)		DhS	7				3	2 526·2	32·7		1 500		
Regentalbahn 8374 Vietach, Bahnhofsplatz 1	4' 8½'' (1·435)	27 (44)	31 (50)		S 4 D 2		D 4 DT 1		8		88·7	12·4 (20·0)			203·3	5·8 (9·4)
Eisenbahn Reinheim-Gross Bieberau (Operated by Deutsche Eb. G)	4' 8½'' (1·435)	2·4 (4·0)	2·6 (2·4)		D	2				2						
Nebenbahn Reutlingen-Gönningen Reutlingen (Operated by Württembergische Nb.AG)	4' 8½'' (1·435)	10 (16)	12·4 (19·5)				D 1				25·6	5·2 (8·4)		130	5·8	5·5 (9·0)
Rhein-Haardtbahn GmbH Bgm Goünzweg-Sor 6700 Ludwigshafen/Rh	3' 3⅜'' (1·00)	E 11 (17)	E 21 (33)	750 V. dc OH	Dh	1	E 14 ET 17		10							
Rhein-Sieg Kreis Eisenbahn Verkehrsbetriebe des Rhein-Siegkreises, 521 Troisdorf, Postfach 4026	4' 8½'' (1·435)	25 (41)	39 (63)		DhL	2				1	189·6	8·3 (13·3)				6·0 (9·7)
Rinteln-Stadthagener Eisenbahn (Operated by Deutsche Eb.G)	4' 8½'' 1·435)	12 (20)	22 (35)		DhL	3				1	8	446·6	7·6 (12·2)				
A.G. Ruhr-Lippe Eisenbahnen Brüderstr 65A, 477 Soest/Westf	4' 8½'' (1·435)	23 (37)	33 (53)		Dh	6				13	519·5	6 276 700 ton-km				
*****Salzgitter Eisenbahn** Verkehrsbetriebe Peine-Salzgitter GmbH Am Hillenholz 28, Postfach 100670, 3320 Salzgitterl	4' 8½'' (1·435)	24 (39) 74 (119)	82 (132) 197 (318)		Dh 62 Dm 13		D 1		9	1 346	39 232	274 354 000 ton-km		2 600	612	5·9 (9·5)
Schleswiger Kriesbahn Verkhersbetriebe des Kreises Schleswig 238 Schleswig, Konigstr 1	4' 8½'' (1·435)	47 (76)	65 (104)		D	5	D 3		5	5	229·6	6·2 (10·0)		500	232·7	7·9 (12·8)
Siegener Kreisbahn GmbH 59 Siegen, Friedrichstr 47	4' 8½'' (1·435)	18 (30)	25 (41)		DhL	9				1	803·1	3·4 (5·5)	3 610 800 ton-km			
Steinhuder Meer-Bahn GmbH 3050 Wunstorf, Hindenburgstr 49 (Operated by Osthannoversche Eb)	4' 8½'' (1·435)	4 (6)	5 (8)		D	2					145·8					
Sudwestdeutsche Eisenbahnen AG 7630 Lahr/Schwarzwald, Friedrichstr 59 Operates 12 lines: Achern-Ottenhöfen Biberach-Oberharmersbach Bruchsal-Hilsbach-Menzingen Haltingen-Kandern Krozingen-Munstertal-Sulzburg Möckmuhl-Dörzbach Neckerbischofsheim-Huffenhardt Wiesloch-Schattausen-Waldengelloch Bregtalbahn Kaiserstuhlbahn Mittelbadische Eisenbahnen Mülheim-Badenweiler																
Tecklenburger Nordbahn 44 Münster (Westf), Koslinerstr 11	4' 8½'' (1·435)	30 (49)	39 (63)		D	3				2	117·1	148·8 (23·8)				
Tegernsee-Bahn AG 8180 Tegernsee, Bahnhofsplatz 5	4' 8½'' (1·435)	7 (12)	9 (15)		SL 1 DhL 2				5		9·9			220	498·5	6·0 (9·6)
Teutoburger Wald Eisenbahn (Operated by Deutsche Eb.G)	4' 8½'' (1·435)	63 (102)	76 (123)		DhL 8 DS 2		D 3 T 2		5	27	919	25·7 (41·3)				7·5 (12·0)
Uetersener Eisenbahn AG 2082 Uetersen, Bahnstr 15	4' 8½'' (1·435)	3 (5)	6 (10)		D	2					73·0	3·1 (5·0)				
Nebenbahn Vaihingen-Enzweihingen Vaihingen (Enz) (Operated by Württembergische Eb.G)	4' 8½'' (1·435)	4·5 (7·2)	5·0 (8·2)				D 1 T 1				67·2	3·4 (5·7)		300	62·3	3·0 (5·0)
Verden-Walsroder Eisenbahn 309 Berden (Aller), Bahnhof Verden-Süd	4' 8½'' (1·435)	16 (25)	20 (32)		D	4					221·7	3·0 (4·8)				
Vorwohle-Emmerthaler Verkersbetriebe GmbH 3452 Bodenwerder	4' 8½'' (1·435)	20 (32)			D	3	D 1		2	6	98·9	2 069 200 ton-km			28·5	9·3 (15·0)
Bahngesellschaft Waldhof Sandoferstr 176, Mannheim-Waldhof	4' 8½'' (1·435)	3 (5)	4 (7)		D	3				19	558·1	1·3 (2·1)				
Wanne-Herner Eisenbahn Am Westhafen 27, 4690 Herne 2	4' 8½'' (1·435)	9 (14)	23 (37)		DhL	9				394	7 426·1	33 776 158 ton-km				

* Operated jointly with Peiner Eisenbahn

Average Speeds			Financial Data	Braking	Couplers	Buffers	Rails	Sleepers (crossties)		Curvature max.	Gradient max. (U=not compensated)	Axle load max.	Altitude max.	Staff employed. Total no. (inclu. workshop)	Names of officials. Extended lists can be found at the end of the individual country in the report section immediately following
Freight Train	Pass. Train	Speed max.	Revenue Expenses	(continuous)	Type and Height above rail	Centres and Height above rail	Weight	Type and thickness	Spacing Number per mile or centres						
mph (km/hr)	mph (km/hr)	mph (km/hr)	in 1 000s		ins (mm)	ins (mm)	lb. per yd (kg/m)	ins (mm)	ins (mm)			tonnes	feet (m)		
		24·9 (40) / 28·9	DM 25·9 / 28·9	Air W'hse Knorr	Screws 23⅝ (600)	Ht. 23⅝ (600)	82/40 (41/20)	Wood	26″ (650)	22°	2·5% / 3·1% **U**	11		6	Dipl. Ing. Bernhard Pohlig
28 (45)	26 (42·5)	37 (60)	DM 32 100·0 / 33 900·0	Air W'hse Knorr	Standard	Standard	100/80 (49/40)	Wood Metal	24·4″ (620)	8·2°	1·67%	20		634	Gen. Man: Dr. Jur. H. W. Wolff
														36	Gen. Man: Gunter Wrietz
25 (40)		37 (60)		Air Knorr	Scharffenberg	Plunger	100/130 (49/54)	Wood 6¼ (160)	26″ (650)	5·8°	0·41%	30	426 (130)	1 600	Dir: D. Werner Jurisch
		15 (25)					99 (49)	Wood 6¼ (160)	1 550 km	6·0°	1·3% / 2·66% **U**	20	1 109 (338)	70	Man: Alwin Schmidt
														26	Dipl. Ing. Hans Reinfelder
				Knorr W'hse	Standard	Standard									
		25 (40)		W'hse Knorr			49·2 (24·4)	Wood 6 (150)	25½″ (650)	9·7°	2·63%	18	1 703 (519)	11	Gen. Man: Jakob Schwenkglenks
	24·2 (39)	31 (60)		Siemens Electric	Scharffenberg 17⅞ (450)	27⅞ (710)	80 (41)	Wood 6 (150)	25½ (650)	13·5°	2·0%	10	10 449 (3 185)	60 (10)	Dir: Dipl. Ing. O. Frione Tr. Man: Dipl. Ing. K. Krustpape
														13	Adolf Becker
		20 (32)		Air Knorr	Standard	Standard	100/83 (49/41)	Wood 6¼ (160)	26″ (650)	5·8°	1·4% **U**	20	443 (135)	34 (2)	Dr. jur: Frank Niethemmer
		20 (32)	DM 17 446 / 17 284	W'hse Knorr	Standard	Standard	99/79 (49/39)	Wood 6 (150)	28⅜″ (670)	7·8°	1·25	15		60 (6)	Dir: H. Helmutelliger
25 (40)		37 (60)		W'hse Knorr Air	Scharffenberg	Standard	99 (49·4)	Wood 6 (150)	26″ (650)	9·2°	2·5%	35	426 (130)	1 600	D. Werner Jurisch
				Kunze Knorr Air	Screw 37¾ (960) / (1 750)	(1 040)	A.99 (49) B.47 (23)	Wood 5½ (140)	30¾″ (780)	9·7°	2·08%	A.18* B.14	159 (49)	60	Gen. Man: Gustav Wode
														143	Karlheinz Forster
														15	Gen. Man: Oskar Tramitz
														32	Gen. Man: Werner Otte
18·6 (30)	25 (40)	37 (60)	DM 2 330·0 / 2 362·0	Knorr W'hse	Screw (1 100)	(1 200) / (850)	S41, S49	Pine	25½″ (650)	7·7°	3·0%	18	2 722 (830)	43	Gen. Man: Dr. P. F. Von Aretin
		25 (40)		Air	Standard	Standard	99/60 (49/30)	Wood 5½ (140)	2 350 (1 470)	7·0°	1·25% **U**	20/18		153	Gen. Man: Dr. K-H. Geuckler
				Knorr Air	Standard	Standard	99/68·6 (49/34)	Wood 6 (150)	26⅜″ (670)	17·5°	0·92%	18		15	Gen. Man: Gerhard Knorr
		31 (50)		W'hse. Knorr	Standard	Standard	67·4 (33·4)	Wood 6 (150)	25½″ (650)	8·7	2·0%	18	843 (257)	11	Dipl. Ing. Ständebach
														37	Gen. Man: K-H. Sievers
														27	Gen. Man: Kurt Santelman
9·3 (15)	12·5 (20)						Type 8	Wood	27½″ (700)	9·7°		25	325 (99)	20	Gen. Man: Luthar Reiss
21·7 (35)		24·9 (40)		Knorr Air	Standard	Standard 39⅜ (1 000)	99/87 (49/43)	Oak 6¼ (160)	26″ (660)	9·7°	0·8% / 1·4% **U**	22·5	180 (55)	224	Gen. Man: Dipl. Kfm R. Görl

NAME OF COMPANY ADDRESS	Gauge ft. in. *(metres)*	Route length incl. E=Electrified miles *(km.)*	Track length incl. E=Electrified miles *(km.)*	Elect. system and type of conductor	Locomotives L=Line S=Shunt Steam Electric Diesel De=elec. Dh=hyd.	Railcars Electric Diesel Trailer Railbus Multiple Unit set	Pass. train cars	Freight train cars Containers	Freight movement: Total Volume carried. Thousands of tonnes	Freight movement: Av'ge haul per ton miles *(km.)*	Freight movement: Av'ge net train load tonnes	Freight movement: Max. trailing load tonnes	Passengers: Total number carried in 1 000s	Passengers: Average journey miles *(km.)*
GERMANY, FEDERAL REPUBLIC *(contd.)*														
Wendelsteinbahn GmbH *(6 km rack)* 8204 Brannenburg, Rosenheimerstr 88	3′ 3⅜″ *(1·00)*	**E** 4 *(7)*	**E** 5 *(8)*	1 500 V. d.c. OH	**E** 4		8	4	1·0		1 500 ton-km		154·2	4·4 *(7·1)*
Werne-Bockum-Höveler Eisenbahn 4618 Kamen, Lünenerstr 219	4′8½″ *(1·435)*	8 *(12)*	11 *(17)*		**S** 1		1		470·6		5 647 300 ton-km		0·4	
Westerwaldbahn D5241 Steinbach/Bindweide uber Betzdorf/Sieg	4′ 8½″ *(1·435)*	13·6 *(21·6)*	16·7 *(27·2)*		**DhL** 4				259·9	6·8 *(11·0)*	460 600 ton-km	2 400		
Westfälische Landes-Eisenbahn AG 478 Lippstadt, Südertor 6 *(Operates 6 lines):* Lippstadt-Warstein Lippstadt-Neubeckum Soest-Brilon Stadt Neubeckum-Westkirchen Neubeckum-Munster (Westf) Borken (Westf)-Burgsteinfurt	4′ 8½″ *(1·435)*	127 *(205)*	199 *(320)*		**SL** 1 **DhL** 12 **DeL** 3 **SS** 1 **DhS** 5 **DS** 2	**D** 3 **T** 4	15	152	20 051·0	21·7 *(35·0)*		1 500	1 578·0	9·3 *(15)*
Nebenbahn Wiesloch-Schatthausen-Waldangelloch *(Operated by Sudwestdeutsche Eb.AG)*	4′ 8½″ *(1·435)*	12 *(20)*	15 *(25)*		**DL** 1	**D** 4	5		62·4	3·7 *(6·1)*			731·2	3·5 *(5·7)*
Wilstedt-Zeven Tostedter-Eisenbahn 2148 Zeven, Bahnhofstr 62	4′ 8½″ *(1·435)*	40 *(64)*	48 *(77)*		**DL** 3	**D** 2 **T** 1	2	6	94·1	21 *(35·9)*	49 500 *train-km*		129·6 *(12·5)*	7·8
Wittlager Kreisbahn AG 4508 Bohmte *(Operated by Bentheimer)*	4′ 8½″ *(1·435)*	24 *(39)*	25 *(41)*		**D** 2	**D** 2 **T** 1	2	8	84·6	7·5 *(12·0)*				
Württembergische Eisenbahn-Ges 7000 Stuttgart 1, Königstr 1 B *Operates 7 lines:*														
Amstetten-Gerstetten		*(20)*	*(23)*						24·6			80·5		
Amstetten-Laichingen		*(20)*	*(23)*						14·9			216·9		
Gaildorf-Untergröningen	4′ 8½″	*(16·5)*	*(18·5)*						64·6			190·0		
Ebingen-Onstmettingen	*(1·435)*	*(8·2)*	*(11)*						22·1			112·7		
Jagstfeld-Ohrnberg		*(22·6)*	*(25)*						55·2			124·3		
Nürtingen-Neuffen		*(8·9)*	*(10)*						624·0			778·6		
Vaihingen-Enzweihingen		*(7·2)*	*(8)*						62·5			49·6		
Württembergische Nebenbahnen GmbH 7000 Stuttgart 1, Königstr 1 B *Operates 2 lines:*														
Korntal-Weissach	4′ 8½″	*(22·3)*	*(25)*						50			427·9		
Reutlingen-Gönningen	*(1·435)*	*(16·5)*	*(19)*						16·6			1·8		
Nebenbahn Zell—Todtnau *(Operated by Mittelbadische Eb)*	3′ 3⅜″ *(1·00)*	12 *(19)*	14·3 *(23)*		**SL** 3	**D** 1	8	10	11·7	7·3 *(11·8)*	19	310	360·1	5·8 *(9·4)*
GHANA														
***Ghana Railway Corporation (GR)** PO Box 251, Takoradi	3′ 6″ *(1·067)*	592 *(953)*	801 *(1 289)*		**SL** 84 **SS** 26 **DeL** 70 **DeS** 15 **DhS** 10		259	3 689	1 626·0	110 *(177)*	130	1 200	7 273·3	28·4 *(45·7)*
GREECE														
***Hellenic Railways Organisation Ltd (CH)** Organisme des Chemins de Fer Helléniques SA 1-3 Karolou Street, Athens	4′ 8½″ *(1·435)*	1 596 *(2 572)*	1 661 *(2 672)*		**D** 188		522	10 170			930 667 000 tonne-km		12 466	72 *(115)*
	3′ 3⅜″ *(1.00)*	597 *(961)*	672 *(1 078)*											
Rack	2′ 5½″ *(0.75)*	13 *(22)*	14 *(23)*											
	1′ 11⅝″ *(0.60)*	18 *(29)*	19 *(30)*											
Athens-Piraeus Electric Railway 67 Athinas Street, Athens	4′ 8½″ *(1·435)*	22 *(36)* **E** 22 *(26)*		600 V. Third Rail	**E** 5 **P** 7	**E** 58 **ET** 77								
GUATEMALA														
Ferrocarriles Guatamaltecos (FEGUA) 18 Calle y 10a avenida, Zona 1, Guatemala	3′ 0″ *(0·914)*	509 *(819)*	595 *(958)*		**S** 90 **D** 17	**D** 2	153	2 155	1 219·4	155·7 *(250·6)*	99	1 085	3 463·6	50 *(80)*
Bandegua *(United Fruit Company)* Cia de Desarrollo, Tiquisate Bananero de Guatemala	3′ 0″ *(0·914)*		74 *(119)*		**S** 44 **D** 7			612						
United Fruit Company Railways Bananera, Izabal	3′ 0″ *(0·914)*	56 *(90)*	94 *(151)*		**DeL** 7 **DhS** 4	**D** 5 **R** 16	16	22		22 *(35)*	250	300	350·0	28 *(45)*
Verapez Railway Livingston, Izabal	3′ 0″ *(0·914)*	30 *(48)*												
GUINEA														
***C.F. de la Guinee** PO Box 581, Conakry														
C.F. Conakry-Fria Compagnie Friguia BP 554, Conakry	3′ 3⅜″ *(1 000)*	90 *(144)*	96 *(155)*		**De** 5	**D** 2		53 **C** 15			1 000	1 900		

* See main entry

Average Speeds			Financial Data	Braking (continuous)	Couplers	Buffers	Rails	Sleepers (crossties)		Curvature max.	Gradient max. (U=not compensated)	Axle load max.	Altitude max.	Staff employed. Total no. (inclu. workshop)	Names of officials. Extended lists can be found at the end of the individual country in the report section immediately following
Freight Train	Pass. Train	Speed max.	Revenue Expenses		Type and Height above rail	Centres and Height above rail	Weight	Type and thickness	Spacing Number per mile (per km) or centres ins (mm)						
mph (km/hr)	mph (km/hr)	mph (km/hr)	in 1 000s		ins (mm)	ins (mm)	lb. per yd (kg/m)	ins (mm)				tonnes	feet (m)		
Rk. 6 (9) Ord 9.5 (15)	Rk. 6 (9) Ord 9.5 (15)	Rk. 6.5 (10) Ord 9.5 (15)		W'hse Air	26¾ (680)	Centre (500)	48/40 (24/20)	Wood Steel	W. (800) St. (700)	25.0°	23.7%	10.2	5 653 (1 723)	31	Gen. Man: Ing Rüdigen Dietrich
		18.6 (30)		Kunze Knorr	Standard	Standard	(99/83) (49/44)	Wood		9.75°	3.0%	20		49	Dipl. Ing. Heinz Stolle
		18.6 (30)		Air	WIEDB	WIEDB	(6·400)	Type F51	27½" (700)	8.7°	2.5%	18	1 860 (567)	26 (4)	Dipl. Ing. Ständebach
19 (30)	25 (40)	37 (60)		Air Knorr; W'hse	Standard	Crs.68⅞" (1 750) Ht. 41¼" (1 050)	109/67 (54/33)	Wood 6 (150)	25½" (650)	13°	2.0%	20	1 404 (428)	615 (100)	Directors: Dipl-Kfm Wienand Dr. Ing Müller
8.7 (14.0)	15.5 (25.0)	31 (50)		Knorr Air	Standard	Standard	66/48 (33/24)	Wood 5½ (140)	(650-850)	9.7°	1.67% U	18	578 (176)	118	Gen. Man: Siegfried Funk
														47	Gen. Man: Dr. zum Felde
15.5 (25)		31 (50)		Knorr Air		Ht. 37" (940) and 41⅞" (1 065)		Wood 5½ (140)	937 (1 500)	8.7°		20	40 (4)	38 (13)	Gen. Man: Diedrich Vagt
															} Gen. Man: Josef Sowa
10.4 (16.8)	18.4 (29.6)	31 (50)		Hardy Vac	Bolt (650)	Central (650)	67/49 (33/24)	Steel	23½" (600)	25.0°	2.9% U	18	2 106 (642)	37 (3)	
12 (19)	28 (45)	Frt. 35 (56) Pass 40 (64)	NC 9 684.3 13 815.2	Vac Brake Co	Auto. Central Buffer-coupling 34½ (876)	E.S. Co Alliance	80/60 (40/30)	Wood 5 (127); Steel	2 200 (1 370)	660 ft. (201 m)	1.0%	16	938 (286)	15 524 (12 499)	Gen. Man: P. O. Aggrey
25 (40)	32.3 (52)	62 (100)		W'hse Hilde-brand Knorr Knorr Hardy	Standard European 21.7 (550) 20.9 (530)	Standard European	93 (46)	Steel	23⅜ (600)	5.8°	2.7% 2.5% U	20	2 523 (769)	12 901 (3 202)	Gen Dirs: S. Keramidas I. Kazantzoglou
							65 (32)	Wood	(600/750)	14.6°	3.0% 2.5% U	13.5	2 671 (814)		
						Central 750 mm	40 (20)	Wood		38°	3.4%	4.5	2 362 (720)		
						Central 530 mm	32 (16)	Wood		44°	3.0%	6.0	951 (290)		
	22 (35)	43.5 (70)		Knorr Air	Schafen-berg 36⅝ (930)	Crs. 68⅞ (1 750) Ht. 39⅜ (1 000)	104/78 (52/39)	Wood 6¼ (160)	27½' (700)	7.2	3.0% 2.7%U	18	162 (269)	203 (103)	Gen. Mans: N. Vlangalis and S. Andreadis
				Triple K-KI-KII-F-H. W'hse	Auto: Tower; Sheran; Alliance Atlas 26 (660)		75/60 (37/30)	Wood 6 (152)	Average 2 900 (1 800)	279 ft (85 m)	3.7%	15			
					70/54 (35/27)			Wood 6 (153)	2 600 (1 615)	4.0°	2.0%	14			Man: R. C. Wells
20 (32)	17 (27)	25 (40)	185.4 498.3	Air W'hse	Gregg Standard 30 (762)		60/40 (30/20)	Pine 6 (153)	24" (608)	18.0°	1.1% U	10	230 (70)	197 (72)	Gen. Man: B. E. Taylor
17 (37)		34 (55)		Vac W'hse	Willison auto 29½ (750)		93 (46)	Metal	2 400 (1 500)	984 ft. (300 m)	1.2%	17	722 (220)	80	Gen. Man: Lancei Traorè

NAME OF COMPANY ADDRESS	Gauge ft. in. (metres)	Route length incl. E=Electrified miles (km.)	Track length incl. E=Electrified miles (km.)	Elect. system and type of conductor	Locomotives L=Line S=Shunt Steam Electric Diesel De=elec. Dh=hyd.		Rail-cars Electric Diesel Trailer Railbus Multiple Unit set		Pass. train cars	Freight train cars Con-tainers		Total Volume carried. Thousands of tonnes	Av'ge haul per ton miles (km.)	Av'ge net train load tonnes	Max. trailing load tonnes	Total number carried in 1 000s	Average journey miles (km.)
GUINEA *(contd.)*																	
C.F. de la Cie. miniero du Conakry Conakry	4′ 8½″ (1·435)	9 (14)			De	2					12						
C.F. de Boke *(Under construction)*																	
GUYANA																	
Demba Railroad Demerara Bauxite Co. Linden	3′ 0″ (0·914)	50 (80)			DL DS	18 19			12	646	754	25 (40)	400	550	18·5	10 (16)	
HAITI																	
National Railroad Company of Haiti *(Ceased operation)*																	
Cie. des C.F. de La Plaine du Cul-de-Sac *(Ceased operation)*					S E D	3 2 5					371						
HONDURAS																	
F.C. Nacional de Honduras la Calle No. 2, San Pedro Sula	3′ 6″ (1·067)	79 (127)	126 (203)		DeL SS	8 2	RD	3	16	517	382·9	30 234 400 ton-km	460	1 200	130·1	31·8 (51·2)	
Standard Fruit Company's Railway Head Office: PO Box 50830, 2 Canal St., International Trade Mart, New Orleans, La., USA Local office: Apart. 96 and 101, La Ceiba	3′ 0″ (0·914)		258 (458)		EL De	16 5			26	718			390	390			
Tela Railroad Co. *(United Fruit Co., 80 Federal Street, Boston, Mass., USA)* La Lima	3′ 6″ (1·067)	103 (166)	217 (350)		DeL DhS	13 12	R	21	22	1 584	1 420·0	44·7 (72·0)		1 500	1 350·0	29·8 (48·0)	
HONG KONG *Kowloon-Canton Railway *(British Section)* Hung Hom, Kowloon, Hong Kong																	
HUNGARY *Hungarian State Railways Magyar Allamvasutak (MAV) Budapest VI, Népköztársaság Utja 73-75	5′ 0″ (1·524) 4′ 8½″ (1·435) 2′ 6″ (0·76)	5 480 (7 483) 4 934 (7 550) E 795 (1 280)	7 960 (12 523) E 1 760 (3 211)	16 000 V and 25 000 1/50	NA		NA		NA	NA C 3 607	134 114	24 187 000 000 ton-km			30 445 000	25 (40)	
Budapest Suburban Railway Budapesti Helyi Erdekü Vasut Akácfa v. 15, Budapest VII *(Now part of the Budapest Traffic Board: Budapesti Közlekedési Vállalat)* *(Operates the following lines):*	4′ 8½″ (1 435)	10 (17) E 63 (101)	179 (289)	1 000 V dc OH Fischer-Jellinek	E De	41 13	E D	162 3	353	420	1 598·0				163 210·0		
Zsigmond tér-Szentendre	4′ 8½″ (1 435)	E 2 (3)		1 000 V dc OH F-J													
Vágóhid-Rákeve (Electric only to Tököl)	4′ 8½″ (1 435)	10 (17) E 15 (24)		1 000 V dc OH F-J													
Gyártelep-Taksony	4′ 8½″ (1 435)	E 5 (8)		1 000 V dc OH F-J													
Borároster-Csepel Tanacshaz tér (Rapid line)	4′ 8½″ (1 435)	E 4 (7)		MAV-Kando													
Csepel-Pesterzsébet Határút	4′ 8½″ (1 435)	E 2 (4)		1 000 V dc OH F-J													
Ors vezér ter-Gödöllö	4′ 8½″ (1 435)	E 18 (29)		1 000 V dc OH F-J													
Cinkota-Csömör Beke tér		E 3 (5)		1 000 V dc OH F-J													
Györ-Sopron-Ebenfurti-Vasut Szilagyi Deszsö-ter, 1, Budapest 1 *(Operates 2 lines):*																	
Györ-Csorna-Fertöszentmiklos-Sopron Offices: Györ	4′ 8½″ (1 435)	53 (85)			S De	21 13											
Celldömölk-Fertöszentmiklos-Mekszikopuszta (for Fertö-videki Helyiérdeku Vasut) Offices: Sopron	4′ 8½″ (1·435)	39 (63)															

* See main entry

Average Speeds			Financial Data	Braking (continuous)	Couplers	Buffers	Rails	Sleepers (crossties)		Curvature max.	Gradient max. (U=not compensated)	Axle load max.	Altitude max.	Staff employed. Total no. (inclu. workshop)	Names of officials. Extended lists can be found at the end of the individual country in the report section immediately following
Freight Train	Pass. Train	Speed max.	Revenue Expenses		Type and Height above rail	Centres and Height above rail	Weight	Type and thickness	Spacing Number per mile or centres						
mph (km/hr)	mph (km/hr)	mph (km/hr)	in 1 000s		ins (mm)	ins (mm)	lb. per yd (kg/m)	ins (mm)	ins (mm)			tonnes	feet (m)		
							102 (50)	Metal 2 400 (1 500)							
12 (19)	15 (24)	25 (40)		W'hse Air	Greggs 23¼		90/60 (45/30)	Hardwood (Mora) 4 (100)	26" (660)	722 ft (220 m)	1·0° U	15	260 (79)	157 (30)	Gen. Man: J. V. Rabbeck
21·7 (35)		31·0 (50)	$ 5 192·3 5 237·9	W'hse Air	AAR Autos 24 (610)		75/60 (37/30)	Wood 6 (150)	20" (508)	886 ft (270 m)	1·5%		769 (213)	223	Gen. Man: Ing. D. Panting Mena
15 (25)	22 (35)	37 (60)		W'hse	Knuckle	22 (560)	76/50 (37/25)	Wood 8 (200)	2 800 (1 750)	886 ft (270 m)	1·0% 0·72% U	15	142 (43)	528 (100)	Gen. Man: H. H. Lacombe
11·6 (16·4)	22·6 (36·6)	75 (120)	Forint 30 762 000 29 006 000	Air Hildebrand-Knorr	U.I.C.	Crs. 67⅞ (1 750) Ht. 39⅜ (1 000)	108/96 (54/48)	Wood Conc 7½ (190)	23⅝ (600)	4·3°	4·0%	23	1 345 (410)	126 346 (18 585)	Gen. Man: Zoltan Szucs
		43 (70)			Auto	95·5/67 (48/34) 67 (23)					3·5%	20			
		50 (80)													

NAME OF COMPANY ADDRESS	Gauge ft. in. (metres)	Route length incl. E=Electrified miles (km.)	Track length incl. E=Electrified miles (km.)	Elect. system and type of conductor	Locomotives L=Line S=Shunt Steam Electric Diesel De=elec. Dh=hyd.	Rail-cars Electric Diesel Trailer Railbus Multiple Unit set	Pass. train cars	Freight train cars / Containers	Total Volume carried. Thousands of tonnes	Av'ge haul per ton miles (km.)	Av'ge net train load tonnes	Max. trailing load tonnes	Total number carried in 1 000s	Average journey miles (km.)
INDIA														
*Indian Government Railways Ministry of Railways (Railway Board), Rail Bhavan, New Delhi 1	5' 6" (1·676)	18 667 (30 041) E 2 497 (4 025)	26 532 (42 755) E 6 130 (9 865)	1 500 V 3 000 V dc OH 25 000 V 1/50	S 5 475 De 864 Dh 102 E 619	D 26 DT 6 E 525 ET 1 189	15 443		33 900 000 000 tonne-km				148 916 000	29·3 (47·4)
	3' 3⅜" (1·00)	15 876 (25 550) E 103 (166)	21 690 (34 907) E 183 (294)	1 500 V dc OH	S 3 355 De 257 Dh 27 E 20	D 45 DT 6 E 43 ET 129	12 176							
Narrow gauges are 2' 6" (762) and 2' 0" (610)	Narrow	2 781 (4 476)	3 125 (5 028)		S 392 Dh 38	D 19 DT 12	1 547							
	Total all gauges	37 324 (60 067) E 2 456 (3 952)	62 018 (99 808) E 6 313 (10 160)		S 9 222 De 1 121 Dh 167 E 639	D 90 DT 24 E 568 ET 1 318	29 166							
Arrah-Sasaram Light Railway Calcutta	2' 6" (0·762)	60 (97)	66 (107)		S 12 D 2		39	147	29·0	32·2 (51·9)			3 106·0	17·0 (27·0)
Bhilai Steel Plant Bhilai-1 (M.P.)	5' 6" (1·676)		91 (146)		SL 5 SS 4 DeS 41 DS 6 Oth 2			565	8 323	2·5 (4)	1 500	3 200		
Bombay Port Trust Ramjibhai Kamami Marg, Ballard Estate, Bombay-400 038	5' 6" (1·676)	7 (11)	133 (214)		S 15 Dh 20			330	2 905·7	24 272 320 tonne-km				
Calcutta Port Trust Railway 15, Strand Rd, Calcutta 700001	5' 6" (1 676)	22 (36) E (1·75)	221 (350) E (44)	2 500 V. ac 50Hz single phase	SS 33 Dh 29			730	2 800					
Dehri-Rohtas Light Railway	2' 6" (0·762)	42 (67)	64 (103)		S 27	D 3 Pet 2	18	752	779·0	34·9 (56·2)			472·0	16·7 (26·9)
Fatwah-Islampur Railway 12 Mission Row, Calcutta 700001	2' 6" (0·762)	27 (43)	29 (47)		S 4		18	33	20·0	19·3 (31·0)			1 886·0	12·4 (19·9)
Madras Port Trust Railway South Beach Road, Madras	5' 6" (1·676) 3' 3⅜" (1·00 m)		11 (18) 29 (46)		SS 11 DhS 22				3 017·3					
Visakhapatnam Port Trust Andhra Pradesh	5' 6" (1 676)		75 (120)		De 6 Dm 11				7 403·8	10 (16)		1 000		
	2' 6" (0·672)		5·5 (9)		S 4 D 2									
INDONESIA														
*Indonesian State Railways Perusahaan Jawatan Kereta Api Jalan Gereja 1, Bandung, Java	3' 6" (1·067)	3 970 (6 389) E 48 (77)	4 500 (7 246) E 63 (101)	1 500 V dc OH	SL 202 EL 4 DeL 75 DhL 84 DhS 137	D 10	2 423	22 279	4 679·9	706 000 000 ton-km			19 978	49·3 (79·3)
	2' 5½" (0·750) 1' 11⅝" (0·600)	314 (505) 65 (105)	326 (525) 57 (92)											
IRAN														
*Iranian State Railways 49 West Takhte-Djamshid Ave, Teheran	4' 8½" (1·435) 5' 6" (1·676)	2 802 (4 525) 57 (92)	2 962 (4 766)		DeL 226 DeS 33 DhS 2 DmS 44		343	7 999	6 347·1	5 309 188 849 ton-km			6 457·5	314·4 (506)
IRAQ														
*Iraqi Republic Railways Baghdad	4' 8½" (1·435)	767 (1 235)			S 19 De 163		240	3 280	1 853 000 000 tonne-km					
IRELAND														
*Coras Iompair Eireann Heuston Station, Dublin 8	5' 3" (1·60)	1 361 (2 190)	1 930 (3 106)		DeL 196 DhS 33	D 57	485	6 519 C 1 197	3 477	585 189 257 tonne-km			13 607	35 (56)
ISRAEL														
*Israel Railways Central Station PO Box 44, Haifa	4' 8½" (1·435)	462 (647)	550 (886)		DeL 35 DhS 22		114	2 095	3 650	462 000 000 tonne-km			3 040	54·7 (88)
ITALY														
*Italian State Railways (Ferrovie dello Stato Italia) Piazza della Croce Rossa, 00100 Rome	4' 8½" (1·435) 3' 1⅝" (0·95)	9 950 (16 014) E 4 919 (7 916)	18 051 (29 070) E 11 140 (17 928)	3 600 V 3/16⅔ and 3 000 V dc OH	SL 691 SS 233 EL 1 798 ES 70 DeL 231 DeS 84 DhL 21 DhS 517 DmS 227 *Narrow* SL 15 DdS 2	E 434 ET 310 D 1 068 DT 187 EM 23 DM 8 *Narrow* D 24 DT 5	10 031	118 261 C 31 820	48 433	16 375 000 000 ton-km			390 070	58·8 (94·6)

* See main entry

Average Speeds			Financial Data		Couplers	Buffers	Rails	Sleepers (crossties)							Names of officials.
Freight Train	Pass. Train	Speed max.	Revenue Expenses	Braking (continuous)	Type and Height above rail	Centres and Height above rail	Weight	Type and thickness	Spacing Number per mile (per km) or centres	Curvature max.	Gradient max. (U=not compensated)	Axle load max.	Altitude max.	Staff employed. Total no. (inclu. workshop)	Extended lists can be found at the end of the individual country in the report section immediately following
mph (km/hr)	mph (km/hr)	mph (km/hr)	in 1 000s		ins (mm)	ins (mm)	lb. per yd (kg/m)	ins (mm)	ins (mm)			tonnes	feet (m)		
S. 7·5 (12·0) D. 14·2 (22·9) E. 15·6 (25·2)	20·4 (32·9)	62 (100) ‡‡	(Crores) 1 767·01 1 609·62	Air and Vac	Screw; also AAR 43½–41 (1 105–1 040)	Crs. 77 (1 956) Ht. (1 105–1 040)	105/90 (52/45) C.I. and	Wood 5 (127) steel conc	Main 26·8″ (680) Branch 33″ (840)	574 ft (175 m)	2·94%	22·9			Chairman: G. P. Worrier
S. 8·1 (13·1) D. 11·6 (18·7) E. 11·7 (18·9)	17·1 (27·5)	47 (75)		Air and Vac	ABC 23 (584)		75/60 (37/30)	Wood 4½ (114) C.I. and steel	Main 26·3″ (670) Branch 33″ (840)	358 ft (109 m)	2·70% (Rack section 8·15%)	12·2			
S. 7·9 (12·7) D. 8·4 (13·5)	11·7 (18·9)	31 (50)		Air and Vac	ABC		60/30 (30/15)	Wood 4 (102)		2′ 6″ g 112 ft (34 m) 2′ 0″ g 43 ft (13 m)		Varies with weight of rail	7 407 (2 258)	1 391 000 (414 000)	
														576	Gen. Man: C. S. Mehta
	4 (7)			Compressed Air	41⅜ (1 050)	Central 76⅞ (1 956) Ht. 43½ (1 105)	105/86 (52/43)	5 (127)		10·0°	15%	40	1 020 (316)	642	
	25 (40)		Rs. 16 672 17 881	Air & Vac W'hse			90/75 (45/37)	Wood 6 (150)			22·5		Sea level	1 700 (308)	Manager: K. M. Rao
4 (6)	6 (10)		Lakhs 432·95 655·64				90/75 (44/37)	Wood 5 (130)	(1300)	14°		20	20 (6)		Chr: Shr. S. R. Dars, IAS Traffic Man.: Shr. B. A. Tikku Shr. B. A. Chatterjee
														827	Sec: J. K. Jain
														233	Chf. Eng. B. B. Mukherjee
3 (5)	5 (8)	10 (16)	Rs. 9 227·1 10 625·1				90/75 (44·6/37)	Wood 5 (127)		14°	0·25%	22·5		643 (112)	Gen. Man: Shri K. N. Chennabassappa
5 (8)	9 (15)			Vac and Air	Screw; Henricot Auto		90/75 (44·6/37) 40/30 (20/15)	Wood 5 (127) Steel	N+3	8·0°	0·67%	BG 20 NG 7·5		635	Traffic Manager: K. Sridharan
17·4 (28)	43 (70)	62 (100)	Rs. 22 222 23 103	W'hse Air and Vac	Henricot Sumitomo 30 (760)		1 067 g 85/52 Narrow 33/25 (16/12·4)	Teak 4¾ (120) (42/56) Some metal	Main 26⅞″ (680) Branch 31½″ (800)	Main 492 ft (680) Branch 328 ft (100 m)	4·0% Rack (150 m)	Main 13·5 8·0% Branch 8-10	Java 4 088 Sumatra 3 788	70 795 (6 178) (1 246)	Chief Dir: R. Soemali
25 (40)	32 (51)	50 (80)	Rials 10 249 129 10 700 568	Air Knorr W'hse	Screw and auto 41¾ (1 060)	Crs 68⅞ (1 750) Ht as coupler	101/79 (50/38)	Conc Steel; Wood 6 (150)	23⅝″ (600)	722 ft (220 m)	2·8%	20	6 946 (2 177)	29 693	Pres: F. Mahmoodian
St 31 (50)	St 37 (60)	St 50 (80)		W'hse Air Vac	Auto & Screw 41¾ (1 060) 23 (584)	68⅞ Crs (1 750)	90/75 (45/37) 75/60 (37/30)	Wood 5 (127) Wood 4½ (114)	N+4 N+3	Standard 4° 34′ Metre 5°	0·8% 0·5%	17 12	1 377		Director General: Ibrahim Mahmoud
13 (21)	Main 39 (63) Suburb 23 (37)	75 (121)	£ 23 262 44 960	Vac G. & C.	P. Screw Fr. 3-link 42 (1 067)	75 (1 905) 42 (1 067)	Main 101/85 (50/42)	Wood 5 (127) and Concrete	32½″ (826)	275 ft (84 m)	2·0% 1·67% U	20	630 (192)	9 123 (2 050)	Gen Man: J. F. Higgins
17 (27)	32 (52)	65 (105)	£Is	Air Knorr W'hse	Standard UIC 41¾ (1 060)	Crs 68⅞ (1 750) Ht 41¾ (1 060)	101/76 (50/37·5)	Wood 6 (150) conc Steel	2 680 (1 670)	13·1°	2·0% U 2·5%	21	2 625 (800)	1 837 (637)	Gen. Man: Zvi Tsafriri
28 (45)	57 (92)	112 (180)	Lira 1 864 638 000 2 740 420 000	Air Breda W'hse	Standard UIC	Standard UIC	121/101/ 99 (60/50/ 49)	Wood 6 (150) Conc 6/7½ (150/190)	60 kg RI (1 666) 50 kg RI (1 445-1 666) 49 kg RI (1 390-1 430)	Radius 820 ft (250 m)	3·1%	20	1 503 (1 375)	159 693 (28 492)	Dir Gen: Doff Ercole Semenza

NAME OF COMPANY ADDRESS	Gauge ft. in. *(metres)*	Route length incl. E=Electrified miles *(km.)*	Track length incl. E=Electrified miles *(km.)*	Elect. system and type of conductor	Locomotives L=Line S=Shunt Steam Electric Diesel De=elec. Dh=hyd.	Railcars Electric Diesel Trailer Railbus Multiple Unit set	Pass. train cars	Freight train cars Containers	Freight movement: Total Volume carried. Thousands of tonnes	Freight movement: Av'ge haul per ton miles *(km.)*	Freight movement: Av'ge net train load tonnes	Freight movement: Max. trailing load tonnes	Passengers: Total number carried in 1 000s	Passengers: Average journey miles *(km.)*
ITALY *(contd.)*														
Ferrovia dell Alto-Pistoiese S. Marello Pistoiese	3′ 1½″ *(0·95)*	**E** 10 *(17)*	**E** 11 *(18)*	1 200 V d.c. OH	**E** 2	**E** 3	5	16	3·7				432·2	
Ferrovia Biella-Novara Piazza Lombardia 6, Biella	4′ 8½″ *(1·435)*	32 *(52)*	40 *(64)*		**S** 5	**D** 7	3	15	12·2	16 *(26)*	80	310	669·6	
Ferrovie Calabro-Lucane Via Nizza 35, Rome	3′ 1½″ *(0·95)*		339 *(545)*		**SL** 3 **SS** 7 **DeL** 7 **DhL** 72	**D** 32 **T** 89	84	540	21·1	553 456 ton-km	70	480	7 630·5	13·7 *(20·3)*
Ferrovia Circumvestnea Catania 330141-330704	3′ 1½″ *(0·95)*	71 *(114)*	75 *(120)*		**S** 1 **De** 3 **DS** 9	**D** 3	9	59						
Ferrovia Circumvesuviana Strade Ferrate Secondarie Meridionali, Corso Garibaldi 387, Naples 80142	3′ 1½″ *(0·95)*	**E** 47 *(157)*	**E** 116 *(188)*	1 200 V dc OH	**DhS** 2 **Dm** 1	**R** 4 **EM** 85	8	40					42 481·9	10·6 *(17·1)*
Ferrovia Cumana (SEPSA) Naples 44 Via Cisterna dell Olio	4′ 8⅞″ *(1·445)*	**E** 16 *(26)*		3 000 V dc OH	**D** 2 **E** 1 **De** 3 **Dh** 1	**E** 11		31			77	110	11 000·0	6·2 *(10)*
Società Emiliana Ferrovie, Tramvie ed Automobili (SEFTA) Piazza Manzoni, Medena	4′ 8½″ *(1·435)*	**E** 25 *(41)*	**E** 38 *(61)*	3 000 V dc OH	**EL** 4 **DS** 1	**E** 10	29	80 **C** 98	100·0	15·2 *(24·5)*	500	580	1 191·5	11·0 *(17·5)*
Ferrovia Genova-Casella Genoa	3′ 3⅜″ *(1·00)*	**E** 15 *(25)*		2 600 V dc OH	**E** 3	**E** 3	5	16	1·4	5·4 *(8·7)*			433·3	
Guidovia Santuario della Guardia Genova S. Quirico	3′ 3⅜″ *(1·00)*	7 *(11)*	7 *(11)*		**De** 11 **DhS** 2			2					158·6	
S.A. La Ferroviaria Italiana Arezzo	4′ 8½″ *(1·435)*	**E** 52 *(84)*	**E** 60 *(96)*	3 000 V dc	**E** 2	**E** 3	10	28	21·7				1 788·0	
Metropolitana Termini-Laurentina	4′ 8½″ *(1·435)*	**E** 7 *(11)*	**E** 17 *(27·5)*	1 500 V dc OH		**E** 40 **T** 8							23 152·0	
Ferrovia Napoli-Piedimonte Matese Cia delle Ferrovie del Mezzogiorno d'Italia 80137 Naples, Piazza Carlo 3 *(Operates 2 lines):*														
Napoli-S. Maria C.V. (S. Andrea)	3′ 1½″ *(0·95)*	**E** 24 *(39)*	**E** 25 *(41)*	11 000 V 1/25	**E** 2	**E** 9	13	22						
S. Maria C.V. (F.S.)— Piedemonte	4′ 8½″ *(1·435)*	25 *(40)*	28 *(46)*		**Dh** 2	**D** 5 **T** 4		22						
Società Nazionale Ferrovie e Tranvie Iseo *(Operates 2 lines):* Brescio-Iseo-Edolo, and Iseo-Rovato	4′ 8½″ *(1·435)*	68 *(109)*	79 *(127)*		**S** 12 **D** 1	**D** 12	39	105	286·3				1 516·5	
Ferrovie Nord Milano Piazzale Luogi Cadorna 14, 20123 Milan	4′ 8½″ *(1·435)*	135 *(218)* **E** 124 *(200)*	230 *(370)* **E** 216 *(348)*	3 000 V dc OH Copper	**SL** 1 **EL** 9 **DeL** 5 **DeS** 2	**E** 50 **ET** 57	279	37	214·6	9·0 *(14·5)*	46	800	32 989·1	12·9 *(20·8)*
Gestione Governativa Ferrovie Padane Via Foro Boario 27, C.A.P. 44100 Ferrara	4′ 8¹¹⁄₁₆″ *(1·445)*	32 *(52)*	39 *(62)*		**Dm** 3	**D** 9	9	28	13·2	424 443 ton-km		600	770·1	16·9 *(27·3)*
Ferrovie Reggiane V. Trento Trieste 9, Reggio Emilia	4′ 8½″ *(1·445)*	47 *(76)*	54 *(86)*		**S** 4 **D** 2					10·7 *(17·3)*				
Societa Romana per le Ferrovie del Nord Via di Villa Ruffo 5, Rome	4′ 8½″ *(1·435)*	**E** 63 *(102)*	**E** 76 *(123)*	3 300 V dc OH	**E** 14	**E** 10	32	93	0·8		100	220	1 946·5	10·7 *(17·2)*
Ferrovia del Renon Balzano *(4·2 km. Rack rail)*	3′ 3⅜″ *(1·00)*	**E** 7 *(12)*		800 V dc	**E** 4	**E** 5	2	10	5·6				352·8	
Società Ferrovie Elettriche di Roma (STEFER) Via dei Radiotelegrafisti 44, Rome *(Operates 3 railways):*														
Ferrovie Roma-Fiuggi-Alatri	3′ 1½″ *(0·95)*	**E** 59 *(96)*		1 500 V dc OH	**E** 3	**E** 2 **EMU** 34	3	60	0·4		58	165	14 116·5	17 *(27·3)*
Ferrovie Roma-Lido	4′ 8¼″ *(1·435)*	**E** 18 *(29)*	**E** 40 *(65)*	1 500 V dc OH	**EL** 9 **DS** 2	**E** 4	48	34	8·3	12·4 *(19·9)*		500	10 055·9	11·8 *(19·1)*
Ferrovia Sangritana Soc. per le Ferrovie Adriatico-Appennino, Lanciano	4′ 8½″ *(1·435)*	**E** 68 *(100)*	**E** 74 *(119)*	3 200 V dc	**E** 3	**E** 9	6	14	6·8				1 162·3	
Società Ferrovie Complementari Della Sardegna Cagliari	3′ 1½″ *(0·95)*	319 *(513)*			**S** 58 **D** 3	**D** 26	89	327	30·2				524·4	
Strade Ferrate Sarde SA Via Sicilia 20, Sassari	3′ 1½″ *(0·95)*	139 *(224)*	148 *(238)*		**S** 19	**D** 11	84	159	7·1				876·2	
Ferrovie Meridionali Sarde Iglesias (Cagliari)	3′ 1½″ *(0·95)*	70 *(113)*	90 *(145)*		**SL** 32	**D** 10	15	330	267·0	9 *(15)*	440	760	520·0	14 *(22)*
Società Subalpina di Imprese Ferroviarie P.O.B. 60, Domodossola *Operates 2 lines:* Domodossola-Swiss Border (1·0 m)	3′ 3⅜″ *(1·00)*	**E** 21 *(33)*	**E** 22 *(36)*	1 500 V dc OH		**E** 6 **D** 2 **EMU** 7	10	32			13 719 ton-km		488·6	
Spoleta-Norcia (0·95 m)	3′ 1½″ *(0·95)*	**E** 32 *(51)*	**E** 34 *(55)*	3 000 V dc OH		**E** 5	7	34	1·7				105·5	

Average Speeds			Financial Data		Couplers	Buffers	Rails	Sleepers (crossties)		Curvature max.	Gradient max. (U=not compensated)	Axle load max.	Altitude max.	Staff employed. Total no. (inclu. workshop)	Names of officials. Extended lists can be found at the end of the individual country in the report section immediately following
Freight Train	Pass. Train	Speed max.	Revenue Expenses	Braking (continuous)	Type and Height above rail	Centres and Height above rail	Weight	Type and thickness	Spacing Number per km or centres ins (mm)						
mph (km/hr)	mph (km/hr)	mph (km/hr)	in 1 000s		ins (mm)	ins (mm)	lb. per yd (kg/m)	ins (mm)				tonnes	feet (m)		
							50·4 (25)			50·0°	4·2%				
				W'hse Air	Standard	Standard	73 (36·1)	Wood 5½ (140)	30" (770)	5·7°	2·0%	16			
20 (40)	25 (40)	43 (70)		W'hse Air	Screw 24½ (620)	Central Crs. 33½ (855)	55/50 (27/25)	Wood 5½ (140)	29½" (750)	17·5°	10% U 6·0%	11	(1 406)	3 200	Dir. Gen: J. Bari
15 (25)	22 (35)	72 (45)		W'hse Air			55 (27·3)			9·2°	2·3%	10	3 202 (976)	382 (80)	
	25 (40)	56 (90)	Lire 68 52·0 375 12·0	W'hse Air	Auto 32·6 (829)	Central 34·2 (870)	73 (36)	Oak 5½ (140)	29" (630)	11·5°	3·0%	12		1 371 (332)	Dir: Dott. Ing. U. Paci
18·6 (30)	49·7 (80)	55·9 (90)		W'hse Air		41⁵/₁₆ (1 050)	92 (46)	Wood 5½ (140)	2 000 (1 250)	11·3°	1·35%	18	141 (43)	290 (100)	Gen. Man: Dott. Ing Angelo Brofferio
				W'hse Air	24½ (620)	Central 33½ (855)	55 (27·3)	Wood 4¾ (120)	2 140 (1 330)	29·0°	4·5%	8			
							18·2 (9)			70·0°	8·3%				
25 (40)	34 (55)	37 (60)	L. 192 601·1 520 760·4	W'hse Air	Standard	Standard	55 (27·3)	Wood 4¾ (120)	32¾" (833)	8·75°	1·2%	15	397 (121)	167 (65)	Pres: Sig Y. Morselli
							56·5 (28)			5·8°	1·7%				
	24 (38)	50 (800)	L. 1 108 180·0 2 254 611·0	Air W'hse	29" (740)		93 (46·3)	Wood 6 (150)	25⅛" (640)	8·7°	3·5%U		151 (46)	194	Ing. L. Catanoso
															Dr. Ing. Marcello Rossetti
	19 (30)	37 (60)	L. 79 239·6 1 397 731·4	W'hse Air			60/44 (30/22)	Wood 5½ (140)		22·0°	3·6%			182 (35)	
	43 (70)	50 (80)	L. 101 018·5 796 205·4	Air			72·5 (36)	Wood 5½ (140)		5·8°	2·5%			93 (16)	
				W'hse	Standard	Standard	72·6 (36)	Wood 5⅛ (130)	29½" (750)	7·0°	2·4% 2·2% U	18			
10 (16)	26 (42)	50 (80)	L. 11 006 098·9 48 300 104·0	W'hse. Air	Draw-hook 42" (1 065)	69 (1 750) 42 (1 065)	93/60 (46/30)	Wood 5⅛/5½ (130/140) Conc.	24-28½" (600-725)	4·6°	3·0%	16	1 266 (386)	2 270 (330)	Op. Man: Dott. Ing. Carlo Gaifami
25 (40)	43 (70)	56 (90)	L. 343 188·5 1 413 359·2	W'hse Air	Standard Bagnara	Standard	55 (27·3)	Oak 7 (180)	29½" (750)	7·7°	0·6%	18	30 (9)	177	Dir: Dr Paolo Fiorini
				W'hse	Standard	Standard	72/60 (36/30)	Wood 5½ (140)	31½" (800)		1·2%	14·5			
72 (45)	88 (55)	43 (70)	L. 253 579·8 1 709 117·8	W'hse Air	Draw-hook 41¼ (1 050)	67½ (1 720) 41¼ (1 050)	72/60 (36/30)	Wood 5⅛ (130)	31½" (800)	17·5°	3·0%	15	1 476 (450)	401 (66)	Gen Man: Dr. Ing. Piero Dionisi Vici
										35·0°					
	21·9 (35·3)	43 (70)	L. 742 443·0 4 883 626·0	Air W'hse	33½" (850)	Buffer-Coupler	72/56 (36/28)	Wood 5⅛ (130)	25⅛ (640)	35·0°	6·0%U	10	213 (700)	803 (185)	Ing. L. Catanoso
	30 (49)	53 (85)	L. 951 988·0 3 209 018·0	Air W'hse			93 (46·3)	Wood 6 (150)	25⅛ (640)	6·3°	1·9%U	16	132 (40)	609 (191)	Ing. L. Catanoso
							55·4 (28)			17·5	4·0%				
							55/42 (27/21)			22·0°	3·0%				
							55/42 (27/21)			17·5°	2·5%				
12 (20)	28 (45)	50 (80)		W'hse Air	21 (530)	Central 31 (785)	55/50 (27/25)	Wood 5½ (140)	29½" (750)	17·5°	2·5%	10	984 (300)	532 (94)	
28 (45)	37 (60)	37 (60)	L. 305 155·8 1 219 886·3	W'hse Air	23 (600)	23 (600)	55/50·4 (27·3/25)	Wood 5⅛ (130)	27½" (700)	35·0°	6·0%	4·9	2 723 (830)	107	Gen. Man: Dr. Z. Paolo
							50·4 (25)			25·0°	4·5%				

NAME OF COMPANY ADDRESS	Gauge ft. in. (metres)	Route length incl. E=Electrified miles (km.)	Track length incl. E=Electrified miles (km.)	Elect. system and type of conductor	Loco-motives L=Line S=Shunt Steam Electric Diesel De=elec. Dh=hyd.		Rail-cars Electric Diesel Trailer Railbus Multiple Unit set		Pass. train cars	Freight train cars Con-tainers	Total Volume carried. Thous-ands of tonnes	Av'ge haul per ton miles (km.)	Av'ge net train load tonnes	Max. trailing load tonnes	Total number carried in 1 000s	Aver-age jour-ney miles (km.)
ITALY *(contd.)*																
Ferrovie del Sud-est, SpA Via Ravenna 14, Rome *Local Office: 70122 Bari*	4' 8½'' (1·435)	294 (473)	342 (550)		DeL DhL DhS	13 1 5	D T	42 24	30	279	170·3	23·2 (37·3)	82	900	7 160·5	15·1 (24·4)
Ferrovia Suzzara-Ferrara Corso Porta Reno 65, Ferrara	4' 8¹¹/₁₆'' (1·440)	51 (81)	59 (95)		DhL DhS	2 2	D T	20 7		22	57·1	18·6 (30)	50	800	937·9	28 (45)
S.A. It. Ferrort amviaria Via Napoli 161, Bari	4' 8½'' (1·435)	E 5 (8)	E 5 (8)	1 200 V dc	D	1	E	2	4	10	1·3				311·1	
Ferrovia Elettrica Transatesina Corso Italia 30, Bolzano	4' 8½'' (1·435)	E 8 (13)	E 10 (16)	1 350 V dc			E	4	8	11	14·4				699·1	
Ferrovie Torino Nord Corso Giulio Cesare 15, Turin	4' 8⅞'' (1·445)	55 (88) E 27 (43)	68 (110) E 35 (56)	4 000 V dc	S E	14 5	E D	2 5	32	50	157·4				5 332·4	
SM Strade Ferrate Umbro Aretine Largo Cacciatori delle Alpi, Perugia	4' 8½'' (1·435)	E 59 (95)	E 67 (107)	3 000 V dc	S De	12 1	E ET	2 9	13	78	72·5	3 187 308 ton-km			5 907·2†	10 (16)
Ferrovia Elettrica Val di Fiemme Bolzano	3' 3⅜'' (1·00)	E 31 (50)	E 37 (59)	2 400 V dc	E	3	E	3	6	92	8·0				183·5	
Ferrovia Valle Caudina Soc. Italiana Strade Ferrate Sovvenzionate, Benevento	4' 8½'' (1·435)	30 (48)	32 (51)		S D	4 1	D	8	16	38	7·5				983·2	
Societa Veneta Autoferrovie Via Enrico degli Scrovegni 1, Padova *Operates 3 lines:*	4' 8½'' (1·435)	76 (122)	81 (1·30)		DeL DhL DS	7 1 2	RD	14	12		84·2	1 729 207 ton-km			1 494·2	
Udine	4' 8½'' (1·435)	22 (36)	24 (39)		SL DeL	5 1	D	3	7	9	39·8	9·3 (15)	60	380	697·4	8·7 (14)
Piove di Sacco	4' 8½'' (1·435)	36 (58)	42 (67)		SL DeL	2 3	D	5	20	44	40·5	6·8 (11)	100	380	1 170·8	12·4 (20)
Bologna	4' 8½'' (1·435)	46 (74)	55 (89)		SL DL DeL	3 1 3	D DT	6 3	21	59	81·3	11·2 (18)	150	380	1 031·0	11·2 (18)
Societá Veneta per Imprese e Costruzioni Pubbliche Via Enrico depli Scrovegni 1, Padova. Local Office: Parma	1·435	44	50		De	2	D	5	4		17·8	404 128 tonne-km			729·3	
IVORY COAST																
*****Regie des Chemins de Fer Abidjan-Niger** PO Box 1394, Abidjan	3' 3⅜'' (1·000)	730 (1 173)	817 (1 318)		D	63	D T	18 33	87	1 247	962	200-650		1 800	2 828	63 (102)
JAMAICA																
*****Jamaica Railway Corporation** PO Box 489, 142 Barry Street, Kingston	4' 8½'' (1·435)	205 (330)	228 (367)		DeL Dh	23 2	D T	6 11	23	382	4 009·5				1 106·0	29 (46)
Alpart Railway Alumina Partners of Jamaica Spur Tree	4' 8½'' (1·435)	11 (18)	13 (21)		DeL DeS	4 1				343	1 500·0	11 (18)	1 200			
Kaiser Bauxite Company Discovery Bay	4' 8½'' (1·435)	16 (25)	23 (37)		DeL DeS	4 2				88	5 000·0	11 (18)	1 700			
JAPAN																
*****Japanese National Railways** 1-6-5 Marunouchi, Chiyoda-ku, Tokyo	3' 6'' (1·067)	13 232 (21 307) E 4 988 (8 032)	25 426 (40 927) E 11 888 (19 132)	20 000 V 1/50 & 1/60; 600 V & 1 500 V dc OH	E D	1 978 2 160	E D	14 899 5 233	6 567	101 042 C 47 774	133 342	40 412 000 000 ton-km			6 996 000	17·4 (28·0)
Hanshin Electric Railway Co Ltd 8 Umeda-cho, Kita-Ku, Osaka	4' 8½'' (1·435)	E 45 (72)	E 105 (169)	600 V dc OH			E T EMU	265 45 28	7						226 129·4	6·6 (10·6)
Jozankei Railway Co 108, 9-chome, 3-Jou, Toyohira, Sapporo City	3' 6'' (1·067)	E 17 (27)	E 67 (108)	1 500 V dc OH	E	2		24	29	52·2	7·3 (4·3)		510	1 752·6	7 (12)
Hankyu Corporation 8-8 Kakuta-cho, Kitaku, Osaka	4' 8½'' (1·435)	E 88 (141)	E 171 (276)	1 500 dc OH	EL 2		E ET	684 512	28			21 551 600 train-km			696 718·1	8·4 (13·6)
Keihin Electric Express Railway Co 17 Shiba Takanawa-Minami-cho, Minato-ku, Tokyo	4' 8½'' (1·435)	E 50 (80)	E 114 (183)	1 500 V dc OH	E	120		443	24						173 565·0	7 (12)
Kei-Hin Electric Railway Co Tenmabashi, Higashi-ku, Osaka	4' 8½'' (1·435)	E 55 (88)	E 124 (200)	600 V dc OH			E ET	324 312	402						172 529·8	7·8 (12·6)
Kei-Sei Electric Railway Co Gojo-machi, Taito-ku, Tokyo	4' 6'' (1·372)	E 52 (83)			E	2	E T	103 155	16							

* See main entry
† Total for combined rail and bus services

Average Speeds			Financial Data		Couplers	Buffers	Rails	Sleepers (crossties)		Curvature max.	Gradient max. (U=not compensated)	Axle load max.	Altitude max.	Staff employed. Total no. (inclu. workshop)	Names of officials. Extended lists can be found at the end of the individual country in the report section immediately following
Freight Train	Pass. Train	Speed max.	Revenue Expenses	Braking (continuous)	Type and Height above rail	Centres and Height above rail	Weight	Type and thickness	Spacing Number per mile (per km) or centres						
mph (km/hr)	mph (km/hr)	mph (km/hr)	in 1 000s		ins (mm)	ins (mm)	lb. per yd (kg/m)	ins (mm)	ins (mm)			tonnes	feet (m)		
15·5 (25)	30 (50)	56 (90)		Air W'hse Breda	Standard	Standard	73/55 (36/27)	Wood 5½ (140)	29½" (750)	7·0°	1·3% 2·4% U		1 486 (453)	2 500 (250)	Ing. Renato De Marco Ing. Guglielmo Zoldester
15·5 (25)	32 (52)	56 (90)	L. 533 934·0 1 024 000·7	W'hse Air	Standard	Standard	101/55 (50/27·6)	Wood 5½ (140) Conc.	29½" (750)	3·8°	1·0%	14·5	80 (24·5)	149 (35)	Dr. Ing. Luciano Puccetti
							54·5 (27)			17·5°	2·9%				
										14·5°	6·2%				
										8·7°	E 3·5% S 1·8%				
19 (31)	25 (41)	31 (50)	L. 4 978 821·1 5 167 231·8	W'hse Air	Standard	Standard	73/55	Oak 5½ (140)	28¼ (720)	5·9°	0·8% 0·2% U	16	1 380 (420)	460 (195)	Ing. Raffaele Roasali Ing. Carlo Simoncelli
							44·4 (22)			29·5°	4·4%				
							72·6 (36)			5·8°	2·0%				
28 (45)	46 (75)	46 (75)	L. 831 603 3 727 738	W'hse Air	Standard	Standard	70/75 (30/36)	Wood 6 (150)	984 ft (750 m)	7·0°	0·7%	20	130	192	Pres: Dr. T. Calore
		43 (70)		W'hse Air	Standard	Standard	60 (30)	Wood (140)	31½" (800)	7·0°	1·6% U	15	1 191 (363)	63 (26)	
		43 (70)		W'hse Air	Standard	Standard	60 (30)	Wood (140)	33⅞" (860)	5·8°	1·2% U	15	16 (5)	137 (49)	
		47 (75)		W'hse Air	Standard	Standard	60 (30)	Wood (140)	33½" (850)	11·7°	1·0% U	15	171 (52)	50 (38)	
45	75	75	L 292 841 1 372 466	W'hse Air	Standard	Standard	36	Wood (140)	750	7·0°	0·8%	20	59		Gen. Man.: Dr. Ing. U. Polettini
			F. 6 170 000 6 060 000	Willison auto All 29¾ (755)								A. 1·0 B. 2·5	A. 15 B. 13		
	23 (37)	40 (25)	$J 6 262·0 7 296·0	W'hse Air	AAR 34½ (876)		80/60 (40/30)	Wood & Conc. 6 (153)	26" (660)	300 ft (92 m)	3·0% U	17	1 705 (443)	1 454 (235)	Chairman: John Allgrove Gen. Man: A. B. Tapper
15 (24)	20 (32)			Air W'hse	Type E AAR 34½ (876)		106/90 (53/45)	Wood 7 (178)	22" (560)	886 ft (270 m)	2·2%	31·5	700 (213)	36	Gen. Man: Noel Choplin
20 (32)	25 (40)			Air W'hse	Type F AAR Standard		115 (57)	Wood 7 (178)	22" (560)	886 ft (270 m)	3·0%	32	1 600 (488)		
Express 32 (52) Local 17 (28)	Express 46 (74) Local 27 (44)	75 (120)		Air; Nippon ABC; Mitsubishi Electric	Auto 34⅔ (880)	None	101·8/ 60·6 (50·4/ 30·1)	Wood 5½ (140) Conc 6½ (170)	Track Class (1) 22⅞ (580) (2) 26 (660) (3) 26 (660) (4) 27⅛ (690)	Track Class (1) 800 m (2) 600 m (3) 400 m (4) 300 m	Track Class (1) 1·0% (2) 1·0% (3) 2·0% (4) 2·5%	18	4 511 (1 375)	426 697 (25 942)	President: Famio Takagi
	100·9 (162·2)	130 (210)		Air	Auto 33⅜ (1 000)		123/107 (60·8/ 53·8)	Conc 7½ (190)	2 780 (1 725)	8 200 ft (2 500 m)	1·5%	16	571 (174)		
		68 (110)	Yen 10 778 619·3 8 652 990·8	Air Electro Magnet	Van Dorn 25⅜ (645)		101/60 (50/30)	Wood 6 (150) & Conc	2 480/ 2 400 (1 540/ 1 490)	11·0°	3·03%	13	62 (19)	3 291 (557)	Gen. Man: Chuziro Noda
16·2 (26·1)	24 (39)	43 (70)	Yen 124 406·0 300 738·0	Air Mitsubishi	(Sibata) 32 (830)		60 (30)	Wood 8¼ 322	26¼" (690)	11·0°	3·3%	14·4	912 (278)	904 (150)	Gen. Man: Tadao Ebina
	46 (74)	68 (110)	Yen 51 208 000·0 45 151 000·0	Air	Auto 34¼ (880)		60/112 (30/60)	Wood 6 (150) Conc	2 560 (1 600)	17·5°	4·0%	17·78	368 (112)	5 894	Pres: Sadao Shibatani
34 (55)	27* (43)	65 (105)	Yen 8 429 031·1 6 179 036·1	Air AMM Elec HSCD	NCB 34¼ (870)	Crs 54 (1 435) Ht. 43 (70)	101 (50)	Wood 5½ (140)	23" (580)	15·9°	2·0% 3·05% U	12	312 (96)	5 300 (600)	Gen. Man: Haruo Sato
	Express 33 (54) Local 25 (41)	Keihan 62 (100) Oten Line 37 (60)		Air	Auto 31 (790)		100/60 (50/30)	Wood 6 (150) Conc	(1 680– 1 800)	Keihan 14·3° Oten 56·0°	Keihan 3·3% Oten 6·67%	15·5	626 (191)	3 142 (433)	Gen. Man: Shiro Muraoka
				Air	Auto		101 (50)	Wood 6 (150)	27½" (700)	14·6°	4·0%				

* Excludes special express trains: 38 mph (61 km/h) and ordinary express trains: 32 mph (52 km/h)

NAME OF COMPANY ADDRESS	Gauge ft. in. (metres)	Route length incl. E=Electrified miles (km.)	Track length incl. E=Electrified miles (km.)	Elect. system and type of conductor	Locomotives L=Line S=Shunt Steam Electric Diesel De=elec. Dh=hyd.		Rail-cars Electric Diesel Trailer Railbus Multiple Unit set		Pass. train cars	Freight train cars Containers	Total Volume carried. Thousands of tonnes	Av'ge haul per ton miles (km.)	Av'ge net train load tonnes	Max. trailing load tonnes	Total number carried in 1000s	Average journey miles (km.)
JAPAN *(contd.)*																
Kinki Nippon Railway Company (Kintetsu Corporation) 581, 6-chome, Uehommachi, Tennoji-ku, Osaka 543	4' 8½'' (1·435) 3' 6'' (1·067) 2' 6'' (0·762)	E 364 (586)	E 711 (1 129)	750 & 1 500 V dc OH	E	13	E T	865 725		94	325·5	18 705 889 ton-km			727 071·1	
Nagano Electric Railway Gondo-cho 2201, Nagano City Nagano	3' 6'' (1·067)	E 44 (71)	E 58 (94)	1 500 V dc OH	EL	3	E ET	47 5		3	77·6	15·6 (25·1)	2 597 548 ton-km	400	14 734·0	9·3 (15)
Nagoya Railroad Co 1-223, Sasashima-cho, Nakamura-ku, Nagoya City	3' 6'' (1·067)	E 325 (523)	487 (785)	600 & 1 500 V dc OH	EL ES DhS	14 2 5	E D ET	521 12 171		75	539·2	7 358 037 ton-km			369 692·8	9·8 (15·8)
Nara Electric Railway Co 184 Mikanomija Monzen, Fushimi-ky, Kyoto	4' 8½'' (1·435)	E 35 (56)		600 V dc OH												
Nishi Nippon Railroad Co 11-17 Tenjin 1-chome, Fukuoka City, Fukuoka	4' 8½'' (1·435) 3' 6'' (1·067)	E 59 (95) E 13 (21)	E 122 (196)	1 500 V and 600 V dc	ES	1	E T	163 88							106 000·0	
Odakyu Electric Railway Co 2-28-12, Yoyogi, Shibuya-ku, Tokyo	3' 6'' (1·067)	E 69 (111)	E 160 (257)	1 500 V dc OH	EL ES	4 1	E T	400 212		33	1 410·7	18·9 (30·4)	660		400 137·0	10·1 (16·1)
Seibu Railway Co 16-15, 1-chome, Minami-Ikebukuro, Toshima-ku, Tokyo 171	3' 6'' (1·067)	111 (179) E 109 (175)	227 (366) E 224 (361)	1 500 V dc OH	EL DS Bat	15 1 6	E T	349 343	25	308	1 231·0	25 (40)	300	600	471 192·0	7·1 (11·4)
Takamatsu Kotohira Electric RR Co 320 Sakuramachi, Takamatsu City	4' 8½'' (1·435)	E 37 (66)	E 42 (68)	1 500 & 600 V dc OH			E	51							12 717·9	6 (9)
Tobu Railway Co. 2/1, 1-chome, Oshiage, Sumida-ku, Tokyo	3' 6'' (1·067)	301 (485) E 295 (474)	593 (955) E 587 (945)	1 500 V dc OH	E	43	E ET D	613 442 3		784	6 638·0	25 (40)	140	500	568 832·0	8·7 (14)
Tokyu Corporation 26-20 Sakuragoka- Cho, Shibuya-ku, Tokyo 150	3' 6'' (1·067)	E 55 (88)	E 113 (182)	1 500 V dc			E	683							59 664 894 pass-km	
JORDAN *Hedjaz Jordan Railway PO Box 582, Amman Note: This is the Jordanian section of the Hedjaz Railway which runs from Damascus (Syria) to Ma'an. The continuation from Ma'an to Medina (Saudi Arabia) is being rebuilt.*	3' 5⅜'' (1·050)	310 (500)	350 (550)		SL SS DeL	13 2 5	D T	2 24	6	330	56·0	28 210 800 ton-km			7·0	
KAMPUCHEA *Phnom-Penh*	3' 3⅜'' (1·00)	(1 800)	403 (649)		SL DeL DeS	24 13 10			67	688	117·4	11 512 900 ton-km			1 027	
KOREA *Korean National Railroad 168 Bongrae-Doug, Jung-ku, Operates all lines in South Korea; no information available regarding railways in North Korea.*	4' 8½'' (1·435) 2' 6'' (0·762)	2 323 (3 744) 125 (78)	2 448 (3 822)		S De E	68 306 90	D E	122 171	1 785	16 208	31 550·9	7 841 000 000 ton-km			131 001·0	45 (72)
LEBANON *C.F. de l'Etat Libanais PO Box 109, Souk el Arwam, Beirut*	4' 8½'' (1·435) 3' 5¼'' (1·050)	208 (335) 51† (82)	300 (483)		SL SS DeL	14 18 6			15	881	659·8	45 (72)	350		72·6	71 (114)
LIBERIA *Lamco J. V. Operating Co Roberts International Airport*	4' 8½'' (1·435)	167 (270)	205 (330)		DeL DeS	14 10	D	5		591	9 080·0	2 360 000 000 ton-km	8 100		40·0	168 (270)
Bong Mining Co PO Box 538, Monrovia	4' 8½'' (1·435)	48 (78)	57 (92)		DeL DhS	4 6	D	2		219	7 200		3 250	3 200		
LUXEMBOURG *Soc. Nat. des C.F. Luxembourgeois 9, Place de la Gare*	4' 8½'' (1·435)	168 (271) E 86 (138)	415 (668) E 213 (344)	3 000 V dc OH and 25 000 V 1/50 OH	EL DeL DhL	19 151 16	D DMU C	17 9 207	77	3 419		865 993 000 ton-km			13 391·6	12·4 (19·9)
MADAGASCAR *Reseau National des C.F. Malagasy Ave de l'Indépendance, Antananarivo*	3' 3⅜'' (1·00)	548 (883)	—		DeL DeS	31 32	D	13	112	1 049	953	258 500 000 ton-km			296 390	

* See main entry
† Of which 20 miles (*32 km*) are rack-rail ABT system

Freight Train mph (km/hr)	Pass. Train mph (km/hr)	Speed max. mph (km/hr)	Revenue Expenses in 1 000s	Braking (continuous)	Couplers Type and Height above rail ins (mm)	Buffers Centres and Height above rail ins (mm)	Rails Weight lb. per yd (kg/m)	Sleepers Type and thickness ins (mm)	Spacing Number per mile (per km) or centres ins (mm)	Curvature max.	Gradient max. (U=not compensated)	Axle load max. tonnes	Altitude max. feet (m)	Staff employed. Total no. (inclu. workshop)	Names of officials
	46 (75)	68 (110)	Yen 101 921 808 / 81 443 928	Air AMA NAB	Sumitomo Tightlock 340 (880)		101/75 (50/37)	Wood 6 (150)	19⅝" (500)	11·5°	3·5% / 3·3% U	18	1 187 (362)	12 600	Chairman: Isamu Saheki President: Eizo Imazato
21 (33)	Express 33 (53) Local 25 (40)	56 (90)	Yen 2 221 071 / 2 516 591	Air dynam	Auto 34⅝ (880)		80/60 (40/30)	Wood 5½ (140)	30⅜/15 (770/380)	8·75°	4·0%	13	2 129 (649)	514 (69)	Pres: M. Miyazawa
21·1 (34)	Express 46 (74) Local 25 (40)	68 (110)	Yen 34 884 573·0 / 29 515 904·0	Air dynam	Auto 34⅝ (880)		100 (50)	Wood 5½ (140)	19⅝" (500)	10·9°	3·5%	13		4 107	President: Kotaro Takeda
		59 (95)	Yen 5 086 000·0 / 4 784 000·0	W'hse AMAR-D AMM-R	Tomlinson Tightlock (648/880)		101/60 (50/30)	Wood 5½ (140) Conc	26" (660)	Rad 558 ft (170 m)	3·3% U	12	1 075 (146)		President: Hirotsugu Yoshimoto
20 (32)	Express 42·5 (68·4) Local 53 (85)	Express 68 (110)	Yen 16 229 000·0 / 13 080 000·0	Air dynamic regen	Auto (880)		100 (50)	Wood 5½ (140) Conc 6¼ (160)	2 640 (1 640)	8·75°	2·5%	15	564 (171·9)	3 592 (420)	Pres: Soh Hirota Man. Dirs: Y. Hayashi H. Miki
20 (32)	Express 33 (54) Other 29 (47)	56 (90)	Yen 15 630 000·0 / 12 380 000·0	Air Tokorozawa	Auto 34⅝ (880)		101/75 (50/37)	Wood 5½ (140)	28" (710)	11·0°	2·5% U 3·5%	12	377 (115)	3 631	President: Shojiro-Kojima
					Auto (880)		60 (30)	Wood 5½ (140)	2 570 (1 600)	22·0°	2·5% U	9			
20 (32)	40 (65)	68 (110)	Yen 20 278 251·0 / 20 802 039·0	Air Nippon A.B. Co	Auto 34⅝ (880)		100/60 (50/30)	Wood 5½ (140) Conc	29½/24" (750/620)	19·1°	2·5% / 3·3% U	12·7	1 772 (540)	16 712	Gen. Man: Kaichiro Nezu
	Express (51) Slow (41)	Express (90) Slow (85)	Yen 25 395 000 / 23 093 000	Air Nippon AMA & HSC	Auto 34⅝ (880)		100 (50)	Wood 5½ (140) Conc	22" (575)	525 ft (160 m)	3·5%	15·5	226 (69)	2 934 (319)	Gen. Man: Seija Egawa
19 (30)	25 (40)	31 (50)	JD 368 881 / 369 745	Vac	Screw 29 (740)	Centre 29 (740)	43 (21·5)	Steel	27½" (700)	328 ft (100 m)	1·7% / 2·0% U	10·5	5 059 (1 542)	686 (196)	Gen. Man: Mohammad R. Qoseini
			$C 265 118 / 411 966												Pres: In Nhel
16 (25)	25 (40)	68 (110)	Won 33 514 / 33 514	Air	Auto 34⅝ (880)	AAR	101/60 (50/30)	Wood 7 (180) 6 (150) Conc 7¼ (185)	Wood 22" (560) Conc 25" (630)	4·25°	2·5% U	18·0	2 319 (707)	39 776 (32 348)	Director General: Kim, Jai Hyun
23 (45)	23 (45)	34 (55)		Air & Vac. Oerlikon Knorr, Jourdain Monneret	Jourdain Monneret		75/60 (37/30)	Conc. 82 (220) Wood 5 (130) Metal 138 (223)		8·0% (1 435 m) 17·5% (1·05 m)	7·0% (Rack) 2·0% U	16 (1 435 m) 13 (1·05 m)	4 879 (1 487)	1 305	Dir. Gen: M. Antoine Barouki
Loaded 30 (49) Empty 33·6 (54)	50 (80)	Loaded 37 (60) Empty 43 (70)		Knorr Air	Type F AAR 36 (914)		132 (65·5)	Wood 7 (180)	21½" (545)	1 640 ft (500 m)	Loaded 0·5% Empty 1·7%	30	1 853 (565)	294	Man: H. N. Bas Koenen Chief Eng. (Operations): Brian R. Hughes Chief Eng. (Maintenance) Björn Ekrem
19 (30)	43 (70)		£L 120 000	Knorr Air	Scharfenberg rotary		98 (49)	Wood 6¼ (160) Steel	25" (630)	3 280 ft (1 000 m)	0·25% / 1·0% U	25	492 (150)	100	Supt: Karl Gouase
37 (60)	50 (80)	68 (110)	Fr. 4 220 220·5 / 4 377 325·7	Air W'hse Knorr Oerlikon	Standard	Standard	108/92 (54/46)	Wood 6 (150) Conc 8¼ (210)	24½/25½" (620/650)	Main 984 ft (300 m) Branch 820 ft (230 m)	1·5%	22	1 640 (500)	4 323 (934)	Gen. Man: Justin Kohl
20 (32)	25 (40)	37 (60)	Fmg. 3 823 / 3 756	Air	—	—	—	Wood/Steel	1 250/1 800 per/km	164 ft (50 m)	3·5%	12·5	1 684 m	4 675	Gen. Man: Adolphe Rakotoarivony

NAME OF COMPANY ADDRESS	Gauge ft. in. (metres)	Route length incl. E=Electrified miles (km.)	Track length incl. E=Electrified miles (km.)	Elect. system and type of conductor	Locomotives L=Line S=Shunt Steam Electric Diesel De=elec. Dh=hyd.	Rail-cars Electric Diesel Trailer Railbus Multiple Unit set	Pass. train cars	Freight train cars	Freight movement: Total Volume carried. Containers / Thousands of tonnes	Av'ge haul per ton miles (km.)	Av'ge net train load tonnes	Max. trailing load tonnes	Passengers Total number carried in 1 000s	Average journey miles (km.)
MALAWI *Malawi Railways Ltd., Central Africa Railway Co. Ltd. PO Box 5144, Limbe	3' 6" (1·067)	420 (677)	451 (727)		DeL 14 DhS 5 DhL 11	D	2	23	649					45·8 (73·7)
MALAYSIA *Malayan Railway Administration PO Box No. 1, Kuala Lumpur	3' 3⅜" (1·00)	1 035 (1 665)	1 338 (2 153)		SL 84 DL 91 DS 41	D 26 T 15	375	6 450	4 500	1 164 200 000 ton-km			598 700 000 pass-km	66·2 (106·5)
MALI *Regie du C.F. du Mali BP 260, Bamako	3' 3⅜" (1·000)	399 (642)	426 (685)		DeL 15 DeS 7	D 3 T 28	24	330	291·5	299 (481)	250	800	624·3	78 (126)
MAURITANIA *C.F. Mauritania Head office: SA des Mines de Fer de Mauritanie Rue La Boétie 87, Paris 8e, France Local office: PO Box 42, Nouadhibov	4' 8½" (1·435)	404 (650)	454 (730)		DeL 26 DeS 11			1 084	8 750·0	401 (645)	13 400	18 500		
MEXICO *F.C. Nacionales de Mexico Avenida Central No. 140 Col. Guerrero, Mexico DF3	4' 8½" (1·435) 3' 0" (0·914)	8 636 (13 901) 191 (309)			DeL 975 DeS 124	D	38	663	32 122 56 225·0		25 647 000 train-km		22 218·0	
F.C. de Chihuahua al Pacifico de C.V. PO Box 46, Chihuahua, Chih.	4' 8½" (1·435)	941 (1 515)	1 083 (1 742)		DeL 54 DeS 5	D	13	65	2 057 2 510·0	228 (367)	570		602·0	137 (221)
F.C. Coahuila y Zacatecas, AG Apartado 116, Saltillo, Coah.	3' 0" (0·914)	101 (162)	120 (193)		De 3		6	164						
Cia. del F.C. Inter-California Mexicali, B. CFA	4' 8½" (1·435)	52 (84)	72 (116)		D 2									
F.C. Mexicano del Pacifico PO Box 14, Los Mochis, Sinaloa	4' 8½" (1·435)	10 (16)	10 (16)		S 3			13						
F.C. Occidental de Mexico Culiacan, Sinaloa	4' 8½" (1·435)	19 (31)	24 (38)		S† 2			40						
F.C. del Pacifico, SA de CV 15-M, Guadalajara, Jalisco	4' 8½" (1·435)	1 359 (2 279)	1 699 (2 733)		DeL 108 DeS 15	R	6	162	4 256 7 128·1	395 (640)	1 005	1 984	1 740·1	449 (722)
F.C. Industrial el Potosi y Chihuahua AP 13, Chihuahua, Chih	4' 8⅜" (1·435)	E 14 (22)	E 17 (27)	600 V dc OH	EL 5	E 110		12		9 (14·5)	180	300		
F.C. Sonora-Baja California Ulises Irigoyen Final, Mexicali, BC,	4' 8½" (1·435)	376 (605)	437 (703)		DeL 16		34	109	713	294 959 733 ton-km			513	164 (264)
F.C. del Sureste Merged into F.C. Unidos del Sureste, September 1968														
F.C. Unidos del Sureste Av. Colon 212, Coatzacacos, Veracruz	4' 8½" (1·435) 3' 0" (0·914)	576 (927) 262 (422)	628 (1 011) 272 (438)		DeL 18 DeS 6 DeL 6 DeS 3	De 1	68 42	848 136	839·0	236 (380)	929	3 000	2 348·5	61·9 (99·6)
F.C. Unidos de Yucatan Merged into F.C. Unidos del Sureste, Sept. 1968	4' 8½" (1·435) 3' 0" (0·914)													
MONGOLIA Mongolian State Railways Ulan-Bator	5' 0" (1·524) 4' 8½" (1·435)	868 (1 397)												
MOROCCO *Office National des CF du Maroc 19 Avenue Allal Ben Abdallah, Rabat	4' 8½" (1·435)	1 091 (1 756) E 440 (708)		3 000 V dc OH	EL 57 DeL 82 DS 46	DMU 4	221		3 143 175 000 ton-km		1 090	4 000	4 128·0	87·9 (141·5)
Also operates: Cie. Franco-Espanole des C.F. de Tanger a Fez				Included in C. F. du Maroc										
C.F. de la Mediterranee au Niger	4' 8½" (1·435)	170 (273)			D 5	D		300						
MOZAMBIQUE *Caminhos de Ferro de Mozambique C.P. No. 276, Maputo	3' 6" (1·067) 2' 5½" (0·75)	1 857 (2 999) 92 (148)	2 355 (3 791)		S 84 DeL 32 DhL 5 DhS 6	D	11	188			1 000	2 200	4 746	32 (52)
Trans-Zambesia Railway Co., Ltd. C.P. 61, Beira	3' 6" (1·067)	180 (289)	195 (316)		SL 9 DeL 15 DhS 3	D	2	11	459 1 510·6	147 (236)	642	1 900	437·7	83·3 (134)

* See main entry
† Oil burning

Average Speeds			Financial Data	Braking (continuous)	Couplers	Buffers	Rails	Sleepers (crossties)		Curvature max.	Gradient max. (U=not compensated)	Axle load max.	Altitude max.	Staff employed. Total no. (inclu. workshop)	Names of officials. Extended lists can be found at the end of the individual country in the report section immediately following
Freight Train	Pass. Train	Speed max.	Revenue Expenses		Type and Height above rail	Centres and Height above rail	Weight	Type and thickness	Spacing Number per mile (per km) or centres ins (mm)						
mph (km/hr)	mph (km/hr)	mph (km/hr)	in 1 000s		ins (mm)	ins (mm)	lb. per yd (kg/m)	ins (mm)				tonnes	feet (m)		
24 (38)	24 (38)	35 (56)	MK 7 573 6 244	Vac D & M	Auto AAR E.S.C. 34 (864)		80/40 (40/20)	Wood 5 (127); steel; conc.	32½" (826)	363 ft (111 m)	2·5% U	16·5	3 805 (1 160)	3 597 (693)	Gen. Man: G. G. Geddes
	45 (72)	60 (96)	$M 75 540 000 84 150 000	W'hse Vac	Type M.C.A. 22¾ (578)	Buffer-coupler	80/60 (40/30)	Wood 5 (127)	30" (762)	11·1°	1·75% U	16	412 (126)	13 386 (2 193)	Gen. Man: Waad bin Jamaluddin
15 (24)	28 (46)	46 (75)	F.M. 3 771 000 3 478 000	Air W'hse	Unic Oferom	Crs. 49¼ (1 250) Ht. 29¾ (755)	60 (30)	Metal	2 400 (1 500)	948 ft (300 m)	2·4% 2·6% U	15	1 463 (446)	1 605 (360)	Gen. Man: Djibril Diallo
24 (38)	Loaded 31 (50) Empty 37 (60)			Knorr Air	Willison Auto. 36 (920)		109 (54)	Steel UIC28 Wood 6 (150)	23⅝" (600)	3 280 ft (1 000 m)	0·5% (loaded) 1·0% U (empty)	25	1 148 (350)	1 240 (500)	Man: Jean Audibert
12 (25)	28 (46)	62 (100)		Air W'hse	AAR		100/115	Wood	1 859	14°	4·0%	30	3 174 m	62 493	Gen. Dir: Luis Gómez Zepeda
22 (35)	31 (50)	37 (60)		W'hse	AAR		60/40 (30/20)	Wood 6 (153)	20" (508)	10·3°	4·0%				Gen. Man: Ing. Alfredo Magallanes R
							90/62 (45/31)	Wood 7 (178)	22" (559)	7·5°		31			
							60/56 (30/28)	Wood 6 (153)			1·5%			15	Pres: Ing. Mario Zamora Cortes
								Wood 8 (203)	20" (508)	2·3°	0·5%				Pres: E. Batiz
21 (34)	32 (52)	59 (95)	$ Mex 518 055 819 712	W'hse Air	Type E 34½ (876)		112/100 (56/50)	Wood 7 (178)	21½" (546)	8·0°	2·6%	11	5 268 (1 606)	6 798 (1 388)	Gen. Man: Luis Gomez Zepeda
9 (15)		11 (18)		W'hse Air	Auto 18 (457)		45 (22·3)	Wood 6 (153)	24" (610)	58·0°	3·77% U	15	6 138 (1 871)	25 (6)	Gen. Man: John A. Engstrom
29·1 (46·9)	38·2 (61·5)	P. 43 (70) F. 56 (90)	$ Mex 87 327·0 141 559·0	W'hse Air	AAR 34½" (876)		90/80 (45/40)	Wood 7 (178)	20" (508)	6·0°	0·7% 1·3% U		2 345 (715)	1 374 (366)	Gen. Man: Ing. R. I. Hernandez
17·7 (28·5)	32·7 (52·6)	53 (85)		W'hse Air	AAR 34½" (876)		90/70 (45/35)	Wood 7 (178)	3 200 (2 000)	8·0°	1·12%	30	459 (140)	3 373 (532)	Gen. Man: Ing. Gelasio Luna y Luna
25 (40)	45 (72)	DMU 72 (115)	(DH millions) 302·52 349·15	Air W'hse	Standard European	Standard European	111/73 (55/36)	Wood 6 (150) Metal conc	1 880- 2 770 (1 166- 1 722)	984 ft (300 m)	1·23% 1·5% U	22	4 288 (1 306)	8 455	Dir. General: Moussa Moussaoui
25 (40)	37 (60)	50 (80)		Vac W'hse	Atlas and Alliance	35¼ (896)	90/60 (45/30)	Wood 5⅛ (130)	2 400 (1 500)	984 ft (300 m)	2·0% 1·8% U	18	4 468 (1 362)	34 275	Gen. Man: Eng. L. M. Alcantara Santos
24 (39)	33 (54)	50 (80)	Esc. 2 351 286 1 454 297	Vac W'hse	Alliance English Steel Co. 33½ (850)		75/40 (37/20)	Wood 5 (127) steel	2 350- 2 080 (1 460- 1 300)	800 ft (244 m)	1·1% U	16	1 188 (362)	1 764 (313)	Exec. Man. (Beira): Eng Fernando Teixeira

NAME OF COMPANY ADDRESS	Gauge ft. in. (metres)	Route length incl. E=Electrified miles (km.)	Track length incl. E=Electrified miles (km.)	Elect. system and type of conductor	Locomotives L=Line S=Shunt Steam Electric Diesel De=elec. Dh=hyd.	Rail-cars Electric Diesel Trailer Railbus Multiple Unit set	Pass. train cars	Freight train cars / Containers	Freight movement Total Volume carried. Thousands of tonnes	Av'ge haul per ton miles (km.)	Av'ge net train load tonnes	Max. trailing load tonnes	Passengers Total number carried in 1000s	Average journey miles (km.)
NEPAL														
*Nepal Government Railway Birganj, PO Raxaul, Dist. Champaran (via India)	2' 6'' (0·762)	6·2 (10)	32 (51)		S 4		1	18	50·0	29 (46)	130	200	250·0	25 (40)
*Nepal Jaynagar-Janakpur Railway Jaynagar (Darbhanga) via India	2' 6'' (0·762)	33 (53)	40 (64)		SL 9		15	60	9·1		100	250	306·0	11·5 (18·5)
NETHERLANDS														
*N.V. Nederlandse Spoorwegen NS Moreelsepark, Utrecht	4' 8½'' (1·435)	1 758 (2 825) E 1 091 (1 754)	4 440 (7 146) E 2 368 (3 812)	1 500 V dc OH	EL 112 DeL 249 DeS 218	E † 33 De 30 EMU 549 DMU 86	297	15 663 C 575						26·4 (42·5)
Hoogovens Steel Works Koninklijke Nederlandsche Hoogovens en Staalfabrieken NV Hoogovens, Ijmuiden	4' 8½'' (1·435)	104 (167)	132† (214)		S 2 DhS 26 DeS 20		5	1 140	30 000·0	45 000 000 ton-km				
NEW ZEALAND														
*New Zealand Government Railways Bunny Street, Wellington	3' 6'' (1·067)	2 809 (4 536) E 62 (100)	4 290 (6 904) E 151 (243)	1 500 V dc OH	S 2 EL 14 DeL 285 DeS 90 DhS 65 DS 36	E 49 ET 79 D 136	412	29 530 C 720	12 577·2	8 382 095 000 ton-km (passenger and freight)			20 035·3	16·4 (26·4)
NZ Forest Products Ltd. Whakatane Board Mills Division Private Bag, Whakatane	3' 6'' (1·067)	7 (11)	14 (22)		DmL 2			NZR Stock	135·0	12 290 000				
Ohai Railway Board PO Wairio	3' 6'' (1·067)	9 (14)	10 (16)		DL		2		300	8 (13)	500	800	3·0	8 (13)
Stuart Chapman Ltd. Ross to Duffers Creek		15 (24)												
NICARAGUA														
F.C. del Pacifico de Nicaragua Apartado Postal No. 5-Managua	3' 6'' (1·067)	217 (350)	240 (387)		DeL 9	D 1	1	185	65·7	9 209 321 tonne-km			537·4	18·6 (30)
NIGERIA														
*Nigerian Railway Corporation Ebute Metta, Lagos	3' 6'' (1·067)	2 178 (3 505)	2 680 (4 313) (3 523)		SL 133 SS 43 DeL 130 DeS 39 DhL 8 DhS 2	D 2	515	4 800					6 219	45 (72·5)
NORWAY														
*Norwegian State Railways Norges Statsbaner (NSB) Storgt. 33, Oslo 1	4' 8½'' (1·435)	2 635 (4 240) E 1 516 (2 440)	3 405 (5 479) E 1 952 (3 141)	15 000 V. 1/16⅔ OH	EL 147 Es 17 DeL 35 DhS 146	E 84 D 45 ET 192 DT 37 EMU 49	843	8 758	26 645·0	2 650 800 000 tonne-km			34 100	37 (60)
Hydro Transport a.s., Rjukanbanen 3661, Rjukan	4' 8½'' (1·435)	E 10 (16)	E 14 (22)	15 000 V. 1/16⅔ OH	EL 4 DhS 3			209	200·9	3 200 000 tonne-km	650			
PAKISTAN														
*Pakistan Railway Shara-e-Sheikh Abdul Hameed Bin Badees, Lahore	5' 6'' (1·676)	4 665 (7 507) E 178 (286)	6 798 (10 940) E 321 (516)	25 000 V 1/50	S 623 D 337 E 29	D 71 DT 117	2 815	35 893			464	2 000		
	3' 3⅜'' (1·00) 2' 6'' (0·762)	277 (446) 380 (612)	343 (552) 453 (729)		S 46 S 41		158 160	1 073 564	11 924·8	388·4 (626·7)	74 50	875 265	131 861·7	46·9 (75·5)
PANAMA														
Chiriqui Land Company Railways Puerto Armuelles Div, Chiriqui (Subsid of United Brands Co)	3' 0'' (0·914)	82 (130)	84 (135)		De 14 Dh 2 D 1	D 9	11	650	27·7	691 900 ton-km			331·0	
Armuelles Division Puerto Armuelles, Chiriqui	3' 0'' (0·914)	78 (126)	104 (167)		De 13 Dm 3	D 3	6	788	4·8	14·1 (22·7)				
Bocas Division Changuinola	3' 0'' (0·914)	60 (96)	160 (257)		DeL 14 DeS 10	D 22	13	508					297·6	
F.C. Nacional de Chiriqui Apartado 12-B, David, Chiriqui	3' 0'' (0·914)	78 (125)	81 (130)		Dh 2 Dm 3	D 4	6	130	14·6				543·6	

* See main entry
† Includes 835 switches

Freight Train mph (km/hr)	Pass. Train mph (km/hr)	Speed max. mph (km/hr)	Revenue Expenses in 1 000s	Braking (continuous)	Couplers Type and Height above rail ins (mm)	Buffers Centres and Height above rail ins (mm)	Rails Weight lb per yd (kg/m)	Sleepers Type and thickness ins (mm)	Sleepers Spacing Number per mile (per km) or centres ins (mm)	Curvature max.	Gradient max. (U=not compensated)	Axle load max. tonnes	Altitude max. feet (m)	Staff employed. Total no. (inclu. workshop)	Names of officials
					A.B.C. 19½-21½		30 (15)	Wood 4½ (115)	(860)	16·0°	1·0% U	14			
10 (16)	15 (24)	20 (32)			A.B.C. 19½-21½	Buffer-coupler	30 (15/12)	Wood 4½ (115)	(925)	4·0°	1·0%	14	1 000 (305)	171 (41)	Gen. Man: Bhuban Bahadur Pradhan
40 (65)	78 (125)	87 (140)	Hfl 1 797 153 / 1 797 153	Air Auto	Standard except trainsets Auto Multi-Servo	Central 68·8 (1 750) Ht 41·6 (1 060)	127/93 (63/46)	Wood 6 (150) and Conc 11½ (290)	Main (2 680) (1 666) Branch 2 150 (1 333) Conc (1 433)	900 ft (275 m)	2·0% 1·43% U	20	597 (182)	27 886 (4 929)	Pres: M. G. de Bruin
9 (15)		19 (30)		Air W'hse.	Atlas (880) SA-3 (1 100)	Crs. 68¾'' (1 750) Ht. 42⅜'' (1 080)	128/98 (64/49)	Oak 6 (150)	21½'' (550)	312 ft (95 m)	2·38%	60	sea level	390	Man Harbours and Transport: T. Ensink Sup Rail Transport: W. A. Salverda
16·70 (26·27)	28·71 (46·19)	Freight Bogie 55 (88) 4-wh. 35 (56) Passenger Train 55 (88) Railcar 60 (96)	$ 170 206·6 / 233 160·1	W'hse. Air	Buffer-coupler 30 (762) Mainly "Norwegian" some Alliance auto.		100/55 (50/28) New rail 91 (45)	Wood Hard 4½ (114) Soft 6 (153) conc. 7 (190)	Main Wood 2 600 (1 625) Conc. 2 112 (1 320) Branch 2 400 (1 500)	Rad. 460 ft (140 m)	Main 3·0% Branch 4·1%	14·5 up to 16 for special wagons, locos	2 671 (814)	20 899 (3 937)	Gen. Man: T. M. Hayward
15 (25)	25 (40)		$ 0 / 116·0	W'hse. Air	NZR standard 25 (648)	25 (648)	55 (27)	Wood 6 (150)	24'' (610)	Rad. 321 ft. (98 m)	1·5%	10	50 (15)	15	Gen. Man: R. C. Sparrow
25 (40)	30 (48)			W'hse. Air	30 (760)	30 (760)	70 (35)	Wood 5 (127)	2 386	230 ft (70 m)	0·66%	14	600 (183)	12 (2)	Directors: R. G. Stark F. J. Gaitt
12 (20)	R'car 28 (46) DeL 22 (35)	R'car 31 (50) DeL 26 (42)	Cordobas 4·3 6·6	Air W'hse.	Type E 28 (711)		60/40 (30/20)	Wood 7 (178)	22'' (560)	Main 10·0° Branch 15·0°	Main 2·8% Branch 3·0% U	12	1 914 (583)	820	Dir. Gen: A. Somoza D.
11·4 (18·3)	12·0 (19·3)	40 (64)	$N 20 860 / 52 542	Vac	ABC Buffer-coupler 34 (864)		80/60 (40/30)	Wood, steel, Conc	2 336- 2 112	575 ft (175 m)	2·0%	Locos 18 Wagons 20	4 496 (1 370)	29 731	Gen. Man.: K. C. Bansal
37 (60)	40 (64)	75 P (120) 56 F (90)	Kroner 1 670 200 / 2 191 300	Air Knorr KE Hildebrand Knorr (Hik)	Standard European 41⅜ (1 050)	Standard European 41⅞ (1 065)	Main 128/72 (64/35) Branch 72/50 (35/25)	Wood 5½ (140) and Conc 6¼ (160)		Main 590 ft (180 m)	Main 2·5% Branch 5·5%	18 (25 on Ofoten line)	4 265 (1 300)	18 323 (2 048)	Gen. Man: R. F. Nordén
27 (43)	34 (55)		Kr. 3 695·5 / 3 265·1	Air Hik KF	Standard	Standard	99 (49)	Wood 5⅛ (130)	2 576 (1 600)	590 ft (180 m)	1·8%	18	995 (303)	51	Ch. Eng: H. Thorbjornsen
10 (16) / 8 (13) 10 (16)	* / 19 (30)	65 (104) / 35 (56) 25 (40)	Rs 726 422·2 / 513 596·8	Vac	BG Screw MG Buffer-Coupler 42½ (1 080)	BG Crs. 77 (1 702) Ht 43½'' (1 105)	100/60 (50/30)	Wood; BG 5'' M & NG 4½'' metal; conc	N+1 to N+8	BG = 10·42° MG = 6·0° NG 2·4°	BG 4·0% MG 0·8% NG 3·5%	BG 22·5 MG 10 NG 7·6	6 398 (1 950) 210 (64) 7 291 (2 222)	134 887	Chairman: A. H. Akhoond Vice-Chairman: K. T. Kidwai
15 (25)	15 (25)	20 (32)	Guavanies 247 669·4 / 209 056·9	K-14F	Type E 25⅜ (645)	55/70	(27/35)	Wood 6 (150)	(1 600)					142	Manager: Dr. Modesto Ali
		30 (48)		Air W'hse	AAR 25 (635)		70/55 (35/27)	Wood 6 (150)	2 600 (1 615)	10·0°	0·75%	14		203	Gen. Man: Victor Heyl
15 (24)	15 (24)	40 (64)			AAR Type 10A 25 (635)		75/45 (37/22)	Wood 7 (178)	2 320 (1 440)	1·2% U		17·5	98 (30)	246 (36)	Gen. Man: B. D. Walker
9 (15)	22 (35)	25 (40)					70/55 (35/27)	Wood		12·0°	3·0%				

NAME OF COMPANY ADDRESS	Gauge ft. in. (metres)	Route length incl. E=Electrified miles (km.)	Track length incl. E=Electrified miles (km.)	Elect. system and type of conductor	Loco-motives L=Line S=Shunt Steam Electric Diesel De=elec. Dh=hyd.	Rail-cars Electric Diesel Trailer Railbus Multiple Unit set	Pass. train cars	Freight train cars Con-tainers	Total Volume carried. Thous-ands of tonnes	Av'ge haul per ton miles (km.)	Av'ge net train load tonnes	Max. trailing load tonnes	Total number carried in 1 000s	Aver-age jour-ney miles (km.)
PANAMA *(contd.)*														
Panama Railroad Division of Panama Canal Company Box 5067, Cristobal, Canal Zone	5' 0'' (1·524)	47 (75)	117 (188)		DeL 3 DeS 3		24	391	231 000				864 000	
PARAGUAY														
*F.C. Presidente Carlos Antonio Lopez PO Box 453, Calle Mexico 145, Asuncion	4' 8½'' (1·435)	273 (440)	274 (441)		SL 17 SS 5	10	13	196	144·3	32 503 998 ton-km			207·6	12·7 (20·4)
F.C. del Norte Villa Concepcion	3' 3⅜'' (1·00)	35 (56)			S 4		3	29						
Industrial Railways Christopherson	2' 0'' (0·610)	11 (18)												
Fassardi Ltda.	2' 5½'' (0·750)	21 (34)												
International Products	3' 3⅜'' (1·00)	59 (95)												
La Azucarera	2' 6'' (0·762)	25 (40)												
Puerto Casado	2' 6'' (0·762)	99 (159)												
Puerto Guarani	2' 5⅞'' (0·760)	57 (92)												
Puerto Ibapoba	2' 6'' (0·762)	20 (32)												
Puerto Sastre	2' 5½'' (0·75)	56 (91)												
PERU														
*Empresa Nacional de Ferrocarriles del Peru (ENAFER-PERU) Direction General, Ancash 207 Lima Formed on 1 December 1972 to operated on behalf of the Government, the lines formerly owned by the Peruvian Corporation and the Peruvian State Railways. The integrated railways are formed into the following two operating groups:-					SL 4 SS 3 DeL 32 DeS 1 DhS 3		77	855 C 71	812 607				807·5	
* **Ferrocarril del Centro** Jr. Ancash 201, Estaciòn Desamparados Lima	4' 8½'' (1·435) 3' 0'' (0·914)	238 (384) 80 (129)	303 (488) 84 (136)		SL 1 DeL 31 Dm 2	D 10	54	1 279	1 508·2			350	1 202	
* **Ferrocarril del Sur** Apartado 194, Arequipa	4' 8½'' (1·435) 3' 0'' (0·914)	574 (924) (192)	688 (1 108) (181)		SL 6 DeL 42 DeS 1 DhS 3 Dm 3	R 12	122	900 C 71	845·2		125	350	2 233	
F.C. Supe-Barranca-Alpas Barranca, Supe	1' 11⅝'' (0·60)	29 (46)			S 5			20						
F.C. Eten-Chichayo-Patapo *(Empresa del Ferrocarril y Muelle de Eten.)* Puerto de Eten	4' 8½'' (1·435)	42 (67)	46 (74)		S 8		14	105	81·4	18·3 (29·4)			738·6	7·2 (11·6)
Ilo-Toquepala Railway Southern Peru Copper Corp., Casilla 2640 Lima	4' 8½'' (1·435)	177 (189)	119 (192)		De 8			233	722·7	117 (189)		4 286		
F.C. Pimental-Pomaico Pimental, Chicago *(Cia del F.C. y Muelle de Pimental)*	3' 0'' (0·914)	43·5 (70)			SL 10 SS 5		5	425	342·6	31·0 (50)	300		3·7	8 (13)
Empresa Minera del Centro del Peru Augusto N, Wiese 891, Lima	4' 8½'' (1·435)	132 (212)	150 (242)		SL 2 DeL 8 DeS 4		13	689	998·8	117 700 534 ton-km	1 500		498·2	46·5 (74·9)
PHILIPPINES														
*Philippine National Railways 943 Claro M. Recto Ave., Manila	3' 6'' (1·067)	658 (1 060)	730 (1 175)		DeL 53 DeS 20 DhS 3	D 37 DT 34	238	1 723	790·8	70 199 188 ton-km			9 674·6	73 (110·7)
Phividec Railways Inc PO Box 300, Ioilo City	3' 6'' (1·067)	73 (117)	92 (148)		De 8 Dh 1	R 11	19	326	165 201·2	6 (10)	52·1	600	3 189·4	170 (274)
POLAND														
*Polish State Railways (Polskie Koleje Panstwowe—P.K.P.) Ministry of Transport, Chalubinskiego 4, Warsaw *Narrow gauges in operation* 600, 750, 785 and 1 000 mm	4' 8½'' (1·435) (23 953) E (6 308) Narrow (2 880)		3 000 V dc OH						481 056·0 13 219	167 (269)	702	2 700	1 151 703 19 699·0	21·9 (35·3)

* See main entry

Average Speeds			Financial Data	Braking (continuous)	Couplers	Buffers	Rails	Sleepers (crossties)		Curvature max.	Gradient max. (U=not compensated)	Axle load max.	Altitude max.	Staff employed. Total no. (inclu. workshop)	Names of officials. Extended lists can be found at the end of the individual country in the report section immediately following
Freight Train	Pass. Train	Speed max.	Revenue Expenses		Type and Height above rail	Centres and Height above rail	Weight	Type and thickness	Spacing Number per mile or centres ins						
mph (km/hr)	mph (km/hr)	mph (km/hr)	in 1 000s		ins (mm)	ins (mm)	lb. per yd (kg/m)	ins (mm)	(mm)			tonnes	feet (m)		
40 (64)	45 (72)	50 (80)	$3 381 000 / 3 231 000	W'hse	AAR D. & E.		100/90 (50/45)	Wood 8 (203)	20 (508)	7·0°	1·25%	15	273 (83)	232 (48)	Pres: Col. R. Hunt / Man: F. R. Call
			$C 247 669·3 / 209 056·9				60·8 (31)	Wood 5 (127)		4·0°	2·0%			915 (150)	Gen. Man: Dr. Modesto Ali
			397 122·4 / 448 320·0												Director-Gen de FFCC Ing. Luis Praeli
19 (30)	22 (50)	Standard 50 (80) Narrow 37 (60)	P. 363 032·9 / 357 020·6	W'hse Air	Type AAR 34½'' (876) 26'' (660)		St. 80/70 (40/35) N 75/50 (37/25)	St. Wood 6 (153) * N. Wood 6 (153)	St. 26'' (660) N. 25'' (635)	St. rad. 330 ft (100 m) N. rad. 246 ft (75 m)	St. 4·37% N. 3·5%	18·5	2 074 15 806 (4 818)		Manager: Jose Baigorria P.
18 (28)	24 (38)	F. 37 (60) P. 50 (80)		Air W'hse	AAR 34½ (876) 26'' (660)		St. 80/60 (40/30) N. 75/5 (37/25)	Wood 6 (150) Conc 6 (150)	23⅝'' (600)	St. rad. 330 ft. (100 m) N. rad. (60 m)	St. 3·7% U N. 3·27% U	St. 18·3 N. 14	14 685 (4 476)	3 437	Dep. Gen. Man: Verner C. Foulkes
							20/18 (10/9)	Wood 6 (150)	2 640 (1 650)	63·0°	3·0%				
						60 (30)		Wood 6 (150)	2 250 (1 400)	9·7°	0·6%	9			
20 (32)		45 (72)		Air W'hse	Type E		90 (45)	Wood 6 (150)	22'' (560)	20°	3%	35	9 500 (2 896)	135 (38)	
24·9 (40)	24·9 (40)						45 (22·3)	Wood 6 (150)	2 640 (1 650)	11·5°	0·5%		820 (250)	180 (53)	
M'line 24 (40)	31 (50)	44 (70)	120 736·9 / 119 807·3	Air W'hse	Sharon A.A.R. 10A 33 (839)		90/70 (45/35)	Wood 6 (150) & Conc	21⅝'' (550)	10·5°	4·73% 4·15% U	10·5	15 190 (4 630)	492	Cyril Kocerhav
18·6 (30)	25 (40)	31 (50)	P. 9 282·0 / 7 548·1	Air W'hse	Junior-Major 33½ (851)	35 (889)	75/70 (37/35)	Wood 5 (127)	18 (458)	5·0°	·5%	13·0	275 (84)	480	Gen. Man: A. T. Viray
23·7 (38·1)	29·7 (47·8)	68 (110)	Revenue zlotys 67 093 411·0	Air W'hse LUV Oerlikon	Screw and Scharfenberg 41½ (1 050)	Standard European Crs 66⅛ (1 750) Ht 37-41½ (940-1 065)	98/84 (49/42)	Wood 6 (150) and Conc 7⅞ (200)	25⅝'' (650)	590 ft (180 m)	2%	21	2 736 (834)	369 757	Minister of Communications: Mieczyslaw Zajfryd, MTS

	Gauge ft. in. (metres)	Route length incl. E=Electrified miles (km.)	Track length incl. E=Electrified miles (km.)	Elect. system and type of conductor	Locomotives L=Line S=Shunt (Steam / Electric / Diesel De=elec. Dh=hyd.)	Rail-cars (Electric / Diesel / Trailer / Railbus / Multiple Unit set)	Pass. train cars	Freight train cars / Containers	Total Volume carried. Thousands of tonnes	Av'ge haul per ton miles (km.)	Av'ge net train load tonnes	Max. trailing load tonnes	Total number carried in 1 000s	Average journey miles (km.)
PORTUGAL														
*Companhia dos Caminhos de Ferro Portugueses (CP) Calcada do Duque, 20 Lisbon	5' 5·55" (1·665)	1 744 (2 807) E 252 (406)	2 386 (3 841) E 520 (837)	25 000 V 1/50 OH	SL 55, EL 46, DeL 162, DeS 34, DhS 36, DmS 6	E 81, ET 196, D 44, DT 51	468	5 318	4 403·0				110 338·0	16·8 (27)
	3' 3⅜" (1·00)	472 (760)	524 (843)		Metre	Metre: D 33, DT 29, R 16, S 36, DeL 17	Metre 89	Metre 593						
Sociedade "Estoril" Estaçäo do Cais do Sodré, Lisbon	5' 5·55" (1·665)	E 16 (26)	E 34 (63)	1 500 V dc OH	EL 3	EMU 31		6	26·0	7·5 (12·0)		300	43 380·8	11·2 (18·0)
PUERTO RICO														
Ponce and Guayama Railroad Aguirre 00608	3' 3⅜" (1·00)	60 (92)	81 (132)		DeL 3, DhL 11, DhS 2, DS 6			1 280	562·0		7 357 073 tonne-km		1 100	
ROMANIA														
Romanian State Railways (Caile Ferate Románe) (CFR) Calea Grivitei 193 B, Bucharest 12	5' 0" (1·524) / 4' 8½" (1·435) / Narrow gauges	21 (34) / 6 424 (10 340) E 348 (560) / 393 (632)	11 818 (19 019) E 889 (1 431)	25 kV 1/50					193 740·0	153·9 (247·7)			361 467·0	34·7 (55·8)
SABAH														
Sabah State Railways PO Box 118, Kota Kinabalu	3' 3⅜" (1·00)	86 (138)	92 (148)		DhL 8, DhS 4, DS 3	R 11, DMU 6	22	148	84·6		3 170 529 ton-km		825·5	22·8 (36·7)
SAUDI ARABIA														
*Saudi Government Railroad Organisation Dammam	4' 8½" (1·435)	357 (575)	455 (733)		DeL 9, DeS 17	D 4	25	1 144	1 307·6		191 887 488 ton-km		132·6	222·8 (385·5)
SENEGAL														
*C.F. du Sénégal Cité Ballabey, Thies	3' 3⅜" (1·00)	641 (1 032)	736 (1 184)		De 33, DeS 4, DhL 4, DhS 17	D 10, T 21	86	1 051	1 806·0		326 240 000 ton-km		3 825·3	49 (78)
SIERRA LEONE														
Marampa-Pepel Mineral Railway Sierra Leone Development Ltd. Co. Brook House, Chertsey Road, Woking, Surrey, GU21 5BJ, England	3' 6" (1·067)	52 (84)	60 (92)		DeL 4, DeS 2, DhS 2, Dh 2, D 2	D 2		200	2 750·0		169 124 000 ton-km			
SOUTH AFRICA														
*South African Railways & Harbours Administration Paul Kruger Building, Wolmarans St., Johannesburg-2001	3' 6" (1·067) / 2' 0" (0·610)	13 572 (22 622) E 4 042 (6 779) / 420 (705)		3 000 V dc OH single phase ac 25+ 50 Hz	SL 1 659, SS 140, EL 1 766, ES 24, DeL 1141, DeS 100, Dh 9	E 1 261, TE 3 165	6 096	187 956 C 581	163 016·0		190 546 398 train-km		621 836·9	
Iscor Private Siding 1143 PO Box 19, Pretoria 0001	3' 6" (1·067) E 1·3 (2·0)	6 (10) E 1·3 (2·0)	120 (193)	3 000 V dc OH	DeS 13, DhS 22, † 9			1 234	6 052·7		16 500 ton-km		200	950
Iscor Private Siding 1414 PO Box 2 Vanderbijlpark	3' 6" (1·067)	8 (13)	180 (289)		DeL 68, DhL 2			1 137			3·0 (4·8)		900	3 000
Iscor Private Siding 2227 PO Box 2, Newcastle 2940	3' 6" (1·067) E 4·3 (7)	9 (14) E 10 (17)	30 (210)	3 000 V. d.c. OH	DeL 8			150	11 780·0		194 ton-km			
Union Lime Company Ltd. PO Box 6810, Johannesburg	3' 6" (1·067)	5 (8)	10 (16)		De 2									
SPAIN														
*Red Nacional de Los Ferrocarriles Españoles (RENFE) Plaza de los Sagrados Corazones, 7, Madrid-16	5' 5·67" (1·668)	8 326 (13 497) E 2 274 (3 665)	12 365 (19 927) E 4 231 (6 816)	1 350 V 1 500 V & 3 000 V dc 6 000 V 3/25	EL 391, DeL 343, DeS 307, DhL 42, DhS 14, DmS 46	R 212, D 68, DT 231, EMU 349, DMU 59	2 126	36 897	37 000·0		10 693 000 000 tonne-km		199 600·0	50·3 (80·9)
Compañia F.C. Estratégicos Secundarios de Alicante Av. Villajoyosa, Alicante	3' 3⅜" (1·00)	60 (97)	60 (97)		S 9	2	38	116	21·9		37 (60)		497·2	19 (30)

* See main entry
† Fireless locomotives

Average Speeds			Financial Data		Couplers	Buffers	Rails	Sleepers (crossties)							
Freight Train	Pass. Train	Speed max.	Revenue Expenses	Braking (continuous)	Type and Height above rail	Centres and Height above rail	Weight	Type and thickness	Spacing Number per km or centres	Curvature max.	Gradient max. (U=not compensated)	Axle load max.	Altitude max.	Staff employed. Total no. (inclu. workshop)	Names of officials. Extended lists can be found at the end of the individual country in the report section immediately following
mph (km/hr)	mph (km/hr)	mph (km/hr)	in 1 000s		ins (mm)	ins (mm)	lb. per yd (kg/m)	ins (mm)	centres ins (mm)			tonnes	feet (m)		
12 (20)	24 (40)	B.G. 75 (120) N.G. 43 (70)	Escudos 2 733 905·5 3 479 618·2	Vac Clayton Air W'hse	UIC 41¾ (1 060) Ht 41¾ (1 060) Scharfenberg	Crs 78¾ (2 000)	*Broad* 111/40 (55/20) *Metre* 73/40 (36/20)	*Broad* Wood 5⅛ (130) *Metre* Wood 4¾ (120)	*Broad* 23⅝" (600) *Metre* 29½" (750)	*Broad* 984 ft (300 m) *Metre* 197 ft (60 m)	*Broad* 2·0% 1·8% **U** *Metre* 2·8% 2·5% **U**	*Broad* 20 *Metre* 14	*Broad* 2 667 (813) *Metre* 2 789 (850)	24 267 (7 796)	President: Eng Emilcar Marques
19 (30)	37 (60)	56 (90)	Es. 111 986·7 64 557·9	Air Jourd. Monneret	Scharf 39 (990) Crs. 76¾ (1 950) Ht. 41⅜ (1 050)		98/80 (49/40)	Conc. Type RS 7⅞ (200)	24½" (620)	1 066 ft (325 m)	1·24%	18	92 (28)	677 (110)	Gen. Man: Duate M. A. Bello
		19 (30)		Air W'hse.	Gould Type V		60/75 (30/37)	Wood 6 (150)	22" (560)	13·5°	0·75% **U**	12	100 (30)	170 (37)	Gen. Man: J. M. Mitchelhill
	14·0 (22·5)	24·9 (40·1)									1·3%			237 522 (16 158)	Head of Railway Dept: Ionel Diaconescu
16 (27)	25 (40)	45 (72)	M$ 2 768·1 4 590·5	Vac Air	Alliance 34¾ (883)		60/30 (30/15)	Wood 4½ (114)	30" (762)	330 ft (101 m)	2·0% 3·0% **U**	12	650 (198)	750	Gen. Man: Datuk Wong Len Hin
31 (50)	50 (80)	62 (100)	44 541·4 53 281·6	W'hse air	Type E 34½ (876)		115/80 (57/40)	Wood 6 (150)	2 980 (1 850)	3·0°	1·0%	29	1 900 (579)	1 521 (507)	Gen. Man: Omar A. Fakieh
38 (45)	38 (60)	50 (80)		Vac Jordain Monn	29¾ (755)	Crs. 49½ (1 250) Ht. 29¾ (755)	72/40 (36/20)	Metal Conc 6⅞ (175)	2 520- 2 220 (1 566- 1 375)	984 ft (300 m)	1·0%	15	236 (72)	4 028 (1 591)	Gen. Man: Khalilou Sall
25 (40)	30 (48)			Vac	Auto AP type F 34½ (876)		80/65 (40/32)	Steel, Pandrol clips	24½" (622)	820 ft (250 m)	Loaded 0·80% Empty 1·75%	17	350 (107)	320	Technical Director: S. D. M. Robertson
13-24 (21-39)	27-38 (44-62)	*Main* 56 (90) *	R 2 371 000·0 2 326 000·0	Vac S.A.R.	Auto 35¼ (895)		115/61 (57/30) Min. on N. gauge 44 (22)	Conc Steel: Wood 5 (127)	27¼" (700) *Branch* 31½" (800)	Min rad *Existing* 300 ft (91·4 m) *New* 550 ft (167·6 m)	*Existing* 3·3% *New* 2·0%	22·5	6 871 (2 094)	227 820 (32 020)	Gen. Man: J. G. H. Loubser
7 (11)	25 (40)		Expenses 1976: R 5 768·1	Vac W'hse	Atlas; Alliance 32 (813)	32 (813)	96/81 (48/40)	Steel; Wood 5 (127)	32" (813)	330 ft (100 m)	1·33% 2·5% **U**	30	4 550 (1 387)	600	Man: P. Leroux
10 (16)	15 (24)		Expenses 1978: R 6 771·0	Vac W'hse	Atlas 29½ (749)		96 (48)	Steel; Wood 5 (127)	32" (813)	330 ft (100 m)	4·16% 1·43% **U**	20	4 909 (1 496)	551 (60)	Gen. Wks. Man: D. W. Lamont
25 (40)	25 (40)		R 982·1	Vac W'hse	Bell 35 (889)		96/80 (48/40)	Wood 5 (127)	32 (813)	300 ft (92 m)	1·0% 1·43% **U**	15	3 890 (1 186)	150	Gen. Wks. Man: C. J. C. J. van Vuuren
															Chairman: H. Byland Admin. Man: M. G. McGlashan
15·0 (24·1)	29·2 (47·0)	87 (140)	Pesetas 38 100·0 44 200·0	Air W'hse Knorr and Vac Jourd Monneret	Screw 41¾ (2 000) Ht. 41¾ (1 060)	Crs. 78¾ (2 000)	*Main* (54/45) *Branch* (42·5/32)	Wood 5½ (140) and conc	23⅝" (600)	820 ft (250 m)	1·6%	25		77 820	
					Buffer coupler	29½ (750)	70/60 (35/30)	Wood 4¾ (120)	(600- 750)	492 ft (150 m)	2·0%	10			

					Loco-motives L=Line S=Shunt Steam Electric Diesel De=elec. Dh=hyd.	Rail-cars Electric Diesel Trailer Railbus Multiple Unit set			Freight movement				Passengers	
NAME OF COMPANY ADDRESS	Gauge ft. in. (metres)	Route length incl. E=Electrified miles (km.)	Track length incl. E=Electrified miles (km.)	Elect. system and type of conductor			Pass. train cars	Freight train cars Con-tainers	Total Volume carried. Thousands of tonnes	Av'ge haul per ton miles (km.)	Av'ge net train load tonnes	Max. trailing load tonnes	Total number carried in 1 000s	Aver-age journey miles (km.)

SPAIN *(contd.)*

Company	Gauge	Route	Track	Elect.	Locos	Railcars	Pass cars	Freight cars	Vol	Av haul	Net load	Max load	Total pass	Av journey
Ferrocarril de Astillero a Ontaneda Santander	3' 3⅜'' (1·00)	22 (35)			S 5	2	12	64	36·1				381·9	
Ferrocarriles Económicos de Asturias Avda. Santander, Oviëdo	3' 3⅜'' (1·00)	71 (115)			S 29	D 2 / T 2	46	975	603·7	50 (80)	300	430	1 723·1	16·8 (27)
Ferrocarril de las Minas de Aznal-collar al Guadalquiver Av. Queipo de Llano No. 15, Seville	3' 3⅜'' (1·00)	27 (43)	30 (48)		S 6		10	175	83·9	15·5 (25)	260	450		
Ferrocarriles del Bidasoa Irun	3' 3⅜'' (1·00)	32 (52)		S 7	3	7	58		14·3				116·3	
Ferrocarriles Y Transportes Surburbanos de Bilbao SA Bilbao	3' 3⅜'' (1·00)	E 37 (59)	E 47 (67)	1 500 V dc OH	S 3	E 18 / EMU 10	50	172	206·9				15 658·0	6·5 (10·4)
Ferrocarril de Minas de Cala Bailen 9, Bilbao	3' 3⅜'' (1·00)	91 (146)												
Ferrocarril del Cantabrico Plaza de las Estaciones, Santander	3' 3⅜'' (1·000)	65 (105)	88 (141)		S 26 / D 1	D 2 / T 3	56	818	880·8	32·3 (52)	260	300	1 852·5	13·7 (22)
Ferrocarril de Carreño Marques de San Estaban 2, Gijon	3' 3⅜'' (1·00)	E 12 (20)	14 (23)	650 V dc	D 1	E 9 / T 14	7	56	172·9	5·7 (9·2)	24	127	4 001·3	6·8 (11)
Cia. Gen. de Ferrocarriles Catalanes SA Calle de la Diputacion 239-3, Barcelona	3' 3⅜'' (1·00)	124 (200) E 35 (56)	93 (150) E 37 (60)	1 500 V dc OH	EL 4 / DL 10 / DS 4 / Dh 1	E 33 / ET 24 / D 15 / DT 3	50	864	626	44 (71)	200	600	12 350	8 (13)
Ferrocarriles de Cataluña S.A. F.C. de Sarriá a Barcelona Plaza de Cataluña No. 1, Barcelona 2	4' 8½'' (1·435)	E 25 (41)	E 39 (63)	1 300 V dc OH		E 62 / T 13		1	1·1				46 355·1	4 (7)
Explotacion de Ferrocarriles por El Estado Ferrocarriles de Via Estrecha (FEVE) General Rodrigo 6, Madrid *Operates the following narrow-gauge lines:*		1 087 (1 757) E 238 (384)		1 200 V dc OH 600 V dc OH 1 500 V dc OH					5 298·6				56 323·7	
Alicante-Gandia Avenida Villajoyosa, 2, Alicante	3' 3⅜'' (1·00)	78 (125)	99 (160)		DhL 4 / DhS 1	D 14 / T 7							892·1	15·5 (24·9)
Amorebieta-Guernica-Bermeo Estacion F.C. Guernica, Vizcaya	3' 3⅜'' (1·00)	19 (30)	21 (34)		DeL 3 / DhS 1	D 3 / T 2	15						1 090·5	8·5 (13·7)
Cartagena-Los Blancos Estaciòn F. C. Cartagena	3' 5¾'' (1·06)	10 (16)	14 (22)			D 6 / T 2							793·7 8·1	5·0
Ferrocarril Gijon Estación F.C. El Ferrol del Caudillo Estación F.C. Muros de Nalón (Asturias)	3' 3⅜'' (1·00)	187 (301)	199 (321)		DhL 3 / DhS 2	D 27 / T 18							1 578·4	16·1 (26·0)
F.C. de Mallorca Estación F.C., Palma de Mallorca	3' 0'' (0·914)	67 (107)	85 (136)		DhL 2	D 8 / T 7							1 288·1	15·7 (25·3)
Santander-Bilbao Calle Bailén 5, Bilbao	3' 3⅜'' (1·00)	111 (179)	117 (188)		DeL 4 / DhL 11 / DhS 2	D 26 / T 19	55	825	112·6	42·2 (67·9)			4 441·2	14·4 (23·1)
Ferrocarriles de Valencia Cronista Rivelles 1, Valencia	3' 3⅜'' (1·00)	E 71 (115)	E 85 (136)	600 V dc OH	EL 12	E 50 / T 74							30 606·1	4·2 (6·7)
Ferrocarril Secundario de Guardiola a Castellar d'en Huch *(Ceased operation)*	1' 11⅝'' (0·60)	8 (12)												
Ferrocarril Secundario de Haroa a Ezcaray Haro (Logrono)	3' 3⅜'' (1·00)	21 (34)			S 3		13	61						
Ferrocarril de Langreo en Asturias Av. Menendez Pelayo 67, Madrid	4' 8½'' (1·435)	40 (64)	43 (70)		S 27		36	2 024	2 841·7				2 630·6	
F.C. Estragetico de Leon a Matallana *(Operated by F.C. de la Robla)*														
Ferrocarriles Suburbanos de Málaga Plaza de Queipo de Llana 1, Malaga	3' 3⅜'' (1·00)	65 (105)	80 (130)		S 11	R 3 / T 3	25	182	156·2	6·4 (10·3)	13·9	160	539·6	10·6 (17·0)
Manresa a Olván Santa Isobel 44, Madrid	3' 3⅜'' (1·00)	31 (50)	32 (52)		S 13 / D 3	D 3		178	791·0	(16)			305·1	(17·8)
F.C. de Montaña a Grandes Pendientes Paseo de Gracia 36, Barcelona 6 *Routes:* Ribas-Caralps-Nuria (Rack) Montserrat-San Juan (Funicular) Montserrat-San Cueva (Funicular)	3' 3⅜'' (1·00)	E 7·5 (12)	8 (13)	1 500 V dc OH	E 4		150	14	0·7	8 (13)			177·3	7 (11·5)
F.C. de Ponferrada a Villablino Minero Siderurgica de Ponferrada, SA Ruiz de Alarcon, 11 Madrid-14	3' 3⅜'' (1·00)	40 (64)	56 (91)		SL 20 / SS 2		21	603	1 327·6	211 (341·9) train-km	497 300	650	31·4	40·5 (36·6)
F.C. E. de Reus a Salou Carreterra Salou, Reus	3' 3⅜'' (1·00)	5 (9)	6 (10)		S 4		20		3·9		17		229·9	
Ferrocarriles de la Robla Bailen 5, Bilbao	3' 3⅜'' (1·00)	211 (340)	242 (390)		SL 35 / SS 8 / DeL 18 / DhS 8		82	1 084	773·0	76 (122·3)	170	900	932·0	29 (50)
Les Minas de Union Explosives Rio Tinto SA Minas de Rio Tinto, Huelva	3' 6'' (1 067)	57 (92)	202 (326)		SL 7 / SS 70 / DhS 1 / De 4		20	65	1 200·0	33·4 (53·8)	116	2 324	5·0	50 (80)
Ferrocarril Secundario de Sadaba a Gallur Gallur, Zaragozo	3' 3⅜'' (1·00)	35 (56)			S 5	2	9	96	58·4				118·0	

Average Speeds			Financial Data		Couplers	Buffers	Rails	Sleepers (crossties)							Names of officials. Extended lists can be found at the end of the individual country in the report section immediately following
Freight Train	Pass. Train	Speed max.	Revenue Expenses	Braking (continuous)	Type and Height above rail	Centres and Height above rail	Weight	Type and thickness	Spacing Number per mile (per km) or centres	Curvature max.	Gradient max. (U=not compensated)	Axle load max.	Altitude max.	Staff employed. Total no. (inclu. workshop)	
mph (km/hr)	mph (km/hr)	mph (km/hr)	in 1 000s		ins (mm)	ins (mm)	lb. per yd (kg/m)	ins (mm)	ins (mm)			tonnes	feet (m)		
11 (18)	21·7 (35)				Buffer coupler	Central 29½ (750)	71/61 (35/30)	Oak 5⅛ (130)	25½″ (650)	328 ft (100 m)	1·8%	10			
12·4 (20)				None	Hook & chain	Central 29½ (750)	62/59 (31/28)	Oak 4¾ (120)	23⅝″ (600)	328 ft (100 m)	0·25%	7·5			
				Vac & Air	Screw 29½ (750)		71/91 (35/45)	Wood 4¾ (120)	27½″ (700)	328 ft (100 m)	2·2%	12			
18·6 (30)	31 (50)			W'hse	21 (530)	29¾ (755)	90/60 (45/30)	Wood 5⅛ (130)	23⅝″ (600)	328 ft (100 m)	2·0%	12			
12·4 (20)	22 (20)	(35)		W'hse Air			90/70 (45/35)	Wood 5⅛ (130)	27½″ (700)	328 ft (100 m)	26·5%	13			
19 (30)	31 (50)	43 (70)		W'hse Air	35⅜ (900)	Central 41⅜ (105)	90/60 (45/30)	Oak 4¾ (120)	23⅝″ (600)	328 ft. (100 m)	2·5%	14	2 365 (721)	677 (195)	Gen. Man: Don Joaquin de Tord
	25 (40)	56 (90)	P. 268 142·2 221 739·4	W'hse Air	Tomlinson 25⅝ (650)	Central 43⅜ (1 100)	110 (54)	Oak 5½ (140)	24″ (600)	492 ft (150 m)	0·44%	12	971 (296)	800 (280)	Gen Man: Don Ramón Montagut y de Miquel
			P. 985 670·2 1 586 861·5												Director: D. Mariano Pascual Laguna
	30 (48)	43 (70)	P. 133 042·0 205 925·0	W'hse Air	Willison 26 (660)		70/60 (35/30)	5″ (130)	26″ (660)	9·5°	1·9%	5	597 (182)	226	Evilio Portillo
	31 (50)	37 (60)	P. 10 872·0 30 177·0	Vac	17⅝ (550)		70·6 (35)	Oak 4¾ (120)	26″ (660)	7·6°	2·25%	12	485 (148)	67	Alfonso Martinez Alvarez
	30 (48)	43 (70)	P. 5 889·0 14 393·0	Air	Willison 29½ (747)		85 (32·5)	Oak 5 (130)	25½″ (650)	6·75°	3·6%	5	462 (141)	60	Evilio Portillo
	29 (47)	50 (80)	P. 30 546·0 49 227·0	Knorr Air	Scharf. 27½ (700)		109/85 (54/42)	Wood 4¾ (120)	2 740 (1 700)	7·6°	2·0%	8	843 (257)	148	José Ma López Martin
	30 (48)	43 (70)	P. 28 026·0 63 961·0	Knorr Air	Scharf. 27½ (700)		65 (32·5)	4¾ (120)	26″ (660)	3·9°	1·2%	8	502 (153)	244	Sebastian Alvear Criado
25 (40)	34 (55)	40 (65)	P. 88 809·0 147 518·0	Vac	21·7 (550)		91/85 (45/42)	5 (130)	26″ (660)	7·6°	2·0%	8	879 (268)	571	G. Pérez Cossio Regato
	25 (40)	31 (50)	P. 133 042·0 205 925·0	W'hse Air	29·5 (750)		91/65 (45/32)	Oak 5½ (140)	26″ (660)	7·6°	1·8%	8	482 (147)	938	Evelio Portillo Hernández
9·3 (15)	12·4 (20)			W'hse Air	Screw 15¾ (400)	Central 23 (580)	70/46 (35/23)	Wood 5½ (140)	30¼″ (770)	17·5°	1·5%	11			
					26½ (675)	34 (875)	70·6 (35)	Wood 5 (130)	25½″ (650)	328 ft. (100 m)	2·96%	11			
Pass and Frt 18 (30) Rack 8 (13) Funicular			P. 6 116·6 5 709·8	Air			40 (20) Rack 30 (15) Funicular			22·0°	8% 15%U		6 442 (1 964)	34	
16 (25)	25 (40)	29 (45)	P. 197 999·9 369 050·6	W'hse Air	Buffer-Coupler	Central 29½ (750)	108/91 (54/45)	Oak 5 (130)	27½/24¾ (700/630)	19·5°	1·88% U	12·5	3 159 (963)	475	Antonio Pachón Ruiz
				None	Central	None	64·6 (32)	Oak 6 (150)	25½″ (650)	19·5°	2·3% U	7			
18 (28)	26 (42)	43·5 (70)	P. 111 228·0 113 592·0	Clayton Vac	Buffer coupler 29½ (750)	Central 29½ (750)	109/70 (54/35)	Oak 5⅛ (130)	20/30″ (500/700)	14·5°	2·6% 2·3% U	16	3 904 (1 190)	1 009 (171)	Gen. Man: A. Zurita
15·5 (25)	15·5 (25)	30 (48)		Vac Gr. & Cl.	Central 27½ (700)	Buffer coupler	90/65 (45/32)	Wood 5⅛ (130)	27½/31½″ (700/800)	17·5°	2·0%	13	1 319 (420)	597	Gen. Man: Don Antonio de Torres Espinosa

NAME OF COMPANY ADDRESS	Gauge ft. in. *(metres)*	Route length incl. E=Electrified miles *(km.)*	Track length incl. E=Electrified miles *(km.)*	Elect. system and type of conductor	Locomotives L=Line S=Shunt Steam Electric Diesel De=elec. Dh=hyd.	Railcars Electric Diesel Trailer Railbus Multiple Unit set	Pass. train cars	Freight train cars Containers	Freight movement: Total Volume carried. Thousands of tonnes	Freight movement: Av'ge haul per ton miles *(km.)*	Freight movement: Av'ge net train load tonnes	Freight movement: Max. trailing load tonnes	Passengers: Total number carried in 1 000s	Passengers: Average journey miles *(km.)*
SPAIN *(contd.)*														
Sociedad Explotadora de Ferrocarrarriles y Tranvias (S.E.F.T) Peñaflorida 6, San Sebastian	3' 3⅜'' *(1·00)*	E 13 *(21)*	E 19 *(31)*	500 V dc OH	EL 2	E 10	30	6	0·4	14 *(23)*		150	3 263·5	4·1 *(6·6)*
Ferrocarril de Soller, SA Castañer 7, Soller, Majorca A=Palma Section B=Puertode Soller Section	3' 0'' *(0·914)*	E 20 *(32)*	E 22 *(35)*	1 200 V dc OH	E 1	E 8	17	0·5	2·6	16·8 *(27·1)*			A.640·9 B.735·6	A.16·0 *(25·7)* B.2·9 *(4·6)*
Ferrocarril del Tajuna, SA Avenida Mendendez Pelayo 67, Madrid 9	3' 3⅜'' *(1·00)*	27 *(44)*	32 *(52)*		DeL 6 DeS 1	D 3	0	158	1 204·5	19·8 *(32)*	200	600		
Ferrocarril de Tharsis a Rio Odiel Cia. de Azufre y Cobre de Tharsis Ltda. Minas de Tharsis, Huelva	4' 0'' *(1·219)*	28 *(46)*	48 *(80)*		DhS 5 DL 5	R 2		80	900	27 *(43)*	600			
Urola (Ferrocarril de Zumarraga a Zumaya) Palcio Diputacion Provincial, San Sebastian	3' 3⅜'' *(1·00)*	E 23 *(37)*	E 27 *(44)*	1 600 V dc OH		E 10†	20	120	38·3	14 *(22·6)*	59	320	898·0	7·2 *(11·6)*
Ferrocarriles Vasco-Asturiana Jovellanos 17, Ovieda	3' 3⅜'' *(1·00)*	65 *(105)*	84 *(135)*		S 38		53	1 663	1 859·7	36 *(57·9)*	117	5 209	2 929·0	10·8 *(17·5)*
Ferrocarriles Vascongados Achuri 8, Bilbao	3' 3⅜'' *(1·00)*	E 98 *(158)*	E 105 *(169)*		S 7 E 17	E 18 D 2	136	895	537·1				7 947·1	
F.C. Electrico de Vigo a La Ramallosa Tranvias Electricos de Vigo, SA Ave. de la Florida 2, Vigo (Pontevedra)	3' 3⅜'' *(1·00)*	E 13 *(21)*				E 10	10	10						
SRI LANKA														
***Sri Lanka Railways** PO Box 355 Colombo 10	5' 6'' *(1·676)*	925 *(1 496)*	1 153 *(1 856)*		DeL 39 DhL 66 DeS 9 DhS 34	D 18	BG 916 NG 99	BG 3 895 NG 199	1 941·7	39 046 100 ton-km			68 460·5	20·8 *(33·5)*
SUDAN														
***Sudan Railways** PO Box 43 Atbara	3' 6'' *(1·067)*	2 970 *(4 780)*	3 379 *(5 441)*		SL 96 SS 31 DeL 102 DeS 5 DhS 54 DhL 1	D 6 TD 3	392	5 577	2 380·2	2 389 336 000 ton-km			2 541 851	501 *(806)*
SURINAM *(Dutch Guiana)*														
Surinam Government Railways Oneverwacht, Paramaribo	3' 3⅜'' *(1·00)*	53 *(86)*			S 8	D 3 T 6	16	58						
SWAZILAND														
***Swaziland Railways** PO Box 475, Mbabane	3' 6'' *(1·067)*	196 *(317)*	222 *(358)*		SL 16			703	2 012·6	336 100 ton-km				
SWEDEN														
***Swedish State Railways (Statens Järnvägar) (S.J.)** S-105 50 Stockholm	Total all gauges	7 072 *(11 379)* E 4 390 *(7 063)*	11,117 *(17 957)* E 6 860 *(11 038)*		EL 618 ES 133 DeL 157 DhL 58 DhS 393 DmS 11 Mu 133	E 40 D 160 ET 38 DT 58	1 592	3 803 Cont *small* 9 788 *large* 684	54 400	287	396			
	4' 8½'' *(1·435)*	6 959 *(10 750)* E 4 390 *(7 063)*	10 750 *(17 298)* E 6 800 *(11 038)*	16 kV 1/16⅝ OH									65 900	119 *(188)*
	2' 11'' *(0·891)*	114 *(185)*	344 *(554)*											
Gränges TGOJ Fack, S-631 01 Eskilstuna	4' 8½'' *(1·435)*	E 186 *(300)*	343 *(552)* E 312 *(503)*	16 000 V. 1/16⅔ OH	EL 27 ES 5 DhS 15 DS 5	D 13	8	2 064	5 597·0	107 *(172)*	2 100	2 700	1 085·0	15 *(24)*
Malmö-Limhans Järnvägs Box 30022, S20061 Malmö	4' 8½'' *(1·435)*	30 *(5·0)*	68 *(11)*		Dh 2		21	36 173	350				6 162	train-km
Nora Bergslags Järnväg Box 29, 71300, Nora Stad	4' 8½'' *(1·435)*	104 *(168)*	107 *(173)*		DhL 3 DS 5			228	315·0					
Nordmark-Klarälvens Järnvägar S-683 01 Hagfors	2' 11¹⁄₁₆'' *(0·891)*	E 68 *(110)*		16 000 V 1/16⅔ OH	EL 6 ES 3 DhS 4			475	385·9	21 313 382 ton-km				
SWITZERLAND														
***Swiss Federal Railways (Schweizerische Bundesbahnen) (SBB) (Chemins de Fer Fédéraux Suisses) (CFF)**	4' 8½'' *(1·435)*	4 684 *(2 913)* E 4 684 *(2 913)*	11 089 *(6 893)* E 11 089 *(2 913)*	15 000 V 1/16⅔ OH	EL 714 ES 171 DeS 103	E 181	3 607	37 780	47 640 000	7 140 000 000 ton-km			223 900	23·0 *(37·0)*
(Ferrovie Federali Svizzere) (FFS) Hochschulstr 6, CH-3030 Bern	3' 3⅜'' *(1·00)*	E 46 *(74)*	63 *(102)* E 58 *(93)*		EL 2	E 16	115	220						

* See main entry
† Seven passenger, three freight

Average Speeds			Financial Data	Braking	Couplers	Buffers	Rails	Sleepers (crossties)		Curvature max.	Gradient max. (U=not compensated)	Axle load max.	Altitude max.	Staff employed Total no. (inclu. workshop)	Names of officials. Extended lists can be found at the end of the individual country in the report section immediately following
Freight Train	Pass. Train	Speed max.	Revenue Expenses	(continuous)	Type and Height above rail	Centres and Height above rail	Weight	Type and thickness	Number per mile (per km) or centres						
mph (km/hr)	mph (km/hr)	mph (km/hr)	in 1 000s		ins (mm)	ins (mm)	lb. per yd (kg/m)	ins (mm)	ins (mm)			tonnes	feet (m)		
16 (25)	17 (27)	22 (35)		Air	Chain and hook 30⅜ (770)	Ht. 29½" (750)	90/70 (45/35)	Wood 4¾ (120)	25½" (650)	17·5°	1·2%	5		121 (21)	Gen. Man: Don Francisco Allende Ordorica
A. 21·7 (35) B. 9·3 (15)	A. 21·7 (35) B. 9·3 (15)	37 (60)	P. 38 670·2 38 606·0	Vac	Screw 19⅝" (500)	Central 27½ (700)	70/45 (35/22·5)	Pine & oak 4¾ (120)	23⅝" (600)	6·4°	2·3% U	9	784 (239)	106 (23)	President: D. Jose Puig Morell Dir. Gen: D. Miguel Colom Rullán
19 (30)			P. 34 394·6 33 479·0	W'hse. Vac	Henricot Auto 29½ (750)		90 (45)	Oak 7⅞ (200)	23½" (600)	11·5°	2·6% U	15	2 296 (700)	95 (23)	Gen. Man: Don Enrique Zamacola Urtizberea
18 (30)		22 (35)		W'hse Vac	Link 30 (762) Ht. 29½ (750)	Crs. 35½ (900) Ht. 29½ (750)	90/70 (45/35)	Pine and Oak 6 (150)	27½" (700)	12·5°	2·86%	14	761 (232)	226	
12·4 (20)	21·4 (34·5)			Vac			65 (32·2)	Oak 5½ (140)	2 400 (1 500)	17·5°	2·9%	12			
					29½ (750)	Buffer coupler	71/60 (35/30)	Oak 5⅛ (130)	27½" (700)	11·6°	1·6% U	12	1 696 (517)		
20 (48)	35 (56)	Steam 50 (80)		Air and Vac W'hse	Alliance 41½ (1 060)	Crs. 77 (1 956) Ht. 45" (1 153) BG 34½" (877) NG	88/80 (44/39) Narrow 46 (23)	Wood 5 (127) Narrow 4½ (114)	2 480 (1 441) Narrow 2 112 (1 305)	Broad 17·5° Narrow 25·0°	Broad 2·3% U Narrow 3·45% U	18	6 226 (1 898)	4 064	Gen. Man: V. T. Navaratne
31 (50)	31 (50)	37 (60) Expenses 50 (80) Railcars	$S 25 441 038 29 529 449	Vac Gr & Cr	Auto Alliance 35 (889)	Buffer-coupler 35 (889)	90/50 (45/25)	Wood: 6 (153)	2 100 (1 300)	1 452 ft (443 m)	1·0%	16·5 (75 lb) 12·5 (50 lb)	3 038 (926)	41 099 (8 548)	Gen. Man: Mohamed Al Rahman Wasfi
18 (29)	43 (70)	43 (70)	E. 6 522·0 6 693·0	Vac	Alliance 36 (914)		81 (40)	Wood 5 (127)	30" (762)	690 ft (210 m)	2·0%	18	4 525 (1 379)	852	Ch. Exec. Officer: A. L. Weidemann
(a) 28 (45) (b) 45 (72)	(a) 34 (55) (b) 65 (105)	80 (130)	Skr. 5 386 000 5 499 000	Air Knorr	Standard except railcars Scharff Ht. 40¾ (1 040) Railcars 19½" (500)	Standard	101/86 (50/43·2)	Wood 6 (150) and conc type 101 8¼ (210) type LS 5¼ (133)	Crs. Main 25½" (650) Secondary 29½" (750) Ore Line 19⅝" (500)	Main 3 280 ft (1 000 m) Secondary 1 968 ft (600 m) Other lines 984 ft (300 m)	High speed lines 1·0% U (1·25%U) Med. speed lines 1·6% U (2·0%U)	20 (25 on Kiruna-Riksgränsen line)	1 971 (601)	38 280 (4 940)	Gen. Man: Bengt Furbäck
43 (70) ore 31 (50)	55 (90)	62 (100)	Kr. 76 500·0 62 800·0	Air Knorr W'hse	Standard except railcars Scharff 19⅝ (500)	Standard	101/87 (50/43)	Wood 6½ (165)	30⅜" (770)	4·0°	1·7%	20	945 (288)	907 (147)	Gen. Man: A. Karlstrom
			Kroner 528 6 635												Man. Dir: Malte Jeppsson
28 (45)	31 (50)		Kr. 9·1 10·4	Air Knorr	Screw 41 (1 040)	68⅝ (1 750) 41 (1 040)	87/66 (43/33)	Pine 6¼ (160)	31½-34" (800-865)	7·25°	2·08%	18		100	Gen. Man: R. Renntun
25 (40)	50 (80)		Kr. 6 718·5 9 896·7	Air	Automatic 29 (735)		83/50 (41/25)	Wood 6/6½ (150/165)	27½-33 (710-830)			10		105	Gen. Man: Einar Severin
		TEE 87 (140) Main line 78 (125)	Fr. 2 224 700 2 242 400	Air Oerlikon Charmilles	Standard	Standard	108/72 (54/46)	Wood, 5·9 (150) Concrete 8·6 (220) Steel 3·5 (90)	25½" (650)	Main line 656 ft (200 m) Narrow 377 ft (115 m)	Main line 3·8% Narrow 12·0%	20	3 747 (1 142)	41 561	Pres: Ing Roger Desponds

NAME OF COMPANY ADDRESS	Gauge incl. E=Electrified ft. in. (metres)	Route length incl. E=Electrified miles (km.)	Track length incl. E=Electrified miles (km.)	Elect. system and type of conductor	Locomotives L=Line S=Shunt Steam Electric Diesel De=elec. Dh=hyd.		Railcars Electric Diesel Trailer Railbus Multiple Unit set		Pass. train cars	Freight train cars Containers	Total Volume carried. Thousands of tonnes	Av'ge haul per ton miles (km.)	Av'ge net train load tonnes	Max. trailing load tonnes	Total number carried in 1000s	Average journey miles (km.)

SWITZERLAND (contd.)

Aarau-Schöftland-Bahn (Merged with Wynentalbahn)

Company	Gauge	Route	Track	Elect.	Loco L/S		Railcars		Pass	Freight	Total Vol	Av'ge haul	Av'ge net load	Max load	Total carried	Avg journey
C.F. Aigle-Leysin (AL) Avenue de la Gare 38, CH 1860 Aigle (Part ABT Rack)	3' 3⅜'' (1·00)	E 4 (6)	E 5·5 (8·8)	1 300 V dc	EL ES	2 1	E	5	6	21	899	6 055 ton-km			262 865	3·5 (5·5)
C.F. Aigle-Ollon-Monthey Champery (Morgins) (AOMC) 38 rue de la Gare 6, CH 1860 Aigle (Strub rack rail on 2 miles)	3' 3⅜'' (1·00)	E 14 (23)	E 15 (25)	750 V dc OH			E	7	5	14	1 071	7·7 (12·3)		70	695 486	4·4 (7·1)
C.F. Aigle-Sepey-Diablerets (ASD) Avenue de la Gare, 38, CH 1860 Aigle	3' 3⅜'' (1·00)	E 14 (22)	E 15 (24)	1 300 V dc	EL	5	E	5	5	17	631	12·3 (19·8)	15 580 ton-km		180 013	11·1 (17·9)
Appenzeller-Bahn (AB) Bahnhofareal, CH-9100, Herlsau. 10	3' 3⅜'' (1·00)	E 20 (32)	E 27 (43)	1 500 V dc	ES DhS SL	1 1 1	E D T	9 1 2	34	40	10·9				1 324 693	
Arth-Rigi Bahn (ARB) Postfach 32 CH-6410 Goldau (Riggenback rack)	4' 8½'' (1·435)	E 5·3 (8·6)	E 5·8 (9·3)	1 500 V dc	EL	1	MUE	6	14	7	1·8		1 796 ton-km		322·9	5·3 (8·5)
C.F. des Alpes Bernoises Bern-Lötschberg-Simplon (BLS) 11 Genfergasse, 3001 Berne Also operates C.F. Berne-Neuchâtel; Gürbetal-Berne-Schwarzenburg-Bahn; and Simmentalbahn	4' 8½'' (1·435)	E 71 (115)	E 142 (228)	15 000 V 1/16⅔ OH	EL ES DeS DhS	42 8 9 11	ER EMU	3 3	126	306	3 964·8	3 866 010 train-km			7 580·6	13·7 (24·3)
Vereinigte Bern-Worb Bahnen (VBW) Postfach 28, 3048 Worblaufen	3' 3⅜'' (1·00)	E 16 (25)	E 18† (29)	800 V dc OH	EL	3	E T	10 7	1	2 plus 23 tonne	94	(4·9)	40	240	4 745	3·9 (6·5)
C.F. Berne-Neuchâtel (BN) (See Bern-Lötschberg-Simplon)	4' 8½'' (1·435)	E 27 (43)	E 33 (54)	15 000 V 1/16⅔ OH	EL EeS DhS	4 3 2	E EMU	2 6	20	31	858·3	973·3 train-km			3 409·7	9· (15·5)
Berner Oberland-Bahnen (BOB) Hoheweg 3800 Interlaken A=adhesion, R=Riggenbach rack	3' 3⅜'' (1·00)	E 15 (24)	E 22 (35)	1 500 V dc OH	ES DhS	5 1	E	8	44	46	16·04	399 563 train-km			1 397·9	8·8 (13·8)
C.F. Biasca-Acquarossa (BA) Biasca	3' 3⅜'' (1·00)	E 9 (14)		1 200 V dc			E	4	2	13						
Biel-Täuffelen-Ins Bahn (BTI) Tauffelen	3' 3⅜'' (1·00)	E 14 (22)	E 15 (25)	1 300 V dc OH	E	10	E ET	9 7	18	10	15	5·7 (9·0)		100	900	6·0 (9·7)
CF Bex-Villars-Bretaye (BEX) La Ruaz, CH 1880	3' 3⅜'' (1·00)	10·5 (17)	13·6 (22)	700 V dc OH	EL ES	2 1	E	14	9	27	9 081				990	
C.F. Bière-Apples-Morges (BAM) 1143 Apples	3' 3⅜'' (1·00)	E 19 (30)	E 22 (35)	15 000 V 1/16⅔OH			E	5	9	31	34·9			70	325·6	9·3
Birsigthalbahn A.G. (BTB) Weidenstr 27, CH-4142, Münchenstein	3' 3⅜'' (1·00)	E 10 (16)	E 13 (21)	940 V dc			E ET	9 7	8				3 081·7	4·3		(7·0)
Bodensee-Toggenburg-Bahn (BT) Bahnhofplatz la, CH-9001 St. Gallen	4' 8½'' (1·435)	E 41 (66)	E 45 (73)	15 000 V 1/16⅔	S EL D	1 6 3	E	8	57		489·6	6 600 000 ton-km		600	4 589·9	8·6 (13·9)
Bremgarten-Dietikon-Bahn (BD) CH-5620 Bremgarten Also operates: Wohlen-Meisterschwanden-B	4' 8½'' (1·435)	E 11·7 (18·8)	E 10 (17)	1 200 V dc	DeL DeS	2 1	E	11		14	19·8	173 668 ton-km			1 150·7	5·7 (9·3)
Brienz-Rothorn-Bahn (BRB) CH-3855, Brienz, Bernese Oberland Abt rack system; line climbs 5 525 ft (1 846 m) in 4·7 miles (7·6 km)	2' 7½'' (0·80)	4·7 (7·6)	5·3 (8·6)		D S	3 7			15	3	249·0	2·5 (4)			147 307	4·3 (7)
C.F. Brig-Visp-Zermatt (BVZ) CH-3900 Brig (Part Abt rack)	3' 3⅜'' (1·00)	E 26 (43)	31 (51)	11 000 V 1/16⅔OH	SL EL DeS Dm	1 6 2 2	E T	5 4	55	80	54·7	1 921 739 tonne-km			2 098·5	
Emmental-Burgdorf-Thun-Bahn (EBT) Bucherstr 1 CH-3400 Burgdorf (Also operates Solothurn-Münster-Bahn and Vereinigte Huttwil-Bahnen)	4' 8½'' (1·435)	E 47 (76)	E 80 (128)	15 000V 1/16⅔	EL ES D	10 14 4	E M	9 9	37		1 756 891	25 568 599 ton-km			4 358 748	11·0 (17·7)
Forchbahn (FB) Postfach 8023 Zurich 1	3' 3⅜'' (1·00)	E 9·5 (15)	E 11 (17)	600/1 200‡ V dc OH			E ET	12 8	3		2·1	29 917 ton-km			2 387 ·1	
Frauenfeld-Wil-Bahn (FW) CH-8570 Weinfelden	3' 3⅜'' (1·00)	E 11 (18)	E 13 (20)	1 300 V dc OH	E	1	E	3	7	43	13·7	158 541 ton-km		140	617·2	5·4 (8·6)
C.F. Fribourgeois (GFM) Perolles 3, 1700 Fribourg (Operates 3 lines)																
Gruyère	3' 3⅜'' (1·00)	E 31 (49)	E 36 (59)	900 V dc	E	4	E EMU	11 3	26	113	⎫				⎫	
Fribourg-Morat-Anet	4' 8½'' (1·435)	E 21 (33)	E 21 (33)	15 000 V 1/16⅔	E	3	E EMU	9 3			⎬ 610	83 000 000 ton-km			⎬ 1 900	6 (9·7)
Bulle-Romont	4' 8½'' (1·435)	E 11 (18)	E 13 (21)	15 000 V 1/16⅔					9	35	⎭				⎭	
Furka-Oberalp-Bahn (FO) P.B. 97, 3900 Brig (Valais) (Part ABT rack)	3' 3⅜'' (1·00)	E 62 (100)	E 71 (114·4)	12 000 V 1/16⅔ OH	SL EL ES DeL DS	1 11 1 2 1	E	4	39	89	201·89	16 (26·9)		100	1 298·3	10 (17·7)

† Includes 2.8 miles (4.5 km) of dual gauge (metre and standard) track
* 600V in Zurich, 1200V elsewhere

Average Speeds: Freight Train mph (km/hr)	Average Speeds: Pass. Train mph (km/hr)	Speed max. mph (km/hr)	Financial Data: Revenue Expenses in 1 000s	Braking (continuous)	Couplers: Type and Height above rail ins (mm)	Buffers: Centres and Height above rail ins (mm)	Rails: Weight lb. per yd (kg/m)	Sleepers (crossties): Type and thickness ins (mm)	Sleepers (crossties): Spacing Number per mile (per km) or centres ins (mm)	Curvature max.	Gradient max. (U=not compensated)	Axle load max. tonnes	Altitude max. feet (m)	Staff employed. Total no. (inclu. workshop)	Names of officials. Extended lists can be found at the end of the individual country in the report section immediately following
4·7 (7·5)	8·7 (14)	9·3 (15)	F. 1 400 1 915	W'hse Air	Central 19⅝ (500)	Central	117/50 (58/25)	Metal	29½″ (750)	18·5°	23·0%	8	4 767 (1 453)	13 (10)	Dir: René Perréaz
16 (25)	17 (28)	37 (60)	F. 1 591 2 952	W'hse Charmilles	Central 29½ (750)	Central 29½ (750)	120/60 (58/30)	Wood & Metal	27½″ (700)	30·0°	6·5% (Rack 13·5%)	14	3 445 (1 050)	50 (5)	Dir: René Perréaz
	18·6 (30)	22 (35)	F. 9 170 1 911	W'hse Air	Central 29½ (750)	Central	60 (30)	Metal	29½″ (750)	18·5°	6·0%	8	3 773 (1 154)	33 (6)	René Perréaz
		40 (65)	F. 3 616·5 5 599·1	Oerlikon Air	Buffer coupler	Central 29½ (750)	72/61 (36/30·1)	Wood 6 (150) & Metal	24¾″ (630)	7·5°	3·7%	10	2 959 (902)	100 (15)	Dir: J. Hardegger
		Up (14) Down (17)	F. 2 497·7 2 330·9	SLM	G.F. Auto	Central 29½ (750)	52·4 (26)	Metal	29½″ (750)	10·9°	20·0%	11	5 895 (1 797)	38 (16)	Gen. Man: Joseph Jütz
		77 (125)	F. 140 224·5 140 009·4	Oerlikon Air and Rheost	Standard	Standard	108/92 (54/46)	Wood 6 (150) and steel	23⅝″ (600)	7·9° (220 m)	2·7%	20	4 067 (1 240)	1 931 ¶	Gen. Man: Dr. F. Anliker
22 (35)	31 (50)	40 (65)	F. 6 095 8 665	Air Charm.	S.I.G. Centre 19⅝ (500)		72/50 (36/25)	Wood 6″ (150) Steel	23⅝″ (600)	Rad. 98 ft (30 m)	3·6%**U**	10	2 021 (616)	122 (32)	Gen Man: Dr J. Fahm Com Man: B. Fink
		78 (125)	F. 12 330·9 16 820·6	Air Rheost	Standard	Standard	92 (46)	Wood/ Steel 6 (150)/ 3½ (90)	23⅝″ (600)	6·1° (285 m)	1·8%	20	1 903 (580)		Gen Man: Dr. F. Anliker
		A. 40 (65) R. 20 (32)	F. 10 035·8 13 381·3	Air Charmilles	G.F. Auto	Central (650)	90/60 (45/30)	Metal; Wood	35½ (900)	19·5°	R. 13 381·3 A. 3·4%	12	3 392 (1 034)	270	Dir: Dr. Roland Hirni
											17·0%		1 750 (538)		
19 (30)	19 (30)	37 (60)	F. 1 160 2 550	Vac Hardy	Fischer Autom	18½ (470)	72·5 (36)	Wood 7⅛ (182)	28⅝″ (600)	25·0°	4·8%	12	1 644 (501)	35	Gen Man: J. Mathys
10 (16)	11 (18)	15·5 (25)	F 2 985·0 4 455·0		G.F. Auto	Central	52·4 (26)	UST		25·0°	200%	14	6 000 (1 807)	54	Dir: René Perrész
32 (50)	43 (65)	43 (65)	F. 1 293·9 2 863·7	W'hse Air	G.F. Auto	24½ (620)	40/60/72 (23/30/ (36)	Wood 6 (150)	26″ (660)	17·5°	3·5%	12	2 339 (713)	48	Gen Man: Pierre Gaillard
	16 (25)	40 (65)	F. 7 798·1 10 095·9	Charmilles Air	Buffer Coupler 23⅝ (600)		60/50 (30/25)	Wood 7 (180)	25⅝ (640)	35·0°	2·8%	8·5	1 293 (394)	80	Dir: P. E. Matzinger
43 (70)	50 (80)	62 (100)	F. 17 750·0 19 560·0	Oerlikon Air	Standard	Standard	92 (46)	Wood & Metal	25⅛″ (640)	600 ft. (30 m)	2·4%	20	2 618 (798)	270	Gen. Man: Dr. W. Kesselring
34 (55)	34 (55)	43 (70)	F. 1 898·9 4 437·6	Air W'hse	Buffer Coupler (560)		60/90 (30/45)	Wood & Metal	23⅝ (600)	98 ft (30 m)	5·3%	20	1 804 (550)	67	Dir: W. Zurcher
		5·6 (9)	F. 1 460 108 1 439 704			Central 17¾ (450)	40 (20)	Metal	31½″ (800)	29·5°	25·0%	6·5	7 386 (2 252)	40	Man: P. Cosandier
25 (40)	28 (45)	31 (50)	F. 20 343·3 16 246·0	Air W'hse and Hardy	Screw Hook	Central 24½ (630)	72/30 (36/30)	Steel Concrete Wood	A 28¼ (720) R 26 (660)	22·0°	A 2·5% R 12·5%	13	5 266 (1 605)	212	Dir: R. Perren
25 (40)	37 (60)	62 (100)	F. 23 385 28 553	Oerlikon Air	Standard	Standard	93/73 (46/36)	Steel Wood 6 (150)	23½″ (600)	7·0°	2·5%	20	2 516 (767)	473 (90)	Gen. Man: Dr Ch Kellerhals
		37 (60)	F. 2 914·6 5 503·2	Air Charmilles	GF Semi- Auto.	None	72·4 (35·9)	Metal	28¼″ (720)	20·0°	7·0%	9	2 250 (686)	44	Gen. Man: H. Hartmann
	21 (34)	34 (55)	SwF. 1 409·4 3 101·2	Vac	G.F. Auto	19⅝ (500)	50·4 (24·8)	Oak	26⅜″ (680)	50·0°	4·6%	10	1 873 (571)	41 (7)	Dir: Dr. R. Sax
			10 000 12 200												Gen. Man: Dr. G. Dreyer
		40 (65)		Vac			60/48 (30/24)	Metal	29½″ (750)	19·5°	5·0%	11	2 815 (858)	267	
		56 (90)		W'hse Oerlikon Air	Standard	Standard	92/72 (46/36)	Metal Metal	24⅞/27½″ (630/700)	8·75°	3·0%	20	2 743 (836)		
		34 (55)	F. 5 834·9 8 155·4	Vac Hardy	Screw S.L.M. 23½ (605)	Central 17⅞ (450) Ht. 23½	70 (35)	Metal	25 5/16″ (650)	22·0°	11·0% **U** 17·9% *	12	7 085 (2 160)	220 (44)	Gen. Man: Dr. S. Zehnder

NAME OF COMPANY ADDRESS	Gauge ft. in. (metres)	Route length incl. E=Electrified miles (km.)	Track length incl. E=Electrified miles (km.)	Elect. system and type of conductor	Loco-motives L=Line S=Shunt Steam Electric Diesel De=elec. Dh=hyd.		Rail-cars Electric Diesel Trailer Railbus Multiple Unit set		Pass. train cars	Freight train cars Containers	Total Volume carried. Thousands of tonnes	Av'ge haul per ton miles (km.)	Av'ge net train load tonnes	Max. trailing load tonnes	Total number carried in 1 000s	Average journey miles (km.)

SWITZERLAND *(contd.)*

NAME OF COMPANY ADDRESS	Gauge	Route length	Track length	Elect. system	Loco L=S=		Rail-cars		Pass. cars	Freight cars	Total Volume	Av'ge haul	Av'ge net load	Max. load	Total number	Avge journey
C.F. Glion-Rochers de Naye (GN) Rue du Lac 36, 1815, Clarens	2' 7½'' (0·800)	E 4·5 (7·6)	E 5 (8)	850 V dc OH	E	2	E	8	5	11	3 249	1 249 959 ton-km			268·1	3 (4·5)
Gornergrat-Bahn (GGB) PO Box 254, CH-3900, Brig *(Abt rack system)*	3' 3⅜'' (1·00)	E 5·8 (9·3)	E 9 (14·6)	725 V 3/50	EL	3	E	16		4	4·6				233·0	
Gürbetal-Bern-Schwarzenburg-Bahn (GBS) *(Operated by Bern-Lötschberg-Simplon.)*	4' 8½'' (1·435)	E 32 (52)	E 38 (61)	15 000 V 1/16⅔ OH	EL 4 DhS 2		E EMU	1 5	10	40	386·3	890 200 train-km		2 000	2 933·9	(13·8)
Vereingte Huttwil-Bahnen (VHB) *(Operated by Emmental-Burgdorf-Thun-Bahn.)*	4' 8½'' (1·435)	E 41 (67)	E 42 (68)	15 000 V 1/16⅔ OH	ES 2 DS 5		E M	5 3			407	13 261 406 ton-km			1 839	6·0 (9·8)
Jungfrau-Bahn (JB) 3800 Interlarken *(Operated by BOB)* *(Strub rack system)*	3' 3⅜'' (1·00)	E 5·6 (9)	E 7 (12)	1 100 V 3/50 OH	E	5	E	10	19	15	0·342	113 359 train-km			724·7	
C.F. du Jura (CJ) 1 rue Général Voirol, 2710 Tavannes	4' 8½'' (1·435)	E 7 (11)	E 8 (13)	15 000 V 1/16⅔	DS	2			} 11	} 26	68·0	7·3 (11·7)	747 949 ton-km	469	873·9	8·1 (13·1)
	3' 3⅜'' (1·00)	E 45 (74)	E 50 (81)	1 500 V dc	EL 14 D 1											
Oberaargau-Jura Bahn (OJB) Grubenstr 12, CH-4900 Langenthal	3' 3⅜'' (1·00)	E 15 (25)	E 16 (26)	1 200 V dc	EL 2 ES 4		E T	6 2	2	8	31·9		150 201 ton-km	230	504·4	4·3 (7)
Kriens Luzern Bahn (KLB) Verkehrsbetrieb der Stadt Luzern Tribschenstr 65, 6000 Lucerne 12	4' 8½'' (1·435)	3 (4·3)	4 (5·6)		Dh	5					80·0		285 929 ton-km			
C.F. Lausanne-Echallens-Bercher (LEB) CH 1040 Echallens	3' 3⅜'' (1·00)	E 0·6 (1)	E 16 (26)	1 500 V dc OH			R	6	9						1 259·1	8·0 (12·8)
C.F. de Lausanne à Ouchy (LO) CP568, CH-1001 Lausanne *(Abt rack system)*	4' 8½'' (1·435)	E 1·7 (2·8)	E 3 (5)	*	E	5†	E (rack)	4	5		31·0	0·6 (1·0)			8 000	
Bergbahn Lauterbrunnen-Mürren (BLM) *(Operated by Berner Oberland)*	3' 3⅜'' (1·00)	E 2 (3) E 1 (1·5)	=cable	550 V dc			E	4	2	4 2	5·2	3·7 (6·1)	169 021 train-km		569·0	3·5 (5·7)
Leuk-Lukerbadbahn (LLB) *(Operating omnibuses only since 1967)*																
Ferrovia Lugano-Ponte Tresa (FL) 6900 Lugano	3' 3⅜'' (1·00)	E 8 (12)		1 200 V dc			E	6	5	4	3·0	6·2 (10)			1 181	5·5 (8·9)
Ferrovia Lugano-Tesserete (LT) *(Operating omnibuses only since 1967)*																
C.F. de Martigny au-Châtelard (MC) Martigny *(Part Strub rack rail)*	3' 3⅜'' (1·00)	E 12 (19)	E 14 (21)	830 V dc OH 3R			E T	10 9	19	18	19·7	274 525 ton-km			350·2	4·3 (6·9)
C.F. Martigny-Orsières (MO) Martigny-Ville	4' 8½'' (1·435)	E 16 (25)		15 000 V 1/16⅔ OH			E	5	9	2	43·5	11·6 (18·7)			466·7	10·7 (17·3)
Mittel-Thurgau Bahn (MThB) 8570 Weinfelden	4' 8½'' (1·435)	E 26 (42)	E 28 (45)	15 000 V 16⅔	D 1 S 2 E 1 De 1		D E EM	2 3 2	3		418·4	7 022 688 ton-km		2 000	1 025	9·5 (15·2)
Cie des C.F. des Montagnes Neuchâteloises (CMN) La Chaux-de-Fonds	3' 3⅜'' (1·00)	E 12½ (20)		1 500 V dc	S	1	E	5	4	24	1·6	(12·8)			551·7	4·2 (6·8)
Ferrovia Del Monte Generoso (MG) 6825 Capolago, Nt. Lugano *(Abt rack system)*	2' 7½'' (0·80)	6 (9)			DhL 1 DL 2		D	4 (3)	6	3		6 (9)	1·0	16	113·1	6 (9)
Münster-Lengnau-Bahn (MLB) *(Operated by B.L.S.)*	4' 8½'' (1·435)															
C.F. Montreux-Oberland Bernois (MOB) Rue du Lac 36, 1815 Clarens *(Operates Montreaux-Glion and Glion aux Rochers de Naye)*	3' 3⅜'' (1·00)	E 47 (75)	E 55 (89)	900 V dc OH	EL 2 DeL 1		E	23	39	120	30·4	567 100 tonne-km			1 640·0	11·4 (18·3)
C.F. Nyon-St. Cergue-Morez (NST-CM) Chemin de Bourgogne 16, 1260 Nyon	3' 3⅜'' (1·00)	E 17 (27)	E 18·6 (30·6)	2 200 V dc	E	7	T	7	13	27	4·96	66 892 ton-km			350·1	10 (15·7)
Oensingen-Balsthalbahn (OeBB) Balsthal	4' 8½'' (1·435)	E 3 (4)		15 000 V 1/16⅔	ES 2 S 2		E	2	9		79	278 026 ton-km			450	
C.F. Orbe-Chavornay (OC) Rue de la Poste 2, CH 1350	4' 8½'' (1·435)	E 3 (4)	E 3·2 (5·2)	750 V dc OH	EL	2	E	4	3		125	1·9 (3·0)		600	133·4	3 (4)
Pilatus-Bahn (PB) Grendelstr 2, 6002 Lucerne *(Locher rack)*	2' 7½'' (0·50)	E 2·9 (4·6)	E 3·2 (5·2)	1 550 V dc OH			E	10			0·310	2·6 (4·2)			238·2	2·6 (4·2)
Cie du C.F. Pont-Brassus (PBr) rue de la Gare 8 1347 Le Sentier	4' 8½'' (1·435)	E 11·8 (19)	E 9 (13)	15 000 V 1/16⅔							18 298	198 822 ton-km			195 300	4·5 (7·3)
Rhätische Bahn (RhB) Bahnhofstr 25, CH-7000 Chur	3' 3⅜'' (1·00)	E 308·8 (391)	E 242 (497)	11 000 V 1/16⅔ OH ‡	SL 2 EL 51 DeL 2 DeS 4		E MU	39 4	261	990	653·0	32 517 000 ton-km			7 275·5	13·8 (22·2)
Rheinech-Walzenhausen-Bahn (RhW) Walzenhausen *(part Riggenbach rack)*	3' 11¼'' (1·200)	E 1·2 (2)					E	1								

* 700V dc Lausanne-Ouchy: 1.5 km
  700V dc Lausanne-Gare Flon: 0.3 km
  15V 16⅔ Hz Flon-Sébeillon: 1.0 km
† 4 rack, 2 adhesion
‡ Excluding Chur Aroso electrified at 2 400 V dc (16 miles; *26 km*), Castione-Mesocco at 1500V (19 miles; *31 km*), and St. Moritz-Tirano at 100V (38 miles; *61 km*)

Average Speeds: Freight Train mph (km/hr)	Average Speeds: Pass. Train mph (km/hr)	Speed max. mph (km/hr)	Financial Data: Revenue Expenses in 1 000s	Braking (continuous)	Couplers: Type and Height above rail ins (mm)	Buffers: Centres and Height above rail ins (mm)	Rails: Weight lb. per yd (kg/m)	Sleepers (crossties): Type and thickness ins (mm)	Sleepers (crossties): Spacing Number per mile (per km) or centres ins (mm)	Curvature max.	Gradient max. (U=not compensated)	Axle load max. tonnes	Altitude max. feet (m)	Staff employed. Total no. (inclu. workshop)	Names of officials. Extended lists can be found at the end of the individual country in the report section immediately following
	6·8 (11)	11 (17·5)		Electric	19½" (500)	19½" (500)	Abt. rack system		35½ (900)	29·0°	22·0%	5·0	6 801 (1 973)	20 (5)	Gen. Man: R. Widmer
5 (8)	10 (16)	10 (16)	F. 9 951·3 8 226·9	Regen	Buffer coupler	Ht. 24⅞ (630)	60/40 (30/20)	Metal	25⅞/35½ (660/900)	22·0°	20·0%	6·75	10 132 (3 089)	93	Dir: R. Perren
		59 (95)	F.11 046·6 17 809·0	Air Rheost	Standard	Standard	93/73 (46/36)	Wood 6 (150)	24⅞" (630)	9·8°	3·5%	20	2 598 (792)		Gen. Man: Dr. F. Anliker
25 (40)	37 (60)	56 (90)	F. 8 481·2 11 644·5	Air Oerlikon	Standard	Standard	93/73 (46/36) Type V	Metal & Wood 6 (150)	23½" (600)	9·5°	2·8%	20	2 444 (745)	173 (5)	Gen. Man: Dr. Ch. Kellerhals
		39 (63)	F.8 779·9 8 044·9	Regen	Buffer-Coupler	Central (520)	41·6 (20·6)	Metal	39⅜" (1 000)	17·5	25·0%	8	11 333 (3 454)	112	Gen. Man: Dr. Roland Hirni
22 (35)	28 (45)	43 (70)	F. 3 085 6 558	W'hse Char-milles	Screw (1 050) Semi-auto. 23⅛ (600)	Crs. 56½ (1 435) Central (600)	72/40 (36/20)	Metal & Wood 6 (150)	28⅜" (720)	29·5°	5·0%	St. 20 M. 14	3 517 (1 072)	118	Gen. Man: J. von Kaenel
11 (18)	17 (28)	37 (60)	F. 1 642 3 078	Air Oerlikon	G.F. Auto. 19½ (500)		72/48 (36/24)	Metal Wood	26" (670)	25·4°	6·5%	20	1 722 (524)	59	Dir: J. Mathys
		19 (30)	F. 561·7 572·3				60/90 (30/45)	Metal & Wood	31⅞" (800)	17·5°	3·4%	18	1 604 (489)	6	Dir: Kurt Frei
37 (30)			F. 1 658·2 3 121·5		G.F. Auto.	20½ (520)	60·2 (30)	Metal	31⅞" (800)	4·4°	4·0%	8		36	
13 (20)	19 (30)		F. 3 108·1 2 756·4	Char-milles Air	G.F. Auto.		72·6 (36)	Metal & Wood 6 (150)	35½" (900)	3·6°	12·0%	16	1 575 (480)	79 (10)	Gen. Man: J. Perret
				Air							5·0% 60·6%		4 859 (1 481)	42	Gen. Man: Dr. Roland Hirni
															Pres: Aw. Dott Demetrio Balestra
										29·0°					
			F. 2 130 2 253	Char-milles W'hse	Scharff. 28⅜ (720)		51 (36)	Oak 5½ (140)	2 280 (1 416)	10·0°	7·0% 20·0%		4 028 (1 228)	58	
			F. 191·3 187·5							7·3°	4·0%		2 959 (902)	63	
24·8 (40)	31·0 (50)	49·7 (80)	F. 6 107·6 5 792·3	W'hse	Standard	Standard	90/73 (45/36)	Wood 6/9½ (150/240)	24⅞" (630)	7·2°	20%	20	1 873 (571)	96	Dir: Dr. R. Sax Dir: A. Welter
							72/40 (36/20)				4·0%		3 657 (1 115)		
9 (14)	9 (14)	9 (14)	F. 675 0 1 002·9	W'hse Air	MG 24 (620)		36 (18)			22°	120%	5	5 315 (1 620)	11	Ch. H. Hochstrasser
11 (18)	25 (40)	47 (75)	F. 6 395·2 8 601·7	Hardy Vac	Screw 19⅝ (500)	Central 29½ (750)	61/48 (30/24)	Wood 6 (150) Concrete 8½ (220) & Metal	25½" (650)	22°	7·2%	11	4 183 (1 275)	226 (35)	Eng: E. Styger
24·8 (40)	24·8 (40)	24·8 (40)	F. 1 133·8 1 814·3	Air W'hse	19⅝ (500)	Central 23·6 (650)	40 (20/36)			45 m	6·0%		4 044 (1 233)	36	Dir: F. Girard
			F. 1 371 1 361·7								12·0%		1 614 (492)		D. Müller
17 (30)	22 (35)	31 (50)	F. 977 1 274	Oerlikon			101/73 (50/36)		(1 500)	11·6°	3·0%	20	1 552 (473)	18 (3)	Dir: E. Maire
		Down 5·6 (9) Up 7·5 (12)	F. 2 458·1 2 347·6	Electric			Locher Rack System			2·0°	48%		6 791 (2 070)	38	Gen. Man: H. Vonwyl
37 (60)	37 (60)	40 (60)	F. 711 1 040	Air	39·3 (1 000)		92 (46)	SBB 1 SBB 2 steel	(1 666)	17·5°	2·8%		3 445 (1 050)	15	Dir: R. Armand
23 (37)	28 (45)	56 (90)	F. 83 642·8 95 005·3	Vac Hardy	Screw 24⅜" (620)	Centre 24⅜ (620)	60/50 (30/25)	Oak 6 (150) Metal	26¾-32¼ (680-820)	39·0°	See foot note	12	7 405 (2,257)	1 450	Dir: Dr. O. Wieland
											25%				

NAME OF COMPANY ADDRESS	Gauge ft. in. *(metres)*	Route length incl. E=Elec- trified miles *(km.)*	Track length incl. E=Elec- trified miles *(km.)*	Elect. system and type of con- ductor	Loco- motives L=Line S=Shunt Steam Electric Diesel De=elec. Dh=hyd.	Rail- cars Electric Diesel Trailer Railbus Multiple Unit set	Pass. train cars	Freight train cars Con- tainers	Total Volume carried. Thous- ands of tonnes	Av'ge haul per ton miles *(km.)*	Av'ge net train load tonnes	Max. trailing load tonnes	Total number carried in 1 000s	Aver- age jour- ney miles *(km.)*

SWITZERLAND *(contd.)*

Rigi-Bahn *(See Arth-Rigi-Bahn)*

Rorschach-Heiden-Bahn (RHB) Heiden *(Riggenbach rack system)*	4' 8½'' *(1·435)*	E 4 *(6)*		15 000 V 1/16⅔		E 3	13	14						
St. Gallen-Gais-Appenzell- Alstätten-Bahn (SGA) 9053 Teufen, (Appenzell) A=adhesion, R=rack.	3' 3⅜'' *(1·00)*	12 *(19·48)*† 3·4 R*(5·5)*		1 500 V dc OH		EL 8 ES 1	25	49	8 050	107 013 ton-km			1 404 104	5·1 *(8·3)*
St. Gallen-Speicher-Trogen (TB) 9042 Speicher, AR	3' 3⅜'' *(1·00)*	E 6 *(10)*	8 *(13)*	1 000 V dc		E 8	12	17	4·7	5 *(8·6)*	6·5	29	850·0	5·0 *(8·1)*

Schöllenenbahn (SB) *(Merged into Furka-Oberalp-Bahn)*

Schweizerische Südostbahn (SOB) CH-8820 Wadenswil	4' 8½'' *(1·435)*	E 30 *(40)*	E 36 *(58)*	15 000 V 1/16⅔	EL 3 ES 1	E 14	24	20	124 000				2 800	5·4 *(8·7)*
Schynige Platte-Bahn (SPB) *(Operated by Berner Oberland Bahnen.)* *(Riggenbach rack system.)*	2' 7½'' *(0·80)*	E 4·5 *(7·2)*	E 5·3 *(8·5)*	1 500 V dc	S 1 E 11		22	10		36 808 train-km				
Sensetalbahn (STB) 3177 Laupen B.E.	4' 8½'' *(1·435)*	E 7 *(11)*	9·3 *(15)*	15 000 V 1/16⅔ OH	S 1 D 1	E 3	4		73·1	2·7 *(4·3)*			370·0	3·3 *(5·3)*
Simmentalbahn (SEZ) *(Spiez-Erlenbach-Zweisimmen)* *(Operated by Bern-Lotschberg-Simplon)*	4' 8½'' *(1·435)*	E 22 *(35)*	E 27 *(43)*	15 000 V 1/16⅔ OH	EL 1 DhS 1	EMU 4	8	16	72·9		507 810 train-km	2 000	976·7	13 *(21)*
Solothurn-Münster-Bahn (SMB) *(Operated by Emmental-Burgdorf-Thun-Bahn.)*	4' 8½'' *(1·435)*	E 14 *(22)*	E 16 *(26)*	15 000 V 1/16⅔	EL 2 OS 1	E 2 M 1	8		109·5		2 245 536 ton-km		596	4·9 *(8·1)*
Solothurn-Niederbipp-Bahn (SNB) Grubenstr 12, CH-4900 Langenthal	3' 3⅜'' *(1·00)*	E 10 *(16)*	E 11 *(17)*	1 200 V dc	EL 2 ES 1	R 17 E 5 T 2	2	6	43·0		131 712 ton-km	300	577·1	4·7 *(7·5)*
Solothurn-Zollikofen-Bern-Bahn (SZB) Postfach 28, 3048 Worblaufen	3' 3⅜'' *(1·00)*	E 23 *(38)*	E 34 *(55)*	1 250 V dc	EL 3 DeS 2 SL 1	E 10 ET 11 EMU 12	11	13‡	188·7	7·4 *(8·2)*	24	240	76 738	6·5 *(10·2)*
Luzern-Stans-Engelberg Bahn (LSE) CH-6362 Stansstad. *(Riggenback rack)*	3' 3⅜'' *(1·00)*	E 16 *(25)* Rack *(1·5)*	E 17 *(28)*	15 000 V 1/16⅔ OH	DhS 2 DS 1 DhL 1	E 7 ET 7	11	4	33·5		248 786 ton-km	450	1 210·1	6·2 *(10)*
Ferrovie Autolinee Regionali Ticinesi (FART) 6601 Locarno	3' 3⅜'' *(1·00)*	E 12 *(20)*	E 14 *(23)*	1 300 V dc OH		E 6	8	17	0·5					
Sihltal-Zürich-Uetliberg-Bahn (SZU) Sihlamstr 5, CH-8039 Zürich Selnau	4' 8½'' *(1·435)*	E 16·7 *(27)*	E 17·3 *(30)*	15 000 V 1/16⅔ OH (18 km) 1·2 kV dc (9 km)	SL 1 EL 2 DeL 2 DhL 1 DmL 1	E 14 ET 14	18	4	183·1		1 017 356 ton-km		3 858·5	5·1 *(8·2)*
Sursee-Triengen-Bahn (ST) Betriebsleitung, 6234 Triengen	4' 8½'' *(1·435)*	5·6 *(9)*			SL 2 DeL 1		22	2	250	4·5 *(7·1)*	61	100	161	4·5 *(7·2)*
C.F. Régional du val de Travers (RVT) Fleurier (Neuchâtel)	4' 8½'' *(1·435)*	E 9 *(14)*		15 000 V 1/16⅔ OH	E 1 D 1	E 2 D 1	10	21	78·6	4·9 *(7·9)*			989·1	3·5 *(5·7)*
C.F. Electriques Veveysans (CEV) 4 avenue de Gilamont, 1800 Vevey *(Stub rack)*	3' 3⅜'' *(1·00)*	E 7 *(11)*	E 8 *(13)*	800 V dc OH	EL 3	R 10	12	7	0·823	4 643 ton-km		791·8	3·7	*(5·8)*
Waldenburgerbahn AG (WB) 4437 Waldenburg	2' 5½'' *(0·75)*	E 8 *(13)*	E 10 *(16)*	1 500 V dc OH	SL 1 E 3		10	22	2·7	34 779 ton-km			670·2	5·8 *(9·3)*
Wengernalp-Bahn (WAB) 3800 Interlaken *(Operated by BOB) (Riggenbach rack system.)*	2' 7½'' *(0·800)*	E 12 *(19)*	E 17 *(28)*	1 500 V dc	EL 8	E 24	40	54	31·6	488 553 train-km			2 530·4	4·8 *(7·7)*
Wohlen-Meisterschwanden-Bahn (WM) 5620 Bremgarten *(Operated by Bremgarten-Dietikon-B)*	4' 8½'' *(1·435)*	E 5 *(8)*	E 7 *(11)*	15 000 V dc	DeS 2	E 2	2		105·1	337 846 ton-km			295·9	3·5 *(5·7)*
Wynental-und Suhrentalbahn (WSB) Hintere Bahnhofstrasse 85, Aarau	3' 3⅜'' *(1·00)*	E 21 *(33)*	E 25 *(40)*	750 V dc OH		E 19	21	27	71·8	6·8 *(10·9)*	88	165	3 991·7	4·2 *(6·8)*
C.F. d'Yverdon — Ste. Croix Quai de la Thièle 32, CH-1400, Yverdon	3' 3⅜'' *(1·00)*	E 15 *(24)*	E 14·9 *(24)*	15 000 V. 1/16⅔ OH	EL 1	E 4	8	15	13·1		199 394	402·4	386·9	9 *(14·2)*

SYRIA

| ***Syrian Railways** Chemins de Fer Syriens BP 182, Aleppo | 4' 8½'' *(1·435)* | 565 *(910)* | | | SL 34 SS 2 DL 10 | D 11 | 123 | 1 106 | | 303 229 000 ton-km | | | 519·2 | |

***Hedjaz Railway Administration** Direction Général des C.F. du Hedjaz PO Box 134, Damascus

Operates two railways

| **Hedjaz Railway** | 3' 5¼'' *(1·050)* | 157 *(253)* | 173 *(279)* | | SL 26 SS 9 | R 4 | 24 | 313 | 101·5 | 82·4 *(136)* | 165 | 275 | 311·0 | 30 *(48)* |
| **Damascus-Serghaya Railway** | 3' 5¼'' *(1·050)* | 42 *(67)* | 45 *(72)* | | SL 9 SS 1 | | 24 | 139 | 74·5 | 37 *(62)* | 84 | 140 | 232·3 | 22 *(35)* |

* See main entry
† Including 2.7 miles *(4.4 km)* Ribbenbach rack and 2 miles *(3.3 km)* of Strub rack
‡ Plus 30 specials for transport of standard-gauge rail wagons

Average Speeds: Freight Train mph (km/hr)	Average Speeds: Pass. Train mph (km/hr)	Speed max. mph (km/hr)	Financial Data: Revenue Expenses in 1 000s	Braking (continuous)	Couplers: Type and Height above rail ins (mm)	Buffers: Centres and Height above rail ins (mm)	Rails: Weight lb. per yd (kg/m)	Sleepers (crossties): Type and thickness ins (mm)	Sleepers (crossties): Spacing Number per mile (per km) or centres ins (mm)	Curvature max.	Gradient max. (U=not compensated)	Axle load max. tonnes	Altitude max. feet (m)	Staff employed. Total no. (inclu. workshop)	Names of officials. Extended lists can be found at the end of the individual country in the report section immediately following
										14·5°	9·0%		2 605 *(794)*		
		55	F. 3 717·6 5 864·6	Air Oerliken						59·0°	R.16·0% A. 5·9%		3 054 *(931)*	100	Pres: E. Vitzthum Dir: Hardegger
	16 *(25)*	31 *(50)*		Char- milles Air	Screw 17′ 7″ *(450)*	Centre 27½ *(700)*		Metal	26½″ *(680)*	58·0°	7·5%		3 136 *(956)*	48 *(16)*	Gen. Man: D. Brugger
	28 *(45)*	50 *(80)*	F. 9 284 9 169	Air Oerlikon			93 *(46)*	Wood Metal & Conc.		8·2°	5·0%	20	3 035 *(925)*	158 *(23)*	Dir: E. A. Gross
	6·8 *(11·0)*		F 1 478·2 1 414·8					Metal			26·0%		6 453 (1 967)	incl. in BOB	Dr. Roland Hirni
18·6 *(30)*	22·3 *(36)*	47 *(75)*		Air W'hse	R.J.V. *(1 060)*	41¾ *(1 060)*	90/60 *(45/30)*	Wood Metal	*(550-650)*	9·7°	3·6%	20	1 811 *(552)*	35 *(5)*	Gen. Man: Hans Spring Pres: Dr. Willi Marki
		47 *(75)*	F. 5 853·6 9 939·4	Vac Rheost	Standard	Standard	94/74 *(46/36)*	Wood 6 *(150)*	26¼″ *(666)*	8·7°	2·5%	20	3 090 *(942)*		Gen. Man: Dr. F. Anliker
25 *(40)*	37 *(60)*	50 *(80)*	F. 2 364·1 3 722·6	Oerlikon	Standard	Standard	93/73 *(46/36)* Type V.	Metal Wood 6 *(150)*	23½ *(600)*	6·25°	2·8%	16	2 359 *(719)*	35 *(15)*	Gen. Man: Dr. Ch. Kellerhals
15 *(25)*	19 *(31)*	37 *(60)*	F. 1 045 1 903	Air	Central 19⅝ *(500)*		60/50 *(30/25)*	Metal Wood	35½″ *(900)*	25·5°	4·5%	20	4 757 *(1 450)*	27	Gen. Man: J. Mathys
22 *(35)*	37 *(60)*	47 *(75)*	F. 13 238·9 17 530·9	Char- milles Air	G.F. Auto 19⅝ *(500)*		72/60 *(36/30)*	Metal Wood & Conc.	23⅝″ *(600)*	Rad. 295 ft *(90 m)*	2·7%*	12	1 837 *(560)*	242 *(45)*	Gen. Man: Dr. J. Fahm Com. Man: B. Fink
22 *(35)*	28 *(45)*	47 *(75)*	F. 5 440·5 5 430·6	Char- milles Air	Auto Fischer 25⅝ *(650)*		73/60 *(35/30)*	Metal & Wood 6 *(150)*	24⅞″ *(630)*	25·0°	5% **U** 25% **U** Rack	16	3 287 *(1 002)*	77 *(6)*	Gen. Man: J. Neuhaus
	25 *(40)*	37 *(60)*	F. 2 234 3 162	Air	Buffer- Coupler	23⅝ *(600)*	61/48 *(30/24)*	Metal 7⅞ *(200)*	2 240 *(1 570)*	29·5°	6·1%	10	1 801 *(549)*	95 *(41)*	Gen. Man: Marco Pessi
37 *(60)*	37 *(70)*	43 *(70)*	F. 7 534·8 11 478·9	Oerlikon Air	Standard *(1 050)*		92/72 *(46/36)*	Wood 6 *(150)*	24½″ *(620)*	7·7°	2·8%	20	1 690 *(515)*	150	Gen. Man: H. Tempelmann
		31 *(50)*	F. 369·3 771·6	W'hse Air	Standard		72·6 *(36)*		1 035 *(1 666)*	8·25°	1·5%	20	1476 *(450)*	17 *(2)*	Gen. Man: B. Jakob
							72·5 *(36)*			11·6°	1·7%		2 522 *(769)*		
		24 *(40)*	F. 1 228·7 2 345·8	Vac Hardy	GF		50/83 *(25/36)*			29·5°	5·0% 20·0 rack	12	4 450 *(1 356)*	39	Gen. Man: E. Lehmann
27 *(45)*	34 *(55)*	34 *(55)*	F. 1 276·6 1 416·9	Char- milles Air	GF 15¼ *(388)*	17⅞ *(440)*	61/50 *(25/30)*			25·0	3·0%	7·5	1 082 *(330)*	29	Gen. Man: A. Fuchs
6·8 *(11)*	13 *(21)*	46 *(74)*	F. 16 736·8 14 917·4	SLM type	Buffer- Coupler	Central *(530)*	51/40 *(20/25·5)*	Metal	39⅜″ *(1 000)*	29·0°	25·0%	8	6 762 *(2 061)*	222	Dr. Roland Hirni
31 *(50)*	22 *(35)*	40 *(65)*	F. 1 062·0 1 840·7	Air Oerlikon	4 *(104)*	7·2 *(185)*	92 *(46)*	Wood & Metal	23⅝″ *(600)*	14·5°	4·2%	20	1 765 *(538)*	30 *(7)*	Dir: W. Zurcher Gen. Man: W. Fink
		40 *(65)*		Air Char- milles	GF auto. *(600)*		72/60 *(36/30)*	Metal CTU	27½″ *(700)*	65·0°	3·7%	10	1 798 *(548)*	170	Dir: Dipl. El.-Ing. P. Diem
(37·5)	*(37·5)*	31 *(50)*	F. 1 215·9 2 693·4	Air	Central 10⅛ *(260)*		60 *30)*	Steel & Wood 7 *(180)*		17·5°	4·4%		3 508 *(1 069)*	62	Dir: Chevalley Marcel
21·7 *(35)*	21·7 *(35)*	*N. Line* 37 *(60)* *S. Line* 31 *(50)*	£S 12 000·0 14 000·0	Air W'hse Knorr	UIC	UIC	74/60 *(37/30)*	Metal *(7/14 mm)*	N. *(1 249)* S. *(1 257/ 1 152)*	N. Line 4·35° S. Line 5·8°	N. Line 2·5% **U** S. Line 2·0% **U**	N. 16·7 S. 15·0°	N. 2 024 *(617)* S. 1 762 *(526)*	1 452 *(346)*	Gen. Man: Ing. Ing Abdel Jabbar Koundakji
															Gen. Man: Fahmi Kosara
22 *(35)*	25 *(40)*	31 *(50)*		Vac Hardy	Air 31 *(800)*	Air 31 *(800)*	50/43 *(25/21·5)*	Metal	27½″ *(700)*	17·5°	2·4% 2·0%**U**	10·5	2 428 *(740)*	865 *(488)*	Gen. Man: Fahmi Kossara
12 *(30)*	15 *(25)*	22 *(35)*		Vac Hardy	UIC 31 *(800)*	UIC 31 *(800)*	55 *(27·6)*	Metal	35½″ *(900)*	17·5°	3·4% 3·0%**U**	11·5	4 609 *(1 405)*		

NAME OF COMPANY ADDRESS	Gauge ft. in. (metres)	Route length incl. E=Electrified miles (km.)	Track length incl. E=Electrified miles (km.)	Elect. system and type of conductor	Locomotives L=Line S=Shunt Steam Electric Diesel De=elec. Dh=hyd.	Rail-cars Electric Diesel Trailer Railbus Multiple Unit set / Con-tainers	Pass. train cars	Freight train cars	Total Volume carried. Thousands of tonnes	Av'ge haul per ton miles (km.)	Av'ge net train load tonnes	Max. trailing load tonnes	Total number carried in 1 000s	Average journey miles (km.)
TAIWAN														
*Taiwan Railway Taiwan Ry. Administration, 2 Yenping Rd. North, Taipei	3' 6'' (1·067) 2' 6'' (0·762)	512 (824) 109 (176) E 307 (495)	1 193 (1 926·5) 149 (240)	60 Hz single phase 25 kV	De 161 SL 141	D 63 T 10 MUD 42	1 150	7 172 C 1 619	15 619·7	297 29 214 454 train-km			115 576·1	
TANZANIA														
*Tanzania Zambia Railway Corporation (TAZARA) PO Box 2834, Dar-es-Salaam *(Responsible for the Tanzam Railway)*														
THAILAND														
*State Railway of Thailand Krung Kasem Rd, Bangkok	3' 3⅜'' (1·00)	2 392 (3 855)	2 746 (4 428)		SL 220 SS 21 D 243	DMU 57	962	9 398	5 116·7	2 504 583 616 ton-km			61 408·5	52·7 (84·9)
TOGO														
Réseau des Chemins de Fer du Wharf du Togo PO Box 340, Lomé	3' 3⅜'' (1·00)	275 (442)	310 (499)		DeL 11 DhL 2 DhS 2 Dm 6	R 5 D 5 C 2	63	378	5 368 000 000 tonne-km			77 502 000 pass-km	31 (50)
TUNISIA														
*Societe Nationale des Chemins de Fer Tunisiens (S.N.C.F.T.) 67 Avenue Farhat Hached, Tunis	4' 8½'' (1·435) 3' 3⅜'' (1·00)	1 200 (1 928)	1 292 (2 089)		De 122	D 60 T 10 C 283	111	5 387	7 367·4	1 521 783 960 ton-km			18 783·5	18·7 (30·1)
TURKEY														
*Turkish State Railways (TCDD) Türkiye Cumhuriyeti Devlet Demiryollar TCDD Isletmesi, Genel Müdürlügü, Ankara	4' 8½'' (1·435)	5 128 (8 253) E 68 (109)	6 109 (9 831) E 157 (253)	25 000 V 1/50 OH	SL 719 SS 100 EL 12 DeL 122 DhL 9 DhS 61	E 30 D 14 DMU 27 R 25	1 175	19 168	17 041·8	7 932 271 000 ton-km			112 956·6	29·4 (47·2)
UGANDA *(See East Africa)*														
USSR														
*Soviet Railways Ministry of Communications Moscow 107104 Novo Basmannaia 2	4' 11⅞'' (1·520) 4' 8½'' (1·435) 3' 6'' (1·067) 1' 11⅝''- 3' 3⅜'' (0·60- 1·0)	84 700 (136 300) E 22 475 (36 170)		25 000V 1/50 OH 1 500 V dc OH 3 000 V dc OH					3 329 400	3 236 500 000 ton-km			3 306 400	56 (90)
UK														
*British Rail British Railways Board 222 Marylebone Road, London NW1 6JJ	4' 8½'' (1·435) 1' 11½'' (0·597)	11 326 (18 190) E 2 365 (3 800) 12 (19)	29 387 (47 153)	25 kV 1/50 OH 1·5 kV dc OH 1·2 kV dc 3R 650/750 Vdc 3R 630/650 Vdc 4R	S 3 EL 333 DeL2 444 DeS 985 DhL 73 DhS 3 DmS134	D 28 EM 7 173 DM 3 440 ET 4 514 DT 1 424 C 5 039	7 168	248 682	195 820				728 270	
Bluebell Railway Ltd. Sheffield Park Stn, Uckfield, Sussex	4' 8½'' (1·435)	5 (8)	10 (16)		SL 20 PS 1 SS 3		30	20					279·9	8 (13)
British Steel Corporation 33 Grosvenor Place, London SW1	4' 8½'' (1·435)												
Scunthorpe Division Scunthorpe Works	4' 8½'' (1·435)		248 (399)		DE 69 DH 16				2 600					
Shelton Works			26 (42)		DE 8 DH 4				569					
Monks Hall Work			1 (1·8)		DE 2				4					
Warrington Works			1 (1·8)		DE 3									
Irlam Works			4 (6)		DE 4				16					

* See main entry

Average Speeds			Financial Data		Couplers	Buffers	Rails	Sleepers (crossties)							Names of officials.
Freight Train	Pass. Train	Speed max.	Revenue Expenses	Braking (continuous)	Type and Height above rail	Centres and Height above rail	Weight	Type and thickness	Spacing Number per mile (per km) or centres ins (mm)	Curvature max.	Gradient max. (U=not compensated)	Axle load max.	Altitude max.	Staff employed. Total no. (inclu. workshop)	Extended lists can be found at the end of the individual country in the report section immediately following
mph (km/hr)	mph (km/hr)	mph (km/hr)	in 1 000s		ins (mm)	ins (mm)	lb. per yd (kg/m)	ins (mm)				tonnes	feet (m)		
			US$ 5 030 574 (revenues only)	Semi-auto 34⅝ (880)			W 10/75 (50/37) E 44 (22)	W Wood 5½ (140) Conc E 4 (100)	2 785 (1 732)	W 5·8° E 17·5°	W 2·31% E 3·04%	Coopers E 33			Man. Director: J. Fan
		P 50 (80) F 37 (60)	Baht 1 395 308 1 436 690	R'cars Air Trains Vac	Auto US Type 33½ (850)		80/50 (40/25)	Wood 6 (150) and Conc	25½/27½ (650/700)	590 ft (180 m)	2·3% 2·6% U	Diesel loco 13·75 Steam 10·5 R'stock 12·0	1 886 (575)	33 976 (6 212)	Gen. Man: Sanga Navicharern
28 (45)	28 (45)	44 (70)		Vac Jordain Monneret	Willison	Central Buffer Coupler	66/40 (33/20)	Metal	2 400 (1 490)	8·7°; in yards 22·0°	1%	12·5	1 083 (330)	1 072	Gen. Man: W. Eiden
25 (40)	37 (60)	68 (110)	D 16 541·5 17 964·9	Air W'hse Vac	Screw St. 41 (1 040) M. Ht. 30" (775)	Standard (1 720) (1 050) M. Central (800)	94/60 (46/30)	Oak (120-140) Conc. (190) Steel	22½-29½" (575-750)	Standard 9·75° Metre 11·3° 11·75°	2·0%	Standard 21 Metre 18	1 066 (325)	7 239 (1 217)	Gen. Man: Mohamed Ali Soussi
19 (30)	39 (63)	78 (125)	T.L. 7 004 039 7 197 462	Oerlikon Knorr air	Standard	Standard	109/90 (54/45)	Wood 6¼ (160) Conc B 55	2 575 (1 600)	Min rad 656 ft (200 m)	2·9% 2·75% U but general 2·5%	20	7 402 (2 256)	63 502 (36 774)	Gen. Director: Orhan Acartar
20·9 (33·7)	28·7 (46·2)	100 (160)	Milliard Roubles 15·6 8·8	Air	SA-Z Auto 42⅛ (1 070)		151/104 (75/51·6) mainly 104 (51·6)	Wood 6¼ (160) 7 (180) Conc.	3 013 (1 872)	Main Line 2 132 ft (650 m) general some 1 148 ft (350 m)	Class I and II 1·5% Class III 2·0% Class IV 3·0%	23		2 031 200	Min of Communications: Boris Pavlovich Beschev
		100 (161)		Vac Air on diesel and electric locos and MU trains	P *Main* Buckeye P *Sub* Screw F *Fast* Screw or Instanter F *Slow* 3-link or Instanter Ht 41¼ (1 048)	Crs 68¼ (1 734) Ht 41¼ (1 048)	*Main* 110 (55)	Wood 5 (127) Conc 5½" (140) at centre 8" (203) at rails	30" (762)	*Main* 2 640 ft (805 m)	*Main* 2·70%	22·5	1 484 (452)	196 635 (33 001)	Chairman: Peter Parker MVO
10 (16)	20 (32)	25 (40)	103 813 102 403	Vac	Screw		Bullhead	Wood Conc.	2 112 (1 312)	2·2°	1·75%	17		7	Supt: B. J. Holden
															Head of Transport: P. A. Thompson

UK (contd.)

NAME OF COMPANY ADDRESS	Gauge ft. in. (metres)	Route length incl. E=Electrified miles (km.)	Track length incl. E=Electrified miles (km.)	Elect. system and type of conductor	Loco-motives L=Line S=Shunt / Steam Electric Diesel De=elec. Dh=hyd.	Rail-cars Electric Diesel Trailer Railbus Multiple Unit set	Pass. train cars	Freight train cars / Containers	Total Volume carried. Thousands of tonnes	Av'ge haul per ton miles (km.)	Av'ge net train load tonnes	Max. trailing load tonnes	Total number carried in 1 000s	Average journey miles (km.)
Sheffield Division														
River Don Works	4' 8½" (1·435)	0·5 (0·8)	8 (13)		DM 8, DH 4			78						
Grimesthorpe Works		0·5 (0·8)	2 (3·2)		DM 1			10						
Cyclops Works			1 (1·8)		DM 1			1						
Stocksbridge Works		1 (1·8)	19 (30·5)		DE 10			450						
Stocksbridge Railway		2 (3·2)	8 (13)		DE 1			44						
Tinsley Park Works		3 (4·8)	16 (26)		DM 2, DH 4, DE 1			196						
Panteg Works		1 (1·8)	6 (9·6)		DE 1, DH 3			100						
Shepcote Lane Works			1 (1·8)		DM 1									
Bilston Works		5 (8)	22 (35)		DE 15			634						
Wolverhampton Works		—	1 (1·8)		DE 1									
Craigneuk Foundry Works		—	3 (4·8)		DE 2			22						
Fullwood Works		—	1 (1·8)		DE 1, DM 1			13						
Distington Works		4 (6·4)	5 (8)		DE 2			72						
Dowlais Works		1 (1·8)	2 (3·2)		DM 2			35						
Landore Works		2 (3·2)	3 (4·8)		DH 3			41						
Rotherham: Templeborough Works		2 (3·2)	50 (80)		DE 16			787						
Rotherham: Aldwarke Works		4 (6·4)	50 (80)		DE 14, DH 3			382						
Trafford Park Works		1 (1·8)	10 (16)		DH 2			45						
Scottish Division														
Ravenscraig Works	4' 8½" (1·435)		50 (86)		DH 22			230						
Dalzell Works		2 (3·2)	10 (16)		DH 4, DE 3			478						
Clydebridge Works		5 (8)	13 (21)		DE 7			221						
Glengarnock Works		4 (6·4)	18 (29)		DH 3, DE 4			200						
Lanarkshire Works		1 (1·6)	12 (19)		DH 3, DE 2			267						
Victoria Works		0·5 (·8)	1 (1·6)											
Hallside Works					DE 2, DE 2									
Teesside Division														
Barrow Works	4' 8½" (1·435)	4 (6·4)	7 (11·2)		DE 2			192						
Consett Works		25 (40)	38 (61)		DH 25, DE 1			502						
Hartlepool Works		16 (25)	40 (64)		DH 21, DE 2			678						
Jarrow Works			2 (3·2)		DM 2			4						
Skinningrove Works		5 (8)	8 (12·8)		DH 3			12						
South Teesside Works		118 (174)	152 (245)		DH 65			1 818						
Workington Works		38 (61)	44 (71)		DH 10, DE 12			755						
Tubes Division														
British Works	4' 8½" (1·435)	0·5 (·8)	2 (3·2)											
Calder Works		0·5 (·8)	2 (3·2)					2						
Clydesdale Works		3 (4·8)	14 (22)		D 3, DE 3			53						
Imperial Works		0·5 (·8)	2 (3·2)		D 2									
Tollcross Works		0·5 (·8)	2 (3·2)											
Bromford Works		0·5 (·8)	2 (3·2)		DE 3			33						
Stanton Works		2·5 (4)	25 (40)		DH 12			940						
Staveley Works		5·5 (8·8)	17 (27)		DE 7			505						
Holwell Works		1 (1·6)	7 (11)		DH 3			140						
Corby Works			152 (245)		DH 52			2 912						
Welsh Division														
Shotton Works	4' 8½" (1·435)		68 (109)		DE 1, DH 23, DM 3			1 581						
Llanwern Works			50 (86)		DH 15, DE 5			253						
Port Talbot Works			111 (179)		DE 28			1 002						
Orb Works			4 (6·4)		DE 1, DM 1									
Whiteheads Works			5 (8)		DE 2, DH 2			25						
Ebbw Vale Works			55 (88)		DH 17			260						
Trostre			4 (6·4)		DE 2			9						
Velindre			3 (4·8)		DE 2			—						
East Moors					DH 18									

Average Speeds			Financial Data			Couplers	Buffers	Rails	Sleepers (crossties)		Curva-ture max.	Gradient max. (U=not compen-sated)	Axle load max.	Alti-tude max.	Staff em-ployed. Total no. (inclu. work-shop)	Names of officials. Extended lists can be found at the end of the individual country in the report section immediately following
Freight Train	Pass. Train	Speed max.	Revenue Expenses		Braking (con-tinuous)	Type and Height above rail	Centres and Height above rail	Weight	Type and thick-ness	Spacing Number per mile *(per km)* or centres ins *(mm)*						
mph *(km/hr)*	mph *(km/hr)*	mph *(km/hr)*	in 1 000s			ins *(mm)*	ins *(mm)*	lb. per yd *(kg/m)*	ins *(mm)*				tonnes	feet *(m)*		

NAME OF COMPANY ADDRESS	Gauge ft. in. (metres)	Route length incl. E=Electrified miles (km.)	Track length incl. E=Electrified miles (km.)	Elect. system and type of conductor	Loco-motives L=Line S=Shunt Steam Electric Diesel De=elec. Dh=hyd.		Rail-cars Electric Diesel Trailer Railbus Multiple Unit set	Pass. train cars	Freight train cars Con-tainers	Freight movement				Passengers	
										Total Volume carried. Thous-ands of tonnes	Av'ge haul per ton miles (km.)	Av'ge net train load tonnes	Max. trailing load tonnes	Total number carried in 1 000s	Aver-age jour-ney miles (km.)
UK *(contd.)*															
BSC (Chemicals) Ltd Orgreave and Brookhouse Works, Sheffield Clarence Works, Middlesbrough	4' 8½" *(1·435)*		9 *(14)*	DE	4				422						
British Steel Service Centres Meadow Hall Works, Sheffield	4' 8½" *(1·435)*	·15 *(·8)*	25 *(2)*	Dh	1				110·0	86 819 ton-km					
Scottish Division Ravenscraig	4' 8½" *(1·435)*		50 *(80)*	D	24				230						
Dalzell		2 *(3·2)*	10 *(16)*	DH DE	4 3				478						
Clydebridge		5 *(8)*	13 *(20)*	DH DE	5 1				221						
Glengarnock		4 *(6·4)*	18 *(29)*	DH DE	3 4				200						
Lanarkshire		1 *(1·6)*	12 *(19)*	DH	3				267						
Victoria		·5 *(·8)*	11 *(18)*	Nil					Nil						
Mossend Eng		1 *(1·6)*	4·1/4 *(6·6)*	DE	2				12						
Clyde Iron		7 *(11·2)*	15 *(24)*	DH DE	4 3				Nil						
Gartcosh		2 *(3·2)*	5.1/2 *(8·8)*	DE	3				Nil						
Duport Steelworks PO Box 15, Briton Ferry, Neath, Glamorgan (Works and railway abandoned 1978)															
Brown Bayley Steels Ltd. *Incorporating* Rotherham-Tinsley Steel Ltd. Leeds Rd, Sheffield S9 3TT	4' 8½" *(1·435)*		3 *(4·8)*	S DS	3 1										
Central Electricity Generating Board *Southern Division (Swindon and Earley power stations)* Swindon Power Station, Purton Rd, Swindon, Wilts.	4' 8½" *(1·435)*		1 *(1·6)*	Batt	1										
Darlington & Simpson Rolling Mills Ltd PO Box 9, Rise Carr Rolling Mills, Darlington, Co Durham	4' 8½" *(1·435)*		3 *(5)*	Dh	2										
Derwent Valley Railway Co Layerthorpe Station, Yorks.	4' 8½" *(1·435)*	4·2 *(6·8)*	6 *(10)*	D DL	2 1			3			58·0				
Esso Petroleum Co Ltd Victoria St, London SW1 24 refineries plants and depots with private sidings	4' 8½" *(1·435)*		21 *(34)*	DhS	9				3 200* C 20	4 000	90 *(145)*	450	1 300		
Felixtowe Dock & Rly Co The Dock, Felixtowe, Suffolk IP11 8SY	4' 8½" *(1·435)*	1·9 *(2·5)*	4 *(7)*	DeS	1					50·28					
Festiniog Railway Portmadoc, N. Wales	1' 11½" *(600)*	14 *(21)*	17 *(27)*	SL DhL DS	6 2 5			31	175					389·2	9 *(12·8)*
Firth Brown Ltd Atlas Works, Sheffield S4 7US	4' 8½" *(1·435)*		8 *(13)*	DhS	5				259	411·8	0·5 *(0·8)*	75	671		
Fishguard and Rosslare Railways and Harbours 163/203 Eversholt St, London NW1 1BG	Wales: 4' 8½" Eire: 5' 3"		1 *(1·6)* 75 *(120)*	Operated in Wales by British Railways and in Ireland by Coras Iompair Eireann.											
Ford Motor Co Ltd Dagenham, Essex	4' 8½" *(1·435)*	6 *(9·6)*	23 *(32)*	DhS	6				400			300			
Guest Keen & Nettlefolds (South Wales) Ltd. PO Box 40, Castle Works, East Moors Rd, Cardiff CF1 1TQ	4' 8½" *(1·435)*	4·5 *(7·2)*	25 *(40·2)*	DeS	14				460	1 500 000					
Imperial Chemical Industries Ltd															
Agricultural Division Severnside Works, Halen, Bristol	4' 8½" *(1·435)*		4 *(6)*	DeS	2										
Mond Division PO Box 7, Winnington, Northwich Cheshire	4' 8½" *(1·435)*	3·5 *(5·6)*	41 *(66)*	De	10				488	230·0	0·8 *(1·3)*	700	1 000		
Aricultural Division PO Box 8, Billingham, Cleveland	4' 8½" *(1·435)*	12 *(19)*	36 *(58)*	DeS	4				255	778·2	2 *(3·2)*	250	600		
Wilton Works Middlesbrough, Cleveland	4' 8½" *(1·435)*	6 *(10)*	16 *(25)*	DeS DS	1 1	D	1						700		
Isle of Man Railway Co Terminal Bldg, Strathallan Cres Douglas	3' 0" *(0·914)*	16 *(25)*		SL	5	D	2	28						117·9	10 *(16)*
Kent & East Sussex Railway *(Operator Tenterten Railway Co Ltd)* Tenterten Town Station, Tenterten, Kent TN30 6ME	4' 8½" *(1·435)*	4 *(6·5)*	4·5 *(7·5)*	SL SS DmS DhS	7 1 1 1	D	1	10						80·0	
Lever Brothers Ltd Port Sunlight, Wirrell, Merseyside L62 4XN	4' 8½" *(1·435)*	5 *(8)*	7 *(11)*	D	2					25·0		120	250		

* 1 100 on loan

Average Speeds — Freight Train mph (km/hr)	Average Speeds — Pass. Train mph (km/hr)	Average Speeds — Speed max. mph (km/hr)	Financial Data — Revenue Expenses in 1 000s	Braking (continuous)	Couplers — Type and Height above rail ins (mm)	Buffers — Centres and Height above rail ins (mm)	Rails — Weight lb. per yd (kg/m)	Sleepers (crossties) — Type and thickness ins (mm)	Sleepers — Spacing Number per mile (per km) or centres ins (mm)	Curvature max.	Gradient max. (U=not compensated)	Axle load max. tonnes	Altitude max. feet (m)	Staff employed. Total no. (inclu. workshop)	Names of officials
															Dir. Gen. Man: R. K. Fox
							95 (47)	Wood Standard							
								Wood 9'' (228)	30'' (762)						
20 (32)		25 (40)	£41·0 37·7	Air			B.H. 80 (40)	Wood 5 (127)	42'' (1 067)	1·45°	0·67%	12		8	Gen. Man: J. Acklam
22 (35)		60 (96)		Vac G & C	Screw 41½ (1 060)	Crs. 68 (1 750) Ht. 41½ (1 060)	98 (48)	Wood 10 (250)	30 (762)	29°		25			
	15 (25)			Air W'hse		Various	75 (37)	Wood 5 (127)	28'' (712)	14·5°	Nil	25	12 (3·6)		Man. Dir: J. G. Parker
13 (30)	20 (32)			Vac G & C	Norweg 18 (457)	Central Buffer	75/50 (37/25)	Wood 5 (127)	29'' (737)	49·0°	1·25%	6	800 (244)	55	Gen. Man: A. G. W. Garraway
4·5 (7)	5 (8)				Standard	Standard	B.H. 95 (42)	Wood 5 (127)	30'' (762)	11·5°	2·6%	50	140 (42)	64	Traffic Man: J. B. Bishop
12 (19·3)				Air	3-link 10½ (267)	Crs. 68 (1 750) Ht. 42 (1 069)	95 (47)	Wood 6 (153)	30	62·0°	5·0%			4	
5 (8)	10 (17)				3-link	Standard	F.B. 98/75 (49/37)	Wood 4½ (115)	30'' (800)	65·0°	1·0%	25		46 (16)	Man: M. R. Vale
6 (9·9)	10 (17)				as BR	as BR		Wood 5 (130)		58°	Level	25	77	100	Traffic Man: D. G. Mathew
	20 (32)						95 (47)	Wood 5 (130)	30'' (762)	17·5°	1·5%	18		3	
10 (16)	12 (19)			Air	Standard	Standard	95 (47)	Wood 5 (130)	31'' (787)	17·5°	2·1%	18	125 (38)	42 (37)	Rail Trans. Man: A. C. Smith
10 (16)	20 (32)		Expenses only £383·4	None	as BR	as BR	95 (42)	Wood 5 (130)	26'' (662)	43°	2·3% U	22·5	40 (12)	96 (45)	Trans. Op. Man: J. F. R. Moddrel
	10 (16)				as BR	as BR	95 (47)	Wood 5 (130)	31'' (787)	12·5°	2·03%	22·5		5 (2)	Trans. Op. Man: H. A. Chapman
	18 (29)	25 (40)	£30·4 34·2	Vac	Norwegian 27 (686)	Buffer-couplers	60 (30)	Wood 5 (130)	36'' (915)	8·75°	1·5%	7	210 (64)	27 (6)	Chf. Exec: W. Jackson
	19 (30)	25 (40)	£41·0 35·0	Vac	Buckeye Standard	Standard	95/91¼ (47/45)	Wood & Steel	29'' (737)	10·5°	2·0%	10	250 (76)	23	Chairman: S. G. N. Bennett
9 (14·5)	15 (24)				Standard	Standard	95/90 (47/45)	Wood 5 (127)	33'' (838)	67·0°	1·1%	25	50 (15)		

NAME OF COMPANY ADDRESS	Gauge ft. in. (metres)	Route length incl. E=Electrified miles (km.)	Track length incl. E=Electrified miles (km.)	Elect. system and type of conductor	Locomotives L=Line S=Shunt Steam Electric Diesel De=elec. Dh=hyd.		Rail-cars Electric Diesel Trailer Railbus Multiple Unit set		Pass. train cars	Freight train cars Containers	Total Volume carried. Thousands of tonnes	Av'ge haul per ton miles (km.)	Av'ge net train load tonnes	Max. trailing load tonnes	Total number carried in 1 000s	Average journey miles (km.)
UK *(contd.)*																
Leighton Buzzard Narrow Gauge Railway Pages Park Station, Billington Rd, Leighton Buzzard Beds LU7 8TN	2' 0'' (0·61)	3·5 (5·6)	7 (11)		S Dm Petrol	6 9 1			7						1 165·6	3 (4·8)
Lincolnshire Coast Light Rly. North Sea Lane Station, Humberston, Grimsby, DN 36 4EP Lincs.	1' 11⅝'' (0·60)	1 (1·6)	1·25 (2)		SL Dn	2 5			4	6					2 900·0	1 (1·6)
Manchester Ship Canal Co. Ship Canal House, King St, Manchester M2 4WX	4' 8½'' (1·435)		50 (80)		DeL DhL D	2 8 8					1 134·5	5 (8)	200	1 000		
Manx Electric Rly Board 1 Strathallan Crescent, Douglas, IoM	3' 0'' (0·914) 3' 6'' (1·067)	E 18 (29) E 5 (8)	E 36 (58) E 10 (16)	560 V dc OH			E T	16 16						316·5		
Middleton Railway Middleton Railway Trust Garnet Rd, Leeds LS11 5JY	4' 8½'' (1·435)		2 (3)		SS DS	8 4				5	1·0		1 100 ton-km		8·0	2·0 (3·2)
National Coal Board Hobart House, Grosvenor Place, SW1																
Northumberland Area Ashington, Northumb	4' 8½'' (1·435)		110 (177)		S De Dh	18 12 23										
North East Area Coalhouse, Team Valley, Gateshead, Tyne and Wear	4' 8½'' (1·435)	31 (50) E 3 (48)	112 (180) E 11 (18)	500 V dc Trolley Wire	S E De Dh D	1 10 8 38 15					1 112·5					
North Durham Area Whitburn, Co. Durham	4' 8½'' (1·435)		165 (265)		S E Dm	3 12 25										
South Durham Area Spennymoor, Co. Durham	4' 8½'' (1·435)		78 (126)		S Dh Dm	11 5 20										
Northern Ireland Railways Central Station, East Bridge St. Belfast BT1 3PB	5' 3'' (1·60)	203 (327)	355 (571)		DeL DhS	3 3	DMU	33	13	20 C 13	3 900 000 train-km				720	5 633·0
The Ravenglass and Eskdale Railway Co Ltd Ravenglass, Cumbria	1' 3'' (0·381)	7 (11)	8 (13)		SL DhL D	4 1 2	D T	1 2	41	12					300·0	6·5 (10·2)
Romney, Hythe and Dymchurch Light Rly Co New Romney, Kent	1' 3'' (0·138)	13 (21)	23 (37)		SL DS	10 1			60	30				40	301·5	8 (13)
Sittingbourne and Kemsley Light Railway	2' 6'' (0·762)	2 (3)	3 (5)		SL Dh Dm	7 1 1			8	50					13·0	4 (6·4)
Snowdon Mountain Railway Ltd Llanberis, Gwynedd, Wales	2' 7½'' (0·800)	4·6 (7·4) Abt rack	5 (8)		SL	7			7	2					153·4	8 (13)
Shell UK Ltd Shell Centre, London SE1 7NA																
Ardrossan Refinery	4' 8½'' (1·435)		1 (1·6)		D	1										
Stanlow Refinery	4' 8½'' (1·435)		17 (22)		D	8										
Shell Haven Refinery	4' 8½'' (1·435)		12 (13)		D	6										
Teesport Refinery	4' 8½'' (1·435)		8 (7)		D	3										
Southend Pier Railway* Southend-on-Sea, Essex	3' 6'' (1·067)	E 1·2 (1·6)	E 1·2 (1·6)	600 V. dc 3rd rail			E T	8 6							1 500·3	2·3 (3·7)
Talyllyn Railway Co Wharf Station, Tywyn, Gwynedd LL36 9EY	2' 3'' (0·686)	7 (11)	8 (13)		SL DhL DmL DmS	6 1 1 1			20	45					1 652·3	
Trafford Park Company Estate Office, Trafford Park, Manchester M17 1AU *(Operated by Manchester Ship Canal Co)*	4' 8½'' (1·435)		6 (10)		D	5					885·6					
Volks Railway 285 Madeira Drive, Brighton, Sussex	2' 8½'' (0·82)	E 1·25 (2·1)	E 1·5 (2·4)	3rd† rail			E T M	9 1 4	9						428·2	2·5 (4)
Welshpool and Llanfair Light Railway Preservation Co Ltd Llanfair Caereinion Station, Powys, Wales	2' 6'' (0·76)	5·5 (8·8)	6 (9)		SL SS DL DS	6 1 1 1			14	21					24·7	6 (10)

* Ceased operation October 1978
† 400V mains input, rectified to 15V dc to track

Average Speeds			Financial Data	Braking (continuous)	Couplers	Buffers	Rails	Sleepers (crossties)		Curvature max.	Gradient max. (U=not compensated)	Axle load max.	Altitude max.	Staff employed. Total no. (inclu. workshop)	Names of officials. Extended lists can be found at the end of the individual country in the report section immediately following
Freight Train	Pass. Train	Speed max.	Revenue Expenses		Type and Height above rail	Centres and Height above rail	Weight	Type and thickness	Spacing Number per mile (per km) or centres ins (mm)						
mph (km/hr)	mph (km/hr)	mph (km/hr)	in 1 000s		ins (mm)	ins (mm)	lb. per yd (kg/m)	ins (mm)				tonnes	feet (m)		
4 (6)	10 (16)		£19 008 21 820		Centre Hudsons 18 (985)		40 (20)	Wood Standard	30" (762)	40°	3·3%	3·5	250 ft (107)	All Volunteers	Chairman: A. P. Tomkins Traffic. Man: R. W. Hughes
	10 (16)	12 (19)	£1·6 0·9			Buffer-Coupler 18" (458)	25/20 (13/10)	Wood	24"-36" (610-915)	30°	None	2·5	Sea level	1	Man. Dir: W. Woolhouse
5 (8)		10 (16)		Air	Standard	Standard	95/110 (47/55)	Wood 5 (127)	31" (787)	25·0°	2·5%	25		43	Railway Supt: B. Valentine
				Air and Ratchet			62/50 (31/25)						1 950 (594)	100	Chief Exec: W. Jackson
5 (8)	8 (13)	10 (16)			Standard 3-link	Standard	95 (47)	Wood 5 (127)	30" (762)	17·5°	3·0%	16		All voluntary	Chairman: J. K. Lee Sec: J. D. Edwards
							45 (22·5)	Wood 5 (127)							Trans. Eng: R. Lowther
							98 (49)	Wood 5 (127)	30 (762)	12·5°	2·8%	15	204 (56)		
		70 (113)	£342·3 2 573·8	Air & Vac. W'hse	P. Screw F. 3-link 41 (1 041)	75 (1 905) 41 (1 041)	92/85 (46/42)	Wood 5 (127)	30" (760)	1 370 ft (418 m)	1·33%	18	375 (114)	1 229 (1 047)	Chief Exec: R. P. Beattie
15 (25)	12 (19)	20 (32)	£133·0 1 380	Air W'hse	Link & Pin	9½ (241)	30/35 (15/18)	Wood 5 (127)	36" (914)		2·77%		170 (51)	25	Gen. Man: D. M. E. Ferreira Ch. Eng: I. Smith
	12 (19)	25 (40)	£188·7 180·3	Vac V.B. Co	Instanta 13 (360)	23½ (597) 14½ (369)	F.B. 24 (11·8)	Wood 4½ (115)	22	12·5°	0·67%	2	Sea Level	28	Man. Dir: J. B. Snell
	12 (20)	15 (24)	£7·0 6·0		Central buffer & hook		60 (30)	Wood 6 (152)	24 (600)	82°		6	20 (6)	All Volunteers	Sec: G. Stickler Lite Hjem, Woodlands Estate, Blean, near Canterbury, Kent
5 (8)	5 (8)			SLM Abt type			39·75 (19·7)	Steel	36" (914)	24·0°	18·2%	6	3 560 (1 075)	40	Gen. Man: M. R. Lane
															Works Man: Clifford C. Williams
															Man: F. W. A. Paterson
															Man: S. J. Gallacher
															Man: F. E. Hixon
															Man: G. G. Rose
	16 (26)	18 (28)	$ 70 000 140 000	Air and Elec	Type AB 24 (610)	Centre 11 (250)	45 (22·5)	Wood 4½ (115)				2·5	Sea Level	23	Foreshore Off: D. Tyler
	11 (16)	15 (24)	£63·9 55·7	Nil	Screw 18 (457)	Centre 36 (915) Ht. 18 (457)	40/61 (20/31)	Wood 5 (127)	33" (838)	22·0°	1·67U	5	230 (70)	18	Traf. Man: D. Woodhouse Ch Eng: J. L. H. Bate Man Dir: W. H. D. Faulkner
		10 (16)	£10·4 46·9		BR	BR	95/75 (47/37)	Wood 5 (127)	30" (762)	29·2°		16		5	Dir: N. G. Westbrook (Chairman) Gen Man: A. D. Lennie Eng: J. Carnley
		12 (20)		Hand	Own	17·4 (444)	50 (25)	Wood & Conc 5 (127)	36" (914)	17·5°		7·5	Sea Level	20 (3)	Dir: A. J. Hewison
	9 (14)	15 (24)			Link & Pin		45 (23)	Wood 5 (127)	27" (686)	29·0°	3·1% 3·5%U	8	600 (183)		Gen. Man: R. T. Russell Sec: J. Dickenson

NAME OF COMPANY ADDRESS	Gauge ft. in. (metres)	Route length incl. E=Electrified miles (km.)	Track length incl. E=Electrified miles (km.)	Elect. system and type of conductor	Loco-motives L=Line S=Shunt Steam Electric Diesel De=elec. Dh=hyd.	Rail-cars Electric Diesel Trailer Railbus Multiple Unit set	Pass. train cars	Freight train cars Con-tainers	Total Volume carried. Thous-ands of tonnes	Av'ge haul per ton miles (km.)	Av'ge net train load tonnes	Max. trailing load tonnes	Total number carried in 1 000s	Aver-age journey miles (km.)
USA														
Aberdeen & Rockfish Railroad Co PO Box 917 Aberdeen, NC 28315	4′ 8½″ (1·435)	47 (76)	62 (100)		De 3			100	1 065·5					
Abilene & Southern Railway Co (Merged into Missouri Pacific 1978)	4′ 8½″ (1·435)	39 (63)												
Ahnapee & Western Railway Co PO Box 91, Algoma, WI 54201	4′ 8½″ (1·435)	14 (23)	18 (29)					200						
Akron & Barberton Belt RR Co PO Box 712, 43 2nd St NW Barberton, Ohio 44203	4′ 8½″ (1·435)	23 (37)	43 (69)		DeS 2				35 157 loads					
Akron, Canton & Youngstown RR 8 N. Jefferson St, Roanoke, Va 24011	4′ 8½″ (1·435)	171 (275)	229 (368)		DeL 11 DeS 4		0	1 756	3 425	293 111 ton miles			0	
Alabama Great Southern RR (Included on Southern Railway System)	4′ 8½″ (1·435)	327 (527)	773 (1 244)		DeL 71 DeS 26		23	3 517	8 289·1	156 (251)	2 100		111·8	160 (257)
Alameda Belt Line PO Box 24352, Oakland, Calif, 94623	4′ 8½″ (1·435)	3·5 (5·6)	19 (30·5)		DeS 1			4	12 500 carloads					
***Alaska Railroad** The Alaska Railroad, Pouch 7-2111, Anchorage, Alaska 99510	4′ 8½″ (1·435)	478 (769)	536 (862)		DeL 32 DeS 31		38	1 626	2 131·6	529 917 000 ton-miles	6 000		84·5	162·9 (262)
Alexander Railroad Co PO Box 277, 145 2nd ave NE. Taylorsville, NC 28681	4′ 8½″ (1·435)	19 (31)	20 (32)		DeS 3				155·9	10 (16)		400		
Algers, Winslow & Western Ry Co PO Box 188, Oakland City, Ind 47660	4′ 8½″ (1·435)	16 (26)	24 (39)		DeL 5									
Aliquippa and Southern R.R. Co. PO Box 280, Aliquippa, Pa 15001	4′ 8½″ (1·435)	47 (76)			DeS 19			998	15 140·8					
Almanor Railroad Co. 909 Terminal Sales Bldg, Portland Oreg 97205	4′ 8½″ (1·435)	13 (21)	16 (25)		De 1				94·6	14 (20)	280			
Alton and Southern Railway Co 1000 S 22nd St E Louis, Ill 62207	4′ 8½″ (1·435)	32 (53)	130 (209)		DeS 20			390	1 390·0					
Amador Central Railway Co PO Box 8498, San Francisco, Ca 94119	4′ 8½″ (1·435)	12 (19)	15 (25)		DeL 2			3	98 100	12 (19)	140	340		
American Rail Heritage Ltd 514 North Market St, Marion, Ill 62959	4′ 8½″ (1·435)	8·5 (13·6)	10 (16)		S 2			5 100						
***Amtrak** **National Railroad Passenger Corp** 400 North Capitol St, Washington, DC 20024	4′ 8½″ (1·435)	26 144† (42 073) E 401 (645)		1 100 V 25 Hz	EL 66 DeL 310 DeS 13	RD 11 ER 61 Turbo79	2 057						18 614 510	
Angelina & Neches River RR Co PO Box 1328, Lufkin, Texas 75901	4′ 8½″ (1·435)	12 (20)			De 2			159	530·9	5 (8)	737	2 100		
Ann Arbor Railroad Co (Operator is Michigan Interstate Railway Co.) P.O. Box 619, Owosso MI48867	4′ 8½″ (1·435)	299 (481)	412 (663)		DeL 15			496	4 800·8	195 (314)	2 356			
Apache Railway Co. PO Box E, Snowflake, Ariz 85937	4′ 8½″ (1·435)	74 (119)	90 (144·8)		DeL 7			491	1 186·6					
Apalachicola Northern Railroad Co 803 Florida National Bank Building, Jacksonville, Fla 32201	4′ 8½″ (1·435)	96 (154)	123 (198)		DeL 11			231	1 647·0	96 (154)				
Arcade & Attica Railroad Corp 278 Main St, Arcade, NY 14009	4′ 8½″ (1·435)	15 (24)	17 (27)		SL 2 DeL 2		7	22		5 (8)			41·0	15 (24)
Arcata & Mad River Railroad Co PO Box 368, Blue Lake, Cal 95525	4′ 8½″ (1·435)	7·5 (12)	9·4 (15)		DeL 3			20	7 000 cars	6·1 (9·8)				
Arkansas & Louisiana Missouri Ry Co PO Box 1653, Monroe, La 71201	4′ 8½″ (1·435)	55 (88)	64 (103)		DL 3 DeS 1			31						
Arkansas Western Rly Co 114 W 11th St, Kansas City, Mo 64105 (Subsidiary of KCS Rly Co)	4′ 8½″ (1·435)	35 (56)												
Aroostook Valley Railroad Co. (Canadian Pacific Railway) PO Box 509, Presque Isle, Mont 04769	4′ 8½″ (1·435)	32 (51)	45 (72)		DeS 3				98·7	11·5 (18·5)	500	2 100		
Ashley, Drew & Northern Railway Co. Box 757, Crossett, Ark 71635	4′ 8½″ (1·435)	41 (66)	53 (85)		DeL 2 DeS 5				1 765·0	23 (37)	4 000	8 300		
***Atchison, Topeka & Santa Fe Rly Co** 80 East Jackson Blvd, Chicago, Ill 60604	4′ 8½″ (1·435)	12 321 (19 800)	21 506 (34 611)		DeL 1 598 DS 93			68 939	90 000	58 900 00 ton-miles				
Atlanta & Saint Andrews Bay Rly 514 E Main St, PO Box 729, Dothan, Ala 36302	4′ 8½″ (1·435)	88 (142)	138 (222)		DeL 10 DeS 2			829	2 836·0	195 038 456 ton-miles				
Atlanta and West Point RR Co 1590 Marietta Blvd NW, Atlanta GA 30318	4′ 8½″ (1·435)	225 (362)			DL 11 DS 13			1 209	6 154·6	71·5 (115)				

* See main entry
† Track owned by Amtrak is 1 661 miles (2 687 km); remainder is the track over which operations are carried out

Freight Train mph (km/hr)	Pass. Train mph (km/hr)	Speed max. mph (km/hr)	Revenue Expenses in 1 000s	Braking (continuous)	Couplers Type and Height above rail ins (mm)	Buffers Centres and Height above rail ins (mm)	Rails Weight lb. per yd (kg/m)	Sleepers Type and thickness ins (mm)	Spacing Number per mile or centres ins (mm)	Curvature max.	Gradient max. (U=not compensated)	Axle load max. tonnes	Altitude max. feet (m)	Staff employed. Total no. (inclu. workshop)	Names of officials. Extended lists can be found at the end of the individual country in the report section immediately following
35 (56)	40 (64)		$ 778·5 572·7	Air			90/70 (45/35)	Wood		10°	3·5%			65 (5)	Ex Vice Pres: R. Veasey
15 (25)				Air			70 (35)	Wood 6 (153)	2 880 (1 790)					20	Pres: S. E. Muma
6 (9·5)	25 (41)			W'hse			100 (49·6)	Oak 6 (153)	22″ (560)	11·8°	2·28% U			70 (16)	Pres: R. W. Coffey
16 (26)	50 (79)		$ 8 931·2 7 341·0	Air	Type E 33″ (839)		115/90 (57/45)	Wood 6 (153)	22″ (560)	5·3°	East 0·63% West 0·56%	30·0		352 (61)	Pres and Gen Man: J. R. McMichael
			$ 12 676 8 769												
				W'hse	AAR Standard		110/70 (54/35)	Fir (Imp.) 7 (178)	20″ (508)	17·3°	0·6%	20	Sea Level	29 (14)	Pres: R. W. Walker
34 (55)	30·8 (49·5)	49 (79)	$ 29 337·9 32 051·5	W'hse NYAB	Type E 28½″ (724)	Cr. 42¾ (1 086) Ht. 50 (1 270)	115/70 (57/35)	Impreg. Fir & Hemlock 7 (178)	19½″ (495)	14·0°	3·0% (S) 2·2% (N)	30	2 363 (720)	825 (190)	Gen. Man: W. L. Dorcy
20 (32)	25 (40)		$ 389·7 185·4	Air			85/60 (42/30)	Wood 7 (178)	27″ (690)				1 250 (381)	11 (1)	Pres: S. J. Zachary
							90 (44·6)	Wood 6 (153)	22½″ (572)	12·0°	2·0%	25			Pres: L. S. Crane
							115 (57)	Wood 7 (178)	22″ (560)	28·7°	0·74% 3·7% U			565	Gen. Supt: J. J. Deyak
15 (24)				Air BW	Standard	None							4 700 (1 439)		Pres: A. C. Goudy
20 (32)	35 (56)			Air W'hse			115/85 (57/42)	Oak 7 (178)	21″ (533)	12·5°	3·55%	31·5		623 (50)	Pres: A. D. Demoss
10 (16)	12 (19)			Air W'hse	Type E 33½″ (851)		80/40 (40/20)	Wood 6 (153)	20″ (508)	20·0°	4·5%U	30	1 535 (468)	10 (1)	Gen. Man: Russel Evitt
															Pres: H. W. Crane
	47 (76)	105 (169)	$ 278 000 719 000	Air E. Pneu	F & H		59/76 (119/152)	Wood 7 (178)	1932/km	8·0°	1·34%	25		20 000	Pres: Paul Reistrup
30 (48)							113/90/75 (50/37)	Wood 6 (153)	19″ (483)		3·0%				Pres: M. E. Kurth
	45 (73)			Air W'hse	Type E		115/85 (57/42)	Wood 6 (153)	19½″ (495)	10·2°	1·6% 1·4%U		1 382 (421)	459 (75)	Pres: C. W. Chapman
25 (40)	35 (57)			Air W'hse	Auto		131/110 (65/54·6)	Wood 6 (153)	20″ (508)	7·0°	2·4% 2·1%U	17·5	7 300 (2 225)	58	Pres: R. Salatka
				Air W'hse	Type E		132/90 (65·5/45)	Wood 7 (178)	18″ (457)	4·0°	1·5%U			90 (18)	Pres: E. Ball
	15 (24)			Air W'hse			70 (35)	Wood 6 (153)	24″ (610)			25	1 900 (579)	17 (2)	Pres: J. A. Yansiels
15 (24)							70 (35)	Fir 6 (153)		25·0°	1·0%			18	Pres: G. L. Oswald
25 (40)	35 (56)			W'hse Air	Auto		90/60 (45/30)	Wood 7 (178)	20″ (508)	16°	1·0%			87 (9)	Pres: J. L. Keller
15 (24)	30 (48)		$ 215·0 204·0	NY AB			85/70 (42/35)	Wood 6 (153)	1 165 (2 600)	12·0°	2·0%U	30	648 (198)	17 (2)	Pres: G. E. Benoit
15 (24)	40 (64)		$5 800 —	Air W'hse	AAR	AAR Standard	90/85 (45/42)	Oak & Pine 7 (178)	21″ (533)	10·0°	4·0%	35	165 (50)	75	Pres: S. R. Tedder
							136/90 (68/45)	Wood 7 (178)	3 200 (2 000)					39 740	President: L. Cena
27·7 (44)	51·5 (83)		$ 1 349·0 1 103·7												
		49 (79)	$ 8 127·4 5 459·8	Air W'hse	Type E 34″ (867)	Standard	115/90 (57/45)	Wood 7 (178)	3 200 (2 000)	4·0°	1·0%U	36·0	356 (108)	167	Pres: A. V. Hooks
							100 (50)	Oak 7 (178)	20″ (508)	3·0°	1·0%				Pres: M. S. Jones

NAME OF COMPANY ADDRESS	Gauge ft. in. (metres)	Route length incl. E=Electrified miles (km.)	Track length incl. E=Electrified miles (km.)	Elect. system and type of conductor	Locomotives L=Line S=Shunt Steam Electric Diesel De=elec. Dh=hyd.		Rail-cars Electric Diesel Trailer Railbus Multiple Unit set	Pass. train cars	Freight train cars Containers	Total Volume carried. Thousands of tonnes	Av'ge haul per ton miles (km.)	Av'ge net train load tonnes	Max. trailing load tonnes	Total number carried in 1 000s	Average journey miles (km.)

USA *(contd.)*

NAME OF COMPANY ADDRESS	Gauge	Route length	Track length	Elect.	Locos		Rail-cars	Pass.	Freight	Total Volume	Av'ge haul	Av'ge net	Max. trailing	Total number	Average journey
Atlanta Stone Mountain and Lithonia RR Co 717 5th Ave, New York, NY 10022	4' 8½" (1·435)	4·3 (6·6)			DeL	1									
Atlanta Terminal Co PO Box 1808, Washington DC 20013	4' 8½" (1·435)		5·3 (8·6)												
Atlantic & Danville Railway Co *(See Norfolk, Franklin and Danville Rly)*															
Atlantic & East Carolina Rly Co PO Box 1808, Washington DC 20013	4' 8½" (1·435)	94 (151)	128 (206)		D	7			220						
Atlantic & Western Railway Co PO Box 1208, Sandford, NC 27330	4' 8½" (1·435)	4 (6·4)	3 (5)		DeS	2			483	47 549					
Atlantic Coast Line Railroad Co *(See Seaboard Coast Line RR)*															
Augusta & Summerville Railroad Co. 1590 Marietta Blvd NW, Atlanta Ga 30318	4' 8½" (1·435)	2·7 (4·7)	5 (8)												
Aurora Elgin & Fox River Electric Co. PO Box 44 So., Elgin, Ill 60177	4' 8½" (1·435)	1·3 (2·1)	5 (8)		De	1									
Auto Train Corp 1801 K St, NW, Washington DC 20005	4' 8½" (1·438)	1 685 (2 710)			DeL DeS	11 4		89	83						
Baltimore & Annapolis RR Co 801 Baltimore-Annapolis, Bvd, Glen Burnie, Md 21061	4' 8½" (1·435)	28 (45)	30 (48)		De	1									
Baltimore & Ohio Chicago Terminal R.R. Co. 2 N. Charles St, Baltimore Md. 21201 *(Subsidiary of Baltimore and Ohio)*	4' 8½" (1·435)	350 (563)	356 (573)												
Baltimore & Ohio Railroad Co B & O Building, 2 North Charles St, Baltimore, Md 21201 *(See Chessie)*	4' 8½" (1·435)	5 433 (8 730)	10 229 (16 623)		DeL DeS	790 243		6	52 157	110 778·1	225 (410)	1 837	20 000		
Bangor & Aroostook Railroad Co. Northern Maine Junction Park, RR2 Bangor, Maine 04401	4' 8½" (1·435)	543 (874)	790 (1 271)		DeL DeS	42 3		2	3 865	3 575·8					
Bath & Hammondsport Railroad Co Water St, Hammondsport, NY, 14840	4' 8½" (1·435)	9 (14)	11 (18)		DeL	2			1	55	8 (13)	106			
Bauxite & Northern Railway Co PO Box 138, Bauxite Ark, 72011	4' 8½" (1·435)	3 (4·8)	19 (30)		De	2									
Beaufort & Morehead Railroad Co PO Box 300, 16 Broad St, Beaufort, NC 28516	4' 8½" (1·435)	4° (6)	17 (27)		DL	3			2	190	4 (6)	1 200			
Beech Mountain RR PO Box 1319, Maryville, Tenn. 37801	4' 8½" (1·435)	8 (13)	8 (13)		DeL	1				364·1					
Belfast & Moosehead Lake RR Co 11 Water St, Belfast, Me 04915	4' 8½" (1·435)	33 (53)	37 (59)		DeL	4			3	182·6	4 766·6 ton-miles (7 016 ton-km)				
Bellefonte Central Railroad Co P.O. Box 236, Bellefonte, Pa 16823	4' 8½" (1·435)	5 (8)	7 (12)		DeS	2				165·0	825·0 ton-miles				
Belton RR Co PO Box 836, Denison, Tx 75020	4' 8½" (1·435)	7 (11)	7 (11)		De	1									
Belt Railway Co of Chicago 6900 S Central Ave, Chicago, Ill 60638	4' 8½" (1·435)	27 (43)	430 (692)		DeS	48			29	1 381·8					
Bessemer & Lake Erie RR Co 600 Grant St., P.O. Box 536, Pittsburgh, Pa 15230	4' 8½" (1·435)	205 (330)			DeL DeS	71 2			9 781	28 600·0	8·55 (137·5)				
Bevier & Southern Railroad Co PO Box 51, Bevier, Macon County, Miss 63532	4' 8½" (1·435)	10 (16)	15 (24)		DeL	1				858·6	10 (16)	1 500	2 000		
Birmingham Southern Railroad Co PO Box 579, Fairfield, Ala 35064	4' 8½" (1·435)	91 (146)	91 (146)		DeS	26			1 147	6 576·0					
Black Hills Central Railroad Hill City, SD 57745	4' 8½" (1·435) 3' 0" (916)	32 (51)	32 (51)		S Pet	6 7		23	13						
Black River and Western Corp PO Box 83, Ringoes, NJ 08551	4' 8½" (1·435)	19 (30)	19 (30)		S	DeS 4 1			14	6					
Bonhomie & Hattiesburg Southern RR Co PO Box 1546, Hattiesburg, Miss 39401 *(See Illinois Central Gulf)*	4' 8½" (1·435)	27 (43)	30 (49)		DeL	2		0					2 700	0	
***Boston & Maine Corporation** Iron Horse Park, N. Billerica, Ma 01862	4' 8½" (1·435)	970 (1 561)	1 105 (1 770)		DeL DeS	119 52			3 464	12 748·4	5 393 057 000 ton-miles				4 248·5
Brandon Corp 28th and N St, Omaha, Ne 68107															
Brooklyn Eastern District Terminal 334 Furman St., Brooklyn, NY 11201	4' 8½" (1·435)	11 (18)	14 (23)		DeL	6			8	1 000·0					

* See main entry

Average Speeds — Freight Train mph (km/hr)	Pass. Train mph (km/hr)	Speed max. mph (km/hr)	Financial Data — Revenue Expenses in 1 000s	Braking (continuous)	Couplers — Type and Height above rail ins (mm)	Buffers — Centres and Height above rail ins (mm)	Rails — Weight lb. per yd (kg/m)	Sleepers (crossties) — Type and thickness ins (mm)	Spacing Number per mile or centres ins (mm)	Curvature max.	Gradient max. (U=not compensated)	Axle load max. tonnes	Altitude max. feet (m)	Staff employed. Total no. (inclu. workshop)	Names of officials
															Pres: L. S. Crane
															Pres: L. Stanley Crane
							85 (42)	Wood 7 (178)		8·67°	0·5%	26			
			$ 97·8 / 269·3	Air			70/50 (35/20)	Oak 7 (178)	2 640 (1 650)					8 (1)	Pres: T. G. Proctor, Jr
															Pres: M. S. Jones Jr
15 (24)															Pres: F. D. Lonnes
															Pres: E. K. Garfield
		25 (40)													Pres. and Gen. Man: E. J. Jubb
															Gen. Supt: M. O. Benson
18·6 (29·9)	28·7 (46·2)	*Freight* 60 (96) *Pass.* 70 (113)	$ 648 383 / 444 661	W'hse & NYAB Air	AAR Types E & F 34½" (867)		140/90 (70/45)	Wood 7 (178)	22" (560)	*Main* 12·0° *Branch* 22·0°	2·84% 3·0%U		2 694 (821)	20 000 (5 800)	Pres. and Chief Exec Officer: H. T. Watkins, Jr
16 (25)		49 (79)	$ 19 200·0 / 19 678·0	W'hse Air	Type E 34½" (876)		115/70 (57/35)	Wood 6 (153)	3 000 (1 865)	10·0°		33	748 (228)	783 (220)	Pres: W. E. Travis Chairman: F. C. Dumaine
			$ 179·2 / 162·7				90/60 (45/30)	Wood 7 (178)		22·0°					Pres: K. M. Honeyman
20 (32·1)	35 (56)						115/85 (57/42)	Oak 7 (178)	21" (533)	9·4°	2·05%	31·5		35	Pres: W. Murray
5 (8)	10 (16)						30 (15)								Leasee: A. T. Leary
5 (8)	8 (13)		$ 181·1 / 343·7	Air	AAR Standard		85 (42)			Rad 15 m	5%	25	2 600 (792)	8	Pres: D. C. Semonite
10 (16)	10 (16)		$ 593·0 / 611·5	W'hse Air	AAR Standard		90/67 (45/33)	Cedar 6 (153)	14" (360)	14·0°	2·2% U	32·8	498 (152)	30 (13)	Pres: H. H. Hutchings Jr Gen. Man. and Auditor: W. I. Hall
15 (24)	20 (32)		$ 112·0 / 110·0	N. York AB Co Air	Standard 34" (864)		130/100 (64·5/50)	Oak 6 (153)	21" (686)	11·0°	2·4%		1 179 (359)	5 (1)	Gen Man: James E. Miller
															Pres. F. H. Guffy
25 (40)	30 (48)		$ 18 496·3 / 16 274·7	W'hse Air	Type E 34½" (877)		115 (57·5)	Oak 7 (178)	19½" (495)	8·0°	2·5% U	36·0	630 (192)	1 000	Pres & G. M.: R. E. Dowdy Vice Pres: R. G. Rubino
			$ 53 998 / 36 353												Gen. Man: M. S. Toon
25 (40)			$ 341·7 / 291·8	W'hse AB	Type E		90 (45)	Pine 6 (153)	20" (510)	30·0°	1·5%			30 (4)	Pres: Mrs C. F. Agee
				W'hse AB	Type E Nat. Mall		100 (49·6)	Oak 7 (178)	21" (533)	12·0°	1·5%	30			Pres: M. S. Toon
															Pres. and Gen. Man: W. B. Heckman
25 (40)	25 (40)			Air			75/85 (37/42·5)	Wood 6 & 7						20 (3)	Gen. Man: T. J. Pittman
15·7 (25·2)			$ 86 200 / 93 500	N York AB Co	Types E & H		131/85 (65/42)	Wood 7 (178)	20" (508)	18·0°	1·38% U	31		3 200	Trustee: R. W. Meserve
				W'hse	M.C.B.		159/60 (79/30)	Wood 7 (178)		38·0°	7·0% on float bridges			150	Gen. Man: F. F. Dayton

NAME OF COMPANY ADDRESS	Gauge ft. in. (metres)	Route length incl. E=Electrified Diesel miles (km.)	Track length incl. E=Electrified Diesel miles (km.)	Elect. system and type of conductor	Locomotives L=Line S=Shunt Steam Electric Diesel De=elec. Dh=hyd.	Rail-cars Electric Diesel Trailer Railbus Multiple Unit set	Pass. train cars	Freight train cars / Containers	Total Volume carried. Thousands of tonnes	Av'ge haul per ton miles (km.)	Av'ge net train load tonnes	Max. trailing load tonnes	Total number carried in 1 000s	Average journey miles (km.)
USA *(contd.)*														
Buffalo Creek Railroad PO Box 2046 Buffalo 5, NY *(See Conrail)*	4' 8½" *(1·435)*	6 *(10)*	35 *(56)*		DeS 7				1 240					
***Burlington Northern Inc** (Merger of CB & Q, GD, NP, and SP & S) 176 E Fifth Street, St Paul Minn 55101	4' 8½" *(1·435)*	24 639 *(39 599)*			De 2 895		119	96 072	181 185·3	609 *(1 033)*		21 000	12 845	18·4 *(29)*
Butte, Anaconda & Pacific Rly Co PO Box 1421, 300 West Commercial Ave, Anaconda, Mont 59711	4' 8½" *(1·435)*	56 *(90)*	108 *(174)*		DeL 9 DeS 1			500	1 729·4	75 109 369 train-km				
Cadillac and Lake City Ry 7707 Lyndon Ave, Detroit, Mi 48238	4' 8½" *(1·435)*	4·5 *(7)*	5·0 *(8)*		DeL 1			25						
Cadiz Railroad Co. 303 S Cascade, Colorado Springs, Colo 80906	4' 8½" *(1·435)*	10 *(16)*	12 *(20)*		DeS 2			150	34·3	10 *(16)*				
California Western Railroad Foot of Laurel St, Fort Bragg, Cal 95437	4' 8½" *(1·435)*	40 *(64)*	49 *(79)*		SL 2 DeL 4	D 2	10		92·9	36 *(63)*	800	1 700	110·7	39·1 *(63)*
Camas Prairie Railroad Co PO Box 1166, 13th & Main St, Lewiston, Idaho 83501 *(Operating Co for NP and UP)*	4' 8½" *(1·435)*	256 *(411)*	315 *(507)*		DeL 16 DeS 4									
Cambria & Indiana Railroad Co. 1275 Daly Ave, Bethlehem, Pa 18015	4' 8½" *(1·435)*	38 *(61)*	62 *(99)*		DeS 19			912						
Camino, Placerville & Lake Tahoe RR Co PO Box L, Camino, Cal 95709	4' 8½" *(1·435)*	9 *(15)*			DeS 2			1	80·0	8 *(13)*	155			
Campbell's Creek Railroad Co. Port Amherst, Charleston, W Va	4' 8½" *(1·435)*	14 *(22)*	20 *(32)*		D 1			110						
CP Rail Canadian Pacific Ltd. *(Lines in Maine)*	4' 8½" *(1·435)*	234 *(376)*												
Cananea Con Copper Cos R Cananea, Sonora, Mx	4' 8½" *(1·435)* 3' 0" *(0·914)*	32 *(51)*	32 *(51)*		DeS 2			137						
Canton Railroad Co PO Box 447, Baltimore, Md 21203	4' 8½" *(1·435)*	5·5 *(10)*	40·4 *(64)*		DeS 17				1 166·5			2 450		
Cape Fear Railways Inc PO Box 70090, Fort Bragg, NC 28307	4' 8½" *(1·435)*	5·910 *(10)*	34		DeL 2			2	101					
Carbon County Railway Co PO Box 1007, E. Carbon Utah 84520	4' 8½" *(1·435)*	11 *(18)*			D 2			125						
Carrollton Railroad PO Box 116, Carrollton, Ky 41008	4' 8½" *(1·435)*	16 *(25)*			DeS 4				150·0	8·8 *(14·16)*				
Cedar Rapids & Iowa City Ry Co PO Box 351, Cedar Rapids, Iowa 52406	4' 8½" *(1·435)*	27 *(43)*	54 *(86)*		DeS 7			47	1 330·6	25 *(40)*		3 600		
Central California Traction Co 526 Mission St, San Francisco, Cal 94105	4' 8½" *(1·435)*	52 *(84)*	72 *(116)*		De 4				11 877·9	23 *(37)*				
Central of Georgia Railway Co 99 Spring St, SW Atlanta, Ga 30303 *(Southern Railway System)*	4' 8½" *(1·435)*	2 208 *(3 553)*			DeL 114 DeS 23			4 160						
Central New York RR Corp 1 Railroad Ave, Copperstown, NY 13326														
Central Vermont Railway Inc 2 Federal St, St Albans, Vt 05478 *(Canadian National)*	4' 8½" *(1·435)*	381 *(590)*	509 *(817)*		DeL 13 DeS 1			1 064	2 291·9	265 626 000 ton-miles			234	
Chattahoochee Indus RR POB 253, Cedar Springs, Ga 31732	4' 8½" *(1·435)*	15 *(24)*			DeS 6			822	2 645·9	20 300 train-km				
Chattahoochee Valley Railway Co PO Box 111, West Point, Ga 31833	4' 8½" *(1·435)*	10 *(16)*	10 *(16)*		DeS 2				259·5	10 *(16)*	235	1 300		
Chesapeake & Ohio Railway Co Terminal Tower, Cleveland, Ohio 44101 *(See Chessie)*	4' 8½" *(1·435)*	4 086 *(6 576)*	10 059 *(16 000)*		DeL 885 DeS 100			72 411	111 884·4	258 *(415)*	2 364	24 000		
Chesapeake Western Railway PO Box 231, 141 W Bruce St, Harrisonburg, Va 22801	4' 8½" *(1·435)*	53 *(85)*	54 *(87)*		DeS 2				301·58	23·4 *(37·6)*				
***Chessie System** The Terminal Tower, Cleveland, Ohio 44101	4' 8½" *(1·435)*	11 000 *(17 700)*	21 412 *(34 600)*		De 1 623			111 298	52 703 000 000 ton-miles					
Chestnut Ridge Railway Co Palmerton, Pa. 18071	4' 8½" *(1·435)*	11 *(18)*	14 *(23)*		DeS 1									
Chicago & Eastern Illinois RR Co 72 West Adams St, Chicago, Ill 60603 *(Owned 45·2% by Missouri Pacific)*	4' 8½" *(1·435)*	643 *(1 035)*	872 *(1 403)*		DeL 36 DeS 6		42	3 314 C 24	15 652·2	184·5 *(296)*		1 955		234 *(377)*
Chicago Heights Terminal Transfer RR *(Chicago & E. Illinois RR)* 72 West Adams St, Chicago, Ill 60603	4' 8½" *(1·435)*	7 *(11)*	36 *(58)*		DeS 2			2 223	134·4					

* See main entry

Freight Train mph (km/hr)	Pass. Train mph (km/hr)	Speed max. mph (km/hr)	Revenue Expenses in 1 000s	Braking (continuous)	Couplers Type and Height above rail ins (mm)	Buffers Centres and Height above rail ins (mm)	Rails Weight lb. per yd (kg/m)	Sleepers Type and thickness ins (mm)	Spacing Number per mile (per km) or centres ins (mm)	Curvature max.	Gradient max. (U=not compensated)	Axle load max. tonnes	Altitude max. feet (m)	Staff employed. Total no. (inclu. workshop)	Names of officials. Extended lists can be found at the end of the individual country in the report section immediately following
															Gen. Man: J. L. Morey
22·2 (35·7)	34·6 (56)	79 (127)		Air W'hse	Types E.F.H.		140/56 (69/28)	Wood 7 (178)	19·5-22 (496-559)	12·3°	2·2%	33	6 323 (1 927)	50 262	Chairman and Chief Executive Officer: Louis W. Menk Vice Chairman and Chief Operating Officer: Robert W. Downing
25 (40)	35 (56)			Air W'hse			115/75 (57/37)	Wood 7 (178)	22" (560)	10·0°	1·0%	30	6 205 (1 891)	20	Pres. and Gen. Man: L. V. Kelly
							75/85 (37/425)	Wood							Chairman: G. W. Flanders
10 (16)	25 (40)		$ 178·0 177·0	Air			85/60 (42/30)	Oak 6 (153)	21" (533)					10	Pres. and Gen. Man: H. S. White
13 (21)	20 (32)	25 (40)	$ 772·6 1 009·5	Air W'hse	AAR		112/75 (56/37)	Wood 6/7 (153/180)	22" (560)	22·0°	3·0%	25	1 740 (530)	55 (8)	Pres. and Dir: R. B. Pamplin
25 (41)	40 (64)			W'hse Air	Type E 33½" (851)	Crs. 36½	90 (45)	Wood 7 (178)	14 (356)	16·0°	3·0% U		3 720 (1 200)	220	Pres: T. P. Rogers
															Gen. Man: R. N. Young
							60 (60)	Fir 6 (153)	20" (508)	16·0°	3·5%				Pres: V. S. Lindgren
				Air W'hse	Type E		131/70 (65/30)	Wood 7 (178)	22" (560)	16·0°	3·25%	30			
			$ 9 506 8 375												
6 (10)	10 (16)		$ 2 470·5 2 778·0	Air W'hse	Type E		90 (44·6)	Oak 7 (178)	22" (560)	20·0°	1·5% 2·0%U		70 (22)	203 (14)	Pres: R. W. Dale, Jr
														20	Exec. Vice Pres. & Gen. Man: J. Odom
							90 (44·6)	Wood 7 (178)		12·0°	1·67% 0·5%U				Pres: M. S. Toon
25 (40·2)							101 (50·1)	Oak 7" (177·8)	20" (508)	9°	3·0%U			7	Gen Man: R. D. Tigar
12 (19)	35 (56)		$ 1 660·3 823·0	W'hse Air	AAR 32½" (825)		100/90 (50/45)	Oak 6 (153)	21" (533)	6·0°	1·5%	40	685 (209)	69 (9)	Gen. Man: D. Arnold
20 (32)	30 (48)		$ 1 632·3 1 484·7	Air	Type E		75/70 (37/35)	Wood 6 (153)	22" (559)	6·0°	0·7%				Pres: R. G. Flannery
17·5 (28·2)	57 (92)	79 (127)	$ 106 355 76 556	N York AB	AAR 34½ (876)		132/56 (66/28)	Wood 7 (178)	20" (508)	6·0°	2·21% 2·05%U	32	1 070 (326)	1 253 (77)	Pres: R. E. Franklin
35 (56)	50 (80)	55 (88)	$ 13 266 10 997	AB-ABD	E 32½ (825)		90/115 (45/57)	Wood 7 (178)	3 200		1·9%	25	1 008 (303)	378	Pres and Chairman: R. A. Bandeen Gen Man: P. C. Larson
															Pres: B. P. Ellen
12 (19)	20 (32)		$ 409·4 403·0	W'hse Air	Type E Beth'm		80/70 (40/35)	Oak 7 (178)	22" (560)	11·0°	2·0%	30	600 (183)	29 (4)	Pres: G. W. Neal
17·7 (38·6)	42·2 (67·9)	F. 60 (97) P. 70 (113)	$ 568 830 415 650	W'hse NYAB	Types E & F 34½ (876)		140/85 (69·4/42)	Wood 7 (178)	21" (538)	Main 10·0° Branch 18·0°	Main 2·76% Branch 4·3%U	39·3	Main 2 082 Branch 3 408	23 000 (5 000)	Chairman of Board and Chief Exec. Officer: Hays T. Watkins
20 (32)	20 (32·18)			W'hse	Standard		80/85 (40/42)	Wood 6 (153)	3 168 (1 980)	6·0°	6·0%			25	Pres: R. F. Dunlap
															Pres: Hays T. Watkins
			$ 1 539 000 1 442 000												
							80 (40)	Wood 7 (178)	22" (560)	10·0°	3·0%				Gen. Man: A. F. Halmi
22 (35)	47 (75)	79 (127)	$ 44 367 32 484	N York AB Co	Type E & H Tightlock 34½ (876)		115/90 (57/45)	Wood 6 (153)	20" (508)	8°	0·9%	30	769 (234)		Pres: J. H. Lloyd
				N York AB Co	Type E		112/90 (56/45)	Wood 6 (150)	20" (508)	12°	1%	30	620 (204)	24 (0)	

NAME OF COMPANY ADDRESS	Gauge ft. in. (metres)	Route length incl. E=Electrified miles (km.)	Track length incl. E=Electrified miles (km.)	Elect. system and type of conductor	Locomotives L=Line S=Shunt Steam Electric Diesel De=elec. Dh=hyd.	Railcars Electric Diesel Trailer Railbus Multiple Unit set	Pass. train cars	Freight train cars Containers	Total Volume carried. Thousands of tonnes	Av'ge haul per ton miles (km.)	Av'ge net train load tonnes	Max. trailing load tonnes	Total number carried in 1 000s	Average journey miles (km.)
USA *(contd.)*														
Chicago & Illinois Midland Ry Co PO Box 139, Springfield, Ill 62705	4' 8½" *(1-435)*	121 *(195)*	175 *(281)*		DeL 15 DeS 6			837	9 549·9			13 000		
Chicago & Illinois Western RR 233 N. Michigan Ave, Chicago, Ill 60601 *(Illinois Central Railroad)*	4' 8½" *(1-435)*	12 *(19)*	36 *(58)*		DS 4									
***Chicago, Milwaukee, St Paul & Pacific RR Co** 516 W. Jackson Blvd, Chicago, Ill 60606	4' 8½" *(1-435)*	10 200 *(16 410)* E 662 *(966)*		3 000 V dc OH	EL 38 DeL 264 DeS 232		69	30 125	42 640·3		1 569			
The Chicago & North Western Transportation Company 400 W. Madison St, Chicago, Ill 60606	4' 8½" *(1-435)*	9 603 *(1 565)*	14 864 *(24 000)*		DeL 837 DeS 121		18	35 125			3 500		24 942	
Chicago Produce Terminal Co 233 N Michigan Ave, Chicago, Ill 60601														
Chicago River & Indiana Railroad Co. 680 Union Station, Chicago, Ill 60606	4' 8½" *(1-435)*	15 *(25)*	138 *(220)*		DeS 17									
Chicago, Rock Island & Pacific RR 332 South Michigan Ave, Chicago, Ill 60604	4' 8½" *(1-435)*	7 385 *(11 870)*	11 070 *(17 816)**		DeL 452 DeS 157		132	25 818 C 58	49 125·0	420 *(675)*				
Chicago Short Line Railway Co 9746 Avenue N, Chicago, Ill 60617	4' 8½" *(1-435)*	29 *(47)*	35 *(56)*		D 4			67						
Chicago South Shore & South Bend RR North Carroll Ave., Michigan City, Ind 46360	4' 8½" *(1-435)*	E 73·8 *(117)*	E 93·6 *(149)*	1 500 V dc OH	EL 3 DeL 11	E 49 T 6		30	4 223·8	73·6 *(165)*			1 473·5	31 *(50)*
Chicago & Western Indiana RR Co 80 E. Jackson Blvd, Chicago 5, Ill 60604	4' 8½" *(1-435)*	27 *(43)*	137 *(220)*											
Chicago, West Pullman & Southern RR Co 2728 E 104th St, Chicago, Ill 60617	4' 8½" *(1-435)*	30 *(48)*	31 *(50)*		DeS 10			396						
Cincinnati, New Orleans & Texas Pacific Rly Co *(Southern Rly System)*	4' 8½" *(1-435)*	337 *(542)*	817 *(1 315)*		DL 124 DS 48		46	8 098	14 360·2	184 *(296)*	1 690		137·8	256 *(412)*
City of Prineville Railway 10th and Main Sts, PO Box 338, Prineville, Oreg 97754	4' 8½" *(1-435)*	18 *(29)*	27 *(43)*		DeL 3			402†	356·9	6 546 500 ton-km				
Claremont and Concord Rly Co 100 Federal St, Boston, Ma 02110 Claremont, NH	4' 8½" *(1-435)*	14 *(23)*			DeS 2			10						
Clarendon & Pittsford RR Co 267 Battery St, Burlington, Vt 05401	4' 8½" *(1-435)*	20 *(32)*	23 *(37)*		De 1			60	100·8	5·1 *(8·0)*	325			
Cliffside Railroad Co 1201 Maple St, Greensboro, NC 27405	4' 8½" *(1-435)*	4 *(6)*	4 *(6)*		DeS 2				21·7					
Clinchfield Railroad Co 229 Nolichucky Ave, Erwin, Tenn 37650 *(Subsidiary of Seaboard Coast Line RR)*	4' 8½" *(1-435)*	275 *(442)*	490 *(788)*		DeL 91 DeS 5			6 134			2 347			
Colorado & Southern Railway Co 1405 Curtis St, Denver, Colo 80202 *(Subsidiary of BN)*	4' 8½" *(1-435)*	683 *(1 099)*	1 103 *(1 791)*		DeL 94 DeS 10			2 878	9 326·6	2 516 637 ton-km				
Colorado & Wyoming Railway Co PO Box 316, Pueblo, Colo. 81002	4' 8½" *(1-435)*	39 *(63)*	117 *(188)*		DeL 6 DeS 13			799	4 745·1	7·7 *(12·4)*				
Columbia & Cowlitz Railway Co PO Box 188, Longview, Wash 98632	4' 8½" *(1-435)*	8 *(13)*	15 *(24)*		DeL 2			78	704·3	6·5 *(10·5)*				
Columbia, Newberry & Laurens R. R. Co. 500 Water St, Jacksonville, Fla 32202 *(Subsidiary of Seaboard)*	4' 8½" *(1-435)*	75 *(121)*	88 *(142)*		DeL 5				1 660·0	61·3 *(98·7)*	1 117	1 830		
Columbus & Greenville Railway Co 1302 Main St, Columbus Miss 39701 *(Merged into Illinois Central Gulf in Sept 1972)*	4' 8½" *(1-435)*	168 *(270)*	225 *(351)*		DeL 12 DeS 8			345			3 000	6 000		
Conemaugh & Black Lick Railroad Co 1275 Daly Ave, Bethlehem, Pa 18015	4' 8½" *(1-435)*	9 *(14)*	47 *(76)*		DeS 27			25						
***Conrail Consolidated Rail Corp** Six Penn Center Plaza, Philadelphia, Pa 19104	4' 8½" *(1-435)*	16 835 *(27 050)* E 597 *(960)*	35 313 *(56 829)* E 1 456 *(2 342)*		DeL3 397 EL 112 ES 9 DeS 902			132 804	258 408·1	421 *(700)*			110 007·9	

* See main entry
† 200 freight cars leased

Average Speeds			Financial Data	Braking	Couplers	Buffers	Rails	Sleepers (crossties)		Curvature max.	Gradient max.	Axle load max.	Altitude max.	Staff employed.	Names of officials. Extended lists can be found at the end of the individual country in the report section immediately following
Freight Train	Pass. Train	Speed max.	Revenue Expenses	(continuous)	Type and Height above rail	Centres and Height above rail	Weight	Type and thickness	Spacing Number per mile (per km) or centres	max.	(U=not compensated)		tude	Total no. (inclu. workshop)	
mph (km/hr)	mph (km/hr)	mph (km/hr)	in 1 000s		ins (mm)	ins (mm)	lb. per yd (kg/m)	ins (mm)	ins (mm)			tonnes	feet (m)		
25 (40)	40 (64)		$ 13 826·0 12 171·0	W'hse N York Air	Type E AAR 33½ (851)		132/75 (65·5/ 37)	Wood 6 (153) 7 (178)	3 000 (1 860)	10°	1·64% U	26·3	616 (188)	482	Pres: Carl D. Forth Vice Pres and Gen Man: William G. Harvey
				AB N York	Type E		90 (45)	Oak 6 (153)	24" (610)	8·0°	0·61%				Pres: J. F. Palmer
21·8 (35)	45·0 (72·4)	100 (160)	$ 454 984·0 497 071·8	Air	AAR		132/115 (66/57)	Wood 7 (178)	3 250 (2 030)	15·33°	1·0% Electric 2·2%		6 317 (1 925)	16 470 (6 012)	Trustee: Stanley Hillman
17 (27·4)	34·9 (56·2)		$ 651 612 535 064	Air W'hse. N York AB Co	Types D.E.F. 32½/34½ (825/876)		115/60 (57/30)	Wood 6/7 (153/178)	20½/23 (520/585)	Main 3·0° Branch 6·0°	Main 1·35% Branch 2·5% U	33·5	6 028 (1 837)	15 252 (6 220)	Pres: J. R. Wolfe
			$ 4 394 3 601·5	Air			105 (52)	Wood 8 (203)	23" (585)			23	16 (5)	258 (21)	Pres: K. E. Smith
21·5 (34·6)	43·4 (69·8)	90 (145)	$ 384 835 650 660	Air AB	Types E.F.H. and Tightlock 34½ (876)		136/60 (68/30)	Wood 7 (178)	21" (530)	12·2°	Main 1·0% Branch 3·6%	Coopers E 60	6 880 (2 097)	14 354 (2 765)	Pres: William J. Dixon
							90 (45)	Oak 6 (153)	21" (533)						Trustee: William M. Gibbons Pres. and Chief Ext. Officer: John W. Ingran
40 (64)	60 (96)	79 (128)	$ 10 324·7 10 617·0	Air W'hse	AAR 33 (874)		115/100 (57/50)	Oak 6 (153)	3 250 (2 030)	14·4%	2·5%		826 (252)	413 (45)	Pres. and Gen. Man: A. W. Dudley
	60 (96)						115/80 (57/40)	Wood 7 (178)	20" (508)	13·5	2·4%	36	580 (177)	732 (115)	Pres: J. H. Park
														200	Pres. and Gen. Man: J. E. Rice
			$ 76 265 47 725	W'hse 14 E.L.											Man: G. S. Gray
15 (24)	20 (32)		$ 867 666	W'hse	Type E 32½ (825)		90/60 (45/30)	Fir 6 (153)	22" (559)	10·0°	3·5%	25	2 800 (850)	25	Pres: Nello Giovanini
															Vice Pres: K. H. Lemnah
	30 (48)			Air W'hse 14 EL	Type E Nat. Mal.		80/70 (40/35)	Wood 6 (153)	18" (458)	18·0°	4·5%	33·5	600 (183)	10	Pres: H. T. Filskov
10 (16)	20 (32)														Pres: P. C. Gratale
20 (32)	55 (86)		$ 39 225 24 833	Air W'hse	31½/34½ (800/876)		132/115 (126/57)	Wood 7 (180)	19½ (500)	14°	1·2% 1·5% U	36	2 630 (802)	1 207 (225)	Gen. Man: J. W. Thomas
21·5 (34·6)	49 (79)		$ 29 323·9 29 323·6	W'hse Air	Tightlock 34½ (876)		112/90 (56/45)	Wood 7 (178)	Main 3 168 (1 910) Branch 2 756 (1 660)	15·0°	2·0% U	31	11 320 (3 450)	874 (89)	Pres: G. F. Defiel
								Wood 7/9 (178/229)		10·0°	2·0%	33·4			Pres: F. H. Jones
20 (32)			$ 1 918·3 1 589·9	Air 26 L			90/85/112 (45/42/56)	Wood 7 (178)	(3 000)	14°	2·5%	30		24	Pres: J. H. Wilkinson Vice Pres. and Gen. Man: Tom S. Brace
14 (22·5)	40 (64)			Air W'hse	Auto 34½ (876)		115/75 (51/37)	Wood 7 (178) 6 (153)	19½" (495)	6°	1·3%	30		46 (0)	Pres: P. F. Osborn
30 (48·2)	45 (72)			W'hse N York	Type E 34½ (876)		85/60 (42/30)	Wood 8 (203)	24" (610)	12·0°	1·6%	19	447 (136)	175	Pres: H. C. Bitner
														534	Pres: R. J. Kent
		110 (180)	$ 3 506 000 3 891 000				65 (33)	Wood 7 (178)	(2 014)	—	1·92%			94 000	Chairman and Chief Exec: E. G. Jordan

NAME OF COMPANY ADDRESS	Gauge ft. in. (metres)	Route length incl. E=Electrified miles (km.)	Track length incl. E=Electrified miles (km.)	Elect. system and type of conductor	Locomotives L=Line S=Shunt Steam Electric Diesel De=elec. Dh=hyd.	Rail-cars Electric Diesel Trailer Railbus Multiple Unit set	Pass. train cars	Freight train cars	Total Volume carried. Containers	Con-tainers Thous-ands of tonnes	Av'ge haul per ton miles (km.)	Av'ge net train load tonnes	Max. trailing load tonnes	Total number carried in 1 000s	Aver-age jour-ney miles (km.)
USA *(contd.)*															
Conway Scenic RR Inc Norcross Circle, N Conway, NH 03860	4' 8½" (1·435)	7·5 (12)	7·5 (12)		SL 2 De 1		10	4						75	11
Coopers Town and Charlotte Valley R Corp 1 Railroad Ave, Cooperstown, NY 13326	4' 8½" (1·435)	16 (26)			SL 1 DeL 1		6	23							
Corinth & Counce RR Co PO Box 128, Highway 57, Counce, Tenn 38326	4' 8½" (1·435)	26 (40)	26 (40)		DeS 3			547	1 670·5	48 655 000 000 train-km					
Curtis Milburn & Eastern R.R. PO Box 540, Cheholis Wash 98532	4' 8½" (1·435)	11 (18)			DeL 2										
Cuyahoga Valley Railway Co 315 Clark Ave, Cleveland, Ohio 44101	4' 8½" (1·435)	10 (16)	15 (24)		DeS 14			215	5 500·0						
Dansville & Mount Morris RR Co Dansville, NY 14437	4' 8½" (1·435)	10 (16)	12·2 (19)		DeL 2		0		58·6		10 (16)		1 000		
Dardanelle & Russellville RR Co 101 Sth Front St, PO Box 150, Dardenelle, Ark 72834	4' 8½" (1·435)	5 (8)	7 (11)		DeL 3 Dh 1				214·0		2·4 (4)	611			
Davenport, Rock Island & North-Western Rly Co 1025, Harrison St, Davenport, Iowa 52801	4' 8½" (1·435)	48 (76)			DeS 7			10							
Delaware & Hudson Railway Corp Delaware & Hudson Bldg, 40 Beaver St, Albany, NY 12207	4' 8½" (1·435)	1 400 (2 253)			DeL 178			5 341				1 997			
Delray Connecting Railroad Co QO Box 266, Detroit, Miky 48232	4' 8½" (1·435)(6·5)	4·1 (29)	18·5		DeS 3			160	975·8		3·0 (4·8)		1 050		
Delta Valley & Southern Railway 1 Park St, Wilson, Ark 72395	4' 8½" (1·435)	2 (3)	4 (6)		DeL 1		0	0	75·0		1·5 (2·4)	450			
***Denver & Rio Grande Western RR Co** PO Box 5482, 1515 Arapahoe St, Denver, Colo 80217	4' 8½" (1·435) Narrow gauge	13 848 (2 973) 45 (72)	3 230 (5 197)		DeL 246 DeS 20 SL 10		40	10 330	30 511·8		336 (509)	2 006	12 000	261·1	74·2 (119·4)
Denver Union Terminal Rly Co 233 Union St, Denver, Colo 80202	4' 8½" (1·435)		6 (10)												
De Queen and Eastern RR Co 810 Whittington Ave, Hotsprings, Ark 71901															
Des Moines Terminal Co 205 Hubbell Bldg, Des Moines, Iowa 50309	4' 8½" (1·435)		9 294 (14 980)												
Des Moines Union Railway Co 902 Walnut Street, Des Moines, Iowa 50309 *(CMSt P & P and N & W own 50% each)*	4' 8½" (1·435)	6 021 (10)	39·6 (68)		DeS 4										
Detroit and Mackinac Railway 120 Oak St, Tawas City, Mich 48763	4' 8½" (1·435)	398 (641)	453 (729)		DeL 10		5	964	2 476·0	294 407 000 ton-km				0	
Detroit Terminal Railroad Co Detroit 12, Mich	4' 8½" (1·435)	18 (29)	158 (254)		DeS 10			11							
Detroit, Toledo & Ironton RR Co One Parkland Boulevard, Dearborn, Mich 48126	4' 8½" (1·435)	476 (766)	758 (1 220)		DeL 69			4 237	13 070·4		110 (177)	1 377			
Detroit & Toledo Shore Line 131 W. Lafayette Ave, Detroit 26, Mich	4' 8½" (1·435)	59 (95)	174 (280)		DeL 10 DeS 6			841	4 944·4		46 (74)	963·9	9 000		
Duluth, Missabe & Iron Range Rly Co Missabe Bdg, Duluth, Minn 55802	4' 8½" (1·435)	462 (744)	599 (970)					8 559							
Duluth & North-Eastern RR Co Ave C & Arch St, Cloquet, Minn 55720	4' 8½" (1·435)	11 (18)	18 (29)		DeL 4				440·1		11 (18)				
Duluth, Winnepeg & Pacific Rly *(Canadian National)* 131 W. Lafayette Blvd, Detroit, Mich 48226	4' 8½" (1·435)	43 (69)	165 (265)		DeL 8 DeS 5			1 391	7 977·0	2 434 000 000 ton-miles					
Durham & Southern Rly Co 500 Water St, Jacksonville, Fla 32202	4' 8½" (1·435)	59 (95)		DeL 4			50								
East Cooper and Berkeley RR PO Box 279, Charlestown, SC 29402															
East Camden & Highland RR PO Box 3180, East Camden, Ark 71701	4' 8½" (1·435)	25 (40)													
East Erie Commercial Railroad 1030 Lawrence Parkway, Erie, Pa 16510 *(General Electric Co.)*	4' 8½"† (1·435)	12½ (20) E 3 (5)	12½ (20) E 3 (5)	Caten-ary and third rail	DeS 3			60	23·0						
East Jersey Railroad & Terminal Co. East 22nd St, Bayonne, NJ	4' 8½" (1·435)	3 (5)			DeS 2										
Edgmoor & Manetta Railway	4' 8½" (1·435)	3 (5)			De 1										
El Dorado & Wesson Railway Co PO Box 46, El Dorado, Ark 71730	4' 8½" (1·435)	6 (10)	12 (20)		D 3			2							

* See main entry
† Seven other gauges used for locomotive testing on electrified line

Average Speeds — Freight Train mph (km/hr)	Pass. Train mph (km/hr)	Speed max. mph (km/hr)	Financial Data — Revenue Expenses in 1000s	Braking (continuous)	Couplers — Type and Height above rail ins (mm)	Buffers — Centres and Height above rail ins (mm)	Rails — Weight lb. per yd (kg/m)	Sleepers (crossties) — Type and thickness ins (mm)	Spacing Number per mile (per km) or centres ins (mm)	Curvature max.	Gradient max. (U=not compensated)	Axle load max. tonnes	Altitude max. feet (m)	Staff employed. Total no. (inclu. workshop)	Names of officials. Extended lists can be found at the end of the individual country in the report section immediately following
		20 (32)		W'hse 6 ET			75/85 (37/42)	Wood	22" (559)	3·0°	3·25%	30	525 (160)	30	Pres: D. A. Smith
															Pres: W. G. Rich
25 (32)	25 (40)		$ 3 851 / 1 575·5	Air Ny-6BL	AAR Type E 34" (860)		115/85 (57/42)	Wood 6 (153) 7 (180)	20" (508)	8·0°	1·5%	32·8	496 (151)	40	Pres: C. W. Byrd
															Pres: J. R. Callaghan
															Pres: L. E. Smith
6 (9·7)							115 (57)								
5 (8)	35 (58)		$ 241·5 / 120·5	Air W'hse	Type D BSC		90/60 (45/30)	Wood 7" (178)	2 820 (1 762)	22°	2·0%	33		13 (3)	Gen Man: R. F. Hart
10 (16)	20 (32)		$ 166·0 / 156·0	Air	Standard		75/65 (37/33)	Wood 6 (150)	24" (610)			33		16 (2)*	Pres: D. C. Phelps
															Gen Man: B. A. Webster
17·1 (27·5)	32·5 (52·3)		$ 88 098 / 101 752	N York AB Co			132/80 (66/40)	Wood 7 (178)	20" (508)	14·0°	0·88% 1·36%U			1 899	Pres: K. P. Shoemaker
5 (8)				Air W'hse	Type E 34½ (876)		115/80 (57/40)	Wood 6 (153)	22" (559)			25		59 (25)	Pres: Chas. A. O'Brien
15 (24)				Air W'hse			75/56 (37/28)	Wood 7 (178)					220 (67)	8	Gen Man: M. A. Davisor
26·2 (42·2)	38 (61)	P. 70 (113) F. 70 (113)	$ 218 016·0 / 179 755·0	Air W'hse.	Types E and P		136/112 (67/56)	Wood 8 (203) 9 (229)	19½" (495)	12·8°	3·0%	36	10 221 (3 115)	3 502 (654)	Pres: W. J. Holtman
															Pres: W. J. Holtman
															Pres: R. G. Beers
			$ 1 162·6 / 1 735·6	Air	AAR		115/75 (57/37)	Oak 7 (178)	16" (407)					109 (15)	Pres: M. Garelick
25 (41)	35 (56)		$ 4 828·0 / 3 967·0	Air	AAR		100/85 (50/42)	Wood 6 (150)	20" (508)	1·0°	1·0%U			150	Chr: C. A. Pinkerton Jr
15 (24·14)							100/30 (50/40)	Wood 6" (153)	21½" (547)	4°	0·8%U	35		180	Pres: W. Galvin
10 (16)	49 (79)		$ 45 213·0 / 36 322·0	N York AB Co W'hse.	Type E 34½ (876)		140/85 (69-4/ 42·5)	Wood 7 (178)	22" (559)	16·0°	1·8%U	38	1 217 (371)	1 623 (484)	Pres: R. A. Sharp
20 (32)	49 (79)		$ 7 062 / 6 286	Air	Auto. 34½ (876)		100 (50)	Wood 7 (178)	18" (460)	4·3°	0·33%	35	599 (183)	360 (70)	Pres: R. F. Dunlap
			$ 59 674 / 38 013	W'hse	Type E		115 (57)	Wood 7 (178)	21" (533)	6·0°	0·6%			1 602	Pres: M. S. Toon
20 (33)	25 (40)		$ 1 144 / 994	Air W'hse			100/80 (50/40)	Wood 7 (178)	22" (559)					30 (18)	Pres and Gen. Man: R. N. Congreve
35 (50)	45 (72)		$ 28 267 / 20 288		Type E 33½ (851)		100/115 (50/51)	Wood 7 (178)				26		436	Pres: J. H. Burdakin
															Pres: A. Paul Funkhouse
															Pres: R. S. O'Connor
		80 (129)	$ 486	Air Various	AAR Standard 34" (860)		100 (50)	Oak 7 (178)	22" (559)	19°	2·5%U	33	750 (229)	24 (9)	Pres and Gen Man: D. E. Sheeran
															Pres: T. P. Connelly
															Pres: W. Heath
															Pres: H. D. Reynolds

* Daily average

USA (contd.)

NAME OF COMPANY ADDRESS	Gauge ft. in. (metres)	Route length incl. E=Electrified miles (km.)	Track length incl. E=Electrified miles (km.)	Elect. system and type of conductor	Loco-motives L=Line S=Shunt Steam Electric Diesel De=elec. Dh=hyd.	Rail-cars Electric Diesel Trailer Railbus Multiple Unit set	Pass. train cars	Freight train cars Con-tainers	Total Volume carried. Thous-ands of tonnes	Av'ge haul per ton miles (km.)	Av'ge net train load tonnes	Max. trailing load tonnes	Total number carried in 1 000s	Aver-age jour-ney miles (km.)
Elgin, Joliet & Eastern Ry Co 208 S. Lasalle St, Chicago, Ill 60690	4' 8½'' (1·435)	200 (320)	1 000 (1 600)		DeL 44 DeS 59			11 242			1 376			
Erie Western Ry Co PO Box 510, Huntington, Ind 46750														
Escanaba & Lake Superior RR Co 827 Wells Bldg, Milwaukee, Wis 53202	4' 8½'' (1·435)	63 (101)	87 (135)		DeS 5			79	192·0					
El Paso Union Passenger Dept Co Rm 2, Union Depot, El Paso Tex 79901	4' 8½'' (1·435)	3·25 (5·2)	3·25 (5·2)											
Everett Railroad Co. PO Box 96, Everett, Pa 15537	4' 8½'' (1·435)	3·6 (5·6)	4·9 (8·1)		DeL 1									
Fairport, Painesville & Eastern Rly. Co. PO Box 229, Painesville, Ohio 44077	4' 8½'' (1·435)	20 (32)			DeS 8			85						
Feliciana Eastern RR Co PO Box 47127, Dallas, Tx 75247	4' 8½'' (1·435)	0·5 (0·8)			DeL 2									
Ferdinand Railroad Co. PO Box 6, Ferdinand, Ind 47532	4' 8½'' (1·435)	6 (10)	7 (11)		DeL 1					24·2	14 (12)	130		
Florida East Coast Railway Co 1 Malaga St, St. Augustine, Fla 32084	4' 8½'' (1·435)	530 (680)	1 029 (1 640)		DL 53 DS 4			1 490	6 828·7	197 (317)				
Fonda, Johnstown & Gloversville RR 111 W. Fulton St., Gloversville, NY 12078	4' 8½'' (1·435)	20 (32)	31 (50)		DeL 2			260	73·0	11 (18)	250			
Fordyce & Princeton R.R. Co. PO Box 660, Fordyce, Ark 71742	4' 8½'' (1·435)	1·5 (2)	2·4 (4)		DeS 1						300	400		
Fore River Railroad Corp 145 East Howard S., Quincy, Mass 02169	4' 8½'' (1·435)		3 (5)		DeS 2									
Fort Smith & Van Buren Rly Co 114 W. Eleventh St, Kansas City, Mo 64105	4' 8½'' (1·435)	21 (24)												
Fort Worth Belt Railway Co North Fort Worth, Tex (Subsidiary of Missouri Pacific)	4' 8½'' (1·435)	3 (5)	18 (29)		D 1									
Fort Worth & Denver Railway Co Union Station Building, Denver, Colo. 80217	4' 8½'' (1·435)	1 241 (2 001)			DL 12 DS 8			1 370						
Frankfort & Cincinnati RR Co Union Passenger Depot, Frankfort, Ky. 40601	4' 8½'' (1·435)	7 (11)			DeS 4									
Gainesville Midland Railroad Co 500 Water St, Jacksonville, Fla 32202 (Subsidiary of Seaboard)	4' 8½'' (1·435)	42 (68)	51 (82)		DeS 1			1						
Galveston, Houston & Henderson RR Co PO Box 28, Galveston, Tex, 77550	4' 8½'' (1·435)	49 (79)	105 (169)											
Galveston Wharves PO Box 328, Galveston, Tex 77553 (Owned by City of Galveston)	4' 8½'' (1·435)	45 (72)	50 (80)		DeS 6									
Garden City Western Railway Co PO Box 597, Garden City, Kans 67846	4' 8½'' (1·435)	14 (23)	17 (27)		DeL 2					164·4	8 (12·9)			
Genesee and Wyoming RR Co 3846 Retsof Road, NY 14539	4' 8½'' (1·435)	12 (19)	23 (37)		DeL 4 DeS 2		1	233	2 150·0	11 (18)	5 000			
Georgetown RR Co PO Box 529, Georgetown, Tx 78626														
Georgia Northern Railway Co PO Box 152, Moultrie, Ga 31768	4' 8½'' (1·435)	68 (109)			DeS 1									
Georgia Railroad 1590 Marietta Blvd, NW Atlanta, Ga 30318 (Subsidiary of Seaboard Coast Line RR)	4' 8½'' (1·435)	331 (533)	521 (838)		DL 18 DS 15		2	1 407						
Georgia, Southern & Florida Ry Co (Southern Railway System)	4' 8½'' (1·435)	397 (639)	565 (909)		DL 44 DS 4			46			1 041			
Gettysburg RR Co Box 631, Gettysburg, Pa 17325	4' 8½'' (1·435)	23 (37)			DeL 4		5	4						
Grafton & Upton Railroad Co Depot St, Hopedale, Mass 01747	4' 8½'' (1·435)	15 (24)			DeL 1 DeS 1									
Graham County Railroad Co Oil City, Pa	4' 8½'' (1·435)	12 (19)			D 1			2						
Grand Trunk Western RR Co (Subsidiary of Grand Trunk Corp) 131 W. Lafayette Blvd., Detroit, Mich. 48226	4' 8½'' (1·435)	930 (1 497)	1 235 (1 987)		DeL 122 DeS 62		17**	9 344	84 782·7	8 557 189 000 ton-miles			402·1	14 (23)
Graysonia, Nashville & Ashdown RR Co 210 S. Front St, Nashville, Ark 71852	4' 8½'' (1·435)	32 (51)	50 (80)		DeS 3			14	523	7 846 321 ton-km				

Average Speeds			Financial Data	Braking	Couplers	Buffers	Rails	Sleepers (crossties)		Curvature max.	Gradient max. (U=not compensated)	Axle load max.	Altitude max.	Staff employed. Total no. (inclu. workshop)	Names of officials. Extended lists can be found at the end of the individual country in the report section immediately following
Freight Train	Pass. Train	Speed max.	Revenue Expenses	(continuous)	Type and Height above rail	Centres and Height above rail	Weight	Type and thickness	Spacing Number per mile (per km) or centres ins (mm)						
mph (km/hr)	mph (km/hr)	mph (km/hr)	in 1 000s		ins (mm)	ins (mm)	lb. per yd (kg/m)	ins (mm)				tonnes	feet (m)		
		45 (72)	$ 90 471 61 040				131/80 (65/40)	Wood 6 (153)	3 200 (2 000)	*Main* 3·0°	1·2%	32·5		3 000 (500)	Pres: M. S. Toon
25 (40)	35 (56)		$ 545·8 493·7	W'hse	Type E		90/75 (45/37)	Wood 6 (153)	3 000 (1 870)	6·0°		30	1 397 (426)	26 (6)	Pres: N. A. Lemke Vice Pres. & Gen. Man: L. L. Hamilton
															Pres: R. O. Coltrin
5 (8)	10 (16)	20 (32)	$ 23 626·9 19 902·4		Standard		100/70 (50/35)	Wood 6 (153)	24″	6·0°	2·08%				Pres: Donald S. Laher
															Pres: A. P. Ford
							90/75 (45/37)	Wood 6 (153)	21″ (530)	4·0°	2·75% U				Pres: R. O. Evans
13 (21)	20 (32)		$ 42·3 33·5	Air NYBL			56 (28)	Woood 6 (150)	18″ (457)		4·0%	33		4	Gen. Man: L. R. Greaves
		60 (96)	$ 50 000 30 000	Air	Automatic		132/90 (65/45)	Wood Conc. 7 (178)	21″/24″	8·5°	3·17%	65	42 13)	1 030 (201)	Pres: W. L. Thornton
15 (26)							80/60 (40/30)	Wood 6 (153)	21″ (533)	14·0°	2·75%	Coopers E-60	850 (259)	26 (3)	Pres: W. Rich
6 (10)	15 (24)		$ 43·9 41·8	Air W'hse	AAR	AAR	60/85 (30/42)	Wood 7 (178)	21″ (534)	12°	1·0% U	27·5		3	Pres: R. Tedder Supt: Tom Branch
							85 (42)	Wood 9 (229)							Pres: C. L. Hartshorn
															Pres: G. F. Defiel
			$ 36 849 27 462												Gen. Man: B. A. Raine
															Pres: P. F. Osborn
25 (40)							115/90 (57/45)	Pine 7 (178)	19½″ (495)	4·0°	0·75%	Coopers E-52	53 (16)	67 (8)	Gen. Man: J. M. Bynum
			$ 1 146 825 1 382 111				112/70 (56/35)	Wood 8 (203)	14″ (356)	20·0°	1·0% 1·0% U			430 (13)	Chairman Board of Trustees: J. Yarborough Gen. Man: C. S. Devoy
15 (24)	30 (48)						85/70 (42/35)	Wood 6 (153)	20″ (508)					5	Pres: W. F. Stoeckly
30 (48)	40 (64)		$ 1 984·5 1 697·2	Air W'hse	Standard 30½ (775)		130/80 (64/40)	Wood 6 (153)	21″ (534)	12·0°	1·12% 1·12% U	33	763 (233)	66	Pres: G. E. Johnson
															Pres: W. L. Pippin
			$ 11 258 10 100				100 (50)	Oak 7 (173)	20″ (508)	3·0°	1·0%				Gen. Man: M. S. Jones Jnr.
			$ 21 943 12 858	W'hse.											Gen. Man: S. Cornell
															Gen. Man: F. H. Abbott
															Oper. Man: H. E. Chandler
25 (40)	60 (96)	84 (135)	$ 175 900·0 174 200·0	W'hse	E.F.H. 34½ (876)		132/100 (65/50)	Oak 8 (203)	18″ (457)	14·3°	0·5% U	33	1 023 (312)	2 014	Pres: J. H. Burdakin Exec. Asst. & Corp. Sec: E. G. Fontaine
							85 (42)	Pine 6 (153)	21″ (533)		1%		40		Pres: A. F. Backus

NAME OF COMPANY ADDRESS	Gauge ft. in. (metres)	Route length incl. E=Electrified miles (km.)	Track length incl. E=Electrified miles (km.)	Elect. system and type of conductor	Loco-motives L=Line S=Shunt Steam Electric Diesel De=elec. Dh=hyd.	Rail-cars Electric Diesel Trailer Railbus Multiple Unit set	Pass. train cars	Freight train cars Con-tainers	Total Volume carried. Thous-ands of tonnes	Av'ge haul per ton miles (km.)	Av'ge net train load tonnes	Max. trailing load tonnes	Total number carried in 1 000s	Aver-age jour-ney miles (km.)
USA (contd.)														
Great Southwest RR Inc 1169 109th St, Grand Prairie, Tx 75050	4' 8½" (1·435)		22 (35)		DeS 2									
Great Western Railway Co PO Box 537, Loveland, Colo 80537	4' 8½" (1·435)	58 (93)	77 (124)		DeL 4 DeS 2			44	287·1					
*__Green Bay & Western Railroad Co__ 2155 Hutson Rd., PO Box 2507, Green Bay, Wis 54306	4' 8½" (1·435)	255 (410)	305 (526)		DeL 19			1 772	2 604·4	275 810 000 ton-miles				
Green Mountain Railroad Corp PO Box 468, Bellows Falls, Vermont, 05101	4' 8½" (1·435)	52 (80)	56 (90)		DeL 3 DeS 3		3	251	109·0 (61)	38	515	850	33·9 (18)	11
Greenville & Northern Railway Co Depot Sq, Barre, Ut 05641	4' 8½" (1·435)	14 (22)	16 (26)		DeS 3			10						
Greenwich & Johnsville Ry Co Greenwich, NY 12834														
Hampton & Branchville RR Co PO Box 56, Hampton, SC 29924	4' 8½" (1·435)	17 (27)	49 (79)		DeL 4	D 1								
Harbor Belt Line Railroad 340 Water St., Wilmington, Cal 9044 (Terminal Switching Line for Santa Fe, Southern Pacific and Union Pacific)	4' 8½" (1·435)		120 (193)		D 3									
Hartford and Slocomb RR PO Box 2243, Dothan, Ala 36301	4' 8½" (1·435)	20 (32)	24 (38)		DeL 2			100	63 124	18 (29)	5 000			
Hartwell Railway Co Box 429, Hartwell, Ga 30643	4' 8½" (1·435)	10 (16)	11 (18)		DeS 2									
Helena Southwestern Railroad Co PO Box 2517, West Helena, Ark 72390	4' 8½" (1·435)	5 (8)	5 (8)		DeS 1			12	Yard Switch-ing only					
High Point, Thomasville & Denton RR Co PO Box 1855, High Point. NC 27260	4' 8½" (1·435)	34 (55)					4							
Hillsboro & Northeastern RR Co Hillsboro, Wis	4' 8½" (1·435)	5 (8)			DeL 1									
Hillsdale County Rly Co 50 Monroe St, Hillsdale, Mich 49242	4' 8½" (1·435)	59 (95)			DeL 2			65						
Hollis & Eastern RR Co PO Drawer C, Duke, Ok 73532	4' 8½" (1·435)	14 (22)			DeL 1									
Holton Inter-Urban Railway Co. (Southern Pacific System)	4' 8½" (1·435)	10 (16)												
Houston Belt & Terminal Railway Co 202 Union Station Bldg, Houston, Tex 77002 (Subsidiary of Missouri Pacific)	4' 8½" (1·435)	53 (85)	235 (378)		DeS 23				switching service only					
Hutchinson & Northern Railway Co 1800 E Carey Blvd, Hutchinson, Kans 67501	4' 8½" (1·435)	E 5 (10)	E 6½ (11)	OH 600 V dc	DeL 2									
*__Illinois Central Gulf Railroad__ **Illinois Central Industries** 233 N Michgan ave, Chicago, Ill 60601 (Merged with GM & O RR)	4' 8½" (1·435)	9 003 (10 350) E 38 (61)	14 329 (23 084) E 127 (204)	1 500 V dc OH	DeL 909 DeS 158	E 163	5	46 388 95 160·8		30 000 000 ton-miles				
Illinois Terminal Railroad Co PO Box 7282, St Louis, Mo 63177	4' 8½" (1·435)	387 (620)	547 (880)		DeL 16 DeS 20			2 662	6 469·1	71·6 (115·2)	2 121			
Indiana Harbor Belt RR Co (New York Central System)	4' 8½" (1·435)	114 (183)	566 (911)		DeS 103			83						
Indiana Interstate Ry Co Inc 1483 Joliet St, Dyer, In 46311	4' 8½" (1·435)													
Indianapolis Union Rly Co 31 E. Georgia St, Indianapolis Ind 46204	4' 8½" (1·435)	16 (26)	65 (105)		DS 12									
Iowa Termal RR Co (Elec) PO Box 486, Charles City, Ia 50616														
Iowa Transfer Ry Co 9th and Walnut St, Des Moines, Ia 50310														
Johnstown & Stony Creek RR Co PO Box 536, Johnstown, Pa 15230	4' 8½" (1·435)	3 (5)	6 (10)		DeS 3									
Joplin Union Depot Co 114 West 11th St, Kansas City, Mo 64105	4' 8½" (1·435)		5 (8)											
Kansas City Connecting RR Co 1600 Genesee St, Kansas City, Mo, 64102	4' 8½" (1·435)	1·9 (3·1)	11 (18)											
Kansas City Southern Lines 114 West 11th St, Kansas City, Mo 64105 (Consists of):														
*__Kansas City Southern Ry. Co.†__ 114 West 11th St., Kansas City, Mo 64105	4' 8½" (1·435)	1 618 (2 640)			DeL 161 DeS 94			8 281 28 510	7 690 000 000 ton-miles				6 877 087 000	
Kansas City Terminal Railway Co 207 Union Station Building, Kansas City, Mo, 64108 (Switching and Terminal Co)	4' 8½" (1·435)	10·8 (17·5)	131 (210)		DeS 10			11						

* See main entry
† Incorporates Louisiana and Arkansas Rly Co.

Average Speeds			Financial Data	Braking (continuous)	Couplers	Buffers	Rails	Sleepers (crossties)		Curvature max.	Gradient max. (U=not compensated)	Axle load max.	Altitude max.	Staff employed. Total no. (inclu. workshop)	Names of officials. Extended lists can be found at the end of the individual country in the report section immediately following
Freight Train	Pass. Train	Speed max.	Revenue Expenses		Type and Height above rail	Centres and Height above rail	Weight	Type and thickness	Spacing Number per mile (per km) or centres ins (mm)						
mph (km/hr)	mph (km/hr)	mph (km/hr)	in 1 000s		ins (mm)	ins (mm)	lb. per yd (kg/m)	ins (mm)				tonnes	feet (m)		
															Gen. Man: J. F. Robinson
		25 (40)	$ 580·1 677·6	W'hse			100/60 (50/30)	Wood 6 (153)	20" (508)	8·0°	1·82%	31·25	5 280 (1 609)	12	Pres: Emil Ramat
45 (72)		49 (78)	$ 11 194 11 294	Air W'hse	E' Type 33½ (851)		90 (45)	Wood 9 (228)	22"	7·0°	0·98%	33	1 186 (362)	405 (80)	Pres: Joseph R. Galassi
30 (48)	30 (48)	45 (72)		Air W'hse	Janney 34½ (876)		105/80 (52/40)	Wood 7 (178)	21" (533)	4°	2·6% 1·9% U	35	1 278 (390)	15 (3)	Pres and Supt: R. W. Adams
20 (32)	30 (48)	45 P (72)	$ 146·8 110·3				70/56 (35/28)	Wood 7 (178)	18-24"	10·0°	1·9%			11	Gen. Man: C. M. Ledford
															Pres: E. O. Lightsey
															Gen. Man: D. R. Stanton
20 (32)		60 (96)		Air W'hse			70 (35)	Oak 7 (178)	22" (560)					9	Pres: G. F. Fischer
							85/56 (42/28)	Wood 6 & 7	24" (610)			18		5 (2)	Pres: M. G. Pfaender
				Air			85/56 (42/28)	Oak 7 (178)	3 168 (1 968)	None	Level			4 (1)	Vice Pres and Gen. Man: R. Rich
															Pres: J. P. Fishwick
															Pres: R. S. Krower
															Pres: J. H. Marino
															Pres: P. Simpson
															Pres: R. L. King
							115/75 (57/37)	Wood 6 (153) 9 (225)	18-22"	Neglig-able	1·75%				Pres and Gen. Man: L. B. Griffin
		10 (16)	$ 99·5 84·4	Air W'hse.	AAR		90/70 (45/35)	Wood 6 (153)	24" (610)	16·0°	Level		25 (8)	8 (1)	Pres: C. N. Bowler
50 (82)	69 (111)		$ 679 570 674 492	ABDW	E & F 34½ (875)		90 (45)	Wood 6 (153) 9 (225)	3 259/km	10°	2%		18	20 181	Pres. and Chief Operating Officer: William J. Taylor
			$ 14 632·0 11 749·0	Air			90 (45)	Wood 6 (153)	20" (508)	18·5°	1·25% U	32	516 (93)		Pres: E. B. Wilson Vice Pres and Gen. Man: D. E. Visney
															Gen. Man: A. B. Cravens
															Pres: L. S. Crane
							115/70 (57/35)	Wood 7 (178)							Pres: M. S. Toon
															Pres: T. S. Carter
							90/80 (45/40)	Wood 7 (178)						17	Pres, A. W. Letzig Jr
			$ 48 135 33 952												Vice Pres. and Gen. Man: R. J. Blair
35 (56)	40 (64)		$ 9 497·9 38 344·0	AB	Type E		146/85 (67/42)	Oak 6 & 7	19½" (496)	10·0°	1·8%	30	1 650 (503)	3 161	Gen. Man: J. E. Gregg
25 (40)	45 (72)		$ 5 916·1 5 895·5	W'hse AB	Type		131/90 (65/45)	Oak 7 (178)	3 140 (1 950)	17·15°	2·0% U	33	855 (261)	1 000	Pres. and Gen Man: V. E. Coe

NAME OF COMPANY ADDRESS	Gauge ft. in. (metres)	Route length incl. E=Electrified miles (km.)	Track length incl. E=Electrified miles (km.)	Elect. system and type of conductor	Locomotives L=Line S=Shunt Steam Electric Diesel De=elec. Dh=hyd.	Rail-cars Electric Diesel Trailer Railbus Multiple Unit set	Pass. train cars	Freight train cars Containers	Freight movement Total Volume carried. Thousands of tonnes	Av'ge haul per ton miles (km.)	Av'ge net train load tonnes	Max. trailing load tonnes	Passengers Total number carried in 1 000s	Average journey miles (km.)
USA (contd.)														
Kansas & Missouri Rly & Terminal Co 1709 Minnesota ave, Kansas City, Kans 66102 (Kansas City Southern System)	4' 8½" (1·435)	E 5 (8)	E 11 (18)											
Kansas City Public Service Freight Operation 8641 Highland ave, Kansas City, Mo 64131	4' 8½" (1·435)	10 (16)			DeS 2									
Kansas, Oklahoma & Gulf Railway Co (Subsidiary of Missouri Pacific)	4' 8½" (1·435)	327 (526)	368 (592)		De 15									
Kelly's Creek & Northwestern RR Co 700 Westgate Tower, Cleveland, Ohio 44116 (Owned by Valley Camp Coal Co)	4' 8½" (1·435)	7 (11)			DeS 5				200					
Kentucky & Indiana Terminal RR Co 2910 Northwestern Parkway, Louisville, Ky 40212	4' 8½" (1·435)	8 (13)	131 (211)		DeS 16									
Kentucky & Tennessee Railway Stearns, McCreary County, Ky 42647	4' 8½" (1·435)	10 (16)	17 (28)		DeL 4			4	571·0	10 (16)	800	1 500		
†**Lackawanna & Wyoming Valley RR Co** Scranton, Pa 18053	4' 8½" (1·435)	19 (31)	23 (37)		D 1									
Lake Erie & Eastern Railroad Co P & LE Ter. Bdg., Pittsburgh, Pa. 15219 (Owned jointly by Pittsburgh and Lake Erie RR and Mahoning Coal RR, operated by P. and L. E. with P. and L. E. equipment)	4' 8½" (1·435)	15 (24)	130 (209)											
Lake Erie and Fort Wayne RR Co 8N. Jefferson St, Roanoke, Va 24011	4' 8½" (1·435)	4 (6)	4 (6)							1·4 (2·2)				
Lake Erie, Franklin & Clarion RR Co PO Box 430, 1062 Wood St, Clarion, Pa 16214	4' 8½" (1·435)	15 (24)	24 (39)		DeS 3				50	12·4	5 (8·5)			
Lakefront Dock & RR Terminal Co Two North Charles St, Baltimore Md 21201 (Owned jointly by Penn Central and Baltimore and Ohio)	4' 8½" (1·435)	3 (5)	63 (101)											
Lake Superior Terminal & Transfer Rly Co 17 Washington Ave, Minneapolis, Minn 55401	4' 8½" (1·435)	5 (8)	24 (38·6)		DeS 6				5					
Lake Superior & Ishpeming RR Co 105, E. Washington St., Marquette, Mich 49855	4' 8⅜" (1·435)	98 (157)			DeL 16				2 409					
Lake Terminal Railroad Co PO Box 536, Pittsburgh, Pa 15230	4' 8½" (1·435)	4 (6·4)	22 (35)		DeS 14			329	2 684·5					
Lamoille Valley RR Co 1 Stafford Ave, Morrisville, Vermont, Vt 05661	4' 8½" (1·435)	98 (157)	—		De 4			600	181·2	75 (120)	900			
Lancaster & Chester Railway Co PO B 230, Lancaster, SC 29720	4' 8½" (1·435)	29 (47)	37 (60)		De 2			48	283·9					
Laona & Northern Railway PO B 126-Laona, Wis 54541	4' 8½" (1·435)	8 (13)	12 (19)		SL 1 / DeL 2		3	23	61·9	7·5 (12)	200	300		
La Salle & Bureau County RR Co PO Box 497, La Salle, Ill 61301	4' 8½" (1·435)	10 (16)	15 (24)		DeLS 2			51	225	5 (7)	700			
Laurinburg & Southern RR Co PO Box 546, Laurinburg, NC 28352	4' 8½" (1·435)	28 (45)	39 (63)		DeL 6 / Dh 1			31	341·1	1 309 133 ton-miles				
Lenawee County RR Co 708 E Michigan St, Adrian, Mi 49224	4' 8½" (1·435)	31 (30)	35 (56)		DeS 2			130	—	3·0 (5·0)	—			
Little Rock Port Railroad 7500 Lindsey Rd, Little Rock, Ar 72206	4' 8½" (1·435)	5·0 (8·0)	9·7 (15·9)		DeS 1									
Live Oak Perry & South Georgia Railroad Co 920 15th St. N.N., Washington 6, DC 20005	4' 8½" (1·435)	58 (93)	73 (117)		DeL 2 / DeS 1		0	3						
Livonia Avon & Lakeside R.R. Corp 3401 Rochester Rd, Lakeville, New York NY 14480	4' 8½" (1·435)	13 (21)			De 2 / SL 1		6	1						
*****Long Island Railroad Co** 93-02 Sutphin Blvd., Jamaica, NY 11435	4' 8½" (1·435)	321 (519) E 121 (266)	531 (856) E 266 (429)	700 V dc Third rail	DeL 59 / DeS 8	E 800	229		2 179·4				69 463	26 (42)
Longview, Portland & Northern Ry Co PO Box 579, Longview, Wash 98632	4' 8½" (1·435)	42 (68)			DeL 4									
Los Angeles Junction Railway Co. 4521 Produce Plaza, Los Angeles, Cal 90058	4' 8½" (1·435)	28 (45)	58 (93)		DeS 5									

* See main entry
† Taken over by Conrail 1 April 1977

Average Speeds			Financial Data	Braking (continuous)	Couplers	Buffers	Rails	Sleepers (crossties)		Curvature max.	Gradient max. (U=not compensated)	Axle load max.	Altitude max.	Staff employed. Total no. (inclu. workshop)	Names of officials. Extended lists can be found at the end of the individual country in the report section immediately following
Freight Train	Pass. Train	Speed max.	Revenue Expenses		Type and Height above rail	Centres and Height above rail	Weight	Type and thickness	Spacing Number per mile (per km) or centres						
mph (km/hr)	mph (km/hr)	mph (km/hr)	in 1 000s		ins (mm)	ins (mm)	lb. per yd (kg/m)	ins (mm)	ins (mm)			tonnes	feet (m)		
							85 (42)	Wood 6 (153)	1 718 (2 750)					2	Gen. Man: D. W. Henry
															Tfc Man: J. G. Ashley
				Air	Type E		115/75 (57/37)	Oak 6 & 7	22″ (559)	7·0°	1·0%				
															Pres: H. S. Richey
				Air W'hse	Type E 34½″ (876)		100 (50)	Wood 7 (178)	22″ (559)	13·0°	1·24%	35	489 (149)	500	Pres. and Gen. Man: J. J. Gaynor
15 (24)	25 (40)		$ 242·0 185·0	Air W'hse	AAR 32		90/80 (45/40)	Wood 9 (229)	2 600 (1 620)	22·0°	3·0%	36	900 (274)	19 (4)	Gen. Man: E. R. Tindle
			$ 130·9 112·5				90 (45)	Wood 6 (153)	24″ (610)	26·0°	2·5%			11	Gen. Man: H. J. Fawley
16 (26)	20 (32)		$ 1 500·2 1 620·1				132/131 (65·5/65)	Oak 7 (178)	19½″ (495)	4·0°	0·30% 0·25% U	33	888 (271)		Pres: C. W. Owens
			$ 68·0 2 289·6	Air W'hse			90/85 (45/42)	Wood 6 (153)	22″ (560)					4	Pres: R. F. Dunlap
12 (19)	25 (40)		$ 2 289·6 898·0	Air W'hse			115/80 (57/40)	Oak 7 (178)	2 728 (1 705)		2·4%			30 (4)	Pres: J. F. Miller
								Wood	21¼″ (533)	12·0°	0·3%			31	Pres: J. T. Colinson
	20 (32)		$ 351·7 1 201·8	Air W'hse	Standard		115/75 (57/37)	Wood 8 (204)	3 052 (1 907)	16·0°	0·5%		641 (195)	125 (3)	Pres: W. S. Burn
12·5 (19·5)	35 (56)		$ 6 341 5 766	Air W'hse	Type E Nat. Mal. Cast. Co.		132/80 (66/40)	Wood 7 (178)	3 000 (1 860)	12·3°	1·9% U	27·5	1 500 (457)	259 (68)	Pres. and Gen. Man: J. J. Scullion
			$ 446·7 440·7	AB			115 (57)	Wood 7 (178)	17″ (431·8)	32·0°	2·5% U				Pres: M. S. Toon
25 (40)			$ 1 032 1 032	Air			85/115 (42/57)	Wood		10·0°	2·1%	33	1 700 (500)	35	Gen. Man: S. A. Snyder
			$ 730·9 777·9				112/60 (56/30)	Wood 6 (153)	22″ (560)					32	Pres: J. B. Bethea
6 (9·7)	20 (32)			Air W'hse	Type E ACF		75/56 (37/23)	Wood 6 (153)	23″ (585)	6·0°	2·5%	12·5	1 000 (305)	7 (1)	Gen. Man: J. S. Mason
20 (32)			$ 201·0 186·9				100/85 (50/42)	Oak 6 (153)	2 600 (1 620)	14·0°	1·5%		300 (91)	16 (3)	Gen. Man: E. T. Barnes Jr.
15 (24)	25 (40)		$ 759·3 678·7	Air			90/56 (45/28)	Wood 8 (204)	21″ (533)			32·8		24	Vice Pres. and Gen. Man: W. S. Jones
10 (16)			$ 178·7 —	Air W'hse	Type E		100 (50)	Wood 6 (153)	3 160		0·4%	32·0			Chairman: H. D. White
10 (16)	15 (24)		$ 170·0 183·6	Air			85/90 (50/55)							5	Agent: M. J. Rayney
				Air			100/90 (50/40)	Wood 7 (178)	22″ (560)	5·0°	2·0%			31	Pres: L. Stanley Crane
															Pres: C. A. Haak
35 (56)	45 (72)	80 (128)		W'hse Air	Mod. Sharon No. 10D 34½″ (876)		100 (50)	Wood 8 (200)	21″ (535)	7·5°	2·0%	Coopers E 72	238 (72·5)	6 585 (2 344)	Pres: Francis S. Gabreski
							110/60 (55/30)	Fir 7 (178)							Pres: B. H. Wills
															Pres: R. W. Walker

NAME OF COMPANY ADDRESS	Gauge ft. in. (metres)	Route length incl. E=Electrified miles (km.)	Track length incl. E=Electrified miles (km.)	Elect. system and type of conductor	Loco-motives L=Line S=Shunt Steam Electric Diesel De=elec. Dh=hyd.	Rail-cars Electric Diesel Trailer Railbus Multiple Unit set	Pass. train cars	Freight train cars Con-tainers	Total Volume carried. Thous-ands of tonnes	Av'ge haul per ton miles (km.)	Av'ge net train load tonnes	Max. trailing load tonnes	Total number carried in 1 000s	Aver-age jour-ney miles (km.)
USA *(contd.)*														
†**Los Angeles Union Passenger Terminal** 800 N Alameda St, Los Angeles, Cal 90012	4' 8½'' *(1·435)*		7 *(11)*											
Louisiana & Arkansas Railway Co *(See Kansas City Southern Lines)*	4' 8½'' *(1·435)*	746 *(1 200)*												
Louisiana Eastern RR PO Box 742, Amite, La 70422	4' 8½'' *(1·435)*	6 *(9·5)*	8 *(13)*		DeL 1 DeS 2				600	55				
Louisiana Midland Ry Co PO Box 110, Jena, La 71342														
Louisiana & North West RR Co Homer, La 71040	4' 8½'' *(1·435)*	62 *(100)*			DeL 5			10						
Louisiana & Pine Bluff Railway Co *(See Arkansas and Louisiana Missouri Rly)* PO Box 1653, Monroe, La 71201	4' 8½'' *(1·435)*	3 *(5)*			DeL 2				3					
Louisiana Southern Railway Co *(Southern Railway System)*	4' 8½'' *(1·435)*	16 *(26)*			D 2									
Louisville & Nashville RR Co 908 West Broadway, Louisville, Ky 40201 *(98% owned by Seaboard Coast Line RR)*	4' 8½'' *(1·435)*	6 574 *(10 579)*	10 076 *(16 216)*		DeL 877 DeS 164			65 873	122 338·2	265 *(426)*				
Louisville, New Albany & Corydon RR Co Box 10 Corydon, Ind 47112	4' 8½'' *(1·435)*	8 *(13)*	10 *(16)*		DeL 1			925	10·9	8·6 *(13·8)*	315			
Louisville & Wadley RR Co 416 E. Broad St, Louisville Ga 30434	4' 8½'' *(1·435)*	10 *(16)*						50						
Lowville & Beaver River RR Co Beaver Falls, NY 13305	4' 8½'' *(1·435)*	11 *(18)*	14 *(23)*		De 2			1	42·3	9 *(14)*	6 cars	13 cars		
Ludington & Northern Rly 2840 Bay Rd, Saginaw, Mi 48603	4' 8½'' *(1·435)*	4 *(7)*			DeL 1									
Lykens Valley RR Co PO Box 81, Milersburg, Pa 17061														
Madison Ry Co, Inc 511 State St, Madison, Ind 47250					DeL 1			4	33·0330					
Magma Arizona Railroad Co PO Box 37, Superior, Ariz 85273	4' 8½'' *(1·435)*	28 *(45)*	35 *(56)*		DeL 3				91·6	28 *(45)*				
*****Maine Central Railroad Co** 242 St. John St, Portland, Maine 04102	4' 8½'' *(1·435)*	850 *(1 367)*	1 002 *(1 680)*		DeL 42 DeS 19			4 209	8 147·8	1 911 384 000 ton miles				
Manitou & Pike's Peak Railway Co PO Box 1329, Colorado Springs, Colo 80901 *(Abt system rack railway)*	4' 8½'' *(1·435)*	9 *(14)*	10 *(16)*		DeL 3 Dh 1		3	1					14·0	9 *(14)*
Manufacturers' Junction Rly Co 2335 S Cicero ave, Cicero, Ill 60650	4' 8½'' *(1·435)*	2 *(3)*	11 *(18)*		DeS 2			90						
Manufacturers' Railway Co 2850 S Broadway, St. Louis, Mo 63118	4' 8½'' *(1·435)*	42 *(67)*			DeS 11			1 225						
Marinette, Tomahawk & Western RR Co PO Box 315, Tomahawk, Wis 54487	4' 8½'' *(1·435)*	14 *(22)*			DeL 2			600						
Maryland & Penna RR Co 490 E. Market St, York, Pa 17403	4' 8½'' *(1·435)*	90 *(145)*			DeS 6			1 371	120·0	26 *(42)*				
Massena Terminal Railroad Co 410 One Allegheny Sq, Pittsburg, Pa 15212	4' 8½'' *(1·435)*	2 *(3)*	9 *(14)*		DeS 2									
McCloud River Railroad Co Drawer A. McCloud, Cal 96057	4' 8½'' *(1·435)*	94 *(151)*	111 *(179)*		DeL 4		2	7	532·6					
McKeesport Connecting Railroad PO Box 536, Pittsburgh, Pa 15230	4' 8½'' *(1·435)*	5 · *(8)*	16 *(26)*		DeS 5			159						
Mercersburg Rly Inc. PO Box 82, Lee Masters Pa 17231	4' 8½'' *(1·435)*	13·6 *(22)*	14·7 *(24)*		DeS 2									
Meridian & Bigbee River Railroad PO Box 551, Meridian, Miss 39301	4' 8½'' *(1·435)*	51 *(82)*	57 *(92)*		DeL 4			126						
Michigan Northern Rly Co PO Box 869, Cadillac Mich 49601	4' 8½'' *(1·435)*	248 *(399)*			DeL 10									
Middletown & Hummelstown RR Co PO Box G, Hummelstown, Pa 17036	4' 8½'' *(1·435)*	6·5 *(10·4)*												
Middletown & New Jersey Rly Co 140 East Main St, Middletown, NY 10940	4' 8½'' *(1·435)*	15 *(24)*	17 *(27)*		DeS 2									
Midland Valley Railroad Co *(Merged with MoPac)*	4' 8½'' *(1·435)*													
Minneapolis Eastern Railway Co 325, South First St, Minneapolis, Minn 55401	4' 8½'' *(1·435)*	2 *(3)*			DeS 1									
Minneapolis, Northfield & Southern Rly 911 Hennepin ave, Minneapolis, Minn 55403	4' 8½'' *(1·435)*	77 *(123)*			DeL 2 DeS 8			546	1 664·5	48·9	1 342·5	6 000		

* See main entry
† Operating agency of Southern Pacific, Santa Fe and Union Pacific

Freight Train mph (km/hr)	Pass. Train mph (km/hr)	Speed max. mph (km/hr)	Revenue Expenses in 1000s	Braking (continuous)	Couplers Type and Height above rail ins (mm)	Buffers Centres and Height above rail ins (mm)	Rails Weight lb. per yd (kg/m)	Sleepers Type and thickness ins (mm)	Spacing Number per mile (per km) or centres ins (mm)	Curvature max.	Gradient max. (U=not compensated)	Axle load max. tonnes	Altitude max. feet (m)	Staff employed. Total no. (inclu. workshop)	Names of officials
															Supt: R. L. Pfister
			$ 30 487 20 567												Chairman: W. N. Deram
25 (40)				Air W'hse			90 (45)	Wood 8 (203)	26'' (660)					10 (2)	Pres: A. E. Morse
							75 (37)	Wood 6 (153)	3 200 (2 000)	2·8°					Pres: M. M. Salzberg
															Pres: J. D. Mullins
20·3 (32·7)	60 (96)		$ 504 687 384 304	Air W'hse	Type E 33¼ (851)		130/75 (64/37)	Wood 7 (178)	3 100 (1 930)	17·3%	2·5%U	33	2 150 (655)		Pres: Prime F. Osborn
15 (24)	30 (48)						90/65 (45/32)	Wood 7 (178)	24'' (610)	12·0°	3·2% 1·8%U			10	Chairman: W. Buchanan Gen. Man: W. Saulman
															Pres: B. D. Gibson
							80/60 (40/30)	Wood 6 (153)	2 800 (1 740)	6·0°	2·5%				Pres: A. J. Turnbull
															Pres: Miss M. L. Sargent
10 (16)			$85·0 —				100 (50)								Gen. Man: J. M. Bishop
15 (24)	20 (32)			Air W'hse	Standard		70 (35)	Wood 6 (153)	18'' (460)	13·5°	3·7%		2 800 (853)		Pres: R. B. Wright
13·2 (21·2)	60 (96)		$ 47 976·1 46 258·7	Air W'hse	AAR Type E 34½ (876)		115/75 (57/37)	Wood 6 & 7 (153/4)	21'' (533)	Main 9·0° Branch 15·0°	2·85%U	32·8	1 893 (577)	1 402 (206)	Pres. and Chairman: E. Spencer Miller
7·5 (12·0)	10 (16)			Electro-dynamic	Roller G.E. 27% (699)		40 (20)	Wood 7 (178)	20'' (508)	16·0°	25·0%	12	14 110 (4 300)	60	Man: John E. Oldberg
			$ 1 036·7 403·3	Air	AAR Type E		100/80 (50/40)	Wood 6 (153)	20'' (508)					13 (2)	Pres: M. C. Kirby
															Pres: R. W. Chapman
															Pres: P. J. Fluge
15 (24)	20 (32)		$ 421·9 309·0	Air	Type E		90/70 (45/35)	Wood 7 (178)	22'' (560)	20·0°	2·5% 3·5%U	30	700 (213)	27 (6)	Pres: H. Lazarus
20 (32)	35 (56)						15/85 (57/42)	Oak 6 (153)	21'' (533)	10°	0·5%	31·5		10	Pres: W. Murray
10 (16)	35 (56)		$ 2 004·1 1 299·7	Air W'hse	Type E Miner 33½ (851)		90/70 (45/35)	Fir 8 (204)	3 100 (1 930)	13·0°	4·0%	30	4 600 (1 398)	65 (9)	Pres: Carl T. Hester
10 (16)			$ 2 204 1 381	AB W'hse	AAR Type E		130/100 (65/50)	Wood 7 (178)	22'' (560)	41·0°	Level	21		102 (82)	Pres: M. S. Toon
	10 (16)	10 (16)		Air	AAR		85/115 (40/57)	Wood 7 (178)	(2 600)	6°	1·25%				Vice Pres: R. C. Hunt
40 (64)				NY 6 BL	Type E		110/90 (55/45)	Oak 7 (178)	21'' (533)	6·0°	1·0%	37·5			Pres: J. W. Bard
															Pres: Elizabeth Andrus
															Pres: W. J. Dillinger
							80/70 (40/35)	Wood 6 (153)		4·0°	2·3%				Pres: R. T. Rasmussen
															Pres: T. P. Heffelfinger
30 (48)	45 (72)		$ 5 214·9 4 454·1	Air W'hse	Type E 32½'' (825)		100/80 (50/40)	Wood 7 (178)	21¼'' (540)	Main 10° Br. 20°	Main 2% Br. 3·5%	28	1 038 (317)	165	Pres: D. J. Boyer

USA (contd.)

Name of company / Address	Gauge ft.in. (metres)	Route length incl. E=Electrified miles (km.)	Track length incl. E=Electrified miles (km.)	Elect. system and type of conductor	Locomotives L=Line S=Shunt (Steam / Electric / Diesel De=elec. Dh=hyd.)	Railcars	Pass. train cars	Freight train cars / Containers	Total Volume carried (Thousands of tonnes)	Av'ge haul per ton miles (km.)	Av'ge net train load (tonnes)	Max. trailing load (tonnes)	Total number carried (in 1 000s)	Average journey miles (km.)
Minnesota, Dakota & Western Rly Co PO Box 19, International Falls, Minn 56649	4' 8½" (1·435)	4 (6)	17 (27)	DeS	5			1 190	1 104·0	3 (5)				
Minnesota Transfer Railway Co 2071 University Ave, St Paul, Minn 55104 (Switching Line only)	4' 8½" (1·435)	13 (21)	75 (121)	DeS	5									
Mississippi & Skuna Valley RR Co PO Box 265, Bruce. Ms 38915	4' 8½" (1·435)	22 (35)	26 (42)	DeL	2			82	4 000	22 (35·4)	249·3			
Mississippian Railway PO Box 446, Amory, Miss 38821	4' 8½" (1·435)		24 (39)	De	2									
Missouri & Illinois Bridge & Belt RR Co (C.B. & Q. and Mo. Pac.)	4' 8½" (1·435)	3 (5)	5 (8)											
Missouri-Illinois Railroad Co (Subsidiary of Missouri Pacific)	4' 8½" (1·435)	324 (522)												
*****Missouri-Kansas-Texas RR Co** 101 East Main St, Denison Texas 75920	4' 8½" (1·435)	2 168 (3 492)	1 682 (2 870)	DeL 142 DeS 37				7 806						
*****Missouri Pacific Railroad** 210 N. 13th St, St Louis, Miss 63103	4' 8½" (1·435)	11 501 (18 509)	16 965 (27 303)	DeL 1 045 DeS 195				55 755						
Mobile & Gulf Railroad Co 409 Commonwealth Bldg, Louisville, Ky	4' 8½" (1·435)	11 (18)	15 (24)	DL	1					11 (18)	100			
Modesto & Empire Traction Co PO Box 3106, Modesto, Cal 95353	4' 8½" (1·435)	5 (8)	28 (45)	DeS	7				1 250·3	5 (8)				
Monongahela Connecting Railroad 3540 Second ave, Pittsburgh, Pa 15219	4' 8½" (1·435)		47 (76)	DeS	22			643	15 000·0					
Monongahela Railway Co 53 Market St, Brownsville, Pa 15417	4' 8½" (1·435)	171 (275)	254 (408)	DeL	11				7 178·1	54 (87)		19 000		
Montour Railroad Co (Owned by P.C. and Pitts. and L. Erie RR) 1 429 Fourth Ave, Coraopolis, Pa 15108	4' 8½" (1·435)	50·6 (81·4)	79 (127)	DeS	14				343					
Montpelier & Barre RR PO Box 314, Barre, Vt	4' 8½" (1·435)	14 (22)		D	5				40					
Morristown & Erie Railroad Co PO Box 2206-R, Morriston, NJ, 07960	4' 8½" (1·435)	11 (18)	15 (24)	DeL 2 DeS 1			3	1	864·8	4 (6)		8 000		
Moscow, Camden & San Augustine Railroad PO Box 77, Camden, Tex	4' 8½" (1·435)	7 (11)	7·8 (12·6)	DeS	1		1						3·9	7 (11)
Moshassuck Valley Railroad Co Saylesville, RI	4' 8½" (1·435)	2 (3)	5 (8)	DeL 1 DeS 1				15						
Muncie & Western Railroad Co 1425 E 12th St, Muncie, Ind 47302	4' 8½" (1·435)		4·2 (7·0)	DeS	2									
Narragansett Pier Railroad Co Inc 1, Railroad St, Peace Dale, RI	4' 8½" (1·435)	6 (10)	7 (11)	DeL	2		1	25	400	5 (8)		400	0·2	
National Railroad Passenger Corp (See under Amtrak)														
Nevada Northern Railway Co PO Box 476, East Ely, Nev 89315	4' 8½" (1·435)	162 (260)	190 (306)	DeL 2 S 1				23	361	121 (198)	2 600	8 000		
Newburgh & South Shore Railway Co PO Box 536 Pittsburgh, Pa 15230	4' 8½" (1·435)	5 (8)	42 (68)	DS	11			298						
New Jersey, Indiana & Illinois RR Co 8 N Jefferson St, Roanoke, Va 24011	4' 8½" (1·435)	11 (18)	31 (50)	DeL			0	515		11 (18)				
New Orleans Public Belt Railroad 1247 International Trade Mart Buildings, New Orleans, La, 70130	4' 8½" (1·435)	24 (35)	153 (246)	DeS	9			3						
New Orleans Union Passenger Terminal 1001 Loyola Ave, New Orleans, La 70113 (Subsidiary of Southern Rly)	4' 8½" (1·435)	6 (10)	25 (40)	DS	2		None	None						
New York Dock Railway 34 Furman St, Brooklyn, NY 1120	4' 8½" (1·435)		8 (13)	DeS	4				6 075 Cars					
New York, Susquehanna & Western RR Co One River Road, Edgewater, NJ 07020	4' 8½" (1·435)	65 (105)	65 (105)	DeL	15		1	26	5 794·2	16 (26)				
Nezperce Railroad Co Nezperce, Idaho	4' 8½" (1·435)	14 (23)	15·3 (24·6)	DeL	4					14 (23)	250			

* See main entry

Freight Train mph (km/hr)	Pass. Train mph (km/hr)	Speed max. mph (km/hr)	Revenue / Expenses in 1000s	Braking (continuous)	Couplers Type and Height above rail ins (mm)	Buffers Centres and Height above rail ins (mm)	Rails Weight lb. per yd (kg/m)	Sleepers Type and thickness ins (mm)	Spacing Number per mile or centres (per km) or (mm)	Curvature max.	Gradient max. (U=not compensated)	Axle load max. tonnes	Altitude max. feet (m)	Staff employed. Total no. (inclu. workshop)	Names of officials
10 (16)	20 (32)		$ 2 041·0 / 1 762·0	Air W'hse	Various		100/60 (50/30)	Wood 8 (200)	18" (460)	Main 8° Secondary 20°				82 (18)	Pres: Robert H. Schwarz Vice Pres: J. S. Gendron
10 (16)	30 (48)						115/85 (57/42)	Wood 6 (153)	22" (560)	3·0°	1·0%			150 (14)	Pres: C. R. Grogan
10 (16)	15 (24)		$ 1 019·0 / 615·0	Air W'hse			90/70 (45/35)	Wood 7 (178)	20" (508)				600 (183)	15	Pres: J. C. Jessop
															Pres: R. W. Wetherby
			$ 6 949 / 6 928												
33 (53)			W'hse	W'hse	Types E,F	119/52 (59/26)		Wood 7 (178)	3 200 (2 000)	8·0°	1·4%	32	1 106 (337)	2 491	Pres: H. L. Gastler
22·4 (36)			$ 1 260 218 / 1 074 000	Air W'hse	AAR 34½" (876)		Up to 136	Wood 7 (178)		19°	2·9%	35	4 611 (1 405)	21 945	Pres: W. J. Gessner
10 (16)	15 (24)			Air										7	
10 (16)	20 (32)		3 978·3 / 3 162·0	Air W'hse	AAR 34½ (876)		160/50 (79/24)	Wood 6 (153)	22" (560)	12·3°	1·0%		125 (38)	66	Pres: R. F. Olsen
5 (8)	12 (19)		$ 7 468 / 4 951	Air W'hse	Type E 34½ (876)		115 (57)	Oak 7 (178)	21" (533)	48·0°	2·25% 2·0%U	35	800 (244)	798 (239)	Gen Super: R. L. McCombs
		35 (56)	$ 10 291·6 / 7 402·7	W'hse. AB	Types D & E		140/85 (70/41)	Wood 6 & 7	22" (560)	Main 10·0° Branch 20·0°	Main 0·5% Branch 2·18%	30	1 207 (368)	240 (43)	Pres: H. G. Allyn Jr
15 (24·1)	25 (40)		$ 3 123·0 / 2 555·2	6 BL W'hse	AAR 34½" (876)		132/90 (65/45)	Oak 7 (178)	20" (508)	11·3°	M: 1·2% Br: 2·44	26	1 225 (373)		Pres: L. E. Smith
															Gen. Man: R. Coxon
15 (24)	20 (32)		$ 445·6 / 350·8	Air W'hse	AAR T peE 33½ (851)		100/80 (50/40)	Wood 7 (150)	24" (610)	18·0°				40	In trusteeship
15 (24)	15 (24)		$ 57·9 / 64·2	Air	Auto	Standard	50 (25)	Oak 6 (150)	3 334 (2 080)	10·0°	3·0%		322 (98·1)	9	Pres: N. C. T. Hester
															Pres: P. J. O'Toole
10 (16)				Air	Yoke		100/70 (50/35)	Wood 6 (153)	2 640 (1 640)				927 (283)	6	Pres: A. M. Bracken
15 (24)	20 (32)	30 (48)	$ 0·48 / 0·42	Air W'hse	AAR Standard		70/60 (35/30)	Wood 6 (153)	3 000 (1 870)	4·0°	2·5%	25	380 (116)	2	Pres: Dr. P. J. Miller Jr.
22 (35)	30 (48)		$ 1 068 / 977	W'hse Air	National Type E 32½ (825)		115/60 (57/30)	Fir 8 (206)	22" (560)	12·0°	3·0%	28	7 000 (2 133)	95 (28)	Pres: H. H. Kremmer
			$ 3 125·1 / 2 404·1	W'hse Air			115/90 (57/45)	Wood 6 & 7	22"-24" (560-610)	20·0°	1·18% U	35		210 (57)	Gen. Man: J. W. Read
15 (24)	45 (72)		$ 508·8 / 730·3	W'hse Air	Type E 30½ (775)		90/80 (45/40)	Wood 7 (178)	24" (616)	5·0°	1·29% U	33	884 (269)	24 (4)	Pres: R. F. Dunlap
15 (24)	25 (40)		$ 5 406·7 / 3 925·2	Air W'hse	AAR Type E 32½/34 (825/864)		115/80 (57/40)	Wood 6 (153)	20" (508)	13°	1·25%	30		264	Gen. Man: P. A. Webb Jnr.
	30 (48)						115/90 (57/45)	Wood 7 (178)	21" (533)	10·0°	1·0%			150	
							159/70 (79/35)	Oak 6 (150)	2 900 (1 800)	5·0°	0·87% U	38·8	112 (48)	48 (8)	Pres: O. Carey
8 (13)	40 (64)		$2 679·2 / 2 574·0	Air NYAB	Type E 33½ (851)		112/80 (56/40)	Wood 6 (153)	22" (559)	7·3°	2·0%	30	1 024 (311)	85	Pres: I. Maidman
		15 (24)					60/50 (30/25)	Wood 8 (200)	20" (510)					6 (0)	Pres: J. Lux

USA (contd.)

Name of Company / Address	Gauge ft. in. (metres)	Route length incl. E=Electrified miles (km.)	Track length incl. E=Electrified miles (km.)	Elect. system and type of conductor	Locomotives L=Line S=Shunt (Steam / Electric / Diesel De=elec. Dh=hyd.)	Railcars (Electric / Diesel / Trailer / Railbus / Multiple Unit set)	Pass. train cars	Freight train cars / Containers	Total Volume carried. Thousands of tonnes	Av'ge haul per ton miles (km.)	Av'ge net train load tonnes	Max. trailing load tonnes	Total number passengers carried in 1 000s	Average journey miles (km.)
Norfolk & Portsmouth Belt Line RR Co, Terminal Bldg, Norfolk 10, Va	4' 8½" (1·435)	27 (43)	82 (132)		D 15									
*Norfolk & Western Railway Co, 8 North Jefferson St, Roanoke, Va 24042	4' 8½" (1·435)	7 659 (12 450)	14 868 (22 529)		DeS 133; DeL 1 366; Others 20		18	94 812	30 404·9	17 528 944 train-miles			402·9	
Norfolk, Franklin & Danviwwe Rly Co, 181 South Main St, Suffolk, Va 23434 (Subsidiary of Norfolk & Western)	4' (1·435)	7-2.7233 (333)	(375)		DeL6			233	1 614·3	60 (96)	646			
Norfolk Southern Railway Co, PO Box 2210, Raleigh, NC	4' 8½" (1·435)	592 (953)	750 (1 207)		DL 29; DS 8		None	2 353	5 163·3	120 (193)	873			
North Lousiana & Gulf RR Co, PO Drawer 550, Hodge, Louisiana 71247	4' 8½" (1·435)	40 (64)	44 (71)		DeS 4			50	749·5	40 (64)				
Northwestern Pacific Railroad Co, PO Box 629, Willits, Cal 95490 (Subsidiary of Southern Pacific Co)	4' 8½" (1·435)	273 (440)	409 (650)		DeL 41; DeS 11				2 819			11 200		
Oakland Terminal Railway, 1925 Sherman St, Alameda, Cal	4' 8½" (1·435)		26 (42)		DeS 1				11 700 carloads					
Ogden Union Railway & Depot Co, 198 West 28th St, Ogden, Utah	4' 8½" (1·435)	5 (2)	116 (186)											
Omaha, Lincoln & Beatrice Rly Co, Box 80268, 1815 Y St., Lincoln, Neb—68501	4' 8½" (1·435)	4 (7)	6 (10)		DeS 2				12·6 cars switched					
Oregon & Northwestern RR Co, PO Box 557, Hines, Ore 97738	4' 8½" (1·435)	51 (82)	51 (82)		DeL 4			395			780	2 200		
Oregon, Pacific & Eastern Rly Co, Cottage Grove, Ore	4' 8½" (1·435)	24 (39)	30 (48)		De 2									
Otter Valley RR, Proctor, Vermont 05765	4' 8½" (1·435)	4·5 (7·0)	4·5 (7·0)		DeL 1		4	4		6 720 train miles			45·0	
Paducah & Illinois RR Co (Illinois Central Railroad)	4' 8½" (1·435)	15 (24)												
Patapsco & Back Rivers Railroad Co, Sparrows Point Bvd, Sparrows Point, Md 21219	4' 8½" (1·435)		103 (166)		DeS 55			100						
Pearl River Valley Railroad Co, Picayune, Miss	4' 8½" (1·435)	5 (8)	6 (10)		DeS 1			6	101·2	5 (8)				
Pecos Valley Southern Railway Co, PO Box 349, Pecos, Texas	4' 8½" (1·435)	40 (64)	48 (77)		DeS 2			2	172·4	12 (19·3)	678	1 500		
Pennsylvania-Reading Seashore Lines, 22 Federal St, Camden, NJ 08103	4' 8½" (1·435)	318 (512)	428 (689)	D	DeL 15; DeS 11	10		0	4 927·0	24·2 (39·0)			117·3	48·1 (77·4)
Petaluma & Santa Rosa Railroad Co (Subsidiary of Southern Pacific), PO Box 629, Willits, Cal 95490	4' 8½" (1·435)	26·4 (42)	31·9 (51)					6	32·8			3 000		
Philadelphia, Bethlehem & New England Railroad Co, 1275 Daly Avenue, Bethlehem, Pa 18015	4' 8½" (1·435)	3 (5)	61 (98)		DeS 24			51						
Pickens Railroad Co, 402 Cedar Rock St, Pickens, SC 29671	4' 8½" (1·435)	9 (14)	10 (16)		De 1			1 066	29·7	291 600 ton-km			325	
Piedmont & Northern Railway Co, PO Box 480, Charlotte, NC 28201 (Subsidiary of Seaboard Coast Line)	4' 8½" (1·435)	150 (241)	164 (263)		DeL 12; DeS 6			16		39·5 (64)				
Pioneer & Fayette Railroad Co, 414, E. Main St, Fayette, Ohio 43521	4' 8½" (1·435)	0·5 (0·8)			DeS 1									
Pittsburgh, Allegheny & McKees Rocks RR Co, 180 Nichol Ave, McKees Rocks, Pa.	4' 8½" (1·435)		13 (21)		D 2			2						
Pittsburgh, Chartiers & Youghiogheny Ry Co, McKees Rocks, Pa 15136	4' 8½" (1·435)	13·5 (21·8)	29 (46)		DeS 4			3				9 600		
Pittsburgh & Lake Erie Railroad Co, P. and L.E. Ter. Bldg, Smithfield and Carson Streets, Pittsburgh, Pa 15219	4' 8½" (1·435)	274 (440)	865 (1 392)		DeL 28; DeS 67		5	15 992						
Pittsburgh & Ohio Valley Rly Co, Neville Island, Pittsburgh, Pa 15225	4' 8½" (1·435)	7 (11)	20·7 (82·9)		DeS 4				1 306·2					
Pittsburg & Shawmut Railroad Co, RD 2-Middle St, Brookville, Pa 15825	4' 8½" (1·435)	88 (142)	137 (220)		DeL 9			1 400	2 800·0	48 (77)	4 000	10 000		
Point Comfort & Northern Railroad, 410 One Allegheny Sq, Pittsburgh, Pa 15212	4' 8½" (1·435)	13 (21)	16 (25)		DeL 3									
Port Huron & Detroit Railroad Co, 2100 Thirty-Second St, Port Huron, Mich	4' 8½" (1·435)	20 (32)	30 (48)		D 2				342·2	10 (16)		2 100		
Portland Terminal Company (Switching Terminal for Maine Central), 242 St John St, Portland, Maine 04102	4' 8½" (1·435)	†23 (37)	99 (159)		DeS 14		50							
Port Terminal Railroad Assn., PO Box 9504, Houston, Tex 77011	4' 8½" (1·435)	31·6 (50·6)	156 (251)		DeS 16									

* See main entry
† Includes mainline leased from BN

Freight Train mph (km/hr)	Pass. Train mph (km/hr)	Speed max. mph (km/hr)	Revenue Expenses in 1000s	Braking (continuous)	Couplers Type and Height above rail ins (mm)	Buffers Centres and Height above rail ins (mm)	Rails Weight lb. per yd (kg/m)	Sleepers Type and thickness ins (mm)	Sleepers Spacing Number per mile (per km) or centres ins (mm)	Curvature max.	Gradient max. (U=not compensated)	Axle load max. tonnes	Altitude max. feet (m)	Staff employed. Total no. (inclu. workshop)	Names of officials
							131/70 (65/35)	Wood 6 & 7	22″ (559)	14·0°	0·5%				Pres: F. S. Morrison
18 (29)	40 (64)	78 (125)	$ 1 135 501 826 904	Air W'hse	E. 34½ (876)		132/115 (78/42)	Wood 7 (178)	19½″ (495)	18·2°	1·4% 1·9% U	32·8	3 577 (1 090)	27 668	Pres: J. P. Fishwick
35 (56)			$ 2 164·0 2 083·0	Air W'hse	Type E 34½ (876)		85/70 (42/35)	Wood 7 (178)	20″ (508)	5·0°	1·92%	31·25		111	Gen Man: F. K. Turner
		40 (64)	$16 186 14 004				100 (50)	Wood 7 (178)	20″ (508)	8·0°	2·9%	25		765	Pres: Henry Oeljen
18 (29)	30 (48)			Air Various	A.A.R. Standard		90/65 (45/32)	Wood 7 (178)	3 200 (2 000)					51 (8)	Pres: J. Hannigan
12 (20)	45 (72)		$ 12 792 9 539				136/90 (67|)	Wood 6 (153)	19½″ (495)	15°	3·04%	25		471	Pres: A. D. Demoss
8 (12·9)				W'hse	AAR Standard		110/70 (55/35)	Imp. Fir. 7 (178)	20″ (508)	17·3°	0·6%	40	20 (6)	30 (3)	Pres: R. G. Flannery
														1 032 (42)	Supt: R. O. Bills
5-10 (8-16)	35 (56)						100/75 (50/37)	Wood 6 (153)	24″ (610)	30·0°			1 918 (365)	3 (0)	Pres: J. W. Hewitt
25 (40)	35 (57)			W'hse Air	Type E		90/70 (45/35)	Fir 7 (178)	3 000 (1 870)	12·0°	2·5%	22·5	4 800 (1 463)	19	Pres: H. H. Howard Supt: R. L. Roy
							80/75 (40/37)								Pres: W. B. Kyle
15 (24)	20 (32)	20 (32)		Air	Knuckle 34½ (876)		80/85/90 (40/42/45)	Wood 6 (153)		16°	5·0%			15	
							115/112 (57/42)	Wood 7 (178)	18″ (508)	7·3°	0·97% U	33	397 (457)		Supt: L. Hogan
															Gen. Man: J. A. Emery
20 (32)	30 (48)			N York AB			85 (42)	Wood 6 (153)	24″ (610)	3·0°	Level			25 (2)	Pres: T. L. Crosby
15 (24)	20 (32)			W'hse			110/40 (55/20)	Wood 8 (203)	24″ (610)	12·5°	1·4%	30	2 960 (902)	28 (2)	Gen. Man: H. L. Cox
35 (56)	60 (96)	70 (112)	$ 9 828 11 478	Air W'hse NYAB	AAR Type E 34½ (876)		133/70 (66/35)	Wood 7 (178) 9 (228)	19½″ (495)	7·0°	3·0% 3·0% U	32·8	167 (51)	511	Gen. Man: R. E. Blosser
6 (10)	15 (24)		$ 166 151				90/70 (45/35)	Wood 6 (153)	19½″ (495)	30°	3·04%	22·5			Pres: A. D. Demoss
														671	Vice Pres. and Supt: R. N. Henning
15 (24)	15 (24)		$ 5 105·7 4 169·4	Air W'hse	AAR Type E		100/85 (50/42)	Wood 7 (178)	2 600 (1 615)		3·0%			7	Pres: Jane Gillespie
	49 (79)		$ 6 694 3 704											355 (37)	Gen. Man: F. Sellers
															Pres: R. C. Repp
							90 (45)	Wood 6 (153)	22″ (560)						Pres: W. H. Moser
15 (24)	20 (32)		$ 2 512 1 709	W'hse	Type E		115 (57)	Oak 7 (178)	22″ (560)	17·5°	1·85% U	30·8			Pres: C. W. Owens
28 (45)	30 (48)	50 (80)/F 65 (105)/P	$ 87 929·2 76 772·9	Air W'hse	AAR 34½ (876)		132/100 (66/50)	Oak 7 (178)	20″ (508)	10·0°	0·6% 0·3% U	39	916 (279)	2 970 (740)	Pres: H. G. Allyn Jr
	15 (24)		$ 238·3 163·3	Air W'hse.	AAR 34½ Type D		130/80 (65/40)	Wood 7 (178)	21/24″ (533/610)	18·0°	0·75%	33	735 (224)	33	Pres: T. H. Connolly
30 (48)	40 (64)		$ 3 715·0	W'hse	Type E		131/85 (65/42)	Wood 7 (178)	21″ (533)	9·0°	1·0%	31·0	1 642 (501)	135	Pres: W. R. Weaver
20 (32)	35 (56)						115/85 (57/42)	Oak 6 (153)	21″ (533)	6·5°	0·47%	31·5	40 (12·2)	32	Pres: W. Murray
				W'hse			80 (40)	Wood 6 (153)	24″ (610)	9·0°	3·0%	30·5			Pres: G. Y. Duffy
30 (49)	40 (64)		$ 9 872·6 (expenses only*)	Air W'hse	AAR Type E 34½ (876)		115/75 (57/37)	Wood 6 & 7	21″ (533)	15·0°	1·5% U	32·8	111 (33·8)	322 (64)	Pres: E. Spencer Miller
	30 (48)						115/75 (57/37)	Oak 6 (153)	19½″ (495)	9·1°	1·04% 0·86% U	32·8	40 (12·2)	400 (80)	

* Shared by Maine Central and Boston and Maine

NAME OF COMPANY ADDRESS	Gauge ft. in. (metres)	Route length incl. E=Electrified miles (km.)	Track length incl. E=Electrified miles (km.)	Elect. system and type of conductor	Locomotives L=Line S=Shunt Steam Electric Diesel De=elec. Dh=hyd.	Rail-cars Electric Diesel Trailer Railbus Multiple Unit set	Pass. train cars	Freight train cars Containers	Total Volume carried. Thousands of tonnes	Av'ge haul per ton miles (km.)	Av'ge net train load tonnes	Max. trailing load tonnes	Total number carried in 1 000s	Average journey miles (km.)

USA *(contd.)*

NAME OF COMPANY ADDRESS	Gauge	Route length	Track length	Elect. system	Locos	Rail-cars	Pass. cars	Freight cars / Containers	Total Volume	Av'ge haul	Av'ge net train load	Max. trailing load	Total number carried	Average journey
Port Townsend Railroad Joshua Green Bldg, Seattle 1, Wash	4′ 8½″ (1·435)	12 (19)			D 2									
Prescott & Northwestern RR Co PO Box 579, Prescott, Ark 71857	4′ 8½″ (1·435)	32 (51)	38 (61)		DeL 3				200	18 (29)	900			
Quincy Railroad Co Inc PO Box 420, Quincy, Cal 95971	4′ 8½″ (1·435)	4 (5)	4 (7)		DeL 2				63·9	3 (5)	150			
Rahway Valley Co Blvd & Market St, Kenilworth, NJ 07033	4′ 8½″ (1·435)	11 (18)	15 (24)		D 2				118·8	2·7 (4·3)				
Raritan River Railroad Co 170 John St, South Amboy, NJ	4′ 8½″ (1·435)	17 (27)	34 (55)		DeS 6				901·1	6 (10)	500			
Reader Railroad PO Box 9, Malvern, Arkansas 72104	4′ 8½″ (1·435)	3·1 (4·8)	4·4 (7·1)		SL 1		4							
***Richmond, Fredericksburg and Potomac Railroad Co.** 2134 West Laburnam Ave., PO Box 11281, Richmond, Virginia 23230	4′ 8½″ (1·435)	109 (180)	472 (780)		DeL 25 DeS 14			1 387	10 987·0					
River Terminal Railway Co 3100 East 45th St, Cleveland, Ohio	4′ 8½″ (1·435)		27 (43)		D 18			244						
Rockdale, Sandow & Southern RR 410 One Allegheny Sq, Pittsburg, Pa 15212	4′ 8½″ (1·435)	6 (10)	8 (12)		De 2									
Roscoe, Snyder & Pacific Rly Co PO Box 68, Roscoe, Tex 79545	4′ 8½″ (1·435)	30 (48)	39 (57)		DeL 2			766	665·20·63	625 (1·1)	4·92			
St Joseph Belt Railway Co South St. Joseph, Mo *(Subsidiary of Missouri Pacific)*	4′ 8½″ (1·435)	2 (3)	18 (29)											
St Joseph Terminal Railroad Co 803 South 4th St, St. Joseph, Mo	4′ 8½″ (1·435)		9 (14)		DS 2		None	None						
***St Louis-San Francisco Railway Co** *("Frisco" Lines including QA & P)* 906 Olive St, St Louis, Mo 63101	4′ 8½″ (1·435)	4 674 (7 210)	6 584 (10 700)		DeL 339 DeS 92			15 724	40 785·6					
St Louis Southwestern Railway Lines 408 Pine St, St. Louis, Mo 63162 *(Southern Pacific)*	4′ 8½″ (1·435)	1 441 (2 318)	2 240 (3 605)		DeL 190 DeS 53			19 085						
St Mary's Railroad Co PO Box 528, St. Marys, Ga	4′ 8½″ (1·435)	11 (18)	20 (32)		D 3			56	8 824·3	11 (18)	1 800	5 800		
St Paul Union Depot Co 2071 University ave, St Paul, Minn 55104 *(Switching line)*	4′ 8½″ (1·435)	1·54 (2·3)												
Sacramento Northern Railway *(In conjunction with Tidewater Southern RR)* 526 Mission St, San Francisco, Cal	4′ 8½″ (1·435)	349 (583)	470 (785)	600 V dc OH	De 13		None	233	949·4	50 (80)	445			
Salt Lake, Garfield & Western Rly Co 11th West and South Temple, Salt Lake City, Utah 84116	4′ 8½″ (1·435)	17 (27)	20 (32)		DeL 3		5	3	106·0	9 (15)	350	840	3·5	30 (48)
Sandersville Railroad Co PO Box 269, Sandersville, Ga	4′ 8½″ (1·435)	(14)	22 (35)		DeS 3			248	400·0	5 (8)	2 000			
San Diego & Arizona Eastern Ry Co *(Transferred to Metropolitan Transit Development Board in 1979)* 45 12th Ave., San Diego	4′ 8½″ (1·435)	138 (222)	166 (267)		DeS 5			16						
San Francisco Belt Railroad Ferry Bdg., San Francisco, Cal 94111	4′ 8½″ (1·435)	8·5 (14)	60 (96)		DeS 4				5 742 cars					
San Luis Central Railroad Co PO Box 1249, Evanston, Ill 60204	4′ 8½″ (1·435)	13 (21)	16 (26)		DeS 1			449	44·1	10	214	2 000		
San Manuel Arizona Railroad Co San Manuel, Ariz 85631	4′ 8½″ (1·435)	30 (48)	30 (48)		DeL 6			4	1 030·8	29·4 (46·8)		3 000		
Santa Maria Valley RR Co PO Box 340, Santa Maria, Cal 93456	4′ 8½″ (1·435)	18 (29)	28 (45)		DeL 8			3	1 322·0					
***Seaboard Coast Line Railroad Co** 3600 West Broad St, Richmond, Va 23230 *(part of The Family Lines System)*	4′ 8½″ (1·435)	9 028 (14 514) 8 960 (14 410)	9 380 (15 106)		DeL1 196			62 386 (C 3 546)	319 500					
Sierra Railroad Company 781 S. Washington St, Sonora, Cal 95370	4′ 8½″ (1·435)	56 (92)	67 (124)		S 2 DeL 3		15	23	484·1	45·7 (73)	900	1 200		
Sioux City Terminal Railway Co 340 Livestock Exch Bldg, Sioux City, Iowa 51107	4′ 8½″ (1·435)	2·5 (4)	12 (19)		DeS 3									
Skaneateles Short Line Railroad Corp 32 Fennell St, Skaneateles, NY	4′ 8½″ (1·435)	5 (8)	6 (10)		DL 2			2	87·7	2 (3·2)				
***Soo Line RR Company** 800 Soo Line Building, Minneapolis, Box 530, Minn 55440	4′ 8½″ (1·435)	4 589 (7 370)	6 103 (9 822)		DeL 197 DeS 30			11 500	22 592·0	10 169 000 000 ton-miles				

* See main entry

Average Speeds: Freight Train mph (km/hr)	Pass. Train mph (km/hr)	Speed max. mph (km/hr)	Financial Data: Revenue Expenses in 1000s	Braking (continuous)	Couplers Type and Height above rail ins (mm)	Buffers Centres and Height above rail ins (mm)	Rails Weight lb. per yd (kg/m)	Sleepers Type and thickness ins (mm)	Spacing Number per mile or centres ins (mm)	Curvature max.	Gradient max. (U=not compensated)	Axle load max. tonnes	Altitude max. feet (m)	Staff employed Total no. (inclu. workshop)	Names of officials. Extended lists can be found at the end of the individual country in the report section immediately following
12 (19)			$ 600·0 400·0				85/56 (42/27)	Wood 6 (153)	22" (560)	6·0°	1·6%	35	250 (76)	21 (4)	Gen Man: H. B. Graham
5 (8)	10 (16)		$113·1 73·6	Air W'hse			75/45 (37/22)	Fir 6 (153)	22" (560)	14·0°			3 550 (1 082)	4	Pres: A. A. Emerson
10 (16)	25 (40)		$ 192·5 166·7	Air			70 (36)	Oak					175 (53)	14	Pres and Gen Man: B. J. Cahill
	20 (33)			W'hse			100 (50)	Wood 7 (178)	24" (610)	12·0°	1·82%	33		57 (5)	Vice Pres: Robert G. Kipp
12 (19)	12 (19)	25 (40)		Air			85/52 (42/26)	Wood						21 (3)	Gen Man: R. A. Grigsby
55 (89)	—	55 (89)			Type E 50/51										Pres: S. Shumate
							115/85 (57/42)	Wood 7 (178)	20" (508)					Gen.	Man: T. E. Malloy
20 (32)	35 (56)						115/85 (57/42)	Oak 6 (153)	21" (533)	5·1°	1·6%	31·5	537	16	Pres: W. Murray
25 (40)	45 (72)		$ 1 812·1 1 408·6	Air W'hse	AAR Standard Type E		75/56 (37/27)	Wood 6 (155)	22" (560)	12·0°			22 (7)	51 (1)	Pres: R. B. Mize
							90 (45)	Wood 6 (153)	25" (635)	20·0°	0·54%U				Pres: K. D. Hestes
							90 (45)	Wood		18·0°				65	Supt: H. T. Hinman
55 (89)	65 (105)		$ 388 964·3 368 852·6	Air	AAR Standard AB		132/90 (66/45)	Wood 7 (178)	3 250 (2 030)	10·4°	2·35% 2·15%U	39	3 195 (1 228)	8 221	Chairman of Board and Pres: R. C. Grayson
	70 (112)		$ 163 405 123 258				136/80 (68/40)	Wood 7 (178)	20" (508)	4·0°	1·0% 1·0% U	32·5	860 (262)		Pres: D. K. McNear
	40 (64)			Air W'hse			90 (45)	Wood 7 (178)	21" (533)	8·0°	0·5%			31 (4)	Vice Pres. and Man: R. W. Chaplin
										15·0°					Pres: C. R. Hussey
	30 (48)		$ 3 228·5 1 815·7	Air W'hse	Type E & F 34½ (876)		100/60 (50/30)	Wood 6 (153) 7 (178)	2 880 (1 790)	20·0°	1·3% 1·1%U	27·5	200 (61)	123	Pres: R. G. Flannery
30 (48)	35 (56)	40 (64)		Air W'hse	AAR		60 (29·8)	Fir 7 (178)	20" (508)	10·0°	1·0%	33	4 235 (1 292)	10	Vice Pres. and Gen Man: Rex N. Firth
							90 (45)	Wood 7 (178)	22" (559)						Gen Man: B. J. Tarbutton Jr
	30 (48)						90/75 (45/37)	Wood 6 (153)	22" (559)	20·0°	2·2%	26·2	3 360 (1 200)		Pres: A. D. Demoss
6 (10)	10 (16)		$ 187·3 485·4	Air W'hse	Type D 33 (850)		174/85 (86/42)	Wood 7 (178)	2 285 (1 420)	25·0°	5·0%			24 (11)	Pres: W. B. Kyle
10 (16)	10 (16)		$ 358 892 358 321	Air W'hse	E and F 34½" (876)		56 (28)	Wood 6 (153)	22" (559)	1·0°	0·1%	33	7 650 (2 332)	8	Pres: G. C. Betke, Jr.
20 (32)	35 (56)			Air W'hse			90 (45)	Wood 8 (204)	21" (534)	6°	2·0% U	35	3 200 (975)	44	Pres: W. L. Parks
							90/75 (45/37)	Fir 7 (178)	3 168 (1 970)					46	Pres: Marian H. Barry Vice Pres: Sue J. Sword
60 (96)	79 (127)		$ 1 903 700 1 727 300	Air W'hse NY Co	E 34½" (876)		100/131 (49/65)	Wood 7 (178)	2 960 (1 850)	10·0°	1·8%	24		19 802	Pres. and Chief Executive Officer: Prime F. Osborn III
15 (24)	25 (40)	35 (56)	$ 474·6 310·0	Air W'hse			110/90 (55/45)	Fir 7 (178)	21" (534)	18·0°	3·0%	19	1 769 (547)	25 (14)	Pres: Charles Crocker Gen. Man: D. J. Franco
							90/85 (45/42)	Oak 6 (153)	18" (457)	26·0°	4·0%	20	1 135 (346)	35	Pres: Ray. A. Rodeen
30 (48)				Air W'hse			70 (34·7)	Wood 7 (178)	18" (457)					7	Pres: G. A. Coffenberg
21 (34)	40 (64)		$ 217 251·0 164 964·0	Air	E & F 35½" (902)		131/52 (65/26)	Wood 6/7	20-22	6·0°	2·9% 3·2% U	32	2 550 (777)	4 582	Pres: L. H. Murray

	Gauge	Route length incl. E=Electrified	Track length incl. E=Electrified	Elect. system and type of conductor	Locomotives L=Line S=Shunt Steam Electric Diesel De=elec. Dh=hyd.	Railcars Electric Diesel Trailer Railbus Multiple Unit set	Pass. train cars	Freight train cars Containers	Freight movement				Passengers	
NAME OF COMPANY ADDRESS	ft. in. (metres)	miles (km.)	miles (km.)						Total Volume carried. Thousands of tonnes	Av'ge haul per ton miles (km.)	Av'ge net train load tonnes	Max. trailing load tonnes	Total number carried in 1 000s	Average journey miles (km.)

USA *(contd.)*

South Brooklyn Railway Co 990 Third ave, Brooklyn, NY 11232	4' 8½" *(1·435)*	6 *(10)*	12 *(20)*		DL 2									
South Buffalo Railway Co 2558 Hamburg Turnpike, Lackawanna 18, NY	4' 8½" *(1·435)*	30 *(48)*	75 *(121)*		DeS 46		0	69	24 000·0	3 *(4·8)*	2 000	7 500		
Southern Industrial Railroad Inc PO Box 358, Centreville, Iowa 52544	4' 8½" *(1·435)*	15 *(24)*	20 *(32)*		D 2									
***Southern Pacific Transportation Company** One Market Plaza, San Francisco, Cal 94105	4' 8½" *(1·435)*	13 601 *(21 762)*	21 300 *(34 200)*		De 2 422		184	82 932						
***Southern Railway System** 920 15th St, NW, Washington DC 20005	4' 8½" *(1·435)*	10 494 *(16 732)*	17 282 *(27 537)*		DeL 1 203 DeS 188			74 099 C 4 405	149 739·0				194·8	382 *(507)*
Southern San Luis Valley Railroad PO Box 98, Blanca, Colo 81123	4' 8½" *(1·435)*	1·3 *(2·1)*	2·6 *(4·2)*		DhS 1				13·8	0·9 *(1·4)*	100	300		
Spencerville and Elgin RR Co PO Box 75, Spencerville, Oh 45887														
Spokane International Railroad Co 1416 Dodge St, Omaha, Nebr 68102	4' 8½" *(1·435)*	150 *(241)*						85	2 516·9	511 285 084 ton miles				
Springfield Terminal Railway Co Clinton St, Springfield, Vt 05156	4' 8½" *(1·435)*	6 *(10)*	7·5 *(12)*		DeS 1				Switching only					
Staten Island Rapid Transit Ry Co 25 Broadway, New York, NY 10004 *(Subsidiary of Baltimore & Ohio Railroad)*	4' 8½" *(1·435)*	27 *(43)* E 14 *(23)*	145 *(233)* E 29 *(47)*	600 V dc 3 rail	DeS 8		55		1 509·9	10·6 *(17)*	1 217		4 839·2	6·5 *(10·6)*
Steelton & Highspire Railroad Co Steelton, Pa 17113	4' 8½" *(1·435)*	3	28 *(55)*		DeS 8									
Stewartstown Railroad Co Stewartstown, Pa	4' 8½" *(1·435)*	7 *(11)*			D 1 Pet 1									
Stockton Terminal & Eastern RR 1330 N. Broadway Ave, Stockton, Cal 95205	4' 8½" *(1·435)*	14 *(22)*	19 *(30)*		DeL 3				606·0		1 800			
Strasburg Railroad Co† PO Box 96, Strasburg, Pa 17579	4' 8½" *(1·435)*	4·5 *(7·2)*	5 *(8)*		S 5 De 1 Gas 1		14	4	600·1	4·5 *(7·5)*			250·0	4·5 *(7·5)*
Strouds Creek and Muddlety RR Grafton, W Va	4' 8½" *(1·435)*	23 *(37)*			D 1									
Sumter & Choctaw Railway Co Bellamy, Ala 36901	4' 8½" *(1·435)*	4 *(6)*	4·9		De 1¶			24		92	170			
Sunset Railway Co *(Southern Pacific Affiliated Co)*	4' 8½" *(1·435)*	51 *(82)*												
Tacoma Municipal Belt Line Railway PO Box 11007, Tacoma, Wash 98424	4' 8½" *(1·435)*		33 *(53)*		DeS 6				60 000 carloads					
Tavares & Gulf Railroad Co Box 1007, Tavares, Fla	4' 8½" *(1·435)*	38 *(61)*												
Tennessee, Alabama & Georgia Rly Co 1478 Market St, PO Box 6508, Sta "B", Chattanooga Tenn 37408	4' 8½" *(1·435)*	93 *(150)*	104 *(167)*		DeLS 4			115	1 279·1	80 *(129)*	1 728			
Tennessee Railroad Co PO Box 498, Oneida, Tenn 37841	4' 8½" *(1·435)*	57 *(92)*	71 *(114)*		D 6				940·4	30·5 *(49·0)*	3 200	6 500		
Terminal Railroad Assn of St. Louis 18th & Market St, St. Louis Mo 63103	4' 8½" *(1·435)*	53 *(87)*	378 *(608)*		DeS 93			75	740 033 carloads					
Terminal Railway of the Alabama State Docks Department Box 1588, Mobile, Ala 36601	4' 8½" *(1·435)*		75 *(121)*		DeS 11				111 344 carloads	6 *(10)*				
Texas City Terminal Railway Co PO Box 591, Texas City, Tex 77590 *(Subsidiary of Missouri Pacific, Santa Fe and the M-K-T railroads)*	4' 8½" *(1·435)*	32 *(53)*	32 *(53)*		DeS 3				18 555 carloads					
Texas Mexican Railway Co 1200 Washington St, PO Box 519, Laredo, Tex 78040 *(Subsidiary of Nat. Rlys of Mexico)*	4' 8½" *(1·435)*	157 *(252)*	240 *(386)*		DeL 13 DeS 14			262	4 128·3	4 128 300 train-km				
Texas, Oklahoma & Eastern RR Co PO Box 1060, Hot Springs, Ark 71901	4' 8½" *(1·435)*	40 *(64)*	46 *(74)*						697·2	38·8	3 400			
Texas Pacific-Missouri Pacific Terminal RR of New Orleans New Orleans 13, La *(Subsidiary of Missouri Pacific)*	4' 8½" *(1·435)*	60 *(96)*	155 *(249)*											
Texas South-Eastern RR Co Diboll, Tex	4' 8½" *(1·435)*	21 *(34)*	27 *(43)*		DeS 3			1	225·1	13·5 *(21·7)*	722			
Tidewater Southern Railway Co 1025 19th St, Sacremento, Cal *(In conjunction with Sacramento Northern)*	4' 8½" *(1·435)*	57 *(92)*	70 *(113)*		DeL 3			93						
Toledo, Angola & Western Rly Co PO Box 307, Sylvania, Ohio 43560	4' 8½" *(1·435)*	8 *(13)*	10 *(16)*		DeS 1				200·0	8 *(12·8)*	400	20 Cars		
Toledo, Peoria & Western RR Co ("The Peoria Road") 2000 E. Washington St, East Peoria, Ill 61611	4' 8½" *(1·435)*	301 *(484)*	393 *(632)*		DeL 19 DeS 4			640	5 492·0	107·5 *(172·5)*	2 944		26	37 *(59·5)*

* See main entry
† Primarily steam (90%) hauled passenger line

Average Speeds			Financial Data	Braking	Couplers	Buffers	Rails	Sleepers (crossties)		Curvature max.	Gradient max. (U=not compensated)	Axle load max.	Altitude max.	Staff employed Total no. (inclu. workshop)	Names of officials. Extended lists can be found at the end of the individual country in the report section immediately following
Freight Train mph (km/hr)	Pass. Train mph (km/hr)	Speed max. mph (km/hr)	Revenue Expenses in 1 000s	(continuous)	Type and Height above rail ins (mm)	Centres and Height above rail ins (mm)	Weight lb. per yd (kg/m)	Type and thickness ins (mm)	Spacing Number per mile or centres ins (mm)			tonnes	feet (m)		
															Pres: J. G. de Roos
6 (9.6)	25 (40)	25 (40)	$ 11 420·0 / 8 802·5		34 (864)		115/105 (57/52)	Wood 7 (178)	22" (559)	38·0°	2·0% / 2·0% U	30	611 (983)	1 200 (65)	Pres: R. J. Kent
25 (40)		79 (127)	$ 2 280 000 / 2 163 800	Air AB	AAR Type E		136/113 (67/53)	Wood 9 (229)	19½" (497)	14·0°	2·8%	35	7 032 (2 143)	43 900	Chair. & Chief Ex. Off: B. F. Biaggini Pres: D. K. McNear
20·8 (33.5)	44 (71)	79 (127)	$ 1 301 716 / 1 120 796	Air W'hse	Types E & F		132/70 (66/35)	Wood 7 (178)	3 250 (2 030)	6·0°	4·36% / 4·21% U	35	3 360 (1 024)	24 312	Pres: L. S. Crane
8 (13)	13 (22)		$ 17·3 / 15·2	Air			65 (32)	Wood 7 (180)	30" (672)		2·0%		7 820 (2 384)		Pres. and Gen. Man: George M. Oringdulph
16 (26)				Air	AAR		131/72 (65/36)	Wood						124	Pres: J. C. Kenefick
10 (16)	30 (48)			Air W'hse	34½" (878)		85/70 (42/35)		15" (381)					12 (3)	Tres: W. O. Moeser
12·5 (20)	20 (32)			W'hse	H2A W'hse		100 (49.6)	Wood 7 (178)	22" (559)	16·0°	1·86%	25			Exec. Vice Pres: J. T. Collinson
															Pres: R. J. Kent
															Pres: J. H. Anderson
5 (8)	10 (16)			W'hse	AAR		90/60 (45/30)	Pine 8 (203)	24" (610)	24·0°	2·0%	20	Sea level	51 (1)	Gen Man: L. Hardaway Jr
29 (47)	29 (47)	29 (47)	$ 544·0 / –	Air W'hse	AAR		85/90 (42/45)	Wood 6 (153)	22" (599)	18·0°	2·0% U	30·0	345 (105)	50	Pres: W. M. Moedinger
															Man: J. E. Sell
6 (8)	10 (16)		$ 67 834 / 66 337	Air	AAR		85/56 (42/28)	Wood 7 (178)	18" (458)			66		3	Pres: J. W. Bard
															Pres: R. L. King
				Air W'hse	Type E 34" (860)		100/60 (50/30)	Wood 8 (200)	22" (560)	12°	level	33	Sea level	50 (2)	Gen Man: Donald E. Carlson
	40 (64)						100 (50)	Wood 7 (178)	21" (533)	8·5°	1·3%	30	954 (291)	85	
20 (32)	25 (40)		$ 582·4 / 493·1	Air W'hse	F National		112/70 (55/35)	Wood 7 (178)	18" (458)	16°	3·5% U	30	1 510 (460)	81 (4)	Gen Man & Co-Receiver: Tom Gentry
25 (40)				Air W'hse	AAR 33" (850)		115/100 (57/50)	Wood 6 & 7	21" (533)		2·6%	32·8	621 (189)	1 965 (100)	VP & Gen Man: O. R. Bailey Jr
10 (16)	30 (48)		$ 2 600·9 / 2 442·0	Air NYAB 14 KL	AAR		90/100 (45/50)	Wood 6 (153)	21" (553)	9°	1·0%	Coopers 72K	30 (9)	175 (18)	Gen Man: A. B. McKenzie
5 (8)			$ 4 068·7 / 3 791·6		AAR		112/60 (56/30)	Wood 6 (153)	2 600 (1 615)	17·0°			20 (6)	95 (12)	Gen Man: J. B. Wimberley
	45 (72)		$ 10 691·0 / 9 722·6		AAR		100/90 (50/45)	Wood 7 (178)	3 168 (1 930)	6·0°	0·75%		800 (244)	22	Pres: A. R. Ramos
	35 (56)		$ 527·6 / 233·3				90/75 (45/37)	Wood 6 (153)	22" (560)	6·0°			480 (146)	23	
							75/60 (37/30)	Wood 6 (153)	20" (508)	10·0°	1·5%				
20 (32)															
	30 (48)			Air W'hse. NYAB			141/56 (70/28)	Wood 6 & 7	2 880 (1 790)	10·0°	1·0%	27	117 (36)	30 (0)	VP and Gen Man: L. D. Michelson
15 (24)			$ 118 000 / 113 000		AAR		75 (37)	Oak 6 (153)	22" (560)	15·0°	2·0%		660 (210)	9	Pres: C. L. Pattison
	49 (79)		$ 21 435·9 / 16 494·5	W'hse	AAR		131/80 (65/40)	Oak 6 (153)	20" (508)	6·0°	1·3% U	33	770 (1 239)	450	Chairman: J. Russel Coulter

NAME OF COMPANY ADDRESS	Gauge ft. in. (metres)	Route length incl. E=Electrified miles (km.)	Track length incl. E=Electrified miles (km.)	Elect. system and type of conductor	Locomotives L=Line S=Shunt Steam Electric Diesel De=elec. Dh=hyd.	Rail-cars Electric Diesel Trailer Railbus Multiple Unit set	Pass. train cars	Freight train cars / Con-tainers	Total Volume carried. Thousands of tonnes	Av'ge haul per ton miles (km.)	Av'ge net train load tonnes	Max. trailing load tonnes	Total number carried in 1 000s	Average journey miles (km.)
USA *(contd.)*														
Toledo Terminal Railroad Co 3648 Hoffman Rd, PO Box 5148, Toledo, Ohio 43611	4' 8½" (1·435)	29 (47)	88 (142)		De 7									
Tooele Valley Railway Co 35 Nth, Broadway, Tooele, Utah 84074	4' 8½" (1·435)	7 (11)	9 (14)		DeLS 1				1·4	7 (11)		750	900	
Trona Railway Co Box 427, Trona, Cal 93562	4' 8½" (1·435)	31 (50)	34 (55)		DeL 4			1	1 176·9				125	
Tucson, Cornelia & Gila Bend RR Co. Box 400, Ajo, Ariz	4' 8½" (1·435)	44 (71)	48 (77)		De 2		1	13	219·5					
Tulsa Sapulpa Union Railway PO Box 520 Sapulpa, Okla 74066	4' 8½" (1·435)	10 (16)	12 (19)		De 3				170·8	5 (8)		576	900	
Tuscola & Saginaw Bay Ry Co Inc 538 East Huron St, Vassar, Mi 48768														
Union Belt of Detroit *(Track owned by PRR, C & O and Wabash RR) (Switching only)*	4' 8½" (1·435)	115 (185)												
***Union Pacific Corporation** 1416 Dodge St, Omaha Neb 68179	4' 8½" (1·435)	9 432 (15 176)	15 836 (25 430)		DeL 1 413 DeS 126			68 540	89 679·9	659·3 (1 060)			1 876	
Union Railway Co (Memphis) *(Subsidiary of Missouri Pacific)*	4' 8½" (1·435)	18 (29)												
Union Terminal Co (Dallas) 400 S Houston St, Dallas, Tex 75202	4' 8½" (1·435)	2 (3)	14·3 (22)											
Upper Merion & Plymouth RR Co PO Box 112, Conshohocken, Pa 19428	4' 8½" (1·435)	16 (26)	16 (26)		DeS 9			126						
Utah Railway Co 1770, University Club Bldg, 136 East S Temple, Salt Lake City, Utah 84111	4' 8½" (1·435)	94 (151)			DeL 14			194		2 158 655 ton-km				
Valdosta Southern RR PO Box 1147, Valdosta, Ga 31601	4' 8½" (1·435)	28 (45)			D 2									
Ventura County Railroad Co PO Box 432, Oxnard, Cal 93032	4' 8½" (1·435)	10 (16)	12 (19)		D 3			2	350·0	10·7 (16)				
Virginia Blue Ridge Railway Piney River, Va 22964	4' 8½" (1·435)	10 (16)	11 (17)		DeL 2			3	59·9	8 (13)		75		
Virginia Central Railway PO Box 239, Fredericksburg, Va 22401	4' 8½" (1·435)	1 (1·6)	2 (3·2)				1		20·0	1 (1·6)		50	50	
Visalia Electric Railroad Co *(Southern Pacific Affiliated Co)*	4' 8½" (1·435)	34 (55)	45 (72)											
Wabash Valey RR Co 1403 Eldorado, Decatur, Ill 62521														
Walla Walla Valley Railway Co 176 E. Fifth St, St Paul, Minn 55101	4' 8½" (1·435)	19 (30)	28 (45)		DeS 2				83·6	8 (13)				
Ware Shoals Railroad Co Ware Shoals, SC	4' 8½" (1·435)	5 (8)			D 1									
Warren & Ouachita Valley Rly Co 325 West Cedar St, PO Box 150, Warren, Ark 71671	4' 8½" (1·435)	16 (26)	17 (28)		DeL 1				185·5	15 (24)				
Warren & Saline River Railroad Co PO Box 390, Warren, Ark 71671	4' 8½" (1·435)	16 (25·7)	17 (27·3)		DeS 2	R 2		1	70·5	2·2 (3·5)				
Warrenton Railroad Co PO Box 518, Warrenton, NC 27589	4' 8½" (1·435)	3 (5)	3·8 (7·2)		DeL 2			250	6·5					
Warwick Railway Co Box 2262, Edgewood 5, RI	4' 8½" (1·435)	1 (2)			D 2									
Washington, Idaho & Montana Rly Co Lewiston, Idaho	4' 8½" (1·435)	50 (80)	64 (103)											
Washington Terminal Co Union Station, Washington, DC	4' 8½" (1·435)	52 (84)	50 (80) E 17 (27)		DeS 7									
Waterloo Railroad Co Waterloo, Iowa *(ICGR)*	4' 8½" (1·435)	67 (108)	92 (148)		DeS 4		8							
Wellsville, Addison & Galeton RR Galeton, Pa	4' 8½" (1·435)	80 (129)	133 (214)		D 4			135						
West Virginia Northern Railroad Co PO Box 458, Kingswood, W Va	4' 8½" (1·435)	17 (27)	22 (35)		DeS 3									
Western Maryland Railway Co 2 N Charles St, Baltimore, Md 21201	4' 8½" (1·435)	860 (1 181)	1 380 (2 247)		DeL 115 DeS 4									
***Western Pacific Railroad Co** 526 Mission St, San Francisco, Cal	4' 8½" (1·435)	1 187 (1 910)	1 695 (2 727)	OH	DeL 138 DeS 15	9		5 943 C 274	11 877·9	555 (893)			1 650	
White Sulphur Springs & Yellowstone Park Railway Co Box 30, White Sulphur Springs, Mont 59645	4' 8½" (1·435)	23 (37)	48 (37)		De 1 S 1		5							

* See main entry

Freight Train mph (km/hr)	Pass. Train mph (km/hr)	Speed max. mph (km/hr)	Revenue Expenses in 1 000s	Braking (continuous)	Couplers Type and Height above rail ins (mm)	Buffers Centres and Height above rail ins (mm)	Rails Weight lb. per yd (kg/m)	Sleepers Type and thickness ins (mm)	Spacing Number per mile or centres ins (mm)	Curvature max.	Gradient max. (U=not compensated)	Axle load max. tonnes	Altitude max. feet (m)	Staff employed Total no. (inclu. workshop)	Names of officials
							112/100 (56/50)	Oak 6 (153) 7 (178)	21" (533)	6·0°	0·83%	Coopers E-70		136	
6 (9·7)		18 (29)	$ 2 384·0 86 729·0	Air W'hse	Type E 34½ (876)		85 (42)	Wood 7 (178)	15" (381)	14·0°	2·4%	31	4 950 (1 509)	23 (2)	Pres: D. H. Lee
14 (22·5)		25 (40)	$ 1 466·0 843·3	Air W'hse	Type F 32 (813)		112/75 (56/37)	Wood 7 (178)	18" (458)	30·5°	1·85%	2·5	3 248 (990)	52	Pres: J. S. Latham
			$ 671·7 484·1												
10 (16)	15 (24)		$ 209·0 208·3	Air W'hse			90/60 (45/30)	Oak 8 (203)	18" (457)		2·0%			19 (9)	Gen. Man: E. M. Grosvener
32 (51·5)	52·2 (84)		$ 2 989 400·0 2 591 000·0	Air W'hse	Type E		133/75 (66/37)	Wood 7 (178)			2·21%		8 240 (2 511)	27 763	Pres: J. C. Kenefick
		25 (40)		Air			100/90 (50/45)	Wood 6 (153)	25" (635)	12·0°	0·54% U		424 (129)	108 (1)	Gen. Man: D. E. Walker
6 (9)		10 (16)	$ 2 526·7 2 124·1	Air			115/90 (57/45)	Wood	2 344 (1 465)					116 (24)	Pres: W. F. Finley Gen. Supt: V. P. Perone
							115/75 (57/37)	Wood 7 (178)	22" (560)	8·0° Br. 12·0°	2·0% Br. 3·9%	31·5		8	Pres: O. K. Curtis
10 (16)	15 (24)						90/60 (45/30)	Wood 6 & 8	22" (560)	13·0°	1·0% U				Gen. Man: C. C. O'Hara Cont: W. Graf
15 (24)	20 (32)		$ 216·6 154·3				80/75 (40/37)	Wood 9 (229)	2 600 (1 600)					14 (1)	Gen. Supt: J. M. Drumheller
10 (16)	15 (24)		$ 19·5 27·3	W'hse	AAR 32½" (877)		100/60 (50/30)	Wood 6 (153)	21" (534)	20·0°	40% U	35	96 (26)	3	Gen. Man: F. Freeman Funk
							80/60 (40/30)	Fir 6 (153)	18" (457)	13·0°	1·0% U				
12 (19)	20 (32)		$ 173·0 177·9		Standard		100/56 (50/28)	Wood 6 (153)	2 816 (1 760)	14·0°	1·0%		1 000 (305)	18 (2)	Gen. Man: K. E. Schneidmiller
10 (16)														8	Pres: R. J. Lane
5 (8)	20 (32)		$ 115·5 137·7	NY Air			75/60 (37/30)	Wood 6 (153)	3 000 (1 875)	3·0°	1·6%	25	Sea level	11 (1)	Gen. Man: H. B. Graham
	20 (32)		$ 27·0 —	Air			70/60 (35/30)	Wood 6 (153)	2 640 (1 640)					3	Pres: W. Formyduvale
							70 (35)	Wood 7 (178)	18" (457)						
		30 (48)					140/100 (70/50)	Wood 7 (178)	20-24" (508/610)						Gen Man: C. W. Shaw Jr
															Sen VP: J. C. Humbert
15 (24)	25 (40)			N.York AB	Auto		115/85 (57/42)	Wood 7"/9" (178/229)	22" (560)	29·0°			2 300 (702)	15 (3)	Gen Man: J. D. Everly
10 (16)		55 (89)	$74 165 000 49 551 000	Air W'hse	Type E, F and H 34½ (876)		132/115 (66/57)	Oak 7 (178)	21" (533)	30·0°	1·75% 3·75%U	Coopers E-72	4 066 (1 233)	2 730	Pres: W. P. Coliton
29·9 (48·2)	52·8 (86·6)	79 (127)	$ 89 578 74 474	Air	Type E 34¼ (876)		136/75 (68/37)	Wood 7 (178)	3 250 (2 020)	10·0°	1·0%	35	5 903 (1 799)	3 051 (632)	Pres: R. G. Flannery
		12 (19)		Air			85/65 (42/32)	Fir 7 (178)	20" (508)	12·0°	1·25%			5	Pres: K. Willson

NAME OF COMPANY ADDRESS	Gauge ft. in. (metres)	Route length incl. E=Electrified miles (km.)	Track length incl. E=Electrified miles (km.)	Elect. system and type of conductor	Loco-motives L=Line S=Shunt Steam Electric Diesel De=elec. Dh=hyd.		Rail-cars Electric Diesel Trailer Railbus Multiple Unit set		Pass. train cars	Freight train cars Con-tainers	Total Volume carried. Thousands of tonnes	Av'ge haul per ton miles (km.)	Av'ge net train load tonnes	Max. trailing load tonnes	Passengers Total number carried in 1 000s	Average journey miles (km.)

USA (contd.)

NAME OF COMPANY ADDRESS	Gauge	Route length	Track length	Elect.	Loco.		Railcars		Pass	Freight	Volume	Av haul	Av load	Max load	Passengers	Av journey
Wichita Union Terminal Rly 1537 Barwise, Wichita, Kans 67214	4' 8½" (1·435)	9 (15)														
Wilkes-Barre Connecting RR Co Hudson, Pa	4' 8½" (1·435)	9 (14)														
Winchester & Western Railroad Co Piccadilly and Kent Sts, PO Box 264, Winchester, Va 22601	4' 8½" (1·435)	18 (29)	18 (29)		DeL	1					118·5	18 (29)	600		1 200	
Winfield Railroad Co† Cabot, Penn 16023	4' 8½" (1·435)	9 (14)	10·95 (17·7)		DeL	1					17·7	9 (14)	300		950	
Winifrede Railroad Co Winifrede, W Va	4' 8½" (1·435)	7 (11)	12 (19)		DeL	1				75	916·6	7 (11)	1 300			
Winston-Salem Southbound Ry Co PO Box 205, Winston-Salem, NC	4' 8½" (1·435)	99 (159)			D	4				42						
Wrightsville & Tennille RR Co Tennille, Ga (Subsidiary of Central of Georgia)	4' 8½" (1·435)	36 (58)			S	1				5						
Wyandotte Southern RR 4655 Biddle ave, Wyandotte, Mich 48192 (Switching only)	4' 8½" (1·435)	4 (6·4)	4 (6·4)		DeS	1										
Wyandotte Terminal Railroad Co 43 Perry Place, Wyandotte, Mich 48192	4' 8½" (1·435)	9 (14)	12 (19)		DeS	5				35	588·4					
Yakima Valley Transportation Co 104 West Yakima ave, Yakima Wash 98902	4' 8½" (1·435)	E 21 (34)	E 27 (43)	d.c.	EL	2										
Yancey Railroad Co. Box 547, Burnsville, NC 28714	4' 8½" (1·435)	13 (21)	15 (24)		DeL	2					37·0	12 (19)				
Youngstown & Northern Railroad Co. 1131 Waverley St, Youngstown, Ohio	4' 8½" (1·435)	5 (8)	8 (13)		DeS	10				345						
Youngstown & Southern Railway Co. (Subsidiary of Montour RR Co) 7891 Southern Blvd, Youngstown, Ohio 44512	4' 8½" (1·435)	49 (79)	60 (96)													
Yreka Western Railroad Co 300 E. Miner St, Yreka, Cal 96097	4' 8½" (1·435)	9 (15)	11 (18)		S DeL	2 2						9 (15)	675		12	

URUGUAY

***Administración de Ferrocarriles del Estado** La Paz 1095, Montevideo	4' 8½" (1·435)	1 866 (3 008)	2 047 (3 294)		S D	19 101	D T	21 3	94	1 571	2 039·5	137 (221)	352		8 581·1	35·8 (57·6)
Administración Nacional de Puertos Montevideo	4' 8½" (1·435)		19 (31)		S D	5 2				143						

VENEZUELA

***Venezuelan State Railways** Instituto Autonomo Administración de Ferrocarriles del Estado Ave Principal los Ruices, Edif Stemo, Pisos 1/3, Caracas	4' 8½" (1·435)	107 (173)	164 (264)		DeL DeS	8 3	R T	5 10	15	323	116·2	13 652 109 ton-km				381·7

VIET-NAM

***Viet-Nam Railway System** Regie des CF du Viêtnam 2, Công-Trường, Diên-Hồng Ho Chi Minh City (Part Rack rail)	3' 3⅜" (1·00)	872 (1 404) (a)	879 (1 415)		S DeL DhS DmS	7 35 10 2	D	1	106	660 C 1 230	35·1				3 945·7	18·6 (30)
North Vietnam Railways No official information Unofficial reports assess route length between 450 and 500 miles (725–800 km)	3' 3⅜" (1·00)															

YUGOSLAVIA

***Yugoslav Railways** General Management, Nemanjina 6, Belgrade	4' 8" (1·435)	7 367 (11 856) E 938 (1 510)	9 433 (15 181) E 981 (1 605)	3 000 V dc OH and 25 000 V 1/50 dc OH	SL 1 432 E 162 De 280 Dh 74		R E TD EMU EMD	266 2 4 1 24 9	4 0002	63 300					Stand-ard 742	163 217·0 40 (64)
	3' 3⅜" (1·00) 2' 6" (0·76) 1' 11⅝" (0·60)									70 198	156·5 (252)		184 (296)	Nar-row 225·9		

* See main entry
† The line was to be sold or abandoned in 1979/80

Average Speeds			Financial Data		Couplers	Buffers	Rails	Sleepers (crossties)		Curvature max.	Gradient max. (U=not compensated)	Axle load max.	Altitude max.	Staff employed. Total no. (inclu. workshop)	Names of officials. Extended lists can be found at the end of the individual country in the report section immediately following
Freight Train	Pass. Train	Speed max.	Revenue Expenses	Braking (continuous)	Type and Height above rail	Centres and Height above rail	Weight	Type and thickness	Spacing Number per mile (per km) or centres						
mph (km/hr)	mph (km/hr)	mph (km/hr)	in 1 000s		ins (mm)	ins (mm)	lb. per yd (kg/m)	ins (mm)	ins (mm)			tonnes	feet (m)		
															Pres: H. C. Briscoe Vice Pres: J. C. Davis
10 (16)	35 (56)		$ 180·6 206·7	Air W'hse	AAR		100/65 (50/32)	Oak 6 (153)	2 800 (1 750)	15°	2·0%	33	945 (288)	10 (5)	Pres: Lemvel W. Brown
5 (8)	8 (13)		$ 25 960·00 50 924·00	Air W'hse	BSC Co.		100/85 (50/42)	Oak 6 (153)		14·0°	1·0%	33	965 (294)	2	Pres: Jerome Castle
15 (24)	25 (40)			Air W'hse	AAR 34½ (876)		100 (50)	Oak 7 (178)	22″ (559)	25·0°	7·0%	35	1 060 (323)	20 (3)	
6 (9·6)	6 (9·6)			Air W'hse	Auto 27 (684)		105/90 (52/45)	Wood 6 (153)	12″ (305)	19·0°	Level	50	579 (176)	15	Pres: H. J. Withers Vice Pres: N. E. Sylvander
5 (8)	10 (16)		$ 1·7 0·9											35	Pres: Earl F. Schuknecht
30 (49)	35 (56)						60/75 (30/37)	Wood 7 (180)	18″ (457)	52°				10 (1)	Man: J. L. Price Supt: R. B. Hardin Ch Eng: G. W. McDonald
	15 (24)						60 (30)	Wood 6 (153)	18″ (457)					10 (8)	Pres: W. H. Banks
															Pres: Edward J. Bernard Jr
20 (32)				Air			100/90 (49/44)	Wood 7 (178)	20″ (508)	8°	2%		1 240 (378)	36	Man: R. A. Weller
20 (32)	40 (64)		$ 175·0 169·7	Air W'hse	Auto		75 (37)	Fir 6 (153)	18″ (457)	16·0°	2·2%		2 620 (799)	15 (None)	Gen Man: L. Cecil
16·3 (26·1)	27·8 (44·8)			W'hse Vac. except railcars air	Screw 41 (1 040) except railcars auto: 34½ (877)	Crs. 68 (1 725) Ht. 41 (1 040)	80/56 (40/28)	Wood 4¾ (120) Some metal and conc	2 100– 2 400 (1 300– 1 500)	8·75°	2·17%	4		9 985	Gen. Man: Ing. Delfino Fros Torres
				Steam Vac Diesel air	33 (990)	Crs. 67⅜ (1 710) Ht. 33 (990)	80 (39·7)						12		
25 (40)	25 (40)	62 (100)	Bs 8 812·0 19 864·0	Air W'hse K/AB/ ABD	Auto 34½ (877)		100 (50)	Wood 7 (180) (1 723)	23½″ (800)	5·8°	10%	31.75	1 938	741 (591)	Gen. Man: Roberto Agostini C.
19 (30)	19 (30)	44 (70)		Vac Jourdain-Monn W'hse	Auto & Draw-hook 22½/34½ (570/876)	Central 32½ (825)	60/50 (30/25)	Steel; pre-str Conc	28¾″ (730)	984 ft (300 m)	Adhes 1·5% Rack 11·5%	13	2 750 (838)		Gen. Man:
12 (19·1)	25 (40)	74·5 (120)	Dinars 5 204 000·0 2 811 000·0		Standard 41¾ (1 060)	Cr. 68¼ (1 750) Ht. 41¾ (1 060)	98/70 (49/35)	Wood & Conc	600 (750)	820 ft (250 m)	3·0% 2·5% U	20	2 854 (870)		Gen. Man: Nikola Filipovic

NAME OF COMPANY ADDRESS	Gauge ft. in. (metres)	Route length incl. E=Electrified miles (km.)	Track length incl. E=Electrified miles (km.)	Elect. system and type of conductor	Loco-motives L=Line S=Shunt Steam Electric Diesel De=elec. Dh=hyd.	Rail-cars Electric Diesel Trailer Railbus Multiple Unit set	Pass. train cars	Freight train cars Con-tainers	Total Volume carried. Thous-ands of tonnes	Av'ge haul per ton miles (km.)	Av'ge net train load tonnes	Max. trailing load tonnes	Total number carried in 1 000s	Average journey miles (km.)
ZAÏRE														
*Société Nationale des Chemins de Fer Zourois (SNCZ) B.P. 297, Lubumbashi	3' 6'' (1·067)	2 224 (3 579) E 533 (858)	2 622 (4 720) E 643 (1 035)	25 000 V. 1/50 OH	D 15 EL 56 ES 5 DeL 56 DhL 8 DhS 61		188	5 166	4 164				1 199·0	131·7 (212)
Office Zairois des C.F. des Grands Lacs PO Box 230, Kalemie, Zaire	3' 6'' (1·067)	596 (959)	657 (1 058)		SL 7 SS 15 DhL 13 DhS 8		52	487	2 192		227·1	690	472·7	
	3' 3⅜'' (1·00)	78 (125)	87 (140)		DhL 3		8	83						
C.F. de Matadi a Kinshasa Office National des Transports (ONATRA) Boulevard du 30 juin, 98, Kinshasa	3' 6'' (1·067)	254 (409)	418 (673)		De 27 DeS 20 DhS 12 DS 4	D 3	63	2 940	1 629·7		300	500	1 290·1	71·5 (115)
C.F. du Mayumbe ONATRA Zone du Mayumbe a Boma	2' 0¼'' (615)	85 (136)	93 (150)		DeL 4 DhL 4 DS 6			370	120·4	47 (75) Up 42 (68) Down				
Ste. des C.F. Vicinaux du Zaire Aketi, Province Orientale	1' 11⅝'' (0·60)	639 (1 023)	(871)		SS 3 DL 21 DhS 4	D 3	17	350						
ZAMBIA														
*Zambia Railways PO Box 935, Kabwe	3' 6'' (1·067)	649 (1 044)	1 000 (1 609)		DeL 79 DhS 18		86	128	26 486	919 401 000 ton-km			1 014·0	
ZIMBABWE														
*Rhodesia Railways PO Box 596, Metcalfe Square, Bulawayo	3' 6'' (1·067)	2 100 (3 368)	2 802 (4 510)		S 165 Dh 6 DeL 79		608	14 458 C 4	11 955	5 588 000 000 ton-km			2 227	

* See main entry

Average Speeds			Financial Data		Couplers	Buffers	Rails	Sleepers (crossties)							Names of officials. Extended lists can be found at the end of the individual country in the report section immediately following
Freight Train	Pass. Train	Speed max.	Revenue Expenses	Braking (continuous)	Type and Height above rail	Centres and Height above rail	Weight	Type and thickness	Spacing Number per mile (per km) or centres	Curvature max.	Gradient max. (U=not compensated)	Axle load max.	Altitude max.	Staff employed. Total no. (inclu. workshop)	
mph (km/hr)	mph (km/hr)	mph (km/hr)	in 1 000s		ins (mm)	ins (mm)	lb. per yd (kg/m)	ins (mm)	ins (mm)			tonnes	feet (m)		
13·7 (22·0)	13·9 (22·3)	*Elec.* 32 *(52)* *other* 28 *(45)*	Zaires 92 971·4 120 833·6	Vac Jourdain Monn (Air on el locs)	Henricot Atlas 34⅝ (880)		80·6/59/49 (40/29/24)	Metal and Wood	1 500/1 300 (1 500)	656ft (200 m)	1·25% (Special cases to 2·3%)	15; Special cases 20	5 295 (1 614)	16 500	Op. Dir: R. Bandour
28 (45)	31 (50)	37 (60)		Vac and air	Henricot Atlas 34⅝ (880)		59/49 (29·3/ 24·4)	Metal & wood 5⅛ (130)	2 400- 2 100 (1 500- 1 300)	328 ft (100 m)	1·25% 2·0% **U**	15	3 510 (1 070)	4 538 (1 348)	Dir. Gen: R. Cherrier Man: G. Mugana Tech. Dir: J. Stas
		31 (50)									2·0% **U**	12·5			
18 (29)	20 (32)	37 (60)		Vac W'hse	Henricot Atlas 34⅝ (880)	Ht 34⅝ (880)	80·6/67 (40/33·4)	Metal	2 800- 2 400 (1 750- 1 500)	508 ft (155 m)	1·7% **U**	16·5	2 444 (745)		Gen. Man: Kanyama Kanana
		22 (35)			Hook 12⁵⁄₁₆ (312)		36·4 (18)	Metal	2 250 (1 400)	98 ft (30 m)	3·2% **U**	8			Gen. Man: J. F. Iyeki
		28 (45)		W'hse Oerlikon	Buffer-coupler	19⅝ (500)	66/20 (33/10)	Metal	2 400 (1 500)	656 ft (200 m)	1·5%	8	2 756 (840)	3 471	
15 (24)	30 (48)	55 (88)		Vac Gresham and Craven	Alliance 35¼ (900)		91/80 (44·6/ 39·7)	Wood Metal 5 (127)	2 240 (1 392)	656 ft (200 m)	1·6%	17	4 527 (1 380)	7 800 (525)	Gen. Man: H. J. Fast
19·8 (31·8)	31·9 (51·4)	56 (90)	Z$ 81 322 80 772	Air Vac	Auto Alliance *and* Atlas 35¼ (896)		109 (54)	Steel; Conc *Wood* 5 (127)	2 348- 2 112 (1 460- 1 305) (1 500 per km)	330 ft (106 m)	2·0%	18·6	5 538 (1 688)	19 538 (2 600)	Ch'man: W. F. Sievwright

INDEX

Printed in England by Netherwood Dalton & Co. Ltd., Huddersfield